THE AFRICAN AMERICAN ALMANAC

NINTH EDITION

THE
AFRICAN
AMERICAN
ALMANAC

NINTH EDITION

Formerly

The

Negro

Almanac

Jeffrey Lehman

Editor

Foreword by

Andrew P. Jackson (Sekou Molefi Baako)

GALE®

THOMSON

Detroit • New York • San Dieg[o] • London • Munich

THOMSON

GALE

The African American Almanac, Ninth Edition

Project Editor
Jeffrey Lehman

Editorial
John H. Harper, Brian J. Koski, Rebecca Parks, Jennifer M. York, Ralph G. Zerbonia.

Editorial Standards
Trish Yancey

Permissions
Margaret Chamberlain

Imaging and Multimedia
Randy Bassett, Mary K. Grimes, Christine O'Bryan, Robyn V. Young

Product Design
Michael Logusz, Jennifer Wahi

Composition and Electronic Capture
Evi Seoud, Mary Beth Trimper

Manufacturing
Rita Wimberley

ISBN 0-7876-4020-4
ISSN 1071-8710

Printed in the United States of America
10 9 8 7 6 5 4 3 2 1

Contributors

Donald F. Amerman Jr., *Editorial Consultant, A&M Editorial Services*

Stephen W. Angell, *Professor of Religion, Florida A&M University*

Gerry Azzata, *Editorial Consultant*

Calvert Bean, *Associate Editor,* International Dictionary of Black Composers

Alaiyo Bradshaw, *Professor of Art History and Studio Art, Parsons School of Design and Long Island University, Brooklyn*

Rose M. Brewer, *Associate Professor of Afro-American and African Studies, University of Minnesota, Twin Cities*

Christopher A. Brooks, *Associate Professor of Music and African-American Studies, Virginia Commonwealth University*

Linda M. Carter, *Associate Professor of English and Language Arts, Morgan State University*

Myla Churchill, *Associate Professor, Long Island University and New York University*

Paulette Coleman, *Executive Director, Exchange Club Family Center, Inc.*

DeWitt S. Dykes Jr., *Professor of History, Oakland University*

James Gallert, *Author and Jazz Historian*

Joseph Guy, *Jazz and Touring Coordinator, Southern Arts Federation*

Verna J. Henson, *Assistant Professor, Department of Criminal Justice, Southwest Texas State University*

Tracey Desirnaí Hicks, *Development Officer, Charles H. Wright Museum of African American History*

Phyllis J. Jackson, *Associate Professor of Art History and Black Studies, Pomona College*

Kristine Krapp, *Editor,* African American Firsts in Science and Technology

Kevin C. Kretschmer, *Reference Librarian, Public Library of Des Moines*

Guthrie P. Ramsey Jr., *Assistant Professor of Music, University of Pennsylvania*

Houston B. Roberson, *Assistant Professor of History, University of the South*

Gil L. Robertson IV, *Founder, The Robertson Treatment*

Kelle S. Sisung, *Editorial Consultant*

Jessie Carney Smith, *Librarian and Professor of Humanities, Fisk University*

Audrey Y. Williams, *Professor Emeritus, Zicklin School of Business, Baruch College, City University of New York*

Raymond A. Winbush, *Director, Institute for Urban Research, Morgan State University*

Michael D. Woodard, *President, Woodard & Associates*

Linda T. Wynn, *Assistant Director for State Programs, Tennessee Historical Commission; Lecturer, Department of History, Fisk University*

Contents

Foreword

The late master historian Dr. John Henrik Clarke said many times in his lectures and writings, "History is a clock that tells a people their historical time of day. It is a compass that people use to locate themselves on the map of human geography. A people's history tells a people where they have been and what they have been, where they are and what they are. More importantly, a proper understanding of history tells a people what they still must be and where they still must go." I've always felt this to be such a dynamic statement on the importance of history in relation to our lives. It is vital to the development, progress, and empowerment of a people for them to have access to their recorded history and culture through written sources such as the *African American Almanac.*

One of the most important freedoms earned by African Americans in 1865, following 400 years of enslavement, was the right to a formal education. Through education, former slaves were empowered to make choices for and about their future and that of their families. Freedom to read a book gave access to secrets that slaves felt were stored between its covers. Freedom to learn "their letters," to write words and sentences, instilled a sense of pride in their ability to communicate in the narrative; to read a newspaper or write a letter, all without fear or persecution. These freedoms created an environment where the African American could reap the benefits of the country he helped build with the knowledge, craft skills, learned talents and creativity brought from his homeland. Education gave the word *freedom* meaning and significance. Education allowed the African American to experience the liberty entitled to all human beings. This freedom came at a high cost. It would only be maintained with constant struggle and vigilance.

Knowledge is power! We have all heard this quote expressed many times in many lectures to students and young people. Knowledge of self, appreciation of one's history and culture, and understanding how knowledge relates to personal and communal progress are integral to the struggle for true freedom. Yet, even now, in the twenty-first century, there is difficulty getting historical information about the culture and contributions of African Americans included as an integral part of the American History curriculum throughout our country. Librarians, teachers and educators share a common mission to provide greater access to the tools and resources that make the quest for knowledge and understanding an enriching journey and a life changing experience.

The founder of Black History Month, Dr. Carter G. Woodson, wrote, "If a race has no history, if it has no worthwhile traditions, it becomes a negligible factor in the thought of the world and stands in danger of being exterminated." Early documentation of the black experience from the oral tradition of the griot in ancient Africa, folktales from the islands of the Caribbean and in the southern tradition of America, gave birth to music in the form of slave ditties and spirituals that gave hope to slaves toiling under the inhuman conditions of the "peculiar institution." Slave narratives documented their experiences in books and speeches to ensure clarity and understanding of the strange legacy of an era of historical significance to a new American culture. The nineteenth century struggles for human rights, from slavery and Reconstruction through the civil rights movement of the twentieth century, are an important chapter in America's story of freedom. This tumultuous journey of a people, from kidnapped Africans to American citizens, is a freedom thread in the fabric of the American flag that waves so proudly across our country.

In Harlem Renaissance poet Langston Hughes's profound poem, "Let America Be America Again," he speaks of America as "A dream— / Still beckoning to me!" In his most famous speech, civil rights activist Martin Luther King Jr. also expounded his vision of the American dream. Meanwhile, Human rights activist Malcolm X referred to it as an "American nightmare." However one evaluates the African American chapters from America's history book, the rights and privileges our new citizens and recent immigrants enjoy is a testament to those struggles and hardships past generations of African Americans overcame. Today's immigrants are the benefactors of passed legislation, lawsuits, marches, sit-ins, civil rights statutes, and affirmative action policies making America a better land for us all. These gains have created greater equality for all of us. It's not completely level yet, but it is getting better. These stories must be told, the history unveiled, the truth written.

The most potent weapon in the hands of the oppressor is the mind of the oppressed. —Steven Biko

Andrew P. Jackson (Sekou Molefi Baako)

Introduction

Since the first edition of *The Negro Almanac* was published in 1967, the work, now titled *The African American Almanac*, has been hailed as the most comprehensive reference product of its kind. It was cited by *Library Journal*, in conjunction with the American Library Association, as "Outstanding Reference Source." Now in its ninth edition, it continues to provide students, teachers, researchers, and interested readers with insight into the history, growth, and achievements of African Americans.

The *Almanac* brings together information on topics that previously required research in specialized archives and library collections. While other publications have followed its pioneering trail, it has continued to grow and refine its coverage to serve the interests and needs of the widest possible audience. It offers a comprehensive and accurate survey of black culture in the United States and around the world.

New Features in This Edition

All material appearing in the eighth edition of *The African American Almanac* was extensively reviewed by the editor and, where appropriate, updated or expanded. In many instances completely new topics were added to the existing essays. As a result, all of the chapters have been reviewed and 19 substantially revised by subject experts—usually the chapter author from the eighth edition. The remaining chapters underwent more moderate updates.

All of the more than 1,000 biographies were reviewed and nearly 600—virtually all of the living individuals—were updated with new information. With the help of the chapter authors, more than 50 new biographies were added. In a new feature, cross-references within the biographical sections were added to assist users looking for such "crossover" successes as Will Smith (pointing from "Film & Television" to "Popular Music") and Mabel K. Staupers (pointing from "Civil Rights" to "Science & Technology").

All directory information is current up to 2002, including entries for federal and state civil rights agencies; national organizations; black federal judges; Congressional Black Caucus members; African Americans holding endowed university chairs, chairs of excellence, or chaired professorships; research institutions; Internet sites of interest to African Americans; print and broadcast media; important films; and museums and galleries exhibiting African American art.

The "Chronology" (chapter 1) contains 50 new events, most since 1999; "African American Firsts" (chapter 2) has been bolstered by more than 100 new entries; and "Landmarks" (chapter 4) now possesses updated contact information—including Internet and e-mail addresses, when available—as well as 25 new entries. The country information in "Africa and the Black Diaspora" (chapter 5) has been made current and the histories include events since the late 1990s.

"Civil Rights" (chapter 7) contains the most recent information on hate crimes and police brutality; "Black Nationalism" (chapter 8) covers the Reparations movement; "Law" (chapter 10) has improved the context for the many cases cited, including dates, places, and names of individuals involved; "Politics" (chapter 11) has added a short section on the role of African Americans in the Election 2000 fiasco as well as a discussion of African Americans in the new Bush administration.

Although most chapters were affected by the 2000 census, "Population," "Employment & Income," "Entrepreneurship," "Education," and "Family" (chapters 12–16) rely on this data most heavily; therefore, explanation of what the new numbers mean has been incorporated into the essays.

"Literature" (chapter 18) has a new section devoted to women writers. Short subsections on architecture/architects and designers (fashion as well as engineering types) were added to "Visual/Applied Arts" (chapter 26).

Approximately half of the images appearing in this work were not published in the previous edition. More than 40 new statistical tables, charts, and graphs, compiled by the Bureau of the Census and other governmental organizations from the 2000 census, appear in pertinent chapters. Finally, the name and keyword index continues to provide improved access to the contents of *The African American Almanac*.

Content and Arrangement

Information in this edition of *The African American Almanac* appears in 29 subject chapters. Many open with an essay focusing on historical developments or the contributions of African Americans to the subject area, often followed by concise biographical profiles. Although the biographies represent only a small portion of the African American community, each subject embodies excellence in their field. Individuals who made a significant contribution in more than one area appear in the subject area for which they are best known. *See* references have been added to simplify the location of biographies.

More than 550 photographs, illustrations, maps, and statistical charts aid the reader in understanding the topics and people covered in the reference work. African American recipients of selected awards and honors—formerly lumped together in the Appendix—have been placed into appropriate chapters. For example, Pulitzer Prize-winning authors appear in "Literature" (chapter 18) and federal judges appear in "Law" (chapter 10). Many chapters also contain a directory of organizations/institutions relevant to their subject matter. This information comes from the most recent Gale databases or was gathered by chapter authors and compiled specifically for this publication.

In order to facilitate research, a bibliography is provided at the end of the *Almanac*. It includes more than 350 recent titles deemed most useful in the further study of African Americana. They are arranged alphabetically by author under categories indicative of their subject matter.

Comments Welcome

Although considerable effort was taken to ensure the accuracy and currency of the information presented in this edition, mistakes and omissions in a work of this magnitude are inevitable. Therefore, the editor welcomes all feedback related to the content of *The African American Almanac*. All comments and suggestions will be considered in the preparation of subsequent editions. They can be sent to:

The African American Almanac
Gale Group
27500 Drake Rd.
Farmington Hills, MI 48331–3535

Acknowledgments

Special Thanks

The editor thanks the many contributors who remained as flexible and reliable as we have grown to depend upon and the Gale staff members who cheerily pitched in, especially Shelly Dickey and Rebecca Parks for their terrific suggestions for improvements. Extra special thanks must be extended to Andrew P. Jackson (Sekou Molefi Baako) for valiantly writing the foreword when our backs were to the wall.

Photographic Credits

The following list—in order of appearance—acknowledges the copyright holders who have granted us permission to reprint the hundreds of images in this work.

Chronology

The Mine of "El Mina" (fortress with pointed domed towers), Gold Coast, Ghana, Africa, 18th century engravings. The Granger Collection, New York. Reproduced by permission. **African slave trade (Africans chained and yoked),** 19th century wood engraving. The Granger Collection, New York. Reproduced by permission. **Slave ship stowage layout,** line drawing. Library of Congress. **Slave women sitting in pile of cotton,** photograph. Library of Congress. **First black slaves arriving in Jamestown,** Virginia, engraving. Library of Congress. **Building where Nat Turner and his men were confined prior to trial and sentencing,** photograph. Public domain. **Joseph Cinque,** overseeing the mutiny and execution of Captain Ferrer, etching. *Harper's Weekly.* The Library of Congress. **Title page from *Uncle Tom's Cabin*** by Harriet Beecher Stowe, Boston, 1852, print. The Granger Collection, New York. Reproduced by permission. **Anthony Burns** (wearing black bow tie, white shirt, black vest and suit jacket), engraving by R.M. Edwards. Prints and Photographs Division. Library of Congress. **"Ho for Kansas,"** (copyprint of broadside, historic American Buildings Survey), illustration. Prints and Photographs Division. Library of Congress. **Dred Scott** (portrait, full head of dark hair with widow's peak), illustration. Library of Congress. **Barges with African Americans on canal,** Richmond, Virginia, photograph. Library of Congress. Reproduced by permission. **Freed slaves waiting for work opportunities,** photograph. U.S. Signal Corps, National Archives and Records Administration. ***The Crisis, A Record of the Darker Races,*** edited by W.E.B. DuBois, cover for November 1910, print. **Black soldiers (on train),** photograph. National Archives, U.S. War Department General Staff. **Oscar DePriest,** photograph. Fisk University Library. Reproduced by permission. **Haywood Patterson (Scottsboro Trials),** photograph. National Archives and Records Administration. **U.S. Army Buffalo Division** (black soldiers at attention), 1945, photograph. National Archives and Records Administration. **George E.C. Hayes, Thurgood Marshall, and James M. Nabrit,** Washington, D.C., 1954, photograph. Library of Congress. **Three demonstrators seated at counter while crowd harasses them,** photograph. AP/Wide World Photos. Reproduced by permission. **Burning bus,** freedom riders, Anniston, Alabama, 1961, photograph. AP/Wide World Photos. Reproduced by permission. **Martin Luther King Jr.** (at the Washington Monument), photograph. AP/Wide World Photos. Reproduced by permission. **March on Washington** (man walking backwards leading), 1963, Washington, D.C., photograph. National Archives and Records Administration. **Martin Luther King Jr.** (being congratulated by King Olav of Norway), 1964, photograph. National Archives (286-MP-NOR-1306). **Civil Rights protest (Selma violence),** Harlem, New York, 1965, photograph. National Archives and Records Administration. **Civil rights workers (slain),** photograph. Reuters/Corbis-Bettmann. Reproduced by permission. **Watts race riots** in Los Angeles. Public Domain. **Lyndon B. Johnson,** (seated, signing Civil Rights Bill), photograph. Library of Congress. **Harold Washington,** with wife at podium, photograph. AP/Wide World Photos. **Martin Luther King Middle School students** celebrating MLK's birthday, 1996, San Francisco, California, photograph. AP/Wide World Photos. Reproduced by permission. **Jesse Jackson Sr.,** photograph. Source unknown. **Tom Bradley,** 1986, Los Angeles, CA, photograph. AP/Wide World Photos. Reproduced by permission. **Rodney King,** (being beaten by police officers), photograph. AP/Wide World Photos. Reproduced by permission. **Mike Espy** (hand on chest), 1994, photograph by Wilfredo Lee. AP/Wide World Photos. Reproduced by permission. **Reginald Denny,** Johnnie Cochran (sitting together on talk show), Los Angeles, CA, 1993, photograph by Nick. AP/Wide World Photos. Reproduced by permission. **Joycelyn Elders** (speaking), Washington, DC, 1994, photograph. AP/Wide World Photos. Reproduced by permission. **O.J. Simpson,** Johnnie Cochran, and Robert Shaprio (Simpson wearing bloody gloves), Los Angeles, CA, 1995, photograph by Sam Mircovich. Archive Photos, Inc. Reproduced by permission. **Nathaniel Grey Jr.,** Chicago, IL, 1995, photograph. AP/Wide World Photos. Reproduced by permission. **Tiger Woods** (kicking out right foot), Augusta, GA, 1997, photograph by John Kuntz. Archive Photos. Reproduced by permission. **President Bill Clinton** (clapping, smiling), Goree Island, Senegal, Africa, 1998, photograph by Greg Gibson. AP/Wide World Photos. Reproduced by permission. **Venus Williams** (playing tennis), photograph. Reuters/Blake Sell/Archive Photos. Reproduced by permission. **Shaquille O'Neal** (hanging on basketball rim after dunking), photograph by Mark J. Terrell. AP/Wide World Photos. Reproduced by permission.

African American Firsts

P.B.S. Pinchback (looking right in dark suit), photograph. Library of Congress. **Jack Johnson** (fists clenched, boxing pose), photograph. Library of Congress. **Jane M. Bolin,** (dark jacket trimmed in contrasting mini pleats), 1939, photograph. Fisk University Library. Reproduced by permission. **Roy Campanella,** (in stadium, wearing baseball uniform), 1952, photograph. AP/Wide World Photos. Reproduced by permission. **Ralph J. Bunche,** photograph. AP/Wide World Photos. Reproduced by permission. **Lorraine Hansberry,** John McClain, Friedrich Duerrenmatt, Robert Dhery, New York City, 1959, photograph. UPI/Corbis-Bettmann. Reproduced by permission. **Robert C. Weaver,** Washington, DC, 1964, photograph. AP/Wide World Photos. Reproduced by permission. **Vanessa Williams,** (Miss America) and Suzette Charles, Atlantic City, NJ, 1983, photograph. AP/Wide World Photos. Reproduced by permission. **Guion S. Bluford Jr.,** Ronald E. McNair, Frederick Gregory, and Charles F. Bolden Jr., photograph. U.S. National Aeronautics and Space Administration (NASA). **Mae C. Jemison** (holding a model of a NASA aircraft), photograph. National Aeronautics and Space Administration. **Tubby Smith,** (being carried off court by players Jeff Sheppard, Steve Masiello, and Jamaal Magloire), photograph by Eric Draper. AP/Wide World Photos. Reproduced by permission. **J.C. Watts** (dark jacket, smiling), photograph. AP/Wide World Photos. Reproduced by permission.

Significant Documents in African American History

Slave cell, photograph. Library of Congress. *The Liberator,* newspaper masthead. Library of Congress. **Henry Highland Garnet,** 1881, photograph. The Granger Collection, New York. Reproduced by permission. **Escaped slaves being returned,** engraving. Library of Congress. **Sojourner Truth,** (holding knitting yarn falling across lap), portrait. National Portrait Gallery, Smithsonian Institution. Reproduced by permission. **Abraham Lincoln giving the first reading of the Emancipation Proclamation** to his Cabinet, published c.1866, mezzotint by A.H. Ritchie after a painting by F.B. Carpenter. Library of Congress. **Frederick Douglass,** photograph. Library of Congress. *Lynch Law in Georgia,* by Ida B. Wells-Barnett, illustration. Rare Book and Special Collections Division. Library of Congress. **Black segregated school,** five boys at table, photograph. Library of Congress. **Federal troops escorting four black students,** Little Rock, AR, photograph. AP/Wide World Photos. Reproduced by permission. **Black Panthers (demonstrating outside of courthouse),** photograph. New York Amsterdam News. Reproduced by permission. **Million Man March (overview of march),** photograph by

Greg Newton. Reuters/Greg Newton/Archive Photos, Inc. Reproduced by permission. **John Hope Franklin,** (sitting), photograph. Fisk University Library. Reproduced by permission.

African American Landmarks

Karen Thurman (U.S. Representative), Gov. Roy Romer, and U.S. Rep. John Lewis, walking across the Edmund Pettus Bridge during the 33rd annual commemoration of the Bloody Sunday March in Selma, AL, Sunday, March 8, 1998, photograph by Kevin Glackmeyer. AP/Wide World Photos. Reproduced by permission. **Federal troops escorting black students,** Little Rock, AR, photograph. Corbis-Bettmann. Reproduced by permission. **Jeff Liberty,** (small metal grave marker), photograph. Source unknown. *The Spirit of Freedom,* the African American Civil War Memorial, bronze sculpture by Ed Hamilton, front view showing three black infantry soldiers and a sailor, cast in high relief, dedicated July, 1998, photographed 2001, Washington, D.C, photograph by Leitha Etheridge-Sims. "Cedar Hill" (two story house of Frederick Douglass), photograph. National Park Service, Department of the Interior. **Memorial depicting Lincoln breaking a slave's chain,** Lincoln Park, Washington, DC, photograph. **Martin Luther King Jr. Memorial,** photograph. Michael Ochs Archives/Venice, Calif. Reproduced by permission. **Jean Baptiste Point Du Sable,** portrait, and aerial view of the landscape where Chicago was built, lithograph. **Levi Coffin,** (turned slightly to his left) from *Reminiscences of Levi Coffin,* engraving. Public domain. **Black pioneers in front of sod house,** Nicodemus, KS, photograph. Denver Public Library-Wester Collection. **Crispus Attucks monument** (broken chain, eagle, flag), photograph. AP/Wide World Photos. Reproduced by permission. **Plaque of a soldier on horseback and marching band,** Fort Shaw, Montana, photograph. Source unknown. **Sojourner Truth,** (gravesite), photograph. Source unknown. **Front view of Motown Museum,** 2648 W. Grand Blvd, Detroit, MI, 1996, photograph by Layne Kennedy. Corbis Corporation. Reproduced by permission. **Old Courthouse at Jefferson National Expansion Memorial,** St. Louis, MO, 1998, photograph by Richard Cummins. Corbis Corporation. Reproduced by permission. **Apollo Theater marquee,** "See You Soon," photograph. AP/Wide World Photos. Reproduced by permission. **Madame C.J. Walker,** (house where she lived [Villa Lewaro]), photograph. Prints and Photographs Division. Library of Congress. **Frederick Douglass,** statue in Rochester, NY, photograph by J.H. Kent. Schomburg Center for Research in Black Culture. Reproduced by permission. **Harriet Beecher Stowe House,** 1996, Cincinnati, OH,

photograph. AP/Wide World Photos. Reproduced by permission. **Wilberforce University** (exterior of building), pen and ink drawing. Daniel A.P. Murray Pamphlet Collection. Rare Book and Manuscript Division. Library of Congress. **Nat Love,** (foot on saddle, holding rifle), photograph. Denver Public Library. **Beale Street during May Music Festival,** Memphis, TN, 1997, photograph. AP/Wide World Photos. Reproduced by permission. **Hampton University,** photograph. Reproduced by permission of the Hampton University Archives. **Shenandoah and Potomac Rivers** at Harpers Ferry, WV, July 1865, photograph by James Gardner. National Archives and Records Administration.

Africa and the Black Diaspora

Map of eastern Africa showing important anthropological sites excavated by the Leakey family, illustration by XNR Productions. The Gale Group. **Map of the Middle East in the mid-600s AD** showing the growth of Muslim territories in the years following the death of Mohammed in 632. The Gale Group. **Map of Africa showing the African Kingdoms in 1400 and 1500.** The Gale Group. **Africa,** map by XNR Productions Inc. The Gale Group. **Map of Africa** (Mediterranean Sea, Red Sea). The Gale Group. **Kilimanjaro (mountain),** Tanzania, photograph by Cory Langley. Reproduced by permission. **Three San (Bushman) women** of the Kalahari gathering edible roots, photograph by Jason Laure. Reproduced by permission. **Ladysmith Black Mambazo,** Shabalala, Joseph (Shabalala dancing the "bump" with group member), 1994, photograph by Jack Vartoogian. Reproduced by permission. **Map of South America** (Caribbean Sea, Oceans). The Gale Group. **Map of the Caribbean** (Bahamas to Trinidad). The Gale Group. **Seven Angolan male children swimming,** (some show victory sign with fingers), photograph by J.P. Laffont. United Nations. **African market along river,** photograph by Cory Langley. Reproduced by permission. **Three Mossi males working in the fields with two oxen,** Toma, Burkina Faso, 1992, photograph by David Johnson. Reproduced by permission. **Mask,** Kilum Mountain-Rain Forest, Cameroon, Oku, photograph by David Johnson. Reproduced by permission. **Congolese government troops patrol streets of Kinshasa,** photograph. AP/Wide World Photos. Reproduced by permission. **Woman weaving beneath a tree,** photograph by Jason Laure. Reproduced by permission. **Women in white garb crossing street,** Eritrea, photograph by Cory Langley. Reproduced by permission. **Modern church,** Axum, Ethiopia, photograph by Cory Langley. Reproduced by permission. **Masai warriors,** women and children at wedding in traditional dress, Kenya, photograph by David Johnson. Global Learning, Inc. Reproduced by permission. **Four women and a man (sitting outside of a barn),** Madagascar, photograph by Cory Langley. Reproduced by permission. **Man working on fishing net (canoes on river),** Malawi, photograph by Cory Langley. Reproduced by permission. **Malian clay fortification,** photograph. Picture Collection, The Branch Libraries, The New York Public Library. **Nomadic family** (mother, father and baby), Mauritania, photograph by Jason Laure. Reproduced by permission. **Ancient part of city (including ornate archway),** Fez, Morocco, photograph by Cory Langley. Reproduced by permission. **Namibian children,** photograph by Cory Langley. Reproduced by permission. **Camel carrying woven millet,** Niamey, Niger, West Africa, photograph by Carolyn Fischer. Reproduced by permission. **Uniformed guards before the presidential palace in Dakar, Senegal,** photograph by Ken Estell. Reproduced by permission. **Independence Monument,** Seychelles, Africa, photograph by Barbara Beach. Reproduced by permission. **Somalis stroll past airline offices and shops** offering cheapest international telephone calls in Africa, photograph. AP/Wide World Photos. Reproduced by permission. **South African village of Cross Roads,** photograph. United Nations. Reproduced by permission. **Three-foot high drum with intricate carving,** Swaziland, photograph by Cory Langley. Reproduced by permission. **Tanzanian man loading bananas onto his bike,** photograph by Cory Langley. Reproduced by permission. **Broom vendor in street (wearing blue and yellow dress),** photograph by Cory Langley. Reproduced by permission. **Tunisian women,** photograph by Cory Langley. Reproduced by permission. **Victoria Falls** (bare tree branches in upper right hand corner), Zambia, photograph by Cynthia Bassett. Reproduced by permission. **Bahamas celebration,** photograph by Cory Langley. Reproduced by permission. **Food vendor on beach (wearing orange hat),** Rio De Janeiro, Brazil, photograph by Cory Langley. Reproduced by permission. **Costa Rican boy in the stern of a boat gutting and cutting fish,** photograph by Cory Langley. Reproduced by permission. **Postcard vendor (wearing light jacket with dark sleeves),** Havana, Cuba photograph by Cory Langley. Reproduced by permission. **Slums on hillside,** Santo Domingo, Dominican Republic, photograph. United Nations. Reproduced by permission. **Open air market in Pointe-a-Pitre, Guadeloupe,** photograph. Unknown source. **Clock tower in center of Linstead Market,** Jamaica, photograph. Jamaican Tourist Board. Reproduced by permission. **People shopping on a street in**

Martinique, photograph by Carolyn Fischer. Reproduced by permission. **Group of West Indian musicians playing steel drums on the beach,** Trinidad, photograph. Susan D. Rock. Reproduced by permission.

Africans in America: 1600 to 1900

Group of slaves disembarking (three-masted ship in distance), engraving. Library of Congress. **Crispus Attucks,** painting. Library of Congress. **British soldiers herding captured slaves onto ship,** drawing. Library of Congress. **Man pulling a plow that is guided by woman in the rice field,** in Savannah, GA, 1870s, photograph by O. Pierre Havens. Schomburg Center for Research in Black Culture. Reproduced by permission. **Slave family** (men, women and children outside of cabin), photograph by T.H.O. Sullivan. Library of Congress. **Missouri Compromise** (map showing boundaries of slave states and free states), drawing by Eric Wisniewski. The Gale Group. **Handbill offering reward for return of slaves,** illustration. Library of Congress. **Slave catcher handbill,** Boston, April 24, 1851, print. Library of Congress. **Escaped slaves** (resting outside an Underground Railroad stop), Cumberland Landing, VA, 1862, photograph by James Gibson. Library of Congress. **Map showing the routes of the Underground Railroad,** illustration. The Gale Group. **Nat Turner,** (confession, the leader of the Late Insurrection in Southampton, VA), 1832, illustration. Rare Book and Special Collection Division. Library of Congress. **Map of United States depicting slave and free territory.** The Gale Group. *Waiting for the Hour,* (painting of African Americans in church on New Year's Eve), painting by Heard and Moseley. Prints and Photographs Division. Library of Congress. **Joseph Cinque,** (lithograph in the *New York Sun,* 1839), lithograph by Moses Y. Beach. Prints and Photographs Division. Library of Congress. **Olaudah Equiano,** (turned right, facing front, book in right hand), photograph. Library of Congress. **Lemuel Haynes,** photograph. Source unknown.

Civil Rights

NAACP anti-lynching poster, photograph. Archive Photos. Reproduced by permission. **Rosa Parks,** age 43, riding in the front of a bus, Montgomery, Alabama, 1956. Corbis-Bettmann. Reproduced by permission. **Protestors sitting on sidewalk get hosed,** Birmingham, AL, 1963, photograph. AP/Wide World Photos. Reproduced by permission. **Dr. Martin Luther King Jr.** (speaking before bank of microphones), Washington, DC, 1963, photograph. UPI/Corbis-Bettmann. Reproduced by permission. **Group showing support for**

deceased street vendor Amadou Diallo's family, photograph by Mark Lennihan. AP/Wide World Photos. Reproduced by permission. **Hate Crimes: Incidents, Offenses, Victims, and Known Offenders by Bias Motivation in 2000,** table created by GGS Information Services for The Gale Group. U.S. Census Bureau. **Ralph D. Abernathy,** (fist raised), New York, NY, photograph. Corbis/Bettmann. Reproduced by permission. **Kwame Toure,** and Dr. Maulana Karenga (seated), 1996, photograph. AP/Wide World Photos. Reproduced by permission. **James Farmer,** (seated on wall outdoors), 1990, Fredericksburg, VA, photograph. AP/Wide World Photos. Reproduced by permission. **Jesse Jackson Sr.** (seated, left hand on table, checkered jacket), photograph. Library of Congress. **Martin Luther King III** (wearing white shirt, print tie, suit jacket), Yeshiva University, New York, 1998, photograph by Ed Betz. AP/Wide World Photos. Reproduced by permission. **Ralph Abernathy,** Fred Shuttlesworth, Martin Luther King Jr. (marching, arms interlocked), photograph. AP/Wide World Photos. Reproduced by permission. **Mary Eliza Church Terrell,** photograph. The Granger Collection, New York. Reproduced by permission. **William Monroe Trotter,** photograph. Fisk University Library. Reproduced by permission. **Ida B. Wells-Barnett,** (wearing square-necked dress with lace and fringe trim), drawing. Source unknown.

Black Nationalism

Title page from *A brief Account of the Settlement and Present Situation of the Colony of Sierra Leone in Africa,* by Paul Cuffe, New York, 1812, photograph. Library of Congress. Reproduced by permission. **Title page from** *Incidents of Hope for the Negro Race in America: A Thanksgiving Sermon,* November 26, 1895, by Rev. Alexander Crummell, Washington, DC, 1895, photograph. Library of Congress. **Marcus Garvey,** (wearing military uniform, plumed hat), 1922, photograph. **Edward Wilmot Blyden,** (seated in armchair, open book on his lap), photograph. Library of Congress. **Rev. Alexander Crummell,** drawing. *Harper's Weekly,* April 14, 1866. **James Forten,** (wearing white shirt and dark jacket with collar turned up), drawing. Charles L. Blockson Collection, Afro American Collection, Temple University. Reproduced by permission. **Audley Moore,** photograph. AP/Wide World Photos. Reproduced by permission. **Khallid Abdul Muhammad** (wearing full embroidered robe and cap), 1998, photograph. AP/Wide World Photos. Reproduced by permission. **Henry McNeal Turner,** (wearing white collar and black cassock), engraving. Public domain. **Malcolm X,** photograph. AP/Wide World Photos. Reproduced by permission.

National Organizations

Richard Allen, engraving. New York Public Library Picture Collection. **W.E.B. Du Bois,** F.H.M. Murray, L.M. Hershaw, and William Monroe Trotter, Niagara Movement meeting, 1906, Harpers Ferry, WV, photograph. **James Farmer,** (standing in front of poster, facing front), photograph. Library of Congress. **Elmer "Geronimo" Pratt,** (wearing print shirt, and glasses), photograph by Nick Ut. AP/Wide World Photos. Reproduced by permission. **Jamil Abdullah Al-Amin (H. Rap Brown)** (on storefront sidewalk), 1990, Atlanta, GA, photograph. AP/Wide World Photos. Reproduced by permission. **Marian Wright Edelman,** photograph. AP/Wide World Photos. Reproduced by permission. **Myrlie Evers-Williams,** (speaking at podium), NAACP, New York, 1995, photograph. AP/Wide World Photos. Reproduced by permission. **Title page from** *A Charge,* Delivered to the African Lodge, June 24, 1797, at Menotomy, by Prince Hall, Boston, photograph. Library of Congress. **George Edmund Haynes,** photograph. Fisk University Library. Reproduced by permission. **Benjamin L. Hooks,** (seated in center of first row), photograph. Library of Congress. **Vernon Jordan,** (facing left, striped tie), photograph. Library of Congress. **Suzanne de Passe (1),** standing with John H. Johnson, and Jewell Jackson McCabe at Seventh Annual Candace Awards. AP/Wide World Photos. Reproduced by permission. **Floyd B. McKissick,** (sign in back reads, "Freedom Now…"), photograph. AP/Wide World Photos. Reproduced by permission. **Dr. Frederick D. Patterson,** (wearing glasses), photograph. Reproduced by permission of Dr. Frederick D. Patterson. **A. Philip Randolph,** (wearing tweed suit, dark hair), 1942, photograph. Library of Congress. **Bayard Rustin,** (wearing dark suit and tie), photograph. Library of Congress. **Faye Wattleton,** photograph. AP/Wide World Photos. Reproduced by permission. **Walter Francis White,** (looking to right with hands on table), photograph. Library of Congress.

Law

Slave catching apparatus (mask, shackles), woodcut. Library of Congress. **O.J. Simpson,** (pointing), Carl Douglas, Johnnie Cochran Jr., Robert Shapiro, Los Angeles, CA, 1995, photograph by Reed Saxon. AP/Wide World Photos. Reproduced by permission. **Mumia Abu-Jamal,** (leaving courthouse), photograph by Chris Gardner. AP/Wide World Photos. Reproduced by permission. **"The First Vote (black males lined up),"** cover illustration from *Harper's Weekly,* November 1867. National Archives and Records Administration. **"Negro Man Entering Movie Theatre by 'Colored'**

Entrance," photograph by Marion Post Wolcott. Prints and Photographs Division. Library of Congress. **Lloyd Gaines,** seated at desk, photograph. National Association for the Advancement of Colored People. Reproduced by permission. **Handbill advertising public meeting concerning the *Dred Scott* decision,** print. Public domain. **Newspaper depiction of a runaway slave** (running, carrying stick with bundle), engraving. Public domain. **Derrick Bell,** (wearing glasses), photograph. Reproduced by permission of Derrick Bell. **Johnnie Cochran,** photograph by A. Horvathova. Archive Photos. Reproduced by permission. **Archibald H. Grimké,** photograph. Fisk University Library. Reproduced by permission. **Charles Hamilton Houston,** (looking to the left), photograph. Fisk University Library. Reproduced by permission. **Gabrielle Kirk McDonald,** (wearing light colored suit jacket with stand up collar), photograph by Kerwin Plevka. *Houston Chronicle*/AP/Wide World Photos. Reproduced by permission. **Thurgood Marshall,** (wearing judicial robes), photograph by Joseph Lavenburg, National Geographic. Collection of the Supreme Court of the United States. **Bernard Parks,** photograph. The Los Angeles Police Dept. **Clarence Thomas,** (wearing judicial robe, head and shoulders), photograph. U.S. Supreme Court. **Jail Inmates by Sex and Race: 1990 to 1999,** table created by GGS Information Services for The Gale Group. U.S. Bureau of Justice Statistics, through 1994, *Jail Inmates,* annual; beginning 1995, *Prison and Jail Inmates at Midyear,* annual. **Prisoners Under Sentence of Death by Characteristic: 1980 to 1998,** table created by GGS Information Services for The Gale Group. U.S. Bureau of Justice Statistics, *Capital Punishment,* annual.

Politics

"The First Colored Senator and Representatives (41st and 42nd Congress of the U.S.)," drawing by Currier and Ives. Prints and Photographs Division. Library of Congress. **Ebenezer D. Bassett,** minister to Haiti, 1869, photograph by J.W. Hurn. Schomburg Center for Research in Black Culture. Reproduced by permission. **Congressional Black Caucus members at a news conference,** 1971, photograph. United Press International. Reproduced by permission. **Black leaders urging sanctions against South Africa,** photograph. AP/Wide World Photos. Reproduced by permission. **Charles Rangel,** photograph. AP/Wide World Photos. Reproduced by permission. **Marion Barry,** (smiling victoriously), Washington, DC,

1992, photograph. AP/Wide World Photos. Reproduced by permission. **Sharon Belton,** Minneapolis Mayor points to map, photograph. AP/Wide World Photos. Reproduced by permission. **Mary Berry,** (gesticulating with right hand), 1979, photograph. Library of Congress. **Julian Bond,** (standing at podium), photograph. Library of Congress. **Tom Bradley,** (looking right with lips closed), Washington, DC, 1969, photograph. Library of Congress. **Ron Brown,** (sitting with hands on table top), 1982, photograph. Library of Congress. **Ralph Bunche,** photograph by Carl Van Vechten. The Estate of Carl Van Vechten. Reproduced by permission. **Chaka Fattah,** (head and shoulders, dark suit, striped tie), photograph. **Patricia Roberts Harris,** (sitting with head leaning forward), Washington, DC, 1977, photograph. Library of Congress. **Congresswoman Sheila Jackson Lee** speaking to a crowd at the crew-welcoming ceremony at Ellington Field on the day following the completion of the STS-101 mission, photograph. U.S. National Aeronautics and Space Administration. **Barbara Jordan,** (chain around neck, earrings), photograph. Library of Congress. **Alan Keyes,** (at podium, campaigning), 1995, Green Bay, WI, photograph. AP/Wide World Photos. Reproduced by permission. **John Mercer Langston,** (sitting on wooden chair), photograph. Library of Congress. **John Robert Lewis,** photograph. Public domain. **Kweisi Mfume,** photograph by Barry Thumma. AP/Wide World Photos. Reproduced by permission. **Adam Clayton Powell,** (seated, hands clasped on table), photograph. Library of Congress. **Charles B. Rangel,** (facing front, smiling), photograph. Library of Congress. **Hiram Rhodes Revels,** (arm resting on table), photograph. U.S. Senate Historical Office. **Edith Sampson,** (presenting coin to ambassador), 1951, photograph. United Nations. Reproduced by permission. **Robert Smalls,** (seated, wearing suit, vest, watch chain and bow tie), photograph. Library of Congress. **Louis Sullivan,** (holding up book), photograph. AP/Wide World Photos. Reproduced by permission. **Robert C. Weaver,** (sitting at desk, looking down), Washington, DC, 1942 photograph by Pat Terry. Library of Congress. **Coleman Young,** (at podium, holding papers), photograph. AP/Wide World Photos. Reproduced by permission. **Chart No. 482. Political Party Identification of the Adult Population, by Degree of Attachment, 1972 to 1994, and by Selected Characteristics, 1994,** illustration. The National Election Studies, Center for Political Studies, University of Michigan. **Local Elected Officials by Sex, Race, Hispanic Origin, and Type of Government: 1992,** table created by GGS Information Services for The Gale Group. U.S. Census Bureau, 1992 Census of Governments, Popularly Elected Officials, (GC92(1)-2).

Population

Population by Race and Hispanic Origin for the United States: 2000, table by GGS Information Services for The Gale Group. U.S. Census Bureau. **Black or African American Population: 2000,** table created by GGS Information Services for The Gale Group. U.S. Census Bureau, Census 2000 Redistricting Data (Public Law 94–171) Summary File, Table PL1. **Haitian refugees on boat,** 1994, photograph. AP/Wide World Photos. Reproduced by permission. **Children in a field of sugar cane in Louisiana,** 1890s, photograph. Schomburg Center for Research in Black Culture. Reproduced by permission. **Kitty Cloud Taylor,** with her daughter (Enterpe), sister, and niece, photograph. The Denver Public Library Photography Collection. Reproduced by permission. **Distribution of the Black Population by State: 1999,** map created by GGS Information Services for The Gale Group. U.S. Census Bureau, July 1, 1999 estimates. **Metropolitan and nonmetropolitan residence by race in 1999,** results in percentages, graph created by GGS Information Services for The Gale Group. U.S. Census Bureau, Current Population Survey, March 1999.

Employment and Income

Civilian Labor Force Participation Rates by Sex, Race and Hispanic Origin: 2000, (aged 16 and older), bar graph created by GGS Information Services for The Gale Group. U.S. Census Bureau. **Physician and patient (in office),** photograph. Index Stock Imagery. Reproduced by permission. **Airline representative speaking with passenger,** photograph. Index Stock Imagery. Reproduced by permission. **Women laundry workers on strike,** photograph. Library of Congress. **Median Income for Households and Average Income per Household Member by Race and Hispanic Origin of Householder: 1999,** bar graph created by GGS Information Services for The Gale Group. U.S. Census Bureau, Current Population Survey, March 2000. **Percent change in labor force, projected 1998–2008,** bar graph created by GGS Information Services for The Gale Group. Bureau of Labor Statistics. **Lawrence Caw,** standing examining an aircraft panel, photograph. U.S. National Aeronautics and Space Administration (NASA). **Employed Civilians by Occupation, Sex, Race, and Hispanic Origin: 1983 to 1999,** parts 1–4, tables created by GGS Information Services for The Gale Group. U.S. Bureau of Labor Statistics, *Employment and Earnings*, monthly, January issues; and unpublished data. **Unemployed and Unemployment Rates by Educational Attainment, Sex, Race, and Hispanic Origin: 1992 to 1999,** table created by GGS Information Services for The Gale Group. U.S. Bureau

of Labor Statistics, unpublished data. **Civilian labor force participation rate and unemployment rate by sex and race in 1999,** bar graph created by GGS Information Services for The Gale Group. U.S. Census Bureau, Current Population Survey, March 1999. **Comparison of Summary Measures of Income by Selected Characteristics: 1993, 1999, and 2000,** table created by GGS Information Services for The Gale Group. U.S. Census Bureau, Current Population Survey, March 1994, 2000, and 2001. **Median Household Income by Race and Hispanic Origin: 1967 to 2000,** chart created by GGS Information Services for The Gale Group. U.S. Census Bureau, Current Population Survey, March 1968–2001. **Earnings by Highest Degree Earned: 1999,** table created by GGS Information Services for The Gale Group. U.S. Census Bureau, Current Population Reports, P20–528. **Poverty Rates by Race and Hispanic Origin: 1959 to 2000,** graph created by GGS Information Services for The Gale Group. U.S. Census Bureau, Current Population Survey, March 1960–2001. **People in poverty by age, sex, and race in 1998,** categorized by all ages, under 18 years, and 65 years and older, in both men and women, bar graph created by GGS Information Services for The Gale Group. U.S. Census Bureau, Current Population Survey, March 1999.

Entrepreneurship

Three escutcheon plates, (identified as brass hinges), photograph. Ploski-Negro. Reproduced by permission. **Cobbler on the Levee,** photograph. Schomburg Center for Research in Black Culture. Reproduced by permission. **Slave Crafts—Chest,** photograph. Ploski-Negro. Reproduced by permission. **Black-Owned Firms by Amount of Receipts: 1997,** chart created by GGS Information Services for The Gale Group. U.S. Census Bureau. **Black-Owned Firms as a Percentage of Total Firms in State: 1997,** map created by GGS Information Services for The Gale Group. U.S. Census Bureau. **Percentage Distribution of Black-Owned Firms by Industry Division: 1997,** chart created by GGS Information Services for The Gale Group. U.S. Census Bureau. **Woman sitting at computer,** photograph. Index Stock Imagery. Reproduced by permission. **James Beckwourth,** (standing), photograph. Library of Congress. **Arthur Gaston,** photograph. AP/Wide World Photos. Reproduced by permission. **La-Van Hawkins,** (holding up sample meals), Atlanta, 1994, photograph. AP/Wide World Photos. Reproduced by permission. **Freedom National Bank,** photograph by Andy Roy. Reproduced by permission. **Madame C.J. Walker,** (wearing long white dress), photograph. Library of Congress.

Family and Health

Generation family portrait, photograph by Bill Bachmann. Index Stock Imagery. Reproduced by permission. **Family Type by Race and Hispanic Origin of Householder: 2000,** bar graph, Married Couples, Female-maintained, no husband present, and Male-maintained, no wife present, (March 2000 Survey), illustration created by GGS Information Services for The Gale Group. U.S. Census Bureau. **Brother and sister painting (outdoors),** photograph. Index Stock Imagery. Reproduced by permission. **Family dinner,** photograph. Index Stock Imagery. Reproduced by permission. **Father and daughter hugging (outdoors),** photograph. Index Stock Imagery. Reproduced by permission. **Mother and children on hammock (outdoors),** photograph. Index Stock Imagery. Reproduced by permission. **Herman Shaw,** (seated), being helped up by President Clinton and Vice-President Al Gore, 1997, photograph. AP/Wide World Photos. Reproduced by permission. **Paula Giddings,** (leaning against wall, arms folded), photograph. MasterMedia Limited Speakers Bureau. Reproduced by permission. **Charleszetta "Mother" Waddles,** photograph. AP/Wide World Photos. Reproduced by permission. **Phill Wilson,** photograph. Office of Public Policy. Reproduced by permission of Phill Wilson. **Family size by type and race of householder in 1999,** results by percent of families, bar graph created by GGS Information Services for The Gale Group. U.S. Census Bureau, Current Population Survey, March 1999. **Family Groups with Children under 18 Years Old by Race and Hispanic Origin from 1980 to 1999,** table created by GGS Information Services for The Gale Group. U.S. Census Bureau, Current Population Reports, P20–515, and earlier reports; and unpublished data. **Family income by family type and race of householders in 1998,** results are by percent of families, categorized by married couples, female households, and male households, bar graph created by GGS Information Services for The Gale Group. U.S. Census Bureau, Current Population Survey, March 1999. **Living Arrangements of Persons 15 Years and Over by Selected Characteristics, 1999,** table created by GGS Information Services for The Gale Group. U.S. Census Bureau, unpublished data. **Marital Status of the Population by Sex, Race, and Hispanic Origin from 1980 to 1999,** table created by GGS Information Services for The Gale Group. U.S. Census Bureau, Current Population Reports, P20–491, and earlier reports; and unpublished data. **Live Births by Race and Type of Hispanic Origin— Selected Characteristics from 1990 to 1998,** table created by GGS Information Services for The Gale Group. U.S. National Center for Health Statistics; *Vital Statistics of the United States,* annual; *National Vital Statistics Report* (NVSR) (formerly *Monthly Vital Statistics Report*); and unpublished data. **Expectation of Life at Birth from 1970 to 1998 and Projections for 1999 to 2001,** table created by GGS Information Services for The Gale Group. U.S. Census Bureau. Except as noted, U.S. National Center for National Statistics, *Vital Statistics of the United States,* annual, and *National Vital Statistics Reports* (NVSR) (formerly *Monthly Vital Statistics Reports*). **Deaths by Selected Causes and Selected Characteristics, 1997,** table created by GGS Information Services for The Gale Group. U.S. National Center for Health Statistics, *Vital Statistics of the United States,* annual. **Percentage of Adults Engaging in Leisure-time Physical Activities: 1998,** table created by GGS Information Services for The Gale Group. U.S. National Center for Chronic Disease Prevention and Health Promotion, unpublished data. **Health Insurance Coverage Status by Selected Characteristics:1990 to 1998,** table created by GGS Information Services for The Gale Group. U.S. Census Bureau, Current Population Reports, P60–208; and unpublished data.

Education

New York African Free School No. 2, engraving. Photographs and Prints Division, Schomburg Center for Research in Black Culture, The New York Public Library, Astor, Lenox and Tilden Foundations. Reproduced by permission. **Large classroom filled with students sitting on benches,** Tuskegee Institute, Tuskegee, AL, 1902, photograph. Library of Congress. **Emily Smith on her college graduation day,** photograph. Schomburg Center for Research in Black Culture, Photographs and Prints Division. Reproduced by permission. **High School and College Graduates by Race and Hispanic Origin (aged 25 and older): 2000,** bar graph created by GGS Information Services for The Gale Group. U.S. Census Bureau. **Marva Collins,** Chicago, IL, 1982, photograph. AP/Wide World Photos. Reproduced by permission. **Malcolm X Academy school,** photograph. © Bruce Giffin. Reproduced by permission. **Educational attainment by sex and race in 1999,** percent of population 25 and over, bar graph created by GGS Information Services for The Gale Group. U.S Census Bureau, Current Population Survey, March 1999. **Mary McLeod Bethune,** (wearing suit jacket open with two buttons showing), photograph by Carl Van Vechten. The Estate of Carl Van Vechten. Reproduced by permission. **Charlotte Hawkins Brown,** portrait. Fisk University Library. Reproduced by permission. **Nannie Helen Burroughs,** portrait. Fisk University Library. Reproduced by permission. **Joe Clark,** (holding book), New

York, NY, 1989, photograph. AP/Wide World Photos. Reproduced by permission. **Septima Clark,** photograph. AP/Wide World Photos. Reproduced by permission. **Johnnetta Cole,** (holding African figure), photograph. AP/Wide World Photos. Reproduced by permission. **Anna Julia Haywood Cooper,** side profile, photograph. The Granger Collection, New York. Reproduced by permission. **John Hope Franklin,** (facing left, clear glasses, dotted tie), photograph. Library of Congress. **E. Franklin Frazier,** photograph. Fisk University Library. Reproduced by permission. **Charles S. Johnson,** photograph. Library of Congress. **Mordecai Johnson,** (third from right), with five unidentified men, photograph. Charles L. Blockson Collection, Afro American Collection, Temple University. Reproduced by permission. **Laurence Clifton Jones,** photograph. Fisk University Library. Reproduced by permission. **Dr. Alain Locke,** (seated in armchair, right profile, hands touching), photograph. Library of Congress. **Carter G. Woodson,** (standing in front of bookshelf, wearing a dark suit), photograph. Schomburg Center for Research in Black Culture. Reproduced by permission. **School Enrollment by Race, Hispanic Origin, and Age: 1980 to 1998,** table created by GGS Information Services for The Gale Group. U.S. Census Bureau, Current Population Reports, P20–521; and earlier reports. **High School Dropouts by Race and Hispanic Origin: 1975 to 1998,** table created by GGS Information Services for The Gale Group. U.S. Census Bureau, Current Population Reports, P20–521. **College Population by Selected Characteristics: 1998,** table created by GGS Information Services for The Gale Group. U.S. Census Bureau, Current Population Reports, P20–521. **Degrees Earned by Level and Race/Ethnicity: 1981 to 1997,** table created by GGS Information Services for The Gale Group. U.S. National Center for Education Statistics, *Digest of Education Statistics,* annual.

Religion

Mother Bethel African Methodist Church, Philadelphia, PA, illustration. Archive Photos. Reproduced by permission. **Three African American men behind podium,** Cincinnati, OH, illustration. Archive Photos. Reproduced by permission. **Juliann Jane Tillman,** (wearing white bonnet, white blouse, black open front top), engraving by Peter Duval. Prints and Photographs Division. Library of Congress. **Parade of men,** opening of the annual convention of the Provisional Republic of Africa in Harlem, carrying banners and a painting of the "Ethiopian Christ," banner above street: "Summer Chatauqua of the Abyssinian Baptist Church," New

York, photograph by George Rinhart. Corbis Corporation. Reproduced by permission. **African American congregation,** woman crying out as she is "touched by the Spirit," photograph. © Bettmann/Corbis. Reproduced by permission. **Gardner C. Taylor,** photograph. AP/Wide World Photos. Reproduced by permission. **A.M.E. Church Reunion,** photograph. Stanley B. Burns M.D. and the Burns Archive. Reproduced by permission. **George Clements,** photograph. AP/Wide World Photos. Reproduced by permission. **Arson investigators at Matthews Murkland Presbyterian Church,** 1996, Charlotte, NC, photograph. AP/Wide World Photos. Reproduced by permission. **Congressman Rev. Floyd Harold Flake** during a sermon on August 3, 1997, photograph by Emile Wamsteker. AP/Wide World Photos. Reproduced by permission. **Absalom Jones,** resting hand on a book, photograph. Fisk University Library. Reproduced by permission. **Bishop Stephen Gill Spottswood,** in clerical garb, head and shoulders, photograph. AME Zion Church. **Iyanla Vanzant,** photograph by Joyce Ravid. Reproduced by permission of Joyce Ravid.

Literature

Inside page of book, *The Interesting Narrative of The Life of Olaudah Equiano or Gustavus Vassa, The African,* photograph. Library of Congress. **Richard Wright,** photograph. AP/Wide World Photos. Reproduced by permission. **Nikki Giovanni,** photograph. Courtesy of Nikki Giovanni. Reproduced by permission. **William Wells Brown,** (wearing frock coat of textured cloth), drawing or engraving. Fisk University Library. Reproduced by permission. **Rita Dove,** photograph. AP/Wide World Photos. Reproduced by permission. **Paul Laurence Dunbar,** photograph. Library of Congress. **Rudolph Fisher,** (wearing dark suit and tie, white handerchief in breast pocket), photograph. The Beinecke Rare Book and Manuscript Library. Reproduced by permission. **Alex Haley,** (head only), photograph. Fisk University Library. Reproduced by permission. **Lorraine V. Hansberry,** photograph. Library of Congress. **Frances E.W. Harper,** portrait. Fisk University Library. Reproduced by permission. **James Weldon Johnson,** photograph. Library of Congress. **Audre Lorde,** (leaning forward, head wrapping), photograph. Library of Congress. **Claude McKay,** photograph. Library of Congress. **Terry McMillan,** photograph by Marion Ettlinger. Unknown source. **Walter Dean Myers,** photograph by David Godlis. Reproduced by permission of Walter Dean Myers. **Gloria Naylor,** photograph. Jennifer Waddell. Reproduced by permission. **Dorothy West,** (standing in front of red painted fence), Martha's Vineyard, MA, 1995, photograph. AP/Wide World Photos. Reproduced by permission.

Media

The North Star, (front page of newspaper founded by Frederick Douglass, 1847), illustration. Library of Congress. **Afro-American Building in Baltimore,** MD, photograph. Source unknown. **Mal Goode,** (holding news copy and microphone), photograph. Courtesy of ABC-TV. **Charlayne Hunter-Gault,** (sitting at desk, left hand on her cheek), photograph. AP/Wide World Photos. Reproduced by permission. **Robert L. Johnson,** speaking at podium, during press conference, announcing the launch of a Web site catering to African Americans, photograph. AP/Wide World Photos. Reproduced by permission. **Robert S. Abbott,** (head and shoulders), photograph. Fisk University Library. Reproduced by permission. **Don Barden,** (close-up, dark suit, geometric tie), 1997, photograph. AP/Wide World Photos. Reproduced by permission. **Les Brown,** photograph. Les Brown Enterprises, Inc. Reproduced by permission. **Ron Buckmire,** photograph. Reproduced by permission of Ron Buckmire. **Samuel E. Cornish,** (short curly hair wearing cravat), 19th century line engraving. The Granger Collection, New York. Reproduced by permission. **T. Thomas Fortune,** drawing. Fisk University Library. Reproduced by permission. **Earl G. Graves,** (arms folded, smiling), photograph. *Black Enterprise Magazine.* Reproduced by permission. **Bill Clinton, Delano Lewis (president and CEO of National Public Radio [left]), and Edward McCracken,** chairman, photograph. AP/Wide World Photos. Reproduced by permission. **Al Roker,** (standing on White House Lawn), photograph by Wilfredo Lee. AP/Wide World Photos. Reproduced by permission. **John B. Russwurm,** (three-quarter view from his left, greying hair), illustration. Library of Congress. **Bernard Shaw,** (holding his Ace Award), photograph. AP/Wide World Photos. Reproduced by permission. **Susan Taylor,** (speaking, pointing right index finger), Cherry Hill, NJ, 1986, photograph. AP/Wide World Photos. Reproduced by permission. **Montel Williams,** (wearing tie that reads, "Think"), 1996, photograph by Richard Drew. AP/Wide World Photos. Reproduced by permission.

Film and Television

Scene from the movie ***Birth of a Nation,*** 1915, photograph. The Kobal Collection. Reproduced by permission. **Paul Robeson, as Brutus Jones,** in a scene from 1933 film *The Emperor Jones,* photograph. ©

Underwood & Underwood/Corbis. Reproduced by permission. **Sidney Poitier** (close-up of face, young, wearing light suit), photograph. Library of Congress. **Scene from the film *Sweet Sweetback's Baadassss Song,*** 1971, photograph. The Kobal Collection. Reproduced by permission. **Cicely Tyson and Maya Angelou in *Roots,*** 1977, photograph. AP/Wide World Photos. Reproduced by permission. **Scene from the film *Hallelujah!,*** 1929, photograph, directed by King Vidor. The Kobal Collection. Reproduced by permission. **Scene from the documentary film *Hoop Dreams,*** 1994, photograph. The Kobal Collection. Reproduced by permission. **Lynn Whitfield,** (wearing sleeveless cocktail dress), New York, NY, 1997, photograph by Mitchell Gerber. Corbis Corporation. Reproduced by permission. **Allen and Albert Hughes,** 1993, photograph by Darren Michaels. The Kobal Collection. Reproduced by permission. **Don Cheadle,** (standing close to wall), photograph by Susan Sterner. AP/Wide World Photos. Reproduced by permission. **Richard Roundtree (l) and Christopher St. John** in the film *Shaft,* 1971, photograph. The Kobal Collection. Reproduced by permission. **Halle Berry,** (wearing lavender dress), 1996, photograph. Archive Photos. Reproduced by permission. **Bill Cosby** (seated), photograph. Library of Congress. **Ruby Dee,** photograph. AP/Wide World Photos. Reproduced by permission. **Morgan Freeman,** photograph. AP/Wide World Photos. Reproduced by permission. **Samuel L. Jackson,** (wearing collarless shirt and suit jacket), photograph © 1993 Deidre Davidson. Archive Photos. Reproduced by permission. **Spike Lee,** directing the film *Crooklyn,* photograph. Archive Photos. Reproduced by permission. **Eddie Murphy,** (talking to rat in a doctor's office), in the movie *Dr. Dolittle,* 1998, photograph by Phil Bray. The Kobal Collection. © 20th Century Fox. Reproduced by permission. **Chris Rock,** (swinging two Emmy awards), Pasadena, CA, 1997, photograph by Kevork Djansezian. AP/Wide World. Reproduced by permission. **John Singleton,** (*Boyz* hat), photograph. Reuters/Corbis-Bettmann. Reproduced by permission. **Wesley Snipes,** (close-up of face, narrow glasses, serious), photograph. AP/Wide World Photos. Reproduced by permission.

Drama, Comedy, and Dance

An elderly man, walking with his banjo in left hand, photograph by V.G. Schreck. Schomburg Center for Research in Black Culture, Photographs and Prints Division. Reproduced by permission. **Bert Williams and George Walker** (both smiling, wearing dark suits), photograph. Fisk University Library. Reproduced by permission. **August Wilson,** photograph. AP/Wide World Photos. Reproduced by permission. **Savion**

Glover, (center, with other cast members), performing a number from *Bring in Da Noise, Bring in Da Funk* at the 50th Annual Tony Awards, 1996, photograph. AP/Wide World Photos. Reproduced by permission. **Katherine Dunham,** (striped costume, off shoulders, left hand on hip), photograph. Library of Congress. **Alvin Ailey,** (dancing), photograph. Library of Congress. **Arthur Mitchell,** photograph. AP/Wide World Photos. Reproduced by permission. **Peter Brook standing with Pearl Bailey,** photograph. Library of Congress. **Eubie Blake,** (96-years-old, playing piano), 1979, photograph. AP/Wide World Photos. Reproduced by permission. **John W. Bubbles,** (seated onstage in pinstripe suit and hat), 1979, Newport Jazz Festival, New York, photograph. AP/Wide World Photos. Reproduced by permission. **Charles S. Gilpin,** photograph. Fisk University Library. Reproduced by permission. **Whoopi Goldberg,** Kathy Najimy and Wendy Makkena, from a scene of *Sister Act 2*, photograph. The Kobal Collection. Reproduced by permission. **Dick Gregory,** (turned to his right, loosened tie at collar), photograph. Library of Congress. **Richard B. Harrison,** photograph. Fisk University Library. Reproduced by permission. **Noble Sissle (1) and Frederick O'Neal,** presenting Ethel Waters with an award for her work in *Pinky*, photograph. AP/Wide World Photos. Reproduced by permission.

Classical Music

Francis (Frank) Johnson (sheet music cover for *Boone Infantry Brass Band Quick Step*), illustration. Library of Congress. **Louis Moreau Gottschalk,** (seated next to piano), sheet music cover, lithograph by Sarony. Library of Congress. **Marian Anderson,** (eyes looking up, wearing metallic striped dress), photograph. Courtesy of Hurok Attractions. **Martina Arroyo,** photograph by Camera Press Ltd. Archive Photos. Reproduced by permission. **Grace Bumbry,** photograph. AP/Wide World Photos. Reproduced by permission. **Anthony Davis,** photograph. © AP/Wide World Photos. Reproduced by permission. **R. Nathaniel Dett,** photograph. Fisk University Library. Reproduced by permission. **Leslie Dunner,** (holding Beethoven's "Complete Piano Concertos"), 1992, photograph. AP/WideWorld Photos. Reproduced by permission. **Yolanda King and Simon Estes,** at the premiere of the NBC television production *King*, photograph. © Liaison Agency. Reproduced by permission. **Denyce Graves,** (singing at the White House), photograph by Wilfredo Lee. AP/Wide World Photos. Reproduced by permission. **Roland Hayes,** (turned to his left, suit with vest), photograph. Library of Congress. **Ann Hobson-Pilot,** photograph by Susan Wilson. Reproduced by permission of Susan

Wilson. **Robert Jordan,** photograph. Reproduced by permission of Robert Jordan. **Ulysses Kay,** (gray suit and dark striped tie), photograph by Oscar White. Corbis. Reproduced by permission. **Tania León,** photograph. AP/Wide World Photos. Reproduced by permission. **Bobby McFerrin,** photograph. AP/Wide World Photos. Reproduced by permission. **Awadagin Pratt,** photograph by Marty Reichenthal. AP/Wide World Photos. Reproduced by permission. **Paul Robeson,** performing in the play *Othello*, 1943, photograph. AP/Wide World Photos. Reproduced by permission. **André Watts at the piano,** 1967, photograph by Alix B. Williamson. Reproduced by permission.

Sacred Music Traditions

"Down in the Lonesome Valley: Shout Song of the Freedmen of Port Royal" (title page of sheet music), illustration. Music Division. Library of Congress. **Thomas Dorsey,** photograph. AP/Wide World Photos. Reproduced by permission. **Tabernacle Choir, performing at KFC Music Competition,** photograph. *The Detroit News.* Reproduced by permission. **Yolanda Adams,** photograph. Reproduced by permission of Yolanda Adams. **Andrae Crouch,** photograph. AP/Wide World Photos. Reproduced by permission. **Thomas A. Dorsey,** (wearing an academic robe), photograph. Fisk University Library. Reproduced by permission. **Kirk Franklin,** (holding award, wearing velvet suit), photograph by Pacha. Archive Photos. Reproduced by permission. **Mahalia Jackson,** photograph by Carl Van Vechten. The Estate of Carl Van Vechten. Reproduced by permission. **The Winans Family** (eight men and four women, posed), 1992, photograph by Ameen Howrani. Reproduced by permission of Warner Brothers Records, Inc.

Blues and Jazz

Muddy Waters (seated, singing into a microphone, wearing a light suit), 1980, photograph. AP/Wide World Photos. Reproduced by permission. **Louis Armstrong,** (playing trumpet, age 65), 1965, photograph. AP/Wide World Photos. Reproduced by permission. **Duke Ellington,** (striped suit, hand broom), New York, 1943, photographed by Gordon Parks. Library of Congress. **John Coltrane,** (holding saxophone), photograph. Library of Congress. **Gil Scott-Heron,** photograph. AP/Wide World Photos. Reproduced by permission. **Count Basie,** (playing piano, in light suit), photograph. Library of Congress. **Clarence "Gatemouth" Brown,** (in Western attire, playing guitar), 1995, photograph by Jack Vartoogian. Reproduced by permission. **Cab**

Calloway, (right hand on side of his face), photograph. Fisk University Library. Reproduced by permission. Nat "King" Cole, (crossed arms resting on knees, smiling), photograph. Library of Congress. Miles Davis, (seated, holding trumpet in lap), photograph. Library of Congress. James Reese Europe, (standing, holding wand), photograph. National Archives/U.S. War Department Staff Photo. Ella Fitzgerald (l-r), Oscar Peterson (piano), Roy Eldridge, and Max Roach, 1952, photograph. Bettmann. Reproduced by permission. Lionel Hampton, (at xylophone), photograph. AP/Wide World Photos. Reproduced by permission. W.C. Handy, at his New York publishing office, 1949, photograph. AP/Wide World Photos. Reproduced by permission. Coleman Hawkins, (playing saxaphone), photograph. Library of Congress. Billie Holiday, photograph. AP/Wide World Photos. Reproduced by permission. B.B. King, (playing "Lucille" [guitar]), photograph by Jack Vartoogian. Reproduced by permission. Charles Mingus, photograph. AP/Wide World Photos. Reproduced by permission. Thelonius Monk, (playing piano, wearing a skullcap), 1969, photograph by Jack Vartoogian. Reproduced by permission. Charlie "Bird" Parker, (playing sax, wearing suspenders and striped pants), photograph. Archive Photos. Reproduced by permission. Ma Rainey, (with an unidentified actor), photograph. AP/Wide World Photos. Reproduced by permission. Sonny Rollins, (on stage playing saxophone, leaning to his left), 1996, photograph by Jack Vartoogian. Reproduced by permission. Bessie Smith, (dancing, in costume), photograph. New York Public Library. Billy Taylor, 1993, photograph. AP/Wide World Photos. Reproduced by permission. Dinah Washington, (posing with fingers interlocked), photograph. UPI/Corbis-Bettmann. Reproduced by permission.

Popular Music

Chuck Berry (leaf print shirt), 1994, photograph by Jack Vartoogian. Reproduced by permission. James Brown, (elbow on knee, watch, ring), photograph. Library of Congress. Barry Gordy, photograph by Ron Frehm. AP/Wide World Photos. Reproduced by permission. George Clinton, (on stage blowing bubbles), photograph by Ken Settle. Reproduced by permission. Queen Latifah, (looking up to sky), photograph. AP/Wide World Photos. Reproduced by permission. Erykah Badu, (on stage, performing), photograph by David McNew. Reuters/Archive Photos. Reproduced by permission. Mary J. Blige, (on stage in leather clothes and hat), photograph. AP/Wide World Photos. Reproduced by permission. Ray Charles, (seated at piano), photograph. Library of Congress. Dr. Dre (wearing cap with embroidered marijuana leaf), 1992, photograph by Daniel Jordan. Interscope Records, Inc. Reproduced by permission. Babyface (holding two Grammys), Los Angeles, CA, photograph. AP/Wide World Photos. Reproduced by permission. Aretha Franklin, (close-up, singing, eyes closed, right hand up), 1998, Newport Jazz Festival, photograph. AP/Wide World Photos. Reproduced by permission. Fugees (in crowd performing), photograph. AP/Wide World. Reproduced by permission. Isaac Hayes, (sitted at piano), photograph. AP/Wide World Photos. Reproduced by permission. Ice Cube with Omar Epps in the film *Higher Learning,*" photograph. AP/Wide World Photos. Reproduced by permission. Janet Jackson, accepting Award of Merit at 28th Annual American Music Awards, photograph. AP/Wide World. Reproduced by permission. Etta James, (in dark gown and jacket with metallic embroidery), photograph by Spencer Lennox-Purcell. Private Music. Reproduced by permission. Quincy Jones, (holding up Entertainer of the Year award), 1996, photograph. AP/Wide World Photos. Reproduced by permission. Chaka Khan, (holding Grammy Award), photograph by Doug Pizac. AP/Wide World Photos. Reproduced by permission. Patti LaBelle, (singing), photograph by Jack Vartoogian. Reproduced by permission. Master P (wearing snake skin suit, large medallion), 1999 American Music Awards, photograph by Mark J. Terrill. AP/Wide World Photos. Reproduced by permission. Notorious B.I.G. (at Billboard Music Awards), photograph Mark Lennihan. AP/Wide World Photos. Reproduced by permission. Chuck D. of the rap group Public Enemy (talking to Columbia University students), New York, 1998, photograph. AP/Wide World Photos. Reproduced by permission. Salt 'n' Pepa, Spinderella (Grammy Awards), Los Angeles, 1995, photograph. AP/Wide World Photos. Reproduced by permission. Tupac Shakur, in the film *Poetic Justice,* 1993, photograph by Eli Reed. The Kobal Collection. Reproduced by permission. Luther Vandross, (in an embroidered black jacket), photograph by Ken Settle. Reproduced by permission. Nancy Wilson, (on stage singing, wearing dark beaded floral gown), 1994, photograph by Jack Vartoogian. Reproduced by permission.

Visual and Applied Arts

Yaure mask, carved wood, Ivory Coast, photograph. The University of Iowa Museum of Art, The Stanley Collection, x1986.482. Reproduced by permission. *Newspaper Boy,* painting by Edward Mitchell Bannister, 1869. National Museum of American Art, Washington, DC/Art Resource, NY. Reproduced by permission. *Wedding Day,* photograph by James Van Der Zee, New York City, 1926. Library of Congress. Faith Ringgold, (with painting), photograph by C Love. Reproduced by permission of Faith Ringgold. ***Roots Odyssey,*** photograph of painting. © Romare Bearden Foundation/ Licensed by VAGA, New York, NY. Reproduced by permission. ***Jim,*** plaster sculpture by Selma Burke, photograph by Manu Sassoonian. Schomberg Center for Research in Black Culture. Reproduced by permission. **Barbara Chase-Riboud,** photograph by Jerry Bauer. Reproduced by permission. ***The Awakening of Ethiopia,*** sculpture by Meta Warrick Fuller, photograph. Schomburg Center for Research in Black Culture, New York Public Library/Art Resource, NY. Reproduced by permission. ***In Celebration,*** serigraph on paper by Sam Gilliam, 1987, Smithsonian American Art Museum, Washington, DC, photograph. Art Resource, NY. Reproduced by permission. **Tyree Guyton,** standing in the midst of his installation piece called the *Heidelberg Project,* Detroit, MI, 1997, photograph. AP/ Wide World Photos. Reproduced by permission. ***Ezekiel Saw the Wheels,*** painting by William H. Johnson, photograph. Library of Congress. ***John Brown Series: Drilling Negroes,*** 1942, painting by Jacob Lawrence, photograph. © Francis G. Mayer/Corbis. Reproduced by permission. **Gordon Parks,** with his son, Gordon Jr., (filming *The Giving Tree*), photograph. AP/Wide World Photos. Reproduced by permission. **Marion Perkins,** photograph. AP/Wide World Photos. Reproduced by permission. **Horace Pippin,** (receiving check, painting in background), Philadelphia, 1946, photograph. Corbis-Bettmann/International News Photos. Reproduced by permission. ***Old Mole,*** sculpture by Martin Puryear, after 1941, photograph. © Philadelphia Museum of Art/Corbis. Reproduced by permission. ***Lift Every Voice and Sing,*** sculpture by Augusta Savage, photograph. UPI/Corbis-Bettmann. Reproduced by permission. **Norma Sklarek,** photograph by Mark Schurer. Reproduced by permission of Norma Sklarek. **Willi Smith** pointing to the hemline of a micro-mini skirt he designed, photograph. Bettmann/Corbis. Reproduced by permission. ***Sand Dunes at Sunset, Atlantic City,*** 1885 oil painting by Henry Ossawa Tanner, to hang in the Green Room of the White House, photograph. AP/Wide World Photos. Reproduced by permission. ***Eternal Presence,*** sculpture by John Wilson, photograph. Reproduced by permission of John Wilson.

Science and Technology

Benjamin Banneker, (*Pennsylvania, Delaware, Maryland and Virginia Almanack and Ephemeris, for the Year of Our Lord 1792*), illustration. Rare Book and Special Collections Division. Library of Congress. **Doctor giving physical exam (stethoscope on back) to young boy,** photograph. © 1994 T. McCarthy. Custom Medical Stock Photo, Inc. Reproduced by permission. **Charles Richard Drew,** (with microscope), photograph. AP/Wide World Photos. Reproduced by permission. **Guion S. Bluford Jr., Ronald E. McNair, Frederick Gregory and Charles F. Bolden Jr.,** photograph. U.S. National Aeronautics and Space Administration (NASA). **Shirley Ann Jackson,** (wearing glasses, speaking), photograph. AP/Wide World Photos. Reproduced by permission. **Meredith Gourdine,** (working with research experiment), photograph. AP/Wide World Photos. Reproduced by permission. **Marjorie Lee Browne,** (close-up, bluish cast), photograph. Source unknown. **Dr. Ben Carson,** (with model human brain), photograph. AP/Wide World Photos. Reproduced by permission. **Jewel Plummer-Cobb,** (wearing white blouse under darker jacket), photograph. Reproduced by permission of Jewel Plummer-Cobb. **Matthew A. Henson,** (head and shoulders, wearing fur jacket), illustration. Library of Congress. **Mae C. Jemison,** (holding a model of a NASA aircraft), photograph. U.S. National Aeronautics and Space Administration. **Elijah J. McCoy,** painting, photograph. Fisk University Library. Reproduced by permission. **Norbert Rillieux,** print. Fisk University Library. Reproduced by permission. **Vivien Thomas,** photograph. © The Alan Mason Chesney Medical Archives of Johns Hopkins Medical Institutions. Reproduced by permission.

Sports

Jackie Robinson (sitting sideways, head turned to his right, in uniform), photograph. Archive Photos. Reproduced by permission. **Barry Sanders,** (running with the ball), photograph by Tim Shaefer. AP/Wide World Photos. Reproduced by permission. **Wilt Chamberlain and Bill Russell** (go up to the hoop), Boston, MA, 1969, photograph. Corbis/Bettmann. Reproduced by permission. **Michael Johnson,** (showing his gold medal), photograph by Wolfgang Rattay. Reuter/Archive Photos. Reproduced by permission. **Arthur Ashe,** holding Wimbledon trophy over head, photograph. AP/ Wide World Photos. Reproduced by permission. **Tiger Woods,** Sydney, Australia, 1996, photograph. AP/Wide World Photos. Reproduced by permission. **Lisa Leslie,** (defended by Kym Hampton), photograph by Jeff Geissler. AP/Wide World Photos. Reproduced by permission. **Dominique Dawes,** (performing on balance beam), photograph by Amy Sancetta. AP/Wide World Photos. Reproduced by permission. **Howard Cosell talking with Muhammad Ali,** photograph. Library of Congress. **Jim Brown,** (at microphones, "BROWNS" banner behind), 1998, Cleveland, OH, photograph. AP/ Wide World Photos. Reproduced by permission. **Cynthia Cooper,** (playing basketball with Tracy Reid), photograph by Rick Havner. AP/Wide World Photos. Reproduced by permission. **George Foreman,** (weighing in), Atlantic City, NJ, 1997, photograph by Charles Rex Arbogast. AP/Wide World. Reproduced by permission. **Chamique Holdsclaw** playing basketball, photograph by Wade Payne. AP/Wide World Photos. Reproduced by permission. **Earvin "Magic" Johnson,** during news conference, photograph by Helvio Romero. AP/Wide World Photos. Reproduced by permission. **Jackie Joyner-Kersee,** (on winner's platform), 1992, Barcelona Olympics, photograph. AP/Wide World Photos. Reproduced by permission. **Carl Lewis,** (during long jump event), Barcelona, 1992, photograph. AP/Wide World Photos. Reproduced by permission. **Jesse Owens,** (on winner's platform), Berlin Olympics, with Lutz and Tajiman, 1936, photograph. AP/Wide World Photos. Reproduced by permission. **Eddie Robinson,** (coaching his last home game), 1997, Grambling, LA, photograph. AP/Wide World Photos. Reproduced by permission. **O.J. Simpson,** playing for the Buffalo Bills, Buffalo, NY, photograph. AP/Wide World Photos. Reproduced by permission. **John Thompson,** photograph by Khue Bui. AP/Wide World Photos. Reproduced by permission. **Lenny Wilkens,** during a news conference in Springfield, MA, October 2, 1998, photograph by Elise Amendola. AP/Wide World Photos. Reproduced by permission.

Military

Unidentified sailor, (standing next to railing, in uniform), photograph. Gladstone Collection, Prints and Photographs Division. Library of Congress. **Military camp,** African American soldiers facing cannons, Jacksonville, TN, photograph. Library of Congress. Reproduced by permission. **Christian A. Fleetwood,** (wearing military uniform), photograph. Manuscript Division. Library of Congress. **Henry O. Flipper,** (wearing uniform with white collar), photograph. National Archives and Records Administration. **African American 24th Infantry** leaving Salt Lake City, UT, for Chattanooga, TN, photograph. Gladstone Collection. Prints and Photographs Division. Library of Congress. **Large group of midshipmen reading around table,** photograph. U.S. War Department, National Archives and Records

Administration. **Black soldiers file past tank,** Ponasacco, Italy, 1944, photograph. U.S. Army Photograph. **Female riveter working on assembly line,** photograph. National Archives and Records Administration. **Benjamin O. Davis Jr. with Lee Rayford** (Tuskegee Airmen, standing next to airplane), photograph by Toni Frissell. Prints and Photographs Division. Library of Congress. **Four soldiers (in foxhole with machine gun),** Korea, 1950, photograph. U.S. Army Photograph. **Young Vietnamese woman welcomes black American soldier with garlands of flowers,** photograph. National Archives and Records Administration. **William H. Carney,** photograph. Fisk University Library. Reproduced by permission. **Benjamin O. Davis Sr.** (wearing dress uniform), 1944, photograph. U.S. Army photograph. **Major Charity Adams,** photograph. National Archives and Records Administration. **Marcelite J. Harris,** 1990, photograph. AP/Wide World Photos. Reproduced by permission. **Hazel Johnson with Clifford Alexander,** photograph. AP/Wide World Photos. Reproduced by permission. **Dorie Miller,** (in naval uniform), photograph. Schomburg Center. Reproduced by permission. **J. Paul Reason,** (wearing full military uniform), photograph. U.S. Navy. **Roscoe Robinson,** wearing Army general's uniform, photograph. AP/Wide World Photos. Reproduced by permission. **Department of Defense Manpower: 1980 to 1997,** table created by GGS Information Services for The Gale Group. U.S. Dept. of Defense, *Selected Manpower Statistics,* annual. **Ready Reserve Personnel Profile by Race and Sex: 1990 to 1999,** table created by GGS Information Services for The Gale Group. U.S. Dept. of Defense, *Official Guard and Reserve Manpower Strengths and Statistics,* annual.

Cover

African American congregation, woman crying out as she is "touched by the Spirit," photograph. © Bettmann/Corbis. Reproduced by permission. **Dr. Ben Carson,** (with model human brain), photograph. AP/Wide World Photos. Reproduced by permission. **Marion Jones** at Penn Relays (1,600 meter relay), photograph. AP/Wide World Photos. Reproduced by permission.

1

Chronology

1492. Blacks are among the first explorers to the New World. Pedro Alonzo Niño, identified by some scholars as a black man, arrives with Christopher Columbus.

1501. The Spanish throne officially approves the use of African slaves in the New World.

1502. Portugal brings its first shipload of African slaves to the Western Hemisphere, selling them in what is now Latin America.

1513. Spain authorizes the use of African slaves in Cuba. Thirty black men accompany Balboa when he discovers the Pacific Ocean.

1526. The first group of Africans to set foot on what is now the United States is brought by a Spanish explorer to South Carolina to erect a settlement. The African captives soon flee to the interior, however, and settle with Native Americans.

1538. Estevanico, a black explorer, leads an expedition from Mexico into what is now Arizona and New Mexico.

1562. Britain enters the slave trade when John Hawkins sells a large cargo of African slaves to Spanish planters.

1600. Historical records indicate that by the year 1600 over 900,000 slaves have been brought to Latin America. In the next century, 2,750,000 are added to that total. Slave revolts in the sixteenth century are reported in Hispaniola, Puerto Rico, Panama, Cuba, and Mexico.

1618. The Gambian government grants monopolies to a group of companies established for the purpose of slave trading.

1619, August. Twenty African indentured servants arrive in Jamestown, Virginia, aboard a Dutch vessel. Most indentured servants are released after serving one term, usually seven years in duration, and are allowed to own property and participate in political affairs. The arrival of these indentured servants is the precursor of active slave trade in the English colonies.

1624. The Dutch, who had entered the slave trade in 1621 with the formation of the Dutch West Indies Company, import Africans to serve on Hudson Valley farms.

1629. African slaves are imported into Connecticut. Five years later, the first African slaves in Maryland and Massachusetts arrive. New Amsterdam's first African slaves come ashore in 1637.

1630. Massachusetts enacts a law protecting slaves from abusive owners.

1639. New England enters the slave trade when Captain William Pierce sails to the West Indies and purchases a group of African slaves.

1640. The increasing use of sugar as a cash crop leads to a rapid rise in the African slave population in the West Indies although growth in mainland English colonies remains slow. The African slave population in Barbados, for example, grows from a few hundred in 1640 to 6,000 in 1645. In contrast, there are 300 slaves in Virginia in 1649 and 2,000 by 1671.

1640. Punitive fugitive laws applying to both indentured servants and slaves are enacted in Connecticut, Maryland, New Jersey, South Carolina, and Virginia. The Virginia law, passed in 1642, penalizes violators 20 pounds of tobacco for each night of refuge granted to a fugitive slave. Slaves are branded after a second escape attempt.

1641. Massachusetts becomes the first colony to legalize slavery, adding a modification that forbids capture by "unjust violence." This provision was subsequently adopted by all of the New England colonies.

1643. The groundwork is laid for eighteenth and nineteenth century fugitive slave laws in the United States when an intercolonial agreement of the New England Confederation declares that mere certification by a magistrate is sufficient evidence to convict a runaway slave.

1651. Anthony Johnson, a black man, imports five servants and qualifies to receive a 200-acre land grant

The Portuguese/Dutch fortress, "El Mina," where innumerable captured Africans were gathered for the European slave trade.

along the Puwgoteague River in North Hampton, Virginia. Others soon join Johnson and attempt to launch an independent African community. At its height, the settlement has 12 African homesteads with sizable holdings.

1662. The Virginia colony passes a law providing that the slave or free status of children be determined by the lineage of the mother.

1663. Maryland settlers pass a law stipulating that all imported Africans are to be given the status of slaves. Free white women who marry black slaves are also considered slaves during the lives of their spouses; children of such unions are also to be classified as slaves. In 1681, a law is passed stipulating that children born from a union of a white servant woman and an African are free citizens.

1670. Voting rights are denied to recently freed slaves and indentured servants in Virginia. All non-Christians imported to the territory "by shipping" are to be slaves for life. Slaves who enter Virginia by land route, however, are to serve until the age of 30 if they are children and for 12 years if they are adults when their period of servitude commences.

1672. A Virginia law is enacted providing for a bounty on the heads of Maroons—black fugitives who form communities in the mountains, swamps, and forests of Southern colonies. Many members of Maroon communities attack towns and plantations.

1685. The French *code noir* is enacted in the French West Indies. The code requires religious instruction for African slaves, permits intermarriage, outlaws working of slaves on Sundays and holidays, but forbids emancipation of mulatto children who have reached the age of 21 if their mothers are still enslaved. The code is largely ignored by the French settlers, however.

1688. Mennonites in Germantown, Pennsylvania, sign an anti-slavery resolution, the first formal protest against slavery in the Western Hemisphere. In 1696, Quakers importing slaves are threatened with expulsion from the society.

1700. The population of black slaves in the English colonies is estimated at 28,000. Approximately 23,000 of these slaves reside in the South.

1704. Elias Neau, a French immigrant, opens a "catechism school" for slaves in New York City, New York.

Africans also participated in the European slave trade by capturing and selling fellow Africans for goods and weapons.

1705. The Virginia assembly declares that "no Negro, mulatto, or Indian shall presume to take upon him, act in or exercise any office, ecclesiastic, civil or military." African Americans are forbidden to serve as witnesses in court cases and are condemned to lifelong servitude, unless they have been either Christians in their native land or free men in a Christian country.

1711. The colonial legislature, after receiving intense pressure from the Mennonite and Quaker communities, outlaws slavery in the Pennsylvania colony but is overruled by the British Crown.

1712, April 6. The Maiden Lane slave revolt in New York City claims the lives of nine whites and results in the execution of 21 slaves. Six others commit suicide.

1723. The colony of Virginia enacts laws to limit the rights of freed African Americans. Free African Americans are denied the right to vote and forbidden to carry weapons of any sort.

1739. Three South Carolina slave revolts occur, resulting in the deaths of 51 whites and many more slaves. One of the insurrections results in the death of 30 whites.

1740. The South Carolina colony passes a slave code which forbids slaves from raising livestock, provides that any animals owned by slaves be forfeited, and imposes severe penalties on slaves who make "false appeals" to the governor on the grounds that they have been placed in bondage illegally.

1744. The colony of Virginia amends its 1705 law declaring that African Americans cannot serve as witnesses in court cases; it decides, instead, to admit "any free Negro, mulatto, or Indian being a Christian," as a witness in a criminal or civil suit involving another African American, mulatto, or Indian.

1746. Slave poet Lucy Terry writes *Bars Fight*, a commemorative poem recreating the Deerfield (Massachusetts) Massacre. Terry, generally considered the first African American poet in America, later tries unsuccessfully to convince the board of trustees at Williams College to admit her son to the school.

1747. The South Carolina assembly commends slaves for demonstrating "great faithfulness and courage in repelling attacks of His Majesty's enemies." It then makes provisions for the utilization of African American recruits in the event of danger or emergency.

1749. Prohibitions on the importation of African slaves are approved in a Georgia law, which also attempts to

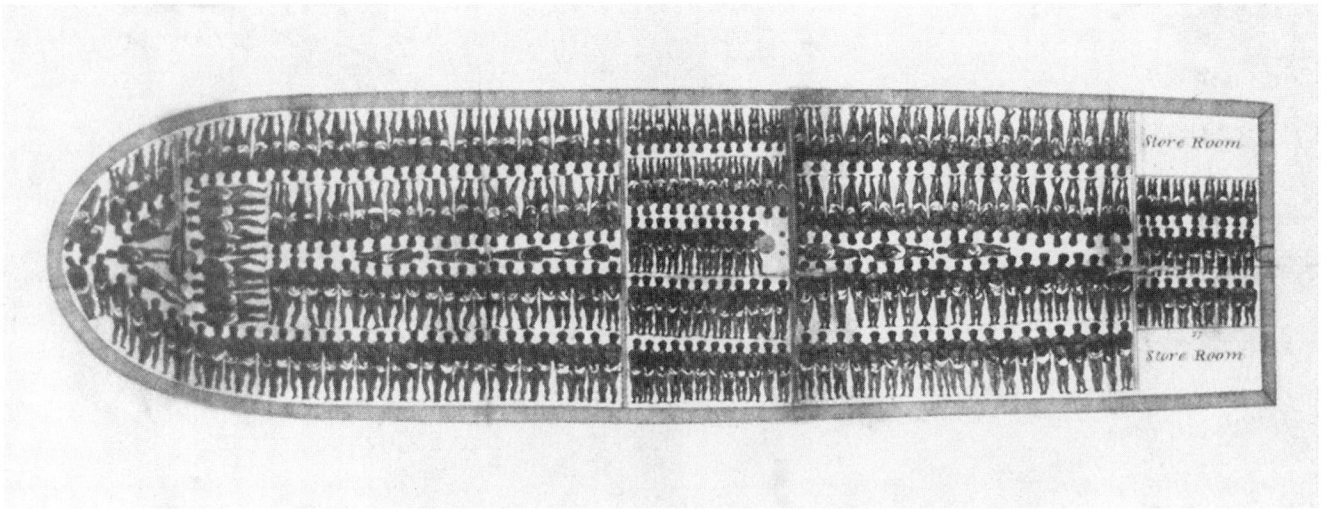

Diagram of the British slave ship, *Brookes,* illustrating the regulated stowing of African slaves.

protect slaves from cruel treatment and from being hired out.

1750. The slave population in the English colonies reaches 236,400, with over 206,000 of the total living south of Pennsylvania. Slaves comprise about 20 percent of the population in the colonies.

1752. George Washington acquires his estate at Mount Vernon, Virginia. Prior to Washington's arrival, there are 18 slaves at Mount Vernon. This number eventually swells to 200. Records indicate that while Washington was concerned for the physical welfare of slaves, he also utilized their services on many occasions and did not advocate their freedom from servitude.

1754. A Quaker, John Woolman, publishes *Some Considerations on the Keeping of Negroes,* an exhortation to fellow members of the Society of Friends to consider emancipating their slaves on grounds of morality. Three years later, some Quakers take legal action against members who ignore this plea.

1760. Jupiter Hammon, an African American poet, publishes *Salvation By Christ With Penitential Cries.*

1767. Phillis Wheatley, a 14-year-old slave, writes *A Poem by Phillis, A Negro Girl, On the Death of Reverend Whitefield.* It is printed in 1770 by the University of Cambridge in New England.

1769. In the Virginia House of Burgesses, Thomas Jefferson unsuccessfully presses for a bill to emancipate African slaves.

1770, March 5. Boston, Massachusetts. Crispus Attucks is shot and killed during the Boston Massacre, becoming one of the first casualties of the American Revolution.

1770. Philadelphia, Pennsylvania. Led by Anthony Benezet, the Quakers open a school for African Americans.

1773. Savannah, Georgia. George Liele and Andrew Bryan organize the first Baptist Church for African Americans in the state.

1774. The Continental Congress demands elimination of the trans-Atlantic slave trade and economic embargoes on all countries participating in it. Rhode Island enacts a law prohibiting slavery. However, this law does not apply to slaves brought into Rhode Island before 1774.

1775. Bunker Hill, Massachusetts. Peter Salem, Salem Poor, and other African Americans fight heroically during the Battle of Bunker Hill.

1775. A German publisher prints Johann Friedrich Blumenbach's article refuting the theory that blacks are racially inferior; it is the first such theory ever in print. In *On the Natural Variety of Mankind,* Blumenbach asserts that the skulls and brains of African Americans are the same as those of Europeans. Blumenbach's paper serves as a counter to the views of French author Voltaire, Scottish philosopher David Hume, and Swedish botanist Carl von Linné (Carolus Linnaeus) that African Americans are akin to apes.

1775. Philadelphia, Pennsylvania. The Continental Congress bars African Americans from serving in the army during the American Revolution.

1775. Philadelphia, Pennsylvania. The first abolitionist society in the United States is organized.

1775. Lord Dunmore, British governor of Virginia, offers freedom to all male slaves who join the loyalist forces. General George Washington, originally opposed to the enlistment of African Americans, is alarmed by the response to the Dunmore proclamation and orders recruiting officers to accept free African Americans for service.

1776. Trenton, New Jersey. Two African Americans, Prince Whipple and Oliver Cromwell, cross the Delaware with George Washington en route to an attack on the British and their Hessian mercenaries in Trenton, New Jersey.

1776. Philadelphia, Pennsylvania. The amended form of the Declaration of Independence, which omits Thomas Jefferson's proposal denouncing slavery, is adopted.

1776. Long Island, New York. French general Marquis de Lafayette praises African American soldiers for successfully assisting Washington's retreat to Long Island. African Americans also help assist Washington's retreat at Trenton and Princeton.

1777. Vermont becomes the first state to abolish slavery.

1778. An African American battalion consisting of 300 former slaves is formed. They are compensated on a par with their white comrades-in-arms and promised freedom after the war. The battalion kills 1,000 Hessians and takes part in a battle at Ponts Bridge in New York.

1779. New York. Alexander Hamilton endorses the plan of South Carolina's Henry Laurens to use slaves as soldiers in the South. "I have not the least doubt that the Negroes will make very excellent soldiers," says Hamilton, ". . . .for their natural faculties are as good as ours." Hamilton reminds the Continental Congress that the British will make use of African Americans if the Americans do not. In Hamilton's words: "The best way to counteract the temptations they will hold out, will be to offer them ourselves."

1780. The Pennsylvania assembly enacts a law providing for the gradual emancipation of slaves.

1782. Thomas Jefferson's *Notes on the State of Virginia* exhibits a curious mixture of perception and naivete with regard to African Americans. On the one hand, Jefferson believes that "the whole commerce between master and slave is a perpetual exercise of the most boisterous passions," On the other hand, he invents the fantasy that African American "griefs are transient."

1783. Slavery in the Commonwealth is abolished by the Massachusetts Supreme Court; African Americans in taxable categories are granted suffrage.

1783. At the end of the American Revolution, some 10,000 African Americans have served in the continental armies—5,000 as regular soldiers.

1787. New York City, New York. The African Free School is opened by the New York Manumission Society.

1787. Congress passes the Northwest Ordinance which forbids the extension of slavery into this area.

1787. Philadelphia, Pennsylvania. African American preachers Richard Allen and Absalom Jones organize the Free African Society.

1787. The Constitution of the United States is adopted. In it, importation of slaves cannot be prohibited before 1808, and five slaves are considered the equivalent of three free men in congressional apportionment.

1790. According to the first census, there are 757,000 African Americans in the United States, comprising 19 percent of the total population. Nine percent of African Americans are free.

1790. Dominican Republic. African Americans comprise seven-eighths of the island's 529,000 inhabitants. Less than 3 percent are free. Mulattoes in French Santo Domingo own 10 percent of the slaves and land.

1790. Chicago, Illinois. Jean Baptiste Pointe du Sable, the son of a French mariner and an African slave mother, establishes the first permanent settlement at what is to become the city of Chicago.

1791. Washington, DC. On the recommendation of Thomas Jefferson, Benjamin Banneker—astronomer, inventor, mathematician, and gazetteer—is appointed to serve as a member of the commission charged with laying out plans for the city of Washington.

1791. Toussaint L'Ouverture, a self-educated Haitian slave, leads an unsuccessful uprising.

1791. Twenty-three slaves are hanged and three white sympathizers deported, following suppression of a Louisiana slave revolt.

1791. Philadelphia, Pennsylvania. Congress excludes African Americans and Indians from serving in peacetime militias.

1793. Mulberry Grove, Georgia. Eli Whitney patents the cotton gin, which strengthens slavery by vastly increasing profits in cotton growing.

1793. Philadelphia, Pennsylvania. Congress passes the Fugitive Slave Act, which makes it a criminal offense to harbor a slave or prevent his or her arrest.

1793. The state of Virginia passes a law that forbids free African Americans from entering the state.

1794. Philadelphia, Pennsylvania. The First African Church of St. Thomas, the first African American Episcopal Congregation in the United States, is dedicated. This same year, Richard Allen organizes the Bethel Church, an African American Methodist Episcopal Church.

Slaves working on a cotton plantation in Beaufort, South Carolina, c.1860.

1795. Several slave uprisings are suppressed with some 50 African Americans killed and executed.

1796. Tennessee. Tennessee is admitted to the Union as a slave state. The state's constitution, however, does not deny suffrage to free African Americans.

1797. North Carolina. Congress refuses to accept the first recorded anti-slavery petition seeking redress against a North Carolina law which requires that slaves, although freed by their Quaker masters, be returned to the state and to their former condition.

1798. Washington, DC. Secretary of the Navy Stoddert forbids the deployment of African American sailors on man-of-war ships, in violation of a nonracial enlistment policy which had been operative in the U.S. Navy for many years. Nevertheless, a few African Americans slip past the ban including William Brown, who serves as a "powder monkey" on the *Constellation* and George Diggs, quartermaster of the schooner *Experiment*.

1799. Mount Vernon, Virginia. George Washington dies. His last will and testament declares: "It is my will and desire that all the slaves which I hold in my right, shall receive their freedom."

1800. Richmond, Virginia. Gabriel Prosser, a slave insurrectionist, plans to lead thousands of slaves in an attack on Richmond. The plan fails and Prosser and 15 of his followers are arrested, tried, and hanged.

1800. Washington, DC. By a vote of 85–1, Congress rejects a petition by free African Americans in Philadelphia to gradually end slavery in the United States.

1803. South Carolina. The state legislature, which had been trying to limit importation of slaves, reopens the slave trade with Latin America and the West Indies.

1804. New Jersey. New Jersey passes an emancipation law. All states north of the Mason-Dixon Line now have laws forbidding slavery or providing for its gradual elimination.

1804. Ohio. The legislature enacts the first of a group of laws restricting the rights and movements of African Americans. Other western states soon follow suit. Illinois, Indiana, and Oregon later have anti-immigration clauses in their state constitutions.

1807. New Jersey. The state alters its 1776 constitution by limiting the vote to free white males.

A group of Africans disembarking from a slave ship in Jamestown, Virginia.

1808, January 1. Congress bars the importation of any new slaves into the territory of the United States (effective January 1, 1808). The law is widely ignored.

1808. The 1807 ban on the importation of slaves is scheduled to take effect. There are one million slaves in the country.

1810. Louisiana. Courts declare in *Adelle v. Beauregard* that an African American is free unless it is otherwise proven.

1811. Delaware. The state forbids the immigration of free African Americans and declares that any native-born free African American who has lived outside of Delaware for more than six months will be deemed a nonresident.

1811. Louisiana. U.S. troops suppress a slave uprising in two parishes (counties) of Louisiana, some 35 miles from New Orleans. The revolt is led by Charles Deslands. Some 100 slaves are killed or executed.

1811. Westport, Connecticut. Paul Cuffe, son of African American and Indian parents and later a wealthy shipbuilder, sails with a small group of African Americans to Sierra Leone to underscore his advocacy of an African American return to Africa.

1812. Louisiana. Louisiana is admitted to the Union as a slave state. State law enables freed men to serve in the state militia.

1815. Fort Blount, Florida. African Americans and Creek Indians capture Fort Blount from Seminoles and use it as a haven for escaped slaves and a base for attacks on slave owners. An American army detachment eventually recaptures the fort.

1816. Baltimore, Maryland. Bethel Charity School is founded by Daniel Coker, an African American.

1816. Louisiana. State laws are enacted which prohibit slaves from testifying against whites and free blacks, except in cases involving slave uprisings.

1816. New Orleans, Louisiana. James P. Beckwourth, an African American and one of the great explorers of the nineteenth century, signs on as a scout for General William Henry Ashley's Rocky Mountain expedition.

1816. Philadelphia, Pennsylvania. The African Methodist Episcopal Church is organized.

1816. Virginia. A slave rebellion led by George Boxley, a white man, fails.

1816. Washington, DC. The American Colonization Society, which seeks to transport free African Americans to Africa, is organized. Protest meetings are subsequently held by many free African Americans in opposition to the society's efforts.

1817. Mississippi. Mississippi enters the union as a slave state. New York passes a gradual slavery abolition act.

1818. Connecticut. African Americans are denied the right to vote in Connecticut.

1818. Philadelphia, Pennsylvania. Free African Americans form the Pennsylvania Augustine Society "for the education of people of colour."

1819. Alabama. Alabama enters the Union as a slave state, although its constitution provides the legislature with the power to abolish slavery and compensate slave owners. Other measures include jury trials for slaves accused of crimes above petty larceny and penalties for malicious killing of slaves.

1820. Liberia. The *Mayflower of Liberia* sails for the West African nation of Sierra Leone with 86 African Americans aboard.

1820, March 3. The Missouri Compromise is enacted. It provides for Missouri's entry into the Union as a slave state and Maine's entry as a free state. There are thus 12 slave and 12 free states in the United States. All territory north of latitude 36°30' is declared free; all territory south of that line is open to slavery.

1821. New York City, New York. The African Methodist Episcopal Zion Church is founded with James Varick as its first bishop.

1821. New York. The state constitutional convention alters the voting requirements of 1777 by establishing higher property and longer residence requirements for African Americans.

1822. Charleston, South Carolina. The Denmark Vesey conspiracy, one of the most elaborate slave revolts on record, fails. Vesey, a sailor and carpenter, and 36 collaborators are hanged, an additional 130 blacks and four whites are arrested, and stricter controls are imposed on free African Americans and slaves. Following this insurrection, slave states adopt laws to further restrict the mobility of African Americans.

1822. Rhode Island. Free African Americans are denied the right to vote in Rhode Island.

1822. Liberia. Liberia is founded by African Americans with the aid of the American Colonization Society.

1823. Mississippi. A law is enacted in Mississippi which prohibits the teaching of reading and writing to African Americans and meetings of more than five slaves or free African Americans.

1824. As the United States moves toward universal male suffrage, more states in the North and West as well as the South move to deny the vote to African Americans. Illinois, Indiana, Iowa, and Michigan require African Americans to post bond in guarantee of good behavior.

1825. Maryland. Josiah Henson leads a group of slaves to freedom in Kentucky. Henson later crosses the border into Ontario and becomes leader of a community of former slaves.

1826. Virginia. Thomas Jefferson dies. His will stipulates that only five of his many slaves should be freed. The remainder are bequeathed to his heirs.

1827, March 16. New York City, New York. *Freedom's Journal*, the first African American newspaper, begins publication.

1827, July 4. New York. Slavery is abolished in New York.

1828. Bennington, Vermont. William Lloyd Garrison, a journalist and reformer, writes his first anti-slavery article in the *National Philanthropist*.

1829. Boston, Massachusetts. David Walker, a free African American, publishes the anti-slavery pamphlet *An Appeal to the Colored People of the World*, which is distributed throughout the country and arouses a furor among slaveholders.

1829. Cincinnati, Ohio. After a riot in which whites attack black residents in Cincinnati and loot and burn their homes, 1,200 blacks flee to Canada.

1829. Philadelphia. The first National Negro Convention convenes.

1830. North Carolina. Slavemasters, in compliance with a state law, transfer control of more than 400 slaves to Quaker residents of North Carolina. The Quakers retain theoretical ownership, but allow slaves virtual freedom until they can afford to transport them to free states.

1830. Philadelphia, Pennsylvania. The first National Negro Convention meets on September 20 at Philadelphia's Bethel Church. The four-day convention launches a church-affiliated program to improve the social status of African Americans.

1830. In an attempt to counter the increasing strength of the abolitionist movement, a number of states pass laws restricting the education, legal safeguards, and citizenship rights of slaves and free African Americans. Many states require the deportation of free African Americans; slave codes are enforced more strictly and the number of slave emancipations decline.

1830. The U.S. Census Bureau reports that 3,777 African American heads of families own slaves, mostly in Louisiana, Maryland, Virginia, North Carolina, and South Carolina.

1831, January 1. Boston, Massachusetts. *The Liberator*, an abolitionist newspaper, is founded by William Lloyd Garrison.

1831. Philadelphia, Pennsylvania. The first Annual Convention of the People of Color meets at Wesleyan Church, where delegates from five states resolve to study African American conditions, explore settlement possibilities in Canada, and raise money for an industrial college in New Haven. Delegates oppose the American Colonization Society and recommend annual meetings.

1831, August. Southampton County, Virginia. Nat Turner leads the biggest slave rebellion in history. Some 60 whites are killed and the entire South is thrown into panic. Turner is captured on October 30 and hanged in Jerusalem, Virginia, 12 days later.

1831. Virginia. Thomas Dew, a legislator, proudly refers to Virginia as a "Negro-raising state" for the nation. Between 1830 and 1860, Virginia exports some 300,000 slaves, and South Carolina exports 179,000. The price of slaves increases sharply due to expanding territory in which slaves are permitted and a booming economy in products harvested and processed by slave labor.

1832. Boston, Massachusetts. The New England Anti-Slavery Society is established by 12 whites at the African Baptist Church on Boston's Beacon Hill.

1833. Philadelphia, Pennsylvania. Black and white abolitionists organize the American Anti-Slavery Society.

1834. South Carolina. South Carolina enacts a law prohibiting the teaching of African American children, either free or slave.

1834. Great Britain. Parliament abolishes slavery in the British Empire; 700,000 slaves are liberated at a cost of 20 million British pounds sterling.

1835. North Carolina. North Carolina, the last Southern state to deny suffrage to African Americans, repeals a voting rights provision of the state constitution. The state also makes it illegal for whites to teach free blacks.

1835. Washington, DC. President Andrew Jackson seeks to restrict the mailing of abolitionist literature to the South.

1836. Washington, DC. The U.S. House of Representatives adopts the "gag rule" which prevents congressional action on anti-slavery resolutions or legislation.

1837. Alton, Illinois. Elijah P. Lovejoy, an abolitionist, is murdered by a mob in Alton after refusing to stop publishing anti-slavery material.

1837. Boston, Massachusetts. A series of abolitionist works are published including Reverend Hosea Eaton's *A Treatise on the Intellectual Character and Political Condition of the Colored People of the United States.*

1837. Canada. African Americans are given the right to vote in Canada.

1839. Montauk, New York. The slaveship *Amistad* is brought into Montauk by a group of Africans who have revolted against their captors. The young African leader, Joseph Cinque, and his followers are defended before the U.S. Supreme Court by former President John Quincy Adams and awarded their freedom.

1839. Warsaw, New York. The first anti-slavery political organization, the Liberty Party, is founded. African American abolitionists Samuel R. Ward and Henry Highland Garnet are among its leading supporters. The party urges boycotts of Southern crops and products.

1839. Washington, DC. The U.S. State Department rejects an African American's application for a passport on the grounds that African Americans are not citizens.

1840. Massachusetts. Massachusetts repeals a law forbidding intermarriage between whites and blacks, mulattoes, or Indians.

1840. New York. These states institute a law advocating jury trials for fugitive slaves.

1840. Pope Gregory XVI declares the Roman Catholic Church's opposition to slavery and the slave trade.

1841. Massachusetts. Frederick Douglass begins his career as a lecturer with the Massachusetts Anti-Slavery Society.

1841. Throughout the country, increasingly restrictive segregation statutes are enacted. The New York state legislature grants school districts the right to segregate their educational facilities. South Carolina forbids white and black mill hands from looking out the same window. Whites and blacks in Atlanta are required to swear on different Bibles in court.

1841. Hampton, Virginia. Slaves aboard the vessel *Creole* revolt en route from Hampton, Virginia, to New Orleans. The slaves overpower the crew and sail the ship to the Bahamas, where they are granted asylum and freedom.

1842. Boston, Massachusetts. The capture of George Latimer, an escaped slave, precipitates the first of several famous fugitive slave cases straining North-South relations. Latimer is later purchased from his master by Boston abolitionists.

1842. Rhode Island. African Americans are granted the right to vote in Rhode Island.

This building was used to hold Nat Turner and other participants in the largest slave rebellion in U.S. history.

1842. Washington, DC. In the case *Prigg v. Pennsylvania*, the U.S. Supreme Court finds a Pennsylvania anti-kidnapping law unconstitutional, claiming that the authority to regulate the recapture of fugitive slaves was an exclusive power of Congress. The case arises when Edward Prigg is convicted of kidnapping for his recapture of an escaped slave.

1843. Buffalo, New York. Henry Highland Garnet calls for a slave revolt and general strike while addressing the National Convention of Colored Men. Garnet, Samuel R. Ward, and Charles Ray participate in the Liberty Party convention, becoming the first African Americans to take part in a national political gathering.

1843. Massachusetts. The Massachusetts and Vermont state legislatures defy the Fugitive Slave Act and forbid state officials from imprisoning or assisting federal authorities in the recapture of escaped slaves.

1843. Washington, DC. The Webster-Ashburton Treaty, in which Britain and the United States agree to prevent slave ships from reaching the African coast in order to suppress the slave trade there, is approved. No agreement is reached, however, to restrict slave trade within the Western Hemisphere.

1845. Washington, DC. The U.S. Congress overturns the gag rule of 1836. Texas is admitted to the Union as a slave state.

1847. New York. The plan of abolitionist Gerritt Smith to parcel up thousands of acres of his land in New York fails to attract prospective African American farmers. Lack of capital among African Americans and the infertility of the land doom the project.

1847. Rochester, New York. Frederick Douglass publishes the first issue of his abolitionist newspaper *The North Star.*

1847. St. Louis, Missouri. Dred Scott files suit for his freedom in the Circuit Court of St. Louis.

1848. Buffalo, New York. The convention of the Free Soil Party is attended by a number of African American abolitionists.

1848. Virginia. Postmasters are forced to inform police of the arrival of pro-abolition literature and turn it over to authorities for burning.

A depiction of the execution of Captain Ferrer by the African slaves aboard the *Amistad* in 1839.

1849. Maryland. Harriet Tubman, soon to be a conductor on the Underground Railroad, escapes from slavery. Tubman later returns to the South no less than 19 times to help transport more than 300 slaves to freedom. In the same year, the Maryland legislature enacts laws to override restrictions on the importation of slaves.

1849. Maryland. The Maryland Supreme Court establishes the "separate but equal" doctrine in response to a suit brought by Benjamin Roberts to have his daughter admitted to a white school.

1850. New York. Samuel R. Ward becomes president of the American League of Colored Laborers, a union of skilled African American workers who train African American craftsmen and encourage African American-owned business.

1850. Washington, DC. The Compromise of 1850, also known as Clay's Compromise, is enacted, strengthening the 1793 Fugitive Slave Act. Federal officers are now offered a fee for the slaves they apprehend. California is admitted to the union as a free state.

1851. Virginia. New laws require freed slaves to leave Virginia within a year or be enslaved again.

1852. Akron, Ohio. Sojourner Truth addresses the National Women's Suffrage Convention.

1852. Boston, Massachusetts. The first edition of Harriet Beecher Stowe's controversial *Uncle Tom's Cabin* is published.

1853. London. William Wells Brown publishes *Clotel, Or, The President's Daughter: A Narrative of Slave Life in the United States*, the first published African American novel.

1853. Oxford, Pennsylvania. Lincoln University, the first African American college, is founded as Ashmum Institute.

1854. Boston, Massachusetts. Anthony Burns, a fugitive slave, is arrested and escorted through the streets of Boston by U.S. troops prior to being returned to his master. His master refuses an offer of $1,200 from Boston abolitionists attempting to purchase his freedom.

1854. The New England Emigration Society is founded to help settle former slaves in Kansas.

1854. Under the Kansas-Nebraska Act, the territories of Kansas and Nebraska are admitted to the Union

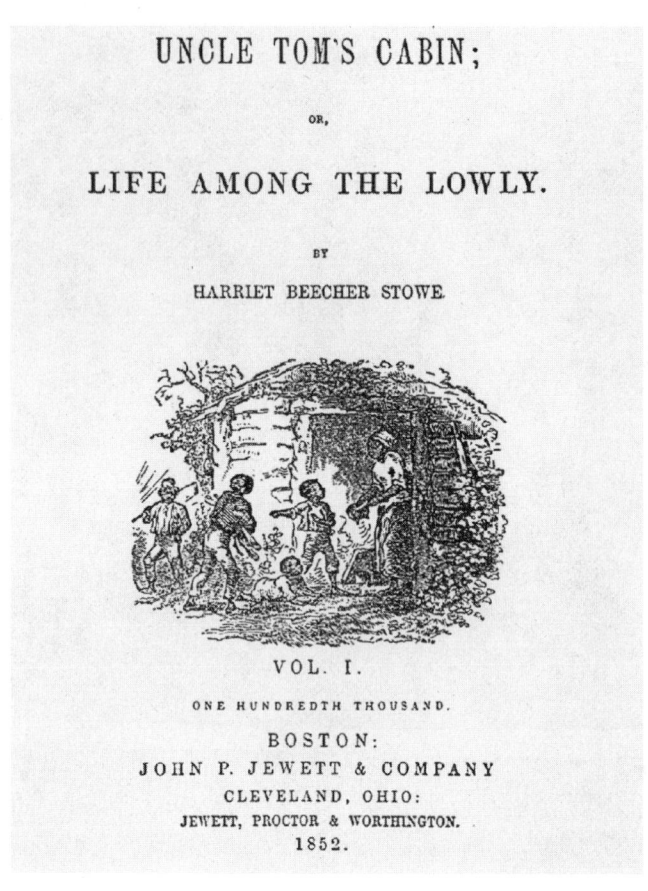

Title page from Harriet Beecher Stowe's *Uncle Tom's Cabin.*

Anthony Burns.

without slavery restrictions, in direct contradiction to the provisions of the Missouri Compromise of 1820.

1855. Maine and Massachusetts.   The slavery issue is further polarized by enactment in these states of laws forbidding state officials from aiding the federal government in enforcement of the fugitive slave laws. The Massachusetts legislature abolishes school segregation and integration proceeds without incident.

1855. New York.   The Liberty Party nominates Frederick Douglass for secretary of the U.S. State Department.

1856. Kansas.   Pro-slavery forces sack the town of Lawrence, noted for its abolitionist, free-soil sentiment.

1857. Maine.   Maine, in defiance of the fugitive slave laws, grants freedom and citizenship to people of African descent.

1857, March 6. Washington, DC.   In the *Dred Scott v. Sandford* decision, the U.S. Supreme Court, by a 6–3 vote, opens federal territory to slavery, denies citizenship rights to African Americans, and decrees that slaves do not become free when taken into free territory. The *Dred Scott* decision is followed by a ruling that African Americans are not entitled to land grants.

1858. Vicksburg, Mississippi.   The Southern Commercial Convention calls for reestablishment of the slave trade, despite opposition from Tennessee and Florida delegations.

1859. Baltimore, Maryland.   Businessmen attending a slaveholders convention complain that free African American laborers and entrepreneurs monopolize some service industries. However, a resolution to expel free African Americans from the state fails.

1859, October 16. Harpers Ferry, West Virgina. John Brown and his followers seize the U.S. Armory. Two African Americans are killed, two are captured, one escapes. Brown is captured and hanged at Charles Town, West Virginia.

1859. Washington, DC.   In the case of *Ableman v. Booth*, the U.S. Supreme Court upholds the Fugitive Slave Act of 1850. The case arises when Sherman Booth rescues a fugitive slave from a Wisconsin jail and is charged by federal marshals with violating federal law.

1860.   As the Civil War approaches, the United States is sharply divided between pro- and anti-slavery forces. In Virginia, a law stipulates that free African Americans

Ho for Kansas!

Brethren, Friends, & Fellow Citizens:

I feel thankful to inform you that the

REAL ESTATE

AND

Homestead　Association,

Will Leave Here the

15th of April, 1878,

In pursuit of Homes in the Southwestern
Lands of America, at Transportation
Rates, cheaper than ever
was known before.

For full information inquire of

Benj. Singleton, better known as old Pap,

NO. 5 NORTH FRONT STREET.

Beware of Speculators and Adventurers, as it is a dangerous thing
to fall in their hands.

Nashville, Tenn., March 18, 1878.

This advertisement served to encourage African Americans to migrate to the Nicodemus, Kansas settlement.

Dred Scott was the plaintiff in one of America's most important legal cases regarding the status of slavery.

can be sold into slavery for committing imprisonable offenses. Maryland forbids emancipation of slaves. President James Buchanan advocates a constitutional amendment confirming the Fugitive Slave Acts. The Democratic party platform supports the *Dred Scott v. Sandford* decision. The Republican platform opposes the expansion of slavery into the western territories, and Abraham Lincoln, still a moderate on the subject of abolition, is elected president. On December 17, South Carolina secedes from the Union.

1861. Fort Sumter, South Carolina. Confederate forces attack Fort Sumter, South Carolina, marking the beginning of Civil War. Jefferson Davis is elected president of the Confederate States of America and defends slavery as necessary to "self-preservation." The Confederates conscript slaves for military support jobs. Some Confederate states use free African Americans in their armed forces.

1861. Washington, DC. The secretary of the U.S. Navy solicits enlistment of African Americans into the Union Army, but most African American offers to help militarily are rejected. Federal policy toward liberated

slaves is erratic, depending mostly on the viewpoint of individual commanders. Lincoln moves warily, counter-manding General Freemont's order that slaves of masters who fight against the Union are to be "declared free men."

1862. New York. The National Freedmen's Relief Association, one of many groups dedicated to assist slaves in making the transition to freedom, is formed. Groups in Philadelphia, Cincinnati, and Chicago are eventually consolidated as the American Freedmen's Aid Commission.

1862. Washington, DC. The U.S. Congress authorizes the enlistment of African Americans for military service in the Union Army.

1862. Washington, DC. President Abraham Lincoln proposes a plan for the gradual, compensated emancipation of slaves. Included is a provision to subsidize emigration to Haiti or Liberia. Lincoln's cautious policies are clarified in a letter to Horace Greeley in which he states his paramount objective as saving the Union "not either to save or destroy slavery." However, Lincoln does sign bills abolishing slavery in the territories and freeing slaves of masters disloyal to the United States. Military commanders are forbidden from returning fugitive slaves to owners and, in September, Lincoln issues an ultimatum giving hostile areas until January 1 to cease fighting or lose their slaves.

1863. Cow Island, Haiti. Lincoln sends a ship to bring back 500 African American settlers after a colonization attempt in Haiti fails.

1863. New York. In anti-draft riots, 1200 people, mostly African Americans, are killed. The riot is spurred in part by the provision that exemption from military service can be bought for $300, a provision bitterly resented by poor white immigrants who vent their frustrations on blacks.

1863, January 1. Washington, DC. Lincoln issues the Emancipation Proclamation, declaring freedom for all slaves in rebellious areas.

1864. Louisiana. The Louisiana legislature, elected under auspices of occupying Union forces, votes to abolish slavery. However, it denies suffrage to African Americans.

1864. Virginia. Fourteen African American soldiers are awarded the Medal of Honor by President Lincoln.

1865. Montgomery, Alabama. Jefferson Davis authorizes the enlistment of African Americans into the Confederate Army. However, Davis stipulates that the number of African American troops cannot exceed 25 percent of the able-bodied slave population.

1865. Appomattox, Virginia. The Confederacy surrenders. Of the 179,000 African Americans who served in the Union Army, 3,000 were killed in battle, 26,000 died from disease, and 14,700 deserted. African Americans represented nine to ten percent of the Union's armed forces.

1865. Tennessee. The Ku Klux Klan is formed with the purpose of reasserting white supremacy in the South.

1865. All-white legislatures in many states enact black codes. These codes impose heavy penalties for "vagrancy," "insulting gestures," "curfew violations," and "seditious speeches." South Carolina requires African Americans entering the state to post a $1,000 bond in guarantee of good behavior and entitles employers to whip African American employees.

1865. Wisconsin. Wisconsin, Connecticut, and Minnesota deny suffrage to African Americans.

1865. Washington, DC. Abraham Lincoln is assassinated. The new president, Andrew Johnson, calls for ratification of the Thirteenth Amendment, but opposes African American suffrage. The Thirteenth Amendment, abolishing slavery and involuntary servitude in all of the United States, is ratified December 16, 1865.

1865, December 6. Washington, DC. Congress establishes the Freedmen's Bureau and passes the Thirteenth Amendment to the Constitution which abolishes slavery.

1866. Memphis, Tennessee. In a race riot in Memphis, 48 blacks and 2 white sympathizers are killed. Also, 35 blacks are killed in a riot in New Orleans.

1866. Washington, DC. Congress passes civil rights legislation despite President Johnson's veto. The act is intended to nullify the black codes. In the District of Columbia, a referendum is held on African American suffrage. Over 6,500 vote against extension of the franchise to African Americans; only 35 favor it. The Fourteenth Amendment passes the House and Senate despite opposition from Johnson.

1867. Iowa. Iowa and the Dakota Territory grant suffrage to African Americans.

1868. Hampton, Virginia. Samuel Chapman Armstrong, a former Union officer, founds Hampton Institute.

1868. Nine states grant suffrage to African Americans, but two deny it. The Republican party platform omits demand for African American suffrage in Northern states.

1868. Many states are readmitted to the Union. The Alabama legislature votes to racially segregate all state schools.

1868. Louisiana. Oscar Dunn, a former slave and captain in the Union Army, is elected lieutenant governor of Louisiana.

1868. South Carolina. The South Carolina House is the first state legislature to have a majority of African Americans. Blacks outnumber whites 87 to 40 in the South Carolina legislature, but whites maintain a majority in the state Senate.

1868. Washington, DC. The Fourteenth Amendment is ratified, establishing the concept of "equal protection" for all citizens under the U.S. Constitution. President Johnson's veto of the bill granting vote to African Americans in the District of Columbia is overridden by Congress.

1869. Washington, DC. The Colored National Labor Union is organized and advocates purchase and distribution of land.

1870. Washington, DC. Recruitment of African Americans for the U.S. Cavalry intensifies. By 1890, 14 African American cavalrymen had received Medals of Honor for bravery in campaigns in the West.

1870. Washington, DC. The Fifteenth Amendment to the Constitution, guaranteeing all citizens the right to vote, is ratified.

Following the arrival of Union troops, African American slaves fled Richmond, Virginia, by means of barges.

1871. Washington, DC. Congress enacts the Ku Klux Klan Act to enforce the provisions of the Fourteenth Amendment.

1874. Washington, DC. Reverend Patrick F. Healy is named president of Georgetown, the oldest Catholic university in the United States.

1875. Kentucky. Oliver Lewis, an African American jockey, rides the horse Aristides to victory in the first Kentucky Derby.

1875. Washington, DC. Congress passes civil rights legislation prohibiting discrimination in such public accommodations as hotels, theaters, and amusement parks.

1876. Hamburg, South Carolina. Federal troops are sent by President Ulysses S. Grant to restore order after five African Americans are killed.

1876. Washington, DC. In *United States v. Cruikshank*, the Supreme Court declares that the Fourteenth Amendment provides African Americans with equal protection under the law but does not add anything "to the rights which one citizen has under the Constitution against another." The Court rules that

"the right of suffrage is not a necessary attribute of national citizenship."

1878. Washington, DC. In the case *Hall v. DeCuir*, the U.S. Supreme Court rules that states cannot prohibit segregation on public transportation.

1878. Washington, DC. The U.S. attorney general reveals widespread intimidation of African Americans attempting to vote and stuffing of ballot boxes in several Southern states.

1879. Frustrated by poverty and discrimination, large numbers of African Americans start to emigrate north and west. A leader of the emigration movement is Benjamin "Pap" Singleton, a former slave who had earlier escaped to Canada and favors separate African American communities. Emigration is vigorously opposed by many whites, some of whom prevent ships from transporting blacks on the Mississippi River.

1879. Washington, DC. Upon hearing the case of *Strauder v. West Virginia*, the U.S. Supreme Court rules that the Fourteenth Amendment ensures blacks all rights that, under law, are enjoyed by whites. In a separate case, the Court rules that one of the purposes of both the Thirteenth and Fourteenth Amendments is

Recently freed African Americans searching for employment opportunities.

to raise the condition of blacks to one of perfect equality with whites.

1881. Tennessee passes a "Jim Crow" railroad law which sets a trend soon taken up by Florida (1887), Mississippi (1888), Texas (1889), Louisiana (1890), and a host of other Southern and border states.

1881. Tuskegee, Alabama. Booker T. Washington opens Tuskegee Institute with a $2,000 appropriation from the Alabama legislature.

1883. Washington, DC. Upon hearing a set of cases challenging the Civil Rights Act of 1875, the U.S. Supreme Court declares the act unconstitutional.

1884. New York. The first issue of the *New York Age* is published by T. Thomas Fortune.

1884. Washington, DC. Former Reconstruction Representative John Roy Lynch is elected temporary chairman of the Republican convention—the first African American to preside over a national political gathering.

1884. Memphis, Tennessee. Fiery journalist Ida Wells-Barnett is successful in her suit against the Chesapeake, Ohio, and Southwestern Railroad Company for racial segregation on a trip from Memphis to Woodstock.

The Tennessee Supreme Court reverses the decision on April 5, 1887.

1888. Richmond, Virginia. Two African American banks are founded—the Savings Bank of the Grand Fountain United Order of True Reformers in Virginia and the Capital Savings Bank in Washington, DC.

1889. Washington, DC. Frederick Douglass is appointed U.S. Minister to Haiti.

1890. Mississippi. The Mississippi constitutional convention begins the systematic exclusion of African Americans from the political arena by adopting literacy and other complex "understanding" tests as prerequisites to voting. Seven other Southern states follow suit.

1890. Washington, DC. In the *In re Green* decision, the U.S. Supreme Court sanctions control of elections by state officials, thus weakening federal protection for Southern black voters. In the case *Louisville, New Orleans and Texas Railway v. Mississippi*, the Court permits states to segregate public transportation facilities.

1891. Baffin Bay, Greenland. Matthew Henson accompanies Admiral Robert E. Peary in his exploration of the Arctic.

1891. Chicago, Illinois. Daniel Hale Williams, physician and surgeon, founds Provident Hospital with the first training school for African American nurses in the United States.

1895. Atlanta, Georgia. Booker T. Washington delivers his famous "Atlanta Compromise" speech at the Cotton States International Exposition.

1896. Cambridge, Massachusetts. W. E. B. Du Bois publishes *Suppression of the African Slave Trade*, the first of some 20 annual sociological studies of African Americans in the United States.

1896. Washington, DC. The National Association of Colored Women, a politically active self-help group, is formed.

1896. Washington, DC. The U.S. Supreme Court in the *Plessy v. Ferguson* decision upholds the doctrine of "separate but equal," paving the way for segregation of African Americans in all aspects of life.

1898. Louisiana. The addition of a "grandfather clause" to the state constitution enables poor whites to qualify for the franchise while curtailing black voter registration. In 1896, there were over 130,000 African American voters on the Louisiana rolls. Four years later, that number has been reduced to roughly 5,000.

1898. Santiago, Cuba. Four African American regiments in the U.S. Army compile an outstanding combat record in and around Santiago during the Spanish-American War. Five African Americans receive Medals of Honor. At the close of the war, over 100 African Americans are promoted to officer status.

1900. Boston, Massachusetts. Booker T. Washington organizes the National Negro Business League.

1900. London, England. W. E. B. Du Bois attends the conference of the African and New World Intellectuals, where he delivers an address incorporating his famous dictum: "The problem of the twentieth century is the problem of the color line." Du Bois also attends the first Pan-African Congress, an international body of concerned African nations protesting Western imperialism and promoting the concept of self-government among colonized peoples.

1902. Richmond, Virginia. Virginia joins other Southern states in adopting the "grandfather clause" as a means of denying African Americans access to the polls.

1903. Georgia. Whites attack blacks in riots, which are spurred by charges that blacks have murdered whites.

1903. Washington, DC. Upon hearing the case *Giles v. Harris*, the U.S. Supreme Court rules that it cannot remedy discrimination in voter registration.

1904. Atlanta, Georgia. Financier Andrew Carnegie brings together a group of prominent African American leaders, including Booker T. Washington and W. E. B. Du Bois, who discuss "the interests of the Negro race." The personal and ideological differences between Washington and Du Bois are evident at the meeting, though there is agreement that the group should press for "absolute civil, political, and public equality." The group shows little fire in advancing familiar proposals for African American self-help.

1905. Fort Erie, New York. Twenty-nine militant African American intellectuals from 14 states organize the Niagara Movement, a forerunner of the National Association for the Advancement of Colored People (NAACP).

1906. Atlanta, Georgia. An extended riot, in which respected African American citizens are killed, brings the city to a standstill for several days. After the riot, interracial groups are formed which attempt to improve conditions for African Americans. Despite the efforts of these groups, many African Americans decide to leave Georgia.

1906. Brownsville, Texas. Several African American soldiers of the 25th Infantry Division are involved in a riot with Brownsville police and merchants. Following the incident, President Theodore Roosevelt dishonorably discharges three companies of African American troops. These dishonorable discharges are finally reversed by the U.S. Army in 1972. The lone survivor from these companies is awarded $25,000 by the U.S. Army in 1973.

1907. Washington, DC. The U.S. Supreme Court upholds the right of railroads to segregate passengers traveling between states, even when this runs counter to the laws of states in which the train is traveling.

1908. Washington, DC. The U.S. Supreme Court, in the case *Berea College v. Kentucky*, upholds a state statute requiring segregation in private institutions.

1909. New York City, New York. The NAACP is founded in New York. The signers of the original charter of incorporation include Jane Addams, John Dewey, W. E. B. Du Bois, William Dean Howells, and Lincoln Steffens. Ida Wells-Barnett is placed on the executive committee.

1909. Matthew Henson places the flag of the United States at the North Pole. Henson, an African American, was part of Admiral Robert E. Peary's expedition.

1910. On separate lecture tours of Great Britain, W. E. B. Du Bois and Booker T. Washington paint contrasting pictures of the African American condition in the United States. Washington tells the British that blacks are making progress; Du Bois underscores injustices and accuses Washington of acquiescing to powerful white interests.

THE CRISIS

A RECORD OF THE DARKER RACES

Volume One   NOVEMBER, 1910   Number One

Edited by W. E. BURGHARDT DU BOIS, with the co-operation of Oswald Garrison Villard, J. Max Barber, Charles Edward Russell, Kelly Miller, W. S. Braithwaite and M. D. Maclean.

CONTENTS

PUBLISHED MONTHLY BY THE

National Association for the Advancement of Colored People
AT TWENTY VESEY STREET   NEW YORK CITY

The first edition of *The Crisis, A Record of the Darker Races,* magazine published by W. E. B. Du Bois in November 1910.

1910. New York City, New York. The first edition of *Crisis* magazine, edited by W. E. B. Du Bois, is published. Only 1,000 copies are in print, but before the end of the decade circulation of the magazine increases one hundred-fold.

1910. New York City, New York. The National Urban League is founded. The new organization stresses employment and industrial opportunities for African Americans. Eugene Kinckle Jones serves as the first executive secretary.

1911. Jamaica. Marcus Garvey forms the Universal Negro Improvement Association.

1912. New York City, New York. James Weldon Johnson's *The Autobiography of an Ex-Colored Man* is published, spurring white recognition of black culture and the advent of the Harlem Renaissance.

1913. Washington, DC. President Woodrow Wilson refuses to appoint a National Race Commission to study the social and economic status of African Americans.

1915. Spurred by boll weevil devastation of cotton crops, the great migration of African Americans to the North begins. Carter G. Woodson establishes the Association for the Study of Negro Life and History.

1915. New York City, New York. The NAACP establishes the Spingarn Medal to recognize annually "the highest achievement of an American Negro."

1915. Washington, DC. The U.S. Supreme Court in *Guinn v. United States* declares the Oklahoma "grandfather clause" unconstitutional.

1917. East St. Louis, Illinois. A riot erupts after African Americans are hired at a local factory. Forty African Americans are killed.

1917, July 28. New York City, New York. Over 10,000 African Americans parade down Fifth Avenue in New York, New York, to protest lynchings and the East St. Louis riot. Marchers in the Silent Protest Parade include W. E. B. Du Bois and James Weldon Johnson. Women and children protesters dress in white and men wear black arm bands.

1917. The United States enters World War I. Joel Spingarn presses the War Department to establish an officer training camp for African Americans. Spingarn's proposal alienates many of his NAACP colleagues who feel that such a camp would only perpetuate segregation and validate theories of African American inferiority. Others concede that the move is prudent, since it is the only way for African American officers to be trained. The NAACP ultimately approves of separate training camps. In October, over 600 African Americans are

commissioned officers, and 700,000 African Americans register for the draft.

1917. Washington, DC. In the case of *Buchanan v. Warley*, the U.S. Supreme Court declares that a Louisville "block" segregation ordinance is unconstitutional.

1918. France. Two African American infantry battalions are awarded the Croix de Guerre and two African American officers win the French Legion of Honor. African Americans are in the forefront of fighting from 1917 until the defeat of Germany in 1918.

1919. Membership in the NAACP approaches 100,000 despite attempts in some areas to make it illegal.

1919. Washington, DC. The U.S. Supreme Court rules in the case *Strauder v. West Virginia* that African Americans should be admitted to juries.

1920. New York City, New York. James Weldon Johnson becomes the first African American secretary of the NAACP and campaigns for the withdrawal of U.S. troops occupying Haiti.

1921. Tulsa, Oklahoma. Twenty-one blacks and ten whites are killed in a riot.

1922. Washington, DC. Republicans in the Senate vote to abandon the Dyer Anti-Lynching Bill, which imposed severe penalties and fines on "any state or municipal officer convicted of negligence in affording protection to individuals in custody who are attacked by a mob bent on lynching, torture, or physical intimidation." The bill, which was approved by the House of Representatives, had also provided for compensation to the families of victims.

1923. New York City, New York. Marcus Garvey is sentenced to a five-year term for mail fraud.

1924. Washington, DC. Congress passes the Immigration Act which excludes people of African descent from entering the country.

1924. Washington, DC. New York Representative Emanuel Cellar introduces legislation to provide for the formation of a blue-ribbon panel to study racial issues. The idea is met with disdain from the African American press, particularly the *Chicago Defender*, which editorializes: "We have been commissioned to death.... We have too many studies and reports already." *The Defender* asserts that African Americans need only to look after their own interests through the creation of a strong party vehicle and potent political leadership in the halls of Congress.

1925. A. Philip Randolph founds the Brotherhood of Sleeping Car Porters.

1926. New York City, New York. Controversy rages among the African American intelligentsia after publication of *Nigger Heaven* by white writer Carl van

African American soldiers leaving by train to serve in World War I.

Vechten. The book glamorizes the free-wheeling style of Harlem life amid the general contention that African Americans are less ashamed of sex and more morally honest than whites. W. E. B. Du Bois finds the assumptions deplorable; James Weldon Johnson, on the other hand, believes the book is neither scandalous nor insulting.

1926. New York City, New York. Langston Hughes, writing in *The Nation* magazine, urges black artists to write from their experience and to stop imitating white writers.

1926. Washington, DC. Negro History Week is introduced by Carter G. Woodson and the Association for the Study of Negro Life and History.

1926. Washington, DC. President Coolidge tells Congress that the country must provide "for the amelioration of race prejudice and the extension to all of the elements of equal opportunity and equal protection under the laws, which are guaranteed by the Constitution." Twenty-three African Americans are reported lynched during 1926.

1927. Atlanta, Georgia. Marcus Garvey is released from prison and deported to the British West Indies.

1927. Chicago, Illinois. The National Urban League organizes a boycott of stores that do not hire African Americans. In 1929, boycotts are started in several other Midwest cities.

1927. Washington, DC. In the case of *Nixon v. Herndon*, the U.S. Supreme Court strikes down a Texas law which bars African Americans from voting in party primaries. Texas goes on to enact a law allowing local committees to determine voter qualifications.

1928. Illinois. Oscar DePriest, a Republican, is elected as the first African American Representative from a Northern state.

1930. Detroit, Michigan. W. D. Fard founds the Temple of Islam, later to become the Nation of Islam.

1930. Washington, DC. A NAACP campaign helps prevent confirmation of U.S. Supreme Court nominee John H. Parker, a one-time, self-admitted opponent of the franchise for African Americans. The NAACP also helps unseat three of the senators who voted for him in later congressional elections.

1931. Alabama. The first trial of the Scottsboro Boys results in a battle between the NAACP and the International Labor Defense, a Communist-controlled group,

Oscar Stanton DePriest.

for the right to represent the young defendants who are charged with rape. The case, which becomes a worldwide *cause celebre* and important propaganda weapon for Communists, drags on for 20 years despite the recanting of a charge by one of the two plaintiffs and medical testimony that rape was not committed.

1932. Washington, DC. Following the Supreme Court's 1927 ruling in *Nixon v. Herndon* the state of Texas passes a statute authorizing the state Democratic party to set up its own rules regarding primary elections. As a result, the state of Texas adopts a resolution that denies African Americans the right to vote in Democratic Party primaries. However, the Supreme Court's ruling in rules that such legislation violates provisions of the Fourteenth Amendment.

1934. Chicago, Illinois. The headquarters of the Nation of Islam are established with Elijah Muhammad as leader.

1934. Washington, DC. A bill that prohibits lynching fails, as President Roosevelt refuses to support it.

1935. New York City, New York. Mary McLeod Bethune founds the National Council of Negro Women.

1935. St. Louis, Missouri. The NAACP bitterly criticizes President Franklin Delano Roosevelt for his failure to present or support civil rights legislation.

1935. Washington, DC. In the case of *Grovey v. Townsend*, the U.S. Supreme Court upholds a Texas law that prevents African Americans from voting in the Texas Democratic primary. The decision is a setback to the NAACP, which has waged several effective legal battles to equalize the ballot potential of the African American voter.

1936. Berlin, Germany. Jesse Owens wins four gold medals in the 1936 Olympics, but is snubbed by the Chancellor of Germany, Adolf Hitler.

1936. Washington, DC. In the case of *Gibbs v. Montgomery County*, the U.S. Supreme Court requires Maryland University to admit an African American student, Donald Murray, to its graduate law school.

1937. New York City, New York. Richard Wright becomes editor of *Challenge*, changes the title to *New Challenge*, and urges African Americans to write with greater "social realism."

1937. Pennsylvania. A new Pennsylvania state law denies many state services to unions discriminating against African Americans.

1937. Spain. Between 60 to 80 of the 3,200 Americans who fight for the Republican side in the Spanish Civil War are African American. Oliver Law, an African American from Chicago, commands the Lincoln Battalion.

1938. Boxer Joe Louis defends his heavyweight title against Max Schmeling.

1938. New York City, New York. Adam Clayton Powell Jr. and other black leaders convince white merchants in Harlem to hire blacks and to promise equal promotion opportunities.

1938. Pennsylvania. Crystal Bird Fauset of Philadelphia, the first African American woman state legislator, is elected to the Pennsylvania House of Representatives.

1939. Miami, Florida. Intimidation and cross-burning by the Ku Klux Klan in the black ghetto of Miami fail to discourage over 1,000 of the city's registered African American voters from appearing at the polls. The Klan parades with effigies of African Americans who will allegedly be slain for daring to vote.

1939. New York City, New York. Jane Bolin is appointed Judge of the Court of Domestic Relations in New York, New York, by Mayor Fiorello LaGuardia, becoming the first African American woman judge in the United States.

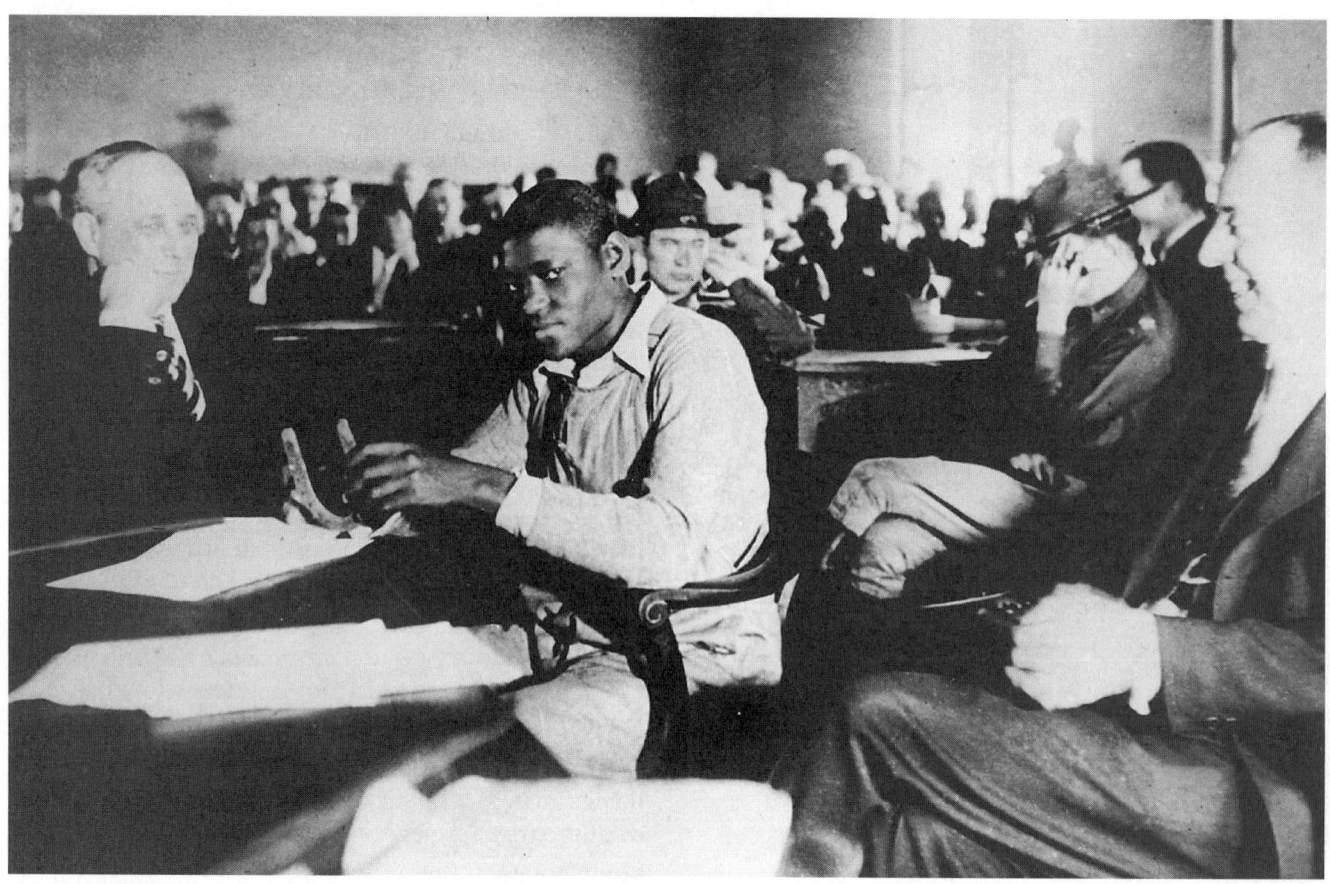

Haywood Patterson, one of the "Scottsboro Boys," on trial in 1931.

1939. Washington, DC. Marian Anderson, denied the use of Constitution Hall by the Daughters of the American Revolution, sings on Easter Sunday before 75,000 people assembled at the Lincoln Memorial.

1940. New York. In a mass meeting, West Indians oppose the transfer of West Indian islands to the United States.

1940. Eighty thousand African Americans vote in eight Southern states. Five percent of voting-age African Americans are registered.

1940. The 1940 census places life expectancy for blacks at 51 years, compared with 62 years for whites. Nearly one-fourth of blacks live in the North and West.

1940. Virginia. The Virginia legislature chooses "Carry Me Back to Ole Virginia," written by African American composer James A. Bland, as the official state song.

1940. Washington, DC. Benjamin O. Davis Sr. is appointed as the first African American general in the history of the U.S. armed forces. Responding to NAACP pressure, President Franklin Roosevelt announces that African American strength in the armed forces will be proportionate to African American population totals. Several branches of the military service and several occupational specialties are to be opened to African Americans. However, Roosevelt rules out troop integration because it will be "destructive to morale and detrimental to . . . preparation for national defense." At the start of Selective Service, less than 5,000 of 230,000 men in the U.S. Army are African American and there are only two African American combat officers. Approximately 888,000 African American men and 4,000 African American women are to serve in the armed forces during World War II. African Americans are mostly confined to service units.

1940. Washington, DC. The U.S. Supreme Court rules that black teachers cannot be denied wage parity with white teachers.

1941, December 7. Pearl Harbor, Hawaii. Dorie Miller, messman aboard the *USS Arizona*, mans a machine gun during the Pearl Harbor attack, downs four enemy planes, and is awarded the Navy Cross.

1941. Washington, DC. Charles R. Drew, an African American physician, sets up the first blood bank.

1941. Washington, DC. Robert Weaver is appointed director of the government office charged with integrating African Americans into the national defense program.

1941. Washington, DC. The threat by African Americans to stage a massive protest march on the nation's capital results in the issuance of Executive Order No. 8802, prohibiting discrimination in the defense establishment.

1941. Washington, DC. In the case of *Mitchell v. United States*, the U.S. Supreme Court rules that separate facilities in railroad travel must be substantially equal. The case is brought before the Supreme Court by African American congressman Arthur Mitchell.

1942. Chicago, Illinois. The Congress of Racial Equality (CORE), a civil rights group dedicated to a direct-action, nonviolent program, is founded. In 1943, CORE stages its first "sit-in" in a Chicago restaurant.

1942. Washington, DC. The Justice Department threatens to file suit against a number of African American newspapers which it believes are guilty of sedition because of their strong criticism of the government's racial policies in the armed services. The NAACP steps in to suggest guidelines which will satisfy the Justice Department.

1944. The United Negro Fund is founded.

1944. The NAACP secures the release of servicemen detained for protesting discrimination in the armed forces.

1944. The European Theater of War. The African American 99th Pursuit Squadron flies its 500th mission in the Mediterranean Theater. Another African American unit, the 92nd Division, enters combat in Italy. On June 6,500 African Americans land on Omaha Beach as part of the D-Day invasion of northern France. Among them is the 761st Tank Battalion which spends 183 days in action and is cited for conspicuous courage. Also cited in January of 1945 is the 969th Field Artillery Battalion for their support in the defense of Bastogne.

1944. The restriction of African American seamen to shore duty ends, as is the exclusion of African Americans from the coast guard and marine corps. The War Department officially ends segregation in all army posts, but the order is widely ignored.

1944. Washington, DC. In the case of *Smith v. Allwright*, the U.S. Supreme Court rules that "white primaries" violate the provisions of the Fifteenth Amendment.

1945. Italy. African American troops are at the forefront of victorious assaults in Germany and northern Italy. The use of African American troops in World War II, however, is more limited than in World War I or the Spanish-American War. Despite efforts by some enlightened naval officers, over 90 percent of African Americans in the U.S. Navy are still messmen when the war ends.

1945. New York. The first state Fair Employment Practices Commission is established in New York as a result of the Ives-Quinn Bill.

1945. Washington, DC. Congress denies funds to the federal Fair Employment Practices Commission, which was established during the war to enforce fair employment policies.

1946. Washington, DC. The U.S. Supreme Court rules in *Morgan v. Commonwealth of Virginia* that segregation on interstate buses is unconstitutional.

1947. Jackie Robinson becomes the first African American to play major league baseball, breaking the national pastime's color barrier.

1947. Atlanta, Georgia. The Southern Regional Council releases figures that demonstrate that only 12 percent of the African Americans in the Deep South (nearly 600,000) meet voting qualifications. In the states of Louisiana, Alabama, and Mississippi, the figure is approximately 3 percent. In Tennessee, more than 25 percent of adult African Americans meet the state voting requirements.

1947. CORE's first "freedom ride" travels through Southern states to press for the integration of transportation facilities.

1947. Tuskegee, Alabama. Statistics indicate that 3,426 African Americans have been lynched in the United States in the period 1882–1947. Of these, 1,217 were lynched in the decade 1890–1900. From 1947 to 1962, 12 African Americans were lynched.

1947. Washington, DC. The Truman Committee on Civil Rights formally condemns racial injustice in America in the widely-quoted report *To Secure These Rights*.

1948. California. The California Supreme Court declares the state statute banning racial intermarriage unconstitutional.

1948. New York City, New York. Ralph Bunche is confirmed by the United Nations Security Council as acting U.N. mediator in Palestine.

1948. Washington, DC. The U.S. Supreme Court in *Shelley v. Kraemer* rules that federal and state courts may not enforce restrictive covenants. However, the Court does not declare such covenants illegal. In a separate case, *Sipuel v. University of Oklahoma*, the Court holds that states are required to provide blacks with the same educational opportunities as whites. President Truman issues Executive Order No. 9981 directing "equality of treatment and opportunity" in the

The U.S. Army's "Buffalo Division," c.1945, facing inspection.

armed forces and creates the Fair Practices Board of the Civil Service Commission to deal with complaints of discrimination in government employment.

1949. Connecticut. Connecticut becomes the first state in the Union to extend the jurisdiction of the Civil Rights Commission into the domain of public housing.

1949. Washington, DC. Representative William L. Dawson becomes the first African American to head a Congressional committee when he is named chairman of the House Committee on Government Operations.

1950. Yech'on, Republic of Korea. The African American 24th Infantry Regiment recaptures the city of Yech'on, the first American victory in the Korean War.

1950. New York City, New York. Edith Sampson is appointed an alternate delegate to the United Nations.

1950. Oslo, Norway. Ralph Bunche wins the Nobel Peace Prize.

1950. The 1950 census places the net ten-year African American emigration from the South at 1.6 million.

1950. Washington, DC. Several U.S. Supreme Court decisions open university facilities to African Americans. In the case of *Henderson v. United States*, the Court rules that segregated tables on dining cars violate the provisions of the Interstate Commerce Act. A special committee reports to President Harry S. Truman that African American servicemen are still barred from many military specialties and training programs, but that the armed forces has largely been desegregated.

1952. In a series of legal maneuvers, the NAACP and other African American groups succeed in desegregating a number of colleges and high schools in Southern and border areas. In addition, public housing projects are opened to African Americans in some Northern and Midwestern cities and desegregation is achieved in several businesses and unions. A public swimming pool is integrated in Kansas City, a golf course in Louisville, and Ford's Theater in Baltimore.

1952. Tuskegee, Alabama. A Tuskegee report indicates that, for the first time in its 71 years of tabulation, no lynchings have occurred in the United States.

1953. Washington, DC. District of Columbia Commissioners order the abolition of segregation in several district agencies. The fire department is among those which escape the mandate. The Defense Department orders an end to segregation in schools on military bases and in veterans hospitals.

1953. New York City, New York. Hulan Jack is sworn in as borough president of Manhattan.

1953. Washington, DC. The U.S. Supreme Court asks to re-hear five school segregation cases first argued in 1942. Sensing a major opportunity, the NAACP puts 100 lawyers, scholars, and researchers to work in preparation. The NAACP also files a complaint with the Interstate Commerce Commission to execute earlier Supreme Court desegregation orders in transportation facilities.

1954, March 4. Washington, DC. President Dwight D. Eisenhower appoints an African American, J. Ernest Wilkins, as undersecretary of labor.

1954, May 17. Washington, DC. By a unanimous vote, the U.S. Supreme Court in the case of *Brown v. Board of Education of Topeka, Kansas* declares that "separate but equal" educational facilities are "inherently unequal" and that segregation is therefore unconstitutional. The decision overturns the "separate but equal" doctrine that has legalized segregation since 1896. In the case of *Hawkins v. Board of Control*, the Court rules that the University of Florida must admit African Americans regardless of any "public mischief" it might cause.

1954, September. In the autumn following the *Brown* decision, 150 formerly segregated school districts in

George Hayes (left), Thurgood Marshall (center), and James M. Nabrit (right) celebrate the *Brown v. Board of Education of Topeka, Kansas* landmark decision.

eight states and the District of Columbia integrate. However, a number of groups opposing integration emerge in the South. Most prominent among these are white citizens councils that soon claim 80,000 members and propose constitutional amendments reinstating segregation.

1954, October 1. Baltimore, Maryland. White parents and students protest the admission of black students to Baltimore's Southern High School. Anti-desegregation demonstrations are also staged in nearby Washington, DC.

1954, October 1. Florida. State Attorney General Richard Ervin files a brief with the U.S. Supreme Court warning that violent resistance would result from any effort to force desegregation in Florida schools.

1954, October 30. Washington, DC. The Department of Defense reports the end of "all-Negro" units in the U.S. Army. However, some bases still refuse to integrate. The Veteran's Administration announces their hospitals have been desegregated, but the Department of Health, Education and Welfare declares it will continue to give funds to segregated hospitals.

1954, November 13. Boca Raton, Florida. Governors attending the Southern Governors Conference pledge to uphold state control over schools and warn that forced school desegregation will create unrest which they claim does not currently exist in their states.

1955, May 31. Washington, DC. The U.S. Supreme Court orders school boards to draw up desegregation procedures. The Court asserts that school authorities have the responsibility of assessing and solving desegregation problems and must do so "with all deliberate speed." The decision reenforces the Court's ruling in *Brown v. Board of Education of Topeka, Kansas.* Reactions to this ruling in the South are mixed. Kansas, Missouri, Oklahoma, and Texas desegregate their school systems with minimal disruption. Georgia's Board of Education adopts a resolution revoking the license of any teacher who teaches integrated classes. Mississippi repeals its compulsory school attendance law and establishes a branch of government for the sole purpose of maintaining segregation. White citizens councils in Mississippi initiate economic pressures against blacks who try to register to vote, while more extreme groups resort to direct terror.

1955, July 14. Richmond, Virginia. The U.S. Circuit Court of Appeals rules that segregation on city buses is illegal. The court claims that the same principle which outlawed segregation in public schools should be applied.

1955, August 31. Greenwood, Mississippi. Two white men are arrested in Greenwood on charges of kidnapping, beating, and shooting 15-year-old Emmett Till. Till, who allegedly whistled at and insulted a white woman, was found dead in the Tallahatchie River. Jurors acquit the defendants on grounds that the body could not be positively identified.

1955, November 25. Washington, DC. In accordance with U.S. Supreme Court edicts, the Interstate Commerce Commission outlaws segregated buses and waiting rooms for interstate passengers. However, many communities ignore the order.

1955, December 1. Montgomery, Alabama. Rosa Parks takes a seat in the front of a city bus, refuses to surrender it to a white man, and is arrested. Four days later, the Reverend Martin Luther King Jr. urges the city's African American community to boycott the buses. This marks the beginning of the Montgomery bus boycott, which leads to the desegregation of Montgomery's city bus system the following year.

1956. Washington, DC. In the case of *Flemming v. South Carolina Electric,* the U.S. Supreme Court strikes down a state statute requiring segregation on public transportation.

1956, February 3. Tuscaloosa, Alabama. Autherine Lucy is admitted to the University of Alabama by court order, but riots ensue and she is expelled on a technicality.

1956, March 11. Washington, DC. Southern members of the Senate, led by Harry Byrd of Virginia, launch a fight against school integration. Byrd obtains the signatures of 100 congressmen on a "Southern Manifesto", attacking the rulings of the U.S. Supreme Court.

1956, July 13. Washington, DC. Southern members of the House of Representatives unite in opposition to an Eisenhower administration-sponsored civil rights bill. The bill would provide for the investigation of civil rights complaints and permit action by the U.S. attorney general in federal courts.

1956, September. By September of 1956, approximately 800 school districts containing 320,000 African American children are desegregated in compliance with the U.S. Supreme Court's 1954 decision. However, nearly 2.5 million African American children remain in segregated schools and there are still no desegregated districts in Virginia, North and South Carolina, Georgia, Florida, Mississippi, Alabama, and Louisiana.

1956, November 13. Washington, DC. The U.S. Supreme Court rules that the segregation of city buses is unconstitutional.

1957, February 14. New Orleans, Louisiana. The Southern Christian Leadership Conference (SCLC) is formed by Martin Luther King Jr. and others to coordinate the activities of nonviolent groups devoted to integration and citizenship for African Americans.

1957, February 26. Little Rock, Arkansas. Governor Orval Faubus signs four segregation bills enabling parents to refuse to send their children to desegregated schools, authorizing the use of school district funds to pay legal expenses incurred in integration suits, creating a committee to make anti-integration studies, and requiring organizations such as the NAACP to publish membership rosters.

1957, April 9. Madison, Wisconsin. The state Supreme Court rules that African Americans can be refused membership in trade unions, since such organizations are voluntary associations.

1957, September 4. Little Rock, Arkansas. Nine black students are turned away from Central High School by a white mob and the Arkansas National Guard when they arrive for classes. The National Guard, which was called to Little Rock by Governor Orval Faubus, is forced by court order to withdraw on September 20. As mobs of angry whites assemble outside of the school and the threat of mob violence escalates, President Dwight Eisenhower issues a proclamation on September 23 ordering an end to any obstruction to court-ordered integration. On September 24, the president issues Executive Order No. 10730 authorizing the use of federal troops to assist in the integration of Central High School.

1957, September 9. Washington, DC. President Dwight D. Eisenhower signs a civil rights bill. The bill provides for the creation of a commission on civil rights to investigate allegations of civil rights and voting rights violations.

1958, February 19. New Orleans, Louisiana. The U.S. Court of Appeals rules that segregation on buses and streetcars in New Orleans is illegal. The Louisiana state assembly later passes a bill which stipulates that the first person seated in a bus's double seat can decide whether a rider of a different race may sit in the adjoining seat. The bill is vetoed by Governor Earl Long because it would require a white rider to request permission to sit next to a black rider.

1958, April 14. Jackson, Mississippi. Governor J. P. Coleman asserts that African Americans in Mississippi are not ready to vote and vetoes a bill which would have given control of voter registration to a court-appointed registrar.

1958, July 16. Baton Rouge, Louisiana. Governor Earl Long signs a bill requiring that blood plasma be labeled according to the race of donor.

1960, February 1. Greensboro, North Carolina. Four African American students refuse to leave a segregated lunch counter, marking the beginning of "sit-in" protests throughout the South.

1960, April. Atlanta, Georgia. The Student Non-Violent Coordinating Committee (SNCC) is formed to organize student protest activities. Church "kneel-ins" and beach "wade-ins" soon join lunch counter and bus station "sit-ins" as effective means of protesting segregation.

1960, April 24. Biloxi, Mississippi. Rioting erupts when a group of African Americans attempt to swim at the city's 26-mile whites-only beach. A curfew is ordered by the mayor and riot police patrol the city. On April 27, the state legislature passes a law authorizing prison terms for anyone convicted of inciting a riot.

1960, May 6. Washington, DC. President Eisenhower signs the Civil Rights Act of 1960. This act authorizes judges to appoint referees who can help African Americans register to vote in federal elections. The act also prohibits intimidation of African American voters through bombing and mob violence.

1960, July 31. New York City, New York. Black Muslim leader, Elijah Muhammad, calls for the creation of a black state either in America or in Africa.

1960, August. As of August 1, "sit-ins" have led to the successful desegregation of lunch counters in 15 American cities.

1960, September 8. New York City, New York. New York Governor Nelson Rockefeller, in an address at the National Urban League Conference, declares that the "sit-ins" are "an inspiration to the nation."

1960, October 3. The SCLC organizes voter "stand-ins" in several American cities to protest against the remaining barriers to African American voter registration.

1960, November 10. New Orleans, Louisiana. The city approves a plan to admit black students to an all-white school. Meeting in a special session, the state legislature votes to take control of the city's school system and to have the schools closed on the day the African American students are scheduled to arrive. On November 14, U.S. marshals escort four black students to the selected schools. On November 15, 11 whites are arrested in disturbances; on November 17 the city experiences severe rioting.

1960, November 14. Washington, DC. In the case of *Gomillion v. Lightfoot,* the U.S. Supreme Court rules that a law designed to redraw the city boundaries of Tuskegee, Alabama, is unconstitutional. The case was brought before the Court after the city of Tuskegee redrew its borders, which excluded all but four or five of the city's 400 African American residents. The Court asserted that such legislation was in violation of the Fifteenth Amendment.

1960, November 23. Baton Rouge, Louisiana. At its annual convention, the Louisiana Teachers Association vows to resist all attempts to integrate the state's public schools.

1961, May 4. Washington, DC. Several busloads of "freedom riders," organized by the Congress of Racial Equality (CORE), embark on a journey through the South to test the compliance of bus stations with the Interstate Commerce Commission's desegregation order. Many of the "freedom riders" are arrested or encounter angry mobs as they travel throughout the South.

1961, May 20. Montgomery, Alabama. A bus carrying "freedom riders" is attacked by a mob and set on fire. U.S. Attorney General Robert Kennedy orders federal marshals into Montgomery to maintain order. On May 21, a mob forms outside of the First Baptist Church, where Martin Luther King Jr. and Ralph Abernathy, pastor of the church, are conducting a meeting. The situation in Montgomery becomes so volatile that Governor John Patterson is forced to deploy the Alabama National Guard and declares martial law in the city.

1961, May 22. Washington, DC. Upon hearing the case *Louisiana ex rel. Gremillion v. NAACP,* the U.S. Supreme Court unanimously rules that two Louisiana laws designed to harass the National Association for the Advancement of Colored People are unconstitutional. The laws required that organizations disclose

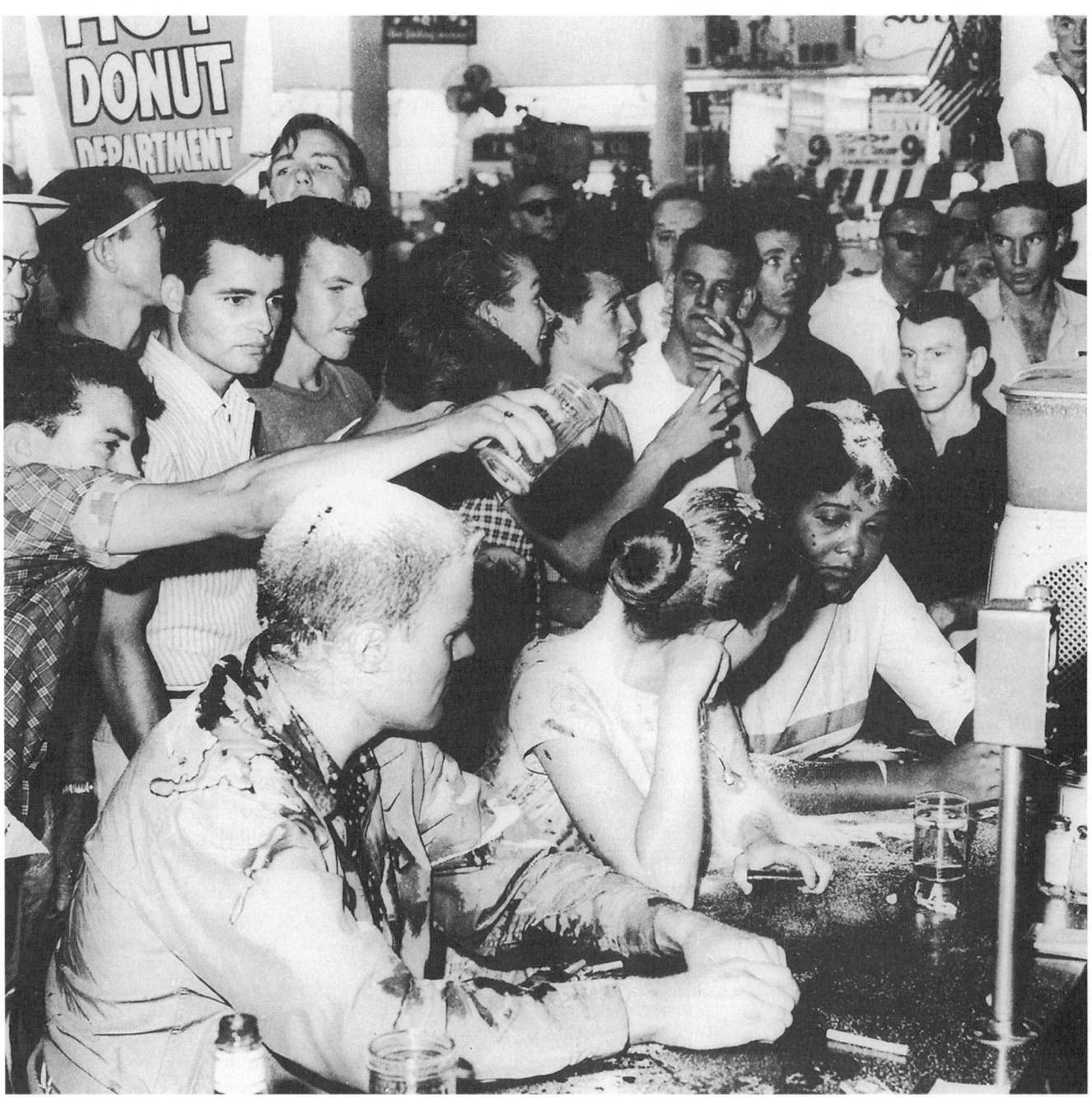

Sit-in demonstrators, like those shown here, faced harassment but effectively protested the segregation of public places.

members' names and attest that its officers are not affiliated with subversive activities.

1961, June 2. Montgomery, Alabama. Federal Judge Frank Johnson Jr. issues a restraining order to prevent "freedom riders" from traveling through the state.

1961, September 29. Atlanta, Georgia. The Southern Regional Council reports that business establishments in more than 100 cities have been desegregated as a result of "sit-ins."

1961, December 11. Washington, DC. Ruling on its first cases pertaining to student "sit-ins", the U.S. Supreme Court decides unanimously to reverse the conviction of 16 African American students. The cases *Briscoe v. Louisiana, Garner v. Louisiana,* and *Hoston v. Louisiana* result from a Baton Rouge lunch counter "sit-in" staged in March of 1960. The students, who had not been asked to leave by the proprietor, had refused a police order to leave and were charged with "disturbing

Freedom riders pictured here in Anniston, Alabama, escaped a fire-bombing.

the peace."

1962, February 26. Washington, DC. The U.S. Supreme Court rules on a suit challenging Mississippi laws that require segregation in intrastate transportation. The case *Bailey v. Patterson* is remanded to district court since, as the Court contends, the issue is no longer litigable; no state may require racial segregation in either inter- or intrastate transportation.

1962, March 24. Columbia, South Carolina. The NAACP files suit in district court to prohibit the Orangeburg Regional Hospital from operating segregated facilities.

1962, May 2. Biloxi, Mississippi. A U.S. district court finds nine Mississippi laws requiring segregated travel accommodations unconstitutional.

1962, September 30. Jackson, Mississippi. Riots erupt on the campus of the University of Mississippi when James Meredith, a 29-year-old African American veteran, is admitted to the university by court order. Federal troops are sent to restore order.

1962, November 20. Washington, DC. The Kennedy administration issues orders banning segregation in federally-financed housing.

1963, April 3. Birmingham, Alabama. Martin Luther King Jr. targets Birmingham for a drive against discrimination. The protesters are driven back by police armed with water hoses and attack dogs. The confrontation, which has been captured on film, awakens public opinion across the country.

1963, June 12. Jackson, Mississippi. Civil rights leader Medgar Evers is assassinated in the doorway of his home. Thousands attend a march mourning the death of Evers on June 15.

1963, August 28. Washington, DC. Some 250,000 people gather at the Lincoln Memorial to demonstrate on behalf of the civil rights bill pending in Congress. The march has been organized by several civil rights organizations including the National Association for the Advancement of Colored People, SCLC, CORE, the Urban League, and the Negro American Labor Council. Martin Luther King Jr., one of many scheduled speakers, gives what will become his most famous speech "I Have a Dream."

1963, September. The South. Less than ten percent of African American public school students attend integrated classes in the fall term. Governor George Wallace of Alabama declares: "I draw the line in the dust and toss the gauntlet before the feet of tyranny and I say 'segregation now, segregation tomorrow, segregation forever.'"

Martin Luther King Jr. waving to the massive crowd at the 1963 March on Washington while holding notes from his famous speech.

1963, September 15. Birmingham, Alabama. Four African American children are killed in the bombing of the 16th Street Baptist Church.

1963, November 22. Dallas, Texas. President John F. Kennedy, a major advocate of civil rights, is assassinated in Dallas, Texas. Kennedy's successor, Vice President Lyndon B. Johnson, promises to continue support for civil rights legislation.

1964, January 23. The Twenty-fourth Amendment to the Constitution is ratified, prohibiting the use of poll taxes in federal elections.

1964, March 8. New York City, New York. Malcolm X leaves the Black Muslim organization, Nation of Islam, to form the Organization for Afro-American Unity—an organization emphasizing black nationalism and social action.

1964, June 2. Washington, DC. A major civil rights bill, forbidding discrimination in public accommodations and employment, is signed into law by President Johnson.

1964, June 25. St. Augustine, Florida. A mob attacks marchers protesting the city's pro-segregation policies. State police watch as some 50 African Americans are prevented from using the city beach.

1964, July–August. New York and New Jersey. On July 18 riots erupt in the Harlem section of New York City. One person is killed, 140 injured, and 500 arrested. This is the first of many large riots to strike urban African American neighborhoods during the 1960s. Shortly after the Harlem disturbances, riots erupt in Brooklyn, New York; Rochester, New York; Jersey City, New Jersey; and Paterson, New Jersey.

1964, August 4. Philadelphia, Mississippi. Three young civil rights volunteers—James Chaney, Michael Schwerner, and Andrew Goodman—are murdered. A number of arrests on federal charges less severe than murder follow. Among the 19 suspects are the sheriff and a deputy sheriff of Neshoba County. No convictions are obtained and charges are dismissed in December.

1964, December 10. Oslo, Norway. Martin Luther King Jr. is awarded the Nobel Peace Prize.

1965, January 2. Selma, Alabama. Reverend Martin Luther King Jr. announces his intention to call for demonstrations if African Americans in Alabama are not permitted to register to vote in appropriate numbers. Twelve African Americans, including King himself, book rooms on January 18 at Selma's Hotel Albert, becoming the first blacks accepted at this formerly all-white hotel. While signing the guest register, King is accosted by a white segregationist who is later fined $100 and given a 60-day jail sentence. On January 19, Sheriff James G. Clark arrests 62 African Americans in Selma after they refuse to enter the Dallas County courthouse through an alley door. Clark and his deputies arrest 150 other African American voter registration applicants the next day. A federal district court order issued on January 23 bars law enforcement officials from interfering with voter registration and warns that violence against African American voters will not be tolerated.

1965, January 15. Philadelphia, Mississippi. A federal grand jury hands down indictments for the June 1964 slaying of three civil rights workers—James Chaney, Andrew Goodman, and Michael Schwerner—in Philadelphia, Mississippi. The following day 18 men, including two law enforcement officers, are arrested. On February 25, U.S. District Court Judge W. Harold Cox dismisses a federal indictment against 17 of the accused.

1965, January 18. Washington, DC. Ruling on the case *Cox v. Louisiana*, the U.S. Supreme Court reverses the conviction of protesters charged with disturbing the peace.

Nearly 250,000 people from across the nation "March on Washington" on August 28, 1963, protesting for increased civil rights.

1965, February 1. Selma, Alabama. Reverend Martin Luther King Jr. and some 770 African Americans are arrested during protest demonstrations. King remains in jail for four days before posting bond. During this time, more than 3,000 persons are arrested. On February 4, a federal district court bars the county board of registrars from administering a literacy test to voter applicants or from rejecting their application on petty technicalities.

1965, February 21. New York City, New York. Malcolm X, a 39-year-old black nationalist leader and former member of the Black Muslim sect, is shot to death in the Audubon Ballroom as he is about to deliver an address before a rally of several hundred followers. Following the murder, Black Muslim headquarters in New York and San Francisco are burned, and most Muslim leaders are placed under heavy police guard. Three African Americans—Talmadge Hayer, Norman 3X Butler, and Thomas 15X Johnson—are later taken into custody and charged with first-degree murder. The trio is convicted and sentenced to life imprisonment on March 10, 1966.

Martin Luther King Jr. (bottom right) being congratulated by King Olav of Norway as King receives the 1964 Nobel Peace Prize.

1965, March 26. Washington, DC. President Lyndon B. Johnson announces the arrest of four Ku Klux Klan members in connection with the murder of Viola Gregg Liuzzo. Liuzzo, a 39-year-old white civil rights worker from Detroit, was slain on a Lowndes County highway during the Selma-to-Montgomery Freedom March. The president declares war on the Klan, calling it a "hooded society of bigots." Robert M. Shelton Jr., Imperial Wizard of the United Klans of America, Inc., answers the president's charges by branding him "a damn liar." On March 30, the House Un-American Activities Committee votes to open a full investigation of the activities of the Klan. The committee chairman, a Louisiana Democrat, asserts that the Klan is committing "shocking crimes."

1965, July 13. Washington, DC. Thurgood Marshall is nominated as Solicitor General of the United States, the first African American person to hold this office.

1965, August 6. Washington, DC. President Johnson signs the 1965 Voting Rights Act, providing for the registration by federal examiners of those black voters turned away by state officials.

1965, August 11. Los Angeles, California. The arrest and alleged mistreatment of a black youth by white policemen sparks an orgy of looting, burning, and

A 1965 protest in Harlem of violence against law abiding civil rights workers and demonstrators.

rioting in the predominantly African American section of Watts. Thousands of National Guardsmen and state police rush to quell the violence. The rioting which lasts six days claims the lives of 35 people and causes nearly 46 million dollars in property damage. On August 20, President Johnson denounces the Los Angeles rioters, comparing them to Ku Klux Klan extremists. He declares that the existence of legitimate grievances in Watts is no justification for lawlessness. "We cannot . . . in one breath demand laws to protect the rights of all our citizens, and then turn our back . . . and . . . allow laws to be broken that protect the safety of our citizens."

1966. Oakland, California. Huey P. Newton and Bobby Seale found the Black Panther party.

1966, January 13. Washington, DC. President Lyndon B. Johnson names Robert Weaver as head of the Department of Housing and Urban Development. Weaver is the first African American appointed to serve in a presidential cabinet in U.S. history. Lisle Carter, also African American, is named as an assistant secretary in the Department of Health, Education and Welfare. Constance Baker Motley, former NAACP lawyer and borough president of Manhattan, becomes the first

African American woman to be named to a federal judgeship.

1966, February 7. Lowndes County, Alabama. A federal court finds Lowndes County, Alabama, guilty of "gross, systematic exclusion of members of the African American race from jury duty." County officials are ordered to prepare a new jury list. Lowndes County is also ordered to desegregate its school system within two years, to close 24 "blacks only" schools, and to introduce remedial programs designed to close the educational gap between white and black students.

1966, February 23. Washington, DC. In the case of *Brown v. Louisiana*, the U.S. Supreme Court reverses the convictions of five blacks charged with disturbing the peace when they refused to leave a whites-only reading room in a public library.

1966, March 25. Washington, DC. In the case of *Harper v. Virginia State Board of Elections*, the U.S. Supreme Court outlaws the use of poll taxes in state elections. The ruling upholds the Twenty-Fourth Amendment which bars the use of such taxes in federal elections.

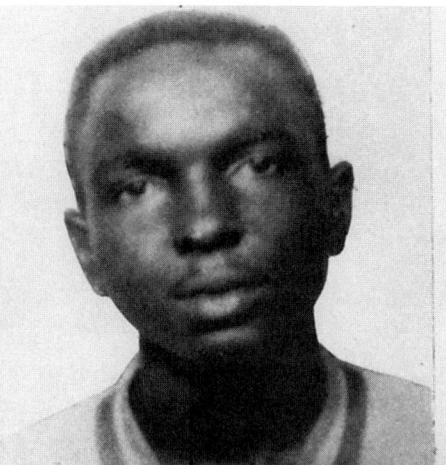

Civil rights workers Michael Schwerner, James Earl Chaney, and Andrew Goodman were murdered in Mississippi in 1965.

1966, June 6. Tennessee. James Meredith is shot shortly after beginning a 220-mile voting rights pilgrimage from Memphis, Tennessee to Jackson, Mississippi. Aubrey James Norvell, 40, is arrested at the scene and taken to jail where, according to authorities, he admits to the shooting. Meredith suffers multiple injuries, but recovers.

1966, June 26. Jackson, Mississippi. The march begun by James Meredith ends with a rally in front of the state capitol in Jackson. Addresses are delivered by Meredith, Martin Luther King Jr., and Stokely Carmichael, who urges the 15,000 African Americans in attendance to "build a power base . . . so strong that we will bring them [whites] to their knees every time they mess with us." The march results in the registration of about 4,000 African American voters.

1966, July 10. Chicago, Illinois. Martin Luther King Jr. addresses a predominantly African American crowd of 30,000 to 45,000 at Soldier Field and launches a drive to make Chicago an "open city." The rally is sponsored by the Coordinating Council of Committee Organizations, a coalition consisting of some 45 local civil rights groups. From July 12 to 15, violence erupts on Chicago's west side in protest of a decision by Chicago police to shut off a fire hydrant which had been opened illegally to give African American children relief from the stifling heat. Two African Americans are killed, scores of police and civilians wounded, and 372 persons are arrested.

1966, July 18. Cleveland, Ohio. Shootings, fire-bombings, and looting spread throughout Cleveland's east side. Four people are killed and 50 are injured.

Most of the 164 persons arrested are charged with looting. The riot results in widespread property damage.

1967, January. Washington, DC. Representative Adam Clayton Powell Jr. of New York is stripped of his chairmanship of the House Committee on Education and Labor and barred from assuming his seat in the Ninetieth Congress. A congressional committee investigating the case later proposes public censure, loss of seniority, and a $40,000 fine. Powell and his lawyers indicate their intention to challenge the constitutionality of this decision in federal court.

1967, February 15. Washington, DC. President Lyndon B. Johnson asks Congress to pass new civil rights legislation pertaining to the sale and rental of housing. In a special address to Congress, Johnson outlines the scope of the proposed bill. The bill, Johnson states, is designed to end discrimination in jury selection, permit the Equal Employment Opportunity Commission to issue cease-and-desist orders, extend the life of the Commission on Civil Rights, and authorize $2.7 dollars in appropriations for the Community Relations Service. The bill would enable individuals to file damage suits in housing discrimination cases. Violators of the bill would be subject to court orders and fines issued by the secretary of the Department of Housing and Urban Development.

1967, March 1. Washington, DC. By a vote of 307–116, the U.S. House of Representatives bars Adam Clayton Powell Jr. from the Ninetieth Congress. Powell immediately files suit in U.S. district court to combat his ouster, asserting that he has met all citizenship, age, and residency requirements for House membership.

The first major U.S. race riot of the 1960s occurred in 1965 in the Watts section of Los Angeles, where an estimated 10,000 rioters participated.

The congressman also charges that his constituency is left without representation and, therefore, vulnerable to discrimination.

1967, March 29. The Fifth Circuit Court of Appeals upholds the legality of revised federal school desegregation guidelines. The court, in an 8–4 ruling, calls for the desegregation of all students, teachers, school transportation facilities, and school-related activities in six Southern states. The guidelines establish rough percentage goals to be used in determining compliance with the Civil Rights Act of 1964.

1967, May 3. Montgomery, Alabama. A federal district court overturns an Alabama statute designed to prevent school desegregation. The court rules that no state may nullify the action of "a federal department or agency without initiating Court action" which only the U.S. Supreme Court can review.

1967, May 10. Jackson, Mississippi. An African American delivery man, Benjamin Brown, is shot and killed during riots on the campus of Jackson State College. Within full view of police, Brown is left at the scene unattended until he is taken to the University Hospital by African American bystanders. The police, unable to contain the demonstrators, are reinforced by more than 1,000 National Guardsmen.

1967, June 2. Boston, Massachusetts. Rioting erupts in Boston's predominantly African American section of Roxbury. The disturbance occurs in the wake of an attempt by welfare mothers to barricade themselves inside a building as a protest against police brutality. The rioting results in the arrest of nearly 100 people, while scores of others are severely injured.

1967, June 12. Newark, New Jersey. The "long hot summer" begins in earnest in Newark, New Jersey, scene of the most devastating riot to sweep an urban center since the 1965 Watts uprising.

1967, June 13. Washington, DC. Thurgood Marshall is appointed an associate justice of the U.S. Supreme Court, the first African American so designated.

1967, June 19. Washington, DC. U.S. District Court Judge J. Skelly Wright rules that *de facto* segregation of African Americans in the District of Columbia is unconstitutional and orders the complete desegregation of the district's schools by the fall.

1967, June 27. Buffalo, New York. Three days of rioting result in more than 85 injuries, 205 arrests, and property damage estimated at $100,000.

1967, July 19. Washington, DC. The U.S. House of Representatives passes legislation which states that it is a federal crime to cross state lines or to use interstate facilities for the purpose of inciting a riot. The bill is aimed at alleged professional agitators who travel from city to city to inflame the people. New York's Emanuel Celler finds the bill "neither preventive nor curative" and fears it will only arouse African American hostility even further.

1967, July 20. Newark, New Jersey. Despite objections by New Jersey Governor Hughes, a four-day conclave of African American leaders, many of them Black Power advocates, convenes in Newark. Militancy and a call for separate nationhood dominate the meeting. One participant at the conference, Alfred Black of the Newark Human Relations Commission, states that "the black today is either a radical or an Uncle Tom. There is no middle ground."

1967, July 22. Detroit, Michigan. Rioting erupts in the morning hours of July 22. By July 29, over 7,000 persons are arrested and 43 persons killed.

1967, July 27. Washington, DC. President Lyndon B. Johnson appoints a blue-ribbon panel to "investigate the origins of the recent disorders in our cities." The president instructs the commission to set aside political considerations and concern itself solely with the health and safety of American society and its citizens. On August 10, the National Advisory Commission on Civil Disorders urges President Johnson to increase the number of African Americans in the army and air national guard. The panel also recommends increased riot-control training for the guard, as well as a review of promotion procedures. The recommendations, delivered in a letter to President Johnson, are forwarded to U.S. Defense Secretary Robert McNamara.

1967, August 14. Dorchester County, Maryland. H. Rap Brown is indicted *in absentia* by a grand jury on charges of inciting to riot, arson, and other related actions which threaten the public peace. Brown is arrested in New York on August 19 and charged with carrying a gun across state lines while under indictment. After strenuous objections are voiced by his white lawyer, William Kunstler, Brown's bail is reduced to $15,000. On August 22, he is released from jail in time to address a crowd of 100 blacks on the steps of the Foley Square courthouse. Pointing to whites nearby, Brown says: "That's your enemy out there. And you better not forget, because I ain't going to."

1967, August 19. New Haven, Connecticut. Nearly 450 persons are arrested during five days of looting, arson, and vandalism. No serious injuries are reported, and no shots are fired by police despite frequent curfew violations.

1967, October 20. Philadelphia, Mississippi. An all-white federal jury of five men and seven women returns a guilty verdict in a retrial for the 1964 murder of three civil rights workers near Philadelphia, Mississippi. Seven men are convicted of conspiracy. However, eight defendants are acquitted, and three are declared victims of a mistrial. Among the guilty are Chief Deputy Sheriff Cecil Price and Sam Bowers, Imperial Wizard of the Ku Klux Klan.

1968, February 5. Orangeburg, South Carolina. Three African American youths are shot to death and more than 30 people are wounded in a racial outburst involving police and students at South Carolina State College. The violence is the culmination of student protests against the segregation of a local bowling alley. On February 7, the campus is sealed off and classes are suspended in the wake of rock and bottle-throwing incidents. On February 8, three students are fired on by police who mistakenly believe one of their troopers has been shot. In reality, the trooper was knocked down by a piece of lumber thrown by a demonstrator. On February 9, Governor McNair orders a curfew and attributes the violence to "Black Power" advocates. On February 11, local blacks call for the removal of the National Guard and announce plans for a boycott of white businesses. The city leaders counter by establishing a Human Relations Commission which resolves to prevent further outbreaks of violence. On February 24, the Southern Regional Council issues a report analyzing the Orangeburg upheaval. The report blames the outbreak of violence on the emotional appeal of black power to young blacks, overreaction by white citizens and police, feelings of hopelessness among blacks, and the expectations by whites that police power and military force must be utilized to cope with all forms of public demonstrations.

1968, February 29. Washington, DC. President Lyndon B. Johnson's National Advisory Commission on Civil Disorders issues an exhaustive report on the causes of the civil disorders that disrupted the nation in 1967. The commission identifies the major cause of the rioting as the existence of two separate bodies in America—"one black, one white, separate and unequal." It charges that white racism, more than anything else, was the chief catalyst in the already explosive mixture of discrimination, poverty, and frustration that ignited so many urban ghettos in the tragic summer of 1967. It reminds white America how deeply it is implicated in the existence of the ghetto. "White institutions created it, white institutions maintain it, and white society condones it." To overcome this terrible and crushing legacy, the commission implores the nation to initiate a massive and sustained commitment to action and reform, and it appeals for unprecedented levels of "funding and performance" in housing, education, employment, welfare, law enforcement, and the mass media.

1968, March 11. Washington, DC. The U.S. Senate passes the Civil Rights Bill of 1968. Among its major provisions are sweeping housing and anti-riot measures which go far beyond the federal protection offered to civil rights workers in the 1967 House version of the bill.

1968, March 29. Memphis, Tennessee. A teenage African American youth is slain after a protest march led by Martin Luther King Jr. deteriorates into violence and looting. The march marks the culmination of six weeks of labor strike activity involving the sanitation workers of the city—90 percent of whom are African American. Civil rights leaders and African American ministers call for a boycott of downtown businesses and urge massive civil disobedience to express support for the strikers. Such action broadens the focus of the strike and transforms it into a general civil rights action. On the day of the march, disturbances begin

Edward W. Brooke (hands folded, left of center) and Thurgood Marshall (2nd from right) attend President Johnson's signing of the 1968 Civil Rights Act.

almost immediately. Some African American students who have been refused the right to leave school and participate in the march begin pelting police with bricks; others smash department store windows along Beale Street. Most of the 6,000 to 20,000 marchers demonstrate peacefully. City and county police join the National Guard in quelling the disturbances. After King is spirited away to safety at the nearby Lorraine Motel, tear gas is fired at the crowds. More than 150 people are arrested, 40 of them on looting charges.

1968, April 4. Memphis, Tennessee. The world is shocked by the assassination of Martin Luther King Jr. Felled by a single bullet, King is pronounced dead at St. Joseph's Hospital at 7:05 P.M. CST, barely one hour after the shooting. Attorney General Ramsey Clark, on hand to conduct the preliminary investigation in person, declares that the early evidence points to the crime as being the work of a single assassin. Witnesses report seeing a white man running from the doorway of a rooming house at 420 South Main Street minutes after the shooting. The killing triggers a wave of violence in over 100 cities including such urban centers as Baltimore, Chicago, Kansas City, Missouri, and Washington,

DC. Some 70,000 federal troops and National Guardsmen are dispatched to restore order. Official figures report 46 dead: 41 blacks, five whites. Thousands are injured and arrested. On April 5, Reverend Ralph Abernathy is named to succeed King and discloses that SCLC's first public gesture will be to lead the march King himself was planning. Three days later, Coretta Scott King takes her place in the front ranks of the marchers, locking arms with two of the 42,000 people on hand for the demonstration. King's body is put on public view at Ebenezer Baptist Church in Atlanta, Georgia, on April 6. He is buried at South View Cemetery on April 9 after funeral services are held at the church and a general memorial service is conducted at Morehouse College, his alma mater.

1968, April 10. Washington, DC. The assassination of Martin Luther King Jr. moves the U.S. House of Representatives to submit to President Johnson a Senate-passed civil rights bill prohibiting racial discrimination in the sale or rental of 80 percent of the nation's housing. Johnson signs the measure on April 11 and counsels the nation to stay on the road to progress by recognizing "the process of law."

1968, May 11. Washington, DC. Caravans of people representing the Poor People's Campaign begin arriving in Washington, DC. The Defense Department alerts "selected troop units" to help District of Columbia police in the event of violence. On Mother's Day, May 12, Coretta Scott King leads a march of welfare mothers from 20 cities and declares at a subsequent rally that she will try to enlist the support of all the nation's women "in a campaign of conscience." The next day Ralph Abernathy, clad in blue denims and using carpenter's tools, presides at the christening of Resurrection City, the plywood shanty town erected within walking distance of the White House and the Capitol. Abernathy is able to report, as the campaign draws to a close, that certain gains have been recorded. The Department of Agriculture, for instance, agrees to "provide food to the neediest counties in this country." The U.S. Senate approves a bill to increase low-income housing construction and the Office of Economic Opportunity (OEO) allocates $25 million for expanded programs including one encouraging participation from poor people.

1968, June 5. Los Angeles, California. Senator Robert Kennedy, a champion of civil rights, is shot and killed moments after leaving a rally celebrating his victory over Eugene McCarthy in the California Democratic primary.

1968, June 8. London. James Earl Ray, alleged assassin of Martin Luther King Jr. is arrested.

1968, July 23. Cleveland, Ohio. Racial violence erupts in Cleveland's Glenville district, resulting in the deaths of eleven persons, eight of them black, and three white policemen. Mayor Carl Stokes helps to restore order after a night of burning and looting which results in over $1 million worth of property damage. Over 3,000 National Guardsmen are on the scene, but they are not widely utilized. Ahmed (Fred) Evans, a 37-year-old antipoverty worker and head of the Black Nationalists of New Libya, is blamed for starting the disturbances. On June 26, Ahmed Evans is arraigned on three charges of first-degree murder.

1968, July 27. Washington, DC. The Kerner Commission releases preliminary findings that indicate a sharp rise in the number of African Americans who accept urban riots as a justifiable or inevitable response to conditions prevailing in the nation's ghettos.

1968, August 7. Miami, Florida. Two days of looting, fire bombing, and shooting in the black section of Miami culminate in Florida Governor Claude Kirk's decision to summon the National Guard to quell the disorders. Despite Ralph Abernathy's plea for an end to the violence, crowds of African Americans battle police over an eight-block area. On August 8, three African Americans are killed in gun battles with law enforcement officials. Although Dade County Mayor Chuck Hall accuses outsiders of instigating the trouble, the ten percent unemployment rate among African Americans in the 16–22 age bracket is cited as a major factor contributing to the violence.

1968, September 8. California. Black Panther Huey P. Newton is tried and convicted of manslaughter in the October 28, 1967, shooting death of a white policeman. Nearly three weeks later, Newton is sentenced to 2–15 years imprisonment. The trial and the conviction introduce the nation at large to a new and formidable Black Panther Party.

1968, October 8. Washington, DC. Some 250 African Americans protest the fatal shooting of an African American pedestrian by a policeman. Demonstrators set fires and block traffic until police reinforcements disperse them with tear gas. The policeman is eventually exonerated of all charges by a federal grand jury.

1968, December 1. New Jersey. Three members of the Black Panthers are arrested on charges of carrying out a machine gun attack on a Jersey City police station on November 29. A Black Panther spokesman claims that a December 1 bombing of party headquarters in Newark is in response to the Jersey City attack. A police sergeant cites the arrest of seven Newark Panthers on November 28 as the cause of the precinct attack.

1969, January 3. Washington, DC. After a long and bitter debate concerning his qualifications and conduct, the House of Representatives votes to seat Adam Clayton Powell Jr. The House, however, fines him $25,000 for alleged misuse of payroll funds and travel allowances and demotes him to freshman status by stripping him of his seniority rank.

1969, February 6. Washington, DC. President Nixon appoints James Farmer as an assistant secretary of the Department of Health, Education and Welfare; Arthur Fletcher as an assistant secretary of the Department of Labor; and William Brown III, as chairman of the Equal Employment Opportunity Commission.

1969, June 6. Houston, Texas. Testimony released in a federal court indicates that the telephones of Martin Luther King Jr. and Elijah Muhammad were tapped by the FBI, despite the fact that President Lyndon B. Johnson had ordered a halt to all wiretaps in 1965.

1969, June 16. Washington, DC. The U.S. Supreme Court rules that the suspension of Representative Adam Clayton Powell Jr. by the House of Representatives is unconstitutional.

1969, July 6. New York City, New York. James Forman of the National Black Economic Development Conference receives a check for $15,000 from the

Washington Square United Methodist Church. The church is the first predominantly white organization to support Forman's demand that American churches pay $500 million in reparations for helping to perpetuate slavery.

1969, August 1. Washington, DC.   The U.S. Justice Department files suit against the state of Georgia to end segregation in its schools. Governor Lester G. Maddox condemns the action as criminal and declares the state will "win the war against these tyrants."

1969, August 19. California.   Black Panther leader Bobby Seale is arrested for the May 19 murder of alleged Panther informer Alex Rackley in New Haven, Connecticut. Bobby Seale's defense attorney accuses the Justice Department of initiating a national campaign to intimidate and harass the Black Panther Party. Seale is later extradited to Connecticut.

1969, August 25. Pittsburgh, Pennsylvania.   Five construction sites are closed by several hundred black construction workers and members of the Black Construction Coalition to protest "discriminatory hiring practices." Four hundred angry white workers stage counter demonstrations on August 28 and 29 to protest the work stoppage.

1969, September 2. Hartford, Connecticut.   After a relatively quiet summer, the nation is stunned when Hartford becomes the scene of widespread civil disorders including fire bombings and sniping. Scores of people are placed under arrest, and a dusk-to-dawn curfew is imposed.

1969, September 23. Washington, DC.   Secretary of Labor George P. Schultz orders federally-assisted construction projects in Philadelphia to follow the guidelines for minority hiring suggested in the so-called "Philadelphia Plan."

1969, October 29. Washington, DC.   Ruling in the case of *Alexander v. Holmes County Board of Education*, the U.S. Supreme Court orders an end to all school segregation. The decision replaces the Warren Court's doctrine of "all deliberate speed," and is regarded as a setback for the Nixon administration.

1970, January 2. Washington, DC.   FBI director J. Edgar Hoover claims that, in 1969, there were over 100 attacks on police by "hate-type" African American groups such as Black Panthers.

1970, January 3. Mississippi.   Governor John Bell Williams announces his intention to submit to the state legislature a proposal to authorize income tax credits of up to $500 a year for contributors to "private" educational institutions. The plan is designed to create a "workable alternative" to school desegregation. That same day, the Department of Health, Education and Welfare reports that a comprehensive survey indicates

that 61 percent of the nation's black students and 65.6 percent of its white students attended segregated schools in 1968. On January 5, black children are enrolled in three formerly all-white Mississippi districts under the watchful eyes of federal marshals and Justice Department officials. Scores of white parents picket the schools, while others keep their children home or send them to private schools.

1970, January 10. Georgia.   Four Southern governors, Maddox of Georgia, Brewer of Alabama, McKeithen of Louisiana, and Kirk of Florida, promise to reject all busing plans designed for their states by the federal government or the courts. Maddox asks the state legislature to abolish compulsory attendance; McKeithen reveals no plan, but describes himself as "drawing the line in the dust;" Brewer denies that the courts have the constitutional authority to order busing as a device to achieve racial balance and promises to use his full executive powers to prevent it; Kirk vows to issue an executive order to block further desegregation of Florida schools.

1970, January 12. Washington, DC.   The U.S. Supreme Court refuses to review the ruling of an Ohio state court which upholds an equal employment plan comparable to the Nixon administration's "Philadelphia Plan." The plan requires state contractors to give assurances that they will employ a specified number of African American workers in projects constructed with federal funds or sponsored completely by the federal government. The Ohio contractor who brought suit in the case had refused to provide such assurances.

1970, January 15.   Though it is not yet a national holiday, the birthday of Martin Luther King Jr. is celebrated with impressive ceremonies, eulogies, and church services in many parts of the country. Public schools are closed in many cities; in others, they are kept open for formal study of King's life and work. In Atlanta, Coretta Scott King dedicates the Martin Luther King Jr. Memorial Center, which includes his home, the Ebenezer Baptist Church, and the crypt housing his remains.

1970, January 19. Washington, DC.   G. Harrold Carswell's nomination to the U.S. Supreme Court draws the immediate fire of civil rights advocates. On January 21, the NAACP condemns Carswell's "pro-segregation record." Two days later, the SCLC's Ralph Abernathy sends a telegram to Senate leaders pleading for "reassurance to the black community that there is. . . understanding and support. . . for our needs." AFL-CIO President George Meany calls the appointment "a slap in the face to the nation's black citizens." Testifying before the Senate Judiciary Committee on January 27, Carswell states: "I am not a racist. I have no notions, secretive or otherwise, of racial superiority." This statement contrasts sharply with a 1948 remark that Carswell would yield to no man "in the firm, vigorous belief in the principles of white supremacy."

1970, February 6. Denver, Colorado. Approximately one-third of Denver school buses are destroyed by bombs in an attempt by segregationists to disrupt the city's school integration plans.

1970, February 16. Washington, DC. President Richard M. Nixon establishes a Cabinet-level task force to assist and counsel local school districts which have been ordered to desegregate their school immediately. The objective is to spare the public school system undue disruption while, at the same time, insuring compliance with the law. On February 18 the Senate passes, by a 56–36 vote, an amendment to deny federal funds to school districts whose racial imbalance is the result of residential segregation. On February 19, Southerners in the House and Senate incorporate riders into two appropriation bills designed to restore "freedom-of-choice" school plans and to prevent the federal government from resorting to busing as a vehicle to promote racial balance.

1970, February 21. Texas. Texas Governor Preston Smith recommends a statewide referendum to give voters the opportunity to approve or reject integrated public school busing. Governors Maddox of Georgia and McKeithen of Louisiana sign bills prohibiting busing and student/teacher transfers to achieve racial balance. Governor Brewer calls a special session of the legislature to sponsor a similar bill for Alabama.

1970, February 28. Washington, DC. A memo written by Daniel Patrick Moynihan to President Richard M. Nixon is revealed. In the memo, Moynihan, domestic advisor to the president, counseled him that "the time may have come when the issue of race could benefit from a period of benign neglect." Moynihan later claims that the memo was intended to suggest ways that the "extraordinary black progress" in the last decade could be "consolidated." However, African American leaders, including Bayard Rustin and Representative John Conyers, charge that the memo is "symptomatic of a calculated, aggressive, systematic effort of the Nixon administration to wipe out civil rights progress of the past twenty years."

1970, March 6. Mississippi. The state Senate approves a tax relief bill designed to grant financial support to white parents who intend to enroll their children in private academies.

1970, March 9. Washington, DC. The U.S. Supreme Court orders the Memphis school system to end racial segregation and remands the case to a lower court where it issues instructions to develop an effective desegregation plan.

1970, April 7. Detroit, Michigan. The school board approves a busing plan for some 3,000 high school students and announces the initiation of a decentralization plan aimed at dispersing white students among the city's secondary schools. In Detroit, 63 percent of the system's 294,000 students are non-white, as are 42 percent of the teachers.

1970, May 12. Augusta, Georgia. Six African Americans are shot and twenty other people are wounded during a night of violence punctuated by looting, burning, and sniper activity. The immediate cause of the violence is said to be the killing of an African American youth in a county jail a few days earlier. Autopsies of African Americans slain during the protests indicate that they were shot in the back. The *New York Times* later reports that at least three of the dead were unarmed bystanders.

1970, May 14. Jackson, Mississippi. Two African American students are shot and killed after a night of violence outside a women's dormitory at Jackson State College. Witnesses charge that police simply moved in and indiscriminately blasted the residence hall with shotguns. President Richard M. Nixon dispatches Justice Department officials to search out the facts, but contradictory explanations make it impossible to assemble a wholly-coherent story. On May 17, the Mississippi United Front vows to provide students and other groups with independent protection.

1970, May 23. Atlanta, Georgia. A five-day, 100-mile march against repression ends in downtown Atlanta with a rally by the Southern Christian Leadership Conference and the NAACP. Speakers at the rally include Ralph Abernathy, Coretta Scott King, and Senator George McGovern. The speakers condemn racism, the Vietnam War, student killings at Kent State and Jackson State, and alleged police brutality in Augusta.

1970, July 10. Washington, DC. The Internal Revenue Service announces its intention to tax private academies practicing racial discrimination in their admissions policies. The greatest impact of the policy is expected to be felt in the South. The new policy promises these schools sufficient flexibility to avoid immediate revocation of their tax-exempt status.

1970, August 7. San Rafael, California. A dramatic shootout results in the death of Superior Court Judge Harold Haley and three African Americans on trial. Later investigation traces the sale of the weapons used in the shootout to Angela Davis, controversial UCLA professor and self-admitted Communist. Davis flees the state following the trial and is placed on the FBI's ten most wanted list.

1970, September. Some 300,000 African American children are integrated in over 200 Southern school districts. However, parental boycotts and delaying tactics by states and cities slow the pace of desegregation. Whites who are opposed to desegregation are encouraged by the Nixon administration's "Southern policy," which has delayed enforcement of integration orders. Nevertheless, the Internal Revenue Service continues to revoke the tax-exempt status of all-white private academies that refuse to admit black students.

1970, October 13. New York City, New York. Angela Davis is arrested and arraigned in federal court on charges of unlawful flight to avoid prosecution for her alleged role in the August 7 killing of Superior Court Judge Harold Haley.

1970, November 5. Henderson, North Carolina. Violence erupts when African Americans protest the reopening of a segregated school. The National Guard is called out to restore order and over 100 arrests are made.

1970, December 30. Philadelphia, Pennsylvania. The U.S. Court of Appeals for the Third Circuit rules that the Department of Housing and Urban Development must promote fair housing when it considers applications for mortgage insurance and rent supplements.

1971, February 4. Washington, DC. Eight African American federal employees file suit in federal court claiming that the Federal Service Entrance Examination, the principal test for qualifying college graduates for civil service posts is "culturally and racially discriminatory."

1971, March 8. Media, Pennsylvania. Files are stolen from a Federal Bureau of Investigation (FBI) office and released to the press reveal that in November of 1970, J. Edgar Hoover ordered an investigation of all groups "organized to project the demands of black [college] students, because they posed a threat to the nation's stability and security."

1971, March 29. Washington, DC. President Richard M. Nixon meets with the Congressional Black Caucus, which had been trying to schedule a meeting with him for several months. The African American members of Congress request increased attention to welfare services, desegregation, housing, and social justice programs. President Nixon reportedly promises stronger enforcement of civil rights laws.

1971, May 5. Brooklyn, New York. A riot erupts in the Brooklyn's Brownsville section after thousands of residents take to the streets to protest cuts in state welfare, Medicaid, food stamps, and educational programs. One policeman is shot, 12 are injured.

1971, May 17. Washington, DC. Senator George McGovern of South Dakota urges the government to divert $31 billion of current federal spending in an effort to end racial discrimination by the end of the century. Milton Eisenhower, former chairman of President Lyndon B. Johnson's Commission on Causes and Preventions of Violence, warns that the United States faces a racial war if it does not remedy the social injustice, inequitable law enforcement, and the availability of firearms in American society.

1971, June 1. Washington, DC. By a vote of 5–4, the U.S. Supreme Court declares unconstitutional a Cincinnati city ordinance making it unlawful for small groups of people to loiter in an annoying manner in public places. Many African Americans claimed that such ordinances had been used by police to harass them.

1971, June 4. Washington, DC. The Department of Labor announces that it is removing support from the voluntary "Chicago Plan," which was to hire 4,000 African Americans and Spanish-speaking Americans for construction jobs on federal projects. After 18 months, less than 900 African Americans had been accepted in training programs and only a few had been admitted to Chicago construction unions.

1971, June 28. Washington, DC. By an 8–0 vote, with Justice Thurgood Marshall abstaining, the U.S. Supreme Court overturns draft evasion charges against Muhammad Ali. In its decision, the Court agreed that Ali, a Muslim, was objecting to military service on religious grounds, rather than on a political basis, as the Department of Justice had charged.

1971, July 24. Columbus, Georgia. Fifteen African Americans are arrested and several hospitalized during racial disturbances following the dismissal of eight African American policemen. Fire bombings and sniping are reported. State troopers are summoned to maintain order.

1971, August 7. Georgia. State Representative Julian Bond tours the state to spark the political interests of African Americans who remain unregistered six years after the passage of the Voting Rights Act. Bond notes that due to a blend of apathy and activism, many African Americans do not perceive the ballot as an effective political weapon that can be used to bring change in their lives. Bond cites as an example the failure of African Americans in 1970 to elect African American officials in a district where they represented a majority of the registered voters. Nevertheless, leaders of the SCLC announce that their goal of electing a Southern black to Congress is feasible in view of the redistricting in a number of Southern states.

1971, August 18. Jackson, Mississippi. Eleven members of the Republic of New Africa, a black separatist organization, are charged with murder and assault of federal officers after the death of Lieutenant I. Skinner, a Mississippi policeman. Skinner was shot when police and FBI agents raided the organization's headquarters in order to serve fugitive warrants on three members. The county district attorney requests that a special grand jury charge the separatists with treason and that the Justice Department allow these charges to take precedence over any federal prosecution.

1971, August 21. San Quentin, California. George Jackson, author of *Soledad Brothers* and a folk hero to many black and white radicals, is killed during a prison break. Some supporters of Jackson claim he was "set-up" for assassination, while others feel the official version of Jackson's death is essentially correct.

1971, October. Chicago, Illinois. "Black Expo," a four-day cultural and business exposition, attracts some 800,000 people. The exposition is conducted by Jesse Jackson and a number of African American businessmen.

1972, January 10. Richmond, Virginia. A federal judge orders the consolidation of Richmond's predominantly black school system with two all-white suburban systems. Judge Robert Mehirge bases his decision on the failure of state officials to take positive action to reverse *de facto* segregation.

1972, January 10. Baton Rouge, Louisiana. Two Black Muslims and two white police officers are killed in a shootout. Disturbances following the shootings injure 31 people and the National Guard is called in to restore order.

1972, March. Gary, Indiana. Some 8,000 African Americans representing a wide spectrum of political views attend the first National Black Political Convention. The convention is chaired by Imamu Amiri Baraka with Mayor Richard Hatcher of Gary, Indiana, as the keynote speaker. The group approves a political platform, the "Black Agenda" that demands reparations, proportional congressional representation for African Americans, an increase in federal spending to combat crime and drug trafficking, reduction of the military budget, and a guaranteed annual income of $6,500 for a family of four.

1972, March 16. Washington, DC. President Nixon proposes a moratorium on all court-ordered busing until July of 1973. African American members of Congress charge that the president is suggesting a return to "separate but equal" schools.

1972, June 4. San Jose, California. After 13 hours of deliberation, a jury of eleven whites and one Mexican-American acquits Angela Davis of murder and other charges in connection with a 1970 courthouse shootout in San Rafael, California.

1972, June 6. Richmond, Virginia. A U.S. Appeals Court, by a 5–1 vote, overturns a plan which would have required the busing of school children between Richmond and two nearly all-white suburbs.

1972, July 12. Miami Beach, Florida. Senator George McGovern of South Dakota wins the presidential nomination at the Democratic party's national convention. African American delegates make up approximately 15 percent of the total delegates in attendance. New York Representative Shirley Chisholm, the first African American woman to seek a presidential nomination, receives 151 votes.

1972, August. Washington, DC. Attorney General Richard Kleindienst files suit against the cities of Los Angeles, California, and Montgomery, Alabama, for discrimination in hiring for public service jobs.

1972, November. Cincinnati, Ohio. The Association for the Study of Black Life History, meeting for its 57th annual convention, changes its name to the Association for the Study of African American History. The change is based on a mail ballot of the Association's membership, some two-thirds of whom opt to substitute "African-American" for "black" in the title. Prominent speakers at the convention include: Andrew F. Brimmer, a governor of the Federal Reserve Board; Representative Louis Stokes of Cleveland; John Hope Franklin, professor of history at Duke University; and Rayford W. Logan, professor of history at Howard University.

1972, November. Richard M. Nixon is reelected president in a landslide victory over Senator George McGovern, despite the fact that some 86 percent of the African American vote went to McGovern. However, African Americans achieve a number of electoral successes as the number of African Americans in Congress increases from 12 to 15; Barbara Jordan of Houston, Texas, and Andrew Young of Atlanta become the first Southern African Americans elected to Congress since Reconstruction. Senator Edward Brooke, an African American Republican from Massachusetts, wins reelection and African American representation in state legislatures increases dramatically.

1972, November 16. Baton Rouge, Louisiana. Two young African American men, Denver A. Smith and Leonard Douglas Brown, are killed on the campus of Southern University during a confrontation between students and police. The students had been pressing for the resignation of the university's president G. Leon Netterville, whom they charged with arbitrarily dismissing teachers he regarded as militant and for being unreceptive to student demands for better living and academic facilities. Following the shootings, Louisiana Governor Edwin W. Edwards closes the school and sends the National Guard to the Baton Rouge campus.

1972, December 14. Washington, DC. In the case of *Banks v. Perks*, the U.S. Supreme Court rules unanimously that residents of racially-segregated housing projects can sue to have them integrated. In its opinion, the Court states that white residents living in segregated housing projects suffer the same social and economic injuries as those denied access to these facilities.

1973, April 28. Washington, DC. A government panel releases its final report determining whether the Tuskegee Syphilis Study, conducted between 1932 and 1972 by the Public Health Service, was justified. The study involved observing the effects of untreated syphilis on 430 African American men living in rural Macon County, Alabama. The panel found no evidence that participants in the study had been given any type of informed consent. The panel concluded that the study was unjustified on both scientific and humanitarian grounds and that all policies regarding research on humans be reformed.

1973, May 29. Los Angeles, California. Thomas Bradley is elected mayor of Los Angeles after defeating the incumbent Sam Yorty by 100,000 votes. Yorty had defeated Bradley in the 1969 mayoral election.

1973, June. Washington, DC. The Joint Center for Political Studies reports that as of April of 1973, 2,621 African Americans held elective offices in the United States at every level from school boards to the Congress. When the first list was compiled, in 1969, the total was only 1,185.

1974. Henry Aaron breaks Babe Ruth's long-standing record and hits his 715th home run.

1974, March. Washington, DC. The Department of Justice releases memos revealing that in the 1960s and early 1970s, the FBI had waged a campaign designed to disrupt, discredit, and neutralize black nationalist groups including the Black Panther party. A major objective of the effort, according to the memo, was to prevent the emergence of an African American leader capable of uniting disparate factions and inspiring violence. Jesse Jackson remarks that the documents implicate the FBI in the deaths of Martin Luther King Jr., Malcolm X, and Fred Hampton.

1974, March 15. Little Rock, Arkansas. The second Black National Political Convention is held. Mayor Richard B. Hatcher of Gary, Indiana, and Imamu Amiri Baraka are among the speakers. Delegates to the convention approve several resolutions including the establishment of a fund to provide money for civil rights causes and a resolution voicing support for African liberation movements.

1974, June. Washington, DC. A draft report from the Senate committee investigating the "Watergate" scandal indicates that the Nixon administration tried to gain the support or neutrality of prominent African Americans during the 1972 presidential campaign by withholding federal funds for government programs. Among those contacted by the Nixon administration were Jesse Jackson, head of Operation PUSH, and James Farmer, an administration official during Nixon's first term.

1974, July 25. Washington, DC. In the case of *Milliken v. Bradley*, the U.S. Supreme Court nullifies an attempt to implement the "metropolitan integration" of predominantly African American schools in Detroit with those of nearby white suburbs. Chief Justice Warren Burger, writing for the majority, declares that segregation in a city's schools does not justify its combination with schools in its suburbs. Justice Thurgood Marshall calls the Court's decision "an emasculation of the constitutional guarantee of equal opportunity."

1974, November. The number of African American elected officials increases at the federal, state, and local levels. African American members of Congress are reelected and one new member, Harold Ford of Memphis, Tennessee, is added. African Americans are also elected to the post of lieutenant governor in California and Colorado.

1974, December 11. Boston, Massachusetts. Violence erupts between supporters and opponents of public school integration.

1975, January 16. Washington, DC. William T. Coleman is named secretary of transportation by President Ford, becoming the second African American in the nation's history to hold a Cabinet post.

1975, January 25. The *New York Times* reports that the FBI had wiretapped conversations of civil rights leaders including Martin Luther King Jr.

1975, May 3. Department of Labor figures report the national unemployment rate at nine percent, the African American rate at 15 percent. Vernon L. Jordan Jr. of the National Urban League reports that the African American rate is actually 26 percent.

1975, August 18. Washington, DC. District of Columbia Appellate Court Judge Julia Cooper is confirmed by the Senate, becoming the highest-ranking African American woman in the federal courts.

1975, August 20. Washington, DC. Senator Edward Brooke calls for a $10 billion federal employment program to end the economic "depression" in black America by creating one million public service jobs.

1975, August 29. Washington, DC. General Daniel James Jr. becomes commander-in-chief of the North

American Air Defense Command (NORAD). On the same day, he is promoted and becomes the first African American four-star general in U.S. history.

1975, September 27. Washington, DC. The Congressional Black Caucus holds its fifth annual dinner. The major theme of the affair is "From Changing Structures to Using Structure—1879–1976." Panelists recommend the federal takeover of the welfare system and poverty assistance, that the states assume more fiscal responsibility for education, and that Caucus-directed programs develop a national African American position on matters of policy.

1975, December. Washington, DC. U.S. Attorney General Edward Levy opens an official review of the Martin Luther King Jr. assassination. Although James Earl Ray was convicted of the crime, many facts point to a conspiracy and suggest that those really responsible for the murder are still at large.

1976, April 26. New York City, New York. The Metropolitan Applied Research Center, a major African American research organization founded to serve as an advocate for the urban poor, announces that it must close due to declining funds.

1976, August 31. Mississippi. A chancellery court orders the NAACP to pay the sum of $1,250,058 to 12 white Port Gibson merchants. The money is compensation for the financial hardships inflicted on the merchants due to the NAACP's successful boycott of white businesses in 1966.

1976, November 2. African American voters play a vital role in Jimmy Carter's victory over President Gerald Ford in the presidential election. Carter received about 94 percent of some 6.6 million African American votes.

1976, November 14. Plains, Georgia. The congregation of President-elect Jimmy Carter's Baptist church votes to drop its 11-year ban on attendance by African Americans.

1976, December 16. Washington, DC. President-elect Jimmy Carter appoints Andrew Young as chief delegate to the United Nations and Patricia Roberts Harris as secretary of the Department of Housing and Urban Development.

1977, January 20. Washington, DC. Clifford Alexander Jr. is sworn in as the first African American secretary of the U.S. Army. President Carter appoints 19 African Americans to his Cabinet, while 37 other African Americans obtain executive positions within the Carter administration.

1977, April 19. New York City, New York. Author Alex Haley receives a Pulitzer Prize for his book *Roots*.

1977, July 29. St. Louis, Missouri. Roy Wilkins, a 42-year veteran of the NAACP, announces his retirement during the organization's 68th annual convention.

1977, September 4. New York City, New York. At a meeting of the National Urban League, 15 African American members agree to form a loose coalition to combat perceived anti-African American sentiment within the nation and seek greater job opportunities for African Americans.

1978, January 17. Major Guion S. Bluford Jr., Major Frederick D. Gregory, and Ronald E. McNair join the space program and begin training as astronauts for future space missions.

1978, May 29. Washington, DC. Files made public by the FBI reveal that an unidentified African American leader worked with the agency during the 1960s in an effort to remove Martin Luther King Jr. from national prominence in the Civil Rights movement. The information released is from the files of the late J. Edgar Hoover.

1978, June 28. Washington, DC. Hearing the case *University of California v. Bakke*, the U.S. Supreme Court, in a 5–4 decision, orders that white student Allan P. Bakke be admitted to the medical school at the University of California, Davis. The Court rules that the refusal to admit Bakke is tantamount to reverse discrimination and that the use of racial or ethnic quotas is an improper means of achieving racial balance. The Court also holds that the college's affirmative action program is invalid since it had the effect of discriminating against qualified white applicants, although the court perceived the goal of attaining a diverse student body as constitutional and permissible.

1978, December 3. The U.S. Census Bureau reports that from 1960 to 1977, the number of African Americans living in suburban areas increased from 2.4 million to 4.6 million, and that 55 percent of the 24.5 million African Americans in the United States live in central cities, indicating a decline from the 1970 figure of 59 percent.

1979, February 27. Washington, DC. The Department of Housing and Urban Development announces that it will foreclose on the financially-troubled Soul City, a new town in rural North Carolina that was to have been controlled by African Americans but open to members of all races. Since 1969, when Floyd B. McKissick announced the idea for the city, $27 million had been spent by federal, state, and local sources. McKissick vows to continue efforts to keep the project alive.

1979, May 2. Washington, DC. The Congressional Black Caucus and delegates from 11 Southern states set up an "action alert communications network." This network is designed to exert pressure on at least 100 white congressional representatives from predominantly black districts to vote with the caucus on important issues.

1979, June 19. The U.S. Census Bureau announces a study indicating that although blacks have made enormous advances in employment, income, health, housing, political power, and other measures of social well-being, they remain far behind white Americans.

1979, June 25. Washington, DC. Amalya L. Kearse becomes the first woman to receive an appointment to the U.S. Court of Appeals.

1979, June 29. Washington, DC. In the case of *United States Steel v. Brian Weber,* the U.S. Supreme Court rules that private employers can legally give special preference to black workers to eliminate "manifest racial imbalance" in traditionally white jobs.

1979, August 1. Washington, DC. The U.S. House of Representatives votes 408–1 to place a bust of the late Martin Luther King Jr. in the Capitol. The bust is the first work of art in the Capitol honoring an African American.

1979, August 16. New York City, New York. Andrew Young resigns as the chief U.S. delegate to the United Nations after being publicly criticized for conducting unauthorized talks with the Palestine Liberation Organization in New York. The resignation sets off a storm of controversy and animosity between segments of the Jewish and African American communities.

1979, December 22. Washington, DC. The Joint Center for Political Studies reveals that between 1978 and 1979, the number of African Americans elected to public office increased by 104. This two percent increase is considered meager, especially because such officials were elected in states with substantial African American populations.

1980, February 6. Washington, DC. The Congressional Black Caucus criticizes President Carter's fiscal 1981 budget proposals because they increase the amount of military spending while reducing the funding for social programs. Caucus members promise to initiate legislation to reduce military spending increases and pronounce the budget "an unmitigated disaster for the poor, the unemployed and minorities."

1980, April 22. Washington, DC. Hearing the case *City of Mobile, Alabama v. Wiley L. Bolden,* the U.S. Supreme Court, in a 6–3 decision, overturns a lower court ruling that an at-large city electoral system is unconstitutional because it dilutes the voting strength of African Americans.

1980, May 11. Washington, DC. Early primary results reveal that the African American community is supporting President Carter's second-term bid despite criticism of his record by national African American leaders, according to reports. The "resounding" victories won by Carter in the Southern primaries are interpreted as African Americans lacking faith in their ability to enact a "Great Society-style social renewal" agenda as proposed by Senator Edward M. Kennedy.

1980, May 14. Birmingham, Alabama. J. B. Stoner, a white supremacist, is convicted for the 1958 bombing of an African American church in Birmingham, Alabama.

1980, May 18. Miami, Florida. The African American Liberty City area and predominantly African American Coconut Grove section of Miami erupt into riotous violence, ending with nine dead and 163 injured, following the acquittal of four white Dade County police officers in the beating death of a black man. In the night-long unrest, stores are looted, property burned, and whites fatally beaten. During the violence, African Americans are heard screaming the name "McDuffie" (Arthur), the African American insurance executive beaten to death following a high-speed chase with Dade County police officers for a traffic violation. Dade County officials impose an 8 p.m. to 6 a.m. curfew; 350 National Guard troops set up headquarters in an armory with 450 more enroute from Orlando.

1980, May 29. Fort Wayne, Indiana. Vernon E. Jordan Jr., president of the National Urban League, is shot and seriously wounded by an unknown assailant. Stating that the shooting evidenced "an element of premeditation," director of the FBI William H. Webster says, "the shooting was not accidental, and was in furtherance of an apparent conspiracy to deprive Vernon Jordan of his civil rights." The shooting occurred just outside Jordan's motel room.

1980, July 3. Washington, DC. A ruling authorizing Congress to impose racial quotas to remedy past discrimination against minority contractors in federal jobs programs is upheld by the U.S. Supreme Court in a 6–3 vote. It validates the ten percent minority set-aside of federal public works contracts, challenged by white contractors in *Fullilove v. Klutznick.*

1980, July 3. Cincinnati, Ohio. In a consent decree with the Justice Department, the city of Cincinnati agrees to hire and promote more African Americans and women within the police department. The decree permanently enjoins the city from engaging in any employment discrimination. Over a five-year period, 34 percent of new police officer vacancies will be filled by African Americans and 23 percent by women. The fire department of the city of Chicago, in a similar action

(April 2, 1980), was permanently prohibited from discrimination against any candidate for promotion on the basis of race or national origin. The settlement of this discrimination action was filed in federal district court and resulted from a suit charging violations of the Civil Rights Act of 1964 and the Federal Sharing Act of 1972. In New York City, the U.S. Court of Appeals (August 1, 1980) overturned a lower court ruling that 50 percent of all new police officer hires be African American or Hispanic. The appeals court, however, ruled that the written test used for hiring had "significant disparate racial impact" in violation of the Civil Rights Act of 1964. It concluded that until a new test was implemented, one-third of all newly hired police must be African American or Hispanic.

1980, September 3. St. Louis, Missouri. St. Louis schools are desegregated peacefully after eight years of struggle. Over 16,000 students are bused on the first day of classes under court orders. No violence is reported.

1980, September 26. Detroit, Michigan. Federal district judge Horace W. Gilmore invalidates the 1980 census on the grounds that it undercounts African Americans and Hispanics, thus violating the one-person, one-vote principle. The action was precipitated by a suit initiated by the city of Detroit with support from dozens of other cities. The census was later upheld in higher courts.

1980, September 26. Washington, DC. The Congressional Black Caucus marks its tenth anniversary with its annual legislative weekend. The group of bipartisan representatives cite as their major achievements the Humphrey-Hawkins Full Employment Bill and the ten percent "minority-set-aside" law established to ensure minority firms a nearly representative share of federal contracts. The caucus identifies its current concern as the potential reapportionment of congressional districts affected by the outcome of the 1980 census.

1980, September 29. New York City, New York. The Schomburg Center for Research in Black Culture opens a new $3.8 million building in Harlem.

1980, September 30. Washington, DC. The first annual Black College Day is attended by 18,000 African American students. Speeches on the preservation of African American colleges and universities are given by African American officials and student leaders. The march is organized by African American journalist Tony Brown in an effort to draw public attention to the impact of integration and merging of African American private and public colleges and universities. Brown contends seven out of ten blacks attending predominantly white colleges do not graduate.

1980, November 23. Philadelphia, Pennsylvania. About 1,000 people from 25 states attend a convention and form the National Black Independent Party. The idea grows out of a National Black Political Assembly in Gary, Indiana, in 1972.

1980, December 12. Washington, DC. African American leaders of the nation's major civil rights organizations meet with President-elect Ronald Reagan who says he will defend the civil rights of minorities. The leaders urge him to appoint an African American to a Cabinet position in his administration. Present at the meeting are Vernon E. Jordan Jr., president of the National Urban League; Benjamin Hooks, executive director, NAACP; and Dorothy I. Height, president of the National Council of Negro Women.

1980, December 18. San Antonio, Texas. A federal grand jury acquits Charles Veverka of four counts of violating the civil rights of Arthur McDuffie, an African American who was beaten to death while in police custody. The jury deliberates for 16 hours, finally breaking an 11–1 deadlock that threatened a mistrial. Veverka was indicted following violent riots in Miami resulting from the acquittal of four white police officers accused of executing the fatal beating.

1980, December 23. Washington, DC. Samuel R. Pierce Jr. is named by President-elect Ronald Reagan to the Cabinet post of secretary of the Department of Housing and Urban Development. As such, Pierce is the highest-ranking African American appointee of the new administration. According to reports, Pierce is a life-long Republican, widely respected in legal, financial, and civil rights circles.

1981, February 7. Miami, Florida. Three Miami youths are convicted of murder in connection with the beating deaths of three whites during the Liberty City riots in May of 1980. A fourth youth who was tried with the others is acquitted. Attorneys for the defendants announce plans to appeal the verdicts.

1981, May 7. Washington, DC. Representative Robert S. Walker, a Republican from Pennsylvania, introduces a bill which prohibits the use of numerical quotas devised to increase the hiring or school enrollment of minorities and women. Entitled the "Equal Employment Opportunity Act," it seeks to amend the Civil Rights Act of 1964 and prevents the federal government from imposing rules on employers or schools to hire workers or to admit students on the basis of race, sex, or national origin. In effect, the proposal no longer requires companies and educational institutions to make up for past discrimination by taking on a set number of minorities and women within a specified time frame.

1981, May 13. Washington, DC. The Labor Department proposes revisions of Executive Order No. 11246 (prohibiting employment discrimination by federal contractors based on race, sex, color, national origin, or religion) in its continuing effort to ease job-discrimination rules for federal contractors. The contents of an internal memorandum reveal the effort seems targeted toward reducing the record-keeping and affirmative action requirements for small contractors and eliminating "unnecessary confrontations" with all contractors. Timothy Ryan, Labor Department solicitor, says that the revisions make the program more manageable and cut the number of companies covered by two-thirds for certain requirements. Secretary Raymond Donovan maintains that a final decision on revisions within the Office of Federal Contracts Compliance Programs has not been made. Administration officials plan to alter the proposal before its effective date of June 29.

1981, May 23. Washington, DC. Calling them "ineffective" and unfair remedies to discrimination, Attorney General William French Smith announces that the Justice Department will no longer continue its vigorous pursuit of mandatory busing and the use of racial quotas in employment-discrimination cases. It also considers amendments which would make "reverse discrimination" illegal under the Civil Rights Act of 1964.

1981, June 10. Washington, DC. The House once again approves an anti-busing provision by a vote of 265 to 122, forbidding the Justice Department from taking any direct or indirect action to require the busing of students to schools other than those closest to where they live with the exception of cases involving special education needs. The provision is known as an "anti-busing rider" because of its attachment to the department's $2.3 billion authorized bill.

1981, June 16. Washington, DC. The Reagan administration, in a letter to Attorney General William French Smith, requires the Justice Department to determine whether the political rights of minority Americans are best served by the Voting Rights Act of 1965. Stating that the act marks the nation's commitment to full equality for all Americans, the administration says that what must be answered is whether the act continues to be the most appropriate means of guaranteeing their rights. The completed report is due October 1.

1981, September 9. New York City, New York. Roy Wilkins, former head of the NAACP and one of the key players in the Civil Rights movement of the 1960s, dies at New York University Medical Center at the age of 80.

1981, September 10. New York City, New York. Vernon Jordan announces his plans to resign as executive director of the National Urban League to join the Dallas-based law firm of Akin, Grump, Hauer, and Field. Jordan's office will be in Washington, DC.

1981, October 7. Washington, DC. A House vote, 389–24, in favor of extending the Voting Rights Act of 1965, seems to ensure the likelihood of an equally strong measure in the Senate, according to Capitol Hill analysts. The House version makes the pre-clearance provisions of the act permanent (requiring six Southern states and Alaska to submit proposed changes in election laws to the Justice Department before implementation), but also features the so-called bailout provision that exempts jurisdictions from the requirement if they can prove a clean ten-year voting rights record and efforts to encourage minority voting.

1981, November 28. Washington, DC. The nomination of Clarence M. Pendleton, president of the Urban League of San Diego, to head the U.S. Commission on Civil Rights results in divided opinion over his suitability for the post. Pendleton's selection is controversial because of his promotion of private industry as a cure-all for African American economic problems and because of his opposition to other positions taken traditionally by the Civil Rights movement on issues such as busing and affirmative action.

1981, December 8. Washington, DC. William Bradford Reynolds, assistant attorney general of the Justice Department's civil rights division, announces plans to seek a ruling by the Supreme Court which would find it unconstitutional to give minorities and women preference in hiring and promotion. Reynolds wants a reversal of the High Court's decision in *Weber v. Kaiser Aluminum and Chemical Corp.*, which upheld the legality of affirmative action hiring and promotion practices negotiated by the company and the United Steel Workers of America. Reynolds contends the *Weber* decision was "wrongly decided" and that different sets of rules for the public sector and the private sector should not exist. Under his direction, the Justice Department has ceased such hiring preferences; the action sought by Reynolds would prohibit individuals, the Labor Department, or the Equal Employment Opportunity Commission from seeking such preferences.

1982, January 2. Los Angeles, California. Los Angeles Mayor Tom Bradley opens his campaign to become the first African American governor of California. The 64-year-old former policeman has been elected as the city's mayor three times.

1982, January 20. Alabama. Two African American civil rights workers, Julia Wilder and Maggie Bozeman, are charged with vote fraud.

1982, February 1. New York City, New York. Representative Shirley Chisholm, a Democrat from New York and the first African American woman to win a seat in Congress, announces that she will not seek another term. She has served the Brooklyn communities of Bedford-Stuyvesant and Bushwick since 1968.

1982, February 1. Washington, DC. The Justice Department proposes that the city of Chicago be allowed to try to desegregate its schools following a plan that would rely mainly on voluntary student transfers rather than mandatory busing.

1982, February 6. Alabama. A small band of Southern civil rights workers, followed by 300 sympathizers, start a 140-mile march in support of the Federal Voting Rights Act and in protest against the vote fraud conviction of two African American political activists. The marchers travel from Carrollton, Alabama, through Selma to the state capitol, Montgomery, a route made famous in early civil rights marches.

1982, February 14. Alabama. Hundreds of voting rights marchers going from Carrollton to Montgomery march peacefully across the Edmund Pettis Bridge.

1982, April 4. Washington, DC. The Bureau of Census reports that the 1980 census missed counting 1.3 million African Americans and that the undercount represented 4.8 percent of the nation's 28 million African Americans. The bureau says that in 1970 the census missed 1.9 million out of 24.4 million African Americans.

1983. Washington, DC. A test case of the Justice Department to eliminate court-ordered busing to desegregate public schools is rejected by the U.S. Supreme Court. It was the contention of the Justice Department that a desegregation plan in Nashville, Tennessee, was contributing to "white flight" from the city.

1983. Louisiana. Louisiana repeals the United States' last racial classification law.

1983, January 12. Washington, DC. A majority of the U.S. Civil Rights Commission charges that the Reagan administration's Justice Department has been moving in the direction of getting judicial approval to end affirmative action. The two-and-a-half-page text issued by the majority asserts that cases in several cities, given the current position of the Justice Department, could result in continued discrimination. The committee's assertion is opposed by the chairman of the committee, Clarence Pendleton, an African American Reagan appointee.

1983, April 13. Chicago, Illinois. Harold Washington becomes the first African American mayor of Chicago. Washington received 656,727 votes (51 percent), while his opponent, Bernard Epton, received 617,159 votes (48 percent). The voting followed racial lines with 90 percent of the votes in black areas going to Washington, as well as some 44 percent of the vote in the city's white liberal areas.

1983, April 22. Greensboro, North Carolina. After 29 months of investigation, a federal grand jury indicts six Ku Klux Klansmen and three members of the American Nazi Party in the deaths of five members of the Communist Workers Party who participated in a "Death-to-the-Klan" rally in Greensboro, North Carolina, in 1979.

1983, May 18. New York City, New York. Benjamin L. Hooks, executive director of the NAACP, is suspended indefinitely by the association's chairman, Margaret Bush Wilson. The controversy was said to have begun with Wilson's criticism of some internal aspects as to how well the organization was doing.

1983, May 25. Washington, DC. In an 8–1 decision the Supreme Court rules that private schools which discriminate on the basis of race are not eligible for tax exemptions. The ruling in *Bob Jones University v. IRS* rejects the Reagan administration's contention that because there is nothing in the Internal Revenue Service code banning such exemptions, they are permissible. The opinion, rendered by Chief Justice Warren E. Burger, stated that racial discrimination in education violates widely accepted views of elementary justice and "that to grant tax exempt status to racially discriminatory educational entities would be incompatible with the concepts of tax exemption."

1983, May 26. Washington, DC. President Ronald Reagan presents three nominees to replace three current members of the U.S. Commission on Civil Rights. If confirmed, the administration would have a majority of its appointees on the six-member commission. A storm of protest and controversy arises from civil rights groups and members of Congress accusing the president of efforts to pack the commission. The three nominees are John H. Bunzel, Morris B. Abram, and Robert A. Destro. The commissioners to be replaced are Mary Frances Berry, Rabbi Murray Saltzman, and Blandina Cardenas Ramirez. However, lawyers from various private and governmental agencies indicated that the president probably does not have the legal authority to dismiss personnel who in effect are members of an independent bipartisan deliberative body with no powers. Jack Greenberg of the NAACP Legal Defense and Educational Fund stated that it was illegal for the president to do what he proposes and that the Fund would represent the commissioners if they decided to mount a challenge.

1983, May 28. New York City, New York. The NAACP's executive director Benjamin L. Hooks is reinstated to his post after an eight-day suspension by board chairman Margaret Bush Wilson. Wilson states that the objective of the action has been achieved and its continuance no longer serves a useful purpose.

Harold Washington (right) addressing an audience after his victory in the 1983 Chicago mayoral race.

1983, August. Washington, DC.   Surveys in the state of Mississippi indicate a probability that enforcement of the Voting Rights Act will be extremely difficult in many counties. As a result, Assistant Attorney General William Bradford Reynolds announces that he will send 300 federal observers into the state to see that the act is enforced. Many civil rights leaders believe the response to be totally inadequate and Jesse Jackson believes that the planned observers are untrained and will be unable to see or understand many violations.

1983, October 20. Washington, DC.   By a vote of 78–22, action is completed in the Senate and the president signs into law a bill making the third Monday of each January a day honoring the memory of slain civil rights leader Martin Luther King Jr. Initially opposed by President Ronald Reagan, many prominent Republican senators urged and got the president's support of the bill, thus insuring passage in the Senate. The bill had previously passed in the house by a margin of 338–90. Senator Jesse Helms (Republican, North Carolina) leads an effort to defeat the bill. Helms accuses King of "Marxist" ways. Helms also attempts to have controversial FBI tapes on King opened and made public in the hope that such disclosure would create public

scandal. Senator Edward Kennedy (Democrat, Massachusetts) is outraged by Helms and asks for a renunciation of the senator in the nation and in his home state.

1983, October 25. Washington, DC.   In a surprise move President Ronald Reagan fires three members from the U.S. Commission on Civil Rights because their views are critical of many aspects of the administration's policies in this area. Those fired were Mary Frances Berry, a professor of history and law at Howard University; Blandina Cardenas Ramirez of San Antonio; and Rabbi Murray Saltzman of Baltimore—all highly regarded as effective spokespersons for minorities.

1983, November 10.   In general elections throughout the nation, African Americans make some significant gains. Wilson Goode is elected mayor of Philadelphia, becoming that city's first African American to serve in such capacity and making his city the fourth of the nation's six largest cities to have an African American as chief executive. Other African American winners are Democrat Harvey Gantt who becomes the first African American elected mayor of Charlotte, North Carolina; James A. Sharp Jr., the first elected African

American mayor of Flint, Michigan; Thirman Milner who wins a second term in Hartford, Connecticut; and Richard Hatcher who wins a fifth term in Gary, Indiana.

1983, December 1. Washington, DC. In a supposed compromise bill President Ronald Reagan signs into law a newly reorganized U.S. Commission on Civil Rights comprised of four presidential and four congressional appointees. As the first of his appointments, Reagan reappoints Clarence M. Pendleton Jr. as chairman of the new commission.

1984. The Centers for Disease Control releases figures on the homicide rate for young African American males. Between 1984 and 1988, the homicide rate among African American males ages 15 to 24 had risen 68 percent.

1984, June 6. Washington, DC. Margaret Bush Wilson, former chairperson of the NAACP, loses the battle to get herself reinstated as a member of the association's governing board. Wilson was the first African American woman chairperson of the NAACP and had been a member of the national board of directors since 1963.

1984, June 13. Washington, DC. In a 6–3 decision the U.S. Supreme Court invalidated a U.S. district court decision that allowed the layoff of three white firefighters who had seniority over three black firefighters. The Supreme Court decided that affirmative action employment gains are not preferential when jobs must be decreased and that "legitimate" seniority systems are protected from court intervention. However, a dissenting opinion by Justices Blackmun, Brennan, and Marshall argued that under Title 7 of the Civil Rights Act of 1964, race-related preferential practice was an acceptable application. As a result of the Court's decision, the Justice Department announces that it will reexamine all federal anti-discrimination settlements and will advise government agencies to not continue the practice of using racial employment quotas when negotiating affirmative action plans.

1984, July 6. Washington, DC. Secret tapes of President John F. Kennedy are made public and demonstrate a sincere effort by Kennedy to get mayors, governors, and congressmen to accept integration and support his civil rights programs. The recordings made during the Kennedy presidency also reveal a dramatic conversation with Martin Luther King Jr. in which King, after a bombing in Birmingham, Alabama, that killed four children at an African American church, calls upon the president to send federal troops into the city to protect the African American community and to prevent riots.

In a conversation with mayor Allen Thompson of Jackson, Mississippi, the president urges him to hire African American police officers. After the mayor assures the president that he will hire African Americans, he said to Kennedy "don't get your feelings hurt" about public statements he may have to make about the president, to which Kennedy replies "well, listen I give you full permission to denounce me in public as long as you don't do it in private."

1984, November 14. Washington, DC. The Supreme Court rules that redistricting plans and election laws that have discriminatory results are affirmed to be illegal under a provision of the 1982 Voting Rights Act. The ruling came as a result of a Mississippi redistricting plan.

1984, November 12. Atlanta, Georgia. The Reverend Martin Luther King Sr. dies of a heart ailment at the age of 82. For 44 years he had been pastor of the Ebenezer Baptist Church and was one of the South's most influential African American clergymen.

1985, January 5. South Africa. Senator Edward Kennedy visits South Africa at the invitation of Noble Peace Prize-recipient Bishop Desmond Tutu. Kennedy also visits Winnie Mandela, the wife of jailed black nationalist Nelson Mandela, but his request to meet with the imprisoned leader is refused by the government.

1985, February 21. New York City, New York. As a cost-savings measure the NAACP will move from its headquarters in New York City to Baltimore, Maryland, by 1986. The association is negotiating the purchase of a suitable building for $2 million in Baltimore after being unable to find a suitable and economically-sound location in New York City.

1985, February 26. Washington, DC. The U.S. Commission on Civil Rights gives enthusiastic support to a Supreme Court decision giving existing seniority systems preference over affirmative action programs even though the African Americans were hired to remedy previously contended discriminatory hiring practices. U.S. Civil Rights Commissioners Mary Frances Berry and Blandina Cardenas Ramirez, in heated disagreement with the Supreme Court and the Civil Rights Commission's report, state that civil rights laws are designed to protect blacks, minorities, and women, not white men. The statement creates new controversy as to the meaning of the existence of the Civil Rights Commission.

1985, March 7. Washington, DC. Charging that the U.S. Commission on Civil Rights had already decided to oppose such measures as timetables and quotas, national civil rights groups boycott hearings on the use of such goals to achieve racial balance or to remedy discriminatory hiring practices.

1985, March 13. Washington, DC. Clarence Pendleton, chairman of the U.S. Commission on Civil Rights, estimates that after the issue of preferential treatment is settled, the Civil Rights Commission should be abolished. Responsibility for civil rights, says Pendelton, should be in the hands of the Justice Department and the Equal Employment Opportunity Commission.

1985, May 1. Washington, DC. A statue of Martin Luther King Jr. is dedicated at the Washington Cathedral as a memorial to his comprehensive contributions and celebrated leadership in the struggle for civil rights.

1985, May 6. Washington, DC. The federal government and the state of Maryland reach tentative agreement on a plan to desegregate the state's public colleges and universities. White enrollment at traditionally black colleges will be increased to 19 percent and black enrollment at predominantly white schools will reach 15 percent from 11 percent. The implementation of this plan is to take five years.

1985, August 2. Washington, DC. Because of the policy of apartheid in South Africa, the U.S. House of Representatives gives final approval to a bill imposing economic sanctions against the South African government by a vote of 380–48. The Reagan administration remains opposed to the legislation.

1985, December 6. Yonkers, New York. Stating that "discriminatory housing practices" on the part of Yonkers, New York, were responsible for the segregation of blacks from whites in the city's schools, U.S. District Court Judge Leonard B. Sand indicated for the first time in school desegregation cases that a city's housing policies are inextricably linked to school segregation. Judge Sand held that since 1949 Yonkers public housing had been deliberately built in low-income neighborhoods which had the effect of confining students to "inferior and racially unmixed schools." The Justice Department in 1980 charged the city of Yonkers with bias in housing and schools and received from the city a tentative plan in 1984 to build public housing in predominantly white East Yonkers. The case could have landmark implications since busing had been the primary means for cities to comply with desegregation rulings.

1985, December 23. Birmingham, Alabama. Federal District Judge Sam Pointer Jr. dismisses a reverse discrimination suit instituted on behalf of 14 white firefighters in Birmingham, Alabama. It was claimed that the 14 whites were denied advancement because of a city hiring and promotion plan favoring less-qualified blacks. Judge Pointer ruled that the city accepted the consent decree along with the Justice Department in 1981, and therefore the decree is valid; he also ruled that the firefighters failed to prove that the plan violated that agreement.

1986, January 11. Richmond, Virginia. L. Douglas Wilder becomes the first African American lieutenant governor of the state of Virginia. Wilder, the grandson of a slave, was a Bronze Star recipient in the Korean War and a former member of the state senate.

1986, January 20. Martin Luther King Jr.'s birthday is observed for the first time as a federal holiday.

1986, March 19. Washington, DC. The Supreme Court in *Wygant v. Jackson Board of Education*, the first of three major affirmative action decisions, rules 5–4 that broad affirmative action plans including hiring goals are permissible if they are carefully tailored to remedy past discrimination. In a ruling involving teachers laid off in Jackson, Michigan, the Court sends a mixed signal by deciding that public employers cannot give affirmative action plans as a substitute for seniority when reducing their work forces.

1986, June 16. Norfolk, Virginia. The U.S. Supreme Court denies an injunction sought by African American parents that would prevent the Norfolk, Virginia, school board from ending school busing to stem "white flight" from the city's public schools. According to the petition, the change would result in "a general resegregation of the public schools of the South."

1986, July 2. Cleveland, Ohio. The U.S. Supreme Court ruling on an action regarding Cleveland printers and New York sheet metal workers upholds the use of affirmative action plans designed to remedy past discrimination. The decision in *Sheet Metal Workers International v. EEOC* rejects the Reagan administration's argument that only specific victims of discrimination are entitled to such relief.

1986, August 5. Washington, DC. African American leaders representing major African American organizations meet to urge the passage of legislation that would impose more stringent economic sanctions on South Africa.

1986, September 11. South Africa. Coretta Scott King visits South Africa, meets with Archbishop Desmond Tutu, cancels a meeting with the prime minister, and later visits Winnie Mandela, wife of the imprisoned South African anti-apartheid leader.

1986, October 3. Washington, DC. In an effort to win Senate support for his veto of a sanctions bill

San Francisco middle school students honoring the inaugural Martin Luther King Jr. Day in 1986.

against South Africa for their apartheid policies, Ronald Reagan appoints an African American career diplomat, Edward J. Perkins, to be the new American ambassador to that country. The bill had been overridden by a wide majority (313–83) in the House. The Senate, despite the appointment, votes with the House by a vote of 78–21 to override the veto.

1986, October 7. Washington, DC.   The 32-year-old case of *Brown v. Board of Education of Topeka, Kansas* is reopened by the original plaintiff and others who maintain that the school district has failed to integrate fully its schools or to eradicate the remaining elements that permitted racial separation in the past. Richard Jones, the lawyer for the plaintiffs, says he will show that the school board approved boundaries that perpetuate racially-separate schools and allowed white parents to avoid compliance with desegregation efforts by offering school attendance alternatives.

1986, October 20. Baltimore, Maryland.   Four days of dedication ceremonies commence as the NAACP opens its new headquarters. The NAACP was founded in New York in 1909 and maintained its headquarters there until this move. There is official indication that

the organization will begin new and diverse programs including business development, in addition to its more fundamental activities such as voter registration and protest demonstrations in its general goal of social and economic justice.

1986, November 4. Norfolk, Virginia.   The Supreme Court declines to review two school desegregation cases, one which allows the city of Norfolk to end its busing plan, and another that attempts to sanction the authority of the Oklahoma City School Board to end busing for students in grades one through four. It is speculated that some high court justices want to leave the lower courts with the means of interpreting law on a local and regional basis. In the Norfolk case, African American parents had claimed that the lower court ruling ending busing would have the effect of reinstating school segregation.

1986, December 21. Queens, New York.   Michael Griffith, a 23-year-old black male, is struck by a car and killed while seeking safety from a white mob beating him with bats and fists. The incident occurred in the white community of Howard Beach, Queens. The whites were reported shouting, "Niggers, you don't belong here!" Griffith and two companions were in the neighborhood looking for a tow for their disabled car.

1987, January 7. Washington, DC. New regulations are issued to strengthen the federal government's authority to reject changes in local election laws that have a discriminatory result. No longer does the legal process have to prove that the intent of the local law was to discriminate, it need only demonstrate that it could have a discriminatory result.

1987, February 11. Queens, New York. In Howard Beach, three white teenagers who participated in a racial attack against three black youths are charged with murder as a result of the death of one of the black youths who was killed by a car along an adjacent parkway as he attempted to escape from his white attackers.

1987, April 5. Washington, DC. Representative Charles Rangel (Democrat, New York) introduces two measures in Congress to have the late revolutionary civil rights leader Marcus Garvey exonerated of mail fraud charges of which he was convicted in 1924. The move by Rangel came after Robert Hill, editor of the Marcus Garvey papers project at the University of California at Los Angeles, discovered new evidence which could indicate that Garvey's conviction may have been politically-motivated. In 1927 Garvey's sentence was commuted by President Calvin Coolidge after which he was deported to Jamaica, his place of birth.

1987, April 7. Chicago, Illinois. Mayor Harold Washington wins reelection to a second four-year term and his supporters win control of the city council for the first time. Voting was along strong racial lines with Washington receiving 97 percent of the black vote cast, and his white opponent Edward R. Vrdolyak receiving 74 percent of the white vote. Hispanics cast 57 percent of their vote for Washington.

1987, April 18. Los Angeles, California. Al Campanis, vice president of personnel for the Los Angeles Dodgers, is pressured to resign from his job after stating that African Americans might not be qualified to be managers or hold executive positions in baseball. The remarks were made by Campanis on the ABC News program "Nightline."

1987, April 25. Fort Smith, Arkansas. A federal grand jury indicts ten white supremacists on charges of conspiring to assassinate federal officials, including a judge, and to kill members of ethnic groups through bombings. Richard Girnt Butler, the leader of the Aryan Nations Church, was named in the indictment, along with nine others affiliated with the church and other white supremacist groups such as the Order and the Ku Klux Klan.

1987, May 3. Washington, DC. Japanese Prime Minister Yasuhiro Nakasone meets with the Congressional Black Caucus and other African American leaders after being accused of making racial slurs in a speech angering African Americans and other ethnic groups. Following the meeting Nakasone agreed to pursue Japanese investments in minority-owned American banks, to set up exchange programs between Japanese colleges and African American colleges, and to locate Japanese companies in predominantly African American areas.

1987, July 1. Phoenix, Arizona. As a result of his decision to rescind state observance of Martin Luther King Jr.'s birthday, Governor Evan Mecham (Republican) faces a citizens' effort to recall him as the governor of the state. The plan has strong state support from both parties and many Republicans wear "Recall Mecham" buttons.

1987, July 28. Montgomery, Alabama. After 15 years a tentative settlement is reached between the Alabama State Police Department and the Justice Department. Accordingly there will be an increase in the number of African Americans at various ranks on the force to as high as 25 percent over a three-year period. The department will promote 15 African Americans to the rank of corporal in a month and will eventually have African Americans comprise 20 percent of its sergeants, 15 percent of its lieutenants, and 10 percent of its captains. Federal District Judge Myron Thompson, who originally ordered the police department to hire one black officer for every white officer hired, has to approve the suggested settlement.

1988. Jesse Jackson receives 1,218 delegate votes at the Democratic National Convention.

1988, August 15. Dallas, Texas. The predominantly African American Bishop College, at one time the largest African American college in the West, closes its doors, unable to pay creditors $20 million. Founded in 1881 in Marshall, Texas, Bishop moved to Dallas in 1961. In 1967, Bishop had an enrollment of 1,500; in 1987 its enrollment had dwindled to 300.

1988, August 26. Boston, Massachusetts. In an effort to prevent a housing settlement between the city of Boston and the U.S. Department of Housing from being implemented, the NAACP files suit to have the agreement blocked, stating that a housing settlement, among other things, should include monetary compensation for people previously denied public housing

Jesse Jackson greeting African American voters during the 1988 presidential campaign.

because of their race and therefore forced to pay higher rent. The Housing Authority of the city of Boston was the largest housing authority in the country to enter into a fair housing voluntary compliance agreement with the federal government.

1988, October 4. Washington, DC. The General Accounting Office of the federal government makes public a report charging that the Equal Employment Opportunity Commission failed to properly investigate as many as 82 percent of the claims made regarding job

discrimination filed with the commission during a three-month period.

1988, November 26. Chicago, Illinois. As tensions increase between Jews and African Americans, the Reverend Jesse Jackson meets with Jewish leaders in an effort to reduce the anger and heal the wounds. The Congregation Hakafa turns out to overflow capacity to hear Reverend Jackson deliver the evening sermon and say, "The sons and daughters of the Holocaust, and the sons and daughters of slavery, must find common ground again." The tension between Jews and African Americans reached a zenith in May when Mayor Sawyer of Chicago was severely criticized for taking a week to condemn the anti-Semitic remarks made by Steve Cokley, an aide to the mayor. Underlying the problem is the political struggle for power in Chicago. In 1983, Jews gave Harold Washington almost 50 percent of their votes and helped give Chicago its first African American mayor; in that race Washington defeated the white Republican candidate, Bernard Epton, who was Jewish.

1988, December 1. Washington, DC. Lieutenant General Colin Powell, President Reagan's national security advisor and the top African American official in the administration, is nominated to become one of ten four-star generals in the U.S. Army. Along with the rank goes the assignment to command all U.S. troops in the continental borders of the country and to be responsible for mainland defense. The new rank also puts General Powell in a strong position to become chief of staff as early as 1991 when the post becomes vacant with the retirement of General Carl E. Vuono. General Powell is credited with helping President Reagan's summit meetings in Moscow and Washington, DC, to become diplomatic successes.

1989, January 16. Miami, Florida. Rioting erupts on the evening of January 16 in the predominantly African American neighborhood of Overtown, following the killing of Anthony Lloyd, a 23-year-old African American, by an Hispanic police officer. On January 18, Miami Mayor Xavier Suarez announces that an independent panel would be appointed to investigate the killing.

1989, January 23. Decatur, Alabama. Six members of the Ku Klux Klan receive jail sentences and fines for their part in harassing African Americans in a civil rights march conducted ten years earlier in Decatur, Alabama. The May 1979 march had been to protest the jailing of Tommy Lee Hines, a retarded black man convicted of raping three white women. Hines's 30-year jail sentence was overturned in 1980, and he was committed to a Montgomery mental hospital.

1989, January 23. Washington, DC. Hearing the case *City of Richmond v. J. A. Croson Co.*, the Supreme Court strikes down a law in Richmond, Virginia, which required 30 percent of public works funds to be channeled to minority-owned construction companies. The landmark decision was decried by minority leaders, hailed by anti-quota officials, and predicted to have national impact on affirmative action and set-aside programs. The "Richmond decision," which was written by Associate Justice Sandra Day O'Connor and carried by a 6–3 majority, said set-aside programs were

only justified if they redressed "identified discrimination." O'Connor specifically suggested that "rigid numerical quotas" be avoided, in order to avoid racially-motivated hirings of any kind. The ruling only pertains to the disposition of federal, state, and local government contracts and does not affect affirmative action programs in private industry.

1989, January 26. Richmond, Virginia. Lieutenant Governor L. Douglas Wilder announces his candidacy for governor of Virginia. If successful, he would become the nation's first African American elected to a governorship.

1989, February 7. The American Council on Education reports that the number of African American men attending college is declining. In 1976, 470,000 African American males were enrolled in college. Ten years later, that number dropped to 436,000. Meanwhile the number of African American female students grew during the same period, from 563,000 in 1976 to 645,000 in 1986. Reasons for the decline of African American male collegians were military enrollment, prohibitive college costs, "school phobia," and the seduction of crime or drugs.

1989, February 10. Washington, DC. Washington lawyer Ronald H. Brown, who held high-level positions in the presidential campaigns of Senator Ted Kennedy and Reverend Jesse Jackson, is elected chairman of the Democratic National Committee. The election of Brown marks the first time an African American has been chosen to lead a major American political party.

1989, February 10. Washington, DC. FBI Director William Sessions orders sweeping changes in the bureau's affirmative action program after finding that the bureau had discriminated against minority employees. African American and Hispanic agents were immediately placed on lists for promotions. Sessions then ordered that FBI employees receive training in racial sensitivity and that the equal employment office budget be increased. Ironically, the FBI is the agency charged with enforcing the nation's civil rights laws.

1989, February 10. Washington, DC. Louis W. Sullivan, on sabbatical leave as president of Morehouse School of Medicine in Georgia, becomes secretary of the Department of Health and Human Services. He is the only African American selected in the first round of Cabinet posts in the Bush administration.

1989, March. Washington, DC. Statistics show that the nation's capital has already taken the lead for having the highest homicide rate in the country. Local police figures show the homicide rate as 55.1 percent higher than the same time in 1988. Figures from the District of Columbia Office of Criminal Justice said 80 percent of the time, the motive for the murders was related to drug activity.

1989, April. Los Angeles, California. Mayor Tom Bradley wins reelection to a fifth term by a total of 157,000 votes.

1989, April 21. New Orleans, Louisiana. The nation's first nonpartisan African American summit convenes April 21–23. Its purpose is to discuss "an African American agenda for the next four years and onto the year 2000," said general chairman and Democratic party leader Richard Hatcher. More than 4,000 delegates from the United States, the District of Columbia, and the Virgin Islands were invited.

1989, March 6. Washington, DC. The U.S. Supreme Court declares a second affirmative action plan unconstitutional in the case *Milliken v. Michigan Road Builders Association.* The Michigan law required that seven percent of state contracts be awarded to minority-owned businesses.

1989, March 7. Washington, DC. A student "sit-in" at Howard University results in the resignation of Republican National Committee Chairman Lee Atwater from the university's board of trustees four days following

Tom Bradley.

his appointment. The students claim that Atwater's stand on civil rights is the cause for the protest.

1989, June 5. Washington, DC. In the case *Wards Cove Packing Co. v. Antonio,* the U.S. Supreme Court toughens the requirements for proof of discriminatory impact in job discrimination suits. The Court also declares in such cases that an employer might justify policies which have a discriminatory impact by providing a reasonable business explanation.

1989, June 12. Washington, DC. In *Martin v. Wilks,* the Supreme Court rules by a 5–4 majority that white workers claiming unfair treatment due to affirmative action settlements can seek compensation under civil rights legislation. The case involved white fire fighters in Birmingham, Alabama, who claimed that affirmative action had deprived them of promotions. Civil rights leaders call the decisions a civil rights setback.

1989, July 2. Washington, DC. The Reverend George A. Stallings Jr. conducts the first Mass of the Imani Temple African American Catholic Congregation.

1989, August 6. Washington, DC. The National Urban League holds its annual conference. Addressing the conference, President George H. W. Bush remarks that he will not strive for stronger affirmative action legislation. He claims that the 1990s will see a surplus of available jobs and a shrinking worker pool.

1989, August 23. Brooklyn, New York. Yusuf K. Hawkins, black youth, is fatally shot by five white youths in Brooklyn's predominantly white Bensonhurst section igniting racial tension throughout the New York City area. The attack is regarded as the most serious racial incident in the city since 1986. On August 31, marches are held protesting the killing. On September 2, blacks protesting in Bensonhurst are confronted by white residents. Of the five youths charged with the killing of Hawkins, only one is convicted.

1989, October 12. The publication of Ralph Abernathy's book *And the Walls Came Tumbling Down* is greeted with outrage. The book claims that Martin Luther King Jr. spent the night before his murder with two women. Twenty-seven African American leaders issue a statement denouncing Abernathy's book.

1989, November 5. Montgomery, Alabama. The first memorial dedicated to the Civil Rights movement is unveiled. The memorial is commissioned by the Southern Poverty Law Center and designed by Maya Lin, who also created the Vietnam War Memorial in Washington, DC.

1989, November 7. New York City, New York. African American candidates do well in elections. In Virginia, L. Douglas Wilder becomes the first elected African American governor in U.S. history. In New York City, David N. Dinkins is elected the city's first African

American mayor. In Detroit, Coleman A. Young is reelected to a fifth consecutive term as mayor. Michael R. White is elected as mayor of Cleveland. African American mayors are also elected in Seattle, Washington; New Haven, Connecticut; and Durham, North Carolina, for the first time in history.

1990, January 9. The United States. The Quality Education for Minorities Project releases its report and recommendations aimed at making schools more responsive to the needs of minority students. The project concludes that minority students are taught in "separate and decidedly unequal" schools resulting in a "gap between minority and non-minority educational achievements."

1990, January 18. Washington, DC. Mayor Marion S. Barry Jr. is arrested after being videotaped purchasing and smoking crack cocaine. Following a split verdict, Barry is sentenced to six months in prison. The arrest generates speculation that Jesse Jackson will enter the 1990 Washington, DC, mayoral race.

1990, February 8. Selma, Alabama. African American students stage a "sit-in" following the firing of the city's first African American school superintendent, Norward Roussell, on February 5. The firing is viewed as a battle to control the city's school board—white school board members outnumber black members six to five, while 70 percent of Selma's student population is African American. The conflict ends after six days of protest. The board amends its position to permit Roussell to stay on as superintendent until the end of his contract.

1990, February 23. Dallas, Texas. Bishop College, founded in 1881 by a group of freed slaves and once the largest African American college in the western United States, is sold at a bankruptcy auction.

1990, March 6. Washington, DC. Clarence Thomas, chairman of the Equal Employment Opportunity Commission, is appointed judge on the U.S. Circuit Court of Appeals for the District of Columbia.

1990, April 18. Washington, DC. By a 5–4 majority, the U.S. Supreme Court upholds the authority of federal judges to order local governments to increase taxes to finance school desegregation in the case *Missouri v. Jenkins*. The case arose when U.S. District Court Judge Russell G. Clark adopted a desegregation plan which would create magnet schools to lure whites back into the inner city. To support this plan, Clark ordered that 75 percent of the costs be paid by the state and 25 percent by the district.

1990, June 27. Washington, DC. The U.S. Supreme Court, by a 5–4 majority, upholds federal affirmative action policies created to increase the number of broadcast licenses held by minorities and women in the case *Metro Broadcasting v. FCC*.

1990, August 9. Georgia. The state's runoff primary system is challenged by the Justice Department. The Justice Department claims that the system is biased against black candidates who often win a plurality of the vote in multi-candidate primaries, but lose when matched with a single white candidate in a runoff election. While seven Southern states have similar primary systems, Georgia is targeted in the lawsuit because, statistically, African Americans make up 26 percent of the population but hold only 10 percent of all elected positions.

1990, August 11. Chicago, Illinois. Operation PUSH (People United to Save Humanity) calls for a boycott of Nike products. The organization reveals that African American consumers purchase approximately 30 percent of all Nike products, but are not represented on Nike's board of directors or in upper management. Nike is one of the country's largest manufacturers of athletic gear.

1990, August 21. Washington, DC. Paul R. Philip, the FBI's highest-ranking African American agent, is chosen to investigate racial discrimination within the bureau. The investigation centers around charges made by a black agent against several white agents in the Chicago and Omaha offices.

1990, September 26. The U.S. Census Bureau releases its annual report on household income. The bureau reports that the average household income of blacks is $18,083; Hispanics, $21,921; whites, $30,406; and Asians, $36,102. Ten percent of whites live in poverty, while 26.2 percent of Hispanics and 30.7 percent of blacks live in poverty. Fifty percent of African American children below age six are classified as poor.

1990, September 27. Washington, DC. At its annual conference, members of the Congressional Black Caucus charge law enforcement officials with targeting African American politicians for harassment and investigation. The prosecution of Washington, DC, mayor Marion Berry is cited as an example.

1990, October 12. Cook County, Illinois. The Illinois Supreme Court validates a lower court decision to bar the Harold Washington Party from the ballot. The court cited an inadequate number of nominating signatures as the reason for its decision. The party, a mostly African American third party slate of candidates, is named for the late mayor of Chicago. Cook County Democrats had expressed concern that the Harold Washington party would take votes from their candidates and guarantee the election of Republicans.

1990, October 22. Washington, DC. President George H. W. Bush vetoes the Civil Rights Act of 1990. On October 16, the Senate passed the bill by a vote of 62–34; the House of Representatives passed the bill on

October 17 by a 273–154 vote. The legislation was designed to reverse the Court's 1989 decision in the case *Wards Cove Packing Co. v. Antonio*, which made it more difficult for minorities and women to prove job discrimination. Bush cites his fear of the introduction of quotas in the workplace as his reason for rejecting the act. On October 24, an attempt to override the veto in the Senate falls one vote short of the two-thirds majority needed.

1990, November 6. Arizona. Voters in Arizona defeat two initiatives to reestablish a Martin Luther King Jr. holiday. The holiday had been a source of conflict since the Democratic governor, Bruce Babbitt, marked the day in 1986 by an executive order only to see it rescinded in 1987 by his successor, Republican Evan Mecham.

1990, December 12. The Department of Education announces that it will bar colleges and universities that receive federal funds from awarding minority scholarships. The department claims that race-specific scholarships are discriminatory and violate federal civil rights laws. On December 18, the department revises the policy, allowing schools that receive federal funds to award minority scholarships if the money comes from private sources or federal programs designed to aid minority students. On March 20, 1991, the policy is reversed completely.

1990, December 18. Mississippi. Byron de la Beckwith is charged for the third time with the 1963 murder of civil rights leader Medgar Evers. Beckwith was tried twice in 1964 with both trials ending in a deadlock.

1991, January 8. Results from a nationwide survey sponsored by the National Science Foundation reveals that white Americans continue to hold negative stereotypes of blacks and Hispanics. Three-quarters of the whites surveyed felt that blacks and Hispanics are more likely to prefer welfare to work. A Census Bureau report shows the household worth of whites with families to average eight times that of Hispanic households and ten times that of black households.

1991, January 15. Washington, DC. In a 5–3 decision, the U.S. Supreme Court puts an end to court-ordered busing in the Oklahoma City school district. Ruling in the case *Oklahoma City Board of Education v. Dowell*, the Court declares that the reemergence of single-race schools, resulting from shifting housing patterns, does justify continued court-ordered busing. The decision overturns an appeals court ruling refusing to turn the once-segregated school district over to local control.

1991, January 20. A *New York Times*/CBS poll of public support for military action in the Persian Gulf reveals that only 47 percent of blacks polled compared to 80 percent of whites favored intervention. One theory on the difference in support points to the disproportionate number of blacks to whites serving in the armed forces. While accounting for only 12 percent of the total U.S. population, African Americans represent 24.6 percent of the U.S. troops in the Gulf. Many African Americans point to the problems of drugs and crime as good places to direct government resources.

1991, February 26. Detroit, Michigan. By a 9–1 majority, the Detroit Board of Education approves the creation of an all-male school for kindergarten through grade eight. The school's goal would be to provide African American male students with an improved learning environment by focusing on the unique problems facing the African American male. Critics of the school label the program discriminatory. The American Civil Liberties Union and the National Organization for Women Legal Defense Fund both file suit in federal district court. On August 15, the court rules that such a school must also be open to girls.

1991, March 3. Los Angeles, California. Black motorist Rodney King is severely beaten by several white police officers after being stopped for a speeding violation. The incident is videotaped by a witness watching from his apartment balcony.

1991, May 6. Washington, DC. The creation of a National African American Museum within the Smithsonian Institution is approved by the institution's board of regents. The museum will include print and broadcast images of African Americans, along with African American art and artifacts.

1991, May 12. Hampton, Virginia. Students at Hampton University hold a silent protest while President George H. W. Bush gives the commencement address. The students point to the administration's policies regarding civil rights as a reason for the demonstration.

1991, May 14. The Washington-based Urban Institute releases its study on job discrimination. The study, conducted in Washington, DC, and Chicago, Illinois, reveals that whites seeking entry-level positions were three times more likely to receive favorable treatment than equally qualified blacks.

1991, June 3. Washington, DC. In the case of *Edmonson v. Leesville Concrete Co.*, the U.S. Supreme Court rules that potential jurors cannot be excluded from civil cases on the basis of race. The Court had, in two earlier cases, ruled that jurors could not be excluded because of race in criminal cases.

1991, June 4. Washington, DC. After defeating two other civil rights bills, the U.S. House of Representatives passes a civil rights bill by a vote of 273–158. The bill is an effort by Congress to reverse the Supreme

One frame of the 1991 video-taped beating of Rodney King by Los Angeles police officers.

Court's 1989 ruling in *Wards Cove Packing Co. v. Antonio* and make it easier for victims of job discrimination to sue for damages. President George H. W. Bush opposes such legislation, claiming that it will force employers to set quotas for hiring minorities in order to protect themselves from possible discrimination suits.

1991, June 20. Washington, DC. The U.S. Supreme Court, hearing in two separate cases *Chison v. Roemer* and *Houston Lawyers v. Texas*, rules that the Voting Rights Act of 1965 is applicable to judicial elections. The cases arose from lower court rulings in Louisiana and Texas which claimed that judges were not representatives and, therefore, the election of such was not covered by the act.

1991, June 27. Washington, DC. U.S. Supreme Court Justice Thurgood Marshall, citing his poor health and advancing age, announces his plans to retire from the bench. Marshall, appointed to the Court by President Lyndon B. Johnson in 1967, was the first African American to serve on the nation's highest court.

1991, July. Washington, DC. President George H. W. Bush nominates African American Court of Appeals

Judge Clarence Thomas to replace the retiring Justice Thurgood Marshall. Thomas, a conservative and former chairman of the Equal Employment Opportunity Commission, was appointed by Bush in 1990 to the federal appeals court. Stating that while chairman of the EEOC, Thomas failed to display sensitivity regarding affirmative action, major national organizations including the NAACP, the NAACP Legal Defense Fund, the Leadership Conference on Civil Rights, and the Congressional Black Caucus voice opposition to the Thomas nomination.

1991, July 4. Memphis, Tennessee. The National Civil Rights Museum, housed in the former Lorraine Motel, is dedicated. Martin Luther King Jr. was shot at the Lorraine Motel on April 4, 1968.

1991, August 19. Brooklyn, New York. Tensions between African Americans and Jews in Brooklyn's Crown Heights section increase, when seven-year-old Gavin Cato is struck and killed by a car driven by a Jewish driver. Rioting erupts, and a Jewish rabbinical student is stabbed to death.

1991, September 13. Richmond, Virginia. Governor L. Douglas Wilder announces his plans to run for the 1992 Democratic presidential nomination. However, by January of 1992, Wilder withdraws from the race. In 1989, Wilder became the first African American elected governor in U.S. history.

1991, September 29. The Department of Justice releases its report on death row inmates. The report reveals that 40 percent of the inmates awaiting execution in the United States are African American, whereas African Americans constitute only 12.1 percent of the general population.

1991, October 11. Los Angeles, California. Korean grocer Soon Ja Du is convicted of voluntary manslaughter for the death of Latasha Harlins. The shooting exacerbates racial tension between African Americans and Koreans.

1991, October 30. Washington, DC. The U.S. Senate approves a new civil rights bill.

1991, November 1. Washington, DC. In a public ceremony, Judge Clarence Thomas is formally seated as the 106th associate justice of the U.S. Supreme Court.

1991, November 2. Washington, DC. Jesse L. Jackson announces he will not seek the 1992 Democratic presidential nomination.

1991, November 5. Washington, DC. In the case *Hafer v. Melo*, the U.S. Supreme Court rules in a unanimous vote that state officials can be sued as individuals acting in an official status and be held personally liable in civil rights suits.

1991, November 7. Washington, DC. The House of Representatives passes Senate Bill 1745, which was passed by the Senate on October 30. President George H. W. Bush signs the bill into law on November 21. However, the signing ceremony for the long-anticipated law is dominated by controversy over a proposed presidential directive that tried to impose a conservative interpretation on the new legislation. Immediately after circulation of the draft, civil rights leaders, senators, and Cabinet members condemn it as an attack on all civil rights progress.

1991, December 30. Alabama. U.S. District Court Judge Harold L. Murphy orders the Alabama state university system to rectify racial discrimination in its hiring, admissions, and financing practices. It is ruled that Alabama's higher education system, divided into predominantly white and predominantly black schools, fosters inferior funding for the predominantly African American universities. Judge Murphy states he will retain jurisdiction over the case for ten years to ensure his orders are carried out.

1992, January 2. Washington, DC. A lawsuit filed by the National Treasury Employees Union challenges the Equal Employment Opportunity Commission's policy which states that the 1991 Civil Rights Act does not apply to job discrimination lawsuits filed prior to the law's enactment in November of 1991.

1992, January 17. Atlanta, Georgia. President George H. W. Bush visits the Martin Luther King Jr. Center for Nonviolent Social Change to sign a proclamation officially declaring Martin Luther King Jr.'s birthday as a national holiday.

1992, January 19. The American Council on Education releases their tenth annual report confirming the number of minority students attending college increased during the 1980s. The report shows 33 percent of black, 29 percent of Hispanic, and 39.4 percent of white high school graduates were attending college in 1990, up respectively from 21.6 percent, 26.1 percent and 34.4 percent in 1985.

1992, January 20. Denver, Colorado. The seventh commemoration of Martin Luther King Jr.'s birthday as a national holiday triggers violence in Denver between civil rights supporters and members of the Ku Klux Klan following a Klan rally. Civil rights supporters throw bricks and bottles at a bus carrying Klan members away from the rally.

1992, February 10. Seattle, Washington. Alex Haley, the Pulitzer Prize-winning author of *Roots* and *The Autobiography of Malcolm X*, dies of heart failure.

1992, February 15. Baltimore, Maryland. The NAACP's Benjamin L. Hooks announces his plans to resign from his position as the organization's director. The announcement is made after Hazel Dukes, the national president, and several other prominent board members are denied reelection.

1992, March 31. Washington, DC. In the case of *Freeman v. Pitts*, the U.S. Supreme Court rules unanimously that school districts operating under court-supervised desegregation orders can slowly be released from court supervision to local control as they achieve racial equality. Reaction to the ruling by educators and civil rights experts is mixed, with general uncertainty as to how the decision will be applied by district courts reviewing individual desegregation orders.

1992, April 29. Los Angeles, California. Riots erupt in Los Angeles following the acquittal of four white police officers in the beating of black motorist Rodney King. The suburban Simi Valley jury that acquitted the police officers had no African American members. The videotaped beating was broadcast around the world and provoked outrage condemning police brutality. With the announcement of the verdict, looting and violence break out across the South Central section of Los Angeles. By the end of the first day, 12 people are dead and more than 100 arson fires engulf the area.

Mayor Tom Bradley declares a local state of emergency and Governor Pete Wilson orders the National Guard to assist local police in controlling the increasing violence. President George H. W. Bush orders the deployment of 1,500 Marines and 3,000 U.S. Army troops to Los Angeles. Many of the shops targeted for looting are those owned by Korean immigrants. Tension between Los Angeles African Americans and Koreans had been rising since the 1991 fatal shooting of a young African American girl, Latasha Harlins, by a Korean grocer. The Bush administration blames the riots on urban decay, crime, and welfare dependency that it claims grew out of the social welfare programs passed by Congress in the 1960s and 1970s.

1992, June 13. Washington, DC. Governor Bill Clinton speaks at the Rainbow Coalition convention and criticizes questionable statements made by rap singer Sister Souljah (Lisa Williamson) in reference to the Los Angeles riots. The Reverend Jesse Jackson, founder of the Rainbow Coalition, says he thinks Clinton's comments were intended to embarrass and provoke him.

1992, June 26. Washington, DC. In the case of *United States v. Fordice*, the U.S. Supreme Court rules 8–1 that the state of Mississippi has not sufficiently desegregated its public universities. Despite "race-neutral" admissions standards, certain policies are targeted as causing informal segregation. Examples include wording of mission statements and higher admissions standards at the predominantly white colleges.

1992, July 23. Washington, DC. The 1990 U.S. Census shows black median household incomes at $19,758 compared to $31,435 for whites and $30,056 for the national median average. The statistics show that blacks earn 63 percent of the median white income, only slightly better than the 62 percent earned by blacks ten years prior.

1992, August 29. Washington, DC. The FBI's Uniform Crime Reports gives the rate of violent offenses by juveniles (ages 10 to 17) as 430 out of 100,000 in 1990. Black arrests are 1,429 out of 100,000, five times the amount of whites arrested.

1992, September 3. Washington, DC. A 1991 U.S. Census Bureau report finds that the number of Americans below the poverty level is the highest number since 1964. In 1991, 14.2 percent of Americans were in poverty compared to 13.5 percent in 1990. In 1991, 32.7 percent of African Americans were in poverty compared to 31.9 percent in 1990.

1992, September 16. Washington, DC. The U.S. Department of Education's report on high school dropout rates shows a 13.6 percent dropout of black students (ages 16 to 24) in 1991 compared to 21.3 percent in 1972. The dropout rate of Hispanics rose from 34.3 percent to 35.3 percent, whereas the rate for whites dropped from 12.3 percent to 8.9 percent.

1992, September 28. Berkeley, California. The University of California at Berkeley Law School is found in violation of federal civil rights laws by the U.S. Department of Education Office for Civil Rights. It is discovered that minority applicants to the school receive preferential treatment over other candidates. As a result of this ruling, the school's admission policies are revised.

1992, October 8. Boston, Massachusetts. A study conducted by the Federal Reserve's regional bank shows evidence of bank discrimination against minorities applying for mortgages. The study measures black, Hispanic, and white rejection rates when all applicants had similar application criteria. The findings show 17 percent rejection of minorities compared to 11 percent rejection of whites. This study is the first to investigate loan application criteria.

1992, November 3. The presidential election brings 16 new African American members to Congress for a total of 38. Senator Earl F. Hilliard is the first African American Alabaman elected to Congress. The District of Columbia's Marion Barry wins a seat on Washington's city council. Florida's first three African American representatives—Corrine Brown, Carrie Meek, and Alcee Hastings—benefit from court-ordered redistricting. In Georgia, three African Americans join Congress: Senator Nathan Deal, Representative Jackie Barrett, and Representative Cynthia McKinney. McKinney is the first African American woman voted into the Georgia House of Representatives.

1992, November. Detroit, Michigan. Two Detroit policemen are charged with murder and two policemen are charged with lesser criminal charges in the beating death of black motorist Malice Green. Larry Nevers and Walter Budzyn, two white police officers, pulled Green out of his car and beat him on the head with metal flashlights. Sergeant Freddie Douglas, a black policeman, is charged with failing to stop the beating. White policeman Robert Lessnau is charged with participating in the beating and aggravated assault. Innocent pleas are entered for all four officers.

1992, November 6. Washington, DC. U.S. Labor Department figures show a decrease in unemployment rates from 7.5 percent in September to 7.4 percent in October. In September, jobless rates drop from 6.7 percent to 6.5 percent for whites, from 11.9 percent to 11.8 percent for Hispanics, and rose to 13.9 percent from 13.7 percent for blacks.

1992, November 7. An outline for one of Martin Luther King Jr.'s speeches is purchased at an auction for $35,000 by New Jersey Group, Kaller and Associates. The King estate filed a lawsuit requesting the return of the document plus $5 million in punitive damages from the dealer, Superior Galleries. King rarely made outlines or notes for his speeches, which explains the inflated worth.

1992, November 18. *Malcolm X*, Spike Lee's motion picture based on Alex Haley's biography of the slain civil rights leader, opens in theaters nationwide.

1992, December 12. Washington, DC. President Bill Clinton's Cabinet and White House appointments include five African American men and one African American woman. They are Clifton R. Wharton Jr. as deputy secretary of the Department of State; Hazel R. O'Leary as secretary of the Department of Energy; Mike Espy as head of the Agriculture Department; Ron Brown, the former Democratic National Committee Chairman, as secretary of the Department of Commerce; Jesse Brown as Veterans Affairs secretary; and Joycelyn Elders, as surgeon general.

1993, January 5. Washington, DC. The House of Representatives passes by 22 votes a rules change that

Michael Espy was appointed Secretary of Agriculture in 1992.

will allow an increase in voting rights to delegates from Washington, DC, and the U.S. territories of American Samoa, Guam, Puerto Rico, and the U.S. Virgin Islands. (The District of Columbia and the Virgin Islands have large black populations.) In the past, the delegates took part in committee actions and votes, but not votes on the House floor, which were restricted to representatives from "the states" because the Constitution stipulated that only "the states" should have legislative authority. Delegates may now participate in all but the final votes affecting legislation.

1993, January 7. Washington, DC. Senator Carol Moseley Braun is one of two women elected to the Senate Judiciary Committee. Braun claimed she was inspired to run partly as a result of angry feelings over the Anita Hill-Clarence Thomas hearings in 1991. The all-male Judiciary Committee had been admonished by the public for its role in the handling of the hearings.

1993, January 8. Washington, DC. The unemployment rate for December of 1992 reaches 7.3 percent, according to U.S. Labor Department figures.

1993, January 24. Bethesda, Maryland. Thurgood Marshall, the first African American Supreme Court justice and lifelong supporter of civil rights, dies of heart failure.

1993, January 18. New Hampshire renames its January holiday from Civil Rights Day to King Day. This is the first time all 50 states have a holiday for Martin Luther King Jr.

1993, March 2. Washington, DC. In the case of *Voinovich v. Quilter*, the U.S. Supreme Court rules that the authority to create voting districts dominated by ethnic minorities is held by individual states. The issue was brought before the Court because of concern over the reorganization practices of Ohio's state legislative voting districts in 1990.

1993, April 9. Baltimore, Maryland. Civil rights champion Benjamin F. Chavis Jr. is elected as executive director of the National Association for the Advancement of Colored People.

1993, April 17. Los Angeles, California. In a civil suit, two of the four Los Angeles police officers charged in the beating of African American motorist Rodney King are convicted, while the other two are acquitted. Officer Lawrence M. Powell is convicted of violating King's rights to an arrest without "unreasonable force." Powell delivered the majority of hits to King with his baton. Sgt. Stacey C. Koon is convicted of allowing the violation by Powell to occur. Officers Theodore J. Briseno and Timothy E. Wind are found not guilty on all charges. As a result of the riots in 1991, the people of

Los Angeles were on edge awaiting the new verdict. Riot training for 7,000 Los Angeles police officers and advance notice of the verdict to the police prepared them for the possibility of further rioting.

1993, May 17. Washington, DC. The U.S. Supreme Court sends the case of *American Family Mutual Insurance Co. v. National Association for the Advancement of Colored People* back to the lower courts. Until decisions by the lower courts, the federal Fair Housing Act may be interpreted to extend coverage toward homeowner's insurance. The NAACP charged that the insurance company refused to sell to African Americans or charged them exorbitant fees. The practice is also known as "redlining."

1993, May 23. Washington, DC. *The Washington Post* begins publishing portions of the late Supreme Court Justice Thurgood Marshall's papers. Immediately following Marshall's death, his papers are made available for use by "researchers or scholars engaged in serious research." These conditions were requested by Marshall when he turned his papers over to the Library of Congress after his retirement. Supreme Court Chief Justice Rehnquist wrote Librarian of Congress James H. Billington a letter admonishing him for lack of judgment in releasing the papers so soon. Marshall's friends, family, and colleagues displayed similar feelings of anger at the papers' speedy release.

1993, June 3. Washington, DC. President Bill Clinton retracts his nomination of Lani Guinier for the position of head of the civil rights division in the Justice Department. Guinier, an African American law professor, had expressed some controversial ideas relating to race and voting rights in some previous professional writings. Clinton justifies his decision by explaining that the views expressed in the writings clashed with his own opinions on the same topics.

1993, June 7. Pop star Prince changes his name to a symbol that combines the signs for male and female.

1993, June 26. Woodland Hills, California. Hall of Fame catcher Roy Campanella, one of the first African Americans to play in the major leagues, dies of a heart attack.

1993, July 23. Fayetteville, North Carolina. James Jordan, father of Chicago Bulls star Michael Jordan, is shot and killed during a robbery attempt.

1993, July 27. Waltham, Massachusetts. Boston Celtics guard Reggie Lewis collapses and dies at Brandeis University during a practice.

1993, August 4. Los Angeles, California. A federal judge sentences Sergeant Stacy Koon and Officer Lawrence Powell to two and a half years in prison for violating the civil rights of motorist Rodney King during a 1991 beating.

1993, August 4. New York City, New York. Leonard Jeffries Jr. is reinstated as chairman of City College's black studies department. A judge rules that the decision by college administrators to remove Jeffries following a controversial 1991 speech violated his constitutional right to free speech.

1993, August 23. Detroit, Michigan. Two white officers, Larry Nevers and Walter Budzyn, are convicted of second-degree murder in the beating death of motorist Malice Green.

1993, September 7. West Palm Beach, Florida. Two white men are convicted of kidnapping and setting afire a black tourist on January 1, 1993. The men are also convicted of attempted murder and armed robbery. They are sentenced to life imprisonment on October 22.

1993, September 8. Washington, DC. Joycelyn Elders is sworn in as U.S. surgeon general.

1993, September 14. Philadelphia, Pennsylvania. The University of Pennsylvania decides not to suspend a group of African American students who seized 14,000 copies of the student newspaper *Daily Pennsylvanian*. The students took the newspapers to protest what they viewed as the *Daily Pennsylvanian*'s conservative and racially-biased views.

1993, September 30. Fort Myer, Virginia. Colin L. Powell retires as chairman of the Joint Chiefs of Staff.

1993, October 6. Chicago, Illinois. Chicago Bulls star Michael Jordan announces his retirement from the NBA.

1993, October 8. New York City, New York. Actor Ted Danson is chastised for appearing onstage in blackface and telling several racist and sexist jokes during a Friars Club roast for actress Whoopi Goldberg.

1993, October 18. Los Angeles, California. Two African American men are acquitted of attempted murder in the beating of truck driver Reginald Denny during the 1992 riot.

1993, October 20. Don Cornelius steps down as host of the syndicated television dance show "Soul Train" after 22 years.

1993, November 2. New York City, New York. Mayor David Dinkins is defeated in a mayoral election by former U.S. attorney Rudolph Giuliani.

1993, November 2. Detroit, Michigan. Dennis Archer defeats Sharon McPhail to become mayor of Detroit, succeeding Coleman Young.

1994, February 3. Washington, DC. Nation of Islam leader Louis Farrakhan censures aide Khalid Abdul

Johnnie Cochran (r) and Reginald Denny are interviewed on TV about Denny's case against two African American men who beat him during the L.A. riots in 1993.

Muhammad for anti-Semitic remarks made in a November of 1993 speech.

1994, February 5. Jackson, Mississippi. Byron de la Beckwith, a white supremacist, is convicted of the 1963 murder of civil rights leader Medgar Evers. Beckwith is sentenced to life in prison.

1994, March 1. Berkeley, California. Former Black Panther leader Eldridge Cleaver is hospitalized after suffering a brain hemorrhage.

1994, March 23. Los Angeles, California. Earvin "Magic" Johnson is named coach of the Los Angeles Lakers.

1994, April 12. Washington, DC. Randall Robinson, executive director of TransAfrica, a lobbying group for African and Caribbean issues, begins a liquid fast to protest the U.S. government's "discriminatory policy" on Haiti.

1994, May 24. Santa Ana, California. Denny's Restaurants agree to pay $54 million to settle lawsuits by African Americans who claim they were discriminated against by the restaurant chain.

1994, May 26. Dominican Republic. Pop star Michael Jackson and Lisa Marie Presley, daughter of Elvis Presley, are married.

1994, June 20. Los Angeles, California. Ex-football star O.J. Simpson is arrested and charged with the murder of his wife, Nicole Brown Simpson, and her friend, Ron Goldman.

1994, August 20. Chicago, Illinois. Benjamin F. Chavis is ousted as executive director of the NAACP by the civil rights organization's board of directors. Earl T. Shinhoster is named interim director.

1994, August 30. Detroit, Michigan. Civil rights activist Rosa Parks is beaten and robbed in her home.

1994, October 3. Washington, DC. Mike Espy, secretary of the U.S. Department of Agriculture, resigns following a federal ethics investigation in which Espy is accused of receiving gifts from businesses regulated by the U.S. Department of Agriculture.

1994, October 21. Atlanta, Georgia. Dexter Scott King, the youngest son of the late Reverend Martin Luther King Jr. is named chief executive and chairman of the Martin Luther King Jr. Center for Nonviolent Social Change.

1994, December 9. Washington, DC. Joycelyn Elders resigns as U.S. surgeon general after making controversial statements regarding drug use and sex education.

1994, December 10. New York City, New York. University of Colorado running back Rashaan Salaam wins the Heisman Trophy.

1994, December 14. Washington, DC. Representative Donald M. Payne, a Democrat from New Jersey, is elected to a two-year term as chairman of the Congressional Black Caucus.

1995, January 12. Minneapolis, Minnesota. Qubilah Bahiyah Shabazz, daughter of the late black nationalist leader Malcolm X, is arrested and charged with plotting to kill Nation of Islam leader Louis Farrakhan.

Joycelyn Elders.

1995, March 18. Chicago, Illinois. Chicago Bulls star Michael Jordan announces his return to the NBA after retiring in 1993.

1995, March 25. Plainfield, Indiana. Boxer Mike Tyson is released from prison after serving three years for a 1992 rape conviction.

1995, April 21. Washington, DC. H. Patrick Swygert is named president of Howard University, replacing Franklyn G. Jenifer who resigned on April 22, 1994.

1995, June 21. Washington, DC. The Senate rejects Dr. Henry Foster Jr.'s bid to become U.S. surgeon general. Foster, a gynecologist and obstetrician, is rejected due to pressure from anti-abortion groups and Senate Republicans.

1995, June 29. Washington, DC. The Supreme Court, by a 5–4 vote, rules that electoral districts drawn to ensure fair political representation of African Americans and other minorities are unconstitutional if race is used as the predominant factor in drawing district boundaries.

1995, July 20. Davis, California. The University of California votes to eliminate affirmative action policies in the admission of students.

1995, October 3. Los Angeles, California. O. J. Simpson is acquitted of the murder of his former wife Nicole Brown Simpson and her friend, Ron Goldman. The O.J. Simpson trial was televised daily throughout the United States and fueled extensive debate regarding race relations in America.

1995, October 3. Creve Coeur, Missouri. Eddie Robinson of Grambling State University, Grambling, Louisiana, has 400 wins in 53 seasons to become college football's winningest coach.

1995, October 16. Washington, DC. The Million Man March, organized by Nation of Islam leader Louis Farrakhan, draws African American men to the nation's capital. The purpose of the march is to offer African American men an opportunity to meet for a day of atonement and to pledge their commitment to themselves, their families, and their communities.

1995, November 8. Alexandria, Virginia. Former chairman of the Joint Chiefs of Staff, Colin L. Powell, ends months of speculation by announcing that he will not run for the U.S. presidency in 1996.

1995, December 9. Chicago, Illinois. Kweisi Mfume is unanimously elected as president and chief executive officer of the NAACP.

1995, December 12. Washington, DC. Jesse Jackson Jr., son of civil rights activist Rev. Jesse Jackson, is elected as the representative of Illinois's Second Congressional District. He replaced Representative Mel

O.J. Simpson stands before the jury wearing the bloody gloves last worn by the assailant of Nicole Brown Simpson and Ron Goldman.

Reynolds who resigned from Congress after being sentenced to five years in prison for sexual misconduct.

1996, January 15. Five of the largest African American congregations in the United States announce the formulation of Revelation Corporation of America, a for-profit company designed to improve the buying power of African American consumers.

1996, January 17. Austin, Texas. Barbara Charline Jordan, scholar, educator, and politician, dies in a hospital of pneumonia and complications from leukemia. She had suffered from multiple sclerosis for several years. In 1966, Jordan became the first African American elected state senator in Texas. In 1972, she was elected to the U.S. Congress, becoming the state's first African American and first woman elected to the position. An excellent orator, Jordan gained national attention in 1974 when she called for the impeachment of President Richard M. Nixon for his involvement in the Watergate scandal. Two years later, she became the first African American woman to give a keynote address at the Democratic National Convention.

1996, January 18. Los Angeles, California. Lisa Marie Presley files for divorce from her husband, pop singer Michael Jackson.

1996, January 30. Los Angeles, California. Los Angeles Lakers star Earvin (Magic) announces his return to the NBA after retiring in 1991. He played in 32 of their 40 games remaining. Later that year he was named among the 50 Greatest NBA Players of all time. He retired again and purchased a minority share in the Lakers.

1996, February 20. Washington, DC. Kweisi Mfume is sworn in as the top executive of the NAACP.

1996, March 11. Baltimore, Maryland. Political activist C. DeLores Tucker urges churches to boycott stores that sell "gangsta rap" on the grounds that it glorifies the use of violence and drugs and degrades women.

1996, April 3. Dubrovnik, Croatia. Commerce Secretary Ronald H. Brown and distinguished American business leaders are killed in a plane crash.

1996, April 8. Cleveland, Ohio. After 17 years of busing, a federal judge lifts a school desegregation order which district officials claim will save $10 million.

1996, May 19. Jackson, Mississippi. James Meredith, who integrated the University of Mississippi in 1962, is shot at by whites who yell insults from a passing truck.

1996, May 28. Pensacola, Florida. Donnie Cochran, who in 1994 became the first African American commander of the U.S. Navy's Blue Angels flight demonstration team, resigns. He cites his own shortcomings in flying that could threaten the safety of his pilots and spectators.

1996, June 13. Washington, DC. The U.S. Supreme Court declares unconstitutional two congressional districts in North Carolina and three in Texas because the districts—majority African American and majority Hispanic—were illegally drawn.

1996, June 22. Washington, DC. The Senate approves Vice Admiral J. Paul Reason to become the U.S. Navy's first African American four-star admiral. President Bill Clinton nominated Reason for the promotion on May 13. Reason later assumes command of the U.S. Atlantic Fleet in Norfolk, Virginia.

1996, June 27. Washington, DC. President Bill Clinton signs the Church Arson Bill affecting racially-motivated burnings. The bill authorizes $10 million to be used to help build churches that are underinsured and increases the sentence for such crimes.

1996, July 1. Washington, DC. The U.S. Supreme Court confirms the ruling that race cannot be a factor in admitting students to the University of Texas Law

Father and son participants in the 1995 Million Man March applauding in response to a speech.

School. Previously, separate and lower standards were used to admit African Americans and Hispanics.

1996, August 30. Tripoli, Libya. Louis Farrakhan receives the Gadhafi International Human Rights Award for organizing the Million Man March. However, U.S. law bars him from accepting gifts from terrorists.

1996, September 13. Las Vegas, Nevada. Rap artist Tupac Shakur, a victim of a drive-by shooting, dies. His career had been marked by violence and run-ins with law enforcement agents. Shakur was named after an Incan chief and raised by his mother, Afeni Shakur, a Black Panther Party member who was imprisoned while pregnant with her son. Tupac Shakur sold millions of records of "gangsta"-style rap music. In some of his works, he taunted the police and glorified violence and misogyny. He became a target for groups that aimed to clean up rap lyrics.

1996, September 23. Chicago, Illinois. Talk show host Oprah Winfrey is the highest-paid entertainer, earning $212 million, according to *Forbes* magazine.

1996, October 4. Washington, DC. Congress passes a bill authorizing the creation of 500,000 black Revolutionary War Patriots commemorative coins. They are to depict the 275th anniversary of the birth of Revolutionary War hero Crispus Attucks.

1996, October 25. Tulsa, Oklahoma. J. B. Stradford, who died 60 years earlier, is cleared of charges that he was one of dozens of African Americans accused of inciting the Tulsa riot of May 31, 1921, that ruined 35 city blocks and killed 36 or more people.

1996, November 5. Atlanta, Georgia. Cynthia McKinney, a Democrat from Georgia, is reelected to the U.S. House of Representatives after district lines are redrawn, making her district predominantly white.

1996, November 15. White Plains, New York. Texaco Inc., a major oil company headquartered in White Plains, agrees to a $176.1 million settlement of a federal discrimination lawsuit filed in 1994 by African American Texaco employees—the largest race discrimination lawsuit ever filed. The company also agrees to help create an outside task force to oversee a Texaco diversity program. On November 4, the *New York Times* made public the existence of an audiotape containing Texaco executives' disparaging racial remarks including their reference to African American workers as "black jelly beans." The company has 27,000 employees, more than 1,400 of whom are African American.

1996, November 12. Washington, DC. President Bill Clinton signs legislation creating the Selma-to-Montgomery National Historic Trail in Alabama, marking the route of the civil rights march that Martin Luther King Jr. led in 1965.

1996, December 18. Oakland, California. The school board recognizes black English, or Ebonics, as a separate language rather than slang or dialect. The board subsequently rescinded its decision to make Ebonics a second language.

1997, January 3. New York City, New York. "Today" show anchor, Bryant Gumbel, the longest-serving host in the show's history, resigns after 15 years.

1997, January 13. Washington, DC. President Bill Clinton awards seven African American soldiers Medals of Honor. Joseph Vernon Baker, 77, the only living recipient in the group, attended the awards ceremony. Baker was a second lieutenant in the U.S. Army's 92nd Infantry Division. None of the 433 Medals of Honor awarded to servicemen for acts of gallantry in World War II had been given to African Americans. African American veterans, however, petitioned the Department of the Army to honor African American servicemen as well.

1997, February 13. Washington, DC. David Satcher is sworn in as U.S. surgeon general and assistant secretary for Health at the Department of Health and Human Services. A physician, educator, and former medical school president, he leaves the position he had held since 1993 as head of the Centers for Disease Control in Atlanta. He was the first African American to head the center. President Bill Clinton nominated Satcher for the surgeon general's post on September 12, 1996.

1997, February 17. Richmond, Virginia. The Virginia House of Delegates retires the state song "Carry Me Back to Old Virginia" by unanimous vote. African American composer James A. Bland wrote the song in 1875; it was adopted by the state in 1940.

1997, February 26. Major League Baseball dedicates the season to Jackie Robinson who on April 15, 1947—50 years ago—broke the league's color barrier.

1997, April 2. Nashville, Tennessee. Tennessee ratifies the Fifteenth Amendment 127 years after its ratification by Congress. The amendment guarantees the right to vote regardless of "race, color or previous condition of servitude."

1997, April 13. Augusta, Georgia. Eldrick "Tiger" Woods finishes with the lowest score in tournament history and wins the 61st Masters. He is the first African American and the youngest person to win the Masters.

Tiger Woods celebrating at The Masters in 1997.

1997, April 28. Old Saybrook, Connecticut. Writer Ann Petry, best known for her 1946 novel *The Street*, dies.

1997, May 1. Washington, DC. The U.S. Senate confirms Alexis M. Herman, assistant to President Bill Clinton, as U.S. secretary of labor.

1997, May 15. Washington, DC. President Bill Clinton issues an apology to the few remaining survivors and relatives of the African American men who were involved in the federal government's "Tuskegee Experiment" nearly a quarter of a century earlier.

1997, May 28. Chicago, Illinois. Eighty-four-year-old John H. Stengstacke, owner and editor of the *Chicago Defender*, dies. He founded the Negro Newspaper Publishers Association.

1997, June 13. Baltimore, Maryland. After conducting a survey of the hotel industry as a part of its Economic Reciprocity Campaign, the NAACP gives failing grades to three major hotel chains for their hiring and promotion practices of African Americans and relations with African American businesses. Receiving the grades were Holiday Inn, Westin, and Best Western.

1997, June 14. Washington, DC. President Bill Clinton names seven people to the White House Initiative on Race and Reconciliation and appoints historian John Hope Franklin chair. The panel's charge is to lead a year-long national dialogue about race.

1997, June 14. San Diego, California. President Bill Clinton delivers a speech on race in the United States at the commencement exercises at the University of California, San Diego. He said, "Now we know what we will look like. But what will we be like? Can we be one America, respecting, even celebrating our differences, but embracing even more what we have in common?"

1997, June 23. New York City, New York. Betty Shabazz, college educator and administrator and widow of slain black nationalist Malcolm X, dies after suffering from extensive burns on June 1. The fires causing her death were apparently set by her grandson, Malcolm Shabazz, a troubled 12-year-old, in her Yonkers, New York, apartment. Betty Shabazz held numerous speaking engagements, often addressing such issues as health and education for disadvantaged youth and black self-determination.

1997, June 28. Las Vegas, Nevada. In a heavyweight boxing rematch with Evander Holyfield, Mike Tyson is disqualified after three rounds and thrown out for biting Holyfield twice on his ears. Later the Nevada Commission fined Tyson $3 million and revoked his boxing license.

1997, July 10. Birmingham, Alabama. The FBI reopens investigation into bombings of the 16th Street Baptist Church where four young African American girls were killed on September 15, 1963, while attending Sunday school.

1997, July 24. Washington, DC. The Army Corps of Engineers agrees to settle a race discrimination suit filed by African American deck-hands on the dredge *Hurley* based in Memphis, Tennessee. The Defense Department found that black workers aboard the ship routinely endured racial epithets and jokes from whites and were denied promotions because they were black. The 16 deck-hands each received $62,500 and were given the opportunity to move from part- time to full-time employment.

1997, August 4. Washington, DC. Robert G. Stanton is sworn into office and becomes the first African American director of the Interior Department's National Park Service. He had worked with the park service from 1962 to January of 1967, then retired from the agency's national capital region.

1997, October. Oakland, California. The Black Panther Legacy Tour begins under the leadership of David Hilliard, former chief of staff for the Panthers.

The bus tour winds through the Oakland neighborhood where the Panthers were founded in 1966 and other sites of significance to the history of the group.

1997, October 25. Philadelphia, Pennsylvania. Over 300,000 African American women arrive for the first Million Woman March. Among the speakers are Maxine Waters, Winnie Mandela, and rapper Sister Souljah.

1997, December 6. Houston, Texas. Lee P. Brown, Democrat, veteran law enforcement officer, and former "drug czar," is elected mayor, the first African American to hold the post. The city's population of 1.8 million reports a racial mix of one-third white, one-third black, and one-third Hispanic.

1998, January 15. Atlanta, Georgia. Martin Luther King III succeeds Joseph E. Lowery as head of the SCLC. Lowery held the post for 20 years.

1998, January 16. Maryland. A county school district in Maryland bans Toni Morrison's novel *Song of Solomon.*

1998, January 23. Cambridge, Massachusetts. Harvard University announces the appointment of Lani Guinier as a full tenured professor in the Harvard Law School. She is the first African American woman to receive tenure at the law school and is known for her outspoken stance on issues such as voting rights and affirmative action.

1998, February 2. Washington, DC. Jane E. Smith becomes president of the National Council of Negro Women, succeeding Dorothy I. Height who held the post for 40 years.

1998, February 5. Washington, DC. Documents from Brown & Williamson Tobacco Company relating to marketing strategies aimed at teenagers and minorities are released during a House judiciary hearing. The documents date back to 1972 and had been used in state lawsuits against the tobacco industry. The Brown & Williamson papers document strategies to attract African Americans, suggesting that a Kool-brand basketball "could become an interesting symbol within the inner city."

1998, February 9. Baltimore, Maryland. Myrlie Evers-Williams announces that she will not seek a fourth term as chair of the National Association for the Advancement of Colored People's board of directors. She leaves the organization that she has headed since 1995 with what she calls a surplus of over $2 million and with restored credibility and financial integrity.

1998, February 21. Baltimore, Maryland. Civil rights activist and educator Julian Bond is elected chair of the NAACP's board of directors, succeeding Myrlie Evers-Williams. He announced his aim to continue the organization's progress "on our way to financial health and integrity."

1998, March 21. Jackson, Mississippi. The state of Mississippi releases documents relating to the now-defunct Mississippi State Sovereignty Commission that used spy tactics and intimidation to preserve racial segregation in the state during the civil rights era. Created in 1956, the commission promoted racial segregation in Mississippi and throughout the country. In 1989, U.S. District Judge William H. Barber ordered the files open. The documents show that previously secret files included information on individual civil rights workers, their religious beliefs, sexual behavior, and other details. License plate numbers were recorded outside civil rights meeting places. Many African American informers were used as spies. Some of the documents discuss the use of violence against the civil rights workers.

1998, March 22. Africa. President Bill Clinton begins an historic 12-day tour of sub-Saharan Africa in the accompaniment of such notable African Americans as Jesse Jackson Sr., Congresswoman Maxine Waters, and Camille Cosby.

1998, April 14. Washington, DC. Franklin D. Raines is named chief executive of the nation's largest mortgage financing company, Fannie Mae.

1998, April 23. Nashville, Tennessee. James Earl Ray, convicted killer of Martin Luther King Jr. dies of liver disease.

1998, May 1. In response to written objections concerning the "n——word," *Merriam-Webster Dictionary* officials announce a plan to revise over 200 words regarded as offensive.

1998, May 2. Pomona, California. Eldridge Cleaver, writer, minister, and former leader of the Black Panther party, dies of undisclosed causes.

1998, June 19. Boston, Massachusetts. Columnist Patricia Smith, on staff since 1990, resigns from the *Boston Globe* after admitting that she fabricated sections of her columns.

1998, July. Atlanta, Georgia. Myrlie Evers, who resigned as board chair of the NAACP, is named chairman emeritus at the organization's annual meeting.

1998, July 19. New York City, New York. Historian and African history scholar John Henrik Clarke dies of a heart attack in Harlem at age 83.

1998, July 22. Atlanta, Georgia. A federal judge rules that CBS News is not guilty of copyright infringement for airing film coverage of Martin Luther King Jr.'s famous "I Have a Dream" speech of 1963, and that the deceased leader's speech is in public domain. CBS used the footage in "The 20th Century with Mike Wallace,"

shown in 1994. The King family sued CBS for its use of the film.

1998, July 24. Manning, South Carolina. In the largest award given to the victims of a hate crime, a jury orders the Ku Klux Klan and its grand dragon to pay $37.8 million for the 1995 burning of the Macedonia Baptist Church in Bloomville.

1998, September 7. Atlanta, Georgia. Hundreds of young people attend the Million Youth March supported by such organizations as the NAACP, the Student Christian Leadership Conference, and Operation PUSH (People United to Serve Humanity). A similar march was held earlier in New York City, but without the organizations' support.

1998, September 18. Washington, DC. The White House Initiative on Race and Reconciliation, after 15 months of examination, releases its report and confirms that racism is still a critical problem in the United States.

1998, September 26. Langston, Oklahoma. Prairie View Agricultural and Mechanical University in Texas ends its 80-game losing streak in football by beating Langston University. This is the longest losing streak in National Collegiate Athletic Association history.

1998, September 21. Mission Viejo, California. Olympic star Florence Griffith Joyner, the first woman to win four Olympic medals, dies of an epileptic seizure while sleeping.

1998, November 1. Oxford, England. Genetic evidence, based on blood samples from living descendants of Thomas Jefferson and his slave Sally Hemings, prove it is likely that Jefferson had fathered a son by Hemings. The DNA was analyzed by an Oxford University research team in England and the results published in the November 5 issue of *Nature*.

1998, November 9. Chicago, Illinois. U.S. Senator Carol Mosely Braun loses her bid for reelection to Republican Peter Fitzgerald.

1998, December 2. Washington, DC. Mike Espy, former secretary of the U.S. Department of Agriculture, is acquitted of charges involving gifts received from businesses regulated by the department.

1999, January 13. Chicago, Illinois. Chicago Bulls star Michael Jordan retires from the NBA a second time. He had led the Bulls to their third straight NBA title and their sixth in eight years.

1999, February 2. Berkeley, California. Five civil rights advocacy groups file suit against the University of California at Berkeley, charging that the school discriminates against minorities in its admissions policies. The groups argue that the elimination of race-based admissions places too much importance on grade

President Bill Clinton acknowledging cheers from students during his visit to Goree Island near Senegal in 1998.

point averages (GPA), Scholastic Aptitude Test (SAT) scores, and advanced placement (AP) courses, which they already regard as inherently biased and discriminatory against minorities. The suit follows recent abolition of race-based admissions policies in California's state universities.

1999, February 4. Amadou Diallo, an unarmed African American immigrant from New Guinea, is mistakenly shot and killed by four white policemen in New York City, raising a national outcry. Diallo was hit by 19 shots in a volley of gunfire. Police said they thought the suspect was reaching for a gun when in fact he was attempting to pull out his wallet.

1999, February 19. Washington, DC. Fifty-nine years after his death, President Bill Clinton pardons Henry O. Flipper, the first African American graduate of West Point who was court-martialed in 1881 and dishonorably discharged in 1882. Clinton notes that "This good man now has completely recovered his good name." Flipper was ostracized by his white classmates. Although acquitted of apparently trumped-up charges of embezzling commissary funds, he was found guilty of "conduct unbecoming an officer" for

lying to investigators. In 1976, the army formally exonerated Clipper, changed his discharge to honorable, and reburied him with full honors in his hometown, Thomasville, Georgia. An annual award is now given in his name to an outstanding West Point cadet.

1999, February 25. Jasper, Texas. White supremacist John William King is sentenced to die for his involvement in the murder of James Byrd Jr. on June 7, 1998. Byrd was tied to the rear of a truck and dragged to his death. Trials for two other men accused in the murder, Lawrence Russell Brewer and Shawn Allen Berry, are pending.

1999, March 16. Miami, Florida. Henry Lyons, convicted earlier this month of racketeering and grand theft, resigns as president of the National Baptist Convention USA—a position he had held since 1994. He had survived earlier attempts of his church denomination to oust him from the convention's presidency and retained the support of his parishioners at Bethel Metropolitan Baptist Church—the church he pastored in St. Petersburg, Florida. Lyons was convicted of pocketing $240,000 in donations earmarked to African American churches burned by arson and for swindling over $4 million from corporations seeking business transactions with the convention.

1999, April. The Trenton (NC) Town Council unanimously selects its first black and first woman mayor. Sylvia Willis succeeded white mayor Joffree Legett who resigned under pressure after denouncing blacks as unfit to govern and claiming that blacks would rather be led by whites. Earlier, the town of about 200 residents, 50 of them African American, refused to annex three African American neighborhoods with about 100 residents. Intervention by the NAACP and an African American boycott of Trenton's white-owned businesses persuaded the town to annex the neighborhoods.

1999, April 12. Legendary band leader and composer Edward Kennedy "Duke" Ellington (1899–1974) is posthumously awarded a Pulitzer Prize on the centennial of his birth. The special music citation was given "in recognition of his musical genius, which evoked aesthetically the principles of democracy through the medium of jazz and thus made an indelible contribution to art and culture."

1999, April 14. Washington, DC. Federal District Court Judge Paul L. Friedman approves a settlement that could provide $2 billion for thousands of African American farmers who sued two years ago because their access to government loans and subsidies had been denied. Over 18,000 farmers have signed up for the settlement. Farmers with less documented evidence of discrimination in loan approvals may take a $50,000 settlement, $12,500 for taxes, and have their federal debts forgiven. Those with more evidence may appear before an independent arbitrator to petition for larger amounts in damages.

1999, April 20. San Francisco, California. U.S. District Judge William Orrick orders an end to 16 years of race-based enrollment in the public schools of San Francisco and approves a lawsuit by Chinese Americans denied admission to preferred campuses in the city. Although African Americans and Hispanics protest his decision, Orrick rules that racial admissions violate Chinese Americans' constitutional rights to equal treatment in a school of their choice. The agreement repeals a limit of 45 percent of racial or ethnic enrollment in a single school and 40 percent in magnet schools.

1999, May 1. Belgrade, Yugoslavia. Jesse Jackson wins the release of the three U.S. soldiers—staff sergeants Andrew Ramirez and Christopher Stone and specialist Steven Gonzales—who Yugoslav authorities had held as prisoners of war since their capture on March 31 near the Yugoslavia-Macedonia border.

1999, June 6. Venus Williams, 18, and her sister, Serena Williams, 17, win the French Open women's doubles title against Martina Hingis and Anna Kournikova, 6–3, 6–7, 8–6.

1999, June 15. Under legislation approved by the U.S. Congress on May 3, Rosa Parks receives the Congressional Gold Medal. Congressman John Lewis said that "one, simple, defining act" by Parks, who in 1955 stood up "for what is right and just," stoked the Civil Rights movement nationwide and led to the end of legalized segregation.

1999, June 15. Hattiesburg, Mississippi. A mistrial is declared in the reopened case against Mississippi businessman Charles Noble for the 1966 slaying of NAACP member Vernon Dahmer.

1999, June 23. Springfield, Massachusetts. Former Georgetown University coach John Thompson is elected to the NBA Hall of Fame, along with former basketball player and general manager Wayne Embry.

1999, July 10. Baltimore, Maryland. The U.S. Coast Guard posthumously honors Alex Haley, Pulitzer Prize–winning author of *Roots*, by commissioning a cutter in his name. Haley spent 20 years in the Coast Guard, rising from ship's steward to become the first head of the Guard's public affairs office.

1999, August 4. Former Detroit Pistons basketball player and NBC-TV basketball analyst, Isiah Thomas announces that he has purchased majority ownership of the Continental Basketball Association (CBA). Thomas acquires the nine-team league for approximately $10 million. Organized as an association with approximately 40 owners, Thomas says he plans to reorganize the CBA into a single entity league.

1999, September 10. Judges in Charlotte, North Carolina, put an end to school busing, ruling that forced integration is no longer necessary. The program was originally put into place 30 years ago.

1999, September 11. Seventeen-year-old Serena Williams beats Martina Hingis of Switzerland 6–3, 7–6, to win the U.S. Open championship in tennis. She becomes only the second African American woman to take the title, after Althea Gibson in 1957 and 1958.

1999, September 20. Lawrence Brewer is found guilty of the June 7, 1998, murder of James Byrd Jr. Byrd died after being dragged by a chain behind a truck. Brewer is sentenced to death on September 23. A second man accused in the case, John King, was sentenced earlier in the year.

2000, January 14. Christopher Paul Curtis wins the Newbery Medal and the Coretta Scott King Author award for his book, *Bud, Not Buddy*. Curtis is the first author to win both awards for one book. The awards are announced annually by the American Library Association (ALA): the Newbery is given for "distinguished

Venus Williams, the first number-one ranked African American tennis player.

contribution to American literature for children"; the Coretta Scott King award honors African American authors and illustrators.

2000, January 19. Michael Jordan becomes a partial owner of the Washington Wizards. He will also serve as the new president of basketball operations for the team. Jordan's total stake is approximately 10 percent, which is valued between $20 million and $30 million. He joins the ranks of only five other African Americans who own portions of NBA teams. Former All-Star Earvin "Magic" Johnson has a small stake in the Los Angeles Lakers; Edward and Bettiann Gardner are part owners of Jordan's former team, the Chicago Bulls; and actor Bill Cosby owns a minority percentage of the New Jersey Nets.

2000, January 23. Denzel Washington wins a Golden Globe award for Best Performance by an Actor in a Dramatic Motion Picture for his role in *The Hurricane*. Halle Berry wins a Golden Globe for Best Performance by an Actress in a Miniseries or Television Movie for her work in *Introducing Dorothy Dandridge*.

2000, February 25. The four white plainclothes policeman charged in the February 1999 shooting of African American immigrant Amadou Diallo, are acquitted on all charges. The defense for the officers asked that the trial take place in Albany, New York, instead of New York City to guarantee a fair hearing. The jury was composed of eight whites and four blacks.

2000, April 18. Gustavas A. McLeod is the first man to pilot an open-cockpit plane to the North Pole. His 35,000-mile journey began in Maryland and was made in a former crop duster. There have been numerous flights to the North Pole since the first plane reached the area in 1937, but no one had successfully made the trip in an open cockpit because of the extreme temperatures.

2000, May 2. South Carolina governor Jim Hodges signs a bill to officially make Martin Luther King Jr.'s birthday a holiday for state workers. South Carolina is the last state to finally recognize the date as a state holiday.

2000, June 9. The U.S. Justice Department reports that after extensive investigation it has found no evidence that a conspiracy led to the 1968 assassination of activist Martin Luther King Jr. Some members of the King family called for the special investigation after a

Memphis civil court concluded in 1999 that a federal conspiracy led to the shooting. In addition, James Earl Ray, the man convicted of the crime in 1969, claimed he did not work alone.

2000, July 1. Songwriter and producer Antonio "L.A." Reid takes over as president and chief executive officer (CEO) of Arista Records from founder Clive Davis, who has headed the company since its inception 25 years earlier.

2000, July 1. After major protest rallies and an NAACP boycott of tourism, the governor of South Carolina removes the Confederate flag from the top of the state capitol dome in Columbia. The flag is considered by many to be a symbol of slavery.

2000, July 8. Twenty-year-old Venus Williams wins the singles title at Wimbledon, becoming the first African American woman to do so since Althea Gibson in 1957. She defeated defending champion Lindsay Davenport, 6–3, 7–6.

2000, July 10. George W. Bush, Republican nominee for president, addresses the national convention of the NAACP in Baltimore, Maryland, and promises party support to African Americans. Republican presidential candidates from the two previous elections, Bob Dole in 1996 and George H. W. Bush in 1992, had both declined invitations from the group.

2000, July 11. Reverend Vashti Murphy McKenzie becomes the first woman bishop in the African Methodist Episcopal Church.

2000, July 23. Tiger Woods, age 24, wins the British Open golf tournament in St. Andrews, Scotland. By taking the contest, he becomes the youngest golfer in history to have won all four Grand Slam events: the British Open, the U.S. Open, the Masters, and the PGA Championship. Only four golfers had previously earned this honor: Gene Sarazan, Ben Hogan, Gary Player, and Jack Nicklaus. Some call it the "Tiger Slam" because the young golfer did not take all four trophies in a single calendar year.

2000, July 25. Joetta Clark-Diggs, her sister Hazel Clark, and sister-in-law Jearl Miles-Clark make history when all three win spots on the same U.S. Olympic team. It is also the first time that three members of the same family will compete in the same event. Hazel Clark won the top spot on the women's 800-meter track team, followed by Miles-Clark in second and Clark-Diggs in third.

2000, August 15. Stephanie Ready becomes the first woman to coach a men's professional basketball team when she is named assistant coach of the National Basketball Developmental League's Greenville (South Carolina) Groove.

2000, September 12. James Perkins Jr., a former computer consultant, becomes the first African American mayor of Selma, Alabama. He ousts Joseph T. Smitherman with 57 percent of the vote. Smitherman, age 70, was running for his tenth consecutive term. He was mayor of Selma during the famous 1965 civil rights march.

2000, September 23. The First Annual African American Women's Health Conference is held in Los Angeles, California. The focus of the event is to address the impact of breast cancer on the African American community. Workshops and speeches will focus on education, risk assessment, early education, and alternative medical treatments. According to national statistics, breast cancer is the number one cause of death among African American women, and African American women who develop breast cancer are twice as likely to die than their white counterparts.

2000, September 23. In the 2000 Summer Olympics held in Sydney, Australia, Marion Jones takes the 100-meter dash in 10.75 seconds, making her the fastest woman in the world. By the end of the games, Jones has won three gold and two bronze medals, the most medals won by a woman during a single Olympics.

2000, November 9. When she takes the helm of Brown University in Providence, Rhode Island, Ruth Simmons becomes the first African American president of an Ivy League college. She is also Brown's first woman president. Prior to being appointed, Simmons was on the faculty of Princeton University, where she served as vice provost in the early 1990s. Since 1995, she was president of Smith College.

2000, December 16. General Colin L. Powell is appointed Secretary of State by President George W. Bush. He is the first African American to hold the position.

2000, December 17. President George W. Bush announces the appointment of Condoleezza Rice as national security adviser. Rice, a Stanford University professor, becomes the first African American and the first woman to hold the post.

2001, January 30. The state of Georgia redesigns its state flag by replacing the large Confederate battle cross with the state seal. Although many Southerners see the Confederate flag as a symbol of southern pride, others view it as a reminder of slavery and segregation.

2001, February 2–4. The National Reparations Convention takes place in Chicago. Among those in attendance are Representative Bobby Rush of Illinois and Representative John Conyers of Michigan. The genesis of the convention can be traced back to April 26, 2000, when the issue of slavery reparations was raised at a joint hearing of the Chicago City Council Finance and Human Relations committees. According to Rush, who spoke at the meeting, "The future of race relations will be determined by reparations for slavery."

2001, April 12. The mayor of Cincinnati, Ohio, declares a state of emergency after four days of racial rioting. The riots broke out after a white police officer fatally shot Timothy Thomas, an unarmed African American teenager. City officers have long been accused of racial profiling and using excessive force.

2001, April 17. In a controversial vote, Mississippi residents decide to retain the design of their state flag, which bears the Confederate battle cross. The state of Georgia redesigned its flag earlier in the year, which means that Mississippi is the only state that still prominently displays the "Southern Cross." Other states, including Arkansas and Alabama, incorporate only portions of it in their state flags.

2001, May 1. Thomas E. Blanton Jr., one of four former Ku Klux Klan members charged with the 1963 bombing of the 16th Street Baptist Church in Birmingham, Alabama, that killed four African American girls, is convicted and sentenced to life in prison.

2001, May 25. The 11th U.S. Circuit Court of Appeals in Atlanta rules that author Alice Randall has every right to publish her book *The Wind Done Gone*. The book, which is a parody of Margaret Mitchell's *Gone with the Wind*, has been surrounded by controversy. Representatives of Mitchell's estate tried to stop it from being released, claiming Randall borrowed her plot and characters from Mitchell's 1939 novel, and thus was in violation of copyright. According to the court, an attempt to stop Randall from publishing her book would be "a violation of the First Amendment." Randall's book was published by Houghton Mifflin in June. Approximately one year later, the two sides reached a confidential settlement under which Randall's novel must be subtitled "An Unauthorized Parody."

2001, May 29. In the largest settlement ever in a U.S. racial discrimination suit, the Coca-Cola Company agrees to pay out $192 million to approximately 2,000 African American employees. The suit was brought against the company by employees who worked for Coca-Cola between April 22, 1995, and June 14, 2000, and claimed that the company discriminated against African Americans in hiring and promoting.

2001, June 12–13. Russell Simmons, founder of Def Jam Records, holds the first two-day Hip-Hop Summit in New York City. The goal of the summit is to bring together a cross-section of America, including recording artists and label executives, in an effort to discuss

issues that face rap music. Nation of Islam leader Minister Louis Farrakhan gives the keynote speech.

2001, July 30. Harvard-educated Pamela Thomas-Graham is named president and chief executive officer (CEO) of CNBC. This makes her the most powerful African American in the cable news industry.

2001, September 15. Representative Barbara Lee of California makes the news when she casts the lone dissenting vote allowing President George W. Bush "to use all necessary and appropriate force" against anyone associated with the September 11, 2001, terrorist attacks. The resolution passes unanimously in the Senate (98–0); the tally in the House is 420–1.

2001, September 24. At the Goodwill Games in Brisbane, Australia, Michael Johnson announces his retirement. Considered to be one of the greatest track-and-field athletes in history, Johnson has won five Olympic gold medals and nine World Championship gold medals during his career.

2001, September 25. NBA star Michael Jordan comes out of retirement, and signs a two-year contract to play basketball for the Washington Wizards. In 2000, Jordan had purchased a portion of the team. According to NBA

Los Angeles Lakers center Shaquille O'Neal.

rules, he is forced to sell his shares and step down as owner because current players cannot also own teams.

2001, September 26. Cincinnati police officer Steven Roach is found not guilty for the murder of Timothy Thomas, an unarmed 19-year-old African American who was shot to death in April 2001. Thomas's death touched off four days of rioting in the city. Following the verdict, there are some isolated incidents of violence, causing Cincinnati mayor Charlie Luken to impose a curfew.

2001, September 27. Robert Johnson, founder of Black Entertainment Television (BET), makes it on *Forbes* magazine's annual list of the top 400 richest people in America. He is number 172. Johnson earns the title of "billionaire" after selling his 63 percent of BET stock, worth $1.3 billion, to Viacom, Inc. He is the first African American billionaire in the United States.

2001, October 5. Barry Bonds of the San Francisco Giants hits 73 home runs to beat Mark McGwire's record for most homers in a single season.

2001, October 26. Henry Ford Museum in Dearborn, Michigan, purchases the bus on which Rosa Parks made her famous "stand" in 1955. The bus had been lost for years, but finally came up on the auction block, along with certificates that document the bus's identification number and guarantee its authenticity. The bus is purchased for $492,000, and will be carefully restored by the museum for public viewing.

2001, November 13. Bishop Wilton Gregory of Belleville, Illinois, is elected the first African American president of the U.S. Conference of Catholic Bishops. As president, Gregory will serve as the public voice of Catholic bishops in the United States.

2001, November 19. Thirty-seven-year-old Barry Bonds is named the National League's Most Valuable Player. He becomes the first baseball player to win the honor four times. Bonds won the award in 1990 and 1992 while playing for Pittsburgh. He was playing for the San Francisco Giants when he was honored in 1993.

2002, February 25. Actor and comedian Bill Cosby announces that he will cancel a March 15 performance in Cincinnati, Ohio, to support a boycott of the city by African American groups. Groups such as the Coalition for a Just Cincinnati are targeting the city for its poor response to riots that broke out as a result of the April 2001 shooting of African American teenager Timothy Thomas by a white police officer.

2002, March 25. Halle Berry becomes the first African American woman to win an Oscar for Best Actress, for her performance in *Monster's Ball*. Denzel Washington wins the Best Actor statue for his role in *Training Day*. He is only the second African American actor, following Sidney Poitier in 1963, to win the award.

2002, March 26. Law student Deadria Farmer-Paellmann files a federal lawsuit against FleetBoston Financial, the railroad firm CSX, and the Aetna insurance company. She files the suit on behalf of 35 million African Americans who are descendants of slaves, and who seek reparations for former injustices. According to the charges, all of the named defendants profited from the slave trade at some point in history. Claimants are asking for billions of dollars in compensation. Lawyers representing Farmer-Paellmann promise to bring charges against other corporations and institutions at a later date.

2002, May 22. Former Ku Klux Klan member Bobby Frank Cherry is convicted and sentenced to life in prison for the 1963 church bombing that killed four African American girls in Birmingham, Alabama. He is the last living member to face charges. Robert Chambliss was convicted in 1977, Thomas Blanton was convicted in 2001, and Frank Cash died in 1994 without being charged.

2002, June 16. Tiger Woods wins the 102nd U.S. Open. He becomes the first player since Jack Nicklaus, in 1972, to win the first two majors of the year. Woods won the U.S. Masters on April 14. He does not win the British Open, however, squelching his quest for a true Grand Slam season.

2002, June 17. The Los Angeles Lakers beat the New Jersey Nets 113–107 to take the NBA championship. This is the third year in a row that the team finishes the season in the top spot. At age 23, Laker Kobe Bryant becomes the youngest player to win three NBA championships.

2002, June 19. The Juneteenth freedom march and rally takes place in Washington, D.C. It begins at the historic home of abolitionist Frederick Douglass and ends on the steps of the U.S. Capitol. The goal of the gathering is to urge President George W. Bush to establish Juneteenth as a national holiday. An official holiday in seven states, June 19 marks the date when word was officially brought to Texas by General Gordon Grander that the Civil War was over and slaves in the South were free. The year was 1865, and because of poor communication methods, slavery was still enforced in Texas at the time.

②

African American Firsts

While not comprehensive, the following list covers a wide spectrum of pioneering events and people in history. Many of the individuals and events described hold considerable intrinsic significance—such as the first publication of a novel by an African American author in 1853—while other events listed are merely interesting. Nevertheless, all are trendsetters in African American history.

1619, August 20. At Jamestown colony, the first 20 Africans arrive in English North America from the Caribbean as indentured servants.

1623. The first African American child in the colonies to be baptized a Christian becomes a member of the Anglican Church in Jamestown. The child's name is William, son of Isabel and William.

1624. William Tucker, who is believed to have been the first African American child born in the American colonies, is born in Jamestown, Virginia.

1746. Slave poet Lucy Terry writes *Bars Fight*, a commemorative poem recreating the Deerfield (Massachusetts) Massacre. In doing so, she is considered to be the first African American poet in America.

1746. Organized in Philadelphia, Pennsylvania, the Free African Society is considered the first African American organization in the United States.

1752. Benjamin Banneker builds the first grandfather clock.

1758. Born in 1702 to free parents in Jamaica, Frances Williams graduates from Cambridge University and becomes the first black college graduate in the Western Hemisphere.

1770. While leading fellow patriots in protest against British soldiers, Crispus Attucks is killed, thus becoming the first American to die during the Revolutionary Period. This event is later memorialized as the Boston Massacre.

1773. *Poems on Various Subjects, Religious and Moral* by 17-year-old Phyllis Wheatley is published in London. It is the first book of poetry published by an African American.

1783. James Derham, born a slave in Philadelphia in 1762, becomes the first African American physician in the United States. Having served as an assistant to his master (a doctor by profession), Derham purchases his freedom in 1783 and goes on to develop a thriving practice with both black and white clientele.

1785, May 15. The first African American missionary minister to work with Native Americans is John Morront of New York. He was ordained a Methodist minister in London, England. Among his converts to the Christian faith are a Cherokee chieftain and his daughter.

1786. Lemuel Haynes, who served during the American Revolution as a minuteman in Connecticut, becomes the first African American minister with a white congregation.

1787. Prince Hall organizes the first African American Masonic Lodge in America.

1789. *The Interesting Narrative of the Life of Olaudah Equiano, or Gustavus Vassa, the African, Written by Himself* is published. It is considered to be the first autobiography written by an African American. The work becomes a best-seller, with nine English editions and one American edition including translations in Dutch, German, and Russian.

1794. The First African Church of St. Thomas is dedicated in Philadelphia, Pennsylvania. It is the first African American Episcopal (AME) congregation in the United States.

1816. Richard Allen, founder of the African Methodist Episcopal Church, becomes the first African American bishop.

1817. The African Methodist Episcopal Church organizes the A.M.E. Book Concern in Philadelphia, the first African American-owned book publishing enterprise in the United States. The Book Concern publishes its first book that same year, *The Book of Discipline*.

1821. New York City's free African American community establishes the first African American theater, the African Grove Theatre, located at Mercer and Bleecker streets.

1823. The first play written and produced by an African American, *The Drama of King Shotaway*, is presented by the African Grove Theatre in New York City. The playwright is Henry Brown.

1827. The first African American newspaper *Freedom's Journal* is published in New York City.

1829. The first African American congregation of Catholic nuns, the Oblate Sisters of Providence, is founded in the United States by Mary Rosine Boegues, Mary Frances Balas, Mary Theresa Duchemin, and Elizabeth Lange.

1829. The first National Negro Convention meets in Philadelphia, Pennsylvania.

1831. The first Annual Convention of the People of Color meets at Wesleyan Church in Philadelphia, Pennsylvania. Delegates from five states resolve to study African American conditions, explore settlement possibilities in Canada, and raise money for an industrial college in New Haven.

1834. The first African American believed to have been granted a patent from the U.S. Patent Office is Henry Blair of Greenross, Maryland.

1839. The first anti-slavery political organization, the Liberty Party, is founded in Warsaw, New York. Among its leading supporters are African American abolitionists Samuel R. Ward and Henry Highland Garnet.

1844. Macon Allen becomes the first African American admitted to a state bar. Charlotte Ray later becomes the first African American woman to gain the same distinction.

1845. Macon B. Allen becomes the first African American lawyer formally admitted to the bar after he passes the state bar examination in Worcester, Massachusetts.

1847. Frederick Douglass publishes the first issue of his abolitionist newspaper, *The North Star*, in Rochester, New York.

1847. David John Peck graduates from Rush Medical College, becoming the first African American to graduate from an American school of medicine.

1853. Lincoln University, the first African American college, is founded as Ashmum Institute in Oxford, Pennsylvania.

1853. The first novel written and published by an African American is a work by William Wells Brown, entitled *Clotel, Or, the President's Daughter*.

1854. John Mercer Langston, who is believed to have been the first African American elected to public office, is elected clerk of Brownhelm, Ohio.

1855. Berea College is the first college established in the United States for the specific purpose of educating blacks and whites together.

1860. The first African American baseball team to tour various parts of the country is called the Brooklyn Excelsiors.

1861. Nicholas Biddle becomes one of the first African Americans wounded during the Civil War. An escaped slave, Biddle attaches himself to a troop unit heading for the defense of Washington, but is stoned by an angry mob in Baltimore. He manages to escape death only with the aid of his white comrades-in-arms.

1861. In Boston, Massachusetts, William C. Nell is appointed postal clerk, becoming the first African American to hold a federal civilian post.

1862. Mary Patterson becomes the first African American woman in the United States to earn a master of arts degree, awarded by Oberlin College.

1863. The first African American appointed a chaplain in the U.S. Army is Henry McNeal Turner.

1863, July 18. The first African American recipient of the Congressional Medal of Honor is Sergeant William H. Carney of the 54th Massachusetts Infantry. He is given the honor for combat valor at Fort Wagner, South Carolina.

1864. Rebecca Lee Crumpler, believed to be the first African American woman physician, graduates from New England Female Medical College.

1865. Henry Highland Garnet is the first African American to deliver a sermon in the chamber of the House of Representatives in the U.S. Capitol.

1865. Martin R. Delany becomes the first African American to attain the rank of major in the U.S. Army. A graduate of Howard University Medical School, Delany served in the Medical Corps. He was also a writer.

1865. Alexander T. Augusta becomes the first African American to hold a medical commission in the U.S. Army. A surgeon and physician with the rank of major, he then becomes the highest ranking African American officer in the Civil War on March 13, when he is promoted to brevet lieutenant colonel.

1865. John Rock becomes the first African American lawyer admitted to practice before the U.S. Supreme Court. His admittance is moved by Senator Charles Sumner of Massachusetts. Chief Justice Salmon P. Chase presides.

1865. The first African American newspaper in the South—*The Colored American*—is published in Augusta, Georgia, and edited by J. T. Shutten.

1866. Edward G. Walker and Charles L. Mitchell are elected to the Massachusetts House of Representatives, becoming the first African Americans to serve in a legislative assembly.

1867. Robert Tanner Freeman becomes the first African American to graduate from Harvard University's School of Dentistry.

1868. Howard University opens its College of Medicine, the first African American medical school in the United States.

1869. George Ruffin graduates from Harvard Law School and becomes the first African American to earn an LL.B. from the university—perhaps the first to graduate from a university law school in the United States.

1869. Ebenezer Don Carlos Bassett, believed to be the first African American to receive an appointment in the diplomatic service, becomes U.S. minister to Haiti.

1869. Harriet E. Adams Wilson becomes the first African American to publish a novel in the United States entitled *Our Nig, or, Sketches from the Life of a Free Black, in a Two-Story White House, North, Showing That Slavery's Shadows Fall Even There.*

1870. Richard Greener becomes the first African American to receive a degree from Harvard. Active as a teacher and editor, Greener is admitted to the South Carolina bar in 1876 and becomes dean of Howard University Law School in 1879.

1870. Hiram R. Revels, of Mississippi, becomes the first African American elected to the U.S. Senate. Joseph H. Rainey, of South Carolina, and Jefferson F. Long, of Georgia, are the first black elected members of the House of Representatives.

1871. Alcorn College, now Alcorn State University, is founded as the first African American land grant college.

1872. The first African American midshipman to attend the U.S. Naval Academy is James Henry Conyers of South Carolina. Conyers does not graduate, however, and leaves the academy on November 11, 1873.

1872. Louisiana Lieutenant Governor Pinckney Benton Stewart Pinchback becomes the first African American governor upon impeachment of the incumbent.

1872. The first African American woman lawyer, Charlotte E. Roy, receives her degree from Howard University School of Law in Washington, D.C.

1872. The first African American delegates to the presidential nominating convention of a major party appear at the Republican Convention in Philadelphia.

1873. The first African American municipal judge, Mifflin W. Gibbs, is elected in Little Rock, Arkansas.

1873. Susan McKinney, believed to be the first African American woman to formally enter the medical profession, is certified as a physician. (Records at the medical college of the New York Infirmary indicate that Rebecca Cole was the first African American woman

P.B.S. Pinchback, the first African American governor.

physician in the United States, having practiced from 1872 to 1881.)

1874. Republican Blanche K. Bruce is elected by the Mississippi state legislature to the U.S. Senate. He becomes the first African American to serve a full term in the U.S. Senate.

1875, May 17. Oliver Lewis, an African American riding in the first Kentucky Derby, becomes the race's first winner.

1875, June 10. Reverend James Augustine Healy becomes the first African American Roman Catholic bishop in the United States.

1876. Graduating from Yale University, Edward A. Bouchet becomes the first African American to earn a Ph.D. from an American university.

1877. George Washington Henderson is elected to Phi Beta Kappa, becoming the first African American to gain membership in the honor society.

1877. Henry O. Flipper becomes the first African American to graduate from the U.S. Military Academy at West Point.

1879, August 1. In Boston, Mary E. Mahoney becomes the first African American woman to receive a diploma in nursing from New England Hospital for Women and Children.

1882. The first daily newspaper owned by an African American, *The Cairo Illinois Gazette*, is published by W. S. Scott.

1884. John Roy Lynch becomes the first African American to preside over a national political convention, when he is nominated temporary chairman of the Republican Party's national convention.

1884. Moses Fleetwood Walker becomes the first African American major league baseball player when he plays for Toledo in the American Association.

1885. The first African American state legislator elected to represent a majority white constituency is Bishop Benjamin William Arnett of the African Methodist Episcopal Church.

1885. The first African American professional baseball team, The Cuban Giants, is formed in New York City by Frank Thompson from a group of waiters at a Long Island hotel.

1885. The first African American Protestant Episcopal bishop in the United States, the Reverend Samuel David Ferguson, is elected to the House of Bishops.

1885. Jonathan Jasper Wright becomes the first African American elected to the State Supreme Court of South Carolina. He is also the first African American to be admitted to the bar in Pennsylvania.

1886. Augustine Tolton is ordained as the first African American Roman Catholic priest.

1886. George "Little Chocolate" Dixon becomes the first African American to win a world boxing title.

1890. Thomy Lafon, a real estate speculator and money lender in Louisiana, is believed to have been the first African American millionaire in the United States.

1891. Daniel Hale Williams, physician and surgeon, founds Provident Hospital in Chicago, Illinois, which includes the first training school for African American nurses in the United States.

1892. The first African American college football game is played between Biddle College (now Johnson C. Smith University) and Livingstone College. Biddle wins 4 to 0.

1893. Dr. Daniel Hale Williams becomes the first surgeon to successfully enter the chest cavity and suture the heart of a living patient.

1893, September 19. E. R. Robinson patents the electric railway trolley.

1894. W. E. B. Du Bois becomes the first African American to be awarded a Ph.D. by Harvard University.

1902. *Off Bloomingdale Asylum*, a satirical comedy, is the first film to use African American actors. The film is made in Paris, France.

1903. Maggie Lena Walker becomes the first African American woman bank president when she founds the Saint Luke Penny Thrift Savings Bank in Richmond, Virginia.

1905. The Louisville Free Public Library in Kentucky is established as the first public library in the nation built exclusively for African Americans.

1906. The first African American fraternity, Alpha Phi Alpha, is organized at Cornell University.

1907. John Hope is named president of Atlanta Baptist College. He is the first African American to be appointed president at a Baptist school. As president, Hope expands the college with funds donated by John T. Rockefeller and Andrew Carnegie.

1907. Alain Leroy Locke becomes the first African American awarded a Rhodes Scholarship.

1908. The first African American sorority, Alpha Kappa Alpha, is founded at Howard University in Washington, D.C.

1908. John Baxter Taylor Jr., collegiate champion, sets a world record in the 440-yard relay at the London Olympic Games, becoming the first African American to win a gold medal. Other members of his relay team are Nathaniel Cartmell, Melvin Sheppard, and William Hamilton.

1908. Jack Johnson wins a bout with Tommy Burns to become the first African American heavyweight champion.

1911, November 17. The Omega Psi Phi Fraternity becomes the first Greek-letter fraternity formed by African Americans on an African American college campus. It was founded at Howard University, Washington, D.C.

1912. George Edmund Haynes is the first African American to received a doctorate from Columbia University.

1914. Jesse Edward Moorland donates his private library of African American history to Howard University. The collection was eventually named the Moorland-Spingarn Research Center, and is essentially the first African American research collection at a major American university.

1915. Marine biologist Ernest Everett Just is the first-ever recipient of a Spingarn Medal, the highest honor bestowed by the National Association for the Advancement of Colored People (NAACP).

Jack Johnson.

1915.   The Association for the Study of Negro Life and History sponsors the first Black History Week, the prelude to Black History Month.

1917.   Tenor Roland Hayes becomes the first African American to give a recital in Boston's Symphony Hall.

1917.   Eugene Jacques Bullard, flying for France, becomes the first African American aviator. A member of the French Air Service, he flies his first mission September 8. Denied a commission three-quarters of a century before, the Air Force grants Bullard an Air Force Commission in 1994.

1918.   Starring on the Rutgers football team, Paul Robeson becomes the first African American to receive All-American honors.

1918.   Hugh N. Mulzac becomes the first African American in the United States to earn a shipmaster's license and have the right to take command of a ship. Mulzac, however, is unable to find employment as a shipmaster and instead must take jobs at sea as a cook and steward for the next 24 years. He finally takes command of a ship in 1942, a Liberty cargo vessel transporting troops and supplies into the war zones.

1919.   Fritz Pollard becomes the first African American to play professional football for a major team, the Akron Indians. In 1916, Pollard had been the first African American to play in the Rose Bowl, for Brown University.

1920.   Author, scholar, and activist James Weldon Johnson becomes the first African American secretary of the NAACP.

1923.   Charles Hamilton Houston becomes the first African American to receive a S.J.D. from Harvard University. While attending Harvard, Houston is the first African American editor of the *Harvard Law Review.*

1923.   The first African American basketball team, known as the Renaissance, is organized.

1924, July 8.   William DeHart Hubbard becomes the first African American in Olympic history to win an individual gold medal in the long jump at the Paris games.

1926.   Violette Anderson becomes the first African American woman lawyer to practice before the U.S. Supreme Court.

1926, June 20.   Mordecai Wyatt Johnson becomes the first African American president of Howard University. He retires in 1960.

1927.   Artist Henry Ossawa Tanner becomes the first African American to be elected to the National Academy of Design.

1928.   Oscar DePriest, a Republican from Illinois, is elected as the first African American representative to the U.S. Congress from a northern state.

1930.   Considered one of the most important writers of the Harlem Renaissance, Nella Larsen is the first African American woman to be awarded a Guggenheim Fellowship in creative writing.

1931.   Estelle Massey Osborne becomes the first African American recipient in the United States of a master's degree in nursing education when she graduates from Columbia Teachers College.

1933.   Hemsley Winfield becomes the first African American to dance for the Metropolitan Opera, performing the role of the Witch Doctor in *The Emperor Jones.*

1933.   Florence Price is the first African American female composer to have a symphony played by a major orchestra: *Symphony in E Minor* by the Chicago Symphony Orchestra.

1933.   The first transcontinental flight by African American civilian pilots is made by Charles Alfred Anderson of Bryn Mawr, Pennsylvania, and Albert Ernest Forsythe of Atlantic City, New Jersey.

1934. Willa B. Brown becomes the first African American woman to hold a commercial pilot's license in the United States.

1936. The first African American musician to conduct a major American symphony orchestra is William Grant Still, who conducts the Los Angeles Philharmonic in the Hollywood Bowl.

1936. At the Olympic Games in Berlin with German chancellor Adolph Hitler in attendance, Jesse Owens becomes the first Olympian to win four gold medals, three of which were world record marks.

1937. Self-taught sculptor William Edmondson becomes the first African American to have a one-person exhibit at the Museum of Modern Art (MOMA) in New York City.

1937. William H. Hastie is the first African American appointed to a federal district dourt, serving in the Virgin Islands.

1938, November 8. Crystal Bird Fauset becomes the first African American woman elected to a state legislature in the United States, acquiring this distinction when she is named to the Pennsylvania House of Representatives.

1939. The first African American woman judge, Jane Matilda Bolin, is appointed to the Court of Domestic Relations by Mayor Fiorello LaGuardia of New York City.

1940. Kenneth Clark becomes the first African American to be awarded a Ph.D. in psychology from Columbia University.

1940. Benjamin O. Davis Sr. is promoted to the rank of brigadier general, becoming the first African American to hold this post in the U.S. Army.

1940. The first postage stamp honoring an African American, the ten-cent Booker T. Washington stamp, goes on sale at Tuskegee Institute. The stamp, which is part of the "Famous American" series, is the culmination of a seven-year campaign sponsored by Major R. R. Wright, president of the Citizens and Southern Bank and Trust Company of Philadelphia. (Some seven years later, a three-cent postage stamp honoring George Washington Carver is issued on the fourth anniversary of the renowned scientist's death.)

1940, November 20. For her role as supporting actress in the movie *Gone with the Wind*, Hattie McDaniel becomes the first African American to win an Oscar from the Academy of Motion Picture Arts and Sciences.

1941. David Roy "Little Jazz" Eldridge joins Gene Krupa's big band as a trumpeter and singer, becoming the first black musician to be a featured player in a white band. Before this, Teddy Wilson and Lionel Hampton were members of Benny Goodman's band, but not as featured players.

Jane M. Bolin.

1941. Charles Richard Drew, an African American physician, sets up the nation's first blood bank, in Washington, D.C.

1942. Bernard W. Robinson, a medical student at Harvard, becomes the first African American commissioned an officer in the U.S. Naval Reserve.

1942. The U.S. Army lifts its color barrier and admits African American women into its women's branch, the Women's Army Corps (WACS).

1943. Pianist and composer Dorothy Donegan becomes the first woman, and the first African American, to play Chicago's Orchestra Hall, sharing the bill with Vladimir Horowitz.

1943. The first African Americans to crew a warship sail into the North Atlantic on the *USS Mason*. One of the crew is Thomas W. Young, who becomes the first African American war correspondent on a Navy warship.

1943. The first Liberty ship named for an African American, the *George Washington Carver*, is launched from a New Jersey shipyard to begin its career of carrying war cargo to Europe during World War II. The *USS Harmon* becomes the first fighting ship to be named for an African American. Leonard Roy Harmon won the Navy Cross for his heroism aboard the *USS San Francisco* in a battle with the Japanese near the Solomon Islands. Harmon died of wounds suffered during the engagement.

1943. W. E. B. Du Bois becomes the first African American admitted to the National Institute of Arts and Letters. At the time of his admittance, Du Bois is head of the Department of Sociology at Atlanta University.

1944. Harry McAlpin of Atlanta's *Daily World* becomes the first accredited African American White House news correspondent.

1944, October 19. The U.S. Navy lifts its color band and admits African American women into the Women's Reserves (WAVES) .

1944, December. Charity Adams (later Charity Adams Earley) becomes the first African American WAC to be selected for overseas duty. She commands the newly-formed 6888th Central Postal Battalion in Birmingham, England. The 800-woman unit is responsible for directing all incoming and outgoing mail for the seven million Americans serving in the European Theater of Operations.

1945. Phyllis Mae Daley becomes the first African American nurse commissioned in the Navy Reserve Corps. Daley, a registered nurse from New York City, is sworn in as an ensign.

1945, May 15. Operatic soprano Camilla Williams becomes the first African American to sign a full contract with a major U.S. opera company, the New York City Opera. She performs the title role in *Madame Butterfly*.

1945, October 3. Irvin Charles Mollison becomes the first African American appointed judge in the continental United States when President Harry Truman names him to the U.S. Customs Court.

1946. Charles Spurgeon Johnson is appointed president of Fisk University, the first African American to hold the position. Before becoming president, Johnson served as chairman of Fisk University's Department of Social Sciences and established the Fisk Institute of Race Relations.

1946. Roy Campanella, a catcher for a Nashua, New Hampshire team, becomes the first African American to manage an organized, integrated, professional baseball team when the regular manager Walt Alston is ejected from the field by the umpire. Nashua wins the game when an African American pitcher, Don Newcombe, hits a pinch hit home run.

Roy Campanella.

1946. The first coin honoring African Americans is issued. The coin is a 50-cent piece bearing a relief bust of Booker T. Washington, the founder of Tuskegee Institute.

1947. Jackie Robinson joins the National League's Brooklyn Dodgers and becomes the first African American in major league baseball in the twentieth century. He plays his first game as first baseman on April 15 in Brooklyn's Ebbets Field against the Boston Braves.

1947. Dan Bankhead of the National League's Brooklyn Dodgers becomes the first African American pitcher in the major leagues. The first African American pitcher in the American League, Leroy Satchel Paige, follows in 1948.

1947. Larry Doby becomes the first African American baseball player to play in the American League. He made his debut with the Cleveland Indians on July 5.

1947. Louis Lautier, Washington Bureau chief of the Negro Newspaper Publishers Association, becomes the first African American issued credentials for both the Senate and the House press galleries. Lautier is admitted to the galleries on March 18 after a Senate Rules

Committee overrides the refusal of the Standing Committee of Newspaper Correspondents to grant him the necessary credentials.

1947. John Lee of Indianapolis, Indiana, becomes the first African American commissioned officer in the U.S. Navy. His first assignment upon being commissioned is on the *USS Kearsage*.

1948. Pianist and singer Hazel Scott becomes the first African American to host her own television show.

1948. William Thaddeus Coleman Jr. becomes the first appointed African American clerk of the U.S. Supreme Court when named to the post by Supreme Court Justice Felix Frankfurter.

1948. Alice Coachman wins the gold medal in high jump in the Olympic Games held in London, becoming the first African American woman to win gold and the only American woman to win a track event that year.

1948. Nancy Leftenant-Colon becomes the first African American member of the Regular Army Nurse Corps. She is commissioned in the Nurse Corps at Lockbourne Air Force Base. She gains experience as a flight nurse. In 1989–1991 she becomes the only woman to hold the presidency of the Tuskegee Airmen.

1948. John Earl Rudder becomes the first African American commissioned officer in the U.S. Marine Corps.

1949. Representative William L. Dawson is named chairman of the House Committee on Government Operations, becoming the first African American to head a congressional committee.

1949. William A. Hinton becomes the first African American to be granted a professorship at Harvard Medical School.

1949. Jesse Leroy Brown becomes the first African American pilot in the U.S. Naval Reserve. On December 4, 1950, at Changjin Reservoir in Korea, Brown is the first African American naval pilot killed in action.

1949. Wesley A. Brown becomes the first African American to graduate from the Naval Academy at Annapolis, Maryland.

1949. The University of Oklahoma Law School admits its first African American student, Ada Lois Sipuel (Fisher).

1949. William H. Hastie becomes the first African American judge appointed to the U.S. Circuit Court of Appeals. Hastie is also the first African American appointed governor of the U.S. Virgin Islands.

1949. Jackie Robinson becomes the first African American baseball player to win his league's "Most Valuable Player" award. The first African American to win the award three times is Roy Campanella, who is awarded the title in 1951, 1953, and 1955.

1950. Tennis player Althea Gibson becomes the first African American to play in the U.S. Open at Forest Hills Country Club.

1950. Gwendolyn Brooks is awarded the Pulitzer Prize for her volume of poetry titled *Annie Allen*. She is the first African American poet to win the award and also the first African American woman elected to the National Institute of Arts and Letters.

1950. United Nations Undersecretary Ralph Bunche becomes the first African American to receive a Nobel Peace Prize.

1950. President Dwight D. Eisenhower appoints Archibald T. Carey Jr. as chair of the Committee on Government Employment Policy. Carey becomes the first African American to hold that position.

1950. Arthur Dorrington becomes the first African American professional hockey player when he plays the 1950–1951 season with the Atlantic City Sea Gulls. He made his debut on November 15.

1950. For her supporting role in the musical *South Pacific*, Juanita Hall becomes the first African American to win a Tony Award.

Ralph Bunche examines his Nobel Peace Prize diploma in 1950.

1950, April 15. Charles Cooper signs with the Boston Celtics, becoming the first African American to sign with an NBA team.

1950, October 31. Earl Lloyd of the then Washington Capitals takes the court, becoming the first African American to actually participate in a National Basketball Association (NBA) game.

1951. Janet Collins becomes the first African American woman to dance for the Metropolitan Opera in New York. Collins, signed by an agent of the company, makes her debut in *Aida*.

1951. William L. Rowe becomes the first African American deputy police commissioner. He is appointed to this position in New York by Mayor Vincent Impellitieri.

1952. Soprano Dorothy Leigh Maynor becomes the first African American artist to perform at Constitution Hall in Washington, D.C.

1952. Joe Black, Rookie of the Year, leads the Brooklyn Dodgers to a win over the New York Yankees and becomes the first African American pitcher to win a World Series game.

1952. Frank E. Petersen Jr. becomes the first African American Marine pilot. He becomes the first African American brigadier general in the marines on February 23, 1979, and retires in 1988 with the rank of lieutenant general.

1953. Ralph Ellison, author of *The Invisible Man*, becomes the first African American to receive the National Book Award.

1953. The University of Virginia awards a doctoral degree to Walter Nathaniel Ridley, the first African American to earn a doctoral degree from a traditional Southern white university. Later Ridley is president of Elizabeth City State College (now University) in North Carolina.

1953. Second baseman Marcenia Lyle "Toni" Stone joins the Negro League's Indianapolis Clowns as the first African American woman to play on a regular big league professional baseball team. She plays one season with the Clowns and another with the Kansas City Monarchs. The five-foot seven-inch St. Paul, Minnesota, native was an experienced player on men's teams, first with the San Francisco Sea Lions and next with the New Orleans Creoles.

1954. Norma Sklarek becomes the first African American woman to be licensed as an architect in the United States.

1954. Charles H. Mahoney becomes the first African American appointed a permanent delegate to the United Nations.

1954. Dr. James Joshua Thomas becomes the first African American pastor of the Reformed Dutch Church. He is installed as minister of the Mott Haven Reformed Church in the Bronx, New York City.

1954. Harry Belafonte's performance in *John Murray Anderson's Almanac* earns him a Tony award, the first ever won by an African American man.

1954. The first African American radio network, the National Negro Network, begins programming. The New York outlet is station WOV. The first program of the network, a soap opera titled *The Story of Ruby Valentine*, stars Juanita Hall and is carried on 40 stations. The program, sponsored by Phillip Morris and Pet Milk, runs five days a week.

1954, October 27. Benjamin Oliver Davis Jr. becomes the first African American general in the U.S. Air Force.

1955. Dorothy Dandridge is the first African American woman to receive an Oscar nomination for best actress. She is nominated for her role in the all-African American musical *Carmen Jones* (1954).

1955, April 17. Conductor and musician Everett Lee directs the New York Opera Company's performance of *La Traviata* and becomes the first African American to conduct a professional grand opera or Broadway show in this country.

1956. Charles Dumas, a freshman at Compton College in Compton, California, becomes the first athlete to high jump over seven feet.

1956. Althea Gibson is the first African American to win the French Open. She captures both the women's singles and doubles titles.

1957. Perry H. Young becomes the first African American pilot for a scheduled passenger commercial airline, New York Airways.

1957. Althea Gibson wins the mixed doubles and women's singles titles at Wimbledon, the first African American tennis player to win any title there. She also wins the same two titles at the U.S. Open, also African American firsts.

1957. James Plinton Jr. becomes the first African American named to an executive position by a major airline when Trans World Airlines names him executive assistant to the director of personnel and industrial relations.

1958. Gloria Davy sings *Aida* at New York's Metropolitan Opera House and becomes the first African American to sing at this celebrated location.

1958. Ruth Carol Taylor becomes the first African American flight attendant when she is hired to work for Mohawk Airlines.

1958, January 18. Willie O'Ree breaks racial barriers in professional hockey when he plays the first of only two games during the 1957–1958 season for the Boston Bruins of the National Hockey League. He is sent back to the minor leagues for two seasons, making it back to the NHL for more than 40 games during the 1961 season. Mike Marson, the second black man to play in the NHL, does not get drafted until 1974.

1959. Charlie Sifford is the first African American to be issued a Professional Golf Association (PGA) card as an "approved player."

1959. Lorraine Hansberry's play *A Raisin in the Sun* is the first play by an African American to receive the New York Drama Critics' Circle Award for best American play.

1959. Hal DeWindt becomes the first male model in the Ebony Fashion Fair.

1959. John McLendon becomes the first African American to coach a racially-integrated professional basketball team, the Cleveland Pipers of the National Industrial Basketball League.

Lorraine Vivian Hansberry being presented the Drama Critics Circle Award in 1959.

1959. The Academy of Television Arts and Sciences makes Harry Belafonte the first African American to win an Emmy Award of any kind. His work in *Tonight with Belafonte* is deemed the best as a lead actor in a comedy, variety, or music series.

1960. Wilma Rudolph, who wore leg braces until she was nine years old, becomes the first African American woman to win three gold medals in track and field in a single Olympic year.

1960, May 10. Nashville, Tennessee, becomes the first major U.S. city to begin desegregating its public facilities.

1961. Wilma Rudolph is the first African American to receive the Sullivan Award as the country's top amateur athlete as selected by the Amateur Athletic Union.

1961. Ernie Davis becomes the first African American to be awarded college football's Heisman Memorial Trophy at the Downtown Athletic Club of New York City, Inc.

1961, August 10. President John F. Kennedy appoints James Benton Parsons judge of the U.S. Federal District Court. He is the first African American to hold this position and also the first African American to receive a lifetime appointment in that post.

1962. A. Leon Higginbotham Jr. is the first African American, and the youngest person ever, to hold the post of commissioner on the Federal Trade Commission.

1962. Jackie Robinson becomes the first African American to be inducted into the Professional Baseball Hall of Fame.

1962. Mal Goode becomes the first African American television news correspondent.

1962. Harvey Russell Jr. is named vice president of Pepsico and becomes the first African American man named vice president of a major American corporation.

1962. Lieutenant Commander Samuel L. Gravely Jr. becomes the first African American to command a United States warship when he assumes command of the *USS Falgout*, a destroyer escort.

1962. Former civil rights lawyer Thelton Henderson becomes the first African American to join the U.S. Justice Department's Civil Rights Division.

1963. William "Count" Basie becomes the first African American to win the Grammy Award for record of the year, *I Can't Stop Loving You.*

1963. Katherine Dunham becomes the first African American choreographer to work at the Metropolitan Opera House in New York.

1963. Sidney Poitier becomes the first African American man to win an Oscar, for his leading role in *Lilies of* *the Field.* Poitier is also the first African American to be nominated for an Oscar since Hattie McDaniel in 1939.

1963. Marian Anderson and Ralph Bunche are the first African Americans to receive a Presidential Medal of Freedom.

1963, December 1. In Jacksonville, Florida, Wendell Scott becomes the first African American to win a NASCAR race. The victory was initially granted to a white driver, but justice was served later—after the "victor's" celebration. As of July 2002, no African American has duplicated this feat. He is inducted into the International Motorsports Hall of Fame in 1999, the first African American so honored.

1964. Frederick O'Neal becomes the first black president of Actor's Equity.

1965. The Freedom National Bank is founded. It is Harlem's first African American-chartered and run commercial bank.

1965. President Lyndon B. Johnson appoints Patricia Roberts Harris as U.S. ambassador to Luxembourg. She is the first African American woman ever to be named an American envoy.

1965. Vivian Malone Jones becomes the first African American graduate of the University of Alabama. Jones and James Hood were among the first African American students enrolled in the university in 1963.

1966. The basketball team from Texas Western University becomes the first college team to win the NCAA National Championship with an all-African American starting five. They beat the favored and all-white University of Kentucky.

1966. Norma Sklarek is the first African American woman to be named a fellow of the American Institute of Architects.

1966. Bill Cosby's work on *I Spy* earns him the first Emmy awarded to an African American for a leading role in a dramatic television series. He is only the second African American to win an Emmy of any kind.

1966. Internationally known graphic artist George Olden is the first African American to design a U.S. postage stamp, the Emancipation Proclamation stamp.

1966. Emmett Ashford, the first African American umpire in the major leagues, makes his debut in the American League opening day game between the Cleveland Indians and the Washington Senators. Ashford umpired in the Southwestern International League in 1952 and in the Pacific Coast League where he was umpire-in-chief in 1965.

1966. Constance Baker Motley becomes the first African American to serve as a federal judge.

Robert C. Weaver.

1966. Robert C. Weaver is named as secretary of the newly created Department of Housing and Urban Development, becoming the first African American appointed to serve in a presidential cabinet.

1966. Edward W. Brooke becomes the first African American elected to the U.S. Senate since Reconstruction. He is seated on January 10, 1967.

1966, April 18. Bill Russell, star center of the world champion Boston Celtics, becomes the first African American to direct a major league sports team when he is named to succeed Red Auerbach as coach of the Boston basketball franchise.

1967. Renee Powell becomes the first African American female to be issued a Ladies Professional Golf Association (LPGA) card.

1967. Emlen Tunnell becomes the first African American to be inducted into the Professional Football Hall of Fame.

1967. Sergio Oliva is the first African American to win the Mr. Olympia competition held by the International Federation of Bodybuilders. He successfully defends his title in 1968.

1967. Thurgood Marshall is appointed an associate justice of the U.S. Supreme Court, becoming the first African American to serve on the nation's highest court. On August 11, 1965, he became the first African American solicitor general and held the position until he joined the Supreme Court.

1967, November 13. The first African American elected mayor of a major U.S. city is Carl B. Stokes. He becomes known in the 1960s as a symbol of minority voting strides. Richard G. Hatcher, mayor of Gary, Indiana, is elected in the same year but not sworn in until January 1, 1968, as the city's first African American mayor.

1968. Diahann Carroll plays the title role in _Julia_ to become the first African American lead actress in a network television series.

1968. Arthur Ashe becomes the first African American to win the American Singles Tennis Championship. In 1963 Ashe was the first African American to play on the U.S. Davis Cup team.

1968. Martin Briscoe becomes the first African American professional football player.

1968. Henry Lewis is the first African American director of an American orchestra—the Newark-based New Jersey Symphony.

1968. Shirley Chisholm of New York becomes the first African American woman elected to the U.S. Congress.

1968. Miss Pennsylvania Sandy Williams wins the inaugural Miss Black America pageant, hosted by the J. Morris Anderson Production Company.

1968, August. Xernona Clayton becomes the first African American woman in the South to host a regular television program.

1969. Gail Fisher becomes the first African American to win an Emmy Award.

1969. James Earl Jones is the first African American to win a Tony Award for a lead role in a drama. His performance as boxer "Jack Jefferson"—based on heavyweight champion Jack Johnson—in _The Great White Hope_ garnered the trophy.

1969. Federal Judge A. Leon Higginbotham Jr. is elected a trustee of Yale University, the first African American to be so honored.

1969. Parks Sausage Company becomes the first African American-owned company to become a publicly traded company, having its stock traded on the National Association of Securities Dealers Automated Quotation (NASDAQ) exchange.

1969. The first African American male and the first African American photographer to win a Pulitzer Prize is Moneta J. Sleet Jr. His prize-winning photograph was a portrait of Coretta Scott King and her youngest child, Bernice, taken at the funeral of Martin Luther King Jr.

1969. Joseph L. Searles III becomes the first African American proposed for a seat on the New York Stock Exchange. Searles, former aide in the administration of New York City Mayor John Lindsay, resigned to become one of the three floor traders, as well as a general partner, for Newburger, Loeb and Co.

1969, January. President Richard Nixon appoints Elizabeth Duncan Koontz director of the U.S. Department of Labor, Women's Bureau. This makes her the first African American director. Koontz later becomes deputy assistant secretary for Labor Employment Standards.

1970. Chris Dickerson becomes the first African American to win the title "Mr. America," one of 15 body building titles Dickerson will earn during his career. One of a set of triplets born in Montgomery, Alabama, on August 25, 1939, Dickerson proves to be an outstanding athlete throughout his school years. An early interest in a singing career and the desire to improve his voice quality and breath control led him into bodybuilding in the mid–1960s.

1970. Renard Edwards becomes the first African American musician to play for the Philadelphia Orchestra when he is hired as a violist for the 1970–1971 season. Edwards was formerly with the Symphony of the New World, an integrated orchestra, one-third to one-half of whose members are African Americans.

1971. Known as the "Father of Black Professional Basketball" for his contributions as coach and owner of the barnstorming New York Renassaince (the Rens), Robert L. Douglass (1882–1979) is the first African American inducted into the Naismith Memorial Basketball Hall of Fame.

1971. Johnson Products, which sells items under the Ultra-Sheen label, is the first African American-owned company to trade on a major stock exchange.

1971. Samuel L. Gravely Jr. becomes the first African American admiral in the history of the U.S. Navy.

1972. U.S. Rep. Shirley Chisholm seeks the Democratic nomination for the presidency, thus becoming the first woman ever to do so.

1972. Approximately 8,000 African Americans attend the first National Black Political Convention. Held in Gary, Indiana, the convention is chaired by Imamu Amiri Baraka with Mayor Richard Hatcher of Gary featured as the keynote speaker.

1972, March 18. The U.S. Navy launches the destroyer escort _USS Jesse L. Brown_, marking the first time a Navy ship is named in honor of an African

American naval officer. That officer is Jesse Leon Brown, who was the first African American pilot in the U.S. Naval Reserve and the first African American naval pilot killed in action during the Korean conflict.

1972, November 17. Barbara Jordan wins a seat in Congress, becoming the first woman from Texas elected to Congress.

1973. Andrew Young wins the inaugural Martin Luther King Jr. Nonviolent Peace Prize.

1973. Coleman A. Young is elected mayor of Detroit, Michigan, the first African American to hold the post in the white-majority city. On the same evening, Maynard H. Jackson is elected mayor of Atlanta, Georgia.

1973. Elayne Jones is invited to become the San Francisco Symphony's timpanist. Accepting, she is the first African American female to hold a principal chair in a major orchestra.

1973. For his Pearl Harbor heroics, including shooting down four Japanese planes during the attack on Pearl Harbor, the U.S. Navy honors Dorie Miller by naming a ship after him—the destroyer escort *USS Miller*. This marks the first time that a military vessel is named after an African American enlisted man.

1973. Shirley Ann Jackson is the first African American woman in the United States to earn a Ph.D. in physics, from Massachusetts Institute of Technology (MIT). She is also the first African American woman to receive a Ph.D. from MIT. Jackson received her B.S. degree from MIT in 1968.

1973, May 29. Thomas Bradley, of Los Angeles, becomes the first African American elected mayor of a city with a population exceeding one million. He defeated the incumbent Sam Yorty by 100,000 votes. Yorty had defeated Bradley in the 1969 mayoral election.

1973, November. Attorney and former California state assemblywoman Yvonne Braithwaite Burke becomes the first African American woman from California ever to be elected to the House of Representatives.

1974. The Athletics Congress of the USA inducts Ralph Boston, Lee Calhoun, Harrison Dillard, Rafer Johnson, Jesse Owens, Wilma Rudolph, and Malvin Whitfield into its National Track & Field Hall of Fame.

1974. The Mary McLeod Bethune Memorial is unveiled as the first monument to an African American, or a woman, to be erected on public land in the nation's capital.

1974. Representative Charles Rangel from New York becomes the first African American to serve on the House Ways and Means Committee.

1974. Barbara Hancock becomes the first African American woman White House Fellow.

1974. Cicely Tyson becomes the first African American female to be awarded an Emmy. Her performance as the lead actress in *The Autobiography of Miss Jane Pittman* earned her the honor in the Comedy or Drama Special category.

1974. *The River Niger* by Joseph A. Walker is the first play written by an African American to receive the Tony Award for Best Play.

1974. Leo Miles becomes the first African American to officiate a Super Bowl game.

1974. Joe Gilliam Jr. becomes a trailblazer for African American quarterbacks in modern times. He is the first African American quarterback to start in a NFL game.

1974, November. The Thunderbirds, the U.S. Air Force Aerial Demonstration Squadron, has its first African American member, when General Lloyd W. "Fig" Newton joins the squad.

1975. The U.S. Navy commissions Donna P. Davis as a lieutenant in the Navy's medical corps, making Davis the first African American woman physician in the corps history.

1975. General Daniel "Chappie" James Jr. becomes commander-in-chief of the North American Air Defense Command (NORAD). On the same day, he is promoted in the air force and becomes the first African American four-star general in U.S. history.

1975. Frank Robinson becomes the first African American to manage a major league baseball team and leads his Cleveland Indians to an opening-day victory over the New York Yankees, hitting a home run.

1975. WGPR-TV, in Detroit, goes on the air, becoming the first African American-owned and operated television station in the United States.

1976. Congresswoman Barbara Jordan is the first African American woman to give a keynote address at the Democratic National Convention.

1977. Drew S. Days accepts the post as the head of the Civil Rights Division of the U.S. Department of Justice. He is the first African American to hold the position.

1977. Pauli Murray, a distinguished lawyer and educator, becomes the first African American woman to be ordained a priest in the predominantly white Episcopal Church.

1977. Clifford Alexander Jr. becomes the first African American to be appointed Secretary of the Army.

1977. Former basketball player Wayne Embry becomes the first African American general manager of an NBA team—the Milwaukee Bucks.

1977. Lionel Wilson is elected mayor, the first African American to hold that position. In 1960 he became the first African American judge in Alameda County.

1977. Karen Farmer becomes the first African American member of the Daughters of the American Revolution (DAR). It was the DAR that refused to allow Marian Anderson to perform in concert in Washington, D.C., in 1939.

1977. Patricia Roberts Harris is appointed Secretary of the Department of Housing and Urban Development, becoming the first African American woman to serve in a Cabinet-level position.

1978. Faye Wattleton is elected president of Planned Parenthood, becoming the first African American woman and the youngest person to head the organization.

1978. Wendy Hilliard becomes the first African American member of the U.S. National Rhythmic Gymnastics Team.

1978. When he joins ABC-TV's *World News Tonight*, Max Robinson becomes the first African American network anchor.

1978. Contralto Marian Anderson becomes the first African American to be awarded the Congressional Gold Medal, the highest honor that can be bestowed upon a civilian. The same year, she also becomes the first African American to receive a Kennedy Center Honor from the John F. Kennedy Center for the Performing Arts.

1978. Reverend Emerson Moore Jr. is named the first African American monsignor of the Catholic Church in the United States. Monsignor Moore is pastor of St. Charles Borromeo Church in New York City.

1979. Amalya L. Kearse becomes the first woman to receive an appointment to the U.S. Circuit Court of Appeals.

1979. U.S. Army Second Lieutenant Marcella A. Hayes, a graduate of the University of Wisconsin and the Army ROTC program, earns her aviator wings and becomes the first African American woman pilot in U.S. armed services history.

1979. Audrey Neal becomes the first African American woman (or woman of any ethnic group), longshoreperson. Neal is employed at the Bayonne Military Ocean Terminal in New Jersey.

1979, August 1. The U.S. House of Representatives votes 408–1 to place a bust of the late Martin Luther King Jr. in the Capitol building. This marks the first time that a work of art honoring an African American is placed in the nation's Capitol.

1979, October 30. Council Richard Arrington Jr. is elected major, the first African American ever elected to the post.

1980. Rosa Parks becomes the first woman to receive the Martin Luther King Jr. Nonviolent Peace Prize.

1980. Howard University launches WHMM-TV, becoming the first licensee of a public TV station on an African American campus and the only African American-owned public television station in the nation.

1980. Levi Watkins Jr., an African American surgeon, performs the first surgical implantation of the automatic implantable defibrillator in the human heart. The device corrects an ailment known as ventricular fibrillation or arrhythmia, which prevents the heart from pumping blood.

1980, September 30. The first annual Black College Day is held in Washington, D.C. Organized by African American journalist Tony Brown, the focus of the event is to draw public attention to the impact of integration and the merging of African American private and public colleges and universities.

1981. Charles P. Chapman is the first African American to swim across the English channel

1981. Isabel Sanford becomes the first African American female to be awarded an Emmy for outstanding lead actress in a television comedy series for her performance in *The Jeffersons*.

1981. Pamela Johnson is named publisher of the *Ithaca Journal* and becomes the first African American woman to hold that position with a major newspaper in the United States.

1981. Ruth Love becomes the first African American to serve as superintendent of the Chicago school system. Prior to her appointment to this post, Love held a similar position in Oakland, California.

1982. Bryant C. Gumbel becomes the first African American to co-host the *Today* show on NBC Television.

1982. Ralph Bradley becomes the first African American to complete the Iditarod Sled Dog Race. Though he finishes last in the 1,049-mile race, he wins the Red Lantern prize with a time of 26:13:59:59.

1983. Louis Gossett Jr. is the first African American male to be awarded an Oscar for best supporting actor for his role in *An Officer and a Gentleman*.

1983. Representing New York, Vanessa Williams becomes the first African American Miss America in the 62-year history of the Atlantic City pageant. The first runner-up is Suzette Charles representing New Jersey, who, coincidentally, is also African American and also the first African American Miss New Jersey. When Williams is forced to surrender her title following the discovery of some scandalous photos, Charles is crowned Miss America.

Vanessa Williams (left), first African American to win Miss America pageant; Suzette Charles was first runner-up, both in 1983.

1983. Carla Dunlap is the first African American to win the Ms. Olympia competition held by the International Federation of Bodybuilders. Seven years later Lenda Murray becomes the second African American to win the title and successfully defends it five times.

1983, April 19. Harold Washington is sworn in as mayor of Chicago, becoming the first African American to hold the position.

1983, August 30. Guion Bluford becomes the first African American to travel in space when he serves as a crew member on the space shuttle Challenger. The crew has a six-day flight on the Challenger.

1983, November. James A. Sharp Jr. is the first African American mayor of Flint, Michigan.

1983, November 10. Democrat Harvey Gantt becomes the first African American elected mayor of Charlotte, North Carolina.

1984. Methodist Reverend Leontine Turpeau Current Kelly becomes the first African American woman bishop of a major religious denomination.

1984. W. Wilson Goode takes the oath of office as the first African American mayor of Philadelphia.

1984, April 2. Former Boston Celtics player John Thompson Jr. becomes the first African American coach to win an NCAA Division I basketball championship. He coached the Georgetown University Hoyas, led by center Patrick Ewing, to victory.

1984, September 8. Oprah Winfrey becomes the first African American woman to host a nationally syndicated television talk show.

1985. In the same year, author Ralph Ellison and singer Leontyne Price become the first African Americans to receive the National Medal of Arts award from the National Endowment for the Arts.

1985. Gwendolyn Brooks assumes a one-year post as Poetry Consultant to the Library of Congress, thereby becoming the nation's first black poet laureate.

1986. African American performers are among the first performers enshrined in the newly-opened Rock and Roll Hall of Fame and Museum: Chuck Berry, James Brown, Ray Charles, Sam Cooke, Fats Domino, Robert Johnson, Little Richard, and Jimmy Yancey.

1986. Kay Roberts earns a doctor of musical arts degree from Yale University. She is the first woman and second African American to do so.

1986. Georg Stanford Brown becomes the first African American to win an Emmy for outstanding directing in a drama series. Brown directed the episode titled "Parting Shots" for the highly acclaimed series *Cagney & Lacey.*

1986. Lieutenant Commander Donnie Cochran becomes the first African American pilot in the U.S. Navy to fly with the Navy's elite special flying squadron, the Blue Angels. Two years later he becomes the first African American to head the squad. The precision flight team was formed in the 1940s and has performed its highly sophisticated aerobatics in air shows in the United States and Europe ever since.

1986. Debi Thomas becomes the first African American to win the U.S. Ladies Figure Skating Championship and the World Championship.

1986, January 11. L. Douglas Wilder becomes the first African American lieutenant governor of the state of Virginia.

1986, January 20. The first national Martin Luther King Jr. holiday is celebrated.

1986, November 22. By winning the Brunswick Memorial World Open in Chicago, George Branham III becomes the first African American bowler to win a Professional Bowling Association (PBA) title.

1987. Dain Blanton, in his third professional season, is the first African American to win a major tournament with the Association of Volleyball Professionals. He is the first and only African American on the AVP tour. Blanton and his partner, Canyon Ceman, won the $300,000 Miller Lite/AVP Hermosa Beach, California, Grand Slam. This is the largest AVP tournament ever held and awards the most prize money in the history of the sport.

1987. Former naval pilot Jill Brown becomes the first African American female to pilot for a major airline.

1987. The rap duo D. J. Jazzy Jeff and the Fresh Prince win a Grammy Award for the hit *Parents Just Don't Understand* and becomes the first African American rap group to win a Grammy.

1987, December 8. Kurt L. Schmoke is inaugurated as the first elected African American mayor of Baltimore, Maryland.

1988. Spelman College appoints its first African American woman president, Johnetta B. Cole.

1988. Eugene Antonio Marino becomes the first African American Roman Catholic archbishop in the United States as he is named archbishop of the Atlanta archdiocese. Marino was one of three auxiliary bishops in Washington, D.C.

1988. Doug Williams becomes the first African American to quarterback a Super Bowl team, the Washington Redskins. The Redskins defeat the Denver Broncos 42–10 in Super Bowl XXII.

1988. Florence "Flo Jo" Griffith Joyner becomes the first American woman to win four gold medals in track and field at a single Olympics.

1988. Juanita Kidd Stoutt is appointed to the supreme court of Pennsylvania and becomes the first African American woman to serve on the highest court of any state.

1989. Washington, D.C., native Colonel Frederick Gregory becomes the first African American astronaut to command a space shuttle.

1989. Washington, D.C., lawyer Ronald H. Brown is elected chairman of the Democratic Party's national committee. Brown is the first African American to head a major American political party.

1989. Norm Rice, who became known as "Mayor Nice," is elected mayor of Seattle, Washington, the city's first African American to hold the position.

1989. Episcopal Reverend Barbara C. Harris, an African American, becomes the first woman bishop in the worldwide Anglican communion. The Episcopal Church decided in 1976 that women could be ordained priests.

1989. Rodney S. Patterson, an ordained Baptist minister, starts the first African American congregation in Vermont, which a magazine has dubbed "the whitest state in America" because of its small African American population. Patterson, who moved to Burlington to join the staff at the University of Vermont, names the church the New Alpha Missionary Baptist Church.

1989. Army General Colin L. Powell becomes the first African American to serve as chairman of the Joint Chiefs of Staff and principal military advisor to the president of the United States, the secretary of defense, and the National Security Council.

1989. Former St. Louis Cardinal first baseman Bill White assumes office as president of the National League, becoming the first African American to head a professional sports league.

1989. As a member of a 14-owner consortium of investors that purchased the Texas Rangers, Comer Cottrell becomes the first African American to own a major league baseball franchise. Cottrell uses his position to speak out about affirmative action in professional sports.

1990. Lorna Simpson is the first African American woman to have her work featured in the Venice Biennale, an international art exhibition.

1990. The Wade H. McCree Jr. Professorship is established at the University of Michigan Law School, making it the first endowed chair at a major American law school to be named after an African American.

Guion S. Bluford Jr. (left), Ronald E. McNair, Frederick Gregory, and Charles F. Bolden Jr.

1990. David Dinkins becomes the first African American mayor of New York City.

1990. Carole Gist of Michigan becomes the first African American Miss USA.

1990. In Virginia, L. Douglas Wilder becomes the first African American elected governor of a state.

1990. Sharon Pratt Dixon is elected mayor of Washington, D.C., thus becoming the first African American woman to manage a major U.S. city.

1991. Robert Johnson's company BET Holdings is the first African American-owned business listed on the New York Stock Exchange.

1991. Corporal Freddie Stowers is posthumously awarded the Medal of Honor for serving in France during World War I. Stowers is the first African American to receive the medal for service in either world war. In 1988, the secretary of the army directed the army to conduct a study to determine whether African American soldiers had been overlooked in the recognition process. Research found that Stowers had been recommended for the medal, but for reasons unknown, the recommendation had not been processed.

1991. Former Roman Catholic nun Rose Vernell is ordained a priest of the Imani Temple African American Catholic Congregation by Bishop George A. Stallings Jr. Vernell is the first woman priest in the church. The congregation was founded in 1989 when Stallings broke with the Roman Catholic Church; this was the first split from the Roman Catholic Church in the United States since 1904.

1991. Although it is his last, Lee Haney wins an unprecedented eighth consecutive Mr. Olympia title. In 1998 Ronnie Coleman wins his first of four consecutive Mr. Olympia crowns, an honor he retains through the 2001 competition.

1991. Lynn Whitfield becomes the first African American female to be awarded an Emmy for outstanding lead actress in a miniseries or special for her performance in *The Josephine Baker Story*.

1991. John Singleton garners an Oscar nomination for best director for his film *Boyz N the Hood*. He is the first African American to be nominated for the award, and at age 23, he is also the youngest director to be so honored.

1991, April. Leon Howard Sullivan organizes and co-chairs the first African and African American Summit held at Abidjan, Ivory Coast.

1992. Carol Moseley Braun of Illinois is elected to the U.S. Senate, becoming the first African American woman senator.

1992. Mae C. Jemison, 35, a physician and chemical engineer, is the first African American woman in space on the U.S. space shuttle *Endeavor* mission. The crew studies the behavior of living organisms in a weightless atmosphere and looks for ways to cure space sickness.

1992. Captain William "Bill" Pinckney becomes the first African American to navigate a sailboat single-handedly around the world. His journey on the boat *Commitment* began in Boston in 1990, covered 32,000 nautical miles, and included several stops.

1992. Awadagin Pratt becomes the first African American to win the Naumburg International piano composition.

1992. Bill Cosby is the first African American to win a Hall of Fame Emmy Award from the Academy of Television Arts and Sciences.

Mae C. Jemison.

1992, November 3. Jacquelyn H. Barrett is elected as the first African American woman sheriff of Fulton County, Georgia.

1992, November 3. Earl F. Hilliard is the first African American from Alabama elected to Congress. Cynthia McKinney becomes the first African American woman voted into the Georgia House of Representatives.

1993. Rita Dove is named U.S. poet laureate, a one-year Library of Congress post. She is the first African American and the youngest person ever to earn the appointment.

1993. A physician, educator, and former medical school president, David Satcher is appointed head of the Centers for Disease Control in Atlanta. He is the first African American to hold the post.

1993. Mike Espy is appointed secretary of agriculture by President Bill Clinton, the first African American to hold the position.

1993. Ronald "Ron" Dellums, who has chaired the Defense Policy Panel, becomes the first African American to head the House Armed Services Committee.

1993. President Bill Clinton appoints Ronald H. Brown commerce secretary. He is subsequently confirmed by the U.S. Senate, thus becoming the first African American secretary of commerce.

1993. Joycelyn Elders is named surgeon general of the United States. Elders is the first African American and the second woman to hold this position. She is sworn into office as U.S. surgeon general in a private ceremony. Elders, 59, is the former head of the Arkansas Health Department.

1993. The first African American student from a historically African American college to win a Rhodes Scholarship is Nima Warfield, an English major at Morehouse College. He plans to study at Oxford's School of Modern History and English in fall 1994.

1993. Eleanor Holmes Norton becomes the first voting delegate in the U.S. House of Representatives for Washington, D.C. Previously, delegates representing the District of Columbia and the U.S. Trust Territory were not allowed to vote on the House floor because the Constitution of the United States specifically restricts legislative authority to state representatives.

1993. African American candidates in Selma, Alabama, win a majority of seats on the city council for the first time, despite efforts by white council members to maintain a majority.

1993. South Carolina's Kimberly Clarice Aiken is crowned Miss America, becoming the first African American woman from the South to win the pageant.

1993. Sharon Sayles Belton becomes the first woman and first African American mayor of Minneapolis, Minnesota.

1993. In his 13th year as a National League umpire, Charlie Williams becomes the first African American to call balls and strikes in a World Series game.

1993, November 7. Toni Morrison becomes the first African American to receive a Nobel Prize for literature.

1994. At the U.S. National Championships, Dominique Dawes becomes the first African American to win the all-around title as best gymnast.

1994. William G. Anderson becomes the first African American president of the American Osteopathic Association, a major medical organization in the United States.

1994. Whoopie Goldberg is the first African American to serve as sole host of the Academy Awards and the first African American Oscar winner to host the show.

1994. Donnie Cochran, the only African American pilot in the Blue Angels, the precision flying squad, becomes the squad's first African American commander.

1994. Louis Westerfield is named academic dean at the University of Mississippi, the first African American to hold that position at the university.

1994. Eighteen year-old Eldrick (Tiger) Woods becomes the youngest player and the first African American to win the U.S. Amateur Golf Championship.

1994. Forty-four year old Beverly Harvard becomes the first African American woman to reach the rank of chief of police in a major U.S. city (Atlanta).

1994, February 3. Commander Charles Bolden leads NASA's first American-Russian Space Shuttle Discovery mission.

1995. Atlanta Hawks coach Lenny Wilkins becomes the winningest coach in NBA history.

1995. In June, Lonnie Bristow becomes the first African American president of the 147-year-old American Medical Association.

1995. Marcelite J. Harris, the Air Force's first African American general in 1990, becomes the first woman of her race to receive the rank of major general.

1995. A retired U.S. Army major general, John Stanford becomes the first African American school superintendent in Seattle, Washington.

1995. Ronald Kirk is elected Dallas's first African American mayor and is the first African American to lead a major Texas city.

1995. Gene C. McKinney becomes the first African American sergeant major, the highest non-commissioned officer in the U.S. Army.

1995. Former speaker and 31-year-veteran of the California General Assembly, Willie L. Brown Jr., defeats incumbent Frank Jordan to become San Francisco's first African American mayor.

1995. Chelsi Smith of Texas is the first African American crowned Miss Universe.

1995. Orlando "Tubby" Smith becomes the first African American head basketball coach at the University of Georgia.

1995. Carolyn G. Morris becomes the first African American assistant director and the highest ranking African American woman in the history of the FBI.

1995. Minnesota Vikings quarterback Warren Moon is the first quarterback to eclipse 60,000 yards in career passing.

1995, February 27. Bernard A. Harris Jr., a physician from Houston, Texas, becomes the first African American to walk in space. Winston E. Scott becomes the second African American to make the trek, from a bridge in the cargo bay of space shuttle *Endeavour*.

1995, March 26. Talk-show host Alan Keyes announces his candidacy for the U.S. presidency. In so doing, he becomes the first Republican African American in the twentieth century to run for president. He attracts little support, however, and does not win a primary.

1996. Leslie B. Dunner becomes the first American prizewinner in the prestigious Arturo Toscanini International Conducting Competition.

1996. At the Summer Olympics held in Atlanta, Georgia, Michael Johnson becomes the first man to win the 200-meter and 400-meter races in the same games.

1996. The first African American to head the Office of Management and Budget for the United States is Franklin D. Raines. This is the highest executive post ever held by an African American.

1996. Former U.S. secret serviceman Hubert T. Bell Jr. is confirmed as inspector general of the Nuclear Regulatory Commission, the first African American to hold that position.

1996. BET Holdings, a parent company of the Black Entertainment Network, launches the nation's first African American-controlled cable movie premium channel, BET Movies/STARZ!3.

1996. St. Adolpho A. Birch Jr. is sworn in as the first African American chief justice of the Tennessee Supreme Court. From 1987 until he joined the Supreme Court in 1993, he was the first African American to serve on the Tennessee Court of Appeals.

1996. Darlene Green becomes the first woman elected comtroller in St. Louis.

1996. A member of the Maryland House of Delegates since 1983, Richard N. Dixon is sworn in as Maryland's first African American state treasurer.

1996. Seventy-three-year old composer George Walker wins the 1996 Pulitzer Prize in music, the first African American to win the prize in that category.

1996. Jacquelyn M. Belcher, former president of Minneapolis Community College in Minneapolis, is inaugurated president of Dekalb College in Georgia. She is the first African American woman president of a University System of Georgia school.

1996. The U.S. Navy appoints its first African American four-star admiral, Vice Admiral J. Paul Reason.

1996. The first African American president of the American Association of Retired Persons (AARP) is Margaret A. Dixon.

1996. Sargeant Heather Lynn Johnson of the 3rd U.S. Infantry becomes the first woman to receive the U.S. Army's tomb guard badge to become a sentinel at the Tomb of the Unknown Soldier in Arlington National Cemetery in Arlington, Virginia.

1996. The National Council of Negro Women dedicates its new headquarters office building. The facility is the first African American-owned building on Pennsylvania Avenue between Capitol Hill and the White House.

1996. The White House unveils Henry Ossawa Tanner's painting *Sand Dunes at Sunset, Atlantic City*, an oil on canvas. The acquisition is the first work by an African American artist to become a part of the White House collection.

1996. The University of Southern Mississippi names James Green head basketball coach, making him the first African American to hold the post.

1996. Detroit Lions running back Barry Sanders becomes the first back in NFL history to rush for 1,000 yards in eight consecutive seasons, with 11,271 total yards.

1996. Marcus Allen becomes the NFL's all-time leader in rushing touchdowns and breaks the record held by former Chicago Bears star Walter Payton.

1996. Eighteen-year-old Chantè Lauree Griffin is the first African American to be crowned Miss Teen of America for 1996–1997. She was elected Miss Teen of California in 1995.

1997. The *Sports Illustrated* swimsuit issue features supermodel Tyra Banks. Banks is the first African American model to be solely featured on the magazine cover in its 34-year history.

1997. Eldrick (Tiger) Woods becomes the first African American and the youngest player (21 years old) to win the Masters. He also records the largest victory margin and the lowest 72-hole total in the tournament's history.

1997. Harvey Johnson is sworn in as mayor of Jackson, Mississippi, becoming the first African American mayor in the state's capital. The ceremony is held on the steps of city hall, which was built by slaves before the Civil War.

1997. Wynton Marsalis becomes the first jazz musician to win a Pulitzer Prize for his jazz opera *Blood on the Fields*.

1997. Moses Ector becomes the highest ranking African American in the Georgia Bureau of Investigation. He is also the first African American to be named bureau chief of staff.

1997. Conrad L. Mallett Jr. becomes the first African American chief justice of the Michigan Supreme Court.

1997. Councilman Preston Daniels is the first African American to be elected mayor.

1997. Massachusetts State Appeals Court Justice Roderick Ireland is confirmed as the first African American justice on the state's Supreme Court.

1997. Robert Stanton is sworn in as director of the National Park Service, the first African American to head the service in its 80-year-old history.

1997. Profitts Inc. elects Julius "Dr. J." Erving to its board of directors, making him the first African American on the 13-member board.

1997. The U.S. Army commissions West Point's first African American cadet 123 years after the former slave was expelled from the academy for failing an examination. The certificate is given posthumously to James Webster Smith during a ceremony in Orangeburg, South Carolina.

1997. Alexis Herman is confirmed as U.S. secretary of labor, making her the first African American to head that department.

1997. The first African American woman to serve as chief federal judge of the U.S. District Court for the District of Columbia is Norma Holloway Johnson.

1997. The first African American head of the Federal Communications Commission is William E. Kinnard, who previously served the commission as general counsel.

1997. Former Olympian Chris Campbell is named executive director of U.S. Amateur Boxing, Inc.; he is the first African American to hold the post.

1997. Thurgood Marshall Jr. is appointed assistant to President Bill Clinton and Cabinet secretary, becoming the first African American to serve as Cabinet secretary.

1997. Earnest L. Tate is appointed to the position of chief of police. He is the first African American to hold the position in Selma, a city once known for its intolerance and beating of protest marchers.

1997. Eric Holder becomes the highest ranking African American law enforcement officer in the nation's history when he is sworn in as deputy U.S. attorney general, the second highest-ranking position in the U.S. Justice Department. He is the first African American U.S. attorney for the District of Columbia since 1993.

1997. Dawn Peter becomes the city's first African American mounted police officer. Previously she served as patrol officer and plain clothes officer in the city.

1997. The nation's first known African American sextuplets are born to Jacqueline and Linden Thompson. One daughter was stillborn. The four surviving girls and one boy are born in Georgetown University Medical Center.

1997. Violet Palmer is named referee in the NBA, becoming the first African American in that position. Palmer and Dee Kanter become the league's first two female officials.

1997. The first predominantly defensive player to win football's Heisman Trophy is Charles Woodson, a defensive back for the University of Michigan.

1997. Dorothy Walker, 57, becomes the first person in the country to undergo an experimental new laser heart surgery procedure, thorascopic investigational heart surgery, at Northwestern Memorial Hospital.

1997. The Association of Trial Lawyers of America elects its first African American president, Indianapolis attorney Richard D. Hailey.

1997. Dallas Mavericks forward A. C. Green breaks the NBA's consecutive game streak when he plays his 907th consecutive game.

1997. After coaching at the University of Georgia for two seasons, Orlando "Tubby" Smith, is the first African American head basketball coach at the University of Kentucky. In 1998, he leads Kentucky to the national championship.

1997. The first African American to win the junior women's title at the U.S. Figure Skating Championship is Andrea Gardiner, a 16-year-old Bay City, Texas, native.

1997. Vivian Fuller is named athletic director at Tennessee State University and becomes the country's first African American woman director of athletics at an NCAA Division I program.

1997. Ann Dibble Jordan, co-chair of the inaugural activities for President Bill Clinton's second term in office, is the first African American woman to serve in the command role.

1997. Walter G. Sellers of Wilberforce, Ohio, is unanimously elected president of Kiwanis International and becomes the first African American to serve in that position.

1997, October 22. The first Kwanzaa stamp is made available through the U.S. Postal Service. It was created by African American artist, Synthia Saint James.

1997, October 29. The U.S. Senate confirms William E. Kennard as chairman of the Federal Communications, making him the organization's first African American chairman.

1997, December 6. Democrat Lee P. Brown is elected mayor of Houston, Texas. A veteran law enforcement officer and former "drug czar," he is the first African American to head the city.

1998. The first African American Male Empowerment Summit (AAMES) is held and attracts more than 500 men.

1998. The first African American-owned securities brokerage firm to become a publicly-traded company is Chapman Holdings, Inc.

1998. Ben Ruffin, vice president of R. J. Reynolds Tobacco Company, is elected the first African American chair of the University of North Carolina's board. The board approves policies for the 16 campuses in the system.

1998. The U.S. Navy selects 32-year career Naval officer Captain James A. Johnson for promotion to rear admiral in the Navy Medical Corps, making him the first African American on active duty to hold that post in the 127-year history of the corps.

1998. Glenn Ivey is the first African American to head Maryland's five-member Public Service Commission.

1998. The first African American Republican elected to a leadership post in modern times is J.C. Watts Jr., Oklahoma congressman from the Fourth District. In November he becomes chairman of the Republican Conference, the number-four position in the House. In 1990 he was the first African American in Oklahoma to win statewide elective office, when he captured a seat on the Oklahoma Corporate Commission, which regulates gas and oil utilities. Watts became the first African American to respond to a President's State of the Union Address in 1997, when he followed President Bill Clinton's speech before the nation.

1998. Seven members of the more than 2,000 African American soldiers who, along with whites, fought in front line battles in 1944 during World War II, are awarded the Bronze Star. White soldiers received their awards soon after the war. Vernon Baker, the only surviving member of the group, is the first and only

Tubby Smith, University of Kentucky's first African American head basketball coach, celebrating the 1998 NCAA championship.

African American hero from the war to receive the award; the others are awarded posthumously.

1998. Three-time World Championship calf roper Fred Whitfield is the first African American to cross the $1 million mark in professional rodeo. He is also the fastest cowboy in the history of Professional Rodeo Cowboys Association to cross the mark.

1998. San Francisco Giants outfielder Barry Bonds becomes the only player in Major League Baseball to have 400 home runs and 400 steals in a career.

1998. *Newsweek* promotes managing editor Mark Whitaker to the position of editor of the weekly news magazine. A Harvard graduate, Whitaker joined the magazine's staff in 1977.

1998. Twenty-two-year old Jonathan Lee Iverson becomes the first African American and the youngest person ever to serve as ringmaster for Ringling Brothers and Barnum & Bailey.

1998. Tom Joyner is the first African American to be elected to the Radio Hall of Fame.

1998. Chamique Holdsclaw becomes the first African American woman basketball player to win the Sullivan Award. This award is given to the top amateur athlete in the United States.

1998. Johnathan Lee Iverson takes over as the first black ringmaster in the 129-year history of the Ringling Bros. and Barnum & Bailey Circus. At age 22, he is also the youngest ringmaster.

1998, January 1. Houston, Texas, gets its first African American mayor when Lee Patrick Brown takes office. Brown also served as police chief of the city from 1982 to 1990.

1998, January 23. Lani Guinier is named professor of law in the Harvard University School of Law, and becomes the first African American woman tenured in the law school.

1998, November 19. Drs. Paula Mahone and Karen Drake become the first African American physicians to assist in the delivery of sextuplets—the McCaughey babies.

1998, December 9. Lieutenant General Benjamin O. Davis Jr., former commander of the Tuskegee Airmen during World War II, receives his fourth star in a White

J.C. Watts, the first African American Republican elected to a leadership post in modern times.

House ceremony. Davis, a graduate of West Point Military Academy, is the son of the nation's first African American brigadier general in the army, Benjamin O. Davis Sr.

1999. At the urging of the Black members of the House Agriculture Committee, the Republican chairman schedules and holds two full committee hearings to consider the plight of Black farmers. In 30 years, there had never been an official committee hearing on this issue

1999. Carolyn B. Lewis becomes the first African American to serve as chair-elect of the American Hospital Association.

1999. Terry D. Bolton becomes the first African American named chief of police of the Dallas Police Department. Bolton is one of few black chiefs in the state of Texas.

1999, January 20. Cheryl Mills is the first African American to argue a case before a U.S. Senate impeachment hearing in the case of President William Clinton.

1999, March 15. Chess player Maurice Ashley, a Jamaican immigrant, becomes the first African American to earn grandmaster status in chess during a tournament sponsored by the Manhattan Chess Club.

1999, March 28. Purdue coach Carolyn Peck leads the Lady Boilermakers to victory over Duke University, becoming the first African American female coach to win a national championship in women's college basketball history.

2000. Three judges, Judge Marva L. Crenshaw of the Florida 13th Judicial Circuit, Judge Sandra Edwards-Stephens of the Florida 5th Judicial Circuit, and James E.C. Perry of the Florida 18th Judicial Circuit Court are appointed by Governor Jeb Bush. All three are the first African Americans appointed to these circuit courts and the most number of African American judges ever to be appointed in one state in one year.

2000, November 3. Dr. Ruth J. Simmons, president of Smith College, is selected to become the first African American president of Brown University, effective July 1, 2001.

2000, December Colin Powell is appointed as Secretary of State for the U.S. government. This marks the first time in history that an African American has held such a high governmental position.

2001. Robert L. Johnson, founder and president of Black Entertainment Television (BET), is listed on the *Fortune* 400 as the first African American billionaire. Oprah Winfrey is the first confirmed African American female billionaire.

2001, January 24. Dr. Roderick Paige is sworn in as Secretary of the U.S. Department of Education: he is the first black man to head this department.

2001, April 23. Kenneth I. Chenault is elected chairman of the board and chief executive officer of American Express. This is the first time an African American heads one of the main financial companies. He had served as the company's president since 1997 and as CEO since January 1, 2001, when Harvey Golub stepped down. The vote makes Chenault's position official.

2001, July 2. Robert Tools becomes the first person ever to receive an implant of a self-contained heart. This discovery leads to new break-throughs and advancements in transplant medicine.

2001, December 10 Giants outfielder Barry Bonds becomes the first player to be honored with the MVP award for baseball four times. This came off of Bonds' other first in October of 2001 when he broke Mark McGuire's homerun record with 73 homeruns in one season.

2002. Jarome Iginla, born to a Nigerian father and an American mother but residing in Canada the majority of his life, is the first African American player to lead the National Hockey League in scoring. At the 2002 Winter Olympics he also helps the Canadian squad win the gold medal in ice hockey.

2002. Venus Williams becomes the first African American tennis player to be ranked number one in the world. Serena Williams supplants her in July. They are the first sisters ever to be ranked first and second at the same time.

2002, March 11. Vonetta Flowers becomes the first African American athlete to win a gold medal at a Winter Olympics when she wins the inaugural two-woman bobsled event. Garrett Hines and Randy Jones become the first African American men to win Winter Olympic medals, bringing home the silver as half of the U.S. four-man bobsled team.

2002, March 24. Halle Berry is the first African American woman to win an Academy Award for a leading role.

3

Significant Documents in African American History

The text of proclamations and orders, legislative enactments, speeches, letters, and even poems and songs representing the course of American history display the presence of African Americans in the yesterday of this country and provide a picture of the changing place they have held in the national consciousness. The documents collected here separately capture for a moment in time the African American's role in American society. However, together these documents bear witness to the African American experience.

◆ THE GERMANTOWN MENNONITE RESOLUTION AGAINST SLAVERY (1688)

The Mennonites, a group of Protestant Christians who settled mainly in Pennsylvania and the Northwest Territory, rejected the use of violence, refused to bear arms or take oaths, and advocated the separation of church and state and the separation of their community from society. The Germantown Mennonite resolution against slavery represents one of the earliest protests against slavery in colonial America. It was passed 69 years after the introduction of the first African slaves in America, at a time when the number of slaves in the colonies was comparatively small. It was not until 1775, however, that the Quakers, a religious group similarly opposed to the institution, formed the first anti-slavery society in the colonies.

This is to the monthly meeting held at Richard Worrell's:

These are the reasons why we are against the traffic of men-body, as followeth: Is there any that would be done or handled at this manner? viz., to be sold or made a slave for all the time of his life? How fearful and faint-hearted are many at sea, when they see a strange vessel, being afraid it should be a Turk, and they should be taken, and sold for slaves into Turkey. Now, what is *this* better done, than Turks do? Yea, rather it is worse for them, which say they are Christians; for we hear that the most part of such negers are brought hither against their will and consent, and that many of them are stolen. Now, though they are black, we cannot conceive there is more liberty to have them slaves, as it is to have other white ones. There is a saying, that we should do to all men like as we will be done ourselves; making no difference of what generation, descent, or colour they are. And those who steal or rob men, and those who buy or purchase them, are they not all alike? Here is liberty of conscience, which is right and reasonable; here ought to be likewise liberty of the body, except of evil-doers, which is another case. But to bring men hither, or to rob and sell them against their will, we stand against. In Europe there are many oppressed for conscience-sake; and here there are those oppressed which are of a black colour. And we who know that men must not commit adultery—some do commit adultery *in* others, separating wives from their husbands, and giving them to others: and some sell the children of these poor creatures to other men. Ah! do consider well this thing, you who do it, if you would be done at this manner—and if it is done according to Christianity! You surpass Holland and Germany in this thing. This makes an ill report in all those countries of Europe, where they hear of [it], that the Quakers do here handel men as they handel there the cattle. And for that reason some have no mind or inclination to come hither. And who shall maintain this your cause, or plead for it? Truly, we cannot do so, except you shall inform us better hereof, viz.: that Christians have liberty to practice these things. Pray, what thing in the world can be done worse towards us, than if men should rob or steal us away, and sell us for slaves to strange countries; separating husbands from their wives and children. Being now this is not done in the manner we would be done at; therefore, we contradict, and are against this traffic of men-body. And we who profess that it is not lawful to steal, must, likewise, avoid to purchase such things as are stolen, but rather help to stop this robbing and stealing, if possible. And such men ought to be delivered out of the hands of the robbers, and set free as in Europe. Then is Pennsylvania to have a good report, instead, it hath now a bad one, for this sake, in other countries; especially whereas the Europeans are desirous to know in what manner *the Quaker* do rule in *their* province; and most of them do look upon us with an envious eye. But if this is done well, what shall we say is done evil?

If once these slaves (which they say are so wicked and stubborn men) should join themselves—fight for their freedom, and handel their masters and mistresses, as they did handel them before; will these masters and mistresses take the sword at hand and war against these poor slaves, like, as we are able to believe, some will not refuse to do? Or, have these poor negers not as much right to fight for their freedom, as you have to keep them slaves?

Now consider well this thing, if it is good or bad. And in case you find it to be good to handel these black in that manner, we desired and require you hereby lovingly, that you may inform us herein, which at this time never was done, viz., that Christians have such a liberty to do so. To the end we shall be satisfied on this point, and satisfy likewise our good friends and acquaintances in our native country, to whom it is a terror, or fearful thing, that men should be handled so in Pennsylvania.

This is from our meeting at Germantown, held ye 18th of the 2nd month, 1688, to be delivered to the monthly meeting at Richard Worrell's.

Garret Henderich,

Derick op de Graeff,

Francis Daniel Pastorius,

Abram op de Graeff.

◆ THE DECLARATION OF INDEPENDENCE (1776)

A concept of particular interest to eighteenth-century men and women was the theory of natural rights, the idea that all individuals possess certain fundamental rights that no government can deny. Using this argument as a justification for revolt, the American colonists, on July 4, 1776, formally announced their intention to separate from Great Britain in a Declaration of Independence.

The responsibility of writing this document was given to Thomas Jefferson. In his original draft, Jefferson included among the colonists' grievances the denial of the "most sacred rights of life and liberty"

to African slaves. However, the draft was revised, and the final version of the declaration was accepted by Congress without Jefferson's indictment against slavery.

In Congress, July 4, 1776. The unanimous Declaration of the thirteen United States of America,

When in the Course of human events, it becomes necessary for one people to dissolve the political bands which have connected them with another, and to assume among the Powers of the earth, the separate and equal station to which the Laws of Nature and of Nature's God entitle them, a decent respect to the opinions of mankind requires that they should declare the causes which impel them to the separation.

We hold these truths to be self-evident, that all men are created equal, that they are endowed by their Creator with certain unalienable Rights, that among these are Life, Liberty and the pursuit of Happiness. That to secure these rights, Governments are instituted among Men, deriving their just powers from the consent of the governed, That whenever any Form of Government becomes destructive of these ends, it is the Right of the People to alter or to abolish it, and to institute new Government, laying its foundation on such principles and organizing its powers in such form, as to them shall seem most likely to effect their Safety and Happiness. Prudence, indeed, will dictate that Governments long established should not be changed for light and transient causes; and accordingly all experience hath shown, that mankind are more disposed to suffer, while evils are sufferable, than to right themselves by abolishing the forms to which they are accustomed. But when a long train of abuses and usurpations, pursuing invariably the same Object evinces a design to reduce them under absolute Despotism, it is their right, it is their duty, to throw off such Government, and to provide new Guards for their future security.—Such has been the patient sufferance of these Colonies; and such is now the necessity which constrains them to alter their former Systems of Government. The history of the present King of Great Britain is a history of repeated injuries and usurpations, all having in direct object the establishment of an absolute Tyranny over these States. To prove this, let Facts be submitted to a candid world.

He has refused his Assent to Laws, the most wholesome and necessary for the public good.

He has forbidden his Governors to pass Laws of immediate and pressing importance, unless suspended in their operation till his Assent should be obtained; and when so suspended, he has utterly neglected to attend to them.

He has refused to pass other Laws for the accommodation of people, unless those people would relinquish the right of Representation in the Legislature, a right inestimable to them and formidable to tyrants only.

He has called together Legislative bodies at places unusual, uncomfortable, and distant from the depository of their Public Records, for the sole purpose of Fatiguing them into compliance with his measures.

He has dissolved Representative Houses repeatedly, for opposing with manly firmness his invasions on the rights of the people.

He has refused for a long time, after such dissolutions, to cause others to be elected; whereby the Legislative Powers, incapable of Annihilation, have returned to the People at large for their exercise; the state remaining in the meantime exposed to all the dangers of invasion from without, and convulsions within.

He has endeavoured to prevent the Population of these States; for that purpose obstructing the Laws of Naturalization of Foreigners; refusing to pass others to encourage their migration hither, and raising the conditions of new Appropriations of Lands.

He has obstructed the Administration of Justice, by refusing his Assent to Laws for establishing Judiciary Powers.

He has made Judges dependent on his Will alone, for the tenure of their offices, and the amount and payment of their salaries.

He has erected a multitude of New Offices, and sent hither swarms of Officers to harass our People, and eat out their substance.

He has kept among us, in times of peace, Standing Armies without the Consent of our legislature.

He has affected to render the Military independent of and superior to the Civil Power.

He has combined with others to subject us to a jurisdiction foreign to our constitution, and unacknowledged by our laws; giving his Assent to their acts of pretended legislation:

For quartering large bodies of armed troops among us:

For protecting them, by a mock Trial, from Punishment for any Murders which they should commit on the Inhabitants of these States:

For cutting off our Trade with all parts of the world:

For imposing taxes on us without our Consent:

For depriving us in many cases, of the benefits of Trial by Jury:

For transporting us beyond Seas to be tried for pretended offenses:

For abolishing the free System of English Laws in a neighboring Province, establishing therein an Arbitrary government, and enlarging its Boundaries so as to render it at once an example and fit instrument for introducing the same absolute rule into these Colonies:

For taking away our Charters, abolishing our most valuable Laws, and altering fundamentally the Forms of our Governments:

For suspending our own Legislature, and declaring themselves invested with Power to legislate for us in all cases whatsoever.

He has abdicated Government here, by declaring us out of his Protection and waging War against us.

He has plundered our seas, ravaged our Coasts, burnt our towns, and destroyed the lives of our people.

He is at this time transporting large armies of foreign mercenaries to complete the works of death, desolation and tyranny, already begun with circumstances of Cruelty and perfidy scarcely paralleled in the most barbarous ages, and totally unworthy of the Head of a civilized nation.

He has constrained our fellow Citizens taken Captive on the high Seas to bear Arms against their Country, to become the executioners of their friends and Brethren, or to fall themselves by their Hands.

He has excited domestic insurrections amongst us, and has endeavoured to bring on the inhabitants of our frontiers, the merciless Indian Savages, whose known rule of warfare, is an undistinguished destruction of all ages, sexes and conditions.

In every stage of these Oppressions We have Petitioned for Redress in the most humble terms: Our repeated Petitions have been answered only by repeated injury. A Prince, whose character is thus marked by every act which may define a Tyrant, is unfit to be the ruler of a free People.

Nor We have been wanting in attention to our British brethren. We have warned them from time to time of attempts by their legislature to extend an unwarrantable jurisdiction over us. We have reminded them of the circumstances of our emigration and settlement here. We have appealed to their native justice and magnanimity, and we have conjured them by the ties of our common kindred to disavow these usurpations, which would inevitably interrupt our connections and correspondence. They too have been deaf to the voice of justice and of consanguinity. We must, therefore, acquiesce in the necessity, which denounces our Separation, and hold them, as we hold the rest of mankind, Enemies in War, in Peace, Friends.

We, therefore, the Representatives of the United States of America, in General Congress, Assembled, appealing to the Supreme Judge of the world for the rectitude of our intentions, do, in the Name, and by Authority of the good People of these Colonies, solemnly publish and declare, That these United Colonies are, and of Right ought to be Free and Independent States; that they are Absolved from all Allegiance to the British Crown, and that all political connection between them and the State of Great Britain, is and ought to be totally dissolved; and that as Free and Independent States, they have full Power to levy War, conclude Peace, contract Alliances, establish Commerce, and to do all other Acts and Things which Independent States may of right do. And for the support of this Declaration, with a firm reliance on the Protection of Divine Providence, we mutually pledge to each other our Lives, our Fortunes and our sacred Honor.

◆ THE OMITTED ANTI-SLAVERY CLAUSE TO THE DECLARATION OF INDEPENDENCE (1776)

Thomas Jefferson's attitudes regarding African slaves wavered during the course of his life. In his early years, Jefferson thought Africans to be biologically inferior. Later, spurred by his conviction that natural rights should be accrued to all men, he decided that slavery had a destructive conditioning effect that stamped Africans with "odious peculiarities."

When Jefferson was assigned the task of drafting a declaration calling for separation from Great Britain, he included a short, passionate attack on King George III's indulgence of the slave traffic. However, at the request of delegates from South Carolina and Georgia and of Northern delegates whose ports sheltered and profited from slave ships, the clause was omitted from the final version. Many historians and critics have since argued that the elimination of this passage offers adequate proof that Africans in America were never meant to share in the fruits of independence and equality in their adopted homeland.

He [King George III] has waged cruel war against human nature itself, violating its most sacred rights of life and liberty in the persons of a distant people who never offended him, captivating and carrying them into slavery in another hemisphere, or to incur miserable death in their transportation thither. This piratical warfare, the opprobrium of *infidel* powers, is the warfare of the *Christian* king of Great Britain. Determined to keep open a market where MEN should be bought and sold, he has prostituted his negative for suppressing every legislative attempt to prohibit or restrain this execrable commerce.

◆ THE CONSTITUTION OF THE UNITED STATES, ART.1, SECTIONS 2 AND 9, ART. 4, SECTION 2 (1787)

Drawn up in 1787 and ratified a year later, the Constitution of the United States outlines the fundamental principles upon which the American republic is built. In a historical context, the Constitution and its amendments are a manifestation of the issues that have faced Americans and their attempts at resolving these issues.

Among the concepts important to Americans living during the eighteenth century were the ideas that all people are created equal and are endowed with certain unalienable rights, and that a government derives its power from the consent of those it governs. However, despite the fact that almost twenty percent of the population was bound in slavery, the economic and social arguments of the time regarding the status of African slaves overrode the tenets of natural rights. In 1857, Chief Justice Roger Brook Taney, delivering the Court's opinion in the case Dred Scott v. Sandford, summarized the attitude of the writers of the Constitution toward African slaves.

. . . They are not included, and were not intended to be included, under the word "citizens" in the constitution, and can therefore claim none of the rights and privileges which that instrument provides and secures. . . . On the contrary, they were at that time considered as a subordinate and inferior class of beings. . . .

Specifically, Article I, Sections 2 and 9, and Article IV, Section 2, of the Constitution deal directly with the status of Africans in America.

Preamble

We the People of the United States, in order to form a more perfect Union, establish Justice, insure domestic Tranquility, provide for the common defense, promote the general Welfare, and secure the Blessings of Liberty to ourselves and our Posterity, do ordain and establish this Constitution for the United States of America.

Article I

Section 2. . . . Representatives and direct Taxes shall be apportioned among the several States which may be included within this Union, according to their respective Numbers, which shall be determined by adding to the whole Number of free Persons, including those bound to Service for a Term of Years, and excluding

Indians not taxed, three-fifths of all other Persons. The actual Enumeration shall be made within three Years after the first Meeting of the Congress of the United States, and within every subsequent Term of Ten Years, in such manner as they shall by Law direct. . . .

Section 9. The Migration or Importation of such Persons as any of the States now existing shall think proper to admit, shall not be prohibited by the Congress prior to the Year one thousand eight hundred and eight, but a Tax or duty may be imposed on such Importation, not exceeding ten dollars for each Person. . . .

Article IV

Section 2. The Citizens of each State shall be entitled to all privileges and Immunities of Citizens in the several States.

A Person charged in any State with Treason, Felony, or other Crime, who shall flee from Justice, and be found in another State, shall on Demand of the executive authority of the State from which he fled, be delivered up, to be removed to the State having Jurisdiction of the Crime.

No Person held to Service or Labour in one State, under the Laws thereof, escaping into another, shall, in Consequence of any Law or Regulation therein, be discharged from such Service or Labour, but shall be delivered up on Claim of the Party to whom such Service or Labour may be due.

◆ THE BILL OF RIGHTS (1791)

Ratified in 1791, the first ten amendments to the Constitution of the United States, commonly referred to as the Bill of Rights, further outline the fundamental rights and freedoms of citizens of the United States. This set of additions to the Constitution was a crucial part of the constitutional ratification process (several states had only ratified the Constitution on the condition that a bill of rights would be added), since eighteenth-century Americans held dearly to the concept of personal freedom. Despite these beliefs, it was not until after ratification of the Fourteenth Amendment to the Constitution and several civil rights laws that the freedoms protected in the Bill of Rights were extended to all United States citizens.

Amendment 1

Congress shall make no law respecting an establishment of religion, or prohibiting the free exercise thereof; or abridging the freedom of speech, or of the press; or the right of the people peaceably to assemble, and to petition the government for a redress of grievances.

Amendment 2

A well regulated Militia, being necessary to the security of a free State, the right of the people to keep and bear Arms, shall not be infringed.

Amendment 3

No Soldier, shall, in time of peace be quartered in any house, without the consent of the Owner, nor in time of war, but in a manner to be prescribed by law.

Amendment 4

The right of the people to be secure in their persons, houses, papers and effects, against unreasonable searches and seizures, shall not be violated and no Warrants shall issue, but upon probable cause, supported by Oath or affirmation, and particularly describing the place to be searched, and the persons or things to be seized.

Amendment 5

No person shall be held to answer for a capital, or otherwise infamous crime, unless on a presentment or indictment of a Grand Jury, except in cases arising in the land or naval forces, or in the Militia, when in actual service in time of War or public danger; nor shall any person be subject for the same offense to be twice put in jeopardy of life or limb; nor shall be compelled in any criminal case to be a witness against himself, nor be deprived of life, liberty, or property, without due process of law; nor shall private property be taken for public use, without just compensation.

Amendment 6

In all criminal prosecutions, the accused shall enjoy the right to a speedy and public trial, by an impartial jury of the State and district wherein the crime shall have been committed, which district shall have been previously ascertained by law, and to be informed of the nature and cause of the accusation; to be confronted with witnesses against him; to have compulsory process for obtaining witnesses in his favor, and to have the Assistance of Counsel for his defence.

Amendment 7

In Suits at common law, where the value in controversy shall exceed twenty dollars, the right of trial by jury shall be preserved, and no fact tried by a jury, shall be otherwise re-examined in any Court of the United States, than according to the rules of the common law.

Amendment 8

Excessive bail shall not be required, nor excessive fines imposed, nor cruel and unusual punishments inflicted.

Amendment 9

The enumeration in the Constitution, of certain rights, shall not be construed to deny or disparage others retained by the people.

Amendment 10

The powers not delegated to the United States by the Constitution, nor prohibited by it to the States, are reserved to the States respectively, or to the people.

◆ FUGITIVE SLAVE ACT CH. 7, STAT. 302 (1793)

The Fugitive Slave Act of 1793 was designed to enforce Article IV, Section 2 of the Constitution and incur penalties against those who aided or abetted attempts of slaves to escape bondage.

Section 1. *Be it enacted by the Senate and House of Representatives of the United States of America in Congress assembled,* That whenever the executive authority of any state in the Union, or of either of the territories northwest or south of the river Ohio, shall demand any person as a fugitive from justice, of the executive authority of any such state or territory to which such person shall have fled, and shall moreover produce the copy of an indictment found, or an affidavit made before a magistrate of any state or territory as aforesaid, charging the person so demanded, with having committed treason, felony or other crime, certified as authentic by the governor or chief magistrate of the state or territory from whence the person so charged fled, it shall be the duty of the executive authority of the state or territory to which such person shall have fled, to cause him or her to be arrested and secured, and notice of the arrest to be given to the executive authority making such demand, or to the agent of such authority appointed to receive the fugitive, and to cause the fugitive to be delivered to such agent when he shall appear: But if no such agent shall appear within six months from the time of the arrest, the prisoner may be discharged. And all costs or expenses incurred to the state or territory making such demand, shall be paid by such state or territory.

Section 2. *And be it further enacted,* That any agent, appointed as aforesaid, who shall receive the fugitive into his custody, shall be empowered to transport him or her to the state or territory from which he or she shall have fled. And if any person or persons shall by force set at liberty, or rescue the fugitive from such agent while transporting, as aforesaid, the person or persons so offending shall, on conviction, be fined not exceeding five hundred dollars, and be imprisoned not exceeding one year.

Section 3. *And be it also enacted,* That when a person held to labour in any of the United States, or in either of the territories on the northwest or south of the river Ohio, under the laws thereof, shall escape into any other of the said states or territory, the person to whom such labour or service may be due, his agent or attorney, is hereby empowered to seize or arrest such fugitive from labour, and to take him or her before any judge of the circuit or district courts of the United States, residing or being within the state, or before any magistrate of a county, city or town corporate, wherein such seizure or arrest shall be made, and upon proof to the satisfaction of such judge or magistrate, either by oral testimony or affidavit taken before and certified by a magistrate of any such state or territory, that the person so seized or arrested, doth, under the laws of the state or territory from which he or she fled, owe service or labour to the person claiming him or her, it shall be the duty of such judge or magistrate to give a certificate thereof to such claimant, his agent or attorney, which shall be sufficient warrant for removing the said fugitive from labour, to the state or territory from which he or she fled.

Section 4. *And be it further enacted,* That any person who shall knowingly and willing obstruct or hinder such claimant, his agent or attorney in so seizing or arresting such fugitive from labour, or shall rescue such fugitive from such claimant, his agent or attorney when so arrested pursuant to the authority herein given or declared; or shall harbor or conceal such person after notice that he or she was a fugitive from labour, as aforesaid shall, for either of the said offenses, forfeit and pay the sum of five hundred dollars. Which penalty may be recovered by and for the benefit of such claimant, by action of debt, in any court proper to try the same; saving moreover to the person claiming such labour or service, his right of action for or on account of the said injuries or either of them.

◆ BENJAMIN FRANKLIN'S ADDRESS TO THE PUBLIC (1798)

Despite the framers of the Constitution's handling of the slavery issue, influential opponents to slavery attempted to exert pressure on the Congress to enact an anti-slavery amendment to the Constitution. Among such groups was the Pennsylvania Society for Promoting the Abolition of Slavery and the Relief of Free Negroes Unlawfully Held in Bondage. Over the signature of the president of the Society, Benjamin Franklin, the following "Address to the Public," urging abolition, was made on November 9, 1789.

It is with peculiar satisfaction we assure the friends of humanity that, in prosecuting the design of our association, our endeavors have proved successful, far beyond our most sanguine expectations.

Encouraged by this success, and by the daily progress of that luminous and benign spirit of liberty which is diffusing itself throughout the world, and humbly hoping for the continuance of the divine blessing on our labors, we have ventured to make an important addition to our original plan; and do therefore earnestly solicit the support and assistance of all who can feel the tender emotions of sympathy and compassion, or relish the exalted pleasure of beneficence.

Slavery is such an atrocious debasement of human nature, that its very extirpation, if not performed with solicitous care, may sometimes open a source of serious evils.

The unhappy man, who has long been treated as a brute animal, too frequently sinks beneath the common standard of the human species. The galling chains that bind his body do also fetter his intellectual faculties, and impair the social affections of his heart. Accustomed to move like a mere machine, by the will of a master, reflection is suspended; he has not the power of choice; and reason and conscience have but little influence over his conduct, because he is chiefly governed by the passion of fear. He is poor and friendless; perhaps worn out by extreme labor, age, and disease.

Under such circumstances, freedom may often prove a misfortune to himself, and prejudicial to society.

Attention to emancipated black people, it is therefore to be hoped, will become a branch of our national police; but, as far as we contribute to promote this emancipation, so far that attention is evidently a serious duty incumbent on us, and which we mean to discharge to the best of our judgment and abilities.

To instruct, to advise, to qualify those who have been restored to freedom, for the exercise and enjoyment of civil liberty; to promote in them habits of industry; to furnish them with employments suited to their age, sex, talents, and other circumstances; and to procure their children an education calculated for their future situation in life—these are the great outlines of the annexed plan, which we have adopted, and which we conceive will essentially promote the public good, and the happiness of these our hitherto too much neglected fellow-creatures.

A plan so extensive cannot be carried into execution without considerable pecuniary resources, beyond the present ordinary funds of the Society. We hope much from the generosity of enlightened and benevolent freemen, and will gratefully receive any donations of subscriptions for this purpose which may be made to our Treasurer, James Starr, or to James Pemberton, Chairman of our Committee of Correspondence.

Signed by order of the Society,

B. FRANKLIN, President

Philadelphia, 9th of November, 1789

◆ GEORGE WASHINGTON'S LAST WILL AND TESTAMENT (1799)

By the eighteenth century, the slavery of Africans had become a firmly entrenched institution of American life, particularly in the South where it was justified as an economic necessity. This argument notwithstanding, it was Washington's decision, at the writing of his last will and testament in 1799, to free all those slaves which he held in his "own right."

In the Name of God Amen

I, George Washington of Mount Vernon—a citizen of the United States,—and lately President of the same, do make, ordain and declare this Instrument; which is written with my own hand and every page thereof subscribed with my name, to be my last Will and Testament, revoking all other. . . . Upon the decease of my wife, it is my Will and desire that all the Slaves which I hold in my *own right*, shall receive their freedom. . . . And whereas among those who will receive freedom according to this devise, there may be some, who from old age or bodily infirmities, and others who on account of their infancy, that will be unable to support themselves; it is my Will and desire that all who come under the first and second description shall be comfortably clothed and fed by my heirs while they live;—and that such of the latter description as have no parents living, or if living are unable, or unwilling to provide for them, shall be bound by the Court until they shall arrive at the age of twenty-five year;—and in cases where no record can be produced, whereby their ages can be ascertained, the judgment of the Court upon its own view of the subject, shall be adequate and final.—The Negros thus bound, are (by their Masters or Mistresses) to be taught to read and write; and to be brought up to some useful occupation, agreeably to the Laws of the Commonwealth of Virginia, providing for the support of Orphan and other poor Children.—And I do hereby expressly forbid the Sale, or transportation out of the said Commonwealth of any Slave I may die possessed of, under any pretence whatsoever.—And I do moreover most pointedly, and most solemnly enjoin it upon my Executors hereafter named, or the Survivors of them, to see that this clause respecting Slaves, and every part thereof be religiously fulfilled at the Epoch at which it is directed to take place; without evasion, neglect or delay, after the Crops which may then be on the ground are harvested, particularly as it respects the aged and infirm;—Seeing that a regular and permanent fund be established for their Support so long as there are subjects requiring it; not trusting to the uncertain provision to be made by individuals.—And to my Mulatto man William (calling himself William Lee) I give immediate freedom; or if he should prefer it (on account of the accidents which have befallen him, and which have rendered him incapable of walking or of any active employment) to remain in the situation he now is, it shall be optional in him to do so: In either case however, I allow him an annuity of thirty dollars during his natural life, which shall be independent of the victuals and cloaths he has been accustomed to receive, if he chooses the last alternative; but in full, with his freedom, if he prefers the first;—and this I give him as a testimony of my sense of his attachment to me, and for his faithful services during the Revolutionary War.

◆ ACT TO PROHIBIT THE IMPORTATION OF SLAVES CH. 22, 2 STAT. 426 (1807)

In adherence with the provisions of Article I, Section 9 of the Constitution, Congress passed and President Thomas Jefferson signed into law an act to end the slave trade. The act, however, which went into effect January 1, 1808, was not rigidly enforced. Evidence of this can be found in the fact that, between 1808 and 1860, some 250,000 slaves were illegally imported into the United States.

An Act to prohibit the importation of Slaves into any port or place within the jurisdiction of the United States, from and after the first day of January, in the year of our Lord one thousand eight hundred and eight.

Be it enacted, that from and after the first day of January, one thousand eight hundred and eight, it shall not be lawful to import or bring into the United States or the territories thereof from any foreign kingdom, place, or country, any negro, mulatto, or person of colour, as a slave, or to be held to service or labour.

Section 2. That no citizen of the United States, or any other person, shall, from and after the first day of January, in the year of our Lord one thousand eight hundred and eight, for himself, or themselves, or any other person whatsoever, either as master, factor, or owner, build, fit, equip, load or to otherwise prepare any ship or vessel, in any port or place within the jurisdiction of the United States, nor shall cause any ship or vessel to sail from any port or place within the same, for the purpose of procuring any negro, mulatto, or person of colour, from any foreign kingdom, place, or country, to be transported to any port or place whatsoever within the jurisdiction of the United States, to be held, sold, or disposed of as slaves, or to be held to service or labour: and if any ship or vessel shall be so fitted out for the purpose aforesaid, or shall be caused to sail so as aforesaid, every such ship or vessel, her tackle, apparel, and furniture, shall be forfeited to the United States, and shall be liable to be seized, prosecuted, and condemned in any of the circuit courts or district courts, for the district where the said ship or vessel may be found or seized. . . .

Section 4. If any citizen or citizens of the United States, or any person resident within the jurisdiction of the same, shall, from after the first day of January, one thousand eight hundred and eight, take on board, receive or transport from any of the coasts or kingdoms of Africa, or from any other foreign kingdom, place, or country, any negro, mulatto, or person of colour in any ship or vessel, for the purpose of selling them in any port or place within the jurisdiction of the United States as slaves, or be held to service or labour, or shall be in any ways aiding or abetting therein, such citizen or citizens, or person, shall severally forfeit and pay five thousand dollars, one moiety thereof to the use of any person or persons who shall sue for and prosecute the same to effect. . . .

Section 6. That if any person or persons whatsoever, shall, from and after the first day of January, one thousand eight hundred and eight, purchase or sell any negro, mulatto, or person, of colour, for a slave, or to be held to service or labour, who shall have been imported, or brought from any foreign kingdom, place, or country, or from the dominions of any foreign state, immediately adjoining to the United States, after the last day of December, one thousand eight hundred and seven, knowing at the time of such purchase or sale, such negro, mulatto, or person of colour, was so brought within the jurisdiction of the United States, as aforesaid, such purchaser and seller shall severally forfeit and pay for every negro, mulatto, or person of colour, so purchased, or sold as aforesaid, eight hundred dollars. . . .

Slave cell used to hold newly arrived Africans in America.

Section 7. That if any ship or vessel shall be found, from and after the first day of January, one thousand eight hundred and eight, in any river, port, bay, or harbor, or on the high seas, within the jurisdictional limits of the United States, or hovering on the coast thereof, having on board any negro, mulatto, or person of colour, for the purpose of selling them as slaves, or with intent to land the same, in any port or place within the jurisdiction of the United States, contrary to the prohibition of the act, every such ship or vessel, together with her tackle, apparel, and furniture, and the goods or effects which shall be found on board the same, shall be forfeited to the use of the United States, and may be seized, prosecuted, and condemned, in any court of the United States, having jurisdiction thereof. And it shall be lawful for the President of the United

States, and he is hereby authorized, should he deem it expedient, to cause any of the armed vessels of the United States to be manned and employed to cruise on any part of the coast of the United States, or territories thereof, where he may judge attempts will be made to violate the provisions of this act, and to instruct and direct the commanders of armed vessels of the United States, to seize, take, and bring into any port of the United States all such ships or vessels, and moreover to seize, take, or bring into any port of the U.S. all ships or vessels of the U.S. wheresoever found on the high seas, contravening the provisions of this act, to be proceeded against according to law. . . .

◆ EDITORIAL FROM THE FIRST EDITION OF *FREEDOM'S JOURNAL* (1827)

Freedom's Journal, published by Samuel Cornish and John B. Russwurm, was the first African American owned and edited newspaper to be published in the United States. This editorial, printed here in its entirety, illustrates the Journal's *aim at bringing an end to slavery and discrimination.*

To Our Patrons

In presenting our first number to our Patrons, we feel all the diffidence of persons entering upon a new and untried line of business. But a moment's reflection upon the noble objects, which we have in view by the publication of this Journal; the expediency of its appearance at this time, when so many schemes are in action concerning our people—encourage us to come boldly before an enlightened public. For we believe, that a paper devoted to the dissemination of useful knowledge among our brethren, and to their moral and religious improvement, must meet with the cordial approbation of every friend to humanity.

The peculiarities of this Journal, renders it important that we should advertise to the world our motives by which we are actuated, and the objects which we contemplate.

We wish to plead our own cause. Too long have others spoken for us. Too long has the public been deceived by misrepresentations, in things which concern us dearly, though in the estimation of some mere trifles; for though there are many in society who exercise towards us benevolent feelings; still (with sorrow we confess it) there are others who make it their business to enlarge upon the least trifle, which tends to the discredit of any person of colour; and pronounce anathemas and denounce our whole body for the misconduct of this guilty one. We are aware that there are many instances of vice among us, but we avow that it is because no one has taught its subjects to be virtuous;

many instances of poverty, because no sufficient efforts accommodated to minds contracted by slavery, and deprived of early education have been made, to teach them how to husband their hard earnings, and to secure to themselves comfort.

Education being an object of the highest importance to the welfare of society, we shall endeavor to present just and adequate views of it, and to urge upon our brethren the necessity and expediency of training their children, while young, to habits of industry, and thus forming them for becoming useful members of society. It is surely time that we should awake from this lethargy of years, and make a concentrated effort for the education of our youth. We form a spoke in the human wheel, and it is necessary that we should understand our pendency on the different parts, and theirs on us, in order to perform our part with propriety.

Though not desiring of dictating, we shall feel it our incumbent duty to dwell occasionally upon the general principles and rules of economy. The world has grown too enlightened, to estimate any man's character by his personal appearance. Though all men acknowledge the excellency of Franklin's maxims, yet comparatively few practice upon them. We may deplore when it is too late, the neglect of these self-evident truths, but it avails little to mourn. Ours will be the task of admonishing our brethren on these points.

The civil rights of a people being of the greatest value, it shall ever be our duty to vindicate our brethren, when oppressed; and to lay the case before the public. We shall also urge upon our brethren, (who are qualified by the laws of the different states) the expediency of using their elective franchise; and of making an independent use of the same. We wish them not to become the tools of party.

And as much time is frequently lost, and wrong principles instilled, by the perusal of works of trivial importance, we shall consider it a part of our duty to recommend to our young readers, such authors as will not only enlarge their stock of useful knowledge, but such as will also serve to stimulate them to higher attainments in science.

We trust also, that through the columns of the FREEDOM'S JOURNAL, many practical pieces, having for their bases, the improvement of our brethren, will be presented to them, from the pens of many of our respected friends, who have kindly promised their assistance.

It is our earnest wish to make our Journal a medium of intercourse between our brethren in the different states of this great confederacy: that through its columns an expression of our sentiments, on many interesting subjects which concern us, may be offered to the public: that plans which apparently are beneficial may be candidly discussed and properly weighed; if worth, receive our cordial approbation; if not, our marked disapprobation.

Useful knowledge of every kind, and everything that relates to Africa, shall find a ready admission into our columns; and as that vast continent becomes daily more known, we trust that many things will come to light, proving that the natives of it are neither so ignorant nor stupid as they have generally been supposed to be.

And while these important subjects shall occupy the columns of the FREEDOM'S JOURNAL, we would not be unmindful of our brethren who are still in the iron fetters of bondage. They are our kindred by all the ties of nature; and though but little can be effected to us, still let our sympathies be poured forth and our prayers in their behalf, ascend to Him who is able to succor them.

From the press and the pulpit we have suffered much by being incorrectly represented. Men whom we equally love and admire have not hesitated to represent us disadvantageously, without becoming personally acquainted with the true state of things, nor discerning between virtue and vice among us. The virtuous part of our people feel themselves sorely aggrieved under the existing state of things—they are not appreciated.

Our vices and our degradation are ever arrayed against us, but our virtues are passed by unnoticed. And what is still more lamentable, our friends, to whom we concede all the principles of humanity and religion, from these very causes seem to have fallen into the current of popular feeling and are imperceptibly floating on the stream—actually living in the practice of prejudice, while they abjure it in theory, and feel it not in their hearts. Is it not very desirable that such should know more of our actual condition; and of our efforts and feelings, that in forming or advocating plans for our amelioration, they may do it more understanding? In the spirit of candor and humility we intend by a simple representation of facts to lay our case before the public, with a view to arrest the progress of prejudice, and to shield ourselves against the consequent evils. We wish to conciliate all and to irritate none, yet we must be firm and unwavering in our principles, and persevering in our efforts.

If ignorance, poverty and degradation have hitherto been our unhappy lot; has the Eternal decree gone forth, that our race alone are to remain in this state, while knowledge and civilization are shedding their enlivening rays over the rest of the human family? The recent travels of Denham and Clapperton in the interior of Africa, and the interesting narrative which they have published; the establishment of the republic of Haiti after years of sanguinary warfare; its subsequent progress in all the arts of civilization; and the advancement of liberal ideas in South America, where despotism has given place to free governments, and where many of our brethren now fill important civil and military stations, prove the contrary.

The interesting fact that there are FIVE HUNDRED THOUSAND free persons of color, one half of whom might peruse, and the whole be benefitted by the publication of the Journal; that no publication, as yet, has been devoted exclusively to their improvement—that many selections from approved standard authors, which are within the reach of few, may occasionally be made—and more important still, that this large body of our citizens have no public channel—all serve to prove the real necessity, at present, for the appearance of the FREEDOM'S JOURNAL.

It shall ever be our desire so to conduct the editorial department of our paper as to give offence to none of our patrons; as nothing is farther from us than to make it the advocate of any partial views, either in politics or religion. What few days we can number, have been devoted to the improvement of our brethren; and it is our earnest wish that the remainder may be spent in the same delightful service.

In conclusion, whatever concerns us as a people, will ever find a ready admission into the FREEDOM'S JOURNAL, interwoven with all the principal news of the day.

And while every thing in our power shall be performed to support the character of our Journal, we would respectfully invite our numerous friends to assist by their communications, and our coloured brethren to strengthen our hands by their subscriptions, as our labour is one of common cause, and worthy of their consideration and support. And we most earnestly solicit the latter, that if at any time we should seem to be zealous, or too pointed in the inculcation of any important lesson, they will remember, that they are equally interested in the cause in which we are engaged, and attribute our zeal to the peculiarities of our situation; and our earnest engagedness in their well-being.

◆ EDITORIAL FROM THE FIRST EDITION OF *THE LIBERATOR* (1831)

The Liberator, *one of the most well-known abolitionist newspapers in the nineteenth century, was published weekly out of Boston, Massachusetts between 1831 and 1865. The paper's founder, William Lloyd Garrison, who was also the founder of the*

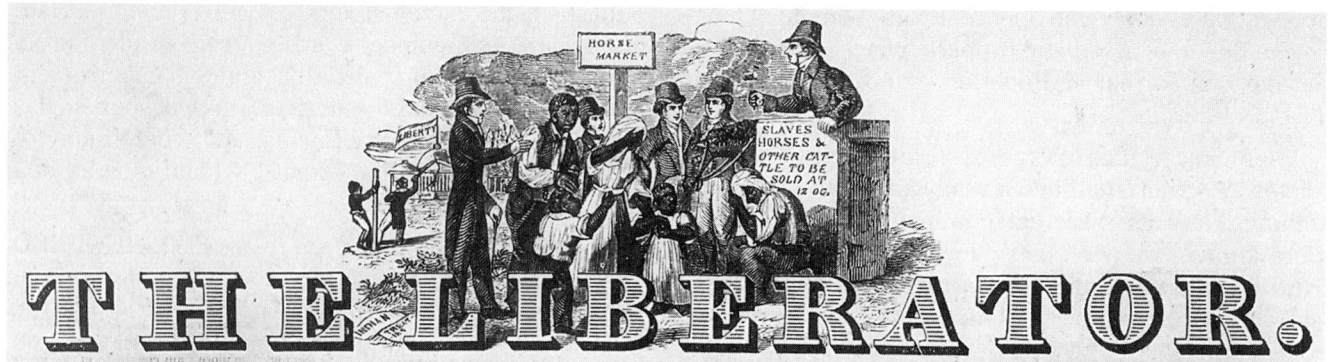

Masthead of William Lloyd Garrison's newspaper, *The Liberator.*

American Anti-Slavery Society, was white. However, most of The Liberator's *subscribers were black. During 34 years of publication, Garrison worked at shifting the sentiment of the nation away from the notion of gradual emancipation toward that of total abolition— as illustrated in this excerpt from the paper's first editorial.*

. . . During my recent tour for the purpose of exciting the minds of the people by a series of discourses on the subject of slavery, every place that I visited gave fresh evidence of the fact, that a greater revolution in public sentiment was to be effected in the free states—and particularly in New England—than at the south. I found contempt more bitter, opposition more active, detraction more relentless, prejudice more stubborn, and apathy more frozen, than among slave owners themselves. Of course, there were individual exceptions to the contrary. This state of things afflicted, but did not dishearten me. I determined, at every hazard, to lift up the standard of emancipation in the eyes of the nation, within sight of Bunker Hill and in the birth place of liberty. That standard is now unfurled; and long may it float, unhurt by the spoliations of time or the missiles of a desperate foe—yea, till every chain be broken, and every bondman set free! Let Southern oppressors tremble—let their secret abettors tremble—let their Northern apologists tremble—let all the enemies of the persecuted blacks tremble.

I am aware that many object to the severity of my language; but is there not cause for severity? I will be as harsh as truth, and as uncompromising as justice. On this subject, I do not wish to think, or speak, or write, with moderation. No! No! Tell a man whose house is on fire to give a moderate alarm; tell the mother to gradually extricate her babe from the fire into which it has fallen;—but urge me not to use moderation in a cause like the present. I am in earnest—I will not equivocate—I will not excuse—I will not retreat a single inch—AND I WILL BE HEARD. . . .

William Lloyd Garrison

◆ THE AMERICAN ANTI-SLAVERY SOCIETY'S *AMERICAN SLAVERY AS IT IS* (1839) (EXCERPT)

In 1839, The American Anti-Slavery Society compiled a massive portfolio of testimonies entitled American Slavery As It Is, *which sought to document the inhumanities of slavery. The introduction, by Theodore D. Weld of New York, written in the style of a prosecutor addressing a court, stirred abolitionist sentiments in the North and was attacked by proslavery forces in the South.*

READER, YOU are empaneled as a juror to try a plain case and bring in an honest verdict. The question at issue is not one of law, but of act—"What is the actual condition of slaves in the United States?"

A plainer case never went to jury. Look at it. TWENTY SEVEN HUNDRED THOUSAND PERSONS in this country, men, women, and children, are in SLAVERY. Is slavery, as a condition for human beings, good, bad, or indifferent?

We submit the question without argument. You have common sense, and conscience, and a human heart— pronounce upon it. You have a wife, or a husband, a child, a father, a mother, a brother or a sister—make the case your own, make it theirs, and bring in your verdict.

The case of Human Rights against Slavery has been adjudicated in the court of conscience times innumerable. The same verdict has always been rendered—"Guilty;" the same sentence has always been pronounced "Let it be accursed;" and human nature, with her million echoes, has rung it round the world in every language under heaven. "Let it be accursed. . . ."

As slaveholders and their apologists are volunteer witnesses in their own cause, and are flooding the world with testimony that their slaves are kindly treated; that they are well fed, well clothed, well housed, well lodged, moderately worked, and bountifully provided with all things needful for their comfort, we propose—first, to disprove their assertions by the testimony of a multitude of impartial witnesses, and then to put slaveholders themselves through a course of cross-questioning which will draw their condemnation out of their own mouths.

We will prove that the slaves in the United States are treated with barbarous inhumanity; that they are overworked, underfed, wretchedly clad and lodged, and have insufficient sleep; that they are often made to wear round their necks iron collars armed with prongs, to drag heavy chains and weights at their feet while working in the field, and to wear yokes and bells, and iron horns; that they are often kept confined in the stocks day and night for weeks together, made to wear gags in their mouths for hours or days, have some of their front teeth torn out or broken off, that they may be easily detected when they run away; that they are frequently flogged with terrible severity, have red pepper rubbed into their lacerated flesh, and hot brine, spirits of turpentine etc., poured over the gashes to increase the torture; that they are often stripped naked, their backs and limbs cut with knives, bruised and mangled by scores and hundreds of blows with the paddle, and terribly torn by the claws of cats, drawn over them by their tormentors; that they are often hunted with blood-hounds and shot down like beasts, or torn in pieces by dogs; that they are often suspended by the arms and whipped and beaten till they faint, and when revived by restoratives, beaten again till they faint, and sometimes till they die; that their ears are often cut off, their eyes knocked out, their bones broken, their flesh branded with red hot irons; that they are maimed, mutilated and burned to death, over slow fires. All these things, and more, and worse, we shall prove. . . .

We shall show, not merely that such deeds are committed, but that they are frequent; not done in corners, but before the sun; not in one of the slave states, but in all of them; not perpetrated by brutal overseers and drivers merely, but by magistrates, by legislators, by professors of religion, by preachers of the gospel, by governors of states, by "gentlemen of property and standing," and by delicate females moving in the "highest circles of society."

We know, full well, the outcry that will be made by multitudes, at these declarations; the multiform cavils, the flat denials, the charges of "exaggeration" and "falsehood" so often bandied, the sneers of affected contempt at the credulity that can believe such things, and the rage and imprecations against those who give them currency. We know, too, the threadbare sophistries by which slaveholders and their apologists seek to evade such testimony. If they admit that such deeds are committed, they tell us that they are exceedingly rare, and therefore furnish no grounds for judging of the general treatment of slaves; that occasionally a brutal wretch in the *free* states barbarously butchers his wife, but that no one thinks of inferring from that, the general treatment of wives at the North and West.

They tell us, also, that the slaveholders of the South are proverbially hospitable, kind, and generous, and it is incredible that they can perpetrate such enormities upon human beings; further, that it is absurd to suppose that they would thus injure their own property, that self-interest would prompt them to treat their slaves with kindness, as none but fools and madmen wantonly destroy their own property; further, that Northern visitors at the South come back testifying to the kind treatment of the slaves, and that slaves themselves corroborate such representations. All these pleas, and scores of others, are build in every corner of the free States; and who that hath eyes to see, has not sickened at the blindness that saw not, at the palsy of heart that felt not, or at the cowardice and sycophancy that dared not expose such shallow fallacies. We are not to be turned from our purpose by such vapid babblings. In their appropriate places, we proposed to consider these objections and various others, and to show their emptiness and folly.

◆ HENRY HIGHLAND GARNET'S ADDRESS TO THE SLAVES OF THE UNITED STATES OF AMERICA (1843) (EXCERPT)

In 1843, Henry Highland Garnet attended the National Convention of Negro Citizens in Buffalo, New York, and on August 16 he delivered a militant oration calling for slave rebellions as the most assured means of ending slavery. It was perhaps the most radical speech by an African American during the

Henry Highland Garnet.

period prior to the Civil War. The proposal moved the delegates and failed by a single vote of being adopted. After reading the speech, anti-slavery advocate John Brown had it published at his own expense in 1848.

Garnet's speech is, for all intents and purposes, addressed to an audience not present to receive it. Garnet speaks "to" the enslaved "on behalf of" the assembled conventioneers. Apologizing for the soft-ness and ineffectiveness of abolitionist efforts, Garnet encourages slaves to "Arise! Strike for your lives and liberties." For Garnet's immediate audience, his mes-sage is one of anger, exasperation, and a summons for heightened militancy.

Brethren and fellow citizens: Your brethren of the North, East and West have been accustomed to meet together in national conventions, to sympathize with each other, and to weep over your unhappy condition. In these meetings we have addressed all classes of the free, but we have never, until this time, sent a word of consolation and advice to you. We have been contented in sitting still and mourning over your sorrows, ear-nestly hoping that before this day your sacred liberties would have been restored. But we have hoped in vain.

Years have rolled on, and tens of thousands have been borne on streams of blood and tears to the shores of eternity. While you have been oppressed, we have also been partakers with you; nor can we be free while you are enslaved. We, therefore, write to you as being bound with you.

Many of you are bound to us, not only by the ties of a common humanity, but we are connected by the more tender relations of parents, wives, husbands and sisters and friends. As such we most affectionately address you.

Two hundred and twenty-seven years ago the first of our injured race were brought to the shores of America. They came not with glad spirits to select their homes in the New World. They came not with their own consent, to find an unmolested enjoyment of the blessings of this fruitful soil. . . . Neither did they come flying upon the wings of Liberty to a land of freedom. But they came with broken hearts from their beloved native land and were doomed to unrequited toil and deep degradation. Nor did the evil of their bondage end at their emancipa-tion by death. Succeeding generations inherited their chains, and millions have come from eternity into time, and have returned again to the world of spirits, cursed and ruined by American Slavery.

[T]he time has come when you must act for your-selves. It is an old and true saying that, "if hereditary bondsmen would be free, they must themselves strike the blow." You can plead your own cause and do the work of emancipation better than any others. The nations of the Old World are moving in the great cause of universal freedom, and some of them at least will, ere long, do you justice. The combined powers of Europe have placed their broad seal of disapprobation upon the African slave trade. But in the slaveholding parts of the United States the trade is as brisk as ever. They buy and sell you as though you were brute beasts. The North has done much; her opinion of slavery in the abstract is known. But in regard to the South, we adopt the opinion of the *New York Evangelist*—"We have advanced so far, that the cause apparently waits for a more effectual door to be thrown open that has been yet." . . . [G]o to your lordly enslavers and tell them plainly that you are determined to be free. Appeal to their sense of justice and tell them that they have no more right to oppress you than you have to enslave them. Entreat them to remove the grievous burdens which they have imposed upon you, and to remunerate you for your labor. . . . Inform them that all you desire is freedom, and that nothing else will suffice. Do this, and forever after cease to toil for the heartless tyrants, who give you no other reward but stripes and abuse. If they then commence the work of death, they, and not you, will be responsible for the consequences. You had far better all die—die immediately—than live slaves and entail your wretchedness upon your posterity. If you would be free in this generation, here is your only hope. However much you and all of us may desire it, there is not much hope of redemption without the shedding of blood. If you must bleed, let it all come at once—rather die freemen than live to be slaves. It is impossible, like the children of Israel, to make a grand exodus from the land of bondage. The Pharaohs are on both sides of the blood-red waters!

Where is the blood of your fathers? Has it all run out of your veins? Awake, awake; millions of voices are calling you! Your dead fathers speak to you from their graves. Heaven, as with a voice of thunder, call on you to arise from the dust.

Let your motto be Resistance! Resistance! Resistance! No oppressed people have ever secured their liberty without resistance. What kind of resistance you had better make you must decide by the circumstances that surround you, and according to the suggestion of expediency. Brethren, adieu! Trust in the living God. Labor for the peace of the human race, and remember that you are three millions!

◆ EDITORIAL FROM THE FIRST EDITION OF *THE NORTH STAR* (1847)

The first edition of Frederick Douglass's newspaper The North Star *was published on December 3, 1847, in Rochester, New York. Douglass, an escaped slave and leader in the abolitionist movement, dedicated his paper to the cause of blacks in America—as displayed in this, the paper's first editorial.*

To Our Oppressed Countrymen

We solemnly dedicate the *North Star* to your cause, our long oppressed and plundered fellow countrymen. May God bless the offering to your good! It shall fearlessly assert your rights, faithfully proclaim your wrongs, and earnestly demand for you instant and even-handed justice. Giving no quarter to slavery at the South, it will hold no truce with oppressors at the North. While it shall boldly advocate emancipation for our enslaved brethren, it will omit no opportunity to gain for the nominally free, complete enfranchisement. Every effort to injure or degrade you or your cause—originating wheresoever, or with whomsoever—shall find in it a constant, unswerving and inflexible foe.

We shall energetically assail the ramparts of Slavery and Prejudice, be they composed of church or state, and seek the destruction of every refuge of lies, under which tyranny may aim to conceal and protect itself. . . .

While our paper shall be mainly Anti-Slavery, its columns shall be freely opened to the candid and decorous discussions of all measures and topics of a moral and humane character, which may serve to enlighten, improve, and elevate mankind. Temperance, Peace, Capital Punishment, Education,—all subjects claiming the attention of the public mind may be freely and fully discussed here.

While advocating your rights, the *North Star* will strive to throw light on your duties: while it will not fail to make known your virtues, it will not shun to discover your faults. To be faithful to our foes it must be faithful to ourselves, in all things.

Remember that we are one, that our cause is one, and that we must help each other, if we would succeed. We have drunk to the dregs the bitter cup of slavery; we have worn the heavy yoke; we have sighed beneath our bonds, and writhed beneath the bloody lash;—cruel mementoes of our oneness are indelibly marked in our living flesh. We are one with you under the ban of prejudice and proscription—one with you under the slander of inferior—one with you in social and political disfranchisement. What you suffer, we suffer; what you endure, we endure. We are indissolubly united, and must fall or flourish together. . . .

We shall be the advocates of learning, from the very want of it, and shall most readily yield the deference due to men of education among us; but shall always bear in mind to accord most merit to those who have labored hardest, and overcome most, in the praiseworthy pursuit of knowledge, remembering "that the whole need not a physician, but they that are sick," and that "the strong ought to bear the infirmities of the weak."

Brethren, the first number of the paper is before you. It is dedicated to your cause. Through the kindness of our friends in England, we are in possession of an excellent printing press, types, and all other materials necessary for printing a paper. Shall this gift be blest to our good, or shall it result in our injury? It is for you to say. With your aid, cooperation and assistance, our enterprise will be entirely successful. We pledge ourselves that no effort on our part shall be wanting, and that no subscriber shall lose his subscription—"*The North Star* Shall live."

◆ FUGITIVE SLAVE ACT CH. 60, 9 STAT. 462 (1850)

For almost 15 years the provisions of the Missouri Compromise had quieted the debate over the expansion of slavery in the United States. However, following the annexation of Texas in 1845 and the ending of

This illustration depicts an escaped slave being returned to his owner in chains.

the war with Mexico in 1848, the question of expansion reignited tensions between pro-slavery forces and opponents to the institution.

With Southern members of Congress threatening to withdraw, a compromise was reached in 1850 between advocates of expression and their rivals. The compromise, a package of five statutes, attempted to address the major points of the sectional conflict. One of the provisions of the compromise, which was supported by many Southerners, was a strengthening of the existing federal fugitive slave law. On September 18, 1850, an act amending the 1793 fugitive slave statute was signed into law. Both the 1850 and the 1793 acts were finally repealed on June 28, 1864.

Section 5. That it shall be the duty of all marshals and deputy marshals to obey and execute all warrants and precepts issued under the provisions of this act, when to them directed; and should any marshal or deputy marshal refuse to receive such warrant, or other process, when tendered, or to use all proper means diligently to execute the same, he shall, on conviction thereof, be fined in the sum of one thousand dollars, to the use of such claimant,. . . and after arrest of such fugitive, by such marshal or his deputy, or whilst at any time in his custody under the provisions of this act, should such fugitive escape, whether with or without the assent of such marshal or his deputy, such marshal shall be liable, on his official bond, to be prosecuted for

the benefit of such claimant, for the full value of the service or labor of said fugitive in the State, Territory, or District whence he escaped: and the better to enable the said commissioners, when thus appointed, to execute their duties faithfully and efficiently, in conformity with the requirements of the Constitution of the United States and of this act, they are hereby authorized and empowered, within their counties respectively, to appoint,. . . any one or more suitable persons, from time to time, to execute all such warrants and other processes as may be issued by them in the lawful performance of their respective duties. . . .

Section 6. That when a person held to service or labor in any State or Territory of the United States, has heretofore or shall hereafter escape into another State or Territory of the United States, the person or persons to whom such service or labor may be due,. . . may pursue and reclaim such fugitive person, either by procuring a warrant from some one of the courts, judges, or commissioners aforesaid, of the proper circuit, district, or county, for the apprehension of such fugitive from service or labor, or by seizing and arresting such fugitive, where the same can be done without process, and by taking, or causing such person to be taken, forthwith before such court, judge, or commissioner, whose duty it shall be to hear and determine the case of such claimant in a summary manner; and upon satisfactory proof being made, by deposition of affidavit, in writing, to be taken and certified by such court, judge, or commissioner, or by other satisfactory testimony, duly taken and certified by some court,. . . and with proof, also by affidavit, of the identity of the person whose service or labor is claimed to be due as aforesaid, that the person so arrested does in fact owe service or labor to the person or persons claiming him or her, in the State or Territory from which such fugitive may have escaped as aforesaid, and that said person escaped, to make out and deliver to such claimant, his or her agent or attorney, a certificate setting forth the substantial facts as to the service or labor due from such fugitive to the claimant, and of his or her escape from the State or Territory in which he or she was arrested, with authority to such claimant,. . . to use such reasonable force and restraint as may be necessary, under the circumstances of the case, to take and remove such fugitive person back to the State or Territory whence he or she may have escaped as aforesaid.

Section 7. That any persons who shall knowingly and willingly obstruct, hinder, or prevent such claimant, his agent or attorney, or any person or persons lawfully assisting him, her, or them, from arresting such a fugitive from service or labor, either with or without process as aforesaid, or shall rescue, or attempt to rescue, such fugitive from service or labor, from the custody of such claimant,. . . or other person or persons lawfully assisting as aforesaid, when so arrested,. . . or shall aid, abet, or assist such person so owing service or labor as aforesaid, directly or indirectly, to escape from such claimant,. . . or shall harbor or conceal such fugitive, so as to prevent the discovery and arrest of such person, after notice or knowledge of the fact that such person was a fugitive from service or labor. . . shall, for either of said offenses, be subject to a fine not exceeding one thousand dollars, and imprisonment not exceeding six months. . . ; and shall moreover forfeit and pay, by way of civil damages to the party injured by such illegal conduct, the sum of one thousand dollars, for each fugitive so lost as aforesaid. . . .

Section 9. That, upon affidavit made by the claimant of such fugitive. . . that he has reason to apprehend that such fugitive will be rescued by force from his or their possession before he can be taken beyond the limits of the State in which the arrest is made, it shall be the duty of the officer making the arrest to retain such fugitive in his custody, and to remove him to the State whence he fled, and there to deliver him to said claimant, his agent, or attorney. And to this end, the officer aforesaid is hereby authorized and required to employ so many persons as he may deem necessary to overcome such force, and to retain them in his service so long as circumstances may require.

◆ ACT TO SUPPRESS THE SLAVE TRADE IN THE DISTRICT OF COLUMBIA CH. 63, 9 STAT. 467 (1850)

Although the importation of new slaves from Africa had been outlawed in 1808, the breeding and trading of slaves was still a big business; the Washington, Maryland, and Virginia area served as headquarters to some of the nation's largest traders.

The renewed debate in Congress over the expansion of slavery during the late 1840s led to what has been referred to as the Compromise of 1850—a package of five resolutions, one of which was the 1850 Fugitive Slave Act. Another of the provisions, a concession to the anti-slavery forces, was an act abolishing the slave trade in the District of Columbia.

Be it enacted,. . . That from and after January 1, 1851, it shall not be lawful to bring into the District of Columbia any slave whatsoever, for the purpose of being sold, or for the purpose of being placed in depot, to be subsequently transferred to any other State or place to be sold as merchandise. And if any slave shall be brought into the said District by its owner, or by the authority or consent of its owner, contrary to the

provisions of this act, such slave shall thereupon become liberated and free.

◆ NARRATIVE OF SOJOURNER TRUTH, "BOOK OF LIFE" (1851) (EXCERPT)

In 1851 Sojourner Truth initiated a lecturing tour in western New York, accompanied by several distinguished abolitionists. To speak against slavery during this period was both unpopular and unsafe. Abolitionist meetings were frequently disrupted by the pro-slavery forces, and their lives threatened. During such times, Sojourner Truth was known to fearlessly maintain her ground, and by her stately manner and well-timed remarks she would disperse the mob and restore order.

After several months in western New York, she traveled to Akron, Ohio, in order to speak before a less-than-receptive audience at a woman's rights convention. Fearing negative publicity through an association with Sojourner Truth and the abolitionist movement, the conventioneers pleaded with Frances D. Gage, presiding member of the convention, not to allow Truth to lecture. On the second day, as the

Sojourner Truth.

conventioneers struggled with the disruptive male clergy of various denominations, Truth slowly rose from her seat and moved towards the podium. Ignoring the requests of her fellow conventioneer, Gage introduced Truth to the audience. A profound hush fell across the audience as Sojourner Truth spoke these words:

Well, children, where there is so much racket there must be something out of kilter. I think that between the Negroes of the South and the women of the North all talking about rights, the white women will be in a fix pretty soon. But what's all this talk about? That man over there says that women need to be helped into carriages and lifted over ditches, and to have the best place everywhere. Nobody ever helps me into carriages, or over mud puddles, or gives me any best place [and raising herself to her full height and her voice to a pitch like rolling thunder, she asked], and ar'n't I a woman? Look at me! Look at my arm! [and she bared her right arm to the shoulder, showing her tremendous muscular power.] I have plowed, and planted, and gathered into barns, and no man could head me—and ar'n't I a woman? I could work as much and eat as much as a man (when I could get it), and bear de lash as well—and ar'n't I a woman? I have borne thirteen children and seen most all sold off into slavery, and when I cried out with a mother's grief, none but Jesus heard—and ar'n't I a woman? [The cheering was long and loud.]

◆ FREDERICK DOUGLASS'S INDEPENDENCE DAY ADDRESS (1852)

In 1852, over three million African Americans were being held as slaves in the United States. Knowing this and understanding the irony implicit in the notion of a holiday commemorating the independence of the United States, Frederick Douglass lost little time in laying bare the contradiction inherent in allowing slavery to exist within a society professedly dedicated to individual freedom.

Fellow Citizens

Pardon me, and allow me to ask, why am I called upon to speak here today? What have I or those I represent to do with your national independence? Are the great principles of political freedom and of natural justice, embodied in that Declaration of Independence, extended to us? And am I, therefore, called upon to bring our humble offering to the national altar, and to confess the benefits, and express devout gratitude for the blessings resulting from your independence to us?

Would to God, both for your sakes and ours, that an affirmative answer could be truthfully returned to these questions. Then would my task be light, and my burden easy and delightful. For who is there so cold that a nation's sympathy could not warm him? Who so obdurate and dead to the claims of gratitude, that would not thankfully acknowledge such priceless benefits? Who so stolid and selfish that would not give his voice to swell the hallelujahs of a nation's jubilee, when the chains of servitude had been torn from his limbs? I am not that man. . .

I am not included within the pale of this glorious anniversary! Your high independence only reveals the immeasurable distance between us. The blessings in which you this day rejoice are not enjoyed in common. The rich inheritance of justice, liberty, prosperity, and independence bequeathed by your fathers is shared by you, not by me. The sunlight that brought life and healing to you has brought stripes and death to me. This Fourth of July is *yours*, not *mine*. You may rejoice, I must mourn. To drag a man in fetters into the grand illuminated temple of liberty, and call upon him to join you in joyous anthems, were inhuman mockery and sacrilegious irony. Do you mean, citizens, to mock me, by asking me to speak today?. . .

Fellow citizens, above your national, tumultuous joy, I hear the mournful wail of millions, whose chains, heavy and grievous yesterday, are today rendered more intolerable by the jubilant shouts that reach them. If I do forget, if I do not remember those bleeding children of sorrow this day, "may my right hand forget her cunning, and may my tongue cleave to the roof of my mouth!" To forget them, to pass lightly over their wrongs, and to chime in with the popular theme, would be treason most scandalous and shocking, and would make me a reproach before God and the world. My subject, then, fellow citizens, is "American Slavery." I shall see this day and its popular characteristics from the slave's point of view. Standing here, identified with the American bondman, making his wrongs mine, I do not hesitate to declare, with all my soul, that the character and conduct of this nation never looked blacker to me than on this Fourth of July. Whether we turn to the declarations of the past, or to the professions of the present, the conduct of the nation seems equally hideous and revolting. America is false to the past, false to the present, and solemnly binds herself to be false to the future. Standing with God and the crushed and bleeding slave on this occasion, I will, in the name of humanity, which is outraged, in the name of Liberty, which is fettered, in the name of the Constitution and the Bible, which are disregarded and trampled upon, dare to call in question and to denounce, with all the emphasis I can command, everything that serves to perpetuate slavery—the great sin and shame of America! "I will not equivocate; I will not excuse"; I will use the severest language I can command, and yet not one word shall escape me that any man, whose judgment is not blinded by prejudice, or who is not at heart a slave-holder, shall not confess to be right and just.

But I fancy I hear some of my audience say it is just in this circumstances that you and your brother Abolitionists fail to make a favorable impression on the public mind. Would you argue more and denounce less, would you persuade more and rebuke less, your cause would be much more likely to succeed. But, I submit, where all is plain there is nothing to be argued. What point in the anti-slavery creed would you have me argue? On what branch of the subject do the people of this country need light? Must I undertake to prove that the slave is a man? That point is conceded already. Nobody doubts it. The slave-holders themselves acknowledge it in the enactment of laws for their government. They acknowledge it when they punish disobedience on the part of the slave. There are seventy-two crimes in the State of Virginia, which, if committed by a black man (no matter how ignorant he be), subject him to the punishment of death, while only two of these same crimes will subject a white man to like punishment. What is this but the acknowledgment that the slave is a moral, intellectual, and responsible being? The manhood of the slave is conceded. It is admitted in the fact that the Southern statute-books are covered with enactments, forbidding, under severe fines and penalties, the teaching of the slave to read and write. When you can point to any such laws in reference to the beasts of the field, then I may consent to argue the manhood of the slave. When the dogs in your streets, when the fowls of the air, when the cattle on your hills, when the fish of the sea, and the reptiles that crawl, shall be unable to distinguish the slave from a brute, then I will argue with you that the slave is a man!

For the present it is enough to affirm the equal manhood of the Negro race. Is it not astonishing that, while we are plowing, planting, and reaping, using all kinds of mechanical tools, erecting houses, constructing bridges, building ships, working in metals of brass, iron, copper, silver, and gold; that while we are reading, writing, and ciphering, acting as clerks, merchants, and secretaries, having among us lawyers, doctors, ministers, poets, authors, editors, orators, and teachers; that while we are engaged in all the enterprises common to other men—digging gold in California, capturing the whale in the Pacific, feeding sheep and cattle on the hillside, living, moving, acting, thinking, planning, living in families as husbands, wives, and children, and above all, confessing and worshipping the Christian God, and looking hopefully for life and immortality beyond the grave—we are called upon to prove that we are men?

Would you have me argue that man is entitled to liberty? That he is the rightful owner of his own body? You have already declared it. Must I argue the wrongfulness of slavery? Is that a question for republicans? Is it to be settled by the rules of logic and argumentation, as a matter beset with great difficulty, involving a doubtful application of the principle of justice, hard to understand? How should I look today in the presence of Americans, dividing and subdividing a discourse, to show that men have a natural right to freedom, speaking of it relatively and positively, negatively and affirmatively? To do so would be to make myself ridiculous, and to offer an insult to your understanding. There is not a man beneath the canopy of heaven who does not know that slavery is wrong *for him.*

What! Am I to argue that it is wrong to make men brutes, to rob them of their liberty, to work them without wages, to keep them ignorant of their relations to their fellow men, to beat them with sticks, to flay their flesh with the lash, to load their limbs with irons, to hunt them with dogs, to sell them at auction, to sunder their families, to knock out their teeth, to burn their flesh, to starve them into obedience and submission to their masters? Must I argue that a system thus marked with blood and stained with pollution is wrong? No; I will not. I have better employment for my time and strength than such arguments would imply.

What, then, remains to be argued? Is it that slavery is not divine; that God did not establish it; that our doctors of divinity are mistaken? There is blasphemy in the thought. That which is inhuman cannot be divine. Who can reason on such a proposition? They that can, may; I cannot. The time for such argument is past.

At a time like this, scorching irony, not convincing argument, is needed. Oh! had I the ability, and could I reach the nation's ear, I would today pour out a fiery stream of biting ridicule, blasting reproach, withering sarcasm, and stern rebuke. For it is not light that is needed, but fire; it is not the gentle shower, but thunder. We need the storm, the whirlwind, and the earthquake. The feeling of the nation must be quickened; the conscience of the nation must be startled; the hypocrisy of the nation must be exposed; and its crimes against God and man must be denounced.

What to the American slave is your Fourth of July? I answer, a day that reveals to him more than all other days of the year, the gross injustice and cruelty to which he is the constant victim. To him your celebration is a sham; your boasted liberty an unholy license; your national greatness, swelling vanity; your sounds of rejoicing are empty and heartless; your denunciation of tyrants, brass-fronted impudence; your shouts of liberty and equality, hollow mockery; your prayers and hymns, your sermons and thanksgivings, with all your religious parade and solemnity, are to him mere bombast, fraud, deception, impiety, and hypocrisy—a thin veil to cover up crimes which would disgrace a nation of savages. There is not a nation of the earth guilty of practices more shocking and bloody than are the people of these United States at this very hour.

Go where you may, search where you will, roam through all the monarchies and despotisms of the Old World, travel through South America, search out every abuse and when you have found the last, lay your facts by the side of the every-day practices of this nation, and you will say with me that, for revolting barbarity and shameless hypocrisy, America reigns without a rival.

♦ *DRED SCOTT V. SANDFORD* 19 HOWARD 393 (1857)

In 1835, Dred Scott, born a slave in Virginia, became the property of John Emerson, an Army doctor, in the slave state of Missouri. From there, he was taken into the free state of Illinois and later to the free territory of Minnesota. In 1847, Scott instituted suit in the circuit court of St. Louis County, Missouri, arguing that he should be given his freedom by virtue of his having resided on free soil. After nine years, his case was certified to the U.S. Supreme Court, where five of the nine justices were Southerners.

Under the terms of the Missouri Compromise, Missouri was allowed to join the Union with a slave population of almost 10,000; Maine was admitted as a free state. However, the compromise also prohibited the expansion of slavery into any part of the Louisiana Territory north of Latitude 36° 30'. It was here, into Illinois and the territory of Wisconsin, that Dred Scott's master brought him, and in 1846 Scott sued his master for his freedom.

After numerous delays, trials, and retrials, the case reached the U.S. Supreme Court in 1856. Hearing this case, the Court was not only faced with the question as to whether Scott was a free man, as a result of his sojourn in a free territory, but it also had to consider whether Congress had the authority under the Constitution to outlaw slavery in the territories. Although each of the nine justices delivered a separate opinion, the opinion of Chief Justice Roger Brooke Taney has been generally accepted as the Court's ruling on the matter.

In delivering his opinion, Chief Justice Roger Brooke Taney declared that, by virtue of both the Declaration of Independence and the Constitution, African Americans could not be regarded as citizens of the United States. Moreover, the Court could not deprive slaveholders of their right to take slaves into any part of the Union, North or South. In effect, therefore, the Missouri Compromise, as well as other anti-slavery legislation, was declared to be unconstitutional.

The question is simply this: Can a negro, whose ancestors were imported into this country and sold as slaves, become a member of the political community formed and brought into existence by the constitution of the United States, and as such become entitled to all the rights, and privileges, and immunities, guaranteed by that instrument to the citizen?. . . .

The words "people of the United States" and "citizens" are synonymous terms, and mean the same thing. They both describe the political body who, according to our republican institutions, form the sovereignty, and who hold the power and conduct the government through their representatives. They are what we familiarly call the "sovereign people," and every citizen is one of this people, and a constituent member of this sovereignty. The question before us is, whether the class of persons described in the plea in abatement compose a portion of this people, and are constituent members of this sovereignty? We think they are not, and that they are not included, and were not intended to be included, under the word "citizens" in the constitution, and can therefore claim none of the rights and privileges which that instrument provides for and secures to citizens of the United States. On the contrary, they were at that time considered as a subordinate and inferior class of beings, who had been subjugated by the dominant race, and, whether emancipated or not, yet remained subject to their authority, and had no rights or privileges. . . .

It is not the province of the court to decide upon the justice or injustice, the policy or impolicy, of these laws. The decision of that question belonged to the political or law-making power; to those who formed the sovereignty and framed the constitution. The duty of the court is to interpret the instrument they have framed, with the best lights we can obtain on the subject, and to administer it as we find it, according to its true intent and meaning when it was adopted.

In discussing this question, we must not confound the rights of citizenship which a State may confer within its own limits, and the rights of citizenship as member of the Union. It does not by any means follow, because he has all the rights and privileges of a citizen of a State, that he must be a citizen of the United States. He may have all of the rights and privileges of the citizen of a State, and yet not be entitled to the rights and privileges of a citizen in any other State. For, previous to the adoption of the constitution of the United States, every State had the undoubted right to confer on whomsoever it pleased the character of citizen, and to endow him with all its rights. But this character of course was confined to the boundaries of the State, and gave him no rights or privileges in other States beyond those secured to him by the laws of nations and the comity of States. Nor have the several States surrendered the power of conferring these rights and privileges by adopting the constitution of United States. . . .

It is very clear, therefore, that no State can, by any act or law of its own, passed since the adoption of the constitution, introduce a new member into the political community created by the constitution of the United States. It cannot make him a member of this community by making him a member of its own. And for the same reason it cannot introduce any person, or description of persons, who were not intended to be embraced in this new political family, which the constitution brought into existence, but were intended to be excluded from it.

The question then arises, whether the provisions of the constitution, in relation to the personal rights and privileges to which the citizen of a State should be entitled, embraced the negro African race, at that time in this country, or who might afterwards be imported, who had then or should afterwards be made free in any State; and to put it in the power of a single State to make him a citizen of the United States, and endue him with the full rights of citizenship in every other State without consent? Does the constitution of the United States act upon him whenever he shall be made free under the laws of a State, and raised there to the rank of a citizen, and immediately clothe him with all the privileges of a citizen in every other State, and in its own courts?

The court thinks the affirmative of these propositions cannot be maintained. And if it cannot, the plaintiff in error could not be a citizen of the State of Missouri, within the meaning of the constitution of the United States, and, consequently, was not entitled to sue in its courts.

It is true, every person, and every class and description of persons, who were at the time of the adoption of the constitution recognized as citizens in the several States, became also citizens of this new political body; but none other; it was formed by them, and for them and their posterity, but for no one else. And the personal rights and privileges guaranteed to citizens of this new sovereignty were intended to embrace those only who were then members of the several State communities, or who should afterwards by birthright or otherwise become members, according to the provisions of the constitution and the principles on which it was founded. . . .

In the opinion of the court, the legislation and histories of the times, and the language used in the declaration of independence, show, that neither the class of persons who had been imported as slaves, nor their descendants, whether they had become free or not, were then acknowledged as a part of the people, nor intended to be included in the general words used in that memorable instrument. . . .

. . . The government of the United States had no right to interfere for any other purpose but that protecting the rights of the owner, leaving it altogether with the several States to deal with this race, whether emancipated or not, as each State may think justice, humanity, and the interests and safety of society, require. . . .

The act of Congress, upon which the plaintiff relies, declares that slavery and involuntary servitude, except as a punishment for crime, shall be forever prohibited in all that part of the territory ceded by France, under the name of Louisiana, which lies north of thirty-six degrees thirty minutes north latitude and not included within the limits of Missouri. And the difficulty which meets us at the threshold of this part of the inquiry is whether Congress was authorized to pass this law under any of the powers granted to it by the Constitution; for, if the authority is not given by that instrument, it is the duty of this Court to declare it void and inoperative and incapable of conferring freedom upon anyone who is held as a slave under the laws of any one of the states. . . .

We do not mean . . . to question the power of Congress in this respect. The power to expand the territory of the United States by the admission of new states is plainly given; and in the construction of this power by all the departments of the government, it has been held to authorize the acquisition of territory, not fit for admission at the time, but to be admitted as soon as its population and situation would entitle it to admission. It is acquired to become a state and not to be held as a colony and governed by Congress with absolute Authority; and, as the propriety of admitting a new state is committed to the sound discretion of Congress, the power to acquire territory for that purpose, to be held by the United States until it is in a suitable condition to become a state upon an equal footing with the other states, must rest upon the same discretion. . . .

But the power of Congress over the person or property of a citizen can never be a mere discretionary power under our Constitution and form of government. The powers of the government and the rights and privileges of the citizen are regulated and plainly defined by the Constitution itself. . . .

These powers, and others, in relation to rights of person, which it is not necessary here to enumerate, are, in express and positive terms, denied to the general government; and the rights of private property have been guarded with equal care. Thus the rights of property are united with the rights of person and placed on the same ground by the Fifth Amendment to the Constitution, which provides that no person shall be deprived of life, liberty, and property without due process of law. And an act of Congress which deprives a citizen of the United States of his liberty of property, without due process of law, merely because he came himself or brought his property into a particular territory of the United States, and who had committed no offense against the law, could hardly be dignified with the name of due process of law. . . .

It seems, however, to be supposed that there is a difference between property in a slave and other property and that different rules may be applied to it in expounding Constitution of the United States. And the laws and usages of nations, and the writings of eminent jurists upon the relation of master and slave and their mutual rights and duties, and the powers which governments may exercise over it, have been dwelt upon in the argument.

But, in considering the question before us, it must be borne in mind that there is no law of nations standing between the people of the United States and their government and interfering with their relation to each other. The powers of the government and the rights of the citizen under it are positive and practical regulations plainly written down. The people of the United States have delegated to it certain enumerated powers and forbidden it to exercise others. It has no power over the person of property of a citizen but what the citizens of the United States have granted. And no laws or usages of other nations, or reasoning of statesmen of jurists upon the relations of master and slave, can enlarge the powers of the government or take from the citizens the rights they have reserved. And if the Constitution recognizes the right of property of the master in a slave, and makes no distinction between that description of property and other property owned by a citizen, no tribunal, acting under the authority of the United States, whether it be legislative, executive, or judicial, has a right to draw such a distinction or deny to it the benefit of the provisions and guaranties which have been provided for the protection of private property against the encroachments of the government.

Now, as we have already said in an earlier part of this opinion, upon a different point, the right of property in a slave is distinctly and expressly affirmed in the Constitution. The right to traffic in it, like an ordinary article of merchandise and property, was guaranteed to the citizens of the United States, in every state that might desire it, for twenty years. And the government in express terms is pledged to protect it in all future time if the slave escapes from his owner. That is done in plain words—too plain to be misunderstood. And no word can be found in the Constitution which gives Congress a greater power over slave property or which entitles property of that kind to less protection than property of any other description. The only power conferred is the power coupled with the duty of guarding and protecting the owner in his rights.

Upon these considerations it is the opinion of the court that the act of Congress which prohibited a citizen from holding and owning property of this kind in the territory of the United States north of the line therein mentioned is not warranted by the Constitution and is therefore void; and that neither Dred Scott himself, nor any of his family, were made free by being carried into this territory; even if they had been carried there by the owner with the intention of becoming a permanent resident. . . .

◆ THE EMANCIPATION PROCLAMATION NO. 17, 12 STAT. 1268 (1863)

In an attempt to bring an end to the Civil War, President Abraham Lincoln, acting on his authority as commander-in-chief, on September 22, 1862 issued a warning that slavery would be abolished in any state that continued to rebel. With the war still raging, Lincoln issued the Emancipation Proclamation on January 1, 1863, freeing slaves in those states that had seceded from the Union. The proclamation did not apply, however, to those areas occupied by Union forces—there remained some 800,000 slaves unaffected by the provisions of the document.

By the President of the United States of America: A Proclamation

Whereas on the 22d day of September, A.D. 1862, a proclamation was issued by the President of the United States, containing, among other things, the following, to wit:

"That on the 1st day of January, A.D. 1863, all persons held as slaves within any State or designated part of a State the people whereof shall then be in rebellion against the United States shall be then, henceforward, and forever free; and the executive government of the United States, including the military and naval authority thereof, will recognize and maintain the freedom of such persons and will do no act or acts to repress such persons, or any of them, in any efforts they may make for their actual freedom."

President Abraham Lincoln seated with several other men during the first reading of the Emancipation Proclamation.

"That the executive will on the 1st day of January aforesaid, by proclamation, designated the States and parts of States, if any, which the people thereof, respectively, shall then be in rebellion against the United States; and the fact that any State or the people thereof shall on that day be in good faith represented in the Congress of the United States by members chosen thereto at elections wherein a majority of the qualified voters of such States shall have participated shall, in the absence of strong countervailing testimony, be deemed conclusive evidence that such State and the people thereof are not then in rebellion against the United States.":

Now, therefore, I, Abraham Lincoln, President of the United States, by virtue of the power in me vested as Commander-in-Chief of the Army and Navy of the United States in time of actual armed rebellion against the authority and government of the United States, and as a fit and necessary war measure for suppressing said rebellion, do, on this 1st day of January, A.D. 1863, and in accordance with my purpose so to do, publicly proclaimed for the full period of one hundred days from the first day above mentioned, order and designate as the States and parts of States wherein the people thereof, respectively, are this day in rebellion against the United States the following, to wit:

Arkansas, Texas, Louisiana (except the parishes of St. Bernard, Plaquemines, Jefferson, St. John, St. Charles, St. James, Ascension, Assumption, Terrebonne, Lafourche, St. Mary, St. Marti, and Orleans, including the city of New Orleans), Mississippi, Alabama, Florida, Georgia, South Carolina, North Carolina, and Virginia (except the forty-eight counties designated as West Virginia, and also the counties of Berkeley, Accomac, Northampton, Elizabeth City, York, Princess Anne, and Northfolk, including the cities of Norfolk and Portsmouth), and which excepted parts are for the present left precisely as if this proclamation were not issued.

And by virtue of the power and for the purpose aforesaid, I do order and declare that all persons held as slaves within said designated States and parts of States are, and henceforward shall be, free; and that the Executive Government of the United States, including the military and naval authorities thereof, will recognize and maintain the freedom of said persons.

And I hereby enjoin upon the people so declared to be free to abstain from all violence, unless in necessary self-defense; and I recommend to them that, in all cases when allowed, they labor faithfully for reasonable wages.

And I further declare and make known that such persons of suitable condition will be received into the armed service of the United States to garrison forts, positions, stations, and other places, and to man vessels of all sorts in said service.

And upon this act, sincerely believed to be an act of justice, warranted by the Constitution upon military necessity, I invoke the considerate judgment of mankind and the gracious favor of Almighty God.

◆ FREEDMEN'S BUREAU ACT CH. 90, 13 STAT. 507 (1865)

On March 3, 1865, Congress passed legislation designed to provide basic health and educational services to former slaves and to administer abandoned land in the South. Under the act, the Bureau of Refugees, Freedmen and Abandoned Lands, commonly referred to as the Freedmen's Bureau, was created.

An Act to Establish a Bureau for the Relief of Freedmen and Refugees

Be it enacted, That there is hereby established in the War Department, to continue during the present war of rebellion, and for one year thereafter, a bureau of refugees, freedmen, and abandoned lands, to which shall be committed, as hereinafter provided, the supervision and management of all abandoned lands and the control of all subjects relating to refugees and freedmen from rebel states, or from any district of country within the territory embraced in the operations of the army, under such rules and regulations as may be prescribed by the head of the bureau and approved by the President. The said bureau shall be under the management and control of a commissioner to be appointed by the President, by and with the advice and consent of the Senate.

Section 2. That the Secretary of War may direct such issue of provisions, clothing, and fuel, as he may deem needful for the immediate and temporary shelter and supply of destitute and suffering refugees and freedmen and their wives and children, under such rules and regulations as he may direct.

Section 3. That the President may, by and with the advice and consent of the Senate, appoint an assistant commissioner for each of the states declared to be in insurrection, not exceeding ten in number, who shall, under the direction of the commissioner, aid in the execution of the provisions of this act.... And any military officer may be detailed and assigned to duty under this act without increase of pay of allowances....

Section 4. That the commissioner, under the direction of the President, shall have authority to set apart, for the use of loyal refugees and freedmen, such tracts of land within the insurrectionary states as shall have been abandoned, or to which the United States shall have acquired title by confiscation or sale, or otherwise, and to every male citizen, whether refugee or freedman, as aforesaid, there shall be assigned not more than forty acres of such land, and the person to whom it was so assigned shall be protected in the use and enjoyment of the land for the term of three years at an annual rent not exceeding six per centum upon the value of such land, as it was appraised by the state authorities in the year eighteen hundred and sixty, for the purpose of taxation, and in case no such appraisal can be found, then the rental shall be based upon the estimated value of the land in said year, to be ascertained in such manner as the commissioner may by regulation prescribe. At the end of said term, or at any time during said term, the occupants of any parcels so assigned may purchase the land and receive such title thereto as the United States can convey, upon paying therefor the value of the land, as ascertained and fixed for the purpose of determining the annual rent aforesaid....

◆ AMENDMENT THIRTEEN TO THE UNITED STATES CONSTITUTION (1865)

Ratified December 18, 1865, the Thirteenth Amendment formally abolished slavery within the United States.

Section 1. Neither slavery nor involuntary servitude, except as a punishment for crime whereof the party shall have been duly convicted, shall exist within the United States, or any place subject to their jurisdiction.

Section 2. Congress shall have power to enforce this article by appropriate legislation.

◆ BLACK CODES OF MISSISSIPPI (1865)

Following emancipation many states sought to impose restrictions on African Americans to prevent them from enjoying equal social status with whites. These restrictions were designed to not only hold African Americans in a subordinate condition, but to impose restrictions upon them not unlike those which prevailed before the Civil War. Black codes imposed heavy penalties for "vagrancy," "insulting gestures," curfew violations, and "seditious speeches." In November of 1865, Mississippi was the first state to enact such laws.

An Act to Confer Civil Rights on Freedmen, and for other Purposes

Section 1. All freedmen, free negroes and mulattoes may sue and be sued, implead and be impleaded, in all the courts of law and equity of this State, and may acquire personal property, and choses in action, by descent or purchase, and may dispose of the same in the same manner and to the same extent that white persons may: Provided, That the provisions of this section shall not be so construed as to allow any freedman, free negro or mulatto to rent or lease any lands or tenements except in incorporated cities or towns, in which places the corporate authorities shall control the same.

Section 2. All freedmen, free negroes and mulattoes may intermarry with each other, in the same manner and under the same regulations that are provided by law for white persons: Provided, that the clerk of probate shall keep separate records of the same.

Section 3. All freedmen, free negroes or mulattoes who do now and have herebefore lived and cohabited together as husband and wife shall be taken and held in law as legally married, and the issue shall be taken and held as legitimate for all purposes; and it shall not be lawful for any freedman, free negro or mulatto to intermarry with any white person; nor for any person to intermarry with any freedman, free negro or mulatto; and any person who shall so intermarry shall be deemed guilty of felony, and on conviction thereof shall be confined in the State penitentiary for life; and those shall be deemed freedmen, free negroes and mulattoes who are of pure negro blood, and those descended from a negro to the third generation, inclusive, though one ancestor in each generation may have been a white person.

Section 4. In addition to cases in which freedmen, free negroes and mulattoes are now by law competent witnesses, freedmen, free negroes or mulattoes shall be competent in civil cases, when a party or parties to the suit, either plaintiff or plaintiffs, defendant or defendants; also in cases where freedmen, free negroes and mulattoes is or are either plaintiff or plaintiffs, defendant or defendants. They shall also be competent witnesses in all criminal prosecutions where the crime charged is alleged to have been committed by a white person upon or against the person or property of a freedman, free negro or mulatto: Provided, that in all cases said witnesses shall be examined in open court, on the stand; except, however, they may be examined before the grand jury, and shall in all cases be subject to the rules and tests of the common law as to competency and credibility.

Section 5. Every freedman, free negro and mulatto shall, on the second Monday of January, one thousand eight hundred and sixty-six, and annually thereafter, have a lawful home or employment, and shall have written evidence thereof as follows, to wit: if living in any incorporated city, town, or village, a license from the mayor thereof; and if living outside of an incorporated city, town, or village, from the member of the board of police of his beat, authorizing him or her to do irregular and job work; or a written contract, as provided in Section 6 in this act; which license may be revoked for cause at any time by the authority granting the same.

Section 6. All contracts for labor made with freedmen, free negroes and mulattoes for a longer period than one month shall be in writing, and a duplicate, attested and read to said freedman, free negro or mulatto by a beat, city or county officer, or two disinterested white persons of the county in which the labor is to be performed, of which each party shall have one: and said contracts shall be taken and held as entire contracts, and if the laborer shall quit the service of the employer before the expiration of his term of service, without good cause, he shall forfeit his wages for that year up to the time of quitting.

Section 7. Every civil officer shall, and every person may, arrest and carry back to his or her legal employer any freedman, free negro, or mulatto who shall have quit the service of his or her employer before the expiration of his or her term of service without good cause; and said officer and person shall be entitled to receive for arresting and carrying back every deserting employee aforesaid the sum of five dollars, and ten cents per mile from the place of arrest to the place of delivery; and the same shall be paid by the employer, and held as a set off for so much against the wages of said deserting employee: Provided, that said arrested party, after being so returned, may appeal to the justice of the peace or member of the board of police of the county, who, on notice to the alleged employer, shall try summarily whether said appellant is legally employed by the alleged employer, and has good cause to quit said employer. Either party shall have the right of appeal to the county court, pending which the alleged deserter shall be remanded to the alleged employer or otherwise disposed of, as shall be right and just; and the decision of the county court shall be final.

Section 8. Upon affidavit made by the employer of any freedman, free negro or mulatto, or other credible person, before any justice of the peace or member of the board of police, that any freedman, free negro or mulatto legally employed by said employer has illegally deserted said employment, such justice of the peace or member of the board of police issue his warrant or warrants, returnable before himself or other such officer, to any sheriff, constable or special deputy, commanding him to arrest said deserter, and return him or her to said employer, and the like proceedings shall be had as provided in the preceding section; and it shall be lawful for any officer to whom such warrant shall be directed to execute said warrant in any county in this State; and that said warrant may be transmitted without endorsement to any like officer of another county, to be executed and returned as aforesaid; and the said employer shall pay the costs of said warrants and arrest and return, which shall be set off for so much against the wages of said deserter.

Section 9. If any person shall persuade or attempt to persuade, entice, or cause any freedman, free negro or mulatto to desert from the legal employment of any person before the expiration of his or her term of service, or shall knowingly employ any such deserting freedman, free negro or mulatto, or shall knowingly give or sell to any such deserting freedman, free negro or mulatto, any food, raiment, or other thing, he or she shall be guilty of a misdemeanor, and, upon conviction, shall be fined not less than twenty-five dollars and not more than two hundred dollars and costs; and if the said fine and costs shall not be immediately paid, the court shall sentence said convict to not exceeding two months imprisonment in the county jail, and he or she shall moreover be liable to the party injured in damages: Provided, if any person shall, or shall attempt to, persuade, entice, or cause any freedman, free negro or mulatto to desert from any legal employment of any person, with the view to employ said freedman, free negro or mulatto without the limits of this State, such costs; and if said fine and costs shall not be immediately paid, the court shall sentence said convict to not exceeding six months imprisonment in the county jail.

Section 10. It shall be lawful for any freedman, free negro, or mulatto, to charge any white person, freedman, free negro or mulatto by affidavit, with any criminal offense against his or her person or property, and upon such affidavit the proper process shall be issued and executed as if said affidavit was made by a white person, and it shall be lawful for any freedman, free negro, or mulatto, in any action, suit or controversy pending, or about to be instituted in any court of law equity in this State, to make all needful and lawful affidavits as shall be necessary for the institution, prosecution or defense of such suit or controversy.

Section 11. The penal laws of this state, in all cases not otherwise specially provided for, shall apply and extend to all freedmen, free negroes and mulattoes. . . .

An Act to Regulate the Relation of Master and Apprentice, as Relates to Freedmen, Free Negroes, and Mulattoes

Section 1. It shall be the duty of all sheriffs, justices of the peace, and other civil officers of the several counties in this State, to report to the probate courts of their respective counties semiannually, at the January and July terms of said courts, all freedmen, free negroes, and mulattoes, under the age of eighteen, in their respective counties, beats, or districts, who are orphans, or whose parent or parents have not the means or who refuse to provide for and support said minors; and thereupon it shall be the duty of said probate court to order the clerk of said court to apprentice said minors to some competent and suitable person on such terms as the court may direct, having a particular care to the interest of said minor: Provided, that the former owner of said minors shall have the preference when, in the opinion of the court, he or she shall be a suitable person for that purpose.

Section 2. The said court shall be fully satisfied that the person or persons to whom said minor shall be apprenticed shall be a suitable person to have the charge and care of said minor, and fully to protect the interest of said minor. The said court shall require the said master or mistress to execute bond and security, payable to the State of Mississippi, conditioned that he or she shall furnish said minor with sufficient food and clothing; to treat said minor humanely; furnish medical attention in case of sickness; teach, or cause to be taught, him or her to read and write, if under fifteen years old, and will conform to any law that may be hereafter passed for the regulation of the duties and relation of master and apprentice: Provided, that said apprentice shall be bound by indenture, in case of males, until they are twenty-one years old, and in case of females until they are eighteen years old.

Section 3. In the management and control of said apprentices, said master or mistress shall have the power to inflict such moderate corporeal chastisement as a father or guardian is allowed to infliction on his or her child or ward at common law: Provided, that in no case shall cruel or inhuman punishment be inflicted.

Section 4. If any apprentice shall leave the employment of his or her master or mistress, without his or her consent, said master or mistress may pursue and recapture said apprentice, and bring him or her before any justice of the peace of the county, whose duty it shall be to remand said apprentice to the service of his or her master or mistress; and in the event of a refusal on the part of said apprentice so to return, then said justice shall commit said apprentice to the jail of said county, on failure to give bond, to the next term of the county court; and it shall be the duty of said court at the first term thereafter to investigate said case, and if the court shall be of opinion that said apprentice left the employment of his or her master or mistress without good cause, to order him or her to be punished, as provided for the punishment of hired freedmen, as may be from time to time provided for by law for desertion, until he or she shall agree to return to the service of his or her master or mistress: Provided, that the court may grant continuances as in other cases: And provided further, that if the court shall believe that said apprentice had good cause to quit his said master or mistress, the court shall discharge said apprentice from said indenture, and also enter a judgment against the master or mistress for not more than one hundred dollars, for the use and benefit of said apprentice, to be collected on execution as in other cases.

Section 5. If any person entice away any apprentice from his or her master or mistress, or shall knowingly employ an apprentice, or furnish him or her food or clothing without the written consent of his or her master or mistress, or shall sell or give said apprentice spirits without such consent, said person so offending shall be guilty of a misdemeanor, and shall, upon conviction there of before the county court, be punished as provided for the punishment of persons enticing from their employer hired freedmen, free negroes or mulattoes.

Section 6. It shall be the duty of all civil officers of their respective counties to report any minors within their respective counties to said probate court who are subject to be apprenticed under the provisions of this act, from time to time as the facts may come to their knowledge, and it shall be the duty of said court from time to time as said minors shall be reported to them, or otherwise come to their knowledge, to apprentice said minors as hereinbefore provided.

Section 9. It shall be lawful for any freedman, free negro, or mulatto, having a minor child or children, to apprentice the said minor child or children, as provided for by this act.

Section 10. In all cases where the age of the freedman, free negro, or mulatto cannot be ascertained by record testimony, the judge of the county court shall fix the age. . . .

An Act to Amend the Vagrant Laws of the State

Section 1. All rogues and vagabonds, idle and dissipated persons, beggars, jugglers, or persons practicing unlawful games or plays, runaways, common drunkards, common night-walkers, pilferers, lewd, wanton, or lascivious persons, in speech or behavior, common railers and brawlers, persons who neglect their calling or employment, misspend what they earn, or do not provide for the support of themselves or their families, or dependents, and all other idle and disorderly persons, including all who neglect all lawful business, habitually misspend their time by frequenting houses of ill-fame, gaming-houses, or tippling shops, shall be deemed and considered vagrants, under the provisions of this act, and upon conviction thereof shall be fined not exceeding one hundred dollars, with all accruing costs, and be imprisoned, at the discretion of the court, not exceeding ten days.

Section 2. All freedmen, free negroes and mulattoes in this State, over the age of eighteen years, found on the second Monday in January, 1866, or thereafter, with no lawful employment or business, or found unlawfully assembling themselves together, either in the day or night time, and all white persons assembling themselves with freedmen, free negroes or mulattoes, or usually associating with freedmen, free negroes or mulattoes, on terms of equality, or living in adultery or fornication with a freed woman, freed negro or mulatto, shall be deemed vagrants, and on conviction thereof shall be fined in a sum not exceeding, in the case of a freedman, free negro or mulatto, fifty dollars, and a white man two hundred dollars, and imprisonment at the discretion of the court, the free negro not exceeding ten days, and the white man not exceeding six months.

Section 3. All justices of the peace, mayors, and aldermen of incorporated towns, counties, and cities of the several counties in this State shall have jurisdiction to try all questions of vagrancy in their respective towns, counties, and cities, and it is hereby made their duty, whenever they shall ascertain that any person or persons in their respective towns, and counties and cities are violating any of the provisions of this act, to have said party or parties arrested, and brought before them, and immediately investigate said charge, and, on conviction, punish said party or parties, as provided for herein. And it is hereby made the duty of all sheriffs, constables, town constables, and all such like officers, and city marshals, to report to some officer having jurisdiction all violations of any of the provisions of this act, and in case any officer shall fail or neglect any duty herein it shall be the duty of the county court to fine said officer, upon conviction, not exceeding one hundred dollars, to be paid into the county treasury for county purposes.

Section 4. Keepers of gaming houses, houses of prostitution, prostitutes, public or private, and all persons who derive their chief support in the employments that militate against good morals, or against law, shall be deemed and held to be vagrants.

Section 5. All fines and forfeitures collected by the provisions of this act shall be paid into the county treasury for general county purposes, and in case of any freedman, free negro or mulatto shall fail for five days after the imposition of any or forfeiture upon him or her for violation of any of the provisions of this act to pay the same, that it shall be, and is hereby, made the duty of the sheriff of the proper county to hire out said freedman, free negro or mulatto, to any person who will, for the shortest period of service, pay said fine and forfeiture and all costs: Provided, a preference shall be given to the employer, if there be one, in which case the employer shall be entitled to deduct and retain the amount so paid from the wages of such freedman, free negro or mulatto, then due or to become due; and in case freedman, free negro or mulatto cannot hire out, he or she may be dealt with as a pauper.

Section 6. The same duties and liabilities existing among white persons of this State shall attach to freedmen, free negroes or mulattoes, to support their indigent families and all colored paupers; and that in order to secure a support for such indigent freedmen, free negroes, or mulattoes, it shall be lawful, and is hereby made the duty of the county police of each county in this State, to levy a poll or capitation tax on each and every freedman, free negro, or mulatto, between the ages of eighteen and sixty years, not to exceed the sum of one dollar annually to each person so taxed, which tax, when collected, shall be paid into the county treasurer's hands, and constitute a fund to be called the Freedman's Pauper Fund, which shall be applied by the commissioners of the poor for the maintenance of the poor of the freedmen, free negroes and mulattoes of this State, under such regulations as may be established by the boards of county police in the respective counties of this State.

Section 7. If any freedman, free negro, or mulatto shall fail or refuse to pay any tax levied according to the provisions of the sixth section of this act, it shall be *prima facie* evidence of vagrancy, and it shall be the duty of the sheriff to arrest such freedman, free negro, or mulatto, or such person refusing or neglecting to pay such tax, and proceed at once to hire for the shortest time such delinquent taxpayer to any one who will pay the said tax, with accruing costs, giving preference to the employer, if there be one.

Section 8. Any person feeling himself or herself aggrieved by judgment of any justice of the peace, mayor, or alderman in cases arising under this act, may within five days appeal to the next term of the county court of the proper county, upon giving bond and

security in a sum not less than twenty-five dollars nor more than one hundred and fifty dollars, conditioned to appear and prosecute said appeal, and abide by the judgment of the county court; and said appeal shall be tried *de novo* in the county court, and the decision of the said court shall be final. . . .

◆ CIVIL RIGHTS ACT CH. 31, 14 STAT. 27 (1866)

This act, enacted April 9, 1866, was designed to protect recently freed African Americans from black codes and other repressive state and local legislation. It was intended to provide all citizens with basic civil rights including the right to make and enforce contracts, to bring suits in court, to purchase and sell real and personal property, and to enjoy security of person and property.

An Act to protect all Persons in the United States in their Civil Rights, and furnish the Means of their Vindication

Be it enacted. . . That all persons born in the United States and not subject to any foreign power, excluding Indians not taxed, are hereby declared to be citizens of the United States; and such citizens, of every race and color, without regard to any previous condition of slavery or involuntary servitude, except as a punishment for crime whereof the party shall have been duly convicted, shall have the same right in every State and Territory in the United States, to make and enforce contracts, to sue, be parties, and give evidence, to inherit, purchase, lease, sell, hold, and convey real and personal property, and to full and equal benefit of all laws and proceedings for the security of person and property, as is enjoyed by white citizens, and shall be subject to like punishment, pains, and penalties, and to none other, any law, statute, ordinance, regulation, or custom, to the contrary notwithstanding.

Section 2. *And be it further enacted,* That any person who, under color or any law, statute, ordinance, regulation, or custom, shall subject, or cause to be subjected, any inhabitant of any State or Territory to the deprivation of any right secured or protected by this act, or to different punishment, pains, or penalties on account of such person having at any time been held in a condition of slavery or involuntary servitude, except as a punishment for crime whereof the party shall have been duly convicted, or by reason of his color or race, than is prescribed for the punishment of white persons, shall be deemed guilty of a misdemeanor, and, on conviction, shall be punished by fine not exceeding one thousand dollars, or imprisonment not exceeding one year, or both, in the discretion of the court. . . .

◆ AMENDMENT FOURTEEN TO THE UNITED STATES CONSTITUTION (1868)

This amendment, ratified July 23, 1868, provided a definition of both national and state citizenship. When the Supreme Court heard the case Dred Scott v. Sandford *in 1857, it ruled that Africans imported into this country as slaves, and their descendants, were not and could never become citizens of the United States. The passage of the Fourteenth Amendment resolved the question of African American citizenship.*

The amendment also reversed what had been the traditional federal-state relationship in the area of citizen's rights. The Fourteenth Amendment provides for the protection of the privileges of national citizenship, and basic civil rights, and guarantees for all citizens equal protection under the law. It also provides the federal government with authority to intervene in cases where state governments have been accused of violating the constitutional rights of individuals.

Section 1. All persons born or naturalized in the United States, and subject to the jurisdiction thereof, are citizens of the United States and of the State wherein they reside. No state shall make or enforce any law which shall abridge the privileges or immunities of citizens of the United States; nor shall any State deprive any person of life, liberty, or property, without due process of law; nor deny to any person within its jurisdiction the equal protection of the laws.

Section 2. Representatives shall be apportioned among the several States according to their respective numbers, counting the whole number of persons in each State, excluding Indians not taxed. But when the right to vote at any election for the choice of electors for President and Vice President of the United States, Representatives in Congress, the Executive and Judicial officers of a State, or the members of the Legislature thereof, is denied to any of the male inhabitants of such State, being twenty-one years of age, and citizens of the United States, or in any way abridged, except for participation in rebellion, or other crime, the basis of representation therein shall be reduced in the proportion which the number of such male citizens shall bear to the whole number of male citizens twenty-one years of age in such State.

Section 3. No person shall be a Senator or Representative in Congress, or elector of President and Vice President, or hold any office, civil or military, under the United States, or under any State, who, having previously taken an oath, as a member of Congress, or as an office of the United States, or as a member of any State legislature, or as an executive or judicial officer of any State, to support the Constitution of the United States, shall have engaged in insurrection or rebellion against the same, or given aid or comfort to the enemies thereof. But Congress may by a vote of two-thirds of each House, remove such disability.

Section 4. The validity of the public debt of the United States, authorized by law, including debts incurred for payment of pensions and bounties for services in suppressing insurrection or rebellion, shall not be questioned. But neither the United States nor any State shall assume or pay any debt or obligation incurred in aid of insurrection or rebellion against the United States, or any claim for the loss or emancipation of any slave; but all such debts, obligations and claims shall be held illegal and void.

Section 5. The Congress shall have power to enforce, by appropriate legislation, the provisions of this article.

◆ AMENDMENT FIFTEEN TO THE UNITED STATES CONSTITUTION (1870)

The Fifteenth Amendment, ratified March 30, 1870, was intended to protect the right of all citizens to vote. However, the amendment was not successful in ending techniques designed to prevent African Americans from voting; many state and local governments continued to employ such tactics as the use of grandfather clauses, literacy tests, "white primaries," and poll taxes as prerequisites to, or deterrents to voting.

Section 1. The right of citizens of the United States to vote shall not be denied or abridged by the United States or by any State on account of race, color, or previous conditions of servitude.

Section 2. The Congress shall have power to enforce this article by appropriate legislation.

◆ KU KLUX KLAN ACT CH. 22, 17 STAT. 13 (1871)

Following the Civil War, white terrorist groups began to spring up throughout the South. These early organizations, consisting mainly of Confederate veterans still obsessed with the goals and aspirations of their Southern heritage, terrorized blacks who sought increased participation in their communities and whites who aided them. Known as the Knights of the White Camelia, the Jayhawkers, or the Ku Klux Klan, by 1871 these groups had become well organized. The Ku Klux Klan Act of 1871 was an attempt by Congress to end intimidation and violence by such organizations. The law, however, failed to exterminate the Klan or to eliminate the continued use of terrorist tactics against blacks and those whites who gave support to black concerns.

Be it enacted . . . that any person who, under color of any law, statute, ordinance, regulation, custom, or usage of any State, shall subject, or cause to be subjected, any person within the jurisdiction of the United States to the deprivation of any rights, privileges, or immunities secured by the Constitution of the United States; shall any such law, statute, ordinance, regulation, custom, or usage of the state to the contrary notwithstanding, be liable to the party injured in any action at law, suit in equity, or other proper proceeding for redress; such proceeding to be prosecuted in the several district or circuit courts of the United States, with and subject to the same rights of appeal, review upon error, and other remedies provided in like cases in such courts, under the provisions of the [Civil Rights Act of April 9, 1866] . . . and the other remedial laws of the United States which are in their nature applicable in such cases.

Section 2. That if two or more persons within any State or Territory of the United States shall conspire together to overthrow, or to put down, or to destroy by force the government of the United States, or to levy war against the United States or to oppose by force the authority of the government of the United States, or by force, intimidation, or threat to prevent . . . any person from accepting or holding any office or trust or place of confidence under the United States, or from discharging the duties thereof . . . or to injure him in his person or property on account of his lawful discharge of the duties of his office, or to injure his person while engaged in the lawful discharge of the duties of his office, or . . . to deter any party or witness in any court of the United States from attending such court, or from testifying in any matter pending in such court fully, freely, and truthfully, or to injure any party or witness in his person or property on account of his having so attended or testified, or by force, intimidation, or threat to influence the verdict, presentment, or indictment, of any juror or grand juror in any court of the United States, or to injure such juror in his person or property on account of any verdict, presentment, or indictment lawfully assented to by him, or on account of his being or having been such juror, or shall conspire together, or go in disguise upon the public highway or upon the premises of another for the purpose, either directly or indirectly, of depriving any person or any class of persons of the equal protection of the laws, or of equal privileges or immunities under the laws, or for the purpose of preventing or hindering the constituted authorities of any State from giving or securing to all persons within such State the equal protection of the laws, or shall conspire together for the purpose of in any manner impeding, hindering, obstructing, or defeating the due course of justice in any State or Territory, with the intent to deny to any citizen of the United States the due and equal protection of the laws, or to injure any person in his person or in his property for lawfully enforcing the right of any person or class of persons to the equal protection of the laws, or by force, intimidation, or threat to prevent any citizen of the United States lawfully entitled to vote from giving his support or advocacy in a lawful manner . . . or to injure any such citizen in his person or property on account of such support or advocacy, each and every person so offending shall be deemed guilty of a high crime. . . .

Section 3. That in all cases where insurrection, domestic violence, unlawful combinations, or conspiracies in any State shall so obstruct or hinder the execution of the laws thereof, and of the United States, as to deprive any portion or class of the people of such State of any of the rights, privileges, or immunities, or protection, named in the Constitution and secured by this act, and the constituted authorities of such State shall either be unable to protect, or shall from any cause fail in or refuse protection of the people in such rights, such facts will be deemed a denial by such State of the equal protection of the laws to which they are entitled under the Constitution of the United States; and in all such cases, or whenever any such insurrection, violence, unlawful combination, or conspiracy shall oppose or obstruct the laws of the United States or the due execution thereof, or impede or obstruct the due course of justice under the same, it shall be lawful for the President, and it shall be his duty to take such measures, by the employment of the militia or the land and naval forces of the United States, or either, or by other means, as he may deem necessary for the suppression of such insurrection, domestic violence, or combinations; and any person who shall be arrested under the provisions of this and the preceding section shall be delivered to the marshal of the proper district, to be dealt with according to law.

Section 4. That whenever in any State or part of a State the unlawful combinations named in the preceding section of this act shall be organized and armed, and so numerous and powerful as to be able, by violence, to either overthrow or set at defiance the constituted authorities of such State, and of the United States within such State, or when the constituted authorities are in complicity with, or shall connive at the unlawful purpose of, such powerful and armed combinations; and whenever, by reason of either or all of the causes aforesaid, the conviction of such offender and the preservation of the public safety shall become in such district impracticable, in every such case such combinations shall be deemed a rebellion against the government of the United States, and during the continuation of such rebellion, and within the limits of the district which shall be so under the sway thereof, such limits to be prescribed by proclamation, it shall be lawful for the President of the United States, when in his judgment the public safety shall require it, to suspend the privileges of the writ of habeas corpus, to the end that such rebellion may be overthrown. . . .

Section 6. That any person, or persons, having knowledge that any of the wrongs conspired to be done and mentioned in the second section of this act are about to be committed, and having power to prevent or aid in preventing the same, shall neglect or refuse so to do, and such wrongful act shall be committed, such person or persons shall be liable to the person injured, or his legal representatives, for all damages caused by any such wrongful act which such first-named person or persons by reasonable diligence could have prevented; and such damages may be recovered in an action on the case in the proper circuit court of the United States, and any number of persons guilty of such wrongful neglect or refusal may be joined as defendants in such action. . . .

◆ CIVIL RIGHTS ACT OF 1875 CH. 114, 18 STAT. 335 (1875)

The Civil Rights Act of 1875 concerned itself primarily with the prohibition of racial discrimination in places of public accommodation. Eight years later, however, the U.S. Supreme Court addressed the issue. Ruling in a set of disputes, which came to be known as the Civil Rights Cases, the Court declared the law unconstitutional, stating that Congress did not have the authority to regulate the prevalent social mores of any state.

An Act to Protect All Citizens in Their Civil and Legal Rights.

Whereas it is essential to just governments we recognize the equality of all men before the law, and hold that it is the duty of government in its dealings with the people to mete out equal and exact justice to all, of whatever nativity, race, color, or persuasion, religious or political; and it being the appropriate object of legislation to enact great fundamental principles into law: Therefore, *Be it enacted,* That all persons within the jurisdiction of the United States shall be entitled to the full and equal enjoyment of the accommodations, advantages, facilities, and privileges of inns, public conveyances on land or water, theaters, and other places of public amusement; subject only to the conditions and limitations established by law, and applicable alike to citizens of every race and color, regardless of any previous condition of servitude.

Section 2. That any person who shall violate the foregoing section by denying to any citizen, except for reasons by law applicable to citizens of every race and color, and regardless of any previous condition of servitude, the full enjoyment of any of the accommodations, advantages, facilities, or privileges in said section enumerated, or by aiding or inciting such denial, shall, for every such offense, forfeit and pay the sum of five hundred dollars to the person aggrieved thereby . . . and shall also, for every such offense, be deemed guilty of a misdemeanor, and upon conviction thereof, shall be fined not less than five hundred nor more than one thousand dollars, or shall be imprisoned not less than thirty days nor more than one year. . . .

Section 4. That no citizen possessing all other qualifications which are or may be prescribed by law shall be disqualified for service as grand or petit juror in any court of the United States, or of any State, on account of race, color, or previous condition of servitude; and any officer or other person charged with any duty in the selection or summoning of jurors who shall exclude or fail to summon any citizen for the cause aforesaid shall, on conviction thereof, be deemed guilty of a misdemeanor, and be fined not more than five thousand dollars.

Section 5. That all cases arising under the provisions of this act. . . shall be renewable by the Supreme Court of the U.S., without regard to the sum in controversy. . . .

◆ FREDERICK DOUGLASS'S SPEECH ON WOMAN SUFFRAGE (1888) (EXCERPT)

In July 1848 Frederick Douglass was one of the few men present at the initial woman's rights convention at Seneca Falls, New York, and it was he who encouraged outspoken feminist Elizabeth Cady Stanton to press for suffrage and who seconded the resolution proposed by Stanton that it was "the duty of the women of this country to secure to themselves their sacred right to the elective franchise." However, in later years, Douglass split ranks with Stanton and Anthony over philosophical differences regarding the Fifteenth Amendment and other matters. Yet, Douglass remained a staunch advocate for the right of women to vote.

In April 1888, Douglass gave a speech before the International Council of Women in Washington, DC. In his message to the conventioneers, Douglass reflected on his role at the Seneca Falls convention and strongly endorsed woman suffrage. Douglass also insisted that it is women, not men, who should be the

Frederick Douglass.

primary spokespersons for the suffrage cause. The text of Douglass's address appeared in the Woman's Journal *on April 14, 1888.*

Mrs. President, Ladies and Gentlemen:—I come to this platform with unusual diffidence. Although I have long been identified with the Woman's Suffrage movement, and have often spoken in its favor, I am somewhat at a loss to know what to say on this really great and uncommon occasion, where so much has been said.

When I look around on this assembly, and see the many able and eloquent women, full of the subject, ready to speak, and who only need the opportunity to impress this audience with their views and thrill them with "thoughts that berate and words that burn," I do not feel like taking up more than a very small space of your time and attention, and shall not. I would not, even now, presume to speak, but for the circumstances of my early connection with the cause, and of having been called upon to do so by one whose voice in this Council we all gladly obey. Men have very little business here as speakers, anyhow; and if they come here at all they should take back benches and wrap themselves in silence. For this is an International Council, not of men, but of women, and woman should have all the say in it. This is her day in court.

I do not mean to exalt the intellect of woman above man's; but I have heard many men speak on this subject; some of them the most eloquent to be found anywhere in the country; and I believe no man, however gifted with thought and speech, can voice the wrongs and present the demands of women with the skill and effect, with the power and authority of woman herself. The man struck is the man to cry out. Woman knows and feels her wrongs as man cannot know and feel them, and she also knows as well as he can know, what measures are needed to redress them. I grant all the claims at this point. She is her own best representative. We can neither speak for her, nor vote for her, nor act for her, nor be responsible for her; and the thing for men to do in the premises is just to get out of her way and give her the fullest opportunity to exercise all the powers inherent in her individual personality, and allow her to do it as she herself shall elect to exercise them. Her right to be and to do is as full, complete and perfect as the right of any man on earth. I say of her, as I say of the colored people, "Give her fair play, and hands off."

There is to-day, however, a special reason for omitting argument. This is the end of the fourth decade of the woman suffrage movement, a kind of jubilee which naturally turns our minds to the past.

The history of the world has given to us many sublime undertakings, but none more sublime than this. It was a great thing for the friends of peace to organize in opposition to war; it was a great thing for the friends of temperance to organize against intemperance; it was a great thing for humane people to organize in opposition to slavery; but it was a much greater thing, in view of all the circumstances, for woman to organize herself in opposition to her exclusion from participation in government. . . . Men took for granted all that could be said against intemperance, war and slavery. But no such advantage was found in the beginning of the cause of suffrage for women. On the contrary, everything in her condition was supposed to be lovely, just as it should be. She had no rights denied, no wrongs to redress. She herself had no suspicion but that all was going well with her.

There are few facts in my humble history to which I look back with more satisfaction than to the fact, recorded in the history of the woman-suffrage movement, that I was sufficiently enlightened at that early day, and when only a few years from slavery, to support your resolution for woman suffrage. I have done very little in this world in which to glory except this one act—and I certainly glory in that. When I ran away from slavery, it was for myself; when I advocated emancipation, it was for my people, but when I stood up for the rights of woman, self was out of the question, and I found a little nobility in the act.

In estimating the forces with which this suffrage cause has had to contend during these forty years, the fact should be remembered that relations of long standing beget a character in the parties to them in the favor of the continuance.

The relation of man to woman has the advantage of all the ages behind it. Those who oppose a readjustment of this relation tell us that what is always was and always will be, world without end. But we have heard this old argument before, and if we live very long we shall hear it again. When any aged error shall be assailed, and any old abuse is to be removed, we shall meet this same old argument. Man has been so long the king and woman the subject—man has been so long accustomed to command and woman to obey—that both parties to the relation have been hardened into their respective places, and thus has been piled up a mountain of iron against woman's enfranchisement.

The universality of man's rule over woman is another factor in resistance to the woman-suffrage movement. We are pointed to the fact that men have not only always ruled over women, but that they do so rule everywhere, and they easily think that thing that is done everywhere must be right. Though the fallacy of this reasoning is too transparent to need refutation, it still exerts a powerful influence.

All good causes are mutually helpful. The benefits accruing from this movement for the equal rights of woman are not confined or limited to woman only. They will be shared by every effort to promote the progress and welfare of mankind everywhere and in all ages.

◆ IDA B. WELLS-BARNETT'S SPEECH ON THE LYNCH LAW IN ALL ITS PHASES (1893) (EXCERPT)

Ida B. Wells-Barnett began organizing and lecturing in support of an international campaign against lynching after a mob destroyed the offices of her newspaper the Memphis Free Speech *on May 27, 1892. In both her speeches and writings, she used graphic, detailed descriptions of certain lynchings and scrutinized the media accounts through which her audiences were most likely to have heard of them. In her speech in Boston's Tremont Temple on February 13, 1893, Wells-Barnett again speaks out against lynchings and suggests a remedy for ending the heinous practice.*

Lynch Law in Georgia.

BY

IDA B. WELLS=BARNETT

A Six-Weeks' Record in the Center of Southern Civilization, As Faithfully Chronicled by the "Atlanta Journal" and the "Atlanta Constitution."

ALSO THE FULL REPORT OF LOUIS P. LE VIN,

The Chicago Detective Sent to Investigate the Burning of Samuel Hose, the Torture and Hanging of Elijah Strickland, the Colored Preacher, and the Lynching of Nine Men for Alleged Arson.

Lynch Law in Georgia was one of numerous publications released by anti-lynching crusader Ida B. Wells-Barnett.

The race problem or negro question, as it has been called, has been omnipresent and all-pervading since long before the Afro-American was raised from the degradation of the slave to the dignity of the citizen. It has never been settled because the right methods have not been employed in the solution. . . . The operations of law do not dispose of negroes fast enough, and lynching bees have become the favorite pastime of the South. As excuse for the same, a new cry, as false as it is foul, is raised in an effort to blast race character, a cry which has proclaimed to the world that virtue and innocence are violated by Afro-Americans who must be killed like wild beasts to protect womanhood and childhood.

In the past ten years over a thousand colored men, women and children have been butchered, murdered and burnt in all parts of the South. The details of these horrible outrages seldom reach beyond the narrow world where they occur. Those who commit the murders write the reports, and hence these lasting blots upon the honor of a nation cause but a faint ripple on the outside world. They arouse no great indignation and call forth no adequate demand for justice. The victims were black, and the reports are so written as to make it appear that the helpless creatures deserved the fate which overtook them.

Persons unfamiliar with the condition of affairs in the Southern States do not credit the truth when it is told to them. They cannot conceive how such a condition of affairs prevails so near them with steam power, telegraph wires and printing presses in daily and hourly touch with the localities where such disorder reigns.

The right of the Afro-American to vote and hold office remains in the Federal Constitution, but is destroyed in the constitution of the Southern states. Having destroyed the citizenship of the man, they are now trying to destroy the manhood of the citizen. All their laws are shaped to this end;—school laws, railroad car regulations, those governing labor liens on crops,—every device is adopted to make slaves of free men and rob them of their wages. Whenever a malicious law is violated in any of its parts, any farmer, any railroad conductor, or merchant can call together a posse of his neighbors and punish even with death the black man who resists and the legal authorities sanction what is done by failing to prosecute and punish the murders. The Repeal of the Civil Rights Law removed their last barrier and the black man's last bulwark and refuge. The rule of the mob is absolute.

Those who know this recital to be true, say there is nothing they can do—they cannot interfere and vainly hope by further concession to placate the imperious and dominating part of our country in which this lawlessness prevails. Because this country has been almost rent in twain by internal dissension, the other sections seem virtually to have agreed that the best way to heal the breach is to permit the taking away of civil, political, and even human rights, to stand by in silence and utter indifference while the South continues to wreak fiendish vengeance on the irresponsible cause. They pretend to believe that with all the machinery of law and government in its hands; with the jails and penitentiaries and convict farms filled with pretty race criminals; with the well-known fact that no negro has ever been known to escape conviction and punishment for any crime in the South—still there are those who try to justify and condone the lynching of over a thousand black men in less than ten years—an average of one hundred a year. The public sentiment of the country, by its silence in press, pulpit and in public meetings has encouraged this state of affairs, and public sentiment is stronger than law.

Do you ask the remedy? A public sentiment strong against lawlessness must be aroused. Every individual can contribute to this awakening. When a sentiment against lynch law as strong, deep and mighty as that roused against slavery prevails, I have no fear of the result. It should be already established as a fact and not as a theory, that every human being must have a fair trial for his life and liberty, no matter what the charge against him. When a demand goes up from fearless and persistent reformers from press and pulpit, from industrial and moral associations that this shall be so from Maine to Texas and from ocean to ocean, a way will be found to make it so.

◆ BOOKER T. WASHINGTON'S "ATLANTA COMPROMISE" SPEECH (1895)

Booker T. Washington, a major voice in the movement for the advancement of African Americans, was often criticized for encouraging blacks to cultivate peaceful coexistence with whites. Washington advocated the use of technical and industrial self-help programs—even if such programs tended to discount the importance of the cultivation of intellectual and aesthetic values. In an address to the 1895 Atlanta Exposition, Washington outlined his philosophy.

Mr. President and Gentlemen of the Board of Directors and Citizens:

One-third of the population of the South is of the Negro race. No enterprise seeking the material, civil, or moral welfare of this section can disregard this element of our population and reach the highest success. I but convey to you, Mr. President and Directors, the sentiment of the masses of my race when I say that in no way have the value and manhood of the American Negro been more fittingly and generously recognized than by the managers of this magnificent Exposition at every stage of its progress. It is a recognition that will do more to cement the friendship of the two races than any occurrence since the dawn of our freedom.

Not only this, but the opportunity here afforded will awaken among us a new era of industrial progress. Ignorant and inexperienced, it is not strange that in the first years of our new life we began at the top instead of at the bottom; that a seat in Congress or the State Legislature was more sought than real estate or industrial skill; that the political convention or stump speaking had more attractions than starting a dairy farm or truck garden.

A ship lost at sea for many days suddenly sighted a friendly vessel. From the mast of the unfortunate vessel was seen a signal: "Water, water; we die of thirst!" The answer from the friendly vessel at once came back: "Cast down your bucket where you are." A second time the signal, "Water, water; send us water!" ran up from the distressed vessel, and was answered: "Cast down your bucket where you are." And a third and fourth signal for water was answered: "Cast down your bucket where you are." The captain of the distressed vessel, at last heeding the injunction, cast down his bucket, and it came up full of fresh, sparkling water from the mouth of the Amazon River. To those of my race who depend on bettering their condition in a foreign land, or who underestimate the importance of cultivating friendly relations with the Southern white man, who is their next door neighbor, I would say: "Cast down your bucket where you are"—cast it down in making friends in every manly way of the people of all races by whom we are surrounded.

Cast it down in agriculture, mechanics, in commerce, in domestic service, and in the professions. And in this connection it is well to bear in mind that whatever other sins the South may be called to bear, when it comes to business, pure and simple, it is in the South that the Negro is given a man's chance in the commercial world, and in nothing is this Exposition more eloquent than in emphasizing this chance. Our greatest danger is, that in the great leap from slavery to freedom we may overlook the fact that the masses of us are to live by the productions of our hands, and fail to keep in mind that we shall prosper in proportion as we learn to dignify and glorify common labor, and put brains and skill into the common occupations of life; shall prosper in proportion as we learn to draw the line between the superficial and the substantial, the ornamental gewgaws of life and the useful. No race can prosper till it learns that there is as much dignity in tilling a field as in writing a poem. It is at the bottom of life we must begin, and not at the top. Nor should we permit our grievances to overshadow our opportunities.

To those of the white race who look to the incoming of those of foreign birth and strange tongue and habits for the prosperity of the South, were I permitted, I would repeat what I say to my own race, "Cast down your bucket where you are." Cast it down among the 8,000,000 Negroes whose habits you know, whose fidelity and love you have tested in days when to have proved treacherous meant the ruin of your firesides. Cast down your bucket among those people who have, without strikes and labor wars, tilled your fields, cleared your forests, builded your railroads and cities, and brought forth treasures from the bowels of the earth, and helped make possible this magnificent representation of the progress of the South. Casting down your bucket among my people, helping and encouraging them as you are doing on these grounds, and, with education of head, hand and heart, you will find that they will buy your surplus land, make blossom the waste place in your fields, and run your factories. While doing this, you can be sure in the future, as in the past, that you and your families will be surrounded by the most patient, faithful, law-abiding, and unresentful people that the world has seen. As we have proved our loyalty to you in the past, in nursing your children, watching by the sick bed of your mothers and fathers, and often following them with tear-dimmed eyes to their graves, so in the future, in our humble way, we shall stand by you with a devotion that no foreigner can approach, ready to lay down our lives, if need be, in defense of yours, interlacing our industrial, commercial, civil, and religious life with yours in a way that shall make the interests of both races one. In all things that are purely social we can be as separate as the fingers, yet one as the hand in all things essential to mutual progress.

There is no defense or security for any of us except in the highest intelligence and development of all. If anywhere there are efforts tending to curtail the fullest growth of the Negro, let these efforts be turned into stimulating, encouraging, and making him the most useful and intelligent citizen. Effort or means so invested will pay a thousand percent interest. These efforts will be twice blessed—"blessing him that gives and him that takes."

There is no escape through law of man or God from the inevitable:

The laws of changeless justice bind Oppressor with oppressed; And close as sin and suffering joined We march to fate abreast.

Nearly sixteen millions of hands will aid you in pulling the load upwards, or they will pull against you the load downwards. We shall constitute one-third and more of the ignorance and crime of the South, or one-third its intelligence and progress; we shall contribute one-third to the business and industrial prosperity of the South, or we shall prove a veritable body of death, stagnating, depressing, retarding every effort to advance the body politic.

Gentlemen of the Exposition, as we present to you humble effort at an exhibition of our progress, you must not expect over much. Starting thirty years ago with ownership here and there in a few quilts and pumpkins and chickens (gathered from miscellaneous sources), remember the path that has led from these to the invention and production of agricultural implements, buggies, steam engines, newspapers, books, statuary, carving, paintings, the management of drug stores and banks, has not been trodden without contact with thorns and thistles. While we take pride in what we exhibit as a result of our independent efforts, we do not for a moment forget that our part in this exhibition would fall far short of your expectations but for the constant help that has come to our educational life, not only from the Southern States, but especially from Northern philanthropists, who have made their gifts a constant stream of blessing and encouragement.

The wisest among my race understand that the agitation of questions of social equality is the extremist folly, and that progress in the enjoyment of all the privileges that will come to us must be the result of severe and constant struggle rather than of artificial forcing. No race that has anything to contribute to the markets of the world is long in any degree ostracized. It is important and right that all privileges of the law be ours, but it is vastly more important that we be prepared for the exercise of those privileges. The opportunity to earn a dollar in a factory just now is worth infinitely more than the opportunity to spend a dollar in an opera house.

In conclusion, may I repeat that nothing in thirty years has given us more hope and encouragement, and drawn us so near to you of the white race, as this opportunity offered by the Exposition; and here bending, as it were, over the altar that represents the results of the struggle of your race and mine, both starting practically empty-handed three decades ago, I pledge that, in your effort to work out the great and intricate problem which God has laid at the doors of the South, you shall have at all time the patient, sympathetic help of my race; only let this be constantly in mind that, while from representations in these buildings of the product of field, of forest, of mine, of factory, letters, and art, much good will come, yet far above and beyond material benefits will be that higher good, that let us pray God will come, in a blotting out of sectional differences and racial animosities and suspicions, in a determination to administer absolute justice, in a willing obedience among all classes to the mandates of law. This, coupled with our material prosperity, will bring into our beloved South a new heaven and a new earth.

◆ *PLESSY V. FERGUSON 163 US 537* (1896)

On February 23, 1869, the Louisiana state legislature enacted a law prohibiting segregation on public transportation. In 1878, ruling in the case Hall v. DeCuir, *the U.S. Supreme Court declared that state governments could not prohibit segregation on common carriers. Twelve years later, the Court hearing the case* Louisville, New Orleans and Texas Railway v. Mississippi *approved a state statute requiring segregation on intrastate carriers.*

In 1896, the Court once again faced the issue of segregation on public transportation. Homer Adolph Plessy, an African American traveling by train from New Orleans to Covington, Louisiana, was arrested when he refused to ride in the "colored" railway coach; Louisiana state law required that "separate but equal" accommodations be maintained in public facilities for blacks and whites. In its majority opinion, the Court declared that "separate but equal" accommodations constituted a "reasonable" use of state police power and that the Fourteenth Amendment "could not have been intended to abolish distinctions based on color, or to enforce social. . . equality, or a commingling of the two races upon terms unsatisfactory to either."

In effect, the Court's ruling had significantly reduced the authoritativeness of the Fourteenth and Fifteenth Amendments to the Constitution, which were designed to provide African Americans specific rights and protections. The "separate but equal" doctrine paved the way for segregation of African Americans in all walks of life and stood until the Brown v. Board of Education of Topeka, Kansas *decision of 1954.*

Justice Brown delivered the opinion of the Court.

This case turns upon the constitutionality of an act of the General Assembly of the state of Louisiana, passed in 1890, providing for separate railway carriages for the white and colored races. . . .

The constitutionality of this act is attacked upon the ground that it conflicts both with the Thirteenth Amendment of the Constitution, abolishing slavery, and the Fourteenth Amendment, which prohibits certain restrictive legislation on the part of the states.

1. That it does not conflict with the Thirteenth Amendment, which abolished slavery and involuntary servitude, except as a punishment for crime, is too clear for argument. Slavery implies involuntary servitude—a state of bondage; the ownership of mankind as a chattel, or at least the control of the labor and services of one man for the benefit of another, and absence of a legal right to the disposal of his own person, property, and services. . . .

A statute which implies merely a legal distinction between the white and colored races—a distinction which is founded in the color of the two races, and which must always exist so long as white men are distinguished from the other race by color—has no tendency to destroy the legal equality of the two races, or reestablish a state of involuntary servitude. Indeed, we do not understand that the Thirteenth Amendment is strenuously relied upon by the plaintiff in error in this connection.

2. By the Fourteenth Amendment, all persons born or naturalized in the United States, and subject to the jurisdiction thereof, are made citizens of the United States and of the state wherein they reside; and the states are forbidden from making or enforcing any law

which shall abridge the privileges or immunities of citizens of the United States, or shall deprive any person of life, liberty, or property without due process of law, or deny to any person within their jurisdiction the equal protection of the laws. . . .

The object of the amendment was undoubtedly to enforce the absolute equality of the two races before the law, but in the nature of things it could not have been intended to abolish distinctions based upon color, or to enforce social, as distinguished from political, equality, or a commingling of the two races upon terms unsatisfactory to either. Laws permitting, and even requiring, their separation in places where they are liable to be brought into contact do not necessarily imply the inferiority of either race to the other, and have been generally, if not universally, recognized as within the competency of the state legislatures in the exercise of their police power. The most common instance of this is connected with the establishment of separate schools for white and colored children, which has been held to be a valid exercise of the legislative power even by courts of states where the political rights of the colored race have been longest and most earnestly enforced. . . .

So far, then, as a conflict with the Fourteenth Amendment is concerned, the case reduces itself to the question whether the statute of Louisiana is a reasonable regulation, and with respect to this there must necessarily be a large discretion on the part of the legislature. In determining the question of reasonableness it is at liberty to act with reference to the established usages, customs, and traditions of the people, and with a view to the promotion of their comfort, and the preservation of the public peace and good order. Gauged by this standard, we cannot say that a law which authorizes or even requires the separation of the two races in public conveyances is unreasonable or more obnoxious to the Fourteenth Amendment than the acts of Congress requiring separate schools for colored children in the District of Columbia, the constitutionality of which does not seem to have been questioned, or the corresponding acts of state legislatures.

We consider the underlying fallacy of the plaintiff's argument to consist in the assumption that the enforced separation of the two races stamps the colored race with a badge of inferiority. If this be so, it is not by reason of anything found in the act, but solely the colored race chooses to put that construction upon it. The argument necessarily assumes that if, as has been more than once the case, and is not unlikely to be so again, the colored race should become the dominant power in the state legislature, and should enact a law in precisely similar terms, it would thereby relegate the white race to an inferior position. We imagine that the white race, at least, would not acquiesce in this assumption. The argument also assumes that social prejudices may be overcome by legislation and that equal rights cannot be secured to the Negro except by an enforced commingling of the two races. We cannot accept this proposition. If the two races are to meet upon terms of social equality, it must be the result of natural affinities, a mutual appreciation of each other's merits, and a voluntary consent of individuals. . . .Legislation is powerless to eradicate racial instincts or to abolish distinctions based upon physical differences, and the attempt to do so can only result in accentuating the difficulties of the present situation. If the civil and political rights of both races be equal, one cannot be inferior to the other civilly or politically. If one race be inferior to the other socially, the Constitution of the United States cannot put them upon the same plane.

It is true that the question of the proportion of colored blood necessary to constitute a colored person, as distinguished from a white person, is one upon with there is a difference of opinion in the different states, some holding that any visible admixture of black blood stamps the person as belonging to the colored race. . . others that it depends upon the preponderance of blood. . . and still others that the pre-dominance of white blood must only be in the proportion of three-fourths. . . .But these are questions to be determined under the laws of each state and are not properly put in issue in this case. Under the allegations of his petition it may undoubtedly become a question of importance whether, under the laws of Louisiana, the petitioner belongs to the white or colored race.

The judgment of the court below is therefore, *Affirmed.*

Justice Harlan Dissenting

In respect of civil rights, common to all citizens, the Constitution of the United States does not, I think, permit any public authority to know the race of those entitled to be protected in the enjoyment of such rights. Every true man has pride of race, and under appropriate circumstances with the rights of others, his equals before the law, are not to be affected, it is his privilege to express such pride and to take such action based upon it as to him seems proper. But I deny that any legislative body or judicial tribunal may have regard to the race of citizens when the civil rights of those citizens are involved. Indeed, such legislation, as that here in question, is inconsistent not only with that equality of rights which pertains to citizenship, national and state, but with the personal liberty enjoyed by everyone within the United States.

The Thirteenth Amendment does not permit the withholding or the deprivation of any right necessarily inhering in freedom. It not only struck down the institution of slavery as previously existing in the United States, but it prevents the imposition of any burdens or disabilities that constitute badges of slavery or servitude. It decreed universal civil freedom in this country. This Court has so adjudged. But that amendment having been found inadequate to the protection of the rights of those who had been in slavery, it was followed by the Fourteenth Amendment, which added greatly to the dignity and glory of the American citizenship, and to the security of personal liberty, by declaring that "all persons born or naturalized in the United States, and subject to the jurisdiction thereof, are citizens of the United States and of the state wherein they reside," and that "no state shall make or enforce any law which shall abridge the privileges or immunities of citizens of the United States; nor shall any state deprive any person of life, liberty, or property without due process of law, nor deny to any person within its jurisdiction the equal protection of the laws." These two amendments, if enforced according to their true intent and meaning, will protect all the civil rights that pertains to freedom and citizenship. Finally, and to the end that no citizen should be denied, on account of his race, the privilege of participating in the political control of his country, it was declared by the Fifteenth Amendment that "the right of citizens of the United States to vote shall not be denied or abridged by the United States or by any state on account of race, color, or previous condition of servitude."

These notable additions to the fundamental law were welcomed by the friends of liberty throughout the world. They removed the race line from our governmental systems.

It was said in argument that the statute of Louisiana does not discriminate against either race but prescribes a rule applicable alike to white and colored citizens. But this argument does not meet the difficulty. Everyone knows that the statute in question had its origin in the purpose, not so much to exclude white persons from railroad cars occupied by blacks, as to exclude colored people from coaches occupied by or assigned to white persons. Railroad corporations of Louisiana did not make discrimination among whites in the matter of accommodation for travelers. The thing to accomplish was, under the guise of giving equal accommodation for whites and blacks, to compel the latter to keep to themselves while traveling in railroad passenger coaches. No one would be wanting in candor as to assert the contrary. The fundamental objections, therefore, to the statute is that it interferes with the personal freedom of citizens. If a white man and a black man

choose to occupy the same public conveyance on a public highway, it is their right to do so, and no government, proceeding alone on grounds of race, can prevent it without infringing the personal liberty of each.

It is one thing for railroad carriers to furnish, or to be required by law to furnish, equal accommodations for all whom they are under a legal duty to carry. It is quite another thing for government to forbid citizens of the white and black races from traveling in the same public conveyance, and to punish officers of railroad companies for permitting persons of the two races to occupy the same passenger coach. If a state can prescribe, as a rule of civil conduct, that whites and blacks shall not travel as passengers in the same railroad coach, why may it not so regulate the use of the streets of its cities and towns as to compel white citizens to keep on one side of a street and black citizens to keep on the other? Why may it not, upon like grounds, punish whites and blacks who ride together in streetcars or in open vehicles on a public road or street? Why may it not require sheriffs to assign whites to one side of a courtroom and blacks to the other? And why may it not also prohibit the commingling of the two races in the galleries of legislative halls or in public assemblages convened for the consideration of the political questions of the day? Further, if this statute of Louisiana is consistent with the personal liberty of citizens, why may not the state require the separation in railroad coaches of native and naturalized citizens of the United States, or of Protestants and Roman Catholics?

The answer given as the argument to these questions was that regulations of the kind they suggest would be unreasonable and could not, therefore, stand before the law. Is it meant that the determination of questions of legislative power depends upon the inquiry whether the statute whose validity is questioned is, in the judgment of the courts, a reasonable one, taking all the circumstances into consideration? A statute may be unreasonable merely because a sound public forbade its enactment. But I do not understand that the courts have anything to do with the policy or expediency of legislation. The white race deems itself to be the dominant race in this country. And so it is, in prestige, in achievements, in education, in wealth, and in power. So, I doubt not, it will continue to be for all time, if it remains true to its great heritage and holds fast to the principles of constitutional liberty. But in view of the Constitution, in the eye of the law, there is in this country no superior, dominant, ruling class of citizens. There is no caste here. Our Constitution is color-blind and neither knows nor tolerates classes among citizens. In respect of civil rights all citizens are equal before the law. The humblest is the peer of the most powerful. The law regards man as a man and takes no account of his surroundings or of his color when his civil rights, as guaranteed by the supreme law of the land, are involved. It is, therefore, to be regretted that this high tribunal, the final expositor of the fundamental law of the land, has reached the conclusion that it is competent for a state to regulate the enjoyment by citizens of their civil rights solely upon the basis of race. . . .

The sure guarantee of the peace and security of each is the clear, distinct, unconditional recognition by our governments, national and state, of every right that inheres in civil freedom, and of the equality before the law of all citizens of the United States without regard to race. State enactments, regulating the enjoyment of civil rights, upon the basis of race, and cunningly devised legitimate results of the war, under the pretense of recognizing equality of rights, can have no other result than to render permanent peace impossible, and to keep alive a conflict of races, the continuance of which must do harm to all concerned. . . .

The arbitrary separation of citizens, on the basis of race, while they are on a public highway, is a badge of servitude wholly inconsistent with the civil freedom and the equality before the law established by the Constitution. It cannot be justified upon any legal grounds.

If evils will result from the commingling of the two races upon public highways established for the benefit of all, they will be infinitely less than those that will surely come from state legislation regulating the enjoyment of civil rights upon the basis of race. We boast of the freedom enjoyed by our people above all other peoples. But it is difficult to reconcile that boast with a state of the law which, practically, puts the brand of servitude and degradation upon a large class of our fellow-citizens, our equals before the law. The thin disguise of "equal" accommodations for passengers in railroad coaches will not mislead anyone, nor atone for the wrong this day has done. . . .

I am of opinion that the statute of Louisiana is inconsistent with the personal liberty of citizens, white and black, in that state, and hostile to both the spirit and letter of the Constitution of the United States. If laws of like character should be enacted in the several states of the Union, the effect would be in the highest degree mischievous. Slavery, as an institution tolerated by law, would, it is true, have disappeared from our country, but there would remain a power in the states, by sinister legislation, to interfere with the full enjoyment of the blessings of freedom; to regulate civil rights, common to all citizens, upon the basis of race, and to place in a condition of legal inferiority a large body of American citizens, now constituting a part of the political community called the People of the United States, for whom, and by whom through representatives, our government is administered. Such a system is inconsistent with the guarantee given by the Constitution to each state of a republican form of government, and may be stricken down by congressional action, constitutional or laws of any state to the contrary notwithstanding.

For the reasons stated, I am constrained to withhold my assent from the opinion and judgment of the majority. . . .

◆ "LIFT EVERY VOICE AND SING" (1901)

Originally intended for use in a program given by a group of Jacksonville, Florida school children to celebrate Lincoln's birthday, "Lift Every Voice and Sing" has become known as the "black national anthem." The song's words, written by poet and civil rights leader James Weldon Johnson, serve as a tribute to African American heritage. The song's music was composed by Johnson's brother and songwriting partner, J. Rosamond Johnson.

Lift every voice and sing Till earth and heaven ring, Ring with the harmonies of Liberty; Let our rejoicing rise High as the listening skies, Let it resound loud as the rolling sea. Sing a song full of the faith that the dark past has taught us, Sing a song full of the hope that the present has brought us, Facing the rising sun of our new day begun Let us march on till victory is won.

Stony the road we trod, Bitter the chastening rod, Felt in the days when hope unborn had died; Yet with a steady beat, Have not our weary feet Come to the place for which our fathers sighed? We have come over a way that with tears has been watered, We have come, treading our path through the blood of the slaughtered Out from the gloomy past, Till now we stand at last Where the white gleam of our bright star is cast.

God of our weary years, God of our silent tears, Thou who has brought us thus far on the way; Thou who has by Thy might Led us into the light, Keep us forever in the path, we pray. Lest our feet stray from the places, our God, where we met Thee, Lest, our hearts drunk with the wine of the world, we forget Thee; Shadowed beneath Thy hand, May we forever stand, True to our God, True to our native land.

◆ MARCUS GARVEY'S SPEECH AT LIBERTY HALL, NEW YORK CITY (1922)

Marcus Garvey, black nationalist and founder of the Universal Negro Improvement Association, dedicated his life to uplifting Africans throughout the world. In this 1922 address, Garvey outlined the goals of the Universal Negro Improvement Association.

Over five years ago the Universal Negro Improvement Association placed itself before the world as the movement through which the new and rising Negro would give expression of his feelings. This Association adopts an attitude not of hostility to other races and peoples of the world, but an attitude of self-respect.

. . . Wheresoever human rights are denied to any group, wheresoever justice is denied to any group, there the U.N.I.A. finds a cause. And at this time among all the peoples of the world, the group that suffers most from injustice, the group that is denied most of those rights that belong to all humanity, is the black group. . . even so under the leadership of the U.N.I.A., we are marshalling the 400,000,000 Negroes of the world to fight for the emancipation of the race and of the redemption of the country of our fathers.

We represent a new line of thought among Negroes. Whether you call it advanced thought or reactionary thought, I do not care. If it is reactionary for people to seek independence in government, then we are reactionary. If it is advanced thought for people to seek liberty and freedom, then we represent the advanced school of thought among the Negroes of this country. We of the U.N.I.A. believe that what is good for the other folks is good for us. If government is something that is worth while; if government is something that is appreciable and helpful and protective to others, then we also want to experiment in government. We do not mean a government that will make us citizens without rights or subjects without consideration. We mean a kind of government that will place our race in control, even as other races are in control of their own government.

. . . The U.N.I.A. is not advocating the cause of church building, because we have a sufficiently large number of churches among us to minister to the spiritual needs of the people, and we are not going to compete with those who are engaged in so splendid a work; we are not engaged in building any new social institutions,. . . because there are enough social workers engaged in those praiseworthy efforts. We are not engaged in politics because we have enough local politicians,. . . and the political situation is well taken care of. We are not engaged in domestic politics, in church building or in social uplift work, but we are engaged in nation building.

In advocating the principles of this Association we find we have been very much misunderstood and very much misrepresented by men from within our own race, as well as others from without. Any reform movement that seeks to bring about changes for the benefit of humanity is bound to be misrepresented by those who have always taken it upon themselves to administer to, and lead the unfortunate. . . .

. . . The Universal Negro Improvement Association stands for the Bigger Brotherhood; the Universal Negro Improvement Association stands for human rights, not only for Negroes, but for all races. The Universal Negro Improvement Association believes in the rights of not only the black race, the white race, the yellow race and the brown race. The Universal Negro Improvement Association believes that the white man has as much right to be considered, the yellow man has as much right to be considered, the brown man has as much right to be considered as the black man of Africa. In view of the fact that the black man of Africa has contributed as much to the world as the white man of Europe, and the brown man and yellow man of Asia, we of the Universal Negro Improvement Association demand that the white, yellow and brown races give to the black man his place in the civilization of the world. We ask for nothing more than the rights of 400,000,000 Negroes. We are not seeking, as I said before, to destroy or disrupt the society or the government of other races, but we are determined that 400,000,000 of us shall unite ourselves to free our motherland from the grasp of the invader. . . .

The Universal Negro Improvement Association is not seeking to build up another government within the bounds or borders of the United States of America. The Universal Negro Improvement Association is not seeking to disrupt any organized system of government, but the Association is determined to bring Negroes together for the building up of a nation of their own. And why? Because we have been forced to it. We have been forced to it throughout the world; not only in America, not only in Europe, not only in the British Empire, but wheresoever the black man happens to find himself, he has been forced to do for himself.

To talk about Government is a little more than some of our people can appreciate. . . .The average man. . . seems to say, "why should there be need for any other government?" We are French, English or American. But we of the U.N.I.A. have studied seriously this question of nationality among Negroes—this American nationality, this British nationality, this French, Italian or Spanish nationality, and have discovered that it counts for nought when that nationality comes in conflict with the racial idealism of the group that rules. When our interests clash with those of the ruling faction, then we find that we have absolutely no rights. In times of peace, when everything is all right, Negroes have a hard time, wherever we go, wheresoever we find ourselves, getting those rights that belong to us in common with others whom we claim as fellow citizens; getting that consideration that should be ours by right of the constitution, by right of the law, but in the time of trouble they make us all partners in the cause, as happened in the last war. . . .

We have saved many nations in this manner, and we have lost our lives doing that before. Hundreds of thousands—nay, millions of black men, lie buried under the ground due to that old-time camouflage of saving the nation. We saved the British Empire; we saved the French Empire; we saved this glorious country more than once; and all that we have received for our sacrifices, all that we have received for what we have done, even in giving up our lives, is just what you are receiving now, just what I am receiving now.

You and I fare no better in America, in the British Empire, or any other part of the white world; we fare no better than any black man wheresoever he shows his head. . . .

The U.N.I.A. is reversing the old-time order of things. We refuse to be followers anymore. We are leading ourselves. That means, if any saving is to be done. . . we are going to seek a method of saving Africa first. Why? And why Africa? Because Africa has become the grand prize of the nations. Africa has become the big game of the nation hunters. Today Africa looms as the greatest commercial, industrial and political prize in the world.

The difference between the Universal Negro Improvement Association and the other movements of this country, and probably the world, is that the Universal Negro Improvement Association seeks independence of government while the other organizations seek to make the Negro a secondary part of existing governments. We differ from the organizations in America because they seek to subordinate the Negro as a secondary consideration in a great civilization, knowing that in America the Negro will never reach his highest ambition, knowing that the Negro in America will never get his constitutional rights. All other organizations which are fostering the improvement of Negroes in the British Empire know that the Negro in the British Empire will never reach the height of his constitutional rights. What do I mean by constitutional rights in America? If the black man is to reach the height of his ambition in this country—if the black man is to get all of his constitutional rights in America—then the black man should have the same chance in the nation as any other man to become president of the nation, or a street cleaner in New York. If the black man in the British Empire is to have all his constitutional rights it means

that the Negro in the British Empire should have at least the same right to become premier of Great Britain as he has to become a street cleaner in the city of London. Are they prepared to give us such political equality? You and I can live in the United States of America for 100 more years, and our generations may live for 200 years or for 5000 more years, and so long as there is a black and white population, when the majority is on the side of the white race, you and I will never get political justice or get political equality in this country. Then why should a black man with rising ambition, after preparing himself in every possible way to give expression to that highest ambition, allow himself to be kept down by racial prejudice within a country? If I am as educated as the next man, if I am as prepared as the next man, if I have passed through the best schools and colleges and universities as the other fellow, why should I not have a fair chance to compete with the other fellow for the biggest position in the nation?. . .

We are not preaching a propaganda of hate against anybody. We love the white man; we love all humanity. . . . The white man is as necessary to the existence of the Negro as the Negro is necessary to his existence. There is a common relationship that we cannot escape. Africa has certain things that Europe wants, and Europe has certain things that Africa wants. . . it is impossible for us to escape it. Africa has oil, diamonds, copper, gold and rubber and all the minerals that Europe wants, and there must be some kind of relationship between Africa and Europe for a fair exchange, so we cannot afford to hate anybody.

The question often asked is what does it require to redeem a race and free a country? If it takes man power, if it takes scientific intelligence, if it takes education of any kind, or if it takes blood, then the 400,000,000 Negroes of the world have it.

It took the combined power of the Allies to put down the mad determination of the Kaiser to impose German will upon humanity. Among those who suppressed his mad ambition were two million Negroes who have not yet forgotten how to drive men across the firing line. . . when so many white men refused to answer to the call and dodged behind all kinds of excuses, 400,000 black men were ready without a question. It was because we were told it was a war of democracy; it was a war for the liberation of the weaker peoples of the world. We heard the cry of Woodrow Wilson, not because we liked him so, but because the things he said were of such a nature that they appealed to us as men. Wheresoever the cause of humanity stands in need of assistance, there you will find the Negro ever ready to serve.

He has done it from the time of Christ up to now. When the whole world turned its back upon the Christ, the man who was said to be the Son of God, when the world cried out "Crucify Him," when the world spurned Him and spat upon Him, it was a black man, Simon, the Cyrenian, who took up the cross. Why? Because the cause of humanity appealed to him. When the black man saw the suffering Jew, struggling under the heavy cross, he was willing to go to His assistance, and he bore that cross up to the heights of Calvary. In the spirit of Simon, the Cyrenian, 1900 years ago, we answered the call of Woodrow Wilson, the call to a larger humanity, and it was for that we willingly rushed into the war. . . .

We shall march out, yes, as black American citizens, as black British subjects, as black French citizens, as black Italians or as black Spaniards, but we shall march out with a greater loyalty, the loyalty of race. We shall march out in answer to the cry of our fathers, who cry out to us for the redemption of our own country, our motherland, Africa.

We shall march out, not forgetting the blessings of America. We shall march out, not forgetting the blessings of civilization. We shall march out with a history of peace before and behind us, and surety that history shall be our breast-plate, for how can a man fight better than knowing that the cause for which he fights is righteous?. . . Glorious shall be the battle when the time comes to fight for our people and our race.

We should say to the millions who are in Africa to hold the fort, for we are coming 400,000,000 strong.

◆ EXECUTIVE ORDER NO. 8802, 3 C.F.R., 1938–1943 COMP. P. 957 (1941)

Issued by President Franklin D. Roosevelt on June 25, 1941, Executive Order 8802 was intended to eliminate discriminatory practices in the defense industry during World War II (1941–1945).

Whereas it is the policy of the United States to encourage full participation in the national defense program by all citizens of the United States, regardless of race, creed, color, or national origin, in the firm belief that the democratic way of life within the Nation can be defended successfully only with the help and support of all groups within its borders; and

Whereas there is evidence that available and needed workers have been barred from employment in industries engaged in defense production solely because of considerations of race, creed, color, or national origin, to the detriment of workers' morale and of national unity:

Now, Therefore, by virtue of the authority vested in me by the Constitution and the statues, and as a prerequisite to the successful conduct of our national defense

production effort, I do hereby reaffirm the policy of the United States that there shall be no discrimination in the employment of workers in defense industries or Government because of race, creed, color, or national origin, and I do hereby declare that it is the duty of employers and of labor organizations, in furtherance of said policy and of this order, to provide for the full and equitable participation of all workers in defense industries, without discrimination because of race, creed, color, or national origin;

And it is hereby ordered as follows:

1. All departments and agencies of the Government of the United States concerned with vocational and training programs for defense production shall take special measures appropriate to assure that such programs are administered without discrimination because of race, creed, color, or national origin;

2. All contracting agencies of the Government of the United States shall include in all defense contracts hereafter negotiated by them a provision obligating the contractor not to discriminate against any worker because of race, creed, color, or national origin;

3. There is established in the Office of Production Management a Committee on Fair Employment Practice, which shall consist of a chairman and four other members to be appointed by the President. The Chairman and members of the Committee shall serve as such without compensation but shall be entitled to actual and necessary transportation, subsistence and other expenses incidental to performance of their duties. The Committee shall receive and investigate complaints of discrimination in violation of the provisions of this order and shall take appropriate steps to redress grievances which it finds to be valid. The Committee shall also recommend to the several departments and agencies of the Government of the United States and to the President all measures which may be deemed by it necessary or proper to effectuate the provisions of this order.

◆ EXECUTIVE ORDER NO. 9981, 3 C.F.R. 1943–1948 COMP. P. 720 (1948)

Signed by President Harry S. Truman on July 26, 1948, Executive Order 9981 ended segregation in the Armed Forces of the United States.

Whereas it is essential that there be maintained in the armed services of the United States the highest standards of democracy, with equality of treatment and opportunity for all those who serve in our country's defense:

Now, therefore, by virtue of the authority vested in me as President of the United States, by the Constitution and the statutes of the United States, and as Commander-in-Chief of the armed services, it is hereby ordered as follows:

1. It is hereby declared to be the policy of the President that there shall be equality of treatment and opportunity for all persons in the armed services without regard to race, color, religion or national origin. This policy shall be put into effect as rapidly as possible, having due regard to the time required to effectuate any necessary changes without impairing efficiency or morals.

2. There shall be created in the National Military Establishment an advisory committee to be known as the President's Committee on Equality of Treatment and Opportunity in the Armed Services, which shall be composed of seven members to be designated by the President.

3. The Committee is authorized on behalf of the President to examine into the rules, procedures and practices of the armed services in order to determine in what respect such rules, procedure and practices may be altered or improved with a view to carrying out the policy of this order. The Committee shall confer and advise with the Secretary of the Army, the Secretary of the Air Force, and shall make such recommendations to the President and to said Secretaries as in the judgment of the Committee will effectuate the policy hereof.

4. All executive departments and agencies of the Federal Government are authorized and directed to cooperate with the Committee in its work, and to furnish the Committee such information or the services of such persons as the Committee may require in the performance of its duties.

5. When requested by the Committee to do so, persons in the armed services or in any of the executive departments and agencies of the Federal Government shall testify before the Committee and shall make available for the use of the Committee such documents and other information as the Committee may require.

6. The Committee shall continue to exist until such time as the President shall terminate its existence by Executive order.

◆ BROWN V. BOARD OF EDUCATION OF TOPEKA, KANSAS 347 U.S. 483 (1954)

Beginning in the late 1930s, the U.S. Supreme Court began to review numerous cases dealing with

Prior to *Brown v. Board of Education of Topeka, Kansas,* African American children were often subjected to inferior educational facilities like the one pictured.

segregation in public education; by the 1950s it had become evident that segregated educational facilities were not equal.

In 1938, ruling in the case Missouri ex rel. Lloyd Gaines v. Canada, *the Court ruled that states were required to provide equal educational facilities for African Americans within its boundaries. (The state of Missouri at that time had maintained a practice of providing funds for African Americans to attend graduate and professional schools outside of the state, rather than provide facilities itself.) Taking an even greater step, in 1950 the Court in* Sweatt v. Painter *ruled that a separate law school for African Americans provided by the state of Texas violated the equal protection clause of the Fourteenth Amendment.*

In 1952, five different cases, all dealing with segregation in public schools but with different facts and from different places, reached the U.S. Supreme Court. Four of the cases, Brown v. Board of Education of Topeka, Kansas, Briggs v. Elliott *(out of South Carolina),* Davis v. Prince Edward County School Board *(out of Virginia), and* Gebhart v. Belton *(out of Delaware) were considered together; the fifth case* Bolling v. Sharpe *coming out of the District of Columbia, was considered separately (since the district is not a state).*

After hearing initial arguments, the Court found itself unable to reach an agreement. In 1953, the Court heard reargument. Thurgood Marshall, legal counsel for the National Association for the Advancement of Colored People Legal Defense and Education Fund, presented arguments on behalf of the African American students. On May 17, 1954, the Court unanimously ruled that segregation in all public education deprived minority children of equal protection under the Fourteenth Amendment. (In the Bolling *case, the Court determined that segregation violated provisions of the Fifth Amendment, since the Fourteenth Amendment is expressly directed to the states.)*

Chief Justice Warren delivered the opinion of the Court.

These cases come to us from the States of Kansas, South Carolina, Virginia and Delaware. They are premised on different facts and different local conditions, but a common legal question justifies their consideration together in this consolidated opinion.

In each of these cases, minors of the Negro race, through their legal representatives, seek the aid of the courts in obtaining admission to the public schools of their community on a nonsegregated basis. In each instance, they had been denied admission to schools attended by white children under laws requiring or permitting segregation according to race. This segregation was alleged to deprive the plaintiffs of the equal protection of the laws under the Fourteenth Amendment. In each of the cases other than the Delaware case, a three-judge federal district court denied relief to the plaintiffs on the so-called "separate but equal" doctrine announced by this Court in *Plessy v. Ferguson*. Under that doctrine, equality of treatment is accorded when the races are provided substantially equal facilities, even though these facilities be separate. In the Delaware case, the Supreme Court of Delaware adhered to that doctrine, but ordered that the plaintiffs be admitted to the white schools because of their superiority to the Negro schools.

The plaintiffs contend that segregated public schools are not "equal" and cannot be made "equal," and that hence they are deprived of the equal protection of the laws. Because of the obvious importance of the question presented, the Court took jurisdiction. Argument was heard in the 1952 Term, and reargument was heard this Term on certain questions propounded by the Court.

Reargument was largely devoted to the circumstances surrounding the adoption of the Fourteenth Amendment in 1868. It covered exhaustively consideration of the Amendment in Congress, ratification by the states, then existing practices in racial segregation, and the views of proponents and opponents of the Amendment. This discussion and our own investigation convince us that, although these sources cast some light, it is not enough to resolve the problem with which we are faced. At best, they are inconclusive. The most avid proponents of the post-War Amendments undoubtedly intended them to remove all legal distinctive among "all

persons born or naturalized in the United States." Their opponents, just as certainly, were antagonistic to both the letter and the spirit of the Amendments and wished them to have the most limited effect. What others in Congress and the state legislatures had in mind cannot be determined with any degree of certainty.

An additional reason for the inconclusive nature of the Amendment's history, with respect to segregated schools, is the status of public education at that time. In the South, the movement toward free common schools, supported by general taxation, had not yet taken hold. Education of white children was largely in the hands of private groups. Education of Negroes was almost non-existent, and practically all of the race were illiterate. In fact, any education of Negroes was forbidden by law in some states. Today, in contrast, many Negroes have achieved outstanding success in the arts and sciences as well as in the business and professional world. It is true that public school education at the time of the Amendment had advanced further in the North, but the effect of the Amendment on Northern States was generally ignored by the congressional debates. Even in the North, the conditions of public education did not approximate those existing today. The curriculum was usually rudimentary; ungraded schools were common in rural areas; the school term was but three months a year in many states; and compulsory school attendance was virtually unknown. As a consequence, it is not surprising that there should be so little in the history of the Fourteenth Amendment relating to its intended effect on public education.

In the first cases in this Court construing the Fourteenth Amendment, decided shortly after its adoption, the Court interpreted it as proscribing all state imposed discriminations against the Negro race. The doctrine of "separate but equal" did not make its appearance in this Court until 1896 in the case of *Plessy v. Ferguson*... involving not education but transportation. American courts have since labored with the doctrine for over half a century. In this Court, there have been six cases involving the "separate but equal" doctrine in the field of public education. In *Cumming v. County Board of Education*... and *Gong Lum v. Rice*... the validity of the doctrine itself was not challenged. In more recent cases, all on the graduate school level, inequality was found in that specific benefits enjoyed by white students were denied to Negro students of the same educational qualifications. In none of these cases [*Missouri ex rel. Gaines v. Canada, Sipuel v. University of Oklahoma, Sweatt v. Painter,* and *McLaurin v. Oklahoma State Regents for Higher Education*] was it necessary to reexamine the doctrine to grant relief to the Negro plaintiff. And in *Sweatt v. Painter . . .* the Court expressly reserved decision on the question whether *Plessy v. Ferguson* should be held inapplicable to public education.

In the instant cases, that question is directly presented. Here, unlike *Sweatt v. Painter*, there are findings below that the Negro and white schools involved have been equalized, or are being equalized, with respect to buildings, curricula, qualifications and salaries of teacher, and other "tangible" factors. Our decision, therefore, cannot turn on merely a comparison of these tangible factors in the Negro and white schools involved in each of the cases. We must look instead to the effect of segregation itself on public education.

In approaching this problem, we cannot turn the clock back to 1868 when the Amendment was adopted, or even to 1896 when *Plessy v. Ferguson* was written. We must consider public education in the light of its full development and its present place in American life throughout the Nation. Only in this way can it be determined if segregation in public schools deprives these plaintiffs of the equal protection of the laws.

Today, education is perhaps the most important function of state and local governments. Compulsory school attendance laws and the great expenditures for education both demonstrate our recognition of the importance of education to our democratic society. It is required in the performance of our most basic public responsibilities, even service in the armed forces. It is the very foundation of good citizenship. Today it is a principal instrument in awakening the child to cultural values, in preparing him for later professional training, and in helping him to adjust normally to his environment. In these days, it is doubtful that any child may reasonably be expected to succeed in life if he is denied the opportunity of an education. Such an opportunity, where the state has undertaken to provide it, is a right which must be made available to all on equal terms.

We come then to the question presented: Does segregation of children in public schools solely on the basis of race, even though the physical facilities and other "tangible" factors may be equal, deprive the children of the minority group of equal educational opportunities? We believe that it does.

In *Sweatt v. Painter* in finding that a segregated law school for Negroes could not provide them equal educational opportunities, this Court relied in large part on "those qualities which are incapable of objective measurement but which make for greatness in the law school." In *McLaurin v. Oklahoma State Regents for Higher Education . . .* the Court, in requiring that a Negro admitted to a white graduate school be treated like all other students, again resorted to intangible considerations: ". . . his ability to study, to engage in discussions and exchange views with other students, and, in general, to learn his profession." Such considerations apply with added force to children in grade and high schools. To separate them from others of similar age and qualifications solely because of their race generates a feeling of inferiority as to their status in the community that may affect their hearts and minds in a way unlikely ever to be undone. The effect of this separation on their educational opportunities was well stated by a finding in the Kansas case by a court which nevertheless felt compelled to rule against the Negro plaintiffs:

"Segregation of white and colored children in public school has a detrimental effect upon the colored children. The impact is greater when it has the sanction of the law; for the policy of separating the races is usually interpreted as denoting the inferiority of the negro group. A sense of inferiority affects the motivation of a child to learn. Segregation with the sanction of law, therefore, has a tendency to [retard] the educational and mental development of Negro children and to deprive them of some of the benefits they would receive in racial[ly] integrated school systems."

Whatever may have been the extent of psychological knowledge at the time of *Plessy v. Ferguson*, this finding is amply supported by modern authority. Any language in *Plessy v. Ferguson* contrary to this finding is rejected.

We conclude that in the field of public education the doctrine of "separate but equal" has no place. Separate educational facilities are inherently unequal. Therefore, we hold that the plaintiffs and others similarly situated for whom the actions have brought are, by reason of the segregation complained of, deprived of the equal protection of the laws guaranteed by the Fourteenth Amendment. This disposition makes unnecessary any discussion whether such segregation also violates the Due Process Clause of the Fourteenth Amendment.

Because these are class actions, because of the wide applicability of this decision, and because of the great variety of local conditions, the formulation of decrees in these presents problems of considerable complexity.

On reargument, the consideration of appropriate relief was necessarily subordinated to the primary question—the constitutionality of segregation in public education. We have now announced that such segregation is a denial of the equal protection of the laws. In order that we may have the full assistance of the parties in formulating decrees, the cases will be restored to the docket, and the parties are requested to present further argument on Questions 4 and 5 previously propounded by the Court for the reargument this Term. The Attorney General of the United States is again invited to participate. The Attorneys General of the states requiring or permitting segregation in public education will also be permitted to appear as amici curiae upon request to do so by September 15, 1954, and submission of briefs by October 1, 1954.

It is so ordered.

◆ THE SOULS OF BLACK FOLKS: ESSAYS AND SKETCHES BY W.E.B. DU BOIS (1955) (EXCERPT)

Many scholars believe that among prominent civil rights leader W.E.B. Du Bois's greatest achievements, his writings truly stand out. Throughout his lifetime, he penned many books and essays expressing his beliefs about racial assimilation, cooperation, and the use of education to end prejudice. Among these notable writings is The Souls of Black Folk, *an extremely popular analysis of the problem of race as it relates to African Americans throughout society.*

After the Egyptian and Indian, the Greek and Roman, the Teuton and Mongolian, the Negro is sort of seventh son, born with a veil, and gifted with second-sight in this American world,—a world which yields him no true self-consciousness, but only lets him see himself through the revelation of the other world. It is a peculiar sensation, this double-consciousness, this sense of always looking at one's self through the eyes of others, of measuring one's soul by the tape of a world that looks on in amused contempt and pity. One ever feels his two-ness,—an American, a Negro; two souls, two thoughts, two unreconciled strivings; two warring ideals in one dark body, whose dogged strength alone keeps it from being torn asunder.

The history of the American Negro is the history of this strife,—this longing to attain self-conscious manhood, to merge his double self into a better and truer self. In this merging he wishes neither of the older selves to be lost. He would not Africanize America, for

America has too much to teach the world and Africa. He would not bleach his Negro soul in a flood of white Americanism, for he knows that Negro blood has a message for the world. He simply wishes to make it possible for a man to be both a Negro and an American, without being cursed and spit upon by his fellows, without having the doors of Opportunity closed roughly in his face.

◆ MARY MCLEOD BETHUNE'S LAST WILL AND TESTAMENT (1955) (EXCERPT)

Prior to her death on May 18, 1955, educator and Bethune-Cookman College founder Mary McLeod Bethune composed her "Last Will and Testament," which was published posthumously in Ebony *magazine. Although a tireless fighter for equality and educational opportunities for African Americans, she continuously eschewed rhetorical militancy in favor of a doctrine of universal love, as demonstrated by the following text.*

Sometimes as I sit communing in my study I feel that death is not far off. I am aware that it will overtake me before the greatest of my dreams—full equality for the Negro in our time is realized. . . . The knowledge that my work has been helpful to many fills me with joy and great satisfaction.

Sometimes I ask myself if I have any other legacy to leave. Truly, my worldly possessions are few. . . . Perhaps in them there is something of value. So, as my life draws to a close, I will pass them on to Negroes everywhere in the hope that an old woman's philosophy may give them inspiration. Here, then, is my legacy.

I leave you love. Love builds. It is positive and helpful.

I leave you great hope. The Negro's growth will be great in the years to come.

I leave you the challenge of developing confidence in one another. As long as Negroes are hemmed into racial blocs by prejudice and pressure, it will be necessary for them to band together for economic betterment.

I leave you a thirst for education. Knowledge is the prime need of the hour.

I leave you a respect for the uses of power. We live in a world which respects power above all things. Power, intelligently directed, can lead to more freedom.

I leave you faith. Faith is the first factor in a life devoted to service. Without faith, nothing is possible.

With it, nothing is impossible. Faith in God is the greatest power, but great, too, is faith in oneself.

I leave you racial dignity. I want Negroes to maintain their human dignity at all costs. We, as Negroes, must recognize that we are the custodians as well as the heirs of a great civilization.

I leave you a desire to live harmoniously with your fellow men. The problem of color is world-wide. It is found in Africa and Asia, Europe, and South America. I appeal to American Negroes—North, South, East and West—to recognize their common problems and unite to solve them.

I leave you finally a responsibility to our young people. The world around us really belongs to youth, for youth will take over its future management.

If I have a legacy to leave my people, it is my philosophy of living and serving. As I face tomorrow, I am content, for I think I have spent my life well. I pray now that my philosophy may be helpful to those who share my vision of a world of Peace, Progress, Brotherhood and Love.

◆ CIVIL RIGHTS ACT OF 1957, PUB.L. NO. 85–315, 71 STAT. 634 (1957)

This act, signed by President Eisenhower on September 9, 1957, was the first piece of comprehensive legislation in the area of civil rights since the Civil Rights Act of 1875, which the Supreme Court in 1883 declared unconstitutional. The new act provided for the creation of a Commission on Civil Rights, extended the jurisdiction of the federal district courts to include civil action arising out of the act, and empowered the U.S. Attorney General to take action in cases where rights secured by the act were believed to have been violated.

An Act to provide means of further securing and protecting the civil rights of persons within the jurisdiction of the United States.

Part I—Establishment of the Commission on Civil Rights

Sec. 101. (a) There is created in the executive branch of the Government a Commission on Civil Rights (hereinafter called the "Commission").

(b) The Commission shall be composed of six members who shall be appointed by the President by and with the advice and consent of the Senate. Not more than three of the members shall at any one time be of the same political party.

(c) The President shall designate one of the members of the Commission as Chairman and one as Vice Chairman. The Vice Chairman shall act as Chairman in the absence or disability of the Chairman, or in the event of a vacancy in that office.

(d) Any vacancy in the Commission shall not affect its powers and shall be filled in the same manner, and subject to the same limitation with respect to party affiliations as the original appointment was made. . . .

Part IV—To Provide Means of Further Securing and Protecting the Right to Vote

Sec. 131. Section 2004 of the Revised Statutes (42 U.S.C. 1971), is amended as follows:

. . . No person, whether acting under cover of law or otherwise, shall intimidate, threaten, coerce, or attempt to intimidate, or coerce any other person for the purpose of interfering with the right of such other person to vote as he may choose, or of causing such other person to vote, for, or to vote as he may choose, or of causing such other person to vote for, or not to vote for, any candidate for the office of President, Vice President, presidential elector, Member of the Senate, or Member of the House of Representatives, Delegates or Commissioners from the Territories or possessions, at any general, special, or primary election held solely or in part for the purpose of selecting or electing any such candidate.

. . . Whenever any person has engaged or there are reasonable grounds to believe that any person is about to engage in any act or practice which would deprive any right or privilege secured by subsection (a) or (b), the Attorney General may institute for the United States, or in the name of the United States, a civil action or other proper proceeding for preventive relief, including an application for a permanent or temporary injunction, restraining order, or other order. In any proceeding hereunder the United States shall be liable for costs the same as a private person. . . .

◆ EXECUTIVE ORDER NO. 10730, 3 C.F.R. 1954–1958 COMP. P. 388 (1957)

In September of 1957, Arkansas Governor Orval Faubus mobilized the Arkansas National Guard in an

Federal troops escorting African American students to class at Little Rock's Central High School.

effort to prevent African American students from entering Little Rock's Central High School. As a result, on September 24, President Dwight D. Eisenhower issued an executive order authorizing the use of the National Guard and the Air National Guard of the United States to assist in desegregation in Little Rock.

Whereas on September 23, 1957, I issued Proclamation No. 3204 reading in part as follows:

Whereas certain persons in the State of Arkansas, individually and in unlawful assemblages, combinations, and conspiracies, have wilfully obstructed the enforcement of orders of the United States District Court for the Eastern District of Arkansas with respect to matters relating to enrollment and attendance at public schools, particularly at Central High School, located in Little Rock School District, Little Rock, Arkansas; and

Whereas such wilful obstruction of justice hinders the execution of the laws of that State and of the United States, and makes it impracticable to enforce such laws by the ordinary course of judicial proceedings; and

Whereas such obstruction of justice constitutes a denial of the equal protection of the laws secured by the Constitution of the United States and impedes the course of justice under those laws;

Now, therefore, I, Dwight D. Eisenhower, President of the United States, under and by virtue of the authority vested in me by the Constitution and Statutes of the United States, including Chapter 15 of Title 10 of the United States Code, particularly sections 332, 333 and 334 thereof, do command all persons engaged in such obstruction of justice to cease and desist therefrom, and to disperse forthwith, and

Whereas the command contained in that Proclamation has not been obeyed and wilful obstruction of enforcement of said court orders still exists and threatens to continue:

Now, therefore, by virtue of the authority vested in me by the Constitution and Statutes of the United States, including Chapter 15 of Title 10, particularly sections 332, 333 and 334 thereof, and section 301 of Title 3 of the United States Code, it is hereby ordered as follows:

Section 1. I hereby authorize and direct the Secretary of Defense to order into the active military service of the United States as he may deem appropriate to carry out the purposes of this Order, any or all of the units of the National Guard of the United States and of the Air National Guard of the United States within the State of Arkansas to serve in the active military service of the United States for an indefinite period and until relieved by appropriate orders.

Section 2. The Secretary of Defense is authorized and directed to take all appropriate steps to enforce any orders of the United States District Court for the Eastern District of Arkansas for the removal of obstruction of justice in the State of Arkansas with respect to matters relating to enrollment and attendance at public schools in the Little Rock School District, Little Rock, Arkansas. In carrying out the provisions of this section, the Secretary of Defense is authorized to use the units, and members thereof, ordered into the active military service of the United States pursuant to Section 1 of this Order.

Section 3. In furtherance of the enforcement of the aforementioned orders of the United States District Court for the Eastern District of Arkansas, the Secretary of Defense is authorized to use such of the armed forces of the United States as he may deem necessary.

Section 4. The Secretary of Defense is authorized to delegate to the Secretary of the Army or the Secretary of the Air Force, or both, any of the authority conferred upon him by this Order.

◆ CIVIL RIGHTS ACT OF 1960, PUB.L. NO. 86–449, 74 STAT. 86 (1960)

This act, signed by President Eisenhower on May 6, 1960, further defined civil rights violations and outlined penalties connected with such violations. It guaranteed the provision of criminal penalties in the event a suspect crosses state lines to avoid legal process for the actual or attempted bombing or burning of any vehicle or building, and provided penalties for persons who obstructed or interfered with any order of a federal court.

An Act to enforce constitutional rights, and for other purposes.

Title II

Sec. 201. Chapter 49 of title 18, United States Code, is amended by adding at the end thereof a new section as follows:

Section 1074. Flight to avoid prosecution for damaging or destroying any building or other real or personal property.

. . . Whoever moves or travels in interstate or foreign commerce with intent either (1) to avoid prosecution, or custody, or confinement after conviction, under the laws of the place from which he flees, for willfully attempting to or damaging or destroying by fire or explosive any building, structure, facility, vehicle, dwelling house, synagogue, church, religious center or educational institution, public or private, or (2) to avoid giving testimony in any criminal proceeding relating to any such offense shall be fined not more than $5,000 or imprisoned not more than five years, or both.

. . . Violations of this section may be prosecuted in the Federal judicial district in which the original crime was alleged to have been committed or in which the person was held in custody or confinement. . . .

Sec. 203. Chapter 39 of title 18 of the United States Code is amended by adding at the end thereof the following new section:

Section 837. Explosives; illegal use or possession; and, threats or false information concerning attempts to damage or destroy real or personal property by fire or explosives.

. . . Whoever transports or aids and abets another in transporting in interstate or foreign commerce any explosive, with the knowledge or intent that it will be used to damage or destroy any building or other real or personal property for the purpose of interfering with its use for educational, religious, charitable, residential, business, or civic objectives or of intimidating any person pursuing such objectives, shall be subject to imprisonment for not more than one year, or a fine of not more than $1,000 or both; and if personal injury results shall be subject to imprisonment for not more than ten years or a fine of not more than $10,000, or both; and if death results shall be subject to imprisonment for any term of years or for life, but the court may impose the death penalty if the jury so recommends.

. . . The possession of an explosive in such a manner as to evince an intent to use, or the use of, such explosive, to damage or destroy any building or other real or personal property used for educational, religious, charitable, residential, business, or civic objectives or to intimidate any person pursuing such objectives, creates rebuttable presumptions that the explosive was transported in interstate or foreign commerce or caused to be transported in interstate or foreign commerce by the person so possessing or using it, or by a person aiding or abetting the person so possessing or using it: Provided, however, that no person may be convicted under this section unless there is evidence independent of the presumptions that this section has been violated.

. . . Whoever, through the use of the mail, telephone, telegraph, or other instrument of commerce, willfully imparts or conveys, or causes to be imparted or conveyed, any threat, or false information knowing the same to be false, concerning an attempt or alleged attempt being made, or to be made, to damage or destroy any building or other real or personal property for the purpose of interfering with its use for educational, religious, charitable, residential, business, or civic objectives, or of intimidating any person pursuing such objectives, shall be subject to imprisonment for not more than one year or a fine of not more than $1,000, or both.

◆ EXECUTIVE ORDER NO. 11053, 3 C.F.R. 1959–1963 COMP P.645 (1962)

On September 30, 1962, riots erupted on the campus of the University of Mississippi when Governor Ross Barnett attempted to block the court-ordered admission of African American student James H. Meredith. President John F. Kennedy quickly responded by authorizing the use of federal troops to restore order.

Whereas on September 30, 1962, I issued Proclamation No. 3497 reading in part as follows:

Whereas the Governor of the State of Mississippi and certain law enforcement officers and other officials of that State, and other persons, individually and in unlawful opposing and obstructing the enforcement of orders entered by the United States District Court for the Southern District of Mississippi and the United States Court of Appeals for the Fifth Circuit; and

Whereas such unlawful assemblies, combinations, and conspiracies oppose and obstruct the execution of the laws of the United States, impede the course of justice under those laws and make it impracticable to enforce those laws in the State of Mississippi by the ordinary course of judicial proceedings; and

Whereas I have expressly called the attention of the Governor of Mississippi to the perilous situation that exists and to his duties in the premises, and have requested but have not received from him adequate assurances that the orders of the courts of the United States will be obeyed and that law and order will be maintained:

Now, therefore, I, John F. Kennedy, President of the United States, under and by virtue of the authority vested in me by the Constitution and laws of the United States, including Chapter 15 of Title 10 of the United States Code, particularly sections 332, 333 and 334 thereof, do command all persons engaged in such obstructions of justice to cease and desist therefrom to disperse and retire peaceably forth-with; and

Whereas the commands contained in that proclamation have not been obeyed and obstruction of enforcement of those court orders still exists and threatens to continue:

Now, therefore, by virtue of the authority vested in me by the Constitution and laws of the United States, including Chapter 15 of Title 10, particularly Sections 332, 333 and 334 thereof, and Section 301 of Title 3 of the United States Code, it is hereby ordered as follows:

Section 1. The Secretary of Defense is authorized and directed to take all appropriate steps to enforce all orders of the United States District Court for the Southern District of Mississippi and the United States Court of Appeals for the Fifth Circuit and to remove all obstructions of justice in the State of Mississippi.

Section 2. In furtherance of the enforcement of the aforementioned orders of the United States District Court for the Southern District of Mississippi and the United States Court of Appeals for the Fifth Circuit, the Secretary of Defense is authorized to use such of the armed forces of the United States as he may deem necessary.

Section 3. I hereby authorize the Secretary of Defense to call into the active military service of the United States, as he may deem appropriate to carry out the purposes of this order, any or all of the units of the Army National Guard and of the Air National Guard of the State of Mississippi to serve in the active military service of the United States for an indefinite period and until relieved by appropriate orders. In carrying out the provisions of Section 1, the Secretary of Defense is authorized to use the units, and members thereof, ordered into the active military service of the United States pursuant to this section.

Section 4. The Secretary of Defense is authorized to delegate to the Secretary of the Army or the Secretary of the Air Force, or both, any of the authority conferred upon him by this order.

◆ THE BIRMINGHAM MANIFESTO (1963) [EXCERPT]

In 1963, a series of events in Birmingham, Alabama made known the plight of African Americans to

the nation at large. African American citizens were arrested en masse during peaceful demonstrations—demonstrations which were crushed by police dogs and firehoses. The Manifesto, dated April 3, 1963, embodied the hope of the African American community in Birmingham that law, order, and peace would somehow prevail.

The patience of an oppressed people cannot endure forever. The Negro citizens of Birmingham for the last several years have hoped in vain for some evidence. . . [of the]. . . resolution of our just grievances.

Birmingham is part of the United States and we are bona fide citizens. Yet the history of Birmingham reveals that very little of the democratic process touches the life of the Negro in Birmingham. We have been segregated racially, exploited economically, and dominated politically. Under the leadership of the Alabama Christian Movement for Human Rights, we sought relief by petition for the repeal of city ordinances requiring segregation and the institution of a merit hiring policy in city employment. We were rebuffed. We then turned to the system of the courts. We weathered set-back after set-back, with all of its costliness, finally winning the terminal, bus, parks and airport cases. The bus decision has been implemented begrudging and the parks decision prompted the closing of all municipally-owned recreational facilities with the exception of the zoo and Legion Field. . . .

We have always been a peaceful people, bearing our oppression with superhuman effort. Yet we have been the victims of repeated violence, not only that inflicted by the hoodlum element but also that inflicted by the blatant misuse of police power. . . . For years, while our homes and churches were being bombed, we heard nothing but the rantings and ravings of racist city officials.

The Negro protest for equality and justice has been a voice crying in the wilderness. Most of Birmingham has remained silent, probably out of fear. In the meanwhile, our city has acquired the dubious reputation of being the worst big city in race relations in the United States. Last fall, for a flickering moment, it appeared that sincere community leaders from religion, business and industry discerned the inevitable confrontation in race relations approaching. Their concern for the city's image and commonwealth of all its citizens did not run deep enough. Solemn promises were made, pending a postponement of direct action, that we would be joined in a suit seeking the relief of segregation ordinances. Some merchants agreed to desegregate their restrooms as a good faith start, some actually complying, only to

retreat shortly thereafter. We hold in our hands now, broken faith and broken promises. We believe in the American Dream of democracy, in the Jeffersonian doctrine that "all men are created equal and are endowed by their Creator with certain inalienable rights, among these being life, liberty and the pursuit of happiness."

Twice since September we have deferred our direct action thrust in order that a change in city government would not be made in the hysteria of a community crisis. We act today in full concert with our Hebraic-Christian traditions, the law of morality and the Constitution of our nation. The absence of justice and progress in Birmingham demands that we make a moral witness to give our community a chance to survive. We demonstrate our faith that we believe that the beloved community can come to Birmingham. We appeal to the citizenry of Birmingham, Negro and white, to join us in this witness for decency, morality, self-respect and human dignity. Your individual and corporate support can hasten the day of "liberty and justice for all." This is Birmingham's moment of truth in which every citizen can play his part in her larger destiny. . . .

◆ MARTIN LUTHER KING'S SPEECH AT THE LINCOLN MEMORIAL, WASHINGTON, DC (1963)

On August 28, 1963, some 250,000 people gathered at the Lincoln Memorial in Washington, DC, in order to raise the nation's consciousness and to demonstrate on behalf of the civil legislation being debated in Congress. It was during this demonstration that Dr. Martin Luther King Jr. gave the "I Have a Dream" speech.

I am happy to join with you today in what will go down in history as the greatest demonstration for freedom in the history of our nation.

Five score years ago, a great American, in whose symbolic shadow we stand today, signed the Emancipation Proclamation. This momentous decree came as a great beacon of light of hope to millions of Negro slaves who had been seared in the flames of withering injustice. It came as a joyous daybreak to end the long night of their captivity.

But one hundred years later, the Negro is still not free. One hundred years later, the life of the Negro is still sadly crippled by the manacles of segregation and the chains of discrimination. One hundred years later, the Negro lives on a lonely island of poverty in the midst of a vast ocean of material prosperity. One hundred years later, the Negro is still languished in the corners of American society and finds himself an exile in his own land. So we have come here today to dramatize a shameful condition.

In a sense we have come to our nation's capitol to cash a check. When the architects of our republic wrote the magnificent words of the Constitution and the Declaration of Independence, they were signing a promissory note to which every American was to fall heir. This note was a promise that all men, yes black men as well as white men, would be guaranteed the unalienable rights of life, liberty, and the pursuit of happiness. It is obvious today that America has defaulted on this promissory note insofar as her citizens of color are concerned. Instead of honoring this sacred obligation, America has given the Negro people a bad check: a check which has come back marked "insufficient funds." But we refuse to believe that the bank of justice is bankrupt. We refuse to believe that there are insufficient funds in the great vaults of opportunity of this nation. So we have come to cash this check—a check that will give us upon demand the riches of freedom and the security of justice.

We have also come to this hallowed spot to remind America of the fierce urgency of now. This is not the time to engage in the luxury of cooling off or to take the tranquilizing drug of gradualism. Now is the time to make real the promises of democracy. Now is the time to rise from the dark and desolate valley of segregation to the sunlit path of racial justice. Now is the time to lift our nation from the quicksands of racial injustice to the solid rock of brotherhood. Now is the time to make justice a reality for all of God's children.

It would be fatal for the nation to overlook the urgency of the moment and to underestimate the determination of the Negro. This sweltering summer of the Negro's legitimate discontent will not pass until there is an invigorating autumn of freedom and equality. Nineteen hundred and sixty-three is not an end, but a beginning. Those who hope that the Negro needed to blow off steam, and will now be content will have a rude awakening if the Nation returns to business as usual. There will neither be rest nor tranquility in America until the Negro is granted his citizenship rights. The whirlwinds of revolt will continue to shake the foundations of our Nation until the bright day of justice emerges.

But there is something that I must say to my people who stand on the warm threshold which leads into the palace of justice. In the process of gaining our rightful place we must not be guilty of wrongful deeds. Let us not seek to satisfy our thirst for freedom by drinking from the cup of bitterness and hatred.

We must forever conduct our struggle on the high plane of dignity and discipline. We must not allow our creative protest to degenerate into physical violence. Again and again we must rise to the majestic heights of meeting physical force with soul force. The marvelous new militancy which has engulfed the Negro community must not lead us to a distrust of all white people, for many of our white brothers, as evidenced by their presence here today, have come to realize that their destiny is tied up with our destiny and their freedom is inextricably bound to our freedom. We cannot walk alone.

And as we walk, we must make the pledge that we shall always march ahead. We cannot turn back. There are those who are asking the devotees of civil rights, "when will you be satisfied?" We can never be satisfied as long as the Negro is the victim of the unspeakable horrors of police brutality. We can never be satisfied as long as our bodies, heavy with the fatigue of travel, cannot gain lodging in the motels of the highways and the hotels of the cities. We cannot be satisfied as long as the Negro's basic mobility is from a smaller ghetto to a larger one. We can never be satisfied as long as our children are stripped of their self-hood and robbed of their dignity by signs reading "For Whites Only." We can never be satisfied as long as a Negro in Mississippi cannot vote and a Negro in New York believes he has nothing for which to vote. No. No, we are not satisfied, and we will not be satisfied until justice rolls down like waters, and righteousness like a mighty stream.

I am not unmindful that some of you have come here out of great trials and tribulations. Some of you have come fresh from narrow jail cells. Some of you have come from areas where your quest for freedom left you battered by the storms of persecution and staggered by the winds of police brutality. You have been the victims of creative suffering. Continue to work with the faith that unearned suffering is redemptive.

Go back to Mississippi, go back to Alabama, go back to South Carolina, go back to Georgia, go back to Louisiana, go back to the slums and ghettos of our northern cities, knowing that somehow this situation can and will be changed. Let us not wallow in the valley of despair.

I say to you today, my friends, that in spite of the difficulties and frustrations of the moment, I still have a dream. It is a dream deeply rooted in the American dream. I have a dream that one day this nation will rise up and live out the true meaning of its creed: "We hold these truths to be self-evident—that all men are created equal."

I have a dream that one day on the red hills of Georgia the sons of former slaves and the sons of former slaveowners will be able to sit down together at the table of brotherhood. I have a dream that one day even the state of Mississippi, a desert state sweltering with the heat of injustice and oppression, will be transformed into an oasis of freedom and justice.

I have a dream that my four little children will one day live in a nation where they will not be judged by the color of their skin but by the content of their character.

I have a dream today.

I have a dream that one day the state of Alabama, whose governor's lips are presently dripping with the words of interposition and nullification, will be transformed into a situation where little black boys and black girls will be able to join hands with little white boys and white girls and walk together as sisters and brothers.

I have a dream today.

I have a dream that one day every valley shall be exalted, every hill and mountain shall be made low, the rough places will be made plain, and the crooked places will be made straight, and the glory of the Lord shall be revealed, and all flesh shall see it together.

This is our hope. This is the faith with which I return to the South. With this faith we will be able to transform the jangling discords of our nation into a beautiful symphony of brotherhood. With this faith we will be able to work together, to pray together, to struggle together, to go to jail together, to stand up for freedom together, knowing that we will be free one day.

This will be the day when all of God's children will be able to sing the new meaning "My country 'tis of thee, sweet land of liberty, of thee I sing. Land where my fathers died, land of the pilgrim's pride, from every mountainside, let freedom ring."

And if America is to be a great nation this must become true. So let freedom ring from the prodigious hilltops of New Hampshire! Let freedom ring from the mighty mountains of New York! Let freedom ring from the heightening Alleghenies of Pennsylvania!

Let freedom ring from the snowcapped Rockies of Colorado!

Let freedom ring from the curvaceous peaks of California!

But not only that; let freedom ring from Stone Mountain of Georgia!

Let freedom ring from Lookout Mountain of Tennessee.

Let freedom ring from every hill and mole hill of Mississippi. From every mountainside, let freedom ring.

When we let freedom ring, when we let it ring from every village and every hamlet, from every state and every city, we will be able to speed up that day when all God's children—black men and white men, Jews and Gentiles, Protestants and Catholics—will be able to join hands and sing in the words of that old Negro spiritual, Free at last! Free at last! Thank God almighty, we are free at last!

◆ AMENDMENT TWENTY-FOUR TO THE UNITED STATES CONSTITUTION (1964)

By 1964, when the Twenty-Fourth Amendment was ratified, most states had already discontinued the use of the poll tax, which had proved to be one of the most effective means of keeping African Americans from the polls—only the states of Alabama, Arkansas, Mississippi, Texas, and Virginia still implemented such a tax. The amendment, proposed in 1962, banned the use of poll taxes as a prerequisite to participating in federal elections; ruling in the case Harper v. Virginia Board of Elections, *the U.S. Supreme Court banned the use of poll taxes in state elections.*

Section 1. The right of citizens of the United States to vote in any primary or other election for President or Vice President, for electors for President or Vice President, or for Senator or Representative in Congress, shall not be denied or abridged by the United States or any State by reason of failure to pay any poll tax or other tax.

Section 2. The congress shall have power to enforce this article by appropriate legislation.

◆ CIVIL RIGHTS ACT OF 1964, PUB. L. NO. 88–352, 78 STAT. 241 (1964)

This civil rights act was signed by President Lyndon B. Johnson on July 2, 1964, although it had been initiated by President John F. Kennedy in June of

1963. More comprehensive than previous acts, the 1964 act contained 11 titles covering the areas of voting rights, access to public facilities, federal aid to schools engaged in the process of desegregation, discrimination in federally funded programs, and discrimination in employment. The act also strengthened earlier voter registration protection; made racial discrimination in restaurants, hotels, and motels illegal; provided for equal access to public parks, pools, and other facilities; outlined unlawful employment practice; and mandated the creation of a federal Equal Employment Opportunity Commission.

An Act to enforce the constitutional right to vote, to confer jurisdiction upon the district courts of the United States to provide injunctive relief against discrimination in public accommodations, to authorize the Attorney General to institute suits to protect constitutional rights in public facilities and public education, to extend the Commission on Civil Rights, to prevent discrimination in federally assisted programs, to establish a Commission on Equal Employment Opportunity, and for other purposes.

Title I—Voting Rights

Sec. 101. Section 2004 of the Revised Statutes (42 U.S.C. 1971). . . is further amended as follows:. . . .

. . . "No Person acting under color of law shall—"

"(A) In determining whether any individual is qualified under State law or laws to vote in any Federal election, apply any standard, practice, or procedure different from the standards, practices, or procedures applied under such law or laws to other individuals within the same county, parish, or similar political subdivision who have been found by State officials to be qualified to vote;"

"(B) deny the right of any individual to vote in any Federal election because of an error or omission on any record or paper relating to any application, registration, or other act requisite to voting, if such error or omission is not material in determining whether such individual is qualified under State law to vote in such election; or"

"(C) employ any literacy test as a qualification for voting in any Federal election unless (I) such test is administered to each individual and is conducted wholly in writing, and (II) a certified copy of the test and of the answers given by the individual is furnished to him within twenty-five days of the submission of his request

made within the period of time during which records and papers are required to be retained and preserved pursuant to title III of the Civil Rights Act of 1960 (42 U.S.C. 1974–74e; 74 Stat. 88). . . ."

Sec. 201. (a) All persons shall be entitled to the full and equal enjoyment of the goods, services, facilities, privileges, advantages, and accommodations of any place of public accommodation, as defined in this section, without discrimination or segregation on the ground of race, color, religion, or national origin.

(b) Each of the following establishments which serves the public is a place of public accommodation within the meaning of this title if its operations affect commerce, or if discrimination or segregation by it is supported by State action:

(1) any inn, hotel, motel, or other establishment which provides lodging to transient guests, other than an establishment located within a building which contains not more than five rooms for rent or hire and which is actually occupied by the proprietor of such establishment as his residence;

(2) any restaurant, cafeteria, lunchroom, lunch counter, soda fountain, or other facility principally engaged in selling food for consumption on the premises, including, but not limited to, any such facility located on the premises of any retail establishment; or any gasoline station;

(3) any motion picture house, theater, concert hall, sports arena, stadium or other place of exhibition or entertainment; and

(4) any establishment (A)(I) which is physically located within the premises of any establishment otherwise covered by this subsection, or (II) within the premises of which is physically located any such covered establishment, and (B) which holds itself out as serving patrons of such covered establishment. . . .

(e) The provisions of this title shall not apply to a private club or other establishment not in fact open to the public, except to the extent that the facilities of such establishment are made available to the customers or patrons of an establishment within the scope of subsection (b).

Sec. 206. (a) Whenever the Attorney General has reasonable cause to believe that any person or group of persons is engaged in a pattern or practice of resistance to the full enjoyment of any of the rights secured by this title, and that the pattern or practice is of such a nature and is intended to deny the full exercise of the rights herein described, the Attorney General may bring a civil action in the appropriate district court of the United States. . . .

Title IV—Desegregation of Public Education

Sec. 407. (a) Whenever the Attorney General receives a complaint in writing—

(1) signed by a parent or group of parents to the effect that his or their minor children, as members of a class of persons similarly situated, are being deprived by a school board of the equal protection of the laws, or

(2) signed by an individual, or his parent, to the effect that he has been denied admission to or not permitted to continue in attendance at a public college by reason of race, color, religion, or national origin and the Attorney General believes the complaint is meritorious and certifies that the signer or signers of such complaint are unable, in his judgment, to initiate and maintain appropriate legal proceedings for relief and that the institution of an action will materially further the orderly achievement of desegregation in public education, the Attorney General is authorized, after giving notice of such complaint to the appropriate school board or college authority and after certifying that he is satisfied that such board or authority has had a reasonable time to adjust the conditions alleged in such complaint, to institute for or in the name of the United States a civil action in any appropriate district court of the United States against such parties and for such relief as may be appropriate. . . .

Title VI—Nondiscrimination In Federally-Assisted Programs

Sec. 601. No person in the United States shall, on the ground of race, color, or national origin, be excluded from participation in, be denied the benefits of, or be subjected to discrimination under any program or activity receiving Federal financial assistance. . . .

Title VII—Equal Employment Opportunity

Sec. 703. (a) It shall be an unlawful employment practice for an employer—

(1) to fail or refuse to hire or to discharge any individual, or otherwise to discriminate against any individual with respect to his compensation, terms, conditions, or privileges of employment, because of such individual's race, color, religion, sex, or national origin; or

(2) to limit, segregate, or classify his employees in any way which would deprive or tend to deprive any individual of employment opportunities or otherwise adversely affect his status as an employee, because of such individual's race, color, religion, sex, or national origin.

(b) It shall be an unlawful employment practice for an employment agency to fail or refuse to refer for employment, or otherwise to discriminate against, any individual because of his race, color, religion, sex, or national origin, or to classify or refer for employment any individual on the basis of his race, color, religion, sex, or national origin.

(c) It shall be an unlawful employment practice for a labor organization—

(1) to exclude or to expel from its membership, or otherwise to discriminate against, any individual because of his race, color, religion, sex, or national origin;

(2) to limit, segregate, or classify its membership, or to classify or fail or refuse to refer for employment any individual, in any way which would deprive or tend to deprive any individual of employment opportunities, or would limit such employment opportunities or otherwise adversely affect his status as an employee or as an applicant for employment, because of such individual's race, color, religion, sex, or national origin; or

(3) to cause or attempt to cause an employer to discriminate against an individual in violation of this section.

(d) It shall be an unlawful employment practice for any employer, labor organization, or joint labor-management committee controlling apprenticeship or other training or retraining, including on-the-job training programs to discriminate against any individual because of his race, color, religion, sex, or national origin in admission to, or employment in, any program established to provide apprenticeship or other training.

(e) Notwithstanding any other provision of this title, (1) it shall not be an unlawful employment practice for an employer to hire and employ employees, for an employment agency to classify, or refer for employment any individual, for a labor organization to classify its membership or to classify or refer for employment any individual, or for an employer, labor organization, or joint labor-management committee controlling apprenticeship or other training or retraining programs to admit or employ any individual in any such program, on the basis of his religion, sex, or national origin in those certain instances where religion, sex, or national origin is a bona fide occupational qualification reasonably necessary to the normal operation of that particular business or enterprise. . . .

Sec. 705. (1) There is hereby created a Commission to be known as the Equal Employment Opportunity Commission, which shall be composed of five members, not more than three of whom shall be members of the same political party, who shall be appointed by the President by and with the advice and consent of the Senate. . . .

◆ EXECUTIVE ORDER NO. 11246, 3 C.F.R., 1964–1965 COMP. P.339–348 (1965)

On September 24, 1965, President Lyndon B. Johnson issued the following executive order, prohibiting discrimination in government employment and government contracting.

Under and by virtue of the authority vested in me as President of the United States by the Constitution and statutes of the United States, it is ordered as follows:

Part I—Nondiscrimination in Government Employment

Section 101. It is the policy of the Government of the United States to provide equal opportunity in Federal employment for all qualified persons, to prohibit discrimination in employment because of race, creed, color, or national origin, and to promote the full realization of equal employment opportunity through a positive, continuing program in each executive department and agency. The policy of equal opportunity applies to every aspect of Federal employment policy and practice.

Section 102. The head of each executive department and agency shall establish and maintain a positive program of equal employment opportunity for all civilian employees and applicants for employment within his jurisdiction in accordance with the policy set forth in Section 101.

Section 103. The Civil Service Commission shall supervise and provide leadership and guidance in the conduct of equal employment opportunity programs for the civilian employees of and applications for employment within the executive departments and agencies and shall review agency program accomplishments periodically. In order to facilitate the achievement

of a model program for equal employment opportunity in the Federal service, the Commission may consult from time to time with such individuals, groups, or organizations as may be of assistance in improving the Federal program and realizing the objectives of this part.

Section 104. The Civil Service Commission shall provide for the prompt, fair, and impartial consideration of all complaints of discrimination in Federal employment on the basis of race, creed, color, or national origin. Procedures for the consideration complaints shall include at least one impartial review within the executive department or agency and shall provide for appeal to the Civil Service Commission.

Section 105. The Civil Service Commission shall issue such regulations, orders, and instructions as it deems necessary and appropriate to carry out its responsibilities under this Part, and the head of each executive department and agency shall comply with the regulations, orders, and instructions issued by the Commission under this Part.

Part II—Nondiscrimination In Employment By Government Contractors And Subcontractors

Section 201. The Secretary of Labor shall be responsible for the administration of Parts II and III of this Order and shall adopt such rules and regulations and issue such orders as he deems necessary and appropriate to achieve the purposes thereof.

Section 202. Except in contracts exempted in accordance with Section 204 of this Order, all Government contracting agencies shall include in every Government contract hereafter entered into the following provisions:

"(1) The contractor will not discriminate against any employee or applicant for employment because of race, creed, color, or national origin. The contractor will take affirmative action to ensure that applicants are employed, and that employees are treated during employment, without regard to their race, creed, color, or national origin. Such action shall include, but not be limited to the following: employment, upgrading, demotion, or transfer; recruitment or recruitment advertising; layoff or termination; rates of pay or other forms of compensation; and selection for training, including apprenticeship. The contractor agrees to post in conspicuous places, available to employees and applicants for employment, notices to be provided by the contracting officer setting forth the provisions of this nondiscrimination clause."

"(2) The contractor will, in all solicitations or advertisements for employees placed by or on behalf of the contractor, state that all qualified applicants will receive consideration for employment without regard to race, creed, color, or national origin. . . ."

Part III—Nondiscrimination Provisions In Federally Assisted Construction Contracts

Section 301. Each executive department and agency which administers a program involving Federal financial assistance shall require as a condition for approval of any grant, contract, loan, insurance, or guarantee thereunder, which may involve a construction contract, that the applicant for Federal assistance undertake and agree to incorporate, or cause to be incorporated, into all construction contracts paid for in whole or in part with funds obtained from the Federal Government or borrowed on the credit of the Federal Government pursuant to such grant, contract, loan, insurance, or guarantee, or undertaken pursuant to any Federal program involving such grant, contract, loan, insurance, or guarantee, the provisions prescribed for Government contracts by Section 202 of this Order or such modification thereof, preserving in substance the contractor's obligations thereunder, as may be approved by the Secretary of Labor, together with such additional provisions as the Secretary deems appropriate to establish and protect the interest of the United States in the enforcement of those obligations. . . .

◆ VOTING RIGHTS ACT OF 1965 PUB.L. NO. 89–110, 79 STAT. 437 (1965)

Signed by President Lyndon B. Johnson on August 6, 1965, the Voting Rights Act was an outgrowth of the protest demonstrations organized by African Americans to draw attention to discriminatory voter-registration practices in several Southern states. The 1965 law abolished literacy, knowledge, and character tests as qualifications for voting; empowered federal registrars to register potential voters in any county where, in the judgments of the Attorney General of the United States, registrars were indeed necessary to enforce the Fifteenth Amendment; and gave the Attorney General of the United States the right to take whatever legal action be deemed necessary to eliminate any equivalent of the poll tax.

Although the single aim of the Voting Rights Act of 1965 was African American enfranchisement in the South, obstacles to registration and voting faced by all minorities were affected. Its potential as a tool for Hispanic Americans, however, was not fully realized for nearly a decade.

An Act to enforce the Fifteenth Amendment to the Constitution of the United States, and for other purposes.

Section 2. No voting qualification or prerequisite to voting, or standard, practice, or procedure shall be imposed or applied by any State or political subdivision to deny or abridge the right of any citizen of the United States to vote on account of race or color.

Section 4. (a) To assure that the right of citizens of the United States to vote is not denied or abridged on account of race or color, no citizen shall be denied the right to vote in any Federal, State, or local election because of his failure to comply with any test or device in any State with respect to which the determinations have been made under subsection (b) or in any political subdivision with respect to which such determinations have been made as a separate unit, unless the United States District Court for the District of Columbia in an action for a declaratory judgment brought by such State or subdivision against the United States has determined that no such test or device has been used during the five years preceding the filing of the action for the purpose or with the effect of denying or abridging the right to vote on account of race or color: *Provided,* That no such declaratory judgment shall issue with respect to any plaintiff for a period of five years after the entry of a final judgment of any court of the United States, other than the denial of a declaratory judgment under this section, whether entered prior to or after the enactment of this Act, determining that denials or abridgments of the right to vote on account of race or color through the use of such tests or devices have occurred anywhere in the territory of such plaintiff. . . .

(d) For purposes of this section no State or political subdivision shall be determined to have engaged in the use of tests or devices for the purpose or with the effect of denying or abridging the right to vote on account of race or color if (1) incidents of such use have been few in number and have been promptly and effectively corrected by State or local action, (2) the continuing effect of such incidents has been eliminated, and (3) there is no reasonable probability of their recurrence in the future. . . .

Section 10. (a) The Congress finds that the requirement of the payment of a poll tax as a precondition to voting (I) precludes persons of limited means from voting or imposes unreasonable financial hardship upon such persons as a precondition to their exercise of the franchise, (II) does not bear a reasonable relationship to any legitimate State interest in the conduct of elections, and (III) in some areas has the purpose or effect of denying persons the right to vote because of race or color. Upon the basis of these findings, Congress declares that the constitutional right of citizens to vote is denied or abridged in some areas by the requirement of the payment of a poll tax as a precondition to voting. . . .

Section 11. (a) No person acting under color of law shall fail or refuse to permit any person to vote who is entitled to vote under any provision of this Act or is otherwise qualified to vote, or willfully fail or refuse to tabulate, count, and report such person's vote.

(b) No person, whether acting under color of law or otherwise, shall intimidate, threaten, or coerce, or attempt to intimidate, threaten or coerce any person for voting or attempting to vote, or intimidate, threaten, or coerce, or attempt to intimidate, threaten, or coerce any person for urging or aiding any person to vote or attempt to vote, or intimidate, threaten, or coerce any person for exercising any powers or duties under section 3 (a), 6, 8, 9, 10, or 12 (e). . . .

Section 14. (1) The terms "vote" or "voting" shall include all action necessary to make a vote effective in any primary, special, or general election, including, but not limited to, registration, listing pursuant to this Act, or other action required by law prerequisite to voting, casting a ballot, and having such ballot counted properly and included in the appropriate totals of votes cast with respect to candidates for public or party office and propositions for which votes are received in an election. . . .

Sec. 17. Nothing in this Act shall be construed to deny, impair, or otherwise adversely affect the right to vote of any person registered to vote under the law of any state or political subdivision. . . .

♦ THE BLACK PANTHER MANIFESTO (1966)

The Black Panther Party relied on a strict and uncompromising regimen to mold its members into a unified and cohesive revolutionary force. Similar to the Nation of Islam, the party denounced all intoxicants, drugs, and artificial stimulants "while doing party work." The intellectual fare of every party member was the ten-point program, which every member was obliged to know, understand, and even to commit to memory.

1. We want FREEDOM. We want power to determine the destiny of our Black Community.

We believe that black people will not be free until we are able to determine our destiny.

2. We want full employment for our people.

We believe that the federal government is responsible and obligated to give every man employment or a guaranteed income. We believe that if the white American businessman will not give full employment, then the means of production should be taken from the businessmen and placed in the community so that the people of the community can organize and employ all of its people and give a high standard of living.

3. We want an end to the robbery by the CAPITALIST of our Black Community.

We believe that this racist government has robbed us and now we are demanding the overdue debt of forty acres and two mules. Forty acres and two mules was promised 100 years ago as restitution for slave labor and mass murder of black people. We will accept the payment in currency which will be distributed to our many communities. The Germans are now aiding the Jews in Israel for the genocide of the Jewish people. The Germans murdered six million Jews. The American racist has taken part in the slaughter of over fifty million black people, therefore, we feel that this is a modest demand that we make.

4. We want decent housing, fit for shelter of human beings.

We believe that if the white landlords will not give decent housing to our black community, then the housing and the land should be made into cooperatives so that our community, with government aid, can build and make decent housing for its people.

5. We want education for our people that exposes the true nature of this decadent American society. We want education that teaches us our true history and our role in the present-day society.

We believe in an educational system that will give to our people a knowledge of self. If a man does not have knowledge of himself and his position in society and the world, then he has little chance to relate to anything else.

6. We want all black men to be exempt from military service.

We believe that Black people should not be forced to fight in the military service to defend a racist government that does not protect us. We will not fight and kill other people of color in the world who, like black people, are being victimized by the white racist government of America. We will protect ourselves from the

Black Panthers demonstrating outside a Manhattan Criminal Court during the trial of the "Harlem Six".

force and violence of the racist police and the racist military, by whatever means necessary.

7. We want an immediate end to POLICE BRUTALITY and MURDER of black people.

We believe we can end police brutality in our black community by organizing black self-defense groups that are dedicated to defending our black community from racist police oppression and brutality. The Second Amendment to the Constitution of the United States gives a right to bear arms. We therefore believe that all black people should arm themselves for self-defense.

8. We want freedom for all black men held in federal, state, county and city prisons and jails.

We believe that all black people should be released from the many jails and prisons because they have not received a fair and impartial trial.

9. We want all black people when brought to trial to be tried in court by a jury of their peer group or people

from their black communities, as defined by the constitution of the United States.

We believe that the courts should follow the United States Constitution so that black people will receive fair trials. The 14th Amendment of the U.S. Constitution gives a man a right to be tried by his peer group. A peer is a person from a similar economic, social, religious, geographical, environmental, historical and racial background. To do this the court will be forced to select a jury from the black community from which the black defendant came. We have been, and are being tried by all-white juries that have no understanding of the "average reasoning man" of the black community.

10. We want land, bread, housing, education, clothing, justice and peace. And as our major political objective, a United Nations-supervised plebiscite to be held throughout the black colony in which only black colonial subjects will be allowed to participate, for the purpose of determining the will of black people as to their national destiny.

When, in the course of human events, it becomes necessary for one people to dissolve the political bands which have connected them with another, and to assume, among the powers of the earth, the separate and equal station to which the laws of nature and nature's God entitle them, a decent respect to the opinions of mankind requires that they should declare the causes which impel them to the separation.

We hold these truths to be self-evident, that all men are created equal; that they are endowed by their Creator with certain inalienable rights; that among these are life, liberty, and the pursuit of happiness.

That, to secure these rights, governments are instituted among them, deriving their just powers from the consent of the governed; that, whenever any form of government becomes destructive of these ends, it is the right of the people to alter or to abolish it, and to institute a new government, laying its foundation on such principles, and organizing its powers in such form, as to them shall seem most likely to effect their safety and happiness.

Prudence, indeed, will dictate that governments long established should not be changed for light and transient causes; and, accordingly, all experience hath shown, that mankind are more disposed to suffer, while evils are sufferable, than to right themselves by abolishing the forms to which they are accustomed. But, when a long train of abuses and usurpations, pursuing invariably the same object, evinces a design to reduce them under absolute despotism, it is their right, it is their duty, to throw off such government, and to provide new guards for their future security.

♦ CIVIL RIGHTS ACT OF 1968 PUB.L. NO. 90–284, TITLES VIII & IX, 82 STAT. 284 (1968)

Title VIII of Public Law 90–284, the Civil Rights Act of 1968, is better known as the Fair Housing Act. It was signed by President Lyndon B. Johnson on April 11, 1968, and created a national housing policy. The act made discrimination in the sale or rental or financing of housing illegal, and empowered the U.S. Attorney General to take action in such cases.

Title VIII—Fair Housing

Sec. 801. It is the policy of the United States to provide, within constitutional limitations, for fair housing throughout the United States.

Section 804. As made applicable by section 803 and except as exempted by sections 803(b) and 807, it shall be unlawful—

(a) to refuse to sell or rent after the making of a bona fide offer, or to refuse to negotiate for the sale or rental of, or otherwise make unavailable or deny, a dwelling to any person because of race, color, religion, or national origin.

(b) to discriminate against any person in the terms, conditions, or privileges of sale or rental of a dwelling, or in the provision of services or facilities in connection there-with, because of race, color, religion, or national origin.

(c) to make, print, or publish or cause to be made, printed, or published any notice, statement, or advertisement, with respect to the sale or rental of a dwelling that indicates any preference, limitation, or discrimination based on race, color, religion, or national origin, or an intention to make any such preference, limitation, or discrimination.

(d) to represent to any person because of race, color, religion, or national origin that any dwelling is not available for inspection, sale, or rental when such dwelling is in fact so available.

(e) for profit, to induce or attempt to induce any person to sell or rent any dwelling by representations regarding the entry or prospective entry into the neighborhood of a person or persons of a particular race, color, religion, or national origin.

Sec. 805. After December 31, 1968, it shall be unlawful for any bank, building and loan association, insurance company or other corporation, association, firm or enterprise whose business consists in whole or in part in the making of commercial real estate loans, to deny a loan or other financial assistance to a person applying therefor for the purpose of purchasing, constructing, improving, repairing, or maintaining a dwelling, or to discriminate against him in the fixing of the amount, interest rate, duration, or other terms or conditions of such loan or other financial assistance, because of the race, color, religion, or national origin of such person or of any person associated with him in connection with such loan or other financial assistance or the purposes of such loan or other financial assistance, or of the present or prospective owners, leases, tenants, or occupants of the dwelling or dwellings in relation to which such loan or other financial assistance is to be made or given. . . .

Title IX—Prevention of Intimidation in Fair Housing Cases

Section 901. Whoever, whether or not acting under color of law, by force or threat of force willfully injures, intimidates or interferes with, or attempts to injure, intimidate or interfere with—

(a) any person because of his race, color, religion or national origin and because he is or has been selling, purchasing, renting, financing, occupying, or contracting or negotiating for the sale, purchase, rental, financing or occupation of any dwelling, or applying for or participating in any service, organization, or facility relating to the business of selling or renting dwellings; or

(b) any person because he is or has been, or in order to intimidate such person or any other person or any class of persons from—

(1) participating, without discrimination on account of race, color, religion or national origin, in any of the activities, services, organizations or facilities described in subsection 901(a). . . .

◆ BARBARA JORDAN'S SPEECH ON PRESIDENTIAL IMPEACHMENT PROCEEDINGS (1974) (EXCERPT)

On July 25, 1974, Congresswoman Barbara Jordan appeared on television to offer her position on the impeachment of the President of the United States, Richard Nixon. Solemn, exhausted, she hunched over four annotated amended pages of her personal notes, as well as four pages of historical impeachment criteria set against the president's conduct. Her black-rimmed glasses reflected the glare of the lighting in the room as she examined her notes. At that moment, she improvised her speech while looking into the television cameras.

"We the people"—it is a very eloquent beginning. But when the Constitution of the United States was completed on the seventeenth of September in 1787, I was not included in that "We the people." I felt for many years that somehow George Washington and Alexander Hamilton just left me out by mistake. But through the process of amendment, interpretation, and court decision, I have finally been included in "We the people."

It is wrong, I suggest, it is a misreading of the Constitution for any member here to assert that for a member to vote for an Article of Impeachment means that the member must be convinced that the President should be removed from office. The Constitution doesn't say that. The powers relating to impeachment are an essential check in the hands of this body, the legislature, against and upon the encroachment of the Executive. In establishing the division between the two branches of the legislature, the House and the Senate, assigning to one the right to accuse and the other the right to judge, the framers of this Constitution were very astute. They did not make the accusers and the judges the same persons.

We know the nature of impeachment. We have been talking about it for a while now. "It is chiefly designed for the President and his high ministers" to somehow be called into account. It is designed to "bridle" the Executive if he engages in excesses. It is designed as a method of national "inquest into the conduct of public men. . . ." The nature of impeachment is a narrowly channeled exception to the separation of powers maxim; the Federal Convention of 1787 said that. It limited impeachment to "high crimes and misdemeanors" and discounted and opposed the term "maladministration."

The drawing of political lines goes to the motivation behind impeachment; but impeachment must proceed within the confines of the constitutional term "high crimes and misdemeanors."

What the President did know on the twenty-third of June was the prior activities of E. Howard Hunt, which included his participation in the break-in of Daniel Ellsberg's psychiatrist, which included Howard Hunt's participation in the Dita Beard ITT affair, which included Howard Hunt's fabrication of cables, designed to discredit the Kennedy administration.

We have heard time and time again that the evidence reflects payment to the defendants of money. The President has knowledge that these funds were being paid and that these were funds collected for the 1972 presidential campaign.

Beginning shortly after the Watergate break-in and continuing to the present time, the President has engaged in a series of public statements and actions designed to thwart the lawful investigation by government prosecutors. Moreover, the President has made public announcements and assertions bearing on the

Watergate case which the evidence will show he knows to be false. . . .

James Madison said, again at the Constitutional Convention: "A president is impeachable if he attempts to subvert the Constitution."

The Constitution charges that President with the task of taking care that the laws be faithfully executed, and yet the President has counseled his aides to commit perjury, willfully disregarded the secrecy of grand jury proceedings, concealed surreptitious entry, attempted to compromise a federal judge while publicly displaying his cooperation with the processes of criminal justice. . . .

If the impeachment provision in the Constitution of the United States will not reach the offenses charged here, then perhaps that eighteenth-century Constitution should be abandoned to a twentieth-century paper shredder. Has the President committed offenses and planned and directed and acquiesced in a course of conduct which the Constitution will not tolerate? That is the question. We know that. We know the question. We should now forthwith proceed to answer the question. It is reason and not passion which must guide our deliberations, guide our debate, and guide our decision.

◆ PRESIDENT GEORGE BUSH'S MESSAGE TO THE SENATE RETURNING WITHOUT APPROVAL THE CIVIL RIGHTS ACT OF 1990 26 WEEKLY COMP. PRES.DOC. 1632–34 (OCT. 22, 1990)

In June of 1989, the U.S. Supreme Court delivered opinions in several cases dealing with seniority systems and racial discrimination in employment. Ruling in the cases Lorance v. ATT Technologies Inc., Martin v. Wilks, Patterson v. McLean Credit Union, *and* Wards Cove Packing Co. v. Antonio, *the Court appeared to reverse earlier civil rights rulings. Civil rights organizations were quick to protest the rulings; opponents of the ruling, including the NAACP Legal Defense and Educational Fund, the Leadership Conference on Civil Rights, the American Civil Liberties Union, and the National Organization of Women, argued that the Court had undermined the protection granted by federal civil rights and equal employment legislation.*

On October 16 and 17, 1990, both houses of Congress approved a bill designed to reverse the Court's ruling. On October 22, President Bush vetoed the bill, claiming that the bill's provisions would encourage employers to establish hiring quotas.

To the Senate of the United States.

I am today returning without my approval [Separate Bill] 2104, the "Civil Rights Act of 1990." I deeply regret having to take this action with respect to a bill bearing such a title, especially since it contains certain provisions that I strongly endorse.

Discrimination, whether on the basis of race, national origin, sex, religion, or disability, is worse than wrong. It is a fundamental evil that tears at the fabric of our society, and one that all Americans should and must oppose. That requires rigorous enforcement of existing antidiscrimination laws. . . .

. . . Despite the use of the term "civil rights" in the title of S. 2104, the bill actually employs a maze of highly legalistic language to introduce the destructive force of quotas into our Nation's employment system. Primarily through provisions governing cases in which employment practices are alleged to have unintentionally caused the disproportionate exclusion of members of certain groups, S. 2104 creates powerful incentives for employers to adopt hiring and promotion quotas. These incentives are created by the bill's new and very technical rules of litigation, which will make it difficult for employers to defend legitimate employment practices. In many cases, a defense against unfounded allegations will be impossible. Among other problems, the plaintiff often need not even show that any of the employer's practices caused a significant statistical disparity. In other cases, the employer's defense is confined to an unduly narrow definition of "business necessity" that is significantly more restrictive than that established by the Supreme Court in *Griggs v. Duke Power Co.* and in two decades of subsequent decisions. Thus, unable to defend legitimate practices in court, employers will be driven to adopt quotas in order to avoid liability.

Proponents of S. 2104 assert that it is needed to overturn the Supreme Court's *Wards Cove Packing Co. v. Antonio* decision and restore the law that had existed since the Griggs case in 1971. S. 2104, however, does not in fact codify Griggs or the Court's subsequent decisions prior to Ward Cove. Instead, S. 2104 engages in a sweeping rewrite of two decades of Supreme Court jurisprudence, using language that appears in no decision of the Court and that is contrary to principles acknowledged even by the Justice Stevens's dissent in Wards Cove: "The opinion in Griggs made it clear that a neutral practice that operates to exclude minorities is nevertheless lawful if it serves a valid business purpose."

I am aware of the dispute among lawyers about the proper interpretation of certain critical language used in this portion of S. 2104. The very fact of this dispute suggests that the bill is not codifying the law developed by the Supreme Court in Griggs and subsequent cases. This debate, moreover, is a sure sign that S. 2104 will lead to years—perhaps decades—of uncertainty and expensive litigation. It is neither fair nor sensible to give the employers of our country a difficult choice between using quotas and seeking a clarification of the law through costly and very risky litigation.

D. 3205 contains several other unacceptable provisions as well. One section unfairly closes the courts, in many instances, to individuals victimized by agreements, to which they were not a party, involving the use of quotas. Another section radically alters the remedial provisions in Title VII of the Civil Rights Act of 1964, replacing measures designed to foster conciliation and settlement with a new scheme modeled on a tort system widely acknowledged to be in a state of crisis. The bill also contains a number of provisions that will create unnecessary and inappropriate incentives for litigation. These include unfair retroactivity rules; attorneys fee provisions that will discourage settlements; unreasonable new statutes of limitation; and a "rule of construction" that will make it extremely difficult to know how courts can be expected to apply the law. In order to assist the Congress regarding legislation in this area, I enclose herewith a memorandum from the Attorney General explaining in detail the defects that make S. 2104 unacceptable.

Our goal and our promise has been equal opportunity and equal protection under the law. That is a bedrock principle from which we cannot retreat. The temptation to support a bill—any bill—simply because its title includes the words "civil rights" is very strong. This impulse is not entirely bad. Presumptions have too often run the other way, and our Nation's history on racial questions cautions against complacency. But when our efforts, however well intentioned, result in quotas, equal opportunity is not advanced but thwarted. The very commitment to justice and equality that is offered as the reason why this bill should be signed requires me to veto it. . . .

George Bush

The White House,

October 22, 1990

◆ CIVIL RIGHTS ACT OF 1991 PUB.L. NO. 102–166, 105 STAT 1071 (1991)

After vetoing Congress's 1990 civil rights legislation, the Bush administration joined both houses of Congress in working on alternative bills. Following months of negotiation, the Senate passed Senate Bill 1745 on October 30; the House passed the bill on November 7. On November 21, President George Bush signed the Civil Rights Act of 1991.

This act is designed to provide additional remedies to deter harassment and intentional discrimination in the workplace, to provide guidelines for the adjudication of cases arising under Title VII . . . and to expand the scope of civil rights legislation weakened by Supreme Court decisions, particularly the Court's ruling in *Wards Cove Packing Co. v. Antonio*, 490 US 642 (1989).

Sec. 2. Findings

The Congress finds that—

(1) additional remedies under Federal law are needed to deter unlawful harassment and intentional discrimination in the workplace;

(2) the decision of the Supreme Court in *Wards Cove Packing Co. v. Antonio*, 490 U.S. 642 (1989) has weakened the scope and effectiveness of Federal civil rights protections; and

(3) legislation is necessary to provide additional protections against unlawful discrimination in employment.

Sec. 3. Purposes.

The purposes of this Act are—

(1) to provide appropriate remedies for intentional discrimination and unlawful harassment in the workplace;

(2) to codify the concepts of "business necessity" and "job related" enunciated by the Supreme Court in *Griggs v. Duke Power Co.*, 401 U.S. 424 (1971), and in the other Supreme Court decisions prior to *Wards Cove Packing Co. v. Antonio*, 490 U.S. 642 (1989);

(3) to confirm statutory authority and provide statutory guidelines for the adjudication of disparate impact suits under title VII of the Civil Rights Act of 1964 (42 U.S.C. 2000e et seq.); and

(4) to respond to recent decisions of the Supreme Court by expanding the scope of relevant civil rights statutes in order to provide adequate protection to victims of discrimination.

Title I—Federal Civil Rights Remedies

Sec. 105. Burden of Proof in Disparate Impact Cases.

(a) Section 703 of the Civil Rights Act of 1964 (42 U.S.C. 2000e–2) is amended by adding at the end the following new subsection:

. . . An unlawful employment practice based on disparate impact is established under this title only if—

. . . A complaining party demonstrates that a respondent used a particular employment practice that causes a disparate impact on the basis of race, color, religion, sex, or national origin and the respondent fails to demonstrate that the challenged practice is job related for the position in question and consistent with business necessity. . . .

. . . With respect to demonstrating that a particular employment practice causes a disparate impact as described in subparagraph

(A)(I), the complaining party shall demonstrate that each particular challenged employment practice causes a disparate impact, except that if the complaining party can demonstrate to the court that the elements of a respondent's decisionmaking process are not capable of separation for analysis, the decisionmaking process may be analyzed as one employment practice.

. . . If the respondent demonstrates that a specific employment practice does not cause the disparate impact, the respondent shall not be required to demonstrate that such practice is required by business necessity. . . .

Sec. 106. Prohibition Against Discriminatory Use of Test Scores.

Section 703 of the Civil Rights Act of 1964 (42 U.S.C. 2000e–2) (as amended by section 105) is further amended by adding at the end of the following new subsection:

. . . It shall be an unlawful employment practice for a respondent, in connection with the selection or referral of applicants or candidates for employment or promotion, to adjust the scores of, use different cutoff scores for, or otherwise alter the results of, employment related tests on the basis of race, color, religion, sex, or national origin. . . .

Title II—Glass Ceiling

Sec. 202 Findings and Purpose.

(a) Findings—Congress finds that—

(1) despite a dramatically growing presence in the workplace, women and minorities remain underrepresented in management and decision-making positions in business;

(2) artificial barriers exist to the advancement of women and minorities in the workplace;

(3) United States corporations are increasingly relying on women and minorities to meet employment requirements and are increasingly aware of the advantages derived from a diverse work force;

(4) the "Glass Ceiling Initiative" undertaken by the Department of Labor, including the release of the report entitled "Report on the Glass Ceiling Initiative," has been instrumental in raising public awareness of—

(A) the underrepresentation of women and minorities at the management and decision-making levels in the United States work force;

(B) the underrepresentation of women and minorities in line functions in the United States work force;

(C) the lack of access for qualified women and minorities to credential-building developmental opportunities; and

(D) the desirability of eliminating artificial barriers to the advancement of women and minorities to such levels;

(f) the establishment of a commission to examine issues raised by the Glass Ceiling Initiative would help—

(A) focus greater attention on the importance of eliminating artificial barriers to the advancement of women and minorities to management and decision-making positions in business; and

(B) promote work force diversity. . . .

◆ THE MILLION MAN MARCH/DAY OF ABSENCE MISSION STATEMENT (1995) (EXCERPT BY DR. MAULANA KARENGA)

I. Introduction

The Black men and women, the organizations and persons, participating in this historic Million Man March and Day of Absence held in Washington, DC, on October 16, 1995, on the eve of the 21st century, and supported by parallel activities in cities and towns throughout the country: *conscious* of the critical juncture of history in which we live and the challenges it poses for us; *concerned* about increasing racism and the continuing commitment to white supremacy in this country; deteriorating social conditions, degradation of the environment and the impact of these on our community, the larger society and the world; *committed* to the ongoing struggle for a free and empowered community, a just society and a better world; *recognizing* that the country and government have made a dangerous and regressive turn to the right and are producing policies with negative impact on people of color, the poor and the vulnerable; *realizing* that every man and woman and our community have both the right and responsibility to resist evil and contribute meaningfully to the creation of a just and good society; *reaffirming* the best values of our social justice tradition which require respect for the dignity and rights of the human person, economic justice, meaningful political participation, shared power, cultural integrity, mutual respect for all peoples, and uncompromising resistance to social forces and structures which deny or limit these; *declare* our commitment to assume a new and expanded responsibility in the struggle to build and sustain a free and empowered community, a just society

Aerial view of the Million Man March.

and a better world. We are aware that we make this commitment in an era in which this is needed as never before and in which we cannot morally choose otherwise.

In doing this, we self-consciously emphasize the priority need of Black men to stand up and assume this new and expanded responsibility without denying or minimizing the equal rights, role and responsibility of Black women in the life and struggle of our people.

Our priority call to Black men to stand up and assume this new and expanded sense of responsibility is based on the realization that the strength and re-sourcefulness of the family and the liberation of the people require it;

that some of the most acute problems facing the Black community within are those posed by Black males who have not stood up; that the caring and responsible father in the home; the responsible and future-focused male youth; security in and of the com-munity; the quality of male/female relations, and the family's capacity to avoid poverty and push the lives of its members forward all depend on Black men's standing up;

that in the context of a real and principled brother-hood, those of us who have stood up, must challenge others to stand also; and that unless and until Black men stand up, Black men and women cannot stand together and accomplish the awesome tasks before us.

II. The Historical Significance of the Project

This Million Man March, forming a joint project with its companion activity, The Day of Absence, speaks to who we are, where we stand and what we are com-pelled to do in this hour of meeting and posing chal-lenges. Its significance lies in the fact that:

1. It is a timely and necessary state of challenge both to ourselves and the country in a time of increasing racism, attacks on hard won gains, and continually deteriorating conditions for the poor and vulnerable and thus an urgent time for transformative and progres-sive leadership;

2. It is a declaration of the resolve of Black men, in particular and the Black community in general, to mobilize and struggle to maintain hard won gains, resist evil and wrong wherever we find it and to continue to push our lives and history forward;

3. It is a reaffirmation of our self-understanding as a people that we are our own liberators, that no matter how numerous or sincere our allies are, the greatest burdens to be borne and the most severe sacrifices to be made for liberation are essentially our own;

4. It is an effective way to refocus and expand discussion on critical issues confronting our people, this country and the world and put forth our posi-tions on them;

5. It is both an example and encouragement of operational unity; unity in diversity, unity without uni-formity, and unity on principle and in practice for the greater good;

6. It is a galvanizing and mobilizing process to raise consciousness, cultivate commitment and lay the ground-work for increased positive social, political and eco-nomic activity;

7. And finally, it is a necessary continuation of our ancient and living moral tradition of speaking truth to power and seeking power for the vulnerable, justice for the injured, right for the wronged and liberation for the oppressed. . . .

VII. Continuing Practice and Projects

38. The Million Man March and Day of Absence can only have lasting value if we continue to work and struggle beyond this day. Thus, our challenge is to take the spirit of this day, the process of mobilization and the possibilities of organization and turn them into ongoing structures and practices directed toward our liberation and flourishing as a people.

39. Central to sustaining and institutionalizing this process is:

a. the follow-up development of an expanded Black political agenda and the holding of a Black Political Convention to forge this agenda for progressive politi-cal change;

b. a massive and ongoing voter registration of Black people as independents; using our vote to insist and insure that candidates address the Black agenda; and creating and sustaining a progressive independent po-litical movement;

c. the building and strengthening of Black united fronts and collective leadership structures like the National African American Leadership Summit to prac-tice and benefit from operational unity in our address-ing local, national and international issues;

d. the establishment of a Black Economic Develop-ment Fund to enhance economic development, culti-vate economic discipline and cooperative practices and achieve economic self-determination;

e. the reaffirmation and strengthening of family through quality male/female relations based on princi-ples of equality, complementarity, mutual respect and shared responsibility in love, life and struggle; and through loving and responsible parenthood that insists on discipline and achievement, provides spiritual, moral and cultural grounding and through expanding rites of passage programs, mentorships and increasing adoptions;

f. the ongoing struggle for reparations in the fullest sense, that is to say: public admission, apology and recognition of the Holocaust of African Enslavement and appropriate compensation by the government; and support for the Conyers Reparations Bill on the Holocaust;

g. the continuing struggle against police abuse, government suppression, violations of civil and human rights and the industrialization of prisons; and in support of the freedom of all political prisoners, prisoners' rights and their efforts to transform themselves into worthy members of the community;

h. the critical task of organizing the community as a solid wall in the struggle against drugs, crime and violence in the community which we see as interrelated and which must be joined with the struggle to reduce and end poverty, increase employment, strengthen fatherhood, motherhood and family, support parents, provide education and prevention programs, and expose and reject those who deal in death for the community.

None of this denies external sources of drugs nor stops us from demanding uniform sentencing and penalties for those involved in the drug trade on the local, national and international level, but it compels us to stand up and take responsibility for the life we must live in spite of external impositions;

i. continuing and expanding our support for African-centered independent schools through joining their boards, enrolling our children, being concerned and active parents, donating time, services and monies to them and working in various other ways to insure that they provide the highest level of culturally-rooted education; and intensifying and broadening the struggle for quality public education through heightened parental concern and involvement and social activism which insist on a responsible administration, professional and committed teachers, continuing faculty and staff development; safe pleasant, encouraging and fully-equipped campuses and an inclusive and culture-respecting curriculum which stresses mastery of knowledge as well as critical thinking, academic excellence, social responsibility and an expanded sense of human possibility;

j. continuing and reinforced efforts to reduce and eliminate negative media approaches to and portrayals of Black life and culture; to organize a sustained and effective support for positive models, messages and works; to achieve adequate and dignified representation of Blacks in various media and in various positions in these media; to expand support for and development of independent Black media; and to challenge successful and notable African Americans in various media to support all these efforts;

k. strengthening and supporting organizations and institutions of the Black community concerned with the uplifting and liberation of our people by joining as families and persons, volunteering service, giving donations and providing and insisting on the best leadership possible;

l. building appropriate alliances with other peoples of color, supporting their liberation struggles and just demands and engaging in mutually supportive and mutually beneficial activities to create and sustain a just and good society;

m. standing in solidarity with other African peoples and other Third World peoples in their struggles to free themselves, harness their human and material resources and live full and meaningful lives;

n. reaffirming in the most positive ways the value and indispensability of the spiritual and ethical grounding of our people in accomplishing the historical tasks confronting us by freeing and renewing our minds and reaffirming our commitment to the good, the proper and the beneficial, by joining as families and persons the faith communities of our choice, supporting them, living the best of our traditions ourselves and challenging other members and the leadership to do likewise and constantly insisting that our faith communities give the best of what we have to offer to build the moral community and just society we struggle for as a people;

o. and finally, embracing and practicing a common set of principles that reaffirm and strengthen family, community and culture, The Nguzo Saba (The Seven Principles): Umoja (Unity); Kujichagulia (Self-Determination); Ujima (Collective Work and Responsibility); Ujamaa (Cooperative Economics); Nia (Purpose); Kuumba (Creativity); and Imani (Faith).

For full text of the Mission Statement, contact University of Sankore Press, 2560 W. 54th St., Los Angeles, CA 9004; phone (800) 997–2656; fax (213) 299–0261.

◆ THE PRESIDENT'S INITIATIVE ON RACE—THE ADVISORY BOARD'S REPORT TO THE PRESIDENT (1998) (EXCERPT)

On June 13, 1997, President Clinton established the seven-member President's Advisory Board to the President's Initiative on Race. Headed by historian John Hope Franklin, the advisory board was given the

John Hope Franklin served as head of the President's Initiative on Race.

responsibilities of promoting national dialogue on race issues, increasing the nation's understanding of the history and future of race relations, identifying and creating plans to calm racial tension and promote increased opportunity for all Americans, and addressing crime and the administration of justice.

On September 18, 1998, the advisory board concluded its work and presented its recommendations to President Clinton. Its report One America in the 21st Century: Forging a New Future *recommended that the president institute a standing advisory board to build upon its foundation and for a public education program to underscore the "common values" of a diverse multiracial nation.*

Introduction

America's greatest promise in the 21st century lies in our ability to harness the strength of racial diversity. Our greatest challenge is to work as one community to define ourselves with pride as a multi-racial democracy. At the end of the 20th century, America has emerged as the worldwide symbol of opportunity and freedom through leadership that constantly strives to give meaning to the fundamental principles of our Constitution. Those principals of justice, opportunity, equality, and inclusion must continue to guide the planning for our future.

The Advisory Board and Its Mandate

Members of the Advisory Board to the President's Initiative on Race have spent the past 15 months engaged in a process designed to examine race relations in America. Through study, dialogue, and action we have begun to engage the American people in a focused examination of how racial differences have affected our society and how to meet the racial challenges that face us. Our task was to take this necessary first step in the President's effort to articulate and realize a vision of a more just society.

In June 1997, through Executive Order No. 13050, President Clinton appointed Dr. John Hope Franklin (chairman), Linda Chavez-Thompson, Reverend Dr. Suzan D. Johnson Cook, Thomas H. Kean, Angela E. Oh, Bob Thomas, and William F. Winter to serve as members of the Advisory Board.

. . . [T]he Board forged ahead to meet the objectives set out by the President through his Executive Order. Those objectives included the following:

Promote a constructive national dialogue to confront and work through the challenging issues that surround race.

Increase the Nation's understanding of our recent history of race relations and the course our Nation is charting on issues of race relations and racial diversity.

Bridge racial divides by encouraging community leaders to develop and implement innovative approaches to calming racial tensions.

Identify, develop, and implement solutions to problems in areas in which race has a substantial impact, such as education, economic opportunity, housing, health care, and the administration of justice.

In addition, the Advisory Board examined issues related to race and immigration, the impact of the media on racial stereotyping, and enforcement of civil rights laws.

We wish to make it clear that this Report is not a definitive analysis of the state of race relations in America today. . . . Rather, we were engaged in the task of assisting with the initial stages of this new America's journey toward building a more just society in the 21st century.

Accomplishments, Challenges, and Opportunities

. . . Many challenges lie ahead. As America's racial diversity grows, the complexity of giving meaning to the promise of America grows as well. It is these challenges that signal where opportunities may exist. This report attempts to frame the challenges, identify the opportunities, and recommended action. It provides an overview of information gathered from communities across the Nation, including diverse points of view about racial differences and controversial issues that are currently being debated and ideas for how strong leadership can continue to move our Nation closer to its highest aspirations.

Report Overview

. . . Although this Report concludes our year-long exploration of race and racism, our work is only the foundation for building one America. The work that lies ahead cannot be accomplished by a single group. Our experience has provided the Nation with the chance to identify leaders in many parts of this country, working in numerous fields, who will promote a vision of a unified, strong, and just society. The Race Initiative affirmed the efforts of Americans who have been, are, and will continue to give meaning to the words "justice," "equality," "dignity," "respect," and "inclusion." We urge bold and decisive action to further the movement toward "redeeming the promise of America."

4

African American Landmarks

As far back as the establishment of first permanent European settlement in America, African Americans have made significant contributions to the social, economic, scientific, and cultural development of this country. The American landscape is covered with sites commemorating this African American experience. From the war for independence, through the conflicts fought on the western frontier, and on to more recent battles, sites have been established to commemorate African American participation in the defense of this nation. The African American quest for knowledge has been embodied at the first institutions organized to educate them in this country. The trail from slavery to freedom can be retraced by way of the many markers noting stations along the Underground Railroad. Other sites commemorate the achievements of African Americans in the arts and sciences or in pursuit of equal rights. Landmarks, unlike most textual documents, stand through time as public testaments to the strength and courage of African Americans.

◆ ALABAMA

Birmingham

Sixteenth Street Baptist Church
1530 Sixth Ave. at Sixteenth St., N.
(205) 251–9402

Wallace A. Rayfield, a local African American architect, designed the present sanctuary, and in 1911 Windham Brothers Construction Company, a local African American contractor, constructed the building. The church has continued to serve as a center for activities in the community. The church received national attention during the middle of the racial unrest of the 1960s, when four African American children— Addie Mae Collins, Denise McNair, Cynthia Wesley, and Carol Robertson—were killed in a bomb explosion near the sanctuary on September 15, 1963. The tragedy spurred Birmingham to address its racial problems and led to greater racial unity nationwide. The building was declared a national historic landmark on September 17, 1980.

Florence

William Christopher Handy Birthplace, Museum, and Library
620 W. College St.
(256) 760–6434

W. C. Handy, composer of "St. Louis Blues," was born in 1873. The cabin in which he was born was moved from its original site to its current location in Florence, Alabama. The restored cabin, constructed circa 1845, contains his piano, trumpet, and other mementos.

Montgomery

Civil Rights Memorial
400 Washington Ave., corner of Hull St.

This black granite monument is presented as a wall with water cascading over the words of Martin Luther King Jr., "Until justice rolls down like waters and righteousness like a mighty stream." The names of 40 civil rights martyrs are inscribed on a circular stone that is also presented. The memorial, commissioned by the Southern Poverty Law Center, was designed by architect Maya Lin and dedicated in 1989.

Dexter Avenue King Memorial Baptist Church and Pastorium
Church, 454 Dexter Ave.; Pastorium, 309 S.
  Jackson St.
(334) 263–3970
<www.dexterkingmemorial.org>

The Dexter Avenue King Memorial Baptist Church, erected in 1878, was the church where Martin Luther King Jr. organized the 1955 boycott of Montgomery's segregated bus system. Although the pastorium was damaged by a bomb on January 31, 1956, the boycott continued and spurred the 1956 Supreme Court ruling that bus segregation was illegal. It was this boycott that brought King into national prominence as a civil rights leader.

King pastored at the church from 1954 to 1959. The church houses a mural depicting scenes of the civil rights movement, as well as a library that includes personal mementoes of King and his family. The church was declared a national historic landmark on July 1, 1974.

Selma

Brown Chapel African Methodist Episcopal Church and King Monument
410 Martin Luther King Jr. St.
(334) 874–7897

The church is housed in an imposing red brick structure with twin towers. It was organized in 1866 and moved to its present site in 1908. Brown Chapel was closely allied with the civil rights movement of the 1960s; in 1965 it became the center for the Southern Christian Leadership Conference's (SCLC) voting rights campaign. Early in 1965 the church served as headquarters for the SCLC, housed rallies for Martin Luther King Jr. and other SCLC leaders, and was the site for planning demonstrations including the ill-fated demonstration on March 7 known as "Bloody Sunday." The voting campaign spurred the passage of the Voting Rights Act of 1965. A monument to King, which is located in front of the chapel, was dedicated in 1979. Brown Chapel was declared a national historic landmark on February 4, 1982.

Edmund Pettus Bridge
Broad St., U.S. 80

On Sunday, March 7, 1965, 300 civil rights demonstrators started out from Selma, Alabama, on what was to be a 55-mile march to Montgomery, Alabama, protesting the denial of voting rights to African Americans who had attempted to register in Selma. Reaching the Edmund Pettus Bridge, the marchers were met by state troopers—the orders to deploy the troopers had been issued by Governor George Wallace to enforce his executive order forbidding such demonstrations. The unarmed marchers were turned back by tear gas and night sticks resulting in numerous injuries.

On March 21, a second march started out, organized by the Rev. Martin Luther King Jr.; this march concluded five days later on the steps of the state capitol building in Montgomery. The two demonstrations aroused national concern and hastened Congress to pass a new voting rights bill.

Built in 1940, the Pettus Bridge marks the site of an important era in African American history. It is part of the Selma to Montgomery National Historic trail. A marker depicting the struggle at the bridge is located near Broad Street.

Talladega

Talladega College and Swayne Hall
627 W. Battle St.
(256) 362–0206
<www.talladega.edu>

The first college for African Americans in Alabama, Talladega College was founded by the American Missionary Association in 1867 as a primary school. The school pursued a liberal arts program at a time when vocational education dominated African American institutions. Its Savery Library houses three fresco panels known as the celebrated *Amistad Murals* by Hale Woodruff, who studied in France under the renowned Henry Ossawa Tanner.

Swayne Hall, built in 1857, is the oldest building on the campus of Talladega College. The building was constructed by slave labor before the school was established and transferred to the college in 1867. It was declared a national historic landmark on December 2, 1974.

Tuskegee

Tuskegee University
(800) 622–6531
<www.tusk.edu>

Tuskegee Institute (now Tuskegee University), a world-renowned center for agricultural research and extension work, first opened on July 4, 1881, with a $2,000 appropriation from the Alabama state legislature. It consisted of a single shanty, a student body of thirty, and one teacher—Booker T. Washington. Tuskegee functioned originally as a normal school for the training of African American teachers, the first of its kind established in the United States. Eventually, it specialized in agricultural and manual training, areas which were to make both the school and Booker T. Washington famous.

In 1882, Washington moved the school to a 100-acre plantation and began a self-help program that enabled students to finance their education. Most of the early buildings were built with the aid of student labor.

The 33rd annual commemoration of the Bloody Sunday March in Selma, Alabama, including U.S. Congresswoman Karen Thurman, Colorado Governor Roy Romer, and U.S. Congressman John Lewis (holding umbrella), 1998.

Next to Washington, the most notable person to be associated with the institute was George Washington Carver, who became its director of agricultural research in 1896. Carver persuaded many Southern farmers to cultivate peanuts, sweet potatoes, and other crops instead of cotton, which was rapidly depleting the soil. Ultimately, Carver's research programs helped develop 300 derivative products from peanuts and 118 from sweet potatoes. At one point, he even succeeded in making synthetic marble from wood pulp.

Today, Tuskegee covers nearly 5,000 acres and has more than 150 buildings. There are more than 27 landmarks associated with Washington and Carver. Places to visit include the Founder's Marker (i.e., the site of Washington's original shanty), the Oaks (i.e., Washington's home), the Booker T. Washington Monument, gravesites for Washington (and two of his wives) and Carver, and the George Washington Carver Museum, which houses the scientist's plant, mineral, and bird collections and exhibits of various products that he

developed. Tuskegee is also home to the George Washington Carver Foundation, a research center founded by Carver in 1940. Tuskegee was declared a national historic landmark on June 23, 1965.

◆ ALASKA

Fairbanks

Mattie Crosby's Home

One of the few African American pioneers of Alaska, Mattie Crosby first came to the territory in 1900 with a Maine family that adopted her. During this period, some African Americans came into the territory during the era of the Gold Rush, while others were occasionally seen on board ships that brought in supplies. However, for nearly 17 years, Mattie Crosby lived in Fairbanks, Alaska, without meeting another African American.

◆ ARIZONA

Tombstone

John Swain Grave Site
Boot Hill Cemetery
U.S. 80
(602) 457–3311

Born a slave in 1845, John Swain went to Tombstone, Arizona, in 1879 as a cowhand in the employ of John Slaughter. Swain was an expert rider and one of several African Americans to work for Slaughter.

In 1884, Swain is said to have fought and lost a one-round boxing match with John L. Sullivan, then heavyweight champion of the world. He died just three months short of his 100th birthday and was buried with honors by the citizens of Tombstone. A special tablet stands on the grave site, commemorating the close ties between Swain and Slaughter.

◆ ARKANSAS

Little Rock

Central High School
1500 Park St., corner of Fourteenth and Park Sts.
(501) 374–1957
<home.swbell.net/chmuseum>

In the fall of 1957, the first major confrontation over implementation of the Supreme Court's 1954 ruling in outlawing racial segregation in public schools took place at Central High School in Little Rock, Arkansas. The school was built in 1927.

Upon their arrival for classes on September 23, 1957, African American students were turned away by the Arkansas National Guard on the order of Arkansas Governor Orval Faubus. President Dwight D. Eisenhower responded to the crisis by issuing an executive order on September 24, which called for the use of federal troops to enforce the court's order to desegregate public schools.

Because of the influx of visitors to the school, the Central High School Museum and Visitor Center opened in September 1997. It is located next to the high school at 2125 W. Fourteenth St.

Ish House
1600 Scott St.

The home of Jefferson Ish was constructed in 1880. Jefferson Ish worked to ensure high quality education for African Americans in the area. After his death, the Ish School was established in the city to honor him. One of his sons, G. W. Ish, became an innovative physician and provided health care for local residents, as well as students at Philander Smith College. G. W. Ish also introduced isoniazid and streptomycin to treat pulmonary tuberculosis. The Ish home was designated a national historic landmark on January 3, 1978. It is a private residence.

Philander-Smith College
812 W. 13th St.
(501) 375–9845

In 1877 this institution was opened under the sponsorship of the African Methodist Episcopal Church as Walder College in Little Rock, Arkansas. After receiving a large donation that enabled the school to construct a permanent brick edifice, the college was renamed.

◆ CALIFORNIA

Allensworth

Allensworth Colony
Star Route 1, Box 148
(661) 849–3433

Established as an all-African American community, the town of Allensworth was founded by Allen Allensworth in 1910. Now a state park, this landmark serves as a memorial to its founder.

Allen Allensworth, as a slave just prior to the Civil War, was a well-known racing jockey in Louisville, Kentucky. With the beginning of the Civil War, Allensworth was allowed to enter the Navy, where he advanced to the rank of chief petty officer. Following the war, Allensworth studied for the ministry and returned to the military service as chaplain of the famed 24th U.S. Infantry. Around 1900 he migrated to California, where he dedicated himself to improving the status of African Americans.

Beckwourth

Beckwourth Pass
<www.beckwourth.org>

Beckwourth Pass, which runs through the Sierra Nevada Mountains in Beckwourth, California, was discovered by Jim Beckwourth, one of a number of African American traders and trappers dubbed "mountain men" by chroniclers of American history. The log cabin

Little Rock Central High School on the day it was integrated.

that he built as his home in 1852 still stands near the Plumas County hamlet named for him.

Hornitos

Gold Mining Camp

This ghost town was the home of Moses Rodgers, a successful and affluent African American mine owner who was one of the finest engineers and metallurgists in the state. Rodgers was one of several African American miners who struck it rich in gold and quartz.

Red Bluff

Oak Hill Cemetery

This is the burial place of Aaron Coffey, the only black member of the Society of California Pioneers. Coffey, the descendant of an officer who fought under Jackson at New Orleans, came to California as a slave in 1849. By day, he worked for his master; by night, as a

cobbler, he accumulated money toward his $1,000 emancipation fee. Betrayed by his owner, he was forced to return to Missouri, where he was again sold. Coffey pleaded with his new master to allow him to return to California and earn the necessary money to free himself and his family, which he had left behind as collateral. Upon accomplishing that mission, Coffey returned to Red Bluff, took up farming, and settled down to a contented family life.

Sacramento

St. Andrew's African Methodist Episcopal Church
2131 Eighth St.
(916) 448–1428
<www.standrewsamechurch.org>

St. Andrew's was the first African Methodist Episcopal congregation in California. Organized in a private residence in 1850, within four years the congregation had founded a school for African, Asian, and Native American children in the church's basement.

San Francisco

Leidesdorff St.

This street in San Francisco, California, is named for William Alexander Leidesdorff, a wealthy and influential California pioneer of African and Danish ancestry and a native of the Danish West Indies. A merchant, Leidesdorff operated the first steamer to pass through the Golden Gate Strait. Leidesdorff was later appointed U.S. vice-consul and ultimately became a civic and educational leader in San Francisco.

♦ COLORADO

Central City

"Aunt Clara" Brown's Chair

Central City Opera House, 621 17th St.
(303) 292–6500

"Aunt Clara" Brown, believed to have been the first African American resident of the Colorado Territory, was born a slave in Virginia. Brown moved to Missouri, where her husband and children were sold before she gained freedom through her master's last will and testament. From Missouri, she headed for Kansas and then for the gold fields of Colorado, where she opened the territory's first laundry. She soon began putting aside money from her earnings towards the purchase of her family's freedom.

Even when the Emancipation Proclamation set her immediate family free, she nonetheless returned to Missouri and brought a group of 38 relatives back to Central City. She remained in the mining community for the rest of her life, nursing the sick and performing other charitable works.

Brown died in 1877 and was buried with honors by the Colorado Pioneers Association, of which she was a member. The Central City Opera House Association dedicated a chair to her in 1932.

Denver

Inter-Ocean Hotel

16th and Market Sts.

Built by Barney Ford, the Inter-Ocean Hotel in Denver, Colorado, was once a showplace for millionaires and presidents. Ford, an African American entrepreneur active during the Gold Rush days, joined the fight over the organization of the Colorado Territory and the question of statehood. Originally allowed to vote, Ford saw this privilege abrogated by the territorial constitution and, as a result, sought to delay statehood for the territory until African American voting rights were reinstated. Enlisting the aid of the famed Massachusetts abolitionist Senator Charles Sumner, Ford urged President Andrew Johnson to veto the bill for statehood.

After Ford retired, he spent the remainder of his life in Denver, where he died in 1902. He is buried alongside his wife, Julia, in Denver's Riverside Cemetery.

Justina Ford House/Black American West Museum

3091 California St.
(303) 292–2566
<www.blackamericanwest.org>

Justina Ford was the first African American doctor in Denver. Upon her arrival in 1902 until 1952, she remained the city's only African American woman doctor. Unable to practice in the local hospital at first, her home, built in 1890, became her office as well. Ford, a family doctor and general practitioner, attracted patients from various races. During her career of over 50 years, she delivered more than 7,000 babies and became known as "the baby doctor." The Black American West Museum purchased the Ford home in 1986 to house the museum and to preserve the memory of Ford and her work. The museum includes photographs, memorabilia, and other documents on African American cowboys. The museum also shows how African Americans helped settle the West.

Pueblo

El Pueblo Museum

119 Central Plaza
(719) 583–0453
<www.coloradohistory.org/hist_sites/ElPueblo/
ElPueblo.htm>

The El Pueblo Museum houses a replica of the Gantt-Blackwell Fort, which Jim Beckwourth, African American explorer, scout, and trader, claimed to have founded in 1842. The validity of the claim has not been established, as Beckwourth had something of a reputation as a teller of tall tales. As of 2002, the museum was closed for renovation.

♦ CONNECTICUT

Canterbury

Prince Goodin Homestead

This parcel of land in Canterbury was once the home of Prince Goodin, a free African American who fought with the British against the French in the French and

Indian War. Goodin enlisted in 1757, after hearing a fiery speech by Canterbury's Rev. James Cogswell that stressed the danger of encroachment against "properties, liberties, religion, and our lives." While serving at Fort William Henry, he was captured during a French attack upon the fort and taken to Montreal, where he was sold into slavery. After three years of captivity, Goodin was freed when the British took the city in 1760.

Prudence Crandall House
Junction of Connecticut Rtes. 14 and 169
(860) 546–9916

The Crandall House, built in 1805, became a school for Canterbury residents in 1831. The admittance of Sarah Harris, a black woman, caused local resentment. Subsequently, Prudence Crandall dismissed her white students and converted the school into a training facility for prospective black teachers. Twenty such students were in residence in 1833. Still in protest, local shopkeepers refused to sell goods to Crandall. The Connecticut General Assembly passed a black law in May 1833 restricting African Americans from outside instruction in private schools without town approval. Crandall ignored the law and, though she was jailed, her conviction was set aside due to technical errors. She closed the school in September 1834. The Crandall House was designated a national historic landmark on July 17, 1991. It is now home to the Prudence Crandall Museum.

Enfield

Paul Robeson Residence "The Beeches"
1221 Enfield St., Rte. 5

Purchased by Paul Robeson and his wife in 1940, this residence served as their home until 1953. Robeson, a singer, actor, and civil rights activist, is best known for his roles in the film *The Emperor Jones* and the musical and film version of *Show Boat*.

Farmington

First Church of Christ
75 Main St.
(860) 677–2601

When in 1839 the mutinied Cuban slave ship *Amistad* landed off the coast of Connecticut, abolitionists in the area demanded protection for the Africans. The First Church of Christ in Farmington, Connecticut, served as the center of community life for the *Amistad* insurrectionists while they awaited trial. The church was designated a national historic landmark on December 8, 1976.

Washington

Jeff Liberty Grave Site
Judea Cemetery
Judea Cemetery Rd.

Here lies the grave of Jeff Liberty, an African American soldier who served in the Continental Army during the American Revolution. His grave marker, erected by the Sons of the American Revolution, states simply "in remembrance of Jeff Liberty and his colored patriots." Liberty, a slave at the time of the rebellion, asked his owner to be allowed to serve in the struggle for independence. His request granted, he fought throughout the revolution with an all-black regiment and was granted freedman status at the end of the war.

◆ DELAWARE

Wilmington

Asbury Methodist Episcopal Church
Third and Walnut Sts.
(302) 655–7060

Jeff Liberty's grave marker in Washington, Connecticut.

The Asbury Methodist Episcopal Church was dedicated in 1789 by the distinguished orator Bishop Francis Asbury. Tradition has it that on one occasion a number of the town's leading citizens, many of whom were eager to hear Asbury preach, but considered Methodism socially beneath them, stayed outside within hearing distance of the sermon, refusing to enter the church. The listeners were impressed by the eloquence of the man they heard—but, as it turned out, the voice they heard was not that of the bishop, but of his African American servant Harry Hosier (also known as "Black Harry") whose compelling testimony reached heir ears and inspired their admiration. In its early years, the church welcomed African American members. However, by 1805 African Americans had left this church, driven out by the decision of white worshippers to confine African American members to the gallery.

◆ DISTRICT OF COLUMBIA

African American Civil War Memorial
Vermont Ave. and U St., NW
<www.afroamcivilwar.org>

Ed Hamilton's bronze sculpture, *The Spirit of Freedom,* at the African American Civil War Memorial.

The "Spirit of Freedom" statue was unveiled on July 18, 1998, in the Shaw neighborhood of Northwest Washington, D.C. It is the centerpiece of the African American Civil War Memorial. Designed by sculptor Ed Hamilton of Louisville, Kentucky, who won a nationwide competition to do the work, the monument is the first to honor and salute African American soldiers and their white officers who fought and died in the Civil War. The memorial, designed by Paul S. Devrouax and landscape architect Edward D. Dunson, is located in a pie-shaped site nearly one block long. The "Spirit of Freedom" is a nine-foot-high 3,000-pound bronze sculpture in a semicircular arc and high relief. The exterior consists of three infantrymen and a sailor working together to fight for family and freedom. The "Spirit of Freedom," depicted as a woman with eyes closed and hands crossed over her chest, is positioned above the men to guide and protect them. In addition to the statue, the granite walls of the memorial are inscribed with nearly 209,000 names of Civil War veterans.

The African American Civil War Memorial Freedom Foundation Museum and Visitors Center, which opened in January 1999, is located two blocks west of the memorial at the corner of Vermont and U streets NW.

Mary McLeod Bethune Memorial
Lincoln Park

The Mary McLeod Bethune Memorial, unveiled in 1974, is the first monument to an African American or a woman to be erected on public land in the nation's capital. Bethune, an educator, was concerned about the children of the laborers working on the Florida East Coast Railroad. Thus, in 1904, she established the Daytona Normal and Industrial Institute for African American girls. In 1926, she merged the institute with the Cookman Institute of Jacksonville to form the Bethune-Cookman College.

The monument, located in Lincoln Park, D.C., is inscribed with the following words:

> I leave you love, I leave you hope. I leave you the challenge of developing confidence in one another. I leave you a thirst for education. I leave you respect for the use of power. I leave you faith. I leave you racial dignity.

Mary McLeod Bethune Council House
1318 Vermont Ave., NW
(202) 673–2402
<nps.gov/mabe/bethune/welcome/frame.htm>

The Mary McLeod Bethune Council House was opened in November 1979, and was granted national historic site status in April 1982. It is home to the Bethune Museum and Archives, which is dedicated to documenting the contributions made by African American women to society and to enriching the lives of America's children through educational materials, programs, and other services. The Council House was built circa 1885. It was Mary McLeod Bethune's last official Washington, D.C., residence, and served as the first headquarters of the National Council of Negro Women.

Blanche K. Bruce House
909 M St., NW

Blanche K. Bruce, from Mississippi, was the first African American to serve a full term in the U.S. Senate. Born in Farmville, Virginia, Bruce learned the printer's trade in Missouri. In 1861, prior to the Civil War, he escaped to Hannibal, Missouri, and set up a school for African Americans. He studied at Oberlin College in Ohio and, after moving to Mississippi, became a wealthy planter. A Republican, Bruce was elected by the Mississippi state legislature to the U.S. Senate in 1874. The Blanche K. Bruce House was designated a national historic landmark on May 15, 1975. It is a private residence.

Ralph Bunche House
1510 Jackson St., NE

Ralph Bunche had a long association with Howard University, where he served on the faculty and organized the political science department. While living in the District of Columbia, he commissioned local African American architect Holyard Robinson to design his residence. Later, Bunche was appointed undersecretary general of the United Nations. He won the Nobel Peace Prize in 1950. The house was designated a national historic landmark on September 30, 1993. In 2001, it was placed on the D.C. Preservation League's Most Endangered Places list. It is a private residence.

Mary Ann Shadd Cary House
1421 W St., NW

Between 1881 and 1886, this three-story brick house, located in Washington, D.C., served as the residence of Mary Ann Shadd Cary, the first African American woman to co-edit a newspaper *The Provincial Freeman*. In 1883, she became one of the first African American women to earn a law degree. Cary, a lecturer, writer, educator, lawyer, and abolitionist, appeared before audiences throughout the country, usually speaking on the topics of slavery and women's suffrage. The house was designated a national historic landmark on December 8, 1976. It has since been demolished.

Frederick Douglass National Historic Site
1411 W St., SE
(202) 426–5961
<www.nps.gov/frdo/index.htm>

Cedar Hill, the 20-room colonial mansion in which Frederick Douglass lived for the last 13 years of his life, has been preserved as a monument to the great nineteenth-century abolitionist. In 1988, it was declared a national historic site. Credit for the restoration and preservation of the home belongs largely to the National Association of Colored Women's Clubs, which worked hand-in-hand with the Douglass Association.

Edward Kennedy "Duke" Ellington Birthplace
2129 Ward Place NW

Born April 29, 1899, Duke Ellington was one of the world's great jazz composers, pianists, and bandleaders. It has been said of him that "the man is the music, the music is the man." The house where Ellington was born has been razed, but a plaque to commemorate the spot was installed on April 29, 1989.

Emancipation Statue
Lincoln Park
E. Capitol St.

Former slaves were responsible for financing and erecting the oldest memorial to Abraham Lincoln in the Washington, D.C., area. Following Lincoln's assassination in 1865, the first five dollars for the statue were donated by a Mrs. Charlotte Scott of Marietta, Ohio. Contributions were soon pouring in, whereupon Congress finally set aside grounds for Thomas Ball's statue depicting Lincoln breaking slavery's chains. The memorial was dedicated on April 14, 1876—the 11th anniversary of Lincoln's assassination.

Charlotte Forten Grimké House
1608 R St., NW

Charlotte Forten Grimké, born of wealthy free African American parents in Philadelphia, was among the first wave of Northerners engaged in educating African Americans in the occupied Union territories of the South. Her activities as an activist, writer, poet, and educator forged a path for other African American women. The house, built circa 1880, was designated a national historic landmark on May 11, 1976. It is a private residence.

"Cedar Hill," Frederick Douglass's home in Washington, D.C.

General Oliver Otis Howard House (Howard Hall)

604 Howard Pl., Howard University

Howard University is named in honor of Union General Oliver Otis Howard, once head of the Freedmen's Bureau, and his residence is one of four original university buildings still standing at this institution. The restored house—a brick residence with a mansard roof, dormer windows, and three and one-half-story tower—was privately built for General Howard between 1867 and 1869. It was declared a national historic landmark on February 12, 1974.

Howard University

2400 Sixth St., NW
(202) 806–6100
<www.howard.edu>

Howard University, founded in 1867, is the largest institution of higher learning established for African Americans immediately following the Civil War.

Covering more than 50 acres, the campus is situated on one of the highest elevations in the District of Columbia. Among the historic buildings are Andrew Rankin Memorial Chapel (1895), Freedmen's Hospital (1909), and the Founders Library. Founders Library contains more than 300,000 volumes and includes the Moorland-Spingarn Collection, one of the finest collections on African American life and history in the United States.

LeDroit Park Historic District

Boundary approximates Florida and Rhode Island Aves., 2nd and Elm Sts., and Howard University.

A subdivision created in 1873, the land was part of that purchased as a site for Howard University and the excess was then sold to Amzi L. Barber, the school's acting president and son-in-law of real estate brokers LeDroit Langdon and Andrew Langdon. Approximately 65 houses had been built in the park by 1887 and included various styles from Italianate villas to Gothic cottages. Originally an exclusive white community, in 1893 the area became racially integrated. Afterwards, many whites moved out, and it was almost totally occupied by African Americans. Among the African American residents were Judge Robert H. Terrell and his wife, Mary Church Terrell, Paul Laurence Dunbar, and much later Mayor Walter Washington. The park

Emancipation Statue in Washington, DC.

was declared a national historic landmark district on February 25, 1974.

Lincoln Memorial
Foot of Twenty-third St. NW, in W. Potomac Park
    on the Mall
<www.nps.gov/linc/home.htm>

The Lincoln Memorial, dedicated in 1922, has been the site of several important events underscoring African Americans' quest for dignity and struggle for equal opportunity. In 1939, when singer Marian Anderson was refused permission to appear at Constitution Hall by the Daughters of the American Revolution, she performed an Easter Sunday concert on the steps of the Lincoln Memorial before a crowd of 75,000. Her rendition of "Nobody Knows the Trouble I've Seen" prompted NAACP Executive Secretary Walter White to foresee the advent of "a new affirmation of democracy." Another such pivotal event involved the 1963 March on Washington, which was climaxed by the Rev. Martin Luther King Jr.'s "I Have A Dream" speech. The memorial was designated a national historic landmark on October 15, 1966.

Metropolitan African Methodist Episcopal Church
1518 M St., NW

Completed in 1886, this Victorian, Gothic-style church was designed by architect George Dearing. The church had two forerunners: Israel Bethel A.M.E. (1821) and Union Bethel A.M.E. (1838). On July 6, 1838, Union Bethel was officially sanctioned by the Baltimore Conference, marking the founding of the Metropolitan AME Church. In 1872 the name was officially changed to Metropolitan African Methodist Episcopal Church. The new church building, which, according to the conference, had to be built "in close proximity" to the Capitol, was dedicated on May 30, 1886. Present at the ceremony were Bishop Daniel Payne, Frederick Douglass, and Francis Cardozo. The building has been the site of funeral services for many prominent African Americans, as well as the place for church service during the inauguration of President Bill Clinton. These services were an official part of the inaugural events, the first to be held at an African American church. It was declared a national historic landmark on July 26, 1973.

Miner Normal School
2565 Georgia Ave., NW

Myrtilla Miner's School for Colored Girls was established in 1851 as a model teaching facility for young African American women. It was the district's only school dedicated solely to teacher training. Although the Miner School, as it was known, operated for a time in different locations, in 1875 it was temporarily affiliated with Howard University's Normal Department. The District of Columbia built a new Miner School—a semipublic school—in 1877 and ten years later it was incorporated into the local public school system. Congress expanded the school into a four-year degree-granting institution in 1929, known as Miner Teachers College. In 1955, the school merged with the local white teachers college to become the District of Columbia Teachers College. This operation ceased in 1977, when the college merged with two other institutions to become the University of the District of Columbia. The school was designated a national historic landmark on October 11, 1991.

M Street High School
128 M St., NW

The Fifteenth Street Presbyterian Church was the birthplace of M Street High School in 1870. The school was originally known as the Preparatory High School for Colored Youth. It moved to several locations until Congress saw a need for an elite school for its African

American population and appropriated money to construct a facility for this purpose. The building was completed in 1891 and was one of the first high schools in the nation built with public funds to serve African Americans. The faculty was well educated and the school offered business and college preparatory classes that were superior to lower level programs in many U.S. colleges and universities. Graduates who became distinguished leaders included Carter G. Woodson and Rayford Logan. Among the early principals were Robert Terrell, Anna Julia Cooper, and Mary Church Terrell. The new Dunbar High School, built in 1916, became the new high school for African Americans, while M Street took junior high school status. School integration in 1954 eliminated the need for a separate facility for African Americans. The school was designated a national historic landmark on October 23, 1986. The building is state-owned and presently vacant.

National Museum of African Art

950 Independence Ave., SW
(202) 357–4600
<www.nmafa.si.edu>

A part of the Smithsonian Institution, the National Museum of African Art maintains exhibitions, research components, and public programs on the art and culture of sub-Saharan Africa. The museum was established in 1964 and incorporated as a bureau of the Smithsonian in 1979.

St. Luke's Episcopal Church

5th and Church Streets, NW

From 1879 until 1934, the pulpit of St. Luke's Episcopal Church was filled by Alexander Crummell, an African American scholar who became a leading spokesman for African and African American liberation. He was the founder of the American Negro Academy, established with the intention of forming a cadre of African American intellectuals and scholars. The church, located in Washington, D.C., was designated a national historic landmark on May 11, 1976.

Mary Church Terrell House

326 T St., NW

Built in 1907, this house served as the residence of Mary Church Terrell, who achieved national prominence as an early educator, the first president of the National Association of Colored Women, and a civil rights and women's rights activist. She spoke at the 60th anniversary of the First Women's Rights Convention in Seneca Falls, New York. Her lecture in German delivered in 1903 at the International Congress of Women led her to the nationwide lecture circuit. The Terrell

House was designated a national historic landmark on May 15, 1975. The building, which is badly deteriorated, is owned by Howard University and is not in use.

Tidal Basin Bridge

Designed and constructed by African American engineer Archie Alphonso Alexander, the Tidal Basin Bridge is one of Washington's major tourist attractions. Alexander, born in Ottumwa, Iowa, in 1888, later became the first Republican governor of the U.S. Virgin Islands in 1954.

Carter G. Woodson House and the Association for the Study of Negro Life and History

1538 Ninth St., NW

Founded in 1915, the Association for the Study of Negro Life and History was formed to study and preserve the historical record of African American culture. The pioneer behind the association was Carter G. Woodson, who operated the organization out of his home until his death in 1950.

A scholar and lecturer, Woodson began publication of the *Journal of Negro History* in 1916. Ten years later, Woodson initiated the observance of "Negro History Week," to be celebrated in February as close as possible to the birthdays of both Frederick Douglass and Abraham Lincoln, during which African American leaders would be appropriately honored. Negro History Week has grown into what is now Black History Month.

The Woodson house, built circa 1890, was designated a national historic landmark on May 11, 1976. Today, the organization is headquartered at 1401 14th Street, NW, and is known as the Association for the Study of Afro-American Life and History. In 2001, the Woodson house was placed on the National Trust for Historic Preservation's list of the most endangered places in the United States. The National Park Service is attempting to obtain national historic site designation.

◆ FLORIDA

Daytona Beach

Bethune-Cookman College

640 Dr. Mary McLeod Bethune Blvd.
(386) 255–1401
<www.bethune.cookman.edu>

One of the leading institutions in the South for the training of African American teachers, Bethune-Cookman College was founded in 1904 by Mary McLeod

Bethune on "faith and a dollar-and-a-half." The school was first known as Daytona Normal and Industrial Institute for Negro Girls.

Bethune served as advisor to Presidents Franklin D. Roosevelt and Harry S. Truman and directed the Division of Negro Affairs in Roosevelt's National Youth Administration. She was one of the most influential women in the United States between the two world wars.

Mary McLeod Bethune House
Bethune-Cookman College
(904) 255–1401

The two-story frame house belonging to the African American activist and educator Mary McLeod Bethune was built in 1920 on the campus of the school that she established in 1904. The house was proclaimed a national historic landmark on December 2, 1974. A virtual tour of the house is available through the college Web site at www.bethune.cookman.edu.

Eatonville

Eatonville, Zora Neale Hurston Memorial Park and Marker
11 People St.

Incorporated in 1887, Eatonville claims to be one of the oldest all-African American communities in America. The fourth mayor of the town, John Hurston, a former slave, was the father of the town's most celebrated resident, Zora Neale Hurston. She is highly recognized today as a folklorist, anthropologist, and noted writer of the Harlem Renaissance. Still virtually all-African American, Eatonville is the site of the Zora Neale Hurston festivals held each January to celebrate Hurston's life and work. In addition, a marker has been placed in the Zora Neale Hurston Memorial Park.

Fort Pierce

Zora Neale Hurston House
1734 School Court St.

Zora Neale Hurston lived and worked in this one-story concrete house in Fort Pierce. Her gravesite in a segregated cemetery in Fort Pierce was unmarked until August 1973, when writer Alice Walker placed a stone at the approximate site of her burial. The home in which she lived from 1957, when she worked as reporter and journalist for a local African American weekly newspaper and continued to write until she died in 1960, was designated a national historic landmark on December 4, 1991. It is a private residence.

Key West

Fort Jefferson
Dry Tortugas National Park
<www.nps.gov/drto>

African American artisans and laborers worked in the construction of Fort Jefferson, a fort in Key West, Florida, which helped control the Florida straits. The largest all-masonry fortification in the western world, it served as a prison until 1873. Among the prisoners was Samuel A. Mudd, a physician who had set John Wilkes Boothe's broken leg after the assassination of Abraham Lincoln.

Fort George Island

Kingsley Plantation
(904) 251–3537

Zephaniah Kingsley traded extensively in slaves, and the headquarters for his operation was on this plantation on Fort George Island. The oldest known plantation in Florida, the Kingsley Plantation was established in 1763. The plantation, which has been restored as a museum, displays exhibits and furnishings that depict the plantation and island life during the period from 1763 to 1783. The site was added to the national park system on February 16, 1988, a part of the Timucuan Ecological and Historic Preserve. On September 29, 1970, it was designated a national historic landmark.

Franklin County

Fort Gadsen State Historic Site
(904) 670–8988

In 1814, the British built the fort as a base for recruiting Seminole Indians and runaway slaves during the War of 1812. The British abandoned it to their allies in 1815, along with its artillery and military supplies. It became known as the Negro Fort and British Fort and served as a beacon for rebellious slaves and a threat to supply vessels on the river. On May 15, 1975, the British fort (only ruins remain) was named a national historic landmark.

Olustee

Olustee Battlefield Historic Memorial
U.S. 90
(904) 752–3866

This site commemorates the largest Civil War battle in Florida's history. Also known as the Battle of Ocean Pond (1864), many African American troops fought bravely for the Union cause. The site was acquired by the state of Florida in 1909. The monument was built in 1912 and dedicated in 1913, just 49 years after the battle.

◆ GEORGIA

Andersonville

Andersonville Prison
GA Rte. 49
(229) 924–0343
<www.nps.gov/ande>

Andersonville, the infamous Confederate prison in Andersonville, Georgia, where thousands of Union soldiers perished as a result of the brutal manner in which they were confined, is now a national monument. Corporal Henry Gooding of the black 54th Massachusetts regiment was imprisoned here, where he died on July 19, 1864. It was Corporal Gooding who had started a protest regarding the pay of African American soldiers, going over the heads of military brass to write President Lincoln. At that time the pay of African Americans was a flat $7 per month. For whites, it ranged from $9 to $30. Encouraged by Colonel Robert Shaw, the African American soldiers of the 54th refused to accept any remuneration unless it were equal to that of white comrades. This financial inequity was subsequently rectified, but Corporal Gooding died at Andersonville without ever having drawn a day's pay.

Atlanta

Clark Atlanta University Center District
(404) 880–8000
<www.cau.edu>

Atlanta University was founded in 1865, holding its first classes for freed slaves in abandoned railway cars. Clark College was founded four years later. The two schools were incorporated in 1988. The Clark Atlanta University System includes the other traditionally African American colleges located in the immediate vicinity: Morris Brown (1881), Morehouse (1867), and Spelman (1881), and the Interdenominational Theological Seminary (1946).

Fountain Hall (formerly Stone Hall), built in 1882 and located on the Morris Brown campus, is the oldest building in the complex. It was named a national historic landmark on December 2, 1974.

Ebenezer Baptist Church
407 Auburn Ave., NE
(404) 688–7263

A Gothic-revival building constructed in 1922, Ebenezer Baptist Church had as its associate pastor the Rev. Martin Luther King Jr. It was from this church that King's movement radiated outward to the rest of the South, organizing chapters of the Southern Christian Leadership Conference (SCLC), the civil rights coalition of which he served as president.

When King was assassinated on April 4, 1968, funeral services were held in this church. As millions watched on television, mourners lined up for miles behind the mule-drawn wagon that carried King from Ebenezer to Morehouse College, his alma mater. There, the eulogies were delivered, and more than 150,000 mourners paid their last respects.

Martin Luther King Jr. National Historic District
Auburn Ave.
(404) 331–6922
<www.nps.gov/malu>

The district, which consists of several blocks of Atlanta's Auburn Avenue and Boulevard, includes Martin Luther King Jr.'s birthplace—a two-story Queen Anne style house built in 1895—and grave site, and the church where King served as assistant pastor. The environs of his childhood are largely intact. Private efforts to create a living monument to King and his beliefs have been carried on primarily through the Martin Luther King Jr. Center for Non-Violent Social Change, Inc. The Martin Luther King Historic District was designated a national historic landmark on May 5, 1977. In 1980, the district was designated a National Historic Site and Preservation District, and thus became a unit of the national park system.

South View Cemetery

Martin Luther King Jr., was laid to rest in South View Cemetery, where a marble crypt was inscribed with the words he used to conclude his famous speech delivered on the occasion of the 1963 March on Washington— "Free at last, free at last, thank God Almighty I'm free at last." In the early 1970s, Dr. King's body was moved from the South View Cemetery to a site next to the Ebenezer Baptist Church and the King Center in Atlanta.

South View cemetery was founded in 1886 by African Americans who balked at a prevailing policy requiring that they be buried in the rear of the municipal cemetery.

Sweet Auburn Historic District
Auburn Ave.

Although only a remnant of its original one-mile expanse has survived, the Sweet Auburn district typified the rapid growth of African American enterprise in

Martin Luther King Jr. memorial in Atlanta, Georgia.

the post-Civil War period. Forced to adjust to segregated residential and commercial patterns, wealthy African Americans settled in the area once known as Wheat Street and the "richest Negro street in the world." The district survives as a center of African American business and social activity. The district was designated a national historic landmark district on December 8, 1976. It is now included in the Martin Luther King National Historic Site and Preservation District.

Augusta

Laney-Walker North Historic District

Bounded by D'Antignac; Seventh, Twiggs, Phillips, and Harrison Sts., Walton Way, and Laney-Walker Blvd.

Developed during the nineteenth century as a self-sufficient, working-class community, the Laney-Walker district includes good examples of such houses as the plantation plain, shotgun, double pen, Victorian cottage, and an indigenous Augusta house. Prominent African American residents of the area were novelist

Frank Yerby, educator and Haines Normal and Industrial Institute-founder Lucy C. Laney, minister and church-founder Charles T. Walker, and numerous physicians, merchants, builders, and business people. Businesses in the district are important landmarks in Augusta's African American community. Examples are the Pilgrim Health and Life Insurance Company (1898) and the Penny Savings Bank (1910). The area was designated a national historic landmark district on September 5, 1985.

Columbus

"Blind Tom" Marker
U.S. Rte. 27A

This marks the grave site of the famous African American pianist "Blind Tom" Wiggins. Born Thomas Green Bethune, son of a slave, he was a prodigy whose astonishing talent brought him into the salons of Europe, where royalty marveled at his virtuoso performances.

Gertrude Pridgett "Ma" Rainey House
805 5th Ave.

The Rainey House was the retirement residence of Ma Rainey, who was recognized as "Mother of the Blues." She made her singing debut at age 14. In 1904, she married William "Pa" Rainey of the Rabbit Foot Minstrels and became known as "Ma." The team performed with various minstrels until they separated.

Ma Rainey worked out of Chicago during the 1920s and early 1930s and continued to tour the South. She had already won a national following as a gospel and blues performer long before she made her first recording in 1924. Rainey retired in 1934. She returned to Columbus in 1935 and lived in the house that she had earlier purchased for her mother. She died in 1939 and was buried in the local Porterdale Cemetery. The Rainey House was declared a national historic landmark on November 18, 1992. In 2002, the house was undergoing renovation by the Friends of Ma Rainey Blues Museum Inc.

Bragg Smith Grave Site and Memorial
Porterdale Cemetery
Fourth St. and Seventh Ave.

This memorial, located in Porterdale Cemetery, was built in memory of Bragg Smith, who was killed while attempting to rescue a city engineer trapped in a caved-in structure. The marble memorial is believed to have been the first civic memorial in the country dedicated to an African American.

Savannah

First Bryan Baptist Church
575 W. Bryan St.

The land on which Bryan Church was built is considered the oldest real estate in the country continuously owned by African Americans. Deeds for the land are dated September 4, 1793. Andrew Bryan formed the First African Baptist Church in Savannah on January 20, 1788, and pastored the congregation that became First Bryan Baptist Church in 1799. He remained there until his death in 1812.

Inside the First Bryan Baptist Church is a memorial dedicated to the Rev. George Liele, a former slave and the first African American Baptist missionary. His work took him up and down the Savannah River, from Augusta to Savannah, several times a year, where he preached to slaves. One of the slaves that he converted and baptized was Andrew Bryan, for whom the church was named.

Woodbury

Red Oak Creek Covered Bridge
North of Woodbury on Huel Brown Rd.

This 1840 structure is 412 feet long and was built by African American bridge builder Horace King, a former slave. King continued to work for his white master, John Goodwin, a contractor, after he was freed in 1848. One of the few extant in the state, the bridge is believed to be the oldest structure of its type in Georgia and the longest wooden bridge span in the state. King built other bridges in west Georgia as well as the bridge across the Chattahoochee River in Columbus. The Red Oak Creek Covered Bridge was designated a national historic landmark on May 7, 1973.

◆ ILLINOIS

Chicago

Robert S. Abbott House
4742 Martin Luther King Dr.

This house was occupied by Robert Stengstacke Abbott from 1926 until his death in 1940. Under Abbott, the *Chicago Defender*, a newspaper targeted to African American readers, encouraged African Americans in the South to migrate northward, particularly to Chicago. Probably more than any other publication, the *Defender* was responsible for the large northward migration of African Americans during the first half of the twentieth century. The house was named a national

historic landmark on December 8, 1976. It is a private residence.

Chicago Bee Building
3647–3655 S. State St.

The *Chicago Bee* Building was the last major structure built in Chicago's Black Metropolis, near State and 35th streets on the Near South Side. African American entrepreneur Anthony Overton had the structure built to house his newspaper, the *Chicago Bee*. Opened in 1931, the building also housed his Overton Hygenic Manufacturing Company. It was the first building designed in the late 1920s Art Deco style and was one of the most picturesque structures in the metropolis. The building was designated a national historic landmark on April 30, 1986. It was purchased by the city of Chicago and it now houses a Chicago Public Library branch.

Oscar Stanton DePriest House
4536–4538 S. Dr. Martin Luther King Jr. Dr.

This house served as the residence of the first African American elected to the House of Representatives from a northern state. Oscar DePriest was born in Florence, Alabama, but moved with his family to Kansas and later to Chicago. While in Chicago, he worked as a real estate broker and, in 1928, he was elected to the U.S. House of Representatives, where he served three terms. Following his tenure, he returned to the real estate business, but remained politically active in Chicago—including serving as vice-chairman of the Cook County Republican Committee. The DePriest house was designated a national historic landmark on May 15, 1975. It is a private residence.

Milton L. Olive Park
Lake Shore Dr.

Milton L. Olive Park was dedicated by Chicago Mayor Richard Daley in honor of the first African American soldier to be awarded a Congressional Medal of Honor during the Vietnam War. Olive died in action after exhibiting extraordinary heroism, having saved the lives of several other soldiers exposed to a live grenade.

Jean Baptiste Point Du Sable Homesite
401 N. Michigan Ave.

Jean Baptiste Point Du Sable, born in Haiti to a French mariner father and a black mother, immigrated to French Louisiana and became a fur trapper. He established trading posts on the sites of the present cities of Michigan City, Indiana; Peoria, Illinois; and Port Huron, Michigan—but the most important post was on the site of Chicago, Illinois. This site, where he

Jean Baptiste Point Du Sable and the area where he founded Chicago.

constructed a log home for his wife and family, is recognized as the first settlement in the Chicago area. In 1796, Du Sable sold his Chicago home and went to live with his son in St. Charles, where he died in 1814.

The homesite was designated a national historic landmark on May 11, 1976. The site of Du Sable's home is marked by a plaque on the northeast approach to the Michigan Avenue Bridge. Two other plaques recognizing Du Sable exist—one in the Chicago Historical Society, the other in the lobby of Du Sable High School, at 49th and State Streets.

Provident Hospital and Training School
500 E. 51st St. and Vincennes Ave.
<www.cchil.org/cch/providen.htm>

The original Provident Hospital and Training School was established as the first training school for African American nurses in the United States. It was founded by Daniel Hale Williams, the renowned surgeon who performed one of the first successful operations on the human heart in 1893. The current hospital was opened in 1933.

Quinn Chapel of the AME Church
2401 S. Wabash Ave.
<www.ci.chi.il.us/landmarks/q/quinnchapel.html>

Quinn Chapel is the oldest African American congregation in Chicago. Its history dates to 1844, when several local African Americans organized a weekly, nonsectarian prayer group that met in a member's home. The group was organized in 1847 as a congregation of the AME Church and was named for William Paul Quinn, bishop, circuit rider, and key figure in the western advance of the church. The church would serve as a focal point for the social and humanitarian life of Chicago's elite African Americans. Erected in 1892, the church structure was declared a national historic landmark on September 4, 1979.

Underground Railroad Marker
9955 S. Beverly Ave.

This marks one of many transit points used by slaves escaping from the South to Canada.

Victory Monument
35th St. and King Dr.

Sculpted by Leonard Crunelle, Victory Monument honors the African American soldiers of Illinois who served in World War I. The monument and tomb of Stephen A. Douglas, once the owner of much of the land in the area, is also located near 35th Street. The Victory Monument was designated a Chicago landmark on September 9, 1998.

Ida B. Wells-Barnett House
3624 S. Dr. Martin Luther King Jr. Dr.

This house was the home of the 1890s fiery journalist, civil rights advocate, and crusader for African American women, Ida Wells-Barnett. Wells-Barnett was exiled from the South after writing scathing articles about lynchings and race relations in Memphis, Tennessee, where her career in journalism began. She organized women's clubs in New England and Chicago and the Alpha Suffrage Club in Chicago. Wells-Barnett was a founder of the National Association for the Advancement of Colored People (NAACP). The Wells-Barnett House was designated a national historic landmark on May 30, 1974. It is a private residence.

Daniel Hale Williams House
445 E. 42nd St.

This house was the home of one of America's first African American surgeons, whose accomplishments include performing one of the first successful heart operations in 1893 and establishing quality medical facilities for African Americans. Daniel Hale Williams was born in Hollidaysburg, Pennsylvania. He had managed a barber shop prior to apprenticing under Henry Palmer, who was surgeon-general of Wisconsin. Williams received his medical degree from Chicago Medical College in 1883 and later opened an office in Chicago; he was the first African American to win a fellowship from the American College of Surgeons. The Williams house was designated a national historic landmark on May 15, 1975. In 1993, the house was severely damaged by fire. It is a private residence.

Quincy

Father Augustine Tolton Grave Site
St. Peter's Cemetery
Broadway and 32nd St.

The Father Augustine Tolton grave site marks the resting place of the first African American to be ordained as a Roman Catholic priest. Ordained in 1886, Father Tolton opened a school for African American children, was pastor at St. Joseph's Church in Quincy, and later served as pastor at St. Monica's Church in Chicago. He died in 1897.

◆ INDIANA

Bloomingdale

Underground Railroad Marker
U.S. Rte. 41

This marks one of several points once used to assist fugitive slaves seeking freedom and safety into Canada. One such slave, William Trail, liked Indiana so much he decided to stay and go into farming. His efforts were

successful, and he became one of many prosperous farmers active in Union County, Indiana.

Fountain City

Levi Coffin House
113 U.S. 27, N.
(765) 847–2432
<www.waynet.wayne.in.us/nonprofit/coffin/htm>

Born in North Carolina in 1798, Levi Coffin, a Quaker abolitionist who was also known as "The President of the Underground Railroad," used his own home in Fountain City as a way station for runaway slaves. Between 1827 and 1847, Coffin hid more than 300 slaves heading for Illinois, Michigan, or Canada. The home was built in 1839, altered in 1910, then restored to its former design.

Coffin left Fountain City for Ohio, where he continued his activities, eventually helping over 3,000 slaves escape from the South—he was still engaged in the resettlement of former slaves long after the Civil War had ended. Coffin died in Avondale, Ohio, in 1877.

Levi Coffin was known as "The President of the Underground Railroad"; his home in Fountain City, Ind., has been preserved in memory of his good deeds.

Indianapolis

Madame C. J. Walker Building
617 Indiana Ave.
(317) 236–2099
<walkertheatre.org/about_us.htm>

The Walker Building was constructed in 1927, the headquarters for the prosperous firm of Madame C. J. Walker (1867–1919). The Art Deco structure was architecturally significant and incorporated African, Egyptian, and Moorish motifs in its design. It housed a number of businesses, including a theater, pharmacy, ballroom, and the Walker Beauty College, where thousands of Walker's successful beauty agents were trained.

Walker's firm manufactured 75 beauty products, as well as training programs, beauty schools, and shops nationwide. Her hair care business catapulted her into fame and wealth, and many called her the nation's first African American woman millionaire. She also gave generously to various charities. The Walker Building was designated a national historic landmark on July 17, 1991. It now houses the Madame Walker Theatre Center.

◆ IOWA

Clinton

Underground Railroad Marker
Sixth and S. Second Sts.

Before the Lafayette Hotel was built, the small house that once stood at this location had been a point of shelter and sustenance for fugitive slaves escaping from Missouri (Iowa was a free territory by virtue of both the Northwest Ordinance of 1787 and the Missouri Compromise of 1820). Many Quakers, who had come to the state before the Civil War, took great pains to maintain an efficient and effective Underground Railroad network.

Des Moines

Fort Des Moines Provisional Army Officer Training School
Southwest Ninth St.
<www2.cr.nps.gov/pad/defenders/fortdm2.htm>

Fort Des Moines Provisional Army Officer Camp was opened on June 15, 1917, for the purpose of training talented African American soldiers for officer's rank. On October 14, 1917, 639 African American soldiers were commissioned as second lieutenants and assigned to the American Expeditionary Forces being sent to France to fight in World War I. African American units, led by men trained at the school, were assembled in France as the 92nd Division. The camp was abandoned at the end of the war, and the site was designated a national historic landmark on May 30, 1974.

Sioux City

Pearl Street

Sioux City was a refuge for many slaves escaping from Missouri. Pearl Street, once the city's main thoroughfare, was named for an African American who had arrived in the town by boat more than a century earlier and achieved widespread popularity as a cook.

◆ KANSAS

Beeler

George Washington Carver Homestead Monument

Along Route K–96 in Ness County lies the plot of land once homesteaded by George Washington Carver, the famed African American agricultural scientist. He spent two years here before attending college in Iowa.

Early migrants to the Nicodemus, Kansas, settlement (courtesy of Denver Public Library, Western Collection).

The homestead was designated a national historic landmark on November 23, 1977, and is indicated by a stone marker and bronze plaque.

Nicodemus

Nicodemus Historic District
U.S. 24 (Site approximates North St., E. Bend Rd., South St., and Seventh St.)

Located two miles west of the Rooks-Graham county line, the Nicodemus Historic District is the last of three now virtually deserted colonies that were founded by the Exodusters—a group of African American homesteaders that migrated from the South to Kansas during the 1870s. A principal leader of the mass migration was Tennessee's former slave Benjamin "Pap" Singleton, who established 11 colonies in Kansas between 1873 and 1880. The name "Nicodemus" was derived from a slave who, according to legend, foretold the coming of the Civil War.

Arriving in 1877, the first settlers lived in dugouts and burrows during the cold weather. From the outset, they were plagued by crop failures. Although never more than 500 in number, they managed nonetheless to establish a community with teachers, ministers, and civil servants. The state of Kansas has commemorated this site with a historical marker located in a roadside park in Nicodemus. The district was designated a national historic landmark on January 7, 1976.

Osawatomie

John Brown Memorial State Park
Tenth and Main Sts.
(913) 755–4384

This state park, named in honor of insurrectionist John Brown, contains the cabin in which he lived and engaged in abolitionist activities during his brief sojourn in Kansas. The cabin, built in 1854 on a site about one mile west of town, was dismantled, moved, and reconstructed in the park in 1912. In 1928 it was covered with a stone pergola. The park was designated a national historic landmark on March 24, 1971.

Topeka

Brown v. Board of Education of Topeka, Kansas National Historic Site
330 Western Ave.
(785) 354–4273
<www.nps.gov/brvb>

The historic area includes Sumner and Monroe elementary schools, both associated with the landmark Supreme Court case. In 1951, Linda Brown, who at first traveled a considerable distance to study at the all-African American Monroe Elementary School, was refused enrollment in Sumner Elementary School because she was African American. What followed was the landmark case *Brown v. Board of Education of Topeka, Kansas.* Upon hearing the case, the U.S. Supreme Court concluded that "separate education facilities are inherently unequal," striking down the 1896 *Plessy v. Ferguson* decision and giving the legal basis for desegregation in public schools. Sumner was designated a national historic landmark on May 4, 1987, and Monroe was included in 1991. The combined area was designated a national historic site on October 26, 1992, and thus became part of the national park system.

♦ KENTUCKY

Berea

Lincoln Hall
Berea College
(859) 985–3000
<www.berea.edu/galleryV/lincolnH.html>

Opened in 1855, Berea College was the first college established in the United States for the specific purpose of educating blacks and whites together. The school's Lincoln Hall, built in 1887, was designated as a national historic landmark on December 2, 1974.

Louisville

Kentucky Derby Museum
Churchill Downs, 704 Central Ave.
(502) 637–7097
<www.derbymuseum.org>

Materials relating to early African American jockeys, who played an important part in racing history, are in the museum. Isaac Murphy, the first jockey to ride three Kentucky Derby horses to victory, is among those represented.

Louisville Free Public Library, Western Colored Branch
604 S. 10th St.
<www.lfpl.org/branches/weste.htm>

The library, established in 1905, was the first public library in the nation built exclusively for African Americans. It was financed by Andrew Carnegie and played an important role in advancing African American culture in Louisville. Thomas F. Blue, the first librarian, opened a library education program at the facility in 1908 to prepare African Americans for positions in the library. The building was declared a national historic landmark on December 6, 1975.

Simpsonville

Lincoln Institute Complex
Off U.S. Rte. 60
(502) 722–8862

Lincoln Institute was Kentucky's leading center for the education of African American students in secondary school between 1908 and 1938. Whitney M. Young Sr. directed the school. When a state law in 1904 ordered Berea College to close its doors to biracial education, the college founded the Lincoln Institute. Kentucky's schools were integrated in the 1950s and the institute became obsolete; it closed in 1965. On December 12, 1988, the complex was designated a national historic landmark. It currently is home to the Whitney M. Young Jr. Job Corps Center.

Whitney M. Young Jr. Birthplace
Off U.S. Rte. 60
(502) 585–4733

Whitney M. Young Jr. was born in a simple, two-story frame building near Simpsonville. He grew up on the campus of the Lincoln Institute. Later, Young worked with the Urban League in Minnesota and Omaha, then became dean of social work at Atlanta University (now Clark Atlanta). In 1961, Young was appointed executive director of the National Urban League, a position he held until 1971, when he died in Lagos, Nigeria. On April 27, 1984, the house in which he was born and lived was declared a national historic landmark.

◆ LOUISIANA

Alexandria

Arna Wendell Bontemps House
1327 3rd St.
(318) 473–4692
<www.arnabontempsmuseum.com>

Arna Wendell Bontemps was born in this modest Queen Anne Revival style cottage in 1906 and remained there until his family relocated to California. Bontemps relocated to New York City in 1923 and became active

as a Harlem Renaissance writer. Later he taught in Huntsville, Alabama, and in Chicago. He moved to Nashville, Tennessee in 1943, to become head librarian at Fisk University and remained there until he retired in 1965. He was then professor at the University of Illinois, Chicago Circle, as it was known then, and curator of the James Weldon Johnson Collection at Yale University. He returned to Fisk as writer-in-residence, the position that he held when he died on June 4, 1973. In his lifetime he wrote numerous books, poems, and articles. His birthplace, now a museum, was designated a national historic landmark on September 13, 1993.

Melrose

Melrose Plantation
Rte. 119
(318) 379–0055
<www.natchitoches.net/melrose/index.html>

The Yucca Plantation, known after 1875 as Melrose Plantation, was established in 1794 by Marie Therese Coincoin, a former slave and wealthy businesswoman. The African House located on the plantation, a unique structure with an umbrella-like roof, is believed to be of direct African derivation. Melrose is also associated with Clementine Hunter, one of its African American workers, whose paintings of the plantation and its activities made her a famous folk painter. The site and its various buildings were declared a national historic landmark on April 16, 1984. It is a private residence.

New Orleans

James H. Dillard House
571 Audubon St.

This house served as the home of James Dillard from 1894 to 1913. Dillard played an important role in African American education in the nineteenth century, strengthening vocational and teacher training programs. Dillard's home was designated a national historic landmark on December 2, 1975. Dillard University, founded in 1869, was named for this educator.

Flint-Goodridge Hospital of Dillard University
Intersection of Louisiana Ave. and LaSalle St.

The hospital was founded in 1911 and became the medical unit of Dillard University in 1932. In the 1930s the hospital was the only institution in the state that offered internships to African American students preparing to become doctors. Flint-Goodrich was also the city's sole health care facility that admitted African Americans. It was significant for its contributions to tuberculosis testing and treatment, infant and maternal care, and syphilis treatment. The hospital closed in 1983 and was designated a national historic landmark on January 13, 1989.

Port Hudson

Port Hudson Siege Marker

Located near the Mississippi River some 25 miles north of Baton Rouge, Port Hudson was the scene of many heroic acts by African American soldiers during the Civil War including Louisiana's celebrated regiment of African Americans, the Native Guards.

◆ MAINE

Portland

John B. Russwurm House
238 Ocean Ave.

Russwurm, the second African American to receive a college degree, graduated from Bowdoin College in 1826. He co-edited the nation's first African American newspaper *Freedom's Journal*, then emigrated to Liberia. The historic house where he lived from 1812 to 1827, the only surviving structure closely tied to Russwurm, was designated a national historic landmark on July 21, 1983. It is a private residence.

◆ MARYLAND

Annapolis

Banneker-Douglass Museum
84 Franklin St.
(410) 974–2893

This museum, located in the city's historic district, is dedicated to the African American surveyor and inventor Benjamin Banneker and the abolitionist Frederick Douglass, both born in Maryland.

Matthew Henson Plaque
Maryland State House

The Matthew Henson Plaque, located inside the Maryland State House, honors the memory of the only man to accompany Admiral Robert E. Peary on all of his polar expeditions. On April 6, 1909, Henson became the first man actually to reach the North Pole. Peary himself, barely able to walk, arrived after Henson had taken a reading of his position and proudly planted the U.S. flag.

Thurgood Marshall Statue
North of Statehouse Circle

A seven-foot bronze statue of Supreme Court Justice Thurgood Marshall was unveiled in Annapolis in November 1996. It is the state's first memorial dedicated to an African American.

Baltimore

Benjamin Banneker Marker
Westchester Ave. at Westchester School

This marker is a tribute to Benjamin Banneker, the black mathematician, astronomer, and inventor who, in 1792, produced an almanac regarded as among the most reliable. His scientific knowledge led to his assignment as a member of the surveying and planning team that helped lay out the nation's capital.

Beulah M. Davis Collection
Soper Library
Morgan State University
(443) 885–3458
<www.library.morgan.edu/depart/spec/homel.htm>

Morgan State University houses an interesting collection of artifacts on Benjamin Banneker, noted astronomer, compiler of almanacs, and—together with Pierre-Charles L'Enfant—surveyor of the District of Columbia. It also houses a number of artifacts on Frederick Douglass and Matthew Henson.

Frederick Douglass Monument
Morgan State University

On the campus of Morgan State University is the Frederick Douglass memorial statue created by the noted African American sculptor James Lewis. The work, completed in 1956, stands 12 feet tall with pedestal. Its simple inscription reads "Frederick Douglass 1817–1895 Humanitarian, Statesman."

Rockville

Uncle Tom's Cabin

This is the site of the log cabin believed to have been the birthplace of Josiah Henson, the escaped slave immortalized as Uncle Tom in Harriet Beecher Stowe's famous abolitionist work of fiction.

Born in 1789, Henson was sold at auction at an early age and transferred among many masters until he managed to escape in 1830. After setting up a community for fugitive slaves in Dawn, Canada, Henson frequently returned to the South to liberate others. Meeting with Stowe, Henson outlined his slave experiences, which later formed the bases for her celebrated story—in the introduction to Henson's autobiography, published some years later, she acknowledged his story as the source of her own tale.

◆ MASSACHUSETTS

Boston

Abiel Smith School and Museum of Afro-American History
46 Joy St.
(617) 725–0022
<www.afroammuseum.org/index.htm>

Now housing the Museum of Afro-American History, this building, built in 1834, was the site of the city's first school for African American children.

African Meeting House
8 Smith Court
(617) 725–0022
<www.afroammuseum.org/site14.htm>

This is the site of the first black church in Boston and oldest surviving black church building in the United States. It was designated a national historic site on May 30, 1974, and is a part of the Boston African American National Historic Site.

Boston African American National Historic Site
14 Beacon St.
(617) 742–5415
<www.nps.gov/boaf/home.htm>

This site includes the Black Heritage Trail and contains the largest concentration of pre-Civil War African American history sites anywhere in the United States. Among them are the African Meeting House (the oldest extant African American church building in New England), the Smith Court residences (typical of African American families and built between 1799 and 1853), the Abiel Smith School (built in 1834), and the home of Lewis Hayden (the most documented of Boston's Underground Railroad stations). Hayden was an escaped slave from Kentucky who helped recruit the all-black 54th Massachusetts Regiment. Congress authorized the African American National Historic Site on October 10, 1980. The National Park Services coordinates its components; the site is federally-owned.

Bunker Hill Monument
(617) 242–5641
<www.nps.gov/Bunker_Hill.htm>

Standing in the Charlestown district of Boston, Massachusetts, the Bunker Hill Monument commemorates the famous Revolutionary War battle which—contrary to popular belief—was actually fought on Breed's Hill on June 17, 1775. A number of African Americans fought alongside the colonists during the battle including Peter Salem, Salem Poor, Titus Coburn, Cato Howe, Alexander Ames, Seymour Burr, Pomp Fiske, and Prince Hall, founder of the Negro Masonic order.

Crispus Attucks Monument

The Crispus Attucks Monument, located in the Boston Common, was dedicated in 1888 to the five victims of the Boston Massacre—Crispus Attucks, Samuel Maverick, James Caldwell, Samuel Gray, and Patrick Carr. The site of the massacre is marked by a plaque on State Street, near the Old State House.

Attucks is believed by many historians to have been the same man who, in 1750, was advertised as a runaway black slave from Framingham, Massachusetts. Although a stranger to Boston, he led a group that converged on a British garrison, which was quartered in King Street to help enforce the Townshend Acts. One of the soldiers of the garrison panicked and fired, and Attucks was the first to fall. Gray and Caldwell were also killed on the same spot; Maverick and Carr died later of wounds sustained during the clash. The British soldiers were later tried for murder but acquitted. The five men are buried a few blocks away in Granary Burying Ground, together with such famous Revolutionary figures as John Adams and John Hancock, as well as Governor William Bradford of Plymouth Colony.

William C. Nell House
3 Smith Court

From the 1830s to the end of the Civil War, William C. Nell was one of the leading African American abolitionists. Born in Boston, he studied law in the office of William I. Bowditch. Nell refused to take an oath to be admitted to the bar because he did not want to support the Constitution of the United States, which compromised on the issue of slavery. He then began organizing meetings and lecturing in support of the anti-slavery

Crispus Attucks Monument in Boston, Mass., memorializes the victims of the Boston Massacre.

movement. The Nell house was designated a national historic landmark on May 11, 1976. It is a private residence.

Colonel Robert Gould Shaw Monument
Beacon and Park Sts.
<www.nps.gov/boaf/site1.htm>

Executed by the famed sculptor Augustus Saint-Gaudens, the Shaw monument depicts Colonel Robert

Gould Shaw and the 54th Massachusetts Volunteers, an African American regiment that served in the Union Army during the Civil War. The regiment particularly distinguished itself in the battle for Fort Wagner, July 18, 1863, during which Colonel Shaw was killed. Sergeant William H. Carney's valiant exploits during this battle later earned him the Medal of Honor.

Cambridge

Maria Baldwin House
196 Prospect and H Sts.

This house was the permanent address of Maria Baldwin from 1892 until her death in 1922. Baldwin served as principal and later as "master" of the Agassiz School in Cambridge, as a leader in such organizations as the League for Community Service, as a gifted and popular speaker on the lecture circuit, and as a sponsor of charitable activities such as establishing the first kindergarten in Atlanta, Georgia. Baldwin exemplified the achievements that were attainable by an African American in a predominantly white society. The house was designated as a national historic landmark on May 11, 1976. It is a private residence.

Phillis Wheatley Folio
Harvard University

During her celebrated trip to England in 1773, Phillis Wheatley was presented with a folio edition of John Milton's *Paradise Lost*, which now is housed in the library of Harvard University in Cambridge, Massachusetts.

Wheatley, who came to America in 1761 as a child aged seven or eight, made rapid strides in mastering the English language and, by the time she was 14, had already completed her first poem. Always in delicate health, she died in Boston on December 5, 1784.

Central Village

Paul Cuffe Memorial

Paul Cuffe, son of a freedman, was born in 1759 and became a prosperous merchant seaman. Cuffe resolved to use his wealth and position to campaign for the extension of civil rights to African Americans. On one occasion, he refused to pay his personal property tax on the grounds that he was being denied full citizenship rights. A court of law eventually upheld his action, whereupon he was granted the same privileges and immunities enjoyed by white citizens of the state. In

Plaque honoring Union Colonel Robert Gould Shaw and the famed 54th Massachusetts Volunteers.

1815, Cuffe transported 38 African Americans to Sierra Leone in what was intended to launch a systematic attempt to repatriate the African American inhabitants of the United States. However, with the growth of abolitionist sentiment, the repatriation movement lost favor.

Dorchester

William Monroe Trotter House
97 Sawyer Ave.

Built in the late 1880s or 1890s, this balloon-frame rectangular-plan house was the primary home of William Monroe Trotter, journalist, civil rights activist, insurance agent, and mortgage broker. He was a bitter opponent of Booker T. Washington and had a confrontation with Washington in Boston on July 3, 1903, that came to be known as the "Boston riot." Trotter formed the Boston Suffrage League and, in 1901, cofounded and became editor and publisher of the crusading newspaper *The Guardian*. His home was designated a national historic landmark on May 11, 1976. It is a private residence.

Great Barrington

W. E. B. Du Bois Homesite
Rte. 23

This location served as the boyhood home of William Edward Burghardt Du Bois from 1868 to 1873. Du Bois, the prominent African American sociologist and writer, was a major figure in the civil rights movement during the first half of the twentieth century. Du Bois fought discrimination against African Americans through his writing, as a college professor, and as a lecturer. The Du Bois homesite was designated on May 11, 1976, as a national historic landmark. The ruins of the original house are located two miles west of Great Barrington on the north side of Route 23.

Lynn

Jan Ernst Matzeliger Statue
Pine Grove Cemetery

The Matzeliger Statue is one of the few extant memorials to this African American inventor, whose shoelace machine revolutionized the industry and made mass-produced shoes a reality in the United States. A native of Dutch Guiana, Matzeliger came to the United States in 1876, learned the cobbler's trade, and set out to design a machine that would simplify shoe manufacturing. Always sickly, he died at an early age, unable to capitalize on his successful patent, which was purchased by the United Shoe Machinery Company of Boston. After his death, Matzeliger was awarded a gold medal at the 1901 Pan-American Exposition.

New Bedford

New Bedford Whaling Museum
18 Johnny Cake Hill
(508) 997–0046

The museum maintains a treasury of whaling artifacts and information including the names and histories of African Americans who participated in the whaling industry. The museum also houses versions of the toggle harpoon—invented by Lewis Temple, an African American metalsmith—which revolutionized the whaling industry.

Westport

Paul Cuffe Farm and Memorial
1504 Drift Rd.

Paul Cuffe was a self-educated African American who became a prosperous merchant. He was a pioneer in the struggle for minority rights in the eighteenth and early nineteenth centuries and was active in the movement for black resettlement in Africa. The Paul Cuffe Farm was designated a national historic landmark on May 30, 1974. It is a private residence.

◆ MICHIGAN

Battle Creek

Sojourner Truth Grave Site
Oakhill Cemetery

This site in the Oak Hill Cemetery marks the resting place of one of the most powerful abolitionists and lecturers of the nineteenth century, Sojourner Truth. Sojourner settled in Battle Creek after the Civil War, but continued to travel on lecture tours until a few years before her death on November 26, 1883.

Cassopolis

Underground Railroad Marker
Rte. M–60

Sojourner Truth's gravesite in Battle Creek, Michigan.

This marks one of many rest places used by slaves escaping from the South to Canada. The marker is located approximately two miles east of Cassopolis.

Detroit

Douglass-Brown Marker
William Webb House
E. Congress St.

The Douglass-Brown Marker indicates the site of the William Webb House, where fellow abolitionists Frederick Douglass and John Brown met in March of 1859 to map out the strategy for the raid on the federal armory at Harpers Ferry, West Virginia. Douglass was strongly opposed to this course of action. Nevertheless, on October 16, 1859, Brown's forces seized the fort, only to be overtaken by federal troops two days later.

Ralph Bunche Birthplace
5685 W. Fort St.

A plaque marks the site of the birthplace of the undersecretary general of the United Nations and Nobel Peace Prize winner, Ralph Bunche, who was born in 1927. Bunche, the first African American to receive this honor, was awarded the prize in 1950 for his work as a United Nations mediator following the Arab-Israeli war of 1948.

Dunbar Hospital
580 Frederick St.
<www.cr.nps.gov/nr/travel/detroit/d28.htm>

The hospital is a landmark in the East Ferry Historic District. In 1918, the townhouse structure became the city's first nonprofit hospital for African Americans, who had inadequate access to mainstream hospitals in Detroit. African American physicians established the Allied Medical Society (later known as the Detroit Medical Society) and raised funds to establish a medical facility, Dunbar Hospital. In 1928, the hospital moved to Brush and Illinois streets and operated as Parkside Hospital until it was lost to urban renewal in 1960. Built in 1892 as a private residence, in 1928 the old Dunbar building served as the home of Charles C. Diggs Sr. and housed his undertaking business. Later his son, Charles Jr., made the home his residence. The building was designated a national historic landmark on June 19, 1979. The Detroit Medical Society recently renovated the building. It is now used as their headquarters. A museum is also on site, which is open to the public.

Elmwood Cemetery
1200 Elmwood Ave.
(313) 567–3453

Elmwood Cemetery contains the grave sites of 14 members of the 102nd U.S. Colored Regiment.

Elijah McCoy Home Site
5730 Lincoln

A plaque marks the site of one of Elijah McCoy's residences. McCoy, born in Ontario, Canada, settled in the Detroit area, opening a manufacturing company in 1870. McCoy is best known for his self lubricating device for locomotives and engines.

Motown Museum
2648 W. Grand Blvd.
(313) 875–2264

This location served as the early headquarters of Motown Records, founded in 1958 by songwriter and independent record producer Berry Gordy Jr. Performers including the Four Tops, Marvin Gaye, the Jackson Five, Martha and the Vandellas, Smokey Robinson, the Supremes, the Temptations, Mary Wells, and Stevie Wonder all played an important part in the early success of Motown. In 1972, the company moved its headquarters from Detroit to Los Angeles, California, but a museum containing restored sound studios and mementos is maintained at this site.

National Museum of the Tuskegee Airmen
Historic Fort Wayne
6325 W. Jefferson Ave.
(313) 843–8849

The museum houses memorabilia of the Tuskegee Airmen, an all-African American unit of fighter pilots active during World War II. The airmen, who were trained at Alabama's Tuskegee Institute (as it was known then), played an important role in the fight against racial discrimination in the armed forces.

Underground Railroad Marker
Second Baptist Church
441 Monroe

One of many stops along the Underground Railroad, the basement of the Second Baptist Church was used to hide runaway slaves. The church, founded in 1836, is one of the oldest African American congregations in the Midwest.

Motown Museum in Detroit, Michigan.

Marshall

Crosswhite Boulder
Michigan Ave. and Mansion St.

The Crosswhite Boulder marks the site of two confrontations that occurred in 1846 in defense of Adam Crosswhite, a fugitive slave who had fled from Kentucky. The Crosswhite case is said to have been instrumental in the enactment of the Fugitive Slave Law of 1850.

◆ MINNESOTA

Minneapolis-St. Paul

Fort Snelling State Park
1 Post Rd.
(612) 725–2389

Fort Snelling was the outpost in the Wisconsin Territory to which the slave later to become known as Dred Scott was transported from Illinois in 1836. Scott met and married his wife Harriet at the fort and saw his first child born there. Later taken to Missouri by his master, he filed suit for his freedom and became a national figure as his case was tried from 1847 to 1857 before numerous tribunals en route to the U.S. Supreme Court. Scott argued that he should be considered free by virtue of his having previously resided in Illinois and at Fort Snelling.

◆ MISSISSIPPI

Jackson

Farish Street Neighborhood Historic District
Approximate boundary Amite, Mill, Fortification,
 and Lamar Sts.
<www.ibinetwork.com/farishst/farishst.htm>

The district, comprising 695 buildings on 125 acres in downtown Jackson, is the state's largest African American community. A segregated area for African American residents in the 1890s, it soon became known for professionals of local or national prominence. The district gives excellent examples of the vernacular buildings of the period 1860 through the 1940s, although most of the buildings were erected between 1890 and 1930. The district was designated a national historic landmark site on March 13, 1980. After that, the boundary increased to include Amite, Lamar, Mill, and Fortification streets and embraced structures built by local African American contractors. The expanded site was designated a national historic landmark on September 18, 1980.

Lorman

Alcorn State University Historic District
Alcorn State University campus
(601) 877–6100
<www.alcorn.edu>

Alcorn State University, founded in 1871, is the oldest African American land grant college in the United States. Land grant status was designated in 1878, and the legislature changed the college's name to Alcorn Agricultural and Mechanical College. The state selected for its first president Hiram R. Revels, a distinguished leader during Reconstruction and the first African American to serve in the U.S. Congress. Buildings in the historic district include Lanier Hall, the Administration Building, and Harmon Hall. The Alcorn district was designated a national historic landmark site on May 20, 1983.

Oakland Chapel on the Alcorn University campus was built in 1838 as one of the first buildings of Oakland College, a white institution. In 1871 the state purchased the school to educate African Americans. The chapel was designated a national historic landmark on May 11, 1976.

Mound Bayou

Isiah Thornton Montgomery House
W. Main St.

This location served as the home of Isiah Thornton Montgomery, who in 1887 founded Mound Bayou—a place where African Americans could obtain social, political, and economic rights in a white supremacist South. The house, a two-story red brick structure built in 1910, was declared a national historic landmark on May 11, 1976. It is a private residence.

Natchez

Natchez National Cemetery
41 Cemetery Rd.
(601) 445–4981

This cemetery, established in 1840, is the final resting place of many African American war dead including landsman Wilson Brown, a Medal of Honor recipient during the Civil War. Brown and seaman John Lawson received their medals for courage in action while serving aboard the U.S.S. *Hartford* in the Mobile Bay engagement of August 5, 1864.

Piney Woods

Piney Woods Country Life School
5096 MS49, 20 miles south of Jackson
(601) 845–2214
<www.pineywoods.org>

Lawrence Clifton Jones established the school in 1909 to provide education for African Americans in Mississippi's back woods. The curriculum combined industrial education and academics. In the early 1920s the junior college program prepared future teachers. Jones gained nationwide attention in the 1950s as "The Little Professor of Piney Woods," when he was featured on the television program *This Is Your Life*. Today, enrolled students originate from both Mississippi and distant states as well.

◆ MISSOURI

Diamond

George Washington Carver Birthplace and National Monument
U.S. Rte. 71
(417) 325–4151
<www.nps.gov/gwca>

Located in a park in Diamond, Missouri, Carver National Monument commemorates the place where the great African American scientist George Washington Carver was born and spent his early childhood. The cabin of his birth no longer exists.

Kidnapped when he was just six weeks old, Carver was eventually ransomed for a horse valued at $300. Raised in Missouri by the family of Moses Carver, his owner, he made his way through Minnesota, Kansas, and Iowa before being "discovered" by Booker T. Washington in 1896. That same year, Carver joined the faculty of Tuskegee Institute, where he conducted most of the research for which he is now famous.

The monument, one of the first created in honor of an African American, consists of a statue of Carver as a boy and encloses several trails leading to places of which he was particularly fond. The park also houses a visitors' center and a museum displaying many of his discoveries and personal belongings. The monument was added to the national park system on October 15, 1966.

Kansas City

American Jazz Museum
18th St. and Vine Ave.
<www.americanjazzmuseum.com>

The museum opened in September 1998 as a monument to the music of the city that flourished between the 1920s and 1940s, as well as to spur redevelopment of the abandoned neighborhood where it is located.

Mutual Musicians Association Building
1823 Highland Ave.
(816) 471–5212

This building served as the home of the American Federation of Musicians Local 627 from the 1920s to the 1940s. Its members created the Kansas City style of jazz and included such greats as Count Basie, Hershel Evens, Lester Young, and Charlie Parker.

Jefferson City

Lincoln University
(800) 521–5052
<www.lincolnu.edu>

The more than $6,000 raised by the 62nd and 65th U.S. Colored infantries constituted the initial endowment for a 22-square-foot room in which classes were held in 1866 at what is now Lincoln University. Known then as the Lincoln Institute, the school began receiving state aid to expand its teacher training program in 1870. It became a state institution nine years later, and instituted college-level courses in 1887. It has been known as Lincoln University since 1921 and has offered graduate programs since 1940.

St. Louis

Scott Joplin House
2685 Delmar Blvd.; office, 2754 Bacon St.
(800) 334–6946
<www.mostateparks.com/scottjoplin.htm>

A composer known as "king of ragtime," Scott Joplin was born in Texarkana, Texas, but he left home to earn a living when he was 14 years of age. In his music he combined Midwestern folk and African American traditions within Western and European forms and provided an important foundation for modern American music. Joplin played piano in the St. Louis and Sedalia, Missouri area, and this house built in the 1890s is the last surviving residence of Joplin. The house, a two-story row house separated into flats, was declared a national historic landmark on December 8, 1976.

Old Courthouse
Broadway and Market Sts.
<www.nps.gov/jeff/och.htm>

It was in the Old Courthouse in 1847 that Dred Scott first filed suit to gain his freedom; for the next ten years,

The Old Courthouse in St. Louis, Missouri.

the Dred Scott case was a burning political and social issue throughout America. In 1857, the case reached the Supreme Court, where Chief Justice Roger Taney handed down the decision that slaves could not become free by escaping or by being taken into free territory nor could they be considered American citizens. Ironically, a few weeks after the decision was rendered, Scott was set free by his new owner. He died a year later. The site was designated a national historic landmark on May 27, 1987.

Homer G. Phillips Hospital
26101 Whittier St.

Built between 1932 and 1936, the hospital provided for the health care of local African Americans. It was also one of the few well-equipped facilities for African Americans from across the country where medical technicians, doctors, and nurses could be trained. The hospital was named for the attorney who was successful in the fight to establish the facility. Inadequate municipal support resulting in budgetary problems forced the hospital to close as an acute care facility on August 17, 1979. The building was designated a national historic landmark on September 23, 1982.

◆ MONTANA

Big Horn Station

Fort Manuel Marker

Captain William Clark and his party, which included a slave named York, camped at this site on July 26, 1806, a year before Manuel Lisa established Montana's first trading post. This site also was chosen by Major Andrew Henry as the Rocky Mountain Fur Company's first trading post; the leader of that expedition was Edward

Rose, another of the famed African American mountain men and explorers active in the territory.

◆ NEVADA

Reno

Beckwourth Trail
<www.beckwourth.org/Trail>

In the early days of pioneer settlement, the barren stretch of trail between Reno and the California line was the last obstacle before passing through to the West Coast. The original trail was laid out by an African American explorer, Jim Beckwourth, one of the legendary mountain men.

◆ NEW HAMPSHIRE

Jaffrey

Amos Fortune Grave Site

This grave site marks the resting place of the eighteenth-century African slave Amos Fortune, who purchased his freedom in 1770 at the age of 60 and went on to become one of the leading citizens of Jaffrey, his adopted hometown. Nine years after purchasing his freedom, Fortune was able to buy freedom for his wife, Violet Baldwin, and his adopted daughter, Celyndia. In 1781, he moved to Jaffrey and worked as a tanner, employing both black and white apprentices. In 1795, six years before his death, Fortune founded the Jaffrey Social Library and, in his will, directed that money be left to the church and to the local school district. (The school fund begun by Fortune is still in existence.)

The Fortune house and barn still stand intact, and both Fortune and his wife lie in the meeting house burial ground. Fortune's freedom papers and several receipt slips for the sale of his leather are on file at the Jaffrey Public Library.

◆ NEW JERSEY

Lawnside

Site of Free Haven

Located just east of the city of Camden, New Jersey, is the town of Lawnside, originally known as Free

Haven. The town served as a major stop on the Underground Railroad, and following the Civil War attracted a large population of freed slaves from the South.

Red Bank

T. Thomas Fortune House
94 W. Bergen Pl.

From 1901 to 1915, this location was the home of African American journalist T. Thomas Fortune. Born a slave in Marianna, Florida, Fortune was freed by the Emancipation Proclamation in 1863. He received training as a printer and founded the *New York Age* newspaper. The Fortune House, built between 1860 and 1885, was designated a national historic landmark on December 8, 1976. It is a private residence.

◆ NEW MEXICO

Lincoln

Old Court House
(505) 653–4372

During the Lincoln County Cattle War of 1877–1878, Billy the Kid, the notorious outlaw, was held in custody at the Old Court House in Lincoln, New Mexico, now a frontier museum. African American cowhands were involved on both sides of this struggle and, on one occasion, a group of African American cavalry men is said to have surrounded Billy the Kid during a particularly bloody battle.

Zuni

Zuni Pueblo
(505) 782–4481

Zuni Pueblo was discovered in 1539 by Estevanico, a Moorish slave, who was one of the original party of Spanish explorers to land in Tampa Bay in 1528.

Having heard of the legend of the Seven Cities of Gold, reputed to be located in the Southwest, Estevanico signed on as an advance scout for an expedition led by a Father Marco. Often traveling ahead of the main party, Estevanico sent most of his messages back via friendly Indians. His last message—a giant cross emblematic of a major discovery—led the expedition to the Zuni Pueblo, which Estevanico apparently thought formed part of the legendary Seven Cities. By the time the expedition arrived, however, the suspicious Zuni had already put Estevanico to death. Today, Estevanico is credited with the European discovery of the territory comprising the states of Arizona and New Mexico.

◆ NEW YORK

Albany

Emancipation Proclamation
New York State Library
(518) 474–5355
<www.nysl.nysed.gov/library/features/ep>

The New York State Library houses President Abraham Lincoln's original draft of the Emancipation Proclamation, which was issued in September 1862. The draft was purchased by Gerritt Smith, a wealthy abolitionist and patron of the famed revolutionary John Brown. The January 1, 1863, version of the proclamation resides in the National Archives of Washington, D.C.

Auburn

Harriet Tubman House
180–182 South St.
(315) 252–2081
<www.nyhistory.com/harriettubman>

Born a slave in Maryland, Harriet Tubman escaped from slavery at the age of 25, only to return to the South at least 19 times to lead others to freedom. Rewards of up to $40,000 were offered for her capture, but she was never arrested nor did she ever lose one of her "passengers" in transit.

During the Civil War, she served as a spy for Union forces. At the close of the war, Tubman settled in this house in Red Bank, New Jersey, years after it had outlived its original function as a major way station on the northbound freedom route of fugitive slaves. In 1953, the house was restored at a cost of $21,000. The house now stands as a monument to the woman believed to have led some 300 slaves to freedom via the Underground Railroad. The house was designated a national historic landmark on May 30, 1974.

Brooklyn

Ronald McNair Monument
Ronald McNair Park

A nine-foot granite monument of Ronald McNair, African American astronaut who lost his life in the space shuttle *Challenger* accident in 1986, was unveiled in a dedication ceremony in McNair Park in 1994. Created by Brooklyn artist Ogundipe Fayomi, the monument consists of three bronze plaques showing images from his life and achievements. McNair's quote is engraved on one side: "My wish is that we would allow this planet to be the beautiful oasis that she is, and allow ourselves to live more in the peace she generates."

Greater New York City

Abyssinian Baptist Church
132 Odell Clark Place
(212) 862–7474
<www.abyssinian.org>

The Abyssinian Baptist Church is one of the oldest and largest African American Baptist congregations in the United States. The church building was completed in 1923, under the leadership of the Rev. Adam Clayton Powell Sr. In 1937, Powell retired and was succeeded by his son Adam Clayton Powell Jr., who was elected to the U.S. Congress in 1960.

Amsterdam News Founding Place
2293 Seventh Ave.

The *Amsterdam News* was founded on December 4, 1909, in the home of James H. Anderson on 132 West 65th Street in New York City. At that time one of only 50 African American "news sheets" in the country, the *Amsterdam News* had a staff of ten, consisted of six printed pages, and sold for two cents a copy. Since then, the paper has been printed at several Harlem addresses. This building was designated a national historic landmark on May 11, 1976.

Apollo Theater
253 W. 125th St.
(212) 749–5838

The Apollo Theater in Harlem, once an entertainment mecca for all races, is one of the last great vaudeville houses in the United States. Erected in 1914, the building was designated a national historic landmark on November 17, 1983.

Louis Armstrong House
3456 107th St., Corona, Queens
(718) 997–3670
<www.satchmo.net>

For years this was the home of Louis Armstrong, the famous jazz musician whose talents entertained millions throughout the world. Whenever Armstrong was at his Corona home in Queens, New York, on a break from his concert dates, he was a favorite with neighborhood youngsters, often entertaining them in his home and on the street. The house was designated a national historic landmark on May 11, 1976.

Ralph Bunche House
115–125 Grosvenor Rd., Kew Gardens, Queens

The house served as the home of Ralph Bunche, the distinguished African American diplomat and undersecretary general to the United Nations. In 1950, Bunche was awarded the Nobel Peace Prize for his contribution to peace in the Middle East. The house was designated a national historic landmark on May 11, 1976. It is a private residence.

Will Marion Cook Residence
221 W. 138th St.

This residence in New York City served as the home of the early twentieth century African American composer Will Marion Cook, whom Duke Ellington called "the master of all masters of our people." Cook was born in Washington, D.C. He began studying violin at 13 years of age and, at 15, won a scholarship to study with Joseph Joachim at the Berlin Conservatory. Syncopated ragtime music was introduced to theatergoers in New York City for the first time with Cook's operetta *Clorinda.* The residence was designated a national historic landmark on May 11, 1976. It is a private residence.

Duke Ellington Statue
Fifth Ave. and 110th St.

A 25-foot high cast bronze monument featuring an eight-foot high statue of Duke Ellington was unveiled on July 1, 1997, on the northeast corner of Central Park. Designed by sculptor Robert Graham, it is the first public monument in the country honoring the jazz legend and composer. Bobby Short, cabaret performer who led the drive to erect the memorial, said that the location is "a bridge between Duke Ellington's two worlds: The sophisticated world of the Upper East Side and the street world of Harlem."

Edward Kennedy "Duke" Ellington Residence
935 St. Nicholas Ave., Apt. 4A

When Duke Ellington recorded "Take the A Train" to Harlem, he meant just that, because the A train express stops on St. Nicholas Avenue and was the quickest way for Ellington to get home. This St. Nicholas Avenue address was the long-term residence of Ellington, who has been regarded by critics as the most creative African American composer of the twentieth century. The residence was designated a national historic landmark on May 11, 1976. It is a private residence.

Fraunces Tavern
Broad and Pearl Sts.
(212) 425–1778
<www.frauncestavernmuseum.org>

One of the most famous landmarks in New York City, Fraunces Tavern was bought in 1762 from a wealthy Huguenot by Samuel Fraunces, a West Indian of black and French extraction. Known as the Queen's Head Tavern, it served as a meeting place for numerous patriots.

The Apollo Theater in Harlem remains a great entertainment venue.

On April 24, 1774, the Sons of Liberty and the Vigilance Committee met at the tavern to map out much of the strategy later used during the war. George Washington himself was a frequenter of the tavern, as were many of his senior officers. Washington's association with Fraunces continued for a number of years, with Fraunces eventually coming to be known as Washington's "Steward of the Household" in New York City. It was at Fraunces Tavern, in fact, that Washington took leave of his trusted officers in 1783 before retiring to Mount Vernon.

Much of the tavern's original furnishings and decor are still intact. The third floor, now a museum, contains several Revolutionary War artifacts, while the fourth floor holds a historical library featuring paintings by John Ward Dunsmore. A restaurant is maintained on the ground floor.

Freedom National Bank
275 W. 125th St.

Freedom National Bank, Harlem's first African American-chartered and -run commercial bank, was founded in 1965. The bank is no longer in business, having closed in 1990.

Harlem Historic District
Approximating the northern tip of Manhattan

Once the political and cultural hub of black America in the twentieth century, Harlem is primarily known as the major site of the literary and artistic "renaissance" of the 1920s and 1930s. Following the migration of blacks from the South and Caribbean to Harlem in the initial decade of the twentieth century, the city became a nurturing ground for pioneering black intellectual (i.e, literature, art, and black nationalism) and popular (i.e, dance and jazz) movements, as well as a vibrant nightlife centered around such nightclubs as the Cotton Club, Smalls Paradise, and the Savoy Ballroom.

Matthew Henson Residence
Dunbar Apartments, 246 W. 150th St.

This residence served as the home of Matthew Henson, the African American explorer who was an assistant to Robert E. Peary. Henson's best known achievement came in 1909, when he became the first man to reach the North Pole. The residence was designated a national historic landmark on May 15, 1975. It is a private residence.

Hotel Theresa
2090 Seventh Ave. at 125th St.

Built in 1913, the Hotel Theresa was once a luxury hotel serving white clientele from lower Manhattan and accommodating "white only" dinner patrons in its luxurious Skyline Room. In 1936, a corporation headed by Love B. Woods tried to take over the hotel and transform it into an African American business establishment. This move failed when Seidenberg Estates, the realtor, set a price beyond the reach of the group. Woods, however, was eventually able to purchase the hotel, which now serves as an office building.

James Weldon Johnson Residence
187 W. 135th St.

From 1925 to 1938, this was the New York City residence of James Weldon Johnson, the versatile African American composer of popular songs as well as poet, writer, general secretary of the NAACP, and civil rights activist. Johnson is best known for composing the song "Lift Every Voice and Sing," which has been called the Negro National Anthem. Johnson was born in Jacksonville, Florida, and studied at Columbia University. The residence was named a national historic landmark on May 11, 1976. It is a private residence.

Maiden Lane—The First Slave Revolt in New York

In 1712, on Maiden Lane and William Street, the first organized slave revolt in New York City occurred. Approximately 30 slaves joined and attempted to fight their way to freedom. Many people were injured in the melee that ensued as the slaves escaped to the woods with the militia close behind. Surrounded in the woods, several slaves committed suicide. The rest were captured and subsequently executed.

Malcolm X Residence
23–11 97th St., East Elmhurst, Queens

African American Muslim leader Malcolm X resided at this location with his family from 1954 until his death in 1965. The house, which was owned by the Nation of Islam while he and his family lived there, was the scene of a fire bombing on February 13, 1965. Malcolm X and his family escaped without injury.

Claude McKay Residence
180 W. 135th St.
(212) 281–4100

From 1941 to 1946, this residence in New York City was the home of the African American poet and writer Claude McKay, who has often been called the father of the Harlem Renaissance. McKay was born in Jamaica, British West Indies, and was in Kingston's constabulary prior to coming to the United States. His residence was named a national historic landmark on December 8, 1976. The building currently houses the Harlem YMCA.

Florence Mills Residence
220 W. 135th St.

This residence was the home of the popular African American singer who in the 1920s achieved stardom both on Broadway and in Europe. The Florence Mills' residence was designated a national historic landmark on December 8, 1976. It is a private residence.

Paul Robeson Residence
555 Edgecomb Ave.

This residence in New York City was the home of the famous African American actor and singer Paul Robeson. In the 1940s and the 1950s, Robeson suffered public condemnation for his socialist political sympathies, even while he was widely acclaimed for his artistic talents. The residence was named a national historic landmark on December 8, 1976. It is a private residence.

John Roosevelt "Jackie" Robinson House
5224 Tilden St., Brooklyn

This house served as the home of Jackie Robinson, the baseball player who in 1947 became the first African American to play in the major leagues in the twentieth century. His baseball contract broke down the color barrier to African American participation in professional sports. While a Brooklyn Dodger, Robinson lived for many years in the same borough of New York City where he played baseball. The residence was designated a national historic landmark on May 11, 1976. It is a private residence.

St. George's Episcopal Church
Third Ave. and First St.

Located in New York City, this was the church home of Harry Thacker Burleigh, the African American composer, arranger, and singer who helped establish the black spiritual as an integral part of American culture. The church was designated a national historical landmark on December 8, 1976.

Schomburg Center for Research in Black Culture
515 Malcolm X Blvd.
(212) 491–2200
<www.nypl.org/research/sc/sc.html>

Part of the New York Public Library System, the Schomburg Center for Research in Black Culture is devoted to documenting the black experience around the world. The collection is built around the private library of Arthur A. Schomburg, a Puerto Rican of African descent. It contains books, pamphlets, manuscripts, photographs, art objects, and recordings that cover virtually every aspect of black life—from ancient Africa to present-day United States. The building was designated a national historic landmark on September 21, 1978.

Sugar Hill, Harlem

Sugar Hill is a handsome residential section in uptown Harlem, New York. It is bordered on the west by Amsterdam Avenue, on the north by 160th Street, on the east by Colonial Park, and on the south by 145th Street. An area of tall apartment buildings and private homes, it is peopled largely by middle-class African Americans, sometimes referred to as the "black bourgeoisie." Its only counterparts in the area of central Harlem are Riverton and Lenox Terrace.

Booker T. Washington Plaque
New York University

Booker T. Washington, educator and founder of Tuskegee Institute, is the only African American honored by a plaque in the Hall of Fame at New York University.

Roy Wilkins House
147–15 Village Rd., Jamaica, Queens

This location served as the home of civil rights leader and former NAACP executive secretary Roy Wilkins from 1952 until his death in 1981. Wilkins had served as executive secretary of the NAACP for 22 years before retiring in 1977. It is a private residence.

Greenburgh

Villa Lewaro

Designed by the noted African American architect Vertner Woodson Tandy for Madame C. J. Walker, the

Madame C.J. Walker's house in Greenburgh, New York.

successful cosmetics manufacturer, Villa Lewaro illustrates the achievements of African Americans in both architecture and business. The Villa Lewaro, built in 1918, was declared a national historic landmark on May 11, 1976. The Building was sold in 1998 and will be used as a tourist attraction.

Lake Placid

John Brown Farm and Grave Site
(518) 523–3900
<www.cr.nps.gov/nr/travel/underground/ny4.htm>

Just six miles south of Lake Placid on Route 86A is the farm Brown purchased after he had left Ohio, now the location of his grave. The farm was part of 100,000 acres set aside for both freedmen and slaves by Gerritt Smith, a wealthy abolitionist. Smith hoped to build an independent community peopled by former slaves who had learned farming and other trades. Brown joined Smith in the venture, but the idea failed to take hold and was eventually abandoned. Brown lived there until he joined the free-soil fight in Kansas.

Rochester

Frederick Douglass Monument
Central Ave. and Paul St.
(716) 546–3960

New York Governor Theodore Roosevelt dedicated the Frederick Douglass Monument in 1899, four years after Douglass' death. In Rochester, Douglass edited his newspaper *The North Star*. Douglass was buried in Mount Hope Cemetery, not far from the memorial.

Frederick Douglass Museum and Cultural Center Foundation
300 Main St.

Opened to the general public in April 1999, this museum pays tribute to one of Rochester's most esteemed citizens of the eighteenth century. Among the artifacts contained in the museum are pews from the church in which Douglass was memorialized following his death in 1895.

South Granville

Lemuel Haynes House
Parker Hill Rd., off Rte. 149

This house, located in South Granville, Washington County, New York, was built in 1793. It served as the home of Lemuel Haynes from 1822 to 1833, the first

Frederick Douglass statue in Rochester, New York.

African American ordained minister in the United States. Haynes was also the first African American to minister to a white congregation. The South Granville home site was declared a national historic landmark on May 15, 1975.

◆ NORTH CAROLINA

Durham

North Carolina Mutual Life Insurance Company
114–116 W. Parish St.

This Parish Street address is the home office of North Carolina Mutual Life Insurance Company, an African American-managed enterprise that was founded in 1898 and achieved financial success in an age of Jim Crow. The business was first located in the Mechanics and Farmers Bank, a six-story structure that symbolized the city's affluent African Americans. Among the outstanding leaders associated with the firm were John Merrick, Charles Clinton Spaulding, and Asa T. Spaulding. The site was declared a national historic landmark on May 15, 1975.

Milton

The Yellow Tavern
Main St., between Lee St. and Farmer's Alley

For more than 30 years, the Yellow Tavern (also known as Union Tavern and the Thomas Day House) was the workshop of Tom Day, one of the great African American artisans and furniture makers of the Deep South prior to the Civil War. Day began making hand-wrought mahogany furniture in 1818 and, within five years, accumulated enough money to convert the old Yellow Tavern into a miniature factory. Both white apprentices and black slaves were taught this skilled trade under his tutelage. Day's artistry was so revered by the citizens of Milton that they went to great pains to secure a special dispensation from a North Carolina law that made it illegal for any free black or mulatto to migrate into the state. The Yellow Tavern, built circa 1910, was declared a national historic landmark by the Department of the Interior on May 15, 1975. Examples of Day's furniture can be seen in the North Carolina State Museum and at North Carolina Agricultural and Technical University in Greensboro.

Raleigh

John Chavis Memorial Park
E. Lenoir and Worth Sts.
(919) 831–6989

This park is named after John Chavis, an African American educator and preacher who founded an interracial school in Raleigh, which later numbered among its graduates several important public figures including senators, congressmen, and governors. As a result of the abortive Nat Turner slave rebellion in 1831, however, African Americans were barred from preaching in North Carolina, obliging Chavis to retire from the pulpit. He died in 1838.

Sedalia

Palmer Memorial Institute Historic District
6135 Burlington Rd., near Rock Creek Dairy Rd.

Charlotte Hawkins Brown, a North Carolina native, founded a school at this site on October 10, 1902, and named it for her friend and benefactor, Alice Freeman Palmer Institute. The school stressed academics, industrial, and vocational education. The school was incorporated on November 23, 1907. By 1916 the school had four buildings and had begun to make its presence felt nationwide. By 1922 it was one of the nation's leading preparatory schools for African American students. The school changed its focus in the 1930s, after the public school system for African Americans improved, and Palmer closed its elementary department and functioned largely as a finishing and college preparatory school. The school closed in 1971. In 1987 the state purchased the site to develop it as a commemorative for African American education. Canary College, the former residence of the school's founder, is the focal point of the site. The site was declared a national historic landmark on October 24, 1988.

◆ OHIO

Akron

John Brown Monument

The John Brown Monument was built in honor of the abolitionist whose ill-fated Harpers Ferry revolt led to his conviction for treason and execution by hanging in 1859.

Cincinnati

Harriet Beecher Stowe House
2950 Gilbert Ave.
(513) 632–5120

The Harriet Beecher Stowe House has been preserved as a memorial to the internationally known author of *Uncle Tom's Cabin*. The house served as the Beecher family residence from 1832 to 1836.

Dayton

Paul Laurence Dunbar House
219 N. Dunbar St.
(800) 860–0148

Paul Laurence Dunbar, the first African American poet after Phillis Wheatley to gain anything approaching a national reputation in the United States, was also the first to concentrate on dialect poetry and exclusively African American themes. His first collection of poetry *Oak and Ivy* was published before he was 20 years old. By 1896, his book *Majors and Minors* had won critical favor in a *Harper's Weekly* review. The Dunbar House was built circa 1890, but Dunbar bought it for his mother in 1903 and lived in it with her until only three years before his death. Dunbar contracted tuberculosis in 1899, and his health continued to fail until his death on February 9, 1906. The house was designated a national historic landmark on June 30, 1980.

Harriet Beecher Stowe's home in Cincinnati, Ohio.

Oberlin

John Mercer Langston House
207 E. College St.

Elected township clerk in 1855, John Mercer Langston is believed to have been the first African American to be elected to public office. Langston later served for the Freedman's Bureau, became the first dean of the Howard University Law School, and served as a U.S. Minister Resident to Haiti. The Langston House, which served as Langston's home from 1856 to 1867, was designated a national historic landmark on May 15, 1975. It is currently occupied by the Oberlin Student Cooperative Association.

Oberlin College
(800) 622–6243
<www.oberlin.edu>

Before the Civil War, Oberlin was one of the centers of underground abolitionist planning. The college was one of the first institutions to graduate African Americans and women; three of John Brown's raiding party at Harpers Ferry were identified as African Americans from Oberlin.

After the war, Oberlin was able to devote more time to its stated mission: providing quality education to all regardless of race. Among the distinguished alumni of Oberlin was Blanche K. Bruce, who served a full term in the U.S. Senate (1875–1881).

Ripley

John Rankin House and Museum
Off U.S. 62, west of Ripley
(513) 392–1627

An Underground Railroad station prior to the Civil War, the John Rankin House in Ripley, Ohio, is believed to have been the haven of the fugitive slave on whose story the novelist Harriet Beecher Stowe based the flight incident in *Uncle Tom's Cabin*. The house was built in 1828.

Wilberforce

Colonel Charles Young House
Rte. 42 between Clifton and Stevenson Rds.

This address was the residence of the highest ranking African American officer in World War I and the first African American military attache. Colonel Charles Young was the son of former slaves and was born in Mays Lick, Kentucky. The Army had declared Young unfit physically because of high blood pressure; to prove that he was physically fit, he rode horseback 500 miles from Wilberforce to Washington, D.C., in 16 days. The Army, however, still stuck by its ruling. The house was declared a national historic landmark on May 30, 1974. It is a private residence.

Wilberforce University
(937) 376–2911
<www.wilberforce.edu>

Established by the Methodist Church in 1856, Wilberforce University is named for William Wilberforce, an English abolitionist. In 1863, the school was purchased by the African Methodist Episcopal Church; in 1981, the institution was sold to the state of Ohio. Wilberforce is the site of the National Afro-American Museum.

◆ OKLAHOMA

Boley

Boley Historic District
Approximating Seward Avenue, Walnut and Cedar
  streets, and the southern city limits

This is the largest of the all-African American towns established in Oklahoma to provide African Americans with the opportunity for self-government in an era of white supremacy and segregation. The town was established in 1903 and named for a white official of the Fort Smith and Western Railway, who encouraged a development for the African American railway workers. Residents migrated from Georgia, Texas, Louisiana, Mississippi, Alabama, and Florida. The Boley Historic District was designated a national historic landmark on May 15, 1975.

Ponca City

101 Ranch

During the latter part of the nineteenth century, the 101 Ranch was one of the largest and most famous in the West. The ranch was established in 1879 and, in its prime, it employed several African American cowhands, the most celebrated of whom was Bill Pickett.

The originator of the art of bulldogging or steer wrestling, Pickett also perfected a unique style unlike any used by contemporary rodeo participants. In March 1932, though then in his seventies, Pickett was still active—the last of the original 101 hands. He died on April 21, 1932, after being kicked by a horse, and was buried on a knoll near the White Eagle Monument. The ranch was declared a national historic landmark on May 15, 1975.

◆ PENNSYLVANIA

Erie

Harry T. Burleigh Birthplace

A friend of famed Czech composer Antonin Dvorak and a composer/arranger in his own right, Harry T. Burleigh was born in 1866 in Erie, Pennsylvania. Burleigh set to music many of the stirring poems of Walt Whitman and arranged such unforgettable spirituals as *Deep River*. He died in 1949.

Lancaster

Thaddeus Stevens Grave Site
Schreiner's Cemetery
W. Chestnut and N. Mulberry Sts.

Senator Thaddeus Stevens of Pennsylvania, a white abolitionist and civil rights activist, was one of the chief architects of the Fourteenth Amendment to the Constitution. Upon his death in 1868, five black and three white pallbearers escorted the body to Washington, D.C. Stevens's body lay in state on the same catafalque that had borne the body of Lincoln and was guarded by African American soldiers of the 54th Massachusetts Regiment. Two days later the body was returned to Lancaster, where over 10,000 African Americans attended the funeral. Stevens was buried in Schreiner's Cemetery, a cemetery for African Americans—in his will, he had rejected burial in a white cemetery because of segregationist policy.

Montgomery County

James A. Bland Grave Site
Merion Cemetery

In the Merion Cemetery in Montgomery County, Pennsylvania, lies the grave of African American composer James A. Bland, who wrote "Carry Me Back to

Wilberforce University in Wilberforce, Ohio.

Old Virginny," now the state song of Virginia. Bland was one of the most popular African American minstrels of the nineteenth century.

Philadelphia

Frances Ellen Watkins Harper House
1006 Bainbridge St.

This was the home of the African American writer and social activist Frances Ellen Watkins Harper, who participated in the nineteenth-century abolition, woman's suffrage, and temperance movements. Harper occupied the residence from 1870 to 1911. The house was named a national historic landmark on December 8, 1976.

Mother Bethel African Methodist Episcopal Church
419 Sixth St.
(215) 925–0616

The current building was erected in 1859; it is the fourth church to be erected on the site where Richard

Allen and Absalom Jones founded the Free African Society in 1787. This organization later grew into the African Methodist Episcopal Church, one of the largest African American religious denominations in the United States.

Allen, the first African American bishop, was born a slave and became a minister and circuit rider after winning his freedom. In 1814, he and James Forten organized a force of 2,500 free African Americans to defend Philadelphia against the British. Sixteen years later, Allen organized the first African American convention in Philadelphia and was instrumental in getting the group to adopt a strong platform denouncing slavery and encouraging abolitionist activities. Allen died in 1831 and was buried in the church crypt.

As for Forten, he had been born free in 1766 and, despite his youth, served aboard a Philadelphia privateer during the Revolutionary War. In 1800, he was one of the signers of a petition requesting Congress to alter the Fugitive Slave Act of 1793. Opposed to the idea of resettling slaves in Africa, Forten chaired an 1817 meeting held at Bethel to protest existing colonization schemes. In 1833, he put up the funds that William

Lloyd Garrison needed to found *The Liberator*. After his death, Forten's work was continued by his successors, who remained active in the abolitionist cause throughout the Civil War and fought for African American rights during Reconstruction. The Forten home served as a meeting place for many of the leading figures in the movement. The church was named a national historic landmark on May 30, 1974.

Negro Soldiers Monument

West Fairmount Park
Lansdowne Dr.

The Negro Soldiers Monument was erected by the state of Pennsylvania in 1934 to pay tribute to its fallen African American soldiers.

Henry O. Tanner House

2903 W. Diamond St.

Born in Pittsburgh in 1859, Henry Ossawa Tanner was the first African American to be elected to the National Academy of Design. He became an internationally recognized painter of the nineteenth Century. The Diamond Street residence was the artist's boyhood home. The site is important also to commemorate the work of Tanner's father, Benjamin Tucker Tanner, bishop in the African Methodist Episcopal Church and editor of the *A.M.E. Church Review*. The homesite, a three-story structure, became Tanner's residence about 1872. The house was designated a historical landmark on May 11, 1976. It is a private residence.

Bessie Smith Residence

7003 S. Twelfth St.

This location served as home to blues singer Bessie Smith from about 1926 until her death in 1937. It is a private residence.

◆ RHODE ISLAND

Portsmouth

Portsmouth served as the site of the only American Revolutionary battle in which an all-African American unit, the First Rhode Island Regiment, participated in 1778.

◆ SOUTH CAROLINA

Beaufort

Robert Smalls House

511 Prince St.

Robert Smalls, a former slave, served in both the state legislature and the U.S. Congress. While in office, Smalls was an advocate for the rights of African Americans. He had lived in Beaufort, South Carolina, both as a slave and as a free man. The Smalls house, a large frame two-story structure built in 1843, was designated a national historic landmark on May 30, 1973. It is a private residence.

Charleston

Avery Normal Institute

125 Bull St.
(843) 953–7609

Founded by the American Missionary Association in 1865, the institute moved to Bull Street and provided college preparatory education and teacher training for Charleston's African American community. Francis Cardozo developed it into a prestigious private school. The school closed in 1954, due to financial difficulties. Today the historic building houses the Avery Research Center for African American History, founded in 1985.

Dubose Hayward House

76 Church St.

Dubose Hayward, the author of *Porgy*, the book upon which George Gershwin's opera *Porgy and Bess* was based, lived here from 1919 to 1924. It was designated a national historic landmark on November 11, 1971.

Old Slave Mart

6 Chalmers St.

The mart was built in 1853 to be used for the auction of slaves and other goods. Originally the mart included two additional lots and three buildings. The buildings were holding points for slaves who were to be sold. The structure that remains is the only known extant facility used as a slave auction gallery in the state. It now houses an African American museum and a gift shop. The building was designated a national historic landmark on May 2, 1975. In 2002, the city-owned structure was closed for renovations.

Denmark Vesey House

56 Bull St.

This was the residence of Denmark Vesey, a free black Charleston carpenter whose hard work earned him substantial wealth and respect among Charleston's African American community. He planned a slave insurrection, carefully selecting leaders and participants who were believed to be his supporters. His plot for July 14, 1822, was uncovered and Vesey was sentenced to death 12 days before the scheduled coup. The Denmark Vesey House was declared a national historic landmark on May 11, 1976.

Columbia

Chapelle Administration Building, Allen University
1530 Harden St.
(800) 254–4165

The Chapelle Administration Building is located at Allen University, a school founded in 1881. Named for Bishop Richard Allen, the school was established primarily to educate clergy for the African Methodist Episcopal church. The Chapelle building is one of the finest works of John Anderson Lankford, a pioneer African American architect who helped gain recognition for African American architects among the architectural community. The building was named a national historic landmark on December 8, 1976.

Frogmore

Penn Center Historic District
Rte. 37

Penn School was founded in 1862 and supported by northern missionaries and abolitionists. Ellen Murray of the Pennsylvania Freemen's Relief Association and her friend, Laura Towne, opened the school in Murray's house. As enrollment expanded, the school relocated to Brick Church, then to a site adjacent to the church. The new school was named Penn School. The school provided exceptional education to local African American residents who were denied admission to the white schools. The school also addressed health, agricultural, and financial needs of the African American residents of St. Helena. It collected and preserved the artifacts, musical recordings, oral history, and heritage of the residents. The school closed in 1948, but its buildings still serve the community. The traditions of the facilities are carried on by Penn Community Services, Inc. On December 2, 1974, the area was designated a national historic landmark district.

Georgetown

Joseph H. Rainey House
909 Prince St.

Joseph Hayne Rainey (1832–1887), a former slave, was the first African American to serve in the U.S. House of Representatives. His election, along with the election of Hiram R. Revels, the first African American

citizen to be elected to the U.S. Senate in 1870, marked the beginning of African American participation in the federal legislative process. The house, built circa 1760, was designated a national historic landmark on April 20, 1984. Rainey lived in the facility from 1832 to 1887. It is now a private residence.

Rantowles

Stono River Slave Rebellion Historic Site

This was the site of a 1739 slave insurrection, during which some 100 slaves escaped. The site, located in Rantowles, South Carolina, was named a national historic landmark on July 4, 1974.

♦ SOUTH DAKOTA

Deadwood

Adams Museum and House
Corner of Sherman and Deadwood Sts.
<www.adamsmuseumhouse.org>

Founded by W.E. Adams to honor the pioneers who settled the Black Hills of South Dakota, including one of the claimants to the legendary title, "Deadwood Dick." Nat Love, an African American, can back up his assertion, however, with a colorful autobiography that takes the reader through his childhood in slavery, his early bronco-busting efforts, and his fabled life as a range rider and fighter in the old West. Love claimed he won the title "Deadwood Dick" during a public competition held in Deadwood on July 4, 1876. The presence of other African American cowboys, gambling house operators, and escort soldiers in the area during those years, as well as the convincing style of Love's narrative, lend a high degree of credibility to his adventurous tales—although, like Jim Beckwourth, he may have been given to moments of wanton exaggeration.

♦ TENNESSEE

Henning

Alex Haley House
Haley Ave. at S. Church St.
(901) 738–2240

Nat Love, part of the colorful history of South Dakota's Black Hills.

Best known for the television adaptation of his Pulitzer Prize-winning book *Roots*, author Alex Haley has awakened both black and white Americans to the richness of African and African American history and culture. The house, built in 1918 by Haley's grandfather, served as his home from 1921 to 1929 and was where he heard many of the stories that inspired him to write *Roots*. Today the house serves as a museum.

Jackson

Casey Jones Home and Railroad Museum
<www.caseyjones.com>

On Chester Street in Jackson, Tennessee, is found the Casey Jones Railroad Museum, which is filled with memorabilia of a bygone era. Jones was immortalized through the song about Casey Jones' legendary train ride. The song, which became popularized in vaudeville and music halls, was written by Wallace Saunders, an African American fireman aboard Jones' locomotive.

The Railroad Museum serves to remind us of the enormous unsung contributions of African Americans to the railroad industry in the United States.

Memphis

Beale Street Historic District
Beale St. from Second to Fourth Sts.
<www.bealestreet.com>

The "blues," a unique black contribution to American music, was born on a Beale Street lined with saloons, gambling halls, and theaters. The street was immortalized by William Christopher Handy, who composed "Beale Street Blues." Beale Street, located in Memphis, Tennessee, was designated a national historic landmark on October 15, 1966.

William Christopher Handy Park

The city of Memphis, Tennessee, pays tribute to famed blues composer William Christopher Handy in the form of a park and a heroic bronze statue overlooking the very same Beale Street that he immortalized in the tune "Beale Street Blues." The statue, showing Handy standing with horn poised, was executed by Leone Tomassi of Italy and was dedicated in 1960, at the close of a memorial campaign instituted by the city shortly after Handy's death in 1958.

Tom Lee Memorial
Riverside Dr., south of Beale St.

The 30-foot high Tom Lee granite memorial was erected in 1954 to honor an African American who, on May 8, 1925, saved the lives of 32 passengers aboard the *M. E. Norman*, an excursion boat that had capsized some 20 miles below Memphis near Cow Island. Alerted to the disaster, Lee pulled 32 people from the water onto his skiff. He was honored for his feat by the Memphis Engineers Club, which provided him with money for the duration of his life. A fund was also raised to purchase him a home. After his death in 1952, a committee raised the money needed to erect the memorial.

Lorraine Hotel
406 Mulberry St.
(901) 521–9699

Beale Street in Memphis, Tennessee.

It was on the balcony of the Lorraine Hotel that Martin Luther King Jr. was assassinated, while emerging from a second-floor room in the presence of a pair of his trusted advisers, Ralph Abernathy and Jesse Jackson. King died in the emergency room of St. Joseph's Hospital on April 4, 1968. The Lorraine closed for business in 1988. It is now operated as the National Civil Rights Museum.

Nashville

Fisk University Historic District

(615) 329–8500

<www.fisk.edu>

Opened on January 9, 1866, and incorporated on August 22, 1867, Fisk University was founded in Nashville, Tennessee, following the Civil War, by the American Missionary Association to provide a liberal arts education for children of former slaves. Fisk School, as it was known then, began operation in former Union army barracks. In 1873, the campus was moved to a new site, the old Fort Gillem. In 1978, the 40-acre campus was designated a national historic landmark district. Among the historic buildings on campus are the residences once occupied by Arna Bontemps, Elmer S. Imes, Robert Hayden, and John W. Work. Several are Victorian design.

A bronze statue of illustrious Fisk graduate W. E. B. Du Bois, standing with book in hand, is located on the campus.

Jubilee Hall, a Victorian Gothic structure, is the South's first permanent structure built to educate African American students. The Fisk Jubilee Singers set out from Nashville in 1871 to raise money for their school, and in their concerts they introduced the Negro spiritual to the world. The singers raised enough money to save the school and to erect Jubilee Hall, which was dedicated on January 1, 1876. The hall was named a national historic landmark on December 9, 1971.

James Weldon Johnson House

911 D.B. Todd Blvd.

Writer and civil rights leader James Weldon Johnson resided at this location from about 1930 until his death in 1938, teaching literature and writing at Fisk University. Johnson was born in 1871 in Jacksonville, Florida. Johnson, in collaboration with his brother J. Rosamond Johnson, was responsible for creating the song "Lift Every Voice and Sing." Johnson's death mask is in the Fisk University Library, Special Collection. This is a private residence.

◆ TEXAS

Houston

Freedmen's Town Historic District
Approximate boundaries: I-45, Dallas Ave, Taft and
　W. Gray Sts.

This historic district, also known as the Fourth Ward, is the oldest existing post-Civil War African American community in the United States. Between 1910 and 1930, the area was the economic center for Houston's African American population. Many of the buildings in the district no longer exist, having fallen prey to developers and decay. In the interest of preserving some of the area's history, the Freedmen's Town home of Rutherford B. H. Yates, the first African American printer in Houston, is being renovated. It will serve as the Rutherford B. H. Yates Museum.

◆ VIRGINIA

Alexandria

Franklin and Armfield Office
1315 Duke St.

From 1828 to 1836, the office of the Franklin and Armfield slave trading company in Alexandria, Virginia, was the South's largest slave-trading firm. (During the company's operation, Alexandria was part of the District of Columbia.) The building was designated a national historic landmark on June 2, 1978.

Colonial National Historical Park
(757) 898–2410
<www.nps.gov/colo>

Jamestown Island, located in Colonial National Historical Park, is where the first African American slaves arrived in the American colonies in 1619. In addition,

the park served as the site of the Battle of Yorktown in 1781, a struggle in which three African Americans held combat positions in patriot militia units and worked for the Hessian forces as musicians and servants.

Arlington

Benjamin Banneker SW9 Intermediate Boundary Stone
18th and Van Buren Sts.

The boundary stone in Arlington, Virginia, commemorates the accomplishments of Benjamin Banneker, who helped survey the city of Washington, D.C., and who was perhaps the most well-known African American in colonial America. Banneker, a mathematician and scientist, was born in Ellicott Mills, Maryland, and received his early schooling with the aid of a Quaker family. Banneker was a national hero for African Americans, and many schools have been named after him. The boundary stone was declared a national historic landmark on May 11, 1976.

Charles Richard Drew House
2505 First St., S.

Located in Arlington, Virginia, this house served as the home of Charles Richard Drew from 1920 to 1939. Drew, a noted African American physician and teacher, is best remembered for his pioneer work in discovering means to preserve blood plasma. The house was named a national historic landmark on May 11, 1976. It is a private residence.

Chatham

Pittsylvania County Courthouse
U.S. Business Rte. 29

The Pittsylvania County Courthouse in Chatham, Virginia, was closely associated with the 1878 case *Ex parte Virginia*. This case, held upon the issue of African American participation on juries, stemmed from a clear attempt by a state official to deny citizens the equal protection of law guaranteed by the Fourteenth Amendment to the Constitution. The courthouse was designated a national historic landmark on May 4, 1987.

Capahosic

Holly Knoll House

From 1935 to 1959, this house served as the retirement home of Robert R. Moton. Moton, who succeeded

Booker T. Washington as head of Tuskegee Institute in 1915, guided the school's growth until 1930. He was an influential educator and active in many African American causes. The house now serves as the central building of the Moton Conference Center.

Glen Allen

Virginia Randolph Home Economics Cottage
2200 Mountain Rd.
(757) 727–5000

As the first supervisor of the Jeanes Fund, set up by a wealthy Philadelphia Quaker to aid African American education, Virginia Randolph worked to upgrade African American vocational training. The cottage in Glen Allen, Virginia, was named a national historic landmark on December 2, 1974. It houses a museum, which is open to the public.

Hampton

Hampton University
(757) 727–5000
<www.hamptonu.edu>

Founded in 1868 as Hampton Normal and Industrial Institute, this was one of the earliest institutions of higher learning for African Americans in the United States. Samuel Chapman Armstrong, an agent of the Freedmen's Bureau, persuaded the American Missionary Association to purchase land for the school. Booker T. Washington was one of its graduates who later founded Tuskegee Institute in Alabama, modeling it after the Hampton tradition. Washington also taught for a time at Hampton. The Hampton area and several of its buildings were designated a national historic landmark district on May 30, 1974.

Handy

Booker T. Washington National Monument
(540) 721–2094
<www.nps.gov/bowa>

The Burroughs plantation, on which educator and scholar Booker T. Washington was born, can be found in a 200-acre park located 22 miles southeast of Roanoke, Virginia. Born a slave, Washington lived here until the end of the Civil War, when he and his mother moved to Malden, West Virginia.

Lynchburg

Anne Spencer House
1313 Pierce St.
(804) 845–1313

Anne Spencer, poet and librarian, was friend and confidante of many Harlem Renaissance luminaries. Her poetry was published largely in the 1920s, when the Harlem Renaissance was in full blossom. She maintained her relationship with the African American cultural leaders of Harlem, and they visited her in the garden that she provided for them. The Spencer home was designated a national historic landmark on December 6, 1976.

Norfolk

Black Civil War Veterans' Memorial
Elmwood Cemetery
Princess Anne Rd.

In a section of Norfolk's Elmwood Cemetery marked by a granite monument lie the grave sites of several African American soldiers who served during the Civil War.

Richmond

Arthur Ashe Statue
Monument Ave.

A 12-foot bronze statue of tennis legend Arthur Ashe was unveiled in his hometown in July 1996. The statue depicts Ashe in a warm-up suit holding books over his head in one hand and a tennis racket in the other. The inscription, taken from a Bible verse, is the opening passage of his autobiography *Days of Grace*: "Since we are surrounded by so great a cloud of witnesses, let us lay aside every weight, and the sin which so easily ensnares us, and let us run with endurance the race that is set before us."

Jackson Ward Historic District

Bounded by Fourth, Marshall, and Smith Streets and the Richmond-Petersburg Turnpike, this was the foremost African American community of the nineteenth and early twentieth centuries and an early center for ethnic social organizations and protective banking institutions. The district was named a national historic landmark on June 2, 1978.

Hampton University, one of the earliest places for African Americans to receive a higher education.

Maggie Lena Walker National Historic Site
110–A E. Leigh St.
(804) 771–2017
<www.nps.gov/malw>

In 1903, Maggie Lena Walker, an African American woman, founded the successful Saint Luke Penny Savings Bank and became the first woman to establish and head a bank. In addition to being the first woman president of a bank, she was editor of a newspaper considered to be one of the best journals of its class in America. The house is located in the Jackson Ward

Historic District of Richmond; it was declared a national historic landmark on May 12, 1975, and it became a part of the national park system on November 10, 1978.

St. Luke Building
900 St. James St.

The Edwardian building, completed in 1903, is national headquarters for the Independent Order of St. Luke, an African American benevolent society founded in Baltimore by Mary Prout, a former slave. The organization helped to ease the transition from slavery to

Harpers Ferry, West Virginia, c.1865, where six years earlier John Brown led his famed abolitionist siege.

freedom, providing financial aid and guidance to newly freed slaves. The oldest African American-affiliated office building in the city, it houses the Maggie Lena Walker office now preserved as a memorial. The structure was remodeled and enlarged between 1915 and 1920. It was designated a national historic landmark on September 16, 1982.

◆ WASHINGTON

Centralia

George Washington Park

This park is named after a liberated slave who escaped from slavery in Virginia when he was adopted by a white couple and taken to Missouri. He then left Missouri with a wagon train heading for the Pacific Northwest, settling on a homestead along the Chehalis River. Once the location was reached by the Northern Pacific Railroad, Washington laid out a town, setting aside acreage for parks, a cemetery, and churches.

Soon over 2,000 lots were in the hands of a thriving population that formed the nucleus of Centerville.

◆ WEST VIRGINIA

Harpers Ferry

Harpers Ferry National Historic Park
(304) 535–6298
<www.nps.gov/hafe>

Harpers Ferry derives its historical fame from the much publicized anti-slavery raid conducted by John Brown and a party of 18 men, including five African Americans, from October 16th to 18th, 1859. Brown hoped to set up a fortress and refuge for slaves that he could transform into an important way station for black fugitives en route to Pennsylvania.

Brown lost two of his sons in the battle and was himself seriously wounded. Later tried and convicted of treason, he was hanged at Charles Town on December 2, 1859.

Malden

Booker T. Washington Monument
U.S. Rte. 60

This monument, erected in 1963, marks the site where Booker T. Washington labored for several years in the salt works. At the time, Washington credited his employer, Mrs. Violla Ruffner, with having encouraged him to pursue a higher education at Hampton Institute.

♦ WISCONSIN

Milton

Milton House and Museum
18 S. Jamesville St.
(608) 868–7772
<www.miltonhouse.org>

The Milton House, the first structure made of poured concrete in the United States, was once used as a hideaway for fugitive slaves escaping by means of the Underground Railroad.

Portage

Ansel Clark Grave Site
Silver Lake Cemetery

Ansel Clark, "born a slave, died a respected citizen," settled in Wisconsin after the Civil War, in which he served as an impressed laborer in the Confederate cause before escaping. Brought to Portage by a man to whom he had tended in a Union hospital, Clark served as town constable and deputy sheriff. For 30 years he worked in law enforcement, standing up to the town's rough characters and keeping them in line with his "firmness and dignity."

5

Africa and the Black Diaspora

♦ A Brief History of Africa ♦ The Modern Day People of Africa
♦ Black People in the Western Hemisphere ♦ Country Profiles

by Donald F. Amerman Jr.

According to renowned Kenyan scholar Dr. Ali Mazrui, author of *The Africans: A Triple Heritage* (1986), modern Africa has been heavily influenced by three main forces—indigenous traditions, the tenets of Islam, and Western culture including Christianity—with both positive and negative results. Among the benefits are a strong sense of continuity and regard for heritage, moral order, and membership in the global village. However, the mingling of such dynamic and divergent threads has caused a clash of cultures with an aftermath of "inefficiency, mismanagement, corruption, and decay of the infrastructure."

♦ A BRIEF HISTORY OF AFRICA

Archaeologists have come to believe that early humans, called *Hominidae*, originated in Africa some eight million years ago and migrated to other continents. Throughout much of the continent there flourished, 15 million to 25 million years ago, a number of families of Dryopithecine apes widely believed to be the forerunners of both humans and more recent ape species. Members of the genus *Australopithecus*, remains of which have been found in southern Africa, are the earliest known hominids and are believed to have developed about eight million years ago. Intermediary forms of human beings—*Homo habilis* and *Homo erectus*—ranged over large portions of the African continent before and during the Pleistocene age. The earliest forms of *Homo sapiens*, the species of modern man, began to appear about one-half a million years ago.

By the time of the Middle Stone Age, three distinct groups of people had evolved in Africa—Bushmanoid, Pygmoid, and Negroid. Only a few Bushmen, as well as a limited number of related Hottentot people, are still found in parts of the southwest portion of the continent, and a few isolated Pygmy groups have survived, mainly in the Congo forests. However, it was the Negroid group that became dominant on the continent. Thus, a number of distinct African races had developed by the close of the Pleistocene period.

The unification of the kingdom of Egypt, a civilization then in its infancy, occurred about 3000 BC. For the next three millennia, Egypt flourished along the Nile, giving rise to some of the most impressive accomplishments of early civilization. These accomplishments include the Pyramids of Giza and the Lighthouse of Alexandria, both of which are included among the Seven Wonders of the Ancient World. The construction by early man of such mammoth building projects as the Pyramids and the Sphinx continues to inspire wonder in today's visitors to these sites. The ancient Egyptians managed to cultivate much of the desert countryside of Egypt through innovative methods of irrigation until most of North Africa fell under Roman control in 146 BC.

Additional sophisticated societies began to develop in sub-Saharan Africa, among them the Kush, which flourished in Nubia, south of Egypt, between 700 BC and 200 AD. Others included the ancient Ghana, Kanem, Mali, Songhai, and the Haissa states. In the Congo, the kingdoms of Lunda, Lula, Bushong, and Kongo were founded, probably between the sixteenth and eighteenth centuries. On the Guinea Coast, the city states of Benin, Ite, Oyo, Ashanti, and Yoruba date back to the fifteenth century. These states traded extensively in gold, ivory, salt, and livestock.

Western Africa was home to the earliest trading empires. Between the fifth and eleventh centuries AD, the empire of Ghana dominated trade in the Sahara region in slaves, gold, and kola nuts. Along the shores of Lake Chad, the empire of Kanem-Bornu developed contemporaneously with Ghana, flourishing there until the seventeenth century. Of the Muslim empires that

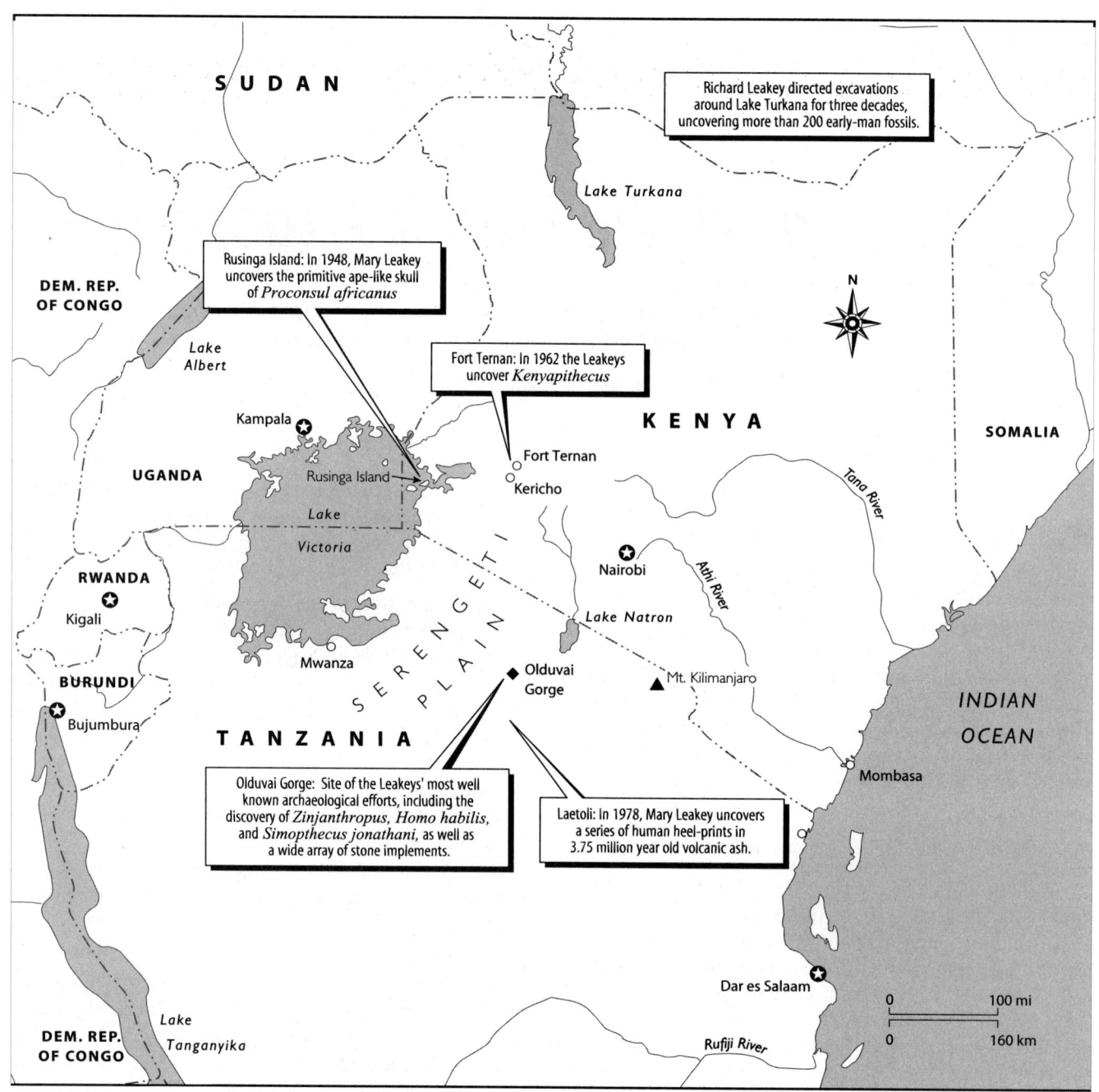

Richard Leakey directed excavations around Lake Turkana for three decades, uncovering more than 200 early-man fossils.

Rusinga Island: In 1948, Mary Leakey uncovers the primitive ape-like skull of *Proconsul africanus*

Fort Ternan: In 1962 the Leakeys uncover *Kenyapithecus*

Olduvai Gorge: Site of the Leakeys' most well known archaeological efforts, including the discovery of *Zinjanthropus, Homo habilis,* and *Simopthecus jonathani,* as well as a wide array of stone implements.

Laetoli: In 1978, Mary Leakey uncovers a series of human heel-prints in 3.75 million year old volcanic ash.

Major archeological finds supporting the evolutionary theory that humans first evolved in Africa.

developed in western Africa, the greatest by far was the Mali, which was dominant from about 1250 to 1400 AD. Succeeding the Mali empire was the Songhai empire of Gao, which flourished throughout most of the fifteenth and sixteenth centuries.

Beginning in the seventh century AD, most of northern Africa fell to Arab invaders, who quickly established the newly founded religion of Islam in African. To control the conquered areas, the Muslims imposed an Islamic governmental structure called the caliphate, which remained in force until the thirteenth century. Muslim traders then became aware of Africa's largely untapped potential in natural resources. By the ninth century, Muslim merchants from North Africa began to trade regularly with the peoples of West Africa, at first exchanging North African salt for gold from West Africa. The merchant class in West Africa was the first major group in the region to fall under the spell of Islam. The

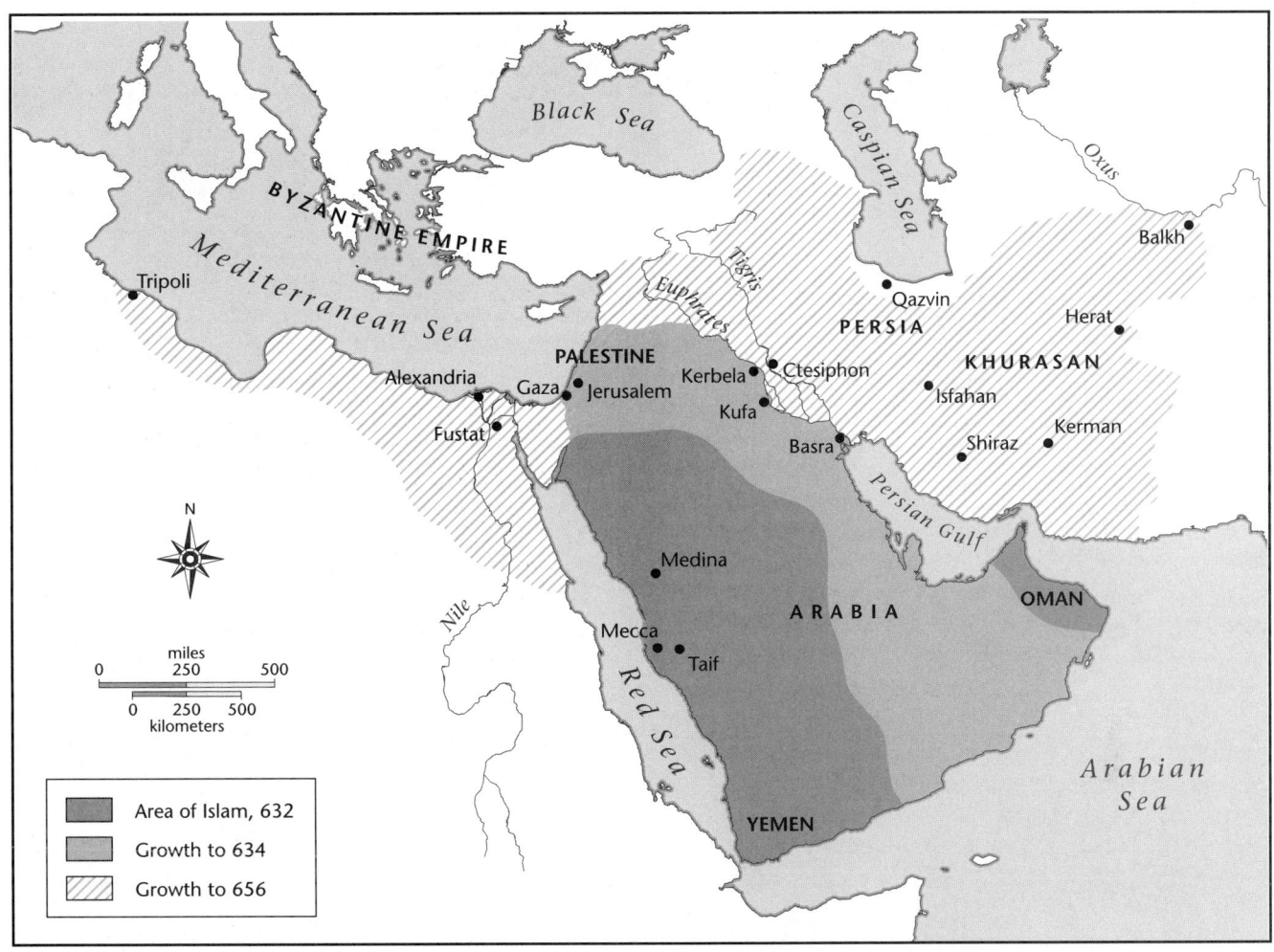

The influence of Islam on Africa is evident in this map of its spread during the Medieval period.

West African merchants were soon joined in their conversion to Islam by tribal leaders. Arab traders first began to set up trading outposts along the East African coast in the twelfth century. These coastal trading centers became part of an intricate trading network that linked Arabia with the markets of China and Southeast Asia.

Trade with Europe began around the fifteenth century, with the slave trade playing an important role. An estimated ten to 30 million people were sold into slavery by the mid-nineteenth century. The slave trade had a devastating effect upon the local societies from which the slaves were drawn and Africa as a whole. Slave traders knew well that growers in the Americas and elsewhere wanted the youngest and strongest to work their fields, so it was those individuals for whom they hunted, leaving the older and weaker behind. The interior of Africa was first exposed to Europeans in

the eighteenth century by missionaries, traders, and adventurers.

Although the British government declared the slave trade illegal in 1807, such human commerce continued to some degree through most of the nineteenth century. Some African territories, stung by the British ban on the slave trade, turned to other European nations to continue such trading. When the British fleet was deployed along the coast of West Africa to enforce that country's ban on the slave trade, slave traders simply shifted their operations to areas not under surveillance. Slaves were even shipped from East African ports to the Americas.

Until the middle of the nineteenth century, the European colonial presence in Africa was confined largely to British and Dutch settlers in South Africa. However, with the opening of the Suez Canal in 1869 and the contemporaneous discovery of diamonds in South Africa, European interest in Africa's natural wealth and

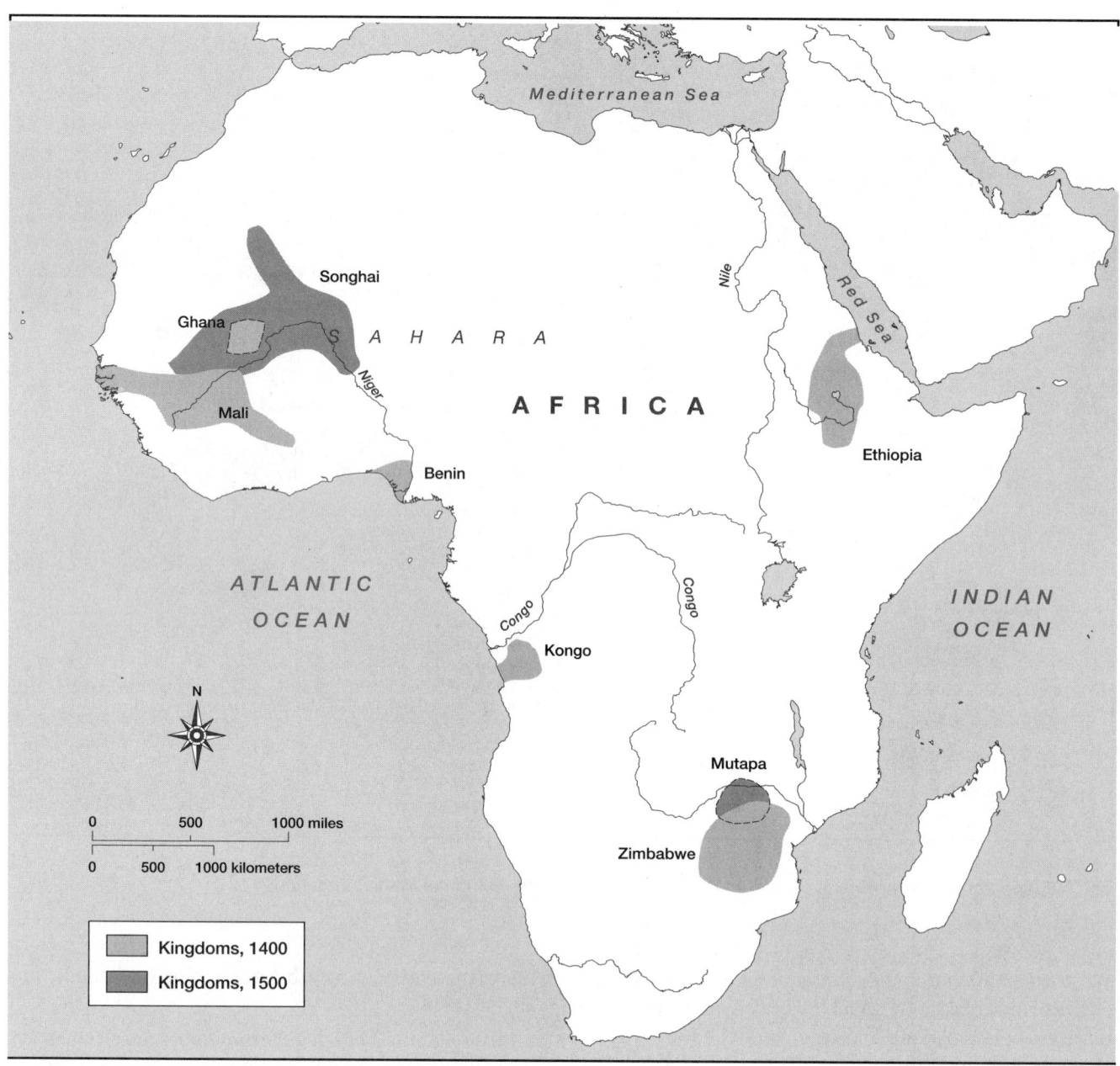

African kingdoms in the 15th and 16th centuries AD.

strategic location increased exponentially. European powers rushed to seize as big a chunk of the continent for themselves as possible. In the final two decades of the nineteenth century, Britain, France, Belgium, Germany, and Portugal scrambled to either conquer African territory or negotiate agreements with African leaders that allowed for mutual control. Only Ethiopia and Liberia escaped European colonization. Germany, however, lost its African territories after World War I.

Although the colonial powers varied to some degree in their treatment of African colonies, almost all did relatively little to improve the quality of life for their African subjects. They concentrated instead on finding more efficient ways to extract raw materials from the colonies or selling European products to them. European rule in Africa proved short-lived. In 1922, Egypt was granted independence from Britain. North Africa became a major arena of World War II, and, after the collapse of France, much of French North Africa was occupied in 1942 by Anglo-American forces. There followed a series of strategic battles between Allied and Axis forces across the sweep of North Africa.

As the tide of nationalism swept across Africa in the mid-twentieth century, the colonial powers, drained by World War II, proved unable to resist. In 1957, the Gold Coast won its independence from Britain and was renamed Ghana. The following year, France gave Guinea its freedom. Over the next few years, Britain and France granted independence to almost all of their other colonies in Africa.

The road to independence for Portugal's African colonies proved a good deal more torturous than most of the territories under British and French control. It took a revolution at home and years of guerrilla warfare in Africa to gain independence for the Portuguese colonies of Angola and Mozambique. Even France and Britain experienced some difficulties in extricating themselves from their colonial holdings in Africa. France was forced to endure a long and costly war with nationalists in Algeria before finally agreeing to independence for the colony in 1962. A unilateral declaration of independence by the white minority of Southern Rhodesia in 1965 led to a 15-year standoff between the colony and Britain. The situation was finally resolved in 1980, when agreement was reached to establish the multiracial nation of Zimbabwe. Africa's last colony, Southwest Africa, was granted independence as Namibia in late 1988, after 73 years of South African control.

The collapse of communism in Eastern Europe and the end of the Cold War had a profound effect on Africa. In the years since independence, many of the new African nations, almost all of which could be classified as developing countries, chose socialist systems, selecting the Soviet Union as their model for economic and political development. Embracing the notion of centrally-planned economies, many of these countries developed into single-party dictatorships. Almost all African countries in the socialist sphere closely aligned themselves with the Soviet Union, which provided for substantial military and economic assistance. When the Soviet Union disintegrated in the early 1990s, many socialist African states were left without a major source of support. Socialism quickly fell into disfavor, with most countries in Africa turning to Western Europe and the United States for help. To curry favor in Western capitals and also in the hope of reinvigorating their failing economies, many of these African nations took aggressive steps to install market mechanisms.

The collapse of the Soviet Union and most of its client states cut off much of the financial support for revolutionary movements in such African countries as Angola and Mozambique. With the Soviets and their allies largely out of the picture, the United States gradually withdrew its support for many African countries' opposition to these Soviet-financed wars of liberation. Among the countries torn apart by these continuing internal struggles was Somalia, which fell into anarchy as multiple warlords battled each other for effective control of the country. In 1992, the United Nations was forced to send nearly 30,000 troops into the country in an effort to restore order.

The early 1990s witnessed the collapse of several dictatorial African regimes as the forces of democratization swept across the continent. The socialist leadership of Benin was forced out, the dictator of Mali was overthrown, and Zambian President Kenneth Kaunda was defeated in 1991. Three years later, Malawi's dictator, Hastings Banda, also met defeat at the polls. In other quarters, chaos still reigned—Angola continued to be torn apart by civil war, and ethnic warfare in Rwanda took a staggering toll in human lives. A shaky peace took hold in Liberia after a bloody civil war, only to be shattered in 1998 by a resumption of internal strife. Further exacerbating Liberia's problems in 2001 was the imposition of UN sanctions because of the government's support of Sierra Leone's Revolutionary United Front rebels.

Undoubtedly, the brightest news from Africa in the final decade of the twentieth century was the end of apartheid in South Africa and the country's first all-race, multiparty elections in 1994. Long-time political prisoner Nelson Mandela was elected president in those historic elections. In June 1999, Mandela, who had decided not to seek a second term in the presidency, was succeeded by Thabo Mbeki.

Prominent African Nationalist Movements

The faces of African nationalism are many and, although most first emerged in the twentieth century, some were well established even earlier. In the late nineteenth century, the Afrikaner nationalism movement was born, fanned by the radical Afrikaner nationalist mythology of Stephen Jacobus Du Toit in his newspaper *Die Afrikaanse Patriot*. Du Toit, founder of the rabidly anti-British Afrikaner Bond, an organization dedicated to driving the British out of South Africa, told his followers that the Afrikaners, also known as Boers, were God's chosen people. The Afrikaners' defeat at the hands of the British in the Boer War in 1902 helped to fuel nationalism among the Afrikaners.

The troubled relationship between South Africa's Afrikaners and the British continued. The two divided over the issue of racial segregation between 1910 and 1939. During both World War I and World War II, many in the Afrikaner community opposed any support of Britain against Germany. Between 1924 and 1933, the

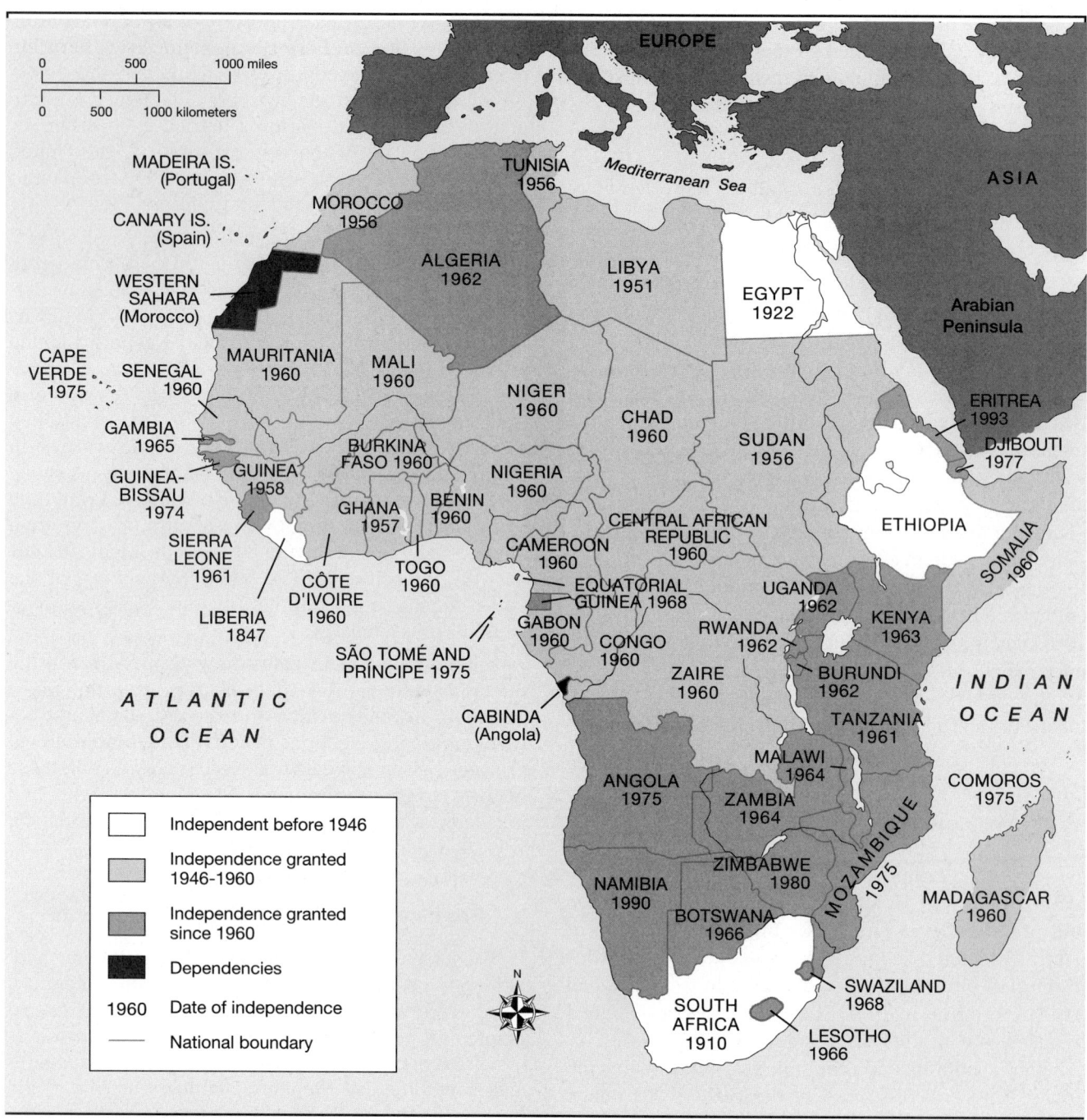

Modern African countries and the years they became independent nations.

National Party, led by Prime Minister J. B. M. Hertzog, promoted bilingualism (English and Afrikaans) in South Africa. Aligning itself with the Dutch Reformed Church, the Afrikaner nationalist movement was steadfast in its opposition to race mixing in South Africa. Three years after the end of World War II, the National Party, led by Daniel Malan, won a stunning victory and immediately imposed the policy of racial separation known as apart-

heid. Afrikaner nationalism continued strong until the late 1970s when it became apparent that Afrikaners could not contain the rising nationalism of the country's black African majority.

The major force for nationalism among South Africa's black majority, the African National Congress (ANC), was founded in 1912 as a nonviolent civil rights organization dedicated to the promotion of black African interests. Drawing largely from the country's middle class, the ANC first worked for change through constitutional means. In a 1940 attempt to revitalize the organization, President Alfred B. Xuma began recruiting new members including Nelson Mandela, Oliver Tambo, and Walter Sisulu. Membership in the ANC swelled substantially in the 1950s after the imposition of apartheid. In the late 1950s, members of the ANC who felt that the country belonged only to black Africans broke away from the organization and formed the Pan-Africanist Congress (PAC). PAC's program of mass demonstrations led in 1960 to the Sharpeville Massacre. The government responded by banning all black political organizations including the PAC and the ANC.

In 1961, elements within the ANC set up a military wing called Umkhonto we Sizwe, which launched a program of sabotage against the government. The unrest that followed led to the arrests of Mandela and Sisulu, both of whom were sentenced to life in prison. Tambo left the country to set up an external wing of the ANC. A 1976 revolt in Soweto reinvigorated languishing black nationalist sentiments in South Africa, leading to an increase in the ANC's membership rolls. In 1990, the government lifted its ban on black political organizations, allowing the ANC once again to operate out in the open. The government also freed Mandela from prison in 1990, setting in motion feverish politicking that led to all-race elections in 1994. In that election, Mandela was elected the country's first president. Three years later, Mandela stepped down as the leader of the ANC and was succeeded by Thabo Mbeki, who in June 1999 was elected president.

A strong believer in African liberation, Kwame Nkrumah led Britain's West African colony of Gold Coast to independence as Ghana in 1957. The son of a goldsmith, Nkrumah was born in Nkroful in the Gold Coast. He was trained as a teacher and, in 1935, went to the United States to continue his studies. While studying in England in 1945, he helped to organize the fifth Pan-African Congress, which drew together African intellectuals and leaders from all over the continent. Returning to Gold Coast in 1947, he became general secretary of the United Gold Coast Convention, but abandoned it two years later to organize the more radical Convention People's Party. Imprisoned briefly in 1950 for his involvement in a campaign of nonviolent protests, he was released to form a government after the CPP swept the colony's elections in 1951. After leading the colony to independence as Ghana in 1957, Nkrumah was instrumental in the founding of the Organization of African Unity in 1963. The following year, he formed a one-party government at home and named

himself president for life. He was overthrown by the Ghanaian military in 1966 and spent the rest of his years in exile, dying in Bucharest, Romania, in 1972.

The nationalist movement in Kenya, which won its independence from Britain in 1963, was led by Jomo Kenyatta, a Kikuyu born in Gatundu in the 1890s. Educated by missionaries, Kenyatta moved to Nairobi in the early 1920s and joined the Kikuyu Central Association, eventually assuming the editorship of the KCA's newspaper. Kenyatta traveled to England in 1929 and 1931 to press, unsuccessfully, KCA demands for the return of Kikuyu land lost to Europeans. For the next 15 years, Kenyatta studied throughout Europe, publishing a number of articles about his native Kenya and the difficulties of its people under colonial rule. His book *Facing Mount Kenya* explored Kikuyu tribal society and the effects of colonialism. In 1945, Kenyatta helped to organize the fifth Pan-African Congress in London. In June 1947, he became president of the Kenya African Union (KAU), a political organization formed a few years earlier. Kenyatta led KAU's unsuccessful campaign for Kenya's self-government under African leadership. Although Kenyatta professed to oppose the use of violence in achieving African nationalist goals, colonial authorities linked him to the Mau Mau terrorist network of the early 1950s and jailed him for nearly nine years. Assuming the leadership of the Kenya African National Union (KANU) shortly after his release from prison, Kenyatta led his party to victory in May 1963 elections, which were held in advance of independence. He led his country to independence in December of 1963 and was elected president of the Republic of Kenya a year later.

◆ THE MODERN DAY PEOPLE OF AFRICA

Geography

The second largest continent on the globe, Africa is bisected by the equator and bordered to the west by the Atlantic Ocean and to the east by the Indian Ocean. Roughly the shape of an inverted triangle—with a large bulge on its northwestern end and a small horn on its eastern tip—it contains 52 countries and six islands that together make up about 20 percent of the world's land mass or 11.5 million square miles.

Africa is essentially a huge plateau divided naturally into two sections. Northern Africa, a culturally and historically Mediterranean region, includes the Sahara desert—the world's largest expanse of desert, coming close to the size of the United States. Sub-Saharan, or so-called "Black Africa," also contains some desert land, but is mainly tropical, with rain forests clustered

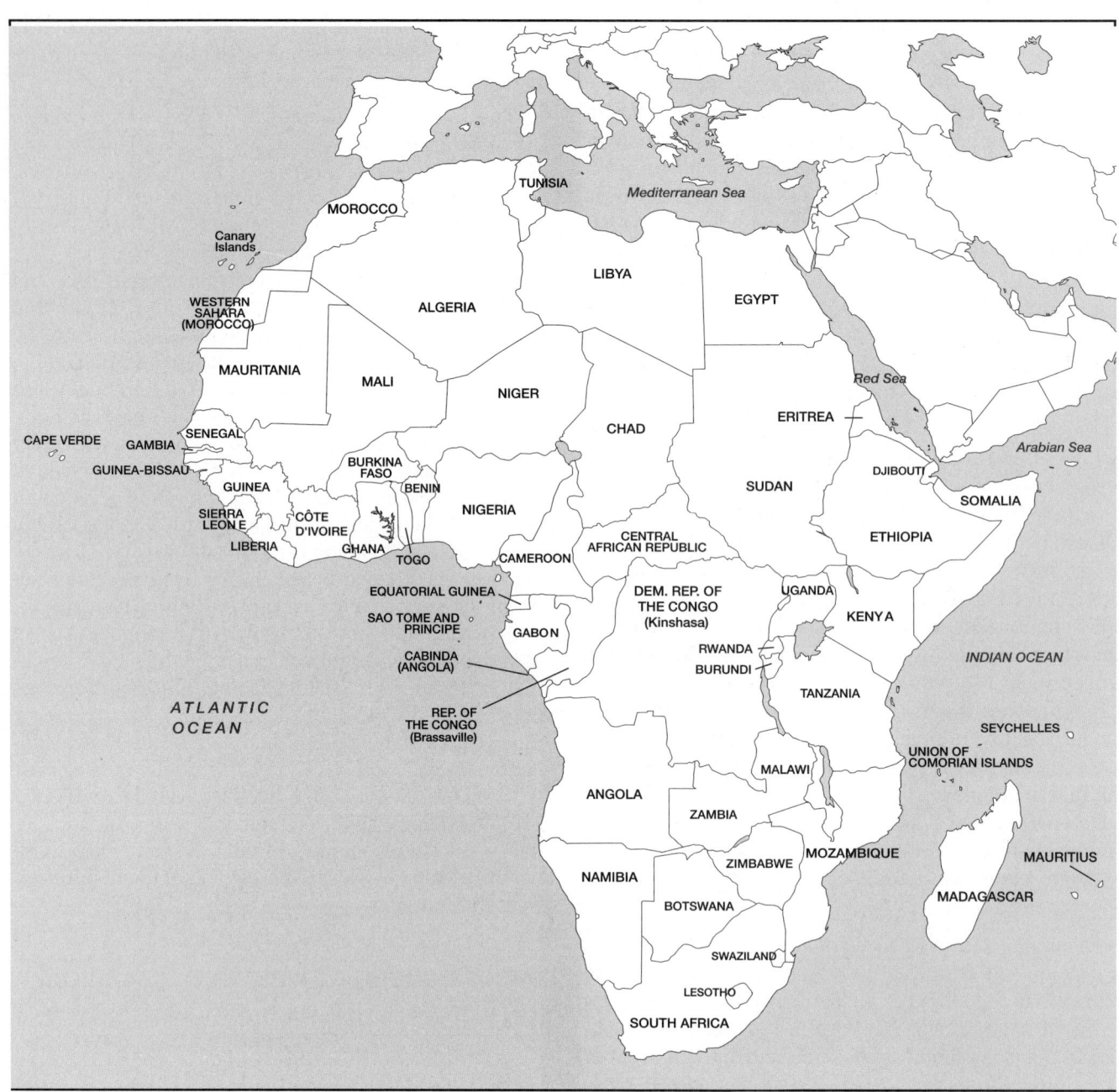

Africa.

around the equator; vast savanna grasslands covering more than 30 percent of continent and surrounding the rain forests on the north, east, and south; some mountainous regions; and rivers and lakes that formed from the natural uplifting of the plateau's surface.

Notable geographical marvels in Africa include Mts. Kenya and Kilimanjaro (the latter of whose highest peak is one of the tallest in the world); the rivers Niger, Senegal, Congo, Zambezi (home of the mile-wide Victoria Falls, one of the world's seven natural wonders),

Orange, Limpopo, Malawi, and Nile (the longest river in the world); lakes Tanganyika, Albert, Rudolf, and Victoria (the second largest freshwater body in the world); and the Libyan, Nubian, and Kalahari deserts.

Economics/Natural Resources

A mineral-rich continent, Africa is a prime source of copper, diamonds, gold, manganese, oil, uranium, zinc,

Mount Kilimanjaro in Tanzania.

and several other deposits. The equatorial forests produce ebony, teak, and rosewood, while cash crops include bananas, cocoa, coffee, cloves, cotton, sisal, sugar cane, tobacco, yams, and all kinds of nuts including cashews and groundnuts. In fact, agriculture has formed the basis of most African economies for centuries. Despite such a wealth of resources, many African nations rank among the poorest in the world. Tribal and political wars, illiteracy, droughts, lack of technological prowess, and the commonality of corruption among government officials all contribute to the weak economy encountered in much of the continent.

Though Africa does have booming urban and industrial centers—for example, Johannesburg, South Africa; Lagos, Nigeria; Dakar, Senegal; Harare, Zimbabwe—the continent is better known to visitors for the national parks and reserves of East and southern Africa. Wildlife concentrations in these locations vary but include antelope, impala, Thompson's gazelles, and wildebeests; buffalo, hippos, and rhinos; elephants; giraffes; zebras; crocodiles; a variety of bird species; hyenas, jackals, and wild dogs; cheetahs, leopards, and lions.

Kenya, located in East Africa, is one of the oldest and most popular game-viewing destinations for safari-seeking tourists. The Samburu National Reserve, Lake Nakuru (also known as the "pink lake" because of an abundance of flamingos), Masai Mara National Reserve, and Amboseli are all favored spots. Nearby, Tanzania offers Lake Manyara National Park, Serengeti National Park, and Ngorongoro Crater (a natural amphitheatre that was formed by the collapse of a volcano). Uganda features Bwindi Forest, home of the Buhoma Gorilla Camp. In the southern region of Africa, South Africa contains ostrich farms; Kruger National Park, one of the continent's largest reserves; Cango Caves; and Kirstenbosch Botanical Gardens. Zimbabwe contributes man-made Lake Kariba, a permanent water source for monkeys, warthogs, waterbuck, and other species including birds; Hwange, a game reserve filled with more than 107 species; and the Zambezi Nature Sanctuary and Crocodile Farm.

Population

The African population is most heavily concentrated in Nigeria; southern Ghana; along the Gulf of Guinea;

San women of the Kalahari Desert gathering edible roots in Botswana.

Benin and Togo; the Nile Valley; in northern Sudan; the East Africa highlands of Ethiopia, Kenya, and Tanzania; eastern Democratic Republic of the Congo; the eastern and southern coasts; and the inland High Veld of South Africa. The desert and mountain regions are largely uninhabited.

In recent years, the population of African has grown rapidly. In 1950, the total population was estimated at 281 million, but, by 2001, the population had reached an estimated 823 million, making it the second most populous continent on the planet. No African nation has developed an effective population control program, and such practices as having multiple wives and early marriages continue. By the year 2020, the population of sub-Saharan Africa alone is expected to reach 1.2 billion.

Until recently, almost 90 percent of Africa's population lived in rural areas. African cities with populations exceeding one million include Accra, Ghana; Addis Ababa, Ethiopia; Cape Town and Johannesburg, South Africa; Cairo, Egypt; Maputo, Mozambique; Ibadan and Lagos, Nigeria; and Congo-Kinshasa. In addition to indigenous Africans, about five million people are of predominantly European descent and one million are of Asian descent.

During a 1959 archaeological expedition in Olduvai Gorge, Tanzania, Kenyan-born anthropologist L. S. B. Leakey and his wife Mary discovered a skull of a species thought to date back more than two million years called *Australopithecus boisei*, *Zinjanthropus*, or "Nutcracker Man" in popular vernacular. Within the next ten years they also unearthed *Homo habilis*, also estimated to date between 1.5 to 2 million years ago, and *Kenyapithecus africanus*. Fossils of early hominoids resembling man have been found in Ethiopia, Kenya, and South Africa by other scientists. The remains are believed to be predecessors of our own human species *Homo sapiens*.

Language

The diversity of Africa's people is underscored by the existence of more than 2,000 languages and dialects including Africanized forms of English, French, and Portuguese. Some fifty major languages are spoken by groups of one million or more people. The major language groups include Arabic (spoken mainly in north Africa), Fula, Hausa, Lingala, Malinke, Nguni (which includes SiNdebele, Xhosa, and Zulu), SeTwana-SeSotho, Swahili, and Yoruba.

"African-language" names are often derived from the names of the ethnic tribes that speak them. For example, Zulu is spoken primarily by Zulus, and Kibondi is the language of the Bondi tribe. Swahili, the most widely spoken language on the continent, is the only one that breaks the pattern. A commercial language originally used among traders and business people, it evolved from Portuguese, Arabic, and Bantu.

As many languages were never translated into written form, Africa acquired a very long and rich oral tradition. In many cases, the oral tradition was the only method of passing literature and history from generation to generation in ancient times. After the fourteenth century, the use of Arabic by educated Muslim blacks was extensive, and some oral literature was subsequently reduced to a more permanent written form. But in spite of the Arab influence, the oral heritage of Africans remained strong, serving not only as an educational device, but as a guide for the administration of government and the conduct of religious ceremonies.

A wealth of proverbs from African culture have survived through the generations. Some of the more popular ones are: if you want to know the end, look at the beginning; when one door closes, another one opens; if we stand tall it is because we stand on the backs of those who came before us; two men in a burning house must not stop to argue; where you sit when you are old shows where you stood in youth; you must live within your sacred truth; the one who asks questions doesn't lose his way; if you plant turnips you will not harvest grapes; god makes three requests of his children: do the best you can, where you are, with what you have now; you must act as if it is impossible to fail; some would be great drinkers but they haven't got the wine; some great eaters but they haven't got the food.

Literature

It is impossible to consider the literature of Africa without including the great body of oral literature for which the continent is so famous. The relationship between oral and written literature is complex and not easily analyzed. It certainly is not simply a matter of evolution that brings us from the oral tradition to the commitment of some of these tales to the written word. In fact, the oral tradition is alive and well today in many small villages throughout Africa.

Of all the arts, literature—both oral and written—is probably the one most highly esteemed in African tradition. Literature for our purposes must be considered to include not just novels and short stories but folk tales, myths, legends, proverbs, and poetry. Much of the folklore of Africa is available only in the oral form. One of the best examples of oral literature is the epic of *Sundiata*, founder of the West African kingdom of Mali in the thirteenth century. However, written literature is not without its own rich history in Africa. For centuries, written literature in Amharic, Arabic, Hausa, and Swahili has existed and, more recently, there has been a sharp increase in African literature written in the languages of the European colonial powers.

The West Coast of Africa, with its long tradition as a breeding ground for the arts, is home to some of the most important of today's African writers. Among these, Nigerian Chinua Achebe, author of *Man of the People*, the story of a newly independent African state strangely reminiscent of his own country, rails against corruption and the cult of personality. All of his work, which includes *Things Fall Apart*, *Arrow of God*, *No Longer at Ease*, and *Home and Exile*, voices a concern for the loss of native culture in the flood of imported European values. Other Nigerian writers making a name for

themselves include Cyprian Ekwensi, Tanure Ojaide, Funso Aiyejina, Amos Tutuola, and Oruora Nzekwu. In Nzekwu's *Blade Among the Boys*, the clash between his native Ibo religion and imported Christian ideals causes confusion in the life of a sensitive young man.

Most of the best-known literature out of South Africa during the twentieth century has come from white authors uneasy about their country's racist policies. William Plomer's *Turbott Wolfe*, published in 1925 well before the imposition of apartheid, argued for a mixing of white and black blood in South Africa to prevent a future in which the country's whites dominated the country. Probably the best-known of the anti-apartheid novels is Alan Paton's *Cry, the Beloved Country*. Other South African authors such as Doris Lessing, Dan Jacobson, J.M. Coetzee, André Brink, and Nadine Gordimer have elevated this literature of protest to a new level of excellence. Gordimer received the Nobel Prize for Literature in 1991, following fellow Africans Wole Soyinka of Nigeria in 1986, and Naguib Mahfouz of Egypt in 1988. Among the better known black writers of South Africa are Sindiwe Magona, Zakes Mda, and Mandla Langa.

Other of Africa's best-known authors include Cameroon's Mongo Beti; Ghana's Ayi Kwei Armah and J.E. Casely-Hayford; Kenya's Ngugi wa Thiong'o; Lesotho's Thomas Mofolo; Nigeria's Ken Saro-Wiwa; Senegal's Sembène Ousmane and Lèopold Sédar Senghor; Somalia's Nuruddin Farah; South Africa's Bessie Head, Ezekiel Mphahlele, and Lewis Nkosi; Uganda's Okot p'Bitek and Moses Isegawa; and Zimbabwe's Dennis Brutus.

Unfortunately for journalists, freedom of the press is a scarce commodity in much of Africa, with many of those who dare to report the truth about government corruption or abuse of human rights being forced into exile or constantly threatened and harassed if they stay. For that reason, many Africans learn more about their neighbors—both locally and continentally—through Western media. But among Africa's most courageous and well-respected journalists are Liberia's Kenneth Y. Best and Isaac Bantu, Ghana's Ben Ephson, and South Africa's Percy Qoboza.

Film

Film is a relatively new art form to Africa, but it has been embraced eagerly as yet another medium through which to tell the many stories of the continent. Perhaps more than any other section of the continent, West

Africa, particularly the former French-speaking colonies, has been drawn to the production of motion pictures. Among West Africa's leading filmmakers are Senegal's Ousmane Sembène and Moussa Touré, Burkina Faso's Idrissa Ouédraogo, Drissa Touré, Gaston Kaboré, and Dani Kouyaté, and Mali's Cheik Oumar Sissoko and Abdoulaye Ascofare. From Cameroon have come the motion pictures of Jean-Marie Teno and Bassek Ba Kkobhio, while Côte d'Ivoire has produced the films of Roger Gneon M'Bala.

The former English-speaking colonies of Africa have managed to turn out a large number of well-received films as well. Among the more successful filmmakers in this group are Moses Adejumo, Afolabi Adesanya, Awala Bayo, and Fred Chagu of Nigeria, John Akomfrah of Ghana, Simon Bright of Zimbabwe, and Barry Feinberg, Athol Fugard, and Peter Goldsmid of South Africa.

There was a sharp jump in the number of Africans engaged in filmmaking between 1980 and 1990. Another significant change has been the increasing involvement of African women in motion pictures. The major political changes in South Africa over the last decade have helped to open that market to a much wider range of "alternative" films and videos than was possible before.

In 1993, the films coming out of Africa were few in number but notable in quality. Among them, *Samba Traore*, directed by Idrissa Ouédraogo, employed an age-old plot line quite effectively: the flight of a young criminal to avoid punishment for his crime. Burundian director Leonce Ngabo cooperated with French and Swiss filmmakers in the production of *Gito the Ungrateful*, the tale of a youth searching for his identity. Director Roger Gneon M'Bala of the Côte d'Ivoire explored the subject of religion in his *In the Name of Christ*. One of the few notable African films of 1994 was *Le Ballon d'or*, directed by Cheik Boukouré of Guinea, which related the story of a young boy's dream of becoming a world-class soccer player.

Some of the most impressive African films of 1995 came from the tiny West African country of Burkina Faso. These included Drissa Touré's *Haramuya*, Dani Kouyaté's *Keita, Voice of the Griot*, and Idrissa Ouédraogo's *Africa, My Africa*. From Cameroon came *The Great White of Lambarene*, an African evaluation of missionary/doctor/philosopher/musician Albert Schweitzer. Also from Cameroon came one of the best African films of 1996: *Clando*, the story of a young foe of a repressive African regime who emigrates illegally to Germany. Burkina Faso's film community produced some of the most notable motion pictures of 1997.

Foremost among these were Idrissa Ouédraogo's *Kini and Adams*, which told the story of the relationship between two poor farmers, and Gaston Kaboré's *Buud Yam*, the tale of a young man's quest to find medicine for his ailing foster sister. Stirring up controversy in 1997 was Guinea's *Dakan*, director Mohamed Camara's exploration of homosexuality, the first African motion picture to tackle the subject.

Significant African films of the late 1990s and early years of the new millennium included South African music video director Akin Omotoso's *God Is African*, recounting the death of Nigerian writer Ken Saro-Wiwa; and Senegalese director Joseph Gaï Ramaka's *Karmen Gei*. Also impressive were Guinea's *Temporary Registration;* Senegal's *L'Afrance* and *And So Angels Die;* Zimbabwe's *One Sunday Morning;* and Gabon's *Dollar*.

Music

Despite the Western stereotype that associates the beating of tribal drums with the whole of traditional music, African music is incredibly diverse and reflective of the vast array of peoples, cultures, and traditions. Confined to localities, some of the world's greatest and most unheralded musicians—many self-taught—play to crowds in Africa. In the past few decades, "cross-over" artists have breached the boundaries of their homeland to win acclaim and fans in the United States and Europe. The irony is that these so-called "African superstars" may not even be stars in their own countries, let alone on the rest of the continent.

Nonetheless, such contemporary American musical forms as blues and jazz have been heavily influenced by African styles and polyrhythms carried over by slaves. In fact, the African lute evolved into the modern-day guitar. Guitars form the basis of *benga* music (popular in Kenya); *juju* (a Nigerian music also replete with talking drums and vocal call and response); palm wine music (an acoustic form popular in regions of West Africa, where palm wine is a favorite elixir); highlife (a jazzy, complex West African dance music punctuated by horns); and *soukous* (derived by the French word for "shake," a peppy dance form originating mainly in Congo-Brazzaville and Congo-Kinshasa). Percussion-based music includes: *apala* (a street-form emergent from Islamic music); *mbalax* (a modern dance style popularized in Senegal); and *jit* (a Zimbabwean hybrid of traditional *chimurenga* guitar, disco-style drum beats, highlife, and *soukous*). *Kora* features a 21-string harp, *kwela* incorporates a penny whistle, and *mbira* got its moniker from the Zimbabwean name for a finger piano. Cameroonians may jive to *makossa* while those in Sierre Leone pop their fingers to *milo* jazz and Cape Verdeans release their troubles with the deep blues of *morna*. South Africans may party to *mbaqanga* on one night and get spiritual with the choral vocals of *mbube* the next. Permutations of once solely African music include *salsa* (Spanish folk music combined with African drums and Cuban rhythms), *soca* (African music with a heady dose of English and Latin folk music), and *zouk* (a mix of French, African, and Guadeloupian music).

Some of Africa's biggest artists, "cross-over" or otherwise, include Angola's Kuenda Bonga (a political-minded singer-songwriter) and Ruy Mingas (a famous Portugeuse-African vocalist and current minister of culture of that country); Burkino Faso's Farafina (a group led by *balafon* virtuoso Mahama Konaté); Cape Verde's Cesaria Evora ("The Barefoot Diva"); Congo-Kinshasa's Mbilia Bel (one of Africa's most successful female singers), 4 Etoiles (featuring *soukous* guitarist Syran Mbenza), Ricardo Lemvo & Makina Loca (an Afro-Latino vocalist), Les Bantous (a *rhumba* band), Tabu Ley (a *soukous* master), Sam Mangwana (known as "Le Pigeon," since his travels and music have produced mixtures of Cuban, Portuguese-African, and Caribbean rhythms), Tshala Muana ("Queen of Mutuashi," a dance form), Papa Wemba (one of the world's greatest singers), and Zap Mama (an all-female group led by poet Marie Daulne); Gabon's Pierre Akendengue (a blind singer, guitarist, poet, and playwright); Guinea's Bembeya Jazz National (featuring Sekou "Diamond Fingers" Diabate); Mali's Toumani Diabate (considered the world's greatest *kora* player), Oumou Sangare (the country's favorite female "praise singer"), and Ali Farka Toure ("The Bluesman of Mali"); Nigeria's King Sunny Ade ("The King of Juju") and Fela Anikulapo Kuti (an outspoken social critic, pianist, saxophonist, and singer); Senegal's Baaba Maal (known as "The Nightingale" because of his clear high-pitched voice), Youssou N'Dour (produces an exciting blend of mbalax, reggae, jazz, and calypso music), and Orchestre Baobab de Dakar; Sierre Leone's Abdul Tee-Jay (a London-based studio guitarist adept at several forms including highlife, *soukous*, *makossa*, and *soca*); South Africa's Ladysmith Black Mambazo (an a capella group led by tenor vocalist Joseph Shabalala), Mahlathini (legendary, deep-voiced "King of the Groaners"), the Mahotella Queens (*mbaqanga* mavens), Miriam Makeba ("The Empress of African Song"), Hugh Masekela (trumpet and flugelhorn playing jazz legend), West Nkosi (multitalented musician, arranger, producer, and bandleader), and The Soul Brothers (one of the nation's biggest-selling groups); Tanzania's Zuhura Swaleh (a female *taarab* singer); and Zimbabwe's Thomas Mapfumo (credited with having created *chimurenga*, or liberation music) and Stella Chiweshe ("The Queen of Mbira").

Family

Family is the social backbone of Africa. Within most African cultures, family impacts all realms of everyday living, both politically and economically. Familial obligations are not restricted to just immediate family; tribal conflict notwithstanding, in Africa each individual is regarded as a dear cousin. In fact, the Western method of breaking familial relationships down to degrees—e.g., first cousin, great-great grandfather twice removed—is virtually nonexistent. Either two people are related or not; and more often then not, without even looking, those individuals will find ties. This unique kinship is inclusive of ancestors. The dead are forever remembered among the living, and the elderly are held with a special regard. Rather than being hidden away or considered burdens, older Africans are viewed as storehouses of wisdom and are a welcome part of society. Women, too, are highly esteemed in much of African tradition, particularly in the agri-based cultures. Often women, not men, are heads of households.

Among Africans, marriage represents a union of two families, not just a bride and groom. Parents and extended family members offer emotional support to a couple throughout their marriage. The bonding of families begins when a man obtains formal permission to marry a prospective bride. In some cultures, bride prices or dowries are still negotiated as are pre-arranged marriages. In true oral tradition, Africans often deliver the news of their upcoming nuptials by word of mouth. Any offspring are extremely valued, and additions to the family are cause for celebration.

Health

Diseases that have been successfully monitored and controlled in Western nations—diphtheria, measles, pertussis, poliomyelitis, tetanus, and tuberculosis—continue to be a problem in many parts of Africa. Diarrhea and tuberculosis account for one-half of all deaths in children. In addition, the fatal yet curable, indigenous sleeping sickness, or African Trypanosomiasis (spread by tsetse flies that carry a parasite, the trypanosome, from human to human), has become a surging epidemic in the Sudan and may spread to the Congo and the Central African Republic. By no coincidence, these three countries have recently

Ladysmith Black Mambazo (performing in 1994) is one of Africa's biggest musical groups.

undergone civil warfare and tremendous political upheaval.

The emergence of Acquired Immune Deficiency Syndrome (AIDS) has had a devastating effect on the continent as well. As of the end of 1999, nearly 15 million sub-Saharan Africans had died from AIDS or AIDS-related illnesses since the disease first emerged. Even more ominous was the news that sub-Saharan

Africa was home in 1999 to 7.3 out of 10 adults newly infected with Human Immunodeficiency Virus (HIV). The region, as of December 31, 1999, was also home to about 70 percent of the 36 million people living with HIV/AIDS worldwide. The demographic impact of AIDS is most immediate and serious in two geographic areas: Central-Austral Africa and West Africa, specifically in the country of Côte d'Ivoire. In both regions, falling life expectancy and increasing infant and child mortality have already been observed. Given the high proportion of the population already infected —up to 30 percent of young adults in some urban areas—and the high mortality resulting from the disease, a further impact over the next two decades is inevitable in these areas. The impact may eventually become as serious in several other geographical areas, but this will depend foremost on whether the spread of HIV can be contained.

In the mid-1990s, Ebola outbreaks wreaked havoc in the Democratic Republic of the Congo, Liberia, Gabon, and the Ivory Coast. After a mid-1996 outbreak in Gabon, there was a temporary lull on the Ebola front until northern Uganda was struck by an outbreak in the fall of 2000. Spread through contact with bodily fluids, the virus is hardy and can survive on moist surfaces such as bodies or food for long periods. The deadly virus disintegrates the membranous linings of blood vessels and organs, usually leading to heart and other organ failure. Each eruption of the modern-day plague has warranted strict quarantines. Ebola is one of the most contagious and lethal viruses known to mankind, and the international scientific community has come together in trying to locate the sources of contamination in hopes of bringing an end to a virus whose newer strains have increased the fatality rate of the afflicted from 80 percent to 97 percent since earlier outbreaks dating back to the 1970s in the Sudan and former Zaire.

Senegalese microbiologist Soulyemane Mboup and other African researchers have made significant contributions to the fight against AIDS. While Mboup is credited as one of the discoverers of the HIV–2 virus, other African scientists seem to have developed a method of using interferon, an immune system-enhancing protein, to alleviate the symptoms of both Ebola and AIDS. In some cases, researchers have claimed to completely eradicate the presence of these diseases in affected patients.

Food shortages caused by drought and civil conflicts continue to cause mass starvation and malnutrition in Ethiopia, Somalia, Mozambique, as well as in parts of western Africa. In the late 1980s and into the 1990s, the international community has joined forces to try to alleviate the situation by sending food and aid to the needy and even resorting to peacekeeping military personnel in situations caused by ongoing civil disturbances.

The practice of female circumcision or genital mutilation—one of many varying rites of passage performed in parts of Africa—has been denounced by Western society as the harbinger of medical problems for women later in life including the inability to walk, chronic infections, and difficult childbirth. While an African and Western effort to stamp out the sometimes fatal ritual is growing, many others decry what they deem to be cultural interference. Tradition holds that the surgery preserves the chastity of those upon whom it is performed.

Medicine and medical advice are often dispensed by traditional healers in Africa, often referred to as "witch doctors" by skeptical Westerners. Diviners and healers treat mental disorders as well as physical ones. They also provide advice for resolving social disputes.

Cuisine

Food plays a large role in African traditions, customs, and beliefs. Africans make liberal use of fresh, locally grown foods in their cooking. Papayas, coconuts, avocados, mangos, guavas, and other "exotic" fruits are abundant and, along with other fruits and vegetables, are eaten much more liberally than in the United States, and many, such as yams and cassava root, are used as staples. For example, maize, cassava, and plantains are often dried and ground into flour. Legumes are also prevalent in African meals. Particularly in the coastal nations, seafood, including shark, is frequently eaten fresh, dried, or smoked. Bat, beef, chicken, goat, monkey, pigeons, and pork are just some of the meats that can be found in different regions. Most Africans enjoy very spicy, hot food. An African pepper that goes by many names *pilli-pilli, piri-piri, and beri-beri* is frequently used. Much hotter than cayenne pepper, *pilli-pilli* does more than increase the palatability of a meal. Similar to garlic, pepper is thought to enhance the body's immune system. Coconut flesh is incorporated into many dishes as is coconut milk, which is also imbibed as a refreshing beverage. African beer, wine, and liquor, both homemade and commercial, are available.

In many African cultures, food is served in one large common bowl; diners then eat with their hands, thus reinforcing the idea of community.

◆ BLACK PEOPLE IN THE WESTERN HEMISPHERE

The Caribbean and Latin American regions of the New World were the first areas of the Western Hemisphere to be settled by African immigrants, some of whom may have arrived in the Americas on the maiden voyage of Christopher Columbus in 1492. Free blacks, many of whom were natives of Spain and Portugal, traveled with Columbus and other early Spanish and Portuguese explorers on voyages to the Americas. This first trickle of blacks of African ancestry into the

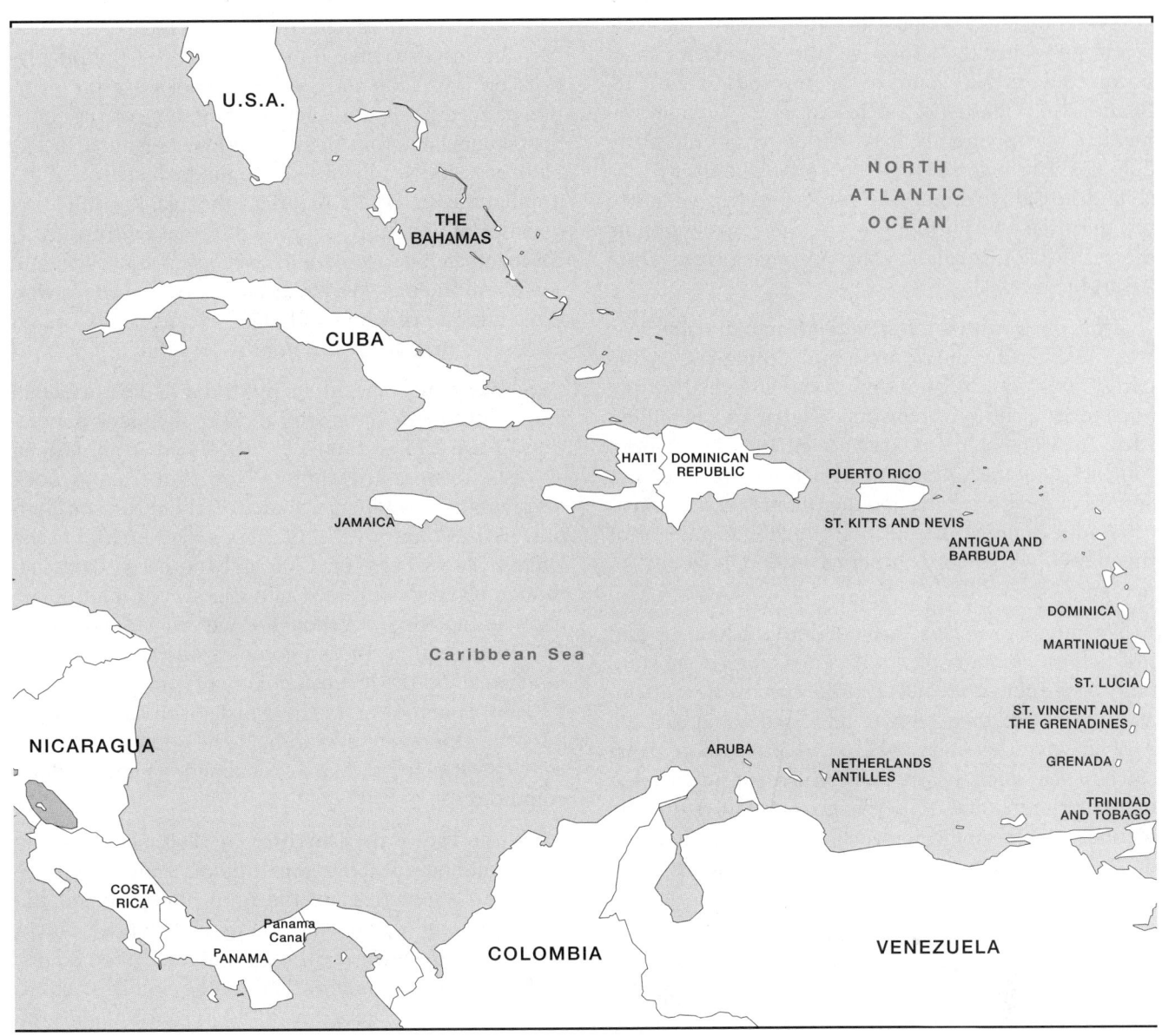

The Caribbean.

New World was soon followed by a flood of enslaved Africans who were brought to work on European settlements.

The very earliest blacks to settle in the Americas included Pedro Alonso Niño, a navigator on the first voyage of Columbus to the New World, and a group of black settlers who joined with Spanish explorer Nicolás de Ovando to establish the first Western settlement on Hispaniola. Some of the blacks accompanying Spanish explorers on their missions to the Americas were indeed slaves, as was the case with Nuflo de Olano, who was present when Vasco Nuñez de Balboa first sighted the Pacific Ocean in 1513. Blacks also were present in the expeditions of both Hernán Cortés and Francisco Pizarro.

Among the so-called Iberian blacks was Estevanico, a survivor of Pánfilo de Narváez's ill-fated 1527 expedition to Florida. On an eight-year overland trip, he made his way with three other survivors to Mexico City, learning a number of Native American languages along the way. He was later killed in a confrontation with members of the Zuñi tribe in what is now New Mexico. Juan Valiente, a black slave of the Spaniards, fought so valiantly with his masters against the Araucanian people of Chile in the 1540s that he was rewarded with his freedom and an estate near Santiago.

As the number of Spanish settlements in the New World grew quickly, so too did the demand for manpower to work the estates of the new settlers. In 1518, Spain's King Charles I gave his approval to the movement of slaves directly from Africa to the American colonies. The Spanish crown controlled the slave trade, selling the right to import slaves to merchants willing to pay the price. The Portuguese, who were busily settling the vastness of Brazil, had begun bringing slaves from Africa by the 1530s.

From the time that the slave trade into the Americas was launched by the Spanish and Portuguese in the early 1500s until its abolition in the latter half of the nineteenth century, an estimated ten to 30 million Africans were sold into slavery in the New World. Almost half of that number, or 47 percent, were put into service in the Caribbean and the Guianas of northeastern South America. Brazil took roughly 38 percent of the slaves, while North America took only about 4.5 percent of the total.

The number of slaves brought into the Spanish and Portuguese colonies of the Americas varied substantially according to the needs of the colony. New Spain, as Mexico was then known, imported about 120,000 African slaves between 1519 and 1650, or about 1,000 slaves a year, most of whom were pressed into service in the colony's mines. Between 1650 and 1810, the number of slaves imported each year was cut almost in half, as more Native Americans became available to work the mines.

Most of the early black population in Latin America and the Caribbean was involved in domestic service or farm labor. Perhaps one-fifth of the black population found work as street vendors, artisans, sailors, miners, and wet nurses. Throughout the Spanish and Portuguese colonies, a number of masters voluntarily set their slaves free, while others encouraged their slaves to purchase their freedom on a sort of installment plan called *coartación*. Life for the slaves of the New World, however, was generally harsh and unpleasant, and the frustration over the elusiveness of freedom sometimes boiled over into unrest and even outright revolt. Such was the case in the colony now known as Haiti, where nearly 500,000 slaves led by François Toussaint L'Ouverture revolted in 1791, throwing off British and Spanish control. In 1801, Toussaint L'Ouverture conquered Santo Domingo, which had been ceded by Spain to France in 1795, and thus he governed the entire island. Following a hard-fought resistance to French colonial ambitions in the Western Hemisphere, Toussaint L'Ouverture struck a peace treaty with Napoleon in 1802.

Today on many islands of the Caribbean, persons of African descent make up the majority of the population; on Barbados and Jamaica, blacks are the overwhelming majority. In other areas, notably on the continental mainland from Mexico south to Argentina, blacks have been largely absorbed into the mainstream of the population. In South America, the black population consists of a mixture of many different cultures: Africans and Indians, known as *zambos;* Caucasians and American Indians, known as *mestizos;* and those who are a mixture of white and black are, as in the United States, referred to as *mulattos.*

Similar to the blacks who live today in the Caribbean and Latin American regions, most of the black population of the United States is descended from African slaves who were brought into North America to work on plantations and farms, particularly in the southern part of the country. Most of these slaves arrived in the United States between 1700 and the early 1800s, although slavery continued into the second half of the nineteenth century. Although slaves were found in all 13 of the original British colonies as well as French Louisiana and the Spanish colony of Florida, the need for slave manpower in the North decreased sharply after the American Revolution. In the South, which was heavily agricultural, slaves remained a highly valued commodity.

On the eve of the Civil War in 1860, blacks in the South numbered about four million, making up approximately one-third of the total population of the region. At the same time, there were about half a million free blacks living throughout the United States, slightly more than half of them in the South. The free black population was a powerful force working for the abolition of slavery in this country. In 1997, African Americans in the United States numbered 32.3 million, accounting for 12.0 percent of the total population.

In recent years, the Caribbean basin has been a major source of black immigration into the United States, with immigrants primarily from Jamaica and Haiti entering the country in search of work. In 1980, the Mariel boatlift brought a significant amount of Cuban refugees to the United States. More recently, thousands of Haitians have attempted, with little success, to emigrate to the United States, since the September of 1991 coup that ousted President Jean-Bertrand Aristide, who was later reinstated with the aid of the U.S. government. Efforts by the United States to foster economic recovery in Haiti have been largely unsuccessful, and attempts to nurture the fledgling democracy, thus far, have yielded limited results.

◆ COUNTRY PROFILES

Notes on Profiles Data

"Area" values are given in square kilometers as that is the unit of measurement most common to the countries covered. To figure the area in square miles, multiply the number by 0.3861.

Most of the statistical data in the country profiles comes from the U.S. Central Intelligence Agency's publication, *World Factbook 2001*.

"Income" values for each nation are the gross domestic product per capita figures as measured using the *purchasing power parity* (PPP) method, which attempts to determine the relative purchasing power of different currencies over equivalent goods and services. For example, if it costs someone in the United States US$300 to buy a month's worth of groceries, but it costs someone in Ghana only US$100 to buy the same amount of groceries, then the person in Ghana can purchase three times as much for the same amount of money. This means that, though the average citizen of Ghana may earn less money than the average citizen of the United States, that money buys more because goods and services cost less in Ghana. Note: GDP figured at purchasing power parity may be three or more times as large as GDP figured at exchange rate parity.

In preparing this latest edition of *The African American Almanac*, editors considered the possibility of removing from its Country Profiles those countries with small or negligible populations of African descent. In the end, it was decided that such deletions would deprive readers of a comprehensive overview of those regions that generally have strong African ties. As a result, this edition continues to provide complete coverage of all countries within Africa and the Americas regardless of the percentage of population of African descent.

Africa

Algeria

Official name: Democratic and Popular Republic of Algeria

Independence: 5 July 1962 (from France)

Area: 2,381,740 sq km

Form of government: republic

Capital: Algiers

International relations: ABEDA, AfDB, AFESD, AL, AMF, AMU, CCC, ECA, FAO, G-15, G-19, G-24, G-77, IAEA, IBRD, ICAO, ICC, ICFTU, ICRM, IDA, IDB, IFAD, IFC, IFRCS, IHO, ILO, IMF, IMO, Inmarsat, Intelsat, Interpol, IOC, IOM, ISO, ITU, MONUC, NAM, OAPEC, OAS (observer), OAU, OIC, OPCW, OPEC, OSCE (partner), UN, UNCTAD, UNESCO, UNHCR, UNIDO, UNMEE, UPU, WHO, WIPO, WMO, WToO, WTrO (observer)

Currency: Algerian dinar (DZD)

Income: US$5,500 (2000 est. of purchasing power parity)

Population: 31,736,053 (July 2001 est.)

Ethnic groups: Arab-Berber 99%, European less than 1%

Religious groups: Sunni Muslim (state religion) 99%, Christian and Jewish 1%

Languages: Arabic (official), French, Berber dialects

Literacy: 61.6% (age 15 and over can read and write; 1995 est.)

Exports: petroleum, natural gas, and petroleum products 97%

Primary export partners: Italy 22%, United States 15%, France 12%, Spain 11%, Brazil 8%, Netherlands 5% (1999)

Imports: capital goods, food and beverages, consumer goods

Primary import partners: France 30%, Italy 9%, Germany 7%, Spain 6%, United States 5%, Turkey 5% (1999)

Since the period of 5 BC, the area that makes up what is now Algeria has been populated by indigenous tribes who have been progressively pushed back from the coast by invaders. As a result, the country's boundaries have shifted during various stages of the conquests. Nearly all Algerians are Muslim of Arab, Berber, or mixed stock.

French colonization began in 1830 and continued until 1954, when the indigenous population staged a revolt. The revolution was launched by a small group of nationalists who called themselves the National Liberation Front (FLN). Negotiations led to a cease-fire signed by France and the FLN on March 18, 1962; France then declared Algeria independent on July 3.

Mohammed Ben Bella became Algeria's first post-independence president, only to be ousted three years later by Col. Boume'dienne. After he died, Chadi Benjadid became the head of state. In 1991, Algeria held its first free election after 30 years of a one-party system, and the National Liberation Front was defeated by the fundamentalist Islamic Salvation Front (FIS) in the first round of voting for the National Assembly. When it appeared clear that the fundamentalist group would win a majority in the second round of voting scheduled for January 1992, the government and army intervened to cancel the elections. Mohammed Boudiaf, a former dissident in the FLN, was installed as president of the ruling State Supreme Council. In May 1992, Boudiaf was assassinated, allegedly by an FIS gunman while delivering a speech in Annaba, continuing the ongoing conflict between the government and the fundamentalist Muslims of the FIS. Algeria has since been in a declared state of emergency.

In 1994, Liamine Zeroual became president and greatly increased the power of that office through constitutional changes approved by voters. The conflict with religious extremists and the FIS continued as both groups boycotted the next round of elections in 1997. This move allowed the military government to consolidate its hold on power as the level of violence increased in the country, as evidenced by the bloody Ramadan massacres and random killings of that same year. After a flawed election in April 1999, Abdelaziz Bouteflika became president. The new president struck a peace accord with rebels and won approval for an amnesty plan in a September 1999 referendum. Violence flared again in the spring of 2001, when the country was swept by violent protests, mostly by members of the country's Berber minority.

Angola

Official name: Republic of Angola

Independence: 11 November 1975 (from Portugal)

Area: 1,246,700 sq km

Form of government: transitional government, nominally a multiparty democracy with a strong presidential system

Capital: Luanda

International relations: ACP, AfDB, CCC, CEEAC, ECA, FAO, G-77, IAEA, IBRD, ICAO, ICFTU, ICRM, IDA, IFAD, IFC, IFRCS, ILO, IMF, IMO, Intelsat, Interpol, IOC, IOM, ITU, NAM, OAS (observer), OAU, SADC, UN, UNCTAD, UNESCO, UNIDO, UPU, WFTU, WHO, WIPO, WMO, WToO, WTrO

Currency: kwanza (AOA)

Income: us$1,000 (2000 est. of purchasing power parity)

Population: 10,366,031 (July 2001 est.)

Ethnic groups: Ovimbundu 37%, Kimbundu 25%, Bakongo 13%, mestico (mixed European and Native African) 2%, European 1%, other 22%

Religious groups: indigenous beliefs 47%, Roman Catholic 38%, Protestant 15% (1998 est.)

Languages: Portuguese (official), Bantu and other African languages

Literacy: 42% (age 15 and over can read and write; 1998 est.)

Exports: crude oil 90%, diamonds, refined petroleum products, gas, coffee, sisal, fish and fish products, timber, cotton

Primary export partners: United States 54%, South Korea 14%, Benelux 11%, China 7%, Taiwan 6% (1999)

Imports: machinery and electrical equipment, vehicles and spare parts; medicines, food, textiles, military goods

Primary import partners: South Korea 16%, Portugal 15%, United States 13%, South Africa 10%, France 8% (1999)

Angola's boundaries were formally established by the Berlin West Africa Congress of 1884–1885. Following World War II, Portuguese interest in colonizing Angola increased, leading to the establishment of a strict and harsh colonial rule.

Discontent over Portuguese unwillingness to concede eventual independence led to the formation of the Popular Movement for the Liberation of Angola (MPLA), the National Front for the Liberation of Angola (FNLA), and the National Union for the Total Independence of Angola (UNITA). In January 1975, the Portuguese and the three liberation movements worked out a complicated agreement—the Alvor Accord—that provided for a transitional government composed of all three groups and for elections in preparation for independence in November of 1975.

The departure of the Portuguese in late 1975 left Angola in the midst of a fierce struggle for power between the three divided liberation movements. Fueling the civil war was the involvement of such foreign powers as the United States, South Africa, the Soviet Union, and Cuba. South African troops, encouraged by the United States, which backed the FNLA-UNITA alliance, actually invaded Angola but were repelled. The Marxist MPLA was finally able to establish control of the country under Augustinho Neto who ruled as the newly independent country's first president until his death in 1979. Neto was succeeded by José Eduardo Dos Santos, but the MPLA government, weakened by continuing South African incursions into Angolan territory and its own inflexible economic policies, had lost territory in the south of the country to UNITA by the early 1980s.

By the late 1980s, the embattled MPLA government was forced to abandon some of its most stridently Marxist economic policies, which opened the door to more cordial relations with Western countries. Hope

Some of these young Angolan boys are making the sign for their people's recent victory over the Portuguese in 1975.

for a lasting peace increased in 1991, when peace accords were signed between the MPLA and UNITA. However, war again erupted the following year, when UNITA refused to acknowledge its defeat in multiparty elections. The struggle between MPLA and UNITA for control of Angola continued into the late 1990s.

In 1997, a plan to install a government of national unity had to be abandoned when Jonas Savimbi, leader of UNITA, refused to come to Luanda because he feared for his life. Savimbi also balked at proposals that he surrender UNITA's control over most of the country's diamond business, arguing that the MPLA controlled all of Angola's lucrative oil trade. In 1998, escalating political and military tension between the Angolan government and UNITA again threatened to flare into a full-scale civil war. In August 1998, the Angolan government sent thousands of troops into neighboring Congo-Kinshasa (now known as the Democratic Republic of the Congo) in support of the regime of Laurent Kabila. As the civil war within Angola continued to rage, the United Nations in March 1999 withdrew its mission from the country. The devastating toll of Angola's civil

war, as of 2001, was estimated by the UN at 1 million lives and another 2.5 million left homeless. An August 2001 UNITA ambush of a train left more than 250 dead.

Angolans are almost entirely Bantu of various ethnic subgroupings. The Ovimbundu subgroup in central and southeastern Angola is the largest, consisting of about 37 percent of the population. The Kongo, concentrated in the northwest but also living in areas adjacent to the Congo as well as Cabinda, constitute about 13 percent. The Mbundu, about 22 percent of the population, are concentrated in the area around Luanda and out toward the east.

Benin

Official name: Republic of Benin

Independence: 1 August 1960 (from France)

Area: 112,620 sq km

Form of government: republic under multiparty democratic rule; dropped Marxism-Leninism December 1989; democratic reforms adopted February 1990; transition to multiparty system completed 4 April 1991

Vendors selling their wares at a market in Benin.

Capital: Porto-Novo is the official capital; Cotonou is the seat of government

International relations: ACCT, ACP, AfDB, CCC, ECA, ECOWAS, Entente, FAO, FZ, G-77, IAEA, IBRD, ICAO, ICFTU, ICRM, IDA, IDB, IFAD, IFC, IFRCS, ILO, IMF, IMO, Intelsat, Interpol, IOC, IOM, ISO (subscriber), ITU, MIPONUH, MONUC, NAM, OAU, OIC, OPCW, UN, UNCTAD, UNESCO, UNIDO, UNMEE, UNTAET, UPU, WADB, WADB (regional), WAEMU, WCL, WFTU, WHO, WIPO, WMO, WToO, WTrO

Currency: Communaute Financiere Africaine franc (CFAF)

Income: US$1,030 (2000 est. of purchasing power parity)

Population: 6,590,782

Ethnic groups: African 99% (42 ethnic groups, most important being Fon, Adja, Yoruba, Bariba), Europeans 5,500

Religious groups: indigenous beliefs 50%, Christian 30%, Muslim 20%

Languages: French (official), Fon and Yoruba (most common vernaculars in south), tribal languages (at least six major ones in north)

Literacy: 37.5% (age 15 and over can read and write; 2000)

Exports: cotton, crude oil, palm products, cocoa

Primary export partners: Brazil 14%, Libya 5%, Indonesia 4%, Italy 4% (1999)

Imports: foodstuffs, tobacco, petroleum products, capital goods

Primary import partners: France 38%, China 16%, United Kingdom 9%, Côte d'Ivoire 5% (1999)

During the precolonial era, Benin was a collection of small principalities, the most powerful of which was the Fon Kingdom of Dahomey. By the seventeenth and eighteenth centuries, the Portuguese and other Europeans established trading posts along the coast. From these posts thousands of slaves were shipped to the New World, primarily to Brazil and the Caribbean. This part of West Africa became known as the Slave Coast.

In 1892, the King of Dahomey was subjugated, and the country organized as the French protectorate of Dahomey. It remained a French colony until independence in 1960, when the name was changed to the Republic of Dahomey, and Hubert Maga became president. Three years later, he was overthrown by military commanders. Mathieu Kérékou took over in 1975. In the same year, the name of the country was changed to the People's Republic of Benin. When the government reverted to civilian control in 1980, Kérékou was reelected president of the republic. Facing formidable internal dissent, Kérékou in 1989 abandoned his Marxist-Leninist ideology. A new constitution, adopted in 1990, laid the groundwork for the establishment of a multiparty republic. Nicéphore Soglo defeated Kérékou in presidential elections in 1991, Benin's first free ballot in 30 years. Although the country's economy improved under Soglo, his personal popularity declined, and he was defeated by Kérékou in 1996 presidential elections. In his second term, Kérékou has largely abandoned his socialist vision, instead pursuing policies of economic liberalization. Kérékou's policies apparently won favor with the country's electorate, winning him reelection in a March 2001 runoff.

The population of Benin comprises about 20 sociocultural groups. Four groups—the Fon, Aja (who are related), Bariba, and Yoruba—account for more than half of the population.

Botswana

Official name: Republic of Botswana
Independence: 30 September 1966 (from United Kingdom)
Area: 600,370 sq km
Form of government: parliamentary republic
Capital: Gaborone
International relations: ACP, AfDB, C, CCC, ECA, FAO, G-77, IBRD, ICAO, ICFTU, ICRM, IDA, IFAD, IFC, IFRCS, ILO, IMF, Intelsat, Interpol, IOC, ISO, ITU, NAM, OAU, OPCW, SACU, SADC, UN, UNCTAD, UNESCO, UNIDO, UPU, WFTU, WHO, WIPO, WMO, WToO, WTrO
Currency: pula (BWP)
Income: us$6,600 (2000 est. of purchasing power parity)
Population: 1,586,119
Ethnic groups: Tswana (or Setswana) 79%, Kalanga 11%, Basarwa 3%, other, including Kgalagadi and white 7%
Religious groups: indigenous beliefs 50%, Christian 50%
Languages: English (official), Setswana
Literacy: 69.8% (age 15 and over can read and write; 1995 est.)
Exports: diamonds 72%, vehicles, copper, nickel, meat (1998)
Primary export partners: EU 77%, Southern African Customs Union (SACU) 18%, Zimbabwe 3% (1998)
Imports: foodstuffs, machinery and transport equipment, textiles, petroleum products

Primary import partners: Southern African Customs Union (SACU) 76%, Europe 10%, South Korea 5% (1998)

Europeans made first contact with the area in the early nineteenth century. In the last quarter of the century, hostilities broke out between the Botswana and the Afrikaners from South Africa (Transvaal). Following appeals by the Botswana for assistance, the British government in 1885 proclaimed "Bechuanaland" to be under British protection. In 1909, despite South African pressure, inhabitants of Bechuanaland, Basutoland (now Lesotho), and Swaziland demanded and received British agreement that they not be included in the proposed Union of South Africa.

In June 1964, the British government accepted proposals for a form of self-government for Botswana that would lead to independence. Botswana became independent on September 30, 1966, and Seretse Khama was installed as the prime minister after the Bechuanaland Democratic Party (BDP) won majority votes. The country was later named Botswana, and upon Khama's death in 1980, Quett Ketumile Joni Masire assumed the presidency, an office to which he was reelected three times. Constitutional reforms in 1994–1995 allowed more political parties to participate in the government and greatly reduced the power of the central government. However, the retirement of President Masire and the orderly succession of his vice president, Festus Mogae, to the presidency in 1998 appeared to extend the BDP's firm grip on power.

Since winning independence, Botswana has maintained a nonaligned foreign policy. Although it opposed the former racist policies of neighboring South Africa, Botswana maintained close economic ties. Large deposits of diamonds have been discovered in Botswana in recent years, making the country one of the world's major producers of the valuable gemstone. Also contributing to the country's economic growth are cattle raising and the mining of copper and nickel. Casting something of a cloud over the country's long-term prospects is the UN's estimate that about one-third of Botswana's adult population is afflicted with HIV/AIDS.

Some 75 percent of the country's population is made up of the Tswana tribe (Botswana), which is divided into eight subgroups: Bamangwate, Bakwena, Batawana, Bangwaketse, Bakgatla, Bamalete, Barolong, and Batlokwa. The Kalanga, Herero, Bushmen (Basarwa), Yei, and Kgalagadi are minorities.

Burkina Faso (formerly Upper Volta)

Official name: none
Independence: 5 August 1960 (from France)
Area: 274,200 sq km
Form of government: parliamentary

Three Mossi men working the land in Toma, Burkina Faso, 1992.

Capital: Ouagadougou

International relations: ACCT, ACP, AfDB, CCC, ECA, ECOWAS, Entente, FAO, FZ, G-77, IAEA, IBRD, ICAO, ICC, ICFTU, ICRM, IDA, IDB, IFAD, IFC, IFRCS, ILO, IMF, Intelsat, Interpol, IOC, IOM, ISO (subscriber), ITU, MONUC, NAM, OAU, OIC, OPCW, UN, UNCTAD, UNESCO, UNIDO, UPU, WADB, WAEMU, WCL, WFTU, WHO, WIPO, WMO, WToO, WTrO

Currency: Communaute Financiere Africaine franc (CFAF)

Income: us$1,000 (2000 est. of purchasing power parity)

Population: 12,272,289

Ethnic groups: Mossi over 40%, Gurunsi, Senufo, Lobi, Bobo, Mande, Fulani

Religious groups: indigenous beliefs 40%, Muslim 50%, Christian (mainly Roman Catholic) 10%

Languages: French (official), native African languages belonging to Sudanic family spoken by 90% of the population

Literacy: 19.2% (age 15 and over can read and write; 1995 est.)

Exports: cotton, animal products, gold

Primary export partners: Italy 13%, France 10%, Indonesia 8%, Thailand 7% (1999)

Imports: machinery, food products, petroleum

Primary import partners: Côte d'Ivoire 30%, France 28%, Spain 3%, Benelux 3% (1999)

Until the end of the nineteenth century, the history of Burkina Faso was dominated by the Mossi, who are believed to have come from central or eastern Africa in the eleventh century. When the French arrived and claimed the area in 1896, the Mossi resisted but were defeated when their capital at Ouagadougou was captured. After World War II, the Mossi renewed their pressure for separate territorial status, and Upper Volta became an autonomous republic in the French Community on December 11, 1958. It achieved independence on August 5, 1960, under President Maurice Yaméogo. Austerity measures imposed by the Yaméogo government at the end of 1965 led to a confrontation between the nation's trade unions and the government. In the opening days of 1966, power was seized by General Sangoulé Lamizana, the army chief of staff. He named himself president and suspended the constitution. In 1980, Lamizana was ousted in a bloodless coup, which was followed by two more coups over the next three years. In August 1984, one year after the coup that brought Captain Thomas Sankara to power as head of the National Revolutionary Council, the country's name was changed from Upper Volta to Burkina Faso.

Sankara was overthrown and executed in an October 1987 coup led by Blaise Campaoré. In 1990, Campaoré introduced some democratic reforms and the following year was reelected. His party won a legislative majority in May 1992 legislative elections. During the mid-1990s, Burkina Faso actively supported revolutionary movements in Gambia and Liberia, alienating it from its neighbors and most Western powers. However, in 1998, Burkina Faso hosted the African Cup of Nations soccer tournament, Africa's biggest sporting event. The nation received favorable international media coverage for its efforts.

The country experienced extensive political and social unrest in the wake of the December 1998 deaths of journalist Norbert Zongo and three companions. At the time of his death, Zongo had been investigating the 1997 death in detention of the driver of the president's brother. In May 1999, President Campaoré promised a full investigation into Zongo's death. A month later several presidential guards were arrested and charged with Zongo's murder. In August 2000 three of five soldiers on trial for Zongo's murder were convicted.

Each year, hundreds of thousands of Burkina Faso's citizens migrate to Côte d'Ivoire and Ghana in search of work. This has contributed to strained relations with Côte d'Ivoire. Despite a July 2001 meeting between the two countries' heads of state called to resolve conflicts, border tensions between Burkina Faso and Côte d'Ivoire continued throughout 2001.

The majority of the population belong to two major West African cultural groups, the Voltaic and the Mande. The Voltaic are far more numerous and include the Mossi, which make up about one-half of the population. The Mossi are still bound by the traditions of the emperor, the Mogho Naba, who holds court in Ouagadougou. Burkina Faso is one of the poorest nations in the world, with most inhabitants subsisting on agriculture and animal husbandry.

Burundi

Official name: Republic of Burundi
Independence: 1 July 1962 (from UN trusteeship under Belgian administration)
Area: 27,830 sq km
Form of government: republic
Capital: Bujumbura
International relations: ACCT, ACP, AfDB, CCC, CEEAC, CEPGL, ECA, FAO, G-77, IBRD, ICAO, ICRM, IDA, IFAD, IFC, IFRCS, ILO, IMF, Intelsat (nonsignatory user), Interpol, IOC, ITU, NAM, OAU, OPCW, UN, UNCTAD, UNESCO, UNIDO, UPU, WHO, WIPO, WMO, WToO, WTrO
Currency: Burundi franc (BIF)
Income: US$720 (2000 est. of purchasing power parity)
Population: 6,223,897
Ethnic groups: Hutu (Bantu) 85%, Tutsi (Hamitic) 14%, Twa (Pygmy) 1%, Europeans 3,000, South Asians 2,000
Religious groups: Christian 67% (Roman Catholic 62%, Protestant 5%), indigenous beliefs 23%, Muslim 10%
Languages: Kirundi (official), French (official), Swahili (along Lake Tanganyika and in the Bujumbura area)
Literacy: 35.3% (age 15 and over can read and write; 1995 est.)
Exports: coffee, tea, sugar, cotton, hides
Primary export partners: Germany 17%, Belgium 14%, United States 8%, France 6%, Switzerland 4% (1999)
Imports: capital goods, petroleum products, foodstuffs
Primary import partners: Belgium 20%, Zambia 11%, Kenya 8%, South Africa 5%, France 4% (1999)

Prior to the arrival of Europeans, Burundi was a kingdom with a highly stratified, feudal social structure. Rulers were drawn from princely dynastic families or *ganwa*, from whom a king or *mwami* was chosen. A *mwami* continued to rule even after independence was granted.

European explorers and missionaries began making brief visits to the area as early as 1858. However, Burundi did not come under European administration until the 1890s, when it became part of German East Africa. In 1916, Belgian troops occupied the country, and the League of Nations mandated it to Belgium in 1923 as part of the Territory of Ruanda-Urundi, now the nations of Rwanda and Burundi. Burundi became independent on July 1, 1962. Just ten years after independence, an abortive coup d'état provoked brutal massacres, claiming the lives of more than 100,000 people.

Burundi's population is made up of three ethnic groups—Hutu, Tutsi, and Twa. Hutus, who make up 85 percent of the population, are primarily farmers whose Bantu-speaking ancestors migrated into Burundi 800 to 1,000 years ago. The Tutsi, who make up 14 percent of the population, are a pastoral people who migrated from Ethiopia several hundred years later. Years of dispute with neighboring Rwanda have continued into the 1990s. Ethnic conflict between the Hutus and Tutsis has led to many atrocities, most notably an explosion of violence in 1993 that claimed tens of thousands of lives and displaced nearly three-quarters of a million Burundians, both Tutsi and Hutu. A military coup in July 1996 increased ethnic strife within Burundi. In December 1999, former South African President Nelson Mandela mediated peace talks that ultimately led to a provisional peace treaty, signed by most of the warring parties in August 2000 and witnessed by Mandela and U.S. President Bill Clinton. Coup attempts in April and July 2001 were suppressed.

Cameroon

Official name: Republic of Cameroon

Independence: 1 January 1960 (from French-administered UN trusteeship)

Area: 475,440 sq km

Form of government: unitary republic; multiparty presidential regime (opposition parties legalized in 1990)

Capital: Yaounde

International relations: ACCT, ACP, AfDB, BDEAC, C, CCC, CEEAC, CEMAC, ECA, FAO, FZ, G-19, G-77, IAEA, IBRD, ICAO, ICC, ICFTU, ICRM, IDA, IDB, IFAD, IFC, IFRCS, ILO, IMF, IMO, Inmarsat, Intelsat, Interpol, IOC, ISO (correspondent), ITU, NAM, OAU, OIC, OPCW, UN, UNCTAD, UNESCO, UNIDO, UNITAR, UPU, WCL, WFTU, WHO, WIPO, WMO, WToO, WTrO

Currency: Communaute Financiere Africaine franc (CFAF)

Income: us$1,700 (2000 est. of purchasing power parity)

Population: 15,803,220

Ethnic groups: Cameroon Highlanders 31%, Equatorial Bantu 19%, Kirdi 11%, Fulani 10%, Northwestern Bantu 8%, Eastern Nigritic 7%, other African 13%, non-African less than 1%

Religious groups: indigenous beliefs 40%, Christian 40%, Muslim 20%

Languages: 24 major African language groups, English (official), French (official)

Literacy: 63.4% (age 15 and over can read and write; 1995 est.)

Exports: crude oil and petroleum products, lumber, cocoa beans, aluminum, coffee, cotton

Primary export partners: Italy 24%, France 18%, Netherlands 10% (2000 est.)

Imports: machines and electrical equipment, transport equipment, fuel, food

Primary import partners: France 29%, Germany 7%, United States 6%, Japan 6% (2000 est.)

The earliest inhabitants of Cameroon were probably Pygmies, who still inhabit the southern forests. However, Bantu-speaking people were among the first to

Cameroonian ceremonial mask adorned by the people of the Kilum Mountain Rainforest.

invade Cameroon from equatorial Africa, settling in the south and later in the west. The Muslim Fulani from the Niger basin arrived in the eleventh and nineteenth centuries and settled in the north. Europeans first made contact with the area in the 1500s. For the next three centuries, Spanish, Dutch, and British traders visited the area.

In July of 1884, Germany, the United Kingdom, and France each attempted to annex the area. A 1919 declaration divided Cameroon between the United Kingdom and France, with the larger, eastern area under France. In December of 1958, the French trusteeship was ended, and French Cameroon became the Republic of Cameroon on January 1, 1960.

The Republic of Cameroon consisted of a federal system integrating the French-controlled south and the British-controlled north under the leadership of its first president, Ahmadou Ahidjo. The country depends heavily on foreign capital and has been faced with internal problems, both ethnic and social, under the leadership of Ahidjo's successor, Paul Biya. Despite sometimes violent confrontations between the nation's political parties, Biya was reelected in 1997 presidential elections, which were boycotted by the three main opposition parties. Despite recent health problems, relative economic prosperity and strong-arm tactics against opponents have enabled Biya to withstand both international and domestic opposition.

President Biya in mid-2001 moved to defuse reports of growing discontent within the country's military by ordering a total reorganization of the Cameroonian armed forces. He also disbanded the Operational Command (OC), a paramilitary crime-fighting unit Biya had created in February 2000, in response to public anger at reports the OC had carried out hundreds of summary executions of suspected criminals.

Cameroon has about 200 tribal groups and clans, speaking at least as many languages and dialects.

Cape Verde

Official name: Republic of Cape Verde

Independence: 5 July 1975 (from Portugal)

Area: 4,033 sq km

Form of government: republic

Capital: Praia

International relations: ACCT, ACP, AfDB, CCC, ECA, ECOWAS, FAO, G-77, IBRD, ICAO, ICFTU, ICRM, IDA, IFAD, IFC, IFRCS, ILO, IMF, IMO, Intelsat, Interpol, IOC, IOM (observer), ITU, NAM, OAU, OPCW, UN, UNCTAD, UNESCO, UNIDO, UNTAET, UPU, WHO, WIPO, WMO, WTrO (observer)

Currency: Cape Verdean escudo (CVE)

Income: US$1,700 (2000 est. of purchasing power parity)

Population: 405,163 (July 2001 est.)

Ethnic groups: Creole (mulatto) 71%, African 28%, European 1%

Religious groups: Roman Catholic (infused with indigenous beliefs); Protestant (mostly Church of the Nazarene)

Languages: Portuguese, Crioulo (a blend of Portuguese and West African words)

Literacy: 71.6% (age 15 and over can read and write; 1995 est.)

Exports: fuel, shoes, garments, fish, bananas, hides

Primary export partners: Portugal, United Kingdom, Germany, Spain, France, Malaysia

Imports: foodstuffs, industrial products, transport equipment, fuels

Primary import partners: Portugal, Netherlands, France, United Kingdom, Spain, United States

Located in the north Atlantic Ocean, the Cape Verde archipelago remained uninhabited until the Portuguese visited it in 1456 and African slaves were brought to the islands to work on Portuguese plantations. As a result, Cape Verdeans have mixed African and Portuguese origins.

In 1951, Portugal changed Cape Verde's status from a colony to an overseas province. In 1956, the African Party for the Independence of Guinea-Bissau and Cape Verde (PAIGC) was organized to bring about improvement in economic, social, and political conditions in Cape Verde and Portuguese Guinea. The PAIGC began an armed rebellion against Portugal in 1961. Acts of sabotage eventually grew into a war in Portuguese Guinea that pitted 10,000 Soviet Bloc-supported PAIGC soldiers against 35,000 Portuguese and African troops.

In December of 1974, the PAIGC and Portugal signed an agreement providing for a transitional government composed of Portuguese and Cape Verdeans. On June 30, 1975, Cape Verdeans elected a National Assembly, which received the instruments of independence from Portugal on July 5, 1975. After winning independence, the country voted for a union with Guinea-Bissau. In 1980, the link ended when João Vieira seized power in Guinea-Bissau. The PAIGC was dissolved and replaced by PAICV (African Party for the Independence of Cape Verde). Pedro Pires, Cape Verde's prime minister and a prominent nationalist, was elected president in 1986. Under him, Cape Verde followed a socialist path with programs of nationalization and agrarian reform. In the country's first free presidential elections made possible by political reforms, Antonio Mascarenhas Monteiro was elected in 1991. A new constitution, firmly establishing the country's new multiparty system, was adopted the following year. In 1996, Mascarenhas was reelected to another five-year term as president.

Cape Verde's privatization program, launched as part of the government's efforts to comply with World Bank/IMF recommendations for economic structural reform, came under fire in 2000 from the PAICV as well as certain members of the ruling Movement for Democracy. This rift within the ruling party eventually gave birth to a new party, the Democratic Renovation Party. The major issue in the 2001 legislative elections was the country's troubled economy. The PAICV captured the majority of the seats, winning for the party's leader, José Maria Neves, the office of prime minister. The PAICV prevailed again in the 2001 presidential elections, as its candidate, Pedro Pires, narrowly won the presidency.

The official language is Portuguese. However, most Cape Verdeans speak a Creole dialect, Crioulo, which consists of archaic Portuguese modified through contact with African and other European languages. Leading contemporary Afro-Cape Verdeans include Cesaria Evora, an internationally renowned singer.

Central African Republic

Official name: Central African Republic
Independence: 13 August 1960 (from France)
Area: 622,984 sq km
Form of government: republic
Capital: Bangui
International relations: ACCT, ACP, AfDB, BDEAC, CCC, CEEAC, CEMAC, ECA, FAO, FZ, G-77, IBRD, ICAO, ICFTU, ICRM, IDA, IFAD, IFC, IFRCS, ILO, IMF, Intelsat, Interpol, IOC, ITU, NAM, OAU, OIC (observer), OPCW, UN, UNCTAD, UNESCO, UNIDO, UPU, WCL, WHO, WIPO, WMO, WToO, WTrO
Currency: Communaute Financiere Africaine franc (CFAF)
Income: us$1,700 (2000 est. of purchasing power parity)
Population: 3,576,884
Ethnic groups: Baya 34%, Banda 27%, Sara 10%, Mandjia 21%, Mboum 4%, M'Baka 4%, Europeans 6,500 (including 1,500 French)
Religious groups: indigenous beliefs 24%, Protestant 25%, Roman Catholic 25%, Muslim 15%, other 11%
Languages: French (official), Sangho (lingua franca and national language), Arabic, Hunsa, Swahili
Literacy: 60% (age 15 and over can read and write; 1995 est.)
Exports: diamonds, timber, cotton, coffee, tobacco
Primary export partners: Benelux 64%, Côte d'Ivoire, Spain, China, Egypt, France (1999)
Imports: food, textiles, petroleum products, machinery, electrical equipment, motor vehicles, chemicals, pharmaceuticals, consumer goods, industrial products
Primary import partners: France 35%, Cameroon 13%, Benelux, Côte d'Ivoire, Germany, Japan (1999)

The first Europeans to settle in the area that is now the Central African Republic were the French, who established an outpost at Bangu. United with Chad in 1906, the outpost formed the Oubangui-Chari-Chad colony.

In 1910, it became one of the four territories of the Federation of French Equatorial Africa, along with Chad, Congo (Brazzaville), and Gabon. However, a constitutional referendum of September 1958 dissolved the federation. The nation became an autonomous republic within the newly established French Community on December 1, 1958, and acceded to complete independence as the Central African Republic on August 13, 1960. The first president and the founder of the Central African Republic was Bathelemy Boganda.

Boganda's successor, David Dacko, was overthrown in 1966 by Gen. Jean-Badel Bokassa, who embarked on a reign of terror, proclaiming himself emperor. A 1981 coup d'état put Dacko back in power. Gen. André Kolingba succeeded Dacko, and a multiparty state was established in 1991. The results of multiparty legislative and presidential elections, held in October 1992, were thrown out by the country's supreme court, which cited multiple irregularities. In September 1993 elections, Ange-Felix Patassé was elected president, succeeding Kolingba, who released Bokassa from prison as one of his last official acts. Patassé was at odds with the military for much of the 1990s, and French troops were needed to put down military mutinies in the late 1990s. In early 1998, the United Nations sent an all-African peacekeeping force to the Central Africa Republic to enforce the so-called Bangui Accords of 1997, which called for an armistice and new elections. Despite opposition party claims of election rigging, incumbent President Patassé was reelected to office in September 1999.

In February 2000, the remaining UN peacekeeping troops stationed in the country withdrew. Political tensions in the capital, however, continued to run high. Although President Patassé promised to seek national reconciliation by bringing together representatives of all major political parties, a conference date was never set. A coup attempt in late May 2001 by army rebels loyal to former President Kolingba was successfully put down. In the wake of the failed coup, Kolingba's political party was ordered disbanded. In late August 2001, Kolingba's wife and children, who had sought refuge in the French Embassy in Bangui, were abducted. Their fate has never been determined.

The Central African Republic is made up of more than 80 ethnic groups, each with its own language. About 70 percent of the population comprises Baya-Mandjia and Banda, with approximately seven percent M'Baka. Sango, the language of a small group along the Oubangui River, is the national language spoken by the majority of Central Africans. The country is one of the poorest nations in Africa, with a high mortality rate and widespread malnutrition and illiteracy.

Chad

Official name: Republic of Chad
Independence: 11 August 1960 (from France)
Area: 1.284 million sq km
Form of government: republic
Capital: N'Djamena
International relations: ACCT, ACP, AfDB, BDEAC, CEEAC, CEMAC, ECA, FAO, FZ, G-77, IBRD, ICAO, ICFTU, ICRM, IDA, IDB, IFAD, IFC, IFRCS, ILO, IMF, Intelsat, Interpol, IOC, ITU, NAM, OAU, OIC, OPCW, UN, UNCTAD, UNESCO, UNIDO, UPU, WCL, WHO, WIPO, WMO, WToO, WTrO

Currency: Communaute Financiere Africaine franc (CFAF)

Income: US$1,000 (2000 est. of purchasing power parity)

Population: 8,707,078 (July 2001 est.)

Ethnic groups: Muslims, commonly referred to as "northerners" or "gorane" (Arabs, Toubou, Hadjerai, Fulbe, Kotoko, Kanembou, Baguirmi, Boulala, Zaghawa, and Maba); non-Muslims, commonly referred to as "southerners" (Sara, Ngambaye, Mbaye, Goulaye, Moundang, Moussei, Massa) including nonindigenous 150,000 (of whom 1,000 are French)

Religious groups: Muslim 50%, Christian 25%, indigenous beliefs (mostly animism) 25%

Languages: French (official), Arabic (official), Sara and Sango (in south), more than 100 different languages and dialects

Literacy: 48.1% (age 15 and over can read and write French or Arabic; 1995 est.)

Exports: cotton, cattle, textiles

Primary export partners: Portugal 38%, Germany 12%, Thailand, Costa Rica, South Africa, France (1999)

Imports: machinery and transportation equipment, industrial goods, petroleum products, foodstuffs, textiles

Primary import partners: France 40%, Cameroon 13%, Nigeria 12%, India 5% (1999)

The region that is now Chad was known to Middle Eastern traders and geographers as far back as the late Middle Ages. Since then, Chad has served as a crossroads for the Muslim peoples of the desert and savannah regions and the animist Bantu tribes of the tropical forests.

The Sao people populated the Chari River basin for thousands of years, but their relatively weak chiefdoms were overtaken by the powerful chiefs of what were to become the Kanem-Bornu and Baguirmi kingdoms. At their peak, these two kingdoms and the kingdom of Ouaddai controlled a good part of what is now Chad, as well as parts of Nigeria and Sudan.

The French first made contact with the region in 1891. The first major colonial battle for Chad was fought in 1900 between the French major Lamy and the African leader Rabah. Although the French won that battle, they did not declare the territory for themselves until 1911, and thereafter armed clashes between colonial troops and local bands continued for many years. Although Chad joined the French colonies of Gabon, Oubangui-Charo, and Moyen Congo to form the Federation of French Equatorial Africa in 1910, Chad did not have colonial status until 1920.

In 1959, the territory of French Equatorial Africa was dissolved, and four states—Gabon, the Central African Republic, Congo (Brazzaville), and Chad—became autonomous members of the French Community. In 1960, Chad became an independent nation under its first president, François Tombalbaye. He was faced with the pressure of resolving the ongoing conflict between the Muslim north and the black south and responded by instituting authoritarian rule. Backed by Libya, FRONAT (Front de Libération Nationale) guerrillas of the north gained power, naming Goukouni Oueddei as head of state. In 1982, he was succeeded by Hisséne Habré, but civil war broke out one year later.

In 1990, Habré was ousted by a rebel group with Libyan support. Rebel leader Idriss Déby assumed the presidency. In January 1992, the Déby government claimed to have put down an uprising by forces loyal to Habré. An understanding was reached in 1994, ending the long-standing battle between the government and Habré forces. In mid-1996 elections under a newly adopted democratic constitution, Déby was elected president. After several postponements, Déby's party dominated legislative elections in 1997. Though Déby's defeated opponents claimed electoral fraud, international observers declared the elections free and fair.

Prospects for Chad's economy improved significantly in mid-2000 when the World Bank approved the country's proposed $3.4-billion oil-development project, which will carry crude oil from the Doba Basin in the south of Chad to the sea through a pipeline passing through Cameroon. One major threat to the project, tentatively scheduled to be completed by 2004, is the continuing rebellion in the country's northern Tibesti region. President Déby handily won reelection in May 2001. Charges from opposition parties that the election had been rigged were rejected by Chad's constitutional court. Déby's heavy-handed repression of subsequent protest demonstrations by the opposition cost him support both domestically and internationally.

Chad is made up of more than 200 ethnic groups. Those in the north and east are generally Muslim, while most southerners are animists and Christians. Ethnic and religious divisions continue to run deep in Chad. The government continues to face armed resistance from rebels in the south demanding regional autonomy, and, in 1998, Amnesty International charged the government with arbitrarily killing civilians from the south.

Comoros

Official name: Federal Islamic Republic of the Comoros

Independence: 6 July 1975 (from France)

Area: 2,170 sq km

Form of government: independent republic

Capital: Moroni

International relations: ACCT, ACP, AfDB, AFESD, AL, CCC, ECA, FAO, FZ, G-77, IBRD, ICAO, ICRM, IDA, IDB, IFAD, IFC, IFRCS (associate), ILO, IMF, InOC, Intelsat, Interpol, IOC, ISO (subscriber), ITU, NAM, OAU, OIC, OPCW, UN, UNCTAD, UNESCO, UNIDO, UPU, WHO, WMO, WTrO (applicant)

Currency: Comoran franc (KMF)

Income: us$720 (2000 est. of purchasing power parity)

Population: 596,202 (July 2001 est.)

Ethnic groups: Antalote, Cafre, Makoa, Oimatsaha, Sakalava

Religious groups: Sunni Muslim 98%, Roman Catholic 2%

Languages: Arabic (official), French (official), Comoran (a blend of Swahili and Arabic)

Literacy: 57.3% (age 15 and over can read and write; 1995 est.)

Exports: vanilla, ylang-ylang, cloves, perfume oil, copra

Primary export partners: France 50%, Germany 25% (1998)

Imports: rice and other foodstuffs, consumer goods; petroleum products, cement, transport equipment

Primary import partners: France 38%, Pakistan 13%, South Africa 8%, Kenya 8% (1998)

Located off the northwestern coast of Madagascar, Portuguese explorers visited the archipelago in 1505. In 1843, the sultan of Mayotte was persuaded to relinquish the island of Mayotte to the French. By 1912, France had established colonial rule over the additional islands of Grande Comore, Anjouan, and Mohéli and placed them under the administration of the governor general of Madagascar. After World War II, the islands became a French overseas territory and were represented in France's National Assembly. On July 6, 1975, the Comorian Parliament passed a resolution declaring unilateral independence. However, the deputies of Mayotte abstained; it remains under French administration. As a result, the Comorian government has effective control over only Grande Comore, Anjouan, and Mohéli. This was followed by a extended period of political upheaval in Comoros including a series of political insurrections and coup d'états.

In 1996, Mohamed Taki Abdulkarim was elected president and unveiled a new constitution extending the powers of the president and making Islam the state religion. In 1997, the islands of Anjouan and Mohéli announced their intention to secede: in light of the relatively high standard of living enjoyed by Mayotte, they wished to return to French administration. After initially affirming its willingness to reincorporate the islands, France urged the Organization of African Unity (OAU) to find a peaceful settlement to the conflict. The OAU later worked out a framework agreement whereby the islands would have their own government within a new entity to be named the Union of Comorian Islands, which would have a separate administration. At an April 1999 peace conference in Madagascar, representatives of Grand Comore, Mohéli, and the Comoros government signed the agreement; the Anjouan delegation did not. Shortly afterwards, army officers took over the Comoros Republic in an apparent coup, bringing to power Col. Azali Assoumani.

The dominant issue in the first years of the new millennium continued to be the secession of Anjouan Island. In early 2000, after a referendum on Anjouan overwhelming supported the island's refusal to sign an OAU-brokered agreement, the OAU imposed sanctions on the island and later voted to support armed intervention to end the secession. In early 2001, the OAU led talks between Anjouan and federal government officials that produced an agreement providing greater autonomy for Comoros' individual island governments but reserved foreign policy and defense for the national government. After an August 2001 coup unseated Anjouan's ruler, Lieut. Col. Said Abeid Abdermane, Col. Mohamed Bacar took over as the island's head of state. In December 2001, Anjouan's voters overwhelmingly supported a new Comoros constitution formalizing the terms set forth in the OAU-brokered reconciliation agreement.

The Comorians inhabiting the islands of Grande Comore, Anjouan, and Mohéli (about 86 percent of the population) share African-Arab origins. Islam is the dominant religion, but a substantial minority of the citizens of Mayotte (the Mahorais) are Catholic and have been influenced strongly by French culture. The most common language is Shikomoro, a Swahili dialect. French and Malagasy are also spoken.

Congo, Democratic Republic of the

Independence: 30 June 1960 (from Belgium)

Area: 2,345,410 sq km

Form of government: dictatorship; presumably undergoing a transition to representative government

Capital: Kinshasa

International relations: ACCT, ACP, AfDB, CCC, CEEAC, CEPGL, ECA, FAO, G-19, G-24, G-77, IAEA, IBRD, ICAO, ICFTU, ICRM, IDA, IFAD, IFC, IFRCS, IHO, ILO, IMF, IMO, Intelsat, Interpol, IOC, IOM (observer), ISO (correspondent), ITU, NAM, OAU, OPCW, PCA,

After days of hiding from civil war in Kinshasa, citizens return to the market as well as government troops (truck in foreground).

SADC, UN, UNCTAD, UNESCO, UNHCR, UNIDO, UPU, WCL, WFTU, WHO, WIPO, WMO, WToO, WTrO
Currency: Congolese franc (CDF)
Income: US$600 (2000 est. of purchasing power parity)
Population: 53,624,718
Ethnic groups: over 200 African ethnic groups of which the majority are Bantu; the four largest tribes—Mongo, Luba, Kongo (all Bantu), and the Mangbetu-Azande (Hamitic)—make up about 45% of the population
Religious groups: Roman Catholic 50%, Protestant 20%, Kimbanguist 10%, Muslim 10%, other syncretic sects and indigenous beliefs 10%
Languages: French (official), Lingala (a lingua franca trade language), Kingwana (a dialect of Kiswahili or Swahili), Kikongo, Tshiluba

Literacy: 77.3% (age 15 and over can read and write French, Lingala, Kingwana, or Tshiluba; 1995 est.)
Exports: diamonds, copper, coffee, cobalt, crude oil
Primary export partners: Benelux 62%, United States 18%, South Africa, Finland, Italy (1999)
Imports: foodstuffs, mining and other machinery, transport equipment, fuels
Primary import partners: South Africa 28%, Benelux 14%, Nigeria 9%, Kenya 7%, China (1999)

The area that is now the Democratic Republic of the Congo or Congo-Kinshasa is believed to have been populated as early as 10,000 years ago. An influx of peoples arrived in the seventh and eighth centuries, when Bantu people from present-day Nigeria settled, bringing with them knowledge of the manufacture and use of metals. In 1482, the Portuguese arrived at the mouth of the Congo River. They found an organized society—the Bakongo Kingdom—that included parts of present-day Congo-Brazzaville, Congo-Kinshasa, and Angola. The Portuguese named the area Congo. At the Berlin Conference of 1885, King Leopold's claim to the greater part of the Zaire River basin was recognized. The Congo Free State remained his personal possession until he ceded it to the Belgian State in 1907, when it was renamed the Belgian Congo.

Following riots in Leopoldville in 1958, Belgian King Bedouin announced that the colony could look forward to independence. Roundtable conferences were convened at Brussels in January 1960, and Belgium granted independence on June 30, 1960. Parliamentary elections were held in April of 1960. The Congolese National Movement (MNC) obtained a majority of the seats, and Patrice Lumumba was named prime minister. After much maneuvering, the leader of the Alliance of the Bakongo (ABAKO) Party, Joseph Kasavubu, was named president.

Chaos started right after independence. Moise Tshombe, premier of Katanga Province, declared Katanga (rich with copper) independent. Belgian military intervened, and, soon after, U.N. troops arrived to help normalize the situation. Meanwhile, Lumumba was assassinated. Tshombe served as prime minister until 1965, when Joseph Mobutu organized a coup d'état. While amassing great personal riches, Mobutu managed to bring resource-rich Congo-Kinshasa (then known as Zaire) to the brink of bankruptcy during the more than 30 years that he held power. The country's increasingly fragile economy and pressures from a sharp influx in refugees all contributed to growing dissatisfaction with Mobutu's regime.

Anti-Mobutu guerrilla fighter Laurent-Désiré Kabila, leader of the Alliance of Democratic Forces for the Liberation of Congo, led rebel forces in seizing large portions of the country in the fall of 1996. In May 1997, as rebels neared Kinshasa, Mobutu stepped down and fled the capital, later dying in exile. The rebels took control of the country, which they renamed the Democratic Republic of the Congo. Kabila's regime has faced heavy criticism from the international community, who suspect that his troops were responsible for the disappearance and assumed massacre of thousands of Hutu refugees. In addition, the political favoritism exhibited by Kabila has led to serious civil strife that threatens to spark a broad regional conflict beyond Congo-Kinshasa's borders.

Attempts to quell the rebellion in the eastern provinces of the Congo in early 2000 were frustrated by President Kabila's demand that Uganda and Rwanda must unconditionally withdraw their troops from the region. Fighting intensified in late 2000. In January 2001, Laurent Kabila was assassinated, reportedly by one of his bodyguards. He was succeeded by his son, Joseph, who seemed more amenable than his father to dealing with eastern Congo rebel leaders in an effort to end the continuing conflict. The younger Kabila also moved quickly to root out corruption at the higher levels of government. In May 2001, Kabila met with leaders of three rebel groups and struck an agreement that created a framework for further dialogue. An October 2001 peace conference in Addis Ababa failed to make much progress, but delegates agreed to continue their efforts to resolve the crisis. Fighting in the eastern provinces was sharply reduced, and Uganda and Rwandan troops began withdrawing from the region.

As many as 250 ethnic groups in the Democratic Republic of the Congo have been distinguished and named. The largest group, the Kongo, may include as many as 2.5 million persons. Other socially and numerically important groups are the Luba, Lunda, Bashi, and Mongo. Some groups, including the aboriginal Pygmies, occupy isolated ecological niches and number only a few thousand.

Approximately 700 local languages and dialects are spoken; four serve as official languages. Lingala developed along the Congo River in the 1880s, in response to the need for a common commercial language. Swahili, introduced into the country by Arabs and especially the Zanzibari Swahilis during the nineteenth century slaving operations, is spoken extensively in the eastern half of the country. Kikongo is used primarily in the area between Kinshasa and the Atlantic Ocean, as well as in parts of Congo and Angola. Tshiluba is spoken primarily by the tribal groups of the south-central Democratic Republic of the Congo.

Congo, Republic of the

Independence: 15 August 1960 (from France)

Area: 342,000 sq km

Form of government: republic

Capital: Brazzaville

International relations: ACCT, ACP, AfDB, BDEAC, CCC, CEEAC, CEMAC, ECA, FAO, FZ, G-77, IBRD, ICAO, ICFTU, ICRM, IDA, IFAD, IFC, IFRCS, ILO, IMF, IMO, Intelsat, Interpol, IOC, IOM (observer), ITU, NAM, OAU, OPCW, UN, UNCTAD, UNESCO, UNIDO, UPU, WCL, WFTU, WHO, WIPO, WMO, WToO, WTrO

Currency: Communaute Financiere Africaine franc (CFAF)

Income: us$1,100 (2000 est. of purchasing power parity)

Population: 2,894,336

Ethnic groups: Kongo 48%, Sangha 20%, M'Bochi 12%, Teke 17%, Europeans NA%; note: Europeans estimated at 8,500, mostly French, before the 1997 civil war; may be half that of 1998, following the widespread destruction of foreign businesses in 1997

Religious groups: Christian 50%, animist 48%, Muslim 2%

Languages: French (official), Lingala and Monokutuba (lingua franca trade languages), many local languages and dialects (of which Kikongo has the most users)

Literacy: 74.9% (age 15 and over can read and write; 1995 est.)

Exports: petroleum 50%, lumber, plywood, sugar, cocoa, coffee, diamonds

Primary export partners: United States 23%, Benelux 14%, Germany, Italy, Taiwan, China (1998)

Imports: petroleum products, capital equipment, construction materials, foodstuffs

Primary import partners: France 23%, United States 9%, Belgium 8%, United Kingdom 7%, Italy (1997 est.)

The early history of the Congo is believed to have focused on three tribal kingdoms—the Kongo, the Loango, and the Teke. Established in the fourth century, the Kongo was a highly centralized kingdom that later developed a close commercial relationship with the Portuguese, who were the first Europeans to explore the area.

With the development of the slave trade, the Portuguese turned their attention from the Kongo Kingdom to the Loango Kingdom. By the time the slave trade was abolished in the 1800s, the Loango Kingdom had been reduced to many small, independent groups. The Teke Kingdom of the interior, which had sold slaves to the Loango Kingdom, ended its independence in 1883, when the Teke king concluded a treaty with Pierre

Savorgnan de Brazza, placing the Teke lands and people under French protection. The area then became known as Middle Congo.

In 1910, Middle Congo became part of French Equatorial Africa, which also included Gabon, the Central African Republic, and Chad. A constitutional referendum in September 1958 replaced the Federation of French Equatorial Africa with the French Community. Middle Congo, under the name Republic of the Congo, and the three other territories of French Equatorial Africa became fully autonomous members within the French Community. On April 15, 1960, it became an independent nation but retained close, formal bonds with the community.

President Fulbert Youlou instituted a dictatorship for the first three years following independence and then was succeeded by a revolutionary government headed by Alphonse Massamba-Debat. In 1968, the military seized control of the nation under Gen. Marien Ngouabi, who declared the Congo a republic to be governed under a one-party system. Assassinated in 1977, Ngouabi was succeeded as president by General Joachim Yhombi-Opango. Two years later, Yhombi-Opango was succeeded by Denis Sassou-Nguesso, who was reelected to the presidency in 1984 and 1989.

The 1990s brought increasing dissatisfaction with the Sassou-Nguesso regime, which was forced in 1992 to adopt a new constitution, making the country a multiparty democracy. In August 1992, Sassou-Nguesso lost in presidential elections to Pascal Lissouba, but the latter's government was soon plagued by accusations of ethnic favoritism. Clashes between various private militias exploded into civil war, killing between 6,000 and 10,000 people and largely destroying Brazzaville. Many of the country's citizens rallied behind opposition forces led by Sassou-Nguesso who, with considerable Angolan assistance, overthrew Lissouba in late 1997. Continuing to maintain power, Sassou-Nguesso has promised national reconciliation, a return to civilian rule, and a professional military.

Civil war again broke out in January 1999 when rebel militias loyal to Lissouba began attacks in and around the capital city of Brazzaville. By the end of the year, army representatives signed a truce agreement with rebel leaders. In March 2001, President Sassou-Nguesso launched talks to draft a new constitution that would help restore peace in the country. Despite opposition charges that the new constitution placed too much power in the hands of the president, the document was adopted by the Congolese parliament in September 2001.

Côte d'Ivoire (Ivory Coast)

Independence: 7 August (1960) (from France)

Area: 322,460 sq km

Form of government: republic; multiparty presidential regime established 1960

Capital: Yamoussoukro; note: although Yamoussoukro has been the official capital since 1983, Abidjan remains the administrative center; the United States, like other countries, maintains its Embassy in Abidjan

International relations: ACP, AfDB, CCC, ECA, ECOWAS, Entente, FAO, FZ, G-24, G-77, IAEA, IBRD, ICAO, ICC, ICFTU, ICRM, IDA, IFAD, IFC, IFRCS, ILO, IMF, IMO, Intelsat, Interpol, IOC, IOM, ISO (correspondent), ITU, NAM, OAU, OIC (observer), OPCW, UN, UNCTAD, UNESCO, UNHCR, UNIDO, UPU, WADB, WADB (regional), WAEMU, WCL, WFTU, WHO, WIPO, WMO, WToO, WTrO

Currency: Communaute Financiere Africaine franc (CFAF)

Income: US$1,600 (2000 est. of purchasing power parity)

Population: 16,393,221

Ethnic groups: Akan 42.1%, Voltaiques or Gur 17.6%, Northern Mandes 16.5%, Krous 11%, Southern Mandes 10%, other 2.8% (1998)

Religious groups: Christian 34%, Muslim 27%, no religion 21%, animist 15%, other 3% (1998)

Languages: French (official), 60 native dialects with Dioula the most widely spoken

Literacy: 48.5% (age 15 and over can read and write)

Exports: cocoa 33%, coffee, tropical woods, petroleum, cotton, bananas, pineapples, palm oil, cotton, fish (1999)

Primary export partners: France 15%, United States 8%, Netherlands 7%, Germany 6%, Italy 6% (1999)

Imports: food, consumer goods; capital goods, fuel, transport equipment

Primary import partners: France 26%, Nigeria 10%, China 7%, Italy 5%, Germany 4% (1999)

The French made their initial contact with Côte d'Ivoire in 1637, when missionaries landed at Assinie near the Gold Coast (now Ghana) border. However, these early contacts were limited. In 1843 and 1844, France signed treaties with the kings of the Grand Bassam and Assinie regions, placing their territories under a French protectorate. French explorers, missionaries, trading companies, and soldiers gradually extended the area under French control until 1893, when Côte d'Ivoire was officially made a French colony.

In December of 1958, Côte d'Ivoire became an autonomous republic within the French Community. Côte d'Ivoire became independent on August 7, 1960. Félix Houphouët-Boigny led the country under a one-party system. He maintained strong ties with Europe, which helped bring about rapid development and economic stability. In October 1990, Houphouët-Boigny was elected to his seventh term as president in the country's first multiparty elections. He died in 1993 and was succeeded by Henri Konan Bédié, head of the National Assembly. Bédié was again elected to office in 1995 elections that were boycotted by opposition parties protesting the government's political restrictions. Continuing the policies of his predecessor, Bédié has helped build a nation of political stability and limited economic prosperity. At the same time, he has maintained a neocolonial dependence on France and blocked effective democratic reforms.

In December 1999, a military coup ousted Bédié from power, replacing him with Gen. Robert Gueï. In an attempt to broaden support for the new government, the military junta formed a coalition first with former Prime Minister Alassane Ouattara's Rally of Republicans, which was further strengthened in early 2000 when four members of the Ivorian Popular Front party agreed to join the cabinet. Gueï lost to Ivorian Popular Front candidate Laurent Gbagbo in the October 2002 presidential elections. At first, Gueï halted the vote count in a vain attempt to hold on to the presidency. He was soon forced from office by a popular revolt, and Gbagbo assumed office, despite strong opposition from some quarters. Political turmoil continued into 2001, and, in early January, a coup was mounted against the Gbagbo regime. It was quickly put down. Later in the year, Gbagbo proposed reconciliations talks that would bring together warring political leaders of the past and present. Such talks were eventually held in November 2001.

Côte d'Ivoire's more than 60 ethnic groups usually are classified into seven principal divisions—Akan, Krou, Lagoon, Nuclear Mande, Peripheral Mande, Senoufo, and Lobi. The Baoule in the Akan division is probably the largest single subgroup, with perhaps 20 percent of the overall population. The Bete in the Krou division and the Senoufo in the north are the second and third-largest groups, with roughly 18 and 15 percent of the national population, respectively.

Djibouti

Official name: Republic of Djibouti
Independence: 27 June 1977 (from France)
Area: 22,000 sq km
Form of government: republic
Capital: Djibouti
International relations: ACCT, ACP, AfDB, AFESD, AL, AMF, ECA, FAO, G-77, IBRD, ICAO, ICFTU, ICRM, IDA, IDB, IFAD, IFC, IFRCS, IGAD, ILO, IMF, IMO, Intelsat (nonsignatory user), Interpol, IOC, ITU, NAM, OAU, OIC, OPCW, UN, UNCTAD, UNESCO, UNIDO, UPU, WFTU, WHO, WMO, WToO, WTrO
Currency: Djiboutian franc (DJF)
Income: us$1,300 (2000 est. of purchasing power parity)
Population: 460,700 (July 2001 est.)
Ethnic groups: Somali 60%, Afar 35%, French, Arab, Ethiopian, and Italian 5%
Religious groups: Muslim 94%, Christian 6%
Languages: French (official), Arabic (official), Somali, Afar
Literacy: 46.2% (age 15 and over can read and write; 1995 est.)
Exports: reexports, hides and skins, coffee (in transit)
Primary export partners: Somalia 53%, Yemen 23%, Ethiopia 5%, (1998)
Imports: foods, beverages, transport equipment, chemicals, petroleum products
Primary import partners: France 13%, Ethiopia 12%, Italy 9%, Saudi Arabia 6%, United Kingdom 6% (1998)

The region, which now makes up the Republic of Djibouti, was first settled by the French in 1862 as a result of growing French interest in British activity in Egypt. In 1884, France expanded its protectorate to include the shores of the Gulf of Tadjourah and the hinterland, designating the area French Somaliland. The boundaries of the protectorate, marked out in 1897 by France and Emperor Menelik II of Ethiopia, were affirmed further by agreements with Emperor Haile Selassie I in 1945 and 1954.

In July of 1967, a directive from Paris formally changed the name of the territory to the French Territory of Afars and Issas. In 1975, the French government began to accommodate increasingly insistent demands for independence. In June of 1976, the territory's citizenship law, which had favored the Afar minority, was revised to reflect more closely the weight of the Issa Somali majority. In a May of 1977 referendum, the electorate voted for independence, and the Republic of Djibouti was inaugurated on June 27, 1977. Independence was followed by a republican form of government.

Since independence, the country has been led by Hassan Gouled Aptidon, the republic's first and only president. Beginning in the 1980s, however, Gouled's tenure was marred by political repression, ethnic hostilities, and serious international debt. Opposition to the Gouled government sparked a sizeable Afar resistance movement in the 1990s; negotiations with the government led to a comprehensive treaty in December

Djiboutian women sitting beneath a tree in northeast Africa.

1994. When Gouled had to leave the country from December 1995 until February 1996 to seek medical treatment in France, a destabilizing struggle for succession ensued. Upon his return, he suspended the civil rights of prominent opposition leaders and restated his intention to remain in office until his term expires in 1999. Gouled's ruling party nominated Ismail Omar Guelleh, nephew of the retiring president, to run for Gouled's post, which he handily won in a face-off with Moussa Ahmed Idriss, who represented a coalition of opposition parties. After his inauguration in May 1999, Omar released a number of political prisoners but still came under fire from human rights organizations for the harassment of journalists, including Moussa Ahmed, who was arrested in September 1999.

In February 2000, Omar's government signed an agreement with rebel leaders of the Front for the Restoration of Unity and Dignity (FRUD) to end nearly a decade of fighting. The following month, Djibouti restored diplomatic relations with Eritrea and also sought to play peacemaker between warring factions in neighboring Somalia. In May 2001, the Omar government reached a peace accord with the radical wing of

FRUD, following which FRUD fighters voluntarily disarmed.

The indigenous population of the Republic of Djibouti is divided between the majority Somalis (predominantly of the Issa tribe with minority Ishaak and Gadaboursi representation) and the Afars and Danakils.

Egypt

Official name: Arab Republic of Egypt

Independence: 28 February 1922 (from United Kingdom)

Area: 1,001,450 sq km

Form of government: republic

Capital: Cairo

International relations: ABEDA, ACC, ACCT (associate), AfDB, AFESD, AL, AMF, BSEC (observer), CAEU, CCC, EBRD, ECA, ESCWA, FAO, G-15, G-19, G-24, G-77, IAEA, IBRD, ICAO, ICC, ICRM, IDA, IDB, IFAD, IFC, IFRCS, IHO, ILO, IMF, IMO, Inmarsat, Intelsat, Interpol, IOC, IOM, ISO, ITU, MINURSO, MONUC, NAM, OAPEC, OAS (observer), OAU, OIC, OSCE (partner), PCA, UN, UNAMSIL, UNCTAD, UNESCO, UNIDO, UNITAR, UNMIBH, UNMIK, UNMOP, UNOMIG, UNRWA, UNTAET, UPU, WFTU, WHO, WIPO, WMO, WToO, WTrO

Currency: Egyptian pound (EGP)

Income: US$3,600 (2000 est. of purchasing power parity)

Population: 69,536,644 (July 2001 est.)

Ethnic groups: Eastern Hamitic stock (Egyptians, Bedouins, and Berbers) 99%, Greek, Nubian, Armenian, other European (primarily Italian and French) 1%

Religious groups: Muslim (mostly Sunni) 94%, Coptic Christian and other 6%

Languages: Arabic (official), English and French widely understood by educated classes

Literacy: 51.4% (age 15 and over can read and write; 1995 est.)

Exports: crude oil and petroleum products, cotton, textiles, metal products, chemicals

Primary export partners: EU 35%, Middle East 17%, Afro-Asian countries 14%, United States 12% (1999)

Imports: machinery and equipment, foodstuffs, chemicals, wood products, fuels

Primary import partners: EU 36%, United States 14%, Afro-Asian countries 14%, Middle East 6% (1999)

Egypt has endured as a unified state for more than 5,000 years, and archaeological evidence indicates that a developed Egyptian society has existed much longer.

In about 3100 BC, Egypt was united under a ruler known as Mena, or Menes, who inaugurated the 30 pharaonic dynasties into which Egypt's ancient history is divided—the Old and Middle Kingdoms and the New Empire.

In 525 BC, the Persians dethroned the last pharaoh of the 26th dynasty. The country remained a Persian province until the conquest of Alexander the Great in 332 BC. After Alexander's death in 323 BC, the Macedonian commander, Ptolemy, established personal control over Egypt, assuming the title of pharaoh in 304 BC. The Ptolemaic line ended in 30 BC with the suicide of Queen Cleopatra. The Emperor Augustus then established direct Roman control over Egypt, initiating almost seven centuries of Roman and Byzantine rule.

Egypt was invaded and conquered by Arab forces in 642 AD and a process of Arabization and Islamization ensued. The French arrived in Egypt in 1798 until an Anglo-Ottoman invasion force drove out the French in 1801. Following a period of chaos, the Albanian Muhammad Ali obtained control of the country.

In 1882, the British occupied Egypt and declared a formal protectorate over Egypt on December 18, 1914. In deference to growing nationalist feelings, Britain unilaterally declared Egyptian independence on February 28, 1922. King Faud I ruled after independence until 1952, when he was overthrown by Gamal Abdel Nasser. Upon Nasser's death, Anwar el-Sadat took over the leadership until he was assassinated in 1981 and succeeded by Hosni Mubarak.

The Mubarak government has come under increasing fire from Muslim fundamentalists who, in 1992, began launching violent attacks against tourists, Coptic Christians, and government officials. Shortly before parliamentary elections in 1995, Mubarak accused the opposition Muslim Brotherhood of aiding and abetting some of the Muslim fundamentalist groups. A number of members of the Muslim Brotherhood were arrested and imprisoned. Mubarak's National Democratic Party won an overwhelming victory in the parliamentary balloting. Since that time, Egypt has refused to release any of the religious zealots, and violence against tourists and Coptic Christians has increased. Yet, Mubarak's continued reliance on the military and his ban on Islamist political opposition threatens his regime's stability, particularly when ordinary Egyptians continue to face economic hardship.

The Mubarak government continued to vigorously prosecute the country's militant Islamic organizations, in April 1999 sentencing more than 85 members of the al-Jihad organization to a variety of punishments, including lengthy prison terms and execution. The action seemed only to fuel the militants' determination to continue its jihad against the government. In September 1999, an Islamic militant attempted to assassinate Mubarak but was unsuccessful. Later that same month, Mubarak was reelected to his fourth six-year term as president. Throughout 1999 and well into the new millennium, Mubarak continued his attempts to play mediator in the off and on peace talks between Israel and the Palestinian Authority.

The Egyptian population is fairly homogenous—Mediterranean and Arab influences appear in the north, as well as some mixing in the south with the Nubians of northern Sudan. Ethnic minorities include a small number of Bedouin Arab nomads dispersed in the eastern and western deserts and in the Sinai, as well as some 50,000 to 200,000 Nubians clustered along the Nile in Upper Egypt.

Equatorial Guinea

Official name: Republic of Equatorial Guinea

Independence: 12 October 1968 (from Spain)

Area: 28,051 sq km

Form of government: republic

Capital: Malabo

International relations: ACCT, ACP, AfDB, BDEAC, CEEAC, CEMAC, ECA, FAO, FZ, G-77, IBRD, ICAO, ICRM, IDA, IFAD, IFC, IFRCS, ILO, IMF, IMO, Intelsat, Interpol, IOC, ITU, NAM, OAS (observer), OAU, OPCW, UN, UNCTAD, UNESCO, UNIDO, UPU, WHO, WIPO, WToO, WTrO (applicant)

Currency: Communaute Financiere Africaine franc (CFAF)

Income: US$2,000 (2000 est. of purchasing power parity)

Population: 486,060 (July 2001 est.)

Ethnic groups: Bioko (primarily Bubi, some Fernandinos), Rio Muni (primarily Fang), Europeans less than 1,000, mostly Spanish

Religious groups: nominally Christian and predominantly Roman Catholic, pagan practices

Languages: Spanish (official), French (official), pidgin English, Fang, Bubi, Ibo

Literacy: 78.5% (age 15 and over can read and write; 1995 est.)

Exports: petroleum, timber, cocoa

Primary export partners: United States 62%, Spain 17%, China 9%, France 3%, Japan 3%, (1997)

Imports: manufactured goods and equipment

Primary import partners: United States 35%, France 15%, Spain 10%, Cameroon 10%, United Kingdom 6% (1997)

The first inhabitants of the region that is now Equatorial Guinea are believed to have been Pygmies, of whom only isolated pockets remain in northern Rio Muni. Bantu migrations between the seventeenth and nineteenth centuries brought the coastal tribes and the Fang people to the area.

The Portuguese, seeking a route to India, landed on the island of Bioko in 1471. The Portuguese retained control until 1778, when the island and adjacent islets were ceded to Spain. From 1827 to 1843, Britain established a base on the island to combat the slave trade. Conflicting claims to the mainland were settled in 1900 by the Treaty of Paris.

In 1959, the Spanish territory of the Gulf of Guinea was established. In 1963, the name of the country was changed to Equatorial Guinea. In March 1968, under pressure from Equatoguinean nationalists and the United Nations, Spain announced that it would grant independence to Equatorial Guinea. In September 1968, Macias Macías Nguema was elected first president of Equatorial Guinea, and independence was granted in October. A military coup occurred in 1979 deposing Nguema, who was put to death for "crimes against humanity." Lieutenant Colonel Teodoro Obiang Nguema Mbasogo, leader of the coup that brought down Nguema, succeeded him as president. Although Obiang Nguema's government made a show of various political reforms over the past few decades, outside observers remain harshly critical of the regime's repressive policies. In addition, Obiang Nguema's government has been sharply criticized for the mishandling of the national economy including the oil boom of the 1990s.

Although Equatorial Guinea's oil production increased sharply during the late 1990s and into the new millennium, making the country's economy the fastest growing in the world in 2001, the benefits reached relatively few of its citizens. As the health of President Obiang Nguema deteriorated in 2001, many observers felt the scene was set for a power struggle between the president's two eldest sons, Teodorin Nguema Obiang Mangué and Gabriel Nguema Lima. However, the family seemed to be leaning toward Gen. Agustin Ndong Ona as a possible successor.

The majority of the Equatoguinean people are of Bantu origin. The largest tribe, the Fang, constitute 80 percent of the population and are divided into about 67 clans. Those to the north of Rio Benito on Rio Muni speak Fang-Ntumu, and those to the south speak Fang-Okak, two mutually intelligible dialects. The Bubi, who form 15 percent of the population, are indigenous to Bioko Island. In addition, several coastal tribes exist, who are sometimes referred to as "Playeros," and include the Ndowes, Bujebas, Balengues, and Bengas on the mainland and small islands, and Fernandinos, a Creole community, on Bioko. These groups comprise five percent of the population.

Eritrea

Official name: State of Eritrea

Independence: 24 May 1993 (from Ethiopia)

Area: 121,320 sq km

Form of government: transitional government

Capital: Asmara (formerly Asmera)

International relations: ACP, AfDB, CCC, ECA, FAO, IBRD, ICAO, ICFTU, IDA, IFAD, IFC, IGAD, ILO, IMF, IMO, Intelsat (nonsignatory user), Interpol, IOC, ITU, NAM, OAU, OPCW, UN, UNCTAD, UNESCO, UNIDO, UPU, WFTU, WHO, WIPO, WMO, WToO

Currency: nakfa (ERN)

Income: us$710 (2000 est. of purchasing power parity)

Population: 4,298,269 (July 2001 est.)

Ethnic groups: ethnic Tigrinya 50%, Tigre and Kunama 40%, Afar 4%, Saho (Red Sea coast dwellers) 3%

Religious groups: Muslim, Coptic Christian, Roman Catholic, Protestant

Languages: Afar, Amharic, Arabic, Tigre and Kunama, Tigrinya, other Cushitic languages

Literacy: 25%

Exports: livestock, sorghum, textiles, food, small manufactures

Primary export partners: Sudan 27.2%, Ethiopia 26.5%, Japan 13.2%, UAE 7.3%, Italy 5.3% (1998)

Imports: machinery, petroleum products, food, manufactured goods

Primary import partners: Italy 17.4%, UAE 16.2%, Germany 5.7%, United Kingdom 4.5%, Korea 4.4% (1998)

Eritrea was an integral part of the kingdom of Aksum and has shared its destiny with Ethiopia. Islamic colonists became established in the coastal area and dominate the region until the later half of the nineteenth century, when Egyptians settled in the area. Founded in 1890 by the Italians, the colony of Eritrea was annexed by Ethiopia after World War II. For years, the Eritrian People's Liberation Forum waged a struggle for independence that was eventually won on May 25, 1993.

Since independence, neighboring Sudan and Eritrea have frequently swapped charges that one was helping opposition groups seeking the overthrow of the other's government. This growing enmity resulted in a severing of diplomatic relations between the two in December

Eritrean women dressed in traditional clothing.

1994. In 1996 Eritrea skirmished briefly with both Djibouti over a contested border and with Yemen over ownership of a collection of small Red Sea Islands. Perhaps most seriously though, armed conflict with Ethiopia erupted again in June 1998. The immediate cause of the fighting was again a disputed border, but tensions over trade issues had been building for months. Despite efforts by the United States, the Organization of African Unity, and neighboring African countries to resolve the conflict diplomatically, both sides continued to arm themselves.

Eritrea's border war with Ethiopia continued throughout 1999, slowing Eritrea's economic performance significantly. In May 2000, Ethiopian forces occupied previously undisputed areas in central and western Eritrean while consolidating their control over such disputed areas as Badme and Zela Ambesa. In July 2000, the newly established United Nations Mission in Ethiopia and Eritrea (UNMEE) deployed 4,200 peacekeeping forces in the disputed region, and, in December 2000, both countries signed a peace agreement in Algiers. The regime of President Isaias Afwerki came under increasing criticism, some of it from high-profile government officials. Afwerki cracked down viciously on one group of 15 outspoken critics, known as G-15, which helped to increase the disaffection of average Eritreans with their government.

Ethiopia

Official name: Federal Democratic Republic of Ethiopia

Independence: oldest independent country in Africa and one of the oldest in the world—at least 2,000 years

Area: 1,127,127 sq km

Form of government: federal republic

Capital: Addis Ababa

International relations: ACP, AfDB, CCC, ECA, FAO, G-24, G-77, IAEA, IBRD, ICAO, ICRM, IDA, IFAD, IFC, IFRCS, IGAD, ILO, IMF, IMO, Intelsat, Interpol, IOC, IOM (observer), ISO, ITU, NAM, OAU, OPCW, UN, UNCTAD, UNESCO, UNHCR, UNIDO, UNU, UPU, WFTU, WHO, WIPO, WMO, WToO

Currency: birr (ETB)

Income: us$600 (2000 est. of purchasing power parity)

A church in Axum, Ethiopia.

Population: 65,891,874

Ethnic groups: Oromo 40%, Amhara and Tigre 32%, Sidamo 9%, Shankella 6%, Somali 6%, Afar 4%, Gurage 2%, other 1%

Religious groups: Muslim 45%–50%, Ethiopian Orthodox 35%–40%, animist 12%, other 3%–8%

Languages: Amharic, Tigrinya, Oromigna, Guaragigna, Somali, Arabic, other local languages, English (major foreign language taught in schools)

Literacy: 35.5% (age 15 and over can read and write; 1995 est.)

Exports: coffee, gold, leather products, oilseeds, qat

Primary export partners: Germany 16%, Japan 13%, Djibouti 10%, Saudi Arabia 7% (1999 est.)

Imports: food and live animals, petroleum and petroleum products, chemicals, machinery, motor vehicles

Primary import partners: Saudi Arabia 28%, Italy 10%, Russia 7%, United States 6% (1999 est.)

Ethiopia is the oldest independent country in Africa and one of the oldest in the world. Herodotus, the Greek historian of the fifth century BC, describes ancient Ethiopia in his writings, and the Old Testament of the Bible records the Queen of Sheba's visit to Jerusalem. Missionaries from Egypt and Syria introduced Christianity in the fourth century AD Europeans did not make contact with Ethiopia until the Portuguese in 1493.

In 1930, Haile Selassie was crowned emperor. His reign was interrupted in 1936 when Italian fascist forces invaded and occupied Ethiopia. The emperor was eventually forced into exile in England despite his plea to the League of Nations for intervention. Five years later, the Italians were defeated by British and Ethiopian forces, and the emperor returned to the throne. After a period of civil unrest, which began in February 1974, the aging Haile Selassie was deposed on September 13, 1974. After deposing Selasie, the military, led by Col. Mariam Haile Mengistu, took over the government and nationalized nearly all the country's economic institutions.

Discontent had been spreading throughout Ethiopian urban elites, and an escalating series of mutinies in the armed forced, demonstrations, and strikes led to the seizure of state power by the armed forces coordinating committee, which later became the Provisional Military Administrative Council (PMAC). The PMAC formally declared its intent to remake Ethiopia into a socialist state. It finally destroyed its opposition in a program of mass arrests and executions known as the "red terror," which lasted from November 1977 to March 1978. An estimated 10,000 people, mostly in Addis Ababa, were killed by government forces. Mengistu's failure to respond to growing national problems—droughts, civil war with Eritrea and Tigray, and declining Soviet aid—ended his rule. Early in 1991, he was forced into exile in Zimbabwe by forces of the Ethiopian People's Revolutionary Democratic Front (EPRDF), led by Meles Zenawi.

In 1994, the economy stagnated, the government's heavy regulation of commerce discouraged agricultural production and food distribution, and famine threatened Ethiopia. International assistance saved many lives, however, and, in 1995, the government finally established a process for returning nationalized land to private control. This redistribution of land appeared to improve Ethiopia's agricultural fortunes: the country enjoyed good harvests in both 1996 and 1997.

In the mid-1990s, Ethiopia also witnessed significant political achievements: delegates to a new legislative body, the Council of People's Representatives, were elected and a new constitution giving special rights to several ethnic rights was also adopted. The name of the country was officially changed to the Federal Democratic Republic of Ethiopia in August 1995—the same month that Meles Zenawi was elected prime minister by the new legislature. However, the late 1990s were marked by ethnic strife and violent raids carried out by soldiers discharged at the end of Ethiopia's long civil war. In 1998, a border dispute with neighboring Eritrea threatened to end Ethiopia's peaceful recovery from years of warfare. The border conflict expanded in 1999, spreading into areas that were previously undisputed. It was not until June 2000 that a cease-fire agreement was reached between the two countries. In December 2000, a comprehensive peace accord was signed in Algiers.

Political turbulence marked the early years of the new millennium. In the spring of 2001, the ruling Ethiopian People's Revolutionary Democratic Front (EPRDF) coalition experienced a critical split within its Tigrayan People's Liberation Front (TPLF) faction. Twelve TPLF members opposing the pro-capitalist policies of the government were ousted from the party and held under house arrest. President Negasso Gidada, siding with the TPLF dissidents, was thrown out as party leader. In October 2001, the country's parliament elected Girma Wolde-Giorgis president, but the political infighting had left the EPRDF regime decidedly weakened.

Ethiopia's population is highly diverse. Most of its people speak a Semitic or Cushitic language. The Amhara, Tigreans, and Oromo make up more than three-fourths of the population, but there are more than forty different ethnic groups within Ethiopia.

Gabon

Official name: Gabonese Republic

Independence: 17 August 1960 (from France)

Area: 267,667 sq km

Form of government: republic; multiparty presidential regime (opposition parties legalized in 1990)

Capital: Libreville

International relations: ACCT, ACP, AfDB, BDEAC, CCC, CEEAC, CEMAC, ECA, FAO, FZ, G-24, G-77, IAEA, IBRD, ICAO, ICFTU, IDA, IDB, IFAD, IFC, IFRCS (associate), ILO, IMF, IMO, Inmarsat, Intelsat, Interpol, IOC, ITU, NAM, OAU, OIC, OPCW, UN, UNCTAD, UNESCO, UNIDO, UPU, WCL, WHO, WIPO, WMO, WToO, WTrO

Currency: Communaute Financiere Africaine franc (CFAF)

Income: us$6,300 (2000 est. of purchasing power parity)

Population: 1,221,175

Ethnic groups: Bantu tribes including four major tribal groupings (Fang, Eshira, Bapounou, Bateke), other Africans and Europeans 154,000, including 10,700 French and 11,000 persons of dual nationality

Religious groups: Christian 55%–75%, animist, Muslim less than 1%

Languages: French (official), Fang, Myene, Bateke, Bapounou/Eschira, Bandjabi

Literacy: 63.2% (age 15 and over can read and write; 1995 est.)

Exports: crude oil 75%, timber, manganese, uranium (1998)

Primary export partners: United States 47%, France 19%, China 8%, Japan 1.3% (1999)

Imports: machinery and equipment, foodstuffs, chemicals, petroleum products, construction materials

Primary import partners: France 64%, United States 4%, United Kingdom 2%, Netherlands 2% (1999)

Gabon's first European visitors were Portuguese traders who arrived in the fifteenth century. The coast became a center of the slave trade. Dutch, British, and French traders later came in the sixteenth century. France assumed the status of protector by signing treaties with Gabonese coastal chiefs in 1839 and 1841. In 1910, Gabon became one of the four territories of French Equatorial Africa, a federation that survived until 1959. The territories became independent in 1960 as the Central African Republic, Chad, Congo

(Brazzaville), and Gabon, which was led by Léon M'ba after independence. Upon his death in 1967, Albert (later known as Omar) Bongo took over as head of state. Reelected in 1973, 1979, and 1986, Bongo faced growing opposition inside Gabon as the 1990s began. The Bongo administration moved toward establishment of a multiparty system, but early attempts in 1990 were rejected by opposition parties that charged Bongo's regime with fraud. A constitution adopted in 1991 formalized the multiparty system, and, in the first elections under the new system in December 1993, Bongo received 51.5 percent of the presidential vote. Unrest soon broke out in reaction to these widely regarded fraudulent elections. This led to mediation and all opposition parties being brought into the government. In 1996, a new constitution was approved by voters adding a senate to the legislature.

Reelected as president in December 1998, Bongo in late January 1999 named Jean-Francois Ntoutome-Emane prime minister. The rest of Bongo's cabinet was dominated by ministers close to the president and included no members from opposition parties. Bongo's appointments came at a time of violent student protests and was followed shortly thereafter by widespread labor strikes triggered by the drop in world oil prices. The government's announcement in late 1999 that it would privatize the postal and telecommunications sectors set off further labor unrest. Despite widespread criticism, the ruling Gabonese Democratic Party won 84 of 120 seats up for grabs in December 2001 legislative elections.

Almost all Gabonese are of Bantu origin. Gabon has at least forty tribal groups, with separate languages and cultures; the largest group is the Fang. Other tribes include the Myene, Bandjabi, Eshira, Bapounou, Bateke/Obamba, and Okande.

Gambia

Official name: Republic of Gambia
Independence: 18 February 1965 (from United Kingdom)
Area: 11,300 sq km
Form of government: republic under multiparty democratic rule
Capital: Banjul
International relations: ACP, AfDB, C, CCC, ECA, ECOWAS, FAO, G-77, IBRD, ICAO, ICFTU, ICRM, IDA, IDB, IFAD, IFC, IFRCS, ILO, IMF, IMO, Intelsat (nonsignatory user), Interpol, IOC, ITU, NAM, OAU, OIC, OPCW, UN, UNCTAD, UNESCO, UNIDO, UNMEE, UPU, WCL, WFTU, WHO, WIPO, WMO, WToO, WTrO
Currency: dalasi (GMD)

Income: US$1,100 (2000 est. of purchasing power parity)
Population: 1,411,205 (July 2001 est.)
Ethnic groups: African 99% (Mandinka 42%, Fula 18%, Wolof 16%, Jola 10%, Serahuli 9%, other 4%), non-African 1%
Religious groups: Muslim 90%, Christian 9%, indigenous beliefs 1%
Languages: English (official), Mandinka, Wolof, Fula, other indigenous vernaculars
Literacy: 47.5% (age 15 and over can read and write; 2001 est.)
Exports: peanuts and peanut products, fish, cotton lint, palm kernels
Primary export partners: Benelux 59%, Japan 20%, United Kingdom 7%, Spain 2% (1999)
Imports: foodstuffs, manufactures, fuel, machinery and transport equipment
Primary import partners: China (including Hong Kong) 49%, United Kingdom 15%, Netherlands 11.6%, Brazil 10%, Senegal 10% (1997)

Gambia was once part of the Empire of Ghana and the Kingdom of Songhai. When the Portuguese visited in the fifteenth century, it was part of the Kingdom of Mali. By the sixteenth century, Portuguese slave traders and gold seekers had settled and had sold exclusive trade rights on the Gambia River to English merchants. During the late seventeenth century and throughout the eighteenth century, England and France struggled continuously for political and commercial supremacy in the regions of the Senegal and Gambia Rivers.

In 1807, slave trading was abolished throughout the British Empire, and the British tried unsuccessfully to end the slave traffic in Gambia. An 1889 agreement with France established the present boundaries, and Gambia became a British Crown colony. Gambia achieved independence on February 18, 1965, as a constitutional monarchy within the British Commonwealth. In 1970, Gambia became a republic. Several attempts were made to establish a post-independence union with Senegal. A contingent of Senegalese soldiers were stationed in Gambia, but the arrangement soured. Coupled with mounting economic problems, the confederation collapsed in 1989, although a new friendship treaty between the two countries was signed in 1991. Sir Dawda K. Jawara, who had led the country since independence in 1965, was overthrown by the military in July 1994. The leaders of the coup set up a provisional ruling council headed by Yayeh Jammeh. Pressured to restore democracy, Jammeh adopted a new constitution in August 1996 that was widely criticized for the restrictions imposed on opposition parties. Jammeh retired from the military and ran successfully for president in September 1996.

Criticism of the Jammeh government in 1999 was being led by Ousainou Darboe of the opposition United Democratic Party. Darboe charged that the Jammeh regime was not only dictatorial but also inefficient. In July 2000, Darboe and other members of his party were charged with murder and put on trial after a supporter of the ruling party was killed during campaigning in the eastern portion of the country. Gambia's relations with neighboring Senegal deteriorated during 2000. In October 2001, Jammeh won reelection as president, defeating Darboe, who had since been cleared of the murder charge.

Ghana

Official name: Republic of Ghana
Independence: 6 March 1957 (from United Kingdom)
Area: 238,540 sq km
Form of government: constitutional democracy
Capital: Accra
International relations: ABEDA, ACP, AfDB, C, CCC, ECA, ECOWAS, FAO, G-24, G-77, IAEA, IBRD, ICAO, ICC, ICFTU, ICRM, IDA, IFAD, IFC, IFRCS, ILO, IMF, IMO, Inmarsat, Intelsat, Interpol, IOC, IOM (observer), ISO, ITU, MINURSO, NAM, OAS (observer), OAU, OPCW, UN, UNCTAD, UNESCO, UNIDO, UNIFIL, UNIKOM, UNITAR, UNMEE, UNMIBH, UNMIK, UNMOP, UNMOT, UNTAET, UNU, UPU, WCL, WFTU, WHO, WIPO, WMO, WToO, WTrO
Currency: cedi (GHC)
Income: US$1,900 (2000 est. of purchasing power parity)
Population: 19,894,014
Ethnic groups: black African 99.8% (major tribes—Akan 44%, Moshi-Dagomba 16%, Ewe 13%, Ga 8%), European and other 0.2%
Religious groups: indigenous beliefs 38%, Muslim 30%, Christian 24%, other 8%
Languages: English (official), African languages (including Akan, Moshi-Dagomba, Ewe, and Ga)
Literacy: 64.5% (age 15 and over can read and write; 1995 est.)
Exports: gold, cocoa, timber, tuna, bauxite, aluminum, manganese ore, diamonds
Primary export partners: Togo, United Kingdom, Italy, Netherlands, Germany, United States, France (1998)
Imports: capital equipment, petroleum, foodstuffs
Primary import partners: United Kingdom, Nigeria, United States, Germany, Italy, Spain (1998)

The first contact between Europe and the Gold Coast dates to 1470 when a party of Portuguese arrived. For the next three centuries, the English, Danes, Dutch, Germans, and Portuguese controlled various parts of the coastal areas. In 1821, the British government took control of the British trading forts on the Gold Coast. In 1844, Fanti chiefs in the area signed an agreement with the British. Between 1826 and 1900, the British fought a series of campaigns against the Ashantis, whose kingdom was located inland. By 1902, the British had succeeded in colonizing the Ashanti region.

On March 6, 1957, the United Kingdom relinquished its control over the Colony of the Gold Coast and Ashanti, the Northern Territories Protectorate, and British Togoland. The Gold Coast and the former British Togoland merged to form what is now Ghana. Focusing on anti-imperialism and pan-Africanism, Ghana became a model for the whole continent. Kwame Nkrumah, which had led Ghana to independence, was idolized throughout the continent. However, in the years that followed, Nkrumah turned increasingly dictatorial. In 1966, he was overthrown and went into exile in nearby Guinea. When Jerry Rawlings, who had masterminded two successful coups in 1979 and 1981, became head of state in 1982, he promised to return the country to pluralism. In 1992, he was elected to the presidency in a multiparty election and won reelection in 1996. With an improved economic and political climate, the appointment of Kofi Annan to head the United Nations in 1997, and President Clinton's historic 1998 visit, Ghana's prominence among African nations has been restored.

President Rawlings announced early in 1999 that he would not run for reelection in 2000. He personally selected Vice President John Evans Atta Mills as his heir apparent, resulting in a split within the ruling National Democratic Congress and the formation of a new party, the National Reform Movement. Mills' leading opponent at the polls in 2000 was John Kufuor, leader of the New Patriotic Party. In the December 2000 presidential elections, neither Mills nor Kufuor received enough votes to score an outright victory, but, in a later runoff race, Kufuor won handily, with 57 percent of the vote. Kufuor assumed power in January 2001 and immediately turned his attention to the country's struggling economy.

Most Ghanaians descend from migrating tribes that probably came down the Volta River valley in the thirteenth century. Ethnically, Ghana is divided into small groups speaking more than fifty languages and dialects. Among the more important linguistic groups are the Akans, which include the Fantis along the coast and the Ashantis in the forest region north of the coast; the Guans, on the plains of the Volta River; the Ga and Ewe-speaking peoples of the south and southeast; and the Moshi-Dagomba-speaking tribes of the northern and upper regions.

Guinea

Official name: Republic of Guinea

Independence: 2 October 1958 (from France)

Area: 245,857 sq km

Form of government: republic

Capital: Conakry

International relations: ACCT, ACP, AfDB, CCC, ECA, ECOWAS, FAO, G-77, IBRD, ICAO, ICFTU, ICRM, IDA, IDB, IFAD, IFC, IFRCS, ILO, IMF, IMO, Intelsat, Interpol, IOC, IOM, ISO (correspondent), ITU, MINURSO, NAM, OAU, OIC, OPCW, UN, UNAMSIL, UNCTAD, UNESCO, UNIDO, UPU, WCL, WFTU, WHO, WIPO, WMO, WToO, WTrO

Currency: Guinean franc (GNF)

Income: us$1,300 (2000 est. of purchasing power parity)

Population: 7,613,870 (July 2001 est.)

Ethnic groups: Peuhl 40%, Malinke 30%, Soussou 20%, smaller ethnic groups 10%

Religious groups: Muslim 85%, Christian 8%, indigenous beliefs 7%

Languages: French (official), each ethnic group has its own language

Literacy: 35.9% (age 15 and over can read and write; 1995 est.)

Exports: bauxite, alumina, gold, diamonds, coffee, fish, agricultural products

Primary export partners: United States, Benelux, Ukraine, Ireland (1999)

Imports: petroleum products, metals, machinery, transport equipment, textiles, grain and other foodstuffs

Primary import partners: France, Belgium, United States, Côte d'Ivoire (1999)

The empires of Ghana, Mali, and Songhai spanned the period from about the tenth to the fifteenth centuries. French military penetration into the area began in the mid-nineteenth century. By signing treaties with the French in the 1880s, Guinea's Malinke leader, Samory Toure, secured a free hand to expand eastward. In 1890, he allied himself with the Toucouleur Empire and Kingdom of Sikasso and tried to expel the French from the area. However, he was defeated in 1898, and France gained control of Guinea and the Ivory Coast (now Côte d'Ivoire).

Guinea became an independent republic in 1958 and voted against entering the French community. Se'kou Touré was the first president until his death in 1984. Shortly after his death, the interim government was ousted in a military coup led by Colonel Lansana Conté, who became president and leader of the Military Committee for National Rectification. He took ambitious steps to democratize the nation and dismantle the existing socialist state. In 1993, Conté was elected president in the country's first multiparty elections. A military mutiny in 1996 took some 60 lives before the president was able to negotiate a truce with his troops. In an attempt to restore confidence in his ability to improve the financial situation of the country, Conté appointed an economist, Sidya Touré, to the office of prime minister that same year.

In mid-December 1998, Conté was elected to his second term as president. Shortly thereafter, he named Lamine Sadimé as the country's new prime minister. Border tensions escalated between Guinea and the neighboring countries of Liberia and Sierra Leone. In March 1999, Guinean forces attacked Sierra Leone rebels holding large sections of the Kambia district, prompting a retaliatory attack by the rebels on two Guinean border towns. Guinea responded to the border attacks by launching a counterattack into Sierra Leone. Liberian President Charles Taylor, meanwhile, accused Guinea of harboring Liberian rebels. These continuing conflicts eventually created a refugee problem in Guinea. Efforts by President Conté's party to modify the constitution to allow a president to serve more than two terms further exacerbated political tensions within the country.

Guinea consists of four main ethnic groups—Peuls (Foulah or Foulani), who inhabit the mountainous Fouta Djallon; Malinkes (or Mandingos), in the savannah regions; Soussous in the coastal areas; and Forestal tribes in the forest regions.

Guinea-Bissau

Official name: Republic of Guinea-Bissau

Independence: 24 September 1973 (unilaterally declared by Guinea-Bissau); 10 September 1974 (recognized by Portugal)

Area: 36,120 sq km

Form of government: republic, multiparty since mid-1991

Capital: Bissau

International relations: ACCT (associate), ACP, AfDB, ECA, ECOWAS, FAO, FZ, G-77, IBRD, ICAO, ICFTU, ICRM, IDA, IDB, IFAD, IFC, IFRCS, ILO, IMF, IMO, Intelsat (nonsignatory user), Interpol, IOC, IOM, ITU, NAM, OAU, OIC, OPCW, UN, UNCTAD, UNESCO, UNIDO, UPU, WADB (regional), WAEMU, WFTU, WHO, WIPO, WMO, WToO, WTrO

Currency: Communaute Financiere Africaine franc (CFAF); previously the Guinea-Bissau peso (GWP) was used

Income: us$850 (2000 est. of purchasing power parity)

Population: 1,315,822 (July 2001 est.)

Ethnic groups: African 99% (Balanta 30%, Fula 20%, Manjaca 14%, Mandinga 13%, Papel 7%), European and mulatto less than 1%

Religious groups: indigenous beliefs 50%, Muslim 45%, Christian 5%

Languages: Portuguese (official), Crioulo, African languages

Literacy: 53.9% (age 15 and over can read and write; 1997 est.)

Exports: cashew nuts 70%, shrimp, peanuts, palm kernels, sawn lumber (1996)

Primary export partners: India 59%, Singapore 12%, Italy 10% (1998)

Imports: foodstuffs, machinery and transport equipment, petroleum products (1996)

Primary import partners: Portugal 26%, France 8%, Senegal 8%, Netherlands 7% (1998)

The rivers of Guinea and the islands of Cape Verde were one of the first areas in Africa explored by the Portuguese in the fifteenth century. Portugal claimed Portuguese Guinea in 1446. In 1630, a "captaincy-general" of Portuguese Guinea was established to administer the territory. With the assistance of local tribes, the Portuguese entered the slave trade, exporting large numbers of Africans to the New World through Cape Verde. The slave trade declined in the nineteenth century, and Bissau, originally founded as a fort in 1765, became the major commercial center.

In 1956, the African Party for the Independence of Guinea and Cape Verde (PAIGC) was organized by Amilcar Cabral and Raphael Barbosa. Despite the presence of more than 30,000 Portuguese troops, the PAIGC exercised influence over much of the country; the Portuguese were increasingly confined to their garrisons and larger towns. The PAIGC National Assembly declared the independence of Guinea-Bissau on December 24, 1973, the same year that PAIGC leader Amilcar Cabral was assassinated by the Portuguese secret police. Portugal granted *de jure* independence on September 19, 1974, when the United States recognized the new nation. Luís de Almeida Cabral, Amilcar's brother, became president of Guinea-Bissau and Cape Verde. Cape Verde later broke away from Guinea-Bissau and its leader, João Bernardo Vieira, who had overthrown Cabral in November 1980.

Vieira, who survived a coup attempt in November 1985, was elected to five-year terms as president in 1984, 1989, and 1994. However, his administration was criticized for entrenched corruption. During a five-month civil war in 1998, rebel forces seized most of the country and part of Bissau. In November 1998, Vieira agreed to a peace accord that called for new elections and the disarmament of the presidential guard. After the presidential guard refused to disarm though, a breakaway army faction drove Vieira from office in May 1999. He first sought refuge in the Portuguese Embassy but was later allowed to leave the country.

After Vieira left office, he was replaced by interim President Malam Bacai Sanhá, president of the national assembly and leader of an anti-Vieira faction of the African Party for the Independence of Guinea-Bissau and Cape Verde (PAIGC). In a runoff presidential election in January 2000, however, Sanhá was defeated by Kumba Ialá of the Party for Social Renewal (PRS). In early 2001, the coalition between the PRS and the Guinea-Bissau Resistance-Bah Fatah Movement collapsed. In the wake of the coalition's breakup, the government's credibility eroded, and calls mounted for the resignation of Ialá and his cabinet. Ialá also came under fire for his treatment of the Ahmadiyya Islamic group, the leaders of which he deported in 2001. Public dissatisfaction with Ialá's rule mounted as 2001 neared an end.

The population of Guinea-Bissau comprises several diverse tribal groups, each with its own language, customs, and social organization. The Fula and Mandinka tribes in the north and northeast of the country are mostly Muslim. Other important tribal groups are the Balanta and Papel, living in the southern coastal regions, and the Manjaco and Mancanha, occupying the central and northern coastal areas.

Kenya

Official name: Republic of Kenya

Independence: 12 December 1963 (from United Kingdom)

Area: 582,650 sq km

Form of government: republic

Capital: Nairobi

International relations: ACP, AfDB, C, CCC, EADB, ECA, FAO, G-77, IAEA, IBRD, ICAO, ICFTU, ICRM, IDA, IFAD, IFC, IFRCS, IGAD, ILO, IMF, IMO, Inmarsat, Intelsat, Interpol, IOC, IOM, ISO, ITU, MINURSO, MONUC, NAM, OAU, OPCW, UN, UNAMSIL, UNCTAD, UNESCO, UNIDO, UNIKOM, UNMEE, UNMIBH, UNMIK, UNMOP, UNTAET, UNU, UPU, WHO, WIPO, WMO, WToO, WTrO

Currency: Kenyan shilling (KES)

Income: US$1,500 (2000 est. of purchasing power parity)

Population: 30,765,916

Ethnic groups: Kikuyu 22%, Luhya 14%, Luo 13%, Kalenjin 12%, Kamba 11%, Kisii 6%, Meru 6%, other African 15%, non-African (Asian, European, and Arab) 1%

Religious groups: Protestant 38%, Roman Catholic 28%, indigenous beliefs 26%, Muslim 7%, other 1%

Languages: English (official), Kiswahili (official),
　numerous indigenous languages
Literacy: 78.1% (age 15 and over can read and write;
　1995 est.)
Exports: tea, coffee, horticultural products,
　petroleum products, fish, cement
Primary export partners: Uganda 18%, United
　Kingdom 15%, Tanzania 12%, Pakistan 8% (1999)
Imports: machinery and transportation equipment,
　petroleum products, iron and steel
Primary import partners: United Kingdom 12%, UAE
　8%, Japan 8%, United States 7% (1999)

The Cushitic-speaking people, who occupied the area that is now Kenya around 1000 BC, were known to have maintained contact with Arab traders during the first century AD. Arab and Persian settlements were founded along the coast as early as the eighth century AD. By then, Bantu and Nilotic peoples also had moved into the area. The Arabs were followed by the Portuguese in 1498, by Islamic control under the Imam of Oman in the 1600s, and by British influence in the nineteenth century. In 1885, European powers first partitioned East Africa into spheres of influence. In 1895, the British government established the East African Protectorate.

From October 1952 to December 1959, Kenya was under a state of emergency, arising from the Mau Mau rebellion against British colonial rule. The first direct elections for Africans to the legislative council took place in 1957, and then Kenya became fully independent on December 12, 1963. Jomo Kenyatta, a member of the predominant Kikuyu tribe and head of the Kenya African National Union, became Kenya's first president. He adopted a moderate, pro-Western policy and pursued capitalism internally, allowing Kenya to achieve a higher level of economic prosperity than its neighbors. Kenyatta died in 1978 and was succeeded by

Masai warriors wearing traditional costumes at a Kenyan wedding in the Amboseli Game Reserve.

Daniel arap Moi, who, in his first few years as president, pursued a populist course. However, in 1982, the constitution was modified to make the country a one-party state. Mounting opposition to his repressive rule through the 1980s put increasing pressure on Moi, who, in December 1991, agreed to legalize opposition political parties. Moi was reelected in 1992, although he continued to be the target of criticism from opposition parties upset by cumbersome restrictions on their activities. In December 1997, Moi was again returned to office, leading to widespread violence and continual accusations of corruption, ethnic favoritism, and human rights abuses.

Criticism of Moi's leadership increased in 1999. His appointment of Francis Masakhalia as finance minister and his reinstatement of George Saitoti as vice president particularly incensed Moi's critics. Masakhalia was eventually replaced in August 1999 by former Energy Minister Chris Okemo. Concern over high-level corruption within the Kenyan government was the dominant theme of 2000 as well. In January 2001, Moi joined with the leaders of Tanzania and Uganda to launch a new East African Economic Community. In March 2001, Richard Leakey resigned as head of the Kenyan Civil Service, giving rise to fears that it might signal an end to efforts to root out government corruption, which had been led by Leakey. Even more alarming to Moi's opponents was his engineering of a merger between his ruling Kenya African National Union and the National Development Party, the country's second largest opposition party. The opposition fired back in June 2001 by forming a new party, the National Party of Kenya.

Lesotho

Official name: Kingdom of Lesotho
Independence: 4 October 1966 (from United
　Kingdom)
Area: 30,355 sq km
Form of government: parliamentary constitutional
　monarchy
Capital: Maseru
International relations: ACP, AfDB, C, CCC, ECA,
　FAO, G-77, IBRD, ICAO, ICRM, IDA, IFAD, IFC,
　IFRCS, ILO, IMF, Intelsat (nonsignatory user),
　Interpol, IOC, ISO (subscriber), ITU, NAM, OAU,
　OPCW, SACU, SADC, UN, UNCTAD, UNESCO,
　UNHCR, UNIDO, UPU, WFTU, WHO, WIPO,
　WMO, WToO, WTrO
Currency: loti (LSL); South African rand (ZAR)
Income: US$2,400 (2000 est. of purchasing power
　parity)
Population: 2,177,062

Ethnic groups: Sotho 99.7%, Europeans, Asians, and other 0.3%,

Religious groups: Christian 80%, indigenous beliefs 20%

Languages: Sesotho (southern Sotho), English (official), Zulu, Xhosa

Literacy: 83% (age 15 and over can read and write; 1999 est.)

Exports: manufactures 75% (clothing, footwear, road vehicles), wool and mohair, food and live animals (1998)

Primary export partners: South African Customs Union 65%, North America 34% (1998)

Imports: food; building materials, vehicles, machinery, medicines, petroleum products (1995)

Primary import partners: South African Customs Union 90%, Asia 7% (1998)

Until the end of the sixteenth century, Basutoland, now Lesotho, was sparsely populated by bushmen (Qhuaique). Between the sixteenth and nineteenth centuries, refugees from surrounding areas gradually formed the Basotho ethnic group. In 1818, Moshoeshoe I consolidated various Basotho groupings and became king. During his reign from 1823 to 1870, a series of wars with South Africa resulted in the loss of extensive lands, now known as the "Lost Territory." Moshoeshoe appealed to Queen Victoria for assistance, and, in 1868, the country was placed under British protection.

In 1955, the Basutoland Council asked that it be empowered to legislate on internal affairs and, in 1959, a new constitution gave Basutoland its first elected legislature. On October 4, 1966, the new Kingdom of Lesotho attained full independence. Three years later, Leabua Jonathan became the head of state and embarked on repressing internal opposition. Years later, when he appeared to be losing the presidential elections, he seized power in order to retain his leadership. In 1986, Jonathan was overthrown by the military. On an interim basis, executive and legislative powers were vested in King Moshoeshoe II, although most powers were exercised by a military council. Moshoeshoe II was exiled in March 1990 and replaced by his son, who was enthroned as Letsie III. After Letsie came under increasing criticism from leaders of neighboring states, he abdicated in 1995 and returned the crown to his father, Moshoeshoe II. The following year, Moshoeshoe was killed in an auto accident, and Letsie III returned to the throne.

Violent anti-government protests prompted South Africa and Botswana to send troops into Lesotho in September 1998. Although those troops were withdrawn by late spring 1999, the impact of their intervention continued to be felt long after their departure. The intervention left the Lesotho Congress for Democracy government of Prime Minister Bathuel Pakalitha Mosisili in power, but it set up the Interim Political Authority (IPA), made up of representatives from the country's 12 major political parties. This set up a conflict between the LCD government and the IPA over what form the country's future electoral system should take. This debate continued until February 2001 when all parties endorsed a plan drafted by the Independent Election Commission for the holding of elections, the first of which was scheduled for 2002.

Liberia

Official name: Republic of Liberia

Independence: 26 July 1847

Area: 111,370 sq km

Form of government: republic

Capital: Monrovia

International relations: ACP, AfDB, CCC, ECA, ECOWAS, FAO, G-77, IAEA, IBRD, ICAO, ICFTU, ICRM, IDA, IFAD, IFC, IFRCS, ILO, IMF, IMO, Inmarsat, Intelsat (nonsignatory user), Interpol, IOC, IOM, ITU, NAM, OAU, OPCW, UN, UNCTAD, UNESCO, UNIDO, UPU, WCL, WFTU, WHO, WIPO, WMO

Currency: Liberian dollar (LRD)

Income: US$1,100 (2000 est. of purchasing power parity)

Population: 3,225,837 (July 2001 est.)

Ethnic groups: indigenous African tribes 95% (including Kpelle, Bassa, Gio, Kru, Grebo, Mano, Krahn, Gola, Gbandi, Loma, Kissi, Vai, and Bella), Americo-Liberians 2.5% (descendants of immigrants from the United States who had been slaves), Congo People 2.5% (descendants of immigrants from the Caribbean who had been slaves)

Religious groups: indigenous beliefs 40%, Christian 40%, Muslim 20%

Languages: English 20% (official), some 20 ethnic group languages, of which a few can be written and are used in correspondence

Literacy: 38.3% (age 15 and over can read and write; 1995 est.); note: these figures are increasing because of the improving school system

Exports: diamonds, iron ore, rubber, timber, coffee, cocoa

Primary export partners: Belgium 53%, Switzerland 9%, United States 6%, France 4% (1999)

Imports: fuels, chemicals, machinery, transportation equipment, manufactured goods; rice and other foodstuffs

Primary import partners: South Korea 30%, Italy 24%, Japan 15%, Germany 9% (1999)

It is believed that the forebears of many present-day Liberians migrated into the area from the north and east between the twelfth and seventeenth centuries. Portuguese explorers visited Liberia's coast in 1461, and, during the next 300 years, European merchants and coastal Africans engaged in trade.

The history of modern Liberia dates from 1816, when the American Colonization Society, a private organization, was given a charter by the United States Congress to send freed slaves to the west coast of Africa. The United States government, under President James Monroe, provided funds and assisted in negotiations with native chiefs for the ceding of land for this purpose. The first settlers landed at the site of Monrovia in 1822. In 1838, the settlers united to form the Commonwealth of Liberia, under a governor appointed by the American Colonization Society.

In 1847, Liberia became Africa's first independent republic. The republic's first 100 years have been described as a "century of survival" due to attempts by neighboring colonial powers, particularly France and Britain, to encroach on Liberia. Independence gave power to the black elite of American origin and technically excluded the indigenous population, creating social tension. In 1980, Sargent Samuel Doe and his Council of Popular Redemption came to power in a bloody coup. Doe leaned on the Soviet Union and established himself as a dictator. He was killed, however, during an insurrection led by the National Patriotic Front, a rebel group led by Charles Taylor. Taylor's group pitted itself against the Liberian army, a monitoring group from the Economic Community of West African States (ECOWAS), and the United Liberation Movement of Liberia for Democracy (ULIMO), a group made up of former Doe allies. Several attempts at ending the civil war were unsuccessful, and the strife continued well into the 1990s. Finally, in 1997, a program to disarm warring factions was declared a success. In July of that year, Taylor was elected president by a landslide. He has worked to rebuild the nation's economy, shattered by years of civil war.

Taylor's government came under fire in early 1999 from a number of its neighbors, who charged that Liberia was supporting Revolutionary United Front (RUF) rebels in Sierra Leone. Taylor's denials failed to satisfy opposition members of the country's National Assembly or Britain and the United States, both of which threatened to suspend aid shipments. Although the country's civil war officially ended in January 1999, Liberia continued to experience extensive political instability. The unrest exploded in fighting in the northern part of the country, where government troops battled against rebels. Relations with Guinea deteriorated nearly to the point of war after Taylor charged

Guinea with supporting the northern rebels. Similarly strained were relations with western governments. The European Union in June 2000 suspended aid to Liberia, and, in October, the United States imposed diplomatic sanctions on Taylor and his associates. Foreign approbation grew in March 2001 when the UN Security Council voted to impose sanctions on Liberia unless it halted its support for RUF rebels in Sierra Leone. The military was kept busy throughout 2001 battling rebels in the northern region.

Libya

Official name: Great Socialist People's Libyan Arab Jamahiriya

Independence: 24 December 1951 (from Italy)

Area: 1,759,540 sq km

Form of government: Jamahiriya (a state of the masses) in theory, governed by the populace through local councils; in fact, a military dictatorship

Capital: Tripoli

International relations: ABEDA, AfDB, AFESD, AL, AMF, AMU, CAEU, CCC, ECA, FAO, G-77, IAEA, IBRD, ICAO, ICRM, IDA, IDB, IFAD, IFC, IFRCS, ILO, IMF, IMO, Inmarsat, Intelsat, Interpol, IOC, ISO, ITU, MONUC, NAM, OAPEC, OAU, OIC, OPEC, UN, UNCTAD, UNESCO, UNIDO, UPU, WFTU, WHO, WIPO, WMO, WToO

Currency: Libyan dinar (LYD)

Income: US$8,900 (2000 est. of purchasing power parity)

Population: 5,240,599

Ethnic groups: Berber and Arab 97%, Greeks, Maltese, Italians, Egyptians, Pakistanis, Turks, Indians, Tunisians

Religious groups: Sunni Muslim 97%

Languages: Arabic, Italian, English, all are widely understood in the major cities

Literacy: 76.2% (age 15 and over can read and write; 1995 est.)

Exports: crude oil, refined petroleum products

Primary export partners: Italy 33%, Germany 24%, Spain 10%, France 5%, Turkey 4%, Tunisia 4% (1999)

Imports: machinery, transport equipment, food, manufactured goods

Primary import partners: Italy 24%, Germany 12%, Tunisia 9%, United Kingdom 7%, France 6%, South Korea 5% (1999)

In the seventh century AD, Arabs conquered the area that is now Libya. In the following centuries, most of the inhabitants adopted Islam and the Arabic language and culture. The Ottoman Turks then conquered the country in the sixteenth century. Libya remained part of their empire—although, at times, virtually autonomous—until Italy invaded in 1911 and, after years of resistance, incorporated Libya as its colony.

King Idris I, Emir of Cyrenaica, led a Libyan resistance to Italian occupation between the two world wars. Under the terms of the 1947 peace treaty with the Allies, Italy relinquished all claims to Libya. On November 21, 1949, the United Nations General Assembly passed a resolution stating that Libya should become independent before January 1, 1952. Libya declared its independence on December 24, 1951.

In a military coup of 1969, King Idris was overthrown by Muammar al-Qaddafi, who nationalized all the petroleum resources and embarked on a program of support for international terrorism against the Western countries. Some of Qaddafi's activities have also created friction with neighboring countries, and, in 1986, the United States bombed Tripoli and Benghazi. Five years later, during the Persian Gulf War, Libya opposed Iraq's seizure of Kuwait as well as the use of force against Iraq by the United States and its allies. In 1992, the United Nations imposed sanctions against Libya for its refusal to extradite two suspects in the 1988 bombing of Pan Am Flight 103 over Scotland. Those sanctions were lifted in 1999 when Libya turned the suspects over to the UN for trial by a Scottish court. Despite five unsuccessful coup attempts and considerable international animosity, Qaddafi remains firmly in office as leader of Libya.

Qaddafi in the late 1990s and early years of the new millennium seemed to moderate his harsh attitude toward the west and particularly toward the United States. Most significantly, it appears that Qaddafi's Libyan regime has distanced itself from terrorism in the years since the imposition of UN sanctions in 1992. Nowhere was this change in policy more evident than in Qaddafi's response to the September 11, 2001, terrorist attacks on the United States. The Libyan leader called the attacks "horrifying" and urged Muslim charitable agencies to provide aid to the United States. The Libyan regime also has reportedly shared intelligence with U.S. officials about Libyan Islamist militants with ties to al-Qaeda.

Madagascar

Official name: Republic of Madagascar

Independence: 26 June 1960 (from France)

Area: 587,040 sq km

Form of government: republic

Capital: Antananarivo

International relations: ACCT, ACP, AfDB, CCC, ECA, FAO, G-77, IAEA, IBRD, ICAO, ICC, ICFTU, ICRM, IDA, IFAD, IFC, IFRCS, ILO, IMF, IMO, InOC, Intelsat, Interpol, IOC, IOM (observer), ISO (correspondent), ITU, NAM, OAU, OPCW, UN, UNCTAD, UNESCO, UNHCR, UNIDO, UPU, WCL, WFTU, WHO, WIPO, WMO, WToO, WTrO

Currency: Malagasy franc (MGF)

Income: US$800 (2000 est. of purchasing power parity)

Population: 15,982,563 (July 2001 est.)

Ethnic groups: Malayo-Indonesian (Merina and related Betsileo), Cotiers (mixed African, Malayo-Indonesian, and Arab ancestry—Betsimisaraka, Tsimihety, Antaisaka, Sakalava), French, Indian, Creole, Comoran

Religious groups: indigenous beliefs 52%, Christian 41%, Muslim 7%

Languages: French (official), Malagasy (official)

Literacy: 80% (age 15 and over can read and write; 1990 est.)

Exports: coffee, vanilla, shellfish, sugar; cotton cloth, chromite, petroleum products

Primary export partners: France 41%, United States 19%, Germany 13%, United Kingdom 8%, Japan 6% (1999)

Imports: intermediate manufactures, capital goods, petroleum, consumer goods, food

Primary import partners: France 34%, Hong Kong 6%, China 6%, Japan 5%, Singapore 4% (1999)

Located east of the African mainland in the Indian Ocean, Madagascar is home to people who arrived from Africa and Asia during the first five centuries AD. Three major kingdoms ruled the island—Betsimisaraka, Merina, and Sakalava. In the seventh century AD, Arabs established trading posts in the coastal areas of what is now Madagascar. Portuguese sighted the island in the sixteenth century and, in the late seventeenth century, the French established trading posts along the east coast.

In the 1790s, the Merina rulers succeeded in establishing hegemony over the major part of the island including the coast. The Merina ruler and the British governor of Mauritius concluded a treaty abolishing the slave trade, which had been important in Madagascar's economy, and, in return, the island received British military assistance. British influence remained strong for several decades. The British accepted the imposition of a French protectorate over Madagascar in 1885. France established control by military force in 1895, and the Merina monarchy was abolished. The Malagasy Republic was proclaimed on October 14, 1958, as an autonomous state within the French Community. A period of provisional government ended with the adoption of a constitution in 1959 and full independence in 1960.

Madagascar pursued a moderate policy after independence, and collaboration with France continued until 1972 when a military coup installed a socialist

Vendors selling their wares in Madagascar.

government headed by General Gabriel Ramanantsoa. Ramanantsoa, who aligned his government with the East Bloc, was ousted and replaced by Lieutenant Commander Didier Ratsiraka in 1975. Late that year, the country was renamed the Democratic Republic of Madagascar. Through the 1980s and into the early 1990s, Ratsiraka's government faced growing opposition, and, in August 1991, the government promised to make democratic reforms. A year later, a new constitution was approved by popular vote. Ratsiraka was defeated by Albert Zafy in a presidential runoff election in 1993. Zafy was impeached in 1996 for failure to reach agreement with the International Monetary Fund on the Malagasy franc's exchange rate, stepped down in October 1996, and ran unsuccessfully against Ratsiraka for the presidency in December 1996.

Vanguard of the Malagasy Revolution, the country's ruling party, in 1999 faced a new challenger in the form of the Gó Alliance, a coalition of opposition parties. All parties to the new opposition coalition were united in their dissatisfaction with the policies of President Ratsiraka but remained divided on other key issues, including the economy. In the December 2001 presidential elections, Ratsiraka trailed opponent Marc Ravalomanana, mayor of the capital city, but since neither candidate had a majority, the outcome of the election remained in question. The upshot was a political struggle between Ratsiraka and Ravalomanana that split the country. In May 2002, a court declared Ravalomanana winner of the election, but Ratsiraka rejected the court ruling and continued to press his claim to power.

Madagascar's population is predominantly of Asian and African origin. The largest groups are the Betsimisaraka (one million), the Tsimihety (500,000), and the Sakalava (500,000).

Malawi

Official name: Republic of Malawi
Independence: 6 July 1964 (from United Kingdom)
Area: 118,480 sq km
Form of government: multiparty democracy
Capital: Lilongwe
International relations: ACP, AfDB, C, CCC, ECA, FAO, G-77, IBRD, ICAO, ICFTU, ICRM, IDA, IFAD, IFC, IFRCS, ILO, IMF, IMO, Intelsat, Interpol, IOC, ISO (correspondent), ITU, NAM,

OAU, OPCW, SADC, UN, UNCTAD, UNESCO, UNIDO, UNMIK, UPU, WFTU, WHO, WIPO, WMO, WToO, WTrO

Currency: Malawian kwacha (MWK)

Income: US$900 (2000 est. of purchasing power parity)

Population: 10,548,250

Ethnic groups: Chewa, Nyanja, Tumbuko, Yao, Lomwe, Sena, Tonga, Ngoni, Ngonde, Asian, European

Religious groups: Protestant 55%, Roman Catholic 20%, Muslim 20%, indigenous beliefs

Languages: English (official), Chichewa (official), other languages important regionally

Literacy: 58% (age 15 and over can read and write; 1999 est.)

Exports: tobacco, tea, sugar, cotton, coffee, peanuts, wood products

Primary export partners: South Africa 16%, Germany 16%, United States 15%, Netherlands 7%, Japan (1999)

Imports: food, petroleum products, semimanufactures, consumer goods, transportation equipment

Primary import partners: South Africa 43%, Zimbabwe 14%, United Kingdom 5%, Germany 5%, Zambia, Japan, United States (1999)

Hominid remains and stone implements dating back more than 1 million years have been identified in Malawi. Early humans are believed to have inhabited the area surrounding Lake Malawi 50,000 to 60,000 years ago.

Malawi derives its name from the Maravi, a Bantu people who came from the southern Congo about 600 years ago. By the sixteenth century, the two divisions of the tribe had established a kingdom stretching from north of today's Nkhotakota to the Zambezi River in the south and from Lake Malawi in the east to the Luangwa River in Zambia in the west.

The Portuguese first reached the area in the sixteenth century. David Livingston reached the shore of Lake Malawi in 1859. By 1878, a number of traders, mostly from Scotland, formed the African Lakes Company to supply goods and services to the missionaries. In 1891, the British established the Nyasaland Protectorate. Nyasaland joined with Northern and Southern Rhodesia in 1953 to form the Federation of Rhodesia and Nyasaland.

Throughout the 1950s, pressures were exerted within Nyasaland for independence. In July 1958, Dr. H. Kamazu Banda returned to the country after a long stay in the United States (where he had obtained his medical degree at Meharry Medical College in 1937), the United Kingdom, and Ghana. He assumed leadership of the

Men mending their fishing nets in Malawi.

Nyasaland African Congress, which later became the Malawi Congress Party (MCP). In 1959, Banda was sent to Gwele Prison for his political activities but was released in 1960.

On April 15, 1961, the MCP won an overwhelming victory in elections for a new legislative council. In a second constitutional conference in London in November of 1962, the British government agreed to give Nyasaland self-governing status the following year. Dr. Banda became prime minister on February 1, 1963, although the British still controlled Malawi's financial security and judicial systems. The Federation of Rhodesia and Nyasaland was dissolved on December 31, 1963, and Malawi became fully independent on July 6, 1964. Two years later, Malawi adopted a new constitution and became a republic with Dr. Banda as its first president. In 1994, in the country's first multiparty elections, Bakili Muluzi, leader of the United Democratic Front and a former cabinet minister, defeated Banda. Muluzi freed political prisoners and closed three prisons. In 1995, Banda and a top aide went on trial for the 1983 murders of four government officials: both were acquitted in December 1995.

Twice postponed, presidential elections were finally held on June 15, 1999. President Muluzi managed to hold on to the presidency, besting his nearest opponent, Gwanda Chakuamba, by the narrowest of margins. In October 2000, the president dismissed his entire cabinet after a report implicated cabinet ministers in widespread corruption. The government continued to root out corruption in 2001, arresting a total of six government officials in February on charges of embezzlement from the Ministry of Education.

The Chewas constitute 90 percent of the population of the central region; the Nyanja tribe predominates in the south and the Tumbuka in the north. In addition, significant numbers of the Tongas live in the north; Ngonis—an offshoot of the Zulus who came from South Africa in the early 1800s—live in the lower northern and lower central regions; and the Yao, who are mostly Muslim, live along the southeastern border with Mozambique.

Mali

Official name: Republic of Mali
Independence: 22 September 1960 (from France)
Area: 1.24 million sq km
Form of government: republic
Capital: Bamako
International relations: ACCT, ACP, AfDB, CCC, ECA, ECOWAS, FAO, FZ, G-77, IAEA, IBRD, ICAO, ICFTU, ICRM, IDA, IDB, IFAD, IFC, IFRCS, ILO, IMF, Intelsat, Interpol, IOC, IOM, ISO (subscriber), ITU, MIPONUH, MONUC, NAM, OAU, OIC, OPCW, UN, UN Security Council (temporary), UNAMSIL, UNCTAD, UNESCO, UNIDO, UPU, WADB, WAEMU, WFTU, WHO, WIPO, WMO, WToO, WTrO
Currency: Communaute Financiere Africaine franc (CFAF)
Income: US$850 (2000 est. of purchasing power parity)
Population: 11,008,518 (July 2001 est.)
Ethnic groups: Mande 50% (Bambara, Malinke, Soninke), Peul 17%, Voltaic 12%, Songhai 6%, Tuareg and Moor 10%, other 5%
Religious groups: Muslim 90%, indigenous beliefs 9%, Christian 1%
Languages: French (official), Bambara 80%, numerous African languages
Literacy: 31% (age 15 and over can read and write; 1995 est.)
Exports: cotton 50%, gold, livestock (1999 est.)
Primary export partners: Italy 18%, Thailand 15%, Germany 7%, Portugal 4% (1999)
Imports: machinery and equipment, construction materials, petroleum, foodstuffs, textiles
Primary import partners: Côte d'Ivoire 19%, France 19%, Senegal 4%, Benelux 3% (1999)

Mali is the cultural heir to succession of ancient African empires—Ghana, Malinke, and Songhai—that occupied the West African savanna. The Ghana empire, dominated by the Soninke people and centered in the area along the Malian-Mauritanian frontier, was a powerful trading state from about 700 to 1075 AD. The Malinke kingdom of Mali, from which the republic takes its name, had its origins on the upper Niger River in the eleventh century. Expanding rapidly in the thirteenth century under the leadership of Soundiata Keita, it reached its height about 1325, when it conquered Timbuktu and Gao. The Songhai empire expanded its power from its center in Gao during the period of 1465 to 1530. At its peak under Askia Mohammad I, it encompassed the Hausa states as far as Kano (in present-day Nigeria) and much of the territory that had belonged to the Mali Empire in the west. It was destroyed by a Moroccan invasion in 1591.

French military penetration of the area began around 1880. A French civilian governor of Soudan (the French name for the area) was appointed in 1893, but resistance to French control was not abrogated until 1898 when the Malinke warrior, Samory Toure, was defeated after seven years of war. In January 1959, Soudan joined Senegal to form the Mali Federation, which became fully independent within the French Community on June 20, 1960. The federation collapsed on August 20, 1960, when Senegal seceded. On September 22, Soudan proclaimed itself the Republic of Mali and withdrew from the French Community.

The first head of state—Modibo Keita—followed a socialist orientation and gradually increased his authoritarian leadership. In 1968, the Military Committee of National Liberation coup overthrew Keita's government and set up a ruling junta led by Lieutenant Moussa Traoré. Although the Traoré government did little to advance the country's economy, Traoré was returned to office in 1979 and 1985. However, a military coup in March 1991 deposed Traoré. In January 1992, a new constitution was adopted, and Alpha Oumar Kounaré was elected president in multiparty elections in April 1992. He was reelected to office in May 1997.

Former President Traoré, his wife, and brother-in-law were sentenced to death in January 1999 after being convicted of economic crimes. However, in September of that year, President Konaré commuted those death sentences to life imprisonment. The government also launched a drive in Septemer to root out government inefficiency and corruption. On May 7, 2001, Mali and Namibia became the first two OAU member states to join the Pan-African Parliament, a key component of

This clay fort was built in the time of King Mansa Musa (ruled 1307–1332), whom some consider the most significant of the Mali kings.

the new organization scheduled to replace the OAU. President Konaré canceled a December 2001 referendum that would have given him immunity from prosecution after widespread criticism of this proposed reform.

Mali's population consists of diverse sub-Saharan ethnic groups, sharing similar historic, cultural, and religious traditions. Exceptions are the Tuaregs and Moors, desert nomads, who are related to the North African Berbers.

Mauritania

Official name: Islamic Republic of Mauritania
Independence: 28 November 1960 (from France)
Area: 1,030,700 sq km
Form of government: republic
Capital: Nouakchott
International relations: ABEDA, ACCT (associate), ACP, AfDB, AFESD, AL, AMF, AMU, CAEU, CCC, ECA, ECOWAS, FAO, G-77, IBRD, ICAO, ICFTU, ICRM, IDA, IDB, IFAD, IFC, IFRCS, IHO (pending member), ILO, IMF, IMO, Intelsat, Interpol, IOC, ITU, NAM, OAU, OIC, OPCW, UN, UNCTAD, UNESCO, UNIDO, UPU, WCL, WHO, WIPO, WMO, WToO, WTrO
Currency: ouguiya (MRO)
Income: us$2,000 (2000 est. of purchasing power parity)
Population: 2,747,312 (July 2001 est.)
Ethnic groups: mixed Maur/black 40%, Maur 30%, black 30%
Religious groups: Muslim 100%
Languages: Hasaniya Arabic (official), Pular, Soninke, Wolof (official), French
Literacy: 46.7% (age 15 and over can read and write; 1998 est.)
Exports: iron ore, fish and fish products, gold
Primary export partners: Japan 18%, France 17%, Italy 16%, Spain 11% (1998)
Imports: machinery and equipment, petroleum products, capital goods, foodstuffs, consumer goods
Primary import partners: France 27%, Benelux 9%, Germany 7%, Spain 7% (1998)

Archaeological evidence suggests that Berber and Negroid Mauritanians lived beside one another before the spread of the desert drove them southward. Migration of these people increased during the third and fourth centuries AD, when Berber groups arrived seeking pasture land for their herds and safety from political unrest and war in the north. The Berbers established a loose confederation, called the Sanhadja, and trading towns to facilitate the trade of gold, ivory, and slaves.

In the tenth century, conquests by warriors of the Soudanese Kingdom of Ghana broke up the Berber confederation. In the eleventh century, the conquest of the Western Sahara regions by a Berber tribe decimated the Ghanaian kingdom and firmly established Islam throughout Mauritania. However, these people were defeated by Arab invaders in the sixteenth century.

French military penetration of Mauritania began early in the twentieth century. However, the area did not come under French control until about 1934. Until independence, the French governed the country largely by relying on the authority of the tribal chiefs, some of whom, such as the Emirs of Trarza and Adrar, had considerable authority. Under French occupation, slavery was legally abolished.

Mauritania became a French colony in 1920. The Islamic Republic of Mauritania was proclaimed in November 1958. Mauritania became independent on November 28, 1960, and withdrew from the French Community in 1966.

Mokhtar Ould Daddah, leader of the Mauritian People's Party was the first head of state, but a series of coups took place: the first, in 1978, replaced Daddah with Col. Moustabpha Ould Mohammed Salek, who was then replaced by Prime Minister Mohammed Khouma Ould Haidalla. In 1984, another coup, this one led by Haidalla deputy Maawiya Ould Sid'Ahmed Taya, unseated Haidalla. Under increasing pressure to democratize, Taya in 1991 adopted a new constitution creating a multiparty state. In a disputed January 1992 election, Taya was chosen executive president. Even though important U.S. aid has been cut off due to a poor human rights record and allegations of slave trading, Taya was returned to office in 1996.

President Taya's ruling party and its allies easily won control of all local councils in two-stage local elections held in early 1999, largely because the balloting was boycotted by major opposition parties. In March of that year, prominent opposition leader Ahmed Ould Daddah, runner-up to Taya in the 1992 election, was charged with inciting intolerance and seeking to disrupt public order. In 2001 legislative elections, the ruling Democratic and Social Republican Party won 64 of 81 seats in the National Assembly.

Moors, heterogeneous groups of Arab-Berber people who speak Hassaniya dialects, make up an estimated three-quarters of the population and are traditionally nomadic pastoralists. The country's black population—the Toucouleur, Soninke, Bambara, and Wolof—are mainly cultivators and are concentrated along the Senegal River.

Mauritius

Official name: Republic of Mauritius
Independence: 12 March 1968 (from United Kingdom)
Area: 1,860 sq km
Form of government: parliamentary democracy
Capital: Port Louis
International relations: ACCT, ACP, AfDB, C, CCC, ECA, FAO, G-77, IAEA, IBRD, ICAO, ICFTU, ICRM, IDA, IFAD, IFC, IFRCS, ILO, IMF, IMO, Inmarsat, InOC, Intelsat, Interpol, IOC, ISO,

Nomadic family of Mauritania.

ITU, NAM, OAU, OPCW, SADC, UN, UN Security Council (temporary), UNCTAD, UNESCO, UNIDO, UPU, WCL, WFTU, WHO, WIPO, WMO, WToO, WTrO

Currency: Mauritian rupee (MUR)

Income: US$10,400 (2000 est. of purchasing power parity)

Population: 1,189,825 (July 2001 est.)

Ethnic groups: Indo-Mauritian 68%, Creole 27%, Sino-Mauritian 3%, Franco-Mauritian 2%

Religious groups: Hindu 52%, Christian 28.3% (Roman Catholic 26%, Protestant 2.3%), Muslim 16.6%, other 3.1%

Languages: English (official), Creole, French, Hindi, Urdu, Hakka, Bojpoori

Literacy: 82.9% (age 15 and over can read and write; 1995 est.)

Exports: clothing and textiles, sugar, cut flowers, molasses

Primary export partners: United Kingdom 32%, France 19%, United States 15%, Germany 6%, Italy 4% (1999 est.)

Imports: manufactured goods, capital equipment, foodstuffs, petroleum products, chemicals (1996)

Primary import partners: France 14%, South Africa 11%, India 8%, United Kingdom 5% (1999 est.)

Portuguese sailors first visited Mauritius in the early sixteenth century, although the island was known to Arabs and Malays much earlier. Dutch sailors, who named the island in honor of Prince Maurice of Nassau, established a small colony in 1638, but abandoned it in 1710. The French claimed Mauritius in 1715, renaming it Ile de France. In 1810, Mauritius was captured by the British, whose possession of the island was confirmed four years later by the Treaty of Paris. After slavery was abolished in 1835, indentured laborers from India brought an additional cultural influence to the island. Mauritius achieved independence on March 12, 1968. Sir Seewoosagur Ramgoolam, head of the Mauritius Labor Party (MLP), led the country for the first 14 years of independence. The opposition Mauritian Military Movement (MMM), under the leadership of Aneerood Jugnauth, came to power in 1982. Pushed from power in an internal MMM struggle, Jugnauth formed a new opposition party, the Mauritian Socialist Movement (MSM). The MSM joined with the MLP in 1983 to win a parliamentary majority. The MSM-MLP coalition was again victorious in both 1987 and 1991. In 1992, the country became a republic, and Cassam Uteem was elected president by the national assembly. In December 1995, Jugnauth was replaced as prime minister by Navin Ramgoolam, son of Seewoosagur Ramgoolam.

The island was rocked in early 1999 by three days of rioting by members of the Creole community, triggered by the death of a popular reggae singer in police custody. An opposition alliance of the Mauritian Militant Movement (MMM) and the Mauritian Socialist Movement (MSM) won a sweeping victory in September 2000 legislative elections, capturing all but eight of the 62 legislative seats. The opposition's victory brought MSM leader Sir Anerood Jugnauth into the prime minister's office. Under the terms of the alliance between the MSM and MMM, Paul Berenger, leader of the MMM, was to take over the final two years as prime minister after Jugnauth had served the first three. Despite rumors of mounting tensions between Jugnauth and Berenger, their ruling coalition remained intact throughout 2001.

Twenty-seven percent of Mauritians are of mixed European and African descent, tracing their origins to the plantation owners and slaves who were the first to exploit the island's potential for growing sugar. Descendants of the Indian immigrants constitute 68 percent of the population and are the principal laborers in the sugar industry.

Mayotte (Mahoré)
Official name: Territorial Collectivity of Mayotte
Independence: none (territorial collectivity of France)
Area: 374 sq km
Form of government: NA
Capital: Mamoutzou
International relations: FZ
Currency: French franc (FRF); euro (EUR)
Income: US$600 (1998 est. of purchasing power parity)
Population: 163,366 (July 2001 est.)
Ethnic groups: NA
Religious groups: Muslim 97%, Christian (mostly Roman Catholic)
Languages: Mahorian (a Swahili dialect), French (official language) spoken by 35% of the population
Literacy: NA
Exports: ylang-ylang (perfume essence), vanilla, copra, coconuts, coffee, cinnamon
Primary export partners: France 80%, Comoros 15%, Reunion
Imports: food, machinery and equipment, transportation equipment, metals, chemicals

Primary import partners: France 66%, Africa 14%, Southeast Asia 11% (1997)

Part of the Comoros archipelago, Mayotte shares its history with the Comoros Federal Islamic Republic. When Comoros declared independence in 1975, Mayotte voted to remain an overseas territory of France. Although Comoros has since claimed Mayotte, the French have promised the islanders that they may remain French citizens for as long as they wish. Both the United Nations and the Organization of African Unity, however, have recognized Mayotte as part of the Comoros.

Morocco
Official name: Kingdom of Morocco
Independence: 2 March 1956 (from France)
Area: 446,550 sq km
Form of government: constitutional monarchy
Capital: Rabat
International relations: ABEDA, ACCT (associate), AfDB, AFESD, AL, AMF, AMU, CCC, EBRD, ECA, FAO, G-77, IAEA, IBRD, ICAO, ICC, ICFTU, ICRM, IDA, IDB, IFAD, IFC, IFRCS, IHO, ILO, IMF, IMO, Intelsat, Interpol, IOC, IOM,

Classic Arab architecture serves as an entranceway to Fez, Morocco.

ISO, ITU, MONUC, NAM, OAS (observer), OIC, OPCW, OSCE (partner), UN, UNCTAD, UNESCO, UNHCR, UNIDO, UPU, WCL, WHO, WIPO, WMO, WToO, WTrO

Currency: Moroccan dirham (MAD)

Income: US$3,500 (2000 est. of purchasing power parity)

Population: 30,645,305 (July 2001 est.)

Ethnic groups: Arab-Berber 99.1%, other 0.7%, Jewish 0.2%

Religious groups: Muslim 98.7%, Christian 1.1%, Jewish 0.2%

Languages: Arabic (official), Berber dialects, French often the language of business, government, and diplomacy

Literacy: 43.7% (age 15 and over can read and write; 1995 est.)

Exports: phosphates and fertilizers, food and beverages, minerals

Primary export partners: France 35%, Spain 9%, United Kingdom 8%, Germany 7%, United States 5% (1999)

Imports: semiprocessed goods, machinery and equipment, food and beverages, consumer goods, fuel

Primary import partners: France 32%, Spain 12%, Italy 7%, Germany 6%, United Kingdom 6% (1999)

Arab forces began occupying Morocco in the seventh century AD, bringing with them Arab civilization and Islam. Morocco's location and resources led to early competition among Europeans in Africa, beginning with successful Portuguese efforts to control the Atlantic coast in the fifteenth century. France showed a strong interest in Morocco as early as 1830. The Treaty of Fez (1912) made Morocco a protectorate of France. By the same treaty, Spain assumed the role of protecting power over the northern and southern (Saharan) zones. The Kingdom of Morocco recovered its political independence from France on March 2, 1956, and by agreements with Spain in 1956 and 1958.

Morocco's claim to sovereignty over the Western Sahara, also known as Spanish Sahara, is based largely on the historical argument of traditional loyalty of the Saharan tribal leaders to the Moroccan sultan as spiritual leader and ruler. The International Court of Justice, to which the issue was referred, delivered its opinion in 1975 that while historical ties exist between the inhabitants of the Western Sahara and Morocco, they are insufficient to establish Moroccan sovereignty.

Morocco, however, exerted pressure on Spain in 1974 and 1975 to relinquish the Western Sahara. When the Spanish left the territory in 1976, they ceded the northern two-thirds to Morocco and the southern one-third to Mauritania. However, the disposition of the territory was disputed by the Polisario Front, a nationalist guerrilla organization. Polisario declared the territory an independent nation. All claimants skirmished over the territory for years, until a cease-fire was declared in 1991. The dispute, however, continued to simmer late in the 1990s. In 1998, the United Nations scheduled a referendum for self-determination for Western Sahara, which is currently occupied by UN peacekeeping forces.

King Hassan II ruled Morocco from 1961 until his death in July 1999. Although he offered strong support for the Arab cause during the 1967 war with Israel, Hassan was identified by Arab extremists as soft on Israel, and several attempts were made on his life. In the late 1990s, Islamic extremists forced Hassan to create a new parliamentary body. Upon his death, Hassan's son, Mohamed VI, assumed the throne.

One of the first indications of the shape Mohamed VI's rule would take came in 1999, when he began to strip power from Interior Minister Driss Basri, his father's closest adviser. By November 1999, the new king had dismissed Basri from office altogether. Mohamed VI's proposals in 2000 for a new family code met strong opposition from the country's Islamist movements. They were particularly outraged by plans to outlaw polygamy and give women greater equality with men. The progress of political liberalization slowed significantly during 2001, signaled by a crackdown on the press and the king's cancellation of a scheduled meeting with officials of the International Federation for Human Rights.

Mozambique

Official name: Republic of Mozambique

Independence: 25 June 1975 (from Portugal)

Area: 801,590 sq km

Form of government: republic

Capital: Maputo

International relations: ACP, AfDB, C, CCC, ECA, FAO, G-77, IBRD, ICAO, ICFTU, ICRM, IDA, IDB, IFAD, IFC, IFRCS, IHO, ILO, IMF, IMO, Inmarsat, Intelsat, Interpol, IOC, IOM (observer), ISO (correspondent), ITU, NAM, OAU, OIC, OPCW, SADC, UN, UNCTAD, UNESCO, UNHCR, UNIDO, UNTAET, UPU, WFTU, WHO, WIPO, WMO, WToO, WTrO

Currency: metical (MZM)

Income: US$1,000 (2000 est. of purchasing power parity)

Population: 19,371,057

Ethnic groups: indigenous tribal groups 99.66% (Shangaan, Chokwe, Manyika, Sena, Makua, and others), Europeans 0.06%, Euro-Africans 0.2%, Indians 0.08%

Religious groups: indigenous beliefs 50%, Christian 30%, Muslim 20%

Languages: Portuguese (official), indigenous dialects

Literacy: 42.3% (age 15 and over can read and write; 1998 est.)

Exports: prawns 40%, cashews, cotton, sugar, citrus, timber; bulk electricity (2000)

Primary export partners: EU 27%, South Africa 26%, Zimbabwe 15%, India 12%, United States 5%, Japan 4% (1999 est.)

Imports: machinery and equipment, mineral products, chemicals, metals, foodstuffs, textiles (2000)

Primary import partners: South Africa 44%, EU 16%, United States 6.5%, Japan 6.5%, Pakistan 3%, India 3% (1999 est.)

Mozambique's first inhabitants were Bushmanoid hunters and gatherers, ancestors of the Khoisani peoples. During the first four centuries AD, waves of Bantu-speaking peoples migrated from the north through the Zambezi River Valley and then gradually into the plateau and coastal areas. When Portuguese explorers reached Mozambique in 1498, Arab trading settlements had existed along the coast for several centuries. Later, traders and prospectors penetrated the hinterland seeking gold and slaves.

After World War II, while many European nations were granting independence to their colonies, Portugal clung to the concept that Mozambique and other Portuguese possessions were "overseas provinces." In 1962, several Mozambican anti-Portuguese political groups formed the Front for Liberation of Mozambique (FRELIMO) that, in September 1964, initiated an armed campaign against Portuguese colonial rule. After ten years of sporadic warfare and major political changes in Portugal, Mozambique became independent on June 25, 1975.

Samora Machel led Frelimo to independence in 1975 and immediately faced civil war with RENAMO (Mozambique National Resistance). More than 600,000 were killed in the civil war; farms, roads, and railways were destroyed; and half of the population was dislocated. After Samora was killed in an air crash, Joaquím Chissano became head of state. A cease-fire was reached with RENAMO in 1992, and the country's first multiparty elections were held in October 1994. Chissano was elected president, and FRELIMO, his party, won 129 of 250 assembly seats. A United Nations peacekeeping force, which had been deployed in December 1992, was withdrawn from Mozambique in early 1995. Privatization of industries has led to massive foreign investment by international corporations and the World Bank.

President Chissano won reelection in presidential elections held in late 1999. The results, however, were disputed by opposition leader Afonso Dhlakama, head of RENAMO. In 2000, RENAMO struck back at Chissano by charging that the president was responsible for the painfully slow arrival of foreign relief after massive flooding caused by Cyclone Eline earlier in the year. Widespread political unrest and sporadic fighting followed. Late in the year, Chissano and Dhlakama met in an effort to resolve the differences between the government and RENAMO. Floods struck Mozambique again in early 2001. President Chissano announced in mid-2001 that he would not run for reelection in 2004.

The ten major ethnic groups living in Mozambique are divided into subgroups with diverse languages, dialects, cultures, and history; the largest are the Majua and Tsonga.

Namibia

Official name: Republic of Namibia

Independence: 21 March 1990 (from South African mandate)

Area: 825,418 sq km

Form of government: republic

Capital: Windhoek

International relations: AfDB, C, CCC, ECA, FAO, G-77, IAEA, IBRD, ICAO, ICRM, IFAD, IFC, IFRCS, ILO, IMF, IMO, Intelsat, Interpol, IOC, IOM (observer), ISO (correspondent), ITU, NAM, OAU, OPCW, SACU, SADC, UN, UNCTAD, UNESCO, UNHCR, UNIDO, UNMEE, UNTAET, UPU, WCL, WHO, WIPO, WMO, WToO, WTrO

Currency: Namibian dollar (NAD); South African rand (ZAR)

Income: us$4,300 (2000 est. of purchasing power parity)

Population: 1,797,677

Ethnic groups: black 87.5%, white 6%, mixed 6.5%

Religious groups: Christian 80% to 90% (Lutheran 50% at least), indigenous beliefs 10% to 20%

Languages: English 7% (official), Afrikaans common language of most of the population and about 60% of the white population, German 32%, indigenous languages: Oshivambo, Herero, Nama

Literacy: 38% (age 15 and over can read and write; 1960 est.)

Exports: diamonds, copper, gold, zinc, lead, uranium; cattle, processed fish, karakul skins

Primary export partners: United Kingdom 43%, South Africa 26%, Spain 14%, France 8%, Japan (1998 est.)

Imports: foodstuffs; petroleum products and fuel, machinery and equipment, chemicals

Primary import partners: South Africa 81%, United States 4%, Germany 2% (1997 est.)

Namibian children.

In 1878, the United Kingdom annexed Walvis Bay on behalf of Cape Colony, and the area was incorporated into the Cape of Good Hope in 1884. In 1883, a German trader, Adolf Luderitz, claimed the remainder of the coastal region after negotiations with a local chief. German administration ended during World War I, when the territory was occupied by South African forces in 1915.

On December 17, 1920, South Africa undertook the administration of South West Africa under the terms of Article 22 of the Covenant of the League of Nations and a mandate agreement confirmed by the League Council. The mandate agreement gave South Africa full power of administration and legislation over the territory as an integral part of South Africa. During the 1960s, as other African nations gained independence, pressure mounted on South Africa to do so in South West Africa.

In 1966, the United Nations General Assembly revoked South Africa's mandate. Also in 1966, the South West Africa People's Organization (SWAPO) began guerrilla attacks on Namibia, infiltrating the territory from bases in Zambia. In a 1971 advisory opinion, the International Court of Justice upheld United Nation

authority over Namibia, determining that the South African presence in Namibia was illegal and that South Africa, therefore, was obligated to withdraw its administration from Namibia immediately. In 1977, the United Nations approved Security Council Resolution 435 that called for the holding of elections in Namibia under U.N. supervision and the cessation of hostile acts by all parties. South Africa agreed to cooperate in achieving implementation of Resolution 435. Nevertheless, in December 1978, in defiance of the U.N. proposal, it unilaterally held elections in Namibia that were boycotted by SWAPO and other political parties.

Intense discussions between the concerned parties continued during the 1978–1988 period. In May 1988, a U.S. mediation team brought negotiators from Angola, Cuba, and South Africa and observers from the Soviet Union together in London. On April 1, the Republic of South Africa agreed to withdraw its troops. Implementation of Resolution 435 officially began on April 1, 1989. The elections held November 7–11, 1989, were certified as free and fair by the special representative, with SWAPO taking 57 percent of the vote; the Democratic Turnhalle Alliance, the principal opposition party, received 29 percent of the vote. By February 9, 1990, the constituent assembly had drafted and adopted a constitution. March 21 of that same year was set as the date for independence. SWAPO's Sam Nujoma won elections, and he became the first head of state in 1990. For the next four years, until February 1994, South Africa continued to administer a small Namibian enclave containing the nation's major seaport, Walvis Bay. In 1994 elections, SWAPO won 53 of 72 seats in the National Assembly. However, dissatisfaction with SWAPO and Nujoma has increased. The international community has criticized Nujoma's plans to run for a third term as president (which the constitution does not permit) as well as his government's lavish spending habits. Meanwhile, Namibia's strong labor unions have prevented significant cuts in the large state bureaucracy.

In December 1999 presidential elections, Nujoma won reelection to a third term in a landslide, capturing more than 75 percent of the votes cast. His nearest rival in the election was Ben Ulenga, whose party, the Congress of Democrats, took over in early 2000 as the main opposition party. Nujoma's decision to allow Angolan armed forces to operate in the northern part of Namibia ensnared the country in the Angolan civil war. The resulting destabilization of northern Namibia continued through most of 2001.

Namibia is one of the least populated countries in Africa. Namibia's indigenous Africans are of diverse linguistic and ethnic origins. The principal groups are the Ovambo, Kavango, Herero/Himba, Damara, mixed race ("Colored" and Rehoboth Baster), white (Afrikaner, German, and Portuguese), Nama, Caprivian (Lozi), Bushman, and Tswana. The minority white population is primarily of South African, British, and German descent. Approximately 60 percent of the white population speaks Afrikaans (a variation of Dutch), 30 percent German, and ten percent English.

Niger
Official name: Republic of Niger
Independence: 3 August 1958 (from France)
Area: 1.267 million sq km
Form of government: republic
Capital: Niamey
International relations: ACCT, ACP, AfDB, CCC, ECA, ECOWAS, Entente, FAO, FZ, G-77, IAEA, IBRD, ICAO, ICFTU, ICRM, IDA, IDB, IFAD, IFC, IFRCS, ILO, IMF, Intelsat, Interpol, IOC, ITU, MIPONUH, MONUC, NAM, OAU, OIC, OPCW, UN, UNCTAD, UNESCO, UNIDO, UPU, WADB, WAEMU, WCL, WFTU, WHO, WIPO, WMO, WToO, WTrO
Currency: Communaute Financiere Africaine franc (CFAF)

Income: us$1,000 (2000 est. of purchasing power parity)
Population: 10,355,156 (July 2001 est.)
Ethnic groups: Hausa 56%, Djerma 22%, Fula 8.5%, Tuareg 8%, Beri Beri (Kanouri) 4.3%, Arab, Toubou, and Gourmantche 1.2%, about 1,200 French expatriates
Religious groups: Muslim 80%, remainder indigenous beliefs and Christians
Languages: French (official), Hausa, Djerma
Literacy: 13.6% (age 15 and over can read and write; 1995 est.)
Exports: uranium ore 65%, livestock products, cowpeas, onions (1998 est.)
Primary export partners: France 45%, Nigeria 27%, United Kingdom 11% (1999)
Imports: consumer goods, primary materials, machinery, vehicles and parts, petroleum, cereals
Primary import partners: France 22%, Côte d'Ivoire 15%, Nigeria 8%, United States 3% (1999)

Considerable evidence indicates that, about 600,000 years ago, humans inhabited what has since become the desolate Sahara of northern Niger. Niger was an important economic crossroads, and the empires of Songhei, Mali, Gao, Kanem, and Bornu, as well as a number of Hausa states, claimed control over portions of the area.

During recent centuries, the nomadic Taureg formed large confederations, pushed southward and, siding with various Hausa states, clashed with the Fulani empire of Sokoto, which had gained control of much of the Hausa territory in the late eighteenth century. In the nineteenth century, the first European explorers reached the area searching for the mouth of the Niger River.

Although French efforts at colonization began before 1900, dissident ethnic groups, especially the desert Taureg, were not defeated until 1922. On December 4, 1958, after the establishment of the Fifth French Republic, Niger became an autonomous state within the French Community. Following full independence on August 3, 1960, however, membership was allowed to lapse. Hamani Diori was overthrown in a military coup and replaced by Col. Seyni Kountché as president. Thirteen years later, Ali Saibou succeeded him. More recently, Ibrahim Barré Mainassara in July 1996 was confirmed in elections as president, a post he had assumed in January of 1996 after ousting Mahamane Ousmane.

President Mainassara was assassinated outside Niamey in early April 1999, after which the military assumed control of the country. Major Daouda Malam Wanké, commander of the presidential guard suspected of gunning down Mainassara, was named military ruler,

Woven millet being transported via camelback in Niamey, Niger.

and he promised an early return to civilian rule. In presidential elections later that year, retired Army Colonel Tandja Mamadou was elected the new civilian president. In early 2000, Mamadou installed a 24-member government and called for emergency action to revitalize the country's economy. The country experienced extensive civil unrest throughout 2001, much of it traceable to the continuing food crisis and the government's decision to reduce grants for university students.

The two largest ethnic groups in Niger are the Hausa, who also constitute the major ethnic group in northern Nigeria, and the Djerma-Songhai. Both groups are farmers who live in the arable, southern tier. The rest of the population consists of nomadic or semi-nomadic livestock-raising peoples, which include the Fulani, Tuareg, Kanouri, and Toubou.

Nigeria

Official name: Federal Republic of Nigeria

Independence: 1 October 1960 (from United Kingdom)

Area: 923,768 sq km

Form of government: republic transitioning from military to civilian rule

Capital: Abuja; note: on 12 December 1991, the capital was officially transferred from Lagos to Abuja; most federal government offices have now made the move to Abuja

International relations: ACP, AfDB, C, CCC, ECA, ECOWAS, FAO, G-15, G-19, G-24, G-77, IAEA, IBRD, ICAO, ICC, ICFTU, ICRM, IDA, IFAD, IFC, IFRCS, IHO, ILO, IMF, IMO, Inmarsat, Intelsat, Interpol, IOC, ISO, ITU, MINURSO, MONUC, NAM, OAU, OIC, OPCW, OPEC, PCA, UN, UNCTAD, UNESCO, UNHCR, UNIDO, UNIKOM, UNITAR, UNMEE, UNMIBH, UNMIK, UNMOP, UNMOT, UNTAET, UNU, UPU, WFTU, WHO, WIPO, WMO, WToO, WTrO

Currency: naira (NGN)

Income: us$950 (2000 est. of purchasing power parity)

Population: 126,635,626

Ethnic groups: Nigeria, which is Africa's most populous country, is composed of more than 250 ethnic groups; the following are the most populous and politically influential: Hausa and Fulani 29%, Yoruba 21%, Igbo (Ibo) 18%, Ijaw 10%, Kanuri 4%, Ibibio 3.5%, Tiv 2.5%

Religious groups: Muslim 50%, Christian 40%, indigenous beliefs 10%

Languages: English (official), Hausa, Yoruba, Igbo (Ibo), Fulani

Literacy: 57.1% (age 15 and over can read and write; 1995 est.)

Exports: petroleum and petroleum products 95%, cocoa, rubber

Primary export partners: United States 36%, India 9%, Spain 8%, Brazil 6%, France 6%, (1999)

Imports: machinery, chemicals, transport equipment, manufactured goods, food and live animals

Primary import partners: United Kingdom 11%, Germany 10%, United States 9%, France 8%, China 6% (1999)

Evidence shows that, more than 2,000 years ago, the Nok people, who lived in what is now the Plateau state, worked iron and produced sophisticated terra cotta sculpture. In the centuries that followed, the Hausa kingdom and the Bornu empire near Lake Chad prospered as important terminals of north-south trade between North African Berbers and forest people who exchanged slaves, ivory, and kola nuts for salt, glass beads, coral, cloth, weapons, brass rods, and cowrie shells used as currency. In the southwest, the Uoruba kingdom of Oyo, which was founded about 1400 and reached its height between the seventeenth and nineteenth centuries, attained a high level of political organization and extended as far as modern Togo. In the south central part of present-day Nigeria, as early as the fifteenth century, the kingdom of Benin had developed an efficient army, an elaborate ceremonial court, and artisans whose works in ivory, wood, bronze, and brass are prized throughout the world today.

Between the seventeenth and nineteenth centuries, European traders established coastal ports for the increasing traffic in slaves destined for the Americas. In 1855, British claims to a sphere of influence in that area received international recognition, and, in the following year, the Royal Niger Company was chartered. In 1900, the company's territory came under the control of the British government. In 1914, the area was formally united as the "Colony and Protectorate of Nigeria." Nigeria was granted full independence on October 1, 1960, as a federation of three regions.

Since independence, Nigeria has faced numerous coups. The Ibos tried to secede, and tension between various ethnic groups increased while the country began a rapid economic development based on oil production. Yakubu Gowon, who had managed to stay in power, was overthrown in 1976 by Mohammed Murtala, followed by Gen. Olusegun Obasanjo. A return to civilian rule came in 1979 under Shehu Shagari; however the military returned in 1984 under Mohammed Buhari and then again under Maj. Gen. Ibrahim Babangida. Defense Minister Sani Abacha ascended to power on November 17, 1993: his government was internationally denounced for widespread human rights abuses including numerous executions. Under increasing domestic and international pressure, Abacha promised to implement a new constitution (drafted by a constitutional commission in 1995) following presidential elections in October 1998. However, Abacha died of a heart attack in June 1998. His successor, Gen. Abdulsalam Abubakar, met with several opposition and foreign diplomats, promised to respect the election timetable, and released many political prisoners. Following riots due to the death of famed political prisoner Moshood Abiola, Abubakar announced a new transition program that called for the military's withdrawal in May 1999.

In the country's first democratic elections in years, held in late May 1999, Olusegun Obasanjo, leader of the People's Democratic Party, was elected president. As his first order of business, Obasanjo focused on rooting out widespread government corruption. To help hasten Nigeria's transition to democracy, Obasanjo in 2000 continued his assault on government corruption and announced a major reform of the country's military. Ethnic and religious violence was widespread from 2000 throughout 2001. In April 2001, Obasanjo replaced the leaders of all of the branches of Nigeria's armed forces

The most populous country in Africa, Nigeria accounts for one-quarter of sub-Saharan Africa's people. The dominant ethnic group in the northern two-thirds of the country is the Hausa-Fulani, most of whom are Muslims. Other major ethnic groups of the north are the Nupe, Tiv, and Kanuri. The Yoruba people are predominant in the southwest. About half of the Yorubas are Christian and half are Muslim. The predominately Catholic Ibos are the largest ethnic group in the southeast, with the Efik, Ibibio, and Ijaw comprising a substantial segment of the population in that area as well.

Reúnion

Official name: Department of Reúnion

Independence: none (overseas department of France)

Area: 2,512 sq km

Form of government: NA

Capital: Saint-Denis

International relations: FZ, InOC, WFTU

Currency: French franc (FRF); euro (EUR)

Income: us$4,800 (1998 est. of purchasing power parity)

Population: 732,570 (July 2001 est.)

Ethnic groups: French, African, Malagasy, Chinese, Pakistani, Indian

Religious groups: Roman Catholic 86%, Hindu, Muslim, Buddhist (1995)

Languages: French (official), Creole widely used

Literacy: 79% (age 15 and over can read and write; 1982 est.)

Exports: sugar 63%, rum and molasses 4%, perfume essences 2%, lobster 3%, (1993)

Primary export partners: France 74%, Japan 6%, Comoros 4% (1994)

Imports: manufactured goods, food, beverages, tobacco, machinery and transportation equipment, raw materials, and petroleum products

Primary import partners: France 64%, Bahrain 3%, Germany 3%, Italy 3% (1994)

The island of Reúnion, located in the Indian Ocean, remained uninhabited until 1654, when the French East India Company established bases and brought in slaves from Africa and Madagascar. France governed the island as a colony until 1946, when it was granted department status. In 1974, France changed Reúnion's status to that of administrative region. Reúnion sends five directly elected representatives to the French National Assembly and three indirectly elected representatives to the Senate. Although groups have occasionally called for the island's independence, the proposals have generally received little support from Réunion citizens who are well aware of the economic advantages gained through territorial ties to France.

The population of Reúnion is of mixed African, French, Indian, and Chinese origin.

Rwanda

Official name: Rwandese Republic

Independence: 1 July 1962 (from Belgium-administered UN trusteeship)

Area: 26,338 sq km

Form of government: republic; presidential, multiparty system

Capital: Kigali

International relations: ACCT, ACP, AfDB, CCC, CEEAC, CEPGL, ECA, FAO, G-77, IBRD, ICAO, ICFTU, ICRM, IDA, IFAD, IFC, IFRCS, ILO, IMF, Intelsat, Interpol, IOC, IOM (observer), ISO (correspondent), ITU, NAM, OAU, OPCW, UN, UNCTAD, UNESCO, UNIDO, UPU, WCL, WHO, WIPO, WMO, WToO, WTrO

Currency: Rwandan franc (RWF)

Income: us$900 (2000 est. of purchasing power parity)

Population: 7,312,756

Ethnic groups: Hutu 84%, Tutsi 15%, Twa (Pygmoid) 1%

Religious groups: Roman Catholic 52.7%, Protestant 24%, Adventist 10.4%, Muslim 1.9%, indigenous beliefs and other 6.5%, none 4.5% (1996)

Languages: Kinyarwanda (official) universal Bantu vernacular, French (official), English (official), Kiswahili (Swahili) used in commercial centers

Literacy: 48% (age 15 and over can read and write; 1995 est.)

Exports: coffee, tea, hides, tin ore

Primary export partners: Germany, Belgium, Pakistan, Italy, Kenya

Imports: foodstuffs, machinery and equipment, steel, petroleum products, cement and construction material

Primary import partners: Kenya, Tanzania, United States, Benelux, France, India

Hutus farmed the area that is now Rwanda until the fifteenth century when Tutsi herders settled in the area. In 1899, the court of Mwami submitted to a German protectorate with resistance. Belgian troops from the Congo occupied Rwanda in 1916, and, after World War I, the League of Nations mandated Rwanda and its southern neighbor, Burundi, to Belgium as the Territory of Ruanda-Urundi. Following World War II, Ruanda-Urundi became a United Nations trust territory with Belgium as the administering authority. The Party of the Hutu Emancipation Movement (PARMEHUTU) won an overwhelming victory in a U.N. supervised referendum.

The PARMEHUTU government, formed as a result of the September 1961 election, was granted internal autonomy by Belgium on January 1, 1962. A United Nations General Assembly resolution terminated the Belgian trusteeship and granted full independence to Rwanda (and Burundi) effective July 1, 1962. Gregiore Kayibanda, leader of the PARMEHUTU Party, became Rwanda's first elected president.

While ethnic clashes continued with neighboring Burundi, Gen. Juvenal Habyarimana, who had been a military head of state, returned to power in the presidential elections of 1978 and 1983 (having been the only candidate in both). In 1994, shortly after ending peace talks with the Tutsi-backed Rwandan Patriotic Front (RPF), President Habyarimana and Burundian President Cyprien Ntaryamira were killed together when their plane was shot down near Kigali. Rwanda exploded in ethnic violence, and the Hutu-dominated Rwandan army went on a rampage, reportedly killing between 500,000 and 1 million Rwandans, mostly Tutsis and Hutus sympathetic to the Tutsi cause. Forces of the

RPF and the Rwandan army soon were in a full-blown civil war. A cease-fire was established in July 1994, and a government backed by the RPF was installed in Kigali. Promises of amnesty failed to convince many of the Hutus, who had fled into the former Zaire (now the Democratic Republic of the Congo), to return.

Regional instability continued to threaten Rwanda's recovery, as exhibited by the renewed fighting along the Democratic Republic of the Congo border in mid-1998. Many Tutsi on both sides of the border aided Laurent-Désiré Kabila to oust then-Zaire's President Mobutu. But Kabila, facing pressure within his own country, purged his military of Rwandan and Congolese Tutsi in 1997. This breach of trust, combined with the continuing agitation of Hutu refugees in Congo, led Rwanda's government to support an armed rebellion against Kabila's government in the Democratic Republic of the Congo during 1998.

Rwanda remained caught up in the conflict in the neighboring Democratic Republic of the Congo throughout 1999. The Rwanda government, led by President Pasteur Bizimungu, repeatedly accused Congo President Laurent Kabila of sheltering and supporting Rwanda's extremist Hutu militia. Rwanda vowed to fight with anti-Kabila rebels to overthrow the Kabila regime. In March 2000, after conflicts with the predominantly Tutsi ruling party over cabinet appointments, President Bizimungu, himself a moderate Hutu, resigned and was replaced by Major General Paul Kagame. In May 2001, ethnic violence flared up again when Hutu rebels launched attacks in Rwanda's northwest. The government was successful in putting down the insurgency.

The indigenous population consists of three ethnic groups. The Tutsi (14 percent) are a pastoral people of Nilotic origin. The Hutus, who comprise the majority of the population (85 percent), are farmers of Bantu origin. The Twa pygmies (1 percent) are thought to be the remnants of the earliest settlers of the region.

Saint Helena

Official name: none
Independence: none (overseas territory of the United Kingdom)
Area: 410 sq km
Form of government: NA
Capital: Jamestown
International relations: ICFTU
Currency: Saint Helenian pound (SHP)
Income: us$2,500 (1998 est. of purchasing power parity)
Population: 7,266 (July 2001 est.)
Ethnic groups: African descent 50%, white 25%, Chinese 25%

Religious groups: Anglican (majority), Baptist, Seventh-Day Adventist, Roman Catholic
Languages: English
Literacy: 97% (age 20 and over can read and write; 1987 est.)
Exports: fish (frozen, canned, and salt-dried skipjack, tuna), coffee, handicrafts
Primary export partners: South Africa, United Kingdom
Imports: food, beverages, tobacco, fuel oils, animal feed, building materials, motor vehicles and parts, machinery and parts
Primary import partners: United Kingdom, South Africa

The islands of Saint Helena, Ascension, and Tristan da Cunha lie about one-third of the way from Africa to South America in the South Atlantic Ocean. The islands remained uninhabited until they were first explored by the Portuguese navigator, João de Nova, in 1502. In 1659, the British East India Company established a settlement on Saint Helena and, in 1673, was granted a charter to govern the island. Napoleon was exiled to Saint Helena from 1815 until his death in 1821.

São Tomé and Príncipe

Official name: Democratic Republic of São Tomé and Príncipe
Independence: 12 July 1975 (from Portugal)
Area: 1,001 sq km
Form of government: republic
Capital: São Tomé
International relations: ACCT, ACP, AfDB, CEEAC, ECA, FAO, G-77, IBRD, ICAO, ICRM, IDA, IFAD, IFRCS, ILO, IMF, IMO, Intelsat (nonsignatory user), Interpol, IOC, IOM (observer), ITU, NAM, OAU, UN, UNCTAD, UNESCO, UNIDO, UPU, WCL, WHO, WIPO, WMO, WToO, WTrO (observer)
Currency: dobra (STD)
Income: us$1,100 (2000 est. of purchasing power parity)
Population: 165,034 (July 2001 est.)
Ethnic groups: mestico, angolares (descendants of Angolan slaves), forros (descendants of freed slaves), servicais (contract laborers from Angola, Mozambique, and Cape Verde), tongas (children of servicais born on the islands), Europeans (primarily Portuguese)
Religious groups: Christian 80% (Roman Catholic, Evangelical Protestant, Seventh-Day Adventist)
Languages: Portuguese (official)
Literacy: 73% (age 15 and over can read and write; 1991 est.)
Exports: cocoa 90%, copra, coffee, palm oil

Primary export partners: Netherlands 18%, Germany 9%, Portugal 9% (1998)

Imports: machinery and electrical equipment, food products, petroleum products

Primary import partners: Portugal 42%, United States 20%, South Africa 6% (1998)

These uninhabited islands were first visited by Portuguese navigators between 1469 and 1472. The first successful settlement of São Tomé was established in 1493. Príncipe was settled in 1500. By the mid-1500s, with the help of slave labor, the Portuguese settlers had turned the islands into Africa's foremost exporter of sugar. São Tomé and Príncipe were taken over and administered by the Portuguese crown in 1522 and 1573, respectively. By 1908, São Tomé had become the world's largest producer of cocoa, still the country's most important crop.

The rocas system, which gave the plantation managers a high degree of authority, led to abuses against the African farm workers. Although Portugal officially abolished slavery in 1876, the practice of forced paid labor continued. Sporadic labor unrest and dissatisfaction continued well into the twentieth century, culminating in an outbreak of riots in 1953 in which several hundred African laborers were killed.

By the late 1950s, a small group of São Tomés had formed the Movement for the Liberation of São Tomé and Príncipe (MLSTP). In 1974, Portuguese representatives met with the MLSTP in Algiers and worked out an agreement for the transfer of sovereignty. After a period of transition, São Tomé and Príncipe achieved independence on July 12, 1975, choosing as its first president the MLSTP Secretary General Manuel Pinto da Costa. Four years after independence, da Costa consolidated his power by eliminating the position of prime minister and assuming those duties himself. He served until 1991, when Miguel Trovoada was elected as president. A coup by military officers on August 15, 1995, removed Trovoada from office, but only briefly. He was reinstated as president seven days later after he agreed to amnesty for the officers engineering the coup. In 1996, he was reelected to a five-year term.

In March 1999, Prime Minister Guilherme Posser da Costa pledged the government to a renewed program of economic stability, aimed principally at reducing inflation, which was running at a rate of more than 20 percent in early 1999. In May 2000, da Costa reshuffled his cabinet after two ministers resigned. Although President Trovoada of the Independent Democratic Action (ADI) party was unable to run for a third term in the country's July 2001 presidential election, the race was won by ADI candidate Fradique de Menezes. Shortly after taking office, de Menezes called for a cabinet reshuffle. When da Costa balked at some of the new president's suggestions, he was replaced by Evaristo Carvalho as prime minister.

São Tomé and Príncipe's population consists of people descended from groups that have migrated to the islands since 1485. Six groups are identifiable: mestizo, of mixed-blood, descendants of African slaves brought to the islands during the early years of settlement from Benin, Gabon, Congo, and Angola; Anglares, reputedly descendants of Angolan slaves who survived a 1540 shipwreck and now earn their livelihood fishing; Forros, descendants of freed slaves; Servicais, contract laborers from Angola, Mozambique, and Cape Verde, living temporarily on the islands; Tongas, children of servicais born on the islands; and Europeans, primarily Portuguese.

Senegal

Official name: Republic of Senegal

Independence: 4 April 1960 (from France); complete independence was achieved upon dissolution of federation with Mali on 20 August 1960

Area: 196,190 sq km

Form of government: republic under multiparty democratic rule

Capital: Dakar

International relations: ACCT, ACP, AfDB, CCC, ECA, ECOWAS, FAO, FZ, G-15, G-77, IAEA, IBRD, ICAO, ICC, ICFTU, ICRM, IDA, IDB, IFAD, IFC, IFRCS, ILO, IMF, IMO, Inmarsat, Intelsat, Interpol, IOC, IOM, ITU, MINURSO, MIPONUH, MONUC, NAM, OAU, OIC, OPCW, PCA, UN, UNCTAD, UNESCO, UNIDO, UNIKOM, UNMIBH, UNMIK, UNTAET, UPU, WADB, WAEMU, WCL, WFTU, WHO, WIPO, WMO, WToO, WTrO

Currency: Communaute Financiere Africaine franc (CFAF)

Income: US$1,600 (2000 est. of purchasing power parity)

Population: 10,284,929 (July 2001 est.)

Ethnic groups: Wolof 43.3%, Pular 23.8%, Serer 14.7%, Jola 3.7%, Mandinka 3%, Soninke 1.1%, European and Lebanese 1%, other 9.4%

Religious groups: Muslim 92%, indigenous beliefs 6%, Christian 2% (mostly Roman Catholic)

Languages: French (official), Wolof, Pulaar, Jola, Mandinka

Literacy: 33.1% (age 15 and over can read and write; 1995 est.)

Exports: fish, ground nuts (peanuts), petroleum products, phosphates, cotton

Guards outside the presidential palace in Dakar, the capital of Senegal.

Primary export partners: France 17%, India 17%, Italy 12%, Spain 6%, Mali 6%, Côte d'Ivoire 4% (1999)

Imports: foods and beverages, consumer goods, capital goods, petroleum products

Primary import partners: France 30%, Nigeria 7%, Italy 6%, Thailand 5%, Germany 4%, United States 4% (1999)

Archaeological findings throughout the area indicate that Senegal was inhabited in prehistoric times. Islam established itself in the Senegal River valley during the eleventh century. In the thirteenth and fourteenth centuries, the area came under the influence of the great Mandingo empires to the east, during which the Jolof empire of Senegal was founded. The Empire comprised the states of Cayor, Baol, Oualo, Sine, and Soloum until the sixteenth century, when they revolted for independence.

The Portuguese were the first Europeans to trade in Senegal, arriving in the fifteenth century. They were soon followed by the Dutch and French. During the nineteenth century, the French gradually established control over the interior regions and administered them as a protectorate until 1920 and as a colony thereafter.

In January of 1959, Senegal and the French Soudan merged to form the Mali Federation, which became fully independent on June 20, 1960. Due to internal political difficulties, the federation broke up on August 20, 1960; Senegal and Soudan (renamed the Republic of Mali) each proclaimed separate independence. Leopold Sedar Senghor, an internationally renowned poet, politician, and statesman, was elected Senegal's first president in August of 1960. Senghor guided the nation and instituted a multiparty system in 1976. Senghor stepped down in 1980, naming Abdou Diouf, prime minister since 1970, as his successor. Senegal joined with Gambia in 1982 to form the confederation of Senegambia, headed by Diouf. The confederation collapsed at the end of the 1980s, although the two countries in 1991 signed a new treaty of cooperation. Over time, the Senegalese public became increasingly disenchanted with Diouf and his Socialist Party's grip on power. In 1991, Diouf initiated electoral reforms, though the changes failed to satisfy opposition leaders. Diouf was again elected to a seven-year term as president in

1993. President Bill Clinton's 1998 visit to Senegal signaled a greater U.S. interest in the country.

Presidential elections in February 2000 produced no clear-cut victor, forcing a runoff election between incumbent Diouf and Abdoulaye Wade, a longtime opposition leader. Wade easily defeated Diouf and assumed the presidency on April 1, 2000. Just over a year later, on April 29, 2001, Wade led a coalition of 40 parties to victory in parliamentary elections, winning 89 of 120 seats in the National Assembly. Late in the year, Léopold Sédar Senghor, Senegal's first president, died at his retirement home in Normandy, France.

Seychelles

Official name: Republic of Seychelles
Independence: 29 June 1976 (from United Kingdom)
Area: 455 sq km
Form of government: republic
Capital: Victoria
International relations: ACCT, ACP, AfDB, C, CCC, ECA, FAO, G-77, IBRD, ICAO, ICFTU, ICRM, IFAD, IFC, IFRCS, ILO, IMF, IMO, InOC, Intelsat (nonsignatory user), Interpol, IOC, ITU, NAM, OAU, OPCW, SADC, UN, UNCTAD, UNESCO, UNIDO, UPU, WHO, WIPO, WMO, WToO, WTrO (observer)
Currency: Seychelles rupee (SCR)
Income: us$7,700 (2000 est. of purchasing power parity)
Population: 79,715 (July 2001 est.)
Ethnic groups: Seychellois (mixture of Asians, Africans, Europeans)
Religious groups: Roman Catholic 90%, Anglican 8%, other 2%
Languages: English (official), French (official), Creole
Literacy: 58% (age 15 and over can read and write; 1971 est.)
Exports: fish, cinnamon bark, copra, petroleum products (reexports)
Primary export partners: France, United Kingdom, Netherlands, Italy, China, Germany, Japan
Imports: machinery and equipment, foodstuffs, petroleum products, chemicals
Primary import partners: South Africa, United Kingdom, China, Singapore, France, Italy

In 1742, the French governor of Mauritius sent an expedition to the islands. A second expedition in 1756 reasserted formal possession by France. The Seychelles islands were captured and freed several times during the French Revolution and the Napoleonic wars, then passed officially to the British under the Treaty of Paris in 1814. Negotiations with the British resulted in an agreement by which Seychelles became a sovereign republic on June 29, 1976. After independence, Seychelles had a multiparty government, but, one year later, Albert René instituted his People's Progressive Front as the only party. Despite several coup attempts during the 1980s, René was able to hold onto power, and, in 1991, the government turned toward a multiparty state. René was elected to a fourth term in 1993. Since then, René has begun to implement a number of free-market reforms, promoting the islands as a center for offshore banking. In addition, several national industries have been privatized.

The formation of a new political party, the Social Democratic Party, was announced in April 1999 by Guy Morel, former governor of the central bank. Morel, formerly a member of the ruling Seychelles People's Progressive Front, said the government's failure to deal effectively with economic problems was the primary motivation for his move. President René managed to hold on to his office in September 2001 presidential elections in which the country's faltering economy was the key issue.

Most Seychellois are descendants of early French settlers and the African slaves brought to the Seychelles

Independence Monument in the Seychelles.

in the nineteenth century by the British, who freed them from slave ships on the East African coast. Indians and Chinese account for the other permanent inhabitants.

Sierra Leone

Official name: Republic of Sierra Leone
Independence: 27 April 1961 (from United Kingdom)
Area: 71,740 sq km
Form of government: constitutional democracy
Capital: Freetown
International relations: ACP, AfDB, C, CCC, ECA, ECOWAS, FAO, G-77, IAEA, IBRD, ICAO, ICFTU, ICRM, IDA, IDB, IFAD, IFC, IFRCS, ILO, IMF, IMO, Intelsat (nonsignatory user), Interpol, IOC, ITU, NAM, OAU, OIC, OPCW, UN, UNCTAD, UNESCO, UNIDO, UPU, WCL, WFTU, WHO, WIPO, WMO, WToO, WTrO
Currency: leone (SLL)
Income: US$510 (2000 est. of purchasing power parity)
Population: 5,426,618 (July 2001 est.)
Ethnic groups: 20 native African tribes 90% (Temne 30%, Mende 30%, other 30%), Creole 10% (descendants of freed Jamaican slaves who were settled in the Freetown area in the late-eighteenth century), refugees from Liberia's recent civil war, small numbers of Europeans, Lebanese, Pakistanis, and Indians
Religious groups: Muslim 60%, indigenous beliefs 30%, Christian 10%
Languages: English (official, regular use limited to literate minority), Mende (principal vernacular in the south), Temne (principal vernacular in the north), Krio (English-based Creole, spoken by the descendants of freed Jamaican slaves who were settled in the Freetown area, a lingua franca and a first language for 10% of the population but understood by 95%)
Literacy: 31.4% (age 15 and over can read and write English, Mende, Temne, or Arabic; 1995 est.)
Exports: diamonds, rutile, cocoa, coffee, fish
Primary export partners: Belgium 38%, United States 6%, Italy 4%, United Kingdom 4% (1999)
Imports: foodstuffs, machinery and equipment, fuels and lubricants, chemicals
Primary import partners: United Kingdom 34%, United States 8%, Italy 7%, Nigeria 5% (1999)

Sierra Leone was one of the first West African British colonies. Foreign settlement did not occur for another two centuries, when the British laid plans for a refuge within the British Empire for freed slaves. In 1787, the site of Freetown received the first 400 freedmen from Great Britain. Disease and hostility from the indigenous people almost eliminated this first group. Five years later, however, another group of settlers, 1,000 freed slaves who had fled from the United States to Nova Scotia during the American Revolution, arrived under the auspices of the newly formed British Sierra Leone Company. In 1800, about 550 blacks arrived from Jamaica via Nova Scotia; these were the maroons, escaped slaves who maintained their independence in the mountains of Jamaica.

The 1951 constitution provided the framework for decolonization. Independence came in April 1961, and Sierra Leone became a parliamentary system within the British Commonwealth. In April 1971, it adopted a republican constitution, cutting the link to the British monarchy but remaining with the Commonwealth. Siaka Stevens, who fought for government control of the country's major resources, namely iron and diamonds, led the country until his retirement in November 1985. He was succeeded as president in January 1986 by Major General Joseph Saidu Momoh. Guerrillas, spilling over into Sierra Leone from the Liberian civil war, captured some border towns in 1991. These border skirmishes eventually evolved into a civil war within Sierra Leone. Momoh was ousted by a military coup in April 1992 and was replaced by Captain Valentine Strasser. Strasser, criticized for the brutality of his regime, was removed from office in a 1996 bloodless coup. Ahmed Tehan Kabbah was elected president in late February 1996. A military junta deposed Kabbah in May 1997, but he was restored to office in March 1998. However, fighting between the government and rebel forces continued into the new millennium.

UN peacekeeping forces arrived in Sierra Leone late in 1999 to monitor implementation of a cease-fire agreement reached in Lomé, Togo, earlier in the year. However, the failure of Revolutionary United Front (RUF) rebels to disarm soon rendered the Lomé agreement effectively meaningless. The United Nations Mission in Sierra Leone (UNAMSIL) tried throughout 2001 to put into effect a peace accord based on the Lomé agreement and did manage to suppress fighting in several areas of the country. However, violence continued in some regions.

Eighteen ethnic groups make up the indigenous population of Sierra Leone. The Temne in the north and the Mende in the south are the largest. About 60,000 are Creoles, descendants of black settlers from Great Britain or North America.

Somalia

Official name: none
Independence: 1 July 1960 (from a merger of British Somaliland, which became independent from the United Kingdom on 26 June 1960, and Italian

Somaliland, which became independent from the Italian-administered UN trusteeship on 1 July 1960, to form the Somali Republic)

Area: 637,657 sq km

Form of government: parliamentary

Capital: Mogadishu

International relations: ACP, AfDB, AFESD, AL, AMF, CAEU, ECA, FAO, G-77, IBRD, ICAO, ICRM, IDA, IDB, IFAD, IFC, IFRCS, ILO, IMF, IMO, Intelsat, Interpol, IOC, IOM (observer), ITU, NAM, OAU, OIC, UN, UNCTAD, UNESCO, UNHCR, UNIDO, UPU, WFTU, WHO, WIPO, WMO, WTrO (observer)

Currency: Somali shilling (SOS)

Income: us$600 (2000 est. of purchasing power parity)

Population: 7,488,773

Ethnic groups: Somali 85%, Bantu, Arabs 30,000

Religious groups: Sunni Muslim

Languages: Somali (official), Arabic, Italian, English

Literacy: 24% (age 15 and over can read and write; 1990 est.)

Exports: livestock, bananas, hides, fish (1999)

Primary export partners: Saudi Arabia 53%, Yemen 19%, UAE 14%, Italy 5%, Pakistan 2% (1999)

Imports: manufactures, petroleum products, foodstuffs, construction materials (1995)

Primary import partners: Djibouti 24%, Kenya 14%, Brazil 13%, Saudi Arabia 10%, India 9% (1999)

The British East India Company's desire for unrestricted harbor facilities led to the conclusion of treaties with the sultan of Tajura as early as 1840. It was not until 1886, however, that the British gained control over northern Somalia through treaties with various Somali chiefs. The boundary between Ethiopia and British Somaliland was established in 1897 through treaty negotiations between British negotiators and Emperor Menelik II.

In 1855, Italy obtained commercial advantages in the area from the sultan of Zanzibar and, in 1889, concluded agreements with the sultans of Obbia and Caluula, who placed their territories under Italy's protection. Between 1897 and 1908, Italy made agreements with the Ethiopians and the British that marked out the boundaries of Italian Somaliland. In June 1940, Italian troops overran British Somaliland and drove out the British garrison. In 1941, British forces began operations against the Italian East African Empire and quickly brought the greater part of the Italian Somaliland under British control.

From 1941 to 1950, while Somalia was under British military administration, transition toward self-government had begun. Elections for the Legislative Assembly were held in February 1960. The protectorate became independent on June 26, 1960; five days later, on July 1, it joined Italian Somaliland to form the Somali Republic. Gen. Mohammed Siad Barre led a military coup in 1969 and established a Marxist political system. Years later, Barre concentrated power in his own family and clan. In 1991, he was toppled, but opposing factions continued fighting for power. After years of civil war and severe drought, the United Nations, with U.S. leadership, introduced forces into Somalia in late 1992 in an attempt to restore order and feed the country's many starving inhabitants. Attempts failed in the late 1990s to gather hundreds of warring clan leaders in an effort to hammer out some sort of truce. Pakistani forces took over the leadership of the UN mission, which finally retreated in March 1995.

Somalia remained without a functioning government until late in 2000. In May, a reconciliation conference, meeting in nearby Djibouti, agreed on a plan for a three-year transitional government (TNG) and a transitional national assembly. The transitional government was finally seated in October with Abdiqassim Salad Hassan as president and Ali Khalif Galaid as prime minister. Although the country now had a nominal government, it seemed largely unable to deal with the continuing tensions between clans, some of which supported TNG, while others bitterly opposed it. In December 2001, an agreement was signed between warring factions in Nairobi, Kenya, but it too failed to bring to an end the country's long-simmering internal conflicts.

The Somali people are herders and farmers. The largest group in the country is the Somali, who are nomadic or seminomadic herders. The remaining population consists of Jiiddu, Tunni, and Maay.

South Africa

Official name: Republic of South Africa

Independence: 31 May 1910 (from United Kingdom)

Area: 1,219,912 sq km

Form of government: republic

Capital: Pretoria; note: Cape Town is the legislative center and Bloemfontein the judicial center

International relations: ACP, AfDB, BIS, C, CCC, ECA, FAO, G-77, IAEA, IBRD, ICAO, ICC, ICFTU, ICRM, IDA, IFAD, IFC, IFRCS, IHO, ILO, IMF, IMO, Inmarsat, Intelsat, Interpol, IOC, IOM, ISO, ITU, MONUC, NAM, NSG, OAU, OPCW, PCA, SACU, SADC, UN, UNCTAD, UNESCO, UNHCR, UNIDO, UNITAR, UNMEE, UPU, WCL, WFTU, WHO, WIPO, WMO, WToO, WTrO, ZC

Currency: rand (ZAR)

Income: us$8,500 (2000 est. of purchasing power parity)

The mixture of Western and African styles can be seen on this street in Mogadishu, Somalia.

Population: 43,586,097

Ethnic groups: black 75.2%, white 13.6%, Colored 8.6%, Indian 2.6%

Religious groups: Christian 68% (includes most whites and Coloreds, about 60% of blacks and about 40% of Indians), Muslim 2%, Hindu 1.5% (60% of Indians), indigenous beliefs and animist 28.5%

Languages: 11 official languages, including Afrikaans, English, Ndebele, Pedi, Sotho, Swazi, Tsonga, Tswana, Venda, Xhosa, Zulu

Literacy: 81.8% (age 15 and over can read and write; 1995 est.)

Exports: gold, diamonds, other metals and minerals, machinery and equipment

Primary export partners: United Kingdom, Italy, Japan, United States, Germany

Imports: machinery, foodstuffs and equipment, chemicals, petroleum products, scientific instruments

Primary import partners: Germany, United States, United Kingdom, Japan

Of the present inhabitants of South Africa, the earliest were Bushmen and Hottentots who are members of the Khoisan language group. In 1488, the Portuguese were the first Europeans to reach the Cape of Good Hope. Permanent white settlement began when the Dutch East India Company established a provisioning station in 1652. In subsequent decades, French Huguenot refugees, Dutch, and Germans settled in the Cape area to form the Afrikaner segment of the modern population.

Britain seized the Cape of Good Hope at the end of the eighteenth century. Partly to escape British political rule and preserve cultural hegemony, many Afrikaner farmers (Boers) undertook a northern migration (the "Great Trek") beginning in 1836. This movement brought them into contact with several African groups, the most formidable of which were the Zulu. Under their powerful leader, Shaka (1787–1828), the Zulu conquered most of the territory between the Drakensberg Mountains and the sea (now Natal). The Zulu were defeated at the Battle of Blood River in 1838.

The independent Boer republics of the Transvaal (the South African Republic) and the Orange Free State

Cross Roads, a Black South African village.

were created in 1852 and 1854. Following the two Boer wars from 1880 to 1881 and 1899 to 1902, British forces conquered the Boer republics and incorporated them into the British Empire. A strong resurgence of Afrikaner nationalism in the 1940s and 1950s led to a decision, through a 1960 referendum among whites, to give up dominion status and establish a republic. The republic was established on May 31, 1961. The National Party extended racial segregation, or the policy of apartheid, through passage of a number of legislative acts. In the 1960s and the 1970s, other laws were passed to further restrict every black African.

The African National Congress (ANC), a predominantly black South African political and paramilitary organization founded in 1912, is the oldest organization opposing legalized racism and white rule in South Africa. It was banned by the South African government from 1960 to 1990, operating underground and in exile.

In December 1988, under great international pressure, the government commuted the death sentences of the Sharpeville Six, who were convicted of murder for their presence in a crowd that killed a black township official. President F. W. de Klerk took several steps, beginning in 1989, to demonstrate his commitment to ending apartheid, including the release of ANC leader Nelson Mandela, imprisoned in 1962 and sentenced to life in 1964 for treason and sabotage, and other political prisoners and detainees; and unbanning the ANC and 32 other anti-apartheid organizations. The tide of social and political changes instigated by de Klerk led to a new constitution and eventually multiparty elections in April 1994 that put Mandela in power as the first black African president of the nation. In April 1996, the Truth and Reconciliation Commission (TRC), the body responsible for investigating crimes committed during the apartheid era in South Africa, began its hearings. Despite misgivings about both its impartiality and its effectiveness, most observers agree that the TRC, which continued to work past its original 18-month deadline, has helped reconcile the new South Africa with its past.

In late 1997, Mandela retired as head of the ANC and was replaced by Thabo Mbeki. Mandela, who announced in 1996 he would not seek a second term as president, had groomed Mbeki to succeed him. Mbeki won the 1999 election, and the ANC was able to form a coalition to give it a two-thirds majority, which is necessary to amend the constitution.

Early on, it became clear that Mbeki was very much his own man, putting his focus on "transformation" rather than the "reconciliation" that had been Mandela's major goal. However, it was also readily apparent that Mbeki lacked the incredible charisma of Mandela, coming under fire from both domestic and international quarters by 2000. His position that the HIV virus was not the only factor behind AIDS brought Mbeki widespread criticism. The new president's push for privatization brought him and the ANC into increasing conflict with their traditional allies, the Congress of South African Trade Unions and the South African Communist Party. In addition to his continuing privatization drive, Mbeki vowed in 2001 to combat corruption within his government.

South Africa's apartheid classification system, which ended in the early 1990s, divided the nation's population into four major racial categories—Africans (blacks), whites, "coloreds," and Asians. The Africans, who comprise 72 percent of the population, are mainly descendants of the Sotho and Nguni peoples, who migrated southward centuries ago. The largest African ethnic groups are the Zulu (nearly 6 million) and Xhosa (about 5.8 million). The white population consists primarily of descendants of Dutch, French, English, and German settlers, with smaller mixtures of other European peoples, and constitutes about 14 percent of the total population. "Coloreds" are mostly descendants of indigenous peoples and the earliest European and Malay settlers in the area. "Coloreds" comprise 9 percent of the population and live primarily in Cape Province. Asians, mainly descendants of the Indian workers brought to South Africa in the mid-nineteenth century to work as indentured laborers on sugar estates in Natal, constitute about 3 percent of the population.

Sudan

Official name: Republic of the Sudan

Independence: 1 January 1956 (from Egypt and United Kingdom)

Area: 2,505,810 sq km

Form of government: transitional—ruling military junta took power in 1989; government is dominated by members of Sudan's National Islamic Front (NIF), a fundamentalist political organization, which uses the National Congress Party (NCP) as its legal front

Capital: Khartoum

International relations: ABEDA, ACP, AfDB, AFESD, AL, AMF, CAEU, CCC, ECA, FAO, G-77, IAEA, IBRD, ICAO, ICRM, IDA, IDB, IFAD, IFC, IFRCS, IGAD, ILO, IMF, IMO, Intelsat, Interpol, IOC, IOM, ISO (correspondent), ITU, NAM, OAU, OIC, OPCW, PCA, UN, UNCTAD, UNESCO, UNHCR, UNIDO, UNU, UPU, WFTU, WHO, WIPO, WMO, WToO, WTrO (observer)

Currency: Sudanese dinar (SDD)

Income: US$1,000 (2000 est. of purchasing power parity)

Population: 36,080,373 (July 2001 est.)

Ethnic groups: black 52%, Arab 39%, Beja 6%, foreigners 2%, other 1%

Religious groups: Sunni Muslim 70% (in north), indigenous beliefs 25%, Christian 5% (mostly in south and Khartoum)

Languages: Arabic (official), Nubian, Ta Bedawie, diverse dialects of Nilotic, Nilo-Hamitic, Sudanic languages, English

Literacy: 46.1% (age 15 and over can read and write; 1995 est.)

Exports: oil and petroleum products, cotton, sesame, livestock, groundnuts, gum arabic, sugar

Primary export partners: Saudi Arabia 16%, Italy 10%, Germany 5%, France 3%, Thailand 3% (1999)

Imports: foodstuffs, manufactured goods, machinery and transport equipment, medicines and chemicals, textiles

Primary import partners: China 14.7%, Libya 14.7%, Saudi Arabia 8.9%, United Kingdom 8.7%, France 6.7% (1999)

From the beginning of the Christian era until 1820, Sudan existed as a collection of small, independent states. In 1881, a religious leader named Mohammed Ahmed ibn Abdalla proclaimed himself the Mahdi, or "expected one," and began to unify tribes in western and central Sudan. The Mahdi led a nationalist revolt culminating in the fall of Khartoum in 1885. He died shortly thereafter, but his state survived until overwhelmed by Anglo-Egyptian forces in 1898. In 1899, Sudan was proclaimed a condominium under Anglo-Egyptian administration. In February 1953, the United Kingdom and Egypt concluded an agreement providing for Sudanese self-government. Sudan achieved independence on January 1, 1956. In 1969, Col. Gaafar Muhammad al-Nimeiry, leading a group of army officers, seized power and set up government under a revolutionary council. Elected president in 1972, Nimeiry first turned to the Soviet Union and Libya for support. However, after several coup attempts, allegedly backed by Libya and local communists, Nimeiry turned to Egypt and the West for assistance. Nimeiry was elected to a third term as president in 1983 but was removed from office two years later in a bloodless coup. After a year of military rule, Sadiq al-Mahdi was elected prime minister. Mahdi's regime was toppled in June 1989 by a military coup led by Omar Hassan al-Bashir. In 1993,

Bashir took some steps toward establishment of a multiparty state, most of which were dismissed as cosmetic by the opposition. In 1996, Bashir and his party swept presidential and legislative elections. Meanwhile, a civil war continued to rage between the Arab peoples of the north and the black Africans in the south of Sudan.

Despite widespread skepticism, Sudan's introduction of multiparty politics at the beginning of 1999 showed early signs of success. A number of longtime opposition leaders were quick to form their own political parties. In December 1999, President Hassan al-Bashir declared a state of emergency, fearing his authority was under threat from former ally Hassan al-Turaibi. The state of emergency continued in force through 2001, although al-Turaibi, the president's principal foe, was arrested in February 2001 for allegedly signing a memorandum of understanding with rebels of the Sudanese People's Liberation Army.

Swaziland

Official name: Kingdom of Swaziland

Independence: 6 September 1968 (from United Kingdom)

Area: 17,363 sq km

Form of government: monarchy; independent member of Commonwealth

Capital: Mbabane; note: Lobamba is the royal and legislative capital

International relations: ACP, AfDB, C, CCC, ECA, FAO, G-77, IBRD, ICAO, ICFTU, ICRM, IDA, IFAD, IFC, IFRCS, ILO, IMF, Intelsat, Interpol, IOC, ITU, NAM, OAU, OPCW, SACU, SADC, UN, UNCTAD, UNESCO, UNIDO, UPU, WHO, WIPO, WMO, WToO, WTrO

Currency: lilangeni (SZL)

Income: us$4,000 (2000 est. of purchasing power parity)

Population: 1,104,343

Ethnic groups: African 97%, European 3%

Religious groups: Protestant 55%, Muslim 10%, Roman Catholic 5%, indigenous beliefs 30%

Languages: English (official, government business conducted in English), siSwati (official)

Literacy: 76.7% (age 15 and over can read and write; 1995 est.)

Exports: soft drink concentrates, sugar, wood pulp, cotton yarn, refrigerators, citrus and canned fruit

Primary export partners: South Africa 65%, EU 12%, Mozambique 11%, United States 5% (1998)

Imports: motor vehicles, machinery, transport equipment, foodstuffs, petroleum products, chemicals

Primary import partners: South Africa 84%, EU 5%, Japan 2%, Singapore 2% (1998)

The people of the present Swazi nation migrated south before the sixteenth century to what is now Mozambique. After a series of conflicts with people living in the area that is now Maputo, the Swazi settled in northern Zululand in about 1750. Unable to match the growing Zulu strength there, the Swazi moved gradually northward in the early 1800s and established themselves in the area of modern Swaziland. The Swazi consolidated their hold in this area under several able leaders. The most important of these was Mswati, from whom the Swazi derive their name. Under his leadership in the 1840s, the Swazi expanded their territory to the northwest and stabilized the southern frontier with the Zulus.

The first Swazi contact with the British came early in Mswati's reign when he asked the British agent general in South Africa for assistance against Zulu raids into Swaziland. Agreements made between the British and the Transvaal (South Africa) governments in 1881 and 1884 provided that Swaziland should be independent. In 1903, Britain formally took over the administration of Swaziland.

An intricately carved drum in Swaziland.

Sobhuza II became head of the Swazi Nation in 1921. By the 1960s, political activity intensified, partly in response to events elsewhere in Africa. Several political parties were formed that agitated for independence. The traditional Swazi leaders, including King Sobhuza and his council, formed the Imbokodvo National Movement. In 1966, the British agreed to hold talks on a new constitution. The constitutional committee, consisting of representatives of the king and of the Swazi National Council, other political parties, and the British government agreed on a constitutional monarchy for Swaziland, with self-government to follow parliamentary elections in 1967. Swaziland became independent on September 6, 1968. In 1973, Sobhuza II repealed the constitution, dissolved the political parties, and assumed full power until his death in 1982. Mswati III became king in 1986.

In 1993, Mswati III called for Swaziland's first general election in 20 years, though he retained a great deal of political power; pro-democratic forces viewed the elections as inadequate. More recently, Swaziland has been affected by waves of general strikes, most of them organized by the Swazi Federation of Trade Unions (SFTU). The last major strike, in early 1996, led to the formation of a Constitutional Review Commission, which Mswati promised would deliver several democratic reforms. But Mswati limited membership on the commission to his own appointees, prompting the SFTU and its allies to reject the commission and call for further strikes.

Political unrest increased in 1999 as opposition groups calling for the establishment of a multiparty democracy grew more militant. Bombings of a number of government facilities were credited to these opposition groups. In August 2001, after years of delay, the Constitutional Review Commission submitted its recommendations to the king. The report was intended to provide a framework for the writing of a new constitution. Towards the end of 2001, the government eased its restrictions on political activities, allowing the public promotion of campaigns for local elections.

Tanzania

Official name: United Republic of Tanzania

Independence: 26 April 1964; Tanganyika became independent 9 December 1961 (from United Kingdom-administered UN trusteeship); Zanzibar became independent 19 December 1963 (from United Kingdom); Tanganyika united with Zanzibar 26 April 1964 to form the United Republic of Tanganyika and Zanzibar; renamed United Republic of Tanzania 29 October 1964

Area: 945,087 sq km

Form of government: republic

A Tanzanian street scene.

Capital: Dar es Salaam; note: legislative offices have been transferred to Dodoma, which is planned as the new national capital; the National Assembly now meets there on regular basis

International relations: ACP, AfDB, C, CCC, EADB, ECA, FAO, G- 6, G-77, IAEA, IBRD, ICAO, ICC, ICFTU, ICRM, IDA, IFAD, IFC, IFRCS, ILO, IMF, IMO, Inmarsat, Intelsat, Interpol, IOC, IOM, ISO, ITU, MONUC, NAM, OAU, OPCW, SADC, UN, UNCTAD, UNESCO, UNHCR, UNIDO, UNMEE, UPU, WFTU, WHO, WIPO, WMO, WToO, WTrO

Currency: Tanzanian shilling (TZS)

Income: us$710 (2000 est. of purchasing power parity)

Population: 36,232,074

Ethnic groups: mainland—native African 99% (of which 95% are Bantu consisting of more than 130 tribes), other 1% (consisting of Asian, European, and Arab); Zanzibar—Arab, native African, mixed Arab and native African

Religious groups: mainland—Christian 45%, Muslim 35%, indigenous beliefs 20%; Zanzibar—more than 99% Muslim

Languages: Kiswahili or Swahili (official), Kiunguju (name for Swahili in Zanzibar), English (official, primary language of commerce, administration, and higher education), Arabic (widely spoken in Zanzibar), many local languages

Literacy: 67.8% (age 15 and over can read and write Kiswahili (Swahili), English, or Arabic; 1995 est.)

Exports: coffee, manufactured goods, cotton, cashew nuts, minerals, tobacco, sisal (1996)

Primary export partners: India 20%, United Kingdom 10%, Germany 8%, Japan 8%, Netherlands 8%, Belgium 4% (1998)

Imports: consumer goods, machinery and transportation equipment, industrial raw materials, crude oil

Primary import partners: South Africa 8%, Japan 8%, United Kingdom 8%, Kenya 7%, India 6%, United States 5% (1998)

The area that is now Tanzania is believed to have been inhabited originally by ethnic groups using a click-tongue language similar to that of southern Africa's Bushmen and Hottentots. Although remnants of these early tribes still exist, most were gradually displaced by Bantu farmers migrating form the west and south and by Nilotes and related Northern peoples.

The coastal area first felt the impact of foreign influence as early as the eighth century. By the twelfth century, traders and immigrants came from as far away as Persia (now Iran) and India. The Portuguese navigator, Vasco da Gama, first visited the East African coast in 1498 on his voyage to India, and, by 1506, the Portuguese claimed control over the entire coast. This control was nominal, however, for the Portuguese did not attempt to colonize the area or explore the interior. By the early eighteenth century, Arabs from Oman had assisted the indigenous coastal dwellers in driving out the Portuguese from the area north of the Ruvuma River. They established their own garrisons at Zanzibar, Pemba, and Kilwa and carried on a lucrative trade in slaves and ivory.

German colonial interests were first advanced in 1884. Karl Peters, who formed the Society for German Colonization, concluded a series of treaties by which tribal chiefs in the interior accepted German protection. In 1886 and 1890, Anglo-German agreements were negotiated that delineated the British and German spheres of influence in the interior of East Africa. In 1891, the German government took over direct administration of the territory from the German East Africa Company and appointed a governor with headquarters at Dar es Salaam. German colonial administration provided African resistance, culminating in the Maji Maji rebellion of 1905 to 1907. German colonial domination of Tanganyika ended with World War I. Control of most of the territory passed to the United Kingdom under a League of Nations mandate.

In the following years, Tanganyika moved gradually toward self-government and independence. In 1954, Julius K. Nyerere, a schoolteacher educated abroad, organized the Tanganyika African Union (UANU). In May 1961, Tanganyika became autonomous, and Nyerere became prime minister under a new constitution. Full independence was achieved on December 9, 1961. On April 26, 1964, Tanganyika united with Zanzibar to form the United Republic of Tanganyika and Zanzibar, renamed the United Republic of Tanzania on October 29, 1964. Nyerere in November 1985 became one of the few leaders on the continent to retire peacefully. He was succeeded by Ali Hassan Mwinyi as president. Opposition parties were legalized in 1992, paving the way for Tanzania's first multiparty elections in October 1995. The Revolutionary Party's Benjamin Mkapa was elected president and his party won the majority of the seats in the National Assembly. Continuing strife in countries bordering Tanzania fueled a surge in the flow of refugees into the country during the mid-1990s. In 1997, Tanzania began a repatriation plan to return the refugees to their homelands.

Continuing economic weakness forced Tanzanian officials in 1999 to reconsider its hesitancy to endorse the proposed revival of the East African Community with neighboring Kenya and Uganda. In November 1999 Tanzania and its neighbors agreed to reestablish the community but put off a decision on a timetable for the commencement of free trade between the member states of the community. Former President Julius Nyerere died in October 1999. President Mkapa was reelected in a landslide in October 2000 elections. The Tanzanian islands of Pemba and Zanzibar experienced an explosion of civil unrest in late January 2001. The protests were led by members of the opposition Civic United Front (CUF) party calling for new presidential elections. Tensions continued between CUF and the ruling Chama Cha Mapinduzi party throughout 2001, despite a peace accord signed by both parties in October.

Tanzania's population consists of more than 120 ethnic groups, of which only the Sukuma has more than one million members. The majority of Tanzanians, including such large tribes as the Sukuma and the Nyamwezi, are of Bantu stock. Groups of Nilotic or related origin include the nomadic Masai and the Luo, both of which are found in greater numbers in neighboring Kenya. Two small groups speak languages of the Khoisan family peculiar to the Bushman and Hottentot peoples. Cushitic-speaking peoples, originally from the Ethiopian highlands, reside in a few areas of Tanzania.

Togo

Official name: Togolese Republic

Independence: 27 April 1960 (from French-administered UN trusteeship)

Area: 56,785 sq km

Form of government: republic under transition to multiparty democratic rule

Capital: Lome

International relations: ACCT, ACP, AfDB, CCC, ECA, ECOWAS, Entente, FAO, FZ, G-77, IBRD, ICAO, ICC, ICFTU, ICRM, IDA, IDB, IFAD, IFC, IFRCS, ILO, IMF, IMO, Intelsat, Interpol, IOC, ITU, MIPONUH, NAM, OAU, OIC, OPCW,

UN, UNCTAD, UNESCO, UNIDO, UPU, WADB, WAEMU, WCL, WFTU, WHO, WIPO, WMO, WToO, WTrO

Currency: Communaute Financiere Africaine franc (CFAF)

Income: us$1,500 (2000 est. of purchasing power parity)

Population: 5,153,088

Ethnic groups: native African (37 tribes; largest and most important are Ewe, Mina, and Kabre) 99%, European and Syrian-Lebanese less than 1%

Religious groups: indigenous beliefs 59%, Christian 29%, Muslim 12%

Languages: French (official and the language of commerce), Ewe and Mina (the two major African languages in the south), Kabye (sometimes spelled Kabiye) and Dagomba (the two major African languages in the north)

Literacy: 51.7% (age 15 and over can read and write; 1995 est.)

Exports: cotton, phosphates, coffee, cocoa

Primary export partners: Nigeria, Brazil, Canada, Philippines (1999)

Imports: machinery and equipment, foodstuffs, petroleum products

Primary import partners: Ghana, China, France, Côte d'Ivoire (1999)

A broom vendor on a city street in Togo.

The Ewe people first moved into the area that is now Togo from the Niger River Valley between the twelfth and fourteenth centuries. During the fifteenth and sixteenth centuries, Portuguese explorers and traders visited the coast. For the next 200 years, the coastal region was a major raiding center for Europeans in search of slaves, earning Togo and the surrounding region the name "the Slave Coast."

In a 1884 treaty signed at Togoville, Germany declared a protectorate over the area. In 1914, Togoland was invaded by French and British forces and fell after a brief resistance. Following the war, Togoland became a League of Nations mandate divided for administrative purposes between France and the United Kingdom. By statute in 1955, French Togo became an autonomous republic within the French Union. In 1957, the residents of British Togoland voted to join the Gold Coast as part of the new independent nation of Ghana. On April 27, 1960, Togo severed its juridical ties with France, shed its United Nations trusteeship status, and became fully independent. The first president, Sylvanus Olympia, was overthrown three years after independence. Nicholas Grunitzky headed the government for a short period and, in 1976, Col. Gnassingbé Eyadéma seized power and instituted a one-party state. Reelected in 1979 and 1986, Eyadéma in August 1991 agreed to share power

with a transitional government until multiparty elections could be scheduled. Though troops loyal to Eyadéma reportedly tried repeatedly to overthrow the interim regime, Eyadéma was reelected in multiparty elections in 1993.

Since 1994, the Togolese economy has seen a partial recovery. But the current political scene is less promising: in 1997, Eyadéma's government blocked the creation of an independent electoral commission, and, after military harassment of opposition leaders marred the 1998 presidential campaign, Eyadéma's claim to have won reelection for another five years led to opposition protests and rioting. Political unrest stemming from the disputed 1998 presidential election intensified during 1999. Most opposition parties boycotted March 1999 parliamentary elections, giving the ruling Rally of the Togolese People party all but two of the 81 seats in parliament.

With tensions rising between the government of President Eyadéma and major opposition parties, the government in early 2000 limited freedom of the press, subjecting any journalist found guilty of defaming the head of state to heavy fines and three months imprisonment. Shortly after Prime Minister Eugene Koffi Adoboli lost a vote of confidence in August 2000, he resigned and was replaced by Gabriel Agbéyomé Kodjo, speaker of the national assembly. In January 2001, the government announced that new parliamentary elections would be held later in the year, but the promised legislative vote was postponed at the last minute.

Togo's population is composed of about 21 ethnic groups. The two major ones are the Ewe in the south and the Kabye in the north.

Tunisia

Official name: Republic of Tunisia
Independence: 20 March 1956 (from France)
Area: 163,610 sq km
Form of government: republic
Capital: Tunis
International relations: ABEDA, ACCT, AfDB, AFESD, AL, AMF, AMU, BSEC (observer), CCC, ECA, FAO, G-77, IAEA, IBRD, ICAO, ICC, ICFTU, ICRM, IDA, IDB, IFAD, IFC, IFRCS, IHO, ILO, IMF, IMO, Inmarsat, Intelsat, Interpol, IOC, IOM, ISO, ITU, MIPONUH, MONUC, NAM, OAS (observer), OAU, OIC, OPCW, OSCE (partner), UN, UN Security Council (temporary), UNCTAD, UNESCO, UNHCR, UNIDO, UNMEE, UNMIBH, UNMIK, UPU, WFTU, WHO, WIPO, WMO, WToO, WTrO
Currency: Tunisian dinar (TND)
Income: us$6,500 (2000 est. of purchasing power parity)
Population: 9,705,102 (July 2001 est.)
Ethnic groups: Arab 98%, European 1%, Jewish and other 1%
Religious groups: Muslim 98%, Christian 1%, Jewish and other 1%
Languages: Arabic (official and one of the languages of commerce), French (commerce)
Literacy: 66.7% (age 15 and over can read and write; 1995 est.)
Exports: textiles, mechanical goods, phosphates and chemicals, agricultural products, hydrocarbons
Primary export partners: Germany 28%, France 22%, Italy 17%, Belgium 5%, Libya 4% (1999)
Imports: machinery and equipment, hydrocarbons, chemicals, food
Primary import partners: France 23%, Germany 23%, Italy 15%, Belgium 3% (1999)

Tunisians are descended mainly from indigenous Berber tribes and from Arab tribes that migrated to North Africa during the seventh century AD. Recorded history in Tunisia begins with the arrival of Phoenicians, who founded Carthage and other North African settlements. In the seventh century, the Muslim conquest transformed North Africa and Tunisia became a center of Arab culture until its assimilation in the Turkish Ottoman Empire in the sixteenth century. In 1881, France established a protectorate there, only to see a rise of nationalism lead to Tunisia's independence in 1956.

One year after independence, Habib Bourguiba deposed the president and instituted a socialist system, later declaring himself president for life. In late 1987, Bourguiba was declared senile, and he was replaced as president by Prime Minister Zine al-Abidine Ben Ali, who took steps to democratize the country. In April 1989 elections, Ben Ali was elected to a full term as president. In 1994, he ran unopposed for president and was reelected. Ben Ali continued to crack down on growing Muslim fundamentalism throughout the 1990s.

President Ben Ali won a resounding reelection victory in October 1999. Habib Bourguiba, Tunisia's founding father, died at the age of 96 in April 2000. Ben Ali's government in 2000 and 2001 came under increasing criticism for its record on human rights. Under growing pressure from within and outside the country, the president in 2001 promised to improve his record on human rights and, as a step in that direction, introduced a liberalized press law in August 2001. Even so, at year's end, Tunisia was listed as one of the 10 countries most hostile to a free press.

Uganda

Official name: Republic of Uganda
Independence: 9 October 1962 (from United Kingdom)
Area: 236,040 sq km
Form of government: republic
Capital: Kampala
International relations: ACP, AfDB, C, CCC, EADB, ECA, FAO, G-77, IAEA, IBRD, ICAO, ICFTU, ICRM, IDA, IDB, IFAD, IFC, IFRCS, IGAD, ILO, IMF, Intelsat, Interpol, IOC, IOM, ISO (correspondent), ITU, NAM, OAU, OIC, OPCW, PCA, UN, UNCTAD, UNESCO, UNHCR, UNIDO, UPU, WFTU, WHO, WIPO, WMO, WToO, WTrO
Currency: Ugandan shilling (UGX)
Income: us$1,100 (2000 est. of purchasing power parity)
Population: 23,985,712
Ethnic groups: Baganda 17%, Karamojong 12%, Basogo 8%, Iteso 8%, Langi 6%, Rwanda 6%, Bagisu 5%, Acholi 4%, Lugbara 4%, Bunyoro 3%, Batoro 3%, non-African (European, Asian, Arab) 1%, other 23%

Tunisian women walking together.

Religious groups: Roman Catholic 33%, Protestant 33%, Muslim 16%, indigenous beliefs 18%

Languages: English (official national language, taught in grade schools, used in courts of law and by most newspapers and some radio broadcasts), Ganda or Luganda (most widely used of the Niger-Congo languages, preferred for native language publications in the capital and may be taught in school), other Niger-Congo languages, Nilo-Saharan languages, Swahili, Arabic

Literacy: 61.8% (age 15 and over can read and write; 1995 est.)

Exports: coffee, fish and fish products, tea; electrical products, iron and steel

Primary export partners: Spain, Germany, Belgium, Netherlands, Hungary, Kenya (1999)

Imports: vehicles, petroleum, medical supplies; cereals

Primary import partners: Kenya 27.5%, United States 21.2%, France 19.3, United Kingdom 5%, India 4% (1999)

Arab traders moving inland from Indian Ocean coastal enclaves reached the interior of Uganda in the 1830s and found several African kingdoms, including the Buganda kingdom, that had well-developed political institutions dating back several centuries.

In 1888, control of the emerging British sphere of interest in East Africa was assigned by royal charter to the Imperial British East Africa Company, an arrangement strengthened in 1890 by an Anglo-German agreement confirming British dominance over Kenya and Uganda. In 1894, the Kingdom of Uganda was placed under a formal British protectorate. The British protectorate period began to change formally in 1955 when constitutional changes leading to Uganda's independence were adopted. The first general elections in Uganda were held in 1961, and the British government granted internal self-government to Uganda on March 1, 1962, with Benedicto Kiwanuka as the first prime minister.

In February of 1966, Prime Minister Milton Obote suspended the constitution, assumed all government powers, and removed the president and vice president. On January 25, 1971, Obote's government was ousted in a military coup led by armed forces commander Idi Amin Dada. Amin declared himself president, dissolved the parliament, and amended the constitution to give himself absolute power. Idi Amin's eight-year rule produced economic decline, social disintegration, and massive human rights violations. In 1978, Tanzanian forces pushed back an incursion by Amin's troops. Backed by Ugandan exiles, Tanzanian forces waged a war of liberation against Amin. On April 11, 1979, the Ugandan capital was captured, and Amin and his remaining forces fled. There followed a chaotic year or so, during which three provisional presidents led the shattered country. In December 1980, Obote was once again elected to the presidency and then overthrown by military coup. The military regime that followed was short-lived. In January 1986, National Resistance Army leader Yoweri Museveni seized power. Museveni, most recently elected president in 1996 in the country's first presidential elections in 16 years, has done much to nurse Uganda's economy back to health.

Widely praised for its progress in revitalizing the economy, Uganda's government in 1999 received pledges of $2.2 billion in additional foreign aid over the following three years. Early in 2000, the presidents of Uganda and Sudan signed an agreement pledging to halt aid to rebels fighting against each country, but the accord proved largely ineffective. Despite a credible challenge mounted by Kiiza Besigye, a former associate of President Museveni, the incumbent won a resounding reelection victory in March 2001 presidential elections.

Bantu, Nilotic, and Nilo-Hamitic peoples constitute most of Uganda's population. The Bantu are the most numerous and include the Baganda, with more than one million members. The Nilo-Hamitic Iteso is the second-largest group, followed by the Banyankole and Basoga, both of Bantu extraction.

Zambia

Official name: Republic of Zambia
Independence: 24 October 1964 (from United Kingdom)
Area: 752,614 sq km
Form of government: republic
Capital: Lusaka
International relations: ACP, AfDB, C, CCC, ECA, FAO, G-19, G-77, IAEA, IBRD, ICAO, ICFTU, ICRM, IDA, IFAD, IFC, IFRCS, ILO, IMF, Intelsat, Interpol, IOC, IOM, ITU, MONUC, NAM, OAU, OPCW, PCA, SADC, UN, UNAMSIL, UNCTAD, UNESCO, UNIDO, UNMEE, UNMIK, UNTAET, UPU, WHO, WIPO, WMO, WToO, WTrO
Currency: Zambian kwacha (ZMK)
Income: us$880 (2000 est. of purchasing power parity)
Population: 9,770,199
Ethnic groups: African 98.7%, European 1.1%, other 0.2%

Religious groups: Christian 50%–75%, Muslim and Hindu 24%–49%, indigenous beliefs 1%
Languages: English (official), major vernaculars—Bemba, Kaonda, Lozi, Lunda, Luvale, Nyanja, Tonga, and about 70 other indigenous languages
Literacy: 78.2% (age 15 and over can read and write English; 1995 est.)
Exports: copper, cobalt, electricity, tobacco
Primary export partners: Japan, Saudi Arabia, India, Thailand, South Africa, United States, Malaysia (1997)
Imports: machinery, transportation equipment, fuels, petroleum products, electricity, fertilizer; foodstuffs, clothing
Primary import partners: South Africa 48%, Saudi Arabia, United Kingdom, Zimbabwe (1997)

About 2,000 years ago, the indigenous hunter-gatherer occupants of Zambia began to be displaced or absorbed by more advanced migrating tribes. By the fifteenth century, the major waves of Bantu-speaking immigrants arrived, with the greatest influx occurring between the late seventeenth and early nineteenth centuries. These groups came primarily from the Luba and Lunda tribes of southern Zaire and northern Angola but were joined in the nineteenth century by Ngoni peoples from the south. By the latter part of that century, the various peoples of Zambia were largely established in the areas they currently occupy.

Except for an occasional Portuguese explorer, the area lay untouched by Europeans for centuries until the mid-nineteenth century, when it was penetrated by European explorers, missionaries, and traders. In 1888, Northern and Southern Rhodesia were proclaimed a British sphere of influence. In 1953, both Rhodesias were joined with Nyasaland to form the Federation of Rhodesia and Nyasaland.

Northern Rhodesia was the center of much of the turmoil and crises that characterized the federation in its last years. At the core of the controversy were insistent African demands for greater participation in government. A two-stage election held in October and December 1962 resulted in an African majority in the Legislative Council. The council passed resolutions calling for Northern Rhodesia's secession from the federation and demanding full internal self-government. On December 31, 1963, the federation was dissolved, and Northern Rhodesia became the Republic of Zambia on October 24, 1964. Led by Kenneth Kaunda for nearly 30 years, the country in 1991 held its first multiparty elections. Frederick Chiluba, leader of the Movement for Multiparty Democracy, defeated Kaunda by a wide margin. In 1996, a new constitution prevented Kaunda from running for president, as it introduced a provision that a candidate's parents must be Zambian-born (Kaunda's parents were Malawian). Chiluba's party easily won elections that same year, amidst widespread student riots and widespread popular dissent.

In March 2000, former President Kaunda announced that he was retiring from politics and stepping down as leader of the United National Independence Party. Kaunda was succeeded as party leader by Francis Nikhoma, a former governor of the central bank. President Chiluba's ruling party's regulations had forbidden a party member from seeking more than two terms as president, but, in April 2001, the rules were changed to permit Chiluba to run for a third term in late 2001 elections. Only a month later, however, Chiluba reversed himself and said he would not run for reelection, largely in response to growing opposition within his own party. Lawyer Levy Mwanawasa was named the ruling party's candidate, and he handily won election to the presidency in late 2001.

Zambia's population comprises more than 70 Bantu-speaking tribes. Some tribes are small, and only two have enough people to constitute at least ten percent of the population.

Zimbabwe

Official name: Republic of Zimbabwe
Independence: 18 April 1980 (from United Kingdom)
Area: 390,580 sq km
Form of government: parliamentary democracy
Capital: Harare
International relations: ACP, AfDB, C, CCC, ECA, FAO, G-15, G-77, IAEA, IBRD, ICAO, ICFTU, ICRM, IDA, IFAD, IFC, IFRCS, ILO, IMF, Intelsat, Interpol, IOC, IOM (observer), ISO, ITU, NAM, OAU, OPCW, PCA, SADC, UN, UNCTAD, UNESCO, UNIDO, UNMIK, UNTAET, UPU, WCL, WFTU, WHO, WIPO, WMO, WToO, WTrO
Currency: Zimbabwean dollar (ZWD)
Income: US$2,500 (2000 est. of purchasing power parity)
Population: 11,365,366
Ethnic groups: African 98% (Shona 71%, Ndebele 16%, other 11%), mixed and Asian 1%, white less than 1%
Religious groups: syncretic (part Christian, part indigenous beliefs) 50%, Christian 25%, indigenous beliefs 24%, Muslim and other 1%
Languages: English (official), Shona, Sindebele (the language of the Ndebele, sometimes called Ndebele), numerous but minor tribal dialects

Literacy: 85% (age 15 and over can read and write English; 1995 est.)
Exports: tobacco 29%, gold 7%, ferroalloys 7%, cotton 5% (1999 est.)
Primary export partners: South Africa 10%, United Kingdom 9%, Malawi 8%, Botswana 8%, Japan 7%, (1999 est.)
Imports: machinery and transport equipment 35%, other manufactures 18%, chemicals 17%, fuels 14% (1999 est.)
Primary import partners: South Africa 46%, United Kingdom 6%, China 4%, Germany 4%, United States 3% (1999 est.)

Archaeologists have found Stone Age implements and pebble tools in several areas of Zimbabwe, suggesting human habitation for many centuries. The ruins of stone buildings also provide evidence of early civilization.

In the sixteenth century, the Portuguese were the first Europeans to attempt colonization of south-central Africa, but the hinterland lay virtually untouched by Europeans until the arrival of explorers, missionaries, and traders some 300 years later. In 1888, the area that became Southern and Northern Rhodesia was proclaimed a British sphere of influence. The British South Africa Company was chartered in 1889, and the settlement of Salisbury (now Harare) was established in 1890.

In 1895, the territory was formally named Rhodesia. In 1923, Southern Rhodesia's white settlers were given the choice of being incorporated into the Union of South Africa or becoming a separate entity within the British Empire. The settlers rejected incorporation, and Southern Rhodesia was formally annexed by the United Kingdom. In September 1953, Southern Rhodesia was joined with the British protectorates of Northern Rhodesia and Nyasaland. The federation was dissolved at the end of 1963 after much crisis and turmoil with Northern Rhodesia, and Nyasaland became the independent states of Zambia and Malawi in 1964.

Although prepared to grant independence to Rhodesia, the United Kingdom insisted that the authorities at Salisbury first demonstrate their intention to move toward eventual majority rule. Desiring to keep their dominant position, the white Rhodesians refused to give such assurance. On November 11, 1965, after lengthy and unsuccessful negotiations with the British government, Prime Minister Ian Smith issued a Unilateral Declaration of Independence (UDI) from the United Kingdom. The British government considered the UDI unconstitutional and illegal but made clear that it would not use force to end the rebellion. The British government imposed unilateral economic sanctions on Rhodesia and requested other nations to do the same. On

Victoria Falls, on the border of Zambia and Zimbabwe.

December 16, 1966, the United Nations Security Council, for the first time in its history, imposed mandatory economic sanctions on a state.

In the early 1970s, informal attempts at settlement were renewed between the United Kingdom and the Rhodesia administration. In 1974, the major African nationalist groups—the Zimbabwe African People's Union (ZAPU) and the Zimbabwe African National Union (ZANU), which split away from ZAPU in 1963—were united into the "Patriotic Front" and combined their military forces. In 1976, the Smith government agreed in principle to majority rule and to a meeting in Geneva with black nationalist leaders. Blacks represented at the Geneva meeting included ZAPU leader Joshua Nkomo, ZANU leader Robert Mugabe, UANC chairman Bishop Abel Muzorewa, and former ZANU leader, the Rev. Ndabaningi Sithole. However, the meeting failed.

On March 3, 1978, the Smith administration signed an internal settlement agreement in Salisbury with Bishop Muzorewa, Rev. Sithole, and Chief Jeremiah Chirau. The agreement provided for qualified majority rule and elections with universal suffrage. Following

elections in April 1979, in which his UANC part won a majority, Bishop Muzorewa assumed office on June 1, becoming Zimbabwe's first black prime minister. However, the installation of the new black majority government did not end the guerrilla conflict that had claimed more than 20,000 lives.

The British and the African parties began deliberations on a Rhodesian settlement in London on September 10, 1979. On December 21, the parties signed an agreement calling for a cease-fire, new elections, a transition period under British rule, and a new constitution implementing majority rule while protecting minority rights. The elections were supervised by the British government. Robert Mugabe's ZANU Party won an absolute majority and was asked to form Zimbabwe's first government. The British government formally granted independence to Zimbabwe on April 18, 1980. In 1985, Mugabe's party won by a landslide in the country's first general election since independence. He was reelected in 1990 and 1996.

Zimbabwe's population is divided into two major language groups, which are subdivided into several tribal groups. The Mashona (Shona speakers), who constitute about 80 percent of the population, have lived in the area the longest and are the majority language groups. The Matabele (Sindebele speakers), representing about 19 percent of the population and centered in the southwest near Bulawayo, arrived within the last 150 years. An offshoot of the South African Zulu group, they had maintained control over the Mashona until the white occupation of Rhodesia.

President Mugabe came under fire in early 1999 for his aggressive land-reform and black-empowerment programs, particularly his threats to seize farms owned by absentee British owners and turn them over to black Zimbabweans. In April 2000, Mugabe's land redistribution scheme exploded into violence when supporters launched attacks on white farmers. In legislative elections in June 2000, Mugabe's ruling Zimbabwe African National Union-Patriotic Front (ZANU-PF) party won a narrow majority of the 120 contested seats but was assured continued domination because of the president's right to nominate an additional 30 members. The elections were marred by extensive violence against supporters of the leading opposition party. In March 2002 elections that many observers contended were conducted in an atmosphere of fear and intimidation, Mugabe claimed victory once again. Shortly thereafter, the Commonwealth suspended Zimbabwe for 12 months after the group's observers accused Mugabe of using his powers as incumbent to steal the election.

Western Hemisphere

Anguilla

Official name: none
Independence: none (overseas territory of the United Kingdom)
Area: 91 sq km
Form of government: NA
Capital: The Valley
International relations: CARICOM (associate), CDB, Interpol (subbureau), OECS (associate), ECLAC (associate)
Currency: East Caribbean dollar (XCD)
Income: US$8,200 (1999 est. of purchasing power parity)
Population: 12,132 (July 2001 est.)
Ethnic groups: black
Religious groups: Anglican 40%, Methodist 33%, Seventh-Day Adventist 7%, Baptist 5%, Roman Catholic 3%, other 12%
Languages: English (official)
Literacy: 95% (age 12 and over can read and write; 1984 est.)

Exports: lobster, fish, livestock, salt
Primary export partners: NA
Imports: NA
Primary import partners: NA

According to legend, this slender island, named in Spanish for the eel its shape suggests, got that name from no less a figure than Christopher Columbus, who is said to have sailed through this area of the Caribbean on one of his early voyages of discovery at the end of the fifteenth century. Some historians dismiss this story as fanciful and contend that the French were the first Europeans to visit these shores. Whatever the story, it is certain that the first colonial settlement was established by the British in 1650. Unlike many other islands in the region, Anguilla remained under the power of the British for the entire colonial period.

The British settlers quickly established farms on the island, although these agricultural holdings were less expansive than the plantation-size holdings found on some of the other Caribbean islands held by the British. This was because the island itself was relatively small and its soil less fertile than on other British-held islands. To work these farms, however, the British imported slaves. Because the island was small, the British decided in the early nineteenth century to link its colonial administration with that of Saint Christopher, better known as Saint Kitts, and Nevis, both of which lie to the south of Anguilla. The three-island colony's local administration was located on Saint Kitts, the largest of the islands.

The British abolished slavery in all of its colonial holdings in 1834, but most of the former slaves continued to work in farming or fishing for many years thereafter. In time, the harvesting of salt emerged as another major occupation for the former slaves. One of the slave traditions that lives on in contemporary celebrations is known as the "jollification." In this observance, Anguillans of both sexes dressed as field workers parade together to a location where a field is planted. Songs of Afro-Caribbean origins are sung as they proceed along their route and begin their field work.

In the late 1960s, as Saint Kitts and Nevis clamored for their independence from Britain, Anguillans decided their future would be brighter if they became a separate dependent territory tied to Britain. In 1967, the island issued a unilateral declaration of independence from Saint Kitts and Nevis, triggering a mini-invasion by British troops to quell the rebellion. In the early 1970s, the island was accorded the British crown colony status that it sought.

In March 1999, the ruling coalition of the Anguilla United Party and the Anguilla Democratic Party retained power, when each party won two of the seven seats in the National Assembly. The remaining three seats were won by the opposition Anguilla National Alliance party.

Antigua and Barbuda

Official name: none

Independence: 1 November 1981 (from United Kingdom)

Area: 442 sq km (Antigua 281 sq km; Barbuda 161 sq km)

Form of government: constitutional monarchy with United Kingdom-style parliament

Capital: Saint John's

International relations: ACP, C, CARICOM, CDB, ECLAC, FAO, G-77, IBRD, ICAO, ICFTU, ICRM, IFAD, IFC, IFRCS, ILO, IMF, IMO, Intelsat (nonsignatory user), Interpol, IOC, ITU, NAM (observer), OAS, OECS, OPANAL, UN, UNCTAD, UNESCO, UPU, WCL, WFTU, WHO, WIPO, WMO, WTrO

Currency: East Caribbean dollar (XCD)

Income: us$8,200 (1999 est. of purchasing power parity)

Population: 66,970 (July 2001 est.)

Ethnic groups: black, British, Portuguese, Lebanese, Syrian

Religious groups: Anglican (predominant), other Protestant, some Roman Catholic

Languages: English (official), local dialects

Literacy: 89% (age 15 and over has completed five or more years of schooling; 1960 est.)

Exports: petroleum products 48%, manufactures 23%, machinery and transport equipment 17%, food and live animals 4%, other 8%

Primary export partners: OECS 26%, Barbados 15%, Guyana 4%, Trinidad and Tobago 2%, United States 0.3%

Imports: food and live animals, machinery and transport equipment, manufactures, chemicals, oil

Primary import partners: United States 27%, United Kingdom 16%, Canada 4%, OECS 3%

Christopher Columbus first visited the islands of Antigua and Barbuda in 1493. Missionaries attempted to settle on the island, but were hindered by the fierce Carib Indians, who inhabited the islands, and the absence of natural freshwater springs. In 1632, the British successfully established a colony. Sir Christopher Codrington established the first large sugar estate in Antigua in 1674, bringing slaves from Africa's west coast to work the plantations. Although Antiguan slaves were emancipated in 1834, they remained bound to their plantation owners. Economic opportunities for the new freemen were limited by a lack of surplus farming land, no access to credit, and an economy built on agriculture rather than manufacturing.

The majority of modern-day Antiguans are descended from the African slaves imported by the British to work the island's sugar plantations. Although the sugar estates were extremely profitable for both their owners and Britain, generating more wealth in the 1780s than all of Britain's New England colonies combined, life for the island's slaves was very harsh indeed. The harshness of life and work on the sugar plantations led to slave riots including one in 1831, just three years before the British ended slavery on the island.

Led by Chief Minister Vere Cornwall Bird Sr., Antigua began to push for independence in the late 1960s. There was a separate push by Barbudans for their independence, but neither the Antiguan nor the British government supported this movement. Antigua and Barbuda became a single, fully independent nation in 1981. Antigua and Barbuda entered the twenty-first century ruled by its black majority.

The ruling Antigua Labor Party of Prime Minister Lester Bird won the general election in March 1999, ensuring Bird another five-year term in office. In May 2001, Bird fired Attorney General Errol Cort and Health Minister Bernard Percival for "a lapse of good judgment" in handling the government's medical benefits scheme. Throughout 2000 and 2001, the country was widely criticized from abroad for its lax attitude toward the problem of money laundering.

Argentina

Official name: Argentine Republic

Independence: 9 July 1816 (from Spain)

Area: 2,766,890 sq km

Form of government: republic

Capital: Buenos Aires

International relations: AfDB, Australia Group, BCIE, BIS, CCC, ECLAC, FAO, G-6, G-11, G-15, G-19, G-24, G-77, IADB, IAEA, IBRD, ICAO, ICC, ICFTU, ICRM, IDA, IFAD, IFC, IFRCS, IHO, ILO, IMF, IMO, Inmarsat, Intelsat, Interpol, IOC, IOM, ISO, ITU, LAES, LAIA, Mercosur, MINURSO, MIPONUH, MTCR, NSG, OAS, OPANAL, OPCW, PCA, RG, UN, UNCTAD, UNESCO, UNFICYP, UNHCR, UNIDO, UNIKOM, UNMEE, UNMIBH, UNMIK, UNMOP, UNTSO, UNU, UPU, WCL, WFTU, WHO, WIPO, WMO, WToO, WTrO, ZC

Currency: Argentine peso (ARS)

Income: us$12,900 (2000 est. of purchasing power parity)

Population: 37,384,816 (July 2001 est.)

Ethnic groups: white (mostly Spanish and Italian) 97%, mestizo, Amerindian, or other nonwhite groups 3%

Religious groups: nominally Roman Catholic 92% (less than 20% practicing), Protestant 2%, Jewish 2%, other 4%

Languages: Spanish (official), English, Italian, German, French

Literacy: 96.2% (age 15 and over can read and write; 1995 est.)

Exports: edible oils, fuels and energy, cereals, feed, motor vehicles

Primary export partners: Brazil 24%, EU 21%, United States 11% (1999 est.)

Imports: machinery and equipment, motor vehicles, chemicals, metal manufactures, plastics

Primary import partners: EU 28%, United States 22%, Brazil 21% (1999 est.)

Though traditionally known for its early Spanish and nineteenth-century Italian and German heritage, Argentina had a large black population during much of the colonial and independence periods. Today the Afro-Argentine population is estimated at a few thousand.

The first slaves were brought into Argentina in the final two decades of the sixteenth century. By 1680, nearly 23,000 slaves had been imported legally, although those brought into the country illegally would certainly swell that figure considerably. Most of the slaves brought into Argentina originated in what is now the Congo and Angola. Although the local government banned the importation of slaves in 1813, illegal trade in slaves continued for nearly 30 more years until a treaty with Britain in 1840 finally cut off this commerce in human cargo. As in most of the Americas, the slaves brought into Argentina were employed as farm workers or domestic servants. Ownership of one or more slaves was considered a status symbol among Argentina's ranchers.

Until relatively recently, Argentina's African heritage has received little attention, due perhaps in part to the scarcity of Afro-Argentines. The limited number of blacks in the country have allowed the country's historians and sociologists to indulge in a bit of revisionism, insisting that blacks are of little historical relevance in Argentina. Regrettably, racist attitudes are not uncommon in modern-day Argentina. When the country's soccer team has faced opposing teams made up largely of blacks, headlines in the sports pages have sometimes referred to these opponents in a derogatory and decidedly racist manner. A handful of contemporary scholars have attempted to preserve the history of the African contributions to the development of Argentina.

Through most of the 1980s, the country's economy stagnated and was battered by high levels of inflation. The 1989 election of Carlos Menem, a member of the Partido Justicialista, better known as the Peronist party, brought a period of rapid economic growth for several years. However, the Menem administration's failure to deepen economic reforms eventually led to a period of economic decline and paved the way for the election in 1999 of Fernando de la Rua. The new president was unable to halt the economic decline, and his government collapsed after two years in a climate of growing civil unrest. At the beginning of 2002, Peronist Eduardo Duhalde was elected president.

Aruba

Official name: none

Independence: none (part of the Kingdom of the Netherlands)

Area: 193 sq km

Form of government: parliamentary democracy

Capital: Oranjestad

International relations: CARICOM (observer), ECLAC (associate), Interpol, IOC, UNESCO (associate), WCL, WToO (associate)

Currency: Aruban guilder/florin (AWG)

Income: US$28,000 (2000 est. of purchasing power parity)

Population: 70,007 (July 2001 est.)

Ethnic groups: mixed white/Caribbean Amerindian 80%

Religious groups: Roman Catholic 82%, Protestant 8%, Hindu, Muslim, Confucian, Jewish

Languages: Dutch (official), Papiamento (a Spanish, Portuguese, Dutch, English dialect), English (widely spoken), Spanish

Literacy: 97%

Exports: live animals and animal products, art and collectibles, machinery and electrical equipment, transport equipment

Primary export partners: United States 42%, Colombia 20%, Netherlands 12% (1999)

Imports: machinery and electrical equipment, crude oil for refining and reexport, chemicals; foodstuffs

Primary import partners: United States 63%, Netherlands 11%, Netherlands Antilles 3%, Japan (1999)

Aruba is one of the few Caribbean islands whose people are still largely descended from an original indigenous population. More than 85 percent of Arubans are of mixed Arawak Indian and European ancestry. A majority of the remaining 15 percent are black immigrants from other Caribbean islands who have come to Aruba to fill some of the many available jobs in thriving tourist and oil industries.

The island's arid climate and relatively barren soil prevented the development of any major agricultural cultivation on Aruba. This lack of large-scale farming helps to explain the absence of any significant slave heritage on the island. When the first oil refineries began to spring up on Aruba in the 1930s, workers, many of them black, were imported from other islands in the Caribbean.

Though their numbers are relatively small, particularly when viewed against the backdrop of the Caribbean as a whole, the blacks of Aruba have made significant contributions to the island's culture in the relatively short time they have been present on the island. Papiamento, the local language, draws on elements of several European languages, the native Arawak tongue, and several African dialects.

In 1997, the legislature of Aruba was dissolved when a conflict broke out between the senior and junior members of the ruling coalition led by Prime Minister Henny Eman. However, in elections in December 1997, the coalition retained power in the legislature with a 12–9 majority over the opposition People's Electoral Movemement (MEP). Four years later, the opposition party wrested power from the coalition, taking 12 of the 21 seats in the legislature and bringing MEP leader Nelson Oduber to power as prime minister.

Bahamas, The

Official name: Commonwealth of The Bahamas
Independence: 10 July 1973 (from United Kingdom)
Area: 13,940 sq km
Form of government: constitutional parliamentary democracy
Capital: Nassau
International relations: ACP, C, CARICOM, CCC, CDB, ECLAC, FAO, G-77, IADB, IBRD, ICAO, ICFTU, ICRM, IFC, IFRCS, ILO, IMF, IMO, Inmarsat, Intelsat, Interpol, IOC, ITU, LAES, NAM, OAS, OPANAL, OPCW, UN, UNCTAD, UNESCO, UNIDO, UPU, WHO, WIPO, WMO, WTrO (observer)
Currency: Bahamian dollar (BSD)
Income: US$15,000 (2000 est. of purchasing power parity)
Population: 297,852
Ethnic groups: black 85%, white 12%, Asian and Hispanic 3%
Religious groups: Baptist 32%, Anglican 20%, Roman Catholic 19%, Methodist 6%, Church of God 6%, other Protestant 12%, none or unknown 3%, other 2%
Languages: English, Creole (among Haitian immigrants)
Literacy: 98.2% (age 15 and over can read and write; 1995 est.)
Exports: pharmaceuticals, cement, rum, crawfish, refined petroleum products

Primary export partners: United States 22.3%, Switzerland 15.6%, United Kingdom 15%, Denmark 7.4% (1998)
Imports: foodstuffs, manufactured goods, crude oil, vehicles, electronics
Primary import partners: United States 27.3%, Italy 26.5%, Japan 10%, Denmark 4.2% (1998)

Christopher Columbus first visited the islands of the Bahamas in 1492 when he landed in the Western Hemisphere, either at Long Bay, Samana Cay, San Salvador Island, or one of a number of other islands. In 1647, the first permanent European settlement was founded. In 1717, the islands became a British crown colony. Most of these British colonists were not large landowners, so African slavery developed more slowly in the Bahamas than in several nearby islands. But it did develop, and, over time, blacks came to dominate the islands, accounting today for about 85 percent of the total population.

Britain's abolition of slavery in all its territories set free some 10,000 former slaves scattered across the Bahamas. Under the terms of the British edict ending slavery in 1834, the newly freed slaves were apprenticed to their former owners and required to remain with those owners as apprentices for a period of four years. Many of the former slaves continued to pursue occupations in farming and fishing, even after their apprenticeships had ended. Eventually a black middle class developed on the islands as individual blacks managed to obtain a higher education and enter such professions as doctors, lawyers, and educators.

Eighty-five percent of Bahamians are of African descent. Many of their ancestors arrived in the Bahamas when it was a staging area for the slave trade and when Bermuda forced out free blacks and slaves. Later, black slaves were brought into the islands by the thousands of British loyalists who fled the American colonies during the Revolutionary War.

The twentieth-century boom in South Florida and the promise of better-paying jobs lured many black Bahamians to the United States, despite the racial discrimination they encountered upon their arrival. A psychological and cultural barrier developed between those Bahamians who left their homeland in an attempt to better themselves and those who chose to remain in the islands. A similar division was seen between those who were attracted to Nassau and the more rapidly developing islands and those who opted for the quiet life on the outer islands.

The Bahamas were granted self-government through a series of constitutional and political steps, culminating in independence on July 10, 1973. The Progressive Liberal Party led the Bahamas to independence and

Bahamian musicians adorned in celebratory costumes performing in the streets.

remained in power until the early 1990s. In August 1992, the Free National Movement (FNM) won parliamentary elections, and its leader, Hubert Ingraham, became prime minister. In March 1997 elections, Ingraham and the FNM were reelected.

The Ingraham government's privatization policy hit a snag in the spring of 1999 when telecommunications workers rejected the government's retrenchment package. Also troublesome for the Bahamian economy was the country's high crime rate, a potential threat to the country's critically important tourism industry. In 2000, the country's offshore banking business was rocked by charges that it was not moving aggressively enough against money laundering, triggering a new government effort to step up its cooperation with other jurisdictions. In May 2002, the ruling Free National Movement, with Tommy Turnquest now at its helm, replacing retiring Ingraham, lost in parliamentary elections to the Progressive Liberal Party (PLP), which won 29 of 40 seats in the House of Assembly. The election brought PLP leader Perry Christie to power as prime minister.

Barbados

Official name: none

Independence: 30 November 1966 (from United Kingdom)

Area: 430 sq km

Form of government: parliamentary democracy; independent sovereign state within the Commonwealth

Capital: Bridgetown

International relations: ACP, C, CARICOM, CCC, CDB, ECLAC, FAO, G-77, IADB, IBRD, ICAO, ICFTU, ICRM, IFAD, IFC, IFRCS, ILO, IMF, IMO, Intelsat, Interpol, IOC, ISO, ITU, LAES, NAM, OAS, OPANAL, UN, UNCTAD, UNESCO, UNIDO, UPU, WFTU, WHO, WIPO, WMO, WTrO

Currency: Barbadian dollar (BBD)

Income: US$14,500 (2000 est. of purchasing power parity)

Population: 275,330 (July 2001 est.)

Ethnic groups: black 80%, white 4%, other 16%

Religious groups: Protestant 67% (Anglican 40%, Pentecostal 8%, Methodist 7%, other 12%), Roman Catholic 4%, none 17%, other 12%

Languages: English

Literacy: 97.4% (age 15 and over has ever attended school; 1995 est.)

Exports: sugar and molasses, rum, other foods and beverages, chemicals, electrical components, clothing

Primary export partners: United Kingdom 14.8%, United States 11.6%, Trinidad and Tobago 7.6%, Venezuela 6.1%, Jamaica 5.8% (1998)

Imports: consumer goods, machinery, foodstuffs, construction materials, chemicals, fuel, electrical components

Primary import partners: United States 30.7%, Trinidad and Tobago 10.2%, Japan 8.3%, United Kingdom 7.7%, Canada 2.2% (1998)

It should hardly come as a surprise that Barbados is considered the most British of the Caribbean islands. For more than 300 years, the island was under the control of the British, whose institutions became firmly entrenched in the Barbadian culture and economy. The first British colonists arrived in 1627, bringing with them ten slaves of African ancestry. The slave population remained relatively limited for the first few years, as most colonists were unable to afford to purchase slave labor and instead worked the land themselves or with the help of indentured servants from Europe. Although the number of slaves on the island was small, their role in the island's economy was pivotal. African slaves, along with some of the native Amerindian people who had been enslaved, were forced to handle the most challenging tasks by their owners.

With the rise of the sugar industry, beginning in the 1640s, Barbados became more heavily involved in the slave trade. Between 1645 and 1685, the number of African slaves on the island skyrocketed from about 5,700 to nearly 60,000. By 1700, the slave population on Barbados was estimated at close to 135,000. Drawn mostly from West Africa, these slaves spoke a variety of languages and represented a staggering number of ethnic groups including the Fon, Fante, Ga, Asante, and Yoruba peoples. By the early eighteenth century, many of the European-born indentured servants who had carried much of the workload in the colony's early years began leaving Barbados in waves. This aggravated the problem of racial imbalance, worrying the white landowners and resulting in tough, new regulations to control the slave population.

Despite the imposition of strong regulations to prevent unrest among the huge slave population, Barbados experienced three major slave rebellions in 1649, 1675, and 1692. Colonial justice was harsh. Rebellious slaves were tortured in an attempt to get them to name confederates. Of those captured and tried, most were sentenced to be executed, often by somewhat barbarous methods including being burned alive. Little slave resistance was recorded in the eighteenth century, but the British Parliament's 1807 ban on the international

slave trade, the Haitian Revolution that brought blacks to power, and the visits of abolitionists to the island culminated in the so-called Easter Rebellion in 1816. As many as 1,000 slaves were killed in the fighting, nearly 150 were executed after the rebellion was put down, and another 120 slaves or so were deported from the island. So shaken by the uprising was the British government that it pressured Barbadian colonists to relax their hold on the slave population. In 1833, the British Parliament voted to end slavery in all British territories.

From 1958 to 1962, Barbados was one of ten members of the West Indies Federation. Barbados negotiated its own independence at a constitutional conference with the United Kingdom in June 1966. The country attained self-rule on November 30, 1966. Since that time, Barbados has been a member of the British Commonwealth of Nations and has assumed a leadership role in the Caribbean Community (CARICOM). Owen Arthur, a member of the Barbados Labour Party, assumed the prime ministership in 1994, after former Prime Minister Erskine Sandiford lost a vote of confidence in the National Assembly. Leading contemporary Afro-Barbadians include George Lamming, a novelist, critic, essayist, and educator.

The ruling Barbados Labour Party emerged victorious from January 1999 legislative elections, winning all but two of the 28 seats in the National Assembly. A move was made in early 2000 to modernize the country's constitution, moving the government to a republican form of government. Prime Minister Arthur in August 2001 proposed measures to stimulate economic growth, aimed principally at reducing the country's high rate of unemployment, hovering in 2002 at about 10 percent.

Ethnically, the population of Barbados is 80 percent African, 16 percent mixed, and 4 percent European.

Belize

Official name: none

Independence: 21 September 1981 (from United Kingdom)

Area: 22,966 sq km

Form of government: parliamentary democracy

Capital: Belmopan

International relations: ACP, C, CARICOM, CDB, ECLAC, FAO, G-77, IADB, IBRD, ICAO, ICFTU, ICRM, IDA, IFAD, IFC, IFRCS, ILO, IMF, IMO, Intelsat (nonsignatory user), Interpol, IOC, IOM, ITU, LAES, NAM, OAS, OPANAL, UN, UNCTAD, UNESCO, UNIDO, UPU, WCL, WHO, WIPO, WMO, WTrO

Currency: Belizean dollar (BZD)

Income: US$3,200 (2000 est. of purchasing power parity)

Population: 256,062 (July 2001 est.)

Ethnic groups: mestizo 43.7%, Creole 29.8%, Maya 10%, Garifuna 6.2%, other 10.3%

Religious groups: Roman Catholic 62%, Protestant 30% (Anglican 12%, Methodist 6%, Mennonite 4%, Seventh-Day Adventist 3%, Pentecostal 2%, Jehovah's Witnesses 1%, other 2%), none 2%, other 6% (1980)

Languages: English (official), Spanish, Mayan, Garifuna (Carib), Creole

Literacy: 70.3% (age 15 and over can read and write; 1991 est.); note: other sources list the literacy rate as high as 75%

Exports: sugar, bananas, citrus, clothing, fish products, molasses, wood

Primary export partners: United States 42%, United Kingdom 33%, EU 12%, CARICOM 4.8%, Canada 2%, Mexico 1% (1999)

Imports: machinery and transportation equipment, manufactured goods; food, beverages, tobacco; fuels, chemicals, pharmaceuticals

Primary import partners: United States 58%, Mexico 12%, United Kingdom 5% EU 5%, Central America 5%, CARICOM 4% (1998)

Belize, known until 1973 as British Honduras, is the only country in Central America in which blacks have made up a majority of the population throughout the twentieth century. The country did not achieve full independence until September 21, 1981. Originally peopled largely by a succession of native American peoples, including the Maya, Belize passed between British and Spanish control throughout the seventeenth century. A treaty between the two countries in 1765 maintained Spain's claim to the land but recognized the British right to maintain coastal settlements for the harvesting of logwood, which was valued for its use in producing dyes. As the British log harvesting efforts expanded, slaves were brought in from Africa and other British colonies in the Caribbean to assist with the effort.

Once the presence of the British wood-harvesting enclave had been established by treaty, the woodcutters graduated from cutting logwood and began to go after mahogany. The nature of this work had a profound effect on slave life in the colony. Trusted slaves roamed the forests of the land, often with little or no supervision, hunting for mahogany trees to be felled. Once found, these slaves known as huntsmen reported to axmen, a team of slaves that would then cut down the trees. Although the slaves employed in mahogany harvesting enjoyed somewhat more freedom to range through the rain forest, the treatment of these slaves overall was not noticeably more humane than that accorded slaves involved in agriculture.

The British established the colony of British Honduras in 1840; it became a crown colony in 1862. Self-government was granted in January 1964. The official name of the territory was changed from British Honduras to Belize in June of 1973, and full independence was granted on September 21, 1981, with George C. Price of the People's United Party installed as the head of government. In December 1984 elections, voters elected Manuel Esquivel prime minister. Five years later, Price was again elected prime minister, a post that was recaptured by Esquivel in 1993 elections. Leading contemporary Afro-Belizeans include Zee Edgell, a writer who has concentrated her writings on the Belizean independence movement, the nation's multiethnic traditions, and the lives of women in Belize.

In August 1998 elections, the ruling United Democratic Party was soundly defeated by the People's United Party, bringing Said Musa to power as prime minister. Esquivel, who had served for 15 years as prime minister, stepped down August 31, 1998. Musa, in his September 1999 state of the union message, pointed to the progress made in building up Belize's economic infrastructure during his first year in office. In March 2000 municipal elections, the governing People's United Party retained control of six of the country's seven municipalities. The country was hit hard in 2000 and 2001 by Hurricanes Keith and Iris, respectively, both of which left thousands homeless.

Most Belizeans are of multiracial descent. Nearly 40 to 45 percent of the population is of African ancestry; more than 25 percent is of mixed local Indian and European descent (mestizo). Another one-fifth of the population is composed of Carib, Mayan, or other Amerindian ethnic groups.

Bermuda

Official name: none

Independence: none (overseas territory of the United Kingdom)

Area: 58.8 sq km

Form of government: parliamentary British overseas territory with internal self-government

Capital: Hamilton

International relations: CARICOM (observer), CCC, ICFTU, Interpol (subbureau), IOC

Currency: Bermudian dollar (BMD)

Income: us$33,000 (2000 est. of purchasing power parity)

Population: 63,503 (July 2001 est.)

Ethnic groups: black 58%, white 36%, other 6%

Religious groups: non-Anglican Protestant 39%, Anglican 27%, Roman Catholic 15%, other 19%

Languages: English (official), Portuguese

Literacy: 98% (age 15 and over can read and write;
1970 est.)

Exports: reexports of pharmaceuticals

Primary export partners: United Kingdom 29.5%,
United States 9.8% (1997)

Imports: machinery and transport equipment,
construction materials, chemicals, food and live
animals

Primary import partners: United States 34%, United
Kingdom 9%, Mexico 8% (1997)

Located in the Atlantic Ocean about 650 miles east of
North Carolina, Bermuda is relatively isolated. The first
Europeans to visit Bermuda were Spanish explorers in
1503. In 1609, a group of British explorers became
stranded on the islands and their reports aroused great
interest about the islands in England. In 1612, British
colonists arrived and founded the town of Saint George,
the oldest, continuously inhabited English-speaking
settlement in the Western Hemisphere.

Slaves from Africa were brought to Bermuda soon
after the colony began. Although the island's soil and
area were ill-suited for large-scale farming, the slaves
were put to work as fishermen, tradesmen, and, to a
limited extent, as field hands. The slaves of Bermuda
rose up against their masters on several occasions,
most notably in 1730, after which the accused ring-
leader, Sarah Bassett, was burned at the stake. Thirty
years later, between 600 and 700 slaves were accused
of plotting a large-scale rebellion. A number of those
were tried and subsequently executed. The slave trade
was outlawed in Bermuda in 1807, and all slaves were
freed in 1834.

Unfortunately for the newly freed slaves of the
island nation, employment opportunities in the tobacco, shipbuilding, and salt mining industries, all of
which had been mainstays of the Bermudian economy,
began to shrink dramatically as those industries themselves started to end. The island economy got a temporary shot in the arm during the U.S. Civil War when
Union ships blockaded the ports of the Confederacy.
Southern importers arranged to have their incoming
goods off-loaded at Bermuda and then smuggled through
the blockade in smaller ships. However, with the end of
the war, this temporary economy boost disappeared.
Bermudians, with an area of less than 21 square miles,
turned to small-scale agricultural ventures to produce
income. The cultivation of onions, potatoes, and Easter
lilies eventually proved so successful and profitable
that indentured servants had to be brought in from
Portugal to help handle part of the workload.

For most of its first 300 years, the government of
Bermuda was composed exclusively of wealthy white
landowners or appointees of the British Crown. Not
until 1963 were the protests of black Bermudians heeded

and universal adult suffrage introduced. Landowners
still had an edge, however, as the law provided them
each with two votes. A new constitution in 1868 gave
the locally elected government complete control over
Bermuda's affairs. Sentiment against independence for
Bermuda remains strong, as reflected in the most recent referendum on the issue; 73 percent voted against
independence in 1995.

Defeated in the November 1998 general election by
the Progressive Labour Party for the first time in 30
years, the opposition United Bermuda Party, led by
former Prime Minister Pamela Gordon, worked in 1999
to broaden its appeal to voters. In October 2001, Gordon stepped down as leader of the United Bermuda Party.

Nearly two-thirds of the Bermudians are of African
descent. An estimated 7,000 U.S. citizens live on the
island; approximately 2,800 of them are military personnel and their dependents.

Bolivia

Official name: Republic of Bolivia

Independence: 6 August 1825 (from Spain)

Area: 1,098,580 sq km

Form of government: republic

Capital: La Paz (seat of government); Sucre (legal
capital and seat of judiciary)

International relations: CAN, CCC, ECLAC, FAO,
G-11, G-77, IADB, IAEA, IBRD, ICAO, ICRM,
IDA, IFAD, IFC, IFRCS, ILO, IMF, IMO, Intelsat,
Interpol, IOC, IOM, ITU, LAES, LAIA, Mercosur
(associate), MONUC, NAM, OAS, OPANAL,
OPCW, PCA, RG, UN, UNCTAD, UNESCO,
UNIDO, UNMIK, UNTAET, UPU, WCL, WFTU,
WHO, WIPO, WMO, WToO, WTrO

Currency: boliviano (BOB)

Income: us$2,600 (2000 est. of purchasing power
parity)

Population: 8,300,463 (July 2001 est.)

Ethnic groups: Quechua 30%, Aymara 25%, mestizo
(mixed white and Amerindian ancestry) 30%,
white 15%

Religious groups: Roman Catholic 95%, Protestant
(Evangelical Methodist)

Languages: Spanish (official), Quechua (official),
Aymara (official)

Literacy: 83.1% (age 15 and over can read and write;
1995 est.)

Exports: soybeans, natural gas, zinc, gold, wood

Primary export partners: United Kingdom 16%,
United States 12%, Peru 11%, Argentina 10%,
Colombia 7% (1998)

Imports: capital goods, raw materials and semimanufactures, chemicals, petroleum, food

Primary import partners: United States 32%, Japan
24%, Brazil 12%, Argentina 12%, Chile 7%, Peru 4%,
Germany 3%, other 6% (1998)

Although blacks make up only about two percent of
Bolivia's population, their history extends back to the
first half of the sixteenth century when the first slaves
were brought into the country. These blacks were
imported from Peru to help supplement the labor of the
indigenous native American population, many of whom
had succumbed to diseases introduced by European
settlers. The African origins of these slaves is the
subject of debate, with some contending that they came
from an area of the West African coast between the
Senegal and Niger rivers, while others maintain they
were brought from Angola. This question of the earliest
Afro-Bolivians' origins is unlikely ever to be resolved,
since Spain maintained no West African trading centers
and thus drew slaves from a wide area and also because
the record keeping of those moving the slaves left much
to be desired. Frequently there was an assumption that
the slaves came from an area close to their port of
embarkation in Africa, but often this was not the case.

The slaves of African origin brought into Bolivia did
not fare well at high elevations and under the stressful
working conditions of the mines. By 1554, most of the
African slaves had been replaced in the country's silver
mines by indigenous labor. The blacks were then put
into other lines of work, including as domestic servants. Some were even apprenticed to artisans skilled
in the crafting of silver and other metals. The majority
of the black slaves were moved to rural areas and
pressed into service as cultivators of crops to feed the
country's growing population. Within Bolivia, many of
the black slaves eventually mixed with other ethnic
groups. Children of mixed African and European ancestry were sometimes classified as mulattos, while
those of African and native American descent were
called zambos. Calculating the African or African-mixed
population in Bolivia's past is difficult because of the
haphazard manner in which records were kept.

Although their numbers were few, Afro-Bolivians
joined the country's struggle to win its independence
from Spain. Independence was achieved in 1825, and
soon thereafter the country's founding constitution
called for the emancipation of all its slaves. However,
not all blacks and native Americans in bondage were
set free. As of 1831, the country's constitution contained a "free-womb" statute that decreed that no one
born after independence could be considered a slave,
but continued to recognize those previously in bondage
as slaves. Complete liberation of the slaves did not
come until 1851.

Never particularly active on the political front, Afro-
Bolivians have had some impact on contemporary
culture, given their dwindling numbers. In the early
1980s, a group of students from Coroico, Nor Yungas,
formed a dance troupe to preserve some of the original
Afro-Bolivian dance forms of the region. Called the
Grupo Afroboliviano, the troupe performed throughout
the country, helping to create an awareness among
their countrymen of the distinct Afro-Bolivian culture.
This, in turn, has sparked a number of efforts to preserve this culture.

Dissatisfaction with the administration of President
Hugo Bánzer erupted into nationwide protests in April
2000. Bánzer's plan to privatize water service in
Cochabamba was the principal cause of the protests.
The president on April 8, 2000, declared a state of
emergency, which was lifted on April 20. Shortly thereafter Bánzer replaced his finance and defense ministers. Protests over the government's policies continued, however, well into 2001. In poor health, Bánzer
resigned on August 6, 2001, and was replaced by Jorge
Quiroga Ramirez, a former IBM executive.

Brazil

Official name: Federative Republic of Brazil

Independence: 7 September 1822 (from Portugal)

Area: 8,511,965 sq km

Form of government: federative republic

Capital: Brasilia

International relations: AfDB, BIS, CCC, ECLAC,
FAO, G-11, G-15, G-19, G-24, G-77, IADB, IAEA,
IBRD, ICAO, ICC, ICFTU, ICRM, IDA, IFAD,
IFC, IFRCS, IHO, ILO, IMF, IMO, Inmarsat,
Intelsat, Interpol, IOC, IOM (observer), ISO, ITU,
LAES, LAIA, Mercosur, NAM (observer), NSG,
OAS, OPANAL, OPCW, PCA, RG, UN, UNCTAD,
UNESCO, UNHCR, UNIDO, UNITAR, UNMOP,
UNTAET, UNU, UPU, WCL, WFTU, WHO, WIPO,
WMO, WToO, WTrO

Currency: real (BRL)

Income: us$6,500 (2000 est. of purchasing power
parity)

Population: 174,468,575

Ethnic groups: white (includes Portuguese, German,
Italian, Spanish, Polish) 55%, mixed white and
black 38%, black 6%, other (includes Japanese,
Arab, Amerindian) 1%

Religious groups: Roman Catholic (nominal) 80%

Languages: Portuguese (official), Spanish,
English, French

Literacy: 83.3% (age 15 and over can read and write;
1995 est.)

Exports: manufactures, iron ore, soybeans,
footwear, coffee

Primary export partners: United States 23%, Argentina 11%, Germany 5%, Netherlands 5%, Japan 5% (1999)

Imports: machinery and equipment, chemical products, oil, electricity

Primary import partners: United States 24%, Argentina 12%, Germany 10%, Japan 5%, Italy 5% (1999)

Brazil was formally claimed in 1500 by the Portuguese and was ruled from Lisbon as a colony until 1808. Brazil successfully declared independence on September 7, 1922. Four major groups make up the Brazilian population: indigenous Indians of Tupi and Guarani language stock; the Portuguese; Africans brought to Brazil as slaves; and various European and Asian immigrant groups that have settled in Brazil since the mid-nineteenth century.

Slavery was introduced into Brazil in the 1530s and expanded greatly when sugar became important. It grew rapidly between 1580 and 1640, when Spain controlled the country. Estimates of the total number of slaves brought to Brazil varies from six million to twenty million. Slavery did not finally end in Brazil until 1888. Though slavery in Brazil was often extremely brutal, and the death rate of blacks on sugar, coffee, and cotton plantations was enormous, large numbers of Africans achieved freedom. About 25 percent of Brazil's blacks were free during slavery.

During the nineteenth century, free blacks intermarried so rapidly that their numbers fell from about 400,000 in 1800 to 20,000 by 1888, when slavery was finally abolished. Free blacks enjoyed full legal equality during both the period of slavery and after it was abolished.

In Brazil, slaves who served masters in cities were often allowed to seek part-time and temporary employment elsewhere. They were able to read and write and develop employable skills. Blacks became important to the development and economy of the country, and some became prominent in public life. Black Brazilian Nilo Pecanha served as vice president and briefly as president of Brazil in the first decade of this century. Blacks also achieved fame in Brazil's intellectual and artistic life.

In the early twentieth century, a new black consciousness emerged in response to the appearance of a number of Afro-Brazilian publications. Also springing up during this period were a number of organizations that aspired to right some of the wrongs faced by the nation's black population. White Brazilians in the years following the abolition of slavery embarked on a policy of "whitening" the country's population through intermixing with Afro-Brazilians. The Brazilian program of "branqueamento" was based on the notion that the presence of European blood in an individual was sufficient to make him or her white. It was against the discrimination and poverty stemming from this racist policy that the Afro-Brazilian organizations fought in the early twentieth century.

The black population of Brazil is the largest in the Americas. Only Nigeria in Africa has a larger population of blacks. The African influences on both the population and the culture of Brazil are all-pervasive. Perhaps no single event better illustrates the scope of the African contribution to Brazilian life than Carnival. However, behind the laughter and goodwill of this annual four-day celebration, the truth is somewhat less reassuring for those who would assume that racism is long dead in Brazil. In fact, Brazilians of African descent lack clout on both the political and the economic level. Afro-Brazilians lag behind their fellow countrymen in terms of education, housing, employment, and health. Activists within the Afro-Brazilian community continue the struggle to achieve complete equality for everyone in the country, regardless of race. Leading contemporary Afro-Brazilians include: musicians Jorge Benjor, Carlinhos Brown, Gilberto Gil, husband and

Brazilian vendor selling food along the beaches of Rio de Janeiro.

wife duo Airto Moreira and Flora Purim, and Milton Nascimento; literary figure Abdias do Nascimento; and internationally recognized sports figure Pelé.

After years of military rule, democracy returned to Brazil in 1985. Three years later, a new constitution was drafted. In the presidential elections of October 1998, Fernando Henrique Cardoso won a second term as president. One of Cardoso's first moves in his second term was to order a devaluation of the real in January 1999. The country's economy showed signs of recovery in 1999 and 2000. However, a difficult external environment in 2001 limited growth and worsened public solvency indicators.

Canada

Official name: none

Independence: 1 July 1867 (from United Kingdom)

Area: 9,976,140 sq km

Form of government: confederation with parliamentary democracy

Capital: Ottawa

International relations: ABEDA, ACCT, AfDB, APEC, ARF (dialogue partner), AsDB, ASEAN (dialogue partner), Australia Group, BIS, C, CCC, CDB (non-regional), CE (observer), EAPC, EBRD, ECE, ECLAC, ESA (cooperating state), FAO, G- 7, G-10, IADB, IAEA, IBRD, ICAO, ICC, ICFTU, ICRM, IDA, IEA, IFAD, IFC, IFRCS, IHO, ILO, IMF, IMO, Inmarsat, Intelsat, Interpol, IOC, IOM, ISO, ITU, MINURCA, MIPONUH, MONUC, NAM (guest), NATO, NEA, NSG, OAS, OECD, OPCW, OSCE, PCA, UN, UNCTAD, UNDOF, UNESCO, UNFICYP, UNHCR, UNIKOM, UNMEE, UNMIBH, UNMIK, UNMOP, UNTAET, UNTSO, UNU, UPU, WCL, WFTU, WHO, WIPO, WMO, WToO, WTrO, ZC

Currency: Canadian dollar (CAD)

Income: US$24,800 (2000 est. of purchasing power parity)

Population: 31,592,805 (July 2001 est.)

Ethnic groups: British Isles origin 28%, French origin 23%, other European 15%, Amerindian 2%, other, mostly Asian, African, Arab 6%, mixed background 26%

Religious groups: Roman Catholic 42%, Protestant 40%, other 18%

Languages: English 59.3% (official), French 23.2% (official), other 17.5%

Literacy: 97% (age 15 and over can read and write; 1986 est.)

Exports: motor vehicles and parts, newsprint, wood pulp, timber, crude petroleum, machinery, natural gas, aluminum, telecommunications equipment, electricity

Primary export partners: United States 86%, Japan 3%, United Kingdom, Germany, South Korea, Netherlands, China (1999)

Imports: machinery and equipment, crude oil, chemicals, motor vehicles and parts, durable consumer goods, electricity

Primary import partners: United States 76%, Japan 3%, United Kingdom, Germany, France, Mexico, Taiwan, South Korea (1999)

Blacks make up a tiny portion—only about two percent—of Canada's total population, but their contributions to the country's founding and its history far outweigh their meager numbers. Africans are believed to have participated in a number of the early exploratory missions to the country. Legend holds that one of the crew members on Jacques Cartier's expedition was an African. However, it is known for certain that a Mathieu de Coste (sometimes rendered as da Costa) served the governor of Acadia as an interpreter to the local Micmac indigenous peoples. Early records indicated that the first slave brought directly to Canada from Africa was a child, brought to Quebec in 1628 by Englishman David Kirke and sold to a local resident upon Kirke's departure the following year. The child was baptized Olivier Le Jeune in May 1633. According to records, he died in 1654.

Between 1628 and the British conquest of 1759, New France imported 1,132 slaves of African origin. Most of these slaves came from the French West Indies or the British colonies elsewhere in North America. A governor of New France had petitioned Paris to permit a trade in African slaves but was turned down, so there was no direct importation of slaves from Africa. The number of slaves living in the British-held colonies of Canada was relatively small until the time of the American Revolution. Loyalists fleeing the new American republic brought with them some 2,000 black slaves. About 1,200 of that number went to the Maritimes including New Brunswick, Nova Scotia, and Prince Edward Island. Of the remaining 800, about 300 went to Lower Canada, as Quebec was then known, and 500 went to Upper Canada (Ontario). Even more influential in Canada's development was the arrival of some 3,500 free black Loyalists, who fled to Canada following the American Revolution. Most of these black Loyalists settled in Nova Scotia and New Brunswick.

Slave codes were more severe in the British-held territories than in New France, where slaves could marry, own property, and maintain parental rights. However, the British were not to sustain slavery for long. London had divided Canada into two governments, Upper Canada and Lower Canada. The governor of Upper Canada, Colonel James Simcoe, an ardent abolitionist, induced the area's legislature to pass laws forbidding importation of slaves and freeing every slave born in the area by the age of 25. As a result, slavery in Upper Canada soon collapsed.

Similar legislation was not enacted in Lower Canada. However, by 1800, the courts, through complex legal decisions, established the principle that a slave could leave his master whenever he wished. In the Maritime Provinces, courts also acted to eliminate slavery in fact if not in theory. Slavery was formally abolished in Canada in 1833.

Meanwhile, starting slowly in the eighteenth century, Canada was becoming a haven for slaves fleeing across her southern borders. Slaves who had served with the British in the American War for Independence came to Halifax from New York in large numbers in 1782 and 1783. Though many were to migrate to Freetown on the West Coast of Africa, others stayed. In 1826, Canada defied the United States and formally refused to return fugitive slaves. In 1829, the legislature of Lower Canada announced that every slave that entered the province was immediately free, a declaration that gave impetus to the Underground Railroad and stimulated moves for resettlement by blacks in Canada.

The passage of the Fugitive Slave Act in 1850 meant that any escaped slave who remained in the United States was to be returned to his owner. Within a year after passage of the law, some 10,000 slaves arrived in Canada, welcomed by a majority of Canadians who provided communities and services for them.

African Americans were accepted into the mainstream of Canadian life, were allowed to choose separate or integrated schools, and were elected to local office and served as officers in the Canadian Army. Black laborers contributed substantially to the expansion of the Canadian Pacific Railroad, as immigrants from Eastern and Southern Europe were to contribute to the development of railroads in the United States. Black skilled laborers were much in demand. By 1861, at the outbreak of the Civil War in the United States, there were 50,000 blacks in Canada. However, after the Civil War, feelings of fear among white Canadians led to discrimination in employment and schools. Many African Americans re-emigrated to the United States, feeling that, with slavery outlawed there, a bright future awaited them. By 1871, the black population of Canada dipped to about 20,000.

Canada, the most sparsely populated country in the world with 1.5 persons per square mile, has become a haven for so many refugees that it has earned awards for outstanding achievement from human rights organizations. In fact, so many immigrants from Asia, Africa, the Caribbean, and elsewhere have moved to Canada, that the established British-Caucasian population has expressed fears it will become extinct (assimilated) within 100 years. Toronto alone has become one of the world's most cosmopolitan cities with more than 100 cultural or ethnic groups.

Although Canada is officially a constitutional monarchy with the governor-general acting as Canadian representative of the British crown, the nation's House of Commons is actually the sovereign. The Liberal Party has won Canada's last three general elections, in October 1993, June 1997, and November 2000, and its leader, Jean Chretien, serves as the country's prime minister. The next general election is scheduled for November 2005.

Cayman Islands

Official name: none
Independence: none (overseas territory of the United Kingdom)
Area: 259 sq km
Form of government: British crown colony
Capital: George Town
International relations: CARICOM (observer), CDB, Interpol (subbureau), IOC, UNESCO (associate)
Currency: Caymanian dollar (KYD)
Income: US$24,500 (1997 est. of purchasing power parity)
Population: 35,527 (July 2001 est.)
Ethnic groups: mixed 40%, white 20%, black 20%, expatriates of various ethnic groups 20%
Religious groups: United Church (Presbyterian and Congregational), Anglican, Baptist, Roman Catholic, Church of God, other Protestant
Languages: English
Literacy: 98% (age 15 and over has ever attended school; 1970 est.)
Exports: turtle products, manufactured consumer goods
Primary export partners: mostly United States
Imports: foodstuffs, manufactured goods
Primary import partners: United States, Trinidad and Tobago, United Kingdom, Netherlands Antilles, Japan

During his fourth visit to the Caribbean in 1503, Christopher Columbus sighted these islands and dubbed them Las Tortugas for the large number of sea turtles he saw in the area. Later in the sixteenth century, Europeans passing through the area began calling the islands Las Caymanas, the Carib Amerindian term for crocodiles. However, it is believed that it was the island's many iguanas, rather than real crocodiles, that inspired this name change. In any case, apart from brief visits to pick up fresh water and turtle meat, Europeans had little to do with these islands until the middle of the seventeenth century when the first European settlement was made. The earliest settlements on the islands were made by a rather disreputable blend of characters including pirates, army deserters, debtors, and shipwrecked sailors. Under the Treaty of Madrid, the Caymans came under British control in 1670. It was more than 60 years before the British established their first permanent settlement, made up largely of planters who had previously been located on Jamaica. Because of this relationship between Jamaica and the Caymans, the islands were considered dependencies of the former until 1962.

These earliest of British settlers first imported African slaves into the islands, using them largely as domestic servants, fishermen, and subsistence farmers. The islands, not particularly fertile, were never considered an ideal setting for farming, so the large-scale agricultural undertakings the planters had enjoyed in Jamaica could not be duplicated in the Caymans. The absence of a plantation-type system and the relative proximity within which the planters and the newly imported slaves lived led in time to a good deal of intermarriage between the two groups. Nearly half of the population of the Caymans today is made up of islanders of mixed European and African descent. As elsewhere throughout the British territories, slavery was abolished in 1834.

When Jamaica won its independence in 1962, the Caymans became a directly held colony of Britain. Under the new arrangements with the United Kingdom, the islanders were given a new constitution and a larger measure of control over their internal affairs. A tourist board launched in 1966 proved extremely successful in attracting tourists to the islands. By 1994, more than one million tourists, close to 70 percent of them from the United States, were visiting the islands annually. Another major source of income for the Caymans came from offshore banking. Shortly after its change in status with Jamaica, Cayman Islanders enacted new legislation to encourage company registration, offshore banking, and trust-company formation in the islands. Today, more than 500 banks do business in the Caymans, and the companies registered there number in the thousands. Prospering under existing conditions, islanders have made no major push for independence.

Long a major center for offshore banking, the Caymans came under increasing scrutiny in 1999 after accusations that the islands' government knowingly abetted tax evasion. Despite vehement denials by government officials, the Financial Action Task Force (FATF) blacklisted the Caymans as one of several countries around the world that had been determined to be uncooperative on matters of money laundering. In June 2001, the FATF eventually relented and removed the islands from its money laundering blacklist.

Chile

Official name: Republic of Chile
Independence: 18 September 1810 (from Spain)
Area: 756,950 sq km
Form of government: republic
Capital: Santiago
International relations: APEC, CCC, ECLAC, FAO, G-11, G-77, IADB, IAEA, IBRD, ICAO, ICC, ICFTU, ICRM, IDA, IFAD, IFC, IFRCS, IHO, ILO, IMF, IMO, Inmarsat, Intelsat, Interpol, IOC, IOM, ISO, ITU, LAES, LAIA, Mercosur (associate), NAM, OAS, OPANAL, OPCW, PCA, RG, UN, UNCTAD, UNESCO, UNHCR, UNIDO, UNITAR, UNMIBH, UNMOGIP, UNTAET, UNTSO, UNU, UPU, WCL, WFTU, WHO, WIPO, WMO, WToO, WTrO
Currency: Chilean peso (CLP)
Income: US$10,100 (2000 est. of purchasing power parity)
Population: 15,328,467 (July 2001 est.)
Ethnic groups: white and white-Amerindian 95%, Amerindian 3%, other 2%
Religious groups: Roman Catholic 89%, Protestant 11%, Jewish NEGL%
Languages: Spanish
Literacy: 95.2% (age 15 and over can read and write; 1995 est.)
Exports: copper, fish, fruits, paper and pulp, chemicals
Primary export partners: EU 27%, United States 16%, Japan 14%, Brazil 6%, Argentina 5% (1998)
Imports: consumer goods, chemicals, motor vehicles, fuels, electrical machinery, heavy industrial machinery, food
Primary import partners: United States 24%, EU 23%, Argentina 11%, Brazil 6%, Japan 6%, Mexico 5% (1998)

Africans first came to Chile with the expedition of Spanish explorer Diego de Almagro in 1536. Some served the expedition as slaves, while others served as soldiers. One such member of the expedition was Juan Valiente, a slave from Mexico who was permitted to join Almagro as a soldier. He later distinguished himself in battle and in time rose to captain of the expedition's infantry. The earliest slaves brought into Chile were used to supplement the labors of indigenous workers in construction, farming, and the mining of gold. Relatively hard-strapped for money, Chile could not afford to import large numbers of slaves.

Despite the economic limits on the importation of slaves, the country's black population, both free and slave, grew fairly dramatically during the final three decades of the sixteenth century. From a population of 7,000 among a total Chilean population of 624,000, the number of blacks surged by 1590 to a total of 20,000, among an overall population of 586,000. Both in the rural countryside and in Chile's growing cities, free and slave blacks found livelihoods. In the cities, most black slaves worked as domestic servants, while outside the cities, they toiled as miners, sheepherders, and cowboys. Free blacks drove coaches, made saddles, and reportedly even served as executioners. Even though the colonial Spanish law accorded blacks the lowest status possible, local authorities often saw fit to circumvent the Spanish crown and gave some slaves positions with supervisory responsibility. A select number of black slaves so distinguished themselves as soldiers that they received land grants. Juan Valiente, the slave from Mexico who served the Almagro expedition as a soldier, became the first black in the Americas known to receive such a land grant.

At about the same time, Chileans first declared their independence from Spain in 1810, talk of an abolition of slavery began to surface. It was not until 1823, however, that Chile became the first Spanish American republic to totally abolish slavery. Since the time of emancipation, the influence of the Afro-Chilean on the country's culture and development seems to have virtually disappeared. Unlike what has happened in many neighboring countries, there has been no Afro-Chilean cultural revival nor any organized involvement in politics by Afro-Chileans. The Chilean census of 1940 revealed a population of only 1,000 blacks and 3,000 mulattos. Some observers and scholars of the Chilean social scene suggest that continuing intermarriage and intermixing have combined to virtually wipe out the black population of the country.

In a December 1988 referendum, longtime military ruler Augusto Pinochet failed to win the majority he needed to remain in office for another eight years. A year later, Patricio Aylwin, leader of the center-left Concertacion de Partidos por la Democracia coalition, was democratically elected to the presidency for a term of four years. He was succeeded in early 1994 by Concertacion candidate Eduardo Frei, who was elected to a six-year term. Frei, in turn, was replaced in March 2000 by Ricardo Lagos, also a Concertacion candidate.

Colombia

Official name: Republic of Colombia
Independence: 20 July 1810 (from Spain)
Area: 1,138,910 sq km
Form of government: republic; executive branch dominates government structure
Capital: Bogota

International relations: BCIE, CAN, CARICOM (observer), CCC, CDB, ECLAC, FAO, G- 3, G-11, G-24, G-77, IADB, IAEA, IBRD, ICAO, ICC, ICFTU, ICRM, IDA, IFAD, IFC, IFRCS, IHO, ILO, IMF, IMO, Inmarsat, Intelsat, Interpol, IOC, IOM, ISO, ITU, LAES, LAIA, NAM, OAS, OPANAL, OPCW, PCA, RG, UN, UN Security Council (temporary), UNCTAD, UNESCO, UNHCR, UNIDO, UNU, UPU, WCL, WFTU, WHO, WIPO, WMO, WToO, WTrO
Currency: Colombian peso (COP)
Income: US$6,200 (2000 est. of purchasing power parity)
Population: 40,349,388 (July 2001 est.)
Ethnic groups: mestizo 58%, white 20%, mulatto 14%, black 4%, mixed black-Amerindian 3%, Amerindian 1%
Religious groups: Roman Catholic 90%
Languages: Spanish
Literacy: 91.3% (age 15 and over can read and write; 1995 est.)
Exports: petroleum, coffee, coal, apparel, bananas, cut flowers
Primary export partners: United States 50%, EU 14%, Andean Community of Nations 16%, Japan 2% (2000 est.)
Imports: industrial equipment, transportation equipment, consumer goods, chemicals, paper products, fuels, electricity
Primary import partners: United States 35%, EU 16%, Andean Community of Nations 15%, Japan 5% (2000 est.)

The diversity of ethnic origins in Colombia results from the intermixture of indigenous Indians, Spanish colonists, and African slaves. In 1549, the area was established as a Spanish colony with the capital at Bogota. In 1717, Bogota became the capital of the viceroyalty of New Granada, which included what is now Venezuela, Ecuador, and Panama. On July 20, 1810, the citizens of Bogota created the first representative council to defy Spanish authority. Total independence was proclaimed in 1813, and, in 1819, the Republic of Greater Colombia was formed.

The African contributions to the population and culture of Colombia are many and varied. The high rate of intermarriage has resulted in a racially diverse population with close to 70 percent of its people classified as mestizos. The terminology used to refer to people of African ancestry or of mixed ancestry is somewhat complicated. The term black, or "negro" in Spanish, is common but avoided by many Colombians because of its sometimes disparaging connotations. More common are the terms "moreno" (brown) and "gente de color" (colored people). In the rural area of the country near the Pacific coast, some of the people of African ancestry refer to themselves as "libres," or free people, terminology that dates back to colonial times. Some people refer to blacks as "costenos" since many of the country's coastal residents are Afro-Colombians.

African slaves were first imported into communities along the northern coast of New Granada, a portion of which later became Colombia, in the 1520s. The port of Cartagena on the Caribbean coast developed into the principal slave trading port. The slaves brought into New Granada were used mostly in mining gold, although some saw service as domestic servants and farmworkers. The supply of native Americans, who had first been pressed into service in the mines, was rapidly being depleted, and the importation of African slaves was deemed necessary to keep the mines operating.

Even during the years of slavery, there was a considerable amount of intermarriage and intermixing between the peoples of colonial New Granada. It is estimated that by the 1770s about 60 percent of the population was classified as "free people of color." As in most territories where slaves were held, masters sometimes decided to set some or all of their slaves free, which turned out often to be a mixed blessing for those who could not find work on their own. Colombia won its independence in 1819, but slavery was not officially abolished until 1851. In the late twentieth century, Colombia's black population was concentrated in three main areas of the country: the upper central portion of the Cauca Valley, which is heavily planted in sugar cane; the Pacific coast; and the Caribbean coastal region. In the 1990s, Pledad Corboda de Castro became the first black woman to be elected to the Colombian Senate in the 1990s. In 1993, she wrote a law instituting equal rights for Afro-Colombians. Other leading contemporary Afro-Colombians include Totó la Momposina, a singer, dancer, and performer of traditional rhythms, and Manuel Zapata Olivella, a writer, physician, anthropologist, diplomat, and leading intellectual and artist of twentieth-century Latin America.

For much of its history as a republic, Colombia has experienced intermittent periods of violence. Some of the earlier violence was reduced in the early 1960s after the country's liberals and conservatives struck power-sharing agreements. However, the peaceful interval was short indeed as new political factions, now marginalized by such agreements, took to guerrilla warfare to press for their various goals. Economic growth spurted in the early 1990s after economic liberalization measures were enacted in 1991, but the country's tight monetary policy and low business confidence significantly slowed growth in the latter half of the decade. President Andrés Pastrana Arango, the first conservative chief executive after 12 years of liberal leadership, faced increasing pressure from leftist guerrilla groups from the late 1990s into the new millennium. Valiant attempts by Pastrana to advance the country on multiple fronts were either frustrated or doomed to failure by the country's continuing preoccupation with violence in the countryside.

Costa Rica

Official name: Republic of Costa Rica
Independence: 15 September 1821 (from Spain)
Area: 51,100 sq km
Form of government: democratic republic
Capital: San Jose
International relations: BCIE, CACM, ECLAC, FAO, G-77, IADB, IAEA, IBRD, ICAO, ICFTU, ICRM, IDA, IFAD, IFC, IFRCS, ILO, IMF, IMO, Inmarsat, Intelsat, Interpol, IOC, IOM, ISO, ITU, LAES, LAIA (observer), NAM (observer), OAS, OPANAL, OPCW, PCA, UN, UNCTAD, UNESCO, UNIDO, UNU, UPU, WCL, WFTU, WHO, WIPO, WMO, WToO, WTrO
Currency: Costa Rican colon (CRC)
Income: US$6,700 (2000 est. of purchasing power parity)

A young boy fishing to help support his family in Costa Rica.

Population: 3,773,057 (July 2001 est.)

Ethnic groups: white (including mestizo) 94%, black 3%, Amerindian 1%, Chinese 1%, other 1%

Religious groups: Roman Catholic 76.3%, Evangelical 13.7%, other Protestant 0.7%, Jehovah's Witnesses 1.3%, other 4.8%, none 3.2%

Languages: Spanish (official), English spoken around Puerto Limon

Literacy: 94.8% (age 15 and over can read and write; 1995 est.)

Exports: coffee, bananas, sugar; pineapples; textiles, electronic components, medical equipment

Primary export partners: United States 54.1%, EU 21.3%, Central America 8.6% (1999)

Imports: raw materials, consumer goods, capital equipment, petroleum

Primary import partners: United States 56.4%, EU 9%, Mexico 5.4%, Japan 4.7%, (1999)

In 1502, on his fourth and last voyage to the New World, Christopher Columbus made the first European landfall in the area. Settlement of Costa Rica began in 1522. In 1821, Costa Rica joined other Central American provinces in a joint declaration of independence from Spain. Unlike most of their Central American neighbors, Costa Ricans are largely of European rather than mestizo descent, and Spain is the primary country of origin. The indigenous population today numbers no more than 25,000. Blacks, descendants of nineteenth-century Jamaican immigrant workers, constitute a significant English-speaking minority of about 30,000 concentrated around the Caribbean port city of Limon.

The greatest influx of slaves into Costa Rica began during the late 1700s when Spanish colonists began importing slaves from neighboring colonies and directly from Africa to replace the dwindling labor force of indigenous Amerindian peoples, many of whom had contracted and died from diseases introduced by Europeans. The census of 1801, the first to provide figures on the black population, reported that 17 percent of the colony's population was made up of blacks or those of mixed-black descent, including mulattos, the result of black-white intermixing, and zambos of black and Amerindian descent.

More significant than the earlier importation of slaves was the movement to what is now Costa Rica by a substantial number of free black laborers from the islands of the Caribbean, particularly Jamaica. This wave of immigrants began arriving in the late nineteenth century and came to help build the railroad designed to carry coffee from the country's interior to ports along its Atlantic Coast. When this construction project had been completed, many of these West Indian laborers stayed on and took work in the banana plantations of the United Fruit Company. Since the majority of these workers had come from English-speaking islands in the Caribbean and continued to speak English among themselves after coming to Costa Rica, they were considered more valuable employees by United Fruit managers, most of whom were English-speaking as well. In the 1920s, when the banana plantations of eastern Costa Rica experienced problems, United Fruit began concentrating on production from western Costa Rica. Most West Indian blacks, whose population was concentrated along the Atlantic coast, showed little interest in relocating westward. Additionally, the government of Costa Rica, feeling the effects of the worldwide Great Depression, enacted laws giving preferential treatment to Costa Rican nationals. Since most of the West Indian workers had never become citizens, they were left without the agricultural work to which they were accustomed. Many moved into cities to make a living. This gradual disintegration of the black coastal enclaves helped to speed black assimilation into the local culture.

Despite a small elite of black intellectuals, the average Afro-Costa Rican in the late twentieth century was poor and worked in subsistence farming or as a wage laborer. Although there was some organized effort by the elite to achieve equality for the country's blacks, few Afro-Costa Ricans ever have achieved political power. The population of blacks in Costa Rica in the early 1990s was estimated at about 64,000, or two percent of the country's population. Leading contemporary Afro-Costa Ricans include Quince Duncan, a writer of West Indian descent.

Costa Rica's longtime border squabble with Nicaragua broke into the open once again in 1999 when Nicaragua accused Costa Rica of violating the 1858 Cañas-Jerez Treaty that separated the two countries. Later in 1999, a group of lawyers from both countries urged that the treaty be revised. The administration of President Miguel Angel Rodríguez Echeverría came under fire for some of its measures to stimulate long-term economic growth, which triggered civil protests and work stoppages. In April 2002, Abel Pacheco of the ruling Social Christian Unity Party won the country's presidency.

Cuba

Official name: Republic of Cuba

Independence: 20 May 1902 (from United States)

Area: 110,860 sq km

Form of government: Communist state

Capital: Havana

International relations: CCC, ECLAC, FAO, G-77, IAEA, ICAO, ICC, ICRM, IFAD, IFRCS, IHO, ILO, IMO, Inmarsat, Intelsat (nonsignatory user), Interpol, IOC, IOM (observer), ISO, ITU,

Cuban vendor selling postcards in Havana.

LAES, LAIA, NAM, OAS (excluded from formal
participation since 1962), OPCW, PCA, UN,
UNCTAD, UNESCO, UNIDO, UPU, WCL, WFTU,
WHO, WIPO, WMO, WToO, WTrO

Currency: Cuban peso (CUP)

Income: US$1,700 (2000 est. of purchasing power
parity)

Population: 11,184,023 (July 2001 est.)

Ethnic groups: mulatto 51%, white 37%, black 11%,
Chinese 1%

Religious groups: nominally 85% Roman Catholic
prior to CASTRO assuming power; Protestants,
Jehovah's Witnesses, Jews, and Santeria are also
represented

Languages: Spanish

Literacy: 95.7% (age 15 and over can read and write;
1995 est.)

Exports: sugar, nickel, tobacco, fish, medical
products, citrus, coffee

Primary export partners: Russia 23%, Netherlands
23%, Canada 13% (1999)

Imports: petroleum, food, machinery, chemicals,
semifinished goods, transport equipment,
consumer goods

Primary import partners: Spain 18%, Venezuela 13%,
Canada 8% (1999)

Cuba is a multiracial society with a population of
mainly Spanish and African origins. When Columbus
first visited the island in 1492, he found it inhabited by three native American groups: the Ciboneys,
Guanahuatabeys, and Taino Arawaks. As Spain developed its colonial empire in the Western Hemisphere,
Havana became an important commercial seaport. Settlers eventually moved inland, devoting themselves
mainly to sugar cane and tobacco farming. As the
native Indian population died out, African slaves were
imported to work on the plantations, the first such
shipment arriving in 1526. These first slaves were used
largely to work the island's sugar and coffee plantations. A 1774 census counted 96,000 whites, 31,000 free
blacks, and 44,000 slaves in Cuba.

The slave trade grew rapidly during the final third of
the eighteenth century and the first quarter of the
nineteenth century. Among the factors contributing to
this dramatic growth were the collapse of the sugar
trade out of Haiti following its revolution and Spain's
decision to allow Cuba to trade with the outside world.

By the early nineteenth century, the slave population of Cuba was estimated at more than a million individuals. Most of the indigenous population had fallen victim to disease or died in conflict with European settlers, so that left the Spaniards and the slaves of African ancestry as the two main population groups within Cuba. Relations between the two groups were at times strained. In 1812, Jose Antonio Aponte, a free black working as a carpenter in Havana, plotted a conspiracy to overthrow colonial rule and abolish slavery. A major factor militating against social advancement by blacks in Cuba was the fear of an uprising by slaves such as had occurred in Haiti. The impact of this phobia is best illustrated by the colonists' savage repression of the so-called Ladder Conspiracy in 1844. In its wake, colonial authorities, widely supported by the European population, executed thousands of blacks and mulattos.

Blacks were allowed to form councils called "cabildos." At first these groups were set up to correspond to the various sections of Africa from which the slaves had originally come. In time, the councils evolved into all-African organizations, accepting members who had originated in all parts of the continent. Eventually, these cabildos developed into the twentieth century clubs and mutual aid societies.

Afro-Cubans played a crucial role in the country's fight for independence from Spain, beginning with the Ten Years' War that began in 1868.. The rebels' 1866 constitution declared that all residents of the republic who took up arms against the Spanish were to be considered free. Following that lead, the rebels' Central Assembly of Representatives proclaimed the abolition of slavery. However, the underlying fear of blacks felt by most white Cubans was exploited by Spanish forces to plant seeds of doubt in the minds of rebel leaders. Rebels were asked to consider the true intentions of blacks who rose through the ranks of the rebel military. Again, visions of a Haiti-type insurrection arose. The resulting divisions among rebel forces led eventually to the failure of their push for independence. The treaty with Spain ending the Ten Years' War provided for freedom only for the blacks who had fought in the revolution. A subsequent uprising, dubbed the Little War of 1879–1880, was discredited in the Spanish press as being racist in nature because many of its leaders were black. Although colonial authorities abolished slavery in 1880, they replaced it with a system called "patronato," under which former slaves were apprenticed to their owners for a period of eight years. In 1886, the system of patronato was ended prematurely, bringing freedom to all.

During the twentieth century, Fidel Castro, who seized power in 1959, transformed Cuba into a socialist nation with the aid of the Soviet Union. Castro became a champion of anti-colonialism, which made him popular in third world countries struggling for independence. The collapse of the Soviet Union and the loss of its extensive aid to Cuba have exacerbated the island's economic difficulties. This, along with the politically repressive nature of the Castro regime, continues to prompt many Cubans to attempt to flee their country. Leading contemporary Afro-Cubans include: musical performers Alfredo "Chocolate" Armenteros, Rubén González, Pablo Milanés, Lázaro Ros, and Jesús (Chucho) Valdés; artists María Magdalena Campos-Pons and Manuel Mendive; film director Gloria Rolando; and literary figures Marcelino Arozarena, Nancy Morejón, and Excilia Saldaña.

Long-strained relations between Cuba and the United States eased somewhat in 1999. U.S. President Bill Clinton announced policy changes that allowed Americans to travel to Cuba and to explore the island's business opportunities. He also allowed U.S. citizens to sue foreign companies for conducting business on confiscated American properties in Cuba. In late July 1999, Fidel Castro urged the United States to cooperate with Cuba in the war on drugs. The first half of 2000 saw a deterioration in U.S.-Cuban relations as the two countries battled over the custody of six-year-old Elián Gonzalez, rescued off the coast of Florida in November 1999 after a disastrous crossing from Cuba in which his mother and several others had drowned. The child was eventually returned to the custody of his father, who took him back to Cuba. In 2001, Cuba was alive with speculation about who would succeed Castro as president. Relations with the United States took another hit when President George W. Bush appointed anti-Castro exiles to high-level government positions.

Dominica

Official name: Commonwealth of Dominica

Independence: 3 November 1978 (from United Kingdom)

Area: 754 sq km

Form of government: parliamentary democracy; republic within the Commonwealth

Capital: Roseau

International relations: ACCT, ACP, C, CARICOM, CDB, ECLAC, FAO, G-77, IBRD, ICFTU, ICRM, IDA, IFAD, IFC, IFRCS, ILO, IMF, IMO, Interpol, IOC, ITU, NAM (observer), OAS, OECS, OPANAL, OPCW, UN, UNCTAD, UNESCO, UNIDO, UPU, WCL, WHO, WIPO, WMO, WTrO

Currency: East Caribbean dollar (XCD)

Income: US$4,000 (2000 est. of purchasing power parity)

Population: 70,786 (July 2001 est.)

Ethnic groups: black, Carib Amerindian

Religious groups: Roman Catholic 77%, Protestant 15% (Methodist 5%, Pentecostal 3%, Seventh-Day Adventist 3%, Baptist 2%, other 2%), none 2%, other 6%

Languages: English (official), French patois

Literacy: 94% (age 15 and over has ever attended school; 1970 est.)

Exports: bananas, soap, bay oil, vegetables, grapefruit, oranges

Primary export partners: CARICOM countries 47%, United Kingdom 36%, United States 7% (1996 est.)

Imports: manufactured goods, machinery and equipment, food, chemicals

Primary import partners: United States 41%, CARICOM countries 25%, United Kingdom 13%, Netherlands, Canada (1996 est.)

Dominica was first visited by Europeans on Columbus's second voyage in 1493. Spanish ships frequently landed on Dominica during the sixteenth century but failed to establish a stronghold on the island. In 1635, France claimed Dominica. As part of the 1763 Treaty of Paris that ended the Seven Years' War being fought in Europe, North America, and India, the island became a British possession.

In 1763, the British established a legislative assembly, representing only the white population. In 1831, reflecting a liberalization of official British racial attitudes, the "Brown Privilege Bill" conferred political and social rights on nonwhites. Three blacks were elected to the Legislative Assembly the following year, and, by 1838, the recently enfranchised blacks dominated that body. Most black legislators were smallholders or merchants, who held economic and social views diametrically opposed to the interests of the small, wealthy English planter class. Reacting to a perceived threat, the planters lobbied for more direct British rule. In 1865, after much agitation and tension, the colonial office replaced the elective assembly with one in which half of the members were appointed.

The power of the black population progressively eroded until all political rights for the vast majority of the population were effectively curtailed. On November 3, 1978, the Commonwealth of Dominica was granted independence by the United Kingdom. Almost all 81,000 Dominicans are descendants of African slaves imported by planters in the eighteenth century.

In 1980, Mary Eugenia Charles became the first woman to come to power in the Caribbean as well as the only black woman to lead an independent nation. Her longevity and determination earned her the nickname "The Iron Lady of the Caribbean." Trained as a lawyer, Charles rose through the ranks of government, spending most of her career in politics. After serving three terms as prime minister, she was succeeded in 1995 by Edison C. James.

In January 2000 general elections, the Dominica Labour Party (DLP) failed to win a majority, capturing only 10 of 21 seats, but was able to form a government after forming a coalition with the Dominica Freedom Party, who won two seats. Roosevelt Douglas, leader of the DLP, became the island's new prime minister. In October 2000, Douglas suffered a fatal heart attack and was replaced by Pierre Charles, former minister of communications and works. In July 2001, the IMF applied pressure to Dominica to reduce government spending and find ways to increase its revenues.

Dominican Republic

Official name: Dominican Republic

Independence: 27 February 1844 (from Haiti)

Area: 48,730 sq km

Form of government: representative democracy

Capital: Santo Domingo

International relations: ACP, CARICOM (observer), ECLAC, FAO, G-11, G-77, IADB, IAEA, IBRD, ICAO, ICFTU, ICRM, IDA, IFAD, IFC, IFRCS, IHO, ILO, IMF, IMO, Intelsat, Interpol, IOC, IOM, ISO (subscriber), ITU, LAES, LAIA (observer), NAM (observer), OAS, OPANAL, OPCW, PCA, UN, UNCTAD, UNESCO, UNIDO, UPU, WCL, WFTU, WHO, WIPO, WMO, WToO, WTrO

Currency: Dominican peso (DOP)

Income: US$5,700 (2000 est. of purchasing power parity)

Population: 8,581,477 (July 2001 est.)

Ethnic groups: white 16%, black 11%, mixed 73%

Religious groups: Roman Catholic 95%

Languages: Spanish

Literacy: 82.1% (age 15 and over can read and write; 1995 est.)

Exports: ferronickel, sugar, gold, silver, coffee, cocoa, tobacco, meats

Primary export partners: United States 66.1%, Netherlands 7.8%, Canada 7.6%, Russia 7.4%, United Kingdom 4.5% (1999 est.)

Imports: foodstuffs, petroleum, cotton and fabrics, chemicals and pharmaceuticals

Primary import partners: United States 25.7%, Venezuela 9.2%, Mexico 4%, Japan 3%, Panama 2.6% (1999 est.)

The island of Hispaniola, of which the Dominican Republic forms the eastern two-thirds and Haiti the remainder, was originally occupied by members of the Taino tribe when Columbus and his companions landed there in 1492. Brutal colonial conditions reduced the Taino population from an estimated one million to about 200 in only 50 years.

Improvised housing in Santo Domingo, Dominican Republic.

Santo Domingo, as the territory was known under Spanish rule, has long been considered the "cradle of blackness in the Americas" because it served as the port of entry for the first slaves traded to the Western Hemisphere. Beginning shortly after the first visit of Columbus, the slave trade brought in waves of Christianized blacks, known as "ladinos," and "bosales," as blacks imported directly from Africa were known. At first these slaves were put to work in the country's gold mines. However, these soon gave out, and efforts were undertaken to cultivate sugar cane on a large scale. Once the sugar business had been successfully established, after a period of fits and starts, progressively more slaves were brought in to work the fields.

From early in the colony's history, blacks outnumbered whites by a significant margin. In 1542, only 50 years after the first visit of Columbus, the population was made up of 30,000 blacks, 6,000 whites, and only 200 Tainos. By the close of the sixteenth century, blacks represented 61 percent of the total population, followed by whites at 23 percent and mulattos at 15 percent. Eventually, sugar cultivation's position as the colony's main cash crop was overtaken by livestock raising and the cultivation of ginger. These changes had

a number of effects on the slave population, among those the fact that fewer slaves were needed to raise livestock than were needed in the cultivation of sugar cane. The reduction in the need for slave labor was timely, because the late sixteenth and early seventeenth centuries saw the loss of a significant number of slaves to disease.

Living conditions for the slaves of Santo Domingo were harsh. The colonial powers, worried by the possibility of a large-scale uprising by blacks, enacted a system of laws that closely regulated every aspect of the lives of slaves. These laws, however, failed to altogether eliminate slave revolts, of which several occurred in the early years of the colony. In the wake of the Haitian Revolution, Toussaint L'Ouverture, a former Haitian slave who had become a military leader, seized control of Santo Domingo, bringing all of Hispaniola under his control. He abolished slavery throughout Santo Domingo. The following year, French soldiers invaded, taking control of Santo Domingo for France, which retained control until the War of Reconquest in 1809. Under French rule, slavery was reinstated. The War of Reconquest, plotted by creoles with the support of the Spanish governor of nearby Puerto Rico, returned Santo Domingo to Spanish control. In 1822, Haitian President Jean-Pierre Boyer seized the colony and maintained control for the next 22 years. Once again, slavery was abolished in Santo Domingo. Independence from Haiti was finally achieved in 1844.

One of the dominant figures in twentieth-century Dominican Republic history was dictator Rafael Trujillo, who ruled the country with an iron hand for more than 30 years. After Trujillo's dictatorship ended in a 1961 assassination, Joaquín Balaguer took over as president and instituted a police state. In 1962, former exile Juan Bosch was elected president in the country's first free elections in four decades. Criticized for being too soft on communism, Bosch was deposed in September 1963 and replaced by a three-man civilian junta. When pro-Bosch elements in the military rebelled against the government, U.S. forces intervened. Voters in 1966 returned Balaguer to the presidency. He won reelection easily in 1970 and 1974. However, in 1978 elections, Balaguer was unseated by Silvestre Antonio Guzmán. In July 1982, Salvador Jorge Blanco was elected to succeed him. Balaguer was returned to the presidency in 1986 elections. He was reelected in 1990 and 1994 but agreed to serve only two years of the last term to which he was elected after charges of election fraud. In 1996, Leonel Fernández Reyna was elected president.

Economic progress on the Dominican Republic was the big news of 1999. The country, with a growth rate of more than 6 percent for several years, was singled out as the best economic performer of the entire Latin American region. Much of its economic growth was credited to the aggressive campaign by President Fernández to attract foreign investment. The president elections of May 2000 brought to power Hipólito Mejía Dominguez, leader of the Dominican Republic Party, which had last been in power in 1986. In 2001, the failure of the Mejía administration to continue the robust economic growth of the recent past caused widespread disillusionment.

Leading contemporary Afro-Dominicans include literary figures Manuel del Cabral and Blas Jiménez and musicians Juan Luis Guerra and Johnny Ventura.

Ecuador

Official name: Republic of Ecuador
Independence: 24 May 1822 (from Spain)
Area: 283,560 sq km
Form of government: republic
Capital: Quito
International relations: CAN, CCC, ECLAC, FAO, G-11, G-77, IADB, IAEA, IBRD, ICAO, ICC, ICFTU, ICRM, IDA, IFAD, IFC, IFRCS, IHO, ILO, IMF, IMO, Intelsat, Interpol, IOC, IOM, ISO, ITU, LAES, LAIA, NAM, OAS, OPANAL, OPCW, PCA, RG, UN, UNCTAD, UNESCO, UNIDO, UPU, WCL, WFTU, WHO, WIPO, WMO, WToO, WTrO
Currency: U.S. dollar (us$)
Income: us$2,900 (2000 est. of purchasing power parity)
Population: 13,183,978 (July 2001 est.)
Ethnic groups: mestizo (mixed Amerindian and white) 65%, Amerindian 25%, Spanish and others 7%, black 3%
Religious groups: Roman Catholic 95%
Languages: Spanish (official), Amerindian languages (especially Quechua)
Literacy: 90.1% (age 15 and over can read and write; 1995 est.)
Exports: petroleum, bananas, shrimp, coffee, cocoa, cut flowers, fish
Primary export partners: United States 37%, Colombia 5%, Italy 5%, Chile 5%, Peru 4% (1999)
Imports: machinery and equipment, raw materials, fuels; consumer goods
Primary import partners: United States 30%, Colombia 13%, Venezuela 6%, Japan 5%, Venezuela 6%, Mexico 3% (1998)

Together with Colombia, its neighbor to the north, and Panama, Ecuador shares a region that makes up the so-called Pacific Lowlands Black Culture. This region stretches from Panama's Darién province in the north through Colombia's Cauca Valley on to Esmeraldas province in Ecuador in the south. The Pacific coastal area stretching through the three countries developed its high concentration of Afro-Hispanics through the migration patterns of blacks and a tradition of racial intermixing that began in colonial times. Although the three-nation Pacific coastal area is notable for its size, blacks historically settled in all three major geographical areas of Ecuador: the Pacific coast, the Amazon lowlands in the eastern part of the country, and the highlands.

As in much of Latin America, Ecuador's Spanish colonial rulers followed a policy of racial and cultural whitening, encouraging widespread racial mixing as a logical avenue to reach that goal. Even in the late twentieth century, remnants of that philosophy can be found in Ecuador. So deeply ingrained is the policy of whitening that even some black groups strongly advocate greater cultural and racial blending.

African slaves were first brought to Ecuador in the middle of the sixteenth century. Most were pressed into service as farm workers in portions of the colony where Indian labor was either scarce or nonexistent. An enclave of blacks grew up in the northwest coastal province of Esmeraldas, after a small party of slaves being transported by ship between Panama and Peru escaped and settled in the area. The escaped slaves mixed freely with the Indians of the region, and the resulting zambos of mixed black and Indian blood came to dominate this region. Although some blacks who joined in the fight for Ecuador's independence from Spain were freed in return for their war efforts, an official proclamation ending slavery did not come until 1851. Even so, an involuntary form of slavery survived until 1894.

Ecuador was beset with increased political instability throughout the final decade of the 20th century and into the new millennium. Although the country has been a presidential democracy since 1979, its political institutions are notoriously fragile. Gustavo Noboa in January 2000 became the sixth president since 1996 after a coup ousted President Jamil Mahuad. Noboa's term as president was to end in January 2003.

Leading contemporary Afro-Ecuadorians include literary figures Nelson Estupiñán Bass and Antonio Preciado Bedoya.

El Salvador

Official name: Republic of El Salvador
Independence: 15 September 1821 (from Spain)
Area: 21,040 sq km
Form of government: republic
Capital: San Salvador
International relations: BCIE, CACM, ECLAC, FAO, G-77, IADB, IAEA, IBRD, ICAO, ICFTU, ICRM, IDA, IFAD, IFC, IFRCS, ILO, IMF, IMO, Intelsat, Interpol, IOC, IOM, ISO (correspondent), ITU, LAES, LAIA (observer), MINURSO, NAM (observer), OAS, OPANAL, OPCW, PCA, UN, UNCTAD, UNESCO, UNIDO, UPU, WCL, WFTU, WHO, WIPO, WMO, WToO, WTrO
Currency: Salvadoran colon (SVC); U.S. dollar (us$)
Income: us$4,000 (2000 est. of purchasing power parity)
Population: 6,237,662 (July 2001 est.)
Ethnic groups: mestizo 90%, Amerindian 1%, white 9%
Religious groups: Roman Catholic 86%
Languages: Spanish, Nahua (among some Amerindians)
Literacy: 71.5% (age 10 and over can read and write; 1995 est.)
Exports: offshore assembly exports, coffee, sugar, shrimp, textiles, chemicals, electricity
Primary export partners: United States 63%, Guatemala 11%, Honduras 7%, Costa Rica 4% (1999)
Imports: raw materials, consumer goods, capital goods, fuels, foodstuffs, petroleum, electricity
Primary import partners: United States 52%, Guatemala 9%, Mexico 6%, Costa Rica 3% (1999)

In the final days of the twentieth century, the black population of El Salvador was negligible, the lowest proportion of African-descended residents to be found anywhere in Central America. During the colonial period, some African slaves were imported by El Salvador's Spanish rulers to help fill labor shortages created by the wholesale exportation of the indigenous Amerindian peoples to South America and Mexico. However, Central America's needs for slave labor was not as great as in other of Spain's New World colonies, largely because the mines in the region produced relatively modest yields and large-scale agriculture was virtually nonexistent. Without the profits from such enterprises, most landowners in El Salvador could ill afford the cost of importing African slaves, particularly since in most cases the available Amerindian labors were sufficient to fill their needs.

By the early 1800s, the number of slaves was so low that it was difficult to find residents who identified themselves as having African roots. Between the low number of slaves and the high rate of intermixing between European, indigenous, and the few blacks in the colony, it had become virtually impossible to distinguish between those with African blood and the mestizos of mixed European and Indian ancestry. By 1824, the Central American Federation, from which the countries of Costa Rica, El Salvador, Guatemala, Honduras, and Nicaragua were eventually formed, had won its independence from Spain. Because the number of slaves throughout the area was small, particularly when compared with other territories in the New World, abolition of slavery was achieved without a great deal of trauma on all parties involved.

Former philosophy professor Francisco Flores Pérez of the conservative National Republic Alliance was elected president in March 1999, roundly defeating his nearest opponent, Facundo Guardado of the Farabundo Marti Front for National Liberation. As his first order of business, Flores pledged to increase the country's standard of living and reduce its rising crime rate. The new president's failure to deliver quickly on his economic promises gave rise to a number of labor actions and protests in 2000. Toward the end of the year, however, indicators pointed to a more promising outlook for the country's economy. In January 2001, a major earthquake caused widespread destruction in an around the nation's capital. El Salvador in March 2001 joined with Guatemala, Honduras, and Mexico in a new free-trade agreement.

French Guiana

Official name: Department of Guiana
Independence: none (overseas department of France)

Area: 91,000 sq km
Form of government: NA
Capital: Cayenne
International relations: FZ, WCL, WFTU
Currency: French franc (FRF); euro (EUR)
Income: us$6,000 (1998 est. of purchasing power
parity)
Population: 177,562 (July 2001 est.)
Ethnic groups: black or mulatto 66%, white 12%,
East Indian, Chinese, Amerindian 12%, other 10%
Religious groups: Roman Catholic
Languages: French
Literacy: 83% (age 15 and over can read and write;
1982 est.)
Exports: shrimp, timber, gold, rum, rosewood
essence, clothing
Primary export partners: France 62%, Switzerland
7%, United States 2% (1997)
Imports: food (grains, processed meat), machinery
and transport equipment, fuels and chemicals
Primary import partners: France 52%, United States
14%, Trinidad and Tobago 6% (1997)

The first European visitor to what is now French
Guiana was Christopher Columbus, who stopped off
there during the course of his third voyage to the New
World. Struck the beauty of the region, he wrote glow-
ingly of its wonders. His writings later inspired other
European explorers to visit the area, many of whom
were convinced that the mythical Eldorado, the golden
city, was to be found within the territory's interior. The
French first visited the area in 1604, looking not only for
gold but for territory that could be claimed for their
country. It was not until 1652 that the first slaves were
brought into Guiana. Because the colony was fairly
sparsely settled, the slave population grew very slowly.
By 1765, Guiana's slave population totaled only about
5,700. Sixty-five years later, in 1830, it reaches its peak
of just over 19,000.

Although most of the African slaves had come from
tropical climates themselves, many fell victim to tropical diseases in Guiana. Others fled their masters in the
more heavily settled coastal zone and escaped into the
interior where they reverted to a lifestyle as hunter-
gatherers, much as they had done in their home countries. Although French attempts to establish agricultural plantations in Guiana failed, the colonial powers
were undaunted in their determination to develop the
territory. The abolition of slavery in 1848 sounded the
death knell for Guiana's two main industries—lumber
and sugar—collapsed. To give the colony a raison
d'étre, the French decided to transform Guiana into a
penal colony. Between 1852 and 1939, France shipped
more than 70,000 prisoners to the colony. Tropical

diseases, including malaria and yellow fever, took an
enormous toll on the prisoners, claiming the lives of
nearly 90 percent of them.

Among the notable French Guianans of African descent, Félix Eboué stands out for his significant contributions as an adviser to General Charles de Gaulle
during World War II. Born in 1884, Eboué was the
descendant of African slaves. He first distinguished
himself through his reforms of the French colonial
administration. Poet Léon-Gontran Damas is the country's most famous writer. In the late twentieth century,
a number of elements of the Afro-Guianan community
were actively seeking to revive and preserve black
culture in the country.

Grenada

Official name: none
Independence: 7 February 1974 (from United
Kingdom)
Area: 340 sq km
Form of government: constitutional monarchy with
Westminster-style parliament
Capital: Saint George's
International relations: ACP, C, CARICOM, CDB,
ECLAC, FAO, G-77, IBRD, ICAO, ICFTU, ICRM,
IDA, IFAD, IFC, IFRCS, ILO, IMF, IMO, Interpol,
IOC, ISO (subscriber), ITU, LAES, NAM, OAS,
OECS, OPANAL, OPCW, UN, UNCTAD, UNESCO,
UNIDO, UPU, WHO, WIPO, WTrO
Currency: East Caribbean dollar (XCD)
Income: us$4,400 (2000 est. of purchasing power
parity)
Population: 89,227 (July 2001 est.)
Ethnic groups: black 82% some South Asians (East
Indians) and Europeans, trace Arawak/Carib
Amerindian
Religious groups: Roman Catholic 53%, Anglican
13.8%, other Protestant 33.2%
Languages: English (official), French patois
Literacy: 98% (age 15 and over can read and write;
1970 est.)
Exports: bananas, cocoa, nutmeg, fruit and
vegetables, clothing, mace
Primary export partners: CARICOM 32.3%, United
Kingdom 20%, United States 13%, Netherlands
8.8% (1991)
Imports: food, manufactured goods, machinery,
chemicals, fuel (1989)
Primary import partners: United States 31.2%,
CARICOM 23.6%, United Kingdom 13.8%, Japan
7.1% (1991)

Similar to the rest of the West Indies, Grenada was
originally settled to cultivate sugar, which was grown

on estates using slave labor. Most of Grenada's population is of African descent; little trace of the early Arawak and Carib Indians remains.

Columbus first visited Grenada in 1498. Grenada remained uncolonized for more than 100 years after the first visit by Europeans, and British efforts to settle the island were unsuccessful. In 1650, a French company purchased Grenada from the British and established a small settlement. By 1753, the island's population was dominated by slaves, who numbered close to 12,000, against a total of 1,262 whites and 179 free blacks. Most of the free blacks were of mixed European-African descent, the result of intermixing between the island's French planters and their slaves. The island remained under French control until captured by the British more than a century later during the Seven Years War. Slavery was outlawed in 1833, the same year Grenada was made part of the British Windward Islands Administration. In 1958, the Windward Islands Administration dissolved. Grenada became an associated state on March 3, 1967, but sought full independence, which the British government granted on February 7, 1974.

The New Jewel movement led by Maurice Bishop assumed power in 1979. He was overthrown and killed in 1983 when Bernard Coard took over the country. The United States, along with forces from other English-speaking Caribbean countries invaded to restore order. The country was then governed by an interim advisory council until parliamentary elections in December 1984. Those elections established Herbert A. Blaize as Grenada's new prime minister. After Blaize's death, Nicholas Brathwaite was elected prime minister. Brathwaite's popularity plummeted in the wake of an economic slowdown in the early 1990s, and he announced he would resign as prime minister in 1995. He was succeeded by George Brizan in February 1995, who in late June 1995 turned over power to Keith Mitchell, established as prime minister in parliamentary elections earlier that month.

A new election was held in January 1999, two months after the ruling New National Party of Prime Minister Mitchell lost its parliamentary majority upon the resignation of Foreign Minister Raphael Fletcher. Mitchell and his party regained their majority. Despite aggressive action earlier in 2001 to close down rogue offshore banks, Grenada in September was added to the blacklist of the Financial Action Task Force in its worldwide crackdown on money laundering.

The island faced new economic troubles in the mid-1990s when the banana crop failed and an infestation of mealybugs severely damaged the cocoa crop. Grenada is one of four former English colonies in the Caribbean considering the formation of a federation to ease financial pressures on all member countries. The others countries discussing joining in this federation are Dominica, St. Lucia, and St. Vincent and the Grenadines. One of the major success stories in Grenada during the 1990s has been the growth experienced by the island's tourism industry. Grenada has proved particularly popular with divers, snorkelers, and sailors in recent years. Also a major player in the island's economy is the spice industry, which continues to turn in a strong performance. The island produces more spices per square mile than anywhere else on earth.

Guadeloupe

Official name: Department of Guadeloupe

Independence: none (overseas department of France)

Area: 1,780 sq km

Form of government: NA

Capital: Basse-Terre

International relations: FZ, WCL, WFTU

Currency: French franc (FRF); euro (EUR)

Income: US$9,000 (1997 est. of purchasing power parity)

Population: 431,170 (July 2001 est.)

Ethnic groups: black or mulatto 90%, white 5%, East Indian, Lebanese, Chinese less than 5%

Religious groups: Roman Catholic 95%, Hindu and pagan African 4%, Protestant 1%

Languages: French (official) 99%, Creole patois

Literacy: 90% (age 15 and over can read and write; 1982 est.)

Exports: bananas, sugar, rum

An open-air market in Guadeloupe.

Primary export partners: France 60%, Martinique 18%, United States 4% (1997)

Imports: foodstuffs, fuels, vehicles, clothing and other consumer goods, construction materials

Primary import partners: France 63%, Germany 4%, United States 3%, Japan 2%, Netherlands Antilles 2% (1997)

Columbus sighted Guadeloupe in 1493. The area was permanently settled by the French in the seventeenth century. The first slaves were brought from Africa to work the plantations around 1650, and the first slave rebellion occurred in 1656. Guadeloupe was poorly administered in its early days and was a dependency of Martinique until 1775.

The slaves of Guadeloupe were slow to react to news of the French Revolution. The French abolition of slavery less than five years later was not preceded by any major uprisings on the island, although a handful of minor revolts did occur. Two members of the French Republican Convention, who brought the abolition decree to Guadeloupe, also recruited freed slaves to help drive out British invaders, who had occupied the island while France was preoccupied with its revolution at home. In the wake of the rout of British occupying forces, many white landowners and merchants sympathetic to the British cause were executed or exiled. As a result, the white ruling class was considerably weakened and depleted in numbers. In the years following the British occupation of the island, whites made up only about 10 percent of the population, compared to about 33 percent in 1735. As the white population was weakened, the black merchant class gained strength. Blacks and those of mixed African and European descent were welcomed into the colony's military.

A number of black soldiers in 1802 revolted against troops sent to the Caribbean by Napoleon Bonaparte to reinstitute slavery. Their resistance was quickly overcome, and France reimposed a particularly brutal brand of enslavement on its islands for the next 46 years. By 1835, 13 years before abolition, free blacks on the island outnumbers whites by a margin of 19,000 to 12,000. In the wake of Britain's ban on slavery in its Caribbean colonies, attempts were made in the French island to make slavery less dehumanizing, as if indeed that were possible. The hope was that by so doing the institution of slavery could be preserved. Despite legislated measures to give slaves some basic rights, the effort was a failure, since individual slave owners were free to deal with their slaves as they wished.

The new millennium brought signs that Guadeloupe and other French overseas departments might soon win greater autonomy in the management of their local affairs. French President Chirac in March 2000 hinted strongly that the highly centralized relationship between Paris and its overseas department might be relaxed in favor of a less restrictive arrangement. Violent protests erupted on Guadeloupe in June 2001 after a number of island shopkeepers refused to observe the anniversary of slavery's abolition on the island.

Most Guadeloupeans are of mixed Afro-European and Afro-Indian ancestry (descendants of laborers brought over from India during the nineteenth century). Several thousand metropolitan French reside there, including civil servants, business people, and their dependents. Leading contemporary Afro-Guadeloupeans include literary figures Jean Louis Baghio'o, Maryse Condé, and Simone Schwartz-Bart.

Guatemala

Official name: Republic of Guatemala

Independence: 15 September 1821 (from Spain)

Area: 108,890 sq km

Form of government: constitutional democratic republic

Capital: Guatemala

International relations: BCIE, CACM, CCC, ECLAC, FAO, G-24, G-77, IADB, IAEA, IBRD, ICAO, ICFTU, ICRM, IDA, IFAD, IFC, IFRCS, IHO, ILO, IMF, IMO, Intelsat, Interpol, IOC, IOM, ISO (correspondent), ITU, LAES, LAIA (observer), NAM, OAS, OPANAL, OPCW, PCA, UN, UNCTAD, UNESCO, UNIDO, UNU, UPU, WCL, WFTU, WHO, WIPO, WMO, WToO, WTrO

Currency: quetzal (GTQ), U.S. dollar (us$), others allowed

Income: us$3,700 (2000 est. of purchasing power parity)

Population: 12,974,361 (July 2001 est.)

Ethnic groups: Mestizo (mixed Amerindian-Spanish or assimilated Amerindian—in local Spanish called Ladino), approximately 55%, Amerindian or predominantly Amerindian, approximately 43%, whites and others 2%

Religious groups: Roman Catholic, Protestant, indigenous Mayan beliefs

Languages: Spanish 60%, Amerindian languages 40% (more than 20 Amerindian languages, including Quiche, Cakchiquel, Kekchi, Mam, Garifuna, and Xinca)

Literacy: 63.6% (age 15 and over can read and write; 2000 est.)

Exports: coffee, sugar, bananas, fruits and vegetables, cardamom, meat, apparel, petroleum, electricity

Primary export partners: United States 51.4%, El Salvador 8.7%, Honduras 5%, Costa Rica 3.4%, Germany 2.7% (1998)

Imports: fuels, machinery and transport equipment, construction materials, grain, fertilizers, electricity
Primary import partners: United States 42.8%, Mexico 9.9%, Japan 4.8%, El Salvador 4.3%, Venezuela 3.8% (1998)

Although blacks make up a very small percentages of Guatemala's population, there are traces of African influence to be found in the Central American country. Among these are a popular folk dance called the marimba, based on rhythms and steps brought to the country by African slaves.

Beginning in the first half of the sixteenth century, steps were taken by Guatemalan whites to limit the number of blacks allowed into the colony. The heavy concentrations of Amerindian indigenous peoples provided an adequate labor supply for most of Guatemala, thus reducing the need for the importation of African slaves. The Guatemalan town of Tianguey enacted an ordinance in 1537 prohibiting the entry of blacks or those of mixed-black ancestry without express permission from town officials. The aim was to prevent any intermixing with the indigenous peoples of the area. Even in the twentieth century, the country's government has attempted to legislate against immigration by blacks. Guatemala's 1945 constitution official bans "immigration of individuals of the black race."

The late 1990s were marked by widespread violence and human rights abuses in Guatemala. A survey of Guatemalans taken in mid-1999 showed that 88 percent felt administration of justice in the country was inadequate. In November 1999 general elections, Alfonso Portillo Cabrera was elected president, and he assumed office in mid-January 2000, promising to revitalize the economy and reduce the power of the country's military. Scandals undermined support for the Portillo administration in 2001, and the president himself came under increasing fire for the continuing high crime rate and his frequent foreign journeys.

Guyana

Official name: Co-operative Republic of Guyana
Independence: 26 May 1966 (from United Kingdom)
Area: 214,970 sq km
Form of government: republic within the Commonwealth
Capital: Georgetown
International relations: ACP, C, CARICOM, CCC, CDB, ECLAC, FAO, G-77, IADB, IBRD, ICAO, ICFTU, ICRM, IDA, IFAD, IFC, IFRCS, ILO, IMF, IMO, Intelsat (nonsignatory user), Interpol, IOC, ISO (subscriber), ITU, LAES, NAM, OAS, OIC, OPANAL, OPCW, PCA, UN, UNCTAD, UNESCO, UNIDO, UPU, WCL, WFTU, WHO, WIPO, WMO, WTrO

Currency: Guyanese dollar (GYD)
Income: us$4,800 (2000 est. of purchasing power parity)
Population: 697,181
Ethnic groups: East Indian 49%, black 32%, mixed 12%, Amerindian 6%, white and Chinese 1%
Religious groups: Christian 50%, Hindu 33%, Muslim 9%, other 8%
Languages: English, Amerindian dialects, Creole, Hindi, Urdu
Literacy: 98.1% (age 15 and over has ever attended school; 1995 est.)
Exports: sugar, gold, bauxite/alumina, rice, shrimp, molasses, rum, timber
Primary export partners: United States 22%, Canada 22%, United Kingdom 18%, Netherlands Antilles 11%, Jamaica (1999)
Imports: manufactures, machinery, petroleum, food
Primary import partners: United States 29%, Trinidad and Tobago 18%, Netherlands Antilles 16%, United Kingdom 7%, Japan (1999)

Guiana was the name given the area sighted by Columbus in 1498, comprising modern Guyana, Suriname, French Guiana, and parts of Brazil and Venezuela. The Dutch settled in Guyana in the late sixteenth century. Dutch control ended when the British became the de facto rulers in 1796. In 1815, the colonies of Essequibo, Demerara, and Berbice were officially ceded to the British by the Congress of Vienna and, in 1831, were consolidated as British Guiana.

Slave revolts, such as the one in 1763 led by Guyana's national hero, Cuffy, stressed the desire to obtain basic rights and were underscored by a willingness to compromise. Following the abolition of slavery in 1834, indentured workers were brought primarily from India but also from Portugal and China. A scheme in 1862 to bring black workers from the United States was unsuccessful.

Independence was achieved in 1966, and Guyana became a republic on February 23, 1970, the anniversary of the Cuffy slave rebellion. Between 1968 and 1972, Guyana was ruled by the PNC party. In 1975, Guyana gained unfortunate international recognition after a religious cult in Jonestown was led into mass suicide by its leader, Jim Jones.

Although the black population of Guyana trails that of the Indo-Guyanese, who make up slightly more than 50 percent of the population and a sharply higher percentage in the late twentieth century government, the African influences upon the country's culture are significant. Blacks played a major role in the development of modern-day Guyana, from the mid-seventeenth century when the first African slaves were sold to

Dutch planters through the early years after independence, when the country was ruled by authoritarian black governments. Forbes Burnham, an Afro-Guyanese led the country from 1968 until 1985. When Burnham died in office in 1985, he was succeeded by Desmond Hoyte, who held office until 1992. In the country's first free elections since 1964, Cheddi Jagan, the first leader of the country after independence, was again voted into office. Jagan died suddenly in office in January 1997 and was succeeded by his widow, Janet, who, in December 1997, won the presidency on her own. Other influential Afro-Guyanese include literary figures Martin Carter and Theodore Wilson Harris.

Citing failing health, President Janet Jagan stepped down in August 1999 and was replaced by Finance Minister Bharrat Jagdeo. In early 2000, the country joined most of its neighbors in passing legislation that made money laundering a crime. In March 2001, general elections, Jagdeo won another five-year term as president. The elections were followed by brief period of civil unrest, which Jagdeo and the leader of the major opposition party sought to calm through reconciliation talks. In July 2001, Guyana's longstanding border conflict with Venezuela boiled over once again when a Venezuelan official denounced the 1899 treaty that ceded the disputed Essequio region to Guyana.

Haiti

Official name: Republic of Haiti
Independence: 1 January 1804 (from France)
Area: 27,750 sq km
Form of government: elected government
Capital: Port-au-Prince
International relations: ACCT, ACP, CARICOM (observer), CCC, ECLAC, FAO, G-77, IADB, IAEA, IBRD, ICAO, ICRM, IDA, IFAD, IFC, IFRCS, ILO, IMF, IMO, Intelsat, Interpol, IOC, IOM, ITU, LAES, OAS, OPANAL, OPCW, PCA, UN, UNCTAD, UNESCO, UNIDO, UPU, WCL, WFTU, WHO, WIPO, WMO, WToO, WTrO
Currency: gourde (HTG)
Income: US$1,800 (2000 est. of purchasing power parity)
Population: 6,964,549
Ethnic groups: black 95%, mulatto and white 5%
Religious groups: Roman Catholic 80%, Protestant 16% (Baptist 10%, Pentecostal 4%, Adventist 1%, other 1%), none 1%, other 3% (1982)
Languages: French (official), Creole (official)
Literacy: 45% (age 15 and over can read and write; 1995 est.)
Exports: manufactures, coffee, oils, mangoes
Primary export partners: United States 89%, EU 8% (1999)

Imports: food, machinery and transport equipment, fuels, raw materials
Primary import partners: United States 60%, EU 13% (1999)

Columbus first visited the Island of Hispaniola in 1492. In 1697, Spain ceded the western third of Hispaniola to France. During this period, slaves were brought from Africa to work the sugar cane and coffee plantations. Several decades later, a major revolt erupted—white French planters, African slaves, and free mulattoes (some of whom owned slaves) clashed over issues of rights, land, and labor, as the forces of France, Britain, and Spain manipulated the conflict. At first, the slaves and mulattoes shared the goals of the French revolution in opposition to the royalist French planters, but with time a coalition of planters and mulattoes arose in opposition to the slaves.

Toussaint L'Ouverture became the leader of the revolutionary slave forces, which by mid-1790s consisted of a disciplined group of 4,000 mostly ex-slaves. He successfully waged a campaign against the British. At the height of L'Ouverture's power and influence in 1796, Gen. Rigaud, who led the mulatto forces, sought to reimpose slavery on the black islanders. L'Ouverture quickly achieved victory, captured Santo Domingo, and, by 1801, had virtual control of the Spanish part of the island. In 1802, a French expeditionary force was sent to reestablish French control of the island. Following a hard-fought resistance to French colonial ambitions in the Western Hemisphere, Toussaint L'Ouverture struck a peace treaty with Napoleon. However, L'Ouverture was tricked, captured, and sent to France where he died on April 7, 1803, under inhumane conditions.

In the wake of its victorious struggle for independence, Haiti became a model for much of the black world. However, it was not long before the black-ruled country began to face enormous pressure, both from within the country and abroad. The country's new rulers were ill-prepared for the responsibility of leading a nation, thus keeping the country in a state of instability. It had no other country to which it could turn for either moral or financial support, because it was regarded as an outcast in a world that was largely controlled by whites. The very idea of slaves overthrowing their masters to seize control of a country was frightening to most white-controlled governments. The country was in ruins in the wake of its battle to banish the French, and Dessalines made a critical error when he pressed all Haitians who were not in the military into agricultural service on some of the surviving plantations. Further exacerbating problems for the new black republic was the growing enmity that developed between the country's black majority and the mulatto elite. After the death of Dessalines, control of the island was split between the blacks, who held the northern part of Haiti, and the mulattos, who were in control of the South.

In the twentieth century, the country languished under nearly 30 years of despotic rule by the Duvalier family. François Duvalier was elected president in 1957. In the 1960s, he declared himself president for life. Upon his death in 1971, he was succeeded by his son, Jean-Claude. During this period, much of the Western world, including the United States, cut off foreign assistance to Haiti to express its collective unhappiness over the political situation there. In the 1980s, popular dissatisfaction with the Duvalier rule grew stronger, and, early in 1986, the young Duvalier was forced to flee the country. A politically tumultuous period followed, with one corrupt leader quickly succeeding another, until the election in December 1990 of Jean-Bertrand Aristide. Only eight months after his inauguration in February 1991, Aristide was ousted in a coup led by Brigadier General Raoul Cedras. Following Aristide's ouster, thousands of Haitians attempted to emigrate to the United States, with little success. In 1994, U.S. forces took control, and Aristide was returned to power. He handed power over to Rene Preval, his hand-picked successor, in December 1995. The country was in an economic and political shambles into the late 1990s.

President René Préval effectively established one-man rule in early 1999 when he dissolved Parliament. Parliamentary elections originally scheduled for late 1999 were postponed until May 2000. Although the integrity of the voting process was widely questioned, the results showed an overwhelming majority for the Lavalas Family party of former President Jean-Bertrand Aristide. In November 2000 presidential elections, Aristide won 91 percent of the vote. The former president returned to power in early 2001 against a backdrop of continuing economic decline and rapid deterioration of the country's economic infrastructure.

Almost 95 percent of the Haitians are of black African descent; the rest of the population are mostly of mixed African-Caucasian ancestry (mulattos). Leading contemporary Afro-Haitians include: Manno Charlemagne, a protest singer and politician; Franck Etienne, a poet, playwright, novelist, teacher, and politician; and literary figure Paulette Poujol-Oriol.

Honduras

Official name: Republic of Honduras
Independence: 15 September 1821 (from Spain)
Area: 112,090 sq km
Form of government: democratic constitutional
 republic

Capital: Tegucigalpa
International relations: BCIE, CACM, ECLAC, FAO, G-77, IADB, IBRD, ICAO, ICFTU, ICRM, IDA, IFAD, IFC, IFRCS, ILO, IMF, IMO, Intelsat, Interpol, IOC, IOM, ISO (correspondent), ITU, LAES, LAIA (observer), MINURSO, NAM, OAS, OPANAL, OPCW, PCA, UN, UNCTAD, UNESCO, UNIDO, UPU, WCL, WFTU, WHO, WIPO, WMO, WTrO
Currency: lempira (HNL)
Income: us$2,700 (2000 est. of purchasing power parity)
Population: 6,406,052
Ethnic groups: mestizo (mixed Amerindian and European) 90%, Amerindian 7%, black 2%, white 1%
Religious groups: Roman Catholic 97%, Protestant minority
Languages: Spanish, Amerindian dialects
Literacy: 72.7% (age 15 and over can read and write; 1995 est.)
Exports: coffee, bananas, shrimp, lobster, meat; zinc, lumber
Primary export partners: United States 35.4%, Germany 7.5%, El Salvador 6.4%, Guatemala 5.8%, Nicaragua 4.8% (1999)
Imports: machinery and transport equipment, industrial raw materials, chemical products, fuels, foodstuffs
Primary import partners: United States 47.1%, Guatemala 7.4%, El Salvador 5.9%, Mexico 4.8%, Japan 4.7% (1999)

The first shipment of African slaves—a group of 165—arrived in Honduras in 1540. About five years later, the number of slaves within the colony had risen to 5,000, most of them brought in to replace Indian workers who had been claimed by disease. Most of these Africans were employed as domestic servants or laborers on small farms that were cultivated solely to produce food for consumption within the colony. The absence of plantation-scale farming and mines kept the region's slave population from growing dramatically. The black population grew more after Honduras won independence, when a large number of West Indian blacks of mixed African and Carib Indian ancestry arrived in the country. Up to 5,000 of these newly arrived immigrants known as Garifuna relocated from the Caribbean island of Saint Vincent to the island of Roatán, off the coast of Honduras, at the end of the eighteenth century. Over time most of these Garifuna moved to the mainland.

Another influx of black slaves arrived in Honduras in the 1830s when a group of white settlers from the Cayman Islands, fearful about their fate if Britain's plans to abolish slavery materialized, began settling in the Honduran Bay Islands. A number of these white Cayman Islanders brought their slaves with them. By the mid-nineteenth century, about 700 blacks from the Cayman Islands had moved to this island group, once again outnumbering the white population. When U.S. fruit companies established vast plantations in the eastern portion of the country, both the black Cayman Islanders and many of the Garifuna went to work for them. The new employment opportunities offered by the fruit estates eventually attracted further black immigration from throughout the Caribbean.

Honduras focused in 1999 on rebuilding from the destruction caused by Hurricane Mitch in October 1998. In 2000, Honduras became the second Latin American country to qualify for debt relief under the Highly Indebted Poor Countries program, which cleared the way for the World Bank, IMF, and other international lenders to forgive portions of the country's debt and restructure other debts. In February, a border conflict with Nicaragua exploded into violence and later brought sanctions from both countries against one another. In November 2001, national elections, the presidency was won by Ricardo Maduro of the National Party, who took office in January 2002.

Jamaica

Official name: none

Independence: 6 August 1962 (from United Kingdom)

Area: 10,990 sq km

Form of government: constitutional parliamentary democracy

Capital: Kingston

International relations: ACP, C, CARICOM, CCC, CDB, ECLAC, FAO, G-15, G-19, G-77, IADB, IAEA, IBRD, ICAO, ICFTU, ICRM, IFAD, IFC, IFRCS, IHO (pending member), ILO, IMF, IMO, Intelsat, Interpol, IOC, IOM (observer), ISO, ITU, LAES, NAM, OAS, OPANAL, OPCW, UN, UN Security Council (temporary), UNCTAD, UNESCO, UNIDO, UPU, WFTU, WHO, WIPO, WMO, WToO, WTrO

Currency: Jamaican dollar (JMD)

Income: US$3,700 (2000 est. of purchasing power parity)

Population: 2,665,636 (July 2001 est.)

Ethnic groups: black 90.9%, East Indian 1.3%, white 0.2%, Chinese 0.2%, mixed 7.3%, other 0.1%

Religious groups: Protestant 61.3% (Church of God 21.2%, Baptist 8.8%, Anglican 5.5%, Seventh-Day Adventist 9%, Pentecostal 7.6%, Methodist 2.7%, United Church 2.7%, Brethren 1.1%, Jehovah's Witness 1.6%, Moravian 1.1%), Roman Catholic 4%, other, including some spiritual cults 34.7%

Linstead market in Jamaica.

Languages: English, Creole

Literacy: 85% (age 15 and over has ever attended school; 1995 est.)

Exports: alumina, bauxite; sugar, bananas, rum

Primary export partners: United States 35.7%, EU (excluding United Kingdom) 15.8%, United Kingdom 13%, Canada 10.5% (1999)

Imports: machinery and transport equipment, construction materials, fuel, food, chemicals, fertilizers

Primary import partners: United States 47.8%, CARICOM countries 12.4%, Latin America 7.2%, EU (excluding United Kingdom) 4.7% (1999)

Jamaica was first visited in 1494 by Christopher Columbus and settled by the Spanish during the early sixteenth century. In the 1650s, British forces seized the island and, in 1670, gained formal possession under the Treaty of Madrid.

Sugar and slavery were important elements in Jamaica's history and development. By the early 1830s, the affairs of the colony were dominated by the island's white minority. As international pressure for an end to slavery began to build, events within Jamaica made clear that the days of slavery were numbered. In 1832, in a revolt known as the Baptist War, more than 20,000 slaves rose up in an effort to break the bonds of slavery. So expansive and violent was this insurrection that it caught the attention of the world outside Jamaica. Conjuring up images of a slave revolution, such as had occurred in Haiti about 30 years earlier, the Jamaican uprising hastened action in Britain's Parliament to abolish slavery. The vote that came in August 1833 freed more than 300,000 slaves in Jamaica. However, provisions of emancipation provided for a gradual transition from bondage to complete freedom. For most slaves, this meant a lengthy period of apprenticeship to their former masters. With the abolition of slavery, the settlers were forced to recruit other sources of cheap labor, resorting to the importation of Asian Indian and Chinese farm hands.

In 1958, Jamaica joined nine other British territories in the West Indies Federation, but withdrew when, in a 1961 referendum, Jamaican voters rejected membership. Jamaica gained independence from the United Kingdom in 1962 but remained a member of the Commonwealth. In the country's first election following independence, Alexander Bustamante, a leader of the Labor Party, was elected prime minister. Bustamante retired five years later and passed power to Hugh Shearer. After a number of years under the Jamaican Labor party, the 1972 elections put Michael Norman Manley in power. Manley, who steered the country toward socialism, served until 1980, when voters selected Edward Seaga as prime minister. In 1989, voters returned Manley to the prime ministership, but he stepped down in March 1992 because of ill health. His successor, Percival J. Patterson, handily won reelection in 1993.

Jamaica's debt crisis worsened in 1999 as loan repayments plus interest were estimated to account for more than 60 percent of the country's budget expenditures. In April 2000, Prime Minister Patterson announced that Jamaica would not borrow additional funds from the IMF but would ask the international agency to monitor its monetary and fiscal policies for the next two years. Throughout the period, the country's high crime rate remained a source of serious concern. In Spring 2001, tourism suffered a body blow when four cruise lines dropped Jamaica from their itineraries. In July 2001, at least 25 persons were killed in gang violence in West Kingston.

A new phenomenon has become particularly apparent in Jamaica, a country that has lost nearly 30 percent of its population to the United States. Though prevalent in all countries that experience heavy emigration, tens of thousands of Jamaican parents have gone abroad, leaving behind children whom they hope to one day be able to summon. The youngsters have acquired the nickname "barrel children" from the barrels filled with goodies—food, clothing, and photographs—the parents send back whenever possible. Though these children have not actually been abandoned, they are often passed from relative to relative or to friends or strangers. Highly at risk, the children are often susceptible to abuse from their supposed benefactors, many drop out of school, and some get into trouble with the law.

Leading contemporary Afro-Jamaicans include novelist and sociologist Erna Brodber, painter and sculptor Everald Brown, reggae musician Jimmy Cliff, novelist and playwright John Hearne, and poet and music producer Mutabaruka.

Martinique

Official name: Department of Martinique

Independence: none (overseas department of France)

Area: 1,100 sq km

Form of government: NA

Capital: Fort-de-France

International relations: FZ, WCL, WFTU

Currency: French franc (FRF); euro (EUR)

Income: US$11,000 (1997 est. of purchasing power parity)

Population: 418,454 (July 2001 est.)

Ethnic groups: African and African-white-Indian mixture 90%, white 5%, East Indian, Chinese less than 5%

Religious groups: Roman Catholic 95%, Hindu and pagan African 5%

Languages: French, Creole patois

Literacy: 93% (age 15 and over can read and write; 1982 est.)

Exports: refined petroleum products, bananas, rum, pineapples

Primary export partners: France 45%, Guadeloupe 28% (1997)

Imports: petroleum products, crude oil, foodstuffs, construction materials, vehicles, clothing and other consumer goods

Primary import partners: France 62%, Venezuela 6%, Germany 4%, Italy 4%, United States 3% (1997)

Christopher Columbus first visited Martinique in 1502 on his fourth voyage to the New World. The island's indigenous Carib Indian population was largely decimated by disease in the wake of Columbus's visit. The area was permanently settled by the French in the seventeenth century. Except for three short periods of British occupation, Martinique has been a French possession since 1635.

A shopping district in Martinique.

As sugar plantations sprang up on Martinique, the need for slave labor grew quickly, particularly since the island's indigenous Carib Indians had been all but wiped out by disease introduced by the first European visitors. The island's population in 1789 was estimated at 12,000 whites, 65,000 slaves, and 5,000 free blacks. In 1848, less than 60 years later, the slave population had moved up by only about 12 percent to 73,000, while the total of free blacks had soared by almost 700 percent. The white population, meanwhile, had shrunk to about 9,000. In the spring of 1848, the slaves of Martinique staged a large-scale revolt that precipitated abolition of slavery in the French colonies one month later.

The island witnessed a number of dramatic changes during the twentieth century. The political realm, once large restricted to Martinique's white minority, began to open up to those of African ancestry. In 1945, black poet and intellectual Aimé Césaire was elected as a Martinican deputy to the French parliament. In addition to his continuing involvement in the politics of his country, Césaire was instrumental in jump-starting the country's cultural renewal with his book of poetry *Cahier d'un retour au pays natal* (*Notebook of a Return to My Native Land*) published in 1947. A strong supporter of Martinique's existing status as an overseas department of France, Césaire has fallen out of favor with some of Martinique's young intellectuals for his failure to call for independence from France.

The outlook for greater local autonomy brightened considerably in March 2000 when French President Jacques Chirac hinted that France's highly centralized relationship with its overseas departments might soon be relaxed. Chirac said that the era of "uniform status" was past and that overseas departments such as Martinique and Guadeloupe might soon enjoy greater local control over their destiny.

About 95 percent of the people of Martinique are of Afro-European or Afro-European-Indian descent. The rest are traditional white planter families, commonly referred to as békdés or creoles, and a sizable number of metropolitan French work in administration and business. Leading contemporary Afro-Martinicians include literary figures Aimé Césaire, Patrick Chamoiseau, Raphaël Confiant, and Joseph Zobel.

Mexico

Official name: United Mexican States

Independence: 16 September 1810 (from Spain)

Area: 1,972,550 sq km

Form of government: federal republic

Capital: Mexico

International relations: APEC, BCIE, BIS, CARICOM
(observer), CCC, CDB, CE (observer), EBRD,
ECLAC, FAO, G-3, G-6, G-11, G-15, G-19, G-24,
IADB, IAEA, IBRD, ICAO, ICC, ICFTU, ICRM,
IDA, IEA (observer), IFAD, IFC, IFRCS, ILO,
IMF, IMO, Inmarsat, Intelsat, Interpol, IOC,
IOM (observer), ISO, ITU, LAES, LAIA, NAM
(observer), NEA, OAS, OECD, OPANAL, OPCW,
PCA, RG, UN, UNCTAD, UNESCO, UNIDO,
UNITAR, UNU, UPU, WCL, WFTU, WHO, WIPO,
WMO, WToO, WTrO

Currency: Mexican peso (MXN)

Income: us$9,100 (2000 est. of purchasing power
parity)

Population: 101,879,171 (July 2001 est.)

Ethnic groups: mestizo (Amerindian-Spanish) 60%,
Amerindian or predominantly Amerindian 30%,
white 9%, other 1%

Religious groups: nominally Roman Catholic 89%,
Protestant 6%, other 5%

Languages: Spanish, various Mayan, Nahuatl, and
other regional indigenous languages

Literacy: 89.6% (age 15 and over can read and write;
1995 est.)

Exports: manufactured goods, oil and oil products,
silver, fruits, vegetables, coffee, cotton

Primary export partners: United States 88.6%,
Canada 2%, Spain 0.9%, Germany 0.9%, Japan
0.6%, United Kingdom 0.6%, Netherlands Antilles
0.5%, Switzerland 0.3% Venezuela 0.3%, Chile 0.3%
(2000 est.)

Imports: metal-working machines, steel mill
products, agricultural machinery, electrical
equipment, car parts for assembly, repair parts
for motor vehicles, aircraft, and aircraft parts

Primary import partners: United States 73.6%, Japan
3.7%, Germany 3.3%, Canada 2.3%, South Korea
2%, China 1.6%, Taiwan 1.2%, Italy 1%, Brazil 1%
(2000 est.)

When Hernán Cortes stepped ashore in Mexico in
1519, he was accompanied by a free black named Juan
Garrido, who later participated in the Spanish toppling
of Tenochtitlán, the Aztec capital. By the middle of the
sixteenth century, it is estimated that there were almost
150,000 black slaves in the country. One of the earlier
slaves, Estevanico, is credited with opening up the
northern interior lands—of what is now New Mexico
and Arizona—to Spanish conquest. During the sixteenth and seventeenth centuries, black Mexicans were
believed to have outnumbered whites by a ratio of two
to one. However, both groups were vastly outnumbered by the indigenous peoples of Mexico.

Beginning in the early part of the eighteenth century,
the country's Afro-Mexican population started to decline, in part because of new Spanish restrictions on
the slave trade. Although the imported African slaves
proved more resistant to many of the European-borne
diseases than the indigenous peoples, many did suc-
cumb to foreign diseases including tuberculosis, yellow fever, and syphilis. Some of the enslaved blacks
were simply worked to death. Furthermore, many of
the African slaves brought into the colony intermixed
with indigenous peoples and whites. The reasons for
this large-scale intermixing was twofold: the Spaniards
purposely limited the number of female slaves they
brought into Mexico, and the prevailing caste system
gave individuals with a lighter skin color a higher
standing. In 1829, Mexico abolished slavery in all its
states except Texas, allowing it to remain there to
pacify the United States. As slavery in the United States
moved westward into Texas, Mexico became a haven
for escaped slaves who slipped into the heart of the
country and blended with the population.

Some 100,000 blacks, about 0.5 percent of the population, live in Mexico today, mostly in the port cities of
Veracruz and Acapulco. Blacks in lesser numbers live
in Mexico City and in border cities across the Rio
Grande River from Texas.

For more than seven decades, Mexico was governed
by the Partido Revolucionario Nacional (PRI). The
PRI's longstanding dominance of the Mexican political
scene ended in July 2000 when Vicente Fox Quesada of
the center-right Partido Accion Nacional (PAN) was
elected president. Although it lost control of the presidency, the PRI held on to its dominant position in the
Congress.

Montserrat

Independence: none (overseas territory of the
United Kingdom)

Area: 100 sq km

Form of government: NA

Capital: Plymouth (abandoned in 1997 due to
volcanic activity; interim government buildings
have been built at Brades, in the Carr's Bay/Little
Bay vicinity at the northwest end of Montserrat)

International relations: Caricom, CDB, ECLAC
(associate), ICFTU, Interpol (subbureau),
OECS, WCL

Currency: East Caribbean dollar (XCD)

Income: us$5,000 (1999 est. of purchasing power parity)

Population: 7,574

Ethnic groups: black, white

Religious groups: Anglican, Methodist, Roman Catholic, Pentecostal, Seventh-Day Adventist, other Christian denominations

Languages: English

Literacy: 97% (age 15 and over has ever attended school; 1970 est.)

Exports: electronic components, plastic bags, apparel, hot peppers, live plants, cattle

Primary export partners: United States, Antigua and Barbuda (1993)

Imports: machinery and transportation equipment, foodstuffs, manufactured goods, fuels, lubricants, and related materials

Primary import partners: United States, United Kingdom, Trinidad and Tobago, Japan, Canada (1993)

When the Leeward Islands (Antigua, Anguilla, Barbuda, Montserrat, Nevis, and Saint Kitts) were first visited by Christopher Columbus in 1493, they were inhabited by Carib Indians. Montserrat was first colonized in 1632 by English settlers who moved to the island from nearby Saint Kitts and Nevis. The island's first slaves were believed to have arrived in Montserrat in 1651. By the early 1670s, there were about 1,000 slaves on the island, a figure that jumped to nearly 6,000 by 1729. At that time, blacks outnumbered whites by about five to one.

The lives of slaves on Montserrat were closely regulated. Colonial laws prohibited slaves from becoming masons, shinglers, sawyers, tailors, coopers, or smiths. Furthermore, blacks were forbidden to plant indigo, ginger, cocoa, cotton, or coffee, the main cash crops of the region, although they could grow vegetables for their own use in small gardens. These restrictions ensured that few slaves would ever be able to make and set aside enough money to purchase their freedom. In 1768 and 1770, the island's whites were alarmed by rumors of planned slave revolts. Neither rumored uprising, however, actually took place.

Throughout the 18th century, the British and French warred for possession of Montserrat, which was finally confirmed as a British possession by the Treaty of Versailles (1783). By the early 19th century, Montserrat had a plantation economy, but the abolition of slavery in 1834, the elimination of the apprentice system, the declining market for sugar, and a series of natural disasters brought the downfall of the sugar estates.

Today, most of Montserrat's population is an intermixture of European settlers and the descendants of West African slaves. In 1997, the 3,000-foot Soufriere Hills volcano erupted repeatedly, causing widespread devastation to property and virtually collapsing the island's economy. More than two-thirds of the country's residents sought shelter off the island.

In the wake of the repeated volcanic eruptions during the late-1990s, Montserrat began its return to some semblance of normalcy in 2000, although the volcano remained unstable. The island's population, reduced from 11,000 in 1995 to 3,400 in 1998, had climbed back to about 5,000 by mid-2000. In April 2001 elections, the National People's Liberation Movement, led by former chief minister John Osborne, won control of the island's legislature, capturing seven of nine seats. The ruling party promised to work to restore jobs lost after the series of devastating volcanic eruptions.

Netherlands Antilles

Official name: none

Independence: none (part of the Kingdom of the Netherlands)

Area: 960 sq km

Form of government: parliamentary

Capital: Willemstad

International relations: CARICOM (observer), ECLAC (associate), Interpol, IOC, UNESCO (associate), UPU, WCL, WMO, WToO (associate)

Currency: Netherlands Antillean guilder (ANG)

Income: us$11,400 (2000 est. of purchasing power parity)

Population: 212,226 (July 2001 est.)

Ethnic groups: mixed black 85%, Carib Amerindian, white, East Asian

Religious groups: Roman Catholic, Protestant, Jewish, Seventh-Day Adventist

Languages: Dutch (official), Papiamento (a Spanish-Portuguese-Dutch-English dialect) predominates, English widely spoken, Spanish

Literacy: 98% (age 15 and over can read and write; 1981 est.)

Exports: petroleum products

Primary export partners: United States 17.5%, Guatemala 8%, Costa Rica 6.5%, The Bahamas 4.6%, Jamaica 4.1%, Chile 3.4% (1998)

Imports: crude petroleum, food, manufactures

Primary import partners: Venezuela 35.3%, United States 21%, Mexico 9.8%, Italy 5.4%, Netherlands 4.8%, Brazil 3.1% (1998)

The Spanish first landed in Curaçao in 1499, and, in 1527, they took possession of Curaçao, Bonaire, and Aruba. So poor was the soil on most of the islands that the Spanish called them *islas inutiles*, capturing many of the native Arawak Indians and then transporting them to nearby Spanish islands to work on plantations.

In 1634, the three islands were passed to the Netherlands, where they have remained except for two short periods of British rule during the Napoleonic Wars.

The islands' rich salt deposits, particularly off the coasts of Saint Maarten, Bonaire, and Curaçao, were perhaps the main reason the Dutch had sought to gain their control. However, the mining of salt was both a difficult and labor-intensive job, and there were not nearly enough Dutch colonists willing to do it. The Dutch decided to import African slaves to handle the workload. The first boatloads of slaves, mostly from the Congo and Angola, arrived in Curaçao in 1639. The Dutch West India Company, which handled the slave trading responsibilities for the Netherlands, increased dramatically in size during this period, becoming the second largest slave-trading power in the Atlantic by the 1640s. By 1700, the slave population on Curaçao and Bonaire totaled 4,000 with another 1,000 slaves split between Saint Eustatius and Saint Maarten. A century later, between them Saint Maarten and Saint Eustatius were home to some 9,000 slaves. Both Curaçao and Bonaire had experienced similar increases, although no exact figures from 1800 are available for those islands. Slavery was abolished in 1863.

Today, some 40 nationalities are represented in the Netherlands Antilles and Aruba. The people of the Netherlands Antilles are primarily African or mixed African-European descent.

Political uncertainty characterized the late 1990s and early years of the new millennium. On Curacao, the largest island of the group, no party secured a dominant position in the May 1999 elections. The two main parties, the National People's Party and the Antillean Restructuring Party, each won the same number of seats in the legislature. Neither party was able to put together a coalition with one of the other parties winning seats in the legislature. A June 2001 referendum in Saint Maarten indicated that more than two-thirds of those voting preferred becoming a separate entity within the Netherlands rather than remaining part of the Netherlands Antilles. Dutch authorities, however, quickly said the idea was "out of the question."

Nicaragua
Official name: Republic of Nicaragua
Independence: 15 September 1821 (from Spain)
Area: 129,494 sq km
Form of government: republic
Capital: Managua
International relations: BCIE, CACM, CCC, ECLAC, FAO, G-77, IADB, IAEA, IBRD, ICAO, ICFTU, ICRM, IDA, IFAD, IFC, IFRCS, ILO, IMF, IMO, Intelsat, Interpol, IOC, IOM, ISO (correspondent), ITU, LAES, LAIA (observer), NAM, OAS, OPANAL, OPCW, PCA, UN, UNCTAD, UNESCO, UNHCR, UNIDO, UPU, WCL, WHO, WIPO, WMO, WToO, WTrO
Currency: gold cordoba (NIO)
Income: US$2,700 (2000 est. of purchasing power parity)
Population: 4,918,393 (July 2001 est.)
Ethnic groups: mestizo (mixed Amerindian and white) 69%, white 17%, black 9%, Amerindian 5%
Religious groups: Roman Catholic 85%, Protestant
Languages: Spanish (official)
Literacy: 65.7% (age 15 and over can read and write; 1995 est.)
Exports: coffee, shrimp and lobster, cotton, tobacco, beef, sugar, bananas; gold
Primary export partners: United States 37.7%, El Salvador 12.5%, Germany 9.8%, Costa Rica 5.1%, Spain 2.5%, France 2.1% (1999)
Imports: machinery and equipment, raw materials, petroleum products, consumer goods
Primary import partners: United States 34.5%, Costa Rica 11.4%, Guatemala 7.3%, Panama 6.9%, Venezuela 5.9%, El Salvador 5.5% (1999)

Christopher Columbus first visited what is now Nicaragua in 1502 on his last voyage to the Americas. It was, however, not until Balboa's discovery of the Pacific in 1513 that Spanish efforts to settle the area began in earnest. Because the economy could neither support nor did it require large-scale slave labor, early Spanish colonists brought relatively few African slaves to what is now Nicaragua. However, the early 1600s saw the development of an English enclave along the territory's desolate Atlantic Coast, known as the Mosquito Coast. By the middle of the seventeenth century, these English settlers had begun to import slaves into their enclave to work the area's plantations and assist in harvesting coastal timber. A century later, when Britain was forced to abandon its Mosquito Coast protectorate, most of the blacks remained, creating black Creole villages, such as Pearl Lagoon and Bluefields. So far were these communities from the center of Spanish power in Managua that the blacks enjoyed considerable local autonomy. The abolition of slavery in the British colonies of the Caribbean in the early 1830s set off a new wave of immigration into the Mosquito Coast as the newly freed slaves joined the free blacks on the Nicaraguan coast. Nicaragua did not win its independence from Spain until 1838.

In 1999, Nicaragua was still trying to shake off the devastating impact of Hurricane Mitch, which had struck in October 1998. The administration of President Arnoldo Alemán Lacayo came under fire for its slowness in declaring a national disaster and was further weakened by charges of corruption, mostly directed at the president himself. In November 2001 presidential elections, Liberal candidate Enrique Bolaños Geyer soundly defeated closest rival Daniel Ortega of the Sandinista Party.

Today, Nicaragua's population is comprised of mestizos (69%), whites (17%), blacks (9%), and indigenous peoples (5%).

Panama

Official name: Republic of Panama
Independence: 3 November 1903 (from Colombia; became independent from Spain 28 November 1821)
Area: 78,200 sq km
Form of government: constitutional democracy
Capital: Panama
International relations: CCC, ECLAC, FAO, G-77, IADB, IAEA, IBRD, ICAO, ICFTU, ICRM, IDA, IFAD, IFC, IFRCS, ILO, IMF, IMO, Inmarsat, Intelsat, Interpol, IOC, IOM, ISO, ITU, LAES, LAIA (observer), NAM, OAS, OPANAL, OPCW, PCA, RG, UN, UNCTAD, UNESCO, UNIDO, UPU, WCL, WFTU, WHO, WIPO, WMO, WToO, WTrO
Currency: balboa (PAB); U.S. dollar (us$)
Income: us$6,000 (2000 est. of purchasing power parity)
Population: 2,845,647 (July 2001 est.)
Ethnic groups: mestizo (mixed Amerindian and white) 70%, Amerindian and mixed (West Indian) 14%, white 10%, Amerindian 6%
Religious groups: Roman Catholic 85%, Protestant 15%
Languages: Spanish (official), English 14%
Literacy: 90.8% (age 15 and over can read and write; 1995 est.)
Exports: bananas, shrimp, sugar, coffee, clothing
Primary export partners: United States 42%, Germany 11%, Costa Rica 5%, Benelux 4%, Italy 4% (1999)
Imports: capital goods, crude oil, foodstuffs, consumer goods, chemicals
Primary import partners: United States 39%, Colon Free Zone 14%, Japan 8%, Ecuador 6%, Mexico 5% (1999)

Prior to the arrival of Europeans, Panama was inhabited by Amerindian groups. By 1519, the Spanish had established settlements, killing or enslaving much of the indigenous Indian population. Africans were brought in to replace the Indian slave workforce. Panama was a part of Colombia from the time of independence in 1821 until it broke away as a separate country in 1903.

One of the most dramatic forces of change in Panama has been the construction of the Panama Canal connecting the Atlantic and the Pacific Oceans. Supported by the United States, which desperately wanted to build the canal, Panama seceded from Colombia. Two weeks later the United States and the newly independent Panama signed a treaty permitting the United States to build the canal and enjoy control over a five-mile stretch of Panamanian territory on either side of the waterway. Panama's existing black population was soon increased dramatically as West Indians arrived by the thousands to help in the massive construction project. Working and living conditions for blacks involved in the project were harsh, particularly since many of the American supervisors overseeing the project were natives of the U.S. South. Segregated living arrangements were put in place by these supervisors. Discrimination against blacks and other Panamanians working on the canal was blatant. They were paid less than Spaniards and Italians who had been imported into Panama to perform the same level of manual labor on the project.

In May 1999 presidential elections, Mireya Moscoso of the opposition Arnulfista Party became the first woman in Panamanian history to win the presidency, defeating Martin Torrijos of the ruling Democratic Revolutionary Party. In September 2000, President Moscoso acknowledged that Panama's economic growth had slowed, but her administration seemed unable to do much reverse the country's economic downtrend. The president also clashed with the Legislative Assembly in 2001 over the reorganization of the state-owned water and sewer services company.

Today, most Panamanians are of mixed parentage—Spanish, Indian, or black.

Paraguay

Official name: Republic of Paraguay
Independence: 14 May 1811 (from Spain)
Area: 406,750 sq km
Form of government: constitutional republic
Capital: Asuncion
International relations: CCC, ECLAC, FAO, G-77, IADB, IAEA, IBRD, ICAO, ICFTU, ICRM, IDA, IFAD, IFC, IFRCS, ILO, IMF, IMO, Intelsat, Interpol, IOC, IOM, ISO (correspondent), ITU, LAES, LAIA, Mercosur, NAM (observer), OAS, OPANAL, OPCW, PCA, RG, UN, UNCTAD, UNESCO, UNIDO, UNMEE, UPU, WCL, WHO, WIPO, WMO, WToO, WTrO
Currency: guarani (PYG)
Income: us$4,750 (2000 est. of purchasing power parity)
Population: 5,734,139 (July 2001 est.)
Ethnic groups: mestizo (mixed Spanish and Amerindian) 95%

Religious groups: Roman Catholic 90%, Mennonite, and other Protestant

Languages: Spanish (official), Guarani (official)

Literacy: 92.1% (age 15 and over can read and write; 1995 est.)

Exports: electricity, soybeans, feed, cotton, meat, edible oils

Primary export partners: Brazil, Argentina, EU

Imports: road vehicles, consumer goods, tobacco, petroleum products, electrical machinery

Primary import partners: Brazil, United States, Argentina, Uruguay, EU, Hong Kong

Since early colonial times, people of African descent, most of them brought into the territory as slaves, have played a significant role in the development of Paraguay and its culture. Because the colony lacked the wealth of natural resources of many of its neighbors in South America and also because the indigenous peoples of the region could be pressed into service, the number of slaves imported was on a smaller scale than elsewhere. The nature of the work to which the early African (and Indian) slaves were put was not much different in nature than in other Spanish colonies of the region: farm work, livestock raising, and domestic service. In later years, some blacks were employed for more specialized tasks including road construction and repair and the smelting of iron. As of 1650, surviving records indicate, the African slave population totaled 15,000 out of a total population of 250,000. However, unlike other Spanish-held territories where the slave population continued to grow strongly into the nineteenth century, by 1782, Paraguay's African slaves had dropped to less than 11,000 in number.

A system unique to Paraguay called *amparo* provided that any freed slave who could not pay tribute to the Spanish crown was turned over to the protective custody of the local government or religious orders. Under conditions much like slavery, many of these newly freed slaves were settled into all-black communities and compelled to work for their custodians. In Paraguay's battle for independence from Spain, it was unnecessary to draft the services of Afro-Paraguayans, free or slave. Thus when independence was achieved in 1811, colonial officials were under no obligation to begin freeing slaves in payments for their military services. It was not until 1869 that the government finally ordered the total abolition of slavery.

In 1999, President Raúl Cubas Grau and his mentor, retired General Lino Oviedo, faced off against the Supreme Court, most of Congress, and the vice president in Cubas' refusal to return Oviedo to jail to serve out a jail term for the latter's role in a 1996 coup attempt. As the country moved toward impeachment, Cubas resigned in March 1999. Shortly thereafter, Luis Angel Gonzalez Macchi, president of the legislature, succeeded Cubas as president. Political and socioeconomic crises dogged Paraguay throughout 2000. Corruption scandals related to his family further weakened the administration of President Gonzalez in 2001.

Estimates of the modern-day population of blacks in Paraguay are difficult to obtain, although some have suggested they account for as much as 3.5 percent of the total population of 5.3 million, or about 186,000.

Peru

Official name: Republic of Peru

Independence: 28 July 1821 (from Spain)

Area: 1,285,220 sq km

Form of government: constitutional republic

Capital: Lima

International relations: ABEDA, APEC, CAN, CCC, ECLAC, FAO, G-11, G-15, G-19, G-24, G-77, IADB, IAEA, IBRD, ICAO, ICC, ICFTU, ICRM, IDA, IFAD, IFC, IFRCS, IHO, ILO, IMF, IMO, Inmarsat, Intelsat, Interpol, IOC, IOM, ISO (correspondent), ITU, LAES, LAIA, MONUC, NAM, OAS, OPANAL, OPCW, PCA, RG, UN, UNCTAD, UNESCO, UNIDO, UNMEE, UNTAET, UPU, WCL, WFTU, WHO, WIPO, WMO, WToO, WTrO

Currency: nuevo sol (PEN)

Income: us$4,550 (2000 est. of purchasing power parity)

Population: 27,483,864 (July 2001 est.)

Ethnic groups: Amerindian 45%, mestizo (mixed Amerindian and white) 37%, white 15%, black, Japanese, Chinese, and other 3%

Religious groups: Roman Catholic 90%

Languages: Spanish (official), Quechua (official), Aymara

Literacy: 88.7% (age 15 and over can read and write; 1995 est.)

Exports: fish and fish products, copper, zinc, gold, crude petroleum and byproducts, lead, coffee, sugar, cotton

Primary export partners: United States 29%, EU 25%, Andean Community 6%, Japan 4%, Mercosur 3% (1999)

Imports: machinery, transport equipment, foodstuffs, petroleum, iron and steel, chemicals, pharmaceuticals

Primary import partners: United States 32%, EU 21%, Andean Community 6%, Mercosur 8%, Japan 5% (1999)

To most, Peru is perhaps best known as the home of the Incas, whose rich culture was developed in the mountain strongholds of the Andes. Most students today are also familiar with the Spanish conquistadors who sought out the Incas' riches in gold and silver and toppled their sophisticated empire in the process. What few recognize is the very real contribution made to Peru's conquest and its subsequent development by African slaves and their descendants. Among the best known of the early blacks involved in the conquest of the Incan Empire was Juan Valiente, a slave serving under Diego de Almagro, who himself accompanied Francisco Pizarro into Peru in 1524. For his services, Valiente was eventually rewarded with a land grant and a number of Indians who were required to pay tribute to him. Strangely, Valiente, despite his new found fortune, remained a slave until his death. As his military superiors negotiated with his master for Valiente's freedom, he was killed in an engagement against local Araucanian Indians at Tucapel.

In Peru's early colonial period, relatively few African slaves were imported, since the bulk of the available work was in the mines high in the mountains, an environment for which the colonial authorities thought the Africans ill-suited. Furthermore, there was plenty of Indian labor available for this work. As the country's arid coastal plain was gradually irrigated and put under cultivation, the need for African slaves grew. Obtaining slaves was a monumental challenge, as they had to be shipped from the west coast of Africa, across the Atlantic, around treacherous Cape Horn at the southern tip of South America, and north along the Pacific Coast to Panama, where they were unloaded. So arduous was the voyage that many slaves did not survive. For those importing the slaves, the cost of this trade was very high indeed. However, well into the seventeenth century, Peru's demands for slaves from Africa remained strong. During the campaign of Argentine José de San Martin for Peru's independence in the 1820s, he tried to entice African slaves into military service with promises of freedom for those who joined him. In fact, for most black slaves in Peru, it was not until 1854 that slavery was officially abolished.

In late 1999, President Alberto Fujimori announced his intention to run for a third term the following year. In a widely questioned election in April 2000, Fujimori came out on top, although without a clear-cut majority. After a major opposition candidate dropped out of the race because of what he claimed was fraud in the first balloting, Fujimori easily swept to reelection in a runoff election. A series of scandals later in 2000 forced Fujimori to call for new elections, and, as pressure against him mounted, Fujimori withdrew from politics in November 2000. Valentin Paniagua was named interim president. After two rounds of presidential elections in spring 2001, independent candidate Alejandro Toledo emerged as the victor.

Today, blacks comprise a very small percentage of Peru's population. Leading contemporary Afro-Peruvians include composer, vocalist, and ethnomusicologist Susana Baca and writer, university professor, and journalist Gregorio Martínez.

Puerto Rico

Official name: Commonwealth of Puerto Rico

Independence: none (commonwealth associated with the United States)

Area: 9,104 sq km

Form of government: commonwealth

Capital: San Juan

International relations: CARICOM (observer), ECLAC (associate), FAO (associate), ICFTU, Interpol (subbureau), IOC, WCL, WFTU, WHO (associate)

Currency: U.S. dollar (US$)

Income: US$10,000 (2000 est. of purchasing power parity)

Population: 3,937,316 (July 2001 est.)

Ethnic groups: white (mostly Spanish origin) 80.5%, black 8%, Amerindian 0.4%, Asian 0.2%, mixed and other 10.9%

Religious groups: Roman Catholic 85%, Protestant and other 15%

Languages: Spanish, English

Literacy: 89% (age 15 and over can read and write; 1980 est.)

Exports: pharmaceuticals, electronics, apparel, canned tuna, rum, beverage concentrates, medical equipment

Primary export partners: United States 88% (2000)

Imports: chemicals, machinery and equipment, clothing, food, fish, petroleum products

Primary import partners: United States 60% (2000)

First visited by Columbus in 1493 on his second voyage to the New World, Puerto Rico was soon conquered by Spaniard Ponce de Leon, who was appointed governor of the island in 1509 (it is interesting to note that several African slaves accompanied Columbus on his 1493 visit to the island). The indigenous Carib Indians, almost all of whom were utilized by the Spaniards as plantation laborers, were eventually wiped out by diseases and harsh treatment and replaced by African slaves.

When Spain authorized Puerto Rico's slave trade in 1510, a number of free blacks from Seville immigrated to the island in search of broader opportunities. For the most part, these were *ladinos*, as Christianized blacks were known, who sought jobs as domestic servants or mine workers. Free blacks outnumbered slaves for most of the island's history. The island's population, according to the 1845 census, included 216,083 whites,

175,000 free blacks, and 51,265 black slaves. Slavery on the island was completely abolished on March 22, 1873. Fifteen years later, Puerto Rico gained its independence from Spain and became a protectorate of the United States, as a result of the Spanish-American War.

Many Puerto Ricans today are of mixed black and Spanish ancestry. For the most part, the original Indian inhabitants of the island were exterminated in the sixteenth century. Leading contemporary Afro-Puerto Ricans include literary figures Isabelo Zenón Cruz, Angela María Dávila, and Ana Lydia Vega.

In the late 1990s and early years of the new millennium, the tension between Puerto Rico and the United States over bombing practice on the island of Vieques increased dramatically. An accident in April 1999 resulted in the death of one civilian and injuries to three others. Pedro Rossello, the island's governor, wrote to President Bill Clinton requesting an end to weapons training on Vieques. Clinton ordered a temporary cessation of such practice, but, when word spread in early 2000 that bombing would soon resume, the outcry in Puerto Rico was intense. Bombing eventually resumed in October 2000, but, in June 2001, the U.S. government agreed to stop using Vieques for bombing practice by May 2003. On January 2, 2001, Sila María Calderón of the Popular Democratic Party was sworn in as governor of the commonwealth.

Saint Kitts and Nevis

Official name: Federation of Saint Kitts and Nevis

Independence: 19 September 1983 (from United Kingdom)

Area: 261 sq km (Saint Kitts 168 sq km; Nevis 93 sq km)

Form of government: constitutional monarchy with Westminster-style parliament

Capital: Basseterre

International relations: ACP, C, CARICOM, CDB, ECLAC, FAO, G-77, IBRD, ICFTU, ICRM, IDA, IFAD, IFC, IFRCS, ILO, IMF, Interpol, IOC, OAS, OECS, OPANAL, OPCW, UN, UNCTAD, UNESCO, UNIDO, UPU, WCL, WHO, WIPO, WTrO

Currency: East Caribbean dollar (XCD)

Income: US$7,000 (2000 est. of purchasing power parity)

Population: 38,756 (July 2001 est.)

Ethnic groups: predominantly black some British, Portuguese, and Lebanese

Religious groups: Anglican, other Protestant, Roman Catholic

Languages: English

Literacy: 97% (age 15 and over has ever attended school; 1980 est.)

Exports: machinery, food, electronics, beverages, tobacco

Primary export partners: United States 68.5%, United Kingdom 22.3%, CARICOM countries 5.5% (1995 est.)

Imports: machinery, manufactures, food, fuels

Primary import partners: United States 42.4%, CARICOM countries 17.2%, United Kingdom 11.3% (1995 est.)

Christopher Columbus first visited the islands in 1493 on his second voyage to the area. Although some historians have suggested that Columbus named the larger island San Cristobal (Saint Christopher) in his own honor or for his patron saint, the name actually was given to the island by Spanish sailors. The island's nickname, Saint Kitts, comes from English sailors' slang for Saint Christopher. In 1624, Saint Christopher became England's first settlement in the West Indies, and it was from there that colonists spread to other islands in the region. In 1624, the French colonized part of the island. However, it was ceded entirely to Britain by the Treaty of Utrecht in 1713.

By the 1660s, approximately one-half of the Saint Kitts' population of 6,000 was black. Over the next 100 years, the ratio changed dramatically, so that by the final quarter of the eighteenth century, the island had ten times as many blacks as whites. The only real industry on both Saint Kitts and Nevis was sugar. It was also the central reason for the high concentration of slaves, most of whom were essential for working the sugar cane fields. In 1834, as in most English colonies, slavery was abolished. There followed a mandatory four-year apprenticeship during which the newly freed slaves were obligated to continue to work for their former masters for a small salary. Little changed for most blacks on the islands, as they continued to toil in the sugar fields of their former masters, even after the end of their apprenticeships. However, they now were obligated to pay for housing and their food on the same estates on which they had once been slaves. Many of the islands' blacks left the islands in search of better work elsewhere.

The Federation of Saint Kitts and Nevis attained full independence on September 19, 1983. Today, blacks comprise the largest percentage of Saint Kitts and Nevis's population.

Responding to pressure from Nevis for greater autonomy, the government edged closer toward constitutional reform in September 1999, appointing a select committee to review proposals for such changes. In March 2000 elections, the ruling St. Kitts-Nevis Labour Party, led by Prime Minister Denzil Douglas, captured all eight St. Kitts seats in the National Assembly. The two Nevis-based parties held on to the three assembly seats assigned to smaller island. In August 2001, Douglas reshuffled his cabinet.

Saint Lucia

Official name: none
Independence: 22 February 1979 (from United Kingdom)
Area: 620 sq km
Form of government: Westminster-style parliamentary democracy
Capital: Castries
International relations: ACCT (associate), ACP, C, CARICOM, CDB, ECLAC, FAO, G-77, IBRD, ICAO, ICFTU, ICRM, IDA, IFAD, IFC, IFRCS, ILO, IMF, IMO, Intelsat (nonsignatory user), Interpol, IOC, ISO (subscriber), ITU, NAM, OAS, OECS, OPANAL, OPCW, UN, UNCTAD, UNESCO, UNIDO, UPU, WCL, WFTU, WHO, WIPO, WMO, WTrO
Currency: East Caribbean dollar (XCD)
Income: us$4,500 (2000 est. of purchasing power parity)
Population: 158,178 (July 2001 est.)
Ethnic groups: black 90%, mixed 6%, East Indian 3%, white 1%
Religious groups: Roman Catholic 90%, Protestant 7%, Anglican 3%
Languages: English (official), French patois
Literacy: 67% (age 15 and over has ever attended school; 1980 est.)
Exports: bananas 41%, clothing, cocoa, vegetables, fruits, coconut oil
Primary export partners: United Kingdom 50%, United States 24%, CARICOM countries 16% (1995)
Imports: food 23%, manufactured goods 21%, machinery and transportation equipment 19%, chemicals, fuels
Primary import partners: United States 36%, CARICOM countries 22%, United Kingdom 11%, Japan 5%, Canada 4% (1995)

The timing of the first European visit to the lushly beautiful island of Saint Lucia has been the subject of debate for some time. Many islanders believe the story, perhaps apocryphal, that Christopher Columbus discovered the island on December 13, 1502, the feast day of Saint Lucy. Whatever the truth about its first European visitor and the timing of the visit, it is known that Europeans were unable to gain a foothold on Saint Lucia until the middle of the seventeenth century because of the native Carib Indians' fierce resistance. Once European settlement began, the Spanish, British, and French squabbled over who had claimed the island first. The Spanish failed to press their claim, but the British and the French continued to fight over Saint Lucia until 1814, during which time the island changed hands seven times. This competition for control of the island impeded large-scale development of plantations on Saint Lucia.

French planters are believed to have imported the first African slaves to Saint Lucia in about 1763, a relatively late start for the slave trade, when compared to other French and British colonies in the region. During the years of slavery, the local patois, a mixture of African dialects and French, developed. It is still spoken throughout the island today. When the island officially became a British territory in 1814, this already entrenched French-based patois made it difficult for the British colonists to communicate with the island's blacks. When slavery was abolished throughout the British colonies in 1834, more than 13,000 slaves on Saint Lucia were freed. Most of the newly freed blacks fled their masters' plantations and carved out tiny farms of their own.

Saint Lucia became an independent state within the British Commonwealth on February 22, 1979. Today, visitors from the United States, Canada, and Europe have been attracted by the island's multicultural heritage—Saint Lucia is now inhabited mainly by people of African and mixed African-European descent, with small Caucasian and Asian Indian minorities.

Prime Minister Kenny Anthony in June 1999 announced plans for the redesign of Saint Lucia's capital, Castries. In September 1999, the island's House of Assembly passed legislation making money laundering illegal. In December 2001 legislative elections, the ruling Saint Lucia Labour Party won 14 of 17 seats in the House of Assembly.

Saint Vincent and the Grenadines

Official name: none
Independence: 27 October 1979 (from United Kingdom)
Area: 389 sq km (Saint Vincent 344 sq km)
Form of government: parliamentary democracy; independent sovereign state within the Commonwealth
Capital: Kingstown
International relations: ACP, C, CARICOM, CDB, ECLAC, FAO, G-77, IBRD, ICAO, ICFTU, ICRM, IDA, IFAD, IFRCS, ILO, IMF, IMO, Intelsat (nonsignatory user), Interpol, IOC, ITU, OAS, OECS, OPANAL, OPCW, UN, UNCTAD, UNESCO, UNIDO, UPU, WCL, WFTU, WHO, WIPO, WTrO
Currency: East Caribbean dollar (XCD)
Income: us$2,800 (2000 est. of purchasing power parity)
Population: 115,942 (July 2001 est.)

Ethnic groups: black 66%, mixed 19%, East Indian 6%, Carib Amerindian 2%

Religious groups: Anglican 47%, Methodist 28%, Roman Catholic 13%, Seventh-Day Adventist, Hindu, other Protestant

Languages: English, French patois

Literacy: 96% (age 15 and over has ever attended school; 1970 est.)

Exports: bananas 39%, eddoes and dasheen (taro), arrowroot starch, tennis racquets

Primary export partners: CARICOM countries 49%, United Kingdom 16%, United States 10% (1995)

Imports: foodstuffs, machinery and equipment, chemicals and fertilizers, minerals and fuels

Primary import partners: United States 36%, CARICOM countries 28%, United Kingdom 13% (1995)

Similar to Saint Lucia, its neighbor to the north, Saint Vincent and the Grenadines, a chain of Caribbean islands, saw no permanent European settlement until the seventeenth century. The Carib Indians, then occupying the islands, fiercely resisted European attempts to colonize. A group of African slaves who survived the sinking of a Dutch slave ship on which they were being transported were the first outsiders allowed by the Caribs to settle on the islands. A treaty between the Caribs and Europeans in the early 1700s finally opened the way for European settlement. The first Europeans to gain a foothold on the islands were the French, who managed to coexist relatively peacefully with the Caribs. When the British moved into the islands and began competing with French planters to see who could carve out the larger plantations, friction with the Caribs was inevitable. After a Carib revolt late in the eighteenth century, British colonial authorities captured more than 5,000 Caribs and exiled them off British Honduras. This stripped the islands of much of their free blacks, most of whom had lived among the Caribs. The blacks remaining in the islands were mostly slaves.

In the early nineteenth century, a massive volcanic eruption caused widespread devastation on Saint Vincent, wiping out much of the island's coffee and cacao crops. When slavery was abolished in 1834, many of the newly freed slaves decided to try to carve out small farms for themselves. White plantation owners were forced to import Portuguese and Asian Indian indentured servants to work in the island's sugar cane fields. As the sugar industry began to slump in the final quarter of the nineteenth century, the government opted to turn over more land to small farmers. Well into the twentieth century, the majority of the island's residents were engaged in small-scale agriculture, a prescription for a precarious economy given agriculture's vulnerability to the vagaries of nature.

The islands were granted full autonomy in 1969 and achieved full independence in 1979.

The opposition Unity Labour Party (ULP) of Saint Vincent and the Grenadines, which had been narrowly defeated by the New Democratic Party (NDP) in June 1998 general elections, began 1999 with a new leader, Ralph Gonsalves, who replaced Vincent Beache. A period of civil unrest followed the April 2000 passage of legislation to increase the pensions and gratuities of parliamentarians. In October 2000, Prime Minister Sir James Fitz-Allen Mitchell retired from the leadership of the NDP and was replaced as prime minister by Arnhim Eustace. The general election of March 2001 brought a return to power of the ULP, which captured 12 of the 15 seats in the parliament. ULP leader Ralph Gonsalves replaced Eustace as prime minister.

Suriname

Official name: Republic of Suriname

Independence: 25 November 1975 (from Netherlands)

Area: 163,270 sq km

Form of government: constitutional democracy

Capital: Paramaribo

International relations: ACP, CARICOM, ECLAC, FAO, G-77, IADB, IBRD, ICAO, ICFTU, ICRM, IDB, IFAD, IHO, ILO, IMF, IMO, Intelsat (nonsignatory user), Interpol, IOC, ITU, LAES, NAM, OAS, OIC, OPANAL, OPCW, PCA, UN, UNCTAD, UNESCO, UNIDO, UPU, WCL, WHO, WIPO, WMO, WTrO

Currency: Surinamese guilder (SRG)

Income: US$3,400 (1999 est. of purchasing power parity)

Population: 433,998 (July 2001 est.)

Ethnic groups: Hindustani (also known locally as "East Indians"; their ancestors emigrated from northern India in the latter part of the 19th century) 37%, Creole (mixed white and black) 31%, Javanese 15%, "Maroons" (their African ancestors were brought to the country in the 17th and 18th centuries as slaves and escaped to the interior) 10%, Amerindian 2%, Chinese 2%, white 1%, other 2%

Religious groups: Hindu 27.4%, Muslim 19.6%, Roman Catholic 22.8%, Protestant 25.2% (predominantly Moravian), indigenous beliefs 5%

Languages: Dutch (official), English (widely spoken), Sranang Tongo (Surinamese, sometimes called Taki-Taki, is native language of Creoles and much of the younger population and is lingua franca among others), Hindustani (a dialect of Hindi), Javanese

Literacy: 93% (age 15 and over can read and write; 1995 est.)

Exports: alumina, crude oil, lumber, shrimp and fish, rice, bananas

Primary export partners: United States 23%, Norway 19%, Netherlands 11%, France, Japan, United Kingdom (1999)

Imports: capital equipment, petroleum, foodstuffs, cotton, consumer goods

Primary import partners: United States 35%, Netherlands 15%, Trinidad and Tobago 12%, Japan, United Kingdom, Brazil (1999)

Columbus first sighted the Suriname coast in 1498, and Spain claimed the area in 1593. Suriname became a Dutch colony in 1667. However, the new colony, Dutch Guiana, did not thrive. The colony experienced frequent uprisings by the slave population, which was often treated with extraordinary cruelty. Many of the slaves fled to the interior, where they resumed a West African culture and established the six major Bush Negro tribes in existence today: the Ndjuka and the Saramaka, the two largest groups, and the Paramaka, Aluki, Swinti, and Matawai.

Well into the eighteenth century, the territory was unique in its high percentage of African-born slaves—by the mid-1750s, about one-third of Dutch Guiana's slaves had arrived from Africa. Among the factors contributing to this phenomenon were a high mortality rate among the slaves and the need to keep importing slaves at a fast pace, in part to replace some who had escaped. Suriname experienced less in the way of violent slave revolts, such as those common throughout much of the New World—the most common form of protest among Suriname slaves was escape.

The maroons, as the runaway slaves were called, were not the only ones to take a stand against slavery, however. Although Dutch Guiana saw less of the slave violence common to slave-holding New World colonies, there was a notable uprising in 1832, when much of the colony's capital was put to the torch by slaves. In 1860, virtually the entire slave population of the colony escaped to uninhabited parts of the colony. Bowing to these growing pressures, the Netherlands abolished slavery in 1863.

Starting in 1951, Suriname began to acquire an increasing measure of autonomy from the Netherlands. On December 15, 1954, Suriname became an autonomous part of the Kingdom of the Netherlands and gained independence on November 25, 1975. Désiré Bourtese led a military coup in 1980 and instituted a socialist state. A separate challenge to the government came from a guerrilla movement under the leadership of Ronny Brunswijk. The Surinamese Liberation Army

(SLA), also known as the Maroon or Bush Negro insurgency, began operating in the northeast in July 1986. It struck against various economic targets including the Suriname Aluminium Company. The government responded with repression and the killing of civilians suspected of supporting the insurgency.

Political upheaval continued in spite of the elections held in 1987. International pressure eventually prevailed, and the military relinquished its control of the government. Ronald Venetiaan was elected president in 1991, followed by Jules Wijdenbosch in 1996. These elections marked the first time in independent Suriname's history that one democratically elected government passed peacefully to another.

In July 1999, a court in The Hague, Netherlands, convicted former military dictator Désiré Bourtese in absentia of drug smuggling charges. Seemingly untroubled by the Dutch court's action, Bourtese, leader of the National Democratic Party, remained Suriname's most powerful politician. In the spring of 1999, Bourtese had split with President Jules Wijdenbosch and withdrawn his support for the ruling coalition. On June 1, Wijdenbosch lost a vote of confidence in the National Assembly and was asked to resign. He refused, promising instead to call a general election no later than May 25, 2000. The New Front party swept the May 2000 legislative elections, clearing the way for the election of its leader, Ronald Venetiaan, as the new president in August 2000. The new government under Venetiaan managed to improve the country's fiscal and economic stability through 2001.

Trinidad and Tobago

Official name: Republic of Trinidad and Tobago

Independence: 31 August 1962 (from United Kingdom)

Area: 5,128 sq km

Form of government: parliamentary democracy

Capital: Port-of-Spain

International relations: ACP, C, CARICOM, CCC, CDB, ECLAC, FAO, G-24, G-77, IADB, IBRD, ICAO, ICFTU, ICRM, IDA, IFAD, IFC, IFRCS, IHO, ILO, IMF, IMO, Intelsat, Interpol, IOC, ISO, ITU, LAES, NAM, OAS, OPANAL, OPCW, UN, UNCTAD, UNESCO, UNIDO, UNU, UPU, WCL, WFTU, WHO, WIPO, WMO, WTrO

Currency: Trinidad and Tobago dollar (TTD)

Income: us$9,500 (2000 est. of purchasing power parity)

Population: 1,169,682 (July 2001 est.)

Ethnic groups: black 39.5%, East Indian (a local term—primarily immigrants from northern India) 40.3%, mixed 18.4%, white 0.6%, Chinese and other 1.2%

Trinidadian and Tobagonian musicians playing traditional steel drums.

Religious groups: Roman Catholic 29.4%, Hindu 23.8%, Anglican 10.9%, Muslim 5.8%, Presbyterian 3.4%, other 26.7%

Languages: English (official), Hindi, French, Spanish, Chinese

Literacy: 97.9% (age 15 and over can read and write; 1995 est.)

Exports: petroleum and petroleum products, chemicals, steel products, fertilizer, sugar, cocoa, coffee, citrus, flowers

Primary export partners: United States 39.3%, CARICOM countries 26.1%, Latin America 9.5%, EU 5.7% (1999)

Imports: machinery, transportation equipment, manufactured goods, food, live animals

Primary import partners: United States 39.8%, Venezuela 11.9%, EU 11%, CARICOM 4.8% (1999)

The island of Trinidad was first visited by Columbus in 1498 on his third voyage to the Western Hemisphere. The Spanish made the first successful attempt to colonize Trinidad in 1592. Trinidad continued under Spanish rule until it was captured by the British in 1797. Africans were brought to the islands during the eighteenth century to provide labor on the sugar cane plantations. Following the abolition of slavery, Indian and Chinese labor was imported.

Trinidad was ceded formally to the United Kingdom in 1802, with the island of Tobago following in 1814. In 1888, Trinidad and Tobago emerged to form a single colony. In 1958, the United Kingdom established the autonomous Federation of the West Indies. Jamaica withdrew in 1961, and, when Trinidad and Tobago followed, the federation collapsed. Trinidad and Tobago obtained full independence and joined the Commonwealth in 1962.

Eric Williams became prime minister at independence and held that position until he died in 1981. Williams was succeeded by George Chambers, who had served as his agriculture minister. Chambers was succeeded in 1996 by Arthur Napoleon Robinson. During an abortive coup attempt in July 1990, Robinson and other government officials were held hostage by a group of more than 100 Muslim militants. In December of that year, Patrick Manning was elected prime minister. Black-led since 1956, the two-island nation elected its first Asian Indian prime minister, Basdeo Panday, in 1996. After the ruling United National Congress party lost its majority in the House of Representatives, tying with the opposition People's National Movement (PNM) in the number of seats won (12 each), a period of political uncertainty followed. The two parties agreed to let President Robinson settle the matter. Robinson tapped PNM leader Patrick Manning to replace Basdeo Panday as prime minister.

A major center of African culture in the Caribbean, Trinidad and Tobago gave birth to calypso and steelpan, as the music of the steel drum is known locally. The country's annual Carnival festival is but one of the nation's many celebrations of music and dance. Leading contemporary Afro-Trinidadians include calypso singer Mighty Sparrow, visual artist/novelist Valerie Belgrave, and literary figures Rafael de Boissiere, Dionne Brand, Merle Hodge, and Earl Lovelace.

Turks and Caicos Islands

Official name: none
Independence: none (overseas territory of the United Kingdom)
Area: 430 sq km
Form of government: NA
Capital: Cockburn Town (on Grand Turk)
International relations: CARICOM (associate), CDB, Interpol (subbureau)
Currency: U.S. dollar (us$)
Income: us$7,300 (1999 est. of purchasing power parity)
Population: 18,122 (July 2001 est.)
Ethnic groups: black
Religious groups: Baptist 41.2%, Methodist 18.9%, Anglican 18.3%, Seventh-Day Adventist 1.7%, other 19.9% (1980)
Languages: English (official)
Literacy: 98% (age 15 and over has ever attended school; 1970 est.)
Exports: lobster, dried and fresh conch, conch shells
Primary export partners: United States, United Kingdom
Imports: food and beverages, tobacco, clothing, manufactures, construction materials
Primary import partners: United States, United Kingdom

Two groups of islands in the Atlantic southeast of the Bahamas, the Turks and Caicos were valued by early British settlers for their salt flats, which for hundreds of years were the economic mainstay of the islands. In 1678, English settlers who had come to the islands by way of Bermuda began importing African slaves to work the salt flats. Of this arduous work, Mary Prince, a female slave, wrote in *The History of Mary Prince, A West Indian Slave* (1831): "We . . . worked through the heat of the day; the sun flaming upon our hands like fire, and raising salt blisters in those parts which were not completely covered. Our feet and legs, from standing in the salt water for so many hours, soon became full of dreadful boils, which eat down in some cases to the very bone, afflicting the sufferers with great torment. . . . Oh that Turk's Island was a horrible place!"

Although slavery was abolished on the islands in 1834, as in most of Britain's New World colonies, life remained extremely difficult for the newly emancipated slaves, for the salt trade remained the islands' only major business for decades to come. It was not until well into the twentieth century that the black majority of the Turks and Caicos managed to acquire any degree of political power. After nearly 50 years of control from the Bahamas, from 1799 to 1848, the islands were granted their own local government, but it was controlled firmly by the white minority. This period of local autonomy lasted until 1873.

Between 1874 and 1959, the Turks and Caicos islands were administered as a dependency of Jamaica. In 1962, the islands became a separate colony. In 1985, Norman B. Saunders, the chief minister and two other ministers caused a scandal when they were arrested in Florida on drug charges and later charged, convicted, and jailed. One year later, the ministerial government ended when other ministers were found guilty of "unconstitutional behavior." The islands remain a crown colony. In the general election of 1999, the ruling Peoples Democratic Movement won 10 of 13 seats in the Legislative Council; the opposition Progressive National Party retained its three seats in the council.

Uruguay

Official name: Oriental Republic of Uruguay
Independence: 25 August 1825 (from Brazil)
Area: 176,220 sq km
Form of government: constitutional republic
Capital: Montevideo
International relations: CCC, ECLAC, FAO, G-11, G-77, IADB, IAEA, IBRD, ICAO, ICC, ICRM, IFAD, IFC, IFRCS, IHO, ILO, IMF, IMO, Intelsat, Interpol, IOC, IOM, ISO, ITU, LAES, LAIA, Mercosur, MINURSO, MONUC, NAM (observer), OAS, OPANAL, OPCW, PCA, RG, UN, UNCTAD, UNESCO, UNIDO, UNIKOM, UNMEE, UNMOGIP, UNMOT, UNOMIG, UNTAET, UPU, WCL, WFTU, WHO, WIPO, WMO, WToO, WTrO
Currency: Uruguayan peso (UYU)
Income: us$9,300 (2000 est. of purchasing power parity)
Population: 3,360,105 (July 2001 est.)
Ethnic groups: white 88%, mestizo 8%, black 4%, Amerindian, practically nonexistent

Religious groups: Roman Catholic 66% (less than one-half of the adult population attends church regularly), Protestant 2%, Jewish 1%, nonprofessing or other 31%

Languages: Spanish, Portunol, or Brazilero (Portuguese-Spanish mix on the Brazilian frontier)

Literacy: 97.3% (age 15 and over can read and write; 1995 est.)

Exports: meat, rice, leather products, vehicles, dairy products, wool, electricity

Primary export partners: MERCOSUR partners 45%, EU 20%, United States 7% (1999 est.)

Imports: road vehicles, electrical machinery, metal manufactures, heavy industrial machinery, crude petroleum

Primary import partners: MERCOSUR partners 43%, EU 20%, United States 11% (1999 est.)

The first Africans arrived in what is now Uruguay as early as 1534 in the company of Spanish explorers. These slaves, most of whom were *ladinos*, as Christianized slaves were known in Spain, joined their masters in the exploration of the Rio de la Plata. By the end of the sixteenth century, Spain was importing increasingly larger numbers of its slaves from Angola in southwestern Africa. Most of the slaves destined for use in the New World were shipped to either Mexico or Cartagena, in what is now Colombia, for transshipment to other Spanish colonies throughout the region. The lengthy voyage of the slave ships from Angola to both Mexico and Cartagena took a tremendous toll on their human cargoes, and many slaves died before reaching their destination. The Spanish began shipping some of their slaves to Buenos Aires on the Rio de la Plata in the southeast of South America. By the end of the seventeenth century, the Spanish discovered that Montevideo, also on the Rio de la Plata but 120 miles closer to the Atlantic, had a fine natural harbor. A settlement was begun there in 1724 and before long much of the slave trade to the region had moved from Buenos Aires to Montevideo, the future capital of Uruguay.

Although the numbers of African slaves imported through Montevideo were impressively high, many of these did not remain in Uruguay, but were shipped into other territories in the region where the demand for slave labor was strong. Within what is now Uruguay, there were little in the way of major mining or agricultural enterprises, and most slaves who remained there toiled as domestic servants. The bulk of the slaves in Uruguay remained in the capital of Montevideo. An end to slavery came in fits and starts during the 1840s. Although freed, many slaves continued to work for their former masters under conditions not far removed

from slavery itself. Uruguay's National Statistics Institute conducted a study in the latter half of the 1990s that found about six percent of Uruguayans identify themselves as black.

After an impressive showing by Tabaré Vázquez, presidential candidate of the leftist Broad Front alliance, in the first round of 1999 presidential elections, the Blanco and Colorado parties joined forces. As a result, Jorge Batlle of the Colorados won the presidency in the second round of elections. Batlle assumed office on March 1, 2000. In 2001, the Batlle administration was faced with a worsening economic situation, exacerbated by an outbreak of foot-and-mouth disease that curtailed the country's vital meat exports.

Venezuela

Official name: Bolivarian Republic of Venezuela

Independence: 5 July 1811 (from Spain)

Area: 912,050 sq km

Form of government: federal republic

Capital: Caracas

International relations: CAN, CARICOM (observer), CCC, CDB, ECLAC, FAO, G- 3, G-11, G-15, G-19, G-24, G-77, IADB, IAEA, IBRD, ICAO, ICC, ICFTU, ICRM, IFAD, IFC, IFRCS, IHO, ILO, IMF, IMO, Intelsat, Interpol, IOC, IOM, ISO, ITU, LAES, LAIA, NAM, OAS, OPANAL, OPCW, OPEC, PCA, RG, UN, UNCTAD, UNESCO, UNHCR, UNIDO, UNIKOM, UNU, UPU, WCL, WFTU, WHO, WIPO, WMO, WToO, WTrO

Currency: bolivar (VEB)

Income: us$6,200 (2000 est. of purchasing power parity)

Population: 23,916,810 (July 2001 est.)

Ethnic groups: Spanish, Italian, Portuguese, Arab, German, African, indigenous people

Religious groups: nominally Roman Catholic 96%, Protestant 2%, other 2%

Languages: Spanish (official), numerous indigenous dialects

Literacy: 91.1% (age 15 and over can read and write; 1995 est.)

Exports: petroleum, bauxite and aluminum, steel, chemicals, agricultural products, basic manufactures

Primary export partners: United States and Puerto Rico 57%, Colombia, Brazil, Japan, Germany, Netherlands, Italy (1999)

Imports: raw materials, machinery and equipment, transport equipment, construction materials

Primary import partners: United States 53%, Japan, Colombia, Italy, Germany, France, Brazil, Canada (1999)

In the sixteenth and seventeenth centuries, Caracas was a major center for the importation of slaves. In the early nineteenth century, blacks and mulattos comprised more than half of the population of the Captaincy General of Caracas, as Venezuela was known at that time. In the latter stages of Venezuela's fight for independence from Spain, Simón Bolivar made extensive use of blacks, mulattos, and zambos, admitting them to the ranks of his rebel army. These blacks played a critical role in the defeat of colonists loyal to Spain. By 1821, Venezuela had been largely wrested from Spain's control.

As early as 1819, Bolivar had called for the abolition of slavery, but he was overruled by a coalition of rebel leaders. Several attempts to loosen the bonds of Venezuelan slaves were undertaken, but little real change was effected in the institution. It was not until 1854 that the country's slaves were finally emancipated.

Today, roughly five percent of Venezuela's 23 million people are black, and another 500,000 are zambos of mixed African and Indian descent. Blacks remain a significant element of the country's population because of its proximity to the Caribbean and employment opportunities that have been available in this oil-rich nation.

For about four decades, from 1958 until the mid-1990s, political power in Venezuela alternated between two political parties, Accion Democratica and the Comite de Organizacion Politica Electoral Independiente. Chronic economic weakness and recurrent scandals over government corruption helped to reduce support for both parties, particularly during the late 1980s and early 1990s. In 1998, Hugo Chavez of the Movimiento Quinta Republica was elected president on a platform pledged to radical political reform. The country's 1961 constitution was replaced with a left-leaning charter in a December 1999 referendum. In July 2000, Chavez was reelected with a comfortable majority. An unsuccessful coup was mounted against Chavez in April 2002.

Virgin Islands, British

Independence: none (overseas territory of the United Kingdom)
Area: 150 sq km
Form of government: NA
Capital: Road Town
International relations: CARICOM (associate), CDB, ECLAC (associate), Interpol (subbureau), IOC, OECS (associate), UNESCO (associate)
Currency: U.S. dollar (us$)
Income: us$16,000 (2000 est. of purchasing power parity)
Population: 20,812 (July 2001 est.)
Ethnic groups: black 90%, white, Asian

Religious groups: Protestant 86% (Methodist 45%, Anglican 21%, Church of God 7%, Seventh-Day Adventist 5%, Baptist 4%, Jehovah's Witnesses 2%, other 2%), Roman Catholic 6%, none 2%, other 6% (1981)
Languages: English (official)
Literacy: 97.8% (age 15 and over can read and write; 1991 est.)
Exports: rum, fresh fish, fruits, animals; gravel, sand
Primary export partners: U.S. Virgin Islands, Puerto Rico, United States
Imports: building materials, automobiles, foodstuffs, machinery
Primary import partners: U.S. Virgin Islands, Puerto Rico, United States

Initially visited by Christopher Columbus in 1493, the Virgin Islands (an archipelago of 74 islands) is now divided into two distinct clusters—British Virgin Islands (six main islands, nearly 40 islets) and U.S. Virgin Islands (three main islands, 65 islets). Great Britain obtained title to the islands and islets in 1666 and, until 1960, administered them as part of the Leeward Islands. At present, the government is headed by a Crown-appointed administrator who is assisted by both executive and legislative councils.

During the latter half of the seventeenth century, British settlers discovered that the islands would support the cultivation of both cotton and sugar. However, to work the fields it was necessary to import slave labor from Africa. Life for the slaves in the British islands was particularly harsh, with inhumane penalties exacted for relatively minor infractions of the rules. A slave who refused his master's orders could have part of his body cut off or his nose split. In 1790, slaves in Tortola revolted after rumors spread that Britain had abolished slavery but local slaveowners were withholding freedom. Although Britain abolished the slave trade in 1808, full emancipation did not come for Virgin Island slaves until 1834. Slavery was replaced by a four-year apprenticeship program, under which all slaves were required to remain in the custody of their former masters.

Today, almost the entire population is of African descent.

In 1999, the ruling Virgin Islands Party successfully fought off a challenge from the newly formed National Democratic Party (NDP), capturing seven of the 13 seats in the Legislative Council. In July 2000, Chief Minister Ralph O'Neal accused his deputy, Eileene Parsons, with complicity in a coup plot and dismissed her. In response, Parsons quit the ruling party and joined the NDP.

Virgin Islands, United States

Independence: n/a (territory of the United States)

Area: 352 sq km
Form of government: NA
Capital: Charlotte Amalie
International relations: ECLAC (associate), Interpol (subbureau), IOC
Currency: U.S. dollar (us$)
Income: us$15,000 (2000 est. of purchasing power parity)
Population: 122,211 (July 2001 est.)
Ethnic groups: black 80%, white 15%, other 5%
Religious groups: Baptist 42%, Roman Catholic 34%, Episcopalian 17%, other 7%
Languages: English (official), Spanish, Creole
Literacy: NA
Exports: refined petroleum products
Primary export partners: United States, Puerto Rico
Imports: crude oil, foodstuffs, consumer goods, building materials
Primary import partners: United States, Puerto Rico

The U.S. Virgin Islands—the largest of which are the islands of Saint Croix, Saint John, and Saint Thomas—were originally settled by the Danish West India Company. Saint Thomas was the first to be colonized in 1672; in 1683, Saint John was colonized; and, by 1733, Saint Croix had been acquired from France. Some 20 years later, the holdings of the company were taken over by the Danish crown, which then reconstituted them as the Danish West Indies.

As in the neighboring British Virgin Islands, the Danish West Indies was found to be ideally suited for the cultivation of sugar cane and cotton. The first shipment of African slaves, numbering 103, arrived in Saint Thomas in 1673. The island had some 160 plantations and more than 3,000 slaves by 1715, only 42 years later. The island of Saint John witnessed a major slave uprising in 1733. The life of slaves in the islands was a harsh one indeed, but in the months preceding the Saint John revolt, their situation had been made even more difficult when the island was hit by a drought and two hurricanes. The actual revolt was set off by the passage in September 1733 of a set of harsh new regulations governing slaves. Slave leaders captured the island's only fort and managed to hold it for six months. Slaves in the Danish islands finally won their freedom in 1848.

The United States bought the territory from Denmark in 1917 for some $25 million and granted citizenship to its inhabitants ten years later. In 1931, its administration was transferred from the United States Navy to the Department of the Interior. The first black governor, William H. Hastie, was appointed in 1946. Melvin Evans, appointed governor in 1969, two years later became the first black governor to be elected. He served until 1975 when islanders elected Cyril E. King as their new governor. King died three years later and was succeeded by his lieutenant governor, Juan Luis, who was reelected governor in 1982. Elected governor in 1986 and reelected in 1990 was Alexander Farrelly, who was succeeded by Roy Schneider after the 1994 elections.

In the islands' 1998 gubernatorial elections, Democrat Charles Wesley Turnbull was elected to a four-year term as governor. Turnbull was expected to stand for reelection in 2002 balloting. The island's territorial legislature consists of a single house with 15 members, seven each from St. Croix and St. Thomas and an at-large member who must reside on St. John. The delegate of the U.S. Virgin Islands to the U.S. House of Representatives has no vote except in committee deliberations.

6

Africans in America: 1600 to 1900

♦ Exploration and the First Settlements in the Americas
♦ Slavery in Colonial America: 1619–1787
♦ African American Status in the New Republic ♦ Expansion of Slavery
♦ Anti-Slavery Movements ♦ The Compromise of 1850 ♦ Civil War ♦ Reconstruction
♦ The Advent of Independent African American Institutions
♦ African American Status after Reconstruction ♦ Figures of the Past

by Houston B. Roberson

♦ EXPLORATION AND THE FIRST SETTLEMENTS IN THE AMERICAS

The presence of the first Africans in the Americas is a point of contention among historians. Some scholars assert that Africans established contact with the Americas prior to the Europeans, arguing from archeological, anthropological, botanical, and linguistic evidence that Africans were present in pre-Columbian America; the work of Ivan Van Sertima is notable in this regard. Others mark the advent of the African presence as coinciding with the presence of the Europeans. Pedro Alonzo Niño, an explorer and companion to Christopher Columbus on his exploratory journey of 1492, appears to have been African; and it is known that an African named Estevanico accompanied the Spanish explorers Panfilo de Narvaez and Alvar Nuñez Cabeza de Vaca on trips throughout the American Southwest during the 1500s. Several other European explorers, including Vasco Nuñez de Balboa and Hernán Cortés, also had African members in their parties.

In 1496 Santo Domingo was established as the first permanent European settlement in the Americas. Indigenous Carib Indians were at first used as laborers; however, they were ill-suited to the rigors of the European system of slavery and died in large numbers from either disease or the constant pressure of forced labor. Portuguese explorers first visited the west coast of Africa in the fifteenth century and found that slave trading was an established institution. West Africans had for some time sold each other to Arabic traders from North Africa. By the early sixteenth century the Portuguese and Spanish were supplying newly established colonies in the Americas with African slave labor and, by the seventeenth century, several other European nations had entered the trade. African slaves proved to be a relatively cheap and inexhaustible source of labor and, from about 1501, they were increasingly used as slaves, replacing the dwindling indigenous labor pool.

♦ SLAVERY IN COLONIAL AMERICA: 1619–1787

The Emergence of Slave Status

Twenty Africans accompanied the Europeans who landed at Jamestown, Virginia, in 1619. These people were not slaves but indentured servants and, upon completing their contracts, they were free to enjoy the liberties and privileges of the "free laboring class." By 1650 there were about 300 Africans in the American colonies, most of whom were indentured servants, and some of whom eventually became property holders and active citizens. The first African American born in the colonies, William Tucker, shared with the other settlers the common birthright of freedom. The slave Anthony Johnson apparently became free about 1622 and had by 1651 amassed enough wealth to import five servants of his own, for which he obtained two hundred and 50 acres from the colonial government; the African American carpenter Richard Johnson imported two white servants in 1654 and received 100 acres.

It is unclear when the first African slaves arrived in the North American colonies. From the 1640s Africans were increasingly regarded as chattel (or persons regarded as fixed items of personal property). In 1641 Massachusetts became the first state to make perpetual bondage legal, and the institution gradually spread among the original 13 colonies. Rhode Island had an anti-slavery ordinance, but this was openly violated, and only Pennsylvania maintained a sustained opposition to slavery. By the 1650s Africans were commonly sold for life and, in 1661, the Virginia House of Burgesses formally recognized the institution of African slavery. The erosion of African indentured servitude in Maryland was finalized with the slave law of 1663, which stated specifically that "All negroes or other slaves within the province, [and] all negroes to be hereafter imported, shall serve *durante vita.*"

As white indentured servitude gradually disappeared from the colonial labor market, the flow of African labor into the colonies was accelerated, and planters rigidly institutionalized the perpetual servitude of Africans. One practical reason for this system was that slaves of African origin could be more easily detected than whites should they escape. Among the common rationalizations for the enslavement of Africans was reference to their non-Christian status: it was asserted that Africans were primitive and savage and fit for nothing better than a life of unbroken labor. Even after African Americans became Christianized, their slave status was not altered; in 1667 the Virginia legislature enacted a statute that proclaimed that "baptism doth not alter the condition of the person as to his bondage or freedom."

The Trans-Atlantic Slave Trade

The Dutch West Indies Company began to provide slave labor to the American colonies in 1621. By the late seventeenth century the Royal African Company, an English company whose most profitable commodity was slaves, began to exert powerful influence within the English court and parliament. The British government in turn exerted great pressure upon the American colonies to develop attitudes and laws that would support a slave economy. The influence of the Royal African Company contributed to William Penn's decision to overrule the objections of fellow Quakers and permit slavery in Pennsylvania. The company also drew

the shipping industry of New England into the slave trade. By the time the Royal African Company lost its monopoly on the West African slave trade in 1696, the sea captains of New England were participating in the massive slave incursions into Africa.

The majority of Africans who were transported to the Americas as slaves came from the area comprising the modern nations of Senegal, Gambia, Guinea, Sierra Leone, Liberia, Burkina Faso, Ivory Coast, Ghana, Togo, Benin, Nigeria, Cameroon, Gabon, the Republic of the Congo, and the Democratic Republic of the Congo. The number of Africans who reached the Americas is estimated at between 10 and 20 million. About 600,000 Africans were brought during the sixteenth century, two million in the seventeenth century, five million in the eighteenth century; and three million in the nineteenth century. In addition to those who reached the Americas must be added the enormous number who died in passage. It is estimated that 15 percent of those who were shipped to the Americas died of disease on the overcrowded boats of the "Middle Passage," and that another 30 percent died during the brutal training period faced in the West Indies before shipment to the American mainland.

Slavery Expansion in Colonial America

The colonies of New England played a principal role in the slave trade, despite their having little local need for slave labor. By 1700, African Americans of New England numbered only 1,000 among a population of 90,000. In the mid-Atlantic colonies, the population comprised a larger percentage, as small slaveholdings employed slaves as farm laborers, domestics, and craftsmen. In New York, slaves comprised 12 percent of the population during the mid-eighteenth century. The Quakers of Pennsylvania protested that slavery violated the principles of Christianity and the rights of man and passed laws prohibiting the slave trade in 1688, 1693, and 1696, but the British parliament overruled these statutes in 1712.

Most slaves, however, lived in the South. The Southern colonies were divided between the tobacco-producing provinces of Virginia, Maryland, and North Carolina, and the huge rice and indigo plantations now comprising the Carolinas and Georgia. Tobacco tended to be grown on family farms around the Chesapeake Bay area and, because of this fact, the slave population was not as concentrated as it was on the plantations further to the south.

The growth of a plantation economy and the concentration of a large number of African Americans in the Southern states led first Virginia (1636) and then the

With slave traders and buyers gathered, a group of Africans disembarks from a slave ship.

other states to form all-white militias. The terror of slave uprisings led the slaveholders to institute ever harsher slave codes. Ultimately, a slave could not own anything, carry a weapon, or even leave his plantation without a written pass. Murder, rape, arson, and even lesser offenses were punishable by death; small offenses were commonly punished by whipping, maiming, and branding. In the area where 90 percent of colonial African Americans lived, a slave had no rights to defend himself against a white and, as far north as Virginia, it was impossible for a white to be convicted for the murder of a slave.

The Maiden Lane slave revolt in New York City in 1712 and the public paranoia over the alleged slave conspiracy of 1741 led to the development of slave codes that were in some cases as severe as those in the South, but in general the North was a relatively less oppressive environment. In Pennsylvania the Quakers allowed African Americans a relative degree of freedom, and in New England the slave codes tended to reflect Old Testament law, maintaining the legal status of slaves as persons with certain limited rights.

Maroon Communities Arise throughout the Americas

The African experience of *marronage* or *cimarronaje* (i.e., escape from slavery), its survivors, and their descendants in the New World reflects an important part of the African diaspora in the Americas. However, little has been documented about this aspect of history.

For more than four centuries, thousands of enslaved Africans managed to escape from plantations and mines of European colonizers throughout the Americas, seeking their freedom in the wilderness. Between the early sixteenth and late nineteenth centuries, maroons challenged the colonial powers and violently resisted enslavement, striking hard at the foundation of the plantation economy of the Western Hemisphere.

In remote areas throughout the United States, the Caribbean, Central America, and South America, maroon communities emerged as free and independent societies that oftentimes forced colonial governments to sign treaties and pacts guaranteeing their freedom, land, and political autonomy. These communities emerged as an integration of African, Native American, and European cultural elements. After centuries of struggle, survival, assimilation, and adaptation, these maroon communities were able to develop a unique sense of identity and history, contributing in many ways to the shape of the Western Hemisphere. Today, descendants of some of the original maroon communities live in Oklahoma and Seminole communities in Texas, as well as Mexico, Jamaica, Suriname, French Guyana, Colombia, and the Bahamas.

Military Service before and during the Revolutionary War

Records of King William's War (1689–1697) relate that the first to fall in Massachusetts was "an Naygro of Colo. Tyng," slain at Falmouth. During Queen Anne's War (1702–1713), African Americans were drafted and sent to fight the French and the Indians when white colonists failed to provide the number of requisitioned men. Many armed African Americans fought at Fort William Henry in New York. Slaves sought freedom as their payment for fighting, and those who were already free sought the wider benefits of land and cash payments. The colony of Virginia ended its policy of excluding African Americans from the militia by 1723, and in 1747 the South Carolina Company made slaves eligible for enlistment in the territorial militia according to a quota system in which a 3:1 ratio was maintained between whites and blacks, thus abating the whites' fears of insurrection. African Americans also fought for the British in the French and Indian War.

African American Patriots

In the years leading to the Revolutionary War, it became apparent that, despite the growth of slavery, at least some African Americans were willing to fight alongside white Americans. On March 5, 1770, an African American named Crispus Attucks was one of the first men killed in the Revolutionary War, when British troops fired on a crowd of protesters in the Boston Massacre. Many African American minutemen fought at the defense of Concord Bridge: among them were Lemuel Haynes, a gifted speaker and later a prominent Congregationalist minister, and Peter Salem, who had received his freedom to enlist. Other figures of the Revolutionary War include Pomp Blackman, Caesar Ferrit, and his son John, Prince Estabrook (who was wounded at Lexington), Samuel Craft, and Primas Black and Epheram Blackman (who were members of Ethan Allen's Green Mountain Boys).

Crispus Attucks, the first of the five Americans killed in the Boston Massacre.

The Move to Disarm African Americans

A major issue during the Revolutionary War was whether African American slaves, and even freemen, should be permitted to bear arms. On May 29, 1775, the Massachusetts Committee of Safety, in a move which reflected their desire to strengthen ties with Southern states, proclaimed that the enlistment of slaves "was inconsistent with the principles that are to be supported, and reflect[ed] dishonor on the colony." On July 9, 1775, Horatio Gates, the adjutant general of the Continental Army, issued from General Washington's headquarters the order that recruiting officers should not accept "any stroller, Negro, or vagabond."

The enormous slave populations of certain Southern states meant that many whites lived in perpetual fear of slave uprisings. In South Carolina slaves outnumbered whites, and in Georgia the population was above 40 percent slaves. To minimize the risk of slaves arming themselves, Edward Rutledge of South Carolina introduced a measure in the Continental Congress to discharge all African Americans (whether free or enslaved) from the Continental Army. Although the proposal was rejected, General George Washington's own council of war decided to terminate all African American enlistment two weeks later, and on October 13, 1775, Continental Congress passed the law. Colonial generals such as John Thomas argued that African Americans soldiered as well as whites and had already "proved themselves brave" in action, but their protests went unheeded. At the close of 1775, it was extremely difficult for African Americans to join the revolutionary forces at any level.

However, on November 7, 1775, the British made a political move that forced the Continental Army to reverse its policy. Lord Dunmore, the governor of Virginia, issued a proclamation that stated, "I do hereby declare all indentured servants, Negroes, or others free, that are able and willing to bear arms, they joining his Majesty's troops, as soon as may be, for the more speedily reducing this Colony to a proper dignity." As the leaders of the impending revolution realized the consequences of the wholesale enlistment of slaves in the British Army, they brought an end to their racially exclusionary policy. Local militias that were formerly unable to fill their muster rolls enlisted free African Americans and won the reluctant acceptance of slave owners as slaves were substituted for those white men who bought their way out of service. As the war progressed, slaveowners were compensated for the enlistment of slaves who were then made free. During the course of the Revolution, many colonies granted freedom to slaves in return for military service. Rhode Island passed the first slave enlistment act on February

2, 1778, raising a regiment that participated gallantly in many important battles. In 1780 Maryland became the only Southern state to enroll slave troops, while South Carolina and Georgia refused altogether to even arm their slaves. While slave conscripts were at first assigned to combat support, in the heat of battle they were often armed. African Americans were often enlisted for longer terms than whites and, by the latter years of the war, many of the most seasoned veterans were African American troops.

◆ AFRICAN AMERICAN STATUS IN THE NEW REPUBLIC

Slaves and Freemen after the Revolution

At the end of the war about 5,000 African Americans had been emancipated through military service. In the following years the Northern states abolished slavery: Vermont in 1777, Massachusetts in 1783, Connecticut and Rhode Island in 1784, New York in 1785, New Jersey in 1786, and Pennsylvania in 1789. In the mid-Atlantic state of Virginia, Thomas Jefferson convinced the state legislature to allow slaveowners to manumit their slaves in 1783. In 1790 there were 757,208 African Americans comprising 19 percent of the population of the United States: 697,681 were slave, and 59,527 were free. During this time the free population faced many of the same restrictions as the slave population: they could not walk on the streets after dark, travel between towns without a pass, or own weapons. There was also the danger of being captured and enslaved, whether one was free or not.

The large number of Southern slaves that had responded to the British Army's call to duty and escaped

Following the war, many African American slaves who had fled to British lines during the American Revolution were reenslaved on remaining British-controlled colonies.

to the British lines, on the other hand, met a more disheartening fate. Fighting against the colonies in exchange for their freedom, most of these slaves were returned to their slaveowners after the defeat of Great Britain. In other cases, they were shipped to various British-controlled colonies to continue a miserable life of slavery.

The United States Constitution

The U.S. Constitution, drafted in 1787 and ratified in 1788, provided fundamental political principles for the nation. Key among these principles was the belief that all people share a fundamental equality, that they possess certain inalienable rights, and that government derives its power from the people. But African Americans were not afforded the rights and privileges of the Constitution. At the time, it was generally believed by whites that people of African descent were racially inferior and incapable of being assimilated into society. It was also widely believed that they were not citizens of the new republic. Article I, section 2 of the Constitution specified that all persons who are not free shall be counted as three-fifths a person for the sake of tax purposes, and article I, section 9 authorized the continued importation of slaves until 1808.

Slavery in the New Nation

In 1793 Eli Whitney's invention of the cotton gin, which separated cotton from cotton fiber, led to a subsequent increase in the consumption of cotton, and heightened the demand for slaves in the cotton-producing states. In 1800 there were more than 893,600 African slaves in the United States; by 1810 there were over 1,191,300. Although the slave trade was technically discontinued in 1808, it is estimated that from that date until 1860 more than 250,000 slaves were illegally imported; furthermore, nothing prohibited slaves from being bartered, and the breeding of slaves for sale became a specialized business. Some of the largest slave trading firms in the nation were located in Maryland, Virginia, and the District of Columbia. Such was the expansion of slavery that, between 1800 and 1859, the population of Mississippi grew from 3,489 slaves and 5,179 whites to 309,878 slaves and 295,718 whites, respectively.

By the mid-eighteenth century, three-fourths of the cotton produced in the world came from the United States, and profits from cotton were so great that vast plantations were hacked from the wilderness, allowing armies of slaves to work the fields. By mid-century the states of Georgia, Alabama, Mississippi, and Louisiana annually produced 1,726,349 bales of cotton, 48 million pounds of rice, and 226,098,000 pounds of sugar. With the outbreak of the Civil War, there were nearly four million slaves in the United States, and nearly three-fourths of them worked in cotton agriculture.

Slave Life

Slavery was by its very nature a brutal and exploitative business, and the average slave lived a terribly grim life. The more fortunate slaves tended to work on family-sized farms or had positions as house servants. Whatever one's surroundings, much of one's fortune depended upon the kindness of the master. On the larger plantations slaves were divided between house and field hands. The former group was charged with such assorted tasks as caring for the grounds and garden of the house, maintenance of the rigs and appliances, house cleaning, and caring for the master's children. House servants were frequently allowed to practice trades, such as smithery, masonry, and tailoring; some even became skilled musicians and doctors. Body slaves served their masters as valets and personal messengers, and from this intimacy real friendships sometimes developed.

But house servants were in a sense aristocrats among slaves. Their daily lives had little in common with those of the faceless masses of field hands who confronted the brutal monotony of sowing and reaping without respite or prospect of change. On larger plantations with 25 or more slaves, the only contact between field hands and whites occurred through the overseer, who often employed cruel and vicious brutality to maintain control. Many planters felt that the largest profits were made by working a slave to death in eight or ten years and then buying a new one. Even tenderhearted masters often had little contact with their field workers, and so long as the overseer returned a profit, no questions were asked. In many places slaves were given no free time at all, but were forced to work 14 or 15 hours a day. Louisiana was the only state with a law regarding the amount of work that could be demanded of a slave—the law permitted a slave to be worked 21 hours every day.

Most slaves could only expect to live with the bare necessities of shelter, clothing, and food. Shelter often consisted of a cramped, windowless, mud-floored shack in which a large family was expected to live; clothing was basic in design and made of course materials; and food was often limited to a bucket of rice or corn per week with no meat. The only break in the routine occurred on such holidays as Christmas, though in some cases slaves were able to hunt, fish, or garden in the hours after work.

Miscegenation

The history of the United States is replete with stories of enslaved African American female slaves being forced into sexual liaisons with their masters and bearing children who were often denied their rightful legal inheritances. In such cities as Charleston, South Carolina, Mobile, Alabama, and New Orleans, Louisiana, there was widespread intermixture between white men and African American women. In New Orleans, as some historians have demonstrated, the practice of young white men maintaining young black women in concubinage was so common as almost to gain social acceptability. However, white fathers varied in accepting responsibility for their black children. Some sold them outright into slavery, while others provided them with money, land, and manumission. Census data indicates that on the eve of the Civil War, of the approximately 3.9 million African American slaves, more than 411,000 were counted as mulatto. The actual figure was

Besides cotton production, African American slaves also cultivated rice.

almost certainly higher because census takers strictly went by the physical features that they observed and judged as mixed race. It is therefore likely that mulattos with predominately African American features were not counted.

Perhaps the most famous, troubling, and enduring miscegenation narrative is the story of Sally Hemings, whose own birth was the product of a slave-master relationship, and Thomas Jefferson, author of the Declaration of Independence and third president of the United States. Despite the fear of race mixing that he expressed in his *Notes on Virginia*, recent DNA evidence suggests with almost absolute certainty that Jefferson, possibly his brother, Randolph, or one of Randolph's six sons, fathered at least one child with Sally Hemings, one of Jefferson's many slaves. Oral tradition among African American members of Jefferson's family has insisted for generations that they were biological descendants of Thomas Jefferson. Most historians chose to believe the white Jefferson descendants who have steadfastly denied that Jefferson or his kin would have fathered one of Hemings's children without any special provision for them. Only recently, after genetics tests erased any reasonable doubts, have most historians begun to reconsider their position on this issue. (The descendants of Sally Hemings were finally allowed to attend the Jefferson family reunion at Monticello, the historic home of Thomas Jefferson, in May 1999. Though the Hemings descendants were not formally admitted into the Monticello Association, the family organization agreed to further examine the DNA test results as well as other evidence provided.)

This saga illuminates the difficulty and struggle enslaved African American women faced as victims who, whether the relationship was consensual or forced, ultimately had no freedom over their bodies and no power of securing protection and security for their progeny beyond whatever was deemed appropriate by the slave-master fathers. Interestingly, the scientific confirmation of the Jefferson-Hemings relationship comes at a time when white members and black members of a few American families are beginning to confront their past familial relationship and forge some level of recognition of past exploitation as a means of possible future reconciliation within their families.

Slave Naming Practices

Slaves had purposeful naming practices that were distinctively different from those of their masters. Most slaves were able to choose the names of their children, usually naming their sons after fathers and daughters after female relatives other than their mother, in order to help identify kin relationships and keep track of which cousins one should not marry. (Slaves followed marriage rules that prohibited marrying one's cousin, even though many planters and free African Americans did not.)

Generally, many slaves used English or European names for themselves and their children to satisfy the preferences of masters. Yet, many Africans kept alive their sense of cultural independence and roots by choosing English equivalents of African names or English names that sounded similar to African names. Still, some African slaves used African names all their lives.

In addition to given or first names, slaves could also have surnames distinctive from those of their owners, although owners were usually unaware of the surnames. Normally, slaves chose a surname that represented or identified the first slave owner of the earliest born-in-Africa ancestor who came to North America as a slave. The surname would then be handed down over the generations to help track relations and lineage. Though many slaves had their own surnames or "titles," many did not. After the end of slavery, those who already possessed surnames revealed them, while others chose one for the first time. During and immediately after the Civil War, government agencies often insisted that slaves have surnames to enroll in their programs or receive government benefits. Those whose family had been owned by members of the same family for several generations might have the same last name as the last owner, although the name was originally chosen to identify a more distant owner within the same family. Those who were aware of a slave family surname extending over two or more generations were likely to keep it in order to feel connected with ancestors, even if the name was one associated with a disliked master. Some persons changed names several times to avoid the possibility of reenslavement. Even after a name was chosen, it was often recorded differently at various times, due to the low level of literacy and variations in spelling.

The Denmark Vesey Conspiracy

The mistreatment of slaves in the years after the Revolution led to an atmosphere of suspicion and terror. Masters lived in constant fear of uprisings, and much time was given over to surveillance. Although organized rebellions were rare, there were many instances of angry slaves burning dwellings and murdering their masters. Slave codes became increasingly strict, but no amount of regulation could dissipate the anger of the slaves nor the guilt and unease that many slave owners experienced.

In 1800 an African American named Denmark Vesey purchased his freedom and, from about 1817, he planned

An extended family of slaves outside their quarters in South Carolina.

a slave revolt in Charleston, South Carolina. The revolt was scheduled to begin on July 14, 1822. With the help of five other African Americans, as many as 9,000 slaves were recruited before their plans were uncovered. As word of the revolt began to leak out, Vesey was forced to move the date forward to June 16; again word was leaked. The state militia was mustered, and an intense investigation of the plot was begun. Some 135 slaves were arrested during the course of the investigation; 97 were bound over for trial; 45 were transported out of the country; and Vesey and 34 others were hanged. As news of the conspiracy spread, Southern states further tightened their slave codes.

◆ EXPANSION OF SLAVERY

Slavery in the Northwest Territory

In the early seventeenth century the French began to settle in what comprises present-day Illinois, Indiana,

Michigan, Ohio, and Wisconsin, and part of Minnesota. The British began to settle in the area during the mid-eighteenth century; and, in July of 1787, Congress passed the Northwest Ordinance, which established a government for the Northwest Territory and provided terms under which states could be formed for entrance into the Union. The ordinance also contained controversial provisions: one prohibited slavery and involuntary servitude in the territory, and the other provided for the return of fugitive slaves to the states from which they had escaped. The European farmers who had brought slaves into the territory were angered by the clause prohibiting slavery, and Congress was petitioned for its repeal. The prohibition against slavery was practically circumvented when the Illinois and Indiana territories established a system of indentured servitude under which any person owning slaves could bring them into the region and place them under lifetime indenture. The restrictions placed on these servants were much like the slave codes of the Southern colonies—indentured servants could not travel alone without a pass or attend public gatherings independently.

The Missouri Compromise

In April of 1803 the United States paid $15 million for the Louisiana Territory, an area comprising the entire Mississippi drainage basin, which had been settled by the French in the late seventeenth century. Many Southerners hoped to extend slavery into the vast new territory, and it was widely expected that Missouri would be admitted to the Union as a slave state. A series of heated debates erupted over the extension of slavery in the region, and in 1819 the House of Representatives introduced legislation authorizing statehood for Missouri while prohibiting the further introduction of slavery into the new state. This drew angry protest from pro-slavery supporters. The controversy was further escalated by two events: Alabama was admitted to the Union as a slave state in 1819, making the total number of slave and free states equal, and Maine applied for statehood in 1820. Between 1820 and 1821 the Missouri Compromise was reached, admitting Missouri to the Union as a slave state with a slave population of almost 10,000, and Maine as a free state, with the understanding that the future expansion of slavery would be prohibited above the latitude of 36° 33'N.

Texas and the Mexican-American War

The territory comprising Texas was part of the Louisiana Territory when the United States purchased it in 1803, but, by 1819, it had become part of Mexico. Mexico provided land grants to American settlers (many of whom brought their slaves with them), and soon Americans outnumbered the Mexicans of the region. In 1836, Texas declared its independence from Mexico and requested annexation to the United States. The possibility of another slave state entering the Union stirred fresh debate. On March 1, 1845, President John Tyler signed the joint resolution of Congress to admit Texas as a slave state; the voters of Texas supported the action, and Texas became a slave state on December 29, 1845. In 1846, Mexican and American troops clashed in Texas, and the United States declared war on the Republic of Mexico. The war ended in 1848 with the Treaty of Guadalupe Hidalgo, whereby Mexico relinquished its claims to Texas and the United States acquired all of the land extending to the Pacific Ocean.

The Wilmot Proviso

In 1846 David Wilmot, a Democrat from Pennsylvania, introduced an amendment to a bill appropriating $2 million for President James Polk to use in negotiating a territorial settlement with Mexico; the amendment stipulated that none of the newly acquired land would be open to slavery. Although the amendment received strong support from Northern Democrats and was passed by the House of Representatives, the Senate adjourned without voting on it. During the next session of Congress a new bill providing $3 million for territorial settlement was introduced. Wilmot again proposed an amendment prohibiting the expansion of slavery into the newly acquired territory. The bill was passed by the House of Representatives, but the Senate drew up a new bill excluding the Wilmot Proviso.

Fugitive Slave Laws

Tensions between Northern and Southern politicians continued to mount over the issue of fugitive slaves. Article IV, Section 2 of the Constitution authorized the return of fugitive slaves and provided procedures for recovery, and in 1793 the Fugitive Slave Act was passed. In Northern states that strongly opposed slavery, "personal liberty" laws were passed in order to undermine federal law; liberty laws placed the burden of proof on masters in cases concerning alleged fugitive slaves. Such a law was enacted in Pennsylvania in 1826, requiring state certification before alleged fugitives could be returned. When Edward Prigg, a professional slave catcher, attempted to capture a fugitive slave residing in the state, he was arrested on kidnapping charges for failing to acquire necessary certification.

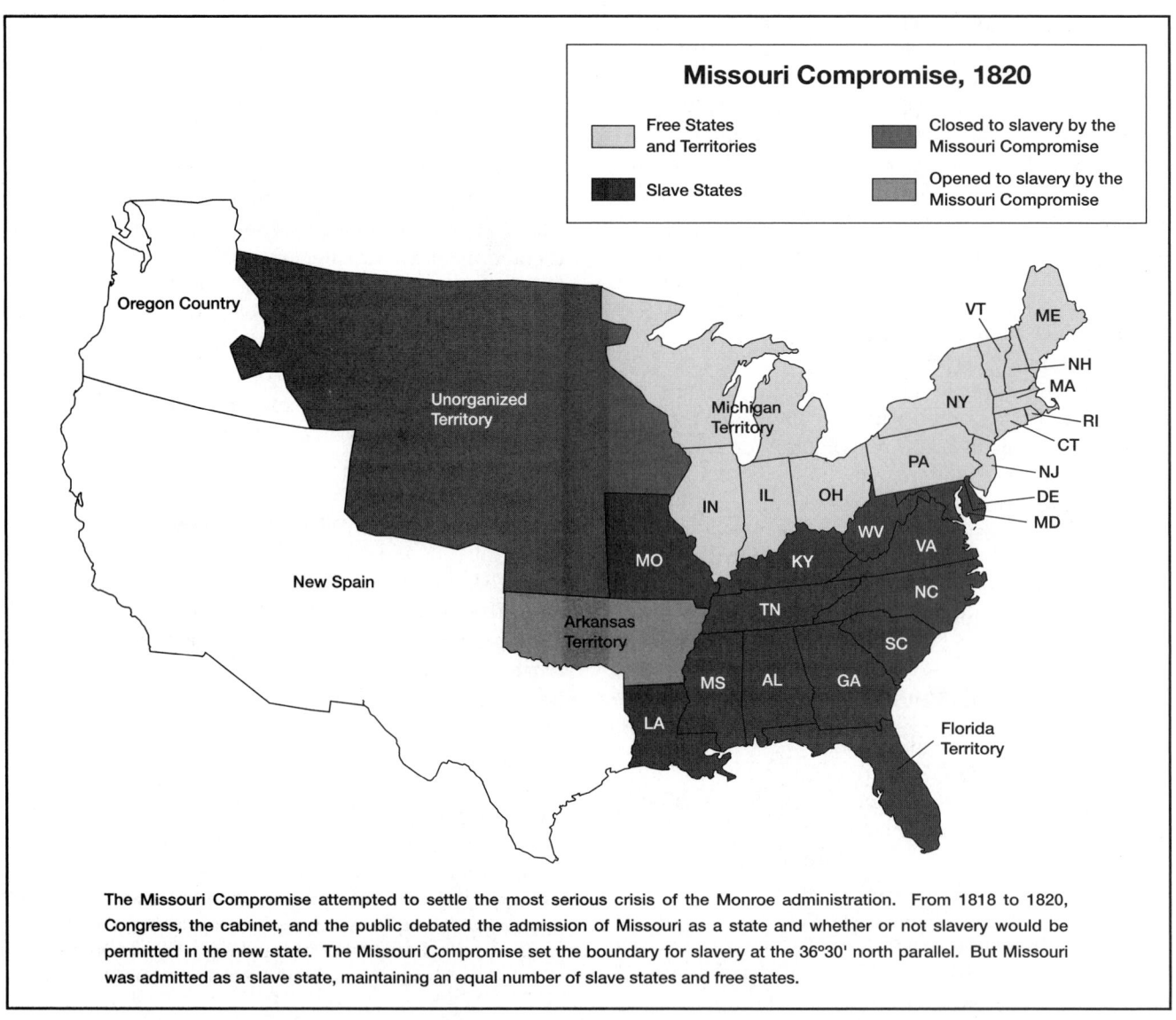

Missouri Compromise, 1820

Free States and Territories

Slave States

Closed to slavery by the Missouri Compromise

Opened to slavery by the Missouri Compromise

The Missouri Compromise attempted to settle the most serious crisis of the Monroe administration. From 1818 to 1820, Congress, the cabinet, and the public debated the admission of Missouri as a state and whether or not slavery would be permitted in the new state. The Missouri Compromise set the boundary for slavery at the 36°30' north parallel. But Missouri was admitted as a slave state, maintaining an equal number of slave states and free states.

The Supreme Court ruled in *Prigg v. Pennsylvania* (1842) that the state's law could not interfere with federal action regarding fugitives and the right of slaveholders to recover property; it also found that states would not be obligated to enforce federal fugitive slave statutes. This led abolitionists to seize upon the idea of not enforcing federal statutes. Following the court's decision several Northern states enacted even more radical personal liberty laws prohibiting the enforcement of the Fugitive Slave Act.

Free African Americans in the South Before 1865

While the majority of the African American population was enslaved before 1865, a sizable number of African Americans were free. The quality of freedom

that African Americans experienced before 1865 generally conformed to the following trajectory: they had a fairly high legal status during the colonial period that was strengthened during the American Revolution, but, almost immediately afterwards, it began to deteriorate. Most notably, the 1790 Alien and Naturalization Act passed under the newly enacted U.S. Constitution disallowed African Americans from becoming citizens and so denied them the federal protections that whites enjoyed.

By the end of the eighteenth century, most Northern states had either abolished slavery or begun programs for gradual emancipation. Slavery had been excluded from the Northwest Territory and, ironically, the American Revolution, with its philosophy of egalitarianism, led to some African Americans gaining their freedom even as other African Americans were increasingly

$200 Reward.

RANAWAY from the subscriber, on the night of Thursday, the 30th of Sepember,

FIVE NEGRO SLAVES,

To-wit: one Negro man, his wife, and three children.

The man is a black negro, full height, very erect, his face a little thin. He is about forty years of age, and calls himself *Washington Reed*, and is known by the name of Washington. He is probably well dressed, possibly takes with him an ivory headed cane, and is of good address. Several of his teeth are gone.

Mary, his wife, is about thirty years of age, a bright mulatto woman, and quite stout and strong.

The oldest of the children is a boy, of the name of FIELDING, twelve years of age, a dark mulatto, with heavy eyelids. He probably wore a new cloth cap.

MATILDA, the second child, is a girl, six years of age, rather a dark mulatto, but a bright and smart looking child.

MALCOLM, the youngest, is a boy, four years old, a lighter mulatto than the last, and about equally as bright. He probably also wore a cloth cap. If examined, he will be found to have a swelling at the navel.

Washington and Mary have lived at or near St. Louis, with the subscriber, for about 15 years.

It is supposed that they are making their way to Chicago, and that a white man accompanies them, that they will travel chiefly at night, and most probably in a covered wagon.

A reward of $150 will be paid for their apprehension, so that I can get them, if taken within one hundred miles of St. Louis, and $200 if taken beyond that, and secured so that I can get them, and other reasonable additional charges, if delivered to the subscriber, or to THOMAS ALLEN, Esq., at St. Louis, Mo. The above negroes, for the last few years, have been in possession of Thomas Allen, Esq., of St. Louis.

WM. RUSSELL.

ST. LOUIS, Oct. 1, 1847.

An 1847 handbill offering a reward for the return of runaway slaves to their owner.

CAUTION!!

COLORED PEOPLE

OF BOSTON, ONE & ALL,

You are hereby respectfully CAUTIONED and advised, to avoid conversing with the

Watchmen and Police Officers of Boston,

For since the recent ORDER OF THE MAYOR & ALDERMEN, they are empowered to act as

KIDNAPPERS

AND

Slave Catchers,

And they have already been actually employed in KIDNAPPING, CATCHING, AND KEEPING SLAVES. Therefore, if you value your LIBERTY, and the *Welfare of the Fugitives* among you, *Shun* them in every possible manner, as so many *HOUNDS* on the track of the most unfortunate of your race.

Keep a Sharp Look Out for KIDNAPPERS, and have TOP EYE open.

APRIL 24, 1851.

Handbill warning African Americans—both enslaved and free—of the ever-present danger of slave catchers and kidnappers.

enslaved. Of course, some enslaved African Americans achieved freedom through escape to the North.

In 1790, it is estimated that there were 59,000 free African Americans (i.e., 27,000 in the North and 32,000 in the South). By 1830, there were approximately 319,000 free African Americans and by 1860, they numbered about 488,000—46 percent of whom lived in the North. Free African Americans were concentrated in the following areas: the tidewater counties of Virginia and Maryland; the Piedmont region of Virginia and North Carolina; and the Southern cities of Baltimore, Washington, Charleston, Mobile, and New Orleans. It is perhaps more accurate to refer to this group of people as non-enslaved African Americans because they faced a myriad of restrictions. In many instances, their freedom of movement was restricted to the county or state in which they lived, they had to carry passes or certificates of freedom, they were barred from certain professions and rarely permitted to vote, and, though they were required to pay local taxes, could not send their children to public schools. Despite these circumscriptions, free African Americans found ways to be productive members of society. Perhaps their greatest advantage over enslaved African Americans was that they possessed more control over their bodies and their labor. They worked in most trades but especially the building, clothing, and food production industries. In fact, the U.S. Census taken between 1820 and 1860 indicated that African Americans were involved in 50 different kinds of occupations.

◆ ANTI-SLAVERY MOVEMENTS

Quakers and Mennonites

The early opposition to slavery was generally based on religious beliefs; Christian ethics were seen as incompatible with slavery. Quakers (or the Society of Friends) and Mennonites were two of first groups to oppose the practice in the United States. Quakers and Mennonites settled mainly in Pennsylvania, though also in the South, and advocated simple living, modest dress, and nonviolence. In 1652 the Quakers passed a resolution against lifetime indenture, and in 1688 the Mennonites did the same. With the continued rise of slavery in the South, many Quakers protested and moved north into Indiana and Ohio.

The Free African Society

In 1787 the Free African Society was organized in Philadelphia by two African Americans, the Rev. Richard Allen and Absalom Jones; Allen later founded the Bethel African Methodist Church, and Jones became the rector of a Protestant Episcopal Church. The society was an important model for political consciousness and economic organization for African Americans throughout the country. It provided economic and medical aid, advocated abolition, and maintained channels of communication with African Americans in the South. Similar to the many other African American organizations that followed, the society was rooted in religious principles. Throughout the nineteenth century, a number of mutual aid societies also sprung up in African American communities of the eastern seaboard, providing loans, insurance, and various other economic and social services to their members and the larger community.

American Colonization Society

In 1816 the American Colonization Society was organized in Washington, D.C., with the objective of encouraging the repatriation of African Americans to Africa. While the idea of returning free African Americans was motivated in part by humanitarian intent, the society was rather moderate in its opposition to slavery. Support for the society came in part from those who feared the possibility of a large, free African American population in the United States.

Congress issued a charter to the society for the transportation of freed slaves to the west coast of Africa, provided funds, and assisted in negotiations with African chiefs who ceded the land that comprised what became Liberia. While Northerners contributed support and donations to the society, Southern patrols threatened freedmen into emigrating. In 1822 the first settlers landed at the site on the western coast of Africa, which was later named Monrovia after President James Monroe. In 1838 the Commonwealth of Liberia was formed and placed under the administration of a governor appointed by the society.

Abolition Societies Formed in Philadelphia and New York

The earliest abolition societies were the Pennsylvania Society for Promoting the Abolition of Slavery, formed in Philadelphia in 1775, and the New York Manumission Society, formed in the city in 1785. Prior to the 1830s a number of anti-slavery societies arose in both the North and the South, and during the 1830s and 1840s numerous abolitionist organizations arose alongside the women's rights organizations as part of the general social reform movement. The American Anti-Slavery Society was formed in Philadelphia in 1833, and after attending one of its meetings, the Quaker abolitionist Lucretia Coffin Mott formed the Philadelphia Female Anti-Slavery Society with the assistance of Elizabeth Cady Stanton. Mott and her husband, James, were active in the Underground Railroad and various other anti-slavery activities, and James served as a delegate to the World Anti-Slavery Convention.

The press served as the primary tool of the anti-slavery movement. In 1827, the journalists Samuel Cornish and John Russwurm launched *Freedom's Journal*, the first African American-owned and edited newspaper; in 1831, William Lloyd Garrison published the first issue of *Liberator;* and other anti-slavery papers followed, including *Anti-Slavery Record;* the *Emancipator; Human Rights;* and the *North Star,* launched by Frederick Douglass.

While many of the anti-slavery organizations were dominated by whites, African American leaders played an important role in the abolition movement. Some of the most notable leaders were Alexander Crummell, Frederick Douglass, Sarah Mapp Douglass, Charlotte Forten, Henry Highland Garnet, Sojourner Truth, and David Walker. Most of these leaders were committed to cooperative relations with whites and opposed separatist doctrines, while some of the more militant abolitionists (i.e., Garnet and Walker) stressed the conditional necessity of violence in the struggle against slavery.

In the South the activities of the abolition movement only hardened the resolve of the slaveholding class to maintain the system of slavery. Depending upon the circumstances, Southern justification of slavery continued along several lines: it was an economic necessity, a means of converting African pagans to Christianity, and a means of controlling an inferior race.

The Underground Railroad Transports Slaves to Freedom

A vast network of individuals and groups developed throughout the country to assist African Americans in escaping from slavery, reaching its height between 1835 and 1865. Abolitionists and free blacks provided "stations"—food, shelter, and financial assistance—while experienced "conductors," who were often themselves runaway slaves, led thousands of "passengers" to freedom in the Northern states, Canada, and Mexico. Two of the most famous conductors were Josiah Henson and Harriet Tubman.

These African Americans were believed to have traveled on the Underground Railroad in order to escape slavery in the South.

Most of the movement occurred at night, with passengers hiding in the barns and homes of sympathetic whites and blacks during the day. Because of the extreme secrecy required to maintain its operation, the precise number of slaves freed by the railroad is unknown. However, its very existence instilled fear in Southern slaveowners and served to further motivate Northern abolitionists in their cause to end slavery.

Nat Turner

In February of 1831, Nat Turner, a slave in Southampton County, Virginia, began to plan a slave revolt, and on August 22, Turner and his co-conspirators killed Turner's master and family. Within 24 hours about 60 whites in the county had been killed. Turner was captured on October 30 and hung on November 11. The incident contributed to the increasing paranoia of Southern society.

Free Labor and Free Soil Movements

Radical Democrats and members of the Whig party who opposed slavery united to form a new political party in Buffalo, New York, in 1848. The party adopted a platform supporting free labor and free soil in response to feelings among Northerners that slavery restricted the freedom of Northern workers to contract for work and should therefore be excluded from the developing regions of the West. Southerners wanted the freedom to expand westward and take their slaves with them. Sen. John C. Calhoun of South Carolina and other Southern delegates maintained that both Congress and the territorial legislatures lacked the authority to restrict the expansion of slavery into the territories. The control of Northern states over the national government led these men to consider secession from the Union.

◆ THE COMPROMISE OF 1850

As the debate over the admission of new Western states continued, Southerners argued that the South should be given guarantees of equal positioning in the territories. In 1850 Senator Henry Clay proposed a compromise in which California would be admitted as a free state, the new territories of New Mexico and Utah would be organized, slavery would be abolished in the

THE ROUTES OF THE UNDERGROUND RAILROAD

District of Columbia, more forceful fugitive slave legislation would be enacted, and the Texas war debt would be resolved. At the time the compromise was hailed by many as the solution to the debate over slavery.

Dred Scott v. Sandford

The slavery debate presented supporters and opponents of the institution with two very important questions: how should fugitives from slavery be treated in jurisdictions where slavery was illegal, and should a slave brought into a free state by his master be viewed as free? The first question was partially addressed by Article IV, Section 2 of the Constitution and by the Fugitive Slave Acts of 1793 and 1850; however the second question had not as yet been addressed. During the 1830s and 1840s a slave by the name of Dred Scott accompanied his master, a surgeon in the U.S. Army on numerous trips to military posts around the country including the free states of Illinois and the territory of Wisconsin. In 1846 Scott sued his master for his freedom, asserting that his sojourns in free jurisdictions made him free. After numerous delays, trials, and retrials, the case reached the Supreme Court in 1856. The court

THE

CONFESSIONS

OF

NAT TURNER,

THE LEADER

OF

THE LATE INSURRECTION

IN SOUTHAMPTON, VA.

AS FULLY AND VOLUNTARILY MADE TO

THOMAS R. GRAY,

In the prison where he was confined, and acknowledged by him to be such, when read before the Court of Southampton: with the certificate, under seal of the Court convened at Jerusalem, Nov. 5, 1831, for his trial.

ALSO,

AN AUTHENTIC ACCOUNT

OF THE

WHOLE INSURRECTION,

WITH

Lists of the Whites who were Murdered,

AND OF THE

Negroes brought before the Court of Southampton, and there sentenced, &c.

RICHMOND:

PUBLISHED BY THOMAS R. GRAY.

In *The Confessions of Nat Turner,* the slave rebel describes the 1831 uprising in Southampton, Virginia.

responded with nine separate opinions, and Chief Justice Roger Brook Taney delivered the deciding opinion. The ruling was both complex and controversial: the Missouri Compromise of 1820 was ruled unconstitutional on the grounds that Congress did not have authority to limit the expansion of slavery; slavery was found to be legal in the territories until the citizens voted for or against it; and Africans and their descendants were found to be ineligible for citizenship in the United States as the framers of the Constitution had not viewed Africans as citizens. Since African Americans were not viewed by the court as citizens, they could not file suit. Despite the finality of the court's decision, the issue of slavery remained unresolved.

John Brown and Harpers Ferry

On October 16, 1859, a white, visionary abolitionist named John Brown led a band of 21 men (five of whom were African Americans) in the seizure of the federal arsenal at Harpers Ferry. After holding the site for several hours, Brown and his followers were captured by federal troops under the command of Robert E. Lee. Southerners were outraged by Brown's actions, interpreting them as symptomatic of a willingness among Northerners to attempt the forcible overthrow of slavery. In December of 1859, Brown was hanged alongside Dangerfield Newby, a runaway slave; John A. Copeland of Carolina; Sheridan Leary, a harness maker and freedman; and Shields Gree, a sailor from South Carolina.

◆ CIVIL WAR

In 1860 Abraham Lincoln, a Northern Republican, was elected president amid continuing polarization over the issue of slavery. Lincoln had voiced opposition to the expansion of slavery in the past, and with his election Southerners became even more fearful of an ideological assault on states' rights and the abolition of slavery nationwide. In 1860 a delegation from South Carolina voted unanimously for the repeal of the state's 1788 ratification of the Constitution and the severing of all relations with the Union; Georgia, Florida, Alabama, Mississippi, Louisiana, and Texas soon followed. In February of 1861, the seven states drew up a constitution and elected Jefferson Davis as president of the Confederate States of America. As Northern leaders sought a means of preserving the nation, Southern troops seized federal installations, post offices, and customs houses, and in April of 1861 Confederate forces took one of the last Union holds in the South—Fort Sumter in Charleston Harbor, South Carolina. Lincoln was forced to retaliate.

African American Soldiers in the Civil War

From the beginning of the war African Americans engaged in the fighting, although Lincoln at first refused to officially employ them in the Union Army. By 1862 Lincoln concluded that the use of African American soldiers was a necessity. An estimated 180,000 African American soldiers served in the Union Army and another 20,000 served in its Navy; however, not all of those African Americans who participated in the war fought on the Union side. There are no accurate records of how many African American soldiers fought for the South, but their numbers grew as white Southerners became more desperate.

Lincoln faced a dilemma in that if he issued an order of universal emancipation, as the abolitionists encouraged him to do, he risked alienating the border states that remained supportive of the Union: these were

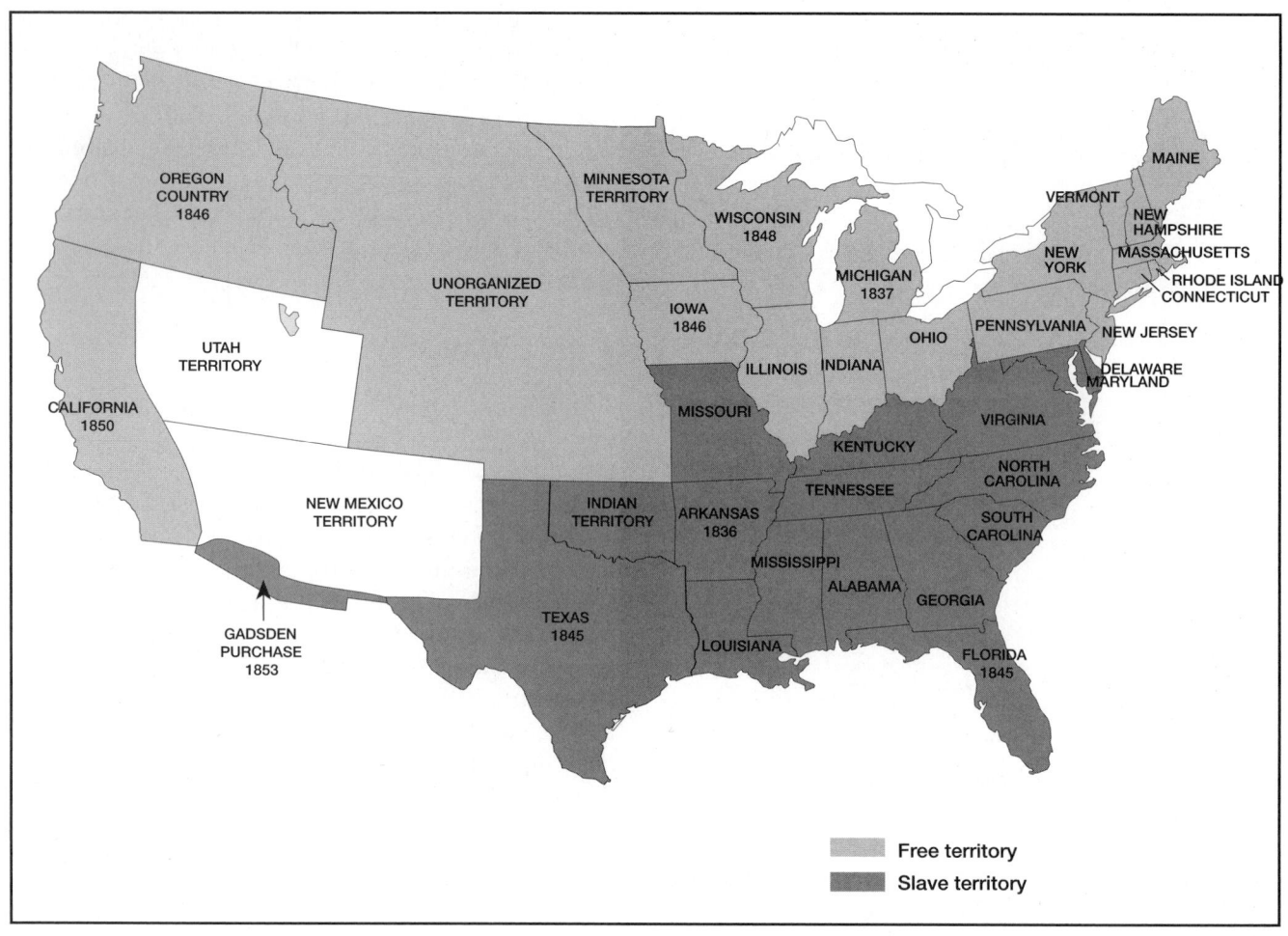

Free territory

Slave territory

Delaware, Maryland, Kentucky, and Missouri. In a letter to Horace Greeley, Lincoln stated:

> If I could save the Union without freeing any slave, I would do it; if I could save it by freeing all the slaves, I would do it; and if I could save it by freeing some and leaving others alone, I would also do that. What I do about slavery and the colored race, I do because I believe it helps save the Union. . . .

During the summer of 1862, Lincoln began to feel that the emancipation of the slaves would be necessary to realizing victory over the South, and on January 1, 1863, he issued the Emancipation Proclamation, freeing slaves in those states that had seceded from the Union. Because the proclamation did not apply to the areas under occupation by Union forces, 800,000 slaves remained unaffected by its provisions. He dared not alienate the slave-owning border states on the Union side, especially in light of the growing antipathy toward African Americans in many Northern cities. In the Draft Riots of July 13–16, 1863, huge mobs of whites in New York City (angry over the provisions of the Conscription Act) attacked blacks and abolitionists, destroying property and viciously beating many to death.

The Civil War lasted from April of 1861 to April 1865, and at the end more than 360,000 Union soldiers and 258,000 Confederate solders were dead. By the end of the war 21 African Americans had received the Medal of Honor, and indeterminate numbers of others had made sacrifices for the cause. On December 18, 1865, the Thirteenth Amendment of the Constitution was ratified, formally abolishing slavery in the United States.

◆ RECONSTRUCTION

Civil Rights and Reconstruction Acts

On March 3, 1865, Congress enacted the first of several acts that set up and empowered the Bureau of Refugees, Freedmen and Abandoned Lands (or the

African Americans gathering for a watch night meeting on the night before the Emancipation Proclamation takes effect.

Freedmen's Bureau). The organization provided former slaves with basic health and educational services and administered land that had been abandoned during the war. In 1866 Congress passed the Civil Rights Act, in which a number of personal liberties were outlined, including the right to make contracts, sue or be sued, own and sell property, and receive the equal benefit of the law. The Reconstruction Act of 1867 outlined the terms under which the Southern states might re-enter the Union—one of these terms required each state to call a convention to draft a new state constitution that would guarantee voting rights for all races. President Johnson vetoed the bill, but Radical Republicans in Congress were able to muster the necessary two-thirds majority needed to override the veto. In addition to abolishing slavery, most new constitutions abolished property qualifications for voting and imprisonment for debt. The state constitutions drawn up in 1867 and 1868 were the most progressive the South had known.

During Reconstruction, more than 200 African Americans held various public offices. South Carolina had two lieutenant governors, Alonzo J. Ransier and Richard H. Gleaves. Jonathan Jasper Wright, the first African American elected to the Pennsylvania bar, traveled to the South and, in 1870, was elected to South Carolina's Supreme Court. Between 1870 and 1901, 20 African Americans served in the U.S. House of Representatives and two African Americans—Hiram R. Revels and Blanche K. Bruce—represented Mississippi in the U.S. Senate. When Bruce's senate term ended, no other African American would be elected to the U.S. Senate until 1966, when Massachusetts elected Republican Edward Brooke.

◆ THE ADVENT OF INDEPENDENT AFRICAN AMERICAN INSTITUTIONS

African Americans' notions of what emancipation entitled contrasted sharply with that of most white Americans. For most whites, it was simply a moment that led to the absence of legalized slavery with few, if any, tacit implications for equality or justice for their erstwhile bondsmen. For African Americans, emancipation was a period of time when they sought to construct the contours of their newly won liberty. It required conscious and intentional acts of self-determination, and, therefore, occasioned a movement to seek political, economic, and social justice and equality.

African Americans, therefore, enjoyed their greatest successes in areas where defining freedom was least dependent upon white control or approval—the family, independent African American churches, and African American colleges.

Family

Though denied the rights and protections of legal marriage, African Americans formed strong familial bonds during slavery. Emancipation allowed some African Americans, forcibly separated during slavery, to rejoin their families; and it permitted African Americans who had been living together as husband and wife to marry legally. Census reports in several Southern states—including Alabama, South Carolina, and Virginia—suggest that by 1870 the proportions of blacks married and involved in family life was comparable to that of whites. Stable family life therefore helped provide an anchor for African Americans in their struggle to live meaningful lives.

Independent African American Churches

Postbellum African American churches functioned not only to meet spiritual yearnings, but also social, economic, and political needs. The churches of African Americans, therefore, helped institutionalize strategies for surviving in an oppressive society. Called the "cultural womb" of the African American community, the church influenced almost all African American institutions and organizations from providing a training ground for musicians and musical forms to founding banks to the more traditional role of instilling moral sensibility. Some historians claim that, collectively, African American churches should be viewed as a "nation within a nation" because these churches played an important political role in the community, as the only "arena of social life in which Negroes could aspire to become leaders . . ." The religious vision and initiative that established these churches were part of an emancipation movement that relied upon African American churches to provide not only spiritual nourishment and moral leadership, but also to serve as a forum to address community concerns.

African American ministers played a crucial role in helping to establish independent churches. As important symbols who presided over the rites of passage—baptisms, marriages, and deaths—ministers were intimately involved in the lives of church members. Ministers participated in helping the Freedmen's Bureau teach newly freed men and women to read and write, find housing and jobs, and even choose new family names. Often they were the best-educated members of their congregations. Most African American preachers had to learn to balance seeking power and opportunity for their congregation with allaying whites' fears of blacks organizing or galvanizing their resources. On the one hand, ministers were in the best position, as respected members of the community, to advocate a liberal interpretation of emancipation. On the other hand, because they had so much power over other African Americans, their very presence posed a threat to white supremacy. African American clergy, therefore, learned the art of negotiating with whites in power. Being too outspoken could cost them their lives; capitulating too much to white authority could eclipse their congregations' freedom.

Between roughly 1865 and the early 1900s, seven major independent African American denominations were founded: the African Methodist Episcopal Church (A.M.E.); the African Methodist Episcopal Church Zion (A.M.E.Z.); the Christian Methodist Episcopal Church (C.M.E.); the National Baptist Convention, USA, Inc.; National Baptist Convention of America Unincorporated; the Progressive National Baptist Convention; and The Church of God in Christ (C.O.G.I.C.). Though some African Americans chose to remain in white majority congregations and denominations, the turn of the twentieth century found most blacks as members of one of the seven independent African American denominations. These institutions worked to define African American emancipation in the broadest possible terms. For example, African American congregations throughout the South embraced a "Gospel of Freedom" that asserted that exercising political and social independence was inextricably tied to controlling institutional expressions of their spirituality.

African American Education

Education was an extremely high priority for African Americans during the postbellum era. This was especially true for African Americans living in Southern cities. Throughout most of the South, African Americans aggressively worked to establish educational facilities—from elementary schools to colleges and universities. Aided in their efforts by Northern missionaries, African Americans eagerly sought to educate themselves and their children. A number of African American colleges were established during these years including: Howard University in Washington, D.C.; Hampton Institute in Virginia; St. Augustine's College in North Carolina; Benedict College in South Carolina; Spelman College, Morehouse College, and the Atlanta University system in Georgia; Alabama State University and Tuskegee Institute in Alabama; and Jackson State College in Mississippi.

Still, the overwhelming majority of African Americans had very little access to any kind of formal education, though many church congregations used their Sunday school programs to teach members how to read the Bible. Education was funded by the state, and states and local school boards openly discriminated against African American schools, chiefly by appropriating less money, providing fewer teachers, and allowing for shorter school terms than that enjoyed by whites (i.e., white schools convened for nine months while most African American schools met for four months). The small number of African Americans who managed to obtain some level of formal education worked with countless others to secure a measure of political, economic, and social freedom.

◆ AFRICAN AMERICAN STATUS AFTER RECONSTRUCTION

The Fourteenth and Fifteenth Amendments

On July 23, 1868, the Fourteenth Amendment was ratified, providing definitions of national and state citizenship, effectively overriding the Supreme Court's decision in *Dred Scott v. Sandford*, and providing for equal privileges of citizenship and protection of the law. On March 30, 1870, the Fifteenth Amendment was ratified to ensure the right to vote. But the amendment proved unsuccessful in its aims, as many state and local governments created voting regulations that ensured African Americans would not vote; these included grandfather clauses, requiring that one's grandfather had voted; literacy tests; poll taxes; and "white primaries," which were held prior to general elections and permitted only whites to vote. In addition, Southern states enacted many laws (known as black codes) that curbed the new rights of the freed slaves: South Carolina made it illegal for African Americans to possess firearms, and other states restricted their right to make and enforce contracts; to marry and intermarry; and even to assemble, "wander," or be "idle."

The Civil Rights Act of 1875

In 1875, Congress attempted to establish a semblance of racial equality by enacting a law that made it illegal to deprive another person of the "full and equal enjoyment of the accommodations, advantages, facilities, and privileges of inns, public conveyance, . . . and other places of public amusement" on account of race. In a number of cases (known as the Civil Rights Cases), the Supreme Court ruled that the Fourteenth Amendment did not authorize Congress to legislate against discriminatory state action, while disregarding discrimination by private individuals including the owners of hotels, theaters, and restaurants.

The Removal of Federal Troops from the South

The U.S. presidential election of 1876 between Samuel J. Tilden and Rutherford B. Hayes was a hotly disputed one. Both Southern Democrats and Northern Republicans claimed the electoral votes of South Carolina, Louisiana, and Florida. So, Congress established an electoral commission to settle the argument. In return for Southerners agreeing to allow presidential Republican candidate Rutherford B. Hayes to become president, a compromise was reached in which the South was promised that all federal troops, assigned to protect African American freedoms and oversee states' readmission into the Union, would be removed. In 1877, soon after taking office, Hayes withdrew all federal troops from the South. This led to an end of federal efforts to protect African Americans' civil rights until passage of the 1964 Civil Rights Act.

Plessy v. Ferguson

In *Hall v. DeCuir* (1878), the Supreme Court decided that states could not outlaw segregation on common carriers, such as streetcars and railroads, and in 1896 the Court again faced the issue of segregation on public transportation in the case of *Plessy v. Ferguson*. The case concerned Homer Adolph Plessy, an African American who was arrested for refusing to ride in the "colored" railway coach while traveling by train from New Orleans to Covington, Louisiana. The law in Louisiana required that "equal but separate" accommodations for blacks and whites be maintained in public facilities, but Plessy challenged this law. Justice Billings Brown delivered the majority opinion that separate but equal accommodations constituted a reasonable use of state police power, and that the Fourteenth Amendment could not have been an effort to abolish social or racial distinctions or to force a co-mingling of the races. In his dissenting opinion, Justice John Marshall Harlan remarked that, "The judgement this day rendered will, in time, prove to be quite as pernicious as the decision made by this tribunal in the *Dred Scott v. Sandford* case. The thin disguise of equal accommodation for passengers in railroad coaches will not mislead anyone nor atone for the wrong this day has done." The ruling paved the way for the doctrine of "separate but equal" in all walks of life, and not until the case of *Brown v. Board of Education of Topeka, Kansas* (1954) would the constitutionality of segregation be seriously challenged.

Racial Nadir

In the wake of almost 35 years of hard earned but seemingly steady progress in successful institution-building within the African American community, the turn of the century ushered in a period of fermented political enervation, economic deprivation, and social segregation for African Americans—what has been dubbed a nadir of postbellum race relations. Despite the efforts of African Americans to establish stable family life, independent churches, and educational facilities, Southern states held conventions in which they rewrote their constitutions to disfranchise African Americans and enforce social segregation. To prevent blacks from voting, whites engaged numerous techniques, including poll taxes, literacy tests, and violence in the form of lynching. Perhaps most indicative of the overthrow of African Americans' gains during Reconstruction was the Wilmington race riot of 1898.

Located on the coast of North Carolina, Wilmington had been a prosperous city known for its naval stores since colonial times. While slavery had existed in Wilmington as in other parts of the South, there had always been a sizable free African American population, many of whom had achieved middle-class status. As late as the 1890s, African Americans held several important positions in the town: three of the ten alderman posts; one of three chairs on the school committee; and a coroner, deputy superior court clerk, justice of the peace, and mail clerk. In addition, there were African American policemen, and the health board was entirely composed of African Americans. On November 10, 1898, the most ghastly offense of the Progressive era occurred in Wilmington as whites took to the streets and refused to allow Republicans—many of whom were African Americans—to take their elected offices. Eventually, President William McKinley had to intervene in the conflict before order could be restored. When the conflict was settled, armed white Democrats had overthrown duly elected Republican officeholders. The physical oppression of slavery had now met its twentieth century incarnation—second-class citizenship.

Accommodation, Confrontational Activism, and Self-Help Movements

In the face of these grave circumstances, African Americans employed several approaches to continue their efforts toward self-determination and self-expression. Some African Americans, following the beliefs and teachings of Booker T. Washington became accommodationists. They worked to develop industrial skills and to make themselves an essential component of the manual labor force and postponed demanding social and political equality, believing that they needed to prove to whites that African Americans were capable of handling the responsibilities and privileges of citizenship. In 1895 at the Atlanta Exposition, Washington made a speech in which he told white philanthropists that if they would support African Americans in their attempt to secure economic means, there would be no concerted effort to push for political rights, and furthermore that "In all things purely social we [blacks and whites] can be as separate as the fingers, yet one as the hand in all things essential to mutual progress."

W. E. B. Du Bois articulated a more confrontational philosophy and strategy. Du Bois and William Monroe Trotter, editor of a Boston newspaper *The Guardian*, argued that as American citizens, African Americans should not have to earn nor prove themselves worthy of rights guaranteed in the Declaration of Independence and U.S. Constitution. Du Bois expressed his fear of the accommodationist approach arguing "if we make technical skill the object of education, we may possess artisans but not, in nature, men." Du Bois and his proponents therefore argued that, led by an elite "talented tenth" of the African American race, African Americans should demand immediate political, social, and economic equality.

The third strategy employed was the self-help movement. Proponents of this movement included white philanthropists, such as John D. Rockefeller and George Peabody, both of whom established education funds that helped to bankroll African American education. Most of the effort in the self-help movement came, however, from such women's organizations as The Colored Women's Federated Clubs, the National Association of Colored Women, and missionary societies of various African American churches. Such women as Ida Wells-Barnett, Susie A. Stone, Henrietta Gibbs, Nannie Helen Burroughs, and Mary Church Terrell were involved in a panoply of activities that included: agitating for women's suffrage, raising money to build schools and hospitals, holding parenting classes, helping to sustain the livelihood of African American churches, and assisting in creating strong, financially solvent state, local, and national church conventions—thereby giving African Americans a national voice. As Mary Church Terrell aptly described this effort, African Americans became involved in the self-help movement with the goal of "Lifting as We Climb."

Historians today debate which of the numerous strategies African Americans employed was most effective, but African Americans living during the time period employed all strategies—often in combination. They engaged accommodation, confrontational activism, and self-help in their effort to secure for themselves and their posterity, the benefits of opportunity, self-expression, and self-determination.

◆ FIGURES OF THE PAST

(Other important figures from this time period appear in specific chapters according to their occupation. For example, mathematician Benjamin Banneker is biographied in the Science & Technology chapter. To locate biographical profiles more readily, please consult the index at the back of the book.)

Alice of Dunk's Ferry (c.1686–1802)
Oral Historian

Alice was born around 1686 in Philadelphia, Pennsylvania, to slave parents brought from Barbados. At the age of ten, she moved to Dunk's Ferry in Bucks County with her master, where she lived out the rest of what proved to be an incredibly long life, spending some 40 of her 116 years collecting tolls at a bridge. Alice's long life, coupled with a remarkable memory, made her an ideal oral historian, recounting for listeners her vivid memories of the early days of the colony. She could remember when the great city of Philadelphia was nothing more than a wilderness, populated by Native Americans and wild animals of the forest. Little is known about her life, although evidence suggests that she remained physically active even past the century mark of her life. She died as a slave just a few miles from Philadelphia in 1802.

Richard Allen. *See* Religion chapter.

Crispus Attucks (c.1723–1770)
Revolutionary Patriot

A runaway slave who lived in Boston, he was the first of five men killed on March 5, 1770, when British troops fired on a crowd of colonial protesters in the Boston Massacre. The most widely accepted account of the incident is that of John Adams, who said at the subsequent trial of the British soldiers that Attucks undertook "to be the hero of the night; and to lead this army with banners, to form them in the first place in Dock Square, and march them up to King Street with their clubs." When the crowd reached the soldiers, it was Attucks who "had hardiness enough to fall in upon them, and with one hand took hold of a bayonet, and with the other knocked the man down." At that point the panicked soldiers fired, and in the echoes of their volley, five men lay dying; the seeds of the Revolution were sown. Attucks is remembered as "the first to defy, the first to die."

James Beckwourth. *See* Entrepreneurship chapter.

Blanche K. Bruce. *See* Politics chapter.

Joseph Cinque (1811–1879)
Insurrectionist

Born in Sierra Leone in 1811 and purchased by Spaniards in Havana, Cuba, in 1838, Cinque was placed aboard the *Amistad* bound for Puerto Principe. When the crew became exhausted from battling a storm, Cinque led the slaves in seizing the ship and killing all but two of the crew, who were kept alive to navigate a course back to Africa. The captive pilots headed north, against the slaves' knowledge, and when the ship was sighted off the coast of Long Island, the slaves were taken to Connecticut and placed in prison. Abolitionists took up the cause of the men and enabled Cinque to raise funds for judicial appeals by speaking on their lecture circuit; his words were translated from Mendi, and he became known as an excellent speaker. In 1841,

Joseph Cinque.

John Quincy Adams won the slaves' case, and they were released and returned to Africa.

Fanny Coppin. *See* **Education chapter.**

Frederick Douglass (1817–1895)
Abolitionist, Editor, Diplomat, Government Official, Legislator, Marshall

Born in Talbot County, Maryland, on February 14, 1817, Frederick Douglass was sent to Baltimore as a house servant at the age of eight, where his mistress taught him to read and write. Upon the death of his master, he was sent to the country to work as a field hand. During his time in the South, he was severely flogged for his resistance to slavery. In his early teens he began to teach in a Sunday school that was later forcibly shut down by hostile whites. After an unsuccessful attempt to escape from slavery, he succeeded in making his way to New York disguised as a sailor in 1838. He found work as a day laborer in New Bedford, Massachusetts, and after an extemporaneous speech before the Massachusetts Anti-Slavery Society, he became one of its agents.

Douglass quickly became a nationally recognized figure among abolitionists. In 1845 he bravely published his *Narrative of the Life of Frederick Douglass*, which related his experiences as a slave, revealed his fugitive status, and further exposed him to the danger of reenslavement. In the same year, he went to England and Ireland, where he remained until 1847, speaking on slavery and women's rights, and ultimately raising sufficient funds to purchase his freedom. Upon returning to the United States, he founded the *North Star*. In the tense years before the Civil War he was forced to flee to Canada when the governor of Virginia swore out a warrant for his arrest.

Douglass returned to the United States before the beginning of the Civil War and, after meeting with President Abraham Lincoln, he assisted in the formation of the 54th and 55th Negro regiments of Massachusetts. During Reconstruction, he became deeply involved in the civil rights movement, and, in 1871, he was appointed to the territorial legislature of the District of Columbia. He served as one of the presidential electors-at-large for New York in 1872 and, shortly thereafter, became the secretary of the Santo Domingo Commission. After serving for a short time as the police commissioner of the District of Columbia, he was appointed marshall in 1871, and held the post until he was appointed the recorder of deeds in 1881. In 1890, his support of the presidential campaign of Benjamin Harrison won him his most important federal post: he became minister resident and consul general to the Republic of Haiti and, later, the charge d'affaires of Santo Domingo. In 1891, he resigned the position in protest of the unscrupulous business practices of U.S. businessmen. Douglass died at his home in Washington, D.C., on February 20, 1895.

Sarah Mapps Douglass. *See* **Education chapter.**

Jean Baptist Point Du Sable. *See* **Entrepreneurship chapter.**

Olaudah Equiano (1750?–1797)
Narrative Writer

Olaudah Equiano was born around 1750 in an Ibo village in southern Nigeria. At the age of 11, he was kidnapped and enslaved in Africa before being shipped to the New World. His masters included a Virginia

Olaudah Equiano, also known as Gustavus Vassa.

plantation owner, a British officer—who gave him the name Gustavus Vassa—and a Philadelphia merchant from whom he eventually purchased his freedom. Equiano then settled in England where he worked diligently for the elimination of slavery. He even went so far as to present a petition to Parliament calling for its abolition.

Equiano's autobiography *The Interesting Narrative of the Life of Olaudah Equiano, or Gustavus Vassa* was published in London in 1789 and went through five editions in five years. It is regarded as a highly informative account of the evils of slavery as it affected both master and slave, as well as the precursor to other important slave narratives, such as the *Narrative of the Life of Frederick Douglass.*

Archibald Grimké. *See* **Law chapter.**

Lemuel Haynes (1753–1833)
Religious Leader

The son of a black father and white mother and born in 1753, he was deserted and brought up by Deacon David Rose of Granville, Massachusetts. He was a

Lemuel Haynes.

precocious child and began writing mature sermons while still a boy. His preparation for the ministry was interrupted by the American Revolution. On April 19, 1775, he fought in the first battle of the war at Lexington, Massachusetts; he then joined the regular forces and served with Ethan Allen's Green Mountain Boys at the capture of Fort Ticonderoga.

James Augustine Healy. *See* **Religion chapter.**

Sally Hemings (1773–1886)
Slave

Sally Hemings was born a slave in Virginia in 1773, the daughter of a white man named John Wayles and a mulatto slave named Elizabeth Hemings. She became the slave and perhaps the concubine of President Thomas Jefferson. While it is known that Hemings bore several mulatto children, there is considerable scholarly debate over whether Thomas Jefferson was their father. One of Jefferson's contemporaries (albeit, a political enemy) accused him of miscegenation in 1802, but the furor over the exact nature of Jefferson's relationship with Sally Hemings did not pick up steam until the late twentieth century, when DNA tests on descendants of Sally Hemings concluded that either Jefferson or a close male relative had fathered Hemings's children. Those who maintain the existence of a sexual relationship between the two figures suggest that Jefferson first seduced Hemings in Paris when she was just 15, and that they maintained a 38-year relationship until his death in 1826.

Josiah Henson (1789–1883)
Educational Administrator, Abolitionist, Religious Leader

Born a slave in a log cabin in Charles County (near Rockville), Maryland, on June 15, 1789, Josiah Henson grew up with the experience of his family being cruelly treated by his master. By the time he was 18 years of age, Henson was supervising the master's farm. In 1825 he and his wife and children were moved to Kentucky, where conditions were greatly improved, and in 1828 he became a preacher in a Methodist Episcopal Church. Under the threat of being sold, he and his family escaped to Ohio in 1830, and the following year entered Canada by way of Buffalo, New York. In Canada he learned to read and write from one of his sons, and he soon began preaching in Dresden, Ontario.

While in Canada he became active in the Underground Railroad, helping nearly 200 slaves to escape to freedom. In 1842 he and several others attempted to start the British-American Manual Labor Institute, but the industrial school proved unsuccessful. Henson related his story to Harriet Beecher Stowe (the author of *Uncle Tom's Cabin*), and it has been disputed whether or not her story is based in part on aspects of his life. He traveled to England three times, where he met distinguished people, was honored for his abolitionist activities and personal escape from slavery, and was offered a number of positions that he turned down in order to return to Canada. He published his autobiography in 1849 and rewrote and reissued it in 1858 and 1879. Henson died in Ontario in 1883.

Harry Hosier (1750?–1806)
Preacher

Most sources report that Harry Hosier (also spelled Hoosier, Hoshur, Hossier), was born a slave near Fayetteville, North Carolina, around 1750. Although little is known as to the circumstances, Hosier experienced both a religious conversion to Methodism and his freedom. He is thought to have met Francis Asbury, the founder of Methodism and evangelist to the slaves, sometime in 1780; Asbury wrote of the meeting that it was "providentially arranged." The two men partnered together to spread the Gospel, with Hosier acting as Asbury's servant, guide, and circuit-riding preacher.

Hosier proved to be an eloquent speaker who, though uneducated, was intellectually alert, creative, and possessed a remarkable memory. Those who heard him preach were instantly impressed with his work. He preached with Asbury at the Fairfax Chapel in Falls Church, Virginia, as early as May 13, 1781. This made him the first black preacher to deliver a sermon to a white Methodist church in America. His fame as a preacher brought him into contact with several other major preachers, including Thomas Coke, who wrote of him, "I really believe he is one of the best Preachers in the world, there is such an amazing power attends his preaching, though he cannot read; and he is one of the humblest creatures I ever saw." Hosier actually resisted learning to read and write throughout his career, relying on his memory for biblical passages and hymns for his listeners. He was present at the historic Christmas conference at the end of 1784, which saw the formal establishment of both the Methodist Episcopal Church and a permanent relationship between black and white Methodists. Although enormously popular,

Hosier was never ordained in the Methodist church, possibly because of his rumored problems with alcohol.

Absalom Jones. *See* **Religion chapter.**

Isaac Lane. *See* **Religion chapter.**

Lucy Laney. *See* **Education chapter.**

John Mercer Langston. *See* **Politics chapter.**

James Armistead Lafayette (b. 1700s)
Spy

Born a slave, he risked his life behind enemy lines collecting information for the Continental Army. He furnished valuable information to the Marquis de Lafayette and enabled the French commander to check the troop advances of British General Cornwallis; this set the stage for General George Washington's victory at Yorktown in 1781 and for the end of the Revolutionary War. In recognition of his services, he was granted his freedom by the Virginia legislature in 1786, although it was not until 1819 that Virginia awarded him a pension of $40 a year and a grant of $100. He adopted the surname "Lafayette" in honor of his former commander, who visited him during a trip to the United States in 1824.

Jarena Lee. *See* **Religion chapter.**

George Liele. *See* **Religion chapter.**

Toussaint L'Ouverture (1743–1803)
Insurrectionist

Born Francois Dominique Toussaint L'Ouverture, a slave on the island of Hispaniola (now Haiti and the Dominican Republic) in 1743, he learned to read and write under a benevolent master. When he was 50 years of age, a violent revolt erupted on the island. White French planters, African slaves, and free mulattoes (some of whom owned slaves) clashed over issues of rights, land, and labor, as the forces of France, Britain, and Spain manipulated the conflict. At first the slaves and mulattoes shared the goals of the French revolution in opposition to the royalist French planters, but with time a coalition of planters and mulattoes arose in opposition to the slaves.

L'Ouverture became the leader of the revolutionary slave forces, which by mid-1790s consisted of a disciplined group of 4,000 mostly ex-slaves. He successfully waged a campaign against the British. At the height of L'Ouverture's power and influence in 1796, General Rigaud, who led the mulatto forces, sought to reimpose slavery on the black islanders. L'Ouverture quickly achieved victory, captured Santo Domingo, and by 1801 had virtual control of the Spanish part of the island. In 1802, a French expeditionary force was sent to re-establish French control of the island. Following a hard-fought resistance to French colonial ambitions in the Western Hemisphere, Toussaint L'Ouverture struck a peace treaty with Napoleon. However, L'Ouverture was tricked, captured, and sent to France where he died on April 7, 1803, under inhumane conditions.

Onesimus (fl. 1700s)
Slave, Scientific Discoverer

Onesimus was a slave in Boston, Massachusetts, during the early 1700s. He had grown up in Africa, a member of the Garamantes tribe, but was enslaved and brought to America. Beginning in 1706, he worked for religious leader Cotton Mather, who also was a contributor to scientific journals such as *Philosophical Transactions of the Royal Society of London*. While reading an article in that magazine, Mather was struck by how closely the recounted practice of inoculation in Turkey resembled what Onesimus had told him about what was done to him in Africa. Mather's description of Onesimus's account was printed in the *Yale Journal of Biology and Medicine* from a letter Mather wrote to the Royal Society. Nevertheless, nothing came of this information for another five years.

In 1721 Boston was hit with a smallpox epidemic. Because of Onesimus's story, Mather insisted that the medical community at least attempt the slave's method of disease prevention. Finally, a country doctor, Zabdiel Boylston, succeeded in saving his six-year-old son and two slaves. Boylston continued to inoculate more and more people safely, keeping careful records. Of the 286 people he inoculated, 2.1 percent died, compared to 14.9 percent of those who acquired smallpox naturally. Boylston reported his findings to the Royal Society, and the medical community became convinced of the value of inoculation.

Through the accurate recounting of the procedure carried out on him, Onesimus helped bring knowledge of inoculation to the Western World. This would remain the primary way of protecting people from the ravages of smallpox until the introduction of Jennerian cowpox vaccination in 1798.

P. B. S. Pinchback. *See* Politics chapter.

Salem Poor (1747–?)
Revolutionary War Soldier

Salem Poor was born a slave in 1747 in Andover, Massachusetts. He spent his childhood and the early years of his adult life on his master's farm in Andover, before purchasing his freedom in 1769. In March of 1774, after the Continental Congress designated certain units of the Massachusetts militia to serve as "Minutemen," the Massachusetts Committee of Safety permitted black volunteers to join town and village companies. A number of free black men promptly enlisted, including Poor. He enlisted in the First Andover Company as a private and, like other militia minutemen, was trained to respond at a minute's notice to British aggression.

When American rebellion against the British turned into open warfare, Poor enlisted under Captain Samuel Johnson in the Fifth Massachusetts Regiment on April 24, 1775. He participated in the Battle of Bunker Hill, and fired the shot that killed British Lieutenant Colonel James Abercrombie. Poor was never far from active duty in the years between 1775 and 1780, and was with some 500 other black sharpshooters in the Continental Army that spent the legendary frozen winter of 1777–78 with General George Washington in his Valley Forge encampment. He also served in the crucial battles of White Plains, New York, and Providence, Rhode Island. Only one instance is recorded of Salem Poor having been commended for his bravery, the submission of the petition of recommendation in December 1775. Two hundred years later Poor's valor was publicly recognized. On March 25, 1975, as part of the United States Postal Service's Revolutionary War Bicentennial series of stamps entitled "Contributors to the Cause," a commemorative ten-cent stamp was issued in recognition of "Salem Poor—Gallant Soldier."

Gabriel Prosser (1775–1800)
Insurrectionist

Gabriel Prosser was born around 1775. He became the coachman of Thomas Prosser of Henrico County, Virginia, and planned a large, highly organized revolt to take place on the last night of August of 1800 around Richmond, Virginia. About 32,000 slaves and only 8,000 whites were in the area, and it was his intention to kill all of the whites except for the French, Quakers, elderly women, and children. The ultimate goal was that the remaining 300,000 slaves in the state would follow his lead and seize the entire state. The revolt was set to coincide with the harvest so that his followers would be spared any shortage of food, and it was decided that the conspirators would meet at the Old Brook Swamp outside of Richmond and marshal forces to attack the city.

The insurrection fell apart when a severe rainstorm made it impossible for many of the slaves to assemble and a pair of house slaves who did not wish their master killed revealed the plot. Panic swept through the city, martial law was declared, and those suspected of involvement were rounded up and hanged; when it became clear that the slave population would be decimated if all of those implicated were dealt with in similar fashion, the courts began to mete out less severe sentences. Prosser was apprehended in the hold of a schooner that docked in Norfolk, Virginia. Brought back in chains, he was interrogated by the governor. When he refused to divulge details of the conspiracy, he was hung.

Joseph H. Rainey. *See* **Politics chapter.**

Hiram Rhodes Revels. *See* **Politics chapter.**

George Ruffin. *See* **Law chapter.**

Dred Scott (1795–1858)
Negotiator

Born in Southhampton, Virginia, in 1795, his first name was simply "Sam." He worked as a farmhand, handyman, and stevedore, and moved with his master to Huntsville, Alabama, and later to St. Louis, Missouri. In 1831 his owner, Peter Blow, died, and he was bought by John Emerson, a surgeon in the U.S. Army. Sam accompanied his new master to Illinois (a free state) and Wisconsin (a territory). Sometime after 1836 he received permission to marry, and by 1848 he had changed his name to Dred Scott. At various times he attempted to buy his freedom or escape but was unsuccessful. In 1843, Emerson died and left his estate to his widow Irene Emerson, who also refused Scott his freedom. He then obtained the assistance of two attorneys who helped him to sue for his freedom in county court.

Scott lost this case, but the verdict was set aside, and in 1847 he won a second trial on the grounds that his slave status had been nullified upon entering into a free state. Scott received financial backing and legal representation through the sons of Peter Blow, Irene Emerson's brother John Sanford, and her second husband, Dr. C. C. Chaffee, all of whom apparently saw the case as an important challenge to slavery. In 1857, the U.S.

Supreme Court ruled against Scott, stating that slaves were not legally citizens of the United States and, therefore, had no standing in the courts. Shortly after the decision was handed down, Mrs. Emerson freed Scott. The case led to the nullification of the Missouri Compromise of 1820, allowing the expansion of slavery into formerly free territories and strengthening the abolition movement.

Sojourner Truth (1797–1883)
Lecturer, Abolitionist

Born Isabella Baumfree in Ulster County, New York, around 1797, she was freed by the New York State Emancipation Act of 1827 and lived in New York City for a time. After taking the name Sojourner Truth, which she felt God had given her, she assumed the "mission" of spreading "the Truth" across the country. She became famous as an itinerant preacher, drawing huge crowds with her oratory—and some said "mystical gifts"—wherever she appeared. She became one of an active group of African American women abolitionists, lectured before numerous abolitionist audiences, and was friends with such leading white abolitionists as James and Lucretia Mott and Harriet Beecher Stowe. With the outbreak of the Civil War she raised money to purchase gifts for the soldiers, distributing them herself in the camps. She also helped African Americans who had escaped to the North to find habitation and shelter. Age and ill health caused her to retire from the lecture circuit, and she spent her last days in a sanatorium in Battle Creek, Michigan.

Harriet (Ross) Tubman (1826–1913)
Lecturer, Abolitionist, Nurse

Born in 1826 in Dorchester County, Maryland, she had the hard childhood of a slave: much work, little schooling, and severe punishment. In 1848 she escaped, leaving behind her husband John Tubman, who threatened to report her to their master. As a free woman, she began to devise practical ways of helping other slaves escape. Over the following ten years she made about 20 trips from the North into the South and rescued more than 300 slaves. Her reputation spread rapidly, and she won the admiration of leading abolitionists—some of whom sheltered her passengers. Eventually a reward of $40,000 was posted for her capture.

Tubman met and aided John Brown in recruiting soldiers for his raid on Harpers Ferry—Brown referred to her as "General Tubman." One of her major disappointments was the failure of the raid, and she is said to have regarded Brown as the true emancipator of her people, not Lincoln. In 1860 she began to canvass the nation, appearing at anti-slavery meetings and speaking on women's rights. Shortly before the outbreak of the Civil War, she was forced to leave for Canada, but she returned to the United States and served the Union as a nurse, soldier, and spy. She was particularly valuable to the army as a scout because of the knowledge of the terrain that she had gained as a conductor on the Underground Railroad.

Tubman's biography, from which she received the proceeds, was written by Sarah Bradford in 1868. Tubman's husband, John, died two years after the end of the war, and in 1869 she married the war veteran Nelson Davis. Despite receiving many honors and tributes, including a medal from Queen Victoria, she spent her last days in poverty, not receiving a pension until 30 years after the Civil War. With the $20 a month that she finally received, she helped to found a home for the aged and needy, which was later renamed the Harriet Tubman Home. She died in Auburn, New York.

Nat Turner (1800–1831)
Insurrectionist

Born a slave in Southampton County, Virginia, on October 2, 1800, he was an avid reader of the Bible who prayed, fasted, and experienced "voices," ultimately becoming a visionary mystic with a belief that God had given him the special destiny of conquering Southampton County. After recruiting a handful of conspirators, he struck at isolated homes in his immediate area, and within 48 hours the band of insurrectionists had reached 60 armed men. They killed 55 whites before deciding to attack the county seat in Jerusalem, but while en route they were overtaken by a posse and dispersed. Turner took refuge in the Dismal Swamp and remained there for six weeks before he was captured, brought to trial, and hanged along with 16 other African American slaves.

James Varick. *See* **Religion chapter.**

Denmark Vesey (1767–1822)
Religious Leader

Born in 1767, Vesey was sold by his master at an early age and later bought back because of epilepsy. He sailed with his master, Captain Vesey, to the Virgin Islands and Haiti for 20 years. He enjoyed a considerable degree of mobility in his home port of Charleston, South Carolina, and eventually purchased his freedom from his master for $600—he had won $1,500 in a lottery. He became a Methodist minister and used his church as a base to recruit supporters to take over Charleston. The revolt was planned for the second Sunday in July of 1822.

Vesey's plans were betrayed when a slave alerted the white authorities of the city. Hundreds of African Americans were rounded up, though some of Vesey's collaborators most likely escaped to the Carolinas where they fought as maroons. After a 22-day search, Vesey was apprehended and stood trial. During the trial he adeptly cross-examined witnesses, but ultimately could not deny his intention to overthrow the city, and he was hung along with several collaborators.

David Walker (1785–1830)
Abolitionist, Civil Rights Activist, Writer

The offspring of a white mother and a black slave father on September 28, 1785, Walker was born free as stipulated by North Carolina law. Though not known how, Walker acquired an education before moving to Boston in the late 1820s. Besides starting a used clothes business, he became an active member of the Massachusetts General Colored Association and an agent for the first African American newspaper *Freedom's Journal*. In 1829, Walker published *Walker's Appeal to the Colored Citizens of the World*, which advocated the violent overthrow of slavery, the formation of African American civil rights and self-help organizations, and racial equality in the United States and independence for the peoples of Africa.

Walker's pamphlet alarmed Southerners who responded by enacting stricter laws against such "seditious" literature and the education of free African Americans. In the North, he also experienced sharp criticism, including from such prominent abolitionists as William Lloyd Garrison and Benjamin Lundy. On June 28, 1830, nine months after publishing his pamphlet, Walker mysteriously died, leaving behind his wife, Eliza. Though never verified, rumor suggests that he was poisoned.

Phyllis Wheatley. *See* **Literature chapter.**

Civil Rights

♦ Early Rights Movements ♦ Civil Rights during the Reconstruction Period
♦ Civil Rights in the Early Twentieth Century
♦ Civil Rights into the Twenty-First Century ♦ Civil Rights Activists
♦ Federal and State Civil Rights Agencies

by Linda T. Wynn

Throughout the history of the United States, African Americans have struggled to obtain basic civil rights. It is a struggle that has spanned several centuries—from the mutinies by Africans during the Atlantic crossing to the insurrections organized by slaves in the New World, from the founding of such organizations as the Free African Society and the abolition movement to the civil rights marches and demonstrations of the twentieth century.

♦ EARLY RIGHTS MOVEMENTS

The Free African Society

In 1787, as a result of segregation and discriminatory practices within the Methodist church, the Reverends Richard Allen and Absalom Jones formed the Free African Society in Philadelphia. (Seven years later, Allen founded the Bethel African Methodist Church, the first African Methodist Episcopal (A.M.E.) Church in America; Jones became the rector of a Protestant Episcopal Church.) The society was an important model for political consciousness and economic organization for African Americans throughout the country. It provided spiritual guidance and religious instruction; economic aid, burial assistance, relief to widows; and medical and financial assistance to orphans. The society also advocated abolition and maintained channels of communication with African Americans in the South. Similar to the many other African American organizations that followed, the society was rooted in religious principles. Throughout the nineteenth century, a number of mutual aid societies sprang up in African American communities in eastern cities, such as New York,

Newport, and Boston, providing loans, insurance, and various other economic and social services to their members and the larger community. The society also helped to facilitate communications between free African Americans throughout the country.

The Abolition Movement

The press and the pulpit served as important tools in the anti-slavery movement. In 1827 Samuel Cornish and John Russwurm founded *Freedom's Journal* in New York, the first African American-owned and operated newspaper in the United States. *Freedom's Journal,* which ceased publication after only three years, was concerned not only with eradicating slavery but also with the growing discrimination and cruelty against free African Americans in both the South and North.

In 1847, abolitionist Frederick Douglass published the first edition of the *North Star,* which eventually became one of the most successful African American newspapers in America prior to the outbreak of the Civil War. Douglass, an escaped slave from Maryland, became one of the best known African American abolitionists in the country. He lectured extensively throughout the United States and England. In 1845, he published his autobiography *Narrative of the Life of Frederick Douglass.*

Although the abolition movement was dominated by whites, numerous African American leaders played a major role in the movement including such figures as Henry Highland Garnet, Harriet Tubman, and Sojourner Truth.

◆ CIVIL RIGHTS DURING THE RECONSTRUCTION PERIOD

Following the Civil War, Republicans, who controlled the U.S. Congress, took up the cause of the newly freed African Americans. Between 1865 and 1875, Congress passed three amendments to the Constitution and a string of civil rights and Reconstructionist legislation. The Thirteenth Amendment, ratified December 18, 1865, abolished slavery and involuntary servitude. The Fourteenth Amendment, ratified July 28, 1868, guaranteed citizenship and provided equal protection under the laws. Ratified on March 30, 1870, the Fifteenth Amendment protected the right of all citizens to vote. In 1866, 1870, 1871, and 1875, Congress passed civil rights legislation outlining and protecting basic rights including the right to purchase and sell property and access to public accommodations. The Reconstruction Acts, passed between 1867 and 1869, called for new state constitutional conventions in those states that had seceded from the Union prior to the Civil War.

Reconstruction eventually produced a wave of anti-African American sentiment, though. White organizations such as the Ku Klux Klan, which aimed at intimidating African Americans and preventing them from taking their place in society, sprang up throughout the North and the South. In 1871, Congress enacted the Ku Klux Klan Act as an effort to end intimidation and violence directed at African Americans. However, the act failed to exterminate the Klan and other terrorist organizations.

The civil rights and Reconstructionist legislation were difficult for many whites to accept and did little to change racist attitudes. The last of the civil rights acts, passed by Congress in 1875, prohibited discrimination in public accommodations. However, by the 1880s the debate as to the constitutionality of such legislation had reached the U.S. Supreme Court. Ruling in a group of five cases in 1883, which became known as the *Civil Rights Cases*, the U.S. Supreme Court concluded that the 1875 Civil Rights Act was unconstitutional on the grounds that the Fourteenth Amendment authorized Congress to legislate only against discriminatory state action and not discrimination by private individuals. The Court's ruling brought about an end to federal efforts to protect the civil rights of African Americans until the mid-twentieth century.

Anti-lynching Efforts

By the late nineteenth and early twentieth century, lynching had become a weapon used by whites against African Americans throughout the country. Between 1882 and 1990, approximately 1,750 African Americans

An NAACP anti-lynching poster.

were lynched in the United States. Victims included women who had been accused of a variety of "offenses" ranging from testifying in court against a white man to failing to use the word "mister" when addressing a white person. Ida B. Wells-Barnett, a journalist and social activist, became one of the leading voices in the anti-lynching crusade by writing and lecturing throughout the United States and England against its practice.

Institutionalized Segregation

Prior to the case of *Plessy v. Ferguson*, the court had started to build a platform upon which the doctrine of "separate but equal" would be based. In 1878, ruling in the case *Hall v. DeCuir*, the court declared that states could not prohibit segregation on common carriers, such as streetcars and railroads. Thereafter, segregation laws sprang up throughout the South.

In 1896, the U.S. Supreme Court faced the issue of segregation on public transportation. At the time, as was the case in many parts of the South, a Louisiana state law was enacted requiring that "separate but equal" accommodations for blacks and whites be maintained in all public facilities. When Homer Adolph Plessy, an African American man traveling by train from New Orleans to Covington, Louisiana, refused to ride in the "colored" railway coach, he was arrested.

With Justice Billings Brown delivering the majority opinion in the *Plessy* case, the Court declared that "separate but equal" accommodations constituted a reasonable use of state police power and that the Fourteenth Amendment of the Constitution could not be used to abolish social or racial distinctions or to force a co-mingling of the two races. The Supreme Court effectively reduced the significance of the Fourteenth Amendment, which was designed to give African Americans specific rights and protections. The ruling in the *Plessy* case, which was termed the "separate but equal" doctrine, paved the way for the segregation of African Americans in all walks of life.

◆ CIVIL RIGHTS IN THE EARLY TWENTIETH CENTURY

Booker T. Washington and W. E. B. Du Bois

During the late nineteenth and early twentieth centuries, two figures—Booker T. Washington and William Edward Burghardt Du Bois—emerged as leaders in the struggle for African American political and civil rights. Washington, an educator and founder of the Tuskegee Normal and Industrial Institute, was a strong advocate of practical, utilitarian education and manual training as a means for developing African Americans. (Founded in 1881, Tuskegee Normal and Industrial Institute was based on a program at Hampton Institute that provided vocational training and prepared its students to survive economically in a segregated society.) In Washington's opinion, education should provide African Americans with the means to become economically self-supporting. Speaking at the Cotton States International Exposition in Atlanta in 1895, Washington outlined his philosophy of self-help and cooperation between African Americans and whites:

> To those of my race who depend on bettering their condition in a foreign land, or who underestimate the importance of cultivating friendly relations with the Southern white man, who is their

next door neighbor, I would say: 'Cast down your bucket where you are'—cast it down in making friends in every manly way of the people of all races by whom we are surrounded.

W. E. B. Du Bois, a young historian and Harvard graduate, challenged Washington's passive policies in a series of stinging essays and speeches. Du Bois advocated the uplifting of African Americans through an educated African American elite, which he referred to as the "Talented Tenth," or roughly a tenth of the African American population. He believed that these African Americans must become proficient in education and culture, which would eventually benefit all. In 1905, Du Bois, along with a group of other African American intellectuals, formed the Niagara Movement. The group drew up a platform that called for full citizenship rights for African Americans and public recognition of their contributions to America's stability and progress. The movement eventually evolved into what became known as the National Association for the Advancement of Colored People (NAACP).

A. Philip Randolph

In 1941, A. Philip Randolph, organizer of an employment bureau for untrained African Americans and founder of the Brotherhood of Sleeping Car Porters, came up with the idea of leading a march of African Americans in Washington, DC, to protest discrimination. On July 25, less than a week before the scheduled demonstration, President Franklin D. Roosevelt issued Executive Order No. 8802, which banned discrimination in the defense industry and led to the creation of the Fair Employment Practices Committee.

◆ CIVIL RIGHTS INTO THE TWENTY-FIRST CENTURY

The Civil Rights movement suffered many defeats in the first half of the twentieth century. Repeated efforts to obtain passage of federal anti-lynching bills failed. The all-white primary system, which effectively disenfranchised Southern citizens of African descent, resisted numerous court challenges. The Depression worsened conditions in rural and in urban areas. On the positive side, the growing political power of African Americans in Northern cities and an increasing liberal trend in the Supreme Court portended the legal and legislative victories of the 1950s and 1960s.

Brown v. Board of Education of Topeka, Kansas

A great deal of the civil rights struggle throughout this period was carried on by the NAACP, which began chipping away at the roots of legalized segregation in a series of successful lawsuits. A major breakthrough for the NAACP came in 1954, when the U.S. Supreme Court ruled in *Brown v. Board of Education of Topeka, Kansas* that discrimination in education was unconstitutional. The *Brown* case involved the practice of denying African American children equal access to state public schools, due to state laws requiring or permitting racial segregation. The U.S. Supreme Court unanimously held that segregation deprived the children of equal protection under the Fourteenth Amendment to the U.S. Constitution, overturning the "separate but equal" doctrine established in *Plessy*.

Civil Rights in the 1960s

Rosa Parks was one of the major catalysts for the 1960s Civil Rights movement. On December 1, 1955, when Parks refused to give up her seat on a Montgomery bus to a white man—as the law required—she was arrested and sent to jail. As a result of Parks's arrest, African Americans throughout Montgomery refused to ride city buses. The Montgomery Bus Boycott led by Martin Luther King Jr. was highly successful and ultimately led to the integration of all Montgomery city buses, when on November 13, 1956, the U.S. Supreme Court in *Gayle v. Browder* ruled that bus segregation in Montgomery was unconstitutional. This case unlike the *Brown* case specifically overturned the Court's *Plessy v. Ferguson* decision because it—like *Plessy*—specifically applied to transportation.

The eventual success of the Montgomery Bus Boycott encouraged a wave of massive demonstrations that swept across the South. Denied service at a Woolworth's lunch counter in Greensboro, North Carolina, freshman students Ezell Blair Jr., Joseph McNeil, Francis McCain, and Davidson Richardson, started the sit-in movement on February 1, 1960. While the North Carolina students received the attention of the national media, a small cadre of Nashville students and adult leaders had tested the city's exclusionary racial policies in the final months of the preceding year. Twelve days after the sit-ins began in North Carolina, African American students in Nashville launched their first full-scale sit-ins. In response to white harassment, Nashville students formulated ten rules of conduct for demonstrators that later became the code of behavior for protest movements in the South. The Nashville student movement was described by Dr. Martin Luther King Jr. as the "best organized and most disciplined movements in the South." On May 10, 1960, Nashville became the first major city to begin desegregating its public facilities. That same year, the Student Non-Violent Coordinating Committee (SNCC) was created and included among its members Julian Bond, H. Rap Brown, Stokely Carmichael, and John Lewis.

The Civil Rights movement of the 1960s galvanized African Americans and sympathetic whites as nothing had ever done before, but was not without cost. Thousands of people were jailed because they defied Jim Crow laws. Others were murdered, and homes and churches were bombed. People lost their jobs and their homes because they supported the movement.

On August 28, 1963, nearly 250,000 people marched in Washington, DC, to awaken the nation's conscience regarding civil rights and to encourage the passage of civil rights legislation pending in Congress. The march was a cooperative effort of several civil rights organizations including the Southern Christian Leadership Conference (SCLC), the Congress of Racial Equality (CORE), the NAACP, the Negro American Labor Council, and the National Urban League. It was during this demonstration that Dr. Martin Luther King Jr., in the shadow of the Lincoln Memorial, gave his well-known and oft-quoted "I Have a Dream" speech. More than an oration about a dream that America would at last practice the tenet expressed in the Declaration of Independence that all people are created equal, King told the nation that as far as African Americans were concerned, it had failed to make payment on its promissory note—one that guaranteed the "unalienable rights of life, liberty and the pursuit of happiness," to all. He stated, "We have come to cash this check—a check that will give us upon demand the riches of freedom and the security of justice." Eighteen days after King's speech, white racists dynamited the occupied Sixteenth Street Baptist Church in Birmingham, Alabama. Four girls attending Sunday School—Denise McNair, 11-years old, and Addie Mae Collins, Carole Robertson, and Cynthia Wesley, all 14 years old—were killed by the explosion. Later King declared, "The innocent blood of these four little girls may well serve as the redemptive force that will bring new light to this dark city. . . . Indeed, this tragic event may cause the white South to come to terms with its conscience."

At its zenith, the Civil Rights movement was the most important event taking place in America. Through demonstrations, "sit-ins," marches, economic boycotts,

Rosa Parks riding in front of white bus passengers after the Supreme Court ruled in 1956 that segregated public accomodations were illegal.

and soaring discourse, the movement aroused widespread public indignation, thus creating an atmosphere in which it was possible to make positive changes in American society.

Justice Brought to Civil Rights Crimes of the 1960s

Four men, believed to be members of the Ku Klux Klan were identified as suspects in the terror campaign against the Sixteenth Street Baptist Church. The Federal Bureau of Investigation (FBI) led the original investigation. It was determined that Robert E. Chambliss, Bobby Frank Cherry, Herman Frank Cash, and Thomas E. Blanton Jr. planted the explosive device. To its credit, the Birmingham FBI office recommended that the suspects be prosecuted. Director J. Edgar Hoover prevented prosecution and court proceedings, however, by refusing the recommendation that the federal prosecutor be given the testimony that identified the suspects. Five years after the Sixteenth Street Baptist Church bombing no charges had been filed and the FBI closed the case.

Firefighters using high pressure hoses to disrupt a 1963 civil rights demonstration in Birmingham, Alabama.

In 1971, Alabama Attorney General, Bill Baxley reopened the case. Six years later, on November 18, Chambliss, also known as "Dynamite Bob," was convicted of murder and sentenced to life in prison. Again, in 1988 and 1997, the case was reopened after informants tipped-off the FBI. Herman Frank Cash, one of the four suspects, died in 1994, however, before a case could be launched against him. On May 17, 2000, the remaining two suspects, Thomas Blanton Jr. and Bobby Frank Cherry were charged with the 1963 murders of Denise McNair, Addie Mae Collins, Carole Robertson, and Cynthia Wesley. Almost a year later, on May 1, Blanton was tried, convicted, and sentenced to life imprisonment.

Almost four decades after the Sixteenth Baptist Church bombing—one of the most heinous acts of terrorism perpetrated against the modern civil rights movement— the final terrorist was put on trial. Bobby Frank Cherry's trial was postponed, however, after Circuit Judge James Garrett initially ruled that he was mentally incompetent and unable to assist his attorney with his defense. In January 2002, Judge Garrett reversed his ruling after "experts" convinced him that Cherry was feigning the disability. Cherry was charged

with four counts of murder and four counts of arson. On May 22, 2002, a jury of nine whites and three African Americans returned a guilty verdict against Cherry, who was later sentenced to life imprisonment.

Other Cases

Throughout the 1990s and into the first decade of the twenty-first century, civil rights cases from the 1960s and 1970s were reopened despite the longing of some white Southerners to conceal the region's racist past. In April 1998, officials in Natchez, Mississippi, reopened the investigation into the 1967 killing of Wharlest Jackson, treasurer of the Natchez NAACP. Jackson, who was killed when a bomb tore asunder his pick-up truck, had been promoted to a position—previously held only by whites—at a local tire plant. No one was ever arrested.

Sam Bowers, former imperial wizard for the Ku Klux Klan, was indicted and convicted in August 1998 for the 1966 murder of Vernon Dahmer Sr., president of the Hattiesburg, Mississippi, NAACP chapter. Dahmer was

Martin Luther King Jr. delivering his famous "I Have a Dream" speech in 1963.

killed by an explosive device detonated at his home. Originally, 14 Klansmen were tried for this murder, but only three were convicted. When authorities brought Charles Nobel, another suspect in the Dahmer case, before the bar of justice in June 1999, the case ended in a mistrial.

Later, in November 1999, Charles Caston, James Caston, and Hal Crimm were sentenced to 20 years in prison for the 1970 murder of Rainey Pool, a one-armed sharecropper from Midnight, Mississippi. Pool was beaten unconscious by a mob and thrown into the Sunflower River. Originally, seven white men were arrested, but the charges were dismissed. Two died, one was acquitted in June 1998, and another, Joe Oliver, pleaded guilty to manslaughter charges in 1999. Charles Caston later died in prison.

The FBI reopened the murder investigations for Charles Eddie Moore and Henry Hezekiah Dee in Natchez, Mississippi, in February 2000. Two men were arrested, but the charges were later dismissed. Four months later, Ernest H. Avants was indicted on federal charges in the June 10, 1966, murder of farmhand Ben Chester White. Authorities reported that White might have been killed in a plot designed to bring Dr. Martin Luther King to Mississippi in an attempt to assassinate the noted leader of the civil rights movement.

In January 2001, the Mississippi attorney general stated that authorities are "vigorously pursuing" possible murder charges in the 1964 slayings of civil rights workers Michael Schwerner, Andrew Goodman, and James Chaney. The following month, officers of the court reviewed the death of black truck driver Ben Brown who was killed on May 11, 1967, during a civil rights protest in Jackson, Mississippi. The FBI reopened its investigation of the 1965 murder of Oneal Moore, killed on a remote stretch of Louisiana's Route 21 in Varnado, and his partner, Creed Rogers. They were the first African Americans hired by the Washington Parish Sheriff's office. A shotgun blast to the back of Moore's head killed him instantly, while Rogers lost an eye and sustained other serious gunshot wounds in the same incident. Shortly after the shooting, police authorities arrested suspected Klansman Earnest Ray McElveen. Although he failed to give a confirmable alibi, McElveen was released and no arrests were ever made in the case.

Two other cases reopened included the 1951 killings in Florida of NAACP members Harry T. Moore and his wife—who died when their home was bombed—and the 1957 murder of Willie Edwards Jr., a resident of Montgomery, Alabama, who jumped off a bridge when Klansmen threatened him with a gun. Prosecutors officially closed both cases.

Perhaps the conviction of Byron de la Beckwith in the Medgar Evers assassination generated a renewed interest in the unsolved civil rights crimes of the 1960s and 1970s. By some counts, since his guilty verdict, approximately 18 crimes from the civil rights era have been re-investigated. Eleven people have been arrested, juries handed down five convictions, one person pleaded guilty, one case resulted in a mistrial, and one ended in acquittal.

Despite the threat of awakening specters of the old South, a new generation of law enforcement officials and officers of the court have become prepared to re-examine civil rights crimes against people of African descent during the 1960s and the 1970s.

Civil Rights Legislation in the 1990s

The Civil Rights movement of the 1950s and 1960s produced significant gains for African Americans. However, historic patterns of hiring and promotion left minorities vulnerable, especially during downward spirals in the national economy. In June 1989, the U.S. Supreme Court delivered opinions in several cases dealing with seniority systems and racial discrimination in employment. Ruling in the cases *Lorance v. AT&T Technologies Inc.*, *Martin v. Wilks*, *Patterson v. McLean Credit Union*, and *Wards Cove Packing Co. v. Antonio*, the Court appeared to reverse earlier civil rights rulings.

Prior to the Court's ruling in *Wards Cove*, the burden of proof in job discrimination suits had been placed on employers, requiring businesses to prove that there was a legitimate business reason for alleged discriminatory practices. With the *Wards Cove* decision, the Court made it more difficult for groups to win such suits by requiring workers to prove that no clear business reason existed for an employer's use of practices that result in discrimination. Civil rights organizations were quick to protest the rulings; opponents of the ruling, including the NAACP Legal Defense and Educational Fund and the Leadership Conference on Civil Rights, argued that the Court had undermined the protection granted by federal civil rights and equal employment legislation.

On October 16 and 17, 1990, both houses of Congress approved a bill designed to reverse the Court's ruling.

The proposed legislation not only reversed the Court's ruling in *Wards Cove*, but it also strengthened provisions of the 1964 Civil Rights Act. On October 22, 1990, President George H. W. Bush vetoed the bill, claiming that its provisions would encourage employers to establish hiring quotas.

This was not the first time that Congress moved to reverse a Court action in the area of civil rights; Congress passed the Civil Rights Restoration Act of 1988 that reversed the Court's ruling in *Grove City College v. Bell* (1984). In the *Grove City College* case, the U.S. Supreme Court ruled that not all programs and activities of an institution were covered by Title IX of the Education Amendments of 1972 (Public Law 89–10, 79 Stat. 27), prohibiting discrimination in educational programs receiving federal financial assistance.

After vetoing Congress's 1990 civil rights legislation, the Bush administration joined both houses of Congress in working on alternative bills. Following months of negotiation, the Senate passed a bill designed to provide additional remedies for deterring harassment and intentional discrimination in the workplace, to provide guidelines for the adjudication of cases arising under Title VII of the Civil Rights Act of 1964, and to expand the scope of civil rights legislation weakened by Supreme Court decisions. The House of Representatives passed the bill on November 7, and on November 21, President George Bush signed the Civil Rights Act of 1991.

The Continuation of Police Brutality in the 1990s

In the late 1960s, incidents of police abuse sparked civil unrest, costly and violent uprisings, and a lingering distrust between minority communities and the police. In an effort to understand the causes of these incidents, President Lyndon Johnson created the National Advisory Commission on Civil Disorders, also known as the Kerner Commission. On July 27, 1968, the commission released its findings: among other things, 12 "deeply held grievances" had been found in the communities that it studies, the most intense being police practices. Unfortunately, as the examples below confirm, major problems in police treatment of minority communities still existed several decades later.

In late 1989, a pregnant white woman, Carol Stuart, was murdered in the racially-divided city of Boston. Her husband told the police that her killer was an African American male. His allegations led police to conduct a manhunt in the predominantly African American neighborhood of Roxbury. African Americans in the community were outraged once it was revealed that Charles Stuart had murdered his wife—Stuart, who was having an extramarital affair and financial problems, subsequently committed suicide—and they charged the police department with applying a "double standard of justice." In response, Boston Mayor Raymond Flynn appointed the St. Clair Commission to examine allegations of abuse of power by the police department.

In 1991, following a high speed chase, African American motorist Rodney King was subdued with extreme force and arrested by officers of the Los Angeles Police Department (LAPD). The broadcast of a videotape of the King beating galvanized international attention on police brutality in Los Angeles. In a subsequent court trial, however, a predominantly white jury found the four officers not guilty of charges filed against them. The verdict ignited one of the worst race riots in the history of the United States. Later, the federal government indicted the officers on charges that they violated King's civil rights. Two of the officers were convicted and incarcerated.

In response to this chain of events, Mayor Tom Bradley created an independent commission to investigate the LAPD. In July 1991, the Christopher Commission released its findings. Documenting the systematic use of excessive force and racial harassment in the department, the report called for structural reforms and the resignation of Los Angeles Police Chief Daryl Gates. "Within minority communities of Los Angeles, there is a widely-held view that police misconduct is commonplace," stated the Christopher Report. "Long standing complaints [are held] by African Americans, Latinos and Asians that LAPD officers frequently treat minorities differently from whites. . . employing unnecessarily intrusive practices such as the 'prone-out,' and engaging in use of excessive force."

Well into the 1990s, scores of other police brutality incidents against blacks surfaced in numerous cities across the nation. These reports included: the 1995 videotaped beating of Corey West in Providence, Rhode Island; the killing of motorist Jonny Gammage in Pittsburgh, Pennsylvania; the 1996 killing of TyRon Lewis in St. Petersburg, Florida; the fatal shooting of unarmed Nathaniel Gaines Jr. in New York City; the 1997 alleged beating of Jeremiah Mearday in Chicago; and the 1998 fatal shooting of Tyisha Miller in Riverside, California.

Many of these incidents, which occurred under questionable circumstances, produced protests and investigations by the U.S. Civil Rights Commission and prompted a national debate on police, race, and the use of deadly force. Civil rights organizations asserted that these incidents mirrored a discriminatory use of deadly force and critical problems ranging from racially-motivated police brutality to unprovoked stops and interrogation of minorities based on racial profiling.

Perhaps, the two most controversial and high profile cases of police brutality occurred in New York within a two-year span. On August 9, 1997, law enforcement officers assaulted Haitian immigrant Abner Louima, who worked as a security guard in Brooklyn, New York. On February 4, 1999, four officers from the New York City Street Crime Unit (SCU), working undercover and patrolling the Soundview neighborhood for a serial rapist, fired 41 shots at Amadou Bailo Diallo, a 22 year-old Muslim immigrant from Guinea, who was outside his apartment.

New York Police Department (NYPD) officers Justin Volpe, Charles Schwarz, Thomas Wiese, and Thomas Bruder from Brooklyn's 70th Precinct arrived at a brawl outside a nightclub at 4:00 A.M. on August 9, 1997. Abner Louima was present, as was his cousin, who struck officer Volpe during the fracas. Volpe mistakenly believed that Louima had thrown the punch and arrested him. According to reports, the Haitian immigrant was beaten by the officers en route to the precinct. Upon arrival, Louima was taken to the restroom where Volpe sodomized him with a wooden stick. Suffering serious internal injuries, he required numerous surgeries and was hospitalized for two months.

The four police officers were indicted for varying levels of involvement in the brutal beating. On December 13, 1999, after pleading guilty, Volpe was sentenced to 30 years in prison, which he appealed. Schwarz was found guilty of holding the Haitian victim down while Volpe assaulted him, but Schwarz, Wiese, and Bruder were acquitted of beating Louima on the way to the precinct. On March 6, 2000, all three were found guilty of conspiracy to obstruct justice. Based on his role in the bathroom assault, Schwarz was convicted for violating Louima's civil rights. On June 27, 2000, District Judge Eugene H. Nickerson of the U.S. District Court for the Eastern District of New York sentenced Schwarz to almost 16 years imprisonment and ordered restitution to Louima in the amount of $277,495.

Retaining attorney Johnnie Cochran, Louima filed a $15.5 million civil rights violation suit against New York City, the Patrolmen's Benevolent Association, and individual officers. It was settled in July 2001 for $8.7 million, the highest settlement that New York has ever paid for a police brutality case.

On February 28, 2002, the Second Circuit Court of Appeals overturned the obstruction of justice convictions against Schwarz, Wiese, and Bruder, and ordered

Protesters gathered to demand fair treatment of African Americans by police after the shooting of Amadou Diallo, 1999.

a new trial for Schwarz on the civil rights charge. Less than a month after the court overturned Schwarz's conviction, he was indicted on two counts of lying under oath. A new trial date for Schwarz was set on June 24, 2002. As of July 13, 2002, Schwarz's fate was still in the hands of the deliberating jury.

In the Amadou Diallo shooting of February 4, 1999, Edward McMellon, Sean Carroll, Kenneth Boss, and Richard Murphy, four officers from the New York City SCU fired 41 shots—19 hits—at the unarmed West African immigrant, who was standing in the vestibule of his Bronx apartment. The officers contended that they suspected Diallo was a sought-after serial rapist and that he had reached for a gun. Some argued that the Diallo shooting was indicative of police brutality carried out by the NYPD toward people of color.

Incensed over the circumstances of the shooting, numerous persons and organizations, including the NAACP, staged a protest rally on March 18, 1999. On

March 26, 1999, the officers were indicted on charges of second-degree murder. Five days later, all pleaded not guilty. They served a 30-day suspension from police duties without pay and were assigned desk duty. The trial began on February 2, 2000. Judge Teresi ruled that the prosecution could not reveal that three of the four officers had fired their weapons at suspects in the past.

In addition to the second-degree murder charge, the jury was allowed to consider manslaughter and criminally negligent homicide. After two days deliberating, though, they returned not guilty verdicts for all the defendants on February 23, 2000. In early March, the U.S. Justice Department investigated whether a federal civil rights case was warranted. It issued a statement on January 31, 2001, that insufficient evidence existed to prove that the officers *intended* to use excessive force, which is a requirement to prove they violated Diallo's civil rights. Therefore, the federal civil rights charges against McMellon, Carroll, Boss, and Murphy were rescinded. On April 18, 2000, Diallo's family filed an $81 million civil suit against the city of New York. This lawsuit was still pending at the time of publication. As a result of the Amadou Diallo killing, however, the issues of police brutality and racial profiling became national concerns. Nevertheless, incidents of police brutality did not diminish.

On Monday, July 8, 2002, the videotape of 16-year-old African American Donovan Jackson being beaten and arrested at a gas station in Inglewood, California, captured national attention. Inglewood police officers were assisting two Los Angeles County sheriff's deputies, who were investigating a car with an expired vehicle registration. According to reports filed by the Associated Press, Koby Chavis—Jackson's father—was cited for driving with a suspended license and was booked for assault on a police officer. In a CNN interview, both father and son said they had no idea why the police questioned them and that they did nothing to provoke the officers. A tourist staying at a motel across the street, captured officer Jeremy Morse picking up the prone, handcuffed Jackson, slamming him face-down onto the trunk of a squad car, and punching him. Morse put a hand on the back of Jackson's neck, punched him with his other hand, and then appeared to choke him. Based on the videotape, two other officers seemed to intervene, with at least one trying to pull Morse away. The Inglewood Police Department, the Los Angeles County Sheriff's Department, and the Los Angeles District Attorney's office all said they were investigating the incident. Morse was suspended—with pay—while the other officers involved were not suspended. Reminiscent of the 1991 beating of Rodney King, the incident elicited cries of racism and demands from civil rights groups for a federal investigation.

Donovan Jackson and Koby Chavis filed a lawsuit against the city of Inglewood, four of its police officers, Los Angeles County, and three of its sheriff's deputies on July 10, 2002. The federal civil rights lawsuit sought unspecified damages and alleged negligence, misconduct, and violation of the constitutional rights of due process and against unreasonable search and seizure. The actions were denounced publicly at all levels: the FBI opened an investigation; U.S. Attorney General John Ashcroft said that he was troubled and worried that the work of law enforcement had gone awry during the incident; and Inglewood Mayor Roosevelt Dorn, who is African American, promised that the conduct captured on tape would not be condoned "under any circumstances."

On the same day that the Inglewood case was brought to the nation's attention, Oklahoma City police officers Greg Driskill and E. J. Dyer were caught on tape striking 50-year old Donald Reed Pete with a police baton. The officers repeatedly hit Pete on the arms, legs, and back. According to news reports, police Captain Jessica Cummins stated that the force appeared appropriate because the officers faced a significant size disadvantage. Pete, who had no prior arrest record in Oklahoma City, reportedly is 6 feet, 3 inches and outweighed Driskill by some 140 pounds. Accused of soliciting prostitution and destroying evidence—by swallowing marijuana—he was arrested on numerous complaints, including assault and battery of a police officer, and held on a $34,000 bond. Under review by a police screening committee, city officials also asked the FBI to conduct a civil rights investigation of the case. Cummins said a police screening committee reviews every case in which an officer uses force to make an arrest. Continuing, she asserted that since the beginning of the year there were 279 incidents, which resulted in 15 disciplinary actions. At the time of publication, no determination or disposition had been made in either civil rights case.

Civil Rights in the Twenty-First Century

Just as the issue of police brutality continued to be an issue in the twenty-first century, civil rights also remained a persistent concern. President George W. Bush, on May 15, 2002, signed into law bipartisan civil rights legislation intended to crack down on discrimination and retaliation in the federal workplace. Known as the Notification and Federal Anti-discrimination and Retaliation Act of 2001 (No Fear), it required agencies to pay for all court settlements or judgments for discrimination and retaliation cases, instead of allowing the agency to use a government-wide slush fund. The bill's notification requirement aimed to improve workforce relations by increasing managers' and employees' knowledge of their respective rights and responsibilities. In addition to the notification requisite, the No Fear act also has mandatory reporting requirements designed to assist in determining if a pattern of misconduct exists within an agency and whether the agency took appropriate action to address any problems.

While the No Fear Act of 2001 focused on the federal work place, race-based affirmative action in college admissions policies remained on the national radar screen. In 1978, the U.S. Supreme Court endeavored to resolve the issue in *Regents of the University of California v. Bakke.* The Court considered the constitutionality of an affirmation action plan used by the University of California-Davis Medical School, which set aside 16 of its 100 openings for disadvantaged and minority applicants. Alan Bakke, a white male applicant, sued the university after it denied him admission. In 1976, the California Supreme Court ruled that Bakke should have been admitted and the U.S. Supreme Court affirmed this decision on June 28, 1978, by a narrow margin of 5–4. On a number of related legal issues, the court divided without a majority number. Only one justice avowed that affirmative action cases should be judged on the same stringent level of scrutiny that applied to "invidious" discrimination. The eight remaining justices stated that race-conscious remedies could be used in some circumstances to correct past discrimination. In essence, the Court used two measurements to sustain affirmative action: a compelling interest must exist for adopting an affirmation action plan and the plan must be narrowly tailored to suit that interest.

After the *Bakke* decision, institutions of higher education tailored their affirmative action plans by abolishing rigid quotas and set-asides. Implementing new plans, school officials began using a multi-factored analysis that permitted admissions officers to consider their school's racial or ethnic diversity as they would consider subjective factors as geographical diversity, life experience, interests and talents, and similar "plus factors." Almost 20 years later, though, with the majority of federal judges appointed by Republican presidents, conservative appellate courts began to strike down "plus factor" plans.

in *Cheryl J. Hopwood, et al v. Texas* (1996), the Fifth Circuit Court of Appeals—which covers Louisiana, Mississippi, and Texas—struck down the University of Texas Law School's "plus factor" affirmative action plan. Four years later, the Ninth Circuit Court of Appeals, in *Katuria Smith, et al v. University of Washington Law School*, upheld the integrity of the admissions policy and allowed the consideration of race as one of the many factors in reviewing applications for admission. The Ninth Circuit stated, "educational diversity is a compelling governmental interest that meets demands of strict scrutiny of race-conscious measures." Covering the states of Alabama, Florida, and Georgia, on August 27, 2001, the Eleventh Circuit Court of Appeals, in *Jennifer L. Johnson, et al. v. Board of Regents of the University of Georgia*, declined to decide whether diversity in education could be a compelling interest. It did, however, strike down as unlawful a University of Georgia admissions policy that awarded "points" to applicants for qualities including minority status. According to Columbia Law School professor Michael C. Dorf, within days of the Eleventh Circuit's decision, the University of Florida said it would cease providing more than 50 minority scholarships. He surmised that further university policy changes would take place in states within the Eleventh Circuit. All of the lead plaintiffs in these cases were white females.

On May 14, 2002, the Sixth Circuit Court of Appeals, which includes Kentucky, Michigan, Ohio, and Tennessee, handed down a narrow decision upholding the affirmative action policies of the University of Michigan Law School. Barbara Grutter, the plaintiff, filed suit against the law school after being denied admission in 1997. The white mother of two, in her forties with a 3.8 grade point average and high scores on the Law School Admission Test (LSAT), alleged that had she been an African American or Hispanic, she would have been admitted. As a "non-traditional student," Grutter argued that she would have brought diversity to the student population. Using the characteristic rationale of reverse discrimination as a consequence of the school's purportedly narrow meaning of "diversity," the litigant challenged the law school's admission's policy that alleged a desire for diversity.

As noted in the case opinion, the University of Michigan Law School's policy explicitly expressed "a commitment to racial and ethnic diversity" with special reference to the inclusion of students from groups historically discriminated against, like African Americans, Hispanics, and Native Americans. The academy acknowledged this guiding principle, in combination with other "soft" variables such as letters of recommendation, the quality of the undergraduate institution, difficulty of undergraduate course selection, the quality of the applicant's essay, residency, leadership and work experience, or unique talents and interests, might result in the admittance of students with relatively low grade point averages and LSAT scores. As cited in the brief, while the University of Michigan Law School sought to enroll a meaningful number, or "critical mass," of under-represented minorities, it denied that such "critical mass" represented any pre-set number or percentage of reserved seats being held for such students.

Upholding the use of race in admissions, the *Grutter v. Bollinger et al.* ruling did little to end the discussion as it was a narrow 5–4 decision with strong dissenting opinions. Furthermore, it supported a ruling made by the Ninth Circuit but contradicted rulings handed down by the Fifth and Eleventh Circuits, which struck down the use of race in admissions. Nevertheless, the Sixth Circuit stated, "We are satisfied that the law school's admission policy sets appropriate limits on the competitive consideration of race and ethnicity."

A decision from the Sixth Circuit is expected soon in *Gratz v. Bollinger et al.*, another admissions lawsuit against an admissions policy at the University of Michigan. Brought by Jennifer Gratz, an unsuccessful applicant in 1995, and Patrick Hamacher, an unsuccessful applicant in 1997, the case ended in a summary judgment—no trial was held—in the university's favor. On December 13, 2000, the judge ruled that the pursuit of diversity as an educational benefit *is* a compelling governmental interest and the university's current admission policy was constitutional. The Center for Individual Rights, which consistently challenges affirmative action policies, appealed the judgment. The University of Michigan cross-appealed regarding its admission policy from 1995 to 1998, which the judge found unconstitutional. Almost a year later, oral argument in the university's undergraduate admissions case was heard in the Court of Appeals.

Many in the higher education and legal arenas expressed beliefs that the incongruities among the various courts provided the vehicle that will move the nation's highest tribunal to issue a definitive decision on the constitutionality of affirmative action programs. Since 1978 the Supreme Court's ruling in *Bakke* had been the guiding standard. Should the Court revisit the *Bakke* decision, there is a large evidentiary body of social science literature that validates diversity as affording tangible benefits to all undergraduate, graduate, and professional school students.

Number of Hate Crimes Against African Americans Increases

Just as police brutality became a national focal point, so, too, did the proliferation of hate crimes against African Americans. (By definition, hate crimes are "crimes against persons or property motivated in whole or in part by racial, ethnic, religious, gender, sexual orientation and other prejudices.") Based on the data collected under the Hate Crime Statistics Acts of 1990 and 1996, the number of hate crimes perpetrated against African Americans and reported to the Federal Bureau of Investigation (FBI) increased from 2,988 in 1995 to 3,838 in 1997. These malicious acts of violence, similar to lynchings of the past, were intended not only to be injurious to individuals but to intimidate and dispirit an entire group of people. An example of such crimes included the destruction of African American churches in the South.

Between 1995 and mid-1996, hundreds of African American churches were set ablaze in the South. These incidents of church arson invoked grievous memories of racist violence during the 1960s, particularly the bombing of Birmingham's Sixth Street Baptist Church in which four small girls were killed on September 15, 1963. In response, President Clinton declared the "investigation and prevention of church arsons to be a national priority."

In June 1996, President Clinton established the National Church Arson Task Force and proposed a three-pronged strategy that called for prosecution of the arsonists, the rebuilding of church edifices, and the prevention of additional fires. In addition, on July 3, he signed the Church Arson Prevention Act of 1996, which passed both chambers of the Congress unanimously. On June 6, 1997, the National Church Arson Task Force released its report: Of the 429 incidents of church burnings, bombings, and attempted bombings investigated, 162 involved African American churches, 75 percent of which were located in the South. The majority of those convicted of destroying African American churches were white males.

Hate crimes were not restricted to the destruction of African American church buildings, though. Three of the more high profile incidents included: the 1995 murder of two African American residents of Fayetteville, North Carolina, by three Army soldiers who identified themselves as "neo-Nazi skin heads"; the 1996 racial harassment of Bridget Ward and her two daughters who moved into a rented home in the virtually all-white Bridesburg neighborhood in Philadelphia; and the 1998 brutal murder of James Byrd Jr. in Jasper, Texas, by three white males who chained him to the back of their pick-up truck and dragged him to his death. One of Byrd's assailants, self-proclaimed white supremacist John William King, was convicted of capital murder, and the jury recommended the death sentence in February 1999.

By the end of the twentieth century, hate crimes against African Americans continued to increase. According to the FBI's 1999 hate crime statistics, the number of incidents involved 9,301 separate offenses, of which 4,295 were motivated by racial bias. There were 2,958 incidents; 3,542 offenses; 3,679 victims; and 2,861 known offenders against African Americans. Over 50 percent of the hate crime victims were attacked because of their race, with the bias against African Americans accounting for 38 percent of all hate crime victims. The following year the trend continued. The 2000 FBI report showed 8,063 incidents reported, involving 9,430 separate offenses, 9,924 victims, and 7,530 known offenders. At 53.7 percent, racial bias represented the largest percentage of single-bias offenses. Taking victims of single-bias motivated hates crimes into consideration, more than 53 percent were attacked because of their race. African Americans accounted for 36 percent of all hate crime victims, decreasing by only two percentage points between 1999 and 2000.

It should be noted that "victim" may refer to a person, business, institution, or society as a whole. The term "known offender" does not imply that the identity of the suspect is known, only that an attribute of the

Incidents, Offenses, Victims, and Known Offenders

BY BIAS MOTIVATION, 2000[1]

Bias motivation	Incidents	Offenses	Victims[2]	Known offenders[3]
Total	8,063	9,430	9,924	7,530
Single-bias incidents	8,055	9,413	9,906	7,520
Race:	4,337	5,171	5,397	4,452
Anti-White	875	1,050	1,080	1,169
Anti-Black	2,884	3,409	3,535	2,799
Anti-American Indian/Alaskan Native	57	62	64	58
Anti-Asian/Pacific Islander	281	317	339	273
Anti-multiracial group	240	333	379	153
Ethnicity/national origin:	911	1,164	1,216	1,012
Anti-Hispanic	557	735	763	694
Anti-other ethnicity/national origin	354	429	453	318
Multiple-bias incidents[4]	8	17	18	10

[1]Because hate crime submissions have been updated, data in this table may differ from those published in *Crime in the United States, 2000.*
[2]The term *victim* may refer to a person, business, institution, or society as a whole.
[3]The term *known offender* does not imply that the identity of the suspect is known, but only that the race of the suspect is identified which distinguishes him/her from an unknown offender.
[4]A *multiple-bias incident* is a hate crime in which two or more offense types were committed as a result of two or more bias motivations.

suspect is identified that distinguishes her or him from an unknown offender.

Modern technology, especially the Internet, has created an opportunity for hate groups to spread their racist beliefs and increase their membership. Data compiled by the Southern Poverty Law Center indicated that the number of Internet hate sites grew from 163 in 1997 to 254 in 1998. According to HateWatch.org, in 2002 there were between 450 and 500 "hard core" hate sites and perhaps as many as 1,750 Web sites that are "problematic."

◆ CIVIL RIGHTS ACTIVISTS

(To locate biographical profiles more readily, please consult the index at the back of the book.)

Ralph D. Abernathy (1926–1990)
Religious Leader, Civil Rights Activist, Organization Executive/Founder

Born March 11, 1926, in Linden, Alabama, the Reverend Ralph David Abernathy was ordained a minister in 1948. He received his bachelor's degree from Alabama State College (now Alabama State University) in 1950 and his master's degree from Atlanta University in 1951. The alliance between Abernathy and Martin Luther King Jr. stretched back to the mid-1950s. While attending Atlanta University, Abernathy had the opportunity to hear King preach at Ebenezer Baptist Church.

After obtaining his master's degree, Abernathy returned to Alabama to serve as a part-time minister at the Eastern Star Baptist Church in Demopolis. In 1951 Abernathy moved to First Baptist Church in Montgomery. Around this time King accepted a position at Montgomery's Dexter Avenue Baptist Church; Abernathy and King became close friends.

In 1955, the two organized the Montgomery Improvement Association to coordinate a citywide bus boycott. The success of the Montgomery Bus Boycott led to the creation of the Southern Negro Leaders Conference; the organization's name was later changed to the Southern Leadership Conference and finally the Southern Christian Leadership Conference (SCLC). In January of 1957, Dr. King was elected the organization's first president.

From the time of Martin Luther King's death in 1968 until 1977, Abernathy served as president of the Southern Christian Leadership Conference. Abernathy continued as a leading figure in the movement until his resignation in 1977, when he made an unsuccessful bid for a U.S. Congressional seat. In 1989, he published his autobiography *And the Walls Came Tumbling Down*, which was criticized by some African American leaders for Abernathy's inclusion of details regarding King's extramarital affairs. Abernathy died of cardiac arrest on April 17, 1990.

Ralph D. Abernathy speaking at the Poor People's Campaign in 1968.

Ella Baker (1903–1986)
Community Activist, Civil Rights Activist, Executive/General Manager

In 1903, Ella Baker was born in Norfolk, Virginia, to Blake and Georgianna Ross Baker, both educated people who worked hard to educate their children. The family and community in which she grew up instilled in her a sense of sharing and community cooperation. Baker's family imbued her with a sense of racial pride and resistance to any form of oppression. Her grandfather, a minister and community leader, was an ardent proponent of civil rights and universal suffrage, and passed his beliefs on to her.

When she was 15, Baker was sent to the Shaw Boarding School (now Shaw University) in Raleigh, where she graduated with a bachelor's degree as valedictorian in 1927. After graduation, she moved to New York City. Baker quickly became involved in progressive politics and attended as many meetings and discussions as she could find. During the Depression, she was outraged at the poverty she saw in the African American areas of the city. Believing in the power of community and group action, she became one of the founders of the Young Negroes Cooperative League, a buying cooperative that bought food in bulk to distribute at low prices to members; in 1931, she became the national director of the League. When President Franklin Roosevelt's Works Progress Administration started, she became involved with their literacy program. Throughout these years she worked closely with other politically aware and motivated people, discussing and evolving a political philosophy of cooperation, equality, and justice.

In the in the late 1930s, Baker began to work for the NAACP. Between 1940 and 1943, she served as a field secretary, traveling all over the country setting up branch offices and teaching people to fight for their rights. During her travels, Baker developed a vast network of contacts in the South that she later relied on when working for the Southern Christian Leadership Conference (SCLC) and the Student Non-Violent Coordinating Committee (SNCC). In 1943, she became the director of branches for the NAACP. During the 1950s, she started fund-raising activities in New York for civil rights struggles in the South. In 1958, Baker moved to Atlanta to work with the SCLC.

Working for the SCLC, Baker became disillusioned with the male clergy-dominated organizational structure of the group. In 1960, she quit the SCLC and took a job with the Young Women's Christian Association. When students began leading sit-ins, the civil rights activist shifted her focus to the development of SNCC. She acted as an unofficial advisor for the group, counseling them to set up their own student-run organization rather than be subsumed under the SCLC or the NAACP. Baker helped launch the Mississippi Freedom Democratic Party that challenged the all-white Democratic delegation at the 1964 presidential convention. She also acted as staff consultant for the interracial SCLC educational fund.

Baker returned to New York City in 1965, but kept working with national and international civil rights organizations. Among her other activities, she raised money to send to the freedom fighters in Rhodesia and South Africa. She remained an active organizer and speaker as long as her health allowed. Baker's belief in the power of communal action and reliance on the workers rather than the leaders had an enormous impact. She worked for all of the major civil rights organizations at their time of greatest need. By the time the SCLC and SNCC were formed, Baker had almost 30 years of civil rights and community organizing experience to offer. She continually strove to keep the movement people-oriented, and she succeeded in helping SNCC remain a student group. Through her philosophy and actions, Ella J. Baker motivated hundreds to act and to help themselves and their neighbors, as she learned to do as a child.

Daisy Bates (1914–1999)
Publisher, Civil Rights Activist, Executive/General Manager

After attending segregated schools where all of the new equipment and up-to-date texts were only reserved for whites, Daisy Lee Gatson Bates spent much of her energy as an adult successfully integrating the schools of Little Rock, Arkansas.

Shortly after their marriage in 1942, Daisy and her husband Lucius Christopher Bates, a journalist, published a newspaper, the *Arkansas State Press*. They made it a point in their paper to keep track and report incidents of police brutality and other racially-motivated violence; their paper became known throughout the state for its campaign to improve the social and economic circumstances of African Americans. Because of their work, the city of Little Rock began to hire African American police officers, and the number of racist incidents decreased.

In 1952, Daisy Bates became the Arkansas president of the NAACP; after the 1954 U.S. Supreme Court decision in *Brown v. Board of Education of Topeka, Kansas*, she became very active in school desegregation. She began taking African American children to white schools to be registered. If the school refused to register the children, she would report it in her paper. In 1957, the superintendent of schools in Little Rock decided to try to integrate the schools and chose nine students, now called the "Little Rock Nine," to be the first African American children to attend Central High, a white school. Most white citizens of Little Rock objected. Bates organized the Little Rock Nine, accompanied them to Central High, and stood with them against the state troopers that Governor Orval Faubus sent to prevent the integration. For days she escorted the children to school, only to be turned away by an angry mob. On September 25, 1957, Daisy Bates entered Central High in Little Rock with the nine children, escorted by 1,000 paratroopers sent by President Dwight Eisenhower: the first steps towards integration were successful. For the rest of their years at Central High,

Bates kept track of the students and acted as their advocate when problems arose, frequently accompanying them and their parents to meetings with school officials.

In October of 1957, one month after she marched into Central High, Daisy Bates was arrested on charges of failing to provide membership information on the NAACP to city officials. The charges were later overturned. Two years later, the *Arkansas State Press* folded, but Bates kept active in the civil rights fight, touring and speaking. She also worked with the Student Non-Violent Coordinating Committee to register voters. Her memoir of the Little Rock crisis, *The Long Shadow of Little Rock*, was published in 1962. In 1985, 26 years after her newspaper ceased production, the *Arkansas State Press* resumed publication. It has continued to serve the needs of the African American community in Little Rock. On November 4, 1999, however, upon Bates's death, then-President Bill Clinton honored her by allowing her body to lie in state at the Capitol.

Julian Bond. *See* Politics chapter.

Stokely Carmichael (1941–1998)
Civil Rights Activist, Nationalist/Repatriationist, Executive/General Manager

If one individual stood at the forefront of the Black Power movement during the 1960s, Stokely Carmichael was that person. He soared to fame as popularizer of the dynamic phrase "Black Power" and as one of the most powerful and influential leaders of the Student Non-Violent Coordinating Committee (SNCC).

Carmichael was born in Trinidad on June 29, 1941, and moved to the United States with his family when he was 11 years of age. As a teenager, Carmichael was jolted by ghetto life in which "black" and "impotent" seemed to be synonymous terms. He was not reassured later when he was admitted to the Bronx High School of Science, encountered white liberals, and felt he had been adopted by them as a mascot. Although he was offered scholarships to predominantly white universities, Carmichael opted to attend Howard University. In 1960, during his first year at the university, he joined the Congress of Racial Equality (CORE) in its efforts to desegregate public accommodations in the South. After graduation in 1964, he rejected scholarship opportunities for graduate school and went south to join SNCC.

Kwame Toure (formerly known as Stokely Carmichael).

As one of their finest organizers, he worked ceaselessly, registering and educating voters in the South. In 1966, he was elected chairman of SNCC; however, as the organization's youngest chair, some members considered his views too radical.

Carmichael's cry for "black power" thrilled many disenfranchised young African Americans, but troubled others, who thought it sounded too violent. He was labeled as potentially violent by the media and the legal authorities. Disagreement with SNCC members arose over the issues of self-defense versus nonviolence and the participation of whites in African American grass roots organizations. In 1967, he resigned as chairperson, and was later expelled from SNCC.

Carmichael spent much of 1968 traveling around the world, speaking to many organizations including some in communist countries. His travels included Ghana, where he joined the Pan-African movement. After returning to the United States, he went to work for the Black Panther party. He was subject to almost constant harassment from the FBI because of his connection with the Panthers, and because he had visited communist countries while traveling. In 1969, he resigned from

the Black Panthers and moved to Guinea, where he had been offered political asylum.

In Guinea, Carmichael turned his efforts to supporting Pan-Africanism; he organized many local chapters throughout the world of the All Afrikan Peoples Revolutionary Party. In 1978, to honor the two men who most influenced his Pan-African philosophical education, SeKou Toure and Kwame Nkrumah, he changed his name to Kwame Toure. Four years after being awarded an LL.D. from Shaw University in recognition for his efforts to free African American people, Kwame Toure died in 1998 from prostate cancer.

Mandy Carter (1948–)
Civil Rights Activist; Gay/Lesbian Rights Activist

Carter was born in Albany, New York, in the late 1940s and spent her childhood in orphanages. She attended community college for a time in Troy, New York, but moved to New York City in 1967 with a savings of $100. There she slept in Central Park before taking a job at drug guru Timothy Leary's League for Spiritual Discovery. She moved to San Francisco later that year and became active in protests against the war in Vietnam. For several years Carter was involved with the War Resister's League. Among these colleagues, she first admitted her sexual orientation. She worked for the group's San Francisco offices during the late 1970s, during which time she first became active in gay and lesbian politics.

In 1982, Carter moved to North Carolina, where she continued her work with the War Resister's League in addition to becoming involved on a national level with gay and lesbian organizations. One of her accomplishments was helping coordinate the 1987 lesbian and gay march on the nation's capital, a role she reprised in 1993. In addition to co-producing an annual festival of women's music and art, Carter has also been instrumental—but ultimately unsuccessful—in campaigns to unseat North Carolina's right-wing Republican senator, Jesse Helms.

Carter has been more successful with smaller tasks such as lobbying against anti-homosexual legislation in Congress, often sponsored by Senator Helms or Robert Dornan (R-Cal.). She has also worked to combat the Christian Right's attempts to infiltrate African American churches in efforts to stymie support of gay and lesbian rights among the congregations; she has done this work first in her role as liaison and later as the director of the Human Rights Campaign Fund's National Black Gay and Lesbian Leadership Forum. Carter has spoken of her political activism in the 1994 volume, *Uncommon Heroes: A Celebration of Heroes and Role Models for Gay and Lesbian Americans*. In the wake of the presidential election fiasco in Florida, Carter was a field organizer for People for the American Way's investigation into minority voter intimidation. This work did not effect a change in the way that Florida conducts its elections, but it did raise awareness of the continued struggle African Americans and other minority groups still face when attempting to exercise even their most basic civil rights.

Septima Clark. *See* Education chapter.

George Crockett. *See* Law chapter.

Angela Y. Davis (1944–)
Women's Rights Activist, Civil Rights Activist, Professor, Lecturer, Author/Poet, Organization Founder

Angela Yvonne Davis was born on January 26, 1944, in Birmingham, Alabama, to middle-class parents, B. Frank and Sallye E. Davis, who stressed academic excellence, political awareness, and activism. Her mother had been politically active since her college days, and Angela participated in demonstrations with her from the time she was in elementary school. To ensure a better education than she would be able to receive in the segregated schools of the South, her parents sent her to Elizabeth Irwin High School, a private progressive school in New York. The school had many radical teachers and students, and Angela soon joined a Marxist study group.

After graduation, Davis continued to seek high quality education. She majored in French at Brandeis College and studied at the Sorbonne in Paris during her junior year. She then pursued graduate studies in philosophy at the Johann Wolfgang von Goethe University in Frankfurt, West Germany. In 1967, she returned to the United States to study at the University of California at San Diego. When she had almost completed her doctorate degree, she took a teaching job at the University of California at Los Angeles.

In 1969, Davis joined the Communist party; the regents of UCLA tried to fire her, but she fought them in court. The following year she became involved with the Black Panther Party. Guns that she had bought for self-defense were used by a member of the Black Panthers in a courtroom shooting. Believing she was involved, the Federal Bureau of Investigation (FBI) sought her arrest. To avoid the federal authorities Davis went underground. She was placed on the FBI's ten most wanted list and was later arrested. In 1972, she was acquitted of all charges, but was not reinstated by the university. Then-California Governor Ronald Reagan

and the state's board of regents decreed that she would never teach in California again.

Following her trial, Davis founded the National Alliance against Racist and Political Repression, a legal group providing defense of minority prisoners. In 1980 and 1984, she ran for vice president of the United States on the Communist party ticket. A writer and philosopher, Davis has written several books including *If They Come in the Morning* (1971), *Women, Race and Class* (1983), *Violence Against Women and the Ongoing Challenge To Racism* (1985), *Angela Davis: An Autobiography* (1988), and *Women, Culture and Politics* (1989).

During the 1990s, Davis remained politically active and a popular yet controversial figure. Her 1995 appointment as presidential chair in charge of developing new ethnic studies courses at University of California-Santa Cruz was heavily opposed by state Republican legislators concerned with her Communist party affiliation. Much sought after, though often protested against, Davis has lectured around the country about "envisioning a new movement" set apart from the radicalism of the 1960s. She continues to write and to support such causes as women's rights, workers' rights, health care, and nuclear disarmament.

W. E. B. Du Bois (1868–1963)
Organization Executive/Founder, Civil Rights Activist, Professor, Author/Editor

An outstanding critic, editor, scholar, author, and civil rights leader, William Edward Burghardt Du Bois is certainly among the most influential African Americans of the twentieth century. Born in Great Barrington, Massachusetts, on February 23, 1868, Du Bois received a bachelor's degree from Fisk University. Upon completion of his academic career at Fisk, Du Bois entered Harvard University where he earned a second bachelor's degree in 1890; a master of arts degree in 1891; and a Ph.D. degree in 1895, making him the first African American to earn a doctorate degree from Harvard. For a time, Du Bois held teaching positions at Wilberforce University, University of Pennsylvania, and Atlanta University.

One of the founders of the National Association for the Advancement of Colored People (NAACP) in 1910, Du Bois served as that organization's director of publications and editor of *Crisis* magazine until 1934. In 1944, he returned from Atlanta University to become head of the NAACP's special research department, a post he held until 1948. Du Bois emigrated to Ghana in 1961 and became editor-in-chief of the *Encyclopaedia Africana*, his enormous Afrocentric publishing venture that was supported by Kwame Nkrumah, since then deposed as president. Du Bois died in Ghana on August 27, 1963, at the age of 95.

Du Bois's numerous books include: *The Suppression of the African Slave Trade to the United States of America, 1638–1870* (1896); *The Philadelphia Negro* (1899); *The Souls of Black Folk: Essays and Sketches* (1903); *John Brown* (1909); *Quest of the Silver Fleece* (1911); *The Negro* (1915); *Darkwater* (1920); *The Gift of Black Folk* (1924); *Dark Princess* (1928); *Black Folk: Then and Now* (1939); *Dusk of Dawn* (1940); *Color and Democracy* (1945); *The World and Africa* (1947); *In Battle for Peace* (1952); and a trilogy *The Black Flame* (1957–1961). It is this enormous literary output on such a wide variety of themes that offers the most convincing testimony to Du Bois's lifetime position that it was vital for African Americans to cultivate their own aesthetic and cultural values even as they made valuable strides toward social emancipation. In this he was opposed by Booker T. Washington, who felt that African Americans should concentrate on developing technical and mechanical skills before all else.

Du Bois was one of the first male civil rights leaders to recognize the problems of gender discrimination. He was among the first men to understand the unique problems of African American women and to value their contributions. He supported the women's suffrage movement and strove to integrate this mostly white struggle. Additionally, Du Bois championed the reproductive freedom of women and women's economic independence from men. He encouraged many African American female writers, artists, poets, and novelists, featuring their works in *Crisis* and sometimes providing personal financial assistance to them. Several of his novels, most notably *The Quest of the Silver Fleece* and *Dark Princess*, feature women as prominently as men, an unusual approach for an author of his day. Du Bois spent his life working not just for the equality of all men, but for the equality of all people.

Medgar Evers (1925–1963)
Civil Rights Activist

Medgar Evers was one of the first martyrs of the Civil Rights movement. He was born in 1925 in Decatur, Mississippi, to James and Jessie Evers. After serving in the U.S. Army during World War II, he enrolled in Alcorn Agricultural & Mechanical College in Mississippi, graduating in 1952. His first job out of college involved traveling around rural Mississippi and selling insurance. He soon grew enraged at the despicable conditions of poor African American families in his state and joined the Mound Bayou Chapter of the NAACP. In 1954, he was appointed Mississippi's first field secretary.

Evers was outspoken and his demands were radical for his rigidly segregated state. He fought for the enforcement of the 1954 U.S. Supreme Court decision of *Brown v. Board of Education of Topeka, Kansas*, which outlawed school segregation. Evers fought for the right to vote, and he advocated boycotting merchants who discriminated against African Americans. He worked unceasingly despite the threats of violence that his speeches engendered. Evers gave much of himself to this struggle, and in 1963, he gave his life. On June 13, 1963, he drove home from a meeting, stepped out of his car, and was mortally shot in the back.

Immediately after Evers's death, the shotgun that was used to kill him was found in nearby bushes, with the owner's fingerprints still fresh. Byron de la Beckwith, a vocal member of a local white supremacist group, was arrested. Despite the evidence against him, which included an earlier statement that he wanted to kill Evers, two trials with all-white juries ended in deadlock decisions, and de la Beckwith walked free. Twenty years later, in 1989, information surfaced that suggested jury tampering in both trials. The assistant district attorney, with the help of Evers's widow, Myrlie Evers-Williams, began putting together a new case. In 1990, Beckwith was arrested once again. On February 5, 1995, a multiracial jury found him guilty of Evers's assassination and sentenced him to life imprisonment.

Evers did not die in vain. His death changed the tenor of the civil rights struggle. Anger replaced fear in the South, as hundreds of demonstrators marched in protest. His death prompted President John Kennedy to ask Congress for a comprehensive civil rights bill, which due to the assassination of President Kennedy in November of 1963, President Lyndon Johnson signed into law in July of 1964. Evers's death, as his life had, contributed much to the struggle for equality.

Myrlie Evers-Williams. *See* National Organizations chapter.

James L. Farmer Jr. (1920–1999)
Civil Rights Activist, Educator, Organization Founder

James Leonard Farmer Jr., the founder of the Congress of Racial Equality (CORE), was born to James L. Farmer Sr. and Pearl Houston Farmer on January 12, 1920, in Marshall, Texas. He attended public schools throughout the South. He earned his B.S. in chemistry from Wiley College in 1938 and and his B.D. in Sacred Theology from Howard University's School of Divinity in 1941. Active in the Christian Youth movement and

James Farmer, 1990.

once vice-chairperson of the National Council of Methodist Youth and the Christian Youth Council of America, Farmer refused ordination when confronted with the realization that he would have to practice in a segregated ministry.

Farmer became a warrior in the struggle to dismantle America's all-encompassing system of racial segregation. In 1941, Farmer accepted a post as race relations secretary for the Fellowship of Reconciliation. Committed to direct, nonviolent protest, Farmer and a group of University of Chicago students became involved in efforts to desegregate Chicago housing. Later in June 1942, he established CORE, the first protest organization in the United States to utilize the techniques of nonviolence and passive resistance advocated by the Indian nationalist Mohandas Gandhi. In June 1943, CORE staged the first successful sit-in demonstration at a restaurant in the Chicago Loop. The organization soon supplemented this maneuver with what came to be known as the standing-line, which involved the persistent waiting in line by CORE members at places of public accommodation where African Americans had been denied admission.

During the early 1960s, under Farmer's leadership, CORE conducted freedom rides, voter registration drives, and protest marches to eradicate racial segregation. In 1961, CORE introduced the freedom ride into the vocabulary and methodology of civil rights protest, dispatching bus riders throughout the South for the purpose of testing the desegregation of terminal facilities. Attacked in Alabama and later arrested in Mississippi, the Freedom Riders eventually succeeded in securing the court-ordered desegregation of bus terminals in 1960 when the U.S. Supreme Court outlawed segregated interstate transportation.

In 1963, when President John F. Kennedy proposed legislation to enact a civil rights bill eliminating racial segregation in public accommodations, Farmer—along with Martin Luther King Jr., Whitney Young, and Roy Wilkins—was one of the Big Four in the Civil Rights movement of the 1960s. As President Johnson shepherded the civil rights bill through Congress in 1964, three CORE workers—Andrew Goodman, Michael Schwerner, and James Chaney—disappeared while registering African American voters in Philadelphia, Mississippi. Outrage over their deaths and other atrocities suffered by Southern citizens of African descent who attempted to register and exercise their right to vote led to the Voting Rights Act of 1965.

In 1966, James Farmer left CORE after serving as national director for five years. Three years later he joined the administration of President Richard Nixon as assistant secretary for administration in the Department of Health, Education, and Welfare. The appointment created a furor in some African American circles, where it was felt that it was inappropriate for a former civil rights leader to serve in the Nixon administration; in other circles, the appointment was praised by those who thought it necessary for African Americans to be represented in all areas. Farmer found that there was little substance to the position, however, and resigned at the end of 1970. During the 1970s, he developed the think-tank, Council on Minority Planning and Strategy (COMPAS), at Howard University and the Fund for an Open Society, a nonprofit organization that granted low-interest mortgages to people planning to live in desegregated neighborhoods. His first book, *Freedom— When?*, was published in 1976, the same year that he broke all ties with CORE. Criticizing its leader, Roy Innis, for such actions as attempting to recruit African American Vietnam veterans as mercenaries in Angola's civil war, Farmer, along with Floyd McKissick, attempted to meet with Innis to reach an agreement on the future of the organization. These discussions failed. Disturbed over the course that the organization had taken, Farmer and a score of former CORE members attempted to create a new racially mixed civil rights organization in 1980.

Farmer entered the arena of higher education as a visiting professor at Mary Washington College in Fredericksburg, Virginia, in 1985. He also wrote *Lay Bare the Heart* in 1985. Farmer was honored for his civil rights achievements and was awarded nearly 20 honorary degrees. In January 1998, President Bill Clinton presented him with the highest civilian honor, the Presidential Medal of Freedom. Farmer, who had been in ill health, died at Mary Washington Hospital in Fredericksburg, Virginia on July 9, 1999.

Fannie Lou Townsend Hamer (1917–1977)
Lecturer, Civil Rights Activist, Organization Executive/Founder

As a poor sharecropper she had only an elementary education, yet Fannie Lou Hamer was one of the most eloquent speakers for the Civil Rights movement in the South. She worked for political, social, and economic equality for herself and all African Americans; Hamer fought to integrate the national Democratic party, and became one of its first African American delegates to a presidential convention.

The youngest of 20 siblings, Hamer was born on October 6, 1917, to Jim and Lou Ella Townsend in Montgomery County, Mississippi. She began picking cotton at the age of six. Because she had to work full-time, Baker dropped out of school in the sixth grade. She began working on the Marlow plantation as a sharecropper. In 1944, when the plantation's owner, W. D. Marlow, learned she was literate, she was given the job as a time and record keeper on the plantation until 1962. In 1962, she lost her job because she tried to exercise her right to vote. Frightened by threats of violent reprisals, Hamer was forced to move away from her home and her family. Angered into action, she went to work for the Student Non-Violent Coordinating Committee (SNCC), helping many African Americans register to vote.

Because the Democratic party refused to send African Americans as delegates to the national presidential convention in 1964, Hamer and others formed the Mississippi Freedom Democratic Party (MFDP). Arguing that the all-white delegation could not adequately represent their state which had a large African American population, Hamer and the MFDP challenged the Democratic delegates from Mississippi for their seats at the convention in Atlantic City, New Jersey. Hamer's speech on their behalf so alarmed the incumbent President Lyndon Johnson that he tried to block the televised coverage of her efforts. The MFDP lost its bid that year, however, their actions did result in a pledge from the national party not to exclude African Americans as delegates in the 1968 convention. In 1968, Fannie Lou Hamer was among the first African American delegates to the Democratic National Convention.

For the next decade, Hamer remained active in the struggle for civil and economic rights. In 1969, she founded the Freedom Farm Cooperative to help needy families raise food and livestock. They also provided basic social services, scholarships and grants for education, and helped fund minority business opportunities. Hamer became a sought after speaker, and in the 1970s, even as her health was failing from cancer, she still toured the country speaking about civil rights for all. Fannie Lou Hamer Hamer died on March 14, 1977.

Jesse L. Jackson Sr. (1941–)
Religious Leader, Civil Rights Activist, Organization Executive/Founder

Jesse Louis Jackson Sr. was born October 8, 1941, in Greenville, South Carolina. In 1959 Jackson left South Carolina to attend the University of Illinois. Dissatisfied with his treatment on campus, he decided to

Jesse Jackson.

transfer to North Carolina Agricultural and Technical College. After receiving his B.A. in sociology, Jackson attended the Chicago Theological Seminary. In 1968, he was ordained a Baptist minister.

Jackson joined the Southern Christian Leadership Conference (SCLC) in 1965. The following year he became involved with the SCLC's Operation Breadbasket. From 1967 to 1971, Jackson served as the program's executive director. Resigning from the SCLC in 1971, he formed his own organization, Operation PUSH (People United to Save Humanity). Through PUSH Jackson continued to pursue the economic objectives of Operation Breadbasket and expanded into areas of social and political development.

Jackson soon became the most visible and sought after civil rights leader in the country. While he described himself as a "country preacher," his magnetic personality had television appeal. Jackson's command of issues and his ability to reach the heart of matters marked him as an individual of intellectual depth. Of all the civil rights leaders, Jackson was the one who could best relate to the young. In a phrase that became his trademark "I am somebody," Jackson was able to bring out the best in them.

From this came Jackson's PUSH-Excel program that sought to motivate young school children to improve academically. In 1981 *Newsweek* magazine credited Jackson with building a struggling community improvement organization into a nationwide campaign to revive pride, discipline, and the work ethic in inner-city schools. With funding from the Carter administration, the PUSH-Excel program was placed in five other cities.

The Jesse Jackson of the 1980s will be best remembered for his two runs for the Democratic nomination for president of the United States. In 1983, many, but not all, African American political leaders endorsed the idea of an African American presidential candidate to create a "people's" platform, increase voter registration, and have a power base from which there could be greater input into the political process. His 1984 campaign was launched under the aegis of the National Rainbow Coalition, Inc., an umbrella organization of minority groups. African American support was divided, however, between Jackson and former Vice President Walter Mondale. During this campaign, Jackson attracted considerable media coverage with controversial remarks and actions, demonstrating a lack of familiarity with national politics.

The 1988 campaign of Jackson showed enormous personal and political growth; his candidacy was no longer a symbolic gesture but was a real and compelling demonstration of his effectiveness as a candidate.

By the time the Democratic convention rolled around, media pundits were seriously discussing the likelihood of Jackson's nomination as the Democratic presidential candidate. "What to do about Jesse" became the focus of the entire Democratic leadership. At the end of the primary campaign, Jackson had finished a strong second to Massachusetts Governor Michael Dukakis. He changed forever the notion that an African American president in America was inconceivable. Jackson took his defeat in stride and continued to campaign for the Democratic ticket until the November election.

Since the 1988 election, Jackson has worked less publicly, but no less energetically. In 1989, he moved with his Rainbow Coalition from Chicago to Washington, DC, believing that the coalition could be more effective in the nation's capital. Jackson continued to write, speak, and lead protests for social change. His primary concerns included crime, violence, drug use, and teenage pregnancy in inner-city neighborhoods, voter registration, health care, affirmative action, and baseball hiring practices. In 1993, Jackson was awarded the Martin Luther King Jr. Nonviolent Peace Prize.

Jackson was active in foreign affairs as well. In 1991, he traveled to Iraq and convinced Saddam Hussein to begin releasing Americans held hostage after Hussein's invasion of Kuwait. In 1994, Jackson met with Fidel Castro in Cuba and, later during the year, President Bill Clinton sent him on a peace mission to Nigeria. Although many expected him to run for president again in 1992 or 1996, Jackson decided against it, saying that he was too tired and the strain on his family too severe. However, he did support his son, Jesse Jackson Jr., who was elected to the House of Representatives (Chicago's 2nd Congressional District) on December 12, 1995. As the decade was coming to a close, Jesse Jackson Sr. continued to be a civil and human rights activist, as well as a political force in American society. As he had done since the mid-1980s in Syria, Cuba, and Iraq, in May of 1999, the Reverend Jesse Jackson Sr. successfully secured the release of three captive U.S. soldiers held as prisoners of war during the Kosovo crisis.

As the new millennium began, Jackson experienced many ups and downs. He received the nation's highest civilian honor, the Presidential Medal of Freedom, from President Bill Clinton on August 9, 2000. Just months later, in January 2001, it was revealed that Jackson had been involved in an extramarital affair, fathering a daughter with the former head of the Rainbow/PUSH Coalition office in Washington, D.C. The scandal threatened to end his public career, yet Jackson seems to have survived the turmoil. In August 2001, Jackson celebrated the 30th anniversary of his Rainbow/PUSH Coalition with a five-day conference in Chicago.

Coretta Scott King (1927–)
Organization Executive/Founder, Civil Rights Activist, Women's Rights Activist, Lecturer, National/International Diplomat, Educator, Community Activist

As the wife of civil rights leader Martin Luther King Jr., Coretta Scott King was ready to continue his work and perpetuate his ideals after his 1968 assassination. While her primary role in the early years of marriage concerned the rearing of their four children, she became increasingly involved in the struggle for civil rights through her husband's activities. After his death, she quickly became a dynamic activist and peace crusader.

Born on April 27, 1927, to Obie Leonard and Bernice McMurray Scott, King is a native of Marion, Alabama. One of three children, during the Depression she was forced to contribute to the family income by hoeing and picking cotton. Early in life she resolved to overcome adversity, seek equal treatment, and achieve a sound education. In 1945, after graduating from the private Lincoln High School, she entered Antioch College in Yellow Springs, Ohio, on a scholarship, majoring in elementary education and music. A teaching career appealed to her; however, she became disillusioned when she was not allowed to practice teaching in the town's public schools. No African American had ever taught there, and Coretta Scott was not destined to be the first to break the tradition.

Musical training in voice and piano absorbed much of her time. After receiving her undergraduate degree from Antioch College, she continued her studies at the New England Conservatory of Music in Boston, where she earned a Mus.B. in voice. In Boston she met Martin Luther King Jr. and they married on June 18, 1953. An exceptional young minister, King's intense convictions and concern for humanity brought her a measure of rare self-realization early in life. Sensing his incredible dynamism, she suffered no regrets at the prospect of relinquishing her own possible career. The Kings had four children: Yolanda Denise (November 17, 1955); Martin III (October 23, 1957); Dexter (January 30, 1961); and Bernice (March 28, 1963).

Completing her studies in 1954, King moved back south with her husband, who became pastor of Dexter Avenue Baptist Church in Montgomery, Alabama. Within a year, the Reverend King led the Montgomery bus boycott and brought forth a new era of civil rights agitation. Two years later, he helped to organize and was elected head of the Southern Christian Leadership Conference (SCLC).

Over the years King gradually became more involved in her husband's work. She occasionally performed at his lectures, raising her voice in song as he did in speech. She became involved in separate activities as well. In 1962, she served as a Woman's Strike for Peace delegate to the 17-nation Disarmament Conference in Geneva, Switzerland. In the mid-1960s, she sang in the multi-arts Freedom Concerts that raised money for the SCLC. As demands on Martin became too much, she filled the speaking engagements he could not keep. After his assassination, Coretta King kept many of the commitments his death left empty. Soon, however, she became a much sought after speaker in her own right.

King's speech on Solidarity Day, June 19, 1968, is often identified as a prime example of her emergence from the shadow of her husband's memory. In it, she called upon American women to "unite and form a solid block of women power" to fight the three great evils of racism, poverty, and war. Much of her subsequent activity revolved around building plans for the creation of a Martin Luther King Jr. Memorial in Atlanta, which she began to work on in 1969. Located in the Martin Luther King Jr. Historic District and designated a national historic landmark on May 5, 1977, the Martin Luther King Jr. historical site became a unit of the National Park Service in 1980. In the same year that she began developing plans for the Martin Luther King Jr. Center for Nonviolent Social Change, King also penned her autobiography *My Life with Martin Luther King Jr.*, a book of reminiscences.

After years of lobbying to have Dr. King's birthday celebrated as a national holiday, she and others were rewarded for their efforts when in November of 1983, President Ronald Reagan signed the bill creating the King holiday. The following year, Coretta Scott King was elected chair of the Martin Luther King Jr. Federal Holiday Commission, established by Congress to formalize plans for the first legal celebration of the King holiday. Beginning on January 20, 1986, the country celebrated the first Martin Luther King Jr. national holiday.

King's activism has extended beyond the borders of the United States. In the mid-1980s, she and two of her children were arrested for demonstrating against apartheid outside of the South African embassy in Washington, DC. In 1986, she visited South Africa for eight days, meeting with businessmen and anti-apartheid leaders. King has also condemned the human rights violations of the Haitian military regime against Haitian citizens. In 1993, she implored the United Nations to reimpose an embargo against the nation.

The well-respected Martin Luther King Jr. Center for Nonviolent Social Change became embattled in an ugly scuffle with the National Park Service over the issue of how best to utilize some of the historic Atlanta district in which the King memorial is located. As chief executive officer (CEO), King was forced to mediate between the family's desire for an interactive museum with exhibitions and programs for children and the National Park Service's plan for a visitor's center on the same site. The dispute was not resolved until April of 1995, a few months after King had officially stepped down as CEO, handing the reigns of leadership over to her son Dexter, who was unanimously voted the center's director and CEO.

Controversy continued to brew. In 1964, Martin Luther King Jr. had given nearly 83,000 documents, including correspondence and other manuscripts, to Boston University. Coretta King had hoped to regain control of that legacy, but in April of 1995, the Massachusetts Supreme Judicial Court ruled in favor of the university.

On a brighter note, Coretta Scott King remains an eloquent and respected spokesperson on behalf of African American and human rights causes and nonviolent philosophy. She is often recognized for keeping her husband's dream alive. In September of 1995, King, along with two other famous civil rights widows—Myrlie Evers-Williams and Betty Shabazz—were honored for their influence by the National Political Congress of Black Women. King has received numerous honorary degrees from colleges and universities, including, Boston University, Morehouse College, Princeton University, and Bates College.

Dexter King (1961–)
Civil Rights Activist, Organization Executive

The youngest son of the King family, Dexter Scott King was born in Atlanta, Georgia, on January 30, 1961. Dexter's early days were filled with his parents' involvement in the nonviolent Civil Rights movement. Not only did his father participate in the movement, but by the mid-1960s his mother, Coretta Scott King, was heavily involved as well.

King's early education was a blend of both private and public academies. In 1979, he graduated from Atlanta's Frederick Douglass High School, where he was recognized not only as the son of the Reverend Martin L. King Jr., but as an individual with a multifaceted identity. His interests included both music and athletics. Offered an athletic scholarship at the nationally recognized University of Southern California, Dexter opted to study at his father's alma mater, Morehouse College.

Dexter did not follow in his father's footsteps by becoming a Morehouse alumnus. Instead, his interest carried him into the world of music video production.

In collaboration with Phillip M. Jones, he produced a music video in observance of the first nationally celebrated Martin Luther King Jr. holiday. That endeavor led to an album in remembrance of Dr. King. Pop icons Prince, Whitney Houston, Run-DMC, and others rendered musical performances. By 1989, Dexter King returned to the civil rights arena when he was named president of the Martin Luther King Jr. Center for Nonviolent Social Change, while his mother remained as the chief executive officer (CEO). Dexter King only remained as president of the center for four months, concerned that he only served as a titular head. However, with the retirement of Coretta Scott King in 1994, Dexter by a unanimous vote of the board of directors, became president and CEO. He was officially installed in January of the following year.

In March of 1997, Dexter King confronted James Earl Ray, the man convicted of his father's assassination, at the Lois DeBerry Special Needs Facility in Nashville, Tennessee. Dexter King asked Ray if he had assassinated Martin Luther King Jr. Ray stated that he had not, and Dexter began working towards Ray's release from prison. However, 13 months after their meeting, James Earl Ray died of liver failure.

Wanting to educate people about his father's nonviolent philosophy, Dexter King's task is finding the most effectual method to bring his father's message of constructive change into the twenty-first century.

Martin Luther King Jr. (1929–1968)
Religious Leader, Civil Rights Activist, Author/Poet, Labor Activist, Organization Executive/Founder, Minister, Anti-war Activist

Any number of historic moments in the civil rights struggle have been used to identify Martin Luther King Jr.—prime mover of the Montgomery bus boycott (1955–1956), keynote speaker at the March on Washington (1963), and the youngest Nobel Peace Prize laureate (1964). However, in retrospect, single events are less important than the fact that King, and his policy of nonviolent protest, was the dominant force in the Civil Rights movement during its decade of greatest achievement, from 1957 to 1968.

King was born Michael Luther King in Atlanta on January 15, 1929—one of the three children of Martin Luther King Sr., pastor of Ebenezer Baptist Church, and Alberta Williams King, a former schoolteacher. (He did not receive the name "Martin" until he was about six years of age.) After attending grammar and high schools locally, King enrolled in Morehouse College in 1944. At this time he was not inclined to enter the ministry, but while there he came under the influence of Dr. Benjamin Mays, a scholar whose manner and bearing convinced him that a religious career could have its intellectual satisfactions. After receiving his B.A. degree in 1948, King attended Crozer Theological Seminary in Chester, Pennsylvania. Graduating in 1951, King was the recipient of the Plafker Award as the outstanding student of the graduating class and the J. Lewis Crozer Fellowship. In 1951, King entered Boston University to pursue his Ph.D. Two years later, he completed his course work. After completing his dissertation for his doctorate in 1955, King was granted a Ph.D. from Boston University.

Married by then, King returned to the South, accepting the pastorate of the Dexter Avenue Baptist Church in Montgomery, Alabama. It was here that he made his first mark on the Civil Rights movement by mobilizing the African American community during a 382-day boycott of the city's bus lines. Working through the Montgomery Improvement Association, King overcame arrest and other violent harassment including the bombing of his home. In 1956, the U.S. Supreme Court declared the Alabama laws requiring bus segregation unconstitutional, thereby granting African Americans equal access on the buses of Montgomery.

A national hero and a civil rights figure of growing importance, King summoned together 115 African American leaders in 1957 and laid the groundwork for a new civil rights organization, now known as the Southern Christian Leadership Conference (SCLC). Elected its president, he soon sought to assist other communities in the organization of protest campaigns against discrimination and to promote voter-registration activities among African Americans.

After the 1958 publication of his first book *Stride Toward Freedom: The Montgomery Story* and a trip to India the following year, where he enhanced his understanding of the non-violent strategies of Gandhi, King returned to the United States and subsequently resigned as pastor of Dexter Avenue Baptist Church. In 1960, he returned to Atlanta where the headquarters of SCLC was located and became co-pastor, with his father of Ebenezer Baptist Church. A sympathizer with the African American Southern student movement, King spoke at the organizational meeting of the Student Non-Violent Coordinating Committee (SNCC) in April of 1960. He soon garnered criticism from the student activists who were intent on maintaining their independence. King was arrested after participating in a student sit-in at Rich's Department Store in Atlanta on October 19, 1960. Similar to the students, he refused to post bail and was incarcerated with the student protesters. Three years later, in Birmingham, Alabama, where

white officials were known for their anti-African American attitudes, King's nonviolent tactics were put to their most severe test. On April 16, King was arrested during a mass protest for fair hiring practices, the establishment of a biracial committee, and the desegregation of department store facilities. Police brutality (i.e., police dogs and fire hoses) used against the marchers dramatized the plight of African Americans to the nation and the world at large with enormous impact. Although arrested, King's voice was not silenced as he issued his classic "Letter from a Birmingham Jail" to refute the criticism of white clergy. In June of 1963, President Kennedy agreed to put sweeping civil rights legislation before the U.S. Congress.

Later that year King was a principal speaker at the historic August 28 March on Washington, where he delivered the "I Have A Dream" speech, one of the most passionate addresses of his career. At the beginning of the next year, *Time* magazine designated him as its Man of the Year for 1963. A few months later he was named recipient of the 1964 Nobel Peace Prize. Upon his return from Oslo, Norway, where he had gone to accept the award, King entered a new battle in Selma, Alabama, where he led a voter registration campaign which culminated in the Selma-to-Montgomery Freedom March. King next brought his crusade to Chicago where he launched a slum rehabilitation and open housing program.

In the North, however, King soon discovered that young and angry African Americans cared little for his pulpit oratory and even less for his solemn pleas for peaceful protest. Their disenchantment was clearly one of the factors influencing his decision to rally behind a new cause and stake out a fresh battleground: the war in Vietnam. Although his aim was to fuse a new coalition of dissent based on equal support for the peace crusade and the Civil Rights movement, King antagonized many civil rights leaders by declaring the United States to be "the greatest purveyor of violence in the world."

The rift was immediate. The National Association for the Advancement of Colored People (NAACP) saw King's shift of emphasis as "a serious tactical mistake"; the Urban League warned that the "limited resources" of the Civil Rights movement would be spread too thin; Bayard Rustin claimed African American support of the peace movement would be negligible; and Ralph Bunche felt King was undertaking an impossible mission in trying to bring the campaign for peace in step with the goals of the Civil Rights movement.

From the vantage point of history, King's timing could only be regarded as superb. In announcing his opposition to the war and in characterizing it as a "tragic adventure" which was playing "havoc with the destiny of the entire world," King again forced the white middle class to concede that no movement could dramatically affect the course of government in the United States unless it involved deliberate and restrained aggressiveness, persistent dissent, and even militant confrontation. These were precisely the ingredients of the civil rights struggle in the South in the early 1960s.

As students, professors, intellectuals, clergymen, and reformers of every stripe rushed into the movement and, in a sense forcing fiery black militants such as Stokely Carmichael and Floyd McKissick to surrender their control over anti-war polemics, King turned his attention to the domestic issue which, in his view, was directly related to the Vietnam struggle: the War on Poverty. At one point, he called for a guaranteed family income, he threatened national boycotts, and spoke of disrupting entire cities by nonviolent "camp-ins." With this in mind, he began to draw up plans for a massive march of the poor on Washington, DC, envisioning a popular demonstration of unsurpassed intensity and magnitude designed to force Congress and the political parties to recognize and deal with the unseen and ignored masses of desperate and downtrodden Americans.

King's decision to interrupt these plans to lend his support to the Memphis sanitation men's strike was based in part on his desire to discourage violence, as well as to focus national attention on the plight of the poor, unorganized workers of the city. The men were bargaining for little else beyond basic union representation and long overdue salary considerations. Though he was unable to eliminate the violence that had resulted in the summoning and subsequent departure of the National Guard, King stayed in Memphis and was in the process of planning for a march that he vowed to carry out in defiance of a federal court injunction, if necessary. On April 3, 1968, the Reverend Dr. Martin Luther King Jr. rendered his last and most foreboding speech "I See the Promised Land," better known as "I've Been to the Mountaintop." Delivered at (the Bishop Charles H.) Mason Temple, King prophesied his demise.

Death came for King on the balcony of the African American-owned Lorraine Hotel just off Beale Street on the evening of April 4. While standing outside with Jesse Jackson and Ralph Abernathy, a shot rang out. King fell over, struck in the neck by a rifle bullet which left him moribund. At 7:05 P.M. he was pronounced dead at St. Joseph's Hospital. His death caused a wave of violence in more than 100 major cities across the country. However, King's legacy has lasted much longer than the memories of those post-assassination riots. In

1969, his widow, Coretta Scott King, organized the Martin Luther King Jr. Center for Non-Violent Social Change. Today, it stands next to his beloved Ebenezer Baptist Church in Atlanta and, with the surrounding buildings, is a national historic landmark under the administration of the National Park Service. Additionally, the Lorraine Hotel, which is listed in the National Register of Historic Places, now serves as the National Civil Rights Museum.

The only twentieth century American accorded a national holiday, Dr. King's birthday is celebrated each year with educational programs, artistic displays, and concerts throughout the United States.

Martin Luther King III (1957–)
Civil Rights Activist, Community Activist, Political Leader, Organization Executive/Founder

Martin Luther King III, the oldest son and second child of the Reverend and Mrs. Martin L. King Jr., was born in Montgomery, Alabama, on October 23, 1957. Reared in Atlanta, M. L. King III received his primary and secondary education in the schools of Atlanta.

Martin Luther King III.

After completing his secondary studies, King entered Morehouse College majoring in political science and history.

A child of the Civil Rights movement, after graduating from his father's alma mater, King III devoted his energies to voter registration campaigns, lobbying to make his father's birthday a national holiday, and pursuing political office. King, a civil and human rights advocate, has been involved in meaningful policy strategies to provide just and equal treatment to citizens throughout the world.

During the administration of President Jimmy Carter, King represented the president on two official delegations to promote peace in foreign countries. In 1984, as a member of the board of directors of the Martin Luther King Jr. Center for Non-Violent Social Change, he went to five poverty- and drought-stricken African nations on a fact-finding mission. This mission produced an initiative to end starvation in Africa. Later, he focused his energy on the injustices of South Africa's system of racial apartheid and joined in the struggle to gain the freedom of Nelson Mandela.

In 1986, King entered the political arena and was elected to office as an at-large representative on the Fulton County Board of Commissioners. Serving until 1993, his tenancy was characterized by enactments regulating minority business participation in public contracting, ethics, purification of the county's natural water resources, and strict hazardous waste disposal provisions. After leaving office, King returned to public speaking, worked with Atlanta youth groups, and continued to be a community and human rights activist. Later, in response to California's Proposition 209, which outlawed policies of affirmative action, he organized Americans United for Affirmative Action (AUAA). A coalition of national groups, the AUAA's purpose is to safeguard affirmative action programs and to maintain the principles of equal opportunity and diversity championed by the Civil Rights movement. A year after founding AUAA, King was appointed president of the Southern Christian Leadership Conference. The Southern Christian Leadership Conference's fourth president and its first lay person, Martin Luther King III was sworn into office on January 15, 1998. In 2001, despite a strong challenge to unseat him as the SCLC's president, King managed to retain the position. He continues to use the platform to speak out against injustices such as the racial profiling of minorities.

Raised among those who were ardently committed to inclusive civil and human rights and a nonviolent fellowship of humanity; Martin Luther King III infuses and applies the belief system into his personal and public life.

John Lewis. *See* **Politics chapter.**

Harry T. Moore (1905–1951)
Educator, Civil Rights Activist, Organization Founder

One of the unknown warriors to give his life for the cause of civil rights and racial justice, Harry Tyson Moore was born on November 19, 1905, in Suwannee County, Florida, to Johnny and Rosa Tyson Moore. He received his education in the schools of Daytona Beach and Jacksonville, Florida. In 1925, Moore graduated from the Florida Memorial College with a high school diploma. After graduation, he taught school in Cocoa for one year. In 1926, Moore served as principal of Titusville Colored School and later as principal of the Mims Elementary School.

A member of the Florida State Teachers' Association, Moore organized the Brevard chapter of the NAACP in 1934. He investigated lynchings and indescribable deeds of mob brutality and launched a campaign against segregated academies of learning and unequal compensation for African American teachers. In 1944, Moore co-founded and became executive secretary of the Progressive Voters' League. Under his leadership, the league successfully inaugurated a state-wide voter registration drive. Because of Moore's activist role in the struggle for civil rights among African Americans in the state of Florida, the Brevard County officials relieved him of his duties as principal in 1946. In May of the same year, he became the first full-time, paid executive secretary of an NAACP state conference.

As the most visible and outspoken African American leader in Florida, Moore received numerous threats. The 1949 alleged rape of a Groveland white woman by four African American men ignited four days of virulent rioting by unrestrained white mobs in African American neighborhoods. A month after the alleged incident, Moore, to no avail, corresponded with President Harry S Truman and Florida's congressional representatives, calling for a review of the Groveland riots and pressing for a special session of Congress to pass laws to protect the civil rights of African Americans. Because Moore sought justice for the accused individuals, he captured the ire of the Ku Klux Klan. His unrelenting campaign for racial equity also placed him at odds with local government officials. When the U.S. Supreme Court reversed the convictions and death sentences of the remaining two defendants in April of 1951, the simmering embers of hostilities over the Groveland case ignited once again.

In the summer of 1951, Moore earned his bachelor's degree from Bethune-Cookman College. Within months of completing his undergraduate studies, the death threats became an absolute reality. Death came to the ever-vigilant warrior for civil rights on December 25, 1951, when a bomb placed beneath his bed exploded. Harry T. Moore, as recorded by Ben Green in his book *Before His Time: The Untold Story of Harry T. Moore, America's First Civil Rights Martyr*, became the first person to lose his life for what became the modern Civil Rights movement. Recognizing his achievements and sacrifices, in 1952 the NAACP posthumously awarded Harry T. Moore the Spingarn Medal, the organization's highest honor.

In 1991, after evidence came to the forefront, then-Florida's Governor Lawton Chiles ordered a re-investigation of the Moore murder. Ironically, this was the same year that Byron de la Beckwith was re-indicted for the 1965 murder of Medgar Evers. By some accounts, Moore's death is as monumentous as those of Evers, Malcolm X, and Martin Luther King Jr.

Diane J. Nash (1938–)
Civil Rights Activist

In the vanguard of the national civil rights and anti-war movements from 1959 to 1967, Diane Judith Nash was born in Chicago, Illinois on May 15, 1938. Reared in a Catholic middle-class home, she received her primary and secondary education in parochial and public schools of Chicago. Nash began her collegiate career at Howard University. Her transfer to Fisk University in Nashville, Tennessee, projected her into the African American struggle for civil rights.

When Diana Nash arrived in the "Athens of the South," racial segregation permeated Nashville. Her personal encounters with the code of "separate but unequal" led Nash to actively seek rectification. Early in 1959 she attended workshops on nonviolence directed by the Reverend James Lawson, under the agency of the Nashville Christian Leadership Conference, an affiliate of SCLC. Nash became imbued with and an ardent supporter of the direct nonviolent protest philosophy.

In November and December of 1959, Nash was among those who "tested" the racial segregation policy of Nashville's downtown lunch counters. Elected chair of the Student Central Committee, she played a pivotal role in Nashville's student sit-in movement. Before the Nashville students could initiate their first full-scale sit-in, North Carolina A&T students staged a sit-in on February 1, 1960, in Greensboro.

When the Nashville students decided on the "jail—no bail" strategy, Nash stated to the judge, "We feel that if we pay these fines we would be contributing to and

supporting the injustice and immoral practices that have been performed in the arrest and convictions of the defendants." Responding to her April 19 query about the immorality of segregation, Mayor Ben West said that lunch counters should be desegregated. On May 10, 1960, Nashville became the first Southern city to begin desegregating its lunch counters.

In April of 1960, Diane Nash was one of the founding students of the Student Non-Violent Coordinating Committee (SNCC). The following February, she participated in the Rock Hill, South Carolina, protests for desegregation. After being arrested, Nash and the other students refused to pay bail. When CORE's original freedom riders were beaten unmercifully in Alabama and aborted the last leg of the ride to New Orleans, John Lewis and Diane Nash determined that permitting the violence of the white mob to overthrow the nonviolence of the demonstrators conveyed the wrong message to the movement's enemies. Nash accepted the responsibility of coordinating this monumental mission.

In May, Nash coordinated the Freedom Rides from Birmingham, Alabama, to Jackson, Mississippi. Three months later, Nash became the director of the direct-action wing of SNCC. Between 1961 and 1965 she worked for SCLC as a field staff person, organizer, strategist, and workshop instructor. Nash was imprisoned for instructing African American children in the techniques of direct nonviolent protest after moving to Jackson, Mississippi. Holding steadfastly to the principles developed in Nashville, she chose jail rather than pay bail.

Nash's ideas were instrumental in initiating the 1963 March on Washington. She and James Bevel conceptualized and planned the initial strategy for the Selma Right-to-Vote Movement that helped produce the Voting Rights Act of 1965. Nash's civil rights activities led her to the Vietnam peace movement. She continued working for political and social transformation through the 1970s and lectured nationally on the rights of women during the 1980s. Nash continues to lecture across the country. Nonviolence was not a tactic for Diane Nash, an unsung but outstanding woman of the Civil Rights movement of the 1960s. For her it became a way of life.

Edgar Daniel Nixon Sr. (1899–1987)
Labor Leader and Civil Rights Activist

Edgar Daniel Nixon Sr., the fifth of eight children, was born in Montgomery, Alabama, on July 12, 1899, to Wesley and Sue Ann (Chappel) Nixon. Nixon's mother died when he was eight years old and he went to live with his paternal Aunt Pinky in Autauga, Alabama. Because of racially segregation and the distance of the one-room school from his aunt's home, Nixon's school attendance was irregular. At age 14, he became self-supporting and worked in Selma and Mobile, Alabama. Subsequent to working in the Union Station baggage room, Nixon was hired as a sleeping-car porter. Later influenced by A. Philip Randolph, he became a member of the Brotherhood of Sleeping Car Porters.

Randolph recognized and helped Nixon polish his organizational skills. However, he was not the wind that propelled Nixon's desire to stir up forces to effect change for the people in the Confederacy's first capital. When he first met Randolph, Nixon was already involved in local efforts to improve the quality of life for Montgomery's African American citizens. Earlier, he had waged an unsuccessful campaign to secure a swimming pool for African Americans after two children drowned while swimming in a drainage ditch. Notwithstanding, it was his indefatigable contributions toward organizing people in the human struggle that was the whirlwind, which fanned Nixon's motivation.

In 1928, with Walter White and Roy Wilkins serving as counselors, the catalyst for change helped establish state and local National Association for the Advancement of Colored People (NAACP) chapters in Alabama. During his tenure as state and local president, 21 branches were added to the state NAACP, and the local membership increased from 500 to approximately 3,000. In the 1930s, Nixon organized the Montgomery Welfare League to assist disadvantaged persons of color secure governmental assistance. When A. Philip Randolph and Baynard Rustin began organizing the 1941 March on Washington to protest against discrimination in the defense industries, Nixon was part of the process that ultimately caused President Franklin D. Roosevelt to issue Executive Order 8802 establishing the Fair Employment Practices Commission.

Later, during the 1940s, Nixon organized the Montgomery Voter's League; served as president of the Progressive Democratic Association, which successfully addressed the issue of African Americans serving on city's police force. He threatened to file suit against city officials on behalf of Oak Park residents who were suffering from city neglect. Also as president of the NAACP, he attempted to challenge the community's binding rule of conduct on Montgomery's city buses that systemically restricted African American seating. However, Viola White, the plaintiff in the test case died while appeals were adjudicated for ten years subsequent to the 1944 filing. In 1944, Nixon persuaded 750 African Americans to march on the courthouse and demand their right of the franchise. The following year, he became the first African American to run for a

political office since Reconstruction when he campaigned for a county seat on the Montgomery Democratic Executive Committee. The civil rights activist was defeated in that election by only 200 votes.

On December 1, 1955, when Rosa Parks was arrested for refusing to relinquish her bus seat to a white man, E. D. Nixon contacted Clifford Durr, a local white attorney, who found out the charges against Parks and the amount of bail money needed to secure her release. Prior to Raymond Parks's arrival, Nixon paid the $100 bail and had Rosa Parks's trial date set for December 5, 1955. He believed that the Parks case should be tested in the courts to nullify Montgomery's bus segregation laws and that African Americans should boycott the bus company. Although he and others made plans for a proposed boycott the Women's Political Council (WPC) set the wheels in motion. The same day of Parks's trial African American citizens staged a boycott of the city buses organized by Alabama State College English professor Jo Ann Robinson, president of the WPC, and others. The one-day sanction imposed by African Americans against the city's transit company proved successful.

Nixon, the Reverends Ralph Abernathy, H. H. Hubbard, and Edgar N. French met and laid the groundwork for a long-term bus boycott and a new organization, which Abernathy named the Montgomery Improvement Association (MIA). At the organizational meeting of MIA, the Reverend Dr. Martin Luther King was elected as president and Nixon as treasurer. During his two-year tenure personally raised approximately $100,000 and wrote checks amounting to almost $500,000 for the MIA and the boycott. He always recognized local whites who supported the movement. When MIA members were indicted for boycott activities, Nixon was the first to be indicted. Adhering to Baynard Rustin's instructions on how to be arrested and throw law enforcement officials off guard, Nixon did not wait for them to come to his home and arrest him, he gave himself up, which demonstrated to the other indicted individuals how to counterbalance law officials' offensive.

For more than a year, thousands of African Americans in Montgomery with "rested souls and weary feet" refused to ride the buses. Eventually, the loss of revenue and a ruling by the U.S. Supreme Court forced the Montgomery Bus Company to desegregate its buses. The boycott took 65 percent of the bus company's business, which caused it to cut schedules, lay off drivers, and increase fares. The city's merchants lost revenue as well. Announced in November 1956, the *Gayle v. Browder* decision, dissimilar from the *Brown* case, specifically overturned the 1896 *Plessy v. Ferguson* decision because it like *Plessy* explicitly applied to transportation. The bus company not only consented to ending segregation but also agreed to hire African American drivers and treat all customers with equal deference. On December 21, 1956, African Americans boarded Montgomery buses and sat wherever they desired.

During his lifetime, Nixon received hundreds of commendations from state and local governments and national organizations. A self-educated person, he was awarded four honorary doctorates, including one from Alabama State University. In 1975, Nixon was appointed to the U.S. Commission on Civil Rights for the state of Alabama of which he served as vice-president.

Edgar Daniel Nixon Sr., who served as Alabama's change agent and played an important role in the civil rights movement, died on February 27, 1987.

Rosa L. McCauley Parks (1913–)
Aide, Civil Rights Activist

Rosa Parks has been called "the Patron Saint," the spark that lit the fire, and the "mother of the movement." Her courage to defy custom and law to uphold her personal rights and dignity inspired African Americans in Montgomery, Alabama, to fight for their rights by staging one of the longest boycotts in history.

Born Rosa Louise McCauley on February 4, 1913, in Tuskegee, Alabama, she was one of two children born to James and Leona Edwards McCauley. Her mother, a schoolteacher, taught Parks until age 11, when she entered Montgomery Industrial School for Girls. Later, she attended Booker T. Washington High School. After attending segregated schools, she went to the all-African American Alabama State College. In 1932, she married Raymond Parks. Eleven years later, she and her husband joined the local National Association for the Advancement of Colored People (NAACP) chapter. One of the first women to join the NAACP, Parks served as the chapter's secretary from 1943 to 1956. Also a member of the Montgomery Voters League, during the summer of 1955, Parks attended workshops at Highlander Folk School, in Monteagle, Tennessee, which had been active in the civil rights struggle since the 1930s.

On December 1, 1955, as Parks was riding the Cleveland Avenue bus home from work, she was ordered by the bus driver to give up her seat to a white man. When she refused to move, the bus driver threatened to call law enforcement officials. Arrested and fined, her case was the last straw for Montgomery's African American citizenry. They were as tired of being underclass citizens as Parks. The Women's Political Council protested her arrest by organizing a boycott of the buses. A young, unknown minister named Martin Luther King Jr. became immediately involved. Realizing the immensity

of the opportunity to begin dismantling the code of Southern segregation, he and other members of the community organized the Montgomery Improvement Association. African Americans and a few whites transported boycotters to and from work, and they continued, despite opposition from the city and state governments, for 382 days.

Following her trial, upon the advice of her attorneys, Parks refused to pay the $14 fine and court costs. Parks's case was appealed all the way to the U.S. Supreme Court. On December 20, 1956, the country's highest tribunal ruled Montgomery's segregated seating unconstitutional. When the boycott ended the following day, both Parks and King were national heroes. Lasting over a decade, the mass movement of nonviolent social change that started in Montgomery culminated in the Civil Rights Act of 1964, the Voting Rights Act of 1965, and the Fair Housing Act of 1968.

Because of the harassment that Rosa and Raymond Parks received during and after the boycott, in 1957 they and her mother moved to Detroit, Michigan. Working in various capacities, she later became a staff assistant in Congressman John Conyers's Detroit office. Parks continued to be involved in the civil rights struggle, giving speeches and attending marches and demonstrations. She marched on Washington in 1963 and into Montgomery in 1965. Parks has received numerous tributes for her dedication and inspiration: in 1979, she received the NAACP's Spingarn Medal; and in 1980, she became the first woman to receive the Martin Luther King Jr. Nonviolent Peace Prize. As she approached retirement, Parks became involved in other activities, such as the Rosa and Raymond Parks Institute for Self-Development. In 1988, the same year that she retired from U.S. Representative Conyers's office, Detroit's Museum of African-American History unveiled her portrait. Two years later, her birthday was celebrated in Washington's Kennedy Center. In addition to being a recipient of the Presidential Medal of Freedom and the inaugural International Freedom Conductor Award, in April 1999, Congress passed legislation authorizing then-President Bill Clinton to award her the Congressional Gold Medal, the country's highest civilian honor.

The honors continued in January 2001. Parks attended the dedication of Troy State University's Rosa Parks Library and Museum in Montgomery, Alabama, featuring a statue in her likeness and an exhibit recounting her history-making conversation with the bus driver who told her to give up her seat in 1955. That same month, her former home in the South was added to the National Register of Historic Places. In 2002, her life story was retold in a made-for-TV movie starring

Angela Bassett and in Douglas Brinkley's biography, *Mine Eyes Have Seen the Glory*. Meanwhile, Parks remained active in the courts fighting the use of her name in the title of a song by OutKast that she considered offensive. Parks's suit was initially dismissed without trial by a U.S. district court judge in 2000, but the issue was brought before an appeals court for reinstatement in May 2001.

A. Philip Randolph. *See* **National Organizations chapter.**

Jo Ann Gibson Robinson (1912–1992)
Civil Rights Activist, Educator, Author

As president of the Montgomery, Alabama, Women's Political Council during the 1950s, Jo Ann Gibson Robinson was one of the several significant originators of the 1955–1956 Montgomery Bus Boycott. The youngest of 12 children, she was born on April 17, 1912, to Owen Boston and Dollie Webb Gibson, near Culloden, Georgia. The first member of her family to obtain a college degree, Robinson graduated from Fort Valley State College and taught for five years in the Macon public schools. Moving to Atlanta, she earned a master's degree in English from Atlanta University.

In 1949, Robinson joined the faculty of Alabama State College as a professor of English. Later, she joined Montgomery's Dexter Avenue Baptist Church and the Women's Political Council (WPC). A young organization, the WPC was founded in the fall of 1946 by Mary Fair Burks, also a member of Alabama State's English Department. Burks was inspired to organize the WPC after a sermon by the Reverend Vernon Johns, then-pastor of the Dexter Avenue Baptist Church, serving as president of the WPC for four years. Organized to protest racial abuse, the WPC developed a program of political action. The programs consisted of four points: voter registration; protest demonstrations of African American abuse on Montgomery city buses; the education of the young about democracy; and literacy programs.

Because she and others came face to face with the degrading effects of racial abuse by drivers of Montgomery city buses, Robinson and the WPC targeted the racial seating practices. On several occasions, the WPC sought a remedy from city officials about African American seating and the imperious conduct of contemptuous city drivers. A year and a half before Rosa Parks refused to give up her seat, in May of 1954—soon after the unanimous Supreme Court decision in the *Brown v.*

Board of Education of Topeka, Kansas case—Robinson corresponded with Mayor W. A. Gayle and alluded to the possibility of a boycott by African Americans of the city's public transportation system if the abuses did not stop. Resultant to Parks's arrest on December 1, 1955, she played a prominent role in the Montgomery bus struggle. A member of the executive board of the Montgomery Improvement Association (MIA), Robinson wrote the organization's newsletter.

Martin Luther King Jr. described Robinson as "apparently indefatigable, she perhaps more than any other person, was active on every level of the protest." Robinson's 1987 memoir *The Montgomery Bus Boycott and the Women Who Started It* took her and other middle-class women from a footnote status to one of centrality within the narrative for open seating on the buses of Montgomery. Joann Gibson Robinson died five years after the publication of her memoir.

Ruby Doris Smith Robinson (1942–1967)
Civil Rights Activist and SNCC Executive Secretary

Ruby Doris Smith, the second of seven children, was born to John Thomas and Alice Banks Smith in Atlanta, Georgia, on April 25, 1942. Smith grew up in a home where her parents were socially conscious and committed to education. The veracity of American racism was no stranger to Smith. However, the images of African Americans walking during the Montgomery bus boycott that flashed across the electronic media's screen sharply focused her resolve, at a young age, to become an active participant in overthrowing the vestiges of Jim Crow. Her parent's commitment to racial justice became a guiding light as Smith matured into a socially conscious being. Under the tutelage of her parents, who stressed education, Smith completed her secondary education and prepared to enter an institution of higher education.

Smith entered Spellman College in 1959. A year later, she became involved in Atlanta's student sit-in movement. One who was cognizant of her "blackness" during the years of segregation, Smith was motivated by the sit-in movement that was ignited by students at North Carolina A&T College in Greensboro, North Carolina. She protested with her older sister and other students from the Atlanta University Center in their attempt to desegregate Atlanta. In April 1960, she joined other students in Raleigh, North Carolina, as they, under the leadership of Ella Baker, established the Student Nonviolent Coordinating Committee (SNCC). A strong advocate of group-centered rather than leader-centered groups, Baker emboldened the conference attendees to institute their own organization rather than become the student branch of the Southern Christian Leadership Conference (SCLC) or other existing civil rights groups. Smith took to heart Baker's exhortation that the liberation movement was more than "the right to eat hamburgers at a lunch counter."

Smith, like other women supporters in the student sit-in movement, led in the transformation of SNCC from a coordinating office into a cadre of activists devoted to expanding the quest for African American civil rights throughout the South. In February 1961, as students honored the first anniversary of the Greensboro sit-ins, she and Diane Nash were among SNCC members who joined the Rock Hill, South Carolina protests, which included the "jail no bail" approach. The Rock Hill "jail no bail" tactic used by the student protesters served as an emotional leap forward for the civil rights movement. A raison d'être based on the Gandhian philosophy, the Rock Hill solution responded to the movement's fiscal crisis of limited bail money. Additionally, the national SNCC organization blended into a local movement, which was a principle of the grass roots organization that later influenced its system of belief.

Bayard Rustin. *See* **National Organizations chapter.**

Al Sharpton (1954–)
Religious Leader, Community Activist, Sports Manager, Public Relations Manager, Organization Executive/Founder

While being shunned by many middle-class African Americans, Al Sharpton draws support from the ranks of the youth and the disenfranchised. Sharpton was born in 1954 in Brooklyn, New York. At the early age of four, Sharpton began delivering sermons and at the age of 13 he was ordained a Pentecostal minister. During and after high school, Sharpton preached in neighborhood churches and went on national religious tours, often with prominent entertainers. Soon he was befriended by a number of well known and influential African Americans including Congressman Adam Clayton Powell Jr., Jesse Jackson Sr., and singer James Brown.

In 1969, Jackson appointed Sharpton youth director of Operation Breadbasket. Around this same time James Brown made Sharpton one of his bodyguards and soon he was doing promotions for the singer. In 1985, Sharpton married singer Kathy Jordan and soon became involved

with fight promoter Don King. Even though Sharpton promoted boxers and entertainers, he had long before put himself in the public spotlight as a social activist. In 1971, he founded the National Youth Movement (later called the United African Movement) ostensibly to combat drug use. The movement, however, soon became a vehicle for Sharpton to draw attention to himself. He urged children to forsake Christmas in favor of a Kwanzaa celebration and the elderly to protest New York City police tactics.

Sharpton made himself part of the publicity surrounding the Bernard Goetz murder trial (1984), the Howard Beach racial killing (1986), the Tawana Brawley debacle (1987), and the Yusef Hawkins-Bensonhurst killing (1989). In 1988, Sharpton was accused of being an FBI informant and passing on information about Don King, reputed organized crime figures, and various African American leaders. In 1989 and 1990, he was acquitted on charges of income tax evasion and embezzling National Youth Movement funds. In 1991, Sharpton was briefly hospitalized after being stabbed by a man wielding a pocket knife.

On August 2, 1994, Sharpton announced the formation of a new political party. He aimed to counter the Liberal Party by reaching African American voters that traditional, mainstream parties have ignored. Sharpton unsuccessfully ran for the U.S. Senate as a candidate of his own Freedom Party, even participating in that year's New York Democratic primary.

Sharpton continues to emerge as an outspoken national political figure. He made headlines with his protest of the U.S. Navy's use of the island of Vieques, Puerto Rico for military bombing operations. He was arrested on May 1, 2001, for trespassing on the island and was sentenced to a 90- day jail term for the offense. While incarcerated, Sharpton went on a highly publicized hunger strike. Shortly after his release, Sharpton announced that he would form an exploratory committee to evaluate a possible bid for the U.S. presidency in 2004.

Fred Lee Shuttlesworth (1922–)
Civil Rights Activist, Clergyman

Born March 18, 1922 in Mugler, Alabama, Fred L. Shuttlesworth was once referred to as "one of the nation's most courageous freedom fighters" by none other than Dr. Martin Luther King Jr. From his 1956 founding of the Alabama Christian Movement for Human Rights through the historic Birmingham demonstrations of 1963, driven by a sense of divine mission, Shuttlesworth pressured Jim Crow restrictions in Birmingham with radically confrontational acts of bravery.

Rev. Fred Shuttlesworth (center) marching with Rev. Ralph Abernathy (left) and Dr. Martin Luther King Jr. (right) in 1965.

His intensive civil rights campaign pitted him against the staunchly segregationist police commissioner Eugene "Bull" Connor and ultimately brought him to the side of Martin Luther King Jr., and to the inner chambers of the White House during the Kennedy administration. Throughout these struggles, Shuttlesworth demonstrated incredible courage and persistence in the face of peril.

When Shuttlesworth sustained only a bump on the head in the 1956 bombing of his home, members of his church called it a miracle. Shuttlesworth took it as a sign that he would be protected on the civil rights mission that had made him a target that night. Standing in front of his demolished home, Shuttlesworth vigorously renewed his commitment to integrate Birmingham's public facilities and police department. The incident transformed him, in the eyes of Birmingham blacks, from an up-and-coming young minister to a virtual folk hero and, in the view of white Birmingham residents, from obscurity to agitator extraordinaire.

Shuttlesworth earned an associate's degree from Selma University and a bachelor's degree from Alabama State College in 1955; in 1969, he received a doctorate of laws degree from Birmingham Baptist College. He has also received a multitude of awards including: Rosa Parks Award from the Southern Christian Leadership Conference (SCLC), 1963; Excellence Award from PUSH, 1974; Martin Luther King Jr. Civil

Rights Award from the Progressive National Baptists, 1975; and the Founders Award from the SCLC, 1977. Since 1966, Shuttlesworth has served as pastor of the Greater New Light Baptist Church in Cincinnati, Ohio.

Mary Modjeska Monteith Simkins (1899–1992)
Civil Rights Activist, Educator

Modjeska Monteith Simkins was a key leader of African American public health and social reforms, and the civil rights movement in South Carolina. Her association with progressive and vanguard groups and movements on the state, regional, and national levels endowed her with a point of view that surpassed the confines of provincialism in the state of her birth. Simkins served in leadership positions that as a matter of course were unavailable to women in the civil rights movement.

Mary Modjeska Monteith, the oldest of eight children, was born on December 5, 1899 to Henry Clarence and Rachel Evelyn (Hull) Monteith in Columbia, South Carolina. Reared in a family with strong work ethics, a strong commitment to education, and a strong religious tradition, the Monteith children were also given a sense of racial pride and taught to be of assistance to those who were less fortunate. From her mother and aunts she learned that community service was important. They helped organize medical care for tubercular patients through their involvement with the women's auxiliary of the Masons and were active members of the National Association for the Advancement of Colored People (NAACP). Active in the Niagara Movement, which was organized by W. E. B. Du Bois, her mother often read to her children from its journal.

Through her entire academic career (from primary through post-secondary) she attended Benedict College in her native city. In 1921, Monteith earned the A. B. degree. Later, she matriculated at Columbia University in New York and Morehouse College in Atlanta, and earned a graduate degree in public health at the University of Michigan at Ann Arbor. After earning her degree from Benedict College, Monteith taught for a year in the college's teacher-training department; the following year she found employment at Booker T. Washington High School in the elementary education department. It was here that her willingness to confront authority and steadfastly hold to her beliefs emerged and characterized the rest of her life. From 1923 to 1929, Monteith taught mathematics at Booker T. Washington High School. In 1929, she married Andrew Whitfield Simkins, an African American businessman who owned real estate and operated a service station in Columbia. Because Columbia's public school system did not allow married women to teach, Modjeska

Monteith Simkins was forced to resign from her teaching position.

In 1931, Simkins entered the field of public health as the director of Negro Work for the South Carolina Anti-Tuberculosis Association (SCATA), and became the state's only full-time African American health worker. By creating alliances with persons of both European and African descent and raising funds, she made a substantial impact on the health of African Americans in South Carolina. Simkins traveled the state educating people about immunizations, maternity and child-care, and sanitation. She published a newsletter and worked with African American teachers and physicians. It was during her 11-year tenure with the Anti-Tuberculosis Association that she became a political activist working with the NAACP and the Civil Welfare League.

Better known as Modjeska Simkins, in the 1930s she became active with and served as secretary of the Civil Welfare League, an organization that set about to improve municipal conditions for Columbia's African American population. They protested against police brutality, the denial of the right to vote, substandard housing, and a multiplicity of other systemic racially discriminatory practices. One of only two women to serve on the state board, she worked with the Columbia branch of the NAACP as publicity director. In 1939, Simkins was one of the founders of the South Carolina Conference of Branches of the NAACP. Two years later, she was elected head of the publicity committee and a member of the speakers' bureau.

Because the conventional, tradition-bound administrators of SCATA considered Simkins's political activism as seditious, they pressured her to discontinue working with the NAACP. When she refused, they discontinued funding for her position, and in effect fired Simkins in 1942. Released from employment, the independent-minded and outspoken Columbia activist came into her own as an agitator for civil rights. The same year of her release from SCATA, Simkins was elected state secretary, a position she held until 1957.

During the time that Simkins held elective office, the South Carolina NAACP undertook lawsuits on behalf of the state's African American populace. The first lawsuit that the civil rights organization undertook concerned equalization of teachers' salaries across the state. When the movement for equity pay for African American teachers was launched in 1943, Simkins was the only woman on a committee of four appointed to raise funds to support the lawsuit. Once the NAACP's Teachers Defense Fund was established, she served as secretary of the project. In 1944, African American teachers won their case in Charleston. The following year, Columbia teachers won a similar case and Simkins actively worked with the city's teachers.

After the NAACP won the teachers' salary cases, it focused its attention on dismantling South Carolina's white primary. In the cases regarding the right of the franchise for African Americans, Simkins participated in planning in-court proceedings and attended courthouse sessions. She kept attorneys abreast of points they might have missed and financially supported George Elmore, the plaintiff in the first voting rights case of *Elmore v. Rice*, which was won in 1947. However, the state's Democratic party instituted strategies to get around the ruling. In an attempt to establish full voting rights for African Americans in South Carolina, the NAACP adjudicated a second case, *Brown v. Baskins,* which it won in July 1948. The same year that the NAACP won the *Elmore v. Rice* case, it filed suit against Clarendon County in an attempt to force the state to provide bus transportation for black as well as white students, which was thrown out on a technicality. Later, however, the case became a demand to end racially segregated education.

The most significant civil rights case in which Simkins played a major role was the suit brought by the NAACP to end racial segregation in South Carolina's public schools and, ultimately, the country's public schools. As secretary, Simkins, the civil rights advocate, assisted Clarendon County's NAACP chapter president, the Reverend Joseph A. Delaine, compose the statement for the school lawsuit that became the *Briggs v. Elliott* case. This case later became one of the five desegregation suits grouped together by the U.S. Supreme Court and decided as the historic 1954 *Brown v. Board of Education of Topeka, Kansas* case. The *Brown* case overturned the Court's 1896 *Plessy v. Ferguson* decision, nullifying its "separate but equal" doctrine and terminating racial segregation in the nation's public schools.

Simkins was active in many organizations that fought against racial discrimination, injustice, and intolerance on the local, regional, and national levels. She worked with political actions groups such as the Columbia Women's Council and the Richland County Citizens Committee. She participated in regional organizations such as the Commission on Interracial Cooperation, the Southern Regional Council, the Southern Conference on Human Welfare, the Southern Organizing Committee for Economic and Social Justice, and the Southern Negro Youth Congress. On the national level, Simkins was a member of the Civil Rights Congress, the National Negro Congress, and the United Negro and Allied Veterans of America.

Considered the matriarch of South Carolina's civil rights movement, Mary Mojeska Monteith Simkins, the woman who could not be bought or sold, died on April 5, 1992. As articulated by Judge Matthew J. Perry during her memorial service, "[She] will be remembered as a woman who challenged everyone. She challenged the white leadership of the state to what was fair and equitable among all people and she challenged black citizens to stand up and demand their rightful place in the state and the nation."

Mabel K. Staupers. *See* **Science & Technology chapter.**

Leon H. Sullivan (1922–2001)
Civil Rights Activist, Organization Founder

Leon Howard Sullivan was born October 16, 1922, in Charleston, West Virginia. Reared by his grandmother after his parents' divorce, Sullivan attended Charleston's segregated elementary and secondary schools. After being ordained a Baptist minister at the age of 17, Sullivan earned a B.A. from West Virginia State College (1943) and an M.A. from Columbia University (1947). He also attended the Union Theological Seminary (1945) and earned a D.D. from Virginia Union University.

At age 21, during the first March on Washington movement (1941–1942) organized by A. Philip Randolph, Leon Sullivan was elected president of the South Orange Council of Churches. As president, Sullivan worked with civil rights leaders such as Bayard Rustin. From 1950 to 1988 Sullivan was the pastor of the Zion Baptist Church in Philadelphia. While there he entered into a lifelong crusade to provide better job opportunities for African Americans. Using the method of direct nonviolent action taught him by Randolph, Sullivan fought racist hiring practices through protest and economic boycott of Philadelphia businesses that employed too few African American employees. Sullivan's campaign experienced some success, but businesses requested workers with technical skills that few African Americans possessed. A promoter of economic self-determination, he provided job training through the Opportunities Industrialization Center. Opening in 1964 with money from a Ford Foundation grant, the Center offered training in electronics, cooking, power-sewing, and drafting. By 1980, the O.I.C. operated programs in 160 cities. Sullivan also founded Zion Investment Associates, which makes seed money available for new African American business ventures. His acceptance within the business community is well symbolized by his long-time membership on the boards of General Motors and Philadelphia's Girard Bank, as well as his association with Progress Aerospace Inc. and Mellon Bank.

Author of *Build Brother Build*, Sullivan is a recipient of the Russwurm Award (National Publisher's Association, 1963); the Philadelphia Fellowship Communion Award (1964); the Philadelphia Book Award (1966); the American Exemplar Medal (1969); the NAACP's Spingarn Medal (1971); and the Franklin D. Roosevelt Four Freedom Medal (1987). In 1991, he received the Presidential Medal of Freedom and the Distinguished Service Award, the Ivory Coast's highest honor.

In the mid-1970s, Sullivan devised the "Sullivan Principles," which successfully encouraged American-owned companies in South Africa to hire more black workers and to treat them equitably in relation to promotions and working conditions. Upon retiring from the Zion Baptist Church in 1988, Sullivan was made pastor emeritus and concentrated his energies on concerns in Africa, especially South Africa's system of apartheid. He called upon American corporations to sell their South African investments and petitioned the U.S. government to bring sanctions against the racially-biased country. Sullivan, however, parted company with President Reagan's "constructive engagement" policy toward South Africa and, in 1987, endorsed a policy of South African divestment. In the same year, Sullivan received the Franklin D. Roosevelt Four Freedoms Medal. Because of Sullivan's efforts, the departure of international businesses, and the sweeping institution of international sanctions, the shackles of South Africa's system of racial segregation were unchained. He founded the International Foundation for Education and Self-Help to combat illiteracy, famine, and joblessness in Africa and to advance the concept of African self-reliance. In April of 1991, Sullivan organized and co-chaired the first African and African American Summit held at Abidjan, Ivory Coast. Six months later, he officiated at the United Nations Day for Africa, a function he inaugurated to bring attention to the issue of debt relief for sub-Saharan African countries.

Leon Howard Sullivan died of leukemia on April 24, 2001, in Scottsdale, Arizona. A pathfinder, Sullivan's achievements made lasting universal contributions to the improvement of humankind throughout the world.

Mary E. Church Terrell (1863–1954)
Organization Executive/Founder, Civil Rights Activist

Mary Eliza Church Terrell, born on September 23, 1863, in Memphis, Tennessee, was the oldest of Robert and Louisa Ayers Church's two children. Because of the racial climate in her native city and its deficient educational facilities for African American children, Church's parents enrolled her in the Antioch College "Model School" in Yellow Springs, Ohio. She attended

Mary Eliza Church Terrell.

articles denouncing racial segregation. Writing under the pseudonym Euphemia Kirk, which she soon discarded, Terrell's treatises were covered in the national and international media. Terrell sought redress for the three companies of African American soldiers dismissed after the 1906 outbreak of racial violence in Brownsville, Texas. In 1909, she was one of two African American women who signed the "Call" for the organizational meeting of the National Association for the Advancement of Colored People. During the Women's Suffrage Movement, Terrell worked with other women for the 1920 ratification of the Constitution's Nineteenth Amendment. In 1940, she wrote her autobiography, *A Colored Woman in a White World.*

After World War II, Terrell aggressively fought racial discrimination. In 1950, she filed suit against Thompson's Restaurant in Washington, DC, for not adhering to the city's 1872 and 1873 public accommodation laws. As chair of the Coordinating Committee for the Enforcement of the District of Columbia Anti-Discrimination Laws, Terrell focused on other segregated facilities. At age 89, she led the picket lines. On June 8, 1953, the Supreme Court ruled Washington's segregated eating facilities unconstitutional in the *District of Columbia v. John R. Thompson* case. This ardent activist fought more than 66 years for gender and racial equality. Mary Church Terrell died on July 24, 1954, two months after the Supreme Court case of *Brown v. Board of Education of Topeka, Kansas* ruled segregation unlawful.

William M. Trotter (1872–1934)
Organization Executive/Founder, Civil Rights Activist, Publisher

William Monroe Trotter was born to James Monroe and Virginia Issacs Trotter on April 7, 1872, near Chillicothe, Ohio. Reared in predominantly white suburban Hyde Park near Boston, he attended and excelled academically at Hyde Park Grammar School and Hyde Park High School. In 1891, Trotter entered Harvard, where he became the university's first African American Phi Beta Kappa. He graduated magna cum laude in 1895 with a B.A. degree. In 1899, after working for various employers, Trotter started his business venture as an insurance agent and mortgage negotiator. Two years later, he, along with William H. Scott and George W. Forbes, founded the *Guardian.* A militant newspaper, it addressed the needs and aspirations of African Americans and served as an organ against racial discrimination. The same year that he co-founded the newspaper, Trotter married Geraldine Louise Pindell who assisted in publishing the *Guardian.*

the public schools in Yellow Springs and in 1879 completed her secondary education in Oberlin, Ohio. Church earned her bachelor's degree from Oberlin College in 1884. The following year she accepted a faculty position at Wilberforce College in Xenia, Ohio. After two years at Wilberforce, Church joined the Colored High School faculty in Washington, DC. She married Robert Heberton Terrell on October 18, 1891. Residing in Washington, the Terrells became the parents of two children, their daughter Phyllis, and Mary, an adopted daughter.

Terrell became active in the feminist movement and founded the Colored Women's League in 1892. Later, this organization merged with the Federation of Afro-American Women and became the National Association of Colored Women (NACW). Organized in 1896, she was elected its first president. In 1895, Terrell was appointed to the school board in the District of Columbia and served until 1901. Her appointment was the country's first for a woman of color. Reappointed in 1906, she held the position for five years.

By 1901, Terrell operated as a leader outside the sphere of women's organizations. She wrote numerous

William Monroe Trotter.

An ideological opponent of the "Wizard of Tuskegee," in 1903, Trotter deliberately disrupted a meeting in Boston at which Booker T. Washington was advocating support of segregation. Subsequently, in 1905, Trotter joined W. E. B. Du Bois in founding the Niagara Movement. However, he refused to move with Du Bois into the National Association for the Advancement of Colored People because he felt it would be too moderate. Neither could he accept the financial and leadership role assumed by whites. Instead, Trotter formed the Negro Equal Rights League. In protest against the segregation policies of President Woodrow Wilson, Trotter led a delegation to the White House to meet with Wilson in 1914. After a heated debate between Trotter and the president, Wilson ordered the group to leave. The following year, he led demonstrations against the showing of D.W. Griffith's racist film *The Birth of a Nation* that glorified the Ku Klux Klan. In 1919, Trotter appeared at the Paris Peace Conference in an unsuccessful effort to have it outlaw racial discrimination. Although the State Department had denied him a passport to attend the conference, he had reached Paris nonetheless by working as a cook on a ship.

Because of his strident unwillingness to work with established groups, chroniclers of the Civil Rights movement have been slow to recognize Trotter. However, many of his methods were adopted in the struggle for racial equality and justice in the late 1950s and 1960s, notably his use of nonviolent protest. Arrested numerous times, Trotter's purpose for consistent direct protest was to eradicate the virulent malevolence of racial segregation.

Booker T. Washington (1856–1915)
Lecturer, Civil Rights Activist, Educational Administrator, Professor, Organization Executive/ Founder, Author/Poet

Booker Taliaferro Washington was born a slave in Hale's Ford, Virginia, on April 5, 1856, to Jane Ferguson, a bonded person. The first nine years of Washington's life was spent in slavery on the farm of James Burroughs, the place of his birth. After emancipation, his family was so poverty stricken that he worked in salt furnaces and coal mines from age nine. Attending school sporadically in Malden, West Virginia, Booker added the surname Washington. Always an intelligent and curious child, he yearned for an education and was frustrated when he could not receive one locally. When he was 16 years of age, his parents allowed him to quit work to go to school. They had no money to help him, so he walked 200 miles to attend the Hampton Institute in Virginia and paid his tuition and board there by working as the janitor.

Dedicating himself to the idea that education would raise his people to equality in this country, Washington became a teacher. He first taught in his hometown, then at the Hampton Institute, and in 1881, he founded the Tuskegee Normal and Industrial Institute in Tuskegee, Alabama. As head of the Institute, he traveled the country constantly to raise funds from both African Americans and whites; soon he became a well-known speaker.

In 1895, Washington was asked to speak at the opening of the Cotton States Exposition, an unprecedented honor for an African American man. His Atlanta Compromise speech explained his major thesis, that African Americans could secure their constitutional rights through their own economic and moral advancement rather than through legal and political changes. Although his conciliatory stand angered some African Americans who feared it would encourage the foes of equal rights, whites approved of his views. Thus his major achievement was to win over diverse elements among Southern whites, without whose support the programs he envisioned and brought into being would have been impossible. Washington penned two autobiographies: *The Story of My Life and Work* (1900) and *Up From Slavery* (1901).

In addition to Tuskegee Institute, which still educates many today, Washington instituted a variety of programs for rural extension work and helped to establish the National Negro Business League. Shortly after the election of President William McKinley in 1896, a movement was set in motion to name Washington to a cabinet post, but he withdrew his name from consideration, preferring to work outside the political arena. One of the most significant leaders among African Americans in the early twentieth century, Booker T. Washington died on November 14, 1915.

Ida B. Wells-Barnett (1862–1931)
Journalist, Lecturer, Civil Rights Activist, Anti-lynching Crusader, Feminist

The oldest of James and Elizabeth Warenton Wells's eight children, Wells-Barnett was born a slave in Holly Springs, Mississippi, on July 16, 1862. The yellow fever epidemic of 1878 claimed the lives of her parents and

Ida B. Wells-Barnett.

youngest brother. At the age of 16, Wells-Barnett assumed responsibility for her siblings. Leaving Shaw University (now Rust College) and passing a teachers' examination, she briefly taught in rural Mississippi to support her brothers and sisters. Wells-Barnett moved to Memphis, Tennessee, and taught in the county and city public school systems.

A train ride from Memphis to Woodstock was the beginning of Wells-Barnett's lifelong public campaign against the injustices faced by African Americans throughout the South. In 1884, after being forcibly removed from the first-class ladies' coach, she filed suit against the Chesapeake, Ohio and Southwestern Railroad. Although she won in the Memphis Circuit Court, the state's Supreme Court reversed the lower court's decision in 1887 because the railroad company had satisfied Tennessee's 1881 statutory requirements to provide "separate but equal" accommodations.

Wells-Barnett published accounts of her experience in the local African American press and wrote for the African American press throughout the country. In 1889, she was elected secretary of the Afro-American Press Association. Wells-Barnett's editorials critical of the Memphis Board of Education led to her dismissal as teacher in 1891. Afterwards, she became a full-time journalist and editor. The March 9, 1892, lynching of three African American male proprietors of the People's Grocery Store caused Wells-Barnett to declare journalistic war on lynching. When her protest writings outraged white men in the South, a mob destroyed her newspaper office on May 27, 1892, and she was banished from the region.

Wells-Barnett moved to New York and continued her struggle against racial injustice and lynching as a columnist for the *New York Age*, edited by T. Thomas Fortune. On June 7, 1892, the *New York Age* published her detailed analysis of lynching, refuting the myth that, by killing African American men, white men intended to shield white women against rape. Her detailed statistics and findings formed the basis of two pamphlets *Southern Horrors* (1892) and *A Red Record* (1895). Lecturing in Great Britain in 1893 and 1894, Wells-Barnett internationalized her anti-lynching campaign.

In 1893, Wells-Barnett focused her attention on the exclusion of African Americans from the World's Columbian Exposition in Chicago. Working with Frederick Douglass, Ferdinand Lee Barnett, and I. Garland Penn, Wells-Barnett co-wrote an 81-page pamphlet entitled *The Reason Why the Colored American is Not in the World's Columbian Exposition—The Afro-American's Contribution to Columbian Literature.* Later in the year, she moved to Chicago and began working for the *Chicago Conservator*, the first African American newspaper in the city, founded by Barnett.

On June 27, 1895, Ida B. Wells-Barnett married Ferdinand L. Barnett and they became the parents of four children. Domesticity did not detract Wells-Barnett from her crusade. Her militant views and support of Marcus Garvey caused her to be branded a radical by the U.S. Secret Service. Wells-Barnett continued to write articles and participate in local and national affairs. In 1898, she and others met with President William McKinley to seek redress for the lynching of an African American postmaster in South Carolina. They also urged passage of a federal anti-lynching bill.

Wells-Barnett was one of two African American women who signed the "Call" for a conference on the Negro. Convening on May 31, 1909, the conference led to the formation of the National Association for the Advancement of Colored People (NAACP).

A champion of women's rights, Wells-Barnett was one of the founders of the National Association of Colored Women. Believing in the power of the ballot box, she founded the Alpha Suffrage Club of Chicago. As a delegate to the National American Woman Suffrage Association's parade in Washington, DC, Wells-Barnett refused to march in the back of the procession. She desegregated the parade by joining the Illinois delegation. Wells-Barnett actively campaigned for Oscar DePriest, the first African American elected as an alderman in Chicago. In 1930, she made an unsuccessful bid for an Illinois State Senate seat.

With a passion for justice, Ida B. Wells-Barnett fought for civil and human rights. One of the most important persons of the late nineteenth and early twentieth centuries, she actively participated in the struggle from the 1890s until her death on March 25, 1931.

Malcolm X. *See* **Black Nationalism chapter.**

Andrew Young. *See* **Politics chapter.**

◆ FEDERAL AND STATE CIVIL RIGHTS AGENCIES

Federal Agencies

Equal Employment Opportunity Commission
1801 L St., NW
Washington, DC 20507
(202)663–4900

U.S. Commission on Civil Rights
624 Ninth St., NW
Washington, DC 20425
(800)552–6843

State Agencies

Alabama Attorney General's Office
State House
11 South Union Street, Third Floor
Montgomery, AL 36130
(334)242–7300

Alaska Human Rights Commission
800 A St., Ste. 2024
Anchorage, AK 99501–3669
(907)274–4692

Arizona Attorney General's Office
1275 W. Washington St.
Phoenix, AZ 85007
(602)542–5025

Arkansas Attorney General's Office
323 Center St., Ste. 200
Little Rock, AR 72201
(501)682–2007

California Attorney General
1300 I St., Ste. 1101
PO Box 944255
Sacramento, CA 94244–2550
(916)322–3360

California Fair Employment and Housing Commission
611 West Sixth Street, Ste. 1500
Los Angeles, CA 90017
(800)884–1684

Colorado Attorney General's Office
1525 Sherman St., 7th Fl.
Denver, CO 80203
(303)866–4500

Connecticut Attorney General's Office
P.O. Box 120
Hartford, CT 06141–0120
(860)808–5318

Delaware Attorney General's Office
Carvel State Office Bldg.
820 N. French St.
Wilmington, DE 19801
(302)577–8400

Florida Attorney General's Office (Legal Affairs Dept.)
The Capitol
Tallahassee, FL 32399–1050
(850)414–3300

Georgia Equal Opportunity Commission
710 Cain Tower
229 Peachtree St.
Atlanta, GA 30303
(404)656–1736

Hawaii Attorney General's Office
425 Queen St.
Honolulu, HI 96813
(808)586–1500

Idaho Human Rights Commission
1109 Main St., 4th Floor
P.O. Box 83720
Boise, ID 83720–0040
(208)334–2873

Illinois Human Rights Department
100 W. Randolph St.
Ste. 10–100
Chicago, IL 60601
(312)814–6200

Indiana Civil Rights Commission
Indiana Government Ctr. North
100 N. Senate Ave., Rm. N-103
Indianapolis, IN 46204–2211
(317)232–2600

Iowa Human Rights Department
Lucas State Office Bldg.
Des Moines, IA 50319
(515)281–7300

Kansas Human Rights Commission
851S Landon State Office Bldg.
900 SW Jackson St.
Topeka, KS 66612–1252
(785)296–3206

Kentucky Human Rights Commission
332 W. Broadway, Ste. 700
Louisville, KY 40202
(502)595–4024

Louisiana Attorney General's Office
Justice Dept.
PO Box 94005
Baton Rouge, LA 70804–9005
(225)342–7013

Maine Human Rights Commission
51 State House Station
Augusta, ME 04333–0051
(207)624–6050

Maryland Human Relations Commission
Sixth St. Paul St., Ste. 900
Baltimore, MD 21202
(410)767–8600

Massachusetts Attorney General's Office
One Ashburton Pl., Rm. 2010
Boston, MA 02108–1698
(617)727–2200

Michigan Attorney General's Office
G. Mennen Williams Building, 7th Floor
525 W. Ottawa Street
PO Box 30212
Lansing, MI 48909
(517)373–1110

Michigan Civil Rights Department
Manpower Bldg., Ste. 101
741 N. Cedar Street
Lansing, MI 48906
(517)334–9335

Minnesota Human Rights Department
Army Corps of Engineers Centre
190 E. Fifth St., Ste. 700
St. Paul, MN 55101
(651)296–5663

Mississippi Attorney General's Office
PO Box 220
Jackson, MS 39205
(601)359–3680

Missouri Human Rights Commission
3315 W. Truman Blvd.
PO Box 1129
Jefferson City, MO 65102–1129
(573)751–3325

Montana Attorney General's Office
Justice Bldg.
215 N. Sanders
PO Box 201401
Helena, MT 59620–1401
(406)444–2026

Nebraska Equal Opportunity Commission
301 Centennial Mall South, 5th Fl.
PO Box 94934
Lincoln, NE 68509–4934
(402)471–2024

Nevada Equal Rights Commission
1515 E. Tropicana Ave., Ste. 590
Las Vegas, NV 89119–6522
(702)486–7161

New Hampshire Human Rights Commission
Two Chenell Dr.
Concord, NH 03301–8501
(603)271–2767

New Jersey Attorney General's Office
Justice Complex
PO Box 080
Trenton, NJ 08625–0080
(609)292–4925

New Mexico Department of Labor
Human Rights Division
1596 Pacheco Street
Santa Fe, NM 87505
(800)566–9471

New York Human Rights Division
One Fordham Plaza, 4th Floor
Bronx, NY 10458
(718)741–8400

North Carolina Human Relations Commission
217 W. Jones St., 4th Fl.
Raleigh, NC 27603–1336
(919)733–7996

North Dakota Attorney General's Office
State Capitol
600 E. Boulevard Ave., Dept. 125
Bismarck, ND 58505–0040
(701)328–2210

Ohio Civil Rights Commission
1111 E. Broad St., 3rd Floor
Columbus, OH 43205–1379
(614)466–2785

Oklahoma Human Rights Commission
2101 N. Lincoln Blvd., Rm. 480
Oklahoma City, OK 73105
(405)521–2360

Oregon Attorney General's Office
Justice Department
Justice Bldg., 1162 Court St., NE
Salem, OR 97310–4096
(503)378–4400

Pennsylvania Human Relations Commission
301 Chestnut Street, Ste. 300
Harrisburg, PA 17101
(717)787–4410

Rhode Island Human Rights Commission
10 Abbott Park Pl.
Providence, RI 02903–3768
(401)222–2661

South Carolina Human Affairs Commission
2611 Forest Drive, Ste. 200
PO Box 4490
Columbia, SC 29240
(803)737–7800

South Dakota Attorney General's Office
State Capitol
500 E. Capitol Ave.
Pierre, SD 57501–5070
(605)773–3215

Tennessee Human Rights Commission
530 Church St., Ste. 400
Cornerstone Square Bldg.
Nashville, TN 37243–0745
(615)741–5825

Texas Attorney General's Office
Price Daniel Sr. Bldg.
PO Box 12548
Austin, TX 78711–2548
(512)463–2100

Utah Attorney General's Office
236 State Capitol
Salt Lake City, UT 84114–0810
(801)366–0260

Vermont Attorney General's Office
Pavilion Office Bldg.
109 State St.
Montpelier, VT 05609–1001
(802)828–3171

Virginia Human Rights Council
Ste. 1202, Washington Bldg.
1100 Bank St.
Richmond, VA 23219
(804)225–2292

Washington Human Rights Commission
711 S. Capitol Way, Ste. 402
PO Box 42490
Olympia, WA 98504–2490
(360)753–6770

West Virginia Human Rights Commission
1321 Plaza East, Room 108A
Charleston, WV 25301–1400
(304)558–2616

Wisconsin Attorney General's Office
PO Box 7857
Madison, WI 53707–7857
(608)266–1221

Wyoming Attorney General's Office
123 Capitol Building
200 W. 24th Street
Cheyenne, WY 82002
(307)777–7841

8

Black Nationalism

◆ The Ideology of Black Nationalism ◆ Early Black Nationalism in the United States
◆ Black Nationalism in the Twentieth Century
◆ Black Nationalists and Pan-African Theorists

by Raymond A. Winbush

◆ THE IDEOLOGY OF BLACK NATIONALISM

Black nationalism is the ideology of creating a nation-state for Africans living in the *Maafa* (a Kiswahili term used to describe the continued suffering of Africans throughout the world). Black nationalism is expressed orally and in writing with its core philosophy being the cultural and political return of African people to a place that would allow for complete self-determination in all aspects of their lives. The earliest protests against American slavery had black nationalistic overtones as evidenced by written narratives that emerged during the last half of the eighteenth century. The nineteenth century would see attempts to establish self-governing homelands for Africans in the *Maafa* that continue today in the United States and Africa. At the core of all black nationalist philosophy is resistance to either cultural or political assimilation into Western culture. The expression of this resistance was seen in revolts of Africans during the Middle Passage within certain countries where displaced Africans resided.

African nationalism is distinguished from Pan-Africanism with the former describing political ideology focusing on Africa, and the latter describing its expression by Africans throughout the *Maafa*. Kwame Nkrumah, Julius Nyerere, and Jomo Kenyatta advocated an "Africa for Africans" when they rebelled against colonialism during the twentieth century. Their ideological ancestors were Paul Cuffe, Martin Delany, Alexander Crummell, and other Pan-Africanists who linked black freedom with Africa.

Since their forced removal from Africa, Africans in the *Maafa* created political and cultural representations of their yearning to return. These creations were often mythological as in the folklore of captured Africans who felt that they could literally fly back to Africa.

Beginning with the horrors of the Middle Passage, Africans created a folklore that emphasized joining forces with their ancestors to defeat their European captors. The oft-repeated but mistaken notion that most of the Africans who jumped from the ships during the Middle Passage were committing suicide ignores the fact that emerging from the folk traditions of many of the captives was the belief that they would reunite with their drowned ancestors and revolt against their enslavers. Similar resistance was seen in the members of the Igbo tribe, who upon being removed from the hull of a slave ship bringing them to the Georgia Sea Islands in 1803 marched slowly but deliberately into the cold Atlantic Ocean and drowned themselves rather than undergo the humiliation of slavery. The resistance aspect of black nationalism is often disconnected from the history of black nationalism, but it is fundamental in understanding how Africans responded to slavery and its aftermath. It explains how the Underground Railroad was a sophisticated resistance movement created by blacks to obtain their freedom, and that while whites participated at several levels, the movement was led by the notion of black self-determination—the cornerstone of black nationalism.

Nationalistic revolts on slave ships frequently took place, reaching their zenith in 1839 with the *Amistad* incident. Sengbe Pieh (renamed Joseph Cinque by his captors), a Mende farmer from Sierra Leone, mutinied aboard the Spanish ship and told its captain to return the ship and its human cargo to Africa. The incident, which garnered international attention, illustrated how black nationalism is more than a political ideology. It is a philosophy centered on resistance and self-determination. It is rooted in the desire for liberation and is reflected in movements as diverse as the Universal

417

Negro Improvement Association of Marcus Garvey, the notion of a unified Africa in the writings of George Padmore, and the Haitian revolution in 1789 led by Touissant L'Ouverture. In Europe, black nationalist thought appeared in the writings of several Africans captured during the Middle Passage. In British African Olaudah Equiano's best-selling book of 1789, *The Interesting Narrative of the Life of Olaudah Equiano, or Gustavus Vassa, the African. Written by Himself,* Equiano saw the return of Africans to Africa as critical to their future.

◆ EARLY BLACK NATIONALISM IN THE UNITED STATES

Most historians consider Paul Cuffe the father of black nationalism in the United States. One of the wealthiest men in the American colonies, Cuffe believed that "commerce furnished to industry more ample rewards than agriculture" and turned to shipbuilding as an expression of his belief. Cuffe acquired enormous wealth after the American Revolutionary War. The crews on his ships were always black, demonstrating Cuffe's belief that the best proof of black excellence was to show that they could manage, work exclusively with one another, and turn out quality products. In 1780 at the age of 21, he and his brother refused to pay taxes since blacks and Native Americans were excluded from voting in Massachusetts.

After his first voyage to Africa in 1811, Cuffe became convinced that economic and cultural exchange was possible between the Africans there and in America. James Forten, Absalom Jones, and Richard Allen supported Cuffe's idea of providing African American workers to Sierra Leone to aid in the resettling of African Americans in Africa. Cuffe would increasingly support these efforts with his generous gifts to the American Colonization Society (ACS), a group dominated by whites who wanted free blacks returned to Africa. Several persons criticized Cuffe and accused him of being used by the ACS. This would be the first time black nationalists would confer with white supremacists in support of their philosophy of separatism. Marcus Garvey, over a century later, would receive similar criticism from W. E. B. Du Bois after meeting secretly with the Ku Klux Klan to solicit their aid in financing a resettlement movement.

In the 1791 Haitian revolt, Toussaint L'Ouverture used Boukman, a Jamaican, as his secretary because L'Ouverture knew of rebellious efforts in Jamaica. Discussion among enslaved Africans throughout the *Maafa* about insurrections were numerous and were influenced by persons such as Gabriel Prosser of Virginia. In 1800, he organized 600 people and nearly

BRIEF ACCOUNT

OF THE

SETTLEMENT AND PRESENT SITUATION

OF

THE COLONY

OF

SIERRA LEONE,

IN AFRICA

This pamphlet dictated by Paul Cuffe described his visit to Sierra Leone from 1811–1812.

consummated what historians believe would have been a successful takeover of the entire state of Virginia by enslaved Africans. Only a last minute thunderstorm and betrayal by nervous conspirators sabotaged the rebellion. Denmark Vesey, though freed in 1800, would later organize 9,000 people in 1822 to lead another nearly successful rebellion. Vesey saw both Prosser and L'Ouverture as inspirational for his quest to free enslaved people in South Carolina.

Maria Stewart of Boston, the first African American woman to record her speeches, spoke about slave rebellions and always referred to herself as an "African." She opposed the white-controlled American Colonization Society—a group that sought to repatriate free African Americans to Liberia—and helped to establish Boston as the seat of early black nationalism. Born in Connecticut in 1803, she remained outspoken about the need for African Americans to "build their own schools and stores." Her essays were published by the white abolitionist William Lloyd Garrison. Her book *Meditations from the Pen of Mrs. Maria Stewart* (1879) outlined her feelings about being an African in America.

The nineteenth century spawned other black nationalists vocal in their denunciation of slavery and their advocacy of an African homeland. In 1829, David Walker published *Walker's Appeal in Four Articles: Together with a Preamble, to the Coloured Citizens of the World, but in Particular, and Very Expressly, to Those of the*

United States of America. Widely known as *Walker's Appeal,* asserted, "it is no more harm for you to kill the man who is trying to kill you than it is for you take a drink of water." The author saw violence as self-defense in the war against slavery. Walker felt that peaceful means of eliminating slavery had failed and that violent retaliation was the only way to succeed. The *Appeal* was denounced by many abolitionists and supporters of repatriation, even by William Lloyd Garrison. The Georgia State Legislature placed a $10,000 reward on Walker's head if he were delivered alive and a $1,000 reward if he was delivered dead. In the South it was illegal to distribute his missive. Walker died mysteriously nine months after the *Appeal* was published.

Walker's Appeal was well-received by Pan-Africanist Martin Delany, the highest-ranking African American in the Union army. His 1852 work *The Condition, Elevation, Emigration, and Destiny of the Colored People of the United States* was the first book that described the conditions of African Americans in the United States from a black nationalist perspective. Delany was strongly in favor of African Americans voluntarily emigrating to Africa, although he denounced the actions of the American Colonization Society as a form of forced emigration. In 1859, he signed a contract with the Nigerian government that allowed cotton production by free West Africans and the eventual repatriation of Africans in the *Maafa.*

Delany's ally Alexander Crummell shared similar emigrationist views. In 1861 he published *The Relations and Duties of Free Colored Men in America to Africa* and argued that because of white supremacist views, blacks should be motivated to return to Africa and support the continent's development. Crummell saw Christianity as a vehicle for achieving that development. In general, however, nineteenth century black nationalists were ambivalent about the role that Christianity played in their liberation. Crummell adopted a traditional view of Christianity and molded it to fit his political views toward black nationalism. Although advocating self-help, which took the form of establishing the American Negro Academy while he taught at Howard University, he was highly critical of Booker T. Washington's obsequious nature toward whites. Crummell's Christianity informed his 1892 book *The Greatness of Christ,* which argued for a social gospel that fused religion and works into the liberation of Africans from slavery. In 1797, Richard Allen and Absalom Jones founded the Free African Society and their subsequent establishment of the African Methodist Episcopal Church reflected the "spiritual nationalism" advocated by nineteenth century black nationalists showing their firm Christianity. Remnants of African

In this 1895 sermon, Reverend Alexander Crummell comments on the struggles of African Americans to achieve full citizenship in the United States.

religious rites were already part of this modified Christianity in the form of music, worship, and scriptural interpretation. They formed the basis for what would be known in the twentieth century as Black Theology. Henry McNeal Turner would expand the membership of Richard Allen's African Methodis Episcopal (AME) Church during the latter half of the nineteenth century and would advocate emigration to Haiti as he grew more disgruntled with the treatment of African Americans after the Civil War. His views would be echoed by Henry Highland Garnet, who—like David Walker—called for violence in the fight to end slavery. He ended his 1843 speech in Buffalo by declaring to the persons at the National Negro Convention:

Let your motto be Resistance! Resistance! Resistance! No oppressed people have ever secured their Liberty without resistance. What kind of resistance you had better make, you must decide by the circumstances that surround you, and according to the suggestion of expediency. Brethren, adieu. Trust in the living God. Labor for the peace of the human race, and remember that you are three millions.

In the speech, Garnet cited the rebellions of Vesey, Turner, and Cinque as examples of the type of resistance that would eventually lead to the freedom of

Africans in America. The use of violence as an alternative was a common thread through many of the writings of early black nationalists.

The century would end with the writings of one of the greatest Pan-Africanist theorists, Edward Wilmot Blyden. Born in the Virgin Islands, Blyden's unwavering devotion to Africa led him to attend school in 1850 in the American Colonization Society's Liberian colony. The publication of *A Vindication of the Negro Race* was one of the earlier treatises that challenged the notion of black intellectual inferiority. Blyden became a Liberian citizen and his devout Christian beliefs resembled those of many nineteenth century black nationalists. Blyden, like Crummell and Walker, saw a love for capitalism, Christianity, and Western education as key to the liberation of Africans in the *Maafa*. The contradictions in this view became the focus of contemporary black scholars such as Wilson Jeremiah Moses and Frances Cress Welsing who saw Christianity as part of the system of white supremacy that had historically oppressed Africans in the *Maafa*.

There was an elitism about nineteenth century black nationalism that would become even more apparent during the colonial struggle against the European powers during the second half of the twentieth century. This elitism would emerge as one of the major deterrents to a "United States of Africa" as advocated by Kwame Nkrumah and Julius Nyerere.

The differences that were emerging among the various factions of Pan-Africanists during the late nineteenth century were set aside in 1884 when German Chancellor Otto von Bismarck convened a meeting in Berlin of 14 European nations regarding the partitioning of Africa. No Africans were invited, and what would become known as the "scramble for Africa" began. The conference gave the European nations the opportunity to expand their political and economic powers without resorting to military conflict in Europe or Africa. From a Pan-African viewpoint, the conference was the most destructive action toward Africa since the advent of slavery. The economic dependency that the Berlin Conference would spawn among African nations is still being felt on the continent.

◆ BLACK NATIONALISM IN THE TWENTIETH CENTURY

Six years after the partitioning summit, Henry Sylvester Williams called the first Pan-African Conference in London as a reaction to what Europeans were doing in Africa. Thirty delegates attended the meeting including a recent graduate of Fisk University named W. E. B. Du Bois who would later be dubbed the "Father of Pan-Africanism." There were discussions about bringing African persons together through better communication but what united the delegation was the anxiety over how the European powers were shaping the destiny of Africans in the *Maafa*. It was in London that Du Bois would first utter his famous phrase that the "problem of the twentieth century was the problem of the color line—the relation of the darker to the lighter races of men in Africa, in America, and the islands of the sea."

Du Bois, along with Marcus Garvey of Jamaica and George Padmore of Trinidad, would dominate the black nationalist movement during the first quarter of the twentieth century. Du Bois drew deeply from the influence of Crummell and Delany, but rejected their amalgam of Christianity in his Pan-Africanism. Garvey and Du Bois would clash despite the similarity of their views. The issue of skin color ran through the early writings of Du Bois, who referred to Garvey as a "fat black monkey." They were opposites in personality, Du Bois seeking links with whites and other progressives interested in the future of Africa and Garvey seeing whites as destroying black self-determination and therefore excluding their participation in the United Negro

Marcus Garvey as photographed by famed African American photographer James Van Der Zee.

Improvement Association (UNIA). Du Bois's founding of the National Association for the Advancement of Colored People (NAACP) in 1909 was an anathema to Garvey. The First Black Parliament held in New York by Garvey in 1916, would rival in size the 1900 London Pan-African Conference. Du Bois countered these large meetings by convening the First Pan-African Conference in Paris in 1919 and several others in following years. It was clear that Du Bois's meetings were more elitist and drew from the European-educated leaders of Pan-Africanism. No amount of editorializing by Du Bois against Garvey during his editorship of the NAACP's *Crisis* magazine affected Garvey's influence over the masses of black people throughout the world. What was even more frustrating to Du Bois was the evidence of Garvey's Pan-Africanism. Ships, businesses, and newspapers flourished under his leadership, whereas Du Bois's vision of Pan-Africanism remained primarily theoretical. Even during Garvey's imprisonment, his wife, Amy Jacques Garvey, ran the UNIA while Henrietta Davis directed the Black Star Line. Du Bois gloated when Garvey was convicted in 1922 by the government and deported in 1926, although their black nationalist goals were nearly identical. Garvey had been successful in mobilizing the largest mass movement ever among African Americans, but the visceral contempt that he and Du Bois had for one another hindered the realization of their dream of an Africa for Africans.

In 1909 Du Bois proposed the publication of an "Encyclopedia Africana," a Pan-African treatise that would examine the world from an African-centered point of view—an important perspective not found in European-centered encyclopedias. Lacking the funds in the United States for its completion, Du Bois would later revive the project at Kwame Nkrumah's invitation during his self-imposed exile in Ghana, but Du Bois would never see it realized. Since that time though, the project has been resurrected by a publishing team in Accra, Ghana, under the title *Encyclopaedia Africana*. According to Grace Bansa, secretary of the project, three volumes have been published with the remaining volumes scheduled for completion by 2009—the 100th anniversary of Du Bois's initial conception of the reference work.

The 1920s would see the emergence of black nationalistic expression throughout the *Maafa*. In the United States it was called the Harlem Renaissance and was led by the poetry and writing of persons such as Claude McKay, Zora Neale Hurston, Countee Cullen, Langston Hughes, Jessie Fauset, and Alain Locke. In Africa, Aime Cesaire, Leon Demas, and Leopold Senghor would create a movement known as Negritude. A reaction against colonialism in general and French colonialism

specifically, the movement had inherent contradictions. While describing an "African personality" common to all black people in the world, it was heavily influenced by a love for the colonial powers and sought to merge the two together in what was really an "African-European" personality. The effects of nearly a half century of colonialism were evidenced in the psychological attachment that many Africans still had toward their European colonizers, and while Negritude reacted to the colonized mentality, many felt it did not go far enough in its denunciation of European domination and support of the nascent freedom struggles beginning in Africa.

Garvey's influence on black nationalism would last for the remainder of the twentieth century and was dynamically linked to several movements. Jamaicans were attracted to his reference to the rise of kings in Africa. In 1928, when Ras Tafari was crowned Haile Selassie I of Ethiopia, another black nationalist religion, Rastafarianism, was born. Rastafarianism would establish its roots in Jamaica but its influence would be global with musicians such as Bob Marley and Peter Tosh teaching others about the white supremacist world of "Babylon." It would emphasize pride in appearance, and the religion's "dreadlocks" hairstyle would become famous around the world.

Garvey's death in 1940 did not subdue his influence on black nationalism. Elijah Poole, a Georgia farmer who had come under the influence of Islam in 1931, began to carve out an urban religion known as the Nation of Islam that would include a mystical theology that described the white man as the "devil" and characterized African Americans as a "lost people" in a strange land. C. L. R. James would fuse Marxism with black nationalism in England and write *Black Jacobins*, a book that provided a Marxist critique of the Haitian Revolution under Touissant L'Ouverture. With Duse Mohammed Ali and Adelaide Hayford, England became the center of black nationalism in Europe. George Padmore befriended Du Bois and Nkrumah as Ghana began its struggle for independence from the United Kingdom. Padmore rejected Marxism when it took a soft approach to the colonization of Africa, and his vocal opposition to its indifference toward the Third World led to his break from the philosophy. His criticism of the Communist Party eventually led to his ouster in 1934, and he spent his final years in England and Ghana.

World War II forced the end of the colonial system. The colonized nations of Africa with their allies in the United States and Great Britain took notice of this and called for a Fifth Pan-African Congress in 1945. This Manchester, England, conference included T. R. Makonnen of Ethiopia, George Padmore of Trinidad,

Kwame Nkrumah of Ghana, Jomo Kenyatta of Kenya, and chairman Peter Millard of British Guiana. Its honorary chair was W. E. B. Du Bois. Padmore advised the politically-minded Nkrumah to return to the Gold Coast and become involved with the rapidly evolving anticolonial waves sweeping the country. Nkrumah's subsequent rise to power in Ghana was heavily influenced by the ideas of Padmore.

Nkrumah made several attempts at uniting Africa's newly independent nations. The Gold Coast attended and was inspired by the final declaration of the 1955 Bandung Conference, where 24 nations called for increased economic, political, and educational cooperation among their countries. The conference also featured a forceful condemnation. In 1958, just one year after becoming Prime Minister of Ghana, Nkrumah called for the first Conference of Independent African States. The eight states in attendance included members above and below the Sahara and discussed the challenges ahead of them as independent states. That same year, Guinea became independent of France under the leadership of Sekou Toure and rejected France's offer to become part of what was referred to as "The New French Community." France's anger led it to order its colonial bureaucrats home, which caused the collapse of the infrastructure of the country. Toure turned to several nations to aid the newly freed Guinea. Nkrumah answered Toure's call and formed a union between the two nations outlined in the Conakry Declaration of 1959. The Central Intelligence Agency added to the chaos of independence by participating in the destabilization of the Congo and the assassination of Patrice Lumumba in 1964. Nkrumah was ousted from Ghana in a coup in 1966.

In the United States, black nationalism took a back seat to integration when the nation began a long period of national introspection over treatment of its African American citizens after the *Brown v. Board of Education of Topeka, Kansas* decision in 1954 declared segregated schools unconstitutional. Rosa Parks and Martin Luther King Jr. became household names as the struggle for liberation in the form of desegregation engulfed the nation. The most significant group espousing black nationalism during this time was the Nation of Islam. Elijah Poole had become Elijah Muhammad and was slowly building a religious group that rejected Christianity as a tool of the white man and encouraged its followers to change their last name to "X."

Before his release from prison in 1952, Malcolm Little discovered the urban prophet's writings and was converted to Islam. The legacy of Marcus Garvey was influential on Malcolm since his father had been an active member of the UNIA in Michigan. Despite his career as a criminal, Malcolm was transformed by the ideology in the teachings of those who told black people in the *Maafa* to look inward for self-determination. Malcolm's attraction to the Nation of Islam and his outspoken critique of white America soon became the subject of newspaper articles and television documentaries. The religion flourished with the attention toward civil rights and through Malcolm's fiery oratory. Television aided the personalization of the Civil Rights movement, and Malcolm provided a counterpoint to Martin Luther King Jr.'s racial inclusiveness in a way similar to that of Du Bois, who had castigated Booker T. Washington. Malcolm's speech, made shortly after the 1963 March on Washington, criticized the entire civil rights establishment, and his story of the "Field Negro" and the "House Negro" captured the black nationalist philosophy of separation. His break with the Nation of Islam and his trips to Africa led him to increase his Pan-African views. He was assassinated in 1965 before these views could be fully articulated in a theory of Pan-Africanism. After the death of Elijah Muhammad in 1975, the Nation of Islam would struggle with internal division but would be revitalized by Louis Farrakhan. His Million Man March in 1995 attracted global attention.

The political assassinations of the 1960s brought a renewed interest in black nationalism due to the cynicism that African Americans felt toward the Civil Rights movement. Stokely Carmichael, H. "Rap" Brown, and others forced integrationists to deal with the issue of black pride and self-determination. The Black Pride movement begun by Malcolm X and exemplified in South Africa by Steven Biko led to the Black Arts movement of the 1960s that saw the most creative expression of black artists since the Harlem Renaissance. Nikki Giovanni, Don Lee, and Gwendolyn Brooks wrote poetry that was uncompromising in its call for black introspection into white supremacy. Plays, books, films, and festivals, celebrated the African roots of the black struggle and created meetings that discussed black self-determination. Maulana Karenga would introduce *Kwanzaa*, an African American holiday that would be celebrated by many African Americans by the end of the century.

A 1972 meeting in Gary, Indiana, established a black political agenda similar to the Negro conventions of the nineteenth century. There were tensions that had always existed between those who wanted a Marxist approach to political empowerment and those who wanted nothing to do with any white philosophy. There had always been a close relationship between blacks and Marxists dating back to the early 1920s. Du Bois, Padmore, Randolph, Baraka, and others had believed that a coalition of labor, progressive whites, and committed blacks could eliminate racial injustice. The most organized though short-lived movement of Black Marxism was the Black Panther Party of the 1960s. Though it is popular to portray it as being all black, the BPP allowed for white membership from its very beginning. Haki Madhubuti, offering a stinging rebuke of Marxism as a viable alternative to black suffering, argued:

> Our major problem is not with the white communists, but with their trained Black ones who are trying to co-op Black nationalism and Pan Afrikanism to make these ideologies and movements something they ain't. There is in our midst the subtle presence of 'Black Marxists' pushing a European socialist analysis of Black nationalism and Pan Afrikanism. The Marxist position is that white racism—which to us is the only functional system of racism in the world—is a result of the profit motive brought on by the European slave trade and that white racism or anti-Black feelings didn't exist before such time. The left (generally described as Marxist-Leninist) whether white or black has always been anti-Black nationalism and this can be documented. Yet, one of the major facts of history is that white racism preceded and advanced itself thousands of years before European capitalism and imperialism was even systematically conceived. It is important to understand that the ideology of white supremacy precedes the economic structure of capitalism and imperialism, the latter of which are falsely stated as the cause of racism.

The conflict between black nationalists and Marxists continued with the formation of the Black Radical Congress (BRC), which convened its first annual meeting in June 1998. Formed immediately after the Million Man March, part of its aim was to regain influence over young black people whom they believed had deserted Marxism in favor of the Afrocentric analysis espoused by Marimba Ani, Molefi Asante, John Henrik Clarke, and Theophile Obenga. The BRC held its first meeting in Chicago and pointedly denounced Louis Farrakhan as being sexist, homophobic, and exclusionary. Attendees included socialists such as Angela Davis, Amiri Baraka, Manning Marable, Cornel West, and Barbara Smith. It was noted by many in attendance that "exclusionary ideologues," such as the Afrocentrists and the Nation of Islam, were absent as main program participants. Black nationalists argue that the absence of spirituality in Marxist ideology is antithetical to religious expression, which is an ever-present factor in most black nationalist ideology. Most black nationalists see spirituality as necessary in a world replete with white supremacy and struggle with a religious expression that will fit their aims. The rise of "urban religions" among young African Americans, such as Ausar Auset, the Five Percent Nation, and the Nation of Islam, reflect the need of a younger generation to embrace faiths that speak to their condition. Contemporary hip hop artists openly mention Louis Farrakhan and the "Mother" (Africa) in their lyrics. Their rhymes reflect the black nationalist tradition of making all things black, including religion.

Toward the end of the twentieth century it became clear that the most significant contribution of Black Nationalism was its work to garner global support for reparations for Africans and people of African descent living in other places. With leaders such as Queen Mother Moore, the Reparations Movement, long thought to be a marginalized black nationalist issue, entered mainstream dialogue when Randall Robinson's book, *The Debt: What America Owes to Black People*, hit the bestseller lists. Robinson had been instrumental in focusing public attention during the 1980s on the anti-apartheid movement. In *The Debt* he eloquently expressed the enormous obligation that the United States owed the descendants of slaves. Groups that had strongly advocated reparations for many years, such as the National Coalition of Blacks for Reparations in America (N'COBRA), National Black United Front (NBUF), and the December 12th Movement (D12), forged ties among their organizations and with traditional civil rights groups.

Added to these developments was the United Nations World Conference Against Racism (WCAR) held in Durban, South Africa, during August and September 2001. Black Nationalists from all over the world succeeded in having the United Nations declare the trans-Atlantic slave trade a crime against humanity at the conference and made reparations one of the gathering's top three issues. Even though the tragic events of September 11, 2001, occurred within one week of the close of the U.N. conference, the issue of reparations became part of the global dialogue on race.

Though in existence prior to the WCAR, the Reparations Coordinating Committee, chaired by Harvard law professor Charles Ogletree and consisting of high profile attorneys such as Johnnie Cochran, Willie Gary, and Alexander Pires, earnestly began to seek legal redress for the impact of slavery upon African Americans. Deadria Farmer-Paellmann, a longtime reparations advocate, filed suit in New York in March 2002 against three corporations, Aetna Life Insurance, CSX Railroad, and Fleet Bank for their active roles in perpetuating American slavery. Another suit quickly followed with the expectation that several more would come to challenge the complicity of private corporations and the U.S. government in the enslavement of Africans.

Reparations activism, anchored firmly in the Black Nationalist tradition, became the most significant social justice movement in the United States since the civil rights era and caught many mainstream human rights groups off guard. Many were forced to balance advocacy for reparations with white board members who saw reparations as an "extremist" movement devoid of civil rights implications. The leaders of these groups, however, knew that at the grassroots level—where Black Nationalism historically has its strongest following—it had grown into an issue that mainstream civil rights groups could not ignore. Furthermore, the international conversation on reparations forged strong bonds between black nationalist groups and traditional civil rights organizations with dialogues that would have been impossible in the late 1990s.

◆ BLACK NATIONALISTS AND PAN-AFRICAN THEORISTS

(To locate biographical profiles more readily, please consult the index at the back of the book.)

Richard Allen. *See* **Religion chapter.**

Edward Wilmot Blyden (1832–1912)
Black Nationalist, Repatriationist

Although he was not American, Edward Blyden had a great influence on American Pan-African philosophy. He wrote about blacks in Africa and America and about Christianity and Islam. Later, he held many different political and diplomatic offices in Liberia.

Blyden was born in 1832 in St. Thomas, Virgin Islands. When he was 12, a white pastor undertook his education and encouraged him to become a minister. When he was 18 he went to the United States, but was unable to find a seminary that would accept a black student. Instead, under the sponsorship of the New York Colonization Society, he went to Liberia to study at the new Alexander High School in Monrovia. Seven years later, he became the principal of the school.

As a writer and editor, he constantly defended his race, championed the achievements of other blacks, attacked slavery, and advocated the repatriation of blacks in Africa. As a teacher, he held many prominent posts at Liberia College. He was a professor of classics from 1862 to 1871 and the school's president from 1880 to 1884. At the same time, Blyden was also a politician and diplomat in Liberia, holding many different offices. He was Secretary of State from 1864 to 1866, Minister of

the Interior from 1880 to 1882, Minister to Britain from 1877 to 1878 and in 1892, and Minister Plenipotentiary to London and Paris in 1905.

Blyden traveled to the United States eight times. In 1861, he was commissioned by the Liberian government to interest Americans in a Liberian education. He returned the following year to recruit African American immigrants to Africa. His last visit in 1895 was in hope of furthering racial accommodation in the South so that racial problems in America would not travel to Africa with new emigrants.

Because of his own religious training, Blyden was interested in Islam as a religion for Africans. Between 1901 and 1906, he was director of education in Sierra Leone. He studied both Christianity and Islam extensively and summed up his views in an influential book *Christianity, Islam and the Negro Race.*

Elaine Brown (1943–)
Political Activist, Author

When Huey Newton, the founder of the Black Panther Party, fled the United States in 1974 to avoid a

Edward Wilmot Blyden.

murder charge, he appointed Elaine Brown as his successor. In the mid-1960s, Brown became involved with the Black Congress, a group of African American organizations in the Los Angeles area that served African Americans. By 1967, Brown had become acquainted with the Black Panther Party, and in 1968, she joined the Southern California chapter.

The Black Panther program combined revolutionary rhetoric, violent actions in the name of self-defense, and a strong commitment to building and strengthening African American communities. It evolved from a black nationalist neighborhood organization under Newton's leadership. However, after his 1968 imprisonment, Eldridge Cleaver made alliances with Marxist organizations advocating a more integrationist approach to worldwide revolution. Building African American communities appealed to Brown, who saw the party as a unifying force.

By the early 1970s, much of the party leadership had been either killed or jailed in police battles. In 1974, with the expulsion of co-founder Bobby Seale, Brown became chairperson of the Black Panther Party. Later that same year, Huey Newton appointed her the Minister of Defense after he fled to Cuba to escape criminal prosecution.

Brown guided the Black Panther Party's efforts to elect an African American mayor in the city of Oakland, California. The party registered 90,000 African American Democrats and secured the endorsement of California Governor Jerry Brown for Black Panther candidate Lionel Wilson in 1976. Wilson won, becoming the first African American mayor of Oakland.

Shortly after the election, Newton was cleared of any charges and returned to Oakland. His return led to the ouster of Brown and her progressive, feminist agenda. Brown left Oakland and immigrated to France in 1977. She lives outside of Paris. In 1992, she wrote her autobiography *A Taste of Power: A Black Woman's Story*. Brown continued to keep tabs on racial struggles throughout the 1990s, and in 2002 published *The Condemnation of Little B*, a story of a 12-year-old black boy put on trial for a murder he might not have committed. The story is based on a true case in the Atlanta court systems. The book has been hailed by critics as a novel that provides a new look at what many people considered a one sided issue.

John Henrik Clarke (1915–1998)
Black Nationalist, Educator

John Henrik Clarke was born on New Year's Day, 1915, in Alabama. His family moved to Georgia when he was four and he was raised in the South. Despite an aptitude for reading, he was forced from school after the eighth grade by poverty. In 1933, he left Georgia to go to Harlem and begin a new life.

In Harlem, Clarke discovered new reading materials on African American history. He studied at New York and Columbia Universities, and found a mentor in Arthur Schomburg. After serving in the Army during World War II, he began to teach African American history at community centers in Harlem. From 1956 to 1958, he taught at the New School for Social Research in New York. He then traveled to West Africa and taught at universities in Ghana and Nigeria.

In 1964, Clarke was licensed to teach at People's College on Long Island and began a career in academia. Clarke was a leading exponent of Afrocentric scholarship and the Black Power movement. In 1969, he began teaching at Hunter College, City University of New York, and in 1970 was appointed a professor in the department of Black and Puerto Rican studies. Clarke retired in 1985.

On July 16, 1998, Clarke died of a heart attack. He made contributions to African and African American studies for more than six decades. He wrote six books and edited or contributed to 17 others in addition to helping found several important black quarterly publications. Besides his academic work, Clarke published more than 50 short stories.

Alexander Crummell (1819–1898)
Black Nationalist, Repatriationist, Minister

Alexander Crummell was born in New York City on March 3, 1819. Crummell began his education at the Mulberry Street School in New York City. In 1831 he began attending high school but transferred in 1835 to a school founded by abolitionists in Canaan, New Hampshire. The school was destroyed by a mob of angry townspeople and Crummell began attending the Oneida Institute in Whitesboro, New York. He later studied in Boston and was ordained into the Episcopal Church in 1844. In 1847 he went to England and studied at Queens College, Cambridge, from 1851 to 1853, and was awarded an A.B. degree.

Crummell then spent several years in Liberia as professor of mental and moral science at the College of Liberia and in Sierra Leone. In 1873 he returned to St. Mary's Mission in Washington, DC, and founded the St. Luke's Protestant Episcopal Church. In 1897 he was instrumental in the founding of the American Negro Academy.

Crummell published three collections of his essays and sermons titled *Future of Africa* (1862), *Greatness of Christ* (1882), and *Africa and America* (1892).

Alexander Crummell.

Crummell died on September 10, 1898, at Point Pleasant, New York.

Paul Cuffe (1759–1817)
Black Nationalist, Repatriationist, Entrepreneur

Cuffe was born January 17, 1759 on Cuttyhunk Island near New Bedford, Massachusetts. He was the son of Cuffe Slocum and Ruth Moses, a Wampanoag Indian.

When Cuffe was 16 he was a sailor on a whaling vessel. After making numerous voyages, he was captured by the British and later released. He then studied arithmetic and navigation, but soon returned to the sea. In 1795 he had his own ship, *Ranger*, and in 11 years he had become a landholder and owner of numerous other sailing vessels. He employed only African Americans on all of his ships because he believed in creating wealth within African American communities and showing whites that blacks were competent in the business of merchant seamanship.

Besides being a merchant seaman, Cuffe was also a black nationalist activist. He discarded his father's slave surname and took his father's Christian first name in its place. He filed suffrage complaints in Massachusetts court; and, although unsuccessful, his legal action laid the groundwork for later civil rights legislation.

Cuffe was also a believer in free blacks repatriating to Africa. In 1811, he sailed to Sierra Leone where he founded the Friendly Society which helped African Americans return to Africa. In 1815, he sailed with 38 colonists for Africa. It was to be his last voyage as he died on September 9, 1817.

Angela Davis. *See* Civil Rights chapter.

Stokely Carmichael. *See* Civil Rights chapter.

Martin Robinson Delany (1812–1885)
Black Nationalist, Repatriationist

Born in Charles Town, Virginia, in 1812, Martin Delany received his first education from a book peddler who also served as an itinerant teacher. Since African Americans were forbidden in the South to learn to read, his family was forced to flee north to Pennsylvania so that their children could continue to study. At the age of 19, he left home to seek further education. He then studied with a divinity student and a white doctor for a time.

As an adult, he became involved in anti-slavery reform and the literacy movement. He began to publish *The Mystery*, a weekly newspaper devoted to news of the anti-slavery movement. When it folded after only a year of publication, Delany became co-editor of the *North Star*, a newspaper started by Frederick Douglass.

In 1848, Delany quit the *North Star* to pursue his medical studies. After being rejected because of his race by several prominent Pennsylvania medical schools, he was able to attend Harvard Medical School. However, after a year he was again expelled due to his race. While he did not receive his degree, he did learn enough to practice medicine the rest of his life. In the 1850s, he saved many lives during a fierce cholera epidemic in Pittsburgh.

Delany became an ardent black nationalist and recommended emigration to establish an independent colony for African Americans in South America or Africa. He wrote on the subject, held several national conventions, and set out on an exploratory expedition to Africa.

After the Emancipation Proclamation of 1863, Delany met with President Abraham Lincoln to discuss the establishment of African American regiments in the army. Lincoln commissioned him as the first African

American major and highest ranking person of color in the United States Army.

After the Civil War, Delany worked with reconstructionists trying to get fair treatment for newly freed slaves and advocated emigration to Africa. He also continued to pursue his scholarship and published *Principal of Ethnology: The Origin of Races and Color* in 1879, in which he discussed the role of black people in the world's civilization. He died in 1885, before he was able to move to Africa.

Wallace D. Fard. *See* **Religion chapter.**

Louis Farrakhan (1933–)
Black Nationalist, Nation of Islam National Minister

Born in New York City in 1933, Louis Farrakhan (then known as Louis Eugene Walcott) was an honor student at Boston English High School and then attended Winston-Salem Teacher's College. Farrakhan was a musician who played the violin and was a calypso singer. While a singer in the 1950s, Farrakhan converted to Elijah Muhammad's Nation of Islam. He quickly worked his way up to a leadership position, becoming the minister of the Boston mosque. He denounced Malcolm X after Malcolm split with Elijah Muhammad in 1963, and assumed leadership of Malcolm's Harlem mosque. After Elijah Muhammad's death in 1975, he briefly supported Muhammad's son and designated successor, Warith Muhammad, as leader of the Nation of Islam. Shortly after Warith Muhammad began accepting whites as members of the Nation of Islam, now renamed the World Community of Al-Islam in the West, Farrakhan split from the group and established a rival organization with about 10,000 members.

Farrakhan's vigorous support for Jesse Jackson's presidential candidacy in 1984 quickly became an issue after Farrakhan made several controversial statements, most notably, calling Judaism a "gutter religion." Overshadowed in the controversy was the involvement of Nation of Islam leaders in American electoral politics for the first time. Previously, Muslims had generally followed Elijah Muhammad's counsel not to vote or to take part in political campaigns.

In January of 1995 Qubilah Bahiyah Shabazz, the daughter of Malcolm X, was arrested and charged with trying to hire FBI informant, Michael Fitzpatrick, to kill Farrakhan whom some believe was involved in the 1965 assassination of her father. Farrakhan publicly defended Shabazz and claimed that the charges were an FBI attempt to entrap her.

On October 16, 1995, African American men from across the United States convened in Washington, DC, for the Million Man March. The march was organized by Farrakhan. Marchers were urged to make a commitment to improve themselves, their families, and their communities. The U.S. Park Service and organizers of the march have conflicted as to how many people actually attended the rally in which Farrakhan challenged the marchers to return home and work to make their communities "safe and decent places to live."

Farrakhan embarked on an 18-nation tour of Africa and the Middle East in early 1996. During the tour, he visited Iran and Libya, nations that the United States believes support international terrorism. Farrakhan, always a lightning rod for criticism, was attacked for the trip.

In 1999, Farrakhan became gravely ill with prostate cancer and sought medical treatment in Phoenix, Arizona. He rebounded in 2000 and continued to be politically active. In June 2001, Farrakhan met with nationally prominent Rabbi Marc Schneier as a first step toward repairing Farrakhan's relationship with American Jews.

Later that same year, the British High Court overturned a 15-year ban on Farrakhan's entering the country. After the September 11, 2001, terrorist attacks on the United States, however, British Parliament began deliberating whether it was safe to have Farrakhan in the country because of his very public views against America's retaliation against Osama Bin Laden and the U.S. bombing of Afghanistan. In 2002, the British ban against Farrakhan was reinstated. In a U.S. court battle, Farrakhan was vindicated in early 2002 when the highest court in Massachusetts ruled that Farrakhan had a legal right to bar women from a speech he gave there in 1994.

James Forten (1766–1842)
Black Nationalist, Entrepreneur

Forten was born to free African American parents in Philadelphia in September of 1766. He studied at a Quaker school but at the age of 15 quit to serve as a powder boy aboard the privateer *Royal Louis* during the American Revolution. He was captured by the British and held prisoner for seven months. He eventually spent a year in England where he was introduced to abolitionist philosophy.

Upon his return to America he apprenticed to a sailmaker. In 1786, he became foreman and by 1798 was owner of the company. The business prospered and in 1832 employed 40 workers.

James Forten.

By the 1830s, Forten had become active in the abolitionist movement and was a strong opponent of African colonization. He became a noted pamphleteer, a nineteenth century form of social activism and was an early fund-raiser for William Lloyd Garrison's *The Liberator*.

Forten was president and founder of the American Moral Reform Society and was active in the American Anti-Slavery Society. He was a vigorous opponent of northern implementation of the Fugitive Slave Act of 1793. Forten died in Philadelphia on March 4, 1842.

Henry Highland Garnet (1815–1882)
Black Nationalist, Religious Leader

Henry Highland Garnet was born a slave in Maryland on December 23, 1815. His family escaped to Pennsylvania and then arrived in New York. In 1826, Garnet attended the African Free School and was first exposed to abolitionism. In 1829, he made several voyages on schooners, working as a steward. When he returned he found his family was in hiding from slave catchers and all their possessions had been taken.

In 1835, Garnet and his friend Alexander Crummell attended the Noyes Academy in Canaan, New Hampshire, until hostile residents destroyed the school. They then attended the Oneida Institute in Whitesboro, New York. Garnet graduated with honors in 1840 from Oneida.

Garnet worked as a Presbyterian minister and abolitionist after his graduation. He also was active in the temperance movement. He became dissatisfied with the moral suasion abolitionists used and urged direct action by slaves against the institution of slavery. He also became active in the American Colonization Society.

Garnet supported the employment of African American soldiers by the Union during the U.S. Civil War, and in 1865, became the first African American to deliver a sermon in the chamber of the House of Representatives in the U.S. Capital. In 1881, he was appointed minister to Liberia. He died there the following year.

Marcus Garvey (1887–1940)
Black Nationalist, Pan-African Theorist

Marcus Garvey was born in St. Ann's Bay, Jamaica, on August 17, 1887. Garvey moved to Kingston at the age of 14, found work in a printshop, and became acquainted with the living conditions of the laboring class. He quickly involved himself in social reform, participating in the first Printers's Union strike in Jamaica in 1907 and in setting up the newspaper *The Watchman*. He left Jamaica to earn money and found similar living conditions for blacks in Central and South America.

Garvey returned to Jamaica in 1911 and began to lay the groundwork of the Universal Negro Improvement Association. Garvey left for England in 1912 to find additional financial backing. While there, he met a Sudanese-Egyptian journalist, Duse Mohammed Ali. While working for Ali's publication *African Times and Oriental Review*, Garvey began to study the history of Africa particularly. He read Booker T. Washington's *Up From Slavery*, which advocated black self-help.

In 1914 Garvey organized the Universal Negro Improvement Association and its coordinating body, the African Communities League. In 1920, the organization held its first convention in New York. The convention opened with a parade down Harlem's Lenox Avenue. That evening, before a crowd of 25,000, Garvey outlined his plan to build an African nation-state. In New York City, his ideas attracted support, and thousands enrolled in the UNIA. He began publishing the newspaper *The Negro World* and toured the United States preaching black nationalism. In a matter of months, he had founded over 30 UNIA branches and launched various business ventures including the Black Star Shipping Line.

In the years following the organization's first convention, the UNIA began to decline in popularity. With the Black Star Line in serious financial difficulties, Garvey promoted two new business organizations, the African Communities League and the Negro Factories Corporation. He also tried to salvage his colonization scheme by sending a delegation to appeal to the League of Nations to transfer the African colonies taken from Germany during World War I to the UNIA.

Mail fraud charges led to Garvey's imprisonment in the Atlanta Federal Penitentiary for a five-year term. In 1927, his sentence was commuted and he was deported to Jamaica by order of President Calvin Coolidge. Garvey then became involved in Jamaican politics. Electoral defeats ended his career. He died on June 10, 1940, in London, England.

Absalom Jones. *See* **Religion chapter.**

Charshee McIntyre (1932–1999)
Educator, Black Nationalist

Charshee McIntyre was born in Andover, Massachusetts, on May 14, 1932, and was raised in Roxbury, Massachusetts. She married jazz instrumentalist Makenda Ken McIntyre and helped George Wein, founder of the Newport Jazz Festival, to bring key jazz figures to the event. In her early thirties, she entered Central State University in Ohio to pursue her education. She transferred to Wesleyan University in Connecticut, majored in African history, and was inducted into Phi Beta Kappa after graduating summa cum laude in 1971. She earned a M.A. in philosophy, a M.A. in African history and a Ph.D. in history from the State University of New York at Stony Brook. She taught at various universities in New York including SUNY Old Westbury, Rutgers, and City College.

McIntyre was the first woman president of the African Heritage Studies Association. She also was active in the National Council for Black Studies and the Association for the Study of Classical African Civilizations (whose membership included John Henrik Clarke), First World, and the African American Heritage of Long Island.

In 1994, McIntyre published a work about the impact of African, Native American, and European worldviews on people of African descent. She believed that the struggle of Africans in the *Maafa* was primarily based on the ancient and sacred relationship between African men and women—a critical bond that had been severely damaged during the period of slavery and its aftermath. Her belief in the male-female bond in Africa influenced many black nationalists to reconsider and, in most cases, abandon their belief in the primacy of males at the expense of women.

When the 1999 African-African American conference convened in Ghana on May 15, 1999, it paused when the news of her death reached the delegates.

Audley Moore (1898–1997)
Black Nationalist, Pan-African Theorist

Audley Moore was born in New Iberia, Louisiana, on July 27, 1898. Her parents were both dead by the time she was 14, and she became the primary support for her two sisters. She worked as a nurse during World War I, and after moving to Anniston, Alabama, organized the first USO for African American soldiers who had been denied entrance by the official USO organization. She also assisted them in receiving medical care and food.

Moving with her sisters and husband to New York City in the 1920s, she became an active member of the Communist Party and help organize support for the 1932 Scottsboro Boys case in Alabama. She was considered the best African American community organizer in

Audley Moore.

the country and helped local groups protest racist policies in housing discrimination, political prosecutions, and unfair employment practices. She created the model for organizing legal redress for political prisoners in the United States.

She became increasingly disenchanted with the Communist Party and resigned her membership in the 1950s. Her roots in Marcus Garvey's teachings could be heard in speeches that encouraged "denegroization" and a demand for reparations for Africans living in the *Maafa*. During the last 20 years of her life she traveled internationally and continued to exhort others to pay attention to the "little people" that needed help against racism in the community. She traveled to Ghana where she was officially installed in an Ashanti ceremony as a "Queen Mother." Nelson Mandela met with her during his visit to New York in 1990. She, Rosa Parks, and Dorothy Height were featured prominently by Louis Farrakhan at the Million Man March.

Many believe that Queen Mother Moore, Marcus Garvey, and Elijah Muhammad are the greatest organizers of black nationalism of the twentieth century. She died on May 2, 1997.

Elijah Muhammad (1897–1975)
Black Nationalist, Nation of Islam Spiritual Leader

Elijah Muhammad was born Elijah Poole in Sandersville, Georgia, on October 10, 1897. His father was a Baptist preacher and former slave. As a boy, Elijah worked as a manual laborer. At the age of 26, he moved with his wife and two children to Detroit. In 1930, he met Fard Muhammad, also known as W. D. Fard, who had founded the Lost-Found Nation of Islam. Poole soon became Fard's chief assistant and in 1932 went to Chicago where he established the Nation of Islam's Temple, Number Two. In 1934, he returned to Detroit. When Fard disappeared later that year, political and theological rivals accused Poole of foul play. He returned to Chicago where he organized his own movement's followers. In the resultant organization, which came to be known as the "Black Muslims," Fard was deified as Allah, and Elijah (Poole) Muhammad became known as Allah's Messenger.

During World War II, Elijah Muhammad expressed support for Japan, on the basis of its being a non-white country, and was jailed for sedition. The time Muhammad served in prison was significant in his later, successful attempts to convert large numbers of black prison inmates, including Malcolm X, to the Nation of Islam. During the 1950s and 1960s, the Nation grew under Muhammad's leadership. Internal differences between Muhammad and Malcolm X, followed by the break between the two men and Malcolm's assassination, provided a great deal of unfavorable media coverage that did not slow the growth of the movement. In the late 1960s and early 1970s, Elijah Muhammad moderated the Nation's criticism of whites. When Muhammad died on February 25, 1975, the Nation was an important religious, political, and economic force among African Americans, especially in this country's major cities.

Elijah Muhammad was not original in his rejection of Christianity as the religion of the oppressor. Noble Drew Ali and the black Jews had arrived at this conclusion well before him. However, Muhammad was the most successful salesman for this brand of African American religion. He was able to build the first strong, African American religious group in the United States that appealed primarily to the unemployed and underemployed city dweller. In addition, his message on the virtues of being black was explicit and uncompromising. He also sought to bolster the economic independence of African Americans by establishing schools and businesses under the auspices of the Nation of Islam.

Khallid Abdul Muhammad (1948–2001)
Black Nationalist, Nation of Islam Lecturer

Muhammad was born Harold Moore Vann in January of 1948 in Houston, Texas. He excelled in academics and athletics as a youth and graduated from high school in 1966. He then spent four years at Dillard University, where his attendance at a 1967 speech given by Nation of Islam figure Louis Farrakhan changed his life. He became one of Farrakhan's original security personnel and soon changed his name to Khallid Abdul Muhammad.

After the death of longtime Nation of Islam leader Elijah Muhammad in 1975, Khallid Muhammad relocated to Uganda to work with black nationalist leader Idi Amin. He returned to the United States upon learning that Farrakhan was reviving the Nation of Islam. By the late 1970s, Muhammad was a minister of the group's Los Angeles mosque. Farrakhan depended heavily on him to help resurrect the Nation of Islam. Beginning in 1978, he and Farrakhan traveled by car throughout the United States establishing study groups and making speeches that eventually led to Farrakhan announcing the rebirth of the Nation in 1981. Muhammad led the Nation's fund-raising, spoke on Farrakhan's behalf, and organized mosques that had deteriorated since the death of Elijah Muhammad. He later headed congregations in New York City and Atlanta. He continued to play a role in the Fruit of Islam, the security team assigned to protect the outspoken Farrakhan. In 1988

Khallid Abdul Muhammad.

Muhammad was charged with the fraudulent use of a Social Security number to obtain a mortgage and spent nine months in prison.

After his release, Muhammad became supreme captain of the Fruits of Islam and in 1991 became Farrakhan's national assistant, a position once held by Farrakhan and Malcolm X under Elijah Muhammad. Muhammad's speeches soon attracted renewed interest in the Nation of Islam, especially among prominent figures in rap music. His discourses often promoted an independent nation for people of African descent. In a 1993 oration in Union, New Jersey, Muhammad uttered fiery pronouncements about black-white relations as well as anti-Semitic remarks, causing a controversy from inside and outside of the Nation. Farrakhan demoted Muhammad soon afterward.

Despite the demotion, Muhammad continued to be popular on the lecture circuit and maintained ties with the Nation. He organized the Million Youth March in New York in October 1998.

From 1998 to his death on February 17, 2001, Muhammad served as national chairman of the New Black Panther Party for Self-Defense, an organization dedicated to self-help and defense of Africans in America. Rooted politically in Huey P. Newton's Black Panther Party of the 1960s, the group is active in the reparations movement. Attorney Malik Zulu Shabbazz was elected to replace Muhammad, his close friend, as the group's chairman after Muhammad's death.

Huey Newton. *See* **National Organizations chapter.**

Kwame Toure. *See* **Stokely Carmichael bio in Civil Rights chapter.**

Bobby Seale *See* **National Organizations chapter.**

Henry McNeal Turner (1834–1915)
Black Nationalist, Repatriationist, Minister

Henry McNeal Turner was born on February 1, 1834, near Abbeville, South Carolina. He was ordained a minister in the African Methodist Episcopal Church in 1853 and as a bishop in 1880. In 1863 Turner became the first African American Army chaplain. He was also president of Morris Brown College for 12 years.

Turner was a leading advocate of repatriation. In 1876 he was elected vice president of the American Colonization Society. He made several trips to Africa and lectured throughout world. Turner was convinced that African Americans had no future in America. Instead, he felt that God had brought African Americans to the New World as a means of spreading Christianity and preparing them to redeem Africa. Turner edited and published several papers including *Voice of Missions* and *Voice of the People*, in which he advocated African American repatriation to Africa. Turner died on May 8, 1915.

Robert F. Williams (1925–1996)
Civil Rights Activist

Robert Franklin Williams was born in Monroe, North Carolina, on February 26, 1925. In 1956, he was elected president of the Monroe NAACP. The organization's membership had dwindled to six. Williams went out and recruited working class people and the unemployed to become members, as opposed to the NAACP's practice of appealing to middle and upper-class professionals.

Henry McNeal Turner.

Williams then targeted institutions in Monroe for desegregation. He tried the county library. It was desegregated without protest. Williams then tried to desegregate Monroe's municipal swimming pool, which failed. In response, Williams led groups of African American youths on sit-ins and other organized protests.

In 1959, responding to the acquittal in Monroe of a white man for the attempted rape of a pregnant African American woman, Williams pronounced: "Since the federal government will not bring a halt to lynching in the South, and since the so-called courts lynch our people legally, if it's necessary to stop lynching with lynching, then we must be willing to resort to that method. We must meet violence with violence." The next day the national office of the NAACP suspended Williams from office for six months. Later in 1959, he was indicted for kidnapping. He became a fugitive and fled to Cuba.

He was reelected president of Monroe's NAACP chapter in 1960. From Cuba, Williams produced a revolutionary radio program "Radio Free Dixie" and produced a Cuba edition of the *Crusader*. In 1966, Williams sought refuge in the People's Republic of China. In 1968, Williams published a pamphlet "Listen Brother!," hoping to dissuade African American servicemen to stop fighting in Vietnam.

In 1968, a group of African Americans, dedicated to establishing a separate African American nation within the United States, formed the revolutionary Marxist-Leninist Republic of New Africa. The RNA elected Williams as its president-in-exile. In 1969, the U.S. embassy granted Williams a passport to return to the United States. Disillusioned with the RNA's internal struggles, he resigned as its president in December of 1969.

Williams won a Black Image Award from a Michigan chapter of the NAACP in 1992. He battled Hodgkin's disease but died on October 15, 1996.

Malcolm X (El-Hajj Malik El-Shabazz) (1925–1965)
Black Nationalist

Born Malcolm Little in Omaha, Nebraska, on May 19, 1925, Malcolm was the son of a Baptist minister who was a supporter of Marcus Garvey's Universal Negro Improvement Association. In 1929, the family moved to Lansing, Michigan. While in Michigan, Malcolm's father was killed. In his autobiography, written with Alex Haley, Malcolm asserted that his father might have been killed by members of the Ku Klux Klan. His mother, stricken by the death of her husband and the demands of providing for the family, was committed to a mental institution.

Malcolm left school after the eighth grade and made his way to New York. He worked as a waiter at Smalls Paradise in Harlem. Malcolm began selling and using drugs. He then turned to burglary and was sentenced to a ten-year prison term on burglary charges in 1946.

While in prison Malcolm converted to the Nation of Islam, headed by Elijah Muhammad. Following his parole in 1952, he soon became an outspoken defender of Muslim doctrines, accepting the basic argument that evil was an inherent characteristic of the "white man's Christian world."

Unlike Muhammad, Malcolm sought publicity by making provocative statements on white supremacy to both black and white audiences. Based on the theology taught by Elijah Muhammad, he branded white people "devils," and spoke of a philosophy of self-defense and "an eye for an eye" when white supremacists attacked African Americans. When, in 1963, he characterized the Kennedy assassination as a case of "chickens coming home to roost," he was suspended from the Nation of Islam by Elijah Muhammad.

Disillusioned with Elijah Muhammad's teachings, Malcolm formed his own organizations, the Organization of Afro-American Unity and the Muslim Mosque

Malcolm X holding an issue of the Black Muslim newspaper *Muhammad Speaks.*

Inc. In 1964 he made a pilgrimage to Islam's holy city, Mecca, and adopted the name El-Hajj Malik El-Shabazz. The pilgrimage gave birth to the views that not all whites were evil and that African Americans could make gains by working through established channels.

His new view brought him death threats. On February 14, 1965, his home was firebombed. A week later, Malcolm was shot and killed at the Audubon Ballroom in Harlem. Although three men were arrested for the crime, there remains a controversy to the present day over who conspired to kill Malcolm.

Malcolm X had a profound influence on both blacks and whites. Many African Americans responded to a feeling that he was a man of the people, experienced in the ways of the street rather than the pulpit or the college campus, which traditionally had provided the preponderance of African American leaders. His emphasis on black pride and doing for self was in the tradition of black nationalism and similar to that of Steven Biko of South Africa. He provided a contrast to Martin Luther King Jr.'s idea of integration.

9

National Organizations

♦ A Brief History ♦ National Organization Leaders ♦ National Organizations

by Jessie Carney Smith

In a dispute between the National Association for the Advancement of Colored People and the State of Alabama, Justice John Marshall Harlan of the U.S. Supreme Court pointed out the significance of association membership, claiming that it is through associations that individuals have sought "to make more effective the expression of their own views." Associations are one of the largest and most influential forces in the United States and have played an important part in the economic, social, and educational development of African Americans. Organizations also have been crucial in developing and disseminating information, ensuring representation for private interests, and promoting social and policy objectives.

♦ A BRIEF HISTORY

Early African American Organizations

Due to restrictive ordinances and limited tolerance by whites, prior to the eighteenth century only the most informal and limited assembling of African Americans was permitted. Often meeting as religious assemblies, African Americans were forced to meet secretly and in small numbers. Thus, the very first African American organizations to exist in the United States cannot definitively be identified.

The Free African Society, organized in Philadelphia in 1787, has been generally accepted as the first African American organization in the United States. Founded by Methodist ministers Richard Allen and Absalom Jones, the Free African Society served as an important source of political consciousness and welfare for African Americans throughout the country by combining economic and medical aid for poor African Americans with support of abolition and sub rosa communication with African Americans in the South.

The abolitionist movement of the nineteenth century produced numerous organizations concerned with issues of importance to African Americans including the American Colonization Society (founded in 1816), the New England Anti-Slavery Society (founded in 1832), and the American Anti-Slavery Society (founded in 1833). Although most of these organizations were

Methodist minister Richard Allen co-founded the Free African Society, the first African American organization.

435

dominated by whites, African American leaders, including Paul Cuffe and Frederick Douglass, played an active role in the movement and in anti-slavery organizations of the time.

During the late nineteenth and early twentieth centuries, many African American organizations came into existence. The primary concern of most of these groups was education, improvement of the race as a whole, and religious training. In 1895, the National Medical Association was founded to further the interests of African American physicians, pharmacists, and nurses. African American women also sought a national network to bring about reform for women and for the race. In 1896, the National Federation of Afro-American Women and the Colored Women's League fused to create the National Association of Colored Women. Mary Church Terrell was its first president. In 1900, Booker T. Washington organized the National Negro Business League to promote commercial development. The success of these organizations stimulated an increase in new African American organizations, such as the National Negro Banker's Association, the National Negro Press Association, and the National Negro Funeral Directors' Association.

The Movement

The Niagara Movement of 1905 marked a turning point in African American history. This new organization was founded by a group of African American intellectuals from across the nation—headed by W. E. B. Du Bois—and approved a "Declaration of Principles," or resolutions calling for full equality for African Americans in American life.

However, the Niagara Movement suffered from weak finances and a policy that restricted membership to African American intellectuals. In 1909, the Niagara Movement was succeeded by a new organization—later known as the National Association for the Advancement of Colored People.

National Association for the Advancement of Colored People

The new organization was largely the brainchild of three people: William English Walling, a white Southerner who feared that racists would soon carry "the race war to the North"; Mary White Ovington, a wealthy young white woman who had attended the 1905 meeting of the Niagara group as a reporter for the *New York Evening Post* and had experience with conditions in the African American ghettos of New York City; and Henry Moskowitz, a New York social worker. The trio

proposed that a conference be called "for the discussion of present evils, the voicing of protests, and the renewal of the struggle for civil and political liberty." The three-day conference was followed by four meetings, the results of which were an increase in membership and the selection of an official name—the National Negro Committee. In 1910, the organization adopted its present name and was incorporated in New York state. By 1914, the association had established some 50 branches throughout the country.

Over the years, the organization has attempted to improve the condition of African Americans through litigation, legislation, and education. *Crisis* magazine, edited by W. E. B. Du Bois, became its chief vehicle for the dissemination of information. Perhaps its most significant legal victory was won in 1954 when the historic *Brown v. Board of Education of Topeka, Kansas* case threw out the "separate but equal" doctrine established by the Supreme Court in *Plessy v. Ferguson* in 1896 and eliminated legal segregation in public education.

NAACP Legal Defense and Educational Fund, Inc.

Established in 1939 by the National Association for the Advancement of Colored People, the NAACP Legal Defense and Educational Fund maintained its own board, program, staff, office, and budget for some 20 years. It has served in the forefront of legal assaults against discrimination and segregation and has an outstanding record of victories. In addition to its litigation, the Legal Defense Fund provides scholarships and training for young lawyers, advises lawyers on legal trends and decisions, and monitors federal programs.

Originally for tax purposes, the NAACP Legal Defense Fund had been maintained as a separate arm of the NAACP, until it officially was divorced from its parent organization in 1959. Following the separation of the organizations, a dispute over identity and the use of the parent organization's name erupted. The National Association for the Advancement of Colored People sued the NAACP Legal Defense Fund for name infringement. After several months of legal wrangling, however, a federal court ruled that the LDF could keep NAACP in its name since the NAACP was its parent organization.

Organizations Concerned with Urban Problems

During the early part of the twentieth century, several organizations concerned with the plight of urban African Americans emerged. In 1906, at the urging of Long Island Railroad President William H. Baldwin, a group of African Americans and whites met for the

William Monroe Trotter (far right) at the 1906 Niagara Movement meeting with W.E.B. Du Bois (seated), F.H.M. Murray (left), and L.M. Hershaw (center).

purpose of studying the employment needs of African Americans. This group, known as the Committee for the Improvement of Industrial Conditions among

Negroes in New York, studied the racial aspects of the labor market—particularly the attitudes and policies of employers and unions—and sought to find openings for qualified African Americans.

At the same time, the League for the Protection of Colored Women was established to provide similar services for African American women in New York and Philadelphia arriving from various parts of the South. These women, who often had no friends or relatives in the North, often fell prey to unscrupulous employment agencies, which led them into low wage jobs.

A third organization, the Committee on Urban Conditions among Negroes, appeared in 1910. It was organized by Ruth Standish Baldwin, the widow of the former Long Island Railroad president, and George Edmund Haynes, one of only three trained African American social workers in the country and the first African American to receive a doctorate from Columbia University. Haynes was named as the first executive secretary of the new agency. A year later, the organization merged with the Committee for the Improvement of Industrial Conditions among Negroes in New York and the National League for the Protection of Colored Women to form the National League on Urban Conditions among Negroes. That name was later shortened to the National Urban League.

From the outset, the organization focused on the social and economic needs of African Americans, seeking training, improved housing, health, recreation, and job assistance for African Americans. The organizational model that the league had established in New York City attracted attention and affiliates were formed in various cities across the United States.

A major goal of the National Urban League was to broaden economic opportunities for African Americans. It was not until the 1960s when Whitney M. Young Jr. became its new leader that the league began to emerge as a force in the civil rights struggle.

Leadership Conference on Civil Rights

The Leadership Conference on Civil Rights was organized in 1950 by A. Philip Randolph, Roy Wilkins, and Arnold Aronson to implement the historic report of President Harry S. Truman's Committee on Civil Rights *To Secure These Rights*. Beginning with only 30 organizations, the conference has grown in numbers, scope, and effectiveness, and has been responsible for coordinating the campaigns that have resulted in the passage of the civil rights legislation of the 1950s and 1960s including the Civil Rights Act of 1957, the Civil Rights Act of 1960, the Civil Rights Act of 1964, the Voting Rights Act of 1965, and the Fair Housing Act of 1968 (also known as the Civil Rights Act of 1968).

The Leadership Conference on Civil Rights currently consists of approximately 157 national organizations representing minorities, women, major religious groups, the handicapped, the aged, labor, and minority businesses and professions. These organizations speak for a substantial portion of the population and together comprise one of the most broad based coalitions in the nation.

Southern Christian Leadership Conference and the Arrest of Rosa Parks

Following the arrest of Rosa Parks, who had refused to give up her seat on a public bus in Montgomery, Alabama, on December 1, 1955, Martin Luther King Jr. and Ralph Abernathy organized the Montgomery Improvement Association that year to coordinate a city wide bus boycott. The success of the boycott led to the creation of a new organization.

This new organization, consisting mainly of African American ministers, met at the Ebenezer Baptist Church in January 1957 and elected King as its first president. Initially called the Southern Negro Leaders Conference and later the Southern Leadership Conference, the Southern Christian Leadership Conference grew to become one of the most influential and effective of all the civil rights organizations.

Organizations and the Court

Although public and private associations of all kinds have traditionally flourished in this country, that has not always been true for African American organizations. The freedom of association—the freedom to assemble, immunity from state scrutiny—similar to the First Amendment freedoms of speech and press, has from time to time been questioned and challenged.

Since the founding of the National Association for the Advancement of Colored People and similar organizations, state and local governments have attempted to prevent the operation of such groups. During the late 1950s, the state of Alabama set out to ban the NAACP from conducting activities within the state, claiming that the association had failed to comply with statutes governing corporations operating within the state. The dispute of *NAACP v. Alabama* was finally resolved by the United States Supreme Court in 1958 in favor of the association. However, the association was met with other interferences—some of the most notable disputes include *Bates v. Little Rock* (1960), *Louisiana ex rel. Gremillion v. NAACP* (1961), and *Gibson v. Florida Legislative Investigating Committee* (1963).

Congress of Racial Equality

The Congress of Racial Equality (CORE), an interracial organization organized to confront racism and discrimination, was founded in 1942 by James Farmer as the result of a campaign protesting discrimination at a Chicago restaurant. From Chicago, the organization spread to other cities and other causes, organizing sit-ins and freedom rides throughout the South.

By the mid-1960s, CORE had changed directions, and Farmer turned leadership of the organization over to a North Carolina lawyer named Floyd McKissick. With McKissick as national director the organization moved toward an exclusively African American membership and staff. In 1967, CORE, at its convention, eliminated the word "multiracial" from its constitution. McKissick left the organization in 1968 and was replaced by the present national director, Roy Innis, the former chairperson of the Harlem chapter.

Student Non-Violent Coordinating Committee

In 1960, a group of African American college students founded the Student Non-Violent Coordinating Committee (SNCC) to coordinate the activities of students engaged in direct action protest. SNCC achieved enormous results in the desegregation of public facilities and earned respect for its determination to act peacefully, no matter how violent or demeaning the provocation.

By 1964, the organization's leader, Stokely Carmichael, had become convinced that the United States could not be turned around without the threat of wholesale violence. In 1967, Carmichael left the organization to join the more militant Black Panther Party. H. Rap Brown, the former minister of justice in the old organization, took over leadership, renaming the organization the Student National Coordinating Committee and promoting violent retaliation in some situations. The organization gradually declined in membership and is now essentially defunct.

Black Panther Party

From its founding by Huey P. Newton and Bobby Seale in 1966, the Black Panther Party was a departure from the platform and tactics of other civil rights organizations. It rejected the institutional structure that, in its view, made American society corrupt, rejected established channels of authority that oppressed the African American community, and middle class values, which it felt contributed to indifference toward, and contempt for, African American urban youth.

The party imposed strict discipline on its members, denouncing the use of intoxicants, drugs, and artificial stimulants "while doing party work." The intellectual fare of every party member is the ten-point program (supplemented by daily reading of political developments), which every member is obliged to know and understand.

By 1970, most of the organization's leadership was either jailed, in exile, or dead—Newton was jailed in 1968 on manslaughter changes; Seale had been jailed on charges stemming from the 1968 Chicago convention riot; Minister of Information Eldridge Cleaver fled to Algeria in 1969 to avoid a prison sentence; and Mark Clark and Fred Hampton were killed during a police raid in 1970.

In June of 1997, former Black Panther leader Geronimo Pratt made headlines when he was released from prison after wrongfully being accused of the 1968 murder of a woman in Santa Monica, California. Throughout his 27 years in prison, Pratt (also known as geronimo ji Jaga) maintained his innocence. In his decision,

Elmer "Geronimo" Pratt.

James Farmer standing in front of one of his organization's posters.

Superior Court Judge Everett W. Dickey held that the prosecution denied Pratt a fair trial in violation of his constitutional rights. The prosecution suppressed material evidence relating to the question of guilt and to the credibility of a material witness, in violation of the 1966 U.S. Supreme Court ruling in *Brady v. Maryland.*

Organizations Providing Community Support

In 1967, the National Urban Coalition was founded to improve the quality of life for the disadvantaged in urban areas through the combined efforts of business, labor, government, and community leaders. Another organization, the National Black United Fund, which provides financial and technical support to projects serving the critical needs of African American communities nationwide, was founded in 1972.

The Reverend Jesse Jackson organized Operation PUSH (People United to Save Humanity, later changed to People United to Serve Humanity) in 1971. The organization has pursued its economic objectives through its Operation Breadbasket Program. It also has worked to motivate young people through its PUSH-EXCEL program which is designed to instill pride and build confidence in young people. Jackson left Operation PUSH to organize another group, the National Rainbow Coalition, Inc., in 1984.

Organizations Responding to Africa and the Caribbean

During the nineteenth and early part of the twentieth centuries, a number of individuals and organizations arose to unite Africans throughout the world. Most notable was the Universal Negro Improvement, founded in 1914 by black nationalist Marcus Garvey. The organization's goals were to instill pride in African American by gaining economic and political power for African Americans in the United States, establishing an independent black colony in Africa, and promoting African nationalism. On February 19, 1918, under the leadership of W. E. B. Du Bois, the first Pan-African Congress was held in Paris. The meeting was attended by blacks from around the world and focused on the problems facing blacks worldwide.

Recently, new organizations have formed to address the concerns of blacks around the world. TransAfrica, founded in 1977 by Randall Robinson, has worked to influence U.S. foreign policy regarding political and human rights in Africa and the Caribbean by informing the public of violations of social, political, and civil rights. Other organizations have also taken a stand on policies affecting blacks around the world.

Greek Letter Organizations

The first Greek letter fraternity established in the United States was Phi Beta Kappa, organized on December 5, 1776, at William and Mary College in Williamsburg, Virginia. At first a secret social club with scholastic, inspirational, and fraternal aims, it abandoned its secrecy in 1826 and became an honorary fraternity based on scholarship. It was not until 1877, however, that Phi Beta Kappa accepted its first African American into membership—George Washington Henderson at the University of Vermont. The undergraduate fraternity movement began to spread throughout colleges in New England and the Middle States. Women's sororities also emerged in the mid-nineteenth century. Although many colleges were racially integrated during this period, their fraternities and sororities were not.

The first decade of the twentieth century was a period of great organizational activity for African Americans, in which organizations dealing with business, education, social, and economic conditions, and other issues were founded. African American colleges and schools of this period also enjoyed the spirit of brotherhood, and their students found social outlet in clubs, literary societies, and other groups. But both on and outside campus, African Americans were confronted by the pressures of racism and sexism and sought relief in a number of ways. African Americans explored ways to form strong social bonds through the founding of their own Greek letter organizations. In time, these organizations became a dominant force in undergraduate college life, as well as in the African American community.

Historical African American Fraternities

Sigma Pi Phi Fraternity, also known as the Boulé, was founded by six African American men in Philadelphia in 1904. It serves as the forerunner of the Greek letter organizations existing in the African American community today. It focuses on the post-college years and historically has been comprised of an elite group of college graduates who have "like attributes, education, skills, and attainments," or who "ha[ve] made places for themselves in their communities through useful service."

Two other well-established Greek letter fraternities were actually founded on white college campuses. Initially organized as a social study club, Alpha Phi Alpha, was founded on December 4, 1906, by a small group of men at Cornell University. The other fraternity, Kappa Alpha Psi, was founded in 1911 at the University of Indiana. Most of the African American Greek letter fraternities and sororities, however, were founded at Howard University in Washington, DC. Other historically prominent African American fraternities include Omega Psi Phi, founded in 1911, and Phi Beta Sigma, established in 1914.

Historical African American Sororities

African American Greek letter sororities date back to 1910, when nine students founded Alpha Kappa Alpha Sorority. Those organizations that followed included Delta Sigma Theta in 1913, organized by 22 young women, and Zeta Phi Beta, established in 1920. Sigma Gamma Rho was founded in 1924 at Butler University in Indianapolis, the only African American sorority founded on a white college campus. The mutual interests of both sororities and fraternities have been promoted by the National Pan-Hellenic Council, established in 1930.

In addition to these organizations, other African American Greek letter organizations were founded as early as 1906 with specialized professional interests in mind. Examples of such groups are Phi Delta Kappa Sorority (education) and Alpha Pi Chi Sorority (business and other professions).

Present-Day African American Fraternities and Sororities

Present-day chapters of Greek letter fraternities and sororities for African Americans have been founded on many traditional white college campuses. Chapters also extend beyond campus grounds into the community, where graduate chapters—sometimes more than one in a city—have been established. Members of both undergraduate and graduate chapters include many well-known individuals who have left their mark on Greek letter organizations as well. For example, in 1914, Mary Church Terrell wrote the "Delta Oath" for Delta Sigma Theta Sorority—an oath that is still recited at formal meetings. Poet and journalist Alice Dunbar-Nelson wrote the lyrics and internationally-known singer Florence Cole Talbert wrote the music for the official Delta Hymn. Historian Charles Wesley wrote the history of Sigma Pi Phi, as well as the history of Alpha Phi Alpha Fraternity.

African American Greek letter organizations continue to focus on various areas of need in the African American community, such as health, education, literacy, housing, juvenile delinquency, teenage pregnancy, family issues, and generally improving the human condition for African Americans. Some have even established non-profit educational foundations to provide for scholarships, research, and foreign travel.

◆ NATIONAL ORGANIZATION LEADERS

(To locate biographical profiles more readily, please consult the index at the back of the book.)

Ralph D. Abernathy. *See* **Civil Rights chapter.**

H. Rap Brown (1943–)
Former SNCC Chairperson

Hubert Rap Brown was born on October 4, 1943, in Baton Rouge, Louisiana. In 1967, he took over leadership of the Student Non-Violent Coordinating Committee, renaming the organization the Student National Coordinating Committee. During his leadership of the committee, Brown was an advocate of violence against the white establishment and used fiery rhetoric in many of his speeches, often saying that "violence is as American as cherry pie." Since the late 1960s, the organization has gradually declined in membership and is now essentially defunct.

In 1968, Brown was charged with inciting a riot in Cambridge, Maryland, and was convicted in New Orleans on a federal charge of carrying a gun between states. In 1969, Brown published the book *Die Nigger Die*. He disappeared in 1970 after being slated for trial in Maryland, and, in 1972, he was shot, arrested, and eventually convicted for a bar holdup in New York City.

While in prison, Brown converted to the Islamic faith and took the name of Jamil Abdullah Al-Amin. After his release, he founded a community grocery store in Atlanta and is currently leader of the Community Mosque in Atlanta.

In August 1994, Al-Amin was arraigned on weapons possession and assault charges stemming from a shooting in an Atlanta city park. Al-Amin claimed that the charges were the result of harassment by federal agents who targeted him because of his radical past and Muslim beliefs.

In March 2000, Al-Amin was arrested in Alabama and charged with murdering a sheriff's deputy. The incident in question occurred in Atlanta, Georgia, on March 16, 2000. Two years later, Al-Amin was convicted of this crime and sentenced to life in jail without parole. At sentencing the jury rejected the prosecution's request for the death penalty.

Benjamin F. Chavis (Muhammad) Jr. (1948–)
Former NAACP Executive Director

Benjamin Franklin Chavis Jr. was born on January 22, 1948, in Oxford, North Carolina. He received a B.A. from the University of North Carolina in 1969, a M.A.

Jamil Abdullah Al-Amin (formerly known as H. Rap Brown).

from the Duke University Divinity School, and a Ph.D. in theology from Howard University in Washington, DC.

He came to national attention in 1971 when, as a civil rights organizer for the United Church of Christ, he was indicted along with nine other people for the fire bombing of a grocery store in Wilmington, North Carolina, during a period of racial unrest. In the controversial trial that followed all of the "Wilmington 10" were found guilty. Chavis was sentenced to a prison term of 29 to 34 years. Chavis was later granted parole and, in 1980, his conviction was reversed amidst conflicting testimony by various witnesses.

Prior to becoming active in the Civil Rights movement, Chavis taught chemistry at the high school level. He also worked as an AFSCME labor organizer (1969), a civil rights organizer for the Southern Christian Leadership Council (1967–1969), as a minister for the United Church of Christ, and as director of their Commission for Racial Justice in Washington, DC (1972). In 1985, he was appointed executive director of the Commission for Racial Justice. Chavis has also served as co-chairperson of the National Alliance Against Racism and Political Repression (1977) and as co-chairperson of the Organizing Committee for Economic and Social Justice.

In 1977, Chavis wrote *Let My People Go: Psalms From Prison*. He received the George Collins Service Award (1977) given by the Congressional Black Caucus, the William L. Patterson Award given by the Patterson Foundation, and the Shalom Award presented by the Eden Theological Seminary. He is also a recipient of the Gertrude E. Rush Distinguished Service Award, J. E. Walker Humanitarian Award, and the Martin Luther King Jr. Freedom Award. Chavis was also active in the South African civil rights struggle.

On April 9, 1993, the National Association for the Advancement of Colored People's board of directors elected Chavis to succeed retiring executive director Benjamin Hooks. Chavis assumed leadership of the NAACP with an agenda designed to increase the membership of young African Americans and revitalize an organization that some people viewed as stagnant. However, Chavis's early initiatives, which included defending "gangsta rap" music, meetings with street gang leaders, and seeking closer ties with controversial Nation of Islam leader Louis Farrakhan, angered many of the NAACP's more traditional members. By the time the NAACP met for its 85th annual convention in July 1994, the NAACP had been split into two factions, one supporting Chavis and the other that believed the organization was being overrun by radical and extremist elements.

In August 1994, it was disclosed that Chavis committed hundreds of thousands of dollars of NAACP money during the preceding autumn to settle a sexual harassment suit against him. On the weekend of August 20, 1994, the NAACP board of directors met and voted to oust Chavis as executive director. Chavis sued the NAACP, claiming that he had been wrongfully terminated. The NAACP settled out of court with Chavis, but he was not reinstated as executive director.

Following his dismissal from the NAACP, Chavis formed a new civil rights organization, the National African American Leadership Summit. He continued his close association with Rev. Louis Farrakhan and together they organized the Million Man March, which convened on October 16, 1995, in Washington, DC. Chavis also serves as a talk show host on Washington, DC's WOL-AM. In 1997, he converted to Islam, took the name Benjamin Chavis Muhammad, and joined the Nation of Islam headed by Rev. Farrakhan. Most recently, Chavis has continued to speak on the benefits of the Nation of Islam and has spoken out against those who look to silence those of color in the United States.

W. E. B. Du Bois. *See* Civil Rights chapter.

Ramona Hoage Edelin (1945–)
National Urban Coalition President and Chief Executive

Born in Los Angeles, California, on September 4, 1945, Ramona Hoage Edelin received her B.A. (magna cum laude) from Fisk University, her M.A. from the University of East Anglia in Norwich, England, and her Ph.D. from Boston University. She has been a lecturer at the University of Maryland, a visiting professor at Brandeis University, and has served as chair of Afro-American studies at Emerson College.

In 1977, Edelin joined the National Urban Coalition as an executive assistant to the president. The National Urban Coalition, an organization to improve the quality of life for the disadvantaged in urban areas, has been active in advocating initiatives designed to encourage youth and promote leadership. Between 1979 and 1982, she moved from director of operations to vice president of operations, then moved to senior vice president of program and policy directing programs in housing, health, education, and advocacy. In 1988, Edelin became the organization's chief executive.

In 1992, Edelin chaired a National Political Congress of Black Women commission in an effort to place black women in prominent positions within the administration of President Bill Clinton. Clinton was so impressed by her that he appointed her to the Presidential Board on Historically Black Colleges and Universities. She was also a member of the 1998 U.S. Delegation to South Africa with President Clinton on his historic mission.

Edelin serves as Treasurer of the Black Leadership Forum, Chair of the Commission on Appointments of African American Women of the National Political Congress of Black Women; Center for Policy Alternatives and the Network for Instructional Television, Inc.; the Federal Advisory Committee for the Black Community Crusade for Children, the Advisory Board of the Civic Network Television, Inc., and a Working Group Member of the National Civic League's Alliance for National Renewal. She chaired the District of Columbia Educational Goals 2000 Panel; served on the District of Columbia Committee on Public Education; chaired the Board of the D.C. Community Humanities Council and the Public Education and Prevention Strategy Team, as well as the District of Columbia Drug Control Policy. She has also served on the D.C. Commission on Budget and Financial Priorities. Edelin has been recognized as a leader in Ebony magazine's listings of 100 Most Influential Black Americans and Organizations; she received the IBM community Executive Program Award; and she is a noted national lecturer, moderating for the Civic Network Television's Building Community Series.

Marian Wright Edelman (1939–)
Children's Defense Fund President

Born in Bennettsville, South Carolina, on June 6, 1939, Marian Wright Edelman received her undergraduate degree from Spelman College in 1960, where she was class valedictorian. That fall, she entered Yale University Law School as a John Hay Whitney Fellow and received her law degree in 1963. Later that year, she joined the NAACP Legal Defense and Education Fund as staff attorney. One year later, she organized the Jackson, Mississippi, branch of the NAACP Legal Defense and Education Fund, serving as its director until 1968 when she founded the Washington Research Project of the Southern Center for Public Policy, which later developed into the Children's Defense Fund.

Wright has served as director of the Harvard University Center for Law and Education, chairperson of the Spelman College board of trustees, a member of the Yale University Corporation, the National Commission on Children, and on the boards of the Center on Budget and Policy Priorities, the U.S. Committee for UNICEF, and the Joint Center for Political and Economic Studies.

As president of the Children's Defense Fund, Edelman has become the nation's most effective lobbyist on behalf of children. Even while social spending was

Marian Wright Edelman.

being cut she has managed to score some victories. In 1986, nine federal programs known as "the Children's Initiative" received a $500 million increase in their $36 billion budget for families and children's health care, nutrition, and early education.

The most visible focus of CDF is its teen pregnancy prevention program. Through Edelman's efforts, Medicaid coverage for expectant mothers and children was boosted in 1984. In 1985, Edelman began holding an annual Pregnancy Prevention Conference, bringing thousands of religious leaders, social and health workers, and community organizations to Washington to discuss ways of dealing with the problem.

In her 1987 book *Families in Peril: An Agenda for Social Change*, Edelman wrote, "As adults, we are responsible for meeting the needs of children. It is our moral obligation. We brought about their births and their lives, and they cannot fend for themselves." Her other books include *Children Out of School in America, School Suspensions: Are They Helping Children?, Portrait of Inequality: Black and White Children in America, Families in Peril: An Agenda for Social Change, The Measure of Our Success: A Letter to My*

Children, and *Guide My Feet: Prayers and Meditations on Loving and Working for Children.*

In 2000, United States President Bill Clinton awarded the Presidential Medal of Freedom to Edelman for her work on the Children's Defense Fund. Edelman spent 2001 working with the Fund as well as testifying to Senate committees on family life and child welfare.

Myrlie Evers-Williams (1933–)
Former NAACP Chair, Civil Rights Activist, Civic Worker

Known for many years as the widow of civil rights worker Medgar Evers, Myrlie Evers-Williams has become prominent in her own right as a civil rights activist, speaker, and the second African American woman to chair the National Association for the Advancement of Colored People's board of directors. As board chair, she rekindled the spirit of the organization, led it to greater fiscal integrity, and increased national membership.

Myrlie Louise Beasley Evers-Williams was born on March 17, 1933, in Vicksburg, Mississippi. In 1950,

Myrlie Evers-Williams.

Evers-Williams enrolled in Alcorn Agricultural and Mechanical College (now University) in Lorman, Mississippi, where she met Medgar Evers on her first day. They married on Christmas Eve of the following year.

The couple lived in the historic, all-African American town of Mound Bayou, Mississippi. During the 1950s and early 1960s, Medgar Evers became active with the NAACP as field secretary. The racially charged atmosphere in Mississippi, as well as the death threats that they received, led the family to take extreme precautions. Their home was firebombed in the spring of 1963. On June 12 of that same year, the death threats became a reality when Medgar Evers was shot in the driveway of his home and died soon afterwards at the University of Mississippi Hospital. Eventually, the home was donated to Tougaloo College. After 30 years of Evers-Williams's dogged determination for justice, on February 5, 1994, Byron De La Beckwith was convicted for the murder of her husband and sentenced to life in prison.

Evers-Williams and her three children moved to Claremont, California, in July 1964. She became highly visible in the NAACP and lectured to branches around the country about her life and the work of her husband. She also continued her education and graduated from Pomona College in 1968 with a B.A. degree in sociology. Later she received a certificate from the Simmons College of Management in Boston, then became director of planning at Claremont College's Center for Educational Opportunity.

From 1973 to 1975, she was vice president for advertising and publicity with the New York-based firm of Seligman and Lapz. In 1975, Evers-Williams moved to Los Angeles and became national director for community affairs with ARCO. She unsuccessfully ran for a seat in California's 24th Congressional District, as well as a seat on the Los Angeles City Council. She married Walter Edward Williams during that same year.

A long-time member of the NAACP, Evers-Williams's work with the organization was acknowledged among its leadership. In 1995, she was elected chairperson of the NAACP's board of directors—the third woman to hold the post. Immediately upon taking office, Evers-Williams faced unpaid organization debts and a cloud of uncertainty among the national membership over the organization's future. Evers-Williams led a successful campaign to restore the NAACP's posture as a viable civil rights organization, strengthen its financial base, and increase membership. After turning around the NAACP, Evers-Williams resigned from the office in 1998 and was succeeded by Julian Bond.

Evers-Williams has been active in other arenas as well. In 1967, she recounted Evers's family life in

Mississippi in her book *For Us, the Living*. She followed this book up in 1998 with *WATCH ME FLY: What I Learned on the Way to Becoming the Woman I Was Meant to Be*, Evers-Williams's adult life story of single motherhood and civil rights battles. She was also a contributing editor to the *Ladies' Home Journal*. Among the many honors that have been bestowed on her is the Spingarn Medal, which the NAACP awarded her in 1998. She continues to lecture widely and appear on radio and television programs.

James Farmer. *See* **Civil Rights chapter.**

Fizzell Gray. *See* **Kweisi Mfume bio in Politics chapter.**

Prince Hall (1735?–1807)
Founder of Black Freemasonry in the United States

Prince Hall is believed to have been born in Bridge Town, Barbados, around 1735. Historians contend that he migrated to the United States in 1765, while others claim that during the late 1740s he had been a slave to William Hall of Boston, Massachusetts, and was freed on April 9, 1770.

In March 1775, Hall, along with 15 other African Americans, were initiated into a lodge of British army freemasons stationed in Boston. The group of African American masons was issued a permit to meet at a lodge on March 17, 1775, and on July 3, 1775, they organized the African Lodge No. 1, with Hall as master of the lodge. The lodge received official recognition from England as a regular Lodge of Free and Accepted Masons in 1784 and was designated the African Lodge 459.

Hall, in addition to leading the organization of African American Freemasonry, was active as an abolitionist. In January 1777, he was the prime force behind an African American petition sent to the Massachusetts state legislature requesting the abolition of slavery in the state. Another important petition, drawn up under his leadership in 1788, called for an end to the kidnapping and sale of free African Americans into slavery. He also actively lobbied for the organization of schools for African American children in Boston. Prince Hall died on December 4, 1807, in Boston.

George E. Haynes (1880–1960)
NUL Co-founder, Sociologist, Educator

A pioneer in the area of social work and an advocate for the urban African American worker, George Edmund

A

CHARGE,

DELIVERED TO THE

AFRICAN LODGE,

JUNE 24, 1797,

In this 1797 address, Prince Hall charges his brother Masons to respect and help each other, work to end slavery, and show love to all mankind.

George E. Haynes.

Haynes helped to found the National Urban League in 1910 and became its first executive director. He also led NUL into its role as advocate for the needs of the African American urban poor.

Born in Pine Bluff, Arkansas, on May 11, 1880, Haynes moved to Hot Springs in search of better educational, social, and vocational opportunities. He was encouraged during a visit to Chicago where he saw a close-knit African American community engaged in discussions about contemporary issues involving their status. After one year of study at the Agricultural and Mechanical College in Normal, Alabama, and a college preparatory course at Fisk University in Nashville, he enrolled in the latter institution in 1899 and received his B.S. in 1903. Haynes received a master's degree in sociology from Yale University in 1904 and then entered the Yale Divinity School. He also enrolled in summer courses at the University of Chicago in 1906 and 1907. In 1912, he became the first African American to received a doctorate from Columbia University. The research for his dissertation was on the working life of African Americans in New York City, culminating in the dissertation topic "The Negro At Work in New York City."

After college, Haynes worked with the Colored Department of the International Committee of the YMCA, but left in 1908 to continue graduate study. In 1911, Haynes founded the Association of Colleges and Secondary Schools and was its first secretary. He was a member of the Fisk University faculty from 1910 to 1921, although he was on leave between 1918 and 1921. At Fisk he chaired the social science department, developed a pioneer program in social work education, and led the university to become a preeminent institution for social work education. He also established affiliate programs in social work education with other African American colleges. In turn, the National Urban League gave fellowships to promising students in the field to pursue advanced degrees in social work.

Haynes had been active in several organizations including three that were the precursors of the National Urban League: the National League for the Protection of Colored Women; the Committee on Urban Conditions among Negroes; and the Committee for Improving Industrial Conditions of Negroes. These organizations merged in 1910 and became the National Urban League. He was the NUL's executive director until 1918.

Haynes became director of Negro economics for the U.S. Department of Labor between 1918 and 1921. From 1921 to 1947, he was executive secretary of the Department of Race Relations of the Federal Council of Churches. Under his leadership, the department established Race Relations Sunday, which is observed nationwide on the second Sunday of each February. From 1942 to 1955, he was a YMCA regional consultant in South Africa, where he collected and disseminated data on the organization's work in these countries. From 1950 to 1959, he was lecturer at the City College of New York.

Throughout his life, Haynes was active in numerous organizations and held membership on boards of trustees at Fisk and Dillard Universities and the State University of New York. His publications included: *Africa: Continent of the Future* (1950); *The Negro at Work during the World War* (1921); *The Trend of the Races* (1929); articles for the *Social Work Yearbook*; and entries on African Americans in the *Encyclopedia Britannica*.

Due to Haynes's efforts, the NUL continues its focus on social work initiatives at local and national levels. After a brief illness, Haynes died in King County Hospital in Brooklyn on January 8, 1960.

Dorothy I. Height (1912–)
National Council of Negro Women Former President

Born in 1912 in Richmond, Virginia, Dorothy Irene Height holds a master's degree from New York University and has studied at the New York School of Social Work. In the fall of 1952, she served as a visiting professor at the Delhi School of Social Work in New Delhi, India. Six years later, she was appointed to the Social Welfare Board of New York by Gov. Averell Harriman and was reappointed by Gov. Nelson Rockefeller in 1961. In 1957, she was named president of the National Council of Negro Women, an organization founded by Mary McLeod Bethune in 1935.

Before becoming the fourth president of the National Council of Negro Women, Height had served on the organization's board of directors. She has also served as associate director for leadership training services for the Young Women's Christian Association, as a member of the Defense Advisory Committee on Women in the Services, as president of Delta Sigma Theta Sorority, as vice president of the National Council of Women, as president of Women in Community Services, Inc., as well as in numerous other organizations. Height is also the founder of the Black Family Reunion, which she created in the 1980s to combat negative media stereotypes of African Americans.

In 1994, President Bill Clinton presented Height and nine other distinguished Americans with the Medal of Freedom, America's highest civilian honor. She was also awarded the Salute to Greatness Award. Height retired from the presidency of NCNW in February 1998 and was named chair and president emeritus of the organization. Jane E. Smith then became NCNW's president and chief executive officer. Height has continued to make appearances on the behalf of the NCNW including lending her voice to a new audiobook focusing on the speeches of Martin Luther King Jr.

Benjamin L. Hooks (1925–)
Former NAACP Executive Director, Minister

Benjamin L. Hooks was born in Memphis, Tennessee, on January 31, 1925, and attended LeMoyne College and Howard University. He received his J.D. from DePaul University in 1948. During World War II, he served in the 92nd Infantry Division in Italy.

From 1949 to 1965, and again from 1968 to 1972, Hooks worked as a lawyer in Memphis. In 1965, Hooks became the first African American judge to serve in the Shelby County (Tennessee) criminal court. As an ordained minister, he preached at Middle Baptist Church in Memphis and the Greater New Mount Moriah Baptist Church in Detroit. As a prominent local businessman, he was the co-founder and vice president of the Mutual Federal Savings and Loan Association in Memphis.

On January 10, 1977, Hooks was unanimously elected executive director of the National Association for the Advancement of Colored People by the board of directors, succeeding the retiring Roy Wilkins.

Under his progressive leadership, the association took an aggressive posture on U.S. policy toward African nations. Among his many battles on Capitol Hill, Hooks led the historical prayer vigil in Washington, DC, in 1979 against the Mott busing amendment, which was eventually defeated in Congress; led in the fight for passage of the District of Columbia Home Rule Bill; and was instrumental in gathering important Senate and House votes on the Humphrey-Hawkins Full Employment Bill.

At the NAACP's national convention in 1986, Hooks was awarded the association's highest honor, the Spingarn Medal. In March 1993, Hooks retired as executive director of the NAACP and was replaced by Benjamin F. Chavis.

Following his retirement, Hooks became senior vice president of Chapman Co., a minority brokerage firm, and returned to the pulpit as minister of Greater Middle Baptist Church in Memphis. He was also installed as professor of social justice at Fisk University with a distinguished chair named in his honor. In 1998, Hooks was selected as one of five judges to sit on a special Supreme Court to rule on the election of appellate judges in Tennessee. When not running special events for the NAACP, Hook continues to teach and preach the values of equality and fairness.

Roy E. Innis (1934–)
CORE Chairperson

Born June 6, 1934, in St. Croix, Virgin Islands, Roy Emile Alfredo Innis has lived in the United States since the age of 12. He attended Stuyvesant High School in New York City and majored in chemistry at City College of New York.

In 1963, Innis joined the Congress of Racial Equality (CORE). In 1965, Innis was elected chairperson of the Harlem branch and went on to become associate national director three years later. In 1968, Innis became national director of the organization. Innis founded the Harlem Commonwealth Council, an agency designed to promote the development of African American owned businesses and economic institutions in Harlem. He also worked in journalism, serving with William Haddad as co-editor of the *Manhattan Tribune*, a weekly featuring news from Harlem and the upper West Side.

Innis's leadership of CORE, however, has been marked with controversy. Numerous members have left the organization, charging that Innis has run the organization as a one-man show. CORE was also the target of a three-year investigation by the New York state attorney general's office into allegations that it had misused charitable contributions. An agreement was reached in 1981 that relieved CORE from admitting to any wrongdoing in its handling of funds, but stipulated that Innis would have to contribute $35,000 to the organization over the next three years. Innis was challenged by a group of former CORE members, headed by James Farmer, the founder and former chairperson of organization, but the effort was unsuccessful and Innis continued as head of the organization. In 1981, Innis became national chairperson of the organization.

While remaining president of the largely inactive CORE, Innis has sought to build a political base in Brooklyn and run for public office on several occasions. In 1986, Innis was a Republican candidate for Brooklyn's 12th Congressional District, but lost the election. He also ran unsuccessfully for the Democratic mayoral nomination in New York City in 1993 against David Dinkins. In 1994, Innis unsuccessfully challenged Mario Cuomo for the governorship of New York. In 2000, Innis was one of the main backers in Alan Keyes campaign for the presidency. He was able to work closely with his son, Niger Innis, who was the New York State Chair of the Keyes 2000 campaign, and a Keyes delegate for New York's 17th Congressional District. Even though Keyes's campaign folded, Innis continues to push for African American's in governmental positions, and hopes to back another African American candidate in 2004.

Benjamin L. Hooks (front row, center) with William Gibson (front, right), (back, l-r) Althea Simmons, Joseph Trevins, John Hope Franklin, and Samuel R. Shepard.

Jesse Jackson Sr. *See* Civil Rights chapter.

John E. Jacob (1934–)
NUL President

Born in Trout, Louisiana, on December 16, 1934, John Edward Jacob grew up in Houston, Texas. He received his B.S. and M.S. in social work from Howard University. During the early 1960s, Jacob worked for the Baltimore Department of Public Welfare, first as a caseworker, then later as a child welfare supervisor. In 1965, he joined the Washington Urban League as director of education and youth incentives.

During his early career with the organization he held a number of increasingly important positions, serving as director of its Northern Virginia Branch in 1966, associate director for administration of the affiliate in 1967, and as its acting executive director from 1968 until 1970. He also spent several months as director of community organization training in the eastern regional office of NUL.

Jacob left the Washington Urban League in 1970 to serve as executive director for the San Diego Urban League, a post he held until his return to the Washington Urban League in 1975. In 1982, Jacob replaced Vernon E. Jordan Jr. as the organization's president, when Jordan retired after ten years as Urban League president.

Jacob has also served on the Howard University board of trustees, the board of the Local Initiatives Support Corporation, the board of A Better Chance, Inc., the Community Advisory Board of New York Hospital, and the National Advertising Review Board, among others.

In 1994, Jacob retired as president of the National Urban League and was succeeded by Hugh B. Price. Jacob is currently an executive vice president for Anheuser-Busch Inc. He has continued to work for Anheuser-Busch throughout the 1990s and into the new millennium. He is responsible for a broad range of worldwide communications activities including public relations, employee communications and the company's efforts to promote responsible alcohol consumption.

He also is a close adviser to Anheuser-Busch Chairman and President August A. Busch III and, more importantly, one of a handful of senior officers who develop strategic directions and strategies for the company.

Vernon E. Jordan Jr. (1935–)
Former NUL President, Presidential Advisor

Vernon Eulion Jordan Jr. was born in Atlanta on August 15, 1935. After graduating from DePauw University in 1957 and from Howard Law School in 1960, he returned to Georgia.

From 1962 to 1964, Jordan served as field secretary for the Georgia branch of the National Association for the Advancement of Colored People. Between 1964 and 1968, Jordan served as director of the Voter Education Project of the Southern Regional Council and led successful drives that registered nearly two million African Americans in the South. In 1970, Jordan moved to New York to become executive director of the United Negro College Fund (now the College Fund/UNCF), helping to raise record sums for its member colleges, until he was selected by the Urban League to become the successor to Whitney M. Young Jr.

Vernon Jordan.

Taking over as National Urban League executive director in January 1972, Jordan moved the organization into new areas, including voter registration in Northern and Western cities, while continuing and strengthening the league's traditional social service programs. An outspoken advocate of the cause of African Americans and the poor, Jordan took strong stands in favor of busing, an income maintenance system that ends poverty, scatter-site housing, and a federally financed and administered national health system. Maintaining that the "issues have changed," since the 1960s, Jordan called for "equal access and employment up to and including top policy-making jobs."

The nation was stunned on May 29, 1980, when Jordan, who had just delivered an address to the Fort Wayne Urban League, was shot by a sniper as he returned to his motel. Jordan was confined to the hospital, first in Fort Wayne and later in New York City, for 90 days.

On September 9, 1981, Jordan announced his retirement, after ten years as head of the National Urban League. During Jordan's tenure, the League increased its number of affiliates from 99 to 118, its staff from 2,100 to 4,200, and its overall budget from $40 million annually to $150 million.

In January 1993, Jordan served as a member of President Bill Clinton's transition team. President Clinton appointed Jordan to his Foreign Intelligence Advisory Board in April 1993. He is also senior partner at the Washington, DC, law firm of Akin, Gump, Strauss, Hauer & Feld and serves on several boards of directors. Many of his achievements were overshadowed by his role in getting intern Monica Lewinsky a job in the White House in 1995.

In 2000, Vernon stepped down from his government position and returned to law full time. In 2001, Jordan was the speaker at Albany State University's commencement in Georgia. Jordan said he had mixed feelings about returning to Albany, where marches and protests in the early 1960s were aimed at ending segregation in that city. He also wrote a memoir called, *Vernon Can Read!: A Memoir*, published in December 2001.

Joseph E. Lowery (1921–)
Former SCLC President, Minister

Joseph E. Lowery was born in Huntsville, Alabama, on October 6, 1921. He holds a Ph.D in divinity and has attended numerous educational institutions including Clark College, the Chicago Ecumenical Institute, Garrett Theological Seminary, Payne College and Theological Seminary, and Morehouse College. Lowery's ministry began in 1952 at the Warren Street Church in Birmingham, where he served until 1961. From there he moved on to become pastor of St. Paul Church from 1964 to 1968.

Lowery was one of the co-founders of the Southern Negro Leaders Conference (which later became the Southern Christian Leadership Conference), serving as vice president.

In 1977, Lowery succeeded Ralph David Abernathy as president of the SCLC. Under his leadership, the SCLC broadened its activities to include: the reinstitution of its Operation Breadbasket; encouraging businesses that earn substantial profits in the African American community to reinvest equitably and employ African Americans in equitable numbers; involvement in the plight of Haitian refugees jailed by the U.S. government; and a march from Selma to Washington, DC, in coordination with the renewal of the Voting Rights Act of 1982. From 1986 until he retired in 1992, Lowery served as pastor of Cascades United Methodist Church in Atlanta, Georgia. Lowery stepped down from the SCLC post in 1997 and was succeeded by Martin Luther King III.

In late 2001, Clark Atlanta University established the Joseph E. Lowery Institute for Justice and Human Rights, a think tank for issues related to civil and human rights. This coincided with Atlanta's Ashby Street being renamed Joseph E. Lowery Boulevard. Both of these events were in honor of Lowery's eightieth birthday in October of 2001.

Jewell Jackson McCabe (1945–)
Former President of the National Coalition of 100 Black Women

Jewell Jackson was born in Washington, DC, on August 2, 1945. McCabe studied at New York City's High School for the Performing Arts as a teen and studied dance at Bard College from 1963 to 1966. She married Frederick Ward, who worked in advertising, while at Bard, whom she later divorced. Her marriage to Eugene McCabe, president of North General Hospital in New York City, also ended in divorce, but she chose to keep his name.

Several years after studying at Bard, McCabe took a job as director of public affairs for the New York Urban Coalition in 1970 and, concurrently, joined an organization called the New York Coalition of 100 Black Women, founded by her mother, businessperson Julia Jackson. At that time, the group was about 75 women shy of the 100 mark; the group reached this goal by the mid-1970s. She left the Urban Coalition in 1973 to become the

public relations officer for Special Services for Children in New York City. In 1975, she took a post as associate director of public information in the Women's Division of the Office of the Governor in New York City and then became director of government and community affairs at WNET-TV in 1977.

From 1975 to 1977, she published *Women in New York* and also donated her time to the United Way, the National Association for the Advancement of Colored People, the United Hospital Fund, and the Association for the Betterment of New York. In 1977, because of her good work, she was named president of the National Coalition of 100 Black Women, a post she held until 1991, when she became chair of the board of directors. By 1981, McCabe had established the organization nationally with chapters in 22 states, attracting some of the most well-known African American women in the United States.

Within two years, McCabe received several prestigious awards including an Eastern Region Urban League Guild Award in 1979, a Seagrams Civic Award, a Links Civic Award, and an outstanding community leadership award from Malcolm/King College, all in 1980. In that same year, she served as deputy grand marshal of the annual Martin Luther King Jr. Parade in New York City. In addition to her chair duties for the coalition, McCabe is president of her own Jewell Jackson McCabe Associates, a firm that does consulting work on government relations, marketing, and events dealing with minority issues. Her client list includes Panasonic, American Express, the NAACP Legal Defense and Education Fund, the Federation of Protestant Welfare Agencies, and the Associated Black Charities.

In 1993, McCabe was a finalist for the position of executive director of the NAACP. McCabe was interviewed by the NAACP's board of directors but was not chosen for the job. Later, to quote Philadelphia Inquirer columnist Claude Lewis, McCabe "asserted. . . that the NAACP's male-dominated board was unwilling to consider seriously a female applicant to head the powerful organization." Her outspokenness on the issue was one of a series of complaints of discrimination based on sex leveled at the NAACP in recent years. McCabe's weighing in on this issue undoubtedly played a part in the 1995 election of Myrlie Evers Williams as chairwoman of the group's board of directors.

Over the years, McCabe has held several gubernatorial appointments in the state of New York. Perhaps the most important of these was chairmanship of the $205-million, 46-member Jobs Training Partnership Council, a program that provides education and skills training to some 50,000 people in New York every year. McCabe has also served on the New York State Council on

Jewell Jackson McCabe (right) at the Candace Awards with Suzanne de Passe and John H. Johnson.

Fiscal and Economic Priorities, the Tax Reform Committee, and the New York State Council on Families, where she was assigned to the Committee on Teen Pregnancy Prevention. In addition to these state affiliations, she has served on the advisory boards of a number of private nonprofit and for-profit corporations, including the Economic Club of New York and the National Alliance of Business.

Floyd B. McKissick (1922–1981)
Former CORE National Director

Born in Asheville, North Carolina, on March 9, 1922, Floyd Bixler McKissick did his undergraduate work at Morehouse and North Carolina Colleges. Having determined that he wanted to become a lawyer, McKissick

applied to the University of North Carolina at Chapel Hill Law School. Since the school was racially segregated at that time, he was denied admission. With the help of NAACP lawyer Thurgood Marshall, McKissick sued the university and became the first African American to earn an LL.B. degree at that institution.

While still in school, McKissick had become an active member of the Congress of Racial Equality (CORE). When McKissick replaced James Farmer as head of CORE on January 3, 1966, he quickly made a name for himself. Under McKissick's direction, the organization moved more firmly into the Black Power movement, refusing to support Martin Luther King's call for massive nonviolent civil disobedience in northern cities, concentrating instead on programs aimed at increasing the political power and improving the economic position of African Americans. In 1967, the

Floyd B. McKissick.

organization moved to eliminate the word "multiracial" from its constitution.

McKissick resigned as national director of CORE in 1968. After leaving CORE, he launched a plan to establish a new community, Soul City, in Warren County, North Carolina. McKissick saw Soul City as a community with sufficient industry to support a population of 50,000. For his venture, he received a $14 million bond issue guarantee from the Department of Housing and Urban Development and a loan of $500,000 from the First Pennsylvania Bank.

Soul City, however, ran into difficulties and despite the best efforts of McKissick the project never developed as planned. In June 1980, the Soul City Corporation and the federal government reached an agreement that would allow the government to assume control of the project. Under the agreement, the company retained 88 acres of the project including the site of a mobile home park and a 60,000 square foot building that had served as the project's headquarters.

McKissick died on April 28, 1981, of lung cancer and was buried at Soul City.

Kweisi Mfume. *See* **Politics chapter.**

Huey P. Newton (1942–1989)
Black Panther Party Co-Founder

The youngest of seven children, Huey P. Newton was born in Monroe, Louisiana, on February 17, 1942. He attended Oakland City College, where he founded the Afro-American Society, and later studied at San Francisco Law School. In 1966, Newton joined forces with Bobby Seale and established the Black Panther Party for Self-Defense.

Newton and his partner almost immediately became targets of police resentment and uneasiness. The hostility came to a climax in 1967, when Newton allegedly killed an Oakland police officer. His eight-week trial was a cause celebre in which more than 2,500 demonstrators surrounded the courthouse chanting Panther slogans and demanding his release. Newton was convicted of voluntary manslaughter and sent to the California Men's Colony. His conviction was later overturned by a California court of appeals.

By the 1970s, the Black Panther Party became a potent political force in California. Co-leader Bobby Seale made an almost successful bid for the mayorship of Oakland in 1973. In 1977, the Panthers helped to elect the city's first African American mayor, Lionel Wilson. Meanwhile, Newton continued to have problems with the law. He was charged with shooting a prostitute, but after two hung juries, the charges were dropped. He was retried and convicted for the 1969 death of the police officer and again the conviction was reversed.

In 1980, he earned his Ph.D. in philosophy from the University of California; his doctoral thesis was "War Against the Panthers: Study of Repression in America." However, this achievement was followed by further problems. He was charged with embezzling state and federal funds from an educational and nutritional program that he headed in 1985. In 1987, he was convicted of illegal possession of guns. In 1989, he was fatally shot by a small-time drug dealer.

Frederick D. Patterson (1901–1988)
UNCF Founder, Former College President

Frederick Douglass Patterson was the force behind the first collective fund-raising efforts among African American colleges—the United Negro College Fund. He was also influential in the development of African American higher education through his presidency of Tuskegee Institute. It was during his administration that the internationally known Tuskegee Airmen was formed.

Frederick D. Patterson.

Patterson was born in the Anacostia neighborhood of Washington, DC, on October 10, 1901. His parents died before young Patterson was two years old, forcing him to live with various family members while attending school. He worked his way through veterinary school, receiving a B.S. in 1923 and an M.S. degree in veterinary medicine in 1927 from Iowa State University. Before and after receiving his master's degree, Patterson taught at Virginia State College (now University) in Petersburg. In 1928, he moved to Tuskegee Normal and Industrial Institute (now University) in Alabama, where he was a teacher and the head of the Veterinary Department. He obtained a Ph.D. in bacteriology from Cornell University in 1932 and returned to Tuskegee as head of the Agriculture Department. A year later, he was named president of Tuskegee. He also chaired the R. R. Moton Memorial Institute and served as director of education for the Phelps-Stokes Fund.

Among Patterson's accomplishments at Tuskegee was the establishment of an accredited school of veterinary medicine. It remains the only such school ever established on an African American college campus. Patterson began a program in commercial aviation in

1939 to train Tuskegee's students as pilots. He was lobbied successfully to have a training program for military pilots at Tuskegee and train commercial aviators as well. His military trainees became the celebrated Tuskegee Airmen, an African American pilots group that fought in World War II. In 1940, Patterson founded the George Washington Carver Foundation to encourage and financially support scientific research by African Americans. In 1948, he started the School of Engineering at Tuskegee.

In 1943, Patterson proposed the creation of an African American college consortium to raise money for their mutual benefit. In 1944, 27 schools came together to form the United Negro College Fund. Some view Patterson's efforts as the most important act during his lifetime. He also was UNCF president from 1964 to 1966. UNCF, now called The College Fund/UNCF, continues as an important national fund-raising effort for the member colleges. Its annual telethons, with singer Lou Rawls as host, raises millions of dollars and promotes financial support for the member colleges locally as well as nationally.

In 1953, Patterson retired from Tuskegee and became president of the Phelps-Stokes Fund, an organization established in 1901 to support the education of African, African American, and Native American students in the United States. He left the fund in 1970 to head the Robert R. Moton Institute, another effort to boost the endowments of African American colleges.

President Ronald Reagan honored Patterson in 1987 with the Presidential Medal of Freedom. Patterson's autobiography *Chronicles of Faith* was completed after his death on April 26, 1988. In recognition of his work, he received the Spingarn Medal from the NAACP posthumously in 1988. Since then, the College Fund/UNCF named its new institute the Frederick D. Patterson Research Institute.

Hugh B. Price (1941–)
NUL President and CEO

When Hugh Price was named president and CEO of the National Urban League in 1994, he inherited an organization with financial problems and a lack of visibility. He proved to be the person to address and eradicate those problems. Price graduated from Amherst in 1963, then received his J.D. from Yale in 1966. Immediately going to work in the inner city, Price worked as an attorney for the New Haven Legal Assistance Association and later as executive director of the Black Coalition of New Haven.

In 1970, Price continued to focus on inner city issues by joining the urban affairs consulting firm of Cogen, Holt & Associates in New Haven, specializing in the analysis of municipal government. After serving as human resources administration director for the city of New Haven, Price was offered the opportunity to express his opinions to a much larger audience on the editorial board of the *New York Times*. Price primarily concentrated on writing about domestic policy issues.

After spending six years at WNET-TV, New York City's public television station, Price became vice president of the Rockefeller Foundation, helping minorities to obtain more opportunities from groups served by the organization. With his extensive background, Price caught the attention NUL board of directors and was named president in 1994.

Price continued to focus on poorly funded schools, inner city youth, and unemployment. He vowed that the Urban League would not be race-specific in its help—it would be need-specific. During his tenure, the Urban League has changed its focus by helping entire urban neighborhoods, instead of singling out a particular race in that neighborhood. This approach has gained Hugh Price much deserved attention in the media. Price continues to be on the front lines for the Urban League and is dedicated to keeping them on track and as useful to all residence who need their assistance He also writes a weekly newspaper column which appears in papers such as *The New York Times, Wall Street Journal, Los Angeles Times, San Francisco Chronicle, Education Week, Review of Black Political Economy,* and *Phi Delta Kappan*.

A. Philip Randolph (1889–1979)
Brotherhood of Sleeping Car Porters and A. Philip Randolph Institute Founder

Asa Philip Randolph was born in Crescent City, Florida, on April 15, 1889. He attended Cookman Institute in Jacksonville, Florida, before moving to New York City.

In New York, Randolph worked as a porter, railroad waiter, and an elevator operator. While attending the College of the City of New York, he was exposed to the socialist movement, and, in 1917, he organized *The Messenger*, a socialist newspaper. In 1925, Randolph founded the Brotherhood of Sleeping Car Porters to help African American railway car attendants working for the Pullman Palace Car Company. After a ten year struggle, Randolph and the union negotiated a contract with Pullman in 1935.

A. Philip Randolph.

Randolph served as a member of New York City's Commission on Race and as president of the National Negro Congress. In 1941, Randolph organized a march on Washington, DC, to bring attention to discrimination in employment. In 1942, he was appointed to the New York Housing Authority and was appointed to the AFL-CIO executive council in 1955.

In 1960, Randolph organized the Negro American Labor Council. He was also one of the organizers of the 1963 March on Washington. In 1964, he founded the A. Philip Randolph Institute in New York City to eradicate discrimination and to defend human and civil rights. He died on May 16, 1979.

Randall S. Robinson (1942–)
TransAfrica Founder and Director

Randall Robinson, brother to the late news anchor Max Robinson, was born in Richmond, Virginia, and is a graduate of Virginia Union University and Harvard Law School. In 1977, Robinson founded TransAfrica to lobby

Congress and the White House on foreign policy matters involving Africa and the Caribbean. Since its creation, the organization has grown from two to over 15,000 members.

In 1984 and 1985, in protest to the policy of apartheid in South Africa, TransAfrica organized demonstrations in front of the South African embassy in Washington, DC; Robinson, along with other protesters including singer Stevie Wonder, were arrested. In addition, the organization has advocated for the cessation of aid to countries with human rights problems. In 1981, TransAfrica Forum, an educational and research arm of TransAfrica, was organized to collect and disseminate information on foreign policy affecting Africa and the Caribbean and to encourage public participation in policy debates.

In 1994, the United States was besieged by scores of refugees seeking to escape Haiti's brutal military dictatorship. Many of these refugees, upon reaching the United States or the U.S. military base in Guantanamo, Cuba, were often sent back to Haiti without receiving asylum hearings. On April 12, 1994, Robinson began a liquid-fast diet in an attempt to increase awareness of the plight of Haitian refugees and to pressure the Clinton administration to change its refugee policy. On May 8, Robinson ended his fast after the Clinton administration announced that it would grant Haitian refugees asylum hearings.

On March 16, 1995, Robinson announced that TransAfrica would lead a group of prominent African Americans to pressure Nigeria's brutal military leaders to step down from power. Along with other demonstrators, Robinson was arrested during protests in front of the Nigerian Embassy in Washington, DC. On November 10, 1995, Robinson, along with notable South African Archbishop Desmond Tutu, announced that they would seek economic sanctions or an oil embargo against Nigeria after its military regime executed a prominent Nigerian writer and eight other minority rights activists.

In 1997, Robinson published his memoirs *Defending the Spirit: A Black Life in America*, which follows Robinson through his triumphs and his hopes for the future. He followed this book up in 1999 with *The Debt: What America Owes to Blacks*, which focuses more on the responsibilities the government of the United States has to the African-American community as well as to people of color around the world. Most recently, in 2002, *The Reckoning: What Blacks Owe to Each Other* hit bookstores. In this companion piece to *The Debt*, Robinson talks directly to the African American community and discusses the ways the community overall needs to improve if they are to be taken seriously by the nation.

Bayard Rustin (1910–1987)
Former A. Philip Randolph Institute Executive Director, Civil Rights Organizer

Bayard Rustin was born in West Chester, Pennsylvania, on March 17, 1910. While in school, he was an honor student and star athlete, experiencing his first act of discrimination when he was refused restaurant service in Pennsylvania while on tour with the football team. He attended Wilberforce University, Cheyney State Normal School (now Cheyney University of Pennsylvania), and the City College of New York.

Rustin was active in various peace organizations, efforts to restrict nuclear armaments, and movements toward African independence. Between 1936 and 1941, Rustin worked as an organizer of the Young Communist League. In 1941, he joined the Fellowship of Reconciliation, a nonviolent antiwar group, and later served as its director of race relations. In 1942, Rustin, along with James Farmer, became active in the Chicago

Bayard Rustin.

Committee of Racial Equality, out of which the Congress of Racial Equality was formed.

Rustin was one of the founding members of the Southern Christian Leadership Conference (SCLC). In 1963, he was named chief logistics expert and organizational coordinator of the March on Washington. From 1964 to 1979, Rustin served as executive director of the A. Philip Randolph Institute in New York City. In 1975, he founded the Organization for Black Americans to Support Israel.

Throughout the 1960s, Rustin maintained support for the nonviolent philosophy to which he had dedicated his life. Nonviolence, he argued, was not outdated; it was a necessary and inexorable plan called for by the African American's condition in the United States. Rustin continued to be active in the Civil Rights movement until his death on August 24, 1987, at the age of 77.

Bobby Seale (1936–)
Black Panther Party Co-Founder

Born Robert George Seale in Dallas, Texas, on October 20, 1936, Bobby Seale, along with Huey P. Newton and Bobby Hutton, was one of the founding members of the Black Panther Party for Self-Defense. His family moved from Dallas to Port Arthur, Texas, before settling in Oakland, California.

After leaving high school, Seale joined the United States Air Force and trained as a sheet-metal mechanic. However, he was discharged for disobeying an officer. Returning home, he found sporadic work as a sheet metal mechanic. In 1959, Seale enrolled at Merritt College and studied engineering drafting. While attending Merritt, Seale joined the Afro-American Association, a campus organization that stressed African American separatism and self-improvement. It was through this organization that Seale met Panther co-founder Huey Newton.

Seale and Newton soon became disenchanted with the association. In 1966, Seale and Newton formed the Black Panther Party for Self-Defense. One of their objectives was to form armed patrols to protect citizens from what they considered racist police abuse.

In March of 1971, Seale was charged with kidnapping and killing Panther Alex Rackley, a suspected police informant. However, a mistrial was declared, and the charges dismissed. Seale began to steer the Panthers away from its revolutionary agenda and toward one of creating community action programs. In 1974, Seale left the party to form Advocates Scene, an organization aimed at helping the underprivileged from grass root political coalitions.

More recently, Seale has served as a community liaison for Temple University's African American Studies Department. He has lectured throughout the country and has written several books including: *Seize the Time: The Story of the Black Panther Party* (1970), *A Lonely Rage: The Autobiography of Bobby Seale* (1978), and *Barbeque'n with Bobby Seale* (1987).

Leon Howard Sullivan. *See* **Civil Rights chapter.**

Mary Church Terrell. *See* **Civil Rights chapter.**

William M. Trotter. *See* **Civil Rights chapter.**

Faye Wattleton (1943–)
Former Planned Parenthood Executive Director, Women's Rights Activist

One of the most influential African American women in the area of reproductive rights, Faye Wattleton propelled Planned Parenthood Association into a high profile, aggressive, and vocal public health organization.

Faye Wattleton.

Born Alyce Faye Wattleton on July 8, 1943, in St. Louis, Missouri, her family, though poor, stressed the importance of helping others who were less fortunate. She graduated from Ohio State University Nursing School in 1964, and then spent two years as a maternity nursing instructor for the Miami Valley Hospital School of Nursing in Dayton. Wattleton received an M.S. degree in maternal and infant health care from Columbia University, as well as certification as a nurse-midwife, after studying on a full scholarship in 1967. While at Columbia, she interned at Harlem Hospital and saw firsthand the risks involved in induced abortions by the untrained. The death of a young woman stressed to her the importance of safe abortions.

Wattleton returned to Dayton in 1967 as assistant director of Public Health Nursing Services. She also joined the local Planned Parenthood board and became its executive director two years later. In 1975, she chaired a council representing executive directors of Planned Parenthood affiliates around the country, increasing her visibility nationally. Three years later, she was elected president of Planned Parenthood, becoming the first African American woman and the youngest person to head the organization.

Immediately after her appointment, Wattleton insisted that the organization become a strong advocate for women's rights and reproductive freedom. She worked to unite the organization's mostly white, middle, and upper class women who belonged to the organization and the mostly poor women who were clients in the parenthood clinics. Wattleton also argued for equal access to the full range of health services by the rich and poor.

She has an impressive list of awards and honors in recognition of her work including the American Humanist Award (1986), Women's Honors in Public Service from the American Nursing Association (1986), Congressional Black Caucus Humanitarian Award (1989), and the American Public Health Association's Award of Excellence (1989).

In January 1992, Wattleton retired from her position with Planned Parenthood and became host of a syndicated talk show that originated in Chicago. In 1996, Wattleton wrote her autobiography *Life on the Line* focusing in on her political background as well as the rights of women. Wattleton continues to tour and speak on the issues of abortion and contraceptives.

Walter White (1893–1955)
Former NAACP Executive Secretary

Walter Francis White was born on July 1, 1893, into a middle class family that lived on the boundary between

Walter White.

an African American and a white neighborhood in Atlanta. His family was modestly successful, allowing him to attend Atlanta University. He eventually came to the attention of the NAACP and began to work for the organization in 1918.

White's light completion and hair color allowed him to conduct several undercover investigations of lynching in the South during the 1920s. This later provided him with material for his novel *The Fire in the Flint*, a brutal depiction of the lynching of an innocent African American doctor. Along with his national efforts to end lynching, the book aroused controversy and brought White greater recognition.

In 1931, White became executive secretary of the NAACP, helping to lift the organization from obscurity to a position of influence in which its support was sought even by U.S. presidents. Under his leadership, the NAACP fought for the right to vote, the right of African Americans to be admitted to professional and graduate schools in state universities, and for equal pay for African American teachers in public schools.

Walter White did not live to see the flowering of the Civil Rights movement in the second half of the 1950s. He died of a heart attack on March 21, 1955. More than 3,000 people attended his funeral, and President Eisenhower praised him as "a vigorous champion of justice and equality."

Roy Wilkins (1901–1981)
Former NAACP Executive Director

Born in St. Louis, Missouri, on August 30, 1901, Roy Wilkins was reared in St. Paul, Minnesota. He attended the University of Minnesota, where he majored in sociology and minored in journalism. He served as night editor of the *Minnesota Daily* (the school paper) and edited an African American weekly, the *St. Paul Appeal*. After receiving his B.A. in 1923, he joined the staff of the *Kansas City Call*, a leading African American weekly.

In 1931, Wilkins left the *Call* to serve under Walter White as assistant executive secretary of the National Association for the Advancement of Colored People. In 1934, he succeeded W. E. B. Du Bois as editor of *Crisis* magazine. Wilkins was named acting executive secretary of the NAACP in 1949, when White took a year's leave of absence from the organization. Wilkins assumed the position as executive secretary of the NAACP in 1955. He quickly established himself as one of the most articulate spokesmen in the Civil Rights movement. He testified before innumerable Congressional hearings, conferred with United States presidents, and wrote extensively.

For several years, Wilkins served as chairperson of the Leadership Conference on Civil Rights, an organization of more than 100 national civic, labor, fraternal, and religious organizations. He was a trustee of the Eleanor Roosevelt Foundation, the Kennedy Memorial Library Foundation, and the Estes Kefauver Memorial Foundation. He was also a member of the board of directors of the Riverdale Children's Association, the John LaFarge Institute, and the Stockbridge School, as well as the international organization, Peace with Freedom. Wilkins died on September 8, 1981.

Carter G. Woodson. *See* Education chapter.

Whitney M. Young Jr. (1922–1971)
Former NUL Director

Whitney Moore Young Jr. was born in Lincoln Ridge, Kentucky, on July 31, 1922. He received his B.A. degree from Kentucky State College (now University) in 1941. He went on to attend the Massachusetts Institute of Technology, and, in 1947, he earned an M.A. degree in social work from the University of Minnesota.

In 1947, Young was made director of industrial relations and vocational guidance for the St. Paul, Minnesota, Urban League. In 1950, he moved on to become executive secretary of the St. Paul chapter. Between 1954 and 1961, Young was dean of the Atlanta University School of Social Work. He also was a visiting scholar at Harvard University through a Rockefeller Foundation grant.

In 1961, the National Urban League's board of directors elected Young as president of the organization. Young instituted new programs such as the National Skills Bank, the Broadcast Skills Bank, the Secretarial Training Project, and an on-the-job training program with the U.S. Department of Labor. Between 1961 and 1971, the organization grew from 63 to 98 affiliates.

In addition to his work with the National Urban League, Young served as president of the National Association of Social Workers and the National Conference on Social Welfare, served on the boards and advisory committees of the Rockefeller Foundation, Urban Coalition, and Urban Institute, as well as on seven presidential commissions. In 1969, Young was selected by President Lyndon B. Johnson to receive the Presidential Medal of Freedom, the nation's highest civilian award. Young wrote two books *To Be Equal* (1964) and *Beyond Racism: Building an Open Society* (1969). He was also coauthor of *A Second Look* (1958). Young died on March 11, 1971, while attending a conference in Africa.

◆ NATIONAL ORGANIZATIONS

100 Black Men of America, Inc.
<www.100blackmen.org>
Founded 1963.

The 100 Black Men of America, Inc. is a national alliance of leading African American men of business, industry, public affairs and government, devoting their combined skills and resources to confronting the challenges facing African America youth. Its mission is to "improve the quality of life of our citizens and enhance educational opportunities for African American youth, in all communities with special emphasis on young African American males." A total of 82 national chapters and 2 international chapters are responsible for mentoring, educational, anti-violence, and economic development programs. These programs nurture creativity, emphasize academic achievement, and reinforce social responsibility.

369th Veteran's Association
369th Regiment Armory
One 369th Plaza
New York, NY 10037
(212) 281–3308
Founded 1953.

Founded to support all patriotic endeavors of the United States and to assist members and their families through charitable programs and community activities. The Association donates funds, equipment, and other supplies to children's camps, needy families, religious institutions, Veterans Administration hospitals, and community and senior citizen centers. It conducts seminar and counseling sessions to assist unemployed veterans and offers study classes to adults for preparation in civil service examinations.

A Better Chance (ABC)
419 Boylston St.
Boston, MA 02116
(617) 421–0950
<www.abetterchance.org>
Founded 1963.

A Better Chance identifies, recruits, and places talented minority students into leading secondary and public schools. Member schools provide financial assistance for those students who are need of assistance. The group also conducts research and technical assistance on expanded opportunities for minority students in secondary and higher education.

A. Philip Randolph Institute
1444 I St., NW, No. 300
Washington, DC 20005
(202) 289–2774
<www.aprihq.org>
Founded 1964.

The Institute promotes cooperation between the African American community and the labor force. The Institute's primary interest is political action through coalition building and the organization of affiliate groups. It also conducts research, runs specialized education programs, and maintains a speakers bureau. Responsible for administering the A. Philip Randolph Educational Fund.

Africa Action
110 Maryland Ave. NE, No. 508
Washington, DC 20002
(202) 546–7961
africaaction@igc.org
<www.africaaction.org>
Founded 2001.

Africa Action works for political, economic and social justice in Africa.

Africa-America Institute
Chanin Bldg., 380 Lexington Ave.
New York, NY 10168–4298
(212) 949–5666
aainy@aaionline.org
Founded 1953.

The Institute works to further development in Africa, improve African American understanding, and inform Americans about Africa. In addition, it engages in training, development assistance, and informational activities. It sponsors African American conferences, media and congressional workshops, and regional seminars.

Africa Faith and Justice Network
3035 Fourth St., NE
Washington, DC 20017
(202) 832–3412
afjn@afjn.org
<afjn.cua.edu>
Founded 1983.

Africa Faith and Justice Network is a Catholic network of individual and group members focused on Africa and the experience of its people. AFJN is committed in faith to collaborate in the task of transforming U.S. mentality and policy on Africa. It seeks to be an instrument of education and advocacy on behalf of justice for Africa.

The Africa Fund
50 Broad St., Ste. 711
New York, NY 10004
(212) 785–1024
<www.prairienet.org/acas/afund.html>
Founded 1966.

Established by the American Committee on Africa to do the following: defend human and civil rights of needy Africans by providing or financing legal assistance; provide medical relief to Africans, particularly refugees; render aid to indigent Africans in the United States, Africa, or elsewhere who are suffering economic, legal, or social injustices; provide educational aid or grants to Africans, particularly refugees; inform the American public about the needs of Africans; and engage in study, research, and analysis of questions relating to Africa.

Africa Inland Mission International

PO Box 178
135 W Crooked Hill Rd.
Pearl River, NY 10965
(845) 735–4014
aim_info@aimint.org
<www.aim-us.org>
Founded 1895.

Africa Inland Mission International's missionaries conduct Bible teaching, community development, education, medical work, and evangelization in Angola, Central African Republic, Chad, Comoro Islands, Kenya, Lesotho, Madagascar, Mozambique, Namibia, Democratic Republic of Congo, Seychelles, Sudan, Tanzania, Uganda, and urban centers in the United States. The group's activities include: theological education; radio and television ministries; youth work; technical assistance services; agricultural and community development; relief work; special, industrial, and secondary education.

Africa Network

PO Box 1894
Evanston, IL 60204–1894
(847) 328–9305
<www2.h-net.msu.edu/~africa/>
Founded 1981.

Network of professors, students, writers, and individuals working to defend just law, freedom, and human rights. Africa Network opposes "the crime of racist, apartheid law," and provides resource materials and information on South Africa. The Network also offers educational outreach programs, in addition to sponsoring programs commemorating important historical events of South Africa, including Sharpeville Memorial Day and Soweto Anniversary Commemoration. The group was originally named for Dennis Brutus, former political prisoner, South African poet, scholar, and anti-apartheid activist, who was granted political asylum in the United States in 1983.

Africa News Service

PO Box 3851
Durham, NC 27702
(919) 286–0747
newsdesk@africanews.org
Founded 1973.

A news agency whose purpose is to supply material on Africa for broadcast and print media. Covers African politics, economy and culture, and U.S. policy and international issues affecting Africa. Obtains news by monitoring African radio stations on short-wave equipment, by subscribing to African publications, and through a network of reporters based in Africa. Also produces investigative stories on U.S. policy and its implications. Provides audio news and programming for radio, articles and graphics for newspapers and magazines, and prints for libraries and institutions. Carries out research for feature articles, news programs, and individuals. Maintains 5000 volume library along with 90 file cabinets of clippings and documents related to Africa.

Africa Travel Association

347 5th Ave., Ste. 610
New York, NY 10016
(212) 447–1926
africatrvl@aol.com
Founded 1975.

The Association conducts regional seminars and trade show exhibitions and sponsors the Africa Guild to help develop a general interest in Africa.

Africa Watch

Human Rights Watch
485 Fifth Ave.
New York, NY 10017–6104
(212) 972–8400
<www.hrwnyc@hrw.org>
Founded 1988.

The Watch monitors and promotes internationally recognized human rights in Africa.

Africa World Press

PO Box 1892
Trenton, NJ 08607
(609) 771–1666
<www.africanworld.com>
Founded 1979.

Founded by scholar activists and members of the African intellectual community. The Press promotes and maintains the development of an independent, democratic, and critical thinking African intellectual community. It also utilizes the scientific knowledge and skills of the community to give service to African peoples and social movements. It further conducts seminars on various subjects, such as the energy crisis, human rights, political repression, and food.

AFRICALINK

c/o USAID
1325 G St. NW Ste. 400
Washington, DC 20005–3121
703235–5415
africalink@info.usaid.gov

AFRICALINK is comprised of individuals and organizations with an interest in the economic and community development of Africa. Promotes sustainable development suitable to local needs and capacities. Identifies and distributes appropriate technologies, facilitates establishment of improved communications networks, and sponsors research and educational programs.

Africamix
8236 Garry Oak Dr.
Citrus Heights, CA 95610
(916) 729–9342
volunteer@africamix.com
<www.africamix.com>

Africamix is a traveling arts and music festival dedicated to promoting public awareness and funding for the prevention of child abuse and neglect in black communities. The group provides residential services and therapeutic foster care for abandoned, abused and neglected children.

African American Breast Cancer Alliance
PO Box 8981
Minneapolis, MN 55408–0981
(612) 825–3675
aabcainc@yahoo.com
<www.geocities.com/aabcainc/>
Founded 1990.

The Alliance is committed to helping Black women, people of color, families and communities cope with breast cancer. It sponsors a breast cancer support group for patients and survivors at various stages of their experiences, and addresses the specific needs of Black women diagnosed with breast cancer. In addition to this work, the Alliance also sponsors celebrations and health events for survivors, families, friends and communities.

African American Cultural Alliance
PO Box 22173
Nashville, TN 37202
(615) 299–0412
kwamefest@aol.com
<www.africanamericanculturalalliance.com>
Founded 1983.

The Alliance seeks to promote African culture and increase public awareness of the cultural and historical heritage of people of African descent by offering educational programs for children through theater, music, dance, history and poetry. AACA conducts research and also maintains speakers bureau.

African American Life Alliance
PO Box 3722
Capitol Heights, MD 20743
forlife@maranatha.net
<blacksforlife.net>
Founded 1991.

Works to educate the African American community about how "sexual promiscuity and illicit moral activities have invaded the communities and are eroding the families, organizations, schools and churches."

African American Museums Association
PO Box 427
Wilberforce, OH 45384
(937) 376–4611
naamcc@erinet.com
<www.artnoir.com/aaam.html>
Founded 1978.

The Association represents museums, scholars, and museum professionals who are concerned with preserving, restoring, displaying, researching, and collecting African American culture and history. The group also provides technical assistance to African American museums, conducting professional training workshops, surveys, and evaluations.

African Chamber of Commerce
2121 Commonwealth Ave., Ste. 200C
Charlotte, NC 28205
(704) 374–0070
acc@africanchamber.org
<www.africanchamber.org>
Founded 1984.

The African Chamber of Commerce promotes African international trade.

African Cradle
509 13th St., Ste. 5
Modesto, CA 95354–2444
(209) 575–1980
info@africancradle.com
<www.africancradle.com>

The African Cradle works with the Ethiopian government to find homes for children in need of adoption, and provides necessary care to infants and children in Ethiopia.

African Development Institute
PO Box 1644
New York, NY 10185
ca498@freenet.buffalo.edu
<www.africainstitute.com>
Founded 1995.

The Institute seeks to find practical solutions to Africa's developmental crisis through non partisan policy research. It conducts study and discussion forums, special events and educational outreach programs.

African-American Labor Center

1925 K St., NW, Ste. 300
Washington, DC 20006
(202) 778–4600
Founded 1964.

The Center assists, strengthens, and encourages free and democratic trade unions in Africa. It has undertaken projects in 43 countries in partnership with African trade unions. Programs are developed upon request and advice of African unions with knowledge of host government. Projects are geared to eventual assumption of complete managerial and financial responsibility by African labor movements. The objective is to help build sound national labor organizations that will be of lasting value to workers and the community, institutions that contribute to the economic and social development of their countries and to Africa's total political and economic independence. Major areas of activity are worker's education and leadership training, vocational training, cooperatives and credit unions, union medical and social service programs, administrative support for unions, and communication and information. The Center sponsors study tours and visitor programs to permit African and American trade unionists to become familiar with each other's politics, economies, and trade union movements; Africans are exposed to technical training not available in their homeland.

African-American Library and Information Science Association

c/o UCLA Center for African-American Studies
    Library
Box 951545
Los Angeles, CA 90095–1545
(310) 825–6060
imz@ucla.edu
Founded 1993.

The Association is comprised of library and information science professionals and others, and is dedicated to empowering people of African descent in the United States and throughout the world. It strives to monitor, evaluate, and report the quality and quantity of library and information service to people of African descent. In addition, it works to assist in the development of collections on the African world community and in the recruitment, placement, retention, and promotion of librarians of African descent. Promotes African American and world community literacy through support of community-based information centers, bookstores, libraries, and other information enterprises.

African-American Music Society

PO Box 2522
Springfield, MA 01101–2522
(413) 734–2555
aamsinc@cs.com
Founded 1988.

Composed of admirers of African American classical music (jazz), the Society seeks to present and preserve the history of jazz and its leading exponents. The Society also conducts educational programs and sponsors concerts.

African-American Natural Foods Association

c/o Cheryl A. Simms
PO Box 497336
Chicago, IL 60649
(773) 363–3939
Founded 1990.

The Association works to increase awareness of natural foods and the nutritional industry in minority communities. It also sponsors seminars and workshops; maintains library and speakers bureau; and plans to establish a natural food resource and information center.

Africare

440 R St. NW
Washington, DC 20001–1935
(202) 462–3614
africare@africare.org
<www.africare.org>
Founded 1971.

Africare seeks to improve the quality of life in rural Africa. It provides health and environmental protection services in rural areas of Africa, works to improve African water and agricultural resources, and conducts public education programs in the United States on African development.

Afro-American Historical and Genealogical Society

PO Box 73086
Washington, DC 20056
(202) 234–5350
badbdw@aol.com
<www.rootsweb.com/~mdaahgs>
Founded 1977.

The Society encourages scholarly research in African American history and genealogy as it relates to

American history and culture. The group also collects, maintains, and preserves relevant material, which the society makes available for research and publication. Conducts seminars and workshops.

Alcoholism in the Black Community

ABC Addiction Services
East Orange General Hospital
East Orange, NJ 07019
(973) 678–8300

All-African People's Revolutionary Party

1738 A St., SE
Washington, DC 20003
Founded 1971.

Founded by Africans and persons of African descent who support Pan-Africanism, "the total liberation and unification of Africa under an all-African socialist government."

Alliance of African American Artists

4936–3 Columbia Rd.
Columbia, MD 21044–2176
(410) 740–0033
joyce@artists4a.com
<www.artists4a.com>

Made up of individuals interested in art. The Alliance works to promote artists of African descent, educate communities about art, and create opportunities for African American artists to display their work.

Alpha Kappa Alpha

5656 S. Stony Island Ave.
Chicago, IL 60637
(773) 684–1282
Founded 1908.

A service sorority founded in 1908.

Alpha Phi Alpha

2313 St. Paul St.
Baltimore, MD 21218
(410) 554–0040
Founded 1906.

A service fraternity founded in 1906.

Alpha Pi Chi

PO Box 255
Kensington, MD 20895
(301) 559–4330
Founded 1963.

A service sorority founded in 1963.

American Association of Blacks in Energy

927 15th St. NW, Ste. 200
Washington, DC 20005
(202) 371–9530
bhill@aabe.org
<www.aabe.org>
Founded 1977.

Founded by African Americans in energy-related professions including: engineers, scientists, consultants, academicians, and entrepreneurs; government officials and public policymakers; and interested students. The Association represents African Americans and other minorities in matters involving energy use and research, the formulation of energy policy, the ownership of energy resources, and the development of energy technologies. It seeks to increase the knowledge, understanding, and awareness of the minority community in energy issues by serving as an energy information source for policymakers, recommending African Americans and other minorities to appropriate energy officials and executives, encouraging students to pursue professional careers in the energy industry, and advocating the participation of African Americans and other minorities in energy programs and policymaking activities. It also updates members on key legislation and regulations being developed by the Department of Energy, the Department of Interior, the Department of Commerce, the Small Business Administration, and other federal and state agencies.

American Baptist Black Caucus

Beth Eden Baptist Church
Tenth and Adeline Sts.
Oakland, CA 94607
(510) 444–1625
Founded 1968.

The Caucus is concerned with reforming the American Baptist Convention in terms of bridging the gap between whites and minority members. It seeks to: develop convention support of scholarship aid for disadvantaged students; resources for business and religious projects in the inner city; adequate representation of minorities in the convention structure; support for African American colleges and universities; and open hiring policies on local, state, and national levels.

American Black Book Writers Association

PO Box 10548
Marina Del Rey, CA 90295
(323) 822–5195
Founded 1980.

The Association represents African Americans in the United States publishing industry. It encourages development of African American authors and works to preserve and advance African American literature. The Association promotes and gives market support to member's works; holds mutual promotions and tours; sponsors cooperative advertising in African American-oriented media; and conducts research on problems affecting African American authors and their works in the United States.

American Committee on Africa

50 Broad St., Ste. 711
New York, NY 10004
(212) 785–1024
<www.prairienet.org/acas/afund.html>
Founded 1953.

Devoted to supporting African people in their struggle for freedom and independence, the Committee focuses on southern Africa and the Western Sahara and support for African liberation movements. It works with legislators, churches, trade unions, and interested students; arranges speaking tours for African leaders; publicizes conditions and developments in Africa; and sponsors research, rallies, and demonstrations.

American Tennis Association

8100 Cleary Blvd.
Plantation, FL 33324–1370
Founded 1916.

Founded by persons interested in tennis, the Association promotes and develops tennis among African Americans. It supports training programs for coaches, sponsors tournaments, and training programs for young players.

American-Southern Africa Chamber of Trade and Industry

1080 Park Ave., Ste. 4W
New York, NY 10128–1167
(212) 410–6560
Founded 1966.

Made up of corporations involved in trade with and within Angola, Botswana, Lesotho, Malawi, Mozambique, South Africa, Swaziland, Zambia, and Zimbabwe, the Chamber furthers the development of trade and investment between the United States and the countries of southern Africa. It also gathers and disseminates information; examines questions pertaining to commercial and industrial relations; and promotes and facilitates economic relations between the countries concerned.

Anti-Repression Resource Team

PO Box 8040
State College, PA 16803–8040
(814) 237–3095
Founded 1979.

The team combats all forms of political repression including police violence and misconduct, Ku Klux Klan and neo-Nazi terrorism, and spying and covert action by secret police and intelligence agencies. It focuses on research, writing, lecturing, organizing, and publishing and conducts training workshops for church, labor, and community organizations.

Association for the Preservation and Presentation of the Arts

2011 Benning Rd. NE
Washington, DC 20002
(202) 529–3244
Founded 1964.

Founded by individuals representing the visual and performing arts and interested others. The organization serves as a vehicle for the promotion of blacks in the arts, as well as seeking to increase public awareness and appreciation of the arts and its representation of African American culture. Other areas of focus include: work on the development of musical and dance productions, production of children's shows, and sponsorship of lectures. Offers scholarships to children and young people interested in the arts.

Association for the Study of African-American Life and History

7961 Eastern Ave., Ste. 301
Silver Spring, MD 20910–4833
(301) 587–5900
asalh@earthlink.net
<www.asalh.org>
Founded 1915.

A sponsor of Afro-American History Month, the Association is comprised of historians, scholars, and students interested in the research and study of black people as a contributing factor in civilization. The Association works to promote historical research and writings, collects historical manuscripts and materials relating to black people throughout the world, and brings about harmony among the races by interpreting one to the other. In addition, it encourages the study of black history and training in the social sciences, history, and other disciplines. Cooperates with governmental agencies, foundations, and peoples and nations in projects designed to advance the study of ethnic history, with emphasis on black heritage and programs for the future. Maintains Carter G. Woodson home in Washington, DC.

Association of African American People's Legal Council

c/o William Bert Johnson
13902 Robson St.
Detroit, MI 48227
(313) 231–6320
Founded 1959.

The Council seeks to achieve equal justice under the law for African Americans and to provide free legal counsel to people of African American descent. It compiles statistics and reports on cases of international inequality and obtains research from public systems on education and its effect on discrimination.

Association of African American Women Scholars

c/o Women's Studies Program
Cavanaugh Hall, Rm. 001C
425 University Blvd.
Indiana University
Indianapolis, IN 46202
(317) 278–2038
aaws@iupui.edu
<www.iupui.edu/˜aaws/>
Founded 1995.

The Association promotes scholarship among women of African descent worldwide, and seeks to form intellectual links among scholars studying Africa, colonialism, and related topics. It serves as a clearinghouse on African history, culture, economics, and development, particularly as these subjects impact women. Additional activities include: Providing information and advice to policy makers; participation in advocacy work; research and educational programs.

Association of African-American Women Business Owners

c/o Brenda Alford
PO Box 13180
Silver Spring, MD 20911–0180
(301) 585–8051
aaawbo@yahoo.com
<www.blackpgs.com/aawboa.html>
Founded 1982.

Made up of small business owners in all industries, particularly business services, the Association seeks to assist in developing a greater number of successful self-employed black women through business and personal development programs, networking, and legislative action. In addition, the group is conducting a two-year project identifying black women business owners as role models and historical figures, and plans to establish an archive.

Association of Black Admissions and Financial Aid Officers of the Ivy League and Sister Schools

PO Box 381402
Cambridge, MA 02238–1402
admissions@cornell.edu
<www.sas.cornell.edu/admissions/aba/
   abafaoilss.htm>
Founded 1970.

The Association was founded by present and former minority admissions and financial aid officers employed at Ivy League or sister schools. These schools include: Brown, Columbia, Cornell, Dartmouth, Harvard/Radcliffe, Massachusetts Institute of Technology, University of Pennsylvania, Princeton, Yale, Barnard, Bryn Mawr, Mount Holyoke, Smith, and Wellesley. The Association aids minority students who wish to pursue a college education and seeks to improve methods of recruitment, admittance, and financial services that support the growth and maintenance of the minority student population at these institutions. It encourages Ivy League and sister schools to respond to the needs of minority students and admissions and financial aid officers.

Association of Black Anthropologists

c/o American Anthropological Association
4350 N. Fairfax Dr., Ste. 640
Arlington, VA 22203–1620
(703) 528–1902
crodrigu@chumal.cas.usf.edu
<www.aaanet.org>
Founded 1970.

The Association works to: formulate conceptual and methodological frameworks to advance understanding of all forms of human diversity and commonality; advance theoretical efforts to explain the conditions that produce social inequalities based on race, ethnicity, class, or gender; and develop research methods that involve the peoples studied and local scholars in all stages of investigation and dissemination of findings.

Association of Black Cardiologists

6849-B2 Peachtree Dunwoody Rd.
Atlanta, GA 30328
(678) 302–4222
abcardio@abcardio.org
<www.abcardio.org>
Founded 1974.

The Association seeks to improve prevention and treatment of cardiovascular diseases.

Association of Black Catholics Against Abortion

1011 1st Ave.
New York, NY 10022
(212) 371–1000
Founded 1988.

The Association conducts educational programs, legislative information, and promotes voter registration.

Association of Black Foundation Executives

1828 L St., NW
Washington, DC 20036
(202) 466–6512
<www.cof.org>
Founded 1971.

The Association encourages increased recognition of economic, educational, and social issues facing African Americans in the grant making field. It seeks to: promote support of African Americans and their status as grant making professionals, increase the number of African Americans entering the grant making field, and helps members improve their job effectiveness. Though involved with grant making organizations, the ABFE itself does not award grants.

Association of Black Nursing Faculty

5823 Queens Cove
Lisle, IL 60532
(630) 969–3809
wesgnld@texas.net
Founded 1987.

The Association works to promote health-related issues and educational concerns of interest to the African American community and ABNF. It serves as a forum for communication and the exchange of information among members, as well as develops strategies for expressing concerns to other individuals, institutions, and communities. It aims to do the following: assists members in professional development; develops and sponsors continuing education activities; fosters networking and guidance in employment and recruitment activities; and promotes health-related issues of legislation, government programs, and community activities.

Association of Black Psychologists

PO Box 55999
Washington, DC 20040–5999
(202) 722–0808
admin@abpsi.org
<www.abpsi.org>
Founded 1968.

The Association aims to do the following: enhance the psychological well-being of African American people; define mental health in consonance with newly established psychological concepts and standards; develop policies for local, state, and national decision-making, which have impact on the mental health of the African American community; support established African American sister organizations and aid in the development of new, independent African American institutions to enhance the psychological, educational, cultural, and economic situation.

Association of Black Sociologists

4200 Wisconsin Ave. NW
PMB 106–257
Washington, DC 20016–2143
(202) 285–4173
evita.bynum@american.edu
<members.aol.com/blacksociology/>
Founded 1968.

Purposes are to: promote the professional interests of African American sociologists; promote an increase in the number of professionally trained sociologists; help stimulate and improve the quality of research and the teaching of sociology; provide perspectives regarding African American experiences, as well as expertise for understanding and dealing with problems confronting African American people; protect professional rights and safeguard the civil rights stemming from executing the above objectives.

Association of Black Sporting Goods Professionals

PO Box 772074
Coral Springs, FL 33077–2074
Founded 1990.

The Association promotes the benefits of diversity, and seeks to facilitate access to career opportunities for its members. It serves as a clearinghouse on the sporting goods industry, and conducts industry research. Additional services and programs include: Job Information Services and Career Awareness Program to encourage increased participation by African Americans in the sporting goods industry; Partners in Progress Program to enhance the understanding of culturally diverse markets among sporting goods executives.

Association of Black Women Attorneys

134 W 32nd St.
New York, NY 10001
(212) 560–3903
abwany@aol.com
Founded 1976.

The Association is an organization for African American women lawyers.

Association of Black Women in Higher Education
c/o Dr. Bettye J. Miller
9203 Tuckehoe Land
Adelphi, MD 20783
(301) 439–7471
drglovermiller@aol.com
Founded 1979.

Comprised of faculty members, education administrators, students, retirees, consultants, managers, and affirmative action officers, the Association's objectives are to nurture the role of black women in higher education, and to provide support for the professional development goals of black women. Association members conduct workshops and seminars.

Association of Concerned African Scholars
c/o Steven Rubert
Department of History
306 Milan Hall
Oregon State University
Corvallis, OR 97331–5104
(541) 737–3661
<www.prairienet.org/acas>
Founded 1977.

The Association facilitates scholarly analysis and opinion in order to impact U.S. policy toward Africa; formulates alternative government policy toward Africa and disseminates it to the public; works to develop a communication and action network among African scholars. It mobilizes support on current issues; participates in local public education programs; stimulates research on policy-oriented issues and disseminates findings; and informs and updates members on international policy developments.

Black Affairs Center for Training and Organizational Development
c/o Margaret V. Wright
10918 Jarboe Ct.
Silver Spring, MD 20901
(301) 681–9827
Founded 1970.

The Center is a multidisciplinary management research organization which promotes social change, educational improvement, organization renewal and goal achievement, systematic problem solving, and multicultural skills development through custom-designed training programs and consultation services.

The Center offers individuals, groups, educational systems, and governmental and community agencies programs such as Equal Employment Opportunity Training; Employee Motivation, Productivity and Improvement Training; Career Education and Development Training. Programs are continually being developed in areas including women's concerns, single parents, youth and sex, drugs and alcoholism, the aging, daycare, sexual harassment, and stress management.

The Black Agenda
PO Box 9726
Columbus, OH 43209
(614) 338–8383
info@blackagenda.com
<www.endarkenment.com/blackagenda/>
Founded 1985.

Dedicated to enhancing the political, economic, social, and cultural status of African Americans, the group fosters communication among members and conducts educational programs.

Black American Cinema Society
3617 Monclair St.
Los Angeles, CA 90018
(323) 737–3292
maymeclayton@webtv.net
Founded 1975.

Made up of faculty members, students, senior citizens, and film and jazz enthusiasts, the Society works to bring about an awareness of the contributions made by African Americans to the motion picture industry in silent films, early talkies, and short and feature films. The Society maintains collection of early black films owned by the Western States Black Research Center. It conducts research projects, film shows, and Black History Month seminars. The Society provides financial support to independent black filmmakers, and compiles statistics; maintains a speakers bureau, and sponsors a traveling film festival.

Black American Response to the African Community
127 N. Madison Ave., Ste. 400
Pasadena, CA 91101
Founded 1984.

The Community is a grass roots organization of entertainers, journalists, clergy, and business, health, and community leaders working to assist the victims of drought and famine in Africa. The group focuses on emergency efforts involving medical needs, water irrigation, housing, and food supplies. In addition, it provides relief for orphans through its Family Network Program, and disseminates current information on drought-stricken areas in Africa. Other activities include: assisting in the development of regeneration projects in affected areas; maintaining the National Education Task Force to educate Americans on the African crisis; sponsoring media updates. The Community raises funds through television documentaries, benefit movie premieres, art exhibits, and collection boxes.

Black Americans for Life

419 7th St. NW, Ste. 500
Washington, DC 20004
(202) 626–8800
nrlc@nrlc.org
<www.nrlc.org>

The group promotes alternatives to abortion for women with crisis pregnancies and strives to be a visible presence defending the rights of the unborn in the African American community. It asserts that African American women are twice as likely as white women to have abortions and believes that abortions are counterproductive to advances made through civil rights efforts.

Black and Indian Mission Office

Commission for the Catholic Missions Among the
　　Colored People and the Indians
2021 H St. NW
Washington, DC 20006–4207
(202) 331–8542
Founded 1884.

The Office coordinates the distribution of funds from the annual Black and Indian Mission Collection in Catholic churches across the United States. These funds go to support priests, nuns, and other religious workers at African American and Native American missions and schools.

Black Awareness in Television

67 Trowbridge St.
Detroit, MI 48202–1337
(313) 867–8790
davidrambeau@hotmail.com
Founded 1970.

The organization produces black media programs for television, video, radio, film, and theatre. It trains individuals in the media and conducts research projects including surveys. In addition, it produces public affairs, cultural arts, soap opera, and exercise programs; sponsors theatre companies; seeks television exposure for black-produced products and black performing artists; and promotes "September is Black Reading Month" program.

Black Broadcasters Alliance

711 West 40th St., Ste. 330
Baltimore, MD 21211
(410) 662–9688
e-mail@thebba.org
<www.thebba.org>
Founded 1997.

The Alliance is comprised of African American broadcasters working to better educate and assist those who seek career opportunities in the industry. It places emphasis on increasing African American representation in ownership, management, engineering and sales. It also exercises the right to inform, lobby and influence not only the public, but also local and national governmental bodies as to equal participation in the industry.

Black Career Women

PO Box 19332
Cincinnati, OH 45219
lindaparker@uc.edu
<www.bcw.org>
Founded 1977.

The group is made up of African American professional women, and promotes professional advancement of its members. The organization also seeks to establish and support "formal Black women's networks." In addition, it provides career development resources and educational courses to members; develops information and research on Black women workers; and serves as a "supportive forum for the Black woman dealing with the complexities of personal and professional development."

Black Caucus of the American Library Association

c/o Gladys Smiley Bell
PO Box 1738
Hampton, VA 23669
(757) 727–5190
webmaster@bcala.org
Founded 1970.

The Association promotes librarianship and encourages active participation of African Americans in library associations and boards and all levels of the profession. It monitors activities of the American Library Association with regard to its policies and programs and how they affect African American librarians and library users. In addition, it reviews, analyzes, evaluates, and recommends to the ALA actions that influence the recruitment, development, advancement, and general working conditions of African American librarians. It facilitates library services that meet the informational needs of African American people, including increased availability of materials related to social and economic concerns, and encourages development of authoritative information resources concerning African American people and dissemination of this information to the public.

Black Coaches Association

PO Box 443
Stone Mountain, GA 30086
bcaexec@mindspring.com
<www.bcasports.org>
Founded 1986.

The Association promotes the creation of a positive environment in which issues such as stereotyping, lack of significant media coverage, and discrimination can be exposed, discussed, and resolved. It provides member services and petitions the NCAA legislative bodies to design, enact, and enforce diligent guidelines and policies to improve professional mobility for minorities.

Black Community Crusade for Children

25 E St. NW
Washington, DC 20001
(202) 628–8787
cdfinfo@childrensdefense.org
<www.childrensdefense.org/bccc.htm>

An organization composed of African American clergy, educators, policy makers, and community leaders that seeks to ensure "no child is left behind, and that every child has a Healthy Start, a Head Start, a Fair Start, a Safe Start, and a Moral Start in life, with the support of caring parents and nurturing communities." The group works to mobilize the Black community on behalf of children. Conducts programs in areas including: community building; spiritual, character, and leadership development; intergenerational mentoring; interracial and interethnic communication; interdisciplinary networking; training. The group organizes Freedom Schools, which provide meals and education and cultural enrichment programs in local communities, operates Student Leadership Network for children (SLNC), and maintains a farm once owned by African American author Alex Haley.

Black Data Processing Associates

9315 Largo Dr. W., No. 260
Largo, MD 20774
nbdpa@ix.netcom.com
<www.bdpa.org>
Founded 1975.

This organization seeks to accumulate and share information processing knowledge and business expertise in order to increase the career and business potential of minorities in the information processing field.

Black Entertainment and Sports Lawyers Association

1129 20th St. NW, Ste. 510
Washington, DC 20036
703683–1800
<www.besla.org>
Founded 1979.

The purpose of the Association is to provide more efficient and effective legal representation to African American entertainers and athletes. It offers a referral system for legal representation and a resource bank for providing information to students, groups, and nonprofit and civic organizations involved in the entertainment industry; and serves as an industry watchdog in protecting the rights of African Americans within the entertainment community.

Black Farmers and Agriculturists Association

PO Box 61
Tillery, NC 27887
(252) 826–2800
tillery@aol.com
<www.coax.net/people/lwf/bfaa.htm>
Founded 1997.

A grass roots organization united in direct response to the decline in African American farmers and landowners.

Black Filmmaker Foundation

670 Broadway, Ste. 300
New York, NY 10012
(212) 253–1690
info@dvrepublic.com
<www.dvrepublic.com>
Founded 1978.

This group fosters audience development by programming local, national, and international film festivals. The Foundation maintains a video library and conducts seminars and workshops.

Black Filmmakers Hall of Fame, Inc.

1322 Wester St., Ste. 400
Oakland, CA 94612
(510) 465–0804
bghfinc@aol.com
Founded 1973.

The Foundation seeks to study, teach, and preserve the contributions of African American filmmakers to American cinema. It fosters cultural awareness through educational, research, and public service programs in the film arts. It also holds film-lecture series, the Black Filmworks Festival, and the annual International Film Competition.

Black Flight Attendants of America, Inc.

1060 Crenshaw Blvd., Ste. 202
Los Angeles, CA 90019
(323) 299–3406
bfaoa@aol.com
<home.attbi.com/ ˜jwreedjr/BFAOA/>
Founded 1974.

This organization of aviation professionals seeks to expand educational opportunities through travel for at-risk communities; supports and mentors aviation professionals; promotes civic and charitable endeavors in African American communities; and assists the corporation in identification of qualified minorities for management and professional positions. The group also sponsors Career Day in inner-city schools.

Black Gold Group

223 Parker St. NE
Washington, DC 20002–3527
(202) 667–0355
Founded 1989.

The Black Gold Group provides support and technical assistance to African American artists.

Black Human Resources Network

1900 L St. NW, Ste. 500
Washington, DC 20036
(202) 775–1669
Founded 1988.

The Network is made up of human resources professionals and practitioners. It promotes the welfare of African American human resource practitioners; encourages development and information exchange among members; monitors legislation pertaining to human resources; and conducts seminars and charitable programs.

Black Informed Professionals

c/o Chante Ramsey
PO Box 586
New York, NY 10159–0586
bipinc_info@yahoo.com
<blackprofessionals.tripod.com/home.html>
Founded 1999.

Comprised of professionals of color, especially those of the African Diaspora, this organization is committed to self-empowerment, networking, and community revitalization.

Black Mental Health Alliance

2901 Druid Park Dr., Ste. A110
Business Ctr. at Park Circle
Baltimore, MD 21215
(410) 837–2642
bhealthall@aol.com
<bmhaec.org>
Founded 1984.

The Alliance seeks to increase clinicians, clergy, educators, and social service professionals' awareness of African American's mental health needs and concerns on such issues as stress, violence, racism, substance abuse, and parenting. Provides consultation, public information, and resource referrals. Conducts a public awareness campaign; educates the community about available resources; develops programs that benefit African American children and families. Offers training to human service workers, teachers, police officers, and other service providers who work with culturally diverse populations. Maintains speakers bureau. The support group provides emotional support, education and interaction for family members experiencing the stresses of caring for and/or living with a mentally ill relative. Provides a resource referral service; maintains an extensive list of African American mental health professionals who are sensitive to and appreciate cultural differences. Offers programs that invest in the needs of African American adult and adolescent females who are at risk of, or have, HIV or AIDS. Offers the "Free Yourself Stop Smoking and Prevention" program.

Black Methodists for Church Renewal

601 W. Riverview Ave.
Dayton, OH 45406
(937) 227–9460
bmcr@bmcr_umc.org
Founded 1968.

The group serves as platform from which African Americans can express concerns to the general church on issues such as: revival and survival of the African American church; involvement of African Americans within the structure of the church; the conduct of the church as it relates to investment policies and social issues; economic support in the African American community; and the support of the 12 African American colleges. It encourages African American Methodists to work for economic and social justice and works to expose racism in agencies and institutions of the United Methodist Church. The group also seeks improvement of educational opportunities for African Americans, the strengthening of African American churches, and an increase in the number of African American persons in Christian-related vocations. It advocates liberation, peace, justice, and freedom for all people and supports programs that alleviate suffering in developing countries.

Black Military History Institute of America

c/o Col. William A. De Shields
PO Box 1134
Fort Meade, MD 20755
(410) 757–4250
bmhia.404@aol.com
Founded 1987.

Made up of individuals interested in promoting the military achievements of African Americans and publicizing other aspects of black history. The organization seeks to: provide archival facilities to collect, preserve, and exhibit materials pertaining to military history; motivate and support underprivileged youths by using military role models as a source of inspiration; foster a spirit of camaraderie and goodwill among all persons sharing an interest in community involvement programs for the underprivileged. The organization also sponsors a slide lectures and photographic exhibit, as well as maintaining a speakers bureau.

Black Pilots of America

PO Box 7463
Pine Bluff, AR 71611
(870) 879–6612
kent5761@earthlink.net
<www.blackpilots-america.org>
Founded 1996.

This organization trains African Americans to participate and advance in various areas within the field of aviation. It also encourages youth to enter the field of aviation, promotes opportunities in field of aviation by lecturing in schools, and encourages recognition of the contributions of blacks in aviation.

Black Psychiatrists of America

c/o Dr. Ramona Davis
1305 Franklin, Ste. 210
Oakland, CA 94612
(510) 834–7103
Founded 1968.

African American psychiatrists, either in practice or training, united to promote African American behavioral science and foster high quality psychiatric care for African Americans and minority group members. The group sponsors public information service.

Black Retail Action Group

c/o Rockefeller Center Station
PO Box 1192
New York, NY 10185
(212) 319–7751
dford1005@onebox.com
<www.bragusa.org>
Founded 1970.

Minorities dedicated to the inclusion of all groups in the mainstream of the American economy.

Black Revolutionary War Patriots Foundation

1612 K St. NW, Ste. 1104
Washington, DC 20006–2802
(202) 452–1776
blkpatr@central.worldweb.net
<www.blackpatriots.org>
Founded 1985.

The Foundation raises private funds for the establishment of a memorial in Washington, DC, to commemorate African American patriots of the American Revolutionary War.

Black Rock Coalition

PO Box 1054, Cooper Sta.
New York, NY 10276
(212) 713–5097
info@blackrockcoalition.org
<www.blackrockcoalition.org>
Founded 1985.

The Coalition promotes, produces, and distributes alternative/African American music and provides information, technical expertise, and performance and recording opportunities for "musically and politically progressive musicians." It also works to increase the visibility of African American rock artists in music media and on college radio stations.

Black Stuntmen's Association

8949 W. 24th St.
Los Angeles, CA 90034
(310) 202–9191
Founded 1966.

Composed of men and women (ages 18 to 50) who are members of the Screen Actors Guild and the American Federation of Television and Radio Artists. The organization serves as an agency for stuntpeople in motion pictures and television, conducts stunt performances at various local schools, and plans to operate school for black stuntpeople. In addition, it also offers placement service.

Black Theatre Network
763 Belmont Pl. E #105
Seattle, WA 98102
352495–2116
mdd3@is8.nyu.edu
<www.btnet.org>
Founded 1986.

The network is made up of individuals involved in higher education and professionals in black theatre. It serves as a networking organization for those with interests in black theater—either in academia or at the professional level—and also organizes workshops.

Black Veterans for Social Justice
665 Willoughby Ave.
Brooklyn, NY 11206
(718) 935–1116
admin@bvsj.xohost.com
Founded 1979.

The group seeks to aid African American veterans in obtaining information concerning their rights, ways to upgrade a less-than-honorable discharge, and Veterans Administration benefits due them and their families. It seeks to prohibit discrimination against African American veterans; provides educational programs; and facilitates veteran's sharing of skills acquired while in service. The group's services include counseling and community workshops on veteran issues and a program to provide services to veterans in local prisons. It also assists veterans who have suffered from the effects of Agent Orange, an herbicide containing dioxin and used as a defoliant in Vietnam until 1969.

Black Women in Church and Society
700 Martin Luther King Dr.
Atlanta, GA 30314
(404) 527–5710
mbellinger@itc.edu
Founded 1981.

Founded to provide: structured activities and support systems for African American women whose goals include participating in leadership roles in church and society; a platform for communication between laywomen and clergywomen. It conducts research into questions and issues pivotal to African American women in church and society and maintains a research/resource center and a library with subject matter pertaining to liberation and African American theology, feminism, and feminist movements.

Black Women in Publishing
PO Box 6275
FDR Station
New York, NY 10150
(212) 772–5951
<www.bwip.org>
baip@baip.org
Founded 1979.

A networking and support group whose purpose is to encourage minorities interested in all sectors of the print industry including book, newspaper, and magazine publishing. It promotes the image of minorities working in all phases of the book, newspaper, and magazine industries; and recognizes achievements of minorities in the media. It works for a free and responsible press and facilitates the exchange of ideas and information among members, especially regarding career planning and job security. Members are kept informed about the publishing industry and their impact on it. The group encourages and works to maintain high professional standards in publishing and collaborates with other organizations in striving to improve the status of women and minorities.

Black Women in Sisterhood for Action
PO Box 1592
Washington, DC 20013
301460–1565
bisa@erols.com
<www.feminist.com/bisas1.htm>
Founded 1980.

BWSA promotes alternative strategies for educational and career development for black women; provides support and social assistance to senior black women in the community; and furnishes role models and mentors to young people, as well as management and leadership skills training, networking, team building, communication techniques, and image building.

Black Women Organized for Educational Development
Black Women's Resource Center
449 15th St., Ste. 310
Oakland, CA 94612
(510) 763–9501
bwoed@pachell.net
Founded 1984.

The Organization fosters self-sufficiency in and encourages empowerment of low-income and socially disadvantaged women by establishing and maintaining programs that improve their social and economic well-being. The group sponsors mentor program for junior high-aged young women in low-income urban areas; and offers support groups, workshops, and seminars. In addition, it maintains the Black Women's Resource Center, an information and referral service for African American women and youth.

Black Women's Roundtable on Voter Participation

1629 K St. NW, Ste. 801
Washington, DC 20006
(202) 659–4929
<www.bigvote.org>
Founded 1983.

A program of the National Coalition on Black Voter Participation. The Roundtable consists of African American women's organizations committed to social justice and economic equity through increased participation in the political process. The Roundtable organizes voter registration, education, and empowerment programs in the African American community; and emphasizes the importance of the women's vote. It seeks to: develop women's leadership skills through nonpartisan political participation; and encourage African American women's involvement in discussions concerning the influence of the women's vote in elections. It supports volunteer coalitions that work on voter registration, voter education, and get-out-the-vote efforts.

Black World Foundation

PO Box 2869
Oakland, CA 94618
(510) 547–6633
blkschlr@aol.com
<www.theblackscholar.org>
Founded 1969.

Composed of African Americans united to develop and distribute African American educational materials and to develop African American cultural and political thought. It offers books in the areas of African American literature, history, fiction, essays, political analysis, social science, poetry, and art. In addition, it maintains a library.

Black Writers Alliance

c/o Tia Shabazz
PO Box 700065
Dallas, TX 75370–0065
tiashabazz@blackwriters.org

The Alliance is dedicated to providing resources and support for black writers through the web medium.

Black, Indian, Hispanic, and Asian Women in Action

1830 James Ave. N
Minneapolis, MN 55411
(612) 521–2986
biha@worldnet.att.net
Founded 1983.

This organization strives to empower Black, Indian, Hispanic, and Asian women through implementation of educational projects. It acts as an advocate for women of color in the areas of family violence, chemical dependence, education, and physical and mental health. The group also works for social change, the health of the family, and advancement of socio-economic status.

Blacks in Government

c/o James Wilson
1820 11th St. NW
Washington, DC 20001–5015
(202) 667–3280
president@bignet.org
<www.bignet.org/big/philosop.htm>
Founded 1975.

Founded by federal, state, or local government employees or retirees concerned with the present and future status of African Americans in government. It develops training and other programs to enhance the liberty and sense of well-being of African Americans in government.

Blacks in Law Enforcement

256 E. McLemore Ave.
Memphis, TN 38106
(901) 774–1118
Founded 1986.

The group seeks to educate the public concerning the contributions made by African Americans in the field of law enforcement. It documents the lives and achievements of the first African Americans to participate in law enforcement in the United States. It also develops programs to improve the public image of law enforcement officers; and has established a short-term training program for law enforcement officers.

Books for Africa

253 E 4th St.
St. Paul, MN 55101
(651) 602–9844
info@booksforafrica.org

This organization seeks to end the book famine in Africa by ensuring the availability of books and educational materials throughout the continent.

Catholic Interracial Council of New York

c/o John Jay College
899 Tenth Ave.
New York, NY 10019
(212) 237–8255
Founded 1934.

The Council works in cooperation with local parishes and governmental and voluntary groups to combat bigotry and discrimination and to promote social justice for all racial, religious, and ethnic groups. It sponsors research, educational forums, workshops, and community action programs. It presents the annual John LaFarge Memorial Award for Interracial Justice to community leaders and the annual Hoey Award to community leaders who have worked to promote objectives of the Council.

Catholic Negro-American Mission Board

2021 H St. NW
Washington, DC 20006–4207
(202) 331–8542
Founded 1907.

The Board supports Catholic sisters' teaching programs among African Americans in the United States.

Center for Constitutional Rights

666 Broadway, Seventh Fl.
New York, NY 10012
(212) 614–6464
Founded 1966.

The Center works in such areas as abuse of the grand jury process, women's rights, civil rights, freedom of the press, racism, electronic surveillance, criminal trials, and affirmative action. It conducts the Ella Baker Student Program, the Movement Support Network, and in Mississippi, The Voting Rights Project.

Center for Educating African-American Males

411 8th St., SE
Washington, DC 20003
Founded 1990.

Comprised of African American males from all walks of life interested in helping young men, the Center works to promote positive attitudes towards school and high levels of academic achievement in African American youth by providing positive adult male role models.

Center for Multicultural Leadership

1028 Dole Human Development Center
University of Kansas
Lawrence, KS 66045
(785) 864–3990
ibldv@dole.lsi.ukans.edu
Founded 1988.

The Center seeks to develop creative leadership and effective management among African Americans for the good of society through research, training, and publication.

Center for Urban Black Studies

Graduate Theological Union
2400 Ridge Rd.
Berkeley, CA 94709
Founded 1969.

The Center provides seminarians and laypersons with resources "to respond to life in the urban community and to represent its oppressed minority people." It develops and offers courses, seminars, and other training programs dealing with issues of race, social justice, urban life, and the African American religious experience. It initiates new ministries; develops and implements community service programs; counsels and assists African American seminarians in placement and in obtaining and developing employment. It also conducts workshops and seminars addressing racial justice, church and race, and urban ministry.

Chi Eta Phi

3029 13th St., NW
Washington, DC 20009
(202) 232–3858
<www.ncat.edu/~nursing/chietaphi.html>
Founded 1932.

Founded by registered and student nurses. Its objectives are to: encourage continuing education; stimulate friendship among members; and develop working relationships with other professional groups for the improvement and delivery of health care services. It sponsors leadership training seminars and offers educational programs for entrance into nursing and allied health fields. It presents scholarships and other financial awards to assist students; sponsors recruitment and retention programs for minority students; and operates speaker's bureau on health education and biographical archives on African American nurses.

Citizens for a Better America
PO Box 7647
Van Nuys, CA 91409–7647
(818) 757–1776
home.earthlink.net/~colaco/
Founded 1975.

Churches and individuals united to create a better America by strengthening individual rights in the United States. The group serves as a public advocacy organization that lobbies for civil rights and environmental legislation. It conducts legal research in civil rights cases and provides research services to communities investigating such issues as fair housing and toxic waste disposal.

Coalition of Black Investors
PO Box 30553
Winston-Salem, NC 27130–0553
(336) 922–6240
Founded 1997.

A national organization that promotes financial literacy among African Americans by addressing issues ranging from savings plans, economic and investment education, and the formation of investment clubs to raising capital for new businesses. It also serves as a link to connect African American investors and investment clubs to communicate ideas and investment strategies.

Coalition of Black Trade Unionists
PO Box 66268
Washington, DC 20036–6268
(202) 429–1203
<www.cbtu.org>
Founded 1972.

Members of 76 labor unions united to maximize the strength and influence of African American and minority workers in organized labor. Activities include: voter registration and education; improvement of economic development; employment opportunities for minority and poor workers; and sponsoring regional seminars.

College Language Association
c/o Dr. Cason Hill
Morehouse College
830 Westu Dr. SW
Atlanta, GA 30314
(404) 681–2800
Founded 1937.

Founded by teachers of English and several foreign languages at historically African American universities.

The Association maintains placement services and a speaker's bureau.

Community Access Producers and Viewers Association
PO Box 68002
Jackson, MS 39286–8002
(601) 362–3431
Founded 1965.

The Association researches the activities of workers, African Americans, and grass roots organizations through the FIS Deep South People's History Project. It maintains extensive Mississippi-centered library and archives; distributes press releases on current southern news; and reprints items on women's liberation and political education.

Conference of Minority Public Administrators
1120 G St., NW, Ste. 700
Washington, DC 20005
(202) 393–7878
<www.aspanet.org>
Founded 1971.

Composed of members of the American Society of Public Administration who belong to a minority group or are interested in the promotion of minorities within public administration.

Congress of National Black Churches
1225 Eye St. NW, Ste. 750
Washington, DC 20005
(202) 371–1091
blong@cnbc.org
<www.cnbc.org>
Founded 1978.

Founded to find answers to problems that confront blacks in the United States and Africa including economic development, family and social support, housing, unemployment, education, and foreign relations. The focus is on religious education and evangelism.

Congress of Racial Equality
817 Broadway, 3rd Fl.
New York, NY 10003
(212) 598–4000
corenyc@aol.com
<www.core-online.org>
Founded 1942.

CORE is the third oldest civil rights groups in the United States and champions equality for all people regardless of race, creed, sex, age, disability, religious, or ethnic background. CORE seeks to establish, in practice, the inalienable right for all people to determine their own destiny, to decide for themselves what social and political organizations can operate in their best interest, and to do so without gratuitous and inhibiting influence from those whose interest is diametrically opposed. CORE administers several major programs including: Project Independence, which is designed to address the lack of skills among inner-city young adults by providing intensive training in office skills and helping them to find meaningful employment; Project Internet Watch; Civil Rights Boot Camp; a legal defense fund; and an immigration program.

Congressional Black Caucus
319 Cannon H.O.B.
Washington, DC 20515
(202) 225–8885
Founded 1971.

Founded by African American members of the U.S. House of Representatives. The Caucus seeks to address the legislative concerns of African American and other underrepresented citizens and to formalize and strengthen the efforts of its members. It establishes a yearly legislative agenda setting forth the key issues that it supports: full employment, national health care, education, minority business assistance, urban revitalization, rural development, welfare reform, and international affairs. It works to implement these objectives through personal contact with other House members, through the dissemination of information to individual African American constituents, and by working closely with African American elected officials in other levels of government. Operates the Congressional Black Caucus Foundation.

Council for African American Progress
1017 W. 15th St.
Little Rock, AR 72202

The Council fosters an appreciation and respect for African American culture and heritage by encouraging African Americans to participate in educational, cultural, social, political, economic, and drug education and prevention issues.

Delta Sigma Theta
1707 New Hampshire Ave., NW
Washington, DC 20009
(202) 986–2400
<www.dst1913.org>
Founded 1913.

A service sorority founded in 1913.

Educational Equity Concepts
114 E. 32nd St., Ste. 701
New York, NY 10016
(212) 725–1803
<www.edequity.org>
Founded 1982.

Organized to create educational programs and materials that are free of sex, race, and disability bias. It offers training programs for parents, teachers, and students; conducts seminars, symposia, and workshops. It also provides conference planning, consulting, and materials development services. Conducts Women and Disability Awareness Project, which discusses and writes on matters concerning disabled women, feminism, and the links between the disability rights and women's movements.

Episcopal Commission for Black Ministries
815 Second Ave.
New York, NY 10017
(212) 867–8400
Founded 1973.

The Commission works to strengthen the witness of African American Episcopalians in the church through programs that include parish and clergy development, scholarships and grants, and international relations. It provides financial assistance and consultations to parishes and church organizations.

Eta Phi Beta
16815 James Couzens
Detroit, MI 48235
(313) 862–0600
Founded 1942.

A professional business sorority founded in 1942.

Executive Leadership Council & Foundation
1010 Wisconsin Avenue, NW, Suite 520
Washington, DC 20007
(202) 298–8226
cmcghee@elcinfo.com
Founded 1986.

A national organization comprised of African American executive officers and large corporations who provide a network for black businesspeople, work to improve opportunities for African American executives, and conduct charitable activities.

Frederick Douglass Memorial and Historical Association

c/o Mary E.C. Gregory
10594 Twin Rivers Rd., Apt. E-1
Columbia, MD 21044
Founded 1900.

Chartered by Congress and administered by the National Park Service, U.S. Department of the Interior, the Association gives daily guided tours of the Frederick Douglass Memorial Home to inform visitors of how Douglass lived and of his contributions to the struggle for liberty, brotherhood, and citizenship. Maintains Douglass's personal library, in addition to sponsoring competitions and operating a speakers bureau.

Free African Liberation Organization-African Liberation Movement

PO Box 644
Adelphi Sta.
Brooklyn, NY 11238
(718) 320–8771
Founded 1989.

An organization comprised of Americans descended from slaves and Africans. The Movement works to bring to African Peoples the attainment of political independence, territorial integrity, national sovereignty and economic reparations.

Frontiers International

6301 Crittenden St.
Philadelphia, PA 19138
(215) 549–4550
Founded 1936.

A multinational group interested in social justice. The group works through member services to assist individual communities focus on constructive action by members in their community.

Global Alliance for Africa

c/o Thomas Derdak, Exec.Dir.
122 S. DesPlaines St.
Chicago, IL 60661
(312) 382–0607
tderdak@globalallianceafrica.org
<www.globalallianceafrica.org>

The Alliance promotes community-based health care development programs for impoverished people living in remote rural areas and urban slums throughout Africa.

Global Coalition for Africa

1919 Pennsylvania Ave. Ste. 550
Washington, DC 20006
(202) 458–4338
<www.gca-cma.org>
Founded 1990.

An intergovernmental policy forum, whose participants include international development and finance organizations. The Coalition seeks to "forge policy consensus on development priorities among African governments and their northern partners," and serves as a catalyst for development action; works to improve cooperation between African and overseas development programs and agencies. It assists African governments in the formulation of public development programs and policies, as well as conducting outreach activities.

Institute for the Advanced Study of Black Family Life and Culture

1484 9th St.
Oakland, CA 94607
(510) 836–3245

The Institute seeks to reunify African American families and to revitalize the African American community. It advocates the reclamation of what the group considers traditional African American culture. In addition, it conducts research on issues impacting the African American Community, such as teenage pregnancy, child-rearing practices, mental health support systems, and the effects of alcohol and drugs. It also maintains HAWK Federation (High Achievement, Wisdom, and Knowledge Federation), a training program employed in school systems to aid in the character development of young African American males. It sponsors in-service training for agencies, school systems, and the juvenile justice system; and develops training curricula for teen parents.

International Association of Black Professional Fire Fighters

8700 Central Ave., Ste. 306
Landover, MD 20785
(301) 808–0804
iabpff@msn.com
<www.iabpff.org>
Founded 1970.

The Association strives to: promote interracial communication and understanding; recruit African Americans for the fire services; improve working conditions for African Americans in the fire services; assist African Americans in career advancement; promote professionalism; and represent African American fire fighters before the community.

International Black Women for Wages for Housework

PO Box 86681
Los Angeles, CA 90086–0681
(323) 292–7405
70742.3012@compuserve.com
<allwomencount.net>

"An independent grass roots network of Black and other women of color. Campaigns for recognition of and compensation for unwaged and low-waged work. Beginning with women of color, we work to make visible the work women do for communities and movements for justice, campaigning against racism and sexism, welfare cuts, rape and other abuse and violence; immigration and asylum laws, police illegalities and other discrimination faced by women and our communities."

International Black Women's Congress

555 Fencher St. Ste. 102
Norfolk, VA 23510
(757) 625–0500
ibwc1609@cs.com
Founded 1983.

The objective is to unite members for mutual support and socioeconomic development through: annual networking tours to Africa; establishing support groups; assisting women in starting their own businesses; assisting members in developing resumes and other educational needs; offering to answer or discuss individual questions and concerns.

International Black Writers

PO Box 437134
Chicago, IL 60643–7134
<www.ibwc.com>
Founded 1970.

The group seeks to discover and support new black writers. It conducts research and monthly seminars in poetry, fiction, nonfiction, music, and jazz. Operates a lending library of 500 volumes on black history for members only, and provides writing services and children's services. The group maintains a speakers bureau; offers referral service; and has plans to establish a hall of fame, biographical archives, and museum.

International Black Writers and Artists

PO Box 43578
Los Angeles, CA 90043
(323) 964–3721
ibwa_2000@yahoo.com
<www.geocities.com/ibwa_2000>
Founded 1974.

Founded by African American writers and artists in the United States and West Indies. It provides encouragement and support to members.

Jack and Jill of America

2802 Gulfstream Ct.
Orlando, FL 32805–5811
(407) 843–6132
New national headquarters to open in Washington, DC, in 2002
jnjinc1938@earthlink.net
<www.jack-and-jill.org/>
Founded 1938.

A parental group designed to help African American parents learn more about their children. The group seeks to increase community awareness and to ensure equal opportunity and advancement for all children.

Kappa Alpha Psi

2322–24 N. Broad St.
Philadelphia, PA 19132
(215) 228–7184
<www.kapsi.org>
Founded 1911.

A social fraternity founded in 1911.

Leadership Conference on Civil Rights

1629 K St., NW, Ste. 1010
Washington, DC 20006
(202) 466–3311
<www.civilrights.org>
Founded 1950.

A coalition of national organizations working to promote passage of civil rights, social and economic legislation, and enforcement of laws already on the books. It has released studies examining former President Ronald Reagan's tax and budget programs in such areas as housing, elementary and secondary education, social welfare, Indian affairs, and tax cuts. It has also evaluated the enforcement of activities in civil rights by the U.S. Department of Justice and reviewed civil rights activities of the U.S. Department of Education.

Minority Business Enterprise Legal Defense and Education Fund

900 Second St., Ste. 8
Washington, DC 20002
(202) 289–1700
<www.mbeldef.org>
Founded 1980.

The Fund serves as an advocate and legal representative for the minority business community.

NAACP Legal Defense and Educational Fund
99 Hudson St., 16th Floor
New York, NY 10013
(212) 219–1900
Founded 1940.

The legal arm of the Civil Rights movement, functioning independently of the National Association for the Advancement of Colored People since the mid-1950s. It works to provide and support litigation on behalf of African Americans, other racial minorities, and women defending their legal and constitutional rights against discrimination in employment, education, housing, and other areas. Also, it represents civil rights groups as well as individual citizens who have bona fide civil rights claims. Contributed funds are used to finance court actions for equality in schools, jobs, voting, housing, municipal services, land use, and delivery of health care services. Has organized litigation campaign for prison reform and the abolition of capital punishment and hosts an annual institute to develop public awareness of new problems being faced by minorities. It also maintains Herbert Lehman Education Fund, through which scholarships are awarded to African American students attending state universities, and sponsors Earl Warren Legal Training Program, which provides scholarships to African American law students.

National Action Council for Minorities in Engineering
350 Fifth Ave., Ste. 2212
New York, NY 10118–2299
(212) 279–2626
<www.nacme.org>
Founded 1980.

The Council seeks to increase the number of minority students enrolled in and graduating from engineering schools. Works with support organizations to motivate and encourage pre-college students to engage in engineering careers. Operates project to assist engineering schools in improving the retention and graduation rates of minority students.

National African American Speakers Association
c/o Dr. Michael V. Wilkins Sr.
3033 Western Ave.
Park Forest, IL 60466–1834
(708) 747–2219
wilkins@4naasa.org
<www.4naasa.org>
Founded 1994.

The Association is made up of professional and in-training speakers learning to inspire, challenge and educate. It offers training programs specifically designed to develop the interpersonal, communication and presentation skills, while enhancing marketable skills.

National Alliance of Black Interpreters
PO Box 70322
New Orleans, LA 70172–0322
(504) 943–6597

National Alliance of Black School Educators
310 Pennsylvania Ave. SE
Washington, DC 20001
(202) 608–6310
nabse@nabse.org
Founded 1970.

The purpose is to promote awareness, professional expertise, and commitment among African American educators. Its goals are to: eliminate and rectify the results of racism in education; work with state, local, and national leaders to raise the academic achievement level of all African American students; increase members' involvement in legislative activities; facilitate the introduction of a curriculum that more completely embraces African America; improve the ability of African American educators to promote problem resolution; create a meaningful and effective network of strength, talent, and professional support. It plans to establish a National Black Educators Data Bank and offer placement service.

National Alumni Council of the United Negro College Fund
8260 Willow Oaks Corporate Dr.
PO Box 10444
Fairfax, VA 22031
(703) 205–3463
<www.uncf.org>
Founded 1946.

The Fund provides a structure for cooperation among African American college alumni groups and friends of African American colleges and works to acquaint the public with the value of African American colleges and higher education. It informs students and the public about contributions of African American college alumni to civic betterment and community progress and recruits students for United Negro College Fund member colleges.

National Association for Black Veterans
PO Box 11432
Milwaukee, WI 53211
(414) 342–5000
<www.mbvets.com>
Founded 1970.

The Association is open to African American and other minority veterans, primarily those who fought in Vietnam. It represents the interests of minority veterans before the Veterans Administration, and operates the Metropolitan Veterans Service to obtain honorable discharges for minority and low-income veterans who, in the organization's opinion, unjustly received a less than honorable discharge. In addition to these services, it defends incarcerated veterans through its Readjustment Counseling Program; operates job creation program; and offers services to geriatric and homeless veterans. The Association also conducts workshops to acquaint lawyers and clinicians with problems associated with Post Traumatic Stress Disorder; sponsors geriatric seminar and training program; operates library of military regulations; compiles statistics; and maintains speakers a bureau.

National Association for Equal Opportunity in Higher Education

8701 Georgia Ave.
Silver Spring, MD 20910
(301) 650–2440
<www.nafeo.org>
Founded 1969.

The Association represents historically African American colleges and universities in their attempt to continue as a viable force in the education community. It seeks to increase funding for member schools through federal and private sources. In addition, it compiles biographical data on schools and individuals, provides placement services, and collects statistics.

National Association for the Advancement of Colored People

4805 Mt. Hope Dr.
Baltimore, MD 21215
(410) 521–4939
leadership@naacp.org
Founded 1909.

Founded by persons "of all races and religions" who believe in the objectives and methods of the NAACP, which are to achieve equal rights through the democratic process and eliminate racial prejudice by removing racial discrimination in housing, employment, voting, schools, the courts, transportation, recreation, prisons, and business enterprises. It offers referral services, tutorials, job referrals, and day care; sponsors seminars; maintains a law library; and awards the Spingarn Medal annually to an African American for distinguished achievement. It also sponsors the NAACP

National Housing Corporation to assist in the development of low and moderate income housing for families.

National Association for the Study and Performance of African-American Music

c/o Orville Wright
35 Blake St.
Mattapan, MA 02126–1003
(617) 361–7460
owright@bellatlantic.net
<www.naspaam.org>
Founded 1972.

The Association's purpose is to foster the creation, study, and promotion of African American-derived music in education. It seeks to heighten public awareness of the problems faced by African American music educators and students and to increase public understanding of those problems. Other services include: Provides a forum for the discussion of concerns; coordinates and disseminates materials concerning African American-derived music in order to assist music teachers in teaching African American music and students; encourages African Americans to aspire to leadership positions and demand inclusion in the development and presentation of Music Educators National Conference activities, including participation in MENC's regional conferences; sponsors collegiate and high school gospel choir competitions; bestows annual national achievement awards to educators successful in demonstrating values inherent in music education. The Association compiles lists of music, books, and related music materials by African Americans.

National Association of African American Chambers of Commerce

750 N St. Paul Place, Ste. 1920
Dallas, TX 75201
(214) 871–3060
naaacc@aol.com
Founded 1983.

Organized to create a strategy for members of local chambers to share in the collective buying power of black minority communities, their primary focus is on the tourism industry, because, according to the Association, African Americans spend approximately $25 billion in the tourism market each year, but African American-owned businesses net very little from this industry. The Association conducts training sessions to acquaint African American business people with the tourism market and marketing strategies. It manages an Advocacy Program, which researches and analyzes issues given priority by local chambers.

National Association of African American Studies

PO Box 865
Morehead, KY 40351–1689
207282–1925
berryl@rocketmail.com
<www.naaas.org>
Founded 1991.

The Association seeks to further the cause of research in African American studies and promote acquaintanceship among those interested in the field. It provides information and support for researchers; serves as a forum for research and artistic endeavors; and conducts educational programs.

National Association of African Americans in Human Resources

c/o Joanne Robinson
PO Box 11467
Washington, DC 20008
856751–2490
joanne.robinson@naaahr.org
Founded 1999.

Founded by human resource professionals, the Association is dedicated to providing a national forum where African Americans can share and gain information, as well as provide leadership on issues affecting individual careers and quality of work life for other African Americans.

National Association of African-American Sportswriters and Broadcasters

308 Deer Park Ave.
Dix Hills, NY 11746
(631) 462–3933
cldavis@suffolk.library.us
Founded 1994.

Founded by African American men and women involved in the sports industry, the Association provides job information in the areas of sports medicine, sports law, and sports management. It also offers children's services along with sponsorship of research and educational programs.

National Association of Black Accountants

7249A Hanover Pky.
Greenbelt, MD 20770
(301) 474–6222
nabaoffice@nabainc.org
<www.nabainc.org>
Founded 1969.

Founded to unite accountants and accounting students who have similar interests and ideals, who are committed to professional and academic excellence, who possess a sense of professional and civic responsibility, and who are concerned with enhancing opportunities for minorities in the accounting profession.

National Association of Black and White Men Together

1747 Connecticut Ave., NW
Washington, DC 20009–1108
(800) NA4-BWMT
(202) 462–3599

National Association of Black Catholic Administrators

1531 W. Ninth St.
Los Angeles, CA 90015–1194
(213) 251–3435
Founded 1976.

Founded to assist the church in its role of evangelization and in defining its mission to the African American community and to provide an inner resource for the social and spiritual needs and concerns of Catholics of African ancestry.

National Association of Black Consulting Engineers

1752 Dallas Dr.
Baton Rouge, LA 70806
(225) 927–7240
mwatson@meljordanlace.com
Founded 1975.

The purpose is to gain recognition and increase professional opportunities for African American consulting engineers by lobbying the federal government.

National Association of Black County Officials

440 1st St. NW, Ste. 410
Washington, DC 20001
(202) 347–6953
nabwinfo@aol.com
Founded 1975.

Black county officials organized the Association to provide program planning and management assistance to counties in the United States. The Association acts as a clearinghouse of technical information exchange to develop resolutions to problems on the local and national levels. It also promotes the sharing of knowledge and methods of improving resource utilization and government operations, and conducts seminars and training sessions.

National Association of Black Customs Enforcement Officers

PO Box 19476
Plantation, FL 33318–9476
(305) 597–2739
Founded 1986.

The Association strives to enhance the welfare of Customs employees by fostering a better employee-management relationship, as well as nurturing and improving the relationship of Customs and the community, particularly the African American community: assuring the equitable hiring, training, assignment, development, promotion and fair treatment of all employees.

National Association of Black Geologists and Geophysicists

c/o U.S. Geological Survey
2255 N. Gemini Dr.
Flagstaff, AZ 86001–1698
(520) 556–7220
<www.nabgg.org>
Founded 1981.

Founded to assist minority geologists and geophysicists in establishing professional and business relationships. It informs minority students of career opportunities in geology and geophysics and seeks to motivate minority students to utilize existing programs, grants, and loans. The Association provides scholarships and oversees the educational careers of scholarship recipients.

National Association of Black Hospitality Professionals

PO Box 8132
Columbus, GA 31908–8132
334298–4802
nabhp@aol.com
Founded 1985.

Founded to develop global educational and economic opportunities for the hospitality industry through the expansion and diversification of minority involvement in the industry. It encourages professional development and opportunity in the industry through the design and implementation of workshops and seminars and seeks to increase the number, size, and capability of minority-owned businesses within the hospitality and tourism industries.

National Association of Black Journalists

8701A Adelphi Rd.
Adelphi, MD 20783–1716
(301) 445–7100
nabj@nabj.org
<www.nabj.org>
Founded 1975.

The Association's aims are to: strengthen the ties between African Americans in the African American media and African Americans in the white media; sensitize the white media to the "institutional racism in its coverage"; expand the white media's coverage and "balanced reporting" of the African American community; and become an exemplary group of professionals that honors excellence and outstanding achievement among African American journalists. It works with high schools to identify potential journalists and awards scholarships to journalism programs that especially support minorities.

National Association of Black Owned Broadcasters

1155 Connecticut Ave., NW
6th Fl.
Washington, DC 20036
(202) 463–8970
nabob@abs.net
<www.nabob.org>
Founded 1976.

The Association represents the interests of existing and potential African American radio and television stations. It is currently working with the Office of Federal Procurement Policy to determine which government contracting major advertisers and advertising agencies are complying with government initiatives to increase the amount of advertising dollars received by minority-owned firms. It conducts lobbying activities and provides legal representation for the protection of minority ownership policies.

National Association of Black Professors

PO Box 526
Crisfield, MD 21817
(410) 968–2393
Founded 1974.

The Association's goals are to: provide a forum for the exchange of information among college professors; enhance education for African American people and enrich the educational process in general; and support and promote intellectual interests of African American students.

National Association of Black Real Estate Professionals

PO Box 21421
Alexandria, VA 22320
Founded 1984.

Founded by African American professionals in real estate, including the areas of design, development, law, engineering, management, and investment, the Association provides a forum for the discussion of information related to the industry. It offers career development and networking opportunities, provides placement and consulting services, and maintains a speakers bureau.

National Association of Black Social Workers

8436 W. McNichols Ave.
Detroit, MI 48221
(313) 862–6700
spirit2749@aol.com
<www.nabsw.org>
Founded 1968.

Founded to support, develop, and sponsor community welfare projects and programs that will serve the interest of the African American community and aid it in controlling its social institutions. It also assists with adoption referrals.

National Association of Black Storytellers

PO Box 67722
Baltimore, MD 21215
(410) 947–1117
Founded 1984.

The Association seeks to establish a forum to promote the African American oral tradition and to attract an audience and works for the reissue of out-of-print story collections.

National Association of Black Women Attorneys

1110 Hamlin St.
Washington, DC 20017
(202) 526–5200
Founded 1972.

Founded to: Advance jurisprudence and the administration of justice by increasing the opportunities of African American and non-African American women at all levels; aid in protecting the civil and human rights of all citizens and residents of the United States; expand opportunities for women lawyers through education; and promote fellowship among women lawyers.

National Association of Black Women Entrepreneurs

PO Box 1375
Detroit, MI 48231
Founded 1979.

Founded by and open to African American women who own and operate their own businesses; are interested in starting businesses; as well organizations and companies desiring mailing lists. The organization acts as a national support system for African American businesswomen in the United States and focuses on the unique problems they face. Its objective is to enhance business, professional, and technical development of both present and future black businesswomen. The group maintains speakers bureau and national networking program; offers symposia, workshops, and forums aimed at increasing the business awareness of black women; and shares resources, lobbies, and provides placement service.

National Association of Blacks in Criminal Justice

North Carolina Central University
PO Box 19788
Durham, NC 27707
(919) 683–1801
office@nabcj.org
<www.nabcj.org>
Founded 1974.

Founded by criminal justice professionals concerned with the impact of criminal justice policies and practices on the minority community. It advocates with local, state, and federal criminal justice agencies for the improvement of minority recruitment practices and for the advancement of minority career mobility within those agencies. It also sponsors regional conferences, career development seminars, and annual training institutes; maintains speakers bureau; and provides financial and in-kind services to community groups.

National Association of Blacks in Government

1820 11th St. NW
Washington, DC 20001–5015
(202) 667–3280
<www.bignet.org>
Founded 1982.

The Association's purpose is to enhance and increase the employability of black officials within government and to prepare black youths for government and private sector careers. It sponsors a yearly seminar to help young people develop management, learning, interpersonal, and specialized skills. In addition, the Association bestows its annual Black Humanitarian Award, as well as compiling statistics.

National Association of Colored Women's Clubs
1601 R St. NW
Washington, DC 20009
(202) 667–4080
Founded 1896.

A federation of African American women's clubs. It carries on civic service, education, social service, and philanthropy programs.

National Association of Investment Companies
733 15th St., NW, Ste. 700
Washington, DC 20005
(202) 289–4336
Founded 1971.

The Association represents the minority small business investment company industry by monitoring regulatory action and collecting and disseminating trade and business information.

National Association of Minority Contractors
666 11th St., NW, Ste. 520
Washington, DC 20004
(202) 347–8259
samcname@aol.com
Founded 1969.

Founded by minority construction contractors and companies interested in doing business with minority contractors. It identifies procurement opportunities. It provides specialized training and serves as a national advocate for minority construction contractors.

National Association of Minority Political Women
6120 Oregon Ave., NW
Washington, DC 20015
(202) 686–1216
Founded 1983.

Founded by professional women interested in the American political process. The Association conducts research and educational programs.

National Association of Minority Women in Business
906 Grand Ave., Ste. 200
Kansas City, MO 64106
(816) 421–3335
Founded 1972.

Founded to serve as a network for the exchange of ideas and information on business opportunities for minority women.

National Association of Negro Business and Professional Women's Clubs
1806 New Hampshire Ave., NW
Washington, DC 20009
(202) 483–4206
<www.nanbpwc.org>
Founded 1935.

Founded by women actively engaged in a business or a profession and who are committed to rendering service through club programs and activities.

National Association of Negro Musicians
11551 S. Laflin St.
Chicago, IL 60643
(312) 568–3818
<www.edtec.morehouse.edu/cgrines/>
Founded 1919.

Founded to promote the advancement of all types of music, especially among young African American musicians. It sponsors annual competitions in which winners compete for scholarships.

National Association of Urban Bankers
1801 K St., NW, Ste. 200-A
Washington DC, 20036
(202) 861–0000
<www.naub.org>
Founded 1975.

Founded by minority professionals in the financial services industry.

National Bankers Association
1802 T St., NW
Washington, DC 20009
(202) 588–5432
Founded 1927.

Founded by minority banking institutions. The Association serves as an advocate for the minority banking industry.

National Bar Association
1225 Eleventh St., NW
Washington, DC 20001
(202) 842–3900
<www.nationalbar.org>
Founded 1925.

Founded by minority attorneys, members of the judiciary, law students, and law faculty. It sponsors educational and research programs.

National Black Alcoholism and Addictions Council

1000 16th St., NW, Ste. 702
Washington, DC 20005–5601
(202) 296–2696
nbac@borg.com
<www.borg.com/~nbac/nbacinfo.htm>
Founded 1978.

The Council works to support and initiate activities that will improve alcoholism treatment services and lead to the prevention of alcoholism in the African American community. It provides training on how to treat African American alcoholics from a cultural perspective and compiles statistics concerning alcoholism among African Americans.

National Black Association for Speech-Language and Hearing

PO Box 50605
Washington, DC 20091
(202) 274–6162
nbaslh@aol.com
<www.nbaslh.org>
Founded 1978.

Comprised of professionals and other individuals concerned with communicatively handicapped blacks, the Association strongly encourages the recruitment and training of African American professionals to work with individuals suffering from speech, language, and hearing problems. It maintains that conditions such as race, socioeconomic class, and cultural differences must be taken into account in order to understand and sensitively study the communicative process, and to treat communicative disorders. The Association supports related research; solicits, and provides, financial support for the training of black students in speech-language pathology and audiology; and disseminates information.

National Black Business Alliance

PO Box 250946
Montgomery, AL 36105
Founded 1979.

The Alliance was founded by African American entrepreneurs and established businessmen. It acts as a national and international support system for black businesses, providing assistance in organizational management and resource development. Holds seminars on bidding for government contracts. Conducts research and educational programs. Provides children's services; sponsors fundraising events; offers placement services; and maintains a speakers bureau.

National Black Catholic Clergy Caucus

321 Walnut St.
PO Box 1088
Opelousas, LA 70571
(318) 942–2392
<www.bcimall.org/nbccc/>
Founded 1968.

Founded by African American priests, brothers, seminarians, and deacons. Its purpose is to support the spiritual, theological, educational, and ministerial growth of the African American Catholic community within the Catholic Church and serves as a vehicle to bring contributions of the African American community to the Catholic Church. It also advances the fight against racism within the Catholic Church and society.

National Black Catholic Congress

320 Cathedral St.
Baltimore, MD 21201–4421
(410) 547–8496
hstanley@nbccongress.org
<www.nbccongress.org>
Founded 1985.

Made up of Catholic dioceses, the Congress works to devise ways and means of improving the condition of African American Catholics both religiously and socially. It conducts an annual pastoral ministry workshop for clergy and others who minister in African American communities and parishes, and sponsors an intensive training program for clergy and lay leaders in the African American apostolate.

National Black Caucus of Local Elected Officials

1301 Pennsylvania Ave. NW, Ste. 550
Washington, DC 20004
(202) 626–3000
inet@nlc.org
<www.nlc.org>
Founded 1970.

Founded by elected African American municipal and county officials united to recognize and deal with problems of members. The Caucus attempts to provide the organizational structure required to better present and respond to issues affecting constituents. It seeks to influence the National League of Cities in the development of policies affecting African Americans; and promotes legislative and economic development initiatives directed toward the needs of the African American community.

National Black Caucus of State Legislators

Hall of States
444 N. Capitol St. NW, Ste. 622
Washington, DC 20001
(202) 624–5457
staff@nbcsl.com
<www.nbcsl.com>
Founded 1977.

Organized to provide more political networking to African American legislators from the federal and state levels. Its goals are to: provide a network through which state legislators can exchange information and ideas on state and national legislation; provide a unified front or platform; serve as a focal point for involvement of African American legislators in the "new federalism." Its activities include arranging meetings between all governmental groups representing African American elected officials and analyzing and forming a position on the "new federalism," conducting seminars, maintaining speakers bureau and biographical archives, and compiling statistics.

National Black Chamber of Commerce

1350 Connecticut Ave. NW, Ste. 825
Washington, DC 20036
(202) 466–6888
info@nationalbcc.org

Founded by African American chambers of commerce organized to create a strategy for members of local chambers to share in the collective buying power of African American minority communities. Its primary focus is on the tourism industry because, according to the association, African Americans spend approximately $25 billion in the tourism market each year, but African American-owned businesses net very little from this industry. It conducts training sessions to acquaint African American businesspeople with the tourism market and marketing strategies.

National Black Child Development Institute

1101 15th St. NW, Ste. 900
Washington, DC 20005
(202) 833–2220
moreinfo@nbcdi.org
<www.nbcdi.org>
Founded 1970.

The Institute conducts direct services and advocacy campaigns aimed at both national and local public policies focusing on issues of health, child welfare, education, and child care. It organizes and trains network of members in a volunteer grassroots affiliate system to voice concerns regarding policies that affect African American children and their families. It stimulates communication between African American community groups, through conferences and seminars, to discuss and make recommendations that will be advantageous to the development of African American children. In addition, it analyzes selected policy decisions and legislative and administrative regulations to determine their impact on African American children and youth. Finally, it informs national policymakers of issues critical to African American children.

National Black Coalition of Federal Aviation Employees

Washington, DC 20026–4392
Founded 1976.

The Coalition's purposes are to: promote professionalism and equal opportunity in the workplace; locate and train qualified minorities for FAA positions; help the FAA meet its affirmative action goals; monitor African American, female, and minority trainees; educate members and the public about their rights and FAA personnel and promotion qualifications; and develop a voice for African American, female, and minority FAA employees.

National Black College Alumni Hall of Fame Foundation

230 Peachtree St. No. 530
Atlanta, GA 30303
(404) 681–4555
nbcahof@onsiteaccess.com
Founded 1984.

Founded by alumni of historical black colleges and universities, the Foundation seeks to increase awareness of importance of historically black colleges and universities. The Foundation also encourages graduates of black colleges and universities to donate funds to their alma maters, and conducts fund raising activities.

National Black Deaf Advocates

PO Box 305288
St. Thomas, VI 00803
340774–5899
rubytim@viaccess.net
Founded 1982.

Advocates for the rights of African American deaf and hearing impaired people. The organization seeks to promote the well-being, culture and empowerment of African Americans who are deaf or hard of hearing. It conducts educational outreach programs; offers leadership training and training for interpreters and transliterators of color; and sponsors the Miss NBDA Pageant.

National Black Gay and Lesbian Leadership Forum (BGLLF)

1219 S. La Brea Ave.
Los Angeles, CA 90019
(323) 964–7820
<www.nblglf.org>

The nation's leading organization addressing the leadership and skill development needs of the African American lesbian and gay communities relative to social, legal, economic, and health issues. The BGLLF maintains the AIDS Prevention Team, an innovative national AIDS education and prevention model. Other major BGLLF programming includes the Women's Caucus and sponsorship of the "Black Lesbian and Gay Leadership Summit: Our Families, Our Communities, Our Lives."

National Black Law Student Association

1225 Eleventh St., NW
Washington, DC 20001
<www.nblsa.org>
Founded 1967.

Founded by African American law students united to meet the needs of African American people within the legal profession and to work for the benefit of the African American community. The Association's objectives are to: articulate and promote professional competence, needs, and goals of African American law students; focus on the relationship between African American students and attorneys and the American legal system; instill in African American law students and attorneys a greater commitment to the African American community; and encourage the legal community to bring about change to meet the needs of the African American community.

National Black Leadership Initiative on Cancer

PO Box 34828
Las Vegas, NV 89133
(702) 655–3752
dorothymkeola@gateway.net
Founded 1994.

Made up of African Americans and health care professionals concerned with the prevention, diagnosis, and treatment of people with cancer, particularly those of African American descent. The organization seeks to facilitate "closing the gap in cancer incidence and mortality and increasing survival from cancer" by increasing awareness among African Americans of cancer and its prevention and treatment. Conducts educational programs to develop volunteer leaders in African American communities, with emphasis on increasing understanding of breast, colorectal, and prostate cancer and the role played by diet in their prevention.

National Black Leadership Roundtable

1023 15 St. NW, Ste. 300
Washington, DC 20036
(202) 589–1710
info@nblr.org
<www.nblr.org>
Founded 1983.

The Roundtable's goals are to: provide a forum for leaders of national African American organizations to discuss and exchange ideas on issues critical to African Americans; aid in the development of political, economic, and networking strategies that are advantageous to the needs of the African American community; and ensure that elected and appointed officials represent and are accountable to the African American community.

National Black MBA Association

180 N. Michigan Ave., Ste. 1400
Chicago, IL 60601
(312) 236–2622
mail@nbmbaa.org
<www.nbmbaa.org>
Founded 1970.

Founded by business professionals, lawyers, accountants, and engineers concerned with the role of African Americans who hold Master of Business Administration degrees. It encourages African Americans to pursue continuing business education; assists students preparing to enter the business world; provides programs for minority youths, students, and professionals including workshops, panel discussions, and Destination MBA seminar; works with graduate schools; and grants scholarships to graduate business students.

National Black McDonald's Operators Association

PO Box 8204
Los Angeles, CA 90008
(323) 296–5495
<www.nbmoa.org>
Founded 1972.

Founded to provide a forum for the exchange of ideas on the improvement of community relations and on the operation and management of restaurants. The Foundation seeks to build and improve the McDonald's restaurant image throughout the community and sponsors training seminars on marketing, better sales practices, labor relations, and profit sharing.

National Black Media Coalition

PO Box 10310
Silver Spring, MD 20914–0310
Founded 1973.

Founded by African American media advocacy groups seeking to maximize media access for African Americans and other minorities in the communications industry through employment, ownership, and programming. It has been recognized by the FCC, Congress, and trade organizations concerned with African Americans and other minorities in the media. Past activities include participating in FCC rule-making proceedings, speaking before university and professional audiences, conducting classes, and negotiating affirmative action plans with large media corporations.

National Black Music Caucus of the Music Educators National Conference
c/o Dr. Ted McDaniel
School of Music, Ohio State University
Columbus, OH 43210
(614) 292–4657
Founded 1972.

The Caucus's purpose is to foster the creation, study, and promotion of African American-derived music in education. It seeks to heighten public awareness of the problems faced by African American music educators and students and to increase public understanding of those problems. In addition, it provides a forum for the discussion of concerns, coordinates and disseminates materials concerning African American-derived music in order to assist music teachers in teaching African American music and students, and encourages African Americans to aspire to leadership positions and to demand inclusion in the development and presentation of Music Educators National Conference activities including participation in MENC's regional conferences.

National Black Nurses Association
8630 Fenton St., Ste. 330
Silver Spring, MD 20910
(301) 589–3200
nbna@erols.com
Founded 1971.

Founded to function as a professional support group and as an advocacy group for the African American community and their health care. It recruits and assists African Americans interested in pursuing nursing as a career.

National Black on Black Love Campaign
9535 S. Cottage Grove Ave.
Chicago, IL 60628–1508
(773) 978–0868
blkonblklove@aol.com
Founded 1983.

Founded by individuals and businesses united to promote the motto "Replace Black on Black crime with Black on Black love" and foster love and respect in all communities where people are, the group believes, inordinately affected by crime. It organizes "No Crime Day" in various communities and "Adopt A Building Program" for businesses. It also sponsors youth organizations and seminars in schools and communities to educate the public in ways of dealing with crime.

National Black Police Association
3251 Mt. Pleasant St. NW
Washington, DC 20010–2103
(202) 986–2070
nbpanatofc@worldnet.att.net
<www.blackpolice.org>
Founded 1972.

The Association seeks to: improve relationships between police departments and the African American community; recruit minority police officers on a national scale; and eliminate police corruption, brutality, and racial discrimination.

National Black Programming Consortium
761 Oak St., Ste. A
Columbus, OH 43205
(614) 229–4399
nbpc@supptec.com
Founded 1979.

Comprised of public telecommunications systems and television stations, academic institutions, and interested individuals. The Consortium's objectives are to: assist the public broadcasting system in supplying programming that serves the needs of all population segments of the United States; serve as a collection, distribution, and archival center for black-oriented television programming; coproduce black programming; serve as a liaison between the black community and telecommunications systems with regard to black programming; provide funds for and encourage more and better black productions. The Consortium also participates in the acquisition and distribution of programs for the cable and international markets, and sponsors children's programs.

National Black Public Relations Society
6565 Sunset Blvd, Ste. 301
Hollywood, CA 90028
(323) 466–8221
nbprs@aol.com
<www.nbprs.org>
Founded 1981.

Founded by African American public relations professionals who are either self-employed or employed by advertising agencies, radio and television stations, businesses, or nonprofit organizations. The organization provides a forum for discussion of topics related to public relations; holds professional development workshops; conducts seminars; and maintains speakers bureau to promote the image of African Americans in business.

National Black Sisters' Conference

3027 4th St. NE
Washington, DC 20017
(202) 529–9250
nbsc@igc.org
<www.bcimall.org/nbsc/nbsc.htm>
Founded 1968.

The Conference seeks to develop the personal resources of African American women; challenges society, especially the church, to address issues of racism in the United States. Its activities include: retreats; consulting, leadership, and cultural understanding; and formation workshops for personnel. It maintains educational programs for facilitating change and community involvement in inner-city parochial schools and parishes and operates Sojourner House to provide spiritual affirmation for African American religious and laywomen.

National Black State Troopers Coalition

c/o Charles Patterson
PO Box 31091
Jackson, MS 39286
Founded 1985.

The coalition promotes communication among minority state troopers; encourages members to participate in self-improvement programs, prepare and compete for promotions, and requests assignments to specialized units to advance careers and better serve communities.

National Black Survival Fund

PO Box 3005
Lafayette, LA 70502–3005
(337) 232–7672
Founded 1982.

A project of the Southern Development Foundation. Its objective is to improve the ability of African American and other minority poor to achieve economic progress through their own effort and initiative. It believes that the economic, cultural, and physical survival of the nation's African American community is endangered due to the recession, discrimination, and government cutbacks in social assistance programs. It seeks to maintain and increase support for programs that can avert the economic and human catastrophe the fund says will result if the opportunities offered to African Americans are undermined by current assistance cutbacks. The Fund also maintains: Food for Survival Program, in which landowners and sharecroppers in Mississippi volunteer land, equipment, and labor to provide food and employment for needy families; Health Care for Survival Program, a cooperative low-cost health center in Mississippi; and Jobs for Survival Program, which has assisted in providing jobs for African American workers in Alabama in construction, farming, and community service.

National Black United Federation of Charities

1212 New York Ave., Ste. 550
Washington, DC 20005
(202) 289–7888
nbufcofc@usbol.com

Comprised of African American charities, the Federation works to help national and local organizations gain resources in order to provide for the needs of African American communities. The group also conducts fundraisers.

National Black United Front

12817 S. Ashland
Calumet Park, IL 60827
(708) 389–9929
<www.nbufront.org>
Founded 1980.

The Front's purpose is to unite African American people of diverse political ideologies, age groups, socioeconomic backgrounds, and religious beliefs in order to build "a viable force for social transformation." Its goals are: the elimination of racism, sexism, bigotry, and racial violence; redistribution of the resources and wealth of the nation to provide abundantly for all citizens; and elimination of the "genocidal mis-education system," police brutality, and denial of human rights nationally and internationally. It believes that current conditions in the United States threaten the survival of African American people as a whole, and urges African Americans to overlook individual differences by working together for common goals. It also addresses such issues as unemployment, police brutality, budget cuts harmful to African American communities, and the resurgence of the Ku Klux Klan. The Front conducts seminars and forums; maintains speakers bureau; offers charitable program; and sponsors competitions and plans to organize boycotts, hold demonstrations, engage in electoral politics, and seek new vehicles for change.

National Black United Fund

40 Clinton St., 5th Fl.
Newark, NJ 07102
(973) 643–5122
nbuf@nbuf.org
<www.nbuf.org>
Founded 1972.

The Fund provides financial and technical support to projects serving the critical needs of African American communities nationwide. Local affiliates solicit funds through payroll deduction to support projects in the areas of education, health and human services, economic development, social justice, arts and culture, and emergency needs. Programs supported by NBUF emphasize self-help, volunteerism, and mutual aid. The Fund maintains the Walter Bremond Memorial Fund Campaign.

National Black Women's Consciousness Raising Association

1906 N. Charles St.
Baltimore, MD 21218
(410) 727–8900
anulane@aol.com
Founded 1975.

Open to African American women interested in women's rights and women's issues. The Association acts as a support group for women, and provides educational and informational workshops and seminars on subjects of concern to black women and women in general. The group annually recognizes individuals, especially for academic achievement.

National Black Women's Health Project

600 Pennsylvania Ave. SE, Ste. 310
Washington, DC 20003
(202) 548–4000
nbwhp@nbwhp.org
<www.BlackWomensHealth.org>
Founded 1981.

The Project encourages mutual and self-help advocacy among women to bring about a reduction in health care problems prevalent among African American women. It urges women to communicate with health care providers, seek out available health care resources, become aware of self-help approaches, and communicate with other African American women to minimize feelings of powerlessness and isolation, and, thus realize, they have some control over their physical and mental health. It points out that higher incidence of high blood pressure, obesity, breast and cervical cancers, diabetes, kidney disease, arteriosclerosis, and teenage pregnancy occur among African American women than among other racial or socioeconomic groups. It also notes that African American infant mortality is twice that of whites and that African American women are often victims of family violence. The Project offers seminars outlining demographic information, chronic conditions, the need for health information and access to services, possible methods of improving the health status of African American women, and sponsors the Center for Black Women's Wellness.

National Black Youth Leadership Council

250 W. 54th St., Ste. 800
New York, NY 10019
Founded 1983.

The Council conducts workshops for groups involved with African American youth and minority student academic and leadership development; and works to reduce the number of minority students that do not finish high school. It provides resources, information, skills, and strategies for fostering such development; advises educators and parents on their role and responsibility to display leadership and success skills to youths they come in contact with; and makes available to educational institutions training and expertise on cultural diversity, multiculturalism, and problems of bigotry and racism. It also sponsors drug abuse awareness programs.

National Business League

2218 Brainard St.
New Orleans, LA 70113
(504) 523–4443
<www.thenbl.com>
Founded 1900.

Founded to encourage minority ownership and management of small businesses and support full minority participation in the free enterprise system.

National Catholic Conference for Interracial Justice

1200 Varnum St.
Washington, DC 20017–1102
(202) 529–6480
Founded 1959.

A Catholic organization working for interracial justice and social concerns in the United States, it initiates programs within and outside the Catholic church to end discrimination in community development, education, and employment.

National Caucus and Center on Black Aged

1200 L St. NW, Ste. 800
Washington, DC 20005
(202) 637–8400
info@ncba-aged.org
<www.ncba-blackaged.org>
Founded 1970.

Founded to seek to improve living conditions for low-income elderly Americans, particularly African Americans. It advocates changes in federal and state laws in improving the economic, health, and social status of low-income senior citizens. It also does the following: promotes community awareness of problems and issues effecting low-income aging population; operates an employment program involving 2,000 older persons in 14 states; sponsors, owns, and manages rental housing for the elderly; and conducts training and intern programs in nursing home administration, long-term care, housing management, and commercial property maintenance.

National Center of Afro-American Artists

300 Walnut Ave.
Boston, MA 02119
(617) 442–8614
Founded 1968.

Open to African American artists; institutions; and interested others. The Center's goals are to: promote cultural activities in African American history and culture; encourage the development of artistic and cultural expression within black communities; increase awareness and appreciation of the achievements of black artists. The center organizes and conducts cultural events, theatrical productions, and concerts. It sponsors workshops on topics such as 19th Century Black America, Introduction to Africa, and the Caribbean.

National Coalition for Quality Integrated Education

1201 16th St., NW
Washington, DC 20036
(202) 822–7708
<www.nfie.org>
Founded 1975.

Founded by national organizations committed to desegregating and improving the quality of elementary and secondary schools in the United States. It serves as a forum for issues and developments pertaining to quality integrated education; and encourages and coordinates citizen involvement in legislative developments.

National Coalition of 100 Black Women

38 W. 32nd St., Ste. 1610
New York, NY 10001–3816
(212) 947–2196
ncloobw@aol.com
Founded 1981.

Founded by African American women actively involved with issues such as economic development, health, employment, education, voting, housing, criminal justice, the status of African American families, and the arts. It seeks to provide networking and career opportunities for African American women in the process of establishing links between the organization and the corporate and political arenas. It encourages leadership development. It also sponsors role-model and mentor programs to provide guidance to teenage mothers and young women in high school or who have graduated from college and are striving for career advancement.

National Coalition of Black Meeting Planners

8630 Fenton St., Ste. 126
Silver Spring, MD 20910
202628–3952
ncbmp@melanet.com
<www.ncbmp.com>
Founded 1983.

The Planners' purposes are to: act as liaison with hotels, airlines, convention centers, and bureaus in an effort to assess the impact of minorities in these fields; assess the needs of the convention industry and how best to meet these needs; enhance members' sophistication in planning meetings; and maximize employment of minorities in the convention industry.

National Coalition of Blacks for Reparations in America

PO Box 62622
Washington, DC 20029–2622
(202) 635–6272
webmaster@ncobra.com
<www.NCOBRA.com>
Founded 1989.

The Coalition seeks to obtain reparations from the U.S. government, other governments, and corporations that profited from the labor of African people who were treated as slaves. It also compiles statistics; offers educational and research programs; and maintains a speakers bureau.

National Coalition on Black Civic Participation
1025 Vermont Ave., NW
Washington, DC 20005
(202) 659–4929
ncbcp@ncbcp.org
<www.bigvote.org>
Founded 1976.

Dedicated to increasing African American participation in civil society, the Coalition's programs of the organization include Operation Big Vote!, Black Youth Vote!, Black Women's Roundtable, Voices of the Electorate, and the Information Resource Center. The Coalition is dedicated to training and engaging African American leaders and community activists in overcoming institutional barriers that have hindered the growth of African American communities politically, socially and economically.

National Conference of Black Lawyers
Two West 125th St., Second Floor
New York, NY 10027
(212) 864–4000
<www.ncbl.org>
Founded 1968.

The Conference maintains projects in legal services to community organizations, voting rights, and international affairs; provides public education on legal issues affecting African Americans and poor people; researches racism in law schools and bar admissions; conducts programs of continuing legal education for member attorneys; maintains general law library; compiles statistics; and maintains lawyer referral and placement services.

National Conference of Black Mayors
1151 Cleveland Ave., Ste. D
East Point, GA 30344
(404) 765–6444
info@blackmayors.org
<www.blackmayors.org>
Founded 1974.

Founded to: improve the executive management capacity and efficiency of member municipalities in the delivery of municipal services; create viable communities within which normal government functions can be performed efficiently; provide the basis upon which new social overhead investments in the infrastructure of municipalities can utilize federal, state, local, and private resources to encourage new industry and increase employment; and assist municipalities in stabilizing their population through improvements of the quality of life for residents and, concurrently, create

alternatives to outward migration. The Conference facilitates small town growth and development through energy conservation.

National Conference of Black Political Scientists
c/o Dr. Lois Hollis
Albany State University
504 College Dr.
Albany, GA 31705
(912) 430–4870
Founded 1969.

Founded by political and social science faculty, lawyers, and related professionals interested in African American politics and related fields. The Conference seeks to encourage research, publication, and scholarship by African Americans in political science; and to improve the political life of African Americans.

National Consortium for Black Professional Development
2142 Belmont Rd.
Louisville, KY 40218–2104
Founded 1974.

Founded by industrial corporations and business firms; universities, including schools of business, science, and math, and public school systems; and affiliates. The Consortium's goal is to increase substantially the number of African American professionals in business administration, communications, applied and natural sciences, engineering, and law. It sponsors a science and engineering competition for African American students and Ph.D. programs in the agricultural sciences and business administration. Maintains a clearinghouse and placement bureau for African American professionals seeking employment; provides recruitment service for universities seeking qualified faculty and students; and services several federal contracts.

National Consortium of Arts and Letters for Historically Black Colleges and Universities
c/o Dr. Walter Anderson
The Westbridge, Ste. 818
2555 Pennsylvania Ave. NW
Washington, DC 20037
(202) 833–1327
Founded 1984.

Founded to encourage academic excellence with an emphasis on cultural growth. The Consortium promotes the study of African American history and culture in the context of the scholarly study of world cultures. It offers no grants, but helps sponsor programs through fundraising efforts.

National Council for Black Studies

California State University
Carson, CA 90747
ncbs@dhvx20.csudh.edu
Founded 1975.

Faculty members, students, and institutions united to promote and strengthen academic and community programs in black and/or African American studies. The Council sponsors undergraduate and graduate student essay contests. It offers professional opportunities referral service; compiles statistics on black studies activities including information on students, faculty, research, and curricula.

National Council of Black Engineers and Scientists

1525 Aviation Blvd., Ste. C-424
Redondo Beach, CA 90278
(213) 896-9779
<www.ncbes.org>
Founded 1986.

The Council represents the interests of African American engineers and scientists. It aims to increase minority participation in technical professions.

National Council of Negro Women

633 Pennsylvania Ave., NW
Washington, DC 20003
<www.usbol.com/ncnw/>
Founded 1935.

Founded by Mary McLeod Bethune to assist in the development and utilization of the leadership of women in community, national, and international life. The Council maintains the Women's Center for Education and Career Advancement, which offers programs designed to aid minority women in pursuing nontraditional careers; also maintains the Bethune Museum and Archives for Black Women's History.

National Counsel of Black Lawyers

116 W. 111 St., 3rd Fl.
New York, NY 10026
(212) 864-4000
Founded 1968.

Attorneys throughout the United States and Canada united to use legal skills in the service of African American and poor communities. Maintains projects in legal services to community organizations, voting rights, and international affairs; provides public education on legal issues affecting blacks and poor people. The Council also researches racism in law schools and bar admissions; conducts programs of continuing legal education for member attorneys; and maintains general law library. It compiles statistics; maintains lawyer referral and placement services. Provides speakers bureau on criminal justice issues, international human rights law, and civil rights practice.

National Dental Association

3517 16th St., NW
Washington, DC 20010
(202) 588-1697
<www.howard.edu/collegealliedhealth.ndamain>
Founded 1913.

The Association was formed by minority health professionals who had been denied access to national associations formed by whites. The association champions the interests and concerns of poor and minority patients and their doctors. The group has several auxiliary chapters and sponsors symposia and student organizations.

National Forum for Black Public Administrators

777 N. Capitol St. NE, Ste. 807
Washington, DC 20002
(202) 408-9300
nfbpa@erols.com
<www.nfbpa.org>
Founded 1983.

Founded to promote, strengthen, and expand the role of African Americans in public administration. The Forum seeks to focus the influence of African American administrators toward building and maintaining viable communities; develop specialized training programs for managers and executives; provide national public administrative leadership resource and skills bank; work to further communication among African American public, private, and academic institutions; and address issues that affect the administrative capacity of African American managers. The Forum maintains an Executive Leadership Institute, which grooms mid-level executives for higher positions in Government; the Mentor Program, which matches aspiring African American managers with seasoned executives over an eight-month period; and the Leadership Institute for Small Municipalities, which provides intensive training for elected and appointed officials from small communities. It offers training programs for black South Africans intent on achieving public administrative positions in the post-apartheid era. It also sponsors the National Minority Business Development Forum to increase the participation of small and minority businesses in local government procurement and contracting programs.

National Funeral Directors and Morticians Association

3951 Snapfinger Dr., Suite 570
Omega World Center
Decatur, GA 30035
(404) 286–6680
<www.nfdma.com>
Founded 1924.

An association of state and local embalmers and funeral directors seeking to promote ethical standards and laws for the profession.

National Hook-Up of Black Women

c/o Wynetta Frazier
1809 E. 71st St., Ste. N
Chicago, IL 60649
(773) 667–7061
cfrazier19@aol.com
Founded 1975.

Black women from business, professional, and community-oriented disciplines representing all economic, educational, and social levels. The group's purpose is to provide a communications network in support of black women who serve in organizational leadership positions, especially those elected or appointed to office and those wishing to elevate their status through educational and career ventures. Works to form and implement a Black Women's Agenda that would provide representation for women, families, and communities and that would help surmount economic, educational, and social barriers. Supports efforts of the Congressional Black Caucus (see separate entry) in utilizing the legislative process to work toward total equality of opportunity in society. The organization seeks to highlight the achievements and contributions of black women, and operates a speakers bureau.

National Medical Association

1012 10th St., NW
Washington, DC 20001
(202) 347–1895
<www.nmanet.org>
Founded 1895.

A professional society formed by African American physicians. The Association maintains 24 separate scientific sections representing major specialties of medicine. It also hosts a symposium and conducts workshops.

National Minority Health Association

PO Box 11876
Harrisburg, PA 17108
(717) 260–0409
Founded 1987.

Founded by health care providers and associations, consumers, executives and administrators, educators, pharmaceutical and health insurance companies, and other organizations with an interest in health. Seeks to focus attention on the health needs of minorities.

National Office for Black Catholics

3025 4th St. NE
Washington, DC 20017
(202) 635–1778
Founded 1970.

Comprised of African American priests, sisters, brothers, and laypersons of the Catholic church. Participating organizations include: National Black Sisters' Conference; National Black Catholic Clergy Caucus (see separate entries). The Office serves as a "foundation for the renewal of the credibility of the church in the black community." It works to coordinate actions designed "to liberate black people and to serve as a unifying strength." Plans to: have specialists and technicians working within the black community to coordinate community organization and development; provide leadership training for youth; attack problems of poverty and deprivation; sensitize blacks to their heritage through historical, cultural, and liturgical experience. Seeks cooperation with groups working toward black liberation. Concerns include: training black and white clergy and religious, Catholic, and non-Catholic laity; influencing decisions involving race and the church; monitoring, in order to prevent, manifestations of racism. Sponsors Pastoral Ministry Institute and African American Culture and Worship Workshop; provides evangelization workshops and leadership training for parish councils and parochial schools.

National Organization for the Professional Advancement of Black Chemists and Chemical Engineers

525 College St. NW
Washington, DC 20059
(202) 667–1699
secretary@nobcche.org
<www.nobcche.org>
Founded 1972.

Founded to aid African American scientists and chemists in reaching their full professional potential; encourages African American students to pursue scientific studies and employment; promotes participation of African Americans in scientific research. The group provides volunteers to teach science courses in selected elementary schools; sponsors scientific field trips for students; maintains speakers bureau for schools;

provides summer school for students of the U.S. Naval Academy. It also conducts technical seminars in Africa.

National Organization of Black College Alumni
PO Box 729
Bluefield, WV 24701
Founded 1982.

Open to graduates, friends, and supporters of the 114 historically black colleges. The organization works to ensure the survival of black colleges by addressing their concerns and needs and providing resources to meet these needs. It coordinates and focuses alumni support for black colleges; strengthens existing alumni associations; urges black youth to obtain a college education; facilitates the exchange of information; and provides consultants.

National Organization of Black County Officials
440 First St., NW, Ste. 500
Washington, DC 20001
(202) 347–6953
<www.nobco.org>
Founded 1982.

Founded by African American county officials to provide program planning and management assistance to selected counties in the United States. The group acts as a technical information exchange to develop resolutions to problems on the local and national levels; promotes the sharing of knowledge and methods of improving resource utilization and government operations; conducts seminars and training sessions; and plans to maintain resource file on the achievements and history of African American county officials.

National Organization of Black Law Enforcement Executives
4609 Pinecrest Office Park Dr., Ste. 2-F
Alexandria, VA 22312–1442
(703) 658–1529
noble@noblenatl.org
<www.noblenatl.org>
Founded 1976.

Founded to provide a platform from which the concerns and opinions of minority law enforcement executives and command-level officers can be expressed; to facilitate the exchange of programmatic information among minority law enforcement executives; to increase minority participation at all levels of law enforcement; to eliminate racism in the field of criminal justice; to secure increased cooperation from criminal justice agencies; and to reduce urban crime and violence. It seeks to develop and maintain channels of communication between law enforcement agencies and the community; and encourages coordinated community efforts to prevent and abate crime and its causes.

National Political Congress of Black Women
8401 Colesville Rd., Ste. 400
Silver Spring, MD 20910
(301) 562–8000
NPCBW@bellatlantic.net
Founded 1984.

The Congress works to encourage African American women to engage in political activities. It offers training in understanding and operating within the political process; strives to develop, educate and encourage African American women to seek office; encourages the appointment of these women at all levels of government.

National Rainbow Coalition, Inc.
1002 Wisconsin Ave., NW
Washington, DC 20006
(202) 333–5270
<www.rainbowpush.org>
Founded 1984.

Founded by the Reverend Jesse L. Jackson Sr. to build a consensus in the area of civil rights, government, politics, labor, education, and business. The Coalition provides a platform for debate and encourages the development of a new political leadership committed to progressive domestic and international policies and programs.

National Society of Black Engineers
1454 Duke St.
Alexandria, VA 22314
(703) 549–2207
info@nsbe.org
<www.nsbe.org>
Founded 1975.

Founded to increase the number of minority graduates in engineering and technology.

National Society of Black Physicists
c/o Dr. Sekazi Mtingwa
1601 E. Market St
North Carolina A & T State University
Greensboro, NC 27411–1086
(336) 334–7646
president@NSBP.org
Founded 1977.

The Society addresses the needs of African American physicists, works to create opportunities for minorities in the field, and sponsors mentor program and lectures on research findings.

National Trust for the Development of African American Men

6811 Kenilworth Ave., Ste. 501
Riverdale, MD 20737–1333
(301) 887–0100
keepthetrust@netzero.net
Founded 1989.

Founded by individuals interested in improving the self-esteem of African American men. The Trust promotes increased understanding of and appreciation for traditional African value systems; works to "create and diffuse a new consciousness in the African rooted people in America." Also conducts research and educational programs, with emphasis on issues facing incarcerated men and their families.

National Urban Coalition

8601 Georgia Ave., Ste. 500
Silver Spring, MD 20910
(301) 495–4999
<www.nucnet.org>
Founded 1967.

The National Urban Coalition seeks to improve the quality of life for the disadvantaged in urban areas through the combined efforts of business, labor, government, and community leaders. It operates programs that work to increase the participation by minority students in science, math, and computer education; and operates the Say Yes to a Youngster's Future program.

National Urban League

120 Wall St.
New York, NY 10065
(212) 558–5300
<www.nul.org>
Founded 1910.

Founded to eliminate racial segregation and discrimination in the United States and to achieve parity for African Americans and other minorities in every phase of American life. The League works to eliminate institutional racism and to provide direct service to minorities in the areas of employment, housing, education, social welfare, health, family planning, mental retardation, law and consumer affairs, youth and student affairs, labor affairs, veterans' affairs, and community and minority business development.

Negro Airmen International

NAI Black Wings in Aviation
PO Box 23911
Savannah, GA 31403
<www.blackwings.com>
Founded February 1967.

Works to increase African Americans' personal and professional mobility through participation in all fields of aviation, especially piloting. Dedicated to educating the public and to improving international service in support of its goals.

NIH Black Scientists Association

c/o Alfred Johnson
PO Box 38
Clarksburg, MD 20871
(301) 402–6425
th112c@nih.gov
<www.nih.gov/science/blacksci/bsaabout.html>

Made up of scientists, physicians, technologists and science administrators at the National Institute of Health (NIH), the Association provides communication and dissemination of information about issues of common interest, development of important personal and professional contacts, career support and enhancement, and group advocacy on issues of importance to underrepresented minorities at NIH and beyond. The group maintains membership database and a speakers bureau.

Office for the Advancement of Public Black Colleges

National Association of State Universities and Land-
    Grant Colleges
1307 New York NW, Ste. 400.
Washington, DC 20005–4722
(202) 478–6040
jpayne@nasulgc.org
<www.nasulgc.org/minority.htm>
Founded 1968.

Founded to collect, organize, interpret, and disseminate data on 35 predominantly African American public colleges. The colleges, located in 18 states, enroll over 135,000 students.

Office of Black Ministries/Episcopal Church Center

c/o Episcopal Church
815 2nd Ave.
New York, NY 10017
(212) 867–8400
<www.ecusa.anglican.org>
Founded 1973.

Comprised of black members of the Episcopal church representing geographically diverse dioceses, including one diocese outside of the United States. The Office works to strengthen the witness of black Episcopalians in the church through programs that include parish and clergy development and international relations. It also provides financial assistance and consultations to parishes and church organizations and compiles statistics. A commission of the Episcopal church.

Omega Psi Phi
2714 Georgia Ave., NW
Washington, DC 20001
(202) 667–7158
Founded 1911.

A social fraternity founded in 1911.

Operation Crossroads Africa
34 Mt. Morris Pk.
New York, NY 10027
(212) 289–1949
oca@igc.apc.org
<www.igc.org/oca>
Founded 1958.

Founded by students and professionals, mostly from the United States, who live and work with African counterparts during July and August on self-help community development projects in Africa. Opportunities are provided for interaction with village elders, educators, and political and other community leaders. The group emphasizes community growth from within a "Third World" structure. Before departure, participants make an intensive study of Africa; after their return, they give speeches about their experiences. Participants pay part of the cost of the project. It organizes work-camp projects for U.S. high school students in the Caribbean and handles the visits of African and Caribbean leaders to the United States. It also sponsors training and exchange programs.

Operation PUSH (People United to Serve Humanity)
930 E. 50th St.
Chicago, IL 60615
(773) 373–3366
Founded 1971.

Founded by the Reverend Jesse L. Jackson Sr. as a national and international human rights organization directed toward education and economic equity and parity for all, particularly African American, Hispanic Americans, and poor people. PUSH seeks to create an ethical atmosphere and encourages self and community motivation and social responsibility. It also sponsors PUSH for Education Program to aid the nation's public schools and restore academic excellence and discipline.

Organization of African-American Veterans
2316 Elmwood Ln.
Sierra Vista, AZ 85635–5050
(602) 458–7245
allengeorgem@cs.com
Founded 1978.

Open to veterans and active personnel of all branches of the U.S. military. The Organization promotes the physical, mental, social, and economic rehabilitation of veterans; works to obtain compensation, medical care, employment, and business assistance for veterans. The group also assists and represents veterans and their families in filing benefit claims, and sponsors and supports beneficial legislation.

Organization of Black Airline Pilots
8630 Fenton St., Ste. 126
Silver Spring, MD 20910
crich757@hotmail.com
<www.obap.org>
Founded 1976.

Founded to enhance minority participation in the aerospace industry. Maintains liaison with airline presidents and minority and pilot associations; conducts lobbying efforts including congressional examinations into airline recruitment practices; provides scholarships; and cosponsors the Summer Flight Academy for Youth at Tuskegee Institute in Alabama.

Organization of Black Designers
300 M St. SW, Ste. N110
Washington, DC 20024
(202) 659–3918
obdesign@aol.com
<www.core77.com/OBD/welcome.html>
Founded 1990.

Comprised of African American designers holding college degrees who are practicing graphic, industrial, fashion, textile, and interior design. The organization provides forum for discussion and educational programs, business, career and economic development. It also sponsors competitions and maintains a speakers bureau.

Phi Beta Sigma
145 Kennedy St., NW
Washington, DC 20011–5294
(202) 726–5424
<www.pbs1914.org>
Founded 1914.

A service fraternity that sponsors the Sigma Beta Club for high school-aged males.

Phi Delta Kappa

408 N. Union St.
PO Box 789
Bloomington, IN 47402–0789
(800) 766–1156
<www.pdkintl.org>

An international organization for professional educators.

Phylaxis Society

c/o Col. Joseph A. Walker Jr.
PO Box 3151
Ft. Leavenworth, KS 66207
Founded 1973.

Founded by Prince Hall Masonic writers and editors of Masonic publications.

Program for Research on Black Americans

50062 Institute for Social Research on Black
   Americans
University of Michigan
PO Box 1248
Ann Arbor, MI 48106–1248
(734) 763–0045
prba@isr.umich.edu
<www.isr.umich.edu/rcgd/prba>
Founded 1976.

The Program collects, analyzes, and interprets empirical data, and disseminates findings based on national and international studies of people of African American and African descent. The group provides research and training opportunities for black social scientists and students. It also fosters high quality research on factors related to mental health and mental disorders among Americans of African descent.

Project Africa

1304 E Lake St.
Minneapolis, MN 55407

The Project was founded by individuals and organizations. Promotes appropriate and sustainable economic and community development in Africa. Conducts educational programs; provides assistance to individuals affected by natural disasters and human conflicts; gathers and disseminates information on development programs.

Project Equality

6301 Rock Hill Rd.
Kansas City, MO 64131
(816) 361–9222
<www.projectequality.org>
Founded 1965.

A nationwide interfaith program enabling religious organizations, institutions, and others to support equal opportunity employers with their purchasing power. Services include: validation of hotels for conventions and meetings of organizations; validations of suppliers to member organizations and institutions; and consultant and educational services to assist employers in affirmative action and equal employment opportunity programs.

Quality Education for Minorities Network

1818 N St., NW, Ste. 350
Washington, DC 20036
(202) 659–1818
<www.qemnetwork.qem.org>
Founded 1987.

Founded to implement the plan developed by the Quality Education for Minorities Project. The Network believes that minorities are under served by the educational system and thus disproportionately lack the skill needed to participate effectively in a society increasingly based on high technology. It plans to work with school systems, communities, universities, and public and private sector institutions to ensure that minority students have equal access to educational opportunities.

Research Institute of African and African Diaspora Arts

3509 Lake Ave., Apt. 1128
Columbia, SC 29206–5110
Founded 1977.

The Institute promotes research into African culture as it relates to African Americans and others of African heritage living outside of Africa. It conducts research and educational programs; provides children's services; maintains speakers bureau and museum; and offers residencies via letter of interest and proposal upon review of residency committee.

Sigma Pi Phi

920 Broadway, Ste. 703
New York, NY 10010
(212) 477–5550
<www.sigma-pi-phi.net>
Founded 1904.

Founded as a social fraternity. It maintains the Boulé Foundation. Sigma Pi Phi is the oldest African American Greek letter society in the United States.

Southern Christian Leadership Conference

334 Auburn Ave., NE
Atlanta, GA 30303
(404) 522–1420
<www.sclcnational.com>
Founded 1957.

A nonsectarian coordinating and service agency for local organizations seeking full citizenship rights, equality, and the integration of African Americans in all aspects of life in the United States and subscribing to the Gandhian philosophy of nonviolence. It works primarily in 16 southern and border states to improve civic, religious, economic, and cultural conditions. It also fosters nonviolent resistance to all forms of racial injustice including state and local laws and practices; conducts leadership training program embracing such subjects as registration and voting, social protest, use of the boycott, picketing, nature of prejudice, and understanding politics; sponsors citizenship education schools to teach reading and writing; helps persons pass literacy tests for voting; provides information about income tax forms, tax-supported resources, aid to handicapped children, public health facilities, how government is run, and social security; and conducts Crusade for the Ballot, which aims to double the African American vote in the South through increased voter registrations.

Southern Coalition for Educational Equity

PO Box 22904
Jackson, MS 39225–2904
(601) 362–6774
Founded 1978.

Founded by a coalition of parents, students, teachers, and administrators that operates in Alabama, Georgia, Louisiana, Mississippi, and North Carolina, with plans to include eight additional states. The Coalition works toward developing more efficient educational programs and eliminating racism and sexism within southern schools. It has organized projects including: Arkansas Career Resources Project, which provides minorities and single heads of households with marketable skills and jobs; New Orleans Effective Schools Project, which attempts to increase school effectiveness through high expectations, stressing academic achievement, and quality instruction; Project MiCRO, which seeks to provide computer access for, and sharpen analytical skills of, minority students; and Summer Program, which focuses on students' reading comprehension skills.

Southern Poverty Law Center

400 Washington Ave.
Montgomery, AL 36104
<www.splcenter.org>
Founded 1971.

Founded to protect and advance the legal and civil rights of poor people, regardless of race, through education and litigation. The Center does not accept fees from clients. It is currently involved in several lawsuits representing individuals injured or threatened by activities of the Ku Klux Klan and related groups and attempts to develop techniques and strategies that can be used by private attorneys. It also operates Klanwatch.

Southern Regional Council

1900 Rhodes Haverty Bldg.
133 Carnegie Way, NW, Ste. 5900
Atlanta, GA 30303
(404) 522–8764
<www.src.wl.com>
Founded 1944.

Founded by leaders in education, religion, business, labor, the community, and the professions interested in improving race relations and combating poverty in the South. The Council comprises an interracial research and technical assistance center that addresses issues of social justice and political and economic democracy. It seeks to engage public policy as well as personal conscience in pursuit of equality. It develops educational programs; provides community relations consultation and field services when requested by official and private agencies; distributes pamphlets pertaining to desegregation of various public facilities and fosters elimination of barriers to African American voting registration; and acts as official sponsor of overseas government officials, leaders, and other visitors who wish to view race relations in the South.

Thurgood Marshall Scholarship Fund

100 Park Ave.
New York, NY 10017
(917) 663–2221
<www.thurgoodmarshallfund.org>

The Fund provides scholarships to students attending the nation's historically black public colleges and universities.

TransAfrica

1744 R St. NW
Washington, DC 20009
(202) 797–2301
info@transafricaforum.org
Founded 1977.

The group is concerned with the political and human rights of people in Africa and the Caribbean, as well as those of African descent throughout the world. It attempts to influence U.S. foreign policy in these areas by informing the public of violations of social, political, and civil rights and by advocating a more progressive attitude in the U.S. policy stance. It supports the work of the United Nations in Africa and sponsors TransAfrica Action Alert to mobilize African American opinion nationally on foreign policy issues by contacting influential policymakers.

TransAfrica Forum
1744 R St. NW
Washington, DC 20009
(202) 797–2301
info@transafricaforum.org
<www.transafricaforum.org>
Founded 1981.

TransAfrica Forum is the research and education arm of its parent organization, TransAfrica. The Forum seeks to provide an independent review of differing perspectives on political, economic, and cultural issues affecting African American communities globally through its publications. It also conducts seminars with scholars and government officials.

Try Us Resources
2105 Central Ave., NE
Minneapolis, MN 55418
(612) 781–6819
<www.tryusdir.com>
Founded 1968.

The group compiles and publishes minority business directories and sponsors minority purchasing seminars.

Union of Black Episcopalians
6105 S. Michigan Ave.
Chicago, IL 60637
(312) 288–0038
<www.afroanglican.org>
Founded 1968.

The Union is dedicated to involving Christians in every facet of church life. It encourages mission, stewardship, education, evangelism, and involvement in church governance and politics.

Unitarian Universalist Association Black Concerns Working Group
25 Beacon St.
Boston, MA 02108
(617) 742–2100
Founded 1985.

Founded to raise denominational public awareness of racism as a current justice issue. It works to implement recommendations regarding racial justice that were adopted by the Unitarian Universalist General Assembly in 1985 and conducts local and regional workshops in an effort to coordinate racial justice work among Unitarian Universalist congregations.

United American Progress Association
701 E. 79th St.
Chicago, IL 60619
(773) 268–1873
Founded 1961.

Comprised of businesses, churches, and organizations in the African American community, the Association promotes and assists African American entrepreneurs. It also encourages business owners to agree to supply goods and services to black communities whose residents support local black-owned firms, and works in conjunction with Operation PUSH and National Black United Front.

United Black Church Appeal
c/o Christ Church
860 Forest Ave.
Bronx, NY 10456
(718) 588–7500
Founded 1980.

Founded to awaken the power of the African American clergy and the African American church in order to provide leadership for the liberation of the African American community. The Appeal is concerned with African American economic development and political power and the strengthening of African American families and churches. It believes pastors in African American churches should reestablish legitimate leadership roles within the African American community. It works with troubled African American youths in the community and rallies against drugs in urban areas. It also supports community betterment projects including surplus food programs and distribution of food to needy families.

United Black Fund of America
1101 14th St. NW, Ste. 601
Washington, DC 20005
(202) 783–0430
Founded 1969.

Comprised of nonprofit agencies that provide human care services to low-income or disabled blacks and other minorities. The Fund assists disadvantaged African Americans and other minorities in becoming self-sufficient by providing funding to member agencies for the establishment of health and welfare programs. It sponsors fundraising activities to support day care service, education, senior citizens, and drug and alcohol rehabilitation programs; monitors the establishment and development of such programs.

United Church of Christ Commission for Racial Justice

c/o United Church of Christ
700 Prospect Ave., E.
Cleveland, OH 44115–1110
(216) 736–2161
Founded 1965.

Founded to ensure racial justice and social equality for ethnic and racial minorities worldwide. It maintains higher education program to provide scholarships to minority college students.

United Negro College Fund

8260 Willow Oak Corporation Dr.
Fairfax, VA 22031
(703) 205–3432
<www.unf.org>
Founded 1944.

Founded as a fund-raising agency for historically African American colleges and universities that are private and fully accredited. It provides information on educational programs, sponsors college fairs for high school and community college students, and administers scholarship awards and corporate and foundation programs.

Visions Foundation

2201 S St. NW
Washington, DC 20008–4013
(202) 462–1779
Founded 1983.

The Foundation promotes understanding of African American culture. It conducts media-related and educational programs to educate the public about the contributions of blacks to society and culture in the United States.

Washington Office on Africa

212 E Capitol St.
Washington, DC 20003
(202) 547–7503
woa@igc.apc.org
<www.woaafrica.org>
Founded 1972.

Founded to monitor and analyze developments in U.S. policy toward southern Africa and work with national and local groups that support the attainment of majority rule. It lobbies on congressional legislation affecting southern Africa.

Young Black Programmers Coalition

PO Box 2661
Mobile, AL 36652–2261
(334) 456–9175
<www.nbpcine.ore>
Founded 1976.

Founded to provide professional training and offer technical assistance to African American entrepreneurs in the broadcast and music industries. The Coalition conducts lobbying activities pertaining to legislation affecting the music industry and provides scholarships to attend African American colleges and universities.

Zeta Phi Beta

1734 New Hampshire Ave., NW
Washington, DC 20009
(202) 387–3103
<www.zpb1920.org>
Founded 1920.

Founded as a service and social sorority in 1920. It maintains the Zeta Phi Beta Sorority Educational Foundation.

10

Law

♦ The Legal Status of African Americans: 1787–1883
♦ African Americans and the Criminal Justice System
♦ African Americans in the Federal Courts
♦ African Americans on the U.S. Supreme Court ♦ Major Federal Legislation
♦ Major U.S. Supreme Court Decisions ♦ Attorneys, Judges, and Legal Scholars
♦ African American Federal Judges by Year of Appointment ♦ Criminal Justice Statistics

by DeWitt S. Dykes Jr.

♦ THE LEGAL STATUS OF AFRICAN AMERICANS: 1787–1883

The attitude toward the legal treatment of African Americans before 1883 was one of ambivalence. An understanding of the treatment of African Americans during the period must begin in 1787 with the adoption of the U.S. Constitution. In addition, the U.S. Supreme Court's treatment of African Americans during this period must be viewed in the context of the history and of the events that gave shape to it.

The United States began in 1776 with a declaration of universal equality. But that promise did not include people of color. The ringing testimony to equality in the Declaration of Independence had its limits. In short, America began with a contradiction that centered on race. The constitutional debates of the 1780s highlighted the nation's contradictory, confusing positions on race questions. The country was founded on the principle of individual liberty, but that liberty did not extend to the African slaves and their progeny. The leading questions of the era were: Should the slaves be counted for purposes of representation? Should Congress be empowered to prohibit slavery and the slave trade? Should an escaped slave be "free" to live among the rest of society?

From its beginning, the United States was mired in a debate over the question of slavery. Southerners wanted slaves counted towards representation in the U.S. House of Representatives, while still insisting that slaves were property. This contradiction led to a compromise in which slaves counted as three-fifths of a person for representational purposes. However, this compromise indicated that the slavery issue would would not easily recede.

Even though the institution of human slavery vexed members of the Constitutional Convention, not once was the word itself used in the document submitted for ratification. The contradiction between the equality espoused by the Constitution and the reality of slavery that the Constitution tolerated would tear the country apart less than 100 years later.

The original Constitution also forbade the new federal government from abolishing the slave trade or otherwise affecting matters of race before the year 1808. Runaway slaves were referred to as "person[s] held to service or labour in one state. . . escaping into another. . . ." This fugitive-slave clause (Article 4, section 2) sought to ensure that the slaveowners' escaped "property," would be returned when found. The purpose of these provisions was to ensure the political superiority of white Americans over the African slaves and their progeny. At the time of the Constitution's framing, African slaves and their descendants were politically inferior to white people.

Even though the framers of the Constitution recognized the peculiar dilemma of racial discrimination, they decided that they could postpone a decision on the "race question." The idea that matters of racial justice and racial equality could be put off was established. With conflicting constitutional antecedents, the Supreme

Court has been enormously conflicted on racial matters. The Court takes its cases as it finds them, and cases on race have never been easily or calmly settled.

The Early Days: *Prigg v. Pennsylvania*

Before the 1800s the Court had very few opportunities to render a decision directly on the question of slavery because it was an accepted institution and feature of American life. The law clearly recognized slaves as property and therefore subject to regulation as other real property might be. This regulation was often justified by citing the fugitive-slave clause of the Constitution. One of the few pre-Civil War cases to address the slavery question and state regulatory powers was *Prigg v. Pennsylvania* (41 US [16 Peters] 539, 1842).

Pennsylvania had enacted a statute prohibiting any person from removing blacks from the state by force or violence with the intention of detaining them as slaves. The Court explained that the fugitive-slave clause "contemplates the existence of a positive, unqualified right on the part of the owner of the slave, which no state law

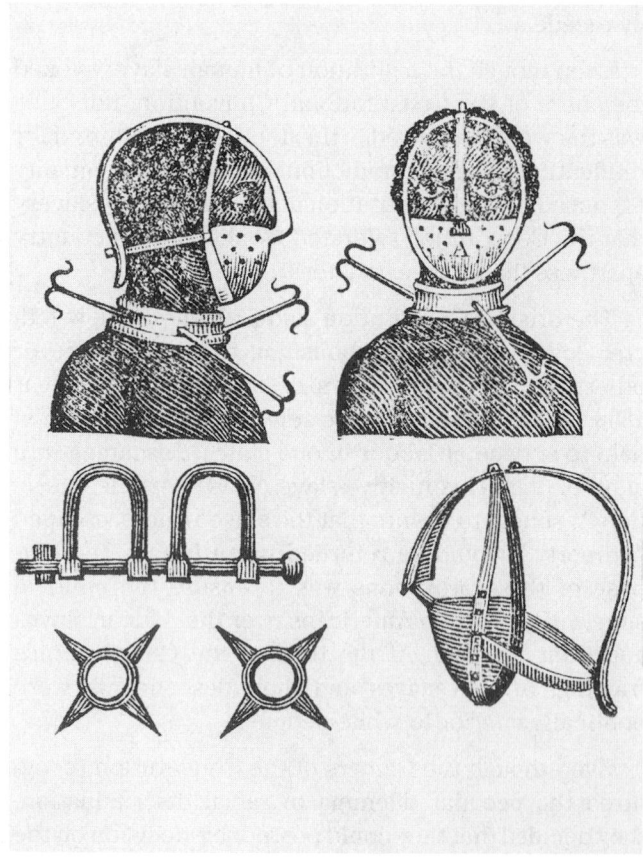

Illustration depicting various slave trading and catching apparatuses.

or regulation can in any way qualify, regulate, control, or restrain." The statute was declared invalid with respect to an escaped slave because, in the words of the Court, "any state law which interrupts, limits, delays, or postpones the right of the owner to the immediate possession of the slave, and the immediate command of his service and labor, operates *pro tanto*, a discharge of the slave therefrom." The Court further held that the clause implicitly vested Congress with the power to assist owners in securing the return of escaped slaves, that Congress had exercised that power by enacting the Fugitive Slave Act of 1793, that this national power was exclusive, and that any state laws regulating the means by which slaves were to be delivered up were unconstitutional.

Prigg announced no landmark policy. It simply affirmed the social and political realities of its time. During the period 1790 to 1883, however, two major cases involving African Americans and the issues of race did reach the Supreme Court: *Dred Scott v. Sandford* (60 US [19 Howard] 393, 1857) and *The Civil Rights Cases* (109 US 18, 1883)—along with the relatively minor case *Strauder v. West Virginia* (100 US [10 Otto] 303, 1880). As a whole, they revealed the abiding ambivalence that consistently has characterized American race relations.

Dred Scott v. Sandford

The 1800s were consumed with sectional strife, primarily strife about race. In 1856 *Dred Scott* was decided. The case would be an impetus toward civil war. Few cases in American judicial history have achieved as much notoriety as *Dred Scott*. The case continues to symbolize the marginal status that African Americans have often held in the nation's social and political order.

Dred Scott was the slave of a U.S. Army surgeon, John Emerson of Missouri. In 1834, Scott traveled with Emerson to live in Illinois, where slavery was prohibited. They later lived in the Wisconsin Territory, where slavery was prohibited by the Missouri Compromise. In 1838, Scott returned to Missouri with Emerson. Emerson later died there in 1843, and three years later Scott sued Emerson's widow for his freedom.

Scott's claim was based on the argument that his former residence in a free state and a free territory, made him a free man. A Missouri state circuit court ruled in Scott's favor, but the Missouri Supreme Court later reversed that decision. Meanwhile, Scott had become legally regarded as the property of John F. A. Sandford of New York. Because Sandford did not live in

Missouri, Scott's lawyers were able to transfer the case to a federal court. The lower federal court ruled against Scott, and his lawyers appealed to the U.S. Supreme Court. By a 7–2 vote, the Supreme Court ruled that Scott could not bring a suit in federal court. The decision was announced on March 6, 1857, two days after the inauguration of President James Buchanan. The *Dred Scott* decision declared that no African American, whether free or slave, could claim U.S. citizenship. It also held that Congress could not prohibit slavery in the U.S. territories. In his opinion, Chief Justice Roger Brooke Taney wrote that African Americans had "no rights which any white man was bound to respect."

This decision—only the second in the nation's history in which the Supreme Court declared an act of Congress unconstitutional—was a clear victory for the political interests that supported slavery. Southerners long had argued that neither Congress nor the territorial legislature had the power to exclude slavery from a territory. Only a state could exclude slavery, they maintained.

The ruling also aroused anger and resentment in the North and other parts of the country and launched the nation further along the course to civil war. It influenced the introduction and the adoption of the Fourteenth Amendment to the Constitution in 1868, which explicitly overruled *Dred Scott*, extended citizenship to former slaves, and sought to give them full civil rights.

Each justice in the majority wrote a separate opinion. Chief Justice Taney's opinion, however, is most often cited because of its far-reaching implications for sectional crisis and for the view of the rights of African Americans that it announced. Speaking for the majority, Chief Justice Taney declared that Scott was not entitled to rights such as the right to vote or to sue in a federal court, because, as an African American, he was not a citizen of the United States. The Court did not dismiss the case after ruling on Scott's citizenship. Because there was a growing national desire for a ruling on the constitutionality of such laws as the Missouri Compromise of 1820, the Taney Court seized the opportunity to express its views on both congressional power and the legal status of African Americans

The Missouri Compromise had forbidden slavery in that part of the Louisiana Territory north of the latitude 36° 30', except for Missouri. Instead of dismissing the suit, the Court discussed this issue as a part of its decision in *Dred Scott*. By the same 7–2 margin, it ruled that the Missouri Compromise, which had been repealed in 1854, was unconstitutional. Taney argued that because slaves were property, Congress could not forbid slavery in territories without violating a slaveowner's right to own property under the Fifth Amendment. As for Scott's temporary residence in the free state of Illinois, the majority ruled that Scott then had still been subject to Missouri law. Dred Scott was sold shortly afterward, and his new owner gave him his freedom two months after the decision.

The *Dred Scott* decision energized the newly created Republican Party, which had been formed to curb the expansion of slavery into the Western territories. The decision forced Democrat Stephen A. Douglas, an advocate of popular sovereignty to devise a system that would enable settlers to ban slavery in their jurisdictions. President Buchanan, the South, and a majority of the Supreme Court had hoped that the decision would end the anti-slavery agitation that consumed the country. Instead, the decision increased antislavery sentiment in the North, strengthened the Republican Party, and fed the sectional antagonisms that finally exploded into war in 1861.

Strauder v. West Virginia and the *Civil Rights Cases*

Between the time of the Civil War and the *Civil Rights Cases*, the only case to protect the rights of African Americans was *Strauder v. West Virginia* (1880). West Virginia permitted only "white male persons who are 21 years of age" to serve on juries in the state. This, of course, meant that it was impossible for African Americans to serve on a jury. The Supreme Court invalidated this provision as a violation of the Fourteenth Amendment's guarantee of equal protection.

The Civil War, caused in part by Justice Taney's decision in *Dred Scott* that Congress could not bar slavery in the territories, actually resulted in the destruction of slavery. Moreover, the war created a completely new balance of power between the national and the state governments. Federalism, unlike it had been understood prior to the Civil War, now would function with a totally new calculus in which the federal government was the dominant power.

The years following the Civil War produced the Thirteenth, Fourteenth, and Fifteenth Amendments to the Constitution. Their purposes were to emancipate and empower the former slaves. These three amendments are compelling evidence of the relationship between the federal and state governments. The text of the Fourteenth Amendment, overturning *Dred Scott*, emphasized the significance of this new relationship and the new power realignments.

U.S. citizenship was redefined as being protected by the national constitution, not as a byproduct of state citizenship. State citizenship was subordinate to national citizenship. Augmented by Congress's enforcement powers, these amendments were the constitutional foundations that supported Reconstruction. A principal legislative result of this period was the passage of the Civil Rights Act of 1875. According to the statute, its purpose was "to protect all citizens in their civil and legal rights." Even though couched in general terms, the statute was designed to aid recently emancipated slaves.

The 1870s became unique years for testing race relations in the United States. During this period there were no state laws requiring the separation of the races in places of public accommodation. Practices in particular establishments or particular jurisdictions were matters of local custom, individual choice, or personal preference. An earlier statute, the Civil Rights Act of 1866, and the ratification of the Fourteenth Amendment in 1868 had spawned cases throughout the country including suits for denying sleeper accommodations to African Americans on a Washington-to-New York train, for refusing to sell theater tickets to African Americans in Boston, for restricting African Americans to front platforms in Baltimore streetcars, and for barring African American women from the waiting rooms and parlor cars of railroads in Virginia, Illinois, and California. There also had been massive resistance on the part of whites to the social integration of the races.

Faced with these challenges, the Republican-controlled Congress enacted the Civil Rights Act of 1875. It invalidated all racially motivated interference with individuals' use of "the accommodations, advantages, facilities, and privileges of inns, public conveyances and theatres" (109 US 9–10). In short, the statute sought to provide legislative specificity to the constitutional norms embodied in the Fourteenth Amendment.

The *Civil Rights Cases* decision resulted from the consolidation of several cases, including *United States v. Singleton*, *United States v. Nichols*, *United States v. Ryan*, *United States v. Hamilton*, and *Robinson v. Memphis & Charleston Railroad*. Five of the cases were criminal prosecutions that directly challenged the constitutionality of the 1875 statute. *United States v. Singleton*, involved the refusal of Samuel Singleton, doorkeeper of New York's Grand Opera House, to honor the tickets of William R. Davis Jr. and his fiancé.

On November 22, 1879, the pair had attempted to see a matinee performance of Victor Hugo's *Ruy Blas*. Davis, the business agent of the African American newspaper *The Progressive-American*, was obviously African American. His fiancée, however, had a light complexion and purchased the tickets earlier. When the couple returned for the performance, they were denied entrance because of Singleton's race.

Stanley involved the refusal of hotelier, Murray Stanley, to serve a meal to Bird Gee, an African American in his Kansas hotel. *Nichols* involved the refusal of the Nichols House in Jefferson City, Missouri, to accept an African American as a guest. In *Ryan*, the doorkeeper at Maguire's Theater in San Francisco denied an African American man entry to the dress circle at the theater. In *Hamilton*, the conductor of the Nashville, Chattanooga & St. Louis Railroad denied an African American access to the ladies' car. Instead, she was relegated to a smoking car.

The sixth case *Robinson v. Memphis & Charleston Railroad* was not a criminal case. It involved travel on the Memphis & Charleston Railroad by a young African American woman, Mrs. Sallie Robinson, and her nephew, Joseph C. Robinson. Mr. Robinson was described as a young African American "of light complexion, light hair, and light blue eyes." The train's conductor attempted forcibly to refuse the two passengers entry to the first-class parlor car for which they had purchased tickets. The conductor mistook the pair for a white man and his paramour. The railroad conceded the constitutionality of the 1875 statute, but argued that it did not apply to the conductor's actions. The trial judge ruled that motive was dispositive under the act. Thus, if the conductor believed Mrs. Robinson to be a prostitute, whether reasonable or not in that assumption, the exclusion was not based on race and the railroad was not liable. The jury found for the railroad and the Robinsons appealed.

The United States, represented before the Supreme Court by Solicitor General Samuel F. Phillips, argued that the act should be upheld in every case. In addition, the government's brief discussed the history of American race relations and the genesis of the Civil War amendments and their statutory descendants. The government stressed particularly the importance of equal access to public accommodations. The solicitor general emphasized that this act was one of several enacted by "a Congress led by men who had fought in the Civil War and had framed the war amendments." Implicit in the solicitor general's position was the idea that Congress understood, as clearly as anyone could, that it was not sufficient to outlaw slavery and to declare equal protection to be the law of the land. Specific statutory protection was necessary to ensure that every vestige of slavery and every reminder of its stigma were eliminated from public life.

The government's arguments, however, did not persuade the Court. It announced its decision on October 15, 1883. The Court ruled 8–1 against the United States. Justice Bradley wrote the opinion of the Court, which asserted two conclusions: the Fourteenth Amendment is prohibitory upon the states only, and the Thirteenth Amendment relates only to slavery and involuntary servitude.

Bradley maintained that the Fourteenth Amendment operated only as a prohibition and restriction against the states. Because the Civil Rights Act of 1875 sought to outlaw acts of private individuals, shopkeepers, and other businesses, it violated the constitution. This "state action" doctrine holds that because the government was not the actor in these cases, the Fourteenth Amendment did not empower Congress to outlaw these practices. Also, Bradley's opinion held that, while Congress was empowered by the Thirteenth Amendment to eliminate slavery and all its vestiges, the denial of access to accommodations in commercial establishments, public conveyances, and public amusements was not a "badge or incident of slavery." The opinion halted the progress of civil rights and limited the ability of the federal government, acting through Congress, to eliminate and eradicate racial discrimination for almost 90 years.

Justice John Marshall Harlan dissented. At the time, Harlan was the Court's only Southerner and a former slaveholder. Although he had been a bitter critic of the Civil War Amendments during the 1860s, he had undergone a transformation. His dissent was not announced on the day of the majority's decision and may not have been written until November. In it, he said that the grounds for the majority's assertions were "too narrow and artificial" and that the majority refused to embrace both "the substance and the spirit" of the Civil Rights Act. "It is not the words of the law but the internal sense of it that makes the law. The letter of the law is the body; the sense and reason of the law is the soul." And, in Justice Harlan's view, the purpose of the act "was to prevent *race* [emphasis in original] discrimination." The majority, as Harlan developed the dissent, betrayed this purpose "by a subtle and ingenious verbal criticism."

Neither the majority of the Supreme Court nor the nation it represented cared to do much else to promote the civil rights of its new African American citizens. Harlan's dissent in the *Civil Rights Cases* forecasted his more famous one in *Plessy v. Ferguson*, as the decision in the *Civil Rights Cases* led to the black codes, Jim Crow laws, and other examples of *de jure* (by law) segregation that came to define American race relations.

The *Civil Rights Cases* revealed the nation's ambivalence on the questions of race. On one hand, Congress had sought to guarantee the rights of the recently freed slaves by proposing constitutional amendments that were ultimately ratified. Congress went further and augmented the constitutional guarantees with additional legislative protections and safeguards. The Supreme Court, however, frustrated these constitutional and legislative initiatives with a constricted reading of the Thirteenth and the Fourteenth Amendments.

◆ AFRICAN AMERICANS AND THE CRIMINAL JUSTICE SYSTEM

Criminal justice in the United States consists of three major components, law enforcement, judicial and legal services, and corrections. Since the 1970s, African Americans have assumed significant leadership roles in both law enforcement and correctional services as evidenced by the rising number of African American judges, prosecutors, and defense attorneys. However, since 1970, the employment of African Americans as judges and prosecutors has not increased at the rate that gives African Americans working in the system a formidable presence.

Law Enforcement

As the largest arm of the criminal justice system, police are the most visible criminal justice servants. As the first point of contact for persons entering the system, officers make discretionary, often quasi-judicial decisions as to whether an arrest should be made when an offense is alleged to have occurred. Law enforcers have been organized and empowered to support the interest of those with means to shape law, a factor that had significant bearing on the prior relationship African Americans had with the police.

Just as any other community, African Americans look to law enforcement for protection from an criminal elements present in their midst. However, until the recent integration of many urban police departments, law enforcement officers were used as agents of segregation and fear in many areas. This legacy still causes problems in African American relations with the police.

Judicial and Legal Services and the Correctional System

In the 1990s, a serious debate on the merits of sentencing and capital punishment arose. Statistics showed that African Americans are likely to receive stiffer penalties for killing whites than whites receive for killing African Americans. This is also true in the administration of the death penalty, which disproportionately is used against African Americans who kill whites. In 1987, the Supreme Court took up the issue in *McKleskey v. Kemp*, and ruled that statistics could not be used to prove the death penalty was being administered in a discriminatory manner. The Court required more evidence and evinced a fear that if they had ruled the other way, that all African Americans on death row would come forward with claims. The issue did not die, however, as in 1999, Illinois announced a moratorium on executions to study the issue.

"The Trial of the Century"

On June 12, 1994, a brutal, double-murder led to one of the most sensational criminal trials of the twentieth century. Nicole Brown Simpson, former wife of African American football legend O. J. Simpson, was brutally slain outside her house along with her friend Ron Goldman. Almost immediately, evidence pointed to O. J. Simpson as the primary suspect. The subsequent, year-long trial was aired on television, allowing viewers to witness the entire spectacle almost as if it were a soap opera.

Prosecutors Marcia Clark and Christopher Darden, an African American, portrayed Simpson as a jealous husband who had been locked in a pattern of domestic abuse. The murder of a spouse by a habitual abuser is common, they argued, and the prosecutors used this as the motive. Simpson's "Dream Team" of defense attorneys focused on an alleged police conspiracy based on race. Simpson was found not guilty in October 1995. Ultimately, the case had little to do with the actual murders. *Broadcasting & Cable* magazine reported that "the verdict. . . broke all previous TV viewing records, with over 150 million people tuning in."

Rather than addressing the crime, the proceedings brought the ugly underbelly of the country's prejudices, fears, and values to light. Polls showed that most whites thought Simpson was guilty, while blacks were divided on the verdict. Many African Americans viewed Simpson as another African American man caught in a judicial system enforced by the bigoted Los Angeles Police Department. The trial was the first in which overwhelming DNA evidence was not persuasive to a jury, as the defense attorneys alleged it had been rendered useless by police errors. The impression that Simpson had purchased his freedom with his high-priced lawyers grew in the years following the trial. Following the verdict, the Brown and Goldman families won a wrongful death civil suit against Simpson, forcing him to sell most of his assets. Simpson became a recluse, innocent in the eyes of the court, but guilty in the eyes of many.

Mumia Abu-Jamal.

The Case of Mumia Abu-Jamal

Though not as big a newsmaker as the O.J. Simpson spectacle, the case of outspoken journalist and former Black Panther Mumia Abu-Jamal caused quite a ripple in the legal system during the mid-1990s. During an altercation between a Philadelphia police officer and Jamal's brother, Jamal claims to have entered the fracas in order to keep his brother from being beaten. Though details are sketchy and contested, the aftermath of the fray left Jamal wounded by a bullet from the officer's gun and the officer dead. Arrested and convicted of murder, Jamal was sentenced to death in 1982.

Groups of national and international supporters advocated for Jamal's release, alleging that aspects of Jamal's case were improperly handled in regards to the U.S. Constitution and correct legal procedure. Many believe Jamal was framed by the Philadelphia police who wanted to keep the blunt and forthright reporter from exposing evidence of corruption within the law enforcement agency.

In December 2001, U.S. District Judge William Yohn invalidated the death sentence. Citing several problems, including the jury instructions, Judge Yohn denied Abu-Jamal's request for a new trial but indicated that he was entitled to a new sentencing hearing.

O.J. Simpson conferring with his team of lawyers (l-r: Carl Douglas, Johnnie Cochran, and Robert Shapiro) during "The Trial of the Century."

◆ AFRICAN AMERICANS IN THE FEDERAL COURTS

Less than 4 percent of all judges are African American. Nonetheless, the amazing fact is that despite a complete lack of legal rights as slaves, African Americans made their first in-roads toward civil rights via the court system. In separate incidents, escaped slave Elizabeth Freeman, New England slave Lucy Prince, and Southern slave Dred Scott, all battled racial barriers with courage and dignity.

African Americans did not enter the courts just as parties to actions, they also participated in the system in professional capacities. In 1844, Macon Allen became the first African American admitted to a state bar. Charlotte Ray later became the first African American woman to gain the same distinction. Other pioneering women followed, including Ellen Craft, Francis Watkins Harper, Laetitia Rowley, Maria Stewart, Mary Church Terrell, and Ida B. Wells-Barnett. John S. Rock became the first African American lawyer to argue a case before the Supreme Court in 1865. In 1873, Mifflin Gibbs became the first African American municipal judge.

Though he only served a single term, his reputation for fairness was legendary, and he was named U.S. consul to Madagascar in 1897. Jonathan Jasper Wright was elected to the South Carolina State Supreme Court in 1870. In 1937, President Franklin D. Roosevelt appointed William H. Hastie to the Territorial Court of the Virgin Islands, making him the first African American federal district court judge. In 1939, Hastie was succeeded by Herman E. Moore, another African American. Jane Matilda Bolin became the first African American female judge when she was appointed Judge of Domestic Relations for the City of New York. In 1945, President Harry Truman appointed Irvin C. Mollison to the U.S. Customs Court (now the U.S. Court of International Trade), thus making him the first African American lifetime appointee to a federal court.

Nominated by the U.S. president and confirmed through Senate hearings, federal judgeships are lifetime appointments. Of the roughly 1,000 active federal judges—including U.S. district courts, U.S. circuit courts, U.S. courts of appeals, and the Supreme Court—by 2002 about 80 were African American. Still, African Americans have received appointments since the early

1960s, beginning with James B. Parsons, who was nominated by President John F. Kennedy to sit on the bench of the U.S. District Court for the Northern District of Illinois in 1961. At that time, the lack of federal African American judges was noticeable. Kennedy appointed Wade Hampton McCree Jr. to the U.S. District Court for the Eastern District of Michigan in 1961, and Thurgood Marshall to the Second Circuit Court of Appeals in 1962. In five years, Marshall would go on to become the first African American appointed to the U.S. Supreme Court.

President Lyndon B. Johnson followed Kennedy's lead, nominating 11 African Americans to federal benches. Among them were A. Leon Higginbotham Jr.—Johnson's first appointee—and Constance Baker Motley. As a member of the U.S. District Court for the Southern District of New York, Motley became the first African American woman to hold a federal judgeship in 1966. The next female appointee did not come for 12 years, when Mary Johnson Lowe was appointed by President Jimmy Carter to the same district court. Carter also chose Amalya Lyle Kearse, in 1979, to become the first African American woman on the U.S. Court of Appeals. She was seated in the same venue in which Thurgood Marshall began his judicial career. Overall, Carter appointed 37 African Americans in four years.

Republican presidents have had the poorest record of nominating African Americans to the federal courts. Richard Nixon only nominated six, and Gerald Ford three, over the combined eight years of their presidential terms. Lyndon Johnson nominated more in half the time. Ronald Reagan only appointed seven African Americans to federal courts in eight years. His successor, President George H. W. Bush, appointed 13 in four years, including U.S. Supreme Court Justice Clarence Thomas. In contrast, Democrat Bill Clinton appointed 63 African Americans to federal courts by August 2000. He tried to appoint more, but the Republican-controlled Senate would not hold hearings or approve many of his judicial nominations, creating numerous vacancies. However, Clinton did help integrate the U.S. Court of Appeals for the Fourth Circuit. After the Senate refused to consider four nominations he made to this court, Clinton nominated an African American lawyer, Roger Gregory, as a "recess appointment" in December 2000. Since the Senate had ended its business for the year, Gregory served through most of 2001 without Senate approval. The maneuver pressured the administration of President George W. Bush to renominate Gregory in May 2001. When Democrats took control of the Senate that spring, the Senate

approved Gregory, who became the first African American lifetime federal judge on the Fourth Circuit Court of Appeals.

◆ AFRICAN AMERICANS ON THE U.S. SUPREME COURT

Thurgood Marshall, a graduate of Lincoln University and Howard University Law School, was admitted to the Maryland Bar in 1933. He later joined the National Association for the Advancement of Colored People (NAACP) as assistant to special counsel Charles Hamilton Houston. In 1938 Marshall succeeded Houston as special counsel, and in 1950, he became director of the NAACP Legal Defense and Educational Fund (LDF). While working for the NAACP and the LDF, Marshall played a major role in some of the Supreme Court's most important cases, including *Smith v. Allwright* (1944), *Morgan v. Commonwealth of Virginia* (1946), *Shelley v. Kraemer* (1948), *Sweatt v. Painter* (1950), and *Brown v. Board of Education of Topeka, Kansas*. Between 1938 and 1961, Marshall argued 32 cases before the U.S. Supreme Court, winning 29.

In 1961, Marshall became the second African American to serve on the U.S. Circuit Court of Appeals, when President John F. Kennedy named Marshall to fill a vacancy. In 1965, President Lyndon B. Johnson appointed Marshall to the post of U.S. solicitor general. With the retirement of Associate Justice Tom Campbell Clark in 1967, Marshall was nominated to fill the vacancy on the high court. Marshall's nomination was met with objections from Southern senators. Nevertheless, he was confirmed, becoming the first African American justice on the U.S. Supreme Court. While on the Court, Marshall served as a supporter of affirmative action, free speech, and the rights of workers. He wrote few famous decisions, but his dissenting opinions in such cases as *Milliken v. Bradley* (1974), and *Regents of the University of California v. Bakke* (1978), are famous.

On June 27, 1991, Justice Marshall announced his plan to retire after 24 years on the U.S. Supreme Court. On July 1, President George H. W. Bush announced that he had chosen Clarence Thomas, a conservative African American appellate court judge, to fill the vacancy created by Marshall. Previously, in 1981, President Ronald Reagan had appointed Clarence Thomas, a graduate of a Holy Cross College and Yale University Law School, to head the civil rights division of the Department of Education. A year later, Thomas was appointed to head the Equal Employment Opportunity Commission. In 1990 Thomas was appointed by President H. W. Bush to fill a vacancy on the U.S. Court of Appeals for the District of Columbia.

In a flurry of controversy, Clarence Thomas was appointed an associate justice of the U.S. Supreme Court in 1991, after being nominated by President George H. W. Bush. Besides Thomas's relative youth and judicial inexperience, his nomination hearings were marred by the accusations from Anita Hill that she had suffered from sexual harassment while under his employ at the Equal Employment Opportunity Commission (EEOC).

The nation, as well as the Senate, seemed divided by Hill's shocking testimony. Thomas denied the allegations and had many of his former co-workers testify for him. After the confirmation votes were counted, Thomas was nominated by the narrow margin of 52–48.

◆ MAJOR FEDERAL LEGISLATION

Emancipation Act (April 1862)
ch.54, 12 state. 376

This law, abolishing slavery in the District of Columbia, was enacted April 16, 1862.

Emancipation Act (June 1862)
ch. 111, 12 Stat. 432

This act, abolishing slavery in all other territories of the United States, was enacted June 19, 1862.

Amendment Thirteen to the U.S. Constitution (1865)

This Amendment, abolishing slavery and involuntary servitude in all of the United States, was ratified December 16, 1865.

Civil Rights Act (1866)
ch. 31, 14 Stat. 27

This act was enacted April 9, 1866, to provide all citizens, especially recently freed slaves, with basic civil rights, including the right to make and enforce contracts, to bring suits in court, to purchase and sell real and personal property, and to enjoy security of person and property.

Amendment Fourteen to the U.S. Constitution (1868)

This Amendment defined U.S. and state citizenship, and provided all citizens with the privileges and immunities of citizenship; the right to life, liberty, and property; and equal protection under the law. It was ratified July 20, 1868.

The Fifteenth Amendment guaranteed that all African American adult males were entitled to vote.

Amendment Fifteen to the U.S. Constitution (1870)

This Amendment prohibited using race, color, or previous condition of servitude to deny anyone the right to vote. It was ratified March 30, 1870.

Civil Rights Act (1870)
ch. 114, 16 Stat. 140

This statute was enacted May 31, 1870, to carry out the provisions of the Fifteenth Amendment. It established penalties for violations of the provisions of the Amendment.

Civil Rights Act (1871)
ch. 99, 16 Stat. 433

This law was enacted February 28, 1871, to further define the protections established in the Fifteenth Amendment.

Civil Rights Act (April 1871)
ch. 22, 17 Stat. 13

This law was enacted April 20, 1871, to further outline the protections provided for by the Fourteenth Amendment. It provided for the vindication of crimes committed under the act in federal court.

Civil Rights Act (1875)
ch. 114, 18 Stat. 335

This act was designed to provide all citizens with equal access to public places. Ruling in 1883 in a set of cases known as the *Civil Rights Cases*, the U.S. Supreme Court invalidated the act.

Civil Rights Act of 1957
Pub.L. No. 85–315, 71 Stat. 634

This act created the Commission on Civil Rights and empowered it to investigate allegations of deprivation of a U.S. citizen's right to vote, to appraise laws and policies of the federal government with respect to equal protection of the law, and to submit a report to the president and to Congress within two years.

Civil Rights Act of 1960
Pub.L. No. 86–449, 74 Stat. 86

This law guaranteed the provision of criminal penalties in the event a suspect crosses state lines to avoid legal process for the actual or attempted bombing or burning of any vehicle or building, and provided penalties for persons who obstructed or interfered with any order of a federal court.

Civil Rights Act of 1964
Pub.L. No. 88–352, 78 Stat. 241

This act prohibited discrimination in the use of public accommodations whose operations involve interstate commerce and provided enforcement measures to ensure equal access to public facilities. It also prohibited racial discrimination in any program receiving federal aid and discrimination on the basis of race, color, religion, sex, or national origin in most areas of employment. It authorized the U.S. attorney general to use lawsuits to desegregate schools and public facilities.

Amendment Twenty-Four to the U.S. Constitution (1964)

This Amendment prohibited the use of a poll tax or any other tax—a common method to keep poorer people, especially African Americans, from voting—as a requirement for voting. It was ratified January 23, 1964.

Voting Rights Act of 1965
Pub.L. No. 89–110, 79 Stat. 437

The Voting Rights Act of 1965 struck down requirements such as literacy and knowledge tests and poll tax payments which had been used to restrict African American participation in voting, and provided for federal registrars to register voters should state registrars refuse to do so. It further stipulated that registered voters cannot be prohibited from voting.

Civil Rights Act of 1968
Pub.L. No. 90–284, 82 Stat. 73

This act provided for open housing by prohibiting discrimination based on race, color, religion, or national origin.

Equal Employment Opportunity Act of 1972
Pub.L. No. 92–261, 86 Stat. 103

This act provided the Equal Employment Opportunity Commission (established by the Civil Rights Act of 1964) with the authority to issue judicially enforceable cease and desist orders in cases involving discriminatory employment practices.

Public Works Employment Act of 1977
Pub.L. No. 95–28, 91 Stat. 116, Title I

The statute provided that 10 percent of funds expended as a result of federal grants be earmarked for minority business enterprises.

Voting Rights Act of 1965 Amendment
Pub.L. No. 97–205, 96 Stat. 131 (1982)

This Amendment was a congressional response to the Supreme Court's ruling in *City of Mobile, Alabama v. Wiley L. Bolden* that required proof of discriminatory intent in voting rights cases. Section 2 of the Voting Rights Act prohibited any voting practice or procedure "imposed or applied by any state or political subdivision in a manner which results in a denial or abridgement of the right of any citizen of the United States to vote on account of race or color."

Civil Rights Commission Act of 1983
Pub.L. No. 98–183, 87 Stat. 1301

This act created an eight-member bipartisan commission with four members appointed by the president, and two by the Senate and House respectively. The commissioners are appointed to four- or six-year terms and can be fired only for neglect of duty or malfeasance in office. The statute was enacted after President Ronald Reagan attempted to fire commissioners who did not express his views on civil rights. The act extended the life of the Civil Rights Commission Authorization Act of 1978, which had been scheduled to expire in 1983.

Civil Rights Restoration Act of 1988
Pub.L. No. 100–259, 102 Stat. 31

The U.S. Supreme Court ruled in 1984 in *Grove City College v. Bell* that not all programs and activities of an institution were covered by Title IX of the Education amendments of 1972 (Public Law 89–10, 79 Stat. 27)

Prior to the Civil Rights Act of 1964, blacks were continually denied access to the same public accommodations as whites.

and that discrimination can be barred only in programs that directly receive federal funds. The act amended portions of the Civil Rights Act of 1964 and refined the definition of programs and activities that were covered by the Civil Rights Act and other legislation. Specifically the amendment addressed Title IX of the Education Amendments of 1972, which prohibits discrimination in educational programs receiving federal financial assistance.

Fair Housing Amendments Act of 1988
Pub.L. No. 100–430, 102 Stat 1619

The Fair Housing Amendments Act of 1988 strengthened laws that resulted from passage of the Fair Housing Act of 1968. The act of 1988 gave the Department of Housing and Urban Development (HUD) the authority to issue discrimination charges, allowed administrative law justices the ability to review housing discrimination cases, and removed the $1,000 limit on punitive damages that a victim of discrimination may receive.

Civil Rights Act of 1991
Pub.L. 102–166, 105 Stat. 1071

This act was designed to provide additional remedies to deter harassment and intentional discrimination in the workplace, to provide guidelines for the adjudication of cases arising under Title VII of the Civil Rights Act of 1964, and to expand the scope of civil rights legislation weakened by Supreme Court decisions, particularly the Court's ruling in *Wards Cove Packing Co. v. Antonio*, 490 US 642 (1989).

Glass Ceiling Act of 1991
Pub.L. 102–166, 105 Stat. 1081

This law was designed to establish a means for studying and addressing the underrepresentation of women and minorities at management and decision making levels in the workforce.

◆ MAJOR U.S. SUPREME COURT DECISIONS

Access to the Polls

United States v. Reese
92 U.S. 214 (1876)

Prior to the Fifteenth Amendment, states regulated all details of state and local elections—they prescribed the qualifications of voters and the manner in which those desiring to vote at an election should make their qualifications known to the election officers. Thus, the Fifteenth Amendment changed the past practice and provided rules not prescribed by state law. However, the Court restricted the scope of the Fifteenth Amendment and the ability of Congress to enforce it by not punishing election officials who unlawfully interfered with, and prevented the free exercise of, the elective franchise.

The federal government indicted two Kentucky election inspectors for refusing to receive and count the vote of an African American citizen. The Supreme Court held that Congress had not yet provided "appropriate legislation"' for the punishment of the offense charged under any sections of the Fifteenth Amendment.

Guinn v. United States
238 U.S. 347 (1915)

In 1910, an amendment to the constitution of Oklahoma restricted voting rights by providing that no illiterate person could be registered. A "grandfather clause," however, granted an exemption for persons who resided in a foreign country prior to January 1, 1866, and had been eligible to register prior to that date, or had a lineal ancestor who was eligible to vote at that time. Since no African Americans were eligible to vote in Oklahoma prior to 1866, the law disenfranchised all African Americans.

The U.S. Supreme Court ruled that the grandfather clause was invalid in Oklahoma or in any other state.

Nixon v. Herndon
273 U.S. 536 (1927)

Dr. L. A. Nixon, an African American, was refused the right to vote in a primary election because of a state statute that prohibited African Americans from participating in Democratic Party primaries in Texas. Nixon filed suit against the election officials and his case ultimately reached the U.S. Supreme Court. Justice Oliver Wendell Holmes wrote, "It is too clear for extended argument that color cannot be made the basis of a statutory classification affecting the right set up in this case." As a result, the Texas statute was declared unconstitutional.

Nixon v. Condon
286 U.S. 73 (1932)

As a result of the U.S. Supreme Court ruling in *Nixon v. Herndon*, the Texas legislature passed a new statute.

This statute empowered the state Democratic executive committee to set up its own rules regarding primary elections. The party promptly adopted a resolution stipulating that only white Democrats be allowed to participate in primaries. Dr. Nixon again filed suit, and his right to vote was again upheld by the U.S. Supreme Court.

Lane v. Wilson
307 U.S. 268 (1939)

In an attempt to restrict voter registration, the Oklahoma legislature stated that all Oklahomans who were already registered would remain qualified voters and that all others would have to register within 12 days (from April 30 to May 11, 1916) or be forever barred from the polls. In 1934, I. W. Lane, an African American, was refused registration on the basis of this statute. The U.S. Supreme Court declared that the statute was in conflict with the Fifteenth Amendment to the U.S. Constitution and was unconstitutional.

Smith v. Allwright
321 U.S. 649 (1944)

The Texas State Democratic Party, during its convention in 1932, limited the right of membership to white electors. As a result, nonwhites were unable to participate in a Democratic Party primary. In *Grovey v. Townsend* (295 US 45), the Supreme Court had upheld this limitation because it was made by the party in convention, not by a party executive committee. In *Smith v. Allwright*, the Court overruled *Grovey*, stating, "[T]he United States is a constitutional democracy. Its organic law grants to all citizens a right to participate in the choice of elected officials without restriction by any state because of race." The Court noted that a political party makes its selection of candidates as an agency of the state. Therefore, it cannot exclude participation based on race and remain consistent with the Fifteenth Amendment.

Gomillion v. Lightfoot
364 U.S. 339 (1960)

African American citizens challenged an Alabama statute that redefined the boundaries of the city of Tuskegee. The statute altered the shape of Tuskegee and placed all but four of Tuskegee's 400 African American voters outside of the city limits, while not displacing a single white voter. The Court struck down the statute as a violation of the Fifteenth Amendment.

Baker v. Carr
369 U.S. 186 (1962)

Baker v. Carr was brought to the Supreme Court by electors in several counties of Tennessee. The electors asserted that the 1901 legislative reapportionment statute was unconstitutional because the numbers of voters in the various districts had changed substantially since 1901. The plaintiffs requested that the Supreme Court either direct a reapportionment by mathematical application of the same formula to the 1960 Census, or instruct the state to hold direct at-large elections. The state district court had dismissed the case on the grounds that it was a political question and did not fall within the protection of the Fourteenth Amendment. The U.S. Supreme Court ruled that the case involved a basic constitutional right rather than a political question and thereby was in the jurisdiction of the U.S. district court and federal courts in general. In later cases, such as *Gray v. Sanders*, 372 U.S. 368 (1963), and *Reynolds v. Sims*, 377 U.S. 533 (1964), the U.S. Supreme Court explained the standards to be applied to voting districts in each state give reasonably equal representation, resulting in a principle popularly referred to as "one man, one vote."

South Carolina v. Katzenbach
383 U.S. 301 (1966)

The Voting Rights Act of 1965 was designed to eliminate racial discrimination in voting, which had influenced the electoral process for nearly a century. The act abolished literacy tests, waived accumulated poll taxes, and allotted the U.S. attorney general vast discretionary powers over regions suspected of discriminatory legislation and practices against African American voters.

South Carolina's petition asserted that the Voting Rights Act encroached on state sovereignty, thus violating the U.S. Constitution. The Supreme Court dismissed the petition because section 1 of the Fifteenth Amendment to the Constitution says, "The right of citizens of the United States to vote shall not be denied or abridged by the United States or by any state on account of race, color, or previous condition of servitude."

Allen v. State Board of Elections
393 U.S. 110 (1969)

The Supreme Court emphasized that subtle as well as obvious state regulations, "which have the effect of denying citizens their right to vote because of their race," are prohibited. The Court confirmed that Section 5 of the Voting Rights Act covered a variety of practices other than voter registration.

Georgia v. United States
411 U.S. 526 (1973)

This case confirmed the propriety of the Voting Rights Act of 1965, which forbids states with a history of racial discrimination (e.g., Alabama, Georgia, Louisiana, Mississippi, North Carolina, South Carolina and Virginia) from implementing any change in voting practices and procedures without first submitting the proposed plan to the U.S. attorney general for approval.

White v. Regester
412 U.S. 755 (1973)

The Supreme Court struck down a Texas multimember districting scheme that was used to prevent African Americans from being elected to public office. The Court upheld a finding that even though there was no evidence that African Americans faced official obstacles to registration, voting, or running for office, they had been excluded from effective participation in the political process in violation of the Equal Protection Clause of the Constitution.

City of Mobile, Alabama v. Wiley L. Bolden
446 U.S. 55 (1980)

A class action suit was filed in the U.S. District Court for the Southern District of Alabama on behalf of African American citizens in Mobile. The suit alleged that the city's practice of electing commissioners at large by a majority vote unfairly diluted the voting strength of African Americans in violation of the Fourteenth Amendment and the Fifteenth Amendment. The district court ruled that the constitutional rights of Mobile's African American citizens had been violated and entered a judgment in their favor. The court also ruled that Mobile's city commissioners be replaced by a municipal government consisting of a mayor and a city council composed of persons selected from single member districts. The lower court decision was upheld.

Thornburg v. Gingles
478 U.S. 30 (1986)

Thornburg v. Gingles was the Supreme Court's first decision interpreting the provisions of the 1982 amendments to section 2 of the Voting Rights Act. The amendments prohibited voting schemes that result in a denial or abridgement of the right to vote due to race or color. In this decision, the Court ruled that the redistricting plan adopted by the North Carolina legislature—which unintentionally led to racially polarized voting by whites and diluted African Americans voting strength—was in violation of the Voting Rights Act. The Voting Rights Act prohibits neutral voting requirements that have a discriminatory effect, as well as those that are intentionally discriminatory.

Shaw v. Reno
509 U.S. 630 (1993)

The Court ruled that using race as a principle of drawing the boundaries of a voting district solely to increase the number of minority voters is a violation of the Equal Protection Clause.

Miller v. Johnson
115 S.Ct. 2475 (1995)

The Court ruled that a congressional district purposely drawn to contain a majority of African American voters is a violation of the Equal Protection Clause.

Hunt v. Cromartie
532 U.S. 234 (2001)

The Supreme Court ruled that evidence that race was a conscious factor in drawing the boundaries of a Congressional district does not automatically make the results unconstitutional if other permissible political reasons were dominant motivating factors. Evidence as to motivation must be presented in court to make a determination of permissibility.

Lloyd Gaines, who won his suit to be admitted to Missouri's School of Law in 1938.

Education

Missouri ex rel. Lloyd Gaines v. Canada
305 U.S. 339 (1938)

Gaines v. Canada was brought before the Supreme Court by Lloyd Lionel Gaines, an African American who had been refused admission to the School of Law of the State University of Missouri. Gaines contended that the University of Missouri's actions were a violation of his rights under the Fourteenth Amendment of the U.S. Constitution.

The University of Missouri defended its action by maintaining that Lincoln University, a predominantly African American institution, would eventually establish its own law school. The Supreme Court of Missouri dismissed Gaines's petition and upheld the university's decision to reject his application. The U.S. Supreme Court, however, reversed this decision, maintaining that the State of Missouri was obliged to provide equal facilities for African Americans or, in the absence of such facilities, to admit them to the existing facility.

Sipuel v. Board of Regents of the University of Oklahoma
332 U.S. 631 (1948)

Ada Lois Sipuel, an African American, was denied admission to the law school of the University of Oklahoma in 1948. Sipuel and the NAACP filed a petition in Oklahoma requesting an order directing her admission.

The petition was denied on the grounds that the *Gaines* decision did not require a state with segregation laws to admit an African American student to its white schools. In addition, the Oklahoma court maintained that the state itself was not obligated to set up a separate school unless first requested to do so by African Americans desiring a legal education. The court's decision was affirmed by the Supreme Court of Oklahoma. The U.S. Supreme Court, however, reversed this decision, and held that the state was required to provide African Americans with equal educational opportunities.

Sweatt v. Painter
339 U.S. 629 (1950)

Heman Marion Sweatt was refused admission to the University of Texas Law School on the grounds that substantially equivalent facilities were already available in another Texas State law school open only to African American students. The U.S. Supreme Court ruled that Sweatt be admitted to the University of Texas Law School. Chief Justice Fred M. Vinson wrote that "in terms of number of the faculty, variety of courses and opportunity for specialization, size of the student body, scope of the library, availability of law review and similar activities, the University of Texas Law School is superior" to those in the state law school for African Americans. Therefore, the refusal to admit Sweatt to the University of Texas Law School was unconstitutional.

McLaurin v. Oklahoma State Regents for Higher Education
339 U.S. 637 (1950)

After having been admitted to the University of Oklahoma, G. W. McLaurin, an African American, was required by school officials to occupy a special seat in each classroom and a segregated table in both the library and the cafeteria because of his race. The U.S. Supreme Court declared unanimously that African American students must receive the same treatment at the hands of the state as other students and could not be segregated.

Gray v. University of Tennessee
342 U.S. 517 (1952)

This case resulted from the refusal of a U.S. district court to force the University of Tennessee to admit African American students. The lone judge to whom the matter was then referred ruled that the African American students were entitled to admission, but did not order the university to enforce this ruling. The Supreme Court was asked to refer the case back to the district court for further proceedings. Pending this appeal, however, one of the students seeking admission was enrolled at the University of Tennessee. Since the Court found no suggestion that persons "similarly situated would not be afforded similar treatment," the case was dismissed as moot.

Brown v. Board of Education of Topeka, Kansas
347 U.S. 483 (1954)

This case involved the practice of denying African American children equal access to state public schools due to state laws requiring or permitting racial segregation. The U.S. Supreme Court unanimously held that segregation deprived the children of equal protection under the Fourteenth Amendment to the U.S. Constitution. The "separate but equal" doctrine of *Plessy v. Ferguson* was overturned. After reargument a year later, the case was remanded (along with its four companion cases) to the district court, which was instructed to enter necessary orders to ensure the admission of all parties to public schools on a racially nondiscriminatory basis.

Hawkins v. Board of Control
347 U.S. 971 (1954)

This case resulted from a ruling of the Florida Supreme Court that denied an African American the right to enter the University of Florida Law School on the grounds that he had failed to show that a separate law school for African Americans was not substantively equal to the University of Florida Law School. The U.S. Supreme Court vacated the judgment and remanded the case to the Florida Supreme Court for a decision in light of the ruling in *Brown v. Board of Education of Topeka, Kansas*, which overruled the separate but equal doctrine.

After two years, the Florida Supreme Court continued to deny Hawkins the right to enter the University of Florida. Also, it had appointed a commissioner to determine if there was a time in the future that Hawkins could be admitted "without causing public mischief." However, the Supreme Court ruled that Hawkins should be admitted to the school promptly, since there was no palpable reason for further delay.

Turead v. Board of Supervisors
347 U.S. 971 (1954)

This case was the result of a provisional injunction requiring the admittance of African Americans to Louisiana State University. The state court of appeals reversed this action, declaring that it required the decision of a district court of three judges. The U.S. Supreme Court vacated this judgment and remanded the case for consideration, in light of *Brown v. Board of Education of Topeka, Kansas*.

Frazier v. University of North Carolina
350 U.S. 979 (1956)

The U.S. Supreme Court affirmed a district court judgment that African Americans may not be excluded from institutions of higher learning because of their race or color.

Cooper v. Aaron
358 U.S. 1 (1958)

The impact of *Brown v. Board of Education of Topeka, Kansas* was very slight until the Justice Department began to initiate its own desegregation lawsuits. Arkansas state officials passed state laws contrary to the Fourteenth Amendment holdings in *Brown I* and *Brown II* that forbid states to use their governmental powers to bar children on racial grounds from attending schools where there is state participation through any arrangement, management, funds, or property. The cases also ordered the states to immediately cease and desist from desegregation practices immediately.

In *Cooper*, the U.S. attorney general filed a petition on behalf of the U.S. government to enjoin the governor of Arkansas and officers of the National Guard from preventing the admittance of nine African American children into Central High School in September 1957 in Little Rock. A law was passed relieving school children from compulsory attendance at racially mixed schools.

The Supreme Court declared that the Fourteenth Amendment outlined in the *Brown* case was the supreme law of the land and could not be nullified by state legislators, executive or judicial officers, or evasive schemes for segregation.

Lee v. Macon County Board of Education
389 U.S. 25 (1967)

The U.S. Supreme Court affirmed a lower court decision ordering the desegregation of Alabama's school districts and declared state school grants to white students attending segregated private schools unconstitutional.

Alexander v. Holmes County Board of Education
396 US 19 (1969)

The U.S. Supreme Court ordered all 33 school districts in Mississippi to desegregate. The Department of Health, Education and Welfare (HEW) had asked that the districts be granted more time to desegregate. This was the first time HEW had sought a delay in integration, but the Court ordered that integration proceed immediately.

North Carolina State Board of Education v. Swann
402 U.S. 43 (1971)

&

Swann v. Charlotte Mecklenburg Board of Education
402 U.S. 1 (1971)

In these two cases the U.S. Supreme Court affirmed the use of busing and faculty transfers to overcome the effects of dual school systems—segregated school systems resulting from residential patterns. Writing the decision, Chief Justice Warren E. Burger noted that "bus transportation has long been a part of all public educational systems and it is unlikely that a truly effective remedy could be devised without continued reliance upon it." The Court declared that segregation resulted from past misconduct and affirmed the lower court's order that the school board transfer students by bus to achieve a racial mix at each school. The ruling, however, left local district judges the authority to decide whether a desegregation plan was constitutionally adequate.

Wright v. City of Emporia
402 U.S. 43 (1971)

&

Cotton v. Scotland Neck Board of Education
407 U.S. 485 (1972)

The Supreme Court held that two towns with heavy concentrations of white students could not secede from a largely African American county school system and form its own school district in an attempt to frustrate integration.

Richmond, Virginia, School Board v. State Board of Education
412 U.S. 92 (1973)

In a 4–4 vote, the Supreme Court declined to reinstate an order to integrate the predominantly African American schools in Richmond with those of two white suburbs. Integrationists expressed concern that permitting *de facto* segregation to stand in this manner would hinder corrective action in other metropolitan areas, perpetuate "neighborhood" one-race schools, and lessen the extent of integration in unitary school systems.

Milliken v. Bradley
418 U.S. 717 (1974)

After failing to reach a decision in *Richmond School Board*, the full Court reached a decision outlawing inter-district remedies to end segregation in schools. The school system of Detroit had become heavily African American due to white flight to the suburbs. Fearing that *Brown v. Board of Education of Topeka, Kansas* would be crippled, the district court ordered busing between the districts of Detroit and its white suburbs.

However, the Court overturned this decision as there was no evidence that the suburbs had contributed to the segregation. Integrationists attacked this decision as the end of *Brown*.

Runyon v. McCrary
427 U.S. 160 (1976)

In a unanimous decision, the Court held that the Constitution places no value on discrimination, and that even though private discrimination was not socially desired by the members of the Court, it may be characterized legally as a form of exercising the freedom of association protected by the First Amendment. The Civil Rights Act of 1866 prohibited racial discrimination in the making and enforcing of contracts, however, argued the families of two African American children who were denied admission to private schools in Virginia. The children's parents sought to enter into a contractual relationship with the private schools on an equal basis to white and nonwhite students.

Regents of the University of California v. Bakke
438 U.S. 265 (1978)

Allan Bakke, a white male who had been denied admission to the University of California Medical School at Davis for two consecutive years, charged that the university's minority quota system—under which only disadvantaged members of certain minority races were considered for 16 of the 100 places in each year's class—denied him equal protection.

The trial court declared that the school could not take race into account in making the admissions decision and held that the challenged admissions program violated the federal and state constitutions and Title VI of the 1964 Civil Rights Act. The university appealed. The Supreme Court ruled that Bakke had been illegally discriminated against and that numerical quotas based on race were unconstitutional, but held that "the State has a substantial interest that legitimately may be served by a properly devised admission program involving the competitive consideration of race and ethnic origin."

Bob Jones University v. IRS
461 U.S. 574 (1983)

Contrary to long-standing IRS policy, the Reagan administration sought to extend tax-exempt status to schools that discriminate on the basis of race. The U.S. Supreme Court recognized the inability of the Justice Department to argue the case fairly, and requested that former Secretary of Transportation William T. Coleman present the argument. The Supreme Court rebuffed the Justice Department's arguments and unanimously agreed with Coleman's position that the IRS could deny tax-exempt status to racially discriminatory schools.

Allen v. Wright
488 U.S. 737 (1984)

Parents of African American children instituted a nationwide lawsuit claiming that the Internal Revenue Service's failure to deny tax-exempt status to racially discriminatory private schools constituted federal financial aid to racially segregated institutions and diminished the ability of their children to receive an adequate education. The U.S. Supreme Court refused to hear the case on the grounds that the plaintiffs did not have "standing" because they failed to show that the injury suffered was "fairly traceable" or caused by the conduct of the IRS. In addition the Court maintained that the remedy was "speculative" since there was no evidence that the withdrawal of tax-exempt status would cause schools to end their racially discriminatory practices.

Oklahoma City Board of Education v. Dowell
498 U.S. 237 (1991)

The Court ruled that when a school district petitioned to end a desegregation order, the petition could be approved if the district has been in good faith compliance with the order from the beginning and if remnants of past discrimination have been eliminated to the degree possible in the situation.

United States v. Fordice
505 U.S. 717 (1992)

The Court ruled that when a state higher education system continues to use educational practices that were started to keep the races segregated and that perpetuate segregation, the practices violate the equal protection guarantee if they can be ended without significantly changing the quality of the education offered.

Jenkins v. Missouri
115 S.Ct. 2038 (1995)

The Court ruled that a federal district court erred in ordering increased salaries for school system employees as part of a program to motivate attendance by non-minority students living outside the district in an effort to increase desegregation.

Employment

Griggs v. Duke Power Co.
401 U.S. 424 (1971)

African American employees challenged their employer's requirement of a high school diploma or passing of intelligence tests as a condition of employment. African Americans were employed only in the labor department where the highest paying jobs paid less than the lowest jobs in the other departments. When the company abandoned its policy restricting blacks to labor in 1965, completion of high school and median scores on two aptitude tests were required to transfer from labor to another department.

The Supreme Court found the objective of Congress in Title III was to achieve equality of employment opportunities and remove barriers that have operated in the past. Under the Act, practices, procedures, or tests neutral on their face and even neutral in their intent cannot be maintained if they operate to "freeze" the status quo of prior discrimination. The employment practice must be related to job performance.

It was determined that neither the high school diploma nor the intelligence tests were demonstrably related to successful job performance. Good intent or absence of discriminatory intent does not redeem employment procedures and practices. The employment policies had a discriminatory effect toward African American employees and were struck down.

Albemarle Paper Co. v. Moody
422 U.S. 405 (1975)

African American employees of a paper mill in Roanoke Rapids, North Carolina, successfully challenged the company's use of written tests that allegedly measured numerical and verbal intelligence. Based upon the standards enunciated in *Griggs v. Duke Power Co.*, the U.S. Supreme Court determined that the tests were discriminatory because they were not job-related and did not predict success on the job. The Court held that the plaintiffs were entitled to "complete justice" and necessary relief that would "make them whole." The Court awarded the African American employees back pay and made it clear that back pay should rarely be denied once there has been a showing of discrimination. The Court also stated that back pay cannot be denied simply because the employer acted in good faith or did not intend to discriminate.

Hazelwood School District v. United States
433 U.S. 299 (1977)

Several African American teachers seeking jobs in suburban St. Louis, Missouri, offered statistical data indicating they had been denied employment opportunities. The plaintiffs attempted to prove their case by showing that the percentage of African American students was greater than the percentage of African American teachers in the school district.

Although the U.S. Supreme Court affirmed that "statistics can be an important source of proof in employment discrimination cases," it rejected the plaintiffs' statistical evidence and called it irrelevant. The Court concluded that relevant statistical data would be the percentage of qualified African American teachers in the relevant geographical area compared with the percentage of African Americans in Hazelwood's teaching staff.

Teamsters v. United States
431 U.S. 324 (1977)

In enforcing the Civil Rights Act of 1964, the Supreme Court held that victims of past union discrimination were entitled to retroactive seniority benefits. The Supreme Court required proof of "intent to discriminate," however, in order to establish that a given seniority system is illegal. Subsequent cases in lower federal courts during the late 1970s entitled discrimination victims to retroactive back pay in addition to retroactive seniority benefits.

Louis Swint and Willie Johnson v. Pullman Standard and the United Steelworkers of America
72 L.Ed. 66 (1982)

African American employees of Pullman Standard brought a lawsuit against Pullman Standard and the United Steelworkers of America. The lawsuit alleged that Title VII of the Civil Rights Act of 1964 was violated by a seniority system. In its decision, the district court ruled "that the difference in terms, conditions or privileges of employment resulting from the seniority system are not the result of an intention to discriminate because of race or color" and held that the system satisfied the requirements of section 703(h) of the Civil Rights Act. This decision was later reversed by the Fifth Circuit Court of Appeals, which stated, "[B]ecause we find the differences in the terms, conditions and standards of employment for black workers and white workers at Pullman Standard resulted from an intent to discriminate because of race, we hold that the system is not legally valid under Section 703(h) of Title VII U.S.C. 2000e-2(h)."

Watson v. Fort Worth Bank and Trust
108 U.S. 2777 (1987)

Clara Watson, an African American woman, alleged that she was repeatedly denied promotion to supervisory positions which were awarded to white employees with equivalent or lesser experience. The bank contended that its promotion decisions were based on various subjective criteria including experience, previous supervisory experience, and the ability to get along with others.

The U.S. Supreme Court held that Watson did not have to prove intentional discrimination. The Court concluded that subjective, facially neutral selection devices that disadvantage African Americans in much the same way as objective criteria (e.g., written tests) are unlawful.

Patterson v. McLean Credit Union
491 U.S. 164 (1989)

An African American female was employed as a teller and file coordinator for ten years until she was laid-off. She alleged that she had been harassed, denied promotion to accounting clerk, and later discharged because of her race. She filed suit asserting violations of section 1981 of the Civil Rights Act.

Racial harassment relating to conditions of employment are not actionable under section 1981, which provides, "All persons. . . shall have the same right to make and enforce contracts. . . as any white citizen," because that provision does not apply to conduct that occurs after the formation of a contract including the breach of the contract's terms and enforcement thereof. Rather, the harassment asserted by the petitioner is past formation conduct of the employer and, therefore, actionable only under Title VII of the Civil Rights Act of 1964.

Wards Cove Packing Co. v. Antonio
490 U.S. 642 (1989)

This case was brought by a class of non-white salmon cannery workers who alleged that their employer's hiring and promotion practices were responsible for the workforce's racial stratification. There were two types of jobs: unskilled cannery jobs, which were filled predominately by non-whites; and non-cannery jobs, mostly classified as skilled positions, which paid more and were held by whites. Statistics were used to show a high percentage of non-whites in cannery jobs and a low percentage in non-cannery positions.

The Supreme Court found that the cannery workforce did not reflect the pool of qualified job applicants or the qualified labor force population. An employer's selection methods or employment practices cannot be said to have a disparate impact on non-whites if the absence of minorities holding such skilled jobs reflects a dearth of qualified non-white applicants. A mere showing that non-whites are underrepresented in the non-cannery jobs will not suffice for a Title VII violation.

Martin v. Wilks
490 U.S. 755 (1989)

In an attempt to remedy past racial discrimination in hiring and promotion practices, the City of Birmingham and its fire department consented to hiring African Americans as firefighters as part of a settlement. White firefighters subsequently challenged the city, alleging that because of their race they were denied promotions in favor of less qualified African Americans in violation of Title VII. Promotion decisions were made on the basis of race in reliance on the consent decree. The Court held that a voluntary settlement between one group of employees and their employer cannot possibly settle the conflicting claims of another group of employees who do not join in the agreement. This settlement would result in persons being deprived of their legal rights in a proceeding to which they were not a party.

Jury Selection and Service

Neal v. Delaware
103 U.S. 370 (1880)

The jury commissioner's conduct was found in violation of the U.S. Constitution when an African American criminal defendant proved that African Americans were excluded from the jury based on their race. Every citizen is afforded the right to equal protection of the laws, including that of juror selection, when jurors will pass judgment upon a defendant's life, liberty, or property. The exclusion of members of the defendant's race is unconstitutional.

Strauder v. West Virginia
100 U.S. 303 (1880)

The Supreme Court overturned the conviction of an African American criminal defendant due to racial discrimination in the selection of jurors. West Virginia passed a state law that prohibited African American men from eligibility to serve as members of a grand jury or a petit jury in the state. The law denied equal protection of the laws to a citizen.

Virginia v. Rives
100 U.S. 313 (1880)

The petitioners asserted that African Americans had never been allowed to serve as jurors in their county in any case where an African American man was involved. Virginia had no formalized or specific statute restricting African American jurors from certain trials. It was held that a mixed jury in a particular case is not essential to the equal protection of the laws and that the right is not given by any state or federal statute.

Hollins v. Oklahoma
295 U.S. 394 (1935)

Hollins, an African American, was charged with rape and convicted at a trial held in the basement of the jail. Three days before the scheduled execution, the NAACP secured a stay of execution. Later the Supreme Court of Oklahoma reversed his conviction.

The U.S. Supreme Court—in a memorandum opinion—affirmed the principle that the conviction of an African American by a jury from which all African Americans had been excluded was a denial of the equal protection clause of the Fourteenth Amendment to the U.S. Constitution.

Hale v. Commonwealth of Kentucky
303 U.S. 613 (1938)

In 1936, Joe Hale, an African American, was charged with murder in McCracken County, Kentucky. Hale moved to set aside the indictment on the grounds that the jury commissioners had systematically excluded African Americans from jury lists. Hale established that one out of every six residents of the county was African

American, and that at least 70 African Americans out of a total of 6,700 persons qualified for jury duty. Still, there had not been an African American on jury duty between 1906 and 1936. Hale's conviction and death sentence were upheld by the Court of Appeals of Kentucky, but both were struck down by the Supreme Court on the grounds that he had been denied equal protection of the law.

Patton v. Mississippi
332 U.S. 463 (1947)

This case involved Eddie Patton, an African American who was convicted of the murder of a white man in Mississippi. At his trial and as part of his appeal, Patton alleged that all qualified African Americans had been systematically excluded from jury service solely because of race. The state maintained that since jury service was limited by statute to qualified voters and since few African Americans were qualified to vote, such a procedure was valid in the eyes of the law. The Supreme Court, however, reversed Patton's conviction on the grounds that such a jury plan, resulting in the almost automatic elimination of African Americans from jury service, constituted an infringement on Patton's rights under the Fourteenth Amendment.

Shepherd v. Florida
341 U.S. 50 (1951)

The Supreme Court reversed the convictions of a Florida state court involving African American defendants solely on the grounds that the method of selecting the grand jury discriminated against African Americans.

Turner v. Fouche
396 U.S. 346 (1970)

The Court affirmed the right of defendants to bring an action in federal court to end discrimination in jury selection.

Castaneda v. Partida
430 U.S. 482 (1977)

The Supreme Court upheld the use of statistical evidence demonstrating that Mexican Americans had been systematically excluded from jury selection, and that such discrimination on the basis of race or color violated the Equal Protection Clause of the Fourteenth Amendment. The principle established in this case, that statistical evidence can be used to prove intentional discrimination, has been used in later cases involving employment, housing, voting, and education.

Batson v. Kentucky
476 U.S. 79 (1986)

Justice Lewis F. Powell, writing for the majority, held that the prosecution in a criminal case may not use its peremptory challenges—challenges to an individual juror for which no cause need be stated—to exclude African American jurors in a case involving an African American defendant.

Turner v. Murray
106 US 1683 (1986)

The Supreme Court expanded the right of African American defendants in capital cases to question potential white jurors to uncover their racial prejudices and biases.

Public Accommodations

Hall v. DeCuir
95 U.S. 485 (1878)

This case involved an unsuccessful attempt of the Louisiana legislature to prohibit segregation in any form of transportation in the state. The statute was attacked as an interference with interstate commerce because it imposed a direct burden and control over common carriers when entering the state. The statute was declared unconstitutional because it required common carriers to transport African American passengers in Louisiana in the same cabin with white passengers.

Civil Rights Cases
332 U.S. 46, 784; 333 U.S. 831; 334 U.S. 834; 378 U.S. 226 (1883)

This group of civil rights cases was heard before the Supreme Court in an effort to determine the constitutionality of the Civil Rights Act of 1875, the first piece of national legislation that attempted to guarantee people of all races "full and equal enjoyment" of all public accommodations including inns, public conveyances, theaters, and other places of amusement. The Court ruled, however, that the act was unconstitutional inasmuch as it did not spring directly from the Thirteenth and Fourteenth Amendments to the Constitution. In the view of the Court, the Thirteenth Amendment was concerned exclusively with the narrow confines of slavery and involuntary servitude. The Fourteenth Amendment did not empower Congress to enact direct legislation to counteract the effect of state laws or policies. The ruling essentially deprived African Americans of the very protections that the three postwar "freedom amendments" were designed to provide.

Plessy v. Ferguson
163 U.S. 537 (1896)

Homer Plessy, an African American, was assigned to the wrong coach on a train traveling within Louisiana. Plessy was arrested for being in the wrong coach. He challenged the 1890 state statute that provided for "separate but equal" railway carriages for whites and blacks.

In the majority opinion of the Supreme Court, "separate but equal" accommodations for African Americans constituted a "reasonable" use of state police power. Furthermore, the Court said that the Fourteenth Amendment "could not have been intended to abolish distinctions based on color, or to enforce social. . . equality or a co-mingling of the two races upon terms unsatisfactory to either."

Morgan v. Commonwealth of Virginia
328 U.S. 373 (1946)

Irene Morgan, an African American, refused to move to the rear seat of a Greyhound bus in which she was traveling from Virginia to Washington, DC. She was convicted in Virginia for violating a state statute requiring segregation of the races on all public vehicles.

NAACP attorneys carried the case through the Virginia courts and on to the U.S. Supreme Court, where it was decided that the Virginia statute could not apply to interstate passengers or motor vehicles engaged in such traffic.

Bob-Lo v. Michigan
333 U.S. 28 (1948)

The operator of a line of passenger ships used to transport patrons from Detroit to an island amusement park was convicted of violating the Michigan Civil Rights Act for refusing passage to an African American. The Supreme Court upheld the application of the Michigan Civil Rights Act.

Rice v. Arnold
340 U.S. 848 (1950)

This case involved the successful attempt to abolish segregation on a Miami, Florida, golf course owned and operated by the city. The U.S. Supreme Court overturned the judgment of the Florida Supreme Court, which had authorized the segregated use of the course.

District of Columbia v. John R. Thompson
346 U.S. 100 (1952)

The Supreme Court unanimously held that a restaurant owner had violated federal law by discriminating against and refusing service to patrons on the basis of race.

Muir v. Louisville Park Theatrical Association
347 U.S. 971 (1954)

In 1954, several African Americans were refused admission to an amphitheater located in a Louisville city park. The park was leased and operated by a privately owned group not affiliated in any way with the city. The Kentucky Court of Appeals found no evidence of unlawful discrimination, but the U.S. Supreme Court overturned this judgment and remanded the case for consideration in the light of the prevailing legal climate as articulated in *Brown v. Board of Education of Topeka, Kansas.*

Mayor and City Council of Baltimore v. Dawson
350 U.S. 377 (1955)

The Supreme Court affirmed a judgment that the enforcement of racial segregation in public beaches and bathhouses maintained by public authorities is unconstitutional.

Holmes v. Atlanta
350 U.S. 859 (1955)

This case involved a suit brought by African Americans to integrate a city-owned and operated golf course in Atlanta, Georgia. The segregated arrangements were deemed constitutionally acceptable by a lower court, but that order was overturned by the U.S. Supreme Court and the case was remanded to the district court with directions to enter a decree for the plaintiffs in conformity with *Mayor and City Council of Baltimore v. Dawson.*

Flemming v. South Carolina Electric
351 U.S. 901 (1956)

This case involved a suit brought by an African American passenger against a bus company for damages due to the bus driver's having required her to change seats in accordance with South Carolina's segregation law. The trial judge dismissed the case on the grounds that the statute in question was valid, but the court of appeals reversed this decision, holding that the "separate but equal" doctrine was no longer valid. The Supreme Court upheld the court of appeals decision.

Gayle v. Browder
352 U.S. 114 (1956)

This case challenged the constitutionality of state statutes and ordinances in Montgomery, Alabama, which required the segregation of whites and blacks on public buses. These statutes were declared unconstitutional by the decision of a three-judge federal district court. The Supreme Court affirmed.

Katzenbach v. McClung
379 U.S. 802 (1964)

&

Heart of Atlanta v. United States
379 U.S. 803 (1964)

The U.S. attorney general sued Ollie's Barbecue Restaurant in Birmingham, Alabama, for its refusal to serve African Americans in its dining accommodations, a direct violation of the anti-discriminatory public accommodations clause of the 1964 Civil Rights Act. The U.S. District Court for the Northern District of Alabama, held that the Civil Rights Act could not be applied under the Fourteenth Amendment to the U.S. Constitution, as there was no "demonstrable connection" between food purchased in interstate commerce and sold in a restaurant that would affect commerce. The U.S. Supreme Court, however, held that "the Civil Rights Act of 1964, as here applied, [is] plainly appropriate in the resolution of what [Congress has] found to be a national commercial problem of the first magnitude."

The *Heart of Atlanta* case dealt with a Georgia motel that solicited patronage in national advertising and had several out-of-state residents as guests from time to time. The motel had already instituted the practice of refusing to rent rooms to African Americans prior to the passage of the 1964 Civil Rights Act and continued this practice afterward. The motel owner filed suit, maintaining that the Act violated his rights under both the Fifth Amendment and the Thirteenth Amendment. The United States countered with the argument that the refusal to accept African Americans interfered with interstate travel, and that Congress, in voting to apply nondiscriminatory standards to interstate commerce, was not violating either amendment. The Supreme Court upheld the right of Congressional regulation, stating that the power of Congress was not confined to the regulation of commerce among the states. "It extends to those activities intrastate which so affect interstate commerce, or the exercise of the power of Congress over it, as to make regulation of them appropriate means to the attainment of a legitimate end."

Bell v. Maryland
378 U.S. 226 (1964)

The Supreme Court ordered a Maryland district court to reconsider its affirmation of a state court conviction of 12 African Americans for trespassing when they refused to leave a restaurant that refused to serve them entirely on the basis of their color.

Evans v. Newton
382 U.S. 296 (1966)

The Supreme Court ruled that the transfer of a city park in Macon, Georgia, from municipal ownership to a board of private trustees did not remove Macon's obligations under the Fourteenth Amendment to guarantee equal rights to use the park by all citizens.

Shuttlesworth v. Birmingham
394 U.S. 147 (1969)

The Supreme Court invalidated Birmingham's Parade-Permit Law, which had been used in 1963 to harass participants in an Easter March organized by Dr. Martin Luther King Jr.

New York State Club Association v. City of New York
108 S.Ct. 2225 (1988)

In a unanimous decision, the Supreme Court upheld the constitutionality of a New York City ordinance that forbids private clubs from discriminating against women and minorities.

Interracial Marriage

Loving v. Virginia
388 U.S. 1 (1967)

This case nullified anti-miscegenation laws. It concerned a white man and an African American woman, residents of Virginia, who married in Washington, DC. Virginia indicted and convicted them of violating its laws against racial intermarriage when the couple returned to Virginia and attempted to reside there, but released them when the couple agreed not to reside in the state for 25 years. The Lovings, however, decided to challenge the agreement and the law. Their appeal was rejected by the Virginia courts but upheld by the U.S. Supreme Court, which ruled the Virginia law unconstitutional. Soon thereafter, federal district courts in other states which forbade intermarriage ordered local officials to issue marriage licenses to interracial couples applying for them.

Requirements for Legislative Membership

Powell v. McCormack
395 U.S. 486 (1969)

According to the Constitution, only three basic factors govern eligibility to serve as a legislator in the U.S. House of Representatives: a minimum age requirement, the possession of U.S. citizenship, and the fulfillment of the state's residency requirement. When U.S. Representative Adam Clayton Powell Jr. was excluded from the 90th Congress on the grounds that he had misused public funds and defied the courts of his home state, he filed suit in federal court in an attempt to force the House of Representatives to review only the necessary credentials for membership.

The district court dismissed the first petition on the grounds that it lacked jurisdiction. By the time the case was heard before the U.S. Supreme Court, the 90th Congress had adjourned. Powell, however, was reelected and finally seated in the 91st Congress, a gesture that did not settle the case or render it moot. The legal point on which the case hinged involved the distinction between "expulsion" and "exclusion." Despite the more than two-thirds majority required for expulsion, the Court ruled that the intent of the House was to "exclude," not to "expel." The Court summation stated flatly that "the House was without power to exclude him from its membership."

Right of Sale and Restrictive Covenants

Buchanan v. Warley
245 U.S. 60 (1917)

The plaintiff brought an action for the performance of a sale of real estate in Louisville, Kentucky. The purchaser, Warley, an African American, maintained that he would be unable to occupy the land since it was located within what was defined by a Louisville ordinance as a white block. The ordinance prohibited whites from living in black districts, and vice versa. Buchanan alleged that the ordinance was in conflict with the Fourteenth Amendment to the U.S. Constitution. The U.S. Supreme Court maintained that the ordinance was unconstitutional.

Shelley v. Kraemer
334 U.S. 1 (1948)

&

Hurd v. Hodge
334 U.S. 26 (1948)

In 1945 an African American family, the Shelleys, received a warranty deed to a parcel of land that was subject to a restrictive covenant barring its sale to African Americans. A lawsuit was subsequently brought in the Circuit Court of St. Louis seeking to divest the Shelleys of the title to the land. The Supreme Court of Missouri directed the trial court to strip the petitioners of their warranty deed. The U.S. Supreme Court reversed this decision, maintaining that restrictive covenants, though valid contracts, could not be enforced by

state courts. In *Hurd v. Hodge*, involving a similar set of circumstances, federal courts were similarly prohibited from enforcing racially-restrictive covenants.

Reitman v. Mulkey
387 U.S. 369 (1967)

In 1964, California voters passed a referendum granting "absolute discretion" to real estate owners in the sale and rental of real property. Lincoln Mulkey filed suit against property owners in Orange County to challenge the validity of the referendum. Mulkey's arguments failed in the lower courts but were accepted by the California Supreme Court on the grounds that the California referendum violated the Fourteenth Amendment of the U.S. Constitution. The U.S. Supreme Court upheld the decision.

Jones v. Alfred H. Mayer, Co.
392 U.S. 409 (1968)

Joseph Lee Jones, an African American, alleged that his race was the sole reason that a real estate agent refused to sell him a home. The Supreme Court held that 42 U.S.C. 1982, a federal statute created during the Reconstruction era to eliminate the vestiges of slavery, prohibits all racial discrimination, public and private, in the sale or rental of property.

Trafficante v. Metropolitan Life Insurance
409 U.S. 205 (1972)

The U.S. Supreme Court ruled that a complaint of racial discrimination in housing may be brought by parties who have not themselves been refused accommodation but who, as members of the same housing unit, allege injury by discriminatory housing practices. The suit had been filed by a black and a white resident of a housing development in San Francisco who contended that the owner of the development was depriving plaintiffs of the right to live in a racially integrated community.

Sentencing and Incarceration

McKleskey v. Kemp
481 U.S. 279 (1987)

Warren McKleskey, a 38-year-old African American man accused of killing a police officer while robbing a furniture store, was sentenced to death by the state of Georgia. In support of his claim that the sentence violated his constitutional rights, McKleskey introduced a sophisticated statistical study that analyzed more than 2,000 murder cases in Georgia. The study demonstrated that there was a disparity in the imposition of capital punishment based on the race of the victim, as well as the race of the defendant.

Defendants charged with killing white persons received the death penalty in 11 percent of the cases, but defendants charged with killing African Americans received the death penalty in only 1 percent of the cases. The study further showed that prosecutors asked for the death penalty in 70 percent of the cases involving black defendants and white victims, and only 19 percent of the cases involving white defendants and African American victims. In sum, the analysis revealed that African Americans who killed whites were 4.3 times more likely to receive a death sentence.

The Supreme Court acknowledged that it had accepted statistics as proof of intent to discriminate in employment, housing, and voting cases. The Court rejected, however, McKleskey's claim that the death penalty in Georgia was applied in a racially discriminatory manner. The Court's reasoning was that although McKleskey showed the existence of racial discrimination in sentencing, he failed to prove that "racial considerations played a part in his sentence." Finally, Justice Powell expressed concern that acceptance of McKleskey's argument would open the floodgates of litigation by African American defendants seeking to introduce statistical evidence to demonstrate that race affected the outcome of their case.

Slavery

Prigg v. Pennsylvania
16 Peters 539 (1842)

After Edward Prigg, a professional slave catcher, captured Margaret Morgan, an escaped slave residing in Pennsylvania, Prigg was tried and convicted under an 1826 Pennsylvania anti-kidnapping statute. Hearing the case, the Supreme Court ruled that the Pennsylvania law was unconstitutional on the grounds that the statute interfered with Congress's power under Art. IV, sec. 2 of the Constitution.

Strader v. Graham
10 Howard 82 (1850)

In 1841, three slaves owned by Christopher Graham of Kentucky, boarded a steamboat owned by Jacob Strader and traveled to Cincinnati. They ultimately escaped to freedom in Canada. Graham sued Strader for the value of the slaves and the expenses incurred while trying to recover them. Graham won the case. Strader appealed, though, claiming that the slaves had become free under Ohio law and provisions of the

Northwest Ordinance. The Supreme Court ruled unanimously that each state had the right to determine the status of slaves within its jurisdiction, that the status of these slaves was to be determined by the state of Kentucky, and that the Northwest Ordinance was no longer in force, since those territories had become states.

Dred Scott v. Sandford
19 Howard 393 (1857)

In 1835, Dred Scott became the property of John Emerson, a U.S. Army doctor, in the slave state of Missouri. From there, he was taken into the free state of Illinois and later to the free territory of Wisconsin. In 1847, Scott initiated suit in the circuit court of St. Louis County, arguing that he should be given his freedom by virtue of having resided on free soil. After nine years, his case came before the U.S. Supreme Court.

In delivering his opinion, Chief Justice Roger Brooke Taney declared that, by virtue of both the Declaration of Independence and the Constitution, African Americans could not be regarded as citizens of the United States. Moreover, the Court could not deprive slaveholders of their right to take slaves into any part of the Union. In effect, therefore, the Missouri Compromise, as well as other antislavery legislation, was declared to be unconstitutional.

Ableman v. Booth
21 Howard 506 (1859)

Abolitionist Sherman Booth was held in a state jail for violating the federal fugitive slave laws by helping a slave escape to freedom. Booth secured a writ of habeas corpus from a state judge who declared the federal laws unconstitutional; the Wisconsin Supreme Court affirmed. The U.S. Supreme Court unanimously upheld Congress's fugitive slave law and all its provisions, ruling that the state court had stepped beyond its sphere of authority. Although the Wisconsin government was deemed sovereign within its territorial limits, it was limited and restricted by the U.S. Constitution. Booth's conviction was upheld.

State and Local Affirmative Action Requirements

United Steelworkers of America v. Brian Weber
433 U.S. 193 (1979)

The United Steelworkers of America and Kaiser Aluminum Company entered into a collective bargaining agreement including a voluntary affirmative action plan designed to eliminate conspicuous racial imbalances in Kaiser's almost exclusively white skilled workforce. The plant in Gramercy, Louisiana, agreed to reserve 50 percent of the openings in the skilled job

Handbill advertising a public hearing to discuss *Dred Scott v. Sandford.*

training programs for African Americans until the percentage of black skilled workers was equal to the percentage of blacks in the local labor force. Brian Weber, a white production worker, who was turned down for the training program although he had more seniority than many accepted blacks, sued the United Steelworkers of America, claiming that the affirmative action program discriminated against whites.

The Supreme Court limited the issue to the narrow question of whether Title VII prohibited private employers and unions from establishing voluntary affirmative action plans. In a 5–2 decision, the Court upheld the affirmative action plan and established three factors to determine the validity of racial preference. The Court approved the plan because it was designed to break down Kaiser's historic patterns of racial segregation, it did not unnecessarily diminish the rights of white employees since it did not require the firing of white employees, and it was a temporary measure not intended to maintain racial balance but simply to eliminate an imbalance.

Fullilove v. Klutznik
448 U.S. 448 (1980)

The Supreme Court upheld a provision of the Public Works Employment Act of 1977 that required a 10 percent set-aside of federal funds for minority business enterprises on local public works projects. The provision had been challenged as a violation of the Equal Protection Clause of the Fourteenth Amendment.

Firefighters Local Union No. 1784 v. Stotts
467 U.S. 561 (1984)

In May 1981, for the first time in its history, the city of Memphis announced layoffs of city employees due to a projected budget deficit. The layoffs, which also affected the fire department, were to be made based on a citywide seniority system that had been adopted in 1973. Carl Stotts, an African American firefighter, sued to stop the layoffs, claiming that since blacks had been hired pursuant to the affirmative action provisions of a 1980 court decree, they would be laid off in far greater numbers than their white coworkers. In a 6–3 decision, the Court held that since the 1980 court decree did not say that African Americans had special protection during a layoff, the layoffs had to be made according to the 1973 seniority system.

An 1837 newspaper depiction of a fugitive slave.

Wygant v. Jackson Board of Education
476 U.S. 267 (1986)

The U.S. Supreme Court dealt a blow to affirmative action in this case involving a public school system's affirmative action plan. The record reflected that the first African American school teacher was not hired in Jackson, Michigan, until 1953. By 1969, only 3.9 percent of the teachers were African American although 15.2 percent of the students were African American. In response, the school board developed an affirmative action plan that protected African American faculty members during layoffs.

Although the U.S. Supreme Court had approved affirmative action plans in prior cases, it rejected the Jackson plan. The Court found that the goal of the plan—to remedy societal discrimination and afford positive role models to African American students—was nebulous and not sufficiently compelling.

Local No. 93, International Association of Firefighters v. City of Cleveland
106 S.Ct. 3063 (1986)

The city of Cleveland, Ohio, which had a long history of racial discrimination, negotiated a consent decree with black firefighters who had filed a lawsuit alleging that they had been unlawfully denied jobs and promotions. The decree included an affirmative action plan with numerical goals for promotion of blacks to the position of supervisor. In response to the union's challenge on behalf of white firefighters, the Supreme Court ruled that the lower courts had broad discretion to approve decrees in which employers settle discrimination suits by agreeing to preferential promotions of blacks, in spite of the objections of white employees.

Local 28, Sheet Metal Workers International Association v. EEOC
106 S.Ct. 3019 (1986)

After finding that the all-white union had discriminated against African Americans and Hispanics seeking to enter the sheet metal trades for more than a decade, the trial court ordered the union to establish a 29 percent non-white membership goal. The court also ruled that the union would have to pay substantial fines if the union failed to meet the goals. After the union failed to reach the goal, the court found the union in contempt and established a new goal of 29.3 percent. The union challenged the court's order.

The Supreme Court upheld the affirmative action goal in light of the union's "persistent or egregious discrimination" and to eliminate "lingering effects of pervasive discrimination." This was the first time the Court expressly approved the use of race conscious relief to African Americans and Hispanics who were not identified victims of discrimination.

United States v. Paradise
480 U.S. 149 (1987)

This case originated in 1972 when the NAACP sued the Alabama Department of Highways because of its long-standing history of racially discriminating employment practices. More than 11 years later, after the department had failed to hire or promote African Americans, the trial court ordered the promotion of one black trooper for every white. The U.S. attorney general challenged the constitutionality of the plan. The U.S. Supreme Court upheld the use of strict racial quotas and found that the plan was "narrowly tailored to serve the compelling government interest" of remedying "egregious" past discrimination against African Americans.

Johnson v. Transportation Agency, Santa Clara County, California
480 U.S. 616 (1987)

The U.S. Supreme Court held that the state transportation agency's voluntary affirmative action plan, under which a female had been promoted to the position of road dispatcher over a male, was consistent with Title VII of the Civil Rights Act of 1964. The Court held that an employer does not have to admit or prove that it has discriminated in order to justify efforts designed to achieve a more racially balanced workforce. The employer only needs to demonstrate that there is a "conspicuous. . . imbalance in traditionally segregated job categories."

City of Richmond v. J. A. Croson Co.
109 S.Ct. 706 (1989)

The Court upheld a court of appeals decision that Richmond's Minority Business Utilization Plan was not sufficiently narrowly tailored to remedy past discrimination in the construction industry. The plan allowed minorities a fixed 30 percent quota of the public contracts based solely on their race.

Adarand Constructors, Inc. v. Peña
115 S.Ct. 2097 (1995)

The Court ruled that affirmative action programs of the federal government that award construction contracts can only be acceptable if they show a compelling interest for the program and the program is narrowly tailored to accomplish this interest.

♦ ATTORNEYS, JUDGES, AND LEGAL SCHOLARS

(To locate biographical profiles more readily, please consult the index at the back of the book.)

Clifford L. Alexander Jr. (1933–)
Attorney, Federal Government Official

Clifford Leopold Alexander Jr. was born in New York City on September 21, 1933. Alexander went to Harvard and earned his B.A. in 1955, graduating *cum laude*. He attended Yale Law School and, in 1958, earned his LL.B. He then became the assistant district attorney of New York County from 1959 to 1961. He was the executive director of the Hamilton Grange Neighborhood Conservation district in Manhattanville from 1961 to 1962. In 1963, he became a staff member of the National Security Council.

Alexander was hired by President Lyndon Johnson as his deputy special assistant in 1964, and quickly rose to become the president's deputy special counsel. He became chairman of the Equal Employment Opportunity Commission in 1967, where he was accused of bullying reluctant employers into complying with federal guidelines for minority employment. In 1969, he left the position.

From 1969 to 1976, Alexander worked for several different law firms. He also became a Harvard overseer. At Harvard, he was involved in working with craft unions to improve minority employment opportunities.

President Jimmy Carter appointed Alexander secretary of the Department of the Army, the first African American to serve in that position. Alexander won the Outstanding Civilian Service Award from the Department of the Army in 1980. Since 1981, Alexander has been president of Alexander Associates, Inc., and served as a consultant on minority hiring practices to Major League Baseball. In the early 1990s, Alexander served as the District of Columbia's chief negotiator in hammering out a deal to build a new stadium for the National Football League's Washington Redskins.

In addition, Alexander has had his own television program *Black on White*, has been director of several Dreyfus money funds, has served on the board of directors for the Mexican-American Legal Defense and Educational Fund, and has taught at Howard University.

Joyce London Alexander (1949–)
Judge

Joyce London Alexander was born in Cambridge, Massachusetts, in 1949. She graduated in 1969 from Howard University after studying there on a scholarship from the NAACP. She worked for U.S. Representative and Speaker of the House, Tip O'Neill (D-Mass.), and then graduated in 1972 from the New England School of Law.

She practiced law for several public foundations and worked as an assistant professor at Tufts University before being appointed to a U.S. district court as a magistrate. In 1996, she was named chief judge, becoming the first African American so honored.

Alexander is known for her activities in the legal community. She has held various positions for the National Bar Association and has founded several educational programs for her peers. In 2002, she served as General Counsel for the Massachusetts Board of Higher Education and as a legal editor for WBZ-TV in addition to remaining an assistant professor at Tufts.

Violette Anderson (1882–1937)
Judge, Attorney

Violette Neatley Anderson was born on July 16, 1882, in London, England. Her family moved to the United States, where she attended North Division High School in Chicago, Illinois, from 1895 to 1899. She then attended the Chicago Athenaeum in 1903, the Chicago Seminar of Sciences from 1912 to 1915, and Chicago

Law School from 1917 to 1920, where she earned her LL.B. in 1920, the same year that she wed Albert E. Johnson.

Anderson worked as a court reporter from 1905 to 1920, which sparked her interest in law. She began a private practice in 1920, becoming the first African American woman to practice law in the U.S. District Court, Eastern Division. From 1922 to 1923, she served as the first female city prosecutor in Chicago.

After five years of practice before the high court of Illinois, Anderson was admitted to practice for the U.S. Supreme Court, becoming the first African American woman to obtain this post. Her admission became a precedent for other African American women.

Anderson also belonged to the Federal Colored Women's Clubs, was the first vice president of the Cook County Bar Association, president of Friendly Big Sisters League of Chicago, and secretary of the Idlewild Lot Owners Association. In addition, she was a member of the executive board of the Chicago Council of Social Agencies. She died on December 24, 1937.

Deborah A. Batts (1947–)
Judge

The first openly lesbian federal judge, Batts was confirmed in 1994 to the U.S. District Court for the Southern District of New York. A graduate of Radcliffe and the Harvard Law School, Batts clerked for a federal judge before joining Cravath, Swaine & Moore, where she worked as a litigator for six years. Next she served as assistant U.S. attorney in New York for five years before accepting a teaching post at Fordham University in 1994.

A supporter of equal rights for gays and lesbians, Batts is known to be an independent thinker unafraid to speak her mind. She was drawn to the legal field after experiencing the political turmoil of the 1960s. She was initially recommended for a federal judgeship during the Bush administration but did not receive a nomination. U.S. Senator Daniel Moynihan recommended her a second time when President Bill Clinton assumed office. Clinton's nomination of Batts was confirmed by the Senate with no challenges on May 6, 1994.

Derrick Albert Bell Jr. (1930–)
Attorney, Educator

Derrick Albert Bell Jr. was born in Pittsburgh, Pennsylvania, on November 6, 1930. He attended Duquesne University and received his LL.B. from the University of Pittsburgh Law School. He married Jewel A. Hairston and the couple has three children. Bell is a member of

Derrick Albert Bell Jr.

the bar in Washington, DC, Pennsylvania, New York, California; the U.S. Supreme Court; the U.S. Courts of Appeals for the Fourth, Fifth, Sixth, Eighth, and Tenth Circuits; and several federal district courts. Bell has written several important books on the law including *Race, Racism and American Law*, (3rd ed., 1992), and *And We Are Not Saved: The Elusive Quest for Racial Justice* (1987). Bell also served as editor of *Desegregation Dialogue, Searching for Remedies Under Brown.*

After graduating from law school, Bell worked for the U.S. Department of Justice from 1957 to 1959, the Pittsburgh Branch of the NAACP as executive secretary from 1959 to 1960, and for the NAACP Legal Defense and Educational Fund as staff attorney from 1960 to 1966. In 1966 he was made deputy assistant to the secretary for civil rights for the Department of Health, Education and Welfare. He also served for a year as the director of the Western Center on Law and Poverty.

Bell began as a lecturer on law at Harvard Law School in 1969, became a professor in 1971, and left in 1980 to be dean of the University of Oregon Law School for five years. After spending one year teaching at

Stanford University, he returned to Harvard Law School in 1986. Four years later, Bell took an unpaid extended leave from his teaching duties at Harvard in protest over the institution's lack of a tenured black woman professor. Bell was formally removed from his position in 1992. His book-length works include: *Faces at the Bottom of the Well: The Permanence of Racism* (1992), *Confronting Authority: Reflections of an Ardent Protester* (1994), *Gospel Choirs: Psalms of Survival in an Alien Land Called Home* (1996), *Afrolantica Legacies* (1998), and a work in progress called *Civil Rights in 2004: Where Will We Be?*

Jane Matilda Bolin (1908–)
Judge, Attorney

At the age of 31, Jane Matilda Bolin was honored by being chosen to be the first African American female judge in the United States. She presided over the Domestic Relations Court of the City of New York (subsequently called the Family Court of the State of New York) for 40 years. Her first ten-year appointment came from Mayor Fiorello La Guardia in 1939. She was appointed to three more successive ten-year terms by mayors William O'Dwyer, Robert F. Wagner Jr., and John Lindsay. After her fourth term, however, Bolin reached the mandatory retirement age.

Bolin was born on April 11, 1908, in Poughkeepsie, New York, her father was the first African American graduate of Williams College. Bolin attended Wellesley College and Yale University School of Law, where she received her LL.B. in 1931. She worked with her father until she passed the New York State Bar examination and then practiced in Poughkeepsie before moving to New York City to practice law with her husband, Ralph E. Mizelle.

In 1937, Bolin was appointed assistant corporation counsel for New York City, a post that she held until she received her appointment to the Domestic Relations Court. Outside of her career, Bolin has taken an active role in the Wiltwyck School for Boys, the Child Welfare League of America, the Neighborhood Children's Center, and the local and national NAACP. She has also traveled extensively and met several heads of state in Africa. Her friends included Eleanor Roosevelt, educator Mary McLeod Bethune, and Judge Waties Waring, who ruled in the first public school desegregation case. Bolin has received honorary degrees from Morgan State University, Western College for Women, Tuskegee Institute, Hampton University, and Williams College.

After her retirement, Bolin became a volunteer reading teacher for the New York City public schools. She received an appointment to the Regents Review Committee of the New York State Board of Regents, which holds hearings involving professional discipline of more than 32 professions. Bolin was honored for her distinguished service by the corporation counsel's office on May 17, 1993.

Yvonne Braithwaite Burke. *See* Politics chapter.

Johnnie Cochran (1937–)
Attorney

Born in Shreveport, Louisiana on October 2, 1937, Johnnie L. Cochran Jr. grew up in Los Angeles. He received a B.A. in 1959 from the University of California. After finishing his law studies at the Loyola Marymount University School of Law in 1963, he passed the California bar exam. Cochran began his law career as prosecutor in the criminal division of the deputy city attorney's office in Los Angeles. In 1965, he left that post to join criminal lawyer Gerald Lenoir in private practice. He then created the firm of Cochran, Atkins & Evans.

During his first stint in private practice, Cochran established himself by defending high-profile African

Johnnie Cochran Jr.

American clients, such as the family of Leonard Deadwyler, a young man shot to death by police while driving his pregnant wife to the hospital, and Geronimo Pratt, a former Black Panther charged with murder. Cochran lost both cases, but he demonstrated how such cases could garner media attention and foment action among the African American community.

Cochran returned to the Los Angeles County district attorney's office in 1978. After two years as a prosecutor, he returned to private practice in 1980. Shortly thereafter, Cochran won a settlement for the family of Ron Settles, who had been strangled by police officers, though his death was originally identified as a suicide.

Cochran's victories increased, and he began representing celebrities such as pop singer Michael Jackson and actor Todd Bridges. Beginning in the summer of 1994, Cochran served as one of the team of defense lawyers for O. J. Simpson, accused of murdering his ex-wife Nicole Brown Simpson and her friend Ronald Goldman. Cochran wore down the prosecution by challenging evidence and concentrating on racially prejudiced officers. Cochran's racially charged closing arguments alleged the police framed O. J. Simpson for murder. In response, the jury acquitted Simpson on all counts.

Following the Simpson case—described in the media as "The Trial of the Century"—Cochran became one of the best known lawyers in the country and was offered a million-dollar advance for his memoirs. Cochran has served as an adjunct professor at both the Los Angeles School of Law and the Loyola University School of Law. He served as chairman of the Rules Committee of the Democratic National Convention in 1984. In 1995, he was awarded the Trumpet Award by the Turner Broadcasting System.

Beginning in 1997, Cochran took part in a daily show for "Court TV." He left the show in 1999 to create "The Cochran Firm," one of the largest personal injury law firms in America, and in 2002 announced that he was organizing yet another firm to look into the possibility of reparations for the descendants of former slaves.

William T. Coleman (1920–)
Civil Rights Activist, Cabinet Officer

William T. Coleman was born in Philadelphia, Pennsylvania on July 7, 1920. Coleman graduated *summa cum laude* in 1941 from the University of Pennsylvania. His law studies at Harvard University were interrupted by World War II, but he returned to the school after the war and, in 1946, received his LL.B., graduating first in his class. He was also the first African American to serve on the editorial board of the *Harvard Law Review.*

In 1948, Coleman became the first African American to clerk for a Supreme Court Justice, when he clerked for Justice Felix Frankfurter. In the mid-1950s, Coleman joined the Philadelphia firm of Dilworth, Paxon, Kalish, Levy & Green. By the mid-1960s, he had become a partner in the firm. In 1959, Coleman served on an employment commission for President Dwight D. Eisenhower, and served Presidents John F. Kennedy, Lyndon B. Johnson, and Richard M. Nixon.

Coleman played an important role in many landmark civil rights cases. He coauthored the brief presented to the court in the 1954 case of *Brown v. Board of Education of Topeka, Kansas* and served as cocounsel on *McLaughlin v. Florida* (1964), which established the constitutionality of interracial marriages. In 1971, he was elected president of the NAACP Legal Defense and Educational Fund.

In 1975, President Gerald Ford appointed Coleman as the secretary of transportation. Coleman reorganized the department and issued a statement of the department's goals. President Ford's defeat in the 1976 election ended his reign at the department. Coleman returned to private practice in Washington, D.C. In 1995, President Bill Clinton presented him with the Presidential Medal of Freedom.

George Crockett Jr. (1909–1997)
Attorney, Judge, Legislator, Civil Rights Activist

Born in Jacksonville, Florida, on August 10, 1909, George William Crockett Jr. began working when he was 12 and graduated from Morehouse College in 1931. After traveling north to Michigan to pursue a law degree, Crockett returned to his hometown and opened a law practice. In 1939, his accomplishments as a lawyer and community activist led him to be chosen as the first African American attorney in the U.S. Department of Justice.

While in Washington, DC, Crockett distinguished himself as counsel for cases concerning the Fair Labor Standards Act, and in 1943, his work led to his appointment by President Franklin D. Roosevelt as an examiner with the Fair Employment Practices Committee. That same year, he was hired by the United Auto Workers in Detroit to serve as director of their Fair Employment Practices Office during a time of increased racial tensions in the city. In 1946, he went into private practice in Detroit in a firm that took on significant civil rights cases. Crockett once argued a case on behalf of accused Communists, which landed him in prison for four months for contempt of court.

Crockett became intensely involved in the civil rights struggle in the South during the 1960s, leaving Michigan for a time to direct the National Lawyers Guild's civil rights effort, Project Mississippi. In 1966, he was elected to Detroit Recorder's Court, a bench that handled the city's criminal docket. In 1969, members of a leftist group who were meeting at an African American church were brought en masse into police custody after a shooting outside the church. Crockett went down to the station in the middle of the night and set up his own impromptu court, releasing most of the people charged on the basis of constitutional law. He was vilified by Detroit's white establishment for his application of the Bill of Rights.

In 1980, two years after he had left the Recorder's Court bench, Crockett was elected as a Democratic Congressional representative for a Michigan district that included part of Detroit. He served in Washington for the next decade, continuing to distinguish himself by speaking out on civil rights issues and even serving another stint in jail for participating in a demonstration against apartheid in South Africa. The legislator was also a vocal opponent of the Reagan administration's policies in Central America, especially during his tenure as chair of the Foreign Affairs Subcommittee on the Western Hemisphere. After his retirement from politics in 1990, Crockett, founder of the National Bar Association Judicial Council, died in 1997.

Drew S. Days III (1941–)
Attorney, Educator

Days was born in Atlanta, Georgia on August 29, 1941. He received his B.A. from Hamilton College in 1963 and continued his studies at the Yale Law School. During his free summer months, Days returned to Georgia to champion civil rights causes and represent the poor as an intern. After graduating in 1966 from law school near the top of his class, Days moved to Chicago to represent minorities in cases of housing discrimination in the city. Later, Days quit practicing law to work in Honduras for the U.S. Peace Corps.

Upon his return to the United States, Days worked in the Legal Defense and Educational Fund for the NAACP. At the same time, he served as an associate professor at Temple University in Philadelphia. In 1977, Days accepted a post as the first African American as the head of the Civil Rights Division of the U.S. Department of Justice. In 1980, Days left the government position to teach at Yale University.

In 1992, President Bill Clinton nominated Days to the position of solicitor general of the United States, the second leading position at the Justice Department. In this position, Days criticized poorly conceived or poorly managed minority assistance programs. In 1995, he argued before the Supreme Court to keep in place minority voting districts in the Deep South. Early in 1996, Days resigned his position at the Justice Department and once again returned to Yale Law School.

Jerome Farris (1930–)
Attorney, Judge

Judge Joseph Jerome Farris was born on March 4, 1930, in Birmingham, Alabama. He earned his B.S. degree from Morehouse College in 1951, and in 1952, joined the U.S. Army Signal Corps. He received a M.S.W. from Atlanta University in 1955 and received his J.D. from the University of Washington in 1958. Farris is married to Jean Shy and has two children.

Farris began his legal career in 1958 with the firm of Weyer, Schroeter, and Sterne. In 1959 he became a partner. He remained in private practice until 1969, when he became a Washington State Court of Appeals judge. Farris served as the chairman of the State Federal Judicial Council of Washington from 1983–1987. In addition, he served as president on the Washington State Jr. Chamber of Commerce from 1965–1966; a trustee with the Pacific Northwest Ballet from 1978–1983; and since 1985, as a regent of the University of Washington.

President Jimmy Carter nominated Farris to the Ninth Circuit Court of Appeals in July 1979. The nomination was confirmed by the Senate on September 26, 1979, and in March 1995, Farris assumed senior status.

Farris has been honored with the Clayton Frost Award from the Jaycees in 1966, received an honorary LL.D. from Morehouse College in 1978, and the Order of the Coif from the University of Washington Law School.

Archibald H. Grimké (1849–1930)
Attorney, Writer, Activist, Diplomat

Archibald Henry Grimké was born on a plantation near Charleston, South Carolina, on August 17, 1849. His father, a white slaveowner, was a successful lawyer. His mother had been a family slave and served as the nurse for Henry Grimké's first wife, Selena. Archibald was considered a slave at the time. He, along with his mother and siblings, were passed on to relatives after his father's death. Grimké attended a special school during his youth. Grimké enrolled in a school directed by Frances Pillsbury and impressed the instructors there with his superior academic abilities. He completed undergraduate studies in only three years and

Archibald H. Grimké.

obtained his master's degree in 1872 from Lincoln University.

Grimké moved to Boston where he practiced law from 1875 to 1883. Beginning in 1885, he presided over the Women's Suffrage Association of Massachusetts. In the early 1890s, Grimké wrote for Boston-area publications, before being appointed the American consul for Santo Domingo (now the Dominican Republic) for four years. He then assumed the presidential role for the Washington chapter of the NAACP while writing, lecturing, and presiding over the American Negro Academy. Grimké wrote several books including biographies of William Lloyd Garrison (1891) and Charles Sumner (1892), numerous essays, and speeches. He died on February 25, 1930.

William H. Hastie (1904–1976)
Attorney, Judge, State Government Official

From 1949 to 1971, William Henry Hastie served as a U.S. Court of Appeals judge for the Third Circuit, the first African American man to hold a federal appellate court position. Hastie was born in Knoxville, Tennessee, November 17, 1904. He was the son of William Henry and Roberta Child Hastie. He received his A.B. from Amherst College in 1925, an LL.B. in 1930, and an S.J.D. in 1933 from Harvard University. He received honorary LL.D.s from many institutions including Rutgers University, Howard University, and Temple University. In 1943, he married Beryl Lockhart. The couple had three children.

Hastie was admitted to the bar in 1930 and was in private practice from 1930 to 1933. In 1933, he became assistant solicitor of the U.S. Department of the Interior, where he served until 1937. In 1937, he became a judge for the District Court of the Virgin Islands, leaving in 1939 to become dean of the Howard University School of Law. In 1942, he was the first civilian aide to the secretary of war. He was governor of the Virgin Islands between 1946 and 1949, before his subsequent position as a U.S. circuit court judge. Hastie was also a trustee of the Amherst College and a fellow of the American Academy of Arts and Sciences. Hastie died on April 14, 1976, in Philadelphia, Pennsylvania.

Joseph W. Hatchett (1932–)
Attorney, Judge, Author

Judge Joseph Woodrow Hatchett was the first African American to be appointed to the highest court of a state since Reconstruction, the first African American to be elected to public office in a statewide election in the South, and the first African American to serve on a federal appellate court in the South.

Born in Clearwater, Florida, on September 17, 1932, Hatchett received his A.B. from Florida A&M University in 1954 and his J.D. from Howard University in 1959. He also has certification in his specialties—a Naval Justice School Certificate in 1973, an Appellate Judge Course in 1977, and an American Academy of Judicial Education Appellate Judge Course in 1978.

From 1959 to 1966, Hatchett was in private practice in Florida, where he also served as the contract consultant for the city of Daytona Beach. He became an assistant U.S. attorney in Jacksonville in 1966, then served as the first assistant of the U.S. Attorney for the Middle District of Florida. In 1971, he became the U.S. magistrate for the Middle District of Florida, and was a justice for the Florida State Supreme Court from 1975 to 1979. A nominee of President Jimmy Carter, Hatchett was a circuit judge for the Fifth Circuit U.S. Court of Appeals from 1979 until his transfer to the Eleventh Circuit on October 1, 1981. In 1996 he became chief judge of the court, serving in that capacity until his retirement on May 14, 1999.

Hatchett was honored with a Howard University Post Graduation Achievement Award in 1977, named Most Outstanding Citizen by the Broward County National Bar Association in 1976, received a Medallion for Human Relations from Bethune-Cookman in 1975, and has been awarded several honorary doctorates. He is the author of multiple publications in the field of law.

A. Leon Higginbotham Jr. (1928–1998)
Judge, Author

Aloysius Leon Higginbotham Jr. was appointed in 1977 by President Jimmy Carter as a judge of the Third Circuit U.S. Court of Appeals and became the circuit's chief judge before his retirement in 1993. He had served on the Federal Trade Commission—the first African American and the youngest person ever to hold the post of commissioner. Born in Trenton, New Jersey, on February 25, 1928, Higginbotham began as an engineering student at Purdue University, but later went to Antioch College to study liberal arts. He received his LL.B. in 1952 from Yale School of Law.

After graduation, he became an assistant district attorney in Philadelphia and later moved into private practice. He was sought out by Pennsylvania Governor David Lawrence to become a member of the Pennsylvania Human Rights Commission. Elected president of the Philadelphia chapter of the NAACP, Higginbotham later earned the honor of "One of the 10 Outstanding Young Men in America" by the U.S. Junior Chamber of Commerce. He was appointed a federal district judge in 1964, where he served until his appointment as a federal appellate judge in 1977. Higginbotham was also a lecturer at Harvard Law School and an adjunct professor at the University of Pennsylvania. In 1993, he was nominated for a position on the New York Times Co. board of directors.

In 1995, a retired Higginbotham levied criticism at Supreme Court Justice Clarence Thomas, whose judicial philosophy differed greatly from his own. While Higginbotham advocated social engineering through legislation, Thomas vigorously held that law should be colorblind. Higginbotham was criticized for what some saw as an unprovoked attack on a colleague.

Higginbotham was known for his writing. He authored more than 100 articles as well as an acclaimed book, *In the Matter of Color: Race and the American Legal Process: The Colonial Period*. He was also praised for his logic and language. In his esteemed career, he won more than 40 honorary degrees. Higginbotham was awarded the nation's highest medal in 1995, when the Presidential Medal of Freedom was bestowed upon him by President Bill Clinton.

Anita Hill (1956–)
Educator, Author, Lecturer

Born on July 30, 1956, in Morns, Oklahoma, Anita Faye Hill was a relatively unknown law professor at the University of Oklahoma until 1991. It was during the Senate confirmation hearings for eventual U.S. Supreme Court Justice Clarence Thomas that Hill became famous. She came forward with sexual harassment charges against Judge Thomas that shocked the nation. Television cameras and viewers watched as she poured out details of Thomas's alleged wrongdoings, purportedly committed when both had worked for the Equal Employment Opportunity Commission. Hill claimed that Thomas repeatedly pressured her to date him, told her plots of pornographic movies, and bragged about his sexual exploits. When asked why she did not quit her job or report Thomas when the incidents occurred during the early 1980s, Hill answered that she feared she would not be able to get another job. Thomas told a conflicting story, and without corroborative evidence for either side, was confirmed by the Senate.

Following the hearings, Hill continued to be hounded by the press. Several books were written and a 76-minute documentary composed of testimony clips entitled *Sex and Justice: The Highlights of the Anita Hill/Clarence Thomas Hearings* was released. Her experience with the hearings changed her life. She decided to take a year-long sabbatical in order to look at the possibility of founding an institute with the purpose of researching racism and sexism. Hill also made many speeches around the country.

Controversy did not escape her on campus. Several lawmakers made news when they requested that Hill be fired. However, the University of Oklahoma dean and other members of the faculty supported her. In 1993, a university professorship to be established in Hill's name was proposed. Though the suggestion met much opposition, the endowed chair was approved two years later. The Anita Faye Hill Professorship, which was dropped in 1999 under renewed political pressure, provided a salary and money for research and travel expenses incurred in the study of women's rights in the workplace.

On March 9, 1995, Hill announced her resignation from the university, but after taking an unpaid leave during which she intended to write, she resumed her teaching post in September of the same year. In 1997, Hill joined the faculty of Brandeis University as a professor of social policy, law, and women's studies in the Heller School for Social Policy and Management.

Race, Gender, and Power in America, co-edited by Hill and Emma Coleman Jordan, was published in 1995.

Hill's second book, *Speaking Truth to Power*, came out in 1997. An autobiography and another title on sexual harassment were in progress in 2002.

Charles Hamilton Houston (1895–1950)
Attorney, Educational Administrator

Charles Hamilton Houston was born in Washington, D.C., on September 3, 1895. After he finished high school at the age of 15, he attended Amherst College and earned his A.B. in 1915 as one of six valedictorians. He briefly taught English, then enlisted in the U.S. Army in 1917, and served in France and Germany. He attended Harvard Law School and became the first African American editor of the *Harvard Law Review*. He received his LL.B. in 1922, and was in the top five percent of his class. He also became the first African American to receive an S.J.D. in 1923 from Harvard University. Later that year he received a Sheldon Fellowship and studied civil law at the University of Madrid. In 1924, he was admitted to the Washington, D.C., bar association in 1924.

Houston was in private practice with his father from 1924 to 1950. Between 1929 and 1935, he was vice dean of the school of law at Howard University. He was special counsel to the NAACP from 1935 to 1940 and a member of the National Legal Aid Committee from 1940 to 1950. He served as the vice president for the American Council on Race Relations from 1944 to 1950, and was a member of the President's Commission on Fair Employment Practices in 1944.

While with the NAACP, Houston teamed with the American Fund for Public Service to direct a program of legal action and education aimed at the elimination of segregation. Former student Thurgood Marshall served under Houston for several years. While in this position, Houston argued several cases before the U.S. Supreme Court including *Missouri ex rel. Lloyd Gaines v. Canada*. The court ruled that Missouri could not keep an African American from attending the white state law school because no such school existed for African Americans.

Historically, Houston's major impact was in his strengthening of Howard University's Law School, as well as his work in civil rights litigation. Many of the cases he argued were instrumental in setting precedents that were to be used in the historic *Brown v. Board of Education of Topeka, Kansas* and *Bolling v. Sharpe* cases that outlawed racial segregation. In addition, he was a columnist for *The Afro-American*.

Houston died April 22, 1950, of a heart ailment and was buried in Lincoln Memorial Cemetery. Five Supreme Court justices attended his funeral. He received a great deal of recognition after his death including the Spingarn Medal awarded by the NAACP.

Norma Holloway Johnson (1932–)
Judge

Born in Lake Charles, Louisiana, Norma Holloway Johnson left Louisiana at the age of 14 to attend high school in Baltimore, Maryland. She was the valedictorian in 1955 at Miner Teacher's College, and graduated in 1962 from the Georgetown Law Center while working as a teacher.

Johnson worked in the Justice Department until 1967, when she became chief of the juvenile division for the District of Columbia. In 1970, President Richard M. Nixon appointed her associate judge for the district's superior court. In 1980, President Jimmy Carter nominated Johnson to fill a vacant seat on the U.S. Circuit Court for the District of Columbia. She was confirmed by the Senate on May 9, 1980. Johnson served as chief judge of the court from 1997 to 2001, and on June 18, 2001, assumed senior status. During her tenure, she rendered many high-profile decisions involving corruption and civil rights.

Charles Hamilton Houston.

Elaine R. Jones (1944–)
Attorney, Organization Executive, Civil Rights Activist

Jones was born on March 2, 1944, in Norfolk, Virginia. She earned a B.A. with honors in 1965 from Howard University, and became the first African American female law student admitted to the University of Virginia School of Law.

Jones received her law degree in 1970 and was offered a job with a prestigious Wall Street firm. She eventually turned down the job on Wall Street and went to work instead for the NAACP Legal Defense and Educational Fund (LDF). The LDF had argued more cases before the Supreme Court than any other organization except the U.S. Department of Justice.

In 1973, Jones became the managing attorney in the LDF's New York City office. In the late 1970s, she helped set up and run the LDF's new Washington, D.C., office. In 1988, Jones was promoted to deputy director-counsel of the LDF, making her second-in-command to the director, Julius Chambers. Jones used this higher profile position to challenge the administrations of Ronald Reagan and George H. W. Bush on their federal judicial appointments. She was an outspoken opponent of both Robert Bork in 1987 and Clarence Thomas in 1991.

Julius Chambers resigned from the LDF directorship in 1993, and the organization's board unanimously chose Jones to succeed him. As president and director-counsel, Jones broadened the organization's agenda to include more cases of environmental and health care discrimination. In addition to litigation, she is concerned with the group's fund-raising efforts.

Nathaniel R. Jones (1926–)
Judge, Civil Rights Activist

Born on May 13, 1926, in Youngstown, Ohio, Nathaniel Raphael Jones is a judge, attorney, and administrator. President Jimmy Carter appointed him to the Sixth Circuit Court of Appeals in Cincinnati, Ohio, on October 5, 1979, where he served until his retirement on March 30, 2002. Prior to that, he was general counsel for the NAACP from 1969 to 1979; executive director of the Fair Employment Practices Commission of the city of Youngstown, Ohio, from 1966 to 1969; in private practice; and a U.S. attorney for the Northern District of Ohio.

While with the NAACP, Judge Jones organized the attack against northern school segregation and also argued in the Supreme Court case *Bradley v. Milliken.*

The Dayton and Columbus, Ohio, school desegregation cases heard before the Supreme Court were also organized by Jones. He has headed a three-man team that investigated grievances of African American servicemen in Germany and responded to the attacks against affirmative action. He was made deputy general counsel to the President's Commission on Civil Disorders in 1967 and co-chairman of the Civilian Military Task Force on Military Justice in 1972.

Jones received a B.A. from Youngstown University in 1951, and an LL.B. in 1956. He has honorary degrees from Youngstown University and Syracuse University. In April 2002, Jones joined the law firm of Blank Rome as senior counsel.

Star Jones (1962–)
Attorney

Star Jones was born Starlet Marie Jones in 1962 and grew up in Trenton, New Jersey. She shortened her name in 1979 upon entering American University. Jones took an active role in college and even served as a national officer of Alpha Kappa Alpha. After earning a law degree from the University of Houston, Jones went to work for the Kings County District Attorney's office, whose jurisdiction included the crime-plagued New York City borough of Brooklyn. She served as a member of its prosecuting staff from 1986 until her promotion to senior assistant district attorney in 1991.

The year 1991 also landed Jones an invitation to appear on Court TV, a cable television network that broadcasts high-profile trials interjected with commentary from experts on the judicial system. The channel soon hired her to appear regularly in conjunction with the William Kennedy Smith rape trial in Florida. Jones's performance earned her network attention.

NBC lured her away from her tough job at the Brooklyn D.A.'s office by offering her its legal correspondent slot. During the two years she appeared on the network, several notable trials attracted the attention of the American viewing public. Jones provided commentary as well as explanation of some of the more complex legal points involved on both the *Today* show and *NBC Nightly News*. The cases included the criminal trial of the Los Angeles police officers charged with beating motorist Rodney King and the rape trial of boxer Mike Tyson.

In 1994, Group W Communications offered Jones her own syndicated television show. Debuting that fall, *Jones & Jury* gave parties to pending "small claims" lawsuits a chance to resolve their disputes on television before a studio audience. Jones would then render the verdict. The show was cancelled in 1995.

The cancellation did not mean the end of Jones's television career, as she became a co-host for the ABC daytime talk show, *The View*, in 1997. Jones has been nominated for the Emmy award for Outstanding Talk Show Host for her continuing analysis and clarification of social and legal events.

In 1998, Jones published a book entitled, *You Have to Stand for Something, or You'll Fall for Anything*, and, in 2002, launched a nonprofit foundation, "The Starlet Fund," aimed at benefitting women and girls around the world.

Amalya Lyle Kearse (1937–)
Judge

Judge Amalya Lyle Kearse was born June 11, 1937, in Vauxhall, New Jersey. She received her B.A. in 1959 from Wellesley College, and her J.D. in 1962 from the University of Michigan. Kearse was in private practice from 1962 to 1969 and worked as an adjunct lecturer for the New York University Law School from 1968 to 1969. On June 21, 1979, President Jimmy Carter appointed her to a judgeship in the U.S. Court of Appeals for the Second Circuit.

Kearse has won the Jason L. Honigman Award for Outstanding Contribution to the Law Review Editorial Board. She has also served on the board of directors for the NAACP Legal Defense and Educational Fund as well as the National Urban League. She was appointed to the President's Commission for the Selection of Judges and served between 1977 and 1978. She served on the executive committee for Civil Rights Under Law for nine years, has been a member of the American Law Institute since 1977, and has been a fellow in the American College of Trial Lawyers since 1979.

Damon J. Keith (1922–)
Judge, Attorney

Damon Jerome Keith was appointed to the U.S. district court by President Lyndon B. Johnson and served from 1967 to 1977. In 1977, he began service as a judge for the Sixth Circuit U.S. Court of Appeals in Cincinnati, Ohio. He assumed senior status in the court on May 1, 1995.

Born on July 4, 1922, in Detroit, Keith attended West Virginia State College and in 1943 received his A.B. Following graduation, he served in the army for three years. He returned to school to earn his LL.B. in 1949 from Howard University. In 1951, Keith took a job as an attorney for the Office of the Friend of the Court in Detroit and held that position from 1951 to 1955. He received an LL.M. from Wayne State University in 1956.

Keith worked for the Wayne County Board of Supervisors from 1958 to 1963 and went into private practice from 1964 to 1967 before being appointed a judge. He has been active in the Michigan Civil Rights Commission, a trustee in the Medical Corporation of Detroit, a member of the Citizen's Advisory Committee on Equal Educational Opportunity, first vice president emeritus of the Detroit Chapter of the NAACP, a member of the management committee of the Detroit YMCA, a member of the Detroit Council of the Boy Scouts of America, a member of the Detroit Arts Commission, and vice president of the United Negro College Fund of Detroit. Keith is also a trustee of the Interlochen Arts Academy and the Cranbrook School.

Judge Keith has been honored with many accolades including being named among 100 Most Influential Black Americans by *Ebony* magazine, in 1971 and 1977. He received a citizen award from Michigan State University and was named a Spingarn Medalist in 1974. He has received honorary degrees from the University of Michigan, Howard University, Wayne State University, Michigan State University, and New York Law School.

Wade Hampton McCree Jr. (1920–1987)
Judge, Attorney

Wade Hampton McCree Jr. was solicitor general under President Jimmy Carter from 1977 to 1981. McCree had already led a distinguished career as a judge and lawyer by the time he reached that position. He died on August 30, 1987. McCree was born in Des Moines, Iowa, on July 3, 1920. He graduated in 1941 from Fisk University, earning his A.B. In 1944 he received his LL.B. from Harvard University. In 1948, he was admitted to the bar in Michigan.

McCree had a private law practice from 1948 to 1952. From 1952 to 1954 he was commissioner of the Michigan Workmen's Compensation Commission. He was a circuit judge for Wayne County, Michigan, from 1954 until 1961. Then he was a judge for the U.S. District Court, Eastern District, in Michigan from 1961 to 1966. McCree had the honor of being the first African American federal judge in the state of Michigan. From 1966 to 1977 he served as a Sixth Circuit U.S. Court of Appeals judge. From 1981 until his death in 1987, he was a member of the faculty at the University of Michigan Law School. In 1984, the Wade H. McCree Jr. Professorship was established at the University of Michigan Law

School, making it the first endowed chair at a major American law school to be named after an African American. McCree was honored with more than 30 honorary degrees in his lifetime including LL.D.s from Howard University, Harvard University, Boston University, Brandeis University, and Tuskegee Institute.

Gabrielle Kirk McDonald (1942–)
Judge

McDonald was born on April 12, 1942, in St. Paul, Minnesota. She attended Hunter College and then, in 1966, graduated *cum laude* from the Howard University School of Law. McDonald worked for the NAACP until 1969 when she went into private practice in Houston, Texas, with her husband.

McDonald earned a reputation as one of the top litigators in the state and won several large settlements for her clients in civil rights cases. Her record attracted national attention and in 1979 President Jimmy Carter appointed her a federal district court judge. In 1988, she resigned from her position and went back into private practice. She also taught at several law schools.

Gabrielle Kirk McDonald.

In 1993, McDonald was the only U.S. citizen elected to the United Nations International War Crimes Tribunal for the former Yugoslavia at the Hague, Netherlands. She was reelected in 1997 and became the presiding judge of the tribunal, a position she held until her resignation on November 17, 1999. In 2001, McDonald was honored by the American Bar Association Commission on Women in the Profession with its Margaret Brent Women Lawyers of Achievement Award.

Theodore McMillian (1919–)
Judge, Educator

Born on January 28, 1919, in St. Louis, Missouri, Theodore McMillian received his B.S. in 1941 from Lincoln University and, in 1949, earned his LL.B. from St. Louis University Law School. He served in the Signal Corps from 1942 to 1946.

McMillian has been a lecturer at St. Louis University Law School as well as a faculty member of Webster College. He became a circuit judge for the State of Missouri and served as an assistant circuit attorney for St. Louis, Missouri, from 1953 to 1956. From 1972 to 1978, he was a judge with the Missouri Court of Appeals. He became a U.S. Circuit Court of Appeals judge for the Eighth Circuit on September 23, 1978.

Judge McMillian has been a member of the board of trustees for Blue Cross, and a member of the Danforth Foundation Advisory Council. He served on the Presidential Council of St. Louis University, and as a board chairman for Human Development Corporation between 1964 and 1977. He has also been a member of the National Legal Aid Advisory Board. He has been honored with an Alumni Merit Award from St. Louis University, an Award of Honor from the Lawyers Association in 1970, and a Man of the Year Award in 1970.

Carmel Carrington Marr (1921–)
Attorney, Diplomat, State Government Official

Carmel Carrington Marr was born in Brooklyn on June 23, 1921, and received her B.A. in 1945 from Hunter College. She earned her J.D. from Columbia University Law School in 1948. As an experienced lawyer in international law, she was appointed by President Harry Truman to the position of legal advisor to the U.S. mission to the United Nations in 1953. She served that position until 1967, keeping in constant contact with missions from other parts of the world and serving on a number of key committees of the U.N. General Assembly.

Marr began her career in private practice from 1949 to 1953. After her position as legal advisor to the United

Nations, she became the senior legal officer of the U.N. Secretariat from 1967 to 1968, and then left to become a member of the New York State Human Rights Appeal Board from 1968 to 1971. Between 1971 and 1986 she served as commissioner of the New York State Public Service Commission. She retired from that position, becoming an energy consultant from 1987 until 1990.

Marr was also the chairperson of the advisory council of the Gas Research Institute between 1979 and 1986, the chairperson of the U.S. Department of Transportation Technology Pipeline Safety Standards Commission from 1979 to 1985, and the chairperson of the National Association of Regulatory Utility Commissioners Gas Commission from 1984 to 1986. She became president of NARUC's Great Lakes Conference of Public Utility Commission and was on the board of the National Arts Stabilization Fund.

Marr has been honored as an Outstanding Community Service by the Brooklyn Urban League and received accolades from the Gas Research Institute, New York State Public Service Commission, American Red Cross, National Council of Churches, and *Mademoiselle* magazine.

Thurgood Marshall (1908–1993)
Judge, Federal Government Official, Attorney, Civil Rights Activist

Thurgood Marshall's long and illustrious career was capped by his 1967 nomination to the U.S. Supreme Court, where he became the first African American to hold the position of Supreme Court Justice. He retired on June 27, 1991. Marshall died at the age of 84 on January 24, 1993. He was laid in state in the Great Hall of the Supreme Court of the United States on the same bier where Abraham Lincoln once rested. More than 20,000 mourners paid their respects.

Born in Baltimore, Maryland, on July 2, 1908, Marshall earned a B.A. from Lincoln University and hoped to become a dentist. He changed his mind, and instead went to Howard University Law School where he graduated in 1933 at the top of his class. He immediately entered private practice in Baltimore. In 1936, Marshall began what was to be a long and fruitful career with the NAACP, starting as an assistant special counsel, and eventually becoming director-counsel of the Legal Defense and Educational Fund (LDF) until 1961. In 1938, as a national special counsel, he handled all cases involving the constitutional rights of African Americans. Then, in 1950, he was named director-counsel of the LDF.

In 1954, Marshall was the lead lawyer for the NAACP before the U.S. Supreme Court in *Brown v. Board of*

Thurgood Marshall.

Education of Topeka, Kansas. He also figured prominently in such important cases as *Sweatt v. Painter* and *Smith v. Allwright.* Of the 32 cases that he argued before the Supreme Court, Marshall won 29.

Marshall was also known for his lifelong support of rights for women. Constance Baker Motley commented that Marshall hired her for an NAACP counsel position when virtually every other employer had turned her down. He also encouraged her when he argued cases before the Supreme Court, and made certain he pointed out other African American women role models.

In 1961, Marshall became a federal circuit judge for the second circuit. In 1946, he was awarded the prestigious Spingarn Medal for his many achievements. He had over 20 honorary degrees to his credit including LL.D. honors in 1960 from the University of Liberia, in 1964 from the University of Michigan, and in 1968 from the University of Otago, in Dunedin, New Zealand. Marshall was also the representative for the White House Conference on Youth and Children, and a member of the National Bar Association. He was sent by President John F. Kennedy to be a personal representative to the independence ceremonies of Sierra Leone.

Constance Baker Motley (1921–)
Federal Government Official, Judge, Civil Rights Activist, Attorney

Born on September 14, 1921, in New Haven, Connecticut, Constance Baker Motley became the first African American woman to become a federal judge. She was appointed in 1966 by President Lyndon B. Johnson to the U.S. District Court for Southern New York.

While still a law student at Columbia University, Motley began working with the NAACP Legal Defense and Educational Fund. In 1946, she was awarded her LL.B. and began to work full-time with the NAACP, eventually becoming an associate counsel. During her 20-year career with the organization, Motley had argued nine successful NAACP cases before the U.S. Supreme Court, and had participated in almost every important civil rights case that had passed through the courts since.

In 1964, Motley made a successful run for the New York State Senate. She became the first African American woman elected to that position. After only a year in the Senate, Motley ran for the position of Manhattan Borough President, emerging the victor by the unanimous final vote of the city council. She thus became the first woman to serve as a city borough president, and, therefore, also the first woman on the Board of Estimate.

Motley was appointed to the U.S. District Court in 1966. In 1982, she was named chief judge of the federal district court that covers Manhattan, the Bronx, and six counties north of New York City. In 1986 she was named senior U.S. district judge.

During her career, Motley received several awards for her contributions to the legal profession and for her role in the advancement of civil rights. She holds more than 20 honorary degrees from prestigious universities including Princeton and Howard. In 1993, Motley was inducted into the National Women's Hall of Fame.

Eleanor Norton. *See* **Politics chapter.**

Charles J. Ogletree Jr. (1952–)
Lawyer

Charles J. Ogletree Jr. was born on December 31, 1952, in Merced, California, and attended Stanford University. In 1974, he received his B.A. and followed it the next year with his M.A. While at Stanford he became involved with the Black Power Movement. He edited a Black Panther newspaper and traveled to Africa and Cuba. His attendance at Angela Davis's trial first attracted him to a career in the law.

Ogletree graduated in 1978 from Harvard Law School and went to work as a public defender in Washington, D.C. He established a reputation as a top trial lawyer and taught at American University and Antioch Law School. In 1985, while in private practice, Ogletree became a visiting professor at Harvard Law School and helped the school develop its trial advocacy workshops.

Ogletree served as Anita Hill's attorney during her testimony before the U.S. Senate concerning the nomination of Clarence Thomas to the Supreme Court. In 1989, he became a full professor at Harvard, where he was named the Jesse Climenko Professor of Law in 1998.

Bernard Parks (1943–)
Police Chief

Bernard C. Parks was born in Beaumont, Texas, on December 7, 1943, but was raised in Los Angeles. After bouncing between jobs, Parks became a police officer in Los Angeles in 1965. Parks received his B.A. in 1973 from Pepperdine University and his M.A. in public

Bernard Parks.

administration in 1976 from the University of Southern California.

Parks steadily moved up the ladder at the Los Angeles Police Department. By 1988 he was the assistant police chief. The Los Angeles riots of 1992 forced incumbent police chief Darryl Gates from his position. Gates was accused by many of racism during his reign as police chief. An African American chief was picked to replace Gates.

The new chief, Willie Williams, clashed frequently with Parks. He demoted Parks in 1994. However, the City Council restored Parks's salary. In 1996, Williams was removed as chief and the next year Parks became the head of the LAPD. Parks held the post until June 2002, retiring after he was denied a second five-year term by the Los Angeles Police Commission in April. During his tenure as chief, Parks attempted reform of the department, implementing changes meant to bring officers closer to their captains. During Parks's term, though, the department was racked by the widely publicized Rampart scandal. The chief also suffered the loss of his grandaughter, Lori Gonzalez, in a gang-related shooting in June 2000.

In July 2002, Parks announced plans to run for Los Angeles City Council in 2003.

James B. Parsons (1911–1993)
Judge

James Benton Parsons was born August 13, 1991, in Kansas City, Missouri. He graduated in 1934 from the James Milliken University and Conservatory of Music and began to teach at Lincoln University. He later taught in Greensboro, North Carolina, until he joined the U.S. Navy in 1942. After World War II, he received an M.A. in political science and a J.D. from the University of Chicago.

Parsons went into private practice and taught constitutional law at the John Marshall Law School. He served as assistant U.S. district attorney for nine years until he became a judge of the Cook County Superior Court. He was appointed a U.S. district court judge in 1961 by President John F. Kennedy. He became the first African American to sit as a federal judge in the continental United States. In 1975, Parsons was named chief judge of the court.

He retired in 1992 after many tributes from other African American judges. Parsons died on June 19, 1993, in Chicago.

Spottswood Robinson (1916–1998)
Attorney, Judge

Spottswood William Robinson III was born July 26, 1916, in Richmond, Virginia. He received his B.A. in 1936 from Virginia Union University and his LL.B. in 1939 from Howard University Law School. He graduated *magna cum laude* from Howard.

Robinson has had a long career in private and public practice. He was an attorney in Richmond until 1960. However, during that time he also taught at the Howard University Law School from 1945 until 1964. He was dean of the school of law from 1960 to 1964. Robinson gained notoriety during the period for his work with the NAACP. He worked alongside Thurgood Marshall for the Legal Defense and Educational Fund from 1948 to 1950. From 1951 to 1960 he was the regional counsel for the NAACP in the southeast.

In 1964, President Johnson appointed Robinson as a federal circuit court judge in Washington, D.C. In 1966, Robinson was promoted to the U.S. Court of Appeals for the District of Columbia Circuit. He also served on the U.S. Civil Rights Commission from 1961 to 1963.

Robinson died on October 11, 1998, in Richmond, Virginia.

George Ruffin (1834–1886)
Judge, Attorney, Civil Rights Activist

George L. Ruffin was born in Richmond, Virginia, in 1834, the first son of free African Americans. In 1853, the family moved to Boston. Ruffin graduated from Chapman Hall school and joined with the Republican Party. He moved for a short while to Liverpool, England, after becoming disillusioned by the *Dred Scott* decision. Returning to Boston, Ruffin worked as a barber. He wrote a review for the *Anglo-African* newspaper in 1863 and attended the National Negro Convention in 1864.

Ruffin also began to read law with a local firm. He graduated in 1869 from Harvard Law School, becoming the first African American to earn an LL.B. from Harvard and, perhaps, the first to graduate from a university law school in the United States. He joined the firm of Harvey Jewell, and then won a seat on the Massachusetts legislature in 1869, becoming the second African American to serve in that body.

Ruffin became known as an exceptional speaker and debater as he focused his attention to the problems in the South. In 1876 and 1877, he won election to the Boston Common Council. He presided over the Negro Convention of New Orleans in 1872. Frederick Douglass was a friend of Ruffin's, and Ruffin was asked to contribute to the introduction to the 1881 revision of *The Life and Times of Frederick Douglass.* Ruffin was appointed in November 1883 as judge of a municipal court in Charlestown. He became the first African American judge in Massachusetts. In 1883, he was made consul resident for the Dominican Republic in Boston. Ruffin's other activities included being named president of the Wendell Phillips Club of Boston, member and president of the Banneker Literary Club of Boston, and superintendent and officer of the Twelfth Baptist Church of Boston. Ruffin died of Bright's disease on November 20, 1886.

Kurt L. Schmoke. *See* **Politics chapter.**

Dred Scott. *See* **Africans in America chapter.**

Robert H. Terrell (1857–1925)
Educator, Judge, Attorney

Robert H. Terrell was born in Charlottesville, Virginia, on November 27, 1857. He worked in a dining hall to pay for his classes at Harvard, where he graduated *magna cum laude* in 1884. He went to work in the Washington, D.C., public schools, and also attended Howard University Law School, earning his LL.B. in 1889 and his LL.M. in 1893. In 1889, he went to work as the chief clerk in the office of the auditor of the U.S. Treasury Department.

Terrell was involved in the private practice of law from 1892 to 1898, until he became a teacher, and later became principal at the M Street High School. He was elected to the Board of Trade in the 1890s. In 1901, he was appointed as a justice of the peace in Washington, D.C. Similar to many African Americans of his day, Terrell was torn between his strongly held civil rights beliefs and Booker T. Washington's conservative ideas. Through Washington's influence, Terrell was nominated by President William H. Taft for the position of judge of the Municipal Court of the District of Columbia in 1910. Despite racial protests in the Senate, Terrell signed the appointment and held the position until his death on December 20, 1925. Terrell suffered two strokes and battled asthma while on the court.

Clarence Thomas (1948–)
Attorney, Supreme Court Justice

Thomas was born June 23, 1948, in Pin Point, Georgia. As a youth, Thomas lived with his maternal grandparents in Savannah. While his grandfather had little education, he was determined that Thomas would go to school and make something of himself. He attended

Clarence Thomas's official U.S. Supreme Court portrait.

various Catholic schools. He intended to enter the priesthood, but left when he encountered a racist seminarian.

Thomas earned his B.A. from Holy Cross College. He was accepted into Yale Law School in 1971 after Yale had adopted an affirmative action program. In 1974, he earned his J.D. After graduating, Thomas became an assistant attorney general for the state of Missouri. Thomas worked briefly at Monsanto Company in St. Louis, specializing in pesticide, fungicide, and rodenticide law. He also worked as a legal assistant for Senator John C. Danforth.

From 1981 to 1982, Thomas was an assistant secretary for civil rights with the Department of Education, then moved on to chair the Equal Employment Opportunity Commission (EEOC) until 1990. His time there was controversial, as he was not allied with either liberals or civil rights leaders, and he did not feel comfortable with the white conservative hierarchy.

After Robert H. Bork resigned his Circuit Court position because he had been rejected for a place on the U.S. Supreme Court, Thomas was appointed to the post. He served there until he was made a justice on the Supreme Court in 1991. Thomas's nomination hearings were marred by accusations of sexual harassment levied against him by former EEOC employee Anita Hill.

Hill became a household name when she came forward with her allegations. The Senate was divided by Hill's testimony. Though Thomas denied the charges and many of his former coworkers testified for him, the case became highly politicized. Thomas was nominated by a vote of 52–48, one of the closest margins in Supreme Court history.

Thomas has gone on to carve out a prominent role as one of the most conservative justices on the Court. Together Justice Antonin Scalia, Thomas forms the right-wing backbone of the Court. In his tenure Thomas has presented strong opinions against affirmative action and desegregation. He also supports limiting the powers of the federal government. In 1992, Thomas was one of ten people to receive the Horatio Alger Award. However, he has consistently been criticized by African American lawyers and judges for his conservative stances. In 1998, he rebuffed his critics at a speech before the National Bar Association.

Evelyn Williams (c.1922–)
Attorney

Williams was born in North Carolina but grew up in Queens, New York, in a close-knit family. After graduating from Brooklyn College, she became a social worker for New York City. Shaken by the poverty she encountered and hoping to take a more active role in helping her community, Williams became a juvenile probation officer, but that also offered little satisfaction.

In the late 1950s, Williams graduated from law school as one of two African Americans in her class. By 1960, she was active in defending those accused of crimes who had little means for expensive legal representation. She also helped raise a niece who eventually became involved with the Black Liberation Army in the early 1970s.

For several years Williams—then working with the New York University Urban Affairs and Poverty Law Program—served as the attorney for her niece, Assata Shakur and her co-defendants against a series of legal charges involving a shootout with police. The case, which included the mysterious death of one of Williams's fellow attorneys, was chronicled in her 1993 autobiography *Inadmissable Evidence: The Story of the African-American Trial Lawyer Who Defended the Black Liberation Army.*

Williams's high-profile defense of Shakur would cost her in more ways than she had imagined. During the 1980s, Williams again entered private practice but became the target of an unsuccessful FBI sting operation. By 1989, she had joined the firm of Stevens, Hinds & White in New York City.

◆ AFRICAN AMERICAN FEDERAL JUDGES BY YEAR OF APPOINTMENT

Appointed by President Franklin D. Roosevelt
1937: William H. Hastie* (District Court, Virgin Islands)
1939: Harnian E. Moore* (District Court, Virgin Islands)

Appointed by President Harry S Truman
1945: Irvin C. Mollison* (U.S. Customs Court)
1949: William H. Hastie* (Court of Appeals, Third Circuit)
1949: Harnian E. Moore (a)* (District Court, Virgin Islands)

Appointed by President Dwight D. Eisenhower
1957: Scovel Richardson* (U.S. Customs Court)
1958: Walter Gordon* (District Court, Virgin Islands)

Appointed by President John F. Kennedy
1961: James B. Parsons* (Senior Judge, District Court, Illinois)
1961: Wade M. McCree* (District Court, Michigan)
1961: Thurgood Marshall* (Court of Appeals, Second Circuit)

Appointed by President Lyndon B. Johnson
1964: Spottswood Robinson* (District Court, District of Columbia)
1964: A. Leon Higginbotham* (District Court, Pennsylvania)
1965: William B. Bryant (Senior Judge, District Court, District of Columbia)
1966: Wade H. McCree* (Court of Appeals, Sixth Court)
1966: James L. Watson (U.S. Customs Court)
1966: Constance B. Motley (Senior Judge, District Court, New York)
1966: Spottswood Robinson* (Senior Judge, Court of Appeals for the Federal Circuit)
1966: Aubrey E. Robinson* (Senior Judge, District Court, District of Columbia)
1967: Damon Keith** (District Court, Michigan)
1967: Thurgood Marshall* (Associate Justice, U.S. Supreme Court)

1967: Joseph C. Waddy* (District Court, District of Columbia)

Appointed by President Richard M. Nixon

1969: Almeric Christian* (District Court, Virgin Islands)

1969: David W. Williams* (Senior Judge, District Court, California)

1969: Barrington D. Parker Sr.* (Senior Judge, District Court, District of Columbia)

1971: Lawrence W. Pierce** (District Court, New York)

1971: Clifford Scott Green (Senior Judge, District Court, Pennsylvania)

1972: Robert L. Carter (Senior Judge, District Court, New York)

1972: Robert M. Duncan** (Military Court of Appeals)

1974: Robert M. Duncan** (District Court, Ohio)

Appointed by President Gerald R. Ford

1974: Henry Bramwell (Senior Judge, District Court, New York)

1976: George N. Leighton** (Senior Judge, District Court, Illinois)

1976: Matthew J. Perry** (Military Court of Appeals)

1976: Cecil F. Poole* (District Court, California)

Appointed by President Jimmy Carter

1978: Almeric Christian (a)* (Chief Judge, District Court, Virgin Islands)

1978: U.W. Clemon (Chief Judge, District Court, Alabama)

1978: Robert F. Collins** (District Court, Louisiana)

1978: Julian A. Cook Jr. (Senior Judge, District Court, Michigan)

1978: Damon J. Keith (Senior Judge, Court of Appeals, Sixth Circuit)

1978: A. Leon Higginbotham* (Senior Judge, Court of Appeals, Third Circuit)

1978: Mary Johnson Lowe* (Senior Judge, District Court, New York)

1978: Theodore McMillian (Court of Appeals, Eighth Circuit)

1978: David S. Nelson* (Senior Judge, District Court, Massachusetts)

1978: Paul A. Simmons (Senior Judge, District Court, Pennsylvania)

1978: Jack E. Tanner (Senior Judge, District Court, Washington)

1979: Harry T. Edwards (Court of Appeals for the Federal Circuit)

1979: J. Jerome Farris (Senior Judge, Court of Appeals, Ninth Circuit)

1979: Joseph W. Hatchett** (Court of Appeals, Eleventh Circuit)

1979: Terry J. Hatter (District Court, California)

1979: Joseph C. Howard* (Senior Judge, District Court, Maryland)

1979: Benjamin T. Gibson** (Senior Judge, District Court, Michigan)

1979: James T. Giles (District Court, Pennsylvania)

1979: Nathaniel R. Jones** (Senior Judge, Court of Appeals, Sixth Circuit)

1979: Amalya L. Kearse (Court of Appeals, Second Circuit)

1979: Gabrielle Kirk McDonald** (District Court, Texas)

1979: John Garrett Penn (Senior Judge, District Court, District of Columbia)

1979: Cecil F. Poole* (Senior Judge, Court of Appeals, Ninth Circuit)

1979: Matthew J. Perry (Senior Judge, District Court, South Carolina)

1979: Myron H. Thompson (District Court, Alabama)

1979: Anne E. Thompson (Senior Judge, District Court, New Jersey)

1979: Odell Horton (Senior Judge, District Court, Tennessee)

1979: Anna Diggs Taylor (Senior Judge, District Court, Michigan)

1979: Horace T. Ward (Senior Judge, District Court, Georgia)

1979: Alcee L. Hastings*** (District Court, Florida)

1980: Clyde S. Cahill Jr. (Senior Judge, District Court, Missouri)

1980: Richard C. Erwin (Senior Judge, District Court, North Carolina)

1980: Thelton E. Henderson (Senior Judge, District Court, California)

1980: George Howard Jr. (District Court, Arkansas)

1980: Earl B. Gilliam* (Senior Judge, District Court, California)

1980: Norma Holloway Johnson (Senior Judge, District Court, District of Columbia)

1980: Consuela B. Marshall (Chief Judge, District Court, California)

1980: George White (Senior Judge, District Court, Ohio)

Appointed by President Ronald Reagan

1981: Lawrence W. Pierce** (Senior Judge, Court of Appeals, Second Circuit)

1982: Reginald Gibson (U.S. Court of Claims)

1984: John R. Hargrove* (Senior Judge, District Court, Maryland)

1984: Henry Wingate (District Court, Mississippi)
1985: Ann Williams** (District Court, Illinois)
1986: James Spencer (District Court, Virginia)
1987: Kenneth Hoyt (District Court, Texas)
1988: Herbert Hutton (District Court, Pennsylvania)

Appointed by President George Bush

1990: Clarence Thomas** (Court of Appeals for the Federal Circuit)
1990: James Ware (District Court, California)
1991: Saundra Brown Armstrong (District Court, California)
1991: Fernando J. Giatan (District Court, Missouri)
1991: Donald L. Graham (District Court, Florida)
1991: Sterling Johnson (District Court, New York)
1991: J. Curtis Joyner (District Court, Pennsylvania)
1991: Timothy K. Lewis** (District Court, Pennsylvania)
1991: Joe B. McDade (Chief Judge, District Court, Illinois)
1991: Clarence Thomas (Associate Justice, U.S. Supreme Court)
1992: Garland E. Burrell Jr. (District Court, California)
1992: Carol Jackson (District Court, Missouri)
1992: Timothy K. Lewis** (Court of Appeals, Third Circuit)

Appointed by President Bill Clinton

1993: Henry Lee Adams (District Court, Florida)
1993: Wilkie Ferguson (District Court, Florida)
1993: Raymond Jackson (District Court, Virginia)
1993: Gary Lancaster (District Court, Pennsylvania)
1993: Reginald Lindsay (District Court, Massachusetts)
1993: Charles Shaw (District Court, Missouri)
1994: Deborah Batts (District Court, New York)
1994: Franklin Burgess (District Court, Washington)
1994: James Beaty Jr. (District Court, North Carolina)
1994: David Coar (District Court, Illinois)
1994: Audrey Collins (District Court, California)
1994: Clarence Cooper (District Court, Georgia)
1994: Michael Davis (District Court, Minnesota)
1994: Raymond Finch (District Court, Virgin Islands)
1994: Vanessa Gilmore (District Court, Texas)
1994: A. Haggerty (District Court, Oregon)
1994: Denise Page Hood (District Court, Michigan)
1994: Napoleon Jones Jr. (District Court, California)
1994: Okla Jones II (District Court, Louisiana)
1994: Blanche Manning (District Court, Illinois)
1994: Theodore McKee (Court of Appeals, Third Circuit)

1994: Vicki Miles-LaGrange (District Court, Oklahoma)
1994: Solomon Oliver Jr. (District Court, Ohio)
1994: Barrington Parker Jr.** (District Court, New York)
1994: Judith Rogers (Court of Appeals for the Federal Circuit)
1994: W. Louis Sands (Chief Judge, District Court, Georgia)
1994: Carl Stewart (Court of Appeals, Fifth Circuit)
1994: Emmet Sullivan (District Court, District of Columbia)
1994: Alvin W. Thompson (District Court, Connecticut)
1994: William Walls (District Court, New Jersey)
1994: Alexander Williams (District Court, Maryland)
1995: R. Guy Cole (Court of Appeals, Sixth Circuit)
1995: Curtis Collier (District Court, Tennessee)
1995: Wiley Daniel (District Court, Colorado)
1995: Andre Davis (District Court, Maryland)
1995: Bernice B. Donald (District Court, Tennessee)
1996: Charles N. Clevert Jr. (District Court, Wisconsin)
1996: Joseph A. Greenaway Jr. (District Court, New Jersey)
1997: Eric L. Clay (Court of Appeals, Sixth Circuit)
1997: Algenon L. Marbley (District Court, Ohio)
1997: Martin J. Jenkins (District Court, California)
1997: Henry H. Kennedy Jr. (District Court, District of Columbia)
1998: Gregory Sleet (District Court, Delaware)
1998: Ivan L.R. Lemelle (District Court, Louisiana)
1998: Sam A. Lindsay (District Court, Texas)
1998: Johnnie B. Rawlinson (District Court, Nevada)
1998: Margaret Seymour (District Court, South Carolina)
1998: Richard Roberts (District Court, District of Columbia)
1998: Gerald Bruce Lee (District Court, Virginia)
1998: Lynn Bush (Court of Federal Claims)
1998: Stephan P. Mickle (District Court, Florida)
1998: Victoria Roberts (District Court, Michigan)
1998: Raner Collins (District Court, Arizona)
1998: Ralph Tyson (District Court, Louisiana)
1999: William J. Haynes Jr. (District Court, Tennessee)
1999: William Hibbler (District Court, Illinois)
1999: Ann Williams (Court of Appeals, Seventh Circuit)
1999: Charles R. Wilson (Court of Appeals, Eleventh Circuit)
2000: George B. Daniels (District Court, New York)
2000: Phyllis J. Hamilton (District Court, California)
2000: Laura Swain (District Court, New York)

2000: Petrese B. Tucker (District Court, Pennsylvania)

2001: Roger L. Gregory (Court of Appeals, Fourth Circuit)

Appointed by President George W. Bush

2001: Barrington Parker Jr. (Court of Appeals, Second Circuit)

2001: Julie A. Robinson (District Court, Kansas)

2001: Reggie B. Walton (District Court, District of Columbia)

2002: Percy Anderson (District Court, California)

2002: Legrome D. Davis (District Court, Pennsylvania)

(a) Reappointment

* Deceased

** No longer serving

*** Impeached and removed from the court

Jail Inmates by Sex and Race: 1990 to 1999

[Data are for midyear. Excludes Federal and state prisons or other correctional institutions; institutions exclusively for juveniles; state-operated jails in Alaska, Connecticut, Delaware, Hawaii, Rhode Island, and Vermont; and other facilities which retain persons for less than 48 hours. As of June 30. Data for 1993 based on National Jail Census; for other years, based on sample survey and subject to sampling variability]

Characteristic	1990	1993	1994	1995	1996	1997	1998	1999
Total inmates [1]	405,320	459,804	486,474	507,044	518,492	567,079	592,462	605,943
Male	368,002	415,600	437,600	455,400	462,500	507,200	(NA)	(NA)
Female	37,318	44,200	48,800	51,600	55,800	59,900	(NA)	(NA)
White non-Hispanic	169,600	180,900	190,100	203,300	215,900	230,300	244,900	249,900
Black non-Hispanic	172,300	203,500	213,400	220,600	213,100	237,900	244,000	251,800
Hispanic	58,100	69,200	74,900	74,400	80,900	88,900	91,800	93,800
Other [1]	5,400	6,200	8,100	8,800	8,600	10,000	11,800	10,400

NA Not available. [1] Includes American Indians, Alaska Natives, Asians, and Pacific Islanders.

SOURCE: U.S. Bureau of Justice Statistics, through 1994, Jail Inmates, annual; beginning 1995, *Prison and Jail Inmates at Midyear,* annual.

Prisoners Under Sentence of Death by Characteristic: 1980 to 1998

[As of December 31. Excludes prisoners under sentence of death who remained within local correctional systems pending exhaustion of appellate process or who had not been committed to prison]

Characteristic	1980	1988	1989	1990	1991	1992	1993	1994	1995	1996	1997	1998
Total[1]	688	2,117	2,243	2,346	2,466	2,575	2,727	2,905	3,064	3,242	3,328	3,452
White	418	1,235	1,308	1,368	1,450	1,508	1,575	1,653	1,732	1,833	1,864	1,906
Black and other	270	882	935	978	1,016	1,067	1,152	1,252	1,332	1,409	1,464	1,546
Under 20 years	11	11	6	8	14	12	13	19	20	17	16	15
20 to 24 years	173	195	191	168	179	188	211	231	264	288	275	267
25 to 34 years	334	1,048	1,080	1,110	1,087	1,078	1,066	1,088	1,068	1,088	1,077	1,101
35 to 54 years	186	823	917	1,006	1,129	1,212	1,330	1,449	1,583	1,711	1,809	1,899
55 years and over	10	47	56	64	73	85	96	103	119	138	151	170
Years of school completed:												
7 years or less	68	180	183	178	173	181	185	186	191	196	205	206
8 years	74	184	178	186	181	180	183	198	195	201	206	217
9 to 11 years	204	692	739	775	810	836	885	930	979	1,040	1,069	1,111
12 years	162	657	695	729	783	831	887	939	995	1,037	1,084	1,120
More than 12 years	43	180	192	209	222	232	244	255	272	282	288	297
Unknown	163	231	263	279	313	315	332	382	422	486	476	501
Marital status:												
Never married	268	898	956	998	1,071	1,132	1,222	1,320	1,412	1,507	1,555	1,641
Married	229	594	610	632	663	663	671	707	718	739	740	749
Divorced[2]	217	632	684	726	746	780	823	863	924	996	1,033	1,062
Time elapsed since sentencing:												
Less than 12 months	185	293	231	231	252	265	262	280	287	306	262	275
12 to 47 months	389	812	809	753	718	720	716	755	784	816	844	813
48 to 71 months	102	409	408	438	441	444	422	379	423	447	456	482
72 months and over	38	610	802	934	1,071	1,146	1,316	1,476	1,560	1,673	1,766	1,882
Legal status at arrest:												
Not under sentence	384	1,207	1,301	1,345	1,415	1,476	1,562	1,662	1,764	1,881	1,957	2,029
Parole or probation[3]	115	545	585	578	615	702	754	800	866	894	880	877
Prison or escaped	45	93	94	128	102	101	102	103	110	112	116	127
Unknown	170	279	270	305	321	296	298	325	314	355	375	419

[1] Revisions to the total number of prisoners were not carried to the characteristics except for race.

[2] Includes persons married but separated, widows, widowers, and unknown.

[3] Includes prisoners on mandatory conditional release, work release, leave, AWOL, or bail. Covers 28 prisoners in 1990, 29 in 1991 and 1992, 33 in 1993 and 1995, 31 in 1994 and 1996, and 30 in 1997.

SOURCE: U.S. Bureau of Justice Statistics, *Capital Punishment,* annual.

Politics

◆ Race, Politics, and Government
◆ Congressional Black Caucus Members (107th U.S. Congress)
◆ Government Officials ◆ Political Statistics

by Paulette Coleman

◆ RACE, POLITICS, AND GOVERNMENT

The history of African American participation in the political process is complex and includes multiple responses to the deliberate and systematic exclusion of African Americans from American life. In colonial times, most African Americans were slaves and thus denied the basic rights of citizenship. Legally, they were prohibited from voting and other means of political expression. Though they could not participate formally in the political process, slaves found other avenues for political expression including various forms of resistance.

A small number of free African Americans were occasionally allowed to vote in certain places. There is evidence that some free African Americans voted in South Carolina's 1701 gubernatorial election. In the early eighteenth century, African Americans petitioned the courts and political leaders for legal protection but with limited success.

Prior to the Revolutionary War, political participation by African Americans was rare. Though slave revolts were an exception, the revolutionary fervor of the times did not go unnoticed by the African Americans. The revolutionary rhetoric resonated with the slaves and served as a catalyst for the filing of petitions with state legislatures and even with Congress to protest slavery. During the Revolutionary War, some freedmen saw military service as a way to be included as citizens in the new nation.

The American Colonization Society, founded by African Americans in 1816, promoted emigration to Africa. Members of this emigration movement eventually established the African nation of Liberia. Meanwhile, others emigrated to Canada, Central and South America, and island nations such as Haiti.

In 1830, free African Americans in Philadelphia convened the National Negro Convention. For two decades the national convention movement continued its development as a mass self-help movement involving African American churches, fraternal organizations, and mutual aid societies. The more militant participants became dominant in the convention by the 1850s. As a result, there was a growing dual determination to build African American institutions while demanding the rights of full participation as citizens of the United States.

The abolitionist movement of the 1830s was part of a multiracial quest for African American emancipation and equality. In addition to campaigning for civil rights through traditional legal means, the abolitionists took a daring step by operating the Underground Railroad system, a covert network of safe havens that assisted fugitive slaves in their flight to freedom in the North. Approximately 50,000 slaves are believed to have escaped to the Northern United States and Canada through the Underground Railroad prior to the Civil War.

In the 1850s, new efforts were made to exclude African Americans from citizenship with the passage of the Fugitive Slave Act. Similarly, the Kansas-Nebraska Act attempted to extend slavery into new territories. The U.S. Supreme Court's decision in the *Dred Scott* case held that African Americans had no rights as U.S. citizens and that a state could not forbid slavery. These legal decisions convinced large numbers of African Americans and others that radical action was necessary. Among them were: Martin Delany and Henry McNeal Turner, who advocated separation from the white race; and John Brown, who believed nothing short of a violent overthrow of the slave system would yield any meaningful results. Frederick Douglass, who opposed efforts like those suggested by Brown, pushed for African Americans to seek rights through assimilation. The ultimate compromise between the two factions was proposed in 1853 when the Colored National Convention in Rochester, New York, advanced the idea of a separate African American society on American soil.

The Union victory in the Civil War and the abolition of slavery under President Abraham Lincoln consolidated African American political support in the Republican Party. This affiliation lasted throughout the end of the nineteenth century and into the early decades of the twentieth century—even after the Republicans began to loosen the reins on the Democratic South in 1876 after the last federal troops were removed.

During the Reconstruction era, from 1865 to 1877, African Americans made significant gains towards increased participation in the political process. Both the Civil Rights Acts of 1866 and 1870 and the Fourteenth Amendment—ratified by the States in 1868—to the Constitution were intended to provide full citizenship with all its rights and privileges to all African Americans. Among the rights that had been denied prior to these acts were the right to sue and be sued, the right to own real and personal property, and the right to testify and present evidence in legal proceedings. The Fifteenth Amendment, ratified in 1870, granted African American men the right to vote. The voting rights amendment failed, however, in its attempts to guarantee African Americans the real freedom to choose at the ballot box. Poll taxes, literacy tests, gerrymandered districts, and grandfather clauses were established by some state and local governments to deny African Americans their right to vote. The poll tax, for example, would not be declared unconstitutional until 1964, with the passage of the Twenty-fourth Amendment. Black codes also restricted the newly won freedom of African Americans by controlling their ability to move about the country, in spite of the fact that the Civil Rights Act of 1875 outlawed racial discrimination in hotels, inns, theaters, and other places of entertainment and public transportation.

Even though these legalized forms of exclusion presented obstacles to African American advancement in the politics of the United States, African Americans were able to achieve a degree of political participation during the Reconstruction era shortly after the end of the Civil War. More than 1,000 African Americans served in local and state elected offices, including 20 African American U.S. Congressmen between 1879 and 1901, two senators, a governor, six lieutenant governors, and numerous state and local officials. In 1869, Ebenezer Don Carlos Bassett became the first African American diplomat when he was appointed consul general to Haiti. In 1870 the Mississippi legislature elected Hiram R. Revels to represent the state in the U.S. Senate after that state was readmitted to the Union. Serving just over a year, Revels was the first African American U.S. senator. Blanche K. Bruce became the first African American elected to the U.S. Senate for a full six-year term in 1874. P. B. S. Pinchback won a U.S. Senate seat in 1873, but a vote by the other senators ousted him in 1876. The same thing happened one year earlier when, in 1875, Pinchback was removed from a House seat to which he had been elected in 1872.

A flashy, colorful individual, Pinchback made enemies because of a gambling habit and his strong stand in support of equal rights for African Americans. Pinchback was the nation's first African American governor. Named lieutenant governor of Louisiana in 1871, Pinchback became acting governor after the impeachment of Governor Warmouth on bribery charges. Pinchback served just 43 days and when the new election was held, Pinchback was defeated.

Reconstruction came to an end in 1877 after considerable controversy about the 1876 presidential election. Rutherford Hayes, the Republican, claimed victory based on the electoral college vote, while Democratic candidate Samuel Tilden made a claim to the presidency due to the popular vote. Furthermore, the

Ebenezer D. Bassett, minister to Haiti.

First African American Senator and Representatives, in the 41st and 42nd Congress of the United States.

election results from Florida, South Carolina, and Louisiana were disputed. Hayes was declared the winner, but the controversy weakened the federal government's role in Southern politics and the civil rights process. As the government in Washington, D.C., withdrew support for the progressive policies on race instituted during the era of Reconstruction, African Americans witnessed a swift decline in their political power and an increased infringement on their civil rights. This assault was expressed in various ways such as the Jim Crow laws, voting rights abuses, and physical violence, including nearly 3,500 lynchings between 1889 and 1922. The lynchings occurred primarily in the southern states of Alabama, Georgia, Louisiana, and Mississippi, but also in some northern cities. After Reconstruction and with the elimination of African Americans from most southern electoral politics by 1889, most Blacks were fighting against disenfranchisement in the South and seeking Congressional support to prevent violations of their hard-won constitutional rights. In the post-Reconstruction period, there were more African Americans appointed to government or political posts than were elected. One exception was Oscar DePriest, who became the first African American elected to Congress in

the twentieth century when he claimed a seat in 1928. His career began in 1915, when he was elected to the Chicago city council with the backing of the Republican machine.

During the nineteenth century most African Americans were supporters of the Republican Party, but as the century drew to a close, a backlash occurred. In the 1890s, a group of white Republicans calling themselves the "Lily Whites" were heavily opposed to rights for African Americans and thus resented the presence of the so-called "Black and Tan Republicans" in their party. African Americans migrating from the south to the north and were becoming increasingly disenchanted with the Republican Party and its efforts to gain support from conservative white voters. Further there was no support from the Republican Party when issues of race arose in northern cities. African Americans began to question what were the benefits of supporting Republican Party and its candidates, although they remained remain locked into a pattern of almost automatic support of Republicans until the late 1920s.

By the turn of the twentieth century, Booker T. Washington had gained prominence as the chief spokesperson on the state of African Americans. Recognized throughout the United States as a prominent African American leader and mediator, he advocated accommodationism as the preferred method of attaining civil rights. His leading opponents included journalist Thomas T. Fortune, an African American historian, and author W. E. B. Du Bois.

Fortune, who had founded the *New York Freeman* newspaper in 1884, attempted to create a national political organization for African Americans. His short-lived, Chicago-based National Afro-American League was aimed at remedying the disenfranchisement of African Americans. Du Bois, on the other hand, felt it was necessary to take more aggressive measures in the fight for equality. In addition to participating in the first Pan-African Conference (London) in 1900, in 1905 he spearheaded the Niagara Movement, a radical African American intellectual forum. Members of the group merged with white progressives four years later to form the National Association for the Advancement of Colored People (NAACP). After Washington's death in 1915, the NAACP became a greater force in the struggle for racial reform.

Women played a significant role at the turn of the century as well, coming together as the National Association of Colored Women in 1896. The female activists met with success in their agitation for rights. Standouts included founder Mary Church Terrell and presidents Ida B. Wells-Barnett and Mary McLeod Bethune. Chief among their causes were speaking out against lynching and the promotion of women's rights.

Racist attitudes, combined with the desperate economic pressures of the Great Depression, exerted a profound effect on politics nationwide during the 1930s. Democrat Franklin Delano Roosevelt won the presidency in 1932 with his reform agenda. He attracted African American voters with his "New Deal" relief and recovery programs. For 70 years African Americans had been faithful to the Republican Party, but their belief in Roosevelt and his New Deal led many to switch to the Democratic Party. African Americans, as well as others benefited from the housing and employment opportunities that came about as a result of Roosevelt's programs. As beneficiaries of these new programs, African Americans saw a direct link between their votes for the Democratic Party and jobs, housing, and other benefits to their community. By 1936, most African Americans had switched to the Democratic Party.

The Communist Party of the United States of America offered an alternative for African Americans alienated by the Republicans and the Democrats. White Communists actively recruited African Americans to their ranks, supporting civil rights through demonstrations and boycotts. They even selected an African American, James Ford, as their vice presidential candidate during the U.S. presidential campaigns of 1932, 1936, and 1940.

World War II ushered in an era of unswerving commitment to the fight for civil rights. As African Americans migrated to the North in search of jobs, several urban entities gained new concentrations of African Americans. In cities such as Detroit, New York, Philadelphia, and Cleveland, African Americans had such a presence that the course of local politics was often swayed by the influence of their vote. At times the African American vote affected the balance of power on the national front as well.

Adam Clayton Powell Jr. was elected to the New York City Council in 1941. By 1944, Powell had gained a seat in the U.S. House of Representatives. As a House member, he challenged a white racist representative who refused to sit next to him. During his tenure he also initiated legislation against lynching, poll taxes, and discriminatory job hiring practices. The so-called "Powell Amendment" referred to his attempts to tack anti-discriminatory measures onto each and every measure that came before the House.

African Americans were advancing in all areas—national associations, political organizations, unions, the federal branch of the U.S. government, and the nation's court system. President Harry S. Truman contributed to African American advancement by desegregating the military, establishing fair employment practices in the federal service, and beginning the trend toward integration in public accommodations and housing. In 1949, Rep. William L. Dawson became the first African American to head a standing committee of Congress when he was elected chairman of House Expenditures. Meanwhile, the civil rights proposals of the late 1940s came to fruition a decade later during President Dwight D. Eisenhower's administration. Eisenhower's administrative aide, E. Frederic Morrow, was the first African American granted an executive position among White House staff.

The Civil Rights Act of 1957, also known as the Voting Rights Act of 1957, was the first major piece of civil rights legislation passed by Congress in more than eight decades. It expanded the role of the federal government in civil rights matters and established the U.S. Commission on Civil Rights to monitor the protection of African Americans' civil rights. The commission determined that unfair voting practices persisted in the South with African Americans still being denied the right to vote in certain Southern districts. Because of these abuses, a second act was passed in 1960 that offered more protection to African Americans at the polls. In 1965, the third Voting Rights Act was passed to eliminate literacy tests and safeguard African Americans' rights during the voter registration process.

The post-war movement for African American rights yielded slow but significant advances in school desegregation and suffrage despite bold opposition from some whites. By the mid- to late-1950s, as the African American fight for equality and progress gained momentum, white resistance continued to mount. The Reverend Martin Luther King Jr. took the helm of the fledgling civil rights movement and launched a multiracial effort to eliminate segregation and achieve equality for blacks through nonviolent resistance. The movement began with the boycott of city buses in Montgomery, Alabama, and by 1960, became a national crusade for black rights. During the course of the next decade, civil rights workers organized economic boycotts of racist businesses and attracted front-page news coverage with African American voter registration drives and anti-segregationist demonstrations, marches, and sit-ins. Bolstered by the new era of independence that was sweeping through sub-Saharan Africa, the movement for African American equality gained international attention.

Racial tensions in the South reached violent levels with the emergence of new white supremacist organizations and an increase in Ku Klux Klan activity. Racially motivated discrimination in all arenas—from housing to employment—rose as Southern resistance to the Civil Rights movement intensified. By the late 1950s, racist hatred had once again degenerated into brutality and bloodshed with African Americans being murdered for the cause, and their white killers escaping punishment.

Democrat John F. Kennedy gained the African American vote in the 1960 presidential elections. His domestic agenda espoused an expansion of federal action in civil rights cases, especially through the empowerment of the U.S. Department of Justice on voting rights issues and the establishment of the Committee on Equal Employment Opportunity. Civil rights organizations continued their peaceful assaults against barriers to integration, but African American resistance to racial injustice was escalating. The protest movement heated up in 1961 when groups such as the Congress of Racial Equality (CORE), the Student Non-Violent Coordinating Committee (SNCC), and the Southern Christian Leadership Conference (SCLC) organized "freedom rides" that defied segregationist policies on public transportation systems.

Major demonstrations were staged in Birmingham, Alabama, under the leadership of King. Cries for equality met with harsh police action against the African American crowds. In 1963, Mississippi's NAACP leader, Medgar Evers, was assassinated. Meanwhile, on August 28, 1963, more than 200,000 black and white demonstrators convened at the Lincoln Memorial to push for the passage of a new civil rights bill. This historic "March on Washington," highlighted by King's legendary "I Have a Dream" speech, brought the promise of stronger legislation from the president.

After Kennedy's assassination that November, President Johnson finally instigated an aggressive civil rights program. The passage of the Civil Rights Act of 1964 sparked violence throughout the country, including turmoil in the cities of New York, New Jersey, Pennsylvania, and Illinois. The Ku Klux Klan stepped up its practice of intimidation with venomous racial slurs, cross burnings, firebombings, and acts of murder.

The call for racial reform in the South became louder early in 1965. King, who had been honored with the Nobel Peace Prize for his commitment to race relations, commanded the spotlight for his key role in the 1965 Freedom March from Selma to Montgomery, Alabama. African Americans were disheartened, however, by the lack of true progress in securing civil rights. Despite the legislative gains made over two decades, economic prospects for African Americans were bleak.

African American discontent over economic, employment, and housing discrimination reached frightening proportions in the summer of 1965, with rioting in the Watts section of Los Angeles. This event marked a major change in the temper of the civil rights movement. Nearly one decade of nonviolent resistance had failed to remedy the racial crisis in the United States and a more militant reformist element began to emerge. "Black Power" became the rallying cry of the middle and late 1960s, and more and more civil rights groups adopted all-black leadership. King's assassination in 1968 only compounded the nation's explosive racial situation. The new generation of African American leaders seemed to champion independence and separatism for African Americans rather than integration into white American society.

Although many African Americans despaired of winning justice within the American political system during this time of turmoil, there were some who continued to work within the system on behalf of their brethren. Through the 1960s, some prominent African Americans served as members of Congress. Shirley Chisholm was elected to the U.S. House of Representatives in 1968, making her the first African American woman to serve in Congress. The next year, Charles Diggs Jr., a member of the U.S. House of Representatives, founded the Democratic Select Committee, a group comprised of the eight other African American members of Congress. Two years later they renamed themselves the Congressional Black Caucus (CBC). Small gains were also made with the elections of Carl

Stokes in 1967 and Richard Hatcher in 1972 as the first African American mayors of Cleveland, Ohio, and Gary, Indiana, respectively.

In 1970 the creation of the Joint Center for Political Studies, geared towards monitoring political developments in the African American community, became the CBC's most important political contribution. Data provided by the Joint Center for Political Studies assisted the Reverend Jesse Jackson during his 1984 presidential campaign. After its founding, the center expanded to include economic studies and currently operates as the Joint Center for Political and Economic Studies. The CBC also laid the groundwork for TransAfrica, a 40,000-person organization dedicated to African American foreign affairs. Founded by Randall Robinson in 1977, TransAfrica came about after the CBC protested against U.S. governmental policy towards minority white rule in such African nations as Rhodesia. Meeting with 130 leaders in September of 1976, the CBC helped Robinson's initiative gain credibility. In the 1990s, the CBC produced such leaders as Kweisi Mfume, who would later head the NAACP.

In the late 1970s, President Jimmy Carter moved stridently to help African Americans. During his tenure he appointed African Americans to key cabinet positions. For example, Andrew Young was named a United Nations ambassador and Patricia Roberts Harris was first the secretary of Housing and Urban Development and then secretary of Health, Education, and Welfare. Fear of black advancement led many whites to shift their allegiance to the Republican Party in the late 1960s. With the exception of Carter's term in office from 1977 to 1981, Republicans remained in the White House for the rest of the 1970s and 1980s. The rise of conservatism gave birth to such important figures as African American conservatives Thomas Sowell, Anne Wortham, and Shelby Steele. A new era of African American liberal activity began with the institution of Reverend Jesse Jackson's Rainbow Coalition. Despite two unsuccessful campaigns for the presidency in the 1980s, Jackson helped swing the pendulum back in favor of liberalism. In 1992, a Democrat, Bill Clinton, was elected president.

After a dozen years of conservatism under Presidents Ronald Reagan and George Bush, Clinton projected a moderate image. Clinton espoused policies that would cut across the lines of gender, race, and economics and offered a vision of social reform, urban renewal, and domestic harmony for the United States. Once in office, Clinton appointed African Americans to key posts in his cabinet, and the African American population began wielding unprecedented influence in government.

In the 1990s, African American participation in government and politics was significant. In 1990, Gary Franks became the only black Republican in Congress when he earned a seat in the U.S. House. He was joined four years later by J. C. Watts Jr., an ordained Baptist minister, but Watts left the Democratic Party in 1989 and declined membership in the liberal CBC.

The year of 1992 saw the election of the first black woman, Carol Mosley Braun, to the U.S. Senate. She shocked political observers by scoring a stunning upset over incumbent Senator Alan Dixon in the Democratic primary on March 17, 1992. In the 1992 November election, she was elected senator. Her term was marred by scandal, however, and she was defeated in 1998 in her bid for reelection.

President Bill Clinton's cabinet included a record number of African Americans. Jesse Brown became the first African American to head the Veterans Affairs Department; Lee P. Brown was selected as head of the Office of National Drug Control Policy; Ron Brown was chosen as secretary of commerce; Dr. Joycelyn Elders was named U.S. surgeon general; Michael Espy was awarded the position of secretary of agriculture; Hazel O'Leary was chosen as secretary of energy; Rodney Slater was appointed secretary of transportation; and Clifton Wharton Jr. became the deputy secretary of the state department. Clinton also nominated a number of African Americans to major positions in federal government agencies including Jacqueline L. Williams-Bridgers to the State Department as inspector general and Shirley A. Jackson to the Nuclear Regulatory Commission as chairperson. As director of the White House Office of Public Liaison, African American Alexis Herman was one of the president's most trusted advisors. Also during Clinton's regime, the Justice Department's Civil Rights Division was headed by Deval Patrick, an African American.

In 1996, Alan Keyes became the first African American Republican in modern times to seek the nomination of the party for the presidency. Keyes attracted little notice, however, and faded from the spotlight. After the reelection of President Clinton, the Supreme Court dealt African Americans a blow in a series of cases that invalidated "Black majority" congressional districts. These gerrymandered districts were created to ensure African Americans were elected to the U.S. House of Representatives. The Court ruled several times—including *Reno, U.S. Attorney General, v. Bossier Parish School Board* in 1999—that race could not be the only factor in creating a district.

1971 U.S. House Black Caucus press conference, including (l-r) George Collins, Ronald Dellums, Shirley Chisholm, William Clay, Charles Diggs, Augustus Hawkins, Parren Mitchell and Walter Fauntroy.

The Democratic Party has relied on African American voters to sustain Democratic candidates in tough elections. In the 1998 congressional elections, the Democrats, crippled by the personal, ethical, and legal scandals surrounding President Clinton, relied on the African American vote to prevent any losses in either chamber of Congress. Republican leaders acknowledged after the election that they needed to reach out to the African American community.

In large part, the presidential election in 2000 confirmed the importance of the African American vote to the Democratic Party and to presidential candidate and then-Vice President Al Gore. Though the election took place on November 7, 2000, the outcome of the election was not official until December 12 when the U.S. Supreme Court decided that hand recounts of votes should be suspended immediately because the recount was unconstitutional. With that decision, the Supreme Court ended the controversy over chads, dimpled and pregnant ballots, and premature calls of the winner of

the presidential election by the major networks. Many voters still feel that Al Gore won the popular vote and that the manual recounts of Miami-Dade, Broward, Palm Beach, and Volusia Counties would have determined his victory. What is known is that many African American and some new immigrant voters experienced unprecedented scrutiny and some harassment in their efforts to vote. Whether there was a conspiracy to deny African Americans and others the right to vote remained hotly debated into the year 2002. As a result of this election debacle, reforms were discussed not only in Florida, but nationally.

George W. Bush, a Republican, became the 45th president of the United States as a result of the hotly-contested election. While he had not appointed as many African Americans and other minorities as President Clinton, his appointments had been in very significant and non-traditional departments. Colin L. Powell, a retired four-star general, became the first African American head of the U.S. Department of State, making him

Leon Sullivan, Coretta Scott King, Randall Robinson, and U.S. Representatives Walter Fauntroy and William Gray meet to advocate for South African sanctions legislation.

the top diplomat in the country. Rodney Paige also was the first African American to hold his post when President Bush named him secretary of the Education Department. Another significant appointment of a high-ranking African American by the Bush administration was his selection of Condoleeza Rice, former provost of Stanford University and a Soviet scholar, as his national security advisor. As a result of these major appointments and the growing number of young, conservative African Americans, there is a re-examining of the African American community's relationship with the Democratic Party. For the foreseeable future, however, African Americans will continue to be closely allied with the Democratic Party while pursuing options to maximize their political interests.

◆ CONGRESSIONAL BLACK CAUCUS MEMBERS (107TH U.S. CONGRESS)

Sanford Bishop
Georgia, 2nd District
2429 Rayburn H.O.B.
Washington, DC 20515

(202) 225–3631

Corrine Brown
Florida, 3rd District
2444 Rayburn H.O.B.
Washington, DC 20515
(202) 225–0123

Julia Carson
Indiana, 10th District
1339 Longworth H.O.B.
Washington, DC 20515
(202) 225–4011

Donna Christian-Christensen
Virgin Islands, Delegate
1510 Longworth H.O.B.
Washington, DC 20515
(202) 225–1790

William "Lacy" Clay Jr.
Missouri, 1st District
415 Cannon H.O.B.
Washington, DC 20515
(202) 225–2406

Members of the Congressional Black Caucus speaking to the press outside the U.S. Capitol in 1980: William Gray, Charles Rangel, Cardiss Collins, Walter Fauntroy, and Bennett Stewart.

Eva Clayton
North Carolina, 1st District
2440 Rayburn H.O.B.
Washington, DC 20515
(202) 225–3101

James Clyburn
South Carolina, 6th District
319 Cannon H.O.B.
Washington, DC 20515
(202) 225–3315

John Conyers
Michigan, 14th District
2426 Rayburn H.O.B.
Washington, DC 20515
(202) 225–5126

Elijah Cummings
1st Vice-Chair
Maryland, 7th District
1632 Longworth H.O.B.
Washington, DC 20515
(202) 225–4741

Danny K. Davis
Illinois, 7th District
1222 Longworth H.O.B.
Washington, DC 20515
(202) 225–5006

Chaka Fattah
Pennsylvania, 2nd District
1205 Longworth H.O.B.
Washington, DC 20515
(202) 225–4001

Harold Ford Jr.
Tennessee, 9th District
325 Cannon H.O.B.
Washington, DC 20515
(202) 225–3265

Alcee Hastings
Florida, 23rd District
2235 Rayburn H.O.B.
Washington, DC 20515
(202) 225–1313

Earl Hilliard
Alabama, 7th District
1314 Longworth H.O.B.
Washington, DC 20515
(202) 225–2665

Jesse Jackson Jr.
Illinois, 2nd District
313 Cannon H.O.B.
Washington, DC 20515
(202) 225–0773

Sheila Jackson-Lee
2nd Vice-Chair
Texas, 18th District
410 Cannon H.O.B.
Washington, DC 20515
(202) 225–3816

William Jefferson
Louisiana, 2nd District
240 Cannon H.O.B.
Washington, DC 20515
(202) 225–6636

Eddie Bernice Johnson
Chair
Texas, 30th District
1511 Longworth H.O.B.
Washington, DC 20515
(202) 225–8885

Stephanie Tubbs Jones
Ohio, 11th District
1516 Longworth H.O.B.
Washington, DC 20515
(202) 225–7032

Carolyn Kilpatrick
Michigan, 15th District
1610 Longworth H.O.B.
Washington, DC 20515
(202) 225–2261

Barbara Lee
California, 9th District
426 Cannon H.O.B.
Washington, DC 20515
(202) 225–2661

John Lewis
Georgia, 5th District
343 Cannon H.O.B.
Washington, DC 20515
(202) 225–3801

Cynthia McKinney
Georgia, 4th District
124 Cannon H.O.B.
Washington, DC 20515
(202) 225–1605

Carrie Meek
Florida, 17th District
2433 Rayburn H.O.B.
Washington, DC 20515
(202) 225–4506

Gregory Meeks
Whip
New York, 6th District
1710 Longworth H.O.B.
Washington, DC 20515
(202) 225–3461

Juanita Millender-McDonald
California, 37th District
125 Cannon H.O.B.
Washington, DC 20515
(202) 225–7924

Eleanor Holmes Norton
District of Columbia, Delegate
2136 Rayburn H.O.B.
Washington, DC 20515
(202) 225–8050

Major Owens
New York, 11th District
2309 Rayburn H.O.B.
Washington, DC 20515
(202) 225–6231

Donald Payne
New Jersey, 10th District
2209 Rayburn H.O.B.
Washington, DC 20515
(202) 225–3436

Charles Rangel
New York, 15th District
2354 Rayburn H.O.B.
Washington, DC 20515
(202) 225–4365

Bobby Rush
Secretary
Illinois, 1st District
2416 Rayburn H.O.B.
Washington, DC 20515
(202) 225–4372

Robert Scott
Virginia, 3rd District
2464 Rayburn H.O.B.
Washington, DC 20515
(202) 225–8351

Bennie Thompson
Mississippi, 2nd District
2432 Rayburn H.O.B.
Washington, DC 20515
(202) 225–5876

Edolphus Towns
New York, 10th District
2232 Rayburn H.O.B.
Washington, DC 20515
(202) 225–5936

Maxine Waters
California, 35th District
2344 Rayburn H.O.B.
Washington, DC 20515
(202) 225–2201

Diane E. Watson
California, 32nd District
2413 Rayburn H.O.B.
Washington, DC 20515
(202) 225–7084

Melvin Watt
North Carolina, 12th District
2236 Rayburn H.O.B.
Washington, DC 20515
(202) 225–1510

Albert R. Wynn
Maryland, 4th District
434 Cannon H.O.B.
Washington, DC 20515
(202) 225–8699

◆ GOVERNMENT OFFICIALS

(To locate biographical profiles more readily, please consult the index at the back of the book.)

Dennis Archer (1942–)
Municipal Government Official, Attorney

Former Michigan State Supreme Court justice Dennis Archer became mayor of Detroit on January 3, 1994. During his campaign he promised better city services, a tougher stance on crime, and increased incentives for businesses choosing to locate in the city. Following Coleman Young's combative reign, Archer represented a distinct change.

Archer was born on January 1, 1942, in Detroit. The family moved to Cassopolis, Michigan, when he was an infant. After graduating from Cassopolis High School in 1959, Archer worked his way through college. Following studies at Wayne State University and the Detroit Institute of Technology, Archer received his B.S. from Western Michigan University in 1965.

For a time Archer worked with emotionally impaired children. While teaching he met Trudy DunCombe, who became his wife in 1967. Archer was able to earn a J.D. from the Detroit College of Law in 1970. He practiced law for several years as a partner with Hall, Stone, Allen, Archer & Glenn and then with Charfoos, Christensen & Archer, until he was appointed to the Michigan Supreme Court by then-Governor James Blanchard.

Archer had been active in Democratic politics in the late 1970s and early 1980s, directing campaigns for Mayor Coleman Young and Congressman George Crocket Jr. His wife, who had also gone through law school and had become a district court judge, supported her husband's decision to run for mayor. Facing Coleman Young, a city fixture, was a daunting proposition, even for one with the impressive political ties Archer had garnered over the years. Archer's tough decision to face Young became a moot point when Young decided not run for a sixth term. Young did, however, back Archer's rival, Sharon McPhail.

The race became sullied when McPhail suggested that Archer, who many considered to be a mild-mannered, upper-class elitist, was the candidate of white businessmen. Archer balanced these assessments by recalling the hard times of his early life as well as by going on record in support of the city's disenfranchised, including children and the homeless. Archer went on to win the election with 57 percent of the vote compared to McPhail's 43 percent, although she had also won 52 percent of the African American vote.

One of Archer's first aims was to heal the racial breaches in the community by bringing his constituents together with common goals. Archer used his influence with the Clinton administration to capture a chunk of federal monies to be used for creating empowerment zones throughout the city. The high profile 1994 G-7 Jobs Conference was held in Detroit. Archer challenged Governor Engler's veto of a decision by Detroit voters to build a casino downtown. He also managed to hammer out a deal with the Major League Baseball's Detroit Tigers, who had threatened to leave the city if a compromise could not be reached in regard to building a new stadium in the city.

Archer's first term was characterized by a robust economy, a balanced budget, a low unemployment rate, and downtown revitalization. Plans began for a new stadium for the Detroit Lions and temporary casinos were built. Perhaps the most important legacy of Archer's first term in office was the restoration of civic pride and confidence in the city and its future. Following his successful first term in office, Archer handily won a second term in 1997 with over 83 percent of the vote.

After his reelection school reform became Archer's priority. His plan required new legislation at the state level that would wrest power and control of the schools from the locally elected school board. Under the reform scheme, the mayor would have the authority to appoint a new school board and the top administrators. Other aspects of the proposal for educational reform include reduced class size; the hiring of 1200 new certified teachers; legislative benchmarks for assessing the school system's success or failure; mandatory summer school in particular cases; a substantial array of after-school programs; technical training for teachers; and site-based decision making.

In the spring of 1999, a group called "The Black Slate" spearheaded the effort to collect enough signatures to recall Archer. Backers of the recall cited factors such as the mayor's handling of a riverfront housing development project, problems with snow removal in January of 1999, damage done to Detroit's People Mover from the implosion of the J. L. Hudson building, and Archer's failure to grant one of Detroit's casino licenses to an African American. The recall effort failed.

Archer announced on April 16, 2001, that he would not seek a third term as mayor of Detroit. Following his tenure, Archer returned to the law firm of Dickinson Wright PLLC. As of 2002, he also served on the board of directors of Johnson Controls and Compuware.

Marion Barry (1936–)
Municipal Government Official

Marion Shepilov Barry was born in Itta Bena, Mississippi, on March 6, 1936, and grew up in Memphis, Tennessee. He earned a B.S. and M.S. in chemistry by 1960, and while a graduate student at Fisk University he became active in NAACP politics and the burgeoning civil rights movement. He eventually co-founded the famous Student Non-Violent Coordinating Committee, a civil rights protest group that made significant gains in erasing the last institutional vestiges of racism in the South. Barry was SNCC's first national chairperson.

After he moved to Washington, D.C., in the mid-1960s, Barry became active in local politics through efforts to move the capital city toward self-government

Marion Barry.

free from congressional interference. Among other achievements, he was instrumental in obtaining federal funding for a citywide youth employment and community service program and was elected to the local school board in 1970. When the "Free D.C." political movement succeeded in loosening congressional rule over the city, Barry ran for a seat on its first council, which he held for three years.

In 1977, Barry was wounded in an altercation involving the seizure of Washington's District Building by radical Muslims. Elected mayor in 1978, over the next few years his administration was marked by both controversy and achievement. His former wife was charged with embezzling federal funds, but Barry himself was never under any suspicion. As mayor, he initiated community-improvement programs to better employment opportunities and housing conditions for Washington's more disadvantaged neighborhoods. During Barry's administration, access increased for contracting opportunities with the city for women- and minority-owned businesses. One of the hallmarks of Barry's tenure as mayor was the launching of large numbers of youth development and summer employment programs.

He was reelected in 1982 and again in 1986. Near the end of his third term, Barry was indicted by a federal grand jury for drug possession. He was convicted of a misdemeanor for usage after being filmed snorting crack cocaine and served the maximum six months.

Despite the setback, Barry's support among his Washington, D.C., constituency did not diminish. In 1992, he again won a city council seat, and he ran successfully for mayor in 1994. His fourth term was sullied when Congress established a financial control board in 1995 to oversee the district's financial recovery. The city faced a growing debt in excess of $722 million. In 1997, Congress and the president extended the control board's power to nearly every facet of the D.C. government, thus stripping Barry of most of his executive power. He did not seek reelection.

Sidney John Barthelemy (1942–)
Sociologist, Municipal Government Official, State Legislator

Sidney Barthelemy was born in New Orleans on March 17, 1942. He attended Epiphany Apostolic Junior College from 1960 to 1963 and received a B.A. from the St. Joseph Seminary in 1967. Two years later he earned a M.S.W. from Tulane University. After graduation, Barthelemy worked in administrative and professional positions in various organizations including Total Community Action, the Parent-Child Development Center, Family Health Inc., and the Urban League of New Orleans. From 1972 to 1974, Barthelemy was the director of the Welfare Department of the City of New Orleans. In 1974, he was elected to the Louisiana State Senate. In 1978, Barthelemy left the state legislature after winning a seat on the New Orleans City Council, where he stayed until his 1986 election as mayor.

Barthelemy has taught at Xavier University as an associate professor of sociology from 1974 to 1986 at Tulane University and the University of New Orleans. He has been the vice-chairman for voter registration for the Democratic National Party, second vice president for the National League of Cities, and president of the Louisiana Conference of Mayors. Barthelemy belongs to the NAACP, National Association of Black Mayors, Democratic National Committee, National Institute of Education, National League of Cities, and the New Orleans Association of Black Social Workers. He has won numerous awards including Outstanding Alumnus of Tulane University, and the 1987 Louisiana Chapter of the National Association of Social Workers' Social Worker of the Year Award. He has also won the American Freedom Award presented by the Third Baptist

Church of Chicago (1987), the 1989 American Spirit Award given by the U.S. Air Force Recruiting Service, and the NAACP's New Orleans Chapter Daniel E. Byrd Award (1990).

In 1993, Barthelemy decided not to seek another term as mayor of New Orleans. He went back to teaching at Tulane and the University of New Orleans.

Sharon Sayles Belton (1951–)
Municipal Government Official

Belton was born in St. Paul, Minnesota, and attended Macalester College. She did not graduate as she dropped out when she became pregnant. Belton worked in the Twin Cities areas as a volunteer, eventually establishing a series of rape shelters in the area.

Her community involvement led her to pursue a city council seat in Minneapolis. She was elected to the city council in 1984, and represented the 8th ward. In 1993, Belton made the decision to run for mayor. She was endorsed by incumbent mayor Don Fraser and won nearly 60 percent of the vote, despite the fact that less than a quarter of the voters were African American.

As mayor, Belton continued to seek to build coalitions to solve the city's problems. This style was her hallmark as a member of city council. She appointed many women and minorities to positions of power within the city government, changing the political culture in Minneapolis. She was reelected to a second term in 1997, but lost a bid for a third in 2000.

In May 2002, Belton joined the University of Minnesota's Humphrey Institute of Public Affairs as a senior fellow in the Roy Wilkins Center for Human Relations and Social Justice.

Mary Frances Berry (1938–)
Educator, Federal Government Official, Civil Rights Activist, Attorney

Mary Frances Berry was born in 1938. She received her B.A. degree from Howard University in 1961 and her M.A. in 1962. In 1966, she received a Ph.D. from the University of Michigan, and her J.D. in 1970. Berry worked for several years as a professor of history and law at several universities throughout the United States. She was appointed assistant secretary of education in the U.S. Department of Health, Education, and Welfare by President Jimmy Carter in 1977. Prior to her service at HEW, Berry was provost at the University of Maryland College Park and chancellor at the University of Colorado at Boulder.

Sharon Sayles Belton.

In 1980 Berry became commissioner and vice-chairan of the U.S. Commission on Civil Rights. She was fired from the commission by President Ronald Reagan in 1983 for criticizing his civil rights policies. She sued him and won reinstatement in federal court. On November 19, 1993, President Bill Clinton named her chair of the Civil Rights Commission. In her role as chair, Berry led the investigation that examined minority voter disenfranchisement in Florida during the 2000 presidential election. She is the Geraldine R. Segal professor of American Social Thought at the University of Pennsylvania where she teaches law and history.

Berry has published numerous books and essays, including *The Pig Farmer's Daughter and Other Tales of American Justice: Episodes of Racism and Sexism in the Courts from 1865 to the Present*, in 1999; *Why ERA Failed: Politics, Women's Rights, and the Amending Process of the Constitution*, in 1986; and *The*

Politics of Parenthood: Child Care, Women's Rights and the Myth of the Good Mother, in 1993.

Unita Blackwell (1933–)
Municipal Government Official, Civil Rights Activist

Unita Blackwell was born on March 18, 1933, in the small Delta town of Lula, Mississippi. The daughter of sharecroppers, Blackwell's family constantly migrated between Arkansas, Mississippi, and Tennessee in search of work This transitory lifestyle lasted well into her early adulthood. Blackwell worked throughout the South at such jobs as chopping cotton and peeling tomatoes, until she finally settled in Mayersville, Mississippi, in 1962.

Initially, Blackwell's eighth-grade education kept her in the fields, but she also became involved with the

Mary Frances Berry.

Student Non-Violent Coordinating Committee's (SNCC) activities in Mississippi. Blackwell began canvassing the state on behalf of the organization, organizing and registering African American voters. In 1964, Blackwell joined fellow-activist Fannie Lou Hamer in the formation of the Mississippi Democratic Freedom Party. The party challenged the white-controlled Democratic political machine in the state, pushing for laws establishing black schools which would teach mathematics and science and preventing black children's employment as sharecroppers. In 1967, Blackwell co-founded Mississippi Action Community Education, an organization which promoted the incorporation of rural districts into towns, enabling them to get government aid in the installation of streetlights and electricity. Her work with the National Council of Negro Women in the early 1970s led to the building of low-income housing units throughout the South and in Puerto Rico.

When Blackwell was elected mayor of Mayersville in 1976, she became the first African American woman mayor in Mississippi. During her tenure, the city has acquired streetlights, paved roads, a fire truck, and a sewer system. She has also instituted an effective food

assistance program, and sponsored the construction of housing for the elderly and disabled. In 1982, Blackwell earned a master's degree in regional planning from the University of Massachusetts at Amherst. She was elected president of the National Conference of Black Mayors in 1990, a position she held until 1992.

Blackwell, who was also a fellow at Harvard University's John F. Kennedy School of Government in 1991, received a MacArthur Foundation "Genius Award" in 1992. She is also the recipient of a 1992 Southern Christian Leadership Award, and the American Planning Association's Leadership Award for elected officials in 1994.

Julian Bond (1940–)
State Representative, Lecturer, Civil Rights Activist, Organization Executive, State Senator, Educator, Media Personality, Media Executive

Throughout his career Julian Bond has been labeled everything from a national hero to a national traitor. He has faced violent segregationists and his own political and personal failures and scandals. He has, however,

Julian Bond.

remained an influential voice in politics, education, and the media.

Bond was born on January 14, 1940. His father, an eminent scholar and president of Lincoln University in Pennsylvania, wanted Julian to follow his footsteps into the world of academics. Although Julian attended fine private schools, he showed little desire for educational pursuits. In 1960, Bond attended Morehouse College in Atlanta where he was a mediocre student. While at Morehouse, however, Bond developed an interest in civil rights activism. He and several other students formed the Atlanta Committee on Appeal for Human Rights (COHAR). Along with other members, Bond participated in several sit-ins at segregated lunch counters in downtown Atlanta. The activities of Bond and his cohorts attracted the attention of Dr. Martin Luther King Jr. and the Southern Christian Leadership Conference. King invited Bond and other COHAR members to Shaw University in North Carolina to help devise new civil rights strategies. At this conference, the Student Non-Violent Coordinating Committee was created. SNCC eventually absorbed COHAR and Bond accepted a position as the SNCC director of communications. By 1965, Bond had grown tired of the SNCC and decided to embark on a new career in politics.

In 1965, Bond campaigned for a seat in the Georgia House of Representatives. He won the election and prepared to take his seat in the Georgia legislature. However, Bond was soon embroiled in a controversy when he announced that he opposed U.S. involvement in Vietnam and supported students who burned their draft cards to protest against the war. These statements outraged many conservative members of the Georgia House of Representatives and on January 10, 1966, they voted to prevent Bond's admission to the legislature. Bond sought legal recourse to overturn this vote and the case eventually went to the U.S. Supreme Court. On December 5, 1966, the Court ruled that the Georgia vote was a violation of Bond's First Amendment right of free speech and ordered that he be admitted to the legislature. The members of the Georgia House of Representatives reluctantly allowed Bond to take his seat, but treated him as an outcast.

In 1968, Bond and several other members of the Georgia Democratic Party Forum protested Governor Lester Maddox's decision to send only six African American delegates out of 107 to the Democratic National Convention. Bond and his supporters arrived at the convention and set up a rival delegation. After several bitter arguments with Georgia's official delegation, Bond's delegation captured nearly half of Georgia's delegate votes. He became the Democratic Party's first African American candidate for the U.S. vice presidency, but he did not meet the minimum age requirement.

From 1974 to 1989, Bond was president of the Atlanta branch of the NAACP. He was elected to the Georgia Senate in 1975 and remained a member until 1987. In 1976, he declined an invitation to become a part of President Jimmy Carter's administration. Bond ran for a seat in the U.S. Congress in 1986 but lost the election to John Lewis. In 1989, he divorced his wife after 28 years of marriage. During the bitter divorce, allegations of Bond's drug use surfaced. Shortly thereafter, he became embroiled in a paternity suit. He initially denied the allegations, but admitted in May of 1990 to fathering the child and was ordered to pay child support.

Bond has served as a visiting professor at Drexel and Harvard Universities. He is a lecturer and writer and is often called upon to comment on political and social issues. Bond has hosted a popular television program *America's Black Forum*, the oldest African American-owned show in television syndication; and narrated the highly acclaimed public television series *Eyes on the Prize*, as well as the 1992 documentary *The American Experience: Duke Ellington—Reminiscing in Tempo*. He has written a nationally distributed newspaper column. In 1994 he became involved in a power struggle with NAACP Board Chairman William Gibson, which cost Bond his position on the board. In 1998, Bond was elected chair of the NAACP board of directors and chair of the board of the NAACP's magazine *The Crisis*. He is currently a distinguished scholar in residence at American University and a lecturer in history at the University of Virginia.

In addition to his role as an active voice in American politics, Bond has written and edited many books, including *Mose T's Slapout Family Album* (1996) and *Lift Every Voice and Sing: A Celebration of the Negro National Anthem* (2000).

Thomas Bradley (1917–1998)
Civil Rights Activist, Municipal Government Official, Organization Executive, City Council Member, Attorney

Bradley was born December 29, 1917, in Calvert, Texas, the son of a sharecropper. In 1924 he moved with his family to Los Angeles. Bradley graduated from Polytechnic High School in 1937 and attended the University of California, Los Angeles, on an athletic scholarship. He excelled at track before quitting college in 1940 and joining the Los Angeles Police Department. While a member of the police force, Bradley worked as a detective, community relations officer, and in the department's juvenile division. In the early 1950s, Bradley began studying law at two Los Angeles

Tom Bradley, former mayor of Los Angeles, California.

colleges, Loyola University and later at Southwestern University. He was awarded an LL.B. from Southwestern University in 1956. Bradley stayed with the LAPD until 1961, when he entered private law practice.

In 1963, Bradley became the first African American elected to the Los Angeles City Council. He was reelected in 1967 and 1971. In the 1973 election Bradley became mayor of Los Angeles, winning 56 percent of the vote. During his time as mayor, Bradley compiled a record and was both lauded and criticized. Bradley's defenders credited him with opening city government to minorities and women, expanding social services to the urban poor, and spurring growth. During Bradley's tenure as mayor, Los Angeles overtook San Francisco as the West Coast's financial center and gained international prominence. Though Bradley is credited with turning Los Angeles into a modern metropolis, his detractors accused him of not keeping up with the city's problems.

One of the toughest situations Bradley faced was the occurrence of the 1992 riots that followed the announcement of "not guilty" verdicts for Los Angeles Police Department officers who were charged with beating African American motorist Rodney King. Bradley was vilified for what some considered to be his lack of response to the incident. Many demanded the firing of Police Chief Daryl Gates. Under the limits of the law, however, Bradley could do no more than ask Gates to resign. Though Gates eventually did leave his post, many considered the situation a serious challenge to Bradley's authority.

Bradley did attempt to heal the community in other ways. Even before the rioting had ended, he set up the nonprofit organization, Rebuild LA. That organization was criticized for creating unreal expectations, but Bradley's Neighbor to Neighbor group was viewed in a positive light. Comprised of nearly 800 volunteers, the outreach group regularly canvassed neighborhoods to give residents an outlet for discussing problems and to help citizens organize themselves in order to solve their own difficulties. In a second trial, two of four LAPD officers charged with violating King's civil rights were found guilty.

One of Bradley's final acts as a city official was to sign a bill that banned smoking in all restaurants. He was honored for his years of service by the U.S. Conference of Mayors in June of 1993. He officially left the mayoral post on July 1, 1993, effectively ending a 30-year public career. After his last term, Bradley returned to the private practice of law. He was then ensnared in a political finance scandal that also caught other California lawmakers, including Governor Pete Wilson and Senator Dianne Feinstein. Laundered campaign funds were traced to Evergreen America Corp., the world's largest container shipping company. Los Angeles's Ethics Commission ordered Bradley and others to repay a total of $15,000, but Bradley refused, claiming he did not know the money had been improperly donated.

Bradley served as president of the National League of Cities and the Southern California Association of Governments. He belonged to the Urban League of Los Angeles and was a founding member of the NAACP's Black Achievers Committee. On the national level he served on President Gerald Ford's National Committee on Productivity & Work Quality and on the National Energy Advisory Council. Bradley won numerous awards and honors including the 1974 University of California's Alumnus of the Year, the 1974 Thurgood Marshall Award, the 1978 Award of Merit given by the National Council of Negro Women, and the NAACP's 1985 Spingarn Medal.

Edward W. Brooke (1919–)
Attorney, Federal Legislator

Edward W. Brooke was born on October 26, 1919, in Washington, D.C. He moved to Massachusetts and, in a state that was overwhelmingly Democratic and in which African Americans constituted only 3 percent of the population, became a popular Republican figure. He first achieved statewide office in 1962 when he defeated Elliot Richardson to become attorney general. His record in that post led to his 1966 election to the Senate over former Massachusetts governor Endicott Peabody.

Born into a middle-class environment, Brooke attended public schools and went on to graduate from Howard. Inducted into an all-African American infantry unit during World War II, Brooke rose to the rank of captain and was ultimately given a Bronze Star for his work in intelligence. Returning to Massachusetts after the war, Brooke attended the Boston University Law School, compiling a top academic record and editing the *Law Review*. After law school, he established himself as an attorney and also served as chairman of the Boston Finance Commission.

Brooke was later nominated for the attorney general's office, encountering stiff opposition within his own party. He eventually won both the Republican primary and the general election against his Democratic opponent. In the Senate, Brooke espoused the notion that the Great Society could not become a reality until it was preceded by the "Responsible Society." He called this a society in which "it's more profitable to work than not to work. You don't help a man by constantly giving him more handouts."

When first elected, Brooke strongly supported U.S. participation in the Vietnam War, though most African American leaders were increasingly opposing it. However, in 1971, Brooke supported the McGovern-Hatfield Amendment that called for withdrawal of the United States from Vietnam. Matters of race rather than foreign affairs were to become Brooke's area of expertise. Brooke was a cautious legislator. However, as pressure mounted from the established civil rights groups and African American militants he decided to attack President Nixon's policies. Brooke was roused into a more active role by the administration's vacillating school desegregation guidelines, its firing of HEW official Leon Panetta, and the nominations to the Supreme Court of judicial conservatives Clement Haynsworth and G. Harrold Carswell.

In 1972, Brooke was reelected to the Senate overwhelmingly, even though Massachusetts was the only state not carried by his party in the presidential election. While Brooke seconded the nomination of President Richard M. Nixon at the 1972 Republican Convention, he became increasingly critical of the Nixon administration. He also began to appear publicly at meetings of the Congressional Black Caucus, a group

he had tended to avoid in the past. Brooke was considered a member of the moderate wing of the Republican Party. In 1978, Brooke's bid for a third term in the Senate was denied by Democrat Paul Tsongas. Brooke, the recipient of more than 30 honorary degrees and various awards, including the NAACP Spingarn Medal and the National Conference of Christians and Jews' Charles Evans Hughes Award, returned to private law practice following his Senate career.

Ron Brown (1941–1996)
Attorney, Federal Government Official, Organization Executive

Ronald H. Brown was born in Washington, D.C., on August 1, 1941, and raised in Harlem, NY. He attended White Plains High School and Rhodes and Walden Preparatory Schools. He graduated from Middlebury College in Middlebury, Vermont, with a B.A. in political science in 1962. Upon graduating, he enlisted in the U.S. Army where he achieved the rank of captain while serving in West Germany and Korea. In 1970, Brown graduated from New York City's St. John's University Law School.

Ron Brown, former Commerce Secretary.

While attending law school, Brown began working in 1988 for the National Urban League's job training center in the Bronx, New York. He continued with them until 1979, working as general counsel, Washington spokesperson, deputy executive director, vice president of Washington operations, and lobbyist. In 1980 he resigned to become chief counsel of the U.S. Senate Judiciary Committee. Largely because of his effectiveness as chief counsel of the Judiciary Committee, he became the general counsel and staff coordinator for Senator Edward Kennedy. Brown also became chief counsel for the Democratic National Committee (DNC) and subsequently the deputy chairman of the DNC. After his term as deputy chairman expired, Brown joined the law firm of Patton, Boggs & Blow.

In 1989 Brown was appointed chairman of the DNC, making him the first African American to head a major American political party. As head of the DNC, Brown proved to be a successful fund-raiser and an effective team builder. During Brown's tenure, Democrats elected an African American governor in Virginia and an African American mayor in New York City. Brown was also considered one of the architects of President Bill Clinton's 1992 election victory. In 1993, President Clinton appointed Brown commerce secretary. He was subsequently confirmed by the U.S. Senate, thus becoming the first African American secretary of commerce.

As commerce secretary, Brown was a leader in developing trade and economic policies which were sometimes controversial. He opened doors that allowed women and minorities to be more involved and aware of business opportunities through the Commerce Department. Brown's service as a cabinet member was marred somewhat by charges of financial impropriety and influence-peddling. An independent counsel was appointed to investigate the allegations. Brown's last official act was leading a group of American businessmen and women to war-torn Croatia so that they might assist in rebuilding the country. Brown died in a plane crash on April 3, 1996, near the Croatian coast.

Blanche K. Bruce (1841–1898)
Federal Government Official, Civil Rights Activist, Federal Legislator

Blanche Kelso Bruce was born a slave in Farmville, Prince Edward County, Virginia. He received his early formal education in Missouri, where his parents had moved while he was young, and may have studied at Oberlin College in Ohio. In 1868, Bruce settled in Floreyville, Mississippi, where he was a successful educator. He later worked as a planter and eventually built up a considerable fortune in property.

In 1870, Bruce entered politics and was elected sergeant-at-arms of the Mississippi Senate. A year later he was named assessor of taxes in Bolivar County. In 1872 he served as sheriff of the county and as a member of the Board of Levee Commissioners of Mississippi. Bruce was nominated for the U.S. Senate from Mississippi in February of 1874. He was elected, becoming the first African American person to serve a full term in the Senate. Bruce became an outspoken defender of the rights of minority groups, including the Chinese and Native Americans. In 1879, he became the first African American to preside over the Senate during a debate. He chaired the investigation into the failure of the Freedmen's Savings and Trust and worked for the improvement of navigation on the Mississippi in the hope of increasing interstate and foreign commerce. Bruce also supported legislation aimed at eliminating reprisals against those who had opposed African American emancipation.

After Bruce completed his term in the Senate in 1881, he failed to win a second term due to the loss of power and influence of the Radical Republicans in the South. He rejected an offer for a diplomatic post to Brazil, because slavery was still practiced there. In 1881, he was named register of the U.S. Treasury Department by President James A. Garfield. Bruce held this position until 1885 when the Democrats regained power. He wrote articles and lectured until 1889, when President Benjamin Harrison appointed him recorder of deeds for the District of Columbia. Bruce served as recorder of deeds until 1893, when he became a trustee for the District of Columbia public schools. In 1897, President William McKinley reappointed him to his former post as register of the treasury. Bruce died on March 17, 1898, in Washington, D.C.

Ralph J. Bunche (1904–1971)
Federal Government Official, Diplomat, Educator

The first African American to win the Nobel Peace Prize, Ralph Bunche was an internationally acclaimed statesman whose record of achievement places him among the most significant American diplomats of the twentieth century. Bunche received the Peace Prize in 1950 for his role in effecting a cease fire in the Arab-Israeli dispute.

Born in Detroit on August 7, 1904, Bunche graduated *summa cum laude* in 1927 with Phi Beta Kappa honors from UCLA. A year later he received his M.A. in government from Harvard. Soon thereafter he was named head of the Department of Political Science at Howard University until 1932 when he resumed his work toward his doctorate from Harvard. He later studied at

Ralph J. Bunche.

Northwestern University, the London School of Economics, and Capetown University. Before World War II broke out in 1939, Bunche did field work with the Swedish sociologist Gunnar Myrdal, author of the widely acclaimed *An American Dilemma*. During the war, he served initially as senior social analyst for the Office of the Coordinator of Information in African and Far Eastern Affairs, and was then reassigned to the African section of the Office of Strategic Services. In 1942, he helped draw up the territories and trusteeship sections ultimately earmarked for inclusion in the United Nations charter.

The single event that brought the name of Ralph Bunche into the international spotlight occurred soon after his appointment in 1948 as chief assistant to Count Folke Bernadotte, U.N. mediator in the Palestine crisis. With the latter's assassination, Bunche continued cease-fire talks between Egypt and Israel. After six weeks of intensive negotiations, Bunche worked out the "Four Armistice Agreements," which brokered an immediate cessation of the hostilities between the two combatants. Once the actual cease-fire was signed, Bunche received numerous congratulatory letters and

telegrams from many heads of state and was given a hero's welcome upon his return to the United States.

Bunche served as undersecretary of Special Political Affairs from 1957 to 1967. By 1968, Bunche had attained the rank of undersecretary general, the highest position ever held by an American at the United Nations. Bunche retired in October of 1971 and died on December 9, 1971. The library of the Department of State was dedicated and renamed in his honor in May of 1997 in recognition of his political and humanitarian contributions.

Yvonne Braithwaite Burke (1932–)
Attorney, State Legislator

Attorney and former California State Assemblywoman Yvonne Braithwaite Burke became the first African American woman from California ever to be elected to the House of Representatives in November of 1972. More than 20 years later, she became the first woman and African American to chair the Los Angeles County Board of Supervisors. Prior to her governmental career, Burke was a practicing attorney, during which time she served as a deputy corporation commissioner, a hearing officer for the Los Angeles Police Commissioner, and an attorney for the McCone Commission which investigated the Watts riots.

Born on October 5, 1932, in Los Angeles, Congresswoman Burke served in the State Assembly for six years prior to her election to Congress. During her final two years, she was chairperson of the Committee on Urban Development and Housing and a member of the Health, Finance and Insurance committees. As a state legislator, Burke was responsible for the enactment of bills that provided for needy children, relocation of tenants, owners of homes taken by governmental action, and which required major medical insurance programs to grant immediate coverage to newborn infants of the insured.

Burke's district, created in 1971 by the California legislature, was about 50 percent African American. In 1972, the district gave 64 percent of its vote to Burke. During Burke's first term in the House, she proved to be an ardent spokesperson for the downtrodden. She became a member of the Committee on Appropriations in December of 1974, and used her position on this committee to advocate an increase in funding for senior citizen services and community nutrition and food programs. Although her proposal for increased spending was defeated by the House of Representatives, Burke's efforts earned the respect of the African American community. In January of 1977, Burke worked diligently for the passage of the Displaced Homemakers Act, which proposed the creation of counseling programs and job training centers for women entering the work force for the first time.

In 1978, Burke resigned to run for attorney general in California. She lost the race but was appointed to the Los Angeles County Board of Supervisors. She resigned from the board in December 1980, and returned to her private law practice. Burke remained a prominent figure in California politics, taking on a number of civic responsibilities, including serving as a member of the University of California Board of Regents. In 1992, Burke was elected as chairperson of the Los Angeles County Board of Supervisors.

Chuck Burris (1951–)
Municipal Government Official

Burris was born in New Orleans in 1951, and was raised in Atlanta. He attended Morehouse College, and in 1971 he received his B.A. In 1975, he received his LL.B. from John Marshall Law School. Burris worked on several of the campaigns of Maynard Jackson and Andrew Young. He worked for the city of Atlanta as a member of the Crime Analyst Team and as budget officer. He was also affiliated with the city's housing department.

While working for the state of Georgia, Burris first discovered the town of Stone Mountain. The city was the birthplace of the modern Ku Klux Klan and had a large monument to the Confederacy carved on Stone Mountain. Burris moved to the town and, in 1991, won election to the city council. Burris was determined to change the town's image from intolerance to inclusiveness.

In 1997, Burris was elected as the mayor of Stone Mountain. The symbolic victory attracted national attention.

Bill Campbell (1954–)
Municipal Government Official

Bill Campbell was born in 1954 in Raleigh, North Carolina. Campbell became mayor of Atlanta in 1992 at the age of 40, signaling a new generation of leadership for the people of Atlanta.

In 1974, Campbell graduated *cum laude* from Vanderbilt University, completing a triple major (history, political science, and sociology) in just three years. He received his J.D. from Duke University in 1977 and went to work for an Atlanta law firm. Campbell worked from 1980 to 1981 for the U.S. Justice Department in Atlanta.

Campbell began his political career in 1981 when he served on the Atlanta City Council. He served three consecutive terms through 1993, co-sponsoring more than 300 pieces of legislation. By 1993, he had become a partner in an Atlanta law firm, along with serving as floor leader of the city council under Atlanta Mayor Maynard Jackson. When Jackson's health began to wane, Campbell was mentioned as a mayoral candidate. The importance of the mayoral election was heightened by the city's preparations for the 1996 Olympics.

The 1993 election for mayor included other city council members, former mayoral candidates, and 12 nonpartisan candidates. Campbell won 49 percent of the vote, shy of the 50 percent needed to win the office outright. He won the runoff election with 73 percent of the vote.

Campbell appointed Beverly J. Harvard the first female police chief of a major American city. He installed mini-police precincts in Atlanta's housing projects, planned alliances between the city and historically African American colleges, and encouraged young people to become active in community services. In 1996, Campbell hosted many dignitaries, including President Bill Clinton, in celebration of the tenth official holiday celebration of Martin Luther King Jr. Day. Campbell proposed a $150 million plan to repair Atlanta's infrastructure before the Olympics. Following the Olympics, Campbell's major efforts focused on downtown redevelopment, privatization of the Water Department, and a transformation of the housing authority in Atlanta from one of the worst in the nation.

Campbell won reelection as Atlanta's mayor in 1997. During his second term, he defended the city's affirmative action program, and won wide praise for his handling of a widely publicized shooting rampage that occurred in the city in 1999. In 2000, it was revealed that Campbell was under federal investigation in a corruption probe. Campbell could not seek a third-term in the office due to term limits. Following the inauguration of mayor-elect Shirley Franklin, Campbell announced that in addition to working in broadcasting, he would be seeking to set up a public policy center at an unspecified historically black college.

Shirley Chisholm (1924–)
Educator, Federal Legislator, Organization Executive, Civil Rights Activist

Shirley Chisholm was born November 30, 1924, in New York City. She graduated *cum laude* from Brooklyn College in 1946 with a B.A. in sociology and in 1952 from Columbia University with an M.A. in elementary education. She had an early career in child care and preschool education, culminating in her directorship of the Hamilton-Madison Child Care Center in New York.

From 1959 to 1964 she was a consultant to the Day Care Division of New York City's Bureau of Child Welfare.

In 1964, Chisholm was elected New York state assemblywoman, representing the 55th district in New York City. In 1968 she became the first African American woman elected to the U.S. House of Representatives, where she served until her retirement in 1982. In 1972, Chisholm announced her candidacy for the Democratic presidential nomination. She campaigned and entered primaries in 12 states, winning 28 delegates and 152 first ballot votes. Chisholm served as a delegate to the Democratic National Mid-Term Conference in 1974 and as a Democratic National Committee member. After retiring from politics Chisholm taught political science at Mount Holyoke College. In 1984, Chisholm co-founded the National Political Congress of Black Women. She spent the next year as a visiting scholar at Spelman College. In 1993, President Bill Clinton nominated Chisholm as ambassador to Jamaica, but due to declining health, she withdrew her name from further consideration.

Chisholm is the author of *Unbossed & Unbought* (1970) and *The Good Fight* (1973). She is a member of the NAACP, the National Association of Colored Women, and the League of Women Voters. She has won numerous awards including the 1965 Woman of Achievement Award presented by Key Women Inc. and the 1969 Sojourner Truth Award given to her by the Association for the Study of Negro Life and History.

William Clay (1931–)
Civil Rights Activist, Federal Legislator

William Clay, the first African American to represent the state of Missouri in the U.S. Congress, was born on April 30, 1931, in the lower end of what is now St. Louis's 1st District. Clay received a degree in political science at St. Louis University, where he was one of four African Americans in a class of 1,100. After serving in the U.S. Army until 1955, Clay became active in a host of civil rights organizations including the NAACP Youth Council and CORE. During this time he worked as a cardiographic aide, bus driver, and insurance agent.

In 1959 and 1963, Clay was elected alderman of the predominantly African American 26th Ward. During his first term, he served nearly four months of a nine-month jail sentence for demonstrations at a local bank. In 1964, Clay stepped down from his alderman's post to run for ward committeeman; he won and was reelected in 1968.

Clay's election platform in 1969 included a number of progressive, even radical, ideas. He advocated that all penal institutions make provisions for the creation of facilities in which married prisoners could set up house with their spouses for the duration of their sentences. He branded most testing procedures and diploma requirements, as well as references to arrest records and periods of unemployment, unnecessary obstacles complicating the path of a prospective employee. In his view, a demonstrated willingness to work and an acceptance of responsibility should be the criteria determining one's selection for a job.

Clay's last job before his election to Congress was as race relations coordinator for Steamfitters Union Local 562. Subjected to considerable criticism from other St. Louis African Americans who labeled the union racist, Clay pointed out that dramatic changes in the hiring practices of the union since he had joined it in 1966 were responsible for the employment of 30 African American steamfitters in St. Louis. Still, Clay conceded that the high-paying job had led him to reduce his active involvement with the civil rights struggle to some degree.

As a congressman, Clay sponsored many pieces of legislation including the Hatch Act Reform Bill, the City Earnings Tax Bill, the IRS Reform Bill, and the Family and Medical Leave Bill, which was the first bill that President Bill Clinton signed into law. In 1993 the Hatch Act, which Clay championed for two decades, was signed into law. Clay has served as chairman of the Subcommittee on Postal Operations and Civil Service, the House Education and Labor Committee, and the House Administration Committee. He has also been a member of the board of directors for Benedict College, Tougaloo College, and the Congressional Black Caucus Foundation. In 1990, Clay's first book, *To Kill or Not to Kill*, was published. In 1993, Clay published *Just Permanent Interests: Black Americans in Congress, 1870–1991*.

Eva Clayton (1934–)
Federal Legislator

Eva M. Clayton was born in Savannah, Georgia. Clayton earned a B.S. in 1955 from Johnson C. Smith University in Charlotte, North Carolina. She earned an M.S. in 1963 from North Carolina Central University. She later attended the University of North Carolina Law School.

Clayton first ran for a congressional seat in 1968 without success. She later worked for the campaign of Jim Hunt who was elected governor. Clayton was rewarded with the post of assistant secretary for community development. Clayton later worked in the Warren County public offices.

In 1992, she was elected representative from the First District of North Carolina. However, her district and others came under fire as racially gerrymandered districts. The district is no longer an African American-majority district. Clayton has still held her seat, and has become a member of the Budget Committee in the House.

Cardiss Collins (1931–)
Accountant, Federal Legislator, Civil Rights Activist

Collins was born Cardiss Robertson on September 24, 1931. She moved to Detroit and graduated from Commerce High School. Collins then moved to Chicago where she worked as a secretary for the state's Department of Revenue. She began studying accounting at Northwestern University and was promoted to accountant and then auditor.

In 1973, Collins was elected U.S. Representative from Illinois' 7th district. She was elected to fill the seat vacated by her husband George Collins, who was killed in an airplane crash. She became the first African American and the first woman to hold the position of Democratic whip-at-large. Collins served on congressional subcommittees dealing with consumer protection, national security, hazardous materials, narcotic abuse and control, and energy concerns. At various points, she also served as active secretary, vice chair, and chair of the Congressional Black Caucus. Collins was a proponent of civil rights, busing, and anti-apartheid legislation.

In 1994, the CBC Foundation elected her the group's chair. Early in 1995, Collins became the top Democrat on the Government Reform and Oversight Committee. On November 8, 1995, Collins announced her decision to retire after 23 years in the House; her 12 terms made her the longest-serving African American female member of Congress. Collins belongs to the NAACP, Chicago Urban League, Northern Virginia Urban League, National Women's Political Caucus, Alpha Kappa Alpha, Congressional Women's Caucus, Alpha Kappa Psi, Black Women's Agenda, and the National Council of Negro Women. Besides the degree she obtained from Northwestern in 1967, she has honorary degrees from Barber-Scotia College, Winston-Salem State University, and Spelman College. The Black Coaches Association (BCA) named Collins Sportsperson of the Year in 1994, after she supported the group's contention that standardized college entrance examinations are racially and culturally biased and, therefore, should not be used by the National Collegiate Athletic Association to establish athletic eligibility.

John Conyers (1929–)
Attorney, Federal Legislator, Federal Government Official, Civil Rights Activist, Organization Executive

Conyers was born in Detroit on May 16, 1929. In 1950, three years after graduating from high school, he enlisted in the U.S. Army as a private and served in Korea before being honorably discharged in 1957 as a second lieutenant. He attended Wayne State University in Detroit, and, after studying in a dual program, he received a B.A. in 1957 and a J.D. in 1958.

Conyers served as a legislative assistant to Congressman John Dingell Jr. from 1958 to 1961 and was a senior partner in the law firm of Conyers, Bell & Townsend from 1959 to 1961. In 1961, he took a referee position with the Michigan Workman's Compensation Department. In 1964, he won election as a Democrat to the U.S. House of Representatives. Conyers had long been active in the Democratic Party, belonging to the Young Democrats, University Democrats, and serving as a precinct delegate to the Democratic Party. After his election, Conyers was assigned to the powerful House Judiciary Committee. From that position he worked on legislation dealing with civil rights, Medicare, immigration reform, and truth-in-packaging laws. He was an early opponent of U.S. involvement in Vietnam and an early proponent of the Voting Rights Act of 1965.

In 1994, Conyers, the most senior African American member of Congress, supported a grass-roots movement comprised of nearly 1,000 individuals seeking reparations from the federal government on behalf of their slave ancestors. The participants held their fifth annual Conference on Reparations in Conyers's hometown of Detroit. Other prominent African Americans lending support included Reverend Jesse Jackson. In 1998 and 1999, Conyers served as the ranking Democrat on the House Committee of Impeachment.

Conyers has been vice-chairman of the National Board of Americans for Democratic Action and the American Civil Liberties Union. He is on the executive board of the Detroit Chapter of the NAACP and belongs to the Wolverine Bar Association. He is the recipient of the 1967 Rosa Parks Award and in 1969 received an honorary law degree from Wilberforce University.

Ronald V. Dellums (1935–)
Social Worker, Federal Legislator, Organization Executive, Lecturer

Ronald Dellums was born in Oakland, California, on November 24, 1935. After attending McClymonds and Oakland Technical High Schools, Dellums joined the U.S. Marine Corps in 1954 and was discharged after two years of service. He returned to school, receiving an associate of arts degree from Oakland City College in 1958, a B.A. from San Francisco State College in 1960, and an M.S.W. from the University of California at Berkeley in 1962.

For the next eight years, Dellums engaged in a variety of social work positions. He was a psychiatric social worker with the Berkeley Department of Mental Hygiene starting in 1962, and then two years later became the Bayview Community Center's program director. Dellums spent one year as director of the Hunters Point Youth Opportunity Center and one year as a consultant to the Bay Area Social Planning Council. In 1967, Dellums worked as a program director for the San Francisco Economic Opportunity Council. From 1968 to 1970, Dellums lectured at San Francisco State College and the University of California's School of Social Work. He also served as a consultant to Social Dynamics Inc.

Dellums was elected to the Berkeley City Council in 1967, and served until his election as a Democrat to the U.S. House of Representatives in 1971. As a representative he chaired the House Committee on the District of Columbia and served on the House Armed Services Sub-committee on Military Facilities and Installations as well as the Sub-committee on Military Research and Development. In 1983, Dellums wrote *Defense Sense: The Search for a Rational Military Policy.*

Dellums, who chaired the Defense Policy Panel, became the first African American to head the House Armed Services Committee on January 27, 1993. Once a militant pacifist, he was recognized as one of the most highly regarded members of Congress to extensively work towards U.S. demilitarization. Dellums chastised U.S. President Bill Clinton for giving in to fear and ignorance, when the president did not follow through on his promise to lift the ban on homosexuals in the military. Dellums retired in 1998 after 27 years in Congress and became president of Healthcare International Management Company.

Oscar Stanton DePriest (1871–1951)
County Commissioner, Federal Legislator

Oscar DePriest was the first African American to win a seat in the U.S. House of Representatives in the twentieth century. Born in Florence, Alabama, in 1871, DePriest moved to Kansas with his family at the age of six. His formal education consisted of business and bookkeeping classes that he completed before running away to Dayton, Ohio, with two white friends. By 1889, he had reached Chicago and become a painter and master decorator.

In Chicago, DePriest amassed a fortune in real estate and the stock market, and in 1904, he entered politics successfully when he was elected Cook County commissioner. In 1908, he was appointed an alternate delegate to the Republican National Convention and in 1915 became Chicago's first African American alderman. He served on the Chicago City Council from 1915 to 1917 and became Third Ward committeeman in 1924. In 1928, DePriest became the Republican nominee for the congressional seat vacated by fellow Republican Martin Madden. DePriest won the November election over his Democratic rival and an independent candidate to become the first African American from outside of the South to be elected to Congress.

Following his election to Congress, DePriest became the unofficial spokesman for the 11 million African Americans in the United States during the 1920s and 1930s. He proposed that states that discriminated against African Americans should receive fewer congressional seats. Also, he proposed that a monthly pension be given to ex-slaves over the age of 75. During the early 1930s, with the United States mired in the Depression, DePriest was faced with a difficult dilemma. Although he empathized with the plight of poor black and white Americans, he did not support the emergency federal relief programs proposed by President Franklin Roosevelt. Rather, DePriest and his fellow Republicans believed that aid programs should be created and implemented by individual states or local communities. DePriest's stance on the issue of federal relief programs dismayed many of his constituents. In 1934, he was defeated by Arthur Mitchell, the first African American Democrat elected to serve in Congress.

DePriest remained active in public life, serving from 1943 to 1947 as alderman of the Third Ward in Chicago. His final withdrawal from politics came about after a dispute with the Republican Party. DePriest returned to his real estate business, and he died on May 12, 1951.

Charles C. Diggs Jr. (1922–1998)
Former Federal Legislator

Charles Cole Diggs Jr. was born in Detroit on December 2, 1922. His father, an undertaker and funeral home owner, was elected into Michigan State Legislature in the 1940s. Diggs attended the University of Michigan and Fisk University in Nashville. After serving in the Air Force during World War II, he earned a B.S. in Mortuary Science from Wayne State University in 1946.

Upon receiving his degree, Diggs joined his father in the family mortuary business and soon followed him into politics. Diggs was elected to his father's seat in the state senate in 1951, and was elected to Congress in 1954 as a representative of Michigan's Thirteenth District.

Diggs was Michigan's first African American representative. During his early years in Congress, he emerged as a strong voice for the civil rights movement, attending the Emmett Till murder trial in Mississippi as an observer, calling for the desegregation of public transportation, and traveling to the flashpoint of Selma, Alabama in the 1960s. In 1969, Diggs was a key player in organizing the Congressional Black Caucus.

In the 1970s Diggs chaired the African Affairs Subcommittee of the House Committee on Foreign Relations. During this period he pressed for the elimination of apartheid segregation in South Africa, and advocated U.S. aid to newly independent African nations. TransAfrica, a "think tank" devoted to African affairs, was founded in Diggs's office in 1978. From 1973–1978 he held the chairmanship of the House District Committee, which was charged with overseeing the affairs of Washington, D.C. His work on the committee played a major role in the establishment of a home-rule government for the District of Columbia.

In 1978, Diggs was charged with illegally diverting $60,000 in office operating funds to pay his own personal expenses. He easily won reelection that year, but was soon convicted of the charges. Diggs was censured by the House and stripped of his committee memberships. He resigned his seat in 1980 after 25 years in Congress.

Following appeals of his conviction, Diggs served seven months in prison. He returned to the mortuary business following his release. During the 1980s, he earned a political science degree from Howard University, and also launched a brief comeback attempt with an unsuccessful run for a Maryland state legislative seat. Diggs died of a stroke in Washington, D.C., on August 24, 1998.

David Dinkins (1927–)
Attorney, Municipal Government Official, State Legislator

In September of 1989, David Dinkins surprised political observers by defeating incumbent Mayor Edward I. Koch in New York City's Democratic mayoral primary. Two months later, in the November election, he defeated Republican contender Rudolph Giuliani. Dinkins's victory marked the first time an African American was elected as mayor of New York. Dinkins thus faced the difficult task of leading a racially polarized and financially troubled city. While many supporters cited Dinkins's calm, professional demeanor as having a soothing effect upon New York's festering racial problems, others chided him for not responding forcefully enough to the many fiscal and social challenges facing the city.

David Dinkins was born in Trenton, New Jersey, in 1927. His parents separated when he was quite young and he moved to Harlem with his mother and sister. He returned to Trenton to attend high school. Following a stint in the U.S. Marines during World War II, he attended Howard University in Washington, D.C., and graduated in 1950 with a B.S. In 1956, Dinkins graduated from the Brooklyn Law School. He became an attorney, and, eventually, a partner in the law firm of Dyett, Alexander, Dinkins, Patterson, Michael, Dinkins, and Jones.

Dinkins's first foray into the world of politics occurred in 1965, when he won an election to the New York State Assembly. He served until 1967, but did not seek reelection after his district was redrawn. In 1972, Dinkins was appointed as president of elections for the City of New York and served for one year. Two years later, in 1975, he was appointed as city clerk and served until 1985. Dinkins ran for the office of Manhattan borough president in 1977 and 1981. He lost both elections by a wide margin. Dinkins ran again in 1985 and was elected. As Manhattan borough president, he was viewed as a mediator who tried to address a myriad of community concerns such as school decentralization, AIDS treatment and prevention services, and pedestrian safety.

As mayor, Dinkins remained true to the issues he had addressed as Manhattan borough president. Other causes he championed included tolerance and acceptance of gays and lesbians, economic parity for women and minorities, and affirmative action. Dinkins set up a program to provide government contracts to businesses owned by women and minorities. Though the program was blemished by faulty bookkeeping and by the complexity of determining which companies were truly eligible, Dinkins's successor kept it in place.

In 1991, when riots erupted between African Americans and Jews in the Crown Heights neighborhood, Dinkins entreated both sides to think about their actions and possible consequences rather than react to the emotional volatility surrounding an incident in which a Jewish man's automobile accidentally struck and killed an African American youth. When riots seized Los Angeles in 1992, most of the nation feared that the violence would spread to other large urban areas with mixed or predominately African American populations. But Dinkins was able to assuage his constituents and prevent the terror and destruction that incapacitated Los Angeles.

In November of 1993, Dinkins's bid for reelection fell short when he was narrowly defeated by Rudolph W. Giuliani. Dinkins left office on December 31, 1993. Poor management had been an Achilles heel of the Dinkins administration. In 1994, the New York Court of Appeals fined the city more than $3.5 million to compensate 5,000 homeless families forced to live in inadequate shelters. In 1994, Dinkins began hosting a radio talk show. Later in the year, he became a member of the AMREP Corp. board of directors and began teaching at Columbia University. Dinkins successfully underwent triple bypass heart surgery in 1995 and continues his professorship in the practice of public affairs in his role as senior fellow at the Barnard-Columbia Center for Urban Policy.

Julian C. Dixon (1934–2000)
Attorney, Federal Legislator, Women's Rights Activist

Julian C. Dixon was born August 8, 1934, in Washington, D.C. He served in the U.S. Army from 1957 to 1960, and received a B.S. in political science from California State University and an LL.B. from Southwestern University Law School in 1967. In 1972, Dixon was elected on the Democratic ticket to the California State Assembly. In 1978, he was elected to the U.S. House of Representatives.

While in the House of Representatives, Dixon served on the House Committee on Standards of Official Conduct, West Point Board of Supervisors, and the Appropriations Sub-Committee on Foreign Operations. He also chaired the Appropriations Sub-Committee on the District of Columbia. This latter appointment made Dixon the first African American to chair an appropriations sub-committee. Dixon was an original co-sponsor of the Equal Rights Amendment and was active in the Congressional Black Caucus.

Julian Dixon died on December 8, 2000, in Los Angeles, California, after suffering a heart attack. He was 66.

Michael Espy (1953–)
Federal Government Official, Attorney

Espy was born November 30, 1953. He received a B.A. from Howard University in 1975, and a J.D. from the Santa Clara School of Law in 1978. After graduating, Espy practiced law in Yazoo City, Mississippi, and managed the Central Mississippi Legal Services from 1978 to 1980. Espy worked for the State of Mississippi as assistant secretary of state for public lands, and from 1984 to 1985, as assistant attorney general for consumer protection.

Espy was elected to the U.S. House of Representatives in 1986, where he served on numerous committees including the House Budget Committee; House Agricultural Committee; Select Committee on Hunger; Sub-Committee on Cotton, Rice & Sugar; Sub-Committee on Conservation, Credit and Rural Development; and the Consumer Relations & Nutrition Committee. In addition, he chaired the Domestic Task Force on Hunger. In 1993, Espy was appointed secretary of agriculture by President Bill Clinton, the first African American to hold this post. However, Espy quickly became the subject of a federal ethics investigation into charges that he accepted gifts from companies that were regulated by the agency he headed. Although he denied any wrongdoing, Espy resigned his post on December 31, 1994. Nearly one year later, charges developed that Espy, while still a cabinet member, had improperly approached an agribusiness lobbyist for money, asking him to help pay off a debt incurred by his brother, who had unsuccessfully run for a House seat.

Espy was the object of a four-year investigation by an independent counsel who charged him with 30 counts of political corruption. The investigation was based on allegations of accepting $33,000 in free gifts, sports tickets, and expensive meals from companies that sought to benefit from good relations with Espy in their dealings with the Department of Agriculture. Espy was exonerated in December 1998 when the jury returned not guilty verdicts on all the counts.

Espy practices law in Mississippi. He is affiliated with the American Bar Association, Mississippi Trial Lawyers Association, and National Conference of Black Leaders, and is on the board of directors of the Jackson Urban League.

Chaka Fattah (1956–)
State Legislator, Civil Rights Activist

Born as Arthur Davenport in Philadelphia, Pennsylvania, on November 21, 1956, Fattah was renamed after the legendary Zulu warrior Chaka by his mother, who with her husband, took new Swahili root names to represent their African heritage. Fattah's mother, Falaka Fattah started the nationally known youth program House of Umoja as a means of combating and controlling gangs. At the age of 14 in an effort to assist his mother, Fattah received 20 abandoned houses in the neighborhood after giving a slide presentation and written proposal to the First Pennsylvania Bank. Falaka

Chaka Fattah.

Fattah used the structures to expand the growing House of Umoja youth program.

Fattah continued to help with the youth program while in high school. With the help of Congressman Bill Gray, Fattah won a federal grant to renovate the houses. Meanwhile at Overbrook High School, Fattah organized the Youth Movement to Clean Up Politics. After attending the Community College of Philadelphia, the University of Pennsylvania, and Wharton Community Education Program, Fattah worked as a special assistant to the managing director of the Office of Housing and Community Development in Philadelphia for two years.

Then in 1982, Fattah decided to run for the Pennsylvania House of Representatives and became the youngest man ever elected to the Pennsylvania General Assembly at the age of 25. While serving as a representative, Fattah earned a master's degree in government administration from Fels School for State and Local Government at the University of Pennsylvania. In 1988, Fattah won an election for state senator in the Seventh District. As a state senator, Fattah raised money for the city of Philadelphia and pioneered programs to rebuild

100 of the country's deteriorating cities. In 1994, Fattah won a seat in the U.S. House of Representatives. He has won an "outstanding contribution award" from the Pennsylvania House of Representatives and the Simpson Fletcher Award for religion and race.

Walter E. Fauntroy (1933–)
Federal Legislator, Religious Leader, Civil Rights Activist

Born February 6, 1933, Walter E. Fauntroy represented the District of Columbia in the House of Representatives from 1971 until 1990. He was Washington, D.C., coordinator for the March on Washington for Jobs and Freedom in 1963, coordinator for the Selma to Montgomery March in 1965, and national coordinator for the Poor People's Campaign in 1969. Fauntroy served as chairman of the caucus task force for the 1972 Democratic National Committee and of the platform committee of the National Black Political Convention. He was the chief architect of legislation in 1973 that permitted the District of Columbia to elect its own mayor and city council and engineered the passage by both the House and Senate of a constitutional amendment calling for full congressional representation for District of Columbia residents in the U.S. Congress.

During his tenure in the House of Representatives, Fauntroy built a record of achievement by playing key roles in the mobilization of African American political power from the National Black Political Convention in 1972 to the presidential elections of 1972 and 1976. For 15 years, Fauntroy chaired a bipartisan congressional task force on Haiti. In November of 1984, Fauntroy and two prominent national leaders launched the "Free South Africa Movement" (FSAM) with their arrest at the South African embassy. He served as co-chair of the steering committee of the FSAM. He was a member of the House Select Committee on Narcotics Abuse and Control and co-sponsored the 1988 $2.7 billion anti-drug bill.

In the 95th Congress Fauntroy was a member of the House Select Committee on Assassinations and chairman of its Subcommittee on the Assassination of Martin Luther King Jr. He was a ranking member of the House Banking, Finance, and Urban Affairs Committee and chairman of its Subcommittee on Government Affairs and Budget. He was also the first ranking member of the House District Committee.

Fauntroy was the recipient of several awards during his political career. In 1984, he was presented with the Hubert H. Humphrey Humanitarian Award by the National Urban Coalition. He also received honorary degrees from Georgetown University Law School, Yale University, and Virginia Union University. After leaving public service, Fauntroy founded Project We Care, a social service located in the Washington, D.C., area. The project is comprised of teams of ministers and church members who canvass neighborhoods in order to serve as conduits between residents and the city. Fauntroy also began his own company.

Fauntroy contracted tuberculosis in the mid-1990s. Through a diligent regimen, however, he remained healthy and actually became an unofficial spokesperson for the disease, urging the public to get tested. Then a discovery was made that he had incorrectly listed a church donation on a disclosure form presented to the Congress. In 1995, Fauntroy was sentenced to a two-year probation, $1,000 fine, and 300 hours of community service after pleading guilty to a misdemeanor charge of falsifying a financial report to Congress.

Continuing his fight for human rights, Fauntroy, a leader of the Free Sudan Movement, was arrested on April 13, 2001, for chaining himself to the gates of the Sudanese Embassy in Washington, D.C., in a protest against Sudan's black slave trade.

Floyd Flake. *See* **Religion chapter.**

Gary A. Franks (1953–)
Federal Legislator, Organization Executive

Gary Franks was born February 9, 1953, in Waterbury, Connecticut. He received a B.A. from Yale University in 1975. Before being elected to the U.S. House of Representatives, Franks was active in local politics and business. He was president of GAF Realty in Waterbury. Franks was also on the Board of Alderman, vice-chairman of the Zoning Board, a member of the Environmental Control Commission, director of the Naugatuck (Connecticut) chapter of the American Red Cross, president of the Greater Waterbury Chamber of Commerce, and a member of the Waterbury Foundation.

In 1991, Franks was elected to the U.S. House of Representatives, thus becoming the only African American Republican in the House until J. C. Watts was elected in 1995. Franks served on the Armed Services Committee, Small Business Committee, and the Select Committee on Aging. In 1993, he was appointed to the highly prized House Energy and Commerce Committee.

Franks has fulfilled a controversial role as an African American opposed to affirmative action and other programs based on preference for women and minorities. With such views, Franks had his share of congressional ruckuses. Formerly the only Republican member of the Congressional Black Caucus, he was actually voted out of the organization in 1993 by members who

did not consider Franks a legitimate African American spokesperson. In 1994, Franks testified in support of a lawsuit to dismantle the African American-majority 11th Congressional District of Cynthia McKinney, an African American Democrat from Georgia. Franks and his political cohorts felt that the district had been improperly designed to increase African American voting strength in the area at the expense of the white electorate.

Franks was known as one of the Republican party's most prominent African American lawmakers. He entered the political landscape at a time when African American Republicans were nonexistent as members of the Senate and absent at municipal and state levels as mayors of major American cities or governors of any states. He was defeated in 1997 after serving three terms. Franks has been named the 1980 Outstanding Young Man by the Boy's Club and Man of the Year by the Negro Professional Women's Club.

Lenora Fulani (1950–)
Political Party Leader, Psychologist, Social Therapist

Born Lenora Branch on April 25, 1950, in Chester, Pennsylvania, she changed her name to Lenora Branch Fulani in 1973. She received a B.S. from Hofstra University. She furthered her education in social therapy with an M.S.T. from Columbia University Teachers College and a Ph.D. from the New York Institute for Social Therapy and Research. Affiliated with the Institute, Fulani opened her own therapy practice in Harlem in the 1970s, the Eastside Center for Short Term Psychotherapy. Concurrently, she founded the National Alliance Party (NAP), a political party for social change.

Fulani has made bids for election as lieutenant governor of New York in 1982 and governor in 1986 and 1990. She also campaigned for election as mayor of New York City in 1985. In 1988 and 1992, she campaigned for election as president of the United States. She made history in 1988 when she became the first woman and the first African American to be included on the presidential ballot in all 50 states. In 1992, she became the first woman to qualify for federal primary matching funds to run her campaign. In 1994, she made a run again for governor of New York, garnering 21 percent of the votes in the primary. Following her gubernatorial defeat, Fulani contributed to the formation of the Patriot Party. The Patriot Party planned to gain wide-range support by appealing to voters independent of the two main political parties in the 1996 elections. The formation of this party was followed by Fulani's creation of the Committee for a Unified Independent Party. In the 2000 presidential election, Fulani made news by backing Reform Party candidate, Pat Buchanan.

Fulani has written widely on the subject of politics. She wrote *Independent Black Leadership in America* in 1990, and *The Making of a Fringe Candidate* in 1992. In the mid-1990s, her newspaper column, "This Way for Black Empowerment" was carried in more than 140 newspapers nationwide. She is the founder and executive producer of the "All-Stars Talent Show," the largest anti-violence program for inner city youth in the country. She hosted her own cable television show *Fulani!*, which aired in more than 20 cities nationwide each week. Fulani remains a leading advocate for the Reform Party and chairs the Committee for a Unified Independent Party.

W. Wilson Goode (1938–)
Municipal Government Official

W. Wilson Goode was born on August 19, 1938, in Seaboard, North Carolina. He received a B.A. in 1961 from Morgan State University. Goode served in the U.S. Army from 1961 to 1963, where he earned a commendation medal for meritorious service and the rank of captain with the military police. In 1968, he earned an M.P.A. from the University of Pennsylvania's Wharton School.

Between 1966 and 1978 Goode held a wide variety of positions including probation officer, building maintenance supervisor, insurance claims adjuster, and president of the Philadelphia Council for Community Advancement. From 1978 until 1980, Goode was chairman of the Pennsylvania Public Utilities Commission and was managing director of the City of Philadelphia from 1980 to 1982. In 1983, Goode was elected the first African American mayor of Philadelphia.

Goode's tenure as mayor of Philadelphia was marred by charges that he was a weak and ineffective leader who was unable to handle the traditionally rough and tumble politics of Philadelphia city government. In May of 1985, during a violent confrontation between the city of Philadelphia and members of MOVE, a radical "back-to-nature" cult that took over a row house in West Philadelphia, Goode ordered police to drop a bomb on the roof of the house to evict MOVE members. A massive explosion and fire resulted that killed 11 people, destroyed 61 homes, and caused $8 million in damage.

Goode barely won reelection in 1987 and was faced with mounting problems. Decades of corruption, racial tension, and urban decay had dampened Philadelphia's civic spirit and created a sense of apathy. Acute tensions between Goode and the city council resulted in a huge budget deficit. In September of 1990, Goode announced that the city was on the verge of bankruptcy. Although a consortium of banks helped to avert disaster, Philadelphia reported a massive $200 million deficit in June of 1991.

Barred by law from seeking a third term, Goode was succeeded as mayor by Edward Rendell in January of 1992. That same year, he wrote his autobiography *In Goode Faith*. After leaving office, Goode started his own company.

William H. Gray III (1941–)
Politician, United Negro College Fund President, Special Envoy to Haiti

Born to a minister and a high school teacher in Baton Rouge, Louisiana, on August 20, 1941, William H. Gray III earned a B.A. from Franklin and Marshall College in 1963, serving during his senior year as an intern for Pennsylvania congressman Robert N. C. Nix. He received a master's of divinity from Drew Theological School in 1966 and a master's of theology from Princeton Theological Seminary in 1970. He also attended the University of Pennsylvania, Temple University, and Oxford University.

Gray served as assistant pastor at Union Baptist Church in Montclair, New Jersey, from 1964 until 1966. He was promoted to senior pastor in 1966 and served in this capacity until 1972. Gray moved to Philadelphia in 1972 to become pastor of Bright Hope Baptist Church.

In 1976, Gray decided to become involved in politics, challenging Robert N. C. Nix for his congressional seat. His first attempt to unseat Nix was unsuccessful. However, in 1978, Gray defeated Nix and was elected to Congress. He became a vocal and influential member of the House, challenging the administration of Ronald Reagan on such issues as social spending and U.S. support for the government of South Africa. He served on the House Budget Committee, becoming chair in 1985 and earned the admiration and respect of even his most implacable political foes. Gray was a member of the House Foreign Affairs Committee for 12 years. For ten of those twelve years, he served on the Appropriations Subcommittee on Foreign Operations. He was also vice-chair of the Congressional Black Caucus. Gray left the House of Representatives in 1991 to head the United Negro College Fund, and he currently serves as president and CEO of that organization.

On May 8, 1994, President Bill Clinton appointed Gray as his special envoy to Haiti. In this capacity, Gray played an instrumental role in the eventual removal of Haiti's brutal military government in October of 1994.

Gray was honored in 1997 as one of four recipients of the "Four Freedoms" Award. He has also served on the board of directors of numerous companies, including Chase Manhattan Bank, EDS Corporation, Visteon Corporation, and Pfizer Corporation.

Patricia Roberts Harris (1924–1985)
Organization Executive, Diplomat, Civil Rights Activist, Federal Government Official, Attorney, Educator

Born in Mattoon, Illinois, on May 31, 1924, Harris received her undergraduate degree in 1945 from Howard University. While at Howard, Harris also served as vice-chairman of a student branch of the NAACP and was involved in early nonviolent demonstrations against racial discrimination. Harris worked for the YWCA in Chicago and served as executive director of Delta Sigma Theta, an African American sorority, from 1953 to 1959. After completing post-graduate work at the University of Chicago and at American University, she earned her Ph.D. in jurisprudence from George Washington University Law School in 1960.

Patricia Roberts Harris, first African American woman to serve in a cabinet post.

An attorney and professor before she entered politics, Harris was appointed co-chairman of the National Women's Committee on Civil Rights by President John F. Kennedy and later was named to the Commission on the Status of Puerto Rico. In 1965, Harris was chosen by President Lyndon B. Johnson to become U.S. ambassador to Luxembourg, the first African American woman ever to be named an American envoy. In 1969 Harris was appointed dean of the Howard University Law School and served in that role until 1970 when she was selected to join a major Washington, D.C., law firm.

Harris served as secretary of the Department of Health and Human Services and also secretary of Housing and Urban Development under President Jimmy Carter. Under President Ronald Reagan, she served as ambassador to Luxembourg, becoming the first African American woman to hold this diplomatic rank in U.S. history. Harris was also the first African American woman to serve in a cabinet post. In 1982, Harris ran an unsuccessful campaign for mayor of Washington, D.C. She became a law professor at George Washington University in 1983 and remained there until her death from cancer on March 23, 1985.

Jesse L. Jackson Jr. (1965–)
United States Congressman, Civil Rights Activist, Organization Executive, Author

U.S. Representative Jesse Louis Jackson Jr. was born to the Reverend Jesse and Jacqueline (Davis) Jackson Sr. on March 11, 1965, in Greenville, South Carolina. He attended Le Mans Academy and St. Albans Episcopal Prep School. After completing his secondary education, Jackson entered North Carolina Agricultural and Technical University in Greensboro, where he graduated magna cum laude in 1987 with a bachelor of science degree in business management. Three years later, he earned the master of arts degree in theology from Chicago Theological Seminary. Jackson continued his education and received the juris doctorate from the University of Illinois College of Law in 1993. Two years before completing his juris doctorate, Jackson married Sandra Lee Stevens.

In 1986, Jackson was arrested for taking part in a demonstration against apartheid at the South African embassy in Washington, D.C. He also participated in protests held in front of the South African consulate in Chicago, Illinois. Jackson's long-time stance against South Africa's system of racial discrimination provided him the unique opportunity of being the only American to share the platform with Nelson Mandela, the major symbol of the struggle for human rights in the Republic of South Africa, following Mandela's February of 1990 release from prison.

During the Democratic National Convention in 1988, Jackson was the last of his siblings to introduce his father, the Reverend Jesse Jackson Sr. The younger Jackson's introduction of his father catapulted him to a successful public speaking career. While pursuing his law degree, Jackson Jr. frequently campaigned for Democratic candidates. After graduating from the University of Illinois College of Law, he became the national field director for the Rainbow Coalition, a political action band conceived by the Reverend Jackson Sr. While serving in this position, Jackson established a nationwide non-aligned program that successfully registered a multitude of new voters. He also inaugurated a voter education program to educate citizens about the importance of participating in the political system including how to utilize technology to win at the polls and to more effectively participate in the political arena. Additionally, he established new local chapters of Operation Push (People United to Save Humanity).

Jackson, born during the African American struggle to obtain the ballot, resigned his position at the Rainbow Coalition in 1995. A Democrat, he entered the world of politics as a candidate for Chicago's Second Congressional District, a seat previously held by Mel Reynolds. After winning the primary and general elections, Representative Jesse L. Jackson Jr. became a member of the 104th Congress in the U.S. House of Representatives on December 12, 1995. Jackson co-wrote the book, *Legal Lynching*, with his father in 1996.

Self-described as "a public servant—not a politician—with a progressive agenda," Representative Jackson is part of a new generation of African American leaders who see their work as an extension of their parents' struggle to eradicate the remaining covert vestiges of discrimination.

Jesse L. Jackson Sr. *See* **Civil Rights chapter.**

Maynard Jackson (1938–)
Attorney, Municipal Government Official, Organization Executive

Jackson was born on March 23, 1938, in Dallas, Texas. At the age of 14 he was admitted to Morehouse College as a Ford Foundation Early Admissions Scholar. He graduated with a B.A. in 1956, with a concentration in history and political science. After graduation, he worked for the Ohio State Bureau of Unemployment Compensation as claims examiner from 1957 to 1958

and as a sales manager and associate district sales manager for P. F. Collier Inc. from 1958 to 1961.

In 1964, Jackson received a J.D. from the North Carolina Central University School of Law and then worked as a lawyer for the National Labor Relations Board. In 1968 and 1969 Jackson was named the managing attorney and director of community relations for the Emory Community Legal Service Center in Atlanta and was a senior partner in the law firm of Jackson, Patterson & Parks from 1970 to 1973.

Jackson had been active in Democratic politics and was the vice-mayor of Atlanta from 1970 to 1974. In 1974, he was elected mayor. At the time of his election to Atlanta's highest office, Jackson was the youngest mayor of a major U.S. city. He remained mayor of Atlanta until 1982. Jackson returned to private life and worked as a bond lawyer before being reelected mayor of Atlanta in 1989. The selection of Atlanta as host of the 1994 Super Bowl and the site of the 1996 Summer Olympic Games were two of the greatest achievements of Jackson's second term.

In 1993, Jackson vetoed domestic partnership legislation, claiming that the City Council did not provide details on funding benefits for partners of city employees. The response of the gay and lesbian community was fervent, as leaders of 40 Atlanta-based lesbian and gay organizations coordinated a barrage of protest actions during that year's Fourth of July holiday. Jackson was also deluged with complaints from angry city taxpayers who felt that Jackson's decision to order more than $45,000 worth of furniture for the mayor's office was government waste in action. Jackson admitted that city purchasing guidelines had not been followed.

Even after leaving office, Jackson has fallen into controversy. Accusations were levied against him that while he was in office, he improperly influenced the manner in which a $1.3 billion financial portfolio was invested as a city audit revealed that nearly 80 percent of the city's 1993 investments were turned over to a firm whose principal was Jackson's 1989 campaign treasurer. Jackson emphatically denied the allegations that he swayed any investment decisions.

Despite the alleged improprieties, Jackson earned a reputation as an aggressive and outspoken mayor. He had the difficult task of leading Atlanta through the difficult transition years from predominantly white leadership to a mixed power structure. Under Jackson's leadership Atlanta made serious gains as a financial center and distribution hub. Expanded international convention facilities turned Atlanta into a major convention center. In 1981, the prestigious *Almanac of Places Rated* named Atlanta the best major city in which to live and work. Jackson had taken advantage of affirmative action programs to improve city housing and social conditions. He also transformed the mass transit system into one of the most modern in the country.

Shortly after his last term, Jackson became chairman of the board and a majority stockholder in Jackson Securities Inc., a banking firm. He also holds interest in Jackmont Hospitality, a group of real estate companies that hoped to stimulate the economy of some of Atlanta's depressed areas. In 1995, Jackson became the principal owner of a joint venture to operate a TGI Friday's restaurant at the city's Hartfield International Airport. Many complained that Jackson's use of Atlanta's affirmative action program to land the premier location was an abuse of a system designed to aid the disadvantaged.

Jackson has served as vice-chairman of the White House Committee on Balanced Growth & Economic Development and the White House Committee on the Windfall Profits Tax. He also served as the National Chairman of the Democratic National Committee's Voting Rights Institute from 2001–2002. He is also the founding chairman of the Atlanta Economic Development Corporation and the chairman of the Atlanta Urban Residential Finance Authority. Jackson belongs to the Georgia and New York Bar Associations, the National League of Cities, and the National Black Caucus of Local Elected Officials.

In 1975, Jackson was named to *Time* magazine's list of 200 young American leaders and *Ebony* magazine's list of 100 Most Influential Black Americans in 1976. In 1994, Jackson and six other Morehouse graduates were honored at the college's sixth annual Candle in the Dark awards dinner.

Sheila Jackson Lee (1950–)
Federal Legislator

Jackson Lee was born in Queens in 1950 and was raised in New York City. She graduated in 1972 from Yale University with a B.A. and then, in 1975, graduated from the University of Virginia Law School with a J.D. Her husband was an official at the University of Houston, and Jackson Lee began her practice in Texas.

Jackson Lee became an associate judge in the Houston court system in 1987, and three years later was elected to the city council. In 1994, she defeated an incumbent Democrat in the congressional primary and was then elected to the seat once held by Barbara Jordan.

Jackson Lee has been associated with Congresswoman Maxine Waters and is a member of the Congressional Black Caucus. In 1997, she was named the

caucus's whip. Jackson Lee served on the House Judiciary Committee that impeached President Clinton and made a name for herself as one of the president's staunchest defenders. She won reelection in 1998 with 90 percent of the vote.

Barbara Jordan (1936–1996)
Educator, Federal Legislator, Civil Rights Activist, State Legislator, Attorney

Barbara Jordan was born on February 21, 1936, in Houston, Texas. Afflicted with multiple sclerosis, she died of viral pneumonia, a complication of leukemia, on January 17, 1996.

Jordan attended Phyllis Wheatley High School, and in 1952, graduated as a member of the Honor Society. In 1956, Jordan received a B.A. from Texas Southern University in history and political science. She went on to Boston University, where she earned a J.D. in 1959. After teaching at Tuskegee Institute for one year, Jordan returned to Houston, where she practiced law and was appointed administrative assistant to a Harris County judge.

Barbara Jordan, the first African American to serve as president *pro tem* of the Texas state senate.

Sheila Jackson Lee congratulates members of NASA's completed STS-101 mission, May 30, 2000.

In 1966, Jordan was elected to the Texas Senate. She was the first African American to serve as president *pro tem* of that body and to chair the important Labor and Management Relations Committee.

In 1972, Jordan was elected to the U.S. House of Representatives, thus becoming the first African American woman from a southern state elected to Congress. As a member of Congress, she served on the Judiciary Committee which heard the impeachment proceedings of President Richard M. Nixon and was the first African American selected as the keynote speaker at the Democratic National Convention in 1976. While a representative, Jordan served on the House Judiciary and Government Operations committees. During her terms in both the Texas Senate and U.S. House, Jordan was known as a champion of civil rights for all and especially minorities and the poor.

From 1979 to 1982, Jordan taught at the Lyndon Baines Johnson School of Public Affairs at the University of Texas. In 1982, she was made holder of the Lyndon Baines Johnson Centennial Chair of National Policy, a post she held until her death. After 15 years out of politics, Jordan was appointed as chair of the

U.S. Commission on Immigration Reform by U.S. president Bill Clinton in 1993. Jordan was credited for her efforts to address the burgeoning U.S. hostility towards immigrants.

Jordan co-authored two books, *Barbara Jordan: A Self-Portrait* (1979) and *The Great Society: A Twenty Year Critique* (1986). She also served on the Democratic Caucus Steering and Policy Committee, and in 1976 and 1992, she was the keynote speaker at the Democratic National Convention.

Jordan belonged to the American Bar Association as well as the Texas, Massachusetts, and District of Columbia bars. She was a member of the Character Counts Coalition, a group whose aim is to address the values of American society, particularly emphasizing youth. She had been on the board of directors of the Mead Corporation and the Henry J. Kaiser Family Foundation. Jordan is the recipient of a long list of awards and honors including the 1984 Eleanor Roosevelt Humanities Award, membership in the Texas Women's Hall of Fame (public service category, 1984), and listing in both the *Ladies Home Journal* "100 Most Influential Women in America" and *Time* magazine's 1976 "Ten

Women of the Year" list. She was bestowed the nation's highest civilian honor in 1994 when President Clinton gave her the Presidential Medal of Freedom for her distinguished career in public service. Jordan had also received 27 honorary doctorate degrees. The LBJ School of Public Affairs has named an endowed chair in her honor and the Barbara Jordan Forum each year in February around the time of her birthday.

Sharon Pratt Kelly (1944–)
Attorney, Municipal Government Official, Media Executive, Educator

Kelly was born Sharon Pratt in Washington, D.C., on January 30, 1944. For a time, she worked under the name Sharon Pratt Dixon, assuming the surname of her former husband. She graduated from Howard University with a B.A. in political science in 1965 and received a J.D. in 1968. In 1967, she edited the Howard University law school journal.

From 1970 through 1971, Kelly was the house counsel for the Joint Center for Political Studies in Washington, D.C. Between 1971 and 1976 she was an associate in the law firm of Pratt and Queen. During this time she also taught at Antioch Law School. In 1976, Kelly began a 14-year association with the Potomac Electric Power Company. While there, she held increasingly responsible positions including associate general counsel, director of consumer affairs, and vice president of public policy.

In 1990, Kelly left the private sector to win the office of mayor of Washington, D.C. In doing so she became the first African American woman elected mayor of a major American city. She was not able to deliver on campaign promises to reform city government and to fire 2,000 middle managers in the D.C. bureaucracy. Her relations with the Democratic Congress were strained and Kelly's administration was perceived as ineffective, which helped pave the way for her 1994 defeat and the comeback of former mayor Marion Barry.

In 1976 and 1977, Kelly was general counsel to the Washington, D.C., Democratic Committee. Between 1985 and 1989, she was treasurer of the Democratic Party and has also sat as a national committeewoman on the Washington, D.C., Democratic State Committee.

Kelly belongs to the American Bar Association and the Washington, D.C., Women's Bar Association. She is affiliated with the Legal Aid Society, the American Civil Liberties Union, and the United Negro College Fund. Kelly was a Falk Fellow at Howard University and has received numerous awards including the 1983 NAACP

Presidential Award, the 1985 United Negro College Fund's Distinguished Leadership Award, and the 1986 Distinguished Service Award presented by the Federation of Women's Clubs.

Alan L. Keyes (1950–)
Federal Government Official, Lecturer, Author

Alan Lee Keyes was born on August 7, 1950, in New York City. Keyes lived in the United States and Italy during his childhood. He began his political career by serving as president of his high school's student council and as the first African American president of the American Legion Boys Nation. Keyes earned a B.A. from Harvard in 1972. He received his Ph.D. in political science from Harvard in 1979.

Following his graduate work, Keyes took a position at the U.S. State Department in 1978. He recruited Jeane Kirkpatrick as a mentor by defending her from verbal attack while serving as U.S. vice-consul in India. At the State Department, Keyes served in the South African Affairs Division, on the Policy Planning Council, in UNESCO (the United Nations Educational, Scientific, and Cultural Organization), and as an assistant

Alan Keyes.

secretary of state for International Organizational Affairs. Keyes was the African American of highest station at the State Department in 1987, but he resigned over a dispute over allocation of U.S. funds to the United Nations.

In 1988 and 1992, Keyes lost senatorial elections in Maryland. In between, he served as president of the Washington, D.C., organization Citizens Against Government Waste from 1989 to 1991. He also served as interim president in 1991 for Alabama A & M University. In 1992, following his second defeat, Keyes started his own talk radio show in Baltimore, *America's Wake-Up Call: The Alan Keyes Show.* Bolstered by the response to his radio show, Keyes announced his candidacy for the U.S. presidency on March 26, 1995. In so doing, he became the first Republican African American in the twentieth century to run for president. He attracted little support, however, and did not win a primary. Despite the showing, Keyes made another unsuccessful run for the GOP nomination in 2000. In 2002, he briefly hosted a televised talk show, *Alan Keyes Is Making Sense.*

Ron Kirk (1954–)
Attorney, Municipal Government Official

Ron Kirk was born on June 27, 1954, in Austin, Texas. He received a B.A. in political science and sociology from Austin College in 1976, during which time he served in 1974 as a legislative aide to the Texas Constitutional Convention. This experience prompted an interest in politics and drove him to complete his law degree in 1979 at the University of Texas School of Law. After two years, Kirk was unsatisfied as a private practice attorney. He moved to Washington, D.C., to work for U.S. Senator Lloyd Bentsen from 1981 to 1983. He returned to Dallas in 1983 to work for the Dallas City Attorney's Office and became the chief lobbyist of Dallas until 1989. He then worked for the firm of Johnson & Gibbs and volunteered for Big Brothers/Big Sisters of America, the Dallas Zoological Society, Dallas Helps, and the North Texas Food Bank among other organizations. In 1994, Kirk took over the Texas secretary of state position from John Hannah. Kirk was elected the mayor of Dallas in 1995 with 62 percent of the vote. In 2001, Kirk announced that he was resigning as the city's mayor in order to seek the nomination as the Democratic candidate for a vacant U.S. Senate seat.

As mayor, Kirk maintained his role as a partner in the law firm of Gardere & Wynn. He was honored in 1992 with a Volunteer of the Year Award from Big Brothers/Big Sisters and a Distinguished Alumni Award from the Austin College Alumni Association. He was named Citizen of the Year by Omega Psi Phi in 1994, the same year that he earned the C. B. Bunkley Community Service Award from the Turner Legal Association.

John Mercer Langston (1829–1897)
Educational Administrator, Federal Legislator, Diplomat, Attorney, Lecturer

Congressman John Mercer Langston was born in Virginia in 1829. Upon the death of his father, Langston was emancipated and sent to Ohio, where he was given over to the care of a friend of his father. Langston spent his childhood there, attending private school in Cincinnati before graduating in 1849 from Oberlin College. Four years later, after getting his degree from the theological department of Oberlin, he studied law and was admitted to the Ohio bar.

Langston began his practice in Brownhelm, Ohio. He was chosen in 1855 to serve as clerk of this township by the Liberty Party. During the Civil War, he was a recruiting agent for African American servicemen, helping to organize such regiments as the 54th and 55th Massachusetts, and the 5th Ohio. In 1867, Langston served as inspector-general of the Freedmen's Bureau

John Mercer Langston, believed to be the first African American ever elected to public office.

and as dean and vice president of Howard University from 1868 to 1875. In 1877 he was named minister resident to Haiti and *charge d'affaires* to Santo Domingo, remaining in diplomatic service until 1885.

Soon after returning to his law practice in the United States, Langston was named president of the Virginia Normal and Collegiate Institute. In 1888, he was elected to Congress from Virginia, but was not seated for two years until vote-counting irregularities had been investigated. He was defeated in his bid for a second term. In 1894 Langston wrote an autobiography *From the Virginia Plantation to the National Capital.* Langston died in 1897.

George Thomas "Mickey" Leland (1944–1989)
Civil Rights Activist, Federal Legislator, Educator

Leland was born on November 27, 1944, in Lubbock, Texas. He graduated from Texas Southern University in 1970 with a B.S. in pharmacy. Leland had been active in the civil rights movement during his student years, and he was elected to the Texas state legislature in 1973. In 1978 he was elected to the U.S. House of Representatives to fill Barbara Jordan's vacated seat. While a representative, Leland served on various committees including Interstate and Foreign Commerce, Post Office and Civil Service, and the committee on the District of Columbia.

In spite of serving on these committees, Leland was devoted to easing the hunger of starving persons in the United States and in other countries, especially African countries. He chaired the House Select Committee on World Hunger and visited starving peoples throughout Africa. In 1989, while traveling to a United Nations refugee camp in Ethiopia the plane on which Leland was traveling crashed near Gambela, Ethiopia, killing all on board.

John Robert Lewis (1940–)
Civil Rights Activist, Federal Legislator, Organization Executive

Committed to nonviolence and the advancement of African Americans, John Lewis was born in Troy, Alabama, on February 21, 1940. He received a B.S. in 1961 from the American Baptist Theological Seminary and a B.A. from Fisk University in 1967. Before entering politics, Lewis was associated with numerous social activist organizations including the Student Non-Violent Coordinating Committee. He served as associate director of the Field Foundation, project director of the Southern Regional Council, and executive director of the Voter Education Project Inc., beginning in 1970.

John Lewis.

In 1982, Lewis was elected Atlanta city councilman-at-large, and voters sent him to the U.S. House of Representatives as a Democrat in 1986. While in the House, Lewis has served on the Public Works, Interior and Insular Affairs committees as well as the powerful House Ways and Means Committee. He has also been a member of the Select Committee on Aging. Lewis's pet project over the years has been the encouragement of a museum bill that would allow for a museum of African American history at the Smithsonian Institution in Washington, D.C.

Lewis denounced the rhetoric of his homophobic colleagues during a House debate that ultimately led to the adoption of legislation to discourage homosexual enlistment in the military. He considered the Republican "Contract With America" as the genesis of a wave of intolerance in American society in the early to mid-1990s. In 1995, Lewis headed a group of nearly 100 trade unionists that interrupted a speech on proposed Medicare changes by House Speaker Newt Gingrich during a conference sponsored by the Congressional Institute. Many of Lewis's critics suggested that the demonstration did little but gain media attention, but Lewis countered that saving Medicare benefits for the elderly was his priority, and he was willing to seize any opportunity to stir up a public debate.

In the 1960s, Lewis was known for his involvement with the U.S. civil rights movement. A strict follower of nonviolent social protest, Lewis was an organizer and participant in numerous sit-ins, freedom rides, and protest marches throughout the South. He abstained from the 1995 Million Man March because he felt that he could not participate in an effort led by Louis Farrakhan. Lewis worked steadfastly in the mid-1990s to help produce a spirit of racial harmony and team spirit in Atlanta as the city prepared for the 1996 Olympics.

Lewis is a 1975 recipient of the Martin Luther King Jr. Non-Violent Peace Prize and has been named to *Ebony*'s "One of the Nation's Most Influential Blacks" list (1991–92) and *Time* magazine's 1974 "One of America's Rising Leaders" list. He belongs to the Martin Luther King Jr. Center for Social Change, the National Democratic Institute for International Affairs, Friends of Vista, and the African-American Institute.

Lewis received a special honor in 2001, the year marking the 40th anniversary of the 1961 Freedom Rides in which he participated, as he was named the winner of a special John F. Kennedy Profile in Courage Award for lifetime achievement.

Kweisi Mfume (1948–)
Federal Legislator, Educator, Civil Rights Activist, Organization Executive

Kweisi Mfume was born Fizzell Gray in Baltimore on October 24, 1948. Mfume once ran the streets and fathered five children out of wedlock. He turned to education and received a B.S. from Morgan State University in 1976, and an M.A. from Johns Hopkins University in 1984.

In 1979, Mfume was elected to the Baltimore City Council by a margin of three votes. He worked hard to diversify city government, improve public safety, enhance minority business development, and divest city funds from South Africa. Active in Democratic politics, Mfume was a member of the Maryland Democratic State Central Committee and a delegate to the Democratic National Conventions in 1980, 1984, and 1988. Mfume was elected to the U.S. House of Representatives in 1987. During his tenure he served on the Banking, Finance and Urban Affairs Committee; the Small Business Committee; the Education and Labor Committee; and the Narcotics Abuse & Control subcommittee. The House speaker chose Mfume to serve on the Ethics Committee and on the Joint Economic

Committee of the House and Senate. He also was vice-chair, and later chairperson, of the Congressional Black Caucus. In addition, Mfume was a member of the Caucus for Women's Issues, the Congressional Arts Caucus, and the Federal Government Service Task Force.

In February 1996, Mfume became president and CEO of the NAACP after the NAACP board of directors unanimously elected him to that post. His priorities were to restore the confidence of members and supporters in this seminal organization, to ensure greater fiscal accountability, and to secure private sector funding. Within weeks of Mfume's appointment, Nissan Motor Corp USA donated $100,000 to the NAACP. Since assuming the chief executive position, Mfume has eliminated the association's debt; set new standards and expectations for NAACP branches nationwide, and diligently worked to engage seasoned local volunteers and a new generation of younger civil rights activists in the mission of the NAACP. In 2000, Mfume led calls for more minority representation on network television. Under his leadership, the NAACP threatened a boycott against the National Broadcasting Company (NBC), but relented when the network agreed to systematically find more minorities to write, produce, and direct its television shows.

Mfume is a trustee of the Baltimore Museum of Art and the Morgan State University Board of Regents, where he previously taught political science and communications. He is also a member of the senior advisory committee of Harvard's John F. Kennedy School of Government and the board of trustees for the Enterprise Foundation.

Arthur W. Mitchell (1883–1968)
Civil Rights Activist, Federal Legislator, Lecturer, Attorney, Organization Executive

Born to slave parents in 1883 in Chambers County, Alabama, Mitchell was educated at Tuskegee Institute and at Columbia and Harvard Universities. By 1929, he had founded Armstrong Agricultural School in West Butler, Alabama, and become a wealthy landowner and a lawyer with a thriving practice in Washington, D.C. When he left the nation's capital that year, it was with the purpose of entering politics and becoming a representative from Illinois.

Mitchell won Democratic approval only after Harry Baker died suddenly. Aided by the overwhelming national sentiment for the Democratic Party during this period, he unseated Oscar DePriest by the slender margin of 3,000 votes. Mitchell's most significant victory on behalf of civil rights came, not in the legislative chamber, but in the courts. In 1937, Mitchell brought

Kweisi Mfume (right) and Gary Franks.

suit against the Chicago and Rock Island Railroad after having been forced to leave his first-class accommodations en route to Hot Springs, Arkansas, and sit in a "Jim Crow" car. He argued his own case before the Supreme Court in 1941 and won a decision which declared Jim Crow practices illegal.

Mitchell proposed that states that discriminated against African Americans should receive fewer congressional seats and advocated strong sanctions against states that practiced lynching. Also, he worked for the elimination of poll taxes to make it easier for African Americans to vote. Following the end of World War II, Mitchell demonstrated that because African Americans fought bravely for the United States, they should be able to vote for their government representatives.

In 1942, Mitchell retired from Congress and continued to pursue his civil rights agenda as a private citizen. He also lectured occasionally and pursued farming on his estate near Petersburg, Virginia, where he died in 1968 at the age of 85.

Marc Morial (1958–)
Municipal Official

Morial was born in 1958 to a prominent, African American family in New Orleans. Morial received his B.A. in 1980 from the University of Pennsylvania and his J.D. three years later from the Georgetown University Law School.

Morial became a supporter of the Reverend Jesse L. Jackson Sr. and worked for Jackson's 1988 campaign for president. In 1991, he was elected to the state senate in Louisiana. Two years later he announced his candidacy for mayor of New Orleans. The election was marred by racial questions and a run-off was needed before Morial could be declared the winner.

Morial battled crime in his first term as mayor, introducing several innovative and controversial reforms within the police department. In 1998, he began his second term as mayor, grabbing national headlines as the city filed a lawsuit against gun manufacturers. In

2001, Morial served as president of the U.S. Conference of Mayors, a position his father had held 16 years before.

Carol Moseley-Braun (1947–)
Attorney, Federal Legislator

Born Carol Moseley in Chicago on August 16, 1947, Moseley-Braun received her B.A. from the University of Illinois in 1969 and her J.D. in 1972 from the University of Chicago Law School. While attending law school, Moseley-Braun worked as a legal intern and an associate attorney for a number of private law firms. After graduating from law school, Moseley-Braun was an assistant U.S. attorney for the northern district of Illinois from 1973 until 1977. In 1979, Moseley-Braun was elected an Illinois state representative from the 25th district, where she became known as an ardent supporter of civil rights legislation. After her bid for the lieutenant governorship was thwarted, Moseley-Braun was elected in 1986 as the Cook County recorder of deeds.

In 1992 Moseley-Braun became the nation's first African American woman elected to the U.S. Senate, making her an icon of the "Year of the Woman." The following year, Moseley-Braun, along with Senator Dianne Feinstein, was selected for the formerly all-male Senate Judiciary Committee. Her first major legislative proposal—an amendment to an omnibus crime bill that would try young offenders implicated in serious crime from the age of 13 and up as adults—was overwhelmingly approved by the Senate.

A recipient of many honors, Moseley-Braun won the 1981 and 1982 Best Legislation Award presented by the Independent Voters of Illinois. She has also won the 1981 National Association of Negro Business & Professional Women's Clubs' Community Recognition Award, the 1981 Chicago Alliance of Black School Educators' Recognition of Excellence in Education Award, the 1982 Afro-American Voters Alliance Community Recognition Award, and a 1993 Essence Award for African American women of achievement. In 1993, she was chosen as the keynote speaker for the annual, prestigious National Urban League dinner. Moseley-Braun belongs to the League of Black Women; Operation PUSH; Federal, Illinois and Chicago Bar Association; and the Women's Political Caucus.

In spite of her national prominence, her celebrity status, and the numerous honors, Moseley-Braun's senate career was dogged by ethical questions which often overshadowed her legislative record. Despite investigations which found no criminal wrongdoing on her part, Moseley-Braun was defeated in 1998.

In 1999, Bill Clinton nominated Moseley-Braun as ambassador to New Zealand. Following her tenure as ambassador, in the fall of 2001 she took a position as visiting professor of politics at Morris Brown College in Atlanta.

Eleanor Holmes Norton (1938–)
Attorney, Federal Legislator, Civil Rights Activist, Organization Executive, Educator

Eleanor Norton was born Eleanor Holmes on April 8, 1938, in Washington, D.C. She attended Antioch College in Ohio but transferred to Yale University and received an M.A. in American Studies in 1963 and a J.D. in 1964 from Yale's law school. After graduating from law school, Norton clerked for a federal judge in Philadelphia before joining the American Civil Liberties Union in 1965 as a litigator specializing in free speech issues. She stayed with the ACLU until 1970, reaching the position of assistant legal director and successfully arguing a First Amendment case before the U.S. Supreme Court. In 1970, she became chairwoman of the New York City Commission on Human Rights, a post she held until 1977, when she headed the Equal Employment Opportunity Commission. In 1981, she was a senior fellow at the Urban Institute. In 1982, she accepted the position of professor of law at Georgetown University. As a tenured professor, Norton still teaches at Georgetown. Norton had previously taught African American history at Pratt Institute in Brooklyn, New York, and law at New York City University Law School.

In 1990 Norton was elected congressional delegate to the U.S. House of Representatives for the District of Columbia. In 1993, the same year she sponsored legislation that would make Washington, D.C., the 51st state, she was allowed to cast a vote in the full house, thus becoming the first resident of the district to vote on the floor of Congress. In 1995, however, the House voted to strip Washington, D.C., of its floor-voting right. Norton protested that she was elected by federal tax-paying citizens who are entitled to full representation. A bipartisan alliance was formed among Norton, Republican House Speaker Newt Gingrich, and Democratic Washington, D.C., Mayor Marion Barry in an effort to save home rule for the district.

Norton is the ranking minority member of the District of Columbia Subcommittee. She is also a member of the Transportation and Infrastructure Committee and the Government Reform and Oversight Committee.

Norton has been named to the *Ladies Home Journal* 1988 "One Hundred Most Important Women" list and the 1989 "One Hundred Most Powerful Women in Washington" list by *Washington* magazine. She is also a recipient of the 1985 Distinguished Public Service Award presented by the Center for National Policy.

Hazel O'Leary (1937–)

Attorney, Federal Government Official, Financial Planner

Hazel O'Leary was born Hazel Reid on May 17, 1937, in Newport News, Virginia. She graduated Phi Beta Kappa in 1959 from Fisk University with a B.A. She received her J.D. in 1966 from Rutgers University School of Law. O'Leary was a utilities regulator under Presidents Ford and Carter, an executive vice president of the Northern States Power Co., and a Washington lobbyist. A proponent of energy conservation and alternative energy sources, she became secretary of energy in President Bill Clinton's administration in 1993.

In addition to formulating energy policy, O'Leary worked to dismantle the nation's nuclear weaponry complex and to help energy producers finance nuclear-waste storage programs. Reorganizing the Department of Energy at the end of the Cold War was one of the first accountabilities assigned to O'Leary. O'Leary campaigned to unveil the expansive network of secret atomic laboratories and weapons plants harbored in the nation. Results of Cold War nuclear tests, radiation releases, and experiments on civilians were also revealed. O'Leary also encouraged domestic resource development.

In the mid-1990s, O'Leary came under heavy scrutiny. First she was criticized for having spent thousands of government dollars on hiring a consultant firm to rank a number of reporters to find out which had given her the most favorable coverage. Then it was disclosed that she had spent much more than other cabinet members on overseas travel. Vice president Al Gore came to O'Leary's defense by noting that her trips had helped create new job opportunities in the United States. For example, O'Leary led a delegation of nearly 100 aides, energy experts, and business leaders to South Africa to uncover possibilities in the newly democratic country.

O'Leary is a certified financial planner, a member of the New Jersey and Washington bars, and has been vice president and general counsel of O'Leary Associates in Washington, D.C. In 1993, the Congressional Black Caucus honored O'Leary for her achievements. After completing her term as secretary of energy, O'Leary resigned and returned to the private sector, where she is currently president and CEO of Blaylock & Partners.

Clarence McClane Pendleton Jr. (1930–1988)

Federal Government Official, Organization Executive

Clarence Pendleton Jr. was born in Louisville, Kentucky, on November 10, 1930. Raised in Washington, D.C., he attended Dunbar High School and received a B.S. in 1954 from Howard University. Pendleton served three years in the U.S. Army and was assigned to a medical unit. After his discharge in 1957, Pendleton returned to Howard University where he received a master's degree in 1961 and coached swimming, football, rowing, and baseball.

In 1968, Pendleton became the recreation coordinator of the Baltimore Model Cities Program and became the director of the Urban Affairs Department of the National Recreation and Parks Association in 1970. Pendleton soon began attracting national attention and in 1972 he headed San Diego's Model Cities Program. In 1975 he became the director of the San Diego Urban League.

By 1980, a change took place in Pendleton's political philosophy. He began to feel that African Americans' reliance on government programs was trapping them in a cycle of dependence and welfare handouts. Pendleton believed that it was in the best interest of African Americans to build strong ties with a strong, expanding private sector and eschew the more traditional ties with liberal bureaucrats and liberal philosophies.

To this end he supported the election of Ronald Reagan to the presidency and was appointed chairman of the Civil Rights Commission by President Reagan in 1981. Pendleton's chairmanship was controversial mostly because of his opposition to affirmative action and forced busing as a means of desegregating schools. Pendleton retained a more liberal philosophy on other matters, however, by supporting the Equal Rights Amendment and the Voting Rights Act. Pendleton died unexpectedly of a heart attack on June 5, 1988, in San Diego.

Pinckney Benton Stewart Pinchback (1837–1921)

Attorney, Federal Legislator, State Government Official, Municipal Government Official

Pinchback was born in Macon, Georgia, on May 10, 1837. Although his mother had been a slave, at Pinchback's birth she had been emancipated by Pinchback's father. Moving to Ohio with his mother, Pinchback attended high school in Cincinnati in 1847, and he began working on riverboats as a cabin boy and then as a steward in 1848.

At the outbreak of the Civil War, Pinchback went to Louisiana and in 1862 enlisted in the Union Army. He soon began recruiting soldiers for an African American unit known as the Louisiana Native Guards or the Corps d'Afrique. Racial problems soon arose with the military hierarchy and Pinchback resigned his commission in protest. After the war Pinchback became active in Louisiana politics. He organized a Republican Club in 1867, and was a delegate to a state constitutional convention in 1868. In that year he was also elected to the state senate and became president *pro-tempore* of that body in 1871. He became lieutenant governor of Louisiana through the line of political succession. In late 1872 and early 1873, Pinchback was governor of Louisiana while the elected official underwent impeachment proceedings. In 1872 and 1873 Pinchback was elected to the U.S. Senate and the U.S. House of Representatives. He was refused seating both times when the elections were contested and his Democratic opponent was named to Congress.

In 1877, Pinchback switched his allegiance to the Democratic Party and in 1882 was appointed surveyor of customs for New Orleans. In 1887, he began attending law school at Straight University in New Orleans and was later admitted to the bar. In 1890, Pinchback moved to Washington, D.C., where he died December 21, 1921.

Adam Clayton Powell Jr.

Adam Clayton Powell Jr. (1908–1972)
Federal Legislator

Born on November 29, 1908, in New Haven, Connecticut, Powell was raised in New York City and graduated in 1930 from Colgate University. In 1931, Powell graduated from Columbia University with a master's degree in religious education. Powell launched his career as a crusader for reform during the Depression. He forced several large corporations to drop their unofficial bans on employing African Americans and directed a kitchen and relief operation that fed, clothed, and provided fuel for thousands of Harlem's needy and destitute. He was instrumental in persuading officials of Harlem Hospital to integrate their medical and nursing staffs, helped many African Americans find employment along 125th Street, and campaigned against the city's bus lines, which were discriminating against Negro drivers and mechanics.

When Powell Sr. retired from Abyssinian Baptist Church in 1936, his son, who had already served as manager and assistant pastor there, was named his successor. In 1939, Powell served as chairman of the Coordinating Committee on Employment, which organized a picket line before the executive offices of the World's Fair in the Empire State Building and eventually succeeded in getting employment at the fair for hundreds of African Americans.

Powell won a seat on the New York City Council in 1941 with the third highest number of votes ever cast for a candidate in municipal elections. In 1942, he turned to journalism for a second time and published and edited the weekly *The People's Voice*, which he called "the largest Negro tabloid in the world." He became a member of the New York State Office of Price Administration in 1942 and served until 1944.

In 1944, Powell was elected to Congress and represented a constituency of 300,000, 89 percent of whom were African American. Identified at once as "Mr. Civil Rights," he encountered a host of discriminatory procedures upon his arrival in the nation's capital. He could not rent a room or attend a movie in downtown Washington. Within Congress itself, he was not allowed to use such communal facilities as dining rooms, steam baths, showers, and barber shops. Powell met these rebuffs head on by making use of all such facilities and insisting that his entire staff follow his lead.

As a first-year legislator, Powell engaged in fiery debates with segregationists, fought for the abolition of discriminatory practices at U.S. military installations, and sought to deny federal funds to any project where discrimination existed. The latter effect was called the Powell amendment and eventually became part of the Flanagan School Lunch Bill, making Powell the first African American congressman since Reconstruction to have legislation passed by both houses.

Powell also sponsored legislation advocating federal aid to education, a minimum-wage scale, and greater benefits for the chronically unemployed. He also drew attention to certain discriminatory practices on Capitol Hill and worked toward their elimination. It was Powell who first demanded that an African American journalist be allowed to sit in the Senate and House press galleries, introduced the first anti-Jim Crow transportation legislation, and the first bill to prohibit segregation in the armed forces. At one point in his career, the *Congressional Record* reported that the House Committee on Education and Labor had processed more important legislation than any other major committee. In 1960, Powell, as senior member of this committee, became its chairman. He had a hand in the development and passage of such significant legislation as the Minimum Wage Bill of 1961, the Manpower Development and Training Act, the Anti-Poverty Bill, the Juvenile Delinquency Act, the Vocational Educational Act, and the National Defense Education Act. The Powell committee helped pass 48 laws involving a total outlay of $14 billion. Powell, however, was accused of putting an excessive number of friends on the congressional payroll, of a high rate of absenteeism from congressional votes, and of living a permissive lifestyle.

In 1967, the controversies and irregularities surrounding him led to censure in the House and a vote to exclude him from his seat in the 90th Congress. The House based its decision on the allegation that he had misused public funds and was in contempt of the New York courts due to a lengthy and involved defamation case which had resulted in a trial for civil and criminal contempt. Despite his exclusion, Powell was readmitted to the 91st Congress in 1968. In mid-1969, the Supreme Court ruled that the House had violated the Constitution by excluding him from membership.

Rather than return to Congress, Powell spent most of his time on the West Indian island of Bimini, where process servers could not reach him. But photographers did and the ensuing photos of Powell vacationing on his boat while crucial votes were taken in Congress affected Powell in his home district. In 1970, he lost the Democratic congressional primary to Charles Rangel by 150 votes. Powell retired from public office and worked as a minister at the Abyssinian Baptist Church. On April 4, 1972, Powell died in Miami.

Joseph H. Rainey (1832–1887)
Civil Rights Activist, Federal Legislator, Federal Government Official

Joseph H. Rainey, the first African American member of the House of Representatives, was born on June 21, 1832, in Georgetown, South Carolina. Rainey's father purchased his family's freedom and moved them to Charleston. During the Civil War, Rainey was drafted to work on Confederate fortifications in Charleston harbor and serve passengers on a Confederate ship. However, Rainey escaped with his wife to the West Indies and remained there until the end of the Civil War in 1865.

Rainey and his wife returned to South Carolina in 1866. In 1868, Rainey was elected as a delegate to the state constitutional convention and was elected to the state senate in 1870. A year later, he was elected to the House of Representatives. As a member of Congress, Rainey presented some ten petitions for a civil rights bill that would have guaranteed African Americans full constitutional rights and equal access to public accommodations. On one occasion, Rainey dramatized the latter issue by refusing to leave the dining room of a hotel in Suffolk, Virginia. He was forcibly ejected from the premises. Rainey was a staunch supporter of legislation that prevented racial discrimination in schools, on public transportation, and in the composition of juries. He supported legislation that protected the civil rights of the Chinese minority in California and advocated the use of federal troops to protect African American voters from intimidation by the Ku Klux Klan. Rainey was reelected in 1872 and, during a debate on Indian rights in 1874, became the first African American representative to preside over a session of Congress. Rainey gained reelection to Congress in 1874 and 1876.

Rainey retired from Congress in 1879. He was appointed as a special agent for the U.S. Treasury Department in Washington, D.C. He served there until 1881, after which he worked for a banking and brokerage firm. After the firm failed, Rainey took a job at a wood and coal factory. In 1886, he returned to Georgetown, where he died on August 2, 1887.

Charles Rangel (1930–)
Federal Legislator

Harlem-born Charles Rangel entered the national spotlight in 1970, when he defeated Adam Clayton Powell Jr. for the Democratic nomination in New York's 18th Congressional District.

Charles Rangel.

Born June 11, 1930, Rangel attended Harlem elementary and secondary schools before volunteering to serve in the U.S. Army during the Korean War. While stationed in Korea with the 2nd Infantry, he saw heavy combat and received the Purple Heart and the Bronze Star Medal for Valor, as well as U.S. and Korean presidential citations. Discharged honorably as a staff sergeant, Rangel returned to finish high school and to study at New York University's School of Commerce, from which he graduated in 1957. In 1960, Rangel received his J.D. while on scholarship at St. John's University.

After being admitted to the bar, Rangel was appointed in 1961 as assistant U.S. attorney in the Southern District of New York. For the next five years, he worked as legal counsel to the New York City Housing and Redevelopment Board, as legal assistant to Judge James L. Watson, as associate counsel to the speaker of the New York State Assembly, and as general counsel to the National Advisory Commission on Selective Service. In 1966, Rangel was chosen to represent the 72nd District, Central Harlem, in the State Assembly. He has served as a member of, and secretary to, the

New York State Commission on Revision of the Penal Law and Criminal Code.

In 1972, Rangel easily defeated Livingston Wingate in the Democratic primary and went on to an overwhelming victory in November. In 1974, he was elected chairperson of the Congressional Black Caucus. In his first term, he was appointed to the Select Committee on Crime and was influential in passing the 1971 amendment to the drug laws that authorized the president to cut off all military and economic aid to any country that refused to cooperate with the United States in stopping the international traffic in drugs. In 1976, Rangel, a leading congressional expert on the subject, was appointed to the Select Committee on Narcotics Abuse and Control.

Rangel served as chairperson of the Congressional Black Caucus from 1974 to 1975 and was a member of the Judiciary Committee when it voted to impeach U.S. President Richard M. Nixon. In 1975, he moved to the Ways and Means Committee, becoming the first African American to serve on the committee. Two years later, his colleagues in the New York Congressional delegation voted him the majority whip for New York State. Rangel, who has served as deputy whip for the House Democratic Leadership, was a speaker at the 1995 Million Man March.

In his capacity as chairman of the Apollo Foundation, Rangel came under fire in the late 1990s for the foundation's management of the historic theatre. In particular, allegations focused on dealings between Rangel and his long-time friend, businessman Percy Sutton. In 1999, both men were cleared of any wrongdoing by New York Attorney General Elliot Spitzer. Following the attorney general's announcement, Rangel left the board in September 1999.

Recently, Rangel has co-sponsored legislation which significantly increases funds for the research of juvenile diabetes, and he made news in 2002 by calling for a significant increase in the number of African American diplomats. Rangel was awarded by the Black Patriots Foundation in 2001.

Kenneth Reeves (1951–)
Municipal Government Official, Attorney

Elected mayor of the city of Cambridge, Massachusetts, in 1992, Kenneth Reeves was the first openly gay mayor in the state. Reeves was popular enough to be elected to a second term in 1994, running on the promise to break down the barriers between city government and local political groups.

Born to Jamaican parents, Reeves grew up in a middle-class Detroit neighborhood. After high school, he attended Harvard College. While there, he was active in community service, working at a housing development in Dorchester, Massachusetts. After graduation, Reeves traveled to the African nation of Benin, studying there for one year before returning to the United States. In 1976, he graduated from the University of Michigan Law School. Seeking a position in Cambridge, Massachusetts, he was hired by the National Consumer Law Center. He ran for public office in a grass-roots effort but lost. He opted to run for city council a second time and was elected in 1989. During that time, he also founded the W. E. B. Du Bois Academy, a mentor program pairing established African American professional men with young African American males for intense tutoring sessions.

Hiram Rhodes Revels (1822–1901)
Federal Legislator

Hiram Rhodes Revels, a native of North Carolina, was the first African American to serve in the U.S. Senate. Revels was elected from his adopted state of Mississippi, and served for approximately one year, from February of 1870 to March of 1871.

Hiram Rhodes Revels.

Born in 1827, in Fayetteville, North Carolina, Revels was educated in Indiana and attended Knox College in Illinois. Ordained a minister in the African Methodist Church, he worked among African American settlers in Kansas, Maryland, Illinois, Indiana, Tennessee, Kentucky, and Missouri before settling in 1860 in Baltimore. There he served as a church pastor and school principal.

During the Civil War, Revels helped organize a pair of Negro regiments in Maryland, and went to St. Louis in 1863 to establish a freedmen school and to carry on his work as a recruiter. For a year he served as chaplain of a Mississippi regiment before becoming provost marshal of Vicksburg. Revels settled in Natchez, Mississippi, in 1866 and was appointed alderman by the Union military governor of the state. In 1870, Revels was elected to the U.S. Senate to replace Jefferson Davis, the former president of the Confederacy. Revels's appointment caused a storm of protest from white Southerners. However, Revels was allowed to take his seat in the Senate.

As a U.S. Senator, Revels quickly won the respect of many of his constituents for his alert grasp of state issues and for his courageous support of legislation which would have restored voting and office-holding privileges to disenfranchised Southerners. He believed that the best way for African Americans to gain their rightful place in American society was not through violent means, but by obtaining an education and leading an exemplary life of courage and moral fortitude. He spoke out against the segregation of Washington, D.C.'s public school system and defended the rights of African Americans who were denied work at the Washington Navy Yard because of their race.

In 1871, Revels left the Senate. He was named president of Alcorn University near Lorman, Mississippi. He left Alcorn in 1873 to serve as Mississippi's secretary of state on an interim basis. In 1876, he returned to Alcorn. That year, he became editor of the *South-Western Christian Advocate*, a religious journal. In 1882, he retired from Alcorn University. Revels lived in Holly Springs, Mississippi, during his later years and taught theology at Shaw University. He died on January 16, 1901.

Condoleezza Rice (1954–)
Government Official, Educator

Condoleezza Rice was born on November 14, 1954, in Birmingham, Alabama. She completed her bachelor's degree in political science in 1974, graduating cum laude and Phi Beta Kappa from the University of Denver. In 1974, she received her master's degree from the University of Notre Dame, and earned a Ph.D. from the Graduate School of International Studies at the University of Denver in 1981.

Rice joined the faculty of Stanford University in 1981 as a professor of political science. At Stanford, Rice's research and teaching interests included the politics of the Soviet Union and Eastern Europe. In 1984, Rice was awarded the Walter J. Gores Award for Excellence in Teaching, and the following year, she was a fellow at the prestigious Hoover Institute.

Rice served as an advisor to the Joint Chiefs of Staff on strategic nuclear policy in 1987. In 1989, she was named director of Soviet and East European affairs on the National Security Council, a position in which she advised President George H.W. Bush during the collapse of the Soviet Union. Following her tenure with the first Bush administration, Rice returned to Stanford. She served as the university's provost from 1993–1999, earning accolades for her handling of the school's finances, and her implementation of new academic programs. Rice left Stanford in 2000 to serve as a foreign policy advisor during the George W. Bush presidential campaign. When Bush was elected, he appointed Rice as his National Security Advisor. She became the first woman and the first African American to hold the position.

Rice's publication credits include: *The Soviet Union and the Czechoslovak Army: 1948–1983* (1984), *The Gorbachev Era* (1986) (with Alexander Dallin), and *Germany Unified and Europe Transformed: A Study in Statecraft* (1995) (with Phillip Zelikow). She has also published numerous articles in journals and magazines such as *Journal of International Affairs, Studies in Comparative Communism, Time, World Politics,* and *Current History.* In addition to her posts in academia and government, Rice has served on the boards of many companies and institutions including, the Chevron Corporation, the University of Notre Dame, the San Francisco Symphony, Hewlett Packard, and San Francisco's public broadcasting network, KQED.

Norm Rice (1943–)
Municipal Government Official

Rice was born on May 4, 1943, in Denver, Colorado, and attended the University of Colorado. He was disappointed by the segregated housing and labor practices, and dropped out in his second year. Moving to Seattle

in 1969, Rice went back to college in the Economic Opportunity Program at the University of Washington, earning a B.A. in communications and an M.P.A. in 1974.

At the age of 35, he ran for Seattle's City Council in 1978 and beat the incumbent. In 1983, Rice was named president of the council, and was encouraged to run for mayor. He was defeated in 1985 but regrouped and ran again in 1989. He became the first African American to become mayor of Seattle. He began his first term by convening an education summit to include all those interested in discussing ways to improve Seattle's public schools. An outgrowth of that summit was the Families and Education Levy, which raised $69 million for student health services, drug and alcohol counseling, and after-school activities.

Because African Americans comprised only 10 percent of Seattle's population, Rice forged a broad-based coalition to win an overwhelming victory in 1993 for reelection. Along with his many duties as mayor of Seattle, Rice also served as president of the Conference of Mayors from 1995–1996.

In March of 1996, Rice announced his candidacy for governor of Washington, but he lost the election. Rice did not seek a third term as mayor in 1997 and took a job in the private sector.

Edith Sampson (1901–1979)
Attorney, Diplomat, Judge, Lecturer

Sampson was born on October 13, 1901, in Pittsburgh, Pennsylvania. The first African American woman to be named an official representative to the United Nations, Sampson served in the United Nations from 1950 until 1953, first as an appointee of President Harry S. Truman and later during a portion of the Eisenhower administration. A native of Pittsburgh, Sampson acquired an LL.B. from the John Marshall Law School in Chicago in 1925 and two years later became the first woman to receive an LL.M. from Loyola University.

A member of the Illinois bar since 1927, she argued in front of the Supreme Court in 1934. During the 1930s, she maintained her own private practice, specializing particularly in domestic relations and in criminal law. After her U.N. appointment, Sampson traveled around the world as a lecturer. She was elected associate judge of the Municipal Court of Chicago in 1962, becoming the first African American woman ever to sit as a circuit court judge. Sampson presided over divorce courts, traffic courts, and landlord-tenant relations courts. In

Edith Sampson, 1951.

1978, she retired from Cook County Circuit Court. Sampson died on October 7, 1979, at Northwestern Hospital in Chicago, Illinois.

Kurt L. Schmoke (1949–)
Attorney, Municipal Government Official, Federal Government Official

Born on December 1, 1949, Kurt L. Schmoke was inaugurated as the first elected African American mayor of Baltimore on December 8, 1987. Schmoke graduated with honors from Baltimore City College High School. In 1967, he won the award as the top scholar-athlete in the city. Schmoke received his bachelor of arts degree from Yale University in 1971, studied at Oxford University as a Rhodes scholar, and earned his law degree from Harvard University in 1976.

After graduating from Harvard, Schmoke began his law practice with the prestigious Baltimore firm of Piper & Marbury, and shortly thereafter was appointed by President Jimmy Carter as a member of the White House Domestic Policy staff. Schmoke returned to Baltimore as an assistant U.S. attorney, where he prosecuted narcotics and white-collar crime cases. He then returned to private practice and was involved in assorted civic activities.

In November of 1982, Schmoke was elected state's attorney for Baltimore, the chief prosecuting office of the city. He created a full-time Narcotics Unit to prosecute all drug cases and underscored the criminal nature of domestic violence and child abuse by setting up separate units to handle those cases. Also, Schmoke hired a community liaison officer to make sure that his office was being responsive to neighborhood questions and concerns.

In his inaugural address, Schmoke set the tone and future direction for his administration when he said that he wanted Baltimore to reduce its large high school dropout and teenage pregnancy rates and combat illiteracy. He has overseen the passage of the largest ever increase in the city's education budget, and, in partnership with Baltimore businesses and community-based organizations, Schmoke developed the Commonwealth Agreement and the College Bound Foundation with the goal of guaranteeing opportunities for jobs or college-entrance to qualifying high school graduates. Since taking office, Schmoke has also begun major initiatives in housing, economic development, and public health. Schmoke proposed educational programs to prepare Baltimore's citizens for high-tech jobs and he has also pushed growth at Baltimore's Inner Harbor. The mayor came under fire in the early 1990s because of Baltimore's persistent crime problems and his failed attempt to privatize nine Baltimore public schools.

Despite being considered the leading contender for the role of Maryland governor, Schmoke decided to run for a third term as Baltimore mayor. Interested in drug reform, Schmoke ran on the platform of decriminalizing drugs to stop related crime. An unexpectedly high turnout of close to 52 percent of registered Democrats gave Schmoke a racially polarized election win in 1995. In December 1998, Schmoke announced he would not seek a fourth term as mayor. Following his final term in office, Schmoke joined the international law firm of Wilmer, Cutler & Pickering.

Throughout his career, Schmoke has been active in the civic and cultural life of the Baltimore community by serving as a member of numerous boards of trustees. In recognition of his commitment to excellence in education and his service to the community, Schmoke has received honorary degrees from several colleges and universities.

Robert Smalls.

and was promoted to captain, the only African American to hold such a rank during the Civil War.

After the war, Smalls was elected to the South Carolina House of Representatives and served from 1868 to 1870. In 1870, Smalls became a member of South Carolina's State Senate and served until 1874. Smalls campaigned for a U.S. Congressional seat in 1874 against an independent candidate and won the election. He took his seat in Congress on March 4, 1875. During his tenure in Congress, Smalls supported a wide variety of progressive legislation including a bill to provide equal accommodations for African Americans in interstate travel and an amendment designed to safeguard the rights of children born to interracial couples. He also sought to protect the rights of African Americans serving in the armed forces.

Smalls won reelection in 1876, an election that was bitterly contested by Smalls's Democratic challenger, George Tillman. Tillman tried unsuccessfully to have Smalls's election to Congress overturned. However, Tillman's supporters were undeterred. In 1877, Smalls was accused of taking a $5,000 bribe while serving as a senator. Although Smalls was exonerated by Governor William D. Simpson, his popularity plummeted. Smalls lost his reelection bid in 1878. In 1880, Smalls ran again for Congress. He lost the election, but maintained that the results were invalid due to vote-counting irregularities. Smalls's charges were substantiated and he was allowed to take his seat in Congress in July 1882. Two months later, another congressional election was held and Smalls lost his seat to fellow Republican Edward W. M. Mackey. However, Mackey died in January of 1884 and Smalls was allowed to serve the remainder of Mackey's term. In 1886, Smalls lost an election to Democratic challenger William Elliott. Though Smalls was no longer a congressman, he remained involved in political activities. From 1889 to 1913, Smalls served as collector of the port of Beaufort. He died on February 22, 1916.

Robert Smalls (1839–1916)
Federal Legislator

Robert Smalls served a longer period in Congress than any other African American Reconstruction congressman. Born a slave in Beaufort, South Carolina, in 1839, Smalls received a limited education before moving to Charleston with the family of his owner. While in Charleston, Smalls worked at a number of odd jobs and eventually became adept at piloting boats along the Georgia and South Carolina coasts.

At the outbreak of the Civil War, Smalls was forced to become a crew member on the Confederate ship *Planter*. On the morning of May 13, 1862, Smalls smuggled his wife and three children on board, assumed command of the vessel, and sailed it into the hands of the Union squadron blockading Charleston harbor. His daring exploit led President Abraham Lincoln to name him a pilot in the Union Navy. He was also awarded a large sum of money for what constituted the delivery of war booty. In December of 1863, during the siege of Charleston, Smalls again took command of the *Planter*

Carl B. Stokes (1927–1996)
Former Municipal Official

Carl Stokes was born in Cleveland, Ohio, on June 21, 1927. Stokes and his older brother, Louis, were raised by their mother following the death of their father in 1929. At the age of 18, he joined the Army and served in Europe near the end of World War II. Following the war, Stokes studied at West Virginia State and Western Reserve University, and served as a liquor enforcement agent from 1950–1953. He returned to school at the University of Minnesota, earning a B.S. in law in 1954. Stokes then completed his J.D. degree at the Cleveland Marshall School of Law.

Along with his brother, Stokes started a law practice in Cleveland in 1957, and a year later was appointed assistant city prosecutor by Cleveland mayor Anthony Celebreeze. Involved in the Civil Rights movement, Stokes served on the executive board of the Cleveland chapter of the NAACP and joined the Urban League. In 1962 he won a seat in the Ohio General Assembly, becoming the first black Democrat to hold that office. He twice won reelection and served until his election as mayor of Cleveland in 1967.

Stokes's victory made him the first African American mayor of a major U.S. city. In the election Stokes won 50 percent of the vote in a city with a 37 percent black population. The Stokes administration was defined by an attempt to increase city services in underserved communities, and an opening of city hall jobs to African Americans. The term was also marked by a deadly shootout in the city during urban riots in July 1968. Further damage was done when it was later revealed money from the mayor's program, Cleveland Now!, had been paid to the black nationalist group implicated in the shootout.

Although Stokes won reelection in 1969, the shootout weakened the good will toward his administration and created a lasting friction among the administration, the police department, and the city council. Stokes, who enjoyed wide national recognition and was elected to the presidency of the National League of Cities in 1970, announced in 1971 that he would not seek a third term as mayor.

In 1972 Stokes left his hometown and became the first African American news anchor in the New York City area. He worked for WNBC television for eight years, serving as urban affairs editor and foreign correspondent in Africa. In 1973, Simon and Schuster published Stokes's political biography, *Promises of Power.* Stokes returned to law practice in Cleveland in 1981. He reentered the political arena in 1983 and was elected as a municipal court judge, a seat he held until 1994, when President Bill Clinton appointed him ambassador to the Seychelles. Stokes left the Seychelles on a medical leave-of-absence after he was diagnosed with cancer of the esophagus in 1995. He died in Cleveland on April 3, 1996.

Louis Stokes (1925–)
Civil Rights Activist, Federal Legislator, Attorney

Stokes was born in Cleveland, Ohio, on February 23, 1925. He was in the U.S. Army from 1943 until 1946. After leaving the service, he attended Case Western Reserve University from 1946 to 1948. He was awarded a J.D. in 1953 from Cleveland-Marshall Law School.

After 14 years in private practice with the law firm of Stokes, Character, Terry and Perry, he was elected as a democrat to the U.S. House of Representatives in 1969.

As Ohio's first African American representative, Stokes served on a number of committees including the Committee on Education and Labor, the House Internal Security Committee, and the Appropriations Committee. He also chaired the House Ethics Committee. As part of the House Assassination Committee, Stokes investigated the deaths of Martin Luther King Jr. and President John F. Kennedy. In 1972 and 1973, Stokes chaired the Congressional Black Caucus, and he was a delegate to the Democratic National Convention in 1972, 1976, and 1980. Stokes was the first African American to chair the Intelligence Committee of the House and the only African American that served on the Iran-Contra Committee. After almost two decades in Congress, Stokes retired in 1999.

Stokes belongs to the Urban League, the American Civil Liberties Union, the American Legion, and the African American Institute. He has served on the board of trustees of the Martin Luther King Jr. Center for Social Change and was vice president of the Cleveland chapter of the NAACP in 1965 and 1966. He is a recipient of the Distinguished Service Award, the William C. Dawson Award, and a Certificate of Appreciation from the U.S. Commission on Civil Rights, of which he was vice-chairman of the Cleveland subcommittee in 1966.

Louis W. Sullivan (1933–)
Educational Administrator, Federal Government Official

Louis W. Sullivan was born on November 3, 1933, in Atlanta, Georgia. On March 1, 1989, the U.S. Senate confirmed Dr. Sullivan as secretary of health and human services by a vote of 98 to 1, making him the first African American appointed to a cabinet position during the administration of U.S. President George Bush.

Instrumental in the development of the Morehouse School of Medicine, which he founded in 1975 as a separate entity from Morehouse College, Sullivan served as professor of biology and medicine and as director and founder of the medical education program at Morehouse College. In 1981, he became Morehouse School of Medicine's first dean and president.

Sullivan graduated from Morehouse College *magna cum laude* with a B.S. in 1954, and received his M.D. in 1958, graduating *cum laude* from Boston University. He completed his internship at New York Hospital Cornell Medical Center and his medical and general pathology

Louis Sullivan speaking before the U.S. Senate Labor and Human Resources Committee.

residencies at Cornell Medical Center and Massachusetts General Hospital. He then fulfilled two fellowships and served in a variety of positions with Harvard Medical School, Boston City Hospital, New Jersey College of Medicine, Boston University Medical Center, the Boston Sickle Cell Center, and others.

Sullivan has been involved in numerous educational, medical, scientific, professional, and civic organizations; has earned advisory, consulting, research and academic positions; and has received many professional and public service awards. Sullivan's research and activities focus on hematology, a branch of biology that deals with the formation of blood and blood-forming organs, and he has authored and coauthored more than 60 publications on this and other subjects. He is also the founding president of the Association of Minority Health Professions.

On January 20, 1989, Sullivan was nominated by President George Bush for the position of secretary of health and human services. He was sworn in on March 10, 1989. In his position, Sullivan was responsible for ensuring the safety of food, drugs, and medical research, and promoting health education. Upon the

expiration of his term in January of 1993, he returned to Atlanta to resume his presidency of the Morehouse School of Medicine. Sullivan served in that capacity until his retirement on May 31, 2002.

Harold Washington (1922–1987)
Federal Legislator, Municipal Government Official, Attorney

Washington was born in Chicago on April 15, 1922. After serving with the Army Air Corps in the Pacific theater during World War II, he received a B.A. from Roosevelt University in 1949. Washington then received a J.D. in 1952 from Northwestern University Law School. After graduation, Washington worked as an assistant city prosecutor in Chicago from 1954 to 1958 and while establishing a private law practice, was an arbitrator with the Illinois Industrial Commission from 1960 to 1964.

Running on the Democratic ticket, Washington was elected to the Illinois House of Representatives in 1965 and served until 1976 when he was elected to the Illinois Senate. He served in the state senate from 1977 to 1980. While a state legislator, Washington helped establish Illinois's Fair Employment Practices Commission, secured passage of consumer protection legislation, and worked to designate Martin Luther King Jr.'s birthday as a state holiday. After the death of longtime Chicago mayor Richard J. Daly in 1977, Washington finished third in the four-man contest for the Democratic nomination for mayor of Chicago. In 1980, Washington was elected to the U.S. House of Representatives and became a member of the 97th Congress. Washington served on the Education and Labor, Government Operations, and Judiciary Committees. Shortly after his reelection to the House, Washington won the Democratic nomination for mayor. In 1983 he won the election to become Chicago's first African American mayor.

Although Washington's mayoralty was marked by political infighting he did manage to institute some reforms including increased city hiring of minorities, deficit reduction, the appointment of an African American police commissioner, and reduction of patronage influence. Washington died while in office on November 25, 1987.

Maxine Waters (1938–)
Federal Legislator, Diplomat, State Representative

Waters was born in St. Louis on August 15, 1938. After graduating from high school, she moved to Los Angeles where she worked at a garment factory and for a telephone company. She eventually attended college and received a B.A. in sociology from California State University. She became interested in politics after teaching in a Head Start program and serving as a delegate to the Democratic National Convention in 1972.

In 1976, Waters was elected to the California State Assembly, where she served on numerous committees including the Ways and Means Subcommittee on State Administration, the Joint Committee of Public Pension Fund Investments, the Joint Legislative Budget Committee, the Judiciary Committee, the Joint Committee on Legislative Ethics, the Select Committee on Assistance to Victims of Sexual Assault, the California Committee on the Status of Women, the Natural Resources Committee, and the Elections, Reapportionment and Constitutional Amendment Committee. As a member of the California Assembly, she created the nation's first statewide child abuse prevention training program, gained passage of a law prohibiting strip searches for nonviolent misdemeanors, and promoted legislation to prevent toxic chemical catastrophes.

In 1990, Waters was elected to the U.S. House of Representatives where she has become an outspoken figure. In addition to holding the position of chair of the Congressional Black Caucus from 1997–1998, Waters has served on the Banking, Finance and Urban Affairs Committee and the Veterans Affairs Committee. She has also served in the influential position of "Chief Deputy Whip" for the Democratic Party since the 106th Congress. Following the 2000 presidential election, Waters was named chair of the "Democratic Caucus Special Committee on Election Reform" by Richard Gephardt. Waters has fought for legislation promoting aid to poor and minority neighborhoods in American cities and combating apartheid in South Africa.

Waters is on the board of directors of *Essence* magazine, and is involved with the National Woman's Political Caucus, the National Steering Committee on Education of Black Youth, and the National Steering Committee of the Center for Study of Youth Policy.

J. C. Watts Jr. (1957–)
Federal Legislator, Religious Leader

Julius Caesar Watts was born on November 18, 1957, in Eufaula, Oklahoma. His father is a minister and Eufaula City councilman, and his uncle once headed Oklahoma's NAACP chapter. Educated at the University of Oklahoma, Watts was a star quarterback and was named Most Valuable Player of the 1980 and 1981 Orange Bowls. He graduated with a journalism degree but chose to continue in athletics, joining the Canadian Football League's Ottawa Rough Riders. He played five years with the Rough Riders and one with the Toronto Argonauts. An ordained minister and motivational speaker for youth and church groups, Watts served as youth director at the Sunnylane Baptist Church at Del City, Oklahoma, and presided over the Watts Energy Corp.

Though he had long considered himself a Democrat, Watts became disenchanted with the direction the party was taking and decided to become a Republican in 1989. The following year he was elected chairperson of Oklahoma's Corporation Commission. The win made him the first African American Oklahoman to win a statewide election. Strongly in favor of welfare reform, defense spending cuts, and a balanced budget, the charismatic Watts built a rapport with his home state that led to his 1994 election victory over the Democratic incumbent to the U.S. House of Representatives. In doing so, Watts became the first African American Republican from a southern state to win a seat in Congress since the Reconstruction, and only the second African American Republican to win a seat in the House in 60 years.

Watts was reelected to Congress in 1996, 1998, and 2000. Shortly after elections of 1998, Watts was elected to become GOP conference chair, the party's fourth-highest position. On July 1, 2002, Watts announced that he would not seek a fifth term in Congress.

Robert C. Weaver (1907–1997)
Lecturer, Federal Government Official, Educator

Robert Weaver became the first African American appointed to a presidential cabinet post when President Lyndon B. Johnson named him head of the newly created Department of Housing and Urban Development (HUD) on January 13, 1966. Previously, Weaver had served as head of the Housing and Home Finance Agency (HHFA) from 1961 to 1966.

Robert Weaver was born on December 29, 1907, in Washington, D.C., where he attended Dunbar High School and worked during his teens as an electrician. Encountering discrimination when he attempted to join a union, Weaver decided to go to college instead and concentrated on economics. Weaver attended Harvard University where he majored in economics, receiving a B.S., an M.S., and a Ph.D. Weaver's grandfather, Dr. Robert Tanner Freeman, was the first African American to earn a D.O. in dentistry at Harvard.

Robert C. Weaver, 1942.

Weaver was one of the academics brought to Washington during the New Deal. From 1934 to 1938, he served in the Department of the Interior in various roles. He was also a part of President Roosevelt's "Black Cabinet." After leaving the Interior Department, Weaver served as a special assistant to the head of the National Housing Authority from 1938 to 1940. From 1940 to 1944, Weaver continued his work with the federal government through the War Production Board and the Negro Manpower Commission.

Weaver left the federal government because he felt implementation of anti-discriminatory measures was moving too slow. He moved in 1944 to Chicago, where he directed the Mayor's Committee on Race Relations. From Chicago he divided his time between teaching and government service.

During the late 1940s and 1950s, Weaver concentrated his energies on the field of education. He became a professor of economics at the Agricultural and Technical College of North Carolina in Greensboro from 1931 to 1932. In 1947, he became a lecturer at Northwestern University and then became a visiting professor at Teachers College (Columbia University) and at the New York University School of Education. During this period, he was also a professor of economics at the New School for Social Research. From 1949 to 1955 he was director of the Opportunity Fellowships Program of the John Hay Whitney Foundation. Weaver also served as a member of the National Selection Committee for Fulbright Fellowships from 1952 to 1954, chairman of the Fellowship Committee of the Julius Rosenwald Fund, and a consultant to the Ford Foundation from 1959 to 1960.

In 1955, Weaver was named deputy state rent commissioner by New York's governor Averell Harriman. By the end of the year, he had become state rent commissioner and the first African American to hold state cabinet rank in New York. From 1960 to 1961, he served as vice chairman of the New York City Housing and Redevelopment Board, a three-man body which supervised New York's urban renewal and middle-income housing programs. Weaver headed the Department of Housing and Urban Development until 1968. From 1969 to 1970, he served as president of Baruch College. Weaver accepted a teaching position at the Department of Urban Affairs at Hunter College in New York in 1971. After he retired from Hunter College in 1978, Weaver continued to serve on the boards of corporations, as well as educational and public institutions. Weaver wrote four books and 185 articles. In 1985, he was elected into the American Academy of Arts and Sciences. Weaver died in his New York City home on July 17, 1997.

Wellington Webb (1941–)
Municipal Government Official

Born February 17, 1941, Webb had to leave his South Side Chicago home to live with his grandmother in Denver, Colorado, due to asthma. After graduating from Colorado State College in 1964 with a B.A. in education, Webb worked in various public service-sector jobs, including welfare caseworker and special education teacher, while obtaining a master's degree.

In 1972, Webb was elected to the Colorado state legislature as a representative from the northeast section of Denver. There he served four years, and rose to prominence within the Democratic Party during the time when, in 1976, Democratic presidential hopeful Jimmy Carter chose Webb to head the state's national election committee. Upon Carter's election, Webb was named a regional director of the U.S. Department of Health, Education, and Welfare. After leaving federal government service in 1981, Webb received an appointment from Colorado's governor as executive director of the Colorado Department of Regulatory Agencies. During his tenure in the early 1980s, Webb was the only African American in the state cabinet.

Webb ran for mayor of Denver first in 1983, but lost. In 1987, he ran successfully for the city auditor post. As city auditor, he was credited with restoring professionalism to the office. In 1991, he faced his city hall colleague, a popular African American district attorney, in another mayoral race. Webb won with 58 percent of the vote, despite being outspent by his well-financed opponent. He was reelected for a second term in 1995. Counted among Webb's accomplishments as mayor are a lower crime rate, a strong economic base, low unemployment, creation of 50,000 jobs, and the completion of a new airport. Webb won a third term in 1999 with a platform promising the revitalization of Denver's poorer neighborhoods, the creation of more affordable housing, and the improved management of traffic congestion.

Webb has served as president of the U.S. Conference of Mayors, as well as head of the National Conference of Black Mayors.

Michael R. White (1951–)
Municipal Government Official

Born and raised on the east side of Cleveland, Ohio, Michael White was elected mayor of Cleveland in 1989. At the time, 40 percent of the city's population was at or below the poverty line.

An alumnus of Ohio State University, White received a B.A. in education and an M.P.A. His political career started in 1974 when he became a special assistant for the mayor's office in Columbus, Ohio. In 1978, White began six years on Cleveland's city council, followed by four years in Columbus as a state senator. In 1989, White entered Cleveland's mayoral race, running against three white candidates and City Council President George Forbes. White won the election.

The central issue for White's administration was the future of Cleveland's young people. Two focal points White worked toward was an upgrade of public education and the development of new jobs programs. White supported the development of the Lake Erie waterfront and the completion of the Rock and Roll Hall of Fame.

When Bill Clinton became president in 1992, White was invigorated by the potential changes with government's relationship to the cities. He was an outspoken supporter of Clinton's plans to get rid of the old welfare system. In 1995, White met with the National Football League Commissioner Paul Tagliabue to try and keep the Browns from moving to Baltimore. White secured a new team which began play in 1999, the same year a new football stadium opened.

In 1999, White launched a major investigation of Cleveland's police department. The inquiry focused on allegations of racism within the force. Despite the appearance of racist graffiti in a number of station locker rooms and accusations that some of the city's officers had worn white supremacist symbols on their uniforms, the investigation ended in March 2000 with White announcing no evidence had been found indicating the operation of hate groups in the department.

Michael White did not seek a fourth term as mayor of the city. He finished serving his third term on December 31, 2001.

Lawrence Douglas Wilder (1931–)
Attorney, State Government Official

Wilder was born on January 17, 1931, in Richmond, Virginia. He graduated from Virginia Union University in 1951 with a B.S. in chemistry. After graduation he was drafted into the U.S. Army and assigned to a combat infantry unit in Korea. During the Korean War he was awarded a Bronze Star for bravery and valor in combat. After being discharged from the army in 1953 Wilder worked as a chemist in the Virginia State Medical Examiner's Office. In 1959 Wilder graduated with a J.D. from Howard University Law School.

Wilder practiced law in Richmond until he became the first African American elected to the Virginia State Senate since Reconstruction. Wilder chaired the important Privileges and Elections Committee and worked on legislation supporting fair-housing, union rights for public employees, and minority hiring. He also voted against capital punishment (a position he has since rescinded). In 1985 Wilder was elected lieutenant-governor and in 1989 he became Virginia's first African American governor, winning the election by a 1/3 of 1 percent of the vote.

As governor, Wilder streamlined the state's budget, eliminated the state's $2.2 billion deficit, and worked to get civil rights legislation passed. Virginia law does not allow its governor to serve consecutive terms. After his term as governor, Wilder remained active in Virginia politics. From 1995–2001, Wilder hosted a popular weekly radio program, *The Doug Wilder Show*. In 1998, he was selected as president of his alma mater, Virginia Union University, but rescinded his acceptance of the position shortly before he was to be inaugurated as president.

In 1979, Wilder won the Distinguished Alumni Award presented by Virginia Union University. In succeeding years, he received the 1982 President's Citation from Norfolk State University, was named the 1993 Alumnus of the Year from the Howard Law School Alumni Association, and earned the 1985 Distinguished Postgraduate Achievement in Law and Politics Award. Wilder belongs to the Richmond Urban League, Richmond Bar Association, American Judicature Society, American Trial Lawyers Association, Virginia Trial Lawyers Association, National Association of Criminal Defense Lawyers, NAACP, and is vice president of the Virginia Human Relations Council.

Wilder continues to work toward the selection of a site and the construction of a slavery museum in his native state. In February 2002, Wilder was appointed by Governor Mark Warner as chairman of a 13-member commission to study the effectiveness and efficiency of Virginia's state government.

Andrew Young (1932–)
Diplomat, Municipal Government Official/
Executive, Federal Legislator, Civil Rights Activist

Andrew Young was born in New Orleans on March 12, 1932, and received a B.S. degree from Howard University and a B.Div. in 1955 from the Hartford Theological Seminary. He was ordained a minister in the United Church of Christ and then served in churches in Alabama and Georgia before joining the National Council of Churches in 1957.

The turning point of Young's life came in 1961, when he joined Reverend Martin Luther King Jr. and became

a trusted aide and close confidante. He became executive vice president of the Southern Christian Leadership Conference (SCLC) in 1967, and remained with King until King's 1968 assassination. During his years with SCLC, Young also developed several programs including antiwar protests, voter registration projects, and other major civil rights drives.

In 1970 Young lost a bid for the U.S. House of Representatives. In the aftermath of the election, Young was appointed chair of the Community Relations Committee (CRC). Though the CRC was an advisory group with no enforcement powers, Young took an activist role, pressing the city government on many issues, from sanitation and open housing to mass transit, consumer affairs, and Atlanta's drug problem. Young's leadership in the CRC led to a higher public profile and answered critics' charges that he was inexperienced in government.

Young launched another bid for a congressional seat in 1972. African Americans comprised only 44 percent of the voters in Young's congressional district. However, Young captured 23 percent of the white vote and 54 percent of the total vote to win by a margin of 8,000 votes. Young was the first African American representative to be elected from Georgia since Jefferson Long in 1870. One year later, in 1973, Young was named the recipient of the Martin Luther King Jr. Nonviolent Peace Prize.

Young was one of the most vocal supporters of his fellow Georgian Jimmy Carter's campaign for the U.S. presidency in 1976. Following President Carter's inauguration, Young left Congress in 1977 to become America's ambassador to the United Nations. Young's tenure there was marked by controversy—his outspoken manner sometimes ruffled diplomatic feathers—as well as achievement, represented primarily in the tremendous improvement he fostered in relations between the United States and lesser developed countries.

Young's career as a diplomat came to an end in 1979 when he met secretly with a representative of the Palestine Liberation Organization (PLO) to discuss an upcoming vote in the UN. America had a policy that none of its representatives would meet with the PLO as long as it refused to recognize the right of Israel to exist as a state. When the news of Young's meeting leaked out, an uproar followed. Young tendered his resignation, which President Carter accepted. The incident badly strained African American-Jewish relations as African Americans felt Jewish leaders were instrumental in Young's removal.

When Maynard Jackson was prevented by law from running for his third term of office as mayor of Atlanta in 1981, Young entered the race. Race entered the campaign when Jackson charged that African Americans who supported the white candidate, State Legislator Sidney Marcus, with "selling out" the civil rights movement. Jackson's remarks were widely criticized, and it was feared that they would create a backlash against Young, too. However, Young ended up with 55 percent of the total vote. He had won 10.6 percent of the white vote, compared to the 12 percent he had won in the primary, and 88.4 percent of the black vote, up from 61 percent earlier.

Young took office at a time when Atlanta was going through several economic and social problems including a shrinking population and a stagnating tax base. In addition, almost a quarter of the city's residents were below the poverty line, and the city was still shaken by the recent murders of 28 African American youths and the disappearance of another. Some critics doubted Young's ability to deal with Atlanta's problems. He was seen as anti-business and a weak administrator. But by 1984, the city had become so successful at attracting new businesses that it was experiencing a major growth spurt. In addition, the crime rate dropped sharply and racial harmony seemed an established fact. Young was decisively reelected.

Limited by law to two terms as mayor, Young ran unsuccessfully for governor of Georgia in 1990. His wife died of cancer four years later. In 1994, Young wrote his autobiography *A Way Out of No Way: The Spiritual Memoirs of Andrew Young.* He was co-chair of the Atlanta Committee for the 1996 Olympic Games and a member of various boards of directors including those of Delta Airlines and Host Marriott Corp. He also remained very active as president of Young Ideas, a consulting firm he founded. In 1995, Young headed up the Southern Africa Enterprise Development Fund, which, in 1996, began offering low-interest loans to small businesses in South Africa and other countries in the same region. In 2001, he attempted to help resolve the issue of forcible land seizure in Zimbabwe from white landowners by black war veterans, meeting with the country's president, Robert Mugabe.

Young has been active in urging fellow Democrats to put away partisanship and pass President George W. Bush's faith-based initiative, which would enable faith-based organizations to apply for various government grants.

Coleman A. Young (1918–1997)
Municipal Government Official

Long-time Detroit icon Coleman Young announced on June 22, 1993, that he would not seek reelection for

Coleman A. Young.

the mayoralty of the city that fall. Young had won each of his mayoral elections by a wide margin. The only mayor in the history of Detroit to serve five consecutive terms led the media to dub him "mayor for life." Once recognized as an urban savior, Detroit's highly publicized problems—crime, declining population, and poor economic standing—had finally instilled doubts in the voters regarding Young's abilities.

Young was born in Tuscaloosa, Alabama, on May 24, 1918. His family moved to Detroit in 1926, after the Ku Klux Klan ransacked a neighborhood in Huntsville, where his father was learning to be a tailor. In Detroit, Young attended Catholic Central and then Eastern High School, graduating from the latter with honors. He had to reject a scholarship to the University of Michigan when the Eastern High School Alumni Association, in contrast to policies followed with poor white students, declined to assist him with costs other than tuition.

Young entered an electrician's apprentice school at the Ford Motor Company. He finished first in the program but was passed over for the only available electrician job in favor of a white candidate. Working on the assembly line, he soon became engaged in underground union activities. Attacked by a company man one day, Young defended himself by hitting his assailant on the head with a steel bar, leading to Young's dismissal.

During World War II, Young was a navigator in the U.S. Army Air Force and was commissioned a second lieutenant. Stationed at Freeman Field, Indiana, he demonstrated against the exclusion of African Americans from segregated officers' clubs and was arrested along with 100 other African American airmen including Thurgood Marshall and Percy Sutton, former president of New York's Borough of Manhattan. Young spent three days in jail. Shortly thereafter, the clubs were opened to African American officers.

After the war, Young returned to his union-organizing activities and was named director of organization for the Wayne County AFL-CIO in 1947. However, the union fired him in 1948 when he supported Henry Wallace, candidate of the Progressive Party, in the presidential election. The union regarded Wallace as an agent of the Communist Party and supported Harry Truman. Young managed a dry cleaning plant for a few years, then founded and directed the National Negro Labor Council in 1951. The council successfully prevailed on Sears Roebuck & Co. and the San Francisco Transit System to hire African Americans. However, they also aroused the interest of the House Un-American Activities Committee, which was in the midst of hunting for alleged communists. When brought before the committee, Young, who denied he was ever a communist, refused to name anyone. Though he emerged from the hearing with his self-respect intact, his council was placed on the attorney general's subversive list. In 1956, the council was disbanded, and charges of Young's communist involvement were used against him, albeit unsuccessfully, during his first mayoral campaign.

After working at a variety of jobs, Young won a seat on the Michigan Constitutional Convention in 1961. The following year he lost a race for state representative but became director of campaign organization for the Democratic gubernatorial candidate in Wayne County (Detroit). He sold life insurance until 1964, when, with union support, he was elected to the state senate. In the senate, he was a leader of the civil rights forces fighting for low-income housing for people dislocated by urban renewal and for bars to discrimination in the hiring practices of the Detroit police force.

Young declared his candidacy for mayor of Detroit in 1973, and mounted a vigorous campaign for the office. He won the office after a racially divisive campaign. Among his early successes in office were the integration of the Detroit police department and promotion of African American officers into administrative positions. The new mayor also created a coalition of business and labor to preserve the industries remaining in Detroit and attract new ones. Young's outspoken and opinionated nature and his fondness for using expletives earned him both passionate supporters and bitter enemies. A Democrat and one of the first big-city mayors to support Jimmy Carter's presidential campaign in 1976, Young had a very close relationship with the Carter administration. He turned down a federal cabinet position offered to him by Carter, but his relationship with the president proved helpful in securing funds for Detroit.

In the 1980s, Young was intensely critical of the administrations of President Ronald Reagan and President George Bush, with their cutbacks in federal aid to urban areas. The federal government seized several opportunities to scrutinize Young as well. Over the years, Young's administration was investigated on more than six different charges including improprieties in the awarding of city contracts and illegal personal use of city funds by the police department; however, Young himself was never personally implicated in the scandals.

Young's popularity was bolstered by a number of citywide improvements credited to him such as the expansion of riverfront attractions, which brought increased convention and tourist traffic to the city and favorable tax abatements that attracted new businesses, including two major automobile plants. Middle-class and white flight to the suburbs, which had begun at the end of the 1960s, continued to rob the city's coffers of essential tax revenue. Some critics argued that Young's attitude toward suburbanites contributed to the phenomenon. Near the end of his tenure, Young endured a barrage of disapproval for autocratic style and his emphasis on cosmetic improvements rather than focusing on true remedies for the decay of the city.

In 1989, Coleman Young won his fifth term as Motor City mayor. Despite a high unemployment rate, a shortage of cash, and a high crime rate, the voters returned the popular Young to office. During 1990, both Detroit and its mayor were targets of highly critical feature stories in the *New York Times* and on CBS. Commentary revolved around Detroit's sagging economy, brutal crime statistics, racial stratification, and a supposed general air of despair. Young countered that under his administration, the city managed to balance its budget despite a dramatic cutback in federal and state aid. He also noted that many neighborhoods had undergone extensive renovation and a new automobile manufacturing plant had opened within the city limits.

In 1993, when Young felt that he no longer had the necessary vitality to run a big city, a major chapter in Detroit politics came to a close. Young turned his attentions towards writing, with Lonnie Wheeler, *Hard*

Stuff: The Autobiography of Coleman Young. After he left politics, Young was a professor of urban affairs at Detroit's Wayne State University, where he continued to raise dialogue about race and class issues. Young was in poor health during his last years and suffered from heart trouble, chronic emphysema, and other respiratory problems. He died on November 29, 1997.

Political Party Identification of the Adult Population, by Degree of Attachment, 1972 to 1994, and by Selected Characteristics, 1994

[In percent. Covers citizens of voting-age living in private housing units in the contiguous United States. Data are from the National Election Studies and are based on a sample and subject to sampling variability; for details, see source]

Year and Selected Characteristic	Total	Strong Demo-crat	Weak Demo-crat	Inde-pendent Demo-crat	Inde-pendent	Inde-pendent Repub-lican	Weak Repub-lican	Strong Repub-lican	Apolitical
1972	100	15	26	11	13	11	13	10	1
1980	100	18	23	11	13	10	14	9	2
1984	100	17	20	11	11	12	15	12	2
1986	100	18	22	10	12	11	15	11	2
1988	100	18	18	12	11	13	14	14	2
1990	100	20	19	12	11	12	15	10	2
1992	100	18	18	14	12	12	14	11	1
1994, total[1]	**100**	**15**	**19**	**13**	**10**	**12**	**15**	**16**	**1**
Age:									
17 to 24 years old	100	9	20	22	10	8	19	10	1
25 to 34 years old	100	11	19	14	12	11	16	16	1
35 to 44 years old	100	13	18	14	12	11	14	18	-
45 to 54 years old	100	15	16	15	7	16	12	17	1
55 to 64 years old	100	18	22	8	8	16	12	15	-
65 to 74 years old	100	28	17	6	8	13	14	15	-
75 to 99 years old	100	19	26	9	9	5	17	13	2
Sex:									
Male	100	13	17	12	11	14	14	18	1
Female	100	18	21	13	10	9	15	13	1
Race:									
White	100	12	19	12	10	13	16	17	1
Black	100	38	23	20	8	4	2	3	1
Education:									
Grade school	100	26	26	7	13	7	11	6	4
High School	100	15	22	14	13	10	13	11	1
College	100	14	16	13	7	13	16	21	-

- Represents zero.
[1]Includes other characteristics, not shown separately.

SOURCE: Center for Political Studies, University of Michigan, Ann Arbor, MI, unpublished data. Data prior to 1988 published in Warren E. Miller and Santa A. Traugott, *American National Election Studies Data Sourcebook, 1952–1986,* Harvard University Press, Cambridge, MA, 1989 (copyright).

Local Elected Officials by Sex, Race, Hispanic Origin, and Type of Government: 1992

Sex, race, and Hispanic origin	Total	General purpose			Special purpose	
		County	Municipal	Town, township	School district	Special district
Total	493,830	58,818	135,531	126,958	88,434	84,089
Male	324,255	43,563	94,808	76,213	54,443	55,228
Female	100,531	12,525	26,825	27,702	24,730	8,749
Sex not reported	69,044	2,730	13,898	23,043	9,261	20,112
White	405,905	52,705	114,880	102,676	73,894	61,750
Black	11,542	1,715	4,566	369	4,222	670
American Indian, Eskimo, Aleut	1,800	147	776	86	564	227
Asian, Pacific Islander	514	80	97	16	184	137
Hispanic	5,859	906	1,701	216	2,466	570
Non-Hispanic	413,902	53,741	118,618	102,931	76,398	62,214
Race, Hispanic origin not reported	74,069	4,171	15,212	23,811	9,570	21,305

SOURCE: U.S. Census Bureau, *1992 Census of Governments, Popularly Elected Officials,* (GC92(1)-2).

Population

♦ The Size of the African American Population ♦ Regional Distribution
♦ African American Towns and Settlements
♦ Contemporary Demographic Characteristics
♦ Population Projections for the Twenty-first Century

by Audrey Y. Williams

The 2000 census was the largest in U.S. history. Between 1990 and 2000 the nation's population increased by 33 million, which was the largest census-to-census increase ever reported. Even though it was the first time that the census allowed respondents to identify themselves by more than one racial category or Hispanic origin, 98 percent identified themselves as belonging to one race. Approximately 70 percent considered themselves non-Hispanic white. A little more than 12 percent identified themselves as Black or African American. Approximately 2 percent identified themselves as members of two racial groups. Of the group reporting being of more than one race, 11 percent reported being both White and Black.

♦ THE SIZE OF THE AFRICAN AMERICAN POPULATION

1619 to 1790

Although there is evidence that Blacks were in South America before Columbus came to the Caribbean, the earliest record of Blacks in what is now the United States is in 1619. A group of African and European indentured servants landed in Jamestown, Virginia, with a small number of British colonists. Historians differ on the exact number, but between 14 and 20 African indentured servants were part of this early settlement. Within a short time, the practice of enslaving Africans began and soon spread throughout the colonies. By 1630, there were 60 enslaved Africans in the American colonies; by 1660, the number increased to 2,920—almost 50 times as much.

By 1680, the colonies were growing and prospering. The strong agrarian society needed strong workers to till the fertile fields. And thus was born the commerce of human flesh, known as the "slave trade." Within 70 years after the first Africans were brought to the colonies the slave population in the American colonies had grown to 16,729. By 1740, the slave population reached 150,000; it increased to 575,000 by 1780. Although a free Black population did exist, it grew at a slower rate than the enslaved population; in 1780, there was only one free Black for every nine slaves.

By the time the Emancipation Proclamation was

Population by Race and Hispanic Origin for the United States: 2000

Race and Hispanic or Latino	Number	Percent of total population
RACE		
Total population	281,421,906	100.0
One race	274,595,678	97.6
White	211,460,626	75.1
Black or African American	34,658,190	12.3
American Indian and Alaska Native	2,475,956	0.9
Asian	10,242,998	3.6
Native Hawaiian and Other Pacific Islander	398,835	0.1
Some other race	15,359,073	5.5
Two or more races	6,826,228	2.4
HISPANIC OR LATINO		
Total population	281,421,906	100.0
Hispanic or Latino	35,305,818	12.5
Not Hispanic or Latino	246,116,088	87.5

SOURCE: U.S. Census Bureau, Census 2000 Redistricting (Public Law 94-171) Summary File, Tables PL1 and PL2.

signed, less than 8 percent of African Americans lived in the Northeast or Midwest. After the Civil War, the percentage of Blacks living in the Northeast declined slightly, and the Midwest percentage rose. By 1900, only 10 percent of all Blacks lived in the Midwest or Northeast.

In 1790 the first official American census was taken, listing 757,000 Blacks. At that time, African descendants constituted 19.3 percent of the nation's population, of which 9 percent or 59,527 were not slaves. By 1790, Pennsylvania, Massachusetts, Connecticut, Rhode Island, New York, New Jersey, and the Northwest Territory had enacted legislation providing for the gradual emancipation of slaves. By 1860, there were almost 4 million persons of African descent in the United States, over 90 percent of them in the South; the freed population, most of whom were in the North, numbered under half a million.

Population Growth Since 1865

The decline and eventual cessation of the slave trade and increased European migration accounted for the population change. In 1900 there were 8.8 million African Americans in the United States, representing 11.6 percent of the total population. Between 1910 and 1930, the African American population declined, reaching a low point in 1930 when the population was only 9.7 percent of the U.S. population. Since 1930, the African American population has grown at a rate faster than the national average. The percent of Blacks living in the South continued to fall until around 1970. At that time, about 39 percent of African Americans were Northerners, 53 percent were Southerners, and about 7.5 percent lived in the West. Thirty years later, the regional distribution of African Americans has changed. According to the 2000 Census Report, the American population numbers approximately 281.4 million, with 19 percent of all Americans living in the Northeast, 22.9 percent living in the Midwest, 35.6 percent living in the South, and 22 percent living in the West. Similar figures for the African American population in 2000 indicate a different settling pattern from the total population: 17.6 percent are in the Northeast, 18.8 percent in the Midwest, 54.8 percent in the South, and 8.9 percent in the West.

By the year 2000, the population percentages indicated a strong growth trend for the African American population. According to the 1990 census, the African American population constituted 12.1 percent of the population, up from 11.7 percent in 1980. By 1997 the African American population in the United States had grown to 32.3 million or 12 percent of the nation's total

resident population. In 2000 the African American population increased to 34.7 million or 12.3 percent of the total population.

The growth of the African American population since the 1980 census is largely due to high birth rates and increased immigration from countries with Black populations. The increase in the number of births over deaths during the past two decades was due mainly to two factors: a larger percentage of African Americans in the childbearing ages, and a reduction in infant mortalities. The African American population has grown from legal and illegal immigration. While streams of Asian and Hispanic migrants to the United States have been more highly publicized, Black immigration has also increased. The Caribbean area is one source of Black immigration, with immigrants primarily from Haiti and Jamaica entering the United States to find work. The Mariel boatlift in 1980 also brought some Blacks from Cuba. Harsh political and economic conditions in Africa, in addition, have provided many people with the incentive to emigrate to the United States. African students overstaying their student visas and working in the United States have contributed to the population figures. Estimations of the size and effects of some of these sources of new population growth are speculative. But according to the U.S. Census Bureau, legal immigration in 1996 from several Caribbean countries, with the exception of Jamaica, Haiti, Dominican

Black or African American Population: 2000

(For information on confidentiality protection, nonsampling error, and definitions, see *www.census.gov/prod/cen2000/doc/pl94-171.pdf*)

Race	Number	Percent of total population
Total population	**281,421,906**	**100.0**
Black or African American alone or in combination with one or more other races	36,419,434	12.9
Black or African American alone	34,658,190	12.3
Black or African American in combination with one or more other races	1,761,244	0.6
Black or African American; White	784,764	0.3
Black or African American; Some other race	417,249	0.1
Black or African American; American Indian and Alaska Native	182,494	0.1
Black or African American; White; American Indian and Alaska Native	112,207	-
All other combinations including Black or African American	264,530	0.1
Not Black or African American alone or in combination with one or more other races	245,002,472	87.1

- Percentage rounds to 0.0.

SOURCE: U.S. Census Bureau, Census 2000 Redistricting Data (Public Law 94-171) Summary File, Table PL1.

Republic, Trinidad and Tobago, and Cuba and African nations amounted to approximately 170,000.

◆ REGIONAL DISTRIBUTION

1790 to 1900

From 1790 until 1900, approximately 90 percent of the African American population lived mostly in rural areas of the South. The abolition of slavery after the Civil War had little impact on the Southern rural character of the African American population. The newly freed slaves were mostly illiterate with agrarian skills. Sharecropping became a way of life for many who agreed to work for very low wages in return for a shelter and a portion of the crop. Sharecropping was not much different from slavery for uneducated African Americans who were easily taken advantage of by dishonest landowners. Once the Reconstruction period ended, some African American leaders urged Blacks to migrate from the South, particularly since former Confederates were still in control in the post-Civil War era.

By 1879 thousands of Blacks from the Deep South had heeded this call by moving to the North and West in order to seek a livelihood free from the sharecropping form of slavery. Henry Adams of Louisiana and Pap Singleton of Tennessee were two African American men who encouraged migration to Kansas. Fifty thousand African Americans alone moved to Kansas from southern Louisiana. One of the towns created by this exodus—Nicodemus, Kansas—still exists today as a small, predominantly African American community. By 1891 several thousand African Americans from South Carolina and Alabama added to the numbers who migrated.

1900 to 1970

In 1900, almost 90 percent of African Americans still lived in the South. Between 1910 and 1920, however, the percentage of African Americans living in the South began to decrease. By 1930, more than 21.2 percent of African Americans resided outside of the South. For the

Between 1991 and 1996, more than 114,000 Haitian refugees fled the political and economic strife in their homeland for the United States.

Even after the end of slavery, many African Americans in the South continued to cultivate the white-owned lands as sharecroppers.

next four decades, the percentage of African Americans living in the South steadily declined. In 1970, approximately 39 percent of African Americans were Northerners, 53 percent were Southerners, and about 7.5 percent lived in the West.

The Great Migration

The exodus of African Americans from the South after the Civil War was not immediately as great a number as some would expect. In some cases uneducated African Americans stayed in the South and worked for low wages out of an ignorance of the alternatives. The emergence of the Black Codes and Jim Crow laws made the new so-called freedom seem more and more like slavery as time went on. As industrialization in the North continued to grow, numbers of European immigrants came to take the jobs, and news of the allegedly more open northern society and the jobs created by industrialization encouraged some to leave the South at the end of the nineteenth century. With the advent of World War I, immigration was curtailed. The repressive Jim Crow laws and life in the South contributed to a decline in the African American population from 1910 to 1920 and far exceeded the population decrease in the South after the entire period following the Emancipation.

Although African American migration from the South was reduced somewhat during the Great Depression of the 1930s, the proportion of African Americans living in the South continued to decrease. The greatest volume of migration of African Americans in the South occurred between 1940 and 1950. This migration was precipitated somewhat by the preparations for World War II. Both World War I and World War II proved strong motivators for African Americans to migrate north. Also, during the 30 years following the end of the Depression—1940 through 1960—the net migration of African Americans from the South totaled about 4.3 million people. After World War II there was a decreased demand for agrarian laborers as farm machinery reduced the need for manual labor.

From 1940 to 1970 the movement of African Americans away from the South was one of the major migrations in U.S. history. In volume, it equals the total Italian immigration to the United States during its peak, the 30-year period from the 1890s to the 1920s. For most African Americans, the exodus from the South meant exchanging a rural life where a person could live off the land with little or no money, to a factory job in cities where everything had to be purchased.

Urbanization

Blacks did not leave the South in great numbers after the Emancipation Proclamation because they had limited access to information about the opportunities in other parts of the country. In 1880 about 13 percent of the African American and 28 percent of the white population lived outside of cities with 25,000 or more people, and therefore were classified as rural. In the late 1800s and early 1900s, white urbanization developed rapidly, and by 1920 the majority of whites were living in urban areas. The increase represented some rural-to-urban migration and a massive wave of immigration from abroad. European immigrants arriving in the 1900s overwhelmingly settled in the cities. Thus the urbanization of the white population from 1880 to 1920 was a reflection of the cities being settled by immigrants.

Urbanization for Blacks and whites declined during the Great Depression of the late 1930s because there was a job shortage. The 1940s, 1950s, and 1960s constituted a period of migration from the South. In 1940, 73 percent of African Americans lived in urban areas compared to 70 percent for whites. By 1987, 86 percent of Blacks and 71 percent of whites lived in cities.

Decline of the African American Farmer

The rapid urbanization of the African American community has been associated with the decline in the Black farmer population. A 1982 Civil Rights Commission Report indicated that if nothing was done to correct the Black farm crisis, Black farmers would no longer exist by the year 2000. In 1920, approximately 49 percent of the Black population lived on farms. Fifty years later only about 2 percent of the nation's Black population lived on farms. In 1987 only 123,000 Blacks lived on farms.

The decrease in the farm population has had a more drastic impact on African Americans than on whites. From 1920 to 1981, the Black farm population fell by 96 percent, whereas the white farm population fell by 79 percent. Until the early 1960s, Blacks were much more dependent than whites on agriculture as a way of making a living, but in the last 20 years whites have been more likely than Blacks to live on a farm. Between 1982 and 1987, Black-operated farms decreased 30.9 percent, while white-operated farms decreased by 6.6 percent. By 1987 only 2.4 percent of whites lived on farms and only 0.4 percent of Blacks did so. In 1999, after 16 years of litigation, Black farmers won a class-action suit against the U.S. Department of Agriculture (USDA) for discriminatory lending practices. The farmers claimed that the unfair and discriminatory practices of the USDA caused them to lose their farms or suffer unnecessary hardships. Each farmer who was able to prove that s/he was discriminated against could be awarded up to $50,000. Cancellation of the USDA debts was also promised. The USDA served as the lender of last resort for Black farmers who were not considered for loans by commercial banks. Delegates attending the 2000 United Methodist General Conference pasted a resolution lamenting the decrease of Black-owned farms and criticizing the agricultural office for practicing "widespread discrimination" with regard to African American farmers.

Migration from 1970 to 1980

The civil rights struggle that highlighted the 1960s was still being waged in the 1970s. As integration, voter registration, voting, and other civil rights issues began to be addressed, the term "New South" started to be used. Children of migrants who came North years before now began to consider relocating to the South to take advantage of the new social and political climate and available jobs. In the early 1970s there were as many African Americans returning to the South as there were African Americans leaving the South to go to the North. By the mid-1980s, southern communities with economies that centered on gas and oil had a decline in jobs, contributing to a decline in the African American migration to the South. In the meantime, the African American presence in the West was growing. In 1910, African Americans were 0.5 percent of the population in the West; by 1990, their numbers increased to 9.4 percent. By 2000, African Americans represented 8.9 percent of the population in the West.

Migration from 1990 to 2000

From 1999 to 2000, 43.4 million Americans moved. Over half of the moves were local or within the same county, 20 percent were between counties in the same state, and 19 percent were moves to a different state. Movers from abroad totaled 4 percent. According to census figures for 1999 to 2000, 15.3 percent of the whites in the United States moved, and of that number 8.5 percent moved within the same county, 3.2 percent within the same state, 3.0 percent a different state, and 0.6 percent moved from abroad. The percentages for African Americans during this period showed that 19.2 percent moved, and of that number 11.7 percent moved within the same county, 3.5 percent within the same state, 3.6 percent moved to another state, and .05 percent moved from abroad.

◆ AFRICAN AMERICAN TOWNS AND SETTLEMENTS

The Cherokee, Choctaw, Chickasaw, Creeks, and Seminole peoples, often called the Five Civilized Nations, were driven from their lands in the South into what is today known as Oklahoma. Between 1830 and 1840 this area was called Indian Territory. These Native American groups brought their slaves with them to set up an agricultural way of life. Some slaves were runaways who were befriended by the Native Americans, and others were personal property. In some instances, Native Americans and African Americans inter-married and had families. After the Civil War, in which both African Americans and Native Americans participated, most of the tribes freed their slaves. The Chickasaws refused to accept the 1866 treaty that required them to adopt their freedmen.

The freedmen and approximately 10,000 African American settlers migrated west to Kansas and Oklahoma establishing between 25 to 27 towns and settlements in the Indian and Oklahoma Territories. Today

During the nineteenth century, some African Americans married and raised families within Native American communities.

there are no traces of most of those towns and settlements. The following is a chronological listing of existing key towns and settlements in Oklahoma and the South.

Nicodemus, Kansas

Nicodemus is the last survivor of the African American communities founded in Kansas after the Civil War. The founding settlers were called "exodusters." Although the exodusters were poor and lacked sufficient tools and seed money, they managed to survive the first winter, some by selling buffalo bones, others by working for the Kansas Pacific railroad at Ellis some 35 miles away. In 1800 the community consisted of an African American population of more than 400. Hopes that the railroad would come their way and add to the town's fortune never materialized. In 1974, Nicodemus was designated as a National Historic Landmark District. In 2000, the population numbered only 20.

Langston, Oklahoma

Edwin P. McCabe, who was the first African American state auditor in Kansas, wanted to make Oklahoma an all-African American state. He founded the town of Langston in 1889. By 1897, Langston had a population of more than 2,000 residents, and the Oklahoma territorial legislature granted the settlement enough land to establish the Colored Agricultural and Normal University, the first African American agricultural and mechanical college. The institution still exists and is the most western of the historically Black colleges and universities. After the land was awarded to the African American community, McCabe tried unsuccessfully to make Oklahoma an all-African American state. According to the 2000 census Langston has an African American population of 1,558, with 55 whites and 21 Native Americans.

Boley, Oklahoma

Boley, Oklahoma, was founded in 1903 on land that was taken from the Creek Nation. Booker T. Washington, a prominent African American leader of the period, encouraged African Americans to migrate to Boley and develop an all-African American town. Washington believed that it was important for African Americans to be self-sufficient and learn crafts and skills to take care of their communities. By 1910 Boley consisted of 80 acres of land and 4,000 inhabitants. It seemed that the social experiment that was providing the opportunity for Black economic, social, and political freedom might just succeed.

African American leaders in Oklahoma urged Congress and President Theodore Roosevelt to prohibit Jim Crow laws being established in the Oklahoma territory. In 1907 the territory was granted statehood without the federal guarantees. Soon Jim Crow laws were enacted to prevent African Americans and Native Americans from voting, and racial violence erupted, making the dreamed-of social experiment a nightmare for people of color. According to the 2000 census, Boley is a small town consisting of 616 African Americans, 401 whites, and 56 Native Americans. Each Memorial Day Boley hosts the Black Rodeo, which brings African Americans from around the region.

The Sea Islands, South Carolina and Georgia

Along the coast of South Carolina and Georgia are a series of islands called the Gullah or Geechee Islands. The climate is warm and humid, much like the tropical coast of West Africa, where the ancestors of today's Gullah people were enslaved and brought to the United States. Their experience in the humid heat and ability to ward off malaria made them excellent candidates to raise the rice crops important to the South. The Gullah people developed a language that is a Creole blend of Elizabethan English and African languages spoken by the Wolof and Fula people. Since there was little chance of the Gullah folk escaping the islands, they were allowed to maintain some of their African traditions. They are said to share many similarities with the people of Sierra Leone. In May, there is a Gullah festival to celebrate the African American heritage. On one of the islands, the Penn Resource Center is maintained with original artifacts, houses, and tools. Teachers, students, and others can visit for the day or spend more time learning about the language, crafts, culture, and history of the Gullah people.

Eatonville, Florida

Located approximately ten miles northeast of downtown Orlando, Eatonville, Florida, is the oldest African American municipality in the United States. In the late 1980s a civic group called Preserve the Eatonville Community was formed to protect and maintain a historic African American community that had a profound history and a celebrity to call its own. Zora Neale Hurston, a Harlem Renaissance writer and anthropologist, mentioned Eatonville in several of her books. Hurston's father served three terms as mayor of Eatonville. Hurston studied at Howard University and was the first African American woman to graduate from Barnard College. The combination of community pride and the support of literary artists like Alice

Walker and Maya Angelou prevented a major highway from cutting through the center of the town. The town now has historic landmark status and holds a "Zora!" festival annually. According to the 2000 census, Eatonville's population consists of 2,172 African Americans and 183 whites.

American Beach, Florida

American Beach, which is about 20 acres of land on Amelia Island, was given its name by Abraham Lincoln Lewis, who purchased the land in 1935. At the time that Lewis bought the land, Jim Crow laws were alive and well in the South. The beaches and resorts for whites only did not allow even millionaires like Lewis to use their facilities. Lewis planned to encourage other well-to-do African Americans to follow his example and eventually build an area for African Americans to enjoy. American Beach, like many small American towns, has had to deter aggressive developers who want to buy up the land for malls and franchises, decimating the town. In 1999 there were 150 permanent residents on American Beach, spanning an area of 78 acres.

Virginia Key, Florida

During the first half of the twentieth century, segregation rules prohibited African Americans from using Florida's scenic beaches. In 1945 the Dade County government made a deserted barrier island, Virginia Key, the only beach for African Americans. It became a vibrant recreational place for community groups, such as churches, fraternities, sororities, families and African American celebrities. In the 1960s, a hurricane destroyed most of Virginia Key's permanent buildings. Also in the 1960s, segregation was outlawed and African Americans could use other public beaches.

In 1999, the city of Miami, the legal owner of Virginia Key, began to consider leasing the beach to developers of upscale campgrounds and hotels. The united effort of environmentalists, historians, and African American activists are fighting that plan. They would prefer that Virginia Key remain undeveloped, with the exception of a civil rights park honoring African American residents who fought against segregation.

◆ CONTEMPORARY DEMOGRAPHIC CHARACTERISTICS

African American Population by State

According to the 2000 Census Report, about 60 percent of all African Americans lived in 10 states that contained almost half the total U.S. population. Census

2000 data on race cannot be accurately compared with data from the 1990 census or earlier, because the 2000 census respondents had the option of identifying their racial group as being more than one group. The states in which 6 out of 10 African Americans lived in 2000 were: New York, California, Texas, Florida, Georgia, Illinois, North Carolina, Maryland, Michigan, and Louisiana. More than 2 million African Americans lived in New York, California, Texas, Florida, and Georgia. North Carolina, Maryland, Louisiana, Virginia, South Carolina, Alabama, and Mississippi each had more than 1 million African American residents in 2000.

In 1960, 64.7 percent of the African American population resided in metropolitan areas in the United States, 51.4 percent of whom resided in central cities, as opposed to suburban areas and rural areas outside the city. In 1970, 74.3 percent of the African American population resided in metropolitan areas, with 58.2 percent living in central cities. By 1990, 83.9 percent of the African American population resided in metropolitan areas, while the proportion residing in central cities declined slightly to 57.3 percent. By 2000, 84.1 percent of the African American population was concentrated in metropolitan areas. The central city population declined to 55.1 percent, while 31.0 percent were living in the metropolitan area outside of the central city.

In 1960, African Americans constituted 16.7 percent of all central city residents; by 1970, African Americans constituted 20.6 percent. According to the 2000 census, the African American population increased faster than the white non-Hispanic majority, but lacked the additional push from immigration to keep up with the Hispanic or Asian American growth rates. African Americans remain the predominant minority group in the South in 2000, while they made up about 12 percent of the total U.S. population.

Although the last decade of the twentieth century saw an increase in the numbers of African Americans leaving the cities for the suburbs, integration often did not happen. In some suburban areas, neighborhoods evolved over time from predominantly white to white/mixed minority to predominantly minority, very similar to the progression that took place in central city areas in the 1990s. Washington, D.C., for example, was two-thirds white and about one-third African American in 1950. In 2000, the city was two-thirds Black and one-quarter non-Hispanic white. In suburban Prince George's County, Maryland, just across the district line, the population was about 85 percent white in 1970. In 2000, the county's population was 24 percent non-Hispanic white and 63 percent Black, reflecting the movement of Blacks from Washington, D.C., into the county.

As a consequence of migration and population shifts, African Americans increasingly became concentrated

Distribution of the Black Population by State: 1999

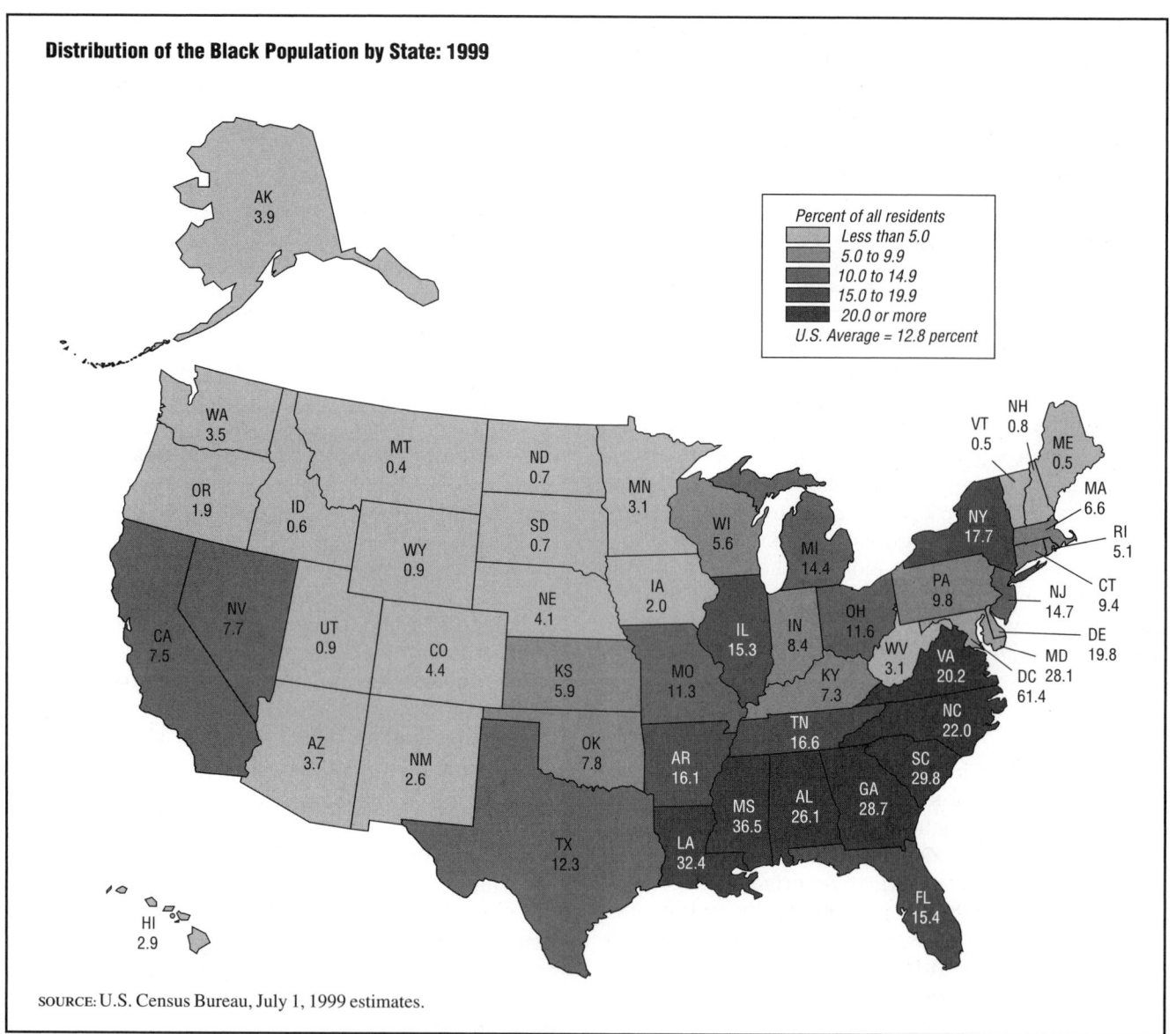

Percent of all residents
- Less than 5.0
- 5.0 to 9.9
- 10.0 to 14.9
- 15.0 to 19.9
- 20.0 or more

U.S. Average = 12.8 percent

SOURCE: U.S. Census Bureau, July 1, 1999 estimates.

in urban areas called ghettos. As in the South, whites that controlled the community from afar frequently owned the land and buildings of the ghettos. These urban areas not only supported segregation between racial groups, but also created intra-group boundaries among African Americans of differing socioeconomic status.

Ghettos offered lower-income African Americans two harsh choices: either dilapidated, privately-owned housing or large public housing projects that posed significant problems, such as poorly maintained facilities, unsafe conditions, and incentives for crime. Later in the century, as African Americans migrated outside large metropolitan areas, many of these problematic housing projects were demolished.

In 1980, African Americans made up 22.5 percent of the total central city population. However, by 1990 this number fell to 22.1 percent. Similar to the white population, though in smaller numbers, the African American population was migrating out of central cities to suburban and rural areas. African Americans moved to the suburbs because there were better options. Middle-class Blacks could afford houses in the suburbs that were unattainable in the cities. Also, some families moved to the suburbs in response to urban renewal programs that were at times termed "African American removal." San Francisco is an example of a city that had a decline in its African American population according to the 2000 census data.. More than 18,500 have left San Francisco since 1990, representing a 23 percent decline. Similarly, Miami lost 21.5 percent of its Black

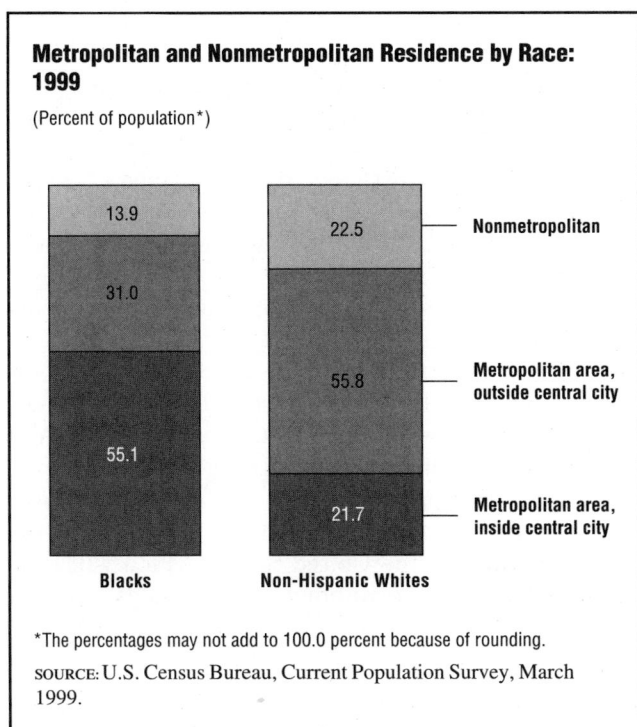

Metropolitan and Nonmetropolitan Residence by Race: 1999

(Percent of population*)

Blacks: Nonmetropolitan 13.9; Metropolitan area, outside central city 31.0; Metropolitan area, inside central city 55.1

Non-Hispanic Whites: Nonmetropolitan 22.5; Metropolitan area, outside central city 55.8; Metropolitan area, inside central city 21.7

*The percentages may not add to 100.0 percent because of rounding.

SOURCE: U.S. Census Bureau, Current Population Survey, March 1999.

population during the 1990s, and Washington, D.C., and Los Angeles also had declines.

Among the 15 cities with the largest African American concentrations, Washington, D.C., and Atlanta had African American majorities by 1970. By 1990, four additional cities—Detroit, Baltimore, Memphis, and New Orleans—had African American majorities, and five of the 11 largest cities in the nation were more than 50 percent African American.

The African American Urban Population

New York City had the largest number of people— 2.3 million—reporting as Black in the 2000 Census. Chicago had 1.1 million, followed by Detroit and Philadelphia, which had between 500,000 and 1 million each. In the Census 2000 report on race and cities, the list of the ten cities with the greatest percentage of African Americans is headed by Gary, Indiana, with 85.3 percent. Gary is followed by Detroit, Michigan, with 82.8 percent; Birmingham, Alabama, with 74.0 percent; New Orleans, Louisiana, with 67.9 percent; Baltimore, Maryland, with 65.2 percent; Atlanta, Georgia, with 62.1 percent; Memphis, Tennessee, with 61.9 percent; Washington, D.C., with 61.3 percent; and Richmond, Virginia, with 58.1 percent.

◆ POPULATION PROJECTIONS FOR THE TWENTY-FIRST CENTURY

The 2000 census revealed the ethnic diversity that will mark the future of the United States. In the 2000 census, nearly 40 percent of the population under 18 years was African American, Asian American, Hispanic American, Native American, or another minority, while 61 percent was non-Hispanic white. The Hispanic category includes a mix of people, some of whom are of African descent, but who identify themselves as Hispanic because of culture and language.

The growth of the minority populations was reflected in the new designations for some states and cities. California as of 2000 became a "minority majority" state, meaning that non-Hispanic whites made up less than 50 percent of the state population. Arizona, California, Hawaii, New Mexico, and Texas and selected counties throughout the country also became minority majorities. In some cases, minority majority communities were clustered around large urban areas; in other cases, these counties identify Native American reservations or non-metropolitan counties with large African American or Hispanic populations.

The projections show the white population decreasing while the population of persons of color increasing. In 2010, the white population is projected to be 241.7 million, or 80.6 percent of the population. That same year, the African American population is estimated to be 39.9 million people, or 13.3 percent of the nation's population. In 2025, the projected white population is 265.3 million, compared to 47.1 million Blacks, which respectively account for 78.5 percent and 13.9 percent of the national population. In 2050, according to the 2000 census data, the African American community will grow to 59.2 million people, representing 14.7 percent of the American population. During the same time period, it is estimated that the white population percentage will decrease. The white population is projected to grow to 302.5 million people, or 74.9 percent of the population.

In the coming decades the elderly population will be much more racially and ethnically diverse than in the 1990s. According to projections, in 2050, of the 80.1 million elderly, 8.4 million will be black, 6.7 million will be races other than white or black, and 12.5 million will be Hispanic, who may be of any race.

In 1990, 28 percent of the white population was age 65 or older. Of that number, 21.7 percent were aged 65 to 79, and 6.3 percent were 80 or older. In contrast for Blacks, 2.5 percent were age 65 or older. Of that number, 2.0 percent were aged 65 to 79, and 0.5 percent were in the over 80 group. For 2050, the projections suggest that all groups will have more people in the elderly groups. For African Americans, 8.4 percent will be in the 65 or older group, 5.9 percent will be aged 65 to 79, and 2.5 percent will be in the over 80 group.

While persons other than white constituted about 1 in 10 elderly persons in 1990, that will change significantly by 2050 when the proportion may increase to 2 of 10. Over this period, the number of elderly Blacks will probably more than triple, and their proportion of the total elderly population will increase from 8 to 10 percent. Asians, Pacific Islanders, Native Americans, Eskimos, and Aleuts combined will increase from less than 2 percent of the total elderly population to 8 percent over the 1990 to 2050 period.

The decrease in the white population and the increase of people of color may change some of the dynamics that were part of the country's history through the twentieth century. The quality and quantity of tension expressed by the many minority groups whose numbers will have increased will have to be addressed. The Hispanic and Asian groups are projected to increase in significant numbers and will vie for their piece of the American pie. Although the multiracial groups were less than 4 percent in the 2000 census, their designation may reduce the percentage of people who are currently counted as Black, Hispanic, or Asian, which were the categories used before the 2000 census. Particularly in Latin America and the Caribbean area, there are multiracial people who may have been counted as Black or white in the past, because the census questionnaire offered a limited choice. The new questions initiated in the 2000 census allow people with multiracial backgrounds to define themselves more specifically. Population figures strongly affect the number of political representatives. The projections suggest that there will be a significant increase in the people of color in the United States, which will have political, social, and economic consequences.

13

Employment and Income

◆ Employment Trends ◆ Labor Force Participation and Unemployment
◆ Federal Government Response to Employment Discrimination ◆ Income Trends
◆ Federal and State Programs that Address Poverty ◆ Status of African Americans
◆ Employment and Income Statistics

by Michael D. Woodard and Verna J. Henson

The last quarter of the twentieth century brought about significant changes in the social and economic status of African Americans. Educated and skilled African Americans experienced considerable upward mobility. Analysts pointed to the passage of equal opportunity legislation during the Civil Rights Era as the primary reason why African Americans with education and skills became able to take advantage of once-denied opportunities in employment and income growth. On the other hand, downsizing, job restructuring, and job dislocation were widespread in the government and private sector. Companies eliminated many blue collar jobs—some by relocating them to countries with cheaper labor—that once provided upward mobility for the less skilled. As a result, African Americans with less education and less skill experiencing decreased income, higher rates of unemployment, or removal from the labor force altogether. In this chapter the employment trends of African Americans will be examined in terms of their employment, occupation, income, and poverty status.

◆ EMPLOYMENT TRENDS

The most significant change in twentieth century American race relations was that African Americans were participating in all areas of employment. Historically, including much of the twentieth century, African Americans were restricted to service jobs in all industry sectors. For example in the corporate arena, the idea of an African American leading a major corporation was not considered. In the entertainment industry,

African Americans were severely underutilized and the roles available to them were limited to buffoonery. African Americans were locked out of professional sports and restricted to segregated leagues, ignored in the arts, and not considered seriously as politicians. By 2002, while still under represented, African Americans headed major corporations and sat on corporate boards of directors. African Americans were well represented in both Democratic and Republican administrations, heading important federal departments and influencing the policy by which this and other countries operate. There was a plethora of African American stars in the music, television, and film industries. In addition, African Americans were increasingly making strides in production and executive positions. Once admitted, African Americans dominated professional sports, including golf and tennis. To say that opportunities did not improve for African Americans would certainly be inconsistent with the facts.

Despite the dramatic changes in the last quarter of the twentieth century, not every segment of the African American population benefitted. The growing African American middle-class experienced a greater range of occupational and economic opportunities than ever before, but an increasing number of African Americans who are disadvantaged were, in effect, locked out of the mainstream of American life. This growing schism in the social and economic conditions among African Americans had serious implications for the way African Americans should be viewed as a group and for the future of the African American community.

◆ LABOR FORCE PARTICIPATION AND UNEMPLOYMENT

In March 2000, there were approximately 16 million African Americans in the civilian labor force comprising 12 percent of the civilian labor force. The labor force participation rate for black men was 68.1 percent and 63.9 percent for black women. The labor force participation rate for white men was 74.3 percent and 60.8 percent for white women. Thus black men were less likely to be in the job market than white men.

Unemployment remained a major problem among African Americans in the labor force as high levels of unemployment have persisted for several decades. Data from the U.S. Bureau of the Census showed that this pattern continued. For example, during the early 1990s, the unemployment rate for African Americans fluctuated but remained above 11 percent. It was not until 1995 that the unemployment rate for African Americans dropped below 11 percent. In 1997, the unemployment rate was 10 percent, and, by 1999, the unemployment rate for African Americans declined to 9 percent. The steady decline in unemployment was attributed to the overall health of the economy. Even with a steady decline, since the 1950s, the unemployment rate for African Americans was consistently twice as high as for whites: 4 percent for white men and 3 percent for white women in 1999.

The Effects of Occupational Discrimination

Much of the variance in unemployment rates between blacks and whites is a direct result of discrimination in the job market, past and present. In fact, for a long time, there were many occupations that African Americans could not hold, regardless of their education level. This resulted in an occupational structure for blacks substantially different from that for whites, remaining in place despite civil rights legislation.

According to the 2000 U.S. census, in 1997, 7.3 percent of all employed African Americans held managerial and professional specialty positions; 15.1 percent were employed as operators, fabricators, or laborers; and 17.6 percent worked in service occupations. African American males were more likely than any other group to be in the most vulnerable blue-collar occupational category, operators, fabricators, and laborers.

Civilian Labor Force Participation Rates by Sex, Race, and Hispanic Origin: 1999

(Percent of population aged 16 and older)

- White non-Hispanic — Men: 74.3 / Women: 60.8
- Black — Men: 68.1 / Women: 63.9
- Asian and Pacific Islander — Men: 74.0 / Women: 59.3
- Hispanic (of any race) — Men: 80.4 / Women: 56.6

■ Men
▢ Women

SOURCE: U.S. Census Bureau, Current Population Survey, March 2000.

In 1997, African Americans comprised 3.6 percent of all health diagnosing occupations.

Furthermore, the occupational marginalization of African American men seemed to be worsening. In 1999, 31 percent of all employed black males held these types of jobs compared to 17 percent of all white males. In addition, 17 percent of employed black males maintained jobs in the lower-paying service sector compared to 8 percent of white males. In contrast, only 17 percent of employed black males held managerial and professional jobs compared to 32 percent for white males. Whereas the operators, fabricators, and laborers category was the largest occupation group for black men, the managerial and professional category was the largest single category for white men. For females, the greatest disparity was in service jobs and managerial and professional jobs: white women had greater representation in managerial and professional jobs (35%); black women had greater representation in service jobs (27%).

Racial discrimination continued to exacerbate African American employment problems. A single-minded focus on racial discrimination in the workplace, however, would neglect and discount the impact of economic changes in the global economy on a skewed occupational distribution, increased joblessness, and lowered real wages among many African Americans in the last quarter century. These economic changes included: the shift from mass production in a manufacturing-based economy to highly computerized data management in an information-based economy; the decrease in the number, quality, and variety of blue-collar jobs; and shifting patterns and location of business and industry.

These economic changes have had an adverse effect on demand for blue-collar labor. Coupled with the cumulative experiences of racial restrictions, the higher number of less-skilled African American workers suffered the most. This circumstance was further compounded for the less-skilled, inner-city African Americans who were geographically isolated from the growing number of jobs shifted to the suburbs and socially isolated from informal job networks that have become a major source of job placement.

Structural changes in labor demand did not just benefit the more educated and highly trained African Americans and white Americans, though. The impact of these structural changes on African Americans were first noted by William J. Wilson in his path-breaking book, *The Declining Significance of Race* (1980) and further elaborated in *The Truly Disadvantaged* (1987). Nevertheless, one cannot ignore the persistent impact of racial discrimination in maintaining disparity between blacks and whites even when education levels are the same.

◆ FEDERAL GOVERNMENT RESPONSE TO EMPLOYMENT DISCRIMINATION

Public Policy on Bias in Employment

The Civil Rights Act of 1964 prohibits discrimination on the basis of race, color, gender, or national origin. This law formed part of an array of public programs that comprised the "Great Society" legislation of the Kennedy and Johnson administrations. Among these measures was the Economic Recovery Act of 1964, which included the Job Corps, the Manpower Training Programs, and many other social interventions. These programs are generally acknowledged as being important to improving the employment prospects of African Americans.

However, according to many policy experts, the Reagan administrations of the 1980s "turned back the clock" to a time of overt and blatant discrimination toward African Americans. They argue that President Ronald Reagan attacked many of the social programs that protected the rights of minorities and used the U.S. Civil Rights Commission to advance his conservative agenda. Indirect support to this claim is the fact that only 4.1 percent of Reagan's political appointments were African American, as compared to 21 percent for President Jimmy Carter. Moreover, experts claim that Reagan's record of recruitment and hiring of African Americans was worse than those of the Johnson, Nixon, and Ford administrations as well. In the estimation of many analysts, the George H. W. Bush administration extended the damaging trends of the Reagan policies into the early 1990s.

The Clinton administration, which enjoyed the widespread support of African Americans, also faced allegations of wrongdoing in the area of racial concerns. In 1997, employees of the Department of Energy leveled accusations against the heads of the department that they skewed data in order to make it appear that they had awarded more minority contracts than they did in reality. While the department had made an impressive 42 percent increase in the number of contracts awarded to minorities, this figure did not approach the 59 percent statistic presented to President Clinton. Other information was deliberately misleading in order to boost the image of the department as being committed to minority business advancement.

Discrimination Lawsuits Decided by the Courts

Although job discrimination does still exist, African Americans found recourse in the court system in the

In 1997, African Americans comprised 17.6 percent of all service industry occupations.

late 1990s as several high-profile lawsuits forced companies to treat their employees equally, regardless of race. In 1996, African American workers won a case against Circuit City after charging that the retailer systematically discriminated against them in promotions at the company's headquarters. That same year Texaco agreed to pay $176 million in the largest race discrimination settlement ever after 1,350 African American employees filed a class action suit to protest the oil company's discriminatory work environment. In addition to the settlement, the company set up diversity workshops for all 20,000 of its employees and boosted its minority hiring from 23 percent to 26 percent.

The federal government has not been exempt from discrimination lawsuits. In 1999, Secretary of Agriculture Dan Glickman settled a class action lawsuit against his department filed by African American farmers in 1997. The settlement attempted to make amends to the thousands of minority farmers who were denied government loans over the years because of their race. According to the terms of the settlement, each farmer would receive $50,000, and any government loans would be forgiven. Many farmers pointed out that their commercial loans—which would not be forgiven and which

carry a higher interest rate than government loans—in general, far exceeded the amount of money being granted, leaving them with significant debts they may not have accrued had they been granted government loans in the first place. In addition, none of the agents who applied discriminatory practices were punished for their past actions.

◆ INCOME TRENDS

The median income for African American families increased throughout the 1990s. In 1993, the median income for African American families was $22,974; by 1999 it had increased to $27,900 ($30,439 in 2000, a 32.5 percent increase). In comparison, median income for white families was $40,195 in 1993 and $44,400 by 1999, a 10.5 percent increase. Although white families experienced a smaller percentage increase over the same period, they started, and remained in 2000, at a level about 50 percent greater ($45,904 as compared to $30,439). Moreover, this disparity has existed for four decades.

The income disparity was even more troubling when factoring educational attainment. Sociological studies

African American female laundry workers staging a strike for improved benefits and wages.

have consistently shown that blacks with comparable levels of education, occupation, and experience tend to earn less than their white counterparts. Data on household income from the U.S. Census Bureau confirm those findings. The table "Earnings by Highest Degree Earned: 1999" presents average income by educational level and reveals that greater education translates into greater income for both blacks and whites. However, the income benefit that white males derive from education far outstrips that for black men and women, as well as for white women. Another troubling pattern is that the amount of disparity between blacks and whites increases as the educational level increases. At the high school graduation level, black men average $22,698 annually while white male high school graduates average $29,782. In other words, black men with a high school diploma earn 76 percent of the income that high school educated white men earn. Black men with a bachelor's degree earn 75 percent of the amount their white counterparts; those with professional degrees earn 61 percent; at the doctorate level, black men earn only 54 percent as much as white men with the same education. To make the point another way, in 1999, black men with a doctorate averaged less income than white men with a bachelor's degree. This table also makes clear that, regardless of race, men derive greater income benefit from their educational accomplishment than women. Therefore, black women receive the smallest financial increase at each level of educational attainment.

The Impact of Family Structure on the Income of African American Families

Family structure also impacts the income potential of African American families. In this section, the income distribution of married-couple, male-headed (wife absent), and female-headed (husband absent) households will be examined.

In 1998, 28 percent of all African Americans had incomes of $50,000 or more, with married couples more likely than other family types to be in this group. Forty-eight percent of African American married couples earned $50,000 or more and 23 percent reported incomes that exceeded $75,000. For white married-couple families, 58 percent had incomes that exceeded $50,000 with 33 percent in excess of $75,000.

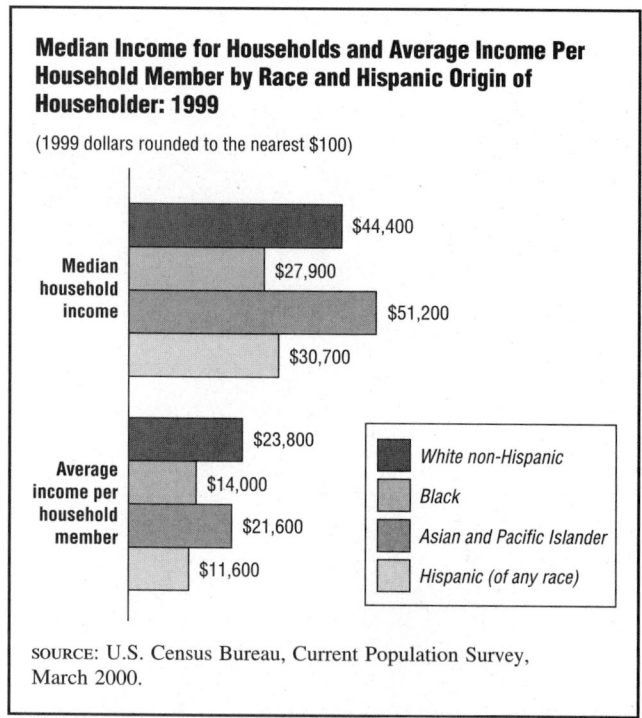

Median Income for Households and Average Income Per Household Member by Race and Hispanic Origin of Householder: 1999

(1999 dollars rounded to the nearest $100)

Median household income
- White non-Hispanic: $44,400
- Black: $27,900
- Asian and Pacific Islander: $51,200
- Hispanic (of any race): $30,700

Average income per household member
- White non-Hispanic: $23,800
- Black: $14,000
- Asian and Pacific Islander: $21,600
- Hispanic (of any race): $11,600

Legend:
- White non-Hispanic
- Black
- Asian and Pacific Islander
- Hispanic (of any race)

SOURCE: U.S. Census Bureau, Current Population Survey, March 2000.

Single parent, female-headed families were concentrated more in the lower income groups. Sixty-seven percent of black female-headed families had incomes of less than $25,000. For white female-headed families, 46 percent earned less than $25,000. For male-headed families, 43 percent of black families had incomes of less that $25,000 while 26 percent of white families earned less than $25,000. Among racial comparisons based on family structure types, black female-headed households fared the worst.

Age of Householder and African American Family Income

Age is a reasonably accurate measure of work experience and therefore one of the most important factors to consider when assessing income. One fact that is often overlooked when considering black-white income differences is the significant variation in the age distributions of the two groups—variation in itself reflecting sociological factors. In other words, it is necessary to compare blacks and whites in the same age categories to obtain a complete picture of the African American income situation. Family income data for 1990 from the U.S. Department of Commerce confirm the relationship between income and age. Generally speaking, family income increases for African Americans as the age of the householder increases. African American householders in the 15- to 24-year-old age category had a median family income of $7,218.

For those between 25 and 34, the median family income was $17,130. Family income gradually rises for African Americans until it peaks at $30,847 for householders between 45 and 54 years old. Beyond that age, there is a gradual and expected decline in income as they withdraw from the labor force. Nonetheless, in no age category do blacks equal whites in median family income. The figures range from 40 percent as much in the 15 to 24 age group to 72 percent as much in the 65 to 74 age group. Overall, black householders under age 65 earn only 59 percent as much as their white counterparts.

Regional Differences in Black Family Income

Income for African American families is likely to vary among different regions of the country. The South continued to have the lowest median household income of any region. At $38,410 the South's average represented about 86 percent of the median household income of the remaining regions. Notably, about half of the African American population resides in this region. The 2000 median household incomes in the other regions were $44,744 in the West, $44,646 in the Midwest, and $45,106 in the Northeast. These differences reflect the variations in regional economies and occupational opportunities for blacks and whites.

Poverty and the African American Community

Employment, unemployment, and income all have an impact on the level of poverty that exists in the African American community. Government statistics on poverty showed a 20 percent decrease in the number of African Americans in poverty since 1960. In 1959, there were 9.9 million blacks living below the poverty line. In 2000 that figure declined to 7.9 million. The major difference was the poverty rates in the two periods. In 1959 the poverty rate was 55.2 percent. The poverty rate for African Americans declined to 22.1 percent in 2000, a historical low. The economic recovery since the 1990–1991 recession accounted for the decline in the poverty rate for blacks.

The difference between the African American poverty rate and the white poverty rate narrowed over the last two decades. In 1980, the poverty rate for whites was 10 percent while the poverty rate for blacks was 33 percent. By 2000, the poverty rate for whites declined to 7.5 percent and the poverty rate for blacks declined to 22.1 percent.

However, a more troubling picture of economic hardship can be seen when examining the depth of poverty. Slightly less than half (3.4 million) of the black poor in 2000 were "severely poor"—that is, they had incomes less than 50 percent of the poverty threshold.

These are the families William J. Wilson described in his book, *The Truly Disadvantaged*, suffering from the relocation of jobs and disproportionately locked in the central city, thus, outside of the job information network. In total some 10.1 million African Americans were near poor in 2000—that is, they had incomes above the poverty threshold but by only 25 percent or less. Taken together, the severely poor, the poor, and the near poor comprised 33 percent of the African American population.

Poverty and African American Teenage Pregnancy

One problem associated with poverty in the African American community is that of single-parent families, of which many teenage mothers made up the most extremely challenged. Rates of pregnancy and nonmarital childbirth are higher for black teenagers than whites, though the gap closed at the end of the twentieth century. Studies indicate that the differences between the two groups can be explained by differences in sexual activity, rates of abortion, the use of contraceptives, and rates of marriage before the child's birth.

Irrespective of the causes of African American teenage pregnancy, the consequences are dramatic for the African American community. Generally speaking, teenage mothers are more likely to be poor and are less likely to finish high school. In more cases than not, the fathers are absent or non-supportive. Thus, it is not unusual for teenage mothers to be dependent on public assistance as a means of support. In large part, this accounts for 38.7 percent of female-headed (spouse absent) households falling below the poverty line in 2000. Teenage mothers tend to be unprepared for the adult responsibilities of parenting. Their children are more likely to be the victims of child abuse and to suffer physical, emotional, and educational problems later on in life.

African American community organizations have attempted to tackle the problem of teenage pregnancy. Groups such as the Children's Defense Fund, the National Urban League, Delta Sigma Theta, and a host of others have developed teenage pregnancy prevention programs. Often these efforts focus on teenage males as well as females.

◆ FEDERAL AND STATE PROGRAMS THAT ADDRESS POVERTY

The issue of African American teenage pregnancy is only one dimension of the overall problem of poverty within the African American community. Many of the programs that address the needs of the poor such as Headstart, Medicaid, Medicare, the Food Stamp Program, and several other forms of assistance were part of a comprehensive effort referred to as the "War on Poverty." Critics argue that these programs were expensive, wasteful, and ineffective. Supporters claim that the programs have not failed, but that America is ambivalent in its determination to provide equal opportunity in employment and the political arena.

Welfare Reform

The most abrupt shift in public policy regarding poverty occurred in 1996 when President Bill Clinton signed sweeping welfare reform legislation into law. Designed to end what critics called an expensive and ineffective bureaucratic system, the legislation called for a mandatory five-year limit for all welfare recipients and stricter rules—such as work requirements—that forced many recipients off the welfare rolls. Within a year, the welfare caseloads in each state had dropped at a startling pace, falling 27 percent nationally from 1994, when the number of recipients was highest. Among the nation's poor, the impact of this legislation was swift, especially in the African American community where poverty is endemic. In early 1997, African Americans accounted for 37 percent of the nation's welfare caseload, even though they only comprised 13 percent of the general population. While the reform caused the welfare load to decline, whites left welfare at a greater rate than blacks—25 percent for whites versus 17 percent decline for blacks. The larger white exodus from welfare roles caused some African American activists to worry that such numbers could reinforce the welfare stereotype of unemployed African Americans.

Three years after the legislation passed, most observers claimed that it was too early to determine whether the reform had a positive or negative impact on the poor. Most studies demonstrated that approximately 50 percent of those who left welfare had jobs, though many of them paid minimum wage only. African Americans had greater obstacles to overcome in becoming financially independent than whites due to a variety of factors, including a greater concentration in inner-cities where jobs are scarce, larger families, and less education.

Affirmative Action Programs Receive Criticism

The social intervention created the greatest backlash against affirmative action. Affirmative action was initiated during the 1960s during the Kennedy and

Johnson era. As such, it provided guidelines and required the establishment of goals and timetables in the hiring of underutilized groups, specifically racial/ethnic minorities, the disabled, and women. The guidelines do not require, however, the hiring of unqualified individuals, despite what opponents argue. Rather, affirmative action rules require the documentation of a good faith effort to hire qualified persons from underutilized groups. Affirmative action rules have been effective in changing hiring practices because they have the weight of the federal government enforcement. As a direct result, a broader range of opportunities became available for African Americans in government, the corporate world, and colleges and universities.

Affirmative action programs have been under particularly heavy attack in the 1990s with several programs being restricted or dismantled altogether. For instance, the 1989 landmark U.S. Supreme Court ruling in *City of Richmond v. J. A. Croson Co.* struck down as unconstitutional under the Fourteenth Amendment a city ordinance of Richmond, Virginia, requiring that 30 percent of each public construction contract be set aside for minority businesses. In June 1995, Adarand Constructors Inc. filed suit against the U.S. Department of Transportation claiming that consideration of "disadvantaged" status—assumed to include women and minorities—in awarding subcontracts violated the equal protection component of the Fifth Amendment's due process clause. The U.S. Supreme Court, in *Adarand v. Peña* remanded the case for further consideration at the appellate level using the "strict scrutiny" criteria established in *Croson.* The Adarand and Croson rulings greatly limited the access of disadvantaged entrepreneurs to procurement opportunities in the private and government sectors.

Studies have documented that while whites support the general principle of equality for all, most do not support the idea of programs and social intervention specifically designed to improve the conditions of African Americans and other minorities. The American belief in rugged individualism leads white Americans to the opinion that social and economic differences between blacks and whites are due to individual factors not systemic factors.

Affirmative action programs have their share of African American critics as well. Many African American conservatives argue that affirmative action programs do not help the disadvantaged. They claim that these programs primarily benefit the African American middle class—a group, they say, that needs no assistance in achieving its economic goals. In addition, critics of affirmative action argue that it unfairly stigmatizes all African Americans, whereby the success of

African Americans in any field is often dismissed as being due to affirmative action. In other words, many whites perceive the need for affirmative action as confirming their belief in the inferiority of blacks.

♦ STATUS OF AFRICAN AMERICANS

The social and economic status of African Americans is complex. It is clear that major improvements have occurred as a result of the civil rights movement, civil rights legislation, and affirmative action policies. Many African Americans are holding more high-status jobs and earn higher incomes than ever before. While the *percentage* of poor African Americans is declining slightly, the number of African Americans who are impoverished remains extremely high. In other words, when one speaks of the future of the African American community, one has to be clear that it is a community that consists of many segments. The lifestyles and opportunities for African Americans in one segment may be vastly different than the conditions experienced by those in another.

Despite the dramatic changes that have occurred within the African American community as a whole, one thing has remained the same: blacks have yet to achieve equality with whites on any measure of social and economic standing. African Americans have consistently had rates of unemployment at least twice as high as those for whites. Blacks who are employed are more likely than whites to hold blue-collar jobs—the type of jobs most likely to be eliminated during the restructuring of the American economy. African Americans are more likely than whites to be among the

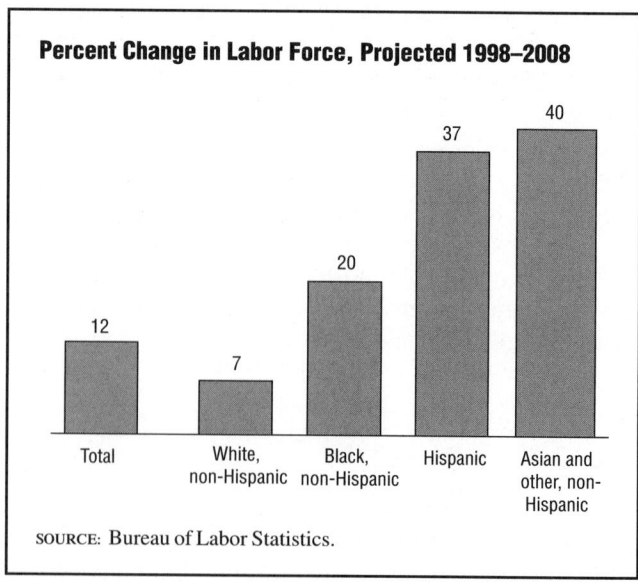

Percent Change in Labor Force, Projected 1998–2008

SOURCE: Bureau of Labor Statistics.

severely poor. The future will continue to be filled with obstacles for African American workers, families, and businesses.

Toward Greater Self-sufficiency

Many of the programs developed to address poverty and racial discrimination in employment were initiated during the 1960s. Generally speaking, these programs have been instrumental in providing opportunities to African Americans that had been denied long after the end of slavery and legalized segregation. At the beginning of the twenty-first century, however, whites have increasingly come to resist and resent programs that secure such opportunities for African Americans and other minorities. As opportunities decline for whites, the competition for good jobs is expected to increase. Blacks and other minority populations are growing at rates that far exceed that of whites. As these populations become better educated, the struggle for desirable jobs will intensify.

The political climate in the New Millennium is such that major social intervention programs are not likely to be initiated by the federal government within the near future. Because of the social and political climate in the United States, many African Americans are advocating a greater emphasis on self-help and internal community development. One sociological model of African American community development is the Black Organizational Autonomy Model. This model maintains that viable African American communities possess community-based organizations with five basic components: economic autonomy; internally developed and controlled data sources; programs to develop and promote African American female leadership; programs that emphasize African American history and culture; and programs that are socially inclusive in leadership. The model proved successful in a case study in Little Rock, Arkansas, of a church-based African American community organization, and has considerable potential for meeting the present and future needs of the African American community.

However, community action may be hampered by a growing schism within the African American community itself. Following on the work of Dr. William Julius Wilson (1980, 1987), Dr. Henry Louis Gates Jr. commented on "the two nations of Black America." Gates sees a troubling divide between African American professionals and the African American underclass in the inner-cities. According to Gates, the African American middle- and upper-classes have more in common with their white colleagues than with the poor of their own race. This disassociation could hinder the upward mobility of the underclass and stagnate community efforts to improve the conditions of the poor if those African Americans with the resources to help feel less inclined to invest in a community of which they are not a part.

African Americans and the Financial Stock Market

African Americans have traditionally steered clear of the investment arena—both in terms of employment and participation in the buying and selling of stocks. Growing up without an understanding of the benefits of long-term investing, most African American children become adults who are leery of putting money into a system they do not understand. A 1998 survey showed that 64 percent of black noninvestors attributed their lack of participation to a "lack of knowledge," compared with 55 percent of whites. When African Americans did choose to invest, they typically selected avenues with low-yield returns such as insurance funds, savings accounts, or real estate—the result being that their money grew at a much slower rate than whites with a substantially greater number of stock portfolios.

The effect of this cautious investment strategy was a gross economic disparity between blacks and whites, particularly in the retirement years. A study of wealth distribution by the Rand Corporation revealed that, among people over 70, blacks have less than 10 percent of the average financial assets available to whites. Many elderly African Americans become overly-dependent on Social Security and fall into poverty. The African American community is already financially handicapped by lower wages and over-representation in blue-collar jobs with few benefits programs such as 401(k) plans; the reluctance to become involved in the stock market has a further crippling effect on African American economic growth.

Towards the end of the 1990s, however, African American distrust of the stock market began to dissolve. Buoyed by a strong market, many African Americans sought out information on how to invest wisely, and investment companies started active minority recruitment programs to entice these new investors. Investment seminars specifically geared towards African American women have been particularly effective in recruiting a group that has typically been too burdened with family concerns to set aside money for investing. In addition, African American groups such as

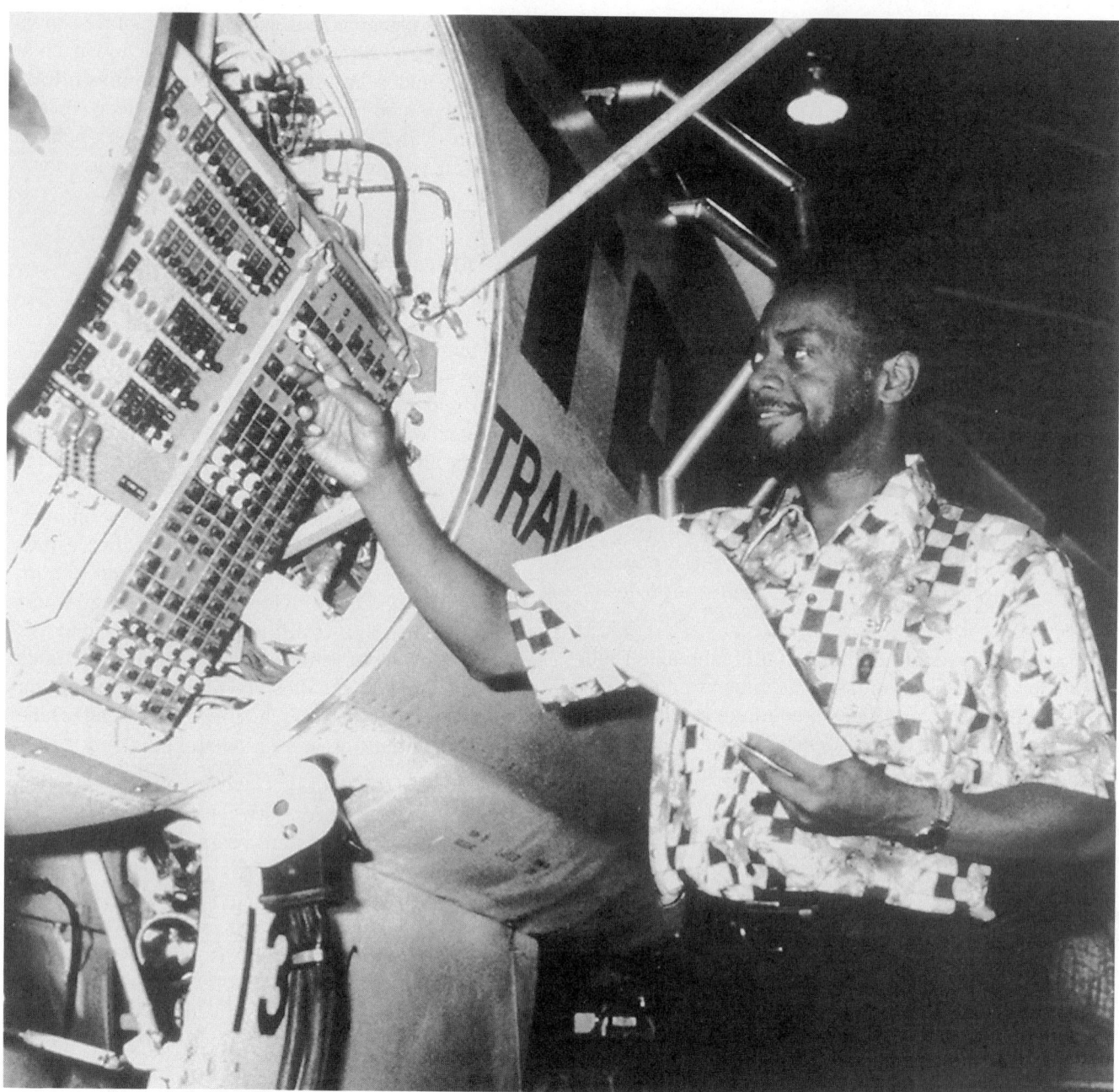

African Americans are holding more well-paying, technical jobs than ever.

the Coalition of Black Investors have formed to promote financial literacy among African Americans and to connect black investors and investment clubs in order to exchange ideas and investment strategies.

Even as blacks close the investment gap, though, they continue to be far outnumbered by whites in investment jobs. Of the country's 90,000 brokers, only 600 were African American in 1998. The percentage of African American employees in the securities industry actually fell from 10.6 percent in 1990 to 8.4 percent in

1996. In 1998, the Reverend Jesse Jackson held a three-day conference with some of the top names on Wall Street to discuss ways to improve minority participation in the financial arena.

Mortgage Lending

African Americans have also experienced racism in the mortgage market. A recent study conducted by the Federal Bank of Boston posited that lending bias against minorities was rampant. In their much-debated findings, the researchers concluded that Boston-area banks rejected 11 percent of mortgage applications by whites and 29 percent of applications by minorities. Such numbers, they argued, proved that discrimination in lending still existed. However, other analysts claim that the study was flawed in its interpretation of the data, and that discrepancies that appear to point to discrimination actually clear up under careful analysis.

Apart from the debate, it is undisputed that there is a far greater rate of white homeowners than African American ones. In spite of the fact that the rate of home ownership reached a record 65.7 percent in 1997, a study found that while 71.3 percent of whites were homeowners, only 43.6 percent of blacks could boast the same. According to a report by the Federal Reserve Board and the Joint Center for Housing Studies at Harvard University, the main reason being "redlining"—banks refusing mortgage loans to low-income buyers, usually minorities. Unable to buy homes, African Americans have frequently been forced to rent in city neighborhoods, which are often destabilized by the lack of homeowners.

Some court decisions and corporate initiatives have been made to address incidents of lending bias. In 1998, three Texas mortgage lenders agreed to make nearly $1.4 billion available to low-income and minority home buyers through 2001 after they were found to have applied discriminatory practices against minority applicants. These civil rights violations were discovered when white federal government housing officials who posed as applicants received better treatment and larger loans than minority applicants of similar financial standing.

Employed Civilians by Occupation, Sex, Race, and Hispanic Origin: 1983 and 1999

[For civilian noninstitutional population 16 years old and over (100,834 represents 100,834,000). Annual average of monthly figures. Based on Current Population Survey. Persons of Hispanic origin may be of any race.]

	1983				1999 [1]			
	Total employed (1,000)	Percent of total			Total employed (1,000)	Percent of total		
Occupation		Female	Black	Hispanic		Female	Black	Hispanic
Total	100,834	43.7	9.3	5.3	133,488	46.5	11.3	10.3
Managerial and professional specialty	**23,592**	**40.9**	**5.6**	**2.6**	**40,467**	**49.5**	**8.0**	**5.0**
Executive, administrative, and managerial[2]	10,772	32.4	4.7	2.8	19,584	45.1	7.6	5.6
Officials and administrators, public	417	38.5	8.3	3.8	655	51.1	14.0	4.9
Financial managers	357	38.6	3.5	3.1	753	51.1	7.0	5.4
Personnel and labor relations managers	106	43.9	4.9	2.6	196	60.4	10.9	6.3
Purchasing managers	82	23.6	5.1	1.4	138	47.4	8.9	5.6
Managers, marketing, advertising and public relations	396	21.8	2.7	1.7	739	37.6	4.8	2.7
Administrators, education and related fields	415	41.4	11.3	2.4	821	62.5	15.0	4.8
Managers, medicine and health	91	57.0	5.0	2.0	716	77.4	8.9	6.6
Managers, properties and real estate	305	42.8	5.5	5.2	577	49.4	6.6	8.9
Management-related occupations	2,966	40.3	5.8	3.5	4,879	57.8	9.8	5.3
Accountants and auditors	1,105	38.7	5.5	3.3	1,658	58.6	9.6	4.9
Professional specialty[2]	12,820	48.1	6.4	2.5	20,883	53.5	8.4	4.5
Architects	103	12.7	1.6	1.5	194	15.7	2.3	4.4
Engineers[2]	1,572	5.8	2.7	2.2	2,081	10.6	4.6	3.5
Aerospace engineers	80	6.9	1.5	2.1	79	11.5	7.5	4.8
Chemical engineers	67	6.1	3.0	1.4	82	16.3	2.7	5.0
Civil engineers	211	4.0	1.9	3.2	287	9.5	5.5	3.3
Electrical and electronic	450	6.1	3.4	3.1	639	10.1	6.1	4.1
Industrial engineers	210	11.0	3.3	2.4	260	16.8	4.1	3.2
Mechanical	259	2.8	3.2	1.1	340	7.1	1.9	2.4
Mathematical and computer scientists[2]	463	29.6	5.4	2.6	1,847	31.1	7.5	3.6
Computer systems analysts, scientists	276	27.8	6.2	2.7	1,549	28.5	7.4	3.4
Operations and systems researchers and analysts	142	31.3	4.9	2.2	241	46.6	8.4	5.2
Natural scientists[2]	357	20.5	2.6	2.1	578	30.1	3.7	3.6
Chemists, except biochemists	98	23.3	4.3	1.2	136	27.4	5.7	3.5
Biological and life scientists	55	40.8	2.4	1.8	109	43.8	3.2	4.1
Medical scientists	(3)	(3)	(3)	(3)	100	44.9	6.1	5.3
Health diagnosing occupations[2]	735	13.3	2.7	3.3	1,071	24.1	4.4	4.1
Physicians	519	15.8	3.2	4.5	720	24.5	5.7	4.8
Dentists	126	6.7	2.4	1.0	173	16.5	1.9	3.1
Health assessment and treating occupations	1,900	85.8	7.1	2.2	3,019	85.7	9.1	3.4
Registered nurses	1,372	95.8	6.7	1.8	2,128	92.9	9.6	3.1
Pharmacists	158	26.7	3.8	2.6	216	49.0	5.6	3.5
Dietitians	71	90.8	21.0	3.7	92	84.0	19.5	4.6
Therapists[2]	247	76.3	7.6	2.7	517	75.8	7.5	4.5
Respiratory therapists	69	69.4	6.5	3.7	90	60.6	17.6	3.3
Physical therapists	55	77.0	9.7	1.5	144	73.2	5.3	5.3
Speech therapists	51	90.5	1.5	-	99	93.1	1.1	4.2
Physicians' assistants	51	36.3	7.7	4.4	67	52.6	4.3	2.6
Teachers, college and university	606	36.3	4.4	1.8	978	42.4	6.5	4.2
Teachers, except college and university[2]	3,365	70.9	9.1	2.7	5,277	74.9	9.9	5.4
Prekindergarten and kindergarten	299	98.2	11.8	3.4	600	98.4	13.4	8.2
Elementary school	1,350	83.3	11.1	3.1	2,072	83.8	10.3	5.1
Secondary school	1,209	51.8	7.2	2.3	1,342	57.5	7.9	5.0
Special education	81	82.2	10.2	2.3	369	84.4	9.1	2.8
Counselors, educational and vocational	184	53.1	13.9	3.2	247	68.7	18.1	5.7
Librarians, archivists, and curators	213	84.4	7.8	1.6	264	82.9	7.6	4.8
Librarians	193	87.3	7.9	1.8	236	83.7	7.7	4.8
Social scientists and urban planners[2]	261	46.8	7.1	2.1	460	58.4	8.1	3.1
Economists	98	37.9	6.3	2.7	141	51.2	6.1	1.9
Psychologists	135	57.1	8.6	1.1	266	64.9	9.9	3.5
Social, recreation, and religious workers[2]	831	43.1	12.1	3.8	1,435	56.4	18.5	6.3
Social workers	407	64.3	18.2	6.3	813	71.4	24.2	7.4
Recreation workers	65	71.9	15.7	2.0	128	66.4	18.0	7.0
Clergy	293	5.6	4.9	1.4	352	14.2	10.3	5.2

[continued]

Employed Civilians by Occupation, Sex, Race, and Hispanic Origin: 1983 and 1999

[For civilian noninstitutional population 16 years old and over (100,834 represents 100,834,000). Annual average of monthly figures. Based on Current Population Survey. Persons of Hispanic origin may be of any race.]

Occupation	1983 Total employed (1,000)	1983 Percent of total Female	1983 Percent of total Black	1983 Percent of total Hispanic	1999[1] Total employed (1,000)	1999[1] Percent of total Female	1999[1] Percent of total Black	1999[1] Percent of total Hispanic
Lawyers and judges	651	15.8	2.7	1.0	964	28.9	5.2	3.9
Lawyers	612	15.3	2.6	0.9	923	28.8	5.1	4.0
Writers, artists, entertainers, and athletes[2]	1,544	42.7	4.8	2.9	2,454	49.9	6.6	5.3
Authors	62	46.7	2.1	0.9	148	55.2	7.3	2.3
Technical writers	(3)	(3)	(3)	(3)	71	60.2	5.7	0.1
Designers	393	52.7	3.1	2.7	722	56.2	3.7	5.5
Musicians and composers	155	28.0	7.9	4.4	172	35.6	9.2	7.1
Actors and directors	60	30.8	6.6	3.4	129	38.8	10.7	5.1
Painters, sculptors, craft-artists, and artist printmakers	186	47.4	2.1	2.3	252	54.8	5.2	3.8
Photographers	113	20.7	4.0	3.4	166	34.5	7.1	8.2
Editors and reporters	204	48.4	2.9	2.1	290	49.8	4.5	2.7
Public relations specialists	157	50.1	6.2	1.9	190	61.0	7.5	4.9
Announcers	(3)	(3)	(3)	(3)	50	21.4	8.9	9.2
Athletes	58	17.6	9.4	1.7	110	28.0	19.0	3.4
Technical, sales, and administrative support	**31,265**	**64.6**	**7.6**	**4.3**	**38,921**	**63.8**	**11.2**	**8.4**
Technicians and related support	3,053	48.2	8.2	3.1	4,355	51.9	10.7	6.4
Health technologists and technicians[2]	1,111	84.3	12.7	3.1	1,701	81.2	14.4	7.3
Clinical laboratory technologists and technicians	255	76.2	10.5	2.9	338	78.5	19.4	5.6
Dental hygienists	66	98.6	1.6	-	106	99.1	2.8	1.5
Radiologic technicians	101	71.7	8.6	4.5	167	74.4	9.7	4.1
Licensed practical nurses	443	97.0	17.7	3.1	357	95.1	18.4	5.8
Engineering and related technologists and technicians[2]	822	18.4	6.1	3.5	973	19.1	9.7	6.2
Electrical and electronic technicians	260	12.5	8.2	4.6	437	14.5	11.3	6.5
Drafting occupations	273	17.5	5.5	2.3	235	18.3	6.5	5.6
Surveying and mapping technicians	(3)	(3)	(3)	(3)	67	11.0	4.5	7.9
Science technicians[2]	202	29.1	6.6	2.8	293	40.8	11.0	7.3
Biological technicians	52	37.7	2.9	2.0	106	64.1	6.8	4.8
Chemical technicians	82	26.9	9.5	3.5	79	28.9	14.9	9.9
Technicians, except health, engineering, and science[2]	917	35.3	5.0	2.7	1,388	41.5	7.0	5.3
Airplane pilots and navigators	69	2.1	-	1.6	143	3.1	2.7	4.3
Computer programmers	443	32.5	4.4	2.1	665	26.3	6.4	3.8
Legal assistants	128	74.0	4.3	3.6	403	83.9	8.7	7.1
Sales occupations	11,818	47.5	4.7	3.7	16,118	50.1	8.7	7.9
Supervisors and proprietors	2,958	28.4	3.6	3.4	4,896	40.9	6.1	6.8
Sales representatives, finance and business services[2]	1,853	37.2	2.7	2.2	2,735	43.9	7.2	5.0
Insurance sales	551	25.1	3.8	2.5	585	44.0	5.8	4.6
Real estate sales	570	48.9	1.3	1.5	769	53.2	5.5	5.0
Securities and financial services sales	212	23.6	3.1	1.1	541	28.5	6.8	3.7
Advertising and related sales	124	47.9	4.5	3.3	187	57.1	11.9	4.1
Sales representatives, commodities, except retail	1,442	15.1	2.1	2.2	1,526	26.8	2.9	5.4
Sales workers, retail and personal services	5,511	69.7	6.7	4.8	6,866	63.9	12.5	10.4
Cashiers	2,009	84.4	10.1	5.4	3,014	77.0	16.7	12.0
Sales-related occupations	54	58.7	2.8	1.3	95	67.7	8.6	3.0
Administrative support, including clerical	16,395	79.9	9.6	5.0	18,448	78.7	13.5	9.4
Supervisors	676	53.4	9.3	5.0	675	57.5	17.5	8.2
Computer equipment operators	605	63.9	12.5	6.0	356	57.0	13.9	7.2
Computer operators	597	63.7	12.1	6.0	350	57.3	13.9	7.3
Secretaries, stenographers, and typists[2]	4,861	98.2	7.3	4.5	3,457	97.9	10.4	7.8
Secretaries	3,891	99.0	5.8	4.0	2,781	98.6	9.5	7.7
Typists	906	95.6	13.8	6.4	556	95.5	15.6	8.5
Information clerks	1,174	88.9	8.5	5.5	2,143	88.3	10.7	11.0
Receptionists	602	96.8	7.5	6.6	1,091	95.4	10.2	10.3
Records processing occupations, except financial[2]	866	82.4	13.9	4.8	1,047	77.8	16.9	10.8
Order clerks	188	78.1	10.6	4.4	270	72.7	21.5	12.0
Personnel clerks, except payroll and time keeping	64	91.1	14.9	4.6	70	83.3	24.6	5.4
Library clerks	147	81.9	15.4	2.5	151	74.4	9.8	11.1
File clerks	287	83.5	16.7	6.1	345	79.2	16.2	11.2
Records clerks	157	82.8	11.6	5.6	202	82.0	15.2	10.3

[continued]

Employed Civilians by Occupation, Sex, Race, and Hispanic Origin: 1983 and 1999

[For civilian noninstitutional population 16 years old and over (100,834 represents 100,834,000). Annual average of monthly figures. Based on Current Population Survey. Persons of Hispanic origin may be of any race.]

	1983				1999[1]			
	Total employed (1,000)	Percent of total			Total employed (1,000)	Percent of total		
Occupation		Female	Black	Hispanic		Female	Black	Hispanic
Financial records processing[2]	2,457	89.4	4.6	3.7	2,181	90.8	8.9	6.4
Bookkeepers, accounting, and auditing clerks	1,970	91.0	4.3	3.3	1,691	91.4	7.6	5.6
Payroll and time keeping clerks	192	82.2	5.9	5.0	146	88.2	8.7	9.3
Billing clerks	146	88.4	6.2	3.9	179	92.0	15.9	8.7
Cost and rate clerks	96	75.6	5.9	5.3	60	83.6	17.9	13.7
Billing, posting, and calculating machine operators	(3)	(3)	(3)	(3)	105	88.1	12.1	7.4
Duplicating, mail and other office machine operators	68	62.6	16.0	6.1	63	56.7	20.2	8.4
Communications equipment operators	256	89.1	17.0	4.4	158	81.7	18.6	13.7
Telephone operators	244	90.4	17.0	4.3	142	83.7	20.2	12.2
Mail and message distributing occupations	799	31.6	18.1	4.5	990	42.2	21.1	8.4
Postal clerks, except mail carriers	248	36.7	26.2	5.2	313	50.8	28.4	7.5
Mail carrier, postal service	259	17.1	12.5	2.7	332	31.8	15.0	5.6
Mail clerks, except postal service	170	50.0	15.8	5.9	194	60.5	24.6	13.5
Messengers	122	26.2	16.7	5.2	151	23.3	15.2	9.6
Material recording, scheduling, and distributing[2,4]	1,562	37.5	10.9	6.6	1,959	45.5	13.2	12.8
Dispatchers	157	45.7	11.4	4.3	274	52.6	14.2	9.2
Production coordinators	182	44.0	6.1	2.2	208	60.2	10.0	4.4
Traffic, shipping, and receiving clerks	421	22.6	9.1	11.1	646	33.7	14.8	17.9
Stock and inventory clerks	532	38.7	13.3	5.5	459	41.8	12.5	11.2
Expediters	112	57.5	8.4	4.3	264	68.1	11.1	13.6
Adjusters and investigators	675	69.9	11.1	5.1	1,802	75.5	18.1	7.9
Insurance adjusters, examiners, and investigators	199	65.0	11.5	3.3	472	71.3	15.4	7.6
Investigators and adjusters, except insurance	301	70.1	11.3	4.8	1,054	77.4	17.8	7.6
Eligibility clerks, social welfare	69	88.7	12.9	9.4	102	85.4	20.8	16.1
Bill and account collectors	106	66.4	8.5	6.5	175	69.8	24.9	6.3
Miscellaneous administrative support[2]	2,397	85.2	12.5	5.9	3,616	83.4	14.4	11.0
General office clerks	648	80.6	12.7	5.2	728	81.4	13.4	12.0
Bank tellers	480	91.0	7.5	4.3	425	87.7	13.3	8.1
Data entry keyers	311	93.6	18.6	5.6	746	81.3	15.6	10.9
Statistical clerks	96	75.7	7.5	3.4	94	83.6	18.2	10.2
Teachers' aides	348	93.7	17.8	12.6	689	91.0	13.8	14.9
Service occupations	**13,857**	**60.1**	**16.6**	**6.8**	**17,915**	**60.4**	**18.3**	**15.2**
Private household[2]	980	96.1	27.8	8.5	831	95.2	15.1	29.3
Child care workers	408	96.9	7.9	3.6	295	97.4	10.2	21.5
Cleaners and servants	512	95.8	42.4	11.8	521	94.4	17.6	33.9
Protective service	1,672	12.8	13.6	4.6	2,440	18.9	19.8	8.2
Supervisors, protective service	127	4.7	7.7	3.1	181	13.2	10.6	5.0
Supervisors, police and detectives	58	4.2	9.3	1.2	96	17.3	8.8	4.8
Firefighting and fire prevention	189	1.0	6.7	4.1	241	2.8	10.6	6.5
Firefighting occupations	170	1.0	7.3	3.8	223	1.9	11.1	5.4
Police and detectives	645	9.4	13.1	4.0	1,108	16.9	18.2	8.1
Police and detectives, public service	412	5.7	9.5	4.4	618	14.2	15.1	9.1
Sheriffs, bailiffs, and other law enforcement officers	87	13.2	11.5	4.0	175	14.4	17.3	3.6
Correctional institution officers	146	17.8	24.0	2.8	315	23.5	24.9	8.7
Guards	711	20.6	17.0	5.6	910	26.7	26.1	9.4
Guards and police, except public service	602	13.0	18.9	6.2	763	20.7	29.0	9.6
Service except private household and protective	11,205	64.0	16.0	6.9	14,644	65.4	18.2	15.5
Food preparation and service occupations[2]	4,860	63.3	10.5	6.8	6,091	57.7	11.8	16.5
Bartenders	338	48.4	2.7	4.4	316	48.4	4.1	12.9
Waiters and waitresses	1,357	87.8	4.1	3.6	1,431	77.4	5.1	10.2
Cooks	1,452	50.0	15.8	6.5	2,078	44.0	17.4	19.9
Food counter, fountain, and related occupations	326	76.0	9.1	6.7	360	64.5	10.3	13.7
Kitchen workers, food preparation	138	77.0	13.7	8.1	293	70.4	13.2	12.6
Waiters' and waitresses' assistants	364	38.8	12.6	14.2	538	49.5	10.6	19.4
Health service occupations	1,739	89.2	23.5	4.8	2,521	89.2	31.7	9.9
Dental assistants	154	98.1	6.1	5.7	213	96.1	6.7	10.4
Health aides, except nursing	316	86.8	16.5	4.8	338	80.5	25.0	10.0
Nursing aides, orderlies, and attendants	1,269	88.7	27.3	4.7	1,970	89.9	35.6	9.8

[continued]

Employed Civilians by Occupation, Sex, Race, and Hispanic Origin: 1983 and 1999

[For civilian noninstitutional population 16 years old and over (100,834 represents 100,834,000). Annual average of monthly figures. Based on Current Population Survey. Persons of Hispanic origin may be of any race.]

	1983				1999[1]			
	Total em-ployed (1,000)	Percent of total			Total em-ployed (1,000)	Percent of total		
Occupation		Fe-male	Black	His-panic		Fe-male	Black	His-panic
Cleaning and building service occupations[2]	2,736	38.8	24.4	9.2	3,021	45.5	21.9	23.2
Maids and housemen	531	81.2	32.3	10.1	663	82.7	25.4	28.1
Janitors and cleaners	2,031	28.6	22.6	8.9	2,118	35.8	21.0	22.1
Personal service occupations[2]	1,870	79.2	11.1	6.0	3,011	80.8	16.1	10.5
Barbers	92	12.9	8.4	12.1	81	20.3	25.1	11.3
Hairdressers and cosmetologists	622	88.7	7.0	5.7	784	90.8	11.7	10.1
Attendants, amusement and recreation facilities	131	40.2	7.1	4.3	247	39.7	11.5	6.9
Public transportation attendants	63	74.3	11.3	5.9	111	83.5	13.1	7.1
Welfare service aides	77	92.5	24.2	10.5	97	83.8	30.2	10.7
Family child care providers	(NA)	(NA)	(NA)	(NA)	469	98.0	13.9	15.5
Early childhood teachers' assistants	(NA)	(NA)	(NA)	(NA)	509	95.3	20.3	10.8
Precision production, craft, and repair	**12,328**	**8.1**	**6.8**	**6.2**	**14,593**	**9.0**	**8.0**	**12.8**
Mechanics and repairers	4,158	3.0	6.8	5.3	4,868	4.8	8.2	10.0
Mechanics and repairers, except supervisors[2]	3,906	2.8	7.0	5.5	4,604	4.5	8.1	10.2
Vehicle and mobile equipment mechanics/repairers[2]	1,683	0.8	6.9	6.0	1,768	1.6	7.2	11.3
Automobile mechanics	800	0.5	7.8	6.0	837	1.4	8.2	13.8
Aircraft engine mechanics	95	2.5	4.0	7.6	147	4.2	7.8	10.4
Electrical and electronic equipment repairers[2]	674	7.4	7.3	4.5	966	11.1	9.3	8.7
Data processing equipment repairers	98	9.3	6.1	4.5	315	15.2	9.4	6.3
Telephone installers and repairers	247	9.9	7.8	3.7	249	13.2	13.2	6.9
Construction trades	4,289	1.8	6.6	6.0	5,801	2.5	7.0	15.0
Construction trades, except supervisors	3,784	1.9	7.1	6.1	4,985	2.6	7.4	16.0
Carpenters	1,160	1.4	5.0	5.0	1,398	1.2	5.1	15.0
Extractive occupations	196	2.3	3.3	6.0	130	0.9	6.3	11.6
Precision production occupations	3,685	21.5	7.3	7.4	3,793	24.3	9.6	13.2
Operators, fabricators, and laborers	**16,091**	**26.6**	**14.0**	**8.3**	**18,167**	**24.1**	**15.7**	**16.6**
Machine operators, assemblers, and inspectors[2]	7,744	42.1	14.0	9.4	7,386	37.2	15.5	18.5
Textile, apparel, and furnishings machine operators[2]	1,414	82.1	18.7	12.5	872	70.8	18.1	28.9
Textile sewing machine operators	806	94.0	15.5	14.5	461	79.9	15.0	33.2
Pressing machine operators	141	66.4	27.1	14.2	79	78.2	20.1	39.0
Fabricators, assemblers, and hand working occupations	1,715	33.7	11.3	8.7	1,995	33.7	14.9	14.7
Production inspectors, testers, samplers, and weighers	794	53.8	13.0	7.7	716	48.3	14.5	19.9
Transportation and material moving occupations	4,201	7.8	13.0	5.9	5,516	9.9	15.9	11.9
Motor vehicle operators	2,978	9.2	13.5	6.0	4,202	11.5	16.1	12.4
Trucks drivers	2,195	3.1	12.3	5.7	3,116	4.9	14.1	12.7
Transportation occupations, except motor vehicles	212	2.4	6.7	3.0	163	2.4	15.0	3.9
Material moving equipment operators	1,011	4.8	12.9	6.3	1,152	5.2	15.5	11.4
Industrial truck and tractor operators	369	5.6	19.6	8.2	544	7.1	21.8	17.4
Handlers, equipment cleaners, helpers, and laborers[2]	4,147	16.8	15.1	8.6	5,265	20.5	15.7	18.8
Freight, stock, and material handlers	1,488	15.4	15.3	7.1	2,060	24.3	17.6	14.7
Laborers, except construction	1,024	19.4	16.0	8.6	1,286	21.6	16.2	17.0
Farming, forestry, and fishing	3,700	16.0	7.5	8.2	3,426	19.7	5.0	23.1
Farm operators and managers	1,450	12.1	1.3	0.7	1,134	24.7	1.0	2.9
Other agricultural and related occupations	2,072	19.9	11.7	14.0	2,135	18.1	7.1	35.1
Farm workers	1,149	24.8	11.6	15.9	757	18.6	5.4	46.0
Forestry and logging occupations	126	1.4	12.8	2.1	107	7.0	5.2	8.0
Fishers, hunters, and trappers	53	4.5	1.8	2.5	50	6.4	5.6	2.3

- Represents or rounds to zero.
NA Not available.
[1]Data not strictly comparable with data for earlier years. See *Employment and Earnings*, issues Feb. 1994, Mar. 1996, Feb. 1997, Feb. 1998, and Feb. 1999.
[2]Includes other occupations, not shown separately.
[3]Level of total employment below 50,000.
[4]Includes clerks.

SOURCE: U.S. Bureau of Labor Statistics, *Employment and Earnings,* monthly, January issues; and unpublished data.

Unemployed and Unemployment Rates by Educational Attainment, Sex, Race, and Hispanic Origin: 1992 to 1999

[As of March (6,846 represents 6,846,000). For the civilian noninstitutional population 25 to 64 years old. Based on Current Population Survey.]

Year, sex, and race	Unemployed (1,000)					Unemployment rate [1]				
	Total	Less than high school diploma	High school graduates, no degree	Less than a bachelor's degree	College graduate	Total	Less than high school diploma	High school graduate, no degree	Less than a bachelor's degree	College graduate
Total: [2]										
1992	6,846	1,693	2,851	1,521	782	6.7	13.5	7.7	5.9	2.9
1995	5,065	1,150	1,833	1,329	753	4.8	10.0	5.2	4.5	2.5
1998[3]	4,463	1,018	1,751	1,111	582	4.0	8.5	4.8	3.6	1.8
1999[3]	3,942	895	1,445	961	640	3.5	7.7	4.0	3.1	1.9
Male:										
1992	4,207	1,151	1,709	854	493	7.5	14.8	8.8	6.4	3.2
1995	2,925	765	1,064	656	440	5.1	10.9	5.7	4.4	2.6
1998[3]	2,461	592	989	575	306	4.1	8.0	5.1	3.7	1.7
1999[3]	2,121	491	782	495	353	3.5	7.0	4.1	3.2	1.9
Female:										
1992	2,639	542	1,142	666	289	5.7	11.4	6.5	5.3	2.5
1995	2,140	385	770	673	313	4.4	8.6	4.6	4.5	2.4
1998[3]	2,002	426	762	537	276	3.9	9.3	4.4	3.5	1.9
1999[3]	1,821	404	663	466	287	3.5	8.8	3.9	3.0	1.9
White:										
1992	5,247	1,285	2,146	1,176	641	6.0	12.9	6.8	5.3	2.7
1995	3,858	831	1,362	1,054	612	4.3	9.2	4.6	4.2	2.3
1998[3]	3,282	711	1,283	814	474	3.5	7.5	4.2	3.2	1.7
1999[3]	2,886	651	1,034	716	484	3.1	7.0	3.4	2.8	1.7
Black:										
1992	1,353	361	619	291	81	12.4	17.2	14.1	10.7	4.8
1995	905	225	377	218	86	7.7	13.7	8.4	6.3	4.1
1998[3]	948	248	402	248	50	7.3	13.4	8.4	6.4	2.1
1999[3]	810	201	321	204	84	6.3	12.0	6.7	5.2	3.3
Hispanic: [4]										
1992	757	408	224	88	36	9.8	13.6	9.6	5.9	4.2
1995	746	393	211	102	40	8.0	10.9	8.1	5.2	3.7
1998[3]	647	337	176	94	41	5.9	8.3	5.5	4.2	2.8
1999[3]	620	315	179	89	36	5.6	7.8	5.5	3.7	2.5

[1] Percent unemployed of the civilian labor force.
[2] Includes other races, not shown separately.
[3] Data not strictly comparable with data for earlier years. See Feb. 1994, Mar. 1996, Feb. 1997, Feb. 1998, and Feb. 1999 issues of *Employment and Earnings*.
[4] Persons of Hispanic origin may be of any race.

SOURCE: U.S. Bureau of Labor Statistics, unpublished data.

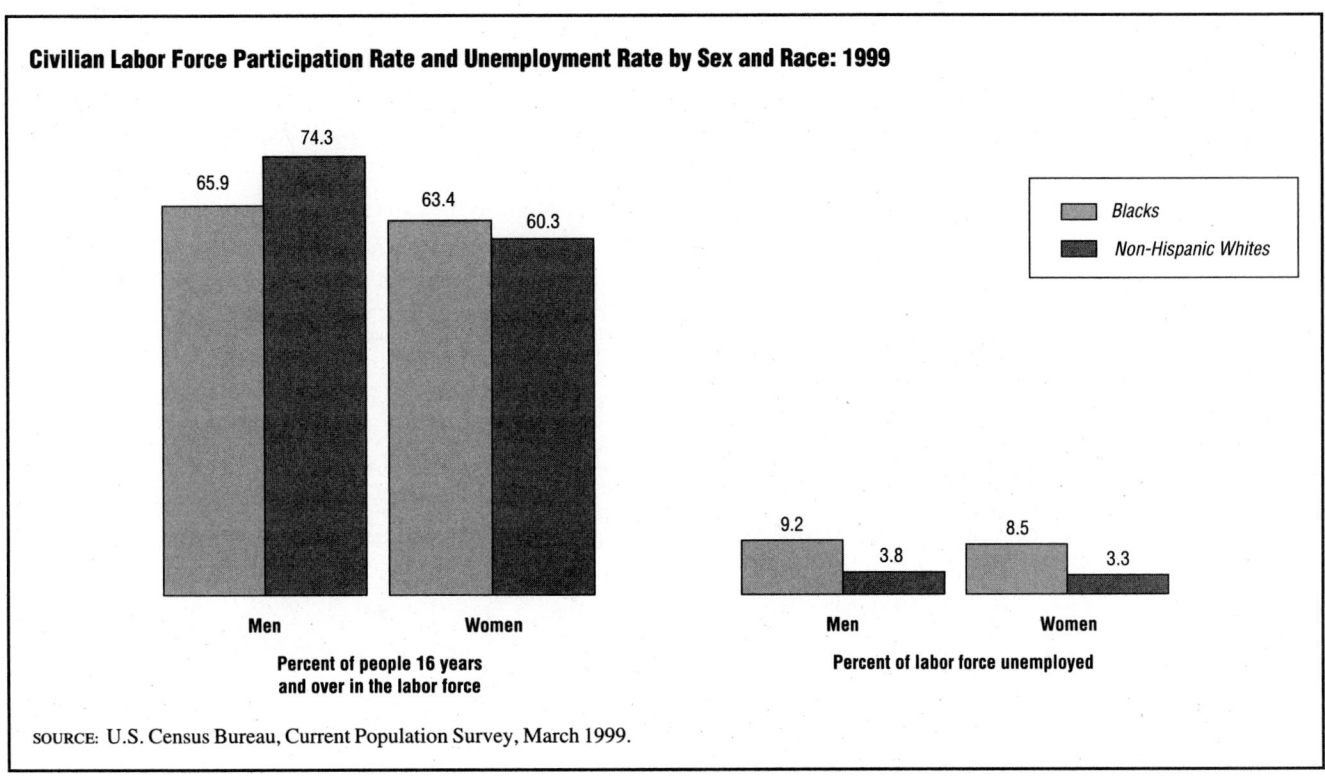

Civilian Labor Force Participation Rate and Unemployment Rate by Sex and Race: 1999

SOURCE: U.S. Census Bureau, Current Population Survey, March 1999.

Comparison of Summary Measures of Income by Selected Characteristics:1993, 1999, and 2000

(Households and people as of March of the following year.)

Characteristic	2000 Number (1,000)	2000 Median income Value (dollars)	2000 Median income 90-percent confidence interval (±) (dollars)	Median income in 1999 (in 2000 dollars) Value (dollars)	Median income in 1999 (in 2000 dollars) 90-percent confidence interval (±) (dollars)	Median income in 1993 (in 2000 dollars) Value (dollars)	Median income in 1993 (in 2000 dollars) 90-percent confidence interval (±) (dollars)	Percent change in real income 1999 to 2000 Percent change	Percent change in real income 1999 to 2000 90-percent confidence interval (±)	Percent change in real income 1993 to 2000 Percent change	Percent change in real income 1993 to 2000 90-percent confidence interval (±)
HOUSEHOLDS											
Race and Hispanic Origin of Householder											
All races[1]	106,417	42,148	324	42,187	325	36,746	282	−0.1	0.9	*14.7	1.2
White	88,545	44,226	452	43,932	406	38,768	371	0.7	1.1	*14.1	1.6
Non-Hispanic	79,376	45,904	434	45,856	474	40,195	387	0.1	1.1	*14.2	1.5
Black	13,352	30,439	757	28,848	882	22,974	747	*5.5	3.4	*32.5	5.4
Asian and Pacific Islander	3,527	55,521	2,443	52,925	3,191	45,105	3,649	4.9	6.4	*23.1	11.3
Hispanic origin[2]	9,663	33,447	1,114	31,767	772	26,919	890	*5.3	3.0	*24.3	5.8
PER CAPITA INCOME											
All races[1]	276,540	22,199	230	21,893	217	18,319	166	*1.4	1.2	*21.2	1.7
White	226,401	23,415	271	23,127	255	19,497	194	1.2	1.4	*20.1	1.8
Non-Hispanic	194,161	25,278	313	24,919	299	20,941	214	1.4	1.5	*20.7	1.9
Black	35,919	15,197	444	14,881	396	11,534	322	2.1	3.4	*31.8	5.3
Asian and Pacific Islander	11,384	22,352	1,221	21,844	1,221	18,456	1,247	2.3	6.7	*21.1	10.5
Hispanic origin[2]	33,863	12,306	377	12,011	416	10,317	354	2.5	3.5	*19.3	5.5

*Statistically significant change at the 90-percent confidence level. NA Not available.
[1]Data for American Indians and Alaska Natives are not shown separately in this table.
[2]Hispanics may be of any race.

SOURCE: U.S. Census Bureau, Current Population Survey, March 1994, 2000, and 2001.

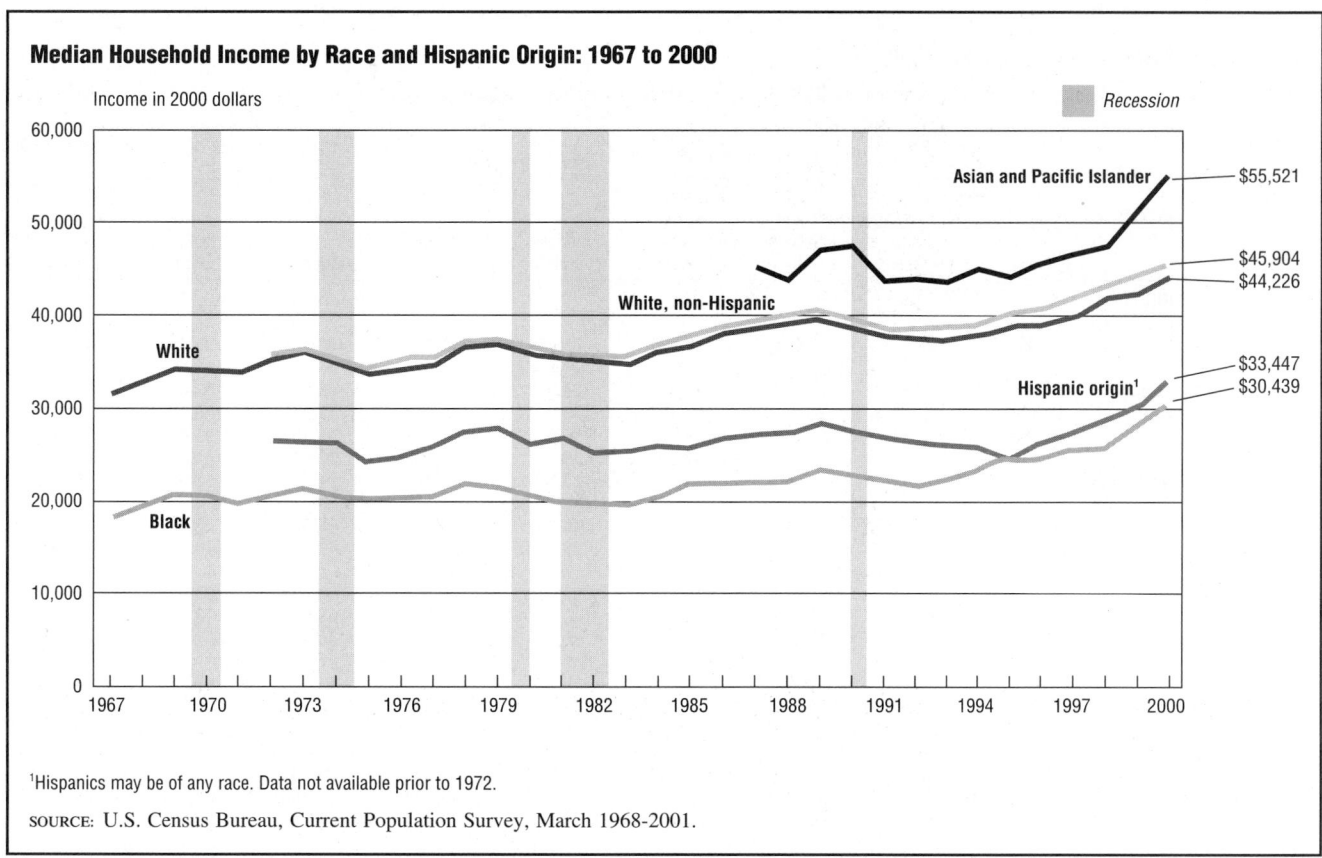

Median Household Income by Race and Hispanic Origin: 1967 to 2000

¹Hispanics may be of any race. Data not available prior to 1972.

SOURCE: U.S. Census Bureau, Current Population Survey, March 1968-2001.

Earnings by Highest Degree Earned: 1999

[For persons 25 years old and over with earnings. Persons as of March. Earnings for prior year. Based on Current Population Survey.]

| Characteristic | Total persons | Level of highest degree | | | | | | | |
		Not a high school graduate	High school graduate only	Some college, no degree	Asso- ciate's	Bache- lor's	Master's	Profes- sional	Doctorate
MEAN EARNINGS (dol.)									
All persons [1]	**30,928**	**16,053**	**23,594**	**25,686**	**32,468**	**43,782**	**52,794**	**95,488**	**74,712**
Age:									
25 to 34 years old	33,084	19,760	26,878	30,515	32,332	42,420	45,930	63,005	65,493
35 to 44 years old	35,823	18,982	26,228	32,100	35,072	48,842	59,892	105,700	70,673
45 to 54 years old	39,285	20,734	27,538	34,775	36,635	53,462	56,651	96,479	86,681
55 to 64 years old	36,410	20,400	26,670	31,998	38,545	47,182	56,078	134,814	85,297
65 years old and over	23,245	12,481	17,165	23,010	28,449	32,974	21,646	82,060	48,205
Sex:									
Male	38,134	19,155	28,742	32,005	40,082	55,057	64,533	108,926	82,619
Female	22,818	11,353	17,898	19,327	25,390	31,452	40,429	65,351	54,552
White	32,057	16,474	24,409	26,357	33,212	44,852	53,497	99,858	77,970
Male	39,638	19,632	29,782	33,041	41,111	56,620	65,637	112,944	85,837
Female	23,213	11,255	18,327	19,390	25,679	31,406	40,679	67,998	55,793
Black	22,829	13,672	19,236	22,148	26,424	36,373	43,054	53,969	46,848
Male	26,090	16,013	22,698	25,807	29,532	42,539	47,951	68,693	46,743
Female	20,026	11,372	15,892	19,269	24,187	31,952	39,760	39,109	46,914
Hispanic [2]	22,117	15,832	20,978	22,151	29,933	35,014	55,581	78,353	69,942
Male	25,534	17,756	24,739	27,145	38,555	40,889	73,362	109,071	90,474
Female	17,461	12,273	15,952	16,941	22,222	29,317	36,589	45,829	33,407

[1] Includes other races, not shown separately.
[2] Persons of Hispanic origin may be of any race.

SOURCE: U.S. Census Bureau, *Current Population Reports,* P20-528.

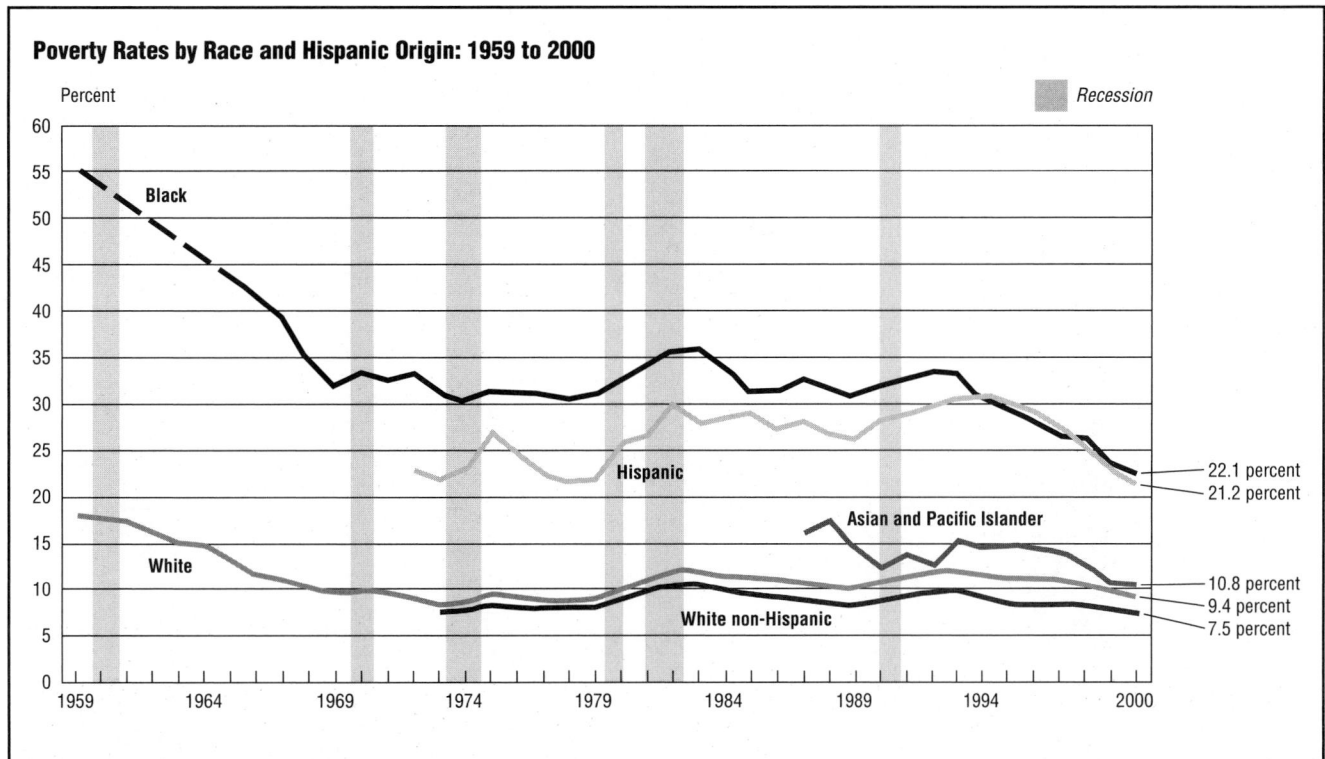

Poverty Rates by Race and Hispanic Origin: 1959 to 2000

Percent

Recession

Black

Hispanic

Asian and Pacific Islander

White

White non-Hispanic

22.1 percent
21.2 percent

10.8 percent
9.4 percent
7.5 percent

Note: The data points represent the midpoints of the respective years. The latest recession began in July 1990 and ended in March 1991. Data for Blacks are not available from 1960 to 1965. Data for the other race and Hispanic origin groups are shown from the first year available. Hispanics may be of any race.

SOURCE: U.S. Census Bureau, Current Population Survey, March 1960-2001.

People in Poverty by Age, Sex, and Race: 1998

(Percent of population)

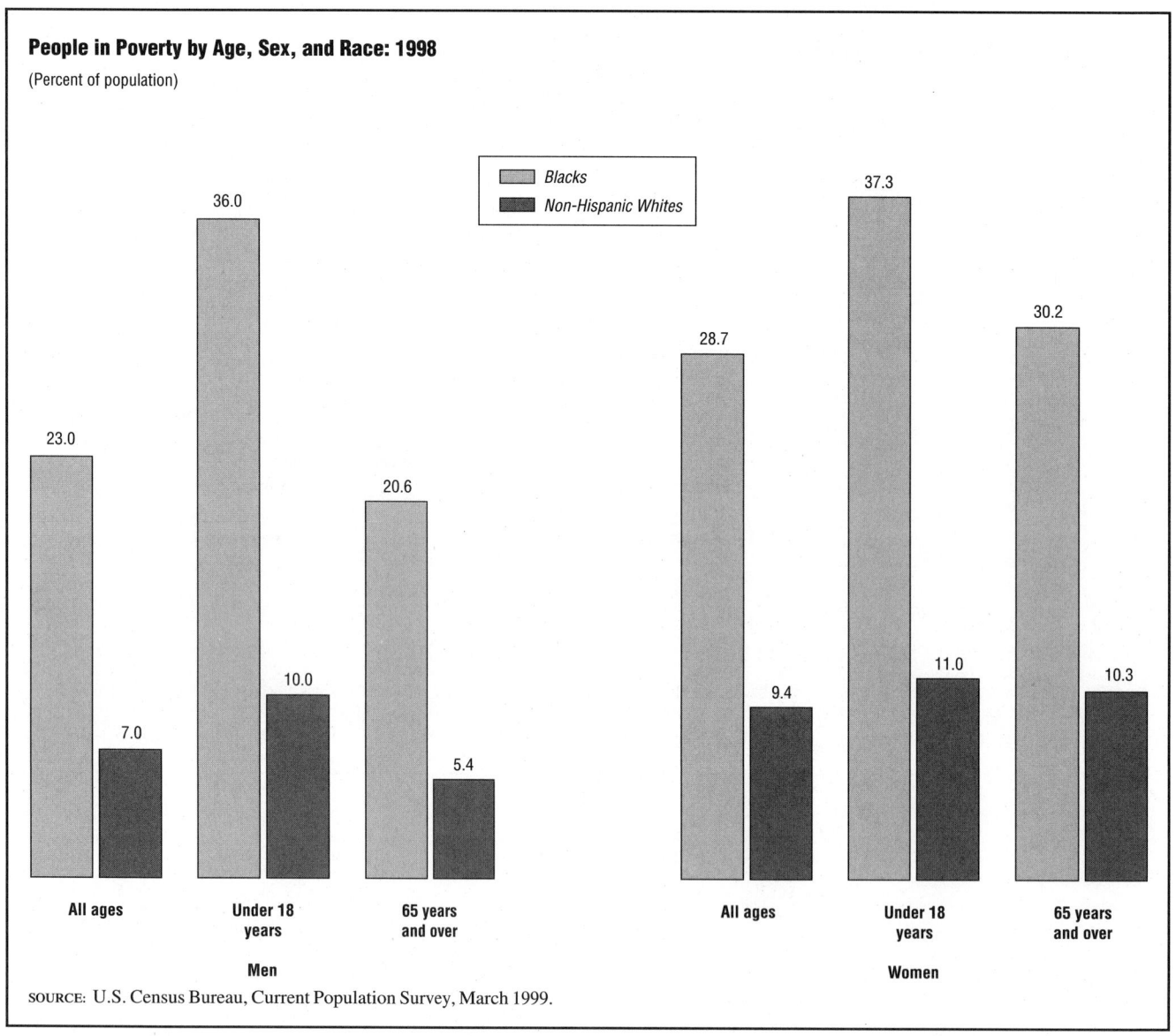

SOURCE: U.S. Census Bureau, Current Population Survey, March 1999.

14

Entrepreneurship

- ◆ Colonial Entrepreneurial Efforts by African Americans
- ◆ African American Entrepreneurship Before the Civil War
- ◆ African American Entrepreneurship in Post-Civil War Era
- ◆ African American Entrepreneurship in the Early Twentieth Century
- ◆ Post-Civil Rights Era Assistance to African American Businesses ◆ Economic Trends
- ◆ Entrepreneurs and Business Executives

by Michael D. Woodard and Hollis F. Price Jr.

African Americans have a long and rich history of entrepreneurship in the United States. Indeed, African Americans have been in business since before the Civil War and continue their entrepreneurial tradition today. Segments of the African American population have exhibited the same entrepreneurial spirit as segments of other ethnic groups who have migrated to this country. Very often, however, the history of African American entrepreneurship has been either overlooked or misconstrued. This essay, which draws heavily from Michael D. Woodard's important book *Black Entrepreneurs in America: Stories of Struggle and Success* (1997), presents an outline of the African American entrepreneurial tradition over time.

◆ COLONIAL ENTREPRENEURIAL EFFORTS BY AFRICAN AMERICANS

As America began to take shape, a number of people of African origin were successful in carving out an economic stake for themselves. Anthony Johnson is believed to be the first person of African descent to have become an entrepreneur in America. Once a slave, Johnson became free around 1622, accumulated substantial property from the Jamestown colonial government, and amassed enough wealth to import five servants of his own by 1651. Other free African Americans soon joined Johnson in an attempt to launch an independent African American community. At its height, the settlement had 12 homesteads with sizeable holdings.

In the early 1770s, entrepreneur Jean Baptiste Du Sable established the first settlement in the area later

called Chicago. Having impressed the British as a well-educated man and capable frontiersman, he was sent to the St. Clair region to manage trade and act as a liaison between Native Americans and the British. Later returning to his original settlement, Du Sable built a bakery, dairy, smoke house, horse mill and stable, workshop, and a poultry house. He also traded, trapped, and served as the local cooper and miller. Through Du Sable's efforts, Chicago became a major center for frontier commerce.

◆ AFRICAN AMERICAN ENTREPRENEURSHIP BEFORE THE CIVIL WAR

While slavery defined the existence of most African Americans prior to the Civil War, two categories of business persons were able to develop and sustain business enterprises. The first group was composed of free African Americans who could accumulate the capital to generate business activity. Numbering about 60,000, free African Americans developed enterprises in almost every area of the business community including merchandising, real estate, manufacturing, construction, transportation, and extractive industries.

The second group consisted of slaves who—as a result of thrift, ingenuity, industry, and/or the liberal paternalism of their masters—were able to engage in business activity. Although the constraints of slavery were such that even highly skilled slaves could not become entrepreneurs in the true sense of the word, some slaves did, during their limited free time, sell their

641

labor and create marketable products. The fact that African American entrepreneurship existed at all during the era of slavery is testimony to an entrepreneurial spirit and determination of a people to achieve economic freedom even under the harshest conditions.

If it was all but impossible for slaves to engage in private enterprise, it was also hazardous for "free" African Americans to do so. Free blacks lived under constant fear of being labeled as "runaway slaves" and being sold into slavery. In addition, in areas where free African Americans lived, laws were passed to restrict their movement and thus their economic freedom. For example, Virginia, Maryland, and North Carolina passed laws by 1835 forbidding free African Americans to carry arms without a license. The right of assembly was also denied African Americans throughout the South—making it illegal for African American civic, business, or benevolent organizations to convene. In addition to reflecting white slaveowners' fears of an African American uprising, such legal restrictions had the purpose and effect of making it difficult for free African Americans to earn a living.

In comparison to the economic exploitation of African Americans in the South, the development of business enterprises by African Americans in the North flourished. In 1838, for example the *Register of Trades of Colored People* in the city of Philadelphia listed 8 bakers, 25 blacksmiths, 3 brass founders, 15 cabinet makers and carpenters, 5 confectioners, 2 caulkers, 2 chair bottomers, 15 tailoring enterprises, 31 tanners, 5 weavers, and 6 wheelwrights. The Philadelphia business register also listed businesses run by African American women. Among these were 81 dressmakers and tailors, 4 dyers and scourers, 2 fullers, and 2 glass and paper makers. The 98 hairdressers registered, comprising the largest trade group, operated some of the most lucrative enterprises.

Another profitable business controlled by African Americans in Philadelphia during the 1820s and 1830s was sailmaking. In 1838, 19 sailmakers were recorded in the business register for that year. Janee Forster, who lived between 1766 and 1841, ran a major sail manufacturing firm. In 1829, Forster employed 40 workers, black and white.

Although several individuals succeeded in the manufacturing trades, the business enterprise that brought prosperity to the largest number of African Americans in Philadelphia was catering. Robert Boyle, an African American waiter, is believed to have developed the idea of contracting to provide formal dinners to serve in domestic entertaining. Catering quickly spread across the developing country, but it was in Philadelphia, the city of its birth, that catering was king.

Significantly, most of the businesses discussed thus far involved the craft or service trades. These were small enterprises that required only a modest capital investment and allowed African Americans to develop an economic niche without threatening larger white-owned businesses.

◆ AFRICAN AMERICAN ENTREPRENEURSHIP IN POST-CIVIL WAR ERA

The promise of freedom and political enfranchisement held out by Lincoln's Emancipation Proclamation of 1863 was soon undermined by racist judicial rulings. In 1877, in *Hall v. DeCuir*, the U.S. Supreme Court ruled that a state could not prohibit segregation on a common carrier. In 1896, with the *Plessy v. Ferguson* ruling, "separate but equal" became the law of the land. Following these decisions, a pattern of rigid segregation of the races was established that remained the norm throughout the nation until the advent of the civil rights movement in the 1960s.

Nevertheless, even within the context of disenfranchisement and segregation, Booker T. Washington saw the possibility of securing African American economic stability through business development. In 1900, Washington spearheaded the development of the National Negro Business League to encourage African American enterprise. During the organization's first meeting, the delegates concluded that: "a useless class is a menace and a danger to any community, and. . . when an individual produces what the world wants, whether it is a product of the hand, heart, or head, the world does not long stop to inquire what is the color of the skin of the producer. . . . [I]f every member of the race should strive to make himself the most indispensable man in his community, and to be successful in business, however humble that business might be, he would contribute much toward soothing the pathway of his own and future generations."

◆ AFRICAN AMERICAN ENTREPRENEURSHIP IN THE EARLY TWENTIETH CENTURY

During the early 1900s, although services continued to be the cornerstone of the African American business community, some African Americans found it easier to raise capital and pursue other entrepreneurial endeavors. One of the finest examples was Madame C. J. Walker. Working as a domestic, Walker developed a hair care system in 1905 that softened and straightened

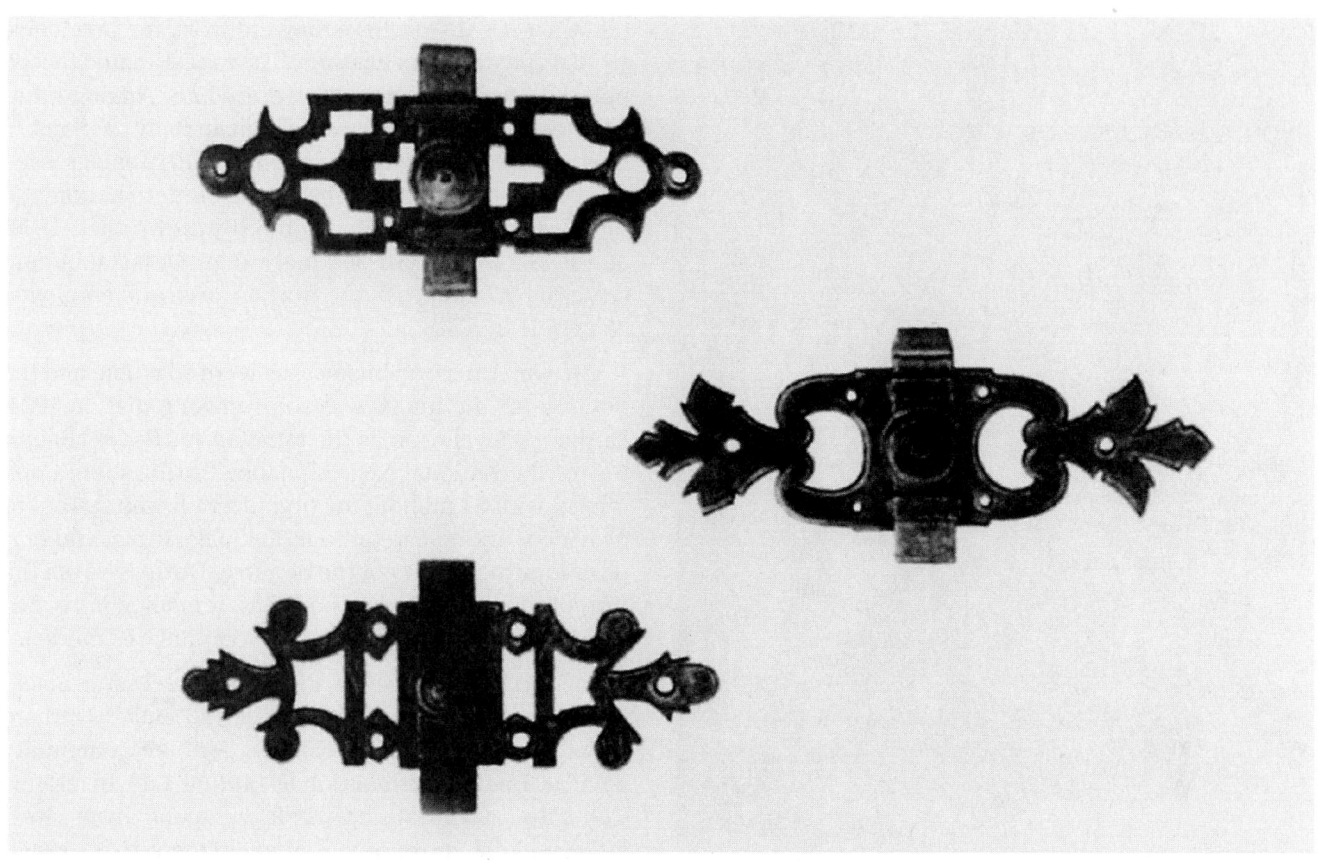

These hinges were crafted by African slaves in the employ of white manufacturers.

hair. She also developed the Wonderful Hair Grower product for women who had experienced hair loss. As an indication of her business acumen, Madame Walker was the first woman to sell products by mail order, and she also formed a national membership of door-to-door agents known as the Madame C.J. Walker Hair Culturists Union of America. To train young women in hair care, Madame Walker opened her own beauty school, the Walker College of Hair Culture. Millions of women, both black and white, throughout the United States, the Caribbean, and South America, became customers of Walker's beauty parlors and products. Before her death in 1919, Madame C.J. Walker had become the first African American female millionaire.

Durham, North Carolina: A Special Case

Turn of the century Durham, North Carolina, represented a special case of enterprise and economic resilience. In publications of the time, Durham was referred to as "The Wall Street of Negro America." By the late 1940s, more than 150 businesses owned by African Americans flourished in Durham. Among these businesses were traditional service providers such as cafes,

movie theaters, barber shops, boarding houses, pressing shops, grocery stores, and funeral parlors. What distinguished Durham, however, was the presence of large African American businesses.

One of the largest and most successful African American businesses in the nation was the North Carolina Mutual Life Insurance Company, which remained the largest African American-owned insurance company in 2002 with assets in excess of $200 million. Surrounding the North Carolina Mutual Life Insurance Company were the Banker's Fire Insurance Company, the Mutual Building and Loan Association, the Union Insurance and Realty Company, the Durham Realty and Insurance Company, the People's Building and Loan Association, the Royal Knights Savings and Loan Association, T. P. Parham and Associates (a brokerage corporation), and the Mortgage Company of Durham. Such businesses established Durham as a "city of enterprise" for African Americans.

Although Durham was a success, external economic pressure and racial hostility made it difficult for African Americans to develop businesses that could compete in the larger economy. Jim Crow laws and segregation

African American shoe cobbler.

forced most African American-owned businesses to limit their market to their own community. Somewhat of an exception, however, was the Durham Textile Mill, the only hosiery mill in the world owned and operated by African Americans at the time. The Durham Textile Mill operated 18 knitting machines and did business in the open market. Their salesmen, who were white, traveled mostly in North Carolina, Indiana, Georgia, South Carolina, and Alabama to market products. The Durham textile manufacturing firm was exceptional in the sense that it was perhaps the first large-scale African American-owned enterprise to compete in the larger economy.

Nevertheless, race relations in Durham were such that the most successful retail and service businesses tended to generate a white clientele. In 1940, for example, Smith's Fish Market, established by the former postal clerk Freeman M. Smith, supplied the Washington Duke, Durham's largest white-operated hotel. Smith was also the major supplier for smaller white and black-owned businesses. In 1940, Smith grossed more than $90,000 and opened four other outlets throughout the city. Similarly, Rowland and Mitchell established a

tailor shop in 1930 where they did work for "exclusive whites and department stores." It was estimated that 80 percent of their customers were white. Among other successful businesses was Thomas Baily & Sons, a meat and grocery store that opened in 1919 and grossed $80,000 a year by 1940. The Home Modernization and Supply Company, founded in 1938 by the brothers U. M. and R. S. George, grossed more than $100,000 in constructing 500 homes in the Durham area and employed 35 people by 1948.

African American businesses were so stable and the outlook for the future was so promising that, in 1924, Durham was chosen as the location for the headquarters of the National Negro Finance Corporation. Capitalized with $1 million, the organization was started to provide working capital to individuals, firms, and corporations in all parts of the country. Durham, from the turn of the century until the 1950s, remained unrivaled as the African American business capital of America.

In the 1990s, some of the most successful black-owned businesses in the country still called Durham "home," including: M & F Bank, Mutual Community Savings Bank, North Carolina Mutual Life Insurance Company, and NCM Capital Management Group. Nevertheless, the entrepreneurial excitement that existed between 1900 and 1950 was impossible to replicate. Indeed, scholars have noted that grassroots entrepreneurship tends to develop quickly by groups who have recently entered their new country's economy, as did African Americans after the abolition of slavery. From generation to generation, however, there is typically a decrease in the entrepreneurship rate as subsequent generations tend to choose the professions over business. In the case of African Americans, a full blown civil rights movement was required to create another surge in the entrepreneurial spirit.

◆ POST-CIVIL RIGHTS ERA ASSISTANCE TO AFRICAN AMERICAN BUSINESSES

The civil rights movement prompted the development of legislation and a number of government agencies to ensure the social, political, and economic rights of African Americans. Perhaps the greatest boost to African American entrepreneurship came in 1967 with the establishment of the U.S. Department of Commerce's Small Business Administration 8(a) program.

Under Section 8(a) of the Small Business Act Amendments (Pub.L. 90–104), the SBA was authorized to enter into contracts with federal agencies on behalf of small and disadvantaged businesses. Participation in the 8(a)

Craftsmen often paid for African slaves to make items like this chest.

program for small and disadvantaged businesses is contingent upon SBA approval of the business plan prepared by the prospective firms. The total dollar value of contracts processed through Section 8(a) had grown from $8.9 million in 1969 to $2.7 billion in 2000. Through the program, many small and African American-owned businesses were able to stabilize and grow. During the early 1980s, however, the Section 8(a) program was criticized because less than 5 percent of the firms had achieved open market competitiveness, implying that the program was assisting the marginal entrepreneur more so than the promising self-employed minority businessperson.

Another product of the civil rights movement was the 1977 Public Works Employment Act (Pub.L. 95–28). It required that all general contractors bidding for public works projects allocate at least 10 percent of their contracts to minority subcontractors. The SBA 8(a) Program and the 1977 Public Works Employment Act constituted the first attempts at "set-asides" to provide access to contracts for small, disadvantaged, and minority businesses. Because of the success of these laws, a strong backlash emerged among white entrepreneurs who were threatened by competition from African American and other disadvantaged groups.

Institutional Adversity: The *Croson* and *Adarand* Decisions

The fundamental concept of set-aside minority assistance programs was called into question during the height of the Reagan-Bush era. In 1989, the landmark U.S. Supreme Court ruling in *City of Richmond v. J. A. Croson Co.* struck down as unconstitutional under the Fourteenth Amendment a city ordinance of Richmond, Virginia, requiring that 30 percent of each public construction contract be set aside for minority businesses. In ruling against the Richmond ordinance, the Supreme Court made the distinction between local/state- and federally-enacted business development programs, holding that the U.S. Congress has far more authority than the states in formulating remedial legislation.

The *Croson* decision had a devastating impact on minority businesses. In Richmond, during the month of July 1987 when a lower court first ruled against the city's set-aside program, 40 percent of the city's total construction dollars were allocated for products and services provided by minority-owned construction firms. Immediately following the court's decision, the minority businesses' share of contracts fell to 15 percent, later dropping to less than 3 percent. In Tampa, Florida, the number of contracts awarded to African American-owned companies decreased 99 percent, and contracts with Latino-owned firms fell 50 percent after *Croson*. Such dramatic decreases in contracts awarded to minority businesses occurred throughout the country. More than 33 states and political subdivisions began taking steps to dismantle their racial/ethnic set-aside programs; more than 70 jurisdictions were conducting studies or holding hearings to review and evaluate their programs in light of *Croson*.

The *Croson* decision legitimated the idea of reverse discrimination in government procurement just as the *Regents of the University of California v. Bakke* (1978) decision did in higher education. This issue would surface again in *Adarand Constructors, Inc. v. Peña* (1995). Adarand filed suit against the U.S. Department of Transportation claiming that consideration of social and disadvantaged status, which was assumed to include women and minority groups, in awarding subcontracts violated the equal protection component of the Fifth Amendment's due process clause. The court of appeals rejected Adarand's claims but in June 1995, the Supreme Court remanded the case for further consideration using the "strict scrutiny" criteria established in *Croson*. Together, the two decisions had the effect of greatly limiting the access of disadvantaged entrepreneurs to procurement opportunities in the private and government sectors.

The government's ambivalence in supporting economic opportunities for African Americans and other minority groups should be viewed as a reflection of society's ambivalence regarding the extent to which African Americans are entitled to economic rights. Nevertheless, the civil rights movement helped African American entrepreneurs gain greater access to capital and to government and private sector procurement opportunities for the first time in history. And as a result, many small African American-owned businesses were able to grow and stabilize.

◆ ECONOMIC TRENDS

The number of African American-owned firms nearly quadrupled in the last quarter of the twentieth century.

Thirty-eight percent of African American-owned firms in 1997 were owned by women. Furthermore, the data showed that African American women were starting businesses at a greater rate than Americans in general.

Gross receipts of African American businesses also increased more than threefold. From 1977 to 1997, receipts of African American businesses grew from less than $20 billion to $71.2 billion. The increase, however, was not evenly distributed across businesses. In 1997, 72 percent of African American-owned businesses had receipts under $25,000, and 18 percent had receipts between $25,000 and $100,000. Meanwhile, 9 percent had gross receipts of more than $100,000, and only a tiny group (1%) had receipts of $1 million or more. Businesses that grossed more than $1 million annually accounted for more than 50 percent of the total receipts for all black-owned firms.

The geographic concentration of African American firms has roughly coincided with the African American population concentration. Six states accounted for 40 percent of the African American population; the same six states claimed 47 percent of African American-owned businesses. In 1997, the state of New York had the greatest number with 86,500, followed by California (79,100), Texas (60,400), Florida (59,700), Georgia (55,800), and Maryland (47,600). While New York had the greatest number of African American-owned firms,

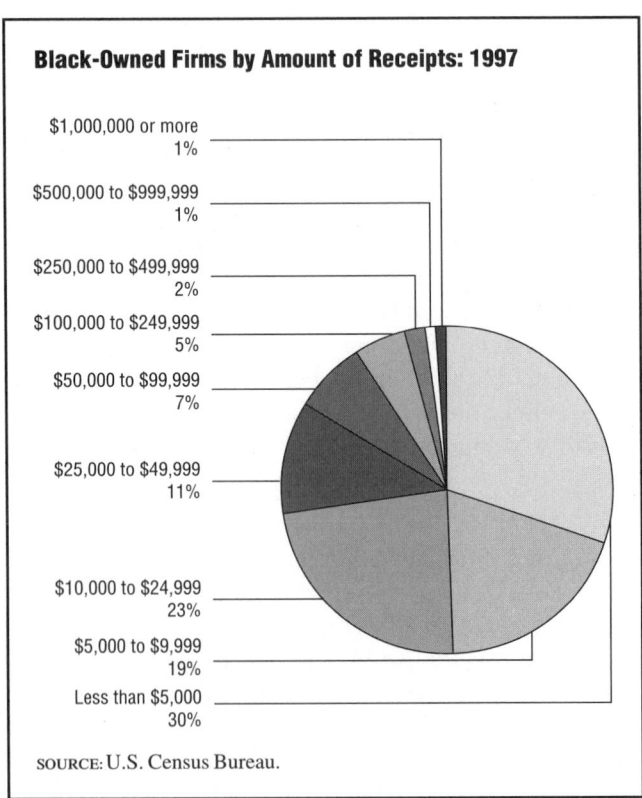

Black-Owned Firms by Amount of Receipts: 1997

$1,000,000 or more — 1%
$500,000 to $999,999 — 1%
$250,000 to $499,999 — 2%
$100,000 to $249,999 — 5%
$50,000 to $99,999 — 7%
$25,000 to $49,999 — 11%
$10,000 to $24,999 — 23%
$5,000 to $9,999 — 19%
Less than $5,000 — 30%

SOURCE: U.S. Census Bureau.

the District of Columbia had the greatest percentage (24%) of such firms: Maryland and Mississippi were the only other states with more than 10 percent of firms owned by African Americans.

African American-owned firms tend to be concentrated in specific metropolitan areas. Reflecting patterns seen in states, 28 percent of all African American-owned firms were located in the following metropolitan areas: Washington, DC-Maryland-Virginia; New York City; Los Angeles-Long Beach in California; Chicago, Illinois; and Atlanta, Georgia.

The location of corporate headquarters in urban areas has provided increased business opportunities for African American business service enterprises. Large cities have become areas where administrative and service functions are the dominant economic activities. The growth in corporate and government administration in central business districts has created a need for complementary advertising, accounting, information technology, computer, legal, temporary human resources, and maintenance business services. African American-owned businesses were distributed throughout the industry sectors of the economy including business services, retail, finance, insurance, real estate, transportation, communications, utilities, and construction.

In the context of the national economy, however, the number of African American-owned businesses and their total revenues continued to be marginal. African Americans composed 12 percent of the population but only 4 percent of all U.S. firms. The average gross receipts for African American businesses were $86,500 compared to $891,000 for all U.S. firms. The $71.2 billion total receipts for African American businesses was dwarfed by the $18.6 trillion gross receipts for all U.S. firms. African Americans participated in manufacturing at one-third the level of all U.S. firms. The number of businesses per 1,000 persons (business participation rate) for African Americans, was 24, the lowest of any ethnic/racial group and less than one-fourth of the overall U.S. business participation rate of 91. Finally, 11 percent of African American firms had paid employees compared to 25 percent of all U.S. firms. In conclusion, while African American businesses have experienced growth, they remained on the margins of the entire U.S. business environment.

AFRICAN AMERICAN-OWNED BUSINESSES IN THE NEW MILLENNIUM

The development of African American-owned businesses in the new millennium likely will continue to reflect their historical experience in business with periods of growth followed by periods of contraction. The implementation of the SBA 8(a) program and other set-asides provided access to a market that was previously closed to black-owned businesses. At the beginning of the twenty-first century, an increasing number of African American entrepreneurs focused on the unique challenges posed by the Information Age. Sixty-two percent of African American-owned businesses were concentrated in business services or communications, transportation, or utilities sectors. Success stories were numerous, and the conventional wisdom still held that continued educational advances, especially in technology and business education, would translate into an increasing number of business successes among aspiring entrepreneurs.

The saliency of race bias in American business remained such that while the size of the economic pie increased, the portion accorded to African American businesspersons remained virtually unchanged. In other words, African American businesses must run extremely hard just to keep pace. While multiple factors may account for this "running in place," the evidence confirmed that the market place is not "race neutral" or "color blind." As stated in *Black Entrepreneurs in*

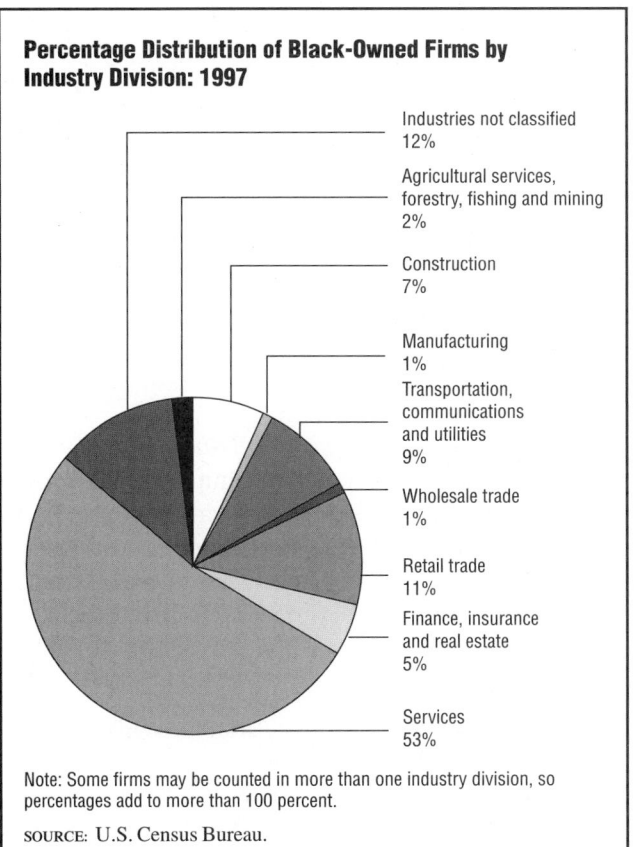

Percentage Distribution of Black-Owned Firms by Industry Division: 1997

Industries not classified
12%

Agricultural services, forestry, fishing and mining
2%

Construction
7%

Manufacturing
1%

Transportation, communications and utilities
9%

Wholesale trade
1%

Retail trade
11%

Finance, insurance and real estate
5%

Services
53%

Note: Some firms may be counted in more than one industry division, so percentages add to more than 100 percent.

SOURCE: U.S. Census Bureau.

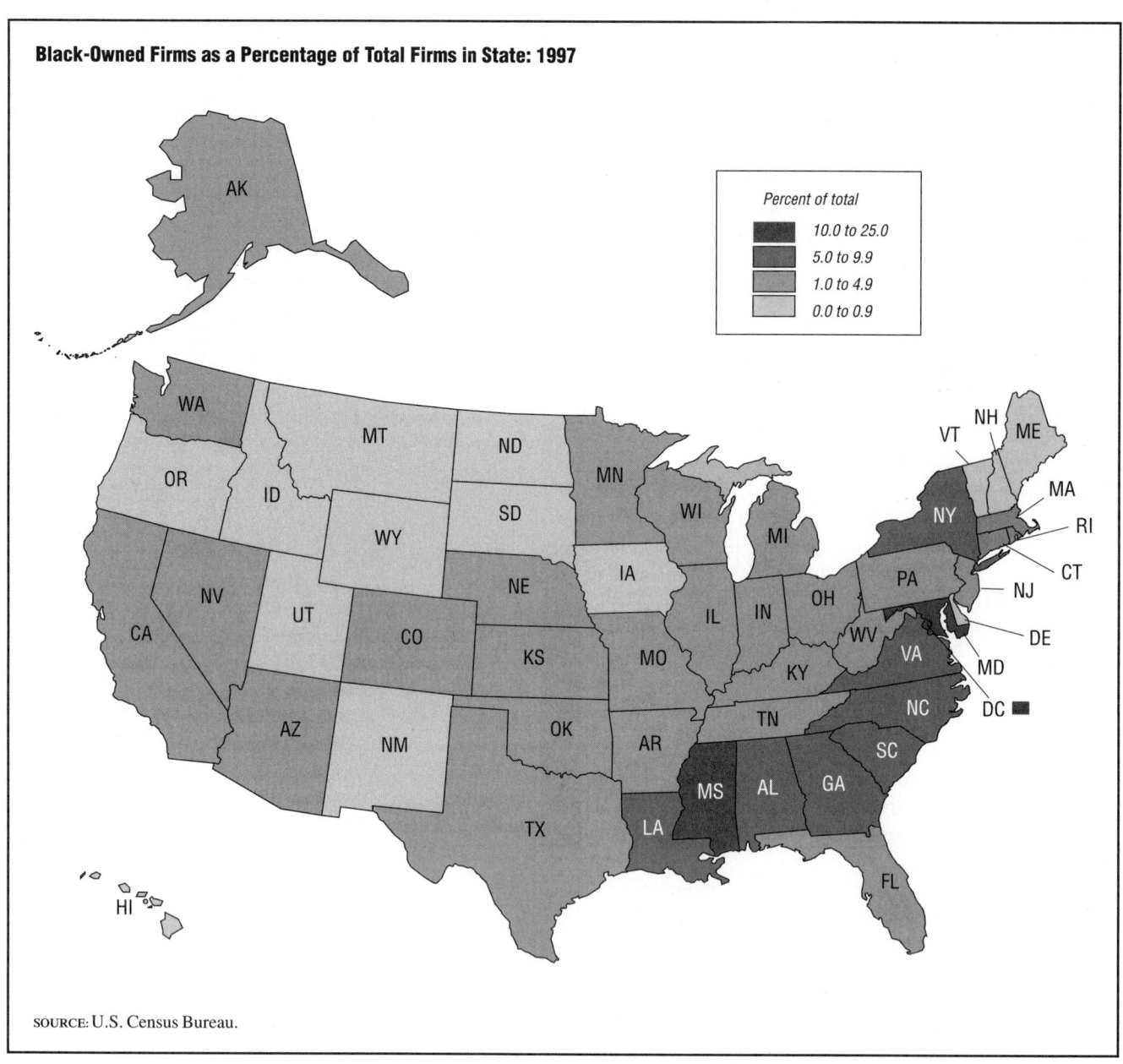

Black-Owned Firms as a Percentage of Total Firms in State: 1997

Percent of total

10.0 to 25.0
5.0 to 9.9
1.0 to 4.9
0.0 to 0.9

SOURCE: U.S. Census Bureau.

America: Stories of Struggles and Success, "the kind of economic detour that negatively impacted the growth of black entrepreneurship in the pre-Civil Rights era has transformed itself but, nevertheless, continues to negatively impact the entrepreneurial experience of African Americans in the post-Civil Rights era."

Greater Entrepreneurial Growth

The relative well-being of the African American community is directly linked to the vitality of its business segment. African American communities must continue to give birth to and grow successful businesses. Indeed, African Americans must strive to increase the rate at which it founds and develops businesses. Even in the face of persistent institutional adversity, the responsibility for greater entrepreneurial growth rests with African Americans. To fulfill this responsibility, African Americans must eliminate so-called "internal barriers." The "successful entrepreneur" must become viewed as an honored career path just as careers as teachers, lawyers, physicians, social workers, and ministers. Fortunately, entrepreneurship has become part of the curriculum or extracurricular activities of many high schools and community organizations. Moreover, parents must explicitly include entrepreneurship in the mix of career options presented to their children. The second internal barrier is commitment. African Americans frequently fail to understand the level of sacrifice necessary to accomplish a goal, especially in business. In addition, entrepreneurs frequently experience fear and have self-doubt about their chances or ability to achieve success. Success in business is difficult to achieve regardless of race. Success in business is enhanced by acquiring the necessary educational background, work experience to be technically competent, and saving sufficient startup capital.

In terms of external barriers, the majority community and government sector must take responsibility for eliminating the artificial barriers to the products and credit markets that have impeded the investment possibilities and profit potential of African American-owned businesses. Analysis conducted by the National Bureau of Economic Research to determine the extent to which minority-owned businesses encountered discrimination in applying for loans concluded that African American-owned businesses faced significant and persistent constraints in the credit market. Furthermore, the study revealed that these constraints extended beyond the availability of credit to also include the cost of credit. In other words, African American-owned businesses paid higher interest rates on their loans than did their majority counterparts.

The Promise of Information Technology

Economic growth in the twenty-first century will occur in the area of information technology. Technological changes will continue to enable smaller businesses to generate, use, and manage information more efficiently, as well as to compete with larger companies. African American entrepreneurs already began participating and benefiting from this Information Revolution. In fact, Tariq K. Muhammad, an acknowledged expert in this area, chronicled the emergence of a class of African American technocrats whom he labeled the "Black Digerati." He stated in his *Black Enterprise* article of the same title that despite appearances to the contrary, "Blacks in the information industry can be found in roles which include inventors, engineers, entrepreneurs, executives, consultants, venture capitalists, lawyers, and headhunters. . . who are masters and creators of the Digital Revolution."

Specifically, the Internet is expected to continue to provide opportunities for success for African American-owned businesses. Anonymity and relatively low startup costs were especially relevant for African American entrepreneurs starting Web-based operations. The former allows entrepreneurs to minimize the possible

The information technology age offers promising business opportunities for African American entrepreneurs.

negative impact that the racial bias of customers, competitors, and potential investors can have on business success, while the latter reduces the capital requirements for launching and operating a business enterprise.

Thus, there is a sound basis for optimism that the information technology sector will afford African American entrepreneurs greater opportunities in obtaining a share of the economic market more commensurate with their population percentage. The accomplishments of African American entrepreneurs in the information technology sector also provides evidence that the entrepreneurial spirit among African Americans burns bright as we move into the new millennium.

Leading Companies and Executives

Earl G. Graves's *Black Enterprise* magazine has compiled lists—the "BE 100s"—of the most successful black-owned companies on an annual basis since 1973. In Graves's introduction to the 2002 issue, he expressed his excitement at how far African American entrepreneurship had grown but also disappointment with how many institutional obstacles still prevent them from achieving their fair share of the entire U.S. marketplace. African American companies on the 2002 list dwarfed those from the first BE 100s: only one of the 1973 listees could have cracked the top 100 industrial/service companies in 2002. The downside, however, was that African Americans remained underrepresented among the biggest U.S. corporations. The largest enterprise of the 2002 lists was not quite 33 percent as profitable as the smallest of the *Fortune* 500 companies.

The top companies reported in their fields were: Camac Holdings Inc. of Houston, Texas, with almost $1 billion in sales (industrial/service top 100); the Harrell Company of Atlanta, Georgia, (auto dealers top 100); Don Coleman Advertising Inc. of Southfield, Michigan (advertising agencies top 20); Carver Federal Savings Bank of New York, New York (banks top 25); North Carolina Mutual Life Insurance Company of Durham, North Carolina (insurance companies top 10); the Williams Capital Group L.P. of New York, New York (investment banks top 15); Ariel Capital Management Inc. of Chicago, Illinois (asset managers top 20); and TSG Capital Group L.L.C. of Stamford, Connecticut (private equity top 10). Complete lists—along with helpful articles about key companies, industries, and individuals—can be found in the June 2002 issue of the magazine.

Similarly, *Fortune* magazine compiled a list in its July 2002 issue called "The 50 Most Powerful Black Executives in America." Among them were more than 10 CEOs of companies, three of whom headed companies ranked by the magazine among the 50 largest in 2001; three CEOs of corporate groups; at least five company presidents and just as many group presidents; two COOs; more than a dozen senior/executive vice presidents; and a handful of various other group or corporate managers or financial officers. The listmakers deemed Stanley O'Neal, president and COO of Merrill Lynch, as the most powerful executive. Others on the list who are covered in this chapter (unless otherwise noted) are: Kenneth I. Chenault, Earl G. Graves (*See* Media chapter), Earvin "Magic" Johnson (*See* Sports chapter), Robert L. Johnson (*See* Media chapter), Vernon Jordan (*See* National Organizations chapter), Richard Parsons, Russell Simmons, John W. Thompson, and Oprah Winfrey (*See* Media chapter). Winfrey was the only woman to crack the top ten, but ten other women joined her in the top 50: Ursula Burns, Lana Corbi, Kim Crawford, Brenda Gaines, Carla Harris, Cathy Hughes, Myrtle Potter, Paula Sneed, Pamela Thomas-Graham, and Jacqueline Woods.

◆ ENTREPRENEURS AND BUSINESS EXECUTIVES

(To locate biographical profiles more readily, please consult the index at the back of the book. For example, media executives appear in the Media chapter.)

Wally Amos Jr. (1937–)
Entrepreneur

Wallace Amos Jr. was born in Tallahassee, Florida, on July 1, 1937, and grew up there until his parents divorced when he was 12 years old. Following his parents's divorce, he went to New York City to live with his Aunt Della. She loved to cook and often made Amos her special chocolate chip cookies. After spending several years in New York City, he dropped out of high school to join the U.S. Air Force, where he earned his high school equivalency degree.

Upon discharge from the Air Force, Amos achieved success as the first African American talent agent for the William Morris Agency. Starting there as a mail clerk, he quickly worked his way up to executive vice president. While there he "discovered" Simon & Garfunkel for the agency and served as agent for such well known acts and entertainers as the Supremes, the Temptations, Marvin Gaye, Dionne Warwick, and Patti Labelle.

In 1975 Amos founded Famous Amos Chocolate Chip Cookies. Based on his Aunt Della's recipe, the cookies became a nationwide success as they spread across the country from his original store on Sunset Boulevard in Los Angeles. By 1980 Amos was selling $5 million worth of cookies each year and his operation had expanded to include a large production facility in Nutley, New Jersey. Amos's success and expansion was enhanced by the backing of such well known entertainers as Bill Cosby and Helen Reddy. In 1985 Amos became vice chairman of the company and served in that capacity until 1989. Amos left the Famous Amos Cookie Corporation in 1989 following a dispute with a group of investors and financial difficulties. He began a new business, Wally Amos Presents. . . Chip & Cookie, in 1990. In 1993, Amos started yet another company, Uncle Noname Cookie Company, and serves as its president. Uncle Noname Cookie Company, based in Honolulu, Hawaii, specializes in five varieties of gourmet cookies. Proceeds from the sale of its cookies are donated to the support of Cities in Schools, a national dropout prevention program of which Amos is a board of directors member.

Amos has donated personal items to the Business Americana Collection at the Smithsonian's Collection of Advertising History and received the Presidential Award for Entrepreneurial Excellence Award from President Ronald Reagan in 1986. In 1987, he received a citation from the Horatio Alger Association. Amos also served as a national spokesperson for Literacy Volunteers of America.

Jim Beckwourth (1798–1866)
Author, Trapper, Entrepreneur

James Pierson Beckwourth was born on April 26, 1798, near Fredericksburg, Virginia. His father was a landowner and member of a prominent Virginia family; his mother was an African American woman, possibly a slave. The family moved to a farm near St. Charles, Missouri, in 1806 and Jim attended school in St. Louis from 1810 to 1814. He was apprenticed to a St. Louis blacksmith but soon found himself heading west. Similar to many other events in Beckwourth's life, there are conflicting stories concerning the dissolution of the apprenticeship. Evidently at this time, Beckwourth also changed the spelling of his last name.

In 1824, Beckwourth joined a westward bound fur trapping and trading expedition under the leadership of William Henry Ashley. Beckwourth soon became known as a man of many adventures and exploits. Although the basis of these stories are factual many, with Beckwourth's approval, have been greatly exaggerated. Nevertheless he undoubtedly embodied the spirit of the legendary mountain men of the American west. In 1827, while still engaged in the fur trade he married a Blackfoot Indian woman. In 1829, he took refuge from a debt collector by hiding with the Crow Indians where he married again. It must be remembered that marriage on the frontier was a much less formal arrangement than it is today. Beckwourth claims he was made a Crow chief in recognition of his fighting prowess against the Blackfeet.

By 1837, Beckwourth was with the U.S. Army in Florida serving as a scout during the Seminole wars. He soon returned to the Rocky Mountains, married a woman in New Mexico, and, in 1842, opened a trading post near what is now Pueblo, Colorado. Between 1844 and 1850, he fought in the California uprising against Mexico and the Mexican-American War. In 1850, Beckwourth joined the California gold rush and while in the Sierra Nevadas discovered a mountain pass that bears his name today. He made the gap more passable, opened an inn, and, by 1851, was guiding wagon trains through the pass.

Beckwourth's memoirs, entitled *Life and Adventures of James P. Beckwourth, Mountaineer, Scout and Pioneer*, were in part ghost written by T.D. Bonner and published in 1856. Beckwourth traveled to St. Louis and Kansas City where the popularity of his book enhanced his reputation and he was regarded as somewhat of a celebrity. Beckwourth returned to Denver, married again, opened a trading post, and was acquitted on a charge of manslaughter. Tiring of city life he signed on with the Army as a scout and fought the Cheyenne Indians. Beckwourth probably died of food poisoning on or around September 25, 1866 while riding to a Crow encampment. Accounts of his purposely being poisoned by Crows are largely discounted today.

James Beckwourth.

Dave Bing (1943–)
Business Executive, Former Professional Basketball Player

Bing was born November 29, 1943, in Washington, DC, where he played basketball at Spingarn High School. He was named to play on a national All-Star team and was voted most valuable player on the tour. Bing attended Syracuse University on a basketball scholarship graduating in 1966 with a B.A. in economics. He was the second overall pick in the 1966 National Basketball Association draft and was chosen by the Detroit Pistons.

During his first season he was the league's top rookie and the league's high scorer his second year. In the 1974–1975 season Bing played for the Washington, DC, Bullets and in the 1977–1978 season he was with the Boston Celtics. Bing was voted the league's Most Valuable Player in 1976 and played in seven NBA All-Star games. The Professional Basketball Writer's Association of America gave him their Citizenship Award in 1977. Bing was named National Minority Small Businessperson of the Year in 1984. In 1989 he was elected to the Naismith Memorial Basketball Hall of Fame.

After being associated with management programs at the National Bank of Detroit, Chrysler Corporation, and Paragon Steel, Bing formed Bing Steel Inc. in Detroit, a very successful steel supplier to the automobile industry. The company eventually came to be known as the Bing Group. In its first five years, the company doubled its revenues. In 2000, a disgruntled employee burned down the main offices and warehouse of the Bing Group, and while the company experienced tough times, Bing rebuilt; the company continues to be a major supplier to most car companies in the Detroit area.

Bing has served on the board of directors of Children's Hospital of Detroit, Michigan Association of Retarded Children and Adults, Black United Fund, Detroit Urban League, and the March of Dimes.

Marie Dutton Brown (1940–)
Entrepreneur

Marie Brown's career is a picture book example of the kind of tenacious nature entrepreneurs need to have, and how to expand on opportunities when they present themselves. She received a degree in psychology in 1962, from Penn State University, where she was part of the one percent of the student body's African American population. She went to work as a social studies teacher in the Philadelphia public school system. Two years later, when a salesperson from a publishing firm in New York came to sell her some of his company's titles for the school, the meeting turned into a job offer to work for Doubleday.

Brown stayed at Doubleday for two years, then moved to Los Angeles with her new husband. She moved back to New York in 1972 and returned to Doubleday as an associate editor. During the 1970s, as an interest in African American literary titles grew, so grew Brown's position, as she brought many ethnic titles to print.

In 1980, Brown quit Doubleday to become founding editor of *Elan* magazine, which focused on the cultural life of the international black community. After only three issues were launched, Brown's financial backers pulled out, leaving Brown jobless. She went to work at a bookstore, giving her firsthand retail experience.

In the fall of 1984, Brown started her own business, Marie Brown Associates, a literary agency that run from her Harlem apartment. Although, similar to any new business venture, times were lean for several years, things started to turn around as Brown began signing more and more writers. As the 1990s began, the larger publishing houses began courting African American writers, but Brown was far ahead of them, as one of only five African American literary agents in the country. Brown still contributes her time to the community, sitting on several boards including the Studio Museum of Harlem.

Malcolm CasSelle (1970–)
Computer Entrepreneur

Born on March 22, 1970, in Allentown, Pennsylvania, CasSelle has accomplished a great deal at a young age. Growing up in Allentown, Pennsylvania, CasSelle developed a passion for writing computer programs in high school. He graduated from Massachusetts Institute of Technology (MIT).

CasSelle left for Japan three days after finishing his undergraduate work in order to enter MIT's Japan program. While overseas, he worked for Shroders Securities and NTT Software Labs. Upon his return to the United States he took a job with Apple Computers. After earning his master's at Stanford, he occupied the position of director of digital publishing and marketing for Blast Publishing. CasSelle would later introduce E. David Ellington, his partner, to the wonders of cyberspace.

Along with Ellington, CasSelle co-founded NetNoir Inc., an African American-oriented online site. Based in San Francisco and available through America Online, NetNoir explores a wide range of news and information. *VIBE* magazine, along with Motown Records and the clothing company Blue Marlin, channel their services and goods through CasSelle's cybersite.

Emma Chappell (1941–)
Banking Executive

Dr. Emma Carolyn Chappell was born in Philadelphia, Pennsylvania, on February 18, 1941. As a member of the Zion Baptist Church, she began to work for the Continental Bank. She took classes at both Temple and Rutgers Universities and slowly moved up the bank's hierarchy. By 1977 she was its first African American female vice president.

Chappell was active in the community during her assent to the top of Continental. She worked for a variety of community action groups that were concerned with redeveloping the inner-city. In 1984 she took time off from Continental to be the treasurer for the presidential campaign of the Reverend Jesse Jackson.

In 1987 Chappell and a group of community business leaders founded the United Bank of Philadelphia, the only African American-owned bank in the city. The bank struggled to find funding in the late 1980s. By March 1992, however, it opened for business with sufficient backing. United struggled upon its opening and, in 1995 and 1996, neared insolvency, but only one year later the bank had reached $106 million in assets. *Black Enterprise* chose it as the financial company of the year in 1995. It also began issuing its own credit cards and embarked on a partnership with American Express to offer investment advice and financial services to its depositors. In June 2000 Chappell stepped down from her duties as chairman of the board and chief executive officer, but United continued its campaign to improve banking services in historically poor neighborhoods of Philadelphia and the surrounding cities. In addition to serving on the boards of Philadelphia-area organizations, she took over executive directorship of the Rainbow/PUSH Coalition's Wall Street Project, which aims to make the businessworld equitable towards African Americans.

Ken Chenault (1951–)
Corporate Executive

Born on June 2, 1951, in Mineola, New York, Kenneth I. Chenault grew up in the town of Hempstead, New York, on Long Island. He attended the upscale, private, untraditional Waldorf School. Following high school, he attended Springfield College on an athletic scholarship. After only one year there, he decided to concentrate more on academics. He transferred to Bowdoin College and received a B.A. in history in 1973, graduating magna cum laude. In 1976, he graduated from Harvard Law School with a juris doctorate.

After graduation, Chenault spent two years working for a corporate law firm before transferring to a firm that specialized in business consultancy. In 1981, he joined American Express. His first position was as a director of strategic planning for the Travel Related Services (TRS) division. He moved up to become vice president of the merchandise services division in 1983, and from 1984 to 1986 served as senior vice president and general manager of marketing for the division. Under his direction, the area saw sales jump from $150 million to $500 million a year. In the second half of the 1980s, Chenault served as executive vice president and general manager for American Express Platinum/Gold division, executive vice president of the personal card division, and president of American Express Consumer Card Group, USA, a post he held until 1991.

That year, Chenault was promoted to president of the American Express Card, and two years later became president of American Express Travel Related Services, USA. With the business on an upswing, Chenault became vice chairman of the company in 1995, making him the highest-ranking African American executive in corporate America. Two years later, he made even more waves when he was named president and chief operating officer. In 2001, Chenault took over as CEO of American Express. Named as the second most powerful African American executive by *Fortune* magazine, Chenault faces the challenges of leading American Express through the country's economic slump.

Comer Cottrell (1931–)
Entrepreneur

Cottrell was born in Mobile, Alabama, on December 7, 1931. He began his sales career at the age of eight, joining his father for visits to clients selling insurance. Cottrell continued his sales career at Sears Roebuck after graduating from the University of Detroit in 1952. Years later, while managing a post exchange at a military base, Cottrell observed that there were no hair products for African Americans. Cottrell decided to form a company that would sell products specifically for hair styles worn by African Americans.

In 1970, Cottrell began his company with an empty Los Angeles warehouse, $600, and a typewriter. He started out marketing hair spray to African American beauticians and barbers. With the moderate success of this product, the Proline company was born. Five years later, Proline opened a distribution center in Birmingham, Alabama. By 1980, Proline had outgrown Los Angeles and moved to Dallas, coinciding with the release of the Curly Kit Home Permanent product. Soon Proline enjoyed sales figures in excess of $11 million and began to expand into overseas markets. By 1989, Proline was ranked nineteenth on *Black Enterprise*'s list of top 100 African American businesses with sales of $36 million annually. Pro-Line had expanded its sales to $104 million in 2000.

In 1989, Cottrell became—as a member of a 14-owner consortium of investors that purchased the Texas Rangers—the first African American to own a Major League Baseball franchise. Cottrell used his position to speak out about affirmative action in professional sports. In 1990, he continued his philanthropy by purchasing the bankrupt Bishop College, a Dallas school founded by free slaves and Baptist missionaries, and he convinced Paul Quinn College to relocate from Waco, Texas, to the Bishop College grounds. In 1994, Cottrell visited South Africa as part of an envoy of African American businessmen sponsored by Langston University's National Institute for the Study of Minority Enterprise to establish links with black-owned businesses there.

Jean Baptiste Point Du Sable (1750?–1818)
Entrepreneur, City Founder

Jean Baptiste Point Du Sable was born in Haiti, reportedly in 1750, to a French mariner and an African-born slave. It is believed that he may have been educated in Paris, France, and worked as a sailor during his young adult years. Du Sable entered North America through either Louisiana or French Canada.

In the early 1770s, entrepreneur Du Sable established the first settlement in the area later called Chicago. Having impressed the British as a well-educated man and capable frontiersman, he was sent to the St. Clair region to manage trade and act as a liaison between Native Americans and the British. Later returning to his original settlement, Du Sable built a bakery, dairy, smoke house, horse mill and stable, workshop, and a poultry house. He also traded, trapped, and served as the local cooper and miller. Through Du Sable's efforts, Chicago became a major center for frontier commerce.

In 1788 Du Sable wedded a Potawatomi woman named Kittihawa, or Catherine, with whom he raised two children. Once married, Du Sable became increasingly involved in the community. His bid in 1800, however, for tribal chieftaincy failed, and soon after he sold his holdings and moved from the Chicago area. Real estate records suggest that he moved to St. Charles, Missouri, and that he probably died there in poverty on August 28, 1818.

E. David Ellington (1960–)
Computer Entrepreneur

Ellington was born in New York, New York, on July 10, 1960. Growing up in Harlem, he was raised primarily by his mother. While earning his undergraduate degree at Adelphi University, which he received in 1981, Ellington worked in the office of a U.S. congressman. In 1983, he received his master's from Howard University, then spent a great deal of his time travelling in such places as Europe, Japan, China, and India. Later, he earned his law degree from Georgetown University. He founded the Law Offices of E. David Ellington and chaired for the International Law Section of the Beverly Hills Bar Association.

In 1995, Ellington and computer entrepreneur, Malcolm CasSelle, cofounded NetNoir Online, an African American-oriented site on the Internet. Billing itself as "The Cybergateway to Afrocentric Culture," NetNoir explores a wide range of news and information. Participants include journalist Charlayne Hunter-Gault and athlete Carl Lewis. Extremely innovative, NetNoir was named one of the "25 Cool Companies of the Year" by *Fortune* magazine. With minority investors, NetNoir News Media Services planned to venture into CD-ROMs and the designing of Web sites in 1996.

Ann Marie Fudge (1951–)
Corporate Executive

Ann Marie Fudge was born April 23, 1951, in Washington, DC. She received a B.A. with honors from Simmons College in 1973 and an M.B.A. from Harvard Business School in 1977. She began her business career at General Electric in 1973 as a manpower specialist. She worked at GE until 1975, when she received a job at General Mills in Minneapolis. There she began as a marketing assistant until she was promoted to assistant product manager in 1977, product manager in 1980, and marketing director in 1983. She remained in that position until she joined Kraft General Foods in 1986.

At Kraft, Fudge started out as the associate director of strategic planning, but by 1989, her worth to the company earned her a vice presidency in charge of marketing and development of the Dinners and Enhancers Division working on products, such as Log Cabin Syrup, Minute Rice, and Stove Top Stuffing. She managed to reposition the products and increase sales in the overburdened food market. She moved up to general manager of that division in 1991, and became executive vice president in 1994. The same year, she became president of the Coffee and Cereals Division.

Fudge has served as president and vice president of the Executive Leadership Council and holds memberships with the National Black MBA Association and the Junior League. She also has served on the board of directors for the Federal Reserve Bank, New York, Allied Signal Inc., General Electric, Liz Clairborne Inc., and Catalyst. She was a COGME Fellow in 1975 and won a Leadership Award from the Young Women's Christian Association in 1979.

S. B. Fuller (1905–1988)
Entrepreneur

S. B. Fuller was born on June 4, 1905, in Monroe, Louisiana. He moved with his family to Memphis, Tennessee, where he dropped out of school after the sixth grade and worked at various jobs. In 1928, he moved to

Chicago and began selling products door-to-door. By the mid 1930s he had established a successful business on the South side of Chicago.

In 1947, he acquired Boyer International Laboratories, a white-owned cosmetics company, and greatly expanded his business. His company grew in size and he became famous for his motivational techniques. However, when whites in the South learned that Boyer was owned by an African American, they boycotted Boyer's products. In 1969, Fuller Products was forced to declare bankruptcy.

Fuller reorganized the company, and it reemerged from bankruptcy in the early 1970s. The company reestablished its sales techniques and grew into a large company again. Fuller died on October 24, 1988, after receiving numerous honors.

Arthur G. Gaston (1892–1996)
Entrepreneur

Arthur George Gaston was the living embodiment of what makes up an entrepreneur. He had stated many times in interviews, that one of his primary rules for

Arthur G. Gaston.

business success is "Find a need and fill it." Gaston's business accomplishments are a testimony to the man's lifelong adherence to this rule.

Gaston was born on July 4, 1892, in Demopolis, Georgia, a small rural town. He started his business career in 1923 by founding the Booker T. Washington Burial Society, guaranteeing African Americans a decent burial. In 1932 it had grown large enough to be incorporated. In 1930, Smith and Gaston Funeral Directors was formed to complement the services of the burial society. The "Smith" was A. L. Smith, Gaston's father-in-law, who helped him financially get started in business.

Finding it hard to staff his growing company with skilled clerical employees, Gaston started the Booker T. Washington Business College in 1939. The college provided a place where African American students could learn proficiency in working on business machines. (The school continues to this day.)

In 1946, Gaston started the Brown Belle Bottling Company, offering Joe Louis Punch. Next came a cemetery in 1947, a motel in 1954, an investment firm in 1955, a savings and loan association in 1957, a senior citizens home in 1963, two radio stations in 1975. In 1986, at the hearty age of 94, Gaston opened the A. G. Gaston Construction Company. From the original burial society in 1923 to his sprawling empire seven decades later, bringing in more than $24 million in revenues in 1991, Arthur Gaston was the quintessential self-made man. He died on January 19, 1996, in Birmingham, Alabama.

Archibald Grimké. *See* Law chapter.

La-Van Hawkins (1960–)
Fast Food Restaurant Entrepreneur

La-Van Hawkins was born and raised in Chicago, Illinois. He suffered as a youth through drug addiction and gang membership. However, after starting to work at McDonald's in downtown Chicago, he turned his life around. He quickly rose through the ranks at McDonald's, becoming director of operations before leaving the company to work for Kentucky Fried Chicken in the late 1970s.

Hawkins managed inner-city projects for KFC and became a district manager. In 1986, he joined T. Boone Pickens in various investment schemes that earned him large amounts of money. In 1990, he began franchising Checkers restaurants. By 1995, the success of this chain had made him a multimillionaire.

La-Van Hawkins.

In 1995, officials for Burger King approached Hawkins about fronting several of their restaurants in urban areas. Hawkins accepted the offer and now owns Burger Kings in various cities and several federal empowerment zones. With more than a dozen Burger Kings in Detroit by 2002, Hawkins continued to add restaurants each year.

Robert Holland Jr. (1940–)
Business Executive

Robert Holland Jr. was born in April of 1940, in Albion, Michigan. Holland earned a bachelor's of science in mechanical engineering from Union College in Schenectady, New York in 1962, and in 1969, he completed a master's of business administration in international marketing at Bernard Baruch Graduate School of Manhattan. In 1968, Holland moved from his job at the Mobil Oil Co. as an engineer and sales manager to join the McKinsey & Co. consulting firm, where he worked as an associate and eventually a partner until 1981. During that time, he worked abroad in the Netherlands, England, Mexico, and Brazil. He returned to Michigan

in 1981 as CEO of City Marketing, a beverage distributor. In 1987, he switched companies again, accepting the chair position for Gilreath Manufacturing, Inc. in Howell, Michigan, a manufacturer of plastic injection molds.

In 1991, Holland started Rohker-J Inc. in White Plains, New York, a company of his own that bought struggling companies, turned them around and sold them. In 1994, Holland's business savvy and his whimsy with poetic verse won him a position as president and CEO of Ben & Jerry's Homemade Ice Cream, Inc. After accomplishing his goals of stabilizing Ben & Jerry's manufacturing operations and bringing more professional management to the company, he resigned in October 1996. In 1997 he founded WorkPlace Integrators, a leading dealer of Steelcase office furniture, in Bingham Farms, Michigan. In addition to his business, Holland has served on the board of directors for the Harlem Junior Tennis Program, UNC Ventures, and Atlanta University Center. He has also served as chairman of the board at Spelman College.

George E. Johnson (1927–)
Business Executive

Johnson was born in Richton, Mississippi, on June 16, 1927. He attended Wendell Phillips High School in Chicago then went to work as a production chemist for a firm that produced cosmetic products for African Americans. While there, he developed a hair straightener for men and began marketing it himself in 1954. By 1957 he had formed Johnson Products and was selling products under the Ultra-Sheen label. The company prospered and, by 1971, its stock was being traded on the American Stock Exchange. Johnson Products was the first African American-owned company to trade on a major stock exchange. In June 1993 Joan B. Johnson, chair and CEO of Johnson Products, announced the sale of the company to Ivax Corp., a white-owned pharmaceutical firm. Johnson Products was officially sold to Ivax in August 1993.

Johnson has served as a director of the Independence Bank of Chicago, the U.S. Postal Service, and the Commonwealth Edison Co. Johnson also is responsible for the George E. Johnson Foundation, which funds charitable and educational programs for African Americans.

Johnson has received the Abraham Lincoln Center's Humanitarian Service Award (1972), *Ebony* magazine's Black Achievement Award (1978), and the public service award presented by the Harvard Club of Chicago. He has also been awarded the Horatio Alger Award (1980) and the Babson Medal (1983).

Johnson has received honorary degrees from many institutions of learning including Chicago State University (1977), Fisk University (1977), and the Tuskegee Institute (1978).

Karl Kani. *See* **Visual and Applied Arts chapter.**

Dennis Kimbro (1950–)
Author, Educator, Motivational Speaker

Dennis Paul Kimbro was born on December 29, 1950, in Jersey City, New Jersey. He graduated from Oklahoma University with a bachelor's in 1972 and later from Northwestern University with a Ph.D. in political economy in 1984, while working as a salesperson at Smithkline Beckman pharmaceutical corporation. In 1987, he left Smithkline to work at ABC Management Consultants Inc., where he worked until 1991. Meanwhile, Kimbro worked at revising a manuscript left to publisher W. Clement Stone written by the late Napoleon Hill, the author of *Think and Grow Rich*. Hill had been working on a version for an African American audience when he died. Stone gave the manuscript to Kimbro. Kimbro interviewed many successful African Americans to chart how they managed to maximize potential and channel positive thinking to build their success.

In 1991, Kimbro's book—co-authored originally by Hill—*Think and Grow Rich: A Black's Choice* was published by Ballantine Books and became the first ever major-release, African American self-help book. In the next two years, the was a best seller among African American audiences, selling more than 250,000 copies and earning Kimbro an Award of Excellence from the Texas Association of Black Personnel in Higher Education in 1992. The same year, Kimbro accepted a post as associate professor and director of the Center for Entrepreneurship at Clark Atlanta University School of Business and Administration. *Daily Motivations for African-American Success*, Kimbro's second book, was published by Ballantine in 1993. In 1997, Kimbro authored *What Makes the Great Great: Strategies for Extraordinary Achievement*, which outlined nine "stones of greatness" that underly true success.

Reginald F. Lewis (1942–1993)
Business Executive

Lewis was born December 7, 1942, in Baltimore, Maryland. He received an A.B. from Virginia State College in 1965 and a law degree from Harvard Law School in 1968. He first worked with the firm of Paul, Weiss, Rifkind, Wharton & Garrison until 1970. He was a partner in Murphy, Thorpe & Lewis, the first African American law firm on Wall Street until 1973. Between 1973 and 1989 Lewis was in private practice as a corporate lawyer. In 1989 he became president and CEO of TLC Beatrice International Holdings Inc. With TLC's leveraged acquisition of the Beatrice International Food Co. Lewis became the head of the largest African American owned business in the United States. TLC Beatrice had revenues of $1.54 billion in 1992.

Lewis was a member of the American and National Bar Associations and the National Conference of Black Lawyers. He was on the board of directors of the New York City Off-Track Betting Corp., the Central Park Conservance, the NAACP Legal Defense Fund, and WNET-Channel 13, the public television station in New York. He was the recipient of the Distinguished Service Award presented by the American Association of MESBIC (1974) and the Black Enterprise Achievement Award for the Professions. Lewis died unexpectedly January 19, 1993, in New York.

J. Bruce Llewellyn (1927–)
Business Executive

James Bruce Llewellyn was born July 16, 1927, in New York City and earned a B.S. from City College of New York. He attended Columbia University's Graduate School of Business and New York University's School of Public Administration before receiving a degree from New York Law School.

Before attending law school, Llewellyn was the proprietor of a retail liquor store. While attending law school he was a student assistant in the District Attorney's Office for New York County from 1958 to 1960. After graduating he practiced law as part of Evans, Berger and Llewellyn. Between 1964 and 1969 he worked in a variety of professional positions for various governmental agencies including the Housing Division of the Housing and Re-Development Board (1964–1965), Small Business Development Corporation (1965), and the Small Business Administration (1965–1969).

In 1969, as part of a syndicate buyout, he became president of Fedco Food Stores of New York. By 1975, the company had grown from 11 to 14 stores and had annual revenues of $30 million and 450 employees.

Llewellyn has served on the boards of the City College of New York and its Graduate Center, American Can Co., American Capital Management Research, and the Freedom National Bank. He has belonged to the Harlem Lawyers Association, the New York Interracial Council for Business Opportunity, and the New York Urban Coalition and its Venture Capital Corporation.

Llewellyn has honorary doctorates from Wagner College, City University of New York, and Atlanta University. He was in the U.S. Army Corps of Engineers from 1944 to 1948. In 2002 he was CEO of Queen City Broadcasting Inc. and chairman of the Philadelphia Coca-Cola Bottling Co., the second largest firm on the "*Black Enterprise* Industrial/Service 100" list.

Samuel Metters (1934–)
Entrepreneur

Dr. Samuel Metters, a native of Austin, Texas, received his B.S. in architectural engineering from Prairie View A&M University, a B.A. in architecture and urban planning from the University of California at Berkeley, a M.S. in systems management and in public administration from the University of Southern California, and a Ph.D. in public administration from USC.

Metters founded Metters Industries Inc. in 1981 after a career that included a stint in the Army. The firm, which has over 350 employees, is a strategic planning and analysis company that works in conjunction with various governmental entities. His customers include the IRS and the U.S. Patent and Trade Office, as well as Northwest Airlines, Howard University, Federal Express, and Fox Studios. Metters has also worked in Saudi Arabia building new cities and handling the logistical problems that go along with any new development. In 2001, Metters began work on a $4.5 million development project in Prairie View, Texas, near the campus of his alma mater. Not surprisingly, Metters Industries ranked among the *Black Enterprise* Industrial/Service 100 leading African American-owned businesses with 2000 sales of $34 million. By 2002, however, annual sales had dropped to $20 million, too low to remain on the BE 100.

In 1987 Metters was selected as a member of the board of directors of the U.S. Black Engineers Publications, Inc. He is also active in the USC Alumni Association, Washington, DC, area Boy Scouts and with Prairie View University.

Rose Meta Morgan (c.1912–)
Entrepreneur

Rose Meta Morgan was born c.1912 in Shelby, Mississippi, but spent most of her growing years in Chicago. She started her own business at the early age of ten, making and selling artificial flowers door-to-door with the assistance of other neighborhood children. By the age of 14, she was earning money styling hair. Morgan claims she was a high school drop out even though she may have actually finished. Either way, she attended Morris School of Beauty, and after graduating,

she rented space in a salon and began styling, grooming, and cutting hair full time. It was during this time that Morgan met Ethel Waters, a famous actress/singer, during a run of performances in Chicago in 1938. Waters invited Morgan to New York because of the stylist's prowess in hair design.

Within six months of moving to New York, Morgan opened her own beauty shop. Later, running out of room, she signed a ten-year lease for an old dilapidated mansion and began to renovate it. Three years later, Morgan's salon—the Rose Meta Morgan House of Beauty—was the most prestigious, most successful African American beauty salon in the world. By 1946, she drew 1,000 customers a week and increased her staff to 29 people including a nurse and masseurs. Morgan began producing and selling a line of cosmetics and hosting fashion shows that matured into major social events at the Renaissance Casino and Rockford Plaza in Harlem. Soon she was considered one of the richest businesswomen in New York. Customers came from all over the country to visit the House of Beauty, and Morgan travelled abroad with her cosmetics, fashion designs, and ideas about beauty and women of color.

In the mid-1950s, Morgan bought and refurbished a new building for the House of Beauty. Thousands of people attended the grand opening and the building was dedicated by the New York City mayor's wife. The new salon offered more features, such as a dressmaking department, a charm school, and a fitness department and later a wig salon to cash in on the renewed popularity in hair pieces. In 1965, Morgan created the Freedom National Bank, New York's only commercial bank run by and for African Americans. In 1972, Morgan created the Trim-Away Figure Contouring business, and shortly thereafter, in the 1980s, she retired with a salon and a set of businesses as a legacy that are the only ones of their kind in the world.

Morgan's marriages were less successful than her businesses. In 1955, she married heavyweight boxing champion Joe Louis, but their marriage was annulled in 1958. Later, Morgan married lawyer Louis Saunders, and though they separated in the early 1960s, Saunders died before they were divorced.

Stanley O'Neal (1951–)
Corporate Executive

Born in Roanoke, Alabama, on October 7, 1951, Stanley O'Neal's family later moved from rural Alabama to Atlanta, Georgia, where O'Neal attended high school. He worked in a General Motors plant while

Freedom National Bank, Harlem's first black commercial bank, was founded in 1965 by Rose Meta Morgan.

studying for his undergraduate degree, which he received from the Kettering Institute in 1974. O'Neal then went on to earn an M.B.A. in Finance from Harvard Business School in 1978. As an executive for General Motors from 1978 to 1986, O'Neal held a succession of financial management jobs in the company's Madrid and New York offices. Ultimately, he served as General Assistant Treasurer, a position giving him responsibility for GM's mergers and acquisitions.

O'Neal left GM to join the investment firm of Merrill Lynch in 1986. As an investment banker at the firm, he made a name for himself in the early 1990s with his resuscitation of the company's junk bond business. O'Neal has held positions as Managing Director and head of Global Capital Markets; Managing Director in Investment Banking and head of the Financial Services Group; co-head of the Corporate and Institutional Client Group; and CEO of the Private Client Group. In 2001, he was named the president and chief operating officer of Merrill Lynch. In its July 22, 2002 issue, *Fortune* magazine named O'Neal the most powerful black executive in the United States. He was scheduled to take over the leadership of Merrill Lynch in December 2002.

Henry G. Parks (1916–1989)
Entrepreneur, Business Executive

Parks was born September 29, 1916, in Atlanta, Georgia. He received a B.S. from Ohio State University and did graduate work there in marketing. After graduating, Parks worked at the Resident War Production Training Center in Wilberforce, Ohio, where he was associated with Dr. Mary McLeod Bethune. In 1939 he was a national sales representative for the Pabst Brewing Co. In addition he became involved in a variety of enterprises, mostly in Baltimore, Maryland, including: theatrical bookings in New York City; a failed attempt at marketing a beverage with former heavyweight boxing champion Joe Louis; real estate; drug store operations; and cement block production.

Parks ultimately bought into Crayton's Southern Sausage Company of Cleveland, Ohio. After becoming familiar with the meat packing industry, he sold his interest in the company for a profit. In 1951 he started H. G. Parks Inc., a sausage packer and distributor with the aid of a group of investors. By 1971 the company had annual revenues of $10.4 million and was distributing its products to more than 12,000 East Coast stores.

Parks served as vice president of the Chamber of Commerce of Metropolitan Baltimore, was on the board of directors of Magnavox, held a seat on the Baltimore City Council, and purchased an interest in Leonard Evans's Tuesday Publications. He died on April 24, 1989, in Towson, Maryland.

Richard Dean Parsons (1948–)
Corporate Executive

Born in the Bedford-Stuyvesant neighborhood of Brooklyn, New York, on April 4, 1948, Richard Dean Parsons grew up in the borough of Queens, New York. He graduated from high school at the age of 16 and attended the University of Hawaii, where he played varsity basketball. He earned a bachelor's from the university in 1968, and continued his education at the Union University of Albany Law School. He graduated at the top of his class and received the highest score on the state bar exam in 1971.

Parsons started his career as a member of New York governor Nelson Rockefeller's legal staff, where he served when Rockefeller became vice president of the United States under Gerald Ford in 1974. He continued in this capacity, also providing legal counsel for President Ford as deputy counsel and then as associate director of the domestic council. He left government service in 1977, to join the New York City law firm, Patterson, Belknap, Webb & Tyler, where he became a partner in 1979. He defended clients, such as Happy Rockefeller and Estee Lauder.

Parsons was appointed chief operating officer of the Dime Savings Bank of New York in 1988, becoming the first African American male to manage a financial institution of Dime's size. Parsons lead the bank to a comeback from severe debt. In 1993, because of Parsons's remarkable leadership skills, newly elected Mayor Rudolph Giuliani chose Parsons to head his transition council and later to be the Deputy Mayor for Economic Development. Parsons instead chose to act as chairman of the Economic Development Corporation for the city. In December 2001, Parsons was named to replace Gerald Levin as the CEO of the AOL Time Warner Corporation.

Parsons, no stranger to sitting on boards of directors, has served on boards for Time Warner Inc., Philip Morris, Tristar Pictures, Howard University, and the Metropolitan Museum of Art. Parsons has also served as a member of the presidential Drug Task Force, as chairperson of Wildcat Service Organization, and as a member of the board of the New York Zoological Society.

Herman J. Russell (1930–)
Housing Construction Entrepreneur

Herman Jerome Russell was born December 23, 1930, in Atlanta, Georgia. At the age of 16, he first went into business—with his father. They bought a small piece of land and built a duplex on it. Russell used the money he accrued from rent to pay for his education at Tuskegee Institute. In 1953, he went to work for his father and, upon his father's death in 1957, took over the family home improvement business.

Russell built a reputation for high quality work that allowed him to break down many racial barriers to success. He began to bid on large construction jobs and has worked on many of the biggest projects built in Atlanta since the 1960s, including Hartsfield International Airport, Coca-Cola Company World Headquarters, and the Georgia Dome. He continued to built afforded housing despite the high-profile success of H. J. Russell & Company.

In 1997, Russell retired from the management of the company, passing it down to his children. He is well known in the Atlanta area for his philanthropy and for his work in the inner-city.

Russell Simmons (1957?–)
Music Company Executive, Producer, Music Promoter

Hollis, Queens, in New York City was the birth place of Russell Simmons. Although he grew up in a middle class neighborhood, Simmons got involved with gangs in his teens. The 1970s brought change to Simmons's life, however, as he enrolled in classes at the Harlem branch of City College of New York. While studying sociology, Simmons began noticing the influence rap music had on young inner-city African Americans. The boasting and story telling skills of various rappers drew crowds on street corners and in neighborhood parks. Simmons found himself in the middle of a movement that would shape the sound of the music, particularly the rap genre. Simmons is married to hip hop clothes designer and model Kimora Lee.

Simmons left college to promote local rap artists. Hard work and perseverance led to the formation of Def Jam Records in 1984. Simmons and his partner, Rick Ruben, signed a deal with CBS Records to distribute their material. Simmons was primarily interested in promoting rap images that displayed the life and style of tough urban streets. Acts such as the Beastie Boys, L.L. Cool J, and Run-DMC pushed Def Jam Records to early success. Other groups such as Public Enemy enjoyed Simmons's input as their careers developed.

The music Simmons involved himself with not only revolutionized hip hop but helped bring fashion to forefront as well. High-top Adidas tennis shoes, black leather jackets, and t-shirts displaying the Def Jam Recording logo flooded the streets. These influences laid a foundation for Simmons own line of clothing called Phat Pharm. Simmons furthered his own professional growth by getting involved in film production. He contributed to *Krush Groove* and *Tougher Than Leather* in the late 1980s. Simmons is CEO of Rush Communications, which in 1992 was the nation's second largest African American-owned entertainment company. Rush is comprised of record labels, management companies, and clothing, radio, film and television divisions. In 1998, Simmons launched an hour-long syndicated series "Oneworld's Music Beat with Russell Simmons." In 2001, Simmons went to Washington to speak out on the behalf of rap artists, promoting the fact that they have brought to the forefront many social issues and that they should not be blamed for the violence that many have associated with their songs. That same year, Simmons published his autobiography *Life and Def: Sex, Drugs, Money, and God* with the help of George Nelson. With 2001 sales of $192 million—16th on the BE Industrial/Service 100—*Black Enterprise* magazine named Rush Communications its Industrial/Service Company of the Year. Simmons was also named a trustee of the National Urban League.

Naomi R. Sims (1949–)
Business Executive, Model

Sims was born March 30, 1949, in Oxford, Mississippi. She attended New York University, where she studied psychology, and the Fashion Institute of Technology, where she graduated in 1967

Sims was a fashion model with the Ford Agency in New York from 1970 to 1973. She was the first African American woman to be a high fashion model and the first to appear in a television commercial. She also appeared on the cover of *Life* magazine.

In 1970 Sims also started lecturing and writing fashion and beauty articles on a freelance basis. In 1973 she co-developed a new fiber for her line of wigs and founded the Naomi Sims Collection which by 1977 had annual revenues of $4 million. Sims has also written a number of books including *All About Health and Beauty for the Black Woman* (1975), *How to Be a Top Model* (1979), *All About Hair Care for the Black Woman* (1982), and *All About Success for the Black Woman.*

In 1969 and 1970 Sims was voted Model of the Year by International Mannequins and won the *Ladies Home Journal* Women of Achievement Award. For her work with underprivileged children in Bedford-Stuyvesant,

she also won an award from the New York City Board of Education. In 1977 Sims was voted into the Modeling Hall of Fame by International Mannequins and made the International Best Dressed List 1971–1973, 1976–1977. Sims has also received recognition for her fund raising efforts for sickle cell anemia and cancer research. She belongs to the NAACP and works closely with drug rehabilitation programs.

In 2002 Sims worked with Naomi Sims Beauty Products Ltd. in New York City.

Percy E. Sutton (1920–)
Business Executive, Attorney

Percy Ellis Sutton was born November 24, 1920, in San Antonio, Texas. He graduated from the Phillis Wheatley High School and attended a number of colleges including Prairie View College, Tuskegee Institute, and the Hampton Institute. His education was interrupted by World War II when Sutton enlisted in the U.S. Army Air Corps. He was promoted to captain and served as a combat intelligence officer in the Italian and Mediterranean theaters. He was decorated with Combat Stars for his service.

After his discharge, Sutton attended law school on the G.I. Bill, first at Columbia University in New York and then Brooklyn Law School where he received an LL.B. in 1950. During the Korean conflict, Sutton reenlisted in the USAF and served as an intelligence officer and a trial judge advocate.

Returning to civilian life, he opened a law office in Harlem with his brother and another attorney. In 1964, he was elected to the New York State Assembly, where he served until 1966. In 1966, he was appointed and later elected to the office of president of the Borough of Manhattan, a post he held until 1977.

With his brother Oliver and Clarence B. Jones, Sutton co-founded the Inner City Broadcasting Corporation in 1971. The company purchased radio station WLIB-AM, making it the first black-owned station in New York City. The company also produced television programs and videos for entertainment companies around the country, including *Showtime at the Apollo.* Sutton retired from the company in 1990, but continued to serve as chairman emeritus.

Sutton has been a civil rights advocate both as an attorney and a politician. He was a national director of the Urban League and a past president of the New York branch of the NAACP. He was voted Assemblyman of the Year by the Intercollegiate Legislative Assembly in 1966. Sutton has also served as a director of the Museum of the City of New York and the American Museum of Natural History.

John W. Thompson (1949–)
Business Executive

John W. Thompson was born April, 24, 1949, in Fort Dix, New Jersey. He graduated from Florida A&M University in 1971 with a bachelor's degree in business administration, and then went on to earn a master's degree in management sciences for Massachusetts Institute of Technology's Sloan School of Management in 1982.

Thompson spent 28 years with industry giant IBM, working his way up from an entry level sales position to occupy one of the company's senior executive posts—general manager of IBM's Americas unit. Though his name was mentioned in some print sources as a possible candidate for IBM's top position, he left the company on April 14, 1999, to be named president and chief executive officer of Symantec Corporation, a Cupertino, California, software company.

The silicon valley company, though long-established and financially viable, was sluggish in its performance. A well-known manufacturer of anti-virus and utility software, Symantec was facing stiff competition. Thompson focused the company's objectives on one area, that of Internet security. Well-publicized technology issues such as looming Y2K system failures, global e-mail viruses, and the activities of hackers helped the company's focus on corporate security solutions pay off. During Thompson's first years as CEO, Symantec revenues picked up substantially, growing from $632 million to $944 million in two years. According to company information, under Thompson's leadership, Symantec served 98 of the *Fortune* 100 companies and more than 100 million customers.

Thompson has served on the board of a number of companies and organizations, including: UPS, NiSource, Inc., Seagate and Crystal Decisions, Florida A&M University Cluster, and the Illinois Governor's Human Resource Advisory Council. He was named as one of *Fortune* magazine's 50 most powerful African American executives in its July 22, 2002 issue.

Madame C. J. Walker (1867–1919)
Entrepreneur

Walker was born Sarah Breedlove near Delta, Louisiana, in 1867. She was orphaned as a child, raised by a sister in Vicksburg, Mississippi, married at the age of 14, and widowed in 1887 at the age of 20.

Walker moved with her daughter to St. Louis where she earned a living by taking in laundry and sewing. By 1905 she had become interested in hair care products for women and began working on a hot comb and her

Madame C.J. Walker.

"Wonderful Hair Grower." In 1906 she moved to Denver and, with $1.50 in her pocket, started a hair preparations company. She soon married C. J. Walker, a newspaperman who taught her the fundamentals of advertising and mail order promotion. In 1908 she moved with her daughter to Pittsburgh where she founded a beauty school, the Walker College of Hair Culture, which trained cosmetologists in the use of her products.

In 1910, with a more central location in mind, she moved to Indianapolis, Indiana, where she established a laboratory and factory and developed a nationwide network of 5,000 sales agents, mostly African American women, known as The Madame C.J. Walker Hair Culturists Union of America.

Her business prospered, and Walker became the first African American female millionaire. She had a townhouse in Harlem and a custom built mansion on the Hudson River near Irvington, New York. She died in New York on May 25, 1919.

Walker was a strong believer in self-reliance and education. She was proud of her accomplishments, especially of providing employment for thousands of African Americans who might otherwise have had less meaningful jobs. Walker was also a genius at marketing, promotion, and mail order sales. Beneficiaries of her estate included Mary McLeod Bethune's school in Daytona, Florida, and other African American schools, the NAACP and the Frederick Douglass home restoration project in Florida.

Maggie Lena Walker (1867–1934)
Banker

Walker was born on or around July 15, 1867, in Richmond, Virginia. She was the daughter of Elizabeth Draper, a former slave, and Eccles Cuthbert, a New York journalist of Irish extraction.

Walker attended Richmond public schools including Armstrong Normal School which functioned as a high school. After graduating in 1883 she taught in the Richmond schools for three years before marrying building contractor Armstead Walker in 1886.

While she had been in school, Walker joined the Grand United Order of Saint Luke, a mutual aid society that served as an insurance underwriter for African Americans. Walker became active in the organization and held a number of lesser positions before becoming the Right Worthy Grand Secretary in 1899. She soon changed the name of the organization to the Independent Order of Saint Luke and moved its headquarters to Richmond.

In 1903, she became the head of the Saint Luke Penny Bank and the first woman in the United States to hold such a position. Although legally separate, the bank had a close financial association with the Independent Order of Saint Luke. The bank later became the Saint Luke Bank and Trust Company and, finally, the Consolidated Bank and Trust Company.

By 1924 under Walker's guidance, the Order had a membership of 100,000, a new headquarters building, more than 200 employees, and its own newspaper—the *Saint Luke Herald.*

Walker was active in many other organizations including the National Association of Colored Women, the Virginia Federation of Colored Women's Clubs, and its Industrial School for Colored Girls. In 1912 she founded the Richmond Council of Colored Women and was a founding member of the Negro Organization Society, a blanket association for African American clubs and organizations.

She was a board member of the NAACP from 1923 to 1934 and the recipient of an honorary degree from Virginia Union University. In 1927 she received the Harmon Award for Distinguished Achievement. Walker died on December 15, 1934.

Terrie M. Williams (1954–)
Business executive

Terrie Michelle Williams was born on May 12, 1954, in Mt. Vernon, New York. She attended Brandeis University where she graduated cum laude in 1975, receiving a bachelor's degree. Williams then earned a master's degree from Columbia University in 1977. Her first job after graduate school was as a medical social worker at New York Hospital. She held this job until 1980 when she became the program administrator of The Black Filmmaker Foundation. In 1982, Williams became vice president and director of corporate communication at Essence Communications, Inc., a position she held until 1987 when she formed her own company, The Terrie Williams Agency.

The multi-faceted Terrie Williams Agency, offers services to individual and corporate clients. In addition to marketing and communications consulting, the agency also offers executive skills training. Among the agency's first clients were giants of the entertainment world such as Miles Davis and Eddie Murphy. The agency has also served clients such as The National Basketball Association, The National Hockey League, Revlon, and the Nickelodeon television network. Williams also works with organizations and programs that provide services for at-risk and underprivileged youth.

Williams is the author of three books: *Personal Touch: What You Really Need to Succeed in Today's Fast-Paced Business World* (1994) (with Joe Cooney); *Stay Strong: Simple Life Lessons for Teens* (2001); and *Plentiful Harvest: Creating Balance and Harmony Through the Seven Living Virtues* (2002). She is the recipient of the Public Relations Society of America (PRSA) New York Chapter's Phillip Dorf Mentoring Award; The New York Women in Communications Matrix Award in Public Relations; and The Citizen's Committee for the New York Marietta Tree Award for Public Service.

15

Family and Health

◆ Family Structure and Stability ◆ Marriage
◆ Gay/Lesbian/Bisexuality/Transgender Issues ◆ Fertility and Births ◆ Children
◆ Health ◆ Life Expectancy ◆ Assessment ◆ Social Activists ◆ Vital Statistics

by Rose M. Brewer

The family, as defined by the U.S. Bureau of the Census, is a group of two or more persons (one of whom is the householder) who are related by birth, marriage, or adoption, and who reside together. In everyday social usage, this definition is usually refined to include diverse family pattern variations, but the American value system has traditionally embraced the concept of lifetime monogamous marriage and prized the "nuclear" family pattern of husband and wife living with their own children in the same household. Yet, with divorce rates hovering at about 50 percent, the prevalence of this idealized pattern has diminished. Remarriages have created increasing numbers of "blended" families comprised of various configurations of stepparents and stepchildren. Formal adoptions of stepchildren and increasing adoptions of children from other countries are also more common. The growth in the numbers of single-parent families headed by women has been called "one of the most startling social developments of the past quarter century."

◆ FAMILY STRUCTURE AND STABILITY

African American families, historically, have been more diverse in family structure than the idealized norm of the nuclear family. Black families have been crafted in the context of the remembered cultures of Africa, cultural creativity within the United States, enslavement, racism, and persistent institutionalized inequality. Family life was central to African cultures and social organization, and enslaved Africans brought this value with them to America. However, the conditions of slavery often prohibited the existence of a stable African American family. Harshness and cruelty,

rape and the severing of family bonds were all too common during enslavement, and slave marriages were not recognized by law. Even so, strong bonds could be formed among enslaved men and women. Herbert Gutman's work *The Black Family in Slavery and Freedom* (1976) indicates that some unions lasted 10, 15, and as many as 25 years depending on the region and the time period. Nonetheless, kin relations rather than marriage were the linchpin of African American families under enslavement. This kin principle remains strong to the present.

Thus, one family pattern that has historically been common among African Americans is that of the "extended" family. This family grouping includes other relatives such as grandparents, aunts, uncles, cousins, nieces, nephews, or other relatives, formally or informally adopted, who share the household temporarily or for a longer time period with a nuclear family. Extended families have long been a strong support system within the African American community. Today, members of extended families may not all live in the same household because of the migratory patterns of family members, but they nonetheless function as a supportive intergenerational kinship unit.

Andrew Billingsley, in his classic work *Black Families in White America* (1968), identified an additional category of families called "augmented" families, which included unrelated persons. In "Understanding African American Family Diversity," an essay from *The State of Black America* (1990), Billingsley describes these supportive, dependable, family—such as networks of relationships. Another classification, "fictive kin," as defined by Carol Stack in *All Our Kin* (1974), includes "play" mothers, brothers, sisters, and so on, who usually do not live together. In some communities, these

Extended families have long been a strong support system within the African American community.

friendship networks resemble and substitute for extended family networks that may no longer exist. Foster families are also a growing phenomenon in the African American community and have been the source of considerable debate. It is usually argued that not enough African American families are sought out to foster African American children. As poverty has increased for many African American families, the issue of bureaucratized foster care will remain a contentious one, and so will the issue of the large number of single female-headed households. This family form is more characteristic of the African American population than of any other American racial or ethnic grouping today.

As Billingsley contends, diversity is and always has been characteristic of African American family life. African American households presently fall into the following categories: (1) married couples with children; (2) married couples without children; (3) extended families (usually those including grandparents); (4) blended families; (5) single-parent families (usually but not always headed by women); (6) cohabiting adults (with or without children); and (7) single-person households (predominantly female).

Number and Size of Families

According to U.S. Census reports, there were 8.7 million African American family households in the United States in 2000, up from 6.2 million in 1980. This increase was most evident in the number of married-couple families and female-headed families with no husband present. In 2000, married-couple families comprised only 47.8 percent of all African American families, contrasted with 1980 when they comprised 56 percent. Forty-four percent of African American families in 2000 were headed by a female householder with no husband present, an increase from the 1980 proportion of 40 percent. The increase in African American female-headed families can be attributed to a multiplicity of factors: racism, the shortage of eligible African American males, the economic vulnerability of African Americans, the shorter life expectancy of African American males, increasing separation and divorce rates among African Americans, the rising rate of out-of-wedlock parenthood, increasing societal permissiveness regarding sexuality, and changing gender roles stressing female autonomy. This emerging American pattern of female autonomy coincides with the existing African

American cultural norm of more egalitarian relationships between women and men than typically found in European American families. Male-headed households with no spouse present represented a mere 8.2 percent of African American families in 2000.

The African American family's structure and status have changed dramatically over the last 40 years, and its configuration, while following the majority population's general post-World War II trends, reflects historical inequities between the races that make the African American family's security especially tenuous as the nation enters the twenty-first century. The same forces that have molded the United States into what it is today have been at work on all facets of African American family life and culture. In that sense, the fortunes of African Americans ebb and flow with the tide of the general economic and social conditions of the nation, especially racial, class, and gender inequities. The African American family also faces dilemmas that emanate from its unique position and identity within American society. African Americans experience problems related to their general minority group status as well as to their unique historical experiences of slavery, oppression, second-class citizenship, and the continuing stigma related thereto.

Furthermore, the political struggles of the Civil Rights movement culminated in increased opportunities for a segment of the African American population, but a significant number of African American families remain locked in poverty. Deindustrialization and globalization of the economy represent a notable structural shift with devastating consequences for many urban and rural African American families. As old city industries close down to settle in white suburbs or out of the country, many African Americans face increasing joblessness.

In fact, the U.S. census data reveal that since the late 1960s the African American unemployment rate has been twice as high as the white unemployment rate, regardless of the economic condition of the country. The 1970s and 1980s, however, were periods of severe economic instability and recession in the United States. African American males were particularly hard-hit by joblessness and underemployment during these decades due to the decline of the manufacturing industries in which many African American males were employed— the automobile and steel industries, for example. This combination of double-digit inflation and high levels unemployment during the 1970s and 1980s disproportionately eroded the purchasing power of African American families. Yet even in the 1990s, during a period of economic expansion and prosperity, many African Americans were still marginalized from the economy.

Income is not the only area in which blacks lag behind whites. According to figures published in *Dollars & Sense* magazine in February of 1996, four of every ten black households have less than $1000 in net worth, and nearly 41 percent of black households are worth less than $11,612 versus 16 percent of white households. Most whites fall into the $25,000 to $49,999 net worth range. The discrepancy is partially attributed to the fact that African Americans tend not to have accumulated assets to pass onto the next generation through inheritance—one of the most significant ways in which people amass wealth.

While disproportionate segments of African American families are poor, significant growth in the number of middle-class and affluent African American families at the upper end of the family spectrum has occurred, particularly of younger, college-educated, dual-income, married-couple families. This growth has occurred since the opening of the opportunity structure in the mid-1960s with the passage of the Civil Rights Act of 1964 and the Voting Rights Act of 1965. Less research has been focused on these upper-strata families than on low-income African American families; as a result, less is known about African American families that are prospering in the current economic climate, though they are one of the largest and fastest-growing segments of the nation's consumer population.

In February of 1996, Stephen Garnett of *Dollars & Sense* noted that "blacks represent less than 13 percent of the American population but exercise a purchasing power that equals the gross national product of the ninth largest country in the world." In 1994, African Americans spent $304 billion—much of it on leisure-oriented goods and services, reflecting a more sophisticated consumer. In the recent past, African Americans tended to spend more on cars, furniture, and home appliances and to devoutly express brand loyalty. In the 1990s, African Americans began to seek superior quality and value rather than blindly purchasing products based on established shopping habits. Support of African American-owned businesses remains an issue, however.

African American families in the lower economic strata are earmarked by the growth in the numbers of households headed by poor, never-married African American females. In 1994, the Center for the Study of Social Policy found that this growth in female-led families correlated almost perfectly with the growth of African American male joblessness. Other issues for these families include: high levels of teenage pregnancies; the shortage of marriageable, employed African American males; disparities between black and white earning power; inadequate housing and social services; and chronic unemployment and underemployment.

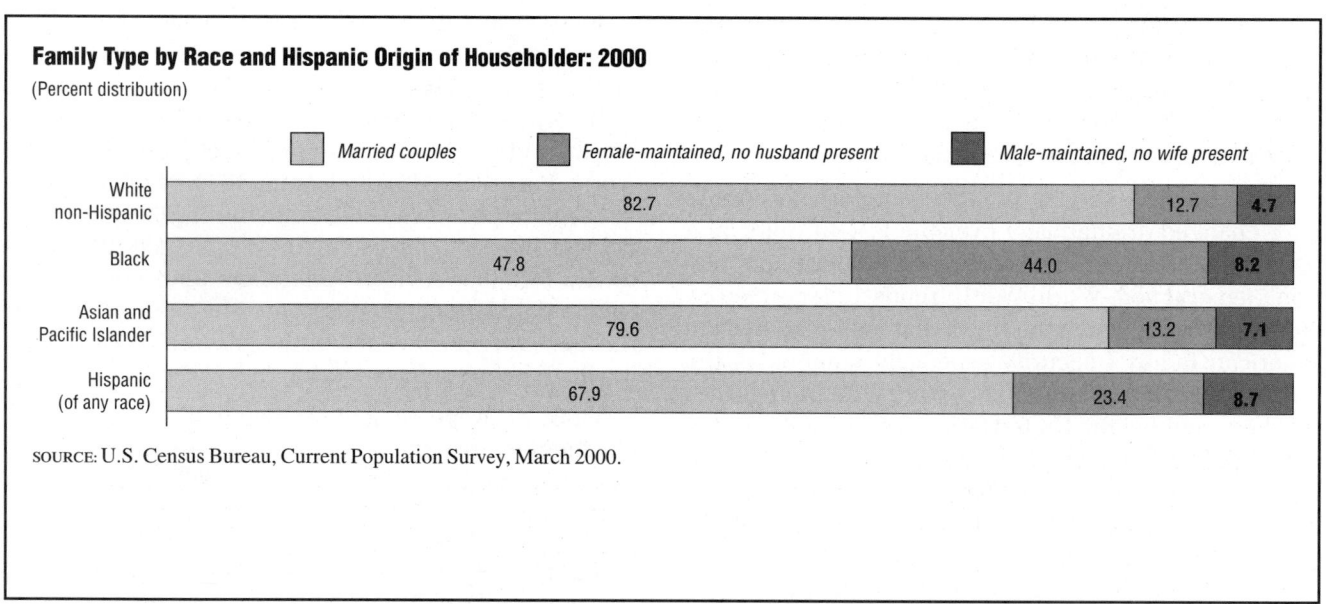

Family Type by Race and Hispanic Origin of Householder: 2000

(Percent distribution)

- Married couples
- Female-maintained, no husband present
- Male-maintained, no wife present

	Married couples	Female-maintained	Male-maintained
White non-Hispanic	82.7	12.7	4.7
Black	47.8	44.0	8.2
Asian and Pacific Islander	79.6	13.2	7.1
Hispanic (of any race)	67.9	23.4	8.7

SOURCE: U.S. Census Bureau, Current Population Survey, March 2000.

Some of the social and psychological costs of these phenomena are the crime, violence, drug abuse, and despair that are frequently endemic in many low-income communities, along with the disproportionate numbers of imprisoned African American males from those communities.

With drug trafficking pervasive in a significant number of inner-city areas, drug-related homicides among African Americans have reached record levels. Young people turn to the illegal economy as the broader economy remains closed to them. Moreover, a disproportionate amount of drugs and guns are brought in from the outside and dumped into these communities. These activities continue to have very negative impacts on African American families and communities.

Some analysts place the primary blame for the deterioration of inner-city African American families on public policies that are inimical to these families, or on the absence of public policies that provide corrective measures that could empower them to help themselves. Representative of those analysts is Robert B. Hill, who in a 1990 essay entitled, "Economic Forces, Structural Discrimination, and Black Family Instability," contended that, "the key economic policies that undermined black family stability have been anti-inflation fiscal and monetary policies, trade policies, plant closings, social welfare, block grants, and federal per capita formulas for allocating funds to states and local areas that have not been corrected for the census undercount."

Particularly crippling in Hill's view was the absence of policy to provide affordable housing for moderate and low-income families, an absence that has a greater impact on African American families because of their unique employment and income problems. One consequence of this shortage is a return to traditional African American extended or augmented family arrangements as dispossessed family members seek temporary housing with relatives and as friends share their abodes with the less fortunate. Another consequence is that increasing numbers of African American families are homeless. Hill estimated the number of homeless individuals and families in 1989 at two to three million. Many of these families, but not all, were single-parent families headed by women.

Other progressive analysts have placed the deterioration of inner-city families squarely on the structural inequality of increasing privatization and the deteriorating employment, income, and wage levels for these families. These analysts also argue that the dismantling of the social welfare state and mandatory work to welfare expectations now in effect will not lift single-parent, female-headed families out of poverty. This dismantling of the U.S. social welfare state through welfare reform is embedded in a fundamental shift in the social contract: increased pursuit of global private profit with little commitment to domestic social programs.

Other analysts, many of them neoconservative or conservative in their sociopolitical orientation, continue to attribute the marked erosion in the social and economic stability of African American families to internal factors within the families themselves, to the welfare system, and to the "Great Society" programs. For example, Irving Kristol noted that, while illegitimate births have increased startlingly since World War

Recreational and leisure time outlets must be made available to African American children, especially in urban areas.

II, among African Americans the rate had risen to 66 percent in 1992, by 1998, this rate stood at 69 percent. Kristol decried the decline in "family values" among these "single moms" who, after having one illegitimate child, opt for and remain on public welfare support as they continue to produce additional children. Daniel Patrick Moynihan alleged that "Great Society" programs destroyed the inner-city black family structure, largely through welfare policies, and argued that social scientists still do not know what public policies will reverse the downward spiral of life conditions of inner-city African American families. Central to Moynihan's analysis and that of his neoconservative successors who have sought to understand changes in African American community and family relations were the relationships between African American family stability and male employment, unemployment, and labor force nonparticipation rates. In 1965, Moynihan and his staff reported strong indicators of change in behaviors of the African American urban poor including a rise in Aid to Families with Dependent Children (AFDC), even as the African American unemployment rate declined, and an increase in the percentage of non-white married women separated from their husbands. As a result of

these factors, Moynihan argued, the African American community had become immersed in "a tangle of pathology" that included family breakdown. Many prominent African Americans disputed Moynihan's conclusions and accused him of "blaming the victims" of social conditions rather than looking at the causes of their problems (i.e., racism, segregation, economic inequities).

K. Sue Jewell continued this line of argument by maintaining that "policies, procedures, and assumptions underlying social and economic programs in the 1960s and 1970s, the "Great Society" years, contributed to the disintegration of black two-parent and extended families and to an increase in black families headed by women." Jewel asserted that "social and economic programs and civil rights legislation could not effectively remove social barriers, which prevent black families from participating fully in mainstream American society." In her view, the liberal social policy of the Great Society era resulted in modest, but not substantial, gains for middle-class African American families. Since Jewell's analysis, welfare reform legislation passed in 1996 which, in effect, ended AFDC. There is a five-year limit on how long families can receive AFDC aid with this legislation (sometimes less, depending on the state) and women are expected to work. This welfare to work feature is known as "workfare." It is too early to determine the long-term impact of these policy changes on African American families, but there is little evidence that the strategy will move a significant number of poor, female-led families out of poverty.

Families in the African American Community

By the mid-1990s, a growing economic differentiation among African American families was increasingly evident; approximately one-third were prospering. Indeed, some African American families—primarily married-couple families headed by highly educated spouses with two or more fully employed earners—are becoming more affluent. These families, who tend to live in suburban areas, are primarily nuclear families, though some are blended units. They may also be part of supportive friendship networks.

Affluent African American families have benefitted from the abolition of segregation and other legal barriers to social, educational, occupational, and residential access and equity. Many of them are headed by persons who are second-, third-, and even fourth-generation college graduates, the beneficiaries of a heritage of education, motivation, and hard work. Nonetheless, such affluent African Americans continue to face "glass ceilings" and attitude-related barriers in many jobs as they seek to move upward in corporate or government hierarchies.

Another third of African American families, the working (middle) class, is comprised of families that are struggling to maintain themselves and provide support systems for their young in the face of reductions in force (RIFs), layoffs, or terminations as the corporations upon which they depend for their livelihood have downsized, moved to different regions of the country, gone out of business, or exported jobs to other countries. The extended or augmented family structure is visible in many of these homes. "Fictive kin" often are part of these family relationships.

The final third includes the nation's poorer African American families. This grouping includes (1) former working-class families who have fallen on hard times; (2) the "working poor," who are employed daily but at minimum wages that do not permit secure or dependable livelihoods; and (3) families of the "underclass," poorest of the poor, most of which are headed by females alone. Many of this latter group have been supported by the welfare system for one or more generations.

Families in Poverty

The debate on cause continues as proportionally greater numbers of black than white families were in poverty in 1998—23 percent, compared with 6 percent of white families. Black families were more than three times more likely to be poor than were white families, a situation which has not changed measurably since 1967. According to U.S. Census Bureau data, of 8.4 million black families in 1998, 2 million were below poverty level, whereas only 3.3 million of 59.5 million white families were in similar circumstances. In absolute numbers, more white families than black ones were poor, but the proportions of poor families was racially lopsided.

While 7 percent of African American families headed by married couples lived in poverty in 1998, poverty was highest among African American families maintained by women with no spouse present—41 percent. The impact of gender inequality, race, and class converge in the lives of these women. Sex segregation in the labor market crowds a disproportionate number of women into the secondary labor market with low wages, few if any job benefits, and poor working conditions. African American women, especially, have faced race and gender inequality in the labor force. Jobs specifically segmented by race/gender have characterized a good deal of the workplace history of these women.

In 1998, 26.4 percent of elderly African American individuals (65 years old and over) were poor. While this marks an improvement over the 1967 figure of 53 percent, proportionally more elderly blacks than whites were poor in both comparison years—8.2 percent of elderly whites were poor in 1998 and 28 percent in 1967. Despite the presence of policies such as Social Security, Medicare, and Supplemental Security Income (SSI), designed to help all elderly Americans, elderly blacks were twice as likely as elderly whites to be poor in 1967, and, in 1998, they were more than three times more likely to be poor.

The Rural Underclass

The findings of O'Hare and Curry-White's 1992 study of rural, inner-city, and suburban underclass populations revealed that approximately three million underclass adults were in these areas in 1990. Using 1990 Current Population Survey (CPS) data on adults aged 19 to 64, they reported that underclass characteristics were much more prevalent in central cities and rural areas than in the suburbs, noting that 2.4 percent of the underclass lived in rural areas and 3.4 percent lived in central cities, yet only 1.1 percent lived in suburban areas. Approximately 32 percent of the rural underclass was African American in 1990, compared to 49 percent of the inner-city underclass. The rate of African American underclass membership was also higher in rural areas—9.1 percent—compared to 7.5 percent in central cities. A sizable body of impoverished rural African Americans live in the South and have higher underclass rates (about one in ten) than do African Americans in large northern cities.

◆ MARRIAGE

In 1999, married-couple families constituted only 47.1 percent of all African American families. 45.1 percent of African American families were headed by a female householder with no husband present. Overwhelmingly, the nation's poor black families fell into this latter category. In 1999, only 38.6 percent of African American women 18 years of age and over were married, compared to 60.3 percent in 1960. The corresponding percentages for African American men were 44.8 percent in 1999 and 63.3 percent in 1960. Clearly issues around sex ratios, redefinition of gender expectations in intimate relations, and alternative life styles such as increasing levels of co-habitation figure into the changes.

The Unavailability of African American Men

The population of African American males aged 15 years old and over in 2000 stood at 12,248,240 compared to 14,181,294 African American females in the same age grouping. The resulting ratio of approximately 86 males to every 100 females makes the matching of every African American female with a same-race male for the traditionally valued lifetime monogamous marriage a numerical impossibility—there simply are not enough African American men alive. When one also removes from consideration those males who are gay, the proportion of eligible African American men for African American women dwindles even more. Further, when one counts the number of African American males who are poorly educated and therefore educationally mismatched for marriage to their relatively more highly educated African American female counterparts, the pool of eligible men shrinks even smaller. High African American male unemployment rates further compound the problem. These factors help to explain the increasing numbers of never-married African American females.

Incarcerated single African American men are unavailable as marriage partners, and African American men in prison who are married are unavailable to be at home with their families and/or provide for them. According to the U.S. Census Bureau's *Statistical Abstract*, in 1999 there were approximately 251,800 African American male inmates in jails alone, not including those in federal and state prisons or juvenile institutions.

Reportedly, many of today's young African American men delay marriage or never marry because of their unemployment or underemployment status, the rationale being that lack of a job or small earnings will not enable them to support families. However, well-educated black men who are employed at good salaries are also less likely to be married than their white counterparts. Marriage outside the race further reduces the number of African American men available for marriage to African American women. In 1999, there were 215,000 marriages of black men to white women, compared to 92,000 marriages of white men to black women. This represented the "loss" of another 123,000 marriageable black men.

In 1997, 9.7 million or 42.4 percent of African American adults (18 years old and over) were married.

In 1997, married couple families comprised only 46 percent of all African American families.

Although not often explored in African American family studies, shifting norms around gender expectations are impacting African American marriage expectations. Validating self through marriage has been challenged. The marriage rate for upper income, highly-educated African American women has traditionally been low and continues to be so. Issues of sexism, male violence, and domestic abuse also figure into the equation in African American women's decisions of whether to marry or not.

Interracial Marriage

In the three decades between 1960 and 1990, interracial marriages more than quadrupled in the United States, but the number remains small. By 1999 less than one percent of all marriages united African Americans with people of another racial heritage. As late as 1967, anti-miscegenation laws prohibiting the marriage of whites to members of another race were still on the books in 17 states; that year, the U.S. Supreme Court finally declared such laws unconstitutional. Surveys indicate that young Americans approaching adulthood

at the dawn of the twenty-first century are much more open to the idea of interracial unions than earlier generations.

Still, according to the 1994 National Health and Social Life Survey, 97 percent of African American women are likely to choose a partner of the same race. Conflict in the United States over black-white relationships stems from the nation's brutal history of slavery, when white men held all the power in society. More than a century after the abolition of slavery, America's shameful legacy of racism remains. According to some observers, high rates of abortion, drug abuse, illness, and poverty among African Americans sparked a movement of African American solidarity in the early 1990s. Many black women—"the culture bearers"—oppose the idea of interracial marriage, opting instead for racial strength and unity through the stabilization of the African American family.

♦ GAY/LESBIAN/BISEXUALITY/ TRANSGENDER ISSUES

African American gays, lesbians, and bisexuals have made some strides in the 1990s in terms of increasing visibility and activism. However, while there appears to be greater awareness of gay and lesbian concerns, there are continuing hate crimes and homophobia. Certainly most would agree that true equality and acceptance have hardly been achieved, but a course has been set for those looking to break the same chains of oppression with which all African Americans—gay or straight—are familiar.

Historically, from Bruce Nugent, "The Bohemian of the Harlem Renaissance" and the first African American writer to deal openly with homosexuality, to James Baldwin and Audre Lorde, African American literature has had its share of gay/lesbian/bisexual representation. In the 1980s and 1990s, the mantle has been passed to Samuel R. Delany, E. Lynn Harris, and Alice Walker's *The Color Purple.* In music and fashion, supermodel/house music maven/actor RuPaul had an impact on the American psyche as has bassist and songwriter Me'Shell NdegeOcello. In Hollywood, Wesley Snipes was unafraid to play a drag queen in the film *To Woo Fong, Thanks For Everything! Julie Newmar,* while Denzel Washington played an extremely homophobic lawyer who has a change of heart after working with a gay client dying of AIDS in *Philadelphia.* The poignant documentary *Paris Is Burning,* a depiction of several cross-dressers and drag queens in New York City, was well-received by audiences and critics alike. Another penetrating documentary, gay African American filmmaker Marlon Riggs's *Black Is . . . Black Ain't,* attempted to peel away the levels of meaning attached to black skin and the impact of those meanings on gay and straight members of the African American community. African American actresses, meanwhile, had prominent roles in the lesbian-focused commercial releases *Go Fish, The Incredibly True Adventures of Two Girls in Love,* and *Bar Girls.*

Outside of the mainstream, the black gay/lesbian/bisexual community is replete with heroes and heroines unknown to the rest of society. Rights activists include: Gregory Adams; Bayard Rustin, Alliance founder and executive director; Derek Charles Livingston, North Carolina Pride Political Action Committee executive director; Gilberto Gerald, African American Gay and Lesbian Studies Center founder and director; Cary Allen Johnson, International Lesbian and Gay Human Rights Commission board member; Ron Simmons, Us Helping Us, People Into Living, Inc. executive director; Paul Davis, Minority AIDS Project of Los Angeles director of education; Nadine Smith, Human Rights Task Force of Florida executive director; Cornelius Baker, National Association of People With AIDS president; Charles W. B. Tarver, IV, the first African American male lobbyist for the Human Rights Campaign Fund

(HRCF); and Keith Boykin, National Black Gay and Lesbian Leadership Forum executive director.

Examples of African American individuals contributing to the visible image of gays in society include: Peter Gomes, Harvard University chaplain; Willa Taylor, the education program coordinator for the Lincoln Center Theater; Sabrina Sojourner, legislative aide to California Congresswoman Maxine Waters; Wynn P. Thomas, production and set designer for director Spike Lee's film production company; H. Alexander Robinson, legal representative for both the American Civil Liberties Union AIDS Project and the Lesbian and Gay Civil Rights Project; Darlene Garner, the first African American elder in the Metropolitan Community Church, a universal fellowship created in 1968 by and for gay Christians; Sherry Harris, Seattle City Council member; Evelyn C. White, *San Francisco Chronicle* reporter and editor of *Black Women's Health Book: Speaking for Ourselves;* Bill E. Jones, president of New York City's Health and Hospitals Corporation, the largest public health network in the United States; Pat Norman, San Francisco Institute for Community Health Outreach executive director and Stonewall 25 Organizing Committee member; Suzanne Shende, director of the Center for Constitutional Rights' Anti-Bias Violence Project; Sandra Robinson, president and CEO of Samaritan College, the international school of ministry for the Universal Fellowship of Metropolitan Community Churches; and Keith St. John, the first African American, openly gay elected official in the United States (Second Ward Alderman, Albany, New York). They are joined in every field and industry and in every region of the country by a host of peers who face challenges because of their sexual orientation, but who do not allow intolerance to hold them back.

◆ FERTILITY AND BIRTHS

Fertility Rates

According to the National Center for Health Statistics, the year 1999 saw 70.1 live births per 1,000 black women aged 15 to 44 years of age, and 65.1 such live births to comparable white women. The 605,970 live births by African American females that year accounted for approximately 15.3 percent of all births nationwide. Black women have had higher fertility rates than white women for the past two centuries; however, birth rates are similar for black and white women with the same level of educational attainment.

The Thompson Sextuplets

On May 8, 1997, in Washington, DC, Linden and Jacqueline Thompson gave birth to the first set of African American sextuplets in the United States. The naturally-conceived pregnancy, which lasted 29 weeks and six days, was the longest gestational period for sextuplets born in the United States. In spite of the remarkable nature of this event, the surviving five babies—four girls and one boy—received little attention from the media until the birth of septuplets to a white Iowa couple a month later. In the wake of the attention and financial support that family received, certain African American groups protested that the Thompsons had not received similar treatment. The National Political Congress of Black Women, Inc. "adopted" the Thompsons, and many companies such as Toys 'R' Us came forward to pledge needed items for the financially-strapped family. For many in the African American community, the neglect of the Thompson family further demonstrated the inherent racism of American society, arguing that if the Thompsons had been white and middle-class, the media would have rushed to publish their story.

Teenage Pregnancy

For a number of years Marian Wright Edelman of the Children's Defense Fund has stressed that teenage pregnancy is a special problem among poor and minority groups who usually have limited opportunities to offer their offspring. Joyce Ladner has explained that the causes of teenage pregnancy range from attempts to find emotional fulfillment and the desire to achieve "womanhood" to ignorance of contraceptives. Political conservatives and neoconservatives maintain that poor teenagers view welfare programs such as Aid to Families with Dependent Children (AFDC) as a viable source of economic support and consequently perceive pregnancy as a means of tapping into the welfare system at an early age. This belief helped shape welfare reform legislation in the 1990s that required adolescent mothers to stay within the households of their families of origin if they are to continue to receive benefits.

Teenage pregnancy is both a national problem and an African American problem. Data from the National Center for Health Statistics reveal that in 1999 the birth rate for all teenagers aged 15 to 19 years old was 49.6 live births per 1,000. Black girls in that age group were over two times more likely than white girls to give birth (83.7 compared with 34.0 per 1,000). For girls between 15 to 17 years old, the birth rate was three times higher among blacks than whites. Furthermore, black girls in the 18 to 19 year old age group had a birthrate of 126.8 live births per 1,000 as compared to 58.9 live births for white girls. This state of affairs and its social, economic, and political ramifications cause great consternation in the African American community as well as in the larger society. Teenage childbearing exacerbates such social problems as high infant mortality, poor physical and mental health, educational insufficiencies, long-term welfare dependency, and poverty. Many teenage mothers do not complete high school, the basic educational expectation in this country; as a result, they are often seriously undereducated and lack marketable skills. Others do not know how to care adequately for their children. By and large, their children will not have the same opportunities as their more advantaged counterparts in any race or ethnic group. Some research, however, suggests that the prospects of these very young mothers are not entirely bleak. For example, research indicates that grandmothers play a significant role in the care and raising of these children.

Various efforts have been aimed at stemming the tide of teenage pregnancy. At the bureaucratic level, some states have decreed punitive measures such as sterilization and/or reduced welfare payments for girls and women on public assistance who have more than one out-of-wedlock birth. African American sororities, fraternities, churches, and civil groups have initiated programs to work directly with African American teenagers. The Children's Defense Fund continues to enlighten the public through a multimedia campaign that urges African American males as well as females to be more responsible for their sexual behavior.

Births of Mixed Racial Parentage

According to the Population Reference Bureau's December of 1992 report, the proportion of mixed-race births for which the race of both parents was known increased from one percent to 3.4 percent between 1968 and 1989; births of children with a black and a white parent increased from 8,700 in 1968 to 45,000 in 1989. This increase was described as "a striking sign of social change" with respect to attitudes about interracial relationships.

Attitudes towards persons with multiracial identities remained volatile in the 1990s, but those with mixed heritages who refuse to be reduced to "black" or "white" became more vocal. A key issue concerned the manner in which the federal government categorizes people. In 1997, new guidelines for designating race on all federal forms were established with five major groups identified: "American Indian/Alaskan Native"; "Asian"; "Native Hawaiian or Other Pacific Islander"; "Black or African American"; and "White." Also added were two categories for ethnicity: "Hispanic or Latino" and "Not Hispanic or Latino." In 1995, the Office of Management and Budget had considered making changes to the existing policy in response to a deluge of complaints from people of all walks of life including European Americans who want to be recognized as more than just white. To address such issues, the government proposed a "multiracial" category. Opponents felt that such a seemingly superficial change could lead to significant cultural difficulties including a hidden caste system like the one already in existence between light- and dark-skinned African Americans. Interestingly, *Newsweek* reported that, at the time, 49 percent of blacks favored the new category versus 36 percent of whites.

◆ CHILDREN

Living Arrangements of Children

In 1998, only 36 percent of African American children lived with both parents, compared to 67 percent in 1960 and 58.5 percent in 1970. This dramatic decline roughly parallels the changes in living arrangements of African American adults resulting from increased divorce and separation rates as well as increases in births to never-married females. By contrast, 74 percent of white children were living with both their parents in 1998, down from 90.9 percent in 1960 and 89.5 percent in 1970. According to a 2001 U.S. Census Bureau report, five percent of black children lived with their grandparents in 1996, compared to one percent of whites and two percent of Hispanics. Black grandparents, particularly grandmothers, are more likely to care for their grandchildren than are whites or Hispanics. Also in 1996, two percent of African American children lived with other relatives, and one percent lived with non-relatives.

In 1999, 65 percent of African American female-headed families had one or more children under 18 years of age present in the household; 38 percent had two or more. These families were more likely to be poor than were married-couple families. Many economic analysts maintain that there is a very strong probability that children from such households will grow up poor and on welfare, be environmentally disadvantaged compared to their middle-class counterparts, drop out of school, have one or more out-of-wedlock births themselves, and be unemployed or unemployable in their adult lives.

Child Support

In years past, when parents have been unable to support their children, extended family members were expected to assist in the process. In today's dismal economic climate, many more mothers than in the past are working in the paid labor force and contributing a larger share of their earned income to their families. Grandparents continue to do and provide what they can, including providing child care while the parent or parents work. Poor families are supported by the welfare system, but with fixed terms of support; this source of income will be phased out for recipients after five years. Many families have been forced to accept unemployment compensation as their support base when one or more member loses a job.

When African American parents divorce, child support becomes a critical issue. In 1989 there were 2,770,000 divorced or separated African American women. Child support payments were court-awarded to only 955,000 (35 percent) of these women. Of those who were supposed to receive child support, only 70 percent actually received payment. The mean child support amount received was $2,263, or 16 percent of total household income. As these figures reveal, in the event of divorce or separation, African American women were primarily responsible for the support of their children. In terms of dollars received, African American women with incomes below the poverty level fared worse than the average in 1989. Of 325,000 such women who were supposed to receive child support, 70 percent actually received payment. Their mean child support sum, a mere $1,674, nevertheless amounted to 32 percent of their total household income.

◆ HEALTH

For African Americans, the incidence of heart disease, high blood pressure, diabetes, obesity, cancer, asthma, and several other conditions is higher than the national average. Another area in which African Americans lag is organ donorship. In 2001, over 32,000 minorities were in need of an organ transplant according to statistics from the United Network for Organ Sharing. In 1995 *CQ Researcher* projected that by 2010, one out of every 20 people will need an organ, tissue, or corneal transplant at some point in their lives. While medical advances have improved survival rates, the best chances for a successful transplant—particularly with bone marrow transplants and skin grafts—are when an organ comes from someone of the same race. Unfortunately, not nearly enough African Americans choose to donate. The lack of available organ donors ultimately means long waits for a compatible organ, death for those who do not receive one, higher costs

In 1995, 31 percent of black children under six years old were regularly left in a relative's care, compared to 18 percent of white children of the same age range.

due to low supply and high demand, and lack of coverage by insurance carriers because of the expense.

The Tuskegee Syphilis Study

At least part of the reason behind the higher rates of disease in African Americans stems from a reluctance to get regular check-ups because of a general distrust of doctors by the African American community. In 1997, a national poll survey conducted for Emory University's Institute of Minority Health Research revealed that 36 percent of African Americans believed it was "very likely" they would unwittingly be used as guinea pigs for medical research. This belief is grounded in an actual instance of the government's exploitation of African American men for the purposes of medical research in the mid-twentieth century. Now known as "The Tuskegee Syphilis Study," the experiment, conducted by government doctors from the Public Health Service, studied the effects of untreated syphilis on 400 African American men in Macon County, Alabama. The doctors never informed the men as to the nature of the study and even withheld medical treatment when it became available in 1942. As a result, over 100 men had died by the time the details of the study were revealed in 1972, and others suffered from serious syphilis-related conditions that could have been relieved by penicillin had it been given to them. Civil rights lawyer Fred Gray brought a class-action lawsuit against the institutions and doctors involved in the experiment in 1973, and the government agreed to a 10 million dollar out-of-court settlement. In 1997, President Bill Clinton formally apologized to the survivors of the experiment.

Medicaid

Many American families receive health care through the federally-funded Medicaid program. Disproportionately high percentages of these families are African American. The total number of Medicaid recipients in the United States increased from 24.3 million in 1990 to 27.9 million in 1998. That year, 7.9 million African Americans were covered by Medicaid.

Herman Shaw, a victim of the Tuskegee Syphilis Study, attends a 1997 press conference in which President Clinton and Vice President Gore apologized for the shameful experiment.

Child Health

Many African American children suffer from the lack of quality health care. In 1990, only about half of inner-city children had been immunized against measles, mumps, and rubella. Measles outbreaks have erupted in many American cities in the 1990s; most were among poor, inner-city children. Nearly 100 deaths from measles were reported in 1990.

A new and growing population of children are born of mothers who used drugs (including alcohol) during their pregnancies. Many of these children experience after-birth withdrawal problems from drugs that affected them *in utero;* they are later more prone to physical and mental disabilities, behavioral problems, and learning impairments when they arrive in the nation's schools. Infants whose mothers drink alcoholic beverages during pregnancy are at risk of Fetal Alcohol Syndrome. Each year, Acquired Immune Deficiency Syndrome (AIDS) afflicts a growing number of children, who usually contract the disease from their mothers before or at birth. Urban children who live in old

and/or poor housing also remain at risk of being exposed to high levels of lead. It has been estimated that 12 million American children, primarily those who are poor, are at risk of lead poisoning and potentially will have their intellectual growth stunted because of exposure to lead. Similar to African American adults and, perhaps due to their affiliation with them, African American children are also at greater risk of accidents, physical abuse, and other violence that may result in disability or death.

HIV/AIDS

African Americans suffer disproportionately from AIDS, the final stage of a disease caused by the Human Immunodeficiency Virus (HIV). The HIV virus severely weakens the body's immune system, leaving HIV-infected people vulnerable to other infections. According to the U.S. Centers for Disease Control and Prevention (CDC), while African Americans represent approximately 12 percent of the U.S. population, 47 percent of all new AIDS cases reported in 2000 were African American. This figure was up from 32 percent in 1990.

The CDC also estimates that African Americans make up close to 38 percent of the total number of reported AIDS cases, and that at the end of 1999, 129,000 African Americans were living with AIDS.

The CDC has kept updated statistics concerning reported cases of AIDS, deaths caused by the disease with breakdowns for various age groups, and various data on the occurrence of AIDS across ethnicities. Data from those organizations showed that in 1996 the age-adjusted AIDS death rate for blacks was higher than that for whites (42.6 percent to 37.5 percent). Data also revealed that, between 1991 and 1996, the number of Africans American AIDS-related deaths increased nearly 8 percent compared to a 13.2 percent decrease in its incidence among gay or bisexual men.

AIDS is spread by viral passage during unprotected sexual intercourse, intravenous drug use, or blood transfusions; it can also be transmitted from mother to child *in utero* or during birth. It is estimated that a clear majority of the AIDS cases among African Americans result from intravenous drug use. While AIDS is fatal, it is preventable if sexually active adults and teenagers engage in "safe sex" practices such as using condoms and avoid behaviors that put them at risk of AIDS infection such as promiscuity, having multiple sex partners, using drugs, and exchanging drug paraphernalia. The African American community and the larger society are saturating the public with information about AIDS in the hope that education will cause people to behave differently and thereby slow the progress of the disease.

Lupus

Lupus is a chronic, autoimmune disorder in which the body's immune system loses the ability to differentiate between itself and foreign substances and forms antibodies that attack healthy tissues and organs. Inflammation of the skin, joints, and kidneys are the most common result, although other areas of the body are subject to swelling as well. The medical community has not yet discovered why the disease overwhelmingly tends to affect women more than men. In fact, nine of every ten sufferers are women. Lupus seemingly targets women of childbearing age, i.e. between the ages of 15 and 40 and is three times more common in black women than white women.

An incurable, excruciating, and often debilitating condition, lupus can present itself in many different forms, making the initial diagnosis difficult. A range of mild to severe symptoms gradually develop including hair and/or weight loss, fatigue, photosensitivity, loss of appetite, fever, nausea, abdominal pain, and pain in any inflamed areas. With improvements in early diagnosis and better treatments, lupus is no longer considered fatal. Most patients are able to continue with their lives and lifestyles. The American Lupus Society (1–800–331–1802) and the Lupus Foundation of America (1–800–558–0121 or <www.lupus.org>) can both offer more information.

Diabetes

Persons with diabetes are unable to convert food sugar, or glucose, into energy that is used by the body's cells or stored for later use. The hormone insulin, produced by the pancreas, plays a crucial role in the conversion. Diabetics either do not produce enough insulin, or any at all, or may produce ineffective insulin. Regardless, the unused glucose collects in the blood and urine and can damage organs such as the kidneys and eyes. The onset of insulin-dependent, or type I diabetes, which usually affects children and young adults, can be very rapid. Symptoms can include frequent urination, excessive thirst, extreme hunger, weight loss, irritability, weakness and fatigue, nausea, and vomiting. Ninety percent of diabetes is noninsulin-dependent. Known as Type II diabetes, the illness most often occurs in adults over the age of 40 and particularly in obese individuals. Symptoms are similar to those associated with the Type I form, however, Type II is also characterized by the chronic presence of wounds that will not heal, stubborn infections, blurred vision, tingling or numbness in the extremities, and burning or itching sensations.

Similar to lupus, diabetes is noncontagious, incurable, potentially debilitating, and disproportionately strikes African Americans. Figures from the American Diabetes Association estimate that blacks are 2 times more likely than whites to contract the condition. In 2002, diabetes afflicted 2.8 million African Americans. African Americans also experience higher rates of serious complications from the disease including blindness, kidney failure, and the need for amputations of the legs or feet. Unfortunately, one-third of those African Americans affected are unaware of their illness, a dangerous statistic because immediate, appropriate medical attention is crucial.

Once informed of their condition, diabetics can maintain relative good health by eating low fat, high carbohydrate meals with a moderate amount of protein; engaging in physical activity that stimulates the body's cells into utilizing glucose; and by tracking their glucose levels. Low blood sugar, or hypoglycemia, is just as much a danger as is the presence of a high glucose level. Overweight individuals are very much encouraged to lose excess weight in order to increase the body's ability to use insulin. Physicians can prescribe medication including insulin shots to help a patient maintain a normal glucose level.

In an effort to reach the African American community, the American Diabetes Association launched the African American Program in 1994. They educate the public through media campaigns and community-based forums such as local churches. For more information contact the American Diabetes Association (1680 Duke St., Alexandria, VA 22314; 1–800-DIABETES or <www.diabetes.org>).

Cigarette, Alcohol, and Drug Use

The use and abuse of cigarettes, alcohol, marijuana, and cocaine (including addiction thereto) is a serious social problem in contemporary American society. The National Center for Health Statistics reports that, in a given month in 1991, four percent of black youth 12 to 17 years old smoked cigarettes, compared with 13 percent of whites and nine percent of Hispanics of the same age. Cigarette smoking has been identified as a major risk factor in lung cancer, cardiovascular disease, and chronic obstructive lung disease. Twenty percent of blacks, 20 percent of whites, and 23 percent of Hispanics in this same age group had used alcohol; 5 percent of blacks and Hispanics and 4 percent of whites had used marijuana; and 0.5 percent of blacks, 0.3 percent of whites, and 1.3 percent of Hispanic youths had used cocaine. In the 18 to 25 year old group in the given month, 22 percent of blacks had smoked cigarettes compared to 36 percent of whites and 25 percent of Hispanics; and 56 percent of blacks had used alcohol compared to 67 percent of whites and 53 percent of Hispanics. Fifteen percent of blacks compared to 14 percent of whites and nine percent of Hispanics, had used marijuana; and 3.1 percent of blacks had used cocaine compared to 1.7 percent of whites and 2.7 percent of Hispanics. It is clear that youths are using these substances as early as age 12 and that usage increases through the young adult period. These percentages represent large numbers of young people. In regard to all age groups, a higher percentage of whites—60 percent—reported alcohol use compared to 42 percent of blacks.

Sickle Cell Anemia

Sickle Cell Anemia (SCA) is a chronic inherited affliction caused by a defect in the hemoglobin component of the blood. It occurs as a result of the mating of two people, each of whom carries the gene for the defective trait, which is passed on to their children. The presence of this abnormal hemoglobin trait can cause distortion (sickling) of the red blood cells and a decrease in their number. The source of SCA seems to be malarious countries; people with sickle cell disease are almost always immune to malaria, so it appears that the sickle cell is a defense mechanism against malaria.

Sickled red blood cells have been found in 1 of every 12 African Americans; but the active disease occurs about once in every 600 American blacks and once in every 1,200 American whites. It is estimated that about 50,000 persons in the United States suffer from the disease. Persons of other races and nationalities are affected by the trait and the anemia including people from Southern India, Greece, Italy, Syria, Caribbean Islands, South and Central America, Turkey, and other countries.

The disease is diagnosed through microscopic and electrophoretic analysis of the blood. The first symptoms of SCA usually appear in children with the disease at about six months of age. Because SCA is a chronic disease, medical management is directed toward both the quiescent and active periods (called "crises") of the malady. Good medical and home care may make it possible for persons with SCA to lead reasonably normal lives. When crises occur, they experience fever, pain, loss of appetite, paleness of the skin, generalized weakness, and sometimes a striking decrease in the number of red blood corpuscles. Complications and infections from these crises can be controlled with antibiotic drugs. A drug, hydroxyurea, has been developed to stimulate fetal hemoglobin to produce more red blood cells and thereby ameliorate SCA crises. However, hydroxyurea is very toxic, and thus far has only been tested on adults with SCA. In other efforts, a female SCA sufferer, also stricken with leukemia, recently received a radical bone marrow transplant from her brother. Since the transplant, she has been free of symptoms from both diseases. This case, the first of its kind, is being closely monitored to determine the mechanisms by which the patient's remission occurred and to see if the results of this procedure can be duplicated with other persons with SCA.

African American people who intend to have children are advised to undergo blood tests to determine whether they are carriers of the sickle cell gene. Two such carriers should agree not to produce children, since half the children will have the trait and one in four the anemia. There is only one chance in four that their child will be free of the disease. Some jurisdictions (Washington, DC, for example) have enacted laws mandating that newborns be screened for sickle cell anemia, along with other diseases. As a result of such legislation, newborns found to be afflicted with SCA can be cared for from birth.

Breast Cancer

The National Cancer Institute has estimated that one in eight women in the United States will develop breast cancer during her life, the risk increasing with age. Breast cancer is the leading cause of cancer death among African American women. Although black women develop breast cancer at slightly lower rates than white women, blacks are twice as likely to die from the disease and at a younger age. Though more research needs to be done, some reasons for the discrepancy include the facts that black women are often in poorer general health than whites; are often less likely to seek out preventive medical care and when they do are less likely to receive adequate medical care; are more likely to have worse prognoses for tumors that do not respond to treatment; and are often pessimistic about their own outlooks. (Studies have shown that maintaining a positive attitude can have an impact on just about any illness.)

African American women must focus on early detection. Approximately 90 percent of breast cancers are discovered via self-examination. Besides self-examinations—which should be conducted monthly, one week after one's menstrual period—the importance of mammograms should not be overlooked. In a recent study, the U.S. Department of Health and Human Services determined that nearly three out of four African American women over the age of 40 had never had a mammogram, though all women regularly should after reaching that age. Many women do not follow early detection guidelines because they can not afford health care, because they have had no prior incidence in their family history, or because they do not display any symptoms, failing to acknowledge that treatment prior to symptoms is more effective. Once discovered, breast lumps may be diagnosed as premenstrual lumpiness or fluid retention caused by hormonal changes; cysts; benign tumors; or cancers.

Treatment programs are determined on a case-by-case basis. In the mid-1990s, the experimental drug tamoxifen was introduced to breast cancer patients. The Cancer Information Service Center (1–800–4-CAN-CER or <www.cis.nci.nih.gov>) can provide more information at as can the Breast Cancer Resource Committee (1765 N St., NW, Ste. 100; Washington, DC 20036–2802; 1–202–463–8040 or <www.afamerica.com/bcrc/>), founded by Zora Brown, an African American.

Prostate Cancer

As the most common cancer in men, prostate cancer afflicts black men more often than whites; in fact, blacks are more than twice as likely to get the disease and are three times as likely to die of the disease. Particularly at risk are those living in rural areas, because they are less likely to regularly visit a physician. As with other forms of cancer, early detection plays a role in treatment and in deterring the likelihood of dying from the disease. Diet is a factor as well; high-fat, low-fiber diets increase the risk of developing cancer. Genetics and personal history are a third factor. In 1996, a new type of radiation treatment option which was 20 percent more effective than conventional radiation was used on patients with early cancer. Called neutron therapy, Seattle's University of Washington and Detroit's Karmanos Cancer Institute were the first two facilities to make the innovative technique available.

◆ LIFE EXPECTANCY

Life expectancy at birth increased substantially during the first 90 years of this century, from 33 years for African Americans of both sexes in 1900 to 71.5 years in 1998. Corresponding figures for both sexes of all races are 47.3 years in 1900 and 76.7 years in 1998. Provisional data of the U.S. National Center for Health Statistics Statistics project a life expectancy of 67.8 years for African American males born in 1998 and 75.0 years for African American females born that year. Corresponding life expectancy projections for white males and females born in 1998 are 74.6 and 79.9 years, respectively, averaged at 77.3 years. That black babies born should have a lower life expectancy at birth than their white counterparts is an ignominious social problem. At the other end of the age continuum, African American males aged 65 years old in 1998 are projected to live 14.4 more years, and African American females 17.5 additional years. This compares with 16.1 more years for white males, and 19.2 additional years for white females. Thus the same pattern holds: white people in the United States continue to have longer life expectancy than African Americans.

These black/white differences can be attributed to a number of factors. African Americans have higher death rates due to the following major causes: accidents, homicides, suicides, heart disease, strokes, liver disease, cancer, diabetes, and AIDS. It is also true that whites, more than blacks, have health insurance coverage of some kind and sufficient personal income to partake of higher-quality health care, both preventive and curative. Whites' higher education and income levels also assure them the greater likelihood of eating nutritionally balanced, healthy meals. Dietary patterns and food choices of low-income African Americans include too many fats and sweets, factors that contribute to obesity and high blood pressure, which carry their own sets of health risks.

Homicide and Death by Accident

Homicide among young African American men is a primary cause for the drop in their life expectancy. In 1999, homicide accounted for 45.3 percent of the deaths among 15 to19 year old African American males, 46.2 percent in the 20 to 24 year old age range, and 26.8 percent for 25 to 34 year old age range. Some social theorists claim that the increasing numbers of African Americans who are poor and hopeless, added to those who are involved in drugs or other substance abuse, account for the homicide rates among African Americans. In 1999, motor vehicle deaths and other accidents accounted for 12,728 deaths among African Americans.

Suicide

Suicide rates are significantly lower among blacks than whites, but black suicide rates are on the rise, a most undesirable form of parity. In 1985, the suicide rate for white males exceeded that for black males by 70 percent; by 1989, the difference had narrowed to 40 percent. Data from the National Center for Health Statistics show that more than 30,000 lives are lost through suicide annually. Among all Americans, the age-adjusted death rate by suicide in 1989 was 11.3 deaths per 100,000. For African American males, the rate was 12.5 per 100,000, and for African American females, it was 2.4 per 100,000. Among African American adolescents and young adults aged 15 to 24 years old, the suicide rate for males was 16.7 per 100,000, and 2.8 per 100,000 for African American females, increases of 49 percent (from 1984 to 1989) and 40 percent (from 1986 to 1989), respectively.

Infant Mortality

Infant mortality rates for African Americans remain more than double that of whites. In 1998, 13.8 deaths per 1,000 live births were reported for black infants, compared to 6.0 deaths per 1,000 live births for whites. The black/white infant death ratios have changed appreciably since 1950, however, when the black infant mortality rate was 43.9 deaths per 1,000 live births and the white rate was 26.8 deaths per 1,000. Progress has been made since 1950, as the infant mortality statistics have improved for both races.

African American women are more likely than whites to give birth to low-weight babies, many of whom fall victim to serious health problems or die during their first year. These babies are particularly susceptible to Sudden Infant Death Syndrome (SIDS), respiratory distress syndrome, infections, and injuries. This phenomenon occurs because disproportionate numbers of African American babies are born to low-income, less-educated teenage mothers who have inadequate prenatal care and poor nutrition, and who smoke, use drugs, or otherwise fail to take care of themselves properly during their pregnancies.

◆ ASSESSMENT

Social Change Possibilities and African American Families

Within the African American community itself, certain attitudinal and behavioral changes are essential. Most significant is economic fairness across racial lines since many problems confronting the African American community stem from poverty. There is also the need for gender justice in the labor market. Salary equity and occupational opportunities which pay a living wage for African American women would make a tremendous difference in poor African American families. Marriage as something other than an fading option could make a difference for many families. Family planning information, including sex education and intervention programs, must be disseminated among teenagers, so that the out-of-wedlock birth rate can be reduced. Substance abuse must be curtailed; people who have hope for the future and who feel that they have some power and control over their lives are less likely to "escape" through drugs or alcohol. At the same time, drug dealers should be severely prosecuted. Children and youth need more adult interaction and supervision in their lives, whether it comes from family members or "significant others" such as mentors provided by such organizations as Concerned Black Men, Inc. or other community service-minded groups.

So many of the problems faced by African American and other low-to-moderate-income families are systemic and interlocking. Action on only one problem will not solve the network of family woes that our society has allowed to accumulate. Once again, the National Urban League has called for a "Marshall Plan for the Cities" to address the totality of current problems. If our society wants to save its cities and a significant portion of its human capital—of which these families comprise a significant part—it must give serious consideration to the formation and implementation of such a plan in both the cities and the rural areas. By so doing, the nation can help all its citizens become productive workers, consistent taxpayers, meritorious parents, and contributing members of stable families.

The Million Man March

On October 16, 1995, The Million Man March, a rally masterminded by Nation of Islam Minister Louis Farrakhan, was held 21 blocks from the steps of the U.S. Capitol Building in Washington, DC. Intended as "a national day of atonement," the thousands of attendees pledged their commitments to family and community. The gathering had spiritual, economic, and political implications for non-marchers as well, including women and children; they were asked to stay home from work/school and spend the day praying and fasting.

The march was organized by the Nation of Islam and promoted by the National African American Leadership Summit. Women, excluded from the actual demonstration, were welcome in the nearly 120 local organizing committees scattered about the country. A grass-roots affair, expenses were covered mostly by donations. Linda Green, appointed as national director of fund-raising, also found financial support for the march. However, a number of African American women such as Angela Davis spoke out publically about the exclusionary nature of the march.

Other forms of support came from a wide range of camps—political, religious, and business-oriented—including civil rights heroine Rosa Parks; former NAACP head Rev. Ben Chavis; Rainbow Coalition leader Rev. Jesse Jackson; Georgia Congresswoman Cynthia McKinney; Southern Christian Leadership Conference (SCLC) executive director E. Randel Osburn; and Melvin Foote and Ambassador Andrew Young, constituency for Africa's executive director and chairperson, respectively. African American colleges scheduled bus trips to the march and the NAACP Youth Councils also encouraged participation from the younger generation. Nonetheless, many African Americans who upheld the tenets of the march distanced themselves from the socio-political action because of Farrakhan's inflammatory views which are often perceived as misogynistic, anti-gay, and anti-Catholic.

Still, the march was deemed a success on many levels given the sheer number of men it reached and the changed representation of African American men it offered, helping to shake the myth of all African American men as convicts, hustlers, and pimps, and replacing it with one of responsible, self-confident, culturally aware men. A number of men registered to vote and a national database of African American male voters was established. The march also spawned a number of spin-off demonstrations including the cross-theological gathering "The New Revival in America: The Emerging Black Male as Man, Husband, Father, and Leader," which took place November 16–18, 1995.

The Million Woman March

The Million Man March was followed by the Million Woman March in Philadelphia, Pennsylvania, on October 25, 1997. Organizers cited their desire to strengthen the cohesiveness of African American women of all walks of life as the primary reason for the march, and key speakers included Winnie Mandela, former wife of South African activist Nelson Mandela, and Congresswoman Maxine Waters. Thousands of women came to Pennsylvania from across the United States to participate in the show of solidarity and to address such issues as the growing number of African American women in prisons, the start of independent African American schools and the hiring of African American women, and the importance of getting more African American women into business and politics.

♦ SOCIAL ACTIVISTS

(To locate biographical profiles more readily, please consult the index at the back of the book. For example, physicians/doctors are located in the Science & Technology chapter.)

Stacey Davis (1960–)
Foundation Executive

As president and chief executive officer of the Fannie Mae Foundation, Stacey H. Davis guides the Foundation's efforts to make home ownership a reality for millions of Americans. Davis received a bachelor's degree in economics from Georgetown University, and later earned a M.B.A. with an emphasis on finance from the University of Michigan Graduate School of Business Administration. After graduate school, Davis worked in a number of investment banking positions. She worked for three years in Merrill Lynch's public finance division; later, she served as a vice president at Pryor McClendon Counts, an Atlanta investment bank.

Davis's tenure with the Fannie Mae Foundation began in 1992. She remained in the southeast and spent three years as the Foundation's director of regional public affairs for the region. From that position, Davis was promoted to vice president for housing and community development for the southeastern region. From 1995 to 1999, while serving in that capacity, Davis put into place innovative home buying programs aimed at helping low- and moderate-income families buy their own homes. In September 1999, Davis was named president and CEO of Fannie Mae, one of the nation's biggest private foundations. Just as she did in her previous posts within the Foundation, Davis has introduced groundbreaking initiatives, such as the introduction of technology driven methods of improving the role that Fannie Mae plays in home ownership and city, community, and neighborhood revitalization.

In addition to her leadership role at the Foundation, Davis has served on the board of a number of organizations, including: Georgetown University, the Distict of Columbia Chamber of Commerce, the Thurgood Marshall Scholarship Fund, and Social Compact. She was the recipient of an honorary degree from Washington, D.C.'s Trinity College in 2001.

Paula Giddings (1947–)
Editor, Educator, Journalist, Social Historian

Paula Giddings has followed a definite focus in her life's work, that of giving a voice to generations of African American women. Through her writings, many issues previously not discussed such as race, gender, and discrimination, came to the forefront of discussion. Beginning at a young age, Giddings knew she wanted to write. She attended Howard University in Washington,

Paula Giddings.

DC, became editor of the literary magazine *Afro-American Review*, and began moving away from creative writing toward journalism and social history. Giddings received an undergraduate degree in English in 1969.

After graduating, Giddings worked as a Random House copy editor during a very exciting time; some of the authors there included the political activists Stokely Carmichael and Angela Davis. A fellow editor was the now-famous author Toni Morrison. In 1984, after five years of extensive research and with the help of a Ford Foundation Grant, Giddings's first book was published, *When and Where I Enter: The Impact of Black Women on Race and Sex in America*. Some of the themes covered in the book include the relationship between sexism and racism, the effect of "double discrimination" on the basis of gender and race on African American women, and the relevance of historical issues to contemporary life.

In 1988, Giddings came out with a second book called *In Search of Sisterhood: Delta Sigma Theta and the Challenge of the Black Sorority Movement*. Giddings has been lauded for her accomplishments by many groups, such as the New York Urban League and the National Coalition of 100 Black Women; Bennett College in North Carolina awarded her an honorary doctorate in humane letters in 1990. In 1992, she was a visiting professor at Princeton University. She earned several fellowships during the next few years and served as a visiting scholar with Phi Beta Kappa in 1995 and 1996. In 2000 Giddings edited a book entitled *Burning All Illusions: Writings from the Nation on Race*, a collection of magazine pieces by great African American writers and thinkers such as W.E.B. Du Bois, Langston Hughes and Ralph Ellison.

Clara and Lorraine Hale
Humanitarian, Educator, Hale House Co-founder

Clara Hale—known affectionately as "Mother Hale"—was born Clara McBride on April 1, 1905, in Elizabeth City, North Carolina. She grew up in Philadelphia, Pennsylvania, where her father was killed during her infancy. Clara's mother struggled to support her three children but died when Clara was only 16. Soon after graduating from high school, she married and moved to New York City. Her husband died of cancer when she was only 27, leaving behind three children, including six-year-old Lorraine E. Hale (1926?–). Mother Hale took both day and evening work as a cleaning person to support the family but was dismayed about leaving her daughter and two sons—one adopted—in childcare facilities. Eventually the elder Hale began taking in children in her own home, and by 1940 she was a foster parent whose modest Harlem apartment often included her own three offspring as well as seven or eight foster children. In all, Mother Hale fostered in excess of 40 children in about 25 years.

Growing up in such an atmosphere, Lorraine became determined to make a difference in her community, earning a B.A. from Long Island University in 1960 and then becoming a public school teacher in New York City. She also pursued her master's degree in special education, and worked variously as a guidance counselor, school psychologist, and special education teacher until 1969.

One spring night that year, Lorraine was driving home from a visit with her mother, who had recently retired as a foster parent. She saw a young woman in obvious distress on a street corner and felt sympathy for both the woman and the baby she had with her. She gave the woman her mother's address and, within a few months, the elder Hale's apartment was again home to children—this time 22 babies born addicted to drugs. For the next year-and-a-half, the Hale children worked overtime to support what would come to be known as Hale House, a pioneering facility in the treatment of babies born to drug-addicted mothers. Their organization received a city grant in 1971 and a federal grant four years later, which helped it move into its own five-story Harlem facilities. Hale House received permission from New York to manage an official "boarding home" on October 5, 1976.

Mother Hale won the Harry S Truman Award for Public Service in 1989 and was personally invited by President Ronald Reagan to attend his State of the Union address in 1985, where she received a standing ovation after being called "a true American hero." She passed away on December 18, 1992, in New York City. Hale House was already renowned for its innovative treatment and research into mother-infant addictions and boasted a tremendous success rate in helping the women overcome their abuse patterns to reunite with their children. Lorraine expanded the foundation's services after her mother's death to assist mothers and children afflicted with AIDS. Hale chronicled this work in her 1992 book *Hale House: Alive With Love*. She also worked toward establishing a hospice retreat for such needs in a rural setting. In 1994 Hale traveled to Zaire under the auspices of the relief organization AmeriCares to provide aid for children in refugee camps. In 2001, however, amid financial investigation by the New York Attorney General's office, Hale resigned her leadership positions to be succeeded by long-time board-member

Edna Wells Handy. She and her husband were indicted in early 2002 on charges relating to improper use of funds.

Charleszetta "Mother" Waddles (1912–2001)
Community Activist, Spiritual Leader

Mother Waddles, as she is commonly known, was born Charleszetta Lena Campbell in St. Louis in 1912, the oldest of seven children of a successful barber. When her father, an upstanding member of his local church, was ostracized after his business failed, his daughter vowed to repudiate the hypocrisy she witnessed in organized religion by promoting truly Christian principles. As a young girl, Waddles worked as a domestic and married at the age of 14. Widowed before she was 20 years of age, she married again and eventually had ten children. She left her second husband, due to his lack of ambition, after they had relocated to Detroit. In 1946, Waddles learned that her neighbor, a single mother of two, was about to be evicted. Waddles collected food from neighboring businesses to enable the woman to feed her children while making immediate payments to keep her home. Soon afterward, Waddles entered a Bible study course and eventually became an ordained Pentecostal minister. Her religious work soon turned into charitable work, however, and in 1950 she opened her Helping Hand restaurant in a

Mother Waddles.

rough area of Detroit, where the indigent could get a sit-down, home-cooked meal for 35 cents. Her third husband, Payton Waddles, provided much support for his wife's work during these years.

In 1956, Waddles expanded the aims of restaurant when she founded the Perpetual Mission for Saving Souls of All Nations, which later became simply the Mother Waddles Perpetual Mission. The center is home to numerous community outreach programs including a medical clinic, a job placement service, and a tutoring program. Staffed entirely by volunteers—sometimes numbering up to 200—and financed solely through the donations Waddles extracts from a supportive local business community, the Mission is famous in Detroit for its decades of service. Still actively involved even though well into her eighties, Waddles sees her work as evidence of Christian principles in action. She has won numerous awards including several presidential commendations and the National Urban League's 1988 Humanitarian Award. Waddles died on July 12, 2001, at her Detroit, Michigan, home. She was 88.

Faye Wattleton. *See* **National Organizations chapter.**

Terrie M. Williams. *See* **Entrepreneurship chapter.**

Phill Wilson (1956–)
Activist, Educator

Phill Wilson was born into a close-knit Chicago family on April 22, 1956. During his formative years, he became an active participant in local African American issues-raising organizations such as Operation PUSH. He graduated from Illinois Wesleyan University with a dual degree in Spanish and theater but forsook law school for marriage and a career with AT&T. Both choices left Wilson with a troubling feeling that there was something lacking, and he ventured into Chicago's gay community in the late 1970s. He met his partner, Chris Brownlie, in 1979, and two years later they relocated to the Los Angeles area where they began an African American-centered giftware company.

The specter of AIDS changed Wilson's life in several ways. He and Brownlie first became politically active in 1986 when they campaigned to win voter rejection of

Phill Wilson.

Proposition 64, a ballot referendum that called for the quarantine of all AIDS patients in California. It was also during this time that Brownlie was diagnosed with AIDS himself and, before he died in 1989, he and Wilson founded the AIDS Health Care Foundation and the National Black Gay and Lesbian Conference and Leadership Forum. Wilson has also been involved as Stop AIDS Los Angeles's director of community outreach and has served as the national director of training for the National Task Force on AIDS Prevention. Of especial import to the activist is the building of recognition and support between the African American community and the gay community, and he was a significant force behind the 1990 "Summit on Homosexuality in the Black Community" symposium at Atlanta's Martin Luther King Jr. Center. Since 1992 Wilson has been the director of public policy for AIDS Project Los Angeles, and, as a spokesperson for gay issues, met with Bill Clinton shortly after his election in 1992.

Wilson is also living with HIV. In 1999 he founded the African American AIDS Policy and Training Institute (AAAPTI). Its main goal, he said, was to develop African American community leaders free of ignorance regarding HIV/AIDS. The institute's Nia Plan—from the Swahili word meaning "purpose"—was rolled out in 18 cities and before critical organizations, including the Congressional Black Caucus and the NAACP. AAAPTI also created the African American HIV University, designed to educate people living with HIV as well as the medical community how to deal with the virus and how to prevent transmission of it. Also in 1999, Wilson coordinated the twelfth World AIDS Conference, held in Geneva, Switzerland. He helped prepare for the 13th conference by setting up educational opportunities in Durban, South Africa.

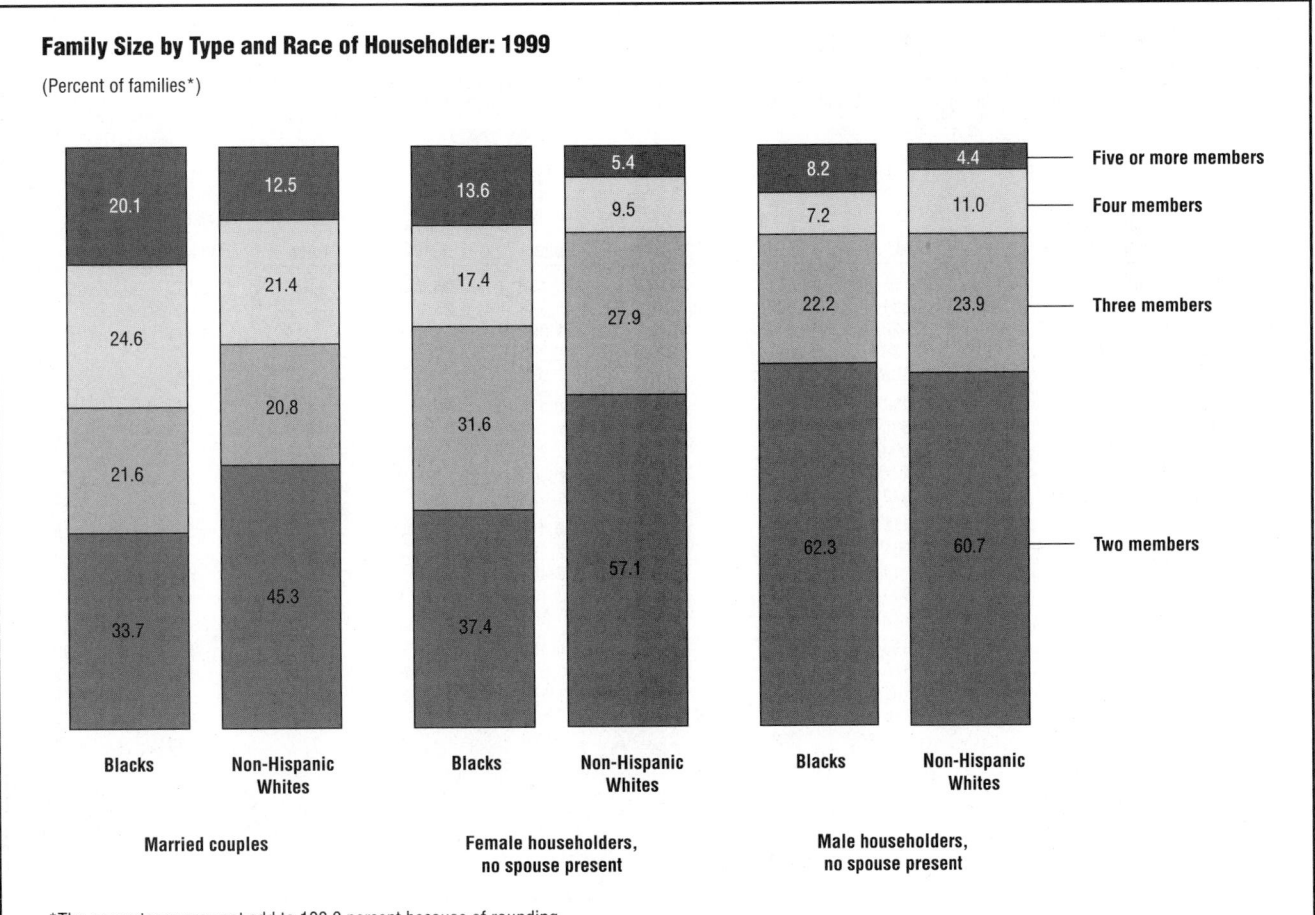

Family Size by Type and Race of Householder: 1999

(Percent of families*)

*The percentages may not add to 100.0 percent because of rounding.

SOURCE: U.S. Census Bureau, Current Population Survey, March 1999.

Family Groups With Children Under 18 Years Old by Race and Hispanic Origin: 1980 to 1999

[In thousands. As of March (32,150 represents 32,150,000). Family groups comprise family households, related subfamilies, and unrelated subfamilies. Excludes members of Armed Forces except those living off post or with their families on post. Based on Current Population Survey.]

Race and Hispanic origin of householder or reference person	1980	1990	1995	1999 Total	1999 Family households	1999 Subfamilies Total	1999 Subfamilies Related	1999 Subfamilies Unrelated
All races, total[1]	**32,150**	**34,670**	**37,168**	**37,430**	**34,613**	**2,816**	**2,328**	**488**
Two-parent family groups	25,231	24,921	25,640	25,538	25,066	472	456	16
One-parent family groups	6,920	9,749	11,528	11,892	9,547	2,344	1,872	472
Maintained by mother	6,230	8,398	9,834	9,841	7,841	1,999	1,591	408
Maintained by father	690	1,351	1,694	2,051	1,706	345	281	64
White, total	**27,294**	**28,294**	**29,846**	**30,132**	**28,240**	**1,892**	**1,475**	**417**
Two-parent family groups	22,628	21,905	22,320	22,139	21,759	379	364	15
One-parent family groups	4,664	6,389	7,525	7,993	6,481	1,512	1,111	401
Maintained by mother	4,122	5,310	6,239	6,368	5,110	1,258	918	340
Maintained by father	542	1,079	1,286	1,625	1,371	254	193	61
Black, total	**4,074**	**5,087**	**5,491**	**5,480**	**4,715**	**768**	**713**	**55**
Two-parent family groups	1,961	2,006	1,962	2,017	1,971	46	46	-
One-parent family groups	2,114	3,081	3,529	3,463	2,744	721	666	55
Maintained by mother	1,984	2,860	3,197	3,139	2,477	663	611	52
Maintained by father	129	221	332	324	267	58	55	3
Hispanic, total[2]	**2,194**	**3,429**	**4,527**	**5,193**	**4,614**	**579**	**497**	**82**
Two-parent family groups	1,626	2,289	2,879	3,354	3,218	136	129	7
One-parent family groups	568	1,140	1,647	1,839	1,396	443	368	75
Maintained by mother	526	1,003	1,404	1,560	1,174	386	319	67
Maintained by father	42	138	243	279	222	57	49	8

- Represents or rounds to zero.
[1] Includes other races, not shown separately.
[2] Hispanic persons may be of any race.

SOURCE: U.S. Census Bureau, *Current Population Reports*, P20-515, and earlier reports; and unpublished data.

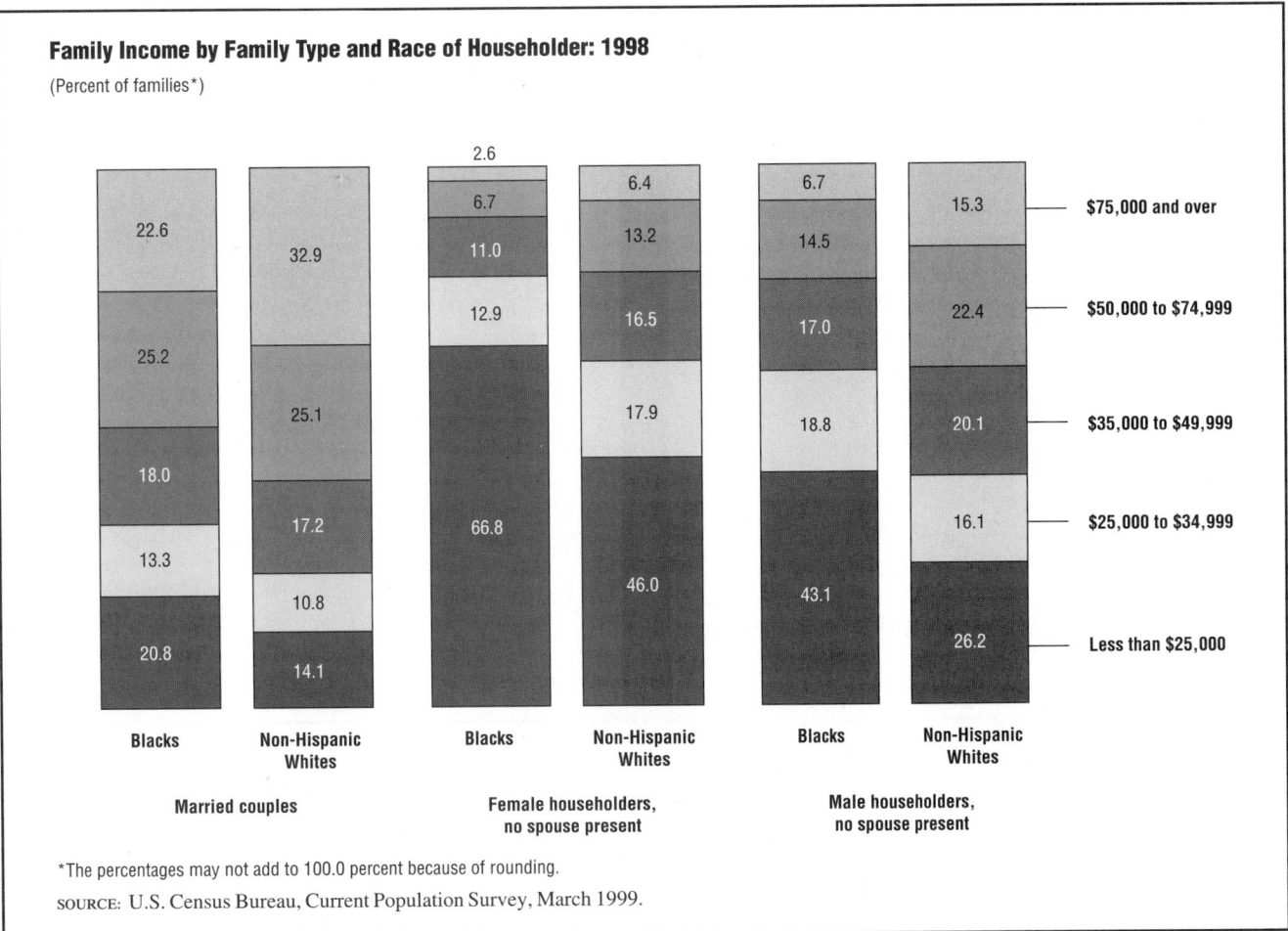

Family Income by Family Type and Race of Householder: 1998

(Percent of families*)

*The percentages may not add to 100.0 percent because of rounding.

SOURCE: U.S. Census Bureau, Current Population Survey, March 1999.

Living Arrangements of Persons 15 Years Old and Over by Selected Characteristic: 1999

[In thousands (211,676 represents 211,676,000). As of March. Based on Current Population Survey which includes members of Armed Forces living off post or with families on post but excludes other Armed Forces.]

Living arrangement	Total	15 to 19 years old	20 to 24 years old	25 to 34 years old	35 to 44 years old	45 to 54 years old	55 to 64 years old	65 to 74 years old	75 years old and over
Total [1]	211,676	19,864	18,058	38,474	44,744	35,232	22,909	17,843	14,551
Alone	26,606	138	1,175	3,714	4,074	4,208	3,549	4,125	5,622
With spouse	111,715	345	3,358	20,350	29,210	24,495	16,047	11,428	6,479
With other persons	73,355	19,381	13,525	14,410	11,460	6,529	3,313	2,290	2,450
White	176,213	15,736	14,397	30,897	36,946	29,754	19,725	15,642	13,118
Alone	22,176	122	908	2,910	3,245	3,372	2,885	3,577	5,158
With spouse	98,374	304	3,028	17,518	25,303	21,402	14,383	10,405	6,032
With other persons	55,663	15,310	10,461	10,469	8,398	4,980	2,457	1,660	1,928
Black	25,446	3,067	2,647	5,257	5,613	3,854	2,285	1,603	1,120
Alone	3,633	10	183	569	692	722	593	455	409
With spouse	8,134	21	198	1,717	2,379	1,865	993	667	295
With other persons	13,679	3,036	2,266	2,971	2,542	1,267	699	481	416
Hispanic origin [2]	21,995	2,837	2,734	5,531	4,630	2,864	1,705	1,092	604
Alone	1,329	27	98	261	211	197	177	212	145
With spouse	10,606	113	744	3,121	2,898	1,844	1,041	590	254
With other persons	10,060	2,697	1,892	2,149	1,521	823	487	290	205

[1] Includes other races and persons not of Hispanic origin, not shown separately.
[2] Persons of Hispanic origin may be of any race.

SOURCE: U.S. Census Bureau, unpublished data.

Marital Status of the Population by Sex, Race, and Hispanic Origin: 1980 to 1999

[In millions, except percent (159.5 represents 159,500,000). As of March. Persons 18 years old and over. Excludes members of Armed Forces except those living off post or with their families on post. Based on Current Population Survey.]

Hispanic origin	Total				Male				Female			
	1980	1990	1995	1999	1980	1990	1995	1999	1980	1990	1995	1999
Total[1]	159.5	181.8	191.6	199.7	75.7	86.9	92.0	95.9	83.8	95.0	99.6	103.9
Never married	32.3	40.4	43.9	47.6	18.0	22.4	24.6	25.8	14.3	17.9	19.3	21.9
Married	104.6	112.6	116.7	118.9	51.8	55.8	57.7	59.0	52.8	56.7	58.9	59.9
Widowed	12.7	13.8	13.4	13.5	2.0	2.3	2.3	2.5	10.8	11.5	11.1	10.9
Divorced	9.9	15.1	17.6	19.7	3.9	6.3	7.4	8.5	6.0	8.8	10.3	11.1
Percent of total	100.0	100.0	100.0	100.0	100.0	100.0	100.0	100.0	100.0	100.0	100.0	100.0
Never married	20.3	22.2	22.9	23.9	23.8	25.8	26.8	26.9	17.1	18.9	19.4	21.0
Married	65.5	61.9	60.9	59.5	68.4	64.3	62.7	61.5	63.0	59.7	59.2	57.7
Widowed	8.0	7.6	7.0	6.7	2.6	2.7	2.5	2.7	12.8	12.1	11.1	10.5
Divorced	6.2	8.3	9.2	9.9	5.2	7.2	8.0	8.9	7.1	9.3	10.3	10.7
White, total	139.5	155.5	161.3	166.8	66.7	74.8	78.1	80.9	72.8	80.6	83.2	85.9
Never married	26.4	31.6	33.2	35.7	15.0	18.0	19.2	20.0	11.4	13.6	14.0	15.6
Married	93.8	99.5	102.0	103.5	46.7	49.5	50.6	51.6	47.1	49.9	51.3	51.9
Widowed	10.9	11.7	11.3	11.3	1.6	1.9	1.9	2.1	9.3	9.8	9.4	9.2
Divorced	8.3	12.6	14.8	16.3	3.4	5.4	6.3	7.1	5.0	7.3	8.4	9.1
Percent of total	100.0	100.0	100.0	100.0	100.0	100.0	100.0	100.0	100.0	100.0	100.0	100.0
Never married	18.9	20.3	20.6	21.4	22.5	24.1	24.6	24.7	15.7	16.9	16.9	18.2
Married	67.2	64.0	63.2	62.0	70.0	66.2	64.9	63.8	64.7	61.9	61.7	60.4
Widowed	7.8	7.5	7.0	6.8	2.5	2.6	2.5	2.6	12.8	12.2	11.3	10.8
Divorced	6.0	8.1	9.1	9.8	5.0	7.2	8.1	8.9	6.8	9.0	10.1	10.6
Black, total	16.6	20.3	22.1	23.6	7.4	9.1	9.9	10.5	9.2	11.2	12.2	13.0
Never married	5.1	7.1	8.5	9.2	2.5	3.5	4.1	4.3	2.5	3.6	4.4	5.0
Married	8.5	9.3	9.6	9.8	4.1	4.5	4.6	4.7	4.5	4.8	4.9	5.0
Widowed	1.6	1.7	1.7	1.8	0.3	0.3	0.3	0.4	1.3	1.4	1.4	1.4
Divorced	1.4	2.1	2.4	2.8	0.5	0.8	0.8	1.1	0.9	1.3	1.5	1.7
Percent of total	100.0	100.0	100.0	100.0	100.0	100.0	100.0	100.0	100.0	100.0	100.0	100.0
Never married	30.5	35.1	38.4	39.2	34.3	38.4	41.7	40.7	27.4	32.5	35.8	37.9
Married	51.4	45.8	43.2	41.4	54.6	49.2	46.7	44.8	48.7	43.0	40.4	38.6
Widowed	9.8	8.5	7.6	7.6	4.2	3.7	3.1	3.7	14.3	12.4	11.3	10.7
Divorced	8.4	10.6	10.7	11.9	7.0	8.8	8.5	10.8	9.5	12.0	12.5	12.8
Hispanic,[2] total	7.9	13.6	17.6	20.3	3.8	6.7	8.8	10.1	4.1	6.8	8.8	10.3
Never married	1.9	3.7	5.0	5.9	1.0	2.2	3.0	3.3	0.9	1.5	2.1	2.6
Married	5.2	8.4	10.4	12.1	2.5	4.1	5.1	6.0	2.6	4.3	5.3	6.1
Widowed	0.4	0.5	0.7	0.8	0.1	0.1	0.2	0.1	0.3	0.4	0.6	0.7
Divorced	0.5	1.0	1.4	1.5	0.2	0.4	0.6	0.6	0.3	0.6	0.8	0.9
Percent of total	100.0	100.0	100.0	100.0	100.0	100.0	100.0	100.0	100.0	100.0	100.0	100.0
Never married	24.1	27.2	28.6	29.0	27.3	32.1	33.8	32.7	21.1	22.5	23.5	25.3
Married	65.6	61.7	59.3	59.4	67.1	60.9	57.9	59.6	64.3	62.4	60.7	59.3
Widowed	4.4	4.0	4.2	4.0	1.6	1.5	1.8	1.5	7.1	6.5	6.6	6.5
Divorced	5.8	7.0	7.9	7.6	4.0	5.5	6.6	6.3	7.6	8.5	9.2	8.8

[1] Includes persons of other races, not shown separately.
[2] Hispanic persons may be of any race.

SOURCE: U.S. Census Bureau, *Current Population Reports,* P20-491, and earlier reports; and unpublished data.

Live Births by Race and Type of Hispanic Origin—Selected Characteristics: 1990 and 1998

[4,158 represents 4,158,000. Represents registered births. Excludes births to nonresidents of the United States. Data are based on Hispanic origin of mother and race of mother. Hispanic origin data are available from only 48 States and the District of Columbia in 1990]

Race and Hispanic origin	Number of births (1,000)		Births to teen-age mothers, percent of total		Births to unmarried mothers, per-cent of total		Prenatal care beginning first trimester		Late or no prenatal care		Percent of births with low birth weight[1]	
	1990	1998	1990	1998	1990	1998	1990	1998	1990	1998	1990	1998
Total	4,158	3,942	12.8	12.5	26.6	32.8	74.2	82.8	6.0	3.9	7.0	7.6
White	3,290	3,119	10.9	11.1	16.9	26.3	77.7	84.8	4.9	3.3	5.7	6.5
Black	**684**	**610**	**23.1**	**21.5**	**66.7**	**69.1**	**60.7**	**73.3**	**10.9**	**7.0**	**13.3**	**13.0**
American Indian, Eskimo, Aleut	39	40	19.5	20.9	53.6	59.3	57.9	68.8	12.9	8.5	6.1	6.8
Asian and Pacific Islander[2]	142	173	5.7	5.4	(NA)	15.6	(NA)	83.1	(NA)	3.6	(NA)	7.4
Filipino	26	31	6.1	6.2	15.9	19.7	77.1	84.2	4.5	3.1	7.3	8.2
Chinese	23	28	1.2	0.9	5.0	6.4	81.3	88.5	3.4	2.2	4.7	5.3
Japanese	9	9	2.9	2.4	9.6	9.7	87.0	90.2	2.9	2.1	6.2	7.5
Hawaiian	6	6	18.4	18.8	45.0	51.1	65.8	78.8	8.7	4.7	7.2	7.2
Hispanic origin[3]	595	735	16.8	16.9	36.7	41.6	60.2	74.3	12.0	6.3	6.1	6.4
Mexican	386	516	17.7	17.5	33.3	39.6	57.8	72.8	13.2	6.8	5.5	6.0
Puerto Rico	59	57	21.7	21.9	55.9	59.5	63.5	76.9	10.6	5.1	9.0	9.7
Cuban	11	13	7.7	6.9	18.2	24.8	84.8	91.8	2.8	1.2	5.7	6.5
Central and South American	83	98	9.0	10.3	41.2	42.0	61.5	78.0	10.9	4.9	5.8	6.5
Other and unknown Hispanic	56	50	(NA)	20.2	(NA)	45.3	(NA)	74.8	(NA)	6.0	(NA)	7.6

NA Not available.
[1]Births less than 2,500 grams (5 lb.-8 oz.).
[2]Includes other races not shown separately.
[3]Hispanic persons may be of any race. Includes other types, not shown separately.

SOURCE: U.S. National Center for Health Statistics; *Vital Statistics of the United States*, annual; *National Vital Statistics Report (NVSR)* (formerly *Monthly Vital Statistics Report*); and unpublished data.

Births to Teens, Unmarried Mothers, and Prenatal Care: 1990 to 1998

[In percent. Represents registered births. Excludes births to nonresidents of the United States. Data are based on Hispanic origin of mother and race of mother. Hispanic origin data are available from only 48 States and the District of Columbia in 1990.]

Characteristics	1990	1993	1994	1995	1996	1997	1998
Percent of births to teenage mothers	**12.8**	**12.8**	**13.1**	**13.1**	**12.9**	**12.7**	**12.5**
White	10.9	11.0	11.3	11.5	11.3	11.2	11.1
Black	23.1	22.7	23.2	23.1	22.8	22.2	21.5
American Indian, Eskimo, Aleut	19.5	20.3	21.0	21.4	20.9	20.8	20.9
Asian and Pacific Islander [1]	5.7	5.7	5.7	5.6	5.3	5.2	5.4
Filipino	6.1	5.8	6.0	6.2	6.1	5.9	6.2
Chinese	1.2	1.0	1.0	0.9	0.9	0.9	0.9
Japanese	2.9	2.7	2.8	2.5	2.5	2.2	2.4
Hawaiian	18.4	18.5	19.6	19.1	18.4	18.6	18.8
Other	(NA)	6.5	6.4	6.3	5.8	5.7	5.8
Hispanic origin [2]	16.8	17.4	17.8	17.9	17.4	17.0	16.9
Mexican	17.7	18.2	18.6	18.8	18.1	17.7	17.5
Puerto Rican	21.7	22.3	23.2	23.5	23.1	22.3	21.9
Cuban	7.7	6.8	7.3	7.7	7.6	7.4	6.9
Central and South American	9.0	9.9	10.4	10.6	10.5	10.5	10.3
Other and unknown Hispanic	(NA)	21.0	20.8	20.1	19.8	19.8	20.2
Percent births to unmarried mothers	**26.6**	**31.0**	**32.6**	**32.2**	**32.4**	**32.4**	**32.8**
White	16.9	23.6	25.4	25.3	25.7	25.8	26.3
Black	66.7	68.7	70.4	69.9	69.8	69.2	69.1
American Indian, Eskimo, Aleut	53.6	55.8	57.0	57.2	58.0	58.7	59.3
Asian and Pacific Islander [1]	(NA)	15.7	16.2	16.3	16.7	15.6	15.6
Filipino	15.9	17.7	18.5	19.5	19.4	19.5	19.7
Chinese	5.0	6.7	7.2	7.9	9.2	6.5	6.4
Japanese	9.6	10.0	11.2	10.8	11.4	10.1	9.7
Hawaiian	45.0	47.8	48.6	49.0	49.9	49.1	51.1
Hispanic origin [2]	36.7	40.0	43.1	40.8	40.7	40.9	41.6
Mexican	33.3	37.0	40.8	38.1	37.9	38.9	39.6
Puerto Rican	55.9	59.4	60.2	60.0	60.7	59.4	59.5
Cuban	18.2	21.0	22.9	23.8	24.7	24.4	24.8
Central and South American	41.2	45.2	45.9	44.1	44.7	41.8	42.0
Percent of mothers beginning prenatal care 1st trimester	**74.2**	**78.9**	**80.2**	**81.3**	**81.9**	**82.5**	**82.8**
White	77.7	81.8	82.8	83.6	84.0	84.7	84.8
Black	60.7	66.0	68.3	70.4	71.4	72.3	73.3
American Indian, Eskimo, Aleut	57.9	63.4	65.2	66.7	67.7	68.1	68.8
Asian and Pacific Islander [1]	(NA)	77.6	79.7	79.9	81.2	82.1	83.1
Filipino	77.1	79.3	81.3	80.9	82.5	83.3	84.2
Chinese	81.3	84.6	86.2	85.7	86.8	87.4	88.5
Japanese	87.0	87.2	89.2	89.7	89.3	89.3	90.2
Hawaiian	65.8	70.6	77.0	75.9	78.5	78.0	78.8
Hispanic origin [2]	60.2	66.6	68.9	70.8	72.2	73.7	74.3
Mexican	57.8	64.8	67.3	69.1	70.7	72.1	72.8
Puerto Rican	63.5	70.0	71.7	74.0	75.0	76.5	76.9
Cuban	84.8	88.9	90.1	89.2	89.2	90.4	91.8
Central and South American	61.5	68.7	71.2	73.2	75.0	76.9	78.0
Percent of mothers beginning prenatal care 3d trimester or no care	**6.0**	**4.8**	**4.4**	**4.2**	**4.0**	**3.9**	**3.9**
White	4.9	3.9	3.6	3.5	3.3	3.2	3.3
Black	10.9	9.0	8.2	7.6	7.3	7.3	7.0
American Indian, Eskimo, Aleut	12.9	10.3	9.8	9.5	8.6	8.6	8.5
Asian and Pacific Islander [1]	(NA)	4.6	4.1	4.3	3.9	3.8	3.6
Filipino	4.5	4.0	3.6	4.1	3.3	3.3	3.1
Chinese	3.4	2.9	2.7	3.0	2.5	2.4	2.2
Japanese	2.9	2.8	1.9	2.3	2.2	2.7	2.1
Hawaiian	8.7	6.7	4.7	5.1	5.0	5.4	4.7
Hispanic origin [2]	12.0	8.8	7.6	7.4	6.7	6.2	6.3
Mexican	13.2	9.7	8.3	8.1	7.2	6.7	6.8
Puerto Rican	10.6	7.1	6.5	5.5	5.7	5.4	5.1
Cuban	2.8	1.8	1.6	2.1	1.6	1.5	1.2
Central and South American	10.9	7.3	6.5	6.1	5.5	5.0	4.9

[continued]

Births to Teens, Unmarried Mothers, and Prenatal Care: 1990 to 1998

[In percent. Represents registered births. Excludes births to nonresidents of the United States. Data are based on Hispanic origin of mother and race of mother. Hispanic origin data are available from only 48 States and the District of Columbia in 1990.]

Characteristics	1990	1993	1994	1995	1996	1997	1998
Percent of births with low birth weight [3]	**7.0**	**7.2**	**7.3**	**7.3**	**7.4**	**7.5**	**7.6**
White	5.7	6.0	6.1	6.2	6.3	6.5	6.5
Black	13.3	13.3	13.2	13.1	13.0	13.0	13.0
American Indian, Eskimo, Aleut	6.1	6.4	6.4	6.6	6.5	6.8	6.8
Asian and Pacific Islander [1]	(NA)	6.6	6.8	6.9	7.1	7.2	7.4
Filipino	7.3	7.0	7.8	7.8	7.9	8.3	8.2
Chinese	4.7	4.9	4.8	5.3	5.0	5.1	5.3
Japanese	6.2	6.5	6.9	7.3	7.3	6.8	7.5
Hawaiian	7.2	6.8	7.2	6.8	6.8	7.2	7.2
Hispanic origin [2]	6.1	6.2	6.2	6.3	7.4	6.4	6.4
Mexican	5.5	5.8	5.8	5.8	5.9	6.0	6.0
Puerto Rican	9.0	9.2	9.1	9.4	9.2	9.4	9.7
Cuban	5.7	6.2	6.3	6.5	6.5	6.8	6.5
Central and South American	5.8	5.9	6.0	6.2	6.0	6.3	6.5

NA Not available.

[1] Includes other races not shown separately.
[2] Hispanic persons may be of any race. Includes other types, not shown separately.
[3] Births less than 2,500 grams (5 lb.-8 oz.).

SOURCE: U.S. National Center for Health Statistics, *Vital Statistics of the United States*, annual; and *National Vital Statistics Reports (NVSR)* (formerly *Monthly Vital Statistics Report*).

Expectation of Life at Birth, 1970 to 1998, and Projections, 1999 to 2010

[In years. Excludes deaths of nonresidents of the United States]

Year	Total			White			Black and other			Black		
	Total	Male	Female	Total	Male	Female	Total	Male	Female	Total	Male	Female
1970	70.8	67.1	74.7	71.7	68.0	75.6	65.3	61.3	69.4	64.1	60.0	68.3
1975	72.6	68.8	76.6	73.4	69.5	77.3	68.0	63.7	72.4	66.8	62.4	71.3
1980	73.7	70.0	77.4	74.4	70.7	78.1	69.5	65.3	73.6	68.1	63.8	72.5
1982	74.5	70.8	78.1	75.1	71.5	78.7	70.9	66.8	74.9	69.4	65.1	73.6
1983	74.6	71.0	78.1	75.2	71.6	78.7	70.9	67.0	74.7	69.4	65.2	73.5
1984	74.7	71.1	78.2	75.3	71.8	78.7	71.1	67.2	74.9	69.5	65.3	73.6
1985	74.7	71.1	78.2	75.3	71.8	78.7	71.0	67.0	74.8	69.3	65.0	73.4
1986	74.7	71.2	78.2	75.4	71.9	78.8	70.9	66.8	74.9	69.1	64.8	73.4
1987	74.9	71.4	78.3	75.6	72.1	78.9	71.0	66.9	75.0	69.1	64.7	73.4
1988	74.9	71.4	78.3	75.6	72.2	78.9	70.8	66.7	74.8	68.9	64.4	73.2
1989	75.1	71.7	78.5	75.9	72.5	79.2	70.9	66.7	74.9	68.8	64.3	73.3
1990	75.4	71.8	78.8	76.1	72.7	79.4	71.2	67.0	75.2	69.1	64.5	73.6
1991	75.5	72.0	78.9	76.3	72.9	79.6	71.5	67.3	75.5	69.3	64.6	73.8
1992	75.8	72.3	79.1	76.5	73.2	79.8	71.8	67.7	75.7	69.6	65.0	73.9
1993	75.5	72.2	78.8	76.3	73.1	79.5	71.5	67.3	75.5	69.2	64.6	73.7
1994	75.7	72.3	79.0	76.4	73.2	79.6	71.7	67.5	75.8	69.6	64.9	74.1
1995	75.8	72.5	78.9	76.5	73.4	79.6	71.9	67.9	75.7	69.6	65.2	73.9
1996	76.1	73.0	79.0	76.8	73.8	79.6	72.6	68.9	76.1	70.3	66.1	74.2
1997	76.5	73.6	79.4	77.1	74.3	79.9	(NA)	(NA)	(NA)	71.1	67.2	74.7
1998, prel[1]	76.7	73.9	79.4	77.3	74.6	79.9	(NA)	(NA)	(NA)	71.5	67.8	75.0
Projections:[2]												
1999	77.0	74.1	79.7	77.5	74.7	80.2	(NA)	(NA)	(NA)	72.2	68.7	75.4
2000	77.1	74.2	79.9	77.7	74.8	80.4	(NA)	(NA)	(NA)	72.4	68.9	75.6
2005	77.8	74.9	80.7	78.3	75.4	81.1	(NA)	(NA)	(NA)	73.5	69.9	76.8
2010	78.5	75.6	81.4	79.0	76.1	81.8	(NA)	(NA)	(NA)	74.5	70.9	77.8

NA Not available.

[1] The 1998 life table values are based upon an 85 percent sample of deaths.

[2] Based on middle mortality assumptions; for details, see source. Source: U.S. Census Bureau, Population Division Working Paper No. 38.

SOURCE: Except as noted, U.S. National Center for Health Statistics, *Vital Statistics of the United States,* annual, and *National Vital Statistics Reports (NVSR)* (formerly *Monthly Vital Statistics Reports).*

Deaths by Selected Causes and Selected Characteristics: 1997

[In thousands (2,314.2 represents 2,314,200). Excludes deaths of nonresidents of the United States. Deaths classified according to ninth revision of *International Classification of Diseases*.]

Age, sex, and race	Total [1]	Heart disease	Cancer	Accidents and adverse effects	Cerebrovascular diseases	Chronic obstructive pulmonary diseases [2]	Pneumonia	Suicide	Chronic liver disease, cirrhosis	Diabetes mellitus	Homicide and legal intervention
ALL RACES [3]											
Both sexes, total [4]	2,314.2	727.0	539.6	95.6	159.8	109.0	85.7	30.5	25.2	62.6	19.8
Under 1 years old	28.0	0.6	0.1	0.8	0.3	0.1	0.4	-	-	-	0.3
1 to 4 years old	5.5	0.2	0.4	2.0	0.1	-	0.2	-	-	-	0.4
5 to 14 years old	8.1	0.3	1.0	3.4	0.1	0.1	0.1	0.3	-	-	0.5
15 to 19 years old	31.5	1.1	1.6	13.4	0.2	0.2	0.2	4.2	-	0.1	6.1
25 to 34 years old	45.5	3.3	4.6	12.6	0.7	0.4	0.5	5.7	0.5	0.6	5.1
35 to 44 years old	89.4	13.2	17.1	14.5	2.8	0.9	1.4	6.7	3.5	1.9	3.7
45 to 54 years old	144.9	35.3	45.4	10.4	5.7	2.8	2.2	4.9	5.6	4.3	1.9
55 to 64 years old	232.0	66.0	86.3	7.1	9.7	10.1	3.7	2.9	5.3	8.4	0.9
65 to 74 years old	464.3	139.4	156.7	8.6	24.9	30.6	10.5	2.7	5.8	16.3	0.5
75 to 84 years old	670.5	227.5	156.3	12.1	54.1	42.1	27.2	2.3	3.5	19.6	0.3
85 years old and over	594.1	240.0	69.9	10.7	61.3	21.8	39.3	0.8	0.9	11.4	0.1
WHITE											
Both sexes, total [4]	1,996.4	639.2	468.5	79.9	138.3	100.8	76.2	27.5	21.7	49.9	9.9
Under 1 years old	18.5	0.4	0.1	0.5	0.2	-	0.3	-	-	-	0.2
1 to 4 years old	3.8	0.1	0.3	1.4	-	-	0.1	-	-	-	0.2
5 to 9 years old	2.5	0.1	0.4	1.0	-	-	0.1	-	-	-	0.1
10 to 14 years old	3.3	0.1	0.4	1.4	-	-	-	0.3	-	-	0.1
15 to 19 years old	10.5	0.3	0.5	5.6	0.1	0.1	0.1	1.5	-	-	1.1
20 to 24 years old	12.0	0.4	0.7	5.6	0.1	0.1	0.1	1.9	-	0.1	1.3
25 to 29 years old	13.4	0.7	1.2	4.9	0.1	0.1	0.1	2.3	0.1	0.1	1.2
30 to 34 years old	18.8	1.6	2.4	5.3	0.3	0.1	0.2	2.6	0.3	0.3	1.2
35 to 39 years old	27.6	3.3	4.7	6.0	0.6	0.2	0.4	3.1	1.0	0.5	1.1
40 to 44 years old	37.6	6.2	8.6	5.7	1.1	0.4	0.6	3.0	1.9	0.8	0.9
45 to 49 years old	48.5	10.8	14.3	4.7	1.5	0.7	0.7	2.6	2.3	1.2	0.7
50 to 54 years old	62.9	16.2	22.5	3.6	2.2	1.6	0.9	2.0	2.3	1.8	0.4
55 to 59 years old	78.4	21.6	30.2	3.0	2.8	3.0	1.1	1.6	2.1	2.5	0.3
60 to 64 years old	109.5	31.4	42.0	2.8	4.2	6.0	1.8	1.2	2.3	3.5	0.2
65 to 69 years old	165.6	48.3	60.7	3.3	7.3	11.2	3.1	1.2	2.6	5.3	0.2
70 to 74 years old	234.2	71.2	76.1	4.1	13.1	17.1	5.8	1.3	2.6	7.5	0.2
75 to 79 years old	290.6	94.8	77.1	5.2	20.7	20.5	9.9	1.3	2.0	8.4	0.2
80 to 84 years old	313.0	110.3	63.4	5.8	27.5	19.2	14.6	0.9	1.3	8.0	0.1
85 years old and over	545.3	221.2	62.9	10.0	56.5	20.5	36.4	0.8	0.8	9.7	0.1
BLACK											
Both sexes, total [4]	276.5	77.2	61.3	12.7	18.1	6.9	7.9	2.1	2.8	11.1	9.3
Under 1 years old	8.5	0.2	-	0.2	0.1	-	0.1	-	-	-	0.1
1 to 4 years old	1.4	0.1	0.1	0.5	-	-	-	-	-	-	0.1
5 to 9 years old	0.9	-	0.1	0.4	-	-	-	-	-	-	0.1
10 to 14 years old	0.9	-	0.1	0.3	-	-	-	-	-	-	0.1
15 to 19 years old	3.2	0.1	0.1	0.8	-	-	-	0.2	-	-	1.4
20 to 24 years old	4.6	0.2	0.2	0.9	-	-	-	0.3	-	-	2.1
25 to 29 years old	5.1	0.4	0.3	1.0	-	0.1	0.1	0.3	-	0.1	1.5
30 to 34 years old	6.6	0.6	0.5	0.9	0.1	0.1	0.1	0.3	0.1	0.1	1.1
35 to 39 years old	9.5	1.2	1.2	1.2	0.3	0.1	0.2	0.2	0.2	0.2	0.9
40 to 44 years old	12.2	2.1	2.0	1.2	0.6	0.2	0.2	0.2	0.3	0.3	0.7
45 to 49 years old	14.7	3.3	3.2	1.0	0.8	0.2	0.3	0.1	0.5	0.5	0.4
50 to 54 years old	14.9	4.1	4.2	0.7	0.9	0.3	0.2	0.1	0.4	0.7	0.2
55 to 59 years old	17.3	5.1	5.4	0.6	1.0	0.4	0.3	0.1	0.4	0.9	0.1
60 to 64 years old	21.4	6.5	6.9	0.5	1.3	0.6	0.4	0.1	0.3	1.2	0.1
65 to 69 years old	25.3	7.8	8.1	0.5	1.6	0.9	0.5	0.1	0.3	1.4	0.1
70 to 74 years old	30.6	9.8	9.2	0.5	2.2	1.1	0.8	0.1	0.2	1.6	0.1
75 to 79 years old	30.2	10.0	7.9	0.5	2.4	1.1	1.0	-	0.1	1.5	-
80 to 84 years old	27.1	9.5	5.7	0.4	2.4	0.9	1.1	-	0.1	1.2	-
85 years old and over	42.1	16.2	6.1	0.6	4.1	1.0	2.3	-	-	1.5	-

-Represents zero.
[1] Includes other causes, not shown separately.
[2] Includes allied conditions.
[3] Includes other races, not shown separately.
[4] Includes those deaths with age not stated.

SOURCE: U.S. National Center for Health Statistics, *Vital Statistics of the United States,* annual.

Percentage of Adults Engaging in Leisure-Time Physical Activity: 1998

[In percent. Covers persons 18 years old and over. Based on response to question about physical activity in prior month. Based on a sample survey of approximately 150,000 persons in 50 states, the District of Columbia and Puerto Rico; for details, contact source]

Characteristic	No partici- pation in physical activity	Partici- pates in regular, sustained activity[1]	Partici- pates in regular, vigorous activity[2]	Characteristic	No partici- pation in physical activity	Partici- pates in regular, sustained activity[1]	Partici- pates in regular, vigorous activity[2]
Total	**28.7**	**20.8**	**13.6**	30 to 44 years old	28.2	19.9	14.8
				45 to 64 years old	31.5	19.8	13.2
Male	26.2	21.9	13.3	65 to 74 years old	35.9	20.3	13.0
Female	31.0	19.7	13.8	75 years old and			
				over	47.1	14.9	12.3
White, non-Hispanic	26.7	21.6	14.0				
Black, non-Hispanic	**33.8**	**17.8**	**12.3**	School years completed:			
Hispanic	38.4	17.4	11.4	Less than 12 years	49.7	14.3	8.2
Other	28.8	21.8	14.3	12 years	33.9	18.2	10.7
				Some college (13-15			
Males:				years)	23.9	22.3	13.9
18 to 29 years old	17.6	26.5	12.2	College (16 or more			
30 to 44 years old	24.9	19.0	11.8	years)	16.3	25.7	19.7
45 to 64 years old	30.6	20.5	14.1				
65 to 74 years old	31.1	24.8	14.2	Household income:			
75 years old and				Less than $10,000	42.4	17.8	10.7
over	39.1	22.2	22.0	$10,000 to $19,999	39.8	16.9	10.5
				$20,000 to $34,999	31.3	19.4	12.1
Females:				$35,000 to $49,999	24.4	21.4	14.0
18 to 29 years old	25.1	20.9	14.2	$50,000 and over	16.9	25.5	17.6

[1] Any type or intensity of activity that occurs 5 times or more per week and 30 minutes or more per occasion.
[2] Rhythmic contraction of large muscle groups performed at 50 percent or more of estimated age- and sex-specific maximum cardio-respiratory capacity, 3 times per week or more for at least 20 minutes per occasion.

SOURCE: U.S. National Center for Chronic Disease Prevention and Health Promotion, unpublished data.

Health Insurance Coverage Status by Selected Characteristics: 1990 to 1998

[Persons as of following year for coverage in the year shown (248.9 represents 248,900,000). Government health insurance includes medicare, medicaid, and military plans. Based on Current Population Survey.]

| | Total persons | Number (mil.) Covered by private or government health insurance | | | | | Not covered by health insurance | Percent Covered by private or government health insurance | | | Not covered by health insurance |
| | | Total[1] | Private | | Government | | | Total[1] | Private | | |
Characteristic			Total	Group health[2]	Medicare	Medicaid				Medicaid	
1990	248.9	214.2	182.1	150.2	32.3	24.3	34.7	86.1	73.2	9.7	13.9
1994[3]	262.1	222.4	184.3	159.6	33.9	31.6	39.7	84.8	70.3	12.1	15.2
1995[3]	264.3	223.7	185.9	161.5	34.7	31.9	40.6	84.6	70.3	12.1	15.4
1996[3]	266.8	225.1	187.4	163.2	35.2	31.5	41.7	84.4	70.2	11.8	15.6
1997[3]	269.1	225.6	188.5	165.1	35.6	29.0	43.4	83.9	70.1	10.8	16.1
1998, total[3, 4]	**271.7**	**227.5**	**190.9**	**168.6**	**35.9**	**27.9**	**44.3**	**83.7**	**70.2**	**10.3**	**16.3**
Age:											
Under 18 years	72.0	60.9	48.6	45.6	0.3	14.3	11.1	84.6	67.5	19.8	15.4
Under 6 years	23.7	20.0	15.1	14.4	0.1	5.7	3.7	84.5	63.8	23.9	15.5
6 to 11 years	24.6	21.0	16.8	15.9	0.1	4.9	3.6	85.4	68.2	20.0	14.6
12 to 17 years	23.8	20.0	16.8	15.4	0.1	3.7	3.8	84.0	70.5	15.5	16.0
18 to 24 years	26.0	18.2	15.9	13.1	0.1	2.5	7.8	70.1	61.1	9.8	30.0
25 to 34 years	38.5	29.3	26.7	25.1	0.4	2.5	9.1	76.3	69.5	6.4	23.7
35 to 44 years	44.7	37.0	34.1	32.0	0.7	2.6	7.7	82.8	76.3	5.8	17.2
45 to 54 years	35.2	30.4	28.2	26.4	1.1	1.6	4.8	86.4	79.9	4.6	13.6
55 to 64 years	22.9	19.5	17.2	15.2	2.0	1.4	3.4	85.0	75.0	6.2	15.0
65 years and over	32.4	32.0	20.2	11.2	31.1	3.0	0.4	98.9	62.3	9.1	1.1
Sex: Male	132.8	109.7	94.0	84.3	15.5	11.7	23.0	82.7	70.8	8.8	17.3
Female	139.0	117.7	96.9	84.3	20.4	16.2	21.3	84.7	69.7	11.6	15.3
Race: White	223.3	189.7	163.7	143.7	31.2	18.2	33.6	85.0	73.3	8.2	15.0
Black	35.1	27.3	18.7	17.1	3.7	7.9	7.8	77.8	53.2	22.5	22.2
Hispanic origin[5]	31.7	20.5	14.4	13.3	2.0	5.6	11.2	64.7	45.4	17.6	35.3
Household income:											
Less than $25,000	68.4	51.2	27.5	18.8	18.2	18.6	17.2	74.8	40.2	27.3	25.2
$25,000-$49,999	79.0	64.2	56.0	49.2	10.4	6.2	14.8	81.3	70.9	7.9	18.8
$50,000-$74,999	57.3	50.6	48.0	44.7	3.7	1.8	6.7	88.3	83.7	3.1	11.7
$75,000 or more	67.0	61.5	59.4	55.8	3.6	1.2	5.5	91.7	88.7	1.9	8.3
Persons below poverty	34.5	23.3	8.8	6.0	4.5	14.0	11.2	67.7	25.6	40.6	32.3

[1] Includes other government insurance, not shown separately. Persons with coverage counted only once in total, even though they may have been covered by more that one type of policy.
[2] Related to employment of self or other family members.
[3] Beginning 1994, data based on 1990 census adjusted population controls.
[4] Includes other races not shown separately.
[5] Persons of Hispanic origin may be of any race.

SOURCE: U.S. Census Bureau, *Current Population Reports*, P60-208; and unpublished data.

16

Education

♦ Educational Opportunities in Colonial America
♦ African American Educational Institutions in the Nineteenth Century
♦ Philanthropy and Education ♦ African American Education in the Twentieth Century
♦ Current Educational Trends ♦ Administrators, Educators, and Scholars
♦ Historically and Predominantly African American Colleges and Universities
♦ Research Institutions
♦ African Americans Holding Endowed University Chairs, Chairs of Excellence,
or Chaired Professorships (2001) ♦ Education Statistics

by Jessie Carney Smith

♦ EDUCATIONAL OPPORTUNITIES IN COLONIAL AMERICA

Historically, the attainment of education for African Americans has been a struggle. As far back as the late 1600s to the mid-1700s, there is some evidence of sporadic, systematic instruction of Africans in colonial America. Prior to 1830, some were even taught to read, write, and, in some instances, perform simple arithmetic. However, between 1830 and 1835, stringent laws were passed prohibiting whites from teaching African Americans to read and write. In spite of these laws though, many individuals struggled to provide informal and formal education to African Americans. In addition, churches and charitable organizations also played an important role in the creation of educational institutions for African Americans in the United States.

Early Christian Missionary Endeavors

Early attempts to educate African Americans can be traced back to the missionary efforts of Christian churches in the early 1600s. French Catholics in Louisiana were probably the earliest group to provide instruction to African American laborers. Although the primary goal was to convert them to Christianity, the process often involved general education. In addition, the French *code noir*, a system of laws, made it incumbent upon masters to educate slaves.

Pennsylvania Quakers, who were opposed to the institution of slavery, organized monthly educational meetings for African Americans during the early 1700s, so that they might have the opportunity for improvement. One such Quaker, Anthony Benezet, established an evening school in his home in 1750 that was successful until 1760. In 1774 Quakers in Philadelphia joined together to open a school for African Americans.

The Society for the Propagation of the Gospel in Foreign Parts, organized by the Church of England in 1701 for the purpose of converting African slaves to Christianity, was another organization that provided educational opportunities to African Americans. In 1751 the Society sent Joseph Ottolenghi to convert and educate African Americans in Georgia. Ottolenghi "promised to spare no pains to improve the young children."

♦ AFRICAN AMERICAN EDUCATIONAL INSTITUTIONS IN THE NINETEENTH CENTURY

African Free Schools in New York and Philadelphia

Similar to the churches, the anti-slavery movement played an important part in the creation of schools. In 1787 the Manumission Society founded the New York African Free School; by 1820 more than 500 African American children were enrolled. Support increased as other African Free Schools were established in New York until 1834 when the New York Common Council took over control of the schools.

In the North, there were opportunities for elementary education for African Americans in mostly segregated schools or in schools run in conjunction with African American churches. For example, in 1804 African Episcopalians in Philadelphia organized a school for African American children. In 1848 an African American industrial training school opened in Philadelphia at the House of Industry. Other schools in operation in Philadelphia included the Corn Street Unclassified School (1849), the Holmesburg Unclassified School (1854), and the Home for Colored Children (1859). By the mid-1860s, there were 1,031 pupils in the African American public schools of Philadelphia: 748 in the charity schools; 211 in the benevolent schools, and 331 in private schools. However, high schools in the North were almost inaccessible to African Americans in much of the nineteenth century.

Freedmen's Organizations and Agencies

At the close of the Civil War, hundreds of thousands of newly-freed African Americans were left without homes and adequate resources. As a means for providing temporary assistance to the former slaves, numerous organizations were formed. The American Missionary Association (AMA), established on September 3, 1846, had maintained an interest in African American education before and after the war. The AMA opened its first school for newly-freed slaves on September 17, 1861, at Fortress Monroe, Virginia. Mary S. Peake became the first teacher in an AMA school. The AMA also established a network of elementary schools, normal schools, and colleges throughout the South. In time, however, most of these schools were absorbed into local and state systems of education. Following the AMA's early efforts, other voluntary and denominational groups responded to the need for freedmen's aid and sent teachers into the Southern and border states, established elementary schools on plantations, in small towns, and in larger cities in the South. Although most of the schools were to be racially integrated, few whites attended.

The New England Freedmen's Aid Society, organized in Boston on February 7, 1862, was founded to promote education among free African Americans. Supporters of the organization included Edward Everett Hale, Samuel Cabot, Charles Bernard, William Lloyd Garrison, and William Cullen Bryant. In New York, a similar organization was founded on February 20, 1862,

the National Freedmens Relief Association. The Port Royal Relief Committee, later known as the Pennsylvania Freedmens Relief Association, founded in Philadelphia on March 3, 1862, followed this trend. In 1863 several of these organizations merged to form the United States Commission for the Relief of the National Freedmen, which, in 1865, became the American Freedman's Aid Union.

The federal government responded to the needs of African Americans in the South. During the 1860s, Congress passed several Freedman's Bureau Acts, creating and financing an agency designed to provide temporary assistance to newly freed slaves. Under the acts, the bureau's chief functions were to provide food, clothing, and medical supplies. Working in conjunction with various benevolent organizations, Bureau Commissioner General Oliver Otis Howard established and maintained schools and managed to provide for teachers. By 1870 the Freedman's Bureau operated over 2,600 schools in the South with 3,300 teachers educating 150,000 students; almost 4,000 schools were in operation prior to the abolition of the agency.

Independent Schools in the Late Nineteenth Century

The education of African Americans has been largely a function of independent schools, private institutions founded to meet the educational and employment needs of African Americans. In the second half of the century, these schools filled the gap until African American land grant colleges were founded in 1890. They also supplied many of the African American teachers in the South.

One of the earliest surviving African American independent schools, Tuskegee Normal and Industrial Institute (now Tuskegee University), was established in 1881 by an act of the Alabama general assembly. Booker T. Washington, the school's organizer and first principal, established a curriculum that provided African American students with the means to become economically self-supporting.

Similarly, other independent schools developed around the country. In a lecture room at the Christ Presbyterian Church, Lucy C. Laney opened what would become the Haines Normal and Industrial Institute in Savannah, Georgia in 1883. In 1901 Nannie Helen Burroughs founded the National Training School for Women and Girls in Washington, DC. By the end of the first year the school had enrolled 31 students; 25 years later more than 2,000 women had trained at the school.

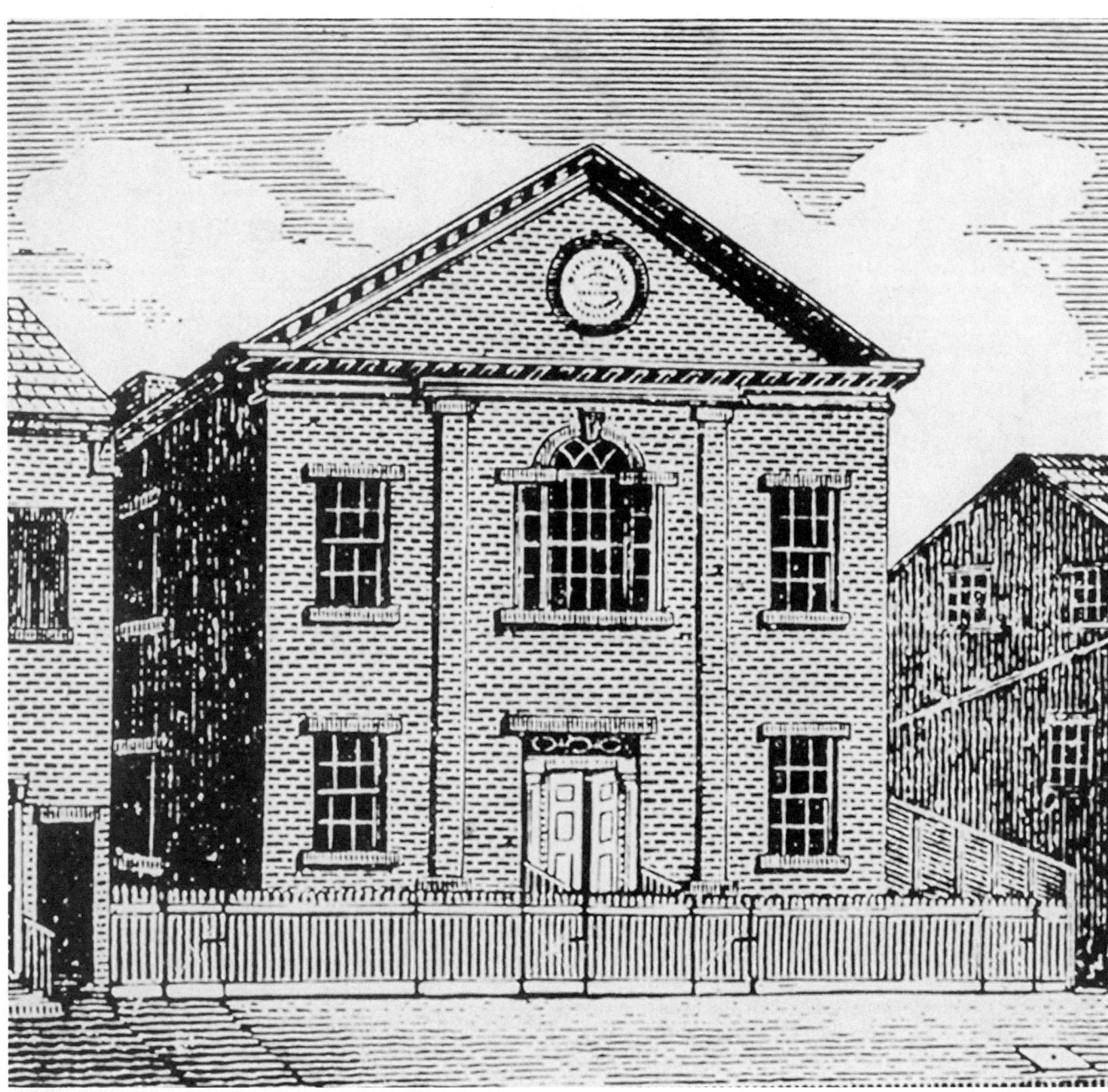

The first New York African Free School opened its doors in 1787. School No. 2 is shown here.

In Sedalia, North Carolina, Charlotte Hawkins Brown founded the Palmer Memorial Institute in 1901.

With only $1.50 and five students, Mary McLeod Bethune founded Daytona Normal and Industrial Institute for Girls (now Bethune-Cookman College) in 1904 in Daytona Beach, Florida. Nineteen years later, the institute merged with the Cookman Institute of Jacksonville, Florida, founded in 1872 by D.S.B. Darnell. Over 2,000 students now study at Bethune-Cookman College.

Early African American Institutions of Higher Education

Lincoln University in Pennsylvania (founded in 1854 as Ashmun Institute) and Wilberforce University (founded in 1856) are often regarded as the oldest of the historically African American institutions of higher education. Wilberforce College, as the latter school was first known, was founded in 1856 by the African Methodist Episcopal Church and named for the English abolitionist William Wilberforce. The school awarded

An American history class at Tuskegee Institute in 1902.

its first degree in 1857. Wilberforce and Lincoln were the first African American colleges to remain in their original location and to develop into degree-granting institutions. The oldest institution in operation today, however, is Cheyney University of Pennsylvania (earlier known as the Institute for Colored Youth and, eventually, Cheyney State College), which was founded in 1837. The primary purpose of these institutions was to train African American youth for service as teachers and ministers.

Between 1865 and 1871, several predominantly African American institutions of higher learning were founded, including Atlanta University (now Clark-Atlanta University), Shaw University and Virginia Union University (1865); Fisk University and Lincoln Institute in Missouri (now Lincoln University) (1866); Talladega College, Augusta Institute (now Morehouse College), Biddle University (now Johnson C. Smith University), Howard University and Scotia Seminary (now Barber-Scotia College) (1867); Hampton Institute (now Hampton University) (1868); Tougaloo College (1869); Alcorn College (now Alcorn State University) and Benedict College (1871). Religious organizations were instrumental in the founding and supporting of these early

African American institutions. The Freedmen's Bureau either founded or aided in the development of Howard University, St. Augustine's College, Lincoln Institute in Missouri, and Storer College (now merged with Virginia Union University). The American Missionary Association founded seven African American colleges; the first of these was Hampton. Other AMA-founded institutions were Atlanta, Fisk, LeMoyne (now LeMoyne-Owen College), Straight (now merged with New Orleans University to become Dillard University), Talladega, Tillotson College (now Huston-Tillotson), and Tougaloo. Benedict College, Shaw University, and Virginia Union were founded and supported by the American Baptist Home Mission Society.

Alcorn College (now Alcorn State University), founded in 1871, was the first African American land grant college. This was made possible under the Morrill Act of 1862, which provided federal land grant funds for higher education. In 1890 Congress passed the second Morrill Act, also known as the Land Grant Act of 1890. The second act stipulated that no federal aid was to be provided for the creation or maintenance of any white

African American female college graduate in the late 1800s.

agricultural and mechanical school unless that state also provided for a similar school for African Americans. As a result, a system of separate, African American land grant institutions developed and became the basis of publicly-supported higher education of African Americans in the South.

African American colleges offered diversity in history, purpose, and curriculums. For example, early in their history, some African American colleges prepared their students for careers in medicine and medical-related fields. Those that prepared students for degrees in dentistry and medicine included Howard University, Meharry Medical College, Shaw University, and New Orleans Medical School. The nation's only degree program in veterinary medicine among historically African American colleges and universities is still offered at Tuskegee University. Bennett College (founded 1873) and Spelman College (founded 1881) are the only two African American women's colleges. At first coeducational, Bennett became a women's two-year college in 1926. Xavier (founded in 1925) is the nation's only Catholic-supported college for African Americans.

By 1900 there were some 34 African American institutions in the United States for higher education and more than 2,000 African Americans with earned degrees.

◆ PHILANTHROPY AND EDUCATION

Pre-Civil War efforts did not fully address the educational needs and desires of African Americans, especially concerning the freed slaves. Northern philanthropy took up some of the burden of improving African American education. Agencies of the antebellum period aided in educating African Americans through their support of private and sectarian schools before and after the Civil War. By the end of the war, however, the South—the region where African Americans were concentrated—still had not addressed the educational needs of African Americans. Neither the newly-freed slaves nor their children had access to free public education. In 1867, a new type of support for education began when Massachusetts merchant George Peabody established the first educational philanthropy in the country. In his concern for the desolate South, he created the Peabody Education Fund to benefit "elementary education to children of the common people." The fund later was credited with stimulating states to develop systems of free schools for the races, "creating favorable public opinion to levy tax to support the schools, and stimulating the development of state teachers associations and normal schools."

So successful was the Peabody effort that in 1882 Connecticut manufacturer John F. Slater, impressed with the developments, created the Slater Fund to uplift the "lately emancipated" people of the South, thus becoming the first philanthropy devoted to the education of African Americans. Through the fund's efforts, private African American colleges and four-year high schools for African Americans were developed. The Fund stimulated vocational and industrial training and established the idea of county training schools. The Daniel Hand Fund, established in 1888, provided for the education of "needy and indigent" African Americans in the South; it was entrusted to the American Missionary Association. By 1914 the Peabody and Slater funds worked in similar areas; Peabody then transferred its assets to Slater.

Anna T. Jeanes further advanced the education of African Americans by giving $1 million to Booker T. Washington of the Tuskegee Institute and Hollis B. Frissell of the Hampton Institute to strengthen rural schools for African Americans in the South in 1907. The gift established the Fund for Rudimentary Schools for Southern Negroes, known as the Jeanes Fund. Initially the Fund supported "industrial teachers" who moved from school to school in the South teaching industrial and utilitarian subjects. The concept was expanded to provide master teachers, known as "Jeanes teachers," to supervise the African American schools. Later the program added new teaching methods, organized in-service training for teachers, and generally improved instruction. The program lasted from 1908 until 1968, when counties took over the Jeanes teachers' work and paid their salaries. Much of the credit for the program was due to Virginia E. Randolph, the first Jeanes teacher. In recognition of her work, the Jeanes teachers established the Virginia Randolph Fund to supplement the Jeanes Fund in 1936.

The Jeanes Fund and the Slater Fund, then working in similar areas, merged in 1937 to form the Southern Education Foundation (SEF). Later that year the Virginia Randolph Fund was incorporated into the SEF. The SEF extended the work of the predecessor funds and ensured that innovative approaches to the education of African Americans continued. From 1937 to 1950, the SEF concentrated on supporting the Jeanes teachers. It also worked with such agencies as the General Education Board (GEB), the Julius Rosenwald Fund, the Carnegie Corporation, and State Agents for Negro Schools. The GEB was a source of support for African American colleges, library collections, and, sometimes, library buildings. It also supported African American teachers and other aspects of education and welfare for African Americans. In its 31-year history, the Julius Rosenwald Fund, established in 1917, helped to build more than 5,000 rural schools for African Americans as a part of regular school systems in 15 Southern states. In various villages and counties, blacks and whites raised additional funds to support these schools. The fund also strengthened African American higher education. Early on, the Carnegie Corporation had provided grants to the Slater and Jeanes programs. Later, the corporation built African American branches of public libraries in various cities in the South. During the first quarter of the twentieth century, several African American colleges received funds from the Carnegie Corporation and Andrew Carnegie himself to support the erection of library buildings. They included the institutions of Atlanta, Cheyney, Fisk, Howard, Tuskegee, and Wilberforce.

In addition, the SEF worked to prepare the South to resolve racial problems. When the *Brown v. Board of Education of Topeka, Kansas* decision was rendered in 1954, bringing about desegregation of public education, the SEF contributed to the decision by conducting studies of African American education in the South largely through support of the Ford Foundation. Its efforts to desegregate public education continued: those Southern states that failed to desegregate higher education were challenged by the lawsuit originally known as

Adams v. Richardson. The SEF supported the Legal Defense Fund in litigation and helped dismantle the dual system of public education. It also supported conferences, studies, and publications dealing with desegregation of higher education. Its report *Miles to Go*, published in 1998, is an example of the SEF's efforts. The study found that over two decades of efforts to desegregate higher education has left blacks in the South and elsewhere out of pace with whites in undergraduate and graduate school enrollment, rates of graduation, faculty diversity, among other areas.

Located in Atlanta since 1948, the SEF is now a public charity that has several interests including programs to increase the supply of minority teachers in the South and to strengthen African American colleges. The SEF, its predecessor agencies, and other private and public agencies, figure prominently in the history and progress of African American education.

◆ AFRICAN AMERICAN EDUCATION IN THE TWENTIETH CENTURY

Early Promoters of African American Studies

From its beginnings, the purpose of African American studies has been to disseminate knowledge about the social, cultural, political, and historical experiences of Africans.

One of the forerunners in the field of African American studies, theologian and educator Reverend Alexander Crummell, along with a group of African American intellectuals, founded the American Negro Academy in Washington, DC, in 1897. The purpose of the organization was to foster scholarship and promote literature, science, and art, among African Americans. The organization's members hoped that through the academy, an educated African American elite would shape and direct society. Crummell first conceived the idea of an American Negro Academy while a student at Cambridge University in England. The organization's founding members included Paul Laurence Dunbar, William Sanders Scarborough, and W.E.B. Du Bois, among other noted educators. Following Crummell's death in 1908, Du Bois was elected president of the academy.

In September of 1915, Carter G. Woodson, a Harvard Ph.D. graduate, organized the Association for the Study of Negro Life and History (now the Association for the Study of Afro-American Life and History). The association's primary purpose was to promote research, encourage the study of African American history, and to publish material on African American history. In 1916, the organization began publishing the *Journal of Negro History,* for which Woodson served as editor until his death in 1950.

Other early scholars of African American studies include: sociologist E. Franklin Frazier (1894–1963); John Edward Bruce (1856–1924); Arthur Schomburg (1874–1938), founder of the Negro Society for Historical Research (1911); and Alain Locke (1885–1954), founder of the Associates in Negro Folk Education (1934).

The End of Legal Segregation in Public Education

In the years that followed the United States Supreme Court's 1896 ruling in *Plessy v. Ferguson*, segregation in public education became the general practice. Prior to the Court's decision in *Brown v. Board of Education of Topeka, Kansas* African American children were often subjected to inferior educational facilities. However, by the 1930s, a string of school desegregation cases reached the Court.

When Lloyd Lionel Gaines, an African American, had been refused admission to the law school of the State University of Missouri in 1936, he applied to state courts for an order to compel admission on the grounds that refusal constituted a denial of his rights under the Fourteenth Amendment of the U.S. Constitution. At that time, the state of Missouri maintained a practice of providing funds for African Americans to attend graduate and professional schools outside of the state, rather than provide facilities itself. The university defended its action by maintaining that Lincoln University, a predominantly African American institution, would eventually establish its own law school, which Gaines could then attend. Until then the state would allow him to exercise the option of pursuing his studies outside the state on a scholarship. Ruling in the case Missouri ex rel. *Gaines v. Canada* in 1938, the United States Supreme Court ruled that states were required to provide equal educational facilities for African Americans within its borders.

Taking an even greater step, in 1950 the United States Supreme Court ruled that a separate law school for African Americans provided by the state of Texas violated the equal protection clause of the Fourteenth Amendment. According to the Court, Herman Marion Sweat's rights were violated when he was refused admission to the law school of the University of Texas on the grounds that substantially equivalent facilities were already available to African Americans at another Texas school. Ruling in the case *Sweatt v. Painter*, the Court ruled that the petitioner be admitted to the University of Texas Law School since "in terms of number of the faculty, variety of courses and opportunity for specialization, size of the student body, scope of the library, availability of law review and similar activities, the University of Texas Law School is superior."

In 1952, five different cases, all dealing with segregation in public schools, reached the United States Supreme Court. Four of the cases *Brown v. Board of Education* (out of Kansas), *Briggs v. Elliott* (out of South Carolina), *Davis v. Prince Edward County School Board* (out of Virginia), and *Gebhart v. Belton* (out of Delaware) were considered together; the fifth case *Bolling v. Sharpe*, coming out of the District of Columbia, was considered separately since the District is not a state.

After hearing initial arguments, the Court found itself unable to reach a decision. In 1953, the Court heard re-argument. Thurgood Marshall, legal consul for the NAACP Legal Defense and Education Fund, presented arguments on behalf of the African American students. On May 17, 1954, the Court unanimously ruled that segregation in all public education deprived minority children of equal protection under the Fourteenth Amendment. (In the *Bolling* case, the Court determined that segregation violated provisions of the Fifth Amendment, since the Fourteenth Amendment is expressly directed to the states.)

African American Colleges and Universities

Many African American students choose to attend Historically Black Colleges and Universities (HBCUs); these schools continue to account for a significant number of African American graduates. According to reports from the U.S. Department of Education, fall enrollment at two-year and four-year HBCUs stood at 274,212 students in 1999. In 1964, over 51 percent of all African Americans in college were still enrolled in historically African American colleges and universities. By 1970 the proportion was 28 percent; 16.5 percent by the fall of 1978; and 6.2 percent by 1998. Yet despite the decline in percentages, as recently as 1999–2000, 24 percent of all African Americans receiving baccalaureate degrees earned them at HBCUs. In 2000, Florida A&M University was the leading producer of African Americans receiving baccalaureate degrees. Between 1991 and 1995, Fisk University was grouped with such large institutions as the University of Michigan, Harvard University, and University of California, Berkeley in the number of African American undergraduates who went on to earn doctorates from the 13 most productive schools. Xavier University in New Orleans has led all colleges and universities in the number of African American students accepted into medical school each year since 1995. The academic and historical significance of HBCUs was honored in 2001 as President George W. Bush proclaimed September 24–30, 2001, National Historically Black Colleges and Universities Week.

The racial composition of some African American colleges has changed dramatically; some of these colleges now have a predominantly white student body. Mandated by court order to raise its white population to 50 percent, the enrollment at Tennessee State University in 1998 was about 30 percent white. Those historically African American institutions with predominantly white enrollments by 1998 are Lincoln University in Missouri (72 percent white), Bluefield State College in West Virginia (89 percent white), and West Virginia State University (85 percent white).

Independent Schools

For years independent schools have been founded in order to exert greater control, ensure quality in education, and to meet the needs of African American children.

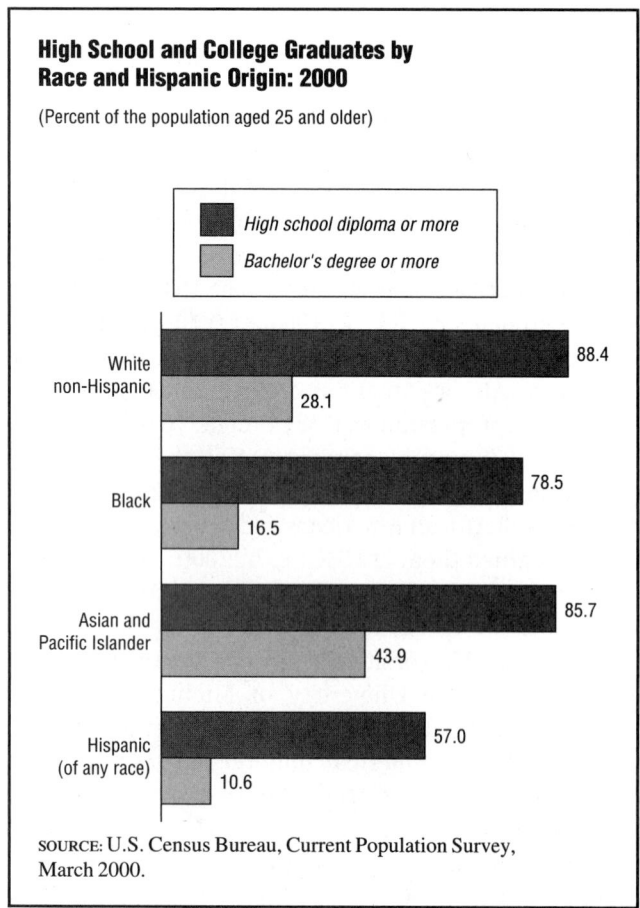

High School and College Graduates by Race and Hispanic Origin: 2000

(Percent of the population aged 25 and older)

- High school diploma or more
- Bachelor's degree or more

White non-Hispanic
88.4
28.1

Black
78.5
16.5

Asian and Pacific Islander
85.7
43.9

Hispanic (of any race)
57.0
10.6

SOURCE: U.S. Census Bureau, Current Population Survey, March 2000.

In 1932, in order to promote religious growth in the African American Muslim community, the Nation of Islam founded the University of Islam, an elementary and secondary school to educate African American Muslim children in Detroit. Clara Muhammad, wife of Elijah Muhammad, served as the school's first instructor. In 1934 a second school was opened in Chicago; by 1965 schools were operating in Atlanta and Washington, DC. The current system of African American Muslim schools, named for Clara Muhammad, is an outgrowth of the earlier University of Islam. There are currently 38 Sister Clara Muhammad schools in the United States.

Gertrude Wilks and other African American community leaders in East Palo Alto, California, organized the Nairobi Day School, a Saturday school in 1966. In 1969 the school became a full-time school. It closed in 1984.

Also founded as a Saturday school program in 1972, the New Concept Development Center in Chicago set out to create an educational institution which promoted self-respect, cooperation, and an awareness of African American history and culture. In 1975 public school teacher and nurse, Marva Collins founded the Westside Preparatory School in Chicago.

In recent years, the educational and social needs of urban youth, particularly African American males, have been given increased attention. Studies show that nearly 40 percent of adult African American males are functionally illiterate, and that the number of African American males incarcerated far outnumbers the number of African American males in college. Addressing these issues, large urban school systems, including Baltimore, Detroit, and Milwaukee, have attempted to create programs that focus on the needs of African American males.

Although African American students have shown improved performance on achievement tests, gaps between black and white students still exist. Progress has been made in the quality of education for African American children, yet inadequacies remain in the provision of resources for the education of African Americans. In recent years, efforts at creating alternative schools designed to meet the needs of African American children and to reflect the culture and social experiences of African Americans have received increased attention. In 1999 the Institute for Independent Education, an organization providing technical assistance to independent neighborhood schools, reported that an estimated 60,000 African American children attended independent community-based schools in the United States.

Marva Collins with her class at the Westside Preparatory School in Chicago in 1982.

◆ CURRENT EDUCATIONAL TRENDS

Afrocentrism

An educational methodology that has sparked both widespread praise and criticism is Afrocentrism. Afrocentrism is based, in part, on the belief that the ancient Greeks stole most of their great philosophical and mathematical thought from the Egyptians, an African people, that the Greek philosopher Aristotle gleaned much of his philosophy from books plundered from the Egyptian city of Alexandria, and that the notable Greek philosopher Socrates was black. Afrocentrists claim that the current educational system in America is deeply flawed and promotes white supremacy. It teaches history, arts, science, and other disciplines from a purely traditional European point of view, while African contributions to these fields of endeavor are ignored entirely or given inadequate consideration. Proponents of Afrocentrism theorize that teaching African American children from an African-centered perspective through the championing of black culture, history, and achievement will increase their feelings of self-worth and give them a greater sense of identity and ethnic pride.

The doctrine of Afrocentrism is not a new phenomenon. Such notable early twentieth century African Americans as activist Marcus Garvey and scholar Carter G. Woodson were among its most ardent supporters. Today, Afrocentrism is championed by African American scholars including, most prominently, Molefi K. Asante. Others include Leonard Jeffries, Asa Hillard, and, until his death, John Henrik Clark. Some public school systems with predominantly African American enrollment, such as Atlanta, New Orleans, Cleveland, Indianapolis, New York, Oakland, and Philadelphia have introduced African-centered principles into their curriculums.

Afrocentrism is not without its critics, however. Among them is Mary Lefkowitz, a professor of humanities at Wellesley College. In her book *Not Out of Africa: How Afrocentrism Became an Excuse to Teach Myth as History* (1996), Lefkowitz disagrees with the assertions of Afrocentrists that the Greeks stole their philosophical and mathematical thought from the Egyptians or that Socrates was black. She argues that Afrocentrist beliefs are based on myth and conjecture, not historical fact, and are designed to promote a political agenda. This criticism is echoed by Arthur Schlesinger, author

A principal with his students of the Malcolm X Academy, an Afrocentric school in Detroit, Michigan.

of *The Disuniting of America* (1991). Schlesinger remarks that African-centered education is divisive, un-American, and promotes the teaching of inaccuracy and distorted history.

Whether one is a supporter or critic, it is clear that Afrocentrism will continue to inspire heated debate for many years to come.

Ebonics

Black English, considered by some as a form of English and not a separate language, came to the forefront of discussion in 1996. While Black English has been explored as early as three decades ago, in 1996 some scholars renamed it Ebonics—a combination of the words ebony and phonics. Its roots are in the African languages that slaves brought to the United States. Some scholars further claim that Ebonics is "characterized by distinct grammar and syntax patterns such as the absence of forms of the verb 'to be.'" When the Oakland, California, school board passed a resolution in 1996 to make Ebonics a second language and declared that all of the teachers in the system should be trained to respect Ebonics—a form of speech

spoken by many African American students, a storm of criticism followed nationally. Opponents contended that Black English, or Ebonics, was substandard grammar and, if regarded as a legitimate language, would be detrimental to African American students. The school board and the superintendent eventually rescinded the decision.

Abandoning Affirmative Action

National debate, lawsuits, and voter reaction over the issue of affirmative action has impacted the education of African American students. Since the U.S. Supreme Court's validation of the use of race as a factor in college and university admissions programs in the case of *Regents of the University of California v. Bakke* (1978), many race-conscious admissions policies have come under attack in courts of law. Recent decisions in federal courts cloud the issue, and may lead to another Supreme Court review of affirmative action policies at institutions of higher learning. In 2001, a decision by the Eleventh Circuit Court of Appeals in *Johnson v. Board of Regents of the University of*

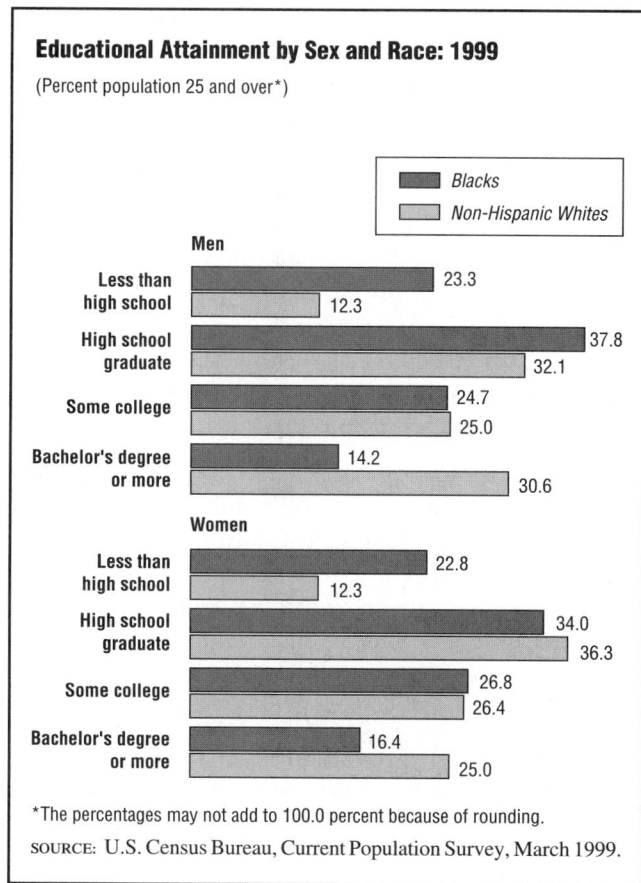

Educational Attainment by Sex and Race: 1999

(Percent population 25 and over*)

■ Blacks
□ Non-Hispanic Whites

Men

Less than high school — Blacks 23.3 / Non-Hispanic Whites 12.3

High school graduate — Blacks 37.8 / Non-Hispanic Whites 32.1

Some college — Blacks 24.7 / Non-Hispanic Whites 25.0

Bachelor's degree or more — Blacks 14.2 / Non-Hispanic Whites 30.6

Women

Less than high school — Blacks 22.8 / Non-Hispanic Whites 12.3

High school graduate — Blacks 34.0 / Non-Hispanic Whites 36.3

Some college — Blacks 26.8 / Non-Hispanic Whites 26.4

Bachelor's degree or more — Blacks 16.4 / Non-Hispanic Whites 25.0

*The percentages may not add to 100.0 percent because of rounding.

SOURCE: U.S. Census Bureau, Current Population Survey, March 1999.

Georgia struck down the race-conscious admissions policy for freshmen at the University of Georgia. The decision mirrored a 1996 Fifth Circuit Court of Appeals ruling that invalidated a similar policy at the University of Texas Law School. On the other hand, the affirmative action admissions policy at the University of Michigan Law School was upheld by a Sixth Circuit Court of Appeals ruling in May 2002.

In a number of states, voter initiatives and executive action have dealt race-conscious admissions policies more setbacks. Voters in California passed Proposition 209 in 1996. The law banned the use of race as a consideration for acceptance to the state's universities. Washington voters passed a similar measure, Initiative 200, in 1998, and Jeb Bush, governor of Florida, instituted the "One Florida Initiative" in 2000. The effects of such measures can be severe in the drop in enrollment of African American students at state institutions of higher learning. A 2002 NAACP Education Department report, "NAACP Call for Action in Education," points out that following the passage of California's Proposition 209, only one African American student enrolled in a class of more than 300 at the University of California, Berkeley's school of law in 1999. The same year, only

two black students were among the entering law school class at the University of California, Los Angeles.

Advocates of race-conscious admission policies, Derek Bok and William G. Bowen, completed a major study that challenges much of the conservative thinking about affirmative action. In their findings, published in the book *The Shape of the River: Long-Term Consequences of Considering Race in College and University Admissions* (1998), the two scholars studied race-conscious admissions in elite higher education and confirmed that such practices "create the backbone of the black middle class."

Voucher Systems and Charter Schools

Some educators regard voucher programs and charter schools as "logical parts of a broad educational mix." The voucher idea originated 40 years ago; it aimed to permit students to transfer from failing public schools to successful private schools. Critics feared, however, that the brightest students, both black and white, would be drawn away, leaving the inner-city schools, in terms of characteristics, African American and poor. They also raised questions about the use of public funds in private institutions, particularly those maintained and operated by churches or religious organizations. Voucher systems have been initiated in a handful of cities, including Cleveland, Milwaukee, and Detroit, and are being considered in about half of the 50 states. The voucher programs that are operational serve low-income, largely African American and Hispanic American children. In July 2002, the U.S. Supreme Court validated the constitutionality of Ohio's voucher program, opening the door for the wider use of school voucher programs throughout the nation.

Charter schools, or independent public schools, may be established by parents, community groups, local or state school boards, colleges and universities, or other individuals or groups. Some charter schools were once private schools, others were converted from existing public schools, and still others are newly established educational institutions. Generally, the schools report directly to the state and bypass local unions or other traditional bureaucracy. They are schools of choice for students and teachers; therefore, they must operate with the highest regard for equity and academic excellence. Supporters have little faith in traditional education systems and look to the charter schools as a viable solution to the problems of public school education. They see charter schools as a means of providing inner-city children the kind of education that students receive in the affluent suburbs. Some educators and parents see the charter school movement as another threat to public school education. By 2001, however, 37 states and the District of Columbia had passed charter school laws.

Single-Sex Schools

The nation has seen a number of single-sex schools opened in recent years. One such school opened in the fall of 1996, when the Young Women's Leadership School, an experimental public school for girls, opened in East Harlem. It emphasizes mathematics and science, subjects in which girls often lag behind boys in performance. The school originally provided for 56 seventh-grade girls, and had expanded to 360 students in grades 7–12 by the year 2000. Advocates of the school based the need on studies that showed that girls, particularly from poor communities, performed better when boys were not present. Some groups, such as the New York Civil Liberties Union, challenged the school, however, arguing that it would violate the U.S. Constitution, as well as the Federal statutory law. The group has challenged plans for other single-sex, single-race schools for young African American men in New York, Detroit, and Milwaukee.

Racial Isolation and Integration in Schools

Nearly a half-century after *Brown v. Board of Education of Topeka, Kansas* segregated public schools continue. Evidence of racial isolation in urban schools, as seen in Hartford, Connecticut, in 1997, led the state's highest court to issue a mandate to desegregate the schools. Under the order, racially-isolated students in urban schools are able to enroll in predominantly white suburban schools on a space-available plan. The Connecticut decision seems to be running counter to the current trend to abandon racial "quotas" in schools, where predominance of one race is not necessarily grounds for legal relief unless the cause lies in segregation patterns of the past. The concern over affirmative action, however, is shifting from colleges and universities to public school districts. Districts that adopted voluntary desegregation plans, such as those in Montgomery County, Maryland, and Arlington, Virginia, wonder if they can continue race-conscious policies.

Desegregation orders imposed by the courts decades earlier are being lifted. In such cities as Nashville, Tennessee; Oklahoma City; Denver; Wilmington, Delaware; and Cleveland, courts have declared that past segregation practices have been remedied and judicial monitoring is no longer needed.

♦ ADMINISTRATORS, EDUCATORS, AND SCHOLARS

(To locate biographical profiles more readily, please consult the index at the back of the book.)

Molefi K. Asante (1942–)
Scholar

Molefi Kete Asante was born Arthur Lee Smith Jr. on August 14, 1942, in Valdosta, Georgia. His name was legally changed to Molefi Kete Asante in 1973. In 1962, Asante graduated with an associate's degree from Southwestern Christian College. He graduated cum laude with a B.A. from Oklahoma Christian College in 1964, received an M.A. from Pepperdine University in 1965, and a Ph.D. from UCLA in 1968.

Asante has taught speech and communications at many universities in the United States. He was an instructor at California State Polytechnic University at Pomona (1966–1967) and California State University at Northridge (1967). In 1968 he accepted an assistant professorship at Purdue University in Lafayette, Indiana, where he remained until 1969 when he began teaching at UCLA. There he advanced from assistant to associate professor of speech and also served as the director of the Center for Afro-American Studies (1970–1973). In 1973 he accepted the position of professor of communications at the State University of New York. He soon became department chairman, a position he held until 1979 when he became a visiting professor at Howard University in Washington, DC (1979–1980). In 1981 and 1982, he was a Fulbright professor at the Zimbabwe Institute of Mass Communications. Since 1980, he has been a professor at Temple University in Philadelphia in the Department of African American Studies.

Asante is a prolific author with over 33 books dealing with both communication theory and the African American experience. Some of his most recent titles include: *Afrocentricity: The Theory of Social Change* (1980); *African Culture: The Rhythms of Unity* (1985); *The Afrocentric Idea* (1987); *Afrocentricity* (1987); *Kemet, Afrocentricity and Knowledge* (1990); *The Historical and Cultural Atlas of African-Americans* (1991); *Colored, on White Campus: The Education of a Racial*

World (1992); *Fury in the Wilderness* (1993); *African American History: A Journey of Liberation* (1995); *African Intellectual Heritage: A Book of Sources* (1996); *The African-American Atlas: Black History and Culture* (1998); *The African American Book of Names and Their Meanings* (1999); *The Painful Demise of Eurocentrism: An Afrocentric Response to Critics* (1999); *The Egyptian Philosophers: Ancient African Voices from Imhotep to Akhenaten* (2000); and (co-editor with Eungjun Min) *Socio-Cultural Conflict Between African American and Korean American* (work in progress as of 2002).

Asante is also a founding editor of the *Journal of Black Studies* and has been a member of the advisory board of the *Black Law Journal* (1971–1973) and *Race Relations Abstract* (1973–1977). Asante has also served as the vice president for the National Council of Black Studies and the African Heritage Studies Association.

Houston Baker. *See* Literature chapter.

Maria Louise Baldwin (1856–1922)
Educator

Born on September 13, 1856, in Cambridge, Massachusetts, Maria Louise Baldwin was one of the most distinguished educators in the United States at the turn of the twentieth century. She was the principal of the Agassiz school in Cambridge, where children of affluent and established white families attended—a rarity for a woman and an African American.

Educated in Cambridge, Baldwin taught first in Chestertown, Maryland, and then was appointed teacher in Agassiz Grammar School. Eventually she taught all grades in the school—from first to the seventh—and in 1889 was promoted to school principal. In 1916, a new school was erected with more grades added and Baldwin's position was changed to master. She strengthened her credentials by enrolling in courses at nearby Harvard University. She remained at Agassiz until 1922.

Baldwin lectured throughout the country on such luminaries as Paul Lawrence Dunbar, Abraham Lincoln, and Thomas Jefferson and on women's suffrage, poetry, and history. During one of her lectures, she collapsed at Boston's Copley Plaza Hotel on January 9, 1922, and died suddenly. The entire nation mourned her death. About a year later, Aggasiz school recognized her by unveiling a tablet created in her memory. Other memorials followed, including the naming in her honor of the Aggasiz school auditorium and a women's residence center at Howard University in Washington, DC.

Lerone Bennett Jr. (1928–)
Scholar

Born on October 17, 1928, in Clarksdale, Mississippi, Lerone Bennett Jr. was educated at Morehouse College, receiving an A.B. in 1949. Bennett worked for the *Atlanta Daily World*, and *Jet* magazine before joining *Ebony* magazine in 1954. He was named executive editor in 1987. Beyond these positions though, Bennett has achieved fame for his essays and other writings.

His 1962 book *Before the Mayflower: A History of the Negro in America* made him one of the best-known and most influential African American historians of the twentieth century. *Before the Mayflower* was revised in 1982 and has been reprinted several times. Bennett's 1964 biography of Morehouse College classmate Martin Luther King Jr., *What Manner of Man*, was welcomed as an evenhanded analysis of the African American leader's life and his role in fundamentally changing the nature of racial dynamics in the United States. Also in 1964, Bennett published *The Negro Mood and Other Essays*, a collection of essays that demonstrated a sharper editorial bite than his previous works. Probing such issues as the failed integration of African Americans into American life and the ways in which African Americans are denied the fruits of society, Bennett takes aim at the white liberal establishment for ignoring the accomplishments of African Americans and for just mouthing the words of racial justice rather acting on that creed. Bennett has also produced a number of other works including *Pioneers in Protest* (1968), *The Shaping of Black America* (1974), and *Wade in the Water: Great Moments in Black History* (1979).

Bennett served as a visiting professor at Northwestern University in 1968–1969. In addition, he was a senior fellow of the Institute of the Black World in 1969. In 2002 Bennett won an American Book Award for lifetime achievement from the American Book Association.

Mary McLeod Bethune (1875–1955)
Founder, Educator

Born on July 10, 1875, near Mayesville, South Carolina, Mary McLeod received a sporadic education in

Mary McLeod Bethune.

local schools. She eventually received a scholarship and studied for seven years at the Scotia Seminary in Concord, North Carolina. In 1893 she went on to study at the Moody Bible Institute in Chicago in lieu of a missionary position in Africa. In 1895 she began teaching at the Haines Institute in Augusta, Georgia. Between 1900 and 1904, she taught in Sumter, Georgia, and Palatka, Florida.

In 1904 she founded her own school in Daytona Beach, Florida—the Daytona Educational and Industrial School for Negro Girls. John D. Rockefeller became an early admirer and supporter of the school after hearing a performance by its choir. Bethune went on to found the Tomoka Missions and, in 1911, the McLeod Hospital. In 1922 her school merged with the Cookman Institute to become Bethune-Cookman College.

Bethune's work received national attention, and she served on two conferences under President Herbert Hoover. In 1936 President Franklin Roosevelt appointed her director of the Division of Negro Affairs of the National Youth Administration. During World War II, she served as special assistant to the Secretary of War,

responsible for selecting WAC officer candidates of African American descent.

Bethune also served on the executive board of the National Urban League and was a vice president of the NAACP. She received the Spingarn Award in 1935, the Frances A. Drexel Award in 1936, and the Thomas Jefferson Medal in 1942. Bethune was also instrumental in the founding of the National Council of Negro Women. She retired from public life in 1950 on her 75th birthday and died five years later on May 18, 1955.

Much of Bethune's philosophy concerned ennobling labor and empowering African Americans to achieve economic independence. Although a tireless fighter for equality, she eschewed rhetorical militancy in favor of a doctrine of universal love.

Charlotte Hawkins Brown (1883–1961)
School Founder, Educator, Civic Leader

Charlotte Hawkins Brown was a pioneer in quality preparatory education for African American youth. She set her ideas and experiments in place at the Palmer Memorial Institute, which she founded in Sedalia, North Carolina, and headed for more than half a century.

Born Lottie Hawkins on June 11, 1883, in Henderson, North Carolina, Hawkins was the granddaughter of slaves. She and 18 members of her family moved to Cambridge, Massachusetts, in 1888 in search of better

Charlotte Hawkins Brown.

social and educational opportunities. By the time of her graduation from Cambridge English School, she had changed her name to Charlotte Eugenia Hawkins. In 1900 she enrolled in State Normal School in Salem, Massachusetts, and left in October 1901, to teach at the American Missionary Association's Bethany Institute near McLeansville, North Carolina. The school closed at the end of the year. Hawkins returned to Cambridge in 1902 and discussed with benefactor Alice Freeman Palmer, whom she met at the end of her high school studies, her plan to start a school in Sedalia, North Carolina. Palmer and other Northern philanthropists provided Hawkins funds for the school and on October 10, 1902, Hawkins founded a school, the Alice Freeman Palmer Institute, which she named in honor of her friend. After Palmer died that fall, the school was renamed Palmer Memorial Institute and was incorporated on November 23, 1907. By then Hawkins had a diploma from Salem Normal School, had studied at Harvard University and Wellesley and Simmons colleges, and married Edward Sumner Brown.

By 1916, the school was housed in four buildings. Fires in 1917 and 1922 destroyed two buildings; one of these, Memorial Hall, was replaced in 1922 with the Alice Freeman Palmer Building. By 1922 the school had built a fine reputation as one of the country's leading preparatory schools for African Americans. The junior college academic program that focused on agricultural and vocational training that Brown introduced in the mid-1920s gave way to secondary and post-secondary education. Later on the school also emphasized good manners and social graces as it prepared youth to assume positions in society. The school's presence, already felt strongly in the South, was now known across the country and students responded by enrolling in the institute in greater numbers. In 1922, Palmer graduated its first high school class.

Brown emerged as a national leader and was recognized for her work in directing the institute as well as her strong resolve in advancing the life of African Americans and African American women in particular. She was a staunch public opponent of lynching. She was an organizer of the North Carolina State Federation of Negro Women's Clubs and was also active in the National African American Women's Club Movement. She persuaded the state to establish homes for African American young women who were in legal difficulty, such as the Efland Home for Wayward Girls. As president of the North Carolina Teachers Association from 1935 to 1937, she helped effect change in the education of the state's African American residents. She was a key figure in the Southern interracial women's movement

and also was the first African American member in the Twentieth Century Club of Boston.

Brown became known for her writings as well. Her works included *Mammy: An Appeal to the Heart of the South* (1919) and *The Correct Thing to Do, to Say, and to Wear* (1940). The latter work, originally used as a guide for Palmer's students, attracted the attention of young people across the country and was reprinted five times.

After 50 years of service, Brown retired as president of Palmer on October 5, 1952, but remained on campus until 1955 as vice-chairman of the board of trustees and director of finances. Wilhelmina Marguerite Crosson replaced Brown as president. By the end of the decade, the school enrolled annually about 200 junior and senior students who came from across the country, the Caribbean, and Africa.

Brown died in Greensboro on January 11, 1961, and was buried at the front of the Palmer campus. Although Brown's spirit and ideals continued for a while, the school began to suffer from declining enrollment, the rising cost of maintenance, and reduced support from benefactors. Another fire in 1971 destroyed the Alice Freeman Palmer Building. In November of that year, Bennett College in nearby Greensboro assumed the institute's debts and took over the site. The home that Brown had built on campus, Canary Cottage, has been preserved and, in 1983, was declared a state historic site. It was declared a national historic landmark in 1988. The institute's campus was designated a state historic site in the previous year.

Nannie Helen Burroughs (1879–1961)
Educator

Born in Orange Springs, Virginia, on May 2, 1879, Nannie Helen Burroughs was one of the most significant Baptist lay leaders of the twentieth century, a lifelong booster of women's education, and a tireless civic organizer. She addressed the National Baptist Convention in Virginia in 1900 on the subject "How the Sisters are Hindered from Helping" and, from that time until her death more than 60 years later, she exercised pivotal leadership. She was elected corresponding secretary for the Woman's Convention, Auxiliary to the National Baptist Convention, U.S.A., Inc., and in 1948 she became president of the Women's Convention.

In 1901 Burroughs founded and presided over the National Training School for Women and Girls, which

Nannie Helen Burroughs.

Joe Clark holding his book, *Laying Down the Law*.

emphasized industrial arts and proficiency in African American history. After only one year, she had recruited 31 students. In honor of her efforts, the school's curriculum was changed to accommodate elementary education, and its name was changed to the Nannie Helen Burroughs School.

Burroughs was active in the anti-lynching campaign and a life member of the Association for the Study of Negro Life and History. She helped organize the Women's Industrial Club of Louisville and was responsible for organizing Washington, DC's first African American self-help program. She also edited such periodicals as the *Christian Banner* and was the author of *Roll Call of Bible Women*. She died on May 20, 1961.

Joe Clark (1939–)
Former Educator, Lecturer, Executive Director

Best known as the feisty, dedicated, baseball bat-wielding school principal portrayed by actor Morgan Freeman in the film *Lean on Me*, Clark has served as an exemplar of school discipline and boasts a distinguished record of achievements and laurels. A 14-year member of the New Jersey Board of Education and an elementary and secondary school principal until 1989, he has been honored by the White House, the NAACP, his alma mater Seton Hall University, and various newspapers and magazines.

Born in Rochelle, Georgia, in 1939, Clark served in the United States Army Reserve from 1958 to 1966. He received a B.A. from New Jersey's William Paterson College in 1960 and his master's degree from Seton Hall in 1974. From 1960 to 1974, Clark served on the board of education in Paterson, New Jersey. He was a coordinator of language arts from 1976 until 1979. Clark became a school principal for the first time in 1979 and quickly earned the admiration and respect of educators for his somewhat controversial, no-nonsense managerial style. In 1983, Clark received the NAACP Community Service Award and was named New Jerseyan of the Year by the *Newark Star Ledger*. The following year, *New Jersey Monthly* honored Clark as outstanding educator. In 1985, Clark appeared in Washington, DC, to receive honors at a presidential conference on academic and disciplinary excellence and also gained awards from Seton Hall and Farleigh Dickinson University. The National School Safety Center gave Clark the Principal of Leadership award in 1986, and the National Black Policemen's Association bestowed their Humanitarian Award upon him in 1988.

In 1989, Clark ended his tenure as principal of Eastside High School in Paterson, New Jersey, and traveled the country as a lecturer. He accepted a job as the director of the Essex County, New Jersey, Youth House, a juvenile detention center in Newark, in August of 1995.

Kenneth Clark (1914–)
Psychologist, Educator, Writer

Born on July 24, 1914, in the Panama Canal Zone, Clark was brought to the United States as a youth by his mother so that he could be educated. He was educated in Harlem and then attended Howard University. He was awarded a B.A. in 1935 and an M.S. in 1936 in psychology. In 1940 he became the first African American awarded a Ph.D. in psychology from Columbia University. He then taught at the Hampton Institute, but left due to its conservative views, moving to City College of New York in 1942, an institution he was to remain at for the rest of his academic career.

Clark was deeply troubled by school segregation and studied its effects with his wife, the former Mamie Phipps. Clark came to the attention of the NAACP during its post-war campaign to overturn legalized segregation. Clark was intimately involved in the long legal struggle which culminated in *Brown v. Board of Education of Topeka, Kansas*. He testified as an expert witness at three of the four cases leading up to the Supreme Court's review of *Brown v. Board of Education* and his report on the psychology of segregation was read carefully by the justices. *Brown v. Board of Education* was not only a milestone in the modern Civil Rights movement, it also made Kenneth Clark into something of an academic superstar. Clark went on to become the most influential African American social scientist of his generation.

In the 1960s Clark was involved with the Great Society's unsuccessful HARYOU program in New York and the MARC Corp.'s program in Washington, DC. Both were efforts to improve integration of public schools and to set test score-based standards for schools and teachers. Both projects, however, were terminated by politics.

In 1975 Clark retired from CCNY and formed his own advisory company to counsel companies on integrating their workforces. Clark has continued to write vehemently on the subject of integration.

Septima Clark (1898–1987)
Educator, Civil Rights Activist

In her unassuming, workmanlike way, Septima Clark made a major impact on the voting rights of thousands of African American Southerners, though many Americans have never heard of her. Clark dedicated her life to education and drove home through her actions a simple concept in which she believed, namely, that before one could get people to register and vote, one had to teach them to read and write. Born on May 3, 1898, in Charleston, South Carolina, Clark was a schoolteacher for most of her life. She dedicated her entire career to educating her community.

In 1937 Clark studied under W. E. B. Du Bois at Atlanta University. She later went on to receive her B.A. at Benedict College in 1942, and her M.A. from Hampton Institute four years later. After teaching for nearly

Septima Clark.

ten years in the Charleston school system, Clark began the "citizenship schools" program, through her position at Tennessee's Highlander Folk School, a center for civil organizing and dialogue in 1956. These citizenship schools taught people to write their names, balance check books, fill out a voting ballot, and understand their rights and duties as U.S. citizens. The schools were a success, and by 1961, had grown too big for Highlander to handle. The Southern Christian Leadership Conference (SCLC) expressed an interest in taking over, so Clark went to work for the SCLC as director of education.

After retiring from the SCLC in 1970, Clark stayed active in civil rights struggles. In 1974, at the age of 76, Clark was elected to serve on the Charleston school board—the same school board that had fired her 20 years earlier for her active involvement with the NAACP. She died in Charleston on December 15, 1987.

Johnnetta B. Cole (1936–)
Spelman College President

A distinguished scholar, Johnnetta Cole has served on the faculties of Washington State University, University of Massachusetts-Amherst, Hunter College, and Spelman College, the historically African American women's institution in Atlanta. Born in Jacksonville, Florida, on October 19, 1936, Cole attended Oberlin College, which awarded her a B.A. in 1957. She went on to earn her master's and doctorate degrees at Northwestern in 1959 and 1967, respectively.

In 1967, Cole began her first teaching assignment at Washington State University, where she taught anthropology and served as director of black studies. The university honored her as Outstanding Faculty Member of the Year for 1969–1970. From 1970 until 1983, Cole was professor of anthropology and African American studies at the University of Massachusetts-Amherst. She left the University of Massachusetts-Amherst in 1983 for a position as professor of anthropology at Hunter College of the City of New York. Cole also served as director of Latin American and Caribbean studies at Hunter College from 1984 until 1987. In 1987, Cole was named president of Spelman College. She retired in 1997 and took a professorship at Emory University in Atlanta. In 2002 she again became president of an historically black women's college, Bennett College in Greensboro, North Carolina.

As an anthropologist, Cole has done field work in Liberia, Cuba, and in the African American community.

A prolific writer, she has published in many mainstream periodicals as well as scholarly journals. Since 1979 she has been a contributor and advising editor to *The Black Scholar*. She is the author of *Conversations: Straight Talk with America's Sister President* (1993) and *Dream the Boldest Dreams: And Other Lessons of Life* (1997). She is a member of the National Council of Negro Women and a fellow of the American Anthropological Association.

Cole has received numerous awards and over 40 honorary degrees. She was presented with the Elizabeth Boyer Award in 1988 and the Essence Award in Education in 1989. In 1990, Cole won the American Women Award, the Jessie Bernard Wise Woman Award, and was inducted into the Working Woman Hall of Fame. In 1994, she received the Jewish National Fund's highest honor, the Tree of Life Award, which is named for the efforts of the Jewish National Fund to reclaim and develop barren land in Israel. She received the Smithsonian's McGovern Behavioral Science Award in 1999.

Marva Delores Nettles Collins (1936–)
Educator

Marva Delores Nettles Collins was born in Monroeville, Alabama, on August 31, 1936. She received a bachelor's degree from Clark College in 1957 and pursued graduate studies at Chicago Teachers College and Columbia University from 1965 until 1967.

Collins' teaching career began at the Monroe County Training School in her hometown in 1958. She taught at Chicago's Delano Elementary School from 1960 until 1975. In 1975, Collins founded the Westside Preparatory School in Chicago and currently serves as its director.

Collins has conducted educational workshops throughout the United States and Europe, and has appeared on several television programs including *60 Minutes*, *Good Morning America*, and *The Phil Donahue Show*. She has served as director of the Right to Read Foundation and has been a member of the President's Commission on White House Fellowships since 1981. Collins has also been a consultant to the National Department of Children, Youth, and Family Services and a council member of the National Institute of Health.

A number of organizations have honored Collins for her distinguished career including the NAACP, the Reading Reform Foundation, the Fred Hampton Foundation, the Chicago Urban League, the United Negro

Johnnetta B. Cole in a gift shop that sells African crafts.

College Fund, Phi Delta Kappa, and the American Institute for Public Service. Among the institutions that have given her honorary degrees are Washington University, Amherst College, Dartmouth University, Chicago State University, Howard University, and Central State University.

Anna Julia Cooper (1858/59–1964)
Educator, Writer, Activist

Anna Julia Cooper was a strong proponent of justice, equality for women, and racial uplift. She was born on August 10, 1858 or 1859, in Raleigh, North Carolina, to a slave mother; her father was possibly the slave owner. Cooper attended Saint Augustine's Normal School and Collegiate Institute (now Saint Augustine's College) in Raleigh and became a teacher at the school when she graduated. She was married briefly to George A. C. Cooper, who died in 1879.

Cooper graduated from Oberlin College in Ohio in 1884, then taught modern languages at Wilberforce University in 1884–1885. The next year she returned to Saint Augustine's and taught mathematics, Latin, and German. In 1888 she received an M.A. degree in mathematics from Oberlin and moved to Washington, DC, where she taught at the Preparatory High School for Colored Youth and was school principal from 1902 to 1906. The school later became the M Street High School, then the Paul Laurence Dunbar High School. She protested the board of education's plan to dilute the school's curriculum and was removed from the principalship. She chaired the languages department at Lincoln University in Missouri from 1906 to 1910, then returned to the M Street School as Latin teacher. On March 23, 1925, at age 66, she successfully defended her doctoral dissertation at the Sorbonne and became the fourth African American woman to earn a doctorate and the first woman to do so in France.

Cooper also became established as a lecturer and writer. As early as 1890, while teaching full-time, she lectured to groups of educators and African American women's groups. In 1900 she lectured on "The Negro Problem in America" at the first Pan-African Conference, then toured Europe. As a writer, she is best

Anna Julia Cooper.

known for *A Voice from the South* (1892); the work marked her as a dedicated feminist and advocate for the African American race. Anna Cooper died on February 27, 1964, when she was 105 years old.

Fanny Coppin (1837–1913)
Educator

Fanny Coppin was born into slavery in 1837 and rose to prominence in the field of education. After her aunt purchased her freedom, Coppin went on to become the second African American woman to receive a degree from Oberlin College.

In 1865, Coppin was appointed principal of the women's department of the Institute for Colored Youth, a high school established by Quakers in 1837, and later principal of the entire school. In 1894 Coppin founded the Women's Exchange and Girls' Home. She served as president of the local Women's Mite Missionary Society and the Women's Home and Foreign Missionary Society and as a vice president of the National Association of Colored Women.

Coppin, an active member of the African Methodist Episcopal Church, served as president of the AME Home Missionary Society and accompanied her husband, Levi J. Coppin, on a missionary venture to South Africa.

Before her death at her Philadelphia home on January 21, 1913, Coppin began writing an autobiography *Reminiscences of School Life, and Hints on Teaching.*

Dolores E. Cross (1938–)
Educational Administrator

Born on August 29, 1938, in Newark, New Jersey, Dolores Evelyn Cross grew up to become the first African American female president of an Illinois state university, when she was appointed the position at Chicago State University. In 1999 she became president of Morris Brown College in Atlanta, Georgia. A veteran educator with more than 20 years of experience, Cross pursued her own education at three prestigious institutions: Seton Hall University, from which she received a B.A. in elementary education in 1963; Hofstra University, from which she earned a master's degree in 1968; and the University of Michigan, from which she garnered a doctorate in 1971. Contact with a fourth well-reputed institution came in 1970, when she began a four-year stint as an assistant professor at Northwestern University.

In 1974, Cross joined the Claremont Graduate School as director of teacher education. After three years, she moved to New York City, where she served as vice chancellor for student affairs and special programs at City University of New York, then spent most of the 1980s as president of the New York State Higher Education Service Corporation. From 1988 to 1990, she was associate provost and associate vice president for academic affairs at the University of Minnesota. Then, in 1990, she was called to the predominantly African American Chicago State University, (CSU) with a dropout rate of 81 percent among enrolled freshman students.

Faced with such a daunting statistic—particularly since nearly one-third of all African American students in Illinois' public institutions attend CSU—Cross embarked on an ambitious program to turn the situation around. She created a model for success for the students, with one of the main tenets being the maintenance of pre-college initiatives going all the way back to elementary school-level children. Meanwhile, improvements to the actual facilities included first-time plans for residence halls and the addition of a $30 million science center. The latter is of grave importance since, in 1993, CSU boasted a nearly 100 percent pass rate for nursing school graduates and the same percentage acceptance rate amongst graduate entrants to medical schools. Meanwhile, enrollment increased 58 percent during Cross's tenure, making CSU the only public university in the state to have significant growth.

Cross left Chicago State in 1997; later she was granted the GE Fund Distinguished Professorship in Leadership and Diversity at the City University of New York Graduate School and University Center. She took over the helm at Morris Brown College in 1999, serving until her resignation in June 2002.

Throughout her career, Cross has been the recipient of several awards including honorary doctorates from Marymount Manhattan (1984) and Skidmore College (1988), the NAACP's Muriel Siverberg Award (1987), and the New York State Commission of Independent Colleges and Universities' John Jay Award (1989).

Howard Dodson Jr. (1939–)
Historian, Educator, Curator

Born in Chester, Pennsylvania, on June 1, 1939, Howard Dodson Jr. was always at or near the top of his class throughout junior high and high school. Out of 89 students at Chester High School, Dodson was one of nine who graduated from college. In 1961, he received a bachelor's of science from West Chester State College and, in 1964, he received a master's degree in history and political science from Villanova University. In 1964, driven by an interest in African people transplanted in the Western Hemisphere, Dodson worked in Ecuador as a member of the U.S. Peace Corps.

In 1969, Dodson entered the doctoral program in Black History and Race Relations at the University of California at Berkeley after spending one year in Puerto Rico. During that time, Dodson studied the socio-political factors behind the Civil Rights and Black Power movements of the time. As part of his doctoral studies, Dodson earned a position at the Institute of the Black World, a research branch of the Martin Luther King Jr. Center for Nonviolent Social Change in Atlanta. Dodson served as director of the Institute from 1974 to 1979.

Dodson's doctoral dissertation "The Political Economy in South Carolina: 1780–1830" demonstrates that African American slave workers were not victims of their circumstances but rather contributors to a complex socio-economic system. In addition to his dissertation, Dodson has written widely on the subject of African American history. He served as editor-in-chief of *Black World View* magazine in 1977, and he has published books including *Thinking and Rethinking U.S. History* (1988), a book for children written with

Madelon Bedell, and *Black Photographers Bear Witness: 100 Years of Social Protest* (1989), a book published by Williams College Museum of Art on which he collaborated with Deborah Willis.

In 1984, Dodson took a post as the head of the Schomburg Center for Research in Black Culture at the New York Public Library. In 1991, due to his ministrations and fund-raising, the Schomburg Center opened an expanded complex. Dodson has served as consultant to the National Endowment for the Humanities, the African American Museums Association, the Library of Congress, the U.S. Department of Education, the Congressional Black Caucus, and the National Council of Churches. He won the Association for the Study of Afro-American Life and History Service Award in 1976 and a Governor's Award for African Americans of Distinction in 1982.

Sarah Mapps Douglass (1806–1882)
Educator

The free-born Sarah Mapps Douglass was an outspoken anti-slavery activist and accomplished educator. She attended the Ladies Institute of the Pennsylvania Medical University. In the 1820s she organized a school for African American children in Philadelphia.

Douglass was an active member of the Philadelphia Female Anti-Slavery Society, which also provided support to Douglass's school. Moreover, she served as vice chairman of the Freedman's Aid Society and was a member of the New York Anti-Slavery Women.

In 1853 Douglass was appointed head of the girls' department at the Institute of Colored Youth (forerunner of Cheney State College). She remained there until her retirement in 1877. Douglass died in Philadelphia on September 8, 1882.

Michael Eric Dyson (1958–)
Educator and Writer

Michael Eric Dyson was born into a middle-class family in Detroit, Michigan, in 1958. He was ordained as a Baptist minister and attended divinity school at Tennessee's Knoxville College, ultimately earning a bachelor's degree in 1982 from Carson-Newman College. Three years later, he accepted a graduate fellowship at Princeton University, obtaining his master's and doctorate degrees by 1993. Dyson went on to become an assistant professor at Brown University. A non-traditional scholar, he chose to target his interests to a larger audience. Dyson reviewed books and films for newspapers, contributed record reviews to *Rolling Stone,* and became a columnist for *Christian Century* and *The Nation. Reflecting Black: African-American Cultural Criticism,* Dyson's first book-length collection of essays, addressed African American pop culture icons.

In 1994 Dyson published *Making Malcolm: The Myth and Meaning of Malcolm X.* The book was written in response to a confrontation with some of Dyson's African American male students at Brown University who objected to the presence of whites in his course on the radical Muslim leader. True to his goal of reaching beyond the scholarly community, Dyson's book was deliberately marketed to a wide, youthful readership. In his third book *Between God and Gangsta Rap,* Dyson attempted to put gangsta rap in its cultural and social perspective and established himself as an authority. As a result, he was asked to testify on the genre before a congressional subcommittee, gained popularity as a lecturer, and became a sought-after guest on talk shows. He continued his writing, producing *Race Rules: Navigating the Color Line* (1996), *I May Not Get There With You: The True Martin Luther King Jr.* (2000), and *Holler if You Hear Me: Searching for Tupac Shakur* (2001). Dyson has been considered one of a group of "new intellectuals." In 1996, he headed the Institute of African American Research at the University of North Carolina in Chapel Hill and continued to address issues of race and culture in both scholarly and popular publications. He next served as a visiting professor at Columbia University before taking a position with DePauw University in Chicago. In 2002, he joined the faculty at Penn State as the Avalon Foundation Professor in the Humanities and African-American Studies.

John Hope Franklin (1915–)
Scholar

Franklin's long and distinguished career includes the publication of numerous books of history and biography, several awards and honorary degrees, and a position of great stature in the scholarly community, and as a leader of a national dialogue about race.

Franklin was born in Rentiesville, Oklahoma, in 1915. He received his bachelor's degree from Fisk University in 1935 and then began graduate work at Harvard, which awarded him a master's in 1936 and a Ph.D. in 1941. He taught history at Fisk and St. Augustine's College while working on his doctorate, later

John Hope Franklin.

moving on to North Carolina College at Durham, Howard University, Brooklyn College (where he chaired the history department), Cambridge University, the University of Chicago, and Duke University.

Among his many publications are such books as *From Slavery to Freedom, A History of Negro Americans, Militant South, Reconstruction After the Civil War, The Emancipation Proclamation, A Southern Odyssey, Race and History: Selected Essays* (1947), and *The Color Line: Legacy for the Twenty-First Century* (1946). Even into his 80s, Franklin continued to produce scholarly works on race. In 1996 he co-wrote *Black Intellectuals: Race and Responsibility in an American Life* for which he won an American Book Award in 1997. He also co-wrote *Runaway Slaves: Rebels on the Plantation, 1790–1860* in 1999.

Twice a Guggenheim Fellow, Franklin received honors from the Fellowship of Southern Writers, Encyclopedia Britannica and many other organizations, was made professor emeritus of history at Duke, and earned the Publications Prize of the American Studies Association established in his name in 1986. Franklin has received over 90 honorary degrees. In 1995, President Clinton awarded Franklin the Presidential Medal of Freedom, America's highest civilian honor. Franklin was honored with a Harold Washington Literary Award in 2000 for his impressive body of work, and that same year was awarded a Lincoln Prize for his distinguished contribution to the study of the Civil War.

In 1997 President Clinton named Franklin as chair of the White House Initiative on Race and Reconciliation, a position that enabled him to lead a year-long dialogue on race held in cities across the nation. He is currently the James B. Duke Professor Emeritus of History at Duke University.

E. Franklin Frazier (1894–1962)
Educator, Sociologist, Activist

E. Franklin Frazier left a 30-year legacy of research and writings on the African American family, youth, the church, and middle class. He combined theory with practice, and his work remains an authoritative source for later generations of scholars.

E. Franklin Frazier.

Born on September 24, 1894, in Baltimore, Maryland, Frazier attended the segregated schools of Baltimore and graduated from the Colored High School. On scholarship, he entered Howard University in Washington, DC, and used income from odd jobs to support his college career. He graduated cum laude in 1915 and a few months later began teaching mathematics at Tuskegee Institute (now Tuskegee University) in Alabama. He left two years later and taught at various African American schools and colleges. After spending some time in military service, he enrolled in Clark University in Worcester, Massachusetts, and graduated in 1920 with a master's degree in sociology.

Frazier was an American Scandinavian Foundation fellow from 1921 to 1922. In the fall of 1922, he moved to Atlanta and held a dual position as director of the School of Social Work and professor of sociology at Morehouse College. He remained productive in research and writing during his Atlanta years. He moved to Chicago and studied full-time for his doctorate at the University of Chicago. In 1929 he moved to Fisk University in Nashville, Tennessee, and in 1931 completed his Ph.D. dissertation "The Negro Family in Chicago," which was regarded as a landmark study. Frazier left Fisk in 1934 and moved to Howard University in Washington, DC, where he remained for 28 years as head of the Department of Sociology. While at Fisk and Howard, he also added to his body of research and writing. Prominent among his publications were *The Negro in the United States* (1949) and his most controversial book *Black Bourgeoise* (1955 and 1957).

Frazier later headed UNESCO's Division of Applied Sciences for two years and traveled and lectured abroad as well. He retired from Howard University as professor emeritus in 1959, but continued to teach there and at Johns Hopkins School of Advanced International Studies. Frazier died on May 17, 1962; his book *The Negro Church in America* was published posthumously that year.

Henry Louis Gates Jr. (1950–)
Literary Scholar, Educator, Critic

Henry Louis Gates Jr. was born on September 16, 1950, in Keyser, West Virginia. He was summa cum laude in 1973 at Yale University, where he earned a bachelor's in history. He went on to receive a master's in 1974 and a Ph.D. in 1979, from Clare College, Cambridge University. He served as a staff correspondent for *Time* magazine in London until 1975. There he studied with Nobel laureate playwright Wole Soyinka of Nigeria. His post-graduate studies examined African American literature as it has derived from the traditions of Africa and the Caribbean. He returned to the U.S. as a guest lecturer for Yale periodically from 1976 to 1979.

In 1979, Gates accepted an assistant professorship in the English department at Yale, where he served as director of the undergraduate Afro-American studies department until 1985. In 1981, the MacArthur Foundation awarded him $150,000 for his critical essays about African American literature. When he republished Harriet E. Wilson's *Our Nig, or, Sketches from the Life of a Free Black, in a Two-Story White House, North, Showing That Slavery's Shadows Fall Even There* in 1983, he vaulted to the top of the world of African American scholarship. He has also been a Rockefeller Foundation fellow and has enjoyed grants from the National Endowment for the Humanities. During this time, he created the PBS television series *The Image of the Black in the Western Imagination*, which aired in 1982. From 1985 to 1990, he served as a professor of English and African Studies at Cornell University and as a W. E. B. Du Bois Professor of Literature at Duke University from 1988 to 1990. He moved to Harvard in 1990, where he was named W. E. B. Du Bois Professor in the Humanities, and in 1991 became chair of the Department of African American Studies.

In 1989, Gates won the American Book Award for *The Signifying Monkey* and an Ainsfield-Wolfe Book Award the same year for *Towards a Theory of Afro-American Literary Criticism*. In 1994, Gates's memoir *Colored People* was published; the work encompasses his experiences growing up in rural West Virginia. In 1996, Gates earned prestige for his African American studies department by attracting some of the country's leading scholars to Harvard. In addition, Gates and Kwame Appiah edited *Encarta Africana*, a multimedia encyclopedia on compact disc released in January 1999.

Other works that Gates has contributed to or edited include: (Contributor) *Facing History: The Black Image in American Art, 1710–1940* (1990); (Introduction) *Josephine Baker and La Revue Negre: Paul Colin's Lithographs of Le Tumulte Noir in Paris, 1927* (1998); (Co-editor) *Pioneers of the Black Atlantic: Five Slave Narratives from the Enlightenment, 1772–1815* (1998); (Co-editor) *Black Imagination and the Middle Passage* (1999); (Co-editor) *The Civitas Anthology of African American Slave Narratives* (1999); (Contributor) *Wonders of the African World* (1999); (Editor) *The Bondswoman's Narrative by Hannah Crafts, a Fugitive Slave, Recently Escaped from North Carolina* (2002).

William L. Hansberry (1894–1965)
Historian, Educator

William Leo Hansberry was born on February 25, 1894, in Gloster, Mississippi. He earned a bachelor's in anthropology in 1921. Determined to eliminate American ethnocentrism regarding Africa, he issued a manifesto to African American schools and colleges titled "Announcing an Effort to Promote the Study and Facilitate the Teaching of the Fundamentals of Negro Life and History." The flier brought Hansberry three job offers from schools, and he accepted a post at Howard University in Washington, DC. Beginning in 1922, he began designing courses on African and African American history.

Despite Hansberry's ability to prove the material taught in his courses, the board of Howard University pulled his financial backing after spurious accusations by colleagues but agreed to keep the African studies program in place. Still, the scuffle cost him much in funds and promotions. Nevertheless, in 1932, Hansberry returned to Harvard to complete his master's in anthropology and history, continuing his studies in the mid-1930s at the University of Chicago's Oriental Institute. His studies won him a Rockefeller Foundation grant that allowed him to study at Oxford University in England from 1937 to 1938, when Howard University finally recognized his achievements with an assistant professorship. But entrenched racial prejudice kept Hansberry from earning more grants and fellowships to continue his work.

Howard University made little effort to compensate him and after over 20 years of service, he remained only an associate professor in 1945. But then the university climate changed and Hansberry was appointed advisor to African students in 1946; in 1950, he was made Emergency Aid to the African Students' Committee at Howard University in addition to his teaching load. Due to increased interest in African studies, Hansberry won a Fulbright scholarship to lecture at Cairo University and to study in Egypt, Ethiopia, and the Sudan in 1953. He also visited Kenya, Uganda, and Zimbabwe. Hansberry died in Chicago on November 3, 1965.

bell hooks (1952–)
Social Activist, Educator, Writer

Feminist educator bell hooks has done her most important work as a teacher in programs that allow a critique of racism that was absent during her own undergraduate years. She contributes essays to a variety of scholarly journals and also publishes fiction and poetry. hooks has gained notoriety as a writer of critical essays on systems of domination, making herself a prominent name in feminist debate. Her titles include: *Talking Back: Thinking Feminist, Thinking Black* (1989); *Black Looks: Race and Representation* (1992); *Killing Rage: Ending Racism* (1995); *Black Is a Woman's Color* (1996); and *Bone Black: Memories of Girlhood* (1996).

Born Gloria Jean Watkins in 1952, hooks grew up with five siblings in Hopkinsville, a small town in rural Kentucky. Despite her family's poverty and hardship, hooks reveled in lessons of diligence and community. She attended segregated public schools, where her role models were single African American female teachers. Verbally and through poetry, hooks began defiantly resisting the sexism she perceived within her neighborhood. Rejecting her expected role as an obedient Southern girl, the writer eventually adopted a pseudonym to represent a new sense of self—a woman who spoke her mind and was not afraid to talk back.

When she won a scholarship to Stanford University, hooks sought out intellectual and political affirmation from the campus feminist movement. Disillusioned and alienated by the absence of material by or discussion about African American women, hooks began criticizing the persistent racism within feminism. Having gained her bachelor's degree in 1973, hooks faced obstacles at the University of Wisconsin and the University of California at Santa Cruz, where male faculty members were determined to prevent her from becoming a university professor. In 1981, hooks published *Ain't I a Woman: Black Women and Feminism*, which was sharply criticized for its defiance of academic convention. Nonetheless, the work became central to discussions of racism and sexism. hooks persisted with her studies, earned a Ph.D. in 1983, and went on to teach African American and women's studies at Yale University, Oberlin College, and City College of New York.

John Hope (1868–1936)
Educator, Activist

The progress made in higher education for African American students has been strongly helped by the efforts of John Hope. His life was committed to improving the school system of his time to afford more minority access. Hope was one of the most influential leaders of his time in the field of higher education.

In 1894, Hope graduated from Brown University in Worcester, Massachusetts, and was elected class orator for the commencement service. In later years, Hope would receive an honorary master of arts and law degree from Brown, along with admittance into the Phi Beta Kappa Society. Upon graduating, Hope accepted a teaching job at Roger Williams University in Nashville, Tennessee. Four years later he accepted a teaching position at Atlanta Baptist College, located in Georgia, the state of his birth. At the college, Hope began a longtime friendship with the educator W. E. B. Du Bois. They both attended the 1895 Macon Convention which turned into the Georgia Equal Rights Convention.

In 1906, John Hope became acting president of Atlanta Baptist College, and the next year he was named president. He was the first African American to be appointed president at a Baptist school. As president, Hope expanded the college with funds donated by John T. Rockefeller and Andrew Carnegie. In 1913, the school was renamed Morehouse College and was very progressive in its stressing of the dignity of its African American students. During the 1920s, the college continued to expand as Hope developed the Atlanta School of Social Work.

In 1929, Hope fulfilled his lifelong ambition to establish a formal relationship among Atlanta's African American schools by having the Atlanta University Affiliation signed by the presidents of Atlanta University, Spelman, and Morehouse College. Hope was appointed president of Atlanta University while continuing as president of Morehouse College. Hope received the Harmon Award in 1930 for distinguished achievement in education. He died in Atlanta on February 20, 1936.

Frederick Humphries (1935–)
College and University President, Educator

Frederick Humphries was born in Apalachicola, Florida, on December 26, 1935. He graduated magna cum laude with a bachelor's degree in chemistry from Florida A&M University in 1957. Following two years as a second lieutenant in the U.S. Army Security Agency, Humphries spent the next five years working on his Ph.D. at the University of Pittsburgh while earning a living as an academic tutor. He received his doctorate in 1964, and took an associate professorship at his alma mater.

In 1967, Humphries became a full professor at Florida A&M after spending two years at the University of Minnesota. Along with the professorship, Humphries also became a program director of the Thirteen-Colleges Curriculum Program, which initially involved 13 historically African American colleges. As director, Humphries advocated new methods of looking at the particular problems facing African American students with the intent of improving students' overall educational progress. Humphries and his colleagues instituted successful experimental curriculum changes that made classrooms "student-centered academic environment(s)." A scientist himself, Humphries also strived to increase African American students' accessibility in math and science.

Tennessee State University hired Humphries as its president in 1974. He served in the post until 1985, when he returned, once again, to his alma mater—this time as its president. Under Humphries, Florida A&M's status as an institute of higher learning was greatly elevated. In 1992, 1995, and 1997, the school attracted more National Achievement Scholars, the nation's top African American students, than any other institution. At the same time, Florida A&M's enrollment more than doubled under the leadership of Humphries; innovative programs that increased the number of African American students going on to pursue graduate studies were implemented. Humphries retired on June 30, 2001.

Charles S. Johnson (1893–1956)
Scholar

Charles Spurgeon Johnson was born in Bristol, Virginia, in 1893. He earned a B.A. from Virginia Union University and worked on a Ph.D. at the University of Chicago.

Johnson occupied a number of diverse positions, from editor to administrator. He served as the assistant executive secretary of the Chicago Commission on Race Relations and as research director of the National Urban League, where he founded the organization's journal *Opportunity.*

In 1928 Johnson was made chairman of Fisk University's Department of Social Sciences. While at Fisk he established the Fisk Institute of Race Relations. In 1933 he was appointed director of Swarthmore College's Institute of Race Relations. In 1946 Johnson was appointed president of Fisk University—the first African American to hold the position.

Johnson wrote several books before his death on October 27, 1956, including *The Negro in American Civilization* (1930), *The Economic Status of the Negro*

Charles Spurgeon Johnson.

(1933), *The Negro College Graduate* (1936), and *Educational and Cultural Crisis* (1951).

Mordecai W. Johnson (1890–1976)
Former College President, Minister

As president of Howard University in Washington, DC, for 34 years, Mordecai W. Johnson became a highly respected minister, educator, and orator of international note. He built the university into a highly visible academic institution that became known as the "Capstone of Negro Education."

Johnson was the son of former slaves. He was born in Paris, Tennessee, on December 12, 1890, and attended Roger Williams University in Nashville and the Howe Institute in Memphis, both of which are now defunct. He transferred to Atlanta Baptist College, now known as Morehouse College, where he completed the secondary and undergraduate programs. He taught at the college for a year, then continued his studies at the University of Chicago where he received a second

Mordecai W. Johnson (fourth from the left).

undergraduate degree. Johnson earned his bachelor of divinity degree from Rochester Theological Seminary in Rochester, New York.

He was pastor of the First Baptist Church in Charleston, West Virginia, for nine years. In 1912 he took a leave of absence to study at Harvard University Divinity School graduating in June of 1922. In 1926, when he was 36-years old, Johnson was elected 11th president and the first African American president of Howard University. Johnson first concentrated on providing financial stability for the school. Starting with the medical school, he received solid support from the Julius Rosenwald Fund and the General Education Board. Then he moved to strengthen the law school and appointed Charles Hamilton Houston as dean of the school; he approached the country's top law schools for recommendations for Howard's law school faculty. One of its most notable

graduates was Thurgood Marshall. The law school also engaged in research and analysis involving important civil rights issues that went before the court. Johnson was awarded the Spingarn Medal in 1928, the NAACP's highest award.

During the first half of his tenure, Johnson faced sharp criticism because he lacked a terminal academic degree and because some faculty and staff opposed his administrative style. He survived the controversy, maintained the support of the board of trustees, and continued fruitful contacts with foundations for financial support. He attracted outstanding scholars to the Howard faculty including philosopher Alain Locke, cell biologist Ernest E. Just, chemist Percy Julian, political scientist Ralph Bunche, historian Rayford Logan, and Charles Drew, who became known for his work with blood plasma. Johnson also erected new buildings and founded several honor societies on campus including a chapter of Phi Beta Kappa.

Johnson traveled widely; his lectures, given without notes, often lasted 45 minutes and held audiences spellbound. His themes often focused on racism, segregation, and discrimination. He retired from the presidency of Howard in 1960 and died on September 10, 1976, when he was 86 years old.

Laurence Clifton Jones (1884–1975)
School Founder, School Administrator

Laurence Clifton Jones founded a school in the deep woods of Mississippi's Black Belt and made it possible for thousands of African American youths to receive elementary and high school education. He uplifted the community as well by helping uneducated men and women to enhance their lives. He became known as "The Little Professor of Piney Woods."

Jones was born on November 21, 1884, in St. Joseph, Missouri, and worked his way to a degree from Iowa State University. Booker T. Washington inspired Jones first through his writings and later when he offered

Laurence Clifton Jones.

Jones a position at his school, Tuskegee Institute (now Tuskegee University). Jones declined and, instead, in 1910 founded what he called a "country life school" in Piney Woods, Mississippi. Officially, the school was established on May 17, 1913. He garnered the moral support of the community, and when the students lacked money for school expenses, he accepted payments in produce.

On June 29, 1912, Jones married Grace M. Allen, whom he had met while he was in college. Together the Joneses enabled the school to grow and engaged in fund-raising activities. Grace taught useful skills to community residents and also became a member of the school's faculty. With the help of the Cotton Blossom Singers—the school's ambassadors of music—the Joneses traveled the United States performing fundraising concerts. Laurence Jones organized the International Sweethearts of Rhythms in the late 1930s and engaged that group in fundraising concerts until the group, which became known worldwide, severed its relationship with the school in April of 1941.

The school then expanded, adding a department for blind children. Jones later became known through the television program *This is Your Life* aired in December of 1954. An appeal for support made during the program resulted in substantial funding for Piney Woods. Jones retired from the presidency in 1974, but continued to travel on official school business until he died in 1975.

E. J. Josey (1924–)
Librarian, Activist, Author

Elonnie Junius Josey was born in Norfolk, Virginia on January 20, 1924. He studied music and played the church organ until 1943, when he was drafted into the U.S. Army, serving for three years. Josey, known simply as E. J., went on to complete his education at Howard University's School of Music, later moving on to Columbia University's master's program in history and the State University of New York's Library School. In 1953, Josey began his career in libraries and rapidly became a leader in confronting segregation within them.

After his initial struggle against the Georgia Library Association when they denied him membership in 1960, Josey persevered in a diverse public and academic library career and gained a reputation as a wise, impassioned speaker on social issues. His publication *The Black Librarian in America* was a pioneering look into conditions for African Americans within librarianship. Its 1994 sequel *The Black Librarian in America Revisited* was an appraisal of changes that had been made in intervening years. Josey helped organize the Black

Caucus of the American Library Association, which combated institutional racism and widespread discrimination both within the profession and in conjunction with library services.

As president of the American Library Association from 1984 to 1985, Josey fostered awareness of the value of libraries as an integral part of the nation's infrastructure. Fighting against severe budget cuts imposed by the Reagan administration, Josey rallied library advocates in Washington, DC, to march with him in protest. Josey has, in addition to his professional achievements, led community advocacy for civil and human rights as a leading member of the NAACP, was a contributor to intellectual development in emerging African countries, and was awarded four honorary doctorates. From the late 1980s until his retirement in 1995, Josey joined the faculty of the School of Library and Information Science at the University of Pittsburgh and devoted himself to achieving a racial balance in library education. For his long service to promoting reading and diverse library selections, Josey was presented with an honorary doctorate of humane letters from Clarion University of Pennsylvania in 2001.

Maulana Karenga (1941–)
Activist-scholar, Educator, Ethicist

Dr. Maulana Karenga is professor and chair of the Department of Black Studies at California State University, Long Beach, where he also chairs the President's Task Force on Multicultural Education and Campus Diversity. He holds Ph.D. degrees in political science from United States International University and in social ethics with a focus on the classical African ethics of ancient Egypt from the University of Southern California. He has also been awarded an honorary doctorate from the University of Durban-Westville, South Africa for his "intellectual and practical work on behalf of African people."

Karenga came to prominence in the 1960s as founder of The Organization Us, a cultural and social change group whose name he explains, "simply means us Black people and stresses the communitarian focus of the organization and its philosophy *Kawaida*, which is an ongoing synthesis of the best of African thought and practice in constant exchange with the world." Karenga and Us have greatly influenced the development of the discipline of black studies, the black arts and black student movements, Afrocentricity, and ancient Egyptian studies. They have also advanced the independent school and rites of passage movements through the *Nguzo Saba* (The Seven Principles of Kawaida).

Moreover, Karenga and Us played important roles in the founding of the initial Black Power conferences in the 1960s and the National Black United Front in the 1980s. More recently they were in the forefront of organizing the National African American Leadership Summit and the Million Man March/Day of Absence. Karenga was a member of the executive council for the landmark 1995 gathering in Washington and authored its mission statement, co-editing the subsequent volume *The Million Man March/Day of Absence: A Commemorative Anthology*. Having celebrated its 33rd anniversary in 1998, The Organization Us continues its declared commitment to "[s]truggle, service and institution-building."

An internationally recognized activist-scholar, Karenga has published numerous scholarly articles and books, among them the widely used *Introduction to Black Studies*; his retranslation and commentary on ancient Egyptian texts; *Selections from the Husia: Sacred Wisdom of Ancient Egypt*; and the influential *Kwanzaa: A Celebration of Family, Community and Culture*. In fact, he created the Kwanzaa celebration now observed throughout the world African community. He has lectured throughout the United States and the world and earned numerous scholarship, leadership, and community service awards.

Elizabeth Duncan Koontz (1919–1989)
Educator, Organizational Official

As teacher, assistant state school superintendent, leader in state and national teachers' associations, and the first African American president of the National Education Association (NEA), Elizabeth Duncan Koontz served the education needs of her constituents. Born on June 3, 1919, in Salisbury, North Carolina, she was the youngest of seven children. She graduated from Livingstone College with honors in 1938 and received a master's degree from Atlanta University in 1941. Beyond this, she studied at the graduate level in several colleges and universities.

Koontz moved from being an elementary school teacher in Dunn, North Carolina, to Aggrey Memorial School in Landis, then to Fourteenth Street School in Winston-Salem, and finally taught special education classes at Price High School in Salisbury. Her participation in the NEA began in 1952, when she was a member of the North Carolina Negro Teachers Association. That group was later admitted to the state chapter of the NEA. She served two terms as secretary, one as vice president, and one as president-elect of the NEA's Department of Classroom Teachers. In 1965, she became the department's first African American president. On July 6, 1968, Koontz was installed as the first

African American president of the NEA. During her tenure, she brought a shift in the association from traditionally conservative to liberal. She supported agitation and, if necessary, strikes to bring about necessary change. She endorsed militant teachers and strongly supported teacher commitment and responsibility.

In January of 1969, President Richard Nixon appointed Koontz as director of the U.S. Department of Labor, Women's Bureau, making her the first African American director. Later she became deputy assistant secretary for Labor Employment Standards. In the latter capacity, she became the U.S. delegate to the United Nation's Commission on the Status of Women. She was active in numerous civic, religious, and educational organizations, and received approximately three dozen honorary degrees from various colleges and universities. Koontz held other positions until she retired in April of 1982. She suffered a heart attack at home in Salisbury and died on January 6, 1989.

Lucy C. Laney (1854–1933)
Educator, School Founder

Lucy Craft Laney spent her life assuring African Americans, particularly women, that they would be educated and had the freedom to educate others. She was born to former slaves on April 11, 1854, in Macon, Georgia. At age 15, Laney entered Atlanta University and graduated in 1873 in the school's first class. She then did graduate study at the University of Chicago during the summer months.

Although virtually penniless, in 1883 Laney opened a school for Augusta, Georgia's African American youth, held in Christ Presbyterian Church. The school was chartered in 1886 under Georgia law as a normal and industrial school. Haines Normal and Industrial Institute established the city's first kindergarten and nurse education department in the early 1890s. Later the nurse education department became the school of nursing at Augusta's University Hospital. By the 1930s, Haines dropped elementary education and offered a four-year high school program and some college-level courses. The Presbyterian Board of Missions, the schools' primary source of funds, withdrew support during the Great Depression. Haines school declined, then closed its doors in 1949. Later, a new public structure, the Lucy C. Laney High School, was built on the site. Laney died on October 23, 1933, in Augusta, and later was recognized as a leading African American educator in the South.

Sara Lawrence-Lightfoot (1944–)
Educator, Sociologist, Writer

Sara Lawrence-Lightfoot's sociological writing has been an attempt to create a clearer picture of the reality of African Americans lives. She has felt much of what has been previously written is a distorted view of who African Americans really are.

Lawrence-Lightfoot's 1994 book *I've Known Rivers: Lives of Loss and Liberation* details life in the African American middle class through interviews with six African American professionals. It was chosen as a Book-of-the-Month Club main choice. In 1978, her book *Worlds Apart* promoted cooperation between parents and teachers for the education of children. Her third book *The Good High School: Portraits of Character and Culture* chronicles the positive methods of six schools in the United States, offering the book as a catalyst for institutional change. She co-wrote a sequel to *The Good High School* in 1997 under the title *The Art and Science of Portraiture*. She also wrote *Respect: An Exploration* in 1999.

Lawrence-Lightfoot departed from her sociological writings to write a personal account of her mother's life in her 1988 book *Balm in Gilead: Journey of a Healer*. She received a MacArthur Award to fund the writing of the book. Along with writing her books, teaching at Harvard University as a professor of education, and conducting her research, Lawrence-Lightfoot gives lectures and serves on numerous committees and national boards, among them the National Academy of Education, the *Boston Globe*, and the John D. and Catherine T. MacArthur Foundation, the last of which she became chair in 2002.

David Levering Lewis (1936–)
Educator, Writer

David Levering Lewis was born May 25, 1936, in Little Rock, Arkansas. He earned a bachelor's in history from Fisk University in 1956 and continued his studies at Columbia University, where he earned a master's degree in 1958. He received his Ph.D. from the London School of Economics and Political Science in 1962. He published his first paper as an undergraduate, titled "History of the Negro Upper Class in Atlanta, Georgia 1890–1958."

Lewis eventually began studying African American history after years as a scholar of French history, teaching at the University of Ghana, Notre Dame University, and Howard University. In 1971, he published a scholarly biography of Martin Luther King Jr., titled *Martin Luther King: A Critical Biography*. Lewis followed this work with one on anti-Semitism called *Prisoners of Honor: The Dreyfus Affair* in 1973 at which time he accepted a teaching post at Federal City College in Washington, DC. In 1974, he became a full professor of history at the University of the District of Columbia.

Throughout the 1970s, he studied the Harlem Renaissance of the 1920s and 1930s, writing a work of definitive scholarship on the subject, published in 1981, as *When Harlem Was in Vogue: The Politics of the Arts in the Twenties and Thirties*. Next, Lewis tackled W. E. B. Du Bois, the great scholar and writer, in his biography *W. E. B. Du Bois: Biography of a Race, 1868–1919*, which won a Pulitzer Prize for biography in 1994 and a National Book Award the same year. In 1999 he accepted a MacArthur Foundation "genius grant" to continue his research, and published *W. E. B. Du Bois: The Fight for Equality and the American Century, 1919–1963* in 2000. By the time his Du Bois biography was published in 1993, Lewis had taken a position as the chair of the history department of Rutgers University, to which he commuted by train from his home on Capitol Hill in Washington, D.C. Lewis contributes regularly to scholarly journals and the *Washington Post*.

Alain Locke (1886–1954)
Scholar

Born on September 3, 1886, in Philadelphia, Locke graduated Phi Beta Kappa with a B.A. degree from Harvard University in 1907. He was then awarded a Rhodes scholarship for two years of study at Oxford University in England and did further graduate study at the University of Berlin (1910–1911). Upon returning to the United States, Locke took an assistant professorship in English and philosophy at Howard University in Washington, DC. He received his Ph.D. from Harvard in 1918 and the same year was made chairman of the philosophy department at Howard where he stayed until his retirement in 1953.

In 1934 Locke founded the Associates in Negro Folk Education. In 1942 he was named to the Honor Roll of Race Relations. A prolific author, Locke's first book was entitled *Race Contacts and Inter-Racial Relations* (1916). His best known works include *The New Negro:*

Alain Locke.

An Interpretation (1925), a book that introduced America to the Harlem Renaissance, and *The Negro in Art: A Pictorial Record of the Negro Artist and of the Negro Theme in Art* (1940). Locke died in New York City on June 9, 1954.

Benjamin E. Mays (1894–1984)
Former Morehouse College President

In addition to occupying the president's office at Morehouse, Benjamin Mays wrote, taught mathematics, worked for the Office of Education, served as chairman of the Atlanta Board of Education, preached in a Baptist church, acted as an advisor to the Southern Christian Leadership Council, and was a church historian.

Born in Epworth, South Carolina, in 1894, Mays attended Bates College and later received his master's and Ph.D. from the University of Chicago. He served as a pastor at Georgia's Shiloh Baptist Church from 1921 to 1924, and later taught at Morehouse College and

South Carolina's State College at Orangeburg. After a stint at the Tampa Urban League, he worked for the YMCA as national student secretary and then directed a study of African American churches for the Institute of Social and Religious Research. From 1934 to 1940, he acted as dean of Howard University's School of Religion, before taking up the presidency of Morehouse from 1940 to 1967. He served in several other distinguished posts including the Atlanta Board of Education chairmanship and positions at HEW and the Ford Foundation. Awards earned by Mays include 43 honorary degrees, the Dorie Miller Medal of Honor, and the 1971 Outstanding Older Citizen Award. He died at his Atlanta home on March 21, 1984.

Jesse Edward Moorland (1863–1940)
Archivist, Clergyman

Jesse Moorland was born on September 10, 1863, in Coldwater, Ohio. Following the untimely death of his parents, Moorland was reared by his grandparents. His early education consisted of sporadic attendance at a small rural schoolhouse and being read to by his grandfather. Moorland eventually attended Normal University in Ada, Ohio, married, and taught school in Urbana, Ohio. He went on to attend Howard University in Washington and graduated with a degree in theology in 1891.

Moorland was ordained a congregational minister and, between 1891 and 1896, he served at churches in South Boston, Virginia, Nashville, and Cleveland. In 1891 he also became active in the YMCA, an association he would maintain for much of his life.

In 1909 Moorland's well-known essay "Demand and the Supply of Increased Efficiency in the Negro Ministry" was published by the American Negro Academy. In it, Moorland called for a more pragmatic ministry, both in terms of the education of its members and its approach to social issues.

By 1910 Moorland had become quite active in the YMCA and was appointed secretary of the Colored Men's Department. In this position, Moorland raised millions of dollars for the YMCA's construction and building fund.

Having reached the mandatory retirement age in 1923, Moorland resigned from the YMCA and began devoting his time and considerable energy to other pursuits. Moorland was active with the Association for the Study of Negro Life and History, the National

Health Circle for Colored People, and the Frederick Douglass Home Association.

From 1907 and onward, Moorland served as a trustee of Howard University. In 1914 he donated his private library of African American history to the university. Out of this gift grew the Moorland Foundation. The collection was renamed the Moorland-Spingarn Collection and later renamed the Moorland-Spingarn Research Center. This collection of documents on African American history and culture was the first African American research collection at a major American university. Moorland died in New York on April 30, 1940.

Rod Paige (1935–)
Secretary of Education

Rod Paige was born on June 17, 1935 in Brookhaven, Mississippi. He attended Lawrence County Training School, where he was a both a solid student and a standout football player. His athletic skills earned him a scholarship to Jackson State University, where Paige earned a bachelor of science degree in 1955, graduating with honors. Following graduation, Paige became a head football coach, first at Utica Junior College, and then at Jackson State from 1962–1969. During this period, he also earned a master of science degree in 1964 and a doctorate in physical education in 1969, both from Indiana University.

In 1971, Paige took the coaching job at Texas Southern University. With it came the position of Athletic Director and a faculty appointment. By 1984, he had risen to the post of dean of the school of education. He served in that capacity through 1990. Paige was elected to the Houston Independent School District Board of Education in 1989. He was named district superintendent in 1994. During his tenure, Paige helped to turn around the state's largest school district by giving more responsibility to effective principals, addressing the issue of unqualified teachers, and making Houston's schools a safe place for students and faculty. Within five years, the district's test scores had risen substantially, and the dropout and violent crime rates had fallen.

Paige was honored in 1999 by the Council of Great City Schools, who named him one of the top two educators in the nation. The next year he was named as the first African-American education secretary by President George W. Bush. In his first two years in the post, Paige helped to create and promote the administration's vision for education reform, which focused on the issues of national assessment testing and school vouchers.

Frederick Douglass Patterson. *See* **National Organizations chapter.**

Benjamin F. Payton (1932–)
Former college president

Born in Orangeburg, South Carolina, in 1932, Benjamin Franklin Payton took a bachelor's degree with honors from South Carolina State College in 1955. He earned a B.D. from Howard University in 1958, a master's degree from Columbia University in 1960, and a Ph.D. from Yale University in 1963. He took a position as assistant professor at Howard University before working for the National Council of Churches as the Commission on Religion and Race's executive director of social justice—a position which he retained even as he took over the presidency of Benedict College in 1967. He left Benedict in 1972 for a position at the Ford Foundation, where he remained until he became the president of Tuskegee University in 1981. Payton has sought to increase the visibility of the university during his tenure, and in 1999 he was instrumental in establishing the nation's first African-American bioethics center on the campus.

Payton holds honorary degrees from Eastern Michigan University, Morris Brown, Benedict, and Morgan State. A recipient of the Napoleon Hill Foundation Gold Medal Award and the Benjamin E. Mays Award, he served as educational advisor to Vice President George Bush on Bush's seven-nation tour of Africa in 1982. Payton has also served as a member of several organizations including the National Association for Equal Opportunity in Higher Education, the Alabama Industrial Relations Council, the National Association of Independent Colleges and Universities, and the Executive Board of the National Consortium for Educational Access.

Arthur A. Schomburg (1874–1938)
Archivist, American Negro Academy President

Born in Puerto Rico in 1874, Arturo Schomburg led a richly varied public life. He worked as a law clerk and was a businessman, journalist, editor, lecturer, New York Public Library curator, and teacher of Spanish.

In 1911 Schomburg co-founded the Negro Society for Historical Research. He was also a lecturer for the United Negro Improvement Association. Schomburg was a member of the New York Puerto Rico Revolutionary Party and served as secretary of the Cuban Revolutionary Party. In 1922 he headed the American Negro Academy, an organization founded by Alexander Crummell in 1879 to promote African American art, literature, and science.

Schomburg, who died on June 10, 1938, collected thousands of works on African American culture over his lifetime. In 1926 Schomburg's personal collection was purchased by the Carnegie Corporation and given to the New York Public Library. In 1973 the collection became known as the Schomburg Collection of Negro Literature and History; the name was later changed to the Schomburg Center for Research in Black Culture.

Shelby Steele (1946–)
Scholar

Steele was born January 1, 1946, in Chicago but grew up in Phoenix, Illinois, a blue-collar suburb of Chicago. He attended high school in Harvey, Illinois, where he was student council president his senior year prior to graduating in 1964. Steele then attended Coe College in Cedar Rapids, Iowa, where he was active in SCOPE—an organization associated with Martin Luther King Jr.'s Southern Christian Leadership Conference. He graduated in 1968 and, in 1971, received an M.S. in sociology from Southern Illinois University. He went on to receive a Ph.D. in English literature from the University of Utah in 1974. While at Southern Illinois University, he taught African American literature to impoverished children in East St. Louis. Steele is currently a professor of English literature at San Jose State University.

In 1990 Steele published *The Content of Our Character: A New Vision of Race in America*, which won the National Book Critics Circle Award. In this controversial book, Steele argued that African-American self-doubt and its exploitation by the white and black liberal establishment is as great a cause of problems for African Americans as more traditional forms of racism. He published *A Dream Deferred: The Second Betrayal of Black Freedom in America* in 1998. Steele has also written articles on this theme for such respected publications as *Harper's*, *New Republic*, *American Scholar*, and *Commentary*.

Because of his beliefs, Steele has been identified as part of an emerging African American neo-conservative movement, but in an interview with *Time* magazine (August 12, 1991), he categorized himself as a classical liberal focusing on the freedom and sacredness of the individual.

H. Patrick Swygert (1943–)
University President, Lawyer

Since taking office as the 15th president of Howard University in Washington, DC, H. Patrick Swygert has worked to craft a strategy to move the institution into the twenty-first century. He aims to place the university on a firmer financial footing and sees Howard's role as one of shaping and implementing an academic and research agenda for African Americans.

Born on March 11, 1943, in Philadelphia, Swygert graduated from Howard University in 1965 with an A.B. degree and received his J.D. from the Howard University School of Law in 1968. After graduation, Swygert was law clerk to Chief Justice William H. Hastie of the U.S. Court of Appeals, Third Circuit in Philadelphia, and later served as administrative assistant to Congressman Charles B. Rangel. He held various positions at Temple University, first as vice president for university administration, then special counsel to the president, and later acting dean of the law school. He was also a full professor on the law school faculty. After serving as visiting professor at the University of Ghana and Tel Aviv University, he was a visiting lecturer in Cairo, Egypt; Rome, Italy; and Athens, Greece.

Swygert has also held several positions with the U.S. government including general counsel to the U.S. Service Commission. He was president of the State University of New York at Albany for five years, until he became president of Howard University on August 1, 1995. He is committed to sustaining Howard's stature among higher education institutions that serve African Americans.

Ivan Van Sertima (1935–)
Scholar

Born in British Guyana in 1935, anthropologist, linguist, and literary critic Ivan Van Sertima is currently professor of African studies at Rutgers University.

In 1977 Van Sertima published *They Came Before Columbus: The African Presence in Ancient America.* Drawing from various disciplines, Van Sertima presents evidence of pre-Columbian contact with the New World by Africans. The book earned him the Clarence

L. Holte Prize in 1981, although it also drew criticism from anthropologists who argued that he ignored critical evidence that would disprove his theory.

In 1979 Van Sertima founded *The Journal of African Civilizations*, which presents a revisionist approach to world history. He is also the author of *Caribbean Writers*, a collection of essays. One of his more recent works is *Early America Revisited*, published in 1998.

Cornel West. *See* Religion chapter.

Clifton R. Wharton Jr. (1926–)
Former University President and Deputy Secretary of State

Clifton R. Wharton, born on September 13, 1926, was the first African American to head the largest university system in the United States—the State University of New York. He was also president of Michigan State University and served as chairman and CEO of the Teachers Insurance and Annuity Association and College Retirement Equities Fund. He also served briefly as President Clinton's deputy secretary of state.

A native Bostonian, Wharton took a bachelor's degree cum laude from Harvard in 1947. He received a master's at Johns Hopkins the following year, as the first African American admitted into the university's School for Advanced International Studies. In 1956 he took a second M.A. from the University of Chicago, which awarded him a Ph.D. in 1958. Between master's degrees he worked as a research associate for the University of Chicago. He then proceeded to the Agricultural Development Council, Inc., where he worked for 12 years. He also held a post as visiting professor at the University of Malaya and served as director and eventually vice president of the American Universities Research Program. Wharton took over the presidency of Michigan State in 1970 and stayed there for eight years; he moved on to the SUNY system from 1978 to 1987. He then became chief executive of the Teachers Insurance and Annuity Association (TIAA), which is the largest pension fund in the world, and later became the first African American to chair the Rockefeller Foundation. Wharton achieved yet another first in 1993 when President Clinton selected him as his deputy secretary of state, the first African American to achieve that post. He was only at the job eight months, however, before he resigned in frustration over political struggles within the administration. He then returned to TIAA as an overseer, and also became a director of the New York Stock Exchange and Harcourt General. As of

2000 he was working as an economist and vice president of the Agricultural Development Council.

Wharton won the President's Award on World Hunger in 1983 and has earned honorary degrees from more than 45 colleges and universities.

Carter G. Woodson (1875–1950)
Association for the Study of Afro-American Life and History Cofounder, Historian, Writer, Publisher, Black History Month Founder

Often called "The Father of Black History," Carter Godwin Woodson was a tireless advocate of African American history in school curriculum, the promotion of African American achievements through the work of the Association for the Study of Negro Life and History that he co-founded, and the promotion of the African American heritage through Negro History Week (now Black History Month).

Woodson was born to former slaves in 1875, in New Canton, Virginia. In 1898, he studied at Berea College in Kentucky, then taught school in Fayette County, West Virginia. In 1900, he was appointed principal of his alma

Carter G. Woodson.

mater, Douglass High School, then returned to Berea until the school, racially integrated at first, was forced to close its doors to African American students because of the state's segregation laws. Woodson then studied at the University of Chicago and returned to Berea after it readmitted African Americans.

Woodson then taught school and later served as school supervisor in the Philippines. He spent a semester at the Sorbonne, where he improved his French-speaking skills. He returned to the University of Chicago, where he received a B.A. in 1907 and M.A. degrees in history, romance languages, and literature in 1908. Woodson began studying for his doctorate at Harvard University in 1908 and later taught at several schools in the District of Columbia; his longest tenure was at the M Street High School where he remained from 1911 to 1917. He completed his dissertation and received his Ph.D. from Harvard in 1912, becoming the second African American man to receive such a degree from that institution (the first was W. E. B. Du Bois).

Deeply devoted to the study and promotion of African American history and to the preservation of the culture of his race, Woodson joined several other men in founding the Association for the Study of African-American Life and History in 1912 (ASALH). Woodson's obsession with the history of African Americans remained foremost throughout his life's work. In 1916, the association began publishing the widely recognized *Journal of Negro History*.

Woodson held several positions in academia in the District of Columbia: principal of Armstrong Manual Training School (1918–1919); faculty member, dean, and head of the graduate faculty at Howard University (1919–1920); and dean at West Virginia Collegiate Institute (1920–1922). After that, he concentrated on the work of the ASALH. In 1921, he organized Associated Publishers, the publishing arm of ASALH. Among his own works issued by the press were *The History of the Negro Church* (1921) and *The Mis-Education of the Negro* (1933).

Woodson remained concerned that young people, teachers, laymen, and others should know about African American history. As a partial solution, beginning February 1926, he promoted a special commemoration, or Negro History Week, to incorporate the birthdays of Booker T. Washington, Abraham Lincoln, and Frederick Douglass. The celebration had national appeal and, later, in 1976, Negro History Week became Black History Month. To further promote African American history among the schools, Woodson founded the Negro History Bulletin in 1937. On April 3, 1950, Woodson died in Washington, DC. In 1976, ASALH changed its name to the Association for the Study of Afro-American Life and History.

♦ HISTORICALLY AND PREDOMINANTLY AFRICAN AMERICAN COLLEGES AND UNIVERSITIES

Alabama A&M University
PO Box 908
Normal, AL 35762
(800) 553–0816
<www.aamu.edu>
Established 1875.

Alabama State University
915 South Jackson Street
Montgomery, AL 36104
(800) 253–5037
<www.alasu.edu>
Established 1867.

Albany State University
504 College Dr.
Albany, GA 31705
(800) 822–7267
<crystal.asurams.edu/asu/>
Established 1903.

Alcorn State University
100 ASU Drive
Lorman, MS 39096
(800) 222–6790
<www.alcorn.edu>
Established 1871.

Allen University
1530 Harden St.
Columbia, SC 29204
(803) 376–5780
Established 1870.
<www.allenuniversity.edu/enter.html>

Arkansas Baptist College
1600 Bishop St.
Little Rock, AR 72202–6099
(501) 374–7856
Established 1884.

Atlanta Metropolitan College
1630 Stewart Avenue, SW
Atlanta, GA 30310
(404) 756–4004
<www.atlm.edu/>
Established 1974.

Barber-Scotia College
145 Cabarrus Ave.
Concord, NC 28025
(800) 610–0778
Established 1867.

Benedict College
Harden and Blanding Sts.
Columbia, SC 29204–1086
(800) 868–6598
<www.benedict.edu>
Established 1870.

Bennett College
900 E. Washington St.
Greensboro, NC 27401–3239
(800) 413–5323
<www.bennett.edu>
Established 1873.

Bethune-Cookman College
640 Dr. Mary McLeod Bethune Blvd.
Daytona Beach, FL 32114–3099
(800) 448–0228
<www.bethune.cookman.edu>
Established 1904.

Bishop State Community College
351 N. Broad St.
Mobile, AL 36603–5898
(334) 438–6801
<www.bscc.cc.al.us>
Established 1965.

Bluefield State College
219 Rock St.
Bluefield, WV 24701
(304) 327–4000
<www.bluefield.wvnet.edu>
Established 1895.

Bowie State University
14000 Jericho Park Rd.
Bowie, MD 20715–3318
(301) 464–3000
<www.bsu.umd.edu>
Established 1865.

Central State University
1400 Brush Row Rd.
Wilberforce, OH 45384–9999
(800) 388–2781
<www.ces.edu>
Established 1887.

Cheyney University of Pennsylvania
Cheyney, PA 19319–0200
(610) 399–2000
<www.cheyney.edu>
Established 1837.

Chicago State University
9501 S. Martin Luther King Jr. Dr.
Chicago, IL 60628–1598
(773) 995–2000
<www.csu.edu>
Established 1867.

Claflin College
College Ave., NE
Orangeburg, SC 29115
(803) 534–2710
<www.icusc.org/cchome.htm>
Established 1869.

Clark Atlanta University
James P. Brawley Dr. at Fair St., SW
Atlanta, GA 30314–4385
(404) 880–8000
<www.cau.edu>
Established 1988.

Clinton Junior College
PO Box 968
Rock Hill, SC 29731
(803) 327–5587
Established 1894.

Coahoma Community College
3240 Friars Point Rd.
Clarksdale, MS 38614–9799
(662) 627–2571
<www.ccc.cc.ms.us/>
Established 1949.

Compton Community College
1111 E. Artesia Blvd.
Compton, CA 90221–5393
(310) 900–1600
gopher://compton.cc.ca.us
Established 1927.

Concordia College
1804 Green St.
Selma, AL 36701
(334) 874–7143
<www.cuis.edu/www/cus/cual.html>
Established 1922.

Coppin State College
2500 W. North Ave.
Baltimore, MD 21216–3698
(410) 383–5400
<www.coppin.umd.edu>
Established 1900.

Cuyahoga Community College
Metropolitan Campus
2900 Community College Ave.
Cleveland, OH 44115
(216) 987–4000
<www.tri-c.cc.oh.us>
Established 1963.

Delaware State University
1200 N. DuPont Hwy.
Dover, DE 19901
(302) 857–6353
<www.dsc.edu>
Established 1891.

Denmark Technical College
Solomon Blatt Blvd.
PO Box 327
Denmark, SC 29042–0327
(803) 793–3301
<www.den.tec.sc.us/>
Established 1948.

Dillard University
2601 Gentilly Blvd.
New Orleans, LA 70122–3097
(504) 283–8822
<www.dillard.edu>
Established 1869.

J.F. Drake State Technical College
3421 Meridian St.
Huntsville, AL 35811
(256) 539–8161
<www.dstc.cc.al.us>
Established 1961.

Charles R. Drew University of Medicine and Science
1621 E. 120th St.
Los Angeles, CA 90059–3025
(323) 563–4800
<www.cdrew.edu>
Established 1966.

Elizabeth City State University
Parkview Drive
Elizabeth City, NC 27909
(800) 347–3278
<www.ecsu.edu>
Established 1891.

Fayetteville State University
1200 Murchison Rd.
Newbold Station
Fayetteville, NC 28301–4298
(800) 222–2549
<www.uncfsu.edu>
Established 1867.

Fisk University
1000 17th Ave., N.
Nashville, TN 37208–3051
(615) 329–8500
<www.fisk.edu>
Established 1866.

Florida A&M University
1500 Wahnish Way
Tallahassee, FL 32307
(850) 599–3000
<www.famu.edu>
Established 1887.

Florida Memorial College
15800 NW 42nd Ave.
Miami, FL 33054–6199
(800) 553–0816
<www.fmc.edu>
Established 1879.

Fort Valley State University
805 State College Drive
Fort Valley, GA 31030–4313
(912) 825–6211
<www.fcsc.edu>
Established 1895.

Grambling State University
100 Main Street
Grambling, LA 71245–3091
(318) 274–2000
<www.gram.edu>
Established 1901.

Hampton University
Hampton, VA 23668–0199
(800) 624–3328
<www.hamptonu.edu/>
Established 1868.

Harris-Stowe State College
3026 Laclede Ave.
St. Louis, MO 63103
(314) 340–3366
<www.hssc.edu/>
Established 1857.

Hinds Community College
Utica Campus
Highway 18 West
Utica, MS 39175–9599
(800) 446–3722
<www.hindscc.edu>
Established 1917.

Mary Holmes College
Hwy. 50 W
PO Drawer 1257
West Point, MS 39773–1257
(601) 494–6820
<www.maryholmes.edu>
Established 1892.

Howard University
2400 6th St., NW
Washington, DC 20059–0001
(202) 806–6100
<www.howard.edu>
Established 1867.

Howard University School of Law
2900 Van Ness St., NW
Washington, DC 20008
(202) 806–8000
<www.law.howard.edu>
Established 1869.

Huston-Tillotson College
1820 East Eighth Street
Austin, TX 78702
(512) 505–3000
<www.htc.edu>
Established 1876.

Interdenominational Theological Center
700 Martin Luther King Jr. Dr., SW
Atlanta, GA 30314
(404) 427–7700
<www.itc.edu>
Established 1958.

Jackson State University
1400 John R. Lynch St.
Jackson, MS 39217
(800) 848–6817
<www.jsums.edu>
Established 1877.

Jarvis Christian College
PO Box 1470
Highway 80 W.
Hawkins, TX 75765–9989
(903) 769–5700
<www.jarvis.edu>
Established 1912.

Kennedy-King College
6800 S. Wentworth Ave.
Chicago, IL 60621–3798
(773) 602–5000
<www.ccc.edu/kennedyking/>
Established 1976.

Kentucky State University
400 E. Main St.
Box PG-92
Frankfort, KY 40601–2355
(502) 227–6000
<www.kysu.edu.>
Established 1886.

Knoxville College
901 College St.
Knoxville, TN 37921
(800) 743–5669
<www.knoxvillecollege.edu/>
Established 1875.

LaGuardia Community College
31–10 Thompson Ave.
Long Island City, NY 11101
(718) 482–5000
<www.lagcc.cuny.edu>
Established 1971.

Lane College
545 Lane Ave.
Jackson, TN 38301
(901) 426–7000
<www.lanecollege.edu/>
Established 1882.

Langston University
PO Box 907
Langston, OK 73050–0907
(405) 466–4000
<www.lunet.edu>
Established 1897.

Lawson State Community College
3060 Wilson Rd., SW
Birmingham, AL 35221
(205) 925–2515
<www.ls.cc.al.us/>
Established 1965.

LeMoyne-Owen College
807 Walker Ave.
Memphis, TN 38126
(901) 774–9090
<www.lemoyne-owen.edu/>
Established 1862.

Lewis College of Business
17370 Meyers Rd.
Detroit, MI 48235
(313) 862–3000
<www.lewiscollege.edu>
Established 1906.

Lincoln University (Missouri)
820 Chestnut St.
Jefferson City, MO 65101–9880
(573) 681–5000
<www.lincolnu.edu>
Established 1866.

Lincoln University of Pennsylvania
Lincoln University, PA 19352
(800) 790–0191
<www.lincoln.ed.>
Established 1854.

Livingstone College
701 W. Monroe St.
Salisbury, NC 28144
(704) 797–1000
<www.lsc.edu>
Established 1879.

**Medgar Evers College of City University
of New York**
1650 Bedford Ave.
Brooklyn, NY 11225
(718) 270–6021
<www.greatcollegetown.com/medgar.html>
Established 1969.

Meharry Medical College
1005 D.B. Todd Jr. Blvd.
Nashville, TN 37208
(615) 327–6000
<www.mmc.edu>
Established 1876.

Miles College
5500 Myron Massey Boulevard
Birmingham, AL 35064
(205) 929–1656
<www.miles.edu>
Established 1905.

Mississippi Valley State University
14000 Hwy. 82 W.
Itta Bena, MS 38941
(662) 254–9041
<www.mcsu.edu>
Established 1946.

Morehouse College
830 Westview Dr., SW
Atlanta, GA 30314–3773
(404) 681–2800
<www.morehouse.edu>
Established 1867.

Morehouse School of Medicine
720 Westview Dr., SW
Atlanta, GA 30310–1495
(404) 752–1500
<www.msm.edu>
Established 1984.

Morgan State University
Cold Spring Lane and Hillen Road
Baltimore, MD 21239
(443) 885–3000
<www.morgan.edu>
Established 1867.

Morris Brown College
643 Martin Luther King Jr. Dr., NW
Atlanta, GA 30314
(404) 738–1000
<www.morrisbrown.edu>
Established 1881.

Morris College
North Main Street
Sumter, SC 29150
(803) 775–9371
<www2.morris.edu/index.asp>
Established 1908.

New York City Technical College
300 Jay St.
Brooklyn, NY 11201
(718) 260–5500
<www.nyctc.suny.edu>
Established 1946.

Norfolk State University
700 Park Avenue
Norfolk, VA 23504–3989
(757) 683–8600
<www.nsu.ed>
Established 1935.

North Carolina A&T State University
1601 E. Market St.
Greensboro, NC 27411–0001
(336) 334–7500
<www.ncat.edu>
Established 1891.

North Carolina Central University
PO Box 19717, Shepherd Station
Durham, NC 27707
(919) 560–6100
<www.nccu.edu>
Established 1910.

Oakwood College
7000 Adventist Road
Huntsville, AL 35896
(256) 726–7000
<www.oakwood.edu>
Established 1896.

Paine College
1235 15th St.
Augusta, GA 30910
(706) 821–8200
<www.paine.edu>
Established 1882.

Prairie View A&M University
PO Box 3089
Prairie View, TX 77446–4019
(936) 857–3311
<www.pvamu.edu>
Established 1876.

Paul Quinn College
3837 Simpson Stuart Rd.
Dallas, TX 75241–4398
(214) 302–3613
<www.pqc.edu>
Established 1872.

Roxbury Community College
1234 Columbus Ave.
Roxbury Crossing, MA 02120–3400
(617) 541–5310
<www.rcc.mass.edu>
Established 1973.

Rust College
150 Rust Ave.
Holly Spring, MS 38635
(662) 252–8000
<www.rustcollege.edu>
Established 1866.

Saint Augustine's College
1315 Oakwood Ave.
Raleigh, NC 27611
(919) 516–4000
<www.st-aug.edu/>
Established 1867.

Saint Paul's College
406 Windsor Ave.
Lawrenceville, VA 23868–9988
(804) 848–3111
<www.saintpauls.edu>
Established 1888.

Savannah State University
3219 Falligant Avenue
Savannah, GA 31404–5255
(912) 356–2336
<www.savstate.edu>
Established 1890.

Selma University
1501 Lapsley St.
Selma, AL 36701
(334) 872–2533
Established 1878.

Shaw University
118 E. South St.
Raleigh, NC 27601
(919) 546–8200
<www.shawuniversity.edu/>
Established 1865.

Shorter College
604 Locust St.
North Little Rock, AR 72114
(501) 374–6305
Established 1888.

Simmons University Bible College
1811 Dumesnil St.
Louisville, KY 40210
(502) 776–1443
<www.sbcollege.edu/>
Established 1879.

Johnson C. Smith University
100 Beatties Ford Rd.
Charlotte, NC 28216
(704) 378–1000
<www.jcsu.edu>
Established 1867.

Philander Smith College
812 W. 13th St.
Little Rock, AR 72202–3799
(501) 370–5310
<www.philander.edu>
Established 1877.

Sojourner-Douglass College
500 N. Caroline St.
Baltimore, MD 21205
(410) 276–0306
<www.sdc.edu/>
Established 1972.

South Carolina State University
300 College St., NE
Orangeburg, SC 29117–0001
(803) 536–7000
<www.scsu.edu>
Established 1896.

Southern University and A&M University at Baton Rouge
PO Box 9901
Baton Rouge, LA 70813
(221) 771–4500
<www.subr.edu>
Established 1880.

Southern University at New Orleans
6400 Press Dr.
New Orleans, LA 70126
(504) 286–5000
<www.suno.edu>
Established 1956.

Southern University at Shreveport
Martin Luther King Jr. Dr.
Shreveport, LA 71107
(318) 674–3312
<www.susbo.edu>
Established 1964.

Southwestern Christian College
200 Bowser Circle
Terrell, TX 75160
(972) 524–3341
<www.swcc.edu/>
Established 1949.

Spelman College
350 Spelman Ln., SW
Atlanta, GA 30314
(404) 681–3643
<www.spelman.edu/>
Established 1881.

Stillman College
PO Box 1430
3600 Stillman Blvd.
Tuscaloosa, AL 35403–1430
(205) 349–4240
<www.stillman.edu>
Established 1876.

Talladega College
627 W. Battle St.
Talladega, AL 35160–2354
(256) 362–0206
<www.talladega.edu>
Established 1867.

Tennessee State University
3500 John Merritt Blvd.
Nashville, TN 37209–1561
(888) 463–6878
<www.tnstate.edu>
Established 1912.

Texas College
2404 N. Grand Ave.
Tyler, TX 75712
(903) 593–8311
<www.texascollege.edu>
Established 1894.

Texas Southern University
3100 Cleburne Ave.
Houston, TX 77004
(713) 313–7011
<www.tsu.edu>
Established 1947.

Tougaloo College
300 E. County Line Rd.
Tougaloo, MS 39174
(601) 977–7700
<www.tougaloo.edu>
Established 1869.

Trenholm State Technical College
1225 Air Base Blvd.
Montgomery, AL 36108
(334) 832–9000
<www.tstc.cc.al.us>
Established 1963.

Tuskegee University
Tuskegee, AL 36088
(334) 727–8500
<www.tusk.edu>
Established 1881.

University of Arkansas at Pine Bluff
1200 University Dr.
Pine Bluff, AR 71611
(800) 264–6585
<www.uapb.edu>
Established 1873.

University of Maryland—Eastern Shore
Princess Anne, MD 21853–1299
(410) 651–2200
<www.umes.umd.edu>
Established 1886.

University of the District of Columbia
4200 Connecticut Ave., NW
Washington, DC 20008
(202) 274–5000
<www.udc.edu>
Established 1976.

University of the Virgin Islands
Charlotte Amalie, St. Thomas
U.S. Virgin Islands 00802
(340) 776–9200
<www.uvi.edu>
Established 1962.

Virginia Seminary and College
2058 Garfield Ave.
Lynchburg, VA 24501
(804) 528–5276
<www.vsu.edu>
Established 1888.

Virginia State University
Petersburg, VA 23806
(804) 524–5000
<www.vsu.edu>
Established 1882.

Virginia Union University
1500 N. Lombardy St.
Richmond, VA 23220
(804) 257–5600
<www.vuu.edu>
Established 1865.

Voorhees College
1411 Voorhees Rd.
Denmark, SC 29042
(803) 703–3351
<www.voorhees.edu>
Established 1897.

Edward Waters College
1658 Kings Rd.
Jacksonville, FL 32209
(904) 366–2715
Established 1866.

Wayne County Community College
801 W. Fort Ave.
Detroit, MI 48226–3010
(313) 496–2500
<www.wccc.edu>
Established 1967.

West Virginia State College
P.O. Box 1000
Institute, WV 25112–1000
(800) 987–2112
<www.wvsc.edu>
Established 1891.

Wilberforce University
1055 N. Bickett Rd.
Wilberforce, OH 45384
(937) 376–2911
<www.wilberforce.edu>
Established 1856.

Wiley College
711 Wiley Ave.
Marshall, TX 75670
(800) 658–6889
<www.wiley.edu>
Established 1873.

Winston-Salem State University
601 Martin Luther King Jr. Dr.
Winston-Salem, NC 27110
(336) 750–2000
<www.wssu.edu>
Established 1892.

Xavier University of Louisiana
7325 Palmetto St.
New Orleans, LA 70125
(504) 486–7411
<www.xula.edu>
Established 1915.

◆ RESEARCH INSTITUTIONS

African Heritage Studies Association
Africana Studies & Research Institute
Queens College
65–30 Kissena Blvd.
Flushing, NY 11367
(718) 997–2845

Anacostia Museum and Center for African American History and Culture
1901 Ft. Pl., S.E.
Washington, DC 20020
(202) 287–3369

Association for Study of Afro-American Life and History, Inc.
7961 Eastern Ave., Ste. 301
Silver Spring, MD 20910
(301) 587–5900
executivedirector@asalh.com
<www.asalh.com>

Bennett College
Women's Leadership Institute
900 E. Washington St., Box C
Greensboro, NC 27401–3239
(336) 370–0436
<www.bennett.edu/wli/wli.htm>

Black Arts Research Center
30 Marion St.
Nyack, NY 10960
barc00@hotmail.com
<barc0.tripod.com/>

Boston University
African American Studies Center
138 Mountfort St.
Brookline, MA 02146
(617) 353–2795
<www.bu.edu/afam/>

Brooklyn College of City University of New York
Africana Studies
2900 Bedford Ave.
3105 James Hall
Brooklyn, NY 11210
(718) 951–5597
<depthome.brooklyn.cuny.edu/africana/>

Brown University
Africana Studies Department
155 Angell St., 2nd Fl.
PO Box 1904, Churchill House
Providence, RI 02912
(401) 863–3137
<www.brown.edu/Departments/African_American_ Studies/>

The Center for the Study of Race and Ethnicity in America
PO Box 1886
Providence, RI 02912
(401) 863–3080
william_simmons@brown.edu
<www.brown.edu/Departments/Race_Ethnicity/ index.shtml>

The Watson Institute
111 Thayer Street
PO Box 1970
Providence, RI 02912–1970
(401) 863–2809
iis@brown.edu
<www.watsoninstitute.org/index2.cfm>

Center for Third World Organizing
1218 E 21st St.
Oakland, CA 94606
(510) 533–7583
ctwo@ctwo.org
<www.ctwo.org>

Charles R. Drew University of Medicine and Science
1621 E 120th St., MP 11
Los Angeles, CA 90059
(310) 668–3177
haward@cdrew.edu

City University of New York
Institute for Research on the African Diaspora in the Americas and the Caribbean (IRADAC)
365 5th Ave., Rm. 7114
New York, NY 10016–4309
(212) 817–2071
iradac@gc.cuny.edu
<www.gc.cuny.edu/research_centers_pages/IRADAC.htm>

Clemson University
Charles H. Houston Center for the Study of Black Experience Affecting Higher Education
213 Martin St.
Clemson, SC 29631–1555
(864) 656–0313
mlorett@clemson.edu
<www.houston.clemson.edu>

College of Staten Island of City University of New York
History Department 2N215
2800 Victory Blvd.
Staten Island, NY 10314
(718) 982–2870
holder@postbox.csi.cuny.edu

Colorado State University
Center for Applied Studies in American Ethnicity
Clark C127
Fort Collins, CO 80523–1790
(970) 491–2418
jxing@lamar.colostate.edu
<www.colostate.edu/Depts/CASAE>

Columbia College
Center for Black Music Research
600 South Michigan Avenue
Chicago, IL 60605–1996
(312) 344–7559

Columbia University
The Institute for Research in African-American Studies
758 Schermerhorn Extension
Mail Code 5512
1200 Amsterdam Ave.
New York, NY 10027
(212) 854–7080
sh2004@columbia.edu
<www.columbia.edu/cu/iraas/>

Cornell University
Africana Studies and Research Center
310 Triphammer Rd.
Ithaca, NY 14853
(607) 255–4625
jet8@cornell.edu

Delaware State University
College of Agriculture and Related Sciences
1200 N Dupont Hwy.
Dover, DE 19901
(302) 857–6400
kbell@dsc.edu

Duke University
Center for Documentary Studies
1317 W Pettigrew St.
Durham, NC 27705
(919) 660–3663
docstudies@duke.edu

Fisk University
Race Relations Institute
1000 17th Ave., N.
Nashville, TN 37208–3051
(615) 329–8575
www.fiskrri.org/

Florida A&M University
PO Box A-19
Tallahassee, FL 32307
(850) 599–3325
nadams2@famu.edu

Florida International University
African-New World Studies Program
University Park
1120 SW 8th St.
Miami, FL 33199–0001
(305) 348–2000
<www.fiu.edu/~africana/>

Florida State University
African American Studies Program
106 Bellamy Bldg.
Tallahassee, FL 32306–2151
blkstudies@mailer.fsu.edu
<www.fsu.edu/~blkstudy/>

Frederick D. Patterson Research Institute
8260 Willow Oaks Corporate Dr.
PO Box 10444
Fairfax, VA 22031–4511
(703) 205–3570
<www.patterson-uncf.org/rbooks.htm>

Harvard University
Civil Rights Project
444 Gutman Library
Cambridge, MA 02136
(617) 496–6367
<www.law.harvard.edu/civilrights/>

The W.E.B. Du Bois Center for Afro-American
    Research
Barker Center
12 Quincy St.
Cambridge, MA 02138
(617) 495–4113
jkendall@fas.harvard.edu

Howard University
The Moorland-Spingarn Research Center
500 Howard Pl. NW
Washington, DC 20059
(202) 806–7240
tbattle@howard.edu
<www.founders.howard.edu/moorland-spingarn/
    default.html>

Indiana State University
Holmstedt Hall, Rm. 315
Terre Haute, IN 47809
(812) 237–2436
psmohad@scifac.indstate.edu

Indiana University Bloomington
Archives of African American Music and Culture
Smith Research Center, Suites 180–181
2805 E. Tenth Street
Bloomington, IN 47408–2601
(812) 855–8547
<www.indiana.edu/~aaamc/>

Neal-Marshall Black Cultural Center
275 N. Jordan Ave. Suite A226
Bloomington, IN 47405
(812) 855–9271

aacc@indiana.edu
<www.indiana.edu/~aacc>

Institute for the Preservation and Study of African-American Writing
PO Box 50172
Washington, DC 20004
(202) 727–4047

Johns Hopkins University
Institute for Global Studies in Culture, Power &
    History
Greenhouse
Johns Hopkins University
Baltimore, MD 21218
(410) 516–7794
igs@jhu.edu
<www.jhu.edu/~igscph>

Joint Center for Political and Economic Studies
1090 Vermont Ave. NW, Ste. 1100
Washington, DC 20005–4961
(202) 789–3500
ewillams@jointcenter.org
<www.jointcenter.org>

Kent State University
101 Oscar Ritchie Hall
Department of Pan-African Studies
Kent, OH 44242–0001
(330) 672–2300
jrowser@kent.edu
<dept.kent.edu/pas/htmfiles/deptpas.htm>

Langston University
Hwy. 33
PO Box 1600
Langston, OK 73050
(405) 466–3346
brblack@lunet.edu
<www.lunet.edu/lib/>

Martin Luther King Jr. Center for Nonviolent Social Change, Inc.
449 Auburn Ave. NE
Atlanta, GA 30312
(404) 526–8900
information@thekingcenter.org
<www.thekingcenter.com>

Morehouse College
Morehouse Research Institute
160 Euhrlee St.
Atlanta, GA 30314
(404) 215–2676
jstanfie@morehouse.edu

**National Afro-American Museum and
Cultural Center**
1350 Brush Row Rd.
PO Box 578
Wilberforce, OH 45384
(937) 376–4944
naamcc@erinet.com

National Black Child Development Institute
1101 15th St. NW, Ste. 900
Washington, DC 20005
(202) 833–2220
moreinfo@nbcdi.org
<www.nbcdi.org>

National Caucus and Center on Black Aged, Inc.
1424 K St. NW, Ste. 500
Washington, DC 20005
(202) 637–8400
samsimncba@aol.com

National Council for Black Studies
College of Arts & Science
California State University, Dominguez Hills
1000 E Victoria St.
Carson, CA 90747
(310) 243–2169
fedwards@csudh.edu
<www.eiu.edu/~ncbs>

National Urban League
Research Department
1111 14th St., NW, 6th Fl.
Washington, DC 20005
(202) 898–1604

New York University
The Institute of African American Affairs
269 Mercer St., Ste. 601
New York, NY 10003–6687
(212) 998–2130
laura.rice@nyu.edu
<www.nyu.edu/gsas/dept/africana/institute-set.html>

Niagara University
Center for the Study and Stabilization of the
    Black Family
PO Box 367
Niagara University, NY 14109
(716) 285–1212

North Carolina Central University
New Education Bldg., Ste. 2027
Durham, NC 27707
(919) 560–6367
fanyanw4@nccu.edu

Northern Illinois University
Center for Black Studies
DeKalb, IL 60115–2854
(815) 753–1709
lgyant@niu.edu
<www.niu.edu/depts/cbs/>

Ohio University
African American Studies Department
300 Lindley Hall
Athens, OH 45701
(740) 593–9178
cambridg@ohiou.edu

Princeton University
The Program in African Amercian Studies at
    Princeton
112 Dickinson Hall
Princeton, NJ 08544–1017
(609) 258–4270
jeanw@princeton.edu
<www.princeton.edu/~aasprog/>

Purdue University
African American Studies and Research Center
1367 Steven C. Beering Hall of Liberal Arts and
    Education (BRNG)
West Lafayette, IN 47907–1367
(765) 494–5680
aasrc@sla.purdue.edu
<www.sla.purdue.edu/academic/idis/african-
    american/>

Rutgers University
Institute of Jazz Studies
Dana Library, 4th Fl.
Newark, NJ 07102
(973) 648–5595
<www.libraries.rutgers.edu/rulib/abtlib/danlib/
    jazz.htm>

**Schomburg Center for Research in Black
Culture**
515 Malcolm X Blvd.
New York, NY 10037–1801
(212) 491–2200
<www.nypl.org/research/sc/sc.html>

Spelman College
Women's Research & Resource Center
350 Spelman Lane, Box 115
Cosby 2nd Floor
Atlanta, GA 30314
404–681-3643 (Ext. 2161)

State University of New York
New York African American Research Foundation
State University Plaza
Central Administration Bldg.
Albany, NY 12246
(518) 443–5798

Temple University
The Center for African American History and
    Culture
Weiss Hall, Ste. B18
1701 N 13th St.
Philadelphia, PA 19122
(215) 204–4851
bcollier@astro.temple.edu
<www.temple.edu/caahc>

Tulane University
Amistad Research Center
6823 St. Charles Ave.
New Orleans, LA 70118
(504) 865–5535
<www.tulane.edu/~amistad/>

**University at Albany, State University
of New York**
Department of Africana Studies
Business Administration 115
Albany, NY 12222
(518) 442–4730
africana@albany.edu
<www.albany.edu/africana/>

University of Alabama
Center for Southern History and Culture
PO Box 870342
Tuscaloosa, AL 35487–0342
(205) 348–7467

University of California at Berkeley
The Department of African American Studies
660 Barrows Hall #2572
Berkeley, CA 94720–0318
(510) 642–7084
<socrates.berkeley.edu/~africam/>

University of California, Los Angeles
Center for African American Studies
160 Haines Hall, Box 951545
Los Angeles, CA 90095–1545
(310) 825–7403
<www.sscnet.ucla.edu/caas/>

Department of Sociology
2201 Hershey Hall
375 Portola Place
Los Angeles, CA 90095–1551
(310) 206–7107

wallen@ucla.edu
<www.sscnet.ucla.edu/soc/index.html>

University of California, Riverside
Center for the Advanced Studies of the Americas
Humanities Bldg., Rm. 3609
Riverside, CA 92521
(909) 787–2196
carlos@chss.ucr.edu
<www.chass.ucr.edu/csbsr/casa.html>

Paul Robeson Center for Legal and Historical
    Research
Humanities Bldg., Rm. 3612
Riverside, CA 92521
(909) 787–2196
lobo@ucrac1.ucr.edu
<www.chass.ucr.edu/csbsr/robeson.html>

University of California, San Francisco
Center for Aging in Diverse Communities
3333 California St., Ste. 335
San Francisco, CA 94143–0856
(415) 476–9933
eliseops@medicine.ucsf.edu
<medicine.ucsf.edu/cadc/>

University of California, Santa Barbara
Center for Black Studies
South Hall, Rm. 4603
Santa Barbara, CA 93106–3140
(805) 893–3914
michel@alishaw.ucsb.edu
<research.ucsb.edu/cbs/>

University of Charleston
Avery Research Center for African American History
    and Culture
125 Bull St.
Charleston, SC 29424
(843) 953–7609
dulaneyw@cofc.edu
<www.cofc.edu/~averyrsc>

University of Chicago
Committee on African and African-American Studies
5828 S. University Ave.
Chicago, IL 60637
(773) 702–0902

University of Cincinnati
The Department of African Amercian Studies
P.O. Box 210370
Cincinnati, OH 45221–0370
(513) 556–0350
afam.studies@uc.edu
<asweb.artsci.uc.edu/afamstudies/>

University of Connecticut
Institute for African American Studies
241 Glenbrook Rd., Box U2162
Storrs, CT 06269–2162
(860) 486–3630
aasadm03@uconnvm.uconn.edu
<www.ucc.uconn.edu/~aasadm03/>

University of Florida
African American Studies Program
330 Little Hall
PO Box 118120
Gainesville, FL 32611
(352) 392–5724
<www.clas.ufl.edu/afam/>

University of Georgia
Institute for African American Studies
312 Candler Hall
Athens, GA 30602
(706) 542–5197
rbmiller@arches.uga.edu
<www.uga.edu/~iaas>

University of Houston
African American Studies Program
Agnes Arnold Hall
College of Liberal Arts & Social Sciences
Houston, TX 77204–3747
(713) 743–2811
jhutchinson@uh.edu
<www.hfac.uh.edu/aas>

University of Illinois at Chicago
Institute for Research on Race and Public Policy
324 CUPPA Hall, M/C 347
College of Urban Planning & Public Affairs
412 S Peoria
Chicago, IL 60607–7066
(312) 996–9145
pjbowman@uic.edu
<www.uic.edu/cuppa/irrpp/>

University of Illinois at Urbana-Champaign
The Afro-American Studies and Research Program
1201 W Nevada St.
Urbana, IL 61801
(217) 333–7781
info@aasrp.uiuc.edu
<www.aasrp.uiuc.edu>

University of Kansas
Institute for Life Span Studies
1028 Dole Center
Lawrence, KS 66045–0048
(785) 864–3990
ibldr@dole.lsi.ukans.edu

University of Maryland at College Park
David C. Driskell Center for the Study of the African
   Diaspora
2114 Tawes Fine Arts Building
College Park, MD 20742–1211
(301) 314–2615

Nyumburu Cultural Center
Bldg. 232, Ste. 1120
Office of the VP for Academic Affairs
College Park, MD 20742
(301) 314–7758
acarswel@accmail.umd.edu
<www.inform.umd.edu/nyumburu>

University of Massachusetts at Boston
The William Monroe Trotter Institute
100 Morrissey Blvd.
Boston, MA 02125–3393
(617) 287–5880
philip.hart@umb.edu
<www.trotterinst.org>

University of Michigan
Center for Afroamerican and African Studies
106 West Hall Bldg.
550 E University
Ann Arbor, MI 48109–1092
(734) 764–5513
caasinfo@umich.edu
<www.umich.edu/~iinet/caas/>

The Program for Research on Black Americans
5062 Institute for Social Research
426 Thompson St.
PO Box 1248
Ann Arbor, MI 48106–1248
(734) 763–0045
prba@isr.umich.edu
<www.isr.umich.edu/rcgd/prba/>

University of Mississippi
Center for the Study of Southern Culture
Barnard Observatory
University, MS 38677
(662) 232–5993
<www.olemiss.edu/depts/south/>

University of Oklahoma
Center for Research on Multi-Ethnic Education
455 Lindsey St., Rm. 804
Norman, OK 73019–0535
(405) 325–4529

University of Pennsylvania
Afro-American Studies Program
3451 Walnut Street
Philadelphia, PA 19104
(215) 898–5000
<www.sas.upenn.edu/afams/>

University of Rochester
Frederick Douglass Institute for African and African-
    American Studies
302 Morey Hall
Rochester, NY 14627–0440
(716) 275–7235

University of Texas at Austin
Center for African and African-American Studies
Jester Center, Rm. A232A
CMC D7200
Austin, TX 78705
(512) 471–1784
caaas@uts.cc.utexas.edu
<www.utexas.edu/depts/caaas/>

University of Virginia
Center for the Study of Civil Rights
1512 Jefferson Park Ave.
Charlottesville, VA 22903
(804) 924–3109

The G. Carter Woodson Institute for Afro-American
    and African Studies
108 Minor Hall
PO Box 400162
Charlottesville, VA 22904–4162
434924–3109
woodson@gwis.virginia.edu
<www.virginia.edu/~woodson>

University of Wisconsin—Madison
The African Studies Program
205 Ingraham Hall
1155 Observatory Dr.
Madison, WI 53706
(608) 262–2380
africa@intl-institute.wisc.edu
<polyglot.lss.wisc.edu/afrst/asphome.html>

Vanderbilt University
Kelly Miller Institute on Black Church Studies
411 21st Ave. S
Nashville, TN 37240
(615) 343–3981
<divinity.library.vanderbilt.edu/kmsi/default.htm>

Wayne State University
Walter P. Reuther Library
5401 Cass Ave.
Detroit, MI 48202
(313) 577–4024
ai6050@wayne.edu

Wesleyan University
Center for African American Studies
343 High St.
Middletown, CT 06459
(860) 685–3568
aducille@wesleyan.edu
<www.wesleyan.edu/afam/>

Western Michigan University
Africana Studies Program
330 Moore Hall
Kalamazoo, MI 49008
<www.wmich.edu/blackamericanstudies/>

Yale University
Gilder Lehrman Center for the Study of Slavery,
    Resistance, and Abolition
PO Box 208206
New Haven, CT 06520–8206
(203) 432–3339
www.library.yale.edu/training/gilderle.htm

◆ AFRICAN AMERICANS HOLDING ENDOWED UNIVERSITY CHAIRS, CHAIRS OF EXCELLENCE, OR CHAIRED PROFESSORSHIPS (2001)

Endowed university chairs are an honor—both for the person for whom the chair is named as well as for the person who is named to the chair. Endowments are bestowed upon academicians of great talent who have distinguished themselves in their careers. Usually an organization separate from a collegiate institution will approach a university in hopes of setting up a chair and endowment fund. According to a report in the Autumn 2001 issue of *The Journal of Blacks in Higher Education*, 18 such chairs have been identified as endowed and named for African Americans including Hannah Diggs Atkins, Sterling A. Brown, Ray Charles, Constance E. Clayton, Bill and Camille Cosby, Charles R. Drew, W. E. B. Du Bois, Benjamin L. Hooks, John E. Jacob, Ernest Everett Just, Martin Luther King Jr., LaSalle D. Leffall Jr., Wade H. McCree Jr., Ronald E. McNair, Willa B. Player, Paul Robeson, and Roy Wilkins.

In 2001, 136 African American professors held endowed chairs, including at least ten of those named for African Americans. Others have either retired from endowed chairs, are professors emeriti, or are deceased, including T. J. Anderson (Tufts University); David C. Driskell (University of Maryland); Edgar G. Epps (University of Chicago); John Hope Franklin (three: Cambridge University, Duke University, and University of Chicago); James Lowell Gibbs Jr. (Stanford University); Edmund Gordon (Columbia Teachers College); Harry E. Groves (University of North Carolina at Chapel Hill); James E. Jones Jr. (University of Wisconsin); Barbara C. Jordan (University of Texas at Austin); C. Eric Lincoln (Duke University and Clark University); Bertha Maxwell-Roddy (University of North Carolina, Charlotte); Samuel DeWitt Proctor (Rutgers University); William H. Peterson (Campbell University); Charlotte H. Scott (University of Virginia); Nathan A. Scott (University of Virginia); John B. Turner (University of North Carolina at Chapel Hill); and Marilyn V. Yarborough (University of North Carolina at Chapel Hill).

Delores P. Aldridge, Grace Towns Hamilton Professor of Sociology and African-American Studies, Emory University.

Gloria Long Anderson, Fuller E. Callaway Professor of Chemistry, Morris Brown College.

Maya Angelou, Reynolds Professor of American Studies, Wake Forest University.

Hannah Diggs Atkins, Hannah Diggs Atkins Professor of Public Service, Oklahoma State University

Regina Austin, William A. Schnader Professor of Law, University of Pennsylvania.

Mario J. Azevedo, Frank Porter Graham Professor, University of North Carolina, Charlotte.

Houston A. Baker Jr., Susan Fox Beischer and George D. Beischer Arts and Sciences Professor of English, Duke University

Oscar A. Barbarin, L. Richardson and Emily Preyer Bicentennial Distinguished Professor for Strenghthening Families, University of North Carolina at Chapel Hill.

Estrada J. Bernard Jr., Van L. Weatherspoon Jr. Professor of Neurosurgery and Chief, Division of Neurosurgery, School of Medicine, University of North Carolina at Chapel Hill.

Mary Frances Berry, Geraldine R. Segal Professor of American Social Thought and Professor of History, University of Pennsylvania.

Joanne M. Braxton, Francis L. and Edwin L. Cummings Professor of American Studies and Professor of English and the Humanities, College of William and Mary.

Frank Brown, Cary C. Boshamer Professor of Education, University of North Carolina at Chapel Hill.

Herrington J. Bryce, Life of Virginia Professor of Business Administration, College of William and Mary.

Roy S. Bryce-Laporte, John D. and Catherine T. MacArthur Professor of Sociology, Colgate University.

John S. Butler, Lawrence D. Gale Professor in Entrepreneurship and Arthur James Douglass Centennial Professor of Entrepreneurship, University of Texas at Austin.

Carolyn M. Callahan, Doris M. Cook Chair of Accounting, Sam M. Walton College of Business, University of Arkansas

Clive O. Callender, LaSalle D. Leffall Professor of Surgery, Howard University College of Medicine.

John O. Calmore, Reef C. Ivey II Research Professor of Law, UNC Law School, University of North Carolina at Chapel Hill.

Loftus C. Carson II, Ronald D. Krist Professor in Law, University of Texas at Austin.

Stephen L. Carter, William Nelson Cromwell Professor of Law, Yale University Law School.

James P. Comer, Maurice K. Falk Professor of Child Psychiatry, Yale University.

William W. Cook, Israel Evans Professor of Oratory and Belles Lettres, Dartmouth College.

Xavier Creary, Charles L. Huisking Professor of Chemistry, University of Notre Dame.

Dolores Cross, General Electric Distinguished Professor in Leadership and Diversity, City University of New York.

William Darity Jr., Cary C. Boshamer Professor of Economics, University of North Carolina at Chapel Hill.

Leon Dash, Swanlund Professor of Journalism, University of Illinois at Urbana-Champaign.

N. Gregson G. Davis, Andrew W. Mellon Professor of the Humanities, Duke University.

Addie Dawson-Euba, Community Coffee/Frank Hayden Professor of Visual and Performing Arts, Southern University.

Charles Edward Daye, Henry P. Brandis Professor of Law, University of North Carolina at Chapel Hill.

Rita Dove, Commonwealth Professor of English, University of Virginia.

Michael Eric Dyson, Ida B. Wells-Barnett University Professor, DePaul University.

Gerald Early, Merle S. Kling Professor of Modern Letters, Washington University in St. Louis.

Harry J. Elam Jr., Christensen Professor for the Humanities, Stanford University

Etta Falconer, Calloway Professor of Mathematics, Spelman College.

Frances Smith Foster, Charles Howard Candler Professor of English and Women's Studies, Emory University.

Oscar H. Gandy Jr., Herbert I. Schiller Professor, Annenberg School for Communication, University of Pennsylvania.

Fannie Gaston-Johansson, Elsie M. Lawler Professor, School of Nursing, Johns Hopkins University.

Henry Louis Gates Jr., W. E. B. Du Bois Professor of the Humanities, Harvard University.

Sylvester James Gates Jr., John S. Toll Professor of Physics, University of Maryland.

Jewelle Taylor Gibbs, The Zellerbach Family Fund Chair in Social Policy, Community Change and Practice, University of California at Berkeley.

Cheryl Townsend Gilkes, MacArthur Associate Professor of Sociology and African-American Studies, Colby College.

Richard A. Goldsby, John Woodruff Simpson Lecturer and Professor of Biology, Amherst College.

Peter J. Gomes, Plummer Professor of Christian Morals, Harvard University.

William B. Gould IV, Charles A. Beardsley Professor of Law, Stanford University.

Pamela Gunter-Smith, Porter Professor of Physiology, Spelman College.

Beverly Guy-Sheftall, Anna Julia Cooper Professor of Women's Studies, Spelman College.

Raymond L. Hall, Orvil Dryfoos Professor of Public Affairs, Department of Sociology, Dartmouth College.

Michael S. Harper, I. J. Kapstein Professor of English, Brown University.

Trudier Harris, J. Carlyle Sitterson Professor of English, University of North Carolina at Chapel Hill.

J. K. Haynes, David Packard Professor of Biology, Morehouse College.

Asa Grant Hilliard III, Fuller E. Callaway Professor of Urban Education, Georgia State University.

Darlene Clark Hine, John A. Hannah Professor of History, Michigan State University.

Matthew Holden Jr., Henry L. and Grace M. Doherty Professor of Government and Foreign Affairs, University of Virginia.

Karla F.C. Holloway, William Rand Kenan Professor of Humanities and Social Sciences, Duke University.

Thomas Holt, James Westphall Thompson Professor, Department of History, University of Chicago.

James O. Horton, Benjamin Banneker Professor of American Civilization and History, George Washington University.

Tasha R. Inniss, Clare Booth Luce Professor of Mathematics, Trinity College, Washington, D.C.

Jacqueline Irvine, Charles Howard Candler Professor of Urban Education, Emory University.

Alex M. Johnson Jr., Mary & Daniel Loughran Professor of Law and vice provost for faculty recruitment and retention, University of Virginia.

Charles Johnson, S. Wilson and Grace Pollock Professorship for Excellence in English, University of Washington.

James H. Johnson Jr., William Rand Kenan Jr. Distinguished Professor of Management, University of North Carolina at Chapel Hill.

Richard A. Joseph, Asa G. Candler Professor of Politics, Department of Political Science, Emory University.

George M. Langford, Ernest Everett Just 1907 Professorship, professor of biological sciences, Dartmouth College.

Sara Lawrence-Lightfoot, Emily Hargroves Fisher Professor of Education, Harvard University.

LaSalle D. Leffall Jr., Charles R. Drew Professor of Surgery, Howard University College of Medicine.

David Levering Lewis, Martin Luther King Jr. Professor of History, Rutgers University.

Richard A. Long, Atticus Haygood Professor, Emory University.

Kenneth R. Manning, Thomas Meloy Professor of Rhetoric and the History of Science, Massachusetts Institute of Technology.

Ali Mazrui, Albert Schweitzer Professor of Political Science, SUNY, Binghamton.

Reuben R. McDonald Jr., Charles and Elizabeth Prothro Regents Chair in Health Care Management, University of Texas at Austin.

John McFaddon, Benjamin Elijah Mays Professor of Education, University of South Carolina.

Donald E. McHenry, University Research Professor of Diplomacy, Georgetown University.

Ruth G. McRoy, Ruby Lee Piester Centennial Professor in Services to Children and Families, University of Texas at Austin.

Ronald E. Mickens, Fuller E. Callaway Professor of Physics, Clark Atlanta University.

Joseph Monroe, Jefferson Pilot/Ronald McNair Professor of Computer Science and Dean of the College of Engineering, North Carolina A&T University.

Ingrid M. Monson, Quincy Jones Professor of African-American Music, Harvard University.

William Moore Jr., A. M. Aikin Regents Chair in Junior and Community College Education Leadership, University of Texas at Austin.

Toni Morrison, Robert F. Goheen Professor, Council of the Humanities, Princeton University.

John Howard Morrow Jr., Franklin Professor of History, University of Georgia.

Valentin Mudimbe, Ruth F. Devarney Professor of Romance Studies and Professor of Cultural Anthropology, Duke University.

Samuel L. Myers Jr., Roy Wilkins Professor, Hubert H. Humphrey Institute of Public Affairs, University of Minnesota.

Robert G. O'Meally, Zora Neale Hurston Professor of English, Columbia University.

Bernard Oliver, Ewing Kauffman/Missouri Chair, School of Education, University of Missouri at Kansas City.

Lucius Outlaw, T. Wistar Brown Professor of Philosophy, Haverford College.

Reginald Owens, F. Jay Taylor Eminent Scholar of Journalism, Louisiana Tech University.

Nell Irvin Painter, Edwards Professor of American History, Princeton University.

Colin Palmer, Dodge Professor of History, Princeton University.

Peter J. Paris, Elmer G. Hornrighausen Professor of Christian Social Ethics, Princeton Theological Seminary.

Nell A. Parker, Herbert G. Kayser Professor of Civil Engineering, City University of New York, City College.

Orlando H. L. Patterson, John Cowles Professor of Sociology, Harvard University.

Gayle Pemberton, William Rand Kenan Professor of the Humanities, Wesleyan University.

Arlie O. Petters, William & Sue Gross Associate Professor of Mathematics, Duke University.

Richard I. Powell, John Spencer Bassett Professor of Art History, Duke University.

Albert Jordy Raboteau, Henry W. Putnam Professor of Religion, Princeton University.

Arnold Rampersad, Sara Hart Kimball Professor in the Humanities, Stanford University.

William J. Raspberry, Knight Professor of Communications and Journalism, Duke University.

Joe Ritchie, Knight Professor of Journalism, School of Journalism, Media and Graphic Arts, Florida A&M University.

Rosalie Richards, Kaolin Endowed Chair in Science, Georgia State University.

Charlotte H. Scott, University Professor of Commerce and Education, University of Virginia.

Lemma W. Senbet, William E. Mayer Professor of Finance, University of Maryland at College Park.

Willis B. Sheftall Jr., Merrill Professor of Economics and Business, Morehouse College.

George Shirley, Joseph Edgar Maddy Distinguished University Professor of Music, University of Michigan.

Diana T. Slaughter-Defoe, Constance E. Clayton Professor of Urban Education, University of Pennsylvania.

Jessie Carney Smith, William and Camille Cosby Professor of the Humanities and University Librarian, Fisk University.

Earl Smith, Dr. Ernest Rubin Distinguished Professor of American Ethnic Studies, Wake Forest University.

Edwin M. Smith, Leon Benwell Professor of Law, University of Southern California.

Barbara J. Solomon, Stein/Sachs Professor, University of Southern California.

Jon Michael Spencer, Tyler and Alice Haynes Professor of American Studies, University of Richmond.

Margaret Beale Spencer, Board of Overseers Professor of Education, University of Pennsylvania.

Claude M. Steele, Lucie Sterns Professor in the Social Sciences, Stanford University.

Chuck Stone, Walter Spearman Professor, School of Journalism and Mass Communication, University of North Carolina at Chapel Hill.

Dorothy S. Strickland, State of New Jersey Professor of Education, Rutgers University.

Ora L. Strickland, State of New Jersey Professor of Education, Rutgers University.

Quintard Taylor, The Scott and Dorothy Bullitt Professor of American History, University of Washington.

Stephen B. Thomas, Philip Hallen Chair in Community Health and Social Justice, School of Social Work, University of Pittsburgh.

Gerald E. Thomson, Samuel Lambert Professor of Medicine, Columbia University.

Lee Thornton, Richard Eaton Professor of Medicine, Columbia University.

Gloria Wade-Gayles, The Eminent Scholar Endowed Chair, Spelman College.

Lonnie H. Wagstaff, M. K. Hage Centennial Professor in Education, College of Education, University of Texas at Austin.

Sheila S. Walker, Annabel Irion Worsham Centennial Professor and director, Center for African and Afro-American Studies, Department of Anthropology, University of Texas at Austin.

Jerry W. Ward Jr., Lawrence Durgin Professor of English, Tougaloo College.

Leland Ward, Louis L. Redding Professor for the Study of Law and Public Policy, University of Delaware.

Isiah M. Warner, Philip W. West Professor of Analytical and Environmental Chemistry, Louisiana State University.

Mary McKelvey Welch, Albert Werthan Professor of Biology, Fisk University.

Cornel West, Class of 1943 University Professor of Religion, Princeton University

Roger W. Wilkins, Clarence J. Robinson Professor of History and American Culture, George Mason University.

James H. Williams Jr., School Engineering Professor of Teaching Excellence, Charles F. Hopewell Faculty Fellow, and professor of applied mathematics, Massachusetts Institute of Technology.

John A. Williams, Paul Robeson Professor of English, Rutgers University.

Lisa R. Williams, Oren Harris Chair in Logistics, Sam M. Walton College of Business, University of Arkansas.

Preston Noah Williams, Houghton Professor of Theology and Contemporary Change, Harvard University.

Walter A. Williams, John M. Olin Professor of Economics, George Mason University.

Scott C. Williamson, Robert H. Walkup Assistant Professor of Theological Ethics, Lousiville Seminary.

Janice D. Willis, Walter A. Crowell University Professor of Social Sciences, Wesleyan University.

William Julius Wilson, Lewis P. and Linda L. Geyser University Professor, Harvard University.

Herbert Graves Winful, The Arthur F. Turneau Professor of Electrical Engineering and Computer Science, University of Michigan.

May L. Wykle, Florence Cellar Professor of Gerontological Nursing, Case Western Reserve University.

School Enrollment by Race, Hispanic Origin, and Age: 1980 to 1998

[As of October (47,673 represents 47,673,000). Covers civilian noninstitutional population enrolled in nursery school and above. Based on Current Population Survey.]

Age	White 1980	White 1990	White 1998	Black 1980	Black 1990	Black 1998	Hispanic origin[1] 1980	Hispanic origin[1] 1990	Hispanic origin[1] 1998
ENROLLMENT (1,000)									
Total 3 to 34 years old	**47,673**	**48,899**	**44,898**	**8,251**	**8,854**	**10,800**	**4,263**	**6,073**	**9,274**
3 and 4 years old	1,844	2,700	2,623	371	452	731	172	249	565
5 and 6 years old	4,781	5,750	4,805	904	1,129	1,321	491	835	1,316
7 to 13 years old	19,585	20,076	17,776	3,598	3,832	4,426	2,009	2,794	4,037
14 and 15 years old	6,038	5,265	5,031	1,088	1,023	1,167	568	739	1,018
16 and 17 years old	5,937	4,858	4,978	1,047	962	1,153	454	592	908
18 and 19 years old	3,199	3,271	3,394	494	596	732	226	329	487
20 and 21 years old	2,206	2,402	2,270	242	305	402	111	213	287
22 to 24 years old	1,669	1,781	1,772	196	274	298	93	121	275
25 to 29 years old	1,473	1,706	1,407	187	162	344	84	130	227
30 to 34 years old	942	1,090	842	124	119	226	54	72	154
35 years old and over	1,104	2,096	2,062	186	238	358	(NA)	145	253
ENROLLMENT RATE									
Total 3 to 34 years old	**48.9**	**49.5**	**56.0**	**53.9**	**51.9**	**59.2**	**49.8**	**47.4**	**50.3**
3 and 4 years old	36.3	44.9	54.2	38.2	41.6	58.3	28.5	29.8	39.7
5 and 6 years old	95.8	96.5	96.0	95.4	96.3	95.3	94.5	94.8	93.3
7 to 13 years old	99.2	99.6	98.9	99.4	99.8	98.6	99.2	99.4	98.9
14 and 15 years old	98.3	99.1	98.9	97.9	99.2	98.8	94.3	99.0	96.8
16 and 17 years old	88.6	92.5	95.1	90.6	91.7	92.9	81.8	85.4	89.1
18 and 19 years old	46.3	57.1	66.8	45.7	55.2	61.1	37.8	44.1	40.3
20 and 21 years old	31.9	41.0	48.9	23.4	28.4	39.9	19.5	27.2	25.6
22 to 24 years old	16.4	20.2	26.3	13.6	20.0	20.8	11.7	9.9	16.3
25 to 29 years old	9.2	9.9	11.5	8.8	6.1	13.9	6.9	6.3	8.7
30 to 34 years old	6.3	5.9	6.3	6.8	4.4	8.8	5.1	3.6	5.5
35 years old and over	1.3	2.1	2.0	1.8	2.1	2.5	(NA)	2.1	2.3

NA Not available.

[1] Persons of Hispanic origin may be of any race.

SOURCE: U.S. Census Bureau, *Current Population Reports*, P20-521; and earlier reports.

Proficiency Test Scores for Selected Subjects, by Characteristic: 1977 to 1996

[Based on The National Assessment of Educational Progress Tests which are administered to a representative sample of students in public and private schools. Test scores can range for 0 to 500. For details, see source]

Test and year	Total	Sex		Race		His-panic origin	Parental education				
		Male	Female	White[1]	Black[1]		Less than high school	High school	More than high school		
									Total	Some college	College graduate
Reading											
9 year olds:											
1979–80	215	210	220	221	189	190	194	213	226	(NA)	(NA)
1987–88	212	208	216	218	189	194	193	211	220	(NA)	(NA)
1993–94	211	207	215	218	185	186	189	207	221	(NA)	(NA)
1995–96	212	207	218	220	190	194	197	207	220	(NA)	(NA)
13 year olds:											
1979–80	259	254	263	264	233	237	239	254	271	(NA)	(NA)
1987–88	258	252	263	261	243	240	247	253	265	(NA)	(NA)
1993–94	258	251	266	265	234	235	237	251	269	(NA)	(NA)
1995–96	259	253	265	267	236	240	241	252	270	(NA)	(NA)
17 year olds:											
1979–80	286	282	289	293	243	261	262	278	299	(NA)	(NA)
1987–88	290	286	294	295	274	271	267	282	300	(NA)	(NA)
1993–94	288	282	295	296	266	263	268	276	299	(NA)	(NA)
1955–96	287	280	294	294	265	265	267	273	297	(NA)	(NA)
Writing[2]											
4th graders:											
1983–84	204	201	208	211	182	189	179	192	217	208	218
1987–88	206	199	213	215	173	190	194	199	212	211	212
1993–94	205	196	214	214	173	189	188	202	(NA)	212	212
1995–96	207	200	214	216	182	191	190	203	(NA)	205	214
8th graders:											
1983–84	267	258	276	272	247	247	258	261	276	271	278
1987–88	264	254	274	269	246	250	254	258	271	275	271
1993–94	265	254	278	272	245	252	250	259	(NA)	270	275
1995–96	264	251	276	271	242	246	245	258	(NA)	270	274
11th grade:											
1983–84	290	281	299	297	270	259	274	284	299	298	300
1987–88	291	282	299	296	275	274	276	285	298	296	299
1993–94	285	276	293	291	267	271	269	279	(NA)	286	293
1995–96	283	275	292	289	267	269	260	275	(NA)	287	291
Mathematics											
9 year olds:											
1977–78	219	217	220	224	192	203	200	219	231	230	231
1985–86	222	222	222	227	202	205	201	218	231	229	231
1993–94	231	232	230	237	212	210	210	225	(NA)	239	238
1995–96	231	233	229	237	212	215	220	221	(NA)	238	240
13 year olds:											
1977–78	264	264	265	272	230	238	245	263	280	273	284
1985–86	269	270	268	274	249	254	252	263	278	274	280
1993–94	274	276	273	281	252	256	255	266	(NA)	277	285
1995–96	274	276	272	281	252	256	254	267	(NA)	278	283
17 year olds:											
1977–78	300	304	297	306	268	276	280	294	313	305	317
1985–86	302	305	299	308	279	283	279	293	310	305	314
1993–94	306	309	304	312	286	291	284	295	(NA)	305	318
1995–96	307	310	305	313	286	292	281	297	(NA)	307	317

[continued]

Proficiency Test Scores for Selected Subjects, by Characteristic: 1977 to 1996

[Based on The National Assessment of Educational Progress Tests which are administered to a representative sample of students in public and private schools. Test scores can range for 0 to 500. For details, see source]

Test and year	Total	Sex		Race		His-panic origin	Parental education				
		Male	Female	White[1]	Black[1]		Less than high school	High school	More than high school		
									Total	Some college	College graduate
Science											
9 year olds:											
1976–77	220	222	218	230	175	192	199	223	233	237	232
1985–86	224	227	221	232	196	199	204	220	235	236	235
1993–94	231	232	230	240	201	201	211	225	(NA)	239	239
1995–96	230	232	228	239	201	207	215	222	(NA)	242	240
13 year olds:											
1976–77	247	251	244	256	208	213	224	245	264	260	266
1985–86	251	256	247	259	222	226	229	245	262	258	264
1993–94	257	259	254	267	224	232	234	247	(NA)	260	269
1995–96	256	261	252	266	226	232	232	248	(NA)	260	266
17 year olds:											
1976–77	290	297	282	298	240	262	265	284	304	296	309
1985–86	289	295	282	298	253	259	258	277	300	295	304
1993–94	294	300	289	306	257	261	256	279	(NA)	295	311
1995–96	296	300	292	307	260	269	261	282	(NA)	297	308
History, 1993–94											
4th graders	205	203	206	215	177	180	177	197	(NA)	214	216
8th graders	259	259	259	267	239	243	241	251	(NA)	264	270
12th graders	286	288	285	292	265	267	263	276	(NA)	287	296
Geography, 1993–94											
4th graders	206	208	203	218	168	183	186	197	(NA)	216	216
8th graders	260	262	258	270	229	239	238	250	(NA)	265	272
12th graders	285	288	281	291	258	268	263	274	(NA)	286	294

NA Not available.

[1] Non-Hispanic

[2] Writing scores revised from previous years; previous writing scores were recoded on a 0 to 400 rather than 0 to 500 scale.

SOURCE: U.S. National Center for Education Statistics, *Digest of Education Statistics*, annual.

High School Dropouts by Race and Hispanic Origin: 1975 to 1998

[In percent. As of October]

Item	1975	1980	1985	1990[1]	1991	1992	1993	1994	1995	1996	1997	1998
EVENT DROPOUTS[2]												
Total[3]	**5.8**	**6.0**	**5.2**	**4.0**	**4.0**	**4.3**	**4.2**	**5.0**	**5.4**	**4.7**	**4.3**	**4.4**
White	5.4	5.6	4.8	3.8	3.7	4.1	4.1	4.7	5.1	4.5	4.2	4.4
Male	5.0	6.4	4.9	4.1	3.6	3.8	4.1	4.6	5.4	4.8	4.9	4.4
Female	5.8	4.9	4.7	3.5	3.8	4.4	4.1	4.9	4.8	4.1	3.5	4.4
Black	8.7	8.3	7.7	5.1	6.2	4.9	5.4	6.2	6.1	6.3	4.8	5.0
Male	8.3	8.0	8.3	4.1	5.5	3.3	5.7	6.5	7.9	4.6	4.1	4.6
Female	9.0	8.5	7.2	6.0	7.0	6.7	5.0	5.7	4.4	7.8	5.7	5.5
Hispanic[4]	10.9	11.5	9.7	8.0	7.3	7.9	5.4	9.2	11.6	8.4	8.6	8.4
Male	10.1	16.9	9.3	8.7	10.4	5.8	5.7	8.4	10.9	9.2	10.4	8.6
Female	11.6	6.9	9.8	7.2	4.8	8.6	5.0	10.1	12.5	7.6	6.7	8.2
STATUS DROPOUTS[5]												
Total[3]	**15.6**	**15.6**	**13.9**	**13.6**	**14.2**	**12.7**	**12.7**	**13.3**	**13.9**	**12.8**	**13.0**	**13.9**
White	13.9	14.4	13.5	13.5	14.2	12.2	12.2	12.7	13.6	12.5	12.4	13.7
Male	13.5	15.7	14.7	14.2	15.4	13.3	13.0	13.6	14.3	12.9	13.8	15.7
Female	14.2	13.2	12.3	12.8	13.1	11.1	11.5	11.7	13.0	12.1	10.9	11.7
Black	27.3	23.5	17.6	15.1	15.6	16.3	16.4	15.5	14.4	16.0	16.7	17.1
Male	27.8	26.0	18.8	13.6	15.4	15.5	15.6	17.5	14.2	17.4	17.5	20.5
Female	26.9	21.5	16.6	16.2	15.8	17.1	17.2	13.7	14.6	14.7	16.1	14.3
Hispanic[4]	34.9	40.3	31.5	37.3	39.6	33.9	32.7	34.7	34.7	34.5	30.6	34.4
Male	32.6	42.6	35.8	39.8	44.4	38.4	34.7	36.1	34.2	36.2	33.2	39.7
Female	36.8	38.1	27.0	34.5	34.5	29.6	31.0	33.1	35.4	32.7	27.6	28.6

[1] Beginning 1990 reflects new editing procedures for cases with missing data on school enrollment.
[2] Percent of students who drop out in a single year without completing high school. For grades 10 to 12.
[3] Includes other races, not shown separately.
[4] Persons of Hispanic origin may be of any race.
[5] Percent of the population who have not completed high school and are not enrolled, regardless of when they dropped out. For persons 18 to 24 years old.

SOURCE: U.S. Census Bureau, *Current Population Reports,* P20-521.

College Population by Selected Characteristics: 1998

[In thousands (209,831 represents 209,831,000), except percent. As of October. For persons 15 years old and over. Based on the Current Population Survey.]

Characteristic	Total population	Enrolled in college							
		Total	Type of school			Percent enrolled full time	Percent employed		
			2-year	4-year	Graduate school		Total	Full time	Part time
Total [1]	209,831	15,546	4,234	8,275	3,037	65.5	63.7	33.6	30.1
Male	101,114	6,905	1,845	3,777	1,284	67.6	62.6	34.7	27.9
Female	108,718	8,641	2,389	4,499	1,754	63.9	64.6	32.8	31.8
White	175,028	12,401	3,389	6,632	2,379	64.6	65.9	34.1	31.8
Black	25,117	2,016	628	1,063	326	63.7	61.9	39.1	22.8
Hispanic origin [2]	21,817	1,363	640	560	164	58.8	62.1	37.0	25.1
15 to 19 years old	19,752	3,793	1,301	2,447	45	88.9	48.6	9.7	38.9
20 and 21 years old	7,131	3,092	701	2,318	73	86.6	56.7	16.8	39.9
22 to 24 years old	10,474	2,561	619	1,406	537	73.8	64.5	30.3	34.2
25 to 34 years old	38,601	3,414	838	1,261	1,314	45.0	75.2	54.6	20.6
35 years and older	133,871	2,685	772	839	1,070	26.4	77.6	63.3	14.3

[1] Includes other races, not shown separately.
[2] Persons of Hispanic origin may be of any race.

SOURCE: U.S. Census Bureau, *Current Population Reports*, P20-521.

Degrees Earned by Level and Race/Ethnicity: 1981 to 1997

[For school year ending in year shown. Data exclude some institutions not reporting field of study and are slight undercounts of degrees awarded]

Level of degree and race/ethnicity	Total						Percent distribution	
	1981	1985	1990	1995	1996	1997	1981	1997
Associate's degrees, total	**410,174**	**429,815**	**450,263**	**538,545**	**553,625**	**563,620**	**100.0**	**100.0**
White, non-Hispanic	339,167	355,343	369,580	419,323	425,028	424,364	82.7	75.3
Black, non-Hispanic	35,330	35,791	35,327	47,142	51,672	55,260	8.6	9.8
Hispanic	17,800	19,407	22,195	36,013	38,163	42,645	4.3	7.6
Asian or Pacific Islander	8,650	9,914	13,482	20,717	23,091	24,829	2.1	4.4
American Indian/Alaskan Native	2,584	2,953	3,530	5,492	5,556	5,927	0.6	1.1
Nonresident alien	6,643	6,407	6,149	9,858	10,115	10,595	1.6	1.9
Bachelor's degrees, total	**934,800**	**968,311**	**1,048,631**	**1,158,788**	**1,163,036**	**1,168,023**	**100.0**	**100.0**
White, non-Hispanic	807,319	826,106	884,376	913,377	904,709	898,224	86.4	76.9
Black, non-Hispanic	60,673	57,473	61,063	87,203	91,166	94,053	6.5	8.1
Hispanic	21,832	25,874	32,844	54,201	58,288	61,941	2.3	5.3
Asian or Pacific Islander	18,794	25,395	39,248	60,478	64,359	67,969	2.0	5.8
American Indian/Alaskan Native	3,593	4,246	4,392	6,606	6,970	7,409	0.4	0.6
Nonresident alien	22,589	29,217	26,708	36,923	37,544	38,427	2.4	3.3
Master's degrees, total	**294,183**	**280,421**	**322,465**	**397,052**	**405,521**	**414,882**	**100.0**	**100.0**
White, non-Hispanic	241,216	223,628	251,690	292,784	297,558	302,541	82.0	72.9
Black, non-Hispanic	17,133	13,939	15,446	24,171	25,801	28,224	5.8	6.8
Hispanic	6,461	6,864	7,950	12,907	14,412	15,187	2.2	3.7
Asian or Pacific Islander	6,282	7,782	10,577	16,842	18,161	18,477	2.1	4.5
American Indian/Alaskan Native	1,034	1,256	1,101	1,621	1,778	1,924	0.4	0.5
Nonresident alien	22,057	26,952	35,701	48,727	47,811	48,529	7.5	11.7
Doctor's degrees, total	**32,839**	**32,307**	**38,113**	**44,427**	**44,645**	**45,394**	**100.0**	**100.0**
White, non-Hispanic	25,908	23,934	25,880	27,826	27,756	28,344	78.9	62.4
Black, non-Hispanic	1,265	1,154	1,153	1,667	1,636	1,847	3.9	4.1
Hispanic	456	677	788	984	999	1,098	1.4	2.4
Asian or Pacific Islander	877	1,106	1,235	2,690	2,646	2,607	2.7	5.7
American Indian/Alaskan Native	130	119	99	130	158	173	0.4	0.4
Nonresident alien	4,203	5,317	8,958	11,130	11,450	11,325	12.8	24.9
First-professional degrees, total	**71,340**	**71,057**	**70,744**	**75,800**	**76,641**	**77,815**	**100.0**	**100.0**
White, non-Hispanic	64,551	63,219	60,240	59,402	59,456	59,852	90.5	76.9
Black, non-Hispanic	2,931	3,029	3,410	4,747	5,016	5,251	4.1	6.7
Hispanic	1,541	1,884	2,427	3,231	3,476	3,553	2.2	4.6
Asian or Pacific Islander	1,456	1,816	3,362	6,397	6,617	7,037	2.0	9.0
American Indian/Alaskan Native	192	248	257	412	463	511	0.3	0.7
Nonresident alien	669	861	1,048	1,611	1,613	1,611	0.9	2.1

SOURCE: U.S. National Center for Education Statistics, *Digest of Education Statistics,* annual.

Religion

- ◆ Origins and History of African American Religious Traditions
  - ◆ African American Female Religious Leadership
  - ◆ African American Churches during Reconstruction
  - ◆ African American Churches in the Twentieth Century
  - ◆ Evolving Trends among African American Churches
  - ◆ African American Denominations ◆ Religious Leaders

by Stephen W. Angell

The first Africans who arrived on North American shores brought their own religious world views with them. While a minority had been Muslims or Christians prior to their kidnapping by slave traders, most adhered to their native African religions. Hundreds of different religions developed, but in general, the Africans believed that the world had been created by a high god who removed himself from direct intervention in worldly affairs after the act of creation.

◆ ORIGINS AND HISTORY OF AFRICAN AMERICAN RELIGIOUS TRADITIONS

Early African American Belief Systems

In Africa, worshipers directed their prayers to intermediary spirits, chief among whom were their ancestors or the "living dead." If proper offering was made to an ancestor, the individual would be blessed with great prosperity, but if the ancestor was slighted, misfortune would result. In addition, the Yorubas worshiped a variety of nature spirits or *orishas*. These spirits often possessed their devotees, who then became mediums of their gods. This kind of spirit-possession is a prominent feature of some modern African American religions, such as *santeria*, which recently has spread across large urban areas including Miami and New York. Also a part of the African worldview, especially among the Bakongo, was the practice of magic, variously known in the New World as *obeah, vaudou (voodoo),* or *conjure.* This magic, designed to help friends (myalism) or to hurt enemies (obeah), at one

time was widely practiced by Africans throughout the Western Hemisphere.

The type of African spirituality that took root in North America merged elements from many African cultures. Since slave masters intentionally mixed Africans from many tribal backgrounds, no "pure" African religion preserving one tradition emerged. Nevertheless, the longstanding scholarly controversy over the extent to which African traditions have been retained in African-based religions is gradually being resolved in favor of those who see extensive survivals. In addition to singing, church music, and preaching style, aspects where an African influence has generally been conceded, scholars have made persuasive arguments for African survivals in family structure, funeral practices, church organization, and many other areas.

Missionary Efforts by Christians

The first sustained effort at converting African Americans to Christianity was made by the Anglican Society for the Propagation of the Gospel in Foreign Parts, which sent missionaries to North America in 1701. These missionaries had little success among the Africans; many mocked those who imitated the whites too closely and, thus, resisted the missionaries. In addition, white slave masters often resented losing slaves' time to church services and feared that slaves would lay a claim to freedom through conversion. The numerous colonial laws, starting with Virginia in 1669, proclaiming that conversion failed to entitle slaves to freedom did not comfort some slave masters, who suspected that Christianity would undermine slave discipline—indeed, some remained unconvinced of the advisability of missionary efforts until emancipation occurred. On the other hand, some slave masters believed the Christianization of Africans to be justification for enslaving them.

Subsequent efforts to convert African Americans to Christianity were more successful. In his seven missionary tours throughout North America between 1742 and 1770, the spellbinding orator George Whitefield effected the conversions of large numbers of both black and white Americans. The ministry of Methodist circuit riders, such as Francis Asbury, was also well received by African Americans at the end of the eighteenth century. Baptist and Methodist churches were the most successful in attracting African American members. Since these churches did not require their ministers to be well educated, doors were opened for aspiring African American ministers, many of whom lived in states where teaching African Americans to read and write was forbidden by law. Furthermore, the Baptists and Methodists were not as hostile to the emotionalism of African American preachers and congregations as were more staid denominations, such as the Episcopalians. Finally, the anti-slavery stance of notable Methodist and Baptist leaders, such as John Wesley, Francis Asbury, and John Leland, and the greater degree of equality nurtured within many Baptist and Methodist congregations were attractive to African Americans.

Early Christian Congregations

Probably the first organizing effort by African Americans to bear fruit in an independent African American congregation was the Silver Bluff Baptist Church in South Carolina, which came into existence between 1773 and 1775. David George, an African American, and seven other men and women formed its organizing nucleus. George Liele, one of George's associates, often preached at the Silver Bluff Church before emigrating to Jamaica in 1782. Andrew Bryan, one of Liele's converts, founded the First African Baptist Church in Savannah, Georgia, in 1788.

Bryan's life well represented the complex predicament faced by African American religious leaders in the antebellum South. In the early years of his ministry, Bryan was whipped and twice imprisoned by whites who feared him. But he bought his freedom, prospered, and eventually came to own much property including eight slaves; his death in 1812 was mourned by blacks and whites alike. While many African American churches continued to be served by white ministers until 1865, African American pastors, licensed ministers, and

exhorters ministering to African American Baptist and Methodist congregations were not at all unusual at this time, either in the South or the North.

Black Catholics

Before the Civil War, African American Catholics were confined largely to Maryland and Louisiana. However, Catholics made greater efforts to convert African Americans after the Civil War. By the end of the nineteenth century, nearly 200,000 African American Catholics were worshiping in the United States, but more Protestant African American ministers existed than did African American priests in the Catholic churches.

Discrimination in White Churches

While white preachers urged African Americans to convert, and many predominantly white congregations welcomed them into membership, racial prejudice was never absent from the religious scene. Although the level of discrimination varied from region to region and congregation to congregation, some factors were relatively constant.

One such factor was the relative paucity of ordained African American clergy. To take the Methodists as an example, some African American ministers were ordained as deacons within the Methodist Episcopal Church prior to 1820, but none in the following four decades. No African American Methodist minister was ordained by the Methodist Episcopal Church to the higher office of elder or consecrated as a bishop prior to the Civil War, unless he was willing to emigrate to Liberia.

Other discriminatory practices also formed part of the religious landscape. The Methodists and many other denominations tried to reserve the administration of sacraments as the exclusive province of white clergy. Segregated seating in churches was pervasive in both the North and the South. Church discipline was often unevenly applied. Of course, racial discrimination in the churches was only a small part of the much larger political and moral controversy over slavery.

Resistance to discrimination took many forms. In the North, Peter Spencer in Wilmington, Delaware, Richard Allen in Philadelphia, and James Varick in New York, led their African American followers out of white Methodist churches and set up independent African American congregations. In Allen's case, his departure was preceded by a dramatic confrontation over segregated seating in Philadelphia's white Methodist church. Each of these men then used his congregation as the nucleus of a new African American Methodist denomination—Spencer formed the African Union Church in

Mother Bethel African Methodist Church, Philadelphia.

1807; Allen, the African Methodist Episcopal Church (AME) in 1816; and Varick, a denomination eventually called the African Methodist Episcopal Zion Church (AME Zion) in 1821.

Meanwhile, in Charleston, South Carolina, a more explosive situation was taking shape. Morris Brown, an African American Methodist minister from Charleston, who had helped Richard Allen organize the African Methodist Episcopal Church, organized an independent African American Methodist church in his home city. The authorities harassed Brown's church and sometimes arrested its leaders. Nevertheless, within a year, more than three-quarters of Charleston's African American Methodists had united with him. The oppression of African Americans in Charleston was so severe that many members of Brown's congregation, including prominent lay leaders, joined the insurrection planned by Denmark Vesey to take over the Charleston armory

and, eventually, the whole environs of Charleston. The conspirators, apprehended before they could carry out their plans, testified that Brown had not known of their scheme, and the minister was allowed to move to Philadelphia, where Richard Allen made him the second bishop of the African Methodist Episcopal Church.

A few African Americans became acquiescent as a result of Christianity. One such example was Pierre Toussaint, a black Haitian slave who fled in 1787 to New York with his white owners, the Berards, just prior to the Haitian Revolution. In 1811, Mrs. Berard manumitted Toussaint on her deathbed. Over the next 40 years, Toussaint became a notable philanthropist, contributing funds to the building of St. Patrick's Cathedral. However, when the cathedral opened, Toussaint did not protest when a white usher refused to seat him for services. Some American Catholics recently revived the controversy over Toussaint, by campaigning for his canonization. Many African American Catholics have strongly objected, seeing Toussaint as passive and servile and thus a poor candidate for sainthood.

Emancipation Efforts of African American Church Leaders

The mid-nineteenth century saw increased anti-slavery activity among many African American church leaders and members. Some gave qualified support to the gradual emancipation program sponsored by the American Colonization Society, which sought to encourage free African Americans to emigrate to Africa in order to Westernize and Christianize the Africans. Virginia Baptist pastor Lott Cary and Maryland Methodist minister Daniel Coker were the two most prominent African American religious leaders to emigrate to Africa in the 1820s. By the 1850s, enough African American Methodists were in Liberia for the Methodist Episcopal Church to consecrate an African American bishop, Francis Burns, to serve the Liberian churches. While some black Americans were emigrating to Africa, others emigrated to the West Indies—Episcopalian Bishop James T. Holly, for example, settled in Haiti to undertake missionary work.

Because of the extreme repression in the slave states, African Americans were unable to openly express their views on political issues. They were, however, often able to make their views clear; for example, a white minister who dwelled too long on the Biblical text that servants should obey their masters was apt to find his African American listeners deserting him. In addition, African American Christians often held secret meetings in "brush arbors," rude structures made of pine boughs, or in the middle of the woods. There they could sing spirituals and pray openly for the quick advent of freedom. Slave revolts, on the other hand, provided a violent outbreak of dissent much feared by whites. The 1831 revolt of Nat Turner, a Baptist preacher, in Northampton County, Virginia, was suppressed only after tremendous bloodshed had been visited upon both African Americans and whites. Frightened whites in the South intensified their surveillance of African American churches in the aftermath of the Turner revolt. Even conservative African American preachers, such as Presbyterian John Chavis in North Carolina and the Baptist "Uncle Jack" in Virginia, were prohibited from preaching.

African American leaders in the North could afford to be more open and forthright in their political stance. Most rejected outright the views of the American Colonization Society in favor of the immediate abolition of slavery. Presbyterian minister Henry Highland Garnet was a prominent abolitionist, urging African American

slaves in 1843 to "let your motto be RESISTANCE! RESISTANCE! RESISTANCE!" African Methodist Episcopal Bishop Daniel Payne and African Methodist Episcopal Zion Bishop Christopher Rush, both emigrants from the Carolinas to the North, were outspoken abolitionists who, after the mid-1840s, became the most prominent leaders in their respective churches. Frederick Douglass was one of the few leading African American abolitionists who did not pursue a ministerial career, and even he had briefly served as an African Methodist Episcopal Zion preacher in New Bedford, Massachusetts. African American clergy were extraordinarily active in recruiting African American men to join the Union armies during the Civil War, after the Emancipation Proclamation opened up the possibility of military service to them. During the Civil War, nearly a dozen African American ministers, including the African Methodist Episcopal Church's Henry McNeal Turner, served as chaplains to African American army regiments.

◆ AFRICAN AMERICAN FEMALE RELIGIOUS LEADERSHIP

Early African American women ministers sometimes served as travelling evangelists, especially within African American denominations. While Sojourner Truth's oratory has become appropriately famous, Maria Stewart, Jarena Lee, Zilpha Elaw, and other early nineteenth century women also spoke eloquently and, in Lee's and Elaw's cases, travelled widely and labored diligently. None of these women were ordained, but Elizabeth (no last name known), a former slave from Maryland whose ministry began in 1796, spoke for many female preachers when she was accused of preaching without a license: "If the Lord has ordained me, I need nothing better." Rebecca Cox Jackson left the African Methodist Episcopal Church in the 1830s when she felt that men denied her the chance to exercise her ministry, and she eventually became head eldress of a predominantly African American Shaker community in Philadelphia.

During the postbellum years, some African American women sought and obtained formal ordination from their denominations. Sarah Ann Hughes, a successful North Carolina evangelist and pastor in the African Methodist Episcopal Church, was ordained by Bishop Henry McNeal Turner in 1885, but complaints from male pastors caused her ordination to be revoked two years later. The AME Church would not ordain another woman until 1948, when Rebecca Glover was ordained. Two women were ordained, however, by African Methodist Episcopal Zion bishops not long after the Hughes controversy—Mary J. Smalls in 1895

A pre-Civil War church service in Cincinnati, Ohio, c. 1853.

as a deacon and in 1898 as an elder, and also Julia A. J. Foote in 1894 and 1900, respectively. Pauli Murray, a distinguished lawyer and educator, in 1977 became the first African American woman to be ordained a priest in the predominantly white Episcopal Church. In 1989, Barbara Harris became the first woman bishop in the history of the Episcopal Church.

Throughout American history, many African American women exercised their ministry through para-ecclesiastical structures, such as women's temperance and missionary societies, while others, such as Anna Cooper and the African Methodist Episcopal Church's Frances Jackson Coppin, became renowned educators.

◆ AFRICAN AMERICAN CHURCHES DURING RECONSTRUCTION

African American church membership grew explosively after the Civil War, especially in the South, where the African American clergy played a prominent part in the Reconstruction governments. African Methodist

Episcopal minister Hiram Revels became the first African American to serve as a U.S. senator, when the Mississippi legislature sent him to Washington, DC, in 1870. However, Revels was only the ground breaker; many African American ministers went on to serve in the Congress or in their state governments. African American participation in Reconstruction politics was effective in large part because ministers in the AME and AME Zion Churches, and many African American Baptist ministers, carefully and patiently educated their congregation members on every civic and political issue. (Although the newly established African American denomination, the Colored Methodist Episcopal Church, largely stayed away from politics during Reconstruction.)

Even though African Americans were largely expelled from Southern state governments after the end of political Reconstruction in the 1870s, many African American ministers and laity continued to play an active political role on such issues as temperance, often campaigning on behalf of prohibition referenda.

Although women were not allowed to become AME church leaders in the early years, they were permitted to teach and preach.

The Southern white campaign of terror, lynching, and disfranchisement steadily reduced African American political power and participation, however, until the onset of mid-twentieth century civil rights movements.

African American Churches' Response to Segregation

As the system of racial segregation imposed in the 1880s and 1890s took hold, African American ministers coordinated a manifold response. First, they forthrightly challenged new segregation laws, engaging in civil disobedience and boycotts. For example, when the city of Nashville, Tennessee, segregated its street cars in 1906, influential Baptist minister R. H. Boyd led an African American boycott of the streetcars, even operating his own streetcar line for a time. No defeat was ever seen as final.

Second, African American ministers helped to nurture a separate set of African American institutions to serve African Americans excluded from white establishments. The Congregationalists, Baptists, and Northern Methodists established schools in the South for African Americans during Reconstruction, but the African Methodist Episcopal, African Methodist Episcopal Zion, and Christian Methodist Episcopal bishops forged ahead with the establishment of their own network of schools. The African American denominations also built up their publishing houses, and the books and periodicals that they published were vital to the black community. Virtually every institution with ties to African American communities received some support from African American churches.

Third, some African American ministers believed that the civil rights retreats of the late nineteenth century should spur African Americans to leave the United States for a destination where their full civil rights would be respected. A "Back to Africa" movement grew to enable African Americans to find a home where they could run governments, banks, and businesses without interference from whites. Thus, Bishop Turner helped to organize a steamship line to carry African Americans back to Africa, and two shiploads of African American emigrants sailed to Liberia in 1895 and 1896 as a result of his efforts. Some African American church leaders, such as Christian Methodist Episcopal Bishop Lucius Holsey and AME Bishop Richard Cain, held views similar to those advocated by Turner, but many more church leaders opposed Turner's emigrationism vigorously. Simultaneously, African American missionary work continued to occupy the attention of African Americans at the end of the nineteenth century. Under the guidance of Bishops Payne and Turner, for example, the African Methodist Episcopal Church had a vigorous missionary presence in Sierra Leone, Liberia, and South Africa.

◆ AFRICAN AMERICAN CHURCHES IN THE TWENTIETH CENTURY

In the twentieth century, African American religious life has become characterized by a far greater degree of diversity and pluralism. At the same time, traditional African American concerns, including the continuing quest for freedom and justice, have been not only maintained but also strengthened. Pentecostalism, which burst on the American scene in 1906, has become a major religious force within the African American community. William Joseph Seymour, a preacher and son of ex-slaves from Louisiana, led an extraordinary interracial revival in Los Angeles from 1906 to 1909 that

Annual convention of the Provisional Republic of Africa in Harlem, New York; marchers from the "Summer Chautauqua of the Abyssinian Baptist Church" carry a painting of the Ethiopian Christ.

enabled Pentecostalism to spread worldwide. The claim that all heavenly gifts that were available to early Christians, including faith healing and speaking in tongues, were available to modern Christians, gave great impetus to the movement. The Pentecostal-oriented Church of God in Christ, founded by Charles H. Mason, who attended Seymour's revival, has become the second largest African American denomination in the United States. In the latter part of the century, the charismatic or Neo-Pentecostal movement has revitalized many congregations within mainline African American denominations.

The liturgy of the African American churches was transformed with the introduction of gospel music in the early part of the twentieth century. Influenced by the work of such composers as Charles Tindley, Charles Price Jones, Lucie Campbell Williams and Thomas

Dorsey, the new music enabled worshipers to praise God with rhythms and harmonies imported from more secular musical genres, such as blues and jazz. This new fusion sparked the creation of compositions that perhaps expressed the deep religious feelings of ordinary worshipers in the pews more appropriately than any previous music. New instruments were brought into the churches for the performance of these new musical compositions including guitars, drums, and, eventually, synthesizers and electronic instruments. This music initially encountered strong resistance in many African American congregations, but the popularity of such performers as Mahalia Jackson and the passage of time have enabled it to win a very wide acceptability. Church choirs and ensembles, such as the Dixie Hummingbirds, helped to gain for gospel music an ever- increasing audience. While both Methodists and Baptists played a part in the spread of gospel

African American congregation, one woman is crying out as she is "touched by the spirit," 1937.

music, the Holiness-Pentecostalist churches stemming from the 1906 revivals in Los Angeles played an especially important role in its increasing popularity.

The black nationalism of Bishop Turner came to full flower in the work of such men as Marcus Garvey (and his chaplain general, George A. McGuire), Elijah Muhammad, and Malcolm X. This black nationalism aided the growth of non-Christian religions, such as Islam and Black Judaism, within the African American community. Black nationalists often rejected Christianity as too complicit with slaveholding and racial oppression. A spectacular rise of storefront churches occurred, some of which were led by flamboyant showmen, such as Father Divine and "Sweet Daddy" Grace. Each of these trends has been significantly aided by the African American migrations after 1915 from southern states to the North, which greatly strengthened African American communities. A somewhat later migration from the

Caribbean provided support for the growth of a diverse range of religions within the African American community including the Episcopal Church, Seventh-Day Adventism, Roman Catholicism, Rastafarianism, santeria, and voodoo. An early Caribbean migrant was Sarah Mae Manning, who brought up her son, Louis Eugene Wolcott, in Boston within the Episcopal Church. He later achieved fame as a Muslim under the name of Louis Farrakhan.

Many black ministers became advocates of a Social Gospel movement. One of the most famous was Rev. Ransom of the African Methodist Episcopal Church, who came into prominence between 1901 and 1904 as pastor of an Institutional Church in Chicago. ("Institutional churches" provided a whole panoply of social services to needy members and neighbors, in addition to regular worship.) Social Gospellers highlighted the reality of collective, societal sin, such as the starvation of children and the denial of human rights, and maintained that Christian repentance of these sins must be followed by concrete actions to rectify injustice and to assist the poor. The Reverend Dr. Martin Luther King Jr. was profoundly influenced by this Social Gospel movement.

Many ministers and congregations maintained a kind of political involvement that built on a long tradition within the African American community and often with Social Gospel concerns in mind. Chicago AME minister Archibald Carey was a behind-the-scenes political organizer early in the twentieth century who effectively represented the interests of the African American community. New York's Adam Clayton Powell Jr. and Floyd Flake and Atlanta's Andrew Young and John Lewis were ministers who achieved election to the U.S. House of Representatives, with Powell rising to the chairmanship of the influential Education and Labor Committee during the 1960s. Other African American ministers, including Malcolm X, Al Sharpton, and Calvin Butts, have played important roles as community organizers, although never serving in elective office. Jesse Jackson's attempts to gain the Democratic nomination for president in 1984 and 1988 brought the electoral clout of the African American church into the spotlight. The African American church's strong involvement in political, economic, and social affairs helps to point out its continuing and central relevance—even indispensability—within the national context.

The Civil Rights movement of the 1960s was deeply influenced by the African American church context from which its most prominent organizer, Martin Luther King Jr., sprang. Its demonstrations, speeches, and movement songs were suffused with biblical images drawn from the Book of Exodus and other parts of the Bible. It was their deep religious faith that made it possible for the movement to keep progressing along a nonviolent path, even when King's home in Montgomery was firebombed or the Ninth Street Baptist Church in Birmingham in 1963 also was bombed, with four young girls the casualties of that violence. In a significant sense, King inherited his activism from his father, Martin Luther King Sr., also a Baptist pastor, who had led rallies and economic boycotts against racial discrimination as far back as the 1930s. But it is also worth recalling that many African American religious leaders in the 1960s thought that King's brand of social activism was too radical. One of King's most determined critics during the 1960s was the theologically conservative president of the National Baptist Convention of the U.S.A., Inc., Joseph H. Jackson. The attempt by King's ministerial allies to unseat Jackson as president of the convention in 1960 and 1961 led to a schism, with King and his supporters forming a new denomination, the Progressive National Baptist Convention. King came under further criticism when, in 1967 and 1968, he made it clear that his advocacy of pacifism extended to opposition to U.S. military involvement in Vietnam.

The Black Theology movement, which grew rapidly after King's assassination, attempted to fashion a critique of the prevalent Christian theology out of the materials that Malcolm X and the Black Power movement provided. African American theologians were skeptical of the integrationist and non-violent thrusts of the Civil Rights movement, calling the African American community toward greater pride in and reliance upon the community's own cultural resources. One such theologian, Albert Cleage, pastor of the Shrine of the Black Madonna in Detroit, argued that Jesus was a black messiah and that his congregation should follow the teachings of Jehovah, a black god. "Almost everything you have heard about Christianity is essentially a lie," he stated. Cleage was representative of many black theologians in arguing that black liberation should be seen as situated at the core of the Christian gospels. In the 1980s, African American women such as Jacquellyn Grant, Delores Williams, and Katie Cannon have formulated "womanist" theologies, which seek to combat the triple oppression of race, class, and gender suffered by most African American women.

Folk Art of Preaching

In most African American congregations, sermonizing is an interpersonal skill that African Americans have elevated to the level of art with such notable elements as call and response and repetition of phrases. The exuberance of all participants is highly dependent upon the tradition within which one worships. For example, in the more highly liturgical traditions such as Roman Catholicism and Eastern Orthodoxy sermons only tend to be instructional. By contrast, non-liturgical Protestant denominations, including Baptist and Pentecostal churches, tend to view sermons as verbal sacraments. In the 1990s, nondenominational churches have reached a new high in popularity, usually centered upon a solitary, charismatic figure. As the medium is the message, performance is as important as the words themselves. Among the most highly regarded "artists" are Gardner C. Taylor, pastor emeritus of Brooklyn, New York's Concord Baptist Church of Christ; Barbara King, founder and minister of Atlanta's nondenominational Hillside Chapel and Truth Center, Inc.; and James Forbes, senior minister of New York City's Riverside Church. They are just a few of those who have been earmarked as the great preachers of the late twentieth century. In 1996, both Forbes and Taylor were deemed two of the twelve most effective preachers by a Baylor University survey, and Taylor was named as one of President Bill Clinton's favorite evangelists.

◆ EVOLVING TRENDS AMONG AFRICAN AMERICAN CHURCHES

As the twenty-first century approaches, African American religions are undergoing substantial changes. The religious searches of prosperous middle-class African Americans has brought about surging enrollment at African American megachurches in many of the nation's metropolitan areas, such as Atlanta, Washington, DC, and Dallas. A growing interest in do-it-yourself spirituality has greatly enlarged the readership of inspirational writers, such as Iyanla Vanzant and T. D. Jakes. There has been an unprecedented interest in racial reconciliation among conservative Christian churches, joining liberal Christians who have pioneered in this area since the 1960s, even while an upsurge in African American church burnings, especially in the rural South demonstrated that the nation still has much work to do in addressing racism. Muslim leader Louis Farrakhan achieved spectacular success with his Million Man March in October 1995, stressing such spiritual themes as atonement, but he has not fashioned an effective follow-up to this headline-grabbing event. Meanwhile, the urban poor, especially young African American men, seem to be staying away from the churches in ever-increasing numbers.

Large African American churches, such as the Ebenezer African Methodist Episcopal Church in Maryland with 12,000 members, have attracted the African American middle-class worshippers in unprecedented numbers. They have done so with very diverse offerings. For example, Ebenezer offers marriage counseling, workshops on financial planning, a ministry to lawyers and a socially involved, intellectually informed ministry. Many of the megachurch ministers, such as Ebenezer's pastor and assistant pastor, have doctoral degrees. African American megachurch members reach out to young African American men who are still in poverty, even though their churches are often in the suburbs, miles away from inner city problems. Some African American churches have traditionally had large memberships, but the new megachurches feature younger pastors who have earned doctorates and are often still in their thirties or forties. Unlike their white counterparts, African American megachurches often seek out social involvement and uplift with the poor. Other African American megachurches can be found in such metropolitan areas as Atlanta, Chicago, Dallas, and Memphis.

Increasingly, African American ministerial leadership is passing from those who were on the front lines of civil rights struggles in the 1960s to their children's generation. Perhaps this reality is best symbolized by recent events in Atlanta. In July 1997, 75-year-old Joseph Lowery, who had helped to found the Southern Christian Leadership Conference with his colleagues Martin Luther King Jr. and Ralph Abernathy, stepped down from the presidency of that organization. Meanwhile, Bernice King, who was five years old when her father was assassinated, has established a successful ministry at the Greater Rising Star Baptist Church in Atlanta. Similar to her father, she preaches a message of forgiveness and reconciliation, and she calls upon churches to commune and fellowship more across racial and ethnic lines. Meanwhile, Atlanta's Ebenezer Baptist Church, where M. L. King Jr. previously preached, opened a new sanctuary seating 1,600 worshipers in March 1999. The old church building, only half as large, will be taken over and maintained by the National Park Service.

African American Churches Address Social Issues

On the whole, African American churches continue to address a wide variety of social problems affecting the African American community. Perhaps most urgently, many churches have strong anti-drug programs. Some congregations have undertaken vigorous action against "crack" houses. Parochial schools, feeding centers, and housing for senior citizens are also part of the African American church's outreach to the community. Many African American ministers have noted, however, the growing division of the African American community along lines of social class and have exhorted middle-class African Americans to give more generously to programs that aid the poor. James Cone, a leading African American theologian, has stated that African American churches need to devote less time and attention to institutional survival and more to finding ways to deal with such pressing issues as poverty, gang violence, and AIDS. In 1997, five historically African American denominations formed Revelation Corporation of America, a partnership between corporations, charities, and churches; the income from the corporation will be used to help to subsidize home

Reverend Gardner Taylor, pastor of Concord Baptist Church in Brooklyn, addressing a protest rally in 1963.

ownership among moderate-income residents of big cities, such as Philadelphia and Memphis.

African American churches have been involved in a wide variety of ecumenical efforts, both with white churches and other African American churches. While mainline Christian organizations, such as the National Council of Churches of Christ, have been involved in efforts for human rights for all and interracial reconciliation since the 1960s, it has only been in the 1990s that evangelical Christian organizations have joined in similar movements. In 1994, predominantly African American and predominantly white Pentecostalist

churches formed an interracial umbrella organization for the first time. The Promise Keepers, a Christian men's movement designed to motivate men to become better husbands and fathers, fully included African Americans in the staff and leadership of the organization. In June 1995, the Southern Baptist Convention adopted a resolution apologizing for its previous defense of slavery and "unwaveringly" denouncing "racism, in all its forms, as deplorable sin." The predominantly white National Association of Evangelicals and the National Black Evangelical Association agreed to hold their future meetings jointly. Still, some racial discontent continued to surface among evangelical Christians. The National Baptist Convention, U.S.A., Inc. withheld its support from one of the Reverend Billy Graham's crusades because of Graham's refusal to support affirmative action. In addition, E. Edward Jones, president of the National Baptist Convention of America, Inc., refused to accept the Southern Baptist Convention's apology for slavery and racism, charging that the resolution was simply a cover for aggressive evangelism in the African American community that would draw members away from historically African American churches.

Dialogues between individual denominations continue to nurture the spirit of cooperation between them, with the result of establishing closer working relationships on the national and community levels. In June 1997, leaders of eight historically African American denominations met in Hampton, Virginia in a week-long conference. The church leaders evinced a remarkable spirit of unity, but agreed to disagree on such issues as whether it could be the church's responsibility to help redeem society by pursuing social and economic change, or the church was only responsible for the salvation of individual souls. African American men from four Methodist denominations met in Atlanta in October 1998, addressing issues relating to families, male mentoring, and reconciliation between their various traditions. Bishops from these four denominations—the predominantly white United Methodist Church and three African American Methodist denominations, the African Methodist Episcopal, the African Methodist Episcopal Zion, and the Christian Methodist Episcopal Churches—continue to explore the possibility of a merger early in the twenty-first century.

African American churches also have found themselves compelled to address issues related to the multiethnic tensions of the 1990s. In the aftermath of the devastating arson attacks on black churches in 1996, white churches and African American churches joined together in some cities to offer workshops against racism. Leading African American pastors in Los Angeles have deplored both the violence of police revealed in the Rodney King incident and the violence of inner city rioters, while advocating urgent attention to the problems of inner-city residents. For example, James Lawson of the Holman United Methodist Church stated that those who burned buildings during the 1992 Los Angeles riots were "responding to a society of violence, not simply a society of racism," and issued "a call to repent." In Queens, New York, an African American Baptist congregation in 1991 warmly welcomed the opportunity to perform an ordination service for a Korean American minister, Chong S. Lee.

Black ministers and congregations have been increasingly opening themselves to frank discussions of human sexuality, impelled in part by the public health threat posed by the AIDS crisis, which has hit African American communities especially hard. In 1999, 5,000 churches participated in the Black Church Week of Prayer for the Healing of AIDS, a hundred percent increase in only ten years. Franklyn Richardson, senior pastor of Grace Baptist Church in Mount Vernon, New York, is one minister who has openly discussed AIDS with his congregation; Richardson's brother died of AIDS in 1993. Some African American congregations are still uncomfortable, however, about augmenting their traditional advocacy of monogamy and pre-marital abstinence with encouragement for sexually active individuals to use condoms to protect themselves from sexually transmitted diseases. Often African American ministers from conservative religious traditions (e.g., many Roman Catholics, Muslims, and Pentecostalists) are able to discuss this matter with their congregations only in an informal manner, if at all.

The cause of gender equality continues to make progress in African American churches. While two predominantly white denominations, the United Methodist and Protestant Episcopal Churches, have elevated African American women to the episcopacy in the past two decades, none of the largest historically African American denominations have done so. Nevertheless, women in some African American churches are achieving more prestigious ministerial assignments. Vashti McKenzie, a former model, disc jockey, and radio program director, has served as pastor of the Payne Memorial AME Church, an "old-line" church in Baltimore, since the early 1990s. Her innovative ministry, she says, is designed to "provide a message of hope for a hurting community." More than 600 female pastors are ensconced in the African Methodist Episcopal Church.

Preaching the gospel in a faithful but relevant fashion remains the most important objective of black churches. In a recent survey, 22 percent of African American clergy considered the most important problem of the African American church to be "lack of evangelism in fulfilling its religious role." That was more than twice the figure for any other problem identified. Ministerial training and financial support is another area needing improvement in many African American churches. African American churches are not in danger of losing sight of their many, vital and extremely significant functions, within both the black community and American society as a whole. It is safe to predict that the African American churches will continue to sustain and develop their important and prophetic witness.

African Methodist Episcopal (AME) Church reunion.

Membership Growth Within African American Churches

While many African American Methodist and Baptist denominations have shown only limited membership growth, other African American denominations are showing marked membership increases. Foremost among these are the Pentecostalist churches, whose lively worship and extensive social ministries are attracting members from all classes within the African American community. The largest of these denominations, the Church of God in Christ, is now estimated to have over three million members. Charismatic congregations, also known as neo-Pentecostalist, within such mainline African American churches as the African Methodist Episcopal Church, are also thriving and for similar reasons.

Other groups that have made substantial membership gains among African Americans include the Roman Catholic and Episcopal Churches and Islam. While estimates differ, apparently more than 1.5 million African Americans now belong to the Roman Catholic Church, which has worked hard in recent years to be sensitive to their needs. In many inner cities, it has maintained churches and schools in predominantly African American neighborhoods, although closings, mostly for financial reasons, are increasing in such dioceses as Detroit. Moreover, the Roman Catholic Church has been receptive to some liturgical variation, allowing gospel choirs and African vestments for priests in African American churches. Nevertheless, Roman Catholics confront some serious problems in serving African American parishioners. Fewer than 300 of the 54,000 priests in the United States are African American, meaning that some African American congregations must be served by white priests. In 1989, George A. Stallings Jr., a priest in Washington, DC, broke away from Catholicism, arguing that the Catholic Church was still racist and did not do enough for its African American members.

In such large cities as New York, Afro-Caribbean immigrants are swelling the ranks of the Episcopal Church. For example, a substantial majority of the 1,300 members of St. Paul's Episcopal Church in Brooklyn are Caribbean immigrants. At least three Episcopal churches in New York City have escaped closing by church authorities because of the influx of members from the Caribbean. The Episcopal Church is not the

More than 1.5 million African Americans belong to the Roman Catholic Church.

only predominantly white denomination to seek to attract new immigrants of African descent to its pews. Presbyterian Church (USA) officials plan to increase their denomination's ethnic minority membership to about 300,000, or about ten percent of total membership, within the next seven years, in part by targeting their outreach to new immigrants of African descent.

Mainstream Islam, despite raising its own complexities, has also made large gains in the United States. Of the six million Muslims in this country, one million are believed to be African American. Most African American Muslims do not distinguish between people of different races and worship cordially side by side with recent Muslim immigrants from Asia and Africa. Louis Farrakhan's Nation of Islam, however, which retains Elijah Muhammad's black separatist teachings, continues to maintain a devoted following. Due to its conservative stance on gender issues, Islam has proven to be more popular among African American men than among African American women. Following Farrakhan's successful Million Man March in 1995, he is quite able to fill the house, even in smaller cities such as Tallahassee, Florida, and hold his audiences spellbound for hours with a mixture of religious prophecy, candid social commentary, and moral exhortation for youth, but surprisingly the march has not achieved for him a sustained national presence. The chief organizer of the Million Man March, Benjamin Chavis Muhammad, converted to the Nation of Islam in April 1997, and then

suffered the termination of his ministerial standing in his former denomination, the United Church of Christ.

African and Afro-Caribbean religions, such as the Yoruba worship of the spirits (orisha), Cuban santeria, and Haitian voodoo, have also been gaining ground in African American communities and on some African American college campuses. Caribbean immigrants to the United States have helped to stimulate the growth of these African-derived traditions. A typical Haitian American voodoo congregation in Brooklyn, New York, was the subject of Karen McCarthy Brown's groundbreaking work *Mama Lola: A Vodou Priestess in Brooklyn*. Some African Americans in the United States are also attracted by the honor shown to ancestors in these African traditions. Iyanla Vanzant, brought up as a Christian but now identifying herself as a Yoruba priestess, has provided low-key advocacy of these traditions in her best-selling works.

Success and Failure Within African American Churches

The most successful African American ministers nowadays employ as many forms of media as possible in order to find and keep their audiences. T. D. Jakes, for example, might seem at first glance to be just a typical pastor of a megachurch, the Potter's House in Dallas, with 15,000 members. But what sets him above the crowd is his authorship of over one dozen books, many of them bestsellers, a popular program on the Black Entertainment Television (BET) cable network, and an active revival schedule that finds him packing venues such as Atlanta's Georgia Dome in July 1998. His popular Internet web page makes his thought widely available to the computer literate. Johnnie Coleman, pastor of the Christ Universal Temple, runs a seminary for pastors and has a radio ministry. Her fellow Chicagoan, Minister Louis Farrakhan of the Nation of Islam, also gets his message out through radio broadcasts and an active publishing program, including a weekly newspaper, *The Final Call*, sold on street corners nationwide. While pastors continue to spread their ideas through sermons on cassette tapes and in print, the most successful find many more ways to reach out.

One prominent African American minister who has encountered some failures is Henry J. Lyons, a St. Petersburg, Florida, Baptist minister who in 1994 became president of the National Baptist Convention of the USA, Inc. On July 9, 1997, Lyons's wife Deborah Lyons was arrested and charged with arson at a Florida home that her husband owned together with Bernice Edwards, director of public relations for his denomination and Henry Lyons's alleged mistress. This eventually led to state and national criminal investigations and indictments against Henry Lyons. Florida authorities charged Lyons with racketeering and grand theft in February 1998. They alleged that he had misappropriated denominational funds and swindled millions of dollars from large corporations by selling bogus membership lists. Five months later, Lyons was indicted by the federal government on 56 counts of extortion, fraud, and tax evasion. Lyons requested forgiveness from his local congregation and his denomination. On February 27, 1999, Lyons was convicted of all three counts brought against him by the state of Florida. On March 16, 1999, he resigned his office as president of the National Baptist Convention, and S. C. Cureton assumed the post until new elections were held. Lyons then pleaded guilty to five charges brought by the federal government on the following day. He was sentenced to five and one half years in a federal penitentiary and had to return $214,500 of donations that he had not distributed.

Increase of Church Burnings in the South

African American churches in the South were under fire—literally—in the 1990s. These incidents of church arson invoked grievous memories of racist violence during the 1960s, particularly the bombing of Birmingham's Sixth Street Baptist Church in which four small girls were killed on September 15, 1963. In 1996, the peak year, 119 of 297 churches affected by arson nationwide were predominantly African American. In other words, while African American churches constituted about six percent of the nation's churches, more than 40 percent of arson cases occurred that year at African American churches.

In response, President Clinton declared the "investigation and prevention of church arsons to be a national priority." In June 1996, President Clinton established the National Church Arson Task Force and proposed a three-pronged strategy that called for prosecution of the arsonists, the rebuilding of church edifices, and the prevention of additional fires. In addition, on July 3, he signed the Church Arson Prevention Act of 1996, which passed both chambers of the Congress unanimously.

Independently, Mac Charles Jones, associate general secretary for racial justice of the National Council of Churches of Christ, met with pastors of more than 30 burned-out churches and heard numerous stories of racist graffiti and threats issued against the pastors. African Americans concerned that the conflagrations are related have taken steps towards fighting the terrorism. To that end, the NAACP urged the Justice Department to investigate; in compliance, a full-scale civil

rights investigation was initiated. The Southern Christian Leadership Conference (SCLC) also instituted a fund for the affected congregations.

Despite federal government involvement though, only 34 percent of the cases have been solved as of November 1998. (Those who have been charged with arson of African American churches have included 68 whites, 37 African Americans, and one Hispanic American.) In addition, neither the Federal Bureau of Investigation (FBI) nor the Bureau of Alcohol, Tobacco and Firearms (ATF)—which together have more than 200 agents on the case—have been able to find a common link among these crimes.

◆ AFRICAN AMERICAN DENOMINATIONS

African-American Catholic Congregation

The Imani Temple, the first African-American Catholic Congregation, was founded in Washington, DC, by George Augustus Stallings Jr., a former Roman Catholic priest, in July of 1989. The schism occurred when Stallings performed a mass based on an experimental rite currently being used in Zaire, in defiance of the prohibition of his archbishop, James Hickey. This was the first schism from the Roman Catholic Church in the United States since 1904. Stallings also voiced a number of criticisms of the Roman Catholic Church at the time of the schism: "There are not enough black priests, not enough black church members, and some of the relatively few black churches that exist are being closed and consolidated. The black experience and black needs are addressed minimally in church services and life." He also asserted that "we could no longer afford to worship white gods in black houses." Thirteen African American Catholic bishops issued a statement denouncing Stallings and accused him of expressing "personal disappointment [and] individually felt frustration" under the cover of charges of racism.

Black Catholic reactions to these developments were mixed. Many expressed sympathy for Stallings's concerns but were unwilling to leave the Roman Catholic Church. Stallings assumed the title of archbishop of Imani Temple in 1991 and, at the same time, ordained a woman to the priesthood of the African American Catholic Congregation. Stallings has also relaxed the Catholic teaching on abortion for his congregation members and has declared the Reverend Dr. Martin Luther King Jr. to be a saint. In forming his denomination, he has experienced some setbacks. Several formerly close associates split with Stallings in 1991, alleging a lack of fiscal accountability in the church and

Reminiscent of the 1960s church bombings, numerous African American churches in the South were destroyed by arson during the 1990s.

accusing him of taking his liturgical innovations too far. In 1994, Stallings dedicated a new cathedral for his denomination in Washington, DC. As of the same year, his denomination claimed 4,200 members in seven cities in the United States and in Lagos, Nigeria.

African Methodist Episcopal Church

The African Methodist Episcopal (AME) Church was founded in 1816 at a conference convened in Philadelphia by Richard Allen, who was elected as its first bishop. In the following years, it grew throughout the North and Midwest and, after the Civil War, expanded quickly throughout the South and the West. In 1991, the church claimed about 3.5 million members, about 1 million of whom are found in churches in Africa, South America, and the Caribbean as a result of successful missionary efforts. It oversees about 8,000 churches, and the AME Church sponsors seven colleges and two seminaries in the United States and several colleges and educational centers in Liberia and South Africa. Payne Theological Seminary is located in Wilberforce, Ohio, at the site of the church's oldest school, Wilberforce University, founded in 1856. Turner Theological Seminary is one of six schools that have joined to form the Interdenominational Theological Center in Atlanta. About one-third of local AME congregations sponsor low-income housing, schools, Job Corps programs, or care for senior citizens. The African Methodist Episcopal Church's chief governing bodies are the General Conference, the Council of Bishops, and the General Board. It publishes the following periodicals: the *Christian Recorder;* the *Voice of Missions,* and the *AME Church Review.*

African Methodist Episcopal Zion Church

Originally known as the African Methodist Episcopal Church, the African Methodist Episcopal Zion Church was founded in 1821 in New York City. James Varick was elected its first "superintendent"; the title of the presiding officer was later changed to bishop. In 1848, the word "Zion" was added to the name of this church in order to avoid confusion with that founded by Richard Allen. It grew slightly prior to 1860, but expanded quickly in such Southern states as North Carolina and Alabama after the Civil War.

As of 1997, the African Methodist Episcopal Zion Church claimed approximately1.3 million members, 100,000 of whom lived in Africa, England, India, South America, or the Caribbean. It possesses nearly 3,100 churches worldwide. The church supports three colleges, two of which are junior colleges, and one seminary. The four-year college and the seminary are Livingstone College and Hood Theological Seminary, both located in Salisbury, North Carolina. The denomination is governed by a general conference, a board of bishops, and a correctional council. Its publications include the weekly *Star of Zion*, the *Quarterly Review*, the monthly *Missionary Seer*, and the quarterly *Church School Herald*.

African Orthodox Church

The African Orthodox Church was founded in 1921 by Archbishop George Alexander McGuire, once a priest in the Protestant Episcopal Church. McGuire was the chaplain for Marcus Garvey's United Negro Improvement Association, but Garvey soon disavowed his chaplain's efforts to found a new denomination. This church is today an autonomous and independent body adhering to an "orthodox" confession of faith. Its nearly 5,100 members worship in some 17 churches.

African Theological Archministry

In 1973 a group of African Americans founded a voodoo kingdom in South Carolina called Oyotunji. This kingdom was run by the leader of the African Theological Archministry, King Efuntola. The king and his followers relocated to South Carolina from Harlem, moving their Shango Temple to Beaufort County. The king received his voodoo training in Nigeria, and his followers worship various gods and deities that represent different forces in life. The affiliated membership of the group is estimated at 10,000.

African Union First Colored Methodist Protestant Church, Inc.

This denomination was formed in 1866 by a merger of the African Union Church and the First Colored Methodist Protestant Church. The African Union Church traced its roots to a Union Church of Africans founded in 1813 by Peter Spencer in Wilmington, Delaware. Today, this denomination has a membership of about 8,000.

Apostolic Overcoming Holy Church of God, Inc.

This Pentecostal denomination, originally known as the Ethiopian Overcoming Holy Church, was incorporated in Alabama in 1920. Evangelistic in purpose, it emphasizes sanctification, holiness, and the power of divine healing. As of 1994, it claimed 173 churches and about 12,000 members.

Bible Way Church of Our Lord Jesus Christ World Wide, Inc.

Founded in 1957, this Pentecostal tradition claimed 300 churches and 250,000 members as of 1994. It publishes *The Bible News Voice* biweekly.

Black Jews

Nearly 100,000 African Americans consider themselves Jewish. Included among these are the Commandment Keepers, founded in Harlem in 1919 by a Nigerian-born man known as "Rabbi Matthew"; the Church of God and Saints in Christ founded in 1896 in Lawrence, Kansas, by William Crowdy; and the Church of God founded in Philadelphia by Prophet F. S. Cherry. In terms of doctrine, these groups share little more than a dislike of Christianity and an affection for the Old Testament. Some black Jews claim descent from the Falasha Jews of Ethiopia, who now reside in Israel. However, few black Jews are recognized as such by orthodox rabbis.

The Church of God and Saints of Christ is probably the largest of these groups, with more than 200 churches and a membership of 38,000. The World African Hebrew Israelite Community—a religious sect that believes blacks in the Western Hemisphere are the descendants of the original Hebrews and, as such, are the rightful heirs of the Holy Land of Israel—has 3,000 members throughout the United States and an additional 1,500 living in Israel. Since the late 1960s, they have been led by the spiritual leader Ben Ami Ben-Israel, formerly a Chicago bus driver named Ben Carter.

Christian Methodist Episcopal Church

The Christian Methodist Episcopal (CME) Church, known until 1954 as the Colored Methodist Church, is the third largest African American Methodist body in the United States. It was founded after the Civil War, when some African American Methodist churches desiring to join neither the African Methodist Episcopal or African Methodist Episcopal Zion Churches successfully petitioned the Methodist Episcopal Church, South, for the right to form their own denomination. The first

CME General Conference was held at Jackson, Tennessee, in 1870. There the church's first two bishops, William H. Miles and Richard Vanderhorst, were elected.

In 1994, the Christian Methodist Episcopal Church estimates its membership at over 1 million persons, of whom 75,000 were located overseas. It possesses about 3,000 churches and maintains five church-affiliated colleges, as well as the Phillips School of Theology, a seminary that is part of the consortium known as the Interdenominational Theological Center in Atlanta. Its periodicals include the bimonthly *Christian Index* and the monthly *Missionary Messenger*.

Church of Christ (Holiness) U.S.A.

This denomination was organized in 1907 by Bishop Charles Price Jones, a renowned and prolific gospel song and hymn writer. The church traces its roots to an 1894 church established by Jones and C. H. Mason, but Jones and Mason parted company thirteen years later after the two men disagreed about whether speaking in tongues was necessary to prove baptism of the Holy Spirit. (Jones insisted that it was not.) Some 160 churches and 9,300 members belong to this denomination, which upholds the possibility of sanctification and Christian perfection. The church operates Christ Missionary and Industrial College, in Jackson, Mississippi.

Church of God by Faith

This Pentecostal denomination was founded in Florida in 1914. Its membership is concentrated in the Southeast.

Church of God in Christ

The Church of God in Christ (COGIC) was organized in 1897 by two former Baptist preachers, Charles H. Mason and C. P. Jones, and was initially strongest in Alabama, Mississippi, and Tennessee. Mason reorganized COGIC in 1907, when he and Jones parted on the issue of speaking in tongues. At that time, Mason was appointed "general overseer and chief apostle" of the Church, as well as its first bishop. It has subsequently expanded very rapidly throughout the United States, especially in African American neighborhoods in the inner cities.

As of 1991, COGIC claimed about 5.5 million members and 15,300 churches. It possesses bible colleges and a junior college, with plans for a university (All Saints University in Memphis) some time in the future. Its Charles H. Mason Theological Seminary is part of the Interdenominational Theological Center in Atlanta. It is governed by a general assembly, a general council

of elders, the board of bishops, and the general board composed of 12 bishops elected by the general assembly to four-year terms. In 1995, Bishop Chandler David Owens was elected presiding bishop over the organization, the fastest-growing Christian group in the United States.

Churches of God, Holiness

This denomination was organized by K. H. Burruss in Georgia in 1914. It split off from the Church of Christ (Holiness) U.S.A. Membership in the group's 40-odd churches totals some 25,000.

Fire Baptized Holiness Church

This church was organized on an interracial basis as the Fire Baptized Holiness Association in Atlanta, Georgia, in 1898; its African American members formed the Fire Baptized Holiness Church in 1908. The church subscribes to standard Pentecostalist doctrines on divine healing, speaking in tongues, and sanctification. As of 1968, it had about 50 churches and a membership of about 9,000.

Nation of Islam

After the death of Elijah Muhammad in 1975, his son Warith D. Muhammad assumed leadership of the movement. Warith Muhammad shifted dramatically away from his father's teachings of black nationalism, stating that whites could become members. He sought to bring his movement in accord with Orthodox Islam, and he eventually succeeded, renaming the Nation of Islam as the World Community of Al-Islam in the West and then as the American Muslim Mission before the merger was accomplished. Three other splinter groups formed, the largest headed by Louis Farrakhan, who split from Muhammad to reestablish the Nation of Islam on the basis of Elijah Muhammad's original black separatist teachings. The remaining two traditions are led by John Farrakhan and Caliph Emmanuel A. Muhammad.

National Baptist Convention of America, Inc.

The National Baptist Convention of America was formed in 1915, as a result of a schism with the National Baptist Convention, USA, Inc. over the issue of control of the denominational publishing house. The supporters of Richard Henry Boyd, chairman of the board of the publishing house, established this convention when Boyd's opponents had attempted unsuccessfully to bring the publishing house more firmly under denominational control. In 1987 it was said to possess 3.5

million members and 2,500 churches. However, more congregations split off in 1988 to form the National Missionary Baptist Association, when the new denomination also tried to assert control over its publishing house. It has missions in Jamaica, Panama, Haiti, the Virgin Islands, and Africa, and supports 15 colleges.

National Baptist Convention of the USA, Inc.

The National Baptist Convention was formed in 1895, through the union of three smaller church organizations, the oldest of which had been founded only 15 years earlier: the Baptist Foreign Mission Convention of the U.S.A.; the American National Baptist Convention; and the National Baptist Educational Convention of the USA. The National Baptist Convention incorporated itself after a dispute over the publishing house led to a schism in 1915.

The National Baptist Convention, Inc., is governed by a 15-member board of directors and a nine-member executive board. It is a supporter of the American Baptist Theological Seminary in Nashville, Tennessee, and of six other colleges. Its publications include the semimonthly *National Baptist Voice*. The convention dedicated its World Center Headquarters in Nashville, Tennessee, in 1989. In 1994, Rev. Dr. Henry J. Lyons was elected as the sixth president of the National Baptists, the largest African American religious order in the United States. On March 16, 1999, Rev. Lyons resigned his office amidst serious state and federal charges against him. S.C. Careton assumed the post of president until new elections were held.

The National Baptist Convention, Inc., as of 1992, claimed 8.2 million members, 100,000 of whom were in foreign countries. Litigation documents concerning its former president, Rev. Lyons, however, established that the denomination's membership in 1998 could be more accurately estimated at one million persons. It possesses 33,000 local churches.

National Missionary Baptist Convention

Founded in 1988, this group boasted 3.2 million members in 1995 and more than 500 churches. Rev. W. T. Snead was elected president of the Convention in 1994.

National Primitive Baptist Convention of America

African American and white Primitive Baptists separated after the Civil War. Although having long avowed opposition to church organization above the congregational level, it was not until 1907 that African American Primitive Baptists formed the National Primitive Baptist Convention. Each congregation is independent, and a decision by officials of a local church is final. Belief in "the particular election of a definite number of the human race" is included within its creed. In 1975, they possessed a membership of 250,000 in 606 churches.

Pentecostal Assemblies of the World, Inc.

An estimated one million members belong to the 1,760 churches of an organization founded in 1906. The church holds that speaking in tongues is vital to spiritual rebirth and that believers should be baptized only in the name of Jesus. Since its origins, it has accepted the ordination of women in the ministry.

Progressive National Baptist Convention, Inc.

The Progressive National Baptist Convention, Inc. was formed in 1961, as a result of a schism in the National Baptist Convention of the U.S.A., Inc. The schism resulted from a dispute over leadership occasioned by differences over tactical strategies in the struggle for civil rights. Those committed to such tactics as nonviolent civil disobedience, including Martin Luther King Jr., left to form the new denomination. The convention's motto is "Unity, Service, Fellowship, and Peace." It is a financial supporter of six colleges. It has active missions in Haiti and Africa. The Convention claims 2.5 million members and more than 2,000 churches and is governed by a 60-member executive board headed by Rev. Bennett Smith Sr. Although it has no publishing house of its own, it does publish a quarterly periodical titled the *Baptist Progress*.

Rastafarians

Members of this religion regard the Ethiopian Emperor Haile Selassie, who died in 1975, a supreme being. Marcus Garvey, a Jamaican-born nationalist who advocated a back-to-Africa movement in the United States in the early 1920s, is also a central figure in the faith. Reggae musician Bob Marley, a Rastafarian, helped to increase the religion's popularity in the United States.

Today, Rastas differ on specific dogma, but they basically believe that they are descended from black Hebrews exiled in Babylon and, therefore, are true Israelites. They also believe that Haile Selassie, whose name before ascending the throne was Lij Ras Tafari

Makonnen, is the direct descendent of Solomon and Sheba, and that God is black. Most white men, they believe, have been worshipping a dead god and have attempted to teach the blacks to do likewise. They hold that the Bible was distorted by King James, and that the black race sinned and was punished by God with slavery. They view Ethiopia as Zion, the Western world as Babylon, and believe that one day they will return to Zion. They preach love, peace, and reconciliation between races, but warn that Armageddon is imminent.

Rastas do not vote, tend to be vegetarians, abhor alcohol, and wear their hair in long, uncombed plaits called dreadlocks. The hair is never cut, since it is part of the spirit, nor is it ever combed. Estimates of their numbers in the United States and around the world vary widely.

Triumph the Church and Kingdom of God in Christ

Founded in 1902, this denomination is identified by their belief in the Pentecostal forms of baptism, but their rejection of speaking in tongues. The type of baptism ceremony in this church is called "fire-baptism."

United Church of Jesus Christ

The United Church of Jesus Christ split from the Church of God in Christ in 1945 over the issue of the Holy Trinity versus a theory of the "Oneness in Godhead," which it follows. This splinter sect was named the Church of God in Christ (Apostolic) and was founded by Bishop Randolph Carr. In 1965, disputes over the lifestyle of Bishop Carr led Monroe Saunders and most of the church's members to leave and found the present-day United Church of Jesus Christ.

◆ RELIGIOUS LEADERS

(To locate biographical profiles more readily, please consult the index at the back of the book.)

Jaramogi Abebe Agyeman (1911–2000)
Founder

Jaramogi Abebe Agyeman was born Albert Cleage Jr. in 1911, in Indianapolis, Indiana. His physician father relocated the family to Detroit a short time later, and Cleage undertook social work as a profession before earning a degree in divinity from Oberlin College in 1943. After his ordination, he headed Congregational churches in Kentucky and Massachusetts; Cleage's work at the latter was notable for the community outreach

and economic programs that he enacted. Returning to Detroit, the minister became head of a Presbyterian congregation that split off into its own church in 1953.

This fellowship, known as the Central United Church of Christ (CUCC), soon became a political powerhouse among Detroit's increasingly significant African American community during the 1950s. Cleage's growing interest in the Black Power movement of the 1960s—and especially the teachings of Nation of Islam leader Malcolm X—led the pastor to create a separate denomination from the CUCC in 1967, based on historical surmisings that Jesus was of African descent. The focal point of the church—and the symbolic gesture that attracted many to it—was a powerful 18-foot mural of the Black Madonna. The Black Christian Nationalist movement and its cornerstone congregation, the Shrine of the Black Madonna, soon became an influential religious, social, political, and economic force in the city.

Basing the church's tenets on both teachings of visionaries, such as Malcolm X, Elijah Muhammad, and Marcus Garvey, Cleage preached economic self-sufficiency to his flock and put the words into action by the creation of numerous social service programs, including a community grocery outlet, in answer to the inflated prices then common to white-owned stores in the African American neighborhoods, and a bookstore stocked with the significant African nationalist literature of the day. The Shrine of the Black Madonna expanded into other American cities over the next several years, but the imprint it left on Detroit was perhaps Cleage's most significant achievement.

In the late 1960s and early 1970s, after contentious 1967 race riots put aside any hopes of smooth integration between a diminishing white population and an increasingly frustrated African American citizenry, Cleage and the church's active membership were credited with helping elect numerous African American political leaders, judges, and school board members who remained a vital force in Detroit well into the 1990s. Cleage authored two books *The Black Messiah* and *Black Christian Nationalism* before taking the name Jaramogi Abebe Agyeman. Cleage died on February 20, 2000, in Calhoun Falls, South Carolina, at the age of 88 due to heart disease.

Noble Drew Ali (1886–1929)
Religious Leader

Noble Drew Ali, whose birth name was Timothy Drew, was born in North Carolina in 1886. He is principally important for his role in establishing the first North American religious movement combining black nationalist and Muslim themes with rejection of Christianity as the religion of whites. In 1913, he established the first Moorish Science Temple in Newark, New Jersey. He taught that African Americans were "Asiatics" who had originally lived in Morocco before enslavement. Every people, including African Americans, needed land for themselves, he proclaimed, and North America, which he termed an "extension" of the African continent, was the proper home for African Americans. The holy book for the Moorish Science Temple was a "Holy Koran," which was "divinely prepared by the Noble Prophet Drew Ali." (This book should not be confused with the Q'uran of Islam.) Every member of the Temple carried a card stating that "we honor all the Divine Prophets, Jesus, Mohammed, Buddha and Confucius" and that "I AM A CITIZEN OF THE U.S.A."

In the 1920s, the Moorish Science Temple expanded to Pittsburgh, Detroit, and Chicago. Noble Drew Ali also started several small businesses, which he ran together with his followers. In 1929 Drew Ali was stabbed to death in his Chicago office, in an apparent strife over the leadership of the Temple. The Moorish Science Temple survived Drew Ali's death, but the Nation of Islam was able to attract some of its followers.

Richard Allen (1760–1831)
Civil Rights Activist, Bishop

Born a slave in Philadelphia on February 14, 1760, Allen converted to Christianity in 1777 and, soon thereafter, bought his freedom. He then travelled widely through the Middle Atlantic States as an exporter. Francis Asbury, the first bishop of the Methodist Episcopal Church, asked Allen to join him as a travelling companion, stipulating that Allen would not be allowed to fraternize with slaves and would sometimes have to sleep in his carriage. Allen refused to accept such an offer, instead settling down in Philadelphia, where he helped to found the Free African Society, an African American society for religious fellowship and mutual aid. One day in the early 1790s, Allen was worshipping in Philadelphia's St. George's Methodist Church when he was pulled off his knees during prayer by white deacons who insisted that Allen was sitting outside the area reserved for African Americans. Allen left, establishing his own church for Philadelphia's African Americans in a converted blacksmith shop in 1794. White Methodists tried to exert their control over his church in various ways, which Allen resisted successfully. In 1816, after the Pennsylvania Supreme Court settled a suit over this church in Allen's favor, Allen called for a conference of African American Methodists. The African Methodist Episcopal Church was founded at this conference, and Allen was consecrated as its first bishop. Allen remained both religiously and politically active in his later years, and he was especially active in

opposing schemes to colonize free African Americans in Africa.

Carl Bean (1946?–)
Clergyman

Since 1985, Bishop Carl Bean, D.M. has been running two projects: the Minority AIDS Project (MAP) and the Unity Fellowship Church for African American gays and lesbians. Starting as a Bible study group, the church quickly took root, with chapters spreading to New York City, Detroit, Washington, DC, Philadelphia, Dallas, and Seattle by 1996. Meanwhile, MAP has become the largest AIDS agency serving African Americans in the United States.

Born and raised as a Baptist in Baltimore, Bean was an avid churchgoer in his youth. He grew up singing gospel, even participating in a Broadway gospel revue. Openly gay, Bean wanted to help liberate ostracized people of color—gay or straight—because he himself had once felt shunned by the church. Reaching out to the disenfranchised, Bean's followers believe that "Love is for everyone."

In 1991, the fellowship embarked on a campaign to work with gangs. Often getting referrals from social workers, Bean's congregation has earned a reputation for doing whatever is required to get people's lives on track. From distributing cash grants for food and bills to paying for funerals, Unity Fellowship members give back to the community.

Sister Thea Bowman (1938–1990)
Writer, Educator, Religious Leader

Born in Canton, Mississippi, in 1938, Thea Bowman, daughter of a medical doctor, joined the Roman Catholic Church at age 12 because of the Catholic education she had received. Three years later, she joined the Franciscan Sisters of Perpetual Adoration. She was extensively educated, earning a Ph.D. in literature and linguistics and was a distinguished teacher who taught elementary and high schools, as well as at colleges. She helped to found the Institute of Black Catholic Studies at Xavier University and was a distinguished scholar known for her writings on Thomas More. But it is probably for the spiritual inspiration that she provided in numerous lectures, workshops and concerts that she will be best remembered. She said that she brought to her church "myself, my black self, all that I am, all that I have, all that I hope to become, my history, my culture, my experience, my African American song and dance and gesture and movement and teaching and preaching and healing."

Calvin O. Butts III (1949–)
Religious Leader

Calvin Butts spent the first eight years of his life on the Lower East Side of New York City, where he was born in 1949. In 1957, the family moved to Queens, New York. During the summer breaks from school, Butts's parents would send him down South to stay with his grandmothers who lived near another in rural Georgia. It was in these early formative years that Butts first became acquainted with church.

After graduating from Flushing High School, where he was class president his senior year, Butts was accepted to Morehouse College. The year was 1967, an explosive time in the American civil rights struggle. Butts attended lectures, rallies, and speeches at Morehouse by Martin Luther King Jr. and other African American leaders. Following one of these very emotional events, Butts found himself immersed in a riot and actually assisted in the firebombing of a local store. Shortly thereafter, he renounced his capitulation to violence.

Just before his graduation from college, Butts was approached by two young seminarians trying to recruit students for their school. Later, he would receive his master's degree in divinity from Union Theological Seminary. While attending the Seminary, Butts raised a few eyebrows through his controversial stance on homosexuality. He has since defended the social and civil rights of gays, which he had once denounced.

Butts was recruited as a junior minister in 1972 by William Epps. During this time, his responsibilities included making hospital visits and conducting funeral services. From the very beginning, though, Butts realized the Abyssinian pulpit provided a great foundation from which to preach. For instance, he was quite vocal in his opposition to police brutality, along with any other form of violence.

Since assuming the pastoral role at Harlem's Abyssinian Baptist Church, which boasts more than 5,000 parishioners, Butts has also been involved the community. He has sat on the board of the Harlem Young Men's Christian Association (YMCA). Also, Butts has supported presidential hopefuls such as Ross Perot. He was the co-chair of Perot's New York campaign. The political arena is one that Calvin Butts will continue to explore. In the 1990s, he showed interest in running for city mayor and for statewide office.

Katie Cannon (1950–)
Presbyterian Minister, Educator, Feminist

Cannon was born January 3, 1950, in Kannopolis, North Carolina. As she approached adulthood, Cannon found that only two roads were available to most African American women in her community—they could work in the local mill or become a school teacher. The teachers that she knew played an important role in the early years of her life; she thrived in the supportive and protective environment of the academic environment, though the bite of racism was still all too real to her. African Americans were prohibited from public places, such as the library and the local pool, and Cannon was determined to escape.

Cannon enrolled in Barber-Scotia College. She graduated with a B.S. in 1971, after rising to the top of her senior class, making the dean's list, and being named Miss Barber-Scotia. The following fall, Cannon went on to study at Johnson C. Smith Seminary of the Interdenominational Theological Center (ITC) in Atlanta, Georgia—one of the two accredited African American seminaries at the time. During her time there Cannon was exposed to every aspect of the ministry. Majoring in Old Testament studies, she was only one of four women in her class. Upon completion of her studies, Cannon received her master's degree in divinity in 1974.

Cannon served as pastor at the Ascension Presbyterian Church in New York City for three years. Her work there was followed by an administrative position at the New York Theological Seminary, then, ready to resume her scholarly endeavors, Cannon decided to attend Union Theological Seminary, where she received her master's degree in philosophy, as well as a Ph.D. As of 1993, Cannon serves as the associate professor of Christian ethics at Philadelphia's Temple University. In 1995, a compilation of previously published essays was released as *Katie's Cannon: Womanism and the Soul of the Black Community.*

Johnnie Coleman (c. 1920–)
Religious Leader, Educator

Coleman grew up in Mississippi during the 1920s. A graduate of Wiley College in Texas and a school teacher in Mississippi and Chicago, Coleman was diagnosed in 1953 with an incurable disease. However, all of her symptoms disappeared after she moved to Kansas City to study at the Unity School of Christianity. Nonetheless, Coleman suffered from racial discrimination at the Unity School. Only her threat to leave the school just short of graduation won her the ability to live on campus and eat in the campus cafeteria. Her south side Chicago church began as a study group in 1956 with only five members. In 1958, she named her church the Christ Universal Temple, and in 1963 she moved to the Chatham section of South Chicago.

In the early 1970s, she served as the first African American president of the Association of Unity

Churches. Nevertheless, she still found racism too prevalent within the predominantly white denomination. Consequently, in 1974, she formed the Universal Foundation for Better Living, Inc., an association of churches devoted to the "positive thinking" derived from the New Thought movement. In the 1970s, she opened the Johnnie Coleman Institute to teach her doctrines derived from New Thought and, in the 1980s, began a broadcast ministry. Teaching her congregation members to discover the power of God within themselves, she has been a long-time advocate of Holy Materialism and Practical Christianity. By 1989, 23 churches belonged to the Universal Foundation, and her own congregation has increased in size to 12,000 members.

James H. Cone (1938–)
Author, Theologian, Educator

Born in Fordyce, Arkansas, in 1938, James Cone received a B.A. from Philander Smith College, a B.D. from Garrett Evangelical Seminary, and an M.A. and Ph.D. from Northwestern University. After teaching at Philander Smith and Adrian Colleges, Cone moved to Union Theological Seminary in 1969. He is currently the Charles A. Briggs Professor of Systematic Theology. Cone is the author of numerous books including *Black Theology and Black Power* (1969); *The Spirituals and the Blues* (1972); *For My People: Black Theology and the Black Church* (1984); and most recently, *Martin and Malcolm and America: A Dream or a Nightmare* (1991).

Perhaps more than any other African American theologian, Cone has provided a systematic exposition of the argument that since God, according to the Bible, is on the side of the poor and oppressed, that in the American context, God is siding with the black liberation struggle. He has made this argument using a diverse set of sources including the writings of modern European theologians such as Karl Barth and the writings and speeches of Malcolm X and Martin Luther King Jr. Cone has worked painstakingly in the past two decades to build ties between black, feminist, and third world liberation theologians.

Suzan Johnson Cook (1957–)
Religious Leader, Author

Reverend Suzan Denise Johnson Cook was born on January 28, 1957. She was raised in the Bronx, New York, and was a communications student at Emerson College when she went to Ghana as an exchange student. There she entertained notions of joining the

ministry. She would later enroll at the United Theological Seminary, where she pursued a doctorate. Just as her role model Presbyterian minister Katie Cannon had found earlier, entering into the pastorship was a task rife with difficulty for a woman, but Cook carved a niche and persevered. Eager to assist other women in pursuing the ministry, she later directed Black Women in the Ministry, sponsored by the New York City Mission Society.

In 1983, Cook began 11 years of preaching at Mariner's Temple, the oldest Baptist facility in Manhattan. Her rapport with the small congregation led her to become the first African American woman elected to senior pastor of a Baptist church in the United States. Her preaching skills have won her recognition as one of the "Fifteen Greatest Black Women Preachers" by *Ebony* (Nov., 1997). During her years with the church membership swelled from 60 to more than one thousand members. Cook became the first woman to be appointed chaplain of the New York City Police Department in 1990, when then-Mayor David Dinkins selected her. Three years later, President Bill Clinton chose her for a White House fellowship, the first female minister to be so recognized. She subsequently served on President Clinton's National Advisory Board on Race. Cook has authored several books, including *Wise Women Bearing Gifts: Joys and Struggles of Their Faith* and *Preaching in Two Voices: Sermons on the Women in Jesus's Life*.

Alexander Crummell. *See* Black Nationalism chapter.

Wallace D. Fard (1877?–1934?)
Religious Leader

W. D. Fard's background is fiercely contested. According to the Nation of Islam, Fard was born in Mecca in 1877 to a black man named Alfonso and a Caucasian woman. Members of the Nation believed that Fard was highly educated, both in England and at the University of Southern California, and that he had been trained as an Arabian diplomat. The Federal Bureau of Investigation, however, contended that Fard was born in New Zealand or Oregon to either Hawaiian or Polynesian parents (possibly one parent was British), and that he was a convicted bootlegger during Prohibition. In 1926, he received a sentence of six months to six years for drug sales in California. Upon his release in 1929, he immediately headed for Detroit.

As a door-to-door salesman, Fard approached African Americans in Detroit, selling silk fabrics and raincoats. Soon he was advising his customers on their diet and health and teaching them about what he said was their true religion, the religion of black people in Africa and Asia. Here Fard was clearly influenced by the teachings of the Moorish Science Temple and by the Ahmaddiya Muslim movement, a Muslim splinter group that preached the imminent arrival of the Mahdi or Messiah. Fard told his listeners of the one true God, Allah. He presented himself as the intermediary between God and humanity. He claimed that Allah was soon to destroy the wicked white world and establish a heaven on earth for his followers. Fard taught his followers that they were not American, owed no allegiance to the American flag, and that they should discard their "slave names." His mission, however, was to achieve "freedom, justice, and equality" for African Americans. He established a University of Islam to teach African Americans the truth about their past, and a paramilitary organization, the Fruit of Islam. Fard attracted numerous followers, perhaps as many as 8,000, within the African American community in Detroit. His most capable follower was a Georgia-born man named Elijah Poole, who was renamed Elijah Muhammad. In 1931, Fard designated Muhammad as his supreme minister.

The already considerable interest of Detroit police in Fard's activities increased further when one of his followers, in November 1932, killed a white neighbor as a sacrifice to Allah. Fard strongly denied that he had ordered the killing, asserting that his teachings had been misunderstood. Still, the police, fearing the growing strength of Fard's movement, put pressure on him to leave Detroit. Lowering his profile, Fard was able to remain in Detroit some months, transferring control of the movement to Elijah Muhammad during that time. But in May 1933, Fard was arrested for disturbing the peace, and he finally assented to demands from the police that he leave Detroit. Fard's later life is as mysterious as his early years. It is said that Fard moved to Chicago and that Elijah Muhammad kept in contact with him for about one year, but his whereabouts after June 1934, were unknown. Following Elijah Muhammad's guidance, however, most members of the Nation of Islam, continued to regard Fard as Allah appearing in person to African Americans.

Father Divine (1879–1965)
Religious Leader, Organization Executive/Founder

Father Divine was born George Baker in 1879 in Rockville, Maryland. In 1902, he moved to Baltimore. Baker visited California in 1906 and attended the Azusa Street Revival, which marked the beginning of Pentecostalism. The following year, after returning to Baltimore, Baker—under the moniker "The Messenger"—became associated with Sam Morris, a Pennsylvania African American man who called himself Father Jehovia, and John Hickerson, also known as Reverend Bishop St. John the Divine, in a house church. All three men had been influenced by the New Thought movement of the Unity Church and considered themselves inwardly divine. After a series of personal and theological quarrels, the three men parted company in 1912.

In 1914, Baker moved to Valdosta, Georgia. Threatened by local authorities, Father Divine left Georgia the same year. After additional travels in the South, he settled in Brooklyn in 1917, where he worked as an "employment agent" for the few followers still loyal to him. His first marriage was to an African American woman named Peninniah, whom he apparently met while living in Brooklyn. Calling his meeting place "Heaven," he soon attracted a larger following and moved to Sayville, Long Island, in 1919. It was at this time that Father Divine began to provide shelter and food to the poor and homeless. Spiritually, Father Divine fostered what amounted to a massive cooperative agency, based on the communal spirit of the Last Supper. His movement practiced complete racial equality. Services included songs and impromptu sermons and were conducted without Scripture readings and the use of clergy. Once he was sentenced to six months in jail as a public nuisance, but the ensuing publicity only enhanced his popularity.

The Divine movement, a non-ritualistic cult whose followers worshiped their leader as God incarnate on earth, grew rapidly in the 1930s and 1940s, with "Father" speaking out across the country and publicizing his views in *New Day*, a weekly magazine published by his organization. He set up "Peace Mission Kingdom"in the United States and throughout the world. After Peninniah's death in 1946, Father Divine married his "Sweet Angel," a 21-year old Canadian stenographer known thereafter as Mother Divine. Father Divine died peacefully at Woodmont, an estate that he had acquired in the Philadelphia suburbs, and his wife pledged to continue the work of the movement.

Louis Farrakhan. *See* Black Nationalism chapter.

Elijah John Fisher (1858–1915)
Community Activist, Minister

Elijah Fisher exemplifies the great charismatic African American preachers of the nineteenth and early twentieth centuries who, with very little formal education, built large religious institutions, counseled racial pride, and expounded the cause of African Americans as a people.

Born in La Grange, Georgia, in 1858, the youngest of eight boys in a family of 17 children, Fisher's father was an unordained preacher of a Baptist congregation that met in a white church. Fisher worked in a Baptist parsonage as a boy slave and was taught to read by a former house slave and a white missionary. In his teens, he worked in mines in Alabama and then as a butler, all the while studying theology on his own time. Though he lost a leg in an accident, Fisher became pastor of several small country churches in his early twenties and then, in 1889, of the Mount Olive Baptist Church in Atlanta. In that year, he enrolled in the Atlanta Baptist Seminary, passed his examinations, and went to preach in Nashville and then Chicago where he led the Olive Baptist Church from 1902 until his death.

Throughout his life, Fisher continued his studies, preached from coast to coast, and involved the churches in youth work, food programs for poor people, and African American businesses. An active member of the Republican party, Fisher strongly criticized African Americans who advised their brethren to rely solely on the good will of whites and publicly criticized Booker T. Washington for not speaking out against lynching.

Floyd Flake (1945–)
Religious Leader, Member of Congress

Born in Los Angeles, Flake came from humble beginnings: he was one of 13 children, and his father was a janitor. He graduated with a B.A. degree from Wilberforce University in 1967 and an M.A. from Payne Theological Seminary in 1970. He subsequently worked as a social worker, marketing analyst, and the dean of students before being called to pastor Allen AME Church in Queens, New York, in 1976. The church prospered under his leadership. By 1986, Allen AME had grown to include 6,000 members. Flake also founded a Christian school at Allen and headed the Allen Home Care Agency for the Elderly. In the latter role, he supervised the construction of a $12 million facility.

In 1986, he ran and won a seat in the U.S. House of Representatives. For 11 years, he served in Congress while remaining pastor of Allen AME Church. He was particularly interested in small business and affirmative action issues and was influential in securing federal government set-asides for minority-owned small businesses. In November 1997, he resigned his seat in Congress so that he could devote his full-time energies again to his church.

Reverend Floyd H. Flake.

Henry Highland Garnet. *See* **Black Nationalism chapter.**

"Sweet Daddy" Grace (1881–1960)
Religious Leader, Sales Agent

Born in 1881 in the Cape Verde Islands, "Sweet Daddy" Grace probably opened his first church in New Bedford, Massachusetts, in 1921, but his first success occurred five years later when he opened a church in Charlotte. Grace's church, the United House of Prayer for All People, had an ecstatic worship style, where speaking in tongues was encouraged. Grace claimed great powers, including the power of faith healing, and he stated that "Grace has given God a vacation, and since God is on His vacation don't worry Him. . . If you sin against God, Grace can save you, but if you sin against Grace, God cannot save you." Even the numerous products that he sold, such as "Daddy Grace" coffee, tea, soaps, and hand creams, were reputed to have healing powers. By the time of his death in 1960, the church had 375 branches and about 25,000 members nationwide.

Barbara C. Harris (1930–)
Executive Director, Bishop, Deacon

Born in Philadelphia in 1930, Barbara Harris, a former public relations executive, was ordained a deacon in the Protestant Episcopal Church in 1979 and a priest one year later. She served as the priest-in-charge of an Episcopalian Church in Norristown, Pennsylvania, the interim pastor of a church in Philadelphia, and the executive director of the publishing company associated with the Episcopal Church. In February of 1989, she was consecrated as suffragan or assistant bishop for the diocese of Massachusetts. She thus became the first woman bishop in the history of the Episcopal Church. She received considerable support, despite the concerns of some that her views were too liberal. Her supporters said that, despite the lack of a college degree or seminary training, she would broaden the outreach of her church.

Lemuel Haynes. *See* **Africans in America chapter.**

James Augustine Healy (1830–1900)
Educator, Religious Leader

James Augustine Healy was the first African American Catholic bishop in the United States. (Healy's brother, Patrick Francis Healy, was a Jesuit priest who served as president of Georgetown University from 1873 to 1882.) For 25 years he presided over a diocese covering the states of Maine and New Hampshire. A native of Macon, Georgia, Healy received his education in the North, first at Franklin Park Quaker School in Burlington, New York, and later at Holy Cross in Worcester, Massachusetts. Healy graduated from the latter with first honors. Healy continued his studies abroad and was ordained in Paris at Notre Dame Cathedral in 1854. He then returned to the United States.

Pastor of a predominantly Irish congregation that was at first reluctant to accept him, Bishop Healy performed his priestly duties with devotion and eventually won the respect and admiration of his parishioners—particularly after performing in his office during a typhoid epidemic. Thereafter, he was made an assistant to Bishop John Fitzpatrick of Boston, who appointed him chancellor and entrusted him with a wide variety of additional responsibilities. In 1875, he was named bishop of Portland, Maine and, in this capacity, he founded 60 parishes, as well as 18 schools.

Joseph Henry Jackson (1904–1990)
Organization Executive/Founder, Theologian, Civil Rights Activist

From 1953 to 1982, Joseph H. Jackson was the president of the National Baptist Convention, U.S.A., Inc., the third largest Protestant denomination in the United States and the largest of the predominantly African American churches. Born in Rudyard, Mississippi, in 1904, Jackson later held a B.A. from Jackson College, a M.A. from Creighton University, and a B.D. from Rochester Colgate School of Divinity. After pastoring churches in Mississippi, Jackson accepted a call to pastor the historic Olivet Baptist Church in 1941. His role in the civil rights movement was a fairly conservative one. He was supportive of the efforts of Martin Luther King Jr. during the Montgomery bus boycott of 1955, but criticized the massive nonviolent civil disobedience campaigns of the early 1960s. Jackson's main emphasis was on the need for African Americans to build a viable economic base. His favorite slogan was "From Protest to Production." He was supportive of Baptist missions in Africa and attempted to finance them by developing farmland in Liberia.

T. D. Jakes (1956–)
Religious Leader, Author

T.D. Jakes, a West Virginia native, began his preaching while as a student at West Virginia State University. After the chemical plant that employed him closed, and his father died of kidney disease, Jakes undertook ministry on a full-time basis. Initially, he ministered in Morganton, West Virginia, and then in Dallas, Texas, where his megachurch congregation today has nearly 15,000 members. He travels widely to undertake revival services. His 1998 revival in Atlanta drew 52,000 attendees. His ministry is also featured on Black Entertainment Television (BET). His books are largely aimed at encouraging and uplifting African American women. His two most popular books, which are filled with extensive passages from and interpretation of the Bible, are *Woman, Thou Art Loosed* and *The Lady, Her Lover and Her Lord.*

Absalom Jones (1746–1818)
Religious Leader

Absalom Jones rose from slavery to become the first African American Episcopal priest and principal founder of St. Thomas, the first African American Episcopal church. Jones was born a slave in Sussex, Delaware, on November 6, 1746. In 1762 his mother, five brothers,

Absalom Jones.

from Union Theological Seminary in Richmond, Virginia, in 1969. She served as a schoolteacher, pastor of Virginia churches, and a staff member of the Virginia Conference of Churches before being elected a bishop in the United Methodist Church in 1984. She presided over the California-Nevada conference, but resigned her office of bishop in 1989. She is married to James David Kelly and has four children. In 2000, Kelly was inducted into the National Women's Hall of Fame in Seneca Falls, New York.

Isaac Lane (1834–1937)
Educational Administrator, Religious Leader

A great religious leader and educator whose life spanned more than a century, Isaac Lane was born a slave in Jackson, Tennessee, in 1834. Self-educated, in 1856 he was granted a license to exhort, a category assigned to African Americans who were forbidden to preach, in the Methodist Episcopal Church South. Lane was ordained a minister in 1865. In 1873 he was made a bishop of the Colored Methodist Episcopal Church (now known as the Christian Methodist Episcopal Church) at a salary so low that he had to raise cotton to supplement his income and support his wife and 11 children. His missionary work was instrumental in establishing the CME Church in Louisiana and Texas. In the 1880s, he established Lane College in Jackson with $9,000 that he raised. He died in 1937.

and sister were sold, and Jones was taken to Philadelphia, where he worked in a store and learned to write. In 1778 he began to ask to purchase his own freedom, but he was not manumitted until 1784.

Jones became a licensed Methodist lay preacher sometime around 1786, focusing on teaching and pastoral work. In May of 1787, Jones joined African American religious leader Richard Allen and others in forming the Free African Society. The African Church of St. Thomas was later dedicated in 1794.

As the unofficial leader of the church, Jones seemed an obvious choice as a lay reader. After becoming lay reader in 1794, he was ordained deacon on August 6, 1795. Jones became the first African American Episcopal priest in 1804. He died in 1818.

Leontine T.C. Kelly (1920–)
Bishop

Leontine T.C. Kelly, the first African American woman bishop in any large U.S. denomination, was born in Washington, DC, in 1920. She received a M.Div. degree

Jarena Lee (1783–1849)
Women's Rights Activist, Minister

Born in 1783, in Cape May, New Jersey, Lee worked as a servant for a family that lived near Philadelphia. She had a conversion experience in 1804, but was unable to find a church with which to unite until she heard Richard Allen, founder of the African Methodist Episcopal Church, preach in Philadelphia. She experienced a call to preach in approximately 1808, and she sought permission to do so from Richard Allen on two occasions. On her first attempt in 1809, Allen refused her request. Eight years later, however, he granted it and licensed her as a preacher. Subsequently, she traveled throughout the North and Midwest, and many of her listeners, especially women, were moved by her eloquent preaching. After Allen's death in 1831, male African Methodist Episcopal preachers in Philadelphia attempted to deny her permission to preach from their pulpits, but she continued her ministry, despite such harassment. In 1848, she attempted to form a connection of female African Methodist Episcopal preachers for mutual support, but her organization soon fell apart.

Many African American women, especially within the African Methodist Episcopal Church, view Jarena Lee as a courageous foremother and a model for church activism.

George Liele (1750–1820)
Educator, Religious Leader

Born a slave in Virginia around 1750, George Liele was sold to a slaveowner in Georgia. He experienced a Christian conversion after hearing a sermon by Matthew Moore, a white preacher, in 1773. Liele began conducting worship services on nearby plantations and, with Moore's sponsorship, soon became the first ordained African American Baptist preacher in America. Liele's slave master, Henry Sharp, granted him his freedom before Sharp was killed in the American Revolution. Liele preached at the Silver Bluff Baptist Church in Silver Bluff, South Carolina, probably the first independent African American congregation formed in North America, as well as a location outside Savannah. One of his notable converts was Andrew Bryan, who founded the First African Baptist Church in Savannah. Some whites attempted to re-enslave Liele, but a British officer in Savannah ensured that he would maintain his freedom. Liele emigrated to Jamaica in 1784, and he started a school and preached to a small Baptist congregation in Kingston. Liele was married a woman that he converted in Savannah, and his four American-born children accompanied him to Jamaica.

Eugene A. Marino (1934–2000)
Archbishop

Born May 29, 1934, in Biloxi, Mississippi, Eugene Marino received his training at Epiphany Apostolic College and St. Joseph Seminary. He was ordained to the priesthood in 1962. The next year Marino was made director of St. Joseph Seminary. He also continued his educational studies at Catholic University, Loyola University, and Fordham University, where he earned a master of arts degree in 1967.

In 1971, Marino was named vicar general of the Josephites and served as an auxiliary bishop in Washington, DC, after his ordination to the episcopate in 1974. Marino became the first African American Roman Catholic archbishop in 1988, when he was appointed to preside over the Atlanta archdiocese. He retired in 1990, in the midst of sex scandal, when an affair he was having with a woman was exposed. In 1993, ex-bishop Marino and Vicki Long, the woman in question, reunited and began a life together. On November 12, 2000, in Manhasset, New York, Marino died of an apparent heart attack. He was 66.

Charles H. Mason (1866–1961)
Religious Leader

Born in 1866 to former slaves on a farm outside Memphis, Tennessee, Charles Mason was converted at the age of 14 and joined a Missionary Baptist church. Mason obtained a preaching license from the Missionary Baptists in 1893 and, in the same year, he claimed to have the experience of entire sanctification, thus aligning himself with the Holiness movement. He had little formal education beyond a brief period of study at the Arkansas Bible College. In 1895, the Baptists expelled him because of his beliefs on sanctification. Mason then held holiness revivals in Mississippi with the help of Charles Price Jones, a prolific writer of hymns and gospel songs, and others. In Lexington, Mississippi, his meetings were held in an abandoned cotton gin house. Despite an armed attack, probably by hostile African Americans, he achieved much success and many new converts with his revival preaching. In 1897, Mason and Jones founded a new Holiness church and called it the Church of God in Christ; they worked together harmoniously over the next decade.

In 1907, Mason attended the Azusa Street Revival conducted by William Seymour in Los Angeles, and he received the gift of speaking in tongues. He believed that the ability to speak in tongues was a necessary precondition for baptism of the Spirit. He and Jones disagreed on this point and parted company. Mason reformed the Church of God in Christ along the lines of his new spiritual insights. Over the next four decades, Mason, as bishop, general overseer, and "chief apostle," shepherded his denomination through a period of tremendous growth. He traveled extensively, preaching at revivals throughout the United States and the world. He was imprisoned for making pacifist statements during World War I. He died in 1961.

Vashti Murphy McKenzie (1947–)
Clergy

Vashti Murphy was born on May 28, 1947, and raised in Baltimore, Maryland. She attended Morgan State University until her junior year, when she married professional basketball player Stan McKenzie. Following a brief period in Phoenix, the couple returned to the Baltimore area. Vashti Murphy McKenzie completed her bachelor's degree at the University of Maryland. After graduation, she worked as a fashion model and a newspaper, radio, and television journalist.

In her late 30s, McKenzie realized that she was called to preach. With the support of her husband and three children, she enrolled in the Howard University School of Divinity, eventually earning a Master of Divinity degree. McKenzie later earned a Doctor of Ministry degree from United Theological Seminary in Dayton, Ohio.

After her graduation from Howard, McKenzie was assigned to a small church in Chesapeake City, Maryland. In 1990, she became the first female pastor of Baltimore's Payne Memorial AME Church. One of the few female senior pastors in the AM at the time, McKenzie had to overcome the all too familiar obstacle of sexism in her first years at the church. During her tenure, the church grew from just over 300 members to nearly 1,700, and established 15 new ministries. McKenzie worked to help the church erase a longstanding division between the itself and the community. The congregation's non-profit community service agency, Payne Memorial Outreach, Inc., built many successful community programs, including summer youth camps, a food pantry, and a job service which supported more than 1,000 clients.

On July 11, 2000, McKenzie was elected as the first female bishop in the 213 year history of the AM church. As bishop, McKenzie leads the 18th Episcopal District in Southeast Africa. The district covers Lesotho, Botswana, Mozambique and Swaziland. In her capacity as bishop, McKenzie planned to address issues including the AIDS crisis, economic development, church membership, and educational development.

McKenzie is the author of *Not Without a Struggle: Leadership Development for African American Women in Ministry* (1996) and *Strength in the Struggle: Leadership Development for Women* (2001). She is the recipient of numerous awards and honors, including: being named in *Ebony* magazine's "Year of the Black Woman" issue in 1992 and as one of the "15 Greatest African-American Female Preachers" by the magazine in 1997; receiving a letter of commendation from the United Nations High Commission for Refugees for Payne Memorial AM church's support of the "Love Baton Project" in 1996; and delivering the closing day invocation at the 2000 Democratic National Convention.

William Henry Miles (1828–1892)
Religious Leader

Born a slave in Kentucky in 1828, Miles was manumitted by his owner in her will. He joined the Methodist Episcopal Church, South, and soon perceived a call to preach. In 1859, he was ordained a deacon. Uncertain about church affiliation after the war, he investigated the possibility of joining the African Methodist Episcopal Zion Church, but soon thought better of it. Thus he remained a preacher in the Methodist Episcopal Church, South, until its African American members, those who had decided not to join the African Methodist Episcopal or African Methodist Episcopal Zion Churches, were allowed to form a separate denomination, the Colored Methodist Episcopal Church. At the initial General Conference of the Colored Methodist Episcopal Church in 1870, Miles was elected one of the denomination's first two bishops. He was an active advocate of African American colleges, especially those affiliated with the CME Church, such as Lane College in Jackson, Tennessee, and Paine Seminary in Atlanta, Georgia. He died in 1892.

Ava Muhammad (1951–)
Religious Leader

Born in 1951, Ava Muhammad grew up in a middle-class, Methodist home in Columbus, Ohio. After graduating from the Georgetown University Law Center in 1975, she became a criminal defense attorney. In 1979, Muhammad was diagnosed with cancer. She began searching for spiritual support, looking first to the church of her youth, but ultimately converting to Islam after hearing Louis Farrakhan speak in New York City.

After joining the Nation of Islam in 1981, Muhammad began to work as Farrakhan's attorney. She defended him in 1986 when he was arrested following his return from a visit to Libya, on which President Ronald Reagan had placed a travel ban. In another high-profile case, she won a defamation lawsuit against the *New York Post*, who in a 1994 story implicated Farrakhan in the assassination of Malcolm X. In addition to her legal work, Muhammad gained prominence and recognition throughout the Nation of Islam, despite the limitations it had historically placed on women. She authored the book, *The Myths and Misconceptions of the Role of Women in Islam* in 1996, and the following year was a key speaker at the Million Women March, speaking on the topic, "The Further Development of Black Women Who Are or Wish to Become Professionals, Entrepreneurs, and/or Politicians."

On July 28, 1998, Muhammad was appointed by Louis Farrakhan as Southern Regional Minister with the Nation of Islam. In this role, Muhammad became the first woman in Islam's 1400-year history to be appointed to a leadership position of the cloth. She has published the books *Real Love* and *Queens of the Planet Earth: The Birth and Rise of the Original Woman*, and currently serves as the national spokeswoman for the Nation of Islam.

Elijah Muhammad. *See* **Black Nationalism chapter.**

Khallid Abdul Muhammad. *See* **Black Nationalism chapter.**

Harold Robert Perry (1916–1991)
Educator, Religious Leader

Harold Robert Perry was consecrated a bishop of New Orleans on January 6, 1966—and thus became the first African American Catholic bishop in the United States in the twentieth century. One of six children, Perry was born the son of a rice mill worker and a domestic cook in Lake Charles, Louisiana in 1916. He entered the Divine Word Seminary in Mississippi at the age of 13, was ordained a priest in 1944, and spent the next fourteen years in parish work. In 1958, he was appointed rector of the seminary. Louisiana has the largest concentration of African American Catholics in the South, some 200,000 in all. In 1989, Perry was one of 13 African American bishops serving Catholic parishes around the nation. He died on July 17, 1991.

Adam Clayton Powell Sr. (1865–1953)
Religious Leader, Community Activist

Adam Clayton Powell Sr., father of the late U.S. representative from Harlem, was largely responsible for building the Abyssinian Baptist Church into one of the most celebrated African American congregations in the world. Born in Virginia in 1865, Powell attended school locally and, between sessions, worked in the coal mines of West Virginia. After deciding to enter the ministry, he began his studies at Wayland Academy (now Virginia Union University), working his way through as a janitor and waiter. He later attended the Yale University School of Divinity and served as pastor of the Immanuel Baptist Church in New Haven.

Powell became pastor of Abyssinian in 1908, when it had a membership of only 1,600 and was fiscally indebted by over $100,000. By 1921, the church had not been made solvent, but was able to move into a $350,000 Gothic structure. (This is its present location on 138th Street in Harlem.) During the Depression, Powell opened soup kitchens for Harlem residents and served thousands of meals. Later he and his son campaigned vigorously to expand job opportunities and city services in Harlem. Powell retired from Abyssinian in 1937 and died in 1953.

Frederick K.C. Price (1932–)
Clergy, Author

Born on January 3, 1932, in Santa Monica, California, Frederick K.C. Price began preaching in a Baptist church in 1955 while also working as a paper cutter. He moved on to pastor AME and Presbyterian churches before finally joining the Christian and Missionary Alliance at West Washington Community Church in 1965. It wasn't until 1970, when he experienced a "baptism of the Holy Spirit," that Price felt satisfied with the direction of his ministry.

In 1973, Price and 300 parishioners moved from West Washington to establish the Crenshaw Christian Center in Inglewood, California. Membership at the church began to grow exponentially as more and more people became interested in Price's neo-Pentecostal message, defined, in part, by speaking in tongues, healing, and prosperity teachings. Price began broadcasting a radio program, *Ever Increasing Faith*, in the mid 1970s, and soon expanded to television. By the early 1980s, the program was broadcast to five major U.S. cities. In 1981, the church purchased the former campus of Pepperdine University and began construction of the 10,146 seat FaithDome, which was dedicated in 1990. By 1999, *Ever Increasing Faith* aired on more than 100 television stations and 42 radio stations, reaching 33 million households in the U.S. and other nations. The Crenshaw Center's congregation had grown to include and estimated 22,000 members by 2002.

Price, who had completed two years of study at Los Angeles City College, returned to school at the Friends International Christian University in Merced, California, earning a bachelor's degree in 1978, a Doctor of Ministry degree in 1988, and a Ph.D. in Religious Studies in 1992. He has authored more than 30 books. Price received a honorary diploma from Rhema Bible Training Center in 1976, and a honorary Doctorate of Divinity from Oral Roberts University in 1982. In 1998, Price received the Horatio Alger Award and the Kelly Miller Smith Interfaith Award from the Southern Christian Leadership Conference.

Joseph Charles Price (1854–1893)
Civil Rights Activist, Minister, Prohibitionist

Born in Elizabeth City, North Carolina, in 1854 to a free mother, Price was educated in the school established for freed African Americans, and later at Shaw and Lincoln Universities, graduating from the latter in

1879. At age 21, he was licensed to preach in the African Methodist Episcopal Zion Church, and he received the ordination of elder six years later. Price was renowned for the eloquence of his public addresses. It was Price who was the most responsible for the African Methodist Episcopal Zion Church's success in establishing a church college—Livingstone College in North Carolina—after ministers in that denomination had failed in several previous attempts. As president of Livingstone College, he quickly gave his school a solid grounding, both academically and financially. For example, he raised $10,000 for his school during a lecture tour of England. He was an active participant in politics, campaigned for civil rights and prohibition, and assumed such offices as chairman of the Citizens' Equal Rights Association of Washington, DC. He died from kidney failure in 1893.

William Joseph Seymour (1870–1922)
Civil Rights Activist, Religious Leader

Born in Centerville, Louisiana, in 1870 to parents who had been slaves, Seymour taught himself to read and write. In 1900, Seymour encountered the prominent promoter of Holiness doctrine, Martin Knapp, and studied under him. He then suffered a bout of smallpox that left him blind in one eye. He was ordained as an evangelist by the "Evening Light Saints," a group that eventually became known by the title Church of God (Anderson, Indiana). Moving to Houston, he sat immediately outside the door of white evangelist Charles Parham's segregated classroom, while Parham lectured on Christian doctrine and, especially, on the importance of speaking in tongues.

In 1906, Seymour moved to Los Angeles to pastor a small African American Holiness church, but his congregation, opposed to Seymour's contention that speaking in tongues was a very important part of Christian experience, dismissed him after one week. Seymour continued to hold religious meetings, attracting an interracial audience. A widely publicized outburst of speaking in tongues brought him an even larger audience, so he moved his "Apostolic Faith Gospel Mission" to a former AME Church building on Azusa Street. The extremely successful meetings that he held before ecstatic, interracial throngs of listeners over the next three years have been universally acknowledged as the beginnings of modern Pentecostalism, both in the United States and around the world. Seymour was greatly saddened when the racial unity displayed in the early stages of Pentecostalism began to break apart under the pressures exerted by racial discrimination in the nation at large. He was holding services at the Azusa Street mission until his death in 1922.

Al Sharpton. *See* **Civil Rights chapter.**

Fred Shuttlesworth. *See* **Civil Rights chapter.**

Amanda Berry Smith (1837–1915)
Organization Executive/Founder, Evangelist/ Missionary

Born in Long Green, Maryland, in 1837, Smith was manumitted during her childhood after her father paid for her freedom. She had a spiritual conversion experience in 1856 and began attending religious meetings faithfully. She resisted identification with any single denomination, and her religious practice was most strongly influenced by Quakers and Methodists. Attendance at the religious meetings of white evangelists Phoebe Palmer and John Inskip introduced her to Holiness doctrine, and she experienced entire sanctification in 1868. Her husband died the following year, and Smith soon became a full-time travelling evangelist. She never sought to breach the barriers against women's ordination erected by male preachers, stating that the calling she had received directly from God was justification enough for her ministry.

From 1878 to 1890, Smith worked as a missionary in England, Ireland, Scotland, India, and Liberia. A Methodist bishop who heard her preach in India stated that he "had never known anyone who could draw and hold so large an audience as Mrs. Smith." On her return to the United States in 1890, she preached widely and wrote her autobiography in 1893, an extremely detailed work now regarded as a classic. Her last 20 years were devoted to the construction and management of the Amanda Smith Orphan's Home for Colored Children in Illinois. She died in 1915.

Stephen Gill Spottswood (1897–1974)
Organization Executive/Founder, Religious Leader, Civil Rights Activist

Bishop of the African Methodist Episcopal Zion Church from 1952 to 1972 and board chairman of the National Association for the Advancement of Colored People from 1961 until his death in 1974, Bishop Spottswood embodied the religious faith and intellectual incisiveness that has produced so many effective African American religious activists.

Spottswood was born in Boston on July 18, 1897, attended Albright College, Gordon Divinity School, and then received a Ph.D. in divinity from Yale University.

Bishop Stephen Spottswood.

As a religious leader, Bishop Spottswood was president of the Ohio Council of Churches and served on the boards of numerous interfaith conferences, as well as heading the African Methodist Episcopal Zion Church. His activity with the NAACP started in 1919, when he joined the organization. He was appointed to the national board in 1955. In 1971, he became the center of a political storm when he chastised the Nixon administration for its policies toward African Americans and refused, under strong pressure from the administration, to retract his comments. He died on December 1, 1974.

George Augustus Stallings Jr. (1948–)
Theologian

Born in New Bern, North Carolina, in 1948, Stallings received his B.A. from St. Pius X Seminary in 1970. He received his B.S. in theology from the University of St. Thomas Aquinas in 1973 and his M.A. in pastoral theology the following year. In 1975, he was granted a licentiate in sacred theology by the University of St. Thomas Aquinas. In 1974 Stallings was ordained and

was named pastor of St. Teresa of Avila in 1976. (St. Teresa of Avila Church is located in one of Washington, DC's poor African American neighborhoods.)

While pastor at St. Teresa, Stallings stressed that the contributions of Africans and African Americans to Christianity should be recognized and that the needs of African Americans must be addressed by the Catholic Church. In an effort to confront what he considered the Catholic Church's racial insensitivity, he made use of what is known as the Rite of Zaire, incorporated jazz and gospel music to the Mass, and added readings by celebrated African American writers to the liturgy. For these actions, Stallings received much criticism. In 1988 he was removed from St. Teresa of Avila and named head of evangelism for Washington, DC.

In 1989 Stallings, still convinced that the Catholic Church was not meeting the cultural, spiritual, and social needs of African American Catholics, announced that he would leave the diocese to found a new congregation, the Imani Temple African-American Catholic Congregation. Stallings not only advocated marriage or celibacy for priests, he also believed that women should be able to serve as priests. In 1991, he ordained former Roman Catholic nun Rose Vernell as a priest in his church. The congregation's membership was estimated at 3,500 members. In 2002, Stallings and his wife, Sayomi, became parents for the first time.

Leon H. Sullivan. *See* Civil Rights chapter.

Gardner C. Taylor (1918–)
Civil Rights Activist, Religious Leader, Community Activist

Rev. Taylor is widely regarded as the dean of the nation's African American preachers. He received a B.A. degree from Leland College in 1937 and a B.D. degree from the Oberlin Graduate School of Theology in 1940. Taylor has long been a community activist: He demonstrated for civil rights and suffered arrest for civil disobedience with Martin Luther King Jr. in the 1960s, and he introduced Nelson Mandela to a New York audience in 1990. He is a trusted counselor to former New York mayor David Dinkins. Taylor served on the New York City Board of Education. He is the past president of the New York Council of Churches and the past vice president of the Urban League in New York City. After 42 years as pastor of the Concord Baptist Church in Brooklyn, Taylor resigned his post in

1990. In 2000 United States President Bill Clinton awarded the Presidential Medal of Freedom to Taylor.

Howard Thurman (1899–1981)
Author, Theologian, Civil Rights Activist, Educator

Born in Daytona Beach, Florida, on November 18, 1899, Thurman studied at Morehouse College, Rochester Theological Center, and Haverford College. Thurman, named by *Life* magazine as one of the 12 great preachers of the twentieth century, served as a pastor to a Baptist church in Ohio and, from 1944 to 1953, to an interracial and interdenominational Fellowship church that he founded in San Francisco. He also served as dean of the chapel at Howard University from 1932 to 1944, as well as Boston University from 1953 until his retirement. Thurman was one of the leading theologians of his time, writing *The Negro Spiritual Speaks of Life and Death* and about his opposition to segregation and support of the Civil Rights movement in *This Luminous Darkness*. Altogether, he authored 19 books including an autobiography published in 1979. He died on April 10, 1981.

Iyanla Vanzant (1954–)
Author, Yoruba Priestess, Lawyer

Vanzant is the author of several books on spirituality that have topped *Blackboard* including *Tapping the Power Within*(1992), *Acts of Faith* (1993), *Interiors: A Black Woman's Healing* (1995), *Value in the Valley* (1995), *The Spirit of a Man* (1996), *In the Meantime* (1998), *One Day My Soul Just Opened Up* (1998), and *Up from Here* (2002). Her own life has served as an inspiration for many of her readers, as it has furnished rich material for her books. Her mother died when she was two years old, and she suffered from rape, spousal abuse, and nervous breakdowns. Yet, she managed to turn her life around. Her years of dependence on welfare ended in 1978, when she matriculated in Medgar Evers College in Brooklyn and subsequently in law school. She served as a public defender in Philadelphia, but left that career behind for public speaking and writing self-help books.

She is currently the director of Inner Visions Life Maintenance Center, headquartered in Silver Springs, Maryland, and dedicated to the spiritual empowerment of African American women and men. Brought up in the Baptist and Pentecostalist faiths, she has since been initiated as a Yoruba priestess. Her writings draw widely from such diverse sources as African spirituality, Christianity, New Thought, and such Eastern religions as Buddhism.

Iyanla Vanzant.

James Varick (1750–1827)
Abolitionist, Bishop, Deacon

Born near Newburgh, New York, around 1750, to a slave mother, Varick was a leader in the movement among African American Methodists in New York to set up a separate congregation. This was accomplished with the formation of the Zion Church in 1796. Ten years later, Varick was ordained a deacon by Bishop Francis Asbury. Varick sought to obtain full ordination as elder for himself and other African American ministers and would have preferred to have received such an ordination within the Methodist Episcopal Church, but this did not prove possible. He did not favor joining Richard Allen's African Methodist Episcopal Church, especially since Allen had been attempting to set up a New York congregation seen by Varick as in competition with the Zion Church. Eventually, Varick participated in setting up the African Methodist Episcopal Zion Church, and he was elected the first superintendent or bishop. He was also deeply involved in issues relating to freedom and human rights, preaching against the slave trade in 1808 and subscribing to the first newspaper in the United States owned by African Americans, *Freedom's Journal.* He died in 1827.

Cornel West (1953–)
Scholar, Educator, Social Critic, Author

The grandson of Rev. Clifton L. West Sr., pastor of the Tulsa Metropolitan Baptist Church, Cornel West was born on June 2, 1953, in Tulsa, Oklahoma. West developed skills of critical thinking and political action almost from birth. By age 17, he was enrolled as an undergraduate student at Harvard. Taking eight courses per semester during his junior year, he was able to graduate *magna cum laude* one year early. He received an A.B. in Near Eastern languages and literature in 1973. Immediately afterward, he completed his M.A. (1975) and Ph.D. (1980) at Princeton University.

Professor of religion and director of Afro-American Studies at Princeton University, Cornel West's analytical speeches and writing on issues of morality, race relations, cultural diversity, and progressive politics have made him a keeper of the prophetic African American religious tradition. West has taught the philosophy of religion at both Union Theological Seminary (1977–1983, 1988) and Yale Divinity School (1984–1987). In 1994 he joined Harvard's faculty, but returned permanently to Princeton in 2002 after a public rift with Harvard's president. A complex individual, he juggles his theological concerns with his political convictions. West serves dual roles as prophet and intellectual within and beyond the African American community. His writings combine a castigation for moral failure with an optimism that insists on the possibility—through struggle—of making a world of stricter morality real.

West's first books were published in the early 1980s, but he wrote many of them in the late 1970s. In the early 1980s, he encountered the Democratic Socialists of America (DSA), an organization that shaped the version of democratic socialism that he would subsequently adopt and promote in his works. Those include *Black Theology and Marxist Thought,* (1979) *Prophesy Deliverance! An Afro-American Revolutionary Christianity* (1982), and *The Ethical Dimensions of Marxist Thought* (1991). West's impassioned and insightful writings also make a resounding appeal for cross-cultural tolerance and unity, while urging individuals to recognize the power of diversity within a society. Following those lines are such works as: *Breaking Bread: Insurgent Black Intellectual Life,* which he co-edited with bell hooks in 1991; *Beyond Eurocentrism and Multiculturalism* (1993); *Race Matters* (1993), perhaps his best known book; and *Jews & Blacks: The Hard Hunt for Common Ground,* co-written with Michael Lerner in 1995. He worked with Lerner on another book in 1996, *Jews & Blacks: A Dialogue on Race, Religion, and Culture in America.* Throughout the 1990s, West teamed up with other well-known public figures to produce books, such as *The Future of the Race* (with Henry Louis Gates Jr., 1996), *Death Blossoms: Reflections from a Prisoner of Conscience* (with Mumia Abu-Jamal, 1997), *The Future of American Progressivism: An Initiative for Political and Economic Reform* (with Roberto Mangabeira Unger, 1998), *The War Against Parents: What We Can Do for America's Beleaguered Moms and Dads* (with Sylvia Ann Hewlett, 1998), *The African-American Century: How Black Americans Have Shaped Our Country* (with Gates, 2000).

⑱

Literature

- ♦ African American Literature of Colonial America
- ♦ African American Literature during the Antebellum Period
- ♦ African American Literature from Reconstruction to the Harlem Renaissance
- ♦ The Harlem Renaissance
- ♦ African American Literature of the Mid-Twentieth Century
- ♦ The Black Arts Movement
- ♦ African American Literature of the Late Twentieth Century and Early Twenty-First Century
- ♦ African American Authors and Literary Critics ♦ Award Winners

by Linda M. Carter

African American literature in the United States reached an artistic pinnacle in the period between World War I and World War II with the Harlem Renaissance. Since then, African American writing has embraced themes that range from the highly-charged and socio-political to private and introspective. The Black Arts movement of the 1960s and 1970s brought acclaim and prominence to many African American writers, and fostered the growth of African American studies at numerous universities around the country. In the 1980s and 1990s, African American writers were working in every genre—from scriptwriting to poetry—as they signed more contracts with major publishing companies, and their works consistently appeared on bestseller lists. During the first decade of the twenty-first century, African American literature maintained the high level of visibility established in the 1980s and 1990s. Black writers continued to explore a diversity of genres as well as themes and to create critically acclaimed works.

♦ AFRICAN AMERICAN LITERATURE OF COLONIAL AMERICA

The African American literary tradition began in 1746 when Lucy Terry, at age 16, created "Bars Fight" and was sustained during the colonial era by individuals such as Jupiter Hammon, Phillis Wheatley, Briton Hammon, James Gronniosaw, and Olaudah Equiano. Although Terry's poem was composed in 1746, it was preserved in song only until its publication in 1855. Thus Jupiter Hammon's "An Evening Thought, Salvation, by Christ, with Penitential Cries," published as a broadside in 1760, was the first poem published by an African American. Thirteen years later, Phillis Wheatley became the first African American—and the second woman—to publish a book in the colonies. Published in 1773, *Poems on Various Subjects, Religious and Moral, by Phillis Wheatley, Negro Servant to Mr. John Wheatley, of Boston, in New England* made a tremendous impact on white colonial America, since many felt that African Americans were not capable of the depth of feeling required to write poetry. Soon after its publication, Wheatley gained such international recognition that she was granted her freedom.

While Terry, Hammon, and Wheatley composed poetry, Briton Hammon, Gronniosaw, and Equiano created autobiographies. In 1760 *The Narrative of the Uncommon Sufferings and Surprizing Deliverance of Briton Hammon, a Negro Man* (1760) was published. Hammon's *Narrative* only contains 14 pages; however, it is considered the first African American autobiography. A more developed autobiography, *A Narrative of the Most Remarkable Particulars in the Life of James Albert Ukawsaw Gronniosaw* was printed in 1770 and reprinted in later editions. Gronniosaw is mentioned in Equiano's two-volume work, *The Interesting Narrative of the Life of Olaudah Equiano, or Gustavus Vassa, the African, Written by Himself* (1789). Gronniosaw and Equiano's autobiographies provided a dual perspective that subsequent slave narratives lacked: life in Africa and life in America. Equiano's autobiography became a bestseller within his lifetime, with nine English editions and one American edition including translations in Dutch, German, and Russian. Equiano died in 1797, yet his autobiography influenced many nineteenth century black autobiographers.

Thefore, these African Americans authors clearly demonstrated that that they could eloquently express themselves in English—a second language for most blacks during the colonial era—and represent themselves effectively in a variety of literary genres.

◆ AFRICAN AMERICAN LITERATURE DURING THE ANTEBELLUM PERIOD

Perhaps the greatest satisfaction for African American writers during the period prior to the Civil War was having the freedom to write. Actually, knowing how to read and write was a tremendous accomplishment for many African Americans. This was due to the fact that only sporadic attempts at systematic instruction of

THE

INTESTING NARRATIVE

OF

THE LIFE

OF

OLAUDAH EQUIANO,

OR

GUSTAVUS VASSA,

THE AFRICAN.

WRITTEN BY HIMSELF.

Behold, God is my falvation ; I will truft, and not be afraid, for the Lord Jehovah is my ftrength and my fong ; he alfo is become my falvation. And in that day fhall ye fay, Praife the Lord, call upon his name, declare his doings among the people. Ifa. xii. 2. 4.

EIGHTH EDITION ENLARGED.

NORWICH:

PRINTED FOR, AND SOLD BY THE AUTHOR.

1794.

PRICE FOUR SHILLINGS.

Formerly fold for 7s.

[*Entered at Stationers' Hall.*]

Olaudah Equiano's autobiography was the first American slave narrative.

Africans in colonial America had been made, and stringent laws were later passed in the nineteenth century that prohibited whites from teaching African Americans to read and write.

The Slave Narratives

Slave narratives are literary milestones. Briton Hammon, James Gronnisaw, and Olaudah Equiano's eighteenth-century autobiographies, along with their nineteenth-century counterparts, are the progenitors of full-length African American prose. These first-person narratives represented more than their individual authors: they provided a literary voice for the silent, enslaved masses who never had opportunities to document their life stories. In doing so, the autobiographers utilized the language of their captors as a method of rebellion. During the nineteenth century, slave narratives established themes and structural considerations that had been previously overlooked. Noted literary critic Frances Smith Foster, in *Witnessing Slavery: The Development of the Ante-Bellum Slave Narrative* (1979), has identified four chronological phases prevalent in slave narratives: (1) the loss of freedom, (2) cognizance of options to slavery and a determination to gain freedom, (3) escape, and (4) freedom realized. Although many readers may consider the narratives by such persons as Frederick Douglass, William Wells Brown, or Harriet Jacobs more political than artistic, the ability to adapt and utilize language in a manner that showed the glaring inconsistencies and inhumanity of slavery must be recognized as an accomplishment of letters. The full extent of these writers' revolutionary thoughts were channeled through these traditional subjects of the Bible and neoclassicism. However, the restructuring and inclusion of the African American perspective created a viable means of resistance and expression.

The three most prominent authors of slave narratives were Frederick Douglass, William Wells Brown, and Harriet Jacobs. Douglass wrote three autobiographies: *Narrative of the Life of Frederick Douglass, An American Slave* (1845), which is considered the preeminent slave narrative; *My Bondage and My Freedom* (1855); and *The Life and Times of Frederick Douglass* (1881). Douglass's fellow abolitionist William Wells Brown also authored three autobiographies: *Narrative of William Wells Brown, A Fugitive Slave* (1847), his most popular autobiography; *Three Years in Europe: Or Places I Have Seen and People I Have Met* (1852); and *My Southern Home* (1880). Harriet Jacobs's *Incidents in the Life of a Slave Girl* (1861) is an important work in that it is the most comprehensive slave narrative by a woman. Douglass, Brown, and Jacobs's autobiographies are currently in print, and they, along with other slave narratives, are available in various collections such as Yusef Taylor's two-volume *I Was Born a Slave: An Anthology of Classic Slave Narratives* (1999) and The Library of America's *Slave Narratives* (2000). The nineteenth-century slave narratives continued the tradition of black self-definition and self-assertion that was established by the eighteenth-century slave narratives. The slave narratives of both centuries served as a preface and a foundation for subsequent expression through fiction, poetry, autobiography, essays, and other genres.

Novels and Other Genres

During the antebellum period, the majority of published African American works were slave narratives; nevertheless, African Americans made significant contributions to other literary genres. Antebellum African American writers, following in the footsteps of their colonial predecessors, continued to create poetry. George Moses Horton, for example, published three volumes of verse: *The Hope of Liberty* (1829); *The Poetical Works of George M. Horton, The Colored Bard of North Carolina* (1845); and *Naked Genius* (1865).

Poetry and slave narratives were genres that African Americans began writing during the eighteenth century. In the nineteenth century, African Americans demonstrated their ability to create fiction. Victor Sejour's short story "The Mulatto" (1837) is the earliest extant work of African American fiction. In 1859 Frances E. W. Harper's "The Two Offers," the earliest known short story by an African American woman, was published.

The first African American novels were published during the antebellum period. The most well known are William Wells Brown's *Clotel, Or, the President's Daughter* (1853), the first African American novel; Frank Webb's *The Garies and Their Friends* (1857); Harriet Wilson's *Our Nig, or, Sketches from the Life of a Free Black, in a Two-Story White House, North, Showing That Slavery's Shadows Fall Even There* (1859), the first published novel by an African American woman; and Martin Delany's *Blake, or, the Huts of America* (1859). In 2002 Hannah Crafts's *The Bondwoman's Narrative* was published. Crafts's handwritten manuscript, dating from the 1850s, was recovered by Henry Louis Gates Jr., and authenticated in 2001. Crafts's work appears to be the first novel written by a female fugitive slave, and it may be the first novel by an African American woman.

The first African American drama, *The Escape, or, a Leap for Freedom*, was published in 1858. Its author is William Wells Brown, the same individual who wrote one of the most influential slave narratives and the first African American novel. He is considered the first African American author of belles lettres.

◆ AFRICAN AMERICAN LITERATURE FROM RECONSTRUCTION TO THE HARLEM RENAISSANCE

With the end of the Civil War and the beginning of the era of Reconstruction, African American writers were eager to address subjects of personal and individual freedom. However, prevalent attitudes forced black writers to continue to address issues of "the master mentality" and "plantation politics." Few writers could support themselves by their writing, and many went unknown.

As the United States moved into the close of the nineteenth century and the first decade of the twentieth century, other African American writers, such as Frances E. W. Harper, Paul Laurence Dunbar, Pauline Hopkins, and Charles Waddell Chesnutt, found an audience that appreciated their works. Among their works published during this period are Harper's novel *Iola Leroy, or, Shadows Uplifted* (1892); Dunbar's volume of verse, *Lyrics of a Lowly Life* (1896), which was his third of 11 volumes; Hopkins's novel *Contending Forces: A Romance Illustrative of Negro Life North and South* (1900); and Chesnutt's short stories *The Conjure Woman* (1899) and *The Wife of His Youth and Other Stories of the Color Line* (1899), as well as his three novels: *The House Behind the Cedars* (1900), *The Marrow of Tradition* (1901), and *The Colonel's Dream* (1905). The most widely known work of this period, Booker T. Washington's *Up From Slavery* (1901), was the best selling slave narrative of the late nineteenth and early twentieth centuries.

White society, however, still controlled much of publishing in America; African American work was often filtered and distorted through this lens. As a result, much of the work published by African Americans attempted to prove that they could fit into America's middle class society. In fact, much of the literature of this era portrayed African Americans as being happy with their assigned lot. Yet some writers—Harper, Dunbar, Hopkins, and Chesnutt, for example—tried to break the chains of this imposed expression. They presented a view of African American life as it really was, not as white America wanted it to be.

The accomplishments of African American writers during the time prior to the Harlem Renaissance attest to both the use of literary forms and the purpose in finding their own voices. Although themes were often muted and subjected to continuous scrutiny, the use of imagery, language, and a new perspective opened the way for African American writers to focus more on the wealth of their culture and the African American experience in a truthful and honest fashion.

◆ THE HARLEM RENAISSANCE

The Harlem Renaissance was the era of prolific African American creativity in literature, art, and music. Resistant to the easy categorization of a timeline, the Harlem Renaissance began around the onset of World War I in 1914 and extended into the early 1930s. It began with the movement of African American artists and writers into Harlem from practically every state in the country. By the 1920s Harlem was the largest community of black individuals in the world, encompassing Africans, people from the West Indies, the Caribbean, and the Americas. This community, similar to many urban communities in the North, saw the collective energies of persons joining together to celebrate the artistic talents of African Americans. While Harlem served as the hub of artistic activity, Washington, D.C., was also a place where many artists congregated to explore the new perspectives and ideas of the time. The largest group of women who were participants in the Harlem Renaissance found their literary identities not so much in Harlem, but in Washington in the company of host poet Georgia Douglas Johnson and other artists.

As African American journals such as W.E.B. Du Bois's *Crisis* and *Opportunity*, edited by Charles S. Johnson, began to flourish, it became possible for African American writers to publish in a style that suited their tastes. Du Bois and Johnson were among the older, established authors, critics, and editors who encouraged younger writers. Jessie Redmon Fauset, who was an author of four novels and editor of *Crisis* magazine, did much to support the work of younger authors as well as women writers. In fact, Langston Hughes and others contend that the Renaissance came about because of the nurturing of older writers including Fauset and Alain Locke, a Howard University professor and literary critic. Also, African American writers discovered that some white patrons in the publishing field were, in fact, interested in promoting their works, and as a result, books by black authors were published with an unprecedented frequency.

In addition to Du Bois and Fauset, important writers of this era include Langston Hughes, Zora Neale Hurston, Wallace Thurman, Countee Cullen, Claude McKay, Nella Larsen, Eric Walrond, Rudolph Fisher, Jean Toomer, and Arna Bontemps. Among the most significant works of the era are Locke's *The New Negro* (1925), an anthology of Harlem Renaissance works; Thurman's *Infants of the Spring* (1932), a novel that satirizes the Harlem Renaissance; and Hughes's *The Big Sea* (1940), his first

autobiography that provides the best account of the Harlem Renaissance by one of its participants. Although free expression was essential to artists of the Harlem Renaissance, stereotypes that permeated the American culture made their writings appear rebellious. The conscious agenda of these mostly young, African American artists concerned the definition and celebration of African American art and culture and a desire to change the preconceived and erroneous notions most Americans had of African American life. Such views are eloquently expressed best in Hughes's essay "The Negro Artist and the Racial Mountain" (1926). Hughes's essay, which was a manifesto for his contemporaries and has served as inspiration for subsequent generations of African Americans, ends with his bold declaration:

> We younger Negro artists who create now intend to express our individual dark-skinned selves without fear or shame. If white people are pleased we are glad. If they are not, it doesn't matter. We know we are beautiful. And ugly too. The tom-tom cries and the tom-tom laughs. If colored people are pleased we are glad. If they are not, their displeasure doesn't matter either. We build our temples for tomorrow, strong as we know how, and we stand on top of the mountain, free within ourselves.

The Harlem Renaissance shifted away from the moralizing work that had been characteristic of much of post-Reconstruction writing that decried racism. W. E. B. Du Bois and Alain Locke realized, as did many of the emerging young writers, that literary efforts that catered to changing the conscience of the United States were no longer useful nor should such efforts be a primary consideration for artists. These writers felt communicating the African American experience through every facet of artistic mediums would, in itself, expound upon ills of a racist world. Issues then could be expressed through the lives of working-class and middle-class characters as the text sought to paint a realistic picture.

In this time of discovery for African Americans of the view from within, many also saw the changing relationships between blacks and whites. Literature reintroduced white America to a people who needed, wanted, and would eventually demand full participation in the society for which they had lived, labored, and died. This perspective would end the goal of convincing white America of African American entitlement and, instead, focus on self-education and exploration of the quality of the African American experience. It paved the way for power through art to inspire the masses and the writers of the 1960s.

◆ AFRICAN AMERICAN LITERATURE OF THE MID-TWENTIETH CENTURY

As the Great Depression of the 1930s deepened, the Harlem Renaissance slowly faded. Richard Wright's publication in 1940 of *Native Son* marked the beginning of a transition period in African American literature that would last until 1955. Writers during this time bridged the richly creative period of the Renaissance with the more intense creativity and socio-political activity that was to define the work produced during the Civil Rights movement.

With the publication of his classic novel *Native Son*, Wright maintained that the era of the Harlem Renaissance—with its motto of art for art's sake'—must end and be replaced with works directly intended to stop racism. He also believed that African Americans were an essential part of American society. These tenets became the foundation for the ideology of the Civil Rights movement.

During this time, other African American writers, notably poets, were taking a different road in their quest to be heard. Such poets as Gwendolyn Brooks, Melvin B. Tolson, Margaret Walker, and Robert Hayden employed classical and mythical themes. Brooks won a Pulitzer Prize in 1950 for her book *Annie Allen* (1949) and was the first African American to receive the award. These poets used a blend of extreme eclecticism with realistic, African American issues. The blend was successful, as their writing was met with acceptance in the university community.

Ann Petry's novel *The Street* (1946); Ralph Ellison's *Invisible Man* (1952), arguably one of the best novels published in the United States during the twentieth century; James Baldwin's novel *Go Tell It on the Mountain* (1953), as well as his essays such as *Notes of a Native Son* (1955), *Nobody Knows My Name: More Notes of a Native Son* (1961), and *The Fire Next Time* (1963), were other books that brought serious African American issues to mainstream culture. In addition, many African American works were gaining acceptance with the mainstream literary establishment.

In 1959, on the "eve" of the Black Arts Movement, Lorraine Hansberry's *A Raisin in the Sun* opened in New York. Hansberry was the first African American woman to have a play produced on Broadway, and the first African American to win the New York Drama Critics Circle Award. Hansberry received inspiration for the drama's title from lines in a Langston Hughes poem, "Dream Deferred." Her play centers around the Younger family's desire to move from Chicago's South Side to a white neighborhood. Thus art imitated reality as *A Raisin in the Sun* mirrored the many efforts to integrate neighborhoods across America during the 1950s.

◆ THE BLACK ARTS MOVEMENT

The Black Arts movement, sometimes called the Black Aesthetics movement, was the first major African American artistic movement since the Harlem Renaissance. Beginning in the early 1960s and lasting through the mid-1970s, this movement was fueled by the anger of Richard Wright, James Baldwin, Ralph Ellison, Ann Petry, and other notable African American writers.

The artistic movement flourished alongside the civil rights marches and the call for the independence of the African American community. As phrases such as "Black is beautiful" were popularized, African American writers of the Black Arts movement consciously set out to define what it meant to be a black writer in a white culture. While writers of the Harlem Renaissance seemed to investigate their identity within, writers of the Black Arts movement desired to define themselves and their era before being defined by others.

For the most part, participants in the Black Arts movement were supportive of separatist politics and a black nationalist ideology. Larry Neal wrote in an essay "The Black Arts Movement" (1968) that the movement was the "aesthetic and spiritual sister of the Black Power concept." Rebelling against the mainstream society by being essentially anti-white, anti-American, and anti-middle class, these artists moved from the Renaissance view of art for art's sake into a philosophy of art for politics' sake.

The Black Arts movement attempted to produce works of art that would be meaningful to the African American masses. Towards this end, popular African American music of the day, including John Coltrane's jazz and James Brown's soul, as well as street talk, were some of the inspirational forces for the movement. In fact, much of the language used in these works was aggressive, profane, and shocking—this was often a conscious attempt to show the vitality and power of African American activists. These writers tended to be revolutionaries, supporting both radical and peaceful protests for change as promoted by Malcolm X and Martin Luther King Jr. In addition, they believed that artists were required to do more than create: artists also had to be political activists in order to achieve nationalist goals.

Leading writers in this movement included Amiri Baraka (Leroi Jones), whose poetry and plays were as well known as his political prowess, and Haki R. Madhubuti (Don L. Lee), a poet and essayist who sold

Richard Wright's *Native Son* marks the end of the Harlem Renaissance.

more than 100,000 copies of his books without a national distributor. On the other hand, Ishmael Reed—an early organizer of the Black Arts movement—later dissented with some of the movement's doctrines and became inspired more by the black magic and spiritual practices of the West Indies (in what he called the "HooDoo Aesthetic"). Other organizers and essayists include Larry Neal, Ethridge Knight, Addison Gale Jr., and Maulana Karenga.

Nikki Giovanni was one of the first poets of the Black Arts movement to receive recognition. In her works, she advocated militant replies to white oppression and demonstrated through her performances that music is an inextricable part of the African American tradition in all aspects of life. Poet Sonia Sanchez was another leading voice of the movement. She managed to combine feminism with her commitment to nurturing children and men in the fight for black nationalism. Sanchez was a member of the Nation of Islam from 1972 to 1975, and through her association with the Black Arts movement, she managed to instill stronger support for the role of women in that religion.

Two major Black Arts presses were run by poets: Dudley Randall's Broadside Press in Detroit and Haki Madhubuti's Third World Press in Chicago. From 1961 to 1976, the most important African American magazine was *Negro Digest* (renamed *Black World* in 1970); its editor, Hoyt Fuller, published the works of the Black Arts poets and prose writers. Landmark publications of the movement include *Black Fire* (1968), an anthology

Nikki Giovanni, a standout poet of the Black Arts movement.

of Black Arts writing edited by Amiri Baraka and Larry Neal; *The New Black Poetry* (1969), edited by Clarence Major; *The Black Woman* (1970), the first major African American feminist anthology, edited by Toni Cade Bambara; *The Black Poets* (1971), edited by Dudley Randall; and *Understanding the New Black Poetry* (1972), an anthology edited by Stephen Henderson.

◆ AFRICAN AMERICAN LITERATURE OF THE LATE TWENTIETH CENTURY AND EARLY TWENTY-FIRST CENTURY

Before the Black Arts movement ended in the mid-1970s, Marvin Gaye's album *What's Going On* (1971) was released. On the album's title track, Gaye sings about the social problems of the late 1960s and early 1970s: the Vietnam War, protest demonstrations, and subsequent police brutality. The title of his classic album was not only a popular greeting but also testimony to the African American literary tradition. Since the end of the Black Arts movement, African Americans have written about "what's going on" in greater numbers and to greater recognition than at any other

time in literary history. Important developments in African American literature during the last three decades of the twentieth century include the overwhelming success of many African American women writers, as well as a growth in the number of authors who have found that they can straddle more than one genre. The works of black writers appear more frequently as bestsellers, and at times, works of several African American authors appear concurrently on the lists. African American writing has become more legitimized in the United States, and African American studies departments have emerged in many universities around the country.

One of the first books of the contemporary renaissance of African American literature was Alex Haley's *Roots* (1976). It was perhaps one of the greatest African American writing coups of the late twentieth century. With Haley's book, as well as the highly popular television miniseries that followed, many black Americans have been encouraged to discover their own African roots. Since then, other books that explore the history of African Americans in the American West, the South, and the North have been published and eagerly received by African Americans.

As a result of the large number of African American literary works that have been published since the 1980s, a multitude of themes are present. Many African American writers have shifted their attention away from writing about the disparity between blacks and whites and toward themes of self-reflection, self-definition, and healing. Numerous African American women write in response to the Black Arts movement, protesting the role that they feel women played in the male-oriented black nationalist movement. Zora Neale Hurston's novel, *Their Eyes Were Watching God* (1937), and her other works have been resurrected and used as inspiration. The women's liberation movement also supports these women by allowing their works to reach a wider audience. In this way, the somewhat female-repressive politics of the Black Arts movement has provoked women writers to express their own unique voices. Alice Walker, Gayl Jones, Toni Morrison, Terry McMillan, and Gloria Naylor are examples of successful women novelists who have become prominent figures in the publishing world. Autobiographer and poet Maya Angelou is another major literary figure.

Since the 1980s, African American women writers have been at the leading edge of the publishing industry—in quality as well as quantity of work. In addition to Walker, Jones, Morrison, McMillan, and Naylor, other prominent women working primarily as novelists include Edwidge Danticat, Gwendolyn Parker, Jamaica Kincaid, Lucinda Roy, Marita Golden, Bernice McFadden, Toni Cade Bambara, Diane McKinney-Whetstone, Helen Lee, Yolanda Joe, Dawn Turner Trice, Pearl Cleage, and Barbara Chase-Riboud. While African American male writers are outnumbered by black women writers, among the contemporary African American male novelists are Ernest Gaines, Ishmael Reed, Walter Mosley, John Edgar Wideman, Albert French, E. Lynn Harris, Colson Whitehead, Darryl Pinckney, Brian Keith Jackson, Trey Ellis, Brent Wade, and Clarence Major. African American novelists often confront issues of identity, offering interpretations of womanhood and manhood. Challenged by W.E.B. Du Bois's statement about dual identity as an American and as a black person, they collectively provide panoramic insight into African American life.

The decade of the 1990s as well as the first decade of the twenty-first century benefited from a broad spectrum of African American works that explored "breath of life" experiences. Themes centered around slavery are prevalent in the works of writers who focus on the African American past. Relationships are of thematic interest to many modern day African American writers. Other important themes in contemporary African American literature relate to family and coming-of-age issues. A number of the coming-of-age novels by African Americans portray their protagonists maturing during the civil rights era.

Barriers have been dismantled in various genres. Rivaling their white contemporaries, Octavia Butler and Samuel Delany create works of science fiction; Tananarive Due crafts supernatural novels; Walter Mosley, Barbara Neely, Valerie Wilson Wesley, and Eleanor Taylor Bland write detective fiction; and August Wilson and Susan-Lori Parks take their plays to Broadway. Clearly, variety exists in contemporary African American novels. Novels of folk history, such as Colson Whitehead's *John Henry Days* (2001), and novels of the urban experience, such as Richard Wright's posthumous novella, *Rite of Passage* (1994), are equally well received. Many artists find that they can straddle more than one genre—Walter Mosley, Alice Walker, Gayl Jones, J. California Cooper, and Andrea Lee are good examples.

With the exception of the novel, the most prolific form of African American writing during the late twentieth and early twenty-first centuries is autobiography. Memoirs and autobiographies have become a popular mode of expression, especially for non-professional writers, entertainers, athletes, educators, ministers, civil rights leaders, politicians, physicians, attorneys, motivational speakers, and relatives of celebrities have written their life stories. A memoir worthy of distinction is Arthur Ashe's *Days of Grace* (1993), a work he co-authored with professor and literary critic Arnold Rampersad. In it, the tennis legend reveals that living with AIDS was not his life's greatest burden; living as a

black person in America was. One of the most popular autobiographies at the end of the twentieth century was *Having Our Say: The Delany Sisters' First 100 Years* (1993), by Sarah (Sadie) L. Delany and A. Elizabeth (Bessie) Delany (with Amy Hill Hearth). Their autobiography was published when Sadie, a former educator, was 104 years old, and Bessie, a former dentist and civil rights activist, was 102. Philanthropist, entrepreneur, and foundation executive Camille Cosby acquired the stage, film, and televison rights to the autobiography. Consequently, *Having Our Say* opened on Broadway in 1995, and was later transformed into a made-for-televison film. During the summer of 2002, *Having Our Say* was recommended reading as the District of Columbia began a program designed to encourage individuals to read.

"Amateur" writers are not the only individuals publishing their memoirs, however. Maya Angelou's first autobiography, *I Know Why the Caged Bird Sings* (1970), is greatly responsible for the revitalization of African American autobiography. Angelou has written five additional autobiographies, including *A Song Flung Up to Heaven* (2002). In 1977, 17 years after Richard Wright's death, his second autobiography, *American Hunger*, was published. Its pages are comprised of the section that Wright's publisher deleted from *Black Boy* (1945).

Poetry, the first genre that African Americans produced, remains a popular vehicle for black expression. A number of poets who began publishing their works in the 1960s—Mari Evans, Amiri Baraka, Sonia Sanchez, Jayne Cortez, Haki Madhubuti, and Nikki Giovanni—along with poets who were first published in the 1970s—such as Maya Angelou, Lucille Clifton, Ai, Toi Derricotte, and Yusef Komunyakaa—have continued to publish in the 1990s and beyond. Joining them are poets who began publishing in the 1980s—Rita Dove and Cornelius Eady—as well as poets who began publishing in the 1990s—Kevin Powell, Elizabeth Alexander, and Kevin Young. Important anthologies that include verse or collections of poetry published since the 1990s include *On the Verge: Emerging Poets and Artists* (1993), edited by Thomas Sayers Ellis and Joseph Lease, and *The Furious Flowering of African American Poetry* (1999), edited by Joanne Gabbin. In 1994, James Madison University hosted the Furious Flower Conference, dedicated to Gwendolyn Brooks. The conference featured three generations of poets, and was acknowledged as the "largest gathering of poets and critics" in more than two decades.

Whether writing in traditional styles such as the sonnet or being influenced by rap or hip-hop, African American creators of verse tackle the same issues as their prose counterparts: identity, racism, sexism, classism, relationships, politics, and urban life. Since the 1980s, poetry has become more popular and more accessible in the United States. Bookstores, universities, and literary groups continue to host established poets who read their verse before audiences. In addition, bookstores and cafés hold poetry slams and open mic nights where amateur poets can present their works. There are a variety of Internet sites that encourage novices to submit their verse.

African American writers and their works continue to be heralded on the national and international levels. Multiple National Book Award winners have been African Americans since the 1980s, including Alice Walker, Charles Johnson, Ai, and Lucille Clifton. Pulitzer Prizes have been awarded to Alex Haley, August Wilson, and Rita Dove, among others. And two African American women writers recorded landmark achievements in 1993: Rita Dove was named U.S. poet laureate and Toni Morrison won the Nobel Prize in literature.

With the arrival of the twenty-first century, African American writers continue to look into their own world for answers rather than letting others define their past, present, or future. Contemporary black authors are the beneficiaries of the vast legacy established by writers of the colonial period, the antebellum period, reconstruction era, Harlem Renaissance, the mid-twentieth century, and the Black Arts movement. Twenty-first century writers, empowered by their talents and their literary ancestors, are expanding and enhancing the African American literary tradition.

◆ AFRICAN AMERICAN AUTHORS AND LITERARY CRITICS

(To locate biographical profiles more readily, please consult the index at the back of the book.)

Raymond Andrews (1934–1991)
Novelist

Born in 1934 in Madison, Georgia, Raymond Andrews left his sharecropper home for Atlanta at 15 years of age. Once establishing himself, he attended high school at night and went on to the U.S. Air Force (1952–1956) and attended Michigan State University before moving to New York City. While working in New York in a variety of jobs: airline reservations clerk, hamburger cook, photo librarian, proofreader, inventory taker, mail room clerk, messenger, air courier dispatcher, and bookkeeper. He also perfected his literary skills.

Andrews's first novel *Appalachee Red* (1978), set in the African American neighborhood of a northern Georgia town called Appalachee, was widely acclaimed. In the opinion of the reviewer for the *St. Louis Globe Democrat*, his work marked the literary debut of a significant modern American novelist of the stature of a Richard Wright or James Baldwin. The following year Raymond Andrews was the first recipient of the annual James Baldwin Prize presented by Dial Press at a ceremony attended by Baldwin.

Andrews's second work *Rosiebelle Lee Wildcat Tennessee: A Novel* (1980) chronicled the 40-year reign beginning in 1906, of the spiritual and temporal leader of the African American community of Appalachee. *Baby Sweets* (1983), Andrews's third novel, which is the name given to the brothel operated by the eccentric son of Appalachee's leading citizen that provides African American prostitutes to the white population. It was published by Dial Press and illustrated by Andrew's brother, Benny, which was the case with all of Andrew's novels. This novel examines how the intermingling of the races affects an entire community, both black and white.

Maya Angelou (1928–)
Novelist, Poet, Actress

Maya Angelou, born Marguerite Johnson on April 4, 1928, is a writer, journalist, poet, actress, singer, dancer, playwright, director, and producer. Angelou spent her formative years shuttling between her native St. Louis; a tiny, totally segregated town in Arkansas; and San Francisco, where she realized her ambition of becoming that city's first African American streetcar conductor. But her true mark came later in life as her words became a symbol of hope that touched the soul of the United States. Perhaps the ultimate recognition of her talent came when President-elect Bill Clinton asked the poet to compose and recite an inaugural poem for his swearing-in ceremony in 1993. Before reaching that point, however, Angelou experienced a great variety of life's offerings, as inspired by her mother, grandmother, and other female role models in her life.

During the 1950s, Angelou studied dance with Pearl Primus in New York City, later appearing as a nightclub singer there, as well as in San Francisco and Hawaii. She toured with the U.S. State Department's production of *Porgy and Bess* in the mid-1950s. She began the following decade in the position of northern coordinator of the Southern Christian Leadership Conference. Angelou went abroad working as an editor for *The Arab Observer*, an English-language weekly published in Cairo. While living in Accra, Ghana, under the black nationalist regime of Kwame Nkrumah, she taught music, drama, and wrote for the *Ghanian Times*. Angelou later went to Sweden to study cinematography.

Angelou became a national celebrity in 1970 with the publication of *I Know Why the Caged Bird Sings*, the first volume of her autobiography, which detailed her encounters with Southern racism and a pre-pubescent rape by her mother's lover. The work was nominated for that year's National Book Award. Four additional volumes of Angelou's autobiography were published: *Gather Together in My Name* (1974); *Singin' and Swingin' and Gettin' Merry Like Christmas* (1976); *The Heart of a Woman* (1981); and *A Song Flung Up To Heaven* (2002).

Angelou's published works also include: *Just Give Me a Cool Drink of Water 'fore I Die: The Poetry of Maya Angelou* (1971); *Oh Pray My Wings Are Gonna Fit Me Well* (1975); *And Still I Rise* (1978); *Shaker Why Don't You Sing?* (1983); *All God's Children Need Traveling Shoes* (1986); and *Wouldn't Take Nothing for My Journey Now* (1993). In addition, Angelou's works include: *Mrs. Flowers: A Moment of Friendship; Now Sheba Sings the Song;* and *Phenomenal Woman: Four Poems Celebrating Women.*

Not limited to writing, Angelou dabbled both in front of and behind the camera. In 1977, she was nominated for an Emmy award for her portrayal of Nyo Boto in the television adaptation of Alex Haley's best-selling novel *Roots.* She also starred in the 1993 made-for-television movie *There Are No Children Here,* which co-starred Oprah Winfrey. That same year, Angelou wrote poetry for John Singleton's *Poetic Justice* and played a small role in the film. The following year, Angelou appeared in a television commercial, reading a version of her poem "Still I Rise" for the United Negro College Fund's Fiftieth Anniversary. She co-starred with Winona Ryder, Anne Bancroft, and Ellen Burstyn in *How to Make an American Quilt* (1995). Also active behind the scenes, she became the first African American woman to have a movie produced with *Georgia, Georgia* (1972), based on one of her books; and directed the films *All Day Long* in 1974 and *Down in the Delta* in 1998.

The 1990s held many highlights for the sought-after poet, who remained as active as she had been earlier in her career. On January 20, 1993, Angelou read her newly-created "On the Pulse of Morning" during the inauguration of President Bill Clinton. This event occurred just a few days after her play *And Still I Rise* was performed in Washington, DC. In 1994, Angelou narrated a World Choir '94 concert held at the Georgia Dome, where the festival featured 10,000 singers from ten different countries. She also gave a reading at the National Black Arts Festival that year. In 1995, Angelou delivered "A Brave and Startling Truth" at a United Nation's fiftieth anniversary ceremony held in San Francisco, read Sterling Brown's "Strong Men" at the inauguration of Washington, DC, Mayor Marion Barry, and was a keynote speaker, along with First Lady Hillary Rodham Clinton, at the 25th anniversary of the Joint Center for Political and Economic Studies.

Angelou has been the recipient of many awards including a Golden Eagle Award for the 1977 documentary *Afro-American in the Arts,* a Matrix Award from Women in Communications, Inc. in 1983, a North Carolina award in literature in 1987, a "best-mannered" citation from the National League of Junior Cotillions in 1993, a Medal of Distinction from the University of Hawaii's Board of Regents in 1994, and a Spingarn Medal from the NAACP that year. In 1981, Wake Forest University gave Angelou a lifetime appointment as Reynolds Professor of American Studies. In 2000, Angelou was awarded the national medal of art by President Bill Clinton. A year later she was honored with the Aaron Davis Hall Harlem Renaissance Award.

Houston A. Baker Jr. (1943–)
Writer, Literary Critic, Scholar, Educator

Houston A. Baker was born in Louisville, Kentucky, on March 22, 1943. In spite of the racist attitudes that permeated his environment, he went on to see himself as more than a victim. He attended Howard University and received a bachelor's degree in English and his master's and doctoral degrees from the University of California at Los Angeles. Out of his youthful experiences he became an advocate for the Black Power movement, which advocated black nationalism in the period of the late 1960s and 1970s.

As a young scholar, Baker shifted his critical perspective toward an African American aesthetic in African American literature. In other words, he considered art an instrument of cultural expression toward the liberation of black people that should be recognized in the study of African American works.

As editor of the book *Black Literature in America* (1971), an anthology of African American writers, he began to produce books that gave voice to artistic and literary experiences found in the study of African American literature. Among others, his books include: *Twentieth-Century Interpretations of Native Son* (1972); *A Many-Colored Coat of Dreams: The Poetry of Countee Cullen* (1974); *No Matter Where You Travel, You Still Be Black* (1979); *The Journey Back: Issues in Black Literature and Criticism* (1980); *Narrative of the Life of Frederick Douglass, An American Slave* (1982); *Blues, Ideology, and Afro-American Literature: A Vernacular Theory* (1984); *Modernism and the Harlem Renaissance* (1987); *Afro-American Poetics: Revision of Harlem and the Black Aesthetic* (1988); *Black Feminist Criticism and Critical Theory* (1988); *Afro-American Literary Study in the 1990's* (1989); *Black Studies,*

Rap and the Academy (1993); *Passing Over* (2000); *Critical Memory: Public Spheres, African American Writing, and Black Fathers and Sons in America* (2001); and *Turning South Again* (2001).

A prolific contributor to numerous scholarly journals and publications as well as president of the Modern Language Association of America in 1992, Baker is considered one of the leading African American intellectuals of his time. As a visiting professor to Duke University and professor and director of the Center for the Study of Black Literature and Culture at the University of Pennsylvania, Baker continues to pursue a more active approach to literary studies.

James Baldwin (1924–1987)
Novelist, Essayist, Playwright

Born in New York City on August 2, 1924, James Baldwin turned to writing after an early career as a boy preacher in Harlem's storefront churches. He attended Frederick Douglass Junior High School in Harlem and later graduated from DeWitt Clinton High School, where he was editor of the school magazine. Three years later, he won a Eugene Saxton Fellowship, which enabled him to write full-time. After leaving the United States, Baldwin resided in France as well as in Turkey.

Baldwin's first novel *Go Tell It on the Mountain* was published in 1953 and received critical acclaim. Two years later his first collection of essays *Notes of a Native Son* again won favorable critical acclaim. This was followed in 1956 by the publication of his second novel *Giovanni's Room*. His second collection of essays *Nobody Knows My Name* established him as a major voice in American literature.

In 1962, *Another Country*, Baldwin's third novel, was a critical and commercial success. A year later, he wrote *The Fire Next Time*, an immediate best-seller and regarded as one of the most brilliant essays written in the history of African American protest. Since then, two of Baldwin's plays *Blues for Mister Charlie* and *The Amen Corner* have been produced on the New York stage where they achieved modest success. His novel *Tell Me How Long the Train's Been Gone* was published in 1968. Baldwin himself regarded it as his first "grown-up novel," but it generated little enthusiasm among critics.

After a silence of several years, the question of whether Baldwin had stopped writing was widely debated. He published the 1974 novel *If Beale Street Could Talk*. In this work, the problems besetting a ghetto family are portrayed with great sensitivity and humor. Baldwin's skill as a novelist is evident as he conveyed his own sophisticated analyses through the mind of his protagonist, a young woman. To many critics, however, the novel lacked the undeniable relevance and fiery power of Baldwin's early polemical essays.

Baldwin's other works during this time include: *Going to Meet the Man* (short stories); *No Name in the Street; One Day When I Was Lost*, a scenario based on Alex Haley's *The Autobiography of Malcolm X; A Rap on Race* with Margaret Mead; and *A Dialogue* with Nikki Giovanni. He was one of the rare authors who worked well alone or in collaboration. Other books by Baldwin include: *Nothing Personal* (1964) with photographs by Richard Avedon; *The Devil Finds Work* (1976), about the movies; his sixth novel *Just Above My Head* (1979); and *Little Man, Little Man: A Story of Childhood* (1977), a book for children. He wrote 16 books in all.

In 1979, Baldwin's novel *Just Above My Head*, which dealt with the intertwined lives from childhood to adulthood of a gospel singer, his brother, and a young girl who is a child preacher, was published. The next year Baldwin's publisher released *Remember This House*, described as Baldwin's "memoirs, history and biography of the civil rights movement" interwoven with the biographies of three assassinated leaders: Martin Luther King Jr., Malcolm X, and Medgar Evers. Meanwhile, in his lectures Baldwin remained pessimistic about the future of race relations.

His last three books were *The Evidence of Things Not Seen* (1985) about the killing of 28 African American youths in Atlanta, Georgia, in the early 1980s; *The Price of the Ticket: Collected Non-fiction 1948–1985* (1985); and *Harlem Quartet* (1987). Baldwin spent most of the remainder of his life in France. In 1986, the French government made him a commander of the Legion of Honor, France's highest civilian award. He died at his home in France, on November 30, 1987, at the age of 63.

Toni C. Bambara (1939–1995)
Writer

Toni Cade Bambara was born Toni Cade in New York City in 1939, and later took on the name of Bambara, after finding the signature "Bambara" on a sketchbook located among the materials in her great-grandmother's trunk. Bambara's mother, who was profoundly influenced by the Harlem Renaissance, strongly encouraged her daughter to explore her creative side and the influences of culture.

Coming of age in the 1960s and 1970s allowed Bambara to participate in both the nationalist and the women's liberation movements. In 1970, Bambara edited *The Black Woman: An Anthology*, which, being the first of its kind, was recognized as beginning the renaissance of African American women's literature. Throughout her career, much of Bambara's writings have explored the experiences of the African American community and, in particular, experiences of African American women.

While working in community focused positions and pursuing her writing, Bambara received her B.A. from Queens College in New York in 1959 and her M.A. from City College of New York in 1964. Bambara's active career in academia and her numerous awards have exemplified her desire to use art to promote the social and political welfare of the African American community—but not at the expense of the African American woman. Her works include: *Gorilla, My Love* (1972); *The Sea Birds Are Still Alive* (1977); *The Salt Eaters* (1980), which received the American Book Award; and *If Blessing Comes* (1987).

On December 9, 1995, Bambara died of colon cancer in Philadelphia. Her last novel *Those Bones Are Not My Child*, was published posthumously in 1999.

Imamu A. Baraka (Leroi Jones) (1934–)
Poet, Playwright, Essayist

Amiri Baraka was born Leroi Jones in Newark, New Jersey on October 7, 1934. He attended Rutgers University in Newark and Howard University in Washington, DC. In 1958 Baraka founded *Yugen* magazine and Totem Press. From 1961 to 1964, Baraka worked as an instructor at New York's New School for Social Research. In 1964 he founded the Black Arts Repertory Theater. He has since taught at the State University of New York at Stony Brook, University of Buffalo, Columbia University, George Washington University, and San Francisco State University, and has served as director of the community theater, Spirit House, in Newark.

In 1961, Baraka published his first book of poetry *Preface to a Twenty Volume Suicide Note*. His second book *The Dead Lecturer* was published in 1964. Fame eluded him, however, until the publication of his play *Dutchman* in 1964, which received the Obie award for the best Off-Broadway play of the season. The shocking honesty of Baraka's treatment of racial conflict in this and later plays became the hallmark of his work.

During the late 1960s Baraka became a leading black power spokesman in Newark. He became head of the Temple of Kawaida, which Baraka describes as an "African religious institution—to increase black consciousness." The Temple and Baraka soon became a focal point of African American political activism in the racially-polarized city. In 1972 Baraka achieved prominence as an African American leader as chairman of the National Black Political Convention.

In 1966, Baraka's play *The Slave* won second prize in the drama category at the First World Festival of Dramatic Arts in Dakar, Senegal. Baraka's other published plays include: *The Toilet* (1964); *The Baptism* (1966); *The System of Dante's Hell* (1965); *Four Black Revolutionary Plays* (1969); *J-E-L-L-O* (1970); and *The Motion of History and Other Plays* (1978). He has edited with Larry Neal *Black Fire: An Anthology of Afro-American Writing* (1968) and *Afrikan Congress: A Documentary of the First Modern Pan-African Congress* (1972). His works of fiction include *The System of Dante's Hell* (novel, 1965) and *Tales* (short stories, 1967). Baraka has also published the following titles: *Black Music; Blues People: Negro Music in White America; Home: Social Essays; In Our Terribleness: Some Elements and Meanings in Black Style* with Billy Abernathy; *Raise Race Rays Raze: Essays Since 1965; It's Nation Time; Kawaida Studies: The New Nationalism, A Black Value System and Strategy and Tactics of a Pan Afrikan Nationalist Party;* and *Funk Lore: New Poems (1984–1995)*.

Arna W. Bontemps (1902–1973)
Poet, Novelist

Arna Wendell Bontemps was one of the most productive African American writers of the twentieth century. Born in Alexandria, Louisiana, on October 13, 1902, and raised in California, Bontemps received his B.A. degree from Pacific Union College in Angwin, California, in 1923 and his M.A. degree from the University of Chicago in 1943. In 1924, his poetry first appeared in *Crisis* magazine, the NAACP periodical edited by W. E. B. Du Bois. Two years later, *Golgotha Is a Mountain* won the Alexander Pushkin Award and, in 1927, *Nocturne at Bethesda* achieved first honors in the *Crisis* poetry contest. *Personals*, Bontemps's collected poems, was published in 1963.

In the late 1920s, Bontemps decided to try his hand at prose, and over the next decade produced such novels as *God Sends Sunday* (1931), *Black Thunder* (1936), and *Drums at Dusk* (1939). His books for young people include *We Have Tomorrow* (1945) and *Story of the Negro* (1948). Likewise of literary merit are such children's books as *Sad-Faced Boy* (1937) and *Slappy*

Hooper (1946). He edited *American Negro Poetry* and two anthologies with Langston Hughes, among others.

In 1968, Bontemps completed the editing of a volume of children's poetry. Other publications included: *One Hundred Years of Negro Freedom* (1961); *Anyplace But Here* (published in 1966 in collaboration with Jack Conroy); *Black Thunder* (1968 reprint); *Great Slave Narratives* (1969); *The Harlem Renaissance Remembered: Essays* (1972, 1984); and *The Old South*. He also edited several anthologies. In 1997 his book *The Pasteboard Bandit* was published posthumously. Bontemps died in Nashville on June 4, 1973, of a heart attack.

Gwendolyn Brooks (1917–2000)
Poet

Gwendolyn Brooks was the first African American to win a Pulitzer Prize. Brooks received this prestigious award in 1950 for *Annie Allen*, a volume of her poetry that had been published one year earlier. Brooks has been associated with the Black Arts movement of the late 1960s. Long a trailblazer, in 1985 she became the first African American woman to be appointed poetry consultant by the Library of Congress.

Brooks was born on June 7, 1917, in Topeka, Kansas, moved to Chicago at an early age, and graduated from Wilson Junior College in 1936. In 1945, she completed a book of poems *A Street in Bronzeville* and was selected by *Mademoiselle* magazine as one of the year's ten most outstanding American women. She became a fellow of the American Academy of Arts and Letters in 1946, and received Guggenheim Fellowships for 1946 and 1947. In 1949, she won the Eunice Tietjen Prize for Poetry in the annual competition sponsored by *Poetry* magazine for the same work that won her that year's Pulitzer. She was named poet laureate of the state of Illinois in 1968.

Brooks's insights into the potential alienation of African American life have been represented in the body of her work, which includes a collection of children's poems *Bronzeville Boys and Girls* (1956); a novel *Maud Martha* (1953); and two books of poetry *The Bean Eaters* (1960) and *Selected Poems* (1963). She has also written *In the Mecca*, winner of the 1968 Anisfield-Wolf Award; *Riot*; *The World of Gwendolyn Brooks*; *Report from Part One: The Autobiography of Gwendolyn Brooks*; *Family Pictures*; *Beckonings*; *Aloneness*; *Primer for Blacks*; *To Disembark*; *Report from Part Two*; and *In Montgomery: New and Other Poems*. Her poems and stories have also been published in magazines and two anthologies *Soon, One Morning* and *Beyond the Angry Black*. The publication of *Selected Poems* in 1964 earned her the Robert F. Ferguson Memorial Award. She has edited *A Broadside Treasury* and *Jump Bad, A New Chicago Anthology*.

Among the other honors Brooks has received, Western Illinois University established The Gwendolyn Brooks Center for African American Literature in 1985. In 1988, she was inducted into the National Women's Hall of Fame. She won an *Essence* Award that year and a Frost Medal from the Poetry Society of America in 1990. In 1994, Brooks was named the year's Jefferson lecturer by the National Endowment for the Humanities, the highest honor for intellectual achievement bestowed by the U.S. government. The same year, Chicago's Harold Washington Library Center unveiled a bronze bust of Brooks prominently located in the facility, and the National Book Foundation awarded her the Medal for Distinguished Contribution to American Letters and $10,000 for her lifetime of achievement. In 1995, Brooks received the National Medal of Arts from U.S. President Bill Clinton.

In 2000, Brooks passed away due to complications from cancer. Survivors include her daughter Nora Brooks Blakely, son Henry Blakely III and a grandson. Her husband, poet and writer Henry Blakely Jr., died in 1996.

Claude Brown (1937–2002)
Novelist

Claude Brown was born in 1937 in New York state. His claim to literary fame rests largely on his best-selling autobiography *Manchild in the Promised Land*, which was published in 1965 when he was 28 years of age. The book is the story of Brown's life in Harlem and, in the process, becomes a highly realistic documentary of life in the ghetto. It tells of Brown's escapades with the Harlem Buccaneers, a "bopping gang," and of his later involvement with the Forty Thieves, an elite stealing division of this same gang.

After attending the Wiltwyck School for emotionally disturbed and deprived boys, Brown returned to New York, was later sent to Warwick Reform School three times, and eventually made his way downtown to a small loft apartment near Greenwich Village. Changing his lifestyle, Brown finished high school and went on to graduate from Howard University in 1965.

Brown began work on his autobiography in 1963, submitting a manuscript of some 1,500 pages that was eventually cut and reworked into the finished product over a two-year period. Brown completed law school in the late 1960s and began practicing in California. In

1976, he published *The Children of Ham* about a group of young African Americans living as a family in a condemned Harlem tenement, begging, stealing, and doing whatever is necessary to survive.

Brown died on February 2, 2002, in New York, of a lung condition. He was 64.

William W. Brown (1815–1884)
Novelist, Playwright

William Wells Brown was the first African American to publish a novel, the first to publish a drama, and the first to publish a travel book. Born a slave in Lexington, Kentucky, on March 15, 1815, and taken to St. Louis as a young boy, Brown worked for a time in the offices of the *St. Louis Times* and then took a job on a riverboat on the Mississippi. In 1834, Brown fled to Canada, taking his name from a friendly Quaker whom he met there. While working as a steward on Lake Erie ships, he educated himself and became well known as a public speaker. In 1849, he went to England and Paris to attend the Peace Congress, remaining abroad for five years.

William W. Brown, a groundbreaker for African American writers. •

Brown's first published work *The Narrative of William W. Brown* (1847) went into three editions within eight months. A year later, a collection of his poems was published *The Anti-Slavery Harp* and in 1852 his travel book *Three Years in Europe* appeared in London. Brown's *Clotel, Or, the President's Daughter*, a melodramatic novel about miscegenation, was first published in London in 1853. As the first novel by an African American (it subsequently went through two revisions), its historical importance transcends its aesthetic shortcomings.

Brown's other books include: the first African American drama *The Escape, or a Leap for Freedom* (1858); *The Black Man: His Antecedents, His Genius, and His Achievements* (1863); *The Negro in the American Rebellion: His Heroism and Fidelity* (1867); and *The Rising Son* (1874).

Ed Bullins (1935–)
Playwright, Essayist, Poet

Ed Bullins was born in Philadelphia on July 2, 1935, and grew up in Los Angeles. Bullins is a writer of drama, and one of the founders of Black Arts/West in the Fillmore District of San Francisco. He patterned this experiment after the Black Arts Repertory Theater School in Harlem, which was founded and directed by Imamu Baraka. In 1977, when *Daddy*, the sixth play in his "Twentieth-Century Cycle," opened at the New Federal Theatre in New York's Henry Street Settlement, Bullins in an interview with the *New York Times* foresaw African American theatrical producers taking plays to cities with large African American populations. A leader of the African American theater movement and creator of more than 50 plays, he has yet to have a play produced on Broadway.

Bullins's main themes are the violence and tragedy of drug abuse and the oppressive life style of the ghetto. He presents his material in a realistic and natural style. Between 1965 and 1968, he wrote *The Rally, How Do You Do, Goin' a Buffalo, Clara's Old Man, The Electronic Nigger*, and *In The Wine Time*. He has also produced *The Fabulous Miss Marie*.

He has been a creative member of Black Arts Alliance, working with Baraka in producing films on the West Coast. Bullins has been connected with the New Lafayette Theater in Harlem where he was a resident playwright. His books include: *Five Plays; New Plays from the Black Theatre* (editor); *The Reluctant Rapist; The New Lafayette Theatre Presents; The Theme Is Blackness; Four Dynamite Plays; The Duplex; The Hungered One: Early Writings*; and *How Do You Do: A Nonsense Drama*.

In 1995 Bullins took up the position of professor of theater, and distinguished artist in residence at Northeastern University. He held this position until 2000.

Octavia E. Butler (1947–)
Novelist

Born in Pasadena, California, on June 22, 1947, Octavia Butler is a graduate of Pasadena City College. She has attended science fiction workshops, including the Clarion Science Fiction Writers' Workshop, and is a member of Science Fiction Writers of America. Her writing has focused on the impact of race and gender on future society. In 1985, Butler won three of science fiction's highest honors for her novella *Bloodchild: Novellas and Stories*: the Nebula, Hugo, and Locus awards. She also won a Hugo in 1984 for her short story "Speech Sounds." The 1987 novella *The Evening and the Morning and the Night* was nominated for a Nebula Award. In 1995, Butler won a MacArthur Foundation fellowship.

Butler's other works include the Patternmaster series, consisting of the novels *Patternmaster* (1976), *Mind of My Mind* (1977), *Survivor* (1978), *Wild Seed* (1980), and *Clay's Ark* (1984); the historical fantasy *Kindred* (1979); the Xenogenesis Trilogy, *Dawn: Xenogenesis* (1987), *Adulthood Rites* (1988), and *Imago* (1989); the dystopian *Parable of the Sower* (1993); and a sequel *Parable of the Talents* (1998). She has also served as a contributor to such science fiction publications as *Clarion*, *Future Life*, and *Isaac Asimov's Science Fiction Magazine*.

Barbara Chase-Riboud. *See* Visual and Applied Arts chapter.

Charles W. Chesnutt (1858–1932)
Novelist

Called the first major African American fiction writer and the first of his race to balance African American and white characters in an African American novel, Charles Waddell Chesnutt holds a prominent place in American literary history. His best fiction dealt with the current issues of his time; he handled satire entertainingly, and he was direct and insightful in his nonfiction works and speeches.

Born in Cleveland, Ohio, on June 20, 1858, Chesnutt moved to North Carolina with his family at the age of eight. Largely self-educated, he was admitted to the Ohio bar in 1887, the same year in which his first story "The Goophered Grapevine" was published in the *Atlantic Monthly*. This was followed in 1899 by two collections of his stories *The Conjure Woman* and *The Wife of His Youth*.

Chesnutt's first novel *The House Behind the Cedars* (1900) dealt with a young girl's attempt to "pass" for white. A year later, *The Marrow of Tradition* examined the violence of the post-Reconstruction period. His final novel *The Colonel's Dream* was published in 1905 and typified Chesnutt's ingratiating approach to his art, one that the writers of the Harlem School were later to reject. Chesnutt also wrote a biography *Frederick Douglass* (1899). He died on November 15, 1932.

Alice Childress (1920–1994)
Playwright, Novelist

Born in Charleston, South Carolina, on October 12, 1920, actress and author Alice Childress studied acting at the American Negro Theatre and attended Radcliffe Institute from 1966 to 1968, through a Harvard University appointment as a scholar-writer. Her plays are *Florence* (one-act play); *Gold Through the Trees; Just a Little Simple* (based on Langston Hughes's *Simple Speaks His Mind*); *Trouble in Mind; Wedding Band; Wine in the Wilderness;* and *When the Rattlesnake Sounds: A Play About Harriet Tubman*.

Childress also edited *Black Scenes* (1971), excerpts from plays in the Zenith series for children. Her other books include: *Like One of the Family: Conversations from a Domestic's Life* (1956); *A Hero Ain't Nothing but a Sandwich* (novel, 1973); *A Short Walk* (1979); *Rainbow Jordan* (1981); and *Many Closets* (1987). Childress's play *Trouble in Mind* won the Obie Award in 1956, as the best original off-Broadway production. In the 1980s she wrote a play based on the life of African American comedienne Jackie (Moms) Mabley. The play was produced in New York City.

Childress's work was noted for its frank treatment of racial issues, its compassionate yet discerning characterizations, and its universal appeal. Her books and plays often dealt with such controversial subjects as miscegenation and teenage drug addiction. Childress died of cancer complications on August 14, 1994.

J. California Cooper (19??–)
Short Story Writer, Novelist, Playwright

Joan California Cooper was born to Joseph and Maxine Cooper in Berkeley, California. She attended a technical high school and studied at San Francisco State College and the University of California. Cooper has also lived in Texas and Alaska; she currently resides in Northern California. Cooper decided to keep her first name silent; thus she uses the initial of her first name. Cooper adopted the name "California" after an individual compared her writing to that of Tennessee Williams who added the name of a state to his nomenclature. Cooper, who believes that age is unimportant, refuses to reveal the year of her birth. Although the public knows little about Cooper's private life, her writing talent has brought her to the attention of the literary world.

Cooper once stated that she could tell stories before she could write. During her childhood, she created plays and performed them for family and friends. To date, she is the author of at least 17 plays including *Everytime It Rains; System, Suckers, and Success; How Now; The Unintended; The Mother; Ahhh; Strangers,* for which Cooper was named San Francisco's Best Black Playwright in 1978; and *Loners,* which is included in Eileen J. Ostrow's *Center Stage* (1981). Her plays have been performed in such theaters as the Berkeley Black Repertory Theatre and the San Francisco Palace of Fine Arts; Cooper's plays have also been performed on college campuses, public television, and radio. After Alice Walker read Cooper's plays, she encouraged her to write short stories. Cooper once commented that her stories could still be in a drawer had it not been for Walker.

Walker's publishing company, Wild Trees Press published Cooper's first collection of short stories, *A Piece of Mine* (1984). In Walker's forward to *A Piece of Mine,* she wrote that "in its strong folk flavor, Cooper's work reminds us of Langston Hughes and Zora Neale Hurston. Like theirs, her style is deceptively simple and direct, and the vale of tears in which some of her characters reside is never so deep that a rich chuckle at a foolish person's foolishness cannot be heard." Cooper's second collection, *Homemade Love* (1986), won the 1989 American Book Award. Her subsequent short story collections are *Some Soul to Keep* (1987), *The Matter Is Life* (1991), *Some Love, Some Pain, Sometime* (1995), and *The Future Has a Past* (2000). Collectively these six volumes contain 52 stories. Her short stories have been reprinted in various publications such as *Daughters of Africa: An International Anthology of Words and Writings by Women of African Descent from the Ancient Egyptian to the Present* (1992), edited by Margaret Busby; and *Cornerstones: An Anthology of African American Literature* (1996), edited by Melvin Donaldson. Cooper has published three novels: *Family* (1991), *In Search of Satisfaction* (1994), and *The Wake of the Wind* (1998).

Cooper's additional awards include the Literary Lion Award and James Baldwin Award, both from the American Library Association, and she was named Woman of the Year by the University of Massachusetts and Best Female Writer in Texas. J. California Cooper is one of today's most popular African American authors.

Countee Cullen (1903–1946)
Poet

Born Countee Porter on May 30, 1903, in Baltimore, he was orphaned at an early age and adopted by Rev. Frederick Cullen, pastor of New York's Salem Methodist Church. At New York University, Cullen won Phi Beta Kappa honors and was awarded the Witter Bynner Poetry Prize. In 1925, while still a student at New York University, Cullen completed *Color,* a volume of poetry which received the Harmon Foundation's first gold medal for literature two years later.

In 1926, Cullie earned his M.A. at Harvard and a year later finished both *The Ballad of the Brown Girl* and *Copper Sun.* This was followed in 1929 by *The Black Christ,* written during a two-year sojourn in France on a Guggenheim Fellowship. In 1927, he edited *Caroling Dusk: An Anthology of Verse by Negro Poets.* The book was reprinted in 1972.

Upon his return to New York City, Cullen began a teaching career in the public school system. During this period, he also produced a novel *One Way to Heaven* (1932), *The Medea and Other Poems* (1935), *The Lost Zoo* (1940), and *My Lives and How I Lost Them* (1942, 1971). In 1947, a year after his death, Cullen's own selections of his best work were collected in a volume published under the title *On These I Stand.* Cullen died of uremic poisoning on January 9, 1946, in New York City.

Samuel R. Delany (1942–)
Novelist

Born in Harlem on April 1, 1942, and a published writer at the age of 19, Samuel Ray Delany has been a prolific writer of science fiction, novelettes and novels. His first book was *The Jewels of Aptor* (1962), followed by *Captives of the Flame* (1963), *The Towers of Toron* (1964), *City of a Thousand Suns* (1965), *The Ballad of Beta-2* (1965), *Babel-17* (1966), *Empire Star* (1966), *The Einstein Intersection* (1967), *Out of the Dead City* (1968), and *Nova* (1968). *Babel-17* and *The Einstein Intersection* both won Nebula awards from the Science Fiction Writers of America, as did his short stories "Aye, and Gomorrah" and "Time Considered as a Helix of Semi-Precious Stones," which also won a Hugo Award at the World Science Fiction Convention in Heidelberg. Delany co-edited the speculative fiction quarterly *Quark, Nos. 1, 2, 3, 4* with his former wife, award-winning poet Marilyn Hacker. He also wrote, directed, and edited the half-hour film *The Orchid.* In 1975, Delany was Visiting Butler Chair professor of English at the State University of New York at Buffalo.

Delany's other books include: *Distant Stars* (1981); *Stars in My Pocket Like Grains of Sand* (1984); *Flight from Neveryon* (1985); *Neveryona* (1986); *The Bridge of Lost Desire* (1988); and the controversial *Hogg* (1996). His non-fiction works include: *The Jewel-Hinged Jaw; The American Shore; Starboard Wine; The Straits of Messina; The Motion of Light in Water* (autobiography, 1988); *The Mad Man* (1994); *They Fly at Ciron* (1995); *Atlantis: Three Tales* (1995); *Times Square Red, Times Square Blue* (1999); and *Shorter Views: Queer Thoughts & the Politics of Paraliterary* (1999).

Rita Dove (1952–)
Poet, Educator

Rita Dove was born on August 28, 1952, in Akron, Ohio. She received a B.A. from Miami University in Oxford, Ohio, in 1973, and an M.F.A. degree from the University of Iowa in 1977. Dove also attended the University of Tubingen in Germany in 1974 and 1975.

Rita Dove.

Dove began her teaching career at Arizona State University in 1981 as an assistant professor. She spent 1982 as a writer-in-residence at Tuskegee Institute (now Tuskegee University). By 1984, she was an associate professor and by 1987, a full professor. Dove, who has served on the editorial boards of the literary journals *Callaloo, Gettysburg Review,* and *TriQuarterly,* joined the University of Virginia's English Department in 1989. She teaches creative writing.

Dove won the 1987 Pulitzer Prize for poetry for a collection titled *Thomas and Beulah.* Her themes are universal, encompassing much of the human condition and occasionally commenting on racial issues. She also published *Yellow House on the Corner* (1980), *Museum* (1983), *Fifth Sunday* (short stories, 1985), *Grace Notes* (1989), *Selected Poems* (1993), *Through the Ivory Gate* (novel, 1993), *Mother Love* (1995), *The Darker Face of the Earth: A Verse Play in Fourteen Scenes* (1995); and *On the Bus With Rosa Parks* (1999).

In addition to the Pulitzer Prize, Dove won many honors including Presidential scholar (1970); Fulbright scholar (1974, 1975); a literary grant from the National Endowment for the Humanities (1978, 1989); Guggenheim fellow (1983, 1984); General Electric Foundation Award for Younger Poets (1987); Ohio Governor's Award (1988); Andrew W. Mellon Fellowship (1988, 1989); University of Virginia Center for Advanced Studies fellow (1989–1992); the Walt Whitman Award (1990); and the Kennedy Center Fund for New American Plays Award for *The Darker Face of the Earth* (1995).

Dove was named U.S. poet laureate, a one-year Library of Congress post, in 1993. She was the first African American and the youngest person ever to earn the appointment. On April 22, 1994, PBS aired a piece entitled "Poet Laureate Rita Dove" on *Bill Moyer's Journal.* She hoped to use the position to revive public interest in serious literature.

Paul Laurence Dunbar (1872–1906)
Poet

The first African American poet to gain a national reputation in the United States, Paul Laurence Dunbar was also the first to use African American dialect within the formal structure of his work. Born of former slaves in Dayton, Ohio, on June 27, 1872, Dunbar worked as an elevator operator after graduating from high school. His first book of poetry *Oak and Ivy* was privately printed in 1893 and was followed by *Majors and Minors,* which appeared two years later. Neither book was an immediate sensation, but there were enough favorable reviews in such magazines as *Harper's* to encourage Dunbar in the pursuit of a full-fledged literary career. In 1896, Dunbar completed

Paul Laurence Dunbar.

Lyrics of a Lowly Life, the single work upon which his subsequent reputation was irrevocably established.

Before his untimely death in 1906, Dunbar had become the dominant presence in the world of African American poetry. His later works included: *Lyrics of Sunshine and Shadow* (1905); *Li'l Gal* (1904); *Howdy, Honey, Howdy* (1905); *A Plantation Portrait* (1905); *Joggin' erlong* (1906); and *Complete Poems*, published posthumously in 1913. This last work contains not only the dialect poems which were his trademark, but many poems in conventional English as well. The book enjoyed such enormous popularity that it has, to this day, never gone out of print. He also published four novels including *The Sport of Gods*, *The Love of Landry*, and *The Uncalled*, and four volumes of short stories.

Ralph Ellison (1914–1994)
Novelist, Essayist

Ralph Ellison's critical and artistic reputation rests largely on a single masterpiece, his first and only novel *Invisible Man*. An instant classic, the novel was given the National Book Award for fiction in 1952 and the Russwurm Award in 1953. Years in the making, the novel's success heralded the emergence of a major writing talent. Ellison worked at a second novel for more than 40 years, but at the time of his death, the untitled work was still incomplete.

Ellison was born in Oklahoma City, Oklahoma, on March 1, 1914, and came to New York City in the late 1930s, after having studied music at Tuskegee Institute (now Tuskegee University) for three years. Initially interested in sculpture, he turned to writing after coming under the influence of T.S. Eliot's poetry and as a direct consequence of his friendship with novelist Richard Wright. He worked for the Federal Writer's Project and wrote for a variety of publications during the late 1930s to early 1940s. In 1942, he became the managing editor of the *Negro Quarterly*. He began writing *Invisible Man* in 1945. During World War II, Ellison worked as a cook in the U.S. Merchant Marines.

In addition to the National Book Award, Ellison won a Rockefeller Foundation Award in 1954; was elected to the National Institute of Arts and Letters; received a Medal of Freedom from President Lyndon Johnson in 1969; was named chevalier de l'Ordre des Arts et Lettres by France in 1969; and was given a National Medal of Arts in 1985. Ellison was the recipient of more than one dozen honorary degrees including doctor of letters degrees from Harvard University (1974) and Wesleyan University (1980). Three years after the publication of *Invisible Man*, the American Academy of Arts and Letters awarded Ellison the Prix de Rome, which enabled him to live and write in Italy until 1957.

Back in the United States, Ellison began an academic career. He taught Russian and American literature courses at Bard College in Annandale-on-Hudson, New York, for three years and spent the early 1960s as a visiting professor at University of Chicago, Yale, and Rutgers, where he was a writer-in-residence. From 1970 to 1980, Ellison was the Albert Schweitzer Professor of Humanities at New York University.

Ellison's second work was a book of essays entitled *Shadow and Act.* Published in 1964, excerpts from the book have been printed in several literary journals. Ellison began writing his second novel *Juneteenth* in 1954 and continued to revise it until he died. (A 1967 fire destroyed 350 pages of his unfinished second novel's manuscript.) In 1982, the thirtieth anniversary edition of *Invisible Man* with a new introduction by Ellison was published. In 1986, a second collection of essays and talks was published as *Going to the Territory*. *The Collected Essays of Ralph Ellison*, edited by John F. Callahan, was published posthumously in 1995.

Ellison died of pancreatic cancer in New York City on April 16, 1994. On May 26, 1994, a memorial tribute to him was held at the American Academy of Arts and Letters in New York.

Mari Evans (1923–)
Poet

Born in Toledo, Ohio, in 1923, Evans studied at the University of Toledo. In 1963, her poetry was published in *Phylon, Negro Digest,* and *Dialog.* Two years later she was awarded a John Hay Whitney Fellowship. One of her better known works is *The Alarm Clock,* which deals with the rude awakening of the African American to the white "establishment." It captures and summarizes the civil rights scene of the 1960s in the United States.

Evans's books include: *I Am a Black Woman; Where Is All the Music?; Black Women Writers (1950–1980): A Critical Evaluation* (1984), edited by Evans, covering 15 African American women poets, novelists, and playwrights; *Nightstar: Poems from 1973–1978* (1980); *J. D.; I Look at Me; Singing Black; The Day They Made Benani; Jim Flying High;* (Co-author) *Mis Taken Brilliance* (1993); (Co-author) *Singing Black: Alternative Nursery Rhymes for Children,* (1998); and *Dear Corinne, Tell Somebody! Love, Annie: A Book about Secrets* (1999).

Jessie Redmon Fauset (1882–1961)
Writer, Editor, Educator

Jessie Redmon Fauset, born April 27, 1882, was a central figure during the Harlem Renaissance not only for encouraging the careers of many of the major writers of the time, but also through her own literary contributions to the movement. In 1919 Fauset became literary editor of *Crisis* magazine, founded by W. E. B. Du Bois and held that position until 1927. As an editor Fauset excelled, for under her leadership, *Crisis* magazine outsold its rival magazine *Opportunity,* started by Charles S. Johnson. She also realized Du Bois's plan for a periodical focusing on children six to sixteen called *The Brownies Book* and was its functional editor.

Fauset's editorial experiences and travel heightened her own sensibilities about the images of African Americans. Her writings professed an awareness of the racism and sexism that existed during the 1920s and 1930s. She contributed numerous short stories, essays,

critiques, poetry, and reviews to the magazine and published her first novel *There is Confusion* in 1924. The book was her response to an unrealistic portrayal of African Americans by white novelist T. S. Stribling. After Fauset's break from *Crisis* in 1927, she established her place as an author and published *Plum Bun: A Novel without a Moral* (1929), *The Chinaberry Tree* (1931), and *Comedy, American Style* (1933).

Fauset, who had received her B.A. from Cornell University in 1905 (Phi Beta Kappa) and her M.A. from the University of Pennsylvania in 1919, taught at both Fisk University in the summer and in high school and college settings. In later years, she returned to teaching, partially because the publishing world was still not ready for an African American, let alone a woman. Fauset died in Philadelphia on April 30, 1961, of hypertensive heart disease. Recently, Fauset's contribution to the dialogue about race, class, and gender have been more fully recognized in her work. She not only challenged the world of publishing with her own work, but by assisting other artists made it possible for unrealistic and negative perceptions of African Americans to be confronted.

Rudolph Fisher (1897–1934)
Writer, Physician, Community Leader

Although he was a radiologist, Rudolph Fisher was best known as a leading writer during the Harlem Renaissance. Fisher wrote short stories and novels that depicted real life in the Harlem community and was also the first African American to write detective fiction.

Fisher was born on May 9, 1897, in Washington, DC. He grew up in a middle-class family who saw that he was rigorously educated at primary and secondary schools in Providence, Rhode Island, and New York City. He graduated Phi Beta Kappa from Brown University with B.A. and M.A. degrees. In 1924, Fisher graduated summa cum laude from Howard University Medical School in Washington. During his medical internship at Freedmen's Hospital in the same city, he published his first short story "The City of Refuge" in the *Atlantic Monthly.*

Continuing his medical education, from 1925 to 1927 Fisher trained at Columbia University's College of Physicians and Surgeons. He entered private practice and continued his writing as well, publishing five short stories in *Atlantic Monthly* and *McClure's,* an essay in *American Mercury,* and an article in the *Journal of Infectious Diseases.*

Fisher published his first novel *The Walls of Jericho* in 1928. In the novel Fisher blends all of Harlem life into one story and bridges the gap between the classes. *The*

Rudolph Fisher.

Conjure-Man Dies: A Mystery Tale of Dark Harlem (1932) was his second novel and the first full-length detective novel with all-African American characters published by an African American author. Fisher published two children's stories in 1932 and 1933, "Ezekiel" and "Ezekiel Learns," and in 1933 he published two short stories "Guardians of the Law" and "Miss Cynthie." The latter work also appeared in *Best Short Stories of 1934.*

In addition to his writing career, Fisher was superintendent of the International Hospital in Manhattan from 1929 to 1932. Between 1930 and 1934, he was a roentgenologist for the New York City Health Department and served in the 369th Infantry. He died of cancer on December 16, 1934, in New York City.

Charles Fuller (1939–)
Playwright

Charles Fuller was born on March 5, 1939, in Philadelphia, Pennsylvania. He became "stagestruck" in his high school days when he went to the Old Walnut Street Theater in his native Philadelphia and saw a Yiddish play starring Molly Picon and Menasha Skulnik. He did not understand a word of it, "but it was live theater, and I felt myself responding to it," he said.

In 1959, Fuller entered the army and served in Japan and South Korea, after which he attended Villanova University and La Salle College. While Fuller was working as a housing inspector in Philadelphia, the McCarter Theater in Princeton, New Jersey produced his first play. The theme concerned interracial marriage, and its creator is quick now to tag it "one of the world's worst interracial plays." However, during this time he met members of The Negro Ensemble Company and, in 1974, he wrote his first play *In the Deepest Part of Sleep* for them. For NEC's tenth anniversary, Fuller wrote *The Brownsville Raid* about the African American soldiers who were dishonorably discharged on President Teddy Roosevelt's orders in 1906 after a shootout in Brownsville, Texas. The play was a hit and Fuller followed it a few seasons later with *Zooman and the Sign*, a melodrama that won two Obie awards.

A Soldier's Play, which won a Pulitzer Prize in 1982, was his fourth play for The Negro Ensemble Company. This drama dealing with a murder set in a backwater New Orleans army camp in 1944, opened NEC's 15th anniversary season in 1981 with a long run and was hailed by the *New York Times* as "tough, taut and fully realized." *A Soldier's Play* became *A Soldier's Story* when it was produced as a film in 1984 by Columbia Pictures. Fuller wrote the screenplay and African American actor Howard E. Rollins Jr. was the film's star. In 1999, Fuller wrote and produced a three part interlocking script called Love Songs for Showtime. The three different sections featured Louis Gossett Jr., Robert Townsend and Andre Braugher

The recipient of the Guggenheim Foundation Fellowship, the Rockefeller Foundation, and the National Endowment for the Arts and CAPS Fellowships in playwrighting, Fuller describes himself as a playwright who happens to be African American, rather than an African American playwright.

Ernest J. Gaines (1933–)
Novelist, Short Story Writer

Ernest J. Gaines was born on a plantation in Louisiana, on January 15, 1933. He moved to California in 1949, where he did his undergraduate study at San Francisco State College. In 1959, he received the Wallace Stegner Fellowship in creative writing. The following year he was awarded the Joseph Henry Jackson Literary Award.

Gaines's first novel was *Catherine Carmier* (1964). Others followed, including *Of Love and Dust* (1967), *Barren Summer* (completed in 1963 but never published), *The Autobiography of Miss Jane Pittman* (1971), *A Warm Day in November* (for young people), and *In My Father's House* (1978). Ironically, the book *The Autobiography of Jane Pittman* was banned in a Conroe, Texas, seventh-grade racial tolerance course in 1995; the school censored the work, citing the liberal use of racial slurs. The 1974 television production of *The Autobiography of Miss Jane Pittman* starring Cicely Tyson boosted Gaines's reputation. Gaines's *A Gathering of Old Men*, published in 1983, was made into a movie as well. In 1994, Gaines's 1993 work *A Lesson Before Dying* won the National Book Critics Circle award for fiction. *A Lesson Before Dying* was also adapted for the small screen by HBO in 1999.

Nikki Giovanni (1943–)
Poet

Nikki Giovanni was born in Knoxville, Tennessee, on June 7, 1943. She studied at the University of Cincinnati from 1961 to 1963 and received her B.A. from Fisk University in 1967. She also attended the University of Pennsylvania School of Social Work for one year and Columbia University School of the Arts for one year in the late 1960s.

In 1969, Giovanni taught at Queens College (CUNY) and Rutgers University before founding a communications and publishing company called NikTom, Ltd. In the mid- to late-1980s, she resumed teaching, spending the year of 1984 as a visiting professor at Ohio State University and the subsequent three years at Mount Joseph on the Ohio as a creative writing professor. Since 1987, Giovanni has taught at Virginia Polytechnic Institute and State University, first as a visiting professor and then as a full professor of English beginning in 1989. That year, she also directed the Warm Hearth Writer's Workshop. From 1990 to 1993, Giovanni served on the board of directors for the Virginia Foundation for the Humanities and Public Policy.

Giovanni's first book of poetry *Black Feeling, Black Talk*, published in the mid–1960s, was followed by *Black Judgment* in 1968. These two works were combined as *Black Feeling, Black Talk, Black Judgment* in 1970. By 1974, Giovanni's poems could be found in many African American literature anthologies, and she also became a media personality through her television appearances, during which she read her poetry. Many of her poems were put to soul or gospel music accompaniment. Such recordings include: *Truth Is on Its Way*, winner of the National Association of Radio and Television Announcers Award in 1972; and *Spirit to Spirit*, a videocassette produced by PBS, winner of the Oakland Museum Film Festival Silver Apple Award in 1988.

A prolific author, Giovanni's books include: *Re: Creation* (poetry); *Spin a Soft Black Song: Poems for Children; Night Comes Softly: Anthology of Black Female Voices* (nonfiction); *My House* (poetry); *Gemini: An Extended Autobiographical Statement* (nonfiction); *Ego Tripping and Other Poems for Young People; A Dialogue: James Baldwin and Nikki Giovanni* (nonfiction); and *A Poetic Equation: Conversations Between Nikki Giovanni and Margaret Walker* (nonfiction). Her other works include: *The Women and the Men: Poems* (1975); *Cotton Candy on a Rainy Day* (poetry, 1978); *Vacation Time: Poems for Children* (1980), dedicated to her son, Tommy, and winner of the Children's Reading Roundtable of Chicago Award; *Those Who Ride the Night Winds* (poetry, 1984); *Sacred Cows . . . and Other Edibles* (nonfiction, 1988), winner of the Ohioana Library Award in 1988; *Grand Mothers: Poems, Reminiscences, and Short Stories About the Keepers of Our Traditions* (1994); *Racism 101* (nonfiction); *Knoxville, Tennessee* (coauthored with Larry Johnson, 1994); *The Selected Poems of Nikki Giovanni* (1995); *Blues for all the Changes* (collection of poems, 1999); and *Grand Fathers: Reminiscences, Poems, Recipes, and Photos of the Keepers of Our Traditions* (1999).

Giovanni won several awards throughout her career including the Highest Achievement Award in 1971 from *Mademoiselle;* life membership to the National Council of Negro Women in 1973; the Outstanding Woman of Tennessee in 1985; the *Cincinnati Post* Post-Corbett Award in 1986; and a Governor's Award in the Arts from the Tennessee Arts Commission in 1999. In addition, Giovanni received honorary degrees from numerous institutions.

Eloise Greenfield (1929–)
Children's Author

Born Eloise Little on May 17, 1929, in Parmele, North Carolina, Greenfield moved to Washington, DC, as a baby and grew up happily in a close-knit, urban neighborhood. After attending Minor Teachers College, she worked in various clerical and secretarial positions. By 1950, she had begun experimenting with creative writing. After years of studying and persevering, Greenfield met fellow writers and made valuable contacts when she joined the District of Columbia Black Writers Workshop in the early 1970s. Soon thereafter, her picture book *Bubbles* was published.

With that initial success, Greenfield established her own niche within the arena of children's books and has published, on average, one book each year. Having a goal of encouraging children to develop positive attitudes about themselves, Greenfield's stories capture both the unique and universal experiences of growing up as an African American. Much of her fiction, as in the novel *Sister*, is concerned with bonding within African American families. Greenfield's biographies of distinguished African Americans and poetic picture books have appeared on "notable" book lists and have placed the author in demand as a speaker at writers' conferences and in classrooms of her young fans.

Greenfield has also recently published *William and the Good Old Days* (1993); *Sweet Baby Coming* (1994); *Honey, I Love* (1995); *On My Horse* (1995); *For the Love of the Game: Michael Jordan and Me.* (1996); *Angels*, (1998); *Water, Water*, (1999); and *I can Draw a Weeposaur*, (2001).

Alex Haley (1921–1992)
Journalist, Novelist

The author of the widely acclaimed novel *Roots* was born Alexander Palmer Haley in Ithaca, New York, on August 11, 1921, and reared in Henning, Tennessee. The oldest of three sons of a college professor father and a mother who taught grade school, Haley graduated from high school at 15 and attended college for two years before enlisting in the United States Coast Guard as a messboy in 1939.

A voracious reader, Haley began writing short stories while at sea, but it took eight years before small magazines began accepting his stories. By 1952, the Coast Guard had created a new rating for Haley—chief journalist—and he began handling United States Coast Guard public relations. In 1959, after 20 years of military service, he retired from the Coast Guard and launched a new career as a freelance writer. He eventually became an assignment writer for *Reader's Digest* and moved on to *Playboy*, where he initiated the "Playboy Interviews" feature.

One of the personalities Haley interviewed was Malcolm X—an interview that inspired Haley's first book *The Autobiography of Malcolm X* (1965). Translated into eight languages, the book has sold more than six

Alex Haley.

million copies. Pursuing the few slender clues of oral family history told to him by his maternal grandmother in Tennessee, Haley spent the next 12 years traveling three continents tracking his maternal family back to a Mandingo youth named Kunta Kinte, who was kidnaped into slavery from the small village of Juffure in Gambia, West Africa. During this period, he lectured extensively in the United States and in Great Britain on his discoveries about his family in Africa and wrote many magazine articles on his research in the 1960s and the 1970s. He received several honorary doctor of letters degrees for his work.

The book *Roots*, excerpted in *Reader's Digest* in 1974 and heralded for several years, was finally published in the fall of 1976 with very wide publicity and reviews. In January 1977, ABC-TV produced a 12-hour series based on the book, which set records for the number of viewers. With cover stories, book reviews, and interviews with Haley in scores of magazines and many newspaper articles, the book became the number one national best-seller, sold in the millions, and was published as a paperback in 1977. *Roots* truly became a phenomenon. It was serialized in the *New York Post* and the *Long Island Press*. Instructional packages, lesson plans based on *Roots*, and other books about *Roots* for schools were published, along with records and tapes by Haley.

Haley's book stimulated interest in Africa and in African American genealogy. The United States Senate passed a resolution paying tribute to Haley and comparing *Roots* to *Uncle Tom's Cabin* by Harriet Beecher Stowe in the 1850s. The book received many awards including the National Book Award for 1976 special citation of merit in history and a special Pulitzer Prize in 1976 for making an important contribution to the literature of slavery. *Roots* was not without its critics, however. A 1977 lawsuit brought by Margaret Walker charged that *Roots* plagiarized her novel *Jubilee*. Another author, Harold Courlander, also filed a suit charging that *Roots* plagiarized his novel *The African*. Courlander received a settlement after several passages in *Roots* were found to be almost verbatim from *The African*. Haley claimed that researchers helping him had given him this material without citing the source.

Haley received the NAACP's Spingarn Medal in 1977. Four thousand deans and department heads of colleges and universities throughout the country in a survey conducted by *Scholastic Magazine* selected Haley as America's foremost achiever in the literature category. The ABC-TV network presented another series *Roots: The Next Generation* in February, 1979 (also written by Haley). *Roots* had sold almost 5 million copies by December, 1978, and had been reprinted in 23 languages.

In 1988, Haley conducted a promotional tour for a novella titled *A Different Kind of Christmas* about slave escapes in the 1850s. He also promoted a drama *Roots: The Gift*, a two-hour television program shown in December, 1988. This story revolved around two principal characters from *Roots* who are involved in a slave break for freedom on Christmas Eve. Haley's drama *Queen*, which he had begun writing before his death, was aired on television in 1998, starring Halle Berry.

Haley died February 10, 1992, of a heart attack.

Virginia Hamilton (1936–2002)
Children's and Young Adult Author

Virginia Hamilton was born on March 12, 1936, into a large extended family in rural Yellow Springs, Ohio. Her career as an author was directly influenced by her parents, who were avid storytellers themselves. She attended nearby Antioch College from 1952 to 1955, ultimately graduating from Ohio State University in 1958. Determined to be a writer, Hamilton settled in New York City and studied the craft at the New School for Social Research. She worked at a variety of jobs and moved back to Yellow Springs before publishing her first book *Zeely* in 1967. Issued during an era of racial strife, *Zeely* was one of the first books for young readers in which African American characters were portrayed as people living with average, universal circumstances as opposed to constantly dealing with politically and racially related problems, such as integration.

After her second novel *The House of Dies Dreary* received the 1968 Edgar Allen Poe Award for best juvenile mystery of the year, Hamilton went on to write and edit more than 30 children's and young adult books within various genres. Her canon includes well-researched historical fiction, contemporary urban novels about teenagers, science fiction and supernatural tales, biographies of the historical figures Paul Robeson and W. E. B. Du Bois, and collections of African American folklore and slavery era "liberation" stories.

Hamilton has been repeatedly honored for her work including winning the Hans Christian Andersen Medal, Newbery Honor Book Award, National Book Award, Coretta Scott King Award, and the MacArthur Foundation Prize in 1995. Many of her works have appeared on notable "best books" lists, and she has inspired an Annual Virginia Hamilton Conference. Hamilton stands as one of the predominant creative forces behind multicultural works for young readers.

On February 19, 2002, Hamilton died in Dayton, Ohio, of breast cancer. She was 65.

Jupiter Hammon (1711–?)
Poet, Tract writer

Jupiter Hammon was born October 17, 1711, probably near Oyster Bay on Long Island, New York. He was one of the first African American poet to have his work published in the United States. *An Evening Thought, Salvation by Christ, with Penitential Cries* appeared in 1761, when Hammon was a slave belonging to a Mr. Lloyd of Long Island, New York. Due to his fondness for preaching, the major portion of Hammon's poetry is religious in tone and is usually dismissed by critics as being of little aesthetic value because of its pious platitudes, faulty syntax, and forced rhymes. Hammon's best-known work is a prose piece *An Address to the*

Negroes of the State of New York delivered before the African Society of New York City on September 24, 1786. This speech was published the following year and went into three editions. He died between 1790 and 1806.

Lorraine Hansberry (1930–1965)
Playwright

Born in Chicago on May 19, 1930, Hansberry studied art at Chicago's Art Institute, the University of Wisconsin, and, finally, in Guadalajara, Mexico. Hansberry wrote the award-winning play *A Raisin in the Sun* while living in New York's Greenwich Village, having conceived the play after reacting negatively to what she called "a whole body of material about Negroes. Cardboard characters. Cute dialect bits. Or hip-swinging musicals from exotic scores." The play opened on Broadway on March 11, 1959, at a time when it was generally held that all plays dealing with African Americans were "death" at the box office. Produced, directed, and performed by African Americans, it was

later made into a successful movie starring Sidney Poitier. It was then adapted into *Raisin*, a musical that won a Tony Award in 1974.

Hansberry's second Broadway play *The Sign in Sidney Brustein's Window* dealt with "the western intellectual poised in hesitation before the flames of involvement." Shortly after its Broadway opening, Hansberry succumbed to cancer on January 12, 1965, in New York City.

Hansberry's books, in addition to the two published plays, include: *To Be Young, Gifted and Black; The Movement: Documentary of a Struggle for Equality;* and *Les Blancs: The Collected Last Plays of Lorraine Hansberry.*

Frances E. W. Harper (1825–1911)
Writer, Poet, Activist

Frances Ellen Watkins Harper, the first African American woman to publish a short story, was one of the most prolific African American women writers of the nineteenth century. She was known also for essays,

Lorraine Hansberry, best-known for her play, *A Raisin in the Sun.*

Frances E. W. Harper, the first African American to publish a short story.

poetry, and for her single novel *Iola Leroy.* Beyond her writings, Harper was an effective traveling lecturer and a supporter of emancipation, the temperance movement, and of the African American women's movement.

Harper was born to free parents in 1825 in Baltimore, Maryland, on September 24, 1825. She was never able to reconcile the death of her mother, a traumatic experience that occurred when Harper was only three years old. She was raised by relatives and attended William Watkins Academy for Negro Youth—a prestigious school in Baltimore that her uncle founded. Uncomfortable in the slave city of Baltimore, Harper moved to Ohio in 1850 and became the first woman teacher at the newly-founded Union Seminary, later a part of Wilberforce University. In 1854, she became a permanent lecturer for the Maine Anti-Slavery Society and spoke throughout New England, Ohio, New York, and elsewhere. "The bronze muse," as she became known, gave fiery speeches and often incorporated her poetry into her lectures. So successful and stirring were her presentations that the Pennsylvania Anti-Slavery Society hired her as a lecturer as well. She held her audiences spellbound and spoke with dignity and composure. Although she wrote and lectured on other topics, her attention to anti-slavery caused scholars to refer to her as an abolitionist poet.

Harper's first volume of poems and prose was published in 1851 as *Forest Leaves,* also printed as *Autumn Leaves.* Her literary career was actually launched in 1854 when she published *Poems on Miscellaneous Subjects;* the work was printed in Boston and Philadelphia and reissued in 1857, 1858, 1864, and 1871. Included in the work were several anti-slavery poems such as "The Slave Mother" and "The Slave Auction," yet most of the poems dealt with women's rights, temperance, religion, and other current issues.

Her writings in the *Christian Recorder* promoted her work as a journalist. Harper's writings in the journal included the serialized novel *Minnie's Sacrifice,* the dramatic poem "Moses: A Story of the Nile," a series of poems by "Aunt Chloe," and the fictionalized essays "Fancy Etchings." She wrote other serials, but it was not until 1892 that she published in book form her first and best-known work *Iola Leroy, or, Shadows Uplifted.* The novel aims to present a true picture of slavery and the Reconstruction, to promote humanity, and to foster a sense of racial pride in African Americans. Her collections of poems that followed included works previously issued but supplemented with other examples of her writings: *The Sparrow's Fall and Other Poems* (c.1894); *Light Beyond Darkness, The Martyr of Alabama* (c.1895); and *Atlanta Offering: Poems* (1895). In 1900 she published *Poems* and, the following year, *Idylls of the Bible.*

Harper's activities also included work with the YMCA, for which she helped develop Sunday schools; the Colored Section of the Philadelphia and Pennsylvania Women's Christian Temperance Union; and the American Women's Suffrage Association. She helped organize the National Association of Colored Women. Harper died in Philadelphia on February 20, 1911.

Robert E. Hayden (1913–1980)
Poet

Robert E. Hayden was born on August 4, 1913, in Detroit, Michigan. A graduate of Detroit City College, now Wayne State University, Hayden was chief researcher on African American history and folklore for the Federal Writers Project in 1936. He went on to do advanced work in English, play production, and creative writing at the University of Michigan. While there, he twice won the Jule and Avery Hopwood Prize for poetry. Hayden also completed radio scripts and a finished version of a play about the Underground Railroad, *Go Down Moses.*

Hayden's first book of poems *Heart-Shape in the Dust* was published in 1940 shortly before he assumed the music and drama critic function for the *Michigan Chronicle.* He taught at Fisk University from 1946 to the early 1970s and later at the University of Michigan. His works include: *The Lion and the Archer* (with Myron O'Higgins); *A Ballad of Remembrance; Selected Poems; Words in the Mourning Time;* and *The Night-Blooming Cereus.* He edited *Kaleidoscope: Poems by American Negro Poets* and *Afro American Literature: An Introduction* (with David J. Burrows and Frederick R. Lapsides). His other books include: *Figure of Time; Angle of Ascent: New and Selected Poems;* and *American Journal* (poems). In 1975, the Academy of American Poets elected him its fellow of the year, and in 1976, he was awarded the Grand Prize for Poetry at the First World Festival of Negro Arts in Dakar, Senegal. From 1976 to 1978, he served as consultant in poetry at the Library of Congress. He was a professor of English at the University of Michigan at the time of his death on February 25, 1980.

Essex Hemphill (1957–1995)
Poet, Essayist, Editor, Gay Rights Activist

Hemphill was born in 1957 in Chicago, but spent parts of his childhood in Indiana, South Carolina, and Washington, DC. After attending the University of Maryland and the University of the District of Columbia, Hemphill began to explore the inner conflicts he experienced as a gay African American male by writing poetry.

For several years Hemphill was a contributor of verse to such journals as *Essence, Black Scholar,* and *Obsidian.* In the late 1980s, he became involved with a project begun by Joseph Beam, an anthology of gay African American poetry called *In the Life.* Hemphill was a contributor to the 1986 volume and took the editorship of its sequel after Beam died of AIDS-related illnesses in 1988. The work was published as *Brother to Brother: New Writings by Black Gay Men* in 1991.

Hemphill became involved in several film projects around this time as well, nearly all of them controversial in some way, which coincided with his aim to make the two communities, the African American and the gay American, enter into a new, more contemporary dialogue with one another. He wrote verse for *Looking for Langston,* a British film that addressed the sexuality of Harlem Renaissance poet Langston Hughes and brought down the ire of the executor of the Hughes estate, and also contributed to and appeared in *Tongues Untied.* This last project, Marlon Riggs's celebratory look at gay African American male culture, was deemed too spicy even for public television at one point.

In 1992, Hemphill saw another book of his own verse published, *Ceremonies: Prose and Poetry.* During the early part of the decade, he became involved in a project interviewing elderly members of the African American gay community in order to provide a glimpse into a period before either gay or civil rights were mentioned. He also contributed to the book *Life Sentences: Writers, Artists, and AIDS.* Hemphill died on November 4, 1995, at the age of 38.

Chester Himes (1909–1984)
Novelist

Born in Jefferson City, Missouri, on June 29, 1909, Chester Himes was educated at Ohio State University and later lived in France and Spain. In 1945, he completed his first novel *If He Hollers Let Him Go,* the story of an African American working in a defense plant. His second book *The Lonely Crusade* (1947) was set in similar surroundings. His other books included: *The Third Generation; Cotton Comes to Harlem; Pinktoes; The Quality of Hurt: The Autobiography of Chester Himes;* and *Black on Black: Baby Sister and Selected Writings.*

Following a stroke that confined him to a wheelchair, Himes and his wife lived in Alicante, Spain. In 1977, they returned to New York City for the publication of the concluding volume of his autobiography *My Life of Absurdity.* Himes died in Spain on November 12, 1984, at the age of 75. A prolific author of almost 20 books, several of his popular novels are being reprinted posthumously in hardcover and paperback editions.

Pauline E. Hopkins (1859–1930)
Writer, Editor, Playwright, Singer, Actress

Although her contemporaries gave her less recognition than modern scholars, Pauline Elizabeth Hopkins became known for promoting racial issues in her short stories, novels, and in her work as editor of the journal *The Colored American.*

Born in Portland, Maine, in 1859, Hopkins moved to Boston when she was still a child and graduated from Girls High School. At age 15 years of age, she entered a writing contest supported by writer William Wells Brown and sponsored by the Congregational Publishing Society in Boston and won a ten-dollar prize for her essay "The Evils of Intemperance and Their Remedies."

Hopkins established the Colored Troubadours and performed with the group for 12 years. On July 5, 1880, in Boston, the Troubadours performed her first play *Slaves' Escape: or the Underground Railroad,* also known as *Peculiar Sam,* which Hopkins had completed a year earlier. During her tenure with the group, she also wrote the play *One Scene from the Drama of Early Days.*

Hopkins helped to establish *The Colored American;* its first issue in May, 1900, published her short story "The Mystery Within Us." Later, the magazine published Hopkins's series of biographical sketches "Famous Women of the Negro Race" and "Famous Men of the Negro Race." About this time the magazine published serialized versions of three of her novels *Hagar's Daughter: A Story of Southern Caste Prejudice* (1901–1902),*Winona: A Tale of Negro Life in the South and Southwest* (1902), and *Of One Blood: or The Hidden Self* (1902–1903). Her first novel, however, *Contending Forces: A Romance Illustrative of Negro Life North and South,* was published by a Boston firm in 1900. She resigned from *The Colored American* in 1904.

In 1905, Hopkins wrote briefly for *Voice of the Negro;* after that her literary career began to decline. She founded her own publishing company, the P. E. Hopkins and Company, and in February and March, 1916, contributed two articles to *New Era Magazine.* She lived in obscurity after 1916 and died on August 13, 1930, as a result of severe burns.

George Moses Horton (1797?–1883?)
Poet

George Moses Horton was the first African American professional man of letters in the United States and one of the first professional writers of any race in the South. He was the first African American southerner to have a volume of poetry published.

Horton was born into slavery in North Carolina around 1797. While growing up on a farm he cultivated a love of learning. With the aid of his mother and her Wesley hymnal, Horton learned to read, although he did not learn to write until years later. While working as a janitor at the University of North Carolina, Horton wrote light verse for some students in exchange for spending money.

Some of Horton's early poems were printed in the newspapers of Raleigh and Boston. When Horton published his first book of poems in 1829, he entitled it *The Hope of Liberty*, in the belief that profits from its sales would be sufficient to pay for his freedom. His hopes did not materialize, however, and he remained a slave until the Emancipation Proclamation. (This book was reprinted in 1837 under the title *Poems by a Slave*.) In 1865, he published "Naked Genius," a poem containing many bitter lines about his former condition that were in sharp contrast to the conformist verse of earlier African American poets. Although he lived in Philadelphia for a while, it appears that he returned to the South where he died around 1883. Richard Walser's *The Black Poet* was written about Horton and published in 1967.

Langston Hughes (1902–1967)
Poet, Novelist, Playwright

Born in Joplin, Missouri, on February 1, 1902, James Langston Hughes moved to Cleveland at the age of 14, graduated from Central High School, and spent a year in Mexico before studying at Columbia University. After roaming the world as a seaman and writing some poetry as well, Hughes returned to the United States. While attending Lincoln University in Pennsylvania, he won the Witter Bynner Prize for undergraduate poetry. In 1930, he received the Harmon Award, and in 1935, with the help of a Guggenheim Fellowship, traveled to Russia and Spain.

The long and distinguished list of Hughes's prose works includes: *Not Without Laughter* (1930); *The Big Sea* (1940); and *I Wonder as I Wander* (1956), his autobiography. To this must be added such collections of poetry as *The Weary Blues* (1926); *The Dream Keeper* (1932); *Shakespeare in Harlem* (1942); *Fields of Wonder* (1947); *One Way Ticket* (1949); *Selected Poems* (1959); and the posthumously published *The Panther and the Lash: Poems of Our Times* (1969).

Hughes was also an accomplished song lyricist, librettist, and newspaper columnist. Through his newspaper columns he created Jesse B. Semple, a Harlem character known as Simple. Simple is the quintessential "wise fool" whose experiences and insights capture the frustrations felt by African Americans. Hughes's Simple

sketches have been collected in several volumes and were adapted for the musical stage in *Simply Heavenly*.

Through much of the 1960s, Hughes edited several anthologies in an attempt to popularize African American authors and their works. Some of these works are *An African Treasury* (1960), *Poems from Black Africa* (1963), *New Negro Poets: U.S.A.* (1964), and *The Best Short Stories by Negro Writers* (1967). Published posthumously was *Good Morning Revolution: Uncollected Writings of Social Protest*. Hughes wrote many plays including *Emperor of Haiti* and *Mulatto*, which was produced on Broadway in the 1930s. He also wrote gospel music plays, such as *Tambourines to Glory Black Nativity* and *Jericho—Jim Crow*. He died on May 22, 1967.

Zora Neale Hurston (1903–1960)
Novelist, Folklorist

Zora Neale Hurston was born on January 7, 1903, in Eatonville, Florida. After traveling north as a maid with a Gilbert and Sullivan company, Hurston acquired her education at Morgan State College, Howard University, and Columbia University. While at Howard under Alain Locke's influence, she became a figure in the Harlem Renaissance, publishing short stories in *Opportunity* and serving with Langston Hughes and Wallace Thurman on the editorial board of the magazine *Fire!*

In 1934, *Jonah's Gourd Vine* was published after her return to Florida. Her most important novel *Their Eyes Were Watching God* appeared three years later. *Moses, Man of the Mountain* (1939) was followed in 1948 by *Seraph on the Suwanee*. Her other three works are two books of folklore, *Mules and Men* (1935) and *Tell My Horse* (1938), and *Dust Tracks on a Road* (1942). Her autobiography was reprinted in 1985 with a new introduction and with several altered chapters restored.

Toward the end of her life, Hurston was a drama instructor at the North Carolina College for Negroes in Durham (now North Carolina Central University). She died in obscurity and poverty on January 28, 1960. Since then, six of her works have been reprinted with new introductions. Hurston is celebrated each year in Eatonville, Florida, where the Zora Neale Hurston Festival is held.

Charles R. Johnson (1948–)
Novelist, Essayist, Cartoonist

Charles Johnson, only the second African American man to win the National Book Award (Ralph Ellison was the first), was born on April 23, 1948, in Evanston, Illinois. He began his career as a political cartoonist in the early 1970s. During the same time period, he was heavily involved in organizations that supported the formation of African American studies as a discipline. Johnson's development as a novelist took shape while receiving his B.A. in 1971 from Southern Illinois University at Carbondale and subsequently his M.A. in philosophy in 1973. Out of these experiences Johnson developed situations in his books that dealt with philosophical discussions about race, identity, and culture.

Johnson's literary works include both novels and short stories, beginning with *Faith and the Good Thing* (1974); *Oxherding Tale* (1982); *The Sorcerer's Apprentice* (short stories 1986); *Middle Passage* (1990), which received the National Book Award that year; and *Dreamer* (1998). He has also ventured into non-fiction with *Africans in America* (1998) and its companion *Soulcatcher and Other Stories*.

Georgia Douglas Johnson (1886–1966)
Poet

As one of the first modern African American women poets to gain recognition, Georgia Douglas Johnson, whose collections of verse were published between 1918 and 1930, is an important link in the chain of African American women lyric poets. Johnson's life spanned most of the literary movements of this century, and her Washington, DC, home was the popular gathering place of early Harlem Renaissance writers.

Johnson was born in Atlanta, Georgia, on September 10, 1886. She was educated in the public schools of the city and at Atlanta University, and she went on to attend Howard University in Washington, DC, and Oberlin Conservatory of Music in Ohio.

Initially, she was interested in musical composition, but gradually Johnson turned to lyric poetry. After teaching school in Alabama, she moved to Washington, DC, with her husband, who had been appointed as recorder of deeds by President William Howard Taft. While in the nation's capital, she too engaged in government work while completing such books as *The Heart of a Woman* (1918), *Bronze* (1922), *An Autumn Love Cycle* (1928), and *Share My World*, published in 1962.

Johnson was a prolific writer; over 200 of her poems were published in her four literary works; other poems and several dramas have appeared in journals and books, primarily edited by African Americans. She died of a stroke on May 14, 1966.

James Weldon Johnson (1871–1938)
Poet, Lyricist, Civil Rights Leader

Similar to W. E. B. Du Bois, African American intellectual James Weldon Johnson played a vital role in the

James Weldon Johnson.

Civil Rights movement of the twentieth century as poet, teacher, critic, diplomat, and NAACP official. Johnson is perhaps most often remembered as the lyricist for "Lift Every Voice and Sing," the song that is often referred to as the African American national anthem.

Born on June 17, 1871, in Jacksonville, Florida, Johnson was educated at Atlanta and Columbia Universities. His career included service as a school principal, a lawyer, and a diplomat (U.S. consul at Puerto Cabello, Venezuela, and later in Nicaragua). From 1916 to 1930, he was a key policymaker of the NAACP, eventually serving as the organization's executive secretary. From 1932 until his death, he was professor of creative writing at Fisk University in Nashville, Tennessee.

In his early days, Johnson's fame rested largely on his lyrics for popular songs, but in 1917 he completed his first book of poetry *Fifty Years and Other Poems*. Five years later, he followed this work with *The Book of American Negro Poetry*, and in 1927, he established his literary reputation with *God's Trombones*, a collection of seven folk sermons in verse. Over the years, this work has been performed countless times on stage and television.

In 1930, Johnson finished *St. Peter Relates an Incident of the Resurrection,* and three years later, his lengthy autobiography *Along This Way* appeared. Johnson died on June 26, 1938, following an automobile accident in Maine.

Gayl Jones (1949–)
Novelist, Poet, Short Story Writer, Educator

Born in Lexington, Kentucky, in 1949, Gayl Jones received a bachelor's degree in English from Connecticut College in 1971 and a master's degree in creative writing from Brown University in 1973. From 1975 to 1981, she was professor of English at the University of Michigan. Jones's work includes four novels *Corregidora* (1975); *Eva's Man* (1976); *Healing* (1998); and *Mosquito* (1998), short stories, and several collections of poetry including *Song for Anninho* (1981), *The Hermit Woman* (1983), *Xarque and Other Poems* (1985), and *Liberating Voices* (1991).

After the release of *Healing* in 1998, Jones's husband Bob Jones had an encounter with the police in Kentucky that resulted in his suicide. This traumatic event caused Jones to step out of the limelight of the literary world and to seek professional therapy for depression. *Mosquito* (1999) was written previous to *Healing* but had never published.

June Jordan (1936–)
Poet, Novelist

Born in Harlem, New York, on July 9, 1936, poet, novelist, essayist, educator, and activist June Jordan attended Barnard College and the University of Chicago. Throughout the 1960s and 1970s, she taught Afro-American literature, English, and writing at several colleges and universities including CUNY, Connecticut College, Sarah Lawrence College, Yale University, and State University of New York at Stoney Brook, where she spent most of her career as director of the poetry center and creative writing program. She left State University in 1989 to teach Afro-American studies and women's studies at the University of California at Berkley. Jordan co-founded and co-directed The Voice of the Children, Inc., a creative workshop.

A prolific writer, Jordan's poems have been published in many magazines, newspapers, and anthologies, and she received a Rockefeller Grant in creative writing in 1969. Her poetry includes: *Who Look at Me* (1969); *Some Changes* (1971); *New Days: Poems of Exile and Return* (1974); *Passion: New Poems, 1977–1980* (1980); *Living Room: New Poems* (1985); *Lyrical Campaigns: Selected Poems* (1989); and *Naming Our Destiny: New and Selected Poems* (1989).

Jordan's books for children and young people include: *His Own Where* (1971), nominated for the National Book Award; *Fannie Lou Hamer* (1972); *Dry Victories* (1972); and *Kimako's Story* (1981).

Author of two plays, Jordan has also published essays including: *Civil Wars* (1981); *On Call: Political Essays* (1985); *Moving Towards Home: Political Essays* (1989); and *Technical Difficulties: African American Notes on the State of the Union* (1992). In addition, she has edited several anthologies, such as *Soulscript: Afro-American Poetry* (1970).

In 2001, Jordan received a Barnes & Noble Writers for Writers Award from the Poets & Writers organization. The award recognized Jordan's Poetry for the People project, which offers poetry workshops to under-served communities. Jordon passed away, on June 14, 2002, at her home in Berkeley, California, of breast cancer. She was 65.

Adrienne Kennedy (1931–)
Writer, Playwright

Born in Pittsburgh, Pennsylvania, on September 13, 1931, Adrienne Lita Hawkins grew up in Cleveland, Ohio. She received a B.A. in education from Ohio State in 1953, and married Joseph C. Kennedy one month later. In 1955, she and her husband moved to New York, and Kennedy studied writing at the American Theatre Wing and at Columbia University, completing her first play *Pale Blue Flowers* which was never produced or published.

In 1960, Kennedy and her husband traveled to Europe and then Ghana on a grant from the Africa Research Foundation. Her writing became more focused, and she published a story in *Black Orpheus* magazine. At the age of 29, Kennedy wrote *Funnyhouse of a Negro,* a one-act play. Edward Albee selected and co-directed the play for production in New York's Circle in the Square. It ran from January 14 to February 9, 1964 at the East End Theatre in New York.

Kennedy's next play *The Owl Answers* produced in 1965, won her a second Stanley Award from Wagner College of Staten Island, New York. Since the mid-1960s, she has written many full-length and one-act plays including *Sun: A Poem for Malcolm X Inspired by His Murder* (1968), *A Movie Star Has to Star in Black and White* (1976), *Black Children's Day* (1980), and *Diary of Lights* (1987). Later, the University of Minnesota Press published collections of her work including *The Alexander Plays* (1992). In 1996, her latest plays *Sleep Deprivation Chamber* and *June and Jean in Concert* were produced at the Joseph Papp Public

Theater and the Susan Stein Shiva Theater, respectively. Kennedy wrote an autobiography that was published in 1987 and titled *People Who Led to My Plays*.

Kennedy's plays are hallmarks of the American experimental theater, avant-garde and non-traditional in the extreme. She has won many awards for her bold and clear vision including an Obie Award in 1964 and a Pierre Lecomte du Novy Award from the Lincoln Center in 1994. In addition to winning many fellowships and grants, Kennedy has been a lecturer at several universities including Yale, Princeton, Brown, Harvard, and at Berkeley of California. She also served as an International Theatre Institute representative in Budapest in 1978.

Recently, Kennedy adapted the Greek tragedy Oedipus for the acting troop the Hartford Footlights. She has also published a collection of all of work appropriately called *The Adrienne Kennedy Reader* in 2001.

John O. Killens (1916–1987)
Novelist, Essayist, Screenwriter

John Oliver Killens was born in Macon, Georgia, on January 14, 1916; he was the son of Charles Myles Sr. and Willie Lee Killens. He attended Edward Waters College, Morris Brown College, Atlanta University, Howard University, Robert H. Terrell Law School, Columbia University, and New York University, and he was a member of the United States Army's South Pacific Amphibian Forces from 1942 to 1945.

Killens attributed his writing career to his paternal great-grandmother who was seven years old when the Emancipation Proclamation was signed. During his childhood, the elderly woman told Killens stories about the past. Sometimes when she finished talking about days gone by, she would tell him, "The half ain't never been told!" Although his original career plans to become a doctor were abandoned when he decided to study law, Killens ultimately accepted his ancestor's challenge to tell parts of the untold half and became a writer.

He was a co-founder and first chairperson of the Harlem Writers Guild, which provided a forum for writers to read their works. *Youngblood* (1954), the first book published by a member of the Harlem Writers Guild and Killens's first novel, is about an African American family's struggle to survive in the South. Four more novels followed: *And Then We Heard the Thunder* (1962), which is based on Killens's encounters with racism in the military during World War II; *'Sippi* (1967), which focuses on struggles over voting rights in the 1960s; *The Cotillion or One Good Bull Is Half the Herd* (1971), which is a satirical interpretation of the

black bourgeoisie; and *Great Black Russian: A Novel on the Life and Times of Alexander Pushkin: A Novel on the Life and Times of Alexander Pushkin* (1989), which is the result of Killens's more than 12 years of research on the life of the poet. In 1968 and 1970, Killens traveled to the Soviet Union where he participated in the Pushkin festivals, conversed with other Pushkin scholars, visited Pushkin's home, and visited the Pushkin museum. While researching and writing *Great Black Russian*, Killens lectured to students and literary groups throughout the United States on Pushkin. Killens's novel was one of the first to consider Pushkin's African ancestry. *Great Black Russian* was completed shortly before Killens's death. Two of the aforementioned novels were nominated for the Pulitzer Prize: *And Then We Heard the Thunder* and *The Cotillion*.

Among Killens's additional works are *Black Man's Burden* (1965), a collection of essays; *Great Gittin' Up Morning: Biography of Denmark Vesey* (juvenile literature, 1972); *A Man Ain't Nothin' But a Man: The Adventures of John Henry* (juvenile literature, 1975); and *Black Southern Voices: An Anthology of Fiction, Poetry, Drama, Nonfiction, and Critical Essays* (1992), a work that was co-edited with Jerry W. Ward Jr. and published after Killens's death. He also wrote screenplays.

Killens, the recipient of many honors and awards, taught at various institutions including Fisk University, Columbia University, Howard University, Bronx Community College, and Medgar Evers College of the City University of New York. On October 27, 1987, Killens died of cancer in Brooklyn, New York.

Jamaica Kincaid (1949–)
Writer

Jamaica Kincaid was born Elaine Potter Kincaid on May 25, 1949, in St. Johns, Antigua. After leaving Antigua at 16 years of age and moving to New York, Kincaid held several positions, while seeking her niche in the United States. Her writing career began as a contributor to the *New Yorker* magazine. Once becoming a staff member, Kincaid had her collection of stories and other short pieces, which mainly ran in the magazine from 1974 to 1976, published under the title *At the Bottom of the River* (1983). It was four years before Kincaid published her first work of fiction *Annie John* (1985). This work was later followed by *A Small Place* (1988), *Annie Gwenn Lilly Pam & Tulip* (1989), *Lucy* (1990), and *Mr. Potter* (2002).

With her lyrical style and semi-autobiographical focus, Kincaid addresses themes about lasting scars from childhood experiences, ambivalence toward parents, the mother-daughter relationship and the search for identity.

Yusef Komunyakaa (James Willie Brown Jr.) (1941–)
Poet, Educator

Yusef Komunyakaa was born James Willie Brown Jr. in 1941, in the segregated, culturally-desolate mill town of Bogalusa, Louisiana. He came to love reading and poetry as a child and at age 16 years of age began pursuing his own talents. After high school graduation, Komunyakaa joined the U.S. Army and was sent to Vietnam to act as a reporter and editor for a military newspaper in 1969. Although he felt estranged from American society upon his return from Vietnam, Komunyakaa enrolled at the University of Colorado and later graduate school at Colorado State University. He received a second master's degree from the University of California at Irvine. A creative writing workshop proved inspirational and his first book of poetry *Dedication and Other Darkhorses* was published in 1977. With the release of his second volume two years later, Komunyakaa accepted a series of fellowships and teaching positions, enabling him to pursue a career as a poet.

While working in New Orleans in 1983, Komunyakaa began to come to terms with his experiences in Vietnam through his writing. This challenge resulted in several sophisticated books filled with cultural influences that portray basic elements of humanity. In 1985, the poet left New Orleans to accept a position as a visiting professor at Indiana University in Bloomington. By 1987, having published two more books of poetry, Komunyakaa became an associate professor in the Afro-American and English studies departments at the university. For personal and religious reasons, the poet changed his name from James Willie Brown Jr. to Yusef Komunyakaa. With the publication of *Neon Vernacular*, he was awarded the 1994 Pulitzer Prize in poetry along with the $50,000 Kingsley Tufts Poetry Award given by the Claremont Graduate School. Komunyakaa's themes of memory and self-definition—as an African American man and a veteran of Vietnam—lend his works a sense of strength and spiritual tenacity.

Recently Komunyakaa has published two new collections of poetry: *Talking Dirty to the Gods* in 2000 and *Pleasure Dome: New and Collected Poems* in 2001. The year 2001 also saw Komunyakaa honored as the winner of the Ruth Lilly Poetry Prize. The award, which includes a cash prize of $100,000, is for lifetime achievement by a United States poet.

Nella Larsen (1891–1964)
Novelist, Librarian, Nurse

Nella Larsen was born in 1891 in Chicago, Illinois, of a Danish mother and a West Indian father. She attended Fisk University's Normal (High) School in Nashville, Tennessee, and from 1909 to 1912, the University of Copenhagen in Denmark. Three years later, she graduated from the Lincoln School for Nurses in New York City. In addition to her writing, she worked alternately as a nurse and librarian, having attended the New York Public Library training school from 1921 to 1923. After one year as head nurse at Tuskegee Institute (now Tuskegee University), she became supervising nurse at the Lincoln Hospital in New York City until 1918, when she joined the city's department of health. During the next 40 years, she worked as a children's librarian at the New York Public Library (1924–1926), Gouverneur Hospital (1944–1961), and the Metropolitan Hospital (1961–1964), all in New York City. Writing, however, is what made her famous.

In the 1920s, Larsen began contributing to children's magazines. At the same time, she found herself immersed in the literary and political activities of the ongoing Harlem Renaissance. Larsen's first novel *Quicksand* (1928) received a bronze medal from the Harmon Foundation. The groundbreaking novel developed themes around African American women's sexuality and about mixed racial identity. Her second major work *Passing* (1929) led to her becoming the first African American woman to be awarded a Guggenheim Fellowship in creative writing (1930). More than 30 years after her death on March 20, 1964, Larsen's novels were reissued, and she finally achieved recognition as one of the most important writers of the Harlem Renaissance.

Julius Lester (1939–)
Writer, Educator

Julius Lester was born in St. Louis, Missouri, in 1939. He grew up in Kansas City, Kansas, and Nashville, Tennessee, where his father led congregations as a Methodist minister. Lester spent the summers of his youth in rural Arkansas, experiencing racism and segregation firsthand. A gifted student, he was an avid musician and aspired to become a writer.

Lester obtained a B.A. in English from Fisk University. He became politically active in the civil rights struggle as a folksinger and photographer of Southern rallies. As a member of the Student Non-Violent Coordinating Committee (SNCC) in the mid-1960s, Lester became head of its photo department and visited North Vietnam to document the effects of U.S. bombing missions. He began publishing ideological books that defended African American militancy including *The Angry Children of Malcolm X* and *Revolutionary Notes*. From 1966 to 1968 Lester served as director of the prestigious Newport Folk Festival and released two record albums himself.

Having achieved fame for his artistic pursuits, Lester was hired to host live radio shows at the public broadcasting station WBAI-FM in New York City. Around the same time, he published two books for children that saw immediate success. *Black Folktales* compiled African legends and slave narratives and *To Be a Slave*, a collection of stories based on oral history accounts, received a Newbery Honor Book citation. In 1971, Lester began hosting the New York public television program "Free Time." His career as an award-winning academician began that same year, when he was hired as professor of Afro-American Studies at the University of Massachusetts-Amherst. He settled there in 1975 and became a full-time professor and author.

Lester flourished as an author by releasing novels and storybooks (with illustrator Jerry Pinkney) that reflected his interests in African American history, folklore, and politics. *Long Journey Home*, a finalist for the National Book Award, explores the everyday lives of African Americans during the Reconstruction period. Lester's *Tales of Uncle Remus: The Adventures of Brer Rabbit*, traditional stories retold in a contemporary southern African American voice, were well-received by teachers and librarians who granted it the Coretta Scott King Award. His 1994 adult novel *And All Our Wounds Forgiven* tracks dramatic events in the 1960s. Lester's individualism and resistance to racial and religious categorization is evident in two autobiographies *All Is Well* and *Lovesong: Becoming a Jew*.

In the second half of the 1990s, Lester flipped back and forth between tales for children and more adult works. His younger audience enjoyed titles such as *Black Cowboy, Wild Horses: a True Story* (1998); *Albidaro and the Mischievous Dream* (2000); and *Ackmarackus: Julius Lester's Sumptuously Silly Fantastically Funny Fables* (2001). More mature audiences were treated to a more historical view of slavery with *From Slave Ship to Freedom Road* (1997) and a dark trip into the psychosis of two young children in *When Dad Killed Mom* (2001).

When he converted to Judaism in mid-life, Lester was ousted from Amherst's renamed African American Studies Department in 1988. Persevering through yet another career change, he moved to the university's Near Eastern and Judaic Studies Department. Since

that time he has also taught in the history and English departments. Lester published a racially-repositioned novelization of *Othello* for young adults in 1995.

Audre Lorde (1934–1993)
Poet

Audre Lorde was born in New York City; graduated with a masters in library science from Columbia University; was poet-in-residence at Tougaloo College; taught at Lehman College, Bronx; and taught at John Jay College and CCNY. She received a National Endowment for the Arts grant and a Cultural Council Foundation grant for poetry.

Her books of poetry included: *Cables to Rage* (1970); *The First Cities* (1968); *From a Land Where Other People Live* (1973); *Coal* (1968); *The New York Head Shop and Museum* (1974); *Between Ourselves* (1976); *The Black Unicorn* (1978); *Chosen Poems–Old and New* (1982); *Zami: A New Spelling of My Name* (1982); *Sister/Outsider: Essays and Speeches* (1984); *Lesbian Poetry: An Anthology* (1982); and *Woman Poet–The East* (1984). Lorde's poetry has been published in many

Audre Lorde.

anthologies, magazines, and lesbian books and periodicals. Lorde died of cancer on November 17, 1992.

Claude McKay (1890–1948)
Poet

Born the son of a farmer in Jamaica (then British West Indies) on September 15, 1890, Claude McKay began writing early in life. Two books of his poems *Songs of Jamaica* and *Constab Ballads* were published just after he turned 20 years of age. In both, he made extensive use of Jamaican dialect.

In 1913, McKay came to the United States to study agriculture at Tuskegee Institute (now Tuskegee University) and at Kansas State University, but his interest in poetry induced him to move to New York City, where he published his work in small literary magazines. McKay then made a trip to England. While there, he completed a collection of lyrics entitled *Spring in New Hampshire*. When he returned to the United States, he became associate editor of *The Liberator* under Max Eastman. In 1922, he completed *Harlem Shadows*, a landmark work of the Harlem Renaissance period.

Claude McKay.

McKay then turned to the writing of such novels as *Home to Harlem* (1928), *Banjo* (1929), and four other books including an autobiography and a study of Harlem. *The Passion of Claude McKay: Selected Prose and Poetry 1912–1948*, edited by Wayne Cooper, was published in 1973. McKay traveled abroad before returning to the United States, where he died on May 22, 1948. His final work *Selected Poems* was published posthumously in 1953.

During World War II, when Winston Churchill addressed a joint session of the United States Congress in an effort to enlist American aid in the battle against Nazism, the climax of his oration was his reading of the famous poem "If We Must Die," originally written by McKay to assail lynchings and mob violence in the South. McKay's *Trial by Lynching* (1967), edited and translated stories, and his *The Negroes in America* (1979 or 1980), edited and translated from the Russian language, have also been published. Many of his works have been reprinted since his death including: *Home to Harlem; Banana Bottom; Banjo* (1970); *A Long Way From Home* (1970); *Harlem: Negro Metropolis* (1972); and *Selected Poems of Claude McKay* (1971). *Songs of Jamaica* and *Constab Ballads* have been bound together as *The Dialect Poems of Claude McKay*. Wayne F. Cooper's *Claude McKay: Rebel Sojourner in the Harlem Renaissance* (1987) is an important book detailing McKay's life and work.

Nellie Y. McKay (c.1940s–)
Literary Critic

Nellie Yvonne McKay, the daughter of West Jamaican parents Harry and Nellie McKay, was born in Harlem c. 1940s. She received three degrees in English and American Literature: a B.A. (cum laude with honors) from Queens College, CUNY in 1969; a M.A. from Harvard University in 1971; and a Ph.D. from Harvard in 1977.

McKay knew how to read before she began her formal education. During her childhood, she decided she wanted to teach. Until two college professors encouraged McKay to teach on the college level, she had planned to become a kindergarten teacher. McKay taught at Simmons College in the 1970s before joining the faculty of the University of Wisconsin-Madison in 1978. Her joint appointment to teach in the African American Studies and English Department was expanded to allow McKay to teach in the Women's Studies Department as well. The departments of African American Studies and Women's Studies were floundering until McKay's arrival. Since then, McKay, one of the most preeminent scholars and literary critics in the United States, has made significant contributions to the departments. Consequently, the University of Wisconsin-Madison has enjoyed national attention in both areas. McKay has declined numerous offers to leave UW-M, including an offer from Harvard, her alma mater.

McKay specializes in nineteenth and twentieth-century African American literature with an emphasis on fiction, autobiography, and black women's writings. Her first book was her doctoral thesis, *Jean Toomer-the Artist: A Study of His Literary Life and Work, 1894–1936* (1984). McKay's other books include *Critical Essays on Toni Morrison* (1988); *The Norton Anthology of African American Literature* (1997), co-edited with Henry Louis Gates Jr.; *Approaches to Teaching the Novels of Toni Morrison* (1997); co-edited with Kathryn Earl; *Beloved: A Casebook* (1998), co-edited with William L. Andrews; and the *Norton Critical Edition of Harriet Jacobs's Incidents in the Life of a Slave Girl* (2000), co-edited with Frances Smith Foster. To date, *The Norton Anthology of African American Literature* is McKay's most prominent publication; McKay and Gates were the general editors and along with nine other African American literary scholars, they created the definitive anthology of African American literature. It presents the works of 120 authors, including 52 women, from 1746 to the present, and 13 major works are reprinted in their entirety. Cornel West has hailed *The Norton Anthology of African American Literature* as "a classic of splendid proportions" while Letty Cottin Pogrebin pointed out, "With the publication of this extraordinary collection, no one can ever again claim ignorance of the rich, rewarding legacy of the African-American literary tradition-and especially of Black women's pre-eminent contribution to this heritage." In addition to her full-length publications, McKay has written essays for literary journals and other books. She has also written various introductions and afterwards to new and recently reprinted books in African American and women's writings.

McKay has received a variety of honors and awards including the Vilas Associate Award, UW-M, 1987–1989; Chancellor's Distinguished Teaching Award, UW-M, 1992; MELUS Award for Contributions to Multi-Ethnic Literatures, 1996; and Honorary Membership in UW-Madison Chapter of Phi Beta Kappa, 1999.

Terry McMillan (1951–)
Novelist

Terry McMillan was born on October 18, 1951, and raised in Port Huron, Michigan. She attended Los Angeles City College, but later transferred to Berkeley and

Terry McMillan.

then to Columbia University to study film. She later enrolled in a writing workshop at the Harlem Writers Guild and was accepted at the MacDowell Colony in 1983. She has taught at the University of Wyoming and the University of Arizona.

McMillan published her first short story when she was 25 years old. Her subsequent novels include *Mama* (1987), *Disappearing Acts* (1989), and *Waiting to Exhale* (1992). She also edited the anthology of contemporary African American fiction entitled *Breaking Ice: An Anthology of Contemporary African-American Fiction* (1992). In 1997 she published *How Stella Got Her Groove Back.* and in 2000 *A Day Late and a Dollar Short* hit the stands.

Waiting to Exhale hit the *New York Times'* bestseller list within one week of being in print and remained there for several months. Hardcover publisher Viking printed 700,000 copies and Pocket Books, which published the paperback version, paid $2.64 million for the rights to the work. In 1995, the novel was adapted into one of the most highly-touted films of the year. Directed by Forest Whitaker, the film version starred Angela Bassett, Whitney Houston, Lela Rochon, and

Loretta Devine. Wesley Snipes and Gregory Hines had smaller roles. *How Stella Got Her Groove Back* was also made into a popular film and *Disappearing Acts* was brought to the small screen.

In 1993, New York Women in Communication gave McMillan a Matrix Award. In 1994, the NAACP Legal Defense and Educational Fund honored McMillan at a luncheon.

James Alan McPherson (1943–)
Short Story Writer

James McPherson, born in Savannah, Georgia, on October 16, 1943, received his B.A. degree in 1965 from Morris Brown College in Atlanta, a law degree from Harvard University in 1968, and an M.F.A. degree from the University of Iowa in 1969. He has taught writing at several universities including the University of Virginia in Charlottesville, where he taught fiction writing. At the present time, he teaches writing at the University of Iowa and is a contributing editor of *Atlantic Monthly*. His short stories have appeared in several magazines. *Hue and Cry*, a collection of short stories published in 1969, was highly praised by Ralph Ellison. Named a Guggenheim fellow in 1972 and 1973, McPherson's second book of short stories *Elbow Room* was published in 1977 and received the Pulitzer Prize for fiction in the following year. McPherson was one of the three African American writers who were awarded five-year grants by the McArthur Foundation of Chicago for exceptional talent in 1981. For 20 years, McPherson taught and put no new literature on the market. Then in 1997, he published the memoir *Crabcakes*. He followed this up in 2000 with a collection of personal essays in *A Region Not Home: Reflections from Exile*.

Haki Madhubuti (Don L. Lee) (1942–)
Poet, Essayist, Publisher

Haki Madhubuti exemplifies the attempt of a person to create a unified self and live a holistic life—not one that is fragmented by the poet, educator, and journalist that Madhubuti has become.

Born Don L. Lee on February 23, 1942, in Little Rock, Arkansas, Madhubuti and his family moved to Detroit a year later. After his father left home and his mother died, he moved to Chicago at age 16 to live with an aunt. He graduated from Chicago City College with an A.A. degree and later received an M.F.A. degree from the University of Iowa.

From 1961 to 1966, Madhubuti prepared to become a writer: he read a book daily and wrote a 200 word review of each book. He published his first volume of poetry *Think Black* in 1966. In 1967, he joined Johari Amini (Jewel Latimore) and Carolyn Rogers in launching the Third World Press; it became the longest continuously-operated African American press in the United States. His other works of poetry published in the 1960s were *Black Pride* (1968) and *Don't Cry, Scream* (1969). Later he taught and served as a writer-in-residence at numerous universities including Chicago State, Cornell, Howard, Morgan State, and the University of Illinois.

In the 1970s he published *Directionscore: Selected and New Poems* and *To Gwen with Love*. His *Dynamic Voices: Black Poets of the 1960s*, published in 1971 by Broadside Press, provided a critical context for writers of the Black Arts movement from one who participated in it. Here the writer defined the role of the African American literary critic and set standards for the critic to follow. The next year he founded *Black Books Bulletin*.

In 1973, Madhubuti changed his name from Don L. Lee to Haki Madhubuti, which, in Swahili, means "justice," "awakening," and "strong." He moved to Howard University that year where he was poet-in-residence. During the 1980s, he began teaching at Chicago State, where he remains as professor of English. His works from the 1970s into the 1990s include: *The Clash of Faces* (1978); *Say That the River Turns: The Impact of Gwendolyn Brooks* (1987); *Killing Memory, Seeking Ancestors* (1987); and *Black Men: Obsolete, Single, Dangerous?*; and *African American Families in Transition: Essays in Discovery, Solution, and Hope* (1990). He also edited *Why L.A. Happened: Implications of the '92 Los Angeles Rebellion* (1993) and *Claiming Earth: Race, Rage, Rape, Redemption: Blacks Seeking a Cultural Enlightened Empowerment* (1994). Although still a poet, in the 1990s he strengthened his skills as an essayist.

Among his honors, Madhubuti has received the DuSable Museum Award for Excellence in Poetry, National Council of Teachers of English Award, the Sidney R. Yates Advocate Award, and the African Heritage Studies Association citation. Later, he was also honored with the Distinguished Writers Award from the Middle Atlantic Writers Association in 1984 and the American Book Award in 1991. In 1984, he was the only poet selected to represent the United States at the International Valmiki World Poetry Festival held in New Delhi, India.

In addition to his teaching duties, Madhubuti is a director of the National Black Holistic Retreat, which he co-founded in 1984. He also remains as publisher and editor of Third World Press. Third World Press also published Madhubuti's two most recent works, *Heartlove: Wedding and Love Poems* in 1998 and *Tough Notes: Letters to Young Black Men* in 2001.

Paule Marshall (1929–)
Writer

Paule Marshall was born Valenza Pauline Burk on April 9, 1929, in Brooklyn, New York. Marshall's parents were emigrants from Barbados, and she grew up in a community with strong West Indian influences. Although Marshall did some writing in her childhood years, her serious devotion to writing began in 1954 as exercise at the end of her work day. The result was her first short story "The Valley Between."

Marshall's work, which centers on people of African descent, sets out to create images that celebrate the human spirit and put asunder all forms of political and social oppression. Marshall has received numerous awards and fellowships and her novels include: *Brown Girl, Brownstones* (1959); *Soul Clap Hands and Sing* (1961); *The Chose Place, the Timeless People* (1969); *Praisesong for the Widow* (1983); *Daughters* (1991); and *The Fisher King* (2000). Short stories and essays are also a part of Marshall's contributions to an African-centered literary experience.

Loften Mitchell (1919–2001)
Playwright

Born on April 15, 1919, in Columbus, North Carolina, and raised in Harlem in the 1920s, Loften Mitchell began to write as a child, creating scripts for backyard shows that he and his brother performed. After completing junior high school, he decided to enroll at New York Textile High because he had been promised a job on the school newspaper. But Mitchell soon realized that he needed the training of an academic high school and, with the help of one of his teachers, transferred to DeWitt Clinton.

Graduating with honors, Mitchell found a job as an elevator operator and a delivery boy to support himself while he studied playwriting at night at the City College of New York. However, he met a professor from Talladega College in Alabama who helped him win a scholarship to study there. He graduated with honors in 1943, having won an award for the best play written by a student.

After two years of service in the U.S. Navy, Mitchell enrolled as a graduate student at Columbia University in New York. A year later, he accepted a job with the city's department of welfare as a social investigator and continued to attend school at night. During this time, he wrote one of his first successful plays, *Blood in the Night*, and in 1957 he wrote *A Land Beyond the River*, which had a long run at an off-Broadway theater and was also published as a book.

The following year Mitchell won a Guggenheim award, which enabled him to return to Columbia University and write for a year. Since then, he has written a new play *Star of the Morning*, the story of Bert Williams, famous African American entertainer.

In 1967 Mitchell published a study of African American theater entitled *Black Drama*. His other books include: *Tell Pharaoh*, a play; *The Stubborn Old Lady Who Resisted Change* (1973), a novel; and *Voices of the Black Theatre* (1976). Mitchell also wrote the books for various Broadway musicals including *Ballads for Bimshire* (1963), *Bubbling Brown Sugar* (1975), *Cartoons for a Lunch Hour* (1978), *A Gypsy Girl* (1982), and *Miss Ethel Waters* (1983).

Mitchell died on May 14, 2001, in Queens, New York. He was 82.

Toni Morrison (1931–)
Novelist, Editor

Born Chloe Anthony Wofford in Lorain, Ohio, on February 18, 1931, Toni Morrison received a B.A. degree from Howard University in 1953, and an M.A. from Cornell in 1955. After working as an instructor in English and the humanities at Texas Southern University and Howard University, Morrison eventually became a senior editor at Random House in New York City, where, for more than 20 years, she was responsible for the publication of many books by African Americans including Middleton Harris's *The Black Book* (edited by Toni Morrison) and books by Toni Cade Bambara, among others. From 1971 to 1972, Morrison was also an associate professor at the State University of New York at Purchase. Throughout the 1970s and 1980s, she wrote and published her novels, in addition to holding visiting professorships at Yale University and Bard College. From 1984 to 1989, she served as Albert Schweitzer Professor of the Humanities at the State University of New York at Albany. In 1989, Morrison became the Robert F. Goheen Professor of the Humanities at Princeton University.

Morrison's first novel *The Bluest Eye* was published in 1969, followed by *Sula*, which won the 1975 Ohioana Book Award and which gained the honor in 2002 of being the final book in Oprah Winfrey's book club. Morrison's third novel *Song of Solomon* (1977) received the 1977 National Book Critics Circle Award and the 1978 American Academy and Institute of Arts and Letters Award. *Tar Baby* was published in 1981, followed by the play *Dreaming Emmett* first produced in Albany, New York, in 1986. *Beloved*, published in 1987, is regarded by some as her most significant work. The historical novel won both the Pulitzer Prize for fiction and the Robert F. Kennedy Award. *Beloved* was also a finalist for the 1988 National Book Critics Circle Award and was one of the three contenders for the Ritz Hemingway Prize in Paris, from which no winner emerged. In addition, *Beloved* was a National Book Award finalist. *Beloved* was also adapted for the silver screen by television talk-show host and actress Oprah Winfrey. In the 1990s, Morrison has written a collection of essays and two novels—*Jazz* (1992) and *Paradise* (1997).

Morrison was elected to the American Institute of Arts and Letters in 1981 and gave the keynote address at the American Writers' Congress in New York City in the fall of that year. She won the New York State Governor's Art Award in 1986. In 1993, the American Literature Association's Coalition of Author Societies founded The Toni Morrison Society, an education group, in Atlanta. Later in the year, Morrison received her highest honor and made history when she became the first African American recipient of the Nobel Prize in Literature, an award that included an $825,000 prize. In 1995, her alma mater, Howard University, bestowed her with an honorary doctorate.

In 2001, Morrison was honored by Alfred A. Knopf and the Toni Morrison Society at a 70th birthday celebration. She is currently working on a set of six illustrated modernized Aesop's fables which she is working on with her son Slade Morrison and the first volume is set to be published in 2003.

Walter Mosley (1952–)
Novelist

Walter Mosley achieved national publicity when, during the 1992 U.S. presidential campaign, Bill Clinton credited him as his favorite mystery writer. Born on January 12, 1952, and raised in the Watts and Pico-Fairfax districts of Los Angeles, Mosely's unique heritage is attributed to an African American father from the deep South and a white, Jewish mother whose family emigrated from Eastern Europe. After drifting among a variety of jobs, including potter, caterer, and computer programmer, he settled in New York City and attended the writing program at City College. By 1987 he had become a full-time writer. Although Mosley's first book, a short psychological novel entitled *Gone Fishin'* (later released in 1997) was turned down by numerous agents, he achieved rapid success in 1990 with *Devil in a Blue Dress*. In the next several years, *A Red Death, White Butterfly,* and *Black Betty* were also greeted with critical acclaim.

Mosley incorporates social and racial issues into gripping novels that authentically portray inner city life in the African American neighborhoods of post-World War II Los Angeles. His creation of the recurring multi-dimensional character, private investigator Ezekiel ("Easy") Rawlins, was heavily influenced by the experiences of Mosley's own father as an African American soldier in World War II and later a southern immigrant in California. With his African American viewpoint and confrontation of shifting societal and moral issues, Mosley has been praised for breaking new ground within the mystery and detective genre and inspiring a new brand of African American fiction. Mosley's success is destined to continue as he is planning nine or ten novels in all for the Rawlins series, eventually bringing the protagonist into the early 1980s.

Mosley received several honors including the John Creasey Memorial Award and Shamus Award for outstanding mystery writing. In 1990, the Mystery Writers of America nominated *Devil in a Blue Dress* for an Edgar Award. The film version of *Devil in a Blue Dress*, with a screenplay penned by the author, was released in 1996. Directed by Carl Franklin, the film starred Denzel Washington as Rawlins. In 1995, Mosely published *R. L.'s Dream*, a fictional meditation on the blues. In the following year, he released *A Little Yellow Dog*. In 1997, he published the book *Always Outnumbered, Always Outgunned*, introducing his most compelling new character since the debut of Easy Rawlins: Socrates Fortlow, a tough, brooding ex-convict determined to challenge and understand the violence and anarchy in his world—and in himself. He continued on with the character of Socrates Fortlow in his 1998 offering *Walkin' the Dog*.

Tackling the e-market, Mosley put out *Whispers in the Dark and the Greatest* in 2000 available solely on the Internet. In 2001 Mosley shifted gears once again, this time introducing narrator and used bookseller Paris Minton in *Fearless Jones*. Mosley went back to the short story format for his 2002 book *Futureland: Nine stories of an Imminent World* about a grim cyber-filled future. He also won a Grammy award in 2002 for best album liner notes for *Richard Pryor. . . And It's Deep Too!: The Complete Warner Bros. Recordings (1968–1992)*.

Walter Dean Myers (1937–)
Young Adult Writer

Walter Milton Myers was born in Martinsburg, West Virginia, in 1937. Upon the death of his mother at age three, he was raised by a foster couple, Herbert and Florence Dean, in Harlem. Myers began writing as a child and was praised in grade school for his academic achievements. Determined to further his education, he joined the U.S. Army at 17 years of age, enabling him to pay part of his college tuition with money from the G.I.

Walter Dean Myers.

Bill. In 1969, upon the publication of his first picture book for children, Myers was determined to become a professional writer. *Where Does the Day Go?* was honored by the Council on Interracial Books for Children and established Myers as an author who addressed the needs of minority children.

Myers worked as a senior editor for the Bobbs-Merrill publishing house, released more picture books, and began writing young adult stories in the 1970s. Since then he has published more than two dozen novels in which he tackles urban social issues, such as teen pregnancy, crime, drug abuse, and gang violence. Myers's authentic dialogue and ability to capture the universal ties and strengthening powers of family and friendship within African American communities prompted great response from teenage readers. Committed to producing quality literature for African American children, he branched into fairy tales, ghost stories, science fiction, adventure sagas, and a popular biography entitled *Malcolm X: By Any Means Necessary.* Myers has won a variety of awards including the Coretta Scott King Award and the Newbery "honor book" citation for *Scorpions.* Myers's novels, particularly

Hoops, Fallen Angels, and *Motown and Didi: A Love Story,* are an enduring presence on both high school and young adult recommended reading lists.

Gloria Naylor (1950–)
Novelist

Gloria Naylor was born in New York City on January 25, 1950, and still lives there. She received a B.A. in English from Brooklyn College in 1981 and an M.A. in Afro-American Studies from Yale University in 1983. She has taught writing and literature at George Washington University, New York University, Brandeis University, Cornell University, and Boston University. In 1983, she won the American Book Award for first fiction for her novel *The Women of Brewster Place,* which was produced for television in 1988. Her second novel was *Linden Hills* published in 1985. Her third novel *Mama Day* (1988) was written with the aid of a grant from the National Endowment for the Arts. In 1988, Naylor was awarded a Guggenheim Fellowship. In 1993, Naylor published a new novel *Bailey's Café.*

In 1998, Naylor returned to familiar ground with her novel *The Men of Brewster Place.* This was a different

Gloria Naylor.

spin on the gritty but secure community that had brought Naylor into the public spotlight, and much like *The Women of Brewster Place* this book was hailed by critics for its characterization and positive messages.

Ann Lane Petry (1912–1997)
Novelist, Short Story Writer

Ann Petry was born in Old Saybrook, Connecticut, on October 12, 1912, where her father was a druggist. After graduating from the College of Pharmacy at the University of Connecticut, she went to New York where she found employment as a social worker and newspaper reporter, studying creative writing at night.

Her early short stories appeared in *Crisis* and *Phylon.* In 1946, after having received a Houghton Mifflin Fellowship, she completed and published her first novel *The Street. The Street* focuses on the lives of African American women in a crowded tenement. Through her exploration of this subject, Petry became the first African American woman writer to address the problems African American women face as they live in the slums. Petry also wrote *Country Place* (1947), *The Narrows* (1953), and *Miss Munel and Other Stories* (1971). Her works for children and young people include *The Drugstore Cat, Harriet Tubman, Tituba of Salem Village, Legends of Saints,* and a fourth book for children and young people. Many of her earlier novels are being reprinted. Petry died on February 28, 1997.

Arnold Rampersad (1941–)
Literary Critic

Arnold Rampersad was born on November 13, 1941, in Trinidad. He received a B.A. and M.A. from Bowling Green State University as well as a M.A. and Ph.D. from Harvard University. Rampersad, who was appointed a MacArthur Foundation fellow from 1991 to 1996, has taught at Stanford University from 1974 to 1983, Rutgers University from 1983 to 1988, Columbia University from 1988 to 1990, and Princeton University from 1990 to 1998. In 1998, Rampersad returned to Stanford University where he is the Sara Hart Kimball Professor in the Humanities.

Rampersad's first book is *Melville's Israel Potter: A Pilgrimage and Progress* (1969). Starting with Rampersad's next book, *The Art and Imagination of W.E.B. Du Bois* (1976), he began chronicling the lives and/or works of the most prominent African American men of the twentieth century. Rampersad is the coauthor of Arthur Ashe's *Days of Grace: A Memoir*

(1993) and author of *Jackie Robinson: A Biography* (1997). Rampersad has edited three books about Richard Wright's writings: *Richard Wright: Early Works: Lawd Today!/Uncle Tom's Children, Native Son* (1991); *Richard Wright's Later Works: Black Boy [American Hunger], The Outsider* (1991); and *Richard Wright: A Collection of Critical Essays* (1994). Rampersad has edited four books on the works of one of Wright's most famous contemporaries, Langston Hughes. These books are *The Collected Poems of Langston Hughes* (1994) as well as *The Collected Works of Langston Hughes: Volume 1: The Poems: 1921–1940* (2001); *Volume 2: The Poems: 1941–1950* (2001); and *Volume 3: The Poems: 1951–1967* (2001). These last three books are the beginning trio of the University of Missouri Press's 18 volume compilation of the poems, novels, plays, short stories, essays, and other works by Hughes, the dean of African American letters. Rampersad is the chair of the four member editorial board for *The Collected Works of Langston Hughes.*

Rampersad is best known for his two-volume *The Life of Langston Hughes: 1902–1941, I, Too, Sing America* (1986), which won the 1987 Anisfield-Wolf Book Award in Race Relations, Cleveland Foundation as well as the 1988 Clarence L. Holte Prize; and *Volume 2: 1941–1967: I Dream a World* (1988), which was a 1989 Pulitzer Prize finalist in biography and winner of a 1990 American Book Award. Rampersad's work is considered the definitive biography of Hughes. Rita Dove, in a *New York Times Book Review*, wrote, "In his superlative study of. . . the most prominent Afro-American poet of our century, Arnold Rampersad has performed that most difficult of feats: illuminating a man who, despite all his public visibility, was quite elusive." John A. Williams commented in the *Los Angeles Times Book Review*, "No other biography of Hughes can match the grace and richness of Rampersad's writing, or his investigative and interpretive abilities." David Nicholson opined in the *Washington Post Book World*, "This may be the best biography of a black writer we have had."

Rampersad has co-edited *Slavery and the Literary Imagination* (with Deborah McDowell, 1989) and *The Norton Anthology of African American Literature* (1997), which is the bench mark compilation of the African American literary tradition by which all subsequent anthologies of black literature will be judged. Henry Louis Gates Jr. and Nellie McKay were the general editors of *The Norton Anthology*, and Rampersad was one of the nine additional editors. He is also a co-editor of the Race and American Culture book series published by Oxford University Press.

Rampersad's impressive publications place him in the forefront as a literary historian/critic.

Ishmael Reed (1938–)
Novelist, Poet

Born in Chattanooga, Tennessee, on February 22, 1938, Ishmael Reed grew up in Buffalo, New York. He attended State University of New York at Buffalo from 1956 to 1960. He worked as a reporter and later as an editor for the *Newark Advance* in New Jersey before co-founding the *East Village Other* in 1965. Reed spent the next few years teaching prose and guest lecturing at different institutions including the University of California at Berkeley. In 1971, he co-founded Yardbird Publishing Co., Inc. After four years as the editorial director, he co-founded Reed, Cannon & Johnson Communications Co., a publisher and producer of videos, and in 1976, the Before Columbus Foundation, which produced and distributed works by unestablished ethnic writers.

A controversial man, Reed has published poetry, novels, plays, and prose. Considered by some to be misogynistic and cynical, others find his work innovative. He is committed to creating an alternative African American aesthetic, which he calls Neo-HooDooism. One hallmark of the movement is the reliance on satire and social criticism.

Reed's works of poetry include: *catechism of d neoamerican hoodoo church* (1971); *Conjure* (1972), which was nominated for the National Book Award; *Chattanooga* (1973); *A Secretary to the Spirits* (1978); and *New and Collected Poetry* (1988). His poetry has also appeared in numerous anthologies and magazines including *The Poetry of the Negro*, *The New Black Poetry*, *The Norton Anthology*, *Cricket*, and *Scholastic* magazine.

Reed's novels include: *The Free-lance Pallbearers* (1967); *Yellow Back Radio Broke Down* (1969); *Mumbo Jumbo*, which also received a National Book Award nomination; *The Last Days of Louisiana Red* (1974); *Flight to Canada* (1976); *The Terrible Twos* (1982); *Reckless Eyeballing; The Terrible Threes* (1989); and *Japanese by Spring* (1992). He also wrote three plays: *The Lost State of Franklin* (1976); *Savage Wilds;* and its sequel *Savage Wilds II.*

Prose works by Reed include: *Shrovetide in Old New Orleans* (1978); *God Made Alaska for the Indians: Selected Essays* (1982); *Writin' Is Fightin': Thirty-seven Years of Boxing on Paper* (1988); and *Airing Dirty Laundry* (1993). He was also the editor of *Multi-America: Essays on Cultural Wars and Cultural Peace* in 1997.

Reed's career has been rich in recognition. In 1974, he won the John Simon Guggenheim Memorial Foundation Award for fiction. The next year he received a Rosenthal Foundation Award and an honor from the National Institute of Arts and Letters. In 1978, Reed earned the Lewis Michaux and American Civil Liberties awards. The following year he was given the Pushcart Prize. He has received fellowships from the Wisconsin Board and Yale University's Calhoun College in 1982; grants have come from New York State, the National Endowment for the Arts, the MacArthur Foundation, and the California Arts Council.

Sonia Sanchez (1934–)
Poet, Playwright

Sonia Sanchez was born on September 9, 1934, in Birmingham, Alabama. She studied at New York University and Hunter College in New York City. She is married to Etheridge Knight, an African American writer of poetry and fiction. She has taught at San Francisco State College and is now teaching in the Black Studies Department of Temple University in Philadelphia. Her plays were published in *The Drama Review* (Summer 1968) and in *New Plays from the Black Theatre* (1969), edited by Ed Bullins. Her poems also have been published in many other magazines and anthologies. Books written or edited by her include ten volumes of poetry: *Homecoming* (1969); *We a Bad People* (1970); *It's a New Day* (1971); *A Blues Book for Blue Black Magical Women* (1973); *Love Poems* (1975); *I've Been a Woman* (1978); *Under a Soprano Sky* (1987); *Wounded in the House of a Friend* (1994); *Like the Singing Coming Off the Drums* (1997); and *Shake Loose My Skin: New and Selected Poems,* (1999). Sanchez has edited two anthologies: *Three Hundred and Sixty Degrees of Blackness Comin at You, An Anthology of the Sonia Sanchez Writers Workshop at Countee Cullen Library in Harlem* (1971); and *We Be Word Sorcerers: Twenty-five Stories by Black Americans* (1973). She has also written *A Sound Investment* (1979), a collection of short stories; and *homegirls and handgrenades* (1984).

Ntozake Shange (1948–)
Playwright, Poet, Novelist

A playwright and poet, Paulette Linda Williams was born in Trenton, New Jersey, on October 18, 1948; she changed her name to Ntozake Shange in 1971. She graduated from Barnard College and received her master's degree from the University of Southern California, where she did other graduate work. She studied Afro-American dance in California and actually performed with the Third World Collective, Raymond Sawyer's Afro-American Dance Company, Sounds in Motion, and West Coast Dance Works.

Shange taught at Sonoma Mills College in California from 1972 to 1975. She went on to teach at CUNY and Douglas College to finish out the 1970s, before becoming the Mellon Distinguished Professor of Literature at Rice University in 1983. For three years she worked as an associate professor of drama at the University of Houston.

Shange's play *For Colored Girls Who Have Considered Suicide/When the Rainbow Is Enuf*, a choreopoem (poetry and dance), was first produced in California, after her dance-drama *Sassafrass* was presented in 1976. Later *For Colored Girls* was produced in New York City, where it had a long run before going on to other cities. It earned Tony, Grammy, and Emmy award nominations in 1977. Among the other works by Shange that have been produced on the stage are *Spell #7, A Photograph: Lovers in Motion* (1979), and *Boogie Woogie Landscapes* (1979). *For Colored Girls* has been published as a book, and Shange's collection *Three Pieces* (1981) contains *Spell #7, A Photograph: Lovers in Motion*, and *Boogie Woogie Landscapes*.

Other books by Shange include: *Nappy Edges* (poetry, 1978); *Sassafrass, Cypress & Indigo* (novel, 1982); *A Daughter's Geography* (poetry, 1983); *From Okra to Greens* (a play, 1984); *See No Evil: Prefaces & Accounts, 1976–1983* (1984); *Betsey Brown* (novel, 1985); *Liliane: Resurrection of the Daughter* (novel, 1994); *I Live in Music* (poetry 1994); and *Whitewash* (children's novel 1997).

A version of *Betsey Brown* for the stage, with music by the jazz trumpeter and composer Baikida Carroll, opened the American Music Theater Festival in Philadelphia, March 25, 1989. Shange directed Ina Cesaire's *Fire's Daughters* in 1993. The Broadway version of *For Colored Girls Who Have Considered Suicide/When the Rainbow Is Enuf* was revived in 1995.

Shange received an Obie Award in 1981 for *Mother Courage and Her Children* and a *Los Angeles Times* Book Prize for poetry that year for *Three Pieces*. A Guggenheim fellow, Shange has been given awards by the Outer Critics Circle and the National Black Theater Festival (1993). She also won the Pushcart Prize.

Lucy Terry (1730–1821)
Poet

Lucy Terry is generally considered one of the first African American poet in the United States. In a ballad that she called "Bars Fight," she recreated an Indian massacre that occurred in Deerfield, Massachusetts, in 1746 during King George's War. "Bars Fight" has been hailed by some historians as the most authentic account of the massacre.

A semi-literate slave in the household of Ensign Ebenezer Wells, she won her freedom and was married to a freed man named Prince. The Prince house served as a center for young people who gathered to listen to their hostess's storytelling. Lucy Terry was a strong woman who argued eloquently for her family's rights in several cases.

Wallace H. Thurman (1902–1934)
Novelist, Playwright, Ghostwriter, Journalist

A caustic critic of African American writing, Wallace Thurman was a member of the New Negro movement known as the Harlem Renaissance. Wallace Henry Thurman, called "Wally" by his friends, was born on August 16, 1902, in Salt Lake City. He graduated from the University of Utah in 1922, having studied premedicine. He did post-graduate work in 1923 at the University of Southern California. He read widely and knew about the Harlem Renaissance then taking place in New York. He attempted a West Coast counterpart of the Harlem Renaissance and established his own short-lived literary magazine *The Outlet*. He moved to New York City the following year.

Thurman was managing editor of the *Messenger* from spring to fall 1926, then moved to *The World Tomorrow*, a white-owned monthly. By now Thurman and Langston Hughes had become good friends. They were a part of a new school known as Harlem Renaissance writers. The group included Arna Bontemps (whom he had known in Los Angeles), Nella Larsen, Dorothy West, Countee Cullen, Jessie Fauset, Aaron Douglas, Zora Neale Hurston, and Gwendolyn Bennett. In the summer of 1926, Thurman and the group established *Fire!*, a short-lived literary magazine that was both obscene and revolutionary. The magazine was to provide another outlet beyond *Crisis* and *Opportunity* magazines for young African American writers to have their works published. He had financed the magazine himself and spent four years paying its debt.

In 1927, many of Thurman's articles were published in prestigious magazines, such as *New Republic* and *Dance Magazine*, further helping to establish him as a critic. The next year, McFadden Publications added Thurman to its editorial staff, and he continued to write. In 1929 he published *The Blacker the Berry the Sweeter the Juice*, an autobiographical novel that embraced intra-race color prejudice and self-hatred. Thurman was also the ghostwriter for several magazines and books. He wrote several plays as well; one of them, *Cordelia the Crude*, premiered on Broadway where it received mixed reviews. It went on to Chicago and Los Angeles .

In 1932, Thurman published two other novels: *Infants of the Spring* and *The Interne*. An alcoholic homosexual, Thurman was often depressed and suicidal. He became ill with tuberculosis and died in New York on December 22, 1934.

Jean Toomer (1894–1967)
Novelist, Poet

Jean Toomer's *Cane*, published in 1923, has been called one of the three best novels ever written by an African American—the others being Richard Wright's *Native Son* and Ralph Ellison's *Invisible Man*. According to Columbia University critic Robert Bone, "Cane is by far the most impressive product of the Negro Renaissance."

A mixture of poems and sketches, *Cane* was written during that period in which most African American writers were reacting against earlier "polite" forms by creating works marked by literary realism. Toomer even went beyond this realm to the threshold of symbol and myth, using a "mystical" approach which is much more akin to the contemporary mood than it was to the prevailing spirit of his own day. *Cane* sold only 500 copies on publication, and it was still little known until reprinted recently with new introductions. Much has been written about Toomer and *Cane* in recent years, including a *Cane* casebook.

Born in Washington, DC, in December of 1894, Toomer was educated in law at the University of Wisconsin and City College of New York before he turned to writing. The transcendental nature of his writings is said to have stemmed in part from his early study under Gurdjieff, the Russian mystic.

Toomer also published quite a bit of poetry. Darwin T. Turner edited *The Wayward and The Seeking: A Collection of Writings by Jean Toomer* (1980), a book of his poetry, short stories, dramas, and autobiography. Other books about Toomer and his writings include: Therman O'Daniel's *Jean Toomer: A Critical Evaluation* (1985); over 40 essays of the most thorough, up-to-date scholarship on Toomer; Robert B. Jones and Margery Toomer Latimer's *The Collected Poems of Jean Toomer* (1988); 55 poems; and Nellie Y. McKay's *Jean Toomer, Artist: A Study of His Literary Life and Work, 1894–1936* (1984, 1987). Toomer died on March 10, 1967.

Alice Walker (1944–)
Poet, Novelist

Alice Walker was born in Eatonton, Georgia, on February 9, 1944. She was educated at Spelman College (1961–1963) and Sarah Lawrence College, from which she received her B.A. in 1965. That year, she worked as a voter registrar in Georgia and worked for the welfare department in New York City. In 1967, she moved to Mississippi, where she was an African American literature consultant for Friends of the Children of Mississippi. From 1968 to 1971, she was a writer-in-residence at Jackson State and Tougaloo Colleges. Moving to Boston, she then lectured at Wellesley and the University of Massachussetts until 1973. While teaching in the early 1970s, she was a Radcliffe Institute fellow.

Walker's work began to be published in the late 1960s, starting with *Once: Poems* in 1968. Two years later she published the novel *The Third Life Grange Copeland*. These two works were quickly followed by a succession of works. Among them were: *Revolutionary Peturnias and Other Poems* (1973), which earned a National Book Award nomination and the Lillian Smith Award; *In Love and Trouble: Stories of Black Women*, recipient of a Richard and Hinda Rosenthal Foundation Award from the American Academy and Institute of Arts and Letters; and *Langston Hughes: American Biography* (for children).

The novel *Meridian* (1976) was followed in 1979 by a book of poetry entitled *Goodnight, Willie Lee, I'll See You in the Morning* and an edited work by Walker titled *I Love Myself When I'm Laughing. . . and Then Again When I Am Looking Mean and Impressive: A Zora Neale Hurston Reader*. The reader was particularly important because it brought about a resurgence of interest in a Harlem Renaissance writer who had been overshadowed by other, better known authors.

In the 1980s, Walker more formally resumed her teaching career, spending the year of 1982 as the Fannie Hurst Professor of Literature at Brandeis University, while also serving as a distinguished writer as the University of California at Berkeley. In 1984, she co-founded Wild Trees Press. That decade's works include: the short story collection *You Can't Keep a Good Woman Down* (1981); two collections of essays and journal entries *In Search of Our Mothers' Gardens: Womanist Prose* (1983) and *Living by the Word: Selected Writings, (1973–1987)*; a book of poetry entitled *Horses Make a Landscape Look More Beautiful* (1984); *To Hell With Dying* (juvenile story, 1988); and the novel *The Temple of My Familiar* (1989). In 1986, she received the O. Henry Award for her short story "Kindred Spirits."

Walker's most well-received work, however, was the 1983 novel *The Color Purple*. Written in the form of a series of letters, the novel was nominated for the National Book Critics Circle Award and won the 1983 Pulitzer Prize as well as an American Book Award. The best-selling book was adapted into an award-winning film featuring Whoopi Goldberg, Danny Glover, Oprah

Winfrey, and Margaret Avery in 1985 and is being revamped for the Broadway stage as a musical in 2002.

In the 1990s, Walker has continued writing. *Possessing the Secret of Joy*, loosely a sequel to *The Color Purple*, was released in 1992. *The Same River Twice: Honoring the Difficult* came out four years later. Her latest novel *By the Light of My Father's Smile* was published in 1998. Walker also published a book of short stories in 2000 entitled *The Way Forward is With a Broken Heart*.

Holder of numerous honorary degrees, Walker has received a Merrill Fellowship for writing, a National Endowment for the Arts grant, a Radcliffe Institute Fellowship, and other honors.

Margaret A. Walker (Margaret Walker Alexander) (1915–1998)
Poet, Novelist

Margaret Walker was born on July 7, 1915, in Birmingham, Alabama, and received her early education in Alabama, Louisiana, and Mississippi. She earned her B.A. from Northwestern University and her M.A. (1940) and Ph.D. (1966), both from the University of Iowa.

In 1942, Walker published *For My People* and, two years later, was awarded a Rosenwald Fellowship for creative writing. She has taught English and literature at Livingston College in North Carolina, West Virginia State College, and Jackson State College in Mississippi. Her novel *Jubilee* appeared in 1965. *For My People* was reprinted in 1969. Her other works are *Prophets for a New Day*, *How I Wrote Jubilee*, *October Journey*, and *A Poetic Equation: Conversations Between Nikki Giovanni and Margaret Walker*. The date of June 17, 1976, was proclaimed Margaret Walker Alexander Day by the mayor of her native Birmingham.

Walker's other works include *Richard Wright: Daemonic Genius* (1988). A second edition of *A Poetic Equation: Conversations Between Nikki Giovanni and Margaret Walker* was published in 1983. She died on November 30, 1998, in Chicago.

Dorothy West (1907–1998)
Writer

Dorothy West was the last surviving member of the Harlem Renaissance, the period of the late 1920s and early 1930s when an outpouring of writing and poetry exuded from the pens and typewriters of African American writers based in Harlem. West was known as "the Kid" by such luminaries as Countee Cullen, Langston Hughes, Richard Wright, and Zora Neale Hurston. West wrote short stories for the *New York Daily News* in the

Dorothy West.

1930s, and twice, during the Great Depression, founded African American literary journals, most notably the *New Challenge*.

West was born on June 2, 1907, in Boston. She later moved to New York City, but eventually returned home, moving into her family's summer home in Oak Bluffs on Martha's Vineyard in 1943. Five years later she wrote her first novel *The Living Is Easy* based on the affluent world of African American achievers. West continued to write short stories for the *Daily News* from her Oak Bluffs home for the next 25 years.

In the 1950s, West began a second novel *The Wedding*, but could not find a publisher interested in handling it. With its theme on interracial marriage, it may have been too hot a topic for the times and was put aside by West in an unfinished state. Instead, West started contributing short pieces to the Vineyard's daily newspaper in the 1970s.

West once again enjoyed fame in the 1990s. In 1992, West's stories caught the eye of former First Lady Jacqueline Onassis, an editor at Doubleday and a summer resident of Martha's Vineyard. Onassis encouraged

West to finish *The Wedding*, and the two of them began meeting weekly. With Onassis acting as West's editor, the novel finally was published in 1995. West dedicated the novel to Onassis. The story was made into a television movie, produced by Oprah Winfrey, and aired in 1998. West died on August 16, 1998.

Phillis Wheatley (1753–1784)
Poet

Born in Senegal in 1753, Phillis Wheatley was brought to the United States as a slave and received her name from Susannah Wheatley, the wife of the Boston tailor who had bought Phillis. Wheatley received her early education in the household of her master. Her interest in writing stemmed from her reading of the Bible and the classics under the guidance of the Wheatley's daughter, Mary.

In 1770, her first poem was printed under the title "A Poem by Phillis, A Negro Girl on the Death of Reverend George Whitefield." Her book *Poems on Various Subjects: Religious and Moral* was published in London in 1773, the first book of poetry published by an African American. She took a trip to England for health reasons, but later returned to the United States and was married. She published the poem "Liberty and Peace" in 1784, shortly before her death. Most of the old books of her poems, letters, and memories about her life were reprinted in the late 1960s and early 1970s. Two books about Wheatley are Julian D. Mason Jr.'s *The Poems of Phillis Wheatley* (1966) and William H. Robinson's *Phillis Wheatley, A Biography* (1981). Robinson also compiled and published *Phillis Wheatley: A Bio-Bibliography* (1981).

Although George Washington was among her admirers (she had once sent him a tributary poem, which he graciously acknowledged), her poetry is considered important today largely because of its historical role in the growth of African American literature. Wheatley's poetry reflects Anglo-Saxon models, rather than her African heritage. It is, nevertheless, a typical example of the verse manufactured in a territory—the British colonies—not yet divorced from its maternal origins. Wheatley died on December 5, 1784.

John Edgar Wideman (1941–)
Writer, Educator

Wideman has been one of the leading chroniclers of life in urban black America, depicting the widening chasm between the urban poor and the white power structure in the United States. He is known for intertwining ghetto experiences with experimental fiction techniques, personal history, and social events to highlight deep cultural conflicts. A prolific writer, Wideman is the only two-time winner of the prestigious PEN/Faulkner Award for literature, one for *Sent for You Yesterday* (1983), and one for *Philadelphia Fire* (1990). In addition to novels, he has written short stories and nonfiction including *Brothers and Keepers* (1984), a juxtaposition of his life and that of his younger brother, incarcerated for taking part in a larceny/murder. The examination of the two brothers' different lives was nominated for the National Book Critics Circle Award.

Born on June 14, 1941, in Washington, DC, Wideman was the first of five children. Growing up in Pittsburgh, where the family moved, Wideman attended highly-regarded Peabody High School. A top student, he was also class president and captain of the basketball team. Enrolling at the University of Pittsburgh on a scholarship, he earned a B.A. in 1963. During his undergraduate career, Wideman made the Big Five Basketball Hall of Fame, won the university's creative writing prize, and was elected to Phi Beta Kappa. He received a Rhodes Scholarship to England's Oxford University, becoming the first African American to receive such recognition in more than 50 years. With a B.A. in philosophy obtained from Oxford's New College in 1966, Wideman began writing and teaching at such institutions as the Universities of Pennsylvania, Wyoming, and, since 1986, Massachusetts at Amherst.

August Wilson (1945–)
Playwright

One of the most important voices in the American theater, playwright August Wilson has become a spokesperson for the black experience in America today. Since his first stage success *Ma Rainey's Black Bottom* in 1984, he has celebrated people of color in several plays, all set in a different decade in the twentieth century. In 1997, he elicited a public debate involving many prominent theater critics on the use of theater as a vehicle for cultural nationalism.

Wilson was born in Pittsburgh, Pennsylvania, in 1945 and the oldest of six children. His mother was a house cleaner, his absent father, a baker. He left school at 15 due to the racist abuse he endured there. But he continued his education in the local library, reading all the literature by African American writers, such as Ralph Ellison, Langston Hughes, Richard Wright, and others. He published a few poems in *Black World* and *Black Lines* in the early 1970s after absorbing the works of Robert Frost, Dylan Thomas, and Amiri Baraka.

It was when Wilson discovered the writings of Malcolm X that he decided to use cultural nationalism,

African American people working toward cultural self-determination, as a basis for playwriting. In 1969, he helped found the African American activist theater company Black Horizons on the Hill which focused on politicizing the community and raising African American consciousness. He staged some early plays through this association, but moved to St. Paul, Minnesota, in 1978 where he says he gained some clarity and became less radicalized. He immediately wrote *Jitney* for the Minneapolis Playwrights Center and won a fellowship prize.

Wilson moved the location of *Jitney* and his next work *Fullerton Street* back to Pittsburgh and produced them at the Allegheny Repertory Theater. After two years of work at the National Playwright Conference, his first major work *Ma Rainey's Black Bottom* caught the eye of Yale Repertory Theater's artistic director Lloyd Richards. Together, they have staged almost all of Wilson's works, Richards directing them himself.

Each of Wilson's plays tells the story of a different segment of the African American experience. *Ma Rainey's Black Bottom* tells how African American entertainers were exploited by whites in the 1920s. His next play *Joe Turner's Come and Gone* discusses the migration of African Americans from rural Southern areas to the industrial cities of the North. *Fences* became an immediate hit when it opened on Broadway in 1987. Actor James Earl Jones played the main character, Troy Maxson, who dreams of playing professional baseball in the 1950s, only to be victimized by white racism. This play won the Pulitzer Prize and other awards for Wilson.

In 1990, August Wilson won his second Pulitzer Prize for *The Piano Lesson*, a play that focuses on a family conflict over selling an heirloom piano once traded for slave ancestors whose portraits are carved into it. Then he produced *Two Trains Running* in 1992, a play about the late 1960s when racial strife and the Vietnam War divided the nation.

Wilson moved to Seattle in the early 1990s. His next play *Seven Guitars* opened in 1996. Set in Pittsburgh in 1948, the unseen main character's death is being mourned at a wake. The seven characters reminisce with music and dream the future. This is another successful production by Wilson and director Lloyd Richards.

The 1997 debate began when Wilson gave a keynote speech to the Theater Communications Group Conference. Entitled "The Ground on Which I Stand," it celebrated the achievements of African American theater and insisted that African American theater was understood and appreciated only by those living the African American experience. He castigated the New York mainstream theater and its critics for lack of support for African American theater. In turn, many New York critics, including Robert Brustein, Frank Rich, and John Simon, published editorial columns analyzing Wilson's speech. Ultimately, a face-to-face debate was held by Wilson and Brustein in January 1998 to discuss the cultural intentions of theater: Wilson/politicization vs. Brustein/universal truth. At the end of the evening the issue remained alive and well. Wilson had revisited his earlier black nationalist beliefs and continues to evoke questions about the African American experience.

In 2001 Wilson was presented with the prestigious Washington Literary Award and in 2002 he was the only American to be honored with an award at the 26th annual Laurence Olivier Awards.

Richard Wright (1908–1960)
Novelist

Born on September 4, 1908, on a plantation near Natchez, Mississippi, Wright drew on his personal experience to dramatize racial injustice and its brutalizing effects. In 1938, under the auspices of the Works Progress Administration Illinois Writers Project, Wright published *Uncle Tom's Children*, a collection of four novellas based on his Mississippi boyhood memories. The book won an award for the best work of fiction by a WPA writer, and Wright received a Guggenheim Fellowship.

Two years later, *Native Son*, a novel of Chicago's African American ghetto, further enhanced Wright's reputation. A Book-of-the-Month Club choice, it was later a successful Broadway production under Orson Welles's direction and was filmed in South America with Wright himself in the role of Bigger Thomas. He published *Twelve Million Black Voices* in 1941.

In 1945, Wright's largely autobiographical *Black Boy* was selected by the Book-of-the-Month Club and went on to become his second best-seller. Wright later moved to Paris where he continued to write fiction and nonfiction including: *The Outsider* (1953); *Black Power* (1954); *Savage Holiday* (1954, 1965); *The Color Curtain* (1956); *White Man Listen* (1957); *The Long Dream* (1958); *Lawd Today* (1963); *Eight Men* (1961); and *American Hunger* (1977), a continuation of Wright's autobiographical work *Black Boy*.

Wright died of a heart attack on November 28, 1960. There are over a dozen books written about him, two casebooks on *Native Son*, a children's book, and a critical pamphlet in a writer's series.

◆ AWARD WINNERS

American Academy and Institute of Arts and Letters Award

1946: Gwendolyn Brooks; Langston Hughes
1956: James Baldwin
1962: John A. Williams
1970: James A. McPherson
1971: Charles Gordone
1972: Michael S. Harper
1974: Henry Van Dyke
1978: Lerone Bennett Jr.; Toni Morrison
1985: John Williams
1987: Ernest J. Gaines
1992: August Wilson
1994: Adrienne Kennedy
2001: Carl Phillips
2002: Charles Johnson

Clarence L. Holte Literary Prize

Co-sponsored by the Phelps-Stokes Fund and the Schomburg Center for Research in Black Culture of the New York Public Library

1979: Chancellor Williams, *The Destruction of Black Civilization: Great Issues of a Race from 4500 B.C. to 2000 A.D.*
1981: Ivan Van Sertima, *They Came Before Columbus: The African Presence in Ancient America*
1983: Vincent Harding, *There Is a River: The Black Struggle for Freedom in America*
1986: John Hope Franklin, *George Washington Williams: A Biography*
1988: Arnold Rampersad, *The Life of Langston Hughes: 1902–1941, I, Too, Sing America*

National Book Award—National Book Foundation

1953: Ralph Ellison, *Invisible Man*, Fiction
1969: Winthrop D. Jordan, *White over Black: American Attitudes toward the Negro, 1550–1812*, History and Biography

1983: Gloria Naylor, *The Women of Brewster Place*, First Novel; Joyce Carol Thomas, *Marked By Fire*, Children's Fiction (Paperback); Alice Walker, *The Color Purple*, Fiction (Hardcover)
1990: Charles Johnson, *Middle Passage*, Fiction
2000: Lucille Clifton, *Blessing the Boats: New and Selected Poems 1988–2000*, Poetry

Nobel Prize

1993: Toni Morrison

PEN/Faulkner Award for Fiction

1982: David Bradley, *The Chaneysville Incident*
1984: John Edgar Wideman, *Sent for you Yesterday*
1991: John Edgar Wideman, *Philadelphia Fire*

Pulitzer Prize

Columbia University Graduate School of Journalism

Biography or Autobiography
1994: *W. E. B. Du Bois: Biography of a Race, 1868–1919*, David Levering Lewis
2001: *W.E.B. Du Bois: The Fight for Equality and the American Century, 1919–1963*, David Levering Lewis

Letters: Fiction
1978: *Elbow Room*, James Alan McPherson
1983: *The Color Purple*, Alice Walker
1988: *Beloved*, Toni Morrison

Letters: Poetry
1950: *Annie Allen*, Gwendolyn Brooks
1987: *Thomas and Beulah*, Rita Dove
1994: *Neon Vernacular*, Yusef Komunyakaa

Letters: Special Awards and Citations
1977: Alex Haley, *Roots*

Journalism: Commentary
1989: Clarence Page
1994: William Raspberry
1996: E. R. Shipp

Journalism: Feature Writing
1999: Angelo B. Henderson

Media

◆ Book Publishers ◆ Newspaper and Magazine Publishers ◆ Broadcasting
◆ African American Media in Cyberspace
◆ Publishing, Radio, and Television Professionals
◆ Print and Broadcast Media Directory

by Tracey Desirnaí Hicks

◆ BOOK PUBLISHERS

There have been more than 100 publishing houses started by African American individuals, organizations, universities and cultural institutions dating back to the early nineteenth century. Some of these entities published volumes of books, while others only published a few. Nevertheless, the publishing industry in the African American community manages to prosper regardless of the obstacles. Since the inception of African American book publishing, three types of publishers have emerged: religious, institutional, and trade publishers.

Religious Publishers

African American religious denominations established religious publishing enterprises in order to publish works that would provide religious instruction and assist the clergy and laity in recording denominational history. Some religious publishers also released books on secular subjects that celebrated some aspect of African American culture or documented African American history.

Prior to the Civil War, two African American religious publishing enterprises existed. The African Methodist Episcopal Church (AME) organized the AME Book Concern in Philadelphia in 1817—the first African American-owned book publishing enterprise in the United States. Publishing its first book in that same year, *The Book of Discipline*, the AME Book Concern published a host of classic religious and secular books until its operations were suspended in 1952 by the General Conference of the African Methodist Episcopal Church. In 1841, the African Methodist Episcopal

Zion Church formed the AME Zion Book Concern in New York City. This firm, which only published religious works, moved to Charlotte, North Carolina, in 1894.

In Jackson, Tennessee, the Colored Methodist Episcopal Church (CME)—known as the Christian Methodist Episcopal Church—started the CME Publishing House in 1870. The CME Publishing House, which only publishes books on religious subjects, is located in Memphis, Tennessee. Another book publishing enterprise owned by African American Methodists is the AME Sunday School Union and Publishing House, established in Bloomington, Illinois, in 1882. It relocated to Nashville, Tennessee, in 1886. Publishing secular and religious books, the AME Sunday School Union and Publishing House remained the oldest publishing unit owned by the AME Church.

One of the most successful African American religious publishers to come into existence during the nineteenth century was the National Baptist Publishing Board (NBPB). Under the leadership of Dr. Richard Henry Boyd and the auspices of the National Baptist Convention, USA, the NBPB was organized in Nashville in 1896. By 1913, this well-managed firm, publishing religious and secular books, grew into one of the largest African American-owned businesses in the country.

In 1915, however, a dispute arose between the National Baptist Convention, USA, and Dr. Richard Henry Boyd over the ownership of the NBPB. In a legal battle, the Tennessee Supreme Court decided in favor of Dr. Boyd. The NBPB—now R.H. Boyd Publishing Corp. in honor of its founder—is owned by the Boyd family. With over 100 years of publishing experience, R. H. Boyd continued to thrive as a religious enterprise by publishing books about family, education, and history, as well as other materials.

In 1907, the Church of God in Christ established the Church of God in Christ Publishing House in Memphis. Restricting its publications to religious books and pamphlets, this publisher met the ever-expanding need for religious literature for one of the fastest-growing African American religious denominations.

Faced with the loss of the NBPB in 1916, the National Baptist Convention, USA, Inc. established the Sunday School Publishing Board of the National Baptist Convention, USA, Inc., in Nashville. Over the years, this firm developed into one of the largest African American-owned publishing enterprises, publishing religious and secular books and pamphlets.

Similar to the Sunday School Publishing Board of the National Baptist Convention, USA, Inc., Muhammad's Temple No. 2, Publications Department, which was founded in 1956 by the Nation of Islam, published religious, as well as secular books. Between 1956 and 1974, this firm issued several books; however, it stopped publishing in 1974.

Institutional Publishers

During the last decades of the nineteenth century and the early decades of the twentieth century, educational, cultural, social, and political institutions were established to meet the specific needs of African Americans. Many of these institutions developed publishing programs.

Colleges and Universities

Hampton Institute became the first African American educational institution to publish books when the Hampton Institute Press was established in 1871. An active publisher until 1940, the Hampton Institute Press published travel books, poetry, textbooks, songbooks, conference proceedings, and *The Southern Workman*, one of the leading national African American periodicals published between its inception in 1871 and its demise in 1939.

In 1896, the Atlanta University Press entered the book publishing market with the release of *Atlanta University Publication Series*, which consisted of monographs reporting on the findings of studies conducted by the university's department of sociology under the direction of Dr. W.E.B. Du Bois. These works represented some of the earliest studies in urban sociology conducted in the South. The Atlanta University Press remained in operation until 1936.

Industrial Work of Tuskegee Graduates and Former Students During the Year 1910, compiled by Monroe

N. Work (1911), was the first book released by the Tuskegee Institute Press. With the publication of this book and other works by the press, Booker T. Washington sought to publicize the success of Tuskegee's program to white philanthropists in the North. The Tuskegee Institute Press, which was active until 1958, published several other important works including John Kenny's *The Negroes in Medicine* (1912) and *Lynching by States, 1882–1958* (1958) by Jessie Parkhurst Guzman.

In 1910, another book publishing enterprise was launched on the campus of Tuskegee Institute—the Negro Yearbook Publishing Company. A partnership consisting of Robert E. Park, the famed white sociologist; Emmett J. Scott, secretary to Booker T. Washington; and Monroe N. Work, a sociology professor, this firm published the first edition of *The Negro Yearbook* in 1912. The most comprehensive reference book to appear to date on African Americans, *The Negro Yearbook* was highly regarded as the definitive work on statistics and facts on blacks worldwide. The enterprise experienced financial trouble in 1929. The Tuskegee Institute financed its operation until 1952. Between 1912 and 1952, *The Negro Yearbook* remained a classic model for most general reference works on blacks.

John W. Work's *The Negro and His Song* (1915) was the first book issued under the Fisk University Press imprint. During the 1930s and 1940s, when Charles Spurgeon Johnson chaired the university's department of sociology, Fisk University Press issued several important studies, including E. Franklin Frazier's *The Free Negro Family* (1932); *The Economic Status of the Negro* by Charles Spurgeon Johnson (1933); and *People versus Property* by Herman Long and Charles Spurgeon Johnson (1947). The last publication released by the Fisk University Press was *Build a Future: Addresses Marking the Inauguration of Charles Spurgeon Johnson* (1949).

Although the board of trustees of Howard University approved the establishment of a university press on February 17, 1919, no university press existed at the university until 1974. Nonetheless, between 1919 and 1974, several books bearing the "Howard University Press" imprint were published, including *The Founding of the School of Medicine of Howard University, 1868–1873* by Walter Dyson (1929); and *The Housing of Negroes in Washington, DC: A Study in Human Ecology* by William H. Jones (1929).

On April 8, 1974, the Howard University Press officially organized as a separate administrative unit within the university. It began with a staff of 12 professionals experienced in book publishing. Its mission remains to support the university by "providing leadership for America and the global community through the publication of noteworthy new scholarship that addresses the contributions, conditions, and concerns of African Americans, other people of African descent, and people of color around the world. The Press publishes a variety of perspectives and disciplines that advance and deepen knowledge in its areas of focus. These include, but are not limited to: political, economic, and social sciences; history; health; education; communications; fine arts; science and technology; literature; and drama.

The Howard University Press's inaugural list of 13 books included such titles as *A Poetic Equation: Conversations Between Nikki Giovanni and Margaret Walker* (1974) and *Saw the House in Half, a Novel* by Oliver Jackman (1974). Releases since 1999 included *Genocide in Rwanda: A Collective Memory* by Carol Pott and John A. Berry, *Mordecai: The Man and His Message, The Story of Mordecai Wyatt Johnson* by Richard I. McKinney, *Black Writers and Latin America Cross Cultural Affinities* by Richard Jackson, and *The Black Seminole Legacy and North American Politics, 1693–1845* by Bruce Edward Twyman. With hundreds of books in print, the Howard University Press—the only African American university press still in existence—continued to flourish as one of the most viable university presses in the country.

Cultural and Professional Organizations and Institutions

African American cultural and professional organizations and institutions have also developed publishing programs that include book publishing. The books published by these organizations document areas of African American history and depict various aspects of African American culture.

Founded in 1897 by the Reverend Alexander Crummell, nineteenth century African American scholar, clergyman, and missionary, the American Negro Academy quickly organized a publishing program that embraced book publishing. The Academy, whose membership included many of the foremost African American intellectuals of the day, released 21 occasional papers as pamphlets and monographs. The American Negro Academy ceased to exist in 1928.

The Association for the Study of Afro-American History and Literature—formerly Association for the Study of Negro Life and History—began its book publishing program in 1918. By 1940, the association had published 28 books. After that year, the book publishing activities of the association declined until 1950, when its founder Carter G. Woodson died and provided in his will for the transfer of the Associated Publishers, Inc. to the association.

Howard University philosophy professor Alain Locke organized the Associates of Negro Folk Education in Washington, DC, with a grant from the American Adult Education Association. The Associates published a series of seven books known as the Bronze Booklets from 1935 to 1940. Written by black scholars on various aspects of African American life and edited by Locke, some of the titles included: *A World View of Race* by Nobel laureate Ralph J. Bunche (1936); *The Negro and Economic Reconstruction* by T. Arnold Hill (1937); and *Negro Poetry and Drama* by Sterling Brown (1937).

Civil Rights, Social Welfare, and Political Organizations

In 1913, five years after its founding, the National Association for the Advancement of Colored People (NAACP) launched its publishing program with three books: *A Child's Story of Dunbar* by Julia L. Henderson; *Norris Wright Cuney* by Maude Cuney Hare; and *Hazel* by Mary White Ovington. In 1914, George Williamson Crawford's *Prince Hall and His Followers* appeared, and in 1919, *Thirty Years of Lynching in the United States, 1889–1918* was released. After 1919, the NAACP published few books, with the organization limiting its publishing to pamphlets, its annual reports, and *Crisis*, a bi-monthly magazine.

Crisis remains dedicated to discussing critical issues confronting people of color, American society, and the world. In addition, it highlights the historical and cultural achievements of these diverse peoples. Through essays, interviews, and in-depth reporting, writers explore past and present issues concerning race and its impact on educational, economic, political, social, moral, and ethical issues. Each issue is also highlighted with a special section, "The NAACP Today," which reports on the news and events of the organization on a local and national level.

In contrast, the National Urban League (NUL) has been a very active book publisher. The League first embarked on book publishing in 1927 when it published *Ebony and Topaz*, an anthology of Harlem Renaissance writers, poets, and artists edited by Charles Spurgeon Johnson. Through the years, NUL released numerous sociological and economic studies on the plight of African Americans, including *Negro Membership in Labor Unions* (1930), *Race, Fear and Housing in a Typical American Community* (1946), and *Power of the Ballot: A Handbook for Black Political Participation* (1973). In addition to these monographs, the organization began publishing *The State of Black America* in 1976. Newer works include *Crime and Justice in Black America* by Christopher E. Stone (1999); a special report entitled *The Impact of Social Security on Child Poverty* by Valerie A. Rawlston (2000); and *The*

Urban League's Assessment of the President's Education Plan (2001) by Hugh B. Price, NAACP President and CEO.

Although the publishing program of the Universal Negro Improvement Association and African Communities League focused on the publication of its newspaper *The Negro World*, this political organization—founded by famed black nationalist leader Marcus Garvey—also published two volumes of *The Philosophy and Opinions of Marcus Garvey*, which were compiled and edited by Amy Jacques-Garvey.

Commercial Publishers

Until the 1960s, most African American commercial book publishing enterprises were short-lived. Two exceptions to this phenomenon existed, however: Broadside Press in Detroit and Third World Press in Chicago. Established by Dudley Randall in 1965, Broadside Press, which remains active, published poetry by African American authors—many of whom became icons later in life—such as Gwendolyn Brooks, Margaret Danner, Robert Hayden, Langston Hughes, Leroi Jones (Amiri Baraka), Don L. Lee (Haki R. Madhubuti), Sonia Sanchez, Melvin Tolson, and Margaret Walker. Following in the footsteps of Randall, in 1967, Haki Madhubuti founded Third World Press. Third World Press is now the oldest continually-operating African American commercial book publisher in the United States. In 1969, Dempsey Travis founded Urban Research Press.

Over the years, African American publishers have learned that a sizable African American readership exists. Since 1970 several major African American publishers have emerged. In 1978, Black Classic Press was founded by librarian Paul Coates to publish obscure, but significant, works by and about people of African descent. In 1981, Open Hand Publishing Inc. was founded by Anna Johnson.

Inspired by the dearth of books for his courses, former Rutgers University African Studies instructor Kassahun Checole founded the Africa World Press in 1983 to publish material on the economic, political, and social development of Africa. By the end of the twentieth century, African World Press, which published nearly 60 titles annually, was the premier publisher of books on African, African American, Caribbean, and Latin American issues. Its sister company, Red Sea Press, established in 1985, was one of the largest distributors of material by and about people of African descent throughout the world.

Just Us Books, Inc., founded by writer Wade Hudson and graphic artist Cheryl Willis Hudson, publishes books and educational material for children that focus on the African American experience. The idea to start the company first came to Cheryl in 1976, when she was unable to find African American images to decorate her daughter's nursery. Just Us Books published its first book in 1988—an alphabet book featuring African American children posed to create the letters. The company had sales of $1.6 million in its 2002 fiscal year.

Newcomers to the publishing industry include: APU Publishing Group, which publishes non-fiction and special interest books, such as autobiography, entrepreneurship, sociology, economy, and educational works; Diaspora Press of America, which publishes African American Diasporic folktales, fiction, non-fiction, poetry, and children's stories; and Amber Books, which publishes self-help and career-guide books. Each was founded in the 1990s.

Independent African American-owned book stores have benefitted from a resurgence of African American authors and an abundance of titles, but major bookstore chains, which are white-owned, make competition stiff. Although African Americans' book buying grew from $181 million in 1990 to $296 million in 1995, with the decline in hardcover sales, publishers were more cautious about placing books with specialty stores for fear that a book would lose mainstream appeal.

With the increasing demand for African American-oriented books, especially those written by African Americans, two diverging opinions arose from the African American literary community. Some believed that the creation of imprints like Strivers Row (Villard/Random House), Amistad (HarperCollins), Harlem Moon (Random House), and Dafina Books (Kensington) diminished the opportunity to showcase different genres. Furthermore, this faction insisted that African American books published by major white companies were too formulaic. Others believed that the abundance of African American books allowed for all kinds of literature; thus, ultimately increasing the number of African American authors published each year. Although the two groups disagreed on the quality of African American literature being published, both agreed that the proliferation of African American writers and the subsequent successful sales of their titles were most important, especially if they retain long-term marketability.

Comic Book Publishers

In the 1990s, African American comics peaked in popularity. Once relegated to a form of children's entertainment, comic books found an audience with young adults in their twenties to thirties. In fact, in 1990, Cable News Network (CNN) noted that sales of multiracial comics had jumped 9 percent, thus accounting for 10 percent of all comic book sales. One reason for the growth among the African American adult readership is collectibility—since most African American series are short-lived, each issue has the potential to become a rarity. Another reason is the fact that African American comics now better reflect the cultural and artistic concerns of the African American community.

African American characters of yore, often grotesquely drawn by whites, were either sidekicks or afterthoughts—never the stars. For example, Ebony, an African American character, paraded around with white superhero, The Spirit, in the 1940s. Meanwhile, Captain America had Falcon, his black version of the Lone Ranger's Native American sidekick, Tonto. Other African American characters were portrayed as ignorant, uneducated, and inept at worst. Blatantly stereotypical, most were created and drawn by white males who did not know much about the reality of African Americans. Over the years, the status of African American comic book characters evolved in the same negative ways that whites' perceptions of blacks did. By the 1960s and 1970s, African Americans were depicted either as drug addicts or Uncle Toms.

True change did not occur until a few enterprising African Americans took matters into their own hands. By 1993, Africa Rising Comics, Afrocentric Books, Dark Zulu Lies, Omega 7 Comics, and UP Comics had created ANIA (the Swahili word for "serve and protect") Comics under the leadership of Eric Griffin. The group's goal was to become a major publishing force by pooling their talents. The mainstream comic book publishers responded by producing comic books that featured black characters to capitalize on the market that ANIA's creators started. Disbanding soon thereafter, ANIA's existence highlighted the growing line of nonwhite superheroes. Their titles included *Brotherman*, *Malcolm 10*, *Heru*, *Zwanna*, *Purge*, and *Ebony Warrior*.

In the mid-1990s, Big City Comics produced *Brotherman*, which revolved around a public defender who also fought crime as "the dictator of discipline." Omega 7 Inc., founded by Alonzo Washington, a former member of ANIA, is based in Kansas City, Kansas. As of 2002, it was the largest independent African American comic book publisher. Omega 7 Inc. introduced fans to *The Original Man*, a champion of morality and supporter and protector of African American women; *The Mighty Ace*, with an anti-drug, anti-gang, anti-violence message; and *Darkforce*, a revolutionary African American hero. Other characters include *Omega Man*, *Original Boy*, *Original Woman*, and *The Omega 7*. Washington develops each comic and writes the storylines.

UP Comics offered *Purge*, which detailed the trials and tribulations of a man whose sole goal was to rid his city of evil. *Lionheart*, from Prophesy Comics, also emphasized morality. In a unique twist, Castel Publications came up with *The Grammar Patrol*, multiethnic heros with a penchant for knowing the rules of speech and writing. Geared towards children, it showed that the medium could be educational as well as entertaining.

Most of these companies were completely African American, from the owners and artists to the storywriters and marketers. Mainstream publishers entered the fray when industry giant DC Comics began distributing Milestone Comics in 1991 as part of their new imprint Milestone Media, formerly an African American-owned, independent publisher run by Derek T. Dingle. With a broad, full-process color system at hand, the company made history as the first major publisher to back African American creators. Among their titles have been *Hardware*, *Blood Syndicate*, *Icon*, *Kobalt*, *Shadow Cabinet*, *Xombi*, and *Static*, the latter featuring a teen hero who also became an animated television program.

Although the desire to read comic books with African American characters and the number of new African American comic books continued to increase, only between 25 and 30 percent of comic book buyers are minorities. Since the demise of ANIA and many other African American independently owned publishers, it became difficult for African Americans to produce their own publications. The two major comic book publishers, DC Comics and Marvel Comics, have both created several or more African American comic book characters and are not usually open to purchasing outside characters unless they can own them outright. In addition, some of the more popular African American comic book characters have been created by whites, for example, *Spawn*, *Luke Cage*, *The Black Panther*, *The Falcon*, and *Blade* (the inspiration for the movies starring Wesley Snipes). Therefore, aspiring African American comic book artists have two options: they can find an independent publisher or self-publish. Since both are usually difficult, many artists opt to work on more established characters, like Superman, Spiderman, or Batman, to ensure their financial stability with the goal of eventually saving enough money to publish their own characters. Two notable exceptions are Alex Simmons, creator of *Blackjack* and P. Skylar Owens, creator of *Knightmare*, *Team Sexecutioner*, and *CyJax*.

◆ NEWSPAPER AND MAGAZINE PUBLISHERS

Newspapers

The African American press is heir to a great, largely-unheralded tradition. It began on March 16, 1827, with *Freedom's Journal*, the first African American newspaper. It was edited and published by Samuel Cornish and

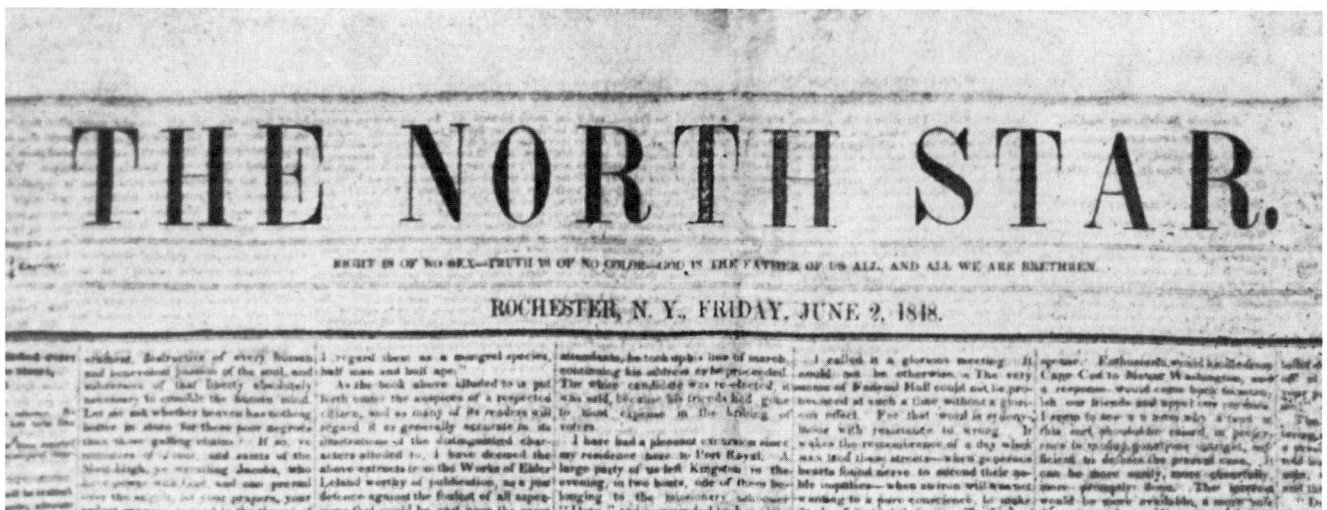

The North Star newspaper was founded by Frederick Douglass in 1847.

John B. Russwurm. *The North Star*, the newspaper of abolitionist Frederick Douglass, first appeared on December 3, 1847.

In the 1880s, African Americans' ability to establish a substantial cultural environment in many cities of the North led to the creation of a new wave of publications including the *Washington Bee, Indianapolis World, Philadelphia Tribune, Cleveland Gazette, Baltimore Afro-American*, and *New York Age*. By 1900, daily papers appeared in Norfolk, Kansas City, and Washington, DC.

Among famous African American newspaper editors were William Monroe Trotter, editor of the *Boston Guardian*, a self-styled "radical" paper that showed no sympathy for the conciliatory stance of Booker T. Washington; Robert S. Abbott, whose *Chicago Defender* pioneered the use of headlines; and T. Thomas Fortune of the *New York Age*, who championed free public schools in an age when many opposed the idea.

In 1940, there were more than 200 African American newspapers, mostly weeklies with local readerships, and about 120 African American magazines in circulation. The *Pittsburgh Courier*, a weekly, had readership of about 140,000 per issue, the largest at the time.

African Americans continue to gain influence as columnists, editorial page editors, assistant managing editors, and reporters on key beats. Although progress has been made in the newsroom, based on a 2002 report by the American Society of Newspaper Editors (ASNE), the prospects of African Americans assuming positions as managers are still low. Exceptions to this overwhelming reality include executive editors Ken Bunting at the *Seattle Post-Intelligencer*; Robert G. McGruder

at the *Detroit Free Press*, who died in 2002; Bennie Ivory at the *Courier-Journal* in Louisville, Kentucky; and Karla Garrett Harshaw at the *Springfield News Sun* in Ohio. The *Denver Post* became the largest U.S. newspaper (highest circulation daily) with an African American executive editor with the appointment of Gregory Moore, formerly the managing editor at the *Boston Globe*. Other African American editors include the managing editors at the *New York Times, Los Angeles Times, Detroit News, Philadelphia Inquirer, Lansing State Journal, Clarion-Ledger* in Jackson, Mississippi, *Press-Enterprise* in Riverside, California, and *News Journal* in Wilmington, Delaware.

The 2002 ASNE report also stated that nearly 2,000 journalists left the newspaper industry in 2001. Despite the loss, however, there was an increase in the percentage of minority journalists working at daily newspapers. This was heartening after a decrease from 11.85 percent to 11.64 percent in the 2001 survey, which was the first decline since ASNE established the annual census in 1978. As it stood in 2002, African Americans comprised approximately 5.29 percent of the staff in U.S. newsrooms.

"These numbers evoke a sigh of relief not exhilaration," said ASNE President Tim McGuire. "I am pleased we are back on the positive track since many people had made dire predictions that the economic downturn was especially harmful to journalists of color. It is obvious editors and publishers were sensitive to these issues when they made cutbacks," he continued. "But this modest increase should prove to us that when the industry starts to hire more journalists we must have programs in place to improve both hiring and retention."

Headquarters of the *Baltimore Afro-American* newspaper.

The lack of minority representation in the newsrooms of mainstream publications has not hindered the rise of the ethnic press, which steadily built circulation and advertising revenue. Traditionally, the survival of the ethnic press depended on classified advertising and advertisements from local auto repair stores, grocers, and travel agents. Some of the more established African American newspapers have always attracted some mainstream advertising, but publications that serve smaller and diverse communities have begun to receive many of the larger billings. Among the largest advertisers were telecommunications companies, airlines, financial services companies, and health care corporations.

The National Newspaper Publishers Association

The National Negro Newspaper Publishers Association was founded in 1940 to represent African American newspaper publishers. The organization scheduled workshops and trips abroad to acquaint editors and reporters with important news centers and news sources. A result was a trend to more progressive and interpretive reporting. In 1956, the association changed its name to the National Newspaper Publishers Association (NNPA),

but oftentimes is also referred to as the Black Press of America. In 1999, the association represented 148 publishers; by 2002 it represented more than 200.

In 2000, the NNPA launched NNPA Media Services—a print and Web advertising-placement and press release distribution service. Last year, in association with the NNPA Foundation, it began building the BlackPressUSA Network—the nation's premier network of local black community news and information portals. BlackPressUSA Network, anchored by BlackPressUSA.com, was the national Web portal for the Black Press of America. According to the association, NNPA Media Services was the gateway to more than 15 million readers with an estimated buying power of $572.1 billion.

The Amsterdam News

Founded in 1909 by James H. Anderson, the *Amsterdam News* became one of the most well-known African American newspapers in the nation. It was first published on December 4, 1909, in Anderson's home on 135 West 65th Street in New York City. At that time, it was one of only 50 African American "news sheets" in the country. The *Amsterdam News* had a staff of ten, consisted of six printed pages, and sold for two cents a copy. In 1935, the paper was sold to two African American physicians, Clilan B. Powell and Phillip M.H. Savory. In 1971, the paper was again sold to a group of investors, this time headed by Percy E. Sutton, Clarence B. Jones, and Wilbert A. Tatum.

During the mid-1970s the *Amsterdam News* took militant positions on civil rights issues, but by the end of the decade it began to focus more moderately on social issues. In 1979, the paper's format was changed from standard or broadsheet size to a tabloid. Following a second labor strike in 1983, the owner-publisher's mantel was assumed by Wilbert Tatum in 1984. Under Tatum's leadership, the paper gained a reputation as an intrepid African American voice on controversial local issues.

Over the course of the past 90 years, a litany of the best and brightest African American personages have written for the paper. They include T. Thomas Fortune, W. E. B. Du Bois, Adam Clayton Powell, Roy Wilkins, and Malcolm X. In 2002, Wilbert A. Tatums's daughter, Elinor, sat at the helm of the paper.

African American Newspapers in the 1990s

A number of newspapers that began publishing in the 1960s, 1970s, and 1980s have gone out of business, mainly due to their inability to attract advertising, both locally and nationally, and because of a general economic decline. In 2002, there were over 200 African American newspapers nationwide. Of these, the papers with the largest paid circulations include New York's *Black American*, the *Hartford Inquirer*, and the *Atlanta Voice*.

Magazines

As early as the 1830s, African American magazines were published in the United States, but the first truly successful magazines did not appear until the 1900s. In 1910, the NAACP began publishing *Crisis*. In November 1942, John H. Johnson launched *Negro Digest*, and in 1945 he published the first issue of *Ebony*. The idea for the new magazine came from two *Digest* writers, and Johnson's wife, Eunice, who contributed the magazine's name. Its first print run of 25,000 copies sold out immediately. The success of *Ebony* led to the demise of *Negro Digest*, and in 1951 the magazine ceased publication. *Ebony* had circulation in 2002 of almost 2 million.

In 1950, Johnson launched the magazine *Tan*, and in 1951 *Jet* magazine. Similar to *Ebony*, *Jet* was an instant success, selling more than 300,000 copies in its first

year. *Tan*, a woman's magazine, later became a show business and personality monthly called *Black Stars*.

Since the founding of *Ebony*, several new and specialized African American magazines have appeared. In 1967, *Black American Literature Review*, a journal presenting essays, interviews, poems, and book reviews, was founded. In the same year, Project Magazines Inc. began publishing *Black Careers*. In 1969, the Black World Foundation published the first edition of *The Black Scholar*.

In 1970, Earl G. Graves, a young businessman, embarked on a concept to publish a monthly digest of news, commentary, and informative articles for African Americans interested in business. Within a few short years, *Black Enterprise* was accepted as the authority on African Americans in business and as an important advocate for an active, socially-responsive, African American middle class. In 2002, it had a monthly subscription rate of 400,000, and a readership of over 3.1 million. *Essence*, a magazine directed at black women, has gained in circulation since its inception in 1970. Featuring health and beauty, fashion, and contemporary living sections, *Essence*, which is part of the Essence Communications Partner conglomerate, is considered one of the top women's magazines. As editor-in-chief for nearly 20 years, Susan L. Taylor was instrumental in the magazine's success. In 2002 the American Society of Magazine Editors voted Taylor into the Magazine Editors' Hall of Fame. Diane Weathers succeeded her as the editor-in-chief. *Essence* boasted a monthly circulation of more than 1 million in 2002, and a readership of 7.6 million, 29 percent of which was male.

In 1980, *Black Family*, a magazine promoting positive lifestyles for African Americans, was founded. In 1986, *American Visions: The Magazine of Afro-American Culture*, the official magazine of the African American Museums Association, was first published. In 1989, *Emerge*, a political magazine that covered hard news, current events, and culture from an African American perspective was introduced. Battling low circulation throughout its existence, it ceased publication in 2000, when Vanguarde Media, Inc. (VMI), a leading multicultural media company specializing in content aimed at, but not limited to, the urban audience, deemed it unprofitable. Vanguarde Media, Inc. was a division of BET Holdings, Inc., which was later sold to Viacom, Inc. VMI was not a part of the sale. *Emerge* was later replaced with *Savoy*, a lifestyle magazine.

In 2000, TV talk-show host and media mogul Oprah Winfrey successfully launched *O, The Oprah Magazine*. The choice for the name was finalized after a series of focus groups were conducted. The overall theme and message of the magazine was to lead women down a path of personal growth. The magazine also offered advice, delved into spirituality, highlighted beauty and fashion, and emphasized health and fitness.

Based on research conducted by a U.S. university, African American-owned magazines—such as *Heart & Soul, VIBE, American Legacy, Honey, Upscale*, and *Black Child*—continued to flourish in harsh economic times because most of their revenue came from subscriptions. Securing high-end advertising, however, remained a problem. Even though African American magazines have made significant progress in attracting automotive, tobacco, and liquor advertisements, whole categories such as fashion, travel, and technology were almost completely absent from their pages. With the increase of the African American middle class, advertising agencies believed that they could reach African Americans through mainstream advertising, in particular through television.

◆ BROADCASTING

Radio

African American radio can be divided into three general periods of historical development: blackface radio (1920–1941), black-appeal radio (1942–1969), and black-controlled radio (1970–). White performers who imitated black humor and music for a predominantly white listening audience was the trademark of blackface radio. During this period, African Americans were essentially outside of the commercial loop, both as radio entertainers and consumers. In the era of black-appeal radio, African Americans entered the industry as entertainers and consumers. The ownership and management of the African American-oriented stations, however, remained mostly in the hands of white businessmen. This situation impelled the development of independent African American radio stations. With the onset of the black-controlled radio era, African Americans began to own and operate their own radio stations, both commercial and public. Nevertheless, the percentage of African American-owned stations lagged far behind the percentage of African American listeners.

While early radio shows featured African American singing groups, they featured no African Americans talking. To Jack L. Cooper, this "was like taxation without representation," and so, on Sunday, November 3, 1929, at 5 P.M., Chicago's white-owned WSBC premiered "The All-Negro Hour" starring Cooper and friends. Born was the concept of African American radio, and Cooper went on to become the nation's first African American radio station executive, the first African American newscaster, the first African American sportscaster, and the first to use radio as a service medium.

Cooper wore many hats. He played second base for a semi-pro baseball team; he had been a singer, a buck-and-wing dancer, and an end man in a minstrel show; he fought 160 amateur boxing bouts; and he managed theaters. Between about 1910 and 1924, he worked as a journalist, writing for a number of African American newspapers including the *Freeman, Ledger*, and *Recorder* in Indianapolis; and the *Bluff City News* and *Western World Reporter* in Memphis. In 1924, he became the assistant theatrical editor of the *Chicago Defender*.

"The All-Negro Hour" was similar to a vaudeville revue on the air, featuring music, comedy, and serials. When it ended its run in 1935, Cooper continued with WSBC, pioneering the African American-radio format by producing several African American-oriented shows. Crucial to that format was local news and public affairs of interest to African Americans.

The first example of public service programming aired December 9, 1938, when Cooper launched the "Search for Missing Persons" show. Aimed at reuniting people who had lost contact with friends and relatives over time, it reportedly had reunited 20,000 people by 1950. According to *Ebony* magazine, Cooper also remodeled a van into a mobile unit to relay on-the-spot news events directly to four radio stations in the Chicago metropolitan area, including news flashes from the *Pittsburgh Courier* and interviews with famous personalities who came to town, such as boxer Joe Louis. Cooper also did play-by-play for African American baseball games from the van.

"Listen Chicago," a news discussion show that ran from 1946 to 1952, provided African Americans with their first opportunity to use radio as a public forum. Following Cooper's lead, between 1946 and 1955 the number of African American-oriented stations jumped from 24 to 600. News was a part of the explosion. "We have learned to do newscasts that answer the question, 'How is this news going to affect me as a Negro?,'" Leonard Walk of WHOD Pittsburgh said in 1954. "We have learned that church and social news deserve a unique place of importance in our daily Negro programming." Yet by and large, these broadcasters were not trained journalists. African American stations did not begin to broadcast news in the modern style until the 1960s.

In 1972, the Mutual Black Network was formed for news and sports syndication under the auspices of the Mutual Broadcasting Network. By the end of the 1970s, the Mutual Black Network had just over 100 affiliates and 6.2 million listeners. The Sheridan Broadcasting Corporation, an African American-owned broadcasting chain based in Pittsburgh, purchased the Mutual Black

Network in the late 1970s, renaming it the Sheridan Broadcasting Network. A second African American radio network, the National Black Network, was formed in 1973. In the 1980s, it averaged close to 100 affiliates and 4 million listeners. Among its regular features was commentary by journalist Roy Wood, which he named "One Black Man's Opinion," and Bob Law's "Night Talk." In January 1992, the American Urban Radio Network was formed, while the National Black Network has since gone out of business.

The networks were a mixed blessing. They provided their affiliates with broadcast-quality programs produced from an African American perspective. This relatively inexpensive access to news, sports, and public affairs features discouraged subscribing stations from producing their own local shows. News and public affairs staffs at the African American-oriented stations remained minimal. There were some notable exceptions, however, including New York's WLIB-AM, which had an African American format that included a highly acclaimed news and public affairs department. A series of shows produced by the station on disadvantaged youth in the city won two Peabody Awards in 1970.

In Washington, DC, the *Washington Post* donated its commercial FM radio license to Howard University in 1971. The new station, WHUR-FM, inaugurated "The Daily Drum," a full hour-long evening newscast that featured special coverage of the local African American community, as well as news from Africa and the Diaspora.

Two major formats have dominated African American-owned commercial radio since the 1970s: "talk" and "urban contemporary." Talk radio formats emerged on African American AM stations in the early 1970s and featured news, public affairs, and live listener call-in shows. By the same time, FM stations dominated the broadcasting of recorded music due to their superior reproduction of high fidelity and stereo signals. In 1972, Inner City Broadcasting initiated the move toward talk radio when it purchased WLIB-AM and the station became "Your Total Black News and Information Station," offering more news and public affairs programming than any other African American-formatted radio outlet in the country.

A pioneer in both "talk" and "urban contemporary" formats, Catherine Liggins Hughes (Cathy Hughes), the founder and owner of Radio One, Inc., owns the largest African American-owned and operated broadcast company in the United States. Radio One's 65 plus broadcast properties include stations in Philadelphia, Washington, DC, Baltimore, Atlanta, and Detroit. Radio One stations are recognized continually for their active community involvement, which is Hughes's trademark.

In 1971, Hughes became a lecturer at Howard University's School of Communication under the direction of Tony Brown. She was instrumental in creating a curriculum that would be accredited by academic associations around the world. In 1973, she began her transition into radio as general sales manager at WHUR-FM, eventually becoming vice president and general manager. Her skills in sales and marketing strategies turned the station into the university's first profit venue in its 100-year history, increasing the station's revenue from $250,000 to $3 million in her first year. In 1975, she developed the now widely-imitated format known as the "Quiet Storm." She purchased her first station, WOL-AM, in Washington, DC, in 1980.

Since the 1970s, the number of African Americans who have entered the public broadcasting arena has increased. In 1990, there were 32 public FM stations owned and operated by African American colleges around the country and another 12 owned by African American community boards of directors. These stations are not subject to the pervasive ratings pressures of commercial radio, thus giving them more latitude in programming news, public affairs, talk, and unusual cultural features. As a result, the growth of African American public radio has expanded the variety and diversity of African American programming now found on the airways, while also increasing the number of African Americans working in radio.

Television

Until the late 1960s, most serious African American journalists were in print journalism rather than in broadcasting. An exception was Lionel Monagas who worked in the early 1950s as a director of CBS-TV network programs, such as *Person to Person* and *Face the Nation*. He had started out as a traffic typist with the CBS affiliate in Washington, DC. In 1956, Monagas became the first African American professional at public station Channel 35 in Philadelphia, later known as WHYY-TV. At WHYY he produced several children's programs including a ten-part series on *The History of the Negro*, narrated by Ossie Davis.

Mal Goode became the first African American network TV reporter in 1962 at ABC-TV. Goode reported that baseball pioneer Jackie Robinson complained to James Hagerty, an ABC vice president hired to set up a competitive news department, that the only two black people he had seen at ABC were "a lady with a white uniform in the lobby dusting and a Negro doorman. [Hagerty's] face got red, and he said we intend to do something about that." Goode was a reporter for the *Pittsburgh Courier* at the time, but in 1949 Pittsburgh's

Mal Goode became the first African American network TV reporter in 1962.

KQV Radio had given the newspaper two 15-minute slots to fill on Tuesday and Wednesday nights. Goode read the news on the program. According to Goode, ABC chose him for the job after spending half a year interviewing 38 African American male candidates. One reason he was chosen, he said, was that he was dark enough to appeal to an African American audience, but light enough so that whites would not feel threatened. Goode went on to work for ABC for 11 years. He was its United Nations correspondent and covered the Cuban missile crisis, the aftermath of Martin Luther King Jr.'s assassination, and the Poor People's March on Washington.

Jobs similar to Goode's were hard to find. In his memoir, *Black Is the Color of My TV Tube,* Emmy-winner Gil Noble of New York's WABC-TV recalled being at WLIB-AM radio during this era: "We would sit in the newsroom and fantasize about earning $300 a week, but few of our number worked at that level. Pat Connell, a former disc jockey at Newark's WNJR, known as 'Pat the Cat,' was anchoring the CBS morning newscast. Mal Goode was reporting for ABC-TV news, as well as for the local station WABC. NBC didn't have any blacks at that time, as far as I can recall, and in the mid-1960s, WNEW-TV had none, nor did WPIX-TV or WOR-TV have any." When Noble went downtown to audition for a major radio station job, he would intone in the ultimate radio voice—"a [Walter] Cronkite delivery that outdid the original"—only to get the familiar brushoff, "Thanks very much. You're fine, but we already have a Negro on staff."

Inside Bedford-Stuyvesant was an innovative show in New York City. Albeit short-lived—on the air from 1968–1970—it was the city's first program written, produced, and presented by African Americans at a time when African Americans were largely unseen on television, except for news footage about protests, riots, or crime. *Inside Bedford-Stuyvesant* offered a unique look into an ignored African American neighborhood and, to a degree, African Americans. In 52 half-hour programs, it was filmed throughout the Bed-Stuy neighborhood, often outdoors. Attracting such major celebrities as singer/actor Harry Belafonte and musician Max Roach, the show mostly revolved around the ordinary people in the neighborhood.

Film scholars and social historians consider *Inside Bedford-Stuyvesant* a rare video time capsule, perhaps the only one of its kind, documenting an African American community. Its creator, Charles Hobson, announced the debut of the show two months after the federal government's Kerner Commission issued a report on race relations, criticizing the media for failing to adequately cover African American communities.

A few African Americans made it onto the white-controlled airwaves. William C. Matney Jr., who had been managing editor of the *Michigan Chronicle,* an African American community paper, and a reporter for the *Detroit News* in 1963, became a TV and radio reporter for WMAQ-TV, the NBC-owned station in Chicago. He joined NBC-TV news in 1966. Veteran newswoman Norma Quarles was hired as a trainee at NBC News in 1966, moving a year later to the NBC station in Cleveland as a reporter and anchor, and ultimately to CNN. Lem Tucker, who died in March 1991, joined NBC News as a copy boy in 1965 and moved up to assistant bureau chief in Vietnam.

In 1967, a self-described "teacher moonlighting as a jazz disc jockey"—who also called play-by-play for basketball games and read the news—applied for a job at soon-to-be all-news WCBS radio in New York. Ed Bradley, who would later co-host CBS-TV's most successful news show *60 Minutes,* impressed a news director by refusing to write copy and record it because, he explained, "You won't learn enough about me that way." Instead, he borrowed a tape recorder, went out on the street, did an update of a story about an anti-poverty program, and got the job. In Portsmouth, Virginia, however, an audacious 25-year-old newscaster named Max Robinson was fired from a UHF station after he broke the rules by showing his face on camera. It was 1964, and only the word "News" was to appear on the screen. White viewers were enraged to see one of "those people" working in the studio. According to news director James Snyder, in 1971 Robinson became the first African American anchor in a major market, at WTOP-TV in Washington, DC. Robinson later became ABC-TV's first African American regular co-anchor.

It took the riots of the 1960s and a stern warning from a federal commission for the broadcast industry to undertake any concentrated hiring of African Americans. When American cities began to burn, African Americans held about 3.6 percent of TV news jobs. White news directors had to scramble to find African American journalists to cover the riots. In 1968, the National Advisory Commission on Civil Disorders, also known as the Kerner Commission, concluded that "the world that television and newspapers offer to their black audience is almost totally white, in both appearance and attitude." "Within a year," wrote Noble, "many of us found ourselves working downtown at major radio and TV stations."

In June 1969, the Federal Communications Commission (FCC) adopted rules prohibiting discrimination in broadcast industry employment and required stations to file annual reports showing the racial makeup of their workforce by job category. African American public affairs shows, such as Noble's *Like It Is*, *Black Journal* hosted by Tony Brown, and Philadelphia's *Black Perspectives on the News*, aired in nearly every city with a substantial African American population. Still, by the time Mal Goode retired in 1973, there were only seven African American reporters at the three networks.

In the 1990s, African Americans began breaking into broadcast management and ownership, yet the numbers remained small. TV general managers included Charlotte Moore English of KSHB-TV, Kansas City; Marcellus Alexander of WJZ-TV, Baltimore; Eugene Lothery of WCAU-TV, Philadelphia; Clarence McKee, CEO and chairman of WTVT-TV, Tampa, Florida; and Dorothy Brunson, owner of a small UHF station, WGTW-TV, Philadelphia.

Ronald Townsend, president of the Gannett Television Group, comprising ten stations, chaired the National Association of Broadcasters' TV board. Jonathan Rodgers became president of the CBS Television Stations Division in August 1990, making him network television's highest-ranking African American news executive. Bryant Gumbel, past co-host of NBC-TV's *Today*,

CBS News correspondent Ed Bradley, and talk show host Oprah Winfrey became three of the highest-paid and most recognized faces on television. ABC-TV's Carole Simpson became a substitute and weekend network TV anchor. African Americans anchored local newscasts in markets around the country.

Another African American-owned broadcasting company that has made great strides in the industry is Granite Broadcasting Corporation. Operating in geographically diverse markets that reach more than 6 percent of the nation's television households, the company's station portfolio consisted of three NBC affiliates, two ABC affiliates, one CBS affiliate, and two major market WB affiliates. Granite is also recognized as an innovator in the development of new media services that combine television broadcasting and Internet platforms.

Still, African Americans, while 12 percent of the population in the 1990 census, represented only 9.8 percent of the television news workforce and 5 percent of the radio workforce. They held 4 percent of the news director positions at commercial TV stations and about 5 percent at commercial radio stations. Those heading news operations included Gary Wordlaw at WJLA-TV in Washington, DC, and Will Wright at WWOR-TV in New York. According to an annual survey by the Center for Media and Public Affairs, most of the news on nightly network television shows continued to be presented by white males. African Americans accounted for only 5 percent of all field reports and anchor stories combined, its 1991 survey found. The most visible African American correspondent was George Strait, ABC-TV health reporter, who tied for 57th in the number of stories filed. Carole Simpson was in sixth place, based on the number of brief news reports read.

In 2001, the Center for Media and Public Affairs diversity survey reported that the proportion of stories covered by minorities fell from 14 percent in 1999 to 11 percent in 2000, a decline of 21 percent. In addition, minorities covered only 8 percent of ABC's stories, their lowest level of representation since 1992; only 14 percent at NBC; and a slightly better 15 percent at CBS. Furthermore, the study noted that the dominance of white males in newscasts continued with only three minority correspondents appearing among the top ten reporters, the most in CMPA's 11 years of tracking. Jim Avila (NBC) ranked 6th on the list of most often-featured correspondents, with Bill Whitaker (CBS) and Byron Pitts (CBS) ranking 7th and 10th, respectively. Only one other minority—ABC's Ron Claiborne ranking 41st—was among the top 50 correspondents. According to CMPA President Dr. Robert Lichter, "Despite the networks' recent commitment to diversity in prime-time entertainment, this attitude has apparently not reached their news bureaus."

The number of African American television and radio owners has decreased because of the consolidation frenzy in the broadcasting industry compounded by the elimination of a federal tax credit that favored minority groups. According to a 1995 survey, of the 1,221 television stations, members of minority groups owned 37; of the 10,191 radio stations, 293 were minority owned. Although the numbers are small, they reflect a significant increase since 1978. That same year, the Federal Communications Commission agreed to grant tax credits to radio and television station owners who sold their properties to minority buyers. The objective of the tax credits benefit was to broaden broadcast ownership and promote more diverse viewpoints. The result effectively lowered the acquisition costs of a television or radio station for a minority.

One benefactor of the tax credit was Ragan A. Henry, an African American lawyer and founder of U.S. Radio. He used the tax break to assemble what had been the largest African American-owned radio group in the nation by 1996 with 25 stations. In 1996, Henry sold U.S. Radio for $140 million to Clear Channel Communications of San Antonio. His financial backers were unwilling to put up more money to buy increasingly expensive stations. It was expected that minority owners would continue to sell their broadcast holdings to white-owned companies as station prices escalated.

Refusing to follow the trend of selling to larger white-owned entities, Ross Love, founder of Blue Chip Broadcasting Ltd., which was established in 1995 in Cincinnati, Ohio, became a part of the Radio One family in 2001. At the time of acquisition, Blue Chip Broadcasting had 15 radio stations in 5 markets—Cincinnati, Columbus, and Dayton, Ohio; Louisville, Kentucky; and Minneapolis, Minnesota. The radio stations owned by Blue Chip in Lexington, Kentucky were sold separately to another party. Additionally, Radio One agreed to operate WDBZ-AM, a Blue Chip urban talk station located in Cincinnati, under a local marketing agreement. Ownership of WDBZ was supposed to transfer to a new company owned principally by Ross Love, Blue Chip's founder and chief executive. In conjunction with this acquisition, Ross Love was nominated to serve on Radio One's board of directors. In the press release announcing Radio One's purchase of Blue Chip Broadcasting, Love expressed his belief that the acquisition would benefit the business's employees and investors by expanding into new markets. Love added, "We share a core expertise in the Urban lifestyle formats and we share a commitment to bettering the communities which we serve."

The tax credit was eliminated in 1995 when Congress swept aside affirmative action policies. The program came under attack because of its use by Viacom to escape $600 million in taxes in a proposed sale of its cable television properties. Viacom had arranged to sell its cable systems to an African American entrepreneur whose company received financial backing from Tele-Communications Inc., the nation's largest cable operator. Since the elimination of the tax credit, the number of minority-owned stations declined slightly.

Although no longer required to adhere to the affirmative action guidelines established by the FCC, the four major networks and several of the largest owners of radio stations have agreed to continue to follow them in their outreach and recruitment efforts. The demise of the affirmative action guidelines came about when it was declared unconstitutional—naysayers believed it would lead to quotas—by a federal court in the spring of 1998.

The list of companies that agreed to continue following the affirmative action guidelines set by the FCC include ABC, CBS, NBC, the Fox network, Time Warner Inc.—which includes CNN, the Tribune Company, and Clear Channel Communications, Inc., the owner of 183 radio stations and 18 television stations. Cox Communications, the Cablevision Systems Corporation, the TCI Group, and Comcast Corporation—all cable outlets—have also agreed. According to BIA, a company that monitors revenues in broadcasting, all of these companies earn roughly one-third of the annual advertising revenue in the broadcast industry.

Radio and Television Advertising

A study conducted in the late 1990s by the U.S. broadcast regulators found that advertisers discriminate against minority-owned radio and television stations or stations that target African American audiences. Furthermore, a recent FCC-sponsored report determined that minority stations earned an estimated 63 percent less in advertising revenue per listener than similar non-minority stations. Many advertisers believed that they could reach African American listeners by sticking to mainstream radio.

It is a general belief that the lack of advertising dollars allocated to African American-formatted stations is due to the lack of minority representation at advertising firms. To remedy this situation, many advertising firms have stepped up their recruitment of minorities. In 1998, minority professionals comprised 11 percent of employees at the nation's 25 leading advertising agencies, up from 7.6 percent in 1995.

Public Television

Begun in the early 1950s, public television failed to realize the hopes of many African Americans for most of its short history. Tony Brown's *Black Journal*, later *Tony Brown's Journal*, was well-received by African American viewers as the only national African American public affairs series on television, but it was constantly threatened with cancellation. After complaints about its anti-administration attitude, the show stayed on the air after it secured underwriting from Pepsi Cola. In its 29th season as of 2002, *Tony Brown's Journal* continued to provide commentary, timely documentaries, and issues of special interest to the African American community.

In 1975, the only African American FCC commissioner, Benjamin Hooks, joined the critics accusing public broadcasters of "arrogance" and of concentrating their efforts on cultured, white cosmopolitans. A 1975 review of public broadcasting stations showed that 108 of 184 public radio licensees (59%) and 52 of the 160 public television licensees (33%) had no minority staff in the top three job categories (officials, managers, and professionals).

In the early 1990s, the highest-ranking African Americans in public television were Jennifer Lawson, who joined PBS in November 1989 as its first executive vice president for national programming and promotion services; Donald L. Marbury, director of the Television Program Fund of the Corporation for Public Broadcasting; and George L. Miles Jr., executive vice president and chief operating officer of WNET-TV New York. Lawson obtained and commissioned the programs that PBS provided to its member stations as well as the promotion of those programs. Marbury managed the $45 million television program fund, which furnished financial support for major series in public television, such as *Frontline*.

The most visible African American journalist on public television has been Charlayne Hunter-Gault, former national correspondent for the *NewsHour with Jim Lehrer*, formerly the *MacNeil/Lehrer NewsHour*. A former *New York Times* reporter noted for her in-depth reporting, Hunter worked for PBS from 1977 to 1997, for NPR from 1997 to 1999, and since 1999 as the Johannesburg (South Africa) Bureau Chief and correspondent for CNN. As of 2002, other African American journalists on television were: Kwame Holman, a Washington correspondent, and Gwen Ifill, senior correspondent and host of *Washington Week*, both on the *NewsHour with Jim Lehrer*; the host of *Life 360*, Michel Martin, a correspondent on ABC News Nightline; and Karen Gibbs, co-host of *Wall $treet Week with FORTUNE*.

Charlayne Hunter-Gault, one of the few African American TV news national correspondents.

One of the most acclaimed pieces of African American journalism on PBS was *Eyes on the Prize*, a history of the civil rights movement produced by Henry Hampton, which aired in 1987, with a sequel in 1990. The network's most controversial production was a one-hour film on African American homosexual men, *Tongues Untied*, by filmmaker Marlon Riggs in 1991. In 2002, *A Huey P. Newton Story*, which was based on the life of assassinated co-founder of the Black Panther Party and produced by Spike Lee, won the George Foster Peabody Award. Produced by Avon Kirkland, *Ralph Ellison: An American Journey* explored the life and work of the influential author whose landmark novel, *Invisible Man*, won him a lifetime of awards and honors; it was nominated for a Literacy In Media Award.

Other programs of note produced by African Americans on PBS between 2000 and 2002, included: *Africa, A Special Presentation Of Nature*, which was the first television series to explore the African continent through the eyes of Africans; *Great Performances—Free To Dance*, which chronicled the crucial role that African American dancers and choreographers played in the development of modern dance as an American art form; and *American Experience—Marcus Garvey*, a program that examined the rise, fall, and global influence of the African American leader.

In 1980, Howard University launched WHMM-TV, becoming the first licensee of a public TV station on an African American campus and the only African American-owned public television station in the nation. On August 31, 1991, San Francisco's Minority Television Project went on the air with KMTP-TV, which became the nation's second African American-owned public television station. One of the principals was Adam Clayton Powell III, son of the late Harlem congressman, Adam Clayton Powell Jr.

Public Radio

Before 1967, there were only two African American educational outlets in the country; by 1990 there were 40 African American public radio stations. Many of them were community radio stations, owned and operated by nonprofit foundations, controlled by a local board of directors, and dependent on listener donations. Others were on college campuses. One of the most successful was WPFW-FM, a 50,000-watt outlet launched in 1977 by the Pacifica Foundation.

Stations such as WCLK-FM at Clark Atlanta University in Atlanta, WBVA-FM in Harrodsburg, Kentucky, and WVAS-FM at Alabama State University in Montgomery, tailored news and public affairs programming to their local African American audiences. WVAS was used as a broadcast journalism lab by students majoring in the field. In the 1990s, on National Public Radio, African American journalists Phyllis Crockett, Vertamae Grosvenor, Cheryl Duvall, and Brenda Wilson won awards for reports on South Africa and issues involving African Americans. Although Crockett and Duvall are no longer with NPR, two new African American journalists, Cheryl Corley and Phillip Davis, have joined the station. Corley's honors include a Chicago Association of Black Journalists award in 2000 for Excellence in Radio (news) and several in 2001, for news, documentary feature, and sports; a Peabody Award as part of the NPR team covering the September 11 attacks; and the Distinguished Service Award (2002) from the American Psychiatric Association Alliance. The National Association of Black Journalists conferred its Award in Excellence to NPR's team coverage of the "UN Conference on Racism," to which Cheryl Corley and Phillip Martin—NPR's former Race Relations Reporter—were a part.

Cable Television

The 1980s saw the explosion of cable television and the decline of television networks. Black Entertainment Television (BET), founded by former congressional aide Robert L. Johnson, made its debut in 1980 and established a news division by the end of the decade. That division produced a weekly news show *BET News* and *Lead Story*, a talk-show featuring African American pundits. In 2000, however, the African American community lost control of one of its largest communications companies when BET became a new property of Viacom Inc., an internationally respected media giant. Johnson drew $1.6 billion out of the package, becoming the first African American billionaire.

In a $3 billion deal, Viacom purchased the BET brand—the core cable channel, BET on Jazz and BET International. For the first time in 20 years, BET's development in these areas will not be controlled by African Americans. Viacom also purchased BET.com and BET's Arabesque Books, the publishing division. The magazine arm, BET's Movies/Starz, BET's Soundstage, jazz club, and other restaurants were not part of the deal. Notably, the company had turned its daily operations of its leading magazines, *EMERGE* and *BET Weekend* over to new partner, Vanguarde Media Inc., owned by former *VIBE* publisher Keith Clinkscales. Clinkscales discontinued both magazines.

The biggest development in cable journalism, however, was the spectacular growth of Ted Turner's Cable News Network (CNN), which went on the air in June 1980. By the time of the 1991 war in the Persian Gulf, CNN had established itself as the station to watch in a crisis. Transmitted across the globe, it became a medium for world leaders to communicate with one another. Until the launching of MSNBC in 1996, CNN had no competition. MSNBC, a massive joint venture between the NBC television network and Microsoft Corporation, was the only service of its kind, combining TV, cable, and the Internet. This news empire claimed an immediate reach of over 25 million households.

Veteran journalist Bernard Shaw, principal Washington anchor, was one of three CNN reporters who captivated the world's audiences with their continuous coverage of the bombing of Baghdad on January 16, 1991, the first night of Operation Desert Storm. Shaw concluded his career as a full-time CNN anchor on *Inside Politics* in 2001. Other African Americans who have worked at CNN include Jay Suber, vice president and executive producer, news features, CNN Newsroom; Graylian Young, Southeast bureau chief;

Robert Johnson of BET Holdings announces the launch of an African American Web site with support from the NAACP and the UNCF.

CNN anchors Andrea Arceneaux, Leon Harris, and Joe Oliver; Cassandra Henderson, anchor for CNN Newsroom; Lyn Vaughn and Gordon Graham, Headline News anchors; and sports anchor Fred Hickman. Correspondent Norma Quarles has been with CNN since 1988. She joined the station after serving 21 years with NBC News and its affiliates.

◆ AFRICAN AMERICAN MEDIA IN CYBERSPACE

African Americans were cruising the information superhighway—a vast electronic communications network comprised of telephones, computers, and televisions—in growing numbers during the late 1990s. An increasing number of African Americans—5.6 million, according to a 1999 Nielsen-CommerceNet study—were using the Internet at home, work, school, and at libraries. This represented an increase of more than 50 percent from 1998. Two years later, Forrester Research, a technology research firm based in Cambridge, Massachusetts, indicated that the popularity of the Internet had not waned within the African American community. More specifically, at that time, approximately 12 million African Americans used the Internet with an

estimated 1 million more expected to go on line each year. Furthermore, this study stated that African American households were getting wired and going online at a faster rate than the country as a whole. Therefore, it was little surprise that an African American was one of the key spokespeople for cyberspace-related equity issues.

Branded "The Net's Conscience," Larry Irving was director of the National Telecommunications and Information Administration. Far from being the only person of color with clout on the Net, though, Irving was one of many experts working in the burgeoning industry to provide access to a wide array of information for educational, business, and entertainment purposes. Other high-ranking African Americans included Andrew C. Barrett, the only black commissioner of the Federal Communications Commission (FCC); Ray Winbush, director of the Bishop Joseph Johnson Black Cultural Center at Vanderbilt University—a network linking black colleges, students, and professors; Jimmy Davies, who partnered with Apple Computer to establish a national electronic bulletin board service for blacks called the African American Information Network; Eugene and Phyllis Tucker Vinson Jackson, founders of the World African Network, a 24-hour, pay cable television network for blacks; and Cleo Manago, founder of the Black Men's Xchange, an Afrocentric national communications clearinghouse.

The World Wide Web comprises a major component of the "highway." Many African American news-oriented Web sites are mentioned below, as well as in the newspaper, magazine, and journal listings in this chapter. Some of the most popular African American Web sites offering information on the various subjects covered in this reference work, can be found in the Bibliography in the back of the book.

www.aawc.com (African American Web Connection)

A gateway to Afrocentric Web sources for the African American community. Topics include art & poetry, black authors, businesses, churches, entertainment, history, organizations, resources in Africa, and publications.

www.abouttimemag.com

Online version of *About Time* magazine. It includes selected full-text articles from recent issues, with archives planned as far back as 1994.

www.Africana.com

Covers African and African American history, current and past politics, music, books, movies, and education on a worldwide scale.

www.Afronet.com

A Web portal for information about the African and African American experience. Topics include legal services, entertainment, health, sports, trading, beauty, and business.

www.Afro-Pages.com

A Web portal for information on African American art, poetry, history, genealogy, and business. Other categories include jobs, auctions, books, music, forums, and videos.

www.BET.com

Online version of the cable station, Black Entertainment Television. Areas of interest include news, music, entertainment, books, food, health, and much more. Highlights about the company and its televised programs are also featured.

www.BlackAmericaWeb.com

A Tom Joyner promoted Web portal targeting African Americans. It features news, business, careers, books, technology, health & fitness, travel, sports, entertainment, and entrepreneur opportunities.

www.black-collegian.com

Online version *Black Collegian*, a national career opportunities magazine. It focuses on education and career information for African American students, as well as providing commentary by leading African American writers, lifestyle and entertainment features, general information on college life, and news on college campuses.

www.blackenterprise.com

Online version of *Black Enterprise*. It offers information about entrepreneurship, technology, personal finance, and other minority business issues.

www.blackfacts.com

An online searchable database for African American history facts.

www.blackhistorypages.com

Provides a wealth of information on a wide variety of topics about people of African descent. With links to other Web sites, topics include Black Indians, civil rights, education, entertainment, genealogy, inventors, lynching, and much more.

www.blackmind.com

Features history, culture, politics, philosophy, and economics all from an African American perspective. Specific topics include shopping, travel, health, insurance, fitness, home, and sports.

www.blackpgs.com (Internet Black Pages)

A listing of African American businesses, churches, schools, organizations, and events in black communities around the world.

www.BlackPlanet.com

Enables African Americans to cultivate meaningful personal and professional relationships, stay informed about the world, and gain access to goods and services that will allow them to do more in life.

www.BlackPressUSA.com

The only national Web site featuring news exclusively from African American journalists and community publications.

www.blackquest.com

An African American history resource established by C. Arthur Blair, the creator of the game, *Black Quest—The Griot*, an educational and heritage game that introduces and reinforces the experiences, achievements, and contributions of African Americans.

www.blacktalk.com

Offers online discussion of numerous topics open to all people.

www.BlackVoices.com

Features a variety of topics, most of them geared toward the African American community, such as national and world news, sports, arts & entertainment, business, health, travel, and an automotive section. Other areas of interest include a career center, chat rooms, and message boards.

www.BlackWebPortal.com

A Web portal to find black businesses, Web sites, and events. It also features discussion boards, chat rooms, weather, and eCommerce.

www.blackworld.com

Provides information on a myriad of topics (business & economy, real estate, society & culture, government, health, travel & tourism, education, recreation, sports, etc.) from places around the world with people of African descent (Africa, the Carribbean, France, and the United Kingdom). General topics of interest such as the lottery, horoscopes, soap opera updates, art, music, car rental, and airline reservations are also included.

www.ebony.com

Online version of *Ebony* magazine. Offers an abbreviated version of the articles and features in the current issue only.

www.essence.com

Online version *Essence* magazine. Targeted toward African American women, topics range from relationships to beauty & style to wellness to food to finance.

The site also features ESSENCE by Mail, ESSENCE at the Mall and ESSENCE Gifts.

www.EverythingBlack.com

An Internet directory and search engine of Web sites specifically targeted to African Americans and persons of African descent worldwide.

www.heartandsoul.com

Online version of *Heart and Soul*, a healthy lifestyle magazine. It features beauty, video, music, and much more.

www.honeymag.com

Online version of *Honey* magazine. It features entertainment news, beauty, fashion, and lifestyle issues aimed at young urban women.

www.jetmag.com

Online version of *Jet* magazine. It features selected stories from the current issue, as well as information on black history, beauty, and movies.

www.MelaNet.com (The Uncut Black Experience)

Dedicated to the intellectual, economic, and spiritual expression of peoples throughout the African Diaspora.

heather.cs.ucdavis.edu/pub/README.html (Minority Affairs Forum)

Created by Professor Norman Matloff in the Department of Computer Science at the University of California at Davis, this site contains articles on minority related topics including immigration, affirmative action, bilingual education, and race relations.

www.montelshow.com

Online version of the *Montel Williams Show*. It features the schedule for upcoming shows and highlights from past shows. There is also an opportunity to learn more about the host, to search for topics of special interest, to submit show ideas, and to pose questions to the show's resident expert.

www.netnoir.com

Under reconstruction as of August 2002. One of the first African American Web sites. Topics of interest include folks & culture, news & information, entertainment, business, education, music, politics, and online shopping.

www.newsavanna.com

Known as the "gravity discussion zone," African Americans can discuss issues relevant to their culture, including race, politics, religion, and entertainment.

www.niaonline.com

One of the premier Internet destinations for African American women. Topics include world news, parenting, health, money, relationships and careers. Top African American opinion-makers and well-known columnists like Jill Nelson, Jewel Diamond Taylor and Harriette Cole also serve as contributors of information.

www.Oprah.com

Online version of the *Oprah Winfrey Show*. It also features information on *O, The Oprah Magazine*, "Oprah's Angel Network," and "Oprah's Book Club," as well as a wide range of other topics of interest to women.

www.savoymag.com

Online version of *Savoy* magazine. It provides cultural news and lifestyle information for African American adults.

www.SeeingBlack.com

Portal focusing on "black opinion, reviews and voice." It provides current articles on film, the visual arts, politics, media and music reviews, as well as chat rooms, subscription services, and a commercial store with specialty merchandise.

www.SOHH.com (Search online Hip-Hop)

Geared towards the hip-hop music industry. Also features entertainment, lifestyle, sports, travel, health & fitness, and technology.

www.soulofamerica.com

The doorway to Afrocentric treasures throughout the nation. Areas of interest include the arts, cultural sites, churches, historic sites, black-owned restaurants, nightclubs, radio stations, and shopping.

www.tavistalks.com

Features all things related to Tavis Smiley, former host of *BET Tonight with Tavis Smiley*, political commentator for the nationally syndicated *Tom Joyner Morning Show* (ABC Radio Networks) and host of *Tavis Talks* on NPR (National Public Radio).

www.tbwt.com (The Black World Today)

Information compiled by journalists, writers, artists, communicators, and entrepreneurs who have banded together to use the information revolution as one means toward the overall empowerment of Black people in the United States and around the world.

www.theconduit.com

Online version of "The Conduit Newsletter," a technological publication targeted towards people of African descent. It provides information about the vast undertakings of African Americans in the world of technology.

www.tjms.com

Online version of the *Tom Joyner Morning Show*, which is aired in over 100 U.S. markets. It features segments from the show, as well as news, entertainment, weather, health, and education.

www.topblacksites.com

Provides a list of the most highly trafficked African American Web sites.

www.upscalemagazine.com

Online version of *Upscale* magazine. Areas of interest include style & beauty, entertainment & arts, and travel & living. Highlights from the current issue and a career corner are also available.

www.vibe.com

Online version of *VIBE* magazine. Loaded with graphics, advertisements, illustrations, and articles on youth-oriented music and culture.

◆ PUBLISHING, RADIO, AND TELEVISION PROFESSIONALS

(To locate biographical profiles more readily, please consult the index at the back of the book.)

Robert S. Abbott (1870–1940)
Newspaper Publisher

A native of St. Simons Island, Georgia, Abbott studied at Beach Institute in Savannah, and later completed

Robert S. Abbott, first publisher of the Chicago *Defender*.

his undergraduate work at Claflin College in Orangeburg, South Carolina. Migrating to Chicago, he attended Kent Law School and took a job in a printing house until he completed his law studies in 1899.

Abbott returned to Chicago and published the first edition of the *Defender* on May 5, 1905, which he initially sold on a door-to-door basis. After Abbott's death, the *Defender* was handed over to his nephew, John H. Sengstacke, who introduced a daily edition of the paper in 1956.

William Banks (1903–1985)
Broadcasting Executive, Attorney, Minister

Born in Geneva, Kentucky, in 1903, William Banks relocated to Detroit as a young man and, after earning a law degree, became a Baptist minister during his forties. Long active in numerous African American community organizations in the city, Banks founded the International Free and Accepted Masons and Eastern Star in 1950 and, under his guidance, the growing group soon became a financially-sound and charity-driven fraternal organization. He continued to work as an attorney in private practice until well past the age of retirement.

In 1964, the Black Masons made their first venture into media ownership with a Detroit FM radio outlet that mixed R&B music and religious broadcasting. Banks's business savvy helped make the station a financial success in the same way that the Masons's other ventures—such as vocational training schools—also caused the organization to thrive. His ties to the Republican community eventually brought him to U.S. President Richard Nixon's White House as a guest in the early 1970s, and the chief executive helped him obtain the first television station license granted to an African American in the United States by the Federal Communications Commission.

The UHF television outlet that Banks and the Masons went on the Detroit airwaves with in 1975 was called WGPR, or "Where God's Presence Radiates." Its first years in operation were shaky, since many members of Banks's team—employees that included his wife, Ivy Bird, and daughter Tenicia Gregory—had little media experience. Within a few years, however, the station gained ratings and financial health. More importantly, WGPR-TV served as a training ground for a legion of African American on-air and behind-the-scenes technical personnel, a group of young people who would eventually go on to figure prominently in Detroit media. Banks died in 1985 at the age of 82. The Black Mason organization that Banks founded owned the station until 1994, when it was purchased by CBS as a local affiliate.

Donald H. Barden (1943–)
Communications Executive

Born on December 20, 1943, Donald Barden struggled in a number of low-wage jobs as an adult, dreaming of one day working for himself in some sort of entrepreneurial venture. A nest egg of $500 helped him to open a record store, then launch a record label, then a public relations firm in Lorain, Ohio. The capital Barden accumulated through these ventures was later parlayed into real estate deals. By the early 1970s, the executive had become a dynamic member of Lorain's business community, owning a newspaper, holding a seat on the city council, and hosting a talk show on Cleveland's NBC affiliate.

Barden's interest in and familiarity with cutting-edge media evolved into his most lucrative undertaking. Foreseeing the rise of the cable industry—and the lack of African American representation within it—Barden invested in Lorain's new cable television provider and used the remunerative rewards to begin his own cable company, Barden Cablevision. He researched and found

Don Barden.

that African American communities were entertaining franchise offers from giants in the industry and offered them a socially-conscious alternative. One of the first cities to award Barden's company a contract was Inkster, Michigan, a suburb of Detroit. His success in wiring the city for cable service and the obvious financial soundness of his company paid off when the city of Detroit awarded Barden Cablevision its much-coveted contract.

Barden launched cable television in Detroit with the help of Canadian financing and began wiring the city in 1986. Always looking into what was on the forefront of the communications industry, Barden's next venture was in the realm of personal communications services, a new messaging technology that would allow small devices to transmit faxes, voice messages, and computer data. He planned to bid on several of the licenses when they were auctioned off for the first time by the Federal Communications Commission in 1994. That same year, he sold his interest in Barden Cablevision for a reported $100 million, reaping a dramatic profit from the company he had started with only a few thousand dollars. In early 1995, it was announced that Indiana authorities had granted Barden a riverboat

casino operating license, one of two to be established in the city of Gary.

With the success of his riverboat casino in Indiana, Barden expressed an interest in obtaining a license for one of the three casinos earmarked for Detroit. When Mayor Archer rejected his bid, Barden recruited celebrity Michael Jackson to help him campaign for a contract in the hopes that Detroit voters would overturn Archer's decision. His billion dollar casino proposal was to be called the "Majestic Kingdom" and included plans for an 800-room hotel, botanical gardens, nightclubs, restaurants, and the Michael Jackson Thriller Theme Park, which would have incorporated advanced technology enabling it to operate regardless of the weather. Despite Barden's vigorous campaigning, Detroit voters rejected his proposal on August 8, 1998.

Barden recently entered into a contract with General Motors to establish an automotive plant in Namibia and South Africa. He, along with his business partner Michael Jackson, took several trips in 1998 to central and southern Africa to investigate other business opportunities in Namibia, Angola, and South Africa. In May 1999, it was announced that Barden has reached a deal to invest in Sengstacke Enterprises, Inc., owner of several African American newspapers in Chicago, Detroit, Pittsburgh, and Memphis.

In 2002 Barden's dream of actually owning a permanent casino came true as he established the Majestic Star casino in Gary, Indiana as well as purchasing three other casinos in Mississippi, Colorado, and Las Vegas. Barden is the first African American to completely own and operate a casino.

Haley W. Bell (c.1895–1973)
Broadcasting Executive

Pioneer, humanitarian, and entrepreneur are just a few of the words that have been used to describe Haley W. Bell. Although a dentist by profession, he was most recognized as the co-founder of the Bell Broadcasting System, which was established in 1955. The other co-founder was his son-in-law, Wendell Cox. The system included WCHB-AM in Inkster (its owners' initials) and WCHD-FM in Detroit, Michigan. Bell's other interests included ownership of a finance company, a tool and die firm, a cemetery, a restaurant, an insurance company, two trade schools, and a funeral home.

As the first African American to ever directly receive a license from the Federal Communications Commission (FCC) to operate a radio station, Bell's stations were the first black-built radio stations in the country. As such, both stations served as training grounds for many local and national media personalities who broke into the airwaves through the black-owned stations. Included among those who once worked at the Bell Broadcasting System were NBC newsman William Matney; Ofield Dukes, a former assistant to Vice President Hubert Humphrey; Trudy Haynes, Detroit's first black weathergirl; Frank Seymour of Seymour & Lundy, a public relations firm; and Martha Jean "the Queen," eventually an announcer on WJLB-FM, but later the owner, president and general manager of WQBH-AM in Inkster, Michigan.

Initially staffed by 23 experienced employees whom Bell admittedly lured away from previous jobs by offering more lucrative wages, the stations adopted the slogan "The Voice of Progress." In accordance with this slogan, the programming on both stations reflected the music, aspirations and accomplishments of Detroit area blacks. While most of the airtime was dedicated to news, religious programs and music (ranging from blues to symphonies), community organizations were also granted a generous hearing.

Often referred to as the "father of Detroit black radio," Bell maintained his dental office in Hamtramck, Michigan until his retirement in 1960. Known for his generosity from both within and outside of the company, Bell believed that if you kept a part of what you earned, you would always be able to give a part of what you had. His belief was further emphasized by the engraved plaque that appeared in his office with the words, "a part of all you earn is yours to keep."

Organizations that benefited from Bell's benevolence included Meharry Medical College, from which he graduated in 1922, the NAACP, the United Negro College Fund, the United Foundation, the Parents Association of Jewish Residential Care, Catholic Charities, Plymouth United Church, and numerous other groups that cut across racial lines.

Born in Brunswick, Georgia, Dr. Haley W. Bell died on March 12, 1973, nine days before he was to be honored by the Detroit Cotillion Club for "his many contributions to charitable and public concerns, including personality-sponsored scholarships for students across the nation."

Ed Bradley (1941–)
Television News Correspondent

Born on January 22, 1941, in Philadelphia, Pennsylvania, Edward R. Bradley received a bachelor of science degree in education from Cheyney State College in 1964. From 1963 to 1967, Bradley worked as a jazz host and news reporter for WDAS radio in Philadelphia. He then spent four years at WCBS radio in New York. His first television assignment was in September of 1971, when he joined CBS as a stringer in the Paris bureau. Within a few months he moved to the Saigon bureau, where he remained until he was assigned to the Washington bureau in June of 1974. From 1974 until 1978, Bradley served as White House correspondent for CBS.

Bradley worked as an anchor for *CBS Sunday Night News* from 1976 until 1981 and as principal correspondent for *CBS Reports*. In 1981, he replaced Dan Rather as a correspondent for the weekly news program *60 Minutes*. In 1992, Bradley became host of the CBS news program *Street Stories*. An avid jazz and blues aficionado, Bradley also is the host of *Jazz from Lincoln Center*. He has hosted the show since 1991.

Due to his outstanding coverage of issues both nationally and internationally, Bradley has received 11 Emmy Awards, two Alfred I. duPont-Columbia University Awards for broadcast journalism, a George Foster Peabody Broadcasting Award, a George Polk Award, and an NCAA Anniversary Award. In 1992, he won an Emmy for his *60 Minutes* segment "Made in China." The National Press Foundation presented Bradley with the Sol Taischoff Award in 1993.

In October of 1995, Bradley filed a report called "The Other America" on *60 Minutes*. In that piece, he examined shantytown homes—known as "colonias"—in the Texas desert along the U.S.-Mexico border. The colonias were designed for low-income, mainly Hispanic families. The woman who built the shanties claimed that Bradley's report wrecked her reputation and falsely accused her and other members of her family of unethical business and political practices. She sued for defamation. However, in late 1997, a Texas jury cleared Bradley of libel in the investigation.

Bradley continued to make a name for himself in the field with his weekly reports on *60 Minutes* as well as other news programs. In 2000, he was inducted into the Deadline Club Hall of Fame run by the New York chapter of the Society of Professional Journalists.

James Brown (1951–)
Sports Anchor

James Brown was born on February 25, 1951, in Washington, DC. Having completed his third season as co-host of *Fox NFL Sunday*, America's most watched, and Emmy Award-winning, pregame show, Brown also served as co-host of *NHL on Fox* studio segments. Brown joined Fox Sports in June of 1994 and is widely recognized as one of the most versatile and multitalented on-air personalities in television.

Prior to entering the communications field, Brown received a bachelor of arts degree in American government from Harvard University in 1973 and then was drafted in the fourth-round by the NBA's Atlanta Hawks. He officially began his broadcasting career in 1984 with WJLA-TV in Washington, DC, and WUSA-TV (1984–1990). He also served as an analyst for the NBA's Washington Bullets local television broadcasts (1978–1983) and co-hosted two weekly Washington area sports programs. At one time, he even hosted a midday program on all-sports radio WTEM in the nation's capital.

In 1984, he joined CBS Sports as a college basketball analyst and co-host of the NCAA basketball championship (1984–1994). Other host roles for CBS included the weekday program during the 1992 Winter Olympics, the Heisman Trophy Award show "CBS Sports Saturday/Sunday" anthology series, and the Emmy Award-winning special *Let Me Be Brave: A Special Climb of Mt. Kilimanjaro.*

Not one to limit himself, in addition to college basketball and NFL play-by-play, Brown has served as a reporter for CBS Sports's coverage of the NBA Finals and Pan American Games. He also delved into other sports areas. He served as commentator of freestyle skiing for CBS at the 1994 Lillehammer Winter Olympics and hosted four *Fox Saturday Night Fight* programs, as well as several pay-per-view boxing events.

Brown is a contributor to the sports magazine program *Real Sports with Bryant Gumbel*, which premiered on HBO in April of 1995 and served as a moderator for a roundtable discussion of the documentary "Hoop Dreams: A Reunion" on PBS. In 2002, Brown joined Sports News Radio to host the the *James Brown Show*. Brown's hard work over the years paid off in fall 2001 when he received the prestigious Sportcaster of the Year Award from the Quarterback Club of Washington for his "outstanding contribution to the world of sports."

Les Brown (1945–)
Motivational Speaker, Talk Show Host, Author

As a renowned motivational speaker, author, and television personality, Les Brown—born Leslie Calvin Brown along with his twin brother Wesley on February 17, 1945—rose to national prominence by delivering a highly-charged message that instructs people on how to shake off mediocrity and live up to their potential.

Brown and his twin brother were born in low-income Liberty City, Florida. They were adopted at six weeks of age by Mamie Brown, a single woman with a heart of gold but little education or money. As a child, Brown lacked concentration, especially in reading. His

Les Brown.

restlessness and inattentiveness, coupled with his teachers's failure to recognize his real potential, resulted in him being labeled as a slow learner. Although this label damaged his self-esteem and stayed with him for many years, he was finally able to overcome it through perseverance and the realization that he was responsible for his destiny. His mother's unyielding belief in his greatness, along with support from a speech and drama teacher in high school, aided him in this journey of discovery.

Brown received no formal education past high school. However, through sheer will, initiative, and persistence, he prides himself on being self-educated. This fact has distinguished him as an authority on human virtue. Brown's insatiable thirst for knowledge and hunger to succeed allowed him to rise from a hip-talking radio announcer to a broadcast manager; from a community activist to a community leader; from a political commentator to three-term legislator; and from a banquet and nightclub emcee to a prominent motivational speaker.

In 1986, Brown entered the public speaking arena on a full-time basis and formed his own company,

Les Brown Unlimited, Inc. The company provides motivational tapes and materials, as well as workshops and personal/professional development programs aimed at individuals, companies, and organizations. He is also the author of *Live Your Dreams* and *It's Not Over Until You Win*. The former host of *The Les Brown Show*, a nationally syndicated daily television talk show that focused on solutions rather than problems, Brown continues to mesmerize audiences with his customized presentations that teach and inspire.

In 1989, Brown was the recipient of the National Speakers Association's highest honor: The Council of Peers Award of Excellence (CPAE). In 1990, he recorded his first in a series of speech presentations entitled *You Deserve*, which was awarded a Chicago-area Emmy. This program eventually became the leading fund-raising program of its kind for pledges to PBS stations nationwide. In addition, in 1992, he was selected as one of the World's Top Five Speakers by Toastmasters International and the recipient of the Golden Gavel Award.

In 1997, Brown resigned from his radio show at WBLS in New York in order to devote more time to his motivational speaking and battling his prostate cancer. Into 1998, Brown's speaking engagements and television appearances brought in about $4.5 million annually. His Detroit-based firm continued to serve high-profile clients such as Chrysler, 3M, and Xerox Corporation. In addition, Brown branched out to train future public speakers, concentrating on promoting the field to more minorities.

Tony Brown (1933–)
Talk Show Host, Producer, Columnist, Author, Film Director

William Anthony Brown, born in Charleston, West Virginia, in 1933, is probably best known as the producer and host of the longest-running minority affairs program in history *Tony Brown's Journal*. The show was selected in the *New York Daily Times* as one of the top ten television shows of all time that presents positive African American images. In 1991, the show was also nominated for the NAACP Image Award for outstanding news, talk or information series/special.

Brown received his bachelor of arts degree in sociology in 1959 and his master's of social work in 1961 from Wayne State University in Detroit. Brown took a job with the *Detroit Courier* as drama critic. During this time he began to be active in the Civil Rights movement, helping to organize the 1963 "March to Freedom" with Dr. Martin Luther King Jr. in Detroit. After leaving the paper, where he had been promoted to the position of

city editor, Brown landed a job with the local PBS station, WTVS, where he became involved in television programming and production. At WTVS, he produced the station's first series aimed at a black audience, *C.P.T.* (Colored People's Time). He joined the New York staff of the PBS program *Black Journal* in 1970 as the show's executive producer and host; in 1977 the show's name was changed to *Tony Brown's Journal* and can still be seen on PBS.

In 1971, Brown founded and became the first dean of Howard University's School of Communications. He continued in that post until 1974. While in this position, he initiated an annual careers conference that is still in place today because of his concern for the lack of African American representation in the communications industry.

Brown has been an advocate of community and self-help programs. In 1980 he organized a "Black College Day," designed to emphasize the importance of historically African American colleges and universities. In 1985 Brown organized the Council for the Economic Development of Black Americans and launched the "Buy Freedom" campaign (now known as the "Buy Freedom Network"), which encourages African American consumers nationwide to patronize African American-owned businesses.

Brown wrote two powerful books *Black Lies, White Lies: The Truth According to Tony Brown* in 1995 and *Empower the People: A 7-Step Plan to Overthrow the Conspiracy That Is Stealing Your Money and Freedom* in 1998. Although both books address problems that cannot be ignored, they also focus on the future and on solutions. Offering innovative plans for making America more competitive through Brown's Team America Concept, the books strive to solve the country's race problem through cultural diversity.

Brown has written, produced, and directed a film *The White Girl*, appeared as a commentator for National Public Radio, and is a syndicated newspaper columnist. He is also host of a radio talk show *Tony Brown* on WLIB in New York, which was to be syndicated nationally. He is a member of the National Association of Black Television and Film Producers, the National Association of Black Media Producers, the National Communications Council, and the National Black United Fund. Brown is the recipient of a Black Emmy Award, an NAACP Image Award, the Educator of the Year Award, and the Communicator of the Year Award from the Academy's national board of trustees. He is president of Tony Brown Productions in New York. In addition to producing movies and television programs, the company also offers a videotape duplication service and markets videos from a collection called *The Library of Black History*.

Ron Buckmire.

Ron Buckmire (1968–)
Mathematician, Internet Directory Founder

Born on May 21, 1968, Ron Buckmire is the creator of the oldest and largest Internet online resource of information about gay, lesbian, bisexual, and transgendered people, The Queer Resources Directory (QRD). Currently, he serves as its executive director and is responsible for its quality control and auditing of user services.

Buckmire spent nearly ten years of his youth in Barbados. In 1986, he relocated to Troy, New York, earning a bachelor of science degree in mathematics (1989), a master of arts degree (1992) and a Ph.D. in applied mathematics (1994), all from Rensselaer Polytechnic Institute. Though the Queer Resources Directory (QRD) was initially started as an electronic archive for the radical group Queer Nation, Buckmire transformed the repository into a broader-based electronic library, featuring news clippings, political contact information, essays, images, and hyperlinks—all dedicated to sexual minorities that have traditionally born the brunt of discrimination.

In addition to his QRD duties, Buckmire is currently an assistant professor in the mathematics department at Occidental College, where he teaches mathematical modeling and complex analysis. Most of his work has been in theoretical aerodynamics and computational fluid dynamics. Buckmire's other activities include participation on the board of directors of the International Gay and Lesbian Human Rights Commission and of Overnight Productions, which is responsible for the international gay and lesbian radio news magazine *This Way Out.*

In 1996, *Out Magazine* listed him among the Top 100 Gay and Lesbian Activists of the Year. In 1997, for its thirtieth anniversary issue, *The Advocate* named him as a member of "Generation Q," 30 activists under age 30 who have made a difference. Buckmire currently teaches at Occidental College, tackling classes in both mathematics and Race and Gender theory.

Edward J. Castleberry (1928–)
Broadcast Journalist

Born July 28, 1928, in Birmingham, Alabama, Castleberry spent two years at Miles College. His career in radio broadcasting includes many stations in the United States. He started as a disc jockey at WEDR and WJLD in Birmingham, Alabama (1950–1955), and has worked in the various capacities of program host, program director, and news personality at WMBM in Miami, Florida (1955–1958), WCIN in Cincinnati, Ohio (1958–1961), WABQ in Cleveland, Ohio (1961–1964), WVKO in Columbus, Ohio (1964–1967), WHAT in Philadelphia, Pennsylvania (1967–1968) and WEBB in Baltimore, Maryland. He then became an anchorman and entertainment editor at the Mutual and National Black Networks.

Castleberry was named Newsman of the Year in 1980 by both the Coalition of Black Media Women and Jack the Rapper Family Affair and received the Outstanding Citizen Award from the Alabama House of Representatives in 1983. In 1985 he was honored by the Smithsonian Institute in Washington, DC. Later, Castleberry was awarded the World War II Victory Medal for his service in the United States Navy.

Spencer Christian (1947–)
Television Weatherperson

Born in Newport News, Virginia, in 1947 and a veteran of the U.S. Army Reserves, Spencer Christian received his bachelor of arts degree in English from

Hampton University in 1970. Upon graduation, he taught English at the Stony Brook School in Long Island, New York before launching his television career.

In 1971, Christian went to work for WWBT-TV in Richmond as a news reporter; from 1972 to 1975 he served as the station's weatherperson. In 1975, he moved to WBAL-TV in Baltimore, where he hosted *Spencer's World*, a weekly, half-hour talk show. He also produced and narrated the Emmy Award-winning, five-part report on declining verbal skills entitled *Does Anyone Here Speak English?* In 1977, he moved to New York's WABC-TV. Christian joined the *Good Morning America* team on ABC in 1986 as weather forecaster. He left the show in 1999 to join a local television station in San Francisco. Most recently, Spencer has been pulling double hosting duties, appearing on the shows *Spencer Christian's Wine Cellar* for the Home and Garden Network and the PBS series *Tracks Ahead*.

During 1988, he was the ABC Television's official on-air spokesperson for the "Readasaurus" campaign, which was part of the company's overall Project Literacy U.S., promoting interest in reading among young children. In 1993, Christian hosted the *Triple Threat* game show on Black Entertainment Television and was inducted into the Virginia Communications Hall of Fame. Later in the same year, he was named Virginian of the Year by the Virginia Press Association. He published *Spencer Christian's Weather Book*, *Spencer Christian's Geography Book*, and, most recently, *Electing Our Government*, a light and lively refresher course on how the United States electoral procedure works. He also co-hosted an experimental, late night series on ABC called *Day's End*, which aired in 27 markets across the country from March through June of 1989.

In 1996, Christian worked on a public education campaign, in conjunction with Everready, that focused on weather emergency preparedness. In addition, he wrote a brochure that contains helpful weather emergency tips. It is available through Energizer and endorsed by the National Weather Service.

Christian worked with a variety of charities in New York and New Jersey. They include Up With People, The March of Dimes, the Huntington's Disease Society of America, Special Olympics, Big Brothers, Make-a-Wish Foundation, and many others. His affiliation with the March of Dimes dates back to 1979 when he served as honorary chair of the North New Jersey chapter.

Xernona Clayton (1930–)
Broadcast Executive

Clayton was born Xernona Brewster on August 30, 1930, in Muskogee, Oklahoma. She received a bachelor of science degree from Tennessee Agricultural and Industrial State University (now Tennessee State University) in 1952 and later pursued graduate studies at the University of Chicago. She also attended the Ru-Jac School of Modeling in Chicago.

Clayton was the first African American woman to have her own television show in the South when she became host of the *Xernona Clayton Show* at WAGA-TV in Atlanta. She has also been a newspaper columnist for the *Atlanta Voice*, taught public school in Chicago and Los Angeles, and dabbled in photography and fashion modeling.

Clayton was active in the Civil Rights movement. Her first husband, now deceased, was the public relations director for Dr. Martin Luther King Jr. Clayton came to the attention of Atlanta officials and was appointed to the position of community relations director of the Model Cities Program. She has also raised funds for sickle cell anemia research and the Dr. Martin Luther King Jr. Birthplace Memorial Restoration Committee.

In 1968, Clayton won the Outstanding Leadership award given by the National Association of Market Developers and a year later the Bronze Woman of the Year in Human Relations award given by Phi Delta Kappa sorority. She is also the recipient of the Georgia Associated Press award for Superior Television Programming 1969–1971. In 1987, Clayton won an Emmy Award for a documentary on juvenile justice. She was named Media Woman of the Year in 1989.

Clayton is the founder of the Atlanta chapter of the National Association of Media Women and a member of the National Academy of Television Arts and Sciences and the National Association of Press Women. She is also a member of the Urban League's board of directors. She co-starred in a major motion picture *House on Skull Mountain*. Clayton married Paul L. Brady, a federal administrative judge, after the death of her first husband. She became the executive producer of Turner Broadcasting's long-running Trumpet Awards show, which honors the achievements of minorities around the world and is broadcast during Black History Month on Turner's flagship network, TBS Superstation.

Don Cornelius (1936–)
Broadcasting Executive

Don Cornelius, the creative mind behind the hit African American dance show *Soul Train* was born in Chicago on September 27, 1936, and grew up on the city's predominantly African American South side. At the age of 30, he fulfilled his dream of becoming a radio announcer when he landed a part-time job as an announcer with WVON in Chicago. Acting as an all-around substitute became too exhausting, however, and he moved to the small UHF television station, WCIU-TV with the seed for *Soul Train* already in mind. Although he initially had trouble convincing sponsors to take a chance on an "ethnic" show, Cornelius was able to get the financial backing he needed, and the first episode of *Soul Train* aired in Chicago on August 17, 1970. The show was essentially a dance party that featured African American performers and dancers and aired once a week.

The inexpensive program, hosted and produced by Cornelius, went national a little over a year later. Cornelius attributed the speed of *Soul Train*'s success to the overall absence of entertainment television programs for African American audiences. The show spawned a record label, Soul Train Records, in 1975, although the label folded after three years. The *Soul Train Music Awards* proved to be a more enduring spin-off; created in 1986, the awards program was the first to be dedicated exclusively to African American musicians. By 1992 *Soul Train* had become the longest-running music program in the history of syndication. Cornelius retired in 1993 as host of the show but he continues to stay active in the television business. In 1995, Cornelius hosted and produced *The Soul Train 25th Anniversary Hall Of Fame Special*. He currently continues to produce *Soul Train* as well as three award shows a year: *The Soul Train Awards*, the *Lady of Soul Awards*, and the *NAACP Image Awards*.

Samuel E. Cornish (1795–1858)
Newspaper Publisher

Samuel Cornish was born in Sussex County, Delaware, in 1795. Ordained as an evangelist by the Presbyterian Church, Cornish acted as an advocate for African Americans through the mouthpiece of the newspaper he co-founded with John Russwurm, *Freedom's Journal*. The paper, which began printing in March of 1827, countered racist propaganda and served as a means of communication for African Americans. He changed the paper's name to *Rights of All* in May of 1829, and the newspaper ceased publication later that year.

Cornish continued editing after the demise of the publication, serving as editor of the *Weekly Advocate* (later changed to *Colored American*) from 1837 to 1838. He was also involved with the African Free

Samuel E. Cornish.

Schools, the Negro Convention movement, the American Anti-Slavery Society, and the American Missionary Society. Cornish died on November 6, 1858, in Brooklyn, New York.

David E. Driver (1955–)
Book Publisher, Writer, Social Activist, Investor

David E. Driver was born on October 17, 1955, and grew up on Chicago's West side. Because of his excellent grades, he attended Lindblom High School, an exceptional public trade school. From there, he earned a bachelor's of arts from Bradley University in Peoria, Illinois, and after he passed the CPA exam, he joined Arthur Young & Company as a staff accountant. In 1978, Driver took a job at the International Hospital Supply Corporation. Until 1980, Driver worked as a finance manager, specializing in foreign currency markets. He moved on to Merrill Lynch Capital Markets where he was promoted to vice president in 1982. While working in stock and bond futures, he received his MBA from the University of Chicago in 1984.

In 1988 with $250,000 and one book that he had written himself—*The Good Heart Book: A Guide to Volunteering*—he founded the Noble Press. Within three years, he had a staff of five, a renovated loft for office space, and books receiving critical attention. The book that earned the Noble Press its reputation was the 1993 release *Volunteer Slavery: My Authentic Negro Experience* by Janet Nelson, that sold 40,000 hardcover copies. Driver sold the paperback rights to Penguin for whom it became a national best-seller and earned an American Book Award in 1994.

By 1993, Noble's annual sales reached the million mark and its distribution outlets grew to number 6,000. Driver founded the Black Literary Society, a book club that posts reading lists on the Internet. Driver also started Young Chicago Authors, a workshop program for aspiring teenage authors. In addition, Driver wrote *Defending the Left: An Individual's Guide to Fighting for Social Justice, Individual Rights and the Environment*, published in 1992. He has served as secretary of the Society of Illinois Book Publishers and is a founding member of the National Association of Black Book Publishers.

Timothy Thomas Fortune (1856–1928)
Newspaper Publisher

Born on October 3, 1856, in Marianna, Florida, Timothy Thomas Fortune was one of the most prominent African American journalists involved in the flourishing African American press of the post-Civil War era. The son of a Reconstruction politician, Fortune was particularly productive before his thirtieth year, completing such works as *Black and White: Land, Labor and Politics in the South* and *The Negro in Politics* while in his twenties.

Fortune attended Howard University for two years, leaving to marry Carrie Smiley of Jacksonville, Florida. The couple went to New York in 1878, with Fortune taking a job as a printer for the *New York Sun*. In time, Fortune caught the attention of *Sun* editor Charles A. Dana, who eventually promoted him to the editorial staff of the paper.

Fortune also edited *The Globe*, an African American daily, and was later chief editorial writer for *The Negro World*. In 1900 Fortune joined Booker T. Washington in helping to organize the successful National Negro Business League. His later activity with Washington gained him more notoriety than his earlier writing, although his written work is more vital in affording him an

T. Thomas Fortune, a prominent antebellum member of the press.

important niche in the history of African American protest.

In 1883, Fortune founded the *New York Age*, the paper with which he sought to "champion the cause" of his race. In time, the *Age* became the leading black journal of opinion in the United States. One of Fortune's early crusades was against segregation in the New York educational system.

Fortune was later responsible for coining the term "Afro-American" as a substitute for Negro in New York newspapers. He also set up the Afro-American Council, an organization which he regarded as the precursor of the Niagara Movement. In 1907 Fortune sold the *Age*, although he remained active in journalism as an editorial writer for several African American newspapers. He died on June 2, 1928.

Malvin R. Goode (1908–1995)
Television News Correspondent

Malvin Russell Goode had been with the *Pittsburgh Courier* for 14 years when in 1962 he joined ABC to cover the United Nations. His first test was the Cuban Missile Crisis, during which Goode distinguished himself with incisive TV and radio reports during the long hours of United Nations debate.

Goode was born in White Plains, Virginia, in 1908; educated in the public schools of Homestead, Pennsylvania; and graduated from the University of Pittsburgh in 1931. He worked for 12 years as a laborer in the steel mills while in high school and college and for five years after graduation. In 1936, he was appointed to a post in juvenile court and became boys work director of the Centre Avenue YMCA, where he led the fight to eliminate discrimination in Pittsburgh branches of the YMCA.

Goode served with the Pittsburgh Housing Authority for six years and in 1948 joined the *Pittsburgh Courier*. The following year he started a career in radio with station KQV, doing a 15-minute news show two nights each week. In 1950, he started a five-minute daily news program on WHOD.

Goode became news director at WHOD in 1952. He and his sister, the late Mary Dee, had the only brother-sister team in radio for six years. He was the first African American to hold membership in the National Association of Radio and TV News Directors and the first African American correspondent on TV network news.

For two months, in 1963, he joined with three colleagues to conduct courses in journalism for 104 African students in seminars at Lagos, Nigeria; Addis Ababa, Ethiopia; and Dar es Salaam, Tanzania.

On September 12, 1995, Goode died of a stroke in Pittsburgh.

Ed Gordon (1960–)
Television Anchor and Host

Born Edward Lansing Gordon III in Detroit, Michigan, the future journalist was inspired to achieve in part by his schoolteacher mother and Olympic gold medalist father, who unfortunately passed away when Gordon was 11. After graduating with a degree in communications and political science from Western Michigan University in 1982, Gordon moved back to Detroit to launch his career in broadcasting.

Taking an unpaid internship with the city's public broadcasting affiliate in 1983 eventually landed him a job as host of its *Detroit Black Journal* a few years later. During that time, he also began freelance reporting from his hometown for an upstart cable network called Black Entertainment Television (BET). In 1988, the Washington, DC-based channel hired him as an anchor and chief correspondent for their weekly news program *BET News*. Gordon left BET in 1996 to join NBC News as host of the Saturday edition of *Internight*, a one-hour talk and interview program on MSNBC. He also serves as a daytime anchor for MSNBC and contributing correspondent for *Dateline NBC*.

Gordon became an increasing presence on the well-regarded alternative to traditional network news, interviewing prominent African Americans on his *Conversations with Ed Gordon* show and hosting programs of special interest such as his *Black Men Speak Out: The Aftermath*, which aired in the wake of the 1992 Los Angeles riots. During his tenure on *Conversations with Ed Gordon*, he interviewed the last two sitting presidents and South African President Nelson Mandela, as well as more outspoken figures, such as the Rev. Al Sharpton and Nation of Islam leader Louis Farrakhan. He also hosted the BET staple *Lead Story*, anchored several BET News specials on a wide range of topics, and hosted the critically acclaimed interview series *Personal Diary*. Though the demands of the job at BET were arduous, Gordon derived a special satisfaction from his work in journalism when young African American males point out to him that they never were interested in news programs before his began airing.

In 1996, Gordon broke out of the mold of cable television news when he was selected as the first journalist to interview O.J. Simpson after Simpson was found not guilty of killing his wife and her lover. This boosted Gordon's overall image as a journalist and showed the public and executives at more prominent news organizations what he was capable of. Later in 1996, NBC hired Gordon on with a three year $1.5 million contract. Gordon continues to work part time at BET and still does BET News specials when time permits.

Earl G. Graves (1935–)
Publisher and Media Executive

In the 1970s, Earl Graves emerged as one of America's leading publishers and exponents of black entrepreneurship. Within a few short years his magazine *Black Enterprise* was accepted as the authority on African Americans in business and as an important advocate for an active, socially responsive, African American middle class. Yearly sales of the magazine are currently over $17 million and increasing. *Black Enterprise* has a circulation of 250,000 and a readership of more than two million.

Born in Brooklyn in 1935, Graves graduated from Morgan State College in 1958 with a bachelor of arts degree in economics. In 1965, he was hired to a position on the staff of Robert Kennedy, then senator from New York. In 1968, he organized Earl Graves Associates, a

Earl G. Graves.

firm which serves as a consultant on urban affairs and African American economic development and publishes *Black Enterprise*. Graves is also president and chief executive officer of Earl G. Graves Ltd., Earl G. Graves Marketing and Research Co., and Earl G. Graves Development Co. In December of 1998, he named his eldest son president of Earl G. Graves Publishing Company.

Graves wrote his autobiography *How to Succeed without Being White* in 1997. His other interests include being president of EGG Dallas Broadcasting, Inc., which operates KNOK-AM and KNOK-FM in Fort Worth, Texas. Graves is also chairman and president of Pepsi-Cola of Washington, DC.

In 1998, Graves started *Black Enterprise Unlimited*, a service that focuses on the business, financial, and lifestyle needs of the African American businessman or woman. The service provided the opportunity for African Americans to access certain areas or products that had formally been unavailable to them. It also sponsored extra-circular activities open to African Americans such as golf and ski outings. In 1999, Graves was honored by the NAACP with the Springarn Medal for his outstanding career in business and commitment to education and support of civil and human rights issues.

Bryant Gumbel (1948–)
Television Anchor

Bryant Gumbel, the popular newscaster who gained fame as co-anchor of the *Today* show, was born in New Orleans, Louisiana, on September 29, 1948, but grew up in Chicago. He received a liberal arts degree from Bates College in Lewiston, Maine, in 1970.

Before embarking on his career in television, Gumbel was a sportswriter. After submitting his first piece to *Black Sports* magazine in 1971, he was given additional freelance assignments and was soon hired as a staff writer. Within eight months, he was elevated to editor-in-chief.

Gumbel began his broadcasting career in October of 1972 when he became a weekend sportscaster for KNBC, the NBC station in Burbank, California. Within a year, he became weekday sportscaster and was appointed the station's sports director in 1976. He remained in that post until 1981. Gumbel made regular sports reports with NBC Sports as host of pre-game programming during coverage of the National Football League, Major League Baseball, and other sports broadcasts. Gumbel debuted as host of HBO's *Real Sports* program on April 2, 1995.

In January of 1982, Bryant Gumbel was named co-anchor of the *Today* show on NBC opposite Jane Pauley, selected as a replacement for Tom Brokaw. In 1997, at the height of the show's ratings, he relinquished his position after 15 years. During his tenure, he distinguished himself as a steadfast anchor, gifted interviewer, and role model for minority journalists. A bidding war for his services erupted between all major networks in the ensuing months following his departure. In the end, Gumbel signed a five-year contract with CBS News that netted him $5 million a year, his own prime-time news magazine *Public Eye With Bryant Gumbel*, which was canceled in 1998, three specials each year, and his own company for syndicated programming development—not to mention CBS stock options. Early in 1999, CBS announced that Gumbel agreed to anchor *This Morning* beginning in the fall of 1999.

In 2000, Gumbel returned to morning television as co-host of the CBS television news show, *The Early Show*. Two and a half years later, Gumbel announced that he was leaving CBS when his contract expired in May of 2002. He will continue to host *Real Sports* for HBO.

Greg Gumbel (1946–)
Radio and Television Sportcaster

The older brother of Bryant Gumbel, Greg Gumbel was born on May 3, 1946, in New Orleans, Louisiana. With his round, friendly face and affable disposition, Gumbel has graced the airways for over 20 years. He has covered local sports for WMAQ-TV in his hometown of Chicago, hosted ESPN's *SportsCenter*, done play-by-play for the Madison Square Garden Network, and served as host for CBS's *The NFL Today.*

Currently employed as a sportcaster at NBC, Gumbel has worked with some of sports television's biggest names including Terry Bradshaw, John Madden, Mike Ditka, Joe Montana, Bill Walton, and Joe Morgan. He has also worked on many large-scale sports events: Super Bowls, World Series, NBA and NCAA basketball championships, and the Olympics, both summer and winter.

Having addressed students at schools across the country, various chambers of commerce and town hall gatherings, as well as Boy Scout organizations, the Anti-Defamation League, and March of Dimes groups, Gumbel entertains and motivates audiences of all ages and types with his comments and videotaped sports highlights.

Ragan A. Henry (1934–)
Broadcast and Newspaper Executive

Ragan A. Henry is president of Broadcast Enterprises National Inc. and former publisher of *The National Leader,* an African American national newspaper launched in May of 1982, both headquartered in Philadelphia. Henry was also founder of U.S. Radio, the largest African American-owned radio group in the nation with 25 stations. In 1996, it was sold for $140 million to Clear Channel Communications of San Antonio, Texas. He is a partner in the Philadelphia law firm of Wolf, Black, Schorr, and Solis-Cohen.

Henry was born in Sadiesville, Kentucky, on February 2, 1934. He received his bachelor of arts degree from Harvard College in 1956 and his L.L.B. from Harvard Law School in 1961. He also attended Temple University Graduate School in 1963. Prior to joining his current law firm, he had been a partner in the Philadelphia firm of Goodis, Greenfield, Henry, and Edelstein from 1964 to 1977.

Henry was a lecturer at LaSalle College from 1971 to 1973 and has been a visiting professor at Syracuse University's S.I. Newhouse School of Communications since 1979. He serves on the boards of directors of Continental Bank, Abt Associates, Inc., National Association of Black Owned Broadcasters (president of the board), LaSalle College, and the Hospital of the University of Pennsylvania. He has been chairman of the John McKee Scholarship Committee Fellowships of the Noyes and Whitney Foundation.

Ragan continues to be active in the community. In 1999, he was elected Vice Chairmen of the Museum's Board of Trustees. In the late 1990s, Ragan was honored by the Broadcasters' Foundation Board of Directors with an American Broadcast Pioneer award, for making an enormous contribution to the broadcasting industry and his community.

Cheryl Willis Hudson (1948–)
Publishing Executive

Cheryl Willis Hudson, publisher, and Wade Hudson, president and chief executive officer, founded Just Us Books, Inc. in 1988 to publish children's books and learning material that focus on the African American experience.

Just Us Books, Inc. is now one of the leading publishers of African American interest books for young people. More than three dozen titles have been published with millions of copies in print. The company has garnered a number of awards and honors including The Parents' Choice Award, the Ben Franklin Award, the Multicultural Publisher's Exchange Award and the American Booksellers Association/Blackboard "Best Seller of 1994."

Hudson is not only the founder of Just Us Books, Inc., but she is also an author herself. Her works include: *Bright Eyes, Brown Skin* (1990); *Good Night, Baby* (1992); *Good Morning, Baby* (1992); and *Hold Christmas in Your Heart: African-American Songs, Poems and Stories for the Holidays* (1995).

A native of Portsmouth, Virginia, Cheryl Willis Hudson graduated (cum laude) from Oberlin College in 1970. She also studied at Northeastern University, the Arts Students League, and Parsons School of Design. Prior to founding Just Us Books, she worked as an art editor and designer for several publishers including Houghton Mifflin, MacMillan Publishing, Arete Publishing, and Paperwing Press/Angel Entertainment.

Wade Hudson (1946–)
Publishing Executive

Wade Hudson is the president and chief executive officer of Just Us Books, Inc., a company that he co-founded with Cheryl Willis Hudson in 1988 to publish children's books and learning material that focus on the African American experience.

A native of Mansfield, Louisiana, he attended Southern University and has worked with numerous civil rights organizations including CORE, the Southern Christian Leadership Conference, and the Society for Opportunity, Unity and Leadership, which he co-founded. He also has worked as a public relations specialist for Essex County and Kean colleges in New Jersey.

As publishing professionals and advocates of diversity in literature, he and his wife conduct workshops and make presentations and appearances on panels across the country. They address topics such as: exploring books for the African American child; entrepreneurship in publishing; the nuts and bolts of building a publishing company; creative packaging of Afrocentric children's books; and publishing multicultural books for children and young adults.

Catherine Liggins Hughes (1947–)
Radio Personality, Broadcasting Executive, Owner & Founder

Born in Omaha Nebraska on April 22, 1947, Catherine Liggins Hughes (Cathy Hughes), formerly Catherine Elizabeth Woods, defines success in terms of the number of African Americans she has given jobs, in particular women, and not in terms of the number of radio stations under her company, Radio One, Inc. As founder and owner of the company, today, Hughes, along with her son Alfred C. Liggins, III, the president and CEO, work side by side running the largest African American owned and operated broadcast company in the nation. Hughes's son is from her first marriage. Headquartered in Lanham, Maryland, Radio One is the first African American company in radio history to dominate in several major markets simultaneously—Atlanta, Baltimore, D.C., Detroit, and Philadelphia—and the first woman-owned radio station to have ranked number one in any major market.

Upon taking the company public in 1999, Hughes became the first African American woman to head a firm publicly traded on a stock exchange in the United States. Radio One's value is currently in excess of two billion dollars. In 2000, *Black Enterprise* named Radio One, "Company of the Year," *Fortune* rated it one of the "100 Best Companies to Work For," and it was inducted into the Maryland Business Hall of Fame.

In August 2000, Radio One purchased KBBT "The Beat" in Los Angeles for $430 million and put actor and comedian Steve Harvey at the helm of the morning slot. The decision to bring on Harvey was carefully researched. After studying the L.A. market, Hughes determined that he was one of the few individuals capable of turning the urban radio market around. Furthermore, she knew that advertisers had begun to realize that urban listeners were consumers with considerable spending power. Her hard work and knowledge about the urban market played a major role in the success of Harvey's show, which is currently one of the top-rated morning shows in the L.A. market.

Moving to Washington, D.C. in 1971 after a successful stint with KOWH, a black ratio station in Omaha, Hughes became a lecturer in the newly established School of Communications at Howard University. She began working for the University's radio station, WHUR-FM, in 1973, as general sales manager and is noted for increasing station revenue from $250,000 to $3 million in her first year. In 1975, she became the first female vice president and general manager of the station. During her tenure, she created the romantic evening radio format known as the "Quiet Storm"—the most listened to nighttime radio format now heard in over 50 markets nationally. Purchasing her first station with her second husband, Dewey Hughes, in 1980, WOL-AM in Washington, D.C., she pioneered yet another innovative format, "24-hour Talk from a Black Perspective."

As creator of the first 24-hour talk radio station to cover news from an African American perspective, Hughes championed black causes. Outspoken, opinionated and oftentimes controversial, as host of her own program on WOL-AM for 14 years, Hughes criticized utility companies for their shut-off policies, encouraged listeners to buy black art and to donate money to charitable causes, and lead on-air protests against negative portrayals of blacks in the media. She also vehemently spoke out on such topics as the loss of black-owned farms, the adoption of black children by non-blacks, and equal pay for women. Her program, which she stopped hosting in 1995, is still one of the most popular talk shows in Washington, D.C.

Hughes's dedication to minority communities, entrepreneurial spirit, and mentoring of women are evident in every aspect of her work and life. As such, she was honored with the Lifetime Achievement Award from the Washington Area Broadcasters Association and The Seventh Congressional District Humanitarian Award. She has been granted the Ron Brown Business of the Year Award by the Department of Commerce, the Baltimore NAACP's Parren J. Mitchell Award, the Mayor's Recognition Award, and the Everett C. Parker Award. In 2001, she received the National Association of Broadcaster's Distinguished Service Award and the Silver Medal Award from the Ad Club for "having furthered the advertising industry's standards, creative excellence and responsibility in areas of social concern."

Remaining steadfast to her decision to purchase black-owned radio stations that are threatened by industry consolidation, Hughes purchased the Bell Broadcasting System based in Detroit in 1997 and Blue Chip

Broadcasting Ltd. based in Cincinnati in 2001. With these purchases, Radio One, now known as a company that can quickly turn around under-performing stations, employs over 1,500 people, owns more than 60 stations that are a mixture of urban contemporary, gospel and talk in nine of the top 20 markets for African Americans across the nation, and reaches over 18 million black listeners daily.

Although the company has grown tremendously over the years, Hughes has said that the foundation of Radio One, Inc. is still based on the spirit of a family that strives to serve as the heart of the community, as well as the pulse of urban radio.

Charlayne Hunter-Gault (1942–)
Journalist

Although now residing in Johannesburg, South Africa, Charlayne Hunter-Gault staked her claim as one of the leading journalists in the United States, having won many of the top honors in her field for excellence in investigative reporting. One of the springboards into her career came when she was the subject of a journalistic investigation at the height of the Civil Rights era. In 1961, she was one of two black students who first broke the color barrier at the University of Georgia. She later went on to receive a bachelor of arts degree from this institution in 1963.

Prior to joining the *MacNeil/Lehrer Report* in 1978 (subsequently the *MacNeil/Lehrer NewsHour* and *The NewsHour with Jim Lehrer*), Hunter-Gault held positions with the *New Yorker*, WRC-TV in Washington, DC, and the *New York Times*. She was the program's first woman anchor. In addition, her personal memoir *In My Place* was published in 1992.

Born on February 27, 1942, in Due West, South Carolina, Hunter-Gault built a reputation as a keen investigator of social injustice, especially among African Americans. Until 1997, she was the national correspondent for *The NewsHour with Jim Lehrer*, the hour-long evening news program broadcast nightly on the Public Broadcasting Service (PBS). She also anchors *Rights and Wrongs: Human Rights Television*, a weekly half-hour newsmagazine on PBS that incorporates news investigative reports, interviews, features, and cultural segments to examine human rights issues worldwide.

She left PBS in the summer of 1997 to join her husband, Ronald Gault, managing director of J.P. Morgan, S.A., and to serve as the South Africa-based correspondent for National Public Radio. In 2000 she became the Johannesburg Bureau Chief for Cable News Network.

Hunter-Gault is the recipient of numerous awards including two national news and documentary Emmy awards and two prestigious George Foster Peabody Award for excellence in broadcast journalism for her work on the *NewsHour's Apartheid People* series on contemporary life in South Africa as well as her coverage of South Africa's move toward a black government with National Public Radio. She was also honored in 2001 by the University of Georgia who named the Holmes-Hunter Academic Building in rememberance of her work to end segregation at the University.

Eugene D. Jackson (1943–)
Broadcast Executive

With over 25 years of experience in communications technology, Eugene D. Jackson began his entrepreneurial career in 1971 by raising $1 million to launch the Unity Broadcasting Network, parent company of the National Black Network (NBN). It is the first hourly news service that is distributed via satellite to over 125 African American-oriented radio stations. He is past president of Unity Broadcasting Network and four radio stations: WDAS-AM and WDAS-FM in Philadelphia and KATZ-AM and WZEN-FM in St. Louis.

Jackson was born in Waukomis, Oklahoma on September 5, 1943. He received a bachelor of science degree in electrical engineering from the University of Missouri at Rolla in 1967 and a master of business administration from Columbia University in 1971.

Jackson was an industrial engineer for Colgate-Palmolive from 1967 to 1968 and a production and project engineer for the Black Economic Union in New York City from 1968 to 1969. From 1969 to 1971, Jackson directed major industry programs for the Interracial Council for Business Opportunity in New York City.

Jackson serves on the boards of directors of the National Association of Broadcasters, the Council of Concerned Black Executives, Freedom National Bank, and Trans Africa (1977). He was a member of the Council on Foreign Relations in 1978 and on the board of governors of the International Radio and Television Society from 1974 to 1976.

Jackson recently divested his interest in broadcasting to develop and invest in cable television, the cellular telephone business, and the Internet. In 1993, he formed the World African Network of which he is chairman and chief executive officer. He is the vice chairman and the largest single shareholder in the Queens Inner-Unity Cable System (QUICS), the $63 million cable system that serves the borough of Queens in New York, as a joint venture with Time Warner, Inc.

John H. Johnson (1918–)
Publisher, Media Executive

One of America's foremost businessmen, John H. Johnson sits at the head of the most prosperous and powerful African American publishing company in the United States. Beginning with *Negro Digest* in 1942 and following with *Ebony* in 1945, Johnson built a chain of journalistic successes that now also includes *Jet, EM: Ebony Man* and most recently, *Ebony South Africa,* which marked the company's foray into international publishing.

Throughout the development of the above publications, he bought and sold three radio stations, started a book publishing division, and produced the former syndicated television show *Ebony/Jet Showcase.* He also created two beauty care lines—Supreme Beauty Products and the world-renowned Fashion Fair Cosmetics—as well as the Ebony Fashion Fair, a spectacular traveling fashion show. In addition, he produces the annual American Black Achievement Awards for television, which first aired in 1978.

Born in Arkansas City, Arkansas, on January 19, 1918, Johnson, at age six, lost his father, a mill worker, and was raised by his mother and stepfather. He attended local segregated schools until the family moved to Chicago. Johnson attended DuSable High School in Chicago, excelling academically and in extracurricular activities, while writing for the yearbook and school paper.

After graduation, an insurance executive heard a speech delivered by Johnson and was so impressed that he offered him a partial scholarship at the University of Chicago. After two years, however, Johnson quit classes and entered the Northwestern School of Commerce in 1938, studying for an additional two years before joining the Supreme Liberty Life Insurance Company. While running the company's house organ, it occurred to Johnson that a digest of weekly or monthly news items of special interest and importance to the African American community might achieve a wide African American readership. The idea resulted in the creation of *Negro Digest*, a periodical containing both news reprints and feature articles. Of the latter, perhaps the most beneficial to circulation was Eleanor Roosevelt's contribution to the feature "If I Were a Negro."

Buoyed by success, Johnson decided to approach the market with yet another offering, a pictorial magazine patterned after *Life.* The first issue of *Ebony* sold out its press run of 25,000 copies and soon became a permanent staple in the world of journalism as large companies began to advertise regularly in it.

In addition to serving as publisher and chief executive officer of Johnson Publishing Company, Inc., Johnson is chairman and chief executive officer of Supreme Life Insurance Company, chairman of WJPC-AM in Chicago and president of Fashion Fair Cosmetics. He has served on the boards of directors of the Greyhound Corporation, Verex Corporation, Marina Bank, Supreme Life Insurance Company, and Zenith Radio Corporation. Johnson also serves as a trustee for the Art Institute of Chicago and United Negro College Fund; on the advisory council of the Harvard Graduate School of Business; as a director for the Chamber of Commerce of the United States; on the advertising council of Junior Achievement and Chicago USO. He has received honorary doctoral degrees from numerous colleges and universities and many honors and awards from civil and professional organizations.

In 1989, Johnson wrote *Succeeding Against the Odds: The Autobiography of a Great American Business.* He has also received a number of awards including: The Medal of Freedom; the Against All Odds award; the Making History award; and the Trumpet award. He has been inducted into the Arkansas Business Hall of Fame and received an honorary doctorate from Harvard University.

Robert L. Johnson (1946–)
Cable Television Executive, Publisher, Businessman

Born on April 8, 1946, in Hickory, Mississippi, Robert L. Johnson graduated from the University of Illinois in 1968 and earned a master's degree in public administration in 1972 from Princeton University. He worked for the Washington, DC-based Urban League, the Corporation for Public Broadcasting, and as a press secretary for the Honorable Walter E. Fauntroy, congressional delegate from the District of Columbia, before joining the National Cable Television Association in 1976.

While serving as vice president of government relations for the association, Johnson came up with the idea of creating a cable channel aimed at African American viewers. In 1979, he took out a $15,000 personal loan to start Black Entertainment Television (BET), a component of the parent company BET Holdings, Inc. As the founder, chairman, and chief executive officer, Johnson molded the station into an extremely popular 24-hour cable station with shows that cater to the interests of African Americans. It reaches over 50 million homes.

BET Holdings, Inc. also operates four other major cable channels: BET On Jazz: The Cable Station; BET On Jazz International, a 24-hour jazz program service that reaches more than two million domestic and one million international subscribers; BET Movies, the first 24-hour, all-black movie channel; and BET Action pay-per-view, which reaches ten million subscribers.

BET Holdings, Inc. has also ventured into other businesses outside of the cable industry including a publishing division responsible for the following publications: *Emerge: Black America's News Magazine; BET Weekend*, the nation's third largest black publication with more than 1.2 million readers; *Heart & Soul*, a health, fitness and beauty magazine; and *Arabesque Books*, the only line of original African American romance novels written by African American authors. Other businesses include: MSBET, an interactive Web site based upon a joint venture with Microsoft Corporation; BET Soundstage, a new music theme restaurant; BET Soundstage Club, a joint venture with Walt Disney World Resort at Disney's Pleasure Island in Orlando, Florida; and BET On Jazz Restaurant, a fine dining restaurant specializing in new world cuisine.

In 1998, Johnson announced that he would soon be starting a venture to make low-budget films with African American stars, financed and produced by African Americans, and largely aimed at the African American urban market. His initial plans included showcasing three motion pictures and ten made-for-television films a year based on the Arabesque books. Johnson also continued to diversify his investments, buying up DC Airlines in 2000, making him the first African American to own a commercial airlines. In 2001, Johnson served on a federal commission to change the Social Security System.

In addition to running BET, Johnson is on the board of directors of US Airways, the Hilton Hotels Corporation, the United Negro College Fund, the National Cable Television Association's Academy of Cable Programming, the American Film Institute, and the Advertising Council. He has received the following major awards: the Business Leader of the Year award from the *Washingtonian* magazine (1998); *Broadcasting & Cable* magazine's Hall of Fame Award (1997); the Business of the Year Award by the Washington, DC. Chamber of Commerce (1985); and the Pioneer award by the Capitol Press Club (1984). Other awards include an NAACP Image Award, a Distinguished Alumni Award from Princeton University, and the President's Award from the National Cable Television Association.

Clarence B. Jones (1931–)
Publishing Executive

Born in Philadelphia in 1931, Jones graduated from Columbia University and Boston University Law School and then practiced as an attorney, specializing in civil rights and copyright cases for a New York City law firm. During this period, he was counsel for Dr. Martin Luther King Jr. and the Southern Christian Leadership Conference. In 1968 and again in 1972, he served as a delegate from New York State to the Democratic Convention. Jones was also an observer at Attica prison during the uprising there in 1971.

In 1971, Jones, as head of Inner City Broadcasting, led a group of investors in the purchase of the New York *Amsterdam News*, the nation's largest African American newspaper. Inner City Broadcasting also owned radio station WLIB and has full ownership of WBLS-FM.

Star Jones. *See* Law chapter.

Tom Joyner (1949?–)
Radio Personality and Announcer

The jingle "oh, oh, oh, it's the Tom Joyner Morning Show" can be heard in more than 100 markets on the four-hour syndicated radio program the *Tom Joyner Morning Show*. Debuting in January of 1994 and hosted by Joyner, it is estimated that over five million listeners tune in daily. In addition, his show reaches more African Americans in the country than any other electronic media. Known as the "Fly Jock, the hardest working man in radio" because he simultaneously hosted the morning show on KKDA in Dallas and the afternoon show for WGCI in Chicago in the 1980s, Joyner keeps audiences captivated with his educational and entertaining material.

Regular program highlights include: "Little Known Black History Facts;" the "It's Your World" soap opera; "Melvin's Lovelines;" comedy bits and news from his co-hosts J. Anthony Brown, Myra J., Ms. Dupree, and Sybil Wilkes; political commentary by Tavis Smiley, host of *BET Tonight with Tavis Smiley*; and the "Old School Breakfast Mix," a music medley of soul classics tailored to Joyner's baby-boomer audience. In addition, there are the "Thursday Morning Mom" and "Real Fathers, Real Men" segments in which people can send in a tribute to an exceptional parent and win that person $500.

Entering radio by accident, Joyner received a job as a newscaster at an African American-owned station in Montgomery, Alabama, not too long after graduating from Tuskegee University. While employed at the station and under the tutelage of Tracy Larkin, he learned that radio needs to be involved in the community. One example of the power of community radio occurred in the early 1970s when Joyner took to the airways to let people know that civil rights activist Stokely Carmichael and his South African wife, Miriam Makeba, needed a ride to a rally in Selma, Alabama. The next day, an entire local entourage was ready to escort them. A more recent example of Joyner's community activism would include the voter registration drive that he and Tavis Smiley coordinated in 1996 that attracted approximately 250,000 African Americans. Through this effort, both gentlemen believe that these additional voters helped to reelect U.S. House members Cynthia McKinney of Georgia and Bennie Thompson of Mississippi after redistricting put them in political jeopardy.

As a graduate of a historically black university, Joyner recently teamed up with the United Negro College Fund and established the Tom Joyner Foundation, a nonprofit organization, to award scholarships throughout the school year to college students in need of financial support to complete their education. Each month, he announces the college or university that will be the beneficiary.

Joyner is the first African American to be elected to the Radio Hall of Fame. He was inducted in 1998. Shortly after, in 2000, Joyner married fitness guru Donna Richardson in Jamaica. Joyner continued to benefit the community when he created an album with various artists, called the "Tom Joyner Allstars," in 2001. All of the proceeds from the album went to the Tom Joyner Foundation.

Delano Lewis (1938–)
Business and Broadcasting Executive

Born in Arkansas City, Kansas on November 12, 1938, Delano Eugene Lewis grew up in Kansas City, Kansas. He received his bachelor or arts degree in political science and history from the University of Kansas in 1960 and a law degree from the Washburn University School of Law in 1963. Fresh out of law school, Lewis became one of only ten African American attorneys in the U.S. Department of Justice in Washington, DC. After two years, he took a post with the Equal Employment Opportunity Commission (EEOC), and after only one year, in 1966, he volunteered for the Peace Corps and went to Nigeria and Uganda. Returning from Africa in 1969, Lewis worked as legislative assistant to various senators and congressmen and donated his time to advisory boards and community service organizations.

In 1973, Lewis left government and entered the private sector. He joined the Chesapeake and Potomac Telephone Company (C&P), a subsidiary of Bell Atlantic, as a public affairs manager in 1973. Subsequently, he held positions of increasing authority and responsibility, culminating in his election as president in July of 1988. In January of 1990, he became the chief executive officer. He then vaulted from the top of the telephone company to the role of president and chief executive officer of National Public Radio (NPR) in 1994. NPR, a membership organization of nearly six hundred public radio stations nationwide, produces and distributes the award-winning programs *All Things Considered, Talk of the Nation, Weekend Edition*, and *NPR's Performance Today*. His goal was to make NPR "the leading provider of high quality news, information and cultural programming worldwide." During his tenure, he focused on three areas: top quality programming, financial strength, and customer service.

At the invitation of Vice President Al Gore, Lewis served as a co-chair of the National Information Infrastructure Advisory Council (NIIAC) from 1994 to 1996. Its members consisted of business, industry, academic, and local government leaders. The NIIAC provided recommendations to the Clinton Administration on how best to develop America's communications network for full citizen participation by 2000.

After a four-year stint as the president and chief executive officer of NPR, Lewis resigned on August 1, 1998 to pursue other interests including teaching, lecturing, and writing a book about his experiences. In 1999, Lewis was chosen by President Clinton to become the U.S. Ambassador to South Africa. He has already focused his efforts on behalf of the United States to such problems as the HIV epidemic, continued integration, and air travel.

Lewis serves on many boards of directors, such as Colgate-Palmolive, Black Entertainment Tonight, Hallburton, and Guest Services, Inc. He is the chairman of the board of the Eugene and Agnes Meyer Foundation, an honorary member of Mainstream, a national board member of Africare, and an emeritus member of the board of the Washington Performing Arts Society. He was named "Man of the Year" by the Greater Washington Board of Trade in 1992, named "Washingtonian of the Year" by *Washingtonian* magazine in 1978, named to the Sovereign Military Order of Malta in 1987, and was awarded the President's Medal from Catholic University in 1978.

Edward T. Lewis (1940–)
Magazine Publisher, Businessman

Edward T. Lewis, who was born on May 15, 1940 in Bronx, New York, is the co-founder, chairman and CEO

Delano Lewis (left), former head of National Public Radio, with former President Clinton.

of Essence Communications Partners (ECP), the corporation that publishes the largest magazine for black women, Essence. However, as of June 28, 2002, he and his partner, Clarence O. Smith, ended their 32-year business partnership. It is believed that this unexpected change in management may be a result of the merger that took place between Essence Communications, Inc. (ECI) and Time, Inc., the nation's largest publisher and a subsidiary of AOL Time Warner, Inc., in 2000.

This historic partnership was forged to broaden the horizons of both companies. For *Essence*, the venture represented a step toward its global initiative to broaden the scope of its brand. For *Time*, the new relationship served as their entree into the burgeoning minority market, more specifically, African American women, a fast growing, but relatively uncharted area. Retaining 51 percent ownership, Lewis remarked that he saw this partnership as "a bright moment in the history of *Essence*" because it would "enable the company (*Essence*) to strengthen its brand in the global marketplace and open the doors to numerous media opportunities, while continuing to provide the best information and inspiration to African American women and people of African ancestry around the world."

A New York banker by profession, Lewis yearned to be on his own. He was just looking for the right opportunity. It arrived in the form of a seminar for aspiring African American entrepreneurs in 1969. At this seminar, someone suggested that a black women's magazine might have potential because it was an untapped market. Knowing nothing about the publication of magazines and even less about black women, Lewis and his four partners, one of which suggested the idea, were intrigued by the prospect. As such, they decided to proceed with the project by creating a magazine that promised, in its May 1970 inaugural issue, to "delight and to celebrate the beauty, pride, strength, and uniqueness of all Black women."

Success did not come as easily nor as quickly as the partners had assumed. The other three partners, all of whom had also attended the seminar, left within four years of the magazine's debut. However, their departures did not deter Lewis and Smith from striving to reach their goal. In actuality, it made both of them more determined because they both believed that the magazine was "right" for the market. They were just waiting for advertisers to realize that African Americans were viable consumers. (The first issue of *Essence* contained only 13 pages of ads out of a total of 100 pages; the next two issues each had only five pages of ads. Today, most profitable magazines aim for at least 50 percent.) Maintaining their unwavering resolve to be the publisher of a premier magazine targeted toward African American women paid off because *Essence* finally broke even in 1976.

In 2002, *Essence* had a monthly circulation of more than 1 million, and a readership of 7.6 million, 29 percent of which was male. Essence, whose readers tend to be between 18 and 50 years old, circulates primarily by subscription. In addition, 35 percent of the readers have a household income of at least $35,000 and 43 percent have attended or graduated from college.

Prior to merging with Time, Inc., Lewis, along with Smith, had expanded the company into a diversified media corporation that included Essence Entertainment, the Essence Music Festival, the Essence Awards television program, Essence Travel, Essence-By- Mail, Essence Art Reproductions, Essence Books, the essence.com Web site, and a host of other ventures.

Having served on numerous arts and educational boards throughout his illustrious career, Lewis's business accomplishments have been recognized by *Black Enterprise* magazine, the National Association of Black Journalists, the American Advertising Federation (Diversity Achievement Role Model Award), the United Negro College Fund (Lifetime Achievement Award), the Democratic Women's Political Caucus (Good Guy Award), the Black Women's Forum (The Men Who Dare Award), Ernst & Young (Entrepreneur of the Year), and many others.

Samuel Logan Jr. (1933–)
Newspaper Publisher

As the former publisher of the oldest and largest African American newspaper in Michigan, the Michigan Chronicle, Samuel Logan Jr. was born on August 31, 1933, in Louisiana. Initially having worked in the cotton fields of Louisiana, Logan moved to Detroit where he found employment in a factory. During the Korean War, he volunteered as a paratrooper with the United States Army, 82nd Airborne Division. After four years of service, he was honorably discharged in 1956. Upon his return to the United States, three men influenced his life: Frank Seymour, who eventually became his role model, Tom Cleveland, and Robert Leatherwood, both owners of Detroit's first African American advertising agency. Logan applied for a position with Cleveland and Leatherwood's agency and was hired to work as a "boy Friday" for $32 a week.

Seymour eventually sold his share of his business to Logan, whose performance had been impressive, which

made him a full partner. Later on, he worked as a sales representative with radio stations WCHB-AM and WCHD-FM, founded by another African American pioneer, Dr. Haley Bell. His next move occurred when he joined the *Michigan Chronicle* as assistant to then-advertising manager, the late Tremaine Shearer. Rising steadily through the ranks, he held the following positions over the years: advertising manager, advertising director, vice president of marketing, and general manager. On his way to the top, Logan took time to acquire a bachelor of arts degree in business administration from the University of Detroit, now the University of Detroit-Mercy, in 1973.

The *Michigan Chronicle* was eventually purchased by by Sengstacke Enterprises, whose headquarters are in Chicago. The company also produced the daily *Chicago Defender*, the *New Pittsburgh Courier*, and the *Tri-State Defender* in Memphis, Tennessee. Logan worked closely with John Sengstack owner of Sengstack Enterprises, and shortly before Sengstack passed away in 1997, the shareholders of Sengstack Enterprises voted Logan in as the new president of the company. However, Logan did not formally take over before Sengstack's death and Norman Trust, John Sengstack's trustee refused to acknowledge Logan's right to the company. He instead passed on the title to Sengstack's children who were left with a great deal of stock in the company. Logan was so angered that he not only stepped down from the presidency, but he left the Michigan Chronicle as well to pursue his own newspaper. In 2001, Logan began African American-oriented *Front Page* which is still published in the Michigan area.

During his time as general manager, the *Michigan Chronicle* was voted the best African American newspaper in the country several times by the National Newspaper Publishers Association. In addition, Logan is a member of the NAACP, the Urban League, the Michigan Historical Commission, and the Central Michigan University Scholarship Fund. He has received awards from the Metropolitan Youth Foundation, The Optimist Club of Central Detroit, Omega Psi Phi Fraternity, Inc., the State of Michigan-Minority Enterprises, and a host of others. In 1993, he was also voted "Publisher of the Year."

Robert C. Maynard (1937–1993)
Journalist, Newspaper Editor, Newspaper Publisher

The youngest of six children, Robert Clyve Maynard was born on June 17, 1937 in Brooklyn, New York. Reared in a family that stressed higher education, only Maynard chose not to pursue a college career. Instead, he cut his high school classes to spend his time at the editorial offices of the *New York Age*, which published his first articles. Although no longer in existence, the newspaper consumed all of Maynard's attention and by the age of 16, he had dropped out of school.

In 1961, Maynard's first big opportunity occurred when Jim Hicks, editor of *York (Pennsylvania) Gazette and Daily*, hired him as a police and urban affairs reporter. Covering a variety of stories, he was eventually assigned to the civil rights movement in the South. Hicks also persuaded him to apply for a one-year Nieman Fellowship for journalists at Harvard University. Maynard was selected for the prestigious award. His second big break occurred at the end of his fellowship. Noticing the broad range of talent that Maynard demonstrated throughout the fellowship program, Ben Bradlee, former editor of the *Washington Post*, hired him, in 1967. As a result, Maynard became the *Post's* first black national correspondent.

Maynard became an immediate success at the *Post*, had a wide range of contacts, and free rein to report local and national news. He originated and wrote a powerful five-part series on the growing black militancy, which was published in September of 1967. In 1972, he helped to cover the Watergate scandal—the illegal break-in of Democratic party offices by the Republican campaign committee during Richard Nixon's presidency—as well as it consequences.

While at the *Post*, Maynard developed a strong interest in developing training opportunities for minority journalists. In 1972, he and Earl Caldwell, a black reporter for the *New York Times*, co-directed a new summer training program in journalism at Columbia University that was funded by the Ford Foundation. When the program was discontinued two years later, Maynard took a leave of absence from the *Post* in 1977 to found a similar program known as the Institute for Journalism Education at the University of California, Berkeley.

Shortly after he founded the Institute, the Gannett newspaper chain hired Maynard as an affirmative action consultant. In 1979, Gannett also appointed him as editor of its newly acquired *Oakland Tribune*, making him the nation's first black director of editorial operations for a major daily newspaper. In spite of his ambitious efforts, the paper struggled financially. When Gannett decided to sale the newspaper in order to pursue other media opportunities, Maynard purchased the *Tribune*. The deal was made possible because of two bank loans and a long-term promissory note to Gannett. As president of the board and owner of 79 percent of the paper's stock, he became the first black in the United States to have a controlling interest in a major, general-circulation city daily.

Though Maynard failed to make the *Tribune* a financial success—primarily because of Oakland's dragging economy and its proximity to prosperous San Francisco and the booming South Bay—his style permeated the newspaper. A symbol of racial pride under Maynard's leadership, the Tribune won a multitude of awards, including a Pulitzer Prize in 1990 for its photographic coverage of the 1989 Bay Area earthquake. For a short time, Maynard was able to sustain the paper with loans and assistance in erasing the original debt from Gannett. However, eventually, matters worsened and he became terminally ill. Consequently, he sold the paper in 1992 to William Dean Singleton, owner of several newspapers in the Bay Area.

Active in many civic organizations, Maynard served on the board of trustees of the Rockefeller Foundation, the Pacific School of Religion, the Bay Area Council, the Associated Press, and the Pulitzer Prize Committee. He was a member of the Oakland Chamber of Commerce, the Council on Foreign Relations, and the Sigma Delta Chi Society of Professional Journalists. He held honorary doctorate degrees from York College in Pennsylvania and the California College of Arts and Crafts.

Upon selling the paper, Maynard kept a busy schedule during his last year of life. He became a faculty member at the Institute for Journalism Education, wrote a syndicated column, and served as a commentator on television news shows. After his death on August 17, 1993, his life was celebrated in both the Bay Area and Washington, D.C.

Robert G. McGruder (1942–2002)
Journalist, Newspaper Editor

A champion of diversity, Robert. G. McGruder, former executive editor of *The Detroit Free Press*, began his distinguished newspaper career in1963 with the now-defunct *Dayton Journal Herald*. Three months later, he joined the *Cleveland Plain Dealer*. The only black reporter in the newsroom, McGruder once said that this was "both a high and low point" in his career. In 1964, he was drafted. After serving in the army for two years in Washington, D.C., he returned to the *Plain Dealer* where he worked as a reporter, city editor, and managing editor.

While at the *Plain Dealer*, McGruder covered Carl Stokes, the first black mayor of a major city and a colorful political character not unlike Coleman A. Young, Detroit's first black mayor. McGruder's aggressive coverage of Stokes's leadership was the impetus for some of the legendary battles that occurred between Stokes and the Cleveland media. He once traveled to the

Bahamas with another reporter to investigate rumors that Stokes was involved in shady business. They found nothing. Eventually, McGruder and Stokes resolved their differences. Later, McGruder helped him write his 1973 autobiography, *Promises of Power*. In another fact-finding mission, he and another reporter examined city financial records and wrote that Cleveland was going broke. Many residents and officials ignored their conclusion, but before long Cleveland became the first big American city to declare bankruptcy.

Before McGruder became an editor at the *Plain Dealer*, he was a labor activist, serving as a negotiator for the Newspaper Guild in its talks with management. He also was one of the leaders of a lengthy strike. As city editor in 1978 and managing editor at 1981, the *Plain Dealer* won numerous local, state and national awards, including two from the National Press Club and one from the Overseas Press Club.

McGruder arrived in Detroit in 1986. It had taken Neal Shine, the longtime managing editor and publisher at the *Detroit Free Press*, more than a decade to hire him. Initially hired as deputy managing editor, he was promoted to managing editor of news in 1987, to managing editor, the second-ranking editor, in 1993, and in 1996, he became the first black executive editor at the Free Press. In 1995, while managing editor at the *Free Press*, McGruder became the first black president of the Associated Press Managing Editors (APME), an association of U.S. and Canadian editors whose newspapers are members of the Associated Press. Since 1931, the organization has been dedicated to the improvement, advancement and promotion of journalism through their newspapers and relationship with the Associated Press.

In each of his positions at the *Free Press*, McGruder talked frequently about the need to diversify newspaper staffs so they could do a better job of covering their constantly evolving communities. He even led a task force for Knight Ridder, the parent company of the *Free Press*, which resulted in major editing hires across the company. Taking his message to the national boards on which he served, McGruder once said that the best moments of his career were the opportunities to promote a number of African Americans to jobs that had never been held by black people.

When McGruder assumed the position of executive editor, the newspaper was in the midst of a bitter strike. Having been a former labor activist, McGruder quickly learned about the other side of the picket line. Maintaining his equilibrium throughout this stressful period, the strike did not end until 2000, McGruder remarked that "the strike was easily the most painful time in his life." Part of his pain was caused by the absence of

many of the minorities he had worked so hard to hire over the years.

In 2001, McGruder won the John S. Knight Gold Medal, the highest honor given to an employee of Knight Ridder. "I stand for diversity," he said when he accepted the medal. "I represent the African Americans, Latinos, Arab Americans, Asians, Native Americans, gays and lesbians, women, and all the others we must see represented in our business offices, newsrooms and newspapers if we truly want to meet the challenge of serving our communities." At the time of the award, Heath Meriwether, publisher of the *Free Press*, called McGruder "a giant in our profession" and praised his leadership at the Free Press and nationally as president of APME, as well as in his role as a member of the board of the American Society of Newspaper Editors (ASNE). Today, many of the people that McGruder hired and nurtured hold important positions at newspapers across the country.

McGruder was a member of the 1986, 1987, 1990, 1991, and 1998 nominating juries for the Pulitzer Prizes and a 1991–92 Knight Ridder/Duke University Fellow. He also served as director of the Michigan Press Association, as a member of the advisory board of the Institute for Minority Journalists at Wayne State University, and as a member of the Accrediting Committee of the Accrediting Council on Education in Journalism and Mass Communication.

Graduating from Kent State University in 1963, McGruder was born on March 31, 1942 in Lousiville, Kentucky. After a 20-month battle with cancer, he died on April 12, 2002. Upon his death, Knight Ridder established the Robert G. McGruder Scholarship Fund in his memory. The Fund will support promising journalism students enrolled at Wayne State University's Journalism Institute for Minorities. The company agreed to match all contributions, dollar for dollar, with a minimum grant of $50,000 to a maximum of $100,000. The *Free Press* also contributed $10,000 to the fund.

John Henry Murphy (1840–1922)
Publisher

John Henry Murphy was born a slave in Baltimore, Maryland, in 1840. He became superintendent of Bethel African Methodist Episcopal Church and founded the Sunday school newspaper, the *Sunday School Helper*. In 1892 he purchased the *Baltimore Afro-American* for $200. By 1922 the *Afro-American* had reached a circulation of 14,000, becoming the largest African American newspaper in the Northeast.

At first, Murphy set the paper's type himself, having acquired this skill in his forties. Throughout, he insisted that his paper maintain political and editorial independence. Murphy died April 5, 1922. The paper grew and is now under the control of Murphy's great-nephew, John H. Murphy III.

Clarence Page (1947–)
Columnist, Author

As a syndicated columnist for Tribune Media Services since 1987, Clarence Page began writing his local column for the *Chicago Tribune* in the mid-1980s. His column, which addresses education, politics, economics, prejudice, housing, hunger and crime, now appears in about 150 papers and in 1989, it won the Pulitzer Prize for Commentary. Based in Washington, D.C., since 1991, Page also does twice-weekly commentary on WGN-TV in Chicago.

Originally joining the *Tribune* as a reporter in 1969, his time with the newspaper was brief because he was drafted into the military. He then rejoined the *Tribune* in 1971 and resumed his journalism career in a variety of beats, including police, rewrite, religion and neighborhood news, with freelance assignments as a rock music critic for *Tempo* at night.

Page eventually became a foreign correspondent in Africa in 1976, an assistant city editor, and an investigative task force reporter in 1979. Growing restless, in 1980, he delved into television by becoming the director of the community affairs department at WBBM-TV, a CBS-owned station. At various times, he also assumed the role of documentary producer, reporter, and planning editor.

The highlight of those years occurred when he was assigned to the protests in 1982 that evolved into the Harold Washington mayoral campaign. As that history-making story rose in prominence, locally and nationally, so did Page's career. Soon thereafter, he was recognized as a "political expert." In 1984, he returned to the *Tribune* as a columnist and a member of the editorial board.

Over the years, Page's writing has been published in *Chicago* magazine, the *Chicago Reader, Washington Monthly, New Republic, The Wall Street Journal, New York Newsday,* and the defunct magazine, *Emerge.* His first book, *Showing My Color: Impolite Essays on Race and Identity,* was published in 1996 and soared to the middle of the best-seller list in Chicago. His television appearances include being a panelist on *The McLaughlin Group* and the *NewsHour with Jim Lehrer*—to which he also contributes essays. He has hosted several documentaries on the Public Broadcasting System and served

as a commentator on National Public Radio's *Weekend Edition Sunday.*

Page's other awards include a 1980 Illinois UPI award for community service for an investigative series titled *The Black Tax* and the Edward Scott Beck Award for overseas reporting of a 1976 series on the changing politics of Southern Africa. Page also participated in a 1972 *Chicago Tribune* Task Force series on vote fraud, which won the Pulitzer Prize. The Illinois and Wisconsin chapters of the American Civil Liberties Union bestowed awards on him for his columns on civil liberties and constitutional rights, and in 1992, he was inducted into the Chicago Journalism Hall of Fame.

Born on June 2, 1947, in Dayton, Ohio, Page earned a Bachelor of Science degree in journalism from Ohio University in 1969. Since that time, he has received honorary degrees from Columbia College in Chicago, Lake Forest College in Illinois, Chicago Theological Seminary, and other institutions of higher education, including his alma mater.

Norma Quarles (1936–)
Television News Correspondent

Born in New York City in 1936, Norma Quarles is an alumna of Hunter College and City College of New York. She first worked as a buyer for a New York specialty shop before moving to Chicago where she became a licensed real estate broker.

In 1965 she began her broadcast career in Chicago at WSDM Radio, working as a news reporter and disc jockey. She later returned to New York where she joined NBC in 1966 for a one-year training program. After three years with WKYC-TV in Cleveland, she was transferred to WNBC-TV in 1970, anchoring the early local news broadcasts during the *Today* show. In 1978, Quarles moved to NBC News as a correspondent based in Chicago, in addition to producing and reporting the *Urban Journal* series for WMAQ-TV. In 1988 Quarles left NBC after 21 years to join Cable News Network's New York bureau. Quarles served as a daytime anchor at CNN until 1990, when she became a correspondent.

Quarles is a member of the National Academy of Television Arts and Sciences, National Association of Broadcast Journalists, Sigma Delta Chi, and a board member of the Governor's National Academy of Television Arts and Sciences. In 1990, Quarles was inducted into the National Association of Black Journalists Hall of Fame. In 1993 Quarles earned a CINE Golden Eagle award as well as two New York Association of Black Journalists Awards for a one-hour CNN special on race relations called *A House Divided*, and for a feature report, "The Delany Sisters."

Dudley Randall (1914–2000)
Publisher, Poet, Librarian

Dudley Randall was born in Washington, DC, on January 14, 1914, and was living in Detroit by the time he was nine years old. An early harbinger of Randall's poetic talent was the appearance of one of his poems in the *Detroit Free Press* at the early age of 13. After serving in the U.S. Army Signal Corps (1942–1946), Randall worked in the foundry at the Ford Motor Company and as a postal carrier and clerk while attending Wayne State University in Detroit. He received his bachelor of arts degree in 1949 and a master of arts degree in library science from the University of Michigan in 1951. He also did graduate work at the University of Ghana.

Randall worked in progressively responsible librarian positions at Lincoln University in Jefferson City, Missouri (1951 to 1954), Morgan State College in Baltimore, Maryland (1954 to 1956), and the Wayne County Federated Library System in Wayne, Michigan (1956 to 1969). From 1969 to 1975, he was a reference librarian and poet-in-residence at the University of Detroit. In 1969, he also served as a visiting lecturer at the University of Michigan.

Randall's love of poetry led to his founding of the *Broadside Press* in 1965. He wanted to make sure that African Americans had an outlet to "speak to and for their people." His works include *Poem Counterpoem* (1966); *On Getting a Natural* (1969); and *A Litany of Friends: New and Selected Poems* (1981). He retired from Broadside Press in 1993; however, it continues to publish new works. In 1980, he founded the Broadside Poets Theater and the Broadside Poetry Workshop.

Randall was active in many Detroit cultural organizations and institutions including the Detroit Council for the Arts and the International Afro-American Museum in Detroit, now the Charles H. Wright Museum of African American History. In 1981, Randall received the Creative Artist Award in Literature from the Michigan Council for the Arts and in 1986 he was named the first poet laureate of Detroit by the late Mayor Coleman A. Young. Randall died on August 5, 2000 in Southfield, Michigan.

Ahmad Rashad (1949–)
Sports Commentator, Television Host

Possessing boyish good looks and a strong athletic frame, many would find it hard to believe that Ahmad Rashad, once known as Bobby Moore, was born on November 19, 1949. As the youngest of six children—three boys and three girls. Born in Portland, Oregon, but reared in Tacoma, Washington, the name change occurred after he converted to Islam in the 1970s while playing professional football for the St. Louis Cardinals. Initially, many of his coaches and teammates viewed the change as silly or pretentious, but they learned to accept it.

Upon leaving St. Louis, Rashad played for Buffalo and Seattle before joining the Minnesota Vikings in 1976. After 11 years of playing professional football, he decided to call it quits in 1983. Despite his early departure, Rashad left his mark on the league. He retired with 495 catches, tenth on the all-time receiving list at the time. Unlike many athletes, prior to announcing his retirement, he had begun to prepare for the next stage in his career: broadcasting. Several times a week after practice, he would go to the CBS affiliate, WCCO-TV in Minnesota, to hone his craft.

His dedication proved to be beneficial because from 1983 to 1988, he worked as a pre-game host for *NFL on NBC*. He also made headline news in 1985 when he proposed during a televised football game to Phylicia Ayers-Allen, better known as Clair Huxtable, the matriarch on the long-running sitcom, *The Cosby Show*. They had one child together, a daughter, but divorced in 2001.

Rashad moved to the booth in 1989 to serve as an analyst. In 1994, he moved back to the studio after being named pre-game show co-host and stayed in that position through the end of the 1997–98 season and Super Bowl XXXII. He lent his talents to *Notre Dame Saturday*, where in 1991 he was a host, and to *NBC Sports Update*, where he served as an anchor and as a commentator for various *SportsWorld* telecasts.

Named executive producer of *NBA Inside Stuff* and NBA Entertainment-produced specials in March 1998, as an Emmy Award-winning sportscaster, Rashad has been the host of *Inside Stuff* on NBC since its inception in 1990. He is also a host for the *NBA on NBC* studio show. In addition to these duties, he extended his duties to include studio hosting, feature reporting, and analysis and commentary for a variety of sports and events, especially NBC's coverage of the NBA.

In between his anchoring assignments, Rashad served as a weekend host and late night correspondent at the 1996 Olympic Games in Atlanta; as one of the hosts of NBC's Olympic TripleCast from Barcelona in 1992; and as studio anchor during coverage of the Seoul Olympics in 1988. His efforts in Seoul earned him an Emmy for writing.

Rashad, a graduate of the University of Oregon, where he was a two-time All-American, was the 1995 recipient of the University's Pioneer Award, the highest honor given to an alumnus. In addition, he served on the university's board of trustees. Holding an honorary degree of Doctor of Journalism from the University of Puget Sound, Rashad was a four-time Pro-Bowl selection for the Minnesota Vikings and was voted to the Vikings All-time 25th Anniversary Team and the 40th Anniversary team. He is also the author of the bestselling book, *Rashad: Vikes, Mikes and Something on the Backside.*

William J. Raspberry (1935–)
Commentator, Journalist

Born in Okolona, Mississippi, on October 12, 1935, Raspberry received his bachelor of science degree in history from Indiana Central College in 1958. While a student, he worked at the *Indianapolis Recorder* as a reporter, photographer, and editorial writer from 1956 through 1960. In 1960, Raspberry was drafted by the Army and served as a public information officer until his discharge in 1962. He began working for the *Washington Post* as a teletypist and soon worked his way up to reporter, assistant city editor, and finally a columnist in 1966. He continues writing today as a nationally syndicated columnist, appearing in 225 newspapers. Raspberry also teaches at Duke University, serving in the Knight Chair in Communications and Journalism.

Raspberry has also appeared as a television panelist and commentator and in 1965 was named Journalist of the Year by the Capital Press Club for his coverage of the Los Angeles Watts riot. In 1967, he received a Citation of Merit in Journalism from Lincoln University in Jefferson, Missouri, for distinction in improving human relations. He is generally regarded as an independent thinker, holding to no particular orthodoxy. His book *Looking Backward at Us*, published in 1991, is very similar to his other writings in that it deals with issues concerning the African American experience and social conditions and race relations in the United States.

Raspberry has taught journalism at Howard University and the University of Maryland School of Journalism. He is also a member of the Poynter Institute for Media Studies board of advisors and the Pulitzer Prize Board, Grid Iron Club, Capitol Press Club, Washington Association of Black Journalists, and Kappa Alpha Psi. Raspberry won the Pulitzer Prize in 1994 for Distinguished Commentary and the Lifetime Achievement Award from the National Association of Black Journalists (NABJ). In 1997, he was named one of the 50 most influential journalists in the national press corps by the *Washingtonian* magazine. In addition, he has been awarded honorary doctorates by 15 educational institutions.

Max Robinson (1939–1988)
Television News Correspondent

Born in Richmond, Virginia, on May 1, 1939, Max Robinson attended Oberlin College, Virginia Union University, and Indiana University. He began his career as a newsreader at WTOV-TV in Portsmouth, Virginia. In 1965, he worked as a studio floor director at WTOP-TV (now WUSA) in Washington, DC, before moving on to WRC-TV to work as a news reporter, and to WTOP-TV, where he worked as anchor.

In 1978, Robinson joined ABC *World News Tonight*, becoming the first African American network anchor. Almost immediately, Robinson took it upon himself to fight racism at whatever cost necessary. ABC management became frustrated with Robinson and moved him to the post of weekend anchor. In 1983, Robinson left ABC for WMAQ-TV in Chicago, where he remained until 1985.

Robinson died of complications from acquired immune deficiency syndrome (AIDS) on December 20, 1988, in Washington, DC. He was the recipient of three Emmy awards, the Capital Press Club Journalist of the Year Award, and the Ohio State Award, as well as an award from the National Education Association. He also taught at Federal City College, in Washington, DC, and the College of William and Mary in Williamsburg, Virginia.

Al Roker (1954–)
Weathercaster, Feature Reporter, Entrepreneur

Delighting visitors from across the country on the sidewalks outside of Studio 1-A with his humor, honesty, outgoing personality, and witty comments, Al Roker is the full-time weatherman for NBC's *Today* show and the weathercaster for News Channel 4's *Live at Five.*

Born Albert Lincoln Roker on August 20, 1954, in New York, New York, Roker began his broadcasting career while still in college by landing a job as a weekend weatherman at WTVH-TV in Syracuse, New York, in 1974. After receiving a bachelor of arts degree in communications from the State University of New York at Oswego in 1976, he moved on to weathercasting jobs in Washington, DC (1976–1978) and Cleveland, Ohio (1978–1983), before becoming the weekend weathercaster at WNBC in New York in 1983. In 1998, his alma mater awarded him an honorary doctorate.

Besides his weathercasting duties, this six-time Emmy Award winner conducts celebrity interviews, cooking segments, and technology updates. Since 1985, he has hosted the annual *Christmas at Rockefeller Center*

Al Roker.

celebration. He has also co-hosted the *Macy's Thanksgiving Day Parade* and the *Rose Bowl Parade*.

In 1994, Roker ventured into the world of entrepreneurship by creating Al Roker Productions, Inc. The multimedia company is involved in the development and production of network, cable, home video, and public televison projects. Two of the most successful projects include the critically acclaimed special on PBS about severe weather *Savage Skies* and a highly rated travel series called *Going Places*. His Web site allows visitors to receive up-to-the-minute weather forecasts, peruse Roker's thoughts on a variety of subjects, laugh at his daily cartoon, write to him, and challenge the mind with some brain-twisting trivia. Another business venture, RokerWare, Inc., is a trademark line of merchandise all personally designed by Roker. Inspired by the birth of his baby girl Leila in 1998, Roker introduced the WeatherBabies line as part of RokerWare, where fans can purchase a baby bib or baby t-shirt.

In 2000, Roker forged into the world of writing with *Don't Make Me Stop This Car!: Adventures in Fatherhood.* He followed this book up in 2001 when *Al Roker's*

Big, Bad Book of Barbecue: 100 Easy Recipes for Backyard Barbecue and Grilling hit the bookshelves.

As an active member of the community, Roker has been honored by many civic and charitable organizations for his professional and community-minded activities and contributions. These include the Children's Defense Fund, the National Urban League Rainforest Alliance, Read Across America, the Arthur Ashe Institute for Urban Health, the Ronald McDonald House, the Hale House, and the Harlem Boys Choir. In addition, he is currently a member of the board of directors of Family AIDS Network and serves as honorary chair for the Susan G. Komen Breast Cancer Foundation Race for the Cure/Three Miles of Men.

Carl Thomas Rowan (1925–2000)
Commentator, Journalist

Carl Rowan was born August 11, 1925 in Ravenscroft, Tennessee. He attended Tennessee A&I (now Tennessee State University) in Nashville and Washburn University in Topeka, Kansas. He received his bachelor of arts degree in mathematics from Oberlin College in 1947 and a master of arts degree in journalism from the University of Minnesota in 1948.

In 1948, Rowan went to work as a copyeditor, then later as a staff writer, for the *Minneapolis Tribune*, where he worked until 1961. In 1961, he was hired by the U.S. Department of State as deputy assistant secretary for public affairs. After three years with the Department of State, Rowan was appointed U.S. ambassador to Finland by President Lyndon Johnson in 1963, and in 1964 he was appointed director of the United States Information Agency (USIA), which operates overseas educational and cultural programs including the worldwide radio service *Voice of America*. In 1965, Rowan resigned from the USIA to work as a columnist for the *Chicago Sun Times*.

Rowan has authored several books including *South of Freedom, Wait Till Next Year, Just Between Us Blacks, Dream Makers, Dream Breakers: The World of Justice Thurgood Marshall,* and a memoir entitled *Breaking Barriers.* He received the Alfred I. DuPont-Columbia University Silver Baton in 1987 for the television documentary *Thurgood Marshall: The Man.* Rowan is a syndicated columnist and his work appears in numerous newspapers across the country.

Rowan has served as a political commentator for the Post-Newsweek Broadcasting Company and has been a frequent panelist on the NBC program *Meet the Press* and the syndicated programs *Agronsky & Co* and *Inside Washington.*

Rowan is the founder of the Project Excellence program, a scholarship program for African American high school students. Scholarships are awarded to students who embrace academic achievement and resist negative peer pressure. Since its inception, the program has awarded more than $52 million in scholarships to more than 2,150 high school graduates.

In 1998, Rowan received the prestigious Victory Award from the National Rehabilitation Hospital in Washington, DC, for overcoming one of the biggest obstacles in his life—that of walking again after having his right leg amputated just below the knee because of a severe foot infection brought on by complications from diabetes. Established in 1986, the award is given to honor individuals who have coped with physical adversity in an exemplary way.

On September 23, 2000, Rowan died of natural causes at Washington Hospital Center in Washington, D.C. He was 75.

John B. Russwurm (1799–1851)
Newspaper Publisher

Born in Port Antonio, Jamaica, on October 1, 1799, Russwurm graduated from Bowdoin College in Brunswick, Maine in 1826. From Brunswick, Russwurm moved to New York, where on March 16, 1827, he and

John Brown Russwurm beside a fragment of *Freedom's Journal.*

Samuel E. Cornish published the first edition of *Freedom's Journal*—the nation's first African American newspaper.

In 1829, Russwurm decided to immigrate to Monrovia, Liberia. From 1830 to 1835, he published the *Liberia Herald.* Cornish, who had left the paper in late 1827, resumed his role as editor in 1830, publishing the paper under the name *Rights of All.*

Russwurm went on to serve as superintendent of education in Monrovia and later as governor of a settlement. He died June 17, 1851.

John Herman Henry Sengstacke (1912–1997)
Publishing Executive

A nephew of the great publisher Robert Abbott, John Sengstacke was born in Savannah, Georgia, on November 25, 1912. He received a bachelor of arts degree from Hampton Institute, now Hampton University, in 1934. Upon graduation, he went to work with Robert Abbott, attended school to learn printing, and wrote editorials and articles for three Abbott papers. In 1934, he became vice president and general manager of the company.

During World War II, Sengstacke was an advisor to the U.S. Office of War Information during a period of severe tension between the government and the African American press. He also presided over the Chicago rationing board.

In 1940, after the death of his uncle, Sengstacke became president of the Robert S. Abbott Publishing Company. In 1956, Sengstacke founded the *Daily Defender,* one of only three African American dailies in the country. In 1940, he founded the Negro Newspaper Publishers' Association, now known as the National Newspaper Publishers Association, and served six terms as president. It is comprised of over 200 African American newspapers. He was president of Tri-State Defender, Inc., Florida Courier Publishing Company, New Pittsburgh Courier Publishing Company, Amalgamated Publishers, Inc., chairman of the Michigan Chronicle Publishing Company and Sengstacke Enterprises, Inc., and treasurer of Chicago Defender Charities, Inc.

Prior to his death on May 28, 1997, after an extended illness, Sengstacke served in leadership positions with many professional, educational, and civic organizations, received a number of presidential appointments, and was the recipient of several academic awards. He held the position of trustee at Bethune-Cookman College and chairman of the board at Provident Hospital and the Training School Association. He was a member of the board of directors of the American Society of Newspaper Editors, on the advisory board of the Boy Scouts of America, and a principal in Chicago United.

Bernard Shaw holding an Ace Award.

Bernard Shaw (1940–)
Television News Anchor

Bernard Shaw was born on May 22, 1940, in Chicago. He was the principal Washington anchor for *News-Stand: CNN & Time*, a weekly primetime investigative newsmagazine on the Cable News Network (CNN). He also co-anchored *Inside Politics*, the nation's only daily program devoted exclusively to political news. Shaw had been on board as the Washington anchor since the cable network went on the air on June 1, 1980, until his recent retirement in 2001. He often reported first-hand on major international news stories. His reporting took him to 46 countries spanning five continents. The awards, honors, and accolades that Shaw has received over the years for his outstanding journalistic aptitude are too numerous to recount.

Shaw was present when the Chinese government's tanks rolled into Tiananmen Square in May of 1989, crushing the student-led pro-democracy movement. In January of 1991, Shaw, along with two other colleagues from CNN, were stranded in Baghdad when allied bombing attacks launched Operation Desert Storm.

From their hotel room, Shaw and the others provided first-hand accounts of the bombing of the city. Shaw covered the outbreak of the Gulf War and the bombing of the Alfred P. Murrah Federal Building in Oklahoma City, Oklahoma, the worst act of terrorism in U.S. history.

As a result of his comprehensive coverage of Operation Desert Storm, Shaw received numerous international, as well as national, awards and honors. In July of 1991, he received the Eduard Rhein Foundation's Cultural Journalistic Award, marking the first time that the foundation has presented this award to a non-German. In October of 1992, the Italian government honored him with its President's Award, presented to those leaders who have actively contributed to development, innovation, and cooperation. In December of the same year, Shaw was the recipient of the coveted David Brinkley Award for excellence in communication from Barry University.

Shaw's first job as a television journalist came in 1971 with CBS News at their Washington bureau where he conducted an exclusive interview with Attorney General John Mitchell at the height of the Watergate scandal. In 1977 he left CBS to join ABC News as Miami bureau chief and Latin American correspondent. Shaw was one of the first reporters to film from location on the Jonestown massacre story in Guyana, and his team provided the only aerial photos of the mass suicide-murder site. ABC sent Shaw to Iran to report on the 1979 hostage crisis at the American embassy in Teheran. He then returned to Washington as ABC's senior Capitol Hill correspondent.

Prior to joining CBS News, Shaw was a reporter for Group W, a Westinghouse Broadcasting Company, based first in Chicago and then in Washington (1966–1971). Shaw served as Group W's White House correspondent during the last year of the Johnson Administration (1968). His other assignments included local and national urban affairs, the struggles of the Mexican Americans and Puerto Ricans, and the plight of the American Indians in Billings, Montana. In 1968, he reported on the aftermath of the assassination of Dr. Martin Luther King Jr. in Memphis and his funeral in Atlanta.

Shaw has been elected a Fellow of the Society of Professional Journalists (SPJ), the highest distinction the society gives to journalists for public service. In June of 1995, he was inducted into the SPJ Hall of Fame. In October of 1996, he received the Paul White Life Achievement Award from the Radio Television News Directors' Association, one of the industry's most coveted awards. One month later, he and his co-anchor Judy Woodruff garnered the 1996 ACE for Best Newscaster of the Year for *Inside Politics*. In April of 1997, he was inducted into the Chicago Journalists Hall of Fame. In September of 1997, he was the inaugural recipient of the Congressional Medal of Honor Society's Tex McCrary Award for journalism, which honors the distinguished achievements of those in the field of journalism.

Shaw hopes in the near future to spend more time with his family, his wife and two adult children, and to get into the literary world, possibly beginning with an autobiography of his career.

Carole Simpson (1940–)
Television News Anchor

Born on December 7, 1940, Carole Simpson graduated from the University of Michigan with a bachelor of arts degree in journalism and did graduate work in journalism at the University of Iowa. She first entered broadcasting in 1965 as a reporter for a local radio station, WCFL, in Morris, Illinois. In 1968, she moved to radio station WBBM in Chicago and in 1970, she went to work as a reporter for the Chicago television station WMAQ.

Simpson made her first network appearance as a substitute anchor for NBC *Nightly News* in 1974 and as anchor on NBC's *Newsbreak* on weekends. In 1982, Simpson joined ABC in Washington as a general assignment correspondent. She is currently the anchor of *World News Sunday* and an Emmy Award-winning senior correspondent for ABC News. She reports most frequently on family and social issues for *World News Tonight With Peter Jennings.* Her reports have also appeared on *20/20*, *Nightline*, and other ABC News broadcasts and specials. She is an occasional contributor to *This Week* and has substituted for Peter Jennings on *World News Tonight.*

Simpson was most recently in the media spotlight in 2001 when she was suspended from reporting on air for two weeks when she made remarks at an Oct. 16 International Women's Media Foundation in which she revealed facts about the identity of the ABC producer whose son apparently contracted anthrax while visiting the network, and spoke about a suspicious letter received by her colleague Cokie Roberts, contradicting earlier network statements. Simpson later said she was sorry for the remarks.

Simpson has served as president of the Radio and Television Correspondents Association, as chairperson of the ABC Women's Advisory Board, and as a member of the board of directors of the Washington chapter of the Society of Professional Journalists. She is also a member of Theta Sigma Phi, the Radio Television News Directors Association, and the National Association of Black Journalists. She has been awarded the Media Journalism Award, the Milestone Award in broadcast journalism from the National Commission of Working Women, the Turner Broadcasting "Trumpet" Award for scholastic achievement, the Leonard Zeidenberg First Amendment Award from Radio and Television News Director Foundation, and the Silver Bell Award from the Ad Council. She was inducted into the University of Iowa Communications Hall of Fame and received the University of Missouri's distinguished journalist award. In 1992, she was named Journalist of the Year by the National Association of Black Journalists. She has established several college scholarships for women and minorities pursuing careers in broadcast journalism at the University of Michigan, as well as the Carole Simpson scholarship administered by the Radio and Television News Directors Foundation (RTNDF). She also established the Carole Simpson Leadership Institute in Dakar, Senegal, for African women journalists in 1998.

Tavis Smiley (1964–)
Host, Executive Producer, Political Commentator

Recognized for his tough interviewing tactics and strong emphasis on issues relevant to the African American community, *Time* selected Tavis Smiley as one of America's 50 most promising young leaders under the age of 40. *Ebony* profiled him as one of Black America's future leaders. *Newsweek* crowned him as among "20 people changing how Americans get their news" and dubbed him one of the nation's "captains of the airwaves." The accolades for the innumerable talents of Tavis Smiley, former host of *BET Tonight with Tavis Smiley*, a live one-hour news and entertainment program on Black Entertainment Television (BET), are endless.

Smiley, born on September 13, 1964 in Gulfport, Mississippi, is the author of *On Air: The Best of Tavis Smiley on the Tom Joyner Morning Show*; the critically acclaimed book *Hard Left: Straight Talk About the Wrongs of the Right*; and *How To Make Black America Better* in 2001. Twice a week, he offers political commentary on the *Tom Joyner Morning Show*, a nationally syndicated radio show. In this role, Smiley led several national radio campaigns which influenced national events, such as Fox Television's decision to return *Living Single* to the lineup, Christie's auction house donation of slavery artifacts to an African American museum, the Katz Radio Group's increased media buys on African American and Hispanic radio, and the honoring of Rosa Parks with the Congressional Medal. In addition to his other on-air roles, Smiley serves as a political analyst on CNN.

Smiley received a bachelor of arts degree in law and public policy at Indiana University in 1986. In 1988, he went to Los Angeles to work for the city's first African American mayor, Tom Bradley. In 1991, he started doing radio segment *The Smiley Report*, which became so popular that it was nationally syndicated a year later. His popularity spread even further when he signed on as the political commentator on the *Tom Joyner Morning Show*. The position was initially designed as a temporary assignment to help Joyner register people to vote. Smiley's few moments on the air were such a success that Joyner extended an invitation to him to regularly comment on the issues of the day.

In the 1990s, Smiley was perhaps best well know for his television show on BET entitled *BET Tonight with Tavis Smiley*, which garnered Smiley three NAACP Image Award for Best "News, Talk or Information Series." In 1999, BET chose not to renew Smiley's contract, and Smiley moved on to work at ABC-TV as a special correspondent for Good Morning America and Primetime Thursday. He also can often be seen as a news correspondent for CNN. Smiley continued to broadcast on the *Tom Joyner Morning Show* and hosted the *The Tavis Smiley Show* for National Public Radio.

Smiley is the recipient of numerous awards, including the Mickey Leland Humanitarian Award, NAMIC in 1998. He maintains memberships with Kappa Alpha Psi Fraternity, Inc., the National Association of Black Journalists, NAACP, and the American Federation of Television and Radio Artists (AFTRA).

Barbara Smith (1946–)
Publisher, Editor, Writer

Barbara Smith was born on November 16, 1946, in Cleveland, Ohio. She earned a bachelor of arts degree from Mount Holyoke College in 1969 and a master's degree from the University of Pittsburgh in 1971. She served as an instructor at the University of Massachusetts from 1976 until 1981, Barnard College in 1983, and New York University in 1985. Together with Myrna Bain, Cherríe Moraga, and Mariana Romo-Carmona, Smith operates Kitchen Table: Women of Color Press, the first publisher in the United States committed to publishing and distributing the work of Third World women.

Smith has co-authored and co-edited numerous books including *Yours in Struggle, Three Feminist Perspectives on Anti-Semitism and Racism, Home Girls, A Black Feminist Anthology, But Some of Us Are Brave, Black Women's Studies*, and *THE TRUTH THAT NEVER HURTS: Writings on Race, Gender, and Freedom.*

Clarence O. Smith (1933–)
Magazine Publisher, Businessman

Clarence O. Smith was born on March 31, 1933. As co-founder of Essence Communications Partners, previously Essence Communications, Inc., Smith was once the driving force behind the success of *Essence* magazine, the company's premier publication targeted toward African American women. On June 28, 2002, however, Smith officially announced his resignation "to pursue other opportunities in existing and new media projects outside of *Essence*." His decision to leave the company marked the end of a 32-year business relationship with Edward T. Lewis, the company's other founder.

Industry experts speculate that his unexpected departure may be a result of the massive corporate restructuring and major staff changes that have taken place since Essence Communications, Inc. (ECI) merged with Time, Inc., the nation's largest publisher and a subsidiary of AOL Time Warner, Inc., in 2000. Regardless of the reason, what was once considered one of the "most successful marriages in black business" abruptly ended. The dissolution of the Lewis and Smith partnership was even more startling because both of them were recently hailed in the June 2002 issue of *Black Enterprise* as "Marathon Men," the management of one of only five companies that have been listed on the BE 100s—the nation's largest black-owned businesses—since the list's inception 30 years ago.

Forever "the salesman," Smith's uncanny ability to attract high-profile advertisers—the lifeblood of consumer publishing—to the magazine in its early years helped to ensure its future, thus making it the household name it is today. Securing ads in the first few years of the magazine proved to be more daunting than Smith had anticipated. Nevertheless, relying on the skills he had acquired as an insurance salesman at the Prudential Life Insurance Company in the early 1960s—when he joined the company there were only two other black agents—Smith eventually established relationships with prestigious advertisers such as Chanel, Giorgio, and Estee Lauder, an account that took him 22 years to close.

Always on the look out for opportunities that would ensure that the company stayed on the cutting edge of business, Smith was instrumental in leading the company beyond publishing into licensing, direct-mail marketing, and television production. He played a key role in the creation of *The Essence Awards*, an annual prime-time network special, and in the production of award-winning programs such as *Essence*, a weekly syndicated magazine and news-service television show. Later, he helped launch Essence-By-Mail, a mail-order catalog catering to African Americans, and Essence Art

Reproductions, a company that markets fine art crafted by African American artists.

In the 1990s, Smith and Lewis ventured into other areas of publishing, starting with the acquisition of *Income Opportunities*, a magazine for people starting new businesses. Three years later, the company entered into a joint venture to publish *Latina*, the first bilingual lifestyle magazine that addressed the interests of Hispanic women in the United States.

Another major triumph for the company occurred in 1995 when the first Essence Music Festival was held in New Orleans. Now an annual event, the four-day festival drew 160,000 attendees to the Superdome during each of its first three years. Yet in 1996, Smith and Lewis nearly cancelled the festival after Louisiana governor M.J. Foster Jr. announced that he was discontinuing affirmative-action programs throughout the state. Governor Foster eventually agreed to meet with Smith, Lewis, and Hugh B. Price, the president of the National Urban League, to discuss plans. After the meeting, Governor Foster issued a new executive order that offered better career opportunities for minorities in Louisiana.

A vigorous advocate for minority representation in the media, Smith has served as the chairman of the Chicago-based African American Marketing and Media Association and as a founding member of the African American Anti-Defamation Association. As with Lewis, Smith has also been recognized by *Black Enterprise* magazine throughout his career for his accomplishments, as well as by Ernst & Young with the Entrepreneur of the Year Award.

Although Smith is no longer with Essence Communications Partners, he will be recognized as president emeritus and co-founder of *Essence* magazine. He will also be credited for generating revenues for the company through the magazine's advertising and developing the company's entertainment division. Lewis will assume his duties.

Thomas Sowell (1930–)
Economist, Professor, Author, Columnist

Since 1980, Thomas Sowell has been the Rose and Milton Friedman Senior Fellow in Public Policy at the Hoover Institution at Stanford University. He has also been associated with three other research centers during his career. From 1972 to 1974, he was project director at the Urban Institute; from 1976 to 1977, he was a fellow at the Center for Advanced Study in the Behavioral Sciences at Stanford University; and from 1975 to 1976, he was an adjunct scholar of the American Enterprise Institute.

A prolific writer—his specialties are economics, history, social policy, and ethnicity—Sowell has published over 25 books, as well as numerous articles and essays covering a wide range of topics from classic economic theory to judicial activism to civil rights to immigration to choosing the right college. His writings have also appeared in scholarly journals in economics, law, and other fields.

In the 1990s, his research focused on cultural history in a world perspective, a subject on which he began writing a trilogy in 1982. The trilogy includes *Race and Culture* (1994), *Migrations and Cultures* (1996) and *Conquests and Cultures* (1998). More recently, he published *Barbarians Inside the Gates* and *The Quest for Cosmic Justice* in 1999. Detouring from his usual style of writing, in 2002, he released his autobiography, *A Personal Odyssey*.

As a nationally syndicated columnist for Creators Syndicate, his column appears in major newspapers throughout the nation. He has also written regular columns for the Scripps-Howard News Service, the *Los Angeles Herald- Examiner*, *New York Times*, *Wall Street Journal*, *Washington Post*, *Los Angeles Times*, *Washington Star*, *Newsweek*, *Newsday*, and *Stanford Daily*. Typically described as a black conservative, some view his writing as groundbreaking for it strongly favors a free-market economic policy. Others, however, strongly disagree with it because his opinions often conflict with those of the minority population.

Born on June 30, 1930 in North Carolina, Sowell grew up in New York, more precisely, in Harlem. As with many others in his neighborhood, he left home early and did not finish high school. The next few years were challenging, but eventually he joined the Marine Corps and became a photographer in the Korean War. After leaving the service, he entered Harvard University where he graduated magna cum laude with a Bachelor of Arts degree in 1958. From Harvard, he went on to receive his Master of Arts degree from Columbia University in 1959 and a Doctor of Philosophy degree from the University of Chicago in 1968. His area of study for each of these degrees was economics.

In the early 1960s, Sowell held jobs as an economist with the Department of Labor and AT&T. Yet, his real interest was in teaching and scholarship and in 1965, he began the first of many professorships at Cornell University. His other teaching assignments include Rutgers University, Amherst University, Brandeis University and the University of California at Los Angeles, where he taught in the early 1970s and again from 1984 to 1989.

Though Sowell had been a regular contributor to newspapers in the late 1970s and early 1980s, he did not begin his career as a newspaper columnist until 1984. Adapting to this style of writing very quickly, he was able to get to the core of issues without the "smoke and mirrors" that so often accompany academic writing.

In 1990, he won the prestigious Francis Boyer Award, presented by the American Enterprise Institute.

Martha Jean Steinberg (c.1930–2000)
Radio Personality, Broadcasting Executive & Owner, Minister

Always coy about her age, Martha Jean Steinberg, better known as "The Queen," acquired this regal title from an announcer early in her career. According to her, when she started out in the business in the 1950s, "every black disc jockey had to have a rhyming, stereotyped name." Although the name was given to her at a time when racism was prevalent in the industry—and under less than desirable conditions—she decided to keep it upon moving to Detroit in the 1960s, thus making it her trademark.

Before she became radio royalty and before she married and divorced a trumpet player named Luther Steinberg, she was Martha Jean Jones of Memphis, Tennessee. Possessing an innate desire to succeed regardless of the circumstances, in 1954, she was hired to work at WDIA-AM in Memphis, a 50,000 watt powerhouse station that blanketed five states. As the first station in the country to air an all black format that included a mix of blues, gospel and black announcers, WDIA-AM became a tremendous hit among black and white listeners, including a young Elvis Presley.

While working at the station, officials noticed Steinberg doing community relations and general work. Based on her outstanding performance in both of these areas, they eventually offered her an on-air job believing she would be a "natural" behind the microphone. Proving them correct, she spoke with supreme authority about her listeners' lives and feelings. It was a tradition she maintained throughout her 40 plus years in the business. Recognizing her contributions to the industry, which included being inducted into the Rock and Roll Hall of Fame and Museum in Cleveland, Ohio (she is the only woman honored among the legendary disc jockeys in the exhibit) and the Black Radio Hall of Fame in Atlanta, Georgia, as well as being featured in the Radio Smithsonian's, *Black Radio: Telling It Like It Was*, a documentary on the history of black oriented radio, a landmark now sits in front of WDIA. Her other accomplishments include being honored at the nation's capitol for her role in black radio; being highlighted in the Radio America series, *Passing It On: Voices from*

Black America's Past, a program that was broadcasted on over 400 radio stations across the country; and narrating the documentary on Berry Gordy and the early years of the Motown Sound, *The Music & The Story* for the Henry Ford Museum in Dearborn, Michigan.

Steinberg's first radio job in Detroit was at WCHB in Inkster, Michigan. She then joined WJLB where her show ruled from 1966–1982. Listening to her show became a must for anybody interested in taking the community's pulse. During the 1967 riots—or rebellion, as she referred to it—she took to the airwaves for 48 hours straight, acting as a peacekeeper. In 1982, she left WJLB to become the vice president and general manager of WQBH. For 14 years, she nurtured and built WQBH, establishing it as the "voice of the community." Her mission was "to bridge the gap between the power structure and the forgotten man" through her daily show, which aired from 11 A.M. to 2 P.M. weekdays. During this time, she tripled the value of the station and on May 12, 1997, purchased it for 3.9 million dollars. Continuing to air her show after purchasing the station, Steinberg's position as a black radio scholar who helped set the guidelines and standards for black radio in America became forever etched in the industry.

While at WQBH, Steinberg experienced a religious conversion and became a self-ordained nondenominational minister. The final outcome of this transformation was the establishment of her own church, the Home of Love, a community center, a low-income housing complex on Detroit's west side, and the "Queen's" Community Workers, a group of individuals who aid senior citizens and youth.

Upon her death on January 29, 2000 from an undisclosed illness, mourners throughout the Detroit metropolitan community commented that Steinberg's greatest gift was her ability to touch the souls of people by offering advice on a full range of human problems. It was a talent that she used on the radio and at her church.

Chuck Stone (1924–)
Journalist, Educator

Chuck Stone was born in 1924 into a family that initially lived in luxurious surroundings due to his father's executive position with a hair care company; however, alcoholism resulted in divorce and Stone's mother moved him and his three younger sisters to Connecticut. After high school, he enrolled in the famed Tuskegee training program for African American bomber pilots during World War II and became a navigator with the U.S. Air Corps. After the war's end, Stone earned degrees from Wesleyan University and the University of Chicago, and for a time worked with an international development agency in Africa.

In 1959, Stone entered the profession of journalism after being hired at the *New York Age*, a Harlem paper. Within a short time, he had become its editor, as well as launched a career noted for his outspoken opinions. During the early 1960s, he became the White House correspondent for the *Washington Afro-American*, for which he often wrote critically of the Kennedy Administration's lack of progress on civil rights issues.

In 1965, Stone joined the staff of Adam Clayton Powell Jr., the controversial Harlem activist who was then serving as a member of the U.S. House of Representatives. When Powell's political career ended amid charges of misuse of public funds two years later, Stone channeled his feelings of anger toward the white political establishment in the fictional chronicle of Powell, *King Strut*. It would be Stone's third book, after the 1968 collection of his newspaper columns, *Tell It Like It Is* and *Black Political Power in America* (1970).

Stone became a regular columnist for the *Philadelphia Daily News* in 1972 and spent the next several years lambasting the city's corrupt political machinery and heavy-handed police force. Equal in his criticisms unleashed first at the administration of former cop Frank Rizzo, and later at the city's first African American mayor, Wilson Goode, Stone's columns—which continued after he became senior editor in 1979—made him both a revered and feared civic personage. In an unusual development, his condemnations of police brutality toward Philadelphia's African American citizenry often prompted suspects to turn themselves in at the columnist's home or office first and wait for authorities to arrest them there.

After nearly two decades, Stone resigned from the *Philadelphia Daily News* to further pursue his career in academia. In 1991, he became the Walter Spearman Professor at the University of North Carolina at Chapel Hill's School of Journalism and Mass Communication. His column continues to be syndicated nationally in over 100 newspapers, and in the spring of 1996 Stone was honored with the Missouri Honor Medal for Distinguished Service in Journalism from the University of Missouri. He joined an impressive roster of past recipients that included Walter Cronkite and Charlayne Hunter-Gault. Stone was also selected to be a torch carrier for the Olympic flame that journeyed across the nation before the opening of the 1996 Summer Games in Atlanta, Georgia.

Currently, Stone is a professor at the University of North Carolina's School of Journalism and Mass Communications. In addition to his teaching duties, Stone is a panelist for the Montreal television program, The Editors and a political analyst for WTVD-TV in Durham.

Pierre Monteau Sutton (1947–)
Broadcast Executive

Pierre Sutton is president of Inner City Broadcasting Corporation in New York City and president of its radio stations in New York and California. He is the son of Percy E. Sutton, chairman of the board of Inner City Broadcasting and former borough president of Manhattan. Inner City Broadcasting has several divisions including Inner City Cable, Inner City Artists Management, and Inner City Broadcasting Corporation-Television (ICBC-TV). ICBC-TV produces *Showtime at the Apollo*, *Apollo Comedy Hour*, and *New Music Report.*

Pierre Sutton was born in New York City on February 1, 1947. He received a bachelor of arts degree from the University of Toledo in 1968. Sutton began his career in 1971 as vice president of Inner City Research and Analysis Corporation, became executive editor of the *New York Courier* newspaper in 1971–1972, later served a public affairs director for WLIB radio from 1972 to 1975, was promoted to vice president of Inner City Broadcasting from 1975 to 1977, and eventually became president in 1977. In 1998, Inner City was ranked 40th on *Black Enterprise*'s top 100 industrial/service companies; in 2002 it ranked 58th.

He has served as a board member of the Minority Investment Fund, first vice president of the National Association of Black Owned Broadcasters, chairman of the Harlem Boy Scouts, member of the board and executive committee of the New York City Marathon, trustee of the Alvin Ailey Dance Foundation, board member of the Better Business Bureau of Harlem, and member of the board of the Hayden Planetarium.

Susan L. Taylor (1946–)
Editor

Susan Taylor was born in New York City on January 23, 1946, and received a bachelor of arts degree from Fordham University. Since 1980, Susan Taylor has been editor-in-chief of *Essence*, a magazine established in 1970 for African American women. The publication has a monthly circulation of one million and a readership of 7.6 million—29 percent of which is male.

A former actress, cosmetologist, and founder of her own cosmetics company, Nequai Cosmetics, Taylor began her relationship with *Essence* magazine as a freelance writer. In 1971, she became the magazine's beauty and fashion editor. She held this position until 1980. Taylor, as editor-in-chief, is also executive coordinator of Essence Communications, Inc. (ECI). ECI is

Susan L. Taylor, editor-in-chief of *Essence*.

a major investor in Amistad Press, an African American-owned book publishing company. The company also has a licensing division that includes Essence Hosery, Essence Eyewear, and Essence Collection by Butterick. Essence Art Reproductions, a distributor of fine art created by African American artists; Essence Television Productions, Inc., producer of the Essence Awards, an annual salute to distinguished African Americans; and the Essence Music Festival, a three-day festival of cultural celebrations and empowerment seminars, also fall under the ECI umbrella.

Taylor is author of the "In the Spirit" column in *Essence* magazine. In 1993, she wrote a book entitled *In the Spirit: The Inspirational Writings of Susan L. Taylor*, a collection of inspirational essays named for and taken from her monthly Essence column. *In the Spirit* has sold over 350,000 copies since its publication. Her most recent book is *Lessons in Living*. In 1999, Taylor became the first African-American woman to receive The Henry Johnson Fisher Award, for lifetime achievement in the magazine industry, from Magazine Publishers of America. She received an even more prestigious honor in 2002 when she was inducted to the

Magazine Editor's Hall of Fame by the American Society of Magazine Editors.

Lemuel Tucker (1938–1991)
Television News Correspondent

Born in 1938 in Saginaw, Michigan, Lemuel Tucker was a graduate of Central Michigan University. Tucker worked as a Washington bureau correspondent for CBS news from 1977 until 1988. Prior to that he was with ABC News as New York City correspondent, from 1972 until 1977. From 1965 through 1972, Tucker was with NBC News where he served for some of that time as assistant bureau chief in Vietnam. He was awarded an Emmy for his reporting on hunger in the United States, a series of seven reports broadcast during 1968 and 1969. He died in March of 1991 in Washington, DC.

Montel Williams (1956–)
Talk Show Host

A former naval intelligence officer who first gained prominence delivering highly-charged, popular motivational speeches to millions of children around

Montel Williams holding a Crystal Apple Award in 1996.

the country, Montel Williams is now a talk show host with a non-traditional background. He began his professional career in the U.S. Marine Corps in 1974. In 1976, Williams became the first African American to attend the prestigious Naval Academy Prep School. At Annapolis, he studied Mandarin Chinese and graduated with a degree in general engineering. He has won numerous awards and distinctions over the course of his long and varied naval career including the Armed Forces Expeditionary Medal and two Meritorious Service Medals.

In 1988, Williams began informally counseling the wives and families of the servicemen in his command. He was later asked to speak to a local group of kids in Kansas City, Missouri, about the importance of leadership and overcoming obstacles. Thus, began his career in motivational speaking. His daily, hour-long talk show, the *Montel Williams Show*, was in its twelfth season in 2002.

Williams's commitment to making a difference resulted in finding solutions to problems by tackling them. Through several episodes in 1997, his show stressed the importance of AIDS education in communities across the country. As a result of the show's ongoing coverage of the AIDS epidemic, the White House Office of National AIDS Policy invited Williams to produce several public service announcements on AIDS prevention. In addition, his After-Care Program arranges for guests to attend psychological treatment, motivational camps, drug and alcohol rehabilitation, and treatment for eating disorders.

In 1999, Williams shocked the broadcasting world by revealing that he had been diagnosed with multiple sclerosis. He vowed to continue to host his talk show in order to be a role model for others with multiple sclerosis and also wanted to use his show to make people aware of the disease as well. He also started the Montel Williams MS Foundation in 1999 to raise money to combat the disease. Williams was in the news again in 2000 when he helped save a 16-year-old boy whose car crashed and burst into flames in Bonners Ferry, Idaho. Williams made the teen a splint from tree branches and a belt, then carried him to safety.

A recipient of several daytime Emmy awards—the most recent in 1996 for outstanding talk show host—the *Montel Williams Show* has been honored with several humanitarian awards. The Entertainment Industry Council, Inc. and the National Institute on Drug Abuse/National Institutes of Health presented the show with a PRISM Commendation for the episode "What Parents Need to Know about Teens and Drugs." The foundation of American Women in Radio and Television granted the show an honorable mention Gracie Award in recognition for excellence in programming

for the positive and realistic portrayal of women. The show also received the Nancy Susan Reynolds Award for the episode "Teenagers Living with AIDS" and the Silver Angel Award for the episode "The Life and Times of Mother Theresa." In 2002, Williams received the first-ever Man of Courage Award at the 7th Annual Race to Erase MS in Los Angeles.

Oprah Winfrey (1954–)
Television Talk Show Host, Actress, Producer

Oprah Winfrey's rise to fame is an inspiring tale. She was born on January 29, 1954, in Kosciusko, Mississippi. Her name was supposed to have been "Orpah" after a biblical figure in the book of Ruth; sources vary as to the origin of the misspelling.

Winfrey was a precocious child who asked her kindergarten teacher to advance her to the first grade; she also skipped the second grade. Her parents, who were not married, separated when she was very young and sent her to live with her grandparents. At the age of six, Winfrey sent to Milwaukee to live with her mother. From the time that she was nine years old, she suffered sexual abuse at the hands of male family members and acquaintances; these events, which she did not discuss publicly until the 1980s, have had a profound effect on her life.

When she was 14 years old, Winfrey went to live with her father in Nashville, Tennessee, and it was there that she got her life back on track. Her father insisted on hard work and discipline as a means of self-improvement, and Winfrey complied, winning a college scholarship that allowed her to attend Tennessee State University. In 1971, she began working part-time as a radio announcer for WVOL in Nashville. Two years later, after receiving a bachelor of arts degree, she became a reporter at WTVF-TV in Nashville. From 1976 to 1983, she lived in Baltimore, working for the ABC affiliate WJZ-TV, progressing from news anchor to co-host of the popular show *People Are Talking*. In 1984, she moved to Chicago and took over the ailing morning show *A.M. Chicago*. By September of the next year, the show was so successful that it was expanded to an hour format and renamed the *Oprah Winfrey Show*. Now in syndication across the country, the *Oprah Winfrey Show* is one of the most popular television programs in history. In 1986, Oprah founded Harpo, Inc., her own production company ("Harpo" is "Oprah" spelled backwards). As such, she is the first African American woman to host a nationally syndicated weekday show, own and produce her own television show, and own a film and a television production company.

A talented actress, Winfrey has appeared in the motion pictures *The Color Purple* (1985), *Native Son*

(1986), and *Beloved* (1998). She has also appeared in the television movies *The Women of Brewster Place* (1989), *There Are No Children Here* (1993), *Before Women Had Wings* (1997), and *Beloved* (1998). As a producer, Winfrey has presented several television and movie specials, most notably *David and Lisa* (1998) *The Wedding* (1998), and *Beloved* (1998), all based on novels.

As a former victim of child abuse, Winfrey is a strong advocate of children's rights. When she heard the tragic story of a four-year-old Chicago girl's molestation and murder, she proposed federal child protection legislation designed to keep nationwide records on convicted child abusers. Her efforts on behalf of abused and neglected children came to fruition on December 20, 1993, when President Clinton signed the "Oprah Bill," a law designed to protect children from abuse.

The Oprah Winfrey Show, in its eighteenth season of syndication in 2002, continued to be the number one talk show on the air and broadcasts in over 130 international territories. It was recently renewed through the year 2004 in over 99 percent of the country, including the top ten markets. Reaching more than 20 million homes a day, the show continued to enlighten, educate, and entertain viewers. In 1998, the show unveiled a new set; premiered a new theme song, "Run on with Oprah" performed by Winfrey herself; and embarked on a new type of programming called "Change Your Life TV," designed to inspire viewers to make small adjustments so that they can create big results in their lives. In the spirit of her "Change Your Life TV" programming, she recently launched a Web site to empower viewers by enabling them to access the experts and use the information and advice offered on the show.

Famous for her candor, forthrightness, and willingness to go the distance, Winfrey successfully won a $12 million slander suit brought against her by Texas cattlemen in 1998. The cattlemen took Winfrey to court over a 1996 show in which one of her guests, an anti-meat activist, suggested that American beef industry practices could cause BSE, or mad cow disease. The cattlemen claimed that because of her influence with viewers, beef prices immediately slumped to a ten-year low. The jury of eight women and four men deliberated close to six hours before rejecting all claims brought by the cattlemen.

In 1998, Winfrey expanded her career to include cable network executive when she launched the Oxygen network, a cable network devoted to women and women's issues. In 2000, she also became a magazine publisher as *O, The Oprah Magazine* hit the newsstands. In 2002, Winfrey's famous book club, started in 1994, came to an end with its 45th and final selection, *Sula* by Toni Morrison. It was also reported in 2002 that

Winfrey will host a new primetime daily show on the Oxygen network called, *Oprah After the Show*, premiering September 16, 2002.

Winfrey continued to win awards for her work in television and film. Accomplishments include receipt of the Horatio Alger Award in 1993 and induction into the Television Hall of Fame in 1994. At the end of the 1995–1996 television season, she received the George Foster Peabody Individual Achievement Award, one of broadcasting's most coveted honors. She was named among "America's 25 Most Influential People of 1996" by *Time* magazine and favorite female television performer at the 1997 and 1998 People's Choice Awards. In 1999, she received the National Book Foundation's 50th anniversary Gold Medal, and in 2001 she was named *Newsweek* magazine's "Woman of the Century." Winfrey has also been honored with seven Emmy awards for Outstanding Talk Show Host and nine for Outstanding Talk Show. In 2002 *Fortune* magazine ranked her the tenth most powerful African American executive; *Savoy* considered her the most powerful African American in the media.

◆ PRINT AND BROADCAST MEDIA DIRECTORY

Publishers

AAIMS Publishers
11000 Wilshire Blvd.
Los Angeles, CA 90024–9577
(213) 968–1195
aaimspub@aol.com

Academica Press, L.L.C.
7831 Woodmont Ave., No. 381
Bethesda, MD 20814
(202) 388–1800
austinlsp1@aol.com

Africa World Press Inc.
PO Box 1892
Trenton, NJ 08607
(609) 844–9583
awprsp@africanworld.com

Afro-Am Publishing/Distributing Company Inc.
1909 W. 95th St.
Chicago, IL 60643–1105
(312) 791–1611

A. G. Halldin Publishing Company Inc.
PO Box 667
Indiana, PA 15701
(412) 463–8450

A.L.A. Black Caucus Publications Committee
499 Wilson Library
University of Minnesota Libraries
Minneapolis, MN 55455
(612) 373–3097

Alpha Kappa Alpha Sorority Inc.
5656 S. Stony Island Ave.
Chicago, IL 60637–1997
(773) 684–1282

Amen-Ra Publishing Co.
PO Box 328642
Columbus, OH 43232

Amistad Research Center
Tulane University
6823 St. Charles Ave.
New Orleans, LA 70118
(504) 865–5535
arc@mailhost.tcs.tulane.edu

Ananse Press
1504 32nd Ave. S.
Seattle, WA 98144
(206) 325–8205

Andre's and Co.
289 Varick St.
Jersey City, NJ 07302

Ankh Enterprises
7850 Sunset Blvd., No. 105
Los Angeles, CA 90046

APU Publishing Group
PO Box 1139
Edgewood, MD 21040
(410) 538–7400
apub@mciworld.com

Arts & Communications Network Inc.
501 Mossy Brook Rd.
High Falls, NY 12440
(914) 687–0767

Associated Publishers, Inc.
1407 14th St. NW
Washington, DC 20005–3704

Atlas Press
3836 Olympiad Dr.
Los Angeles, CA 90043–1130
(213) 295–3036

August Press
108 Terrell Rd.
PO Box 6693
Newport News, VA 23606–2241
(757) 591–2371

Balamp Publishing
2208 Lucerne Dr.
Henderson, NV 89014–4904

Bandele Publications
8314 Greenwood, No. A
Takoma Park, MD 20912
(301) 779–7530

B-Dock Press
PO Box 8
Willingboro, NJ 08046
(609) 877–6018

Beacon Press
25 Beacon St.
Boston, MA 02108
(617) 742–2110

Beckham Publications Group Inc.
PO Box 4066
Silver Spring, MD 20914–4066
(301) 384–7995

Bell Enterprises, Inc.
PO Box 9054
Pine Bluff, AR 71611
(501) 247–1922

Benin Publishing Co.
10 Mosshill Pl.
Stony Brook, NJ 11790

Best Western Press
22220 Bogie St.
Tehachapi, CA 93561–7561
(805) 822–7206

Black Classic Press
PO Box 13414
Baltimore, MD 21203
(410) 358–0980
bcp@charm.net

Black Economic Research Team Inc.
PO Box 13513
Baltimore, MD 21203

Black Entrepreneurs Press
4502 S. Congress Ave., Ste. 254
Austin, TX 78744
(512) 444–9962

Black Fashion Museum
2007 Vermont Ave. NW
Washington, DC 20001
(202) 667–0744
bfmdc@aol.com

Black Graphics International
PO Box 732, Linwood Sta.
Detroit, MI 48206

Black Light Fellowship
2859 West Wilcox St.
Chicago, IL 60612
(773) 826–7790

Black Resource Guide Inc.
501 Oneida Pl. NW
Washington, DC 20011
(202) 291–4373

Black Student Fund
3636 16th St. NW, 4th Fl.
Washington, DC 20010–1147
(202) 387–1414

Blue Diamond Press
Tilden Towers II
801 Tilden St.
Bronx, NY 10467
(718) 882–8160

Bosck Publishing House
3325 Thornridge Tr.
Douglasville, GA 30135
(404) 755–8170

Broadside Press
PO Box 04257
Detroit, MI 48204
(313) 963–8526

Burrelle's Information Services
75 E. Northfield Rd.
Livingston, NJ 07039
(973) 992–6600
directory@burelles.com

CAAS Publications
Center for African-American Studies
160 Haines Hall
PO Box 951545
Los Angeles, CA 90095–1545
(310) 825–7403

Carlisle Press
201 Gale St., No. 303
Mechanicsburg, PA 17055
(717) 697–1642

Carver Publishing Inc.
PO Box 9353
Hampton, VA 23670–0353
(757) 838–1244

Center for Black Music Research
600 S. Michigan Ave.
Chicago, IL 60605–1996
(312) 344–8559
cbmr@cbmr.colum.edu

Charill Publishers
4468 San Francisco Ave.
PO Box 150124
St. Louis, MO 63115
(314) 382–4998

Chatham Bookseller
8 Green Village
Madison, NJ 07940
(973) 822–1361

Christian Methodist Episcopal Publishing House
PO Box 2018
Memphis, TN 38101
(901) 345–4120

Civilized Publications Inc.
2019 S. 7th St.
Philadelphia, PA 19148
(215) 339–0062
76055.3011@compuserve.com

Clarity Press Inc.
3277 Roswell Rd. NE, Ste. 469
Atlanta, GA 30305
(877) 613–1495
clarity@islandnet.com

Cline Transportation Service Ltd.
PO Box 552
Malden, MA 02148
(617) 322–3998

Contemporary Crafts, Inc.
5271 W. Pico Blvd.
Los Angeles, CA 90019

Cottage Books
1801A Duke Dr.
Silver Spring, MD 20902
(301) 649–5123

Council Oak Books
1290 Chestnut St., No. 2
San Francisco, CA 94109
(415) 931–6868

Crescent Imports & Publications
PO Box 7827
Ann Arbor, MI 48107–7827
(734) 665–3492
mumshey@aol.com

DARE Books
33 Lafeyette
Brooklyn, NY 11217–1420
(718) 625–4651

Department of Africana Studies
51 W. Warren Ave., 1001 Faculty/
　　Administration Bldg.
Detroit, MI 48202
(313) 577–2321

Detroit Black Writers Guild Inc.
PO Box 23100
Detroit, MI 48223–0100
(313) 897–2551

Diaspora Press of America
PO Box 200981
Boston, MA 02120–0018
(617) 298–1254
princeyemi36@hotmail.com

Eakin Press
PO Box 90159
Austin, TX 78709
(512) 288–1771
eakinpub@sig.net

ECA Associates Press
PO Box 15004
Chesapeake, VA 23328
(757) 547–5542
eca@melanet.com

Eliza Washington
614 Wilshire Ave.
Waterloo, IA 50701
(319) 234–1460

Essai Seay Publications
PO Box 55
East St. Louis, IL 62202–0055
(618) 271–7890

Evangelist Association
700 W. 55th Ave.
Merrillville, IN 46410
(219) 887–7811

Famous Black Quotations
PO Box 64898
Chicago, IL 60664–0898

Fertile Soil Publishing
PO Box 48066
Oak Park, MI 48237
(313) 534–6358

Fire!! Press
241 Hillside Rd.
Elizabeth, NJ 07208
(908) 289–3714
fire.press@verizon.net

Freeland Publications
PO Box 18941
Philadelphia, PA 19119

Fruits for Knowledge Press
1474 Heather Pl.
Pottstown, PA 19464–1707
(610) 323–2982

General Hall Inc.
5 Talon Way
Dix Hills, NY 11746
(516) 243–0155

Georgia A. Johnson Publishing Co.
2608 Darien Dr.
Lansing, MI 48912–4538
(517) 372–9642

Guild Press
PO Box 22583
Minneapolis, MN 55422
(763) 566–1842

Gumbs & Thomas Publishers Inc.
PO Box 381
New York, NY 10039
(212) 694–6677

Heat Press
PO Box 26218
Los Angeles, CA 90026
(213) 482–8902
artheat@aol.com

Heinemann
361 Hanover St.
Portsmouth, NH 03801–3912
(603) 431–7894
custserv@heinemann.com

Helga M. Rogers
4975 59th Ave. S.
St. Petersburg, FL 33715–1619
(727) 864–3292
helgandrew@aol.com

Heritage Press
PO Box 18625
Baltimore, MD 21216
(410) 728–8521

Historic Florida Keys Foundation Inc.
Old City Hall
510 Greene St.
Key West, FL 33040
(305) 292–6718

Holloway House Publishing Group
8060 Melrose Ave.
Los Angeles, CA 90046
(323) 653–8060
psi@loop.com

House of Nia
4014 Calmoor St.
National City, CA 91950
(619) 479–4425

Howard University Press
2225 Georgia NW, Ste. 720
Washington, DC 20059
(202) 238–2570
howardupress@howard.edu
<www.founders.howard.edu/hupress/>

Institute for Southern Studies
2009 Chapel Hill Rd.
P.O.B. 531
Durham, NC 27702
(919) 419–8311
issinfo@i4south.org

James H. Boykin
1260 NW 122nd St.
Miami, FL 33167–2827
(305) 681–7663

Joint Center for Political and Economic Studies
1090 Vermont Ave. NW, Ste. 1100
Washington, DC 20005–4961
(202) 789–3500

Julian Richardson Associates Publishers
1712 Fillmore St.
San Francisco, CA 94115
(415) 346–4311

Just Us Books Inc.
356 Glenwood Ave. 3rd. Floor
East Orange, NJ 07017
(973) 672–7701
webmaster@justusbooks.com
<www.justusbooks.com>

Kansas City Black Pages
1601 E. 18th St., Ste. 315
Kansas City, MO 64108
(816) 421–0400

Kemp Krafts
288 Flynn Ave., No. 20
Burlington, VT 05401–5374
(802) 862–4418

Khamit Corp.
140 Buckingham Rd.
Brooklyn, NY 11226
(718) 469–3199

Lawrence Hill Books
611 Broadway, Ste. 530
New York, NY 10012
(212) 260–0576

Lindsey Publishing Inc.
2023 W. Carroll Ave., Ste. F241
Chicago, IL 60612
(312) 226–1458
lindseyp@dpliv.com

Lunan-Ferguson Library
4630 Geary Blvd., Ste. 305
San Francisco, CA 94118–2937
(415) 752–6100

M. L. Williams Publishing Co., Inc.
PO Box 53552
1315 Walnut St., Ste. 1624
Philadelphia, PA 19105
(215) 735–1121

Majority Press Inc.
PO Box 538
Dover, MA 02030
(508) 655–5636
writeus@themajoritypress.com

Mankind Publishing Co.
8060 Melrose Ave.
Los Angeles, CA 90046
(323) 653–8060
psi@loop.com

Marcus Horton Sweet African American Culture Center
4 Holly Ln.
Malvern, PA 19355
(610) 647–1481

McNary Publishing
PO Box 62421
St. Louis Park, MN 55426
(612) 650–2952
102114.3141@compuserv.com

Meherrin River Press
301 E. Broad St.
Murfreesboro, NC 27855
(252) 398–3554

Melvett Chambers, Pub.
PO Box 8475
Denver, CO 80201
(303) 321–2955

Michigan State University Press
1405 S. Harrison Rd., Ste. 25
East Lansing, MI 48823–5202
(517) 355–9543
msupress@msu.edu

Middle Atlantic Regional Press
2549 11th St. NW
Washington, DC 20001–3923
(202) 265–7609

Middle Passage Press Inc.
5517 Secrest Dr.
Los Angeles, CA 90043
(213) 298–0266

Mphahlele K. Lukman Inc.
9110 Ave. A
Brooklyn, NY 11236
(718) 485–7009

National Action Council for Minorities in Engineering Inc.
350 Fifth Ave., Ste. 2212
New York, NY 10118–2299
(212) 279–2626
info@nacme.org

National Black Music Foundation
902 42nd Ave. N.
PO Box 90639
Nashville, TN 37209

Native Sun Publishers Inc.
PO Box 13394
Richmond, VA 23225
(804) 233–7768

New Day Press Inc.
Karamu House
2355 E. 89th St.
Cleveland, OH 44106
(216) 795–7070

One Nation Books and Art, Inc.
1969 Dina Ct.
Powell, OH 43065

Open Hand Publishing Inc.
PO Box 20207
Greensboro, NC 27420–0207
(336) 292–8585
openhndl@bellsouth.net

Papyrus Literary Enterprises
100 Prospect Ave.
Hartford, CT 06106
readersndex.com/ple

Path Press Inc.
PO Box 2925
Chicago, IL 60690
(847) 424–1620
PathPressInc@aol.com

Pathfinder Press
410 West St.
New York, NY 10014
(212) 741–0690
pathfinderpress@compuserve.com

Paul G. Partington
7320 S. Gretna Ave.
Whittier, CA 90606
(562) 695–7960

The Place in the Woods
3900 Glenwood Ave.
Golden Valley, MN 55422–5302
(763) 374–2120
placewoods@aol.com

Poets Pay Rent, Too
PO Box 75796, Sanford Sta.
Los Angeles, CA 90075

Popular Press
Bowling Green, OH 43403
(419) 372–7866

Project BAIT Publishing
13217 Livernois
Detroit, MI 48238–3162
(313) 931–3427

R & M Publishing Co.
PO Box 1276
Holly Hill, SC 29059
(803) 279–2262
mackattack07319@cs.com

Raw Ink Press
Southwest Sta.
PO Box 70417
Washington, DC 20024–0417

Rev. Dr. Charles L. Hoskins
St. Matthew's Episcopal Church
1401 MLK Blvd.
Savannah, GA 31401
(912) 234–8126

Richard Bailey Publishers
PO Box 1264
Montgomery, AL 36102–1264
(334) 272–7248
rbail@bellsouth.net

Rufus Shaw Publishing
PO Box 152432
Dallas, TX 75315
(214) 331–1925

Russell Mootry Jr. Associates
810 Grove Ave.
Holly Hill, FL 32117
(904) 255–6871
mootryr@cookman.edu

Schenkman Books Inc.
118 Main St.
PO Box 119
Rochester, VT 05767
(802) 767–3702
schenkma@sover.net

Sea Island Information Group
11022 Belton St.
Upper Marlboro, MD 20772–1402
(301) 350–1360

Sea Urchin Press
PO Box 10503
Oakland, CA 94610–0503
(510) 568–7488

Seymour-Smith Publishers
PO Box 381063
Germantown, TN 38138

Shamal Books Inc.
GPO Box 16
New York, NY 10116
(212) 622–4426

Specialty Promotions Company Inc.
6841 S. Cregier Ave.
Chicago, IL 60649
(312) 721–3177

Spencer's International Enterprises Corp.
PO Box 43822
Los Angeles, CA 90043
(213) 294–7125

Steladon Press
PO Box 4732
Upper Marlboro, MD 20775
(301) 350–3669

Studio Museum in Harlem Museum Shop
144 W. 125th St.
New York, NY 10027
(212) 864–4500

Syracuse Cultural Workers/Tools for Change
PO Box 6367
Syracuse, NY 13217
(315) 474–1132
scw@syrculturalworkers.org

The New Press
450 W. 41st St.
New York, NY 10036
(212) 629–8802
newpress@aol.com

The Peoples Publishing Group Inc.
299 Market St.
Saddle Brook, NJ 07663–5312
(201) 712–0090

Third World Press
PO Box 19730
Chicago, IL 60619
(773) 651–0700
twpress3@aol.com

Tivoli Publishing Co.
2718 Brooklyn Ave.
Kansas City, MO 64109
(816) 923–2546
info@tivolipublishing.com

Tucker Publications Inc.
PO Box 580
Lisle, IL 60532–0580
(630) 969–3809
callen@tuckerpub.com

Unicorn/Fitzgerald
808 Charlotte St.
Fredericksburg, VA 22401
(540) 371–3253

Universal Black Writer Press
328 Sterling Pl., No. 2B
Brooklyn, NY 11238–4433
(718) 398–8941

University of Georgia Press
330 Research Dr.
Athens, GA 30602–4901
(706) 369–6163
books@ugapress.uga.edu

University of Massachusetts Press
PO Box 429
Amherst, MA 01004
(413) 545–2217
umpress.umass.edu

University of Missouri Press
2910 LeMone Blvd.
Columbia, MO 65201
(573) 882–7641

University Place Book Shop
821 Broadway
New York, NY 10003
(212) 254–5998

University Publishers of America
4520 E. West Hwy., Ste. 800
Bethesda, MD 20814–3389
(301) 654–1550
CISinfo@lexis-nexis.com

Uraeus Publishing Inc.
3104 Georgia Ave. NW
Washington, DC 20001

Urban Research Press Inc.
840 E. 87th St.
Chicago, IL 60619
(312) 994–7200

Very Serious Business Enterprises
PO Box 356
Newark, NJ 07101
(609) 641–0776

Waverly House Publishing
PO Box 1053
Glenside, PA 19038
(215) 884–5873
info@natsel.com

Wealth Enterprises
3368-F Governor Dr., No. 105
San Diego, CA 92122

Winston-Derek Publishers, Inc.
PO Box 90883
Nashville, TN 37209–0883
(615) 256–0201
jillmerry@aol.com

Wright-Armstead Associates
2410 Barker Ave., Ste. 14-G
Bronx, NY 10467
(718) 654–9445

Wyndham Hall Press
52857 County Rd. 21
Bristol, IN 46507
(219) 848–4834
whpbooks@aol.com

Newspapers

Alabama

Birmingham World
407 15th St. N.
Birmingham, AL 35203–1877
(205) 251–6523

Campus Digest
Tuskegee, AL 36083
(205) 727–8263

Greene County Democrat
265 Prarie Ave.
Eutaw, AL 35462
(205) 372–3373

Mobile Beacon
2311 Costarides St.
Mobile, AL 36633
(334) 479–0629

National Inner City
1318 Polaris Dr.
Mobile, AL 36633–1545
(334) 602–0210

New Times
PO Box 40536
Mobile, AL 36640–0536
(205) 432–0356

Shoals News Leader
PO Box 427
Florence, AL 35631
(205) 766–5542

Speakin' Out News
1300 Meridian St.
Huntsville, AL 35804
(205) 551–1020
info@speakinoutnews.com

Arizona

Arizona Informant
1746 E. Madison, No. 2
Phoenix, AZ 85034
(602) 257–9300

California

Bakersfield News Observer
1219 20th St.
Bakersfield, CA 93301
(805) 324–9466

Berkeley Tri City Post
PO Box 1350
Oakland, CA 94604–1350
(510) 763–1120

Black Voice News
PO Box 1581
Riverside, CA 92502
(909) 682–6070

California Advocate
1715 E St., No. 108
Fresno, CA 93706
(209) 268–0941

California Voice
270 Francisco St.
San Francisco, CA 94133–2012

Carson Bulletin
349 W. Compton
Compton, CA 90224
(213) 774–0018

Central Star/Journal Wave
2621 W. 54th St.
Los Angeles, CA 90043
(323) 290–3000
wcnpapers@aol.com

Compton Bulletin
349 W. Compton
Compton, CA 90224
(213) 774–0018

Compton Carson Wave
2621 W. 54th St.
Los Angeles, CA 90043
(323) 290–3000
wcnpapers@aol.com

Compton Metropolitan Gazette
14621 Titus St., Ste. 228
Van Nuys, CA 91402
(818) 782–8695

Culver City Star
2621 W. 54th St.
Los Angeles, CA 90043
(323) 290–3000
wcnpapers@aol.com

Ethiopian Mirror
PO Box 6881
Beverly Hills, CA 90212
(323) 939–3059

Firestone Park News/Southeast News Press
4053 Marlton Ave.
Los Angeles, CA 90008
(213) 291–9486

Herald Dispatch
4053 Marlton Ave.
Los Angeles, CA 90008
(213) 291–9486

Inglewood/Hawthorne Wave
2621 W. 54th St.
Los Angeles, CA 90043
(323) 290–3000
wcnpapers@aol.com

Inglewood Tribune
349 W. Compton
Compton, CA 90224
(213) 774–0018

Long Beach Express
14621 Titus St., Ste. 228
Van Nuys, CA 91402
(818) 782–8695

Los Angeles Sentinel
3800 S. Crenshaw
Los Angeles, CA 90008
(213) 299–3800

Lynwood Journal
349 W. Compton
Compton, CA 90224
(213) 774–0018

Lynwood Press
2621 W. 54th St.
Los Angeles, CA 90043
(323) 290–3000
wcnpapers@aol.com

Mesa Tribune Wave
2621 W. 54th St.
Los Angeles, CA 90043
(323) 290–3000
wcnpapers@aol.com

Oakland Post
PO Box 1350
Oakland, CA 94604
(510) 763–1120

Pasadena Gazette
14621 Titus St., Ste. 228
Van Nuys, CA 91402
(818) 782–8695

Precinct Reporter
1677 W. Baseline St.
San Bernardino, CA 92411
(909) 889–0597

Richmond Post
PO Box 1350
Oakland, CA 94604–1350
(510) 763–1120

Sacramento Observer
Box 817
San Leandro, CA 94577

San Bernardino American News
1583 W. Baseline St.
San Bernardino, CA 92411–1756
(909) 889–7677

San Diego Voice and Viewpoint
PO Box 120095
San Diego, CA 92112–0095
(619) 266–2233

San Fernando Gazette Express
14621 Titus St., Ste. 228
Van Nuys, CA 91402
(818) 782–8695

San Francisco Post
PO Box 1350
Oakland, CA 94604–1350
(510) 763–1120

San Francisco
270 Francisco St.
San Francisco, CA 94133–2120
(415) 391–2030

Southwest News Wave
2621 W. 54th St.
Los Angeles, CA 90043
(323) 290–3000
wcnpapers@aol.com

Sun-Reporter
1791 Vancroft Ave.
San Francisco, CA 94124
(415) 931–5778

Watts Star Review
4053 Marlton Ave.
Los Angeles, CA 90008
(213) 291–9486

Westchester Star
2621 W. 54th St.
Los Angeles, CA 90043
(323) 290–3000
wcnpapers@aol.com

Wilmington Beacon
349 W. Compton
Compton, CA 90224
(213) 774–0018

Connecticut

Hartford Inquirer
PO Box 1260
Hartford, CT 06143
(860) 522–1462

Inner City Newspaper
50 Fitch St.
New Haven, CT 06515
(203) 387–0354

District of Columbia

New Observer
811 Florida Ave. NW
Washington, DC 20001
(202) 232–3060

Washington Informer
3117 Martin Luther King Jr. Ave. SE
Washington, DC 20032–1537
(202) 561–4100
informer@usbol.com

Washington New Observer
811 Florida Ave. NW
Washington, DC 20001–3017
(202) 232–3060

Florida

Bulletin
2490 Dr. Martin Luther King Jr. Way
Sarasota, FL 34230–2560
(941) 953–3990

Capital Outlook
602 N. Adams St.
Tallahassee, FL 32301–1114
(904) 681–1852

Daytona Times
427 S. Dr. M. L. King Jr. Blvd.
Daytona Beach, FL 32114
(904) 253–0321

Famuan
309 Tucker Hall
Tallahassee, FL 32307
(904) 599–3159
thefamuan@hotmail.com

Florida Sentinel-Bulletin
2207–21st Ave.
Tampa, FL 33601
(813) 248–1921

Florida Star Times
PO Box 40629
Jacksonville, FL 32203–0629
(904) 766–8834

Miami Times
900 NW 54th St.
Miami, FL 33127
(305) 757–1147
miamit@aol.com

Orlando Times
4403 Vineland Rd., Ste. B-5
Orlando, FL 32855–5339
(407) 841–3710

Pensacola Voice
213 E. Yonge St.
Pensacola, FL 32503–3766
(904) 434–6963

Voice
640 2nd Ave.
Daytona Beach, FL 32115
(904) 255–1401

Weekly Challenger
2500 9th St. S.
St. Petersburg, FL 33705
(727) 896–2922

Westside Gazette
PO Box 5304
Fort Lauderdale, FL 33310
(954) 523–5115

Georgia

Atlanta Daily World
145 Auburn Ave. NE
Atlanta, GA 30303
(404) 659–1110
publisher@atlantadailyworld.com

Atlanta Inquirer
947 Martin Luther King Jr. Dr. NW
Atlanta, GA 30314
(404) 523–6086

Atlanta Voice
633 Pryor St. SW
Atlanta, GA 30314–0405
(404) 524–6426

AUC Digest
PO Box 3191
Atlanta, GA 30302
(404) 523–6136

Columbus Times
2230 Buena Vista Rd.
Columbus, GA 31993–2999
(706) 324–2404

Fort Valley Herald
315 N. Camellia Blvd.
Fort Valley, GA 31030
(912) 822–9714

Metro Courier
PO Box 2385
Augusta, GA 30903
(404) 724–6556

Savannah Herald
1803 Barnard St.
Savannah, GA 31401–8022
(912) 232–4505
savannaherald@earthlink.net

Savannah Tribune
916 Montgomery St.
Savannah, GA 31402
(912) 233–6128
sharon@savannahtribune.com

Southeastern News
302 W. 16th Ave., Ste. D
Cordele, GA 31015
(912) 273–6714

Illinois

Chatham-Southeast Citizen
412 E. 87th St.
Chicago, IL 60619
(312) 487–7700

Chicago Citizen
412 E. 87th St.
Chicago, IL 60619
(312) 487–7700

Chicago Crusader
6429 S. Martin Luther King Dr.
Chicago, IL 60637
(773) 752–2500

Chicago Independent Bulletin
2037 W. 95th St.
Chicago, IL 60643–1129
(312) 783–1040

Chicago South Shore Scene
7426 S. Constance
Chicago, IL 60649
(773) 363–0441

Chicago Standard News
615 S. Halsted
Chicago Heights, IL 60411
(708) 755–5021

Chicago Weekend
412 E. 87th St.
Chicago, IL 60619
(312) 487–7700

Decatur Voice of the Black Community
625 E. Wood St.
Decatur, IL 62523

East St. Louis Monitor
1501 State St.
East St. Louis, IL 62205
(618) 271–0468

Final Call
734 W. 79th St.
Chicago, IL 60620
(312) 602–1230

Hyde Park Citizen
412 E. 87th St.
Chicago, IL 60619
(312) 487–7700

Muslim Journal
929 W. 171st. St.
Hazel Crest, IL 60429–1901
(708) 647–9600

N'DIGO
401 N. Wabash, Ste. 534
Chicago, IL 60611
(312) 822–0202

New Chicago Shoreland News
11740 S. Elizabeth
Chicago, IL 60643
(773) 785–5384

South End Citizen
412 E. 87th St.
Chicago, IL 60619
(312) 487–7700

South Suburban Citizen
412 E. 87th St.
Chicago, IL 60619
(312) 487–7700

South Suburban Standard
615 S. Halsted
Chicago Heights, IL 60411
(708) 755–5021

Tri-City Journal
7115 W. North Ave., No. 308
Oak Park, IL 60302–1002
(312) 346–8123

Indiana

Frost Illustrated
3121 S. Calhoun St.
Fort Wayne, IN 46807–1901
(219) 745–0552

Gary American
PO Box 1199
Gary, IN 46407–0199
(219) 883–4903

Gary New Crusader
1549 Broadway
Gary, IN 46407–2240
(219) 885–4357

Indianapolis Recorder
2901 N. Tacoma Ave.
Indianapolis, IN 46218–2700
(317) 924–5143

Info
1953 Broadway
Gary, IN 46407
(219) 882–5591

Kentucky

Louisville Defender
1720 Dixie Hwy.
Louisville, KY 40210
(502) 772–2591

Suspension Press
PO Box 2064
Covington, KY 41012

Louisiana

Alexandria News Weekly
PO Box 608
Alexandria, LA 71309–0608
(318) 443–7664

Baton Rouge Weekly Press
1283 Rosenwald Rd., Ste. 1
Baton Rouge, LA 70807–4173
(225) 775–2002

Louisiana Weekly
822 Perdido St., Ste 413
New Orleans, LA 70112
(504) 524–5563
louisianaweekly@la-weekly.net

New Orleans Data News Weekly
3501 Napolean Ave.
New Orleans, LA 70125
(504) 822–4433
data@newsweekly.com

Shreveport Sun
PO Box 38357
Shreveport, LA 71133–8357
(318) 631–6222

Maryland

Baltimore Afro-American
2519 N Charles St.
Baltimore, MD 21218
(410) 554–8200

Michigan

Blazer News
PO Box 806
Jackson, MI 49204
(517) 787–3018

Detroit Journal
11000 W. McNichols, Ste. 210
Detroit, MI 48221
(313) 342–1717

Grand Rapids Times
PO Box 7258
Grand Rapids, MI 49510–7258
(616) 245–8737

Michigan Chronicle
479 Ledyard St.
Detroit, MI 48201
(313) 963–5522

Michigan Citizen
211 Glendale, Ste. 216
Highland Park, MI 48203
(313) 869–0033

Minnesota

Minneapolis Spokesman
3744 4th Ave. S.
Minneapolis, MN 55409
(612) 827–4021
srpub2@aol.com

Mississippi

Jackson Advocate
300 N. Fanisha
Jackson, MS 39207–3708
(601) 948–4122

Missouri

Call
PO Box 410–477
Kansas City, MO 64141
(816) 842–3804

Kansas City Globe
615 E. 29th St.
Kansas City, MO 64109
(816) 531–5253

St. Louis American
4242 Lindell Blvd.
St. Louis, MO 63108–2916
(314) 533–8000

St. Louis Argus
4595 Martin Luther King Dr.
St. Louis, MO 63113

St. Louis Crusader
715 Vandeventer Ave.
St. Louis, MO 63108–3527

St. Louis Metro Evening Whirl
PO Box 5088
St. Louis, MO 63115
(314) 535–4033
tpcwhirl@aol.com

Nevada

Las Vegas Sentinel-Voice
900 E. Charleston Blvd.
Las Vegas, NV 89104
(702) 380–8100

New Jersey

Black Voice/Carta Latina
Student Activities Center
New Brunswick, NJ 08901
(732) 445–7025

New York

Afro-American Times
1195 Alantic Ave.
Brooklyn, NY 11216
(718) 636–9500

Afro-Americans in New York Life and History
PO Box 63
Buffalo, NY 14216
(716) 691–4257

Amsterdam News
Frederick Douglass Blvd.
New York, NY 10027
(212) 932–7400

Brooklyn New York Recorder
86 Bainbridge St.
Brooklyn, NY 11233
(718) 493–4616

Buffalo Criterion
623 William St.
Buffalo, NY 14206–1648
(716) 882–9570

Challenger
1303 Fillmore Ave.
Buffalo, NY 14211–1205
(716) 897–0442

City Sun
PO Box 560
Brooklyn, NY 11202–0560
(718) 624–5959

Communicade
104 Magnolia St.
Rochester, NY 14606

Daily Challenge
1360 Fulton St.
Brooklyn, NY 11216
(718) 643–1162

Hudson Valley Black Press
PO Box 2160
Newburgh, NY 12550
(914) 562–1313

Jamaica Shopping & Entertainment Guide
164–11 89th Ave., Ste. 190
Jamaica, NY 11432
(718) 591–7777

New York Beacon
12 E. 33 St., 6th Fl.
New York, NY 10016
(212) 213–8585
hazelsmith24@hotmail.com

New York Evening Express
204 W. 118th St.
New York, NY 10026–1739
(212) 666–5818

New York Sojourner-Herald
PO Box 7263, Capital Sta.
Albany, NY 12224
(518) 448–6072

New York Voice/Harlem U.S.A.
175–61 Hillside Ave.
Jamaica, NY 11432
(718) 206–9866

NY Carib News
15 W. 39th St.
New York, NY 10018
(212) 944–1991

North Carolina

Carolina Peacemaker
400 Summit Ave.
Greensboro, NC 27420–0853
(919) 274–6210

Carolina Times
PO Box 3825
Durham, NC 27702
(919) 682–2913
ctimes@compuserve.com

Carolinian
649 Maywood Ave.
Raleigh, NC 27611
(919) 834–5558

Charlotte Post
1531 Camden Rd.
Charlotte, NC 28230
(704) 376–0496

County News
PO Box 407
Statesville, NC 28687
(704) 873–1054
countnews4you@aol.com

'M' Voice Newspaper
PO Box 8361
Greenville, NC 27834
(919) 757–0365

Star of Zion
PO Box 26770
Charlotte, NC 28269
(704) 599–4630

Wilmington Journal
412 S. 7th St.
Wilmington, NC 28401–1020
(910) 762–5502
wilmjourn@aol.com

Winston-Salem Chronicle
617 N. Liberty St.
Winston-Salem, NC 27101–2912
(336) 722–8624

Ohio

Akron Reporter
PO Box 2042
Akron, OH 44309
(330) 773–4196

Buckeye Review
1201 Belmont Ave.
Youngstown, OH 44501
(330) 743–2250

Call and Post
1949 E. 105 St.
Cleveland, OH 44106
(216) 791–7600

Cincinnati Herald
354 Hearne Ave.
Cincinnati, OH 45229
(513) 961–3331

Toledo Journal
3021 Douglas Rd.
Toledo, OH 43606
(419) 472–4521

Oklahoma

Black Chronicle
PO Box 17498
Oklahoma City, OK 73136
(405) 424–4695

Oklahoma Eagle
PO Box 3267
Tulsa, OK 74101–3267
(918) 582–7124
news@oklahomaeagle.com

Oregon

Portland Skanner
PO Box 5455
Portland, OR 97228–5455
(503) 285–5555
info@theskanner.com

Pennsylvania

Lincolnian
Office of Communications
Lincoln University, PA 19352
(610) 932–8300

New Pittsburgh Courier
315 E. Carson St.
Pittsburgh, PA 15219–1202
(412) 481–8302

Philadelphia New Observer
1930 Chestnut St., Ste. 900
Philadelphia, PA 19103
(215) 665–8400

Philadelphia Tribune Metro Edition
522 S. 16th St.
Philadelphia, PA 19146
(215) 893–4097

Philadelphia Tribune
524–526 S. 16th St.
Philadelphia, PA 19146–1565
(215) 546–1006

South Carolina

Black News
1310 Harden
Columbia, SC 29204
(803) 799–5252

Charleston Chronicle
1109 King St.
Charleston, SC 29413–0548
(803) 723–2785

Charleston Black Times
1310 Harden
Columbia, SC 29211
(803) 799–5252

Orangeburg Black Voice
PO Box 11128
Columbia, SC 29211
(803) 799–5252

Tennessee

Fisk News
1000 17th Ave. N.
Nashville, TN 37208
(615) 329–8710

Memphis Silver Star News
3144 Park Ave.
Memphis, TN 38111

Tennessee Tribune
Tennessee Tribune Bldg.
Nashville, TN 37208
(615) 321–3268

Tri-State Defender
124 E. Calhoun Ave.
Memphis, TN 38103–4598
(901) 523–1818

Texas

African-American News & Issues
6130 Wheatley St.
Houston, TX 77091–3947
(713) 692–1892

African-American News & Issues—Central-Southwest, Texas Edition
6130 Wheatley St.
Houston, TX 77091–3947
(713) 692–1892

African-American News & Issues—Metroplex-North, Texas Edition
6130 Wheatley St.
Houston, TX 77091–3947
(713) 692–1892

African Herald
4300 N. Central Expy., Ste. 201
Dallas, TX 75206
(214) 823–7666

Dallas Post Tribune
2726 S. Beckley
Dallas, TX 75224
(214) 946–7678

Dallas Weekly Newspaper
Anthony T. Davis Bldg.
Dallas, TX 75215
(214) 428–8958

Houston Defender
PO Box 8005
Houston, TX 77288
(713) 663–6996

Houston Forward Times
5407 Chenevert St.
Houston, TX 77288–8346
(713) 526–4727
forwardt@flash.net

Informer & Texas Freeman
PO Box 3086
Houston, TX 77253
(713) 218–7400

Lubbock Southwest Digest
902 E. 28th St.
Lubbock, TX 79404
(806) 762–3612

San Antonio Register
PO Box 1598
San Antonio, TX 78296–1598
(512) 222–1721

Villager
1223-A Rosewood Ave.
Austin, TX 78702
(512) 476–0082

Virginia

New Journal & Guide
362 Campostella Rd.
Norfolk, VA 23523
(757) 543–6531

Roanoke Tribune
PO Box 6021
Roanoke, VA 24017–6021
(540) 343–0326

Washington

Facts Newspaper
2765 E. Cherry St.
Seattle, WA 98122
(206) 324–0552

Northwest Dispatch
PO Box 5637
Tacoma, WA 98415
(253) 272–7587

Seattle Medium
2600 S. Jackson St.
Seattle, WA 98144
(206) 323–3070

Tacoma True Citizen
2600 S. Jackson St.
Seattle, WA 98144
(206) 323–3070

Wisconsin

Milwaukee Times
2254 MLK Jr. Dr.
Milwaukee, WI 53212
(414) 263–5088

Milwaukee Community Journal
3612 N. Martin Luther King Dr.
Milwaukee, WI 53212
(414) 265–5300

Milwaukee Courier
2431 W. Hopkins St.
Milwaukee, WI 53206–1298
(414) 449–4860
editorial@milwaukeecourier.com

Milwaukee Star
3815 N. Teutonia Ave.
Milwaukee, WI 53206
(414) 449–4870
editorial@milwaukeecourier.com

Magazines and Journals

A & T Register
1601 E. Market St.
Greensboro, NC 27411
(910) 334–7700

About. . . Time
283 Genesee St.
Rochester, NY 14611
(716) 235–7150

African American Review
Shannon Hall 119
St. Louis, MO 63103–2007
(314) 977–2705

Afro-American Historical and Genealogical Society Journal
Box 73086
Washington, DC 20056–3086
(202) 234–5350
rootsweb.co/~mdaahg

Afronet Magazine
PO Box 43631
Los Angeles, CA 90043
(310) 205–4123
afronet@afronet.com

Alternative Press Index
PO Box 33109
Baltimore, MD 21218
(410) 243–2471
altpress@altpress.org

American Visions
1101 Pennsylvania Ave. NW, Ste. 820
Washington, DC 20004
(202) 347–3820

Atlanta Tribune: The Magazine
875 Old Roswell Rd., Ste. C-100
Roswell, GA 30076
(770) 587–0501
news@atlantatribune.com

Black Books Bulletin: Words Work
PO Box 19730
Chicago, IL 60619
(773) 651–0700
twpress3@aol.com

Black Dates
Box 83912
Los Angeles, CA 90083–0912
(310) 410–0808
newsroom@blk.com

Black Employment and Education Magazine
Bldg. 56, Ste. 282
Atlanta, GA 30324
(404) 469–5891

Black Enterprise
130 5th Ave.
New York, NY 10011
(212) 242–8000
benyc_ads@blackenterprise.com

Black Health
53 Oakwood Dr.
Madison, CT 06443–1823
(203) 431–3454

Black Tennis Magazine
PO Box 210767
Dallas, TX 75211
(214) 670–7618

Black Careers
PO Box 8214
Philadelphia, PA 19101–8214
(215) 387–1600

Blackfire
Box 83912
Los Angeles, CA 90083–0912
(310) 410–0808
newsroom@blk.com

BLK
Box 83912
Los Angeles, CA 90083–0912
(310) 410–0808
newsroom@blk.com

Clevelandlife Magazine
1729 Superior Ave., No. 400
Cleveland, OH 44114
(216) 771–5433

Creole Culture Magazine
PO Box 92202
Lafayette, LA 70509
(318) 269–1956

Ebony
820 S. Michigan Ave.
Chicago, IL 60605–2191
(312) 322–9200

EM: Ebony Man
820 S. Michigan Ave.
Chicago, IL 60605–2191
(312) 322–9200

Essence
1500 Broadway, 6th Fl.
New York, NY 10036
(212) 642–0600

Footsteps
30 Grove St., Ste. C
Peterborough, NH 03458
(603) 924–7209
custsvc@cobblestone.mv.com

Harmony Magazine
PO Box 81
Brooklyn, NY 11205
culture@mail.idt.net

HealthQuest
200 Highpoint Dr., No. 215
Chalfont, PA 18914
(215) 822–7935

Heart & Soul
315 Park Ave. S., 11th Fl.
New York, NY 10010
(646) 654–4200

Homecoming
100 Bridge St., No. A-3
Hampton, VA 23669
(757) 722–1300

Honey
315 Park Ave. S., 11th Fl.
New York, NY 10010
(646) 654–4200

Ivy Leaf
5656 S. Stony Island Ave.
Chicago, IL 60637–1997
(773) 684–1282

Jet
820 S. Michigan Ave.
Chicago, IL 60605–2191
(312) 322–9200

Journal of Black Psychology
2455 Teller Rd.
Thousand Oaks, CA 91320
(805) 499–0721
info@sagepub.com

Journal of Black Studies
2455 Teller Rd.
Thousand Oaks, CA 91320
(805) 499–0721
info@sagepub.com

Journal of Negro History
1407 14th St. NW
Washington, DC 20005–3704
(202) 667–2822

Journal of the National Medical Association
1012 Tenth St. NW
Washington, DC 20001
(202) 347–1895
ktaylor@nmanet.org

Kuumba
Box 83912
Los Angeles, CA 90083–0912
(310) 410–0808
newsroom@blk.com

Lincoln Review
1001 Connecticut Ave. NW, Ste. 1135
Washington, DC 20036–5504
(202) 223–5112

Living Blues
University of Mississippi
University, MS 38677
(662) 915–5993
cssc@olemiss.edu

Meanderings
157 Primrose Way
Palo Alto, CA 94303

Message
55 W. Oak Ridge Dr.
Hagerstown, MD 21740
(301) 393–3000
editoria@rhpa.org

Minority Business Entrepreneur
3528 Torrance Blvd., Ste. 101
Torrance, CA 90503–4826
(310) 540–9398
mbewbe@mbemag.com

Negro History Bulletin
1407 14th St. NW
Washington, DC 20005–3704
(202) 667–2822

NOMMO
118 Kerkhoff Hall
Los Angeles, CA 90024
(310) 825–9898

NSBE Magazine
1454 Duke St.
Alexandria, VA 22314–3429
(703) 549–2207

Papyrus
100 Prospect Ave.
Hartford, CT 06106
www.readersndex.com/ple

Players
8060 Melrose Ave.
Los Angeles, CA 90046
(213) 653–8060

Prime
7116 Helen C. White Hall
Madison, WI 53706
(608) 262–3262

Pure Heart Magazine
PO Box 11130
Birmingham, AL 35202
(205) 815–2179

Raising Black and Biracial Children
PO Box 30
Burbank, CA 91503–0030
(661) 723–9805

Right On!
233 Park Ave. S.
New York, NY 10003
(212) 780–3500

Savoy
315 Park Ave. S., 11th Fl.
New York, NY 10010
(646) 654–4200

SENGA
7501 Morrison Rd.
New Orleans, LA 70126
(504) 242–6022

The Black Collegian
140 Carondelet St.
New Orleans, LA 70130–2526
(504) 523–0154
leon@black-collegiate.com

The Black Scholar
PO Box 2869
Oakland, CA 94618
(510) 547–6633

The Christian Index
PO Box 2018
Memphis, TN 38101
(901) 345–4120

The Journal of Negro Education
Howard University
Washington, DC 20059
(202) 806–8120

The Review of Black Political Economy
Rutgers—The State University of New Jersey
Piscataway, NJ 08854–8042
meq@meforum.org

The Western Journal of Black Studies
PO Box 645910
Pullman, WA 99164–5910
(509) 335–3518
wsupress@wsu.edu

USBE & Information Technology
729 E. Pratt St., No. 504
Baltimore, MD 21202
(410) 244–7101
ccgmag@aol.com

Vital Issues
600 New Hampshire Ave. NW
Washington, DC 20037
(202) 625–7048

Washington View
6856 Eastern Ave. NW, No. 309
Washington, DC 20012–2165

Your Black Books Guide
912 W. Pembroke Ave.
Hampton, VA 23669
(757) 723–2696
ubus@pinn.net

Radio Stations

Alabama

WAJF-AM
1301 Central Pkwy. SW
Decatur, AL 35601–4817
(205) 340–1490

WARB-AM
PO Box3770
Oxford, AL 36203
(205) 835–1580

WBHK-FM
2301 1st Ave. N., Ste. 102
Birmingham, AL 35203
(205) 322–2987

WBLX-FM
1204 Dauphin St.
Mobile, AL 36604
(334) 432–7609

WDJL-AM
6420 Springfield Rd.
Huntsville, AL 35806
(205) 852–1223

WDLT-FM
280 Hwy. 35
Red Bank, AL 07701

WDLT-FM
PO Box 180426
Mobile, AL 36618–0426
(334) 380–9098

WENN-FM
424 16th St. N.
PO Box 697
Birmingham, AL 35203–0697
(205) 254–1820

WEUP-AM
PO Box 11398
Huntsville, AL 35814
(205) 837–9387

WGOK-AM
Box 1425
Mobile, AL 36633–1425
(334) 432–8661

WJUS-AM
PO Box 930
Marion, AL 36756
(334) 683–2043

WKXN-FM
PO Box 369
Greenville, AL 36037
(334) 382–6555

WMMV-FM
PO Box 901
Spanish Fort, AL 36527–0901

WNPT-FM
5200 Flatwoods Rd.
Northport, AL 35473
(205) 330–5608

WRAG-AM
Hwy. 17 S.
PO Box 71
Carrollton, AL 35447–0071
(205) 367–8136

WSBM-AM
624 Sam Phillips St.
PO Box 932
Florence, AL 35631
(256) 764–8121

WSLY-FM
11474 U.S. Hwy. 11
York, AL 36925
(205) 392–5234

WTUG-FM
142 Skyland Blvd.
Tuscaloosa, AL 35405–4015
(205) 345–7200

WZMG-AM
915 Saugahatchee Lake Rd.
PO Box 2329
Opelika, AL 36803
(334) 745–4656

Arizona

KISO-AM
840 N. Central Ave.
Phoenix, AZ 85004
(602) 258–8181

Arkansas

KCAT-AM
PO Box 8808
Pine Bluff, AR 71611–8808
(501) 534–5001

KCLT-FM
307 Hwy 49B
Box 2870
West Helena, AR 72390
(501) 572–9506

KIPR-FM
700 Wellington Hills Rd.
Little Rock, AR 72211–2026
(501) 663–0092

KLRG-AM
1403 Main St.
North Little Rock, AR 72114–4128
(501) 376–1063

KMZX-FM
1403 Main St.
North Little Rock, AR 72114–4128

KOKY-FM
700 Wellington Hills Rd.
Little Rock, AR 72211
(501) 401–0200

KXAR-FM
2806 Country Club Ln.
Hope, AR 71801
(870) 722–2299

KYFX-FM
13910 Cooper Orbit Cove
Little Rock, AR 72210
(501) 666–9499

California

KACD-FM
1424 Lincoln Blvd.
Santa Monica, CA 90401–2745
(310) 899–6999

KALI-AM
5723 Melrose Ave.
Hollywood, CA 90038–3898
(213) 466–6161

KBLA-AM
1700 N. Alvarado St.
Los Angeles, CA 90026
(213) 665–1580

KDNZ-FM
2130 Fulton St., UC 402
San Francisco, CA 94117
(415) 422–6880

KJLH-FM
161 N. La Brea Ave.
Inglewood, CA 90301
(310) 330–2200

KKBT-FM
6735 Yucca St.
Hollywood, CA 90028
(213) 466–9566

KSRH-FM
185 Mission Ave.
San Rafael, CA 94901
(415) 457–5774

KXBT-AM
3267 Sonoma Blvd.
Vallejo, CA 94590
(707) 644–8944

Colorado

KDKO-AM
4155 Grape Street
Denver, CO 80216
(303) 394–7505

KKMG-FM
6805 Corporate Dr., Ste. 130
Colorado Springs, CO 80919–1977
(719) 593–2700

Connecticut

WKND-AM
544 Windsor Ave.
PO Box 1480
Windsor, CT 06095
(203) 688–6221

WNHC-AM
112 Washington Ave.
North Haven, CT 06473–1707
(203) 234–1340

WQTQ-FM
153 Market St., 8th Fl.
Hartford, CT 06103

WYBC-FM
165 Elm St.
PO Box 209050
New Haven, CT 06520
(203) 432–4118

Delaware

WJKS-FM
First Federal Plaza Bldg.
704 King St.
Ste. 604
Wilmington, DE 19801
(302) 622–8895

District of Columbia

WHUR-FM
529 Bryant St. NW
Washington, DC 20059
(202) 806–3500

Florida

WAMF-FM
Florida A&M University
PO Box 6202
Tallahassee, FL 32312
(904) 599–3083

WEDR-FM
Box 551748
Carol City, FL 33055
(305) 623–7711

WEXY-AM
412 W. Oakland Park Blvd.
Fort Lauderdale, FL 33311–1712
(305) 561–1520

WHBX-FM
PO Box 3168
Tallahassee, FL 32315–3168
(850) 201–3000

WJHM-FM
37 Skyline Dr., Ste. 4200
Lake Mary, FL 32746
(407) 333–0072

WJWA-AM
PO Box 189
West Palm Beach, FL 33402

WPJS-AM
3033 Riviera Dr., Ste. 200
Naples, FL 34103–2748
(813) 248–9040

WPOM-AM
5033 Okeechobee Blvd.
West Palm Beach, FL 33417–4533
(561) 687–1960

WPUL-AM
PO Box 4010
South Daytona, FL 32121–4010
(904) 767–1131

WRBD-AM
PO Box 626
Stuart, FL 34995–0626
(954) 731–4800

WRNE-AM
312 E Nine Mile Rd., Ste. 27
Pensacola, FL 32514–1475
(904) 478–6000

WRXB-AM
2060 1st Ave. N.
St. Petersburg, FL 33713–8802
(727) 327–9792

WSWN-AM
2001 State Rd. 715
PO Box 1505
Belle Glade, FL 33430
(561) 996–2063

WTCL-AM
PO Box 157
Chattahoochee, FL 32324–0814
(904) 663–2323

WTMP-AM
5207 Washington Blvd.
Tampa, FL 33619
(813) 620–1300

WWAB-AM
1203 West Chase St.
PO Box 65
Lakeland, FL 33802–0065
(813) 682–2998

Georgia

WAKB-FM
PO Box 10003
Augusta, GA 30903
(706) 854–0440

WALR-FM
209 CNN Center
Atlanta, GA 30303
(404) 688–0068

WBKZ-AM
386 N. Milledge Ave.
Athens, GA 30601
(706) 543–8074

WBKZ-AM
548 Hawthorne Ave.
PO Box 88
Athens, GA 30606
(706) 548–8800

WCNN-AM
209 CNN Center
Atlanta, GA 30303–2705
(404) 688–0068

WFXA-FM
PO Box 1998
Columbus, GA 31994
(404) 576–3565

WFXM-FM
Atl Hwy. 341
Fort Valley, GA 31030
(912) 827–1273

WGOV-AM
2973 U.S. 84 W.
Valdosta, GA 31601
(912) 242–4513

WHGH-AM
PO BOX 2218
Thomasville, GA 31799
(912) 228–4124

WHVL-FM
120 Liberty St./CD-104
Hinesville, GA 31313
(912) 369–1047

WJGA-FM
PO Box 878
Jackson, GA 30233
(770) 775–3151

WPGA-FM
PO Drawer 980
Perry, GA 31069–0980
(912) 987–2980

WVGS-FM
Georgia Southern University
Box 8016
Statesboro, GA 30460
(912) 681–0877

WVKX-FM
PO Box 569
Irwinton, GA 31042
(912) 946–3445

WVVS-FM
1500 N. Patterson
Valdosta, GA 31698–0002
(912) 333–5600

Illinois

WBCP-AM
904 N. 4th St. Unit D.
Champaign, IL 61820
(217) 359–1580

WEJM-FM
800 S. Wells, Ste.250
Chicago, IL 60607
(312) 360–9000

WEMG-AM
12844 S. Halsted St.
Chicago, IL 60628
(312) 468–1060

WGCI-FM
332 S. Michigan Ave., Ste. 600
Chicago, IL 60604
(312) 427–4700

WOUI-FM
3300 S. Federal St.
Chicago, IL 60616
(312) 567–3087

WPCD-FM
2400 W. Bradley Ave.
Champaign, IL 61821
(217) 351–2450

WVAZ-FM
800 S. Wells, Ste. 250
Chicago, IL 60607
(312) 360–9000

Indiana

WPZZ-FM
645 Industrial Dr.
Franklin, IN 46131–9617
(317) 736–4040

WSYW-AM
1800 N. Meridian St., Ste. 605
Indianapolis, IN 46202–1433
(317) 271–1111

WTLC-FM
2126 N. Meridan St.
Indianapolis, IN 46202
(317) 923–1456

Iowa

KALA-FM
518 W. Locust St.
Davenport, IA 52803–2898
(319) 333–6219

KIGC-FM
William Penn University
201 Trueblood Ave.
Oskaloosa, IA 52577
(641) 673–1095

KRUI-FM
129 Grand Ave. Ct.
Iowa City, IA 52242
(319) 335–9525

KUCB-FM
1404–6th Ave.
Des Moines, IA 50314
(515) 246–1588

KUNI-FM
University of Northern Iowa
Cedar Falls, IA 50614–0359
(319) 273–6400

Kansas

KSWC-FM
Southwestern College
Winfield, KS 67156–2499
(620) 229–6263

Ohio

WIZF-FM
7030 Reading Rd., No. 316
Cincinnati, OH 45237–3839
(513) 351–5900

Louisiana

KBCE-FM
Box 69
Boyce, LA 71409
(318) 793–4003

KFXZ-FM
3225 Ambassador Caffery Pkwy.
Lafayette, LA 70506–7214
(318) 981–0106

KGRM-FM
Drawer K
Grambling, LA 71245

KJCB-AM
413 Jefferson St.
Lafayette, LA 70501–7057
(318) 233–4262

KMEZ-FM
1450 Poydras St.
New Orleans, LA 70112
(504) 593–2171

KNEK-FM
PO Box 598
Washington, LA 70589
(318) 826–3921

KNWD-FM
Northwestern State University
PO Box 3038
Natchitoches, LA 71497
(318) 357–4180

KQXL-FM
650 Wooddale Blvd.
Baton Rouge, LA 70806
(225) 926–1106

KRRQ-FM
3225 Ambassador Caffery
Lafayette, LA 70506
(337) 981–0106

KSCL-FM
2911 Centenary Blvd.
Shreveport, LA 71104
(318) 869–5296

KXZZ-AM
311 Alamo St.
Lake Charles, LA 70601
(318) 436–7277

KYEA-FM
1200 N. 18th St., Ste. D
Monroe, LA 71201–5449
(318) 322–1491

KZWA-FM
PO Box 699
Lake Charles, LA 70602
(318) 491–9955

WEMX-FM
650 Wooddale Blvd.
Baton Rouge, LA 70806
(225) 926–1106

WQUE-FM
2228 Gravier
New Orleans, LA 70119
(504) 827–6000

WXOK-AM
7707 Waco Ave.
Baton Rouge, LA 70806
(504) 926–1106

WYLD-FM
2228 Gravier St.
New Orleans, LA 70119
(504) 827–6000

Maryland

WEAA-FM
Hillen Rd. & Coldspring Ln.
Baltimore, MD 21251
(443) 885–4526

WJDY-AM
1633 N. Division St.
Salisbury, MD 21801–3805
(410) 742–5191

WPGC-FM
4200 Parliament Place, Ste. 300
Lanham, MD 20706
(301) 441–3500

WWIN-FM
100 St. Paul St.
Baltimore, MD 21202
(410) 332–8200

WXYV-FM
1829 Reistertown Rd.
Baltimore, MD 21208
(410) 653–2200

Massachusetts

WAIC-FM
1000 State St.
Springfield, MA 01109
(413) 736–7662

WBOT-FM
60 Main St.
Brockton, MA 02301
(508) 587–9898

WCHC-FM
Holy Cross College
Box G
Worcester, MA 01610
(508) 793–2475

WGAJ-FM
PO Box 248
Deerfield, MA 01342–0248
(413) 774–1850

WILD-AM
90 Warren St.
Boston, MA 02119
(617) 427–2222

WJMN-FM
235 Bear Hill Rd.
Waltham, MA 02451
(617) 290–0009

Michigan

WDZZ-FM
6317 Taylor Dr.
Flint, MI 48507–4683
(810) 767–7300

WGPR-FM
3146 E. Jefferson Ave.
Detroit, MI 48207
(313) 259–8862

WHPR-FM
15851 Woodward Ave.
Highland Park, MI 48203
(313) 868–8812

WJLB-FM
645 Griswold St., Ste. 633
Detroit, MI 48226–4177
(313) 965–2000

WKBZ-FM
592 W. Pontaluna Rd.
Muskegon, MI 49444
(616) 798–2141

WKWM-AM
3777 44th St. SE
Kentwood, MI 49512–3945
(616) 956–3323

WMXD-FM
645 Griswold
Detroit, MI 48226
(313) 965–2000

WNMC-FM
1701 E. Front St.
Traverse City, MI 49686
(616) 922–1091

WQBH-AM
Penobscot Bldg.
Detroit, MI 48226
(313) 965–4500

WQHH-FM
101 Northcrest Rd., Ste. 4
Lansing, MI 48906–1262
(517) 484–9600

WTLZ-FM
3190 Christy Way
Saginaw, MI 48603–2286
(517) 754–1071

WXLA-AM
101 Northcrest Rd., Ste. 4
Lansing, MI 48906–1262
(517) 484–9600

Minnesota

KMOJ-FM
501 Bryant Ave. N.
Minneapolis, MN 55405
(612) 377–0594

KSGS-AM
7001 France Ave. S., No. 200
Minneapolis, MN 55435–4202
(612) 836–1041

Mississippi

WACR-AM
1910 14th Ave. N.
PO Box 1078
Columbus, MS 39703
(662) 328–1050

WACR-FM
1910 14th Ave. N.
PO Box 1078
Columbus, MS 39703
(662) 328–1050

WAID-FM
112 Le Flore Ave.
Box 668
Clarksdale, MS 38614
(662) 627–2281

WBAD-FM
PO Box 4426
Greenville, MS 38704–4426
(662) 335–9265

WBFN-AM
Drawer 70
Quitman, MS 39355
(601) 776–3327

WCLD-FM
Drawer 780
Cleveland, MS 38732
(601) 843–4091

WESE-FM
PO Box 3300
Tupelo, MS 38803
(662) 842–1067

WESY-AM
7 Oaks Rd.
PO Box 5804
Greenville, MS 38704–5804
(662) 378–9405

WJMG-FM
1204 Gravel Line St.
Hattiesburg, MS 39401
(601) 544–1941

WKRA-FM
Hwy. 4 East-C
PO Box 398
Holly Springs, MS 38635
(662) 252–6692

WKXG-AM
Browning Rd.
PO Box 1686
Greenwood, MS 38930
(662) 453–2174

WMXU-FM
PO Box1076
Columbus, MS 39703
(662) 327–1183

WNBN-AM
1290 266–23rd St.
Meridian, MS 39301
(601) 483–7930

WORV-AM
1204 Graveline
Hattiesburg, MS 39401
(601) 544–1941

WQFX-FM
Security Bldg., Penthouse Ste.
PO Box 789
Gulfport, MS 39502

WRJH-FM
1985 Lakeland Dr.
Jackson, MS 39216
(601) 713–0977

WTYJ-FM
20 E. Franklin
Natchez, MS 39120
(601) 442–2522

Missouri

KIRL-AM
3713 Hwy. 94 N.
St. Charles, MO 63301
(314) 946–6600

KJLU-FM
820 Chestnut St.
Jefferson City, MO 65102–0029
(573) 681–5301

KMJM-FM
10155 Corporate Sq. Dr.
St. Louis, MO 63132
(314) 692–5108

KMVC-FM
500 E. College St.
Marshall, MO 65340
(816) 886–6924

Nebraska

KBBX-AM
11128 John Galt Blvd., Ste. 192
Omaha, NE 68137–2321
(402) 556–6700

Nevada

KCEP-FM
330 W. Washington St.
Las Vegas, NV 89106–3327
(702) 648–4218

KOKY-FM
7201 W. Lake Mead Blvd., Ste. 400
Las Vegas, NV 89128
(702) 804–5200

KQXL-FM
7201 W. Lake Mead Blvd., Ste. 400
Las Vegas, NV 89128
(702) 804–5200

KRRQ-FM
7201 W. Lake Mead Blvd., Ste. 400
Las Vegas, NV 89128
(702) 804–5200

WEMX-FM
7201 W. Lake Mead Blvd., Ste. 400
Las Vegas, NV 89128
(702) 804–5200

WLXC-FM
7201 W. Lake Mead Blvd., Ste. 400
Las Vegas, NV 89128
(702) 804–5200

New Hampshire

WSPS-FM
St. Paul's School
Concord, NH 03301
(603) 229–4810

New Jersey

WBLX-FM
280 Hwy. 35
Red Bank, NJ 07701
(732) 758–8900

WRRC-FM
2083 Lawrenceville Rd.
Lawrenceville, NJ 08648
(609) 896–5369

New York

WBLK-FM
712 Main St., Ste. 112
Buffalo, NY 14202
(716) 852–5955

WBLS-FM
3 Park Ave.
New York, NY 10016
(212) 447–1000

WCKX-FM
PO Box2307
Newburgh, NY 12550
(914) 561–2131

WFXK-FM
405 Lexington Ave.
New York, NY 10174
(212) 697–2280

WHCR-FM
City College of New York
138th & Convent Ave.
New York, NY 10031
(212) 650–7481

WNYO-FM
State University of New York at Oswego
9B Hewitt Union
Oswego, NY 13126
(315) 341–2101

WPKF-FM
20 Tucker Dr.
Poughkeepsie, NY 12603
(845) 471–2300

WPTR-FM
6 Johnson Rd.
Latham, NY 12110
(518) 786–6600

WRKS-FM
395 Hudson St. 7th Fl.
New York, NY 10014
(212) 242–9870

WSUC-FM
SUNY Cortland
Brockway Hall
PO Box 2000
Cortland, NY 13045
(607) 753–2936

WWRL-AM
41–30 58th St.
Woodside, NY 11377
(718) 335–1600

WXYV-FM
40 W. 47th St.
New York, NY 10019
(212) 809–2900

North Carolina

WFMC-AM
914 W. Grantham St.
Goldsboro, NC 27530
(919) 734–4211

WFXC-FM
5400 S. Miami Blvd., No. 116
Morrisville, NC 27560

WFXK-FM
3209 Gresham Lake Rd., Ste. 160
Raleigh, NC 27615
(919) 954–1043

WIDU-AM
145 Roman St.
Drawer 2247
Fayetteville, NC 28302
(910) 483–6111

WIKS-FM
207 Glenburnie Dr.
New Bern, NC 28561–2815
(252) 633–1500

WJMH-FM
7819 National Service Rd
Bldg 401
Greensboro, NC 27409
(910) 605–5200

WNAA-FM
NC A&T State University
Price Hall, Ste. 200
Greensboro, NC 27411
(336) 334–7936

WQOK-FM
8001–101 Creedmoor Rd.
Raleigh, NC 27613
(919) 848–9736

WRVS-FM
1704 Weeksville Rd.
CB 790
Elizabeth City, NC 27909
(252) 335–3230

WSMY-AM
PO Box 910
Roanoke Rapids, NC 27870
(919) 536–3115

WSNC-FM
Winston Salem State Univ.
601 MLK Jr. Dr.
Winston-Salem, NC 27101
(910) 750–2324

WXDU-FM
Duke University
Box 90689
Durham, NC 27708
(919) 684–2957

WZFX-FM
106–108 Hay St.
Suite 200
Fayetteville, NC 28301
(919) 486–4991

Ohio

WCKX-FM
510 E. Mound St.
Columbus, OH 43215–5539
(614) 464–0020

WJTB-AM
105 Lake Ave.
Elyria, OH 44035
(216) 327–1844

WLQR-AM
2965 Pickle Rd.
PO Box 167581
Oregon, OH 43616
(419) 691–1470

WRBP-AM
34 Federal Plaza W. Ste. 1200
Youngstown, OH 44503
(330) 744–5115

WZAK-FM
2510 St. Clair Ave.
Cleveland, OH 44114
(216) 621–9300

Oklahoma

KALU-FM
Langston University
Langston, OK 73050
(405) 466–2924

KOKF-FM
7700 N. Council Rd.
Oklahoma City, OK 73132
(405) 728–7717

KVSP-AM
1528 NE 23rd St.
Oklahoma City, OK 73111
(405) 427–5877

KXOJ-AM
2448 E. 81st St., Ste.5950
Tulsa, OK 74137
(918) 492–2660

Pennsylvania

WBUQ-FM
1250 McCormick Center for Human Services
Bloomsburg University
Bloomsburg, PA 17815
(570) 389–3530

WDAS-FM
23 W. City Avenue
Bala Cynwyd, PA 19004
(610) 617–8500

WDNR-FM
PO Box 1000
1 University
Chester, PA 19013
(610) 499–4439

WHAT-AM
2471 N. 54th St.
Philadelphia, PA 19131
(215) 581–5161

WIXQ-FM
Millersville University
SMC Basement
Millersville, PA 17551
(717) 872–3333

WKDU-FM
3210 Chestnut St.
Philadelphia, PA 19104
(215) 895–5920

WLIU-FM
Office of Student Activities
Lincoln University, PA 19352
(610) 932–8300

WPHI-FM
100 Old York Rd., Ste. 2–260
Jenkintown, PA 19046
(215) 884–9400

WPPJ-AM
201 Wood St.
PO Box 626
Pittsburgh, PA 15222
(412) 392–4725

WTCY-AM
PO Box 104
Harrisburg, PA 17108
(717) 238–1041

WUSL-FM
440 Domino Ln.
Philadelphia, PA 19128
(215) 483–8900

Rhode Island

WDOM-FM
Providence College
Joseph Hall, Ste. 106
Providence, RI 02918
(401) 865–2460

WRBU-FM
88 Benevolent St.
Providence, RI 02906
(401) 272–9550

South Carolina

WASC-AM
840 Wofford
PO Box 5686
Spartanburg, SC 29304
(803) 585–1530

WBAW-AM
PO Box447
Barnwell, SC 29812
(803) 259–3507

WDOG-AM
PO Box 442
Allendale, SC 29810
(803) 584–3500

WDOG-FM
PO Box 442
Allendale, SC 29810
(803) 584–3500

WFXA-FM
104 Bennett Ln.
North Augusta, SC 29841
(803) 279–2330

WGCD-AM
PO Box 746
Chester, SC 29706
(803) 581–1490

WKHT-FM
PO Box 1269
Sumter, SC 29151
(803) 775–0753

WLBG-AM
Box 1289
Laurens, SC 29360
(803) 984–3544

WLXC-FM
1801 Charleston Hwy., Ste. J
Cayce, SC 29033
(803) 796–7600

WQKI-FM
PO Box 1742
Orangeburg, SC 29118
(803) 874–2777

WWDM-FM
PO Box 9127
Columbia, SC 29290
(803) 495–2558

WYNN-FM
170 E. Palmetto St.
PO Box 100531
Florence, SC 29501–0531
(803) 662–6364

Tennessee

KJMS-FM
80 N. Tillman
Memphis, TN 38111
(901) 323–0101

WBOL-AM
PO Box 191
Bolivar, TN 38008
(901) 658–3690

WDBL-AM
Box 606
Springfield, TN 37172
(615) 384–5541

WDIA-AM
112 Union Ave.
Memphis, TN 38103
(901) 529–4300

WFKX-FM
111 W. Main St.
Jackson, TN 38301
(901) 427–9616

WFSK-FM
1000 17th Ave. N.
Nashville, TN 37208
(615) 329–8754

WHRK-FM
112 Union Ave.
Memphis, TN 38103
(901) 529–4300

WJMR-AM
150 State Line Rd.
Clarksville, TN 37042
(931) 431–4984

WJTT-FM
409 Chestnut St., Ste. A154
Chattanooga, TN 37402
(423) 265–9494

WMDB-AM
3051 Stokers Ln.
Nashville, TN 37218
(615) 255–2876

WQQK-FM
10 Music Cir. E
Nashville, TN 37203–4338

WVOL-AM
50 Music Sq. W, Ste. 901
Nashville, TN 37203–3228
(615) 227–1470

Texas

KALO-AM
7700 Gulfway
Port Arthur, TX 77642
(409) 963–1276

KAZI-FM
8906 Wall St., Ste 202
Austin, TX 78754–4542
(512) 836–9544

KCOH-AM
5011 Almeda Rd.
Houston, TX 77004
(713) 522–1001

KIIZ-AM
Box 2469
Harker Heights, TX 76543
(817) 699–5000

KKBT-FM
433 E. Las Colinas
Irving, TX 75039
(214) 869–9020

KKDA-FM
PO Box 530860
Grand Prairie, TX 75053
(972) 263–9911

KMHT-FM
1127 Judson Rd., No. 249
Longview, TX 75606

KMJQ-FM
24 Greenway Plaza, No. 1508
Houston, TX 77046
(713) 623–0102

KSHU-FM
Box 2207
Huntsville, TX 77341
(936) 294–3939

KSJL-AM
217 Alamo Plaza, Ste. 200
San Antonio, TX 78205
(210) 271–9600

KSSM-FM
108 East Ave. E
PO Box 607
Copperas Cove, TX 76522
(817) 547–8889

KZEY-AM
PO Box 4248
Tyler, TX 75712
(903) 593–1744

Utah

KLGN-AM
PO Box 3369
Logan, UT 84321
(801) 752–1390

KWCR-FM
Weber State University
3750 Harrison Blvd., Ste. 1906
Ogden, UT 84408–1906
(801) 626–6000

Vermont

WWLR-FM
Lyndon State College
Box F
Lyndonville, VT 05851
(802) 626–6213

Virginia

KMZX-FM
Norfolk, VA (804)622–4600

WAMF-AM
446 Plank Rd.
Farmville, VA 23901
(804) 392–8114

WARR-AM
PO Box610
Hampton, VA 23669–0610

WCDX-FM
2809 Emerywood Pkwy., Ste. 300
Richmond, VA 23294
(804) 672–9299

WCHV-AM
1140 Rose Hill Dr.
Charlottesville, VA 22903
(804) 977–5566

WHOV-FM
Hampton University
Hampton, VA 23668
(757) 727–5670

WJJS-AM
3305 Old Forest Rd.
Lynchburg, VA 24501–2912
(804) 847–1266

WJMH-FM
900 Laskin Rd.
Virginia Beach, VA 23451
(804) 437–9800

WMYK-FM
645 Church St., Ste. 400
Norfolk, VA 23510
(804) 622–9723

WPZZ-FM
645 Church St., No. 400
Norfolk, VA 23510
(800) 873–4600

WWHS-FM
Box 606
Hampden-Sydney College
Hampden Sydney, VA 23943
(804) 223–6809

Washington

KKFX-AM
1509 Queen Anne Ave., N No. 612
Seattle, WA 98109–5730
(206) 728–1250

KRIZ-AM
2600 S. Jackson St.
Seattle, WA 98144
(206) 329–7880

KZIZ-AM
c/o KRIZ-AM
2600 S. Jackson St.
Seattle, WA 98144
(206) 627–1103

Wisconsin

KUWS-FM
1800 Grand Ave.
Superior, WI 54880–2898
(715) 394–8530

WBZN-AM
2400 S. 102nd St.
West Allis, WI 53227
(414) 321–1007

WKKV-FM
2400 S. 102nd St.
West Allis, WI 53227
(414) 321–1007

WKPO-FM
1 Parker Pl., Ste. 485
Janesville, WI 53545
(608) 758–9025

WMCS-AM
2979 N. Mayfair Rd.
Milwaukee, WI 53222
(414) 771–1021

Television Stations

California

KNTV-TV
645 Park Ave.
San Jose, CA 95110
(408) 286–1111

KSEE-TV
5035 E. McKinley
Fresno, CA 93727
(209) 454–2424

Florida

WTVT-TV
3213 W. Kennedy Blvd.
Tampa, FL 33609
(813) 876–1313

Georgia

WGXA-TV
559 Martin Luther King Jr.
Macon, GA 31201
(912) 745–2424

WRDW-TV
PO Drawer 1212
Augusta, GA 30903–1212
(912) 278–1212

Illinois

WEEK-TV
2907 Springfield Rd.
Peoria, IL 61611
(309) 698–2525

Indiana

WPTA-TV
3401 Butler Rd.
Box 2121
Fort Wayne, IN 46801
(219) 483–0584

Louisiana

WNOL-TV
1661 Canal St., Ste. 1200
New Orleans, LA 70112–2861
(504) 525–3838

Maine

WVII-TV
371 Target Industrial Circle
P.O. Box 1101
Bangor, ME 04401
(207) 945–6457

Michigan

WWMT-TV
590 W. Maple St.
Kalamazoo, MI 49008
(616) 388–3333

Minnesota

KBJR-TV
230 E. Superior St.
Duluth, MN 55802
(218) 727–8484

New York

WKBW-TV
7 Broadcast Plaza
Buffalo, NY 14202
(716) 845–6100

WTVH-TV
980 James St.
Syracuse, NY 13203
(315) 425–5555

Tennessee

WFLI-TV
6024 Shallowford Rd., Ste. 100
Chattanooga, TN 37421
(423) 893–9553

Texas

KEYE-TV
10700 Metric Blvd.
Austin, TX 78758
(512) 835–0042

Wisconsin

WJFW-TV
S. Oneida Ave.
PO Box 858
Rhinelander, WI 54501
(715) 369–4700

Film and Television

◆ African Americans in Film ◆ African Americans in Television
◆ Filmography of Selected Feature Films and Documentaries
◆ Actors, Filmmakers, and Film and Television Executives ◆ Award Winners

by Gil L. Robertson IV

As the foremost medium for creative expression, cinema yields a great deal of power and influence in defining images that shape humanity. Although primarily seen as a form of entertainment, it plays a significant role in the manner in which society views itself and the world around it. With regards to the representation of African Americans in cinema, the medium has largely failed in illuminating images that reflect the complete diversity of that experience. Instead, it has largely focused on images that devalue African Americans by confining their representation within an ideological web of myths, stereotypes, and caricatures.

The experiences of African Americans in television have been somewhat less limiting than those realized in film. This has been due, in part, to the fact that television sought to capture an African American audience from the outset. In fact, many of the medium's earliest participants such as Steve Allen publicly stated that the medium's success would certainly benefit by the inclusion of African American performers. Therefore, beginning with the medium's widespread use in the late 1940s and into the present day, television has provided some unique avenues of expression for African Americans in acting, production, and executive roles.

◆ AFRICAN AMERICANS IN FILM

The Silent Film Era

Beginning with the inception of the "moving camera" in the 1890s, African American images in cinema have been positioned, marginalized, and subordinated in every possible manner to glorify and relentlessly hold to America's status quo. In 1898, the first African Americans appeared in film as soldiers heading for battle in the Spanish-American War. Soon afterwards though, the depiction of African Americans began to mirror the racial stereotypes of that time, appearing as criminals, ministers, and, during the period in which American society grew sentimental for the Civil War era, as slaves. The most provocative film of the era in which African Americans were depicted in servitude was D.W. Griffith's *The Birth of a Nation* (1915).

Released at the end of the silent film era, *The Birth of a Nation* unleashed a tremendous amount of ire and controversy that is still discussed in cinematic circles. Although its release represented a technical and artistic triumph for the film community, its unabashed message of racial intolerance and embellished, stereotypical images of African Americans has become symbolic of the tremendous obstacles that African Americans face in cinema. Although other films such as *Uncle Tom's Cabin* (1909) and *The Nigger* (1915) drew upon the same anti-African American propaganda, *The Birth of a Nation*, due to its technological significance, stands out as a fundamental reference to cinema's position on African American images.

Redefining African American Images

In response to the popularity of such films, African Americans during the 1910s and 1920s formed independent film projects and production companies in order to create more realistic images of the African American culture.

Perhaps the best known African American filmmaker of this period is Oscar Micheaux, who managed to generate financial profits from more than 30 silent and sound features that his private studio released. Utilizing a similar distribution system to that created

A scene from *The Birth of a Nation,* a movie reviled for its racist message and stereotypical representation of African Americans.

by African American film producer Noble Johnson, Micheaux personally delivered films to movie theaters across the country, edited films on the road, and obtained money from theater owners by having actors give private performances from scenes of upcoming releases. Despite the fact that many of his films suffered from poor technical skills, Micheaux's expert abilities as a promoter earned him a sizeable following. (Always daring, Micheaux turned the tables on Hollywood by casting his light-skinned actors to play whites in several of his films.) In 1924 the Micheaux movie *Body and Soul* featured Paul Robeson in his film debut.

After recovering from bankruptcy, Micheaux released *The Exile* in 1931—the first African American feature-length sound movie—and *God's Stepchildren* (1937), among other "talkies." As tastes began to shift from what were called "race productions" though, Micheaux saw his audience dwindle. His final film released in 1948, a three-hour epic titled *The Betrayal*, was a commercial failure. While many of his films have been lost, Micheaux maintained control of his prized works, ensuring that they were protected as the legal property of his wife.

There were other African American pioneer filmmakers of this time period—some of whose efforts pre-dated Micheaux's. William "Bill" Foster began using "all-colored" casts in a number of short films in 1913. Through his Foster Photoplay Company, he released several films, the most notable of which were *The Railroad Porter, The Butler,* and *The Grafter and the Maid.* Although Foster genuinely believed in the viability of launching an African American movie company, attempting to secure technical and financial support, not to mention distribution outlets, soon brought about his company's demise.

Headed by Noble Johnson, the Lincoln Motion Picture Company, which was established in the summer of 1915, was perhaps the first company to produce significant films featuring black performers for African American audiences. The company released several films that depicted African Americans in a common, natural manner. In response to distribution problems that often plagued African American studios, Johnson worked out a commission system that engaged African American media personnel across the United States to utilize their business relationships with movie theater owners and show his films. By doing so, Johnson was able to produce such films as *The Realization of a Negro's Ambition* (1916), *The Trooper of Company K* (1917), and *The Law of Nature* (1918). Though somewhat successful, this system could not compete with major Hollywood studios, and after Johnson's defection to Universal Films, the company soon folded.

Another early African American film pioneer was Emmett J. Scott. A former secretary to Tuskegee Institute founder Booker T. Washington, Scott believed that African American cinema could be financially supported through the sale of stock in his production company. Incorporated in July 1916, his Birth of a Race Photoplay Corporation produced *The Birth of a Race* and released the film in December 1918. Although the film did not meet original expectations, it did succeed in establishing a capital-raising tool that would prove instrumental to future African American filmmakers.

In addition, many other African American entrepreneurs took the gamble on producing films with varying degrees of success. The Frederick Douglass Film Company premiered its first film *The Colored American Winning His Suit* in 1916. In 1920, the Royal Gardens Film Company presented *In the Depths of Our Hearts,* and in 1921 the ex-heavyweight champion Jack Johnson starred in *As the World Rolls On* for Andlauer Productions. In each case, however, the African American entrepreneurs behind these ventures succumbed to the insurmountable obstacles dealt to them because of racism.

Breaking into Mainstream Sound Films

Prior to the sound era of cinema, many film producers used white actors in "blackface," or burnt-cork makeup, to portray blacks. As a means of capturing the distinctive dialect and cadence of African Americans though, most producers began to employ African American actors for such limited roles during the new era of sound film. Though short "talkies" by other white filmmakers depicted African Americans in a more authentic manner, little else changed for African American performers, generally appearing as criminals and domestic servants, among other roles. In fact, the film widely heralded for utilizing sound in film *The Jazz Singer* (1927) starred ex-vaudevillian Al Jolson singing in "blackface."

One favorable change for African American performers during this era was the establishment of the movie musical. From the late 1920s through the 1940s, countless movie musicals were made and featured African American performers. For the fortunate few, singing in a film was a real achievement—not only did it guarantee work on a project, but it also enabled performers to showcase broader talents. As the film community reveled in its latest trend, many multitalented African American performers—such as Lena Horne—were discovered.

Already gaining impressive notoriety for her beauty and singing talent, Horne's film career actually began with the black independent film *The Duke Is Tops* as well as some short films. Lured to Hollywood in 1942 by Metro-Goldwyn-Mayer for a major role in *Panama Hattie,* Horne became the first African American performer awarded a major studio contract.

Lena Horne faced some unusual circumstances in Hollywood, though, due to her physical appearance. As a light-skinned African American with long flowing hair, she was viewed by many as something other than black. However, as a staunch supporter of her ethnicity, the actress refused to sacrifice pride in her heritage—such as playing demeaning roles as a slave or servant—for greater opportunities of film stardom. As a result, Horne only appeared in two other major films *Cabin in the Sky* and *Stormy Weather.* Beyond these works, Horne's brief film career mostly consisted of musical numbers that could easily be edited in order to appease Southern viewing audiences.

Another notable performer whose breakthrough came during this era was actor Paul Robeson. Widely respected for his work as a stage actor, Robeson went on to play important roles in nine feature films between 1929 and 1942. By sheer force of talent and charisma, Robeson succeeded where many others had failed in consistently securing roles that were central to the

Paul Robeson (standing, center) as Brutus Jones in *The Emperor Jones.*

theme of the film. In such classic dramas as *The Emperor Jones*, the musical *Show Boat*, and the British film *The Proud Valley*, Robeson created characters that challenged film barriers of that time. Unfortunately, the barriers of prejudice and stereotype continued to exist, and Robeson, after consistently being denied roles worthy of his talent, abandoned Hollywood to pursue a concert career.

African American Actors Endure Racial Stereotypes

Throughout the pantheon of early Hollywood cinema perhaps no other African American caricature was as well-entrenched as the "mammy" figure. Often the source of comic relief, these characters populated films from around 1914 through the late 1950s. No two performers better embodied that image than Louise

Beavers and Hattie McDaniels, since physically, they both met the industry's standards. Although Beavers and McDaniels both enjoyed lengthy film careers, neither was able to discard this stereotype. Beavers, who is best known for her role in the 1934 film version of *Imitation of Life*, also appeared in over 120 films. McDaniels, who earned an Academy Award in 1939 for her role in *Gone with the Wind*, appeared in more than 300 films. Despite the stereotypical roles that each performed, Beavers and McDaniels were both well-respected and seen as successful members of the Hollywood film community.

Between the late 1920s through the mid-1940s, many other African American performers were successful in establishing film careers. Although virtually all had to suffer through gross indignities in pursuit of careers, they nevertheless contributed to the growing African American presence in mainstream films. These actors and actresses included Earl "Rochester" Anderson, Rex Ingram, Ethel Waters, and Nina Mae McKinney.

World War II Propaganda Films Strive for Racial Harmony

With the advent of World War II, leaders of the Civil Rights movement of the early twentieth century seized the opportunity to press the U.S. government to address racial injustice including providing equal opportunity in wartime industry and the military. At the same time, such activist groups as the National Association for the Advancement of Colored People (NAACP) lobbied Hollywood for better film roles for African Americans.

In response, the U.S. War Department produced the groundbreaking film *The Negro Soldier* in 1944. At the same time, Hollywood produced movies that depicted a racially-integrated military, years before President Truman's Executive Order No. 9981 mandated desegregation of the armed forces. For example, in *Crash Dive*, African American actor Ben Carter is shown saving the life of the film's star, Tyrone Power. In the film *Lifeboat* African American actor Canada Lee is shown among a shipwrecked group of civilians whose ship has been destroyed by enemy fire.

Later in the war, the U.S. government commissioned several short civilian films that expressed the theme of racial harmony. One such effort was *The House I Live In*, which won an Oscar Award for best short film in 1947. Documentaries of this period also reflected a liberal attitude toward race relations shortly after wartime. For example, documentarians Loeb and Levitt produced the work *The Quiet One* in 1948 that depicted the concerted effort put forth by white social workers in dealing with disadvantaged black juveniles.

Blacks in Postwar American Films

Films made in post-war America began to feature African Americans in multidimensional roles, as well as more integrated into American life. In fact, a number of films that were released in the late 1940s through the mid-1960s presented African Americans with families, careers, and working towards goals of a better life. Thus, Hollywood films sought, if only slightly, to broaden the scope of the African American experience. One significant cause was the increasing degree of political and economic influence wielded by the African American community.

Making his film debut in the 1950 drama *No Way Out* Sidney Poitier became the cinematic model for integration. Consistently depicted as an educated, intelligent, and well-mannered black man, Hollywood was quick to

Sidney Poitier in 1960, the cinematic model of racial integration.

capitalize on Poitier's appeal. With film credits that include *Cry, the Beloved Country* (1951), *The Defiant Ones* (1958), *A Raisin in the Sun* (1961), *Guess Who's Coming to Dinner* (1967), and *In the Heat of the Night* (1967), Poitier became Hollywood's first bonafide African American film star. In 1963, he won the Academy Award in the best actor category—the first by an African American—for his lead role in *Lilies of the Field*.

Though Poitier's success symbolized the changing industry standards for African American performers during the course of the next two decades, his stardom did not come without a price. Although positioned as a leading actor, Poitier's characterizations often lacked human dimension. For instance, in all but three of the films made during this period, Poitier was never allowed to exhibit any degree of sexuality. Nonetheless, Poitier's career heralded greater acceptance of black actors as equals to their white counterparts.

In 1954, film actress Dorothy Dandridge became the first African American woman to be nominated for an Academy Award in the best actress category for her role in *Carmen Jones*. With unrivaled talent and beauty, it seemed that Dandridge would become the female counterpart to Poitier's leading African American man. However, she was unable to ever find a subsequent role offering the same dimensions as Carmen Jones. While Dandridge repeatedly demonstrated dramatic ability and landed a respectable contract with Twentieth Century Fox, the industry mainly only cast her in films as an exotic native. When the pressures of battling the film industry proved too much, Dandridge drifted from the Hollywood scene and in 1965 died of an apparent suicide.

In the case of actor Harry Belafonte, Hollywood was faced with another dilemma. A naturally romantic hero, the film industry found it difficult to contain Belafonte's sexuality. Similar to Dandridge whom he starred opposite in *Carmen Jones* and *Island in the Sun*, Belafonte's career was therefore largely confined to playing an island native and other unflattering roles. After performing in *Odds Against Tomorrow*, *The World, the Flesh, and the Devil*, and *Buck and the Preacher*, Belafonte began a successful career as a concert performer and prominent civil rights spokesperson, selecting future film projects only with great discretion.

Many other actors and actresses enjoyed success in films and mainstream acceptance. Among those who made a real impact during this period were Diana Sands, Ruby Dee, and Brock Peters. Along with Poitier, Dandridge, and Belafonte, their films marked the advent of the 1960s Civil Rights movement.

Blaxploitation Films

During the 1960s Civil Rights movement and the war in Vietnam, American society was in the midst of a cultural revolution. As a result, films began to reflect the political and social changes brought about by the period's harsh, challenging ideology. Director Melvin Van Peebles's seminal 1971 African American-action film *Sweet Sweetback's Baadasssss Song* seemed to define, more than any other film, this era—one marked with contempt for white social order and its police.

In the wake of the enormous success of Peebles's films, Hollywood rushed to produce similar movies that would capture this new African American audience. Although some of the African American action films, most notably *Shaft* (1971), *Superfly* (1972), and *Coffy* (1973), experienced a great deal of commercial success, this trend was soon dubbed "blaxploitation" by the African American media. In pursuit of increased profits though, Hollywood even remade blaxploitation films from classic horror movies—*Blacula* and *Blackenstein*, both in 1972.

Along with the popularity of African American action films was the emergence of a new wave of serious African American-oriented dramas. While most of these films failed to meet their initial expectations, a number of others did—the 1969 releases of *The Learning Tree*, *Slaves*, *Putney Swope*, and *Sounder* (1972) to name a few.

Finally, more African Americans worked in Hollywood than ever before during this period—many behind the camera as well. Such screenwriters as Richard Wesley, Bill Gunn, and Lonne Elder and directors Gordon Parks Sr., Gordon Parks Jr., Michael Schultz, and Stan Lathan were all called upon to participate in the making of major studio films.

Transitions in African American Film

Although Motown founder Berry Gordy Jr.'s impact on the American music industry is legendary, little credit has been given to him as a film producer/director. Under his Motown Films banner, Gordy produced several films, the most successful being the 1972 release *Lady Sings the Blues* starring Diana Ross and Billy Dee Williams. Gordy's pairing of them was the first time that African American performers were presented as romantic icons. Gordy's 1976 film *Mahogany* was also the first to feature an African American actress as glamorous, independent, and sexual.

African American comedians were enjoying enormous film success as well. Richard Pryor emerged in the late 1970s as a film icon. Best known for his often provocative, iconoclastic stand-up routines, Pryor rose to superstardom through supporting role appearances. After appearing opposite Gene Wilder in the 1976 buddy film *Silver Streak*, Pryor continued to exhibit box-office clout in such films as *Greased Lightning*, *Which Way Is Up*, and *Bustin' Loose*. He later returned to the stage where his two live concert films permanently sealed his position in film history. Other comedians, notably Eddie Murphy in the terrifically successful movie *48 Hours* (1982) later benefitted from Pryor's success.

New African American Cinema Emerges

Towards the mid-1980s African American actors and actresses appeared to be running on empty. With the roles offered by the blaxploitation era long gone, stereotypes of the past began to reemerge. The tragic mulatto, a well-used cinematic device once again appeared as such actresses as Rae Dawn Chong (*American Flyers*), Jennifer Beals (*Flashdance*), and Lisa Bonet (*Angel Heart*) were cast in roles that made no discernable

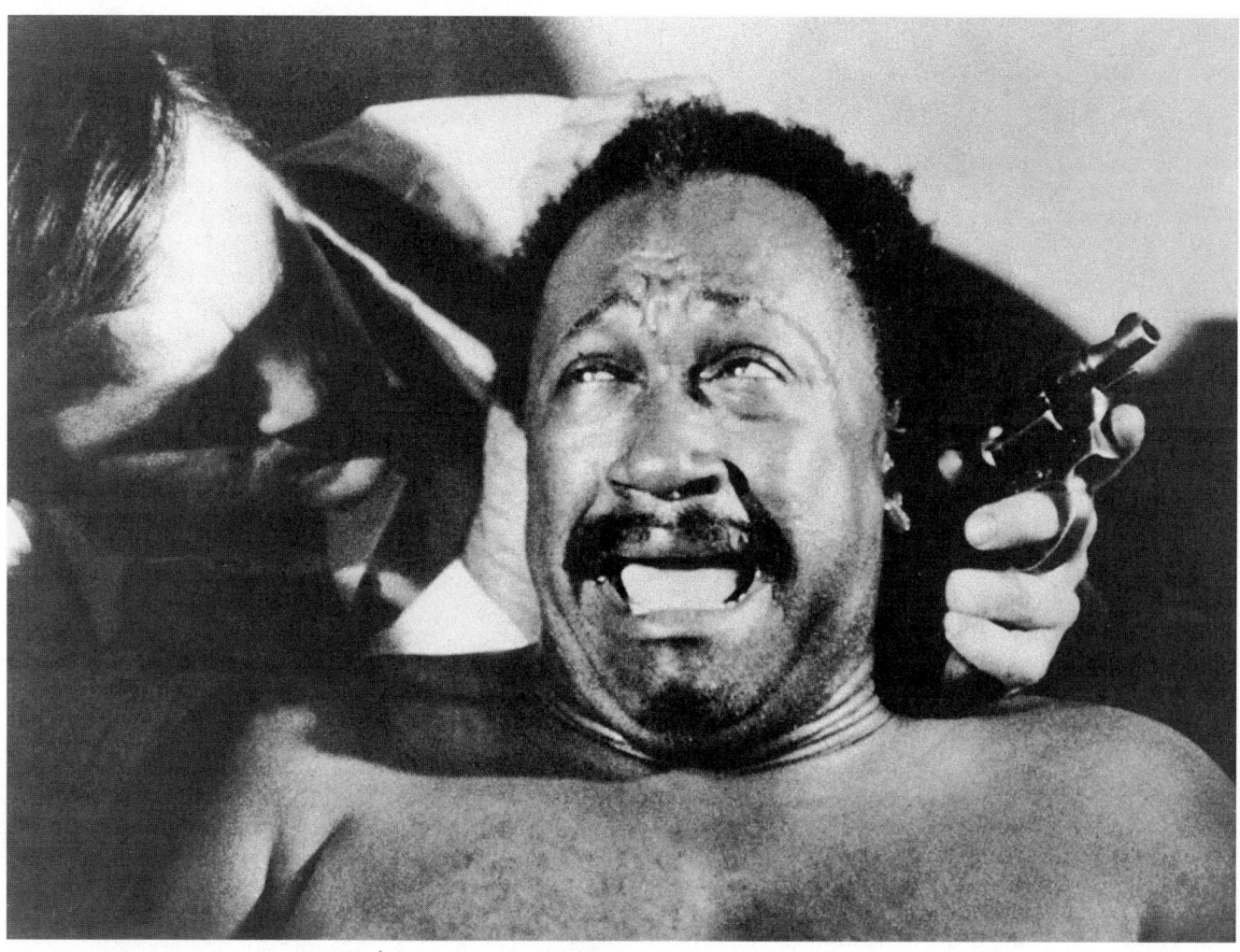

Scene from Melvin Van Peebles's 1971 film *Sweet Sweetback's Baadasssss Song,* which defined its era in film.

mention of their ethnicity. In addition, the African American musical made a brief resurgence in the films *Beat Street, Krush Groove, The Last Dragon, The Cotton Club,* and *Purple Rain.*

Another trend that enjoyed renewed popularity in cinema was "buddy movies." Although cinematic history is filled with various pairings of black and white performers, the film industry in the 1980s perfected the trend with enormous box-office success. Some notable buddy film pairings included Carl Weathers and Sylvester Stallone in the *Rocky* films and Danny Glover and Mel Gibson in the *Lethal Weapon* series.

Meanwhile, a low-budget independent film was released by a recent New York University Film School graduate named Spike Lee. The release *She's Gotta Have It* resulted in the resurgence of African American cinema. Lee managed to gain large audiences for most of his commercial ventures and directed a string of successful Hollywood films including one of the most

politically-charged films of the era, *Do the Right Thing* (1989).

Spike Lee's box-office successes, coupled with the achievements of University of Southern California Film School graduate John Singleton (*Boyz N the Hood, Poetic Justice,* and *Rosewood*) and comedian turned actor/director Robert Townsend, (*Hollywood Shuffle* and *The Five Heartbeats*) seemed to guarantee a viable future for African American filmmakers. Along with the filmmakers, African American actors in Hollywood began to gain steady work.

Promising Future Awaits African Americans in Film

The beginning of the new millenium showed great promise for African American talent in film. For the first time in history African American actors were able to establish solid careers in cinema. Among others,

Angela Bassett, Halle Barry, Danny Glover, Whoopi Goldberg, Morgan Freeman, Samuel Jackson, Martin Lawrence, Eddie Murphy, Wesley Snipes, and Alfre Woodard created a lasting impact on the tapestry of film. A fresh and exciting new crop of talented actors like Taye Diggs and Sanaa Lathan, and directors Malcolm Lee, Patrick Famuyiwa, and Gina Prince-Bythewood, also seemed well on their way to major movie careers.

The proliferation of music artists crossing over into film had grown tremendously. Ice Cube, Queen Latifah, LL Cool J, and especially Will Smith built strongly on their pre-2000 track records. Their multi-media successes spawned opportunities for a new generation of music talent like rappers DMX (*Exit Wounds*) and Eve (*Barbershop*), as well as singer Beyoncé Knowles (*Austin Powers in Goldmember*) and the late Aaliyah (*Queen of the Dammed*).

Action films also broke new ground, producing not one, but two stars of African American descent. The international success of films *The Mummy Returns* and *Scorpion King* turned World Wrestling Entertainment champion The Rock into a major star. Meanwhile the box office success of films like *The Fast and the Furious* and *XXX* catapulted Afro-Italian actor Vin Diesel into the exclusive $20 million club as an actor.

Perhaps the most surprising change took place during the 2002 Academy Awards ceremony when Denzel Washington (*Training Day*) and Halle Berry (*Monster's Ball*) each won Oscars for lead roles. Never had a black woman won for best actress, and only the great Sidney Poitier—40 years earlier—had received the best actor Oscar. As more African American performers gained responsibility for defining African American images in cinema, opportunities for black actors, filmmakers, and industry executives during the twenty-first century seemed to be very promising.

◆ AFRICAN AMERICANS IN TELEVISION

The Early Years of Television

Largely due to the fact that many of the new medium's early stars were lifted from popular radio programs, African American performers began to make advancements within television almost from the start. For example, entertainer and pianist Bob Howard was included in the CBS network's evening broadcast. Another gifted entertainer, jazz pianist Hazel Scott, had her own 15-minute broadcast three days a week. African American performers also appeared on variety and game shows, such as *Your Show of Shows*, *All Star* *Revue*, *Strike it Rich*, and *High Finance*, throughout the late 1940s and into the 1950s. On the ABC television network, musician Billy Daniels was given his own short-lived variety show in the fall of 1952.

Although television did not make use of all the same stereotypes that cinema employed, many negative caricatures did arise. As the medium began to rebroadcast feature films and shorts that appeared in theaters, many grossly unflattering portrayals of African Americans began to appear on television. In fact, such shorts as Hal Roach's *Our Gang/Little Rascals* became television mainstays.

In 1950, veteran actress Ethel Waters appeared on the first television show in which an African American was the central figure. As the star of *Beulah* for the first two seasons, the popular show centered on the weekly trials and tribulations of a black maid or "mammy"—a supporting character on the popular *Fibber McGee and Molly* radio show. (*Beulah* ran until 1953, when protests by the NAACP and other activist groups forced its cancellation.)

Other numerous former radio performers quickly followed in Waters's wake including Eddie "Rochester" Anderson who played opposite Jack Benny on *The Jack Benny Show* and Willie Best who was a regularly featured performer on *The Trouble with Father* and *Oh My Little Margie*. In 1953 actress Lillian Randolph began to reprise the role of a maid that she played on radio for the television series *Make Room for Daddy*. Later, she appeared in the television show *Great Gildersleeve*.

Perhaps no other television show, though, created as much controversy for its negative stereotyping of African Americans as the *Amos n' Andy* show. Based on the very popular 1930s and 1940s radio show *Amos n' Andy* ran from 1951 to 1953. The show was perceived by many, both black and white, as an offensive reminder of the past, and the NAACP initiated lawsuits and boycott threats that were critical in forcing the show's cancellation. After the series was cancelled though, it continued to appear in syndication until the mid-1960s.

Throughout the early 1950s, variety shows hosted by veteran white entertainers, such as Ed Sullivan, Milton Berle, and Steve Allen, occasionally featured African American entertainers. But in 1956, NBC took the bold step of creating a slot for the variety program *The Nat King Cole Show*. Although the variety format had always been very popular with television viewers, and Cole's recording success was undeniable, the network was unable to secure regular sponsors, especially after Cole touched the arm of a white female guest. The show was cancelled after its first season.

Commercial Television Reacts to the 1960s

Throughout the late 1950s and into the 1960s, African Americans appeared in many serious documentaries concerning rural poverty, segregation, and the Civil Rights movement led by the Reverend Martin Luther King Jr. The powerful medium of television provided King and the other leaders the opportunity to increase the white viewing audience's awareness of their civil rights cause.

Commercial television reacted to the changing political, social, and economic climate in the United States much the same way that cinema did—by including more African American performers in its programming. Ensemble television shows soon began to feature African American performers: Otis Young appeared in *The Outcast;* Greg Morris starred in *Mission Impossible;* and Nichelle Nichols was featured in *Star Trek.* However, the most dramatic changes in television's positioning of African American talent occurred when Sheldon Leonard hired Bill Cosby as one of two leads to star in the 1965 television show *I Spy* and actress Diahann Carroll was featured as a widowed nurse and single mother in the drama *Julia.*

While the show only lasted three seasons, *I Spy* marked the first time that an African American television actor was so widely accepted by television viewers—primarily for his inoffensive, perfect image. Consequently, Cosby earned three Emmy Awards for his portrayal of the character, Alexander Scott. Lasting from 1968 to 1971, *Julia* presented Carroll as an African American woman seemingly detached from the reality of the lives led by most African Americans. Though popular with the majority viewing audience, the show was criticized for its bland depiction of an African American. Others, however, viewed Carroll's character as an improvement over past characterizations of African Americans on television.

Blacks also began to appear on television in roles opposite whites in ways that had never before been possible. *Harlem Detective* featured black and white actors cast as equals on the police force. *Eastside/ Westside* and *The Nurses* featured African American actresses Cicely Tyson and Hilda Simms, respectively, in regularly featured roles. Praised for its more balanced portrayal of African Americans, *Eastside/Westside* unfortunately lasted only one season.

As the first successful African American television variety show, *The Flip Wilson Show* was the first weekly program by an African American to feature "racial comedy" as a form of general audience entertainment. The show's rousing success paved the way for the development of the future African American situation comedies.

The Presence of African Americans on Television Expands

During the 1970s television producers, such as Norman Lear with *All in the Family, Sanford and Son,* and *Good Times* and Bud Yorkin with *What's Happenin'* and *Carter Country,* created comedy programming to appeal to African American audiences. Though these shows flourished and made the African American presence on television commonplace, critics referred to them as "new minstrelsy" and derided their perpetuation of stereotypical aspects of African American humor.

One of the most significant changes occurred in children's television programming. The public television series *Sesame Street* featured a multiracial mix of children and adults interacting and learning. In addition, animated programs or cartoons, such as Bill Cosby's *Fat Albert and the Cosby Kids* (1972–1989) and the *Jackson Five,* depicted events in the lives of young African American characters.

In the category of drama, notably made-for-television movies and miniseries, two productions stood out among the rest in the 1970s—*The Autobiography of Miss Jane Pittman* (1974) and *Roots* (1977). Starring actress Cicely Tyson, *The Autobiography of Miss Jane Pittman* was set in 1962 and spanned the life of a 110-year old African American woman from the era of slavery to the 1960s Civil Rights movement. For her outstanding efforts, Tyson was awarded an Emmy for best lead actress in a drama-special program. Based on the Alex Haley novel, *Roots* was the highest-rated miniseries ever, attracting an estimated 130 million viewers. Featuring such prominent African American actors as Louis Gossett Jr., Cicely Tyson, and Maya Angelou, the eight-part epic movie traced Haley's family history from Africa to slavery in the American South.

The Cosby Decade

Throughout the late 1970s and early 1980s, African American actors continued to appear in stereotypical comedies or made-for-television movies with few exceptions. In 1984, however, veteran entertainer Bill Cosby returned to television with a half-hour series called *The Cosby Show.* Although expected to do well, few could have predicted the level of the show's popularity. Consistently rated the top weekly television program, *The Cosby Show* ran for eight seasons and created tremendous opportunities for African American performers. While the phenomenal success of the *Roots* miniseries had proven that all-African American television vehicles could attract a large viewing audience, *The Cosby Show* demonstrated that an audience of similar proportions would also regularly support an

Cicely Tyson and Maya Angelou performing in *Roots,* the hugely popular made-for-television miniseries of the 1970s.

entertaining, family-oriented program centered on African Americans as well.

In the wake of *The Cosby Show's* success, an increasing number of African Americans began producing more African American-themed shows in the late 1980s. Actor Frank Reid produced and starred in the short-lived, Emmy Award-winning show *Frank's Place.* Choreographer Debbie Allen produced *The Cosby Show* spin-off *A Different World,* which depicted academic life at a historical African American university. In addition, Quincy Jones produced *The Fresh Prince of Bel-Air* starring rap artist Will Smith, and *In Living Color,* which was produced by comedian Keenan Ivory Wayans and featured many talented members of the Wayans family.

Burgeoning Television Networks Target African American Audiences

Black Entertainment Television (BET) Holdings, Inc., which began operations in the 1980s, became the first African American-controlled cable entertainment company listed on the New York Stock Exchange in the 1990s. Led by industry giant Robert Johnson, BET targets an estimated 45 million subscribers nationwide by providing original programming on its three cable television channels—BET Cable Network, BET on Jazz, and BET Movies/Starz!3. In addition, the company has diversified its holdings by publishing magazines, marketing clothes and cosmetics, and forming a partnership with Microsoft to offer MSBET, an online service that provides entertainment information to the growing number of African Americans using the Internet. Citing a need to expand market share, as well as improve ad revenue, Robert Johnson sold the pioneering network to Viacom Holdings in November 2000. Although this move was not expected to affect programming, it did mark the end of African American ownership of any major TV concern.

While African American programs have become an increasing rarity on the major television networks which have begun to concentrate on offerings that deliver them the widest possible audience share, the launch of several networks brought new promise for African Americans. Clearly understanding the financial gain that could result, such upstart television networks as Fox, Warner Brothers (WB), and United Paramount

Network (UPN) began to vigorously court African American audiences in the 1990s. Such highly-rated programs as *Roc, Living Single, Martin,* as well as many others were major hits with both black and young white television viewers.

Finally, in the areas of daytime and late night talk shows, several African Americans attained widespread acceptance for the first time in television history: Oprah Winfrey and Montel Williams have produced Emmy Award-winning daytime shows, while Arsenio Hall successfully led many imitators in attempting to revitalize the late night talk show format.

The Future of African Americans in Television

As the television industry headed into the twenty-first century, more African Americans than ever before were involved in television—in acting, production, and executive roles. However, while African Americans have continued to enjoy success in comedic television vehicles, no primetime dramatic series has made it beyond a full television season since the 1970s. Instead, the trend is for African American performers to be cast in ensemble shows, such as *ER, Touched by an Angel,* and *NYPD Blue.* Although most of these shows integrate their African American cast members into their stories well, many African American performers fear that their singular voice is being diluted by an increasingly multiethnic array of characters.

This brand of programming has received mixed reviews from the NAACP and other minority watchdog groups, who in recent years have challenged the networks on the lack of diversity in their programming. In an attempt to counter such fallout, during the 2001 TV season network programmers introduced two new sitcoms (*My Wife and Kids* and *The Bernie Mac Show*) which enjoyed solid ratings and whose success could even spark another "Black Renaissance" on TV.

On the other hand, the monopolies once held by the major networks have in recent years been overrun by the growing cable market, which has increased opportunities for Black talent. Cable programming has countered traditional TV programming with a brand of engaging and often provocative shows that have attracted viewers away from the major networks, as seen by the success of regularly scheduled shows like *OZ, Soul Food* and *The Shield,* and made-for-TV films like *Feast of All Saints, Boycott,* and *The Corner.* Although the sale of BET in November 2000, left a void in terms of black ownership within this market, the cable market does appear to be offering African American talent great growth opportunities as we settle into the new millenium.

Launched amidst great fanfare in January of 1995, the creation of the UPN and WB networks brought new promise for African Americans in Television. Both networks' early programming delivered alternative viewing options to traditional television fare. With a line-up of shows that stressed diversity and leaned heavily on urban themed programming like *Moesha, The Wayans Brothers, For Your Love,* and *The Steve Harvey Show,* both networks were soon well established in the marketplace. Ironically, just as their reputations became established, both networks began to abandon their urban programming initiatives in favor of more "mainstream" fare. Although the UPN has continued to maintain a night dedicated to urban comedies, the network has consistently come under fire from watchdog groups for the stereotypical content being portrayed.

♦ FILMOGRAPHY OF SELECTED FEATURE FILMS AND DOCUMENTARIES

The following filmography includes more than 200 selected feature films and documentaries that are remarkable for their depiction of themes and issues related to the experiences of African Americans throughout history. Ranging from the early silent movie era through major studio releases, documentaries, and made-for-television movies of the 1990s, many of these cinematic works also represent significant milestones for African Americans in the film and television industries.

African Americans in WWII: A Legacy of Patriotism and Valor
(2000)

African American war veterans from all branches of the military describe their personal experiences in World War II. Includes tributes by General Colin Powell and then-President Bill Clinton.

Africans in America: America's Journey through Slavery
(1998)

A four-part television documentary that chronicles the history of racial slavery in the United States from the start of the Atlantic slave trade in the sixteenth century to the end of the American Civil War in 1865. The work examines slavery from philosophical, societal, and economic viewpoints.

Ali
(2001)

Boxer Muhammad Ali is depicted during a contentious decade (1964–1974), in which he converted to Islam, befriended civil rights icons, refused the draft, was stripped of his World Heavyweight Champion title, married four times, and blurred lines between sport, ethics and society. Smith, who received an Oscar nomination for Best Actor for this role, gives an inspired performance in and out of the ring. Another noteworthy is Jaime Foxx as cornerman "Bundini" Brown.

America's Dream
(1995)

Trilogy of short stories covering African American life from 1938 to 1958: "Long Black Song," based on a short story by Richard Wright; "The Boy Who Painted Christ Black," based on a story by John Henrik Clarke; and Maya Angelou's "The Reunion."

Amistad
(1997)

Director Steven Spielberg creates an epic that relates the 1839 account of African captives aboard the slaveship *Amistad*, led by a Mende tribesman named Cinque (Djimon Hounsou), who free themselves and take over the ship in a bloody mutiny. Lengthy legal battles eventually reach the Supreme Court, where the Africans are found to be rightfully freed individuals in the eyes of the law.

The Autobiography of Miss Jane Pittman
(1974)

The history of African Americans in the South is seen through the eyes of a 110-year-old former slave. From the Civil War through the Civil Rights movement, Miss Pittman (Cicely Tyson) relates every piece of African American history, allowing the viewer to experience the injustices. Received nine Emmy Awards; adapted by Tracy Keenan Wynn from the novel by Ernest J. Gaines.

Baby Boy
(2001)

John Singleton returns to the South Central L.A. neighborhood of his breakthrough *Boyz N the Hood* in this candid look at a culture that fosters and tolerates lack of emotional maturity in young African-American males. Jody (Tyrese Gibson) is a 20-year-old manchild who still lives with his mother, has two children with two different women, no job, and cheats on his current girl, Yvette. Jody's life changes when his mother's boyfriend moves in. Melvin (Ving Rhames), an ex-con who's been down the road Jody is heading, shows no tolerance for his attitude. Jody gets a job, but his idea of earning a living is selling stolen dresses at a beauty parlor. Real trouble starts when Rodney (Snoop Dogg), a street thug and Yvette's ex, is released from prison and refuses to leave her house. Singleton toys with two

endings, but finishes the story with the message that the means to fix the problems he's described are within reach.

Beloved
(1998)

Oprah Winfrey's pet project (she had owned the film rights for ten years) is a faithful adaptation of Toni Morrison's Pulitzer Prize-winning novel.

Beverly Hills Cop
(1984)

When a close friend of smooth-talking Detroit cop Axle Foley (Eddie Murphy) is brutally murdered, he traces the murderer to the posh streets of Beverly Hills. There he must stay on his toes to keep one step ahead of the killer and two steps ahead of the law. First of three action-comedies.

Bingo Long Traveling All-Stars & Motor Kings
(1976)

Set in 1939, this film follows the comedic adventures of a lively group of African American baseball players (Billy Dee Williams, James Earl Jones, and Richard Pryor) who have defected from the old Negro National League. The All-Stars travel the country challenging local white teams.

Bird
(1988)

The richly textured biography of jazz saxophone great Charlie Parker (Forest Whitaker), from his rise to stardom to his premature death via extended heroin use. The soundtrack, which features Parker's own solos remastered from original recordings, earned an Academy Award for best sound. Whitaker earned the Cannes Film Festival Award for best actor, while Clint Eastwood garnered the Golden Globe Award for best director.

Birth of a Race
(1918)

Emmet J. Scott's film offers a positive depiction of African Americans during the Civil War. Although the film did not meet original expectations, it proved an inspiration to many African Americans.

Black Girl
(1972)

Directed by Ossie Davis, this intense drama examines the relationship between an African American woman, who feels that she is a failure, and her children.

Black Like Me
(1964)

Based on John Howard Griffin's successful book about how Griffin turned his skin black with a drug and traveled the South to experience prejudice firsthand. Features Roscoe Lee Brown.

Black Rodeo
(1972)

Documentary directed by Jeff Kanew provides a glimpse of an all-African American rodeo held at Triborough Stadium in New York in September, 1971.

Blackboard Jungle
(1955)

Well-remembered urban drama about an idealistic teacher (Sidney Poitier) in a slum area who fights doggedly to connect with his unruly students. Bill Hailey's "Rock Around the Clock" over the opening credits was the first use of rock music in a mainstream feature film.

Blacula
(1972)

The African Prince Mamuwalde (William Marshall) stalks the streets of Los Angeles trying to satisfy his insatiable desire for blood. Mildly successful melding of blaxploitation and horror that spawned a sequel *Scream, Blacula, Scream.*

Blood of Jesus
(1941)

A sinful husband accidentally shoots his newly baptized wife, causing an uproar in their rural town. Director Spencer Williams Jr. later starred as Andy on the *Amos n' Andy* television series. Due to its rare treatment of African American religion, the film was named to the National Film Registry in 1991.

Blue Collar
(1978)

An auto assembly line worker, tired of the poverty of his life, hatches a plan to rob his own union. Starring Richard Pryor and Yaphet Kotto, the film is a study of the working class and the robbing of the human spirit.

Body and Soul
(1924)

The first screen appearance of Paul Robeson has him cast in a dual role as a conniving preacher and his good brother. The preacher preys on the heroine, making her life a misery. Objections by censors to the preacher's character caused him to be redeemed and become worthy of the heroine's love. Directed by African American filmmaker Oscar Micheaux.

Boesman & Lena
(2000)

This adaptation of the apartheid-era play by Athol Fugard follows the travails of downtrodden couple, Boesman (Danny Glover) and Lena (Angela Bassett). Their shanty town home in Cape Town has been bulldozed by the government so they take to the dusty road with their meager belongings, constantly bickering about their plight. The couple construct a makeshift abode for the night, which attracts the attention of an old man even lower on the economic ladder, whom Lena allows to stay to Boesman's displeasure.

Boycott
(2001)

Superb HBO docudrama recreates the Civil Rights movement's early days, from Rosa Parks's (Iris Little-Thomas) refusal to give up her seat to a white man on a segregated Montgomery, Alabama, bus, through the subsequent boycott of the bus system by the city's black population, to the success of the boycott and the rise to prominence of Dr. Martin Luther King Jr. (Jeffrey Wright) as the movement's most eloquent and popular leader. Through the use and mix of many different visual styles, director Clark Johnson uses artful touches to tell the story without overplaying his hand. Wright is fantastic as King, with other outstanding performances turned in by Howard as Ralph Abernathy and Pounder as boycott organizer Jo Anne Robinson.

Boyz N the Hood
(1991)

John Singleton's debut as a writer and director is an astonishing picture of young African American men, four high school students with different backgrounds, aims, and abilities trying to survive Los Angeles gangs and bigotry. Excellent acting throughout, with special nods to Laurence Fishburne and Cuba Gooding Jr. Musical score by Stanley Clarke. Singleton was the youngest director ever nominated for an Oscar.

The Brother from Another Planet
(1984)

A black alien (Joe Morton) escapes from his home planet and winds up in Harlem, where he is pursued by two alien bounty hunters. The humor arises from cultural and racial misunderstandings. Independently-made morality fable by John Sayles.

Brother John
(1970)

An early look at racial tensions and labor problems. An angel (Sidney Poitier) goes back to his hometown in Alabama to see how things are going. Directed by James Goldstone with musical score by Quincy Jones.

The Brothers
(2001)

A chain reaction of male introspection is set off as four successful, young African American men navigate the tricky waters of serious relationships in modern Los Angeles. All the bases are covered: there is the womanizing lawyer, Brian (Bill Bellamy); the one night stand-weary physician, Jackson (Morris Chestnut); the just-engaged Terry (Shemar Moore); and the unhappily married Derrick (D. L. Hughley). Not quite as strong as its female counterpart, the much-praised *Waiting to Exhale*, but the capable comic actors never veer too far away from the exploration of modern sexual politics.

Buck and the Preacher
(1972)

A trail guide (Sidney Poitier) and a con man preacher (Harry Belafonte) and wife (Ruby Dee) join forces to help a wagon train of former slaves who are seeking to homestead out West. Poitier's debut as a director.

Buffalo Soldiers
(1997)

Post-Civil War western concerns the all-black cavalry troops created by Congress in 1866 to patrol the American West. A former slave and by-the-book Army man, Sgt. Washington Wyatt (Danny Glover), leads the chase for Apache warrior Victorio (Harrison Lowe) across the New Mexico Territory while trying to deal with the common degradation suffered by his troops at the hands of white officers.

The Bus
(1964)

Documentary covers Martin Luther King Jr.'s epic 1963 March on Washington.

Cabin in the Sky
(1943)

Based on a Broadway show and featuring an all-African American cast—Ethel Waters, Eddie Anderson, Lena Horne, and Rex Ingram. Lively dance numbers and a musical score with contributions from Louis Armstrong and Duke Ellington.

Carmen Jones
(1954)

George Bizet's tale of femme fatale Carmen with an all-African American cast—Dorothy Dandridge, Harry Belafonte, Diahann Carroll, and Brock Peters. Dandridge's Oscar nomination for best actress was the first ever by an African American in a lead role. The film earned the 1955 Golden Globe Award for best film and was named to the National Film Registry in 1992.

Change of Mind
(1969)

Directed by Robert Stevens, the film portrays an African American male (Raymond St. Jacques) who has a white man's brain transplanted into his head. After the operation, he is accepted by the brain donor's wife as her husband. Music by Duke Ellington.

Charlotte Forten's Mission: Experiment in Freedom
(1985)

Fact-based story set during the Civil War. A wealthy, educated African American woman (Melba Moore), determined to prove to President Lincoln that blacks are equal to whites, journeys to a remote island off the coast of Georgia. There she teaches freed slaves to read and write.

Chuck Berry: Hail! Hail! Rock 'n' Roll
(1987)

Engaging, energetic portrait of one of rock's founding fathers, via interviews, behind-the-scenes footage, and performance clips of Berry at 60 years of age. Songs featured: "Johnny B. Goode," "Roll Over Beethoven," "Maybelline," and more. Appearances by Etta James, Bo Diddley, and Robert Cray, among others.

The Civil Rights Movement: Ordinary Americans
(2000)

Documentary film that juxtaposes contributions of Martin Luther King Jr., Malcolm X, and Presidents Eisenhower, Kennedy, and Johnson with views of rank-and-file protesters. Recommended for Grades 7–12.

Claudine
(1974)

Directed by John Berry, the film depicts a single mother (Diahann Carroll) who attempts to maintain her family of six children. James Earl Jones plays a trash collector and her boyfriend.

Cleopatra Jones
(1973)

Federal government agent (Tamara Dobson) with considerable martial arts prowess takes on loathsome drug lords. Followed by *Cleopatra Jones and the Casino of Gold.*

Clockers
(1995)

Strike (Mekhi Phifer), leader of a group of drug dealers (clockers), engages in a power struggle with his boss (Delroy Lindo), his do-the-right-thing brother Victor (Isaiah Washington), and his own conscience. He is also suspected of murder by relentless narcotics cop Rocco Klein (Harvey Keitel). Poignant and compelling street drama is based on the Richard Price novel. Music by Terence Blanchard.

Color Adjustment
(1991)

Narrated by Ruby Dee, the film documents the modern history of race relations in the United States in the arena of television. Traces the progress of African Americans from caricatures to victims to mainstream as portrayed by television.

The Color Purple
(1985)

Adaptation of Alice Walker's acclaimed book features strong lead from Whoopi Goldberg (her screen debut which earned the 1986 Golden Globe Award for best actress in a drama) and talk show host Oprah Winfrey (also her film debut), among others. Brilliant musical score by co-producer Quincy Jones compliments this strong film.

The Cool World
(1963)

Tough-talking docudrama, set on the streets of Harlem, focuses on a 15-year-old African American youth whose one ambition in life is to own a gun and lead his gang. Named to the National Film Registry in 1994.

Cooley High
(1975)

African American high school students in Chicago go through the rites of passage in their senior year during the 1960s. Film is funny, smart, and much acclaimed. Great soundtrack featuring Motown hits of the era is a highlight. Sequel to the TV series *What's Happenin'.*

Cora Unashamed
(2000)

In this adaptation of the Langston Hughes short story that finds racism and tragedy in a small Iowa town in the 1930s, Cora Jenkins (Regina Taylor) and her mother (CCH Pounder) are the only blacks in the community. Cora works as a housekeeper for the Studevant family and becomes strongly attached to the family's daughter, Jessie. This bond is resented by Jessie's mother, selfish and cold Lizbeth (Cherry Jones), whose exaggerated sense of propriety brings about disaster.

Cornbread, Earl and Me
(1975)

Directed by Joe Manduke, a high school basketball star from the ghetto is mistaken for a murderer by cops and is shot, causing a subsequent furor of protest and racial hatred. Music by Donald Byrd.

The Corner
(2000)

Based on a true story, this miniseries reveals how drugs have infested a Baltimore neighborhood and how the residents are affected. Told semi-narratively by a documentary crew, the story follows the lives of drug addicts and drug dealers. Won several Emmy awards, including Outstanding Miniseries, and Outstanding Directing.

Cosmic Slop
(1994)

Three-part anthology. "Space Traders," based on a story by Derrick Bell, finds a fleet of aliens offering to solve all of American society's most pressing social ills if they can have the entire black population in return (for what purpose is never explained). "The First Commandment" features a Catholic priest in a Latino parish who comes up against his parishoners' beliefs in Santeria. "Tang," based on a story by Chester Himes, finds a poor, desperately unhappy married couple dreaming about what they'll do with the rifle mysteriously delivered in a flower carton to their door.

The Cotton Club
(1984)

An African American musician playing at The Cotton Club falls in love with gangster Dutch Schultz's girlfriend. A black tap dancer falls in love with a member of the chorus line who can pass for white. These two love stories are told against a background of mob violence and music during the early jazz era.

Cotton Comes to Harlem
(1970)

A successful mix of crime and comedy about a suspicious preacher's back-to-Africa scheme that detectives (Godfrey Cambridge and Raymond St. Jacques) suspect is a swindle. Based on the novel by Chester Himes, the film serves as the directorial debut of Ozzie Davis.

The Court Martial of Jackie Robinson
(1990)

True story of a little known chapter in the life of the famous athlete. During his stint in the Army, Robinson (played by Andre Braugher) refused to take a back seat on a bus and subsequently faced the possibility of court martial.

Crisis at Central High
(1980)

A dramatic television recreation of the events leading up to the 1957 integration of Central High in Little Rock, Arkansas. Based on teacher Elizabeth Huckaby's journal.

Crooklyn
(1994)

Director Spike Lee profiles an African American middle-class family growing up in 1970s Brooklyn and focuses on the only girl (Zelda Harris) coming of age. Music by Terence Blanchard.

Darktown Jubilee
(1914)

One of the earliest feature films to star an African American, actor-comedian Bert Williams. This film was controversial because it portrayed African Americans in a positive manner.

Daughters of the Dust
(1991)

Five women of a Gullah family living on the Sea Islands off the Georgia coast in 1902 contemplate moving to the mainland in this emotional tale of change. Family bonds and memories are celebrated with a quiet narrative and beautiful cinematography in Julie Dash's feature-film directorial debut. Honored by the Sundance Film Festival for best cinematography.

The Defiant Ones
(1958)

Thought-provoking story about racism revolves around two black and white escaped prisoners (Sidney Poitier and Tony Curtis) from a chain gang in the rural South. Their societal conditioning to hate each other dissolves as they face constant peril together. Earned several cinematic honors including Academy Awards for best story, screenplay, and best black & white cinematography, as well as the Golden Globe Award for best film—drama.

Devil in a Blue Dress
(1995)

Easy Rawlins (Denzel Washington), an unemployed aircraft worker in 1948 Los Angeles, is hired to find mystery woman Daphne (Jennifer Beals) by a shady businessman. Realism and accuracy in period detail enhance a solid performance by Washington. Based upon the Walter Mosley novel.

Do the Right Thing
(1989)

An uncompromising, brutal comedy written and directed by Spike Lee about the racial tensions surrounding a white-owned pizzeria in the Bed-Stuy section of Brooklyn on the hottest day of the summer, and the violence that eventually erupts.

Down in the Delta
(1998)

Chicago matriarch Rosa Lynn (Mary Alice) tries to prevent her jobless, single-mom daughter Loretta (Alfre Woodard) from succumbing to destructive forces by sending Loretta and her two grandchildren to her brother's home (Morgan Freeman) in the Mississippi delta. Poet-novelist Maya Angelou's first outing as a director skillfully demonstrates the importance of connecting to one's heritage.

A Dream for Christmas
(1973)

Earl Hamner Jr. (best known for writing *The Waltons*) wrote this moving made-for-television story of an African American minister whose church in Los Angeles is scheduled to be demolished.

Driving Miss Daisy
(1989)

Tender and sincere portrayal of a 25-year friendship between an aging Jewish woman and the African American chauffeur forced upon her by her son. The film subtly explores the effects of prejudice in the South. Earned numerous Academy and Golden Globe Awards.

The Duke Is Tops
(1938)

In singer Lena Horne's earliest existing film appearance, she attempts to make the "big-time," while her boyfriend joins a traveling medicine show. The film helped to begin the 1940s swing era.

Dutchman
(1967)

Film presentation of Amiri Baraka's one-act play depicting the claustrophobic reality of the African American male's situation in the late 1960s. Starring Al Freeman Jr., the film earned best honors at the 1967 Cannes Film Festival.

Eight Trey Gangster: The Making of a Crip
(1993)

A provocative documentary that explores the experiences and social environment influencing the life decisions of an African American gang member in Los Angeles.

The Emperor Jones
(1933)

Loosely based on Eugene O'Neill's play, the film portrays the rise and fall of a railroad porter (Paul Robeson) whose exploits take him from a life sentence on a chain gang to emperor of Haiti.

Eve's Bayou
(1997)

Set in Louisiana in 1962 and told in flashback, the film presents a mesmerizing and complex story with haunting visuals about the upper middle-class Batiste family. Impressive, multilayered directorial debut from Kasi Lemmons. Music by Terence Blanchard.

Eyes on the Prize
(1986)

A comprehensive six-part series on the history of the Civil Rights movement from World War II to the present. Includes Rosa Parks and the bus boycott, the leadership of Martin Luther King Jr., and the last great march in Selma, among other moments.

Eyes on the Prize II: America at the Racial Crossroads (1965–1985)
(1987)

The Civil Rights movement, from the mid-1960s to mid-1980s, is traced in this four-volume documentary.

A Family Thing
(1996)

Racial issues are addressed in this character-driven story of two brothers in which Southerner Earl Pilcher (Robert Duvall) learns his biological mother was black and that he also has a half brother, Ray (James Earl Jones), who is black and living in Chicago. The two brothers slowly find common ground.

Fear of a Black Hat
(1994)

A good-natured comedy in which the trio known as NWH (Niggaz With Hats) are touring in support of their album and trying to convince filmmaker Nina Blackburn (Kasi Lemmons) of their street credibility. However, the more the gangsta rappers explain themselves, the less sense they make.

Feast of All Saints
(2001)

Based on the historical novel by Anne Rice, this film depicts nineteenth-century New Orleans, and Gens de Couleurs (Free People of Colour). Caught between the opposing worlds of white privilege and black subjugation, the Free People of Colour are descended from black slaves and white oppressors.

The Five Heartbeats
(1991)

Well-told story of five African American singers in the 1960s, their successes and failures as a group and as individuals. Skillfully directed by Robert Townsend who did research by talking to the Dells. Music by Stanley Clarke.

For Love of Ivy
(1968)

Sidney Poitier is a trucking executive who has a gambling operation on the side. Ivy (Abbey Lincoln) is the black maid of a rich white family who is about to leave her job to look for romance. The two are brought together but the road to true love does not run smooth. Based on a story by Poitier; music by Quincy Jones.

For Us, The Living
(1988)

The life and assassination of civil rights activist Medgar Evers are dramatically presented in this adaptation of the biography written by Evers's widow. Provides insight into Evers's character, not just a recording of the events surrounding his life.

48 Hrs.
(1982)

An experienced San Francisco cop (Nick Nolte) springs a convict (Eddie Murphy) from jail for 48 hours to find a vicious, murdering, escaped con. Film marks Murphy's screen debut.

Fresh
(1994)

Enterprising young man (Sean Nelson) who sells drugs draws life lessons from chess-hustler father (Samuel L. Jackson) and heroin-dealing mentor (Giancarlo Esposito), so he looks for a way out of the dead-end business. First time director Boaz Yakin was awarded the Filmmakers Trophy and Special Jury Prize at the 1994 Sundance Film Festival.

Fundi: The Story of Ella Baker
(1986)

Ella Baker's nickname "Fundi" comes from the Swahili word for a person who passes skills from one generation to another. This film documents Baker's work in the Civil Rights movement of the 1960s, and her friendship with Dr. Martin Luther King Jr.

Get on the Bus
(1996)

Spike Lee looks at the personal side of the Million Man March through a fictional group of men who board a bus in south central Los Angeles and head for Washington, DC. Practically ignoring the event itself, Lee and writer Reggie Rock Bythewood focus on the men who participated, their reasons, and their interaction with each other.

Ghosts of Mississippi
(1996)

Director Rob Reiner tells the story of civil rights leader Medgar Evers, murdered in 1963, and the three trials of Byron De la Beckwith (James Woods), who was finally convicted (after two hung juries) in 1994. Whoopie Goldberg plays the role of Evers's widow, Myrlie; Evers's sons, Darrell and Van, play themselves; and daughter Reena appears as a juror while her character is played by Yolanda King, the daughter of slain civil rights leader Martin Luther King Jr.

Glory
(1989)

A rich, historical spectacle chronicling the 54th Massachusetts, the first African American volunteer infantry unit in the Civil War. Winner of Academy Awards for best cinematography and best sound, the film offers stunning performances throughout, with exceptional work from Morgan Freeman and Denzel Washington who earned both Academy and Golden Globe Awards for best supporting actor.

Go, Man, Go!
(1954)

This film depicts the Harlem Globetrotters at a time when few African Americans competed in professional basketball and the traveling team worked to find its place in American sports with its players' amazing skills and showmanship.

Go Tell It on the Mountain
(1984)

Young African American boy tries to gain the approval of his stern stepfather in this fine adaptation of James Baldwin's semi-autobiographical novel set in the 1930s.

Gone Are the Days
(1963)

Adaptation of the play *Purlie Victorious*. An African American preacher (Ossie Davis) stands up to a segregationist plantation owner from whom he obtains money to establish a church.

Gone with the Wind
(1939)

Based on Margaret Mitchell's novel, this epic Civil War drama traces Scarlett O'Hara's (Vivien Leigh) survival through the tragic history of the South during the Civil War and Reconstruction Period. Hattie McDaniel became the first African American to win an Academy Award for her portrayal of the loyal maid, Mammy. The multiple Academy Award-winning film was named to the American Film Institute Top 100 list in 1998.

Greased Lightning
(1977)

The story of the first African American auto racing champion, Wendell Scott (Richard Pryor), who had to overcome racial prejudice to achieve his success. Co-written by Melvin Van Peebles, the film also starred Pam Grier and Cleavon Little.

The Great White Hope
(1970)

A semi-fictionalized biography of boxer Jack Johnson, played by James Earl Jones, who became the first African American heavyweight world champion in 1910. Jane Alexander makes her film debut as the boxer's white lover, as both battle the racism of the times.

The Greatest
(1977)

Autobiography of Cassius Clay, the boxer who would later become the internationally recognized Muhammad Ali. Ali plays himself, and George Benson's hit "The Greatest Love of All" is introduced.

The Green Mile
(1999)

Paul Edgecomb (Tom Hanks) is the decent head guard at Louisiana's Cold Mountain Penitentiary in 1935. He works E block, which is death row (title refers to the color of the floor). Among his prisoners is hulking black man John Coffey (Michael Clarke Duncan), whose intimidating size belies a sweet nature. And something else—it seems Coffey has the power to heal. The characters are more symbols than human beings; but Duncan's performance earned him acclaim, including Golden Globe and Screen Actor's Guild nominations for best supporting actor.

Green Pastures
(1936)

An adaptation of Marc Connelly's Pulitzer Prize-winning play that attempts to retell biblical stories in black English vernacular of the 1930s. Southern theater owners boycotted the controversial film which had an all-African American cast.

Guess Who's Coming to Dinner
(1967)

Controversial in its time, a young white woman (Katharine Houghton) brings her black fiancé (Sidney Poitier) home to meet her parents (Katharine Hepburn and Spencer Tracy). The situation truly tests their open-mindedness and understanding. Named to the American Film Institute Top 100 list in 1998.

Hallelujah!
(1929)

The first all-African American feature film and the first talkie for director King Vidor was given the go-ahead by MGM production chief Irving Thalberg, though he knew the film would be both controversial and get minimal release in the Deep South. Great music included traditional spirituals and songs by Irving Berlin.

Hangin' with the Homeboys
(1991)

One night in the lives of four young men. Although the Bronx does not offer much for any of them, they have little interest in escaping its confines, and they are more than willing to complain. With characters insightfully written and well-portrayed, the film earned honors for best screenplay at the 1991 Sundance Film Festival.

Hank Aaron: Chasing the Dream
(1995)

Docudrama combines archival footage, interviews, and reenactments to tell the story of the life and career of Henry Aaron, baseball's all-time home run king. Emphasis on personal and societal issues, as well as on-the-field accomplishments.

Harlem Nights
(1989)

Two Harlem nightclub owners in the 1930s battle comically against efforts by the mob and crooked cops to take over their territory. High-grossing effort from Eddie Murphy, who directed, wrote, produced, and starred in this film. Music by Herbie Hancock.

Having Our Say: The Delany Sisters' First 100 Years
(1999)

A made-for-television movie based on the true story of the Delany sisters (played by Ruby Dee and Diahann Carroll), who lived well beyond the age of 100 after having built successful careers at a time when most women, and most African Americans, were being denied opportunities. Produced by Camille O. Cosby.

A Hero Ain't Nothin' but a Sandwich
(1978)

A young urban African American teenager (Larry B. Scott) gets involved in drugs and is eventually saved from ruin. Based on Alice Childress's novel.

Higher Learning
(1994)

Malik (Omar Epps), Kristen (Kristy Swanson), and Remy (Michael Rapaport) are college freshmen who confront issues of racial prejudice and emerging sexuality. Laurence Fishburne plays an instructor in this John Singleton film.

Hollywood Shuffle
(1987)

Robert Townsend's autobiographical comedy about a struggling African American actor in Hollywood trying to find work and getting nothing but stereotypical roles. Written, directed, and financed by Townsend who created this often clever and appealing film on a $100,000 budget.

Home of the Brave
(1949)

A black soldier is sent on a top secret mission in the South Pacific, but finds that he must battle with his

Hallelujah! was the first African American feature film.

white comrades as he is subjected to subordinate treatment and constant racial slurs. Hollywood's first outstanding statement against racial prejudice.

Hoodlum
(1996)

Highly fictionalized tale of 1930s gangster "Bumpy" Johnson (Laurence Fishburne, reprising his role from *The Cotton Club*), who refuses to allow Dutch Schultz (Tim Roth) and Lucky Luciano (Andy Garcia) to muscle into the Harlem numbers rackets.

Hoop Dreams
(1994)

Exceptional documentary follows two inner-city basketball phenoms' lives through high school as they chase their dreams of playing in the NBA. Offers plenty of game footage, but the more telling and fascinating parts of the film deal with the kids' families and home life. Both players encounter dramatic reversals of fortune on and off the court, demonstrating the incredibly long odds they face. Earned numerous honors including the Audience Award at the 1994 Sundance Film Festival.

House Party
(1990)

Light-hearted, African American hip hop version of a 1950s teen comedy with rap duo Kid 'n' Play. Features real-life music rappers and some dynamite dance numbers. Earned best cinematography honors at the 1990 Sundance Film Festival.

How Stella Got Her Groove Back
(1998)

A scene from the award-winning documentary film, *Hoop Dreams*.

A flipside to the May-December romance that is based on the novel by Terry McMillan. Stars Angela Bassett and Whoopi Goldberg, among others.

How U Like Me Now?
(1992)

Daryll Robert's second directorial effort offers a fresh look at African Americans on film with plenty of lively supporting characters and witty dialogue. Music by Chuck Webb.

The Hurricane
(1999)

A moving but truncated true story of middleweight boxing champ Rubin "Hurricane" Carter (Denzel Washington). He spent 20 years in prison after being falsely accused and convicted of murder. Anchored by an Oscar-winning performance by Washington, the film came under fire for its rearrangement of the facts behind the case.

I Know Why the Caged Bird Sings
(1979)

An African American writer's memories of growing up in the rural South during the 1930s. Strong performances from Esther Rolle and Constance Good. Based on the book by Maya Angelou.

I'll Make Me a World: A Century of African American Arts
(1999)

PBS documentary produced by famed documentarian Henry Hampton that honors the achievements of twentieth-century African American writers, dancers, painters, actors, filmmakers, musicians, and other artists who changed forever who Americans are as a nation and culture.

I'm Gonna Git You Sucka
(1988)

Parody of "blaxploitation" films popular during the 1960s and 1970s. A number of stars who made "blaxploitation" films, including Jim Brown, take part in the gags.

Imitation of Life
(1934)

Fannie Hurst novel tells the story of widowed Beatrice Pullman (Claudette Colbert) who uses maid Delilah's (Louise Beaver) recipe for pancakes in order to have the women open a restaurant, which becomes a success. Both mothers suffer at the hands of their willful teenaged daughters.

In the Heat of the Night
(1967)

An African American homicide expert (Sidney Poitier) is asked to help solve the murder of a wealthy industrialist in a small Mississippi town, despite resentment on the part of the town's chief of police (Rod Steiger). Powerful script with underlying theme of racial prejudice is served well by taut direction and powerhouse performances. Won several Academy and Golden Globe Awards.

Introducing Dorothy Dandridge
(1999)

Beautiful, sexy singer/actress Dorothy Dandridge (Halle Berry) was the first African American woman to be nominated for a best actress Oscar for her title role in 1955's *Carmen Jones*. Ten years later, at the age of 42, she was dead from an overdose of antidepressants after suffering a lifetime of tragedies—an abusive childhood, two failed marriages, a brain-damaged child, tumultuous affairs, limited career choices, and bad financial decisions. Berry won a Golden Globe Award for her lead role.

Intruder in the Dust
(1949)

A small Southern community develops a lynch mob mentality when a black man is accused of killing a white man. Powerful, but largely ignored portrait of race relations in the South. Adapted from a novel by William Faulkner.

Jack Johnson
(1971)

Documentary discusses the life of the first African American heavyweight boxing champion, Jack Johnson. Brock Peters provides the voice of Johnson and Miles Davis the musical score.

Jackie Brown
(1997)

Quentin Tarantino finally climbs back into the director's chair with his leisurely but satisfying adaptation of Elmore Leonard's *Rum Punch*. No, it's not *Pulp Fiction*, but it could do for Pam Grier what *Pulp* did for John Travolta. Grier stars as out-of-luck-and-options stewardess Jackie Brown, who runs money to Mexico for ruthless arms dealer Ordell (Samuel L. Jackson). Busted on one of her errands, she comes up with an intricate plan to get out from under, hopefully with the money and without getting caught or killed. Slower and less bloody than Quentin fans are used to, but as usual, he gets killer performances from everybody. Cool dialogue and chronological shifts are again key ingredients, along with a heightened sense of character development. Bridget Fonda and Robert De Niro make the most of small (but crucial) roles, but it's Robert Forster (another '70s whatever-happened-to refugee) who provides the standout performance. The look and feel of the movie reflects the dingy world it inhabits, as well as Tarantino's love of '70s blaxploitation flicks.

The Jackie Robinson Story
(1950)

Chronicles Robinson's rise from UCLA to his breakthrough as the first African American man to play baseball in the major league. Robinson plays himself; the film deals honestly with the racial issues of the time.

Jason's Lyric
(1994)

Director Doug McHenry's intense drama focuses on the stormy relationship between two brothers (Allen Payne and Bokeem Woodbine) whose lives in an impoverished Houston neighborhood lead them along different paths.

Jefferson in Paris
(1994)

Thomas Jefferson (Nick Nolte) confronts the personal and political issues of slavery in America, as well as his feelings for Sally Hemings (Thandie Newton), a Monticello slave brought to Paris by Jefferson's daughter.

Jo Jo Dancer, Your Life Is Calling
(1986)

Richard Pryor directed and starred in this semi-autobiographical price-of-fame story of a comic, hospitalized for a drug-related accident, who must reevaluate his life. A serious departure from Pryor's slapstick comedies. Music by Herbie Hancock.

Joey Breaker
(1993)

Small picture works large message with sense of humor and sincere performances. Dedicated to Fred Fondren who died of AIDS in 1992. Filmed in New York City and St. Lucia.

John Q
(2002)

Denzel Washington is the title's everyman hero who's desperate and gutsy enough to bypass medical bureaucracy altogether to get his 10-year-old son Mike (Daniel E. Smith) the heart transplant he desperately needs to live. John Quincy Archibald's plant has just cut his hours, and when his HMO gives him the run-around, he is forced to come up with the $75,000 for his son's operation. Unable to come up with it, John Q. takes over the emergency room and demands his son be placed at the top of the transplant list.

The Josephine Baker Story
(1990)

Made-for-television biography of exotic entertainer/activist Josephine Baker (played by Lynn Whitfield), an African American woman from St. Louis who found superstardom in pre-WWII Europe, but repeated racism and rejection in the United States.

Juice
(1992)

Day-to-day street life of four Harlem youths as they try to earn respect (juice) in their neighborhood. The gritty look and feel of the drama comes naturally to Ernest R. Dickerson in his directorial debut.

Lynn Whitfield, star of the TV biopic, *The Josephine Baker Story.*

Jungle Fever
(1991)

Married black architect's affair (played by Wesley Snipes) with his white secretary (Annabella Sciorra) provides the backdrop for a cold look at interracial love. Written, produced, and directed by Spike Lee, the film focuses more on the discomfort of friends and families than with the intense world created by the lovers for themselves. Samuel L. Jackson plays a drug-addicted brother.

Kansas City
(1995)

Robert Altman mixes music, politics, crime and the movies in this bittersweet homage to his hometown, set in the jazz-driven 1930s. Styled to imitate the brilliant jazz scores played by the likes of Joshua Redman and James Carter.

King
(1978)

Docudrama with terrific cast follows the life and career of one of the greatest non-violent civil rights leaders of all time, Martin Luther King Jr.

Lady Sings the Blues
(1972)

Jazz artist Billie Holiday's life (depicted by singer Diana Ross) becomes a musical drama depicting her struggle against racism and drug addiction in her pursuit of fame and romance. Billy Dee Williams, Richard Pryor, and Scatman Crothers head the supporting cast.

Laurel Avenue
(1993)

Looks at the life of an extended working-class African American family in St. Paul, Minnesota, over a busy weekend.

Lean on Me
(1989)

Depicts the career of Joe Clark, a tough New Jersey teacher who became the principal of the state's toughest, crime-plagued school and, through controversial hard-line tactics, turned it around.

The Learning Tree
(1969)

A beautifully photographed adaptation of Gordon Park Sr.'s biographical novel about a 14-year-old African American boy in 1920s Kansas. The first feature film financed by a major Hollywood studio to be directed by an African American.

Lethal Weapon
(1989)

Danny Glover and Mel Gibson work well together as a pair of cops who uncover a heroin smuggling ring. Packed with plenty of action, violence, and humorous undertones.

The Liberation of L.B. Jones
(1970)

In this dramatic study of Southern race relations, a wealthy black undertaker (Roscoe Lee Brown) wants a divorce from his wife (Lola Falana) who is having an affair with a white policeman.

Lilies of the Field
(1963)

Five East German nuns enlist the aid of a free-spirited U.S. Army veteran (Sidney Poitier). They persuade him to build their chapel and teach them English. Poitier is excellent as the itinerant laborer and became the first African American man to win an Academy Award for best actor.

Listen Up! The Lives of Quincy Jones
(1991)

A biography of the music legend responsible for various movie scores, record productions, and arrangements for the industry's top stars.

The Long Walk Home
(1989)

Whoopi Goldberg stars in this dramatic story about the relationship between a rich white housewife (Sissy Spacek) and her black maid whom she drives to work during the 1956 Montgomery bus boycott.

Look Out Sister
(1948)

Louis Jordan and an all-African American cast star in this musical satire of westerns. Lots of African American culture, slang, and music from 1940s.

Losing Isaiah
(1994)

A controversial and emotionally-moving story of a social worker (Jessica Lange) who adopts the title character, an African American baby abandoned by his drug-addicted mother (Halle Berry). Four years later, now clean and sober, the natural mother enlists the aid of a lawyer (Samuel L. Jackson) to regain custody of her child.

Lost Boundaries
(1949)

Respected physician Scott Carter (debut role for Mel Ferrer) and his family live and work in a small New Hampshire town, hiding the fact that they are black, passing for white, in their segregated society. But then the truth becomes known. Canada Lee also stars in this film based on a true story.

Love Jones
(1996)

A contemporary Chicago nightclub, the Sanctuary, is the gathering spot for middle-class African American urbanites looking for romance. Earned the Audience Award at the 1997 Sundance Film Festival.

The Mack
(1973)

The Mack is a pimp who comes out of retirement to reclaim a piece of the action in Oakland, California.

Violent blaxploitation film was box-office dynamite at the time of its release.

Malcolm X
(1992)

Marked by strong direction from Spike Lee and good performances (notably Al Freeman Jr. as Elijah Muhammad), it is Denzel Washington's convincing performance in the title role that truly brings this stirring tribute to the controversial African American activist alive. Based on *The Autobiography of Malcolm X* by Malcolm X and Alex Haley.

The Man
(1972)

James Earl Jones plays the president pro tem of the U.S. Senate who becomes the first African American president when all the office holders above him in the presidential succession become victims of accidents and illnesses.

Menace II Society
(1993)

Critically acclaimed portrayal of African American teens living in Watts during the 1990s is realistically captured by 21-year-old twin directors, Allen and Albert Hughes, in their big-screen debut.

Miss Evers' Boys
(1997)

Wrenching docudrama covers a 40-year U.S. Public Health Service study in which African American men suffering from syphilis were monitored but not treated for the disease. Alfre Woodward earned the Emmy Award for outstanding lead actress in a miniseries or special for her role as nurse Eunice Evers.

Mississippi Masala
(1992)

This film portrays an interracial romance that sets off a cultural collision and escalates racial tensions in a small Southern town when Mina (Sarita Choudhury), a sheltered young Indian woman, falls in love with Demetrius (Denzel Washington), an ambitious African American man with his own carpet-cleaning business.

Mo' Better Blues
(1990)

Bleek Gilliam (Denzel Washington) is a handsome, accomplished self-interested jazz trumpeter who divides his limited time between two female lovers (Cynda Williams and Joie Lee). What is interesting is subtle

Allen and Albert Hughes in 1993, the year of their critically-acclaimed debut film, *Menace II Society*.

racial issues his life draws into focus. The Branford Marsalis Quartet provides the music for Bleek's group, scored by Lee's dad, Bill (on whose life the script is loosely based).

Monster's Ball
(2001)

Georgia death-row prison guard Hank (Billy Bob Thornton) is following in his father Buck's footsteps as a guard, and as a bigot. His son also has joined the family business, but doesn't seem to have the heart or stomach for it. When his son throws up during the execution of Lawrence Musgrove (Sean "P. Diddy" Combs), Hank flies into a rage that makes him reexamine his life. Soon after, he helps the waitress, Leticia (Halle Berry) from the diner he frequents after an auto accident. Leticia is Musgrove's widow, unbeknownst to Hank, who begins a relationship with her that changes both of them. A well-done, raw, and unflinching story that the excellent cast inhabit perfectly, especially Berry who won the Best Actress Oscar.

Mr. & Mrs. Loving
(1996)

Fact-based movie, set in the 1960s, follows the interracial romance, marriage, and struggle of Richard Loving (Timothy Hutton) and Mildred "Bean" Jeter (Lela Rochon) and their landmark Supreme Court decision concerning miscegenation laws.

Native Son
(1986)

This second film adaptation of the classic Richard Wright novel tells the story of a poor African American man who accidentally kills a white woman and then hides the body.

New Jack City
(1991)

Director Mario Van Peebles stars in his own film as a police detective who assigns two undercover officers (Ice-T and Judd Nelson) to capture a wealthy Harlem drug lord (Wesley Snipes). Music by Johnny Gill, 2 Live Crew, Ice-T, and others.

No Maps on My Taps
(1979)

A unique African American art form—jazz tap dancing—is shown in rare photos and Hollywood film clips from the 1930s, and in intimate portraits of three surviving dancers: Sandman Sims, Chuck Green, and Bunny Briggs.

No Way Out
(1950)

Sidney Poitier plays an outstanding young actor who treats two white criminals who are wounded in an attempted robbery. After one of the men dies, the other accuses the doctor of murder.

Norman, Is That You?
(1976)

Film adaptation based on the Broadway play about the confused black parents of a homosexual son and his white lover.

Nothing but a Man
(1964)

Duff Anderson (Ivan Dixon) portrays an African American laborer trying to make a life in a small Alabama town. Abbey Lincoln, Yaphet Kotto, and Gloria Foster also star in this unsentimental depiction of the times. Named to the National Film Registry in 1993.

Once Upon a Time . . . When We Were Colored
(1995)

Actor Tim Reid makes a fine directorial debut with the story of an African American youngster growing up parentless in 1950s Mississippi. Nostalgic, sensitive, and heartwarming adaptation of Clifton Taulbert's autobiographical book.

One False Move
(1991)

Not a typical crime thriller, first-time feature director Carl Franklin is more interested in a psychological character study of racism and small-town mores. Earned the 1993 Independent Spirit Award for best director.

One Potato, Two Potato
(1964)

The story of an interracial marriage between white laborer Julie Cullen (Barbara Barrie) and Frank Richards (Bernie Hamilton), an African American man that she meets at the plant where she works.

Panther
(1995)

A highly controversial, fictionalized account of the Black Panther movement in the late 1960s. Directed by Melvin Van Peebles. Music by Stanley Clarke.

Paris Is Burning
(1991)

Jennie Livingston's documentary portrayal of New York City's transvestite balls between 1985 and 1989. This is a compelling look at a subculture of primarily African American and Hispanic men and the one place they can truly be themselves. Winner of the 1991 Sundance Film Festival Grand Jury Prize.

Pastime
(1991)

A bittersweet baseball elegy set in the minor leagues in 1957. A boyish 41-year-old pitcher cannot face his impending retirement and pals around with the team pariah, a 17-year-old African American rookie. Splendidly written and acted, the film won the 1991 Sundance Film Festival Audience Award.

A Patch of Blue
(1965)

A kind-hearted blind girl (Elizabeth Hartman) falls in love with an African American man (Sidney Poitier) without acknowledging racial differences.

Paul Robeson: Tribute to an Artist
(1980)

A documentary that features a look at the tremendous life of actor Paul Robeson.

The Piano Lesson
(1994)

Adaptation of August Wilson's 1990 Pulitzer Prize-winning play set in 1936 concerning the prized heirloom of the Charles family—an 80-year-old, ornately carved upright piano.

Pinky
(1949)

Early Hollywood treatment of the tragic choice made by some African Americans to pass as white in order to attain a better life for themselves and their families. Based on the novel *Quality* by Cyd Ricketts Sumner.

Poetic Justice
(1993)

John Singleton's second directorial effort is about Justice (Janet Jackson in her film debut), a young hairdresser who copes with her boyfriend's brutal murder by writing poetry (provided by poet Maya Angelou). Production stopped on the South Central Los Angeles set during the 1992 riots, but the aftermath provided poignant pictures for later scenes.

Porgy and Bess
(1992)

The Glyndebourne production of Gershwin's folk opera about the denizens of Catfish Row. Simon Rattle conducts the London Philharmonic.

Posse
(1993)

Set during the Spanish-American War, this film revolves around a group of African American soldiers. Following their escape from Cuba with a fortune in gold, they travel towards Freemanville, where the group's leader (director Mario Van Peebles) avenges the death of his father.

Purple Rain
(1984)

A quasi-autobiographical film tells the tale of Prince's struggle for love, attention, acceptance, and popular artistic recognition in Minneapolis. Earned the 1984 Academy Award for best original song score and/or adaptation.

Putney Swope
(1969)

Comedy about a token African American ad man mistakenly elected chairman of the board of a Madison Avenue ad agency who turns the company upside down.

The Quiet One
(1948)

Explores the ghetto's psychological effects on a ten-year-old African American child. The film's commentary was written by James Agee.

Race to Freedom: The Story of the Underground Railroad
(1994)

Story of four fugitive slaves, in 1850, who struggle to get from North Carolina to the safety of Canada through a network of safe houses and people willing to risk smuggling them to asylum.

A Rage in Harlem
(1991)

Set in Harlem in 1956, this film portrays the tale of a beautiful con woman named Imabelle (Robin Givens). Adapted from a book by Chester Himes.

Ragtime
(1981)

From the E.L. Doctorow novel set in 1906 America, a small, unthinking act represents all the racist attacks on an African American man who refuses to back down this time.

A Raisin in the Sun
(1961)

Outstanding story of a black family trying to make a better life for themselves in an all-white neighborhood in Chicago. Based on the Broadway play by Lorraine Hansberry who also wrote the screenplay.

Rebound: The Legend of Earl "The Goat" Manigault
(1996)

The film stars Don Cheadle as the title character, a 1960s Harlem playground basketball phenom who turned his life around. After dropping out of college, turning to heroin, and winding up in prison, he founded his own basketball tournament in Harlem. Music by Kevin Eubanks.

Richard Pryor: Live on the Sunset Strip
(1982)

Filmed live at the Hollywood Palladium, this film captures Richard Pryor at his funniest including his segment about "Pryor on Fire."

The River Niger
(1976)

James Earl Jones is riveting and Cicely Tyson is good in this adaptation of the Tony-award winning play about African American ghetto life. Directed by Krishna Shaw, the film depicts believable characters expressing realistic emotions.

Roots
(1977)

The complete version of Alex Haley's made-for-television saga that follows an African American man's search for his heritage, revealing an epic panorama of America's past. Music by Quincy Jones.

Roots: The Gift
(1988)

Don Cheadle played the title role in *Rebound.*

A made-for-television movie based on the Alex Haley characters featuring Louis Gossett and LeVar Burton, among others.

Roots: The Next Generation
(1979)

Sequel to the landmark television miniseries continuing the story of author Alex Haley's ancestors from the Reconstruction era of the 1880s to 1967, culminating with Haley's visit to West Africa where he is told the story of Kunta Kinte.

Rosewood
(1996)

Based on the true story of the well-off African American community of Rosewood, Florida, which was destroyed by a white mob in 1923. Directed by John Singleton and starring Ving Rhames, the film accurately shows the tensions present between blacks and whites of the time.

Sally Hemings: An American Scandal
(2000)

Soap opera-ish romance based on the relationship between widowed ambassador (and third President) Thomas Jefferson (Sam Neill) and his young mulatto house slave Sally Hemings (Carmen Ejogo)—an affair that lasted for 38 years. (DNA proved Jefferson to be the father of one and possibly all six of Hemings's children.) Sally remains dignified through the years as does Jefferson. The heighth of excitement in this movie is Sally castigating her lover about his contradictory attitudes towards slavery.

Say Amen, Somebody
(1982)

Documentary about gospel music and two of its greatest legends—Willie Mae Ford Smith and Thomas A. Dorsey. Aptly demonstrates the power of music sung from the heart.

Scary Movie
(2000)

The Wayans brothers' parody of *Scream* and all its progeny. Not as focused a satire as *I'm Gonna Git You Sucka* and more likely to offend, still it was a huge box-office success and a hit, with teenagers especially.

School Daze
(1988)

Director/writer/star Spike Lee's second outing is a rambunctious comedy set at an African American college in the South.

Separate but Equal
(1991)

A powerful dramatization of the 1954 *Brown v. Board of Education of Topeka, Kansas* case that resulted in a landmark civil rights decision of the Supreme Court. Features Sidney Poitier as NAACP attorney Thurgood Marshall.

Sergeant Rutledge
(1960)

The story of a court-martial, told in flashback, about an African American cavalry officer on trial for rape and murder. A detailed look at overt and covert racism handled by master director John Ford. Based on the novel *Captain Buffalo* by James Warner Bellah.

Set It Off
(1996)

This film finds four female friends (Jada Pinkett, Queen Latifah, Vivica A. Fox, and Kimberly Elise) in

Los Angeles pushed over the edge and taking up bank robbery to escape poverty and strike a blow against "the system."

Shadows
(1960)

Director John Cassavettes's first independent feature revolves around jazz player Hugh (Hugh Hurd), his brother Ben (Ben Carruthers), and sister Lelia (Lelia Goldoni). Light-skinned enough to pass for white, Lelia gets involved with the white Tony (Anthony Ray) who leaves when he finds out her true heritage. Music by Charles Mingus. The film was named to the National Film Registry in 1993.

Shaft
(1971)

Gordon Parks Sr. directed this sophisticated action film featuring Richard Roundtree as the African American private eye, John Shaft. Academy Award-winning theme song by Isaac Hayes, the first music award from the Academy to an African American. Adapted from the novel by Ernest Tidyman.

Richard Roundtree (left) and Christopher St. John in the 1971 film, *Shaft*.

Shaft
(2000)

John Singleton's updated the 1971 blaxploitation flick with Samuel L. Jackson starring as the nephew of the coolest private dick ever (Richard Roundtree has a cameo in his original role). But Jackson can more than hold his own in the cool department as he tracks down rich-kid murderer Walter Wade Jr. (Christian Bale), who's after the only witness to his crime, a scared waitress (Toni Collette). Wade hires a Latino drug dealer and a couple of bad cops to find the girl and kill Shaft, setting off much gunfire and snappy dialoque. Jackson has charisma to burn, but other characters, as well as potentially interesting plot points, get short shrift.

She's Gotta Have It
(1986)

Spike Lee wrote, directed, edited, produced, and starred in this very popular romantic comedy about an independent-minded African American girl in Brooklyn and the three men and one woman who compete for her attention. Awarded the 1987 Independent Spirit Award for best first feature.

Show Boat
(1936)

The second of three film versions of the Kern/Hammerstein musical (based on the Edna Ferber novel) about a Mississippi showboat and the life and loves of its denizens. The film's musical numbers include Paul Robeson's immortal rendition of "Old Man River." Named to the National Film Registry in 1996.

Silver Streak
(1976)

Energetic Hitchcock parody features successful first pairing of Richard Pryor and Gene Wilder.

Skin Game
(1971)

A fast-talking con artist (James Garner) and his African American partner (Lou Gossett Jr.) travel throughout the antebellum South setting up scams. Finely acted comedy-drama.

Slam
(1998)

After being jailed for possession and suspicion of murdering his supplier, street-smart, low-level drug dealer Ray (Saul Williams) relies on spoken word poetry that he composes to see him through life's challenges. Awarded the Sundance Film Festival Grand Jury Prize in 1998.

Slaves
(1969)

Ossie Davis appears in this remake of *Uncle Tom's Cabin*. Directed by Herbert J. Biberman.

A Soldier's Story
(1984)

An African American U.S. Army attorney (Howard E. Rollins Jr.) is sent to a Southern military base to investigate the murder of an unpopular sergeant. From the Pulitzer-prize winning play by Charles Fuller, with most of the Broadway cast. Fine performances from Denzel Washington and Adolph Caesar. Music by Herbie Hancock.

Sophisticated Gents
(1981)

Nine boyhood friends, members of an African American athletic club, reunite after 25 years to honor their old coach and see how each of their lives has been affected by being black men in American society. Based on the novel *The Junior Bachelor Society* by John A. Williams.

Soul Food
(1997)

Film depicts the lives of three sisters (Vanessa Williams, Vivica A. Fox, and Nia Long) who struggle to hold their family together by keeping up their mother's Sunday dinner tradition after she becomes ill. Boasts many promising debuts including director/writer George Tillman Jr. Produced by music producer Kenneth "Babyface" Edmonds.

Soul of the Game
(1996)

Television movie follows the lives of three talented players in the Negro League during the 1945 season as they await the potential integration of baseball: Flashy, aging pitcher Satchel Paige (Delroy Lindo); mentally unstable catcher Josh Gibson (Mykelti Williamson); and the young, college-educated Jackie Robinson (Blair Underwood).

Sounder
(1972)

The film depicts the struggles of a family of African American sharecroppers in rural Louisiana during the Depression. Cicely Tyson brings strength and style to her role with fine help from Paul Winfield. Adapted from the novel by William Armstrong. Nominated for several Oscars at the 1972 Academy Awards. Music by Taj Mahal.

South Central
(1992)

A low-budget urban drama set in a gang-infested Los Angeles neighborhood. Feature debut of director Steve Anderson. Based on the novel *Crips* by Donald Bakeer.

Stormy Weather
(1943)

In this cavalcade of African American entertainment, the plot is overshadowed by the nearly non-stop array of musical numbers, showcasing this stellar cast (Lena Horne, Bill Robinson, Fats Waller, Dooley Wilson, and Cab Calloway) at their performing peak.

Straight Out of Brooklyn
(1991)

A bleak, nearly hopeless look at a struggling African American family in a Brooklyn housing project. An up-close and raw look at part of society seldom shown in mainstream film. Music by Harold Wheeler. Awarded the Sundance Film Festival Special Jury Prize in 1991.

Sudie & Simpson
(1990)

Heartwarming tale of friendship between a 12-year-old white girl and an adult black man set in rural 1940s Georgia. Based on Sara Flanigan Carter's autobiographical novel.

Sugar Hill
(1994)

Two brothers (Michael Wright and Wesley Snipes) are heroin dealers who have built their own crime empire in the Sugar Hill section of Harlem. Snipes is moved to reconsider his career options when he falls for an aspiring actress (Theresa Randle). Music by Terence Blanchard and Larry Joshua.

Superfly
(1972)

Controversial upon release, pioneering blaxploitation film of the 1970s has Harlem dope dealer (Ron O'Neal) attempt to leave the profession after one last big score. Directed by Gordon Parks Jr. Excellent period tunes by Curtis Mayfield.

Sweet Sweetback's Baadassssss Song
(1971)

An African American man kills two white policemen who beat up a black militant. He uses his streetwise survival skills to elude the law and escape to Mexico. Directed by Melvin Van Peebles.

Take a Giant Step
(1959)

An African American youth (Johnny Nash) struggles with society's attitude towards race and seeks the comfort of his family's maid (Ruby Dee). Directed by Philip Leacock.

They Call Me Sirr
(2000)

Based on the true story of Sirr Parker (Kente Scott), a talented, but poverty-striken high school football player in South Central Los Angeles. After Sirr and his younger brother are abandoned by their mother, Sirr struggles to look after his family (including an ailing grandmother) while keeping his place on the team. But the teen is finally forced to turn to his coach (Michael Clarke Duncan) for help.

A Time to Kill
(1996)

Powerful story of revenge, racism, and the question of justice in the "new South." Based on the John Grisham novel. Samuel L. Jackson earned a Golden Globe Award nomination for best supporting actor.

To Kill a Mockingbird
(1962)

Faithful adaptation of Harper Lee's powerful novel. Gregory Peck's performance as Southern lawyer defending a black man (Brock Peters) accused of raping a white woman is flawless, earning him the Academy and Golden Globe Awards for best actor. The film was named to the National Film Registry in 1995 and the Top 100 list of the American Film Institute in 1998.

To Sir, with Love
(1967)

Skillful and warm performance by Sidney Poitier as an idealistic teacher who wins over his unruly students in London's tough East End. Based on the novel by E.R. Braithwaite.

To Sleep with Anger
(1990)

Danny Glover's best performance as a stranger from the South whose visit divides an African American middle-class family living in Los Angeles. Insightful look into the conflicting values of black America. The film earned the Sundance Film Festival Special Jury Prize in 1990.

Training Day
(2001)

In this drama, Denzel Washington portrays Alonzo Harris, a veteran undercover narc who's become morally bankrupt and works on the "might makes right" theory of justice. Opposing him is rookie Jake Hoyt (Ethan Hawke), who first wants to be a part of Harris's team and then learns just what it will cost him. Washington's ferocious performance won him a Best Actor Oscar.

The Tuskegee Airmen
(1995)

Made-for-television drama based on the formation and World War II achievements of the U.S. Army Air Corps' first squadron of African American combat fighter pilots, the "Fighting 99th" of the 332nd Fighter Group. Based on a story by former Tuskegee airman, Robert W. Williams.

Uncle Tom's Cabin
(1914)

Satisfying version of Harriet Beecher Stowe's tale from the view of a founder of the Underground Railroad. Sam Lucas was the first African American actor to garner a lead role. Subsequent versions of this film were made in 1927 and 1987 (first sound version).

Undercover Brother
(2002)

Funny but padded spoof of secret agents and blaxploitation movies. Brother (Eddie Griffin) is a secret agent from the B.R.O.T.H.E.R.H.O.O.D. sent to rescue General Warren Boutwell, a black war hero turned presidential candidate (the always-cool Billy Dee Williams) who has been brainwashed in a plot by The Man to destroy African American culture. This more-hit-than-miss comedy finds many targets of all stripes to lampoon, and does so with just the right amount of funk.

Uptight
(1968)

In a story set in Cleveland, actor Raymond St. Jacques leads a group of African American well-armed revolutionaries shortly following the assassination of Martin Luther King Jr. Ruby Dee and Julian Mayfield serve as co-stars.

Uptown Saturday Night
(1974)

Two working men (Sidney Poitier and Bill Cosby) attempt to recover a stolen lottery ticket from the African American underworld after being ripped off at an illegal gambling place. Directed by Sidney Poitier.

Waiting to Exhale

(1995)

Popular adaptation of Terry McMillan's novel about four African American women (Whitney Houston, Angela Bassett, Loretta Devine, and Lela Rochon) hoping to enter the right romantic relationship. Music by producer Kenneth "Babyface" Edmonds.

The Walking Dead

(1994)

Preston A. Whitmore II's directorial debut depicts the Vietnam War from the perspectives of four black and one white Marine assigned to rescue prisoners of war from a North Vietnam camp in 1972.

The Watermelon Man

(1970)

The tables are turned for a bigoted white man when he wakes up one morning to discover he has become a black man. Godrey Cambridge takes on both roles. Directed by Melvin Van Peebles.

What's Love Got to Do with It

(1993)

Energetic biographical film of powerhouse songstress Tina Turner (Angela Bassett) and her abusive relationship with husband, Ike (Laurence Fishburne). Based on *I, Tina* by Turner and Kurt Loder. For her performance, Bassett earned the Golden Globe Award for best actress in 1994. Music by Stanley Clarke.

The Wiz

(1978)

An African American version of the long-time favorite *The Wizard of Oz*, based on the Broadway musical. Features all-star cast—Diana Ross, Michael Jackson, Lena Horne, Nipsey Russell, and Richard Pryor. Music by Quincy Jones.

The Women of Brewster Place

(1989)

Excellent, complex script gives each actress in a fine ensemble headed by executive producer Oprah Winfrey (in her dramatic television debut) time in the spotlight. Pilot for the series *Brewster Place*. Based on the novel by Gloria Naylor.

The Wood

(1999)

Based on writer-director Rick Famuyiwa's real life story, the ensemble comedy flashes back between the middle and high school days of three male friends growing up in Inglewood, California, and an eventful wedding day in the late 1990s. Captures the mood and nostalgia of the 1980s through memorable rhythm and blues and hip hop music.

The World, the Flesh, and the Devil

(1959)

Three survivors of a nuclear holocaust form an uneasy alliance and deal with issues of survival and racism. Features actor Harry Belafonte.

Zebrahead

(1992)

Outstanding performances by the young and largely unknown cast, particularly Michael Rapaport and N'Bushe Wright, and an excellent musical score by Taj Mahal enriches the action. Awarded the Sundance Film Festival Filmmakers Trophy.

Zooman

(1995)

The film offers a hard-hitting message on violence and responsibility and features performances by Louis Gossett Jr. and Vondie Curtis-Hall. Based on Fuller's 1978 play *Zooman and the Sign*.

◆ ACTORS, FILMMAKERS, AND FILM AND TELEVISION EXECUTIVES

(To locate biographical profiles more readily, please consult the index at the back of the book.)

Angela Bassett (1959?–)
Actress

Born in St. Petersburg, Florida, in the late 1950s, Angela Bassett was one of two daughters of a single mother and grew up in public housing. Inspired to the acting craft after witnessing a stage performance by James Earl Jones when she was a teenager, Bassett earned top grades and enrolled in Yale University. After receiving a master's degree from its prestigious school of drama in the early 1980s, Bassett settled in New York City and began winning acting roles in an industry not particularly known for a wealth of interesting, non-stereotypical roles offered to African American women.

Bassett found work in television commercials, the CBS daytime television drama *The Guiding Light* and debuted on Broadway in the acclaimed musical *Ma Rainey's Black Bottom*. Film roles were next on the horizon; in 1991, she appeared in two notable films, John Singleton's *Boyz N the Hood*—a casting that came with the good word of her friend, actor Larry Fishburne—and John Sayles's *City of Hope*. Her work attracted the attention of filmmaker Spike Lee, who cast her as Betty Shabazz, wife of Malcolm X, in his 1992 film biography of the slain leader. Bassett's portrayal won high marks from critics for its intensity and sensitivity.

Once again voicing strong support for his acting colleague, Fishburne agreed to play the role of 1960s soul musician Ike Turner in a film on the condition that Bassett won its starring role based on Tina Turner's autobiography. The 1993 film *What's Love Got to Do With It* catapulted Bassett into major stardom and won her rave reviews from critics for the vivid depiction of some of the more harrowing years of the singer's life. She won a Golden Globe Award for her efforts as well as two NAACP Image Awards. Late in 1995, Bassett appeared in a lead role in the cyberspace thriller *Strange Days* (1995), opposite Ralph Fiennes and in the Eddie Murphy comedy *Vampire in Brooklyn* (1995). Later that same year the actress won further critical acclaim for her ensemble-cast part in 1995's *Waiting to Exhale*, the box-office hit based on novelist Terry McMillan's tale of a close-knit quartet of African American women. In 1998 she starred as an older woman who falls in love with a much younger man in *How Stella Got Her Groove Back*. During that same year, she also served as series narrator for the acclaimed PBS documentary titled *Africans in America: America's Journey through Slavery*.

In 1999, Bassett began work on a science fiction movie with director Walter Hill titled *Supernova*. She moved into producing in 2000 with a Showtime original movie *Ruby's Bucket of Blood*, which she also starred in. Also in 2000 Bassett starred in the critically acclaimed *Boesman & Lena*. The year saw Bassett move back towards the mainstream with *The Score* alongside Robert De Niro and Edward Norton. Bassett continued to do what she considered meaningful movies in 2002 with her role in *Sunshine State*, an in-depth personal and political look at the state of Florida and the people who live there.

Harry Belafonte (1927–)
Singer, Actor

Born on March 1, 1927, in New York City, Harry Belafonte moved to the West Indies at the age of eight. At 13, Belafonte returned to New York, where he attended high school. Belafonte joined the Navy in 1944; after his discharge, while working as a janitor in New York, he became interested in drama. He studied acting at Stanley Kubrick's Dramatic Workshop and with Erwin Piscator at the New School for Social Research, where his classmates included Marlon Brando

and Walter Matthau. A successful singing engagement at The Royal Roost, a New York jazz club, led to other engagements around the country. But Belafonte, dissatisfied with the music he was performing, returned to New York, opened a restaurant in Greenwich Village, and studied folk singing. His first appearances as a folk singer in the 1950s "helped give folk music a period of mass appeal," according to John S. Wilson in a 1981 *New York Times* article. During his performances at the Palace Theater in New York, Belafonte had audiences calypsoing in the aisles.

Belafonte produced the first integrated musical shows on television, which both won him two Emmy awards and resulted in his being fired by the sponsor. The famous incident in which white British singer Petula Clark touched his arm while singing a song caused a national furor in pre-civil rights America. When Dr. Martin Luther King Jr. marched on Montgomery, Alabama, and Washington, DC, Harry Belafonte joined him and brought along a large contingent of performers. Touring in the stage musical *Three for Tonight* in which he had appeared on Broadway in 1955, Belafonte was forced to flee in the middle of a performance in Spartanburg, South Carolina, and be rushed to the airport in the mayor's car. Word had come that the Ku Klux Klan was marching on the theater.

Belafonte also appeared on Broadway in John Murray Anderson's *Almanac* (1953), and his movies include: *Carmen Jones* (1954); *Island in the Sun* (1957); *The World, the Flesh, and the Devil* (1958); *Odds Against Tomorrow* (1959); *The Angel Levine* (1969); *Buck and the Preacher* (1972); *Uptown Saturday Night* (1974); and *White Man's Burden* (1995). He also directed the film *Port Chicago*, in 1994.

In the 1980s, Belafonte appeared in his first dramatic role on television in the NBC presentation of *Grambling's White Tiger* and, in 1981, Columbia Records released his first album in seven years, *Loving You Is Where I Belong*, consisting of mostly ballads. He has received numerous awards and honors including the 1982 Martin Luther King Jr. Nonviolent Peace Prize and three honorary doctorates. Belafonte received the Thurgood Marshall Lifetime Achievement Award in 1993 and the National Medal of Arts in 1994. Belafonte received a Distinguished American Award at the John F. Kennedy Library in 2002 as well as a lifetime achievement award from the NAACP, Detroit Chapter.

Halle Berry (1968–)
Actress, Model

Halle Berry was born in Cleveland, Ohio, to an interracial family. After winning the Miss Teen Ohio beauty pageant, Berry enrolled in Cleveland's Cuyahoga

Halle Berry, the first African American woman to win an Oscar for a leading role.

Community College in 1986 to study broadcast journalism. She decided to become an actor and moved to Chicago, where she studied acting and worked as a model.

She relocated to Manhattan in 1988 and landed her first TV role on the television series *Paper Dolls*. Her big break came when she was selected by director Spike Lee to appear in his 1991 film *Jungle Fever* in which she played a crack addict.

Berry was cast in the 1991 social satire *Strictly Business*. Some of her notable film roles include the 1996 action film *Executive Decision*, the 1997 comedy *B.A.P.S.*, and the 1997 made for television movie *Solomon & Sheba*, where she starred playing the Queen of Sheba. She also starred as Dorothy Dandridge in the HBO film *Introducing Dorothy Dandridge* and in the 1998 film *Bulworth*. Her high profile marriage to baseball star David Justice ended in divorce in 1996.

Berry's rise to true fame would begin in the year 2000. She was honored as the Outstanding Actress for her portrayal of Dorothy Dandridge in the HBO special of the same name at the 31st NAACP Image Awards.

Later that same year she would win a Golden Globe and a Screen Actors Guild Award for best TV actress in a mini-series or TV movie for her role in *Introducing Dorothy Dandridge*. A few months later she shocked the entertainment world by revealing that she married singer Eric Benet in a secret ceremony at an undisclosed location. This didn't seem to affect her career, however, which was in high gear. Berry received a Screen Actors Guild Award for outstanding performance by a female actor in a leading role for *Monster's Ball*. A few weeks later, she was awarded the film industries' highest honor when she took home the Academy Award for best actress for her work in *Monster's Ball*.

Andre Braugher (1962?–)
Actor

A Chicago native, Andre Braugher began his career in the highly popular *Kojak* television movies. He received a B.A. from Stanford University and a M.F.A. from the Juilliard School. He has performed numerous productions of Shakespeare in New York for the New York Shakespeare Festival and at the Joseph Papp Public Theatre.

He gained national recognition for his starring role as Detective Frank Pembleton on the long-running serial drama *Homicide: Life on the Street*. In 1998, Braugher earned an Emmy Award for outstanding lead actor in a drama series.

Braugher's other notable television and film roles include *Glory* (1989), *Murder in Mississippi* (1990), *Simple Justice* (1993), *The Tuskegee Airmen* (1995), *Get on the Bus* (1996), *Primal Fear* (1996), *City of Angels* (1998), *Passing Glory* (1999), *All the Rage* (1999), and *Duets* (2000) opposite Gwyneth Paltrow. In 1999, Braugher made his directorial debut with one vignette of the Showtime trilogy *Love Songs*. He also began appearing as a regular on the television series *Gideon's Crossing* which garnered him a nomination in 2000 for a Golden Globe award for best TV actor in a drama.

Diahann Carroll (1935–)
Actress, Singer

Diahann Carroll was born in the Bronx on July 17, 1935, the daughter of a subway conductor and a nurse. As a child, she was a member of the Abyssinian Baptist Church choir; at the age of ten, Carroll won a Metropolitan Opera scholarship. Singing lessons held little appeal for her, however, so she continued her schooling at the High School of Music and Art. As a concession to her parents, Carroll enrolled at New York University, where she was to be a sociology student, but stage fever led her to an appearance on a television talent show, which netted her $1,000. A subsequent appearance at the Latin Quarter Club launched her professional career.

In 1954, Carroll appeared in *House of Flowers*, winning favorable press notices. In that year, she also appeared in a film version of *Carmen Jones*, in the role of Myrt.

Movie and television appearances kept Carroll busy until 1958, the year she was slated to appear as an Asian in Richard Rodgers's *Flower Drum Song*. The part did not materialize. Three years later, Rodgers cast her in *No Strings* as a high fashion model, a role for which she earned a Tony award in 1962.

In the late 1960s, Carroll was cast as lead in the television series *Julia*, in which she played a nurse and war widow. She also appeared in the films *Porgy and Bess* (1959), *Goodbye Again* (1961), *Paris Blues* (1961), *Claudine* with James Earl Jones (1974), *Sister, Sister* (1982), and *The Five Heartbeats* (1991). She has been featured in the television series *Dynasty* and *A Different World* and has written an autobiography.

From 1996 to 1997, Carroll appeared on stage in the Broadway musical *Sunset Boulevard*. In 1998 she played a small role as a voodoo priestess in the movie *Eve's Bayou*. Carroll also battled breast cancer that same year and did many promotional spots for the American Cancer Society. In 1999, Carroll played Sadie Delany in the film adaptation of the play *Having Our Say: The Delany Sisters' First 100 Years.* for CBS. Carroll continued to work on the small screen over the next few years first starring in *Livin' for Love: The Natalie Cole Story*, then winning a role in 2002 as a judge on the short-lived television drama *The Court* opposite Sally Field.

Bill Cosby (1937–)
Actor, Comedian

Born on July 12, 1937, Bill Cosby is one of the most successful performers and businessmen in the United States.

A native of suburban Philadelphia, Cosby left high school to become a medic in the U.S. Navy. As a testament to his commitment to education, he obtained his diploma while in the service. After leaving the military, he entered Temple University, where he played football and worked evenings as a bartender.

While doing this work, Cosby began to entertain the customers with his comedy routines and, encouraged by his success, left Temple in 1962 to pursue a career in show business. He began by playing small clubs around

Bill Cosby performing his comedy routine on stage.

Philadelphia and in New York's Greenwich Village. Within two years, he was playing the top nightclubs around the country and making television appearances on shows hosted by Johnny Carson, Jack Paar, and Andy Williams. In fact, he earned the opportunity to serve as guest host of Carson's *Tonight Show*. In the 1960s Cosby became the first African American to star in a prime time television series; *I Spy* ran from 1965 to 1968 and won Cosby three Emmy Awards.

In the 1970s, Cosby appeared regularly in nightclubs in Las Vegas, Tahoe, and Reno, and did commercials for such sponsors as Jell-O, Del Monte, and Ford. From 1969 until 1972, he had his own television series *The Bill Cosby Show*. During the early 1970s he also developed and contributed vocals to the Saturday morning children's show *Fat Albert and the Cosby Kids*. He appeared in such films as *Uptown Saturday Night* (1974), *Let's Do It Again* (1975), *A Piece of the Action* (1977), and the award-winning television movie *To All My Friends on Shore (1971)*.

In 1975, Random House published his book *Bill Cosby's Personal Guide to Tennis: or, Don't Lower the Lob, Raise the Net.* For several years, he was involved in educational television with the Children's Television Workshop. He returned to college, spending five years at the University of Massachusetts earning a master's degree and then in 1977, a doctorate in education.

He was star and creator of the consistently top-rated *The Cosby Show* from 1985 to 1992, author of two best-selling books *Fatherhood* (1986) and *Time Flies* (1987), and a performer at the top venues in Las Vegas, where he earned $500,000 a week. He also won top fees as a commercial spokesman for Kodak and Coca Cola. He has recorded more than 27 albums and has received five Grammy Awards. Cosby also hosted a new version of the old Groucho Marx game show *You Bet Your Life*. In 1994, Cosby reunited with Robert Culp, his co-star from the *I Spy* show, for a new television movie *I Spy Returns*. He also starred in the short-lived series *The Cosby Mysteries* in 1995. Toward the end of the decade Cosby hosted *Kids Say the Darndest Things*, a show originally hosted by Art Linkletter, and starred in another sitcom entitled *Cosby*.

In 1998 Cosby was an honoree at Kennedy Center Honors. A few years later, Cosby's *Cosby* sitcom took its final bow on CBS in spring of 2000. Cosby has continued to be active behind the scenes with many producing credits and he continues to make public appearances such as when he addressed the 2001 commencement crowd at Ohio State University in Columbus, Ohio. Cosby appeared in rare form, dressed in a t-shirt and sweat pants—with a tassel hanging from his baseball cap.

Cosby and his wife, Camille, live in rural New England. The Cosbys made headlines when they donated $20 million to Spelman College in Atlanta.

Rupert Crosse (1928–1973)
Actor

Born in Nevis, British West Indies, on November 29, 1928, Rupert Crosse moved to Harlem at an early age. Crosse returned to Nevis at the age of seven, after the death of his father. Reared by his grandparents and strongly influenced by his grandfather, a schoolmaster, Crosse received a solid education before returning to New York, where he attended Benjamin Franklin High School. Crosse also later worked at odd jobs before interrupting high school to spend two years in military service in Germany and Japan. Once out of service, Crosse finished high school and entered Bloomfield College and Seminary in New Jersey. Though he intended to become a minister, it was obvious from the jobs he had held—machinist, construction worker, and recreation counselor—that his career plans were not yet definite.

Crosse subsequently enrolled at the Daykarhanora School, studying acting and appearing in the Equity Library Theatre off-Broadway production *Climate of Eden*. He then transferred to John Cassavetes's workshop, where he helped to create *Shadows* (1961), winner of a Venice Film Festival Award. Crosse's first Hollywood role was in a Cassavetes movie *Too Late Blues* (1962). His most important film role was as Ned McCaslin in the screen adaptation of William Faulkner's Pulitzer Prize-winning novel *The Reivers* (1969). Crosse was nominated for an Academy Award as best supporting actor for this outstanding performance. His other film credits include *The Wild Seed* (1965) and *Ride in the Whirlwind* (1965).

Crosse's stage credits are also numerous including appearances in *Sweet Bird of Youth*, *The Blood Knot*, and *Hatful of Rain*. Television viewers saw Crosse in *Dr. Kildare*, *I Spy*, and *The Man from U.N.C.L.E.*, as well as several other series.

Rupert Crosse died of cancer on March 5, 1973, at the age of 45 at his sister's home in Nevis.

Dorothy Dandridge (1922–1965)
Actress

Dorothy Dandridge was born on November 9, 1922, in Cleveland, Ohio; her mother was the actress Ruby Dandridge. As children, Dorothy and her sister, Vivian, performed as "The Wonder Kids," touring the United States. In 1934, they were joined by a third performer, Etta Jones, and the trio became the Dandridge Sisters. The Dandridge Sisters were a popular act, performing at the Cotton Club in Harlem and in the motion picture *A Day at the Races* (1937). By the 1940s, Dorothy Dandridge had struck out on her own, appearing in the "soundies" (musical shorts) *Easy Street*, *Yes, Indeed*, *Cow Cow Boogie*, *Jungle Jig*, *Paper Doll*, and *Sing for My Supper*.

Dandridge married Harold Nicholas (of the famed Nicholas Brothers dance team) in 1942, and had a daughter, Harolyn, in 1943. Harolyn was diagnosed as having a severe developmental disability and was sent to an institution; shortly thereafter, Dandridge divorced Nicholas. She carried on a fairly successful career as a nightclub singer during the 1940s and 1950s. Her greatest triumph, however, came as a film actress, particularly in the all-African American musical *Carmen Jones* (1954) for which she received an Oscar nomination for best actress, becoming the first African American woman to receive this nomination. Another important role was in *Island in the Sun* (1957), where she was paired romantically with a white man, John Justin—a breakthrough in desegregating the screen. In 1959, Dandridge played Bess opposite Sidney Poitier's Porgy in the movie version of *Porgy and Bess*. Ultimately, she appeared in over 25 films.

Dandridge married the white Las Vegas restaurateur Jack Dennison in 1959, but three years later divorced and declared personal bankruptcy. She died of an overdose of a prescription antidepressant on September 8, 1965.

Ossie Davis (1917–)
Actor

Ossie Davis grew up in Waycross, Georgia, and attended Howard University in Washington, DC, where Dr. Alain Locke suggested he pursue an acting career in New York. After completing service in the Army, Davis landed his first role in 1946 in the play *Jeb*, where he met Ruby Dee, whom he married two years later.

After appearing in the movie *No Way Out* (1950), Davis won Broadway roles in *No Time for Sergeants*, *Raisin in the Sun*, and *Jamaica*. In 1961, he and Dee starred in *Purlie Victorious*, which Davis himself had written. Two years later, they repeated their roles in the movie version *Gone Are the Days*.

Davis's other movie credits from this period include *The Cardinal* (1963), *Shock Treatment* (1964), *The Hill* (1965), *A Man Called Adam* (1966), and *The Scalphunter* (1968).

Davis then directed such films as *Cotton Comes to Harlem* (1970) and *Black Girl* (1972). His play *Escape to Freedom: A Play about Young Frederick Douglass*, had its debut at Town Hall in New York and later was published by Viking Junior Books. Davis has also been involved with television scripts and educational programming. *The Ruby Dee/Ossie Davis Story Hour* was produced for television in 1974. The arts education television series *With Ossie and Ruby* appeared in 1981. Davis and Ruby Dee also founded the Institute of New Cinema Artists and the Recording Industry Training Program.

Davis's continued movie appearances include roles in *Let's Do It Again* (1975), *Hot Stuff* (1979), and *Nothing Personal* (1979). Recent film credits include *Harry and Son* (1984), and Spike Lee's *School Daze* (1988) and *Do the Right Thing* (1989). In addition, Davis has appeared on such television series as *The Defenders*, *The Nurses*, *East Side, West Side*, and *Evening Shade*. In 1993, Davis starred in the TV miniseries *Queen*, the sequel to the classic miniseries *Roots*. He also appeared in the TV movie *The Android Affair* in 1995.

Davis has continued to be very active on both the big and small screens. In 1996 he appeared in Spike Lee's *Get on the Bus* as well as the movie *I'm Not Rappaport*. In 1997 he played Juror #2 in a remake of the classic movie *12 Angry Men* and in 1998 he starred in another remake, *Dr. Dolittle*, with Eddie Murphy. For most of 1999 he played small roles in television movies such as *The Soul Collector* and *The Ghosts of Christmas Eve*. He continued to work in television between 2000 and 2002 popping up in mini series such as *Jazz* and *The Feast of All Saints*. In 2000, Davis and his wife Ruby were honored with a Life Achievement Award from the Screen Actors Guild.

Davis is also the author of *Just Like Martin*, a novel for young adults.

Sammy Davis Jr. (1925–1990)
Actor, Comedian, Dancer, Singer

Sammy Davis Jr. was often called "the world's greatest entertainer," a title that attested to his remarkable versatility as singer, dancer, actor, mimic, and musician.

Davis was born in New York City on December 8, 1925. Four years later he was appearing in vaudeville with his father and "uncle" in the Will Mastin Trio. In 1931, Davis made his movie debut with Ethel Waters in *Rufus Jones for President*; this was followed by an appearance in *Season's Greetings*.

Throughout the 1930s, the Will Mastin Trio continued to play vaudeville, burlesque, and cabarets. In 1943, Davis entered the Army and served for two years by writing, directing, and producing camp shows. After his discharge, he rejoined the trio, which in 1946 cracked the major club circuit with a successful Hollywood engagement.

Davis recorded a string of hits ("Hey There," "Mr. Wonderful," "Too Close for Comfort") during his steady rise to the top of show business. In November 1954, he lost an eye in an automobile accident, which fortunately did not interfere with his career. He scored a hit in his first Broadway show *Mr. Wonderful* (1956) and later repeated this success in *Golden Boy* (1964).

In 1959, Davis played Sportin' Life in the movie version of *Porgy and Bess*. Other Davis movies from this period include *Oceans 11* (1960) and *Robin and the Seven Hoods* (1964). His 1966 autobiography *Yes, I Can* became a best seller, and he starred in his own network television series. In addition, he spent time with a coterie of entertainers dubbed "The Rat Pack," who were fixtures of top-dollar nightspots in Los Angeles and Las Vegas throughout the decade.

In 1968, the NAACP awarded Davis its Spingarn Medal. In the 1970s, Davis appeared in films, television, and nightclubs. In 1972, he was involved in a controversy over his support of Richard Nixon which was publicized by a famous photograph of Nixon hugging Davis at the 1972 Republican Convention. In 1974, Davis renounced his support of Nixon and Nixon's programs. In the same year, his television commercials for Japan's Suntory Whiskey won the grand prize at the Cannes Film Festival, and the National Academy of TV Arts and Sciences honored him for his unique contributions to television.

In 1975, Davis became host of an evening talk and entertainment show. In 1980, he marked his fiftieth anniversary as an entertainer and the Friars Club honored him with its Annual Life Achievement Award. During that same decade, Davis embarked on a hugely successful revue tour with Frank Sinatra and Liza Minelli. In 1989, he appeared in his final film *Tap* with Gregory Hines and Harold Nicholas. Later that year, he was diagnosed with throat cancer and died on May 16, 1990. Shortly before his death he was honored with a television special devoted to his life.

Davis married three times. His first marriage was in 1959 to singer Loray White. He married his second wife, actress Mai Britt, in 1961; she is the mother of his three children. In 1970, he married dancer Altovise Gore.

Suzanne de Passe (1948–)
Producer, Entrepreneur

Suzanne de Passe was born in 1948 in Harlem. She graduated from Manhattan High School and attended Syracuse University. She left without receiving her degree and became a booking agent for a New York theater. It was there that Motown Records founder Barry Gordy found de Passe and hired her as his creative assistant. Having discovered the Jackson 5 and the Commodores while working for Motown, de Passe developed a reputation for spotting talent.

In 1973 she received an Oscar nomination for co-writing the screenplay of the movie *Lady Sings the Blues*. In the early 1980s, she became the head of Motown Productions, the film and television division of Motown. Her production of "Motown 25," an anniversary show for the company, earned several Emmy Awards. In 1989, de Passe produced the miniseries *Lonesome Dove*, which won seven Emmy Awards, a Golden Globe, and a Peabody Award. She also served as executive producer to the many spinoffs of the this award-winning miniseries. In 1999, she produced *The Temptations*, the well-received docudrama based on the famous Motown singing group.

De Passe is the CEO of her own production company, de Passe Entertainment. The company has produced the WB shows *Sister, Sister* and *Smart Guy*. In 1986, she was the subject of a study by the Harvard Business School. She has consistently taken less than the normal fee accorded to producers in order to get her projects funded, believing visibility is more important than profit. In 1995 de Passe was awarded the Charles W. Fries Producer of the Year Award for her outstanding contribution to the television industry.

De Passe continued to produce in 1999 with executive producer credits on *Zenon, Girl of the 21st Century*, which aired on the Disney Channel. She worked again with Disney as executive producer of *The Loretta Claiborne Story* for Disney/ABC Sunday Night in 2000. Also in 2000, she was executive producer of *Cheaters* which aired on HBO. She returned to Disney in 2001 to produce *Zenon: The Zequel*. Most recently, de Passe served as executive producer of the *32nd Annual NAACP Image Awards*, which aired March 2001 on the Fox Network.

Ruby Dee (1924–)
Actress

Ruby Dee was born in Cleveland on October 27, 1924, but grew up in Harlem, attending Hunter College in New York. In 1942, she appeared in *South Pacific*

Ruby Dee holding an Emmy Award in 1991.

with Canada Lee. Five years later, she met Ossie Davis while they were both playing in *Jeb*. They were married two years later.

Ruby Dee's movie roles from this period include parts in *No Way Out* (1950), *Edge of the City* (1957), *Raisin in the Sun* (1961), Genet's *The Balcony* (1963), and *Purlie Victorious* (1963), written by Davis. Since 1960, she has appeared often on network television.

In 1965, Ruby Dee became the first African American actress to appear in major roles at the American Shakespeare Festival in Stratford, Connecticut. Appearances in movies including *The Incident* (1967), *Uptight* (1968), *Buck and the Preacher* (1972), *Black Girl* (directed by Davis) (1972), and *Countdown at Kusini* (1976) followed. Her musical satire *Take It from the Top*, in which she appeared with her husband in a showcase run at the Henry Street Settlement Theatre in New York, premiered in 1979.

As a team, Ruby Dee and Ossie Davis have recorded several talking story albums for Caedmon. In 1974, they produced *The Ruby Dee/Ossie Davis Story Hour*, which was sponsored by Kraft Foods and carried by more than 60 stations of the National Black Network. Together they founded the Institute of New Cinema Artists to train young people for jobs in films and television, and then the Recording Industry Training Program to develop jobs in the music industry for disadvantaged youths. In 1981, Alcoa funded a television series on the Public Broadcasting System titled *With Ossie and Ruby*, which used guests to provide an anthology of the arts. Recent film credits include *Cat People* (1982) and, with Ossie Davis, Spike Lee's *Do the Right Thing* (1989). In 1998, she narrated the PBS special *God's Gonna Trouble the Waters*. She was honored, along with husband Ossie Davis, with a Life Achievement Award from the Screen Actors Guild in 2000.

Bill Duke (1943–)
Actor, Producer, Director

Bill Duke was born in Poughkeepsie, New York. He graduated with a B.A. in 1964 from Boston University and in 1968 with an M.A. from New York University. Duke began his career directing off-Broadway plays including the New York Shakespeare Festival's production of *Unfinished Business* for which he won the 1974 Adelco Award.

He made his film debut with *American Gigolo* in 1980, and has worked as an actor in a number of projects for film and television that include *Predator* (1987), *Commando* (1985), *Bird on a Wire* (1990), and *Action Jackson* (1988).

As a director his films include *A Rage in Harlem* (1991), *Deep Cover* (1992), *The Cemetery Club* (1992), *Sister Act 2: Back in the Habit* (1993), and *Hoodlum* (1997).

In 1994, he completed *Black Light: The African American Hero*, a book of photo essays celebrating 90 of the greatest African American heroes of the twentieth century. His most recent work as an author was a 1998 inspirational book entitled *The Journey*. He is currently the head of the School of Performing Arts at Howard University.

Tracey Edmonds (1967–)
Producer

As the president and CEO of Edmonds Entertainment, Tracey Edmonds is involved in virtually every aspect of the entertainment business. With divisions that include a record label, music publishing, film and television production and artist management, Edmonds's power and influence is unique for an African American female in entertainment.

A Southern California native, Edmonds is a 1987 Stanford graduate and former real estate executive who, in 1993, parlayed her business smarts and connections to create Yab Yum Entertainment. Originally established as a music publishing house, the company expanded into filmmaking with the 1996 release *Soul Food*. Grossing $43 million dollars at the box office, the film paved the way for Edmonds's entry into film. Since, Edmonds has produced the romantic comedy *Hav' Plenty*, and teen drama *Light it Up*.

Married to R&B/pop superstar Kenneth "Babyface" Edmonds, Tracey is one half of Edmonds Entertainment which she runs with her husband. Edmonds herself is very involved in the business, most recently serving as executive producer of the hit series *Soul Food* for Showtime based on the movie of the same name produced by Edmonds. She currently splits her time between Edmonds Entertainment and being at home with her two sons, Brandon and Dylan Michael. Edmonds has also won numerous awards for her achievements in the industry, including Turner Broadcasting System's prestigious Tower of Power Award (2000).

Stepin Fetchit (1902–1985)
Actor

Stepin Fetchit's place in movie history is a controversial one. Praised by some critics as an actor who opened doors for other African Americans in Hollywood, he has been berated by others for catering to racist stereotypes and doing little to raise the status of

African American actors. His characters—lazy, inarticulate, slow-witted, and always in the service of whites—have become so uncomfortable to watch that his scenes are sometimes cut when films in which he appeared are shown on television. Even at the height of his career, civil rights groups protested his roles, which they considered demeaning caricatures.

Born Lincoln Theodore Monroe Andrew Perry in Key West, Florida, on May 30, 1902, Stepin Fetchit's early career was in the Royal American Shows plantation revues. He and his partner, Ed Lee, took the names "Step 'n' Fetchit: Two Dancing Fools from Dixie." When the duo broke up, Fetchit appropriated "Stepin Fetchit" for himself.

Fetchit appeared in numerous motion pictures in the 1920s and 1930s including *In Old Kentucky* (1927), *Salute* (1929), *Hearts in Dixie* (1929), *Show Boat* (1929), *Swing High* (1930), *Stand Up and Cheer* (1934), *David Harum* (1934), *One More Spring* (1936), and *Zenobia* (1939). Fetchit earned a great deal of income from these films and spent it wildly. His extravagant lifestyle ended when he filed for bankruptcy in the 1930s.

Fetchit made sporadic appearances in films later in his life, among them *Miracle in Harlem* (1949), *Bend of the River* (1952), *Amazing Grace* (1974), and *Won Ton Ton, The Dog Who Saved Hollywood* (1976).

Laurence Fishburne (1961–)
Actor

Laurence Fishburne made his stage debut at age ten with the Negro Ensemble Theatre. The Augusta, Georgia, native made television history as a member of daytime television's first African American family on *One Life to Live*. Making his film debut at the age of 12 in *Cornbread, Earl and Me*, (1975) Fishburne moved to the Philippines for two years to co-star in the Francis Ford Coppola war classic *Apocalypse Now*. Other notable roles for the actor include: *Rumble Fish* (1983); *The Cotton Club* (1984); *Gardens of Stone* (1987); *King of New York* (1990); *Class Action* (1991); *Deep Cover* (1992); and *Searching for Bobby Fischer* (1993).

Following his star making performance in director John Singleton's *Boyz N the Hood*, Fishburne was nominated for an Oscar for his portrayal of 1960s pop icon Ike Turner in the 1993 film *What's Love Got to Do With It*. In 1995, Fishburne became the first African American to play the title role in the film adaptation of the Shakespeare classic *Othello*. On Broadway, the actor has starred in the August Wilson production *Two Trains Running* and finished a run in the play. In film, Fishburne's projects also include *Fled* (1996), *Hoodlum* (1997), *Event Horizon* (1998), and *The Matrix* (1999).

In 2000, Fishburne expanded his role to author as he wrote, starred in, and produced *Once in the Life*. He has continued to stay active in the film industry, and will be staring in two Matrix sequels which are both slated to appear in theaters in 2003.

Morgan Freeman (1937–)
Actor

Born in Memphis, Tennessee, on June 1, 1937, Morgan Freeman grew up in Greenwood, Mississippi. He joined the U.S. Air Force in 1955, but left a few years later to pursue an acting career in Hollywood, taking classes at Los Angeles City College. He moved to New York City in the 1960s.

Freeman's first important role was in the short-running off-Broadway play *The Nigger-Lovers* in 1967. Soon thereafter, he appeared in the all-African American version of the musical *Hello, Dolly!*

Americans who grew up in the 1970s remember Freeman fondly as a regular on the public television program *The Electric Company* in which he appeared from 1971–1976; his most notable character was the hip

Morgan Freeman.

Easy Reader. More theater roles followed in productions of *The Mighty Gents* (1978), *Othello* (1982), *The Gospel at Colonus* (1983), and *The Taming of the Shrew* (1990).

In 1987, Freeman was cast in the Broadway play *Driving Miss Daisy*. He won an Obie Award for his portrayal of Hoke, the chauffeur for a wealthy white woman in the American South. Freeman recreated his Broadway role for the 1989 movie version of the play, receiving an Academy Award nomination for best actor. In the same year, Freeman appeared in the highly successful movie *Glory* about an all-African American Union regiment in the Civil War. Other film credits include: *Clean and Sober* (1988), *Lean on Me* (1989), *Johnny Handsome* (1989), *Unforgiven* (1993), *The Shawshank Redemption* (1994), *Outbreak* (1995), and *Seven* (1995). Freeman also directed the 1993 film *Bopha!*. In 1995, Freeman was nominated again for an Academy Award for his role in *The Shawshank Redemption*. In 1998, Freeman starred in such movies as *Deep Impact* and *Hard Rain*. He continued to appear on both the large and small screens between 2000 and 2002 in movies such as *Along Came A Spider* and *The Sum of All Fears* and television specials such as *Shawshank: The Redeeming Feature*. In 2000, Freeman received an award from the Hollywood Film Festival for his acting career. Freeman is slated to appear in the Stephen King movie *Dreamcatchers* in 2003.

Danny Glover (1947–)
Actor

Born on July 22, 1947, in San Francisco, California, Danny Glover attended San Francisco State University and trained at the Black Actors Workshop of the American Conservatory Theatre.

Glover went on to appear in many stage productions including *Island, Macbeth, Sizwe Banzi is Dead*, and New York productions of *Suicide in B Flat, The Blood Knot*, and *Master Harold. . . and the Boys*, which won him a Theatre World Award.

Glover's film credits include: *Escape from Alcatraz* (1979); *Chu Chu and the Philly Flash* (1984); *Iceman* (1984); *Witness* (1985); *Places in the Heart* (1985); *The Color Purple* (1985); *Mandela* (1987); *Lethal Weapon* (1987) and its sequels; *Bat 21* (1988); *Predator 2* (1990); *To Sleep With Anger* (1990); *Flight of the Intruder* (1991); *A Rage in Harlem* (1991); *Pure Luck* (1991); *Grand Canyon* (1991); *Bopha!* (1993); *The Saint of Fort Washington* (1993); *Angels in the Outfield* (1994); *Operation Dumbo Drop* (1995); *Lethal Weapon 4.* (1997); *Beloved* (1998); *Boesman and Lena* (2000); and *The Royal Tenenbaums* (2001).

On television, Glover appeared in the hit series *Hill Street Blues*, the miniseries *Chiefs, Lonesome Dove*, and other projects including *Many Mansions, Face of Rage, A Place at the Table, Mandela*, and *A Raisin in the Sun*.

Glover has won numerous awards for his acting including an Honorary Doctorate of Fine Arts Degree from San Francisco State University in 1997. In 1998, Glover was appointed a goodwill ambassador for the United Nations Development Program.

Louis Gossett Jr. (1936–)
Actor

Born in Brooklyn on May 27, 1936, Louis Gossett began acting at the age of 17 when a leg injury prevented him from pursuing his first love—basketball. In 1953, he won out over 445 contenders for the role of a black youngster in *Take a Giant Step*, for which he received a Donaldson Award as best newcomer of the year.

While performing in *The Desk Set* in 1958, Gossett was drafted by the professional basketball team the New York Knicks, but decided to remain in theater. Ultimately, he would appear in more than 60 stage productions including such plays as *Lost in the Stars, A Raisin in the Sun, The Blacks*, and *Murderous Angels*.

On television, Gossett played character roles in such series as *The Nurses, The Defenders* and *East Side, West Side*. In 1977, he won an Emmy for his performance in the acclaimed miniseries *Roots*. He also starred in such films as *Skin Game* (1971), *The Deep* (1977), *An Officer and a Gentleman* (1983), *Iron Eagle* (1986), *Iron Eagle II* (1988), and *Diggstown* (1993). In 1989, Gossett starred in his own television series *Gideon Oliver*.

Gossett has also starred in television movies throughout the 1990s including *Father and Son: Dangerous Relations* (1993); *Ray Alexander: A Taste for Justice* (1994); *The Inspectors* (1998); and *For Love of Olivia* (2001).

Pam Grier (1949–)
Actress

Pamela Suzette Grier was born May 26, 1949, in Winston-Salem, North Carolina. Her father's military career kept the family moving. Grier spent her early years in Europe, until the age of 14, when her family returned to the United States. They settled in Denver, Colorado, where she would enroll in Metropolitan State College with aspirations of a future career in medicine.

In 1967, Grier entered the Miss Colorado Universe contest in hopes of winning prize money to battle the rising tuition costs. There she attracted the attention of an agent with her second-place finish. David Baumgarten, who handled many great talents, invited her to Hollywood to begin a career in acting. Grier was disinclined to go, but she was encouraged by her mother to take the agent up on his offer.

After signing with the Agency of Performing Arts, Grier attended acting classes and worked the office switchboard. Acting roles did not come right away, but she eventually landed a small part in 1969's *The Bird Cage*. Throughout the 1970s, she was a box-office draw, often appearing in blaxploitation movies such as *Coffy* (1973) and *Foxy Brown* (1974). Though she was usually cast as a strong, independent woman and enjoyed being one of the few actresses given the chance to create such portrayals, she felt hemmed in by the stereotypes these films encouraged. One of the few bankable female stars of the time, Grier unofficially retired. Then in 1981, she co-starred in *Fort Apache: The Bronx*.

A demanding film, Grier felt validated by the success of her difficult performance. Since then, Grier has appeared on stage, in films, and on television. She was recognized by the NAACP Image Awards as the best actress in 1986 for *Fool for Love*. In 1993, she received awards from the National Black Theatre Festival and the African American Film Society. In 1997 she made a comeback in Quentin Tarentino's *Jackie Brown*. Since then she has appeared in movies such as *Snowday*; *A Passion in the Dessert*; and the Snoop Dog movie *Bones*.

Henry Hampton (1940–1998)
Documentary Filmmaker

As a force behind the library of documentaries that primarily seek to address the African American experience, Henry Hampton used his vast understanding of the film medium as a tool to bring cultures together. A St. Louis native and son of a prominent surgeon, Hampton received his B.A. in literature in 1961 from Washington University. He has also taught at Tufts University.

In 1968, Hampton founded his production house, Blackside Inc., and initially produced industrial and documentary films. With a focus towards achieving social change through entertainment, Blackside Inc. has produced more than 60 films and media projects since its inception. Notable projects include *The Great Depression, America's War on Poverty, Code Blue,* and "Malcolm X: Make It Plain," an *American Experience* biography. However, Hampton is best known for the critically acclaimed, 14-hour documentary on the Civil Rights movement, *Eyes on the Prize*.

Hampton perfected the art of mixing archival news footage with contemporary interviews, thus giving the events more meaning to his audience. During his career he received numerous awards including six Emmys, an Academy Award nomination, and the Dupont/Columbia Award for excellence in journalism. At the time of his death, he was working on the documentary *I'll Make Me a World*, a six-hour series on African American creative artists which was presented on PBS in memoriam to Hampton in 1999.

Rex Ingram (1895–1969)
Actor

A major movie and radio personality during the 1930s and 1940s, Rex Ingram was born on October 20, 1895, in Cairo, Illinois, aboard the *Robert E. Lee*, a Mississippi riverboat on which his father was a stoker.

Ingram attended military schools, where he displayed an interest in acting. After working briefly as a cook for the Union Pacific Railroad and as head of his own small window-washing business, Ingram gravitated to Hollywood, where in 1919 he appeared in the original Tarzan film. Roles in such classics as *Lord Jim*, *Beau Geste* (1926), *King Kong* (1933), *The Green Pastures* (1936), and *Huckleberry Finn* (1939) followed. During the late 1920s and early 1930s, Ingram also appeared prominently in theater in San Francisco. During the late 1930s, he starred in daytime radio soap operas and in Works Progress Administration theater projects.

Ingram continued with a distinguished career on the New York stage and in film and television. In 1957, he played Pozzo in *Waiting for Godot*. Later film credits include *Elmer Gantry* (1960), *Your Cheating Heart* (1964), *Hurry Sundown* (1967), and *Journey to Shiloh* (1968). He died on September 19, 1969.

Samuel L. Jackson (1949?–)
Actor

Samuel Jackson was born in Chattanooga, Tennessee c. 1949. As a child, Jackson's active imagination had him recreating scenes from his favorite movies. He also acted in various school plays. His first serious involvement in acting came as a student at Morehouse College in Atlanta. After deciding on drama as a major, Jackson began to enroll in theater classes at Morehouse's sister school, Spelman College.

After receiving his Dramatic Arts degree, Jackson and his wife-to-be, La Tanya Richardson, moved to New York City. Jackson performed in various shows and films between the years 1976 and 1981. As a cast

Samuel L. Jackson.

member of Charles Burnett's *A Soldier's Play*, Jackson began to make connections. Morgan Freeman and Spike Lee both encouraged Jackson to keep pursuing his goals. Several years later, Jackson and Lee collaborated on the first of many films the two would film together.

School Daze and *Do the Right Thing*, both directed by Spike Lee, set the stage for the creation of Jackson's reputation which was established in *Jungle Fever*, also directed by Lee. This film highlighted Jackson's versatility as he portrayed a crack addict. The role won Jackson various awards including the Cannes Film Festival's Best Supporting Actor Award. Lead rolls in major Hollywood productions continued to propel Jackson's career forward. In the 1990s, appearances in *Jurassic Park*, *Patriot Games*, and the Hughes brothers' *Menace II Society* all brought the actor praise. The height of all of Jackson's success came in his role in the 1994 blockbuster *Pulp Fiction*.

Despite the accolades and success his films produced, Jackson wished to work on-stage again. His wish came true as he was cast as the male lead in the play *Distant Fires*. Demand for Jackson's work has

kept him busy. Movies such as *Die Hard with a Vengeance* and *The Great White Hype* have kept the actor busy in the mid-1990s. In 1999, he starred in the much anticipated prequel to *Star Wars*, *Star Wars: Episode I-The Phantom Menace*.

In 2000, Jackson played a variety of roles, from the lady-loving detective in *Shaft* to the evil genius in *Unbreakable*. He continued to make movies in 2001 with roles in independent films such as *The Caveman's Valentine* and *The 51st State*. Jackson returned to the mainstream in 2002 with blockbuster hits such as *Changing Lanes* with co-star Ben Affleck, and the long awaited *Star Wars: Episode II: Attack of the Clones*.

James Earl Jones (1931–)
Actor

Jones (whose father Robert Earl Jones was featured in the movie *One Potato, Two Potato*) was born in Tate County, Mississippi, on January 17, 1931, and raised by his grandparents on a farm near Jackson, Michigan. He turned to acting after a brief period as a premedical student at the University of Michigan (from which he graduated cum laude in 1953) and upon completion of military service with the Army's Cold Weather Mountain Training Command in Colorado.

After moving to New York, Jones studied at the American Theatre Wing, making his off-Broadway debut in 1957 in *Wedding in Japan*. Since then, he has appeared in numerous plays, on and off-Broadway, including *Sunrise at Campobello* (1958), *The Cool World* (1960), *The Blacks* (1961), *The Blood Knot* (1964), and *Anyone, Anyone*.

Jones's career as an actor progressed slowly until he portrayed Jack Jefferson in the Broadway smash hit *The Great White Hope*. The play was based on the life of Jack Johnson, the first black heavyweight champion. For this performance, Jones received the 1969 Tony Award for the best dramatic actor in a Broadway play and a Drama Desk Award for one of the best performances of the 1968–1969 New York season.

By the 1970s, Jones was appearing in roles traditionally performed by white actors including the title role in *King Lear* and an award-winning performance as Lenny in Steinbeck's *Of Mice and Men*.

In 1978, Jones appeared in the highly controversial *Paul Robeson*, a one-man show on Broadway. Many leading African Americans advocated a boycott of the show because they felt it did not measure up to the man himself. However, many critics gave the show high praise.

In 1980, Jones starred in Athol Fugard's *A Lesson from Aloes*, a top contender for a Tony Award that year.

He also appeared in the Yale Repertory Theater Production of *Hedda Gabler*. In the spring of 1982, he co-starred with Christopher Plummer on Broadway in *Othello*, a production acclaimed as among the best ever done. In 1987, Jones received a Tony award for his performance in August Wilson's Pulitzer Prize-winning play *Fences*.

Jones's early film credits include *Dr. Strangelove* (1964), *River Niger* (1976), and *The Greatest* (1977). He was the screen voice of Darth Vader in *Star Wars* (1977) and its sequels *The Empire Strikes Back* (1980) and *The Return of the Jedi* (1983). Jones has also appeared in the following movies: *Conan the Barbarian* (1982); *Allan Quartermain and the Lost City of Gold* (1986); *Soul Man* (1986); *Matewan* (1987); *Coming to America* (1988); *Field of Dreams* (1989); *Three Fugitives* (1989); *The Hunt for Red October* (1990); *Patriot Games* (1992); *Sommersby* (1993); *The Sandlot* (1993); *Excessive Force* (1993); *The Meteor Man* (1993); *Clean Slate* (1994); *Clear and Present Danger* (1994); *The Lion King* (1994); *Jefferson in Paris* (1995); *Cry, the Beloved Country* (1995); *A Family Thing* (1996); *Fantasia 2000*; and *Finder's Fee* (2001).

Among numerous television appearances, Jones portrayed author Alex Haley in *Roots: The Next Generation* (1979) and has narrated documentaries for the Public Broadcasting System. During the early 1990s, Jones appeared in the television series *Gabriel's Fire* and the television movies *Percy and Thunder* and *The Vernon Johns Story*. He starred in the CBS series *Under One Roof* in 1995 and in the cable television miniseries *The Feast of All Saints* in 2001. Jones is also well known for his voice which has been heard in numerous commercials, including Verizon Wireless, and in promos for the Cable News Network (CNN).

In 1976, Jones was elected to the Board of Governors of the Academy of Motion Picture Arts and Sciences. In 1979, New York City presented him with the "Mayor's Award of Honor for Arts and Culture." He received an honorary Doctorate of Humane Letters from the University of Michigan in 1971 and the New York Man of the Year Award in 1976. In 1985, he was inducted into the Theater Hall of Fame.

Martin Lawrence (1965–)
Comedian, Actor

Martin Lawrence was born in Frankfurt, West Germany, in 1965. He grew up in Landover, Maryland, and would entertain his mother as a child. Intent on achieving stardom, he appeared on the talent forum *Star Search*, but did not immediately meet with success. In New York City's Greenwich Village, he would tell jokes for handouts.

He went to Hollywood and appeared in the sitcom *What's Happening Now!* before being selected for a role in Spike Lee's popular film *Do the Right Thing*. In the early 1990s he appeared in the films *House Party* (1990), *Talkin' Dirty after Dark* (1991), and *Boomerang* (1992).

Lawrence's comedic style earned him his own sitcom *Martin* on network television. In the series, which ran from 1992 to 1997, Lawrence played a disc jockey whose on-air confidence was at odds with his less successful personal life. In addition to playing the title character, Lawrence also played the character's mother and "Shenehneh," an outspoken young woman. For his role, Lawrence won an NAACP Image Award in 1996.

Lawrence continued to appear in movies including *Life* (1999) with co-star Eddie Murphy, *Blue Streak* (1999), *Big Momma's House* (2000), *What's The Worst That Could Happen* (2001) and *Black Knight* (2001).

Canada Lee (1907–1952)
Actor

Canada Lee was born Leonard Corneliou Canagata in Manhattan, New York, on May 3, 1907. After studying violin as a young boy, he ran off to Saratoga to become a jockey. Failing in this endeavor, he returned to New York and began a boxing career. In 1926, after winning 90 out of 100 fights, including the national amateur lightweight title, he turned professional. Over the next few years, he won 175 out of some 200 fights against such top opponents as Jack Britton and Vince Dundee. In 1933, a detached retina brought an end to his ring career. He had acquired the name Canada Lee when a ring announcer could not pronounce his real name.

In 1934, Lee successfully auditioned at the Harlem YMCA for his first acting role which was in a Works Progress Administration production of *Brother Moses*. In 1941, Orson Welles, who had met Lee in the Federal Theatre's all-African American production of *Macbeth*, chose him to play Bigger Thomas in the stage version of Richard Wright's famed novel *Native Son*.

In 1944, Lee served as narrator of a radio series called "New World A-Comin'"—the first such series devoted to racial issues. That same year, he also appeared in Alfred Hitchcock's film *Lifeboat* and in the Broadway play *Anna Lucasta*. He also worked for the NBC radio network as master of ceremonies for various war-related programming.

Lee's political activism eventually ended his career. He campaigned against racism and discriminatory hiring practices. He also signed a petition urging the expulsion of Mississippi racist Theodore Bilbo from the Senate. Eventually, these efforts led to his blacklisting by the Hollywood establishment for suspicion of being a communist agent. In 1950, he starred in the British production of *Cry, the Beloved Country*—the first film to challenge apartheid and the wretched living conditions of blacks in South Africa. However, the emotional stress of the blacklisting affected his health and in 1952, he died of a heart attack.

Spike Lee (1957–)
Filmmaker

Lee was born March 20, 1957, in Atlanta, Georgia. His family moved briefly to Chicago before settling in New York in 1959. Lee received a B.A. in mass communication in 1979 from Morehouse College. After a summer internship at Columbia Pictures in Burbank, California, Lee enrolled in New York University's prestigious Institute of Film and Television. He received an M.A. in filmmaking in 1983. While at New York University he wrote and directed *Joe's Bed-Stuy Barbershop: We Cut Heads* for which he won the 1982 Student Academy award given by the Academy of Motion Picture Arts and Sciences. The movie was later shown on public television's Independent Focus Series.

Spike Lee directing the film *Crooklyn*.

Notable films by Lee include: *She's Gotta Have It* (1986), which resulted in the resurgence of African American cinema; *School Daze* (1988); *Do The Right Thing* (1989); *Mo' Better Blues* (1990); *Jungle Fever* (1991); *Malcolm X* (1992); *Crooklyn* (1994); *Clockers* (1995); *Girl 6* (1996); *He Got Game* (1998); *Summer of Sam* (1999); and *Bamboozled* (2000). In 2002, Lee tried working for the Public Broadcast station when he directed *A Huey P. Newton Story*, created and performed by Roger Guenveur Smith, based on his play. *She's Gotta Have It* won the Los Angeles Film Critics New Generation award and the Prix de Juenesse at the Cannes Film Festival.

Lee has also written two books: *Spike Lee's Gotta Have It: Inside Guerilla Filmmaking* (1987) and *Uplift the Race* (1988). He has established a fellowship for minority filmmakers at New York University and is a trustee of Morehouse College. Lee's production company, Forty Acres and a Mule Filmworks is located in Brooklyn, New York.

Byron Lewis (1931–)
Producer

Byron Lewis was born in Newark, New Jersey. He received his B.A. in 1953 from Long Island University. He founded the Uni-World corporation in 1969. Lewis recognized early the power behind the buying potential of African Americans and ethnic markets. As the marketing agency for accounts that include powerhouse corporations such as Burger King, Mars Inc. and Quaker Oats, Uni-World generated over 200 million dollars in revenue in 1998.

Lewis is the executive producer of the widely syndicated television show *America's Black Forum* and the founder and executive producer of the Acapulco Black Film Festival. Lewis is a member of the National Urban League and has won many honors for his role in advertising and as a producer. Lewis also spends a great deal of time talking with and teaching younger African Americans about the ways in which some companies are using African-American images and music to sell their products to young people.

Hattie McDaniel (1898–1952)
Actress

Hattie McDaniel was born on June 10, 1898, in Wichita, Kansas, and moved to Denver, Colorado, as a child. After a period of singing for Denver radio as an amateur, she entered vaudeville professionally, and by 1924 was a headliner on the Pantages circuit.

By 1931, McDaniel had made her way to Hollywood. After a slow start, during which she supported herself as a maid and washer woman, she gradually began to get more movie roles. Her early film credits include *Judge Priest* (1934), *The Little Colonel* (1935), *Showboat* (1936), *Saratoga* (1937), and *Nothing Sacred.* Her portrayal of a "mammy" figure in *Gone with the Wind,* a role for which she received an Oscar award in 1940 as best supporting actress, is still regarded as a definitive interpretation. McDaniel was the first African American to receive an Oscar award.

McDaniel subsequently appeared in films such as *The Great Lie* (1941), *In This Our Life* (1942), *Johnny Come Lately* (1943), *Since You Went Away* (1944), *Margie* (1946), *Never Say Goodbye* (1946), *Song of the South* (1946), *Mr. Blandings Builds His Dream House* (1948), *Family Honeymoon* (1948), and *The Big Wheel* (1949).

In addition to her movie roles, McDaniel enjoyed success in radio, in the 1930s, as Hi-Hat Hattie and in the 1940s in the title role of the very successful "Beulah" series. McDaniel died on October 26, 1952.

Butterfly McQueen (1911–1995)
Actress

Butterfly McQueen's portrayal of Prissy in *Gone with the Wind* (1939) rivals Hattie McDaniel's Oscar-winning role as the "mammy," and is certainly as popular with audiences as Vivien Leigh's Scarlett O'Hara or Clark Gable's Rhett Butler.

Born Thelma McQueen on January 8, 1911, in Tampa, Florida, McQueen began her career in the 1930s performing as a radio actress in *The Goldbergs, The Danny Kaye Show, The Jack Benny Show,* and *The Beulah Show.* She also appeared on stage in *Brown Sugar* (1937), *Brother Rat* (1937), and *What a Life* (1938).

After her role in *Gone with the Wind* in 1939, McQueen was cast in other motion pictures such as *I Dood It* (1943), *Cabin in the Sky* (1943), *Mildred Pierce* (1945), and *Duel in the Sun* (1947). She appeared as Oriole on the television series *Beulah* from 1950 to 1952.

Given her outspokenness against racism and discrimination and her refusal to play stereotyped servant roles, McQueen's appearances after this period were sporadic. In 1968, she won accolades for her performance in the off-Broadway play *Curley McDimple.* She was cast in the television program *The Seven Wishes of Joanna Peabody* in 1978, and the film *Mosquito Coast* in 1986. McQueen received a B.A. in Spanish from New York City College in 1975.

On December 22, 1995, McQueen died after being critically burned when a kerosene heater in her cottage caught fire.

Oscar Deveraux Micheaux (1884–1951)
Filmmaker, Author

Micheaux was born in 1884 in Metropolis, Illinois. Little is known about his early years other than he left home at 17 and worked briefly as a pullman porter. In 1904 he began homesteading in Gregory County, South Dakota.

Micheaux was a hard-working farmer who loved to read and had a flair for writing. In 1913 he wrote, published, and promoted *The Conquest: Story of a Negro Pioneer.* This novel was followed by *Forged Note: Romance of the Darker Races* in 1915 and *The Homesteader* in 1917. Much of his writing was melodramatic and probably autobiographical.

In 1918 the Lincoln Picture Company, an independent African American film production company, tried to buy the film rights to *The Homesteader.* When Micheaux insisted that he direct the planned movie, the deal fell through. Micheaux went to New York where he formed the Oscar Micheaux Corp. Between 1919 and 1937 Micheaux made about 30 films including *Body and Soul,* a 1924 movie in which Paul Robeson made his first cinematic appearance.

Although Micheaux was an excellent self-promoter of his books and films, his company went into bankruptcy in 1928. By 1931 however, Micheaux was back in the film business producing and directing *The Exile* (1931), and *Veiled Aristocrats* (1932). Between 1941 and 1943 he wrote four more books *Wind From Nowhere, Case of Mrs. Wingate, Masquerade,* and *Story of Dorothy Stansfield.* In 1948 he made his last film *The Betrayal.* While none of Micheaux's films achieved critical acclaim, they were quite popular with black audiences and attracted a limited white following. While his characters broke with the African American stereotypes of the day, the themes of his movies ignored racial injustice and the day-to-day problems of African Americans.

Micheaux was known as a hard worker and a natty dresser who consumed neither alcohol or tobacco. Although he made a great deal of money, all of it was squandered away. Micheaux died penniless in Charlotte, North Carolina. Conflicting dates are given for his death—March 26, 1951 and April 1, 1951.

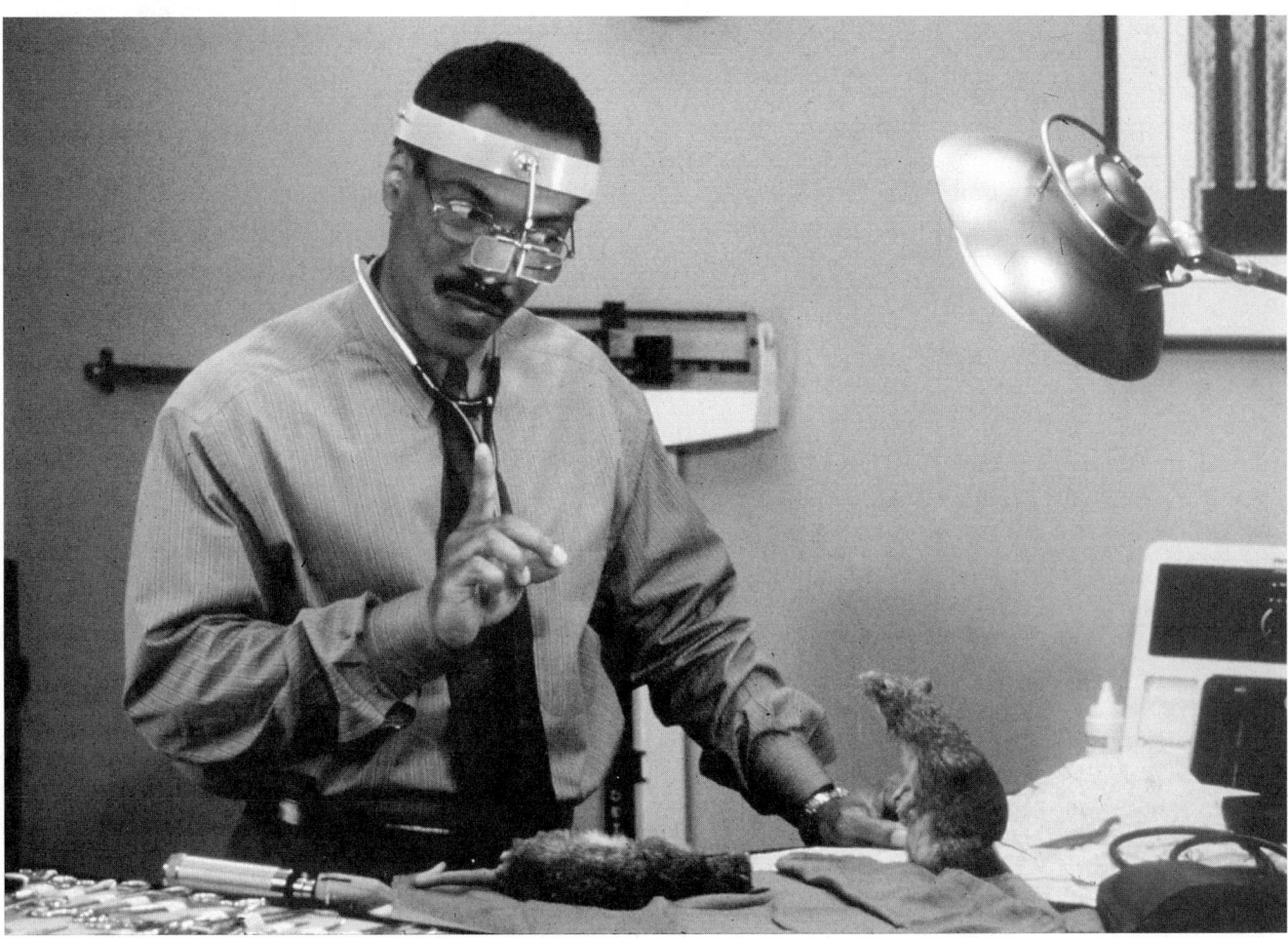

Eddie Murphy as the lead in *Dr. Dolittle*.

Eddie Murphy (1961–)
Actor, Comedian

Eddie Murphy was born on April 3, 1961, in the Bushwick section of Brooklyn, the son of a New York City policeman and amateur comedian. As a youngster, he did imitations of cartoon characters and, as he grew older, began preparing comic routines with impressions of Elvis Presley, Jackie Wilson, Al Green, and the Beatles.

Murphy attended Roosevelt Junior-Senior High School on Long Island and hosted a talent show at the Roosevelt Youth Center before beginning to call local talent agents to secure bookings at Long Island nightclubs. He was a little known stand-up comedian when he made his first appearance on the late-night television show *Saturday Night Live* in 1980. He made a memorable impression, and within three years was hailed as a major new star based on his work in the hit films *48 Hours* (1982) and *Trading Places* (1983).

After his success with the first two Paramount films, Murphy starred in *Beverly Hills Cop* (1985) and its sequel *Beverly Hills Cop II* (1987), which were two of the major box-office hits of the decade. The concert film *Eddie Murphy: Raw* (1987) followed, as well as an effort at light-hearted fantasy *The Golden Child* (1986).

Murphy's film appearances include: *Coming to America* (1988); *Harlem Nights* (1989); *Another 48 Hours* (1990); *Boomerang* (1992); *The Distinguished Gentleman* (1992); *Beverly Hills Cop III* (1994); *Vampire in Brooklyn* (1995); and *Bowfinger* (1999).

In the 1990s, in addition to appearing in the comedies *The Nutty Professor* (1996), *Dr. Dolittle* (1998), and *Life* (1999), Murphy also provided the voice for the main character in television's *The PJs*, an animated sitcom that takes a satirical look at life in a housing project. In 1993, Murphy married model Nicole Mitchell.

In 2000–2001, Murphy capitalized on the success of some of his former movies, staring in *The Nutty Professor II: The Klumps* and *Dr. Dolittle 2*. He also was the voice behind the character of Donkey in the smash animated comedy *Shrek*, for which Murphy was honored with the People's Choice Award for best Comedic Performance in 2002. Murphy continued to stay active in 2002 starring in the movie *Showtime* with Robert De Niro. Murphy also spent time away from Hollywood as he and his wife Nicole, gave birth to their fifth child, daughter Bella Zahra.

Clarence Muse (1889–1979)
Actor, Director

Born on October 14, 1889, Clarence Muse was perhaps best known for his film acting, He was, however, also successful as a director, playwright, and actor on the stage.

The Baltimore native's parents came from Virginia and North Carolina, and his grandfather from Martinique. After studying law at Dickinson University in Pennsylvania, Muse sang as part of a hotel quartet in Palm Beach, Florida. A subsequent job with a stock company took him on tour through the South with his wife and son. Coming to New York, he barely scraped a living together, mostly performing as a vaudevillian.

After several plays with the now-famous Lincoln Theatre group and the Lafayette Players in Harlem, and a Broadway stint in *Dr. Jekyll and Mr. Hyde*, where having white roles played by blacks in white face created quite a controversy, Muse had established himself as an actor and singer.

Muse's first movie role was in *Hearts in Dixie* (1929), produced at the William Fox Studio, in which Muse played a 90-year-old man. Later, he returned to the stage for the role of a butler in the show that was to be called *Under the Virgin Moon*. After Muse wrote the theme song, the title was changed to his *When It's Sleepy Time Down South*. Both the song and the show were hits.

When the Federal Theatre Project in Los Angeles presented Hall Johnson's *Run Little Chillun*, Muse directed the show. After its successful two-year run, Muse made the screen adaption *Way Down South* (1939).

During Muse's career, he appeared in 219 films, and was at one time one of the highest paid African American actors, often portraying faithful servant "Uncle Tom" characters. His movie credits include: *Huckleberry Finn* (1931); *Cabin in the Cotton* (1932); *Count of Monte Cristo* (1934); *So Red the Rose* (1935); *Showboat* (1936); *The Toy Wife* (1938); *The Flame of New Orleans* (1941); *Tales of Manhattan* (1942); *Heaven Can Wait* (1943); *Night and Day* (1946); *An Act of Murder* (1948); *Porgy and Bess* (1959); *Buck and the Preacher* (1971); and *Car Wash* (1976). His last film was *Black Stallion* in 1979. He also appeared over the years in concerts and on radio.

Muse died October 13, 1979, the day before his ninetieth birthday. He had lived in Perris, California on his Muse-a-While Ranch.

Sidney Poitier (1927–)
Actor

Sidney Poitier was born on February 20, 1927, in Miami, but moved to the Bahamas with his family at a very early age. At age 15, he returned to Miami; he later rode freight trains to New York City, where he found employment as a dishwasher. After the attack on Pearl Harbor, he enlisted in the Army and served on active duty for four years.

Back in New York, Poitier auditioned for the American Negro Theater, but was turned down by director Frederick O'Neal. After working diligently to improve his diction, Poitier was accepted in the theater group, receiving acting lessons in exchange for doing backstage chores.

In 1950, Poitier made his Hollywood debut in *No Way Out*, followed by successful appearances in *Cry, the Beloved Country* (1952), *Red Ball Express* (1952), *Go, Man, Go* (1954), *Blackboard Jungle* (1956), *Goodbye, My Lady* (1956), *Edge of the City* (1957), *Band of Angels* (1957), *Something of Value* (1957), and *Porgy and Bess* (1959), among others. Poitier starred on Broadway in 1959 in Lorraine Hansberry's award-winning *Raisin in the Sun*, and repeated this success in the movie version of the play in 1961.

In 1965, Poitier became the first African American to win an Oscar for a starring role, receiving this award for his performance in *Lilies of the Field*. Seven years earlier, Poitier had been the first African American actor nominated for the award for his portrayal of an escaped convict in *The Defiant Ones*.

Subsequent notable film appearances include performances in *To Sir with Love* (1967), *Heat of the Night* (1967), *Guess Who's Coming to Dinner* with Spencer Tracy and Katharine Hepburn (1968), *Buck and the Preacher* (1972), and *A Warm December* (1973), in both of which he acted and directed, *Uptown Saturday Night* (1974), and *A Piece of the Action* (1977). After years of inactivity, Poitier performed in two additional films *Little Nikita* and *Shoot To Kill*, both released in 1988. His directing ventures include *Stir Crazy* with Richard Pryor and Gene Wilder (1980), *Hanky Panky* with Gilda Radner (1982), and the musical *Fast Forward* (1985).

Poitier spent two years writing his memoirs *This Life* published by Knopf in 1980. In 1981, Citadel Press published *The Films of Sidney Poitier* by Alvin H. Marill.

In 1993, Poitier won the Thurgood Marshall Lifetime Achievement Award and the Living Legend Award from the National Black Theater Festival. On December 3, 1995, he was presented with one of the Kennedy Center Honors. In 2000 Poitier received the Screen Actors Guild lifetime achievement award. Poitier diversified his career in 2000 as well by not only writing but recording his second autobiography *The Measure of a Man*. Poitier was awarded a Grammy in 2001 for Best Spoken Word Album for *The Measure of a Man*, from the National Academy of Recording Arts & Sciences. Also in 2001, Poitier received the Hall of Fame Award from the National Association for the Advancement of Colored People (NAACP) at the organization's Image Awards ceremony. Perhaps his biggest honor came in 2002 when the Academy of Motion Picture Arts and Sciences awarded Poitier with a lifetime achievement award for his motion picture career.

Phylicia Rashad (1948–)
Actress

Known to millions as Claire Huxtable from *The Cosby Show*, Phylicia Rashad has led a distinguished acting career on television and the stage. She was born on June 19, 1948, in Houston, Texas, and until 1985 was known as Phylicia Ayers-Allen. Her sister is the famous Debbie Allen; both sisters received early instruction in music, acting, and dance. Phylicia graduated magna cum laude from Howard University in 1970 with a B.F.A. in theater.

Early in her career, Rashad played the character Courtney Wright in the soap opera *One Life to Live*. Her big break came with *The Cosby Show* in which she and Bill Cosby presided over the Huxtable family for seven years, from 1985 to 1992. In 1997, she and Cosby began the new sitcom *Cosby*. Rashad has also appeared in Broadway and off-Broadway productions of *The Cherry Orchard*, *The Wiz*, *Zora*, *Dreamgirls*, *A Raisin in the Sun*, and *Into the Woods*.

Rashad has received two honorary doctorates, one from Providence College in Rhode Island and one from Barber-Scotia College in North Carolina. In 1995, Rashad was named spokesperson for the American Diabetes Association. In 1999, Rashad was honored by the National Council of Negro Women with the Dorothy I. Height Dreammaker Award. In 2001, Rashad and her husband Ahmad Rashad, filed for divorce after 15 years of marriage. This did not slow down Rashad's career, however, as she took to the stage for the PBS production of *The Old Settler* and the critically acclaimed *Blue*.

Chris Rock (1966–)
Comedian, Actor

Chris Rock was born in the late 1960s in Brooklyn, New York. He grew up in the mostly black neighborhood of Bedford-Stuyvesant, but because of a busing policy, he attended school in the predominantly white neighborhood of Bensonhurst. At school Rock had to endure everyday abuse from prejudiced classmates.

Supported by his family, Rock began a stand-up career at a young age. He caught a break when one of his ideals, Eddie Murphy, saw his routine and cast him in *Beverly Hills Cop II*. The role led to another in *I'm Gonna Git You Sucka*, a satire of blaxploitation films of the 1970s. In 1990 Rock auditioned for *Saturday Night Live* and earned a spot on the cast. On the show, Rock became known for his outspoken commentaries during the weekly send-up of the nightly news and for such characters as the talk show host Nat X.

In 1993 Rock left *Saturday Night Live* and became a member of the cast of *In Living Color*. He felt more comfortable on the set of the new show, which provided more opportunities to satirize situations involving African American characters. Unfortunately, the show only lasted for one season with Rock as a member of the cast. After appearing in *CB4* (1993), a movie about the rap industry that he co-wrote, Rock's career entered a dormant period during which his father died. During the off-time, Rock studied the work of other comedians he respected, including Bill Cosby, Eddie Murphy, Richard Pryor, Woody Allen, and Don Rickles.

In the late 1990s Rock found an audience on cable television. He was a popular host of the "MTV Music Video Awards," served as the 1996 presidential election correspondent for Comedy Central's *Politically Incorrect*, and earned two Emmy Awards for his comedy special *Chris Rock: Bring the Pain* (1996). He also has a series, *The Chris Rock Show*, on HBO which won an Emmy for Best Writing in 1999, the same year that Rock played "Rufus," Jesus's 13th apostle, in the controversial Kevin Smith film *Dogma*.

Chris Rock holding two Emmy Awards in 1997.

Between 2000 and 2002, Rock starred in a variety of movies including: *Nurse Betty* (2000); *Down to Earth* (2001); *Pootie Tang* (2001); *Osmosis Jones* (2001); *Jay and Silent Bob Strike Back* (2001); and *Bad Company* (2002).

Richard Roundtree (1942–)
Actor

Richard Roundtree is best known as John Shaft, the tough, renegade detective from the movie *Shaft* (1971). Born in New Rochelle, New York, on July 9, 1942, Roundtree graduated from New Rochelle High School, and attended Southern Illinois University on a football scholarship. After brief stints as a suit salesman and a model, he began a stage career with the Negro Ensemble Company. With *Shaft* (1971) and its sequels *Shaft's Big Score* (1972) and *Shaft in Africa* (1973), Roundtree reached the peak of his career and became a pop icon.

Roundtree subsequently appeared in the films *Embassy* (1972), *Charley One Eye* (1973), *Earthquake* (1974), *Diamonds* (1975), and *Man Friday* (1976). He

appeared in the television miniseries *Roots* (1977) and continues to be cast in various television programs and motion pictures.

In 1995, Roundtree appeared in the films *Seven* and *When We Were Colored*. He has also served as host of the TV show *Cop Files*. He also appeared on the WB network in 1997 in *Rescue 77*, a paramedic-based drama.

In 2000, Roundtree announced that he had fought a seven-year bout with breast cancer and won. Roundtree is now an active member of the American Cancer Society and is working to make people aware of male breast cancer.

John Singleton (1968–)
Filmmaker

Singleton was born in Los Angeles in 1968. After graduating from high school in 1986, he enrolled in the University of Southern California's prestigious Film Writing Program, which is part of their School of Cinema-Television. While there he formed an African

John Singleton.

the 2000 release of the remake of *Shaft*. He followed this up in 2001 with a return to the themes of his college thesis with the critically acclaimed *Baby Boy*.

Will Smith. *See* **Popular Music chapter.**

Wesley Snipes (1962–)
Actor

Born in Orlando, Florida, on July 31, 1962, Wesley Snipes spent his childhood in the Bronx, New York. At the age of 12, he appeared in his first off-Broadway production, a minor role in the play *The Me Nobody Knows*. His interest in dance led him to enroll in New York's High School for the Performing Arts. However, before completing the curriculum, his mother sent him back to Orlando to finish school, where he continued to study drama.

Upon high school graduation, Snipes was awarded a scholarship to study theater at the State University of New York at Purchase. Snipes subsequently appeared in on and off-Broadway productions including Wole Soyinka's *Death and the King's Horsemen*, Emily Mann's *Execution of Justice*, and John Pielmeier's *The Boys of Winter*. He has also appeared in Michael Jackson's video "Bad" and in the HBO production *Vietnam War Story* for which he received cable television's best actor award.

Snipes's film appearances include roles in *Wildcats* (1986), *Streets of Gold* (1986), *Major League* (1989), and *King of New York* (1990). In 1990 Snipes appeared in Spike Lee's *Mo' Better Blues*, with Denzel Washington. This was followed by a role in Mario Van Peebles's *New Jack City* (1991) and in Spike Lee's *Jungle Fever* (1991). His most recent films include *White Men Can't Jump* (1992), *Passenger 57* (1992), *Rising Sun* (1993), *Sugar Hill* (1993), *One Night Stand* (1997), *Blade* (1998), *The Art of War* (2000), *Disappearing Acts* (2000) for HBO, and *Blade 2* (2002).

Robert Townsend (1957–)
Director, Actor

Robert Townsend began his career as an actor with bit parts in such films as *Cooley High* (1975) and *A Soldier's Story* (1984). He was born in Detroit, Michigan, and worked as a stand-up comedian before coming to Hollywood to try acting.

American Film Association and did a six month director's internship for the *Arsenio Hall Show*. He twice won the school's Jack Nicholson Award for best feature length screenplay. Before graduating in 1990, he signed with the well known Creative Artists Agency.

Singleton was soon approached by Columbia Pictures to sell the film rights to *Boyz N the Hood*, his original screenplay and college thesis. Singleton agreed, but only if he would be the movie's director. The movie was released in July of 1991 to mixed critical reviews. Although its first showings were marred by theater violence, it garnered Singleton an Academy Award nomination for best director. He became the first African American and the youngest person to be so honored.

Since *Boyz N the Hood*, Singleton has done a short cable television film for Michael Jackson entitled *Remember the Time*. His second film *Poetic Justice* was released in the summer of 1993. His third film *Higher Learning* was released in 1995 followed the next year by *Rosewood*. Singleton then took a break from movie making as he dealt with his divorce in 1997. Shortly after, Singleton was back in the director's chair with

Wesley Snipes.

In 1987 Townsend responded to the paucity of film roles available to African American actors by creating and financing his own project *Hollywood Shuffle*. The film's success launched Townsend into prominence as a director. Other notable Townsend films include the Eddie Murphy concert film *Eddie Murphy: Raw* (1987), *The Five Heart Beats* (1991), *The Meteor Man* (1993), *B.A.P.S.* (1997); the Lifetime original *Jackie's Back* (1999); and the NBC movie *Little Richard* (2000).

Townsend has won two Cable Ace Awards and multiple NAACP Image Awards. He is best known for his role as the patriarch on the long-running sitcom *Parenthood*. Townsend also served as host on the syndicated variety show *Motown Live*. He had a starring role in the suspense drama *Fraternity Boys*. In 1999 Townsend directed the dramatic trilogy *Love Songs* and the Lifetime cable network made-for-television movie *Jackie's Back*.

Cicely Tyson (1939–)
Actress

During the early 1970s, Cicely Tyson emerged as America's leading black dramatic star. She achieved this through two sterling performances—as Rebecca, the wife of a Southern sharecropper in the film *Sounder* (1972) and as the lead in a television special *The Autobiography of Miss Jane Pittman*, (1974) the story of an ex-slave who, past her 100th year, challenges racist authority by deliberately drinking from a "white only" water fountain as a white deputy sheriff watches.

Cicely Tyson was born in New York City on December 19, 1939, and raised by a very religious, strict mother, who associated movies with sin and forbade Cicely to go to movie theaters. Blessed with poise and natural grace, Tyson became a model and appeared on the cover of America's two foremost fashion magazines *Vogue* and *Harper's Bazaar* in 1956. Interested in acting, she began to study drama and in 1959 appeared on a CBS culture series *Camera Three* with what is believed to be the first natural African hair style worn on television.

Tyson won a role in an off-Broadway production of Jean Genet's *The Blacks* (1961), for which she received the 1962 Vernon Rice Award. She then played a lead part in the CBS series *East Side, West Side*. Tyson subsequently moved into film parts, appearing in *The*

Comedians (1967) and *The Heart Is a Lonely Hunter* (1968). Critical acclaim led to her role as Rebecca in *Sounder* (1972), for which she was nominated for an Academy award and named best actress by the National Society of Film Critics. She won an Emmy television acting trophy for *Jane Pittman* (1974).

Tyson's other film appearances include *The Blue Bird* (1976) and *The River Niger* (1976). On television, she has appeared in *Roots* (1977), *King* (1978), and *Wilma* (1978). She portrayed Harriet Tubman in *A Woman Called Moses*, and Chicago schoolteacher Marva Collins in a made-for-television movie in 1981. Television appearances include *The Women of Brewster Place* (1989). In 1995, Tyson starred in the television series *Sweet Justice*.

In 1979, Marymount College presented Tyson with an honorary Doctor of Fine Arts. Tyson owns a house on Malibu Beach in California. In November 1981, she married jazz trumpeter Miles Davis, but the couple divorced before Davis's death. In 2001 Tyson was honored with a lifetime achievement award at the National Black Theatre Festival.

Melvin Van Peebles (1932–)
Filmmaker, Actor, Writer

Melvin Van Peebles was born on August 21, 1932, in Chicago, Illinois. As a child, Van Peebles's family moved to Phoenix, Illinois, where he graduated from high school. Studying English literature, Van Peebles received his Bachelor in Arts from Wesleyan University in 1953. After spending three and a half years as a flight navigator for the U.S. Air Force, Van Peebles settled in San Francisco.

While in San Francisco, Van Peebles began to dabble in filmmaking. *Three Pickup Men for Herrick*, completed in 1958, is the best known of his early work, but with success in his sight, Van Peebles took his films to Hollywood. Several rejections frustrated Van Peebles, prompting a move to Holland. There Van Peebles's luck changed for a short while. He acted with the Dutch National Theater while studying astronomy at the University of Amsterdam, but troubles with his wife forced Van Peebles to move again. He found a home in Paris, where he wrote several novels in self-taught French.

Experiences in France led to Van Peebles's first international film success. *Story of a Three-Day Pass* (1968) received generally positive criticism as it premiered at the San Francisco International Film Festival. This led to Van Peebles directing a string of films including *Watermelon Man* (1970) and *Sweet Sweetback's Baadasssss Song* (1971) which he wrote, directed, and produced. A smash, the film grossed

nearly $14 million dollars. This film used a mostly black crew and became controversial for its violence, earning an X rating. However, the money the film earned launched the "blaxploitation" film movement in Hollywood.

In 1971, Van Peebles turned his attention toward Broadway. His productions of *Ain't Supposed to Die a Natural Death* and *Don't Play Us Cheap* received mixed reviews. Despite the lack of critical enthusiasm for his work, *Ain't Supposed to Die a Natural Death* closed as the fifth-longest running show on Broadway and *Don't Play Us Cheap* received first prize during a Belgian Festival. Throughout the 1970s, Van Peebles continued to write and direct for films, plays, and television. In 1987, his teleplay *The Day They Came to Arrest the Book* received an Emmy Award.

After a hiatus, Van Peebles returned to directing for the film *Identity Crisis* (1989), featuring his son Mario, who also penned the film. In 1993, the father-son team reversed roles in the film *Posse*, which Mario directed and in which Melvin acted. In the mid-1990s, they continued to develop a variety of projects together including *Panther* (1995), a fictionalized motion picture of the history of The Black Panthers. In 1997, Van Peebles took to the small screen to portray a psychic cook in the remake of Stephen King's *The Shining*.

In 1998, Van Peebles seemed to be everywhere. He served as "honorary president" for the opening of the French Black Roots cultural festival ("Racines Noires '98") organized to coincide with the 150th anniversary of the abolition of slavery in France. He also performed a music-cum-spoken word cabaret show, "Melvin Van Peebles' Roadkill Wid' Brer Soul." In between, Van Peebles continued to work on pre-production and directing for his film *Bellyfull* which came out to rave reviews in 2000. *Bellyfull* won Van Peebles the Acapulco Black Film Festival International Films Competition as well as the Byron E. Lewis Trailblazer award.

Denzel Washington (1954–)
Actor

Born on December 28, 1954, in Mt. Vernon, New York, Denzel Washington attended an upstate private high school, the Oakland Academy, and then entered Fordham University as a pre-med major. Washington did not originally intend to become an actor, but when he auditioned for the lead role in a student production of Eugene O'Neill's *The Emperor Jones*, he won the part over theater majors. His performance in that play, and later in a production of *Othello*, led his drama instructor to encourage Washington to pursue an acting career.

Washington's first major role was in the off-Broadway drama *A Soldier's Story*. Washington re-created his role when the play was adapted into a motion picture in 1984. He played Dr. Phillip Chandler on the television series *St. Elsewhere* and appeared in a string of films including *Carbon Copy* (1980), *Cry Freedom* (in which he portrayed South African activist Steven Biko) (1987), *The Mighty Quinn* (1989), *Glory* which won him an Academy Award for best supporting actor (1989), *Mo' Better Blues* (1990), *Mississippi Masala* (1992), and *Malcolm X* (1992). Washington also starred in *Philadelphia* (1993), playing an attorney for an HIV-positive lawyer played by Oscar winner Tom Hanks. Later, he starred in *Crimson Tide* (1995), *Devil in a Blue Dress* (1995), *Virtuosity* (1995), *Courage Under Fire* (1996), and *He Got Game* (1998).

In 1999, Washington played one of the most important roles of his career as incarcerated boxer Rubin Carter in the movie *The Hurricane*, based on the true story of Rubin "Hurricane" Carter. Washington was honored as the Outstanding Actor for his work in *The Hurricane* at the 31st National Association for the Advancement of Colored People (NAACP) Image Awards. He also received a Golden Globe for best actor in a drama for this role in 2000. Many expected Washington to take the Oscar for best actor as well that year, but he would have to wait another couple of years before he would walk away with that award. In 2001, Washington starred opposite Ethan Hawk in the number-one box office hit *Training Day*. It wasn't long before the awards started to roll in. In 2001 Washington was honored with the best actor award by the Los Angeles Film Critics Association for *Training Day*. Then in 2002, he was awarded the best actor Oscar for *Training Day*, becoming only the second African American to win the award.

In addition to winning two Oscars and a score of Golden Globes, Washington won the Silver Beard Award at the Berlin International Film Festival in 1993. Washington is married to actress Pauletta Pearson.

Damon Wayans (1960–)
Comedian

Damon Wayans was born on September 4, 1960, in New York City. While growing up, Wayans wore leg braces and special shoes to correct problems caused by a foot deformity. As a result, he often found himself teased by fellow classmates. As an adolescent and young adult, he found himself in trouble with the law on a couple of occasions.

In the 1980s Wayans turned to stand-up comedy. His brother Keenan Ivory Wayans was already gaining a following, and Damon quickly became popular on the circuit as well. Headlining appearances in clubs across the country eventually led to his film debut in *Beverly Hills Cop* (1984). In the mid-1980s Wayans was selected as a cast member on *Saturday Night Live*. He returned to stand-up after one year and appeared in several films through the remainder of the 1980s including *Hollywood Shuffle* (1987), *Roxanne* (1987), *Punchline* (1988), and *Earth Girls Are Easy* (1989), in which he starred as one of three aliens.

In the 1990s Wayans joined the cast of *In Living Color*. The show, created by his brother Keenan Ivory Wayans, provided a platform for social commentary. The skits often featured characters that were members of groups that historically faced discrimination. Wayans portrayed a gay movie critic; Homey, a sad-faced, black clown that refused to kowtow to "the [white] man"; and Handyman, a physically challenged superhero.

After three seasons, Wayans left *In Living Color* to pursue film work. He served as the executive producer of *Mo' Money*, a film that he wrote. Wayans also played the main character in the romantic comedy, which tells the story of a man who tries to turn from a life of crime in order to pursue a relationship with a coworker. Wayans appeared in a number of other films in the 1990s including *Major Payne* (1994), *Blankman* (1994), *Celtic Pride* (1996), and *The Great White Hype* (1996). In several of these films, Wayans also served in additional capacities as writer and executive producer.

Wayans returned to television in the 1990s. He created the short-lived drama *413 Hope St.* in 1997 before returning to comedy with *Damon*, a series that reunited him with *In Living Color* co-star David Alan Grier. The series only lasted a year but Wayans was not discouraged. He came back in 2001 with the ABC hit *My Wife and Kids*. The show has been a ratings success and Wayans won the People's Choice Award in 2002 for favorite male performer in a new television series for his acting on the series.

Keenan Ivory Wayans (1958–)
Comedian

Keenan Ivory Wayans was born in New York City on June 8, 1958. He began his career as a stand-up comic at the Improv clubs in New York City and Los Angeles. After appearances on such television series as *Benson*, *Cheers*, *Chips*, and in the movies *Star 80* (1983) and *Hollywood Shuffle* (1987), Wayans struck fame with *I'm Gonna Git You Sucka* (1989)—a hilarious sendup of 1970s "blaxploitation" films—which he wrote and produced. His greatest success was the popular television series *In Living Color*, an irreverent show in which celebrities were often outrageously parodied. *In Living Color* won an Emmy Award in 1990.

Wayans is the oldest of a family of ten; three of his siblings—Damon, Shawn, and Kim—were regulars on *In Living Color*. In the late 1990s he hosted his own television talk show. Most recently, Wayans has been writing and directing the *Scary Movie* trilogy. *Scary Movie* a spoof on horror movies appeared in theaters in 2000 and a year later *Scary Movie 2* followed. Wayans himself appeared in a small role in the first *Scary Movie* and there are rumors that he might show up on screen again in the third installment which is slated to arrive in theaters in 2003.

Billy Dee Williams (1937–)
Actor

A screen, television, and stage actor with impressive credits, Billy Dee Williams has starred in some of the most commercially popular films ever released.

Born William December Williams in Harlem on April 6, 1937, Williams was a withdrawn, overweight youngster who initially planned to become a fashion illustrator. While studying on scholarship at the School of Fine Arts in the National Academy of Design, a CBS casting director helped him secure bit parts in several television shows including "Lamp Unto My Feet" and "Look Up And Live."

Williams then began to study acting under Sidney Poitier and Paul Mann at the Actors Workshop in Harlem. He made his film debut in *The Last Angry Man* (1959), and then appeared on stage in *The Cool World* (1960), *A Taste of Honey* (1960), and *The Blacks* (1962). He later appeared briefly on Broadway in *Hallelujah Baby* (1967) and in several off-Broadway shows including *Ceremonies in Dark Old Men* (1970).

Williams's next major role was in the acclaimed television movie *Brian's Song* (1970), a performance for which he received an Emmy nomination. Motown's Berry Gordy then signed Williams to a seven-year contract after which he starred in *Lady Sings the Blues* (1972) and *Mahogany* (1976) with Diana Ross. His last movie for Gordy was *The Bingo Long Traveling All-Stars and Motor King* (1976).

In the early 1980s, Williams appeared in two of George Lucas's *Star Wars* adventures: *The Empire Strikes Back* (1980) and *Return of the Jedi* (1983). He has appeared in numerous television movies including *Scott Joplin* (1977), *Christmas Lilies of the Field* (1979), and the miniseries *Chiefs*. When he was cast opposite Diahann Carroll in the prime time drama *Dynasty* his reputation as a romantic lead was secured. At the end of the decade, he starred in action films such as *Oceans of Fire* (1986) and *Number One With a Bullet* (1987).

In 1995, Williams played a detective in the TV murder mystery *Falling for You*. He also hosted the Black Theatre Festival in Winston-Salem, North Carolina and the Infiniti Sports Festival. In 1999 he took on another television series *Code Name: Eternity* which only lasted one season. In 2000, Williams began to make a movie comeback starring in such movies as *The Ladies Man* (2000); *The Last Place on Earth* (2000); *Very Heavy Love* (2001); *Good Neighbor* (2001); and *Undercover Brother* (2002). Some of Williams's paintings were featured in a computer screensaver program "Art in the Dark: Extraordinary Works by African American Artists."

Vanessa Williams (1963–)
Model, Singer, Actress

A native of New York City, Vanessa Williams made history in 1983, when she became the first African American woman to be chosen Miss America, and again in 1984, when she was forced to relinquish her title after *Penthouse* published nude photos of her taken years before her crowning.

In the wake of the pageant controversy Williams has gone on to achieve success, signing in 1987 with Mercury/Wing Records. Her debut project *The Right Stuff* achieved gold record status fueled by hit singles such as the titled track and the ballad "Dreamin." More hits have followed in 1992 including "Saving the Best for Last" and "Colors of the Wind," the theme song from the blockbuster Disney animated film *Pocahontas* which went on to win Academy, Golden Globe, and Grammy awards.

Williams made her film debut with *Under the Gun* in 1986, and has gone on to star opposite Arnold Schwarzenegger in *Eraser* (1996) and *Hoodlum*, (1997) alongside Laurence Fishburne. Some of her other notable film roles include the highly successful family drama *Soul Food* (1997) and the romantic dance musical *Dance With Me* (1998). Williams made her Broadway debut in June 1994 in the hit musical *Kiss of the Spider Woman*. On television, Williams has starred in *Stompin' at the Savoy* (1992), *The Jacksons: An American Dream*

(1992), *The Odyssey* (1997), and, most recently, *Don Quixote* (2000). Off screen, Williams gave birth to a baby girl, Sasha Gabriella, in 2000, the first for her and her husband Rick Fox.

Paul Winfield (1941–)
Actor

Born in Los Angeles on May 22, 1941, Paul Winfield grew up in a poor family. Excelling in school, he attended a number of colleges—the University of Portland, Stanford University, Los Angeles City College, and the University of California at Los Angeles—but left UCLA before graduation to pursue his acting career.

Winfield appeared on television shows in the late 1960s and early 1970s—most notably as one of Diahann Carroll's boyfriends in the series *Julia*. His great success in that period was in the film *Sounder* (1972), in which he played a sharecropper father in the nineteenth-century American South. For this role, he received an Academy Award nomination for best actor.

Winfield subsequently appeared in the motion pictures *Gordon's War* (1973), *Conrack* (1974), *Huckleberry Finn* (1974), and *A Hero Ain't Nothing but a Sandwich* (1978). He received accolades for his portrayal of Dr. Martin Luther King Jr. in the NBC movie *King* (1978), for which he received an Emmy nomination. His second Emmy nomination came with his role in the television miniseries *Roots: The Next Generation* (1979).

In the 1980s, Winfield kept busy with appearances on television in *The Charmings*, *The Women of Brewster Place*, *Wiseguy*, and *227*; on film in *Star Trek II: The Wrath of Khan* (1982), *Damnation Alley* (1983), and *The Terminator* (1984); and on the stage in *A Midsummer Night's Dream*, *Othello*, and *The Seagull*. In 1990, he played the sarcastic Judge Larren Lyttle in the movie *Presumed Innocent* and in 1992 appeared on Broadway in the cast of *A Few Good Men*.

Winfield has won several major awards including an NAACP Image Award and election to the Black Filmmakers Hall of Fame. In 1995, Winfield won an Emmy for best guest actor on a drama series for his work in *Picket Fences*, "Enemy Lines." Winfield continued to be active on the large and small screens appearing in movies such as *Mars Attacks!* (1996), *Relax. . . It's Just Sex* (1998), and *Seconds to Die* (2001), and such television series as *Built to Last* (1997) and *Teen Angel* (1997). In 2001, Winfield began to speak publicly about his diabetes and has often been heard encouraging African American men to exercise and to lose weight.

♦ AWARD WINNERS

Academy Awards (Oscars)

Best Performance by an Actor in a Leading Role
1963: Sidney Poitier, in *Lilies of the Field*
2002: Denzel Washington, in *Training Day*

Best Performance by an Actress in a Leading Role
2002: Halle Berry, in *Monster's Ball*

Best Performance by an Actor in a Supporting Role
1982: Louis Gossett Jr., in *An Officer and a Gentleman*
1989: Denzel Washington, in *Glory*
1996: Cuba Gooding Jr., in *Jerry Maguire*

Best Performance by an Actress in a Supporting Role
1939: Hattie McDaniel, in *Gone with the Wind*
1990: Whoopi Goldberg, in *Ghost*

Best Original Score
1984: Prince, for *Purple Rain*
1986: Herbie Hancock, for *'Round Midnight*

Emmy Awards—Primetime

Outstanding Lead Actor in a Drama Series
1966–1968: Bill Cosby, in *I Spy*
1991: James Earl Jones, in *Gabriel's Fire*
1998: Andre Braugher, in *Homicide: Life on the Street*

Outstanding Lead Actor in a Comedy, Variety, or Music Series
1959: Harry Belafonte, in *Tonight with Belafonte*
1985: Robert Guillaume, in *Benson*

Outstanding Lead Actress in a Comedy, Variety, or Music Series
1981: Isabel Sanford, in *The Jeffersons*

Outstanding Lead Actress in a Comedy or Drama Special
1974: Cicely Tyson, in *The Autobiography of Miss Jane Pittman*

Outstanding Lead Actress in a Miniseries or Special
1991: Lynn Whitfield, in *The Josephine Baker Story*
1997: Alfre Woodard, in *Miss Evers' Boys*
2000: Halle Berry, in *Introducing Dorothy Dandridge*

Outstanding Supporting Actor in a Comedy, Variety, or Music Series
1979: Robert Guillaume, in *Soap*

Outstanding Supporting Actor in a Miniseries or Special
1991: James Earl Jones, in *Heatwave*

Outstanding Supporting Actress in a Drama Series
1984: Alfre Woodard, in "Doris in Wonderland" episode of *Hill Street Blues*
1991: Madge Sinclair, in *Gabriel's Fire*
1992: Mary Alice, in *I'll Fly Away*

Outstanding Supporting Actress in a Comedy, Variety, or Music Series
1987: Jackee Harry, in *227*
1988: Jackee Harry, in "The Talk Show" episode of *227*

Outstanding Supporting Actress in a Miniseries or Special
1991: Ruby Dee, in "Decoration Day," *Hallmark Hall of Fame*

Outstanding Directing in a Drama Series
1986: Georg Stanford Brown, in "Parting Shots" episode of *Cagney & Lacey*
1990: Thomas Carter, in "Promises to Keep" episode of *Equal Justice*
1991: Thomas Carter, in "In Confidence" episode of *Equal Justice*
1992: Eric Laneuville, in "All God's Children" episode of *I'll Fly Away*
1999: Paris Barclay, in "Hearts and Souls" episode of *N.Y.P.D. Blue*

Outstanding Producing in a Miniseries or Special
1989: Suzanne de Passe, in *Lonesome Dove*

Outstanding Producing in a Variety, Music, or Comedy Special
1984: Suzanne de Passe, in *Motown 25: Yesterday, Today and Forever*
1985: Suzanne de Passe, in *Motown at the Apollo*

Outstanding Variety, Music, or Comedy Special
1997: *Chris Rock: Bring the Pain*

Outstanding Achievement in Music Composition
1971: Ray Charles, in *The First Nine Months Are the Hardest*
1972: Ray Charles, in *The Funny Side of Marriage*

Outstanding Achievement in Music Composition for a Series
1977: Quincy Jones and Gerald Fried, in *Roots*

Outstanding Choreography
1981: Debbie Allen, for "Come One, Come All" episode of *Fame*
1982: Debbie Allen, for "Class Act" episode of *Fame*
1989: Debbie Allen, for *Motown 30: What's Goin' On!*
1999: Judith Jamison, for *Dance in America: A Hymn for Alvin Ailey (Great Performances)*

Emmy Awards—Daytime

Outstanding Talk Show
1987–89, 1991–92, 1994–1997: *The Oprah Winfrey Show*

Outstanding Talk Show Host
1987: Oprah Winfrey, *The Oprah Winfrey Show*
1991–1996: Oprah Winfrey, *The Oprah Winfrey Show*
1996: Montel Williams, *The Montel Williams Show*
1998: Oprah Winfrey, *The Oprah Winfrey Show*

Sports Awards

Outstanding Sports Personality/Studio Host
1999–2000: James Brown

Outstanding Sports Event Analyst
1997: Joe Morgan

Outstanding Sports Journalism
1995: "Broken Promises" and "Pros and Cons" episodes of *Real Sports with Bryant Gumbel*
1998: "Diamond Buck$" and "Winning at All Costs" episodes of *Real Sports with Bryant Gumbel*

Hall of Fame Award
1992: Bill Cosby
1994: Oprah Winfrey

Drama, Comedy, and Dance

◆ The Origins of African American Performance Art ◆ Minstrelsy
◆ Reclaiming the Black Image: 1890 to 1920
◆ African American Dramatic Theater in the Twentieth Century
◆ African American Musicals in the Twentieth Century
◆ African American Comedy in the Twentieth Century
◆ African American Dance in the Twentieth Century
◆ Stage Actors, Comedians, Choreographers, and Dancers ◆ Award Winners

by Myla Churchill

For more than 200 years, African American performers have appeared on the American stage. Despite the prejudices that they have faced both within the theater community and from the entertainment-seeking public, they have made significant contributions to American performance art. The artistic heritage of today's African American actors, dancers, and comedians can be traced back to the last decades of the eighteenth century.

◆ THE ORIGINS OF AFRICAN AMERICAN PERFORMANCE ART

The Earliest Plays with African American Actors

The first performances by African American actors on the American stage were in plays authored by white playwrights who provided blacks with narrow opportunities to portray shallow characters. Often blacks were cast in the role of the buffoon in order to appeal to the sensibilities of a bigoted public. In 1769, for example, the cast of Lewis Hallam's comedy *The Padlock* included a West Indian slave character named Mongo, who was a clown to be played by a black. Other white-authored plays from the period that depicted blacks in demoralizing roles were *Robinson Crusoe, Harlequin* (1792), and *The Triumph of Love* (1795) by John Randolph, which included the native black character named Sambo. Thus, the earliest appearances of blacks on the American stage were as characters devoid of intellectual and moral sensibilities.

The African Grove Theatre

New York City's free African American community founded the first African American theater in 1821—the African Grove Theatre, located at Mercer and Bleecker streets "in the rear of the one-mile stone on Broadway." A group of amateur African American actors organized by Henry Brown presented *Richard III* at the theater on October 1, 1821. The African Grove Theatre subsequently produced *Othello, Hamlet,* and such lighter works as *Tom and Jerry* and *The Poor Soldier, Obi.*

One of the principal actors at the African Grove Theatre was James Hewlet, a West Indian-born black who distinguished himself in roles in *Othello* and *Richard III.* Hewlet later toured England and billed himself as "The New York and London Colored Comedian." Ira Aldridge, who later distinguished himself as one of the great Shakespearean tragic actors, was also a member of the permanent group that performed at the African Grove Theatre. Aldridge was cast in comic and musical roles as well as in Shakespearean tragedies.

The African Grove Theatre also featured the first play written and produced by an African American. The play was Henry Brown's *The Drama of King Shotaway,* which was presented in June of 1823.

Because of disturbances created by whites in the audience, the local police raided the African Grove Theatre on several occasions. The theater was wrecked by police and hoodlums during one of these raids, which forced its closing in late 1823. The group of black actors affiliated with the African Grove Theatre, determined to preserve their company, continued for several years to present plays at different rented locations throughout New York City.

◆ MINSTRELSY

Talented slaves were among the earliest African American entertainers in colonial and antebellum America. On plantations throughout the South, slave performers—using clappers, jawbones, and blacksmith rasps—danced, sang, and told jokes for the entertainment of their fellow slaves as well as their masters, who often showcased their talents at local gatherings. Some masters hired out talented slaves to perform in traveling troupes.

During the late 1820s and early 1830s, white entertainers, exposed to the artistry of black performers, began to imitate blacks in their routines. Blackening their faces with cork, these white entertainers performed jigs, songs, and jokes with topical allusions to blacks in their lyrics. Thus, the art of minstrelsy as theatrical material was born.

White minstrel troupes in blackface became very popular on the American stage in the 1830s. Among some of the more famous white minstrel performers were Thomas Dartmouth Rice, "Daddy Rice," the original "Jim Crow," Edwin Forrest and Dan Emmett, and the Christy Minstrels.

Some traveling white minstrel troupes used black performers to enhance the authenticity of their productions. One such troupe was the Ethiopian Minstrels, whose star performer was William Henry Lane, an African American dancer who used the stage name "Master Juba." Lane was one of the greatest dancers of his generation. Throughout the United States and England, "Master Juba" was enthusiastically praised by audiences and critics alike. One anonymous English critic, quoted by dance historian Marian Hannah Winter, wrote the following critique of one of Lane's performances:

"Juba exceeded anything ever witnessed in Europe. The style as well as the execution is unlike anything seen in this country. The manner in which he beats time with feet, and the extraordinary command he possesses over them, can only be believed by those who have been present at the exhibition." ("Juba and American Minstrelsy." *Chronicles of the American Dance*, edited by Paul Magriel.)

Although black minstrel troupes began to appear in the 1850s, it was not until after the Civil War that they

Traveling African American minstrels began to appear in the 1850s, serving as a precursor to stage performers.

became established on the American stage. Although black minstrels inherited the negative stereotypes that white minstrels had established, the African American performer won a permanent place on the American stage, providing a training ground for the many black dancers, comedians, singers, and composers to come. Notable among these stage personalities were dancer-comedians Billy Kersands, Bert Williams, Bob Height, Dewey "Pigmeat" Martin, and Ernest Hogan; singers such as Gertrude "Ma" Rainey and Bessie Smith; and composers James Bland and William Christopher Handy. To a great extent, black minstrelsy created a national appreciation for the talent of black stage entertainers, drawing audiences to black shows and other forms of black entertainment for generations to come.

◆ RECLAIMING THE BLACK IMAGE: 1890 TO 1920

By the 1890s, African American producers, writers, and stage performers sought to reform the demeaning images of blacks that were prevalent on the American stage. *The Creole Show*, cast by African American producer Sam Jack in 1891, was the first all-black musical to depart from minstrelsy. *The Creole Show*, which was also notable for its inclusion of a chorus line, premiered in Boston in 1891 and later played at the Chicago World's Fair for the entire season. In 1895, African American producer John W. Ishaw presented *The Octoroon*, another all-black musical that moved away from the minstrel tradition. *Oriental America*, which Ishaw also produced, broke further from minstrel conventions by not closing with the traditional walkaround, but with an operatic medley.

Between 1898 and 1911, 13 all-black musicals opened on Broadway, showcasing the talents of African American musicians, lyricists, directors, producers, and writers.

Trip to Coontown, written and directed by Bob Cole in 1898, completely broke away from the minstrel tradition. The plot of this all-black performance piece was presented completely through music and dance. The first musical produced, written, and performed by African Americans on Broadway, it ushered in a new era for blacks on the American stage.

The highly popular *Clorindy: The Origin of the Cakewalk*, with music by composer Will Marion Cook and lyrics by poet Paul Laurence Dunbar, opened in 1898 at the Casino Roof Garden. Cook engaged the comic-dance duo of Bert Williams and George Walker and built the show around their talents. Comedian-singer Ernest Hogan was also featured. Hogan would later appear on Broadway in both *Rufus Rastus* and *Oyster Man* (1902). Bob Cole, J. Rosamond Johnson, and James Weldon Johnson wrote and performed in *The Shoo-Fly Regiment*, another musical that opened on Broadway in 1902.

Williams and Walker premiered their first Broadway musical, *The Policy Players*, in 1899. This success was followed by the *Sons of Ham*, which played on Broadway for two seasons beginning in September of 1900. Their most famous musical, *In Dahomey*, premiered on Broadway in 1903 and after a long run, toured successfully in England. *The Southerners*, with music by Will Marion Cook, opened on Broadway in 1904 with an interracial cast starring Abbie Mitchell. The Williams and Walker team returned to Broadway in 1906 with a new musical *Abyssinia*, which consistently played to a full house. Williams and Walker appeared in their last Broadway production together entitled *Bandanna Land* in 1908. George Walker fell into ill health after the show closed and died in 1911.

Bert Williams went on to appear in *Mr. Lord of Koal* on Broadway in 1909 and later he was the star comedian performer in the *Ziegfeld Follies*. The last black musical to open on Broadway before the 1920s was *His Honor the Barber* in 1911, with S. H. Dudley in the lead.

Black Vaudeville

The unique world of black vaudeville employed dancers, comics, and pantomimes who, denied access to the American legitimate stage, developed their own revues and routines that reflected the African American popular culture. The white owners of the Theater Owners Booking Association (T.O.B.A.) hired the entertainers to play to black audiences in large and small towns across America from the early 1900s until the Great Depression.

Vaudeville was the stage where dancers such as Bert Williams and Bill "Bojangles" Robinson polished their craft that helped them eventually move into the mainstream white theater. Comic Dewey "Pigmeat" Markham developed his legendary "Here Come Da Judge" routine. Tim Moore was wildly popular, later to be seen on "Amos n' Andy" as the incorrigible "Kingfish."

The cakewalk, a dance of slave origin, was said to be a parody of the showy party manners of slave owner families, but its mimicry delighted the masters and mistresses. The cakewalk became a national and worldwide rage at the end of the nineteenth century, even though the black bourgeoisie condemned it as vulgar.

Just as the cakewalk was developed to make fun of a white dancing style, ragtime was a response to European classical music. Ragtime was derived from minstrel show tunes and New Orleans street marches. Pianists Ben Harvey and Scott Joplin made its distinctive rhythmic syncopation popular in the 1890s. One of the earliest examples of the form is the "Harlem Rag" of 1895.

Humor was used to cope with the pain and frustration of everyday life. Markham's "Here Come Da Judge" routine was a critical farce on a legal system that afforded no justice or protection for African Americans. Ventriloquist Johnnie Woods with his sidekick Little Henry played the circuit as a dapper, prosperous gentleman berating and chiding the incorrigible dummy, dressed in a red check suit with bad manners and poor breeding. These comedy styles were later imitated by white performers such as Eddie Cantor, Al Jolson, and Abbott and Costello, who were a success on the white stage where blacks were not allowed.

What white folks derided as demeaning and vulgar became grist for the comic and satiric black player. They took the white notions of low-class and made a joke of it. The subject of race on the black stage was

The successful vaudeville team of Bert Williams (left) and George Walker.

ground for debate, commiseration, derision, and mockery. But they also condemned bad manners and attitudes among themselves.

Although black performers were often able to bridge the gap from folk and vaudeville entertainment to the musical classics and drama, white audiences typically expected them to restrict themselves to the more "Negroid" comedy routines and minstrel styles. However, the privileged few of high society saw some of the best of the black players at the "colored clubs" such as the Cotton Club, Connie's Inn, and the Club Alabam' in New York. The Cotton Club boasted a Chorus Line of "tall, tan and terrific" black women as well as the hottest black entertainment.

The Black Performer in Europe 1900 to 1920

Many black performers who struggled on the American circuit found great success in Europe. The "black craze" of African American art, music, and dance took Paris by storm in the 1920s. Ballroom dancers such as Fredi Washington and Al Moore, the singers Bessie Smith and Josephine Baker, and producers such as Claude Hopkins found a receptive audience amongst "Roaring Twenties" Parisians. Europe was not as color-conscious as the United States. The elegant and refined Washington and Moore were so light-skinned that they were not totally accepted on the black circuit with their "white style" act. However, Europe welcomed their sophisticated artistry and style.

Hopkins introduced singer Josephine Baker to Paris where she developed her flamboyant and provocative act before appreciative Europeans. In the Folies Bergère, Baker pushed the boundaries of nudity and innuendo in her singing and dancing, and she remained an international sensation throughout her career.

The dancer and pantomime Johnny Hudgins was an enormous hit with black and white audiences both in the United States and Europe. He was filmed by Jean Renoir in a short entitled *Charleston* in the 1920s, which left behind a detailed account of his act. His characters included the Ballroom Dancer, the Ice Skater, and the Pullman Porter. One of his more notable numbers involved him performing the Charleston in a lady's feather-plumed straw hat.

◆ AFRICAN AMERICAN DRAMATIC THEATER IN THE TWENTIETH CENTURY

The Dramatic Theater from 1900 to 1940

Black actors on the American dramatic stage, like the performers in all-black musicals, struggled to shed the demeaning image of the African American projected by most white-produced minstrelsy and drama. The presentation of three plays—*The Rider of Dreams*, *Granny Maumee*, and *Simon the Cyrenian*—by white playwright Ridgely Torrence at the Garden Theatre in Madison Square Garden on April 5, 1917, was an exceptional and highly successful effort to objectively portray the African American on the dramatic stage.

During the Harlem Renaissance years, the African American dramatic actor remained less active than the black performer in musicals, and the image of blacks projected by white playwrights was generally inadequate. For example, although Charles Gilpin starred in Eugene O'Neill's *The Emperor Jones* at the Provincetown Theatre in 1920, critic Loften Mitchell noted that:

> This play, while offering one of the most magnificent roles for a Negro in the American theater, is the first in a long line to deal with the Negro on this level. O'Neill obviously saw in the Negro rich subject matter, but he was either incapable or unwilling to deal directly with the matter. (*Black Drama, the Story of the American Negro in the Theatre*, 1967.)

Nonetheless, African American actors and actresses had to accept the roles in which they were cast by white playwrights. In 1924, the O'Neill play *All God's Chillun' Got Wings* opened at the Provincetown Theatre with Paul Robeson and Mary Blair to mixed reviews because of its interracial theme. Rose McClendon starred in Paul Green's Pulitzer Prize-winning *In Abraham's Bosom* in 1926 and was ably supported by Abbie Mitchell and Jules Bledsoe. Marc Connelly's *Green Pastures* opened on Broadway on February 26, 1930; with Richard B. Harrison playing "De Lawd," it ran for 557 performances and was taken on an extensive road tour.

In the 1930's, Langston Hughes brought the African American voice to the stage. Three of his plays were produced successfully on Broadway. *Mulatto*, which opened in 1935, starred Rose McClendon and Morris McKenney, and had the longest Broadway run of any play written by an African American in the history of the American theater with 373 consecutive performances. The other two plays were *Little Ham* (1935) and *Troubled Island* (1936).

The Federal Theater Project

In the mid-1930s, the Works Progress Administration (WPA) sponsored one of the greatest organized efforts to assist and encourage American actors, especially African American actors. The Federal Theater Project employed a total of 851 African American actors to work in 16 segregated units of the project in Chicago, New York, and other cities from 1935 until 1939, when Congress ended the project. While the project was in operation, African American actors appeared in 75 plays including classics, vaudeville routines, contemporary comedies, children's shows, circuses, and "living newspaper" performances. Notable among the African American actors who worked in the project—and later became stars on Broadway and in film—were Butterfly McQueen, Canada Lee, Rex Ingram, Katherine Dunham, Edna Thomas, Thomas Anderson, and Arthur Dooley Wilson.

In the wake of the Federal Theater Project, The American Negro Theater was established in Harlem by Abram Hill, Austin Briggs-Hall, Frederick O'Neal, and Hattie King-Reeves. Its objective was to authentically portray African American life and to give African American actors and playwrights a forum for their talents. Some of their productions eventually made it to Broadway. In 1944, the theater produced *Anna Lucasta* in the basement of the 135th Street Library in Harlem. It was successful enough to move to Broadway and featured Hilda Simms, Frederick O'Neal, Alice Childress, Alvin Childress, Earle Hyman, and Herbert Henry. Abram Hill's *Walk Hard* opened in Harlem in 1946 and became a Broadway production with Maxwell Glanville in the lead. The American Negro Theater provided a training ground for many African American actors who later became stars on Broadway and in Hollywood including Ruby Dee, Ossie Davis, Harry Belafonte, and Sidney Poitier.

Dramatic Theater in the 1950s

The rise of television in the 1950s generally had an adverse affect on the American theater. Employment for all actors fell sharply, especially for African American actors. Ethel Waters did, however, open on Broadway in 1950 as the lead in *Member of the Wedding*, which was well-received. Louis Peterson's *Take a Giant*

Step opened on Broadway in September of 1953 to critical praise; in the cast were Frederick O'Neal, Helen Martin, Maxwell Glanville, Pauline Myers, Estelle Evans, and Louis Gossett Jr.

One of the most successful all-black plays to appear on Broadway opened in March of 1959: Lorraine Hansberry's *Raisin in the Sun*, which won the New York Drama Critics Circle Award. It was directed by the legendary African American director Lloyd Richards. Its cast included Sidney Poitier, Ruby Dee, Diana Sands, Claudia McNeil, Louis Gossett Jr., Ivan Dixon, Lonnie Elder III, and Douglas Turner Ward. Lorraine Hansberry was hailed a pioneer that paved the way for African American political and social playwrights.

The Dramatic Theater Since 1960

As the Civil Rights movement challenged the national conscience in the 1960s, every facet of African American life changed, including black performing arts. More plays about African Americans by both black and white playwrights were produced, providing increased employment for black actors.

On May 4, 1961, *The Blacks*, by French playwright/author Jean Genet, opened Off-Broadway at the St. Mark's Theater. A play about black Americans written for white audiences, *The Blacks* provided employment for a host of African American actors including Roscoe Lee Browne, James Earl Jones, Louis Gossett Jr., Helen Martin, Cicely Tyson, Godfrey Cambridge, Raymond St. Jacques, Maya Angelou, Charles Gordone, and many others who appeared in its road tours. Subsequently, African American dramatic actors appeared on and Off-Broadway in several major plays by white playwrights. Notable among them were: *In White America* by Judith Rutherford Marechal (1968), with Gloria Foster and Moses Gunn; *The Great White Hope* by William Sackler (1968), starring James Earl Jones; and *So Nice, They Named It Twice* by Neil Harris (1975), featuring Bill Jay and Veronica Redd.

On May 23, 1961, when the Leroi Jones play *The Dutchman* opened at the Cherry Lane Theatre, the black revolutionary play was introduced to theater audiences. African American actors were provided with the opportunity to perform in roles that not only affirmed blackness, but portrayed black political militancy. Several black revolutionary plays followed that afforded opportunities for African American actors including James Baldwin's *Blues for Mr. Charlie* (1964), with Al Freeman Jr. and Diana Sands; and *The Toilet/The Slave*, (1964) by Leroi Jones, starring James Spruill, Walter Jones, Nan Martin, and Al Freeman Jr.

That same year, Jones (Imamu Amiri Baraka) founded the Black Arts Repertory Theatre/School to make theater more accessible by "taking it to the streets." The objective was to promote interaction between the artists and the audience. Baraka and many other playwrights, poets and essayists believed that their primary responsibility was to create work for and about African American people. This philosophy evolved into the Black Arts Movement (BAM). Artists of the BAM raged against theatrical convention and mandated that the only art of worth reflected the cultural, social and political concerns of their communities. In addition to Baraka, some of the award-winning playwrights of the BAM were Ed Bullins, *The Taking of Miss Janie*(1975); Richard Wesley, *The Black Terror* (1972); Sonia Sanchez, *Next Stop the Bronx* (1968), and Adrienne Kennedy, *The Funnyhouse of the Negro* (1964).

The dissident voices of the Black Arts Movement gave rise to a wave of black regional theater companies; such as the Crossroads Theatre in New Jersey; Freedom Theatre in Philadelphia; the Penumbra Theatre in Minnesota; The New Federal Theatre in New York; the Inner City Cultural Center in Los Angeles; Jomandi Productions in Atlanta and the St. Louis Repertory Theatre to name a few. Their focus was to foster the development of playwrights, actors, managers and technicians and to provide the African American community with plays steeped in a cultural context.

The most venerable institution of this Black Theatre Movement was the Negro Ensemble Company (NEC) founded in New York in 1967. This theatrical production company, initially financed by a three-year grant of $1.2 million from the Ford Foundation, was the brainchild of playwright/actor Douglas Turner Ward. Originally housed at the St. Mark's Theater, the company moved to Theater Four. Actor Robert Hooks served as executive director, Gerald Krone as administrative director, and Douglas Turner Ward as artistic director.

The Negro Ensemble staged more than 100 productions and featured the work of many black playwrights including Nobel laureates, Wole Soyinka and Derek Wolcott. The three plays went to Broadway under Ward's direction: Joseph A. Walker's Tony Award-winning drama, *The River Niger* (1973); Leslie Lee's Obie winner, *The First Breeze of Summer* (1975); and Samm-Art Williams' Tony-nominated play, *Home* (1980). NEC also produced Charles Fuller's *A Soldier's Play* (1981), which won a Pulitzer Prize and was adapted into *A Soldier's Story* (1984), a film starring Denzel Washington. Negro Ensemble provided work for a plethora of outstanding African American actors and actresses including Louis Gossett Jr., Charles Brown, Denise Nicholas, Phylicia Rashad, Esther Rolle, Roxie

Roker, Michele Shay, Adolph Ceasar, Frances and Gloria Foster, Moses Gunn and Barbara Montgomery.

Independent of the Negro Ensemble Company, several African American playwrights had plays successfully produced on Broadway. Ntozake Shange's widely acclaimed *For Colored Girls Who Have Considered Suicide/When the Rainbow Is Enuf* (1972) had a cast of seven African American actresses. August Wilson's *Fences*, which opened on March 26, 1987, featured James Earl Jones and won the 1987 Pulitzer Prize in Drama. Wilson's *Two Trains Running*, starred Roscoe Lee Browne and Laurence Fishburne, and received the New York Drama Critic's Award for 1992. *The Piano Lesson*, which opened in 1990, earned Wilson his second Pulitzer Prize, and his *Seven Guitars* premiered in 1996. In 2001, Wilson's *King Hedley* boasted six nominations and a Tony Award for Viola Davis as Best Featured Actress in a Play. Wilson was one of the strongest African American voices in theater at the end of the twentieth century and his influence laid the groundwork for many of the resonant voices in the twenty-first.

Suzan-Lori Parks's *Topdog/Underdog* won the 2002 Pulitzer Prize in Drama under the direction of George C. Wolfe. *Topdog* garnered Tony nominations for the playwright and Broadway star Jeffrey Wright, who won a Tony in 1994 for Best Featured Actor in *Angels in America: Perestroika* also directed by Wolfe.

Other burgeoning playwrights include, Cheryl West (*Play On!*), Regina Taylor (*Oo-Bla-Dee*), Charles Randolph-White (*Blue*) and Keith Glover (*Thunder Knocking On The Door*).

◆ AFRICAN AMERICAN MUSICALS IN THE TWENTIETH CENTURY

Between 1898 and 1911, 13 all-black musicals opened on Broadway. The performances showcased the talents of Ernest Hogan and the comic-dance duo of George Walker and Bert Williams. For nearly a decade after the close of *His Honor the Barber* though, the Broadway stage did not carry exclusively African American musicals.

On May 23, 1921, *Shuffle Along* signaled the return of black musicals to "The Great White Way" and the arrival of the Harlem Renaissance on the American stage. Featuring the talented singer-dancer Florence Mills, *Shuffle Along* was written by Noble Sissle, Eubie Blake, Flournoy Miller, and Aubrey Lyles. Mills quickly became a sought-after performer, appearing in *The Plantation Revue*, which opened on Broadway on July 17, 1922, and later toured England. In 1926, Mills returned to Harlem and played the lead in *Black Birds* at the Alhambra Theatre for a six-week run. Subsequently, Mills performed in Paris for six months.

Noble Sissle and Eubie Blake returned to Broadway on September 24, 1924, with their new musical *Chocolate Dandies*. In 1926, Flournoy Miller and Aubrey Lyles opened on Broadway in *Runnin' Wild*, which introduced the Charleston to the country. Bill "Bojangles" Robinson, starring in *Blackbirds of 1928*, dazzled Broadway audiences with his exciting tap dancing style. Miller and Lyles mounted several other black musicals on Broadway during the 1920s, including *Rang Tang* (1927) and *Keep Shufflin'* (1928), with musical numbers staged by Harlem's preeminent choreographer Leonard Harper. Harper conceived and staged *Hot Chocolates* in 1929, with music composed by Fats Waller and lyrics by Andy Razaf. *Hot Chocolates* introduced the songs "Ain't Misbehavin'" and "Black and Blue," as well as Broadway newcomers Cab Calloway and Louis Armstrong.

Porgy and Bess, opening on Broadway in 1935, became the major all-black musical production of the 1930s. With music by George Gershwin, this adaptation of the novel and play by DuBose and Dorothy Heyward was an immediate success as a folk opera. Todd Duncan was cast as Porgy, with Ann Brown as Bess, and comedian-dancer John Bubbles as the character Sportin' Life.

In the 1940s, black musicals were scarce on Broadway. *Cabin in the Sky*, starring Ethel Waters, Dooley Wilson, Todd Duncan, Rex Ingram, J. Rosamond Johnson, and Katherine Dunham and her dancers, ran for 165 performances after it opened on October 25, 1940. *Carmen Jones*, perhaps the most successful all-black musical of the decade, opened in 1943 with Luther Saxon, Napoleon Reed, Carlotta Franzel, and Cozy Cove; it had a run of 231 performances and was taken on tour. In 1946 *St. Louis Woman*, featuring Rex Ingram, Pearl Bailey, Juanita Hall, and June Hawkins, played a short run to mixed reviews.

The years from 1961 to the mid-1980s constituted one of the most active periods for African American performers in musical theater. Many of the black musicals produced during these years, both on and Off-Broadway, enjoyed substantial runs and extended road tours.

Langston Hughes's musical *Black Nativity* opened on Broadway on December 11, 1961. Directed by Vinnette Carroll, the cast was headed by gospel singers Marion Williams and the Stars of Faith and also featured Alex Bradford, Clive Thompson, Cleo Quitman, and Carl Ford. Although it ran for only 57 performances on Broadway, it went on to tour extensively throughout the United States and abroad.

August Wilson won his second Pulitzer Prize for *The Piano Lesson*.

In 1964, Sammy Davis Jr. dazzled Broadway in Clifford Odets's *Golden Boy*. Davis was supported by a brilliant cast which included Robert Guillaume, Louis Gossett Jr., Lola Falana, and Billy Daniels. *Golden Boy* ran for 586 performances.

Leslie Uggams and Robert Hooks appeared in *Hallelujah Baby*, which opened in New York's Martin Beck Theater on April 26, 1967. *Hallelujah Baby*, a musical look at five decades of black history, received a Tony Award and ran for 293 performances.

Purlie, based on Ossie Davis's 1961 play *Purlie Victorious* opened on May 9, 1970, with Melba Moore and Robert Guillaume in lead roles. *Purlie* received good reviews and enjoyed a run of 688 performances.

Micki Grant's *Don't Bother Me, I Can't Cope*, starring Micki Grant and Alex Bradford, opened on April 19, 1972, to rave reviews. For this musical, which ran for 1,065 performances, Micki Grant received a Drama Desk Award and an Obie Award.

Virginia Capers, Joe Morton, and Helen Martin opened *Raisin*, based on Lorraine Hansberry's play *Raisin in the Sun* on October 13, 1973. *Raisin* received the Tony Award for the best musical in 1974 and had a run of 847 performances.

Despite initially poor reviews, *The Wiz*, a black musical version of *The Wizard of Oz*, became a highly successful show. Opening on Broadway on January 5, 1975, *The Wiz* featured an array of talented performers including Stephanie Mills, Hinton Battle, Ted Ross, Andre De Shields, Dee Dee Bridgewater, and Mabel King. *The Wiz* swept the Tony Award ceremonies in 1975 and became the longest-running black musical in the history of Broadway with 1,672 performances.

Ain't Misbehavin', another popular black musical of the 1970s, opened on May 8, 1978. Based on a cavalcade of songs composed by Thomas "Fats" Waller, *Ain't Misbehavin'* starred Nell Carter, Andre DeShields, Armelia McQueen, Ken Page, and Charlaine Woodard. It played to Broadway audiences for 1,604 performances, and Nell Carter received a Tony Award as Best Featured Actress.

Three spectacular black musicals premiered on Broadway in the 1980s. *Dream Girls*, which opened at the Imperial Theater on December 20, 1981, captivated Broadway audiences with a cast that included Obba Babatunde, Ben Harney, Cleavant Derricks, Loretta Devine, Jennifer Holiday, and Sheryl Lee Ralph. *Dream Girls* ran for 1,522 performances on Broadway and had an extensive road tour. Ben Harney and Jennifer Holiday won Tony Awards for Best Actor/Actress in a Musical. On April 27, 1986, Debbie Allen opened in the lead role of *Sweet Charity*. Reviews were favorable and the musical enjoyed a run of 386 performances, establishing Debbie Allen as a musical theater actress. *Black and Blue* opened on January 26,1989 at the Minskoff Theatre. The show was reminiscent of a 1920's musical revue, spotlighting the illustrious composers of that era. *Black and Blue* ran for 829 performances and won three Tony Awards including Best Actress in a Musical for blues singer, Ruth Brown.

A few new all-black musicals opened in the early 1990s including *Five Guys Named Moe*, a tribute to musician Louis Jordan with Clarke Peters and Charles Augin; *Once On This Island*, a star-crossed love story set in the French Antilles that earned eight 1991 Tony nominations; and *Jelly's Last Jam*, featured Tonya Pinkins who won a Tony Award for Best Featured Actress and Gregory Hines as Jelly Roll Morton won the Tony for Best Actor in a Musical in 1992.

Young African American musical stars hit it big on Broadway in the 1990s. The monumental hit *Bring in 'Da Noise, Bring in 'Da Funk* opened in 1995 starring young tap wizard Savion Glover and directed by George C. Wolfe. It celebrated 300 years of African American history in poetry, music, song and dance. The musical won four 1996 Tony Awards, including one each for Glover and Wolfe and one for Ann Duquesnay as Best Featured Actress for her role as 'Da Singer. *Noise/Funk* continued a long run on Broadway while mounting a highly successful touring company.

A lavish production of *Carousel* opened on Broadway in 1994 in which a young African American actress and singer, Audra McDonald, won a Tony Award as Best Featured Actress in a Musical. She won her second Tony in 1996 for a dramatic role in *The Master Class*; then starred in the musical *Ragtime* and in 1998 and won a third Tony for featured performance.

Lillias White and Chuck Cooper won Best Featured Actress/Actor for their performances in *The Life*, a popular musical which garnered 12 Tony nominations in 1997.

African American choreographer Garth Fagan won the Tony Award for his work on the Disney-produced spectacle *The Lion King*, which also took the Tony for Best Musical in 1998.

In 2000, two African Americans captured the Tony Awards for Best Actress/Best Actor. Heather Headley won for her title role in the musical adaptation of Verdi's opera *Aida*, and Brian Stokes Mitchell won Best Actor in a revival of *Kiss Me Kate*.

◆ AFRICAN AMERICAN COMEDY IN THE TWENTIETH CENTURY

The earliest black comedians in America, like other early black entertainers, were slaves who in their free time entertained themselves and their masters. In the early minstrel shows, white comedians in blackface created comic caricatures of blacks, whom they referred to as "coons." When African Americans began appearing in minstrel shows shortly after the Civil War, they found themselves burdened with the "coon" comic caricatures created by white performers. The dance-comedy team of Bert Williams and George Walker were the most famous of the early black comedians, appearing in numerous black musicals between 1899 and 1909.

In the all-black musicals of the 1920s, a new comic movement emerged: the comedy of style which emphasized such antics as rolling the eyes or shaking the hips. The venom and bite of black folk humor was replaced by a comedy of style that was more acceptable to the white audiences of these all-black musicals.

Real black folk humor, however, did survive and thrive in black nightclubs and black theaters such as the Apollo in Harlem and the Regal in Chicago in the 1930s, 1940s, and 1950s. In these settings, known as the "Chitterlin' Circuit," such African American comedians as Tim Moore, Dusty Fletcher, Butterbeans and Susie, Stepin Fetchit, Jackie "Moms" Mabley, Redd Foxx, and Slappy White performed without restrictions.

African American comedians enjoyed greater exposure during the 1960s. No longer confined to the "Chitterlin' Circuit," comedians such as Jackie "Moms" Mabley, Redd Foxx, and Slappy White began to perform to audiences in exclusive white clubs as well as to audiences within the black community. They used black folk humor to comment on politics, civil rights, work, sex, and a variety of other subjects. Jackie "Moms" Mabley made two popular recordings: *Moms*

Savion Glover performs with *Bring in 'Da Noise, Bring in 'Da Funk* fellow cast members.

Mabley at the UN and *Moms Mabley at the Geneva Conference.* In January of 1972, Redd Foxx premiered on television as Fred Sanford in *Sanford and Son,* which remained popular in syndication.

Several younger African American comedians came into prominence in the early 1960s. Dick Gregory used black folk humor to make political commentary. Bill Cosby specialized in amusing chronicles about boyhood in America. Godfrey Cambridge, although successful, did not rely on black folk humor. During the late 1960s and the early 1970s, Flip Wilson, who parodied historical and social experience by creating black characters who lived in a black world, became extremely popular on television. His cast of characters, which included "Freddy the Playboy," "Sammy the White House Janitor," and "Geraldine," were the epitome of black folk humor as commentary on an array of issues.

Another pivotal African American comedian who began his career in the 1960s was Richard Pryor. His well-timed, risque, sharp folk humor quickly won him a large group of faithful fans. Pryor, who has recorded extensively, also starred successfully in several

films including *Lady Sings the Blues, Car Wash,* and *Stir Crazy.*

During the 1980s, numerous African American comedians became successful in the various entertainment media. Eddie Murphy made his first appearance on the television show *Saturday Night Live* on November 15, 1980. From television, Murphy went on to Hollywood, making his movie debut in the film *48 Hours* in 1982. Starring roles followed in such films as *Beverly Hills Cop,* which was the highest-grossing comedy film in history, and *Trading Places.* Murphy established his own company, Eddie Murphy Productions, to create and produce television and film projects. His recent projects include sequels to his box office hits, *The Nutty Professor* and *Dr. Dolittle.* In 1988, Arsenio Hall was featured with Eddie Murphy in the film *Coming to America* and hosted his own highly successful late-night talk show. Hall came to prominence in 1987 as a successful interim guest host on the *The Late Show.*

After achieving success on the stand-up circuit, several African Americans earned opportunities on television and in films in the 1990s. Keenan Ivory

Wayans and his brother Damon starred with several of their siblings in the critically acclaimed sketch-comedy show *In Living Color*, which provided a vehicle for social commentary. Martin Lawrence appealed to audiences in a self-titled television show that featured him performing not only as himself but also as his mother and another female character, Sheneneh. Chris Rock gained popularity on *Saturday Night Live* with brash, politically-informed characters that helped him earn roles in such movies as *Lethal Weapon 4* (1998), *Dogma* (1999) and *Nurse Betty* (2000). He won a 2000 Grammy Award for his comedy album *Bigger & Blacker* and Rock's HBO program, *The Chris Rock Show* won an Emmy for Best Writing.

Steve Harvey, Bernie Mac, D.L. Hughley and Cedric the Entertainer reign as "The Original Kings of Comedy." Their two-year comedy tour was the most successful in history. It grossed $37 million for the comedians and their promoter, Walter Latham, and brought them to the attention of Spike Lee. In 2000, he produced a documentary of the tour that propelled the "Kings" into the forefront of mainstream media. In 2002, *Cedric the Entertainer Presents* will follow Bernie Mac in the FOX fall line-up, joining the ranks of comedians with self-titled sitcoms.

◆ AFRICAN AMERICAN DANCE IN THE TWENTIETH CENTURY

Black dance, like other forms of black entertainment, had its beginnings in Africa and on the plantations of early America, where slaves performed to entertain themselves and their masters. White minstrels in blackface incorporated many of these black dance inventions into their shows, while dancers in black minstrelsy like "Master Juba" (William Henry Lane) thrilled audiences with their artistry.

Many performers in the early black musicals that appeared on Broadway from 1898 through 1910 were expert show dancers, such as George Walker and Bert Williams. Similarly, in the all-black musicals of the 1920s, performers such as Florence Mills and Bill "Bojangles" Robinson captivated audiences with their show dancing. The musical *Runnin' Wild* (1926) was responsible for creating the Charleston dance craze of the "Roaring Twenties."

By the early 1930s, African American pioneers of modern dance were appearing on the dance stage. Four of these African American innovators were Hemsley Winfield, Asadata Dafore, Katherine Dunham, and Pearl Primus.

Hemsley Winfield presented what was billed as "The First Negro Concert in America" in Manhattan's Chanin Building on April 31, 1931. Two suites on African themes were performed, along with solos by Edna Guy and Winfield himself. In 1933, Winfield became the first African American to dance for the Metropolitan Opera, performing the role of the Witch Doctor in *The Emperor Jones*.

Austin Asadata Dafore Horton, a native of Sierra Leone, electrified audiences in New York with his 1934 production of *Kykunkor*. Dance historian Lynne Fauley Emery concluded that *Kykunkor* "was the first performance by black dancers on the concert stage which was entirely successful. It revealed the potential of ethnic material to black dancers, and herein lay Dafore's value as a great influence on black concert dance" (1988, *Black Dance from 1619 to Today*).

Katherine Dunham had her first lead dance role in Ruth Page's West Indian ballet *La Guiablesse* in 1933. In 1936, Dunham received a master's degree in anthropology from the University of Chicago; her thesis *The Dances of Haiti* was the result of her on-site study of native dances in the West Indies. For the next 30 years, Dunham and her dance company toured the United

Dancer, choreographer, and student of world dance styles, Katherine Dunham.

States and Europe, dazzling audiences with her choreography. During the 1963–1964 season, Dunham choreographed the Metropolitan Opera's production of *Aida*, becoming the first African American to do so.

Pearl Primus, like Katherine Dunham, was trained in anthropology. Her research in primitive African dance inspired her first composition performed as a professional dancer entitled *African Ceremonial*, which she presented on February 14, 1943. On October 4, 1944, Primus made her Broadway debut at the Belasco Theater in New York. Her performance included dances of West Indian, African, and African American origin; the concert was widely acclaimed and launched her career as a dancer. Primus has traveled to Africa many times to research African dances; in 1959 she was named director of Liberia's Performing Arts Center. She later opened the Primus-Borde School of Primal Dance with her husband, dancer Percival Borde, and the Pearl Primus Dance Language Institute in New Rochelle, New York. In 1991, President George H.W. Bush honored Primus with the National Medal of Arts. She died October 29, 1994 at the age of 73.

By the late 1950s, several African American dancers and dance companies were distinguishing themselves on the concert stage. Janet Collins was the "premiere danseuse" of the Metropolitan Opera Ballet from 1951 until 1954. Arthur Mitchell made his debut as a principal dancer with the New York City Ballet in 1955. Alvin Ailey established his company in 1958. In addition, Geoffrey Holder, who made his Broadway debut in 1954 in *House of Flowers*, became a leading choreographer.

Since the early 1960s, two of the leading dance companies in the United States have been headed by African American males and composed largely of African American dancers. They are the Alvin Ailey American Dance Theater and the Dance Theatre of Harlem. In the 1970s, several prominent African American women dancers established schools and trained young dancers in regional companies throughout the United States.

The Alvin Ailey American Dance Theater

The Alvin Ailey American Dance Theater, since its founding in 1958, has performed before more people throughout the world than any other American dance company. With a touring circuit that has included 48 states and 45 countries on all continents, the Alvin Ailey American Dance Theater has been seen by more than 15 million people. Today, the Alvin Ailey organization consists of three components: the Alvin Ailey American Dance Theater, the Alvin Ailey Repertory Ensemble, and the Alvin Ailey American Dance Center.

Between 1958 and 1988, the Alvin Ailey Dance Theater performed 150 works by 45 choreographers, most of whom were African American. Notable among these African American choreographers have been Tally Beatty, Donald McKayle, Louis Johnson, Eleo Romare, Billy Wilson, George Faison, Pearl Primus, Judith Jamison, Katherine Dunham, Ulysses Dove, Milton Myers, Kelvin Rotardier, Geoffrey Holder, and Gary DeLoatch. More than 250 dancers, again mostly African American, have performed with the dance theater. Among its star performers have been Judith Jamison, Clive Thompson, Dudley Williams, Donna Wood, Gary DeLoatch, George Faison, and Sara Yaraborough. A prolific choreographer, Alvin Ailey created numerous works for his dance theater and other dance companies including: *Revelations* (1958); *Reflections in D*, with music by Duke Ellington (1962); *Quintet* (1968); *Cry* (1971); *Memoria* (1974); and *Three Black Kings* (1976). Alvin Ailey choreographed *Carmen* for the Metropolitan Opera in 1973 and *Precipice* for the Paris Opera in 1983.

Alvin Ailey.

The Alvin Ailey Repertory Ensemble (AARE) was established in 1974 as a training and performing company. Many of its graduates advance to the dance theater or perform with other dance companies. In 1988, the AARE had more than 100 members.

Alvin Ailey died in December of 1989, and his belief that a company should exhibit the works of many artists has allowed the three troupes to flourish in the ten years since his death. Judith Jamison has taken over as artistic director and has expanded Ailey's concept of extending dance opportunities as fully as possible.

The Alvin Ailey American Dance Center is the official school of the Ailey organization. It attracts students from across the United States and abroad and offers a certificate in dance. The center's curriculum includes training in ballet, the Dunham Technique, jazz, and modern dance. In 1998, a fully staffed school in New York City had an enrollment of 3,500 students; three intensive summer camps in urban locations taught dance to preteens and awarded scholarships, and an affiliation with Fordham University offers a bachelor in fine arts to eligible dance students.

The Alvin Ailey American Dance Theater celebrated its 40th year in December of 1998 by presenting the works of many choreographers including artistic director Judith Jamison, two current company members, and a French guest. Long-time Ailey choreographer Geoffrey Holder redesigned and restaged his lavish 1967 production of *The Prodigal Prince*, the story of a Haitian folk artist and voodoo priest who painted with a feather, for the anniversary celebration.

The Dance Theatre of Harlem

In 1969, Arthur Mitchell, who had established himself as one of the leading ballet dancers in the United States, and Karel Shook, a white ballet teacher, founded the Dance Theatre of Harlem. It was established after Martin Luther King Jr.'s death to provide the arts of dance and theater to young people in Harlem. The Dance Theatre of Harlem made its formal debut in 1971 at the Guggenheim Museum in New York City. Three of Mitchell's works were premiered at this concert: *Rhythmetron, Tones,* and *Fete Noire.*

Today, the dance theater's repertory is wide-ranging. It includes works in the Balanchine tradition such as *Serenade,* as well as black-inspired works such as *Dougla.* Among the most spectacular works performed by the theater are *Firebird, Giselle, Scheherazade,* and *Swan Lake.* Some of the dancers who have had long associations with the theater are Lowell Smith, Virginia Johnson, Shelia Rohan, and Troy Game. Many of the

Arthur Mitchell co-founded the Dance Theatre of Harlem in 1969.

theater's graduates have gone on to perform with other dance companies in the United States and Europe.

Black Regional Dance Schools

While Ailey and Mitchell built their companies in New York, African American women such as Joan Myers Brown, Ann Williams, Cleo Parker Robinson, Lula Washington, and Jeraldyne Blunden established young, mostly African American dance companies in major American cities. Robinson founded her Cleo Parker Robinson Dance Ensemble in 1970 in her native Denver, the same year that Blunden created her company in Dayton, Ohio, and Brown opened her school in Philadelphia. In 1976, Williams founded the Dallas Black Dance Theater, and in 1980 Washington created a troupe in Los Angeles that is now known as the Lula Washington Dance Theater.

Each institution began as a school with deep roots in African American urban communities they never left behind. They all started on a shoestring with a few eager young dancers. Their focus was on the discipline of dance and the values of integrity and intelligence. Today these troupes are nationally known for the high quality of their dancing and for repertories that include modern dance classics, some by African American choreographers. These five women have developed a cooperative network through which they exchange ideas and dancers. Collectively, they have trained thousands of dancers, some of whom have gone on to major companies.

In 1997, they were honored with a daylong tribute entitled *Dance Women: Living Legends*, in which all five companies performed and celebrated the efforts of these five women in the pursuit of dance.

Between 1960 and 1999, many African American dancers have led distinguished careers in concert dance and show dancing. Among them have been Eleo Pomare, Debbie Allen, Rod Rogers, Fred Benjamin, Pepsi Bethel, Eleanor Hampton, Charles Moore, Garth Fagan, Carmen de Lavallade, and Mary Hinkson. Fagan earned a Tony Award in 1997 for his choreographic work in the stage production of Disney's *The Lion King*. Foremost among African American choreographers have been Geoffrey Holder, Louis Johnson, Donald McKayle, Bebe Miller, George Faison, and Donald Byrd. Prominent among the African American dancers who are reviving the tap dance tradition are Buster Brown, Honi Coles, Hinton Battle, Gregory Hines, Lavaughn Robinson, Nita Feldman, Ted Levy, and Savion Glover. Glover came to prominence in the 1995 Broadway production of *Bring in 'Da Noise, Bring in 'Da Funk*

◆ STAGE ACTORS, COMEDIANS, CHOREOGRAPHERS, AND DANCERS

(Playwrights appear in the Literature chapter. To locate biographical profiles more readily, please consult the index at the back of the book.)

Alvin Ailey (1931–1989)
Dancer, Choreographer

Alvin Ailey was born in Rogers, Texas, on January 5, 1931. He was the founder of the Alvin Ailey Dance Theater and won international fame as both dancer and choreographer. Ailey studied dancing after graduating from high school, where he was a star athlete. After briefly attending college, Ailey joined the stage crew of the Lester Horton Theater in Los Angeles, for which Ailey eventually performed as a dancer. In 1953, after Horton's death, Ailey became the company choreographer. In 1954, Ailey performed on Broadway as the lead dancer in *House of Flowers*.

Ailey formed his own dance group in 1958 and began giving four performances annually. In 1962, the Ailey troupe made an official State Department tour of Australia, receiving accolades throughout the country. One critic called Ailey's work "the most stark and devastating theater ever presented in Australia."

After numerous appearances as a featured dancer with Harry Belafonte and others, Ailey performed in a straight dramatic role with Claudia McNeil in Broadway's *Tiger, Tiger Burning Bright*. Other Broadway appearances included roles in *Ding Dong Bell*, *Dark of the Moon*, and *African Holiday*. Ailey also choreographed or staged several operas including Samuel Barber's *Anthony and Cleopatra*, Leonard Bernstein's *Mass*, and Georges Bizet's *Carmen*. In addition, Ailey created works for various international ballet stars and companies.

In 1965, Ailey took his group on one of the most successful European tours ever made by an American dance company. In London, it was held over six weeks to accommodate the demand for tickets, and in Hamburg it received an unprecedented 61 curtain calls. A German critic called this performance "a triumph of sweeping, violent beauty, a furious spectacle. The stage vibrates. One has never seen anything like it." In 1970, Ailey's company became the first American modern dance group to tour the Soviet Union.

During the mid-1970s Ailey, among his other professional commitments, devoted much time to creating special jazz dance sequences for America's Bicentennial celebration. Among numerous honors including several honorary degrees, Ailey was awarded the NAACP's Spingarn Medal in 1976. Ailey died on December 1, 1989.

Ira Aldridge (1807–1867)
Actor

Born on July 24, 1807, in New York City, Ira Aldridge was one of the leading Shakespearean actors of the nineteenth century. Although he was denied the opportunity to perform before the American public in his prime, the fame that he won abroad established him as one of the prominent figures of international theater.

Aldridge's early dramatic training centered around the African Grove Theatre in New York in 1821. His first role was in *Pizarro*, and he subsequently played a variety of small roles in classical productions before accepting employment as a steward on a ship bound for England.

After studying briefly at the University of Glasgow in Scotland, Aldridge went to London in 1825 and appeared in the melodrama *Surinam, or a Slave's Revenge*. In 1833, he appeared in London's Theatre Royal in the title role of *Othello*, earning wide acclaim. For the next three decades, he toured the continent with great success, often appearing before European royalty.

Aldridge died in Lodz, Poland, on August 7, 1867. He is honored by a commemorative tablet in the New Memorial Theatre in Stratford-upon-Avon, England.

Debbie Allen (1950–)
Actress, Singer, Dancer, Director

Debbie Allen was born on January 16, 1950, in Houston, Texas. From the age of three, she trained as a dancer with the Ballet Nacional de Mexico, the Houston Ballet, and the National Ballet School. A cum laude graduate of Howard University, she became head of the Dance Department at the Duke Ellington School of Performing Arts.

Allen began her career on the Broadway stage in the chorus line of the hit musical *Purlie* (1972). She then portrayed Beneatha in the Tony and Grammy award-winning musical *Raisin* (1973). Other early stage roles were in the national touring company of *Guys and Dolls* and the drama *Anna Lucasta* performed for the New Federal Theatre at the Henry Street Settlement in New York.

Allen was subsequently selected to star in an NBC pilot *3 Girls 3* and then appeared on other television hits including *Good Times* and *The Love Boat*. At this time, her talent as a choreographer recognized, she worked on such television projects as *Midnight Special* as well as two films *The Fish that Saved Pittsburgh* (1979) and *Under Fire* (1981).

The year of 1982 was pivotal for Allen. She appeared in the film *Ragtime* and the television series *Fame*, as well as the Joseph Papp television special *Alice at the Palace*. Allen also starred in a dance performance for the Academy Awards ceremonies.

Allen's career continued with roles in the television special *Ben Vereen: His Roots* and the miniseries *Roots: The Next Generation* (1979). She also appeared on stage again in *Ain't Misbehavin'* (1979) and a revival of *West Side Story* (1980), which earned her a Tony Award nomination and a Drama Desk Award.

As each season passed on *Fame*, Allen became more involved as choreographer and was soon regularly directing episodes of the series. In 1988, she was selected by the producers to become director of the television sitcom *A Different World*. In another acknowledgment of her stature as a performer and creative talent, she starred in her own television special during the 1988–89 season. She choreographed the Academy Awards telecasts for several years in the 1990s.

In 1995, Allen appeared with LL Cool J in the television show *In the House*. She also worked as director of the television program *Out of Sync*. In 1999, Allen returned to television to star in *Michael Jordan: An American Hero*. She appeared in *The Old Settler* (2001) and *The Painting* (2002), both "PBS Hollywood Presents" productions.

In 1998, Allen co-produced the historic film *Amistad* with Steven Spielberg directing, after she had spent ten years looking for someone to champion it. *Amistad* chronicles the 1839 revolt on board a slave ship bound for America. It highlights the courtroom drama about Joseph Cinque, the enslaved African who led the revolt played by Djimon Hounsou. Also in 1998, Allen produced the musical *Brothers of the Knight* for the Kennedy Center. She published a book version of the play in 2000.

Allen made a move to better the community in 2001 when she opened the Debbie Allen Academy. The Academy offers students 12 lessons per week in ballet, modern, jazz, hip-hop and African dance. The school also offers a "pre-academy" preparatory program and plans to establish a professional ensemble that will perform annually. In its first year, the school had 150 students and looks to expand that as time goes on.

Allen is an Executive Committee member of UCLA's School of Theatre, Film and Television. She was awarded an honorary doctorate from her alma mater, Howard University, and the North Carolina School of the Arts.

Eddie "Rochester" Anderson (1905–1977)
Comedian

For many years, Eddie Anderson was the only African American performing regularly on a network radio show. As the character Rochester on the Jack Benny program, he became one of the best-known African American entertainers.

Anderson was born in Oakland, California, on September 18, 1905, the son of "Big Ed" Anderson, a minstrel performer, and Ella Mae, a tightwire walker. During the 1920s and early 1930s, Anderson traveled throughout the Middle and Far West singing, dancing, and performing as a clown in small clubs. On Easter Sunday, 1937, he was featured on Jack Benny's radio show, in what was supposed to be a single appearance; Anderson was such a hit that he quickly became a regular on the program.

Anderson is best known for his work with Benny (in television as well as on radio), but he also appeared in a number of movies including *What Price Hollywood?* (1932), *Cabin in the Sky* (1943), and *It's a Mad, Mad, Mad, Mad World* (1963).

Anderson died on February 28, 1977, at the age of 71.

Pearl Bailey with director Peter Brook.

Pearl Bailey (1918–1990)
Singer, Actress

Born on March 29, 1918, in Newport News, Virginia, Pearl Bailey moved to Philadelphia with her family in 1933. She sang at small clubs in Scranton, Pennsylvania, and in Washington, DC, before becoming the vocalist for the band of Cootie Williams and later for Count Basie. In the early 1940s, Bailey had her first successful New York engagements at the Village Vanguard and the Blue Angel. During World War II, she toured with the USO. Bailey made her New York stage debut in 1946 in *St. Louis Woman,* for which she won a Donaldson Award as the year's most promising new performer. She also appeared in the films *Variety Girl* (1947) and *Isn't It Romantic?* (1948).

During the 1950s Bailey appeared in the movies *Carmen Jones, That Certain Feeling,* and *Porgy and Bess,* and on Broadway in *House of Flowers.* In the 1950s and 1960s, she worked as a recording artist, nightclub headliner, and television performer. In 1967, she received a special Tony Award for her starring role on Broadway in *Hello, Dolly!* In 1969, she published an autobiography *The Raw Pearl.* Her other books include: *Talking to Myself* (1971); *Pearl's Kitchen* (1973); *Duey Tale* (1975); and *Hurry Up, America, and Spit* (1976).

In 1975, Bailey was named a special adviser to the United States Mission to the United Nations. In 1976, she appeared in the film *Norman, Is That You?* with Redd Foxx, and on stage in Washington, DC, in *Something To Do,* a musical saluting the American worker. She also received an award in 1976 from the Screen Actors Guild for outstanding achievement in fostering the finest ideals of the acting profession. Georgetown University made her an honorary doctor of humane letters in 1977.

In January of 1980, Bailey gave a one-night concert at Radio City Music Hall in New York. In 1981, she performed as the voice of the cartoon character "Owl" in the Disney movie *The Fox and the Hound.*

Bailey married the jazz drummer Louis Bellson in 1952. She died on August 17, 1990, in Philadelphia.

Josephine Baker (1906–1975)
Dancer, Singer

Born in St. Louis on June 3, 1906, Josephine Baker received little formal education; she left school at the age of eight to supplement the family income by working as a kitchen helper and baby-sitter. While still in elementary school, she took a part-time job as a chorus girl. At 17, she performed as a chorus girl in Noble Sissle's musical comedy *Shuffle Along,* which played in Radio City Music Hall in 1923. Her next show was *Chocolate Dandies,* followed by a major dancing part in *La Revue Nègre,* an American production that introduced *le jazz hot* to Paris in 1925.

In Paris, Baker left the show to create her most sensational role, that of the "Dark Star" of the Folies Bergère. In her act, she appeared topless on a mirror, clad only in a protective waist shield of rubber bananas. The spectacular dance made her an overnight star and a public figure with a loyal following. In true "star" tradition, she catered to her fans by adopting such flamboyant eccentricities as walking pet leopards down the Champs-Elysées.

In 1930, after completing a world tour, Baker made her debut as a singing and dancing comedienne at the Casino de Paris. Critics called her a "complete artist, the perfect master of her tools." In time, she ventured into films, starring alongside French idol Jean Gabin in *Zouzou* (1934), and into light opera, performing in *La Créole* (1934), an operetta about a Jamaican girl.

During World War II, Baker served first as a Red Cross volunteer, and later did underground intelligence work through an Italian Embassy attaché. After the war, the French government decorated her with the Legion of Honor. She returned to the entertainment world, regularly starring at the Folies Bergère, appearing on French television, and going on another extended international tour. In 1951, in the course of a successful American tour, Baker made headlines by speaking out against discrimination and refusing to perform in segregated venues.

Beginning in 1954, Baker earned another reputation—not as a lavish and provocative entertainer, but as a progressive humanitarian. She used her fortune to begin adopting and tutoring a group of orphaned babies of all races and retired from the stage in 1956 to devote all her time to her "rainbow family." Within three years, however, her "experiment in brotherhood" had taken such a toll on her finances that she was forced to return to the stage, starring in *Paris, Mes Amours,* a musical based in part on her own fabled career.

Baker privately, and without voicing discouragement, survived numerous financial crises. Illness hardly managed to dampen her indomitable spirit. Through her long life, she retained her most noteworthy stage attributes—an intimate, subdued voice, coupled with an infectiously energetic and vivacious manner.

Baker died in Paris on April 12, 1975, after opening a gala to celebrate her fiftieth year in show business.

James Hubert "Eubie" Blake (1883–1983)
Musician, Composer

Eubie Blake was born in Baltimore on February 7, 1883. The son of former slaves, Blake was the last of ten

Eubie Blake performing at the piano during the 1979 Newport Jazz Festival.

children and the only one to survive beyond two months. His mother worked as a laundress, his father as a stevedore.

At the age of six, Blake started taking piano lessons. He studied under the renowned teacher Margaret Marshall and subsequently learned musical composition from Llewelyn Wilson, who at one time conducted an all-black symphony orchestra sponsored by the city of Baltimore. At the age of 17, Blake was playing for a Baltimore night club.

In 1915, Blake collaborated with Noble Sissle. That year, Blake and Sissle sold their first song "It's All Your Fault" to Sophie Tucker, and her introduction of the song started them on their way. Blake and Sissle moved to New York and, together with Flournoy Miller and Aubrey Lyles, created one of the pioneer black shows *Shuffle Along* in 1921; the show was produced again on Broadway in 1952. *Chocolate Dandies* and *Elsie* followed in 1924.

During the early 1930s, Blake collaborated with Andy Razaf and wrote the musical score for Lew Leslie's *Blackbirds*. Out of this association came the hit *Memories of You*. During World War II, Blake was appointed musical conductor for the United Services Organization's (USO) Hospital Unit. In 1946 he announced his retirement and enrolled in New York University.

For many years, Blake's most requested song was "Charleston Rag," which he composed in 1899 and which was written down by someone else because Blake could not then read music. Among his most famous songs were "How Ya' Gonna Keep 'Em Down on the Farm," "Love Will Find a Way," and "You're Lucky to Me." Some of his other works include "I'm Just Wild About Harry," "Serenade Blues," "It's All Your Fault," and "Floradora Girls," with lyrics by Sissle.

Though known as a master of ragtime, Blake always most loved the music of the classical masters. In the intimacy of his Brooklyn studio, Blake rarely played the music for which the world reveres him. In 1978, Blake's life and career were celebrated in the Broadway musical *Eubie!* Several thousand people attended concerts at the Shubert Theatre and St. Peters Lutheran Church celebrating Blake's 100th birthday on February 8, 1983. Blake also received honorary doctorates from numerous colleges and universities. He died on February 12, 1983.

John Bubbles (1902–1986)
Dancer, Singer

John Bubbles, inventor of rhythm tap dancing, was born John William Sublett on February 19, 1902, in

John W. Bubbles performing at the 1979 Newport Jazz Festival.

Louisville, Kentucky. At the age of seven, he teamed with a fellow bowling alley pinboy, Ford "Buck" Washington, to form what became one of the top vaudeville acts in show business. Throughout the 1920s and 1930s, Buck and Bubbles played the top theaters in the country at fees of up to $1,750 a week. The two appeared in several films including *Cabin in the Sky* (1943). Bubbles captured additional fame as Sportin' Life in the 1935 version of *Porgy and Bess*. After Buck's death in 1955, Bubbles virtually disappeared from show business until 1964, when he teamed up with Anna Maria Alberghetti in a successful nightclub act.

In 1979, at the age of 77 and partially crippled from an earlier stroke, Bubbles recreated his characterization of Sportin' Life for a one-night show entitled *Black Broadway* at New York's Lincoln Center. The show was repeated in 1980 for a limited engagement at the Town Hall in New York. In the fall of 1980, Bubbles received a Lifetime Achievement Award from the American Guild of Variety Artists and a Certificate of Appreciation from the city of New York.

Bubbles died on May 18, 1986, at the age of 84.

Ed Bullins. *See* **Literature chapter.**

Anita Bush (1883–1974)
Actress, Singer

Born in 1883, Anita Bush was involved with the theater from early childhood. Her father was the tailor for the Bijou, a large neighborhood theater in Brooklyn, and Anita would carry the costumes to the theater for him, giving her a backstage view of performers and productions. Her singing/acting career took off in her early 20s, when she was in the chorus of the Williams and Walker Company. With Williams and Walker, she performed in such Broadway hits as *Abyssinia* and *In Dahomey*, which also had a successful European tour. When the group split up in 1909, she went on to form the Anita Bush Stock Company, which included her own show of chorus girls and such greats as Charles Gilpin and Dooley Wilson, with whom she also founded the Lafayette Players.

Bush died on February 16, 1974.

Donald Byrd (1949–)
Choreographer

Donald Byrd, one of the most important choreographers in modern dance, has created his own unique style of dance based on the influences of some great predecessors. From the styles and movements of Alvin Ailey, the classic ballet of George Balanchine, and the creations of Twyla Tharp, Byrd has established his own distinct contributions to dance.

Byrd was born on July 21, 1949, in New London, North Carolina, and raised in Clearwater, Florida. He was trained in classical flute and active in school theatrics and the debate team. When he was 16, two dancers from Balanchine's New York City Ballet, Edward Villella and Patricia McBride, conducted a lecture-demonstration in Clearwater, which left a lasting impression on him. An excellent student, Byrd received a scholarship for minority students to Yale University. He majored in philosophy but his exposure to the Yale Theater groups led him to consider being an actor. The racist attitudes of his classmates at Yale discouraged him, and he transferred to Tufts University in Boston.

Through his friend at Tufts, William Hurt, Byrd learned about the Alvin Ailey Dance Theater. At a performance of Alvin Ailey's signature work *Revelations*, Byrd felt the theatrical power of dance. Inspired, he began taking dance classes at Tufts and eventually went to New York in the early 1970s to study with a variety of dance teachers, among them, the Ailey School, Twyla Tharp, and the Gus Solomons Jr. company in

1976. When Solomons was named dean of the dance program at the California Institute of the Arts, he took Byrd along to teach.

While in California, Byrd began receiving acclaim for his choreography. By 1977, he was producing shows of his own work on the West Coast as well as at the Dance Theater Workshop back in New York. Byrd founded his own company, Donald Byrd/The Group in 1978. His style was now a unique blend of classical ballet, modern dance, and urban street dancing. Despite his company's success, Byrd struggled for several years with alcohol and drug dependency. After a scathing review by a supporter of his work in 1985, Byrd entered treatment and soon returned to his career.

In 1987, Byrd choreographed a new piece for the Ailey Repertory Company. The work *Crumble* was well received and from then on, he continued to contribute works to the Ailey companies. Byrd staged his next piece *Shards* in 1988 with strong influences of Balanchine. In 1991, the Ailey Dance Theater debuted *Dance at the Gym*, a work about teen culture. Byrd's own troupe, Donald Byrd/The Group, presented *Prodigal* in 1990, a dance inspired by Balanchine's *Prodigal Son*. The next year they produced a controversial piece about racial stereotypes called *The Minstrel Show*. This show won a Bessie Award for Donald Byrd/The Group in 1992.

The 1990s were creative years for Donald Byrd. He and his company toured the United States and Europe in 1993 presenting a repertoire of works choreographed by Byrd, among them *Bristle*, a long work exploring tensions between the genders. For Christmas of 1994, Byrd developed *The Harlem Nutcracker*, an African American version of the classic *Nutcracker*, using Duke Ellington-style big band arrangements of Peter Tchaikovsky's original music. Byrd's *The Beast* premiered in 1996 at the Brooklyn Academy of Music; the piece examines various types of domestic violence. By 1998, Byrd and his work were honored in a program of dances created by African American male choreographers called *Young Choreographers Defining Dance*. In 2000, Byrd followed up his Ellington inspired *Nutcracker* with another fairy-tale spun to jazz music, this time entitled *Sleeping Beauty* where he played with the notions of what was beautiful and how people viewed beauty in dance.

Godfrey Cambridge (1933–1976)
Actor, Comedian

Godfrey Cambridge was born in New York on February 26, 1933, to parents who had emigrated from British Guiana. He attended grammar school in Nova Scotia, while living with his grandparents. After finishing his schooling in New York at Flushing High School and Hofstra College, he went on to study acting.

Cambridge made his Broadway debut in *Nature's Way* (1956), and was featured in *Purlie Victorious*, both on stage in 1961 and later on screen. He also appeared off-Broadway in *Lost in the Stars* (1958), *Take a Giant Step*, and *The Detective Story* (1960). Cambridge won the Obie Award for the 1960–1961 season's most distinguished off-Broadway performance for his role in *The Blacks*. In 1965, he starred in a stock version of *A Funny Thing Happened on the Way to the Forum*.

As a comedian, Cambridge appeared on the *Tonight Show* and many other variety hours. His material, drawn from the contemporary racial situation, was often presented in the style associated with the contemporary wave of African American comedians. One of Cambridge's most memorable roles was as the star of a seriocomic Hollywood film *The Watermelon Man* (1970) in which the comedian played a white man who changes color overnight. Cambridge has also performed dramatic roles on many television series.

During the mid-1970s, Cambridge remained in semi-retirement, making few public appearances. Cambridge died at the age of 43 in California on November 29, 1976. His death occurred on a Warner Brothers set, where he was playing the role of Ugandan dictator Idi Amin for the television film *Victory at Entebbe*.

Hope Clarke (1943–)
Stage Director, Actress, Choreographer

From duets with Alvin Ailey to a complete revisioning of *Porgy and Bess*, Hope Clarke's career continues to expand the influences of African American culture in the American arts.

Hope Clarke was born in Washington, DC, in 1943. She grew up in a segregated, close-knit African American community. However, her talent and determination propelled her into a career in show business. In 1960 she won a part in the original touring company of Leonard Bernstein's *West Side Story*. From there, she became a principal dancer in two African American dance troupes: the Katherine Dunham Company and the Alvin Ailey American Dance Theater. Her duets with the late Alvin Ailey became legendary. Armed with talent and discipline, she left the company in the 1970s to pursue a new career in acting.

As an actress, Clarke's most notable feature film performance was in the classic film *A Piece of the Action*, starring Bill Cosby and Sidney Poitier. She also appeared in guest roles on numerous television shows

including *The Jeffersons*, *Hill Street Blues*, *Three's Company*, and *As the World Turns*.

Besides acting, Clarke was called in to choreograph various stage and television shows. Her years as a dancer prepared her well. She worked for the New York City-based Opera Ebony, helping to produce *Porgy and Bess* in such unlikely venues as Brazil and Finland. She won a Tony nomination for Best Choreography for her work in the 1992 Broadway hit *Jelly's Last Jam*.

Clarke continued to stage projects as diverse as Dorothy Rudd Moore's *Freedom* and Wolfgang Amadeus Mozart's *Cosi Fan Tutte*. She choreographed the production of *Frida* for the Houston Grand Opera. In 1995 she became the first African American, and the first African American woman, to direct and choreograph a major staging of the George Gershwin opera-musical *Porgy and Bess*, also for the Houston Grand Opera.

This major production of *Porgy and Bess* was staged in celebration of the work's 60th anniversary. Clarke brought to it her African American, feminine, and artistic sensibilities. She based the opera's setting around the Charleston-based Gullahs, an African American group believed to be Angolan in origin. Her characterizations employ the cultural and linguistic integrity of this unique community. In 1995, Clarke received a Tony Award for her work on *Porgy and Bess*. It toured many major American cities including San Diego, Los Angeles, San Francisco, Houston, and Minneapolis. It also played engagements in Japan and at Italy's famed La Scala opera house in Milan.

In 1998, Clarke received a New York Dance and Performance Award, known as a "Bessie," for her outstanding achievements as a performance professional. She continues to direct and choreograph dances and musicals in New York and elsewhere.

Bill Cosby. *See* Film & Television chapter.

André De Shields. (1946–)
Actor, Director, Choreographer

The ninth of 11 children born and reared in Baltimore, Maryland, Broadway veteran André De Shields began his professional career in the Chicago production of *Hair*. This controversial production led to a role in *The Me Nobody Knows* and membership in Chicago's Organic Theatre Company where he created the role of Xander the Unconquerable in *Warp*.

Many doors opened for De Shields in the 1970s. He debuted on Broadway in *Warp* (1973); co-choreographed two Broadway shows for Bette Midler, the critically acclaimed *Bette Midler* (1973) and *Bette Midler's Clams on the Half Shell Revue* (1975); and starred in two Tony Award-winning musicals that made him a Broadway legend, *The Wiz* (1975), a remake of *The Wizard of Oz*, but with an all-black cast, and *Ain't Misbehavin'* (1978), a musical tribute to legendary Fats Waller. In 1982, De Shields won an Emmy Award for his performance as Viper in the television special presentation of *Ain't Misbehavin'*.

De Shields garnered his first Tony and Drama Desk Award nominations in 1997 for his featured role as Jester in *Play On!* In 2001, he received Tony, Drama Desk, and Astaire Award nominations and won an Outer Critics' Circle Award for his performance as Noah T. "Horse" Simmons in *The Full Monty*, a role he also originated in London. Other Broadway credits include *Haarlem Nocturne* (1984) and *Stardust* (1987).

On the concert stage, De Shields performed *Mood Ellington*, an original one-man tribute to the Duke, directed and choreographed by Mercedes Ellington. Other concert stage performances include the cabaret opera *Casino Paradise* and *Songs of Innocence and Experience* at Carnegie Hall and the Royal Festival Hall in London. He has also toured with the Chamber Music Society of Lincoln Center as the narrator for Wynton Marsalis's *A Fiddler's Tale*.

Recent directing credits include a restaging of *Play On!* at the Crossroads Theatre Company, featuring Leslie Uggams and Stephanie Mills. He has also directed at the Denver Center Theatre, the Cortland Repertory Theatre, the Victory Gardens Theatre, and La Mama, E.T.C.

De Shields was featured in the films *Extreme Measures* with Hugh Grant and *Prison* directed by Renny Harlin. His television credits include guest appearances on *Sex and the City, Another World,* and *Law and Order; I Dream of Jeannie—15 Years Later*; and two PBS "Great Performances": *Alice in Wonderland* and *Ellington—The Music Lives On*.

A dedicated educator, De Shields served as director of Carnegie Hall's *Jazzed,* an educational strategy for restoring the arts to the public schools. He was the Dr. Martin Luther King Jr./Rosa Parks/Cesar Chavez Visiting Professor at the University of Michigan, Ann Arbor, and in 2002 was an adjunct professor of Shakespeare at his graduate alma mater, New York University-the Gallatin School of Individualized Study, where he received his first "Distinguished Alumni Award" in 1992. The Alumni Association of his undergraduate institution, the University of Wisconsin-Madison, honored De Shields with the Distinguished Alumni and the Person of the Year awards in 2001.

Katherine Dunham (1910–)
Choreographer, Dancer

Katherine Dunham has for many years been one of the leading exponents of primitive dance in the world of modern choreography.

Born in Joliet, Illinois, on June 22, 1910, Dunham attended Joliet Township Junior College and the University of Chicago, where she majored in anthropology. With funding from a Rosenwald Fellowship, she was able to conduct anthropological studies in the Caribbean and Brazil. She later attended Northwestern University, where she earned her Ph.D.; MacMurray College, where she received a L.H.D. in 1972; and Atlanta University, where she received a Ph.D.L. in 1977.

In the 1930s, she founded the Dunham Dance Company whose repertory drew on techniques Dunham learned while studying in the Caribbean. She has used her training in anthropology and her study of primitive rituals from tropical cultures to create unique dance forms that blend primitive qualities with sophisticated Broadway stage settings. In 1940, she appeared in the musical *Cabin in the Sky,* which she had choreographed with George Balanchine. She later toured the United States with her dance group; after the war, she played to enthusiastic audiences in Europe.

Among Dunham's choreographic pieces are: *Le Jazz Hot* (1938); *Bhahiana* (1939); *Plantation Dances* (1940); *Haitian Suite (II)* (1941); *Tropical Revue* (1943); *Havana 1910/1919* (1944); *Carib Song* (1945); *Bal Negre* (1946); *Rhumba Trio* (1947); *Macumba* (1948); *Adeus Terras* (1949); *Spirituals* (1951); *Afrique du Nord* (1953); *Jazz Finale* (1955); *Ti Cocomaque* (1957); and *Anabacoa* (1963). Under the pseudonym Kaye Dunn, Dunham has written several articles and books on primitive dance. She has been referred to as "the mother of Afro-American dance."

On January 15, 1979, at Carnegie Hall in New York, Dunham received the 1979 Albert Schweitzer Music Award, and selections from her dance repertory from 1938 to 1975 were staged.

In 1982, Dunham founded the Katherine Dunham Center for Arts & Humanities in East St. Louis to promote research and training in the arts and humanities. Its mission is to promote "arts-based communication techniques for people of diverse cultures, and [provide] a multi-art training program to humanize and socialize individuals as well as provide them with marketable skills."

During the 1990s, it was feared that the legacy of Dunham would eventually be lost due to lack of funding and the volume of material that needed to be preserved. But in 2000, the Doris Duke Charitable Foundation gave the Library of Congress $1 million to purchase and preserve the dancer/choreographer's archives. In addition, Illinois set aside a matching $1 million to make sure Dunham's legacy would remain alive in her home state.

Dunham has founded schools of dance in Chicago, New York, Haiti, Stockholm, and Paris. She has also lectured at colleges and universities across the country. Dunham is a winner of the Dance Magazine Award and the Kennedy Center honors.

Garth Fagan (1940–)
Choreographer

Garth Fagan was born on May 3, 1940, in Kingston, Jamaica. He discovered dance by way of gymnastics but was discouraged from a dance career by his father, an academic. However, he studied and danced with Ivy Baxter and the Jamaican National Dance Company, touring throughout Latin American while still in high school.

In 1960, Fagan left Jamaica and enrolled at Wayne State University in Detroit to study psychology. After completing his master's program, he commuted to New York to study with Martha Graham, Jose Limon, and Alvin Ailey. Fagan helped launch several Detroit-based dance companies: Detroit's All-City Dance Company, Detroit Contemporary Dance Company and Dance Theatre of Detroit. Eventually, he moved to Rochester, New York, to become a Distinguished Professor at the State University of New York at Brockport. There he taught young, untrained dancers who became his first company, Garth Fagan Dance.

Fagan always sought to transform dance, using the polyrhythms of Afro-Caribbean dance, modern floor techniques, the theatrics of Alvin Ailey, and the agility of ballet to create new movement. In 1986, Fagan directed and choreographed *Queenie Pie*, the Duke Ellington *street opera* at the Kennedy Center. Since then, he has created pieces for the Dance Theatre of Harlem, *Jukebox for Alvin* for the Alvin Ailey American Dance Theatre, (1993), a solo work for Judith Jamison, and *Never No Lament* for the José Limón Company in 1994.

Fagan's numerous honors include a Guggenheim Fellowship, the three-year Choreography Fellowship from the National Endowment for the Arts, the Dance Magazine Award for "significant contributions to dance during a distinguished career," and the "Bessie" Award (New York Performance Award) for sustained achievement. In 1996 he was named among 25 American scholars, artists, professionals, and public figures to receive the title, Fulbright Fiftieth Anniversary Distinguished Fellow.

In 1998, Fagan received the Tony Award for best choreography for his critically acclaimed work in the Broadway hit *The Lion King*, which also won the Tony for best musical. Fagan himself danced in the show. In 1998, he also received the Drama Desk Award, the Outer Critics Circle Award, and the Astaire Award.

Fagan's *Nkanyit* premiered in 1997 at the John F. Kennedy Center in Washington, DC, and opened at the Joyce Theatre in New York again in November of 1998. The title means "an all-encompassing respect for life, elders, and each other instilled early in childhood." This piece juxtaposes African ancestors dancing to American songs, and modern folk moving to Kenyan percussion. The heart of the work is the dynamic relationship between parent and child and the struggle to create "family." In 2001, Fagan's work was recognized when he received the Samuel H. Scripps American Dance Festival Award. Recent works by Fagan include, *Two Pieces of One: Green* (1998), *Woza* (1999), *Trips and Trysts* (2000), and *Music of the Line / Words in the Shape* (2001). With his ability to produce entertaining, dramatic, and insightful movement, Fagan continues to push the limits, inside and out, of postmodern dance.

Redd Foxx (1922–1991)
Actor, Comedian

Redd Foxx's most famous role was Fred Sanford, the junkman on the popular NBC series *Sanford and Son*, which began in 1972. It was the second most popular role on television after Archie Bunker in *All in the Family*. As a result, Foxx became one of the highest paid actors in show business. In 1976, it was reported that he was earning $25,000 per half-hour episode, plus 25 percent of the producer's net profit.

Sanford is actually Foxx's family name. He was born John Elroy Sanford in St. Louis on December 9, 1922, and both his father and his brother were named Fred. As a boy, he concocted a washtub band with two friends and played for tips on street corners, earning as much as $60 a night. At 14, Foxx and the band moved to Chicago; the group broke up during World War II.

Foxx then moved to New York, where he worked as a rack pusher in the garment district as he sought work in night clubs and on the black vaudeville circuit. While in New York, he played pool with a hustler named Malcolm Little, who was to change his name to Malcolm X.

In the early 1950s, Foxx tried to find work in Hollywood. He had a brief stint with *The Dinah Washington*

Show, but mostly survived by performing a vaudeville act and working as a sign painter. This comedy act contained adult content, which limited his bookings.

Foxx's first real success came in 1955, when he began to record party records. He ultimately made more than 50 records, which sold over 20 million copies. His television career was launched in the 1960s with guest appearances on *The Today Show*, *The Tonight Show*, and other variety programs. He also began to appear in Las Vegas nightclubs.

Throughout the long run of *Sanford and Son*, Foxx disputed with his producers over money. Originally, he was not receiving a percentage of the show's profits, which led him to sit out several episodes; a breach of contract suit filed by the producers resulted. There were racial undertones to these disputes, with Foxx referring to himself as a "tuxedo slave" and pointing to white stars who owned a percentage of their shows. Eventually, Foxx broke with the show and with NBC.

Foxx then signed a multimillion dollar, multiyear contract with ABC, which resulted in a disastrous comedy variety hour that he quit on the air in October of 1977. The ABC situation comedy *My Buddy* which he wrote, starred in, and produced followed. In 1978, however, ABC filed a breach of contract suit. In 1979, Foxx was back at NBC planning a sequel to *Sanford and Son*. He also made a deal with CBS, which in 1981 was suing him for a second time, allegedly to recover advances not paid back.

In 1976, Foxx appeared in the MGM movie *Norman, Is That You?* He continued his appearances in nightclubs in Las Vegas and New York. In 1979, the book *Redd Foxx, B.S.* was published, comprised of chapters written by his friends.

In 1973, Foxx received the Entertainer of the Year Award from the NAACP. In 1974, he was named police chief of Taft, Oklahoma, an all-black village of 600 people. He also ran a Los Angeles nightclub to showcase aspiring young comedians, both black and white. In addition, Foxx did numerous prison shows, probably more than any other famous entertainer, which he paid for out of his own pocket. Foxx died on October 11, 1991.

Al Freeman Jr. (1934–)
Actor

Al Freeman Jr. has won recognition for his many roles in the theater and motion pictures. His title role in the television film *My Sweet Charlie* (1970) earned him an Emmy Award nomination.

Albert Cornelius Freeman Jr. was born in San Antonio, Texas, on March 21, 1934, son of the pianist Al Freeman Sr. and Lottie Coleman Freeman. After attending schools in San Antonio and then Ohio, Freeman moved to the West Coast to study law at Los Angeles City College. Following a tour of duty with the U.S. Army in Germany, Freeman returned to college and decided to change his major to theater arts after being encouraged by fellow students to audition for a campus production.

Freeman did radio shows and appeared in little theater productions in the Los Angeles area before performing in his first Broadway play *The Long Dream* (1960). Other Broadway credits include: *Kicks and Company* (1961); *Tiger, Tiger Burning Bright* (1962); *Blues for Mr. Charlie* (1964); *Conversations at Midnight* (1964); *The Dozens* (1969); *Look to the Lilies* (1970); and *Medea* (1973).

Off-Broadway, Freeman worked in *The Living Premise* (1963), *Trumpets of the Lord* (1963), *The Slave* (1964), and *Great MacDaddy* (1974). He also appeared in *Troilus and Cressida* (1965) and *Measure for Measure* (1966) for the New York Shakespeare Festival. He has also done more than a dozen feature films including: *Dutchman* (1967); *Finian's Rainbow* (1968); *The Detective* (1968); *The Lost Man* (1969); *Castle Keep* (1969); *Malcolm X* (1992); and *Once Upon a Time When We Were Colored* (1995). In 1998, Freeman appeared in the poignant film *Down in the Delta* with Alfre Woodard and Wesley Snipes, which was directed by poet Maya Angelou.

Freeman has appeared in such television series as *The Defenders*, *The FBI*, and *Naked City*, and was featured as Lieutenant Ed Hall in ABC's daytime drama *One Life to Live*. He also appeared on television in Norman Lear's *Hotel Baltimore* (1975).

Charles Gilpin (1878–1930)
Actor

Charles Gilpin was born in Richmond, Virginia, on November 20, 1878. After a brief period in school, he took up work as a printer's devil. In 1890, he began to travel intermittently with vaudeville troupes, a practice that continued for two decades. He worked as a printer, elevator operator, prizefight trainer, and porter during long interludes of theatrical unemployment.

From 1911 to 1914, Gilpin toured with a group called the Pan-American Octette. In 1914 he had a bit part in a New York production *Old Ann's Boy*. Two years later he founded the Lafayette Theatre Company, one of the earliest black stock companies in New York.

After Eugene O'Neill saw Gilpin in *Abraham Lincoln*, he was chosen to play the lead in *The Emperor Jones*, the role in which he starred from 1920 to 1924. In

Charles Gilpin.

1921, Gilpin was awarded the NAACP Spingarn Award for his theatrical accomplishment.

Gilpin lost his voice in 1926 and was forced to earn his living once again as an elevator operator. He died on May 6, 1930.

Savion Glover (1974–)
Dancer, Choreographer

Tap dance wizard Savion Glover was born in Newark, New Jersey, in 1974. His mother noticed his keen sense of rhythm early on, and he began learning percussion at four years old. Ready to try something new, he began tap lessons at the Broadway Dance Center in New York City three years later. By the time he was ten, Glover was the understudy for the lead in *The Tap Dance Kid* and later starred in the role of the Kid. After two years in that show, he went on to perform in *Black and Blue* which opened first in Paris before moving to New York. His work earned him a Tony Award nomination in 1989.

Glover's talent developed quickly as he learned by imitating the techniques and sounds of tap greats such

as Sandman Sims, Harold Nicholas, Jimmy Slyde, and Sammy Davis Jr., who appeared with him in the film *Tap* in 1988. He excelled in "close work" (taps without jumps or leaps), acrobatic tap, and admits to creating moves inspired by Michael Jackson.

Glover next appeared in *Jelly's Last Jam*, which opened on Broadway in 1992, playing the young Jelly Roll Morton and co-starring with Gregory Hines. From Broadway, Glover went to television to appear, from 1991 to 1995, in *Sesame Street* and in several feature shows such as *Dance in America: Tap!*, *Black Filmmakers Hall of Fame*, and performing at the Academy Awards ceremony in 1996 and 1999.

Glover's greatest stage success is *Bring in 'Da Noise, Bring in 'Da Funk* which opened in 1995 and for which Glover was the choreographer and prime performer. The show combined poetry, tap, and musical styles such as blues, rhythm and blues, jazz, hip hop, and street drumming in dramatic and satiric sketches that tell of the black experience in America. Glover won the Tony Award for best choreography in 1996 for *Bring in 'Da Noise, Bring in 'Da Funk*. That same year he earned a Dance Magazine Award, a National Endowment for the Arts award, and was named Best New Theater Star by *Entertainment Weekly*. Since then, Glover has been teaching tap classes for children and has moved to Hollywood to develop further shows to showcase his extraordinary talents.

In 2000, Glover appeared in the Spike Lee film *Bamboozled* as a street dancer who is recruited to play in a minstrel show in order to make fun of network executives. Glover was honored with the Flo-Bert award from the New York Committee to Celebrate National Tap Dance Day. He appeared in the 2002 film *Bojangles*, which also starred Gregory Hines.

Whoopi Goldberg (1955–)
Actress, Comedienne

Born Caryn E. Johnson in Manhattan's Chelsea district on November 13, 1955, Whoopi Goldberg began performing at the age of eight at the children's program at Hudson Guild and Helen Rubeinstein Children's Theatre. After trying her hand at theater, improvisation, and chorus parts on Broadway, she moved to San Diego in 1974 and appeared in repertory productions of *Mother Courage* and *Getting Out*.

Goldberg joined the Black St. Hawkeyes Theatre in Berkeley as a partner with David Schein, and then went solo to create *The Spook Show*, performing in San Francisco and later touring the United States and Europe.

In 1983, Goldberg's work caught the attention of Mike Nichols, who created and directed her Broadway

Whoopi Goldberg (center) and co-stars in *Sister Act.*

show a year later. She made her film debut in *The Color Purple* (1985), winning an NAACP Image Award as well as a Golden Globe Award.

Goldberg's other film credits include: *Jumpin' Jack Flash* (1986); *Burglar* (1987); *Fatal Beauty* (1987); *The Telephone* (1988); *Homer and Eddie* (1989); *Clara's Heart* (1988); *Beverly Hills Brats* (1989); *Ghost* (1990); *The Long Walk Home* (1990); *Soapdish* (1991); *Sister Act* (1992); *The Player* (1992); *Sarafina!* (1992); *Made in America* (1993); *Sister Act 2: Back in the Habit* (1993); *Naked in New York* (1994); *Corrina, Corrina* (1994); *Star Trek: Generations* (1994); *Boys on the Side* (1995); and *Moonlight and Valentino* (1995).

On television, she starred in *Whoopi Goldberg on Broadway, Carol, Carl, Whoopi and Robin, Funny, You Don't Look 200,* and hosted *Comedy Tonight.* She received an Emmy nomination in 1985 for her guest appearance on *Moonlighting,* had a recurring role on *Star Trek: The Next Generation,* and was a founding member of the Comic Relief benefit shows. In 1998, Goldberg also brought the popular *Hollywood Squares* game show back to network television. She stayed with

the show for four seasons leaving in 2002. She both produced and starred in the show. She also produced both *What Makes a Family* for Lifetime Television and *Ruby's Bucket of Blood* for Showtime in 2000.

Goldberg was awarded as Best Supporting Actress for her portrayal of Oda Mae Brown in the film *Ghost.* In 1993, Goldberg received the Woman of the Year Award from Harvard University's Halting Pudding Theatricals organization. She also won People's Choice Awards in 1993 and 1994. In 2000, Goldberg was honored at the Santa Barbara Film Festival with their most prestigious award, the Ruby. In 2001, Goldberg was awarded the Mark Twain Prize for American Humor.

Goldberg served as host of the Academy Awards in 1994, 1996, 1999, and 2002.

Dick Gregory (1932–)
Comedian, Civil Rights Activist, Writer, Nutritional Advocate

Dick Gregory was born on October 12, 1932, in St. Louis. His father left the family in a state of poverty, and

Dick Gregory.

Gregory helped his mother by earning money through doing odd jobs. After high school, he entered Southern Illinois University on an athletic scholarship. In 1954 he was drafted into the U.S. Army. In the military his superiors, who were not fond of Gregory's flippant attitude, challenged him to win a talent show or face court-martial charges. Gregory won the contest and continued his military stint in the Special Service's Entertainment Division.

After his discharge from the army, Gregory went to Chicago and pursued a career as a stand-up comic. He opened a club called the Apex but failed to attract enough business to make the venue successful. The venture was not a total failure: Gregory ended up marrying his financial partner, Lillian Smith. In January of 1961, Gregory received the opportunity to perform at the Playboy Club for a group of Southern executives. Although initially turned away by the club's booking agent, who had assumed that Gregory was white, the comedian insisted on doing his routine. Although the crowd was expectedly resistant at first, Gregory persevered and won them over. The performance resulted in a three-year contract with the club.

During the early 1960s Gregory's popularity grew. His comedy relied upon discussions of himself and included social commentary on such matters as racism and civil rights. Several national commentators acknowledged Gregory as the first black comedian to gain acceptance as a social satirist. In the 1960s, he wrote *Back of the Bus* (1962) and *Nigger: An Autobiography* (1964).

In the 1960s Gregory involved himself in the burgeoning civil rights movement. He committed himself to events that resulted in increases in political fund raising and voter registration. Not one to contribute passively to causes, Gregory was arrested on numerous occasions and risked violence from local police. His views of nonviolent participation, fostered by Martin Luther King Jr., were challenged by his paying witness to a sheriff kicking his wife during a protest in Missouri.

As the 1960s progressed, Gregory withdrew from the entertainment arena and participated more actively in politics. He ran for mayor of Chicago in 1967 and earned nearly 200,000 votes for president as the candidate for the Freedom and Peace Party in the 1968 national election.

Nutritional issues have been a focus for Gregory since he became a vegetarian during the 1960s. At one point in his career, he refused to perform in clubs that allowed smoking and drinking. In the 1970s he co-wrote *Dick Gregory's Natural Diet for Folks Who Eat: Cooking with Mother Nature* (1974) with Alvenia Fulton. In 1984 he founded Health Enterprises, a business focused on marketing a powdered diet drink. Gregory also participated in marathons.

In the 1990s Gregory returned to the stage in Brooklyn to bring his comedy and social views to a new generation. His opinions on such issues as world hunger, "gangsta" rap music, drug use, and warfare come through during his performances. In 1993, he co-authored *Murder in Memphis: The FBI and the Assassination of Martin Luther King* and seven years later he published *Callous on My Soul: The Autobiography of Dick Gregory* in 2000.

Gregory received the *Ebony*-Topaz Heritage and Freedom Award, along with numerous honorary degrees from major universities. He also was honored with the Wellness of You 2001 Tree of Life Award.

Moses Gunn (1929–1993)
Actor

Born on October 2, 1929, in St. Louis, Moses Gunn showed dramatic promise at a young age—reading monologues aloud when he was nine. Six scholarships from other schools were offered to Gunn before he chose to earn a degree in speech and drama from Tennessee State University. There he organized a student troupe called Footlights Across Tennessee, a group that toured the South and Midwest, staging shows written by little-known black playwrights. While completing some graduate work at the University of Kansas, Gunn performed in *Othello*.

With his eye on a career on the New York stage, Gunn raised money by teaching drama at Grambling College in the early 1960s. He served as an understudy for an off-Broadway production, later joining the regular cast. Once he had gained more experience, Gunn gained a reputation as a leading Shakespearian actor. He appeared regularly with the New York Shakespeare Festival and won off-Broadway's Obie Award for his portrayal of Aaron the Moor in a 1967 production of *Titus Andronicus*. During the same era, he became a founding member of the Negro Ensemble Company, whose production of *The First Breeze of Summer* led to the actor's second Obie in 1975.

By the 1970s, Gunn had become a favorite on the national and international scenes. As a maturing performer, he did not limit his appearances to stage. Moviegoers enjoyed his supporting performances in films ranging from *Shaft* to *The Great White Hope*. As Booker T. Washington in *Ragtime*, Gunn earned an Image Award from the NAACP in 1981. Gunn was successful on the little screen, too, appearing in the made-for-television epic *Roots;* he earned an Emmy nomination for his portrayal in *Roots* of Kintango, a seventh-century African secret sect leader. He also did sitcoms and cop shows.

From a sensual Othello to a fiery Booker T. Washington, actor Moses Gunn specialized in crafting strong, memorable characters. His career spanned more than three decades. Beyond his own career, Gunn worked tirelessly as an advocate for other African American actors during a time when the theatrical establishment seemed all too willing to limit their presence both onstage and behind the scenes. He died of asthma complications on December 17, 1993, at the age of 64.

Arsenio Hall (1955–)
Actor, Comedian, Talk Show Host

Born on February 12, 1955, in Cleveland, Ohio, Arsenio Hall started his professional career as a standup comic, making the rounds of clubs and honing his presentation. Soon, he was appearing on television specials as well as touring with noted musical performers.

Hall was selected as a guest host of Fox Television's *Joan Rivers Show* when Rivers left, and soon won over both studio and television audiences. When this show concluded, he went on to star with Eddie Murphy in the movie *Coming To America* (1988). Hall also appeared in the movies *Harlem Nights* (1989) and *Bopha!* (1993).

Paramount then hired Arsenio Hall to be the host of his own show. Within weeks after the show's premiere in 1989, Hall had again built a solid audience following, particularly with young viewers, and provided the most substantial competition established evening talk shows had ever faced. In 1994, due to declining ratings and competition from talk show rivals Jay Leno and David Letterman, *The Arsenio Hall Show* went off the air.

In 1997, Hall appeared on a short-lived television series on ABC titled simply *Arsenio*. In 1998, Hall joined the cast of the martial arts police drama, *Martial Law*. Most recently, Hall was seen in the 2002 movie *Showtime* alongside Robert De Niro and Eddie Murphy.

Juanita Hall (1902–1968)
Singer

Born on November 6, 1902, in Keyport, New Jersey, Hall studied at the Juilliard School of Music after singing in Catholic Church choirs as a child. Hall devoted her life to music as a singer in stage and movie productions and choirs.

Her first major stage appearance was in Ziegfield's *Showboat* in 1927. Her lengthy stage career culminated in her role as Bloody Mary in Rodgers and Hammerstein's *South Pacific* in 1949. Hall went on to appear in *Flower Drum Song* and the movie versions of both shows. She served as a soloist and assistant director of the Hall Johnson Choir (1931–1936), conducted the Works Progress Administration chorus in New York City (1936–1941), and organized the Juanita Hall Choir in 1942.

Hall performed at the Palladium in London and was a guest on the Ed Sullivan and Perry Como television shows. She was the recipient of the Donaldson award and the Tony award. Hall died February 29, 1968, in Bay Shore, New York.

Leonard Harper (1899–1943)
Dancer, Choreographer, Producer

Leonard Harper was born into show business in Birmingham, Alabama. When he was just four years old, he began dancing and picking up stage tricks from his father, vaudeville actor William Harper. When Harper's father died, leaving the family destitute, the ten year-old was thrust into show business full time as the only means of supporting his mother and little brother.

Harper took his act on the road in carnivals and small musical comedy theaters called "Jig Tops." By the age of 12, he teamed up with comedian George Freeman. Together they formed a stock company and produced shows on the southern minstrel circuit. Harper longed for brighter lights, though, so he traveled to Chicago and joined an all-star minstrel show, where he met his future wife and partner, Osceola Blanks.

The new couple formed the vaudeville team of Harper and Blanks that became nationally known for their upscale attire and for introducing the dance craze, "Walking the Dog." Harper and Blanks broke the theatrical color barrier. They were the first black act to tour the Shubert Vaudeville circuit of white theaters. They were billed as "The Smart Set Couple" and performed their act dressed in full formal wear.

In 1922, Harper pioneered a new form of musical production, the intimate nightclub review. He produced *Plantation Days*, featuring Ethel Waters, at the Green Mills Garden, a posh club on Chicago's Gold Coast. The show toured America then sailed off to London to play before the royal family at the Empire Theatre.

When Harper returned to the United States, he was immediately hired as the main floorshow producer at Connie's Inn. His name became synonymous with the popularity of nightclub revues in New York City throughout the 1920s. Harper featured Ethel Waters and put Josephine Baker in top hat and tails for the first time in the Plantation Club's *Tan Town Topics*; mounted Texas Guinan's speakeasy shows with Ruby Keeler; and integrated burlesque by being the first black to produce and direct a whole stage show, *Hollywood Follies*, for Columbia. He also staged the debut floorshow entertainment for famous nightspots such as the Cotton Club, Smalls Paradise, and the Apollo Theatre.

In 1924, Harper opened a dance studio in Times Square and personally trained the Marx Brothers, Mae West, Ruby Keeler, Jack Albert, Fred and Adele Astaire, the Busby Berkeley dancers, and other stars in what became know as the "Leonard Harper System."

On Broadway, Harper starred in Lew Leslie's *Black Birds* with Florence Mills. He staged the musical numbers in *Keep Shufflin'* (1928), and in 1929, conceived and staged *Hot Chocolates* with music composed by Fats Waller and lyrics by Andy Razaf. *Hot Chocolates* featured newcomers Cab Calloway and Louis Armstrong and introduced two numbers that later became the title songs of two Broadway musicals, "Ain't Misbehavin'" and "Black and Blue."

Leonard Harper died while rehearsing a small nightclub show in 1943.

Robin Harris (1953–1990)
Comedian, Actor

Robin Harris was born August 30, 1953, in Chicago, Illinois. He attended Ottawa University in Kansas, where he ran a 4:18 mile on the track team. After college, he pursued a career in comedy rather than athletics, doing stand-up comedy as much as possible while working at Hughes Aircraft and Security Pacific Bank to support himself. Harris's interest in 1970s comedians such as Redd Foxx motivated to create his own act in a similar style. Finally in 1985, after years of hard work, he began to build a name for himself as the master of ceremonies at Comedy Act Theater in Los Angeles. Due primarily to Harris's influence, the Comedy Act Theater became a stopping spot for black celebrities.

Spike Lee was the first in the film industry to recognize Harris's talent and cast him in his 1989 film *Do The Right Thing*, which Harris followed with roles in *I'm Gonna Git You Sucka* and *Harlem Nights*. In 1990, he continued his successfully growing film career playing Pops in *House Party*. His movie career vaulted him into a new level of stardom, and he started playing 2,000-seat auditoriums with his comedy act, though continuing his much smaller and less profitable gigs at the Comedy Act Theater.

In 1990, Harris's life became very hectic between his comedy act gigs, an HBO special, his album and soon-to-be movie *Bebe's Kids*. The schedule proved too much for him, and he died on March 18, 1990, of heart failure in his hometown of Chicago. The animated film version of Harris's comedy album *Bebe's Kids* was released posthumously as was his HBO comedy special.

Richard B. Harrison (1864–1935)
Actor

Richard B. Harrison was one of the few actors to gain national prominence on the basis of one role, his characterization of De Lawd in *Green Pastures*.

Harrison was born in Canada in 1864 and moved to Detroit as a young boy. There he worked as a waiter, porter, and handyman, saving whatever money he could to attend the theatrical offerings playing in town. After studying drama in Detroit, he made his professional debut in Canada in a program of readings and recitations.

For three decades, Harrison entertained black audiences with one-man performances of *Macbeth*, *Julius Caesar*, and *Damon and Pythias*, as well as with poems by William Shakespeare, Edgar Allan Poe, Rudyard Kipling, and Paul Laurence Dunbar. In 1929, while serving on the faculty of North Carolina A & T as drama instructor, he was chosen for the part in *Green Pastures*.

Richard B. Harrison.

By the time of his death in 1935, Harrison had performed as De Lawd 1,656 times. His work earned him the 1930 Spingarn Medal and numerous honorary degrees.

Gregory Hines (1946–)
Actor, Dancer

After a distinguished career as a tap dancer, Gregory Hines made an unusual transition to dramatic actor.

Born in New York City on Valentine's Day, 1946, Hines began dancing with his brother Maurice under the instruction of tap dancer Henry LeTang. When Gregory was five, the brothers began performing professionally as the Hines Kids. Appearing in nightclubs and theaters around the country, they were able to benefit from contact with dance legends such as "Honi" Coles, Sandman Sims, the Nicholas Brothers, and Teddy Hale.

As teenagers, the two performed as the Hines Brothers. When Gregory reached age 18, the two were joined on drums by their father, Maurice Sr. The trio became

known as Hines, Hines and Dad. They performed internationally and appeared on *The Tonight Show*. Eventually, Gregory tired of the touring and settled in California, where he formed the jazz-rock band Severance.

Gregory Hines subsequently moved back to New York and landed a role in *The Minstrel Show* (1978). He would later appear in such Broadway musicals as *Eubie!* (1978), *Sophisticated Ladies* (1981), and *Comin' Uptown* (1990), as well as feature films including *The Cotton Club* (1985), *White Nights* (1985), *Running Scared* (1985), and *Off Limits* (1988). Hines starred in the 1989 Tri-Star film *Tap* with Sammy Davis Jr., not only acting and dancing, but singing as well. Hines has also appeared in the films *White Man's Burden* (1994), *Renaissance Man* (1995), *Dead Air* (1995), and *Waiting to Exhale* (1995).

On television, Hines appeared in the series *Amazing Stories* and the special *Motown Returns to the Apollo*, which earned him an Emmy nomination. His 1997 show *The Gregory Hines Show* was favorably reviewed but short-lived. He also appeared as the lead character in the 2001 television movie *Bojangles*. When not appearing in films or television, he toured internationally with a solo club act. *Gregory Hines*, his first solo album, was released by CBS/Epic in 1988. The album was produced by Luther Vandross, who teamed with Gregory for a single "There's Nothing Better Than Love," which reached number one on the R&B charts in 1987.

Hines has received numerous awards including the Dance Educators Award and the Theater World Award. Hines has been nominated for several Tony Awards, and in 1992 received the award for best actor in a musical for his role in *Jelly's Last Jam*.

Geoffrey Holder (1930–)
Actor, Dancer, Choreographer, Costume Designer, Director

Geoffrey Holder has succeeded as an artist in many areas. Holder was born on August 1, 1930, in Port-of-Spain, Trinidad. At an early age, he left school to become the costume designer for his brother's dance troupe, which he took over in 1948. Holder led the dancers, singers, and steel band musicians through a series of successful small revues to the Caribbean Festival in Puerto Rico, where they represented Trinidad and Tobago. His appearances with his troupe in the mid-1950s were so popular that he is credited with launching the calypso vogue.

Early in his career, Holder appeared in New York as a featured dancer in *House of Flowers* (1954). He later performed with the Metropolitan Opera and as a guest star on many television shows. Film credits include:

Live and Let Die (1973), the James Bond adventure; and *Dr. Dolittle* (1967), the children's classic starring Rex Harrison.

Holder received two Tony Awards in 1976, as director and costume designer for the Broadway show *The Wiz*, the all-black adaptation of *The Wizard of Oz*. In 1978, he directed and choreographed the successful Broadway musical *Timbuktu*. In 1982, Holder appeared in the film *Annie* based on the hit Broadway musical, playing Punjab, a character from the original comic strip.

Holder received a Guggenheim Fellowship to pursue his painting, and his impressionist paintings have been shown in galleries such as the Corcoran in Washington, DC. In 1995, an exhibition of Holder's paintings was held at the State University of New York in Albany. Holder also has written two books. *Black Gods, Green Islands* is a retelling of West Indian legends; his *Caribbean Cookbook* is a collection of recipes that Holder also illustrated.

In 1998, Holder restaged his 1967 production *The Prodigal Prince* for the fortieth anniversary celebration of the Alvin Ailey Dance Theater. In 2000, he appeared along side Mercedes Ellington in a cooking show called *Harmony in the Kitchen*. In 2002, Holder was honored by the International Association of Blacks in Dance for his career.

Holder is married to the ballet dancer Carmen de Lavallade.

Lena Horne (1917–)
Actress, Singer

Lena Horne has been called the most beautiful woman in the world, and her beauty has been no small factor in the continued success of her stage, screen, and nightclub career.

Horne was born on June 30, 1917, in Brooklyn, New York. She joined the chorus line at the Cotton Club in 1933, and then left to tour as a dancer with Noble Sissle's orchestra. She was given a leading role in *Blackbirds of 1939*, but the show folded quickly, whereupon she left to join Charlie Barnett's band as a singer. She made her first records, including the popular *Haunted Town*, with Barnett. In the early 1940s she also worked at New York's Cafe Society Downtown.

Horne then went to Hollywood, where she became the first black woman to sign a term contract with a film studio. Her films included *Panama Hattie* (1942), *Cabin in the Sky* (1943), *Stormy Weather* (1943), and *Meet Me in Las Vegas* (1956). In 1957, she took a break from her film and nightclub schedule to star in her first Broadway musical *Jamaica*. Her popular recordings included "Stormy Weather," "Blues in the Night," "The Lady Is a Tramp," and "Mad about the Boy."

Throughout the 1960s and 1970s, Horne appeared in nightclubs and concerts. Her greatest recent success, however, was on Broadway. On May 12, 1981, she opened a one-woman show called *Lena Horne: The Lady and Her Music* to critical and box-office success. Although it opened too late to qualify for the Tony Award nominations, the show was awarded a special Tony at the June ceremonies. The production ran for two years and the soundtrack produced by Quincy Jones won two Grammy Awards. In December of 1981, she received New York City's highest cultural award, the Handel Medallion.

Horne was married for 23 years to Lennie Hayton, a white composer, arranger, and conductor who died April 24, 1971. She had been married previously to Louis Jones. A generous and gracious woman, Horne has quietly devoted much time to humane causes.

In 1994, Horne released her first recording in a decade entitled *We'll Be Together Again*. This album was followed by *An Evening with Lena Horne* (1995); *Lena Horne at Metro-Goldwyn-Mayer* (1996); and *Being Myself* (1998). In 1999 a gala in her honor was held at New York's Avery Fisher Hall.

Eddie Hunter (1888–1974)
Comedian

Eddie Hunter got his start when working as an elevator operator in a building frequented by the great tenor Enrico Caruso. Hunter had been writing vaudeville comedy parts on the side, and Caruso encouraged and helped him. In 1923, Hunter's show *How Come?*, a musical revue, reached Broadway.

Hunter performed in his own persona in the majority of the shows he wrote. *Going to the Races*, produced at the Lafayette Theatre in Harlem, had Hunter and his partner live on stage, interacting with a movie of themselves playing on the screen. Hunter considered this show one of his best. As one of the principal performers in *Blackbirds*, he toured Europe during the late 1920s. His show *Good Gracious* also toured Europe.

Depicting himself as "the fighting comedian," Hunter developed a reputation for speaking out against racial discrimination in the performing arts. He frequently told of his experience in Phoenix, Arizona, where the male members of the show were forced to sleep in the theater where they were performing; accommodations for blacks simply did not exist at the time. Hunter characterized his European reception as being relatively free of prejudice and felt that he only received the respect and recognition due to him when abroad.

By 1923, Hunter had a full recording contract with Victor Records. His recordings included *It's Human Nature to Complain, I Got,* and *My Wife Mamie.* Shortly thereafter, he suspended his singing career to begin traveling with a new show he had developed. But when "talking" movies came into being, vaudeville fell out of favor. Eddie Hunter thus retired from show business and entered the real estate business in the 1930s.

Earle Hyman (1926–)
Actor

Earle Hyman was born in Rocky Mount, North Carolina, on October 11, 1926. He began his acting career with the American Negro Theatre in New York City.

In 1963, Hyman made his foreign-language acting debut in Eugene O'Neill's *The Emperor Jones* in Oslo, Norway, becoming the first American to perform a title role in a Scandinavian language. Hyman had originally become acquainted with Norway during a European trip made in 1957. He had planned to spend only two weeks in the Scandinavian country, but found himself so enchanted with Norway that he all but forgot the rest of Europe. When Hyman returned to New York, he resolved at once to learn Norwegian, and for practice, began to study the role of Othello (which he was performing for the Great Lakes Shakespeare Festival of 1962) in that language. By sheer coincidence, the director of *Den Nationale Scene* of Bergen, Norway, invited him to play Othello there in the spring of the following year, a performance which marked Hyman's first success in the Norwegian theater.

In 1965, Hyman returned to Norway to play *The Emperor Jones* for a different theater company and received high critical acclaim for his portrayal. Hyman remained in Norway intermittently for six years and has been the subject of several Norwegian radio broadcasts and television interviews. He still spends six months each year in Scandinavia playing Othello and other classical roles. He played Halvard Solness to Lynn Redgrave's Mrs. Alvine Solness in Henrik Ibsen's *The Master Builder* at the National Actor's Theatre in 1992. A bronze bust of the actor as Othello has been erected in the Norwegian theater where Hyman performed, and he has also been presented with an honorary membership in the Norwegian Society of Artists, the third foreigner and first American to be so honored.

Hyman's many on and off-Broadway credits include: *No Time for Sergeants* (1955); *St. Joan* (with Diana Sands at Lincoln Center) (1956); *Mister Johnson* (1956); *Waiting for Godot* (1957); Lorraine Hansberry's *Les Blancs* (1970); Edward Albee's *Lady from Dubuque;* the black version of Eugene O'Neill's *Long Day's Journey into Night* (at the Public Theatre, 1981); and *East*

Texas Hot Links (1994). Among other film and television work, Hyman has appeared on the daytime drama *Love of Life* and *The Cosby Show.* In more recent years, Hyman has been seen in the television movies *Hijacked: Flight 285* in 1996 and *The Moving of Sophia Myles* in 2000.

Judith Jamison (1944–)
Dancer, Choreographer

Born in Philadelphia on May 10, 1944, Judith Jamison started to study dance at the age of six. She was discovered in her early twenties by the choreographer Agnes De Mille, who admired her spontaneous style.

From 1965 to 1980, Jamison was a principal dancer for Alvin Ailey's American Dance Theater for 15 years, performing a wide gamut of roles, especially choreographed for her by Ailey. She has made guest appearances with many other dance companies, including the American Ballet Theatre, and with such opera companies as the Vienna State Opera and the Munich State Opera. In the 1980s, Jamison scored a great success on Broadway in *Sophisticated Ladies,* a musical featuring the music of Duke Ellington. In 1988, she formed the Jamison Project.

Since 1989, Jamison has served as artistic director of the Alvin Ailey Dance Theater. Among her recent dance works are *Hymn* (1993) and *Riverside* (1995). *Hymn* is featured in the PBS documentary *Hymn: Remembering Alvin Ailey* premiering in 1999. Her 1996 work *Sweet Release* was a collaboration with celebrated trumpeter Wynton Marsalis. Her ballet *Echo: Far From Home* opened in New York in December of 1998; *Double Exposure,* another ballet, premiered at the Lincoln Center Festival in 2002.

In 1993, Jamison wrote the book *Dancing Spirit: An Autobiography.* She is the youngest recipient ever to receive the Dance USA Award which was presented at the Spoleto Festival, USA, in May of 1998. In 2000, President Bill Clinton paid tribute to Jamison at the Kennedy Center Honors program in Washington D.C. In 2002, Jamison was named as a recipient of the National Medal of Arts.

Virginia Johnson (1950–)
Dancer

Virginia Johnson was the prima ballerina for the Dance Theatre of Harlem from its very beginning in 1969. Her career started very early. She was born in Washington, DC, on January 25, 1950, and began studying ballet when she was three years old at the Washington School of Ballet. She continued to study there under scholarships throughout high school and performed in productions with the American Light Opera Company and in the annual staging of the Washington Ballet's *The Nutcracker Suite.*

Although black ballerinas were rare, Johnson received a scholarship to study dance at New York University's School of the Arts. However, the emphasis on modern dance there dissatisfied her, so she joined a ballet school in Harlem being run out of a church basement by the former New York City Ballet dancer Arthur Mitchell. At 19, she left NYU to become part of the fledgling company. Mitchell created the Dance Theatre of Harlem (DTH) as a commitment to the Harlem community after the assassination of Martin Luther King Jr. His aim was to establish a company of black dancers and add a new style to contemporary classical ballet. DTH and Johnson were a perfect match.

In 1974, Johnson danced her first solo role for the Dance Theatre of Harlem and became its star ballerina. Emotive, romantic, and long-limbed, Johnson was a natural for legendary choreographer George Balanchine's dances, performing them clearly and smoothly. In her tenure at DTH, she danced many traditional roles such the title role in *Giselle.* The DTH then reset the European tale in the bayous of Louisiana to tell the stories of a community of free Creole blacks. Critics praised Johnson's performances as "glorious and subtle touching and authoritative."

Johnson continued to add modern roles to extend her technical facility. She danced Balanchine's *Serenade* and *Allegro Brilliante,* Glen Tetley's *Voluntaries,* Bronoslava Nijinska's *Les Biches,* and portrayed the Accused (Lizzie Borden) in Agnes de Mille's dramatic *Fall River Legend.*

Johnson toured the world with DTH in her capacity as dance diva. During the late 1980s, Johnson was one of the first American ballerinas to visit the Soviet Union where she performed at the Kirov State Theater of Ballet and Opera in Leningrad. In the early 1990s, Johnson traveled to post apartheid South Africa with the DTH where she strove to be an ambassador of change through the beauty of dance.

Among her television presentations, Johnson has danced in Public Broadcasting Service's (PBS) *Dance in America* series and performed *Creole Giselle* for NBC. She also danced in and choreographed the television film *Ancient Voices of Children.*

Johnson continued to received accolades for her roles in the 1990s: as the Accused (Lizzie Borden) in *Fall River Legend* with the Cleveland Ballet in 1991, and as Blanche in *A Streetcar Named Desire* at the Dance Theatre of Harlem's 25th anniversary season at Lincoln Center in New York City in 1994.

On September 21, 1997, Virginia Johnson retired from the stage at age 47. For 28 years as the Dance Theatre of Harlem's prima ballerina, she brought to her dramatic performances great sensitivity, an intense ferocity, and total generosity to her company and her audiences.

Bill T. Jones (1952–)
Dancer, Choreographer

Jones was born into a family of 12 children in Florida in the early 1950s; eventually his migrant worker parents moved north to New York, where Jones excelled in high school athletics. Jones enrolled in the State University of New York at Binghampton in the early 1970s with the hope of pursuing a career in theater. He was already an accomplished actor, but eventually transferred into the university's dance department. While in college, Jones developed a romantic relationship with fellow dancer Arnie Zane.

Jones and Arnie Zane left Binghampton for the wider pastures of Amsterdam for several years; when they returned to New York City, they founded the American Dance Asylum, whose early mid-1970s performances caused a stir because of the dancers' onstage nudity. Next, Jones and Zane formed a more accessible dance company in 1982. They named the troupe after themselves, and one of their first performances that year earned critical praise at the Brooklyn Academy of Music's innovative Next Wave Festival.

The Bill T. Jones/Arnie Zane dance company continued to thrive until Zane fell ill with AIDS; the principal's inability to tour almost ended the troupe's existence financially, and his death in 1988 added greatly to Jones's burden. However, Jones was able to use the grief to create a dance opus paying homage to his longtime partner, and the 1989 debut of *Absence* received laudatory reviews. The death of another member of the company resulted in another work that addressed issues of loss due to AIDS within the artistic community, *D-Man in the Waters.*

Jones has also addressed issues of the African American cultural experience, especially as experienced by those of alternative sexual orientation, in such productions as *Last Supper at Uncle Tom's Cabin.* He has been candid about his own status as an HIV-positive person. In 1994 he was awarded a MacArthur Foundation fellowship; the following year saw the premier of *Still/Here* at the Brooklyn Academy of Music. Jones coauthored a book, 1995's *Last Night on Earth,* and collaborated with jazz drummer Max Roach and novelist Toni Morrison on a dance piece entitled *Degga* performed at Lincoln Center that same year as well.

Later, *Still/Here* became the subject of media sniping between Jones and *New Yorker* writer Arlene Croce, who termed it "victim art" in early 1996. Jones asserted that the New York media is biased in favor of Jewish matters. In 1997, Jones spoke to the American Dance Therapy Association members at their annual conference about the use of such works as *Still/Here* in dance therapy.

Jones has continued to create such works as *Ursonata* whose name comes from a poem by Dada artist Kurt Schwitters. Another work uses poems recorded by Dylan Thomas. Avant-garde musician Laurie Anderson was commissioned to score his *Harriet and Rhonda Ten Rounds*. In January of 1999, Jones staged *We Set Out Early Visibility Was Poor*, a new work exposing a more ecstatic and less political side of his work. It is symbolic and lyric, mixed with a marked desire for peace after the pain of loss. Jones continues to reach into his emotional life to manifest his art. In 2000, Jones went on a solo tour of America and Europe called *The Breathing Show*. In late October, the Axis theater began performing Jones' latest show, *Fantasy in C Major*.

Adrienne Kennedy. *See* Literature chapter.

Woodie King Jr. (1937–)
Producer, Director, Writer

Born in Mobile, Alabama, but raised in Detroit, Woodie King became interested in acting while in his teens. During his last year at Cass Technical High School, King was offered a scholarship to the Will-O-Way School of Theatre in suburban Bloomfield Hills, Michigan. There he had the opportunity to study with such luminaries as Vincent Price and Helen Hayes; however, frustrated by the lack of roles for black actors in classical plays, King was prompted to produce.

While attending Detroit's Wayne State University, King teamed up with several other black theater students to found Concept-East, a community-based black theater company. King served as director and manager from 1960 to 1963. One of the plays produced, *Study in Color*, received enough widespread praise that King brought a touring production of the show to New York in 1964, where it played at the American Place Theatre. Rather than return to Detroit, King chose to stay in New York, where he continued working at the American Place, staging five plays.

In 1970, King founded a new company, The New Federal Theatre (NFT), named after the Harlem-based, government-funded troupe of the 1930s. Based at the Henry Street Settlement, King envisioned the NFT as a community theater that promoted the work of writers from diverse backgrounds. Playwrights such as J. E. Franklin, *Black Girl*; Ron Milner, *What the Winesellers Buy*; Ed Bullins, *The Taking of Miss Janie*; David Henry Hwang, *Dance and the Railroad*; Damien Leake, *Child of the Sun*; Laurence Holder, *When Chickens Came Home To Roost*; Nikos Kazantzakis, *Christopher Columbus*; Alexis DeVeaux, *No*; and Dr. Endesha Ida Mae Holland, *From the Mississippi Delta* have been brought to national attention because their work was showcased at NFT.

Many notable actors including, Jackee Harry, Morgan Freeman, Denzel Washington, Debbie Allen, Phylicia Rashad, Glynn Turman, Esther Rolle, Samuel L. Jackson, Laurence Fishburne, Robert Downey Jr., Debbie Morgan, and Lynn Whitfield performed in NFT productions.

King also co-produced several plays on Broadway, Leslie Lee's *The First Breeze of Summer* (1975) and Ntozake Shange's *For Colored Girls Who Have Considered Suicide When the Rainbow Is Enuf* (1976). In the 1980s, he executive produced a musical, *Reggae* (1980), and directed the Broadway cast of Ron Milner's *Checkmates* (1988).

King wrote and directed *The Black Theatre Movement: "A Raisin in the Sun" to the Present*, which aired on PBS in 1979, and scripted teleplays for the series *Sanford and Son*. King also edited or co-edited a number of important anthologies, including *Black Drama Anthology*, *Black Short Story Anthology*, and *Black Poets and Prophets: The Theory, Practice and Esthetics of the Pan-Africanist Revolution*. King's collection of essays, *Black Theater: Present Condition*, was published in 1981.

In 1997, King received an Obie Award for Sustained Achievement. *American Visions* dubbed Woodie King Jr., the "king of black theater producers," in its April 2000 issue.

Martin Lawrence. *See* Film & Television chapter.

Jackie "Moms" Mabley (1894–1975)
Comedienne

Mabley was born Loretta Mary Aiken in Brevard, North Carolina, on March 19, 1894, and entered show business as a teenager when the team of Buck and

Bubbles gave her a bit part in a vaudeville skit called "Rich Aunt from Utah."

With the help of comedienne Bonnie Bell Drew, Mabley developed a monologue, and was soon being booked on the black vaudeville circuit. Influenced by such acts as Butterbeans and Susie, she developed her own comic character, a world-weary old woman in a funny hat and droopy stockings, delivering her gags with a mixture of sassy folk wisdom and sly insights.

Her first big success came in 1923 at Connie's Inn in New York. Engagements at the Cotton Club in Harlem and Club Harlem in Atlantic City followed.

Moms Mabley was discovered by white audiences in the early 1960s. Her record album *Moms Mabley at the U.N.* became a commercial success and was followed by *Moms Mabley at the Geneva Conference.* In 1962, she made her Carnegie Hall debut on a program with Cannonball Adderley and Nancy Wilson. Her subsequent Broadway, film, television, and record successes made her the favorite of a new generation.

Moms Mabley died on May 23, 1975, at the age of 78 in a White Plains, New York, hospital.

Bernie Mac (1957–)
Comedian, Actor

Bernard "Bernie Mac" McCullough was born in 1957, one of 15 children, and raised on the South Side of Chicago. Almost from the start he was destined to be a comic. He was just four when he witnessed his mother laughing until she cried as she watched Bill Cosby perform on television. The power Cosby had to elicit such reaction made an impact. By the time he graduated high school, his comic reputation was intact. Voted class clown by his fellow students, Mac turned the title down. "I thought it was an insult," he told *Entertainment Weekly.*

Mac's professional career started slowly. He worked a series of menial jobs to pay the rent and did impromptu stand-up in the subways, eliciting tips for laughs. Mac's first break came in Chicago in 1990 when he won the Miller Lite Comedy Search, which led to a spot on HBO's *Def Comedy Jam.* Damon Wayans was the host that night and was so impressed that he offered Mac a film debut in *Mo' Money* (1992).

Over the next few years, Mac appeared in many films. Often cast as a funny sideman, he proved himself in dramatic roles as well, most notably as "Flip," a homeless ex-basketball star in *Above the Rim* (1994). Mac wrote and starred in his own HBO show, *Midnight Mac,* which was nominated for a Cable Ace Award in

1995. He developed a following because of his recurring role on the TV series *Moesha* and his featured roles in the cult classics *Friday* (1995) and *Life* (1999).

Even as his small and large screen careers were taking off, Mac stepped up his live performance schedule. He went out on the road in 1994 with his own *Who Ya Wit Tour,* which included a ten-piece band and five "Mac-A-Roni Dancers." In 1997, Mac joined four other comics, beginning the tour that would propel him into the realm of comedic royalty. Along with Steve Harvey, D. L. Hughley, and Cedric the Entertainer, Mac embarked on the *Original Kings of Comedy* tour.

The show was the first comedy tour to move from headlining theaters and small arenas to selling out 11,000 seat stadiums. In fact, it became the highest grossing comedy tour in history. The show's success drew the attention of director Spike Lee, and in February of 2000 he headed to the Charlotte, North Carolina, show with 12 cameras, producing one of Hollywood's most unexpected hits, *The Original Kings of Comedy.*

In 2001, Mac was part of an ensemble cast of stars—with Hollywood heavy-hitters such as Matt Damon, George Clooney, and Brad Pitt—in the re-make of *Ocean's Eleven.* Also in 2001, his first book, *I Ain't Scared of You: Bernie Mac on How Life Is,* was published, and FOX launched the *Bernie Mac Show,* which was an instant success. FOX renewed the show for the 2002 fall line-up. Mac had several more films on the horizon, including *Charlie's Angels II* (2003).

Audra McDonald (1970–)
Singer, Actress

Audra McDonald is one of the American theater's outstanding performers. Within only a few years, she has won three Tony Awards as featured or supporting actress for her work in *Carousel* in 1994, *The Master Class* in 1996, and *Ragtime* in 1998.

McDonald was born in Berlin, Germany, on July 3, 1970, and grew up in Fresno, California, as part of a musical family. Her parents were trained singers and her aunts toured with a gospel singing group. McDonald's professional career began at age nine when she performed in dinner theater for young people. She played roles in *Hello, Dolly!, A Chorus Line, Grease,* and *The Wiz.* After graduating from the Roosevelt School of the Performing Arts in Fresno, McDonald enrolled at the prestigious Juilliard School of Music in Manhattan. However, since Broadway was always McDonald's first love, she was discontented at the classically oriented Juilliard. She took a break from her studies and landed a role in *The Secret Garden*, both on Broadway and in the touring company. She eventually went back to Juilliard and completed a bachelor's degree in 1993.

McDonald auditioned several times until she landed a role in the extravagant production of *Carousel*, staged at the Lincoln Center in 1994. She won critical praise for her role as Carrie Pipperidge, as well as the Tony, Drama Desk, Outer Critics Circle and Theatre World awards that year. Her next star turn was as Sharon, an aspiring singer in conflict with the great opera diva Maria Callas in *The Master Class*. In the show, Sharon sings a technically demanding aria from Giuseppi Verdi's *Macbeth*, a feat brilliantly carried off by McDonald. She earned her second Tony Award for her performance as best featured actress in a play.

Next, McDonald won a part in one of the most ambitious productions in Toronto and New York in 1997, the musical *Ragtime* based on E. L. Doctorow's best-selling 1975 novel about New York at the turn of the century. Her character, Sarah, a young black washerwoman who abandons her illegitimate child, is a relatively small but pivotal part. McDonald won her third Tony Award for best featured actress in a musical category in 1998.

McDonald continues to expand her scope of musical projects. In the autumn of 1998, McDonald released her debut solo album *Way Back to Paradise*, featuring new songs by some of the promising young musical theater composers writing today. She regularly performs her musical repertoire at the cabaret at the Joseph Papp Public Theater. Her biggest challenge in 1999 was the production of her own musical, a show called *Marie Christine*, based on *Medea* and set in New Orleans and Chicago in the 1880s. In 2000, McDonald released her second CD titled *How Glory Goes*, as well as taking the stage in a New York Philharmonic Special Edition of *Sweeny Todd*. In 2001, McDonald appeared on the ABC remake of Rodgers and Hammerstein's *South Pacific*, as well as the HBO movie *Wit*, which gained her an Emmy nomination.

Donald McKayle (1930–)
Dancer, Choreographer, Company Director, Writer

Donald Cohen McKayle, born on July 6, 1930 in Harlem, New York, struggled from humble roots to become an eminent and distinguished American choreographer, performer, and director, in dance, theater, film, and television. As a teenager, when McKayle saw a performance by the legendary Pearl Primus, he eagerly auditioned for the New Dance Group and to his surprise, was awarded a scholarship. His voracious appetite for movement led him to take advantage of the multitude of dance offerings—modern, ballet, Haitian, Hindu, and tap.

There were few role models to guide his youthful aspirations, so he relied primarily on his own personal courage and persistence to pursue his dreams in the face of the social and racial restrictions. When he appeared for auditions during the late 1940s and was told no "Negroes" were wanted, he responded, "I am here, and I would like you to see me dance. . . maybe you'll change your mind."

In 1951, McKayle did change minds when he choreographed what would become an American classic, *Games*, based on childhood play, rhymes, and chants. Exploring the light, carefree innocence of youth and the darker social stigmas associated with racial and social divisions, *Games* brought to the concert stage over a century of inequities and prejudice. That same year, McKayle appeared on Broadway in *Bless You All*. Other Broadway performing credits include *House of Flowers* (1954), *Copper and Brass* (1957), and *West Side Story* (1957).

During the 1950s, he danced in the companies of such innovators as Jean Erdman, Mary Anthony, Merce Cunningham, Anna Sokolow, and Martha Graham. He was also artistic director and resident choreographer of Donald McKayle and Company, from 1951 through 1969. His company featured artists who would eventually become prominent leaders and performers in the world dance scene, including Carmen de Lavallade, Arthur Mitchell, Alvin Ailey, Mary Hinkson, and Eliot Feld.

McKayle received five Tony nominations for his work on Broadway including Best Choreographer for, *Golden Boy* (1964), *Doctor Jazz* (1975), *Sophisticated Ladies* (1981), and *Raisin* (1974), which won a Tony award for Best Musical plus earned him another nomination for Best Director.

McKayle's film choreography includes, *The Great White Hope* (1970), *Bedknobs and Broomsticks* (1971), and *The Jazz Singer* (1980). He received Emmy nominations for *Minstrel Man* (1977) and the children's special, *Free To Be You and Me* (1974).

Many international companies perform his master works in concert dance, including the Alvin Ailey Dance Theater; the Batsheva Dance Company of Tel Aviv, Israel; Ballet Nuevo Mundo of Caracas, Venezuela; Ballet Contemporaneo of Buenos Aires, Argentina; and the San Francisco Ballet.

Appointed Claire Trevor Professor of Dance at the University of California, Irvine, McKayle received the UCI medal, the university's highest honor. He has also been named "One of America's Irreplaceable Dance Treasures: The First 100," by the Dance Heritage Coalition of the Library of Congress. McKayle's autobiography, *Transcending Boundaries: My Dancing Life*, was published in 2002 and *Heartbeats of a Dancemaker*, a PBS documentary on him, was scheduled to air in 2003.

Bebe Miller (1950–)
Choreographer, Dancer, Artistic Director

Bebe Miller was born on September 20, 1950, to an elementary school teacher and a ship steward. Although she grew up in the housing projects of South Brooklyn, New York, her arthritic mother took the family to adult dance classes at Manhattan's Henry Street Settlement every Saturday. Soon, Miller was learning creative dance from Murray Louis and Alwin Nikolais who taught children's dance classes there. Miller went on to take traditional ballet classes at the Carnegie Hall school at the age of 13. She soon stopped, unhappy with the formality of classic dance styles.

Miller resumed taking modern dance when she was 20 and studied fine arts at Earlham College in Richmond, Indiana. After graduating from Earlham in 1971, she moved back to New York to resume dance classes with Nikolais. She won a fellowship to study dance at Ohio State University in Columbus and earned a master's degree from there in 1975.

Two years later Miller joined the modern dance company of Nina Wiener, who had studied with Alvin Ailey and Twyla Tharp, and for six years was inspired by Wiener to infuse her technique with fun and intensity. Soon she was creating her own dances, and performing her group and solo pieces at New York City workshops devoted to developing modern dance choreographers. She left Weiner's company in 1982 and formed the Bebe Miller Company two years later.

Miller's dances have always reflected her inner and outer struggles. Her 1984 dance *Trapped in Queens* shows the difficulties of city life. *Two*, her collaborative duet with dancer Ralph Lemon, examines the changing relationships between men and women. Some of the black influences she brings to her dances show up in the accompanying music. She has used reggae (*Jammin'* 1981), gospel (*Heart, Heart* 1986), Duke Ellington (*Spending Time Doing Things* mid-1980s), and Jimmie Hendrix (*The Hendrix Project* 1991) as accompaniment. In addition to music, Miller collaborates with writers, set designers, and visual artists to create her unique performance pieces.

Miller and her company spent much of the mid-1980s touring throughout the United States and earning numerous accolades. She won four National Endowment for the Arts Choreographer's Fellowships, the New York Dance and Performance Award ("Bessie") for choreography for 1986 and 1987, and the American Choreographer Award and John Guggenheim Memorial Fellowship in 1988.

Alvin Ailey commissioned Miller to create new works for his Alvin Ailey Repertory Ensemble in 1987. Miller produced her series of dances called *Habit of Attraction* the next year, another look at the mysteries of relationships. Another work *Allies* was commissioned in 1989 in part by New York's Brooklyn Academy of Music. This was Miller's first appearance at the Academy's Next Wave festival and allowed her to work on a larger scale. *Allies* again studied human interaction and evolving relationships. Alongside *Allies*, Miller danced her signature solo *Rain* which describes in movement some of Miller's own social and spiritual views.

Her 1991 work *The Hendrix Project* tied music by Jimmie Hendrix and Bob Dylan and the vision of the 1960s to the cultural issues of the 1990s. It was danced in Los Angeles and San Francisco in a program titled *Black Choreographers Moving Towards the 21st Century*. Bebe Miller Company then took it to New York and Europe.

In 1993, Bebe Miller conducted a residency class at Walker Art Centre in Minneapolis which performed her work *In Mnemosyne's House, Again and Again* for which she collaborated with environmental sculptor Eve Laramie and the Minneapolis New Dance. The mid-1990s saw the premieres of *Tiny Sisters, Yard Dance, Heaven and Earth, Blessed,* and *Rythem Studies*.

In recent years, Miller has been investigating the combination of theatrical narrative and abstract movement to express the human condition through the physical body. Her newest work in progress, *Map of the Body*, was developed as part of a master's class in September of 1999. In 2000, Miller was named a Bill Como Fellow as part of the New York Foundation for the Arts Artists' Fellowships. 2001 saw Miller premier *Verge* at the Cultural Crossroads 651 performance. *Verge* would go on to win Miller three New York Dance and Performance (Bessie) Awards for choreography.

Florence Mills (1896–1927)
Singer, Dancer

Florence Mills was born in Washington, DC, on January 25, 1896. She made her debut there at the age of five in *Sons of Ham*. In 1903, the family moved to Harlem, and in 1910 she joined her sisters in an act called the Mills Trio. She later appeared with a group called the Panama Four, which included Ada "Brick-top" Smith.

In 1921, Mills appeared in *Shuffle Along*, a prototype for African American musicals, and her success led to a long engagement at the Plantation, a New York night spot. After a successful appearance in London, she returned to the United States in 1924 to star in *From Dixie to Broadway*, in which she performed her trade-mark song "I'm Just a Little Blackbird Lookin' for a Bluebird." Later, her own *Blackbirds* revue was a great success in London and Paris.

Mills returned to the United States in 1927. Exhausted by her work abroad, she entered the hospital on October 25 for a routine appendectomy and died suddenly on November 1.

Abbie Mitchell (1884–1960)
Singer, Actress

Most celebrated as a concert artist, Abbie Mitchell also performed on the stage and in light musical comedy. At the age of 13, she returned to her native New York City from Baltimore, joining Will Marion Cook's Clorindy Company, and later achieving her first real success with the Williams and Walker Company.

By 1923, having performed in almost every European country, Mitchell returned home to give the first of her many voice concerts in the United States. Mitchell also performed with many opera companies and acted in several plays including *Coquette* (with Helen Hayes; 1927), *Stevedore* (1934) and Langston Hughes's *Mulatto* (1937). She also headed the voice department at Tuskegee Institute for three years.

Arthur Mitchell (1934–)
Dancer, Choreographer

Mitchell was born in Harlem on March 27, 1934, and attended New York's famed High School of the Performing Arts. Mitchell was the first African American male to receive the high school's dance award in 1951.

Upon graduation in 1952, Mitchell enrolled as a scholarship student in the School of American Ballet, run by the eminent choreographer George Balanchine, who also directed the New York City Ballet. In 1955, Mitchell was invited by Balanchine to join the New York City Ballet. Before long, he was a principal dancer in the company, performing in such works as *Agon* and *A Midsummer Night's Dream*.

Mitchell left the New York City Ballet in 1969 to establish the Dance Theatre of Harlem, which he founded

to give young African Americans an opportunity to get out of the ghetto through the arts. Mitchell and the studio have received numerous awards and citations including the Changers Award given by *Mademoiselle* magazine in 1970 and the Capezio Dance Award in 1971. Surviving a financial crisis in 1990, the school and company are now back on their feet, though treading carefully due to the precarious state of the arts in the United States.

In 1993, New York City Mayor David Dinkins presented Mitchell with the Handel Medallion, the city's highest cultural honor. He was also one of the winners of the Kennedy Center Honors and the National Medal of Arts in 1993. The School of American Ballet presented Mitchell with a lifetime achievement award at its annual dinner on February 6, 1995. In 1999, Mitchell was inducted into the Dance Hall of Fame and a year later he was the only dancer to win a gold medal at the Sixth New York International Ballet Competition. Mitchell continues to tour with the Dance Theater of Harlem nationally and internationally.

Eddie Murphy. *See* Film & Television chapter.

Fayard (1914–) and Harold (1924–) Nicholas
Dancers

The Nicholas Brothers were one of the great tap dance teams of the first half of the twentieth century. Their acrobatics and precision were admired by the likes of Fred Astaire and George Balanchine, and their appearances in motion pictures provide a record of their astounding abilities.

Fayard Nicholas was born in 1914; Harold in 1924. Their professional debut was, ironically, on the radio program *The Horn and Hardart Kiddie Hour* in 1931. In 1932, they became a featured act at Harlem's Cotton Club. They made their first Broadway appearance in the *Ziegfeld Follies* of 1936; this was followed by *Babes in Arms* in 1937.

The Nicholas Brothers's film debut was in *Pie Pie Blackbird* in 1932, and they appeared in several other movies in the 1930s and 1940s including *The Big Broadcast of 1936* (1936), *The Great American Broadcast* (1941), *Sun Valley Serenade* (1941), *Stormy Weather* (1943), and *The Pirate* (1948). The latter is particularly memorable for the sequence in which they are featured.

Harold Nicholas married actress Dorothy Dandridge in 1942, but the couple later divorced. The two brothers continue to be active in the world of dance: Harold co-starred with Gregory Hines in the movie *Tap* in 1989, and Fayard won a Tony Award for best choreographer for the Broadway musical *Black and Blue* in the same year. In 1992, the Nicholas Brothers were honored by the Kennedy Center. They received awards from *Dance Magazine* in 1995. A gala for the Nicholas Brothers was celebrated at Carnegie Hall in April of 1998 called *From Harlem to Hollywood: A Tribute to the Nicholas Brothers, "Tap Legends."* It starred Gregory Hines, Lena Horne, Savion Glover, Maya Angelou, Maurice Hines, Ben Vereen, and Jimmy Slide, representing the many generations influenced and inspired by these "Tap Legends."

Frederick O'Neal (1905–1992)
Actor

Frederick O'Neal was the first black person to hold the position of president of Actor's Equity, a fitting tribute to his long years of service to the American theater as both actor and teacher.

O'Neal was born on August 27, 1905 in Brookville, Mississippi. After his father's death in 1919, he moved with his family to St. Louis, finishing high school there and appearing in several Urban League dramatic productions.

In 1927, with the help of some friends in St. Louis, O'Neal founded the Ira Aldridge Players, the second African American acting troupe in America. For the next ten years, he played in 30 of its productions. In 1937, he came to New York, and three years later helped found the American Negro Theater. Today, its alumni include such established stars as Sidney Poitier, Earle Hyman, Harry Belafonte, Ruby Dee, Ossie Davis, and Hilda Simms.

O'Neal himself starred in *Anna Lucasta* (1944), for which he won the Clarence Derwent Award and the Drama Critics Award for the best supporting performance by an actor on Broadway. He was later featured in *Take a Giant Step*, *The Winner*, and several other stage productions. His films include *Pinky* (1949) and *The Man with the Golden Arm* (1956). He also appeared on several televised dramatic and comedy shows.

In 1964, O'Neal became the first black president of Actor's Equity. After devoting himself full-time to Actor's Equity, O'Neal was in 1970 elected international president of the Associated Actors and Artists of America, the parent union of all show business performers's unions. He became president and chairman of the board of the Schomburg Center for Research in Black Culture, a position which included such responsibilities as raising money to conserve and preserve materials in the center, soliciting resources for the institution,

and lobbying for the construction of a new building. He was a member of the New York State Council on the Arts, President of the Catholic Interracial Council, chairman of the AFL-CIO Civil Rights Committee, and vice president of the A. Philip Randolph Institute. In 1980, he received the National Urban Coalition's Distinguished Trade Unionist Award. In 1990, he received a special tribute from the Black Filmmakers Hall of Fame. O'Neal died on April 27, 1992.

Pearl Primus (1919–1994)
Dancer, Choreographer

Pearl Primus's anthropological approach to dance made her one of the most purposeful figures in that medium: for her, dance was education, not merely entertainment. Her aim was to show audiences and dancers alike the African roots of dance and to bring the African American experience alive.

Primus was born in Trinidad on November 29, 1919. Originally intending to pursue a career in medicine, she received a bachelor of arts degree in pre-medical sciences and biology from Hunter College, with graduate work in medical education and psychology. But 1940s America did not welcome blacks or women in medicine, and after seeking employment in vain, Primus sought assistance from the government's National Youth Administration. She was put into a youth administration dance group, and by 1941 was accepted into New York City's New Dance Group. Her professional debut was at the Young Men's Hebrew Association in New York City on February 14, 1943. In April of that year, she began appearing at Café Society Downtown, the famed New York City nightclub, but left after ten months for an appearance on Broadway at the Belasco Theater. By this time she had her own dance company, Pearl Primus, Percival Borde, and Company. She toured Africa and the southern United States, and incorporated what she learned into her dance style.

Primus is best known for the dances *African Ceremonial* and *Strange Fruit*, which were incorporated into her *Solos for Performance at the Café Society* (ca. 1944) and *Hard Times Blues* (1945).

Primus died on October 29, 1994.

Richard Pryor (1940–)
Comedian, Actor

Comedian Richard Pryor has had great success as a stand-up comedian, writer, actor, and recording star. He has often used elements of his unconventional upbringing and adult life as material in his comedy routines.

Born Richard Franklin Lennox Thomas Pryor III on December 1, 1940, in New York City, he was raised by his grandmother in the Peoria, Illinois, brothel she ran. His mother worked there as a prostitute. His parents married when he was three years old, but the union did not last. His grandmother was a strict disciplinarian and young Richard was often beaten.

In school Pryor was often in trouble with the authorities. Pryor was expelled from high school for striking a teacher. In 1958 he joined the army and spent two years in Germany. He returned to Peoria after his military service and during the early 1960s began his work as a stand-up comic on a local circuit. He moved to New York City's Greenwich Village in 1963 where he honed his stand-up routine. A 1964 appearance on *The Ed Sullivan Show* led to his first movie role in *The Busy Body* (1966), followed by bit parts in the 1968 films *The Green Berets* and *Wild in the Streets*. During this time Pryor continued to play to live audiences.

In 1972, Pryor played Piano Man in *Lady Sings the Blues* and earned an Academy Award nomination for his performance. Throughout the 1970s, Pryor continued his work as a stand-up comic and also contributed his writing talents to television's *The Flip Wilson Show* and *Sanford and Son*, Mel Brooks's film *Blazing Saddles*, and Lily Tomlin's television special *Lily* for which he won an Emmy Award. He won two of his five Grammy Awards for his comedy albums *That Nigger's Crazy* (1974) and *Bicentennial Nigger* (1976).

Pryor wrote and starred in *Bingo Long Traveling All-Stars — Motor Kings* (1976) and received raves for his work in *Silver Streak* (also 1976). In 1979, the comedian's film *Richard Pryor Live in Concert* brought his stand-up act to millions.

In 1978, Pryor suffered a major heart attack, and in 1980, while freebasing cocaine, he set himself ablaze and suffered severe injuries. He addresses these incidents in his second concert movie *Live on Sunset Strip* (1982). In 1985 Pryor co-wrote, directed and starred in *Jo Jo Dancer, Your Life Is Calling*, a semi-autobiographical tale of a comedian who relives his life immediately following a near fatal accident. Pryor's later films include: *The Toy; Some Kind of Hero; Brewster's Millions; Critical Condition; Stir Crazy; Bustin' Loose; Moving;* and *See No Evil, Hear No Evil*. In 1989 Pryor co-starred with Eddie Murphy in *Harlem Nights*. He teamed with Gene Wilder in the 1991 film *Another You* and appeared in *Lost Highway* later in the decade.

Pryor has been in failing health in recent years. He was diagnosed with multiple sclerosis in 1986 and has had triple bypass heart surgery. He lives a reclusive life in his Bel Air, California, home. In 1993, Pryor was awarded with a star on the Hollywood Walk of Fame.

In 1995, Pryor's collection of memoirs *Pryor Convictions—and Other Life Sentences* was published, detailing his difficult childhood, failed marriages, and battles with cocaine addiction and multiple sclerosis. In 1998 Pryor was honored with the first Mark Twain Prize for American Humor and in 2000 he won the MTV Lifetime Achievement award. In 2002 Pryor sued successfully for the legal rights to the master tapes of his early comedy recordings, in a settlement against Michael Chernow. Chernow had purchased the assets of Laff Records in 1988 and believed erroneously that his company, M. B. Music, held the rights to the Pryor master recordings.

Phylicia Rashad. *See* **Film & Television chapter.**

Lloyd Richards (1923?–)
Theatrical Director, Educator

Lloyd Richards, renowned actor, stage director, and educator, was born in Toronto, Ontario, in the early 1920s. He moved to Detroit while still young where he worked to support his family and eventually studied at Wayne State University, first law and then theater, receiving his degree in 1944. After serving in World War II as one of the first black pilots, he returned to Detroit and became active in radio drama and regional theater.

Soon Richards moved to New York to earn a living acting in plays and television dramas and coaching others in his own studio. In 1959, Sidney Poitier convinced him to direct an important Broadway play, Lorraine Hansberry's classic story *A Raisin in the Sun*. This play, the first by a black woman to be produced on Broadway, explores issues of segregation, thwarted ambition, and family tensions. It ran for 530 performances and made its stars and Richards famous. In the wake of that success, Richards began teaching drama at Hunter College and New York University.

In 1966, Richards was named director of the prestigious playwrights's conference at the Eugene O'Neill Theater in Waterford, Connecticut. He continued to nurture and produce new plays for regional theaters by such promising playwrights as August Wilson, Athol Fugard, John Patrick Shanley, Charles Fuller, and David Henry Hwang. In 1979, Richards became dean of the Yale School of Drama and artistic director of the Yale Repertory Theater.

Many famous plays debuted at the Yale Repertory Theater under Richards's direction. These include South

African playwright Athol Fugard's *Master Harold. . . and the Boys* and two Pulitzer Prize-winning works by August Wilson, *Fences* and *The Piano Lesson*. He won the Tony Award for best director for *Fences* in 1986.

Richards's most creative partnership was with playwright Wilson for whom he directed, not only *Fences* and *The Piano Lesson*, but also *Ma Rainey's Black Bottom*, *Joe Turner's Come and Gone*, and *Two Trains Running*, for which he was awarded the Helen Hayes Award for best director in 1992.

The Yale Repertory Theater also attracted a number of notable actors while Richards was in residence including James Earl Jones, Glenn Close, Jason Robards, Colleen Dewhurst, and Angela Bassett. In 1979, Richards directed Jones in a one-man show about the life and career of black actor Paul Robeson.

Lloyd Richards left the Yale Repertory Theater in 1991 after 12 years as dean and artistic director. However, he continued to direct, lecture, and mentor new talent in the theater. In 1995, he directed a Hallmark Hall of Fame production of *The Piano Lesson* for television, starring Charles S. Dutton and Alfre Woodard.

Among his many honors, Richards was inducted into the Theater Hall of Fame in 1990. Other distinctions include the Directors Award from the National Black Theatre Festival, a National Medal of Arts from President Bill Clinton in 1993, the Huntington Award for lifetime achievement in 1995 and a 1996 Outer Critics Award for best director of Wilson's play *Seven Guitars*.

Bill "Bojangles" Robinson (1878–1949)
Dancer

Bill Robinson was born in May of 1878, in Richmond, Virginia. Having been orphaned early, he was raised by his grandmother, a former slave. By the time he was eight, he was earning his own way by dancing in the street for pennies and working as a stable boy.

In 1887, Robinson toured the South in a show called *The South Before the War*. The following year, he moved to Washington, DC, where he again worked as a stable boy. By 1896, he had teamed up with George Cooper. This act was successful on the circuit until the slump of 1907 caused it to fold. Robinson returned to Richmond and worked as a waiter until a year later when he was taken up by a theatrical manager and became a cabaret and vaudeville headliner.

In 1927, Robinson starred on Broadway in *Blackbirds*, and in 1932 he had top billing in *Harlem's Heaven*, the first all-black motion picture with sound. Later, he scored a Hollywood success by teaching his famous stair dance to Shirley Temple in *The Little Colonel* (1936). Robinson made 14 movies including *The Littlest Rebel* (1935), *In Old Kentucky* (1936), *Rebecca of Sunnybrook Farm* (1938), *Stormy Weather* (1943), and *One Mile from Heaven* (1938).

Throughout his long career on stage and in movies, Robinson was known as the "King of Tap Dancers." Robinson died on November 15, 1949.

Chris Rock. *See* Film & Television chapter.

Ntozake Shange. *See* Literature chapter.

Sinbad (1956–)
Comedian, Actor

The 6-foot, 5-inch Sinbad has delighted audiences with his comedy, which combines street parlance—noticeably free of obscenities—with tales of American life. Born David Adkins on November 10, 1956, in Benton Harbor, Michigan, Sinbad aspired to be a basketball star. He earned a basketball scholarship to the University of Denver, but a serious knee injury caused him to give up basketball, and he left college in 1978. Shortly thereafter, he renamed himself Sinbad, after the heroic character in *The Arabian Nights*, to boost his spirits. He spent three and a half years in the U.S. Air Force, hating every minute until his 1983 discharge.

By that time, Sinbad had decided to try his hand at stand-up comedy. A series of low-paying engagements throughout the United States followed, and his break came when he appeared on the television talent contest *Star Search* seven times in the mid-1980s. He later worked as a warm-up comedian for *The Cosby Show*, and in 1989 he was cast as dorm director Walter Oakes on *A Different World*—a role that was broadened in 1991 when Oakes became a counselor. In 1993, Sinbad starred in his own situation comedy *The Sinbad Show* about a single foster parent. The show only lasted one season. He appeared in the movies *Houseguest* in 1995 and *Jingle All The Way* with Arnold Schwarzenegger in 1996.

In 1997, Sinbad published *Sinbad's Guide to Life: Because I Know Everything*. He also took over as host of the late night talk show *Vibe* in 1997, and Sinbad took a more invested interest in the show when his production company Afros and Bellbottoms agreed to finance the second season of the show. The show was eventually cancelled in 1998 due to low ratings. Since 1998 Sinbad has appeared on such shows as *Hollywood Squares* and *Ready To Run*. In 2000, he hosted the Miss Universe Pageant. Sinbad looks to return to the silver screen in 2002 with roles in *Crazy as Hell* and *Treading Water*.

Noble Sissle (left) and Frederick O'Neal present Ethel Waters with an award from the Negro Actors Guild of America for her role in *Pinky*.

Noble Sissle (1889–1975)
Lyricist, Singer

Noble Sissle was born in Indianapolis, Indiana, on July 10, 1889. He reaped his early successes teamed up with the great Eubie Blake. Sissle wrote the lyrics and sang them in performance; Blake composed and played the music. Together the two created such songs as "I'm Just Wild about Harry," "It's All Your Fault," "Serenade Blues," and "Love Will Find a Way."

In 1921 *Shuffle Along*, the first black musical with a love theme, made Sissle and Blake famous. Joining forces with the writing and comedy team of Flournoy Miller and Aubrey Lyles, Sissle and Blake wrote the words and music to over a dozen songs for the show. *Shuffle Along* became a huge success in the United States and Europe, where it had a prolonged tour. As with most black performers in the early 1900s, Sissle and his troupe would have to travel as far as 20 or 30 miles out of their way to find a place to eat and sleep, since blacks were not welcome in the white hotels of the towns where they played.

Other Sissle and Blake shows included *Chocolate Dandies* (1924) and *Keep Shufflin'* (1928). Noble Sissle died December 17, 1975, at his home in Tampa, Florida.

Lynne Thigpen (1948?–)
Actress

Lynne Thigpen has spent more than 25 years proving that she could make a living working on stage, screen, and television as a professional actress. She grew up in

Joliet, Illinois, "always a singer and always a performer." Her high school English teacher encouraged her theatrical pursuits so, after graduation, she enrolled at the University of Illinois in Champaign-Urbana, where she majored in English and speech. Although pursuing teaching certification, she won an acting fellowship to the University and began a master's degree in theater. After one semester, she left school for New York and Broadway.

Soon after arriving in New York, Thigpen landed a two-year role in the popular musical *Godspell* on Broadway which later led to a role in the 1973 film version. She then worked as a musical performer in various stage productions including *Tintypes*, for which she earned a Tony nomination in 1980. Deciding that singing was not enough, Thigpen switched to acting and won recurring roles on such television shows as *All My Children*, *L.A. Law*, and *Law and Order*. Family shows such as *The Cosby Show*, *Dear John*, and *Roseanne* showcased her comedic talents. She also appeared in many films, among them, *The Warriors*, *Tootsie*, *The Paper*, *Lean on Me*, and *Bob Roberts*.

Serious drama highlighted Thigpen's versatile talents. In 1988, she won the Los Angeles Drama Critic's Award for her role opposite James Earl Jones in August Wilson's *Fences*. She was also honored with an Obie Award for her portrayal of an itinerant South African woman in Athol Fugard's *Bozeman and Lena* in 1992.

In the 1990s, Thigpen was probably best known for her role as the Chief on the Public Broadcasting Service (PBS) children's show *Where in the World Is Carmen Sandiego?* Over her six years in this series, she was nominated four times for Emmys as outstanding performer in a daytime children's television series. In 1999, she filmed a guest part as the head of WASA (the Worms' Air and Space Agency) for *The Muppet Show*.

Thigpen was named associate artistic director of the Circle Repertory Company in New York City in 1995, along with Austin Pendleton, only to decline it a few months later to continue acting full-time. She played the role of a childless Jewish African American woman in Wendy Wasserstein's *An American Daughter* in 1996, winning the 1997 Tony Award for best featured actress.

Thigpen's voice alone has won her recognition. She has narrated numerous documentaries for PBS. She was heard on radio on *The Garrison Keillor Show*. Listeners of books on tape know her melodic voice from thoughtful narrations of works such as *The Autobiography of Miss Jane Pittman*, *Roll of Thunder, Hear My Cry*, *One Better*, and other audio productions.

Lynne Thigpen continues to prove that stretching one's creative muscles in the performing arts can shape a varied and viable career. In 1999 she appeared in the movies *Random Hearts* and *Bicentennial Man*. She also starred in the off Broadway show *Jar the Floor* for which she won an Obie award. In 2000, she took on a role opposite Samuel L. Jackson in the remake of *Shaft* and also appeared as a regular on the television series *The District*. A year later she appeared beside Steve Martin and a cast of other notable actors and actresses in the comedy *Novocaine*.

Leslie Uggams (1943–)
Singer, Actress

Born in the Washington Heights section of New York City on May 25, 1943, Leslie Uggams enjoyed a comfortable childhood. She made her singing debut at the age of six, performing with the choir of St. James Presbyterian Church in New York. Shortly thereafter she debuted as an actress in the television series *Beulah*. A year later, Uggams began performing regularly at the famed Apollo Theatre in Harlem, opening for such legends as Louis Armstrong, Ella Fitzgerald, and Dinah Washington. Uggams developed her poise and stage presence early in life, attending the Professional Children's School, where she was chosen student body president in her senior year.

Uggams subsequently won $25,000 on the popular television quiz show *Name That Tune*, which renewed her interest in a singing career. In 1961, while studying at Juilliard, Uggams became a regular on *The Mitch Miller Show*, a variety show featuring old favorites. She was at the time the only black performer appearing regularly on network television.

Throughout the 1960s, Uggams appeared in numerous nightclubs and had several supper club and television engagements. Her big break came when she was signed as a replacement for Lena Horne in *Hallelujah Baby*, a show that presented a musical chronicle of the civil rights movement. Uggams won instant stardom and received a Tony Award for her performance.

In 1977, Uggams appeared as Kizzy in the television adaptation of Alex Haley's novel *Roots*. In May 1982, she performed in a new Broadway show *Blues in the Night* at the Rialto Theater in New York City. She has also appeared on television in the miniseries *Backstairs at the White House* and *The Book of Lists*; in the film *Skyjacked*; and in the musicals *Jerry's Girls*, *The Great Gershwin*, and *Anything Goes*.

After touring during the early 1990s in *Stringbean*, a musical based on the career of Ethel Waters, Uggams joined the cast of the hit daytime soap opera *All My Children* in 1996. In 1995 she released her latest recording *Painted Mem'ries*. More recently, Uggams appeared at Primary Stages in New York in the title role of the well-reviewed play *The Old Settler* by John Henry Redwood in October of 1998. In 2001, she took the stage again, this time as Ruby in *King Hedley II* a continuation of August Wilson's *Seven Guitars*. She received a Tony Award Best Actress nomination for the role.

Ben Vereen (1946–)
Dancer, Actor

Ben Augustus Vereen was born October 10, 1946, in Miami, Florida. After his family moved to the Bedford-Stuyvesant section of Brooklyn, New York, he attended the High School of Performing Arts in Manhattan. His dancing ability had been discovered almost accidentally after he had been sent to dance school by his mother. Vereen has since been called America's premier song and dance man.

Vereen made his stage debut in 1965 in *The Prodigal Son*. He went on to appear in *Sweet Charity* (1966), *Golden Boy* (1968), *Hair* (1968), and *No Place to Be Somebody* (1970). Vereen is best known for his Broadway role in *Pippin* (1972), which won him a Tony Award. He was also nominated for a Tony for his co-starring role in *Jesus Christ Superstar* (1971). His film appearances include roles in *Funny Lady* (1975), *All That Jazz* (1979), and *The Zoo Gang*.

Vereen has starred in the ABC comedy series *Tenspeed and Brown Shoe* and is known for his television specials; the highly acclaimed *Ben Vereen: His Roots* (1978) won seven Emmy Awards. He also portrayed Louis "Satchmo" Armstrong, and received wide acclaim for his role of Chicken George in television's adaption of Alex Haley's *Roots* (1977) and for his performance in *Jubilee*.

His concert tour in the late 1990s earned Vereen the highest honors awarded by the American Guild of Variety Artists: "Entertainer of the Year," "Rising Star," and "Song and Dance Star." He is the first person to win three of these AGVA awards in one year.

Vereen continued to work in both television and movies throughout the 1990s working on such shows as *OZ* and *Feast of All Saints* and appearing in movies such as *Why Do Fools Fall in Love?* and *I'll Take You There*. Currently Vereen is touring with a production of Herb Gardner's *I'm Not Rappaport* which is expected to return to Broadway sometime in 2002.

Fredi Washington (1903–1994)
Actress, Dancer, Civil Rights Activist

Born Fredericka Carolyn Washington in Savannah, Georgia, on December 23, 1903, Washington and her younger sister were sent to a convent after the death of their mother and subsequent remarriage of their father. As a teenager, she left this sheltered world to live with relatives in New York City in order to pursue a career in the performing arts.

One of Washington's first big breaks came in 1919 when she was cast as a member of the Happy Honeysuckles, the back-up troupe for Josephine Baker. Two years later she began earning a good salary in the stage production of an all-black musical called *Shuffle Along*. Washington was next discovered by Broadway impresario Lee Shubert, who urged her to audition for a play called *Black Boy*. In the 1926 production, she starred—under the stage name Edith Warren—opposite Paul Robeson, but unfortunately much media and audience attention at its debut was focused on Washington's light complexion. Indeed, she was often able to pass as white, especially when traveling in the segregated areas of the South with her first husband, a member of Duke Ellington's orchestra.

During the 1920s Washington continued to appear in stage roles and toured Europe for a time; she also appeared in the 1930 production of *Sweet Chariot*. Moving on to film, Washington again teamed with Robeson when she appeared in the 1933 drama *The Emperor Jones*—but Hollywood censors insisted she wear makeup to darken her complexion during her love scenes with him. The following year Washington appeared in her most acclaimed role in the film *Imitation of Life*, portraying a young woman who forsakes her heritage in order to pass as white.

Unfortunately, Washington found her acting career stymied by a lack of roles for African American women in general and especially for ones with light complexions; she fought for many decades to reverse such attitudes in the film industry in Hollywood. In 1937 she founded the Negro Actors Guild of America, and wrote extensively on the subject for the New York City-based paper *The People's Voice* for which she served as theater critic and columnist. During the 1940s and 1950s she worked as a cast consultant on numerous African American-themed films in Hollywood and continued to appear in stage productions. She died on June 28, 1994, in Stamford, Connecticut.

Ethel Waters (1896–1977)
Actress, Singer

The distinguished career of Ethel Waters spanned half a century. She showed her versatility by contributing to virtually every entertainment medium—stage, screen, television, and recordings.

Ethel Waters was born on October 31, 1900, and spent most of her childhood in her hometown of Chester, Pennsylvania. By the age of 17, she was singing professionally at the Lincoln Theatre in Baltimore. During this early phase of her career, she became the first woman to perform W. C. Handy's "St. Louis Blues" on stage.

After several years in nightclubs and vaudeville, Waters made her Broadway debut in the 1927 review *Africana*. In 1930, she appeared in *Blackbirds*, and in 1931 and 1932 she starred in *Rhapsody in Black*. The following year she was featured with Clifton Webb and Marilyn Miller in Irving Berlin's *As Thousands Cheer*. In 1935, she co-starred with Bea Lillie in *At Home Abroad*, and three years later she played the lead in *Mamba's Daughters*.

In 1940, Waters appeared in the stage version of *Cabin in the Sky*, a triumph which she repeated in the 1943 movie version. Her other film appearances include: *Rufus Jones for President* (1931); *Tales of Manhattan* (1941); *Cairo* (1942); *Stage Door Canteen* (1943); and *Pinky* (1949).

Her autobiography *His Eye Is on the Sparrow* was a 1951 Book-of-the-Month Club selection. The title is taken from a song that she sang in her 1950 stage success *Member of the Wedding*.

Waters died on September 1, 1977, in Chatsburg, California.

Damon Wayans. *See* Film & Television chapter.

Keenan Ivory Wayans. *See* Film & Television chapter.

Bert Williams (1874–1922)
Comedian, Dancer

The legendary Bert Williams is considered by many to be the greatest black vaudeville performer in the history of the American stage.

Born on November 12, 1874, on New Providence Island in the Bahamas, Williams moved to New York with his family, and then on to California, where he graduated from high school. After studying civil engineering for a time, he decided to try his hand at show business.

In 1895, Williams teamed with George Walker to form a successful vaudeville team. Five years later, they opened in New York in *The Sons of Ham* and were acclaimed for the characterizations that became their stock-in-trade—Walker as a dandy and Williams in blackface, complete with outlandish costumes and black dialect. The show ran for two years.

In 1902, their show *In Dahomey* was so popular that they took it to England, where it met with equal success. The partners continued to produce such shows as *The Policy Players*, *Bandanna Land*, and *Abyssinia* until Walker's death in 1909.

Thereafter, Williams worked as a featured solo performer in the *Ziegfeld Follies*, touring America for ten years in several versions of the show. His most famous songs were "Woodman, Spare That Tree"; "O, Death, Where is Thy Sting"; and "Nobody," his own composition and trademark.

Williams died of pneumonia on March 4, 1922.

August Wilson. *See* Literature chapter.

Flip Wilson (1933–1998)
Comedian, Actor

Flip Wilson reached the pinnacle of the entertainment world with a series of original routines and ethnic characters rivaled only by those of Bill Cosby. Wilson's hilarious monologues, seen on a number of network television shows, made him the most visible black comedian of the early 1970s.

Born Clerow Wilson on December 8, 1933, Wilson was the tenth in a family of 24 children, 18 of whom survived. The family was destitute, and Wilson was a troublesome child during his youth in his hometown of Jersey City; he ran away from reform school several times and was ultimately raised in foster homes.

Wilson's comic talents first surfaced while he was serving in the U.S. Air Force. Sent overseas to the Pacific, Wilson entertained his buddies with preposterous routines. Back in civilian life, he worked as a bellhop and part-time showman. Opportunity struck in 1959 when a Miami businessman sponsored him for one year at $50 a week, thus enabling Wilson to concentrate on the evolution of his routine. For the next five years or so, Wilson appeared regularly at the Apollo Theatre in Harlem. In 1965, he began a series of nationwide appearances on *The Tonight Show*. Long-term contracts and several hit records followed in quick sequence, and Wilson became firmly established as one of the truly innovative talents in the comedy profession.

With *The Flip Wilson Show* in the early 1970s, Wilson became the first black to have a weekly prime time television show under his own name. He became famous for his original character creations such as "Geraldine." On January 31, 1972, he appeared on the cover of *Time* magazine. In 1976, he made his dramatic debut on television in the ABC series *The Six Million Dollar Man*.

During the early 1980s, Wilson appeared in numerous nightclubs and television specials. He starred in the television series *People Are Funny* in 1984 and *Charlie & Co.* in 1985. He has also made comedy albums including *The Devil Made Me Buy This Dress*, for which he received a Grammy Award.

Wilson died on December 1, 1998.

George C. Wolfe (1954–)
Playwright, Stage Director, Producer

Wolfe was born September 23, 1954, into a Frankfort, Kentucky, household; his father worked for the state and his mother was an educator and later school principal. Wolfe grew up in an insular African American community that stressed self-sufficiency and achievement, and a visit to New York City as a teenager helped instill a desire for a career in the theater. By 1976 he had earned a degree in theater from Pomona College.

After working for a few years in the Los Angeles theater scene, Wolfe moved to New York City in 1979. After earning a master's degree in musical theater from New York University, he had his first minor recognition with the 1985 off-off Broadway production of his play *Paradise*. Wolfe's 1986 satire on African American cultural icons, *The Colored Museum*, won rave reviews from critics but also weathered criticism as well; eventually the play was staged at New York's Joseph Papp Public Theater and broadcast on PBS.

Wolfe became affiliated with the esteemed Public Theater, which stages the annual New York Shakespeare Festival, and directed several works for it beginning in 1990 including *Spunk* and *The Caucasian Chalk Circle*. With the 1992 Broadway debut of *Jelly's Last Jam*—a musical about the life of 1920s jazz musician Jelly Roll Morton that Wolfe wrote and directed—he rose in prominence in New York's theater community; in 1993 he directed parts one and two of the Pulitzer Prize-winning trilogy by playwright Tony Kushner, *Angels in America*. For his direction of first segment of the drama *Millennium Approaches*, Wolfe won a Tony Award.

Another honor was accorded Wolfe in 1993 when he was named director of the Joseph Papp Public Theater/New York Shakespeare Festival; since then he has been praised for giving the venerable institution a more multicultural focus. Recent works under his directorial aegis include a revival of *The Tempest* and the hit Broadway musical *Bring in 'Da Noise, Bring in 'Da Funk*, which won four Tony Awards, one of them for

Wolfe's direction. In 1998 Wolfe revived another Shakespeare classic *Macbeth* starring Alec Baldwin and Angela Bassett. In 1998 he brought back the classic *On the Town* and in 1999 went back to Shakespeare with *The Taming of the Shrew*. Wolfe did his most recent Shakespeare revival in 2000 with *Julius Cesear*. Then Wolfe went in a new direction, taking on the projects *Topdog/Underdog* in 2001 and *Elaine Stritch at Liberty* in 2002.

Wolfe has been the recipient of the Drama Desk, Outer Critics Circle, Dramalogue and Obie awards. He was named Person of the Year by the National Theater Conference and "a living landmark" by the New York Landmark Conservatory. His alma mater Pomona College gave him an honorary doctorate in 1995.

◆ AWARD WINNERS

New York Drama Critics' Circle Award

Best American Play
1959: *A Raisin in the Sun*, Lorraine Hansberry
1975: *The Taking of Miss Janie*, Ed Bullins
1982: *A Soldier's Play*, Charles Fuller
1992: *Two Trains Running*, August Wilson

Best New Play
1985: *Ma Rainey's Black Bottom*, August Wilson
1987: *Fences*, August Wilson
1988: *Joe Turner's Come and Gone*, August Wilson
1990: *The Piano Lesson*, August Wilson
1996: *Seven Guitars*, August Wilson
2000: *Jitney*, August Wilson

Pulitzer Prize—Drama
1970: *No Place To Be Somebody*, Charles Gordone
1982: *A Soldier's Play*, Charles Fuller
1987: *Fences*, August Wilson
1990: *The Piano Lesson*, August Wilson
2002: *Topdog/Underdog*, Suzan-Lori Parks

Tony Awards

Actor (Dramatic)
1969: James Earl Jones, *The Great White Hope*
1975: John Kani, *Sizwe Banzi*; Winston Ntshona, *The Island*
1987: James Earl Jones, *Fences*

Supporting or Featured Actor (Dramatic)
1982: Zakes Mokae, *Master Harold. . . and the Boys*
1992: Larry Fishburne, *Two Trains Running*
1994: Jeffrey Wright, *Angels in America*
1996: Ruben Santiago-Hudson, *Seven Guitars*

Actor (Musical)

1970: Cleavon Little, *Purlie*
1973: Ben Vereen, *Pippin*
1982: Ben Harvey, *Dreamgirls*
1992: Gregory Hines, *Jelly's Last Jam*

Supporting or Featured Actor (Musical)

1954: Harry Belafonte, *John Murray Anderson's Almanac*
1975: Ted Rose, *The Wiz*
1981: Hinton Battle, *Sophisticated Ladies*
1982: Cleavant Derricks, *Dreamgirls*
1983: Charles "Honi" Coles, *My One and Only*
1984: Hinton Battle, *The Tap Dance Kid*
1991: Hinton Battle, *Miss Saigon*
1997: Chuck Cooper, *The Life*

Supporting or Featured Actress (Dramatic)

1977: Trazana Beverley, *For Colored Girls Who Have Considered Suicide/When the Rainbow Is Enuf*
1987: Mary Alice, *Fences*
1988: L. Scott Caldwell, *Joe Turner's Come and Gone*
1997: Lynne Thigpen, *An American Daughter*
2001: Viola Davis, *King Hedley II*

Actress (Musical)

1962: Diahann Carroll, *No Strings*
1968: Leslie Uggams, *Hallelujah, Baby*
1974: Virginia Capers, *Raisin*
1982: Jennifer Holliday, *Dreamgirls*
1989: Ruth Brown, *Black and Blue*
1996: Audra McDonald, *Master Class*
2000: Heather Headley, *Aida*

Supporting or Featured Actress (Musical)

1950: Juanita Hall, *South Pacific*
1968: Lillian Hayman, *Hallelujah, Baby*
1970: Melba Moore, *Purlie*
1975: Dee Dee Bridgewater, *The Wiz*
1977: Delores Hall, *Your Arms's Too Short To Box with God*
1978: Nell Carter, *Ain't Misbehavin'*
1992: Tonya Pinkins, *Jelly's Last Jam*
1994: Audra McDonald, *Carousel*
1996: Ann Duquesnay, *Bring in 'Da Noise, Bring in 'Da Funk*
1997: Lillias White, *The Life*

Play

1974: *The River Niger*, Joseph A. Walker
1987: *Fences*, August Wilson

Classical Music

♦ Black Musicians in Early America ♦ Classical Music in the Twentieth Century
♦ Studies in African American Music
♦ American Academy and Institute of Arts and Letters Award Winners
♦ Classical Music Composers, Conductors, Instrumentalists, and Singers

by Calvert Bean

When the first Africans arrived in 1619 on the eastern coast of what is now the United States, they brought with them a rich musical heritage. In the culture from which these slaves were torn, music and dance were part of almost every public activity. Each community had expert musicians who transmitted these vital skills, orally and through training, from generation to generation. They brought to the New World not only their songs and dances, but their love of and need for music as an integral part of daily life.

♦ BLACK MUSICIANS IN EARLY AMERICA

As slaves, the Africans absorbed much of the folk and religious music of the white culture—which followed European models—while cherishing their own native practices. The resulting hybrid was a uniquely American style of music adopted by both white and black musicians.

Enslaved Africans sang English psalms and hymns in church as they converted to Christianity. They heard folk and popular tunes in the taverns and in their homes. Some slaves in the South studied with itinerant music teachers. The most talented musicians gained professional skills that were quickly put to use by whites. Both bonded servants and slave musicians, playing instruments such as the violin, flute, and piano, provided much of the recreational music for their masters. On the self-sufficient plantations of the South, the most musically gifted of the domestic slaves provided evening "entertainments." They played at dance

balls and dancing schools. Once public concerts became possible and popular in the New World, a few talented slaves actually gave public concerts.

Early African American Composers and Conductors

Besides instrumentalists, African Americans were dance and military band leaders, composers and arrangers, singers, church choral directors, and entertainers. Free African Americans in Northern cities, such as Boston, Philadelphia, and New York, established remarkable careers and enjoyed wide esteem before the Civil War. One of the best examples is Frank Johnson (1792–1844), an all-around "music man" who was a virtuoso bugler and flutist, a bandmaster whose organizations were in great demand for military ceremonies and public dances, and an arranger of countless tunes and composer of many others. From his home base in Philadelphia, he toured widely with his band, including travel to England (then unprecedented for an African American ensemble), with as much success on the road as at home. Other leading conductors of both social and military bands included James Hemmenway (1800–1849), Aaron Connor (d. 1850), Isaac Hazzard (1804–1865), and William Appo (1808–1887)—all originally working in Philadelphia—and Peter O'Fake (1820–1884) of Newark, New Jersey, and J.W. Postlewaite (1827–1889) of St. Louis. As styles and customs changed, especially with the appearance of ragtime, musicians such as Will Marion Cook (1869–1944) and James Reese Europe (1881–1919) inherited Johnson's legacy in both public acceptance of their music and their anticipation of later musical trends.

Sheet music from Francis Johnson's "Boone Infantry Brass Band Quick Step".

Louis Moreau Gottschalk on sheet music for "Murmures Aeolians," lithograph by Sarony.

African American Pianists

African American pianists found fame in the nineteenth century, beginning with Louis Moreau Gottschalk (1829–1869) of New Orleans, who became an international star as a touring pianist and produced a striking body of piano solos influenced by his African and Cuban backgrounds. "Blind Tom" Bethune (1849–1909) became famous as a virtuoso with a repertoire of thousands of pieces. He was followed by John "Blind" Boone (1864–1927) with similar abilities, who achieved equal if not greater fame as a touring recitalist. Both were child prodigies who produced descriptive showpieces that dazzled audiences. André Watts made a hugely successful debut as a premiere pianist when he was only 16 years of age as soloist with the New York Philharmonic in 1962.

Although other excellent later pianists had varying degrees of success, many of them built their primary careers as teachers in colleges and universities. Hazel Harrison (1883–1969) and Helen Hagan (1891–1964) had long teaching careers after auspicious beginnings as performers, as did Natalie Hinderas (1927–1987).

Finally, African American pianists deserving honorable mention include composer/conductor R. Nathaniel Dett (1882–1943), composer/teacher George Walker (1922–), and Awadagin Pratt (1966–) whom many consider to be the successor to famed performer André Watts.

African American Women Vocalists

While men dominated instrumental music in the nineteenth century and beyond, women achieved renown with vocal music. Elizabeth Taylor Greenfield (c. 1824–1876) was known as the "Black Swan" for her fluid and graceful phrasing, while M. Sissieretta Jones (1869–1933) was called the "Black Patti," after the famous white diva, Adelina Patti. Contralto Marian Anderson (1902–1993) emerged in the twentieth century as one of its highest-achieving and most durable artists. Mid-century, sopranos Leontyne Price and Jessye Norman were two of dozens of outstanding African American singers who conquered recital and opera stages.

Marian Anderson.

♦ CLASSICAL MUSIC IN THE TWENTIETH CENTURY

Racism in Classical Music

During most of the nineteenth century, African American musicians performed for both black and white audiences. Towards the end of the century, however, white audiences began to favor European performers over any American performer, and white musicians over black. Despite their obvious success in classical music, by the beginning of the twentieth century, African Americans were not considered suitable as classical musicians, and white audiences accepted them only on the vaudeville and minstrel stage.

Whites also considered blacks to be unable to contribute to art music as composers. As an example, in response to composer Scott Joplin's attempt to produce his opera *Treemonisha* in New York, the *The New York Age* stated on March 5, 1908, "Since ragtime has been in vogue, many Negro writers have gained considerable fame as composers of that style of music. From the white man's standpoint of view after writing ragtime, the Negro does not figure."

Flutist D. Antoinette Handy wrote in the preface of *Black Women in American Bands and Orchestras* (1981) that her book originated in the mind of a 14-year-old African American girl who decided that she wanted to be a symphony orchestra flutist. She attended a concerto by the New Orleans Philharmonic and proceeded to go backstage afterwards to see the orchestra's first flutist. After inquiring whether the musician was accepting any pupils, she was stunned when the flutist's response was, "Do you mean that you, a Negro, want to study flute?" This attitude unfortunately prevailed in more subtle ways toward the end of the twentieth century: a 1981 survey by the National Urban League disclosed that of the nearly 5,000 musicians playing regularly in 56 leading orchestras, only 70 were African American.

The accomplishments of African Americans are all the more remarkable given the intense racism of the times. The Symphony of the New World (1965–1976) was formed by Elayne Jones and white conductor Benjamin Steinberg as the first racially integrated orchestra in the country. One of its goals was to provide valuable training and experience for instrumentalists striving to be accepted into symphony orchestras. In the 1970s, two national African American opera companies were established. Opera/South was founded in 1970 by Sister Elise, a singer and white member of the Catholic order of the Sisters of the Blessed Sacrament and by members of the Mississippi Inter-Collegiate Opera Guild. The company staged productions of grand opera and of operas by African American composers including *Highway No. 1 USA* and *A Bayou Legend* by William Grant Still and *Jubilee* and *The Juggler of Our Lady* by Ulysses Kay. In 1973, Sister Elise was one of four founders of Opera Ebony; the other three were African American musicians Margaret Harris, Benjamin Matthews, and Wayne Sanders. These companies were effective showcases for African American talent and often provided the first opportunities for individuals to begin careers in opera. Three stage works were also responsible for starting many young artists in successful careers: Virgil Thomson and Gertrude Stein's *Four Saints in Three Acts* premiered in 1934; *Porgy and Bess* by George Gershwin, first produced in 1935; and *Treemonisha* by Scott Joplin, first staged in 1972 in Atlanta.

African American Symphonic Music

African American composers have had increasing numbers of works performed by symphony orchestras from the 1930s and onward. African American symphonic music falls into two categories: black-stream music, synonymous with Gunther Schuller's *Third Stream*, which is serious music influenced by the ethnic background of the composer; and traditional European music created by African American composers. *Afro-American Symphony* by William Grant Still falls into the former category and was the first symphonic work by an African American composer to be performed by a major symphony orchestra—the Rochester Philharmonic—in 1931. Florence Price was the first African American female composer to have a symphony played by a major orchestra: Symphony in E Minor by the Chicago Symphony Orchestra in 1933. A year later, Price conducted her Concerto in One Movement for piano and orchestra at the Chicago World's Fair, with her student Margaret Bonds as soloist and the Women's Symphony of Chicago. In later years, composers such as George Walker, Howard Swanson, Ulysses Kay, Hale Smith, T.J. Anderson, Olly Wilson, Anthony Davis, and David Baker created a large repertoire of music based on Western European styles and forms that were informed or transformed through their racial heritage. To varying degrees, all of these composers have absorbed and expressed features common to African American music by their use of sacred and secular folk music, including the basic African call-and-response pattern, and of popular or vernacular music, including spirituals, ragtime, blues, and jazz.

◆ STUDIES IN AFRICAN AMERICAN MUSIC

Beginnings of Academic Research

African American literature, music, and art were well-established as subjects of academic study by the end of the twentieth century. In music, Eileen Southern's *The Music of Black Americans: A History*, published in 1971, was the first comprehensive presentation of the subject. Its subsequent revisions in 1983 and 1997 show its continuing pertinence as both a textbook and reference source. The breadth and depth of information in this volume demonstrate the great variety of African American music and of its myriad creators and practitioners.

Two precursors of this volume were James Monroe Trotter's *Music and Some Highly Musical People* (1878) that presented the accomplishments of African Americans in European styles, and Maud Cuney Hare's *Negro Musicians and Their Music*, (1936), which was more comprehensive in the styles covered. The ever-increasing quality and quantity of research in African American music herald the development of younger scholars who can use wisely the resources available to them at the beginning of their careers and who will increase those resources steadily as they progress. Thus, a much more accurate picture of the history of American music will result.

Recent Research on African American Music

In more recent years, the Center for Black Music Research was founded in 1983 by Samuel A. Floyd Jr. in Chicago. He is the author of *The Power of Black Music* (1995), among several other publications. Located at Columbia College, the center has as its mission "to research and promote the music of people of African descent throughout the world. . . through education, performance, publication, and scholarly discussion." It has actively contributed to the research publications and performances of contemporary and historic compositions that they have sponsored. They also have an ever-growing library and computer database of resources used by scholars all over the country. In addition, the *International Dictionary of Black Composers* (1999) fills a large gap in study materials on African American music and musicians.

At the end of the twentieth century, the trend toward inclusiveness of all kinds of music in formal study—not jazz, blues, classical, or sacred music as distinct and separate artistic worlds—bodes well for a better understanding of African American music. Certainly twentieth-century African American classical composers have worked in a wide variety of styles, from the vernacular to the avant-garde. A large number of these composers are not bound to one style or another, but rather move freely among them to produce unexpected and challenging works.

◆ AMERICAN ACADEMY AND INSTITUTE OF ARTS AND LETTERS AWARD WINNERS

1974: Olly Wilson
1982: George Walker
1988: Hale Smith
1991: Tania J. León

◆ CLASSICAL MUSIC COMPOSERS, CONDUCTORS, INSTRUMENTALISTS, AND SINGERS

(To locate biographical profiles more readily, please consult the index at the back of the book.)

Adele Addison (1925–)
Singer

Born July 24, 1925 in New York City, soprano Adele Addison completed her musical training at Westminster Choir College in 1946 and studied later at the University of Massachusetts. After making her recital debut at Town Hall in New York City in 1952, she performed recital tours throughout the United States and Canada. In 1963, she toured the Soviet Union under a U.S. State Department cultural exchange program.

While primarily a recitalist, Addison has appeared with the New England, New York City, and Washington opera companies. She gave the premiere performance of John LaMontaine's *Fragments from the Song of Songs* with the New Haven Symphony in 1959 and of Francis Poulenc's *Gloria* with the Boston Symphony in 1961. She was also a soloist during the opening week of concerts at Lincoln Center, New York, in 1962.

Betty Lou Allen (1930–)
Singer, Educator

Born on March 17, 1930, in Campbell, Ohio, Betty Allen studied at Wilberforce University and toured with Leontyne Price in the group the Wilberforce Sisters. She continued her musical studies at the Hartford School of Music and the Berkshire Music Center at Tanglewood and studied voice with Sarah Peck Moore, Paul Ulanowsky, and Zinka Milanov.

Allen made her New York debut in the Virgil Thomson-Gertrude Stein opera *Four Saints in Three Acts* with the New York City Opera in 1953, and made her debut at the Teatro Colón in Buenos Aires in 1964. She has appeared as a soloist with many leading orchestras and conductors including Leonard Bernstein, Antal Dorati, and Lorin Maazel. She held positions on the faculties of the North Carolina School of the Arts, the Curtis Institute of Music, and the Manhattan School of Music. Allen also served as the executive director and chair of the voice department at the Harlem School of the Arts in New York City.

Marian Anderson (1902–1993)
Singer

Born in Philadelphia, Pennsylvania, contralto Marian Anderson was brought up in a family of church musicians, and she began singing publicly as a child. Her professional career began in earnest in the 1920s, but her initial New York debuts were unsuccessful. However, her victory in a performance competition with the New York Philharmonic in 1925 led to further engagements, principally in Europe, where she established her reputation as a leading concert artist. On her return to the United States, her 1935 Town Hall performance in New York won her the acclaim that she deserved.

In 1939, Howard University wished to present Anderson in recital at Constitution Hall in Washington, DC. She was barred from performing there, however, by the Daughters of the American Revolution because of her race. Public reaction to this racially-motivated action was immediate and intense and, through the efforts of First Lady Eleanor Roosevelt (who resigned from the organization in protest), Anderson was invited to sing on the steps of the Lincoln Memorial. For this memorable Easter Sunday concert, the audience was an estimated 75,000 strong.

In 1955 Anderson became the first African American artist to perform with the Metropolitan Opera Company when she sang the role of Ulrica in Verdi's *Un Ballo in Maschera* for one season. Two years later she became a goodwill ambassador for the U.S. State Department, and in 1958 she was named to the U.S. delegation to the United Nations.

As a conclusion to her lengthy career, "the world's greatest contralto" toured the nation in a series of farewell concerts that ended on Easter Sunday of 1965 at Carnegie Hall in New York City. Anderson was not only a great singer but also a humanitarian, one who established fellowships for young singers and who toppled racial barriers for succeeding generations.

T(homas) J(efferson) Anderson (1928–)
Composer, Educator

Born on August 17, 1928, in Coatesville, Pennsylvania, to educator parents, T.J. Anderson began to study piano with his mother at the age of five. He began performing with jazz groups in junior high school, which cemented his love of music. He earned a bachelor of music degree in 1950 at West Virginia State College and a master of music education degree at Pennsylvania State University the following year. He was a music instructor for a few years before pursuing his Ph.D. at the University of Iowa, where he studied with Philip Bezanson and Richard Hervig and which he completed in 1958. He also studied with Darius Milhaud in the summer of 1964 at the Aspen (Colorado) School of Music. Following teaching positions at West Virginia State College, Langston and Tennessee State Universities, and Morehouse College, he joined the faculty of Tufts University in Medford, Massachusetts, where he chaired the music department. He retired as professor emeritus in 1990.

Anderson has received over 25 commissions, beginning in 1961, for a large variety of works—instrumental solos and ensembles, chamber and full orchestra, band, dramatic music, and solo vocal and choral music. A few of his notable compositions are: *Spirit Songs* (commissioned by Yo Yo Ma) for cello; *Transitions: A Fantasy for Ten Instruments* (Berkshire Music Center, Tanglewood, and the Fromm Foundation); *Squares: An Essay for Orchestra* (West Virginia State College); *Thomas Jefferson's Orbiting Minstrels and Contraband: A 21st Century Celebration of 19th Century Form* (for string quartet, woodwind quintet, jazz sextet, dancer, soprano, computer, visuals, keyboard synthesizer); *Variations on a Theme by M.B. Tolson* (soprano, instrumental ensemble); *Soldier Boy, Soldier*, a two-act opera (Indiana University and National Endowment for the Arts); and *Walker*, a one-act opera (Boston Atheneum, on a libretto by South African Derek Walcott, Nobel Prize laureate, based on the death of David Walker in 1830 in Boston).

Anderson's deep knowledge and control of twentieth-century musical techniques and developments—including jazz, big band music, blues, and spirituals—formed his compositional style. For the 1972 premiere of Scott Joplin's opera *Treemonisha* Anderson was the orchestrator and helped in its staging. Another notable event was his conducting the first performance of the Black Music Repertory Ensemble in 1988. Among more than 30 awards and honors, he received four MacDowell Colony fellowships, in addition to honorary doctorates and composer residencies.

Martina Arroyo.

Martina Arroyo (1936–)
Singer, Educator

Martina Arroyo was born to a Puerto Rican father and an African American mother in Harlem. Although encouraged by her mother in artistic pursuits—piano, ballet, church choir—she was expected to enter a profession that could provide a more secure living than one in the arts. After attending Hunter High School, she continued at Hunter College, where she earned a degree in Romance languages in 1956. During her college years, she met the distinguished voice teacher Marinka Gurewich with whom Arroyo trained almost continuously until Gurewich's death in 1990.

As many other African American artists of her generation, Arroyo did not have an easy time breaking into American operatic performance, but found success in European opera houses. In 1965, while visiting her family in New York on vacation from the Zürich Opera Company, she was called to fill in for Birgit Nilsson as Aida at the Metropolitan Opera. Her performance in this demanding Verdi role led to a contract and made her an international star virtually overnight.

Along with frequent opera appearances in the United States and abroad in the 1970s and 1980s, Arroyo had many engagements with leading orchestras, performing music ranging from Handel to Stockhausen. Arroyo officially retired from performing in 1989. Only two years later, however, she agreed to sing the leading female role, written for her by Leslie Adams in his new opera *Blake*, based on a nineteenth-century novel about a slave family. After retirement, Arroyo was in demand as a distinguished visiting professor. Some of the universities where she has taught are the University of California at Los Angeles, Louisiana State University, Wilberforce University, and Indiana University at Bloomington. Arroyo has also served as an honorary member of the Carnegie Hall board and a member of the board of trustees at Hunter College.

David Baker (1931–)
Composer, Instrumentalist, Educator, Author

Born in Indianapolis, Indiana, David Baker was educated in the public schools and Jordan Conservatory of that city. He earned bachelor (1953) and master (1954) degrees in music education at Indiana University at Bloomington and later studied at the Berklee School of Music and the Lenox School of Jazz, from which he received a diploma in 1959. Among his private composition teachers were George Russell, John Lewis, William Russo, and Gunther Schuller. He also studied trombone privately with J.J. Johnson, John Marcellus, and Bobby Brookmeyer, and cello with his Indiana colleague Janos Starker, with Jules Eskin and others.

In the late 1950s and early 1960s, Baker played in the bands of Maynard Ferguson, Quincy Jones, George Russell, Wes Montgomery, and Lionel Hampton. After joining the faculty of Indiana University in 1966 as chairman of the jazz department, Baker continued to perform with various groups, lecture, conduct workshops and clinics, and publish a large number of books and articles in the field of jazz.

Baker's catalog of compositions is very large and includes over 60 commissioned works for solo and ensemble instrumental works, vocal and choral music, pieces for string, chamber, and full orchestra, dramatic music, and well over 150 works for jazz ensembles. Not surprisingly, Baker has issued over 60 books on music improvisation including *Advanced Ear Training for Jazz Musicians; Advanced Improvisation* (two volumes); *Contemporary Techniques for the Trombone* (two volumes); and *Improvisational Patterns: The Bebop Era* (three volumes). In the course of his very active career, he has received over 30 awards and honors. He has participated in many organizations including the National Endowment for the Arts, American Symphony Orchestra League, the National Jazz Foundation, the Afro-American Music Bicentennial, the nominating jury in music for the Pulitzer Prize, and the Smithsonian Institution.

Kathleen Battle (1948–)
Singer

In her high school and early college years, soprano Kathleen Battle, a native of Portsmouth, Ohio, had no ambition to become a professional singer. She studied voice, piano, languages, and dance as she earned her bachelor and master degrees in music education from the University of Cincinnati College-Conservatory. She continued studies during two years of teaching general music in an inner-city school.

An audition with Thomas Schippers, conductor of the Cincinnati Symphony Orchestra and co-founder of the Spoleto (Italy) Festival of Two Worlds, led to her professional debut in Brahms's *German Requiem* in Spoleto. Through Schippers, Battle met James Levine

in 1974, who became her friend, mentor, and counselor. She sang with many orchestras as soloist, studied opera and song literature and acting, and, in 1975, was in the Broadway company of Scott Joplin's opera *Treemonisha*. Her New York City opera debut followed in 1976 as Susanna in Mozart's *The Marriage of Figaro*, and her Metropolitan Opera debut took place in 1978 as the shepherd in Wagner's *Tannhäuser*. Since then she has sung a wide range of roles in opera houses throughout the world, notably in operas by Mozart, Rossini, Massenet, and Richard Strauss.

In 1994, Battle was dismissed from the Metropolitan Opera production of Donizetti's *Daughter of the Regiment*, following a much-publicized dispute with management. The rift proved to be no stumbling block to her career, however, as her recordings have been very successful including the "crossover" discs, such as *So Many Stars, Honey and Rue*, and *Angels' Glory*. In addition, she has also recorded Gershwin along with Herbie Hancock, and baroque arias with trumpeter Wynton Marsalis.

Thomas "Blind Tom" Greene Bethune (1849–1908)
Pianist, Composer

"Blind Tom" was the stage name of pianist Thomas Greene, born a slave in Columbus, Georgia. The surname "Bethune" was the name of the family that owned him and his mother. His musical prowess manifested itself when he was four years old, and he received music lessons from Bethune family members. His remarkable skills, especially his ability to memorize pieces practically on first hearing, have caused speculation that he was autistic, an "idiot savant." Tom began performing for money in public before the Civil War. Colonel John Bethune kept control of Tom and his earnings after slavery was abolished and acted, in effect, as his concert manager. His renown grew rapidly after the war, and he toured throughout the United States and in Europe to great acclaim. His immense repertoire included works by standard classical composers, such as Bach, Beethoven, and Chopin; virtuoso display pieces by Gottschalk and Liszt; improvisations on current ballads and other popular tunes; and his own works that combined elements of the virtuosic and improvisational, and often described weather or military events. *The Battle of Manassas* is an example of one of his most effective works of this kind, a potpourri of well-known melodies with special keyboard effects, such as tone clusters and noises made on the piano.

Tom retired in 1898, some ten years before his death.

Margaret Allinson Bonds (1913–1972)
Composer, Pianist

Margaret Bonds, born in Chicago, grew up in an artistic and creative family. Her first piano teacher was her mother, a church organist. Her family's friends consisted of many distinguished musicians and writers including Florence Price and Will Marion Cook who acted as Bonds's mentors. As a youngster she began to compose, and when she was in her teen years she held jobs as accompanist for nightclub acts and as a music copyist.

Bonds was one of very few African American students at Northwestern University in Evanston, Illinois, from which she received both a bachelor and a master of music degree by the time she was 21 years old. In the latter part of the 1930s, she founded and directed the Allied Arts Academy, which closed in 1939 because of financial difficulties. She moved to New York City, where she resumed study at the Juilliard School of Music, and was active as both solo and duo pianist and accompanist, gave lecture demonstrations, and was involved in many professional and community organizations.

Bonds's compositions reflect jazz influence, as well as spirituals and the blues, and she gained a thorough mastery of the techniques of Western music. The greater portion of her music is vocal and choral, but there are many piano solos and dramatic works as well including *The Ballad of the Brown King* (1954) and *Shakespeare in Harlem* (1959), a play by Langston Hughes.

In 1967, Bonds moved again, this time to Los Angeles where she taught piano and worked with the Inner City Cultural Center and Repertory Theater. Written and premiered in 1972, her *Credo*—dedicated to the memories of soprano Abbie Mitchell and Langston Hughes—was performed by the Los Angeles Philharmonic and conducted by Zubin Mehta shortly after her sudden death.

John William "Blind" Boone (1864–1927)
Pianist, Composer

Born fifteen years later than "Blind Tom" Bethune, "Blind" Boone's upbringing and education were considerably different from his predecessor's, although their careers were very similar. Both had tremendous skill at the keyboard and very large repertoires at their fingertips, and they both toured extensively for many years. Boone, however, had more formal training, and received support from the citizens of Warrensburg, Missouri, who raised money for him to study at the Institute for the Education of the Blind (later, St. Louis School for the Blind), in St. Louis. After less than three years of piano lessons at the school, Boone left in order to begin a career in music.

There were several lean years before Boone met John Lange, a Missouri businessman and entrepreneur who set up the Blind Boone Concert Company, a partnership that provided for the pianist and a stipend for his mother. A typical Boone program, following the pattern of Bethune's, included classical works from Bach to Brahms, his own arrangements of popular ballads and dance tunes, descriptive and concert pieces, and, on occasion, improvisations. Boone, unlike Bethune, performed and wrote ragtime pieces as well. His familiarity with this newly-popular music went back to his days as a student in St. Louis.

With Lange's death in 1916, the fortunes of the company declined and, with burgeoning new entertainment media and an apparent increase in racism, so did performing engagements. Nevertheless, Boone continued his partner's practice of benefiting communities and organizations of African Americans with concert revenues. Boone's "farewell concerts" began in the early 1920s, but his final concert was given shortly before his death in 1927.

Gwendolyn Bradley (1952–)
Singer

Soprano Gwendolyn Bradley was born in New York City but grew up in Bishopville, South Carolina. She was a finalist in the 1977 Metropolitan Opera National Council auditions and a graduate of the North Carolina School of the Arts. She also attended the Curtis Institute of Music and the Academy of Vocal Arts in Philadelphia and studied with Margaret Harshaw and Seth McCoy.

Bradley made her professional operatic debut in 1976 with the Lake George (New York) Opera Festival as Nanetta in Verdi's *Falstaff*. Other companies with which she has appeared include Central City Opera (Colorado), Opera/South, and the Opera Company of Philadelphia. Her Metropolitan Opera debut in 1981 was in the Met's first production of Ravel's *L'Enfant et les Sortilèges*. She has been a soloist with several orchestras including the Philadelphia Orchestra, the Kansas City Philharmonic, the Charleston Symphony, the Los Angeles Philharmonic, and the Seattle Symphony.

Grace Ann Bumbry (1937–)
Singer

A native of St. Louis, Missouri, Grace Bumbry was the first African American to perform in Bayreuth, Germany, the shrine of Richard Wagner. She had the role of Venus in *Tannhäuser* in 1961 and sang to great

Grace Bumbry performing.

acclaim. She had appeared in the operatic capitals of Europe, so the Bayreuth debut served as a boost to a career that was already flourishing. She made her American operatic debut in this role as well at the Chicago Lyric Opera in 1963.

As a teenager, Bumbry had won a scholarship to the St. Louis Institute in a competition, but the segregationist policy of that school kept her out. Later, however, she attended Boston University, Northwestern University, and the Music Academy of the West in Santa Barbara, California, where her primary teacher was the renowned Lotte Lehmann. She also studied with Pierre Bernac.

Fairly early in her career, Bumbry gradually shifted from mezzo soprano to soprano roles, in which she achieved as much success as in the lower voice range. Among them were Lady Macbeth (*Macbeth*, Verdi), Leonora (in both *Il Trovatore* and *La Forza del Destino*, Verdi), *Salome* (R. Strauss), *Tosca* (Puccini), and *La Gioconda* (Ponchielli). She has sung both Amneris and Aida—mezzo and soprano—in Verdi's *Aida*. Virtuoso soprano roles that became part of her repertoire in the 1970s and 1980s are Abigaille (*Nabucco*, Verdi) and Norma (Bellini).

Henry Thacker "Harry" Burleigh (1866–1949)
Singer, Composer, Arranger, Editor

Born in 1866, baritone Harry Burleigh did not leave his hometown of Erie, Pennsylvania, for formal music study until 1892. He went to New York to study at the

National Conservatory of Music from 1892 to 1996, then headed by composer Antonin Dvorak. Dvorak encouraged his students to use folk music and spirituals as the source of their art, which had a decisive influence on Burleigh's musical beliefs and practices. His vocal prowess gained him the position of soloist with a wealthy Episcopal church—where he remained for 50 years—and in the chorus of a synagogue for 25 years, both in New York City. Beginning in 1911, he was also an editor for the Ricordi Publishing Company until 1946.

Besides his lifelong association with sacred music, Burleigh was involved with Broadway musical shows, and he also toured widely as a recitalist including trips to Europe and England. He was a private teacher of voice, music theory, and composition.

As a composer and arranger, Burleigh was the first to arrange spirituals in the style of art songs with the use of chromatic embellishments and nineteenth-century romantic harmonic practice. Arrangements were also made for chorus which were very popular, as were his original art songs that were widely programmed by leading singers of the day. He did not compose in large forms or dramatic music, and his only instrumental works are suites, one each for piano and for violin and piano. A charter member of the American Society of Composers, Authors and Publishers, Burleigh was awarded honorary degrees by Atlanta and Howard Universities.

Frances Elaine Cole (1937–1983)
Violinist, Harpsichordist

Frances Cole studied violin at the Cleveland Institute of Music and at Miami University in Ohio, where she was concertmaster of the orchestra. She earned a doctorate at Teachers College of Columbia University, New York, in 1966, and during her years of study played for the National Orchestral Association. As she was finishing her doctorate, she discovered her interest in the harpsichord and began to study the instrument at the Landowska Center in Connecticut. In 1967, she became resident harpsichordist with the Gallery Players in Provincetown, Massachusetts, appeared on national television programs, and began touring throughout the United States and Europe.

Cole was as well known for her humor and innovation as for her elegant musical interpretations. In 1976, for example, she arrived dressed as Anna Magdalena Bach in a horse-drawn carriage for an outdoor concert at Lincoln Center, New York. She played jazz in a trio and was a cabaret singer under the name of Elaine Frances. She also served on the music faculties of

Queens College and the Westminster Choir College and presented workshops at many colleges and universities.

Will Marion Cook (1869–1944)
Composer, Violinist, Conductor

Will Cook's earliest musical activities focused on the violin and Western concert music. At the age of 15, he left his hometown of Washington, DC, to study at the Oberlin (Ohio) Conservatory and after four years there he travelled to Berlin, Germany, for study with the renowned master violinist Joseph Joachim. A few years after his return to Washington, Cook left for New York, where he studied at the National Conservatory of Music with its director Antonin Dvorak and John White, a virtuoso violinist.

Dissatisfied with the course of his career, which he attributed partly to racial discrimination, Cook took advantage of an opportunity to conduct a newly-formed orchestra in Washington. Soon thereafter, he began to work in the musical theater of New York City with collaborators such as singer Bob Cole, vaudevillians George Walker and Bert Williams, and the writer Paul Laurence Dunbar. Cook was part of some theatrical "firsts": the first all-African American musical comedy on Broadway *Clorindy, or The Origin of the Cakewalk* with Dunbar, a "ragtime operetta" that introduced syncopation to the Broadway musical; and *In Dahomey*, with Williams and Walker, written and performed by African Americans for presentation on Broadway and, subsequently, also the first such show presented in London at Buckingham Palace.

Cook was the composer or co-composer of 17 musical shows in addition to songs that he wrote apart from shows. However, there are only a few piano pieces and no works for violin. Among the several younger musicians to whom he was mentor were Margaret Bonds, Duke Ellington, and Eva Jessye.

Roque Cordero (1917–)
Composer, Educator

Roque Cordero studied clarinet and string instruments as a child growing up in Panama, and he began to write popular songs at an early age before beginning to study composition formally when he was 17. In 1943, he came to the United States to study composition with Ernest Krenek at Hamline University in St. Paul, Minnesota, and conducting with Dmitri Mitropoulos at the

University of Minnesota at Minneapolis. He graduated from the latter magna cum laude with a bachelor of arts degree. Back in his native country, he served on the faculty of the National Institute of Music of Panama, serving as director from 1953 to 1964. He returned to the United States to become assistant director of the Latin American Music Center at Indiana University, Bloomington beginning in 1966. From 1972 to 1987, when he retired, he was professor of music at Illinois State University at Normal.

Cordero has written a large number of solo and ensemble instrumental works and several for orchestra including the prize-winning Second Symphony and Violin Concerto. His style blends elements of Panamanian vernacular music with more formal Western European practices including serialism and polytonality. A balance of these two major aesthetic components is the predominant trait of his musical language.

Among many honors and awards that Cordero has received are a Guggenheim Fellowship, an honorary professorship at the University of Chile, an honorary doctorate from Hamline University, and a Koussevitzky International Recording Award. His commissions, numbering over 20, have come from several countries in South America and prestigious institutions in the United States including the National Endowment for the Arts and the Kennedy Center.

Anthony Curtis Davis.

Anthony Curtis Davis (1951–)
Composer, Pianist, Educator

Anthony Davis's father was the first African American professor at Princeton University and was later chair of the Afro-American studies department at Yale University. Born in Paterson, New Jersey, the young Davis grew up in a cultural environment in which he was encouraged to be creative. He earned a bachelor's degree in music from Yale in 1975; later, he returned to teach in the early 1980s and early 1990s. He has also been a visiting professor or lecturer at Harvard, Cornell, and Northwestern Universities and at the University of California at San Diego. In 1996, Davis was honored with an American Academy of Arts and Letters Award in Music.

Davis, who had studied piano in his teen years, began to play jazz with different groups while at Yale, and after moving to New York City, quickly developed a reputation as an advanced player and highly-proficient improviser. Finally, he founded his own group, Episteme, (which means "knowledge") so that he could work out his compositional ideas. Experience with this group caused him to focus on composition as his primary activity, rather than improvisation. He has written in many media including jazz ensembles, opera, instrumental solos and ensembles to orchestra, and voice to chorus.

By the end of the 1990s, Davis had received over 20 commissions from symphonies, opera and dance companies, choral groups, and other organizations. Three of his four operas are based on real characters and events: *Amistad,* 1997, for the Lyric Opera of Chicago (about a slave revolt aboard a ship and its aftermath); *Tania,* 1992, for the American Music Theater Festival (based on the Patty Hearst kidnapping); and *X: The Life and Times of Malcolm X,* 1986, for the Kitchen Center. About *X,* perhaps the work that has made the biggest impact, critic Andrew Porter praised the "constantly impressive" score and believed that ". . . an 'ordinary' opera goer will be able to respond readily to the music." Davis himself stated that "I hope it will open a door for others to create large works and then realize that this separateness in American culture is just a by-product of race, not a by-product of the art. It's important for me that what I do helps the next generation of musicians."

William Levi Dawson (1899–1990)
Composer, Conductor, Educator

Born in Anniston, Alabama, William Dawson became a student at the age of 15 in the Tuskegee Institute, founded by Booker T. Washington. His studies included piano, composition, and trombone. He moved to Kansas City, Kansas, to teach music in high school, and he excelled as a jazz trombonist during his years there. He was also able to earn a bachelor of music degree at the Horner Institute of Fine Arts in 1925.

In 1926, Dawson moved to Chicago, where he continued to play in jazz ensembles (including Jimmy Noone's Apex Orchestra and the Fourteen Doctors of Syncopation) and to study composition at the American Conservatory of Music and the Chicago Musical College. He received a master of music degree in 1927 from the conservatory. By this time he was publishing arrangements of spirituals and conducting a large church choir. Dawson was invited to Tuskegee to head the Institute's School of Music in 1931 and remained there until retirement in 1955. During his tenure, he strengthened the music curriculum and built the Institute Choir into an organization nationally recognized as outstanding. After his retirement, he remained active as a guest conductor in the United States and abroad.

Dawson's most famous work is the Negro Folk Symphony, premiered in 1934 by the Philadelphia Orchestra and conducted by Leopold Stokowski. It was the first symphony by an African American composer to be premiered by a major U.S. symphony orchestra. It was revised in 1952 after Dawson visited West Africa, where he studied African rhythms and their influence on African American music. His arrangements of spirituals have been staples of the choral repertoire, as have some of his original works. A statement about the symphony made by Dawson is a good short description of the goals of "nationalist" composers: his goal was "to write a symphony in the Negro folk idiom, based on authentic folk music but in the same symphonic form used by the composers of the (European) romantic-nationalist school."

James Anderson DePriest (1936–)
Conductor

Born in Philadelphia, James DePriest studied piano and percussion from the age of ten, but he did not decide on a musical career until he reached his early twenties. After finishing high school, he entered the Wharton School of the University of Pennsylvania and received a bachelor of science in 1958 and a master of arts degree in 1961. He also studied music history and theory and orchestration at the Philadelphia Conservatory of Music and composition with Vincent Persichetti.

In 1962, DePriest was engaged as an American specialist in music for a U.S. State Department cultural exchange tour of the Near and Far East. During this tour, he was stricken with polio and paralyzed in both legs. Within six months of intensive therapy, he had fought his way to the point of being able to walk with the aid of crutches and braces. Courage, determination, and talent carried him to the semifinals of the 1963 Dmitri Mitropoulos International Music Competition for Conductors. After another overseas tour, this time as conductor in Thailand, he returned to the United States and conducted several American orchestras including the Philadelphia and the New York Philharmonic. In 1964, he captured first prize in the Mitropoulos Competition. Another career highlight occurred on June 28, 1965, when he conducted his Aunt Marian Anderson's farewell concert in Philadelphia at Robin Hood Dell.

DePriest has been the music director of the Oregon Symphony and has been a guest conductor in most of the capitals of the United States and Europe.

R(obert) Nathaniel Dett (1882–1943)
Composer, Arranger, Conductor, Pianist

Born of musical parents, a Canadian mother and an American father, in Drummondville, Ontario, Dett studied the piano and played in church from an early age. In 1893, his family moved from Canada to Niagara Falls, New York, where he began playing in public in his teen years. After two years of study at a music conservatory in nearby Lockport, he moved to Oberlin, Ohio in 1903 for baccalaureate studies at the Oberlin Conservatory, where he also began his career as a choral conductor. He received his bachelor of music degree in 1908.

Dett held teaching positions, after graduation, at Lane College (Jackson, Tennessee), Lincoln Institute (Jefferson City, Missouri), and Hampton Institute (Hampton, Virginia) from 1913 to 1932. He raised the standards of the Institute's choir, not only in excellence of performance but also in establishing the spiritual—in arrangements and as the source of original works—as part of the basic choral repertoire. After an unfortunate disagreement with the administration, he moved to Rochester, New York, and earned a master's degree at the Eastman School of Music in 1932. One of his composition teachers there was the school's director, Howard Hanson. After a few more years in Rochester, where he was busy as a choir director and composer, he took a position at Bennett College in North Carolina.

R. Nathaniel Dett.

In 1943, he directed the Women's Army Corps chorus of the United Services Organization, but his life was cut short in October of that year by a fatal heart attack, nine days before his 61st birthday.

Dett's many choral works include collections of Negro spirituals and large-scale dramatic compositions, notably *Chariot Jubilee* (1919) and *The Ordering of Moses: Biblical Folk Scenes*, an oratorio (1932, his master's thesis). There are also several works for piano including: *Cinnamon Grove Suite, Enchantment, In the Bottoms*, and *Magnolia*.

Dett gave very specific prefaces to several of his scores, many of which were definitely of "that class of music known as 'program music' or 'music with a poetic basis.'" Throughout his life he actively supported African American folk music through his writings, arrangements, conducting, and study. For his essay *Negro Music* (1920), he received the Bowdoin Literary Prize from Harvard University. He was a founder of the National Association of Negro Musicians in 1919 and served as its president from 1924 to 1926. Howard University and the Oberlin Conservatory both awarded him honorary doctorates.

Carl Rossini Diton (1886–1962)
Pianist, Singer, Composer

Carl Diton first learned piano from his father, a professional musician. He studied at the University of Pennsylvania and received his bachelor's degree in 1909. Following graduation, he went on to become the first African American pianist to make a cross-country concert tour. He furthered his piano studies in Munich, Germany, with the aid of an E. Azalia Hackley scholarship. In the 1920s, he began voice study and made his concert debut in Philadelphia in 1926. He continued to study voice at the Juilliard School, New York City, where he was awarded an artist's diploma in 1930.

Teaching began to take up more of his time, although he continued to perform. He also began to compose and received several awards including the Harmon Award. Most of his works are art songs and arrangements of spirituals. He was a founding member of the National Association of Negro Musicians in 1919, which has been a source of much support for young musicians through grants and scholarships and has also honored distinguished musicians of all kinds.

Dean Dixon (1915–1976)
Conductor

Born in Manhattan in 1915, Dean Dixon was exposed to classical music by his parents, who often took him to Carnegie Hall. While he was still in high school, he formed his own amateur orchestra at the Harlem YMCA, which soon grew to 70 members and gave regular concerts. He was admitted to the Juilliard School of Music on the basis of a violin audition, and he was awarded the bachelor's degree in 1936. Three years later, he earned a master's degree from the Teachers College of Columbia University.

Dixon's Symphony Society, founded in 1932, received community support, and in 1941 Eleanor Roosevelt was instrumental in setting up a concert that eventually led to his becoming the music director of NBC radio network's summer symphony. Shortly thereafter, he made his debut with the New York Philharmonic, the first African American to conduct that orchestra.

However, Dixon was unable to find a position as music director with an American orchestra, so he went to Europe, where he worked with several orchestras in Sweden and Germany and to Australia for the Sydney Symphony. After his return to the United States in 1970, he was a frequent guest conductor and left a recorded legacy estimated at 20 discs at the time of his death in 1976.

Mattiwilda Dobbs (1925–)
Singer

Mattiwilda Dobbs graduated from Spelman College in Atlanta, Georgia, her hometown, as valedictorian of her class in 1946. She majored in voice and studied at Columbia University Teachers College, where she earned a master's degree. She studied voice privately with Lotte Leonard in New York and, in Paris, with Pierre Bernac on a Whitney Fellowship. Soprano Dobbs won the International Music Competition held in Geneva, Switzerland, in 1951 and later was the first African American to sing a principal role at La Scala in Milan, Italy.

In 1955, Dobbs made her American operatic debut in the lead in the San Francisco Opera's *The Golden Cockerel*, becoming the first African American to play a major role in that company. This career achievement was followed by her debut at the Metropolitan Opera in *Rigoletto*—only the third African American to sing on that stage and the first to sing a romantic lead. Her successful showings in American opera companies led to an even greater international fame as she toured all over the world, including the Soviet Union, where she was the first Met artist to appear at the Bolshoi. At the peak of her career, her active repertoire included more than 200 concert pieces and 20 operatic roles.

In 1974, Dobbs served as artist-in-residence at Spelman College and has likewise taught at Howard University since the 1970s. She was elected to the board of directors of the Metropolitan Opera in 1989.

Robert Todd Duncan (1903–1998)
Singer, Actor, Educator

Baritone Todd Duncan's mother, herself a musician, encouraged him in his ambition to become an opera singer. He was raised in Indianapolis, Indiana, and graduated with a bachelor of music degree from Butler University. He attended Columbia University Teachers College in New York, where he received a master's degree in music. After teaching briefly in a high school, he began college teaching and was on the music faculty of Howard University for some 15 years, where he also served as department head.

Duncan's performance in an all-African American, New York City production of Mascagni's *Cavalleria Rusticana* in 1934 led to his being chosen by George Gershwin to sing the lead role of Porgy in the premiere of his opera *Porgy and Bess*. Duncan also starred in two later revivals. He continued to be active as a concert singer and theatrical performer, and, in the New York City Opera's 1945–1946 season, he became the first African American member of the company with roles in *I Pagliacci*, *Aida*, and *Carmen*. However, he was never invited to sing at the Metropolitan Opera, which would have been the realization of his dream as a singer.

Besides work in films, Duncan appeared in some outstanding Broadway shows including *Cabin in the Sky*, *Show Boat* and Weill's *Lost in the Stars*, in which he created the role of Stephen Kumalo and for which he received both the New York Drama Critics and Tony Awards in 1950. He retired from public performance in 1967 but continued to teach privately in Washington, DC, for many years. Educational institutions with which he was associated during this period are Howard University and the Curtis Institute of Music. Both Valparaiso and Butler Universities awarded him honorary doctorates.

Leslie B. Dunner (1956–)
Conductor, Clarinetist, Composer

A native of New York City, Dunner graduated from Manhattan's High School of Music and Art in 1974. He earned a bachelor's degree in clarinet performance

Leslie Dunner.

from the Eastman School of Music (1978) and continued study at Queen's College (New York) for a master's degree in music theory and musicology (1979). He received a doctorate in orchestra conducting and clarinet performance from the College-Conservatory of Music of the University of Cincinnati (1982).

Dunner's honors include the NAACP's James Weldon Johnson Award in 1991; the 1994 American Symphony Orchestra League Award; and in 1996, becoming the first American prize-winner in the prestigious Arturo Toscanini International Conducting Competition. He was also a semi-finalist in the Herbert von Karajan International Conducting Competition.

Posts held by Dunner include seven seasons with the Detroit Symphony Orchestra as resident conductor, and music director of the Annapolis Symphony Orchestra in Maryland as of December, 1998. He has also served as music director of Symphony Nova Scotia in Halifax, guest conductor with the Warsaw Philharmonic for its tour of South Africa, and guest conductor for the New York City Ballet.

In the late 1980s, Dunner began to work with the Dance Theatre of Harlem and had earlier served with the Pacific Northwest Ballet Company as assistant conductor. He has made appearances with many orchestras as guest conductor and has had the opportunity to work with some of the century's greatest conductors.

Dunner performs as a freelance clarinetist, and several of his compositions have been recorded, including his *Short Rhapsody for Clarinet.*

Simon Estes (1938–)
Singer

Born on February 2, 1938, in Centerville, Iowa, Simon Lamont Estes is the grandson of a slave and the son of a coal miner. An athletic scholarship to the University of Iowa provided him with the opportunity to study voice with Charles Kellis. Estes received a full scholarship to the Juilliard School of Music, New York City, where he studied with Sergius Kagen and Christopher West. In 1964, he received grants that allowed him to travel to Germany, where he was soon given a contract with the Deutsche Oper in West Berlin. Bass-baritone Estes recounted the circumstances of his debut as Ramfis in Verdi's *Aida* in April of 1965: "I didn't have any rehearsal. It was the first time, literally, I had ever been on a stage. I didn't meet the conductor until the curtain parted and I saw him on the podium." Other roles followed, and in 1966 he won the silver medal in the Tchaikovsky Competition in Moscow. His European

Simon Estes with Yolanda King.

career developed rapidly, appearing with the opera companies of Vienna, Munich, Hamburg, Paris, Milan, and Florence. In 1978, Wolfgang Wagner invited him to appear at Bayreuth in the title role of *The Flying Dutchman*, and Estes became the first African American male singer to sing at the shrine of Richard Wagner.

Estes had been singing with various American opera companies, with performances in San Francisco, Boston, and Chicago, and he had a leading role with the Hamburg State Opera in its production of Gunther Schuller's *The Visitation* that played at the Metropolitan Opera House. His debut with the Met company, however, did not take place until 1982, in the role of the Landgrave in Wagner's *Tannhäuser*. Two seasons later, he played Porgy in the Met's first production of Gershwin's *Porgy and Bess*.

Besides singing in opera houses in Europe and America, Estes has been a busy recitalist from the time of his concert debut in 1980 at Carnegie Hall. Among recordings of major works that he has made are Beethoven's Symphony No. 9, Handel's *Messiah*, Fauré's *Requiem*, and *The Flying Dutchman*. He has also recorded spirituals and highlights from *Porgy and Bess*.

Estes has received numerous awards including the Tchaikovsky Medal in 1985 and the Iowa Award of Achievement in 1996.

James Reese Europe. *See* **Blues & Jazz chapter.**

Louis Moreau Gottschalk (1829–1869)
Composer, Pianist

Louis Gottschalk was a native of New Orleans who was a violin prodigy around the age of six. Switching instruments, he soon became an outstanding pianist and studied in Europe with leading teachers when he was in his teen years. In his mid-twenties, he made his New York City debut, having already established a brilliant reputation in Europe. He toured internationally with great success for the rest of his short life.

Gottschalk's compositions for piano reflect the Creole environment of his childhood, and several of them are based in African American- and Cuban-inspired folk music including *Le Bananier* and *Bamboula*. He also wrote characteristic salon pieces. His autobiographical *Notes of a Pianist* provides information about his life, methods of composing, the people he knew, and the places he visited.

Denyce Graves (1965–)
Singer

A native of Washington, DC, mezzo-soprano Denyce Graves was a student at the Duke Ellington School for the Performing Arts in that city. In 1981, she began study with Helen Hodam at the Oberlin College Conservatory (Ohio) and transferred to the New England Conservatory of Music (Boston) in 1984. She received a bachelor of music degree and artist diploma in 1988 and later joined the Houston (Texas) Grand Opera Studio of the University of Houston, where she worked with Elena Nikolaidi.

Some of the prizes Graves won early in her career include awards from the Richard Tucker Music Foundation, Opera Columbus Vocal Competition (the Eleanor Steber Award), the Marian Anderson Award presented by her to Graves in 1991, the Grand Prix Lyrique given once every three years by the Friends of Monte Carlo Opera, and George London and Metropolitan Opera career study grants.

In the 1990s Graves's career as opera and recital singer and orchestra soloist flourished. She has sung the title role in Bizet's *Carmen* in opera houses throughout North and South America and Europe to great

Denyce Graves.

acclaim; she and Placido Domingo opened the Metropolitan Opera's 1997–1998 season in that opera. Another signature role for Graves is Dalila in *Samson et Dalila* (Saint-Saens), which she has also sung at the Met. A few of the works in which she has been soloist with leading orchestras worldwide are Verdi's *Requiem*, *La damnation de Faust* by Berlioz, *Shéhérazade* by Ravel, and Mahler's *Kindertotenlieder* and Eighth Symphony.

Reri Grist (1932–)
Singer

Born in New York City, soprano Reri Grist received her bachelor's degree in music from Queens College (New York) in 1954. Performing the role of Consuela in Bernstein's *West Side Story* brought her national attention. She made an equally strong impression in a very different work—Mahler's Symphony No. 4—which she sang with the New York Philharmonic. Since then, she has sung at many of the world's leading opera houses including La Scala (Milan), Vienna State, Britain's Royal Opera, and the Metropolitan Opera.

In 1960, the stage director of the Met, Herbert Graf, left that company to become director of the Zürich Opera. Grist was one of several artists to go with him. While she was in Europe, Stravinsky asked Grist to sing in *Le Rossignol* under his direction. Besides performing, Grist has taught at the Hochschule für Musik (Germany) and Indiana University.

Emma Azalia Hackley (1867–1922)
Singer, Choral Director, Educator

E. Azalia Hackley did as much to promote African American musicians as she did their traditional music. Growing up in Detroit, she studied voice and piano and began to perform in public at an early age. She received a degree in music at the University of Denver in 1901 and later traveled to Paris, France, for further voice study.

Hackley traveled extensively as a recitalist in the early years of the century but gradually became more occupied with furthering the careers of young African American artists. She established scholarships, sponsored debut recitals, and also helped many young performers to find college-level teaching positions. Hackley founded the Normal Vocal Institute in Chicago in late 1915 and directed it until its demise in 1917. One of her major activities in the latter part of her life was organizing large community concerts to promote the importance of African American folk music and to raise the level of public interest and pride in the African American musical heritage. The Hackley Collection was established by the National Association of Negro Musicians at the Detroit Public Library some 20 years after her death, in order to preserve her papers, memorabilia, and other materials relating to African American music and musicians.

Helen Eugenia Hagan (1893–1964)
Pianist, Composer, Educator

Helen Hagan was born into a musical family: her mother played piano and her father was a baritone. After receiving her early music training from her mother and in the public school system in New Haven, Connecticut, she became the first African American pianist to earn a bachelor of music degree from Yale University in 1912. She was also the first African American to win Yale's Sanford Fellowship, which permitted her to study in Europe with Vincent d'Indy. She earned a diploma in 1914 from the Schola Cantorum and returned to the United States to earn a master's degree from Columbia University Teachers College in New York City.

Between 1914 and 1918, Hagan toured in the United States, often playing her own compositions. In 1918,

she toured Europe, entertaining African American World War I servicemen. When she gave a recital in 1921 at Aeolian Hall, she became the first African American pianist to give a solo performance in a major New York City concert hall. From the 1930s onward, she was a college teacher at Tennessee Agricultural and Industrial State College and Bishop College (Marshall, Texas) and privately in her own New York music studio.

D(orothy) Antoinette Handy (Miller) (1930–)
Flutist, Educator, Author

After studying violin and piano with her mother as a child, Antoinette Handy became determined on a career in music. Flute became her major instrument, and she studied at Spelman College in Atlanta; the New England Conservatory of Music in Boston, where she earned a bachelor of music degree in 1952; and Northwestern University in Evanston, Illinois, where she earned a master of music degree in 1953. Later she studied at the National Conservatory in Paris and received an artist's diploma in 1955.

As was the case with so many African American musicians and vocalists in the mid-twentieth century, Handy could not secure a job as an orchestra musician in the United States because of her race. However, a chance audition during her time in France yielded a position as first-chair flutist with the Orchestre International, an orchestra supported by the French government that toured Germany in the interest of better foreign relations in 1954. This experience served as the beginning of a 25-year career as a symphony musician with such orchestras as the Chicago Civic, Musica Viva Orchestra of Geneva, Switzerland, Symphony of the Air of the NBC radio network, the Symphony of the New World, and the Richmond (Virginia) Symphony.

In addition to performing, Handy devoted much of her life to teaching music history, theory, and arranging at such institutions as Florida A&M University and Tuskegee Institute. She conducted research of her own on the topic of African American music as a Ford Foundation Humanities Fellow in 1971 and has since published numerous articles for professional journals. She is also the author of the books *Black Women in American Bands and Orchestras* (1981), *The International Sweethearts of Rhythm* (1983, revised 1998), *Black Conductors* (1995), and *Jazz Man's Journey* (1999).

In 1990, Handy was appointed director of the National Endowment for the Arts' Music Program, after having served as acting director and assistant program director. The Music Program is one of the Endowment's largest operations, and before her retirement in 1993,

Handy had administered the distribution of between 11 million and 15 million dollars—money that provided backing for up-and-coming musicians and support for the creation of new music and for musical performances, organizations, and training institutions.

Margaret Rosezarion Harris (1943–2000)
Pianist, Conductor, Composer

Margaret Harris was a child prodigy; she first performed in public at the age of three, began touring nationally when she was four, and played with the Chicago Symphony when she was ten. She was a student of conducting and piano at the Curtis Institute of Music, Philadelphia, and received bachelor's and master's degrees from the Juilliard School of Music (1964, 1965).

Harris began conducting Broadway shows in 1970, starting with *Hair*. Other shows included *Two Gentlemen of Verona, Raisin, Guys and Dolls*, and *Amen Corner*. She was a founding member of Opera Ebony and served as its music director. Among major orchestras that she conducted were the symphonies of Chicago, Minneapolis, Detroit, San Diego, St. Louis, and Los Angeles. Harris also taught at the University of West Florida and Bronx Community College of the City University of New York.

Besides having written scores for musical productions and television shows, she composed choral and instrumental works, the scores for two ballets, and two piano concertos. Harris was both soloist and conductor for performances of these concertos.

Margaret Harris died in New York City on March 7, 2000.

Hazel Harrison (1883–1969)
Pianist, Teacher

Hazel Harrison was born in La Porte, Indiana. She showed prodigious musical gifts from early childhood and may have earned a living as a dance-hall pianist, if it were not for her mother's determination that she pursue a serious music career. Because a European debut was essential for an American concert performer, her major teacher, Victor Heinze, arranged a German tour for her in 1904, during which she was a soloist with the Berlin Philharmonic and attracted favorable notices.

A grant allowed Harrison to return to Germany in 1911, when she became the student of the virtuoso pianist and composer Ferruccio Busoni, who was the biggest influence on her musical life. With the onset of World War I she returned to the United States and stunned critics with her impressive concerts. She debuted in New York City at Town Hall in 1930 to glowing reviews. However, segregation largely confined her talent to concerts played in African American churches, high school gymnasia, and on African American college campuses. This racism caused Harrison to focus on a teaching career, and she joined the faculty of Tuskegee Institute in 1931. Other academic positions followed, at Howard University (1936–1955) and at Alabama State College in Montgomery (1958–1963). She gave her final public concert there in 1959. That Harrison never made commercial recordings is probably the main reason that, in spite of glowing reviews and the devotion of generations of her students, her achievements as a performer are now little known.

Roland Hayes (1887–1977)
Singer

Roland Hayes was born to former slave parents in Curryville, Georgia. His father, a tenant farmer, died

Roland Hayes.

when Hayes was 11. His mother, determined that her six children would not share her illiteracy, sent them to Chattanooga, Tennessee, where the brothers would rotate working and attending school. When his turn came for school, Hayes elected to continue working to provide for the family, but he studied at nights including music study. Later, attending Fisk University, he toured with the Jubilee Singers and also traveled to London, England, for further vocal study.

Hayes became an active recitalist beginning around 1915 and was consistently acclaimed as one of the best tenors. In 1917, he became the first African American to give a recital in Boston's Symphony Hall. Three years later, he gave a royal command performance in London and made very successful appearances throughout Europe. His recital programs included Negro spirituals, folk songs, operatic arias, and American art songs. He gave a well-received farewell concert in New York's Carnegie Hall on his 75th birthday in 1962.

During his long career, Hayes received many awards and citations including eight honorary degrees and the NAACP's Spingarn Medal. His success in the concert field, along with that of Marian Anderson and Paul Robeson, played a large role in broadening the opportunities later available to younger African American singers.

Barbara Hendricks (1948–)
Singer

Soprano Barbara Hendricks, born in Stephens, Arkansas on November 20, 1948, graduated from the University of Nebraska with a bachelor of science degree in chemistry and mathematics. She then attended the Juilliard School of Music in New York City and received a bachelor of music degree in voice in 1973. Hendricks made her debut in 1975 with the San Francisco Spring Opera and has since performed with major opera companies and festivals throughout the United States and Europe. Among them are the Boston Opera, the Metropolitan Opera, St. Paul Opera, Santa Fe Opera, Houston Opera, and the Deutsche Oper in Berlin, and at the Aix-en-Provence and the Glyndebourne Festivals. She has performed frequently as an orchestra soloist as well.

Hendricks has received several awards including a French Grammy for best French performer of classical music in 1986, an honorary doctorate from Nebraska Wesleyan University in 1988, and an honorary membership in the Institute of Humanitarian Law in 1990. She has also served as a human rights activist and, beginning in 1987, as a goodwill ambassador for the United Nations High Commission for Refugees. It is in this capacity that Hendricks has travelled to Rwanda, Bosnia, and Southeast Asia.

Ann Stevens Hobson-Pilot (1943–)
Harpist

Ann Hobson-Pilot, born November 6, 1943, in Philadelphia, was one of the first African American women to hold a permanent position in a major national symphony orchestra. She began studying piano with her mother at an early age and took up the harp in high school so that she could play an instrument on which her mother could not judge so easily what she might be doing wrong. Her first major teacher in harp was Marilyn Costello, principal harpist of the Philadelphia Orchestra and teacher at the Philadelphia Music Academy. After her second year at the academy, she attended the Maine Harp Colony (her first application for admission had been rejected on racial grounds), where she met Alice Chalifoux, principal of the Cleveland Orchestra and teacher at the Cleveland Institute of Music. Hobson-Pilot decided to transfer to the Institute. Chalifoux was influential in starting Hobson-Pilot

Ann Hobson-Pilot.

on her professional orchestra career at the National Symphony Orchestra in Washington, DC. Three years later, Hobson-Pilot joined the Boston Symphony as the associate principal harpist.

Hobson-Pilot's other activities have included performing with the Boston Symphony Chamber Players and the New England Harp Trio and making solo appearances with orchestras throughout the country. Besides conducting clinics and workshops, she has taught at the Philadelphia Musical Academy, the New England Conservatory in Boston, and was a member of the board of trustees at the Longy School of Music. Hobson-Pilot has been honored by the Professional Arts Society of Philadelphia, and received an honorary doctorate of fine arts from Bridgewater State College in 1988.

Ben Holt (1955–1990)
Singer

Born in Washington, DC, baritone Ben Holt attended the Oberlin College Conservatory of Music and was a scholarship student at the Juilliard School of Music, where he worked with Sixten Ehrling, Tito Gobbi, and Manuel Rosenthal. He also took master classes with Luciano Pavarotti and worked extensively with renowned pianist and coach Martin Isepp. When he was in the Merola Program of the San Francisco Opera, taking master classes with Elisabeth Schwarzkopf, he was invited to study privately with her at her studio in Zürich, Switzerland.

Holt made his Metropolitan Opera debut in Puccini's *La Bohème* during the 1985–1986 season, and in 1986 he made his debut with the New York City Opera in the title role of *Malcolm X*, by Anthony Davis. Leading roles in Gershwin's *Porgy and Bess* and Mozart's *The Marriage of Figaro* were also in his repertoire. Holt won many competitions, including the Joy of Singing Competition and the D'Angelo Young Artists Competition, and awards from the Oratorio Society of New York and Independent Black Opera Singers.

Isaiah Jackson (1945–)
Conductor

Isaiah Jackson was born in Richmond, Virginia, where he started piano lessons at the age of four, was sent to a private boarding school in Vermont when he was 14 years old, and traveled with his high school class to the former Soviet Union.

Although Jackson had wanted to be a musician, his parents hoped that he would enter the diplomatic corps. Eventually, he enrolled at Harvard University, from which he graduated cum laude in 1966 with a degree in Russian history and literature. Upon graduation, he followed his first inclination and went to Stanford University for studies in music. After earning a master's degree there in 1967, he moved to the Juilliard School of Music in New York City, where he earned a master's and a doctor of musical arts degree, finishing in 1973.

Shortly thereafter, Jackson conducted major American orchestras including the New York and Los Angeles Philharmonics and the Vienna Symphony. He was also conductor for the Dance Theatre of Harlem at the Spoleto Festival in Italy. Jackson held concurrent positions with various regional orchestras and, for 14 years, he was associate conductor of the Rochester Philharmonic. In 1985, he was guest conductor with the orchestra of the Royal Ballet, London, and became the first African American to hold a chief position—music director—with the Royal Ballet in 1987. In that year he also became the first African American conductor of the Dayton (Ohio) Philharmonic. Jackson has served as guest conductor in the United States and abroad and has been principal guest conductor of the Queensland Symphony Orchestra.

Jackson's awards include being honored as the recipient of the first Governor's Award for the Arts in Virginia in 1979. He also received the Signet Society Medal for the Arts from Harvard University in 1991.

Eva Jessye (1895–1992)
Choral Conductor, Composer

Ebony magazine cited Eva Jessye as "the first black woman to receive international distinction as a choral director," and she was the first African American woman to succeed as a professional choral conductor. Because of racial discrimination, she could not attend high school in her hometown of Coffeyville, Kansas, so she went to Kansas City to study at the Quindaro State School for the Colored (now Western University). There she met Will Marion Cook, who influenced her to become a musician. She also studied at Langston University in Oklahoma and, on completing her formal education, taught in public schools and at Morgan State (Baltimore) and Claflin (Orangeburg, South Carolina) Colleges.

With her move to New York City in 1922, Jessye began her career as a choral conductor, and a few years later she became successful in radio with her own choir. After that, she was invited to train a choir for the King Vidor film *Hallelujah* and then directed the choirs for two of the operas that would be very important to the careers of so many young African American singers:

Four Saints in Three Acts (1934) by Virgil Thomson and Gertrude Stein, and Gershwin's *Porgy and Bess*, based on the book by DuBose Heywood (1935). Jessye was involved in many later productions of this opera into the early 1960s. Her choir did not disband until 1970.

Among Jessye's compositions, based largely on spirituals, are the oratorio *Paradise Lost and Regained* (1936) and *The Chronicle of Job*, a folk drama (1936), as well as many arrangements, especially of spirituals. Her very large collection of memorabilia makes up the Eva Jessye Collection of the University of Michigan, Ann Arbor, Afro-American Music Collections. Jessye lived in Ann Arbor for the last ten years of her life.

J(ohn) Rosamond Johnson (1873–1954)
Composer, Performer

J. Rosamond Johnson, born in Jacksonville, Florida, began piano lessons at age four with his mother. At an early age he studied composition and voice with teachers at the New England Conservatory of Music in Boston and, around 1905, privately with Samuel Coleridge-Taylor in London, England, when Johnson was performing there.

Johnson's career as a professional performer began in 1896. In 1899, he went to New York City to work in the musical theater, first in vaudeville. He soon formed a partnership with his brother, writer/poet/political activist James Weldon Johnson (1871–1938) and the established vaudevillian Bob Cole. They were very successful in producing and writing their own works and contributing to many other musicals during the first decade of the century. After Cole's death in 1912, J. Rosamond continued working with his brother and other partners, made several tours in the United States and England, and sang in many stage productions including the original (1935) and subsequent companies of Gershwin's *Porgy and Bess*. Another notable theatrical work in which he performed was *Cabin in the Sky*.

Besides their theatrical collaborations, the brothers Johnson wrote the song "Lift Ev'ry Voice and Sing" premiered in 1900 by a public school chorus in Jacksonville. The song became known as the "Negro National Anthem" and later as the "Black National Anthem." Later, they published two collections of arrangements of spirituals for solo voice and piano (1925, 1926), and J. Rosamond issued two more volumes of arrangements of African American folk music (1936, 1937), the second of which is titled *Rolling Along in Song: A Chronological Survey of American Negro Music*. All of these publications, as well as their works for the musical

stage, reflected James Weldon's concern that "a distinct African-American creative voice" be sustained in artistic works and attest to their interest in, knowledge of, and sense of the need for the preservation of the folk music of African Americans.

Elayne Jones (1928–)
Timpanist

Elayne Jones, born in New York City on January 30, 1928, began to study the piano with her mother when she was six-years-old. She graduated from the High School of Music and Art and then attended the Juilliard School of Music on a scholarship sponsored by Duke Ellington. In 1949, she was hired by the New York City Opera and Ballet Company orchestra at an unusually young age. She worked with many other orchestras in the New York area including the American Symphony Orchestra from 1962, when the orchestra was founded, until 1972. In that year she was invited by the San Francisco Symphony's music director, Seiji Ozawa, to become its timpanist. Accepting, she became the first African American female to hold a principal chair in a major orchestra.

In 1974, Jones was denied tenure with the orchestra, and, on appeal in 1975, was again denied. She lost the fight to retain her position despite her exemplary professional record and the strong support of friends, colleagues, and the San Francisco public. In 1965, she had been one of the movers for founding the Symphony of the New World and was its first president. Additionally, she has worked as a freelance timpanist in the musical theater, films, and television. She has also taught in many institutions in the New York and San Francisco areas and has lectured widely.

In 1993, the National Association of Negro Musicians gave her its Distinguished Service Award. Jones announced in 1994 that she would take a leave of absence from the San Francisco Opera, where she had played since leaving the symphony, in order "to investigate how [to] best use [her] years of experience to benefit young African American people."

Scott Joplin (1868–1917)
Composer, Pianist

Scott Joplin was born in Texarkana in 1868 and received an early musical education in guitar and piano. Leaving home in his teens, he became a travelling musician, settling for some periods of time in Sedalia and St. Louis, Missouri. He worked with minstrel companies and other musical groups and began to be recognized as an outstanding ragtime piano player. His enduringly popular "Maple Leaf Rag" was published in 1899, and publication of many more ragtime compositions followed regularly.

Joplin had ambitions for writing more "substantial" works, however, and his first effort was the opera *A Guest of Honor*, which he took on tour in 1903. This was a financial failure (even though it was a "ragtime opera"), and any performance materials were lost. After Joplin's move to New York in 1907, where his compositions continued to be successfully published, he decided to return to the musical theater and, in 1911, completed *Treemonisha*. He himself undertook publication of the vocal score; the storyline was a sort of parable about education being the key to improve the lot of the African American. No performance was mounted during his lifetime. However, there was a premiere of the work given at the Atlanta Memorial Arts Center in January of 1972, for the Afro-American Music Workshop of Morehouse College. T.J. Anderson orchestrated from the vocal score, and Katherine Dunham was responsible for staging and choreography. Two subsequent orchestrations were made, attesting to the work's popularity and attraction to musicians, and the opera reached Broadway for a run in 1975.

The Complete Works of Scott Joplin was issued in 1981 (the piano works), and there have been numerous articles, books, and dissertations written on Joplin's life and works since the resurgence of interest in ragtime in the early 1970s. In 1976, he was awarded the honorary Bicentennial Pulitzer Prize for contributions to American music.

Robert Jordan (1940–)
Pianist, Educator

Robert Jordan was born in Chattanooga, Tennessee in 1940. He earned a bachelor of music degree in 1962 from the Eastman School of Music in Rochester, New York, where his major teacher was Cecile Genhart; and a master of music degree at the Juilliard School of Music, with Rosina Lhevine as his major teacher, in 1965.

Jordan made a successful New York debut as soloist with the Symphony of the New World in 1971 and as recitalist in the next season at Alice Tully Hall in Lincoln Center. He was a Fulbright Scholar for two years, which he spent studying and performing in Germany. Jordan has performed in Africa, Asia, South America, Europe, and the United States as recitalist and orchestra soloist. In 1980 he joined the faculty of the State University of New York at Fredonia as professor of piano, and he received the Chancellor's Award for Excellence in Teaching. In 1987, he served as Martin Luther King Visiting Professor at Northern Michigan

Robert Jordan.

University in Marquette, and, in 1991, in the same capacity at the University of Michigan, Ann Arbor. Jordan established the Mamie and Ira Jordan Minority Music Scholarship and Scholastic Achievement award at SUNY-Fredoria in 1997.

Ulysses Simpson Kay (1917–1995)
Composer, Educator

From the mid-1940s on, Ulysses Kay composed steadily for instrumental solos and ensembles, string, chamber, and full orchestra, band, voice, chorus, opera, and for film and television. A large number of his works—almost 60—were commissioned. His compositions are strongly based in Western European traditions—he was a student of Howard Hanson and Paul Hindemith—but they are also rooted in African American folk music practices.

Kay was born in Tucson, Arizona, to musical parents, and he benefitted from a number of other musical influences throughout his childhood. His uncle was the legendary cornet player Joseph "King" Oliver, who urged his sister to give the young Ulysses piano lessons

Ulysses Kay.

before starting him on any other instrument. Besides piano, however, he studied violin and saxophone, sang in the school glee club, and played in the marching band and dance orchestra. He attended the University of Arizona, where he earned a bachelor of music degree in 1938. Two years later, he received a master of music degree from the Eastman School of Music in Rochester, New York.

During service in the Navy from 1942 to 1946, Kay wrote the work that first brought him critical attention, *Of New Horizons*, which was performed by the New York Philharmonic in 1944. Kay's *Suite for Orchestra* in 1945 received a prize from Broadcast Music, Incorporated, a company for which Kay later acted as a consultant from 1953 until 1968. This prize was to be the first of many awards, fellowships, and grants, which would allow the gifted composer to concentrate on his music in both Europe and the United States.

Although he served as a visiting professor at Boston University and the University of California at Los Angeles, he did not receive a permanent teaching position until he joined the faculty of the Lehman College of the City University of New York in 1968. In 1988, he retired

from his position as distinguished professor of composition and theory.

Some representative works by Kay are the film score *The Quiet One* (1948), *Six Dances for String Orchestra* (1954), *Choral Triptych* (1962), *Markings* (1966), *Southern Harmony: Four Aspects for Orchestra* (1975), and the opera—one of five—*Frederick Douglass* (1991). Kay received over 25 honors and awards, which include a George Gershwin Memorial Award, Fulbright and Guggenheim Fellowships, a National Endowment for the Arts Grant, and election to the American Academy of Arts and Letters, as well as several honorary doctorates.

Tania León (1943–)
Composer, Conductor, Pianist

Tania Justina León is a native of Havana, Cuba, where she earned both a bachelor's and a master's degree in music from the Carlos Alfredo Peyrellado Conservatory. In 1967, she emigrated to the United States and worked for another bachelor's degree in music education and a master's in composition from New York University. There she studied with Ursula Mamlok and Laszlo Halasz, and later she studied conducting with Seiji Ozawa and Leonard Bernstein at the Berkshire Music Festival at Tanglewood, Massachusetts.

In New York, León's first professional work in music was as an accompanist and then music director of what became Arthur Mitchell's Dance Theatre of Harlem. She went to the Festival of Two Worlds in Spoleto, Italy, with the company in 1971, and there she made her

Tania León.

first appearance as conductor. Additionally, she wrote scores for Mitchell's choreography. With increasing demands on her time for guest conducting, piano performances, and commissions for works, she left the company in 1980. She served as music director for the Alvin Ailey Dance Company for the 1983–84 season, and music director for Broadway musicals from 1978's *The Wiz*, to *The Lion King* in 1996.

León joined the faculty of Brooklyn College in 1985 and became professor in 1994. She was the Revson Composer for the New York Philharmonic from 1993 until 1996, and its new music advisor from 1996 to 1997. She has also served as composer- or conductor/composer-in-residence for many orchestras and educational institutions.

Thoroughly trained in the classical music tradition, León began to incorporate her ethnic backgrounds—encompassing Chinese, African, South American, Cuban, and French—into the creation of unique works with startling juxtapositions, which are informed by her mastery of the contemporary orchestra. Just a few of her colorful works are: *Kabiosile* for piano and orchestra (1988); *Indígena* for chamber orchestra (1991); the chamber opera *Scourge of Hyacinths* for the Fourth Munich Biennale (1994); *Para Viola y Orquesta* (1995); and *Bata* (1995). She has received over 30 commissions and numerous honors and awards including citations from the National Council of the Arts, Havana, the National Endowment for the Arts, Meet the Composer, the Dean Dixon Achievement Award, and a Rockefeller Foundation residency.

Henry Jay Lewis (1932–1996)
Conductor, Double Bassist

Henry Lewis was born in Los Angeles and knew early on that he wanted to be a musician, in spite of his father's disapproval of the profession. He was only 16 years old when he joined the Los Angeles Philharmonic Orchestra in 1948 as a double bassist, becoming the first African American instrumentalist to play with a major American orchestra. In 1954, he was drafted into the U.S. Army. While stationed in Germany, between 1955 and 1957 he conducted the Seventh Army Symphony Orchestra. Following discharge, he returned to the Los Angeles Philharmonic as assistant conductor. Lewis founded the String Society of Los Angeles in 1959 (later known as the Los Angeles Chamber Orchestra) and was engaged as guest conductor with virtually every major American orchestra. From 1965 to 1968 he was also the music director of the Los Angeles Opera Company.

Lewis was selected as conductor and music director of the New Jersey Symphony in 1968 and so became the first African American to serve in that position with a major American orchestra. He conducted the New York Philharmonic in 1972 and became the first African American to conduct the Metropolitan Opera Orchestra. Resigning from the New Jersey Symphony in 1976, Lewis remained active as a guest conductor in the United States and Europe, and made recordings with the Scottish Opera and the Netherlands Radio Symphony Orchestra. In 1991, he was music director of the London production of *Carmen Jones*.

Lewis was founder of the Black Academy of Arts and Letters and a member of the California Arts Commission and the Young Musicians Foundation.

Dorothy Leigh Maynor (1910–1996)
Singer, Administrator

Born in Norfolk, Virginia, Dorothy Mainor (she changed the spelling of her last name when she became a singer) grew up in an atmosphere of music and singing. She intended originally to become a home economics teacher, and, with this in mind, entered the Hampton Institute College Preparatory School in 1924. However, her development as a singer in the school choir prompted her choir director, R. Nathaniel Dett, to convince her to switch to a voice major. She graduated from the Institute with a bachelor's degree in 1933.

Maynor was heard by the director of the Westminster Choir, who made it possible for her to receive a scholarship at the Westminster Choir College in Princeton, New Jersey. She received her bachelor's degree in music in 1935 and went to New York City to continue voice study. At the Berkshire Music Festival in Tanglewood, Massachusetts, in 1939, Boston Symphony Orchestra conductor Serge Koussevitzky immediately took an interest in furthering her career. Maynor was acclaimed by critics on her 1939 Town Hall debut in New York, and thus began her remarkable 25-year career as recitalist, orchestra soloist, and recording artist.

Following her debut, Maynor toured the United States and the rest of the world and performed with the leading orchestras of the day. Additionally, Maynor embarked upon a recording career in which she sang arias, spirituals, and operas. Her interpretations of the latter, however, were limited to the recording studio because no opera company of the time would allow an African American to perform in their productions. Although her singing earned Maynor extremely favorable reviews from critics around the world, she was not allowed to audition for the Metropolitan Opera. In an ironic twist, she would become the first African American member of the Met's board of directors in 1975. In 1952, Maynor became the first African American artist to perform at Constitution Hall in Washington, DC.

Maynor retired from singing after her husband's heart attack in 1963. However, she remained active in the arts through the foundation of what became the Harlem School of the Arts located initially in the St. James Presbyterian Church. By the late 1970s the school boasted more than 40 instructors and over one thousand students. With the school rapidly outgrowing the church, Maynor raised $3.5 million to erect a new building, which opened in 1979, the year she retired as its director.

Bobby McFerrin (1950–)
Singer, Conductor, Songwriter

Robert McFerrin Jr., the son of opera singers Robert and Sara McFerrin, was born on March 11, 1950, in New York City. In 1958, his family moved to Los Angeles, and he attended Sacramento State University and Cerritos College. Dropping out of college, he played piano for several show companies. By 1977 he had decided to concentrate on a singing career, and he was discovered by Jon Hendricks. He performed at jazz festivals and began touring and recording with George Benson and Herbie Hancock, among other jazz greats. His first of

Bobby McFerrin.

many solo albums was called simply *Bobby McFerrin*. He has gone on to win ten Grammy Awards. His song "Don't Worry, Be Happy" topped the popular music charts in 1989.

McFerrin made his conducting debut with the San Francisco Symphony in 1990, and he was appointed conductor and creative chair of the St. Paul Chamber Orchestra. In 2002, he was chosen as a recipient of the prestigious George Peabody Medal for Outstanding Contributions to Music in America. McFerrin is in demand as both vocalist and conductor for orchestras around the country and continues to present innovative programming in both capacities.

Robert McFerrin (1921–)
Singer, Educator

Baritone Robert McFerrin, born on March 19, 1921, in Marianna, Arkansas, was brought up in St. Louis, Missouri, where he attended public schools and sang in his father's church choir. After a year at Fisk University in Nashville, the young Robert attended the Chicago Musical College, where he earned a bachelor's degree.

McFerrin began his professional singing career in Broadway shows including *Lost in the Stars* and *The Green Pastures*. He also sang with the National Negro Opera Company in William Grant Still's *Troubled Island*, the role of Rigoletto with the New England Opera Company in 1950, and, after winning the 1954 Metropolitan Auditions of the Air, he became a member of the regular roster of the Metropolitan Opera for three seasons, the first African American male singer to do so.

McFerrin has been a guest professor of voice at several institutions in Finland, Canada, and the United States, and has performed widely in North and South America and Europe. Both Stowe Teacher's College in St. Louis and the University of Missouri awarded him honorary doctorates.

Lena Johnson McLin (1928–)
Composer, Conductor, Educator

Born September 5, 1928, in Atlanta, Lena McLin was immersed in music as a child, particularly gospel and classical. Her mother, a choir director, gave her piano lessons and exposed her to various kinds of sacred music. This foundation of religious music became even stronger during the years she lived with the family of her uncle, Thomas A. Dorsey, the "father of gospel music," in Chicago. McLin received a bachelor of music degree from Spelman College in Atlanta in 1951, and she moved to Chicago for graduate study in composition and music theory, first at the American Conservatory of Music and then at Roosevelt University, where she also studied electronic music and voice.

In 1959, McLin began a long teaching career in the Chicago public schools, which was distinguished by her development and implementation of a music curriculum for the school system, and included her writing a textbook on music history. She also conducted a variety of church and community choirs; founded an opera company, the McLin Ensemble, in 1957 and the gospel group, the McLin Singers, in 1968; and has served as guest conductor and in workshops for several national organizations and educational institutions.

The varied list of McLin's compositions includes several piano solos and dozens of choral works, among them the commissioned mass *Eucharist of the Soul*, the dramatic oratorio *Free at Last: A Portrait of Martin Luther King Jr.* and *The Torch Has Been Passed*, based on President John F. Kennedy's inaugural address. Her style shows her love for and mastery of all kinds of music—gospel, rock, popular, and past and current traditions of Western concert music—which can be distinct or interwoven in her scores and always make clear and direct statements.

Abbie Mitchell. *See* **Drama, Comedy, & Dance chapter.**

Leona Mitchell (1949–)
Singer

Soprano Leona Mitchell was born in Enid, Oklahoma, and graduated from Oklahoma University in 1971. She made her Metropolitan Opera debut as Micaela in Bizet's *Carmen* in 1975 and also sang the roles of Lauretta in Puccini's *Gianni Schicchi*, Pamina in Mozart's *The Magic Flute*, and Madamoiselle Lidoine in Poulenc's *Dialogues of the Carmelites*.

Her outstanding vocal capabilities have caused her to be regarded as the leading American soprano with a career that has taken her to all the major opera houses of the world. She has likewise performed with several orchestras and, in 1980, sang the role of Bess in the Cleveland Orchestra Blossom Festival production of Gershwin's *Porgy and Bess* and in the subsequent recording. In 1983, she was inducted into the Oklahoma Hall of Fame. Mitchell was one of a select group of subjects considered in Rosalyn M. Story's 1990 book, *And So I Sing: African-American Divas of Opera and Concert.*

Dorothy Rudd Moore (1940–)
Composer, Teacher, Singer

Born in Wilmington, Delaware, Dorothy Rudd Moore attended the Wilmington School of Music as a teenager and, in 1963, received a bachelor of music degree, magna cum laude, in theory and composition from Howard University, where her major composition teacher was Mark Fax. Later, she studied composition privately with Chou Wen Chung in New York City and with Nadia Boulanger at the American Conservatory in Fontainebleau, France. She also studied voice at Howard University and privately, and she has performed frequently as a singer.

Moore taught piano, voice, sight-singing, and ear-training at the Harlem School of the Arts, New York University, and Bronx Community College. Among her works in various media are: *Dirge and Deliverance*, for piano and cello, commissioned by her husband Kermit Moore; *Flowers of Darkness* for tenor and piano, commissioned by William Brown; *Reflections* for concert band; and the opera *Frederick Douglass*, commissioned and premiered by Opera Ebony in 1985, about which *Opera News* reported that she "displays a rare ability to wed musical and dramatic motion, graceful lyric inventiveness, [and] a full command of the orchestral palette."

Kermit Moore (1929–)
Cellist, Conductor, Composer

Kermit Moore's first musical identity was as a cellist. He studied the instrument at the Cleveland Institute of Music and received a bachelor's degree in 1951. He earned a master of arts degree at New York University in 1952, and, in 1956, he attended the Paris National Conservatory and was awarded an artist's diploma. He gave his New York recital debut at Town Hall in 1949 and has concertized internationally in the major capitals of Europe and Asia. He has also made appearances with many orchestras, particularly in Europe.

In 1964, Moore co-founded the Symphony of the New World in New York. Besides performing as cellist with the group, he also conducted occasionally. He was careful to include a wide variety of works by African American composers on his symphonic programs. One of the most unusual, perhaps, was the Concerto for Violin and Orchestra, premiered in 1867 by its composer, the Afro-Cuban Joseph White, and given its first American performance with Ruggero Ricci as soloist in 1974. He has had many engagements as guest conductor in the United States.

In addition to his work with the Symphony of the New World, Moore served as conductor of the Brooklyn Philharmonic beginning in 1984. He was also one of several founders of the Society of Black Composers as well as the Classical Heritage Ensemble. He writes instrumental solos and ensembles including concertos for cello and timpani, and for voice.

Undine Smith Moore (1904–1989)
Composer, Educator

A native of Jarret, Virginia, Undine Smith Moore studied piano in Petersburg and began her college studies at Fisk University in Nashville. In 1926, she was awarded a bachelor of arts degree, cum laude, and a music school diploma, and later attended Columbia University Teachers College, where she earned a master's degree and professional diploma in 1931. She took further graduate studies at several schools including the Juilliard and Eastman Schools of Music.

Moore taught at Virginia State College in Petersburg from 1927 until 1972, when she became professor emerita. Her students included many illustrious contributors to the music world, such as jazz pianist Billy Taylor, opera singer Camilla Williams, conductor Leon Thompson, gospel singer Robert Fryson, music educators Michael V.W. Gordon and James Mumford, and composer Phil Medley. At the university, she co-founded the Black Music Center in 1969 and was co-director until 1972. After retirement, she was a visiting professor at many universities and colleges. Some of her awards include honorary doctorates from Virginia State University and Indiana University, the Seventh Annual Humanitarian Awards from Fisk University, and the National Association of Negro Musicians Award (1975). In 1982, her *Scenes from the Life of a Martyr: To the Memory of Martin Luther King*, an oratorio, was nominated for the Pulitzer Prize.

Moore's style was infused with African American influences and a tonal musical language. Choral music makes up the largest part of her output and there are many works for instrumental solos and ensembles including *Afro-American Suite*, commissioned by Antoinette Handy's Trio Pro Viva. Her 1987 trio *Soweto*, inspired by events in that South African town, was the last work she wrote.

Michael DeVard Morgan (1957–)
Conductor

Born in Washington, DC, Michael Morgan received music training in the public schools he attended, in addition to private piano lessons. He attended the Oberlin College Conservatory of Music from 1975 to 1979. He pursued additional studies in the Vienna master classes of Witold Rowicki and at the Berkshire Music Center at Tanglewood, where he was a conducting fellow and student of Seiji Ozawa and Gunther Schuller. Morgan was selected to work with Leonard Bernstein for one week, which culminated in Morgan's appearance with the New York Philharmonic in September of 1986. From 1980 to 1987, he was Exxon/Arts Endowment assistant conductor of the Chicago Symphony Orchestra and later became affiliate artist conductor; he was also co-resident conductor of the Chicago Civic Orchestra. He became music director of the Oakland East Bay Symphony Orchestra in 1993 and has appeared as a guest conductor with many of the nation's major orchestras and abroad.

The many awards Morgan has earned include first prize in the Hans Swarowsky International Conductors Competition (Vienna, Austria), the first prize in the Gino Marrinuzzi International Conductors Competition (San Remo, Italy), and first prize in the Baltimore Symphony Young Conductors Competition.

Jessye Norman (1945–)
Singer

On September 15, 1945, soprano Jessye Norman was born into a musical family in Augusta, Georgia. Her mother, a schoolteacher, gave her children piano lessons. The young Jessye's musical talents were evident early, and at the age of 16 she entered the Marian Anderson Scholarship competition. She did not win, but her audition at Howard University led to a four-year scholarship. Receiving her bachelor's degree in 1967, she continued study, first at the Peabody Conservatory with Alice Dushak, and then at the University of Michigan with Pierre Bernac and Elizabeth Mannion for a master's degree in 1968. That year, she entered the International Music Competition held in Munich, Germany, and won first place. Her operatic career in Europe was launched, and she made debuts at the Deutsche Oper in Berlin, La Scala in Milan, and the Royal Opera House in Covent Garden, London. Her American opera debut took place at the Hollywood Bowl as Aida, and her stage debut with the Opera Company of Philadelphia in the double bill of Purcell's *Dido and Aeneas* and Stravinsky's *Oedipus Rex* (1982). In 1983, she made her Metropolitan Opera debut as Cassandra in *Les Troyens* by Berlioz.

Taking a break from opera performance, Norman was a busy recitalist and orchestra soloist from 1975 to 1980, with a far-ranging repertoire. She continued these activities after resuming operatic appearances as Ariadne in *Ariadne auf Naxos* by Richard Strauss. Her vocal prowess and the breadth of her musicianship are demonstrated by the variety of operas that she sings including Rameau, Mozart, Meyerbeer, Wagner, Verdi, and

Bartok. Among her numerous recordings are two compact discs of spirituals (one with Kathleen Battle) and many concert works and operas, and even a "crossover" pop album *Lucky to Be Me*. Norman won a Grammy Award in 1984 for her performance on *Songs of Maurice Ravel*. She has also received honorary degrees from Howard University, the Boston Conservatory, and the University of the South.

Coleridge-Taylor Perkinson (1932–)
Composer, Conductor

A native New Yorker, Coleridge-Taylor Perkinson graduated from the High School for Music and Art in that city and, after two years at New York University, transferred to the Manhattan School of Music, where he studied conducting with Jonel Perlea and composition with Vittorio Giannini. He also studied composing at Princeton University with Earl Kim, and conducting at the Berkshire Music Center at Tanglewood, the Mozarteum in Salzburg, Austria, and the Netherlands Radio Union.

Perkinson worked steadily as a composer and music director. Some of the groups with which he has been associated are the Dessoff Choirs as assistant conductor, the Max Roach Jazz Quartet as pianist, the Symphony of the New World, as founding member and associate conductor from 1965 to 1970, and the Negro Ensemble Company as composer-in-residence. He has received many commissions including three from dance companies: Arthur Mitchell Dance Company, 1971; Dance Theatre of Harlem, 1972 and 1987; and the American Dance Theater Foundation, 1984. He has been guest conductor for several orchestras in the United States and abroad.

Perkinson has written a great deal of incidental and commercial music for film and television programs, and he has written and arranged for many different kinds of artists, such as Harry Belafonte, Max Roach, Marvin Gaye, and Melvin Van Peebles. Instrumental works are predominant in his catalog of works, ranging from solos to mixed ensembles to string, chamber, and full orchestras. His works demonstrate his complete knowledge of twentieth-century compositional techniques and his ease in using them for highly-varied expressive purposes. The folk music of African Americans is a basic part of what and how Perkinson writes.

Julia Perry (1924–1979)
Composer, Conductor

Julia Perry, born in Lexington, Kentucky, was raised in Akron, Ohio. As a child, she studied piano and became interested in composing early on. In 1942, she entered the Westminster Choir College in Princeton, New Jersey, and studied composition and conducting, in addition to violin, piano, and voice. After earning a master's degree in 1948, she studied composition at the Juilliard School of Music, where her music was performed for the first time.

In the 1950s, Perry lived mostly in Europe. Having studied with Luigi Dallapiccola at the Berkshire Music Center at Tanglewood, Massachusetts, she continued studies with him in Italy on two Guggenheim Fellowships in 1954 and 1956. She also studied with Nadia Boulanger in Paris during this time and won a Boulanger Grand Prix for her Viola Sonata in 1952. She continued studying conducting as well, and she had many opportunities to conduct some of her works in Europe. She also was a lecturer on American music through the United States Information Service.

With her return to the United States in 1959, Perry continued to compose and was engaged to teach at several colleges. She concentrated on writing instrumental music in the 1960s, whereas earlier she specialized in vocal music including choral. Among her output of orchestral works were 12 symphonies. Whatever the medium, Perry was almost always availing herself of the rich resources of her African American musical heritage, and she was in command of the Western European tradition including the latest techniques that had been developed in Europe and the United States.

Some of her most-performed works are: *Stabat Mater* (1951) for contralto or mezzo-soprano and string quartet or string orchestra; *A Short Piece for Orchestra* (1952), that was premiered by the Turin Symphony conducted by Dean Dixon; and *Homunculus C.F.* (1960), for eight percussionists, harp, celesta, and piano.

A debilitating stroke in 1973 almost incapacitated Perry, and it was no doubt a major factor in her early death.

Evelyn LaRue Pittman (1910–)
Choral Director, Composer

While a senior at Spelman College in Atlanta studying African American history, Evelyn Pittman committed herself to teaching African American history through music. Her first work, a musical play, was produced at Spelman in 1933, the year she graduated. During the years she taught in the public schools in Oklahoma City from 1935 to 1956, she conducted weekly broadcasts with her own professional vocal group, the Evelyn Pittman Choir, on a local radio station. She also directed a 350-voice choir sponsored by the YWCA and directed orchestras, choirs, and operettas in the schools.

She published songs which she composed about African American leaders that she published in the collection *Rich Heritage* in 1944.

In 1948, Pittman went to the Juilliard School of Music in New York City to study composition under Robert Ward. Later, she attended the University of Oklahoma at Norman and studied with Harrison Kerr, receiving a master's degree in 1954. Kerr introduced her to his former teacher, Nadia Boulanger, who became her teacher from 1956 to 1958. During that period, she completed her folk opera *Cousin Esther* written for an African American cast. It was performed many times to favorable reviews in both France and the United States.

Pittman returned to public school teaching in 1958 in New York and continued to compose. After the assassination of Dr. Martin Luther King Jr. in 1968, she wrote the opera *Freedom Child* in his memory. Upon her retirement from teaching, she dedicated herself to directing a touring company of *Freedom Child* and remained committed to improving race relations through music and drama.

Awadagin Pratt (1966–)
Pianist, Conductor, Violinist

Awadagin Pratt was born on March 6, 1966, in Pittsburgh, Pennsylvania, and began studying piano at the age of six. In 1975, his family moved to Illinois, and he attended the University of Illinois, Urbana, at the age of 16, majoring in music. In 1986 he enrolled in the Peabody Conservatory of Music in Baltimore, where he earned performer's certificates in piano and violin in 1989 and a graduate performance diploma in conducting in 1992.

In 1992 Pratt's career as a concert pianist began when he became the first African American to win the Naumburg International piano composition. After several major concert successes, he was awarded the Avery Fisher Career Grant in 1994, and his full-time concert career continued at a rapid pace. He has performed with many major American orchestras, and he has given recitals throughout the United States and in Europe, Africa, and Japan.

Pratt has been interested in the education of younger musicians during his career and has given up to ten master classes a year, beginning in 1992, at such colleges as the Eastman School of Music and the Universities of Washington, Missouri, Minnesota, Texas, and many others. He has served on the boards of the Pratt Music Foundation and the Next Generation Festival.

Pratt's third recording on the EMI recording label was entitled *Live from South Africa* (1997), performed from the stage of the Capetown Opera House. Asked by

Awadagin Pratt.

an interviewer for *Piano and Keyboard* magazine about how he chooses music for performance, Pratt responded that his selections "have to be works that express, that evoke something more than themselves. Music and art are about expressing some sort of joy about all states of experience—a celebration, even, of those states."

Pratt's recordings include, *Play Bach* (2002), *Pratt: Transformations* (1999), *Beethoven: Piano Sonatas* (1996), *Awadagin Pratt: A Long Way From Normal* (1994).

Florence Beatrice Price (1888–1953)
Composer, Pianist, Educator

As a young child, Florence Price studied piano with her mother in her hometown of Little Rock, Arkansas, and was precocious enough to play in public for the first time at the age of four. When she was only 14 years old, she began study with Frederick Converse and George Chadwick at the New England Conservatory of Music in Boston, where she earned diplomas in organ and piano in 1906. She returned to Arkansas to teach at the high school and college levels and moved to Atlanta in 1910 to become head of the music department of Clark College.

In 1912, Florence married attorney Thomas Price in Little Rock, where they lived until moving in 1927 to Chicago—a move prompted by increasing racial tensions in the South. In Chicago she taught privately and took advanced studies at the Chicago Musical College and the American Conservatory. Price had published her first composition in 1899, and, after her move to Chicago, the number of her publications increased notably, especially of organ, piano, and vocal music.

The best-known of her orchestral works is, perhaps, her Symphony in A Minor, No. 1 that won first prize in the 1930 Wanamaker Music Contest; it was performed by the Chicago Symphony Orchestra at the Chicago World's Fair Century of Progress Exhibition in 1933. Three of her other prizewinning compositions in that competition were Piano Sonata in E Minor (first prize) and Piano Fantasie No. 4 and the orchestral *Ethiopia's Shadow in America* (both honorable mentions). Her Concerto in One Movement for piano had several performances, the solo part often played by her student Margaret Bonds. Price was well-known for her songs and arrangements of spirituals, which were performed by such stellar singers as Marian Anderson, Roland Hayes, Leontyne Price, and Blanche Thebom. Anderson championed her setting of Langston Hughes's "Songs to a Dark Virgin."

Price was thoroughly familiar with and comfortable in using African American folk music, both sacred and secular, and her works in standard concert form usually demonstrate this aspect of her style. Overall, her style is usually described as "neoromantic" and "nationalistic."

Leontyne Price (1927–)
Singer

Soprano Mary Violet Leontyne Price was born on February 10, 1927, in Laurel, Mississippi, where her parents encouraged her in music with piano lessons and participation in their church choir. With the idea of teaching music in school, she attended Central State College in Wilberforce, Ohio. Even before her graduation in 1949 with a bachelor's degree in music education, she received a scholarship at the Juilliard School of Music in New York City. Her work there attracted the attention of critic and composer Virgil Thomson, who cast her in her first professional role as Cecilia in a revival of his and Gertrude Stein's opera *Four Saints in Three Acts*. Soon afterwards, she toured in Europe as Bess in a revival of Gershwin's *Porgy and Bess* (1952–1954). Her marriage to co-star William Warfield ended in divorce in 1973.

After the tour was completed, Price made her New York recital debut at Town Hall and took other operatic roles on both stage and television. She was the first African American to perform opera in television when she played Puccini's *Tosca.* Her performance was so well-received that she was invited back to play Pamina and Donna Anna from Mozart's *The Magic Flute* and *Don Giovanni* respectively, and Madame Lidoine in Poulenc's *Dialogues of the Carmelites.* Her Metropolitan Opera debut was as Leonora in Verdi's *Il Trovatore.* Other Verdi roles in which she was brilliantly successful were in *Aida, Un Ballo in Maschera, Ernani,* and *La Forza del Destino.* For the opening of the new Metropolitan Opera House in 1966, she was Cleopatra in the specially-commissioned opera by Samuel Barber, *Antony and Cleopatra.* She has sung many roles with other opera companies as well, especially the San Francisco Opera (she was awarded their medal in honor of the twentieth anniversary of her company debut) and the Lyric Opera of Chicago.

Price has received several honorary doctorates, over 20 Grammy Awards, and a Kennedy Center Honor for lifetime achievement in the arts. She ended her operatic career in 1985 in *Aida* at the Metropolitan Opera but has continued performing. Her recordings are numerous and span a wide range of repertory. There are several collections of arias—operatic and concert—art songs, Christmas and patriotic songs, and a collaboration with Andre Previn on 12 pop songs *Right as the Rain.* In late September 2001, Price emerged from retirement to participate in the Carnegie Hall "Concert of Remembrance," held in honor of the victims of the September 11 terrorist attacks.

Kay George Roberts (1950–)
Conductor, Violinist

Kay Roberts was born in Nashville, Tennessee on September 16, 1950, and began her professional musical career as a violinist when she joined the Nashville Symphony during her last year in high school. She continued to play with the orchestra until she graduated with a bachelor's degree from Fisk University in 1972. In 1971, she represented the Nashville Symphony in Arthur Fiedler's World Symphony Orchestra. She earned a master of music degree in 1975, a master of musical arts in 1976, and a doctor of musical arts degree in 1986 from Yale University—the first woman and second African American to do so. During her second year of residency at Yale, Roberts's talent as a conductor first came to the attention of her instructor and, thereafter, she focused on conducting rather than the violin.

Roberts has guest conducted many orchestras including the symphonies of Nashville, Chattanooga, Indianapolis, Des Moines, Greater Dallas, and Chicago, in addition to the Cleveland Orchestra, the Mystic Valley Chamber Orchestra, and the Bangkok Symphony in Thailand. She became the music director of the New Hampshire Philharmonic in 1982 and of the Cape Ann Symphony Orchestra in 1986.

Roberts began teaching at the College of Music at the University of Massachusetts at Lowell in 1978. She has received numerous awards throughout her career including the 1991 Outstanding Achievement in the Performing Arts Award from the League of Black Women and the 1993 National Achievement Award from the National Black Music Caucus. She served as a fellow at Harvard University's W.E.B. DuBois Institute for Afro-American Research from 1997 through 1999.

Paul Robeson (1898–1976)
Singer, Actor

Born in Princeton, New Jersey, Paul Robeson was the son of a runaway slave who worked his way through

Paul Robeson performing the lead role in the Shakespearean play, *Othello,* in 1943.

Lincoln University and became a minister. Paul Robeson entered Rutgers College (now University) on an athletic scholarship and won a total of 12 letters in track, football, baseball, and basketball. His academic ability gained him another prize: Phi Beta Kappa honors in his junior year.

Robeson moved to New York City after graduation and began the study of law at Columbia University in 1920. He also began to act, and this profession eventually took precedence over a law career (he had been admitted to the New York State bar in 1923). He was cast in Eugene O'Neill's *The Emperor Jones* in 1923 and, two years later, in *All God's Chillun' Got Wings,* gaining excellent reviews for both production. His rich singing voice, coupled with his strong interest in spirituals and international folk songs, led him to concertize in recital, first in New York and later in Europe and England. Besides enjoying great success on the London and Broadway stages, he also acted in several films in the 1930s and early 1940s. He became one of the first African Americans to depart from stereotypical film roles.

Robeson's concern for racial justice came increasingly to the forefront in those years as well, and his travels to the Soviet Union convinced him of the honesty of that country's statements regarding the equal treatment of all people. With the Cold War settling in after World War II, Robeson's freely expressed views brought him into conflict with Congress and federal authorities, and, despite his denials, he was accused of being a communist. His career was effectively ended, and his passport was revoked in 1950—to be restored eight years later by a U.S. Supreme Court decision. He moved to England and traveled widely in Europe and the Soviet Union until 1963, when he returned to the United States. In 1971, his autobiography *Here I Stand* was published. He continued to be active in civil and human rights issues until his health began to fail in the 1970s. In 1998, he was posthumously honored with a Grammy Lifetime Achievement Award.

Philippa (Duke) Schuyler (1931–1967)
Pianist, Composer

Born in New York City to an African American father and a white mother, Philippa Schuyler embodied her parents' desire to prove to the world that the intermingling of the black and white races would result in a hybrid which would draw from the strengths of each lineage. She initially fulfilled their expectations: at the age of two and a half she could read and write; by age four she was composing music; and by age five she was performing Mozart. Her IQ, tested by New York University, was 185. She was given piano lessons at the age of three and early in elementary school she began to study harmony, having already written dozens of piano pieces. She gave her first solo recital at the age of six. While Schuyler was studying throughout her childhood and adolescence, she had relatively little formal composition training, and that ended when she was 15. Among her teachers were Dean Dixon and Antonia Brico in conducting, Josef Hoffman, Paul Wittgenstein, and Gaston Dethier in piano, and Clarence Cameron White in violin.

With her parents pushing her career, the child prodigy wowed the critics in both the excellence of her playing and the quality of her compositions. Schuyler began to perform widely as a teenager and appeared as orchestra soloist and recitalist; several of her works were performed by orchestras including the New York Philharmonic, the Chicago Symphony, and the Detroit Symphony. She made three world tours, at first under U.S. State Department auspices, and received numerous awards throughout her career. Among them was a 1939 World's Fair Medal as one of the "Women of Tomorrow," an Award of Merit from the Fair in 1940, a Distinguished Achievement Award from the National Negro Opera Company Foundation, in 1955, gold and silver medals from Haile Selassie, the Emperor of Ethiopia, in 1955, and, after her death, the establishment of a memorial foundation in her name.

However, despite her successes, Schuyler's appeal to white America faded as soon as she entered young adulthood. Stung by the racism she had not encountered as a child, Schuyler left the United States to travel the world and played for numerous foreign dignitaries. In spite of the acclaim she received outside of the United States, the rejection she experienced in America was a bitter reminder that, regardless of her success abroad, she was still a second-class citizen back home. Her travels became a painful search for identity which she attempted to reconcile through her fiction and nonfiction writing. She even adopted a different identity, claiming to be Felipa Monterro, an Iberian-American, in the hopes of gaining acceptance before white audiences in America. However, initial reviews of her concerts performed in Europe under this new identity were mediocre.

In 1967, Schuyler was killed in a helicopter crash in Da Nang Bay, South Vietnam, where she had gone to help in the rescue of some schoolchildren.

Hale Smith (1925–)
Composer, Educator, Editor

Born on June 29, 1925, Hale Smith is a native of Cleveland, Ohio. He attended the city's public schools and earned bachelor (1950) and master (1952) of music

degrees from the Cleveland Institute of Music. His only composition teacher, Marcel Dick, was a major influence, as were such jazz figures as Duke Ellington and Art Tatum.

In 1958, on his move to New York City, Smith began arranging for and collaborating with many different kinds of musicians including Chico Hamilton, Dizzy Gillespie, and Oliver Nelson. Active as a music editor and consultant from 1961, he worked for several music publishing companies—Marks Music and C.F. Peters, among them. He joined the faculty of the University of Connecticut at Storrs in 1970 and retired in 1984.

Smith has received over 20 commissions and many prestigious awards in the course of his career and has written frequently on many musical subjects. A few of his outstanding compositions are: *Contours* (1961); *Ritual and Incantations* (1974); *Innerflexions* (1977); *Mirrors: Rondo-Variations for Two Pianos* (1988); and *A Ternion of Seasons* for instrumental ensemble (1996). Among several works for concert band, some with pedagogical aims are: *Somersault: A Twelve Tone Adventure for Band* (1964); *Take a Chance: An Aleatoric Episode for Band* (1964); and *Expansions* (1967).

Smith has used the general term "formal music" as a category for his instrumental, band, orchestra, vocal, and choral scores, and within them can be found, in varying degrees, techniques and idioms of African American music. Highly sensitive to instrumental "color" and with a strong dramatic sense, he has consistently conceived of and found new ways to express a broad spectrum of musical ideas.

William Grant Still (1895–1978)
Composer, Conductor

William Grant Still was born in Woodville, Mississippi, and, because of his father's untimely death, his mother moved to Little Rock, Arkansas, where he attended public schools. His family encouraged his interest in music, and he began to take violin lessons as a teenager. He attended Wilberforce University in Ohio but left before receiving a pre-med degree to study at the Oberlin College Conservatory (Ohio).

Still began playing professionally in several bands, spent some time in the U.S. Navy, and moved to New York City to work for the Pace and Handy Music Company Band. He later became director of the classical division and then musical director for the Pace Recording Company. He had many opportunities to play in theater orchestras and to arrange for shows, radio programs, and the movies.

In the 1920s, Still studied with two very different kinds of composers: first, the traditionalist George

Chadwick, who was at the New England Conservatory of Music in Boston, and then Edgard Varèse, a leading member of the avant-garde. This broad experience in Western European music expanded his compositional horizons and complemented his African American musical heritage. He was a student of and apologist for black vernacular music in both his musical and academic writings.

Still believed that folk music was the richest source for sounds needed to make American music stand apart from the European models that had dominated composed music. In his attempt to be instrumental in defining an "American sound," Still spent his life collecting, studying, and analyzing the many melodies and rhythms of the ethnic groups that make up the Western hemisphere. Although he arranged folk songs, especially African American spirituals, for various instrumental and choral combinations, he used the scales and rhythms derived from them as his primary source of inspiration in his larger forms. Still chose to compose his own melodies and to harmonize them using the richly stacked chords of jazz and blues. He wanted to elevate the blues by using its characteristic structures in symphonies, ballets, and operas.

Still's Afro-American Symphony, 1930 (revised 1969), was the first of five symphonies that he wrote. In 1931 it was the first large orchestral work to be performed by a major orchestra, the Rochester Philharmonic under the direction of Howard Hanson. One of his eight operas, *Troubled Island*, was the first by an African American composer to be staged by a major U.S. company, the New York City Center's Opera Company, in 1949. Another opera *Bayou Legend* was the first by an African American composer to be telecast nationally, over the Public Broadcasting Service in 1981. He was one of the most prolific composers of his generation and was active as a composer into the early 1960s.

Still was among the accomplished artists whose work will always be associated with the Harlem Renaissance in the 1920s and 1930s, and he and Duke Ellington are the leading composers of that movement. A term by which he was often characterized is "the dean of Afro-American composers," and his achievements as a composer testify to the validity of that title.

Howard Swanson (1907–1978)
Composer

Howard Swanson was born in Atlanta to a family in which there were several educators, including his mother. He and his siblings were given music lessons and sang in church, however, it was only with the family's move to Cleveland, Ohio, in 1918, that he studied the piano formally. Although Swanson began to work for the U.S. Postal Service after high school in order to help support his family, he entered the Cleveland Institute of Music, where he studied composition with Herbert Elwell and earned a bachelor of music degree in 1937.

Through a Rosenwald Fellowship that he received in 1938, Swanson was able to go to Paris to study with Nadia Boulanger at the American Academy in Fontainebleau. His study was interrupted by World War II, and he returned to the United States in 1941. After the war, he returned to Europe until 1966, when he made his permanent home in New York City. By this time he had been receiving commissions and his works were being performed. In 1950, for example, Marian Anderson sang his setting of Langston Hughes's "The Negro Speaks of Rivers" (1942) at Carnegie Hall, and his Short Symphony (1948) was premiered by the New York Philharmonic. This symphony won the New York Music Critics' Circle Award in 1952. He wrote steadily into the 1970s, and his works continued to be performed by a wide variety of ensembles and soloists. Swanson's work is most often characterized as "neoclassic," yet his heritage of African American music and traditions is the basis of his musical language. The largest percentage of his compositional output is vocal music; he never wrote an opera or music for the theater.

Shirley Verrett (1931–)
Singer, Actress, Educator

Born on May 31, 1931, in New Orleans, Louisiana, Shirley Verrett moved to California at the age of 11. Her father was her first voice teacher, and her earliest musical experiences were in the Seventh Day Adventist Church. She briefly attended Oakwood College and Ventura College, where she majored in business administration.

By the mid-1950s, she began taking voice lessons in Los Angeles and trained her sights on the concert stage. After winning a television talent show in 1955, she enrolled at the Juilliard School on a scholarship and earned her bachelor's of music degree in 1961. She made her New York City opera debut in 1957 in a production of *Lost in the Stars*, and she returned to the city in 1964 to sing the title role in Bizet's *Carmen* at the Metropolitan Opera. By then, she had performed the role in Spoleto, Italy, Moscow, and had appeared in several concert versions of the opera. The *New York Herald Tribune*'s critic claimed her Carmen as one of the finest "seen or heard" in New York for the past generation.

Verrett's yearly recital tours took her to major music centers throughout the country. Between 1983 and

1986, Verrett lived in Paris and had a series of operas staged especially for her by the Paris Opera including, Rossini's *Mose*, Cherubini's *Medee*, and Gluck's *Iphigenie en Tauride* and *Alceste*. She made a triumphant return to the Metropolitan Opera in 1986 as Eboli in *Don Carlo* and also starred that year in a new production of *Macbeth* with the San Francisco Opera. In the 1987–1988 season, Verrett made her long-awaited Chicago Lyric Opera debut as Azucena in *Il Trovatore*.

In the mid-1990s, Verrett turned her career to dramatic acting. She was featured in a major Broadway revival of Rodgers and Hammerstein's *Carousel*. Since 1996 she has held the position of the James Earl Jones Distinguished University Professor of Music at the University of Michigan in Ann Arbor. Verrett also teaches during summer months at Accademia Musicale Chigiana in Siena, Italy.

George Walker (1922–)
Pianist, Educator

George Walker, born into a musical family in Washington, DC, began piano study at the age of five, attended public schools in Washington—during which time he was also a student in the junior division of the Howard University School of Music— and earned a bachelor of music degree at the Oberlin Conservatory of Music (Ohio) in 1941. His graduate education included two artist diplomas—one in piano and one in composition—from the Curtis Institute of Music, where he was a student of Rudolph Serkin and Rosario Scalero in 1945; a diploma from the American Academy at Fontainebleau, France, in piano in 1947 (he also studied there in the 1950s with Nadia Boulanger); and a doctor of musical arts degree and artist diploma from the Eastman School of Music in 1957. He made his debut with the Philadelphia Orchestra conducted by Eugene Ormandy in 1941 in Rachmaninoff's Piano Concerto No. 3, and his New York recital debut at Town Hall in 1945.

Walker's very promising career as a concert artist began to shift toward teaching and composition in the mid-1950s. After brief tenures at Dillard University, the Dalcroze School of Music, the New School for Social Research, Smith College, and the University of Colorado, he joined the faculty of Rutgers University in 1969, where he remained until his retirement in 1992. Besides many works for piano, including four sonatas, he has written for several other instruments, chamber and full orchestra, solo voice, and chorus. Among his numerous honors and awards are several honorary doctorates and two Guggenheim Fellowships, along with a large number of commissions. In 1996, he won the Pulitzer Prize in Music for *Lilacs for Soprano or Tenor and Orchestra*, based on a text by Walt Whitman— the first for a living African American composer. He was inducted into the American Classical Music Hall of Fame in 2000.

A master of twentieth-century musical techniques, Walker shows a deep connection in his works with his African American musical heritage, especially spirituals and jazz. He once stated, "I believe that music is above race. I am steeped in the universal cultural tradition of my art. It is important to stress one's individuality beyond race, but I must do it as a black person who is aspiring to be a product of a civilized society."

William C. Warfield (1920–)
Singer

Baritone William Warfield was born on January 22, 1920, in West Helena, Arkansas, and later moved with his family to Rochester, New York. The son of a Baptist minister, he received early training in voice, organ, and piano and, in 1938, while a student at Washington Junior High School, won the vocal competition at the National Music Educators League Convention in St. Louis, Missouri.

Warfield studied at the Eastman School of Music and received his bachelor's degree in 1942. He made his recital debut at New York's Town Hall in 1950 and, afterwards, made an unprecedented tour of Australia under the auspices of the Australian Broadcasting Commission. A year later he made his film debut in the movie version of Jerome Kern's *Showboat* and also performed the role of Joe on the stage in several productions. He also has appeared on several major television shows and starred in the NBC television version of *Green Pastures*. He became identified with the role of Porgy in Gershwin's *Porgy and Bess* in the 1950s and later. He married his co-star Leontyne Price during the 1952–1954 touring revival of the opera; they were divorced in 1973.

In 1974 Warfield accepted a position as professor of music at the University of Illinois School of Music in Urbana. He retired in 1990 as chairman of the voice faculty and has since been a visiting professor at Eastern Illinois University and an adjunct professor of music at Northwestern University.

Warfield has been active in the National Association of Negro Musicians, serving as its president in 1984. He has served also as a board member of the Lyric Opera of Chicago and the New York College of Music; a trustee of the Berkshire Boys Choir; a member of the music panel of the National Association for the Arts, and a judge for the Whittaker Vocal Competition of the Music Educator's National Conference.

Among honors that Warfield has received are honorary doctorates from the University of Arkansas, Boston University, and Milliken University. He won a 1984 Grammy Award in the spoken word category for his recording of Aaron Copland's *A Lincoln Portrait*. He has appeared frequently with orchestras as soloist and narrator and has been teacher and mentor to many younger singers.

André Watts (1946–)
Pianist

One of America's most gifted pianists, André Watts was the first African American concert pianist to achieve international stardom. Born June 20, 1946, in Nuremberg, Germany, of a Hungarian mother and an African American soldier, he spent the first eight years of his life on U.S. Army posts in Europe before moving to Philadelphia. By the time he was nine years old, he was already performing with the Philadelphia Orchestra. After graduating from Lincoln Preparatory School in Philadelphia

André Watts, 1967.

and attending the Philadelphia Academy of Music, he enrolled at Baltimore's Peabody Conservatory of Music.

In 1962, when Glenn Gould was unable to appear as soloist with the New York Philharmonic, Leonard Bernstein chose Watts as a last-minute replacement. At the conclusion of his performance of Liszt's E-flat Major Piano Concerto, the 16-year-old Watts received a standing ovation, not only from the audience but also from the orchestra.

From the mid-1960s on, Watts has toured the world as a recitalist and has appeared with leading orchestras in the United States and abroad. He has also been a frequent performer of chamber music. His recordings continue to be popular and his performances of works by Liszt and other romantic composers have been especially notable.

Watts was awarded the Lincoln Center Medallion (1971), honorary doctorates from Yale University (1973) and Albright College (1975), and the National Society of Arts and Letters Gold Medal (1982). He performed a concert in 1988 telecast nationally in honor of the 25th anniversary of his New York Philharmonic debut. Watts remains one of the world's "greatest in demand" pianists, both as recitalist and concert soloist.

Clarence Cameron White (1880–1960)
Violinist, Composer, Conductor, Teacher

Clarence Cameron White, born in Clarksville, Tennessee, moved with his widowed mother to his grandparent's house in Oberlin, Ohio. They were musically inclined and encouraged their grandson in his musical interests. With his mother's remarriage, the family moved to Washington, DC, where he studied violin with Will Marion Cook and Joseph Douglass. A period at the Oberlin College Conservatory (Ohio) ended without a degree, and he began working in the Washington public schools and the Washington Conservatory of Music.

White became acquainted through correspondence with the British composer Samuel Coleridge-Taylor and performed with him in concert during one of Coleridge-Taylor's American tours. White later studied with him in London, through the aid of an E. Azalia Hackley scholarship.

After his return from London in 1911, White had a heavy schedule of touring, composing, and teaching. He was a founding member of the National Association of Negro Musicians in 1919. In 1924, he settled at West Virginia State College as head of the music department but left in 1930 to study composition with Raoul LaParra in Paris on a Rosenwald Fellowship. On his return to the United States in 1932, he chaired the music department of Hampton Institute (which was discontinued in 1935).

In 1937 White was named a music specialist for the National Recreation Association, established by President Roosevelt under the aegis of the Works Progress Administration. The association's responsibility was to offer aid in organizing community arts programs.

Through these moves and teaching positions, White's catalog of compositions was growing. He wrote, not surprisingly, many works for violin, some of which are teaching pieces. His most performed works have been *Bandanna Sketches* (1918) and *From the Cotton Fields* (1920). The most ambitious of White's compositions is the opera *Ouanga*, a three act opera with a plot revolving around the historical figure Dessalines who ruled Haiti and attempted to eliminate the practice of voodoo. White used the country's folk music, especially rhythmic dance patterns, with which he had become familiar through a visit to Haiti, while casting its structure in a Western European, late nineteenth-century framework. Completed in 1932, the premiere was staged in 1949 by the Burleigh Musical Association in South Bend, Indiana. White became the first African American to receive the Bispham Medal after a performance in 1932.

Olly Woodrow Wilson (1937–)
Composer, Educator

Olly Wilson, born in St. Louis, Missouri on September 7, 1937, was educated in the city's public schools. He studied the piano and clarinet at an early age and played in his church choir and in the high school band. He graduated from Washington University, in his hometown, with a bachelor's degree, and pursued graduate studies at the University of Illinois at Urbana and the University of Iowa, where he earned a Ph.D. in 1964.

The diversity of Wilson's interests and breadth of his vision are indicated by his study of electronic music in 1967 at the University of Illinois—he won the Dartmouth Arts Council Prize in the International Competition for Electronic Compositions with *Cetus* in 1968—and his trips to Ghana in 1971 and 1978, for study of African music.

In 1970, Wilson joined the faculty of the University of California at Berkeley, where he has held several positions including associate dean of the graduate division and department chair. Not only has he been a prolific composer, but he has also written many articles on various aspects of contemporary music in general and African American music in particular.

Beginning in the 1970s, Wilson has written mostly in the orchestral medium and has received over 20 commissions. Some of them include: *Akwan* for piano/electric piano and orchestra (1972); *Lumina* for orchestra (1981); *Of Visions and Truth* for vocal soloists and chamber orchestra (1990–1991); *Hold On* for orchestra (1997–1998); and *Spirit Song* for soprano, double chorus, and orchestra, which the composer described as "about the evolution and development of the black spiritual." His musical style is all-encompassing. He has mastered the Western European, twentieth-century tradition, African American vernacular music, and African rhythmic and pitch practices.

23

Sacred Music Traditions

- ◆ Early Influences of African American Sacred Music
- ◆ The Emergence of Spirituals in the Nineteenth Century
- ◆ The Rise of Gospel Music in the Twentieth Century
- ◆ Sacred Music Composers, Musicians, and Singers

by Christopher A. Brooks

African American sacred music—slave songs, early religious songs, spirituals, and gospel music—is an expression of African American culture no less significant than blues and jazz. Originally rooted in the enslavement experience of early Africans, African American sacred music was later influenced by evangelical Protestant Christianity and performed at African American churches and camp meeting revivals. As time passed, it took on different forms and gained larger acceptance among European and white American concert audiences. Today through both live performances and commercial recordings, it encompasses a wide range of styles and ensembles, reaches an audience of millions worldwide, and is recognized as a vitally important element in America's cultural heritage.

◆ EARLY INFLUENCES OF AFRICAN AMERICAN SACRED MUSIC

Syncretized Religions of the African Diaspora

Of the 15 million Africans who were brought to the New World, the vast majority of them were enslaved from the sixteenth through the middle of the nineteenth century. Despite the enslavement experience, many Africans maintained and practiced some variation of their traditional beliefs, culture, and musical heritage. An area that combined these customs with some European influences were their religious practices. Many Africans in the New World—especially those in Catholic-colonized areas—became nominal Christians, but continued to practice their traditional African belief systems which they adapted to Western religions. These syncretized religions were fertile ground for maintaining many ritualized African chanting practices and song styles, while the worshipping practices were nominally Christian. Examples of such New World syncretized religions are *candomble* in Brazil, *santeria* in Cuba and Puerto Rico, *vodun* in Haiti, and to a lesser extent, *kumina* in Jamaica. There is still a rich musical tradition associated with many of these religious beliefs, although local musical influences have had an effect as well. Many of these sacred music practices survived in one form or another well into the twentieth century.

American Colonial and Antebellum Periods

Most musical activity in American colonial society was vocal, although there are late eigteenth century paintings that depict enslaved Africans playing string instruments and dancing. Since much of American colonial society—both black and white—was preliterate, the method of collective song teaching (as in a church service, for example) was done by a technique called "lining out." This process involved a leader who sang a line or two of a song or hymn, sometimes over-enunciating the words. The congregation followed by singing the same line after the leader. This method can still be found in some African American churches.

Other indications of African American musical activity during the eighteenth century can be gleaned from chronicle accounts in news journals in Massachusetts, New York, and Virginia. When papers in these areas reported missing or fugitive African Americans, they frequently commented on their musical ability (on a particular instrument, for example), along with some physical description.

The period after the American Revolutionary War saw the emergence of two important African American institutions: the self-help benevolent societies and the African independent church movement. The benevolent societies, such as the African Union Society (Rhode Island), Free African Society (Philadelphia), Brown Fellowship (Charleston), the Society of Free Africans (Washington, DC), and the African Society of Boston, were among several pseudo-religious moral aid groups that were formed to help recently freed African Americans. By the late eighteenth and early nineteenth centuries, several independent African churches began emerging in both southern and northern states. Many churches in the South, however, were either very closely scrutinized or shut down because of uprisings that were planned or carried out by insurrectionists, such as Gabriel Prosser in Richmond, Virginia (1800), Denmark Vesey in Charleston, South Carolina (1822), and Nat Turner outside South Hampton, Virginia (1831).

By the late eighteenth century, Methodism had claimed large numbers of African Americans because of its official anti-slavery stance. The celebrated religious leader and Free African Society founding member Richard Allen established the African Methodist Episcopal (AME) Church in 1794, after a break with the mostly white St. Georges Methodist Church in Philadelphia. (In 1816, the AME Church formally separated from the mother Methodist Church.) In 1801, Allen published a collection of religious songs entitled *A Collection of Spiritual Songs and Hymns from Various Authors*. It eventually became the most widely-used religious songbook in African American Protestant churches around the United States and, by the end of the nineteenth century, the 11th edition was published with notated music.

Another African American religious phenomenon of the early nineteenth century involved the camp meeting. These continuous, outdoor religious services were inspired by the Second Great Awakening movement that spread across the United States in that century. Many African American participants were known to perform dances, such as the "ring shout" and "shuffle step." Such religious behavior was criticized by some purists, such as Richard Allen, but was clearly acceptable among a growing sector of African American worshippers.

◆ THE EMERGENCE OF SPIRITUALS IN THE NINETEENTH CENTURY

Spirituals were perhaps the most significant musical contribution of the enslaved African population of the nineteenth century. They have certainly gained most of the attention of collectors, scholars, and those with a casual interest in the musical genre. Spirituals are an outgrowth of the African American enslavement experience and Protestant Christianity. A similar tradition apparently did not develop on the African continent nor anywhere else within nations of the African Diaspora. So to that degree, the spirituals are, from all existing evidence, uniquely American.

There are few absolute features that can be pointed to when trying to distinguish one spiritual from another. Up-tempo songs such as "A Great Camp Meetin'" might have been called a "jubilee," while an equally spirited "I'm Gonna Lift Up a Standard for My King" might have been regarded as a "shout." The terms "plantation songs" and "slave songs" were also used to describe spirituals. An apparent standard feature of the spiritual, however, was its employment of African American dialect. One of the earliest collections of spirituals was *Slave Songs of the United States* (1867). It was a collaborative work of William Allen, Charles Ware, and Lucy McKim Garrison, all of whom had abolitionist backgrounds. In the preface of the work, they commented on the uniqueness of African American vocal

Sheet music from the African American spiritual, "Down in the Lonesome Valley."

styles and the inability of conventional Western musical notation to accurately transcribe the unique vocal effects such as screams, yodels, falsetto, and glissandi, which they heard when the songs were performed.

It was the apparent disregard of these performance practices, among other things, that would lead some scholars such as George Pullen Jackson, Neuman White, and Donald Wilgus to promote a "white" spiritual theory. They argued that because it was the Europeans who gave Christianity to the enslaved Africans, they also gave them the music with which to worship. This argument has been soundly refuted, however, because Jackson was comparing printed versions of spirituals (i.e., arranged spirituals in Western musical notation) to those of Western European folk songs and saw similarities in melodies and time signatures. This school of thought also neglected the fact that the majority of spirituals employ a call-and-response performance technique, and that was not a traditional feature of Western European folk songs.

Alert and Map Songs

Although they functioned in an entirely different capacity, a tradition related to spirituals was the "alert songs" and "map songs." While the text of these songs was ostensibly religious, the alert songs encoded messages or signals about escape attempts or planned secret meetings of enslaved African Americans. Examples of such songs included "Steal Away to Jesus," "Good News the Chariots Comin," "Wade in the Water," and "I'm Packin' Up." In fact, "Wade in the Water" was known to be a frequently used alert song of the celebrated conductor Harriet Tubman. In addition to the religious meaning of the song, there was a very practical use for "wading in the water." It could also mask any body scent, which made it more difficult for the search dogs to follow those who were escaping. Map songs were designed to give directions to fugitive African American slaves. In the song "Sheep, Sheep, Don't You Know the Road?," the use of the word "road" could have encoded some message about a specific escape route. "Follow the Drinking Gourd" was another map song that was a metaphoric allusion to the Big Dipper, and the escapees were to follow it north to freedom.

It was clear that by the 1870s, the genre known alternately as spirituals, plantation songs, and jubilees was inextricably linked to the African American enslavement experience, and it was viewed by much of the American public as an acceptable form of religious expression. Evidence of this can be seen in the large numbers of spiritual collections that appear throughout the balance of the nineteenth century and well into the twentieth century. Volumes and collections such as *Hampton and Its Students* (1874), *The Story of the Jubilee Singers* (1877), *The Jubilee Singers* (1883), *Jubilee and Plantation Songs* (1884), *Old Plantation Melodies* (1899), *Songs of the Confederacy and Plantation Songs* (1901), *Nine Negro Spirituals* (1918), *Sit Down, Negro Spirituals Arranged by Roland Hayes* (1923), and *Book of Negro Spirituals* (1938), among many others, illustrate this point.

Spiritual Concerts

Attention was being drawn to spirituals not only through the collections, essays, books, and articles, but through live performances as well. By the 1870s, concerts of spirituals had become a fund-raising vehicle for several struggling African American colleges, most notably Calhoun College, Fisk University, Hampton Institute, and to a lesser extent Tuskegee Institute. Several of these groups made highly successful overseas tours in what Paul Fritz Laubenstein referred to as the *ausbreitung* (spreading) around the European continent.

With the frequency and popularity of these overseas tours by the 1890s, European audiences and Americans were exposed to a different kind of African American musical talent, other than what had been featured in minstrel shows. When the celebrated Bohemian composer Antonin Dvorak recognized the uniqueness of this genre and encouraged his students, such as Harry T. Burleigh and Will Marion Cook, to compose and arrange more spirituals, it was given a new level of acceptance and recognition.

Other arranged spirituals came from other composers and arrangers, such as R. Nathaniel Dett. Dett was best known at Hampton Institute for organizing a choir composed of students and community members and transforming the group into an internationally-renowned touring organization that specialized in African American sacred music. Many of the songs that the choir performed were Dett's own compositions or arrangements of spirituals. Among his choristers was the celebrated soprano Dorothy Maynor who became a distinguished concert singer and recitalist.

On several occasions, Dett was compelled to defend his performance of "arranged" spirituals, which were not viewed as authentic as the "folk" versions of the genre that were accompanied by claps, body swaying, and shouts. Several white observers and benefactors such as George Peabody saw the Dett arrangements as imitations of white classical composers and, as such, not as genuine. However, the Hampton group had a highly successful tour of Europe in 1930.

The production of arranged spirituals would continue in the skillful hands of other musical luminaries, such as Hall Johnson, John W. Work, Florence Price, J. Rosamund Johnson, and W.C. Handy, among many others. The live performances and recorded legacy of African American concert singers featuring spirituals in their recitals is a practice that continued throughout the twentieth century in the artistry of singers, such as Marian Anderson, Roland Hayes, Dorothy Maynor, Paul Robeson, Robert McFerrin, Leontyne Price, Shirley Verrett, Jessye Norman, and many others.

Holy Dancing, Church Song Concerts, and Shout Preaching

Although much scholarly and casual interest was directed to the spiritual, other African American sacred music traditions emerged by the end of the nineteenth century as the African American church movement itself gained momentum. By the 1890s, the Holiness and Sanctified Church movement had crystallized. The largest denomination within this tradition, the Church of God and Christ, was founded by the Memphis-based religious leader, Charles Henry Mason, formerly of Lexington, Mississippi. Collectively, the Holiness/Sanctified churches believed in spirit possession, speaking in tongues (i.e., a form of glossolalia), improvisatory singing. "Holy dancing" was also seen as an acceptable form of religious behavior. Certain instruments such as drums, tambourines, triangles, guitars, and cymbals were frequently used to accompany the singing.

A figure at the turn of the century who played a role in what would come to be called "gospel" music was Rev. Charles Albert Tindley. Tindley was a Maryland-born Methodist camp meeting preacher and singer who, in the 1870s, settled in Philadelphia. There he founded the East Calvary Methodist Episcopal Church in 1902. It was later renamed the Tindley Temple. Tindley established a practice of sponsoring periodic concerts of church songs and, consequently, had many of his compositions published in a 1916 collection entitled *The New Songs of Paradise*. Included in this collection were such songs as "Leave It There," "What Are They Doing in Heaven Tonight," "We'll Understand it Better By and By," and "I'll Overcome Someday," which was the melodic basis of the 1960s Civil Rights anthem "We Shall Overcome." The collection was so popular that several subsequent editions would appear by the 1940s.

Although Tindley had the support of his congregation, other religious songwriters received support from such organizations as the National Baptist Convention, which was founded in the 1880s. It became a vehicle for groups to perform and for exposing congregations and individuals to religious music. In 1921, the National Baptist Convention produced a collection of 165 religious songs entitled *Gospel Pearls*. This work was enormously popular in many African American congregations without regard for denomination.

By the 1920s, singing ministers or so-called "shout" preachers began recording brief three to five minute sermons and song performances. These recorded sermons might include a congregation or a small choir. Celebrated names in this tradition were Revs. F.W. McGee of Memphis, J.C. Burnett of Kansas City, Theodore Frye from Mississippi, E.H. Hall of Chicago, and A.W. Nix and J.M. Gates of Atlanta. Gates's style was captured in several recordings that are still extant, such as "The Need of Prayer" (1926), "Down Here Lord, Waiting on You" (1929), and numerous other examples.

♦ THE RISE OF GOSPEL MUSIC IN THE TWENTIETH CENTURY

Although the term "gospel" music did not become a standard phrase in reference to a specific African American sacred musical genre before the 1930s, its predecessors were in place long before that time. Many scholars regard Chicago as the birthplace of gospel music because many of its churches produced pioneering singers and composers. The figure most closely associated with the rise of the so-called blues-based gospel was Thomas A. Dorsey, commonly known as the "Father of Gospel Music."

Thomas Dorsey: Father of Gospel Music

Born in rural Georgia, Dorsey was the eldest child of a Baptist minister whom he frequently accompanied on the keyboard during his father's evangelizing trips. Dorsey eventually moved to Atlanta when he was a teenager and played keyboard in brothels and saloons. In 1916, Dorsey made a stop in Chicago en route to Philadelphia, and it became his home base for the rest of his life. He initially pursued his career as a blues musician and was known at varying points in his career as "Georgia Tom," "Barrelhouse Tommy," and by a few other names. Several of his blues compositions were recorded by jazz greats such as Joseph "King" Oliver (1895–1938), among others. Between 1923 and 1926, he was the official accompanist for the great blues singer, Gertrude "Ma" Rainey. He toured with Rainey and was featured in several of her recordings for the Paramount label. When he married Nettie Harper in 1925, Rainey made her a wardrobe mistress so she could travel with the group.

Although Dorsey had strong credentials as a bluesman, he continued to foster his religious music beginnings from his childhood. He attended the National Baptist Convention in 1920 and had one of his songs "Some Day, Somewhere" published in the Convention's 1921 collection *Gospel Pearls*. Around 1927, he began "peddling" (i.e., Dorsey accompanying a singer at the keyboard) his religious songs in Chicago area churches, but they were rejected by many ministers because of their stylistic affinity to the blues. In 1931, Dorsey experienced a double personal tragedy when his daughter and first wife, Nettie, died in childbirth. Afterwards, he composed "Take My Hand, Precious Lord," which has remained his most celebrated and frequently performed work.

By the 1930s, Dorsey was more devoted to composing and promoting religious music. In 1931, he formed the world's first gospel choir at Ebenezer Baptist Church in Chicago and opened the first publishing company devoted to the sale of gospel music. With his colleague, Sallie Martin, he founded the National Convention of Gospel Choirs and Choruses as a vehicle for training gospel choirs and soloists. More than any single individual, Dorsey was responsible for elevating gospel music to its current professional status.

Willie Mae Ford Smith Influences Future Singers

In addition to Sallie Martin, who also acted as his business manager and was a celebrated name in gospel music in her own right, Dorsey discovered a talented singer, Willie Mae Ford Smith who, in 1936, Dorsey appointed as the director of the Soloists Bureau of the National Convention of Gospel Choirs and Choruses. In this role, she demonstrated the proper style and delivery of gospel songs to a new generation of younger singers. Also influenced by the blues in her childhood, Smith later abandoned what would have been a prominent career as a gospel singer to become an ordained evangelist in the Holiness Church of God Apostolic. As an evangelist, Smith frequently interspersed songs with a brief sermon, a practice that became known as "sermonette and song." Smith and Dorsey were featured in the 1982 gospel music documentary *Say Amen, Somebody*.

Mahalia Jackson Becomes Gospel's International Star

Among Dorsey's other celebrated discoveries was Mahalia Jackson who became gospel music's first international star. Born in New Orleans, Jackson moved to Chicago in the 1920s to pursue a career as a beautician. Dorsey first met her in 1929 and became her official accompanist from 1937 to 1946. Jackson began a recording career in the 1930s, but did not achieve national fame until she recorded the song of the celebrated Memphis minister and composer, Rev. W. Herbert Brewster, "Move On Up a Little Higher," which sold over one million copies. She toured extensively in Europe, gaining a wide following in several countries. Jackson gave a highly successful concert at New York's Carnegie Hall in the early 1950s and was invited to sing at the White House in 1961 by the recently inaugurated President John F. Kennedy.

While the Civil Rights movement was in full swing in the 1960s, gospel music became an unofficial vehicle for the movement because many of its songs became the basis of freedom songs of the era. Mahalia Jackson was a major follower of the Rev. Dr. Martin Luther King Jr. and reached an international audience when she sang at the 1963 March on Washington.

Gospel Quartets and Choirs

By the end of the 1930s, gospel music had established at least two generic performing groups. The first was the all-male "gospel quartet," which was made up of four or five singers dressed in business suits who sang in a cappella barber shop-style harmonies. The second was the "gospel chorus," which could be women and men (or all women) dressed in choir robes who were accompanied by piano or organ. Prominent gospel quartets included such groups as the Golden Gate Jubilee Quartet, the Famous Blue Jay Singers, the Jubilaires, the Mighty Clouds of Joy, the Fairfield Four, the Soul Stirrers, the Five Blind Boys of Mississippi, among many others. Notable gospel choirs included such groups as the Ford Family Quartet, the Roberta Martin Singers, the Clara Ward Singers—another group that Thomas Dorsey would discover and help to promote—and later the Barrett Sisters.

The Golden Age of Gospel

Gospel music experienced a "golden age" from the mid-1940s to the 1950s when, in addition to the numerous recordings that were made, such women as Lucie Campbell, Roberta Martin, Queen C. Anderson, Ruth Davis, Dorothy Loves Coates, Edna Gallmon Looke, and Bessie Griffin were among the most celebrated

Thomas Dorsey performing with the Wandering Syncopators in 1923.

names in the gospel business. Their male counterparts were Julius Cheek, Archie Brownlee, Brother Joe May, Alex Bradford, James Cleveland, Claude Jeter, and Ira Tucker, among others. By the end of this period, gospel music had shaken itself free of its Pentecostal/Holiness roots to reach widespread acceptance in many African American Protestant churches around the United States. Instrumentally, the organ, at this time, also became the standard accompanying instrument for most church-based gospel ensembles.

By the 1960s, gospel was experiencing other changes. As far back as the late 1930s, such religious singers as Sister Rosetta Tharpe had performed gospel music outside of the church by performing in New York's Apollo Theater. However, when such groups as the Clara Ward Singers performed at the Newport Jazz Festival in 1957 and, subsequently, in nightclubs in the early 1960s, gospel music was blended with other popular musical genres and reached a crossover audience. Such gospel groups as the Staple Singers and the Edwin Hawkins Singers scored individual successes. Edwin Hawkins's 1969 recording of "O Happy Day" sold over a million copies on both religious and popular

music charts. Large community-based gospel choirs, such as the Mississippi Mass Choir, the Abyssinian Choir led by Alex Bradford, the Greater Metropolitan Church of Christ Choir led by Isaac Whittmon, the Harold Smith Majestics, the Donal Vail Choraleers, the Charles Ford Singers, the Triboro Mass Choir led by Albert Jamison, the Chicago Community Choir led by Jessy Dixon, the Voices of Tabernacle led by James Cleveland, and the Michigan State Community Choir led by Mattie Moss Clark made successful recordings and/or tours around the United States. Soloists and small groups that emerged in their own right during this era were Shirley Caesar, Marion Williams, who had been a member of the Clara Ward Singers, Albertina Walker, Delois Barrett Campbell and the Barrett Sisters, and the O'Neal Twins.

Contemporary Gospel Sounds

Since the 1970s, gospel music has reached a mainstream audience and become a commercially viable tradition. In vocal harmony music, Sweet Honey in the Rock and Take 6 have continued the tradition of gospel quartets and small choral groups. An a cappella group

Tabernacle Choir, performing at a music competition.

of female vocalists that performs an eclectic mix of political music, folk songs, spirituals, and gospel, Sweet Honey in the Rock's album *Feel Something Drawing Me On* (1989) focused on sacred music. Take 6, a male ensemble of Seventh Day Adventists, won several Grammy awards for its original song "Spread Love" (1988) and for *Take 6* (1988) and *So Much 2 Say* (1991).

The tradition has also produced several popular musicians, such as Sam Cooke, Lou Rawls, Aretha Franklin, Ray Charles, Al Green, Stevie Wonder, Bobby Womack, and Johnnie Taylor, among others. In fact, Sam Cooke, who had been a lead singer with the Soul Stirrers, was among the first gospel singers to have a successful crossover career and achieve equal success as a popular music performer. Other contemporary musicians who have remained more or less within the tradition, while reaching large crossover audiences include Andraè Couch, Tramaine Hawkins, Walter Hawkins, Lynette Hawkins, Jessy Dixon, the celebrated Winans Family, and Kirk Franklin.

During the 1990s, gospel began to be influenced by rap music, although gospel musicians referred to their performances as "street poetry." Large ensembles such

as Sounds of Blackness have used rap music to reinvent sacred songs, while gospel quartets, such as the Williams Brothers, have incorporated synthesizers and percussion overdubs into their modern version of gospel. These innovations have created sizeable controversy among performers and listeners devoted to more traditional styles of gospel music.

Though most gospel music continues to be performed at religious services and African American community events across the United States, it is recognized as a truly significant aspect of America's cultural heritage, as witnessed in such Smithsonian Institution projects as *We'll Understand It Better By and By: Pioneering African American Gospel Composers* (1992) and Smithsonian's gospel music collection *Wade in the Water* (1994).

◆ SACRED MUSIC COMPOSERS, MUSICIANS, AND SINGERS

(To locate biographical profiles more readily, please consult the index at the back of the book.)

Yolanda Adams.

Yolanda Adams (1961–)
Singer

A native of Houston, Yolanda Adams was born on August 27, 1961. She is the oldest of six siblings. Her family offered her a solidly religious upbringing, and as a small child she created for herself an imaginary friend she called "Hallelujah" and sang a solo in church at age three. She grew up with the classic gospel sounds of James Cleveland and the Edwin Hawkins Singers, but hers was also a musically eclectic household. Adams's mother, a pianist who majored in music in college, introduced her daughter to jazz, classical music, and rhythm and blues. Adams joined a gospel choir, the Southeast Inspirational Choir, shortly after her father's death when she was 13 years of age.

Adams hoped to become a fashion model even as she embarked on a career as an elementary school teacher. However, her powerful voice propelled her to the forefront of the Southeast Inspirational Choir's performances; she took a solo on the choir's 1980 hit "My Liberty." In 1986 well-known gospel producer, composer, and pianist Thomas Whitfield heard the choir and wasted no time in approaching Adams. The result was the album *Just as I Am* released in 1987 on Sound of Gospel Records.

Adams signed with the Tribute label in 1990, and between 1990 and 1997 released four successful albums, all of which won Stellar awards, a prestigious gospel music industry honor. Albums *Through the Storm* and *Save the World* produced pieces that Adams still sings in concert, such as "The Battle Is the Lord's," but it was 1995's *More Than a Melody* that really moved her style sharply in the direction of secular urban contemporary music. The album was honored with a Soul Train Lady of Soul award and a Grammy award nomination, and 1996's *Yolanda. . . Live in Washington* also earned the singer a Grammy nomination.

In the years following the release of *More Than a Melody*, honors and opportunities have flowed Adams's way with increasing regularity. She performed on the 1996 Soul Train Music Awards, the 1997 Essence Awards, BET's Teen Summit, and the *Tonight Show*. A special thrill was a performance during the Christmas festivities at the White House in 1995. Adams was also named a national spokesperson for the FILA Corporation's *Operation Rebound* youth outreach program, a post that often takes her on the road to speak with students in inner-city schools.

During the late 1990s, Adams's reputation seemed certain to continue to rise. In 1997 she was featured in the 50-city Tour of Life organized and headed by contemporary gospel sensation Kirk Franklin. That same year, she married stockbroker and former New York Jets football player Tim Crawford at Houston's First Presbyterian Church, and she enrolled in the prestigious divinity program at Howard University in Washington, DC.

In 2001, Adams won the award for R&B/Soul or Rap Song for "Open My Heart" at the Soul Train Lady of Soul Awards. Her album *The Experience* won the Grammy for Best Contemporary Soul Gospel Album in 2002. That same year, she also collected an American Music Award and co-hosted the 33rd annual Dove Awards with NFL-star Kurt Warner.

Vanessa Bell Armstrong (1953–)
Gospel Singer

Armstrong was born Vanessa Bell on October 2, 1953, in Detroit, Michigan. During the late 1980s, her combination of gospel music with the secular stylings of influences such as Aretha Franklin laid the groundwork for successful "crossover" gospel stars like Kirk Franklin, Yolanda Adams, and CeCe Winans.

Armstrong, whose father was a minister, began singing in Detroit churches when she was only four years old. In 1966, the gospel choir leader Mattie Moss Clark heard the young Armstrong perform and took her under her wing. Soon the young singer was performing with such artists as the Rev. James Cleveland, the Mighty Clouds of Joy, and the Winans Family.

After marriage and the birth of five children, Armstrong recorded her debut album, *Peace Be Still*, in 1984. The album was an immediate success, going to the top of the gospel charts and winning Armstrong a recording contract with the R&B label Jive Records. In 1987, she performed the theme song of NBC's television series *Amen* and appeared in the Broadway production *Don't Get God Started*. That year she also released her second album, *Vanessa Bell Armstrong*. The album, which blended gospel with contemporary urban music, had one of its singles&"You Bring Out the Best in Me"& become a hit on the R&B charts, and proved to be a strong seller. At the same time, Armstrong received criticism from some fans of traditional gospel who accused the singer of "selling out" and "backsliding."

In the early 1990s, Armstrong released four albums, *Wonderful One* (1990), *The Truth About Christmas* (1990), *Chosen* (1991), and *Something on the Inside* (1993). In 1995, she chose John P. Kee as the producer of her seventh album, *The Secret Is Out*. In 1998, she released the acclaimed *Desire of My Heart: Live in Detroit*, which featured performances by her father, Elder Jesse Bell, and Perfecting Church's pastor Marvin Winans. The album marked a strong return to traditional gospel themes, a move that pleased many fans. She followed with *Brand New Day* in 2001.

Shirley Caesar (1938–)
Singer

The leading gospel music singer of her generation, Shirley Caesar was born in Durham, North Carolina, in 1938. One of 12 children born to gospel great "Big Jim" Caesar, Shirley sang in church choirs as a child. By age 14, Caesar went on the road as a professional gospel singer, touring the church circuit on weekends and during school vacations. Known as "Baby Shirley," Caesar joined the Caravans in 1958. Featured as an opening act in the show, Caesar worked the audience to a near fever pitch. When Inez Andrews left the Caravans in 1961, Caesar became the featured artist who provided crowds with powerful performances of such songs as "Comfort Me," "Running for Jesus," and "Sweeping Through the City."

After leaving the Caravans in 1966, Caesar formed her own group, the Shirley Caesar Singers. Her sheer energy and determined spirit made her one of the reigning queens of modern gospel. Her first album *I'll Go* remains one of her most critically acclaimed. In 1969, she released a ten-minute sermonette with the St. Louis Choir that earned her a gold record. A ten-time Grammy winner, Caesar conducts weekly sermons at the Mount Calvary Holy Church between performances and recording dates.

Rev. James Cleveland (1932–1991)
Singer, Pianist, Composer

Known by such titles as "King James" and the "Crown Prince," the Rev. James Cleveland emerged as a giant of the postwar gospel music scene. Likened to the vocal style of Louis Armstrong, Cleveland's raw bluesy growls and shouts appeared on more recordings than any other gospel singer of his generation.

Born on December 5, 1932, in Chicago, Illinois, James Cleveland first sang gospel under the direction of Thomas Dorsey at the Pilgrim Baptist Church. Inspired by the keyboard talents of gospel singer Roberta Martin, Cleveland later began to study piano. In 1951 Cleveland joined the Gospelaires, a trio that cut several sides for the Apollo label. With the Caravans, Cleveland arranged and performed on two hits "The Solid Rock" and an up-tempo reworking of the song "Old Time Religion."

By the mid-1950s, Cleveland's original compositions had found their way into the repertoires of numerous gospel groups, and he was performing with such artists as the Thorn Gospel Singers, Roberta Martin Singers, Mahalia Jackson, the Gospel Allstars, and the Meditation Singers. In 1960 Cleveland formed the Cleveland Singers featuring organist and accompanist Billy Preston. The smash hit "Love of God" recorded with the Detroit-based Voices of Tabernacle, won Cleveland nationwide fame within the gospel community. Signing with the Savoy label, Cleveland, along with keyboardist Billy Preston, released a long list of classic albums including *Christ Is the Answer*, and *Peace Be Still*. As a founder of the Gospel Workshop of America in 1968, Cleveland organized annual conventions that brought together thousands of gospel singers and songwriters. A year later, he helped found the Southern California Community Choir.

In 1972, James was reunited with his former piano understudy Aretha Franklin, who featured him as a guest artist on the album *Amazing Grace*. Recipient of the NAACP Image Award, Cleveland also acquired an honorary doctorate from Temple Baptist College. Although the commercial gospel trends of the 1980s had caused a downturn in Cleveland's career, he continued to perform the gutsy blues-based sound that brought him recognition from listeners throughout the world. Cleveland died February 9, 1991, in Los Angeles, California.

Andraè Crouch (1942–)
Singer, Pianist

An exponent of a modern pop-based gospel style, Andraè Crouch became one of the leading gospel singers of the 1960s and 1970s. Born on July 1, 1942, in Los Angeles, Andraè Edward Crouch grew up singing in his father's church. Along with his brother and sister, Crouch formed the Crouch Trio, which performed at their father's services as well as on live Sunday-night radio broadcasts. In the mid-1960s Crouch was "discovered" by white Pentecostal evangelists and subsequently signed a contract with Light, a white religious record label. Over the last four decades, Crouch has written numerous songs, many of which have become standards in the repertoire of modern gospel groups. Among his most famous songs are "I Don't Know Why Jesus

Andraè Crouch.

Loved Me," "Through It All," and "The Blood Will Never Lose Its Power." In recognition for this work, Crouch received an ASCAP Special Songwriter Award.

During the late 1960s Crouch, inspired by the modern charismatic revival movement, began adopting street smart language and informal wardrobe. After forming the Disciples in 1968, Crouch recorded extensively and toured throughout the United States and Europe. His California style of gospel music combines rock, country music, and soul with traditional gospel forms. The Disciples won Grammys in 1975, for *Take Me Back* and in 1979, for *Live in London*, which also received a Dove Award. *This Is Another Day* garnered a Dove Award in 1976, as did Crouch's 1984 solo recording *No Time to Lose*.

Since the 1970s, Crouch's back-up groups have incorporated both electronic and acoustic instruments including synthesizers. The new approach earned Grammys in 1980 and 1981. As the decade ensued, Crouch recorded as a solo artist and was bestowed the Gospel Music Excellence Award for best male vocalist in 1982, for *More of the Best*. During this period, Crouch was also instrumental in helping the Winans Family produce their first recordings.

On September 23, 1995, Crouch assumed the pastorship of the Christ Memorial Church of God in Christ in Pacoima, California, the same pulpit once manned by his father. Nearly one year earlier, Crouch—a two-time NAACP Image Award recipient and one-time Golden Halo awardee—released *Mercy!*, his first album since 1984. His return was well-received, and he has followed it up with more recordings, including *Pray* (1997) and *Gift of Christmas* (1998). In 1998 Crouch was inducted into the Gospel Hall of Fame.

Thomas A. Dorsey (1899–1993)
Composer, Arranger, Music Promoter

Popularly known as the "Father of Gospel Music," Dorsey was born on July 1, 1899, in Villa Rica, Georgia. He sang in church choirs and occasionally traveled with his father, accompanying him on the keyboard during evangelizing trips. When he dropped out of school at around age 13, he began playing in a local saloon and adopted the stage name "Barrelhouse Tommy," which was one of many that he used. In 1916 Dorsey went to Chicago, and it became his home base for the rest of his life. Between 1919 and 1921, he studied at the Chicago School of Composition and Arranging. He worked with the jazz group Will Walker's Whispering Syncopators in local Chicago clubs and scored a triumph when his work "Riverside Blues" was recorded by the great cornettist Joseph "King" Oliver in December 1923.

Thomas Dorsey.

Although Thomas A. Dorsey was a well-known blues musician as a result of his arrangements, compositions, performances and recordings throughout much of the 1920s, his lasting contribution to the history of American music, if not the world, lay in his talent as a sacred music composer. As early as 1920, he experienced a religious rebirth at the National Baptist Convention, and one of his religious songs "If I Don't Get There" appeared in a later edition of the convention's landmark collection *Gospel Pearls* produced in 1921. As early as 1927, he had begun promoting his religious songs in area churches, but was rejected by many ministers because of the arrangements' stylistic affinity to the blues.

In 1930 Dorsey's song "If You See My Savior" was performed at the National Baptist Convention to a tumultuous response. From that point on, he became more committed to composing, arranging, promoting and recording gospel songs. In 1931, along with Theodore Frye, he organized what is generally recognized as the world's first gospel chorus at Chicago's Ebenezer Baptist Church. During this period, Dorsey formed his own publishing company dedicated to selling gospel music and co-founded the National Convention of Gospel Choirs and Choruses, Inc., with his colleague Sallie Martin. The organization became a vehicle for training gospel choirs and coaching soloist. This booming period in Dorsey's career was not without its personal tragedy, however. In 1932, his first wife, Nettie, died in childbirth. After this traumatic event, he composed his most celebrated work "Take My Hand, Precious Lord."

Among Dorsey's most celebrated discoveries was Mahalia Jackson, who became gospel music's first international star. He also served as her official accompanist between the years 1937–1946. Dorsey also promoted Clara Ward, along with many other singers and groups. Dorsey toured extensively in the 1930s and 1940s throughout the United States, Europe, Mexico and North Africa and served as director of the National Convention of Gospel Choirs and Choruses, Inc. into the 1970s.

By the late 1970s, failing health forced him into semi-retirement. Dorsey reemerged in a 1982 documentary *Say Amen, Somebody*, in which he appeared with Mother Willie Mae Ford Smith; the documentary also featured footage of some of Dorsey's historical performances with Ford Smith and several of his protégéges including Mahalia Jackson, the O'Neal twins, Delois Barrett Campbell, and the Barrett Sisters. By the late 1980s he was suffering from the effects of Alzheimer's disease. He died in Chicago, Illinois, in January 1993.

Kirk Franklin (1970–)
Singer, Composer

Born in Fort Worth, Texas, in 1970, Kirk Franklin was reportedly abandoned by his teenage mother when he was an infant; he was adopted by his Aunt Gertrude, who was a strict Baptist. Being raised in a very religious environment, he was teased by his friends who called him "church boy." He began taking keyboard lessons at the age of four and, by the time he was 11 years old, led the Mt. Rose Baptist Church near Dallas. After a troubled adolescence, Franklin eventually returned to his religious roots.

By the mid-1980s, Franklin was attracting the attention of religious music producers with his songs and choral works. In 1991 his compositions appeared on a recording by the Dallas-Fort Worth Mass Choir entitled "I Will Let Nothing Separate Me." By 1993, he had put together a 17-piece vocal group, the Family, and released his debut album *Kirk Franklin and the Family*. Selections from this release caused crossover appeal—Franklin's songs, while religious in text, were being played on rhythm and blues charts. While this caused

Kirk Franklin holding the Soul Train Music Award.

his reputation to spread in many pop music markets, it disturbed many gospel music purists who felt that release was too pop-oriented. Franklin fueled these suspicions further by signing a record deal with B-Rite Records, which also had an association with the rap label, Death Row Records.

In 1995 Franklin and the Family released a Christmas recording, but his next major album *Whatcha Lookin 4* in 1996 took Franklin's combination of rhythm and blues and gospel one further step—the album hit the pop charts running and scored on both the gospel and rhythm and blues charts. As with his first release, it won accolades among pop music followers, much to the disappointment of gospel music's conservative rank. In 1997 he was chosen as *Billboard Magazine's* number one gospel artist and number one contemporary Christian artist and signed a multiyear recording contract with the B-Rite label. In 1998, Franklin released *Nu Nation Project*, which contained biblical references and stylistically was a combination of rap music and gospel. In that same year, his autobiography *Church Boy* was released. With the release of a live album, *The Rebirth of Kirk Franklin* in 2002, Franklin continued to

received critical and popular praise. Franklin is married to former rhythm and blues singer, Tammy Renee Collins, and they have three children.

Tramaine Hawkins (1951–)
Singer

Tramaine Hawkins began singing when she was only four years old in the Ephesian Church of God in Christ in Berkeley, California where her grandfather was pastor. Though Hawkins developed her passion for gospel music during childhood, her career accelerated in 1969 when the Northern California State Choir—which she had joined—recorded "Oh Happy Day." Her first performance with the choir after the song's success was at Madison Square Garden.

As a child, Hawkins sang with the Sunshine Band and later with the Heavenly Tones. After 11 years together, the Heavenly Tones began to get offers to sing at secular jobs, but Hawkins felt her calling was still gospel music. When the Northern California State Choir's name was changed to the Edwin Hawkins Singers and the choir started to do a lot of club dates for entertainers, such as the Jackson Five and Diana Ross, Hawkins chose to leave the group.

For 11 months, she sang with Andraè Crouch's Disciples. Yet Hawkins missed her old group and rejoined it. In 1970, after touring Europe with the Edwin Hawkins Singers, she accepted a marriage proposal from Edwin's brother, Walter Hawkins. During their many years of marriage, she worked side by side with Walter, also a singer, recording artist, composer, arranger, producer, and the pastor of the Love Center Church in Oakland, California. Eventually they divorced, and Tramaine married Tommy Richardson. On occasion, Walter and Tramaine still work together.

Hawkins has a controversial, contemporary style that has been criticized over the years. She raised suspicion in 1985 within the gospel community when her techno-funk hit "Fall Down," from the *Spirit of Love* album, topped the dance charts despite the religious content of its lyrics. In a 1990 concert, Hawkins brought in musicians and singers from outside the gospel field to participate in a live-recording project including rock guitarist Carlos Santana, jazz organist Jimmy McGriff, and jazz tenor saxophonist Stanley Turrentine. Her success with her mixing of traditional gospel, blues, jazz, and other singing styles helped create what is called contemporary gospel.

Altogether, Hawkins has recorded nine solo albums and won numerous awards including two Grammys, two Dove Awards, and two Communications Excellence to Black Audiences (CEBA) Awards.

Mahalia Jackson (1912–1972)
Singer

Hailed as the world's greatest gospel singer, Mahalia Jackson's rich contralto voice became a national institution. Through her many live engagements, recordings, and television appearances, Jackson elevated gospel music to a level of popularity unprecedented in the history of African American religious music.

The third of six children, Jackson was born on October 26, 1912, in New Orleans, Louisiana. Growing up in New Orleans, Jackson absorbed the sounds of parade music and brass bands. She later discovered the blues, a music labeled the "devil's music" by regular churchgoers, and listened secretly to recordings of singers such as Mamie and Bessie Smith.

In 1927, at the age of 15, Jackson moved to Chicago where she joined the Greater Salem Baptist Church. Two years later, Jackson met the gospel musician and songwriter Thomas A. Dorsey who invited her to sing at

Mahalia Jackson (photographed by Carl Van Vechten).

the Pilgrim Baptist Church. In 1937 Jackson recorded four sides for the Decca label including the song "God's Gonna Separate the Wheat From the Tares."

Jackson's big break arrived in 1947 when she released gospel music's first million-selling record "Move on Up a Little." In 1949 her song "Let the Holy Ghost Fall on Me" won the French Academy's Grand Prix du Disque. Soon afterward, she toured Europe and recorded the gospel hit "In the Upper Room." During the 1960s, Jackson became a musical ambassador—not only did she perform at the White House and at London's Albert Hall, but she sang at the historic 1963 March on Washington. She was asked by the Rev. Martin Luther King Jr. to sing at his funeral should she survive him. She sadly fulfilled this engagement after his assassination in 1968.

On January 27, 1972, Jackson died of a heart condition in Chicago, Illinois. At her funeral at Great Salem Baptist, some 45,000 mourners gathered to pay their respects to a woman who brought gospel music into the hearts and homes of millions of listeners.

T. D. Jakes. *See* **Religion chapter.**

Bobby Jones (1939–)
Singer, Televison Host

Bobby Jones, born in Paris, Tennessee, was a schoolteacher in Nashville for a time after earning his master's degree from Tennessee State University. He left his teaching job to become a textbook consultant specializing in elementary education, then began teaching reading skills at Tennessee State University in the early 1970s. Around this same time, he also began a second career as a singer on the gospel circuit and continued his activism in the local civil rights movement and his church. In 1976 he helped create the city's first Black Expo which featured numerous workshops, and also attracted some of its 50,000 attendees with a host of concerts.

Black Expo also attracted the attention of local media executives and inspired Jones to suggest a local gospel show. The *Nashville Gospel Show* was a hit in the area, but Jones jumped ship in 1980 when he was invited by Robert Johnson, founder of the fledgling Black Entertainment Television (BET) network, to bring an hour of gospel television to the new cable network. Similar to its counterparts in pop and soul, the show offers gospel fans live performances by well-known names in the industry along with interview clips and album reviews. The *Bobby Jones Gospel Hour* is also broadcast on the American Christian Network and the Armed Forces radio and television stations, giving Jones an audience of gospel fans around the world.

In 1989 Jones expanded his presence on BET with the half-hour show *Video Gospel*, which he also hosts. Jones himself has also performed internationally, including stops in Israel and Africa, and sang at the White House for President Jimmy Carter; he was also invited to appear before Ronald Reagan in a performance at the Kennedy Center for the Performing Arts.

Jones kept his teaching job at Tennessee State as late as the mid-1980s, and by then had also earned a doctorate in curriculum leadership from Vanderbilt University. He has a record label, GospoCentric, and in addition to his television responsibilities has brought an increased awareness for the music form since 1989 with his live tours known as the "Bobby Jones Gospel Explosions." His "Mini-Explosions" bring gospel music to audiences in smaller cities across the United States as well as in Europe and the Caribbean.

John P. Kee (1962–)
Gospel Singer, Songwriter

Born into a religious family on June 4, 1962, in Charlotte, North Carolina, John P. Kee was the 15th of 16 children. The musically gifted Kee formed his first gospel choir by the age of 13, and studied voice and classical music at the North Carolina School of the Arts in Winston-Salem. Later, while attending California's Yuba College Conservatory of Music, Kee worked with such groups as Cameo and Donald Byrd & the Black-birds. At this time, he also began using and selling cocaine, at one point even going so far as to run a drug operation out of a church.

It wasn't until Kee witnessed the murder of a close friend during a drug deal that he turned away from his wayward lifestyle and returned to religion and gospel music. In 1981, Kee formed the New Life Community Choir in Charlotte. The choir, which consisted of 30 young inner city recruits, was aimed at attracting the young and providing a safe place for them to flourish spiritually. Four Years later, Kee received a break when he recorded "Jesus Can Do It All" and "He's My All and All" for James Cleveland's Gospel Music Workshop of America's (GMWA) annual mass choir album.

Kee and his choir have recorded and performed prolifically since releasing *There Is Hope* in 1990. Their subsequent recordings are: *Churchin' Christmas* (1992),

Churchin' (1992), *Lillies of the Valley* (1993), *Wash Me* (1994), *We Walk by Faith* (1994), *Color Blind* (1994), *Never Shall Forget* (1994), *Just Me This Time* (1994), *Yes Lord* (1994), *Wait on Him* (1994), *Livin' on the Ultimate High* (1995), *Show Up!* (1995), *Stand* (1995), *Christmas Album* (1996), *Thursday Love* (1997), *Strength* (1997), *Any Day* (1998), and *Not Guilty. . . The Experience* (2000). The choir has won two Billboard Music Awards, at least 20 GWMA Excellence Awards, and has been nominated twice for a Grammy Award—for the albums *Show Up!* and *Strength*.

Kee has produced albums by Shawn McClemore and New Image, Drea Randle, Vanessa Bell Armstrong, and the Victory in Praise Mass Choir. In addition to his role as a musician, choir director, and producer, Kee has run an inner-city youth program in Charlotte and served as a full-time minister.

Roberta Martin (1907–1969)
Singer, Pianist

Born in Helena, Arkansas, on February 12, 1907, Martin was a gifted keyboardist with early ambitions of being a concert pianist. After moving to Chicago as a young adult, she became the accompanist for Thomas A. Dorsey and Theodore Frye's historic gospel choir at Ebenezer Baptist Church in the 1930s. From this group she co-founded, along with Frye, the all-male Martin-Frye Quartet in 1933. The group subsequently became known as the Roberta Martin Singers. In the 1940s, she added women to the group, including a young lead soprano named Delois Barrett, and toured extensively. Martin also established a music publishing company and produced several of her many compositions including "Try Jesus, He Satisfies" (1943), "Yield Not to Temptation" (1944), and "God Is Still on the Throne" (1959). Martin was also influential as an accompanist and promoted the careers of several other groups including the Barrett Sisters. She died in Chicago, Illinois, on January 18, 1969, after a brief illness.

Sallie Martin (1896–1988)
Singer

Born in Pittfield, Georgia, on November 20, 1896, Martin traveled to Chicago, Illinois, in 1919. Her church singing took on greater significance after she began a professional relationship with Thomas A. Dorsey. Martin auditioned for his choir at Ebenezer Baptist Church in the early 1930s, and they maintained an association for the next 40 years. She became a song demonstrator for Dorsey, and they co-founded the National Convention of Gospel Choirs and Choruses, Inc. in 1932. Later in 1940, Martin co-founded the Martin-Morris Music Company with musician Kenneth Morris. That same year, she also began touring with her own group, the Roberta Martin Singers, throughout the United States and Europe.

As the Civil Rights movement gained momentum in the late 1950s and early 1960s, gospel music would be heavily identified with the movement. Sallie Martin was an active supporter of both the movement and its figurehead, Rev. Martin Luther King Jr. On several occasions, she represented him in his absence, such as at Nigeria's independence celebration in 1960. After retiring from live performances in the 1970s, she appeared in the French production *Gospel Caravan* in 1979. In 1986, she was honored by the city of Chicago for her achievements as a singer, composer, and promoter of gospel music. She died two years later at the age of 92.

Willie Mae Ford Smith (1906–1994)
Singer

The Ford family moved from Rolling Forks, Mississippi, to Memphis, Tennessee, when Willie Mae, born on April 21, 1906, was a young girl. In the early 1920s, she sang the lead in the Ford family quartet (made up of Ford's sisters), and they appeared at the National Baptist Convention in 1922 singing "Ezekiel Saw the Wheel" and "I'm in His Care." In 1932, she met Thomas A. Dorsey who in 1936 appointed her the director of the Soloists Bureau of the National Convention of Gospel Choirs and Choruses, Inc. In this role she demonstrated the proper style and delivery of gospel songs to younger singers.

Because the Baptist Church did not allow women to preach, Smith left in 1939 and joined the Holiness Church of God Apostolic. She became an ordained evangelist and limited her singing to religious services and revivals. As an evangelist, Smith frequently combined a brief sermon with a song. This practice became known as "sermonette and song." In 1982, she was the subject of a gospel documentary *Say Amen, Somebody* which featured footage of the historic performances of many of her protégés, including Mahalia Jackson, the O'Neal twins, and Delois Barrett Campbell, as well as her own performances. In 1988, "Mother Smith" was honored with a National Heritage Fellowship from the

National Endowment for the Arts. Her last years were spent in a retirement community in Kansas City, Missouri, which is where she died in 1994.

Sister Rosetta Tharpe (1915–1973)
Singer, Pianist, Guitarist

Born Rosetta Nubin on March 20, 1915, in Cotton Plant, Arkansas, Sister Rosetta Singer Tharpe came from a background of religious music—her mother, Katie Bell Nubin, was a singer in the Holiness Church. At a young age, Rosetta learned to sing and play the piano and guitar. By the 1930s, Tharpe began recording and making appearances in nightclubs. For example, she appeared at New York's Cotton Club with Cab Calloway accompanying herself on guitar.

In 1938, Tharpe performed gospel music at John Hammond's concert at Carnegie Hall entitled *From Sprirituals to Swing at Carnegie Hall*. Tharpe subsequently performed with other well-known popular musicians, including Lucky Millinder, Benny Goodman, and eventually such blues musicians as Muddy Waters. However, she was principally known within religious circles for strong gospel singing and guitar playing. Tharpe later performed with the Dixie Hummingbirds and recorded with her mother, Katie Bell Nubin. Their recorded performance of "Daniel in the Lion's Den" became a gospel music classic. For a time, she also had a backup group known as the "Rosettes." As a result of her many bus tours, Tharpe was particularly well known in rural areas of the South. Tharpe eventually settled in Philadelphia, Pennsylvania, where she died on October 9, 1973.

Charles Albert Tindley (1851?–1933)
Composer

Believed to have been born on July 7, 1851, in Berlin, Maryland, Tindley began preaching at outdoor religious gatherings, also known as camp meetings, in Maryland when he was a teenager. In the 1870s, he relocated to Philadelphia to continue his education. He furthered his religious studies by correspondence through Boston Theological Seminary and became an ordained minister in the mid-1880s. After preaching in surrounding states on the East coast, Tindley returned to Philadelphia to pastor the East Calvary Methodist Episcopal Church, later renamed the Tindley Temple in his honor. He held periodic religious music concerts at his church,

The Winans Family is known as "The First Family of Gospel Music".

which frequently featured songs that he had composed. His compositions include such standards as "We'll Understand It Better By and By," "What Are They Doing in Heaven Tonight," "Stand By Me," and "I'll Overcome Someday," which were published in his 1916 collection *New Songs of Paradise*. This hymnal was quickly adopted by several African American churches around the United States.

Frequently cited as a major influence on gospel music great Thomas A. Dorsey, Tindley unequivocally

helped to set the stage for modern gospel music's emergence. He died on July 26, 1933, in Philadelphia, Pennsylvania.

Albertina Walker (1929–)
Singer

Affectionately known as the "Queen of Gospel," Albertina Walker was born and raised on the South side of Chicago, one of nine children in a hardworking

Baptist family. Her mother was a member of the West Point Baptist Church, and Albertina and her sister Rose Marie both sang in the choir there. When Walker was still a little girl, the church's choir director formed a small children's gospel group called the Williams Singers. With this group, and occasionally as a duo, the Walker sisters performed in churches throughout Chicago and the Midwest.

The West Point Baptist Church was the site of many rousing gospel concerts during Walker's youth. She was inspired by the performances of such great gospel singers as Sally and Roberta Martin, Mahalia Jackson, and Tommy A. Dorsey. When Walker entered her teen years, she began to sing at various Baptist and Pentecostal churches; the performances were broadcast on radio, giving Walker an entry into the show business side of gospel music.

Along with remaining members of Robert Anderson's ensemble and keyboardist James Cleveland, Walker created the Caravans. From the group's founding in 1952 until virtually the end of the 1960s, the Caravans dominated traditional gospel, performing all over the United States and Europe and in such celebrated theaters as New York's Apollo, Carnegie Hall, and Madison Square Garden. After the Caravans disbanded in 1967, Walker began to perform as a soloist.

Walker was featured in the 1992 film *Leap of Faith* as a member of a spirited gospel choir. In 1993 she received a Grammy Award nomination for *Albertina Walker Live*, and that same year she performed a concert for Nelson Mandela during his visit to the United States. From her base in Chicago she has been active in politics, working with the Reverend Jesse Jackson and organizing the Operation PUSH People's Choir. Her album *Songs of the Church* brought her a Grammy Award in 1995, and she received a Dove Award two years later for *Let's Go Back: Live in Chicago*. Walker is the founder of and one of the chief contributors to the Albertina Walker Scholarship Foundation, a source of funds for aspiring young gospel singers.

The Winans Family
Gospel Singing Group

Comprised of Benjamin "BeBe," Cecelia "CeCe," Marvin, Carvin, Michael, and Ronald, this Detroit-based gospel singing group has become one of gospel music's first families. The older Winans brothers, Marvin and Carvin, sang at their great-grandfather's Congregational Church of Christ on Detroit's east side. The younger Winans children's musical talents, especially BeBe and CeCe, were further encouraged by their father, David Winans Sr. who was also a minister. He was the first to organize the family into a quartet called the "Testimonials." Under this name the family quartet produced two recordings "Love Covers" (1977) and "Thy Will Be Done" (1978).

The Winanses eventually came to the attention of the celebrated gospel musician, Andraè Crouch, who was instrumental in helping to produce their first national release *Introducing the Winans* (1981). The album was subsequently nominated for a Grammy award. Two years later another release *Long Time Coming* also received a Grammy nomination.

In 1987, BeBe and CeCe launched a duo career with the release *BeBe & CeCe Winans*, singing mostly jazz, rhythm and blues, and a few religious works. Their next release *Heaven* (1988) included the recordings "Heaven," "Lost Without You," and "Celebrate New Life." It reached gold record status, rated highly on national rhythm and blues charts, and earned them four Grammy nominations. Their third album *Different Lifestyles* (1991) reached number one on the national rhythm and blues charts. Since then, BeBe and CeCe have worked together and individually with other celebrated popular artists including Whitney Houston, Bobby Brown, Gladys Knight, Luther Vandross, and Aretha Franklin, among others. The brother-sister duo has also performed at Carnegie Hall, Culturefest in West Africa, and the 1993 inaugural celebration of President Bill Clinton. They have also released two additional albums *Relationships* (1994) and *The Greatest Hits* (1996).

BeBe has recorded three solo albums, including *Love & Freedom* (2000). CeCe's numerous solo recordings include *Everlasting Love* (1998) and the self-titled *CeCe Winans* (2001). The younger Winans sisters, Angie and Debbie, have recorded with the family; together, they garnered several Dove, Stellar, and Soul Train awards.

24

Blues and Jazz

◆ The Blues Tradition ◆ The Jazz Tradition ◆ Women in Blues and Jazz
◆ Jazz Education ◆ The Future of Blues and Jazz
◆ Blues and Jazz Composers, Musicians, and Singers

by Joseph Guy and Jim Gallert

In less than a century, the remarkable American music called jazz has risen from its obscure origins to become the most original, time-loved, admired, and played form of musical expression around the world. Jazz has a long and rich ancestry. Its roots go back to the arrival of the first Africans on American soil and their encounter with European musical traditions. Since then, black music has taken many forms in America, including work songs, gospel and spirituals, and a huge variety of dance music originally popularized by brass bands and traveling minstrel, medicine and vaudeville shows.

◆ THE BLUES TRADITION

Ragtime and Blues

The evolution of African American music has gone through many stages in the last 200 years. The dance music known as ragtime was among the first; it became very popular in the nineteenth century. Ragtime's heavily syncopated rhythms and sprightly melodies, typically played on a piano or by a brass band, had a distinctly African American flavor. Its greatest exponent was Scott Joplin (1868–1917), a pianist known as "the king of ragtime composers."

At about the same time, a brand new form of African American folk music called the blues began coalescing into a 12-bar pattern that remains largely unchanged today. The blues typically use three-line verses sung in a so-called AAB rhyming pattern. This simple and universal pattern proved to be—and still is—highly adaptable to popular songwriting. The blues also displayed a harmonic quality that made it sound quite different from the popular music of that era. It was

derived by "flatting" both the third and seventh notes of the widely-used tempered, or "classical," scale. These two seemingly simple innovations allowed for an infinity of variations which, over the past century, have had a vast impact on modern music, including, jazz, rhythm and blues, soul, rock and roll and, most recently, rap. None of these forms would exist without the invention and popularization of the blues element.

Blues History and Styles

The true origins of the blues remain somewhat murky. The form seems to have sprung up simultaneously in many places across the South around the end of the nineteenth century. From there, the music followed African American Southerners to wherever they migrated, evolving and incorporating whatever musical influences they encountered along the way. While the music clearly came from the country, it was in the city of Memphis, Tennessee that it actually became known as "the blues."

W. C. Handy (1873–1958), the African American bandleader of a minstrel orchestra often credited with "inventing" blues, actually did not do so. But he may well have been the first individual to achieve commercial success playing it. Handy, by his own description, was a folklorist, documenting different styles of music and other cultural indicators he found during his travels. Although the word "blues" was already being widely used to describe an assortment of work songs, field hollers, and folk tunes by around 1910, it was Handy's publication of the composition "Memphis Blues" in 1912 that established the genre as a readily identifiable musical style. Handy's "discovery" of the blues aside, three rural areas—the Mississippi Delta; Texas; and the

1085

Piedmont region (Georgia and the Carolinas)—played the most important roles as blues breeding grounds.

Mississippi Delta Blues

Handy claimed to have discovered the blues at a train station in the sleepy Delta town of Tutwiler, Mississippi in 1903. This "Mississippi style" has been the most instrumental in shaping the blues sound over the decades. Primarily Mississippi Delta blues consisted of a singer accompanying himself on a guitar in a highly percussive manner. The vocal style was both the most speech-like and most passionate of the early regional styles. The guitar technique stressed string-bending; it also frequently employed slides or bottleneck as guitar effects. Handy connected that unique, sliding sound with the sound of Hawaiian guitar playing.

Charley Patton (1887–1934) was probably the most influential of the early Mississippi blues practitioners. Since his day, countless other blues singers have emulated his growling vocal style, which was a direct descendent of field hollers, work songs, and gospel singing. Patton influenced contemporaries such as Willie Brown, Eddie "Son" House, Johnny Shines, and Robert Johnson. Johnson, the best known musician to come out of the Delta blues tradition, was another vital link in the chain of influences leading to modern blues. He inspired another generation of blues artists, including Chicago bluesmen Muddy Waters, Elmore James, John Lee Hooker, and Howlin' Wolf. Interestingly, Robert Lockwood Jr., Johnson's protégé, points out that Johnson had a much broader repertoire than what he recorded. He also played rags, the popular songs of the day.

At this same time, the Beale Street jug band style emerged in Memphis. Popularized by Furry Lewis and Memphis Minnie, this style depended on homemade instruments such as kazoos, washboards, washtubs, spoons, and all manners of percussion devices. Jug band music is one of the best examples of how the blues sounded before it solidified into its classic format— guitar-based and reliant on the twelve-bar format.

Texas Blues

Meanwhile in Texas, Blind Lemon Jefferson (1897–1929) reigned as the undisputed king of the blues. Early Texas blues, as performed by Jefferson, contrasted with the Delta style in several ways. The guitar accompaniment was less percussive; instead, it made more frequent use of melodic lines and embellishments. Texas blues singers tended to enunciate their lyrics more clearly than their Mississippi counterparts. They often sang in a high-pitched voice rather than a growl or moan.

The Texas blues bloodline flows from Jefferson, through such legends as Lightnin' Hopkins, Clarence "Gatemouth" Brown, and T-Bone Walker, and on to such modern blues stars as B.B. King, Johnny Copeland, and Albert Collins. Classic Texas blues have given contemporary blues much of its improvisational element, rhythmic swing and jazzy electric guitar soloists.

Piedmont Blues

The Piedmont blues style varied considerably within its own region. But its common elements, which differentiated it from other blues styles of the era, were its more rhythmic bass lines and its emphasis on the fingerpicking style of guitar playing. Highly syncopated, the style connects closely with earlier string band traditions that integrated ragtime and country dance styles. Early Piedmont practitioners included Blind Boy Fuller and Blind Willie McTell. The legendary duo of Brownie McGhee and Sonny Terry were its best-known modern proponents.

Early Blues Recordings

The commercial success of the female blues performers (see the section entitled "Women in Blues and Jazz") eventually led the record companies to begin recording male artists, whom until then they had completely ignored. In 1924, Okeh made what was probably the first record by a male country blues singer, Ed Andrews. The first male blues recording star, however, was Papa Charlie Jackson, a talented banjo player who performed some of the earliest recorded versions of many country blues standards. Over the next several years, a number of record companies produced field recordings, so named because companies recorded them on location in the rural south with portable equipment, rather than in Northern studios.

Migration of the Blues

During the Great Depression of the 1930s millions of African Americans left the rural South for the cities of the North, and the blues traveled with them. The majority of the bluesmen who made the trek were young. Blues musicians tended to be itinerant, hoboing their way through particular regions. These performers adapted their traditional music to their new surroundings, incorporating the concerns of urban life into their lyrics. Blues scenes began to emerge in Chicago, St. Louis, Detroit, and other Midwestern and Northern cities.

Older musicians tended to stay put in the South. Skip James and Mississippi John Hurt were among the many bluesmen who did not migrate until later, if ever, and whose sounds remained countrified. Even today, those geographical differences remain. Contemporary Delta blues still sound much more like Charley Patton's brand than Buddy Guy's.

The blues players of each region tended to relocate to a particular area as they fled the South. Musicians in the Piedmont region of North Carolina drifted toward New York. Many of the Texans, meanwhile, headed westward to California. T-Bone Walker was one of the most important representatives of this migration, which led to the development of the West Coast blues sound, including use of the electric guitar after 1940, through a lineage that included a number of important piano bluesmen as well as guitarist B. B. King.

Chicago Blues

As blues artists in the Mississippi Delta and other parts of the Deep South headed to Northern cities, a fertile blues scene developed in Chicago. The evolution of Chicago blues hinged on the amplification and re-arrangement for small bands of traditional solo Delta blues. Taking their cue from the work of such Mississippi legends as Robert Johnson, Southern immigrants began establishing a blues scene in Chicago even before the onset of the Depression.

Popular Chicago blues performers during the 1920s and 1930s included Memphis Minnie, Tampa Red, Big Bill Broonzy, and Sonny Boy Williamson. Another, even larger wave of blues Southern musicians after World War II solidified Chicago's position as the center of the blues universe. This generation of artists included Howlin' Wolf, Little Walter, and Muddy Waters.

Eventually, Chicago blues began to incorporate elements of blues styles from other areas. The most obvious input came from the Texas/West Coast guitar soloists who were working in the style of T-Bone Walker. Chicago's modern blues stars Otis Rush, Buddy Guy and Magic Sam were at forefront of this new emphasis on electric lead guitar improvisation.

The Varied Sounds of Blues

Like jazz, the label "blues" covers an incredibly diverse body of music. It defies convenient classification systems. Nevertheless, a number of recognizable styles and movements have emerged within the blues idiom over the years. Some of them are associated with the geographical areas in which they blossomed, while others transcend the boundaries of time and location.

"Jump blues" developed during the 1940s and 1950s, primarily in California. Jump was a jazzier, horn-driven style that relied less on guitar than many other blues forms. The predominant instruments were the alto or tenor saxophone.

Its proponents have included Amos Milburn, Johnny Otis and Louis Jordan. In Louisiana, Lightnin Slim, Slim Harpo, and Lazy Lester championed a laid-back "swamp" style. Louisiana also produced the blues offshoot called "zydeco," which incorporates elements from local Acadian (Cajun) culture. Clifton Chenier, Boozoo Chavis, and Rockin' Dopsie were among its initial, main proponents. The folk-flavored blues of the Carolina Piedmont region spawned the highly underrated Brownie McGhee, who influenced rock and roll, folk, and blues musicians. The term "piano blues" captures a wide variety of music spanning most of the continent and century including the entire progression from barrelhouse to boogie-woogie to hard rocking Chicago blues. Big Maceo Merriweather, Sunnyland Slim, Meade Lux Lewis, Albert Ammons, Professor Longhair, and Otis Spann were some of the most important piano bluesmen.

Muddy Waters.

Two paths that blues have taken in recent years include modern acoustic blues and modern electric blues. Modern acoustic blues is essentially a movement for the revival of the older country blues sounds. Taj Mahal is one of its major proponents. Modern electric blues simply refers to the most contemporary trappings—including horns and more sophisticated studio recording techniques—placed on urban blues. Robert Cray is among its most commercially successful practitioners.

◆ THE JAZZ TRADITION

New Orleans Jazz

Jazz was born when the primarily instrument music of ragtime met the primarily vocal music of blues. Although this process was taking place simultaneously in many parts of America, the basic language of jazz was first widely recognized in New Orleans.

This was due not only to the rich musical tradition of this port city with its international climate, but also because social conditions in New Orleans, while certainly not free from racist elements, were less restrictive and more open than in other large American cities of the time. So musicians of varied ethnic backgrounds, including those with traditions rooted in the rhythms of West Africa and Latin America, mingled and blended their own personal styles. This rich brew of ethnic traditions met head-on with the harmonic structures of European classical and brass band music, the melodic and harmonic qualities of nineteenth century American folk music, as well as religious music, work songs, and minstrel show music.

Many jazz histories mistakenly over-emphasize the importance of the New Orleans red light district called Storyville. While early jazz certainly was performed there, and the word jazz is derived from "jass" or "jas," a reference to this type of district, there were also many other outlets for making music. These included dances, picnics, parades, carnivals, and the traditional New Orleans funerals, for which a brass band would accompany the casket from church to cemetery with mournful strains, and then lead the march back to town with lively, peppy music including ragtime and early jazz. Music was, and still is, an important part of New Orleans' social fabric.

Musicians from New Orleans began to tour the United States from about 1907 onward and had a significant influence wherever they went. Some of them visited Europe, notably the great clarinetist and soprano saxophonist Sidney Bechet (1897–1959), who has been called the first great jazz soloist. However, the intricate style of collective improvisation which Bechet and others of his era reveled in, which gave each instrument in the band its own specific role, was not so easily absorbed and led to some confusion about its quality and true sophistication. It is another myth of jazz history that most of these early jazz players were a special breed of self-taught "naturals"; in fact, almost all of them had good, basic, musical training, and many could read music well. And, indeed, it was a somewhat younger New Orleanian, Louis Armstrong (1901–1971), who would have the biggest impact on the future of jazz.

Armstrong was brought to Chicago—by then a center of jazz activity—in 1922 by his mentor and fellow New Orleans trumpeter Joe "King" Oliver (1885–1938) and made his first records there. Two years later he moved to New York to join the band of Fletcher Henderson (1897–1952), the first musically significant big band in jazz.

Early African American Jazz Recordings

Jazz developed almost simultaneously with the phonograph, and without dissemination on records, it is unlikely that jazz would have spread as quickly as it did. Ironically, the first New Orleans jazz group to make a record was a white group, the Original Dixieland Jazz Band in 1917. African American musicians had already made records by then, but they were not in a jazz idiom. It was approximately five more years before the best African American players from New Orleans, such as Jelly Roll Morton, King Oliver and Louis Armstrong, were able to make records.

By studying recorded performances, musicians anywhere could learn at least the rudiments of jazz, a spontaneous music in which improvisation played a considerable role. "Improvisation" is a much-misunderstood concept. It does not mean inventing music on the spot without guidelines. What it does mean is that musicians, building on shared foreknowledge of musical concepts, particularly harmonic and chordal outlines, added their own personal ideas to that shared framework while they performed together. In addition, a jazz musician's personal style on their chosen instrument depended on tonal qualities, a distinctive approach to rhythm and phrasing, and a personal vocabulary of melodic and thematic characteristics. These crucial and unique ingredients are what allow a seasoned listener to almost immediately identify who is playing in a jazz performance, provided that the musician has developed a personal style.

The Swing Era

Most early New Orleans jazz bands employed trumpet, trombone, and clarinet for lead instruments and piano, guitar (or banjo), bass (string or brass) and drums for a rhythm section. By contrast, the early "big bands" used three trumpets, one or two trombones, three reeds (saxophonists doubling clarinet), and the same rhythm section instruments. These larger ensembles more commonly employed written scores called arrangements, but gave the soloists freedom to improvise their contributions.

Louis Armstrong's 1924 arrival was a revelation to members of Henderson's New York big band. Armstrong's first solos on Henderson's records stand out like diamonds in a tin setting. First and foremost, Armstrong displayed a clearly superior sense of rhythm that made other players sound stiff and clumsy in comparison. He had discovered "swing," the rhythmic element that sets jazz apart from other music. It's a kind of rhythmic thrust that seems to float and soar. Moreover, his trumpet sound was the biggest and most musically appealing of the day. Armstrong's playing also boasted both exceptional range and incredible technique. Furthermore, his gifts of melodic invention were so great that he almost single-handed laid the foundation for jazz as a medium for personal expression by an instrumental soloist.

One of Armstrong's first Henderson colleagues to get the message was tenor saxophonist Coleman Hawkins (1904–1969), who soon created the first influential jazz style on his own instrument. Armstrong also greatly affected that band's chief arranger, Don Redman (1900–1964), who was the first to translate the trumpeter's discoveries to big band arranging. Many others followed suit, especially after Louis, now back in Chicago, began to make records with his own studio groups, the Hot Fives and Hot Sevens from 1925 to 1928. These records gained him national attention and made his reputation as the preeminent jazz soloist.

By the late 1920s, jazz had become a mainstay of American popular dance music and had established a beachhead in Europe as well. African American musicians were touring worldwide, even in such exotic places as China and India. Wherever they went, their brilliant new music left an imprint. Yet there was still quite a gap between jazz at its best and its more commercially acceptable versions. Not until the advent of the so-called "swing era" in the mid-1930s did unadulterated jazz reach a level of true popular acceptance, which to this day remains unmatched. For about 15 golden and exciting years, jazz was indeed America's popular music.

This acceptance was due primarily to the big bands that had reached new heights of artistic maturity. Duke Ellington (1899–1974), rightly called the greatest American jazz composer, was partly responsible for this

success. His unique band, for which he gradually created a perfect balance between written and improvised elements, included such legendary soloists as Johnny Hodges (alto sax), Harry Carney (baritone sax), Barney Bigard (clarinet), Cootie Williams (trumpet), and Rex Stewart (cornet). This band began a most important engagement at Harlem's famous Cotton Club in late 1927. Thanks to its appearances there, regular network radio broadcasts, and many recordings, Ellington's music reached a huge audience. His band visited England for the first time in 1933.

Don Redman and Benny Carter (b.1907), a brilliant multi-instrumentalist and arranger-composer, also accomplished important work at this time. Fletcher Henderson began arranging for big band in the early 1930s and soon became one of the best. Such efforts laid the foundation for the success of Benny Goodman (1909–1986), a white clarinetist and band leader. Wisely, he commissioned the best black arrangers, including Henderson, and also was the first white band leader to hire black musicians, including pianist Teddy Wilson and vibraphonist Lionel Hampton in 1936.

By 1936, the swing era was in full bloom. African American dance styles, developed at such places as Harlem's Savoy Ballroom, swept the nation as young people jitterbugged to the sounds of an astonishing number of excellent bands. Bands led by Jimmie Lunceford (1902–1947) and Count Basie (1904–1984) stood out among the many others. The big bands spawned a host of gifted young players and also brought into the limelight many giants with established jazz reputations such as Armstrong, who led his own big bands from 1929 to 1947.

World War II brought economic and social changes that affected the big bands. Gasoline rationing impaired the constant touring that was one of that tradition's lifeblood. Vocalists, who first gained popularity through their work with the bands, became stars in their own right. A nearly yearlong ban on all recording, imposed by the musician's union in August 1942, further hurt big band popularity. After the war, the advent of television wrought fundamental changes in the ways people entertained themselves. People could stay in the comfort of their own homes and watch the latest offerings from the entertainment world. A second musician's union strike in 1948 further served to popularize vocalists, who were not then considered "musicians" by the union. Together, these changes sounded the death knell for ballrooms and night clubs, and for the bands which relied upon them. The big bands declined rapidly and only a handful survived, among them Ellington's and Basie's. Even though their leaders have long since died, their bands continue to this day.

Louis Armstrong's discovery of "swing" set jazz apart from other kinds of music.

Meanwhile, the music itself had also undergone fundamental changes. The new generation of players who had come up playing in the big bands were eager to express themselves at greater length than most such groups permitted. They were also developing new and potentially radical musical ideas.

The most advanced soloists of the swing era—Roy Eldridge (trumpet), Lester Young (tenor sax), Art Tatum (piano), and Sid Catlett (drums)—had been extending the rhythmic, harmonic, and technical resources of their instruments. Two young geniuses, both doomed to early death by tuberculosis—guitarist Charlie Christian (1916–1942), featured with Benny Goodman, and bassist Jimmy Blanton (1918–1942), featured with Duke Ellington—revolutionized the language of their respective instruments.

Christian was among the many notable players who participated in jam sessions (see Jazz Education section) at Minton's Playhouse, a nightclub in Harlem, in the early 1940s. Here, where pianist Thelonious Monk

and drummer Kenny Clarke were in the regular house band, musical experiments fed new ideas into the new jazz mainstream and led to the advent of modern jazz in 1944–1945.

Bebop Gives Jazz a New Voice

The chief creators of this new jazz language were trumpeter and band leader-composer Dizzy Gillespie and alto saxophonist-composer Charlie Parker, both of whom had played with leading big bands. While working together in the band of pianist Earl Hines—the father of modern jazz piano style—in 1943, they began solidifying their mutually compatible ideas. When they joined forces in a small group, both on records and in person in 1945, bebop, as the new jazz style soon was called, came into first flowering.

Though bebop was solidly grounded in earlier jazz styles, it did not strike the general public that way. Audiences were often unable to follow the intricate rhythmic and harmonic sophistication of the boppers.

Duke Ellington, 1943, considered the greatest American jazz composer.

Furthermore, the bop musicians, unlike most of the jazz players before them, were not interested in pleasing the public. They were more concerned with creating music that fulfilled their own, personal, artistic ambitions. Gillespie, with his irrepressible sense of humor and outgoing personality, had an easy manner with the public and became identified in the general press with bebop.

A New Audience for Jazz

In any case, the advent of bop, which had its beginnings in the swing era, helped accelerate a change in who listened to jazz. By the mid-1930s, small clubs catering to jazz connoisseurs had begun to spring up in most of the larger urban areas. The biggest and most famous concentration was in New York, along two blocks of West 52nd Street, then known as "Swing Street." In such clubs, musicians could perform for knowledgeable listeners without making musical compromises; most of them were too small for dancing, so people came strictly to listen. This was in contrast to

other clubs that offered floor shows complete with a headlining group or entertainer, a comic, dancers, and local singers.

By this time, many people all over the world had become interested in jazz as a serious art form. Some studied and documented its origins and history; others collected, researched, and interviewed older jazz musicians in an effort to identify personnel on records. Jazz bands sprang up in Europe, Asia and South America, among other places. Travelling musicians had settled around the world and spread the jazz message. Indeed, so many African American musicians lived in the Montmarte section of Paris after WWI that it was dubbed "Little Harlem." Publications such as *Downbeat* and *Metronome*, catered to musicians and serious fans. They even conducted polls and presented awards; in 1944 the prestigious magazine *Esquire* presented its awards at a huge all-star jazz concert on the stage of the Metropolitan Opera House in New York.

Jazz concerts were a rarity in the 1920s. But then, in 1938, Goodman staged one at Carnegie Hall; from 1943 through 1948, Duke Ellington also gave annual concerts there. By the late 1940s, jazz concerts were regular events; most famous are the Jazz at the Philharmonic (JATP) all-star tours. In many ways, then, the stage was now set for viewing jazz as something more than mere entertainment or dance music. In the eyes of many, the music had gained parity with "classical" music and deserved serious artistic consideration.

The movement towards more "serious" appreciation for jazz, combined with the ascendancy of new forms of the blues, laid the foundation for the advent of rock and roll music. This new music filled the need for young people to have their own music to dance to at a time when jazz was perceived to have largely abandoned them. Nevertheless, many jazz musicians and fans resented the advent of rock music. Eventually, of course, rock itself spawned its own constituency of "serious" performers, commentators, and magazines.

The Development of Cool Jazz

Toward the end of the 1940s, bop began to trigger a reaction against its nervous energy. This movement, spearheaded by trumpeter Miles Davis (1926–1991), became known as "cool jazz." In contrast with the frenzied pace of bop solos, improvisers in the "cool" camp sought a more relaxed sound. The energy was sensual rather than frenetic and focused on a smooth, legato pace rather than bop's staccato feel.

While cool jazz began to take root primarily on the West Coast, largely among white musicians, black musicians on the East Coast in the 1950s were pioneering the "hard bop" style. Hard bop built on the harmonies and the fiery approach of bop, but added a bluesy, hard-edged element. Tenor saxophonist Sonny Rollins, trumpeter Donald Byrd, pianist Horace Silver, and drummer Art Blakey played major roles in the evolution of hard bop in the second half of the 1950s.

Post-Bop and the Avant-Garde

The trumpeter Miles Davis, who had worked with bop pioneer Charlie Parker and also led his own very influential cool jazz groups, hired a then little-known tenor saxophonist, John Coltrane (1926–1967), in 1956. With Coltrane, who also worked with Thelonious Monk, and pianist Bill Evans, Davis introduced a modal approach (i.e., based on scales rather than harmonies) to jazz improvisation in 1958. Sometimes called simply "modal jazz," this new style eventually became known as "post-bop." Many of the same musicians who had been hard boppers a few years earlier, including Byrd and drummer Max Roach, and younger players such as Wayne Shorter and McCoy Tyner, played key roles in its development.

John Coltrane helped introduce "modal jazz" or "post-bop" with Miles Davis's band.

While bop and post-bop continued to develop, even more radical forms of jazz sprang up in quick succession. In 1959, a young Texas-born alto saxophonist, Ornette Coleman (b. 1930), brought his adventurous quartet to New York and ignited a huge controversy. His music seemed to abandon most of the hitherto known harmonic and structural principles of jazz. Actually Coleman rooted his music deeply in the blues and in well-established improvisational jazz procedures; in time his music gained acceptance as part of the jazz tradition.

By the 1960s, many people viewed the history of jazz as a linear progression toward maximum freedom for the player. Avant-garde jazz was very much in evidence, in many and varied forms. Just as bop had opened new windows of creative opportunity to soloists, each new emerging style that followed stripped away additional layers of constraint. Some saw this trend as the return of African American music to the complete freedom of the field holler; released from the rhythmic and harmonic limitations that had been imported from the classical music of white Europe. And no musician better expressed the raw emotion and lyrical beauty of this approach than John Coltrane. After leaving the Miles Davis group in 1960, Coltrane formed his own group, which took modality much further and extended its improvisations, both in length and intensity, to a point of near ecstasy. The pianist Cecil Taylor (b. 1930), a virtuoso of the keyboard, further stretched the boundaries of jazz with inventive combinations of post-bop jazz, modern classical music, and experimental noise. Another keyboardist who pushed the boundaries of jazz was composer and bandleader Sun Ra (1914–1993) and his Arkestra. Ra and his wildly colorful group combined the music of Fletcher Henderson, Duke Ellington and his own unique and often surrealist compositions into a swirling mix of music, dance and theater. Meanwhile, the bassist and composer Charles Mingus (1922–1979), deeply influenced by Ellington and Parker, found new and imaginative ways of combining written and improvised jazz. Tenor saxophonist Sonny Rollins (b. 1930), while remaining rooted in traditional harmonic ground, dramatically expanded his solo improvisation. And by the end of the 1960s, Albert Ayler (1936–1973), a tenor saxophonist who stripped R&B music to its essentials and played it in "free-form" style, brought another new and intensely personal voice to jazz.

Over the course of the 1960s, many others contributed to the dismantling of the melodic rulebook. Pharoah Sanders, Archie Shepp and Sonny Sharrock were among those who leaned their art toward Coltrane's approach. Ornette Coleman spawned a line of jazz innovators that has included trumpeter Don Cherry and, after he added electric amplification to his sound, bassist Jamaaledeen Tacuma and guitarist James "Blood" Ulmer. Don Pullen and Anthony Braxton were also among the many notable proponents of "free jazz," as avant-garde jazz was then beginning to being called, and its various offshoots. When John Coltrane died suddenly in 1967, jazz was at the height of its experimental, expansionist stage, much of it inspired by the social and political upheavals of the time. But within a few years of Coltrane's passing, the storm began to quiet.

Soul Jazz

The most commercially popular jazz style of the 1960s was not bebop, hard bop, or free jazz, but rather "soul jazz." While the other, more critically acclaimed styles were gaining recognition as an "art form" suitable for concert halls, soul jazz was thriving in bars and clubs and enjoying success with the record buying public. Soul or "funky" jazz differs from bebop and hard bop in that it emphasizes the rhythmic groove. The music's basslines focus on a dance-related back beat rather than a four-to-the-bar walking pattern, while melodies and solos focus on enhancing and extending the central groove. This emphasis on the dance actually hearkens back to the earlier forms of swing jazz.

Pianist Horace Silver, often cited as the first soul jazz practitioner, emerged from the mid-1950s hard bop movement and began infusing his music with elements of blues, gospel, soul, and R&B. Other pianists to follow Silver's lead include Bobby Timmons, Les McCann, Gene Harris, and Ramsey Lewis. In 1956 organist Jimmy Smith exploded onto the jazz scene playing the Hammond B-3 organ. His foot-pedal basslines, percussive left-hand chords, and fiery right-hand solo lines revolutionized his instrument and expanded the soul jazz genre. Those following in Smith's footsteps include Brother Jack McDuff, Shirley Scott, Jimmy McGriff, Big John Patton, and Charles Earland. But pianists and organists were not the only jazz players to find the style appealing. Saxophonists Stanley Turrentine, Eddie "Lockjaw" Davis and David "Fathead" Newman, along with guitarists Grant Green, George Benson, Wes Montgomery and Kenny Burrell, enjoyed tremendous success with soul jazz endeavors.

Fusion and Free Funk

The 1970s saw the development of yet another school of jazz, called "jazz/rock fusion." Miles Davis, again in the forefront of a new jazz development, had already laid the groundwork in the previous decade on such albums as *In a Silent Way* and *Bitches Brew*. Fusion married the rhythms of rock and the virtuosity of the jazz soloist. Other champions of fusion included Wayne Shorter (founder of the group Weather Report), drummer Jack DeJohnette, and keyboardist Herbie Hancock. Another type of fusion that gained popularity in the 1970s was "world fusion," which incorporated rhythmic and melodic elements from a variety of international music, most notably Brazilian and other Latin musical styles. Advocates have included Yusef Lateef (who first incorporated Middle Eastern instruments into his music in the 1950s), Don Cherry, and Ronald Shannon Jackson.

Beginning in the 1980s and building on the jazz/rock fusion model, free funk incorporated the rhythms and sounds of urban funk into a horn-driven, free improvisational framework. Ronald Shannon Jackson, James "Blood" Ulmer, and Jamaaledeen Tacuma—all one-time Ornette Coleman disciples—have been among its best practitioners.

The Return to Traditionalism

In the early 1980s, many younger musicians began turning back to the rich, earlier tradition of jazz for inspiration. These included the gifted trumpeter Wynton Marsalis (also an expert classical player) and several other remarkable musicians from New Orleans, among them Wynton's older brother Branford Marsalis (tenor and soprano saxophones), trumpeter Terence Blanchard, and alto saxophonist Donald Harrison. These players rejected both "fusion," with its elements of electronics and rock, and the practices of "free jazz" and instead looked to the bebop tradition, Louis Armstrong and Duke Ellington for inspiration.

As a way of highlighting their return to earlier jazz traditions, these younger players developed "repertory jazz" in the late 1980s. This refers to the institutional resurrection and performance of big band compositions and arrangements. Wynton Marsalis directs the most notable of these ensembles, the Lincoln Center Jazz Orchestra. It specializes in the music of Ellington and other earlier jazz masters. The Smithsonian Jazz Masterpiece Ensemble, jointly directed by David Baker and Gunther Schuller, two master musicians with classical as well as jazz training, also concentrates almost exclusively on performing the composition of early jazz masters in so called "authentic" styles.

The proponents of traditionalism, the so-called "young lions" of jazz, persisted in their return to jazz roots during the 1990s. Wynton Marsalis has served as a sort of godfather to this group of musicians. Tenor saxophonist Joshua Redman, son of former Ornette Coleman saxophonist Dewey Redman, is one of the most commercially successful of these "young lions." The younger Redman brought his style of hard bop to its largest audience ever—an audience that worships him as a rock star. Other successful players from this school include trumpeter Roy Hargrove; alto saxophonist Antonio Hart; drummer Winard and trumpeter Phillip Harper; bassist Christian McBride, guitarist Mark Whitfield, pianist Marcus Roberts and saxophonist James Carter, whose ever-expanding repertoire incorporates early jazz, funk, and avant-garde. These performers have brought jazz to the attention of its broadest audience in decades through re-affirmation of bop and earlier jazz. This re-affirmation led to the first-ever, all-jazz, music cable channel, BET Jazz, in 1996. Yet some older jazz artists worry that the reluctance of the younger generation to innovate or challenge the musical status quo does more harm than good to the genre. But, at the same time, many of these older musicians are seeing their careers revitalized, largely thanks to those same up-and-comers that they criticize.

Neoclassicism

While their origins are vastly different from those of the "young lions," the many gifted players who emerged from Chicago's 1960s Association for the Advancement of Creative Music (AACM) have also arrived at a similar approach to preserving the accomplishments of their "traditions." In such groups as the Art Ensemble of Chicago, the World Saxophone Quartet, and Lester Bowie's Brass Fantasy, musicians from the AACM school continued to refine their take on free jazz through the 1970s and 1980s, eventually creating a style often called neoclassicism. Neoclassicism applies the freedoms gained through the free jazz movement to more structured compositions. Important neoclassicists have included David Murray, Don Pullen, Roscoe Mitchell and Henry Threadgill. The AACM scene has remained vital, led by, among others, composer and saxophonist Edward Wilkerson.

Acid Jazz

In the mid-1980s disc jockeys (also known as DJs) working in British dance clubs resurrected and began spinning classic soul jazz recordings for their young audiences. Utilizing the more obscure cuts from soul jazz and other "dismissed" jazz explorations such as Miles Davis's electric albums, Donald Byrd's *Black Byrd,* and Herbie Hancock's *Headhunters,* DJs such as Gilles Peterson spawned what became known as the "acid jazz" movement. Albums by the British Hammond B-3 player James Taylor and labels such as Acid Jazz Records in the late 1980s furthered the return to groove-oriented music. The label released a series of compilation albums titled *Totally Wired,* featuring soul jazz

obscurities with overdubbed rhythm and solo tracks created by "acid jazz artists." Other acid jazz artists emerged, including Galliano, Young Disciples, Urban Species, the Stereo MCs, MC Solaar, and Courtney Pine. Acid jazz broke into the mainstream in 1991 when the Brand New Heavies released their first album; it generated several hit singles which, in turn, triggered acid jazz communities around the world.

Jazz Vocalists

Although thought of as primarily an instrumental art form, jazz has a strong vocal tradition. Louis Armstrong started the tradition in 1926 with his jazzy "scat"—substituting nonsense syllables in place of a song's lyrics, approximating the sound of a musical instrument— rendition of "Heebie Jeebies." Armstrong was also a superior interpreter of popular songs and recorded some of the first jazz ballad treatments of several classics, including "Body And Soul" and "Stardust." Other early jazz singers included Cab Calloway, Fats Waller, Ella Fitzgerald and Billie Holiday. Each one had a distinctive style. Holiday recorded a number of records in the mid- and late-1930s that established a beautiful balance between the singer and her instrumental accompanists. Holiday is often cited as the foremost jazz singer of all time.

Although they primarily made their mark as instrumentalists or bandleaders, Louis Armstrong and Billy Eckstine both enjoyed considerable success as crooners over the course of their careers. Joe Williams, a true vocal giant, got his start in the 1930s, and worked with Count Basie in the 1950s. He was responsible for re-establishing Basie's band before the American public with "Everyday I Have The Blues." In the late 1950s the vocal trio of Dave Lambert, Jon Hendricks, and Annie Ross rose to national prominence with their recording *Sing a Song of Basie.* The trio perfected and popularized "vocalese," the art of putting lyrics to a previously recorded jazz solo. In the 1980s, an artist with a similar vision, Bobby McFerrin, blasted onto the scene. His 1984 release *The Voice* made history as the first major label jazz album recorded entirely without accompaniment or overdubbing. A vocal improviser in the truest sense of the word, McFerrin veered away from jazz later in his career. Will Downing, Jon Lucien, and Kevin Mahogany picked up the slack in the 1990s, with Mahogany gaining recognition as the leading figure among them. The vocal sextet Take 6, known for mixing elements of jazz, gospel, and pop, also enjoyed popular success.

The women vocalists, however, have always left the most lasting marks on the jazz vocal tradition. Such giants as Billie Holiday and Ella Fitzgerald emerged in the 1930s, building upon the success of the big band and swing movements. The crop of female vocal stars that followed as bebop took over included Sarah Vaughn, Carmen McRae, Nancy Wilson, and Betty Carter. Carter, with her fertile imagination and amazing technique, applied bop and post-bop techniques to her vocalizing. Dee Dee Bridgewater was one of the few jazz singers to break out of obscurity in the 1970s. Since the 1980s, however, jazz vocals have made a comeback with the emergence of Diane Schuur, Diana Krall and Dianne Reeves, all of whom draw from classic jazz vocalists: Ella Fitzgerald, Carmen McRae, Nat Cole and Ethel Waters. Indeed, to many younger jazz fans these women represent what jazz is. Other currently popular jazz vocalists include Cassandra Wilson, Nnenna Freelon and Shirley Horn.

Spoken Word Jazz and Jazz Rap

As previously discussed, the roots of jazz include work songs, gospel songs, field hollers, and other vocal traditions. While most histories of jazz have focused on the music's instrumental aspects and mainstream jazz vocalists, few have paid attention to the use of spoken word in jazz.

One of the first persons to combine the more modern forms of jazz music with the spoken word was Langston Hughes (1902–1967). An leader of the African American movement in the first half of the twentieth century, Hughes wrote eloquently about both jazz and the blues. In 1958 jazz musician Charles Mingus released *Weary Blues*, an album that featured Hughes performing his poetry. Hughes was also a songwriter, and artists such as Betty Carter, Eric Dolphy, Abbey Lincoln, Taj Mahal, and Nina Simone have performed his songs.

While primarily known for his 1960s essays about jazz and his poetry, Amiri Baraka has also been an active participant in the spoken word and jazz movement, contributing his voice and poetry on albums by Malachi Thompson and David Murray. With a focus on Afro-centric social commentary and feminism, poet and percussionist Jayne Cortez has released a number of fine albums from the 1970s through the 1990s. Similar in approach but aligned more with the avant-garde movement is Amina Claudine Myers. A pianist with ties to the AACM in Chicago, Myers's vocal work draws heavily from the spoken word tradition.

Gil Scott-Heron, a poet who has had considerable success in jazz, rap, and R&B, has also released numerous albums featuring his poetry and music. Beginning with his 1970 release *Small Talk at 125th & Lennox*, which was fashioned with legendary jazz producer Bob

Gil Scott-Heron, a poet with successes in the music world.

Thiele, and through his mid-1990s albums, Scott-Heron's work has always been revealing and poignant. Ishmael Reed is similar to Scott-Heron in many ways, but he focuses on African American evolutionary prose and poetry in combination with Latin-flavored jazz.

In the 1990s two other spoken word and jazz artists emerged on the New York scene. Sekou Sundiata, a Harlem native who teaches English literature at the New School for Social Research, combines his African American consciousness poetry with soulful and jazzy music on his 1997 debut *The Blue Oneness of Dreams*. In a similar vein, Yonkers poet Sha-Key released her jazz and soul-tinged debut album *A Headnaddas Journey to Adidiskizm* in 1994.

The hip-hop world has also discovered. Initially focused on vocalizations or "raps" over beats "scratched" from vinyl records and later derived from electronic sampling, rap music began linking with jazz in the late 1980s. In 1988 the band Stetsasonic sampled fusion pianist Lonnie Liston Smith's track, "Talkin' All That Jazz." The band Gang Starr issued its debut single "Words I Manifest" with a Charlie Parker line as the main melody. In 1990 Gang Starr, along with Branford

Marsalis, Terence Blanchard and Kenny Kirkland, contributed the spoken word/jazz track "Jazz Thing" for the soundtrack to Spike Lee's movie *Mo' Better Blues*.

The late 1980s also saw the rise of Afro-centric/native tongue movement led by hip hop pioneer Afrika Bambaataa. The Jungle Brother's 1988 release *Straight out the Jungle* featured several jazzy textures, and the following year the release of the group De La Soul's debut album *3 Feet High and Rising* further showcased the molding of jazz and rap influences. These two early groups were followed by A Tribe Called Quest, whose album *The Low End Theory* featured jazzy moods and textures along with samples from guitarist Grant Green and the bassist Ron Carter. By 1993 the trio known as Digable Planets released their album *Reachin' (A New Refutation of Time and Space)*, which featured samples from Eddie Harris, Sonny Rollins, and Art Blakey. Following this release the group mounted a tour that featured the pioneering use of live jazz musicians in place of the sampling.

Responding to the prevalence and popularity of hip hop artists using jazz samples in their music, Blue Note Records granted a British production duo named US3 exclusive license to use samples from its catalogue in mid-1993. In early 1994 the duo had a top ten hit with "Cantaloop (Flip Fantasia)," based on samples from Herbie Hancock's "Cantaloupe Island." The most successful fusion of live jazz and rap came in mid-1993 on an album called *Jazzmatazz*. Featuring Roy Ayers, Courtney Pine, Lonnie Liston Smith and the stylings of Gang Starr's rapper Guru, the album was a true synthesis of the two styles. Other such projects followed, including *Stolen Moments: Red Hot + Cool*, Branford Marsalis's *Buckshot Lefonque*, and work by the rap band The Roots.

♦ WOMEN IN BLUES AND JAZZ

While most singers and musicians playing blues on the rural porches and in the taverns of the South were men, women were fulfilling a large role in blues history through other channels. In fact, the first big recording stars of blues were women, performing a style that eventually came to be known as "classic blues." The first blues recording made by a singer was "Crazy Blues," recorded in 1920 by Mamie Smith for Okeh Records. Sales of this record in the black community were significant and quickly led to the formation of Okeh's "Race Record" series, featuring recordings made by and for black consumers. Other labels soon started race record series and several new labels sprang up specifically to record black artists. Record company scouts began scouring cities in search of female blues singers, even as many singers starting singing either blues or popular songs with the word "blues" in the title. Record companies and promoters began marketing many fine singers such as Ethel Waters and Mamie Smith as blues singers even though their repertoire was centered more in popular music. True classic blues singers included Ida Cox, Victoria Spivey, Sippie Wallace, Bessie Smith and Ma Rainey.

Before achieving widespread fame, all of these women got their start in the "tent shows" of the South. These shows traveled to rural locations and did indeed take place in a large, outdoor tents. In urban areas the performances took place in theaters or similar venues. Once a singer achieved fame, she traveled with her own tent and provided an entire show featuring comics, up-and-coming singers, acrobats and a chorus line. During the heyday of classic blues from the mid-1920s to the early 1930s, six or seven piece jazz combos usually backed female singers. A black-formed and owned association called the Theater Owners Booking Association, or TOBA, linked a number of venues around the country into a circuit for black artists.

The Great Depression effectively scuttled the elaborate touring shows of the 1920s and the TOBA circuit. By the early 1930s many of the classic blues singers had re-tooled their repertoires, changed careers or worked piecemeal, struggling to earn a living. Bessie Smith, until her unexpected death in 1937, appeared with big bands and sang fewer blues. Ma Rainey and Sippie Wallace tilted towards gospel music, Ethel Waters appeared in films and spent her later years singing gospel music. Still others, like Alberta Hunter, who inaugurated Paramount Record's race series by recording her composition "Downhearted Blues" in 1921, maintained a parallel career in the theater and also worked as a nurse.

The tradition of women singing the blues continued over the next generations with performers such as Dinah Washington, who became a star with Lionel Hampton's jazz band in 1943. Helen Humes rose to prominence with Count Basie's orchestra in the late 1930s. Both women performed as singles for most of their careers and also included popular material in their repertoire. Many other women blues singers worked in jump blues bands, while others some sang smooth, sexy ballads in trios styled after pianist Nat "King" Cole. Etta James, who counts Billie Holiday as one of her idols, and Koko Taylor, who developed her style after that of Bessie Smith, are among the prominent blues vocalists of the last few decades. As the blues sound percolated into other forms of pop music, listeners could hear its traces in the gospel-inspired voices of such soul and rock artists as Chaka Khan, Tina Turner, and most notably, Aretha Franklin.

Women in Jazz

Woman instrumentalists in jazz during its first decades were uncommon, and woman bandleaders were rare. Those women who did learn to play an instrument generally played the piano and often played for church related activities. This is in accord with an African tradition that held that strings or piano were appropriate for women but horns or drums were better suited for men. Not surprisingly, Lil Hardin Armstrong and Mary Lou Williams, two of the best-known women jazz instrumentalists, were pianists. All-woman bands ("girl bands") were usually regarded as a novelty even though many of the women were excellent musicians and played technically demanding arrangements; some were superb soloists. Women occasionally were featured with male groups, for example the trumpeter/vocalist Valaida Snow, or led male bands, like Lil Hardin Armstrong and pianist Edythe Turnham. Some, like pianist Dorothy Donegan (1924–1998) spent most of their careers as solo performers. Donegan studied with the legendary Art Tatum and, like Tatum, had prodigious technique. In 1943 she became the first woman, as well as the first African American, to play Chicago's Orchestra Hall, sharing the bill with Vladimir Horowitz. In 1992 Donegan was honored with the NEA's American Jazz Master award following trombonist Melba Liston's receipt of the award in 1987. Other notable women instrumentalists before 1940 include trumpeters Ernestine "Tiny" Davis and Dolly Jones.

By the 1940s there were over 300 girl bands across the country, but only a fraction of them made records. The International Sweethearts of Rhythm is generally regarded as one of the best all-girl bands. Originating at the Piney Woods Country Life School in Piney Woods, Mississippi in 1937, the band achieved considerable success which led to a USO tour in 1945. They disbanded in the late 1940s. The Sweethearts left behind some radio broadcast acetates and also some film performances.

By the 1950s women instrumentalists had become more common; male-female jazz combos raised few eyebrows. Detroit's Dorothy Ashby brought the sounds of the harp to bebop, making her first record as a leader in 1956 and recording nine more albums as leader over the next 14 years. Along similar lines, Alice Coltrane (nee McCloud) played in her husband John Coltrane's last group and then went on to record several albums in the late 1960s and 1970s that featured her distinctive piano, harp, organ and composing skills. During the 1980s, the all-woman band Straight Ahead was judged on its musical merits and in the mid-1990s Diva, an all-woman big band, offered a swinging interpretation of the genre.

There are many female jazz stars, including violinist Regina Carter, pianists Renee Rosness, JoAnn Brackeen and Geri Allen, saxophonist/bandleader Jane Bunnett and Jane Ira Bloom, and drummers Cindy Blackman and Terri Lynn Carrington to name only a few. Women playing jazz still face particular issues—as do women in most occupations—but they enjoy a more level playing field than their predecessors.

Perhaps the most successful female jazz instrumentalist to date was pianist, composer and arranger Mary Lou Williams (1910–1981), a musician who adapted her style through every jazz era from ragtime to avant-garde. In 1930 Williams joined Andy Kirk's Twelve Clouds of Joy as its pianist; her swinging and adventurous arrangements sparked the band. Williams arranged for many bandleaders, including Benny Goodman, Earl Hines, and Duke Ellington. In the early 1940s she had her own band featuring a young Art Blakey on drums; she championed and interacted with the younger musicians who developed bebop. During her later career Williams created a foundation to assist musicians, ran her own record label, and was a university professor—all while continuing to compose and perform.

Lil Hardin Armstrong (1898–1971) was a college-educated pianist who made her mark playing in King Oliver's Creole Jazz Band in the early 1920s. She helped her then-husband Louis Armstrong make important career choices, led all-girl and male bands in the early 1930s, and was house pianist at Decca Records in the mid 1930s. Lil worked mainly as a solo pianist around Chicago in her later years and spent time in Europe. She remained active and popular until her sudden death in 1971.

Another fine instrumentalist to emerge in the early 1980s was drummer Cindy Blackman, a classically-trained percussionist who has worked with Jackie McLean, Sam Rivers, and Joe Henderson, in addition to releasing four of her own albums.

Having launched her recording career in 1982, pianist and composer Geri Allen has since released a dozen albums featuring such players as Oliver Lake, Ornette Coleman, Lester Bowie, Betty Carter, Ron Carter, and Dewey Redman. As an indication of her artistic excellence, Allen became the first woman to win the Danish Jazzpar Award in 1996.

Finally, violinist Regina Carter has continued to enjoy considerable success in the 1990s after her involvement with the highly respected, Detroit-based, all-female group Straight Ahead. A talented player with a beautiful tone, it has been suggested that Carter has the potential to become the most significant new violinist in jazz since Jean-Luc Ponty in the late 1960s.

◆ JAZZ EDUCATION

In jazz's earliest years, musicians learned how to play it by emulating the elders they most admired, many of whom had formal musical training. In black communities jazz and many jazz bands were often family affairs that included both immediate and extended family members. For example, both tenor saxophonist Lester Young and bassist Oscar Pettiford learned to play while in their respective family bands.

Both grade and high school teachers have provided significant educational pathways. These teachers themselves received training in college or other formal settings; each teacher usually developed a personal teaching approach that helped create regional stylistic differences. Early teachers cited in jazz literature include Major N. Clark Smith in Kansas City, Missouri and Lloyd Reese in Los Angeles.

Recordings, too, were an essential means for early students to learn jazz. Students could study stylistic details of an admired musician's solo by slowing down the phonograph and learning a solo literally note by note.

The key method of learning jazz, however, was by playing in a local band. Seated alongside seasoned musicians, younger players could learn by careful listening and diligent practicing. Bands often contained established musicians who enjoyed helping youngsters; for example, bassist Milt Hinton learned how to improvise from trumpeter Dizzy Gillespie when both were members of Cab Calloway's orchestra in the late 1930s.

Jam sessions provide significant arenas for transferring information from established players to neophytes. These sessions served as forerunners of formally organized group education activity and hark back to the African traditions of oral and aural history.

Jam sessions may seem like informal affairs, but they are in fact quite structured and controlled. Established players usually determine which newcomers have access to the bandstand. They also usually specify the number of choruses a musician is allowed for his solos, as well as the length of time the neophyte can be on the bandstand.

The newcomer must be familiar with the material and have a basic command of his instrument. Older musicians commonly welcome younger players to sessions and depending upon the youngster's performance may offer praise or criticism, generally in a constructive manner. The neophyte is almost always encouraged to continue learning.

Kansas City jam sessions of the 1930s have taken on legendary status. These often highly competitive gatherings pitted the best players against each other in "cutting contests." The story of tenor saxophone giants Coleman Hawkins and Lester Young trading solos all night long and trying hard to outplay each other by creating music more creative, beautiful or swinging is one of the great stories in jazz lore. Determining the "winner" of a cutting contest depended on who could best sway the opinion of both the crowd and other musicians. But jam sessions today are less significant as a vehicle for teaching jazz.

Formal jazz education goes back at least 80 years to certain college campuses that offered both credit and non-credit courses. Alabama State Normal College was one of the first to offer credited course. Some colleges had dance bands that often toured between semesters to raise money for the school. Students gained practical experience in playing and learned survival skills that helped them survive life "on the road."

Jazz education on campus expanded during the 1940s and several universities, like Alabama State, Tennessee State and the Berklee School (now College) of Music offered credit for jazz ensembles, improvisation and arranging. This expansion continued during the 1950s and 1960s as more than 200 colleges and universities added jazz courses to their curriculum. Instrument companies began sponsoring clinics and school jazz festivals. Today there are thousands of student ensembles and jazz education is an established curriculum at over 500 colleges. Jazz programs now include specialized fields of study, like vocal jazz, rehearsal techniques, performance styles and practices, arranging and improvisation. Many professional or working jazz musicians have become involved in formal education, bringing a different, more real-world perspective to the students. But some professional musicians, like pianist Barry Harris and trumpeter Marcus Belgrave, albeit highly regarded as teachers, generally prefer to work outside the confines of academia. Other musicians, perhaps most notably Art Blakey, Betty Carter and bassist Ray Brown, used their groups as a training ground for promising younger players.

Jazz education has grown apace with the music, and today offers a structured environment in which pupils can master the fundamental skills necessary to play the music. The only drawback to this formalization is a formulaic approach that may stifle individuality.

◆ THE FUTURE OF BLUES AND JAZZ

According to many blues scholars and musicians, contemporary blues music has witnessed a progressive decline in popularity among young African American audiences, whose interests lie in more identifiable musical forms, notably contemporary R&B, rap, and hip hop. At the same time, blues has enjoyed a revival among white, middle-class audiences that frequently attend music festivals and urban nightclubs. Furthermore, despite the emergence of talented newcomers such as Robert Cray, Lucky Peterson, Corey Harris, and Keb' Mo', veteran artists have few apprentices to whom they can pass along their knowledge and skills. Thus, the future of contemporary blues music will be determined by both old and new practitioners' ability to gain greater popularity, notably among African American audiences, and train and inspire emerging artists, while preserving the rich traditions of this important American musical form. As long as human beings live, love, fight and strive, they will get the blues or, as blues great Willie Dixon put it, "The blues is the facts of everyday life." The question is whether the means of expressing those facts in the 21st century will remain within the blues genre.

Jazz continues to influence many forms of music and is now accepted as one of the world's great art forms. Ironically, Jazz, and jazz musicians, are often accorded greater status in countries other than the United States. After a long and remarkable period of intense innovation, the music seems to have reached a point where it is taking stock of its past while looking to the future with such dynamic styles as acid jazz, spoken word jazz, and jazz rap. Certainly, there is no shortage of talented younger musicians who want to play jazz. The only shortage may be an audience for their improvisations.

Whatever the next century may bring, the story of jazz is one of the most remarkable chapters in the history of the twentieth century artistic creativity. Filmmaker Ken Burns' 2001 documentary on the history of jazz won wide acclaim for telling a complex story in a generally cogent manner. Born in the crucible of slavery, jazz has become the universal song of freedom. Perhaps Thelonious Monk put it best when he said, "jazz and freedom go hand in hand."

♦ BLUES AND JAZZ COMPOSERS, MUSICIANS, AND SINGERS

(To locate biographical profiles more readily, please consult the index at the back of the book.)

Muhal Richard Abrams (1930–)
Pianist, Composer, Bandleader

Born September 19, 1930 in Chicago, Abrams began his professional career in 1948, playing with many of the city's best musicians and bands. In 1961, he formed the Experimental Band with Roscoe Mitchell, Eddie Harris, and Donald Garrett, which soon became an informal academy for Chicago's most venturesome players. Under Abram's quiet but firm guidance and

with the addition of Henry Threadgill, Joseph Jarman, Fred Anderson, and Steve McCall, the academy grew into the Association for the Advancement of Creative Music (AACM). The AACM helped young musicians perform and promote their own music, which could not be presented through established venues. Mitchell and Jarman, along with Lester Bowie, Malachi Favors, and Don Moye, later achieved worldwide prominence as the Art Ensemble of Chicago.

Though he never so appointed himself, Abrams was the recognized leader and moral and spiritual force behind the AACM. In 1976, Abrams moved to New York where he performed with Anthony Braxton, Leroy Jenkins, and others and began a long term relationship with the Italian Black Saint label with whom he released 16 albums as leader or co-leader, bringing him national and international recognition. In 1990, he was the first recipient of the prestigious Danish Jazzpar Award, and subsequent recordings include, *Family Talk* (1993), *One Line, Two Views* (1995), and *The Visibility of Thought* (2001).

"Red" Allen (1908–1967)
Trumpeter

Born in New Orleans January 7, 1908, Henry "Red" Allen Jr. learned to play trumpet in his father's brass band at an early age, moving on to play in such famous Crescent City bands as that of George Lewis (1923), John Handy (1925), and the riverboat bands of Fate Marable (1926). Allen joined King Oliver's band in St. Louis in 1927, traveling with Oliver to New York, before returning to Fate Marable's Band in 1928, where he was discovered by representatives of the Victor recording company looking for a performer to compete with Louis Armstrong. Through this association Allen recorded with the Luis Russell band (1929–1932) as lead trumpeter before moving to the bands of Fletcher Henderson (1933–1934) and the Mills Blue Rhythm Band (1934–1937).

After a solo career in which he, along with Louis Armstrong, set the standard for the swing era style of trumpet playing, Allen returned to Russell's band in 1937 before leaving again to record New Orleans style traditional music with Jelly Roll Morton and Sidney Bechet. In the 1940s and 1950s, Allen adapted his style to play with Coleman Hawkins, Pee Wee Russell, J.C. Higginbotham, and others.

Red's early playing, like Armstrong's, over time developed into a fluid, light style that took advantage of the trumpet's timbral range. In early years he used trills, smears, growls, and splattered notes that later inspired free jazz players. His later playing reflected a movement away from traditional and swing styles to tight knit combo style playing with blues influences. The hallmark of Red's playing was that he always sounded "modern" in whatever context he was playing as aptly demonstrated on his 1957 LP *World on a String*.

Lil Armstrong (1898–1971)
Pianist, Singer, Composer

Lillian Hardin Armstrong was born in Memphis, Tennessee, in 1898 but her family moved from Memphis to Chicago somewhere around 1914 or 1915. Hardin was a classically trained musician who received her music education at Fisk University. One of her first jobs was selling sheet music in Jones music store in Chicago. Legend has it that she met Jelly Roll Morton while working there, and it was Morton who influenced her style of hitting the notes "real heavy." She joined Freddy Keppard's band while still in her teens and joined King Oliver's Creole Jazz Band in 1920, where she met her husband Louis Armstrong, who was then second trumpet. Lil and Louie were married in 1924. She led her own band with Louis in 1925 and went on to play and write music for many of Armstrong's Hot Five and Hot Seven concerts and recordings from 1925 to 1928.

The Armstrongs were divorced in 1932, but Lil continued working as an accompanist with such players as Red Allen and Zutty Singleton until she led a series of all-star groups for Decca Records from 1937–1940. In 1952 she went to Europe, appearing with Sidney Bechet and as a solo artist. She returned to the United States in the early 1950s and continued playing until her death. Two of her songs, "Bad Boy" and "Just For a Thrill," became big hits in the 1960s. While playing at a tribute to Louis Armstrong at Chicago's Civic Center Plaza, Lilian Armstrong collapsed and died of a heart attack on July 7, 1971, one day after Louis's death.

Louis Armstrong (1901–1971)
Trumpeter, Singer

Born August 4, 1901, in New Orleans, Louis Armstrong was not only the most influential instrumentalist and vocalist in jazz history, but quite simply, one of the most famous people of the twentieth century.

Raised by his mother in New Orleans's Third Ward, Armstrong was arrested on December 31, 1913, for firing a pistol in the street and was sent to the Colored Waifs Home. It was there that he first learned to play the cornet. His skill increased with the experience that he gained from playing in the Home's band. When he was finally released from the institution, he was already proficient enough with the instrument to begin playing for money.

Befriended by his idol and mentor Joe "King" Oliver, Armstrong quickly began to develop his jazz skills. When Oliver left for Chicago in 1919, a place opened for Armstrong as a member of the Kid Ory band in New Orleans. In 1922, Oliver asked Armstrong to join him in Chicago as second cornet with his Creole Jazz Band, and it was here that Louis made his first appearance on a jazz recording in 1923.

With his skills and reputation growing, Armstrong left Chicago in 1924 to join the Fletcher Henderson band at the Roseland Ballroom in New York City. After a long tour with Henderson, he returned to Chicago in late 1925 to play with the Erskine Tate Orchestra, switching from cornet to trumpet, the instrument he played from then onward. During the next four years he made a series of recordings titled Louis Armstrong's "Hot Five" or "Hot Seven," which showcased his brilliant technique, swinging style, and improvisational ability. These recordings also featured other great players such as pianist Earl Hines, trombonist Kid Ory, and drummer Baby Dodds.

In 1929, Armstrong returned to New York and, in the revue *Hot Chocolates*, scored his first triumph with a popular song Fats Waller's "Ain't Misbehavin'." This success was a turning point in his career, leading Armstrong to begin fronting big bands and to play and sing popular songs rather than blues or original instrumentals.

With his fame growing Armstrong returned to New Orleans in 1931 and in 1932 headlined at the London Palladium, where he acquired the nickname "Satchmo" as a result of the garbling of a previous nickname in a review in London's *Melody Maker* magazine. From 1933 to 1935 he toured Europe returning to the United States to film *Pennies from Heaven* with Bing Crosby. He continued to evolve from the status of musician to that of personality-entertainer, and his singing soon became as important as his playing. In 1947, he formed a sextet that was an immediate success, and he continued to work in this context for the rest of his career, touring throughout the world.

Armstrong continued to develop his multifaceted career appearing in numerous movies, at Newport and other major festivals, and scoring highly in a new phenomenon, music polls. He scored a tremendous success in 1964 with his recording of "Hello, Dolly!", which bounced the Beatles from the top spot on the Top 40 list, a great feat in the age of rock. His style, melodically and harmonically simple compared to those of avant-garde and then free jazz, evolved little, and his improvisations grew more infrequent. Yet his warmth and genuine appeal never faded. Though his health began to decline, he kept up his heavy schedule of international touring. When he died in his sleep at home in Corona, Queens, two days after his seventieth birthday, he had been preparing to resume work in spite of a serious heart attack suffered some three months prior. "The music—it's my living and my life" was his motto.

Louis Armstrong's fame as an entertainer in the later stages of his extraordinary career sometimes made people forget that he remained a great musician to the end. More than any other artist, Louis Armstrong symbolized the magic of jazz, a music unimaginable without his contribution. "You can't play a note on the horn that Louis hasn't already played," said Miles Davis. "I mean even modern." In addition, such contemporary musicians as Wynton Marsalis echo that opinion. As evidence of his lasting influence, in 1988, on the strength of its use in the film *Good Morning Vietnam* Armstrong's recording of "What A Wonderful World" became a surprise hit, climbing to number 11 on the Billboard chart.

"Count" Basie (1904–1984)
Pianist, Bandleader

Born August 24, 1904, in Red Bank, New Jersey, William James Basie received his musical training from his mother and by picking up rudiments watching the pit bands at Harlem movie theaters. He later took informal organ lessons from Fats Waller (often crouching beside Fats in the Lincoln Theater in Harlem) before debuting in the early 1920s as an accompanist to various vaudeville acts. In 1927 Basie was stranded in Kansas City when the vaudeville act he was touring with disbanded. Remaining in Kansas City in 1928 he joined Walter Page's Blue Devils with Jimmy Rushing as the vocalist, melding his New York stride style to the hard-riffing Kansas City sound. After this Page's band broke up, Basie joined the Bennie Moten band, and after Moten's death in 1935, formed his own band around the core of the Moten group. While playing at the Reno Club in Kansas City, William was soon dubbed "Count" by a local radio announcer.

At the urging of critic John Hammond, Basie brought his group to New York City in 1936, and within a year he had cut his first record and was well on his way to becoming an established presence in the jazz world. The Basie trademark was his rhythm section, which in the early years featured Basie's own clean, spare piano style, the drumming of "Papa" Jo Jones, and the bass work of Walter Paige. Outstanding soloists such as saxophonist Lester Young and trumpeter Harry "Sweets" Edison and original arrangements by Basie and other band members added to the band's distinctive sound.

Throughout the 1940s Basie maintained his big band that featured a steam of outstanding soloists including

Illinois Jacquet and J.J. Johnson. Financial constraints led Basie to a small band format with Clark Terry, Wardell Gray, and Buddy DeFranco for the years 1950 and 1951 before he returned to the big band format that he maintained for the rest of his career. In addition to maintaining a rigorous and successful international touring schedule, the Basie band scored two hits in 1955 with "April in Paris" and "Everyday I Have The Blues," featuring the vocals of Joe Williams. In 1957 his band became the first American band to play a royal command performance for the Queen of England and the first African American jazz band ever to play at the Waldorf Astoria Hotel in New York City, completing a 13-week engagement at the hotel. Basie and his band remained active and popular until his death on April 26, 1984.

The legacy of the Count Basie band is far reaching. His rhythm sections keep the pulse strong and propulsive yet uncluttered, providing the perfect springboard for soloists. Basie's own spare piano style laid the groundwork for modern jazz pianists, and the light, airy, and swinging sound of Lester Young's saxophone influenced virtually all jazz players to follow.

Sidney Bechet (1897–1959)
Saxophonist, Clarinetist

Born May 14, 1897, in New Orleans, Sidney Bechet began playing clarinet at age six and by his late teens had played with many of the early New Orleans bands including those of Freddie Keppard and "King" Oliver. After a short stay in Chicago, Bechet relocated to New York where he eventually joined Will Marion Cook's Southern Syncopated Orchestra for a tour of Europe. About this time Bechet began playing the soprano saxophone, which became his signature sound and allowed him to standout in ensembles as only trumpet players had prior been capable. The group received rave reviews, and one such review by conductor Ernest Ansermet resulted in Bechet becoming the first individual jazz player to be seriously accepted as a distinguished musician.

During the early 1920s Bechet made a series of records with Clarence Williams's Blue Five, worked briefly with Duke Ellington (one of his great admirers), Mamie Smith, and others before returning to Europe in the mid-1920s. By this time Bechet's virtuosity and presence as a soloist was unmatched by any other reed player, with Louis Armstrong on trumpet being his only equal. From 1928 to 1938 he worked primarily with Frenchman Noble Sissle, both in Europe and the United States, but saw his popularity decline as the bands of

Count Basie.

Ellington, Basie, and Armstrong gained popular attention. After a Dixieland revival in the late 1930s, Bechet was being hailed once again by critics as a jazz luminary, and in the 1940s he made several records with Louis Armstrong, Jelly Roll Morton, and Earl Hines.

In 1949, Bechet permanently moved to France, where he enjoyed the greatest success of his career and enjoyed celebrity status. He died there of cancer in 1959.

Eubie Blake. *See* **Drama, Comedy, & Dance chapter.**

Art Blakey (1919–1990)
Drummer, Bandleader

Born October 11, 1919, in Pittsburgh, Pennsylvania, Art Blakey was not only one of the greatest drummers

in jazz, he was also one of the music's foremost talent spotters and nurturers. After early experience with Fletcher Henderson (1939) and Mary Lou Williams (1940), he joined Billy Eckstine's (1944–1947) band, where along with Dizzy Gillespie, Charlie Parker, and Miles Davis he took part in the early stirrings of bebop. Known up to that time as a shuffle drummer, Blakey adapted his style to the complex velocities and patterns of bebop and began using triplet figures over 4/4 time. After Eckstine's band dissolved, Blakey worked as a sideman and in his own groups, further developing his style by incorporating African and Afro-Cuban tunings and techniques into his playing.

In 1954 he formed the Jazz Messengers, which met with immediate success. For the next 36 years, Blakey hired and helped to stardom a vast number of gifted players, among them Horace Silver, Lee Morgan, Freddie Hubbard, Benny Golson, Woody Shaw, Wayne Shorter and Wynton Marsalis, to name but a very few.

Blakey had one of the most distinctive sounds in jazz, possessed a near photographic memory for arrangements, and a gift for nurturing talent that produced some of the finest recordings in jazz history.

Jimmy Blanton (1918–1942)
Bassist

Born in St. Louis, Missouri, in 1918, Blanton played with Jeter Pillars and Fate Marable before joining Duke Ellington in 1939. During his short life Blanton made a incalculable contribution in transforming the use of the string bass in jazz. Until his emergence, the string bass rarely played anything but quarter notes in ensemble or solos. By playing the bass more as a horn, Blanton began sliding into eighth- and sixteenth-note runs, introducing melodic and harmonic ideas that were totally new to the instrument. His skill put him in a different class from his predecessors, making him the first true master of the bass and demonstrating the instrument's unsuspected potential as a solo vehicle. Tragically, Blanton died of tuberculosis in 1942.

Buddy Bolden (1868–1931)
Cornetist

Buddy Bolden, a barber by trade, was perhaps the first jazz legend known for his drinking ability, his success with the ladies, and his flamboyant showmanship. Because his career predates the recording of jazz, the evidence of his talent as a cornet player lies in the oral tradition. By 1895 he was leading his own band playing dances, parties, picnics, and by the turn of the century his clear, ringing tone and his use of "blue" phrases and notes was so popular that he was often called upon to sit in with several bands on a single evening. It is unknown whether he applied improvisational techniques to his playing or simply heightened the rhythmic coloring and added melodic embellishments to the jigs, rags, and brass band tunes of the day. What is certain is that his playing and his performance style greatly influenced the players of his day and virtually all of those to follow.

In 1906, Bolden began suffering periods of derangement, perhaps brought on by heavy drinking, and was committed by his family to East Louisiana State Hospital in 1907, where he remained for the last 24 years of his life.

"Big Bill" Broonzy (1893–1958)
Guitarist, Singer

Born Jun 26, 1893, in Scott, Mississippi, William Lee Conley Broonzy was one of a family of 17 who first learned to fiddle on a homemade instrument. Taught by his uncle, he was performing by age ten in church and at social functions before working as a preacher. After a stint with the Army, he moved to Chicago, switched to guitar, and began playing with Papa Charlie Jackson before beginning his recording career with Paramount in 1927. By the early 1930s he was recording hokum and blues and touring with Black Bob and Memphis Minnie as well as working sessions where the powerful new Chicago sound was being developed. He appeared at Carnegie Hall in 1938 for John Hammond's "Spirituals to Swing" series and appeared the following year with Benny Goodman and Louis Armstrong in the film *Swingin' the Dream*. He spent the 1940s barnstorming the South with Lil Green's road show and working in Chicago with Memphis Slim before touring Europe in the early 1950s and developing a worldwide following. He continued to tour and record into the mid-1950s before dying of cancer on August 15, 1958, in Chicago.

Broonzy's impressive musical skill, size and variety of musical repertoire, and influence on contemporaries and their followers make him one of the most important players in blues history. He wrote hundreds of songs including the classics "All by Myself" and "Key to the Highway," and his contributions to the formation of the Chicago blues sound were immense.

Clarence "Gatemouth" Brown (1924–)
Guitarist, Singer

Born April 18, 1924, in Vinton, Louisiana, and raised in Orange, Texas, Clarence "Gatemouth" Brown may have earned his nickname due to his "big as a gate" voice, but it is his guitar wizardry that has earned him a place in the blues pantheon. The son of a Cajun singer who could play accordion, banjo, fiddle, and mandolin, Brown himself became a multi-instrumentalist at an early age. As a youth Brown preferred his father's lively Cajun tunes and the jazz being produced by such musicians as Count Basie and Louis Jordan over the blues. His attitude changed, though, when he was introduced to the jazz-inspired blues of guitar pioneer T-Bone Walker.

Brown's first big break came in 1947, when he was called in as a last-minute replacement for the ailing Walker at a prominent Houston nightclub. The club's owner immediately offered Brown a long-term contract to record for his newly formed label, Peacock Records. Brown recorded more than 50 sides of music for Peacock by 1960, his blistering riffs of string-bending fury inspiring a legion of Texas players such as Albert Collins, Johnny Copeland, and Johnny "Guitar" Watson. Brown's music did not fare well on the rhythm and blues charts though, and only one of his singles "Mary

Clarence "Gatemouth" Brown.

years he often sat in with musicians visiting nearby Philadelphia including Miles Davis and Fats Navarro, both of whom were heavy influences on Brown. He suffered a near fatal car crash in the summer of 1950, but recovered and was soon touring with the R&B band of Chris Powell. He appeared with Tad Dameron and toured Europe with Lionel Hampton's band in 1953. In 1954 he recorded with Art Blakey and so impressed peers and audiences that he soon formed and co-led a group with drummer Max Roach, which included Sonny Rollins on tenor saxophone.

The now legendary Brown-Roach ensemble recorded and performed extensively in 1954–1955, during which Brown's individual style emerged. Often cited for his ability to construct intricate solos akin to those of Dizzy Gillespie, Brown's playing also displayed a bouncy jubilance and soulfulness that defines the post-bop/ hard bop sound. Not just a hot soloist, some of Brown's most compelling work is his masterful feel on ballads. Unfortunately, just as Brown was reaching his creative zenith, he was killed, along with Richie Powell and Powell's wife, in a car crash in the early morning of June 25, 1965.

Raymond Matthews Brown (1926–2002)
Bassist

Born October 13, 1926, in Pittsburgh, Ray Brown studied piano and bass while in high school before playing with Jimmy Hinsley and Snookum Russell in 1944. He moved to New York in 1945 where he played with Dizzy Gillespie, Charlie Parker, and Bud Powell, eventually joining Dizzy Gillespie's big band and making several recordings. In the late 1940s Brown was part of the great Jazz at the Philharmonic (JATP) tours playing with Lester Young and Buddy Rich, among others. In 1948 Ray married Ella Fitzgerald and led a trio for her for a short period of time (Ray and Ella divorced in 1952). In 1951 Brown recorded with Milt Jackson and John Lewis, in what would later become known as the Modern Jazz Quartet, before joining Oscar Peterson's Trio, an association that lasted 15 years. During this time, he and Peterson produced award-winning records and were in constant demand for concerts.

Brown continued to appear on Jazz at the Philharmonic (JATP) recordings, and after leaving Peterson in 1966 he settled in California and began a successful career managing and producing other jazz acts including the Modern Jazz Quartet and Quincy Jones. Brown continued to perform and record, notably a duet with Duke Ellington in 1972, and formed the LA Four in 1974 with Bud Shank and Shelley Mann. During 1976 and 1977, Brown was the musical director of the Concord

is Fine"/"My Time is Expensive" (1949) had nationwide success. But his furious instrumentals, low-down Texas blues, and horn-powered tunes became a foundation of the Texas post-war era. The early 1960s proved to be a difficult time for Brown, so in 1964 he went to Europe, where he toured and recorded widely and attained a sizable following. Rebuilding his career, he returned to the United States when blues began to show signs of resurgence. Despite winning a Grammy Award in 1981 for *Alright Again,* he has never quite become a household name in the United States, although his releases, such as *Standing My Ground* (1989) and *Back to Bogalusa* (2001), have continued to receive acclaim.

Clifford Brown (1930–1956)
Trumpeter, Composer, Bandleader

Born October 30, 1930, in Wilmington, Delaware, Clifford Brown received a trumpet from his father while in high school and studied harmony, theory, trumpet, piano, vibes, and bass with a private teacher. Brown studied mathematics in college, graduating from Maryland State University in 1950. During his college

Summer Festival. He received a National Endowment for the Arts American Jazz Master Fellowship in 1995.

Brown died while on tour in Indianapolis on July 2, 2002 at the age of 75. He is widely regarded as one of the finest jazz bassists in history.

Cab Calloway (1907–1994)
Singer, Dancer, Bandleader, Author

Born Cabell Calloway, III, on December 25, 1907, in Rochester, New York, the second of six children born to an attorney and his teacher-wife. Calloway grew up in Baltimore where he sometimes sang with the Baltimore Melody Boys, and after moving to Chicago with his family, he enrolled in pre-law at Crane College. He appeared in *Plantation Days* at the Loop Theatre with his sister Blanche, who along with older brother Elmer also became bandleaders, and also worked as master of ceremonies and relief drummer at the Sunset Café. In 1928 he took over leadership of an 11-piece band, the Alabamians, which promptly disbanded when its first New York booking at the Savoy Ballroom was a failure. Calloway stayed in New York landing a role in the all-African American revue *Connie's Hot Chocolates*.

Cab Calloway.

In 1929, Calloway took over as leader of another band, the Missourians, where Cab's energetic stage presence ignited the band and its audiences. This group, renamed Cab Calloway and His Orchestra, replaced Duke Ellington's band at the Cotton Club. It was here in 1931 that Calloway, during a radio broadcast, swung into a recently written song called "Minnie the Moocher." According to Calloway, he realized he had forgotten the lyrics and filled in the blanks by scat-singing the first thing that came into his mind: "Hi-de-hi-de-hi-de-ho. Ho-de-ho-de-ho-de-hee." The band played along, the audience hollered back raucously, Calloway had a hit, and his band remained at the Cotton Club for nine consecutive years. It was during this period that Calloway created many of his other signature songs including "Reefer Man" and "Kicking the Gong Around," and he developed his famous scat style of singing. Over the years his band included many great players such as Milt Hinton, Doc Cheatham, Dizzy Gillespie, Ben Webster, Cozy Cole, Mario Bauza, and Chu Berry, all of whom Cab helped in advancing their careers.

After his run at the Cotton Club, Calloway continued to lead his big band, and he also appeared in the 1943 film *Stormy Weather* with Lena Horne. Changing times forced Calloway to disband his orchestra in 1948, and he fronted smaller groups until 1952, when he played the breakthrough role of Sportin' Life in the Broadway revival of *Porgy and Bess*. In addition to continually appearing with jazz bands, Calloway went on to star with Pearl Bailey in the late 1960s all-African American production of *Hello Dolly*, published his autobiography *Of Minnie the Moocher and Me* in 1976, and appeared in the movies *Cincinnati Kid* and the *Blues Brothers*.

Calloway died on November 18, 1994. His official honors include a National Medal of Arts presented by President Clinton. However, his legacy is that of one of the greatest entertainers of all time and as a man who not only withstood the indignities of blatant racism, but inspired, nurtured, and helped promote those with whom he worked.

Benny Carter (1907–)
Saxophonist, Trumpeter, Composer, Bandleader

Bennett Lester Carter, born August 8, 1907, in New York City, is largely a self-taught musician having learned music primarily from his mother. Enrolled in 1925 at Wilberforce College in Ohio to study theology but soon left to join Horace Henderson's traveling band. Late in 1928, he formed his own band which appeared at the Arcadia Ballroom in New York before serving short stints with Fletcher Henderson, Chick Webb, and Charlie Johnson, with whom he recorded in 1929. In 1931 he took the position of musical director for McKinney's

Cotton Pickers and wrote tunes for Benny Goodman before launching his own big band in 1933, which helped shape the language of big band jazz. Alumni of this band include Sid Catlett, Chu Berry, and Teddy Wilson. In addition to his influential work scoring for saxophone sections, Carter had few peers as a trumpeter, appearing as a sideman with Willie Bryant in 1934 before moving to Paris and then London in 1936, where he worked as staff arranger for BBC radio. In 1937 he played a session at a Dutch resort leading an interracial and international big band, the first successful unit of its kind in jazz history.

Returning to New York in 1938, Carter again led his own large and small ensembles including work with Dizzy Gillespie, and in 1944 he moved to Los Angeles where his West Coast band included Max Roach, J.J. Johnson, and Buddy Rich. Carter was the first African American composer to break the color barrier in the Hollywood film studios. He scored many major films including *The Snows of Kilimanjaro*, as well as television shows including *Mod Squad*. During the 1950s and 1960s Benny wrote and arranged for Sarah Vaughn and Abbey Lincoln while continuing to record and perform with his own projects. Carter received an honorary doctorate in music from Princeton University in 1974, and in 1988, he toured Europe, visited Japan with his own band, performed in Brazil for the first time in his career, and recorded three albums. In 1996, Carter was honored with the Kennedy Center Awards for Lifetime Achievement. Carter's recorded legacy documents his talents as a composer-arranger and his alto sax playing which, along with that of Johnny Hodges, remains as one of the most important influences of the 1930s.

Betty Carter (1930–1998)
Jazz Singer

Born Lillie Mae Jones in Flint, Michigan, on May 16, 1930, the jazz vocalist performed under the name Lorene Carter until given the nickname "Betty Bebop" by Lionel Hampton, a moniker that evolved into Betty Carter. As a child, Carter had studied piano at the Detroit Conservatory of Music and became fascinated by jazz while in high school. After entering talent contests and touring small clubs in Michigan and Ohio, Carter began performing with nationally known musicians as they toured the area.

Ultimately, she attracted the attention of swing bandleader Lionel Hampton, who hired her for regular engagements with his band beginning in 1948. Carter performed with the band despite her preference for the more modern sounds of musicians like Dizzy Gillespie. Musical disagreements eventually led to her dismissal

by Hampton in 1951, but not before she had made a well-received appearance at Harlem's Apollo Theater.

After touring small jazz clubs on the East Coast during the early 1950s, Carter began to make a name for herself by carving out a distinctive style. She recorded the album *Meet Betty Carter and Ray Bryant* in 1955. In 1958, she recorded *Out There*, and followed it with the well-received *The Modern Sound of Betty Carter* in 1960. After recording a duet album with Ray Charles—*Ray Charles & Betty Carter* (1961)—that received national recognition, she continued to record, but like many jazz musicians in the 1960s, she saw her career suffer during the ascendancy of rock music.

Despite pressures to release more commercially viable albums, Carter continued to perform and record in the sometimes inaccessible bebop style that she cultivated and loved. During this time, she formed her own label, Bet–Car, and gradually built her audience back up. She performed a New York stage show, *Don't Call Me Man*, in 1975, and appeared at the Newport Jazz Festival in 1977 and 1978. In the 1980s, Carter signed a contract with Verve Records that included the label's rerelease of Bet-Car recordings. Her albums include: *At the Village Vanguard* (1970), *Now It's My Turn* (1976), *Whatever Happened to Love?* (1982), *Look What I Got* (1988), *It's Not About the Melody* (1992), and *I'm Yours, You're Mine* (1996). Widely respected for her artistic integrity and influence, during the 1990s Carter relished her role as a senior figure in jazz, and geared her focus toward jazz education. She died in Brooklyn, New York, on September 26, 1998.

Clifton Chenier (1925–1987)
Singer, Accordionist

Born on June 25, 1925, in Opelousas, Louisiana, Clifton Chenier is generally regarded as the "King of Zydeco," the dance music that combined Cajun two-step and waltzes with blues licks that arose from Louisiana's black French-speaking Creoles. The son of accordionist John Chenier, Clifton took up the instrument at an early age and by the time he was 17 years of age, he and his brother, Cleveland, who played the rub board, were playing weekend gigs.

By the early 1950s Chenier had formed the Hot Sizzlers, a seven-piece combo with electric guitar, piano, tenor sax, bass, and drums added to the brothers' instruments, drastically changing the direction of the music. Chenier was eventually discovered by a talent scout and signed to the Elko record label in 1954. The first session yielded "The Louisiana Stomp" which had some success, but Chenier moved to the Specialty Records label a year later. His first big hit was "Ay, 'Tit Fille" in 1955, which sold well throughout the South and made it to the rhythm and blues charts. Chenier quickly became a big attraction in the Gulf Coast region and toured with Etta James and Jimmy Reed, but elsewhere remained relatively unknown.

Chenier moved to Houston in the early 1960s, where he was "rediscovered," this time by Chris Strachwitz of Arhoolie Records. He released his first album *Louisiana Blues and Zydeco* on Arhoolie in 1964 and recorded a number of dates for Arhoolie and other labels. In the 1970s and 1980s, Zydeco suddenly experienced something of a renaissance, and Chenier was its point man. He became a fixture on college campuses across the United States and eventually toured Europe as well. Although his health began failing in the 1980s, Chenier continued to work until his death on December 12, 1987.

Charlie Christian (1916–1942)
Electric Guitarist

Born in Dallas, Texas, and raised in Oklahoma City, Charlie Christian studied with his father and played in combos around Oklahoma. Jazz critic John Hammond heard Christian in 1939 and recommended him to Benny Goodman (Hammond's brother-in-law), and Christian soon joined Goodman's sextet. Charlie Christian did for the electric guitar what Jimmy Blanton did for the bass, achieving great fame as the first electric guitarist to play single-string solos. For the first time in jazz, a guitar could be heard over the other players and could move from being strictly a rhythm section instrument to a lead instrument. He revolutionized jazz in other ways as well, where sitting in after hours at such Harlem clubs as Minton's with Charlie Parker, Dizzy Gillespie, Kenny Clarke, and Thelonious Monk, Christian participated in the birth of bebop. Tragically, he did not live to enjoy the huge success of the bebop style that he helped create, for in 1941 Christian was hospitalized with tuberculosis and died on March 2, 1942, at the age of 25.

"Klook" Clarke (1914–1985)
Drummer

Born January 9, 1914, Kenneth Spearman Clarke—later known as Liaqa Ali Salaam—was part of a musically inclined Pittsburgh family. Clarke studied vibes, piano, and trombone, as well as musical theory and gained his early professional experience with Roy Eldridge and Edgar Hayes, traveling to Finland and Sweden with Hayes in 1937. In 1939–1940, Clarke played with Teddy Hill before the remnants of that band became the house band at Minton's in Harlem. There, working with Dizzy Gillespie, Charlie Parker, Thelonious Monk, Bud Powell, and Charlie Christian, Clarke helped

develop the early sounds of bebop. It was during this time that Clarke developed his influential style, shifting the basis of timekeeping from the bass drum to the ride cymbal, then using the bass drum and snare to interject accents against the beat, earning him the nickname of "Klook" or "Klook-mop." In addition to his work at Minton's, Clarke also toured with Louis Armstrong and Ella Fitzgerald, played with Benny Carter in 1941–1942, spent a year and a half in Chicago with Red Allen, and led his own band fronted by Coleman Hawkins.

After a stint in the military beginning in 1943, Clarke returned to New York and recorded with virtually all of the bebop players, notably with Dizzy Gillespie in 1946. In 1951, he toured with Billy Eckstine, and in the following year he helped organize the Modern Jazz Quartet, where he remained for the next three years. He moved to France in 1956 where he worked with visiting American talents like Bud Powell and Miles Davis, and co-led a fine "big band" with Belgian pianist and arranger Frency Boland from 1961 to 1972. In addition to his influence on jazz drumming, Clarke is known for co-writing the bop classics "Salt Peanuts" with Dizzy Gillespie and "Epistrophy" with Thelonious Monk. Clarke died on January 26, 1985, in Paris, France.

Nat "King" Cole (1917–1965)
Singer, Pianist

Nathaniel Adams Cole was born on March 17, 1919, in Montgomery, Alabama (The family name was Coles, but Cole dropped the "s" when he formed the King Cole Trio years later.). When he was five, the family moved to Chicago, and he was soon taking piano lessons and playing organ and singing in the church where his father served as minister. While attending Phillips High School, Cole formed his own band and played with other small combos. He made his recording debut in 1936 with Eddie Cole's Solid Swingers, headed by his bassist brother Edward with accompaniment by two other brothers, Fred and Isaac.

Cole soon joined the touring revue *Shuffle Along* and, after the show folded, he found work in small clubs in Los Angeles. In 1939 he formed the King Cole Trio with guitarist Oscar Moore and bassist Wesley Prince. The trio played radio shows, worked nightclubs and recorded for Decca, increasing its popularity with the recording of "Sweet Lorraine" in 1940.

Moving to Capital Records in 1943, the trio recorded "Straighten Up and Fly Right," a national hit selling more than 500,000 copies. The trio's popularity was soaring and in addition to their success with recordings they appeared in two movies and in the first Jazz at the Philharmonic (JATP) concert. Starting with the hit

Nat "King" Cole.

"The Christmas Song" in 1946, Cole begin adding string sections to his records, diminishing his piano playing and focusing on his singing. In 1948–1949 his trio was the first African American jazz combo to have its own sponsored radio series. By the time "Mona Lisa" hit number one in 1950, Cole was an international star.

Over the next decade Cole appeared in a number of movies, toured the world, and in 1956–1957 hosted his own television show. Sadly, the show was canceled due to the lack of a national sponsor in a time of pervasive racism. Cole's career continued to soar until his death of lung cancer in 1965.

Ornette Coleman (1930–)
Saxophonist, Trumpeter, Violinist, Composer

Born on March 9, 1930, in Fort Worth, Texas, Ornette Coleman began his musical career in carnival and R&B bands. Fired by R&B guitarist-singer Pee Wee Crayton for his unconventional style of playing, Coleman eventually settled in Los Angeles, making his living as an elevator operator while studying harmony and theory textbooks on his own time. He began to compose, sat in

jam sessions, and made his first album in 1958. Encouraged by John Lewis, who recommended him for a scholarship to Gunther Schuller's Lennox School of Jazz in the summer of 1959, Coleman and his quartet—Don Cherry, pocket cornet; Charlie Haden, bass; Billy Higgins, drums—opened at the Five Spot in Manhattan in the fall of 1959. The appearance stirred up a firestorm of debate among jazz musicians, critics, and fans. These debates were so furious, some resulting in Coleman being physically threatened, that in 1962 he withdrew from public appearances.

Coleman's music, while abandoning traditional rules of harmony, tonality, and the basing solos on chord changes, obviously was not the senseless noise as some heard it. In fact, the music of the first Coleman quartet, which made many recordings, was very melodic, had a strong blues feeling, and, in retrospect, sounds not so startling. He continued to go his own way in music, teaching himself to play trumpet and violin (the latter left-handed and amplified) and in 1965 his "comeback" saw the unveiling of a system he called "harmolodic," which gave equal weight to harmony, melody, and "the instrumentation of the movement of forms." Eventually, Coleman was accepted by many of his peers, evidenced by his being named a Guggenheim fellow in 1967, and some of his compositions are now considered jazz standards.

In the 1970s, Coleman composed and performed a long work for symphony orchestra and alto sax, "The Skies of America," and debuted Prime Time, a kind of jazz-fusion band with two electric guitars and two drummers. The original quartet was triumphantly reunited at the 1989 JVC Jazz Festival and also recorded again that year.

Coleman's music has influenced many players, most notably Dewey Redman, Steve Coleman, Miles Davis, and James Ulmer. Yet, his music remains a very personal means of expression; as such, it has much beauty and feeling to offer the open-minded listener. In 1993, a box set of Coleman's works entitled *Beauty Is a Rare Thing* was issued. The following year, Coleman, the father of free jazz, received a prestigious MacArthur fellowship, the so-called "genius award." In 1998, Coleman was named Jazz Artist of the Year in the Down Beat International Critics Poll, and he continues to release recordings and makes infrequent performance appearances.

John Coltrane (1926–1967)
Saxophonist, Bandleader

Born September 23, 1926, in Hamlet, North Carolina, John William Coltrane was taught to play clarinet by his father before studying alto saxophone in high school. After graduating, he moved to Philadelphia and studied music at the Ornstein School and played cocktail gigs. After playing in a Navy band in Hawaii in 1945–1946, he started his professional career with R&B bands, joining Dizzy Gillespie's big band on alto saxophone in 1949. When Gillespie broke up the band in 1950 and scaled down to a sextet, he had Coltrane switch to tenor sax and kept him.

After stints with two great but very different alto saxophonists, Earl Bostic and Johnny Hodges, Coltrane was hired by Miles Davis in 1955. At first, some musicians and listeners did not care for what they felt was Coltrane's "harsh" sound, but as the Davis Quintet became the most popular jazz group of its day, Coltrane was not only accepted but began to influence younger players, recording his first albums as leader. Coltrane's mounting drug problems forced Davis to release Coltrane in 1957. Returning to Philadelphia, Coltrane underwent a spiritual reawakening and kicked his drug habit, returning to New York later that year to work with Thelonious Monk. It was during this brief period with Monk that Coltrane began being admired as an innovator as his sound became harmonically "dense." Coltrane began inserting ever more complex chord progressions every two beats as opposed to every measure or two, playing sixteenth notes in the process, and his famous "sheets of sound" style emerged.

Rejoining Miles Davis in 1958, Coltrane participated in the influential *Kind Of Blue* record date, and Miles's experiments with modal improvising (i.e., playing on scales rather than chord changes) set the stage for Coltrane's future work as a leader. In 1959 Coltrane composed and recorded "Giant Steps" from the album of the same name, a piece so harmonically intricate and fast that it staggered most of his fellow saxophonists and propelled Coltrane into superstardom. Coltrane left the Davis group in the spring of 1960 and formed his own group that included pianist McCoy Tyner, bassist Steve Davis, and drummer Elvin Jones. In 1961 this group released the album *My Favorite Things*, featuring the show tune of the same name in a performance that featured his soprano sax and lasted nearly 14 minutes, sparking an renewed interest in the soprano sax and modality. The quartet, with rotating bassists, became one of the most tightly knit groups in jazz history; the empathy between Coltrane and Elvin Jones was astonishing, and in their live performances, the four musicians would sometimes play a single tune for more than an hour, creating music so intense that some listeners compared it to a religious experience.

Still eager to explore new and more challenging territory, Coltrane began experimenting with African and Middle Eastern song forms, unusual instrumentation, and complex arrangements by Eric Dolphy. Two albums from this period, *Africa/Brass* and *Live at the Village Vanguard* feature "Trane," as he was now being called, improvising over bass and drums (no piano) and incorporating braying, squawking, and split tones to convey the emotion of the tunes. Just as Ornette Coleman, Coltrane was moving away from the constraints of melody, steady rhythm, and chord progressions in favor of primal drones and vamps that required his rhythm sections to rethink their roles. He continued to explore these themes, along with more traditional renderings of popular tunes, on numerous releases throughout the early 1960s.

Coltrane was himself a deeply spiritual man and in 1964 he released one of his masterpieces, the suite *A Love Supreme*, an offering of music and poetry that reflects Coltrane's inner peacefulness in the face of the storm of his other musical offerings. But by mid-1965 Coltrane was fully immersed in the avant-garde, free-jazz movement, and albums from this period such as *Ascension* feature three and four saxophonists where minimal thematic material is interspersed with long stretches of collective improvisation. Coltrane had carried the music to where the point was not the notes, but the sounds with which they were voiced. Seemingly on the cusp of breaking further musical ground, Coltrane died of liver cancer on July 17, 1967.

Turiya Alice Coltrane (1937–)
Pianist, Harpist, Composer, Bandleader

Born August 27, 1937 in Detroit Michigan, McLeod began studying classical music at age seven, learning to play both piano and harp. She expanded her skills playing organ in church and playing with R&B bands while in high school before becoming a member of local groups led by Kenny Burrell and Yusef Lateef. McLeod traveled to Paris in 1959 to study with Bud Powell followed by a stint recording and touring with Terry Gibbs. She met saxophonist-composer John Coltrane in 1962, and they were married in 1965. She then replaced McCoy Tyner as pianist in John Coltrane's group the following year and played with Coltrane until his death in 1967.

Coltrane continued her investigation of composition and arrangement and after converting to Hinduism, she began combining classical Indian instrumentation with jazz and classical musical forms. She collaborated with such jazz veterans as Pharoah Sanders, Joe Henderson, Ornette Coleman, and Rashied Ali and released several albums as leader in the late 1960s and throughout the

1970s. Her recording output and performance appearances diminished during the 1980s and 1990s, but in 2002, Coltrane released *Eternity* on the Sepia Tone label.

Miles Davis (1926–1991)
Trumpeter, Composer, Bandleader

Born Miles Dewey Davis Jr. on May 25, 1926, in Alton, Illinois, Davis's family moved to East St. Louis in 1927 where his father, a prominent dentist and substantial landowner, gave him a trumpet for his 13th birthday. Davis played in the high school band and studied with Elwood Buchanan, who encouraged him to develop the warm, vibrato free tone that later became Miles's trademark. In the early 1940s Davis met local star Clark Terry and sat in with his idols Charlie Parker and Dizzy Gillespie when they passed through St. Louis with the Billy Eckstine Band. In 1945, his father sent Miles to the Juilliard School of Music in New York, but within a short time Davis was working the 52nd Street clubs with Charlie Parker and Coleman Hawkins, recording with Parker for the first time in November 1945. In 1946 Parker and Davis left for California where

Miles Davis.

they split (Parker ended up in a sanitarium) and after playing with Charles Mingus, Davis joined the band of Billy Eckstine, bringing him back to New York.

Davis recorded again with Charlie Parker upon Parker's return to New York in 1947, but Davis and drummer Max Roach left in 1948 to pursue a new approach. The new project, a nine–piece band including Lee Konitz, Gerry Mulligan, and John Lewis was short lived, but its recordings had great impact on musicians. Employing such non-traditional instruments as french horn and tuba and using arrangements of rich, complex harmonies and a "cooler" less frenetic sound, the group launched the "cool jazz" movement. The project had no commercial success and the sessions that were recorded were not released in full until years later.

In 1950–1951 Davis recorded his first records for the Prestige label, the first free from the restrictions of the four minute 78 rpm disc and also featuring the playing of both Sonny Rollins and Jackie McLean. Around this time, Davis's addiction to heroin began hampering his career and resulted in erratic behavior that forced his release from the label. He recorded for Blue Note and again with Prestige before kicking his habit in 1953 by moving home, locking himself in a room, and going cold turkey for two weeks. He returned to New York in early 1954, recording two dates with Horace Silver, Percy Heath, and Art Blakey and with a slightly different group a few weeks later that introduced a new Davis style. By infusing his "cool" playing with the hard drive of the blues, these recordings signaled the beginnings of the "hard bop" style of jazz.

More success followed when in 1955 Davis formed a quintet with John Coltrane, Philly Joe Jones, Red Garland, and Paul Chambers that released a flurry of classic records for both Prestige and Columbia Records. Unfortunately drug problems resurfaced, this time with other members of the band, and the group disbanded for good in 1957. Meanwhile, Davis changed his focus again and he made his first record with arranger Gil Evans, *Miles Ahead*. This was followed by two other collaborations with Evans, *Porgy and Bess* and *Sketches Of Spain*, both landmarks in jazz for their lush and innovative arrangements that set off Miles's haunting trumpet solos. In 1958 Davis formed a sextet with Cannonball Adderley on alto sax, Bill Evans on piano, and the return of John Coltrane on tenor. The group recorded several sessions highlighted by the album *Kind Of Blue*, which established modal improvisation in jazz and set the stage for Coltrane's later explorations on his own.

Over the ensuing six years, Davis continued to introduce new ideas and give exposure to new talent. By 1964, he had Wayne Shorter on saxophones, Herbie

Hancock on piano, Ron Carter on bass, and the sensational 18-year-old Tony Williams on drums. This group, Miles's second great quintet, introduced many new ideas, mostly in the realm of rhythmic and harmonic freedom, and over the next three years released a slate of classic albums, most notably *Miles Smiles*. However, in 1968 Davis got restless again, and attracted by the possibilities of electronic instruments, incorporated three electric pianos played by Hancock, Chick Corea, and Joe Zawinul. New bassist Dave Holland, along with John McLaughlin on electric guitar, filled out the ensemble resulting in the albums *In a Silent Way* and *Bitches Brew*, which ushered a new style—jazz fusion. Davis continued to experiment with this style through 1975 when poor health forced a six-year retirement. He returned to performing in 1981, followed shortly by experiments with hip hop and rap before dying on September 28, 1991.

Miles Davis changed the style of his music more often than any other jazz musician of his stature, influencing the course of jazz history and creating controversy with each change. Yet his instrumental abilities, his eye for talent, and his unique personal vision mark him as one of the greatest jazz musicians in history.

Willie Dixon (1915–1992)
Guitarist, Singer, Songwriter

Born July 1, 1915, in Vicksburg, Mississippi, Willie Dixon was selling his songs to local bands by the time he was a teenager, singing with the Union Jubilee Singers. Afterwards he moved to Chicago, won the Illinois State Golden Gloves Championship, and recorded for Bluebird with his group, the Five Breezes, before being jailed for a year as a conscientious objector for refusing military service. By 1945 he was playing bass guitar for late night jam sessions with Muddy Waters and others and was hired as a session bassist by Chess Records in 1948.

As staff writer, arranger, and bass player, Dixon's work was primarily featured on other artists's cuts. When Muddy Waters recorded "Hoochie Coochie Man," followed by Howlin Wolf on "Evil," and Little Walter on "My Babe," Dixon's career as a songwriter was launched. Dixon became the label's tunesmith, recording manager, and bassist until the mid-1960s. Dixon also worked as musical director for a series of American folk-blues festivals in Europe, and Dixon's music caught on with British rock bands such as the Yardbirds and the Rolling Stones. After his association with Chess ended in the late 1960s, Dixon recorded *I Am the Blues*, a collection of his best-known songs, and organized the Chicago Blues All-Stars for tours of Europe, achieving fame in his own right. In the mid-1970s, realizing that he was not receiving his share of song royalties, he sued ARC Music (Chess's publishing company) and artists such as Led Zeppelin for copyright infringement and regained the rights to his songs as well as financial compensation. During the 1980s Dixon helped other artists regain rights to their songs, was the first producer/songwriter honored with a boxed-set retrospective of his career, and published his autobiography. He suffered from poor health later in the decade, losing his leg to diabetes, before dying on January 29, 1992 in Burbank, California.

Willie Dixon's life and enormous body of work are a cornerstone of the blues. He is one of the first professional blues players to gain recognition and success as a songwriter, producer, and performer. His songs and style inspired generations of American and European artists in both the blues and rock and roll genres. Quite simply, Willie Dixon is one of the most important figures in blues history.

Eric Dolphy (1928–1964)
Alto Saxophonist, Clarinetist, Flutist

Born in Los Angeles June 20, 1928, Dolphy took up alto sax in high school. After a 1950–1953 stint in the army, Dolphy first gained recognition with the Chico Hamilton quintet of 1958 to 1959, playing with the band at the 1958 Newport Jazz Festival. In 1960 he moved to New York where he collaborated with Charles Mingus and played club dates with trumpeters Booker Little and Freddie Hubbard. Dolphy was featured on Ornette Coleman's groundbreaking 1960 album *Free Jazz* before his 1961–1962 stint with John Coltrane, where his arranging skills were featured on Coltrane's *Africa/Brass* release. While on tour with Mingus in 1964, Dolphy decided to stay in Europe, where he recorded with Dutch, Scandinavian, and German rhythm sections. He died suddenly in Berlin on June 24, 1964, of a heart attack possibly brought on by diabetes.

Although he died at age 36, Dolphy's impact on jazz was substantial. He was greatly admired by fellow musicians and was honored with numerous awards including *Down Beat* magazine's New Star award for alto, flute, and miscellaneous instruments in 1961. Dolphy produced a sizable body of work due to a prolific recording schedule—from April 1960 to September 1961 he played on 13 recording sessions—while creating a style that extended bop into new harmonic territory leading to free jazz. As well, his mastery of bass clarinet and flute legitimized them as jazz instruments.

Teddy Edwards (1924–)
Saxophonist, Composer

Born April 26, 1924, in Jackson, Mississippi, Theodore Marcus Edwards came from a musical family, his father and grandfather both musicians. Edwards began as an alto player, bouncing between Tampa, Florida, and Detroit, and touring with Ernie Field's orchestra before joining Roy Milton's band in Los Angeles in 1945. Shortly thereafter, he joined Howard McGhee's group and switched to tenor sax. On such classic McGhee recordings as "Up In Dodo's Room," Edwards's helped to define the sound of tenor saxophone in the emerging bebop movement.

During the 1940s and early 1950s, Edwards played with many different artists including Benny Carter, Max Roach, Clifford Brown, Dodo Marmarosa, Dexter Gordon, and Gerald Wilson, helping fashion the West Coast bop sound. In the early 1960s he made some outstanding recordings as leader, playing with Howard McGhee and Phineas Newborn Jr. In the late 1960s and 1970s he composed and arranged for television, radio, and film before reviving his career in the 1990s through work with Tom Waits. Edwards is known for his big, warm sound that work well with bluesy ballads and on soaring solo flights.

"Little Jazz" Eldridge (1911–1989)
Drummer, Trumpeter, Singer

Born January 30, 1911, in Pittsburgh, David Roy Eldridge played his first "job" at the age of six on drums. When he was 15 and had switched to trumpet, he ran away from home with a carnival band. After playing with some of the best bands in the Midwest, he arrived in New York in 1930, impressing the locals with his speed and range and finding jobs with good bands. He made his first record in 1935 with Teddy Hill, and by the next year he was starring in Fletcher Henderson's band. In 1937 he put together his own group and recorded as leader for the first time, introducing a trumpet style influenced by Louis Armstrong, but which assimilated the longer lines and fluid articulation of reed players such as Coleman Hawkins and Benny Carter. Eldridge's style would have a profound influence on the bop players to follow, Dizzy Gillespie in particular.

In 1941, Roy, now known in the world of music as "Little Jazz," joined Gene Krupa's big band as trumpeter and singer, becoming the first black musician to be a featured player in a white band (Teddy Wilson and Lionel Hampton were member's of Benny Goodman's band, but not as featured players). Eldridge's duet of "Let Me Off Uptown" with singer Anita O'Day scored a smash hit for Krupa while his instrumental feature "Rockin' Chair" was hailed as a jazz classic. When Krupa's band dissolved in 1943 Eldridge led his own big band for a while, but joined Artie Shaw in 1944. In the late 1940s he was starring in the Jazz at the Philharmonic (JATP) tours, playing with Charlie Parker, Lester Young, and Buddy Rich. A 1950 tour with the Benny Goodman sextet brought Eldridge to Paris, where he stayed for 18 months. During this time his career was stalled due to the advent of bebop and the trumpet innovations of his former disciple Gillespie.

In the 1950s Eldridge backed Ella Fitzgerald and toured with Jazz at the Philharmonic (JATP) and enjoyed a long association with Coleman Hawkins in addition to making a number of solid recordings throughout the 1960s. A full decade, from 1970 and onward, found Eldridge leading the house band at Jimmy Ryan's club in New York City, but a heart attack in 1980 put an end to his trumpet playing, though he still worked occasionally as a singer and gave lectures and workshops on jazz. He died on February 26, 1989. Often thought of as a stylistic bridge between Louis Armstrong and Dizzy Gillespie, Roy Eldridge's innovations and virtuosity on the trumpet qualify him as an equal.

"Duke" Ellington (1899–1974)
Bandleader, Composer, Pianist

Edward Kennedy Ellington, nicknamed Duke in his teens for his dapper dress style and courtly manners, was born into a middle-class family in Washington, DC, on April 29, 1899. Duke began playing piano at 7 years of age and by age 18 had formed his first band, Duke's Serenaders, and written his first composition "The Soda Fountain Rag." Duke was offered an art scholarship at Pratt Institute in New York, but he already had a taste of band leading and preferred to stay with music. Although he had some success in his hometown by 1923, he felt the urge to go to New York, where careers were made. Initially he did not succeed, but by 1924 he was leading his band renamed the Washingtonians at Club Hollywood and appearing on weekly radio broadcasts. In 1927 the young pianist-composer opened a five-year stint at the Cotton Club, the most famous Harlem night spot.

It was at the Cotton Club that the unique Ellington style evolved as Duke began composing in earnest, producing "Mood Indigo," "Tiger Rag," "The Mooche," and "Black and Tan Fantasy." Their outrageous "Jungle Nights," arranged and overseen by Duke, brought in huge crowds. Unlike most other bands, Ellington's band played mostly his own music and kept the same players with him. He had a great sense for their potential—almost as a great coach knows how to develop an athlete's skills—and many of Duke's bandmates who joined him during this time stayed with him for decades (none longer than baritone saxophonist Harry Carney, in the band from 1927 until 1974). Many became stars in their own right (ex., Johnny Hodges, alto sax; Cootie Williams, trumpet; and Barney Bigard, clarinet), but somehow they always sounded better with Ellington, who knew just what to write for what he called their "tonal personalities."

In 1932 the Ellington band left the Cotton Club and began touring, and in 1933 a larger version of the band completed their first European tour, where they were enthusiastically received. Back home, the band continued to record (Duke being one of the first musicians to truly understand the importance of records, and the fact that making good ones required something different than playing in public) and released such hits as "Solitude," "Sophisticated Lady," and "In a Sentimental Mood." In 1935, deeply touched by the death of his mother, Ellington composed "Reminiscing in Tempo," his longest work to date; most of his output, however, was tailored to the time limit of a little over three minutes imposed by the 78 rpm technology.

In 1939 the addition of three key players, tenor Ben Webster, bassist Jimmy Blanton, and associate composer-arranger Billy Strayhorn (who would stay with Duke until his death in 1967), propelled the band to new heights. With these additions and until a recording ban went into effect in August 1942, the Ellington band produced a string of classics including Strayhorn's "Take the A Train" and "Chelsea Bridge," along with Ellington's "Jack the Bear" and "Bojangles." In 1943 Ellington initiated what would become an annual appearance at Carnegie Hall where he presented his first extended work *Black, Brown and Beige*. The end of the war and the close of the big band era caused the orchestra to struggle with many personnel changes, but Ellington's royalty money kept the band on the road and by the early 1950s the band was back in top form.

A second peak was reached in 1956, when the band gave a tremendous performance at the Newport Jazz Festival. The show, which was recorded, was highlighted by "Crescendo and Diminuendo In Blue," featuring 27 choruses by tenorman Paul Gonsalves, and the 7,000 strong audience nearly rioted. Ellington once again enjoyed renewed popularity appearing on television, touring Europe in 1958 and 1959, playing all the major jazz festivals, and scoring for film. In the 1960s, buoyed by U.S. State Department tours, Ellington again began unveiling such compositional masterworks as *Money Jungle* (1962), *The Far East Suite* (1966), and *The Afro-Eurasian Eclipse* (1971).

Ellington and his astonishing creations have been an inspiration to generations of musicians. Most recently, Wynton Marsalis who both in his own composing and in his efforts to get Ellington's music performed live (as with the Lincoln Center Jazz Orchestra) has done much to keep the Elllington legacy in the forefront of American music. There can be no doubt that Duke Ellington, who was also a brilliant pianist, will stand as one of the greatest composers of the twentieth century. Duke died of cancer on May 24, 1974, four weeks after his 75th birthday.

James Reese Europe (1881–1919)
Bandleader

James Reese Europe was born in Mobile, Alabama, on February 22, 1881, but later moved to Washington, DC, where at ten years of age he studied violin with the U.S. Marine Band. In 1904, he moved to New York and worked as a pianist before organizing the New Amsterdam Musical Association. In 1910 Europe formed the Clef Club, a clearinghouse for African American musicians which also had an orchestra that served as an important incubator for future jazz players. Europe had a concert at Carnegie Hall in 1914 that featured 125 singers and musicians, 25 years before Duke Ellington

James Reese Europe with the Army band.

would debut there. During World War I, Europe directed the 369th Infantry Regimental Band, which performed throughout France and was a major force in the development of jazz in that country. Following his return to the United States, Europe toured the United States with his band. In 1919 he was stabbed to death by a member of his band while on tour.

Ella Fitzgerald (1918–1997)
Singer

Born April 25, 1918, Ella Fitzgerald was discovered in 1934 by drummer-band leader Chick Webb at an amateur contest at Harlem's Apollo Theater in New York City. She cut her first single with Webb, now her legal guardian, a year later. In 1936 she recorded her first efforts at "scat" singing. In 1938 she recorded "A Tisket, A Tasket," a novelty number that brought her commercial success and made her name widely known among the general public. She soon became the first jazz vocalist to hold more popularity than the band with which she sang. Webb died in 1939, and Ella led the band for the next year. Among musicians, however, her reputation rested on her singular ability to use her voice as an instrument, improvising effortlessly in a style filled with rhythmic subtleties. Her bell-like clarity and flexibility of range were equally effective on ballads and up-number tunes.

In the mid-1940s Ella worked with Dizzy Gillespie, witnessing the birth of bop, and recorded with Louis Jordan and Louis Armstrong. In 1948 she married bassist Ray Brown, with whom she worked and recorded *Airmail Special* (1952), which featured a mature scat style. In 1955 Ella began working exclusively with Norman Granz. Given more suitable material and better playing opportunities her career soared. She appeared in several films including *Pete Kelly's Blues* (1955) and *St. Louis Blues* (1958), presented her own concert at the Hollywood Bowl and, in celebration of the release of their four LP collaboration, played Carnegie Hall with Duke Ellington in April 1958.

In the 1960s and the early 1970s, Ella toured the world, playing with more than 40 symphonies in the United States alone, until poor eyesight forced her into semi-retirement. In 1995, Fitzgerald was inducted into the National Women's Hall of Fame. Other career highlights include 11 Grammy Awards, Kennedy Center Honors (1979), Whitney Young Award (1984), National Medal of Arts (1987), France's Commander of Arts and Letters (1990), and the Medal of Freedom (1992), in addition to winning *Downbeat* magazine's best female jazz singer poll for 18 consecutive years.

Since the 1970s, she had been in steadily declining health and had been hospitalized for various ailments.

In 1993, her legs were amputated below the knees as the result of complications from diabetes. Ella Fitzgerald died on June 15, 1997. No other vocalist has been so unanimously acclaimed. Fondly known as "The First Lady of Song," she was the leading jazz interpreter of popular song for more than 50 years.

Tommy Flanagan (1930–2001)
Pianist

Born in Detroit in March 16, 1930, Tommy Flanagan traveled to New York in 1956 as part of the "Motor City" invasion of gifted jazz musicians and soon was playing with Charlie Parker, Dizzy Gillespie, and Ben Webster, who recognized his understated but catchy melodic talents. He was much in-demand as a sideman, recording such classic sessions as *Saxophone Colossus* with Sonny Rollins and *Giant Steps* with John Coltrane. Long stints (1962–1965 and 1968–1978) as Ella Fitzgerald's accompanist and musical director (a role he also filled, much more briefly, with Tony Bennett) kept Flanagan out of the limelight. From the mid-1970s on, as leader of his own fine trios and recording prolifically in the United States, Europe, and Japan, his work met with critical acclaim including his receipt of the 1993 Jazzpar Award. Flanagan was widely known as a modernist with a love of lyricism who could also play bluesy lines that swing. He died of an aneurysm in New York City on November 16, 2001 at the age of 71.

"Blind Boy" Fuller (1908–1941)
Singer, Guitarist

Born July 10, 1908, in Wadesboro, North Carolina, "Blind Boy" Fuller was one of the most recorded early blues artists in the Piedmont blues tradition. Unlike his contemporaries, Big Bill and Memphis Minnie, who recorded for decades, Fuller's recordings were completed over a period of six years prior to his premature death at age 33. Fuller was a fine and expressive vocalist and a masterful guitarist who could play in multiple styles including slide, ragtime, pop, and delta blues. Although his career was spent as a street musician and house party favorite, Fuller's National steel guitar can be heard on such hits as "Rag Mama Rag," "Trucking My Blues Away," and "Step It Up and Go." Much of Fuller's repertoire remains a vital part of the Piedmont tradition still played to this day.

Erroll Garner (1921–1977)
Pianist, Composer

Born in Pittsburgh June 15, 1921, Garner grew up in a musical family and began picking out piano melodies

From left to right: Jazz greats Ella Fitzgerald (vocals), Oscar Peterson (piano), Roy Eldridge (trumpet), and Max Roach (drums).

before he was three years old. He started taking piano lessons at six but played all his assignments by ear instead of learning to read notes. At seven, he began playing regularly on Pittsburgh radio station KDKA. He dropped out of high school to play with a dance band and soon arrived in New York in 1944, playing the famous clubs of 52nd Street. From 1945–1949 Garner freelanced recording for numerous labels. It was in that same year that he recorded "Laura" which sold a half million copies, and his fame began to grow. By 1950 he had recorded with Benny Carter, Charlie Parker, Coleman Hawkins, Teddy Edwards, and others. On March 27, 1950, he gave a solo recital at Cleveland's Music Hall, and in December he performed a concert at New York's Town Hall. Garner's most famous composition "Misty" was a big hit in 1959. During the 1960s and 1970s, Garner appeared with orchestras, scored for film, and toured France, South America, and Asia.

A keyboard artist who played and composed by ear in the tradition of the founding fathers of jazz, Erroll Garner won the international acclaim of jazz lovers, music critics, and the general public. Strong and bouncy left-hand rhythms and beautiful melodies are the trademarks of his extremely enjoyable music. Garner was diagnosed with lung cancer, and he died at age 55 on January 2, 1977.

"Dizzy" Gillespie (1917–1993)
Trumpeter, Bandleader

Born October 21, 1917, John Birks Gillespie received his early musical training in his native South Carolina, studying at the Laurinberg Institute from 1932–1935. After moving to Philadelphia in 1935, he joined Frankie Fairfaxes Orchestra before moving to New York and joining the Teddy Hill band, where he replaced his early idol, Roy Eldridge. He stayed with Hill until 1939 when he joined Cab Calloway's band with whom he remained until 1941. Hill became manager of Minton's Playhouse, and Gillespie was soon sitting in with Kenny Clarke, Thelonious Monk, and Charlie Christian for after hours jams where his bop experimentation was already beginning to develop and his career as an arranger began to emerge. In 1942 Gillespie recorded his first "bop" solo with Les Hite before joining Earl Hines's band in 1943. Shortly he and Charlie Parker joined Billy Eckstine's band, with Parker as lead altoist and Gillespie as musical director. After leaving Eckstine's band in 1945, Parker and Gillespie recorded Gillespie's compositions "Shaw Nuff," "Salt Peanuts," and "Hot House," sounding the first salvo of bebop. In 1946 Gillespie, having split with Parker, formed his own big band. The following year he hired Cuban drummer Chano Pozo,

integrating Pozo's Latin clave feel into the bands rhythmic framework and virtually creating Afro-Cuban jazz.

By 1948 Gillespie's trademark goatee, horn-rimmed glasses, and beret were the personifications of bebop, but Gillespie continued to move into new directions. Famed musicians including pianist John Lewis, drummer Kenny Clarke, trombonist J.J. Johnson, and saxophonist John Coltrane all worked with Dizzy until he dissolved the big band in 1949. He then toured the world with smaller ensembles and steadily increased his reputation until by the 1970s and 1980s he was the puckish elder statesman of jazz. Through it all Dizzy's dazzling speed, harmonic ingenuity, and rhythmic flair marked him as genius of the trumpet. His skills as composer, his use of trans-African clave in swing, and his ability to improvise made him one of the true giants of jazz, with many of his compositions now jazz standards. Dizzy died January 6, 1993, in Englewood, New Jersey.

Dexter Keith Gordon (1923–1990)
Saxophonist, Bandleader

Born in Los Angeles on February 27, 1923, the son of a prominent physician whose patients included famous jazz musicians, Dexter Keith Gordon began playing clarinet at seven, switching to alto and then tenor. He joined Lionel Hampton's newly formed big band in 1940. Section work with Louis Armstrong and Fletcher Henderson followed, and in 1944 Gordon cut his first side with Nat Cole. Later that year, he joined the Billy Eckstine band. After freelancing in New York, he returned home and in 1946 recorded a "tenor battle" titled "The Chase" with Wardell Gray, which became one of the biggest modern jazz hits. He sporadically continued to team up with Gray until 1952, when he was imprisoned for two years for heroin possession. His addiction plagued him for much of the next 15 years.

Gordon made a major comeback in the early 1960s with a series of much-acclaimed recordings. His association with the hard bop movement at Blue Note Records, where he worked with Herbie Hancock, Bobby Hutcherson, Sonny Stitt, and Bud Powell, asserted his role as the premier bop tenor stylist. In 1962, he settled and remained in Copenhagen, Denmark, for the next 14 years, although he released two well-received records in the United States in 1969, and he made brief playing visits to his homeland. In 1977, he permanently moved back to the United States, forming his own group and winning many new fans. In 1986, he starred in the French feature film 'Round Midnight, in which his portrayal of a character based on Lester Young and Bud Powell won him an Oscar nomination as best actor.

Gordon was one of the prime movers behind the hard bop revolution of the 1960s and his rich, robust tenor sound never faltered. He never succumbed to straying into fusion or pop, choosing instead to be an expatriate to play for audiences who appreciated pure jazz. Dexter died April 26, 1990, in Philadelphia.

Johnny Griffin (1928–)
Saxophonist

John Arnold Griffin III was born in Chicago in 1928 and played his first gigs with Lionel Hampton's big band (1945–1947) and in the armed services. Griffin moved to New York and in 1956 recorded his first album for Blue Note Records followed by two more records in 1957, establishing his fast and exuberant bop style of playing. Later in 1957 he joined Art Blakey's Jazz Messengers where he met Thelonious Monk with whom he recorded the next year, followed by collaborations with Eddie "Lockjaw" Davis on "tenor battles." In December 1962, he moved to Europe and played all over the continent. He lived in Paris in the late 1960s and later moved to the Netherlands, where he owned a farm. In the late 1970s, Griffin moved back to the United States, celebrating the occasion with outstanding concerts and recordings with his friend, Dexter Gordon. Sometimes called "The Little Giant" because he is a small man with a very big sound, Griffin remains dedicated to the bop and hard bop styles.

Buddy Guy (1936–)
Guitarist

For the generation of 1960s British rock guitarists such as Eric Clapton, Jeff Beck, Keith Richards, and others who learned their techniques listening to blues in the early 1960s, Buddy Guy was the real thing. Although it was not until the 1990s that his playing was adequately captured on tape, Guy represents a direct link between the earlier generation of Chicago blues musicians that included his mentor, Muddy Waters, and the crop of blues and rock and roll guitarists, both black and white, that presently dominate the genre.

Born on July 30, 1936, in Lettsworth, Louisiana, Guy began playing acoustic guitars as a teenager, emulating the work of Southern blues artists Lightnin Slim and Guitar Slim, before working his first gigs in Baton Rouge in the 1950s with Big Poppa John Tilly. He left the South for Chicago in 1957, and quickly made his mark on the local club scene. Before Guy's arrival, blues guitarists usually played sitting down. Guy not only played while standing, but would throw chairs off the stage, abuse his guitar, and wander outside with the aid of a 150-foot cord, increasing his profile immensely.

Guy cut two singles for Cobra Records in 1958, followed by a number of singles for Chess between 1960–1967, where he also backed Muddy Waters and other blues legends such as Howlin' Wolf, Sonny Boy Williamson, and Little Walter. His singles from this period, including "Let Me Love You Baby" and "Stone Crazy," are some of the most popular blues of the period.

Guy's first album for Vanguard, *A Man & the Blues*, in 1968 followed in the same vein, but his following albums failed to do well. As a live act, however, he became a legend, both in the clubs of Chicago and at festivals around the world. In the 1970s Guy began his long and successful collaboration with harmonica player Junior Wells. In 1983 Guy opened his own blues club, the Checkerboard Lounge, on Chicago's South side. He sold the Checkerboard in 1985, then opened another club called Buddy Guy's Legends in 1989. In 1991 Guy issued his first domestic release in ten years, *Damn Right I've Got the Blues*, which won a Grammy Award, as did his next album *Feels Like Rain*. He released the well-received *Sweet Tea* in 2001, and continues to record and tour. Buddy Guy is indeed Chicago's blues king.

Lionel Hampton (1908–2002)
Vibraphonist, Pianist, Bandleader

Born on April 20, 1908 in Louisville, Kentucky, Lionel Hampton was the first jazz musician to feature the vibraphones or "vibes," an instrument that has since maintained a vital role in jazz. Raised in Chicago, Lionel moved to California in 1928 and played drums with the Paul Howard Orchestra. His first recorded effort on vibes was on the 1930s recording "Memories of You," which featured Louis Armstrong, then fronting the Les Hite band in California. Hampton later left Hite's band to form his own Los Angeles group. When Benny Goodman heard him in 1936, he used him on a record date, along with Teddy Wilson and Gene Krupa, and then persuaded him to join on a permanent basis. This decision established Goodman's band as the first to have an inter-racial lineup, a practice Goodman would maintain.

Hampton continued to play with the Goodman Quartet until 1940, the year he formed his own orchestra. In 1942 the band scored its first big hit "Flyin' Home," which featured a screaming brass section over a driving rhythm section and "Illinois" Jacquet's rhythm and blues solo, creating a whole new school of tenor playing. By the mid-1940s the band adopted elements of the bop sound, but Hampton's style remained essentially one of swing. His bands featured the best of jazz including Dinah Washington, Betty Carter, Dexter Gordon, Clark Terry, Art Farmer, Clifford Brown, and

Lionel Hampton.

Johnny Griffin. In addition to his long-standing big band, Hampton ran his own record labels, publishing house, and other businesses. In 1981, he became a professor of music at Howard University, and he was honored in 1995 at the Kennedy Center Concert Hall with a tribute to his work as a United Nations music ambassador. Hampton continued to tour the world until his death on August 31, 2002.

Herbie Hancock (1940–)
Keyboardist, Composer, Bandleader

Herbie Hancock was born in Chicago on April 12, 1940, and received early training as a classical pianist. After he graduated from college in 1960, he played his first Chicago jazz gigs with Coleman Hawkins and Donald Byrd. Moving to New York he recorded two albums with Byrd before getting his own sessions in 1962 with Blue Note. Hancock's world class compositional skills, "soul bop" style, and excellent sidemen (i.e., Tony Williams, Ron Carter, Freddy Hubbard, and Grant Green) define the "experimental" side of Blue Note in the mid-1960s. Concurrently Hancock became a

part of Miles Davis's band (1963–1969), considered one of the top rhythm sections (again with Williams and Carter) and jazz groups of all-time, a tenure that imprinted heavily on Hancock's artistic development.

From 1969–1972 Hancock's sextet cut three fusion albums, recording two influential "electric jazz" albums with Davis (i.e., *Jack Johnson* and *On the Corner*) before releasing his own groundbreaking *Headhunters* (1974), where his blend of pop, funk, and jazz sets the standard for fusion. In his career Hancock has released numerous albums, many which are considered classics (ex., *Takin' Off* and *Maiden Voyage*), and has become one of the most commercially successful and famous jazz musicians ever, although many consider his music more pop than jazz. Hancock has won Grammys both for jazz composition and rhythm and blues performance, a handful of MTV Video Music Awards for the video of his 1984 hit "Rockit" and an Academy Award for best original score in 1986 for the film *'Round Midnight*. He also co-founded the record label Transparent Music in 2000.

His commercial success aside, Hancock is one of the all-time best jazz pianists who works with integrity, creativity, and is consistently attuned to his audience. In addition to his piano and compositional skills, his use of electronics to communicate his vision firmly establishes him as a major jazz figure.

W. C. Handy (1873–1958)
Trumpeter, Composer, Bandleader

Although he began as a cornetist and bandleader in the 1890s, William Christopher Handy's fame as the "Father of the Blues" rests almost entirely on his work as a composer. Handy was born on November 16, 1873, in Florence, Alabama. After studying at Kentucky Musical College, Handy toured with an assortment of musical groups, becoming the bandmaster of the Mahara Minstrels in 1896. During his travels Handy came into contact with many African American music traditions, and the melodies and song forms from work songs and gospel were then merged into his own brass band compositions. Popular legend has Handy "discovering" the blues in a train station in Tutwiler, Mississippi, in 1903 when he heard a singer accompanying himself on guitar and reciting three-line rhyming verses.

In 1909, during a political campaign in Memphis, Handy wrote "Mr. Crump," a campaign song for E.H. "Boss" Crump. Three years later, the song was published as the "Memphis Blues," establishing the blues as an identifiable category of music. In 1914, Handy published his most famous song "St. Louis Blues" and that same year also wrote "Yellow Dog Blues." Others

W. C. Handy, known as "The Father of the Blues," in 1949.

Coleman Hawkins (playing sax).

songs that have become perennial favorites are "Joe Turner Blues" (1915), "Beale Street Blues" (1916), "Careless Love" (1921), and "Aunt Hagar's Blues" (1922).

In the 1920s, Handy became a music publisher in New York. Despite his failing eyesight, he remained active until his death on March 29, 1958. His songs extended beyond the world of jazz to find their way into the general field of popular music in many forms. Their popularity continues unabated today.

Coleman Hawkins (1904–1969)
Saxophonist

Hawkins was born on November 21, 1904, in St. Louis, Missouri. When Hawkins took up the tenor at the age of nine, he had already had four years of training on piano and cello. He continued his studies at Washburn College in Topeka, Kansas, and in 1922 toured with Mamie Smith's Jazz Hounds. In 1923, he began a ten-year stint with Fletcher Henderson's band where his style defined the sound of the saxophone until the emergence of Lester Young in the mid-1930s and later the "cool jazz" sound of Stan Getz in the 1950s.

Hawkins left Henderson in 1934 to tour England and the European continent, recording with Django Reinhardt, Benny Carter, and others. When he returned to the United States in 1939, he recorded his biggest hit "Body and Soul," establishing himself as a national jazz name and revealing a harmonic sophistication equaled at the time by only pianist Art Tatum. Unlike many of his contemporaries, Hawkins was open to the experimentation of the young bop musicians, and in 1944 he formed an all-star band for the first bop record session including both Thelonious Monk and Max Roach in his own bands. During the remainder of his career, Hawkin's led many of his own groups, recorded for several labels, toured regularly, and won numerous awards. Hawkins died on May 19, 1969.

In addition to being an innovator, Hawkins integrated many elements into his playing style: the "slap tongue" attack and influence of Louis Armstrong, the heavy vibrato and legato pace of cool jazz, and the vertical scaler approach of John Coltrane. Given the position occupied by the tenor saxophone in jazz today, it is difficult to imagine that until Coleman "Bean" Hawkins came along, this instrument was not seriously considered as a suitable jazz vehicle. The full, rich tone that Hawkins brought to the tenor has helped make it one of the most vital instruments in the contemporary jazz ensemble.

Roy Owen Haynes (1926–)
Drummer, Bandleader

Born in Boston on March 13, 1926, Roy Haynes began playing professionally during his late teens with Luis Russell's big band and then joining Lester Young's sextet with whom he established his reputation. Settling in New York, he worked with Charlie Parker and Dizzy Gillespie, then toured for several years (1953–1958) in Sarah Vaughan's trio. Haynes has played and recorded with virtually every jazz great from Thelonious Monk, Miles Davis, and John Coltrane to Eric Dolphy, Chick Corea, and Pat Methany, as well as leading and recording his own bands including his Hip Ensemble.

Haynes is both a fantastic soloist and a great, creative ensemble drummer. His playing has influenced generations of players, and his style of placing more emphasis on the interaction between snare and bass drum and less on the ride cymbal was a major departure from earlier styles. His signature tightly-tuned snare drum and rim shots mixed with displaced beats between cymbals and drums are legendary. Recipient of the 1994 Danish Jazzpar Award, Haynes maintains an active recording and touring schedule well into his seventies.

Fletcher "Smack" Henderson (1897–1952)
Bandleader, Arranger, Pianist

Born in Cuthbert, Georgia, on December 18, 1897, Fletcher Henderson traveled to New York in 1920 to study chemistry, but took a job to earn some extra money as house pianist and musical director for Black Swan, the first African American-owned and operated record company. Chemistry soon took a back seat, and in 1924 he was persuaded by some of his recording studio colleagues to audition their band for a new club. The band earned the job and soon graduated to the Roseland Ballroom on Broadway, where they resided for eight years, while also touring and making hundreds of records.

The Henderson Orchestra was the first big band to achieve its reputation playing jazz, and it became an incubator for some of the greatest stars of all time, among them Louis Armstrong, Coleman Hawkins, and Benny Carter. Arranger and saxophonist Don Redman shaped the band's early style. When he left in 1928,

Carter and others including Fletcher's younger brother Horace, also a pianist and arranger, took over. It was not until 1933 that Fletcher himself began to compose full-time for his band. However, he had such a talent for arranging that he soon became one of the architects of swing. Ironically, just as he hit his stride as a composer, his band fell on hard times, forcing him to dissolve it in 1939. Afterwards, Henderson became a freelance arranger for, among others, Benny Goodman, for whom he wrote numerous charts and gained his widest audience. Henderson led another big band from 1941–1947, through which passed such great players as Ben Webster, Chu Berry, and Roy Eldridge. But Henderson was unable to achieve the same level of success as during the 1920s. Late in his career, he worked as accompanist, arranged and played for *The Jazz Train* review, and led a sextet at the Café Society in New York.

Henderson's main legacy to jazz was his work as an arranger, where his simple style of pitting reed against brass sections and the use of swinging voice-blocked passages defined swing music and soon influenced all popular music. Henderson died on December 29, 1952, after a two-year invalidism brought on by a stroke.

Joe Henderson (1937–2001)
Saxophonist, Composer

Born April 24, 1937, Henderson studied music at Wayne State University in Detroit and played jam sessions with Sonny Stitt and visiting stars before forming his first group in 1960. After military service (1960–1962), he traveled to New York where he co-led a band with trumpeter Kenny Dorham and appeared on more than 30 recordings for Blue Note Records from 1963–1968 that encompassed hard bop to avant-garde styles. He joined the groups of Horace Silver in 1964, Miles Davis in 1967, Freddie Hubbard in 1967, and Herbie Hancock in 1969. Beginning in the 1970s, he led his own groups. Henderson experimented with avant-garde structures, jazz-funk fusion, electronic effects, and at times infused his music with political awareness and social commentary. Although an accomplished and prolific composer, Henderson became known for his reinterpretation of standards such as his Grammy Award-winning 1992 album of Billy Strayhorn compositions entitled *Lush Life*.

Henderson was one of the foremost tenor stylists of the post-Coltrane era with an original and influential solo style that featured intense and fiery playing with a polished tone and melodic complexity. Able to float prettily as Stan Getz or to play with the bluesy feel of T-Bone Walker, Henderson's range was broad and his style immediately identifiable. Henderson had not performed publicly since suffering a stroke in 1998. He died in San Francisco, California, on June 30, 2001.

Earl "Fatha" Hines (1903–1983)
Pianist, Bandleader

Born on December 28, 1903, in Duquesne, Pennsylvania, to a trumpeter father and organist mother, Hines studied piano in Pittsburgh in 1914 and formed his own trio while still in high school. He began to play in local clubs with vocalist Lois Deppe before moving on to Chicago in 1923, where he began working with top Chicago bands. In 1926 Hines met Louis Armstrong, and they began recording together brilliant series of records by 1928 with Louis Armstrong's Hot Five. Hines soon became known as "the trumpet-style pianist." The intricacy of his style was well beyond that of his contemporaries, and his style of right-hand single note improvisations over left-hand counter rhythms served as a touchstone for a successive generation of pianists. His work has a brassy quality that is rhythmically intricate and makes great use of tremolos and multiple octaves.

In 1928, Hines formed his own band at the Grand Terrace in Chicago. For the next 20 years, this band served as a proving ground for many great instrumentalists and innovators of the period—from Bud Johnson and Trummy Young in the early era to Dizzy Gillespie and Charlie Parker in the later years. The Grand Terrace gig ended, and from 1948 to 1951 Hines worked again with Armstrong before his career slumped. In 1964, a series of New York recitals revitalized his career, and he enjoyed great success in Europe, Japan, and in the United States until his death on July 22, 1983.

Milt Hinton (1910–2000)
Bass

Milton J. Hinton was born in Vicksburg, Mississippi, on June 23, 1910, and was considered one of the greatest bass players. He played with many top jazz artists including Cab Calloway, Count Basie, Louis Armstrong, Teddy Wilson, and Benny Goodman. Hinton appeared in concerts throughout the world and on numerous television shows, and he recorded prolifically. Known for his warmth of tone and vitality, Hinton was a master of "slapping" the bass and soloing in a thoroughly modern manner. He was also an accomplished photographer and writer whose autobiography *Bass Lines* appeared in 1988. *Over Time: The Jazz Photographs of Milt Hinton* was published in 1992, and

due to the diversity and longevity of his career, it is a valuable glimpse into jazz history. Hinton died on December 19, 2000, in Queens, New York, after an extended illness. He was 90.

Billie "Lady Day" Holiday (1915–1959)
Singer

Born Eleanora Harris in Baltimore, Maryland, on April 7, 1915, the daughter of jazz musician Clarence Holiday who later abandoned her, Billie was singing in Harlem nightclubs by the time she was 15 years old. Discovered by talent scout John Hammond, she was recommended to Benny Goodman with whom she cut her first recordings in 1933, and from 1935 to 1939 she established her reputation with a series of records made with Teddy Wilson. She also sang with her own band and those of Count Basie and Artie Shaw, and her recordings of the late 1930s with Lester Young—who dubbed her "Lady Day"—and Buck Clayton underscore how much her singing resembled the playing of an instrumentalist.

Holiday's voice was sweet, sexy, and full of the blues. Her distinctive behind-the-beat style of singing

Billie Holiday.

and the way she let her voice trailed off for emotional impact set her apart from all other singers. Her landmark 1939 recording of "Strange Fruit," a protest against lynchings, was released despite her own label's, Columbia Records, refusal to even record the tune. In her song "God Bless the Child," she departed from popular material to depict the personal alienation that she had experienced. By the time of her 1944 release of "Lover Man," she had moved from jazz to a more orchestrated pop setting, and the song is often referred to as the definitive sound of Holiday. By the late 1940s, her long-term addiction to heroin had landed her in jail. Although she returned to performing throughout the 1950s, the effect of her hopeless battle with addiction had greatly diminished her voice, if not her expressiveness.

Holiday brought all of her worldly experience to the stage, and her songs display the vulnerability of a woman who had been betrayed by an unjust and harsh world and herself. Holiday died on July 17, 1959, in New York City, less than a month after her appearance at a benefit concert.

John Lee Hooker (1920–2001)
Singer, Guitarist

John Lee Hooker was born in Clarksdale, Mississippi, on August 17, 1920. He first learned his "Delta licks" from his stepfather, Will Moore, and his colleagues, James Smith and Coot Harris. He traveled to Memphis, Cincinnati, and Detroit, where in 1948 he cut a demo for Bernie Besman, owner of the Sensation label. "Boogie Chillen" and "Sally Mae" were on the first single he recorded for the Sensation label. It became a hit on the rhythm and blues chart in 1948. He followed this record with "Crawling King Snake" in 1949 and "In the Mood for Love" in 1951, both of which were chart toppers. Hooker then recorded for several labels under a number of pseudonyms including Delta John, Johnny Lee, and Birmingham Sam and his Magic Guitar Hooker, before landing at Vee Jay Records under his own name from 1955 to 1964. At Vee Jay, Hooker recorded with a full rhythm section that included Eddie Taylor and Jimmy Reed, and he had several successes including "Baby Lee" in 1956, "I Love You Honey" in 1958, and "Boom, Boom" in 1962. Hooker was idolized by British blues bands and was also popular on the folk coffeehouse circuit.

In the 1970s and 1980s, Hooker collaborated with such popular performers as Canned Heat, Bonnie Raitt, and Van Morrison. He also appeared in the film *The Blue Brothers*, starring John Belushi and Dan Ackroyd in 1980. Long recognized as one of the primary contributors to the blues genre, the prolific Hooker has made more than 40 albums, many of which Chess Records reissued in the 1990s. Rhino released *The Ultimate Collection (1948–1990)* in 1991. Hooker died at the age of 83 on June 21, 2001, in San Francisco, California.

Sam "Lightnin" Hopkins (1912–1982)
Singer, Guitarist

Born March 15, 1912, in Centerville, Texas, Sam "Lightnin" Hopkins was one of the most prolific blues artists of all time, both in the recording studio and on stage. Inspired by Texas predecessor Blind Lemon Jefferson, Hopkins built his first guitar out of a cigar box and chicken wire at the age of eight. While still very young, he left home for a life on the road, singing and playing for money throughout Texas. In 1920 he reunited with Jefferson, serving as his guide and learning his musical licks.

During the late 1920s and much of the 1930s, Hopkins played the Houston bar circuit as a duo with his cousin, legendary Texas blues musician Texas Alexander. After working as a sharecropper near Dallas for a few years, he returned to Houston in 1946 and resumed his beer hall career with Alexander. He was soon discovered by a scout from Aladdin Records and teamed with pianist Wilson "Thunder" Smith to create the duo, Thunder and Lightnin. They recorded "Katie May" in 1946, which became a regional hit, and scored another hit with "Shotgun Blues" in 1948.

Hopkins made the rhythm and blues charts several times in the early 1950s for a variety of labels, but Hopkins's popularity declined over the course of the decade as his rustic style did not compete well with rock and roll. In 1959, however, folklorist Mack McCormick rediscovered him. Introduced to a new audience consisting largely of whites, Hopkins was reinvented as a "folk-blues legend," and he quickly attained a level of acclaim that had previously eluded him. Hopkins recorded and toured constantly across the United States, Canada, and Europe throughout the 1960s and 1970s, and he was featured in a number of books and film documentaries. He died of throat cancer on January 30, 1982. As one of the last great country blues musicians, Hopkins style bridged the gap between rural and urban styles.

"Son" House (1902–1988)
Singer, Guitarist

Born on March 21, 1902, in Riverton, Mississippi, Eddie James House Jr. was preaching the gospel in Baptist churches by the time he was 15 years old, as his family wandered between plantations looking for work. He did not pick up a guitar until he was 25 years of age, once saying he did not even like the sound of a guitar. However, after playing a few house parties, earning some money, and discovering corn whisky, he became a blues musician. His new career was interrupted, however, when he was sentenced to a prison term for killing a man during a drunken party. Released two years later though, he hit the road and soon played with Charley Patton. Although the men were completely dissimilar in style and personal attributes, they shared a love for alcohol and the blues, and by the early 1930s Patton had given House entree to a recording opportunity with Paramount. The sides House cut, including "My Black Mama," "Preachin' the Blues," and "Dry Spell Blues," are some of the darkest, gut-wrenching, and rawest blues ever recorded. The recording hardly sold at the time but those who heard them were enthralled, and in 1941 Library of Congress folklorist Alan Lomax visited House to once again record his music. These recordings, mostly solo, but some with a backing string band, where a glimpse into the future of blues as well as rock and roll.

House moved to Rochester, New York, and did not record again until 1964, when guitarist Alan Wilson (later of the blues-rock group Canned Heat) "rediscovered" House. House began touring again, recorded his work, appeared at Carnegie Hall in 1965, and was the subject of a documentary. House fell ill from Parkinson's and Alzheimer's diseases in the mid-1970s, retired from performing in 1975, and died on October 19, 1988, in Detroit, Michigan.

Son House was a major innovator in the Delta blues tradition and, along with his playing partner Charley Patton, he stands at the top of the blues hierarchy. He was a primary inspiration to both Muddy Waters and Robert Johnson, and was one of the most powerful performers in blues, at once spiritual and demonic in delivery and emotional impact.

Howlin' Wolf (1910–1976)
Singer, Harmonica Player

Blues singer and harmonica player Howlin' Wolf was born Chester Arthur Burnett in West Point, Mississippi, on June 10, 1910. When he was 18 years of age, he met guitarist Charley Patton and, although he never matched Patton's prowess on guitar, Patton's influence was seen in Burnett's later growl of a voice and entertaining ability. He learned to play the harmonica from blues musician Aleck "Rice" Miller (Sonny Boy Williamson II) who married his half-sister Mary, and by the end of the 1930s he was playing local juke joints. After a four-year stretch in the Army he settled down as a farmer and by 1948 was a radio personality in West Memphis, where he and guitarist Willie Johnson debuted their electric band. He made his first recording in 1951 for Sam Phillips where his baying style of singing won him the name Howlin' Wolf, and by 1953 he was picked up by the Chess label in Chicago.

At Chess Howlin' Wolf was paired with guitarist Hubert Sumlin, and the two cut several hits including "Evil" and "Smokestack and Lightning" in 1956. The two were then paired with Willie Dixon, who was Chess's staff writer, and over the next several years the trio had major hits with "I Ain't Superstitious," "The Red Rooster," "Back Door Man," and "Wang Dang Doodle." Most of these songs became blues classics but were also picked up by such British bands as the Rolling Stones. Wolf and Dixon parted ways in 1964, and Wolf recorded his own songs including "Killing Floor." By the end of the decade, such rock and roll idols as the Doors, Cream, and Jeff Beck were recording his material. Throughout the 1970s, Wolf was increasingly ill, suffering several heart attacks. He died from complications of an operation on January 10, 1976.

Alberta Hunter (1895–1984)
Singer

Born April 1, 1895, in Memphis, Tennessee, Alberta Hunter debuted as a club singer in Chicago at around 1912, making her first recording in 1921. She wrote "Down Hearted Blues" which became Bessie Smith's first hit, and on her early 1920s recordings she used such prominent sidemen as Fletcher Henderson, Eubie Blake, Fats Waller, Louis Armstrong, and Sidney Bechet. She starred in the stage show *Showboat* with Paul Robeson in London from 1928–1929 and worked in Paris for many years. After returning to the United States, she worked for the USO in World War II and the Korean War before retiring in 1956 to become a nurse at age 61. She was forced to retire from nursing in 1977 when it was discovered that she was 82 years old—not 65 years of age as she had reported. She made a comeback as a jazz singer, appearing regularly at the Cookery in New York City, until her death in 1984.

Jean-Baptiste "Illinois" Jacquet (1922–)
Saxophonist, Bandleader

Jean-Baptiste Jacquet was born in Broussard, Louisiana, on October 31, 1922, and raised in Texas. Jacquet began playing drums as a teenager before learning soprano and alto saxophones. He began his career as an altoist, but when he joined Lionel Hampton's band in 1942 he switched to tenor. Soon thereafter, Jacquet recorded his famous 64-bar honking solo on Hampton's "Flyin' Home" and made both his own and the Hampton band's name.

After stints with Cab Calloway (1943–1944) and Count Basie (1945–1946), Jacquet joined the Jazz at the Philharmonic (JATP) touring group in which he starred in tenor "battles" with Flip Phillips and others. He soon formed his own swinging little band and became a mainstay in the international jazz circuit. He formed a fine big band, Jazz Legends, in 1984 with which he continues to tour and record.

Jacquet was one of the first to "overblow" the tenor sax, reaching high harmonics that were dismissed by some as a circus stunt but really got to audiences; eventually, of course, such overblowing became part and parcel of the instrument's vocabulary, as in the later work of John Coltrane and the style of David Murray. But Jacquet is also a warm ballad player and is always a swinging tenor.

Elmore James (1918–1963)
Singer, Guitarist

Born on January 27, 1918, in Richland, Mississippi, James adapted to music at an early age, learning to play bottleneck on a homemade instrument made from a broom-handle and a lard can. By the age of 14, he was a weekend musician working diners and juke joints under the names "Cleanhead" or Joe Willie James. He worked with visiting players such as Robert Johnson, Howlin' Wolf, and Sonny Boy Williamson before forming his first band in the late 1930s. He served for three years with the Navy in Guam during World War II, and after his discharge he moved to Memphis where he became one of the first "guest stars" on the "King Biscuit Time" radio show in Helena, Arkansas. James's first recording came in 1951 with "Dust My Broom," which became a surprise top ten rhythm and blues hit and James's signature tune. He then moved to Chicago where over the course of the 1950s he assembled his famous band, the Broomdusters, and recorded numerous sides that made the charts and became blues classics. A regular performer in Chicago's blues clubs and on the radio, James's health began to decline in the late 1950s. After a return to Mississippi, he traveled back to Chicago to record "The Sky is Crying" before legal troubles with record labels and the musicians's union forced him back to Mississippi. He returned again to Chicago in 1963 where on May 24 he suffered a fatal heart attack.

Elmore James was the most influential slide guitarist of the post-war period. His attitude and tone on the guitar updated the sound of Robert Johnson, and his signature guitar licks are a foundation in blues guitar. A radio repairman by trade, James reworked his guitar amplifiers to produce raw, distorted sounds that would inspire the rock and roll movement of the 1960s. His voice was loud, forceful, and prone to break in the high registers, conveying a sense of hysteria. His bands were as loud and powerful as any blues band in Chicago, helping to launch the Electric Chicago Blues movement.

"Skip" James (1902–1969)
Singer, Guitarist, Songwriter

Although Nehemiah Curtis "Skip" James became much more popular during the blues revival of the mid-1960s than ever before, it makes little sense to speak of his "rediscovery." The fact is that he had barely been discovered in the first place. James was born on June 21, 1902, in Bentonia, Mississippi, home to a thriving Delta blues tradition. His father, a Baptist minister, was competent on both organ and guitar. When James became interested in blues—an interest sparked primarily by local player Henry Stuckey—at about age seven, his father was happy to become his first guitar teacher.

In his teens, James moved to Memphis to play dance hall and barrelhouse music. He returned to Mississippi, settling in Jackson in the 1920s. There his unique falsetto vocal stylings and from-the-heart presentation earned him regional fame. In 1931 James was brought North to record 26 songs for Paramount Records. Only a handful of the songs were ever released, and James gradually withdrew from performing.

By the 1940s, James was out of the music business. In addition to becoming an ordained minister, he worked at a variety of non-music jobs during the next couple of decades. He was "rediscovered" from out of nowhere by blues revivalists John Fahey and Bill Barth in 1964, and by the following year he was earning standing ovations at blues festivals from audiences larger than any he had played for during his prime. James's highly personal style had an air of untarnished authenticity, completely devoid of commercial awareness, that was well accepted by the folk purists who made up his new generation of fans. James died on October 3, 1969, in Philadelphia, Pennsylvania.

"Blind" Lemon Jefferson (1897–1929)
Guitarist, Singer

Blind Lemon Jefferson was one of the pioneers of Texas blues. Born poor and blind, music was one of the few career options open to Lemon—which was his given name, not a nickname. Jefferson's performing career began when he was 14 years old. He would make a daily trek on foot into the nearest town, Wortham, where he would sit in front of some store and begin to play for money. He eventually acquired a sizable local following and was invited to play at country picnics and other such events. At 20 years of age, Jefferson moved to Dallas, where he made money playing in brothels and taverns. Among the local adolescents that he hired as guides during this period were the young Lightnin' Hopkins and T-Bone Walker.

In 1925 and 1926, Jefferson made a series of recording trips to Chicago, home of the Paramount record label. His records sold well coast to coast, and he became possibly the very first country blues-recording star. He made a total of about 80 records over the next couple of years. In 1929, the heavy-drinking Jefferson got lost in a blizzard after leaving a party in Chicago and froze to death.

Jefferson was a serious showman who balanced a driving guitar style with a booming two-octave voice. A brilliant improvisor, he often halted at the end of vocal lines to play guitar solos and could play in unusual meters. Too many budding blues musician to mention learned their first licks from these early Jefferson recordings. Long a favorite of American folk fans, Jefferson's songs have since been covered by countless folksingers and rock and roll artists over the years as well, and he was honored in the naming of the rock group Jefferson Airplane in the 1960s.

"J. J." Johnson (1924–2001)
Trombonist, Bandleader

Born January 22, 1924 in Indianapolis, Indiana, James Louis Johnson was the unchallenged master of the modern jazz trombone. He was the first musician to have adapted this instrument to the demanding techniques called for by the advent of Bop. Early in his career, Johnson displayed such skill in performing high speed and intricate solos that those who knew him only from records found it hard to believe that he was actually using a slide—and not a valve—trombone.

Johnson started playing the trombone in 1938 and within three years was playing with "Snookum" Russell. Soon after, he met Fats Navarro who was an early influence. By 1942, he joined Benny Carter and began arranging before joining Count Basie in 1945. Relocating to New York, he played with Dizzy Gillespie, Bud Powell, Miles Davis, and Charlie Parker where participated in the bop movement. During those years, his trombone was as widely imitated as the trumpet and alto saxophone of Gillespie and Parker. In 1952, Johnson retired for a time, only to return in 1954 as partner of fellow trombonist Kai Winding in the popular Jay and Kai Quintet, which released several popular recordings.

Johnson's ability as a composer took over, and by the late 1960s, he had quit performing and concentrated on writing for film and television. Despite his absence from the stage, in 1995 *Down Beat* readers and critics both voted him into the magazine's hall of fame. The man widely considered the greatest jazz trombonist of all time died on February 4, 2001, in his hometown of Indianapolis.

James Price Johnson (1891/94–1955)
Pianist, Composer

James P. Johnson was born on February 1, 1891, in New Brunswick, New Jersey, and studied with his mother and private teachers beginning in childhood. The family moved to New York in 1904, and Johnson was soon working professionally during school breaks. He was soon leading a band at the Clef Club, working vaudeville and cabaret shows, and making piano rolls before releasing his first recordings in 1917. He was musical director for road shows and toured England with *Plantation Days*, before moving to Hollywood to write the classical score for Bessie Smith's *Yamacraw*. In 1928 he appeared at a Carnegie Hall concert before retiring to Jamaica, New York, in the 1930s to concentrate on writing concert music based on traditional African American themes. He completed a tone poem in 1930, the "Symphony Harlem" in 1932, and a symphonic jazz treatment of "St. Louis Blues" in 1936. Johnson was partially paralyzed by a stroke in 1940 and was semi-active until 1951 when another stroke left him bedridden until his death in New York on November 17, 1955.

Johnson's more serious works were neglected due to the lack of respect accorded to African American composers at the time by the classical world. He is more famously known as the master of the "stride piano," an instrumental style which derives its name from the strong, striding, left hand of the player playing bass notes and chords while the right hand plays melody. "Stride piano" came into its own during the 1920s in conjunction with the phenomenon known as the "rent party." Such a party was held for the purpose of raising rent money and involved the payment of an admission fee which entitled a patron to food, drink, conviviality, and a stride piano session. Johnson, along with Fats Waller and Willie "the Lion" Smith, were among the many who sharpened their skills in the rent party training ground.

Lonnie Johnson (1899–1970)
Guitarist, Singer

Johnson was born February 8, 1899, in New Orleans. By 1912 he was playing on the streets with his father who was a violinist. He began developing his unique jazzy style almost from the start. During World War I, Johnson played with a theater troupe that entertained Allied soldiers. In 1920, after 13 members of his family had died in an influenza epidemic, he moved to St. Louis, where he played in theaters and on riverboats. Johnson signed a recording contract with OKeh Records in 1925 after winning a blues contest, and he quickly attained a sizable following among African American buyers of OKeh's "race" Records.

In addition to his blues work, Johnson made recordings with a number of top jazz artists in the 1920s including Louis Armstrong, Duke Ellington, and Eddie Lang. He also played behind several of the classic female blues singers over the next several years. Altogether, Johnson made about 130 recordings between 1925 and 1932. He moved around quite a bit, eventually settling in Chicago, where he began working the bustling nightclub scene around 1937. He recorded for Bluebird during a five-year stint beginning in 1939 before joining King Records in 1947 where he soon had such hits as "Tomorrow Night," "So Tired," and "Confused." In the early 1950s, Johnson toured endlessly, both in the United States and abroad, and recorded regularly.

In spite of his tremendous activity, however, Johnson never achieved major stardom. By the early 1950s, his career was going nowhere, and he took a job as a janitor at a Philadelphia hotel. He was rediscovered in 1960 by jazz scholar Chris Albertson who arranged a new recording contract with the Prestige label. Although Johnson became quite popular with young white audiences in the United States and Europe during the blues revival of the 1960s, these listeners preferred the raw country blues of Skip James, Son House, and others, so major stardom again eluded him. In 1969, Johnson was hit by a car in Toronto, Canada, and he died on June 16, 1970, from the effects of the accident.

It would not be unreasonable to say that Lonnie Johnson was the single most influential guitar player in the history of blues. Johnson not only invented the guitar solo: he invented just about everything else a guitar does in blues, as well as jazz, country, and rock and roll.

Robert Johnson (1911–1938)
Singer, Guitarist

Born on May 8, 1911, in Hazelhurst, Mississippi, Johnson played a bit of harmonica as a teenager but had no real talent, and attempts to sit in with local legends Charley Patton and Son House were at first unsuccessful. He married young and wandered the Delta looking for work, committing himself to being a full-time musician after his wife died during childbirth. After approximately one year of studying with Ike Zinneman, an unrecorded blues musician, Johnson emerged with the astounding abilities to play guitar in a variety of styles and to write carefully constructed songs with original lyrics. These abilities were further honed by his constant work as a street musician and party circuit player that required him to play blues, pop, and hillbilly songs. His quick rise to virtuosity were the source of much of the legend and myth surrounding Johnson. Astounded by his newly found ability, listeners circulated the rumor that Johnson had met the devil at a crossroads, trading his soul for the ability to play guitar.

Johnson did not record as much as his contemporaries Charley Patton, Lonnie Johnson, or Blind Lemon Jefferson, but he traveled more than all of them. After his first recordings were released and "Terraplane Blues" became his signature work, he toured the Delta, Chicago, Detroit, and St. Louis. However, in August 1938 at a juke joint in Three Forks, Mississippi, he was reportedly poisoned by a jealous husband who had given him a jug of tainted liquor, and he died several days afterwards. Johnson's legend remained only among devotees and British rock and roll stars that covered his songs. However, a retrospective of his work was released by Columbia in the mid-1960s. Later, a complete boxed set including the only two known pictures of Johnson was released in 1990, and it became the first blues recordings to sell more than a million units, evidence of Johnson's stature as a blues pioneer.

Johnson's most enduring contribution in style was his ability to accompany himself by playing a boogie bass line on the bottom strings, while playing melody on the top strings. His use of rundowns, turnbacks, and repeats were all new in his day, and his playing inspired many other great blues musicians to follow in his path including Jimmy Reed, Elmore James, and Lightnin Slim. His recordings of "Love in Vain," "Crossroads," and "Sweet Home Chicago" are blues standards that place Johnson at the top of the blues genre.

Elvin Ray Jones (1927–)
Drummer, Bandleader

Born September 9, 1927, in Pontiac, Michigan, the youngest of the remarkable Jones Brothers developed his style in the vibrant jazz scene of Detroit where he cut his first records in 1953 that displayed his already remarkable style. Arriving in New York in 1955, he worked with such notables as J. J. Johnson, Sonny

Rollins, and Donald Byrd before joining John Coltrane's quartet in 1960.

With this group—the most influential of its time—Elvin Jones astonished musicians and listeners with his awesome independence of limbs (keeping four rhythms going at once), amazing drive, and ability to respond within mini-seconds to Coltrane's furious flow of ideas. Elvin Jones left Coltrane in 1965 and soon led his own groups that have featured such fine saxophonists as Frank Foster, George Coleman, and Coltrane's son, Ravi. Among Jones's numerous recordings with these groups are *Mr. Jones* and *Poly-Currents*, 1969; *Love & Peace*, 1978; and *It Don't Mean a Thing*, 1993.

One of jazz's master drummers, Elvin Jones integrated the drums with the frontline (melody) players to a farther extent than anyone had done before, always maintaining the pulse while featuring complex cross-rhythms and atypical resolutions to phrases.

Hank Jones (1918–)
Pianist

The eldest of the three extraordinary Jones brothers, Henry Jones was born in Vicksburg, Mississippi, on July 31, 1918, and raised near Detroit, where he began his professional career as a jazz musician. He traveled to New York City in 1944 and recorded with the great trumpeter and singer Hot Lips Page. His brilliant keyboard technique and skill as both soloist and accompanist soon found him in the company of such giants as Coleman Hawkins and Charlie Parker. He toured with Jazz at the Philharmonic (JATP) and became Ella Fitzgerald's accompanist.

Settling into studio work in New York, Hank Jones became one of the most recorded jazz musicians—he is to piano what Milt Hinton and George Duvivier were to the bass—in all sorts of contexts. Jones joined the CBS Orchestra in 1959 and remained until the ensemble disbanded in 1974. From the 1970s onward, Hank Jones began to do more work in clubs and on tour and to record more as a soloist and trio leader, often billed as "The Great Jazz Trio," with various star bassists and drummers. Jones remains at the head of the pack when it comes to great jazz pianists.

Thad Jones (1923–1986)
Cornetist, Composer, Arranger, Bandleader

Born March 28, 1923, the middle brother of the gifted Jones family, Thaddeus Joseph Jones played in a band led by brother Hank during his teen years before working with Sonny Stitt and a stint in the Army (1943–1946).

Thad played with Billy Mitchell in Detroit and cut his first records there in 1953. Traveling to New York in 1954, he was quickly discovered by Charles Mingus, who recorded him for his Debut label, and then joined Count Basie's band that same year, staying for almost a decade. During this time he honed his writing skills, contributing numerous arrangements and original tunes for the band and providing the solo on Basie's biggest instrumental hit "April In Paris."

In New York in 1963, Thad Jones joined forces with the great drummer Mel Lewis to co-lead what began as a rehearsal band but soon became the most talked about new big band in jazz. As the Thad Jones-Mel Lewis Jazz Orchestra, it gave new life to the language of big band jazz, as Thad Jones blossomed as a composer and arranger of music that was swinging but fresh. Perhaps his best-known composition, however, is the beautiful ballad "A Child Is Born." The band held together until 1979, when Thad Jones moved to Denmark and Mel took over, keeping much of Thad's "book" alive. Thad led his own bands in Scandinavia, then traveled back to the United States briefly in 1984 to take on leadership of the Count Basie Band, returning to Denmark in ill health six months prior to his death on August 20, 1986. Thad possessed great skills as both a trumpeter and a composer-arranger making him one of the few "complete" jazz musicians. A player of great agility and melodic invention, Jones's playing displayed a tart and razor sharp sound.

B. B. King (1925–)
Singer, Guitarist, Bandleader

Riley B. King is one of the most successful artists in the history of the blues. King was born on September 16, 1925, in Indianola, Mississippi. He was first exposed to the blues through an aunt who owned a phonograph. While a teenager, King purchased his first guitar for eight dollars—money he earned working in the cotton fields. At 19 he hitchhiked to Memphis where his cousin, country blues guitarist Bukka White, taught him the basics of blues guitar. After returning home for a while, King returned to Memphis in 1948, playing at the 16th Street Grill for 12 dollars a night. He then found a spot on a newly opened radio station in Memphis called WDIA, where he played for ten minutes each afternoon and later became a disc jockey. The station named him "The Boy from Beale Street" and, thereafter, he was known as B. B. King.

King cut his first record in 1949 for the Bullet label titled "Miss Martha King," named after his wife he had left in Mississippi. He then signed with RPM Records

B.B. King.

and cut several sides for them in Memphis under the supervision of Sam Phillips. Soon King had his first rhythm and blues chart topper in 1951 with "Three O'Clock Blues." King hit the road to promote the song, and it was during this era that he first named his guitar Lucille, after a woman who had inspired a barroom brawl and fire that almost cost King his life. For the course of the 1950s, King was a hit-making force in the rhythm and blues field, with more than 20 of his songs scoring on the charts. He continued his success into the 1960s with his release "The Thrill Is Gone," which received the first of King's multiple Grammy Awards. Soon King won international success, influencing such artists as the Rolling Stones.

In addition to an average of 300 performances around the world each year, King has opened two jazz clubs—one in Memphis and the other in Universal City, California—and co-founded the Foundation for the Advancement of Inmate Recreation and Rehabilitation with lawyer F. Lee Bailey. King's many prestigious honors include an honorary doctorate from Yale University (1977), induction into the Rock & Roll Hall of Fame (1987), the Lifetime Achievement Award from the

National Academy of Recording Arts and Sciences (1987), and the Presidential Medal of the Arts (1990). In 1995 King was one of the recipients of the Kennedy Center Honors.

"Rahsaan Roland" Kirk (1936–1977)
Composer, Flutist, Saxophonist

At first called "gimmicky" by critics, Ronald Theodore Kirk proved to be one of the most exciting jazz instrumentalists. His variety of instruments was matched only by the range of his improvisational styles, often switching in the middle of a number from a dissonant exploration to a tonal solo based on a conventional melody.

Born in Columbus, Ohio, on August 7, 1936, Kirk was technically blind, having been able to see nothing but light from infancy. Educated at the Ohio State School for the Blind, he began picking up horns at the age of nine. At 19 years of age, while touring with Boyd Moore, he started experimenting with playing more than one instrument at a time. Finding obscure horns such as the stritch and the manzello, he worked out a technique for playing three-part harmony (on three horns simultaneously) through the use of false fingering. In 1960, Ramsey Lewis helped Kirk get his first important recording date with Argo Records, and in 1961 he played with Charles Mingus's group, going on the international circuit later that year. Kirk employed whistles, gongs, and toys as improvisational tools, often vocalizing melody lines and encouraging audience participation and providing amusing commentary from the stage. He reached his greatest popularity in the early 1970s before a stroke caused his left side to be paralyzed. He then switched to playing tenor sax with one hand and continued to tour, although in a more smooth jazz form. Kirk died on December 5, 1977, an icon and visionary of post-bop jazz and individual expression. Among his many compositions are "Three for Dizzy," "Hip Chops," "The Business Ain't Nothin' But the Blues," "From Bechet, Byas, and Fats," and "Mystical Dreams."

John Aaron Lewis (1920–)
Pianist, Composer, Bandleader

Born May 3, 1920, in La Grange, Illinois, Lewis was raised in a middle-class environment in Albuquerque, New Mexico. Lewis studied music and anthropology at the University of New Mexico until 1942. After three years in the Army, he went to New York City and soon became pianist and arranger with Dizzy Gillespie's band. Two years later at Carnegie Hall, Gillespie's band performed Lewis's first major work "Toccata for Trumpet and Orchestra."

After a European tour with Gillespie, Lewis returned to the United States to play with Lester Young and Charlie Parker and to arrange for Miles Davis. In 1952, after having finished his studies at the Manhattan School of Music, Lewis founded The Modern Jazz Quartet (MJQ) along with drummer Kenny Clarke, vibes master Milt Jackson, and bassist Percy Heath. After Clarke was replaced by Connie Kay in 1956, the group stayed together until 1974 with occasional reunions thereafter. With the MJQ, Lewis developed his trademark spare, cool sound with a strong classical presence and wrote many compositions including his classic "Django." Lewis has also composed film scores, collaborated with other "Third Stream" proponents including Gunther Schuller, taught jazz, and co-founded the American Jazz Orchestra. Lewis continues to perform and record. Lewis released a well-received solo album entitled *Evolution* in 1999, and followed it up with *Evolution II*, a live recording issued in 2001. His economical piano style recalls that of Count Basie in its perfection of note selection and retention of the blues form.

Abbey Lincoln (1940–)
Singer

Born Anna Marie Wooldridge on August 6, 1930, in Chicago, Lincoln graduated from Kalamazoo Central High School in Kalamazoo, Michigan, and later studied music for a number of years in Hollywood under several prominent vocal and dramatic coaches. She began her professional career in Jackson, Michigan, in 1950, after winning an amateur singing contest. After performing in nightclubs, she began recording in 1956. Throughout the late 1950s and 1960s, she sang in a group led by drummer Max Roach whom she married in 1962 (the couple divorced in 1970). Their recording *Freedom Suite* mingled social and political theory with jazz and entered strongly into the collective mindset of the Civil Rights movement.

As a soloist, Lincoln toured in Africa, Asia, Europe, and the Far East before becoming an assistant professor of African American theater and Pan-African studies at California State University. Lincoln made several film appearances including *The Girl Can't Help It* (1956), *Nothing But a Man* (1964), and *For the Love of Ivy* (1968), earning several awards and induction into the Black Filmmakers Hall of Fame in 1975. That same year, she produced her own play *A Pig in a Poke*. Just as importantly, however, Lincoln has been hailed by many outstanding African American jazz performers, including Coleman Hawkins, Benny Carter, and Charles

Mingus, as a singer with nuance who can shift accents and rhythmic delivery as well as notes, while maintaining a conversational feel to her delivery. Fairly inactive in the 1980s, Lincoln regained her prominence in 1993 via a television documentary entitled *You Gotta Pay the Band: The Words, the Music, and the Life of Abbey Lincoln*, which aired on PBS. Throughout the 1990s, Lincoln contributed to and produced numerous lauded albums including her 1999 release *Painted Lady*. In March 2002, Lincoln performed in a three-concert retrospective sponsored by Jazz at Lincoln Center entitled *Over The Years: An Anthology Of Her Songs*.

Melba Liston (1926–1999)
Arranger, Trombonist

Melba Liston, who has played with the greatest names in jazz, was one of the very few jazz female trombonists. Liston was born in Kansas City, Missouri, on January 13, 1926, but her family later moved to California. Her musical history began in 1937, in a youth band under the tutelage of Alma Hightower. Liston continued her trombone studies, in addition to music composition, throughout high school. She found work with the Los Angeles Lincoln Theater upon graduation. She met band leader Gerald Wilson on the night club circuit, and he introduced her to Dizzy Gillespie, Count Basie, Duke Ellington, Charlie Parker, and Dexter Gordon, with whom she recorded some outstanding work in the mid-1940s. By the late 1940s, Liston was playing alongside John Coltrane and John Lewis in Dizzy's band, and she later toured with Billie Holiday as her assistant musical director and arranger. When the big band era waned, Liston jumped off the music circuit and returned to California, where she passed a board of education examination and taught for four years.

During the late 1950s, she was coaxed back into performing by Dizzy for his great State Department band (1956–1957) and then toured with Quincy Jones (1959–1961). During the next 20 years she led an all-female jazz group and performed freelance arrangements for Ellington, Basie, Dizzy, and Diana Ross. In 1974, she went to Jamaica to explore reggae. When she returned to the United States in 1979, she formed Melba Liston and Company, in which she revived swing, bebop, and contemporary compositions, many of which were her own until a stroke forced her to give up performing in 1985. She subsequently began composing with the aid of a computer and, beginning in the early 1990s, worked with Randy Weston, Abbey Lincoln, and T.S. Monk. She was regarded as a brilliant and creative arranger and an exceptional trombonist who possessed a beautiful, polished tone. Liston died on April 23, 1999, in Inglewood, California, at the age of 73.

Jimmie Lunceford (1902–1947)
Bandleader

Born on June 6, 1902, in Fulton, Missouri, James Melvin Lunceford grew up in Denver and played alto sax with George Morrison in 1922. He received his B.A. at Fisk University, where he met Willie Smith, Ed Wilcox, and Henry Wells, all of whom would eventually work in Lunceford's band for many years. He later studied at City College in New York. After having become proficient on all reed instruments, clarinet, flute, guitar, and trombone, Lunceford began teaching and launched his career as a band leader in Memphis from 1926–1929. By 1934, Lunceford's band was playing at the Cotton Club in Harlem, hosting nightly radio broadcasts, and recording for Decca Records. During the next decade, the Lunceford band was as well known as those of Basie and Ellington. His powerhouse swing/dance band featured flashy costume uniforms, choreographed dance moves by the musicians, and a host of brilliant instrumentalists playing original charts of high-energy jazz. The Lunceford vogue faded after 1944, around the time the band was experiencing changes in personnel. Lunceford died of a heart attack on July 13, 1947, while the band was on tour. Although he hardly ever played an instrument while recording with his band—except flute in his recording of "Liza"—the Lunceford style was one which influenced many band leaders and arrangers up to the 1950s. Furthermore, Lunceford's band stands as one of the leading and most influential of the big jazz orchestras in the 1930s.

Howard "Maggie" McGhee (1918–1987)
Trumpeter

Born on March 6, 1918, in Tulsa, Oklahoma, McGhee was raised in Detroit where he played clarinet in high school before switching to trumpet. His early band dates included stints at the Club Congo in Detroit followed by work with Lionel Hampton and Andy Kirk, with whom he made his first recording *McGhee Special* in 1942. During this time, McGhee also participated in the bop experiment at Minton's Playhouse before a 1945 tour with Coleman Hawkins, which took him to California where he recorded his influential dates with Charlie Parker for Dial Records. After returning to New York, McGhee recorded some classic work with both Milt Jackson and Fats Navarro that helped him become one of the most acclaimed trumpeters by the end of the 1940s. In the 1950s McGhee suffered from drug addiction and became obscure, but returned in the early 1960s to make some very good recordings. Inactive again until 1975 when he recorded another set of solid

efforts, McGhee remained relatively unknown due to his lack of sustained exposure during his career. McGhee died on July 17, 1987, in New York City.

Howard McGhee was one of the most recorded and important trumpeters of the bop era, forging a hard bop trumpet style that would be built upon by Fats Navarro and Clifford Brown. His solo efforts were known for their flow of ideas and hard-blowing style that were always swinging.

Carmen McRae (1922–1994)
Singer, Pianist

Born in Brooklyn on April 8, 1922, Carmen McRae's natural talent on the keyboards won her numerous music scholarships. During her teen years, she carefully studied the vocal style of Billie Holiday and incorporated it into her own style. An early highlight came when Holiday recorded "Dream of Life," one of McRae's compositions. After finishing her education, McRae moved to Washington, DC, and worked as a government clerk by day and a nightclub pianist/singer by night. In the 1944, she worked with Benny Carter and then with Mercer Ellington and Count Basie through the 1940s. She recorded her first solo record in 1954 for Decca, gaining enough attention to be dubbed a "new star" by *Down Beat* magazine.

In 1967, McRae appeared in the film *Hotel*, thus beginning a string of periodic television and film appearances that extended into the 1980s, when she had a part in the 1986 film *Jo Jo Dancer, Your Life Is Calling*. McRae had a flurry of activity in the 1990s, recording six albums between 1990 and 1991 alone. *Carmen Sings Monk* was nominated for a Grammy Award. In 1994 McRae was honored with a National Endowment for the Arts American Jazz Masters Award. Later in the year she suffered a stroke that eventually led to her death on November 10, 1994. McRae was best known for her witty interpretations of songs, smoky voice, and her behind-the-beat phrasing that reflected the influence of Billie Holiday.

Branford Marsalis (1960–)
Saxophonist, Bandleader

Branford Marsalis was born on August 26, 1960, in New Orleans. A very gifted player, he got his start as a member of Art Blakey's Jazz Messengers in 1980. From 1982 to 1985, he played in his brother Wynton's quartet. He has since performed with a multitude of artists from Mile Davis and Dizzy Gillespie to Tina Turner and

Public Enemy. Only 14 months older than his brother, Wynton, Branford has gained equal fame, not least due to his wide exposure as band leader for the *Tonight Show* from 1992 to 1995. An inventive soloist and an imaginative leader-organizer, Marsalis won a Grammy in 1993, formed the group Buckshot LeFonque, a hip hop and jazz ensemble in 1994, and has hosted "JazzSet" on National Public Radio. Marsalis won yet another Grammy in 2001, this time for his album *Contemporary Jazz*.

Branford's interests beyond jazz include mid-1980s touring stints with pop/rock acts Sting, Bruce Hornsby, and the Grateful Dead which brought him increased exposure. Marsalis's forays into acting have included parts in several feature films including *Throw Momma From the Train* (1987) and director Spike Lee's motion picture *School Daze* (1988). Marsalis's quartet provided the music for Lee's *Mo' Better Blues* in 1990. More outgoing than his brother, Wynton, Branford is an open-minded neo-traditionalist who is willing to nurture rather than preserve jazz.

Wynton Marsalis (1961–)
Trumpeter, Bandleader

Born on October 18, 1961, into a musical family in New Orleans—his father, Ellis Marsalis, is a prominent pianist and teacher and brothers, Branford and Delfeayo, are both musicians in their own right—Wynton Marsalis was well-schooled in both the jazz and classical traditions. At 17 years of age, he won an award at the prestigious Berkshire Music Center for his classical prowess; one year later, he left the Juilliard School of Music to join Art Blakey's Jazz Messengers.

After touring and recording in Japan and the United States with Herbie Hancock, he made his first LP in 1981, formed his own group, and toured solo extensively. Soon he made a classical album, and became the first instrumentalist to win simultaneous Grammy awards as best jazz and classical soloist in 1984. He received the Pulitzer Prize in 1997 for his oratorio *Blood on the Fields*—the first jazz-based work to win this coveted prize. *Standard Time, Vol. 5: The Midnight Blues* followed a year later. In 1999, he released *Marsalis Plays Monk: Standard Time, Vol. 4* to coincide with the popular PBS special. Beyond recordings, Marsalis has composed music for films and ballet and co-founded the Lincoln Center Jazz Orchestra.

A brilliant virtuoso of the trumpet with total command of any musical situation in which he chooses to place himself, Marsalis has also made himself a potent spokesman for the highest musical standards in jazz, to which he is firmly and proudly committed. He has urged young musicians to acquaint themselves with the rich tradition of jazz and to avoid the pitfalls of "crossing over" to pop, fusion, and rock. His own adherence to these principles and his stature as a player have made his words effective. In 1994, the same year his septet disbanded, Marsalis published *Sweet Swing Blues on the Road*, a collection of essays about the jazz life. Not content with simply playing, Marsalis also teaches with educational outreach program Project Discovery and at such places as the New England Conservatory of Music.

Memphis Minnie (1897–1973)
Guitarist, Singer

Born Lizzie Douglas on June 3, 1897, in Algiers, Alabama, and raised in Walls, Mississippi, Memphis Minnie learned to played banjo and guitar and moved alone to Memphis in 1910—at the age of 13. She played on the streets, toured the South with medicine shows and circuses, and lived with Casey Bill Weldon who tutored her. In 1929, she married guitarist "Kansas" Joe McCoy, with whom she formed a marvelous, inventive duo with a rural flavor. She recorded some masterpieces of guitar playing such as "Hoodoo Lady," and her style became more urbanized. Her style continued to evolve, and in 1938 she formed a duo with her new lover, guitarist Ernest "Little Son Joe" Lawlars, whose compositions "Digging My Potatoes," "Me and My Chauffeur," and "I'm So Glad," and delicate accompaniment combined with stunning guitar interplay helped to increase Minnie's popularity and success. In the late 1940s and early 1950s, Memphis Minnie tried several comebacks, but asthma and new trends in African American music forced her to retire in 1957. She died on August 6, 1973, in Memphis.

Memphis Minnie earned the respect of her peers throughout her long career with solid musicianship and more than 250 blues recordings over four decades, some of which are still widely performed by contemporary artists. Undoubtedly, she was the most popular and prolific female blues artist outside the vaudeville tradition.

Charles Mingus (1922–1979)
Bassist, Composer, Bandleader

Born on April 22, 1922, in Nogales, Arizona, Mingus grew up in the Watts area of Los Angeles. Starting on trombone and cello, he settled on the bass and studied with Red Callender, a noted jazz player, and Herman

Charles Mingus.

Rheinschagen, a classical musician. He also studied composition with Lloyd Reese. Early in his professional career, he moved to San Francisco and worked with Barney Bigard in a band that included the veteran New Orleans trombonist Kid Ory, and toured briefly in Louis Armstrong's big band. He also led his own groups and recorded with them locally. After a stint in Lionel Hampton's band, which recorded his interesting composition "Mingus Fingers," he joined Red Norvo's trio with which he traveled to New York in 1951.

Settling in New York, he worked with many leading players including Dizzy Gillespie and Charlie Parker and founded the record label Debut with Max Roach. He also formed his first of many so-called jazz workshops in which new music, mostly written by himself, was rehearsed and performed by four to 11 musicians taking verbal cues from Mingus. Mingus believed in spontaneity as well as discipline and often interrupted public performances by his band if the playing did not meet his standards, sometimes firing players on the spot. Although controversial, Mingus inspired loyalty with drummer Dannie Richmond, playing with Mingus from 1956 to 1970 and again from 1974–1977. Other

longtime associates include trombonist Kimmy Knepper, pianist Jaki Byard, and the saxophonists Eric Dolphy, Booker Ervin, and John Handy in the earlier years; later, saxophonist Bobby Jones and trumpeter Jack Walrath.

Mingus's music was as volatile as his temper, filled with ever-changing melodic ideas and textures and shifting, often accelerating, rhythmic patterns. He was influenced by Duke Elllington, Art Tatum, and Charlie Parker, and his music often reflected psychological states and social issues—Mingus was a staunch fighter for civil rights and wrote such protest pieces as "Fables of Faubus," "Meditations On Integration," and "Eat That Chicken." He was also steeped in the music of the Holiness Church ("Better Git It In Your Soul" and "Wednesday Night Prayer Meeting") and in the whole range of the jazz tradition ("My Jelly Roll Soul," "Theme For Lester Young," "Gunslinging Bird," and "Open Letter To Duke"). Himself a virtuoso bassist, he drove his sidemen to their utmost, often with vocal exhortations that became part of a Mingus performance. He composed for films and ballet and experimented with larger forms; his most ambitious work, an orchestral suite called "Epitaph," lasts more than two hours and was not performed in full until years after his death from amyotrophic lateral sclerosis or Lou Gehrig's disease—with which he struggled valiantly, composing and directing from a wheelchair until almost the end of his life. Though he was often in financial trouble and once was evicted from his home, he also received a Guggenheim fellowship in composition and was honored by President Carter at a White House jazz event in 1978.

At its best, Mingus's music—angry, humorous, always passionate—ranks with the greatest in jazz. He also wrote a strange but interesting autobiography *Beneath the Underdog* (1971). A group, Mingus Dynasty, continues to perform his music into the 1990s.

Keb' Mo' (1952–)
Guitarist, Banjo Player, Singer, Songwriter

Born Kevin Moore on October 3, 1951, in Los Angeles, Keb' Mo' was exposed to gospel at an early age. At 21, he joined a rhythm and blues band that was later hired for a tour by Papa John Creach, playing on three of Creach's albums. Keb' Mo' later opened for such jazz and rock and roll artists as the Mahavishnu Orchestra, Jefferson Starship, and Loggins and Messina. These experiences helped broaden Keb' Mo's musical horizons and abilities. In 1980 he recorded a rhythm and blues-based solo album *Rainmaker* for Casablanca, which promptly folded. In 1983, he joined Monk Higgins's band as a guitarist and met a number of blues musicians who collectively increased his understanding of the genre. He subsequently joined a vocal group called the Rose Brothers and worked around the Los Angeles area.

The year 1990 found Moore portraying a Delta blues musician in a local play titled *Rabbit Foot* and later playing Robert Johnson in a docudrama called *Can't You Hear the Wind Howl?* He released his self-titled debut album as *Keb' Mo'* in 1994, featuring two Robert Johnson covers, 11 songs written or co-written by Moore, and his guitar and banjo work. Keb' Mo' performed a well-received set at the 1995 Newport Folk Festival. Keb' Mo's second release on Okeh Records, *Just Like You*, won a Grammy Award and was one of the best-selling blues albums in 1996. He has followed up with the albums *Slow Down* (1998), *The Door* (2000), and *Big Wide Grin* (2001).

Keb' Mo' draws heavily on the old-fashioned country blues style of Robert Johnson, but writes much of his own material, keeping his sound contemporary with touches of soul and folksy storytelling.

Thelonious Monk (1917–1982)
Pianist, Composer

Born on October 10, 1917, in Rocky Mount, North Carolina, Thelonious Sphere Monk's family moved to New York in his infancy. By his early teens, he was providing piano accompaniment for his mother in church. He later toured with an evangelist before studying at Julliard and then working with the Lucky Millender Band (1942), Coleman Hawkins (1943–1945), and Cootie Willaims (1945) who first recorded Monks's "Round Midnight." In addition to these bands and Dizzy Gillespie's big band, Monk was in the house band at Minton's Playhouse, the primary breeding ground for the bop movement. Monk recorded his first dates as a leader in 1947, many of which are considered classics. Monk's career was seriously harmed when he was arrested on drug charges and lost his cabaret card, losing his ability to play in New York clubs for the next six years and forcing Monk to survive on session and out-of-town work. After he regained his right to work in New York in 1957, he had a long run at the Five Spot featuring a quartet that included John Coltrane, and his recordings from this period are often considered to be his best. Monk's fame began to grow and he appeared at numerous festivals, on television, and by the mid-1960s was featured on the cover of *Time* magazine. By the end of the decade, health problems cut into his activities, and his last major tour was from 1971 to 1972.

Thelonious Monk.

When he died on February 17, 1982, he had not played in public for six years.

Although associated with the bop movement and that genre's harmonic advancements, Monk stood apart from bop in his approach to structure, rhythm, and style of improvisation. His lightening fast right-hand figures and compositions that featured unusual and hard to learn changes made him thoroughly modern. He insisted that improvisations should be derived from the melody rather than the chord changes as practiced in bop. Monk has been called the first jazz post-modernist and most important jazz composer since Duke Ellington. Many of his compositions including "Round About Midnight," "Ruby My Dear," "Off Minor," and "Epistrophy" have become jazz standards.

"Jelly Roll" Morton (1890–1941)
Composer, Pianist, Bandleader

Born October 20, 1890, in New Orleans, Ferdinand Joseph Lementhe Morton was playing piano in New Orleans's Storyville brothels by 1902. Restless and ambitious, he hit the road, working in vaudeville and minstrel shows, hustling pool, running gambling halls, and traveling as far as Alaska and Mexico. He finally settled in Chicago in 1923, where he then recorded with his Red Hot Peppers in 1926–1928. These recordings feature his own compositions and arrangements, and they showed that he was a major talent, quite possibly the first real composer in jazz, if not the inventor of the music as he would later claim. These recordings also came just as Louis Armstrong was changing the shape of jazz, and Morton's style which emphasized collective improvisation and polyphony clashed with Armstrong's virtuoso performances and big band-ensemble playing. The result was that Morton was consistently overlooked.

In 1928 he moved to New York and made some very good recordings, but he was considered out-of-date when big band swing came to the fore, although Morton's composition "King Porter Stomp" became a swing anthem. In 1938 he was discovered living in Washington, DC, managing an obscure night club by Library of Congress musical folklorist Alan Lomax who recorded a series of solo performances and reminiscences that revived Morton's career and resulted in a few more sessions. Failing health and restlessness led Morton to drive to California, where he had a lady friend. But the trip made him ill, and he died in his fiftieth year, just before the revival of interest in traditional jazz, which would have given him the break he needed.

Few musicians in jazz were as colorful or talented as Jelly Roll Morton. Morton may not have invented jazz but he certainly was an important bridge between ragtime and jazz. A pool hustler, pimp, and tireless self-promoter, Morton's ego and attitude alienated many people. But his compositions, which were often constructed in three distinct sections and displayed unison melody lines, time choruses, instrumental breaks, and group improvisations are undeniably brilliant. His piano playing influenced many players after him including Earl "Fatha" Hines.

"Fats" Navarro (1923–1950)
Trumpeter

Theodore Navarro was born in Key West, Florida, in 1923. He started on trumpet at age 13 and also played tenor sax around Miami. Navarro was first heard nationally in 1943–1944 as a member of Andy Kirk's band until Dizzy Gillespie recommended him to Billy Eckstine, with whom he played for 18 months. In 1946 Navarro was established as a top soloist, and he left Eckstine to work with Illinois Jacquet, Lionel Hampton, and Coleman Hawkins and to record with smaller and less

constraining groups, first as a leader in 1946–1947 and then with Tadd Dameron, Bud Powell, and Howard McGhee in 1948–1949. These sessions set the course for jazz trumpeting, as Navarro's fat, full sound and rich, melodious solos would later influence the styles of Clifford Brown and Lee Morgan. Inactive for the last year of his life, Navarro died on July 7, 1950, from the effects of drug addiction and tuberculosis.

Herbie Nichols (1919–1963)
Pianist, Composer

Born January 3, 1919 in New York City, Nichols studied with a private teacher as a youth before serving in the Army until 1943. Most of Nichols's experience was with rhythm and blues and Dixieland groups, which were in sharp contrast to his modern and complex composing style. He made his first records for Blue Note in 1955, featuring numerous original compositions and some excellent sidemen such as drummers Art Blakey and Max Roach. Notably lacking in self-promotion and major support, his work did not sell well and Nichols remained unknown. Although his music is quite accessible to listeners, it was difficult for musicians to play, owing to his frequent extension of the 32-bar AABA form that required rehearsal, rather than jam session blowing. Often compared to Thelonious Monk for their similarity in harmonic language and angular melodies, Nichols composing style was distinct and his piano playing, suggestive of Art Tatum's, was virtuosic.

Most jazz fans know Herbie Nichols through his tune "Lady Sings the Blues," which was recorded by Billie Holiday. During his lifetime, though, only four of Nichols's albums, all in trio settings, were released before his death at age 44 from leukemia. It was only after he had died that his work was discovered and promoted by younger New York musicians such as Roswell Rudd, Cecil Taylor, and Steve Lacy. However, the work that has been documented reveals Nichols to be one of the great unsung legacies of jazz.

"King" Oliver (1885–1938)
Cornetist

Born May 11, 1885, in Abend, Louisiana, Joseph Oliver started on trombone but switched to cornet and began playing with the Melrose Brass Band in 1907 before joining the Olympia Brass Band. Oliver first earned the sobriquet "King" in 1917 in Kid Ory's band after establishing himself as the best cornet performer as compared to Freddie Keppard, Manuel Perez, and a host of others. During the Storyville era, Oliver met and befriended Louis Armstrong, becoming Armstrong's mentor. With the closing of Storyville, Oliver left for Chicago in 1919, and Armstrong replaced him in Ory's band. By 1922, Oliver had a steady gig at Lincoln Gardens and summoned Armstrong to Chicago to play in his Creole Jazz Band as second cornetist. In 1923, the Creole Jazz Band made the first important recordings by an African American jazz group. Other sidemen in Oliver's band included Baby Dodds, Johnny Dodds, Barney Bigard, and Lil Armstrong. From 1925–1927 Oliver led the Dixie Syncopators at the Plantation Café and constructed a new type of jazz that combined the skills of well-trained musicians with more spontaneous players associated with the earlier New Orleans styles, placing Chicago at the head of the jazz movement.

Changing tastes, a disastrous tour, business errors, and failing health caused Oliver's career to decline, however. He moved to New York in 1928. Continued dental problems forced him to give up playing, and beginning in 1932 Oliver toured mainly in the South before poor health forced him to end his musical career. He died in Savannah, Georgia, where he worked in a poolroom beginning in 1936 until his death on April 8, 1938. Oliver was one of the major inventors of early jazz who used mutes and buckets to alter the sound of his horn and often imitated vocal sounds with his cornet. His distinctive licks and phrases formed the early vocabulary of the great trumpeters who followed him.

"Kid" Ory (1886–1973)
Trombonist, Bandleader

Edward "Kid" Ory's musical career is in many ways emblematic of the story of New Orleans jazz itself. They both reached a high point during the first two decades of this century. They both moved north during the 1920s, only to lapse into obscurity in the 1930s before being revived in the next two decades.

Ory was born on December 25, 1886, in La Place, Louisiana. He was the best known of the so-called tailgate trombonists—a style that used the instrument for rhythmic effects, fills, and glissandi, and in which solos were played in a rough, forceful style. He led his own bands in New Orleans and Los Angeles, where in 1922 he led Spike's Seven Pods of Pepper as the first African American band to record in the New Orleans style. In 1925 he moved to Chicago to play with King Oliver, Jelly Roll Morton, and with Louis Armstrong's Hot Fives and Hot Sevens with whom he recorded his famous composition "Muskrat Ramble" in 1926.

He returned to the West Coast in 1929 and, after playing for a time with local bands, retired to run a successful chicken ranch from 1930–1939. In the 1940s, he gradually returned to music with Barney Bigard, Bunk Johnson, and other New Orleans notables. He toured Europe successfully in 1956 and again in 1959, and he spent his final years living comfortably in Hawaii before his death on January 23, 1973.

Charlie "Bird" Parker (1920–1955)
Saxophonist

Charles Christopher Parker Jr. was born in Kansas City, Missouri, on August 29, 1920, and took up alto sax, a present from his mother in 1931. Parker left school at 16 to become a professional musician. After an initial lack of success, which some attribute to his early drug use and lack of technique, he found work with pianist Jay McShann and others. Parker first visited New York in 1939, and on return in 1941 he recorded his first sides with McShann and met Dizzy Gillespie who was developing parallel ideas that would emerge in the bop movement some four years later.

In the early 1940s, Parker played with the bands of Earl Hines, Cootie Williams and Andy Kirk, as well as

Charlie Parker.

the original Billy Eckstine band—the first big band formed expressly to feature the new jazz style in both solos and arrangements. In 1945, Parker cut a series of remarkable sides under Gillespie's name that became definitive sides of the bebop style. Although Parker was revered by a host of younger musicians, his innovations, at first, were met with a great deal of opposition from traditionalist jazz musicians and critics.

Moving to California in 1945, Parker, addicted to heroin, suffered a breakdown and was confined to a state hospital in California in 1946. Six months later he recorded two sessions with Erroll Garner for Dial Records that stand as pinnacles of his career—as influential in Parker's day as Armstrong's Hot Fives sides were in the 1920s. From that point onward, he confined most of his activity to working with quintets, at times featuring Miles Davis, Kenny Dorham, Al Haig, Max Roach, and Roy Haynes. Parker also recorded and toured with a string section and visited Europe in 1949 and 1950. During the last five years of his life, Parker went through cycles of illness brought on by his addictions. He made his final appearance in 1955 at Birdland, the club which had been named in his honor, and died a week later of heart seizure at a friend's apartment.

Parker's influence on the development of jazz has been felt not only in the realm of the alto saxophone, which he dominated, but on the whole spectrum of jazz ideas. The astounding innovations that he introduced melodically, harmonically, tonally, and rhythmically made it impossible for any jazz musician from the mid-1940s to present time to develop without reflecting some of Parker's influence, with or without acknowledgment

Charley Patton (1887–1934)
Singer, Guitarist

Charley Patton was one of the very earliest practitioners of the Delta country blues style. As such, he profoundly influenced succeeding generations of blues artist, as the Delta sound evolved into the genre's modern recognizable form. His hoarse and impassioned singing and his fluid guitar style made him the original king of the Delta blues. Born in 1887 in Edwards, Mississippi, Patton received his musical education from members of the Chatmon family, some of whom went on to forge their own recording careers in the 1920s and 1930s.

At around 1897, Patton moved to the plantation of Will Dockery, where music was a constant part of the sharecropper lifestyle. At local juke joints, Patton became one the earliest composers of songs in the 12-bar

pattern that came to be recognized as the standard blues form.

For the next 30 years or so, Patton played wherever he could—at picnics, on the street, or at other plantations. He gradually developed a sophisticated guitar style that helped lay the groundwork for what eventually coalesced into the Delta style. Although his musical skills were polished, his performance style was not. On the stage, Patton was a clown, performing guitar tricks, singing unintelligibly at times, and improvising at will. He was almost as well-known for his hard-drinking ways and constant womanizing as he was for his raw baritone singing voice. But the sound of his whiskey and cigarette voice would inspire a young Howlin' Wolf, and his propulsive guitar beat and keen rhythmic sense would plant the seeds for John Lee Hooker's boogie style.

In 1929 Patton was brought North to record for the Paramount label. He recorded approximately 60 sides for both Paramount and Vocalion over the next few years, but the surviving quality of the recordings makes it difficult to know how Patton really sounded. He is regarded as one of the first to tie the blues to a strong, syncopated rhythm and to utilize the slide for vocal-like effects. In addition, he is thought to have pioneered the popping of his bass strings and using the guitar like a drum to reinforce beats or make counter rhythms. Patton died in Indianola, Mississippi, on April 28, 1934, of heart disease.

Oscar Pettiford (1922–1960)
Bassist

Pettiford was born on September 30, 1922, in Okmulgee, Oklahoma, on a Native American reservation and raised in Minneapolis. Until he was 19 years old, he toured with the family band (father and 11 children) and was well known in the Midwest. In 1943, Charlie Barnet heard him in Minneapolis and hired him to team up with bassist Chubby Jackson. Pettiford left Barnet later that year, frequenting Minton's Playhouse and playing with Roy Eldridge, before he and Dizzy Gillespie led the first bebop group to perform on 52nd Street. Pettiford cut his first sides in 1943 and played with Coleman Hawkins and Duke Ellington, with whom he recorded "Swamp Fire," a fine example of Pettiford's power and attack.

Pettiford's fame grew during the 1950s through his recordings and his tours of Europe and Asia, and he continued to lead his own sextet and big band. In 1958, he settled permanently in Europe, where he continued to work until his death in Copenhagen in 1960. During his peak in the 1940s, Pettiford was a unique bassist who was melodically inventive and technically agile on both bass and cello. Building on the concepts first explored by Jimmy Blanton, Pettiford extended the range and complexity of jazz bass. Pettiford was also a fine composer who wrote "Bohemia After Dark" and "Blues in the Closet."

"Bud" Powell (1924–1966)
Pianist, Composer

Earl Rudolph Powell was born on September 27, 1924, in New York City into a family of musicians. A piano prodigy, he had his first big-time job with trumpeter Cootie Williams's big band in 1943 and became involved in the "birth of bebop" at Minton's Playhouse in Harlem and on 52nd Street.

In 1945 he was severely beaten about the head by Philadelphia police in a racially-motivated incident, and he suffered the first of several nervous breakdowns that plagued him for the rest of his life. He continued to work with Gillespie and took part in bop combo sessions for Savoy Records in the late 1940s, although he was often in the care of a mental hospital. He lived in Paris from 1959 to 1964, frequently working with his old friend Kenny Clarke. He died in New York on August 1, 1966, and reportedly more than 5,000 people attended his funeral in Harlem.

Powell is considered to be the first to transfer the melodic, harmonic, and rhythmic innovations of bop to the piano keyboard, setting the style for modern jazz piano. Although he was greatly influenced by Art Tatum and Teddy Wilson, his rapid right-handed melody lines played to match the horns combined with his random and dissonant left-hand chords were completely his own style.

Sun Ra (1914–1993)
Pianist, Composer, Bandleader

Born Herman Sonny Blount on May 14, 1914, in Birmingham, Alabama, Sun Ra spent the early part of his career in Chicago, where he played rhythm and blues, jazz, and blues. A highlight was playing in Fletcher Henderson's band in 1947 at the Club DeLisa. During the 1950s, while Ornette Coleman, Cecil Taylor, and Miles Davis were carving out niches for their musical visions and personalities, Blount changed his name to Sun Ra and assembled a band to play his unorthodox and challenging music.

Ra's Arkestra had three distinct periods: big band/ hard bop in the 1950s; free jazz in the 1960s; and swing from the mid-1970s onward. It fused African-style polyrhythms, unusual harmonies, and audacious stage performances to create an often spectacular event. The group, which counted more than 100 members over its history, lived communally, first in Chicago and later in Philadelphia, and released records on Ra's own Saturn label.

Ra's music pushed into mystical abstraction and theater, and audiences often participated in the experience. An admirer of American popular music, Ra often incorporated compositions by Ellington, Gershwin, and others into his performance. His interpretations—arrangements, tempos, and unique instrumentation—gave these works a different sound. Sun Ra died on May 30, 1993, following a series of strokes.

"Ma" Rainey (1886–1939)
Singer

Ma Rainey, the "Mother of the Blues" who enveloped the 1920s with her powerful, message-oriented songs, is remembered as a genuine jazz pioneer. Born Gertrude Pridgett in Columbus, Georgia, on April 26, 1886,

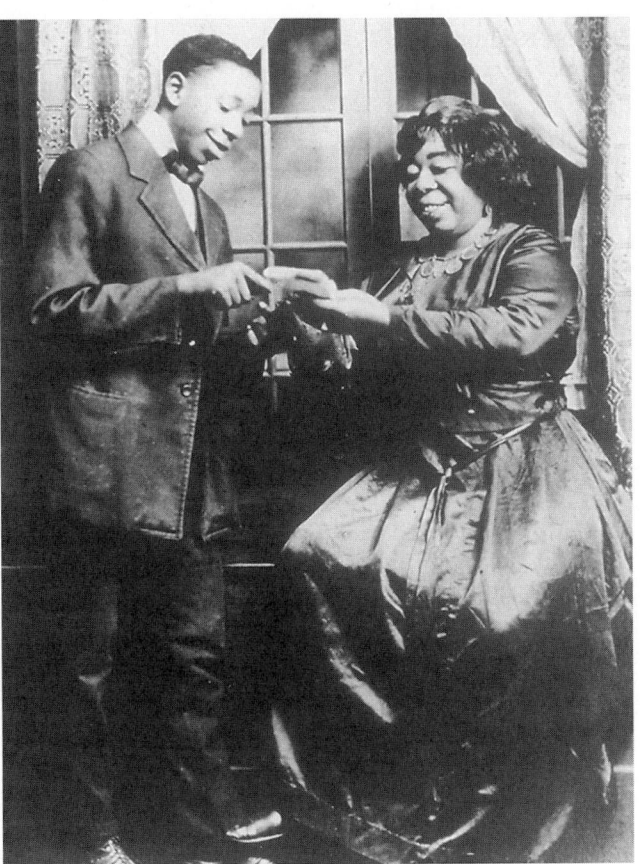

Ma Rainey performs in the musical production, *The Rabbit Foot Minstrels,* with an unidentified actor.

she gave her first public performance as a 12-year-old at the local Springer Opera House. In 1904 she married singer/dancer William "Pa" Rainey, and the duo embarked on a long entertainment career, touring around the South with minstrel shows, circuses, and tent shows.

Around 1912, Rainey introduced a teen-aged Bessie Smith into her act, a move that was later seen as having a major impact on the blues/jazz singing styles. She made her first recording in 1923 for Paramount Records and was soon recording with Fletcher Henderson, Louis Armstrong, and Coleman Hawkins. Between 1923 and 1928 when she stopped recording, she has released over 100 songs including the blues classics "C.C. Rider" and "Bo Weavil Blues." Though she continued to tour the South for a few more years, blues singing by females was less popular than by her male counterparts. She retired in 1935 and, until her death on December 22, 1939, managed the two theaters that she owned in Georgia. Similar to other classic blues singers of her time, Rainey sang pop, minstrel, and blues tunes, but she delivered them with a heavier, tougher, and earthier delivery than the cabaret blues singers that followed her.

Dewey Redman (1931–)
Saxophonist

Born in Fort Worth, Texas, on May 17, 1931, he started playing the clarinet when he was 12, taking private lessons briefly for six months before he turned to self-instruction. At 15, he earned a job with an eight-piece band that performed in church as the minister passed the collection plate. At Prairie View A&M College, Dewey teamed up with a piano and bass player to work in local clubs, found a spot in the Prairie View "swing" band, and graduated in 1953 with a degree in industrial arts and a grasp on a new instrument on which he had experimented—the saxophone. After a stint in the Army, Dewey obtained a master's degree in education at North Texas State University and taught school and directed school bands in western and southern Texas.

In 1959, Redman moved to Los Angeles, where he found the music scene to be very cliquish, and then to San Francisco, where he remained for seven years, studying music, working on his own theories of chord progressions, improvisation, and technique. In 1967, Dewey went to New York City and joined Ornette Coleman who brought him into his group with Dave Izenson on bass and Denardo Coleman on drums.

By 1973, Dewey was dividing his playing time between solo efforts, gigs with Ornette Coleman and

Keith Jarrett, and the composition of "Peace Suite" dedicated to the late Ralph Bunche. Later he co-founded the group, Old and New Dreams. Dewey Redman has spent most of his life in search of a greater knowledge of his instrument—the tenor saxophone—constantly reevaluating his relationship to his music. His son, Joshua, emerged as one of the finest young tenor saxophonists of the early 1990s.

Don Redman (1900–1964)
Saxophonist, Composer

Born in Piedmont, West Virginia, on July 29, 1900, Redman was a child prodigy who played trumpet at the age of three, joined a band at six, and later studied harmony, theory, and composition at Boston and Detroit conservatories. In 1924, he joined Fletcher Henderson's band as lead saxophonist and staff arranger and also recorded as accompanist for such leading blues singers as Bessie Smith, Ma Rainey, and Alberta Hunter. When Louis Armstrong joined the Fletcher band, Redman adopted Armstrong's sense of swing, and in 1928 he became leader of McKinney's Cotton Pickers, having built both of these bands into two of the best in jazz history.

During most of the 1930s, Redman led his own band, regarded as one of the leading African American orchestras of its time and the first to play a sponsored radio series. He also wrote for many other prominent bands, black and white. In 1951, Redman became musical director for Pearl Bailey. From 1954 to 1955, he appeared in a small acting role in *House of Flowers* on Broadway. He continued to arrange and record until his death on November 30, 1964. Redman was the chief architect of the integration of popular orchestral dance music and jazz, using both written and improvised parts to create a swing feel.

Jimmy Reed (1925–1976)
Singer, Guitarist

Born September 6, 1925, in Dunleith, Mississippi, on a plantation, Reed learned the basics of guitar and harmonica from Eddie Taylor, a semi-professional musician. In 1943 Reed moved to Chicago but was soon after drafted into the Navy. After a two-year stint, he moved back to Mississippi to marry before relocating to Gary, Indiana, where he found work in a meat packing plant. In the early 1950s he was working with John Brim's Gary Kings as a harmonica player before the drummer in the band, future guitar legend Albert King, introduced him to Vee Jay Records where he made his first recordings. He was reunited with Taylor— a partnership that lasted the rest of Reed's life—and their third single "You Don't Have to Go" made number five on the rhythm and blues charts. Unfortunately, Reeds severe drinking problem became legendary, and he struggled to even perform or record, often requiring assistance to remember the lyrics or when to play his instruments. With the help of his wife and Taylor, Reed managed to function, even in spite of being diagnosed with epilepsy in 1957, and he placed 11 songs on the Hot 100 chart and 14 on the rhythm and blues charts in the 1950s and 1960s. Reed worked sporadically during the 1970s before becoming a recluse and obtaining treatment for his illnesses. He died in Oakland, California, on August 29, 1976.

Reed's best known songs "Big Boss Man," "Bright Lights, Big City," and "Baby, What You Want Me to Do" are part of the standard blues repertoire and have been played by everyone from garage bands to Elvis Presley. His bottom-string boogie rhythm guitar patterns, two-string turnarounds, country harmonica, and mush mouth vocals served as the first introduction to the blues for many people. While lacking the technical proficiency on his instruments as Son House and Elmore James and also lacking a voice as powerful as Muddy Waters and Howlin' Wolf, Jimmy Reed's simple tunes and laid back feel were a popular contrast, making aspiring players worldwide feel that they could participate in the blues.

Max Roach (1924–)
Percussionist, Composer

Born on January 10, 1924, in New Land, North Carolina, and raised in Brooklyn, New York, Maxwell Lemuel Roach is one of the key figures in the development of modern jazz. He made his record debut in 1943 with Coleman Hawkins and was part of the first group led by Dizzy Gillespie to play bebop on 52nd Street in New York (1943–1944). He later worked with Charlie Parker's finest group (1947–1948). In 1954, he joined the brilliant young trumpeter Clifford Brown as co-leader of the Clifford Brown-Max Roach Quintet, an ensemble that defined the hard bop sound. After Brown's untimely death in a car crash, Roach began to lead his own groups of various sizes and instrumentation including interesting work with solo and choral voices, an all-percussion band, and a jazz quartet combined with a string quartet. His many compositions include "We Insist-Freedom Now," a suite written with his wife at the time, singer Abbey Lincoln, which was one of the first jazz works with a strong and direct political and social thrust.

A phenomenally gifted musician with a matchless percussion technique, Roach developed the drum solo into new heights of structural refinement; he has been an influence on every drummer to come along since the 1940s. Along with Kenny Clarke and Art Blakey, Roach is considered to be one of the founding fathers of bop drumming. Over his career Roach has played with Bud Powell, Miles Davis, Thelonious Monk, and Sonny Rollins. A professor of music at the University of Massachusetts since 1972, Roach became the first jazz artist to receive a MacArthur Fellowship in 1988—the most prestigious and lucrative award in the world of arts and letters.

"Sonny" Rollins (1930–)
Saxophonist, Bandleader

Born on September 9, 1930, in New York City, Theodore Walter Rollins took piano lessons when he was nine but lost interest in music until learning to play the alto sax in 1944. He was soon playing gigs on tenor and made his recording debut at 19 years of age with Babs Gonzalas for Capitol Records. Soon afterwards, he made sessions with trombonist J. J. Johnson, who recorded his first composition "Audubon," and pianist Bud Powell. Distinctively personal from the outset, his style developed through work with pianist Thelonious Monk, Powell, drummer Art Blakey, and trumpeter

Sonny Rollins.

Miles Davis. In 1956 he voluntarily entered the federal penitentiary at Lexington, Kentucky, to kick his drug habit before joining the Clifford Brown-Max Roach Quintet, where he came into his own style. Later that year he recorded *Saxophone Colossus*, marking a major breakthrough with songs such as "St. Thomas" and "Blue 7" that featured his thematic improvisational abilities. Employing a piano-less trio, a form he pioneered, he followed with two more records *Way Out West*, which showcased his love for off-beat pop and show tunes, and *Freedom Suite*, which was built around meditations on the lack of integration of the races in American society. Also during this period, he cut several albums for Blue Note Records that featured his own compositions along with oddball cover tunes made fresh and unique by the quality sidemen (i.e., Philly Joe Jones, Max Roach, J.J. Johnson, Horace Silver, and Thelonious Monk) and Rollins's early hard bop stylings.

In 1959, he took two years off from active playing, studying, and practicing. When he reappeared at the helm of his own quartet in 1961, he surprised even those who already knew the quality of his work with the power and conviction of his playing on *The Bridge*. A string of excellent albums on several labels followed until another "retirement" at the end of the 1960s. He was named a Guggenheim fellow in 1972 and continued to release strong offerings throughout the 1970s and 1980s. Rollins maintained an active schedule into the 1990s, and in 2002, won a Grammy for his album *This Is What I Do*. Known for his impressive endurance and stamina, Rollins has often been called a force of nature akin to a volcano.

Rollins has written many fine tunes in his career, but it is as an instrumentalist and improvisor that he is best known. His robust, almost hard tone, use of grace notes, and the ability to create harmonically imaginative but melodic statements, even at amazingly fast tempos, is unmatched. He is recognized as the first jazz soloist to improvise in terms of a complete pattern of a solo, or as Thelonious Monk once said, "play the melody, not the changes." Rollins stands as one of the most commanding musical voices in jazz history.

Otis Rush (1934–)
Guitarist, Singer

Otis Rush has been a mainstay of the Chicago blues scene for more than 40 years. A pioneer of the "West side" style of blues guitar work, Rush's sound combines the best elements of the South side, delta-influenced approach with the smoother, modern, urban stylings that B.B. King and T-Bone Walker brought to the blues.

One of seven children, Rush was born on April 29, 1934, in Philadelphia, Mississippi. Although he was attracted to the country blues guitar of Lightnin' Hopkins and others, Rush started out as a harmonica player. In 1948 he moved to Chicago, where he continued to develop his harmonica skills while working a day job in the stockyards. He did not begin studying guitar until 1953. Initially, his guitar role model was Muddy Waters, but he gradually began to infuse the more modern phrasing and jazzier feel of Walker and King into the deep Mississippi foundation that he had inherited from Waters.

Rush was noticed playing in the clubs by bassist Willie Dixon, who got him a contract with the newly established Cobra label. His first record for Cobra, "I Can't Quit You Baby," became a hit in 1956, and his work over the next few years was generally well-received. In 1959, Rush signed with Chess Records and recorded the successful single "So Many Roads, So Many Trains." He was unable to sell consistently for Chess, however, and his career slumped badly in the first half of the 1960s. He signed with the Houston-based Duke Records in 1962, but saw only one single released by that company. Meanwhile, he continued to perform regularly on the Chicago club circuit and occasionally in other cities.

Rush's appearance on the 1966 compilation album *Chicago: The Blues Today* revived his flagging career. It gained him a new generation of fans including a number of white rock musicians, and he was much in demand for blues festival gigs. Nevertheless, large scale stardom continued to elude Rush, with the exception of a wildly enthusiastic reception in Japan in 1975. Discouraged, Rush stopped performing for a short spell in the early 1980s. By the middle of the decade, however, blues was enjoying another revival, and a revitalized Rush managed to establish himself as a true giant of the modern blues scene. His 1994 album *Ain't Enough Comin' In* and the 1998 Grammy Award winning *Any Place I'm Going*, along with his continuing live performances, have cemented that reputation.

Jimmy Rushing (1903–1972)
Singer

Born on August 26, 1903, in Oklahoma City, Oklahoma, into a musical family (his father played trumpet and brother and mother were singers), James Andrew Rushing played piano and violin as a youth, but entered music professionally as a singer in the Californian after-hours world in 1925. After that, Rushing was linked with leading bands and musicians: Walter Page (1927–1928); Bennie Moten (1929); and as a mainstay of the famed Count Basie band (1936–1949), where his intense, high-pitched style of blues singing propelled the band to new heights.

Rushing formed his own small group when he left Basie and, in the ensuing years, worked most often solo. Following the upsurge in popularity of the blues in the mid-1950s, Rushing appeared at all the major jazz festivals and made several successful European tours with his own and Benny Goodman's bands, earning him critical acclaim and commercial success. His style endured for more than four decades of jazz, largely due to its great warmth, a sure, firm melodic line, and a swinging use of rhythm. Rushing died of leukemia on June 8, 1972, in New York City. The song "Mister Five by Five," written in tribute to him, is an apt physical description of Jimmy Rushing who was one of the greatest male jazz and blues singers.

Noble Sissle. *See* **Drama, Comedy, & Dance chapter.**

Bessie Smith (1894–1937)
Singer

Bessie Elizabeth Smith was born on April 15, 1894, in Chattanooga, Tennessee. Called "The Empress of the

Bessie Smith.

Blues," she had no peers. Her magnificent voice, sense of the dramatic, clarity of diction, and incomparable time and phrasing set her apart from the competition and made her appeal as much to jazz lovers as to lovers of the blues. Her first recording, Alberta Hunter's "Down Hearted Blues," sold approximately 750,000 copies in 1923—figures that only Caruso and Paul Whiteman were achieving at that time.

By the earlier 1920s, Bessie Smith had been singing professionally for some 15 years. However, records by African American singers had only been made since 1920, and only by much less earthy voices. She already had a sizeable following and had appeared in large shows, so the timing was right—not the least for Columbia Records, whom she pulled out of the red. Before long, she was backed by the best jazz players including Louis Armstrong, and by 1925 she starred in her own touring show that traveled in its own private Pullman car. By 1927, she was the highest paid African American artist in the world. In 1929 she made a short film *St. Louis Blues* that captures for posterity some of her magnetism as a stage performer.

But tastes in music were changing rapidly, and though Bessie Smith remained with the times by adding popular songs to her repertoire, the Depression nearly ended the jazz and blues record business. In 1931, Columbia dropped her, and she soon began touring as a "single." John Hammond brought her back to the studios in 1933. Her singles were wonderful, her singing as powerful and swinging as ever, but they did not sell well and turned out to be her last recordings. She still found plenty of work on the traveling circuit, but it proved to be less financially rewarding. Early one morning on a road in Mississippi, she was fatally injured in a car collision. She died on September 26, 1937, at the age of 42.

Billy Strayhorn (1915–1967)
Composer, Arranger, Pianist

Born in Dayton on November 29, 1915, and raised in Pittsburgh, William Thomas Strayhorn early on showed an unusually sophisticated gift for songwriting, both in terms of music and lyrics. While still in his teens, he wrote "Lush Life," a song he demonstrated to Duke Ellington in 1938. A short time later Ellington recorded the Strayhorn tune "Something to Live For" and by 1939 Strayhorn joined the Ellington entourage in New York. Duke first thought of Strayhorn as a lyricist—something for which he was always searching—but soon found out that Strayhorn had a knack for arranging and was a talented pianist as well.

Before long the two musicians had established a working relationship that remains unique in the history of music. From 1940–1942 Strayhorn contributed many standout tunes to the Ellington repertoire—"Take the A Train," "Passion Flower," "Chelsea Bridge," and "Rain Check." After the mid-1940s, Ellington and Strayhorn began sharing credit for their compositions, and Strayhorn led small group sessions drawn from Ellington's larger band. Strayhorn also co-composed and arranged hundreds of tunes and extended works including "The Deep South Suite," "A Drum is a Woman," "Such Sweet Thunder," and "The Perfume Suite." Strayhorn rarely recorded on his own, and his death from cancer on May 31, 1967, inspired Ellington's great album *And His Mother Called Him Bill.*

A sensitive, swinging pianist Strayhorn is remembered for his great harmonic sophistication and beautiful touch that perfectly complemented Ellington's more percussive and expansive vision.

Art Tatum (1909–1956)
Pianist

Born on October 13, 1909, in Toledo, Ohio, Arthur Tatum was blind in one eye and partially sighted in the other. Although he could read some music with the assistance of braille, he learned primarily by ear. He made his professional debut on radio in Toledo before going to New York City in 1932 as accompanist for singer Adelaide Hall, with whom he cut his first records. He was soon making his own records and appearing on 52nd street. He settled in Chicago, and by the mid-1930s his reputation was international. Known primarily as a soloist, Tatum began working in a 1943 trio patterned after Nat King Cole's group, with Slam Stewart on bass and either Tiny Grimes or Everett Barksdale on guitar. While he maintained this format for most of the rest of his career, in 1953 he began working with Norman Granz, with whom he recorded a monumental 121 unaccompanied solos, and a series of small group sessions with Benny Carter, Buddy DeFranco, and Ben Webster. It is these recordings on which his reputation was built among both critics and musicians. Though he enjoyed a full career and recorded quite prolifically, Tatum lived too soon to benefit from the acceptance that came to jazz as concert hall music, which would have been an ideal medium for him. He died on November 5, 1956, in Los Angeles, California, from uremia.

For sheer technical mastery, Tatum had few peers—perhaps only Earl Hines and Cecil Taylor have come close to matching Tatum's skill. A child prodigy, Tatum seemed to have all the elements of his style in place by early adulthood. His harmonic and linear invention, unusual phrase lengths, radical leaps in logic, lush tone, and relaxed swing were his trademarks. Tatum exerted a strong influence on the bop movement and all who followed. His left-hand figures were reminiscent of such early stride players as Fats Waller, while his intricate right-hand lines and habit of playing with the tempo suggest the technique of Earl Hines. His ability to never abandon the melody line but to change, obscure, and reharmonize it at will are legendary.

Billy Taylor (1921–)
Pianist, Composer, Educator

Born in Greenville, North Carolina, on July 24, 1921, William Taylor Jr.'s career started shortly after graduating from Virginia State College in 1942 with a B.A. in music, when he was employed in Ben Webster's group. He quickly established himself as a pianist on the New York scene, becoming a regular on "Swing Street" and playing with Billie Holiday, Ella Fitzgerald, Coleman Hawkins, Roy Eldridge, and others. A protegee of Art Tatum and Teddy Wilson, Taylor worked with Machito's Afro-Cuban band, toured Europe with Don Redman, and replaced Errol Garner in the Slam Stewart trio. After a 1949–1951 stint as house pianist for the famed Birdland club where he backed visiting stars, Taylor played a year-long engagement at Club Le Downbeat with a trio that included Charles Mingus.

Taylor made recordings with a variety of jazz artists for numerous labels during the 1950s and started his own publishing company before embarking on a campaign to educate the public through radio, television, and print. In 1958, he hosted "The Subject Is Jazz" on the Educational Television Network. He also hosted radio programs on two New York City stations and garnered a Peabody Award for his work. In the 1960s, Taylor served as musical director for Tony Brown's *Black Journal Tonight,* and in 1965 he founded Jazzmobile as part of the Harlem Cultural Council's summer programs. Starting out as an idea for a parade float, Jazzmobile eventually developed into a service that seasonally brought major jazz artists out to poor urban areas for free performances.

From 1968 to 1972, Taylor led an 11-piece band for television's *David Frost Show.* He returned to school, earning a doctorate in music education from the University of Massachusetts in 1975; his dissertation was later published as *Jazz Piano: History and Development* and became the text for a course offered on National Public Radio (NPR). Taylor directed *Jazz Alive!* for NPR from the late 1970s to early 1980s. He also became a regular on *CBS Sunday Morning,* serving as the program's jazz correspondent since 1980; in 1983 he earned an Emmy Award for a segment on

Quincy Jones. Taylor has served on numerous boards and panels including a position with the prestigious National Council on the Arts. In 1994, he was named the Kennedy Center artistic advisor.

Taylor has won several honors in his career. Among them have been recognition for lifetime achievement (1984) from *Down Beat* and induction into the magazine's Hall of Fame; a Jazz Masters Fellowship from the National Endowment for the Arts (1988); induction into the International Association of Jazz Educators Hall of Fame (1991); a Tiffany Award from the International Society of Performing Arts Administrators (1991); a National Medal of the Arts (1992); and Man of the Year from the National Association of Jazz Educators. Few musicians have done more for the cause of jazz than Dr. Billy Taylor, who has been properly credited with obtaining proper respect and recognition for African American music since the 1950s.

Cecil Percival Taylor (1933–)
Pianist, Composer

Born March 15, 1933, in Long Island City, New York, Cecil Percival Taylor attended the New England Conservatory, but said that he learned more from listening to Ellington; another early influence was Bud Powell. Early gigs include work with Hot Lips Page and Johnny Hodges before he made his first recording with Steve Lacy on soprano sax in 1956. The following year he appeared at the Newport Jazz Festival and was also recorded there. Settling in New York City, Taylor often struggled with lack of work and acceptance, but continued to go his own musical way. He worked mostly in live settings with drummer Sonny Murray and alto saxophonist Jimmy Lyons in the early 1960s before releasing a breakthrough album *Unit Structures* in 1966 on Blue Note Records. In the late-1960s, he experimented with larger frameworks for his playing, recording with the Jazz Composers Orchestra. In the early 1970s, he briefly taught at various universities. Meanwhile, he had gained a following in Europe and Japan, and in the 1980s there was more frequent work and a spate of recordings including some brilliant solo efforts. He also teamed for concerts with Mary Lou Williams and Max Roach. In 1988, he was featured in a month-long festival of concerts and workshops in Berlin; some of the results were issued in a lavish 11-CD boxed set. In that decade, Taylor, always fascinated by dance which he sometimes included in his performances, teamed with the famous ballet star Mikhail Baryshnikov in concert. Despite his lack of acceptance in the mainstream, Taylor received a MacArthur Fellowship in 1992. Taylor's recent live recordings, including *Qu'a: Live at the Irridium, Vol. 1* and *Qu'a Yuba:*

Live at the Irridium, Vol. 2 (1998), along with *The Willisau Concert* (2002), have garnered stellar reviews.

Taylor has set his own path in music, combining post-bop, contemporary classical music, and experimental noise into a unique and powerfully personal statement. As one of the leaders of creative-improvised music, Taylor's place in jazz is somewhat similar to John Cage's place in modern classical music. Influenced by Bud Powell, Thelonious Monk, and Duke Ellington, Taylor creates fierce and elegant soundscapes of shifting textures and accents. He once said "approach the keyboard as if it were 88 tuned drums." Taylor continues to stand as a unique force in jazz.

Koko Taylor (1935–)
Singer, Songwriter

As the undisputed "Queen of the Chicago Blues," Koko Taylor has become one of the few women to achieve legendary status in a genre dominated by men wielding electric guitars. Taylor's raspy vocal style is a throwback to the early Delta blues tradition, and she has credited her success to her refusal to dilute her singing to conform to modern fads.

Billy Taylor.

Taylor was born Cora Walton on September 28, 1935, on a farm near Memphis. After her mother died in 1939, her sharecropper father raised her, along with her five older siblings. Working in the cotton fields, the entire family would sing the blues, influenced most strongly by the classic songs played by B.B. King on his radio show. At about the age of 18, she married Robert "Pops" Taylor and moved with him to Chicago, where he had landed a job in a slaughterhouse.

In Chicago, Taylor worked as a domestic during the day and haunted South side blues clubs by night. She frequently joined such legendary Chicago blues musicians as Howlin' Wolf, Buddy Guy, and Junior Wells. Taylor was soon "discovered" by blues star Willie Dixon, who introduced her to Chess Records and wrote three songs for her. One of them, "Wang Dang Doodle," released in 1964 became a huge hit on the rhythm and blues chart.

Taylor quickly became a prominent member of the Chicago blues community. After Chess folded, she signed with Alligator Records, playing a large role in that label's transformation into a major blues outfit. Taylor continues to maintain a hectic tour schedule, and her albums have been regularly nominated for Grammy Awards, winning one in 1984. In addition, she has won numerous Handy awards.

McCoy Tyner (1938–)
Pianist, Composer, Bandleader

Born on December 11, 1938, in Philadelphia, pianist McCoy Tyner attended the Granoff School of Music and then joined the Art Farmer-Benny Golson Jazztet. Moving to New York, Tyner joined John Coltrane's quartet in 1960. During his five years with Coltrane, Tyner developed a unique two-handed, densely harmonic style that matched Coltrane's model approach and could also stand up to Elvin Jones's polyrhythmic drumming. While with Coltrane, he participated in the recordings of such milestone albums as *My Favorite Things*, *Crescent*, *A Love Supreme*, and *Ascension*. He left Coltrane's group in 1965 after the addition of second drummer Rashied Ali and saxophonist Pharoah Sanders, which resulted in his playing being drowned out.

After leaving Coltrane, he made a number of albums as leader of his own groups in various sizes—from trios to a unique big band—for Blue Note, Milestone (1972–1980), and Columbia Records, before signing with Impulse Records in 1995. Undergoing a resurgence of popularity in the 1990s, Tyner's band was named Jazz Big Band of the Year by *Down Beat* readers in 1994. Their recording *Journey* featured such players

as vocalist Diane Reeves and trombonist Slide Hampton. With the 1999 release of *McCoy Tyner and the Latin All-Stars*, Tyner demonstrated his ability to mix his unique style with a Latin rhythm. In 2000, *Jazz Roots: McCoy Tyner Honors Jazz Piano Legends of the 20th Century* was released on the TelArc label.

Tyner is one of the most distinctive and influential pianists in jazz as well as a superb composer and arranger whose own work is often unfairly overshadowed by his work with Coltrane.

Sarah Vaughan (1924–1990)
Singer

Sarah Lois Vaughan was born on March 27, 1924, in Newark, New Jersey. She sang in church, accompanied the choir on the piano, and tried a few pop songs at high school parties. As part of a dare, she entered the Wednesday night amateur contest at Harlem's famed Apollo Theater. Billy Eckstine happened to be backstage, ran out front as soon as he heard her voice, and recommended the young woman to his boss, band leader Earl Hines, who promptly hired her. In the Hines's band at that time were Charlie "Bird" Parker and Dizzy Gillespie. They and Vaughan left Hines when Eckstine decided to start his own big band, the first to feature the new sounds of bop. By 1945, she made her first recordings under her own name including the classic "Lover Man" with Bird and Dizzy, the only singer to record with the two together.

A year later she started her solo career, gained wide recognition as part of the Jazz at the Philharmonic (JATP) tour in 1948, and signed with Columbia in 1949, helping to launch her to international fame. Though she had some big pop hits during her long and rich career, she never strayed from jazz for long, and her 1950 jazz session with Miles Davis is a classic. Between 1954 and 1967, she cut an amazing array of pop and jazz recordings with Clifford Brown, Count Basie, Roy Haynes, Benny Carter, and Gerald Wilson. In the 1970s and 1980s, she continued to record prolifically, exploring Brazilian songs and the Duke Ellington songbook, but rarely working in the jazz format.

Incredibly, as she aged, she got better, losing none of her amazing top range and adding to the bottom, while her mastery of interpretation also increased. Vaughn was a virtuoso who had complete control of pitch, timbre, and dynamics. Able to use her contralto voice as a horn, she embellished melodies with the leaps and structure of an instrumentalist, leading her fans to call her "the Divine One." Sarah died on April 3, 1990, in Los Angeles, California, a mere six months after he last performance.

"T-Bone" Walker (1910–1975)
Guitarist, Songwriter

The electric guitar is now the predominant solo instrument in American pop music, largely due to Aaron Thibeaux Walker. T-Bone Walker was the first blues artist to use amplification as a music-making tool, and his playing represents a bridge between early jazz and modern, guitar-driven rock. He is cited as an important influence by countless guitarists, blues and rock and roll musicians alike.

Walker was born on May 28, 1910, in Linden, Texas, and grew up in Dallas. Both of his parents were working musicians, and Walker was exposed to many different instruments as a youth. Walker also worked for a time as Blind Lemon Jefferson's guide, escorting the legendary guitarist around town. By the time he was 16 years old, T-Bone (a corruption of his middle name) was himself a working professional guitarist.

Recording as Oak Cliff T-Bone, Walker released two singles for Columbia Records in 1929. In 1934 he relocated to Los Angeles, leaving his steady guitar gig to his soon-to-be-famous pal Charlie Christian, who revolutionized the role of guitar in jazz. In Los Angeles, Walker played in small combos at jazz clubs before joining Les Hite's Cotton Club Orchestra as a singer, guitarist, and composer in 1939. With Hite, Walker established himself as one the pioneers of the electric guitar, which he used to successfully compete on equal terms with the band's horn section.

Having established his own reputation, Walker went solo in 1940, recording for Capital Records on such tunes as "Mean Old World" (1942) and "I Got a Break Baby," which featured his fluid, elegant riffs and mellow vocals. Walker signed with Black & White Records in 1946. A year later, he recorded his most famous hit "Call It Stormy Monday," which quickly became a blues standard of the highest order. His jump blues single "T-Bone Jumps Again" from the same session is an up-tempo instrumental that displays his dexterity playing at faster speeds.

Walker continued to record impressive work for a number of labels for most of the 1950s. He toured tirelessly during the 1960s, living the rugged, hard-drinking lifestyle that often goes with touring. However, as so many other of his peers from the post-war rhythm and blues ranks, he had difficulty competing with the advent of rock and roll. His 1970 release *Good Feelin'* won a Grammy Award, but stomach ailments and a stroke in 1974 slowed him down. He died of pneumonia on March 16, 1975, in Los Angeles.

An incurable showman, Walker dazzled audiences with an arsenal of tricks such as behind-the-back guitar playing while doing the splits, that may have influenced rock and roll performer Jimi Hendrix. Modern day electric blues guitar can be traced directly back to Walker, who was its first innovator.

"Fats" Waller (1904–1943)
Composer, Pianist, Singer, Bandleader

Born in Greenwich Village in New York City on May 21, 1904, Thomas Wright Waller's father wanted him to follow in his footsteps as a preacher. However, the younger Waller liked the good times that came with playing the piano well, which he did almost from the start. At 15, he turned pro, backing singers in Harlem clubs and playing piano for silent movies at the Lincoln Theatre. In the early 1920s he became a protégé of stride pianist James P. Johnson who helped him get jobs cutting piano rolls. Waller also accompanied a number of classic blues singers such as Bessie Smith and Alberta Hunter, and began writing songs. By the end of the 1920s Waller was a force in New York, performing on a regular radio broadcast and recording with Fletcher Henderson and Sidney Bechet. A talent for writing songs soon became evident. His first and biggest hit was "Ain't Misbehavin" from 1929; others include "Honeysuckle Rose," "Blue Turning Gray Over You," and "The Jitterbug Waltz." He also wrote "London Suite" for solo piano.

With his own small group and occasional big band, he cut more than 500 sides between 1934 and his untimely death at 39 in 1943. His style really came across on records, and no matter how trite the tune, he transformed it into a jazz gem. He also appeared in films including *Stormy Weather* with Lena Horne, and toured Europe. He also enjoyed playing Bach, especially on the organ, which he was the first to make into a jazz instrument. In 1932, the world-famous Marcel Dupre invited Fats to play the organ at the Notre Dame Cathedral in Paris. On a return train trip from Hollywood, where he had played the Zanzibar Room, to New York City, Waller died of pneumonia on December 15, 1943.

Waller was one of the greatest showmen of jazz, a terrific organist, fine singer, and talented songwriter. Weighing in at over 300 pounds and standing more than six feet tall, Waller came by his nickname naturally. Wherever he went people loved him and his terrific style.

Dinah Washington (1924–1963)
Singer

Washington was born Ruth Lee Jones on August 29, 1924, in Tuscaloosa, Alabama, and got her start singing

Dinah Washington.

gospel music at St. Luke's Baptist Church on Chicago's South side. She toured churches with her mother, playing the piano and singing solos, until another opportunity beckoned—an amateur talent contest at Chicago's Regal Theater. Her triumphant performance led to performances at local nightclubs, and in 1943 the 19 year-old singer successfully auditioned for a slot in Lionel Hampton's band. She was soon discovered by composer and critic, Leonard Feather, and Washington and Feather together created several chart toppers including "Baby Get Lost," "Salty Papa Blues," "Evil Gal Blues," and "Homeward Bound." She then worked with Milt Jackson and Charles Mingus in 1945, and over time her singing moved from the blues to more jazz-oriented material. By the 1950s she was a successful crossover artist, gaining legendary status with "What A Difference A Day Makes" and "Unforgettable." Washington died of an overdose of alcohol and diet pills on December 14, 1963, in Detroit.

Washington's popularity as a blues singer in the tradition of Bessie Smith and her ability to cross over into jazz and pop genres have won her many fans in the decades since her death. Able to sound seductive and

tough at the same time, Washington was an immensely talented vocalist.

Muddy Waters (1915–1983)
Guitarist, Harmonica Player, Singer

Waters was born Morganfield McKinley in Rolling Fork, Mississippi, on April 4, 1915, and grew up in nearby Clarkesdale on Stovall's plantation. He began playing guitar at the age of 17, performing at parties and fish fries. Waters, who idolized Son House, was first captured on tape in field recordings by Alan Lomax in 1941. After running a juke house in the early 1940s, Waters moved to Chicago in 1943, where he played in clubs during the evening and worked as a laborer during the day.

In 1946 Waters cut sides for Columbia Records, but his urban sound was not well-received, and they were not released. Appearing as a sideman in 1947 with Sunnyland Slim, Waters also cut two sides for Chess Records before recording "I Feel Like Going Home" in 1948, which became his first national rhythm and blues hit. On the single, he fronted his own band that included Little Walter on harmonica. In the 1950s, Waters produced such masterpieces as Willie Dixon's "I'm Your Hoochie Coochie Man," "Got My Mojo Working," "Tiger in Your Tank," and "Mannish Boy." Popularized by white British youth, Muddy Waters eventually played on stage with many of them including Eric Clapton and Mike Bloomfield, both of whom considered Waters a guitar master and a living legend.

In the late 1960s and into the 1970s, Waters began receiving the kind of widespread recognition he deserved, including winning three Grammy Awards and a Trendsetter Award and being inducted into the *Ebony* Readers' Poll Black Hall of Fame. The post-war Chicago blues scene would have been incomplete without Muddy Waters. His aggressive, swaggering, Delta-rooted vocal sound and piercing slide guitar attack made him the "Father of Electric Blues." Waters died on April 30, 1983.

Ben Webster (1909–1973)
Saxophonist

Born in Kansas City, Missouri, on March 27, 1909, Benjamin Francis Love Webster was at first a pianist, but switched to saxophone in his late teens. He worked with the family band led by Lester Young's father and with many other Midwestern bands. Ben traveled to New York in 1931 with Bennie Moten and was a featured performer on the landmark recording of "Moten Swing." After gaining a name among musicians as one of the most gifted disciples of Coleman Hawkins, he made many records and toured with many prominent bands including those of Fletcher Henderson, Cab Calloway, Benny Carter, and Teddy Wilson.

When Webster joined Duke Ellington in 1940, along with Jimmy Blanton and Billy Strayhorn, he really blossomed as a tenor soloist and soon became an influence in his own right. When he left Ellington in 1943, he mainly led his own small groups, recorded prolifically, and became one of the first African American musicians to join a network radio musical staff in 1944 with CBS. By the 1950s Webster moved to the West Coast and recorded with Art Tatum, Coleman Hawkins, and Billie Holiday. In 1965, he left on what had been planned as his first brief visit to Europe, but he never returned home. Due to a lack of work in the United States and changing trends in the jazz industry, Webster settled in Copenhagen, Denmark, where he spent the final decade of his life as a revered and beloved elder statesman of jazz. During this period, his always masterful ballad playing ripened to full maturity, and his sound, ranging from a whisper to a gruff roar, became one of the unsurpassed landmarks of classic jazz. He died on September 20, 1973, in Amsterdam, Netherlands. One of the big three tenor saxophone players of the 1930s and 1940s, along with Coleman Hawkins and Lester Young, Webster's full-bodied tone, warm vibrato, and bluesy melodies made him an icon.

Mary Lou Williams (1910–1981)
Pianist, Composer, Arranger

Most women who have achieved fame in jazz have been singers, from Bessie Smith to Betty Carter. An exception to this rule was Mary Lou Williams, dubbed the "First Lady of Jazz." Born in Atlanta on May 8, 1910, and brought up in Pittsburgh, Mary Elfrieda Scruggs had already performed in public at the age of six and was a pro by 13. Three years later she married saxophonist John Williams, with whom she made her record debut. When John joined Andy Kirk's band, she took over his old group. Soon, however, she was writing arrangements for Kirk, and in 1931 she became the band's pianist and musical director.

Though she also wrote for Benny Goodman, Earl Hines, and Tommy Dorsey, she stayed with Kirk until 1942, helping to make the band one of the swing era's best. After a return home to Pittsburgh in 1942, where she formed her own band that included a young Art Blakey, she settled in New York. A champion of modern jazz, she gave advice and counsel to such rising stars as Dizzy Gillespie and Thelonious Monk and contributed scores for Gillespie's big band. Williams joined Duke

Ellington's band and served as staff arranger, contributing some 15 pieces during 1946. She led her own groups (sometimes all female) and began to compose longer works including the "Zodiac Suite," performed at Town Hall in 1946 by the New York Philharmonic Orchestra.

Williams lived in England and France from 1952 to 1954. After returning to the United States, she retired from music for approximately three years, forming a charitable organization to assist musicians with dependency and health problems. Resuming her career, she toured widely including a 1957 appearance at the Newport Jazz Festival with Gillespie, ran her own record label (1955–1963), and wrote several religious works including a jazz mass performed at St. Patrick's Cathedral. In 1977, she became artist-in-residence and teacher of jazz history and performance at Duke University, a position that she held until her death on May 28, 1981, in Durham, North Carolina.

Williams was a highly regarded instrumentalist, primarily in the swing idiom, and a gifted composer. Most importantly, she was the only major jazz artist who lived and adapted her playing style throughout all of the jazz eras including spirituals, ragtime, blues, Kansas City swing, boogie woogie, bop, and avant-garde.

"Sonny Boy" Williamson (1899–1965)
Singer, Harmonica

Most sources have the man who was to become Sonny Boy Williamson as being born on December 5, 1899, in Glendora, Mississippi. However absolutely nothing is known of his early childhood, and even his real name, believed to be Aleck Ford "Rice" Miller, cannot be verified. What is known is that by the mid-1930s, he was traveling the Delta working under the alias of Little Boy Blue with such blues legends as Robert Johnson, Robert Nighthawk, and Elmore James. By the early 1940s he was appearing on "King Biscuit Time," the first live blues radio show. (The sponsor of the show had Miller pose as John Lee "Sonny Boy" Williamson, an established Chicago blues star, in order to increase sales of their product. Apparently the ruse succeeded and when John Lee was murdered, Miller became "the original Sonny Boy.") The show was an immediate hit, but Miller did not record his work until the period of 1951–1954 when his first single "Eyesight to the Blind" became a hit. Miller also participated in Elmore James's "Dust My Broom" session before recording his first session for Chess Records in August 1955, releasing "Don't Start Me To Talkin." In 1963 he headed to Europe and enjoyed tremendous success, recording with British blues-rock groups, the Yardbirds and the Animals, before releasing the hit "Help Me."

Two years later, he returned to the United States, where he died of a heart attack in Helena, Arkansas, on May 25.

Sonny Boy Williamson was one of the great blues legends who enjoyed tremendous popularity among blues purist and rock and roll fans. He wrote and played some of the best blues songs ever. His sly, world-weary vocal delivery, combined with his powerful harmonica playing, made his sound unique.

Teddy Wilson (1912–1986)
Pianist, Bandleader

Born on November 24, 1912, in Austin, Texas, Theodore Wilson's father taught English and his mother was head librarian at Tuskegee Institute. Teddy studied music theory at Talladega College before moving to Detroit in 1929 where he played in local bands before moving to Chicago in 1930. From 1931–33 he played in Louis Armstrong's big band and with others, before he was brought to New York by Benny Carter in 1933.

Two years later, Wilson began to make a series of records with Billie Holiday, Ben Webster, and Johnny Hodges. Meanwhile, he became famous as the first black jazz musician to be featured with a white band when he was hired in 1935 to play with the Benny Goodman Trio and Quartet with whom he stayed until 1939. His marvelously clear, harmonically impeccable piano style was a big influence on the pianists of the swing era. His own big band formed in 1939 was excellent but not a commercial success. From 1940 onward, he mostly led small groups or appeared as a soloist, touring worldwide and making hundreds of records. Though seriously ill, he continued to perform until a week before his death on July 31, 1986, in New Britain, Connecticut. Two of his three sons are professional musicians.

Wilson's style evolved from the early influence of Earl Hines, Art Tatum (who befriended him early in his career), and Fats Waller, but became a neat and quietly swinging style that featured single note lines that was revolutionary at the time. Wilson was also a fine but little known arranger and writer.

"Prez" Young (1909–1959)
Saxophonist

Born August 27, 1909, in Woodville, Mississippi, Lester Willis Young was instructed on trumpet, violin, alto sax, and drums by his father who was a trained musician that studied at Tuskegee. His family moved to New Orleans during Lester's infancy, and by age ten Lester was playing drums in the family band. He spent his youth on the carnival circuit in the Midwest, choosing to concentrate on the saxophone at age 13 (i.e., the C melody saxophone after his idol Frankie Trumbauer). Young's first major job was as baritone with the Bostonians in 1929–1930, before touring all over the Midwest with the bands of King Oliver and Walter Page.

After a brief stint with Count Basie, Young was offered Coleman Hawkin's chair in Fletcher Henderson's orchestra, but he was criticized for not having the same style as his predecessor and he soon left. He returned to Kansas City to play with Andy Kirk, and then with Count Basie from 1936 to 1940. During the Basie years, Young surpassed Hawkins as the vital influences on the tenor. Hardly a tenor man from the mid-1940s through the 1950s achieved prominence without building upon the foundations laid by Lester Young. After leaving Basie's band, Young worked in several small combos in the early 1940s before entering the Army in 1944. During his 15-month service, Young suffered what many characterized as traumatic racial prejudice that affected him for the rest of his life. After his return to civilian life, he worked in numerous small combos and toured with the Jazz at the Philharmonic (JATP) units. He suffered a complete emotional breakdown in 1955, but made a comeback the next year. He died from a combination of mental problems, alcoholism, and malnutrition on March 15, 1959, within hours of returning from a long engagement in Paris.

It was Lester Young who gave Billie Holiday the name "Lady Day" when both were with Count Basie, and it was Holiday, in turn, who christened Lester Young "President" (later shortened to "Prez"). Young is remembered for his style which formed the bridge from hot and swing jazz to bebop and cool jazz. Young transformed the big, full-tone, and dotted eighth- and sixteenth-note phrasing to a moodier, laconic sound utilizing a series of evenly placed eighth notes played legato.

Popular Music

◆ The Rise of Rhythm and Blues ◆ "Crossovers" into Country Music
◆ Sweet Soul Music and Social Revolution ◆ Psychedelic Soul to Disco
◆ Rap: From Subculture to Mass Appeal
◆ New Directions: From Nuevo Soul to Pop-Hip Hop
◆ Popular Music Composers, Musicians, and Singers ◆ Award Winners

by Guthrie P. Ramsey Jr.

◆ THE RISE OF RHYTHM AND BLUES

The appearance of rhythm and blues or "R&B" marks one of the most important developments in American popular music. Before rhythm and blues, the swing style of jazz was considered the most popular music of the day. Artists like Benny Goodman, Duke Ellington, and Count Basie reigned in America's popular imagination and on the record sales charts. Things began to change during the mid-1940s, though. The term "rhythm and blues" describes a number of historically specific styles that have grown out of the African American vernacular music tradition since mid-century. Rhythm and blues laid the foundation for numerous subsequent styles including rock and roll, soul, disco, funk, jazz fusion, rap and, most recently, "smooth" (contemporary) jazz. R&B artists combined the conventions of several popular music styles: swing jazz, boogie woogie, gospel blues, blues, and, in some cases, novelty pop. From the swing tradition, rhythm and blues musicians adopted the riff-based horn arrangements and driving rhythms of groups such as Count Basie and His Orchestra. Gospel and blues music provided a system of dramatic vocal techniques, which were crafted by artists into highly stylized personal mannerisms. Gospel, jazz, and blues also provided musical forms such as 32-bar songs and 12-bar blues patterns to the new style. Unlike the swing era big bands, "jump blues" groups featured fewer horns and a heavy rhythmic approach marked by a walking boogie bass line, honking saxophone solos, and a two-four

drum pattern. Among the greatest exponents of post-war jump blues were guitarist T-Bone Walker, saxophonist Eddie "Cleanhead" Vinson, and blues shouter Big Joe Turner.

Singer and saxophonist Louis Jordan fronted a supremely popular jump blues ensemble that featured his singing, which was a smooth gospel-influenced vocal style. In 1949, the popularity of the style championed by Jordan and others led producer Jerry Wexler, who was working at *Billboard Magazine*, to change its African American pop chart title to rhythm and blues, thus coining the name of this new music. The new sound, originally dubbed "jump blues" and later rhythm and blues, proved extremely popular beyond the African American community, marking one of many important "cross-over" moments in American popular music history. The melding of musical techniques that distinguished rhythm and blues is related to the specific socio-historical context of mid-century America. Due to an ample supply of jobs caused by World War II, black and white Southerners flooded the North seeking new opportunities and life chances. This migration created a dramatic shift in the demographics of major cities in the North, Midwest, and West. The burgeoning U.S. economy during the war provided these migrants with the resources to seek different kinds of entertainment in their new locales.

The lyrics of rhythm and blues songs reflected ways in which some migrants negotiated these changes. Many rhythm and blues lyrics speak of life in the South through a nostalgic lens; others use metaphors that reference country living; and others speak of hardships associated with life in the urban North. As African

Americans pressured the U.S. government to end Jim Crow and the laws of the land that denied them equal rights, the color line between the races became less rigid, and as a result, white and black Americans gained greater access to each other's cultures, especially music. Much as jazz music already was, rhythm and blues was an important source of cultural exchange. In fact, the popularity of rhythm and blues paved the way for rock and roll's replacing jazz as the America's quintessential popular music in the 1950s. But the music remained rooted in the sound of the African American church, though not exclusively. Some of the early recordings exemplifying the gospel influence on rhythm and blues were Cecil Grant's 1945 hit "I Wonder," Roy Brown's 1947 classic "Good Rocking Tonight," and Wynonie Harris's 1949 disc "All She Wants To Do Is Rock."

Dinah Washington was one of the earliest female rhythm and blues singers to make a mark on the entertainment industry during the 1940s. Her song stylings combined jazz, blues, gospel, and pop ballads. During her childhood, Washington honed her musical skills in the Baptist churches in Chicago, although she, as many others, was born in the South. After scoring hits with "Evil Gal Blues" and "Salty Papa Blues" early in her career, she recorded a string of hits for the Mercury label, with which she began an association in 1948. Washington's recorded work sprawls over several categories including rhythm and blues, pop, jazz, and country.

Louis Jordan, however, is considered the most important jump blues or rhythm and blues performer during the 1940s. He formed his group Louis Jordan and His Tympani Five in 1938 with an eye toward entertaining and capturing some of the white market. His repertoire was eclectic: jump blues, ballads, and novelty songs. With titles such as "Beans and Cornbread," "Saturday Night Fish Fry," and "Ain't Nobody Here but Us Chickens," the group's chart busting songs, as writer Nelson George has noted, "suggest country life, yet the subject of each is really a city scene."

It was not long before this kind of raw-edged rhythm and blues emerged from hundreds of independent recording labels that appeared across the country in the postwar era. With the increased availability of rhythm and blues recordings, a handful of African American radio disc jockeys became locally famous as the first promoters and salesmen of this music. Bringing their colorful street language to the airwaves, pioneer African American DJs such as Al Benson and Vernon Winslow not only helped to popularize rhythm and blues, but set the trend for modern pop and African American radio programming.

Rhythm & Blues and the African American Church

In the early 1950s, numerous gospel quartets and street corner singing groups set out to establish careers in the African American popular music scene. Influenced by gospel music groups such as the Golden Gate Quartet and the Harmonizing Four and the secular singing of groups such as the Inkspots, vocal groups appeared that performed complex harmonies in *a capella* style. As they would for rap artists in decades to come, street corners in urban neighborhoods became training grounds for thousands of young aspiring African American artists. This music, known as doo wop, first arrived on the scene with the formation of the Ravens in 1945. Not long afterward, there followed a great succession of doo wop "bird groups" including the Orioles who, in 1953, scored a nationwide hit with "Crying in the Chapel"—a song which, for the first time in African American popular music, walked an almost indistinguishable line between gospel and mainstream pop music. In the same year, Billy Ward formed the Dominoes, featuring lead singer Clyde McPhatter, the son of a Baptist minister.

In the wake of the success of these vocal groups, numerous gospel singers left the church to become pop music stars. In 1952, for example, the Royal Sons became the pop group Five Royales. They later changed their name to the Gospel Starlighters (with James Brown), and finally the Blue Flames. Five years later, a young gospel singer named Sam Cooke landed a number one pop hit with "You Send Me," a song which achieved popularity among both black and white audiences.

The strong relationship between gospel and rhythm and blues was evident in the music of more hard-edged rhythm and blues groups such as Hank Ballard and the Midnighters. Maintaining a driving blues-based sound, Ballard's music, while featuring gospel-based harmonies, retained secular themes, as evidenced in his 1954 hit "Work With Me Annie." However, the capstone of gospel rhythm and blues appeared in the talents of Georgia-born pianist and singer Ray Charles, who in 1954 hit the charts with "I Got a Woman," which was based upon the gospel song "My Jesus Is All the World to Me." Charles's 1958 recording "What I'd Say" is famed for its call-and-response pattern which directly resembled the music sung in Holiness churches.

Rock and Roll

The rise of white rock and roll around 1955 served to open the floodgates for thousands of black rhythm and blues artists longing for a nationwide audience. A term applied to black rhythm and blues and its white equivalents during the mid-1950s, rock and roll represented a label given to a music form by the white media and marketplace in order to attract a mass multiracial audience. Alan Freed, a white DJ from Ohio is credited with being the first to air radio programming dubbed "rock 'n roll," and thus he is remembered in some circles as the "Father of Rock and Roll." While the term itself had been used in black vernacular language for years, it was used by white promoters of rock and roll to distinguish it from rhythm and blues, which was, of course, closely associated with black music culture. Many Southern whites expressed outrage at the growing interest in rhythm and blues and rock 'n roll among white teenagers, and various authorities mounted "Don't Buy Negro Records" campaigns. As African American music writer Nelson George explained, naming this music rock and roll, "dulled down the racial identification and made young white consumers of Cold War America feel more comfortable." Taken from a term common among the Delta and electric blues cultures, rock and roll was actually rhythm and blues rechristened with a more "socially acceptable" title. Of course, the term "rock and roll" had sexual connotations as well; this, along with its roots in black culture, allowed white cultural conservatives of the time to demonize the form.

Thus, the majority of rhythm and blues performers never made the distinction between rhythm and blues and rock and roll. Ike Turner, a talent scout for the pioneering Sun Studios record label, was a formidable bandleader and guitarist; his 1951 cut "Rocket 88" has been considered by some to be the very first rock and roll record. The song's distorted guitar tone was achieved by accident—coming from a broken amplifier speaker—but would influence the gritty sound of many subsequent rock and blues guitarists. Turner achieved mainstream success in collaboration with his wife, singer Tina Turner, whose fame would later eclipse him. One rhythm and blues artist who established a prosperous career in rock and roll was New Orleans-born pianist Antoine "Fats" Domino. Although he had produced a great amount of strong rhythm and blues material before his career in rock and roll, Domino did not hit the charts until 1955 with "Ain't That A Shame," followed by the classics "Blueberry Hill," "I'm Walkin," and "Whole Lotta Loving." Another rhythm and blues pianist/singer to enter the rock and roll field was Little Richard Penniman, a former Pentecostal gospel singer whose career in pop music began in 1956 with the hit "Tutti Frutti." Little Richard's fiery vocalizations featuring screams, hollers, and falsetto whoops was only matched for intensity by his very explosive and rhythmic piano playing, which drew on blues and gospel traditions. Before entering a Seventh Day Adventist seminary in 1959, Little Richard produced a string of hits: "Long Tall Sally," "Rip It Up," "The Girl Can't Help It," and "Good Golly Miss Molly."

In 1955, as Fats Domino's New Orleans style rhythm and blues tunes climbed the charts, a young guitarist from St. Louis named Chuck Berry achieved nationwide fame when his country-influenced song "Maybelline" reached number five on the charts. Backed by bluesman Muddy Waters's rhythm section, "Maybelline" offered a unique form of rhythm and blues, combining white hillbilly, or rockabilly, with jump blues; Berry revolutionized rhythm and blues by featuring the guitar as a lead, rather than a rhythm instrument. Modeled after his blues guitar mentor T-Bone Walker, Berry's double string guitar bends and syncopated up-stroke rhythm created a driving backdrop for his colorfully poetic tales of teenage life. A very eclectic and creative musician, Berry incorporated the sounds of urban blues, country, calypso, Latin, and even Hawaiian music into his unique brand of rhythm and blues. His classic "Johnny B. Goode" recorded in 1958 became a standard in almost every rock and roll band's repertoire including 1960s rock guitar hero Jimi Hendrix. According to popular music scholar Timothy D. Taylor, many African American early rockers like Berry made a concerted effort to court an integrated audience, a notion that is evident in changes he made to a later recording of the song "Johnny B. Goode."

◆ "CROSSOVERS" INTO COUNTRY MUSIC

African American musicians did not remain consigned to styles closely associated with African American culture. Dinah Washington, for example, recorded several pop tunes beginning with the mainstream title "What a Difference a Day Makes" in 1959, her first major hit. She also recorded what were known as "reverse crossovers," songs that originally appeared in the country or pop category but which Washington performs in her patented jazz-blues-gospel manner. In addition, Chuck Berry was not the only African American to take an interest in country music. Ray Charles's crossover into country music in the early 1960s caused controversy in many circles. In 1959, Charles recorded "I'm Moving On," a country tune by Hank Snow. Despite opposition, Charles went on to record a fine collection of songs in 1962 entitled *Modern Sounds in Country Music*. Filled with soulful ballads and backed by colorful string sections, the session produced two classic numbers "You Don't Know Me" and "I Can't Stop Loving You." Its popularity spawned a 1963 sequel *Modern Sounds in Country Music Volume 2*, producing several more hits including Hank Williams's "Your

Chuck Berry.

Cheating Heart" and "Take These Chains From My Heart."

Unlike other mainstream African American country artists, Charles's renditions remained immersed in his unique gospel blues sound. Before Charles's entrance into the country music field there had been many African American country artists such as Dedford Bailey, a partially disabled harmonica player who became a regularly featured performer on the Grand Ole Opry from 1925 to 1941. However, it was not until 1965, when Charley Pride arrived on the country music scene with his RCA recordings "Snakes Crawl at Night" and "Atlantic Coastal Line" that an African American artist emerged as a superstar in the country tradition. Pride's songs were so steeped in the country tradition that many radio listeners were astounded when they found out his racial identity. With the arrival of Pride, there appeared other African American country artists such as Linda Martel from South Carolina, O. B. McClinton from Mississippi, and Oklahoma-born Big Al Downing and Stoney Edwards. The most noted of these artists, Edwards recorded two nationwide hits in 1968 with Jesse Winchester's "You're On My Mind" and Leonard Cohen's "Bird on a Wire."

◆ SWEET SOUL MUSIC AND SOCIAL REVOLUTION

The tremendous social upheavals of the 1960s—including but not limited to the Civil Rights, Black Power, and women's movements and the coalescence of a youth-based counterculture—were paralleled by numerous new musical forms. Perhaps no single genre of popular song encapsulated the highs and lows of this period more than soul music. Soul music drew on several idioms of African American music including gospel, jazz, and blues. According to music scholar David Brackett, gospel vocal techniques that signified spiritual ecstasy in the religious context were transplanted by soul singers into the secular context with important results. The most prominent of these is a sense of raw passion that identified the singers with the songs and the songs with the African American community. Thus, being born in the African American church, where testifying preachers and harmonizing choirs shepherded their congregations to weekly ecstasy, the form was escorted into the secular world by a handful of artists schooled simultaneously in gospel, jazz, country blues, rhythm and blues, and rock and roll.

Although he had precursors such as vocalist Clyde McPhatter, who recorded with the Dominoes and the Drifters, singer keyboardist Ray Charles has been credited as one of the founders of the soul genre. His earliest hits—notably, "What'd I Say" and "I Got a Woman"—brought the emotional testifying and call-and-response arrangements associated with gospel music into a non-religious context. He added the earthy pull of the blues and a jazz-influenced harmonic complexity to his distinctive musical blend. This hybrid of blue groove and spirit was the secular gospel known as soul music. Such innovations were controversial, but the sounds of soul sweetened and enriched rhythm and blues music from then on. Blind "Brother Ray" became a cultural icon in the ensuing decades.

While rhythm and blues had functioned for some time as gospel's sinful, worldly counterpart—focusing largely on the concerns of the body while church music addressed the spirit—soul refused to deny either side of human experience. Even so, the young genre's exuberance and ambition made it ideal for reflecting the growing aspirations of America's black population. Inspired by the teachings and nonviolent organizing of Dr. Martin Luther King Jr. and other civil rights leaders, African Americans also responded to songs that trumpeted change. "People Get Ready" and "We're a Winner" by Curtis Mayfield and the Impressions were early anthems as soul grew and drew many more listeners.

Singer-bandleader James Brown, meanwhile, combined uplift and hard groove, gradually moving from heady soul/rhythm and blues into a new territory called funk with hits such as "I Got You (I Feel Good)" and "Cold Sweat." Brown ran one of the tightest ships around, alternately inspiring and browbeating his musicians; turnover was high, but the ensemble was always a well-oiled machine. Though he would refine the funk style—driving rhythms emphasizing the "one" or first beat of each measure; repetitive vocal phrases and improvised, "churchy" shouts; and minimal, almost dissonant, instrumental figures—during the early 1960s, its content remained largely sexual for some time. Brown's mid-1960s work began laying the musical foundation for funk, and his music primarily celebrated the dynamic tradition of African American social dancing in songs such as "There Was A Time" and "Licking Stick," often naming popular dances such as the "boogaloo" and the "funky chicken" in songs. Brown's political message did not fully materialize until the end of the decade. By then, his funky sermons championed African American economic independence and freedom from addiction. Brown had a seismic affect on pop; not only funk artists but also scores of rock and rap musicians took his work as a point of departure.

James Brown, "The Godfather of Soul."

Following Brown's lead, Sly and the Family Stone—led by Sylvester "Sly Stone" Stewart, a Northern California DJ and producer—lent a psychedelic rock tinge and communal good vibes to the bedrock funk groove. Featuring musicians black and white, male and female, the group offered one of the most inclusive visions in pop history. While "Dance to the Music" mapped out their utopia in musical terms, they trumpeted tolerance and equality in happy hits such as "Everyday People," "Everybody Is a Star," and "You Can Make It If You Try." Stone's vision would darken substantially later on, however.

The syncopated rhythms of New Orleans were also fundamental to the development of modern funk. The Meters began as an instrumental foursome and eventually backed up acts as diverse as singer Lee Dorsey, vocal group The Pointer Sisters, and British popster Robert Palmer. During the 1960s they scored some instrumental hits—notably "Cissy Strut"—before adding vocals in the 1970s. Though they eventually disbanded and were partly subsumed by soul survivors the Neville Brothers, the Meters were profoundly influential.

Soul North and South: Stax/Volt, Atlantic, and Motown

Soul music's increasing hold on the public imagination during the 1960s had a great deal to do with two record companies, the Atlantic Records subsidiary Stax/Volt in the South and Motown in the North. Stax/Volt was a Memphis-based label that introduced the world to the rough-hewn "funky" sound of Southern soul and rhythm and blues. The company's greatest successes came during the 1960s, thanks to a roster of powerful artists, gifted songwriters, and one of the greatest "house bands" in music history. The band in question, led by keyboardist Booker T. Jones, was a formidable mixed race groove machine that not only backed the whole Stax roster and numerous acts on its parent label, Atlantic, but also achieved success as an instrumental recording act, Booker T. and the MG's. Their smoldering workouts "Green Onions" and "Hip Hug-Her" became signature themes of the era.

Stax's roster included vocal duo Sam and Dave, Rufus and Carla Thomas, Eddie Floyd, and Otis Redding. House songwriters Isaac Hayes and David Porter wrote hits such as "Soul Man" and "Hold On, I'm Coming" for Sam and Dave; Hayes himself would later become a pop/soul superstar. Redding was both an extraordinary singer and a gifted tunesmith; he penned the luminous "Dock of the Bay" and the righteous "Respect." The latter song was transformed into an anthem of nascent feminism and African American dignity thanks to the alchemy of Atlantic Records's Aretha Franklin, a gospel-bred singer turned pop maven; Franklin would become the "Queen of Soul" and one of the most enduring figures in popular music. While Franklin made "Respect" and other celebrated recordings—tracks such as "Chain of Fools," the incandescent "(You Make Me Feel Like a) Natural Woman," and "I Never Loved a Man" at the Fame studios in Muscle Shoals, Alabama, other Atlantic soul stars came to Memphis to make their hit records. The Stax crew collaborated with Wilson Pickett on hugely successful singles such as "In the Midnight Hour" and "Land of 1,000 Dances." Ultimately, however, Stax lost its commercial momentum and by the 1970s was struggling to compete with a panoply of rivals.

As soul music gained a mass following in the African American community, an African American-owned and family-run Detroit record company emerged as one of the largest and most successful African American business enterprises in the United States. In 1959, Berry Gordy, a Detroit entrepreneur, songwriter, and modern jazz enthusiast, established the Motown Record Corporation.

Berry Gordy.

With its headquarters located in a modest two-story home, the company proudly displayed a sign on its exterior reading Hitsville USA. Taking advantage of the diversity of local talent, Gordy employed Detroit-based contract teams, writers, producers, and engineers. Motown's studio became a great laboratory for technological innovations, advancing the use of echo, multitracking, and over-dubbing. In the studio, Gordy employed the city's finest jazz and classical musicians to accompany the young singing talent signed to the company.

Unlike the soul music emerging in studios such as Stax and Muscle Shoals, Motown's music was also marketed at the white middle class; Gordy called his music "The Sound of Young America" and sought to produce glamorous and well-groomed acts. "Blues and R&B always had a funky look to it back in those days," explained Motown producer Mickey Stevenson. "We felt that we should have a look that the mothers and fathers would want their children to follow." Indeed, a meticulously controlled and glamorous image was an extremely important component in Berry Gordy's Motown ideology. He required artists signed to the label to attend classes on etiquette, stage presence, and choreography. In fact, the strict division of labor that Gordy established in this company might be compared to the automobile assembly lines for which Detroit is well-known.

Thus, Motown set out to produce a sound, which it considered more refined and less "off-key" than the music played by mainstream soul and blues artists. In its early years of operation, Motown retained a rhythm and blues influence as evidenced in songs such as the Marvelettes' "Please Mister Postman" (1961), Mary Wells's "You Beat Me to the Punch" (1962), and Marvin Gaye's "Pride and Joy" (1963).

One of the main forces responsible for the emergence of a unique "Motown sound" appeared in the production team of Brian and Eddie Holland, and Lamont Dozier, or H-D-H, as they came to be known. Utilizing the recording techniques of Phil Spector's "wall of sound," the H-D-H team brought fame to many of Motown's "girl groups" such as Martha and the Vandellas, and the Supremes, featuring Diana Ross.

During 1966 and 1967, H-D-H began to use more complex string arrangements based upon minor chord structures. This gave rise to what has been referred to as their "classical period." As a result, many Motown songs reflected the darker side of lost love and the conditions of ghetto life. This mood was captured in such songs by the Four Tops as "Reach Out, I'll Be There," "Bernadette," and "Seven Rooms of Gloom."

After the Holland-Dozier-Holland team left Motown in 1968, the company, faced with numerous artistic and economic problems, fell into a state of decline. A year later, Gordy signed the Jackson Five, the last major act to join the label before its demise. The Jacksons landed 13 consecutive hit singles including "ABC" and "I'll Be There," championing a style that might be called "bubblegum soul"—African American music directed at a preteen and young adolescent audience, a legacy that was seen in 1980s and 1990s groups such as New Edition and Boyz II Men. In 1971, Gordy moved the Motown Record Corporation to Los Angeles, where the company directed its efforts toward filmmaking. Through the late 1970s and early 1980s, Motown continued to sign such acts as the Commodores, Lionel Richie, and DeBarge. But in 1984, Gordy entered into a distribution agreement with MCA records and eventually sold Motown to an entertainment conglomerate.

◆ PSYCHEDELIC SOUL TO DISCO

Disillusionment after the deaths of civil rights champion Dr. Martin Luther King Jr. and black power advocate Malcolm X, along with the lingering trauma of the Vietnam War and the worsening plight of America's inner cities, had a marked influence on soul's direction. Curtis Mayfield projected a vision of wary hope in his early 1970s work. His landmark soundtrack for the "blaxploitation" film *Superfly* reflected the new soul paradigm: at once gritty and symphonic, encompassing soul's far-reaching ambition and funk's uncompromising, earthy realism. Isaac Hayes's theme from *Shaft*, another urban action film, earned an Academy Award. Much of the funk and soul of this period drew not only on the percolating rhythms developed by Brown but also on the trailblazing guitar work of Jimi Hendrix.

Hailed by many as the greatest electric guitarist of all time, Hendrix had toiled as a sideman for numerous rhythm and blues acts but emerged as a rocker of the first order during the mid-1960s. By the time of his death in 1970, he had revolutionized lead guitar playing forever; his use of the wah-wah pedal, an effect that lent a powerful percussive dimension to the instrument, became a staple of funk. His melding of psychedelic rock, hard blues, and soul tropes, meanwhile, influenced the "psychedelic soul" that emerged in his wake.

Commercial soul addressed the tenor of the times. Trailblazers Sly and the Family Stone focused less on the rainbow-colored sentiments of the preceding era and more on urban turmoil with their landmark album *There's a Riot Going On*, as did Marvin Gaye with hits such as "Trouble Man" and "What's Goin' On." The O'Jays enjoyed chart success with such anxious singles as "Backstabbers" and "For the Love of Money," and the Temptations wrapped their prodigious vocal chops around inner-city woes on "Papa Was a Rolling Stone," among other smashes.

These commercial laments were outstripped in daring—though not in sales—by the work of Detroit's Funkadelic. Fronted by singer and hairstylist George Clinton, who led a doo wop group called The Parliaments in the 1950s, Funkadelic mixed acid rock's cosmic guitar excursions with funk's relentless grooves; a danger existed in their work that limited its commercial appeal, but profoundly influenced rock and rap.

Eventually, Clinton established another group, Parliament, which focused on horn-driven funk and elaborate, fantasy-oriented concept albums. Funkadelic and Parliament, though manifestly different at first, gradually moved into similar territory as "P. Funk"; the "P" meaning "pure." Soon P. Funk was the umbrella term for a family of bands that included Bootsy's Rubber Band and the Brides of Funkenstein. Clinton scored in the 1980s as a solo artist, most notably with the megahit "Atomic Dog." P. Funk was so influential that for a time Parliament found itself competing with acts that appropriated its sound and themes including hitmakers such as the Ohio Players, Rick James, George Duke,

As front man for Funkadelic, George Clinton's music influenced both rock and rap.

and Earth, Wind and Fire. Though funk declined during the 1980s, artists such as Prince took it in a new, eclectic direction.

The decade did not lack for more traditionally romantic performers, however. Apart from Marvin Gaye, the period's most seductive male vocalists were arguably Al Green and Barry White. Green's rich falsetto and intimate phrasing on hits such as "Let's Stay Together" and "Love and Happiness" quickly established him as a visionary in the genre; though he left pop music to sing gospel music and preach, he remained a beloved figure in the soul world and returned to the fold for a 1995 album. White's bedroom soundtracks, meanwhile, kept lovers in thrall with an intoxicating blend of his baritone vocals and symphonic arrangements. Another funk direction coalesced in the work of jazz-based artists such as Herbie Hancock and Patrice Rushen, both of whom scored hits in the 1970s and 1980s that coincided with the appearance of the so-called "Quiet Storm" format in rhythm and blues radio programming. Each drew on jazz, rhythm and blues, and funk in their recordings, some of them

featuring piano solos that extended them beyond the length of typical rhythm and blues recordings.

During the mid-1970s, club dance floors were increasingly dominated by the pulsating sounds of disco. With its thumping beat and lush arrangements, the music was viewed by many as a saccharine and escapist form that betrayed the mission of funk and soul. While a number of powerful performers emerged from the disco scene, few could approach the star power of diva Donna Summer, who enjoyed a wave of hits before a religious conversion moved her into gospel. Though disco's "crossover" success meant that a number of artists who scored in that format were white, several all-African American acts, notably Chic, Kool and the Gang, and LaBelle, flourished during this period.

♦ RAP: FROM SUBCULTURE TO MASS APPEAL

While funk sold millions of records and received extensive radio airplay in the mid-1970s, rap music emerged within a small circle of New York artists and entertainers in neighborhoods in Upper Manhattan and the South Bronx. Rap music belongs to a larger cultural system known as hip hop, which comprises graffiti writing and breakdancing (and its derivatives) together with rapping itself. Disc jockeys at private parties discovered how to use "little raps" between songs to keep dancers on their feet. From behind the microphone, DJs created a call and response pattern with the audience. Rapping consists of a vocalist performing non- to semi-melodic oral declamations over a rhythmic background, which can be as sparse as a single drum track or an elaborate, multitextured, multiple instrumental track Taking advantage of their master of ceremonies status, they often boasted of their intellectual or sexual prowess. "Soon a division of labor emerged," explained Jefferson Morley. "DJs concentrated on perfecting the techniques of manipulating the turntables, while master of ceremonies (MCs or rappers) concentrated on rapping in rhymes." Through the use of a special stylus, rappers moved records back and forth on the turntable in order to create a unique rhythmic sound, known within the rap culture as needle rocking and later as "scratching." In its short history, both the MC and DJ aspects of rap music having undergone significant changes, and the genre has exploded in many artistic directions and satellite idioms such as hip hop soul, New Jack Swing, and gangsta rap, among other approaches. The subject matter addressed in rap music has been equally eclectic, covering many topics including male and female braggadocio, highly sexualized content, gender relationships, race politics, partying, and youthful leisure.

Long before the modern rap, or hip hop, culture appeared, however, there were African American artists who performed in a rap style idiom. In 1929, for instance, New York singer-comedian Pigmeat Markham gave performances representative of an early rap style.

Rap music is also rooted in the talking jazz style of a group of ex-convicts called the Last Poets. During the 1960s, this ensemble of African American intellectuals rapped in complex rhythms over music played by jazz accompanists. Last Poet member Jalal Uridin, recording under the name Lightning Rod, released an album entitled *Hustler's Convention*. Backed by the funk band Kool and the Gang, Uridin's recording became very influential to the early New York rappers.

Among one of the first New York rap artists of the early 1970s was Jamaican-born Clive Campbell, aka Cool Herc. A street DJ, Herc developed the art of sampling, the method of playing a section of a recording over and over in order to create a unique dance mix. Others to join the New York scene were black nationalist DJ Africa Bambaataa from the southeast Bronx and Joseph Saddler, known as Grandmaster Flash, from the central Bronx. Flash formed the group Grandmaster Flash and The Three MCs (Cowboy, Kid Creole, and Melle Mel). Later he added Kurtis Blow and Duke Bootee who founded the Furious Five.

However, rap music did not reach a broad audience until 1980 when the Sugar Hill Gang's song "Rapper's Delight" received widespread radio airplay. Small record companies began to affect the development of pop for the first time in years. Def Jam spearheaded the rise of influential rappers LL Cool J, Run-DMC, and Public Enemy, while Tommy Boy Records contributed to the rise of electro-funk. As rap groups assembled during the decade, they began to use their art to describe the harsh realities of inner city life. Unlike early rap music which was generally upbeat and exuberant in tone, the rap style of the 1980s exhibited a strong sense of racial and political consciousness. Grandmaster Flash's "The Message" was the first blatantly political rap hit; its yearning and desperation recalled the angst-ridden soul records of the preceding decade and hinted as rap's potential. Toward the end of the decade, rap came to express an increasing sense of racial militancy. Inspired by the Nation of Islam and the teachings of martyred race leader Malcolm X, rap groups such as Public Enemy turned their music into voice supporting black power. Public Enemy's second LP *It Takes A Nation of Millions to Hold Us Back* sold more than 1 million copies. Their song "Fight the Power" appeared in director Spike Lee's film *Do the Right Thing*. The group's third album *Fear of a Black Planet* was released in 1990. While it is a statement against "western cultural supremacy," explained group member Chuck D., it is also "about the coming together of all races" in a "racial rebirth." Rapper KRS-One of Boogie Down Productions provided eloquent, barbed political commentary as well.

Women have also played a role in the shaping of rap music. Rap artists such as Queen Latifah, MC Lyte, and the group Salt-N-Pepa represent a growing number of female rappers who speak for the advancement of black women in American society. Queen Latifah has emerged as critic of male dominance in the music industry and the sexist image of women presented by some male rap artists.

The late 1980s also saw the birth of the "Native Tongues" school of rap, the graduates of which employed an eclectic array of samples and more heavily relied on humor and baroque rhymes than did their hardcore and political counterparts. The best known groups of this school were De La Soul, A Tribe Called Quest, and The Pharcyde; Digital Underground, meanwhile, openly aspired to be "Sons of the P." and wove elaborate Parliament-esque concepts. Artists with a more bohemian bent began to rely heavily on jazz; some, such as Digable Planets and US3, sold briskly. A

Queen Latifah, a leader in the growing number of female rap artists.

few, such as Arrested Development and Spearhead, stayed close to their soul and funk roots.

The biggest story in rap during the 1990s was the rise of "gangsta" rap, which utilized old school funk beats and dwelt on hustling and violence—usually without soul's veneer of guarded optimism. The group N.W.A. (Niggaz With Attitude) upset social conservatives with their megahit "F___ Tha Police," and its alumni Dr. Dre, Ice Cube, and Eazy E would all become major solo artists. Ice-T put a slightly more deliberative spin on his gangster tales, but it was Dre's protégés, Snoop Doggy Dogg and former Digital Underground member Tupac Shakur, who would become the biggest crossover acts of all. Snoop's laid-back style in particular earned him pop status with cuts such as "Gin and Juice," "Murder Was the Case," and "Doggy Dogg World." The crossover success of these recordings was so worrisome to aforementioned conservatives that gangsta rap lyrics became a staple in political speeches, and politicians and activist groups threatened to take action against record companies that released such material. Shakur, Notorious B.I.G. (a.k.a. Biggie Smalls), and his protégé, Lil' Kim, all made impacts on hip hop culture with powerfully explicit lyrics. The murders of Shakur and Notorious B.I.G. sent shock waves throughout the entertainment industry and inspired passionate pleas from insiders to tone down some of the more violent lyrics in some artists' work.

Some pop rappers, such as MC Hammer (who eventually dropped the "MC") and DJ Jazzy Jeff and the Fresh Prince, enjoyed periodic success and then faded from the charts. Those who retained a bit more street-level credibility, on the other hand, such as Naughty By Nature, who had a mega-smash with "O.P.P.," and Coolio, who ruled the charts and scored a Grammy Award for his "Gangster's Paradise," enjoyed a longer reign. Beginning in the mid-1980s and into the 1990s, rap artists such as Will Smith (the Fresh Prince), Ice Cube, Ice-T, Tupac Shakur, and Queen Latifah crossed over successfully into film and television projects (some of them with hip hop themes), confirming the widespread acceptance of these artists throughout American culture. Some of these films such as *Do the Right Thing* and *Boyz N the Hood* enjoyed critical acclaim and popularity.

In the mid-1990s, creative rhyme style and techniques were perpetuated by Das Efx, Fu-Schnickens, Mystikal, Bone Thugs-N-Harmony, Busta Rhymez, and the Fugees, among others. With its array of styles and points of view, rap has emerged as a primary cultural form for young African Americans. Similar to the music of its predecessors, rap is filled with artistic energy and descriptions of the human experience. As a 1999 *Time* magazine cover story exclaims, rap music and hip hop rose in 20 short years from a subcultural expression to one that has changed the course of American popular culture in profound ways.

◆ NEW DIRECTIONS: FROM NUEVO SOUL TO POP-HIP HOP

Perhaps in part to counter the increasing dominance of hardcore hip hop in the marketplace, rhythm and blues and soul moved in a softer direction during the 1980s; as bands were replaced by sequenced keyboards and drum machines, recordings in this genre were increasingly dominated by producers and vocalists. Even longtime soul legends such as Aretha Franklin and Chaka Khan moved in a glossier direction. This period saw the rise of a handful of phenomenally successful singers, notably Whitney Houston, whose mother Cissy had sung with Franklin and others. Following a monster debut, Houston collected a string of hits and awards; her apotheosis came with the gargantuan sales of the soundtrack to the film *The Bodyguard* in which she also had a starring role. Houston's athletic vocal chops paved the way for a number of other new soul divas including Toni Braxton, Mariah Carey, and

Erykah Badu performing at the 1998 Soul Train Awards.

Mary J. Blige. Producers L.A. Reid and Babyface were among the preeminent hitmakers of this era; like Babyface, R. Kelley was successful both as producer and recording artist. Special mention should be made here of producer Teddy Riley, whose "New Jack Swing" combined the soul singing, hip hop grooves, and intermittent rap performances captured dance audiences in the late 1980s and early 1990s. The Minneapolis-based producing team Jimmy Jam and Terry Lewis, also important innovators in the "New Jack Swing" idiom, helped to define the sound of pop-hip hop in the early 1990s. The duo is credited with crafting pop entertainer Janet Jackson's extremely popular sound as her career matured. Perhaps the most successful producer/performer in the pop-hip hop arena has been Sean "Puffy" Combs, who almost singlehandedly defined the sound of mainstream hip hop in the mid- to late 1990s.

While the soft-edged trend continued through the 1990s, some artists within the fold, such as the smash groups TLC and En Vogue, flirted with old school soul. Meanwhile, "alternative" or "nuevo" soul emerged at the margins, thanks to artists such as bassist/singer-songwriter Me'Shell NdegéOcello, Arrested Development refugee Dionne Farris, and Marvin Gaye-disciple D'Angelo. Artists such as Erykah Badu, Lauryn Hill, and Faith Evans enjoyed popularity and critical success, with their unique blends of hip hop sensibilities and soul singing styles. Boyz II Men, Brandy, and Monica updated the bubblegum soul style of previous decades.

Since the year 2000, a new classic soul style emerged that looked back to the early-mid-1970s for its inspiration. Personified best by the gifted vocalist and poet Jill Scott of Philadelphia, this loose network of artists sport hair styles and clothing closely identified with the Black Power Movement. Like an artists collective of the Movement's cultural arm, new classic soul musicians combine poetry, social consciousness, and cultural critique with the sound of live funk bands and other production values of hip-hop, especially acid jazz—à la Earth Wind and Fire, the Ohio Players, and the Gap Band. Themes of romantic love and gospel-drenched vocal techniques also link new classic soul to the past, but the subtle mixture of jazz fusion, funk, poetry, rapping, and soul singing of the highest order demonstrate a healthy eclecticism that has carried African American popular culture into the next century with a roar.

◆ POPULAR MUSIC COMPOSERS, MUSICIANS, AND SINGERS

(To locate biographical profiles more readily, please consult the index at the back of the book.)

Nicholas Ashford (1943–)

Valerie Simpson (1948–)
Singers, Songwriters

One of the most enduring songwriting teams to emerge from Motown is the duo of Nicholas Ashford and Valerie Simpson. For over a quarter of a century, the team has written hit songs for artists from Ray Charles to Diana Ross.

Nick Ashford was born in Fairfield, South Carolina, on May 4, 1943; Valerie Simpson was born in the Bronx section of New York City on August 26, 1948. The two met in the early 1960s while singing in the same choir at Harlem's White Rock Baptist Church. With Ashford's gift for lyrics and Simpson's exceptional gospel piano and compositional skills, the two began to write for the staff of Scepter Records in 1964. Two years later, their song "Let's Go Get Stoned" became a hit for Ray Charles.

In 1962, Ashford and Simpson joined Motown's Jobete Music, where they wrote and produced hit songs for Marvin Gaye and Tammi Terrell including "Ain't Nothing Like the Real Thing," "Good Loving Ain't Easy to Come By," and the "Onion Song." Next, they worked with Diana Ross who had just set out to establish a solo career producing such hits as "Remember Me," "Reach Out (and Touch Somebody's Hand)," and an updated version of "Ain't No Mountain High Enough."

Ashford and Simpson's success as songwriters led them to release their own solo recording *Exposed* in 1971. After signing with Warner Brothers in 1973, they recorded a number of hit LPS: *Is It Still Good To Ya* (1978); *Stay Free* (1979); *A Musical Affair* (1980); and their biggest seller *Solid* in 1985. The duo temporarily retired from recording in the late 1980s but they returned to the recording scene in 1996, when they launched their own label Hopsack and Silk. Their first release was a collaboration with renowned poet Maya Angelou titled *Been Found*. In 1999, the couple celebrated their 25 year wedding anniversary with a gala in New York.

Anita Baker (1958–)
Singer

One of the most sophisticated soul divas to emerge in the 1980s, Baker considers herself "a balladeer" dedicated to singing music rooted in the tradition of gospel music and jazz. Inspired by her idols Mahalia Jackson, Sarah Vaughan, and Nancy Wilson, Baker brings audiences a sincere vocal style which defies commercial trends and electronic overproduction.

Born on January 26, 1958, in Toledo, Ohio, Baker was raised in a single-parent middle class family in Detroit. She first sang in storefront churches, where it was common for the congregation to improvise on various gospel themes. After graduating from Central High School, Baker sang in the Detroit soul/funk group Chapter 8. Although Chapter 8 recorded the album *I Just Want To Be Your Girl* for the Ariola label, the group's lack of commercial success caused it to disband, and for the next three years, Baker worked as a receptionist in a law firm.

In 1982, Baker, after signing a contract with Beverly Glen, moved to Los Angeles, where she recorded the critically acclaimed solo album *Songstress*. Following a legal battle with Glen, Baker signed with Elektra and recorded her debut hit album *Rapture* in 1986. As the album's executive producer, Baker sought "a minimalist approach" featuring simple recording techniques which captured the natural sounds of her voice. The LP's single "Sweet Love" brought Baker immediate crossover success. Baker's follow-up effort, the multiplatinum selling *Giving You the Best I Got* is considered one of the finest pop music albums of the 1990s. Her third effort *Compositions*, recorded in 1990, featured a number of backup musicians including Detroit jazz guitarist Earl Klugh.

After a nearly four-year hiatus, Baker released the double platinum *Rhythm of Love* in 1994. In 1996, Baker filed lawsuits against Elektra, her management and her legal staff. She subsequently joined the Atlantic label, but as of mid-1999 has yet to release an album on that label. Rhino however did put out a compilation album of Baker's in 2002 entitled *The Best of Anita Baker*. Winner of five Grammys, two NAACP Image Awards, two American Music Awards, two Soul Train Awards, and a star on Hollywood's Walk of Fame, Baker has brought her audiences music of eloquence and integrity that sets her apart from most of her contemporaries.

Harry Belafonte. *See* **Film & Television chapter.**

Chuck Berry (1926–)
Singer, Songwriter, Guitarist

The first guitar hero of rock and roll, Chuck Berry's jukebox hits of the 1950s remain some of the most imaginative poetic tales in the history of popular music. Influenced by such bluesmen as Aaron T-Bone Walker and the picking styles of rockabilly and country musicians, Berry's solo guitar work brought the guitar to the forefront of rhythm and blues. His driving ensemble sound paved the way for the emergence of bands from the Beach Boys to the Rolling Stones.

Born on October 18, 1926, in San Jose, California, Charles Edward Anderson Berry grew up in a middle-class neighborhood on the outskirts of St. Louis. Berry first sang gospel music at home and at the Antioch Baptist Church. Although Berry was drawn to the sounds of bluesmen such as Tampa Red, Arthur Crudup, and Muddy Waters, he did not become serious about music until he was given a guitar by local rhythm and blues musician Joe Sherman. Taken by the sounds of rhythm and blues, Berry formed a trio with Johnny Jones on piano and Ebby Harding on drums. Hired to play backyard barbecues, clubs, and house parties, the trio expanded their repertoire to include Nat "King" Cole ballads and country songs by Hank Williams.

By 1955, the 28-year-old Berry had become a formidable rhythm and blues guitarist and singer. While in Chicago, Berry visited a club to hear his idol, Muddy Waters, perform. At the suggestion of Waters, Berry visited Chess Studios where he eventually signed with the label. Berry's first hit for Chess was "Maybelline," a country song formerly entitled "Ida May." In 1956, Berry continued on a path toward superstardom with the hits "Roll Over Beethoven," "Oh Baby Doll," followed by "Rock and Roll Music," and the guitar anthem "Johnny B. Goode."

Released from the Indiana Federal Prison in 1964 after serving a sentence for violating the Mann Act, Berry resumed his musical career, recording "Nadine" and "No Particular Place to Go." Since the 1970s, Berry has continued to record and tour. Berry's 1972 release of the novelty tune "My-Ding-a-Ling" became his best-selling single. In 1988, Taylor Hackford paid tribute to the guitar legend in his film *Hail! Hail! Rock 'n Roll*. Berry was also a featured performer at the opening of Cleveland's Rock and Roll Hall of Fame and Museum in 1995. In 2001 Berry was honored at the Kennedy Center Honors Gala as one of the twentieth century's most influential musicians.

Mary J. Blige (1971–)
Hip Hop Singer

Born in 1971 in Yonkers, New York, Blige was raised in the Schlobohm housing projects. In her youth, Blige was influenced by the rhythm and blues, soul, and funk albums that her mother played, as well as the early lessons her father, a professional jazz musician, gave her. She landed a record deal when Andre Harrell of Uptown Records heard a karaoke tape which she had recorded at age 16.

Called the inventor of "New Jill Swing" by *Stereo Review*, Blige's debut album *What's the 411* (1992) sold more than 3 million copies and her second album *My*

Mary J. Blige.

Life (1994) went multiplatinum, establishing her career as an international recording star. She won a Grammy Award in 1996 for "You're All I Need," which was a duet with the rapper Method Man. Her third project *Share My World* (1997) was also granted multiplatinum status. Blige has also been dubbed the "Queen of Hip Hop Soul," a designation that characterizes the hallmarks her style: soulful melodies over hip hop rhythm tracks.

In 1999, Blige's album *Mary* hit the charts with such singles as "All That I Can Say" and "Sexy." In 2001, Blige released her fifth album *No More Drama*, a deeply personal album that remained a collective effort musically yet reflected more of Blige's songwriting than any of her previous efforts.

Brandy (1979–)
Singer, Actress

Although only a teenager, Brandy became one of the biggest pop stars of the 1990s. Her immense talent came through not only in her singing career, but also in her success as a television and film actress. Born Brandy Rayana Norwood on February 11, 1979, in McComb, Mississippi, Brandy's family moved to Los Angeles when she was four. The daughter of a choir director, Brandy's vocal training began in her church's youth choir. Early on, she and her younger brother, Ray-J, displayed enough talent to be featured in choir performances. By age 11, Brandy had begun singing at local events, and even placed second in an all-ages talent show. Just a year later, she landed a spot as a backup singer for the R&B group Immature.

In 1993, at the age of 14, Brandy signed a recording contract with Atlantic Records. That year she also earned a role on the short-lived ABC sitcom, *Thea*. Brandy released her self-titled debut album in 1994, becoming a sensation with the singles "I Wanna Be Down," "Baby" and "Brokenhearted." She also experienced massive success as a contributor to the soundtracks for the films *Waiting to Exhale* ("Sittin' Up in My Room"), *Batman Forever* ("Where Are You Now?"), and *Set it Off* ("Missing You").

Brandy returned to acting, landing the starring role on the successful UPN sitcom, *Moesha*. The show ran from 1996–2001, earning Brandy an even larger following. In 1997, she appeared in the starring-role of Disney's television film version of *Cinderella*, and in 1999, she appeared alongside Diana Ross in the television movie *Double Platinum*. Brandy also made her feature film debut that year with a role in the film *I Still Know What You Did Last Summer*.

Her second solo album release, *Never S-A-Y Never* (1998), proved to be even more successful than her first. "The Boy Is Mine," a duet with fellow teen-sensation, Monica, topped both the pop and R&B charts for weeks. The single earned the Grammy Award for Best R&B Performance by a Duo or Group. *Never S-A-Y Never* went on to sell more than five million copies. In 2002, Brandy released her third album, *Full Moon*, and caused a stir by anouncing that she had been secretly married for months to producer and songwriter, Robert Smith.

Bobby Brown (1969–)
Singer

Savvy and street smart, singer Bobby Brown possesses a charismatic charm which has earned him numerous million-selling records. Born in Boston in 1969, he was a founding member of the successful group New Edition. Brown remained with the group from 1984 to 1987. His solo debut album *King of Stage* featured the single "Girlfriend." Brown's second release *Don't Be Cruel* produced the single "Don't Be Cruel," and the video hits "My Prerogative" and "Every Little Step."

In 1990, Brown embarked on a worldwide tour after releasing a successful single from the soundtrack to the hit movie *Ghostbusters II*. In July of 1992 Brown married singer/actress Whitney Houston in a star-studded ceremony. Two years later, the two solo artists performed together for the first time on the televised 1994 Soul Train Music Awards program. Aside from maintaining a burgeoning music career, Brown is the owner of B. Brown Productions, as well as his own private recording studio.

Brown's violent temper and brushes with the law were the subject of much publicity in the 1990s, even eclipsing the release of his 1993 recording *Remixes in the Key of B* and the album *Forever* in 1997. In early 1998 he was convicted of drunk driving. Later that year he was arrested for misdemeanor sexual battery, but the charges were eventually dropped In July of 2000, Brown served 65 days in jail for violating his probation. Brown tried to get his career back on track in 2001 by appearing in the movie *Two Can Play at That Game* but has yet to produce any new albums.

James Brown (1933–)
Singer, Bandleader

James Brown's impact on American and African popular music has been of seismic proportion. His explosive onstage energy and intense gospel music and rhythm and blues-based sound earned him numerous titles such as "The Godfather of Soul," "Mr. Dynamite," and "The Hardest Working Man in Show Business." During the 1960s and early 1970s, Brown's back-up group—called the Flames, the Famous Flames, and then the JBS—emerged as one of the greatest soul bands in the history of modern music, one that served as a major force in the development of funk and fusion jazz.

Born in Barnell, South Carolina, on May 3, 1933, Brown moved to Augusta, Georgia, at the age of four. Although he was raised by various relatives in conditions of economic deprivation, Brown possessed an undaunted determination to succeed at an early age. When not picking cotton, washing cars, or shining shoes, he earned extra money by dancing on the streets and at amateur contests. In the evening, Brown watched shows by such bandleaders as Louis Jordan and Lucky Millinder.

At 15, Brown quit school to take up a full-time music career. In churches, Brown sang with the Swanee Quartet and the Gospel Starlighters, which soon afterward became the rhythm and blues group the Flames. During the same period he also sang and played drums with rhythm and blues bands. While with the Flames, Brown toured extensively, performing a wide range of popular material including the Five Royales's "Baby Don't Do It," the Clovers's "One Mint Julep," and Hank Ballard and the Midnighters's hit "Annie Had a Baby."

In 1956, Brown's talents caught the attention of Syd Nathan, founder of King Records. In the same year, after signing with the Federal label, a subsidiary of King, Brown recorded "Please Please Please." After the Flames disbanded in 1957, Brown formed a new Flames ensemble, featuring former members of Little Richard's band. Back in the studio the following year, Brown recorded "Try Me" which became a Top 50 pop hit. On the road, Brown polished his stage act and singing ability, producing what became known as the "James Brown Sound." His 1965 hit "Papa's Got a Brand New Bag" earned him a Grammy for best rhythm and blues recording, a feat he repeated in 1986 with "Living in America," a song that appeared on the soundtrack of the film *Rocky IV*.

After the release of "Out of Sight," Brown's music exhibited a more polyrhythmic sound as evidenced in staccato horn bursts and contrapuntal bass lines. Each successive release explored increasingly new avenues of popular music. Brown's 1967 hit "Cold Sweat" and the 1968 release "I Got the Feeling" not only sent shock waves through the music industry, they served as textbooks of rhythm for thousands of aspiring musicians. In 1970 Brown disbanded the Flames and formed the JBs, featuring Bootsy Collins. The group produced a string of hits such as "Super Bad" and "Sex Machine." *Universal James* (1993) was Brown's 79th album.

Despite the negative publicity generated by the oft "in trouble" performer, Brown's career remained effervescent in the late 1980s to 1990s. Inducted into the Rock and Roll Hall of Fame in 1986, the ever popular Brown received the Ray Charles Lifetime Achievement Award from the Rhythm & Blues Foundation as part of the organization's Pioneer Awards program in 1993. Later that year, he was awarded for his lifetime achievements at the Black Radio Exclusive awards banquet in Washington, DC. Also, Steamboat Springs, Colorado, voted to name a bridge after the soulster and Brown's hometown of Augusta, followed suit by naming a street after him. Perhaps the sweetest tribute paid to Brown has been the naming of the James Brown Cookeez by a Georgia-based cookie company. Many of his recordings were reissued in the 1990s, and hundreds of his records have been sampled by those in rap and hip hop circles, illustrating Brown's continuing musical influence. Brown's most recent appearance was at RFK Stadium in Washington, D.C., in "United We Stand: What More Can I Give," a benefit for victims of the September 11, 2001, terrorist attacks.

Ruth Brown (1928–)
Singer

Born Ruth Weston on January 30, 1928, in Portsmouth, Virginia, Ruth was initially influenced by jazz greats Sarah Vaughn, Dinah Washington, and Billie Holiday. She ran away from home in 1945 with trumpeter Jimmy Brown whom she soon married. Initial career frustrations including a serious car accident that hospitalized her for nine months from 1948–1949, delayed her debut. However, her first recording for Atlantic in 1949, "So Long," was a torch ballad hit. In the early 1950s her seductive vocal delivery placed her on the rhythm and blues charts with such tunes as "Teardrops in My Eyes," "I Know," "5-10-15 Hours," and "He Treats Your Daughter Mean." By 1960 she had a dozen rhythm and blues chart hits before her career declined.

Brown raised two sons and worked a nine-to-five job before reviving her career in the mid-1970s with television, movie, and stage appearances including her 1989 Broadway show *Black and Blue* for which she won a Tony Award. In the 1990s Ruth has issued some fine recordings including: *Fine and Mellow* (1991); *Songs of My Life* (1993); *Live in London* (1996); *R+B=Ruth Brown* (1997); and *Good Day for the Blues*. She also hosted radio shows on National Public Radio, and formed the nonprofit Rhythm & Blues Foundation, an organization that helps musicians recoup their share of royalties (Ruth has personally endured a nine-year fight with Atlantic to win back her royalties). In 1999 Brown published *Miss Rhythm: The Autobiography of Ruth Brown, Rhythm and Blues Legend* chronicling her career and the rise of Blues music.

Ruth's hit-making reign during the 1950s helped establish the prominence of the blues as a market force.

Ray Charles (1930–)
Singer, Pianist, Bandleader

Ray Charles Robinson was born on September 23, 1930, in Albany, Georgia. Blinded by glaucoma at the age of six, Charles received his first musical training at a school for the blind in St. Augustine, Florida. His parents died while he was in his teens, and after playing with local bands Charles moved to Seattle in 1947 where he formed a trio. Influenced by the smooth pop/rhythm and blues style of Charles Brown and Nat King Cole, Charles scored a top ten rhythm and blues hit with "Baby Let Me Hold Your Hand." In the early 1950s he teamed with Guitar Slim and Ruth Brown before scoring a number two rhythm and blues hit with "I Got a Woman" in 1955. This recording was the first to capture Charles's gospel moan and horn-driven arrangements that became his trademarks.

Ray Charles.

Throughout the 1950s Charles released a string of rhythm and blues hits that combined sophisticated arrangements with the emotional grit of rhythm and blues that would become known as "soul" music. Charles also scored his first top ten pop hit with "What'd I Say," which highlighted Charles's pleading church vocals with a rock and roll piano line. His singing and piano playing drew on many sources including jazz, and he cut pure jazz sides with David "Fathead" Newman and Milt Jackson, helping to imbibe a sense of "soul" and instrumental "funkiness" to the jazz idiom.

By the end of the 1950s, Charles switched to ABC Records and gained artistic control of his work. His pop success was assured with "Hit the Road Jack" followed in 1962 by "I Can't Stop Loving You," a country and western song that topped the charts. Charles was immensely popular through the mid-1960s before his career was halted in 1965 by his involvement with drugs. He emerged with more hits in the late 1960s, although he had begun to focus almost entirely on pop music.

Charles was inducted into the Rock and Roll Hall of Fame in 1986, received a National Medal of Arts in 1993, and took part in the 1995 JVC Newport Jazz Festival.

Recipient of more than ten Grammy awards and honorary life chairman of the Rhythm and Blues Hall of Fame, Charles is also an inductee to the Pop Hall of Fame, the Rock and Roll Hall of Fame, and the Songwriters Hall of Fame. He received an honorary doctorate in 1999 from Wilberforce University. In 2001, Charles teamed up with Bally's entertainment to create the first slot machine for the blind. Charles continues to perform and make music, releasing his newest album, *Thanks For Bringing Love Around Again* in 2002, marking his seventh decade in the music business.

George Clinton (1942–)
Singer, Songwriter, Bandleader, Producer

The father of "P. Funk," (i.e., "pure") George Clinton spun the funk formula refined by James Brown into an institution. His groups Parliament and Funkadelic and a panoply of offshoots kept the rest of the rhythm and blues world straining to keep up during the 1970s; by the 1990s, the prodigious body of work recorded under the P. Funk moniker exercised a huge influence on rap, soul, and rock. Though he relied heavily on a group of talented musicians to bring his visions to life, Clinton was the visionary behind the legendary "Parliafunkadelicment Thang."

Born in North Carolina, Clinton moved with his family to New Jersey during his adolescence; there he helped form a doo wop group called The Parliaments. After years of struggling and a move to Detroit, the group managed to sell some songs to other artists, but never achieved success on its own. With the advent of psychedelic rock in the mid-1960s, The Parliaments began to change in form; they morphed into Funkadelic by 1968, adding hard rock guitar and spacey grooves. The early Funkadelic albums, notably *Maggot Brain*, became classics of untamed funk rock.

Clinton deployed Parliament as a slightly more conventional funk vehicle in the early 1970s, emphasizing horns and more dance-oriented arrangements. By the middle of the decade, Parliament had become a major hitmaker with its fantasy-themed concept albums and its circus-like performances. Songs such as "Flash Light," "Bop Gun (Endangered Species)," "Mothership Connection," and "Aqua Boogie" became funk staples.

Funkadelic began to take a more commercial turn, particularly after signing with Warner Bros. Records; its biggest hits came with the albums *One Nation Under a Groove* and *Uncle Jam Wants You*. Clinton helped his bassist Bootsy Collins become a funk legend in his own right, and oversaw albums by such P. Funk enterprises as The Brides of Funkenstein, Parlet, and the P. Funk All-Stars, among many others. He also

released a slew of solo recordings; his biggest hit in this capacity was the boisterous "Atomic Dog." Though business declined for these acts during the 1980s, Clinton's influence was constant in African American pop; by the 1990s, P. Funk recordings were among the most sampled in hip hop. Clinton went so far as to set up an easy licensing system for rap artists who wanted to lift from his work. Thanks to the adoration of everyone from Dr. Dre to rockers such as the Red Hot Chili Peppers, Clinton became a ubiquitous figure on the pop culture scene. He fronted the P. Funk All-Stars at the Lollapalooza Festival and appeared in numerous films and television commercials.

In 1999 Clinton filed a lawsuit against his record company for the rights to his 1960 and 1970s songs. Clinton however lost his lawsuit in 2001 due to a contract that he signed in 1983. George Clinton continues to tour with the P. Funk All-Stars and can often be seen on college campuses and smaller venues.

Natalie Cole (1950–)
Singer

With five gold records and her star on Hollywood Boulevard, Natalie Cole has emerged since the 1980s as a major pop music star. Born on February 6, 1950, in Los Angeles, Natalie was the second daughter of jazz pianist and pop music legend Nat "King" Cole. During the early 1970s, Cole performed in nightclubs, while pursuing a degree in child psychology at the University of Massachusetts. In 1975, she recorded her first album *Inseparable* at Curtis Mayfield's Custom Studios. Her other albums include: *Thankful* (1978); *I'm Ready* (1983); *Good to Be Back* (1989); *Take a Look* (1993); and *Holly and Ivy* (1994), which coincided with her PBS special "Natalie Cole's Untraditional Traditional Christmas."

In 1991, Cole released a 22-song collection of her father's hits. The album, which contains a remixed version of the original title track "Unforgettable," features a duet between Cole and her father and earned her "Record of the Year" and "Album of the Year" Grammys, complementing the Grammys she won in 1976 for best new artist and in 1976 and 1977 for best rhythm and blues female vocal performance. Cole also won two NAACP Image Awards in the mid-1970s and an American Music Award in 1978.

In 1996, Cole released her next album *Stardust*. She put touring with the album on hold so that she could join the cast of the animated movie *Cats Don't Dance* which arrived in theaters in 1997. In 1998, Cole published her autobiography entitled *Angel on My Shoulder* depicting her triumph over drug use and bad marriages. In late 2000, NBC aired *Livin' Large: The Natalie*

Cole Story, a television movie in which Cole actually starred. In 2002, Cole wed Bishop Kenneth H. Dupree and also signed a contract with Verve records to produce her next few albums. Her first Verve album is slated to arrive in stores in fall of 2002.

Sean "Puffy" Combs (1969–)
Music Company Executive, Entrepreneur

Sean Combs was born in New York, New York, in 1969. His ear for rap and hip hop combined with his production skills are a proven combination. He began to be noticed at the age of 19 in New York's hip hop scene. As an intern at Uptown Records, Combs's talents earned him a permanent position. He headed Uptown's Artist & Repertoire department where his primary responsibilities were signing and developing new talents.

In 1991 Combs's luck took a turn for the worse. Anxious fans for a charity basketball game rushed the entrance, killing nine people. The event, staged by Combs, put a black mark on his young career. Media attacks and mayoral investigations pushed Combs into a depression. Unable to work, he confined himself to his Mt. Vernon, New York, home. Within a year, Uptown fired him.

Frustration and rejection inspired Combs to pursue his life's dreams. His talent had earned him a reputation, prompting Arista Records to sign him to a deal. Combs called this division of Arista Records "Bad Boy Entertainment." Success soon followed as Bad Boy released hits by rappers Craig Mack and the Notorious B.I.G., both of whom Combs is credited for discovering.

The ability to find such talent sets Combs apart from most other hip hop producers. The success of Bad Boy's hip hop artists led to the development of new artists. Various projects including the 1996 release of singer Faith Evans's debut kept Combs busy. After the shooting death of his friend, Notorious B.I.G., on March 7, 1999, Combs rewrote some of the lyrics on his own debut album *No Way Out*. The album produced three hit singles including "I'll Be Missing You," a tribute to Notorious B.I.G. Combs continues to be driven to succeed, opening up a soul food restaurant in Manhattan and a clothing label in the late 1990s.

In early 2000, Combs was indicted on two counts of criminal possession of a weapon. Later that year he pleaded not guilty to bribery charges related to a December 1999 shooting at a New York nightclub. Combs's former driver Wardel Fenderson also sued the rap music producer for $3 million. Fenderson claims he suffered personal injuries while helping Combs flee the 1999 shootout in New York. Fortunately for Combs, he was acquitted of all four counts of criminal gun possession and one count of bribing a witness in 2001. Combs' time in court did nothing to slow his music production. Combs's 2001 album, *The Saga Continues* with the Bad Boy Family, peaked at number two on the pop charts. In 2002, Combs was back in court settling a paternity lawsuit brought by his ex-girlfriend, the mother of his three-year-old son. Combs was also back in the studio recording *We Invented the Remix* which debuted at Number 1 on the album charts.

Sam Cooke (1931–1964)
Singer, Songwriter

Sam Cooke's sophisticated vocal style and refined image made him one of the greatest pop music idols of the early 1960s. One of the first gospel music artists to crossover into popular music, Cooke produced songs of timeless quality, filled with human emotion and spiritual optimism.

Born in Clarksdale, Mississippi, on January 2, 1931, Sam Cooke grew up the son of a Baptist minister in Chicago, Illinois. At the age of nine, Cooke, along with two sisters and a brother, formed a gospel group called the Singing Children. While a teenager, he joined the gospel group the Highway QCs which performed on the same bill with nationally famous gospel acts.

By 1950, Cooke replaced tenor Rupert H. Harris as lead singer for the renowned gospel group the Soul Stirrers. Cooke's first recording with the Soul Stirrers, "Jesus Gave Me Water," was recorded for Art Rupe's Specialty label. Although the song revealed the inexperience of the 20-year-old Cooke, it exhibited a quality of immense passion and heightened feeling. Under the pseudonym Dale Cooke, Sam recorded the pop song "Loveable" in 1957. That same year, in a session for producer Bumps Blackwell on the Keen label, Cooke recorded "You Send Me" which climbed to number one on the rhythm and blues charts. On the Keen label, Cooke recorded eight more consecutive hits including "Everyone Likes to Cha Cha Cha," "Only Sixteen," and "Wonderful World," all of which were written or co-written by Cooke.

After his contract with the Keen label expired in 1960, Cooke signed with RCA, and was assigned to staff producers Hugo Peretti and Luigi Creatore. In August, Cooke's recording "Chain Gang" reached the number two spot on the pop charts. Under the lavish production of Hugo and Luigi, Cooke produced a string of hits such as "Cupid" in 1961, "Twistin' the Night Away" in

1962, and "Another Saturday Night" in 1963. Early in 1964, Cooke appeared on the "Tonight Show," debuting two songs from his upcoming LP which included the gospel-influenced composition "A Change Is Gonna Come." On December 11, Cooke checked into a three-dollar-a-night motel where he demanded entrance into the night manager's room. After a brief physical struggle, the manager fired three pistol shots which mortally wounded Cooke. Despite his tragic death, Cooke left behind a catalogue of classic recordings and over 100 original compositions including the hit "Shake," which was posthumously released in 1965.

Sammy Davis Jr. *See* Film & Television chapter.

Fats Domino (1928–)
Singer

Antoine Domino was born on February 26, 1928, in New Orleans. As a teenager, Domino received piano lessons from Harrison Verret. In between playing night clubs, Domino worked at a factory and mowed lawns around New Orleans. At age 20, he took a job as a pianist with bassist Billy Diamond's combo at the Hideaway Club. At some point in his early career, his five-foot five-inch, 200-pound frame led to the nickname "Fats."

In 1949, while playing with Diamond's group, Domino was discovered by producer and arranger David Bartholomew, a talent scout, musician, and producer for the Imperial label. During the following year, Domino hit the charts with the autobiographical tune "Fat Man." After the release of "Fat Man," he played on tour backed by Bartholomew's band.

Although Domino released a number of sides during the early 1950s, it was not until 1955 that he gained national prominence with the hit "Ain't That A Shame." In the next six years, Domino scored 35 top hits with songs such as "Blueberry Hill" (1956), "Blue Monday" (1957), "Whole Lotta Lovin" (1958), and "I'm Walkin" (1959). Domino's recording success led to his appearance in several films in the 1950s including *The Girl Can't Help It*, *Shake Rattle and Roll*, *Disc Jockey Jamboree*, and *The Big Beat*.

After Domino's contract with Imperial expired in 1963, he signed with ABC where he made a number of commercial recordings. In 1965 Domino moved to Mercury and then to Reprise in 1968. In the early 1970s, Domino began to tour with greater regularity than he had during the peak of his career. In 1995, while on tour in England, Domino was hospitalized for infection and exhaustion. Despite suggestions his health is in decline,

Domino continues to work on new material, and honors flow his way. These honors include a Rhythm and Blues Foundation Pioneer Award in 1995 and a National Medal for the Arts in 1998. Domino continues to tour, making special appearances at places such as Harrah's Jazz Casino where he has done shows in 1999, 2000, 2001, and 2002.

Dr. Dre (1965?–)
Rap Singer, Producer

From the time he was four years old, Dr. Dre, born Andre Ramelle Young, was playing DJ at his mother's parties. In 1981, he heard a song by Grandmaster Flash that inspired him to change his name in honor of basketball star Julius "Dr. J." Erving and become a DJ. Dr. Dre began spinning records at a Los Angeles nightclub, producing the dance tapes in the club's four-track studio. In addition to using the rap trademarks of sampling, scratching, and drum machines, he added keyboards and vocals.

In 1982, when Dre was 17 years old, he formed the World Class Wreckin' Cru with another DJ. Their first

Dr. Dre.

independently released single sold 50,000 copies. The following year, Dre graduated from Compton, California's Centennial High School. He was offered a mechanical drafting position with an aircraft firm, but he turned it down to devote himself to music. In 1985, Dr. Dre joined the newly formed group, N.W.A. (Niggaz With Attitude), along with Ice Cube, Eazy E, Yella, M. C. Ren, and Arabian Prince. That year he also produced Eazy E's first platinum album *Eazy-Duz-It.*

N.W.A's successful yet controversial body of work included the multiplatinum *Straight Outta Compton,* released in 1989 on Eazy E and Dr. Dre's Ruthless Records. Dr. Dre produced the D.O.C., a rapper he had discovered in Texas. The result was that the album *No One Can Do It Better* went to number one on *Billboard's* R&B album chart. Dre also produced a platinum album for Michel'le, another number one recording.

In January of 1990, Ice Cube left N.W.A. over a financial dispute; N.W.A. recorded the last of their four recordings without him in 1991. Later that year, Dre left Ruthless to co-found Death Row Records with Suge Knight. Dre's first solo effort *The Chronic* was released in 1993. The work, featuring such budding rap artists as Snoop Doggy Dogg, sold 3 million copies. He went on to produce Snoop's debut *Doggystyle.*

In 1994, Dre received a Grammy Award for best rap solo performance. At the *Source* Awards, he was named best producer, solo artist, and *The Chronic* was named best album. The following year he was named "One of the Top 10 Artists That Mattered Most, 1985–1995" by *Spin.* In 1996, Dre stunned the hip hop community by announcing that he was leaving Death Row. He had hoped that the label would spread into other genres such as jazz and reggae, but rap continued to bring in the money, and others did not share his vision. Instead, Dre started his own label, Aftermath Entertainment. He continues to edit videos, in addition to penning his biography. He also appeared in small acting role in the 1996 film *Set It Off.*

In 2000 Dre joined the rock group Metallica in a legal fight against Napster Inc., the company that produces software which allows Internet users to share music from their computer hard drives. They and other artists succeeded in protecting their copyrighted material from being downloaded from the site. Later that year, Dr. Dre received a Lifetime Achievement Award at the Source Hip-Hop Music Awards. It was the first awards show dedicated to hip-hop music. 2001 was an even more momentous year for Dre. He won Grammys for Best Rap Performance by a Duo or Group for "Forgot About Dre," his duet with Eminem, and Producer of the Year (Non-Classical) from the National Academy of Recording Arts & Sciences. He also was honored with an American Music Award in the "favorite rap/hip hop artist" category.

Eazy E (1963–1995)
Rap Singer

Born Eric Wright in 1963 in Compton, California, Eazy E was a former drug dealer who founded Ruthless Records. He was co-founder of the innovative and controversial group N.W.A. (Niggaz With Attitude) that is credited with establishing the gangsta' strain of rap music in the early 1990s. N.W.A. included Eazy, Dr. Dre, Ice Cube, and DJ Yella. The group released clean and explicit versions of their recordings.

Between 1988 and 1991, N.W.A. had many commercial successes despite (and perhaps because of) their hardcore image including the project *Straight Outta Compton* (1989), which went multiplatinum. Eazy also excelled at production, launching groups such as J.J. Fad, Above the Law, the D.O.C., Michel'le, the Jewish rap group Blood of Abraham, H.W.A (Hoez With Attitude), and Bone Thugs N Harmony. He died of complications from AIDS in 1995.

Kenneth "Babyface" Edmonds (1958?–)
Songwriter, Producer

Edmonds was born in the late 1950s in Indianapolis, Indiana, and spent his high school years finagling interviews with pop star idols such as the Jackson 5 and Stevie Wonder. After performing in a number of rhythm and blues bands, Edmonds began a collaboration with Antonio "L.A." Reid in 1981; they were then members of an act called the Deele, but soon gained acclaim writing and producing songs for other artists such as Shalamar and Bobby Brown.

In 1989, Edmonds and Reid formed their own company, LaFace Records, backed by the Arista label. They continued their success in writing and producing pop, soul, and rhythm and blues hits for such artists as Paula Abdul and Whitney Houston, and Edmonds and Reid are also credited with giving considerable start to the careers of TLC and Toni Braxton. The duo has won numerous Grammy Awards including one for producer of the year for the 1993 soundtrack to the Eddie Murphy film *Boomerang* and have shared several songwriter of the year honors from Broadcast Music Inc. (BMI).

Edmonds is also a popular solo artist and performer in his own right, with three well-received releases to his name including the 1993 release *For the Cool in You,* a platinum seller whose hit "When Can I See You" brought

Kenneth "Babyface" Edmonds holding two Grammy Awards.

him the 1993 Grammy for best male rhythm and blues vocalist. For several months between 1994 and 1995 Edmonds was on the road, performing as an opening act for Boyz II Men, yet another one of the enormously successful groups he has written for and produced. In late 1995 he gained further accolades for producing for the soundtrack to the acclaimed film *Waiting to Exhale*. In 1997 Edmonds released the recording *Babyface: MTV Unplugged* and followed it up with a Christmas album in 1998. In 2001 Edmonds's latest effort as "Babyface," called *Face2Face*, was released. Edmonds continues to flourish as a record mogul, performer, and movie producer.

Roberta Flack (1939–)
Singer, Pianist

Born in Black Mountain, North Carolina, on February 10, 1939, Roberta Flack moved to Washington, DC, with her parents at the age of nine. Three years later she studied classical piano with prominent African American concert musician Hazel Harrison. After winning several talent contests, Flack won a scholarship to Howard University, where she graduated with a bachelors degree in music education. During the early 1960s, Flack taught music in the Washington, DC, public school system.

While playing a club date in 1968, Flack was discovered by Les McCann whose connections resulted in a contract with Atlantic Records. Flack's first album *First Take* appeared in 1970 and included the hit song "The First Time Ever I Saw Your Face." Throughout the 1970s, Flack landed several hits such as "Killing Me Softly With His Song" and "The Closer I Get to You," a duet with Donny Hathaway; both songs earned Grammys, and "Killing Me Softly" was remade in 1996 by the rap group the Fugees. In the early 1980s, Flack collaborated with Peabo Bryson to record the hit "Tonight I Celebrate My Love For You." In 1991, Flack enjoyed another Top 10 hit "Set the Night to Music," a duet with Maxi Priest. More recently, Flack has been involved in educational projects, and in 1994, she recorded the album *Roberta*, a Grammy nominated recording of jazz, blues and pop classics.

Flack's music was brought to a whole new generation in 1996 when the Fugees remade her hit "Killing Me Softly With His Song." She even played the song on her radio show Brunch with Roberta Flack, a two-hour syndicated radio program during which she spins discs and reminisces about her days in the pop limelight. In 1997, she put out her next album of holidays songs simply entitled *Christmas Album*. In 1999, Flack started an international tour and was allowed the honor of singing to Nelson Mandela during her stop over in South Africa. Flack continues to make and perform her music worldwide.

Aretha Franklin (1942–)
Singer, Pianist, Songwriter

During the 1960s, the collaboration of Aretha Franklin and Atlantic Records producer Jerry Wexler brought forth some of the deepest and most sincere popular music ever recorded. As "Queen of Soul," Franklin has reigned supreme since the late 1960s. Her voice brings spiritual inspiration to her gender, race, and the world.

Daughter of the famous Reverend Charles L. Franklin, Aretha was born on March 25, 1942, in Memphis, Tennessee. Raised on Detroit's east side, Franklin sang at her father's New Bethel Baptist Church. Although she began to study piano at age eight, Franklin refused to learn what she considered juvenile and simple tunes. Thus, she learned piano by ear, occasionally receiving instruction from individuals such as the Reverend James Cleveland. Franklin's singing skills were modeled after

Aretha Franklin.

gospel music singers and family friends including Clara Ward and rhythm and blues artists such as Ruth Brown and Sam Cooke.

At 14, Franklin quit school to go on the road with her father's Franklin Gospel Caravan, an endless tour in which the family traveled thousands of miles by car. After four years on the road, Aretha traveled to New York City to establish her own career as a pop artist. In 1960, she signed with Columbia Records talent scout John Hammond. Her six year stay at Columbia Records, however, produced only a few hits and little material that suited Franklin's unique talents.

In 1966, Franklin signed with Atlantic Records, and, in the following year, recorded a session for Wexler that resulted in the hit "I Never Loved a Man (The Way That I Loved You)." That same year, Franklin's career received another boost when her reworking of Otis Redding's song "Respect" hit the charts. Franklin's first LP *I Never Loved a Man* was followed by a succession of artistically and commercially successful albums: *Aretha Arrives*, *Lady Soul*, *Aretha Now!*, and *This Girl's In Love With You*. Her prominence grew so great that Franklin appeared on the cover of *Time* magazine

in 1968. That year she performed at Martin Luther King Jr.'s funeral and at the Democratic National Convention.

During the 1970s, Franklin continued to tour and record. In 1971, she released the live LP *Aretha Live at the Fillmore West*, backed by the horn and rhythm section of Tower of Power. Her next release *Amazing Grace* featured Reverend James Cleveland and the Southern California Community Choir. In 1977, she performed at President Jimmy Carter's inauguration, later doing the same for U.S. president Bill Clinton in 1993.

In 1980, Franklin appeared in the film *The Blues Brothers*. No stranger to television, she appeared in the specials "Aretha," "Aretha Franklin: The Queen of Soul," and "Duets," in 1986, 1988, and 1993, respectively. The 1980s also saw Franklin score her first big commercial success in more than a decade with the album *Who's Zooming Who?*, featuring the single "Freeway of Love." In 1988, she released a double-live LP *One Lord, One Faith*—an effort dedicated to her father who passed away the previous year.

Franklin has won 15 Grammy Awards in her career including the lifetime achievement award, which was bestowed upon her in 1995. Other of her honors include an American Music Award and an *Ebony* magazine American Black Achievement Award, both in 1984; declaration as a "natural resource" of the state of Michigan in 1985; induction into the Rock and Roll Hall of Fame in 1987; an Essence Award in 1993; and a Kennedy Center Honors Award in 1994. Only Janet Jackson has matched Franklin's record of 14 gold singles, the most by a female solo artist.

Franklin has stayed active in the 1990s, a decade in which many of her classic recordings were reissued. She was a headliner at the 1994 New Orleans Jazz and Heritage Festival and lent a track to the 1995 *Waiting to Exhale* soundtrack. In 1995, Franklin embarked on a new venture, launching her own label, World Class Records. Franklin also performed on the 1998 VH-1 concert special "Divas Live," along with Gloria Estefan, Celine Dion, Mariah Carey, Shania Twain, and others. The concert raised money to fund music education in elementary schools. Finally, in a celebrated July 17, 1999 concert of the "Three Tenors"—Luciano Pavarotti, José Carreras, and Placido Domingo—in Detroit, Franklin performed the national anthem. Franklin also received the National Medal of Arts in 1999 from then President Bill Clinton.

In 2000, Franklin published her autobiography *Aretha: From These Roots* with help from Davis Ritz. In 2001, Franklin was saluted during VH1's "Divas Live: The One and Only Aretha Franklin." The event featured Franklin singing with other groups and soloists such as Mary J. Blige, Jill Scott, Celia Cruz, Marc Anthony, Kid Rock, Nelly Furtado, and the Backstreet Boys. Numerous compilation albums of Franklin's will be appearing in 2002, including an album with her and late rock great Otis Redding.

The Fugees
Hip Hop Singing Group

With a sound most often described as "eclectic," the Fugees landed on the hip hop charts in 1993 with their Ruff House debut *Blunted on Reality*. Initially known as the Tranzlator Crew, Lauryn Hill, Prakazrel "Pras" Michel, and Wyclef Jean have been working together since they were teenagers in northern New Jersey. They were forced to change their name when a 1980s new wave band called Translator filed a legal protest.

Released under the name Fugees, their first album *Blunted on Reality* received rave reviews. Sales for the album were moderate, while critics announced that Hill should pursue a solo career.

With sales of 17 million, the trio's second release *The Score* (1996) made them the biggest selling rap act in

history. Produced by Jean and Hill, the album included covers of Roberta Flack's "Killing Me Softly with His Song" and Bob Marley's "No Woman, No Cry." The band made great strides in bringing hip hop with a positive attitude to a new generation.

The Fugees have stated that they plan future releases, but the success of the member's individual projects leave the groups future in doubt. Jean released his multiplatinum solo debut *The Carnival* (1997). The album was well-received in the United States and in his native Haiti, and he followed it up with *The Ecleftic: 2 Sides II a Book* (2000). Michel's solo efforts culminated in *Ghetto Superstar* (1998). Also in 1998, Hill released her debut solo album *The Miseducation of Lauryn Hill*, which brought her an unprecedented five Grammy Awards. Her MTV *Unplugged* appearance was released as *MTV Unplugged No. 2.0* in 2002.

Marvin Gaye (1939–1984)
Singer, Songwriter

The son of a Pentecostal minister, Marvin Gay was born on April 29, 1939, in Washington, DC (the final "e" on his surname was not added until the early 1960s). Raised in a segregated slum-ridden section of Washington DC, Gaye experienced a strict religious upbringing. As Gaye later recalled: "Living with my father was like living with a king, a very peculiar, changeable, cruel, and all-powerful king." Thus Gaye looked to music for release. Around the age of three, he began singing in church. While attending Cardoza High School, Gaye studied drums, piano, and guitar. Uninspired by his formal studies, Gaye often cut classes to watch James Brown and Jackie Wilson perform at the Howard Theatre.

Soon afterward, Gaye served a short time in the Air Force, until obtaining an honorable discharge in 1957. Returning to Washington, DC, Gaye joined the doo wop group the Marquees. After recording for Columbia Record's subsidiary label, Okeh, the Marquees moved to the Chess/Checker label where they recorded with Bo Diddley. Although the Marquees performed their own compositions and toured regularly, they failed to gain popularity. It was not until they were introduced to Harvey Fuqua, who was in the process of reforming Moonglows, that the Marquees attracted notice in the pop music world. Impressed by their sound, Fuqua hired the Marquees to form a group under the new name Harvey and the Moonglows. Still under contract at Chess, Fuqua brought the Moonglows to the company's studio in Chicago to record the 1959 hit the "Ten Commandments of Love."

In 1960, Fuqua and Gaye traveled to Detroit where Fuqua set up his own label and signed with Motown's

The Fugees, (l-r) Wyclef Jean, Pras Michel, and Lauryn Hill.

subsidiary, Anna. After a stint as a backup singer, studio musician, and drummer in Smokey Robinson's touring band, Gaye signed a contract with Motown as a solo artist. Released in 1962, Gaye's first album was a jazz-oriented effort entitled *The Soulful Moods of Marvin Gaye.* With his sights on a career modeled after the ballad singer Frank Sinatra, Gaye was not enthusiastic when Motown suggested he record a dance record of rhythm and blues material. Nevertheless, Gaye recorded the song "Stubborn Kind of Fellow" in 1962; it entered the Top 10 R&B charts. This was followed by a long succession of Motown hits, such as "Hitch Hike," "Pride and Joy," "Can I Get a Witness," and "Wonderful One."

Motown's next projects for Gaye included a number of vocal duets, the first of which appeared with singer Mary Wells on the 1964 album *Together.* In collaboration with singer Kim Weston, Gaye recorded the 1967 hit LP *It Takes Two.* His most successful partnership, however, was with Tammi Terrell. In their two-year association, Gaye and Terrell recorded, under the writing and production team of Ashford and Simpson, such

hits as "Ain't No Mountain High Enough" and "Your Precious Love" and "Ain't Nothing Like the Real Thing" in 1968.

Back in the studio as a solo act, Gaye recorded the hit "Heard It Through the Grapevine." With his growing success, Gaye achieved greater creative independence at Motown, which led him to co-produce the 1971 hit album *What's Going On,* a session producing the best selling singles "What's Going On," "Mercy Mercy (the Ecology)," and "Inner City Blues (Make Me Wanna Holler)."

After his last LP for Motown *In Our Lifetime,* Gaye signed with CBS Records in April 1981, and within the next year released the album *Midnight Lover,* featuring the Grammy Award-winning hit "Sexual Healing." On Sunday, April 1, 1984, after a heated argument, Gaye was fatally shot by his father in Los Angeles, California. Despite his public image, Gaye had suffered from years of inner conflict and drug abuse. "This tragic ending can only be softened by the memory of a beautiful human being," described long-time friend Smokey Robinson. "He could be full of joy sometimes, but at others, full of woe, but in the end how compassionate, how wonderful, how exciting was Marvin Gaye and his music."

Berry Gordy Jr. (1929–)
Music Company Executive

From assembly line worker to impresario of the Motown Record Corporation, Berry Gordy Jr. emerged as the owner of one of the largest African American-owned businesses in American history. A professional boxer, songwriter, producer, and businessman, Gordy has been a self-made man. Through his determination and passion for music, the living legend helped create one of the most celebrated sounds of modern music.

The seventh of eight children, Berry Gordy was born on November 28, 1929, in Detroit. Berry Gordy Sr., the owner of a grocery store, a plastering company, and a printing shop, taught his children the value of hard work and family unity. Despite his dislike for manual labor, Berry possessed a strong desire to become commercially successful. After quitting high school to become a professional boxer, Berry won several contests before leaving the profession in 1950. A year later, Gordy was drafted into the U.S. Army, where he earned a high school equivalency diploma.

Upon returning from a military tour of Korea in 1953, Berry opened the 3-D Record Mart, a jazz-oriented retail store. Forced into bankruptcy, Berry closed the store in 1955, and subsequently took a job as an assembly line worker at the Ford Motor Company. His nightly visits to Detroit's thriving jazz and rhythm and blues scene inspired Gordy to take up songwriting. In 1957, one of Gordy's former boxing colleagues, Jackie Wilson, recorded the hit "Reet Petite," a song written by Berry, his sister Gwen, and Billy Davis. Over the next four years, the Berry-Gwen-Davis writing team provided Wilson with four more hits: "To Be Loved," "Lonely Teardrops," "That's Why (I Love You So)," and "I'll Be Satisfied."

By 1959, Billy Davis and Gwen Gordy founded the Anna label, which distributed material through Chess Records in Chicago. Barret Strong's recording of "Money (That's What I Want)," written by Gordy and Janie Bradford, became the label's biggest selling single. With background as a writer and producer with the Anna label, Gordy decided to start his own company. In 1959, he formed Jobete Music Publishing, Berry Gordy Jr. Enterprises, Hitsville USA, and the Motown Record Corporation. Employing a staff of local studio musicians, writers, and producers, Berry's label scored its first hit in 1961 with Smokey Robinson's "Shop Around."

By the mid-1960s, Gordy assembled a wealth of talent including The Supremes, The Four Tops, The Marvelettes, Marvin Gaye, and Stevie Wonder.

In 1971, Gordy relocated the Motown Recording Corporation to Los Angeles. Although most of the original acts and staff members did not join the company's migration to the West Coast, Gordy's company became one of the country's top African American-owned businesses. Throughout the 1970s and 1980s, Motown continued to produce artists such as the Jackson Five, the Commodores, Lionel Richie, Rick James, and DeBarge. Gordy also tried his hand at producing feature films. *Lady Sings the Blues* (1972), *Mahogany* (1975), and *The Last Dragon* (1985) were not critical successes, but attracted the participation of such celebrities as Diana Ross, Billy Dee Williams, Richard Pryor, and Vanity. Faced with financial problems, Gordy signed a distribution agreement with MCA in 1984 and sold the label in entirety to the giant six years later.

Gordy's induction into the Hall of Fame in 1988 brought recognition to a giant of the recording industry who helped transform the sound of popular music. He was honored with a lifetime achievement award at the 1993 Black Radio Exclusive awards banquet ceremony. Among *Forbes*'s 400 richest Americans in the mid-1980s, Gordy authored his autobiography *To Be Loved: The Music, the Magic, the Memories of Motown* in 1994. In 1997 Berry gained co-composing credits on *I'll Be There*, and *You've Made Me So Very Happy*. Gordy was honored in 1998 at the Essence Awards with the Image Maker award and in 2001, he was inducted into the Independent Music Hall of Fame.

Al Green (1946–)
Singer, Songwriter, Preacher

Possessing one of the supplest voices in popular music, Al Green launched a series of hits up the soul charts during the 1970s. But the Arkansas native turned his back on pop later in that decade, singing gospel and preaching in a Memphis church. His influence on the development of soul was such, however, that he was tempted back to the secular realm for a 1995 album.

Green spent his early years singing gospel in the South, but switched to pop and scored a hit "Back Up Train" in 1967. It was not until he hooked up with producer Willie Mitchell, however, that he found his niche. Recording for Mitchell's Hi Records in Memphis with an ace band, Green managed a remarkable synthesis of intimate, romantic pop and gritty soul. The fruits of this happy union included "Tired of Being Alone," "Love and Happiness," "Let's Stay Together," and "I'm Still in Love With You." His smoldering "Take Me to the River" was covered by numerous other artists.

Though he was "born again" into Christianity in 1973, Green continued to record largely secular music—albeit with a religious tinge—for several years. After founding his own church, the Full Gospel Tabernacle, in Memphis, he returned to gospel music. His recordings won regular honors in gospel circles and even a Grammy Award, but his presence continued to be felt in the soul/rhythm and blues world. Apart from the occasional duet, however, he steered clear of pop until his return in 1995 with *Your Heart's In Good Hands.*

In 2000, Green, with help from Davin Seay, published his autobiography *Take Me To the River.* In 2001, Green was honored at the Rhythm & Blues Foundation holds 12th Annual Awards Gala with a Lifetime Achievement award.

M.C. Hammer (1963–)
Rap Singer

Born Stanley Kirk Burrell in 1963 in East Oakland, California, M.C. Hammer began his career with a group he formed called "The Holy Ghost Boys," in which he performed religious raps during the mid-1980s in Oakland clubs. Hammer recorded his first song "Ring 'Em" in his basement and sold the 12-inch copies out of his car trunk. The song rose to number one in the San Francisco Bay area.

In 1988 Capitol Records re-released his first album, renaming it *Let's Get It Started.* It produced three Top 10 singles and went double platinum. Hammer's second album *Please Hammer, Don't Hurt 'Em*, released in 1990, remained on *Billboard*'s pop chart for 21 weeks. Hammer became internationally known for a "crossover" style rap, colorful costumes, and showy style of dance. His "Can't Touch This" single produced a hit video hailed for its innovative production and Hammer's energetic dancing. Hammer's 1991 *Too Legit to Quit*, which went multiplatinum, leveled a critique at the use of samples in hip hop music, using live musicians and vocalists. Hammer's star rose quickly, and he became a veritable cottage industry in the early 1990s.

Hammer turned to the production end of the business and launched the careers of 3.5.7., Angie B., and Special Generation; he also managed Heavy D & the Boyz, Troop, Ralph Tresvant., and boxer Evander Holyfield for a short time. Hammer's music has been featured in such films as *Rocky V, Teenage Mutant Ninja Turtles*, and *The Addams Family.* He has won many honors including three Grammy Awards, seven American Music Awards, three Soul Train Awards, and two MTV Awards. After a slump in popularity, mounting criticism from the hip hop critics about his blatant commercialism, and ensuing financial problems, Hammer returned to Christian music in 1997, proclaiming a new music ministry of evangelism with the project *Family Affair.* In 2001, Hammer continued his message of hope and religion with his new album *Active Duty.* Hammer filmed a music video by the Washington D.C. Capitol's reflecting pool for the albums first single, "No Stoppin' Us-USA." All of the proceeds from the video and the single went to those affected by the September 11, 2001, terrorist attacks.

Herbie Hancock. *See* Blues & Jazz chapter.

Andre Harrell (1962?–)
Music Company Executive, Producer, Musician

Andre O'Neal Harrell was born in the Bronx, New York. While growing up with hard times in the housing projects there, young Harrell developed a desire to succeed. As a teenager, Harrell teamed up with Alonzo Brown to form the playful rap duo Dr. Jekyll (Harrell) and Mr. Hyde (Brown). Before long, they had three Top 20 hits under their belts and were carving a niche for themselves in rap.

Despite the his early rap success, Harrell enrolled in classes at the Bronx's Lehman College. After three years of study in communications and business management, Harrell met Russell Simmons in 1983. Simmons lured Harrell to come work for him at Rush Management, a company that helped define the hip hop of the day. Within two years, Harrell had worked his way to vice president and general manager and was instrumental in building the career of such rap icons as LL Cool J, Run-DMC, and Whodini.

Success continued to follow Harrell wherever he went. He left Rush Management to begin his own record company, Uptown Records. In 1988, the achievements of Uptown Records prompted a $75,000 record deal from music mega-company MCA. Artists such as Al B Sure!, Guy, and Heavy D all prospered under Harrell's direction. By 1992, Uptown and their artists had blazed a shiny trail of gold and platinum albums and had landed an unprecedented $50 million multimedia agreement with MCA. Soon projects such as the television show "In Living Color" and a showcase of Uptown recording artists including Mary J. Blige and Jodeci on MTV's "Unplugged" were in the works. In 1995, Harrell left the reins of Uptown to become the new president/CEO of Motown Records. He continues to produce chart topping albums such as Babyface's *Face2Face* and Mary J. Blige's *What's the 411.*

Isaac Hayes.

Isaac Hayes (1942–)
Singer, Pianist, Producer

Born on August 20, 1942, in Covington, Tennessee, Isaac Hayes moved to Memphis at age seven, where he was introduced to the sounds of blues, country western, and the music of idol Sam Cooke. Through the connections of saxophonist Floyd Newman, Hayes began a career as a studio musician for Stax Records in 1964. After playing piano on a session for Otis Redding, Hayes formed a partnership with songwriter Dave Porter. Together they were responsible for supplying a number of hits to Carla Thomas, William Bell, and Eddie Floyd.

The first real break for the Hayes-Porter team came when they were recruited to produce the Miami-based soul duo Sam and Dave. In the span of four years, Hayes and Porter succeeded in making Sam and Dave Stax's hottest selling act, producing such hits as "Hold On I'm Coming," "Soul Man," and "I Thank You!" During this period Hayes and Porter continued to perform in a group that established them as an underground legend in the Memphis music scene.

In the late 1960s, Hayes's solo career emerged in an impromptu fashion, when a late night session with drummer Al Jackson and bassist Duck Dunn prompted Stax to release his next effort. *Hot Buttered Soul* went double platinum in 1969. Featuring a soul version of the country song "By the Time I Get to Phoenix," Hayes's rendition set a trend for the disco/soul sound of the 1970s. Following the release of the albums *To Be Continued* and *Isaac Hayes Movement*, Hayes recorded the soundtrack for the "blaxplotation" film *Shaft* and the album *Black Moses*. In 1971, "Theme from *Shaft*" won an Academy Award for best song in a motion picture and Grammy Awards for best instrumental and best original score for a motion picture. *Black Moses* earned a Grammy, too, this one for best pop instrumental performance.

Hayes left the Stax label to join ABC in 1974. Hayes recorded a series of disco albums. In 1977, the commercial downturn in Hayes's career forced him to file bankruptcy. Though he composed Dionne Warwick's "Déjà Vu,"—nominated for a Grammy in 1978—his last gold record "Don't Let Go" was released on the Polydor label in 1979. Hayes moved into the 1980s and 1990s appearing on television shows and in such films as the futuristic thriller *Escape From New York* (1981) and the comedy spoof *Robin Hood: Men in Tights* (1993).

Winner of a 1994 Georgy Award, as bestowed by the Georgia Music Hall of Fame, Hayes has heavily influenced the music of the late 1980s and early 1990s; together with James Brown, Hayes has been one of the most frequently sampled artists by purveyors of rap. Choosing not to jump ship, however, Hayes has stuck to his own brand of "hot buttered soul." In 1995, he issued his first new recordings in seven years—*Branded* and *Raw and Refined*—and contributed a track to the Hughes brothers' film *Dead Presidents*. Hayes has also lent his voice to the role of "Chef" on the Cable Ace Award-winning animated show *South Park*, a role that has introduced him to a new generation of fans.

During 2000 and 2001, Hayes appeared on numerous soundtracks for movies including *Shaft* and *South Park: The Movie*. In 2002 Hayes was inducted into to the Rock and Roll Hall of Fame.

Jimi Hendrix (1942–1970)
Guitarist, Songwriter

When Jimi Hendrix arrived on the international rock music scene in 1967, he almost single handedly redefined the sound of the electric guitar. Hendrix' extraordinary approach has shaped the course of music from jazz fusion to heavy metal.

On November 27, 1942, in Seattle, Washington, Johnny Allen Hendrix was born to an enlisted U.S. Army soldier and a teenage mother. Four years later, Johnny Allen was renamed James Marshall Hendrix. Because of his mother's fondness for night club life and his father's frequent absences, Hendrix was a lonely, yet creative, child. At school he won several contests for his science fiction-based poetry and visual art. At the age of eight, Hendrix, unable to afford a guitar, strummed out rhythms on a broom. Eventually, he graduated to a fabricated substitute made from a cigar box, followed by a ukelele, and finally an acoustic guitar that was purchased by his father.

By the late 1950s, Hendrix began to play in local bands in Seattle. While a teenager, he played along with recordings by blues artists such as Elmore James and John Lee Hooker. After a 26-month stint (1961–1962) in the 101st Airborne Division, Hendrix played in the Nashville rhythm and blues scene with bassist Billy Cox. For the next three years, Hendrix performed under the name Jimi James, backing up acts such as Little Richard, Jackie Wilson, Ike and Tina Turner, and the Isley Brothers.

In 1964 Hendrix moved to New York City where he performed in various Greenwich Village clubs. While in New York he formed the group Jimi James and the Blue Flames. After being discovered by producer and manager Chas Chandler, the former bassist with the Animals, Hendrix was urged to leave for England. Arriving in England in 1966, Hendrix, along with bassist Noel Redding and drummer Mitch Mitchell, formed the Jimi Hendrix Experience. In 1967, after touring Europe, the trio hit the charts with a cover version of the Leaves song "Hey Joe." In the same year, the group released the groundbreaking album *Are You Experienced?*

In 1968 the Experience recorded *Axis Bold As Love* which led to extensive touring in the United States and Europe. On the Experience's next LP *Electric Ladyland*, Hendrix sought to expand the group's trio-based sound. A double record effort, *Electric Ladyland* featured numerous guest artists such as keyboardists Steve Winwood and Al Kooper, saxophonist Freddie Smith, and conga player Larry Faucette. The record also contained "All Along the Watchtower," a song written by Hendrix's musical and poetic idol Bob Dylan.

After the Experience broke up in 1969, Hendrix played the Woodstock Music and Arts Festival with the Gypsy Sons and Rainbows, featuring bassist Billy Cox. Along with drummer Buddy Miles, Hendrix and Cox formed the Band of Gypsys, and in 1970 the group released an album under the same title. Months later, Mitchell replaced Miles on drums. In August, the Mitchell-Cox lineup played behind Hendrix at his last major performance held at England's Isle of Wight

Festival. On September 18, 1970, Hendrix died of a sleeping pill overdose in a hotel room in England. Despite his short career, Hendrix established himself as a major figure in pop music history. In 1992, Hendrix was inducted into the Rock and Roll Hall of Fame.

Lauryn Hill. *See* **The Fugees.**

Whitney Houston (1963–)
Model, Singer, Actress

A multiple Grammy Award winner whose face has graced the covers of magazines from *Glamour* to *Cosmopolitan*, Whitney Houston emerged as one of the most vibrant popular music talents during the 1980s. A talented singer, model, and actress, Houston dominated the pop charts into the 1990s. Her biggest successes were associated with two motion pictures in which she had major roles.

Born on August 9, 1963, Houston grew up in East Orange, New Jersey. As a member of the New Hope Baptist Choir, she made her singing debut at age 11. Later, Houston appeared as a backup singer on numerous recordings, featuring her mother, Cissy Houston, and cousin Dionne Warwick. Despite her success as a fashion model, Houston found the profession "degrading," and, subsequently, quit in order to seek a career in music. She backed up the likes of Chaka Khan, Lou Rawls, and the Neville Brothers.

By age 19, Houston had received several recording contract offers. In 1985, she released her debut album on the Arista label entitled *Whitney Houston*, which produced four hits: "Saving All My Love for You," which won the Grammy for best female pop performance; "You Give Good Love"; "How Will I Know," which earned an MTV Video Music Award for best female video; and "The Greatest Love of All." The album won seven American Music Awards, a feat she would duplicate in 1994. Houston's second LP *Whitney* appeared in 1987, and just as her first effort, the work spawned a number of hits including "I Wanna Dance With Somebody," "Didn't We Almost Have It All," "So Emotional," "Where Do Broken Hearts Go?," and "Love Will Save the Day." The album received four American Music Awards. Following the success of her second record, Houston released *One Moment In Time* (1988) and the slickly produced *I'm Your Baby Tonight* (1990).

In 1992, Houston married singer Bobby Brown and made her acting debut in the film *The Bodyguard*, co-starring Kevin Costner. The first single from the soundtrack, a remake of Dolly Parton's "I Will Always Love You," spent 14 straight weeks on top of the pop singles chart; according to statistics from *Billboard* magazine, Houston set a record for the most time spent at the top of the charts, edging out Boyz II Men's "End of the Road" (13 weeks) and Elvis Presley's "Don't Be Cruel" (11 weeks). Her vocal performance on the soundtrack won her seven American Music Awards including the 1994 Award of Merit; four Grammy Awards including record of the year, album of the year, and best female pop performance; two Soul Train Music Awards including the Sammy Davis Jr. Entertainer of the Year Award and the Female Rhythm and Blues Single Award for "I Will Always Love You;" four NAACP Image Awards; and the National Association of Black Owned Broadcasters's lifetime achievement award. Later in the year, AT&T signed Houston as the spokesperson for the corporation's "True Voice" campaign; Houston sang in two of the company's commercials.

Houston's next offering was not long in coming. With Angela Bassett, Lela Rochon, and Loretta Devine, Houston co-starred in the 1995 film adaption of Terry McMillan's *Waiting to Exhale*. A box office winner, the movie's soundtrack was written by producer Babyface and featured, in addition to Houston, such performers as Aretha Franklin and Toni Braxton. Houston sang the very successful first single "Exhale (Shoop Shoop)." Her most recent film *The Preacher's Wife* allowed Houston to return to her gospel roots. Her latest album *My Love is Your Love* was released in the fall of 1999.

In 2000 Houston released her greatest hits album, *Whitney: The Greatest Hits*. A few weeks later, Houston was officially charged with marijuana possession, stemming from an incident earlier in the year. Her lawyers announce that her marijuana possession case could be dismissed in three months if she met certain probation-like conditions. Houston met those conditions and in March of 2001, the charges against her were dropped. In August of 2001, Houston signed a contract with Arista Records worth over $100 million. Her first album for Artista, *Love, Whitney* came out a few months later.

Phyllis Hyman (1949–1995)
Singer

Phyllis Hyman was a singer of the heart and was appreciated by connoisseurs of both romantic jazz and rhythm and blues singing. She was born in Philadelphia on July 6, 1949, and raised in Pittsburgh. An elementary school teacher noticed and nurtured her vocal talents, but she grew up poor and prepared for a career as a legal secretary.

Nevertheless, Hyman reached New York in her early twenties and soon began working as a vocalist. By 1974 she formed her own band, Phyllis Hyman and the PH Factor. She became a regular at the toney Upper West Side clubs, Rust Brown's and Mikell's. In 1976 she was discovered by percussionist and producer Norman Connors and was a featured performer on his album *You Are My Starship* singing the ballad "Betcha By Golly Wow," which helped Hyman meet the co-writer of the song and her longtime good friend, Linda Creed.

Hyman signed with the record label Arista in 1977, and one of her first releases "Somewhere in My Lifetime" was produced by vocal star Barry Manilow and rose high in the rhythm and blues charts. Her signature hit was the ballad "You Know How to Love Me." Personally, her marriage to manager Larry Alexander in the late 1970s ended in divorce.

Her career took an upswing in the late 1970s when she signed on with the Broadway cast of *Sophisticated Ladies*, a revue of Duke Ellington's music. She sang in the show for three years and earned a Tony nomination for her performance in 1981. Her rendition of "In a Sentimental Mood" is on the original cast album. In 1986 Hyman moved to the Philadelphia International label and made some of her best recordings. *Living All Alone* was soon released and featured her signature lush, sad romantic ballads including a new song written by her friend, Linda Creed. Hyman herself began writing songs that reflected her life story, which is why her songs were so emotionally true and compelling. The 1991 *Prime of My Life* contained songs with such titles as "It's Not About You (It's About Me)," "It Takes Two," and "Why Not Me?"

In 1988, she appeared in the Spike Lee film *School Daze*. She also toured the USA, Europe, and Japan in the late 1980s with a successful show that played the Harlem Apollo, Oakland's Paramount, and the Fox Theatre in St. Louis. She was a stunning performer, tall and dressed in African clothing.

On talk shows though, Hyman was open about her lifelong search for love and admitted to being lonely. When her friend, Linda Creed, died in 1993, it was rumored that Hyman was struggling with alcohol and drugs. On June 30, 1995, before a performance at the Apollo, she died from an overdose of pills. Not forgotten though, her legend continues to grow as five albums have been released since her death including *We Love You Phyllis: A Tribute to Phyllis Hyman* (1998), featuring Norman Connors and Jean Carne.

Ice Cube (1969–)
Rap Singer, Actor

Behind his oft-misogynistic and racist gangster image, rapper Ice Cube is a serious artist. Dedicated to black pride, he is a staunch spokesperson for black nationalism. Ice Cube looks upon his music as a means

Ice Cube.

of launching a "mental revolution" in order to awaken African American youth to the value of education and the creation of private African American economic enterprises.

Born Oshea Jackson, Ice Cube grew up in the west side of South Central Los Angeles. While in the ninth grade Jackson wrote his first rhyme in typing class. Prompted by his parents to pursue an education after high school, he attended a one-year drafting course at the Phoenix Institute in 1988. In the following year, Ice Cube achieved great commercial success as a member of N.W.A. (Niggaz With Attitude). One of the group's founding members, along with Dr. Dre and Eazy E, Ice Cube wrote or co-wrote most of the material for N.W.A.'s first two albums. *Boyz N the Hood* was released in 1986. Ice Cube's authoritative baritone won him a legion of fans for his N.W.A. rap anthem "Gangsta Gangsta." He also scripted much of Eazy's first solo work *Eazy-Duz-It*, followed by N.W.A.'s platinum *Straight Outta Compton*, which included the controversial single "F___ Tha Police."

Though he still worked sporadically with Dr. Dre after leaving N.W.A., Ice Cube released his 1990 solo album *AmeriKKKa's Most Wanted*, produced with Public Enemy's Chuck D. and the Bomb Squad—the recording went gold within three months. He then formed Street Knowledge, a record production company, and produced female rapper Yo Yo's *Make Way for the Motherlode*. During the same year, Ice Cube also made his acting debut in director John Singleton's film *Boyz N the Hood*. The rapper-actor went on to star in a number of films including *Trespass* (1992) with Ice-T; *Higher Learning*, Singleton's vehicle of 1994; the 1995 comedy *Friday*, which he co-wrote and co-produced; Charles Burnett's 1995 work *The Glass Shield; Anaconda* in 1997; and *I Got the Hook Up* in 1997. The late 90s saw Ice Cube in more serious roles in movies such as *The Players Club, Three Kings*, and *Ghost of Mars*. Ice Cube returned to comedy in 2000 with a sequel to his 1995 hit *Friday* entitled *Next Friday* and a third movie *Friday After Next* in 2002.

Having recorded his own *Kill at Will* and *Death Certificate* in 1991, Ice Cube remained active in Yo Yo's career, serving as executive producer of her *Black Pearl* in 1992, and worked with other artists, directing videos including one for blues-rock artist Ian Moore in 1993. Ice Cube stayed on top of his own music game as well, releasing *The Predator* in 1992; the recording debuted at number one on two *Billboard* charts—pop and rhythm and blues—at the same time, the first to do so since 1976 and Stevie Wonder's *Songs in the Key of Life*. In 1992, Ice Cube figured in the lineup of Lollapalooza II, an annual traveling rock festival. 1993's *Lethal Injection* featured the smash single "It Was a Good Day." Ice Cube also issued *Bootlegs & B-Sides*, and, in 1995, he contributed to the *Streetfighter* motion picture soundtrack.

In 1998, Ice Cube released volume one of his hard hitting best-seller *War and Peace*. The album saw Ice Cube collaborating with artists such as a Mister Short Khop, Mack Ten, and Korn. The second volume of *War and Peace* hit music stands in 2000. That same year Ice Cube received a Lifetime Achievement Award at the Source Hip-Hop Music Awards.

Ice–T (1958–)
Rap Singer, Actor

With his image as a street–wise hustler, Ice–T became one of the West Coast's first major rap artists, laying down a style that would later be adopted by "gangsta" rappers such as Dr. Dre and Snoop Doggy Dogg. Ice–T, who became one of the first rappers to have warning labels placed on his albums, also set the tone for much of the controversy that would follow rap music during the 1990s and into the new millenium.

Born Tracey Morrow in Newark, New Jersey, on February 14, 1959, Ice–T moved to Los Angeles following the death of his parents. He attended Crenshaw High School, and took on the name Ice–T after reading the books of Iceberg Slim, a former pimp. Ice–T made several recordings and had minor roles in the films *Breakin'* (1984), *Breakin' 2: Electric Boogaloo* (1984), and *Rappin'* (1985).

In 1987, Ice–T signed a major–label recording contract with Sire Records. He released *Rhyme Pays* the same year. Along with the title track to the movie *Colors* (1988), the album's portrayal of ghetto life, violence, and criminal activity brought Ice–T national attention. He followed with *Power* (1988) and *The Iceberg/Freedom of Speech. . . .Just Watch What You Say* (1989). Ice–T's 1991 release *O.G. Orginal Gangster* proved to be a seminal record in the history of "gangsta" rap. Included on the album was the track "New Jack Hustler," title track of the film *New Jack City* (1991), in which Ice–T starred with Wesley Snipes.

O.G. Orginal Gangster also featured the debut of Ice–T's rap/metal band Body Count, who released a full–length album the following year. *Body Count* (1992) contained the notorious song "Cop Killer." The track sparked protest from policemen and politicians, and earned Ice–T a place on the FBI National Threat list. Finally, after threats of boycotts of stores selling the album, Sire pulled the record and reissued it without the controversial song. The controversy surrounding Ice–T gradually began to fade. He continued to record solo rap albums, including, *Home Invasion* (1993), *The Last Temptation of Ice* (1995), *Cold as Ever* (1996), *VI: Return of the Real* (1996), and *7th Deadly Sin* (1999); but also found success in acting.

Ice–T has made numerous television appearances. In addition to a starring role on the series *Law & Order: Special Victims Unit*, he has also appeared as the host of *Being Tough*. Ice–T's film credits include, *Trespass* (1992), *Surviving the Game* (1994), *Johnny Mnemonic* (1995), *Rhyme and Reason* (1997), *Mean Guns* (1997), *Body Count* (1997), *Crazy Six* (1998), *Urban Menace* (1999), *The Wrecking Crew* (1999), *Leprechaun in the Hood* (1999), *Judgment Day* (1999), *Sonic Impact* (2000), *Ablaze* (2000), *Kept* (2001), and *Gangland* (2001).

Janet Jackson (1966–)
Singer, Actress

The youngest child of a family of talented children, Janet Jackson is a tremendously energetic performer, whose singing and dance styles have reached immense popularity around the world. She is one of the most

Janet Jackson accepting her Award of Merit at the 2001 American Music Awards.

successful of a family of highly talented performers including her brother Michael, the so-called "King of Pop." In the 1990s, she has fully emerged from his shadow and has become a full-fledged sex symbol and role model.

Born on May 16, 1966, in Gary, Indiana, Janet Jackson began performing with her brothers at age six, doing impressions of famous stars such as Mae West and Cher. She made her first professional singing debut at one of the Jackson Five's shows in the Grand Hotel in Las Vegas. Before she was ten years old, Jackson was spotted by television producer Norman Lear, resulting in her appearances on such television shows as "Good Times," "Different Strokes," and "Fame."

In 1982, Jackson's debut album for the A&M label, *Janet*, contained only a few minor hits. Teamed with producers Jimmy Jam and Terry Lewis, Jackson released her more commercially successful LP *Dream Street*. Her 1986 release *Control* scored six hit singles including "What Have You Done For Me Lately," "Nasty," "When I Think of You," "Control," "Let's Wait Awhile," and "Pleasure Principle." Under the direction of Jam and Lewis, Jackson released the dance-oriented album *Janet Jackson's Rhythm Nation 1814* in 1989, which went quadruple platinum. Among the record's numerous singles were "Miss You Much," "Come Back To Me," and "Black Cat."

After an extensive world tour in 1990, Jackson left the A&M label to sign a contract with Virgin Records in 1991. The four-album contract was worth an estimated $80 million with $50 million guaranteed up front. Two years later, she starred alongside Tupac Shakur in John Singleton's *Poetic Justice*. Jackson played a soul-searching hairdresser prone to writing poetry; Maya Angelou, who was also featured in the film, provided the poems Jackson's character read. In 1994, Jackson released *janet*. Critically acclaimed, the album did well commercially, too. The single "Any Time, Any Place" earned Jackson her 14th gold single, the most by any female solo artist other than Aretha Franklin. The following year, Jackson collaborated with her brother Michael on a track entitled "Scream." The visually stunning video associated with the single was one of the most expensive ever made. Later in 1995, her *Design of a Decade: 1986–1996* made a splashy debut. She also contributed a song to the soundtrack for *Ready to Wear*. Her follow up album to *janet*, *The Velvet Rope*, debuted at the number one position in The Billboard 200 chart, a testament to her star power.

In 2000, Jackson's "secret husband" of nine years, Rene Elizondo, made their marriage public by filing for divorce. By 2001, the divorce was final, but did nothing to slow down Jackson's career. In April of 2001 Jackson's seventh album *All For You* was released to critical success. The album won her an American Music Award in the "favorite pop/rock female artist" category as well as a Grammy for Best Dance Recording, for "All For You," from the National Academy of Recording Arts & Sciences.

Jackson has earned much recognition throughout her career. Between 1986 and 1992, she garnered four *Billboard* Awards; seven American Music Awards; two MTV Video Music Awards; one Grammy Award; three Soul Train Awards; a BMI Pop Award; and the 1992 Sammy Davis Jr. Award for entertainer of the year. In 1990, she acquired a star on Hollywood "Walk of Fame," and, in 1992, the NAACP gave her its Chairman's Award. Three years later, she received an Essence Award. Jackson is also the recipient of the Lena Horne Award for outstanding career achievements (1997). In 2001 Jackson received a special Award of Merit at the American Music Awards for her outstanding musical contribution. She also received a Billboard Artist Achievement Award that year for her continued perseverance in the music industry.

Michael Jackson (1958–)
Singer, Composer

From child singing star with the Jackson Five to his success as a solo performer in the 1980s, Michael Jackson has amassed the largest following of any African American singer in the history of popular music. Jackson has an audience that transcends the boundaries of nations and bridges the gaps brought about by generational differences. Despite some missteps in the early 1990s, the "King of Pop" reigns supreme.

The fifth of nine children, Michael Jackson was born on August 29, 1958, in Gary, Indiana. As a child, Michael, along with his brothers Tito, Jermaine, Jackie, and Marlon, comprised the Jackson Five. Under the tutelage of their father, Joe, the five boys learned to sing and dance. On weekends the family singing group traveled hundreds of miles to perform at amateur contests and benefit concerts.

After two years on the road, the group landed an audition with Motown records. Upon signing with the label in 1969, the Jackson Five hit the charts with the number one hit "I Want You Back," a song arranged and produced by Berry Gordy Jr. On recordings and television shows, Michael's wholesome image and lead vocal style attracted fans from every racial and age group. During the group's six-year stay at Motown, the Jackson Five scored 13 consecutive Top 20 singles such as "ABC," "The Love You Save," and "I'll Be There."

While lead vocalist for the Jackson Five, Michael had signed a separate contract with Motown in 1971, formalizing a solo career that produced the hits "Got to Be There" in 1971, "Ben" in 1972, and "Just a Little Bit of You" in 1975. When cast in the role of the scarecrow in the 1975 Motown film *The Wiz*, Jackson met producer Quincy Jones who later collaborated with him to record the 1979 hit LP *Off the Wall* on the Epic label. Two years later, Jackson, guided by the production skills of Jones, recorded the biggest selling album of all time, *Thriller*. The seven hit singles included "Beat It," "Billie Jean," "Wanna Be Startin' Something," and the title track, which featured a voice over by horror cult figure Vincent Price. The video for the song was almost a mini-movie, starring Jackson as a dancing werewolf run amok, with special effects that rivaled any full-length feature film.

In 1985, Jackson co-wrote the song "We Are the World" for the U.S.A. for Africa famine relief fund. After joining Jones to produce *Bad* in 1987, Jackson led the most commercially successful tour in history. Four years later, Jackson released *Dangerous*, which included the hit single "Black or White."

In 1993, Jackson announced that the progressive lightening of his skin has been the result of a skin disorder known as vitiligo and not from intentional bleaching. The public declaration was one of many Jackson would find himself making about various topics in the ensuing years. Scandal-ridden, Jackson hit a backslide in his career following allegations of child molestation—charges that were dropped—and the coming to light of a pain medication addiction brought about by poor health.

Coming on the heels of such devastating disclosures, *HIStory: Past, Present, and Future, Book I* (1995) featured hits from the past as well as new works. Compared to his previous recordings, sales were disappointing and the recording was not considered a commercial success. Fan loyalty to the gifted musician, however, drove some of the new songs into chart contention including "The Earth Song," the controversial "They Don't Care About Us," and the lilting ballad "You Are Not Alone." The compilation also gave Jackson a chance to work with his sister Janet, when the two collaborated on the duet "Scream," the first single to be released. The ensuing video for "Scream" cost $7 million, making it one of the most expensive and eye-catching videos ever produced. Jackson's follow up album to *HIStory, Blood on the Dance Floor* was released in 1997, and is a partly new, partly remixed recording.

In 2001, Jackson gave his fans his first completely original album since 1992's *Dangerous* entitled *Invincible*. 2001 also saw the televised reunion of the Jackson Five during a 30th anniversary tribute to Jackson. Also appearing to honor Jackson were music greats Ray Charles, guitarist Slash, and producer Quincy Jones.

Jackson had made headlines in 1994, when he announced his betrothal to Lisa Marie Presley, daughter of the late rock legend Elvis Presley. The marriage of Jackson and Presley was considered highly unusual, and many critics dismissed it as a publicity stunt. On June 14, 1995, Jackson and Presley were interviewed by Diane Sawyer on ABC's *Prime Time Live*. During the interview, the two insisted they were deeply in love and planned to eventually have children. However, in January of 1996, Lisa Presley announced that she was divorcing Jackson. Jackson remarried later that year to long time friend Debbie Rowe. A son was born to them in early 1997, followed by a daughter in the spring of 1998.

Jackson's business ventures have had more staying power. An astute business man, he entered into a $600 million joint publishing deal with Sony in 1995. The deal combined Sony's music publishing division with Jackson's ATV Music Catalog, which once owned the rights to the entire collection of The Beatles' work.

More importantly, Jackson continues to garner acclaim, despite his setbacks. In 1993, he received three American Music Awards including the first-ever International Artist Award, and was recognized at the World Music Awards ceremony in Monte Carlo, Monaco. In addition, he received special Grammy honors that year. Two years later, he won three MTV Video Awards. In 2002, Jackson was honored with an Artist of the Century award at the American Music Awards. While many argue that his work has been uneven, his contribution to modern pop has been enormous. Indeed, Jackson redefined stardom for the video era. Popular culture will never be the same.

Etta James (1938–)
Singer

Born Jamesetta Hawkins on January 25, 1938, Etta James was a child prodigy, singing gospel music on the radio in Los Angeles by the time she was five. As a teenager in 1950, she formed a singing group called The Creolettes with two friends. The trio was discovered by rhythm and blues star Johnny Otis in 1954. Otis changed the group's name to The Peaches and took the girls on

Etta James.

the road with him. The Peaches recorded their first song "Roll with Me, Henry" which topped the charts in 1955, along with "Good Rocking Daddy." The success of that record led to a tour with rock and roll star Little Richard and studio backup vocal jobs with Marvin Gaye, Minnie Riperton, and Chuck Berry. James signed with Chess and cranked out ten chart-making hits between 1960 and 1963 including "At Last," "Trust in Me," and "Something's Got a Hold on Me." In 1967 she traveled to the famous Muscle Shoals, Alabama studio, where she recorded many of her biggest hits including "I'd Rather Go Blind" and "Tell Mama."

Although successful on the rhythm and blues charts, James did not manage to catch on with wider audiences in the 1960s. With Chess through 1975, James continued to record with moderate success in the gray region between blues, soul, rhythm and blues, and rock. After a recording lapse lasting for much of the 1980s, she recorded the album *The Seven Year Itch* for Island Records in 1988. Despite her inability to establish herself as a mainstream superstar, James has been a major influence on many singers who did attain that status including Diana Ross and Janis Joplin.

In 1993, James was inducted into the Rock and Roll Hall of Fame. In 1995, she co-authored her autobiography with David Ritz entitled *Rage to Survive: The Etta James Story*. She continued to put out albums throughout the 1990s such as *Stickin' to My Guns* (1990); *The Right Time* (1992); *Respect Yourself* (1997); and *The Heart of a Woman* (1999). Her newest studio album *Blue Gardenia* hit stores in 2001.

Quincy Jones (1933–)
Trumpeter, Arranger, Producer

Winner of 20 Grammy Awards and the writer of more than 52 film scores, Quincy Jones is popular music's quintessential musician/producer. Aside from performing trumpet with the likes of jazzmen Lionel Hampton and Dizzy Gillespie, Jones has produced for artists from Frank Sinatra to Michael Jackson.

Quincy Jones was born on March 14, 1933, in Chicago, Illinois. At age ten, Jones moved to Bremerton, Washington. As a member of Bump Blackwell's Junior Orchestra, Jones performed at local Seattle social functions. In 1949, Jones played third trumpet in Lionel Hampton's band in the local Seattle club scene. After befriending jazz bassist Oscar Pettiford, Jones established himself as an able musician and arranger.

From 1950 to 1953, Jones became a regular member of Hampton's band, and, subsequently, toured the United

Quincy Jones.

States and Europe. During the mid-1950s, Jones began to record jazz records under his own name. In 1956, he toured the Middle East and South America with the U.S. State Department Band headed by Dizzy Gillespie.

In 1961, Jones was appointed musical director at Mercury Records. In search of new musical horizons, Jones began producing popular music including Leslie Gore's 1963 hit "It's My Party." Jones's growing prestige at Mercury led to his promotion to vice president of the company, marking the first time an African American had been placed in an executive position at a major label. During this time, Jones also began to write and record film scores. In 1967, he produced the music score for the movie *In the Heat of the Night*. He also produced the music score for Alex Haley's television miniseries "Roots" and co-produced the film adaptation of Alice Walker's *The Color Purple* with Steven Spielberg.

After his production of the 1978 Motown-backed film *The Wiz*, Jones went on to produce the film's star, Michael Jackson, on such recordings as the 1979 release *Off the Wall* and the 1985 record-breaking hit *Thriller*. Jones's 1989 release *Back on the Block*, a

Grammy winner, was praised by critics and was no doubt a sign of Jones's continuing role in the future development of African American popular music. Two years later, Jones sat down with his old buddy Miles Davis. The musical encounter was recorded and released in 1993 as *Miles & Quincy Live at Montreux*, along with a video documentary of the same name. In 1995, Jones released his album *Q's Juke Joint*, featuring updated versions of tunes popularized in post-slavery roadhouses.

Jones is also influential in the media industry. He is chairman of Quest Broadcasting; in 1994, the group partnered with Chicago's Tribune Co. to buy television stations in Atlanta and New Orleans. His joint venture with Time Warner—*VIBE* magazine, which Jones founded—has been very successful. The publication covers urban music and culture and has a high readership among African Americans and Latinos. In the late 1990s, Jones turned to exploring the multimedia realm. He released a CD-ROM, Q's Juke Joint, which, such as his album of the same name, is an examination of African American music.

In 1997, Jones received the WGCI-AM/FM Granville White Lifetime Achievement Award for excellence in the music industry. In 1999, Jones was honored with the James D. Patterson award, which recognizes individuals who have helped to ensure the continued existence of historically Black colleges and universities and the education of Black students. Early in 2001, Jones sold Qwest Records to Warner Music and concentrated full time on his television/movie production company. He also published *Q: The Autobiography of Quincy Jones* in that year. In December of 2001, Quincy was awarded a Kennedy Center honor. His most recent honor came again from the National Academy of Recording Arts & Sciences when he was awarded the Grammy for Best Spoken Word Album for *Q: The Autobiography of Quincy Jones*.

Louis Jordan (1908–1975)
Singer, Alto Saxophonist, Bandleader

Louis Jordan led one of the most popular and influential bands of the 1940s. The shuffle boogie rhythm of his jump blues ensemble, the Tympany Five, had a profound impact on the emergence of rhythm and blues. As guitarist Chuck Berry admitted, "I identify myself with Louis Jordan more than any other artist." For it was Jordan's swinging rhythms, theatrical stage presence, and songs about everyday life that made him a favorite among musicians and listeners throughout the 1940s.

Born in Brinkley, Arkansas, July 8, 1908, Jordan was the son of a bandleader and music teacher. He received his music education in the Brinkley public schools and the Baptist College in Little Rock. Jordan's early music career as a clarinetist included stints with the Rabbit Foot Minstrels and Ruby Williams's orchestra. Soon after moving to Philadelphia in 1932, Jordan joined Charlie Gains's group; sometime around 1936, he joined drummer Chick Webb's band.

After Webb's death in 1938, Jordan started his own group. Because Jordan performed for both white and black audiences, he, to use his own words, learned to "straddle the fence" by playing music ranging from blues to formal dance music. Signing with Decca records during the same year, Jordan began a recording career which, by the early 1940s, produced a string of million selling recordings such as "Is You Is or Is You Ain't (My Baby)," "Choo Choo Ch'Boogie," "Saturday Night Fish Fry," and "Caledonia." Aside from working with artists such as Louis Armstrong, Bing Crosby, and Ella Fitzgerald, Jordan appeared in several films such as the 1949 release *Shout Sister Shout*.

Although failing to achieve the success he experienced during the 1940s, Jordan fronted a big band in the early 1950s. During the 1960s and 1970s, he continued to tour the United States, Europe, and Asia. His career came to an end in 1975 when he suffered a fatal heart attack in Los Angeles. Jordan was inducted into the Rock and Roll Hall of Fame in 1987. He was further celebrated in 1990 in the hit stage production of *Five Guys Named Moe*.

Eddie Kendricks (1939–1992)
Singer

As a member of the Temptations in the 1960s, Eddie Kendricks's articulate soulful falsetto provided Motown with a number of pop music classics. Kendricks's gospel music background "enabled him to bring an unusual earnestness to the singing of love lyrics," wrote music historian David Morse. "He can be compared only with Ray Charles in his ability to take the most threadbare ballad and turn it into a dramatic and completely convincing statement."

Born on December 17, 1939, in Birmingham, Alabama, Kendricks grew up with close friend and Temptations's member Paul Williams. In 1956 Kendricks and Williams quit school and traveled northward to become singing stars in the tradition of their idols Clyde McPhatter and Little Willie John. In Detroit, Kendricks and Williams formed the doo wop singing group the Primes which performed at talent contests and house parties. In 1961 the Primes recorded the songs "Mother of Mine" and the dance tune "Check Yourself" for Berry Gordy's short-lived Miracle label.

Upon the suggestion of Berry Gordy, the Primes changed their name to the Temptations and after adding David Ruffin as lead vocalist, they set out to become one of the most successful groups on the Motown label. Throughout the decade, Kendricks sang lead on several songs including the classics "My Girl" in 1965, "Get Ready" in 1966, and "Just My Imagination (Running Away With Me)" in 1972.

In June of 1971, Kendricks pursued a solo career and eventually recorded two disco-influenced hits "Keep on Truckin'" in 1973 and "Boogie Down" in 1974. Kendricks's career soon fell into decline. Unable to find material to suit his unique artistic sensibility, Kendricks switched record labels several times before reuniting with the Temptations in 1982. After the reunion, Kendricks performed with the Temptations on the Live Aid broadcast and on the album *Live at the Apollo Theater with David Ruffin and Eddie Kendricks*. In 1987 Ruffin and Kendricks signed a contract with RCA and recorded the aptly titled LP *Ruffin and Kendricks*. Stricken by lung cancer, Kendricks died in October 1992.

Chaka Khan.

Chaka Khan (1953–)
Singer

Born in Great Lakes Naval Training Station, Illinois, in 1953, Chaka Khan (neé Yvette Marie Stevens) changed her name after attending the Yuruba Tribe African Arts Center in Chicago, her hometown. She sang with a number of groups including Lyfe, Lock and Chains, Baby Huey and the Babysitters and Ask Rufus, which shortened its name to Rufus and signed to ABC in 1973. After a modest selling debut album, Rufus's sophomore project featured Stevie Wonders's composition "Tell Me Something Good" on the *Rags to Rufus* album (1974). Soon, Khan earned the billing "featuring Chaka Khan," and the group produced a string of successful projects including *Rufusized* (1974), *Rufus featuring Chaka Khan* (1975), and *Ask Rufus* (1977).

Khan embarked on a solo career in 1978. During this time she collaborated with industry giants Quincy Jones ("Stuff Like That") and Joni Mitchell ("Don Juan's Reckless Daughter"). Her efforts as a solo artist featured collaborations with such luminaries as George Benson, The Average White Band, The Brecker Brothers, and Phil Upchurch. Throughout the 1980s, Khan expanded her reputation by recording in eclectic situations including jazz standards, rock, and hard hitting

soul. She collaborated with a dizzying mix of musicians such as Prince, Freddie Hubbard, Chick Corea, and Grandmaster Melle Mel. In the 1990s, the music of her earlier career remained staples in the both the rhythm and blues and smooth jazz radio formats. Her 1998 release *Come 2 My House* is collaborative project with "the artist formerly known as Prince" and features Khan's signature vocal style: a wide range, intense musicality, clarion tone, and sensual feeling. That same year Chaka Khan received ASCAP's first Rhythm & Soul Heritage Award. In 2000, Khan was honored with the Granville White Lifetime Achievement Award

Gladys Knight (1944–)
Singer

Born May 28, 1944, in Atlanta, Georgia, Gladys Knight was raised in a family which valued education and the sounds of gospel music. At age four, Knight began singing gospel music at the Mount Moriah Baptist Church. When she was eight, Knight won first prize on the television program "Ted Mack's Amateur Hour" for a rendition of the song "Too Young." Between the years 1950 and 1953, Knight toured with the Morris Brown Choir of Atlanta, Georgia. Around this same time, Knight joined her sister Brenda, brother Merald, and cousins William and Eleanor Guest to form a local church singing group. In 1957 the group took the name the Pips upon the suggestion of cousin and manager James "Pips" Woods.

Two years later Langston George and Edward Patten replaced Brenda Knight and Eleanor Guest. Though Gladys periodically left the group, she rejoined in 1964. After recording for several record labels, the Pips finally signed with Motown's subsidiary, Soul. Despite the lack of commercial success, the group released a number of fine recordings under the supervision of Motown's talented production staff including Norman Whitfield and Ashford and Simpson. In 1967 the group released the single "I Heard It Through the Grapevine" which reached number two on the Billboard charts. Following a long string of hits on Motown, the Pips signed with the Buddah label in 1973, releasing the album *Imagination*, which provided the group with two gold singles "Midnight Train to Georgia" and "I've Got to Use My Imagination."

By the late 1970s the group, faced with legal battles and contract disputes, began to fall out of popular vogue. For three years the group was barred from recording or performing together. As a result of an out-of-court settlement in 1980, the Pips signed a new contract with CBS, where they remained until 1985. Joined by Dionne Warwick and Elton John, Knight recorded the Grammy Award-winning gold single "That's What Friends Are For" in 1986. Released in 1988, the title cut of the Pip's *Love Overboard* album became their biggest selling single in decades. That same year, Knight recorded the theme for the James Bond film *License To Kill*. Released on the MCA label, Knight's 1991 album *Good Women* features guest stars Patti LaBelle and Dionne Warwick. Knight released another album *Just For You* in 1994. In 1995, Gladys Knight and the Pips were inducted into the Rock and Roll Hall of Fame.

In 1998, Knight put forth the album *Many Different Roads*, her first album to fully focus in on the spiritual side of music. In 2001, Knight returned to more contemporary music with her album *At Last*. She also married business consultant William McDowell that same year. It was her fourth marriage and his second. In 2002, Knight was back in the limelight as she won a Grammy for Best Traditional R&B Vocal Album, for *At Last*,

from the National Academy of Recording Arts & Sciences.

Suge Knight (1966–)
Music Company Executive

Born Marion Knight Jr. in 1966, Knight grew up in the rough neighborhood of Compton, California. Despite being surrounded by violence, Knight picked up the nickname "Suge"—short for "Sugar"—because of his basic good-natured temperament. While in high school, Knight devoted his time to playing football with the hopes of gaining an athletic scholarship to college. Standing over 6 feet tall and weighing nearly 300 pounds, Knight took his talents to the University of Nevada in Las Vegas. There he won several awards including the Rookie of the Year on defense and a spot on the dean's list for academics. After college, Knight was drafted by the NFL's Los Angeles Rams, but decided to pursue different avenues.

A string of run-ins with the law almost put an end to any hopes Knight had. Between the years of 1987 and 1990, Knight was arrested for several crimes including auto theft, battery, and attempted murder. His luck soon changed as he made a name for himself while working as a bodyguard for musicians. Eventually, Knight formed a publication company and made a significant amount of money from ownership rights to several of white rapper Vanilla Ice's songs.

Based on the success of his publishing company, Knight decided to venture into artist management. This led to Knight meeting Dr. Dre, formerly of N.W.A. At that time, Dre was managed by Ruthless Records, but Knight pulled some strings and signed Dre and two other Ruthless artists to new contracts. Controversy surrounded the transaction as Knight was accused of using force to finalize the deal. Together with Dr. Dre, Knight founded Death Row Records. Blistering success quickly followed as the label grossed more than $60 million in 1993. An already impressive artist roster including Dr. Dre, Snoop Doggy Dogg, and Warren G. quickly improved with the signing of Mary J. Blige and Jodeci. With three multiplatinum albums under his belt, Knight began to refer to Death Row Records as the Motown of the 1990s. In luring top artists to Death Row, Knight often doubles their royalty rates, offers more creative control for the musician, and upgrades their contracts. In 1995, Knight even bailed jailed rapper Tupac Shakur out of prison in order to add more talent to the Death Row cluster. In the late 1990s, Knight faced his own legal battles. In 1997, Knight was sentenced to nine years in state prison for conspiracy to illegally possess a firearm, after violating several state probations for weapons charges. This was followed by a federal prison term for his role in a drug case. Knight was granted a new hearing in 1998. Finally, in 2001, Knight was released from a federal prison in Oregon after serving five years of his nine-year sentence for the assault and probation violations.

KRS-One (1965?–)
Rap Singer

A self-described teacher whose Boogie Down Productions (BDP) was an important influence on hardcore rap, KRS-One survived street life, prison, homelessness, the murder of a close friend, and negative criticism to emerge as one of rap's most powerful figures. Born as Lawrence Parker c. 1965 in Brooklyn, New York, KRS-One (initially representative of "Kris, Number One," later an acronym for Knowledge Reigns Supreme Over Nearly Everyone") also went by Krishna Parker or Kris Parker. Leaving home at 13, he lived on the streets, taking odd jobs when available and hanging out in public libraries. Self-educated, he served a short stint in jail for selling marijuana. Upon his release, the 19-year-old met Scott Sterling, a social worker and DJ who worked under the name Scott LaRock. Together the two formed BDP.

BDP recorded one album *Criminal Minded* before LaRock was killed while trying to break up a fight. Persevering, KRS-One kept their music alive, recording several critically acclaimed works with the various musicians who comprised the BDP crew. In 1990, he created H.E.A.L., or Human Education Against Lies, an afrocentric, pro-educational organization. KRS-One also founded Edutainer Records that year. In 1991, he recorded *Live Hardcore Worldwide*, one of the first live rap albums ever, and produced such artists as Queen Latifah and the Neville Brothers. His 1992 album *Sex and Violence* returned to the earlier hardcore sound of BDP, while his 1997 recording *I Got Next* produced raw funk on tracks such as "The MC." KRS-One took a four year sabbatical from the music industry, but returned strongly with his 2001 release *The Sneak Attack*. He then surprised many fans and critics with his 2002 album *Spiritual Minded*, a hardcore gospel record which preaches the ways of a religious lifestyle in rap format.

Patti LaBelle (1944–)
Singer

Born in Philadelphia, Pennsylvania, in 1944, Patti LaBelle (née Patricia Holt) has remained one of the most respected divas of the pop-soul tradition. Known for her dramatic vocalizations and stage presentations,

Patti LaBelle performing in 1990.

LaBelle's career has lasted several decades by keeping up with popular trends without sacrificing her signature vocal gymnastics.

While still a teenager, LaBelle formed the Bluebelles with Cindy Birdsong, Sarah Dash, and Nonah Henderson. They scored a hit in "I Sold My Heart to the Junkman" (1962) and "Down the Aisle" (1963) during the height of the girl group fad in popular music. Shortly thereafter, the group adopted the name Patti LaBelle and the Bluebelles, which was ultimately shortened to LaBelle, and they turned to a harder rock style in the early 1970s. The group scored a million seller hit with the energetic "Lady Marmalade." The group disbanded in 1976, and LaBelle embarked on a solo career.

In the mid-1980s, she recorded the hits "New Attitude" (1985) and "Oh People" (1986) and the Bayer Sayer-Burt Bacharach song "On My Own" (1986), which featured a duet with Michael McDonald of the Doobie Brothers. LaBelle is the recipient of eight Grammy Award nominations and three Emmy Award nominations. In 1992, she received a Grammy for best R&B vocal performance. She produced numerous albums throughout the 1990s including *Burnin'* (1991); *Gems*

(1994); and *Flame* (1997). While her entire body of recordings throughout the 1980s and 1990s were met with mixed commercial success, she has established herself as a sentimental favorite among pop-soul audiences. In 2000, LaBelle put out the studio album, *When a Woman Loves*. In 2001, she was awarded the Lena Horne Award for outstanding career achievement at the *Soul Train*'s Lady of Soul Awards.

Little Richard (1932–)
Singer, Pianist

Flamboyantly dressed, with his hair piled high in a pompadour, Little Richard is a musical phenomenon, an entertainer hailed by pop superstar Paul McCartney as "one of the greatest kings of rock and roll." Richard's image, mannerisms, and musical talent set the trend for the emergence of modern popular music performers from Jimi Hendrix to Prince.

One of 12 children, Richard Wayne Penniman was born on December 5, 1932, in Macon, Georgia. As a child in Macon, Richard heard the sounds of gospel music groups, street musicians, and spiritual-based songs emanating from homes throughout his neighborhood. Nicknamed the "War Hawk" for his unrestrained hollers and shouts, Richard's voice projected with such intensity that he was once asked to stop singing in church. Richard's first song before an audience was with the Tiny Tots, a gospel group featuring his brothers Marquette and Walter. Later Richard sang with his family in a group called the Penniman Singers; they appeared at churches, camp meetings, and talent contests.

In high school, Richard played alto saxophone in the marching band. After school he took a part-time job at the Macon City Auditorium, where he watched the bands of Cab Calloway, Hot Lips Page, Lucky Millinder, and Sister Rosetta Thorpe. At age 14, Richard left home to become a performer in Doctor Hudson's Medicine Show. While on the road, he joined B. Brown's Orchestra as a ballad singer performing such compositions as "Good Night Irene" and "Mona Lisa." Not long afterward, he became a member of the traveling minstrel show of Sugarfoot Sam from Alabama.

Richard's first break came in 1951, when the RCA label recorded him live on the radio, producing the local hit "Every Hour." Traveling to New Orleans with his band the Tempo Toppers, Richard's group eventually played the Houston rhythm and blues scene, where he attracted the attention of Don Robey, president of Peacock Records. After cutting some sides for the Peacock label, Richard sent a demo tape to Art Rupe's Los Angeles-based Specialty label. Under the direction of Specialty's producer Bumps Blackwell, Richard recorded the 1956 hit "Tutti Frutti" at J&M Studios in New Orleans. Richard's subsequent sessions for Specialty yielded a long list of classic hits such as "Long Tall Sally," "Lucille," "Jenny, Jenny," and "Keep a Knocking." In 1957, Richard appeared in the films *Don't Knock Rock* with Billy Haley and *The Girl Can't Help It* starring Jane Mansfield.

In the following year, Richard quit his rock and roll career to enter the Oakland Theological College in Huntsville, Alabama. Between 1957 to 1959 Richard released several gospel recordings and toured with artists such as Mahalia Jackson. In 1962, Richard embarked on a tour of Europe with Sam Cooke. One year later Richard hired a then unknown guitarist, Jimi Hendrix, who went under the pseudonym of Maurice James. In Europe Richard played on the same bills as the Beatles and Rolling Stones.

By the 1970s, Richard pursued a career as a full-fledged evangelist and performer. In 1979, he set out on a nationwide evangelist tour. In the following decade, he appeared in the film *Down and Out in Beverly Hills* and recorded "Rock Island Line" on the tribute LP to Leadbelly and Woody Guthrie entitled *Folkways: A Vision Shared.*

Richard's continuing activity in show business represents the inexhaustible energy of a singer who had a profound impact on the careers of artists such as Otis Redding, Eddie Cochran, Richie Valens, Paul McCartney, and Mitch Ryder. Having earned special Grammy honors in 1993, Richard was honored with a lifetime achievement award by the Rhythm & Blues Foundation the following year. Later that year, he headlined the 1994 New Orleans Jazz and Heritage Festival and he is a charter member of the Rock and Roll Hall of Fame and Museum. He was called upon by the House of Blues Foundation to assist in the organizations Blues School House program in 1995.

Richard continued to tour throughout the 1990s and has appeared in numerous television shows and movies, usually as himself. In 2000, NBC produced a television about his life titled "Little Richard" starring Robert Townsend. Also in 2000, Richard was named the goodwill ambassador to his hometown Macon, Georgia. Most recently Richard was inducted into the National Association for the Advancement of Colored People (NAACP) Hall of Fame.

LL Cool J (1968–)
Rap Musician, Actor

In the mid-1980s, LL Cool J became one of rap music's first major stars. Along with a handful of other musicians, he played a major role in rap's entry and acceptance into the mainstream of American pop music. Even with the enormous shifts and changes in the industry over the past two decades, LL Cool J has remained a successful rap musician. In addition to his long-lived prominence as a rapper, LL Cool J has also cultivated a successful television and film acting career.

Born James Todd Smith on January 14, 1968, LL Cool J (short for "Ladies Love Cool James") grew up in Queens, New York. At the age of 16, he released "I Need A Beat," the first record issued on Russell Simmons and Rick Rubin's Def Jam label. The single proved to be very popular, and he released his debut album, *Radio* (1985), the following year. With the success of the album, LL Cool J was invited to perform a version of his single "I Can't Live Without My Radio" in the film *Krush Groove* (1985). He also appeared as a rapper in the film *Wildcats* (1986).

His second album, *Bigger and Deffer* (1987) proved to be an even bigger hit than *Radio*. The album's single "I Need Love" became the first rap song to top Billboard Magazine's R&B chart, expanding the appeal of rap music to a broader audience. That year, "Going Back to Cali," a single from the soundtrack for the film *Less Than Zero*, proved to be another major hit on the charts. LL Cool J followed with the albums *Walking with a Panther* (1989); *Momma Said Knock You Out* (1990); *14 Shots to the Dome* (1993); *Mr. Smith* (1995); *Phenomenon* (1997); and *G.O.A.T. Featuring James T. Smith* (2001).

The onset of the 1990s saw LL Cool J explore the media of film and television, both as a musician and an actor. He was the first rap artist to appear on MTV's *Unplugged* in 1991, and turned in an impressive performance as an undercover policeman in the *The Hard Way* (1991). A year later, he appeared in the film *Toys* (1992). In 1995, LL Cool J was given his own television series, *In the House*. The sitcom, which premiered on NBC before moving to the UPN network, ran until 1999. LL Cool J's acting credits include roles in the following films: *Out-of-Sync* (1995), *B.A.P.S* (1997), *Caught Up* (1998), *Woo* (1998), *Halloween: H20* (1998), *Deep Blue Sea* (1999), *In Too Deep* (1999), *Any Given Sunday* (1999), *Charlie's Angels* (2000), *Kingdom Come* (2001), and *Rollerball* (2002).

Master P (c.1970–)
Music and Film Company Executive, Rap Singer, Actor

Born Percy Miller, Master P grew up in a housing project in New Orleans's Third Ward, an area with a reputation for a high crime rate and violence. His parents divorced when he was 11 years of age, and his

Master P holding an American Music Award in 1999.

mother moved to California. Though he shuttled back and forth between New Orleans and California, the teenaged Percy settled in the Crescent City, attended Booker T. Washington and Warren Eason high schools, and played basketball at both schools. After graduation, he reportedly earned a basketball scholarship to the University of Houston. However, he was sidelined by a leg injury and headed back home rather than sit out the season. After the death of his brother, Kevin, and with some junior college business courses to his credit, Master P moved to Richmond and opened a small record store, No Limits Records, financing the store with $10,000 that he received as part of a medical malpractice settlement related to the death of his grandfather.

Master P was soon able to turn his successful record store into a powerhouse producer of Southern-influenced gangsta rap albums. He self-produced his first album *The Ghetto's Tryin' to Kill Me* in 1994, selling 200,000 copies out of the trunk of his car. Master P then took the profits from this album and produced two collections of rap music: *Down South Hustlers, Vol. 1* and *West Coast Bad Boys, Vol. 1*. By 1997, the four-year label had a cluster of artists who, while not household names, were well-known to rap fans.

Master P next targeted the film industry. In 1997, he produced, directed, and acted in a low-budget semi-autobiographical film titled *I'm 'Bout It* without any outside backing. The success of this direct-to-video film spawned *I Got the Hook Up* the following year. This time there was no problem signing Dimension Records as a distributor for the film. A third film *MP Da Last Don* soon followed.

No Limit then made a major move to Baton Rouge. It also undertook a number of new enterprises. A sports management company, No Limit Sports Management, was started in 1997 and represents such professional players as Ron Mercer of the Boston Celtics and Derek Anderson of the Cleveland Cavaliers. By 1998, No Limits Records had incorporated 12 businesses in Baton Rouge including a complex called "The Ice Cream Shop," which includes five recording studios, a dorm, a gym, a pool, an aquarium, a sun deck, a movie theater, a domed basketball court, and 15 Hummers for transportation. The Master P Foundation has also been a supporter of the Baton Rouge schools and community.

In 1998, Master P tried out for the Continental Basketball Association's Fort Wayne Furies and was signed as a free agent in October. His performance with the Furies brought an invitation to try out with the National Basketball Association's Charlotte Hornets. While Master P did not make the cut, he intends, as was the case with the other accomplishments in his life, to continue working until he succeeds.

His basketball career temporarily on hold, Master P continued to make music. In 1999 he came out with *Only God Can Judge Me* followed by *Ghetto Postage* in 2000 and *Game Face* in 2002. Master P continues to build his producing credits by managing the career of his son, rap star Lil' Romeo.

Curtis Mayfield (1942–1999)
Singer, Songwriter, Music Producer

Born on June 3, 1942, in Chicago, Illinois, Curtis Mayfield learned to sing harmony as a member of the Northern Jubilee Singers and the Traveling Souls Spiritualist Church. In 1957, Mayfield joined the Roosters, a five-man doo wop singing group led by his close friend Jerry Butler. Renamed the Impressions, the group released the 1958 hit "Your Precious Love," featuring Butler's resonant baritone and Mayfield's wispy tenor. But in the following year, Butler left the group to pursue a solo career. In search of material, Butler collaborated with Mayfield to write the hit songs "He Will Break Your Heart" and "I'm a-Telling You."

In 1960, Mayfield recruited Fred Cash to take Butler's place in the newly reformed Impressions. In the next year the Impressions hit the charts with the sensual soul tune "Gypsy Women." In collaboration with Butler, Mayfield also established the Curtom Publishing Company. With the loss of original members Richard Brooks and Arthur Brooks, the three remaining members of the Impressions, Mayfield, Cash, and Sam Goodman continued to perform as a trio. Under the direction of jazz musician/arranger Johnny Pate, the Impressions recorded "Sad Sad Girl" and the rhythmic gospel-based song "It's All Right," released in 1963.

During this time, Mayfield also wrote a number of songs for his Chicago contemporaries including "Monkey Time" for Major Lance, "Just Be True" for Gene Chandler, and "It's All Over Now" for Walter Jackson. Writing for the Impressions, however, Mayfield turned to more socially conscious themes reflecting the current of the civil rights era. Mayfield's finest "sermon songs" were "People Get Ready" (1965), "We're a Winner" (1968), and "Choice of Colors" (1969).

After leaving the Impressions in 1970, Mayfield released his debut album *Curtis*. On his 1971 LP *Curtis Live!*, Mayfield was accompanied by a tight four-piece backup group, which included guitar, bass, drums, and percussion. Mayfield composed the score for the 1972 hit film *Superfly*. The soundtrack became Mayfield's biggest commercial success, providing him two hits with the junkie epitaph "Freddie's Dead" and the wah-wah guitar funk classic "Superfly." Despite his commercial success, Mayfield spent the remainder of the decade in collaboration with other artists, working on such projects as the soundtrack for the film *Claudine*, featuring Gladys Knight and the Pips, and the production of Aretha Franklin's 1978 album *Sparkle*.

Throughout the next decade, Mayfield continued to record such albums as *Love is the Place* in 1981, and *Honesty* in 1982. Joined by Jerry Butler and newcomers Nate Evans and Vandy Hampton, the Impressions reunited in 1983, for a 30-city anniversary tour. In 1983, Mayfield released the LP *Come in Peace With a Message of Love*. But in August 1990, while performing at an outdoor concert in Brooklyn, New York, Mayfield received an injury that left him paralyzed from the neck down. In the following year, Mayfield's contributions to popular music were recognized when the Impressions were inducted into the Rock and Roll Hall of Fame. In 1994, Mayfield was presented with the Grammy Legend Award. Earlier that year a number of his peers, including Aretha Franklin, got together to record *All Men Are Brothers: A Tribute to Curtis Mayfield*. Despite his injuries, Mayfield triumphed, producing a Grammy nominated album *New World Order* in late 1996. Curtis

Mayfield was inducted into the Rock and Roll Hall of Fame on April 5, 1999. Mayfield dies December 26, 1999, in Roswell, Georgia, at the age of 57.

Bobby McFerrin. *See* **Classical Music chapter.**

Pras Michel. *See* **The Fugees.**

Notorious B.I.G. (1973–1997)
Rap Singer

Notorious B.I.G., also known as Biggie Smalls and B.I.G., was born Christopher Wallace in the Bedford-Stuyvesant section of Brooklyn in 1973. A self-described, former "100 percent hustler" and high school drop out, Notorious B.I.G. became within his short career one of most influential and respected talents in hip hop history.

Noted for his massive six-foot three-inch, 300-plus pound frame, a husky-voiced yet fluid, and rhythmically inventive delivery style and explicit lyrics, he began his career making amateur tapes for fun with the OGB (Old Gold Brothers), when his talents caught the attention of rapper Big Daddy Kane's DJ. He was soon featured in the rap trade magazine *The Source* in its "Unsigned Hype" column, a showcase for new rappers. A record deal with Uptown Records followed shortly thereafter, and he created "Party and Bullshit" for the film *Who's the Man?* After he signed with his business associate and friend Sean "Puffy" Combs's Bad Boy label, Notorious B.I.G. recorded *Ready to Die* in 1994 and the project went platinum. He was named rap artist of year in 1995 at the *Billboard* Awards. Notorious B.I.G.'s star rose quickly within hip hop culture's inner circle, and he became a much sought after guest rapper on numerous recordings. His collaborations include Junior M.A.F.I.A., Mary J. Blige, Total, among others. In 1997 Notorious B.I.G. died a violent death after being shot in a Los Angeles parking lot. Another recording project, ironically titled *Life After Death. . . 'Til Death Do Us Part*, was released posthumously.

Teddy Pendergrass (1950–)
Singer

Born Theodore Pendergrass in 1950 in Philadelphia, the vocalist learned singing from his mother, who performed in nightclubs, and in his childhood apprenticeship in church. Although he became known as one of the most prominent soul balladeers of the late 1970s and 1980s, he began his professional career as a drummer for the group the Cadillacs.

In 1970 Pendergrass moved from his duties as drummer and began singing with Harold Melvin and the Blue Notes, a group that had started as a doo wop group in the 1950s and which signed with the producers Gamble and Huff's label, Philadelphia International, in 1972. Pendergrass's powerful and passionate baritone presentation ultimately earned him the lead spot in the Blue Notes, and for six years his vocals became the group's signature sound. During this period the Blue Notes recorded such hits as "I Miss You" and "If You Don't Know Me By Now," among others, establishing themselves as one the premiere soul groups of the decade.

In 1976, Pendergrass left the group to pursue a successful solo career, remaining with Gamble and Huff and producing a string of hits, such as "I Don't Love You Anymore" (1976) and the number one rhythm and blues single "Close the Door" (1978). Pendergrass became a heartthrob among female fans, mounting successful tours with his Teddy Bear Orchestra and recording albums that were commercially profitable. His career path turned downward following a 1982 near-fatal car crash in Philadelphia that paralyzed him from the neck down. He has maintained a respectable recording career despite these challenges, releasing the album *You and I* in 1997, and some of his recordings over the last decade have done well on the charts. In 1999 Pendergrass published *Truly Blessed* his tell-all biography co-authored with Patricia Romanowski. Pendergrass continues to tour the country performing musically and speaking about the rights of the disabled.

Charley Pride (1939–)
Singer

The first African American superstar of country music, Charley Pride is a three-time Grammy Award winner whose supple baritone voice has won him international fame. He was the first African American with the Grand Ole Opry in 50 years. A prolific artist, Pride has recorded more than 30 albums.

Born on March 18, 1938, in Slege, Mississippi, Charley Pride grew up listening to late night radio broadcasts of the Grand Ole Opry, country music's most famous showcase. Although he taught himself guitar at age 14, Pride soon turned his attention to a professional baseball career. At age 16, he left the cotton fields of Slege for a stint in the Negro American baseball league. During his baseball career, Pride sang on public address systems and in taverns. In 1963, country singer

Notorious B.I.G. holding two Billboard Music Awards in 1995.

Red Sovine heard Pride and arranged for him to attend an audition in Nashville one year later. This led to a recording contract with the RCA label and produced the 1964 hit "Snakes Crawl at Night."

Throughout the 1960s, Pride toured incessantly, appearing at concert dates and state fairs, as well as on radio and television. In 1967, Pride debuted at the Grand Ole Opry and within the same year hit the charts with singles "Does My Ring Hurt Your Finger?" and "I Know One." With the release of *The Sensational Charley Pride* in 1969 and the subsequent year's *Just Plain Charley*, Pride found himself entering the decade of his greatest recognition. By the time he received the Country Music Award for entertainer of the year in 1970, Pride had already achieved tremendous success as a major figure in the popular cultural scene of the United States. Other honors included *Billboard*'s Trendsetter Award and the Music Operators of America's Entertainer of the Year Award.

In the 1980s, Pride not only continued to find success as a music star, he became a successful entrepreneur. Making his home on a 240-acre estate in North Dallas, Texas, Pride emerged as a majority stockholder in the First Texas Bank and part owner of Cecca Productions. Pride made more history in 1993, when he became the first African American to join the cast of the Grand Ole Opry since DeFord Bailey's presence nearly 52 years earlier. The following year, Pride published his autobiography entitled *Pride: The Charley Pride Story*. In 1999, Pride was honored with a star on the Hollywood Walk of Fame for his career. A year later he was the first African American to ever be inducted into the Country Music Hall of Fame.

Prince (1958–)
Singer, Songwriter, Producer

The son of a jazz pianist, Prince Rogers Nelson was born on June 7, 1958, in Minneapolis, Minnesota. By age 14, Prince had taught himself to play piano, guitar, and drums. Drawn to many forms of rock and soul, Prince explained that he never grew up in one particular culture. "I'm not a punk, but I'm not an rhythm and blues artist either—because I'm a middle class kid from Minnesota."

It was his eclectic taste that led to Prince's creation of the Minneapolis sound. After forming the band Grand

Central in high school in 1973, Prince renamed the group Champagne and eventually recruited the talents of Morris Day. In 1978 Prince signed with Warner Brothers and recorded his debut album *For You*. His follow-up album *Prince* featured the hit "I Wanna Be Your Lover." Rooted in the music of Sly and the Family Stone and Jimi Hendrix, Prince's third LP *Dirty Mind* was released in 1980.

Two years later, Prince achieved superstardom with his album *1999*, an effort which was followed by a spectacular tour comprised of Prince and the Revolution, the Time, and the bawdy girl trio Vanity 6. Prince's 1984 film soundtrack *Purple Rain*, which received rave reviews for Prince's portrayal of a struggling young musician, grossed $60 million at the box office in the first two months of its release. Near the end of 1985 Prince established his own record label Paisley Park, the warehouse/studio located in the wooded terrain of Chanhassen, Minnesota. That same year, Prince released the album *Around the World in Day*, featuring the hit singles "Raspberry Beret," "Paisley Park," and "Pop Life."

Prince's next film project *Under the Cherry Moon*, filmed in France, was completed under his direction. The soundtrack *Parade Music From Under the Cherry Moon* produced a number of hit singles including "Kiss" and "Mountains." After reforming the Revolution, Prince released *SPIN of the Times* in 1987, which included a duet with Sheena Easton titled "I Could Never Take the Place of Your Man." Following the LP *Love Sexy*, Prince recorded several songs which appeared on the soundtrack for the film *Batman*. This was followed by another film soundtrack *Graffiti Bridge* in 1990.

In September 1992, Prince signed a six-album contract with Warner Brothers. Backed by his new first rate ensemble the New Power Generation, Prince embarked on a nationwide tour in April 1993 which proved the most impressive since his commercial breakthrough in the early 1980s. Prince has not only become an owner of his own nightclub, the Grand Slam, he has contributed a set of original music to the Joffery Ballet's production of "Billboards" which opened in January of 1993 to rave reviews.

That year, the eccentric performer also changed his name to an unpronounceable symbol and announced the retirement of "Prince" from recording. In 1994, The Artist Formerly Known as Prince (TAFKAP) debuted interactive CD-ROM software and New Power Generation retail establishments. Two years later, the long-time bachelor married on Valentine's Day and commissioned a symphony from his band to commemorate the occasion.

Recording under the title The Artist Formley Known as Prince, Prince produced the albums *Gold Experience* (1995); *Chaos and Disorder* (1996); the mammoth three disc *Emancipation* (1996); the multi-disc outtake album *Crystal Ball* (1998); *New Power Soul* (1998); *Rave Un2 the Joy Fantastic* (1999); and *Rainbow Children* (2001). Prince also received a great deal of radio and television airtime in the year before the millennium when his rock hit "1999" became the theme song for almost all New Year's Eve celebrations.

Public Enemy
Rap Group

As spokesmen of racial pride and proponents of militant public activism, Public Enemy have redefined the sound and the lyrical message of rap music. The formation of Public Enemy centered around Adelphi University in Long Island, New York, where the group's founder Carlton Ridenhour, a.k.a Chuck D., a graphic design major, joined fellow students Hank Shocklee and Bill Stephney at radio station WBAU. First appearing on Stephney's radio show, Ridenhour soon hosted his own three-hour program. Ridenhour's powerful rap voice attracted a number of loyal followers. Ridenhour soon recruited the talents of William Drayton a.k.a Flavor Flav, Norman Rodgers, a.k.a Terminator X, and Richard Griffin, a.k.a Professor Griff to form Public Enemy. Shocklee and his production-oriented peers in the group came to be known as the Bomb Squad and their talents were often sought by other artists.

In 1987, Public Enemy released the debut album *Yo! Bum Rush the Show*, which sold more than 400,000 copies. Two years later Professor Griff, the group's "minister of information," was fired by Chuck D. for making anti-Semitic comments. Under the leadership of Chuck D. the group went on to record the song "Fight the Power" for director Spike Lee's film *Do The Right Thing*. The group's second album *It Takes a Nation of Millions to Hold Us Back* became a million seller.

Public Enemy's 1990 release *Fear of a Black Planet* featured themes regarding a world struggle for the advancement of the black race. The controversial "911 Is a Joke" led to widespread discourse over the song's allegations that emergency personnel respond slower, if at all, to calls originating from inner city or predominantly African American areas. The follow-up album *Apocalypse '91: The Enemy Strikes Black* was a startling statement of social and racial consciousness and featured a collaboration with the heavy metal band Anthrax on "Bring the Noise," a track that originally appeared on *It Takes a Nation*. Another single "By the Time I Get to Arizona" sparked another nationwide

Chuck D of Public Enemy speaks to a class at Columbia University in 1998.

debate over the refusal of Arizona state officials to recognize Martin Luther King Jr.'s birthday as a legal holiday.

Greatest Misses, a hits compilation released in 1992, seemed to signal the end of an era for the Public Enemy camp. In a departure from their earlier work, 1994's *Muse Sick n Hour Mess Age* traded the sonic dissonances of the Bomb Squad for samples from classic soul recordings. Meanwhile, most of the members had established themselves as solo artists or developed other career directions in the early 1990s, but overall the group's popularity seemed to wane as gangsta rap commandeered the airwaves. The group proved that they could incorporate the more modern sounds of hip-hop into their music with the critically innovative album *He Got Game*, the soundtrack for the Spike Lee movie of the same name. However, much like many of their later 1990s offerings, the rap buying audiences passed over this album. The group returned to their hardcore rap roots with their 1999 offering *There's a Poison Going On. . .*, but critics paid more attention to

the album than fans did. Public Enemy however continues to tour and released of their eighth studio album *Revolverlution* in 2002.

Queen Latifah (1970–)
Singer, Actress

Born Dana Owens, rap artist Queen Latifah grew up in East Orange, New Jersey, and began performing in high school as the human beat box for the rap group Ladies Fresh. In 1989, she launched her solo recording career with the album *All Hail the Queen*, an afrocentric, pro-woman work. Her other recordings include: *Nature of a Sista'* (1991), featuring the single "Latifah Had It Up 2 Here"; *Black Reign* (1993), which spawned the feminist anthem "U.N.I.T.Y"; and 1998's *Order in the Court*, which *Entertainment Weekly* called "fun and funky."

Latifah manages the careers of other rap artists through her New Jersey-based Flavor Unit Records and Management Company, of which she is the CEO. In addition, she was a regular on the Fox network's *Living Single*, along with co-stars Kim Fields, Erika Alexander, and Kim Coles. She has also made appearances on *The Fresh Prince of Bel-Air* and in such films as the Hudlin brothers' *House Party II*, Spike Lee's *Jungle Fever*, and Ernest Dickerson's *Juice*. She had lead roles in *Set It Off* (1996) and *Bringing Down the Houze* (2003). In 1998, Latifah gave a bravura perfomance as a sultry jazz singer in the movie *Living Out Loud*. The following year, Latifah was named one of *People* magazine's 50 Most Beautiful People, released an autobiography, *Ladies First: Revelations of a Strong Woman*, and briefly hosted her own television talk show.

Otis Redding (1941–1967)
Singer, Songwriter

Born on September 9, 1941, in Dawson, Georgia, Otis Redding moved with his parents at age three to the Tindall Heights housing project in Macon. In grade school Redding played drums and sang in a church gospel group. A few years later he learned the vocals and piano style of his idol Little Richard. Quitting school in the tenth grade, Redding went on the road with Little Richard's former band, the Upsetters. But Redding's first professional break came when he joined Johnny Jenkins and the Pinetoppers. Redding's debut single was a Little Richard imitation tune "Shout Bamalama." Accompanying Jenkins to a Stax studio session in Memphis, Redding was afforded some remaining recording time. Backed by Jenkins on guitar, Steve Cropper on piano, Lewis Steinburg on bass, and Al Jackson on drums, Redding cut "Hey Hey Baby" and the hit "These Arms of Mine."

Signed to the Stax label, Redding released the 1963 album *Pain in My Heart*. Backed by members of Booker T. and the MGs, Redding's follow-up LP *Otis Blue (Otis Redding Sings Soul)* featured the 1965 hit "Respect." In the next year, Redding broke attendance records at shows in Harlem and Watts. After releasing a cover version of the Rolling Stones's song "Satisfaction" in 1966, Redding embarked on a European tour which included his appearance on the British television show "Ready Steady Go!"

In August 1966, Redding established his own record company, Jotis, which was distributed through the Stax label. Following a few commercially unsuccessful ventures, Redding recorded singer Arthur Conley who provided the label with the million-selling single "Sweet Soul Music." Redding's recordings "Try a Little Tenderness" and the vocal duet "Tramp," featuring Carla Thomas, hit the charts in 1967. On June 16, Redding, backed by the MGs, performed a stunning high-paced set at the Monterey Pop Festival. On December 10,

Redding's career came to an tragic end when the twin engine plane carrying him to a concert date in Wisconsin crashed in Lake Monona, just outside Madison. As if in tribute, Redding's song "Sitting on the Dock of the Bay," released a few weeks after his death, became his first gold record.

Lionel Richie (1949–)
Singer, Songwriter, Pianist

Lionel Brockman Richie was born on June 20, 1949, on the campus of Tuskegee Institute in Alabama. Richie's grandmother Adelaide Foster, a classical pianist, became his music instructor, introducing him to the works of Bach and Beethoven. While a freshman at the Tuskegee Institute, Richie formed the Mighty Mystics who, along with members of the Jays, became the Commodores. Combining gospel, classical, and country-western music, the Commodores emerged as a formidable live act throughout the 1960s and 1970s. After signing with the Motown label, the group landed its first hit in 1974 with the song "Machine Gun." In 1981 Richie recorded the hit theme song for Franco Zefferelli's film *Endless Love*.

A year later, Richie released his first solo album *Lionel Richie*, which featured the hits "Truly," "You Are," and "My Love." His follow-up release *Can't Slow Down* produced five more hits: "All Night Long (All Night)," "Running with the Night," "Hello," "Stuck on You," and "Penny Lover." In collaboration with Michael Jackson, Richie co-wrote "We Are the World" for USA for Africa, the famine relief project organized and produced by Quincy Jones. In 1985 Richie received an Oscar nomination for "Best Original Song" for his composition "Say You, Say Me." A year later, Richie's third album *Dancing on the Ceiling* provided him with the hits "Dancing on the Ceiling," "Love Will Conquer All," "Ballerina Girl," and "Se La."

After taking a hiatus from recording, Richie released *Back to Front* in 1992, which yielded the hit "Do It to Me." This album was followed up by the recording *Time* in 1998 and *Renaissance* in 2001. Richie was inducted into the Songwriters Hall of Fame in 1994. In 1997 he married his long-time girlfriend Diane Alexander and a year later the couple had a daughter, Sophia.

Teddy Riley (1967–)
Producer, Songwriter, Musician

Born of October 8, 1967, Teddy Riley grew up in Harlem, New York. By age ten he could play guitar, bass, several horns, and keyboards. In his early twenties Riley merged aspects of hip hop, pop, and soul to create a new kind of music called "new jack swing." In the mid-1980s Riley formed his first band, Wreckx-N-Effect, with brothers Markell and Brandon Mitchell, which produced the hit single "New Jack Swing" (1984).

In 1987 he formed Guy with Aaron Hall and Timmy Gatling. Their first effort on the Uptown/MCA label, *Guy*, (1988) topped *Billboard*'s rhythm and blues chart and sold over 2 million copies. The group toured, selling out many venues. With their second album *1990s The Future*, Guy had more of a pop feel. *The Future* went platinum and received brilliant reviews.

Success was followed by difficult times. After his younger brother, Brandon Mitchell, was killed in gunfire, Riley decided to move to Virginia Beach. Then Riley and his longtime manager, Gene Griffen, split over a money dispute. Finally, Guy disbanded.

Next Riley formed Blackstreet with Chauncey "Black" Hannibal, Dave Hollister, and Levi Little. After the release of their first album, Hollister and Little left the group and were replaced by Eric Williams and Mark Middleton. They see themselves as role models and keep their music and image clean. The single "No Diggity" (1997) went platinum and topped the charts. Blackstreet won a Grammy Award for the best rhythm and blues performance in 1998. In 1999, Riley and Blackstreet put out their third album *Finally* which included the single "I Got What You On."

Throughout his career Riley has written and produced 10 platinum albums, 22 platinum singles, and 11 gold singles for a variety of artists including Michael Jackson, Keith Sweat, Wreckx-N-Effect, Bobby Brown, and Kool Moe Dee. In 1990 Riley founded Future Records Recording Studio, LOR Records & Management, and Future Entertainment Group Ltd. in Virginia Beach.

Smokey Robinson (1940–)
Singer, Songwriter, Producer

Proclaimed by Bob Dylan as one of America's greatest poets, Smokey Robinson is a pop music legend. He has risen to fame as a brilliant songwriter, producer, and singer. His instantly recognizable falsetto voice continues to bring Robinson gold records and a legion of loyal fans.

William Robinson Jr. was born in Detroit, on February 19, 1940. After his mother died when he was ten years old, Robinson was raised by his sister. Nicknamed "Smokey" by his uncle, Robinson was a bright student who enjoyed reading books and poetry. A reluctant saxophone student, Robinson turned his creative energy to composing songs that he collected in a dime store writing tablet. While attending Detroit's Northern High School in 1954, Robinson formed the vocal group the Matadors, which performed at battle-of-the-band contests and at recreation centers.

Robinson's introduction to Berry Gordy in 1957 resulted in the Matadors's first record contract with George Goldner's End label. Upon joining the newly formed Motown label in 1960, the group changed their name, at Gordy's suggestion, to the Miracles. Although the Miracles's debut album failed to attract notice, they provided Motown with its first smash hit "Shop Around" in 1961, a song written and co-produced by Robinson.

In close collaboration with Gordy, Robinson spent the following decade as one of Motown's most integral singers and producers. With the Miracles he recorded such hits as "You Really Got a Hold On Me" in 1963, "Tracks of My Tears" in 1965, "I Second That Emotion" in 1967, and "Tears of a Clown" in 1970. As a writer he provided the label with hits such as "My Guy" for Mary Wells, "I'll Be Doggone" for Marvin Gaye, and "My Girl" for the Temptations.

In 1972, Robinson left the Miracles to launch a solo career. Despite the moderate success of his records during the disco craze of the 1970s, Robinson continued to perform and record. In 1979, Robinson experienced a comeback with the critically acclaimed hit "Cruisin." Three years later, Robinson appeared on the NBC-TV special *Motown 25: Yesterday, Today, and Tomorrow*. Between 1986 and 1991, Robinson released five more albums including *Smoke Signals*, *One Heartbeat*, and *Love, Smokey*. He was inducted into both the Rock and Roll Hall of Fame and the Songwriters Hall of Fame in 1986, and in 1987, he won a Grammy for his vocal performance on "Just to See Her." Robinson continued to make music through the 1990s with such albums as *Double Good Everything* in 1991 and *Intimate* in 1999. In 1995, Robinson was signed by Music by Design, a U.K. company that solicits artists to create original music for television and radio commercials. Robinson continues to tour and play at events such as his current appearance at the Annual Race to Erase MS.

Diana Ross (1944–)
Singer, Actress

One of six children, Diane Ross was born in Detroit, on March 26, 1944. An extremely active child, Ross swam, ran track, and sang in church. In 1959, she joined the Primettes, a group comprised of Mary Wilson, Florence Ballard, and Barbara Martin. After failing to attract the attention of the Lupine label, the group auditioned for Berry Gordy Jr. who signed them to Motown. Upon the suggestion of Berry, the group changed its name to the Supremes. Released in 1961, the group's song "I Want a Guy," featuring Ross on lead vocals, failed to chart. Not long afterward, following Martin's departure, the trio continued to record with Ross on lead vocal.

The Supremes did not find commercial success on the Motown label until 1964, when they were placed under the guidance of the Holland-Dozier-Holland production team. In 1964, H-D-H turned out the Supreme's first smash hit "Where Did Our Love Go?" followed by numerous hits such as "Baby Love" in 1964, "I Hear a Symphony" in 1965, "You Can't Hurry Love" in 1966, and "Reflections" in 1967. With preferential treatment by Gordy, Ross became the dominant figure of the group. By the mid-1960s Ross's emerging talent prompted Gordy to bill the group as Diana Ross and the Supremes.

In 1970, Ross left the Supremes to launch her solo career. Her debut album *Diana Ross* featured the writing and production talents of Ashford & Simpson, an effort that included the hit "Reach Out and Touch (Somebody's Hand)." One year later she made her film debut in the Motown-sponsored movie *Lady Sings the Blues* in which she won an Oscar nomination for her biographical portrayal of jazz singer Billie Holiday. Her role in the 1975 Motown-backed film *Mahogany* brought her not only an Oscar nomination, but the number one selling single "Do You Know Where You're Going To." In 1978, Ross starred in the film version of *The Wiz*, the last full-scale motion picture to be backed by Motown.

After leaving Motown in 1981, Ross signed a $20 million contract with the RCA label. Her debut album *Why Do Fools Fall in Love?* went platinum. This was followed by four more LP's for RCA including *Silk Electric* in 1982, *Swept Away* in 1984, and *Eaten Alive* in 1985. Two years later, Ross left RCA to sign with the London-based EMI label, which produced the albums *Red Hot Rhythm 'n Blues* in 1987, *Working Overtime* in 1987, and *Greatest Hits, Live* in 1990. Meanwhile, Ross had returned to Motown Records as a recording artist and partial owner in 1989, one year after being inducted into the Rock and Roll Hall of Fame.

In the 1990s, the Grammy and Tony Award-winning Ross continued to enjoy popularity around the world; She achieved tremendous success as the owner of her own multimillion dollar corporation Diana Ross Enterprises. Her autobiography *Secrets of a Sparrow: Memoirs* was published in 1993, and a compilation called *Diana Extended/The Remixes* hit the stores in 1994. Ross continues to occasionally act, appearing as a schizophrenic in the television movie *Out of the Darkness* (1994) and alongside the young star Brandy in *Double Platinum* (1999). In 2000, VH1 honored Ross with their show "Divas 2000: A Tribute to Diana Ross." The show included performances by Mariah Carey, Faith Hill, Donna Summer, RuPaul, Destiny's Child, and Ross herself with the Supremes.

Salt-N-Pepa
Rap Group

Salt-N-Pepa includes Salt (Cheryl James), Pepa (Sandy Denton), Spinderella (Deidre "Dee Dee" Roper), and former Spinderella, Latoya Hanson, and was formed in 1985 in Queens, New York. They were the first female rap group to go platinum and are widely recognized as paving the way for the present generation of female rap stars. Originally named Super Nature, they changed their name to Salt-N-Pepa in 1987.

Salt-N-Pepa's debut project, *Hot Cool and Vicious*, went platinum, setting the stage for a decade of mega hits for the group including "Push It" (1987); *A Salt with a Deadly Pepa* (1988), which was nominated for a Grammy; the single "Expressions" (1989); and *Blacks' Magic* (1990). Their single "Let's Talk About Sex" was used a public service video education the youth community about the dangers of AIDS. The 1993 project *Very Necessary* produced the hits "Whatta Man" and "Shoop." The same year James and Denton appeared in the comedy film *Who's the Man?*. They released their fifth album *Brand New* in 1997. Following the release of the album, James and Denton began to focus more on their acting careers.

Tupac Shakur (1971–1996)
Rap Singer

Born Tupac Amaru Shakur in the Bronx in 1971, Shakur was a multitalented rap artist and actor who became a powerhouse in hip hop culture. He made his acting debut in an Apollo Theater production of *A Raisin in the Sun* in 1984 as a benefit for Jesse Jackson's unsuccessful presidential campaign. After his family moved to Baltimore, Shakur attended the High School of the Performing Arts and wrote his first rap song following the violent death of a friend. He dropped out of high school, moved to California, and began circulating tapes of his music until he landed a job as a roadie with the group Digital Underground, eventually working his way to a guest spot as a rapper in their stage show.

In 1991 he signed with Interscope Records and released his debut project *2Pacalypse Now*. A string of commercially successful and critically acclaimed projects followed, including *Strictly 4 My N.I.G.G.A.Z.* (1993), *Me Against the World* (1995), and *All Eyez On Me* (1996). Shakur's rap style was celebrated for its versatile vocal inflection, rhythmically subtle delivery, and the range of lyrical topics, although the latter was also the source of much criticism because of its frequently explicit content. Shakur also received accolades for his acting in the films, among them, *Juice*

Salt 'n' Pepa.

(1992), *Poetic Justice* (1993), *Above the Rim* (1994), and *Gang Related* (1997). Shakur's career was marred by controversies, which included intermittent trouble with the law for which he spent time incarcerated. Like his contemporary, Notorious B.I.G., Shakur died in a Las Vegas drive-by shooting in 1996.

Russell Simmons. *See* **Entrepreneurship chapter.**

Will Smith (1968–)
Rap Artist, Actor

Born on September 25, 1998, in Wynnefield, Pennsylvania, Will Smith became a successful rap musician in the late 1980s, and had a hit television show during the early 1990s. By the turn of the century, he personified the media mega-star, racking up both multi-platinum selling albums and movie box-office hits.

At the age of 18, Smith and Jeff Townes formed the rap duo DJ Jazzy Jeff and the Fresh Prince. They were successful on the local scene, and after landing a record deal with Jive Records, released *Rock the House* in 1987. Their second album, *He's the DJ, I'm the Rapper*, was released a year later. It became one of the biggest selling rap albums up to that point due mainly to the success of the single, "Parents Just Don't Understand." That year, the single also brought the duo a Grammy Award for Best Rap Performance. DJ Jazzy Jeff and the Fresh Prince went on to release three more albums, *And in This Corner. . .* (1989), *Homebase* (1991), and *Code Red* (1993).

Smith's popularity as a rap musician led to a starring role in the NBC sitcom *The Fresh Prince of Bel-Air*. The show proved successful and ran from 1991–1996, earning Smith a Golden Globe nomination for best actor in a television program in 1992. Smith also began to appear in feature films, landing roles in *Where the Day Takes You* (1992), *Six Degrees of Seperation* (1993), *Made in America* (1993), and *Bad Boys* (1995).

The box-office success of *Independence Day* (1996) established Smith as a major film star capable of utilizing both action and comedy in a role. It was followed by *Men In Black* (1997), *Enemy of the State* (1998), and *Wild Wild West* (1999). His abilities as a dramatic actor were showcased in *The Legend of Bagger Vance* (2000)

Tupac Shakur from his role in the movie *Poetic Justice.*

and *Ali* (2001). In addition to critical praise, Smith received an Oscar nomination for his portrayal of the former heavyweight champion. Smith followed the performance with *Men In Black II* (2002).

In addition to his work as an actor, Smith continued to make well-received rap albums. He released *Big Willie Style* in 1997. The album contained the hit singles "Gettin' Jiggy Wit It," "Miami," and "Just the Two of Us." Smith followed with two more solo albums, *Willenium* (1999) and *Born to Reign* (2002).

Donna Summer (1948–)
Singer

One of the biggest stars of the disco era, Donna Summer first gained notice with a pulsatingly, erotic Euro-hit, then moved on to mainstream popularity. She ruled the charts through the late 1970s, though the fading of disco left her with no choice but to streamline her style. Although her popularity declined in the ensuing years, she became one of the few stars of the era to transcend the kitsch that surrounded it.

Born Donna Gaines in Boston, the singer got her first break when she was cast in a traveling production of a rock musical. While in Germany she met Helmut Sommer, whom she married; she later made the acquaintance of Italian producer Giorgio Moroder, who produced her first hit, the throbbingly sexual "Love to Love You Baby." Summers's moans and groans were her initial route to stardom. Through the late 1970s, however, she continually expanded her range. Her hits included a cover version of the pop standard "Macarthur Park," as well as "On the Radio," "Bad Girls," "Hot Stuff," and "Last Dance."

Summer became a born-again Christian in the early 1980s, and gradually turned toward inspirational music. She earned Grammy Awards for best inspirational performance in 1984 and 1985, but she surfaced less and less frequently in the pop world. Summer continues to produce, and in recent years she has put out more albums, including a recording of her VH1 concert called *VH1 Presents: Live & More Encore!* in 1999 and *Greatest Hits 2001* in 2001.

Tina Turner (1939–)
Singer

With a music career spanning more than 30 years, Tina Turner has come to be known as the "hardest working woman in show business." From soul music star to rock goddess, Turner's vocal style and energetic stage act remain a show-stopping phenomenon.

Born Annie Mae Bullock on November 25, 1939, in Brownsville, Tennessee, Turner moved to Knoxville with her parents at age three. Turner first sang in church choirs and at local talent contests. After moving with her mother to St. Louis at age 16, Turner met pianist Ike Turner, leader of the R&B group the Kings of Rhythm. Hired by the band to sing at weekend engagements, Annie Bullock married Ike Turner in 1958 and took the stage name Tina Turner. When the band's scheduled session singer failed to appear at a recording session in 1960, Tina stepped into record the R&B song "Fool in Love" which became a million seller.

With a major hit behind them, the Turners formed the Ike and Tina Turner Revue, complete with the Ikettes. Major international success came for the Turners in 1966 when producer Phil Spector combined his "wall of sound" approach with a R&B sound to record the hit "River Deep, Mountain High." Subjected to years of physical abuse by her husband, Turner divorced Ike in 1976 and set out on a solo career. That same year she co-starred in The Who's rock opera film *Tommy* as the Acid Queen.

In 1984 Turner's career skyrocketed with the commercial success of the album *Private Dancer*, which featured the hit singles "What's Love Got to Do With It" and "Better Be Good." Turner's sensuously vibrant image soon appeared on high budget videos, magazine covers, and in films such as the 1985 release *Mad Max 3: Beyond the Thunderdome* in which she played the tyrannical Aunty Entity. With the immense commercial success of her 1989 album *Foreign Affair*, Turner closed out the decade as one of the most popular singers on the international music scene.

In 1991, Tina and Ike Turner were inducted into the Rock and Roll Hall of Fame. That same year, Turner released the album *Simply The Best* and, in 1993 a movie based on her life and starring Angela Bassett was released. In 1996, Turner returned to recording with *Wildest Dreams*. Due to the album's popularity, Turner returned to touring in 1997. She continued to tour through 2001 and also found time to put out the album *Twenty Four Seven*. Turner announced in 2001 that when her most current world tour, started in 2000, was over, she would also be finished touring for good. She has not announced plans to retire permanently from music.

Luther Vandross (1951–)
Singer, Composer, Producer

One of the premier pop artists of the 1980s, Luther Vandross was responsible for the emergence of a new school of modern soul singers. Born in New York City on April 20, 1951, Vandross was the son of a gospel singer and a big band vocalist. Vandross received his musical education by listening to recordings of Aretha Franklin and the Supremes. In high school Vandross formed numerous singing groups. Throughout the 1970s, he was great as a background singer, performing with such artists as David Bowie, Carly Simon, and Ringo Starr. He also sang advertising jingles such as AT&T's theme "Reach Out and Touch."

Following the release of his first album *Never Too Much* in 1981, Vandross was called upon to sing duets with a number of pop artists including Aretha Franklin and Dionne Warwick. As a successful writer and producer, Vandross released five albums in the 1990s including the 1991 release *Power of Love*, which went multiplatinum, *Never Let Me Go* in 1993, *Your Secret Love* in 1996, and *I Know* in 1998. Vandross has continued to be prolific in recent years, touring and producing albums like *Smooth Love* in 2000 and the self-titled *Luther Vandross* in 2001. In 2001, Vandross won an American Music Award in the "favorite soul/rhythm & blues male artist" category.

Luther Vandross.

Mary Wells (1943–1992)
Singer

Born in 1943 and raised in Detroit, Michigan, Mary Wells started her music career as a featured soloist in her high school choir. At age 17 Wells signed a contract with Motown. With Smokey Robinson as her main producer and writer, Wells scored a number of hits such as "I Don't Want to Take a Chance" in 1961, "You Beat Me to the Punch" in 1962, and "My Guy" in 1964. In the same year, she recorded the album *Together* with Marvin Gaye and toured England with The Beatles.

At the peak of her career, Wells left the Motown label to become an actress. After relocating in Los Angeles, she signed a contract with the Twentieth Century Fox records. Unfortunately, Wells could never find a producer who equaled Robinson's ability to record her material. Her debut single in 1965 "Use Your Head" achieved only modest commercial success. In the 1970s Wells left music to raise her children. For a brief period she was married to Cecil Womack, brother of the rhythm and blues great Bobby Womack.

During the 1980s, Wells returned to music performing on the oldies circuit. In 1985 she appeared in "Motown's 25th Anniversary" television special. Diagnosed as having cancer of the larynx in August 1990, Wells, without medical insurance to pay for treatment, lost her home. Not long afterward, the Rhythm and Blues Foundation raised over $50,000 for Wells's hospital costs. Funds were also sent by artists such as Bruce Springsteen, Rod Stewart, and Diana Ross. Despite chemotherapy treatments, Wells died on July 26, 1992 and was buried at Forest Lawn Memorial Park in Los Angeles.

Jackie Wilson (1934–1984)
Singer

Between 1958 and 1963, Jackie Wilson reigned as one of the most popular rhythm and blues singers in the United States. Dressed in sharkskin suits and sporting a process hairstyle, Wilson exhibited a dynamic stage performance and a singing range which equaled his contemporaries James Brown and Sam Cooke.

Jack Leroy Wilson was born on June 9, 1934, in Detroit, Michigan. Wilson's mother sang spirituals and gospel songs at Mother Bradley's Church. As a youngster, he listened to the recordings of the Mills Brothers, Ink Spots, and Louis Jordan. In high school he became a boxer, and at age 16 he won the American Amateur Golden Gloves Welterweight title. But upon the insistence of his mother, Wilson quit boxing and pursued a career in music. While a teenager, Wilson sang with the Falcons in local clubs, and at talent contests held at the Paradise Theater. He also worked in a spiritual group with later members of Hank Ballard's Midnighters.

In 1953 Wilson replaced Clyde McPhatter as lead singer of the Dominoes. Wilson's only hit with the Dominoes was the reworking of the religious standard "St. Theresa of the Roses." Upon the success of the recording, Wilson signed a contract as a solo artist with the Brunswick label. Wilson's 1957 debut album *Reet Petite* featured the hit title track song which was written by songwriters Berry Gordy Jr. and Billy Taylor. The songwriting team of Gordy and Taylor also provided Wilson with the subsequent hits "To Be Loved" in 1957, "Lonely Teardrops" in 1958, and "That's Why I Love You So" and "I'll Be Satisfied" in 1959.

During the early 1960s, Wilson performed and recorded numerous adaptations of classical music compositions in a crooning ballad style. This material, however, failed to bring out the powerful talent of Wilson's R&B vocal style. Although Wilson's repertoire contained mostly supper club standards, he did manage to produce the powerful pop classics "Dogging Around"

in 1960 and "Baby Workout" in 1963. Teamed with writer/producer Carl Davis, Wilson also recorded the hit "Whispers" and the rhythm and blues masterpiece "Higher and Higher" in 1967.

Following Wilson's last major hit "I Get the Sweetest Feeling" in 1968, he performed on the oldies circuit and on Dick Clark's "Good Ol' Rock 'n' Roll Revue." In 1975 Wilson suffered a serious heart attack on stage at the Latin Casino in Cherry Hill, New Jersey. Forced into retirement, Wilson spent his last eight years in a nursing home until his death on January 21, 1984.

Mary Wilson (1944–)
Singer

As a member of the Motown supergroup the Supremes, Mary Wilson's musical career represents an American success story. Born on March 6, 1944, in Greenville, Mississippi, Wilson moved to Detroit at age 11. Raised in the Brewster-Douglas housing project on the city's east side, Wilson learned to sing by imitating the falsetto voice of Frank Lyman. Along with Barbara Martin and Betty Travis, Wilson formed the Primettes. Upon the departure of Travis, another neighborhood girl named Diana Ross joined the group. Appearing at talent shows and sock hops, the Primettes went on to win first prize at the 1960 Detroit/Windsor Freedom Festival talent contest. Although the Primettes cut two singles on the Lupine label featuring Wilson on lead vocal, they failed to achieve commercial success.

On January 15, 1961, the 16-year-old Wilson and fellow Primette members Diana Ross, Florence Ballard and Barbara Martin signed with the Motown label as the Supremes. Wilson's effort to win the lead vocal spot, however, soon gave way to the dominance of Diana Ross. Released in 1964, the group's first gold single "Where Did Our Love Go?" made Wilson and the Supremes overnight celebrities. Between 1964 and 1968 Wilson sang background vocals on a number of hits including "Baby Love," "You Can't Hurry Love," and "Reflections." Before leaving the group in 1976, Wilson also sang such recordings as "Love Child," "I'm Living in Shame," and "Someday We'll Be Together."

In 1983 Wilson was briefly reunited with the Supremes on the "Motown's 25th Anniversary" television special. In 1994, Wilson was thrust into the media spotlight when a car she was driving overturned and killed her son. The accident ended her long-standing feud with Diana Ross. In 2000, Wilson considered going on tour again with Ross and the Supremes, but negotiations did not work out. Instead, Wilson decided to go back to school, and in 2001 she earned an associates degree in arts from New York University. Making her home in Los Angeles, Wilson occasionally appears on the oldies circuit and at small Supremes revival shows.

Nancy Wilson (1937–)
Singer

Nancy Wilson was born in Chillicothe, Ohio, in 1937. Her musical talents were first noticed when, as a child, she performed for her family at various gatherings. The performances continued as Wilson became a member of her church choir. Influence from artists such as Billy Eckstine and Nat "King" Cole helped Wilson determine that singing would be her career. As a teen, Wilson and her family moved to Columbus, Ohio. Wilson soon became the host of her own radio show, Skyline Melody, during which she performed phoned in requests.

In 1955, Wilson enrolled in classes at Ohio's Central State College to pursue teaching credentials. Her stint in school was short lived, however, as Wilson dropped out to pursue her singing career. She spent the next three years touring the country as a member of Rusty Byrant's Carolyn Club Band. The experience Wilson gained while touring gave her the courage to go solo. New York City became Wilson's new home as her career skyrocketed.

Shortly after her arrival in the Big Apple, Wilson obtained permanent work at a local night club. Word of her masterful performances soon spread all over the city prompting a recording session with Capitol Records. 1960 marked the release of her debut album *Like in Love* and the recording of her first major hit entitled "Save Your Love for Me." *How Glad I Am* won a Grammy in 1964, beginning a 30-year streak of acclaim.

Wilson's blend of rhythm and blues, jazz, and pop styles captivated thousands of fans around the world. Television executives began to take advantage of Wilson's talents, giving her a weekly variety show. The Emmy Award-winning *The Nancy Wilson Show* was merely the beginning of Wilson's television appearances. Guest spots on the *Tonight Show, Merv Griffin Show,* and *Today Show* soon followed.

During the late 1970s and early 1980s, technology began to influence the fashion in which studio recordings were made. Wilson continued to record and tour despite differences with various recording companies over issues of sound. Nonetheless, she was named Global Entertainer of the Year in 1986 by the World Conference of Mayors and the NAACP bestowed upon her its Image Award that year as well.

Just as much heralded in the 1990s, Wilson's 55th full-length recording was completed in 1997. In 2001, she released her first Christmas album, *A Nancy Wilson Christmas*. With a star on the Hollywood Walk of Fame, an Essence Award, a Martin Luther King Center for Social Change Award, and a Trumpet Award to her name, Wilson's bevy of honors is symbol of her timelessness and a testimony to the loyalty of her fans.

Stevie Wonder (1950–)
Singer, Pianist, Composer

Popular music's genius composer and singer Stevie Wonder has remained at the forefront of musical change. His colorful harmonic arrangements have drawn upon jazz, soul, pop, reggae, and rap-derived new jack rhythms. Wonder's gift to pop music is his ability to create serious music dealing with social and political issues while at the same time revealing the soulful and deeply mysterious nature of the human experience.

Steveland Morris Judkins was born on May 13, 1950, in Saginaw, Michigan. Raised in Detroit, Wonder first sang in the church choir. He was most attracted to the sounds of Johnny Ace and B. B. King, which he heard on late night radio programs. By age eight Wonder learned to play piano, harmonica, and bongos. Through

Nancy Wilson.

the connections of Miracles member Ronnie White, Wonder auditioned for Berry Gordy Jr. who, immediately signing the 13-year-old prodigy, gave him the stage name of Little Stevie Wonder. After releasing his first singles "Thank You (For Loving Me All the Way)" and "Contract of Love" in 1963, "Fingertips, Pt. 2" became the first live performance of a song to reach the top of the pop charts. That year Wonder also became the first recording artist to hold number one slots on the *Billboard* Hot 100, R&B Singles, and album charts, simultaneously. In the following year, Wonder hit the charts with "Hey Harmonica Man."

With the success of his recording career, Wonder began touring more frequently. Motown assigned Wonder a tutor from the Michigan School for the Blind, allowing him to continue his education while on the road. In 1964, he performed in London with the Motown Revue, a package featuring Martha and the Vandellas, the Supremes, and the Temptations. Wonder's subsequent recording of the punchy rhythm and blues single "Uptight (Everything's Alright)" became a smash hit in 1966. Wonder's growing commercial success at Motown brought him greater artistic freedom in the studio. In collaboration with Clarence Paul, Wonder produced a long succession of hits including Bob Dylan's "Blowing in the Wind" in 1966, "I Was Made to Love Her" in 1967, and "For Once in My Life" in 1968. In 1969, President Richard Nixon gave Wonder a Distinguished Service Award from the President's Committee on Employment of Handicapped People. That year, *My Cherie Amour* generated a single of the same name.

After recording the 1970 album *Signed, Sealed & Delivered*, featuring the title track, Wonder moved to New York City, where he founded Taurus Production Company and Black Bull Publishing Company, both of which were licensed under Motown. With complete control over his musical career, Wonder began to write lyrics addressing social and political issues. Through the technique of overdubbing, he played most of the instruments on his recordings including the guitar, bass, horns, percussion, and brilliant chromatic harmonica solos. *Music From My Mind*, *Talking Book*, and *Inversions* all feature Wonder's distinctive synthesizer accompaniment.

Released in 1979, Wonder's *Journey Through the Secret Life of Plants* was an exploratory musical soundtrack for a film documentary. In 1984, Wonder's soundtrack for the film *Woman in Red* won him an Academy Award for best song with "I Just Called To Say I Love You." One year later, Wonder participated in the recording of "We Are the World" for U.S.A for Africa, a famine relief project. He also teamed up with Paul McCartney for the hit single, "Ebony and Ivory." Wonder's 1985 album *Square Circle* produced the hit

singles "Part Time Lover" and "Overjoyed" and won a Grammy. After the 15-time Grammy Award winner was inducted into the Rock and Roll Hall of Fame in 1989, he composed material for the soundtrack to Spike Lee's film *Jungle Fever*. Eight years in the making, 1995's *Conversation Piece* hit fans the same year as did the double-live recording *Natural Wonder*. He also contributed to the tribute recording *Inner City Blues: The Music of Marvin Gaye* and to Quincy Jones's *Q's Jook Joint*. He won an *Essence* Award that year. Wonder has also founded the SAP/Stevie Wonder Vision Awards, which are given to research and products that enable visually-impaired people to enter the workforce. In 2000, President Bill Clinton paid tribute to Wonder at the Kennedy Center Honors program in Washington, D.C. In 2002, Wonder received a lifetime achievement award from the Songwriters Hall of Fame in New York.

◆ AWARD WINNERS

Grammy Awards

Record of the Year
1963: *I Can't Stop Loving You*, Count Basie
1967: *Up, Up and Away*, 5th Dimension
1969: *Aquarius/Let the Sun Shine In*, 5th Dimension
1972: *The First Time Ever I Saw Your Face*,
    Roberta Flack
1973: *Killing Me Softly with His Song*,
    Roberta Flack
1976: *This Masquerade*, George Benson
1983: *Beat It*, Michael Jackson
1984: *What's Love Got To Do with It*, Tina Turner
1985: *We Are the World*, USA For Africa; produced
    by Quincy Jones
1988: *Don't Worry, Be Happy*, Bobby McFerrin
1991: *Unforgettable*, Natalie Cole with Nat
    "King" Cole
1993: *I Will Always Love You*, Whitney Houston

Album of the Year
1973: *Innervisions*, Stevie Wonder; produced by
    Stevie Wonder
1974: *Fulfillingness' First Finale*, Stevie Wonder;
    produced by Stevie Wonder
1976: *Songs in the Key of Life*, Stevie Wonder;
    produced by Stevie Wonder
1983: *Thriller*, Michael Jackson; produced by
    Quincy Jones
1984: *Can't Slow Down*, Lionel Richie; produced by
    Lionel Richie and James Anthony Carmichael
1990: *Back on the Block*, Quincy Jones; produced by
    Quincy Jones
1991: *Unforgettable*, Natalie Cole

1999: *The Miseducation of Lauryn Hill*, Lauryn Hill; produced by Lauryn Hill

Pulitzer Prize

Music: Special Awards and Citations
1976: Scott Joplin
1996: George Walker
1997: Wynton Marsalis
1999: Edward Kennedy "Duke" Ellington (posthmously)

Rock and Roll Hall of Fame
1986: Chuck Berry; James Brown; Ray Charles; Sam Cooke; Fats Domino; Little Richard; Robert Johnson; Jimmy Yancey
1987: The Coasters; Bo Diddley; Aretha Franklin; Marvin Gaye; Louis Jordan; B.B. King; Clyde McPhalter; Smokey Robinson; Big Joe Turner; T-Bone Walker; Muddy Waters; Jackie Wilson
1988: The Drifters; Barry Gordy Jr.; The Supremes
1989: The Ink Spots; Otis Redding; Bessie Smith; The Soul Stirrers; The Temptations; Stevie Wonder
1990: Louis Armstrong; Hank Ballard; Charlie Christian; The Four Tops; Holland, Dozier, and Holland; The Platters; Ma Rainey
1991: La Vern Baker; John Lee Hooker; Howlin' Wolf; The Impressions; Wilson Pickett; Jimmy Reed; Ike and Tina Turner
1992: Bobby "Blue" Bland, Booker T. and the M.G.'s; Jimi Hendrix; Isley Brothers; Elmore James; Doc Pomus; Professor Longhair; Sam and Dave
1993: Ruth Brown; Etta James; Frankie Lymon and the Teenagers; Sly and the Family Stone; Dinah Washington
1994: Willie Dixon; Bob Marley; Johnny Otis
1995: Al Green; Martha and the Vandellas; The Orioles
1996: Little Willie John; Gladys Knight and the Pips; The Shirelles
1997: Mahalia Jackson; The Jackson Five; Parliament
1998: Jelly Roll Morton; Lloyd Price
1999: Charles Brown; Curtis Mayfield; The Staple Singers
2000: Nat "King" Cole; King Curtis; Earth, Wind & Fire; Billie Holiday; James Jamerson; The Moonglows; Earl Palmer
2001: Solomon Burke; The Flamingos; Michael Jackson; Johnnie Johnson
2002: Isaac Hayes

26

Visual and Applied Arts

◆ The African Roots of African American Art ◆ The Formation of an Arts Tradition
◆ The African Legacy Endures Colonial America ◆ Rise of the Professional Artists
◆ African American Arts in the Twentieth Century ◆ Arts-Related Support Professions
◆ Exhibiting African American Art ◆ Architecture and Design Professionals
◆ American Academy and Institute of Arts and Letters Award Winners
◆ Visual and Applied Artists ◆ Museums Exhibiting African American Art
◆ Institutions Specializing in Exhibiting African American Art

by Phyllis J. Jackson

Africans and their descendants have been making objects and creating works of art since the first indentured Africans arrived on the North American continent in 1619. Black artists in the United States have created an extraordinary and distinctive visual tradition despite the social, political, and cultural odds confronting them. Some are such well-known historical figures as Henry Ossawa Tanner, Jacob Lawrence, Elizabeth Catlett, Romare Bearden, and Faith Ringgold, and Martin Puryear. Others including Scipio Moorehead, Mary Edmonia Lewis, James Presley Ball, Robert Duncanson, and Meta Warrick Fuller are only familiar to art specialists. Still, thousands of other artists and their works have gone unrecorded or unheralded despite contributing to America's rich visual legacy. Whether formally trained or self-taught, crafting objects for their personal use, fulfilling public or private commissions, African American artists and artisans have worked in a vast array of media and styles to express themselves aesthetically.

Art produced by African American artists over the centuries includes innumerable drawings, designs, paintings, sculptures, carvings, ceramics, architecture, photographs, prints, cartoons, computer graphics, web pages, furniture, clothing, jewelry, utensils, site-specific installations, performance pieces, and independent cinema. In all its variants, African American art appeals to aesthetic sensibilities, inspires confidence, raises awareness, and challenges long-standing assumptions and representational conventions of mainstream culture. Thus, African American art stands as one of the most important bodies of creative works shaping aesthetic, intellectual, and visual culture throughout the world.

◆ THE AFRICAN ROOTS OF AFRICAN AMERICAN ART

Of the millions of Africans who were brought to the Americas, the majority came from West and Central Africa. Transported by British, French, Dutch, Spanish, and Portuguese slave traders, Africans in the Americas originated from cultures as disparate as the Akan, Bambara, Edo, Fante, Igbo, Kongo, Mandinka, Mende, Wolof, and Yoruba. Despite this ethnic variety, Westerners use the generic and deprecating term "tribe" to describe all African social systems. Generally, this is a misleading term/concept because it obscures the large population numbers, structural complexity, diversity, and long histories of African societies. The term also distorts and diminishes the historical significance of the artistic, aesthetics, and patronage traditions that arose within each society. Rather, these ethnic groups, cultures, kingdoms, and nation-states had varying levels of social, political, and economic accomplishment.

Within each of these ethnic groups, there was a common language, cosmology, spiritual practices, and political-economic history that shaped the related art-making practices. Consequently, a diverse artistic legacy emerged across the African continent, with each society developing its own unique arts traditions (i.e., subjects, forms, styles, iconography, materials and usage). For example, the stylized abstract copper reliquary figures from Gabon differ sharply from the naturalistic Ile Ife terracotta and bronze sculptures.

Africans brought an appreciation for their culture's language, cosmology, spiritual beliefs, ceremonies, rituals, ancestry, and political history. In addition, they brought knowledge of the aesthetic values, artistic practices, and visual customs of their individual cultures. Many carried skills and talents from working as artists and artisans in one of the many gender-segregated workshops and guilds. African art guilds produced objects as varied as sculpture, jewelry, textiles, and pottery, all made from materials as diverse as gold, bronze, wood, ivory, cotton, silk, fur, raffia, clay, beads, and shells. For example, the Edo artists that cast the world-renowned "Benin bronzes" for the Edo royal

A mask made by the Yaure people of the Ivory Coast.

courts of the fourteenth to eighteenth centuries worked within a very different artistic and political tradition than the ivory carvers of saltcellars that were imported from the Congo during the Europe Renaissance. Some art forms, styles, and techniques have survived, others retained in modified versions and adapted to American cultural milieu.

◆ THE FORMATION OF AN ARTS TRADITION

Synthesis and resistance are the cultural and creative hallmarks of African American art. Culturally, African American art is a hybrid tradition of the aesthetic values and artistic practices of Africa, the African Diaspora, Western Europe, and Euro-America. Each of these cultural groups within their historical era has its own set of prevailing social values, economic conditions, and political relations, as well as individual and collective artistic interests. These factors combine to affect the changing proportion of African or European influence on black artists' work. The most formative influence arises from the fusion of so many African ethnic heritages into the revitalized amalgam now known as African American culture.

African and African Diasporic visual arts traditions are dramatically different from Western traditions in both form (medium/material, style/technique) and content (subject/themes, motifs/meaning). The ultimate tension is that Western traditions are based on principles that radically conflict in their regard for African life, art, and culture. African visual tradition assumes the humanity, beauty, intelligence, and worth of African and African-descended people. Conversely, white-European tradition has exploited and manipulated the authority of Western philosophy, aesthetics, social theory, and science to associate full human potential with only people of European descent, especially heterosexual male.

Necessarily, black art is a resilient representational practice that resists cultural oppression. From the colonial period of enslavement to the present day, black artists have had to work within and against a mainstream visual culture that customarily demonizes blackness and devalues all things African. As a result, black artists' work, self-consciously and by its mere existence, undermines European racial mythologies along with the social, political, and economic hierarchies that those European-derived myths justify. Black art, therefore, is an artistic and aesthetic heritage that works to value blackness and black people, particularly as worthy subject matter, while simultaneously redeeming the diverse cultural heritages of Africa.

◆ THE AFRICAN LEGACY ENDURES COLONIAL AMERICA

Africans in colonial America created art and artifacts that revealed their indebtedness to Africa's myriad cultural traditions. The majority of black artists during the seventeenth and eighteenth centuries were enslaved. Works created under this adverse condition fall into two broad categories. First, Africans with technical skills were required to direct most of their time and creative talents to making items for the use and benefit of slaveholders. For example, enslaved Africans built many of the plantation manors along and crafted the interior woodwork and furniture. Their metal crafting skills helped produce beautiful decorative arts as well as the shackles used for bondage. Second, since slaveholders forced Africans to work from sunup to sundown, they only occasionally found time or resources to apply their creative energies to benefit themselves, families, or friends. A standing, wrought iron figure and a decorated wooden drum made in the style of the Akan are the earliest known pieces of art made for themselves, uncovered through archaeological excavations of Virginia plantations.

Generally, early black artists did not have the liberty to make such art as painting and sculpture, nor did they have resources to work in such precious materials as canvas oil, marble, or gold. Rather, they adapted skills and techniques once employed to make objects for daily use, sacred ceremonies, or African royal courts. Artistic and aesthetic Africanisms can be found embedded in the details of architectural ornaments, building designs, handcrafted furniture, quilts, clothing, and tools. African carpenters designed and built their one-room quarters using styles and techniques originating in Africa. These techniques and motifs testify to the cultural and historic difficulties that surface when trying to draw concrete boundaries between what are black arts and what are Euro-American arts.

Early Black Artists Secure Compensation for Their Efforts

Black women and men were often sold and purchased based on their skills. They were often hired out by slaveholders and permitted to keep a small portion of the earned income. In this way, some slaves were able to save enough money to buy their own and family members' freedom. They often worked as anonymous apprentices and journeyman in occupations as varied as pottery, silversmithing, cabinet making, and tailoring.

The proportion of emancipated or even free-born black people and artists was higher in the North than the South. Yet, northeners also lived and labored within all the legal and cultural oppression of white supremacist culture. To secure monetary or material compensation for their work, free black artisans made objects that appealed to the aesthetic sensibilities of the patron class—primarily whites with discretionary funds. Some of what has been preserved and celebrated as Euro-American art and architecture, in many instances, may have been produced by enslaved or free black people.

Prominent Black Artists in Early America

There are, however, art and artisans whose names and works are part of the historical record. Scipio Moorehead is the first black artist with an attributed work. Moorehead was an enslaved African who learned drawing and painting from his slaveholder's wife. He created a 1773 ink drawing *Portrait of Phillis Wheatley*—an engraving of Moorehead's portrait served as the frontispiece of Wheatley's celebrated publication *Poems on Various Subjects, Religious and Moral*. The young poet paid homage to Moorehead's painting skills in a poem titled "To S. M., A Young African Painter, On Seeing His Work." Since none of Moorehead's paintings are extant, Wheatley's description serves as an invaluable description of them.

Dave Drake (c.1780s–1864) was one of the most prolific potters in the Edgefield District of South Carolina. Drake's slaveholder taught him the craft, but Drake quickly developed his own distinctive style for making large, glazed stoneware jars. It is unclear how Drake learned to read and write, but he did so even though it violated South Carolina law. He left his own enduring legacy because he signed his name on dozens of pots. He also enhanced his renowned work by inscribing the exterior of more than 20 with such short, prophetic verse as:

this noble jar will hold 20
fill it with silver then you'll have plenty
(March 31, 1858)

Much later, Harriet Powers (1837–1911), a former slave made two appliquéd quilts in 1886 and 1898. They are sometimes referred to as Bible quilts because most of the individual panels represent Old and New Testament scenes that reveal her creative retention of African design qualities. Powers's quilts are representative of the innovative character of black quilters, both female and male. These self-taught or informally trained artisans produced an important segment of nineteenth-century black arts and crafts.

◆ RISE OF THE PROFESSIONAL ARTISTS

In the late eighteenth and nineteenth centuries, many black people wanted to express themselves creatively in the "fine arts" of painting and sculpture. Among these early black artists, some were born free and others emancipated, but all accepted work when and where they could find it. Generally, these artists worked independently and without the support of artist collectives or the encouragement of black arts movements. More often than not, only Euro-Americans possessed the financial resources to purchase or commission hand-painted portraits, still life studies, history pictures, landscapes, mythological or genre scenes, monumental public sculpture, private garden sculpture, elaborate cemetery markers, or delicate decorative arts. As a result, for black artists working in the fine arts, financial success and artistic accomplishment depended upon a repression of African-derived forms or aesthetics and the avoidance of subject matter that celebrated or respected the humanity of African people and their descendants.

Historical records indicate that Joshua Johnston (1765–1830) was the earliest artist of African descent to work as a professional portrait painter. After being freed in 1796, Johnston worked as a "limner" or self-taught artist. He advertised his services in the newspapers and painted quaint, modest portraits of prosperous merchants and their families in the Baltimore, Maryland area. There are now 80 paintings signed by or attributed to Johnston. This relatively large body of work suggests that Johnston's seemingly naive style met with the conservative and puritanical aesthetic tastes of affluent whites in the early American republic. Only two of Johnston's portraits are of men of African descent and both wear clerics collars. Art, thereby, links Johnston to a class of free-black, anti-slavery activists in his home city. Historians suggest that one painting *Portrait of a Cleric* is of Daniel Coker, a black abolitionist and forefather of the African Methodist Episcopal (A.M.E.) Church. As a founding father of black art, Johnston created works that met the needs of patrons in conflicting classes—a paradoxical legacy that continues today.

Professional African American Artists Depict Their Culture

In terms of subject and style, it is often difficult to distinguish the work of nineteenth-century black painters, sculptors, or photographers from that of their white counterparts. Robert Duncanson's Ohio River style landscape paintings, capturing the grandeur of the American wilderness, provide no indication that the artist is of African ancestry. Similarly, Jules Lion (1810–1866) was a pioneering artist, and one of 50 documented black daguerreotypists who operated successful portrait studios or traveling business in the decades immediately following the invention of daguerreotypes in 1839. Most of their clientele were Euro-Americans looking to permanently capture their image with the new medium. The most notable and important distinction in the art of black and white artists occurs in the small percentage of professional African American artists' work that portrays black people.

Black artists infused their representations of black historical figures as well as fictional ones with a dignity and strength of character foreign to white artists' works. James Presley Ball (1825–1904/05?) and Augustus Washington (1820–75) were ardent abolitionists and used their work to deplore the horrors of slavery. Ball also turned the camera on his own family, capturing polished images of free black people with access to the middle-class comforts before and after the Civil War. Although the family photos are a small percentage of Ball's pictures, they stand in sharp contrast to the tattered and unkempt look customarily used to represent black people by white artists. Patrick H. Reason's engraving of Henry Bibb's portrait is another exquisite example. It is a dignified portrayal of the anti-slavery lecturer and celebrated slave narrative author. Book in hand, Henry Bibb stares boldly out at the viewer. The pose refers to his command of the art of writing and his courage to resist oppression. It is an image that undermines the pro-slavery myths that black people were docile creatures who happily accepted positions of servitude and lacked the capacity to reason.

Edward Mitchell Bannister's *Newspaper Boy* (1869) is an engaging portrait of an industrious black lad. This seemingly uncomplicated portrait is exceptional because white artists either represented black youth as ingratiating servants, or they depicted them as lazy, mischievous, and troublesome thieves. In this and other works, black artists rejected the demeaning facial caricatures and stereotypical scenes favored by Euro-American artists and collectors.

In the aftermath of the Civil War and Reconstruction, white Americans developed so many representations of grinning, deferential black male banjo players that the pictorial theme became a defaming and humiliating staple in the visual vocabulary of American culture. In 1893, however, Henry O. Tanner took up the banjo subject in *Banjo Lesson*, one of his three "genre" paintings portraying African Americans. Tanner's painting of an aged man passing on a cherished skill to a young boy turned a convention of gross caricature into a sensitive representation that respects rather than ridicules black musical talent and familial relations.

Edward Mitchell Bannister's *Newspaper Boy,* 1869.

Under risky circumstances, nineteenth century artists therefore used the visual arts as an arena to exercise their creativity while simultaneously struggling to undermine and rebuke hostile cultural imagery that perpetuated African American oppression.

African American Artists Study in Europe

The most ambitious African American artists throughout the nineteenth century and the first half of the twentieth century sought critical acclaim, patronage, and financial success working as formally trained fine artists. To work in the academic or avant-garde styles of their day, African American artists who had the necessary financial resources or social connections traveled to France, England, German and Italy to train in the academies and studios of prominent painters and sculptors. In many cases, black artists such as the neoclassical sculptor Mary Edmonia Lewis (c.1850–1911) and Henry Ossawa Tanner (1859–1937) preferred to live and work in Europe. Black expatriates found more opportunities and greater acceptance living with racial prejudice in Europe than in segregated America.

◆ AFRICAN AMERICAN ARTS IN THE TWENTIETH CENTURY

During the twentieth century, more and more creative African Americans swelled the ranks of formally trained and professional artists. They built upon the scattered personal efforts of their predecessors, fashioning a modern art tradition as individuals, art collectives, and participants of broad cultural movements. Various intellectual trends, political ideologies, and aesthetic values emerged during the century to demonstrate the look and significance of African American art. Influences as varied as pan-Africanism, modernism, Black power, feminism, Afrocentrism, and postmodernism presented the work of artists as dissimilar as Augusta Savage, Palmer Hayden, Elizabeth Catlett, Norman Lewis, Faith Ringgold, Charles Searles, John Biggers, Renee Stout, Lorna Simpson, and David Hammons.

Twentieth century creative visionaries expanded the form of African American art by working in styles, techniques, and materials considered experimental, innovative, and avant-garde, as well as those deemed conservative and derivative. By broadening the parameters for acceptable subject matter to include representations of black people and black life, these artists dramatically transformed the power of American visual culture. In addition, African American artists and their supporters have engaged in century-long dialogues regarding the role of black artists, the purpose of their work, black artists' relationship to black communities, and their responsibility to try and improve the conditions under which black people live.

The "New Negro" Era

African American artists, who came of age at the turn of the twentieth century, emerged during an era that supported artistic sensibilities and creative concerns focusing on the cultivation and uplift of the "New Negro." As a concept or term, the "New Negro" came to designate an ideology of resistance and a form of progressive social activism that stood against all forms of oppression. This new attitude prompted hundreds of thousands of African Americans to migrate from the rural agrarian South to the urban industrial North to escape dire economic circumstances, the horrors of Jim Crow segregation, white supremacist nightriders, and lynch mob culture. The Great Migrations promoted a surge in political organizing, social mobilization, and cultural renewal usually referred to as the "New Negro" movement, the Negro Renaissance, the Harlem Renaissance.

"New Negro" intellectuals and political leaders embraced a form of race consciousness that allowed them to value black culture and arts, actually celebrating them as integral to America's contemporary richness and future greatness. Their activism gave birth to a generation of modern African American artists with twentieth century, rather than nineteenth-century, artistic concerns. These artists worked in diverse media and styles, yet their aesthetic convictions rested on the assumption that black people and culture were worthy and significant subjects for modern art.

W. E. B. Du Bois routinely urged such African American artists as Henry O. Tanner and Meta Warrick (1877–1968) to develop visual imagery that would rehabilitate the image of black people in the public imagination. He urged artists to produce paintings and sculptures that challenged the European and Euro-American tradition of representing black people in a litany of fine arts servants and advertising stereotypes. Some accepted the call to create art in service of social uplift, while others only wanted to make art as an individual form of expression. Whatever their creative inspiration, "New Negro" era artists' works are revered icons that serve as the collective cornerstone of the twentieth-century African American art and aesthetics.

Meta Warrick Fuller's 1914 bronze sculpture *Ethiopia Awakening* is a landmark artistic statement. It is the earliest example of African American art to overtly validate African arts and cultures. The near life-size personification of Africa wears the headdress of an ancient Egyptian queen. She appears to be emerging from her mummy-like wrapping, though the lower portion of her body remains bound. *Ethiopia Awakening* directly challenged a favored Western visual theme called The Four Continents (Europe, Asia, America and Africa). By convention many white artists portrayed the African continent as asleep, contributing nothing to the development of human civilization with the exception of slave labor. Throughout the twentieth century, however, many artists have become more knowledgeable about Africa and its cultures, allowing them to completely abandon Western-derived assertions that the continent of Africa laid dormant.

James VanDerZee's (1886–1983) photographs captured the vitality of Harlem in its heyday as the "mecca" of African American life and culture. For example, his individual and group portraits of Marcus Garvey and Universal Negro Improvement Association-sponsored parades are meaningful historical documents and creative aesthetic statements. He also permanently fixed the image of thousands of Harlemites whose names have been lost, although their upwardly mobile images continue to testify to the cultural energy of urban life. In addition, such painters as Edward Harleston, Malvin

"Wedding Day," a photograph by James Van Der Zee in Harlem, 1926.

Gray Johnson, William Edouard Scott, and Laura Wheeler Warring captured the vibrancy of black culture in their portraits and pictorial scenes.

The Harlem Renaissance and the Works Progress Administration

The "New Negro" era sparked an intense flowering of artistic creativity among African American writers, musicians, singers, theater performers, and fine artists. When World War I ended in 1918, Harlem, an uptown section of Manhattan, was home to the largest black population in urban America and the cultural heart of this artistic activity. Frequently referred to as the Harlem Renaissance, it was a national and international movement in black arts and culture encompassing other urban centers such as Chicago, Cleveland, and Washington, D.C., as well as in the Caribbean and Europe.

Alain Locke (1885–1954), a Howard University philosophy professor and Rhodes scholar, was a prominent architect of the Harlem-based arts revival. He believed that if black artists demonstrated their creative and intellectual mastery of literature and the fine arts to the American public, they would garner respect for the black race and thereby change white attitudes and improve race relations. To stimulate critical and financial support for black artists, Locke served as guest editor for "Harlem: Mecca of the New Negro," a special issue of the journal *Survey Graphic* (1925). Contributing essayists theorized and celebrated the aesthetics of African art and the achievements of African American arts and culture.

Locke's essay "The Legacy of the Ancestral Arts" urged black artists to draw upon the artistic and cultural legacies of Africa in the creation of their art. Locke maintained that if the stylized abstraction of West African sculpture could inspire avant-garde artists (e.g. Pablo Picasso, George Braque, or Emile Nolde) to create important modern styles such as cubism or German expressionism, it certainly should lead "New Negro" artists to develop a unique visual vocabulary. Locke's and his contributors' ideas were culturally progressive at the time. Yet, they rested on two concepts refuted today: the existence of biologically determined racial essences and a form of romantic primitivism. The later not only cast Africa and Africans as primitive, but as the polar opposite of civilized Europe and Europeans.

Nonetheless, artists as diverse as Aaron Douglas, Palmer Hayden, Sargent Claude Johnson, Archibald Motley Jr., James Lesesne Wells, and Augusta Savage, temporarily or permanently abandoned the conventions of their European style training to experiment with African-inspired styles or subjects. Aaron Douglas is the artist most frequently highlighted as the quintessential Harlem Renaissance artist. A trained portrait painter, Douglas abandoned the realist style, developing instead a stylized Egyptian form of figurative painting that graces numerous Harlem Renaissance publications, including illustrations and designs in Alain Locke's book *The New Negro* and James Weldon Johnson's *God's Trombones: Seven Negro Sermons in Verse* (1927).

The movement generated an unprecedented level of patronage from private individuals and organizations. For example, the National Association for the Advancement of Colored People (NAACP) and the National Urban League instituted important art awards. Their respective publications *Crisis* and *Opportunity* became venues for artists and for critical reviews of "New Negro" art exhibitions. The principal sponsorship of Harlem Renaissance art came from the Harmon Foundation, established by the real estate investor William E. Harmon. The foundation awarded prizes and sponsored juried exhibitions and shows that traveled around the United States. The foundation exercised creative control over the type of art produced or promoted. As a result, the foundation, shows, awards, and even the artists have been subject to social and critical controversy.

Occurring during the high point of the Harlem Renaissance, the stock market crash of 1929 cast the United States into the Great Depression. The Federal Arts Project (1935–1943) was one of the "New Deal" relief programs sponsored by Franklin D. Roosevelt's Works Progress Administration (WPA). The Federal Arts Project (FAP) paid artists to produce works celebrating America and American art styles for the public. The FAP promoted an environment where figuration and social realism were valued over abstraction and allegory. In many ways, FAP funding contributed to black artists' turning away from the stylistic Africanisms encouraged by Locke and the Harmon Foundation, focusing instead on African American folk culture.

A Federal Arts Project assignment employed a young Jacob Lawrence and provided him early support in his career. He subsequently became one of America's most celebrated black artists. Lawrence titled a series of 60 paintings *The Migration of the Negro* (1940–1941). The series secured him critical acclaim, a feature in *Fortune* magazine, a one-man show at the prestigious Downtown Gallery, and the purchase of several of his panels by the Museum of Modern Art. In Chicago, the Southside Community Art Center (SCAC) provided early careers opportunities for such artists as Archibald Motley Jr., Charles Sebree, and Gordon Roger Parks. In addition, Hughie Lee-Smith and Charles Sallee found teaching opportunities and support at Karamu House Artist Association in Cleveland (established 1935). The Karamu House and SCAC are still in operation today.

Clearly, the Federal Arts Project and the Works Progress Administration were important for the development of African American art. Yet, black artists complained that the program administrators routinely discriminated against them. The Harlem Artists Guild (1935–1941), a collective founded by Augusta Savage, Elba Lightfoot, Charles Alston, and Arthur Schomburg, made the redressing of the problems an important organizational goal.

African American Artists Explore Modernistic Art Forms

By the late 1930s and early 1940s, such artists as William H. Johnson, Charles Alston, Hale A. Woodruff, and Norman Lewis were less inspired by social realism and more interested in the formalist concerns of European modernism, especially expressionism and abstraction. Eldzier Cortor and Hughie Lee Smith, for instance, explored the visual power of surrealism in paintings. They preferred the challenge of working in styles that most Americans considered foreign and experimented with such a range of approaches that in some abstract paintings the subject is recognizable while in other paintings the subjects are completely non-presentational. Romare Bearden (1911–1988) was an African American artist that began working with representational abstraction. During the 1940s, however, he moved on to become an early practitioner of abstract expressionism, a modern art movement that catapulted New York onto the world art scene, effectively displacing Paris as the leading center of the art world.

The modernist disdain for realism took hold among American avant-garde artists, critics, and patrons. Thus, an arts environment was cultivated in which Euro-American collectors could "discover" and champion the art of such self-trained African American artists as the painter Horace Pippen and the sculptor William Edmondson, because they did not employ the conventions of representation realism. Collectors believed these self-taught artisans found modernist expression without the struggle of rejecting formal training or attempting to surpass tradition. White collectors and curators commonly referred to these self-taught artists as "folk artists," "native artists," and "Negro-primitives," frequently preferring and promoting them over professionally trained African American artists. Despite the criticism that this was a racist and patronizing practice, twentieth-century self-taught artists have continued to be important contributors to African American art.

From "Black Art" to "Afrocentrism"

The Black Art movement, also referred to as the Black Aesthetic movement, developed during the tumultuous 1960s in defiant opposition to Western or Eurocentric aesthetic values that continued to regulate the appreciation and production of art and culture in the United States. Proponents of the Black Art movement challenged members of the black creative community to redefine the roles of the artist and art in light of an increasingly radicalized black political agenda. Black aestheticism championed the belief that the first step towards black liberation required black people to construct a new world view. It insisted that black people needed to develop a black consciousness or perspective that is Africa-centered rather than Europe-centered as a form of intellectual growth and personal empowerment.

The Black Art debates were heated and polemic. Definitions and interpretations of black aestheticism were conflicting. Addison Gayle's anthology *The Black Aesthetics* (1971) captured the theoretic diversity among literary and visual artists. Yet, proponents universally embraced some qualities. First and foremost, they rejected the notion that art and politics were separate domains of human activity. The late critic and poet Larry Neal, one of the movement's most influential theorists, proclaimed, "the artist and the political activist are one." He maintained that the difference between the Black Arts and Black Power concepts is that "one is concerned with the relationship between art and politics; the other with the art of politics."

Under this theoretic formation, art was not a luxury, but a basic and necessary weapon in black people's struggle against the social and political order of the United States. In theory and practice, those embracing black aestheticism rejected the idea that art was destined for the pedestals and walls of private galleries, public museums, and homes of the affluent. They attacked the modernist doctrine of "art for art's sake" as false and misleading, asserting that art must support and promote a black revolution. Black visual artists across the United States heeded the call, creating a body of paintings, sculptures, prints, assemblages, and public murals that sought to inform and inspire black people to aggressively resist oppression. One stream of black aesthetic artists created works that were inspired by the revolutionary idealism of African liberation struggles against European colonialism. Another stream of Black Arts visionaries de-emphasized the political and focused on celebrating the glory of ancient and contemporary African cultures.

An example of the evolution of community art and its accessibility was represented by the emergence of a group called COBRA: the Coalition of Black Revolutionary Artist. Members of the group collaborated on a community mural project in Chicago, Illinois, creating the Wall of Respect (1967), painting portraits of historical black figures including Frederick Douglas, Marcus Garvey, and Malcolm X. Their celebration of ethnic heritage and identity became beacons for black consciousness murals in Detroit and Boston. COBRA later became known as the AFRI-COBRA: the African Commune of Bad Relevant Artists.

Prior to this period, affluent Euro-Americans were the main collectors, patrons, and consumers of black artists' work. Therefore, black artists' solicitation of a black audience marks a critical turning point in the development of the African American artistic tradition. These artists did not define their work as protest art, because by black aesthetic definitions, protest art plays to the moral conscience of a liberal white audience. Theoretically, the Black Art movement spoke to those who lived the black social and cultural experience.

In 1967 the Faith Ringgold painting titled *US Postage Stamp to Commemorate the Advent of Black Power* indicated her general support for the more militant tendencies of the organized struggle for black human rights over those of the Civil Rights movement. Elizabeth Catlett aligned herself with specific political activists and a particular political organization in her 1969 prints entitled *Malcolm Speaks for Us* and *Homage to the Panthers*. Dana Chandler's paintings *(4)00 More Years* and *Molotov Cocktail* are representative of a group of works that launch a pictorial assault against American cultural symbols such as the United States flag. Other works such as Betye Saar's *The Liberation of the Aunt Jemima* (1972) attack the negative pictorial stereotypes that plague black men, women, and children. Saar revises the "mammy" image with a pistol, rifle, and broom. However, not in her old role as caretaker to the world, but in a new position as an urban warrior. Such artists as Saar, Murry DePillars, Jeff Donaldson, and Joe Overstreet created pieces that

Faith Ringgold.

rob established visual clichés as Aunt Jemima of their widespread cultural currency.

The other stream of artists focused on cultural reclamation rather than political agitation. As more and more African countries gained their independence, beginning with Ghana in 1957, black artists began traveling to the African continent. They produced art honoring legendary African kings and queens, colorful scenes of African villages, and busy marketplaces. They learned about African art and culture from firsthand experience rather than books written by Europeans or Euro-Americans. They produced works such as Thomas Feeling's *Senegalese Woman* and John Bigger's *Ghanian Harvest Festival*, which capture the strength and beauty of African women while emphasizing the vibrancy of their traditional dress. In contrast to this document quality, such artists as Charles Searles and Faith Ringgold created colorful, African-inspired paintings and sculptures, borrowing African formal elements and materials and reworking them into generic stylized visions.

Since the so-called streams were never hard and fast, numerous artists worked in both, self-consciously attempting to balance the formal and the political. The Civil Rights and Black Power movements generated tremendous debates and activity among creative artists, and some critics dismissed the art as angry, romantic, or mere propaganda. As organized activism waned in the mid- to late-1970s, the Black Art movement lost much of it collective momentum. Many artists who emerged during the era are still creating, exhibiting, or teaching art today. Their artistic theories, artistic strategies, and aesthetic concerns helped lay the foundation for African American contemporary arts.

Contemporary Arts

During 1980s and 1990s, there was a virtual explosion in the number of self-taught and formally trained African Americans who created, exhibited, and marketed their art. Contemporary artists have opportunities to work with a diverse array of materials, media, new technologies, and critical concepts. They are able to employ styles, techniques, and approaches unimagined by their creative predecessors.

During this time period, individual African American artists received critical recognition, increased gallery representation, greater inclusion in group and solo museum shows, and became the subject of academic scholarship. The visually engaging art by artists such as Emma Amos, Jean-Michel Basquiat, Robert Colescott, Houston Conwill, Lyle Ashton Harris, Glenn Ligon, Renee Green, Lorraine O'Grady, Howardena Pindell, Alison Saar, and Fred Wilson have been the focus of breathtaking exhibits. African American visual artists have been the recipients of prestigious prizes and awards. In 1987, Romare Bearden was awarded the Presidential Medal of Honor. In recent years, MacArthur Fellowships (somes referred to as the Genius Award) have been awarded to Robert Blackburn, David Hammons, Kerry James Marshall, Martin Puryear, John T. Scott, Kara Walker, and Deborah Willis.

Contemporary African American art manifests as multiple aesthetic and artistic trends, not as a single, consciously constructed art movement. Afrocentricity, feminism, postmodernism are a few of the influential intellectual and cultural currents shaping the work of painters, sculptors, photographers, and video, mixed-media installation, and performance artists. Additionally, individual artists have the insight and liberty to have a multiplicity of interests. They explore issues of race, gender, sexuality, sexual orientation, and class as intersecting rather than mutually exclusive concerns. This stands in contrast to the Harlem Renaissance or Black Arts movement which primarily challenged racism, with the latter movement frequently dismissing feminists' calls to end sexism as hampering racial unity. Today, works by artists such as Lorna Simpson, Carrie Mae Weems, or Adrian Piper build on the groundbreaking feminist work of such artists as Elizabeth Catlett and Faith Ringgold who are themselves still producing.

Carrie Mae Weems and Lorna Simpson combine written text with photographic or figurative imagery. This contemporary practice allows them to create art that can challenge the viewer, pose questions, and offer devastating culture critiques that focus on dismantling racial and sexual mythologies. Simpson is the first African American woman to have a solo exhibit at the Museum of Modern Art, while Weems is the first African American woman to have a major exhibition at the National Museum for Women in the Arts.

Other contemporary artists such as Dawoud Bey, Renee Cox, Anthony (Tony) Gleaton, Fern Logan, and Coreen Simpson use the medium of photography in innovative and profoundly illuminating ways. Following the lead of Roy DeCarava and Gordon Parks, this new generation of artists turns their cameras on people, scenes, and cityscapes, transforming documentary photography into aesthetically stimulating art.

Additionally, there is an important contingent of contemporary African American painters and sculptors who consider abstraction and the emphasis on the skillful manipulation of materials far more rewarding than figuration or overt cultural criticism. Barbara Chase-Riboud, Melvin Edwards, Sam Gilliam, Richard Hunt, Marian Hassinger, Alvin D. Loving Jr., Martin Puryear, Raymond Saunders, and William T. Williams continue to follow the abstractionist path paved by such artists as Alma Thomas (1891–1978), Hale Woodruff (1900–1980), and Norman Lewis (1909–1979).

Charles Bibbs, Varnetta Honeywood, and Synthia Saint James are representative of a group of artists who celebrate African American culture in their work. They create symbolic images about love, strength, fortitude, survival, spirituality, and vitality. Their colorful, figurative works pay tribute to historical figures as well as daily activities that are the heart and soul of African American life and culture. They are heartwarming, esteem-building scenes that recall church and family gatherings, children playing, men laboring, women quilting or braiding hair, people dancing, or lovers embracing. Artists working in this trend self-consciously cultivate an appreciation for African-inspired aesthetics, design principles, forms, concerns, and some subject matter. The National Black Arts Festival, founded in 1988, is a citywide, biannual event held in Atlanta, Georgia, that showcases art of this type.

In many instances, these artists specifically create for popular culture rather than the so-called fine art market where collectors pay high prices for the unique art object. The celebratory images easily translate into accessibly priced reproductions, such as print, posters, cards, mugs, T-shirts, book illustrations, and even Internet pages catering to an African American buying public. It was virtually impossible to find reproductions of African American art in the mid-1980s. A few years into the 21st century, however, art containing black subjects and aesthetics can be purchased from galleries, frame shops, mail order, or web pages.

With the Information Age revolution, computer technology, public media, and visual images have emerged as important forms of expression. Such artists as Leah Gilliam, Glen Ligon, and Betye Saar are creating and appropriating visual images to make computer-generated art for distribution on CD-ROM or display on the Internet. Artists such as Renee Cox and Alonzo Adams even maintain their own Internet sites, allowing them to take African American art directly to a global audience.

◆ ARTS-RELATED SUPPORT PROFESSIONS

Historically, black artists have not had equal and unrestricted access to institutions that support the making, exhibiting, and collecting of art. Despite the modernist myth that art and aesthetics are separate and distinct from the political arena, the making and consuming of art are deeply enmeshed in it. Many arts schools, museums, galleries, as well as private and public patrons followed the Jim Crow and gender segregation dictated by U.S. laws or social customs.

Thus, black men and women have not had equal access to training, severely limiting the number of people who could become artists. Moreover, in the arena of creative expression, white males have had and continue to receive privileges not extended to women of all races or men of color. Fortunately, opportunities increased dramatically during the post-civil rights era, and this exponentially increased the number of black people who chose to train and define themselves as artists and independent craftspeople. Consequently, there was an unprecedented flowering of African American arts and culture during the last three decades of the twentieth and first years of the twenty-first centuries, as countless black women and men opt to use the visual arts as a form of expression.

Despite the upsurge, the majority of African American artists still struggle to find support and encouragement from teachers, curators, dealers, collectors, critics, and historians. There is a need to increase the intelligently informed support for black artists and their work. Black artists must depend upon support from arts-related professionals to promote widespread knowledge and appreciation of their work. These arts-related professionals include art critics who evaluate the merit of art and art shows; curators who acquire, preserve, and exhibit art for public museums and private collectors; commercial art dealers who promote interest in specific artists, sell their original art, and market more accessibly priced reproductions; and art historians who study the types of art that creative people make. Necessarily, art historians are interested in providing insight about the beliefs and philosophies underpinning aesthetic preferences, criticism, patronage, collection, use, and exhibition patterns. They also chronicle the emergence of forms, subjects, styles, conventions, and techniques and try to account for their transformation and change over time.

These arts-related professionals are necessary forces in the development of scholarly and critical literature—including books, catalogues, and journal articles—and exhibitions that showcase black art. Black artists and their work will begin to gain more scholarly and critical attentions, exhibitions, gallery space, and sales as the number of art-related professionals with formal training in African American art expand.

Books and exhibition catalogues are an important source for stimulating interest in African American art. Presently, four illustrated surveys provide comprehensive and up-to-date accounts of African American visual arts. Samella Lewis's *African American Art and Artists* (1994) provides brief historical overviews and artists biographies. Crystal A. Britton's *African American Art: The Long Struggle* (1996) is a narrative of a collective visual tradition. Richard J. Powell's *Black Art*

and Culture in the Twentieth Century (1997) is a more theoretical analysis of themes, trends, and high moments uniting black cultural production. Written as a new addition to the multivolume series *World of Art* published by Thames and Hudson, Powell's book is the first in the collection to focus on African American artists.

In 1998, Oxford University Press released Sharon F. Patton's *African American Art* as an historic addition to its series the *Oxford History of Art*. It is a textbook that includes glossaries, timelines, and penetrating analyses. As the first African American art surveys by major mainstream publishing houses, Powell's and Patton's books are landmark and potentially trendsetting, scholarly publications. In addition, Hampton University Museum publishes a quarterly periodical *The International Review of African American Art*.

◆ EXHIBITING AFRICAN AMERICAN ART

The decades of the 1970s through the 1990s gave birth to a group of influential exhibitions dedicated to resurrecting, presenting, and discussing African American art and artists. Curators organized these special focus exhibits to fill the void left by the institutionalized exclusion of black artists and their work in mainstream shows by public museums or private galleries. Initially, these shows possessed a strong archaeological quality. Curators mined the collections of a wide variety of public and private patrons, excavating and assembling images by artists working in diverse media from many historical eras and stylistic periods.

The first wave of shows and catalogues had a documentary character, focusing on demonstrating the existence of black professional fine artists. Art that had languished in storerooms for generations was made available for public viewing in such shows and catalogues as: *Forever Free: Art by African-American Women, 1862–1980*, an exhibition organized by Arna Bontemps and Jacqueline Fonvielle-Bontemps; Lynda R. Hartigan's *Sharing Traditions: Five Black American Artists in Nineteen-Century America* (1985); Keith Morrison's *Art in Washington and Its Afro-American Presence: 1940–1970* (1985); Bucknell University's *Since the Harlem Renaissance: Fifty Years of Afro-American Art* (1984); David Driskell's *Hidden Heritage: Afro-American Art, 1800–1950* (1985); Edmund Barry Gaither's *Massachusetts Masters: Afro-American Artists* (1988); and *African-American Artists 1880–1987: Selections from the Evans-Tibbs Collection* (1989). These catalogues broke new ground simply in the quality of the richly illustrated color publications. Since exhibitions are temporary, making the reproductions available to a relatively wide audience allowed students and scholars the opportunity to continue to study works that had been hidden from both the contemporary and historical view. The majority of the artists featured are male, yet the works of a few women, such as Edmonia Lewis, Lois Mailou Jones, or Alma Thomas, also appear.

Another group of exhibits focused on the crafts art made by enslaved Africans, as well as those forms of creative expressions made by self-taught artists after the abolition of slavery. John Michael Vlach organized *The Afro-American Tradition in Decorative Arts* (1978), and the catalogue is a foundational text on the arts produced by enslaved people. The exhibited objects and collection of essays edited by Edward Campbell Jr. and Kym S. Rice in *Before Freedom Came: African-American Life in the Antebellum South* are extremely valuable for understanding the material production as well as its archaeological to ideological contexts. In addition, Jane Livingston and John Beardsley's *Black Folk Art in America, 1930–1980* (1982), William Ferris's *Afro-American Folk Arts and Crafts* (1983), and *Baking in the Sun: Visionary Images from the South, Selections from the Collection of Sylvia and Warren Lowe* (1987) discuss folk arts practices through the first half of the twentieth century.

The years leading to the 1976 U.S. Bicentennial gave birth to a recovery movement championing American art and culture. Although primarily celebrating white artists, the recovery movement brought legitimacy to American folk arts, especially female quilting traditions. In the following decade, the folk arts revival converged with the growing interest in African American arts, paving the way for such exhibitions and catalogues as Gladys-Marie Fry's *Stitched From the Soul: Slave Quilts From the Ante-Bellum South*, Cuesta Benberry's *Always There: The African American Presence in American Quilts*, Maude Wahlman's *Signs and Symbols: African Images in African-American Quilts* and Moira Roth's *Faith Ringgold: Change, Painted Story Quilts*, which showcased quilts made by women of African descent from the period of enslavement to the present. These shows placed an important body of art before the public for appreciation and scholarly study. It is worth noting that non-black museums, galleries, and curators supported these quilt shows at a higher rate than they did shows by formally trained, professional black women artists. Furthermore, the curators who created the most conceptually challenging study of African American art organized exhibitions that explored themes, movements, or styles.

A series of exhibitions mounted in the 1980s advanced the scholarship on African American artists. The Studio Museum of Harlem, while under the directorship of Mary Schmidt Campbell, took the lead in the development of such creative, thought-provoking, and historically-based shows as *New York/Chicago: WPA and the Black Artists* (1978); *Ritual and Myth: A Survey of African American Art* (1982); *An Ocean Apart: American Artists Abroad* (1983); *Tradition and Conflict: Images of a Turbulent Decade, 1963–1973* (1985); and the richly illustrated *Harlem Renaissance: Art of Black America* (1987). The catalogues are collaborative efforts, containing sets of essays from a wide range of contributors. Essayists do not explore issues impacting women artists or contrast any of the formal or thematic concerns of women with those of men. The strength of these publications is that the writers discuss the art critically and historically, moving beyond the formula of recounting biographical information and describing the art's formal qualities.

In 1989, a large number of well-financed exhibitions and catalogues appeared after decades of little activity. Gary A. Reynolds and Beryl J. Wright organized *Against the Odds: African-American Artists and the Harmon Foundation*. Richard Powell organized *The Blues Aesthetic: Black Culture and Modernism*. Alvia Wardlow curated *Black Art Ancestral Legacy: The African Impulse in African-American Art*. The California Afro-American Museum opened *Introspectives: Contemporary Art by Americans and Brazilians of African Descent* and *1960s: A Cultural Awakening Re-evaluated 1965–1975;* Deborah Willis and Howard Dodson curated *Black Photographers Bear Witness: 100 Year of Social Protest*. Leslie King-Hammond curated *Black Printmakers and the WPA* for the Lehman College Art Gallery in the Bronx. The catalogues accompanying these shows also reveal tremendous depth in the archival research, the resurrection of buried histories, and the production of historical analyses.

In connection with the 1990 biannual National Black Arts Festival in Atlanta, the Nexus Contemporary Art Center mounted *Africobra: The First Twenty Years*. Regina A. Perry published her long awaited *Free Within Ourselves: African-American Artists in the Collection of the National Museum of American Art* in 1992. *Dream Singers, Story Tellers: An African-American Presence* (1992) with essays and text in both English and Japanese provided a refreshingly new approach for an international audience. Bomani Gallery's *Paris Connections: African American Artists in Paris* (1992) examined production from an international perspective. Curator Thelma Golden organized *Black Male: Representations of Masculinity in Contemporary American Art* for the Whitney Museum of American Art. The art selected for the show examined notions of race and gender in the minds of artists of different races and the public at large. Beryl Wright's catalogues for *African-American Art Twentieth Century Masterworks,*

(1993) and Richard J. Powell's *Exultations: African-American Art Twentieth Century Masterworks, II* (1995) were unapologetically focused on canon building. Debra Willis, *Black: A History of Black Photographers, 1840 To The Present* (2000) and the Brooklyn Museum's *Committed to the Image: Contemporary Black Photographers* (2001) are landmark exhibitions with lushly illustrated catalogues of historical figures and their work as well as cutting-edge, contemporary photographic movements. Likewise, The Studio Museum of Harlem's co-sponsorship of *To Conserve a Legacy: American Art from Historically Black Colleges and Universities* (1999) and organizing of the provocative exhibition *Freestyle* reveal the historical diversity of African American artistic legends, while the latter show focuses on a new generation who came of age in the post-Civil Rights, hip hop heyday of the 1980s and according to curator Thelma Golden create from a post-black aesthetic.

These exhibits and catalogues demonstrate that African American artists have been and continue to be important agents in the struggle for social, political, and economic justice in the United States. African American artists stand among the legions of incredibly resilient, courageous, and visionary black people who acted on their beliefs that the life that they wanted for themselves and others must be free of racial, economic, cultural, and visual barriers. The core of what artists have to say on canvas, in stone or on video, join what artists in literature, music, or theater have been thinking and verbalizing for centuries. In spirit, however, African American visual artists add another dimension to the chorus of voices that celebrate the ways that people of African descent thrive in the United States.

◆ ARCHITECTURE AND DESIGN PROFESSIONALS

Since the early twentieth century, African Americans have carved out careers in the elite fields of architecture and professional design. Julian F. Abele (1881–1950) was the first African-American to graduate from the Pennsylvania School of Fine Arts and Architecture in 1904, and stands as the first major African-American architect. As chief designer of the Philadelphia-based firm Horace Trumbauer & Associates, Abele contributed to designs for Philadelphia's Free Library and Museum of Art, Harvard University's Widener Library, as well as the chapel and many other buildings of Trinity College in Durham, N.C. (which was later renamed Duke University) and the James B. Duke mansion on Fifth Avenue and 78th Street in New York City (now NYU's Graduate Institute of Fine Arts). In 1926, Paul Revere Williams became the first black member of

the American Institute of Architects. He is the most well know African American architect, celebrated for designing part of the Los Angeles International Airport and the L.A. homes of stars like William Holden, Lucille Ball, Frank Sinatra, Bojangles Robinson and Betty Grable. Williams and Howard H. Mackey organized the first juried exhibit of the work of "Negro architects" at Howard University in 1931.

These early architects also worked on projects for affluent African Americans and middle-to-low-income communities. For example: Wallace A. Rayfield designed the 16th Street Baptist Church in Birmingham, Ala. (1911), site of the 1963 bombing that killed four girls; John A. Lankford of Washington, D.C., designed churches and taught at the architecture school at Howard University; George Washington Foster teamed with Vertner Woodson Tandy, the first black person to graduate from Cornell University's architecture school, to create the firm that built St. Philip's Episcopal Church in New York in 1911, and the Harlem townhome of hair-care millionaire Madame C.J. Walker. Clarence W. ("Cap") Wigington (b. 1883) was the first registered African American architect in Minnesota and the first African American municipal architect in the nation. Between 1915 and 1947, in the Office of the City Architect of St. Paul, he designed an array of schools, fire stations, park structures, and municipal buildings that helped define the city's landscape. Wigington's nearly 60 St. Paul buildings comprise one of the most significant collections of works by an early African American architect. Hilyard Robinson designed Langston Terrace, the nation's first public housing program built in Washington, D.C., which opened in 1937. Making up less than 2 percent of the nation's 50,000 registered architects, contemporary designers continue to work in tradition styles and break racial and cultural design barriers. They build on the legacy of early black architects who mastered conventional Western design formulas. With increasing frequency contemporary architects such as Jack Travis incorporate African-inspired design aesthetics. Melvin L. Mitchell's *The Crisis of the African American Architect: Conflicting Cultures of Architecture and (Black) Power* (2001) examines the many concerns they face. African-American professional in the fields of graphic design, visual communications, interior design, fashion design, and industrial design encounter many of the same obstacles. In 1990, David H. Rice founded the Organization of Black Designers (OBD) to address the concerns and promote the work of black architectural, graphic, advertising, product, interior, fashion, and industrial and transportation designers. Currently under the directorship of Shauna Stallworth, the organization has membership of over 6,000. In 1995, Rice penned the essay "What Color is

Design?" As the organization's manifesto, it boldly stated that "Lack of Diversity = Design Sterility." Rice asserted, "In such a highly competitive new world order, we as Americans cannot afford to deny, in any way, the development of the potential of any segment of our citizenry. The creativity of Black Americans has contributed much to the cultural richness of our society even under stringent restrictions. That same creativity lives in the hearts and minds of countless Black youngsters and Black professionals who only need the opportunity to allow its full expression. America can no longer afford to waste human resources. It is no longer a matter of 'divide and conquer,' but 'unite and prosper.' Our future depends upon it."

◆ AMERICAN ACADEMY AND INSTITUTE OF ARTS AND LETTERS AWARD WINNERS

1946: Richmond Barthé
1953: Jacob Lawrence
1963: Raymond Saunders
1966: Romare Bearden
1971: Norman Lewis
2001: Chakaia Booker

◆ VISUAL AND APPLIED ARTISTS

(To locate biographical profiles more readily, please consult the index at the back of the book.)

Charles Alston (1907–1972)
Painter, Sculptor, Muralist

Born in Charlotte, North Carolina, in 1907, Alston received his B.A. and M.A. from Columbia University in New York. He was later awarded several fellowships and grants to launch his painting career.

Alston's paintings and sculpture are in such collections as those of IBM and the Detroit Institute of Arts. His murals depicting the history of medicine adorn the facade of Harlem Hospital in New York, and he was a member of the National Society of Mural Painters. Notable works include: *Exploration and Colonization* (1949); *Blues with Guitar and Bass* (1957); *Blues Song* (1958); *School Girl* (1958); *Nobody Knows* (1966); *Sons and Daughters* (1966); and *Frederick Douglass* (1968).

Benny Andrews (1930–)
Painter

Born in Madison, Georgia, on November 13, 1930, Andrews studied at Fort Valley State College in Georgia and later at the University of Chicago. He was awarded

a B.F.A. from the Art Institute of Chicago in 1958. During his career, he has taught at the New York School of Social Research, New York City University, and Queens College in New York. His works have appeared in exhibitions around the country including the Boston Museum of Fine Arts, the Martha Jackson Gallery in New York City, and other museums and galleries.

Andrews directed the Visual Arts Program for the National Endowment for the Arts from 1982 to 1984. He has also directed the National Arts Program, offering children and adults an opportunity to exhibit and compete for prizes in many cities across the United States.

Other honors include an honorary doctorate from the Atlanta School of Art, 1984; John Hay Whitney Fellowship, 1965 to 1967; New York Council on The Arts Grantee, 1971; NEA Fellowship, 1974; Bellagie fellow, Rockefeller Foundation, 1987; and a National Endowment for the Arts Painting Fellowship, 1986. Notable works include: *The Family; The Boxer; The Invisible Man; Womanhood; Flora;* and *Did the Bear.*

Edward Mitchell Bannister (1828–1901)
Painter

Born in Nova Scotia in 1828, Bannister was the son of a West Indian father and African American mother. Both parents died when he was very young. Bannister moved to Boston in the early 1850s, where he learned to make solar plates and worked as a photographer.

Influenced by the Barbizon style popular at the time, Bannister's paintings convey his own love of the quiet beauty of nature and his pleasure in picturesque scenes with cottages, cattle, dawns, sunsets, and small bodies of water. In 1871, Bannister moved from Boston to Providence, Rhode Island, where he lived until his death in 1901. He was the only nineteenth-century African American artist who did not travel to Europe to study art, believing that he was an American and wished to paint as an American. Bannister became one of the leading artists in Providence in the 1870s and 1880s, and in 1880 he became one of seven founders of the Providence Art Club, which later became known as the Rhode Island School of Design. Notable works include: *After the Storm; Driving Home the Cows;* and *Narragansett Bay.*

Ernie Barnes (1938–)
Painter

Barnes attended North Carolina Central College (now North Carolina Central University) from 1957 to 1960, where he majored in art and played on the football team. Barnes left school without graduating when the Washington Redskins drafted him. After playing for other NFL teams and a Canadian Football League team, Barnes retired due to an injury.

Barnes continued to paint throughout his football career, so his teammates dubbed him "Big Rembrandt." With his experience as a player and his painterly talents, Barnes became a sports artist. He secured a contract to paint for the American Football League and New York Jets owner Sonny Werblin.

He was the official artist for the 1984 Olympic Games in Los Angeles. Barnes paints in a colorful and lively style. He exaggerates the muscularity and physical attributes of his figures. He received national attention when his paintings were used on the 1970s television show *Good Times*. In 1997, he completed *The Dream Unfolds*, his commission for the Naismith Memorial Basketball Hall of Fame in Springfield, Massachusetts.

Barnes has received numerous commissions to paint portraits of athletes and celebrities, including boxer Oscar de la Hoya and film and music star Will Smith. His painting, *In Rapture*, appeared as cover art on B.B. King's album *Making Love is Good For You* (2000). In 2002, the painting *In Remembrance*, a response to the September 11th attack on the World Trade Center, was purchased by the city of Philadelphia. The painting is housed in the city's African American Museum.

Richmond Barthé (1901–1989)
Sculptor

Born on January 28, 1901, in Bay St. Louis, Mississippi, Barthé was educated at the Art Institute of Chicago from 1924 to 1928. He studied under Charles Schroeder and Albin Polasek. Barthé's first love was painting, but it was through his experiments with sculpture that he began to gain initial critical attention in 1927. His first commissions were busts of Henry Ossawa Tanner and Toussaint L'Ouverture. The acclaim resulting from them led to a one-man show in Chicago and a Rosenwald Fellowship for study in New York City.

Barthé's work has been exhibited at several major American museums. The Metropolitan Museum of Art in New York City purchased *The Boxer* in 1943. In 1946, he received the first commission given to an African American artist for a bust of Booker T. Washington for New York University's Hall of Fame. A year later he was one of the committee of 15 artists chosen to help modernize sculpture in the Catholic churches of the United States.

Barthé held membership in the National Academy of Arts and Letters. He died March 6, 1989, at his home in Pasadena, California, at the age of 88. Notable works include: *Singing Slave; Maurice Ens; Lot's Wife;* and *Henry O. Tanner.*

Jean–Michel Basquiat (1960–1988)
Painter

In a brief, tragic career, Jean-Michel Basquiat gained attention from wealthy collectors as a young artist discovered by Andy Warhol and promoted by other art consultants. He was raised in Brooklyn and attracted the New York art world with his trendy personal appearance (tangled dreadlocks) as a musician and artist at the age of 18. His works are autobiographical and deliberately "primitive" in style. In February 1985 he was a featured artist on the cover of the *New York Times Magazine*, shoeless in a suit, shirt, and tie.

The Whitney Museum of American Art in New York City owns many of the six hundred works this artist produced, reportedly valued in the tens of millions of dollars.

Basquiat began his career illegally painting images on buildings throughout the city. SAMO (slang for "same old s___") was his signature and trademark. He often used it in his paintings to preserve his reputation as a street artist. Basquiat was quoted as saying that his subject matter was, "[r]oyalty, heroism, and the streets."

He reportedly died of a drug overdose. Notable works include: *Self Portrait as a Heel #3; Untitled (History of Black People); Hollywood Africans;* and *CPRKR* (in honor of Charlie Parker).

Romare Bearden (1914–1988)
Painter, Collagist

Romare Howard Bearden was born on September 2, 1914, in Charlotte, North Carolina. His family moved to Pittsburgh and later to Harlem. Bearden studied with George Grosz at the Art Students League and, later on the G.I. Bill, went to Paris where he met Henri Matisse, Joan Miro, and Carl Holty. A product of the new generation of African Americans who had migrated from the rural areas of the South to the urban cities of the North, Bearden's work reflected the era of industrialization. His visual images would reflect the city life, jazz, and city people. Bearden's earlier works belonged to the school of social realism, but after his return from Europe his images became more abstract.

In the 1960s, Bearden changed his approach to his picture-making and began to make collages, soon becoming one of the best known collagists in the world.

Roots Odyssey. Romare Bearden, 1976.

His images are montages of his memories of past experiences and of stories told to him by other people. They are for Bearden "an attempt to redefine the image of man in terms of the black experience." Notable works include: *Street Corner; He Is Arisen; The Burial; Sheba;* and *The Prevalence of Ritual.*

John Biggers (1924–2001)
Painter

Born in Gastonia, North Carolina, in 1924, Biggers derived much of his subject matter from the contributions made by African Americans to the development of the United States. As a teacher at Texas Southern University, Biggers became a significant influence on several young African American painters.

Some of his most powerful pieces were created as a result of his study trips to Africa including *The Time of Ede, Nigeria,* a series of works done in the 1960s. Notable works include: *Cradle; Mother and Child; The Contributions of Negro Women to American Life and Education;* and *Shotgun, Third Ward, #1.*

Biggers died January 25, 2001, at his home in Houston, Texas, after suffering a heart attack. He was 76.

Camille Billops (1933–)
Sculptor, Photographer, Filmmaker

A noted sculptor in art and retailing, Camille Billops was born in California in 1933, graduated from California State College in 1960, and then studied sculpture under a grant from the Huntington Hartford Foundation. In 1960, she had her first exhibition at the African Art Exhibition in Los Angeles, followed in 1963 by an exhibit at the Valley Cities Jewish Community Center in Los Angeles. In 1966, she participated in a group exhibition in Moscow. Since then, her artistic talents, which include poetry, book illustration, and jewelry making, have earned the praise of critics throughout the world, particularly in Sri Lanka and Egypt, where she also has lived and worked.

Billops has also taught extensively. In 1975, she was active on the faculties of the City University of New York and Rutgers at Newark, New Jersey. In addition, she has conducted special art courses in the Tombs, a New York City jail. She lectured in India for the United States Information Service on African American artists in 1972. She participated in an exhibit at the New York Cultural Center in 1973. Along with her husband, James Hatch, Billops co-founded the Hatch-Billops Archives of Black American Cultural History. The archives, located in New York City, chronicles the work of black artists in the visual and performing arts.

Billops is a printmaker, filmmaker, and photographer who has also been active in the mail-art movement which has made art more accessible to the public. She has written articles for the *New York Times, Amsterdam News* and *Newsweek.*

Her grants for film include the New York State Council on the Arts, 1987 and 1988; NYSCA and New York Foundation for the Arts, 1989; Rockefeller Foundation, 1991; and National Endowment for the Arts, 1994.

In 1992, Billops won the prestigious Grand Jury Prize for best documentary at the Sundance Film Festival for *Finding Christa,* an edited combination of interviews, home movies, still images, and dramatic acting. Notable works include: *Tenure; Black American; Portrait of an American Indian* (all three are ceramic sculptures); *Year after Year* (painting). *Older Women and Love* (film); *Suzanne, Suzanne* (film); *A String of Pearls* (film); and *The K.K.K. Boutique Ain't Just Rednecks* (film).

Billops is also the author of *The Harlem Book of the Dead,* with James Van Der Zee and Owen Dodson.

Robert Blackburn (1920–)
Printmaker

Robert Blackburn was born in Summit, New Jersey, in 1920. He studied at the Harlem Workshop, the Art Students League, and the Wallace Harrison School of Art. His exhibits include *Art of the American Negro, 1940,* Downtown Gallery, New York and Albany Museum; *Contemporary Art of the American Negro, 1966;* and numerous print shows in the United States and Europe. His work is represented in the Library of Congress, the Brooklyn and Baltimore museums, and the Atlanta University Collections. He has been a member of the faculty of The Cooper Union, New York University, and Columbia University.

Along with his other accomplishments, he founded The Printmaking Workshop as an artist-run cooperative in 1949. In 1971, it was incorporated as a nonprofit printmaking studio for work in lithography, etching, relief, and photo-processes. The workshop, a magnet for Third World and minority artists that reflects Mr. Blackburn's personalty, remains a haven for artists "to turn out prints for the love of it" and to do anything from experimental hodgepodge to polished pieces. In 1988, Bob Blackburn and the Printmaking Workshop were given the Governor's Art Award for making "a significant contribution to the cultural life of New York State." Blackburn received a MacArthur Award in 1992, and has been the recipient of five honorary doctorates. Notable works include *Boy with Green Head* and *Negro Mother.*

Selma Burke (1900–1995)
Sculptor, Educator

Selma Burke was an artist whose career spanned more than 60 years. She was born in Mooresville, North Carolina, on December 31, 1900. She received a B.A. from Winston-Salem University, a R.N. from St. Augustine College in 1924, an M.F.A from Columbia University in 1941, and a Ph.D. from Livingston College in 1970. Burke received her training as a sculptor at Columbia University in New York. She also studied with Maillol in Paris and with Povoley in Vienna.

Burke worked as an instructor in art and sculpture at Friends School/George's School/Forrest House in New York City from 1930 until 1949. From 1963 until 1976, she served as an instructor in art and sculpture at the Sidwell School, Haverford College, Livingston College, and Swarthmore College. The A.W. Mellon Foundation hired Burke as a consultant from 1967 until 1976. Burke

Jim, a plaster sculpture by Selma Burke.

founded New York City's Selma Burke School of Sculpture in 1940 and the Selma Burke Art Center in Pittsburgh in 1968, where she taught and supported many young artists.

In 1987, Burke received the Pearl S. Buck Foundation Women's Award. She also received honorary degrees from Livingston College, the University of North Carolina, and Moore College of Art.

Burke is best known for her relief sculpture rendering of Franklin Delano Roosevelt that was minted on the American dime. On August 29, 1995, she died of cancer.

The Pearl S. Buck Foundation Woman's Award was given to her in 1987 for her professional distinction and devotion to family and humanity. Notable works include: *Falling Angel; Peace;* and *Jim.*

Stephen Burrows (1943–)
Fashion Designer

Stephen Burrows was born on September 15, 1943, in Newark, New Jersey. Burrows began making clothes at a young age. He later studied at the Philadelphia Museum College of Art and the Fashion Institute of Technology in New York City.

With a partner, he opened a boutique in 1968. He worked for Henri Bendel from 1969 to 1973. From 1974 to 1977 he attempted to run a Seventh Avenue firm, but found it unsatisfying and returned to Bendel's in 1977 .

Known for his unique color combinations, he used patches of cloth for decorative motifs in the 1960s. Top-stitching of seams in contrasting threads, top stitched hems, known as "lettuce hems" because of their fluted effect, were widely copied. He preferred soft, clinging, easy-moving fabrics such as chiffon and matte jersey. He also liked asymmetry. During the 1970s he enjoyed immence success as his clothes were adopted readily by disco dancers, for whom he designed using natural fabrics with non-constricting, light and airy qualities. Throughout the 1980s Burrows designed custom-made clothing, juxtaposing the strongest colors, and in 1993 he returned to Henri Bendel to design eveningwear. He won a Coty American Fashion Critics' Award in 1974 and a special Coty Award in 1977.

Elizabeth Catlett (1919–)
Sculptor, Painter

Elizabeth Catlett was born on April 15, 1919. The granddaughter of North Carolina slaves, Catlett was raised in the northwest district of Washington, D.C. As a young woman she attempted to gain admission into a then all-white art school, the Carnegie Institute of Technology in Pittsburgh, Pennsylvania. She was refused entry and instead went to Howard University and graduated as an honor student in 1935. In 1940, she went on to study at the University of Iowa, where she became the first of their students to receive an M.F.A.

Her exhibition history dates back to 1937 and includes group and solo presentations at all the major American art museums as well as institutions in Mexico City, Moscow, Paris, Prague, Tokyo, Beijing, Berlin, and Havana. Catlett's public sculpture can be found in Mexico City; Jackson, Mississippi; New Orleans; Washington, D.C.; and New York. Her work is represented in the permanent collection of over 20 museums throughout the world. The artist resides in Cuernavaca, Mexico.

Catlett accepted teaching positions at various African American colleges in order to earn a living, but by 1946 she had moved to Mexico, where she eventually settled. Always a promoter of human struggle—visually concerned with the recording of economic, social, and political themes—Catlett became involved with the Civil Rights movement so deeply that it contributed greatly to her philosophy of life and art. Between 1941

and 1969, Catlett won eight prizes and honors, four in Mexico and four in America. Notable works include: *Black Unity* (1968); *Target Practice* (1970); *Mother and Child* (1972); and *Woman Resting* (1981). In 1993, Catlett worked with James Weldon Johnson on the book *Lift Every Voice and Sing*.

Catlett was presented with an honorary doctorate of human letters from Morgan State University in 1993. She has received honorary doctorates of fine art from the New School for Social Research, Tulane University, Spelman College, Howard University, and Cornell College.

Dana Chandler (1941–)
Painter

Dana Chandler is one of the most visible African American painters in the United States. Chandler's huge, colorful black power murals can be spotted throughout areas of Boston, a constant reminder of the resolve and determination displayed by the new breed of young African American urban dwellers.

Chandler's easel works are bold and simple. One piece *The Golden Prison* shows an African American man with a yellow and red striped flag "because America has been yellow and cowardly in dealing with the black man." *Fred Hamton's Door* shows a bullet-splintered door bearing a stamp of U.S. government approval.

Born in Lynn, Massachusetts, in 1941, Chandler received his B.S. from the Massachusetts College of Art in 1967. Chandler has worked as a critic of African American art for the *Bay State Banner*, an assistant professor of art and art history at Simmons College in Boston, and an artist in residence at Northeastern University. Chandler also founded and directed an artist collaborative called the African American Master Artists in Residency Program (AAMARP). Notable works include: *Fred Hamton's Door*; *Martin Luther King Jr. Assassinated*; *Death of Uncle Tom*; *Rebellion '68*; *Dynamite*; *Death of a Bigot*; and *The Golden Prison*.

Chandler is a member of the National Conference of Black Artists, Boston Black Artists Association, National Conference of Artists, Boston Union of Visual Artists, and the American Association of University Professors.

Barbara Chase-Riboud (1936–)
Sculptor, Author

Barbara Chase-Riboud was born in Philadelphia, Pennsylvania, in 1936. She received a B.F.A. from Temple University in 1956 and a M.F.A. from Yale University in 1960. Chase-Riboud grew up encouraged to express herself artistically by her jazz musician mother and a

Barbara Chase-Riboud.

Sally Hemmings (1979); *Valide: A Novel of the Harem* (1986); *Echo of Lions* (1989); and *The President's Daughter* (1994). She has published three books of poetry, *From Memphis to Peking* (1974); *Portrait of a Nude Woman as Cleopatra, a Meloloque* (1987); and *Egypt's Nights* (1994).

Chase-Riboud made headlines in 1997 when she brought a lawsuit against the film company DreamWorks, claiming that *Amistad*, a movie directed by Steven Spielberg, plagiarized parts of her novel *Echo of Lions*. She was, in turn, accused of being guilty of plagiarism, as a *New York Times* story alleged that she had taken passages from a 1936 book about harems for one of her novels, *Valide*. The controversy subsided in 1998 when Chase-Riboud settled with DreamWorks for an undisclosed amount.

Robert Colescott (1925–)
Painter

Robert Colescott was born in California in 1925. He received his B.A. from the University of California in 1949 and an M.A. in 1952. In 1953, Colescott studied in Paris with Fernand Léger. His works are found in the collections of numerous museums, including the Metropolitan Museum of Art, the Museum of Modern Art, the Whitney Museum of American Art, and San Francisco Museum of Modern Art.

A controversial artist criticized by both African American groups and traditionalists, Colescott's work questions the "heroic" and "pushes the standards of taste." He has substituted black figures in place of white figures in famous European paintings as he explores racism and sex in his works, along with other taboos and stereotypes. Notable works include: *Homage to Delacroix: Liberty Leading the People; Eat Dem Taters; Shirley Temple Black and Bill Robinson White;* and *The Power of Desire, The Desire for Power.*

Houston Conwill (1947–)
Performance Artist, Environmental Artist

Born in Lexington, Kentucky, in 1947, Conwill spent three years studying for the priesthood. His strong Catholic upbringing and Catholic ritual play a part in his art that draws from both American and African myths and religions. In his explorations, he mostly uses non-traditional materials such as replacing canvas with latex. The environments that he builds, paints, and fills with real chalices, candlesticks, carpets, or sand are works to which he adds his own personal iconography as well as some ancient symbols. Since the late 1980s, many of Conwill's projects have been designed and executed in collaboration with his sister,

father she describes as a "frustrated painter." Enrolled in the Fletcher Art School at the age of seven, she studied piano and ballet as a child. Building on this early training, she majored in art at Temple University in Philadelphia. She then used a fellowship from the John Hay Whitney Foundation to study in Rome for one year. Chase-Riboud returned to the United States and attended Yale School of Art and Architecture. She has lived and worked in Europe as a sculptor and writer since 1961.

Chase-Riboud's mixed-media sculptures combine "soft" and "hard" materials, such as silk cords, juxtaposed to metals, usually bronze cast, in the lost-wax technique. She uses contrasting materials to explore formal concerns and metaphorically comment on issues regarding race and society. Chase-Riboud's work has been exhibited in numerous one-woman shows and group shows such as *Three Generations of African-American Women Sculptors: A Study in Paradox* (1997) and *Explorations in the City of Light: African-American Artists in Paris, 1945–1965* (1996).

In addition to making visual arts, Chase-Riboud writes historical novels and poetry. Her novels include:

Estella Conwill Majozo, a poet, and Italian American architect Joseph DePace.

Conwill's work is included in the collections of the City College of New York; Howard University; Museum of Contemporary Art, Los Angeles; Museum of Modern Art, New York; and Studio Museum in Harlem. He is the recipient of a Guggenheim Memorial Foundation Fellowship and two National Endowment for the Arts fellowships. Notable works include: *The Cakewalk Manifesto; Passion of St. Matthew; East Shout;* and *JuJu Funk.*

Emilio Cruz (1938–)
Painter

Emilio Cruz was born in New York City in 1938. His education includes work at the Art Students' League under Edwin Dickinson, George Grosz and Frank J. Reilly. Cruz has exhibited widely since 1959. Exhibits have included the Anita Shapolsky Gallery, 1986, 1991; The Studio Museum in Harlem, 1987; the Portland Museum of Art in 1987; the Rhode Island School of Design, 1987; the Gwenda Jay Gallery, Chicago, 1991; the G.R. N'amdi Gallery, Birmingham, Michigan, 1991; and Steinbaum Krauss, New York, 1998.

An artist whose works are narrative and formalistic (emphasizing color and forms as the dominant elements), he combines these two theoretical approaches often with figurative subjects.

His awards include: the Cintas Foundation Fellowship, 1965–1966; John Hay Whitney Fellowship, 1964–1965; Walter Gutman Foundation Award, 1962. Notable works include: *Silver Umbrella; Figure Composition 6;* and *Striated Voodoo.*

Roy DeCarava (1919–)
Photographer

Roy DeCarava's existence in New York City prepared him for his work as a photographer. He began as a commercial artist in 1938 by studying painting at Cooper Union. This was followed by classes at the Harlem Art Center from 1940 to 1942, where he concentrated on painting and printmaking. By the mid-1940s, he began to use photography as a convenient method of recording ideas for his paintings. In 1958, DeCarava gave up his commercial work and became a full-time freelance photographer. Edward Steichen began to study his work and suggested that he apply for a Guggenheim Fellowship. Winning this award allowed DeCarava the financial freedom to take his pictures and tell his story. One of DeCarava's photographs from this body of work appeared in Steichen's exhibition *Family of Man* at the Museum of Modern Art. Later, Langston

Hughes worked with DeCarava to create the book *Sweet Flypaper of Life.*

DeCarava has worked as a photographer for *Sports Illustrated* and taught photography at Hunter College, New York. His work can be found in many important collections throughout the United States including: Andover Art Gallery, Andover-Phillips Academy, Massachusetts; Art Institute of Chicago, Chicago, Illinois; Atlanta University, Atlanta, Georgia; Belafonte Enterprises, Inc., New York; Center for Creative Photography, University of Arizona; the Corcoran Gallery of Art, Washington, D.C.; Harlem Art Collection, New York State Office Building, New York; Lee Witkin Gallery, New York; Menil Foundation, Inc., Houston, Texas; Metropolitan Museum of Fine Arts, Houston, Texas; The Museum of Fine Arts, Houston, Texas; Museum of Modern Art, New York; Olden Camera, New York; Joseph E. Seagram & Sons, Inc., New York; and Sheldon Memorial Art Gallery, University of Nebraska, Nebraska.

DeCarava received a Distinguished Career in Photography Award in 1991 from the Friends of Photography. That same year, the American Society of Magazine Photographers presented him with a special citation for photographic journalism. DeCarava has also received honorary doctorates from The Maryland Institute, Rhode Island Institute of Fine Arts, and Wesleyan University.

Beauford Delaney (1910–1979)
Painter

Born in Knoxville, Tennessee, in 1910, Beauford Delaney was described by his elder brother Samuel as a "remarkably dutiful child." For Beauford Delaney, recognition came by way of an elderly white artist of Knoxville named Lloyd Branson. Branson gave him lessons and, after a time, urged him to go to a city where he might study and come into contact with the art world.

In 1924, Beauford Delaney went to Boston to study at the Massachusetts Normal School, later studying at the Copley Society, where he took evening courses while working full-time at the South Boston School of Art. From Boston, Delaney moved on to New York.

It was in New York that Delaney took on the life of a bohemian, living in the village in coldwater flats. Much of his time was spent painting the portraits of the personalities of the day, such as Louis Armstrong, Ethel Waters, and Duke Ellington. In 1938, Beauford Delaney gained national attention when *Life,* in an article on "negroes," featured a photograph of him surrounded by a group of his paintings at the annual outdoor exhibition in Washington Square in New York. In 1945, Henry

Miller wrote the essay "The Amazing and Invariable Beauford Delaney," which was later reprinted in *Remember to Remember*. The essay describes Delaney's bohemian lifestyle in New York during the 1940s and 1950s.

In the 1950s, Delaney left New York with the intention of studying in Rome. Taking the *Ile de France*, he sailed to Paris, next visiting Greece, Turkey, Northern Italy—but he never got to Rome. Returning to Paris for one more visit, Delaney began to paint, make new friends, and create a new social life filled with other artistic figures. Paris was to become Beauford Delaney's permanent home.

By 1961, Delaney was producing paintings at such an intense rate that the pressure began to wear upon his strength, and he suffered his first mental collapse. He was confined to a clinic in Vincennes, and his dealer and close friends began to organize his life, hoping to help relieve some of the pressure. However, the rest of his life, Delaney was to suffer repeated breakdowns and by 1971 was back in a sanitarium, where he was to remain until his death in 1979.

Beauford Delaney's numerous exhibitions took place in such venues as Artists Gallery, New York in 1948; Roko Gallery, New York, 1950–1953; Musée d'Art Moderne, Paris, 1963; American Negro Exposition, Chicago, 1940; and Newark Museum, 1971. His work can be found in the collections of the Whitney Museum of American Art, New York; the Newark Museum, New Jersey; and Morgan State College in Baltimore, Maryland. Notable works include: *Greene Street; Yaddo; Head of a Poet;* and *Snow Scene*.

Aaron Douglas (1899–1988)
Painter, Illustrator

Born in Topeka, Kansas, in 1899, Aaron Douglas achieved considerable eminence as a muralist, illustrator, and academician. As a young man, Douglas studied at the University of Nebraska, Columbia University Teachers College, and l'Academie Scandinave in Paris. He had one-person exhibits at the Universities of Kansas and Nebraska and also exhibited in New York at the Gallery of Modern Art. In 1939, Douglas was named to the faculty of Fisk University and later became head of its department of art.

Douglas died on February 2, 1988. In 1992, Fisk University opened a new gallery in his memory. Douglas is considered one of the most important painter and illustrator of the Harlem Renaissance. Notable works include: murals at Fisk University and in the Countee Cullen branch of the New York City Public Library; illustrations in books by Countee Cullen, James Weldon

Johnson, Alain Locke, and Langston Hughes. Alexander Dumas, Marion Anderson, and Mary McLeod Bethune are among the many African Americans he painted or rendered in charcoal.

David Clyde Driskell (1931–)
Painter, Historian

Born in Eatonton, Georgia, in 1931, Driskell studied at Howard University and earned his M.A. from the Catholic University of America in 1962. He also studied at the Skowhegan School of Painting and Sculpture and the Netherlands Institute for History of Art. He has taught at Talladega College, Fisk University, Institute for African Studies of the University of Ife in Nigeria, and the University of Maryland at College Park.

Driskell has been the curator for the William and Camille O. Cosby Collection—the largest collection of African-American art in the world. In 1997 he served as adviser to President Bill Clinton on the purchase of the first artwork by an African American artist to be added to the White House collection. Driskell is also a major collector of African American art. The 1999 traveling exhibit, "Narratives of African American Art and Identity: The David C. Driskell Collection," included 100 works from his personal collection, including pieces by Romaré Bearden, Henry O. Tanner, and Minnie Evans.

A recipient of many awards including the John Hope Award and prizes from the Danforth Foundation, American Federation of Arts, and Harmon Foundation, Driskell has exhibited at the Corcoran Art Gallery, National Museum, and Rhodes National Gallery in Salisbury, Rhodesia. Notable works include: *Movement; The Mountain; Still Life With Gateleg Table; Memories of a Distant Past* and *Shango Gone*.

Robert Duncanson (1817–1872)
Painter

Robert Duncanson was the son of an African American mother and a Scottish-Canadian father. Born in upstate New York in 1817, he spent much of his childhood in Canada. During his youth, he and his mother moved to Mt. Healthy, Ohio, where in 1840 the Western Freedom's Aid Society, an anti-slavery group, raised funds to send him to Glasgow, Scotland, to study art. Returning to Cincinnati three years later, Duncanson advertised in the local newspaper as the proprietor of a daguerreotype studio. He continued to work at his daguerreotype studio until 1855, when he began to devote all of his time to his painting. Similar to many landscape artists of this time, Duncanson traveled around the United States drawing his compositions from the images of nature before him. In 1853, he made his second trip to Europe—this time to visit Italy, France, and England.

Although Duncanson was active during and after the Civil War, with the exception of his painting of *Uncle Tom and Eva*, he made no attempts to present the turmoil that was taking place within the United States or the social pressures that he experienced. In September 1872, Duncanson suffered a severe mental breakdown and committed suicide in Detroit, Michigan. Notable works include murals in the Taft Museum and *Bishop Payne*.

William Edmondson (1882–1951)
Sculptor

William Edmondson was a stonecutter and self-taught sculptor. Born in Nashville, Tennessee, in 1882, he supported himself working as a hospital orderly and other menial jobs. His work was discovered by Mrs. Meyer Dahl-Wolfe, who had an extensive private collection and brought Edmondson to the attention of the Museum of Modern Art. His work was received extremely well in an exhibition of self-taught artists. In 1937 he was the first African American to have a one-person exhibit at the museum. Private collectors and museums have purchased his few sculptures.

Inspired by biblical passages, Edmondson worked on tombstones and his sculpture, which he did in limestone, at the home he shared with his mother and sister until their deaths. He continued to live alone and work there until his own death in 1951. Notable works include: *Choir Girls; Lion;* and *Crucifixion*.

Elton Clay Fax (1909–1993)
Illustrator, Writer

Born in Baltimore in 1909, he graduated from Syracuse University with a B.F.A., in 1931. He taught at Claflin University from 1935 to 1936 and was an instructor at the Harlem Community Art Center from 1938 to 1939. His work has been exhibited at the Baltimore Art Museum, 1939; American Negro Exposition, 1940; the Metropolitan Museum of Art; and Visual Arts Gallery, New York, 1970. Examples of his work are included in some of the nation's university collections including Texas Southern, the University of Minnesota, and Virginia State University.

Publications by Fax include: *Africa Vignettes; Garvey; Seventeen Black Artists;* and *Black Artists of the New Generation. The Portfolio Black and Beautiful* features his art work, and he has written *Hashar,* a book about the life of the peoples of Soviet Central Asia

and Kazakhstan. Notable works include: *Steelworker; Ethiopia Old and New; Contemporary Black Leaders;* and *Through Black Eyes*.

Elton Fax died in Queens, New York, in May, 1993.

Tom Feelings (1933–)
Illustrator

Born in Brooklyn, New York, on May 19, 1933, Thomas Feelings grew up in the Bedford-Stuyvesant neighborhood. He began to draw cartoons at the age of four, and his art work flourished under the guidance of an African American artist named Thipadeux who encouraged Feelings to draw the people in his neighborhood. After high school, he attended the Cartoonists and Illustrators' School in New York City on a three-year scholarship. Feelings's art studies were interrupted by four years of service for the U.S. Air Force in England, but upon completion of his military service, he continued his art studies at the New York School of the Visual Arts.

While in art school, Feelings produced "Tommy Traveler in the World of Negro History," a comic strip published in *New York Age,* a Harlem newspaper. Completing art school in 1961, Feelings marketed his portfolio to earn freelance assignments and began to get work with magazines of primarily African American readership. In 1964, Feelings traveled to Tema, a city in Ghana, with other African Americans enlisted by the Kwame Nkrumah, then head of Ghanian government, to help direct the newly independent country toward the future. Africa changed Feelings's art on a spiritual and stylistic level. In 1966, he was forced to leave when the Nkrumah government fell.

Feelings returned to the United States hungry for work. There was a huge demand for works by and depicting African Americans, especially children's books. In this new climate, Feelings illustrated such books as *To Be A Slave* (1968) and *Moja Means One: A Swahili Counting Book,* which won a Caldecott Honor Award in 1972. From 1971 to 1974, Feelings administered the Guyanese Ministry of Education's children's book project while living in Guyana. There he wrote his autobiography *Black Pilgrimage,* published in 1972. After returning to the United States, Feelings illustrated more books spread over the next ten years including *Now Sheba Sings the Song* (1987), a collaboration with the poet/writer Maya Angelou.

While serving as an artist in residence at the University of South Carolina, Feelings has completed illustrations for two books. In 1993, he finished illustrations for *Soul Looks Back In Wonder,* a book compiling the poems of many African American authors. Two years later, he completed *The Middle Passage*, which portrays the passage of slave ships from Africa to the Western hemisphere. Both books received Coretta Scott King Awards from the American Library Association.

Feelings has earned many awards for his illustrations including two outstanding achievement awards from the New York School of Visual Arts, Visual Artists Fellowship and National Endowment for the Arts grants, and Distinguished Service to Children Through Art Award from the University of South Carolina (1991). Feelings has earned three Coretta Scott King Awards.

Meta Vaux Warrick Fuller (1877–1968)
Sculptor

Meta Vaux Warrick Fuller was a part of the transitional period between the artists who chose to simulate Euro-American subjects and styles and the later artistic periods. Her African American subjects of *The Wretched*, exhibited at the Paris Salon in 1903 and 1904, did not suit popular tastes.

Born in 1877, in Philadelphia and educated at the School of Industrial Art and the Pennsylvania Academy, Fuller's interest in sculpture led her to study with Charles Grafly and at the Academie Colarossi in Paris with Rodin. She was the first African American woman to become a professional artist.

She married and settled in the Boston area, where in 1910, most of her works were destroyed by fire. The Boston Art Club and the Harmon Foundation exhibited her works, and representative pieces of her sculpture can be found in the Cleveland Museum of Art today.

Sam Gilliam (1933–)
Painter

Born in Tupelo, Mississippi, in 1933, Sam Gilliam produces hanging canvases that are laced with pure color pigments rather than shades or tones. The artist bunches these pigments in different configurations on drooping, drape-like canvases, giving the effect, in the words of *Time* Magazine, of "clothes drying on a line." His canvases are said to be "like nobody else's, black or white."

Gilliam received his M.A. from the University of Louisville in 1961. He was awarded National Endowment of Humanities and Arts grants in National Endowment for the Arts grants in 1967, 1973, 1974, and 1989. He has had one-man and group shows at the Washington Gallery of Modern Art; Jefferson Place Gallery; Adams-Morgan Gallery in Washington, D.C.; the Art Gallery of Washington University, St. Louis, Missouri; the Speed Museum, Louisville; the Philadelphia Museum

Meta Vaux Warrick Fuller's *The Awakening of Ethiopia*, c.1910.

of Art; the Museum of Modern Art; the Phillips Collection and Corcoran Gallery of Art, both in Washington, D.C.; the San Francisco Museum of Art; the Walker Art Center, Minneapolis, and the Whitney Museum of American Art. He is represented in the permanent collection of over 45 American museums.

Among Gilliam's awards and honors are the Longview Foundation Award in 1970; an Order of Merit Award

Sam Gilliam's serigraph on paper, *In Celebration,* 1987.

from the University of Louisville Alumni Association in 1987; and honorary doctorates from the University of Louisville, Memphis College of Art and Design, Corcoran Gallery and School of Art, and Northwestern University.

In 1980, Gilliam was commissioned, with 13 other artists, to design work for installation in the Atlanta, Georgia Airport Terminal, one of the largest terminals in the world and the first to install contemporary artwork on its walls for public viewing. Notable works include: *Watercolor 4* (1969); *Herald* (1965); *Carousel Change* (1970); *Mazda* (1970); *Plantagenets Golden* (1984); and *Golden Element Inside Gold* (1994).

Tyree Guyton (1955–)
Multimedia Artist

Born in Detroit on August 24, 1955, Tyree Guyton

has transformed the blighted urban pocket in which he has spent much of his life into an enormous ongoing art project that utilizes the debris of the abandoned cityscape. Interested in the arts from a young age, after high school Guyton served in the U.S. Army and then worked at Ford Motor Company for several years. He also began a family and in his spare time took art classes.

In 1984, Guyton left his firefighting job to become a full-time artist. He started transforming the small city block in which he and wife, Karen Smith, and their several children lived. His grandfather, a former housepainter, was both a source of early inspiration and an integral contributor to Guyton's artistic project. Using ordinary housepaint, old toys, bicycles, and other found objects they salvaged from the junk piles that plague the city, Guyton transformed Heidelberg Street

Tyree Guyton standing in front of his controversial Heidelberg Project.

into a dynamic and unique art installation. A crack house, one of the many abandoned residences on the street, was painted in wild colors that discouraged the drug sales that even narcotics squad raids had not been able to stop. A tree was nailed several yards high with vintage bicycles. Polka dots decorated the street, Guyton's own home, and nearly every other available surface. The combination of dots, stripes, lively patterning, and re-invention of discarded objects had been inspired by the style in which Guyton's mother had decorated their home on a tight budget when he was growing up.

Long heralded by the international artistic community, Guyton's art has periodically come under criticism, however. Other residents of the eastside Detroit neighborhood dismiss the out-of-town visitors and laudatory praise heaped on the Heidelberg Project by the art critics and harken for the days of a neatly manicured lawn and more placid environs. In the fall of 1991, city bulldozers demolished several of the houses that Guyton had transformed, one of which had been slated for inclusion on a tour of local artistic sites. Ironically, that year he was named the Michiganian of the Year and the following year earned the Governor's Arts Award.

Guyton sued the city—with the support of prominent members of Detroit's artistic community—but dropped the suit when a more sympathetic mayoral administration came into power in 1994. However, action by the Detroit City Council led to partial dismantling of the project by 1999.

Richard Hunt (1935–)
Painter, Sculptor

Richard Hunt was born in Chicago in 1935 and began his formal career after studying at the School of the Art Institute of Chicago, where he received a number of awards.

After graduating in 1957, Hunt was given the James Nelson Raymond Traveling Fellowship. He later taught at the School of the Art Institute of Chicago and at the University of Illinois. From 1962 to 1963, he pursued his craft under a Guggenheim Fellowship.

Hunt's solo presentations have appeared at the Cleveland Museum of Art; Milwaukee Art Center; Museum of Modern Art; Art Institute of Chicago; Springfield Art Museum, Massachusetts; Indianapolis Museum of Art;

Studio Museum, Harlem; and a U.S.I.S.-sponsored show throughout Africa, which was organized by the Los Angeles Museum of African American Art. Hunt sits on the board of governors at the School of the Art Institute of Chicago and the Skowhegan School of Painting and Sculpture; is a commissioner at the National Museum of American Art, Washington, D.C. He has also served on the advisory committee at the Getty Center for Education in the Arts, Malibu.

His works are in the Museum of Modern Art, New York; Cleveland Museum of Art, Ohio; Art Institute of Chicago; Milwaukee Art Center; Baltimore Museum of Art; Martin Gallery, Washington, D.C.; National Museum of American Art, Washington, D.C.; Hirshhorn Museum, Washington, D.C.; Museum of Twentieth Century Art, Vienna, Austria; the Albright Knox Gallery, Buffalo, New York; National Museum of Israel, Jerusalem; Terry Dintenfass Gallery, New York; Dorsky Gallery, New York; Whitney Museum of American Art, New York; and Howard University. He has had many other commissions. Notable works include: *Man on a Vehicular Construct* (1956); *Linear Spatial Theme* (1962); *The Chase* (1965); and *Arching* (1986).

Joshua Johnston (1765–1830)
Painter

Active between 1789 and 1825, Joshua Johnston is the first known African American portrait painter from the Baltimore area. At least two dozen paintings have been attributed to this artist who was listed as a "free house-holder of colour, portrait painter." He was listed in the Baltimore directories in various studio locations.

It is believed Johnston may have been a former slave of Charles Wilson Peale, the artist who is also known for having started a drawing school in Maryland in 1795; or Johnston may have simply known the artist and his works. In either case, Johnston was most likely self-taught. A portraitist in the style of the period, his work now seems quaint. Only one black subject has been attributed to him, *Portrait of a Cleric*. Notable works include *Portrait of Adelia Ellender*, *Portrait of Mrs. Barbara Baker Murphy* and *Portrait of Sea Captain John Murphy*.

Larry Johnson (1949–)
Painter, Illustrator, Editorial Cartoonist

Born in Boston, Massachusetts, in 1949, Larry Johnson attended the School of the Boston Museum of Fine Arts. He became a staff illustrator at *The Boston Globe* in 1968, where he covered many assignments including courtroom sketches, sports events, entertainment, editorial sports cartoons and drawings, and other features. Johnson is now nationally syndicated through Universal Press Syndicate.

Barry Gaither, director of the National Center of African American artists in Boston, says, "Johnson's works can be divided horizontally between commercial illustration and fine art, and vertically between drawings and paintings in acrylics and watercolor." In addition to working for the *Globe*, Johnson worked for the now defunct *National Sports Daily*, has designed book jackets for Little Brown, and has been commissioned by Pepsi-Cola, the *Old Farmer's Almanac*, the National Football League, and *Fortune*, among others. He later left the *Globe* to freelance and run his own company, Johnson Editions, a producer of fine arts prints and other multiples, such as greeting cards. Johnson was awarded the Associated Press Editorial Cartoon Award in 1985. Notable works include *Island Chisel*; *Rainbow*; and *Promises*.

In 1995, several of Johnson's photographs were included in the six-artist exhibition entitled *New Testament*, which was hosted by the Marc Foxx Gallery in Santa Monica, California. The Margo Leavin Gallery in Los Angeles also hosted an exhibition of Johnson's art work in 1995.

Lester L. Johnson (1937–)
Painter, Educator

Born in Detroit, Michigan, in 1937, Johnson attended the University of Michigan, where he received a B.F.A. in 1973, and a M.F.A. in 1974. He teaches at the Center for Creative Studies, College of Art and Design, in Detroit, Michigan.

His works are in many collections including: the Detroit Institute of Arts; Osaka University Arts, Japan; Johnson Publishers and The Masonite Corp., Chicago; Sonnenblick-Goldman Corp., New York; Taubman Co., Inc., Bloomfield Hills, Michigan; and St. Paul Co., St. Paul, Minnesota.

Commissions have included: *Urban Wall Murals*, Detroit, 1974; New Detroit Receiving Hospital, 1980; and Martin Luther King Community Center. Johnson has exhibited at major institutions including the Whitney Museum of American Art Biennial, 1973; National African American Exhibit, Carnegie Institute, Pittsburgh, Pennsylvania; the National Academy of Design, Henry

Ward Ranger National Invitational, 1977; and the Edward Thorp Gallery in New York City, 1994.

Among his awards are the Andrew W. Mellon Foundation Grant, 1982 and 1984; and a Recognition Award, African American Music Art Association.

Sargent Johnson (1888–1967)
Sculptor

Sargent Johnson, who three times won the Harmon Foundation's medal as the nation's outstanding African American artist, worked in stylized idioms, heavily influenced by the art forms of Africa in sculpture, mural bas-reliefs, metal sculpture, and ceramics.

Born in Boston in 1888, he studied at the Worcester Art School and moved to the San Francisco Bay area in 1915, where his teachers were Beniamino Bufano and Ralph Stackpole. He exhibited at the San Francisco Artists Annual, 1925 to 1931; Harmon Foundation, 1928 to 1931, 1933; Art Institute of Chicago, 1930; Baltimore Museum, 1939; and the American Negro Exposition, Chicago, 1940. He was the recipient of numerous awards and prizes.

From the beginning of his career he spoke of his sculpture as an attempt to show the "natural beauty and dignity of the pure American Negro" and wished to present "that beauty not so much to the white man as to the Negro himself. Unless I can interest my race, I am sunk." Notable works include: *Sammy; Esther; Golden Gate Exposition Aquatic Park murals;* and *Forever Free.* He died in 1967.

William Henry Johnson (1901–1970)
Painter

William H. Johnson was a pioneer African American modernist whose work went from abstract expressionist landscape and flower studies influenced by Vincent Van Gogh, to studies of black life in America, and finally to abstract figure studies in the manner of Rouault.

Born in Florence, South Carolina, on March 18, 1901, he studied at the National Academy of Design; Cape Cod School of Art, under Charles Hawthorne; in southern France, 1926 to 1929, and Denmark and Norway, 1930 to 1938. Exhibits include Harmon Foundation (Gold Medal in 1929); Aarlins, Denmark, 1935; Baltimore Museum, 1939; American Negro Exposition, Chicago, 1940. He produced one-person shows in Copenhagen in 1935, and at the Artists Gallery, New York, in

William H. Johnson's *Ezekiel Saw the Wheels*, c.1939.

1938. Notable works include: *Booker T. Washington; Young Man in Vest; Descent from the Cross;* and *On a John Brown Flight.* He died on April 13, 1970.

Ben Jones (1942–)
Painter, Sculptor

Ben Jones was born in Patterson, New Jersey, in 1942, and studied at the School of Visual Arts; New York University, where he received an M.A.; the Pratt Institute; the University of Science and Technology, Ghana; and the New School of Social Research.

Jones is a professor of fine arts at Jersey City State College. As a sculptor, his works made during the height of the Black Arts movement in 1970 were cast in plaster from living models and painted in brightly colored patterns, resembling traditional African symbols. Masks, arms, and legs arranged in multiples or singly seem to have roots in African ceremony ritual and magic.

His pieces are in such collections as: the Newark Museum; Studio Museum in Harlem; Howard University; and Johnson Publications, Chicago. His exhibits have included: The Museum of Modern Art; Studio Museum in Harlem; Black World Arts Festival, Lagos, Nigeria; Newark Museum; Fisk University, Nashville, Tennessee, among others.

Jones's awards have included grants from the National Endowment for the Arts; the New Jersey Arts Council; Delta Sigma Theta Sorority, and others. Notable works include: *Five Black Face Images; High Priestess of Soul;* and *Untitled (6 Arms)*.

Karl Kani (1968?–)
Fashion Designer

Born Carl Williams, Kani was preoccupied with style as a youth. His fashion sense first became noticed on the streets of Flatbush, a neighborhood of Brooklyn, New York. While his peers were buying the latest clothes, Williams was busy purchasing material he would later bring to various tailors, instructing them to make garments exactly how he wanted for a relatively small price. As time passed, people who had seen Williams in one of his "originals" wanted their own made-to-order clothes. Williams began taking orders and supplying the demand.

While working at Seasons Sportswear in south central Los Angeles, Williams developed the name Kani, based on the question "Can I?" as in "Can I do it?" In 1989, Kani met Carl Jones, co-founder of Threads 4 Life. Jones, who had already proven his ability to sell clothes with his Cross Colours line, agreed to help Kani get his designs out to the public. By 1992, the Kani line of clothing had added roughly $35 million dollars to the Threads 4 Life profit margin. Disagreements with Threads 4 Life eventually led Kani to venture off on his own.

Kani began "Karl Kani Infinity" in 1994. While competition for hip hop clothing had become fierce, Kani saw potential in the previously ignored market. Rap stars such as Tupac Shakur began wearing his designs, spreading the Kani name. By 1996, Kani's sales figures were at $54 million dollars and his company was at number 25 on the *Black Enterprise 100s*. Despite constant battles with fashion counterfeiters, Kani's success has continued through his use of unique licensing agreetments. Kani was at number 41 on the *Black Enterprise 100s* in 2001 with sales of $76.9 million. In 2002, Kani launched "Life," a new line of clothing for men and women.

Jacob Lawrence (1917–2000)
Painter

Born on September 7, 1917, in Atlantic City, New Jersey, Jacob Lawrence received his early training at the Harlem Art School and the American Artist School. He worked under the guidance of such artists as Charles Alston, Henry Bannarn, Anton Refregier, Sol Wilson, Philip Reisman, and Eugene Moreley. His rise to prominence was ushered in by his painting of several series of biographical panels commemorating important episodes in African American history. A narrative painter, Lawrence created the "philosophy of Impressionism" within his work. Capturing the meaning and personality behind the natural appearance of a historical moment, Lawrence created a formal series of several dozen small paintings that related to the course of a particular historic event in American history, such as *The Migration Series* ("... and the Migrants keep coming"), which traced the migration of the African American from the South to the North, or the discussion on the course of a man's life (e.g., Toussant L'Ouverture and John Brown).

Lawrence was a visual American historian. His paintings recorded African American in trade, theater, mental hospitals, neighborhoods, or running in Olympic races. Lawrence's works are found in collections at the Metropolitan Museum of Art, Museum of Modern Art, Whitney Museum of American Art, the National Museum of American Art, and the Wadsworth Atheneum in Hartford, Connecticut.

Lawrence lived in Seattle, Washington, where he died on June 9, 2000, at the age of 82. His notable works include: *The Life of Toussaint L'Ouverture* (41 panels, 1937); *The Life of Harriet Tubman* (40 panels, 1939); and *The Negro Migration Northward in World War* (60 panels, 1942). He also produced commissioned book and magazine illustrations, murals, posters, drawings, and prints. Among these are a 1976 print for the U.S. Bicentennial, illustrations for a 1983 special edition of John Hersey's book *Hiroshima* and a 1984 poster for the National Urban League.

In 1970, Lawrence was awarded the NAACP's Spingarn Medal. He received an invitation to paint the 1977 presidential inauguration of Jimmy Carter. President George Bush bestowed on Lawrence the National Medal of Arts in 1990. He was also the recipient of numerous honorary degrees.

Lawrence wrote and illustrated the book *The Great Migration: An American Story* in 1993.

Hughie Lee-Smith (1915–1999)
Painter

Hughie Lee-Smith was born on September 20, 1915, in Eustis, Florida. He studied at the Cleveland Institute

Drilling Negroes (1942) from Jacob Lawrence's *John Brown* series of paintings.

of Art and Wayne State University, where he received his B.S. in art education in 1953.

From childhood, Lee-Smith was encouraged to pursue his art, and he enjoyed a long career. He worked for the Ohio Works Progress Administration and the Ford Factory at River Rouge during the 1930s and 1940s. He did a series of lithographic prints and painted murals at the Great Lakes Naval Station in Illinois. He taught art at Karamu House in Cleveland, the Grosse Pointe War Memorial in Michigan, Princeton Country Day School, Howard University, the Art Students League, and other institutions.

Lee-Smith's works can be seen in museums, schools, galleries, and collections across the United States including the American Negro Exposition, Chicago; Southside Community Art Center; Snowden Gallery; Detroit Artists Market; Cleveland Museum of Art; Whitney Museum of American Art; Museum of Modern Art; the June Kelly Gallery, New York City, and the Evans-Tibbs Collection, Washington, D.C. His painted

environments are often of decaying or ghetto environments in a state of revitalization peopled by a single or sometimes double-figured occupant. His subjects suggest desolation or alienation, but waving banners or balloons in the scene counter the expression in their symbolism of hope and gaiety.

Lee-Smith's one-person shows and exhibitions are numerous. He received more than a dozen important prizes including the Founders Prize of the Detroit Institute of Arts (1953), Emily Lowe Award (1957, 1985), Ralph Fabri Award, Audubon Artists, Inc. (1982), Binny and Smith Award (1983), and Len Everette Memorial Prize, Audubon Artists, Inc. (1986). He was a member of the Allied Artists of America, the Michigan Academy of the Arts, Sciences & Letters, and the Artists Equity Association. Notable works include: *Portrait of a Sailor; Old Man and Youth; Waste Land; Little Diana;* and *Aftermath.*

Lee-Smith died on February 23, 1999 in Albuquerque, New Mexico at the age of 83.

Edmonia Lewis (1845–1890)
Sculptor

Edmonia Lewis was America's first black female artist and also the first of her race and sex to be recognized as a sculptor. Born on July 4, 1845, in Albany, New York, she was the daughter of a Chippewa Indian woman and a free African American man. From 1859 to 1863, under the patronage of a number of abolitionists, she was educated at Oberlin College.

After completing her schooling, Lewis moved to Boston, where she studied with Edmund Brackett and did a bust of Colonel Robert Gould Shaw, the commander of the first black regiment organized in the state of Massachusetts during the Civil War. In 1865, she moved to Rome, where she soon became a prominent artist. Returning to the United States in 1874, she fulfilled many commissions including a bust of Henry Wadsworth Longfellow that was executed for the Harvard College Library.

Her works are fine examples of the neo-classical sculpture that was fashionable during her lifetime. It is believed that she died in Rome in 1890. Notable works include *Hagar in the Wilderness*, *Forever Free*, and *Hiawatha*.

Norman Lewis (1909–1979)
Painter

Norman Lewis was born in New York City in 1909. He studied at Columbia University and under Augusta Savage, Raphael Soyer, Vaclav Vytacil, and Angela Streater. During the Great Depression he taught art through the Federal Art Project from 1936 to 1939 at the Harlem Art Center. He received a Carnegie International Award in Painting in 1956 and has had several one-person shows at the Willard Gallery in New York.

As one of the artists to develop the abstract movement in the United States, Lewis participated in many group shows in such institutions as the Whitney Museum of American Art, the Metropolitan Museum of Art, and the Art Institute of Chicago. Notable works include *Arrival and Departure* and *Heroic Evening*.

Geraldine McCullough (1928–)
Sculptor

Geraldine McCullough's steel and copper abstraction *Phoenix* won the George D. Widener Gold Medal at the 1964 exhibition of the Pennsylvania Academy of Fine Arts. In earning this award, she added her name to a roster of artists who have already won the same honor including Jacques Lipchitz and Theodore Roszak.

A native of Arkansas, McCullough has lived in Chicago since she was three years old and is a 1948 graduate of the city's Art Institute. She also studied at the University of Chicago, DePaul University, Northwestern University, and the University of Illinois.

McCullough taught at Wendell Phillips High School from 1950 to 1964 in Chicago and at Rosary College in River Forest, Illinois. Currently, she works and resides in Oak Park, Illinois. She has received many awards and commissions. Her works are represented in the collections of Howard University and the Oakland Museum of California. She was part of the Smithsonian Institution's exhibition *Three Generations of African American Women Sculptors*. Notable works include: *Bessie Smith; View from the Moon; Todd Hall Front; Atomic Rose; Phoenix;* and *Martin Luther King.*

Ionis Bracy Martin (1936–)
Painter, Printmaker, Educator

Born on August 27, 1936, in Chicago, Illinois, Ionis Bracy Martin attended the Junior School of the Art Institute of Chicago before going to Fisk University, where she studied with Aaron Douglas and earned her B.S. in 1957. Martin received an M.Ed. degree from the University of Hartford (1969) and an M.F.A. from Pratt Institute, Brooklyn, New York (1987). She has served as a trustee of the Wadsworth Atheneum, a co-trustee and chairperson of the Ella Burr McManus Trust for the Alfred E. Burr Sculpture Mall, and a member of the advisory board of the CRT Craftery Gallery, Hartford. In 1972 she co-founded of the Artists Collective along with Jackie McLean, Dollie McLean, Paul Brown, and Cheryl Smith.

In addition to exhibiting in the Hartford area, Martin has been exhibited in New York; Springfield, Boston, and Northampton, Massachusetts; Fisk University, Nashville, Tennessee; and the University of Vermont, Burlington, Vermont. Among her many prizes and honors are a grant from the Connecticut Commission on the Arts (1969); a graduate fellowship in Printmaking, Pratt Institute (1981); a Summer-Six Fellowship from Skidmore College (1987); and a fellowship with the W.E.B. Du Bois Institute, Harvard University (1994).

Martin has been a teacher at Weaver and Bloomfield High Schools and lecturer in African American art at Central Connecticut State University. Martin also lectures on and demonstrates serigraphy. Notable works include: *Mother and Child; Allyn's Garden; Gran' Daddy's Garden;* and *Little Women of the Amistad: Series.*

Evangeline J. Montgomery (1933–)
Jeweler, Photographer, Sculptor

Evangeline Montgomery was born in New York City on May 2, 1933. She received an associate's degree from Los Angeles City College in 1958 and her B.F.A. from the California College of Arts and Crafts in 1969. She also studied at the University of California, Berkeley and California State University.

Montgomery has worked as a freelance artist; an art consultant to museums, community organizations, and colleges for EJ Associates; and program director for Arts America. Known primarily for her metal boxes, incense burners, and jewelry, Montgomery has also been awarded prizes for her photography. Her works are in collections at the Oakland Museum and the University of Southern Illinois.

Active with many organizations, Montgomery has served on the San Francisco Art Commission, the advisory board of Parting Ways Ethnohistory Museum, and the board of directors of the Museum of the National Center of Afro-American Artists. She is currently a member of the Michigan Chapter of the National Conference of Artists, the College Art Association, the American Museums Association, and the Women's Art Caucus. Montgomery is also on the board of directors of the District of Columbia Arts Center.

Her awards have included a Smithsonian Fellowship and a museum grant from the National Endowment for the Arts. In 1989, Montgomery was presented with a Special Achievement Award from Arts America. Notable works include *Ancestor Box 1* and *Justice for Angela Davis*.

Archibald Motley (1891–1980)
Painter

Born in New Orleans in 1891, Motley's artistic talent was apparent by the time he attended high school. His father wanted him to become a doctor, but Archibald insisted on art and began formal education at the Art Institute of Chicago. During this time he worked as a laborer, coming into contact with the drifters, scavengers, and hustlers who are now immortalized in his street scenes. His genre scenes are highly stylized and colorful and are often associated with the *Ash-Can* school of art, a popular style in the 1920s.

In 1928, Motley had a one-person show in downtown New York and became the first artist, black or white, to make the front page of the *New York Times*. He was awarded a Guggenheim Fellowship in 1929 and studied in France. He was the recipient of a Harmon Foundation award for an earlier, more literal portrait. Notable works include: *The Jockey Club*; *The Plotters*; *Parisian Scene*; *Black Belt*; and *Old Snuff Dipper*. Motley died in 1980.

John Wilfred Outterbridge (1933–)
Sculptor

John Wilfred Outterbridge was born in Greenville, North Carolina, on March 12, 1933. He studied at North Carolina A&T University in Greensboro; the Chicago Art Academy; the American Academy of Art, Chicago; and the Art Center School of Design, Los Angeles.

From 1964 until 1968, Outterbridge worked as an artist/designer for the Traid Corporation. He worked as artistic director and co-founder of the Communicative Arts Academy from 1969 until 1975. He has also taught at California State University and Pasadena Art Museum. Outterbridge was director of the Watts Towers Art Center, Los Angeles, from 1976 until 1992.

Outterbridge's sculptures are assemblages constructed from discarded materials. Some of his works are tributes to African ancestors and their descendants in Los Angeles and in other communities. Outterbridge is known for making and helping create "Street Art," a combination of painting, relief sculpture, and construction that incorporates words and symbols expressing community goals and social ideas.

Outterbridge was featured in *Black Artists on Art*, Volume I (Selma Lewis/Ruth Waddy, Los Angeles Contemporary Crafts, 1971, 1976). Notable works include: *Shoeshine Box*; *Mood Ghetto*; and *Ethnic Heritage Group*.

In 1990, Outterbridge was presented with the Malcolm X Freedom Award by the New Afrikan People's Organization and the Lifetime Achievement Award from the First Annual King Blvd. Memorial Project. The National Endowment for the Arts awarded Outterbridge with its Visual Arts Fellowship in 1994. That same year, he was presented with an honorary doctorate of fine arts by the Otis College of Arts and Design and the J. Paul Getty Visual Arts Fellowship.

Gordon Parks (1912–)
Photographer, Composer, Writer, Director

Parks was born on November 30, 1912, in Fort Scott, Kansas. After the death of his mother, Parks went to St. Paul, Minnesota to live with relatives. He attended Central and Mechanical Arts high schools. Despite having fond childhood memories of his father on the family farm, Parks had a dysfunctional upbringing. He worked at a variety of jobs including janitor, busboy, and semi-pro basketball player. Always interested in

Gordon Parks (seated, wearing hat) directing *The Learning Tree* as his son, Gordon Parks Jr., takes still photographs.

the arts, Parks also tried sculpting, writing and touring with a band, but these artistic endeavors were largely without focus.

In 1933, Parks joined the Civilian Conservation Corps and in the late 1930s, while working as a railroad porter, he became interested in photography as a medium on which he could finally concentrate his artistic interests. After purchasing a used camera, Parks worked as a freelance photographer and as a photojournalist. In 1942, he became a correspondent for the Farm Security Administration, and from 1943 to 1945 he was a correspondent for the Office of War Information. After the war he worked for Standard Oil Company of New Jersey, and in 1948 he became a staff photographer for *Life* magazine. He soon achieved national acclaim for his photographs and in the mid-1950s he began doing consulting work on Hollywood productions. In the 1960s Parks began doing television documentaries, and in 1966 he published his biography *A Choice of Weapons*.

Parks has authored numerous books, including: *Flash Photography* (1947); *Camera Portraits: The Techniques and Principals of Documentary Portraiture* (1948);

The Learning Tree (1963); *A Poet and His Camera* (1968); *Born Black* (1971); *Gordon Parks: Whispers of Intimate Things* (1971); *Moments without Proper Names* (1975); *Flavio* (1978); *To Smile in Autumn* (1979); *Shannon* (1981); *Voices in the Mirror: An Autobiography* (1990); *Arias in Silence* (1994); *Glimpses Toward Infinity* (1996); and *Half Past Autumn: A Retropective* (1997). In 1968 Parks produced, directed, and wrote the script and music for the movie production of *The Learning Tree*. Parks also directed and scored the following movies: *Shaft* (1971); *Shaft's Big Score* (1972); *The Super Cops* (1974); *Leadbelly* (1976); *Odyssey of Solomon Northrup* (1984); and *Moments Without Proper Names* (1986).

Parks is a recipient of the NAACP's Spingarn Award (1972), the Rhode Island School of Design's Presidents Fellow Award (1984), and Kansan of the Year (1986). In 1988 President Ronald Reagan presented him with the National Medal for the Arts. That same year, Parks won the World Press Photo Award. In 1989, he was awarded the Library of Congress National Film Registry Classics film honor for *The Learning Tree* in 1989, and was also presented with the New York Mayor's Award and the Artist of Merit Josef Sudek Medal. In 2002, the Jackie Robinson Foundation presented Parks with a Lifetime Achievement Award.

Parks is a member of the NAACP, Urban League, Newspaper Guild, Association of Composers and Directors, Writer's Guild, AFTRA, ASCAP, International Mark Twain Society, American Film Institute, Academy of Motion Pictures Arts and Sciences, and the American Society of Magazine Photographers.

On July 7, 1995, the Library of Congress announced that it had acquired the archives of Gordon Parks. The archives include roughly 15,000 manuscript pages of Parks's poems, novels and screenplays, as well as several thousand photographs and negatives.

Marion Perkins (1908–1961)
Sculptor

Born in Marche, Arkansas, in 1908, Perkins was a self-taught artist. His early works were composed while he tended a newspaper stand on Chicago's South side. He later studied privately with Simon Gordon as the two men became close friends.

Perkins's work has been exhibited at the Art Institute of Chicago, American Negro Exposition (1940), Xavier University, and Rockland College, Illinois (1965). As artist in residence at Jackson State College in Mississippi, where much of his sculpture is housed, Perkins

Self-taught sculptor Marion Perkins at work.

founded a scholarship fund for art students. Perkins died in 1961.

Howardena Pindell (1943–)
Painter

Born in Philadelphia on April 14, 1943, Howardena Pindell received a B.F.A. from Boston University in 1965 and a M.F.A. from Yale University in 1967. She first gained national recognition for her 1969 exhibition *American Drawing Biennial XXIII* at the Norfolk Museum of Arts and Sciences in Virginia. By the mid-1970s, Pindell's work began appearing in such exhibitions as *Eleven Americans in Paris*, Gerald Piltzer Gallery, Paris, 1975; *Recent Acquisitions; Drawings*, Museum of Modern Art, New York, 1976; and *Pindell: Video Drawings*, Sonja Henie Onstad Foundation, Oslo, Norway, 1976.

Pindell began to travel around the world as a guest speaker. Some of her lectures include: "Current American and Black American Art: A Historical Survey" at Madras College of Arts and Crafts, Madras, India, 1975; and "Black Artists, U.S.A.," Academy of Art, Oslo,

Norway, 1976. In 2002, she was a professor of art at State University of New York, Stony Brook.

Her work is part of the permanent collection in over 30 museums including the Brooklyn Museum, High Museum in Atlanta, Newark Museum, Fogg Museum in Cambridge, Massachusetts, Whitney Museum of American Art, Museum of Modern Art, and the Metropolitan Museum of Art. Pindell has received two National Endowment for the Arts Fellowships and a Guggengeim Fellowship.

Pindell has received numerous awards throughout her career. In 1990, she won the College Art Association Award for Best Exhibitor. She received the Studio Museum in Harlem Award and Joan Mitchell Fellowship in 1994. In 1996, the Women Caucus for Art presented Pindell with its Distinguished Contribution to the Profession Award.

Jerry Pinkney (1939–)
Illustrator

Born in Philadelphia on December 22, 1939, Jerry Pinkney studied at the Philadelphia Museum College of Art. Pinkney has exhibited in illustrator shows throughout the country and is best known for his illustrations for children's and text books.

From his studio in his home in Croton-on-Hudson, New York, Pinkney has been a major contributor to the U.S. Postal Service's stamps in the Black Heritage Series. Benjamin Banneker, Martin Luther King Jr., Scott Joplin, Jackie Robinson, Sojourner Truth, Carter G. Woodson, Whitney Moore Young, Mary McLeod Bethune, and Harriet Tubman stamps were designed by Pinkney.

A recipient of many honors, he has created illustrations in children's books such as *The Talking Eggs*, written by Robert San Souci; earned a Caldecott Honor of Medal (Pinkney's second such honor) in 1989, received a Coretta Scott King Honor Book Award; was named an American Library Association Notable Book; and won the Irma Simonton Black Award from the Bank Street College of Education. In 1994, Pinkney won the Caldecott Medal for his illustrations in the book *John Henry*. That same year, he won two Parent's Choice Awards for the books *John Henry* and *The Sunday Outing*.

Pinkney has worked in Boston as a designer and illustrator. He is one of the founders of Kaleidoscope Studio in Boston, where he also worked for the National Center of Afro-American Art. He also was a visiting critic for the Rhode Island School of Design. He has taught at Pratt Institute, the University of Delaware, and in the Art Department at the State University of

New York at Buffalo. Pinkney has illustrated numerous books, including *The Tales of Uncle Remus*; *Call It Courage*; *Self Portrait*; *Sam and the Tigers*; *Minty: A Story of Young Harriet Tubman*; and *The Nightingale*. Pinkney also illustrated *Back Home*, which was written by his wife, Gloria Jean Pinkney.

Horace Pippin (1888–1946)
Painter

Horace Pippin has been ranked in the company of Henri Rousseau due to his accomplishment as a self-taught artist. Born on February 22, 1888, in West Chester, Pennsylvania, Pippin began painting in 1920, and continued until his death on July 6, 1946. Among his most vivid works are battle scenes that he remembered from his own experience in World War I.

Pippin's earliest works are designs burned into wood with a hot poker. He did not make his first oil painting until 1930. This task was complicated by his wartime injury; he had to guide his right arm with his left hand in order to paint. He painted family reunions, Biblical stories, and historical events. Notable works include:

Horace Pippin (right), his painting in background, receiving a check, Philadelphia, 1946.

John Brown Goes to a Hanging; *Flowers with Red Chair*; *The Den*; *The Milk Man of Goshen*; and *Dog Fight Over the Trenches*.

James A. Porter (1905–1971)
Art Historian, Painter

James A. Porter was a painter who also earned acclaim as a writer and educator. Born in Baltimore in 1905, he studied at Howard University receiving a B.S. in 1927; Art Students League, New York; Sorbonne; and received a M.A. from New York University. He was awarded numerous travel grants that enabled him to study African and European art firsthand.

Among his ten one-person shows are exhibits at Port-au-Prince, Haiti, 1946; Dupont Gallery, Washington, D.C., 1949; and Howard University, 1965. His works are in the collections of Howard University; Lincoln University, Missouri; Harmon Foundation; IBM; and others. The first African American art historian, he wrote *Modern Negro Art* (1943), as well as numerous articles.

In 1953, he became chairman of the Department of Art and director of the Gallery of Art at Howard University, a position he held until his death. He was a delegate to the UNESCO Conference on Africa held in Boston in 1961, and to the International Congress of African Art and Culture in Salisbury, Southern Rhodesia, 1962. In 1965, at the 25th anniversary of the founding of the National Gallery of Art, he was named "one of America's Most Outstanding Men of the Arts." His notable works include: *On a Cuban Bus*; *Portrait of F. A. as Harlequin*; *Dorothy Porter*; and *Nude*.

Martin Puryear (1941–)
Sculptor

Martin Puryear was born in Washington, D.C., in 1941. He attended Catholic University of America and received an M.F.A. from Yale University in 1971. He has studied in Sweden and worked in Sierra Leone with the Peace Corps from 1964 to 1966.

Representing the United States in the 1989 São Paulo Bienal in Brazil, he received first prize. His work has been described as post-minimalist, but it really defies categorization. Puryear executes his own large pieces in wood and metal.

Puryear was the only African American artist in the contemporary section of the exhibit "Primitivism in Twentieth-Century Art: Affinity of the Tribal and Modern" at the Museum of Modern Art 1984. In 1991, he collaborated with musician Wynton Marsalis and playwright Garth Fagan in designing a dance production,

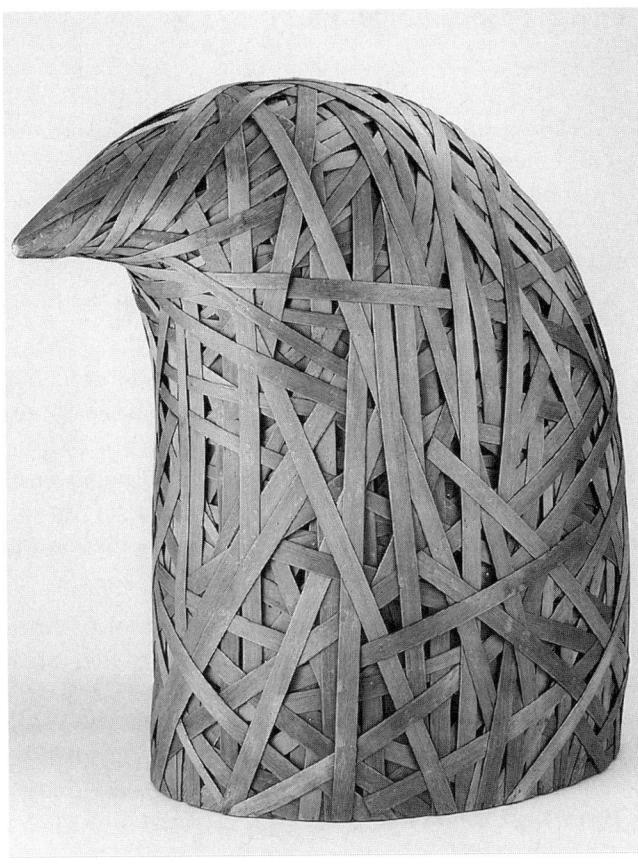

Old Mole sculpture by Martin Puryear, from the Philadelphia Museum of Art.

"Griot New York." Puryear has exhibited throughout the U.S., and his sculpture is in the collections of many major American museums, including the Art Institute of Chicago, Hirshhorn Museum & Sculpture Garden, the Museum of Modern Art, and the National Gallery.

Puryear studied in Japan in 1987 on a Guggenheim Fellowship. He has also been the recipient of a MacArthur Foundation grant. Puryear has taught at the University of Illinois, Chicago, and was the artist in residence at the Penland School of Crafts in North Carolina during the spring of 1997. Notable works include: *For Beckwith; Maroon Desire; and Sentinel.* His works since 1985 have been untitled.

Faith Ringgold (1930–)
Painter, Fiber Artist

Committed to a revolutionary perspective both in politics and in aesthetics, Faith Ringgold is a symbolic expressionist whose stark paintings are acts of social reform directed toward educating the consciousness of her audience. Her most intense focus has been upon the problems of being black in America. Her works highlight the violent tensions that tear at American society including the discrimination suffered by women. Ringgold is also known for her distinctive story quilts. These quilts feature paintings on canvas that are bordered with quilted textiles and handwritten strips of white fabric that contain fanciful stories.

Born in Harlem on October 8, 1930, she was raised by parents who made sure she would enjoy the benefits of a good education. She received her B.S. in 1955 and her M.F.A. in 1959 from the City College of New York. She is a professor of Art at the University of California at San Diego.

Ringgold's boldly political work has been widely shown. Since 1968 she has had several one-person shows and her paintings are included in the collections of the Chase Manhattan Bank, New York City; the Museum of Modern Art, the Bank Street College of Education, New York City; and the Solomon R. Guggenheim Museum.

In 1972, Ringgold became one of the founders of the Women Students and Artists for Black Liberation, an organization whose principal goal is to make sure that all exhibitions of African American artists give equal space to paintings by men and women. In line with her interest in sexual parity, she has donated a large mural depicting the roles of woman in American society to the Women's House of Detention in Manhattan.

Her first quilt *Echoes of Harlem, Tar Beach* was completed in 1980. Other quilts produced by Ringgold include *The Sunflower Quilting Bee at Arles,* and *Who's Afraid of Aunt Jemima.* In 1991, she illustrated and wrote a children's book *Tar Beach.* This book was followed by *Aunt Harriet's Underground Railroad in the Sky* (1992), *My Dream of Martin Luther King* (1996), and *The Invisible Princess* (1998), among others. Notable artistic works include: *The Flag Is Bleeding; Flag for the Moon; Die Nigger; Mommy & Daddy;* and *Soul Sister, Woman on a Bridge.*

Ringgold has received several awards for her work including honorary doctorates from Moore College of Fine Art, Wooster College, Massachusetts College of Art, and City College of Art. In 1996, she received an award from the National Museum of Women in the Arts.

Betye Saar (1926–)
Painter, Sculptor

Betye Saar was born in California on July 30, 1926. She went to college, got married, and raised her children—all while creating artwork built upon discarded pieces of old dreams: postcards, photographs, flowers, buttons, fans, and ticket stubs. Her motifs range from the fetish to the everyday object. In 1978, Saar was one of a select group of American female artists to be discussed in a documentary film entitled *Spirit Catcher: The Art of Betye Saar.* It appeared on WNET-13 in New York as part of "The Originals: Women in Art" series.

Saar studied at Pasadena City College, University of California where she received a B.F.A. in 1949, as well as Long Beach State College, University of Southern California, San Fernando State College, Valley State College, California, and the American Film Institute. She was a teacher-in-residence at Hayward State College, California. She has exhibited throughout the United States. Her works are included in the collections of the Boston Museum of Fine Art; Hirshhorn Museum and Sculpture Garden, Washington, D.C.; Los Angeles County Museum; and the Philadelphia Museum of Art, among others. In 1994, Saar's works were displayed with over 200 other artists at Brazil's Bienal, a biannual art exhibition featuring the works of artists from over 71 countries. Notable works include: *The Vision of El Cremo; Africa; The View from the Sorcerer's Window;* and *House of Gris Gris,* a mixed-media installation created with daughter Alison Saar.

Synthia Saint James (1949–)
Illustrator, Author

Saint James was born in 1949 in Los Angeles, California. She is a self-taught illustrator and author whose work has been exhibited internationally in Stockholm, Sweden, Paris, France, Seoul, Korea, Quebec, Canada, Los Angeles, New York City, and Salt Lake City, as well as the National Museum of Women in the Arts, Washington D.C.

Saint James's colorful figurative images celebrate the daily life and culture of African Americans in her paintings. The stylized silhouettes take shape through the use of broad sweeps of contrasting color. Her pictures grace the covers of over 50 books including those by Terry McMillan, Iyanla Vanzant, and Alice Walker. Dozens of corporations, organizations, and individuals have commissioned Saint James to design work for their licensed products, event, and commemorative posters. The United States Postal Service, commissioned her to create the first Kwanzaa Stamp, made available on October 22, 1997.

Saint James is an award-winning author and illustrator of children's books including *The Gifts of Kwanzaa, Sunday, It's Kwanzaa Time!.* She received a 1997 Coretta Scott King Honor for her illustrations in *Neeny Coming. . . Neeny Going.* Saint James's eighth children's book *No Mirrors In My Nana's House* (1998) was written by Ysaye Barnwell, and her ninth book *Girls Together* (1999) was written by Sherley Anne Williams.

Augusta Savage (1900–1962)
Sculptor

A leading sculptor who emerged during the Harlem Renaissance, Augusta Savage was one of the artists represented in the first all-black exhibition in America, sponsored by the Harmon Foundation at International House in New York City. In 1939, her symbolic group piece *Lift Every Voice and Sing* was shown at the New York World's Fair Community Arts Building.

Savage was born in Green Cove Springs, Florida, on February 29, 1900, and studied at Tallahassee State Normal School at Cooper Union in New York City, as well as France as the recipient of Carnegie and Rosenwald fellowships. She was the first African American to win acceptance in the National Association of Women Painters and Sculptors.

In the 1930s she taught in her own School of Arts and Crafts in Harlem and helped many of her students take advantage of Works Progress Administration projects for artists during the Depression. Notable works include: *Lift Every Voice and Sing; The Chase; Black Women; Lenore; Gamin; Marcus Garvey;* and *W.E.B. Du Bois.*

Charles Searles (1937–)
Painter, Educator

Born in Philadelphia, Pennsylvania, on July 11, 1937, Searles studied at Fleicher Art Memorial, and the Penn Academy of Fine Arts (1968 to 1972). His works have been exhibited at the Dallas, the Brooklyn, Philadelphia, Reading, High, Milwaukee, Whitney, and Harlem Studio Museums; Columbia University; and many other galleries and museums.

Searles has traveled to Europe and Africa. He has taught at the Philadelphia College of Art, the Philadelphia Museum Art Studio Classes, University of the Arts, Brooklyn Museum Art School, Jersey State College, and Bloomfield College in New Jersey.

He was commissioned to execute several murals including the U.S. General Service Administration interior; *Celebration* (1976) for the William J. Green Federal Building; *Play Time* (1976) for the Malory Public Playground; Newark, New Jersey Amtrak Station wall sculpture (1985); and the Dempsey Service Center wall sculpture (1989).

His works are in the collections of the Smithsonian Institute, Washington, D.C.; New York State Office

Augusta Savage's sculpture *Lift Every Voice and Sing* (1939) being installed.

Building; Philadelphia Museum of Art; Federal Railroad Administration; Ciba-Gigy, Inc.; Dallas Museum of Art; Montclair Art Museum; Phillip Morris, Inc.; and Howard University.

The human figure, color, and rhythmic patterns dominate his paintings. Notable works include: *Cultural Mix; Rhythmic Forms; Play Time; Strutting;* and *Celebration.*

Lorna Simpson (1960–)
Photographer, Conceptual Artist

Simpson was born in Brooklyn, New York, on August 13, 1960, and attended the School of Visual Arts, where she earned her B.F.A. in 1982. She received her M.F.A. from the University of California, San Diego, in 1985. Her works are concerned with language and words, especially those with double and contradictory meanings, as well as stereotypes and cliches about gender and race.

Simpson is among the new young photographers who have broken into the mainstream of conceptual based art. Her work has been shown at the Museum of Modern Art and the Wadsworth Atheneum. She has served on the advisory board of the New Museum, New York City, and also on the board of Artists Space.

In 1990, Simpson became the first African American woman to have her work featured in the Venice Biennale, an international art exhibition. Her work has been shown in exhibitions throughout the United States, Europe, Latin America, and Japan. Several institutions have offered exhibitions of her work, among them the Ansel Adams Center in San Francisco, the Whitney Museum of American Art in New York City, and the

Milwaukee Art Museum. Her works have also been exhibited in the Just Above Mid-Town Gallery, Mercer Union (Toronto), and the Wadsworth Atheneum Museum's Matrix Gallery. Notable works include: *Outline; Guarded Conditions; Easy for Who to Say; Flipside; Bio; Untitled ("prefer/refuse/decide");* and the interactive multimedia composition *Five Rooms.*

Norma Merrick Sklarek (1928–)
Architect

Sklarek was born on April 15, 1928, in New York City, and received a B.A. in architecture from the Barnard College of Columbia University in 1950. In 1954, she became the first African American woman to be licensed as an architect in the United States. In 1966, Sklarek became the first African American woman to be named a fellow of the American Institute of Architects.

Sklarek's career began at Skidmore, Owens, Merrill, where she worked as an architect from 1955 until 1960. She also served on the faculty of New York City College from 1957 until 1960. In 1960, she took a position with

Norma Sklarek.

Gruen and Associates in Los Angeles, California, where she worked for the next 20 years. She also served as a faculty member at UCLA from 1972 until 1978. Sklarek became vice president of Welton Becket Associates in 1980 and worked there until 1985. From 1985 until 1989, Sklarek was a partner in the firm Siegel, Sklarek, and Diamond, the largest female-owned architectural firm in the United States. In 1989, she began working as a principal for The Jerde Partnership before retiring in 1992.

Among the notable structures designed by Sklarek are the U.S. Embassy in Tokyo; Courthouse Center, Columbus, Indiana; City Hall, San Bernardino, California; and Terminal One, Los Angeles International Airport.

Moneta Sleet Jr. (1926–1996)
Photographer

Moneta Sleet was born on February 14, 1926, in Owensboro, Kentucky. He studied at Kentucky State College under Dr. John Williams, a family friend, dean of the college, and an accomplished photographer. In 1947, he received his BA from Kentucky State College. He earned a master's degree from New York University in 1950.

Sleet taught photography at Maryland State College from 1948 until 1949. He moved to New York City in 1950 to work as a sportswriter for *Amsterdam News.* He also worked as a photographer for *Our World* from 1951 until 1955. Sleet moved to Chicago and took a job with the Johnson Publishing Company, where he was staff photographer for *Ebony* and *Jet* magazines.

In 1969, Moneta Sleet became the first African American to win a Pulitzer Prize in Photography. Although employed by *Ebony,* he was eligible for the award because his photograph of Coretta Scott King at her husband's funeral was picked up by a wire service and published in daily newspapers throughout the country. He also received awards from the Overseas Press Club of America, National Urban League, and the National Association of Black Journalists. In 1989, the University of Kentucky inducted Sleet into its Kentucky Journalism Hall of Fame.

His work has appeared in several group exhibitions at museums including the Studio Museum in Harlem and Metropolitan Museum of Art. In 1970, solo exhibitions were held at the City Art Museum of St. Louis and at the Detroit Public Library. Other solo exhibitions of Sleet's work have been held at the New York Public

Library, Newark Public Library, Chicago Public Library Cultural Center, Milwaukee Public Library, Martin Luther King Jr. Memorial Library, Albany Museum of Art, New York State Museum, and the Schomberg Center for Research in Black Culture.

Sleet was a member of the NAACP and the Black Academy of Arts and Letters. He died in New York City on September 30, 1996.

Willi Smith (1948–1987)
Fashion Designer

Born on February 29, 1948, in Philadelphia, Pennsylvania, Willi Smith studied at the Parsons School of Design on a scholarship and became popular during the 1960s. He was known for his designer wear in natural fibers that were cross-seasonal and affordable. His clothes were sportswear pieces that mixed readily with Willi-wear from previous years as well as other clothes. Smith was innovative in mixing and matching plaids, stripes, and vivid colors. He designed for both men and women. Smith had his clothes manufactured in India, traveling there several times a year to supervise the making of his functional and practical collections.

Fashion designer, Willi Smith.

In 1983 Willi Smith received the Coty American Fashion Critics Award for Women's Fashion. He died in 1987.

Nelson Stevens (1938–)
Muralist, Painter, Graphic Artist

Born in Brooklyn, New York, in 1938, Stevens received a B.F.A. from Ohio University in 1962 and a M.F.A. from Kent State University in 1969.

An active member of AFRI-COBRA—a group exploring the aesthetics of African American art, which includes the use of the human figure, bright colors, African inspired patterns, text, letters and other symbols relating to the African American experience. He is also a member of the National Conference of Artists.

Stevens is a professor of art at the University of Massachusetts in Amherst, Massachusetts. He has exhibited at the National Center of Afro-American Artists, Boston; The Studio Museum in Harlem; Howard University; and Kent State University. Notable works include: *Madonna and Child*, for a 1993 calendar; *Art in the Service of the Lord; Malcolm—King of Jihad;* and *A Different Kind of Man.*

Henry Ossawa Tanner (1859–1937)
Painter

Alain Locke called Henry Ossawa Tanner the leading talent of the "journeyman period" of African American art. Born in Pittsburgh on June 21, 1859, Tanner chose painting rather than the ministry as a career, overcoming the objections of his father, an African Methodist Episcopal bishop. After attending the Pennsylvania Academy of Fine Arts, he taught at Clark University in Atlanta while working as a photographer. Some of Tanner's most compelling work, such as *The Banjo Lesson* (1890), was produced during this period in which he emerged as the most promising African American artist of his day.

In 1891, Tanner abandoned black subject matter and left the United States for Paris, where he concentrated on religious themes. In 1896, his *Daniel in the Lion's Den*, a mixture of realism and mystical symbolism, won honorable mention at the Paris Salon. The following year, the French government purchased his *Resurrection of Lazarus*. In 1900, Tanner received the Medal of Honor at the Paris Exposition and the Lippincott Prize.

Tanner died in 1937. In 1996, his painting *Sand Dunes at Sunset, Atlantic City*, became the first painting by an African American to be added to the permanent collection of the White House. Other notable

Henry O. Tanner's *Sand Dunes at Sunset, Atlantic City,* became the first painting by an African American artist to become a permanent part of the White House collection in 1996.

works include: *Flight into Egypt; The Annunciation; Thankful Poor;* and *The Sabot Makers.*

Alma W. Thomas (1891–1978)
Painter

Born in Columbus, Georgia, in 1891, Alma Thomas moved to Washington, D.C., as a teenager. She enrolled at Howard University and was the first graduate of its art department in 1924. In 1934 she received her M.A. from Columbia University and later studied at American University.

Retiring after a 38-year teaching career in public schools, Thomas concentrated solely on her painting. She is best known for her non-objective, mosaic-like works that emphasize color, pattern, and space. The optical relationships of her colors in flat shapes create three-dimensional forms, enlivening the painted surfaces with movement and pulsating rhythms. It is this later work that brought her many prizes and awards.

Her works are in the collections of the National Museum of American Art at the Smithsonian Institute, Howard University, Concord Gallery, Metropolitan Museum, La Jolla Museum, and private corporations.

Notable works include: *The Eclipse; Arboretum Presents White Dogwood; Elysian Fields; Red Sunset;* and *Old Pond Concerto.*

Bob Thompson (1937–1966)
Painter

Born in Louisville, Kentucky, in 1937, Thompson studied at the Boston Museum School in 1955 and later spent three years at the University of Louisville. In 1960, Thompson participated in a two-person show at Zabriskie Gallery and two years later received a John Hay Whitney Fellowship. For the next several years, Thompson had several one-person exhibitions in New York and Chicago. His work was also seen in Spain. He died in Rome at the age of 29.

Thompson's work is in several permanent collections around the country including the Chrysler Museum in Provincetown, Massachusetts. In 1970, Thompson's work was featured in the *African-American Artist* exhibition at the Boston Museum of Fine Arts. Notable works include: *Ascension to the Heavens; Untitled Diptych; The Dentist* (1963); and *Expulsion and Nativity* (1964).

James Van Der Zee (1886–1983)
Photographer

James Augustus Joseph Van Der Zee was born on June 29, 1886, in Lenox, Massachusetts. His parents had moved there from New York in the early 1880s after serving as maid and butler to Ulysses S. Grant. The second of six children, James grew up in a family filled with creative people. Everybody painted, drew, or played an instrument, so it was not considered out of the ordinary when, upon receiving a camera in 1900, Van Der Zee became interested in photography.

By 1906 Van Der Zee had moved to New York, married, and took odd jobs to support his growing family. In 1907, he moved to Phoetus, Virginia, where he worked in the dining room of the Hotel Chamberlin in Old Point Comfort, Virginia. During this time he also worked as a photographer on a part-time basis. In 1909, he returned to New York.

By 1915, Van Der Zee had his first photography job as assistant in the Gertz Department Store in Newark, New Jersey. With the money he saved from this job, he was able to open his own studio in 1916. Over the course of a half century, James Van Der Zee would record the visual history of Harlem. His subjects included Marcus Garvey, Sweet Daddy Grace, Father Divine, Joe Louis, Madame Walker, and many other famous African Americans.

In 1969, the exhibition *Harlem On My Mind* produced by Thomas Hoving, then director of the Metropolitan Museum of Art, brought James Van Der Zee international recognition. He died in 1983.

Laura Wheeler Waring (1887–1948)
Painter

Born in 1887 in Hartford, Connecticut, Waring received her first training at the Pennsylvania Academy of Fine Arts, where she studied for six years. In 1914, she won the Cresson Memorial Scholarship, which enabled her to continue her studies at the Academie de la Grande Chaumiere in Paris.

Waring returned to the United States as an art instructor at Cheyney State Teachers College in Pennsylvania. Eventually she became head of the art department. Her work, particularly portraiture, has been exhibited at several leading American art galleries. In 1927, she received the Harmon Award for achievement in fine art. With Betsy Graves Reyneau, Waring completed a set of 24 re-paintings of a variety of their works titled *Portraits of Outstanding Americans of Negro Origin* for the Harmon Foundation in the 1940s.

Waring was also the director in charge of the African American art exhibits at the Philadelphia Exposition in 1926 and was a member of the national advisory board of Art Movements, Inc. She died in 1948. Notable works include: *Alonzo Aden; W.E.B. Du Bois; James; Weldon Johnson;* and *Mother and Daughter.*

Carrie Mae Weems (1953–)
Photographer, Conceptual Artist

Carrie Mae Weems was born in Portland, Oregon, in 1953. She received her B.F.A. from the California Institute of the Arts in 1981, and a M.F.A. from the University of California at San Diego in 1984. Weems also earned an M.A. in African American folklore from the University of California at Berkeley.

A young artist who explores stereotypes, especially those of African American women. Formerly a photo documentarian, Weems also teaches filmmaking and photography at Hampshire College in Amherst, Massachusetts. Her works are "about race, gender, class and kinship."

She has exhibited throughout the U.S., including shows at the Rhode Island School of Design; Wadsworth Atheneum, Hartford, Connecticut; J. Paul Getty Museum of Art, Malibu, California; Museum of Modern Art, New York; and International Center for Photography, New York. Notable works include: *Mirror, Mirror; Black Woman With Chicken; High Yella Girl; Colored People; Family Pictures and Stories;* and *Ain't Jokin'.*

Edward T. Welburn (1950–)
Automobile Designer

Edward T. Welburn is the chief designer of automobiles for the Oldsmobile Studio of General Motors. In 1992, his design for the Olds Achieva was honored as one of the outstanding designs of the model year.

Welburn began his career with the GM Design Staff as a creative designer in 1972, advancing to the positions of senior creative designer and assistant chief designer. While a member of the GM Design Staff, he designed the Cutlass Supreme, Cutlass Ciera, and the Oldsmobile Calais. In 1989, he moved to the Oldsmobile Studio as chief designer.

In 1985, the Indianapolis 500 pace car was designed by a team on which Welburn served. He was named Alumni of the Year in 1989 by the Howard University Student Association. Welburn won the Industrial Designers Society of America Award for Design Excellence for his part in the design for *Oldsmobile Aerotech* in 1992.

Welburn is a member of The Cabinet and the Founders Society of the Detroit Institute of Arts.

James Lesesne Wells (1902–1993)
Artist

Born on November 2, 1902, in Atlanta, James Lesesne Wells was a pioneer of modern American printmaking. After graduating from high school, Wells lived with relatives in New York City and worked for two years to earn money for college. He studied drawing at the National Academy of Design for one term from 1918 to 1919. Wells spent one year at Lincoln University before transferring to Teachers College at Columbia University in 1923 and earned a B.S. in 1927. He received an M.S. from Columbia in 1938.

Immediately after earning his undergraduate degree, Wells created African American print illustrations for magazines. He also made connections with art dealer and gallery owner J. D. Neumann, who included Wells's work in a 1929 exhibition of *International Modernists*. These projects captured the attention of Howard University's James V. Herring, who invited Wells to join the prestigious school's art faculty that year. Thus began a 39-year career at the university, during which Wells established a graphics arts department and taught several soon to be well-known artists including Charles Alston and Jacob Lawrence. Wells taught clay modeling, ceramics, sculpture, metals, and block printing.

During the Great Depression, Wells devoted himself to printmaking involving African American history and industrial themes. Despite a lack of critical recognition, Wells's work won numerous art competitions throughout the 1930s including the George E. Haynes Prize in 1933. At this time, he also served as the director of a summer art workshop that preceded the Harlem Community Art Center.

After World War II, Wells spent a sabbatical year working at Stanley Hayter's famous Atelier 17, then the most innovative center of etching and printmaking in the United States. Wells continued to teach and win awards for his artwork in the 1950s and 1960s. He moved the Washington, D.C., and joined his brother-in-law Eugene Davidson, president of the local NAACP, in segregation protests. The harassment Wells suffered as a result of his outspokenness—a cross was burned in his yard in 1957—may have inspired the religious themes of much of his work from the era. He took first prize in a religious art exhibition sponsored by the Smithsonian in 1958.

After retiring from Howard in 1968, Wells continued to paint and make prints in the 1980s. In 1980, then-U.S. president Jimmy Carter bestowed Wells with a presidential citation for lifelong contributions to American art. Four years later, Washington, D.C., had a "James L. Wells Day." Designated a "living legend" by the National Black Arts Festival in 1991, Wells's work was featured in a retrospective exhibition by the Harmon Foundation, which had recognized him for his artwork as early as 1916, when he took a first prize in painting and second prize in woodworking. He died of congestive heart failure at the age of 90.

Charles White (1918–1979)
Painter

White was born in 1918 in Chicago and was influenced as a young boy by Alain Locke's critical review of the Harlem Renaissance, *The New Negro*. At the age of 23, White won a Rosenwald Fellowship which enabled him to work in the South for two years, during which time he painted a celebrated mural depicting the black people's contribution to American democracy. It is now the property of the Hampton Institute in Virginia.

The bulk of White's work is done in black-and-white, a symbolic motif which he felt gave him the widest possible purview. Notable works include: *Let's Walk Together; Frederick Douglass Lives Again; Women;* and *Gospel Singer.*

Paul Revere Williams (1894–1980)
Architect

Williams was born in Los Angeles, California, on February 18, 1894, and graduated from the University of California at Los Angeles. He later attended the Beaux Arts Institute of Design in Paris and received honorary degrees from Howard, Lincoln, and Atlanta Universities as well as Hampton Institute.

Williams became a certified architect in 1915. After working for Reginald Johnson and John Austin, he opened his own firm in 1923. Williams designed some 400 homes and a total of three thousand buildings including homes for Cary Grant, Barbara Stanwyk, William Holden, Frank Sinatra, Betty Grable, Bill "Bojangles" Robinson, and Bert Lahr.

In 1926 he was the first African American to become a member of the American Institute of Architects. He served on the National Monument Commission, an appointee of President Calvin Coolidge. Notable works include: *Los Angeles County Airport; Palm Springs Tennis Club;* and *Saks Fifth Avenue at Beverly Hills.* He died on January 23, 1980.

William T. Williams (1942–)
Painter

William T. Williams was born in Cross Creek, North Carolina, on July 17, 1942. He received his B.F.A. from Pratt Institute in 1966 and his M.F.A. from Yale University in 1968.

In 1970, Williams taught painting classes at Pratt Institute and at the School of Fine Arts. Since 1971, he has been a professor of art at City University of New York, Brooklyn College. He also served as a visiting professor of art at Virginia Commonwealth University.

Williams has been the recipient of several awards. In 1992, the Studio Museum in Harlem presented him with its Annual Award for Lifetime Achievement. He was also awarded the Mid-Atlantic Foundation Fellowship in 1994.

Exhibitions of Williams's work have been presented at, among others, the Studio Museum in Harlem, Wadsworth Atheneum, Art Institute of Chicago, and the Whitney Museum of American Art. Notable works include: *Elbert Jackson L.A.M.F. Port II*; *Big Red for N.C.*; and *Buttermilk*.

John Wilson (1922–)
Painter, Printmaker

Born in Boston on April 14, 1922, John Wilson studied at the Boston Museum of Fine Arts; Fernand Leger School, Paris; El Instituto Politecnico, Mexico City; and the Escuela de las Artes del Libro, Mexico City. In 1947, Wilson received a B.A. from Tufts University. He has been a teacher at Boston Museum, Pratt Institute, and Boston University.

His numerous exhibits include: the Albany Institute; the Library of Congress National (and International) Print Exhibit(s); Smith College; Carnegie Institute; and the American International College, Springfield, Massachusetts. His work is represented in the collections of the Museum of Modern Art; Schomburg Collection; Department of Fine Arts, French Government; Atlanta University; and Bezalel Museum, Jerusalem. Notable works include: *Roxbury Landscape* (oil, 1944); *Trabajador* (print, 1951); and *Child with Father* (graphic, 1969).

Wilson created the Dr. Martin Luther King Jr. Monument in Buffalo, New York, in 1983 and the Dr. Martin Luther King Jr. Commemorative Statue at the U.S. Capitol in Washington, D.C. In 1987, he completed the monument *Eternal Presence*, which resides at the Museum of the National Center of Afro-American Artists, Boston, Massachusetts.

Hale Woodruff (1900–1979)
Painter, Muralist

Hale Woodruff's paintings were largely modernist landscapes and formal abstractions, but he has also painted rural Georgia scenes evocative of the "red clay" country. Born in Cairo, Illinois, in 1900, he graduated from the John Herron Art Institute in Indianapolis. Encouraged by a bronze award in the 1926 Harmon Foundation competition, Woodruff went to Paris to study at both the Academie Scandinave and the Academie Moderne, as well as with Henry Ossawa Tanner.

In 1931, he became art instructor at Atlanta University and later accepted a similar post at New York University. In 1939, he was commissioned by Talladega College for *The Amistad Murals*, an episodic depiction of a slave revolt.

In 1948, Woodruff teamed with Charles Alston to work on the Golden State Mutual Life Insurance Company Murals in California, which presented the contribution of African Americans to the history of the development of California. Woodruff's last mural assignment came in 1950 when he developed the series of mural panels for Atlanta University entitled *The Art of the Negro*. Other notable works include: *Ancestral Remedies*; *The Little Boy*; and *The Amistad Murals*.

Richard Yarde (1939–)
Painter

Richard Yarde was born in Boston, Massachusetts, on October 29, 1939. He studied at the School of the Museum of Fine Arts and at Boston University, where he received a B.F.A. in 1962 and an M.F.A. in 1964. He has taught at Boston University, Wellesley College, Amherst College, Massachusetts College of Art, Mount Holyoke College, and the University of Massachusetts.

Yarde has received numerous awards for his art including Yaddo fellowships in 1964, 1966, and 1970, McDowell Colony awards in 1968 and 1970, and the Blanche E. Colman Award in 1970.

The Boston Museum of Fine Arts, Wadsworth Atheneum, Rose Art Museum, National Museum of African-American Artists, and Studio Museum in Harlem have all exhibited his works. He has held one-person shows at numerous galleries and universities. His works are in many collections, such as the Wadsworth Atheneum in Hartford, Connecticut. Notable works include: *The Stoop*; *Passage Edgar and I*; *The Corner*; *Paul Robeson as Emperor Jones*; *Head and Hands I*; *Josephine's Baffle Triptych*; and *Richard's Cards*.

John Wilson's clay sculpture, *Eternal Presence,* 1987.

◆ MUSEUMS EXHIBITING AFRICAN AMERICAN ART

Alabama

George Washington Carver Museum
1212 Old Montgomery Rd.
PO Drawer 10
Tuskegee Institute, AL 36087–0010
(334) 727–3200
Fax:(334) 727–4597

Arkansas

Art and Science Center for Southeast Arkansas
701 Main St.
Pine Bluff, Arkansas 71601
(870) 536–3375

California

African American Historical and Cultural Society
Fort Mason Center Bldg. C, No. 165
San Francisco, CA 94123
(415) 441–0640
Fax: (415) 441–2847

African American Museum and Library at Oakland
125 14th St.
Oakland, CA 94612
(510) 238–4980
Fax:(510) 238–2232
<www.oaklandlibrary.org/AAMLO/>

California Afro-American Museum
Exposition Park
600 State Dr.
Los Angeles, CA 90037
(213) 744–7432
Fax:(213)744–2050
<www.caam.ca.gov>

DeYoung Museum
Golden Gate Park
San Francisco, CA 94118
(415) 863–3330
<www.thinker.org/fam/>

Ebony Museum of Art
30 Jack London Village, Stes. 208 and 209
Oakland, CA 94607
(510) 763–0745

Museum in Black
4331 Degnan Blvd.
Los Angeles, CA 90008
(213) 292–9528

Museum of African-American Art
4005 S. Crenshaw Blvd., 3rd Fl.
Los Angeles, CA 90008
(323) 294–7071

Colorado

Black American West Museum and Heritage Center
3091 California St.
Denver, CO 80207
(303) 292–2566
Fax: (303) 382–1981
<www.coax.net/people/wf/bawnus.htm>

Connecticut

Connecticut Afro-American Historical Society
444 Orchard St.
New Haven, CT 06511
(203) 776–4907

Delaware

Afro-American Historical Society of Delaware
512 E. 4th St.
Wilmington, DE 19801
(302) 478–5591

District of Columbia

Anacostia Museum and Center for African American History and Culture
900 Jefferson Dr., SW
Room 1130
Washington, DC 20560

Bethune Museum-Archives, National Historic Society
1318 Vermont Ave., NW
Washington, DC 20005
(202) 673–2402
Fax:(202) 673–2414

Smithsonian Institute, National Museum of African Art
950 Independence Ave., SW
Washington, DC 20560
(202) 357–4600
Fax:(202) 357–4879
<www.si.edu/nmasa>

Florida

African American Museum of the Arts
325 S. Clara Ave.
Deland, FL 32720
(386) 736–4004

Appleton Museum of Art/The Appleton Cultural Center
4333 NE. Silver Springs Blvd.
Ocala, FL 34470
Fax: (352) 236–7136
<www.appletonmuseum.org>

Black Archives Research Center and Museum, Florida A and M University
c/o Florida A and M University
PO Box 809Tallahassee, FL 32307
(850) 599–3020
Fax: (850) 561–2604

Black Heritage Museum
PO Box 570327
Miami, FL 33257–0327
(305) 252–3535
Fax: (305) 252–3535

Museum of African-American Art
1305 N. Florida Ave.
Tampa, FL 33602
(813) 272–2466
Fax: (813) 272–2325

Georgia

Apex Museum
135 Auburn Ave., NE
Atlanta, GA 30303
(404) 521–2739
Fax: (404) 523–3248
<www.apexmuseum.org>

Harriet Tubman African American Museum
340 Walnut St.
Macon, GA 31201
(478) 743–8544
Fax: (478) 743–9063
<www.tubmanmuseum.com>

High Museum of Art
1280 Peachtree St.
Atlanta, GA 30309
(404) 733–4422
Fax: (404) 733–4529
<www.high.org>

King-Tisdell Cottage of Black History Museum
502 E. Harris St.
Savannah, GA 31401
(912) 234–8000
Fax: (912) 234–8100
<www.kingtisdell.org>

Uncle Remus Museum
PO Box 184
Eatonton, GA 31024
(706) 485–6856

U.S. National Park Service, Martin Luther King Jr. National Historic Site and Preservation District
501 Auburn Ave., NE
Atlanta, GA 30312
(404) 331–5190

Illinois

Afro-American Genealogical and Historical Society, Du Sable Museum of African American History
740 E. 56th Pl.
Chicago, IL 60637
(773)947–0600
Fax: (773) 947–0677
<www.dusable.org>

Art Institute of Chicago
111 S. Michigan Ave.
Chicago, IL 60603
(312) 443–3600
Fax: (312) 443–0849
<www.artic.edu/aic/>

Indiana

Indiana University Art Museum
1133 E. 7th St.
Bloomington, IN 47405–7309
(812) 855–5445
Fax:(812) 855–1023
<www.indiana.edu/~iuam>

Kansas

First National Black Historical Society of Kansas
601 N. Water
Wichita, KS 67201
(316) 262–7651
Fax: (316) 265–6953

Maryland

Baltimore's Black American Museum
1765 Carswell St.
Baltimore, MD 21218
(410) 243–9600

Banneker-Douglass Museum
84 Franklin St.
Annapolis, MD 20401
(401) 974–2893
Fax: (401) 974–2553

Great Blacks in Wax Museum
1601–03 E. North Ave.
Baltimore, MD 21213
(410) 563–3404
Fax:(410) 675–5040
<www.gbiw.org>

Maryland Museum of African Art
5430 Vantage Point Rd.
Columbia, MD 21044–0105
(410) 730–7105
Fax:(410) 715–3047

Michigan

Charles H. Wright Museum of African-American History
315 E. Warren Ave.
Detroit, MI 48201–1443
(313) 494–5800
<www.maah-detroit.org>

Detroit Institute of Arts
5205 Woodward Ave.
Detroit, MI 48202
(313) 833–7900
<www.dia.org>

Motown Historical Museum
2648 West Grand Blvd.
Detroit, MI 48208
(313) 875–2264

University of Michigan Art Museum
525 S. State St.
Ann Arbor, MI 48109
(734) 764–0395
<www.umich.edu/˜umma/>

Mississippi

Smith Robertson Museum and Cultural Center
528 Bloom St.
Jackson, MS 39202
(601) 960–1457
Fax: (601) 960–2070

Missouri

Black Archives of Mid-America
2033 Vine St.
Kansas City, MO 64108
(816) 483–1300
Fax:(816) 483–1341
<www.blackarchives.org>

Nebraska

Great Plains Black Museum
2213 Lake St.
Omaha, NE 68110
(402) 345–2212
Fax: (402) 344–7255

New Jersey

African Art Museums of the SMA Fathers
23 Bliss Ave.
Tenafly, NJ 07670
(201) 567–0450
Fax: (201) 541–1280
<www.smafathers.org>

Afro-American Historical Society Museum
1841 Kennedy Blvd.
Jersey City, NJ 07305
(201)547–5262

Newark Museum
49 Washington St.
Newark, NJ 07101–0540
(973) 596–6550
Fax: (973) 642–0459

New York

African-American Institute Museum
380 Lexington Ave.
New York, NY 10168
(212) 949–5666
Fax:(212) 682–6174

African American Museum of Nassau County
110 Franklin St.
Hempstead, NY 11550
(516) 572–0730

Brooklyn Museum of Art
200 Eastern Parkway
Brooklyn, NY 11238–6052
(718) 638–5000
Fax:(718) 638–3731
<www.brooklynart.org/>

El Museo Francisco Oller Y Diego Rivera
91 Allen St.
Buffalo, NY 14202
(716) 884–9693

Studio Museum in Harlem
144 W. 125th St.
New York, NY 10027
(212) 864–4500
Fax:(212) 666–5753
<www.studentmuseuminharlem.ark>

North Carolina

Duke University Museum of Art
PO Box 90732
Durham, NC 27708–0732
Fax:(919) 681–8624
<www.duke.edu/web/dumal/>

NCCU Art Museum
PO Box 19555
Durham, NC 27707
(919) 560–6211
Fax:(919) 560–5012

Ohio

African American Museum
1765 Crawford Rd.
Cleveland, OH 44106
(216) 791–1700
Fax: (216) 791–1774

Allen Memorial Art Museum
Oberlin College
Oberlin, OH 44074
(440) 775–8665
<www.oberlin.edu/~allenart/>

Cincinnati Art Museum
953 Eden Park Dr.
Cincinnati, OH 45202–1596
(513) 639–2995
Fax:(513) 721–0129
<www.cincinnatiartmuseum.org>

National Afro-American Museum and Cultural Center
1350 Brush Row Rd.
PO Box 578
Xenia, OH 45384
(937) 376–4944
Fax: (937) 376–2007
<www.ohiohistory.org>

Oklahoma

Kirkpatrick Center Museum Complex
2100 N.E. 52nd
Oklahoma City, OK 73111
(405) 427–5461
Fax: (405) 424–5106
<www.omniplex.org>

Pennsylvania

African American Museum in Philadelphia
701 Arch St.
Philadelphia, PA 19106
(215) 574–0380
Fax: (215) 236–4255
<www.aampmuseum.org>

South Carolina

Avery Research Center for Afro-American History and Culture
125 Bull St.
College of Charleston
Charleston, SC 29424
(803) 953–7609
<www.cofc.edu/~averyrsc>

I.P. Stanback Museum and Planetarium
South Carolina State University
300 College St., NE
Orangeburg, SC 29117
(803) 536–7174
Fax: (803) 536–8309

Mann-Simons Cottage: Museum of African-American Culture
1403 Richland St.
Columbia, SC 29201
(803) 252–1770

Rice Museum
Intersection of Front and Screven Sts.
PO Box 902
Georgetown, SC 29442
(843) 546–7423
Fax:(843) 545–9093
<www.thestrand.com/rice>

Tennessee

Chattanooga African American Museum
200 E. Martin Luther King Jr. Blvd.
Chattanooga, TN 37203
(423) 266–8658

Texas

African American Museum
3536 Grant Ave.
Dallas, TX 75315
(214) 565–9026
Fax:(214) 421–8204

Utah

Utah Museum of Fine Arts
410 Campus Center Dr.
Salt Lake City, UT 84122
(801) 581–7332
Fax:(801) 585–5198
<www.utah.edu/umfa>

Virginia

Alexandria Black History Resource Center
638 N. Alfred St.
Alexandria, VA 22314
(703) 838–4356
Fax: (703) 706–3999

Black History Museum and Cultural Center
00 Clay St.
Richmond, VA 23219
(804) 780–9093
Fax: (804) 780–9107

Hampton University Museum
Hampton University
Hampton, VA 23668
(757) 727–5308
<www.hamptonu.edu>

Harrison Museum of African American Culture
523 Harrison Ave., NW
Roanoke, VA 24016
(540) 345–4818

♦ INSTITUTIONS SPECIALIZING IN EXHIBITING AFRICAN AMERICAN ART

California

Wilson Brown Gallery
255 G St., Ste. 147
San Diego, CA 92101
(619) 232–8377

Shimawari Gallery
4176 Piedmont Ave.
Oakland, CA 94611
(510) 923–1222
Fax: (510) 923–1104

Steve Turner Gallery
275 S. Beverly Dr. (Suite 200)
Beverly Hills, CA 90212
(310) 271–3721
Fax: (310) 271–3741

Colorado

Mosadi's Collection
Denver, CO 80206
(303) 331–0700
Fax: (303) 331–0300

Connecticut

Artists Collective, Inc.
1200 Albany Ave.
Hartford, CT 06112
(860) 527–3205

District of Columbia

Evans-Tibbs Collection
1910 Vermont Ave., NW
Washington, DC 20001
(202) 234–8164

Howard University Gallery of Art
2455 6th St., NW
Washington, DC 20059
(202) 806–7070
Fax:(202) 806–6503

Sign of the Times Cultural Workshop and Gallery, Inc.
605 56th St., NE
Washington, DC 20019
(202) 399–3400
Fax: (202) 399–5460

Florida

African American Caribbean Cultural Center
1601 S. Andrews Ave.
Ft. Lauderdale, FL 33316
(945) 467–5881

Gallery Antiqua
5138 Biscayne Blvd.
Miami, FL 33137
(305) 759–5355

Georgia

Clark Atlanta University Art Galleries
223 James P. Brawley Dr., SW
Atlanta, GA 30314
(404) 880–6102
<www.cau.edu/artgalleries>

Hammonds House Galleries and Resource Center
503 Peeples St., SW
Atlanta, GA 30310
(404) 752–8730

Herndon Home
587 University Pl., NW
Atlanta, GA 30314
(404) 581–9813
Fax: (404) 538–0239

Martin Luther King Jr. Center, Cultural Affairs Program
449 Auburn Ave., NE
Atlanta, GA 30312
(404) 524–1956
Fax: (404) 526–8901

McIntosh Gallery
One Virginia Hill
587 Virginia Ave.
Atlanta, GA 30306
(404) 892–4023
<www.artnet.com/mcintosh.html>

National Black Arts Festival
236 Forsyth St., Ste. 405
Atlanta, GA 30303
(404) 730–7315

Louisiana

The Neighborhood Gallery
2135 Soniat St.
New Orleans, LA 70115
(504) 891–5573

Stella Jones Gallery
Bank One Center, Place St. Charles
201 St. Charles Ave.
New Orleans, LA 70170
(504) 568–9050
Fax: (504) 568–0840

Maryland

African-American Visual Arts
3402 Millford Mill Rd.
Baltimore, MD 21244
(410) 521–0660
Fax: (410) 521–4053

Alliance of African-American Artists
P.O. Box 1764
Randallstown, MD 2133
(443) 414–1108
<www.artists4a.com>

Morgan State University Gallery of Art
Carl Murphy Fine Arts Center
Morgan State University
1700 E. Coldspring Ln.
Baltimore, MD 21239
(410) 319–3333

Massachusetts

National Center of Afro-American Artists
122 Elm Hill Ave.
Dorchester, MA 02121
(617) 442–8614

Wendell Street Gallery
17 Wendel St.
Cambridge, MA 02138
(617) 864–9294

Michigan

Art on the Avenue
19132 Livernois
Detroit, MI 48221
(313) 863–4221

Black Folk Arts
425 W. Margaret
Detroit, MI 48203
(313) 865–4546

Creative Arts and Frames
1539 East Lafayette Ave.
Detroit, MI 48207
(313) 567–0795

Dell Pryor Gallery
639 Beaubien
Detroit, MI 48226
(313) 963–5977

Detroit Audio and Art
13110 West McNichols
Detroit, MI 48235
(313) 862–8227

Donna Anderson Gallery
135 Pierce
Birmingham, MI 48009
(248) 593–6892

Eric's I've Been Framed
16525 Livernois
Detroit, MI 48221
(313) 861–9263

George R. N'Namidi Gallery
66 East Forest
Detroit, MI 48201
(313) 831–8700

Hi-Line Gallery
Northland Mall
21500 Northwestern Highway
Southfield, MI 48075
(248) 552–1155

J. Rainey Gallery
1440 Service
Detroit, MI 48207
(313) 259–2257

Jo's Gallery
19376 Livernois
Detroit, MI 48221
(313) 864–1401

Linda's Framework Gallery
180 West Nine Mile Road
Ferndale, MI 48220
(248) 546–0987

Sherry Washington Gallery
1274 Library
Detroit, MI 48226
(313) 961–4500

Umoja Fine Arts
16250 Northland Drive
Southfield, MI 48075
(248) 552–1070

Your Heritage House
110 E. Ferry
Detroit, MI 48202
(313) 871–1667

Minnesota

Pillsbury House/Cultural Arts
3501 Chicago Ave. S.
Minneapolis, MN 55407
(612) 824–0708
Fax: (612) 827–5818

Missouri

Vaughn Cultural Center
524 North Grand
St. Louis, MO 63120
(314) 535–9227

New Jersey

Atrium Gallery
Morris County Administration and Records Bldg.,
　5th Floor
Court Street
Morristown, NJ 07960
(973) 540–0615

Harambee Gallery
4 Midland Ave.
Montclair, NJ 07042
(973) 744–9033

VER
PO Box 493
Cherry Hill, NJ 08003
(856) 346–3131
Fax: (856) 346–3251

New York

African-American Cultural Center of Buffalo
350 Masten Ave.
Buffalo, NY 14209
(716) 884–2013
Fax: (716) 885–2590

African-American Culture and Arts Network
2090 Adam Clayton Powell Jr. Blvd.
New York, NY 10027
(212) 749–0827

Archibald Arts
602 Tenth Ave. #2RS
New York, NY 10036
(212) 247–5087
Fax: (212) 247–5387

Bedford-Stuyvesant Restoration Center for Arts and Culture
1368 Fulton, Ste. 4G
Brooklyn, NY 11216
(718) 636–6948
Fax: (718) 636–6902

Bill Hodges Gallery
24 W. 57th St., 6th Fl.
New York, NY 10019
(212) 333–2640
Fax: (212) 333–2644
<www.Billhodgesgallery.com>

Black Filmmaker Foundation
670 Broadway, Ste. 304
New York, NY
(212) 253–1690
Fax:(212) 253–1689

Black Spectrum Theater Co.
Roy Wilkens Park
119–07 Merrick Blvd.
Jamaica, NY 11434
(718) 723–1800
<www.blackspectrum.com>

The Cinque Gallery
560 Broadway (Suite 504)
New York, NY 10012
(212) 966–3464

Community Folk Art Gallery
2223 Genessee St.
Syracuse, NY 13210
(315) 424–8487
Fax: (315) 424–8487

Grinnell Gallery
800 Riverside Dr. (Suite 5E)
New York, NY 10032
(212) 927–7941

Harlem School of the Arts
645 St. Nicholas Ave.
New York, NY 10030
(212) 926–4100
<www.erols.com/nsoa>

Hatch-Billops Collection, Inc.
491 Broadway
New York, NY 10012
(212) 966–3231
Fax: (212) 966–3231

International Agency for Minority Artists Affairs Inc.
163 W. 125th St.
New York, NY 10027
(212) 749–5298
<www.harlem.cc>

June Kelly Gallery
591 Broadway, 3rd Fl.
New York, NY 10012
(212) 226–1660
<www.junekellygallery.com>

Martha Henry, Inc. Fine Art
400 E. 57th St. (Suite 7L)
New York, NY 100022
(212) 308–2759
Fax: (212) 754–4419

Michael Rosenfeld Gallery
24 W. 57th St., 7th Fl.
New York, NY 10019
(212) 247–0082
Fax: (212) 247–0402
<michaelrosenfeldglry.com>

Peg Alston Fine Arts
407 Central Park W. (Suite 6C)
New York, NY 10025
(212) 662–5522
Fax: (212) 662–7495

Schomburg Center For Research in Black Culture
515 Malcolm X Blvd.
New York, NY 10037–1801
(212) 491–2200
<www.nypl.org/research/sc/>

Sragow Gallery
73 Spring St.
New York, NY 10012
(212) 219–1793

UFA Gallery
508–526 W. 26th St., #317
New York, NY 10001
(212) 633–2735
Fax: (212) 367–8166
<www.ufagallery.com>

North Carolina

African-American Atelier
Greensboro Cultural Center
200 N. Davie St.
Greensboro, NC 27401
(336) 333–6885

Afro-American Cultural Center
401 N. Meyers St.
Spirit Square
Charlotte, NC 28202
(704) 374–1565
Fax: (704) 374–9273

Biggers Art Sales Traveling Gallery
1404 N. Oakwood St.
Gastonia, NC 28052
(704) 867–4525

Black Artists Guild
400 N. Queen St.
P.O. Box 2162
Kinston, NC 28501
(919) 523–0003
Fax: (919) 523–1732

Cooper Associates
626 Fearrington Post
Fearrington Village, NC 27312
(919) 542–3457
Fax: (919) 542–5839

Diggs Art Gallery
Winston-Salem State University
601 Martin Luther King Jr. Dr.
Winston-Salem, NC 27110
(336) 750–2458

Huff's Art Studio
2846 Patterson Ave.
Winston-Salem, NC 27105
(336) 724–7581

St. Augustine's College Art Gallery
Dept. of Art
Saint Augustine's College
Raleigh, NC 27611
(919) 516–4026

Shaw University Art Center
Shaw University Dept. of Art
Raleigh, NC 27602
(919) 546–8420

Weatherspoon Art Gallery
North Carolina A and T State University
P.O. Box 26170
Greensboro, NC 27402–6170
(336) 334–5770

Ohio

Afro-American Cultural Center
Cleveland State University
Black Studies Program
2121 Euclid Ave., UC 103
Cleveland, OH 44115
(216) 687–3655
Fax: (216) 687–5446

Arts Consortium
1515 Linn St.
Cincinnati, OH 45214
(513) 381–0645
Fax: (513) 345–3743

Karamu House
2355 E. 89th St.
Cleveland, OH 44106
(216) 795–7070
Fax: (216) 795–7073
<www.karamu.com>

Malcolm Brown Gallery
20100 Chagrin Blvd.
Shaker Heights, Ohio 44122
(216) 751–2955
<www.malcolmbrowngallery>

Resident Art and Humanities Consortium
1515 Linn St.
Cincinnati, OH 45214
(513) 381–0645

Oklahoma

NTU Art Association
2100 N.E. 52nd St.
Oklahoma City, OK 73111
(405) 424–1655

Pennsylvania

African Cultural Art Forum
237 S. 60th St.
Philadelphia, PA 19139
(215) 476–0680

Minority Arts Resource Council
1421 W. Girard Ave.
Philadelphia, PA 19130
(215) 236–2688
Fax: (215) 236–4255

Rhode Island

Rhode Island Black Heritage Society
202 Westminster St.
Providence, RI 02903
(401) 751–3490
Fax: 751–0040

Tennessee

Blues City Cultural Center
205 N. Main St.
Memphis, TN 38103
(901) 523–3031
Fax: (901) 525–7369

Carl Van Vechten Gallery of Fine Arts
Fisk University
Dr. D. B. Todd Blvd. and Jackson St. N.
Nashville, TN 37203
(615) 329–8720

Memphis Black Arts Alliance
985 S. Bellevue
Memphis, TN 38106
(901) 948–9522
Fax: (901) 948–9936
<www.webspawner.com/users/mbaa/>

Tennessee State University Institute for African Studies
Tennessee State University
PO Box 828
Nashville, TN 37209
(615) 963–5561

Texas

Artcetera
PO Box 131914
Houston, TX 77219
(713) 270–4319

Black Art Gallery
5408 Almeda Rd.
Houston, TX 77004
(713) 529–7900

Ebony Fine Art Gallery
631 E. Highway 67
Duncanville, TX 75237
(972) 298–4092

27

Science and Technology

◆ Early African American Inventors ◆ Early African American Scientists
◆ African Americans in Medicine ◆ African Americans in Air and Space
◆ Modern Contributions to Science and Technology
◆ Engineers, Mathematicians, Inventors, Physicians, and Scientists

by Kristine Krapp

◆ EARLY AFRICAN AMERICAN INVENTORS

Perhaps in science more than in other areas, African Americans have been afforded few sanctioned opportunities to offer contributions. However, will and intelligence helped individuals bring their ideas and dreams into the light. The Industrial Revolution swept African Americans along just as dramatically as it did the rest of the world. Though not all of them became household names, African Americans have made their mark in science and technology. For example, when Alexander Graham Bell invented the telephone, he chose Lewis Latimer to draft the plans. Later, Latimer became a member of the Edison Pioneers, a group of inventors who worked for Thomas Edison from 1884 to 1912.

One of the earliest African American stars of science was Benjamin Banneker, a free African American who lived in the 1700s. Considered the first African American scientist, Banneker was an expert in mathematics and astronomy, both of which he studied during his friendship with an influential white Quaker neighbor. In 1754, Banneker constructed what has been considered the first grandfather clock made in the United States. Later, Banneker and the Quaker's son were selected to lay the plans for the city of Washington, DC. Thus, not only was Banneker the first African American to receive a presidential appointment, he was one of the first African American civil engineers. In the early 1790s, his almanac—a year-long calendar loaded with weather and astronomical information that was especially useful to farmers—was published with much success. New editions were issued for several years.

In 1790, the U.S. government passed the U.S. Patent Act, legislation that extended patent rights to inventors including free blacks. Slaves would not have this right until the passage of the Fourteenth Amendment. In one of history's most absurd bureaucratic fiats, slaves could neither be granted patents nor could they assign patents to their masters. The underlying theory was that since slaves were not citizens they could not enter into contracts with their owners or the government. As a result, the efforts of slaves were dismissed or credited to their masters. One can only speculate on the extent to which slaves were active in invention. For example, Joe Anderson, a slave, was believed to have played a major role in the creation of a grain harvester, or reaper, that his master Cyrus McCormick was credited

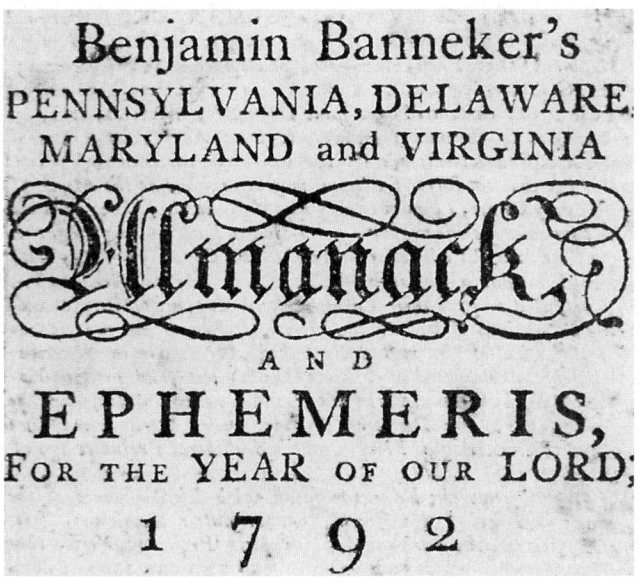

The title page from Benjamin Banneker's 1792 *Almanack*.

with inventing, but available records are insufficient to determine the degree to which Anderson was involved. Similarly, Benjamin Montgomery, a slave belonging to Confederate President Jefferson Davis, is thought to have concocted an improved boat propeller. Since the race of patent-seekers was rarely noted and other African American inventions such as ice cream, created by Augustus Jackson of Philadelphia in 1832, were simply never patented, one cannot be sure how many inventions were made by free blacks either.

The first free blacks to have their inventions recorded were Thomas L. Jennings, whose dry-cleaning methodology received patent protection in 1821, and Henry Blair who invented a seed planter in 1834. Free black Norbert Rillieux patented his sugar refining evaporator, thus revolutionizing the industry. The son of a French planter and a slave woman, Rillieux left his home in New Orleans to study engineering in Paris. After teaching mathematics there and experimenting with steam evaporation, he created his vacuum pan evaporator. With his invention, a single person could do work that once required several people working at once. He returned to the United States and became wealthy as the device was implemented in sugar refineries in his home state and abroad in Cuba and Mexico. However, racial tensions in the United States wore on him, and in 1854, he moved to France, where he spent the remainder of his life.

In 1848, free black Lewis Temple invented the toggle harpoon for killing whales, a major industry at the time. Temple's invention almost completely replaced the type of harpoon formerly used as it greatly diminished the mammal's ability to escape after being hooked. Prior to the Civil War, Henry Boyd created an improved bedframe, and James Forten, one of the few African Americans from that era to gain extreme wealth from an invention, produced a device that helped guide ship sails. He used the money he earned to expand his sail factory.

The Reconstruction era opened the door to creativity that had been suppressed in African Americans. Between 1870 and 1900, a time when nearly 80 percent of African American adults in the United States were illiterate, African Americans were awarded several hundred patents. Elijah McCoy worked as a locomotive fireman on a Michigan line lubricating the hot steam engines during scheduled train stops. After years of work, in 1872, McCoy perfected and patented an automatic lubricator that regularly supplied oil to the engine as the train was in motion. The effect on the increasingly important railway system was profound as conductors were no longer forced to make oiling stops. McCoy adapted his invention for use on ships and in factories. When copycats tried to steal his invention, the phrase "the real McCoy" came into vogue.

In 1884, Granville T. Woods invented an improved steamboiler furnace in his Cincinnati electrical engineering shop. Three years later, Woods patented an induction telegraph or "Synchronous Multiplex Railway Telegraph," that allowed train personnel to communicate with workers on other trains while in motion. He was also responsible for what later became known as the trolley when he produced an overhead electrical power supply system for streetcars and trains. A prolific inventor, Woods, known as "The Black Edison," patented more than 60 valuable inventions including an airbrake, which he eventually sold to George Westinghouse.

Jan Matzeliger came to the United States from South America in 1877. Living in Lynn, Massachusetts, he obtained work in a shoe factory. There he witnessed the tedious process by which shoe soles were attached to shoe uppers by workers known as hand lasters. For six months he secretly labored at inventing a machine to automate the work. Unsatisfied with his original design, he spent several more years tweaking and perfecting his creation so that by the time he was granted a patent in 1883, the equipment was so successful that manufacturers the world over clamored for the gadgetry.

Progress has been a gift from women as well as men. For example, Sarah Goode is credited with creating a folding cabinet bed in 1885; Sarah Boone invented the ironing board in 1892; and photographer Claytonia Dorticus was granted several patents that were concerned with photographic equipment and developing solutions as well as a shoe dye. But Madame C. J. Walker, often regarded only as an entrepreneur, was one of the most successful female inventors. She developed an entire line of hair care products and cosmetics for African Americans, claiming that her first idea had come to her in a dream.

During the next few years, Garrett Morgan patented a succession of products including a hair straightening solution that was still a bestseller in as late as the 1970s; a gas mask, or "breathing device" for firefighters; and an improved traffic signal. Morgan tried to pass himself off as Native American. However, once his identity as an African American was discovered, several of his purchase orders were canceled.

Nonetheless, the early inventors paved the way for future African Americans. These men and women, as well as the countless unknown ones, were forced to endure the byproducts of racism. Whites were oftentimes hesitant to buy African American inventions unless the smell of eventual monetary gains was too strong. McCoy, Woods, and several others died poor, although their creations sold extremely well.

◆ EARLY AFRICAN AMERICAN SCIENTISTS

The contributions of African American scientists are better known than those of African American inventors, partly because of the recognition awarded to George Washington Carver, an agriculturalist, who refused to patent most of his inventions. Born into slavery in 1864, Carver was the first African American to graduate from Iowa Agricultural State College, where he studied botany and agriculture. One year after earning a master's degree, Carver joined Tuskegee Institute's Agriculture Department. In his role as department head, he engineered a number of experimental farming techniques that had practical applications for farmers in the area. Through his ideas, from crop rotation to replenish nutrient-starved soil to his advocacy of peanuts as a cash crop, Carver left an indelible mark in his field. An inventor at heart, he was behind the genesis of innumerable botanical products, by-products, and even recipes. Recognition of his efforts came in several forms including induction into England's Royal Society of Arts and Manufacturing and Commerce in 1916. In 1923, he received an NAACP Spingarn Medal. Six years after his death, in 1949, Carver was the subject of a U.S. postal stamp.

Born approximately ten years before Carver earned his bachelor's degree, Ernest Everett Just was a pioneering marine biologist who had graduated *magna cum laude* from Dartmouth College in 1907. The first-ever recipient of a Spingarn Medal in 1915, his first paper was published as "The Relation of First Cleavage Plane to the Entrance Point of the Sperm" in 1912. The work showed how the location of cell division in the marine worm *Nereis* is determined by the sperm's entry point on an egg. Just did the majority of his research at the Marine Biological Laboratory in Woods Hole, Massachusetts, where he spent many summers. Teaching at Howard for many years, he had a tenuous relationship with the school, paving the way for him to accept an offer to conduct research at the Kaiser Wilhelm Institute for Biology in Berlin, Germany. The first American to be invited to the internationally respected institution and remained there from 1929 to 1933, at which point the Nazi regime was surging to power. Because he preferred working abroad to being shut out of the best laboratories in the United States on the basis of race, Just spent the rest of his career in France, Italy, Spain, and Portugal.

African Americans have had successes in engineering and mathematics as well. In 1876, Edward Bouchet became the first African American to earn a doctorate from a university in the United States, when he acquired a Ph.D. in physics from Yale. In the twentieth century, Elmer Samuel Imes, husband of Harlem Renaissance writer Nella Larsen, received a Ph.D. in physics from the University of Michigan in 1918. In his dissertation, Imes took the works of white scientists Albert Einstein, Ernest Rutherford, and Niels Bohr, one step further, definitively establishing that quantum theory applied to the rotational states of molecules. His efforts would later play a role in space science.

Chemist Percy Julian carved a brilliant career for himself after obtaining a doctorate from Switzerland's University of Vienna in 1931. His specialty was creating synthetic versions of expensive drugs. Much of his work was conducted at his Julian Research Institute in Franklin Park, Illinois. In the 1940s, another scientist, Benjamin Peery, switched his focus from aeronautical engineering to physics while still an undergraduate at the University of Minnesota. After garnering a Ph.D. from the University of Michigan, Peery went on to a lengthy career teaching astronomy at Indiana University, the University of Illinois, and Howard University.

Between 1875 and 1943, only eight African Americans were awarded doctorates in pure mathematics. David Blackwell became the first tenured African American professor at the University of California at Berkeley in 1955. An expert in statistics and probability, he was a trailblazer despite a racially motivated setback he incurred soon after completing his doctoral work at the University of Illinois. Nominated for a Rosenwald Fellowship from the Institute for Advanced Study at Princeton University, Blackwell was rejected because of his race. Undaunted, he went on to become the only African American mathematician to be elected into the National Academy of Sciences.

◆ AFRICAN AMERICANS IN MEDICINE

The medical profession has yielded a number of African Americans of high stature. As early as the 1860s, African Americans had entered medical schools in the North and had gone on to practice as full-fledged physicians. In fact, during the Civil War, Dr. Alexander T. Augusta was named head of a Union army hospital and Rebecca Lee Crumpler became the first female African American doctor by graduating from the New England Female Medical College in Boston. She was able to attend on a scholarship that she received from Ohio Sen. Benjamin Wade, an abolitionist. She used her schooling to provide health care to former slaves in the former confederate capital of Richmond, Virginia. Her 1883 *Book of Medical Discourses* taught women how to address their own health issues, as well as those of their children.

Rebecca J. Cole was the second African American woman to become a physician and the first African American graduate of the Women's Medical College of Pennsylvania. For over 50 years, she devoted her life to improving the lot of the poor. Her positions included performing a residency at the New York Infirmary for Women and Children and running Washington, DC's Government House for Children and Old Women and Philadelphia's Woman's Directory, a medical aid center.

In 1867, Susan McKinney Steward began studying at the New York Medical College for Women. Three years later she earned the distinction of being the third African American female physician in the United States and the first in New York State. She specialized in homeopathic treatments and had black and white patients of both genders as clients. After opening a second office in New York City, she helped co-found the Brooklyn Women's Hospital and Dispensary. She also served at the Brooklyn Home for Aged Colored People. Steward vigorously supported the women's suffrage movement and conducted missionary work with her second husband, a chaplain for the Buffalo Soldier regiment. She ended her career by taking on the role of school doctor at Wilberforce University.

In 1868, Howard University opened its College of Medicine, the first African American medical school in the country. The school nearly failed five years later when monetary problems arose and salaries for faculty were unavailable. Thanks to the efforts of Dr. Charles Purvis, who convinced the school to let him and his peers continue teaching on a non-paid basis, the school survived the crisis. Purvis was later appointed chief surgeon of Washington, DC's Freedman's Hospital by U.S. President Chester Arthur. Purvis was thus the first African American to run a civilian hospital. He did so until 1894, when he began a private practice.

Meanwhile, in 1876, Nashville's Meharry Medical College was founded. Despite the decidedly low number of jobs for African American physicians who were routinely turned away from nearly every facility other than Freedman's Hospital, the school was another sign of the slowly developing progress by African American physicians including Dr. Daniel Hale Williams, who replaced Purvis at Freedman's. Williams advanced Freedman's through internships, better nurses' training, and the addition of horse-drawn ambulances.

Williams had graduated from the Chicago Medical College in 1883, and entered into private practice almost immediately. Business was slow until 1890, when he met Emma Reynolds, an aspiring African American nurse, whose skin color had kept her from gaining admission to any of the nursing schools in Chicago. Inspired by her unfortunate dilemma, Williams decided to operate his own hospital in hopes of initiating his own program for aspiring nurses. With 12 beds, Provident Hospital became the first African American operated facility in the United States, and Reynolds was the first to enroll in Williams's classes. Near the end of his career, Williams was appointed the first African American associate surgeon at Chicago's St. Luke Hospital and later was the only African American charter member of the American College of Surgeons. During his career, Williams helped convince 40 hospitals to treat African American patients.

African Americans in the South also received improved care in the late 1890s, thanks to Alice Woodby McKane and her spouse who was also a doctor. In 1893, they founded the first training school for African American nurses—in Savannah, Georgia. McKane had obtained her medical degree one year earlier from the Women's Medical College of Pennsylvania. In 1895, the couple set up their first hospital in Monrovia, Liberia, before establishing the McKane Hospital for Women and Children in Georgia the following year.

Progress moved westward as another African American woman used her training to benefit the region's African American population, though her patients transcended all racial barriers. Beginning in 1902, Denver's "Baby Doctor," Justina Ford, proudly served her community as the only African American physician in Colorado for over 50 years. An obstetrician, she delivered more than 7,000 babies, conducting most of her business by house calls.

Back in the East, Freedman's Hospital was the training ground for future head trauma authority, Dr. Louis Wright, a Harvard Medical School graduate whose high academic standing meant nothing to Boston area hospitals that refused to hire African Americans. When World War I erupted, Wright enlisted and found himself in charge of his unit's surgical ward. After the war, Wright, who had received a Purple Heart, became the first African American physician to work in a New York City hospital when he was appointed to Harlem Hospital in 1919. Later he became director of surgery, president of the medical board, and was admitted to the American College of Surgeons. Four years before his death in 1952, he founded the Cancer Research Foundation at Harlem Hospital. The son of two physicians, his father and his stepfather, the latter of whom was the first African American graduate of Yale Medical School, Wright had two daughters who continued the family legacy by becoming doctors.

An almost legendary legacy was created by Dr. Charles R. Drew, a star high school athlete whose interest lay in medicine. A pathologist and expert on

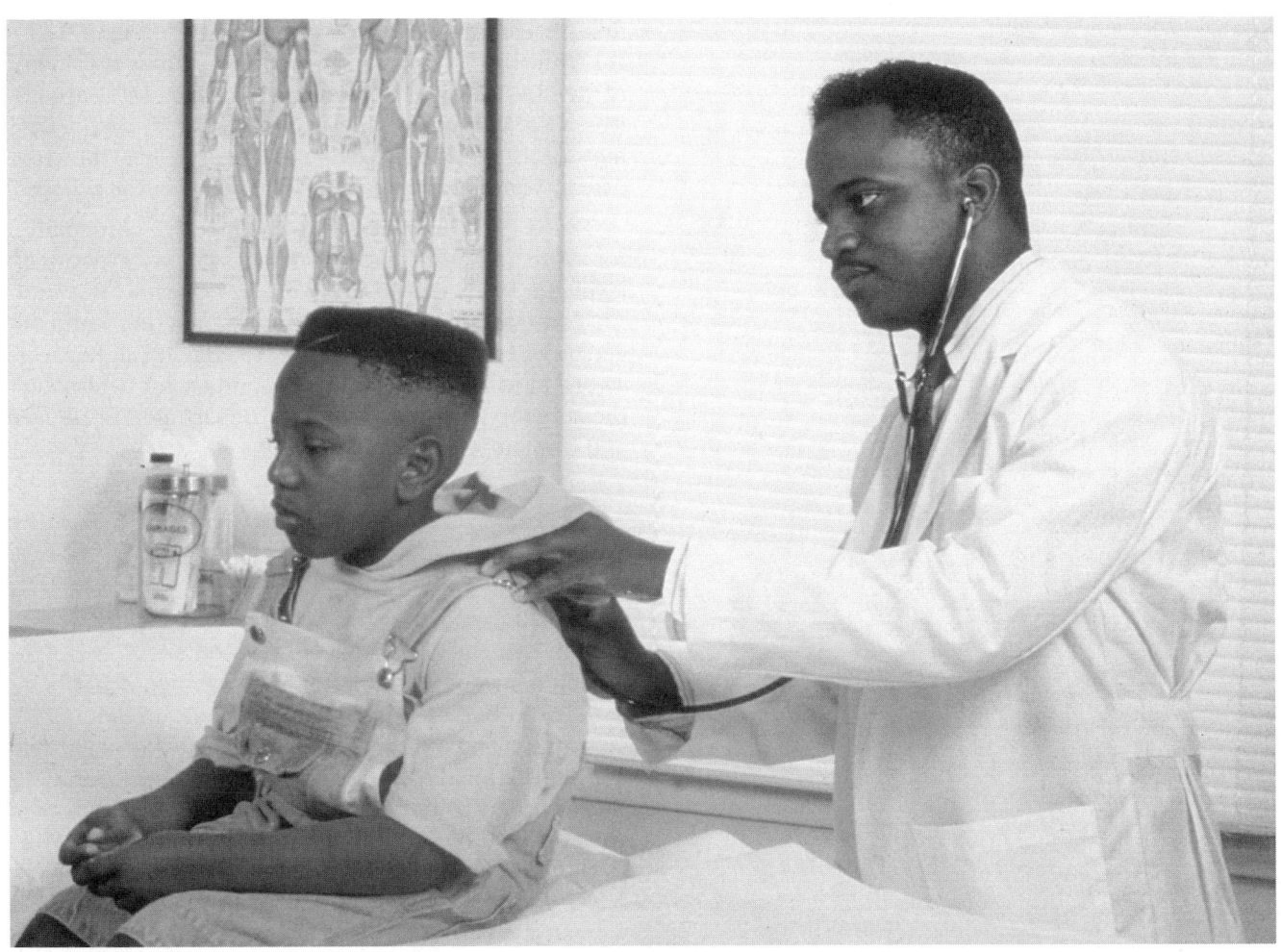

African American doctor and patient, 1994.

blood transfusions, Drew discovered that blood plasma was easier to store than whole blood and was compatible with all blood types. His experiments helped him receive a M.D. in 1940. During World War II, he helped Great Britain develop a national blood collection program, and was later asked to do the same for the U.S. Armed Forces. Unfortunately racism reared its ugly head again—African American donors were first completely excluded from the program, and later were only allowed to donate to other African American servicemen. Frustrated, Drew withdrew from the program, briefly resuming his teaching career at Howard before joining the staff of Freedman's Hospital as medical director.

Howard continued developing new talents. Dr. Roland Scott, a physician at Howard University's College of Medicine, became a pioneer in the study and treatment of sickle cell anemia. His research was pivotal in drawing public attention to the disorder and prompting the U.S. government to devote money to more extensive study. Under the Sickle Cell Anemia Control Act passed in 1972, Congress forced the National Institutes of Health to set up treatment centers for patients. Scott was named director of the program that involved screening as well as treatment for those already afflicted.

In recent years, African Americans have made great strides in the fields of medicine. Alexa Canady became the first African American neurosurgeon in 1975. She continues to be a leader and innovator in the areas of Craniofacial Abnormalities, Epilepsy, Hydrocephalus, Pediatric Neurosurgery, and Tumors of Spinal Cord and Brain. She has also contributed to special research topics such as assist in the development of neuroendoscopic equipment, evaluating programmable pressure change valves in hydrocephalus, head injury, hydrocephalus and shunts, neuroendoscopy, and pregnancy complications of shunts. Another African American neurosurgeon who advanced the field to new heights was Dr. Ben Carson. In 1987, Caron led a 70-member surgical team at Johns Hopkins Hospital to

Charles Richard Drew.

separate Siamese twins who were joined at the cranium. A surgery like this had never been attempted before, but Carson was able to not only perform the surgery but also was able to save both twins with minimal brain damage.

Canady and Carter changed the way the medical profession handled injuries and complications to the brain. Ten years after Carter's ground-breaking surgery, a pair of doctors changed the way that the medical community dealt with the subject of multiple births. Drs. Paula Mahone and Karen Drake are heads of a team of 40 specialists involved in the delivery of the McCaughey septuplets at Iowa Methodist Medical Center, the first set of septuplets to be born and survive in the United States. Mahone, Drake, Canady, and Carter are but a few examples of the major new discoveries and achievements that African Americans have made in the medical field.

African Americans have also begun to break into positions of power and prestige in the medical community. In 1989, Renee Rosilind Jenkins became the first African American president of the Society of Adolescent Medicine. In 1990, Roselyn Epps took over as the

first African American president of the American Medical Women's Association and the first woman president of the DC Medical Society a year later. Dr. Barbara Ross-Lee was named the Dean of Ohio University College of Osteopathic Medicine, making her the first African-American woman to lead a U.S. medical school.

These rises in positions in the medical community for African Americans were also seen on a national level. In 1993, Dr. Joycelyn Elders became the first African American to be appointed as U.S. surgeon general. Six years later, in 1998, Dr. David Satcher was sworn in as both the assistant secretary for health and the surgeon general for the U.S. Department of Health and Human Services.

◆ AFRICAN AMERICANS IN AIR AND SPACE

In 1920, Texan Bessie Coleman was accepted at the French flying school, École d'Aviation des Freres, following a string of rejections from aviation schools in the United States. Having completed seven months of instruction and a rigorous qualifying exam, she earned her international aviator's license from the Federation Aeronautique Internationale the following year and went on to study further with aircraft designer Anthony H. G. Fokker. Known to an admiring public as "Queen Bess," Bessie Coleman was the first African American woman ever to fly an airplane, the first American to earn an international pilot's license, and the first African American female stunt pilot. During her brief yet distinguished career as a performance flier, she appeared at air shows and exhibitions across the country, earning wide recognition for her aerial skill, dramatic flair, and tenacity. The tragic demise of the professional aviatrix occurred in 1926, when she was scheduled to parachute jump from a speeding plane at 2,500 feet. Ten minutes after takeoff, however, the plane careened wildly out of control, flipping over and dropping Coleman, who plunged 500 feet to her death. Though he remained in the aircraft, the pilot was instantly killed when the plane crashed to the ground. Later, a service wrench mistakenly left behind in the engine was found to have been the cause of the accident.

Six years later, in 1932, pilot James Herman Banning and mechanic Thomas C. Allen flew from Los Angeles to New York City in 41 hours and 27 minutes. The transcontinental flight was followed by the first round-trip transcontinental flight the next year. That feat was accomplished by Albert Ernest Forsythe and Charles Alfred Anderson, who flew from Atlantic City to Los Angeles and back in 11 days, foreshadowing the advent of commercial flight.

Willa B. Brown became the first African American woman to hold a commercial pilot's license in the United States in 1934. She was also the first African American woman to ascend to the rank of lieutenant in the Civil Air Patrol Squadron. Brown later founded the National Airmen's Association of America, the first aviators group for African Americans. With her husband, Cornelius R. Coffey, she established the first African American-owned flying school—Coffey School of Aeronautics—and the first African American-owned school to receive certification from the Civil Aviation Authority. Brown became the first African American member of the Federal Aviation Agency's Women's Advisory Council in 1972.

The second African American woman to earn a full commercial pilot's license was Janet Harmon Bragg, a Georgia nurse who took an interest in flying when she began dating Johnny Robinson, one of the first African American aviation instructors. The first woman of any race to be admitted to Chicago's Curtiss Wright Aeronautical University, she was initially denied her commercial license despite having successfully fulfilled all preliminary requirements including the airborne portion of the test. Her white instructor from the Federal Aviation Administration made it quite clear, however, that he would not grant a license to an African American woman. Rather than give up, Bragg merely tested again with another instructor the same year and was granted her license in 1942. Along with a small group of African American aviation devotees, she formed the Challengers Air Pilots Association (CAPA). Together, members of CAPA opened an airport in Robins, Illinois, the first owned and operated by African Americans.

Other African American notables in the field of aviation include: Perry H. Young, who, in 1957 became the first African American pilot for a scheduled passenger commercial airline, New York Airways; Otis B. Young Jr., who, in 1970, was the first African American pilot of a jumbo jet; and former naval pilot Jill Brown, who became the first African American female to pilot for a major airline in 1987.

Military men were the first African Americans to enter into the line of space exploration. In 1961, U.S. Air Force Captain Edward Dwight was invited by Pres. John F. Kennedy to apply to test-pilot school. Two years later, Dwight was in the midst of spaceflight training when Kennedy was assassinated. Without the president's support, Dwight was pretty much ignored by National Aeronautics and Space Administration (NASA). Air Force Major Robert H. Lawrence thus became the first African American astronaut a few years later. A doctor of physical chemistry, Lawrence was killed in a plane crash in December of 1967, just six months after his selection by NASA. African Americans would not make inroads in space until the genesis of the Space Shuttle program.

African American scientists were, however, prevalent. For example, Katherine Johnson joined the National Advisory Committee on Aeronautics, the precursor to NASA, in 1953. Initially all she was asked to do was basic number crunching, but she spent a short period filling in at the Flight Research Division. There her valued interpretation of data helped in the making of prototype spacecraft, and she soon developed into an aerospace technologist. She developed trajectories for the Apollo moon-landing project and devised emergency navigational methods for astronauts. She retired in 1986.

Emergencies of another sort have been tackled by air force flight surgeon Vance Marchbanks, whose research showed that adrenaline levels could affect the exhaustion level of flight crews. His work brought him to the attention of NASA, and he became a medical observer for NASA's Project Mercury. Along with several other personnel scattered about the globe, Marchbanks, stationed in Nigeria, was responsible for monitoring pioneering astronaut John Glenn's vital signs as he orbited the earth in 1962. Later, Marchbanks received the civilian post of chief of environmental health services for United Aircraft Corporation, where he had a hand in designing the space suit and medical monitoring systems used in the Apollo moon shot.

Also specializing in design, aeronautical test engineer Robert E. Shurney spent nearly his entire career, from 1968 to 1990, at the Marshall Space Flight Center, specializing in design utility. His products included refuse disposal units that stored solids in the bottom and liquid in tubes to prevent any materials from floating openly and contaminating an entire cabin. The units were used in the Apollo program, Skylab, and on the first space shuttle missions. He also crafted strong, yet lightweight, aluminum tires for the lunar rover. Much of his experimentation was conducted on KC-135 test planes in order to achieve the condition of weightlessness.

Assertiveness enabled O. S. Williams to bring forth his own achievements. In 1942, Williams talked his way into employment at Republic Aviation Corporation as part of the technical staff. Better known as "Ozzie," he took the experience he earned there to NASA contractor Grumman Corporation. The small rocket engines that he co-developed saved the lives of the Apollo 13 astronauts when the ship's main rocket exploded during flight in 1970.

Three missions later, George Carruthers, a Naval Research Laboratory astrophysicist, designed the far-ultraviolet camera/spectograph for use on Apollo 16.

The semiautomatic device was able to photograph deep space—regions too far to be captured by regular cameras—once set up on the surface of the moon. Carruthers, who earned a Ph.D. in aeronautical and astronautical engineering from the University of Illinois in 1964 and was granted his first patent in 1969 for an electromagnetic radiation image converter.

With a 1965 Ph.D. in atomic and molecular physics from Howard University, Carruther's contemporary, George E. Alcorn, has been one of the most prominent people working with semiconductors and spectrometers. Working for private industry, including IBM and NASA, Alcorn has over 25 patents to his name including secret projects concerning missile systems.

In a less clandestine fashion, aerospace engineer Christine Darden has been a leading NASA researcher in supersonic and hypersonic aircraft. Her main goal has been the reduction of sonic boom, a phenomenon that creates an explosive burst of sound that can traumatize those on the ground. Darden works at manipulating an aircraft's wing or the shape of its nose to try to control the feedback produced by air waves resulting from a plane's flight.

Dealing with people rather than machinery, director of psychophysiology at NASA's Ames Research Center, Patricia Cowings's post-doctoral work has touched upon such fields as aerospace medicine and bioastronautics. Since the late 1970s, she has assisted astronauts by teaching them biofeedback techniques—how to impose mind over matter when zero gravity wreaks havoc with one's system. By studying physical and emotional problems that arise in such a setting, she can seek the cause and prescribe a therapy to alleviate stress. She was also the first woman of any race in the United States to receive astronaut training.

These individuals are joined by numerous others in the field of aviation and space flight including chemical engineer Henry Allen Jr., a liquid and solid rocket fuel specialist; missile expert and inventor extra ordinaire Otis Boykin; health services officer Julian Earls; aerospace technologist Isabella J. Coles; astrodynamicist Robert A. Gordon; and operations officer Isaac Gillam IV, to name a few. Once the Space Shuttle program began in earnest, however, African Americans also took to the skies.

Traveling in the Space Shuttle *Challenger*, U.S. Air Force Colonel Guion "Guy" Bluford was the first African American to fly in space, where he coordinated experiments and was in charge of deploying satellites. After his first mission in 1983, Bluford participated in three more. Astronaut Ronald McNair was aboard the tragic *Challenger* flight of 1986, his second trip on the shuttle. The vehicle exploded 73 seconds after liftoff,

killing all seven crew members. Charles Bolden's first mission was aboard the 1986 flight of the Space Shuttle *Columbia*. He has also flown on the *Discovery*. The first African American to pilot a space shuttle was Frederick Drew Gregory, who did so in 1985, on his first journey to outer space. A veteran pilot of both helicopters and airplanes, Gregory became an astronaut in 1979. Gregory also made history on his fourth flight, when he commanded the first mission comprised of Russians and Americans. Mae Jemison went into space as a science specialist in 1992's joint U.S.-Japanese project on the shuttle *Endeavour*. The following year, Bernard Harris took off in the Space Shuttle *Columbia*. He served as a mission specialist in Spacelab-D2, alongside Germans and Americans.

◆ MODERN CONTRIBUTIONS TO SCIENCE AND TECHNOLOGY

The achievements of African American inventors and scientists of the mid- to late twentieth century have been obscured by reasons more complex than blatant racial prejudice. The main reasons include the advent of government and corporate research and development teams. Such work, whether contracted or direct, often precludes individual recognition, regardless of a person's race. Nonetheless, in the corporate world as well as in academia, African American scientists and engineers play a substantial role in the development of solid state devices, high-powered and ultra-fast lasers, hypersonic flight—2000 to 3000 miles per hour—and elementary particle science. African American engineers employed by NASA in managerial and research positions have made and continue to make considerable contributions.

African American manufacturing and servicing firms in various computer and engineering areas have been established. For example, African American entrepreneur Marc Hannah has made a niche for himself in the field of computer graphics as cofounder of Silicon Graphics Incorporated. Chief scientist and vice president of the company, Hannah has adapted his electrical engineering and computer science know-how to a variety of applications including military flight simulators and CAT scan devices. In addition, his computer-generated, 3-D special effects have been featured in such major films as *Terminator 2* (1991), *Aladdin* (1992), and *Jurassic Park* (1993).

Academia has more African American science and technology faculty members, college presidents, and school of engineering deans than in the past. Many of these academics are serving in the country's most prestigious institutions. However, this progress has not

Guion S. Bluford Jr. (left), Ronald E. McNair, Frederick Gregory, and Charles F. Bolden Jr.

continued, and there is cause for concern in the future. The 1970s was a decade of tremendous growth for minorities in science and engineering. In the eighties, though, there was a progressive decline in the production of African American scientists, even though the numbers of Asian American and women scientists were still growing. In 1977, for example, people of color earned 13 percent of science and engineering doctorates, with Asian Americans at three percent of those. By 1993, 16 percent of the degrees went to people of color, and Asian Americans earned seven percent of those degrees. In addition, women earned 40 percent of science and engineering doctorates in 1993, up from 25 percent in 1977. The numbers of African Americans entering scientific fields has slowly increased since the late 1980s, although they continue to be grossly underrepresented. Another area in which African Americans have been faltering is medicine.

In the mid- to late 1990s, the number of African American applicants to medical school was declining at a high rate. The search for potential African American physicians has been nearing crisis-level status. The repercussions of this shortage includes difficulty for the poor and elderly in finding African American attendants if they so desire. Primary care specialists—internists, pediatricians, obstetricians, gynecologists, etc.—were particularly in demand.

The health care profession began responding to this problem in 1991, when the Association of American Medical Colleges initiated Project 3000 by 2000—the primary aim being to graduate 3,000 minorities by the year 2000. In particular, Xavier University was the top school in the country for African American placement into medical school, gaining a reputation for placing an average of 70 percent of its pre-med seniors into medical schools each year. Meanwhile, African American doctors already in practice were forming cooperatives amongst themselves in order to serve those African American patients who were discriminated against by Health Maintenance Organizations (HMOs) that considered them too poor or sick to be participants.

The situation is not as dire in engineering, perhaps due in part to a mentoring program established in 1975, by the National Action Council for Minorities in Engineering (NACME). With industry backing, the council has focused on youngsters as early as the fourth-grade level. More than 4,700 of their students have acquired engineering degrees and their graduates make up ten percent of all engineers from minority groups. However, there is some indication that fewer African Americans are entering engineering fields since 1980. As of 1996, about 29 percent of the college-age population was made up of African Americans, Latinos, and Native Americans. This same group, though, accounted for less than three percent of engineering doctoral recipients.

Still, the importance of role models with names and faces can not be overlooked. Some African American scientists have entered into the public consciousness; for example, in 1973, Shirley Ann Jackson became the first African American woman in the United States to earn a Ph.D. in theoretical particle physics as well as the first female African American to earn a Ph.D. from the prestigious Massachusetts Institute of Technology (MIT). She has had a distinguished career, culminating with her appointment as chair of the Nuclear Regulatory Commission by President Bill Clinton in 1995.

Another African American rose to the position of National Science Foundation (NSF) director, the highest science-related administrative post in the United

Shirley Ann Jackson, the first female African American to earn a Ph.D. from MIT.

States. Holder of a physics Ph.D. from St. Louis's Washington University, Walter Massey was able to create a number of programs to provide science-oriented training to young African Americans. During his two-year stint at the NSF, from 1991 to 1993, Massey repeated the kind of success he had when he began the Inner City Teachers Science program while teaching at Brown University.

In the field of medical research, Charles Whitten founded the National Association for Sickle Cell Disease in 1971. His work has been complemented more recently by Griffin Rodgers, chief of the Molecular Hematology Unit at the National Institutes of Health. In the 1990s, Rodgers was working on an experimental anti-cancer drug that could possibly provide benefits for sickle cell anemia patients.

Patients with prostate cancer have been encouraged by the work of Detroit-based urologist and oncologist Isaac Powell. In 1995, the Centers for Disease Control and Prevention named his screening program as the outstanding community health project of the year. Powell has been pursuing the idea of advanced diagnostic testing for African American men. Through a partnership with the Karmanos Cancer Institute and area churches, nurses, and hospitals, Powell has been able to educate the public about the importance of undergoing prostate cancer screening. Benefitting from a prostate-specific antigen test, patients have had their cancer caught early enough to undergo successful surgery. In 1996, Powell's program was being exported to other cities in the United States.

The cancer research of a young African American biologist, Jill Bargonetti, has garnered much attention. She discovered a correlation between a specific gene's ability to bind with the genetic matter known as DNA and its ability to suppress tumors. In 1996, she received a $300,000, three-year grant from the American Cancer Society and a $200,000, four-year award from the Department of Defense to pursue her study of breast cancer.

Outside of medical research, one-time Olympic athlete and engineering physicist Meredith Gourdine earned a Ph.D. from the California Institute of Technology in 1960. The Olympic medalist then formed Gourdine Systems, a research and development firm geared towards patenting inventions that use state-of-the-art power sources developed from advanced research in physics. Though blinded by diabetes in 1973, Gourdine went on to launch Energy Innovations the next year. An inventor at heart, he has more than 70 patents in his name and was inducted into the Black Inventors Hall of Fame.

The energy of earthquakes motivates geophysicist Waverly Person. His interest in seismology paid off

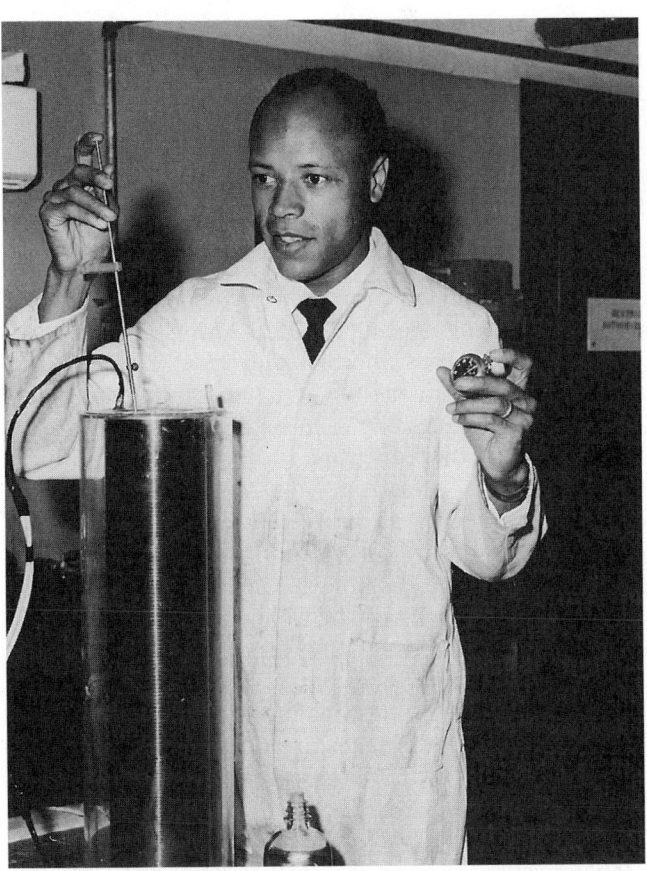

Meredith Gourdine conducting an experiment in magneto-hydrodynamics.

when he was named director of the U.S. Geological Survey's National Earthquake Information Center in 1977. The first African American earthquake scientist, Person is also the first African American in more than 30 years to hold such a prominent position in the U.S. Department of the Interior.

Similarly, meteorologist Warren Washington has been concerned with the earth's climate. Since 1987, the greenhouse effect expert has been director of the Climate and Global Dynamics Division of the National Center for Atmospheric Research. After seven years there, he was elected to a one-year term as the first African American president of the American Meteorological Society. Afterwards, Washington co-founded the Black Environmental Science Trust, introducing African American children to science.

In the 1990s and into the new millennium, personal computers and the World Wide Web have been one of the largest areas of scientific and industrial invention. One of the fathers of the Internet, Philip Emeagwali created a formula in 1989 that used 65,000 separate

computer processors to perform 3.1 billion calculations per second. This feat allowed computer scientists to comprehend the capabilities of computers to communicate with one another. Another innovator is Omar Wasow, the executive director of Blackplanet.com who created the "community" strategy of running Web domains that almost all Internet sites utilize to maximize efficiency. African American's have also used the computer to create programs that are aiding in everyday life and government. One such example is Athan Gibbs who introduced in 2002 the Gibbs' Tru Voter Validation System, a computer touch-screen system that allows voters to touch the picture of the candidate they chose to vote for, eliminating confusion among voters and possible corruption of ballots.

Along with hundreds of other notable African Americans, scientists have been working towards restoring scientific education at all levels. Their presence, whether inside or outside of the public eye, is felt. Younger African Americans who learn of their endeavors are thus encouraged to free their creative science minds.

Rainbow/PUSH Coalition Seeks Greater Minority Representation in Silicon Valley

Having addressed the lack of employment opportunities for African Americans on Wall Street, the Reverend Jesse Jackson used the same policy during 1999 towards the Silicon Valley—a segment of the economy where whites hold more than 90 percent of the chief executive officer jobs and board seats at the top 150 public corporations. Seeking greater African American representation in this prominent high-tech region of California, Jackson's Rainbow/PUSH Coalition purchased approximately $100,000 worth of stock in 50 of the largest high-tech corporation and announced future plans of opening a staffed office in San Jose, assembling an advisory board of influential Silicon Valley executives to suggest methods of increasing African American and Hispanic American participation in the region's workforce, and hosting a conference that will address methods to effectively educate minorities for high-tech careers.

While acknowledging that nearly 31 percent of the high-tech industry's engineers and professionals are Asian American and that Silicon Valley is a major employer of immigrants, Jackson is exerting pressure on corporations to reach beyond their usual networks to work with minority-owned businesses in order to widen their pool of money and talent. With the support of a number of African American chief executive officers—Frank S. Greene of New Vista Capital, Robert E. Knowling of Covad Communications, Roy Clay of Rod-L Electronics; and Kenneth L. Coleman of Silicon

Graphics Inc.—Jackson hopes to end the so-called "color-blind" hiring practices that high-tech corporate executives claim to apply which, in Jackson's opinion, prevents them from recognizing minority markets. (According to *Target Market News*, African Americans annually spend $3.8 billion on computer and consumer electronic gear.)

◆ ENGINEERS, MATHEMATICIANS, INVENTORS, PHYSICIANS, AND SCIENTISTS

(To locate biographical profiles more readily, please consult the index at the back of the book.)

George E. Alcorn (1940–)
Physicist

George Edward Alcorn was born on March 22, 1940. He graduated with a B.A. in physics from Occidental College in 1962, and a M.A. in nuclear physics from Howard University in 1963. In 1967, he earned his Ph.D. from Howard University in atomic and molecular physics. After earning his Ph.D., Alcorn spent 12 years working in industry.

Alcorn left IBM, where he had worked as a Second Plateau Inventor, to join NASA in 1978. While at NASA, Alcorn invented an imaging x-ray spectrometer using thermomigration of aluminum, for which he earned a patent in 1984, and two years later devised an improved method of fabrication using laser drilling. His work on imaging x-ray spectrometers earned him the 1984 NASA/Goddard Space Flight Center (GSFC) Inventor of the Year Award. During this period he also served as deputy project manager for advanced development and was responsible for developing new technologies required for the space station *Freedom*. He also managed the GSFC Evolution Program, concerned with ensuring that over its 30-year mission the space station develops properly while incorporating new capabilities. Since 1992, Alcorn has served as chief of Goddard's Office of Commercial Programs, supervising programs for technology transfer, small business innovation research, and the commercial use of space programs. He managed a shuttle flight experiment that involved Robot Operated Material Processing System, or ROMPS, in 1994.

Alcorn holds over 25 patents. He is a recognized pioneer in the fabrication of plasma semiconductor devices, and his patent "Process for Controlling the Slope of a Via Hole" was an important contribution to the process of plasma etching. This procedure is now used by many semiconductor manufacturing companies. Alcorn was one of the first scientists to present a computer-modeling solution of wet etched and plasma etched structure, and has received several cash prizes for his inventions of plasma-processing techniques.

Archie Alexander (1888–1958)
Civil Engineer

Born in 1888 in Ottumwa, Iowa, Archie Alphonso Alexander graduated from the University of Iowa with a B.S. in civil engineering in 1912. During his collegiate years he was a star football player who earned the nickname "Alexander the Great" on the playing field. His first job was as a design engineer for the Marsh Engineering Company that specialized in building bridges. Two years later, in 1914, Alexander formed his own company, A. A. Alexander, Inc. Most of the firm's contracts were for bridges and sewer systems. So successful was he that the NAACP awarded him its Spingarn Medal in 1928. The following year, he formed Alexander and Repass with a former classmate. Alexander's new company was also responsible for building tunnels, railroad trestles, viaducts, and power plants. Some of Alexander's biggest accomplishments include the Tidal Basin Bridge and K Street Freeway in Washington, DC; a heating plant for his alma mater, the University of Iowa; a civilian airfield in Tuskegee, Alabama; and a sewage disposal plant in Grand Rapids, Michigan.

A member of Kappa Alpha Psi, Alexander was awarded their "Laurel Wreath" for great accomplishment in 1925. Alexander received honorary civil engineering degrees from the University of Iowa in 1925 and Howard University in 1946. The following year, Alexander was named one of the University of Iowa's outstanding alumni and "one of the first hundred citizens of merit." Politically active, Alexander was appointed Governor of the Virgin Islands in 1954 by President Dwight Eisenhower, though he was forced to resign one year later due to health problems. He died at his home in Des Moines, Iowa in 1958.

Benjamin Banneker (1731–1806)
Mathematician/Statistician, Astronomer, Surveyor/Explorer, Publisher

Benjamin Banneker was born on November 9, 1731, on a tobacco farm near Baltimore, Maryland. His mother was a free woman and his father was her slave, whom she purchased and married. At the age of 21, Banneker became interested in watches and later constructed a grandfather clock based upon a pocket watch he had seen, calculating the ratio of the gears and wheels and carving them from wood. The clock operated for more than 40 years.

Banneker's aptitude for mathematics and knowledge of astronomy enabled him to accurately predict the solar eclipse of 1789. By 1791, he began publishing an almanac which contained tide tables, weather information, data on future eclipses, and a listing of useful medicinal products and formulas. The almanac, which was the first scientific book published by an African American, appeared annually for more than a decade. Banneker sent a copy to Thomas Jefferson, and the two corresponded, debating the subject of slavery.

Banneker served as a surveyor on the six-person team that helped lay out the base lines and initial boundaries for Washington, DC. When the chairman of the committee, Major Pierre Charles L'Enfant, abruptly resigned and returned to France with his plans, Banneker was able to reproduce the plans from memory in their entirety. He died on October 25, 1806.

Andrew J. Beard (1849– 1921)
Railroad Porter, Inventor

Inventor Andrew Jackson Beard was born a slave in Eastlake, Alabama. While working in an Alabama railroad yard, Beard had seen men lose hands, arms, legs, and even their lives in accidents occurring during the manual coupling of railroad cars. The system in use involved the dropping of a metal pin at exactly the right moment when two cars met. Men were often caught between cars and crushed to death during this split-second operation. Beard's invention, the "Jenny Coupler," was an automatic device which secured two cars by merely bumping them together. In 1897, Beard received $50,000 for an invention that has since prevented the death or maiming of countless railroad workers.

Guion S. Bluford Jr. (1942–)
Space/Atmospheric Scientist, Aerospace Engineer, Air Force Officer, Airplane Pilot

Guy Bluford was born November 22, 1942, in Philadelphia. He graduated with a B.S. from Pennsylvania State University in 1964. He then enlisted in the U.S. Air Force and was assigned to pilot training at Williams Air Force Base in Arizona. Bluford served as a fighter pilot in Vietnam and flew 144 combat missions, 65 of them over North Vietnam. Attaining the rank of lieutenant colonel, Bluford received an M.S. from the Air Force Institute of Technology in 1974 and a Ph.D. in aerospace engineering in 1978.

In 1979, Bluford was accepted in NASA's astronaut program as a mission specialist. On August 30, 1983, with the liftoff of the *Challenger* shuttle Bluford became the first African American in space. He flew three other space shuttle missions, aboard *Challenger* in 1985, and aboard *Discovery* in 1991 and 1992, for a total of 688 hours in space. Bluford retired from NASA in 1993 to pursue a career in private industry, where he has served as vice president and general manager of Engineering Services Division of NYMA, Inc. In this position, Bluford directs engineers, scientists, and technicians who provide engineering support to NASA's Lewis Research Center.

Bluford has won numerous awards including the Distinguished National Science Award given by the National Society of Black Engineers (1979), NASA Group Achievement Award (1980, 1981), NASA Space Flight Medal (1983), and the NAACP Image Award in 1983. Some of his military honors include the National Defense Service Medal (1965), Vietnam Campaign Medal (1967), Air Force Commendation Medal (1972), Air Force Meritorious Service Award (1978), the USAF Command Pilot Astronaut Wings (1983), and the NASA Distinguished Service Medal (1994).

Charles F. Bolden Jr. (1946–)
Airplane Pilot, Space/Atmospheric Scientist, Marine Officer, Operations and Systems Researcher/ Analyst

Born in Columbia, South Carolina, and a graduate of the U.S. Naval Academy and the University of Southern California, Charles Bolden Jr. has a B.S. in electrical science and a M.S. in systems management. Bolden began his career as a second lieutenant in the U.S. Marine Corps, becoming a naval aviator by 1970. In 1973, he flew more than 100 sorties while assigned in Thailand. Upon return to the United States, Bolden began a tour as a Marine Corps selection and recruiting officer. In 1979, he graduated from the U.S. Naval Test Pilot School and was assigned to the Naval Test Aircraft Directorates.

Bolden was selected as an astronaut candidate by NASA in May of 1980, and, in July of 1981, completed the training and evaluation program—making him eligible for assignment as a pilot on space shuttle flight crews. A veteran of four shuttle missions, Bolden has served as pilot for the Hubble Space Telescope deployment mission and was commander of the first joint American-Russian space shuttle mission. In 1994, he accepted a position at the Naval Academy. Bolden has been awarded the Defense Superior Service Medal, the Defense Meritorious Service Medal, the Air Medal, the Legion of Merit, and the Strike/Flight Medal. His current rank is major general.

In 2002, Bolden was nominated for the position of deputy administrator of The National Aeronautics and Space Administration (NASA). However, due to a

Defense Department order limiting the service of senior military officers in civilian jobs during the U.S. antiterrorism offensive, the highly qualified candidate's nomination was withdrawn from consideration.

Marjorie L. Browne (1914–1979)
Mathematician/Statistician, Educator

Browne was born September 9, 1914, in Memphis, Tennessee. She received a B.S. in mathematics from Howard University in 1935, an M.S. from the University of Michigan in 1939, and a Ph.D. in mathematics, again from the University of Michigan, in 1949. Browne was one of the first two African American women to earn a Ph.D. in mathematics. She taught at the University of Michigan in 1947 and 1948. She accepted the post of professor of mathematics at North Carolina Central University in 1949 and became department chairperson in 1951. In 1960, she received a grant from IBM to establish one of the first computer centers at a minority university.

Browne's doctoral dissertation dealt with topological and matrix groups, and she was published in the *American Mathematical Monthly*. She was a fellow of

Marjorie Lee Browne.

the National Science Foundation in 1958–1959 and again in 1965–1966. Browne was a member of the American Mathematical Society, the Mathematical Association of America, and the Society for Industrial and Applied Mathematics. She died in 1979.

Alexa I. Canady (1950–)
Neurosurgeon

Alexa Irene Canady, the first African American woman to become a neurosurgeon in the United States, was born November 7, 1950, in Lansing, Michigan. Canady was recognized as a National Achievement Scholar while in high school, and attended the University of Michigan where she received a B.S. in 1971 and an M.D. in 1975. As a medical student, she was elected to Alpha Omega Alpha honorary medical society and received the American Medical Women's Association citation.

Canady's internship was spent at the Yale-New Haven Hospital in 1975 to 1976. She gained her landmark residency in neurosurgery at the University of Minnesota from 1976 to 1981. Following her residency, Children's Hospital in Philadelphia awarded Canady a fellowship in pediatric neurosurgery in 1981–1982. In addition to treating patients directly, Canady served as an instructor in neurosurgery at the University of Pennsylvania College of Medicine. In 1982, she accepted a position at Henry Ford Hospital in Detroit. The following year, Canady transferred to pediatric neurosurgery at Children's Hospital of Michigan, where she became the assistant director of neurosurgery at Children's Hospital three years later, and director in 1987.

She began teaching at Wayne State University School of Medicine as a clinical instructor in 1985, and assumed a clinical associate professorship in 1987. Canady retired in 2001, at which point she was the chief of neurosurgery at Children's Hospital of Michigan. Among her numerous honors and awards, Canady has been inducted into the Michigan Women's Hall of Fame, and was named Woman of the Year in 1993 by the American Women's Medical Association.

George R. Carruthers (1939–)
Astrophysicist

Dr. George Carruthers is one of the two naval research laboratory people responsible for the *Apollo 16* lunar surface ultraviolet camera/spectrograph, which was placed on the lunar surface in April 1972. It was Carruthers who designed the instrument while William Conway adapted the camera for the lunar mission. The spectrographs, obtained from 11 targets, include the first photographs of the ultraviolet equatorial bands of atomic oxygen that girdle the earth. The camera was also used on *Skylab* in 1974.

Carruthers, who was born on October 1, 1939, in Cincinnati, Ohio, grew up on Chicago's South Side. He built his first telescope at the age of ten. He received his Ph.D. in aeronautical/astronautical engineering from the University of Illinois in 1964.

In 1966, Carruthers became a research assistant at the Navy's E. O. Hulburt Center for Space Research, where he began work on the lunar surface ultraviolet camera/spectrograph. The images received from the moon gave researchers invaluable information about the Earth's atmosphere, including possible new ways to control air pollution. The images also aided in the detection of hydrogen in deep space—evidence that plants are not the only source of Earth's oxygen.

Carruthers has continued his research, and is currently head of the Ultraviolet Measurements Group in the Space Science Division of the Naval Research Laboratory. He is the recipient of the NASA Exceptional Scientific Achievement medal for his work on the ultraviolet camera/spectrograph. Carruthers also won the Arthur S. Fleming Award in 1971, and the 2000 Outstanding Scientist Award presented by the National Institute of Science.

Ben Carson (1951–)
Neurosurgeon

Born Benjamin Solomon Carson on September 18, 1951, in Detroit, Michigan, Dr. Carson has been recognized throughout the medical community for his prowess in performing complex neurosurgical procedures, particularly on children with pediatric brain tumors his main focus. Among his accomplishments are a number of successful hemispherectomies, a process in which a portion of the brain of a critically ill seizure victim or other neurologically diseased patient is removed to radically reduce the incidence of seizures. Carson's most famous operation took place in 1987, earning him international acclaim. That year he successfully separated a pair of West German Siamese or conjoined twins, who had been attached at the backs of their heads. The landmark operation took 22 hours; Carson led a surgical team of 70 doctors, nurses, and technicians.

Carson was raised in Detroit. A problem student—he almost killed a peer during a knife fight when he was 14 years old—and a failing student, his mother imposed a reading program on him and limited his television viewing until his grades improved. In high school, he continued to excel and was accepted at Yale University

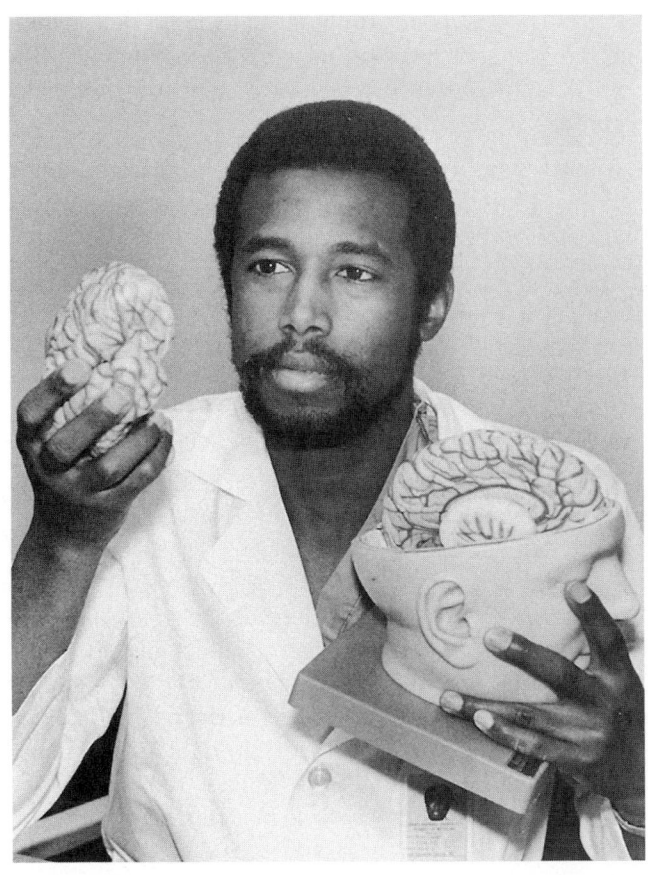

Ben Carson examines a model of the human brain.

in 1969 with a scholarship. With a B.A. from that Ivy League institution, Carson entered the University of Michigan, where he obtained his M.D. in 1977. For one year he served as a surgical intern at the Johns Hopkins Hospital, later doing his residency there. From 1983 to 1984, Carson practiced at the Sir Charles Gairdner Hospital in Perth, Australia. In 1984, at 33 years of age, he became the youngest chief of pediatric neurosurgery in the United States. Then, in 1985, Johns Hopkins named him director of pediatric neurosurgery. Carson is currently Professor of Neurosurgery, Plastic Surgery, Oncology and Pediatrics at Johns Hopkins. He is also the co-director of the Johns Hopkins Craniofacial Center.

Carson has authored three best-selling books: *Gifted Hands* (1990), *Think Big* (1992), *The Big Picture* (1999). He has also established a scholarship fund, USA Scholars Program, with the aid of his wife.

George Washington Carver (c. 1864–1943)
Educator, Agricultural/Food Scientist, Farmer

George Washington Carver devoted his life to research projects connected primarily with Southern agriculture. The products he derived from the peanut and the soybean revolutionized the economy of the South by liberating it from an excessive dependence on cotton.

Born a slave in Diamond Grove, Missouri, sometime between 1861 and 1865, Carver was only an infant when his mother was abducted from his owner's plantation by a band of slave raiders. His mother was sold and shipped away, and Carver was raised by his mother's owners, Moses and Susan Carver. Carver was a frail and sickly child, and he was assigned lighter chores around the house. Later he was allowed to attend high school in a neighboring town.

Carver worked odd jobs while he pursued his education. He was the first African American student admitted at Simpson College, Indianola, Iowa. He then attended Iowa Agricultural College (now Iowa State University) where, while working as the school janitor, he received a degree in agricultural science in 1894. Two years later he received a master's degree from the same school and became the first African American to serve on its faculty. Within a short time his fame spread, and Booker T. Washington offered him a post at Tuskegee Institute. It was at the Institute's Agricultural Experimental Station that Carver did most of his work.

Carver revolutionized the southern agricultural economy by showing that 300 products could be derived from the peanut. By 1938, peanuts had become a $200 million industry and a chief product of Alabama. Carver also demonstrated that 100 different products could be derived from the sweet potato.

Although he did hold three patents, Carver never patented most of the many discoveries he made while at Tuskegee, saying "God gave them to me, how can I sell them to someone else?" In 1940, he established the George Washington Carver Foundation and willed the rest of his estate to the organization, so his work might be carried on after his death. He died on January 5, 1943.

Jewel Plummer Cobb (1924–)
Cell Biologist

Born in Chicago on January 17, 1924, Cobb grew up exposed to a variety of African American professionals through her parents. By 1950, she had completed her M.S. and Ph.D. in biology. As a cell biologist, her focus was the action and interaction of living cells. She was particularly interested in tissue culture, in which cells are grown outside of the body and studied under microscopes. Among her most important work was her study

Jewel Plummer Cobb.

with Dorothy Walker Jones of how new cancer-fighting drugs affected human cancer cells. Cobb also conducted research into skin pigment. She was particularly interested in melanoma, or skin cancer, and melanin's ability to protect skin from damage caused by ultraviolet light.

Cobb noted the scarcity of women in scientific fields, and she wrote about the difficulties women face in a 1979 paper "Filters for Women in Science." In this piece, Cobb argued that various pressures, particularly in the educational system, act as filters that prevent many women from choosing science careers. The socialization of girls has tended to discourage them from pursuing math and the sciences from a very early age, and even those women who got past such obstacles have struggled to get university tenure and the same jobs (at equal pay) as men.

Cobb has been president emeritus of California State University in Fullerton since 1990. She has been active in her community, recruiting women and minorities to the sciences and founding a privately funded gerontology center.

W. Montague Cobb (1904–1990)
Anthropologist, Organization Executive/Founder, Medical Researcher, Educator, Editor

William Montague Cobb was born on October 12, 1904, in Washington, DC. For more than 40 years he was a member of the Howard University Medical School faculty; thousands of medical and dental students studied under his direction. At Howard, he built a collection of more than 600 documented skeletons and a comparative anatomy museum in the gross anatomy laboratory. In addition to a B.A. from Amherst College, an M.D. from Howard University, and a Ph.D. from Case Western Reserve, he received many honorary degrees. Cobb died on November 20, 1990, in Washington, DC.

As editor of the *Journal of the National Medical Association* for 28 years, Cobb developed a wide range of scholarly interests manifested by the nearly 700 published works under his name in the fields of medical education, anatomy, physical anthropology, public health and medical history. He was the first African American elected to the presidency of the American Association of Physical Anthropologists and served as the chairman of the anthropology section of the American Association for the Advancement of Science. Among his many scientific awards is the highest award given by the American Association of Anatomists. For 31 years he was a member of the board of directors of the NAACP and served as the president of the board from 1976 to 1982.

Price M. Cobbs (1928–)
Psychiatrist, Author, Management Consultant

Cobbs was born in Los Angeles, California, on November 2, 1928, and followed in his father's path when he enrolled in medical school after earning a B.A. from the University of California at Berkeley in 1954. He graduated from Meharry Medical College in 1958, and, within a few years, had established his own San Francisco practice in psychiatry.

With his academic colleague at the University of California, William H. Grier, Cobbs authored the groundbreaking 1968 study *Black Rage*. In it, the authors argued that a pervasive social and economic racism had resulted in an endemic anger that stretched across all strata of African American society, from rich to poor; this anger was both apparent and magnified by the social unrest of the 1960s. Cobbs and Grier also co-authored a second book *The Jesus Bag* (1971) that discussed the role of organized religion in the African American community.

A seminar Cobbs held in 1967 with other mental health care professionals eventually led him to found his own diversity training company, Pacific Management Systems. Since its inception, the company has been instrumental in providing sensitivity training for Fortune 500 companies, community groups, law enforcement bodies, and social service agencies. A member of numerous African American professional and community organizations, as well as an assistant clinical professor at the University of California at San Francisco, Cobbs continues to guide PMS well into its third decade. The firm has pioneered the concept of ethnotherapy, which uses the principles of group therapy to help seminar participants rethink their attitudes toward members of other ethnic groups, the disabled, and those of alternative sexual orientations.

Elbert F. Cox (1895–1969)
Educator, Mathematician/Statistician

Cox was born in Evansville, Indiana on December 5, 1895. He received his B.A. from Indiana University in 1917 and his Ph.D. from Cornell University in 1925. His dissertation dealt with polynomial solutions, and made Cox the first African American to be awarded a Ph.D. in pure mathematics. Cox was an instructor at Shaw University (1921–1923), a professor in physics and mathematics at West Virginia State College (1925–1929), and an associate professor of mathematics at Howard University from 1929 to 1947. In 1947, he was made full professor and retired in 1966.

During his career, Cox specialized in interpolation theory and differential equations. Among his professional accolades were memberships in such educational societies as Beta Kappa Chi, Pi Mu Epsilon, and Sigma Pi Sigma. He was also active in the American Mathematical Society, the American Physical Society, and the American Physics Institute. Cox died on November 28, 1969.

Ulysses G. Dailey (1885–1961)
Editor, Health Administrator, Surgeon, Diplomat

From 1908 to 1912, Ulysses Grant Dailey served as surgical assistant to Dr. Daniel Hale Williams, founder of Provident Hospital and noted heart surgeon. Born in Donaldsonville, Louisiana, in 1885, Dailey graduated in 1906 from Northwestern University Medical School, where he was appointed a demonstrator in anatomy. He later studied in London, Paris, and Vienna, and in 1926 set up his own hospital and sanitarium in Chicago. Dailey was associated with Provident Hospital after his own hospital closed in 1932, and he retained a position there until his death.

A member of the editorial board of the *Journal of the National Medical Association* for many years, Dailey traveled around the world in 1933 under the sponsorship of the International College of Surgeons, of which he was a founder fellow. In 1951, and 1953, the U.S. State Department sent him to Pakistan, India, Ceylon, and Africa. One year later he was named honorary consul to Haiti, moving there in 1956 when he retired.

Charles R. Drew (1904–1950)
Educator, Medical Researcher, Health Administrator, Surgeon/Physician

Using techniques already developed for separating and preserving blood, Charles Drew pioneered further into the field of blood preservation and organized procedures from research to a clinical level, leading to the founding of the world's two largest blood banks just prior to World War II. Born on June 3, 1904 in Washington, DC, Drew graduated from Amherst College in Massachusetts, where he received the Messman Trophy for having brought the most honor to the school during his four years there. He was not only an outstanding scholar, but the captain of the track team and a star halfback on the football team.

After receiving his medical degree from McGill University in 1933, Drew returned to Washington, DC, to teach pathology at Howard. In 1940, while taking his D.Sc. degree at Columbia University, he wrote a dissertation on "banked blood," and soon became such an expert in this field that the British government called upon him to set up the first blood bank in England. He also initiated the use of "bloodmobiles," trucks equipped with refrigerators to transport blood and plasma to remote locations.

During World War II, Drew was appointed director of the American Red Cross blood donor project. Later, he served as chief surgeon at Freedmen's Hospital in Washington, DC, as well as professor of surgery at Howard University Medical School from 1941–1950. A recipient of the 1944 Springarn Medal, Drew was killed in an automobile accident on April 1, 1950.

Joycelyn Elders (1933–)
Physician, Endocrinologist, Former U.S. Surgeon General

Dr. Joycelyn Elders was born Minnie Joycelyn Jones, on August 13, 1933, in Schaal, Arkansas. The first of eight children, she grew up working in cotton fields. An avid reader, Jones earned a scholarship to Philander Smith College in Little Rock. Jones studied biology and chemistry in hopes of becoming a lab technician. She was inspired towards greater ambitions after meeting

Edith Irby Jones (no relation), the first African American woman to study at the University of Arkansas School of Medicine. After obtaining her B.A., Jones served as a physical therapist in the U.S. Army in order to fund her post-graduate education. She was able to enroll in the University of Arkansas School of Medicine in 1956. However, as the only African American woman, and one of only three African American students, she and the other African Americans were forced to use a separate university dining facility—the one provided for the cleaning staff.

Having married Oliver B. Elders in 1960, the newly dubbed Joycelyn Elders fulfilled a pediatric internship at the University of Minnesota, then returned to Little Rock in 1961 for a residency at the University of Arkansas Medical Center. Her success in the position led her to be appointed chief pediatric resident, in charge of the all-white, all-male battery of residents and interns. During the next 20 years, Elders forged a successful clinical practice, specializing in pediatric endocrinology, the study of glands. She published more than 100 papers in that period and rose to professor of pediatrics, a position she maintained from 1976 until 1987, when she was named director of the Arkansas Department of Health.

Over the course of her career, Elders's focus shifted somewhat from diabetes in children to sexual behavior. At the Department of Health, Elders was able to pursue her public advocacy in regards to teenage pregnancy and sexually transmitted diseases. In 1993, U.S. president Bill Clinton nominated Elders for the U.S. surgeon general post, making her the second African American and the fifth woman to hold the cabinet position. Though her confirmation was not unchallenged—many decried her liberal stance—she was formally voted into approval for the position by the Senate on September 7, 1993.

During her tenure, Elders attacked Medicaid for failing to help poverty-stricken women prevent unwanted pregnancies and faulted pharmaceutical companies for overpricing contraceptives. Between 1993 and December of 1994, she spoke out in support of the medicinal use of marijuana, in favor of studying drug legalization, family planning, and against toy guns for children. An uproar was raised when Elders was reported to have recommended that masturbation be discussed in schools as part of human sexuality. She was forced to resign by Clinton in December of 1994.

Elders returned to the University of Arkansas Medical School, and resumed teaching, though the state's General Assembly budget committee tried to block her return. In 1995, she was hosting a daily talk show on AM stations KYSG in Little Rock and WERE in Cleveland. That same year, she joined the board of the American

Civil Liberties Union. In 1996, her autobiography, entitled *Joycelyn Elders MD: From Sharecropper's Daughter to Surgeon General of America*, was published. Elders continues to lecture throughout the U.S. on health-related issues.

Philip Emeagwali (1954–)
Mathmatician, Engineer, Computer Scientist

Philip Chukwurah Emeagwali, considered a "father" of the Internet, was born on August 23, 1954, in Akure, Nigeria. A young math prodigy, Emeagwali's high school studies were interrupted when he and his family—members of the Igbo tribe—were forced to flee to eastern Nigeria during the country's civil war. After living in refugee camps and serving as a cook in the Biafran army, Emeagwali entered Christ the King College in Onitsha, and in 1973, earned a general certificate of education from the University of London.

Emeagwali ventured to the United States the following year to pursue further studies. He earned a B.S. in mathematics from Oregon State University in 1977, an M.S. in civil engineering from George Washington University in 1981, a "post master's degree" in ocean, coastal, and marine engineering in 1986, an M.A. in applied mathematics from the University of Maryland in 1986, and a Ph.D. in scientific computing from the University of Michigan in 1993. Emeagwali became a citizen of the United States in 1981 when he married Dale Brown, a renown scientist and cancer researcher.

In the mid-1970s, Emeagwali began working with computers, eventually becoming a supercomputer programer. By 1989, he had set the world's fastest computational record, using 65,000 separate computer processors to perform 3.1 billion calculations per second. The work was important in that it enabled scientists to grasp the capacities of supercomputers, as well as the theoretical uses of linking numerous computers to communicate—an idea that eventually led to the creation of the Internet. For his work, Emeagwali earned the 1989 Gordon Bell Prize, a highly coveted award in the computing world. Later, Emeagwali's background in engineering combined with his knowledge of computers also led to an important breakthrough in the field of petroleum engineering.

Emeagwali, who works as an independent consultant, has performed engineering duties for the Maryland State Highway Commission and the U.S. Bureau of Reclamation. In addition to work as a researcher at the National Weather Service and the University of Michigan during the 1980s, he was a research fellow at the University of Minnesota's Army High Performance Computing Research Center from 1991–1993. He currently

works as an independent consultant, and is the recipient of number awards, including Computer Scientist of the Year, National Technical Association, 1993; Eminent Engineer, Tau Beta Pi National Engineering Honor Society, 1994; and International Man of the Year, Minority Technology Council of Michigan, 1994.

Solomon C. Fuller (1872–1953)
Neurologist, Psychiatrist

Born on August 11, 1872, in Monrovia, Liberia, Fuller was the son of Solomon Fuller, a coffee planter and government official whose father had been a slave in Virginia. In 1889, he sailed to the United States and earned his M.D. from Boston University School of Medicine in 1897.

By 1900, he had started his own study of mental patients, and four years later, traveled to Germany to study with Emil Kraepelin and Alois Alzheimer, the discoverer of the disease that bears his name. During his stay in Germany, Fuller had an opportunity to spend an afternoon with Paul Ehrlich, who in 1908 would win the Nobel Prize for his research in immunology.

Fuller's most significant contribution was in the study of Alzheimer's disease. By the latter part of the twentieth century, scientists still had not reached full agreement as to its cause. At the time of Fuller's work, the prevailing belief was that arteriosclerosis, or hardening of the arteries, caused Alzheimer's. Fuller disagreed and put forth this opinion in the course of diagnosing the ninth documented case of Alzheimer's. Proof of his ideas came in 1953, the year he died, when other medical researchers would confirm the lack of any linkage between arteriosclerosis and Alzheimer's.

Helene D. Gayle (1955–)
Epidemiologist, AIDS Researcher

Helene Gayle was born on August 16, 1955, in Buffalo, New York, the third of five children of an entrepreneur father and social worker mother. After graduating from Barnard College in 1976, she then won acceptance to the University of Pennsylvania's medical school.

Having once heard a speech on the cure of smallpox had inspired Gayle to pursue public health medicine, and her direction would prove a significant one in the years to come as the plague of AIDS came to decimate communities across the globe. She received her M.D. from University of Pennsylvania as well as a master's degree in public health from Johns Hopkins, both in 1981. After a residency in pediatrics, she was selected to enter the epidemiology training program in 1984 at the Centers for Disease Control in Atlanta, Georgia, the nation's top research center for infectious diseases.

For much of the 1980s Gayle was intensely involved in the CDC's research into AIDS and HIV infection through her work first in the center's Epidemic Intelligence Service, and later as a chief of international AIDS research, a capacity in which she oversaw the scientific investigations of over 300 CDC researchers. Gayle has been instrumental in raising public awareness about the disease, and is especially driven to point out how devastating AIDS has been to the African American community. Sex education, better health care for the poor, and substance abuse prevention are some of the proposals Gayle has championed that she believes will help reduce deaths from AIDS.

In 1992, Gayle was hired as a medical epidemiologist and researcher for the AIDS division of the U.S. Agency for International Development, cementing her reputation as one of the international community's top AIDS scientists. Since 1995 Gayle has served as director of CDC's National Center for HIV, STD, and TB Prevention.

Evelyn Boyd Granville (1924–)
Author, Educator, Lecturer

Born in Washington, D.C., on May 1, 1924, Granville attended Smith College from 1941 to 1946, and earned an A.B. and a M.A. in mathematics. She received a Ph.D. from Yale University in 1949, making her one of the first two African American women to be awarded a Ph.D. in pure mathematics.

Granville's first teaching position was as an instructor at New York University (1949–1950). She then moved to Fisk University where she was an assistant professor (1950–1952). From 1956 to 1960, Granville worked for IBM on the Project Vanguard and Project Mercury space programs, analyzing orbits and developing computer procedures. Over the next seven years, Granville held positions at the Computation and Data Reduction Center of the U.S. Space Technology Laboratories; the North American Aviation Space and Information Systems Division; and as a senior mathematician for IBM.

Granville returned to teaching in 1967, taking a position at California State University in Los Angeles and teaching there until her retirement in 1984. In addition to her role as a college level instructor, Granville worked to improve mathematics skills at all levels. From 1985 to 1988, Granville taught mathematics and computer science at Texas College in Tyler. In 1990, she accepted an appointment to the Sam A. Lindsey Chair at the University of Texas at Tyler, and in subsequent years, has continued teaching there as a visiting

professor. Granville is the co-author of *Theory of Applications of Math for Teachers* (1975). She received an honorary doctorate from Smith College in 1989.

Frederick D. Gregory (1941–)
Airplane Pilot, Astronaut

Gregory was born January 7, 1941 in Washington, DC. He is the nephew of the late Dr. Charles Drew, noted African-American blood plasma specialist. Under the sponsorship of United States Representative Adam Clayton Powell, Gregory attended the U.S. Air Force Academy and graduated with a B.S. in 1964. In 1977, he received an M.S.A. from George Washington University.

Gregory was a helicopter and fighter pilot for the USAF from 1965 to 1970, and a research and test pilot for the USAF and National Aeronautics and Space Administration (NASA) in 1971. In 1978, he was accepted into NASA's astronaut program, making him the second African American astronaut in NASA's history. In 1985, he went into space aboard the *Challenger* Space Shuttle as a pilot, a first for an African American. Gregory served with NASA's Office of Safety and Mission Assurance until 2001, when he was named acting associate administrator for the Office of Space Flight.

Gregory, who retired from the Air Force with the rank of colonel, belongs to the Society of Experimental Test Pilots, the Tuskegee Airmen, the American Helicopter Society, and the National Technical Association. He has won numerous medals and awards including the Meritorious Service Medal, the Air Force Commendation Medal, and two NASA Space Flight Medals. He has twice received the Distinguished Flying Cross. He is also the recipient of George Washington University's Distinguished Alumni Award, NASA's Outstanding Leadership Award, and the National Society of Black Engineers' Distinguished National Scientist Award.

Lloyd A. Hall (1894–1971)
Research Director, Chemist

Grandson of the first pastor of Quinn Chapel A.M.E. Church, the first African American church in Chicago, Lloyd Augustus Hall was born in Elgin, Illinois, on June 20, 1894. A top student and athlete at East High School in Aurora, Illinois, he graduated in the top ten of his class and was offered scholarships to four different colleges in Illinois. In 1916, Hall graduated from Northwestern University with a B.S. in chemistry. He continued his studies at the University of Chicago and the University of Illinois.

During World War I, Hall served as a lieutenant, inspecting explosives at a Wisconsin plant. After the war, Hall joined the Chicago Department of Health Laboratories, where he quickly rose to senior chemist. In 1921, he took employment at Boyer Chemical Laboratory. He became president and chemical director of the Chemical Products Corporation the following year. In 1924, he was offered a position with Griffith Laboratories. Within one year, he was chief chemist and director of research.

There Hall discovered curing salts for the preserving and processing of meats, thus revolutionizing the meatpacking industry. He also discovered how to sterilize spices and researched the effects of antioxidants on fats. Along the way, he registered more than 100 patents for processes used in the manufacturing and packing of food, especially meat and bakery products.

In 1954, Hall became chairman of the Chicago chapter of the American Institute of Chemists. The following year, he was elected a member of the national board of directors, becoming the first African American man to hold that position in the institute's 32-year history. Upon his retirement from Griffith in 1959, Hall continued to serve as a consultant to various state and federal organizations. In 1961, he spent six months in Indonesia, advising the Food and Agricultural Organization of the United Nations. From 1962 to 1964, he was a member of the American Food for Peace Council, an appointment made by President John F. Kennedy.

Marc R. Hannah (1956–)
Computer Scientist

Hannah, a native Chicagoan, was born on October 13, 1956. In high school, he took a computer science course that kindled his interest in this relatively new field. Also inspired by the example of an older brother, he earned high grades that would qualify him for a Bell Laboratories-sponsored scholarship to engineering school. He would eventually earn a Ph.D. from Stanford University in 1985.

While at Stanford, he met James Clark, an engineering professor who was a pioneer in computer graphics, having invented a special computer chip that was the heart of an imaging process. Hannah redesigned the chip to operate five times faster, an advance that impressed Clark enough to invite Hannah to join him in founding a computer graphics company—in 1981 Silicon Graphics was born.

Silicon Graphics' technology has been used to enhance many devices, such as military flight simulators and medical CAT scans. Among the most lucrative areas for this technology, and certainly the one best-known, is that of video and film animation. The special effects made possible by three-dimensional imaging in films such as *Star Wars, Terminator II,* and *Jurassic Park.* Hannah is now vice president and chief scientist of the company's Entry Systems Division.

Matthew A. Henson (1866–1955)
Seaman, Explorer/Surveyor, Author

Matthew Henson was born August 6, 1866, in Charles County, Maryland near Washington, DC. He attended school in Washington, DC, for six years, but at the age of 13, signed on as a cabin boy on a ship headed for China. Henson worked his way up to seaman while he sailed over many of the world's oceans. After several odd jobs in different cities, Henson met U.S. Navy surveyor Robert Edward Peary in Washington, DC. Peary, who was planning a trip to Nicaragua, hired Henson on the spot as his valet. Henson was not pleased at being a personal servant, but nonetheless felt his new position held future opportunities.

Peary eventually made seven trips to the Arctic starting in 1893. He became convinced that he could become the first man to stand at the North Pole. Henson accompanied Peary on these trips to Greenland and became an integral part of Peary's plans. The

Matthew Henson.

pair made four trips looking for a passageway to the North Pole. In 1909, Peary and Henson made their final attempt at reaching the Pole. Although Peary was undoubtedly the driving force of these expeditions, he was increasingly reliant on Henson. Henson's greatest assets were his knowledge of the Inuit language and his ability to readily adapt to their culture. He was also an excellent dog driver, and possessed a physical stamina that Peary lacked due to leukemia. Henson felt that he was serving the African American race by his example of loyalty, fortitude, and trustworthiness.

By the end of March of 1909, they were within 150 miles of their goal. Henson, because of his strength, would break trail and set up camp for the night, while Peary followed. On April 6th, Henson thought he had reached the Pole; Peary arrived later to affirm the belief. Henson then had the honor of planting the U.S. flag.

In 1912, Henson wrote *A Negro at the North Pole*, but the book aroused little interest. By the 1930s, however, Henson began receiving recognition for his contributions to arctic exploration. In 1937, he was the first African American elected to the Explorers Club in New York. In 1944, he and other surviving members of the expedition received Congressional medals. In 1954, Henson received public recognition for his deeds from President Eisenhower. Henson died in 1955 and was buried in New York. In 1988, his remains were exhumed and buried with full military honors at Arlington National Cemetery, next to the grave of Robert Peary.

William A. Hinton (1883–1959)
Lecturer, Medical Researcher, Educator

Long one of the world's authorities on venereal disease, Dr. William A. Hinton is responsible for the development of the Hinton test, a reliable method for detecting syphilis. He also collaborated with Dr. J. A. V. Davies on what is now called the Davies-Hinton test for the detection of this same disease.

Born in Chicago on December 15, 1883, Hinton graduated from Harvard in 1905. In 1912, he finished his medical studies in three years at Harvard Medical School. After graduation, he was a voluntary assistant in the pathological laboratory at Massachusetts General Hospital. This was followed by eight years of laboratory practice at the Boston Dispensary and at the Massachusetts Department of Public Health. In 1923, Hinton was appointed lecturer in preventive medicine and hygiene at Harvard Medical School, where he served for 27 years. In 1949, he was the first person of color to be granted a professorship there.

In 1931, at the Boston Dispensary, Hinton started a training school for poor girls so that they could become medical technicians. From these classes of volunteers grew one of the country's leading institutions for the training of technicians. Though he lost a leg in an automobile accident, Hinton remained active in teaching and at the Boston Dispensary Laboratory, which he directed from 1916 to 1952. He died in Canton, Massachusetts on August 8, 1959.

Shirley Ann Jackson (1946–)
Lecturer, Physicist

Born in Washington, DC, on August 5, 1946, Shirley Ann Jackson graduated as valedictorian of her class from Roosevelt High School in 1964. In 1968, she received a B.S. degree from Massachusetts Institute of Technology. In 1973, she became the first African American woman in the United States to earn a Ph.D. in physics, which she also earned from Massachusetts Institute of Technology.

Jackson's first position—as a research associate at the Fermi National Accelerator Laboratory in Batavia, Illinois where she studied large subatomic particles—reflected her interest in the study of subatomic particles. Jackson has worked as a member of the technical staff on theoretical physics at AT&T Bell Laboratories, as a visiting scientist at the European Center for Nuclear Research in Geneva, and as a visiting lecturer at the NATO International Advanced Study Institute in Belgium.

In 1995, President Bill Clinton named Jackson as chair of the Nuclear Regulatory Commission (NRC). Under Jackson's direction, the NRC became more aggressive about inspections and forced some top officials out of office because of their lax enforcement of safety regulations. Jackson has held the post of professor at Rutgers University and is active in many organizations including the National Academy of Sciences, the American Association for the Advancement of Science, and the National Science Foundation. In 2001, she was elected to the board of the Public Service Enterprise Group, just one day after being appointed a director of the AT&T Corporation. Jackson has also been named to seven boards of publicly traded companies since July 1999, when she became president of Rensselaer Polytechnic Institute.

Mae C. Jemison (1956–)
Physician/Surgeon

Mae Jemison was born October 17, 1956, in Decatur, Alabama, but her family moved to Chicago when she was three years old. She attended Stanford University

Mae Jemison became the first African American woman in space in 1992.

on a National Achievement Scholarship and received a B.S. in chemical engineering and a B.A. in Afro-American studies in 1977. She then enrolled in Cornell University's medical school and graduated in 1981. Her medical internship was at the Los Angeles County/ University of Southern California Medical Center in 1982. She was a general practitioner with the INA/Ross Loos Medical Group in Los Angeles until 1983, followed by two years as a Peace Corps medical officer in Sierra Leone and Liberia. Returning to the United States in 1985, she began working for CIGNA Health Plans, a health maintenance organization in Los Angeles, and applied for admission into NASA's astronaut program.

In 1987, Jemison was accepted in NASA's astronaut program. Her first assignment was representing the astronaut office at the Kennedy Space Center in Cape Canaveral, Florida. On September 12, 1992, Jemison became the first African American woman in space on the shuttle *Endeavour*. She served aboard the *Endeavour* as a science specialist. As a physician, she studied the effect of weightlessness on herself and other crew members. Jemison resigned from NASA in

1993 to pursue personal goals related to science education and health care in West Africa. In 1994, Jemison founded the International Science Camp in Chicago to help young people become enthusiastic about science.

In 1988, Jemison won the Science and Technology Award given by *Essence* magazine and in 1990 she was Gamma Sigma Gamma's Woman of the Year. In 1991, she earned a Ph.D. from Lincoln University. She also served on the board of directors of the World Sickle Cell Foundation from 1990 to 1992.

Frederick M. Jones (1893–1961)
Mechanic

In 1935, Frederick McKinley Jones built the first automatic refrigeration system for long haul trucks. Later, the system was adapted to various other carriers including railway cars, ships, and trucks. Previously, foods were packed in ice so slight delays led to spoilage. Jones' new method instigated a change in eating habits of the entire nation and allowed for the development of food production facilities in almost any geographic location. Refrigerated trucks were also used to preserve and ship blood products during World War II.

Jones was born in Kentucky in 1893. His mother left the family when he was a baby, and his father left him at age five to be raised by a priest until he was 16 years of age. There Jones received a sixth grade education. When he left the rectory, he worked as a pin boy, mechanic's assistant, and finally, as chief mechanic on a Minnesota farm. He served in World War I and, in the late 1920s, his mechanical fame spread when he developed a series of devices to adapt silent movie projectors into sound projectors.

Jones also developed an air conditioning unit for military field hospitals, a portable x-ray machine, and a refrigerator for military field kitchens. During his life, a total of 61 patents were issued in Jones's name. He died in 1961.

Percy L. Julian (1899–1975)
Educator, Medical Researcher, Research Director

Born on April 11, 1899 in Montgomery, Alabama, Julian attended DePauw University in Greencastle, Indiana. He graduated Phi Beta Kappa at DePauw University and was valedictorian of his class after having lived during his college days in the attic of a fraternity house where he worked as a waiter. For several years, Julian taught at Fisk, West Virginia State College, and Howard University where he was associate professor and head of the chemistry department.

He left to attend Harvard and the University of Vienna, where he earned a Ph.D. in 1931. Julian then continued his research and teaching duties at Howard.

In 1935, Julian synthesized the drug physostigmine, which is used today in the treatment of glaucoma. He later became director of research, chief chemist and did soybean research at the Glidden Company, where he specialized in the production of sterols, which he extracted from the oil of the soybean. The method perfected by Julian in 1950 eventually lowered the cost of sterols to less than 20 cents a gram and, ultimately, enabled millions of people suffering from arthritis to obtain relief through the use of cortisone, a sterol derivative. Later, Julian developed methods for manufacturing sex hormones from soya bean sterols: progesterone was used to prevent miscarriages, while testosterone was used to treat older men for diminishing sex drive. Both hormones were important in the treatment of cancer.

In 1954, after serving as director of research for the Glidden Company, he founded his own company, the Julian Laboratories, in Chicago and Mexico. Years later, the company was sold to Smith, Kline, and French. In 1947, Julian was awarded the Spingarn Medal and, in 1964, he founded Julian Institute and Julian Associates Incorporated in Franklin Park, Illinois. He was awarded the Chemical Pioneer Award by the American Institute of Chemists in 1968. Julian died on April 19, 1975.

Ernest E. Just (1883–1941)
Editor, Zoologist, Marine Biologist

Born in Charleston, South Carolina, on August 14, 1883, Ernest Just received his B.A. in 1907 with high honors from Dartmouth and his Ph.D. in 1916 from the University of Chicago. His groundbreaking work on the embryology of marine invertebrates included research on fertilization—a process known as parthenogenesis—but his most important achievement was his discovery of the role protoplasm plays in the development of a cell.

Just began teaching at Howard University in 1907 and started graduate training at the Marine Biological Laboratory in Woods Hole, Massachusetts in 1909. He performed most of his research at this site over the next 20 summers. Between 1912 and 1937, he published more than 50 papers on fertilization, parthenogenesis, cell division, and mutation. He also published a textbook in 1939 that was the result of his research in cell functioning and the structure and role of protoplasm within a cell.

A member of Phi Beta Kappa, Just received the Spingarn Medal in 1914 and served as associate editor of *Physiological Zoology, The Biological Bulletin,* and

The Journal of Morphology. In 1930 Just was one of 12 zoologists to address the International Congress of Zoologists and he was elected vice president of the American Society of Zoologists. Just left the United States in 1929 because of racist attitudes that prevented his career from advancing. He died on October 27, 1941.

Samuel L. Kountz (1930–1981)
Physician/Surgeon, Medical Researcher

Born in 1930 in Lexa, Arkansas, Samuel Kountz graduated third in his class at the Agricultural, Mechanical and Normal College of Arkansas in 1952, having initially failed his entrance exams. He pursued graduate studies at the University of Arkansas, earning a degree in chemistry. Senator J. W. Fulbright, whom he met while a graduate student, advised Kountz to apply for a scholarship to medical school. Kountz won the scholarship on a competitive basis and was the first African American to enroll at the University of Arkansas Medical School in Little Rock, graduating with his M.D. in 1958. Kountz was responsible for finding out that large doses of the drug methylprednisolone could help reverse the acute rejection of a transplanted kidney. The drug was used for a number of years in the standard management of kidney transplant patients.

While he was still an intern, Kountz assisted in the first West Coast kidney transplant. In 1964, working with Dr. Roy Cohn, one of the pioneers in the field of transplantation, Kountz again made medical history by transplanting a kidney from a mother to a daughter—the first transplant between humans who were not identical twins. At the University of California in 1967, Dr. Kountz worked with other researchers to develop the prototype of a machine that is now able to preserve kidneys up to 50 hours from the time they are taken from the body of a donor. The machine, called the Belzer Kidney Perfusion Machine, was named for Dr. Folker O. Belzer, who was Kountz's partner. Kountz went on to build one of the largest kidney transplant training and research centers in the nation. He died in 1981 after a long illness contracted on a trip to South Africa in 1977.

Lewis H. Latimer (1848–1928)
Draftsperson, Electrical Engineer

Lewis Howard Latimer was employed by Alexander Graham Bell to make the patent drawings for the first telephone, and later he went on to become chief draftsman for both the General Electric and Westinghouse companies. Born in Chelsea, Massachusetts, on September 4, 1848, Latimer enlisted in the Union Navy at the age of 15 and began studying drafting upon completion of his military service. In 1881, he invented a method of making carbon filaments for the Maxim electric incandescent lamp and later patented this method. He also supervised the installation of electric light in New York, Philadelphia, Montreal, and London for the Maxim-Weston Electric Company. In 1884, he joined the Edison Company.

Theodore K. Lawless (1892–1971)
Physician, Philanthropist

Theodore Kenneth Lawless was born on December 6, 1892, in Thibodeaux, Louisiana. He received his B.S. from Talladega College in 1914 and continued to further his education at the University of Kansas and Northwestern University, where he received his M.D. in 1919. He then pursued a master's in dermatology, which he finished at Columbia University. From there he furthered his studies at Harvard University, the University of Paris, the University of Freiburg, and the University of Vienna.

Lawless started his own practice in the Chicago's predominantly African American South Side upon his return in 1924, which he continued until his death in 1971. He soon became one of the premiere dermatologists in the country and earned great praise for researching treatments and cures for a variety of skin diseases including syphilis and leprosy. During the early years of his career, he taught dermatology at Northwestern University Medical School, where his research was instrumental in devising electropyrexia, a treatment for those suffering cases of syphilis in its early stages. Before he left his role at Northwestern in 1941, he aided in building the university's first medical laboratories.

After leaving Northwestern, Lawless entered the business world beginning as president of 4213 South Michigan Corporation, which sold low-cost real estate, and later as president of the Service Federal Savings and Loan Association. And by the 1960s, he was well-known as one of the 35 richest African American men in the United States. During his lifetime, Lawless served on dozens of boards of directors and belonged to countless organizations. He served on the Chicago Board of Health, as senior attending physician at Provident hospital, as associate examiner in dermatology for the National Board of Medical Examiners, as chairman of the Division of Higher Education, and as consultant to the Geneva Community Hospital in Switzerland. He was also recognized with many awards for his exemplary breakthroughs in medicine, public service, and philanthropy including the Harmon Award in Medicine in 1929, the Churchman of the Year in 1952, the Springarn

Medal from the NAACP in 1954, and the Daniel H. Burnham Award from Roosevelt University in 1963. He died in 1971.

Robert H. Lawrence Jr. (1935–1967)
Astronaut, Airplane Pilot

Air Force Major Robert H. Lawrence Jr. was the first African American astronaut to be appointed to the Manned Orbiting Laboratory. Lawrence was a native of Chicago, and while still in elementary school he became a model airplane hobbyist and a chess enthusiast. Lawrence became interested in biology during his time at Englewood High School in Chicago. As a student at Englewood, Lawrence excelled in chemistry and track. When he graduated, he placed in the top ten percent of the class.

Lawrence entered Bradley University, joining the Air Force Reserve Officer's Training Corps and attaining the rank of lieutenant colonel, making him the second highest ranking cadet at Bradley. Lawrence was commissioned a second lieutenant in the United States Air Force in 1956 and soon after received his bachelors degree in chemistry. Following a stint at an air base in Germany, Lawrence entered Ohio State University through the Air Force Institute of Technology as a doctoral candidate, earning his Ph.D. in 1965. Lawrence's career came to an end in 1967 when his F-104D Starfighter jet crashed on a runway in a California desert.

Elijah McCoy (1843–1929)
Inventor, Machinist

Born in Canada, McCoy traveled to Scotland at age 16. There he was apprenticed to a master mechanic and engineer. After the Civil War, he moved to Ypsilanti, Michigan, where he sought work as an engineer. However, he was only able to obtain employment as a fireman and oiler for Michigan Central Railroad.

McCoy's first invention was a lubricating cup that used steam pressure to drive oil into channels that brought it to a steam engine's moving parts. It was patented in 1872. Before this invention, these parts had to be oiled at the car's intermittent stops, slowing the pace of rail travel considerably. In addition, the automatic device kept the engine better lubricated than was possible with the old method. Variations of this cup came to be used on many types of heavy machinery. Although McCoy received at least 72 patents in his lifetime, little money would reach his pockets as a result of his ideas. Because he lacked the capital to invest in manufacturing, he sold most of his patents for modest sums of money while the manufacturers made millions. Later in his life, he helped found the Elijah

Elijah McCoy.

McCoy Manufacturing Company, but he died just a few years later.

Ronald E. McNair (1950–1986)
Astronaut

Ronald McNair was born on October 21, 1950, in Lake City, South Carolina. He was a graduate of North Carolina A&T State University with a B.S. degree in physics. He also received a Doctorate of Philosophy in Physics from Massachusetts Institute of Technology. He was presented an honorary Doctorate of Laws from North Carolina A&T in 1978.

McNair was working on the use of lasers in satellite communications when he was selected by NASA in 1978 to train as an astronaut. In August 1979, he completed a one-year training and evaluation period that made him eligible for assignment as mission specialist on Space Shuttle flight crews. He presented papers in the areas of lasers and molecular spectroscopy and gave many presentations in the United States and Europe. He was the second African American to orbit the earth on a NASA mission.

Despite the rigorous training in the NASA program, he taught karate at a church, played the saxophone, and found time to interact with young people. McNair was aboard the shuttle *Challenger* that exploded shortly after liftoff from Cape Kennedy and plunged into the waters off the Florida coast on January 28, 1986. The shuttle had a crew of seven persons including two women, a mission specialist, and a teacher-in-space participant.

Walter E. Massey (1938–)
Physicist

Walter Eugene Massey was born in Hattiesburg, Mississippi, on April 5, 1938. At the end of tenth grade, he accepted a scholarship to Morehouse College. He almost quit after a few weeks, but graduated four years later with a B.S. in physics. He completed his Ph.D. in physics in 1966.

Massey's research interests have included solid state theory (study of properties of solid material) and theories of quantum liquids and solids. While still a graduate student, he studied the behavior of both solid and liquid helium-3 and helium-4, publishing a series of papers on this work in the early 1970s. He became a full professor at Brown University in 1975 and was named dean of the college in the same year. Massey's best-known accomplishment at Brown was his development of the Inner City Teachers of Science (ICTOS) program, a program for the improvement of science instruction in inner city schools. He was awarded the American Association for the Advancement of Science's Distinguished Service Citation for his development of ICTOS.

In 1979, the University of Chicago invited Massey to become professor of physics and director of the Argonne National Laboratory, which the university operates for the U.S. Department of Energy. The facility was beset by financial troubles at the time, and Massey has been credited with its successful recovery. In the fall of 1990, Massey was chosen by Pres. George H. W. Bush to head the National Science Foundation (NSF), a position he held until 1993. He was only the second African American to hold that post. Massey has been president of Morehouse College since 1995.

Jan Matzeliger (1852–1889)
Inventor, Shoemaker/Leather Worker

Born in 1852 in Paramaribo, Dutch Guiana, Matzeliger found employment in the government machine works at the age of 10. Nine years later, he left home and eventually immigrated to the United States, settling in Philadelphia, where he worked in a shoe factory. He later moved to New England, settling permanently in

Lynn, Massachusetts in 1877. The Industrial Revolution had by this time resulted in the invention of machines to cut, sew, and tack shoes, but none had been perfected to last a shoe, which involved stretching the leather over a model foot. Observing this, Matzeliger designed and patented a device, one which he refined over the years to a point where it could last the leather, arrange the leather over the sole, drive in the nails, and deliver the finished product—all in one minute's time.

Matzeliger's patent was subsequently bought by Sydney W. Winslow, who established the United Shoe Machine Company. The continued success of this business brought about a 50 percent reduction in the price of shoes across the nation, doubled wages for unskilled workers, and improved working conditions for millions of people dependent on the shoe industry for their livelihood. Between 1883 and 1891, Matzeliger received five patents on his inventions, all which contributed to the shoe making revolution. His last patent was issued in September 1891, two years after his death.

Matzeliger died of tuberculosis in 1889 at the age of 37, long before he had the chance to realize a share of the enormous profit derived from his invention. He never received any money. Instead, he was issued stock in the company that did not become valuable until after his demise.

Garrett A. Morgan (1877–1963)
Inventor

Born in Paris, Kentucky, in 1877, Morgan moved to Cleveland at an early age. Although he was most famous for his invention of the gas inhalator, an early gas mask, he also invented an improvement on the sewing machine that he sold for $150, as well as a hair refining cream that straightened human hair. The cream remained in use for over 40 years. In 1923, having established his reputation with the gas inhalator, he was able to command a price of $40,000 from the General Electric Company for his automatic traffic signal.

In 1912, Morgan developed his "safety hood," a gas inhalator that was a precursor to the gas mask. The value of his invention was first acknowledged during a successful rescue operation of several men trapped by a tunnel explosion in the Cleveland Waterworks, some 200 feet below the surface of Lake Erie. During the emergency, Morgan, his brother, and two other volunteers were the only men able to descend into the smoky, gas-filled tunnel and save several workers from asphyxiation.

Orders for the Morgan inhalator soon began to pour into Cleveland from fire companies all over the nation, but as soon as Morgan's racial identity became known, many of them were canceled. In the South, it was necessary for Morgan to utilize the services of a white man to demonstrate his invention. During World War I the Morgan inhalator was transformed into a gas mask used by combat troops. Morgan died in 1963 in Cleveland—the city that had awarded him a gold medal for his devotion to public safety.

Waverly J. Person (1927–)
Geophysicist

Waverly J. Person, born on May 1, 1927, is the first African American to hold the prominent position of director of the United States Geological Survey's National Earthquake Information Center. A respected geophysicist and seismologist, he was also one of the first African Americans in his field. He also currently encourages minority students to consider the earth sciences as a career.

While a technician at the National Information Earthquake Center, he took up graduate studies. From 1962 to 1973, he held that position and simultaneously completed graduate work at American University and George Washington University. His supervisors increasingly assigned him more challenging tasks that he performed well, gaining notice among his peers. Soon, he was qualified as a geophysicist and transferred to the United States Geological Survey's National Earthquake Information Center in Colorado. In 1977, Person was named director of the Colorado National Earthquake Information Center, and in 1994, was named director of the National Earthquake Information Center.

Person has been honored with many distinguished awards throughout his professional life. These include an Honorary Doctorate in Science from St. Paul's College in 1988; Outstanding Government Communicator in 1988; Meritorious Service Award—United States Department Interior in 1989; and in 1990, the Annual Minority Award from the Community Services Department in Boulder, Colorado. His work at the National Earthquake Information Center has been praised by United States Department of the Interior.

Norbert Rillieux (1806–1894)
Inventor, Mechanical Engineer

Norbert Rillieux's inventions were of great value to the sugar refining industry. The method formerly used called for gangs of slaves to ladle boiling sugarcane juice from one kettle to another—a primitive process

Norbert Rillieux.

known as "the Jamaica Train." In 1845, Rillieux invented a vacuum evaporating pan (a series of condensing coils in vacuum chambers) that reduced the industry's dependence on gang labor, and helped manufacture a superior product at a greatly reduced cost. The first Rillieux evaporator was installed at Myrtle Grove Plantation, Louisiana, in 1845. In the following years, factories in Louisiana, Cuba, and Mexico converted to the Rillieux system.

A native of New Orleans, Rillieux was the son of Vincent Rillieux, a wealthy engineer, and Constance Vivant, a slave on his plantation. Young Rillieux's higher education was obtained in Paris, where his extraordinary aptitude for engineering led to his appointment at the age of 24 as an instructor of applied mechanics at L'Ecole Centrale. Rillieux returned to Paris permanently in 1854, securing a scholarship and working on the deciphering of hieroglyphics.

When his evaporator process was finally adopted in Europe, he returned to inventing with renewed interest— applying his process to the sugar beet. In so doing, he cut production and refining costs in half. Rillieux died in Paris on October 8, 1894, leaving behind a system

that is in universal use throughout the sugar industry, as well as in the manufacture of soap, gelatin, glue, and many other products.

Mabel K. Staupers (1890–1988)
Former National Association of Colored Graduate Nurses President, Nurse, Civil Rights Advocate

As president of the National Association of Colored Graduate Nurses, Mabel Keaton Staupers led a successful drive to integrate the mainstream nursing profession and to end segregation in the U.S. Armed Forces Nurse Corps in World War II.

Staupers was born in Barbados, West Indies, on February 27, 1890, and migrated to the United States in 1903, settling in Harlem. She began her nursing education in 1914 at Freedmen's Hospital School of Nursing (now known as Howard University College of Nursing) in Washington, DC, and in 1917 graduated with class honors. After graduation, she began private-duty nursing until, with the assistance of physicians Louis T. Wright and James Wilson, she helped to found the Booker T. Washington Sanitarium in Harlem in 1922. This served as Harlem's first inpatient center for African American patients with tuberculosis.

With a working fellowship, Staupers spent time at Jefferson Hospital Medical College in Philadelphia, then conducted a survey of health needs in Harlem for the New York Tuberculosis Association. She identified the health care problems of minorities, leading to the establishment of the Harlem Committee of the New York Tuberculosis and Health Association. Ultimately, she served 12 years as executive secretary.

During the 1930s and 1940s, Staupers worked closely with association president Estelle Massey Riddle in a fight to integrate African American nurses into the mainstream of nursing. On January 20, 1945, the surgeon general of the U.S. Army announced that race would no longer be a factor in accepting nurses into the Army Nurse Corps. The U.S. Navy followed five days later by integrating the Navy Nurse Corps.

Later Staupers fought to end the racial barriers of the American Nurses' Association (ANA); in 1948, its House of Delegates opened the organization to African American members. By 1949, however, Staupers persuaded the NACGN's members that the organization had realized its goals and was now obsolete. The organization's convention in that year voted to dissolve the organization, and Staupers presided over the formal dissolution.

In recognition of her leadership and efforts to remove racial barriers for African American women in the military and the ANA, Staupers was widely honored. Among her honors was the Spingarn Medal, which she received from the National Association for the Advancement of Colored People in 1951. She recorded the plight of African American nurses in her book *No Time for Prejudice: A Story of the Integration of Negroes in the United States.* Staupers died on November 29, 1989.

Lewis Temple (1800–1854)
Inventor

The toggle harpoon invented by Lewis Temple improved the whaling methods of the nineteenth century, leading to a doubling of the annual catch. Little is known of Temple's early background, except that he was born in Richmond, Virginia, in 1800 and had no formal education. As a young man he moved to New Bedford, Massachusetts, then a major whaling port. Finding work as a metal smith, Temple modified the design of the whaler's harpoon and, in 1848, manufactured a new version of the harpoon with a barbed and pivoting head, making it much harder for a harpooned whale to escape. Using the "toggle harpoon," the whaling industry soon entered a period of unprecedented prosperity. Temple, who never patented his harpoon, died destitute.

Vivien Thomas (1910–1985)
Surgical Research Technician

Born in Nashville, Tennessee, in 1910, Thomas had dreamed of a career as a physician since childhood. As a teenager, he worked as a carpenter and as an orderly to earn money for college, and enrolled in Tennessee Agricultural and Industrial College in 1929. The stock market crash later that year eradicated Thomas's savings, and he was forced to quit school.

The following year, he was hired for a research assistant post at Vanderbilt University Medical School; he would become trauma researcher and surgeon Alfred Blalock's assistant. For the next decade, Thomas worked long hours in the lab, conducting medical experiments for Blalock that eventually led to lifesaving advances in medicine during World War II, especially in the use of blood transfusions.

When Blalock was hired by the prestigious medical school at Johns Hopkins University in 1940, he would accept the post only if they hired Thomas as well. One of their most significant achievements together was a surgical procedure that restructured the blood vessels around an infant's heart if the child was in danger of death due to poor circulation of blood into the lungs.

Vivien Thomas.

Thomas became a well-known, and well-regarded figure on the campus of Johns Hopkins. He remained at the institution even after his mentor passed away in 1964, and in 1971, was honored by graduates of its medical school for his achievements. He became a medical school faculty member in 1977, and received an honorary degree in 1976. He retired in 1979. Thomas passed away in 1985, the same year a recounting of his life was published titled *Pioneering Research in Surgical Shock and Cardiovascular Surgery: Vivien Thomas and His Work with Alfred Blalock.*

Margaret E. M. Tolbert (1943–)
Analytical Chemist

Margaret E. Mayo Tolbert was born on November 24, 1943, the third of six children raised by their grandmother. She obtained an M.S. in analytical chemistry in one year, and in 1970, she was recruited to join the doctoral program in chemistry at Brown University. Her research on biochemical reactions in liver cells was partially funded by a scholarship from the Southern Fellowship Fund.

In 1979, Tolbert spent five months in Brussels, Belgium, studying how different drugs are metabolized in rat liver cells at the International Institute of Cellular and Molecular Pathology. After her return to the United States, she was appointed director of the Carver Research Foundation. During her tenure, Tolbert was able to bring several large scientific research contracts to the university from the federal government—contracts that expanded the research capabilities of the entire school. From 1990–1993, Tolbert directed the Research Improvement in Minority Institutions Program for the National Science Foundation (NSF), which works to strengthen the infrastructure of research programs at minority colleges and universities.

In 1996, Tolbert was appointed the director of the New Brunswick Laboratory at Argonne National Laboratories. As only the third director in the laboratory's almost 50-year history, Tolbert's position allows her to help the entire country by enhancing nuclear security nationally as well as support international nonproliferation efforts. In addition, Tolbert was elected a fellow of the American Association for the Advancement of Science in 1998. She is a member of Sigma Xi, the American Chemical Society, the Organization of Black Scientists, and the American Association of University Women. She organized the U.S. Department of Energy's Science Education Directors Council in 1994, and served as the council's chair in 1995–1996.

Omar Wasow (1970–)
Computer Programmer, Entrepreneur

Wasow is an Internet analyst for "NewsChannel 4" in New York. His reports appear on the station's various newscasts, and he is a frequent contributor to the station's Web site. He also serves as the Internet analyst for MSNBC. In addition, Wasow is the executive director of BlackPlanet.com at Community Connect Inc., a Web site that facilitates online community among African Americans.

Wasow has become a leading commentator on the challenges and opportunities of new media and the new economy. The founder of New York Online, he was tagged by the *New York Times* as a "pioneer in Silicon Alley," *Newsweek* magazine as one of the "50 most influential people to watch in cyberspace," one of the "Silicon Alley Top 10" by the *Village Voice* and "one of fifty to watch in 1999" by *A-List* magazine.

In 1993, Wasow predicted a shift in online demographics from hackers and academics to mainstream users, and rapidly produced the widely admired local online community New York Online. As his reputation grew, corporate clients like *VIBE, Essence, Consumer Reports, Latina Magazine, The New Yorker,*

United Artists, and Samsung retained his company's expertise to assist them in launching successful Internet ventures of their own.

Wasow is also a member of the Board of Contributors of *USA Today*, and writes an Internet business column for FeedMag.com. Active in a number of social issues, particularly school reform, Wasow is the co-chair of The Coalition for Independent Public Charter Schools. In that capacity, he helped push New York state to pass its recent breakthrough Charter Legislation. He is also a member of several non-profit boards including the New York Software Industry Association, WorldStudio, and The Refugee Project. As a result of Wasow's long standing commitment to civic participation, he was recently selected to be a fellow in the Rockefeller Foundation's Next Generation Leadership program.

Levi Watkins Jr. (1945–)
Surgeon, Educator

Levi Watkins was born in Kansas in 1945 but grew up in Montgomery, Alabama, where through his involvement in local churches he became acquainted with civil rights leaders Dr. Ralph David Abernathy and the Rev. Martin Luther King Jr. Both were prominent members of the Montgomery community, as was Watkins's own father, a college professor. The teenager's participation in civil rights issues did not stop him from excelling academically, as he graduated as valedictorian of his high school class and went on to earn a 1966 honors degree from Tennessee State University.

Watkins's awareness of issues of racial inequality led him to apply to Vanderbilt University Medical School, and he first learned of his acceptance as its first African American student by reading the newspaper headline announcing the breakthrough. He graduated in 1970, and began his internship and surgical training at the prestigious medical school at Johns Hopkins University. Watkins also studied at Harvard University Medical School for a time, and conducted research that led to the lifesaving practice of prescribing angiotensin blockers for patients susceptible to heart failure.

In 1978, Watkins became Johns Hopkins's first African American chief resident in cardiac surgery, and became a faculty member that year as well. Two years later, he made medical history with the first successful surgical implantation of an AID (Automatic Implantable Defibrillator) device, which has been credited with saving countless lives by its ability to restore a normal heartbeat during an attack of arrhythmia. In 1991, he became a full professor of cardiac surgery at Johns Hopkins, another first for the institution. For several years, however, Watkins had been working to increase minority presence at this elite medical school, and he instituted a special minority recruiting drive when he was appointed to the medical school's admissions committee in 1979. He is currently Dean for Postdoctoral Programs and Faculty Development at Johns Hopkins.

Daniel H. Williams (1856–1931)
Surgeon/Physician

A pioneer in open heart surgery, Daniel Hale Williams was born in Hollidaysburg, Pennsylvania, on January 18, 1856. In 1878, he apprenticed to a prominent physician, giving him the training to enter the Chicago Medical College in 1883.

Williams opened his office on Chicago's South Side at a time when Chicago hospitals did not allow African American doctors to use their facilities. In 1891, Dr. Williams founded Provident Hospital, which was open to patients of all races. At Provident Hospital on July 10, 1893, Williams performed the operation upon which his later fame rests. A patient was admitted to the emergency ward with a knife wound in the pericardium, or the membrane enclosing the heart. With the aid of six staff surgeons, Williams made an incision in the patient's chest and successfully repaired the tear. The patient fully recovered and was soon able to leave the hospital.

In 1894, Pres. Cleveland appointed Williams surgeon-in-chief of Freedmen's Hospital in Washington, DC. He completely reorganized and updated procedures at the hospital, adding specialty departments, organizing a system horse-drawn ambulances, and initiating more sanitary medical practices. After some political infighting at Freedmen's, he resigned his post in 1897 to return to Provident.

Williams was instrumental in the forming of the Medico-Chirurgical Society and the National Medical Association. In 1913, he was inducted into the American Board of Surgery at its first convention. Over the course of his career, Williams helped establish over 40 hospitals in 20 states to serve African American communities. He died on August 4, 1931, after a lifetime devoted to his two main interests—the NAACP and the construction of hospitals and training schools for African American doctors and nurses.

O. S. Williams (1921–)
Aeronautical Engineer

Oswald S. "Ozzie" Williams was born on September 2, 1921, in Washington, DC. He was the second African American to receive a degree in aeronautical engineering in 1943, and he earned his master's in the field in 1947.

In 1950, Williams took an engineering position at Greer Hydraulics, Inc. There he was responsible for the development of the first experimental airborne radio beacon, which was used to locate crashed airplanes. However, it was never produced commercially. At Grumman International, where he was hired on as a propulsion engineer in 1961, Williams managed the development of the *Apollo* Lunar Module reaction control subsystem. He was fully responsible for the $42 million effort for eight years. He managed the three engineering groups that developed the small rocket motors that guided the lunar module, the part of the *Apollo* spacecraft that actually landed on the moon. Williams went on to a career in marketing at Grumman, culminating in his election as a company vice president in 1974.

28

Sports

◆ Baseball ◆ Football ◆ Boxing ◆ Basketball ◆ Other Sports ◆ Women in Sports
◆ Athletes, Coaches, and Sports Executives
◆ Winners of Select Prizes and Tournaments

Despite the prejudices of the nineteenth and twentieth centuries, African Americans have excelled in various sports. In addition to accomplishing a multitude of athletic feats, many of the exploits of African American athletes have helped to spur societal changes. The integration of baseball in 1947 by Jackie Robinson and the legacy of heavyweight champion Joe Louis helped to launch the Civil Rights movement. Additionally, the rise in black nationalism of the 1960s and 1970s was projected by the words and deeds of African American athletes, such as Muhammad Ali, Wilt Chamberlain, and Curt Flood.

Professional and some amateur sports have also given African Americans the opportunity for instant fame and wealth afforded by few other venues. For some, success on the athletic field carries over into the private sector, as many African American athletes have used their wealth and clout to start businesses and give back to the community. As the twenty-first century begins, however, a major obstacle exists—few African Americans have been given employment in front office positions or been granted ownership of professional sports teams.

◆ BASEBALL

Professional baseball began in Hoboken, New Jersey, in 1846. The game was dominated by amateurs and roving semi-professionals until the National League was formed in 1876. Initially, there was no prohibition against African Americans playing in the National League or its rivals—the American Association, the Union League, and the Players League. Moses Fleetwood Walker was the first prominent African American professional baseball player during the 1880s for the Toledo Mud Hens of the American Association. However, in an exhibition game with a National League team, the Chicago White Stockings, the "color line" was drawn in baseball for the first time. White Stockings player/manager Cap Anson refused to play on the same field with Walker. Later, when Anson heard an African American was about to be signed in the National League, he used his influence to initiate a "gentlemen's agreement" among the teams not to sign any African American players. This agreement became the standard in organized baseball.

Efforts to sneak African Americans into the major leagues under the guise of being Cuban or American Indians failed. Until the 1920s, the only way for African Americans to play baseball was as semi-professionals touring and playing wherever they got the chance. As the 1920s dawned, an organized, professional Negro League was established by Rube Foster and others to give African Americans the chance to play big league baseball. The Negro League featured teams such as the Detroit Stars, Homestead Grays, New York Elite Giants, and others that played wherever they could find a stadium and funding. They frequently filled Major League Baseball stadiums when given the chance and the quality of their product was evidenced by such Hall of Fame players as Satchel Paige, Josh Gibson, Ray Dandridge, "Cool Papa" Bell, Oscar Charleston, Buck Leonard, and Judy Johnson.

The Negro League was never financially stable, however, and teams frequently folded. Many chose to—or felt their best option was to—play for pay in Cuba or the Dominican Republic. Despite efforts by Major League Commissioner Kenesaw Mountain Landis to stop them, many exhibition games were arranged between Negro League and Major League All-Star teams. The exhibitions were competitive and the Negro League players demonstrated their skill by winning many of the contests. As long as Landis was commissioner of Major League Baseball, however, integration was impossible.

Jackie Robinson, known far and wide as the man who broke Major League Baseball's color barrier.

In 1945, following the death of Landis and the appointment of Happy Chandler as commissioner, Brooklyn Dodger general manager and part-owner Branch Rickey began a search for an African American to integrate Major League Baseball. He settled on UCLA alumnus Jackie Robinson. In 1946, Robinson played for the Dodgers top minor league team in Montreal. In 1947, he integrated baseball despite virulent opposition from players, teammates, and all of the other Major League Baseball owners. Robinson was named the National League's Rookie of the Year in 1947 and won the Most Valuable Player award in 1949. The Cleveland Indians integrated the American League in 1947 with Larry Doby.

By 1958, all Major League Baseball teams had integrated their rosters and African American players became stars in both leagues. In 1975, Frank Robinson became the first African American manager of a Major League Baseball team with the Cleveland Indians. However, baseball's front office positions remained closed to African Americans as the game features few African American managers or general managers. The power structure changed slightly in the 1988 when former player Bill White became the first African American to be president of the National League. White was succeeded in 1994 by another African American, Leonard Coleman.

In addition, many of baseball's top stars have been African American. Hank Aaron became baseball's all-time home run leader and drove in more runs than anyone in history. Rickey Henderson holds the record for most steals, and Lee Smith has more saves than any other player. Additionally, African American players have been the recipients of the Most Valuable Player Award in the American or National League over 35 percent of the time during the last half century.

Curt Flood also changed the face of baseball. In 1969, Flood decided to challenge his trade from the St. Louis Cardinals to the Philadelphia Phillies on the grounds that baseball's reserve clause—binding players to their existing teams—was in violation of federal antitrust laws. A lawsuit brought by Flood was eventually heard by the U.S. Supreme Court, which ruled against Flood and decided that baseball could retain its posture as the only professional sport exempted from federal antitrust legislation. Shortly after the decision, an agreement between the players and management ended the reserve system and established free agency.

The percentage of African American players in Major League Baseball has declined since its peak in the 1970s. One factor responsible for this change is the streamlining of inner city baseball programs and urban little leagues due to financial problems. The economic situation has become so bad in some American cities that even scholastic athletic programs are threatened with cutbacks or dissolution. Nevertheless, many of the game's top players are African American, including Barry Bonds, Mike Cameron, Cliff Floyd, Ken Griffey Jr., Derek Jeter, and Gary Sheffield.

In 1997—the 50th anniversary of the the game being racially integrated—Major League Baseball took action to honor Jackie Robinson's feat. Commissioner Bud Selig retired his number 42 from use by *any* baseball team. President Bill Clinton offered remarks on Robinson's legacy at a ceremony in New York's Shea Stadium. Also that summer, Robinson's widow, Rachel, took part in a ceremony at the Baseball Hall of Fame dedicating a wing to African Americans.

NATIONAL BASEBALL HALL OF FAME
1962: Jackie Robinson
1969: Roy Campanella
1971: Leroy R. "Satchel" Paige
1972: Josh Gibson; Walter "Buck" Leonard
1973: Roberto W. Clemente; Monte Irvin

1974: James T. "Cool Papa" Bell
1975: William "Judy" Johnson
1976: Oscar M. Charleston
1977: Ernest Banks; Martin Dihigo; John H. Lloyd
1979: Willie Mays
1981: Andrew "Rube" Foster; Robert T. Gibson
1982: Hank Aaron; Frank Robinson
1983: Juan A. Marichal
1985: Lou Brock
1986: Willie L. "Stretch" McCovey
1987: Ray Dandridge; Billy Williams
1988: Willie Stargell
1990: Joe Morgan
1991: Rod Carew; Ferguson Jenkins
1993: Reggie Jackson
1995: Leon Day
1996: Bill Foster
1997: Willie Wells
1998: Larry Doby
1999: Orlando Cepeda; Joe Williams
2000: Tony Pérez; Norman "Turkey" Stearnes
2001: Kirby Puckett; Hilton Smith; Dave Winfield
2002: Ozzie Smith

◆ FOOTBALL

Unlike the other major American sports, professional football was integrated from its inception. Beginning in 1919 with Fritz Pollard of the Akron Indians of the American Professional Football League, African Americans participated in professional football. At the peak of hard times brought on by the Great Depression, however, white players complained that African Americans reduced the number of jobs available to them. Team owners then joined into an unwritten pact that African Americans would no longer be allowed to play professionally.

The NFL was bereft of African American players until the Los Angeles Rams signed Kenny Washington and Woody Strode in 1946. Later that same year Cleveland Browns fullback Marion Motley not only became the first black player in the All-American Football League, but he also was the earliest African American pro football star. Motley led the AAFL in rushing, was instrumental in the Browns' multiple AAFL championships, and continued to do the same when the team was absorbed by the NFL. Syracuse University's Jim Brown began his career with the Browns shortly after the retirement of Motley and became the top running back in the league. Brown led the league in rushing for eight of his nine years and held the career yardage mark for 19 years after his retirement.

By the end of Brown's career in the mid-1960s, other African American stars had emerged. New York Giants safety Emlen Tunnel—the first black player for the Giants since re-integration—retired in 1961 with 79 career interceptions, a record that was not eclipsed until 1979. With 14 touchdowns in 1965, rookie Chicago Bears running back Gale Sayers immediately gained notoriety as one of the most exciting running backs of the era. Sayers went on to lead the league in rushing in 1966 and 1969 and became the youngest man ever elected to the NFL Hall of Fame in 1977. Blacks excelled at every position except quarterback, which remained unofficially reserved for white players.

African American stars continued to proliferate in the 1960s and 1970s. Charley Taylor was the first African American to lead the league in receptions twice. Willie Wood was the first to lead the NFL in interceptions. In 1973, the Buffalo Bills' O. J. Simpson became the first player to rush for more than 2,000 yards in a single season. Only three players have managed that feat since, all of them African American, but all of them in 16 games as opposed to the 14 played by Simpson: Eric Dickerson's 2,105 yards in 1984; Barry Sanders's 2,053 in 1997; and Terrell Davis's 2,008 in 1998. The visibility of African Americans in the NFL was demonstrated with the popularity of certain teams' defensive lines and their familiar nicknames. The Minnesota Vikings offered the "Purple People Eaters," including Carl Eller, future state supreme court justice Alan Page, and Jim Marshall. David "Deacon" Jones and Rosey Grier were mainstays on the Los Angeles Rams' "Fearsome Foursome." The great Pittsburgh Steelers defenses of the 1970s were known as the "Steel Curtain" and included "Mean" Joe Greene.

During the 1980s, the New York Giants' Lawrence Taylor revolutionized the position of outside linebacker. In 1984, Walter Payton of the Bears eclipsed Jim Brown's record for career rushing yards and concluded his brilliant career in 1987 with 16,726 yards, more than 1,000 yards ahead of the second most as of the end of the 2002 season. In 1988, the Washington Redskins' Doug Williams became the first African American to quarterback his team to a Super Bowl victory. The 1990s have been dominated by three running backs who have won Most Valuable Player Awards: the now-retired Detroit Lions' Barry Sanders, the Dallas Cowboys' Emmitt Smith, and the Denver Broncos' Terrell Davis. The San Francisco 49ers' wide receiver Jerry Rice holds the record of most touchdowns scored in league history. The Cowboys' now-retired but still flamboyant cornerback Deion Sanders became one of the game's most visible and dominant defensive players, also notably dangerous as a kick and punt returner.

In the late 1990s, African Americans represented approximately 70 percent of those playing in the NFL.

Barry Sanders retired as the second leading rusher in NFL history.

The proportion of African Americans in the coaching ranks and team front offices, however, has not grown at the same pace. African Americans made up less than 20 percent of the head coaches in the league and held none of the upper-level management positions.

This is a similar problem in college football, as most coaching jobs are still held by whites. The major avenue for African Americans in coaching—and at one time in playing—was through historically African American colleges. Grambling's former head coach Eddie Robinson produced several NFL stars as did other predominantly African American colleges. The integration of major Southern universities, however, has weakened the influence of African American colleges.

PROFESSIONAL FOOTBALL HALL OF FAME

1967: Emlen Tunnell
1968: Marion Motley
1969: Fletcher "Joe" Perry
1971: Jim Brown
1972: Ollie Matson

1973: Jim Parker
1974: Richard "Night Train" Lane
1975: Roosevelt Brown; Leonard "Lenny" Moore
1976: Leonard "Len" Ford
1977: Gale Sayers; Bill Willis
1980: Herb Adderley; David "Deacon" Jones
1981: Willie Davis
1983: Bobby Bell; Bobby Mitchell; Paul Warfield
1984: Willie Brown; Charley Taylor
1985: O. J. Simpson
1986: Ken Houston; Willie Lanier
1987: Joe Greene; John Henry Johnson;
　　Gene Upshaw
1988: Alan Page
1989: Mel Blount; Art Shell; Willie Wood
1990: Junious "Buck" Buchanan; Franco Harris
1991: Earl Campbell
1992: Lem Barney; John Mackey
1993: Larry Little; Walter Payton
1994: Tony Dorsett; Leroy Kelly
1995: Lee Roy Selmon
1996: Charlie Joiner; Mel Renfro
1997: Mike Haynes
1998: Mike Singletary; Dwight Stephenson
1999: Eric Dickerson; Ozzie Newsome;
　　Lawrence Taylor
2000: Ronnie Lott
2001: Jackie Slater; Lynn Swann
2002: Dan Hampton; John Stallworth

◆ BOXING

African American athletes have been boxing professionally since colonial times and have dominated the sport—especially in the heavyweight division— since the 1930s. In 1886 George "Little Chocolate" Dixon became the first African American to win a world boxing title. In 1908, Jack Johnson became the first to win the heavyweight title. Joe Walcott—not to be confused with "Jersey" Joe Walcott, a heavyweight contemporary of Joe Louis—lost his only shot at the world lightweight championship in 1897, lost his first bout for the world welterweight championship the next year, but captured the welterweight title in 1901. Throughout Walcott's tumultuous career, he fought in handicap events where he was required to weigh much less than his opponent—and much less than his normal body weight. Walcott also fought light-heavyweights and heavyweights with unbelievable success. Because of this, he was called the greatest welterweight and greatest "pound for pound" fighter of all time by many boxing experts. Middleweight champion "Sugar" Ray Robinson and light-heavyweight Roy Jones Jr. are also mentioned in such discussions. Joe Louis held the world heavyweight title for a record 11 years and 8 months in the 1930s and 1940s. Henry Armstrong held three world titles at once—featherweight, lightweight, and welterweight—during the Great Depression.

Louis, Robinson, and Armstrong were stars in what is considered the first golden age of African Americans in boxing. A new golden age was ushered in on March 8, 1971, when Muhammad Ali and Joe Frazier drew the sport's first multimillion-dollar gate. Ali, a national figure since winning an Olympic gold medal in 1960, was also one of the first athletes to comment on American political and social events despite the danger such a stance could pose to his career.

Other divisions have featured African American stars. During the 1970s and 1980s attention shifted to talented fighters in the middle and welterweight divisions including "Sugar" Ray Leonard, "Marvelous" Marvin Hagler, and Thomas "Hit Man" Hearns. When Ali was no longer able to defend his heavyweight crown, new challengers such as his former sparring partner Larry Holmes and Michael Spinks ascended to the championship ranks.

As purses for major boxing events reached the $100 million mark in the mid-1980s, a new generation of fighters arose. "Iron" Mike Tyson became the best known heavyweight champion since Ali and the wealthiest boxer of all time. His tumultuous reign was ended in Japan with a knockout by James "Buster" Douglas, who in turn lost the title to Evander Holyfield. Even without a title to his name, Tyson continued to be the most visible figure in boxing. In 1992, he was convicted of sexual assault and sentenced to jail. While incarcerated he made headlines for his conversion to Islam and his admissions of youthful indiscressions. After his release, he quickly regained his title until Holyfield won it from him in 1996. In a 1997 rematch, Tyson bit Holyfield twice during the early rounds, prompting Tyson's disqualification and suspension from boxing. Despite the lifting of that suspension, legal troubles and prison time have clouded the career of boxing's most famous figure.

Other stars, including Pernell Whitaker and Roy Jones Jr., have shone brightly in recent years, but none have held the attention of the public like Mike Tyson. Many experts see the lack of a popular heavyweight champion as a sign of the death of the sport of boxing.

Top boxers can conceivably earn as much as $100 million for less than a dozen major ring events. The advent of pay-per-view television and cable network sponsorship has lead to soaring profits for the sport and its practitioners, although declining ratings and public interest threaten this trend. Colorful entrepreneur Don King is the most famous, wealthy, and controversial boxing promoter of the modern era. His powerful position in boxing's ranks and his hold on Tyson have allowed him to control championship boxing, despite frequent troubles with the Internal Revenue Service and complaints from former fighters who worked under King.

◆ BASKETBALL

African American presence in basketball dates to the early days of the sport. College basketball dominated the first half of the twentieth century as no major professional league existed until the late 1940s. In 1916, educators, coaches, and faculty members from Hampton Institute, Shaw, Lincoln, Virginia Union, and Howard University formed the Central Interscholastic Athletic Association, the first African American collegiate conference. Others soon followed, including the Southeastern Athletic Conference, Southwestern Athletic Conference, and Southern Intercollegiate Athletic Conference.

Much of the legacy of African American basketball history lies in its pioneers. Bob Douglas, who founded the Harlem Renaissance in the 1920s, is considered the "Godfather of black basketball." His innovations included monthly player contracts, a custom designed team bus, and tours in the South. John McLendon, a coach during the 1950s and 1960s, is recognized as the strategic architect of the fast break and was the first African American to publish a book detailing his coaching philosophy. He was also the first to coach a professional team. Additionally, McLendon was a prominent advocate of the desegregation of intercollegiate athletics.

For years most top college African American players signed with the Harlem Globetrotters, an internationally known barnstorming team. From their inception in 1926, the Globetrotters have delighted basketball fans worldwide with their unique combination of skill and humor. Famous Globetrotters include "Meadowlark" Lemon, "Curly" Neal, "Goose" Tatum, and Marques Haynes.

Professional basketball organized in the late 1940s as the National Basketball Association and was integrated in 1950. In the same year Chuck Cooper of Duquesne University was the first African American to be drafted in the league. Nat "Sweetwater" Clifton was the first signed to a professional contract. However, on October 31, 1950, when Earl Lloyd of the then Washington Capitols took the court, he became the first African American to actually participate in an NBA game.

Wilt Chamberlain (right) and Bill Russell—two of the most dominant centers in the history of professional basketball.

Basketball grew in the 1950s and 1960s as African American players such as Bill Russell, Wilt Chamberlain, Elgin Baylor, and Oscar Robertson enjoyed success in both college and then as professionals. In 1966, Texas Western University became the first college team to win the NCAA National Championship with an all-African American starting five. They beat the favored and all-white University of Kentucky, a milestone that began the end of segregated basketball teams.

The late 1960s and 1970s featured the rise of two of the great stars of the game—Kareem Abdul-Jabbar and Julius Erving. Abdul-Jabbar starred at UCLA and led the Bruins to three straight NCAA crowns. He then became a professional star with the Milwaukee Bucks and Los Angeles Lakers. Along with Earl Monroe, Willis Reed, Elvin Hayes, and others, African American players began to dominate the league. The rival American Basketball Association began the slam dunk competitions which dominate the NBA All-Star Weekend. Julius Erving became the most popular player in the ABA due to his dunks and acrobatics.

The 1980s and 1990s featured the growth of basketball into one of the most popular sports in the United States and around the world. The huge success of the NCAA Final Four has led to large financial revenues for colleges. In 1982, John Thompson of Georgetown University became the first African American to coach in the Final Four. Two years later his team won the tournament. The talents of Magic Johnson, Isiah Thomas, Charles Barkley, Karl Malone, Alonzo Mourning, and others led to large growth of the college game and the NBA. These players became celebrities as well as athletes.

The most famous player of both decades is Michael Jordan. Considered the greatest basketball player of all time, Jordan's success and personality have made him one of the most famous people in the world. He led the University of North Carolina to an NCAA title in 1982 and led the Chicago Bulls to six NBA titles. His endorsements established Nike athletic shoes as one of the largest apparel companies in the world.

African Americans now occupy more than 80 percent of the spots on NBA rosters including such stars as Shaquille O'Neal, Kobe Bryant, Kevin Garnett, Grant Hill, Allen Iverson, and Tim Duncan. Other areas, especially coaching and management positions, have less representation. The Atlanta Hawks' Lenny Wilkens has won more games than any other coach in history, with more than 1,260 victories. Approximately 15 percent of top management and administrative positions are held by African Americans. In 1990, Bertram Lee and Peter C. B. Bynoe became the first African American owners of a professional sports franchise with the purchase of the Denver Nuggets.

Recent incidents involving high-profile players have dented the popularity and rapid growth of professional basketball. In 1997, Latrell Sprewell, an All-Star player, attempted to strangle his coach, P.J. Carlesimo, at a practice. Following a league suspension, Sprewell returned to the NBA as a player for the New York Knicks. Sprewell's return was delayed along with the NBA season by a labor dispute which resulted in a lock out by NBA owners that did not end until early January 1999, resulting in a shortened season. In February 2002, retired NBA star Jayson Williams was charged with manslaughter in the shooting death of a limousine driver. Months later, Allen Iverson, a league MVP, as well as one of its most visible and talented players, was arraigned on charges that he had threatened two men while armed with a gun.

NATIONAL BASKETBALL HALL OF FAME

1971: Robert L. Douglass (contributor)
1974: Bill Russell
1976: Elgin Baylor; Charles Cooper
1978: Wilt Chamberlain
1979: Oscar Robertson
1981: Clarence Gaines; Willis Reed
1983: Sam Jones
1984: Nate Thurmond

1987: Walt "Clyde" Frazier
1988: Wes Unseld
1989: William "Pop" Gates; K.C. Jones; Lenny
   Wilkins (player)
1990: Dave Bing; Elvin Hayes; Earl "The
   Pearl" Monroe
1991: Nate "Tiny" Archibald
1992: Lusia Harris-Stewart; Connie Hawkins;
   Bob Lanier
1993: Walt Bellamy; Julius "Dr. J" Erving;
   Calvin Murphy
1995: Kareem Abdul-Jabbar; Cheryl Miller
1996: George Gervin; David Thompson
1997: Alex English
1998: Marques Haynes, Lenny Wilkins (re-honored
   as a coach)
1999: Wayne Embry, John Thompson (coach)
2000: Bob McAdoo; Isiah Thomas
2001: John Chaney (coach); Moses Malone
2002: Earvin "Magic" Johnson; the Harlem
   Globetrotters

♦ OTHER SPORTS

African American athletes have excelled in track and field, winning medals at various Olympiads and other competitions. This tradition began at the 1908 London Olympics, when John Baxtor Taylor became the first African American to capture a gold medal as part of the 4x400-meter relay team.

Jesse Owens was the star of the first half of the twentieth century. Owens is best known for his four gold medal performance at the 1936 Olympics in Berlin, Germany. However, it was on May 25, 1935, at Ann Arbor, Michigan, that Jesse Owens provided the greatest performance in track and field history at the Big Ten Championships as a member of Ohio State University. Owens began this day by equalling the world record in the 100-yard dash. He then proceeded to set the world records in the broad jump, 220-yard dash, and 220-yard low hurdles.

Owens began a string of medal-winning performances by African Americans in track and field. At the 1960 Olympics, Ralph Boston broke Owens's long jump record to win the gold medal. In so doing, he also became one of only two track stars to break a world record on six separate occasions. Rafer Johnson won the decathlon in the same Olympics. Bob Beamon, at the 1968 Mexico City Games, leaped 29' 2 1/2" in the long jump competition to win the gold medal and extend the world record by almost two feet. Beamon's record sat unbeaten and presumed out of reach for a quarter of a century, until Mike Powell bested it by 2" at

the 1991 World Track & Field Championships in Tokyo. In 1984, in Los Angeles, Carl Lewis became the first athlete since Owens in 1936 to win four gold medals. Edwin Moses became the greatest 400-meter hurdler in history, winning gold medals in 1976 and 1984 as well as winning 122 straight races. At the 1992 Olympic Games, Michael Johnson became the next African American star, winning the 400-meter dash. At the 1996 Olympics in Atlanta, Johnson became the first man to win the 200-meter and 400-meter races in the same games.

One of the most controversial events in Olympic history occurred in 1968 during an awards ceremony. After finishing first and third respectively, in the 200-meter dash, Tommie Smith and John Carlos, while on the victory stand, raised their arms in unison with black gloves on their clenched fists. This became known as the "Black power salute." Their protest caused them to lose their medals.

Historically, African American Olympic athletes have not fared well at the Winter Games. Debi Thomas was the first to win a medal of any kind—bronze—in 1988 in figure skating. Not until the 2002 Olympiad did another black American ascend the podium for a medal. Jarome

Michael Johnson holding the gold medal that he won at the Olympic Games in 1996.

Iginla won a gold medal with the Canadian men's ice hockey team. More notably, however, Vonetta Flowers won gold with her white teammate for their 2-woman bobsled performance. Similarly, half of the U.S. 4-man bobsled team was African American: Garrett Hines and Randy Jones captured silver medals to become the first African American men to place at a Winter Olympiad.

The professional tennis community was largely devoid of African Americans through World War II, as they were not welcome by the U.S. Lawn Tennis Association (USLTA). In a sport primarily associated with the upper class, the only avenues of competition open for African Americans were universities and colleges, clubs and various minor tournaments. Shortly after the war, the USLTA loosened its discrimination policy and, in 1948, Oscar Johnson became the first African American player to win a USLTA-sanctioned event.

Arthur Ashe, a classy and congenial champion, won the Australian Open in 1970 and the Wimbledon title in 1975, along with several less celebrated tournaments during his career. He represented the United States as a member of the Davis Cup team ten times and was its captain from 1981 to 1984. Ashe also made contributions off the court. He made significant contributions as a human rights activist and retained a dignity and grace during his battle with AIDS. In 1996 MaliVai Washington became the first African American since Ashe to reach the Wimbledon finals.

African Americans' attempts to break into golf prior to World War II paralleled those of their tennis counterparts. However, the Professional Golfers Association (PGA) did not rescind its white-only policy until 1959, when Charlie Sifford became the first African American to be issued a PGA card as an "approved player." In 1967 Renee Powell became the first African American female to be issued a LPGA card. Sifford was the best known of the initial participants on the tour. He was the first to win a predominantly white event with his victory at the 1957 Long Beach Open. In 1975 Lee Elder became the first African American to compete at the Masters tournament. In the 1980s Calvin Peete enjoyed success on the tour and competed in the 1983 Ryder Cup.

However, not until the arrival of Tiger Woods in the mid-1990s did an African American golfer become a superstar. Woods was a child prodigy, winning several junior tournaments before he was a teenager. In 1994 Woods became the first African American to win the U.S. Amateur title. He repeated this feat the next two years, becoming the first man to win the amateur title three years in a row. In 1997, after becoming a professional, Woods won the Masters tournament with a record score. He also rose to the ranking of the world's top player. These accomplishments indicate the level of fame Woods has achieved. He has become the

Arthur Ashe holding the Wimbledon Trophy above his head in 1975.

preeminent African American athlete with the retirement of Michael Jordan and has several endorsement deals.

African American luminaries exist in other sports. By winning the Brunswick Memorial World Open, George Branham III became the first African American bowler to win a Professional Bowling Association (PBA) title. Branham has won four other titles, including the prestigious Firestone Tournament of Champions in 1993, which was the first time an African American had won one of bowling's Triple Crown events. The weightlifter John Davis was the first athlete of any race to win eight consecutive World and Olympic Championships, during a career spanning three decades. Superlative bodybuilder Lee Haney reached the top of his field by winning eight consecutive Mr. Olympia titles from 1984 to 1991. Picking up where Haney left off, Lenda Murray captured every Ms. Olympia title from 1990 through 1995. Following in their footsteps, Ronnie Coleman won the Mr. Olympia title in 1998 and retained it through the 2002 competition. At the turn of the nineteenth century, cyclist Marshall Taylor was among

Tiger Woods.

the three most celebrated African American athletes in the world. During the same era, jockey Isaac Murphy, viewed as the greatest in the world at his craft, was part of a triumphant half century of African American jockeys. Oliver Lewis won the inaugural Kentucky Derby aboard Aristedes, in 1875. However, until Marlon St. Julien rode to a seventh-place finish in the 2000 Derby, no African American had ridden in the Derby since 1911.

One sport on which African Americans have had a negligible influence is auto racing. Willie T. Ribbs is the only African American to drive at the Indianapolis 500 and has failed in his efforts to put together a successful NASCAR team. Julius Erving and former football star Joe Washington are the first African American owners of a NASCAR team but race with a white driver. Wendell Scott is the only African American to win a NASCAR race, with that win coming in the 1960s.

◆ WOMEN IN SPORTS

Although not provided with the same opportunities that have been traditionally afforded to men, African American women have made a significant contribution to the sports world. African American women are on the vanguard of the new opportunities, achieving success in sports as varied as tennis to basketball.

In 1948, Alice Coachman became the first African American woman to capture an Olympic gold medal in the high jump. Wilma Rudolph overcame debilitating childhood illnesses to win three golds at the 1960 Olympiad in Rome. Her teammate, 15-year-old Barbara Jones, became the youngest female to win a gold medal in track and field. In the 1968 games, Wyomia Tyus became the second African American to win more than one gold medal in one Olympiad as well as the first to set world records in two different events. In 1988, Debi Thomas became the first African American woman to win an Olympic medal in figure skating. Florence Griffith Joyner won four medals during the 1988 Olympiad, including three gold medals. Jackie Joyner-Kersee, owner of two Olympic gold medals, and Gail Devers who has overcome the effects of Graves' disease to win a gold medal at the 1992 Olympic Games, are recent stars.

The first female African American athlete to dominate her sport was tennis's Althea Gibson. A superb athlete, Gibson was named 1957's female athlete of the year during which she captured the prestigious Wimbledon singles title and U.S. Lawn Tennis Association championship. She won both titles again in 1958 and was the undisputed number one women's player in the world during those years. She became the first African American woman to capture a Grand Slam event in 1956 with her singles and doubles championships at the French Open. Zina Garrison-Jackson was the next prominent female African American tennis player, eventually reaching a top-ten ranking, and becoming a 1990 Wimbledon finalist.

In the late 1990s the Williams sisters, Venus and Serena, entered the international tennis scene, bringing new attention to the sport among African Americans. Serena, the youngest, became the first of the sisters to win a Grand Slam title, taking the U.S. Open in 1999. Venus followed with back-to-back victories at the U.S. Open and Wimbledon in 2000 and 2001. The sisters have gone on to dominate the sport. In 2002, they became the two highest ranked players on the tour.

Basketball has been a major outlet for African American female athletes. Cheryl Miller is one of the most famous female basketball players. She was named All-American at the conclusion of each of her four years at the University of Southern California, was national player of the year three times, and was inducted in the Basketball Hall of Fame in 1994. The decade of the 1970s featured the great center Lusia Harris, the first woman to be inducted into the Basketball Hall of Fame. Others who have left their marks in basketball annals include University of Kansas star Lynette Woodard, perhaps best known as the first female member of the Harlem Globetrotters in 1985.

In 1997 two professional basketball leagues for women were established. The WNBA, supported by the men's NBA, and the ABL. Both leagues allowed stars such as Cynthia Cooper, Lisa Leslie, Sheryl Swoopes, and Chamique Holdsclaw the chance to exhibit their skills beyond the college level. The ABL folded before it could launch its third season, but the WNBA continued on with much success. The league, which was originally comprised of eight teams, had expanded to 16 by 2000.

Other notables in sports include the late volleyball player Flo Hyman; bodybuilder Lenda Murray, who won the Ms. Olympia title six times; Lyle (Toni) Stone who was the first African American woman to play professional baseball with the Indianapolis Clowns of the Negro American League in 1953; and Olympic gymnast Dominique Dawes. In 1978, Wendy Hilliard became the first African American member of the U.S. National Rhythmic Gymnastics Team.

Dominique Dawes performing at the 1996 Olympic Games in Atlanta.

Lisa Leslie.

Unfortunately, very few of the above mentioned women ever had the opportunity to display their talents on a professional level. Women's athletics has long been hamstrung by the lack of non-amateur forums in which African American female athletes could participate. For many, the Olympic Games or intercollegiate athletics have been the final step of their careers.

Women's athletics received a boost with the enactment of Title IX of the Education Amendment Act of 1972, which stipulated that any university receiving federal funds was obligated to provide an equal or proportionate number of scholarships for women. While the law provides opportunities to women, it has been criticized in its implementation as many universities have cut men's programs to fund scholarships for women.

◆ ATHLETES, COACHES, AND SPORTS EXECUTIVES

(To locate biographical profiles more readily, please consult the index at the back of the book.)

Hank Aaron (1934–)
Baseball Player, Sports Executive

Henry Louis Aaron was born in Mobile, Alabama, on February 5, 1934. He played sandlot ball as a teenager and later played for a local team named the Black Bears. He first played professional baseball with the Indianapolis Clowns of the Negro American League.

In June of 1952, Aaron's contract was purchased by the Boston Braves. The following season, playing for their minor league team in Jacksonville, his .362 average led the South Atlantic League. In 1954 he was promoted to the Braves, then based in Milwaukee.

Aaron enjoyed perhaps his finest season in 1957, when he was named Most Valuable Player and led his team to a world championship. He batted .322, with 44 homers, 132 RBIs, and 118 runs scored.

In 1974 Aaron became the all-time home run leader when he hit his 715th, breaking Babe Ruth's mark of 714 home runs. He played his final two seasons in the American League with the Milwaukee Brewers, completing his career with a total of 755 home runs.

During his career, Aaron won a pair of batting titles and hit over .300 in 12 seasons. He won the home run and RBI crowns four times apiece, hit 40 or more homers eight times, and hit at least 20 home runs for 20 consecutive years, a National League record. In addition, he was named to 20 consecutive All-Star teams.

In January of 1982, Aaron was elected by the Baseball Writers Association to the Baseball Hall of Fame. Since the mid-1990s, he has served as vice president/assistant to the president for the Braves.

Kareem Abdul-Jabbar (1947–)
Basketball Player

Abdul-Jabbar was born Ferdinand Lewis Alcindor Jr. on April 16, 1947, in New York City. In high school, at 7' 1/2" tall, he established a New York City career record of 2,067 points and 2,002 rebounds, leading Power Memorial High School to three straight championships. Power won 95 and lost only six games during his years with the team.

Abdul-Jabbar combined great height with catlike moves and a deft shooting touch to lead UCLA to three consecutive NCAA Championships. Twice, as a sophomore and a senior, he was chosen as the top collegiate player in the country. He finished his career at UCLA as the ninth all-time collegiate scorer, accumulating 2,325 points in 88 games. After leading UCLA to its third consecutive NCAA title, Abdul-Jabbar signed a contract with the Milwaukee Bucks for $1.4 million.

In his rookie season, 1969–1970, he led the Bucks, a recently established expansion club, to a second place finish in the Eastern Division. After being voted Rookie of the Year, he went on to win the scoring championships in 1971 and 1972. He won a world championship in 1971. In 1973, he finished second in scoring with a 30.2 point average, but became dissatisfied with life in Milwaukee. At the end of the 1974–1975 season he was traded to the L.A. Lakers. Abdul-Jabbar enjoyed a very successful career with the Lakers, leading the team to NBA championships in 1980, 1982, 1985, 1987, and 1988.

Abdul-Jabbar converted to the Hanafi sect of Islam while in college, though he did not change his name until 1971. Greatly influenced by the life and struggles of Malcolm X, he believes that the Islamic religion is distinct from the nationalistic Black Muslims.

Abdul-Jabbar announced his retirement after the 1988–1989 season, one year after the Lakers had won back-to-back World Championships. He was elected into the Basketball Hall of Fame in 1994.

Abdul-Jabbar has applied his experience and knowledge of the game to the areas of coaching and scouting. In 2000, he served as an assistant coach for the Los Angeles Clippers, and in 2001 took a position as scout, consultant, and assistant coach for the Indianapolis Pacers.

Muhammad Ali (1942–)
Boxer

Born Cassius Clay, in Louisville, Kentucky, on January 17, 1942, Ali started boxing as a youth. After winning the 1960 Olympic gold medal as light-heavyweight, Clay turned pro. In 1963 he converted to Islam, and changed his name to Muhammad Ali. A year later, Ali won the world heavyweight championship by knocking out Sonny Liston.

After nine successful title defenses, Ali refused to serve in the armed forces during the Vietnam War. He maintained that it was contrary to his Muslim beliefs. Stripped of his title and banned from boxing in the United States, Ali was jailed, but he refused to back down and was finally cleared on a technicality by the U.S. Supreme Court in 1970.

Coming back to the ring after a three and one-half year layoff, he was defeated by heavyweight champion Joe Frazier. In 1974 when neither held a title, Ali defeated Frazier to earn a shot at regaining the title.

Few fans gave Ali a chance against heavyweight champion George Foreman when they met in Zaire on October 30, 1974. A 4–1 underdog at ring time, Ali amazed the boxing world and knocked out his stronger,

Muhammad Ali being interviewed by friend and verbal sparring partner Howard Cosell.

younger opponent. After regaining the crown, Ali defeated Frazier in their third fight in Manilla. Ali then lost his title to Leon Spinks in 1978, briefly regained it, and then retired.

In 1980 Ali came out of retirement to fight his former sparring partner, heavyweight champion Larry Holmes. He was defeated. After a 1981 loss to Trevor Berbick, he retired again.

Forced to fight when he was past his prime, Ali took tremendous beatings late in his career. In the 1980s, the former champion was diagnosed with Parkinson's disease. Despite the disease, Ali has maintained a public presence. This was most notably demonstrated in his being chosen to light the Olympic torch at the 1996 Summer Olympics in Atlanta.

Ali continues to work for various causes including international hunger and poverty relief. In 2001, the National Association of Broadcasters Education Foundation awarded Ali with a Service to America Leadership Award, in part for his founding of the nonprofit Muhammad Ali Center.

Henry Armstrong (1912–1988)
Boxer

The only boxer ever to hold three titles at the same time is Henry Armstrong, who accomplished this feat on August 17, 1938, when he added the lightweight championship to his featherweight and welterweight titles.

Armstrong was born on December 12, 1912, in St. Louis, Missouri. In 1929, while fighting under the name of Melody Jackson, he was knocked out in his professional debut in Pittsburgh. Two weeks later he won his first fight. For the next eight years he traveled from coast to coast, fighting until he was finally given a shot at the featherweight title on October 20, 1937. He won the title when he defeated Petey Sarron.

Less than a year later, on May 31, 1938, Armstrong picked up his second title with a decision over welterweight champion Barney Ross. Within three months he added the lightweight crown, winning a decision over Lou Ambers.

Armstrong was inducted into the Black Athletes Hall of Fame in 1975 and died in 1988.

Arthur Ashe (1943–1993)
Tennis Player, Television Commentator

Born in Richmond, Virginia, Ashe learned the game of tennis at the Richmond Racket Club, which had been formed by local African American enthusiasts. Dr. R. W. Johnson, who had also served as an advisor and benefactor to Althea Gibson, sponsored Ashe's tennis.

By 1958, Ashe reached the semifinals in the under-15 division of the National Junior Championships. In 1960 and 1961, he won the Junior Indoors Singles title. In 1961, Ashe entered UCLA on a tennis scholarship.

While still an amateur, Ashe won the United States Amateur Tennis Championship and the U.S. Open Tennis Championship and became the first African American ever named to a Davis Cup Team.

In 1975, Ashe defeated Jimmy Connors to win Wimbledon and won the World Championship Tennis singles title over Bjorn Borg.

In 1979, at the age of 35, Ashe suffered a heart attack. Following quadruple bypass heart surgery, Ashe retired from active tennis. He began writing a nationally syndicated column and contributed monthly articles to *Tennis Magazine*. He wrote a tennis diary *Portrait in Motion*, his autobiography *Off the Court*, and the book *Advantage Ashe*. In addition, he compiled the historical work *A Hard Road to Glory: A History of the African-American Athlete*.

Ashe was named captain of the U.S. Davis Cup team in 1981. He was a former president and active member of the board of directors of the Association of Tennis Professionals, and a co-founder of the National Junior Tennis League. Late in his career, he also served as a television sports commentator.

In April of 1992, Ashe announced that he had contracted AIDS as the result of a tainted blood transfusion received during heart bypass surgery. He died on February 6, 1993.

Ernie Banks (1931–)
Baseball Player

Born in Dallas, Banks was slightly built at 6'1", 180 pounds, but his powerful wrists help him produce a career total of 512 home runs. His 44 homers and five grand slams in 1955 were single season records for shortstops. His best season was 1958, during which he led the National League in at-bats (617), home runs (47), runs batted in (129), and slugging percentage (.614). He was named the league's Most Valuable Player after the 1958 and 1959 seasons.

Banks, who was moved to first base during the 1961 season and played in 717 consecutive games, may have the somewhat dubious distinction of being the greatest player to never play in a World Series, as his Chicago Cubs rarely produced winning ballclubs during his tenure.

Banks, along with second baseman Gene Baker, formed the majors' first all-African American double play combination. He was the second African American to play for the Cubs, after Baker. Banks was elected to the Baseball Hall of Fame in 1977 and is also a member of the Texas Sports Hall of Fame.

After his playing career, Banks became a bank executive with Seaway National Bank. He remained visible in the community, becoming a board member of the Chicago Transit Authority, the Chicago Metropolitan YMCA, and the Los Angeles Urban League.

Elgin Baylor (1934–)
Basketball Player, Basketball Coach, Sports Executive

Born on September 16, 1934, in Washington, DC, Elgin Baylor first attracted attention while attending Spingarn High School. He became an All-American at Seattle University, leading the Chieftains to the Final Four in 1958. In 1959, Baylor made his professional debut with the Minneapolis Lakers, becoming the first rookie to be named Most Valuable Player in the All-Star Game. He also was named to the All-League team and set a scoring record of 64 points in a single game.

After five years as a superstar, Baylor injured his knee during a 1965 playoff game against the Bullets and never played at the same level again. He totaled 23,149 points in his career, and his scoring average of 27.4 is the fourth highest in NBA history. His best year was 1961–1962, when he averaged 38.2 points a game. When he retired in 1968, Baylor had been an All-Pro nine times and had played in eight consecutive All-Star games.

Baylor was inducted into the Black Athletes Hall of Fame in 1975 and the Basketball Hall of Fame in 1976.

He was head coach of the New Orleans Jazz in 1978–1979. Since 1986, Baylor has been executive vice president of basketball operations for the Los Angeles Clippers.

Dave Bing. *See* **Entrepreneurship chapter.**

Barry Bonds (1964–)
Baseball Player

Barry Bonds was born on July 24, 1964, in Riverside, California. He was exposed to baseball heavily during childhood. Bonds's father, Bobby, and his godfather, Hall of Famer Willie Mays, were Major League outfielders. Bonds played three sports in high school—baseball, basketball, and football. Although he was offered a contract to play with the San Francisco Giants upon graduation, he opted to attend college at Arizona State University.

After success at the collegiate level, Bonds was selected by the Pittsburgh Pirates as the sixth selection in the 1985 baseball draft. He spent a brief time in the minor leagues before being called up by the National League club at the age of 21. During his rookie season, he led all first-year players in home runs, runs batted in, stolen bases, and walks.

In 1990 Bonds earned Most Valuable Player (MVP) honors. He hit 32 home runs, stole 52 bases, batted in 114 runs, scored 104 runs, and earned his first of four consecutive Gold Gloves for defensive play during the year. With Bonds's support the Pirates won the Eastern Division of the National League but ended up losing to the Cincinnati Reds in a postseason series.

The Pirates entered the playoffs during the next two seasons, but met with postseason frustration both years. The 1992 campaign was notable because Bonds earned his second MVP award. Regardless of his success during the regular season, however, Bonds was unable to contribute in the same fashion during the playoffs.

After the completion of the 1992 season, Bonds signed a lucrative deal with the San Francisco Giants. The contract provided him with $43.75 million over the course of six years, making him the highest paid player at the time. Although some critics doubted that any player was worth such a salary, Bonds quieted them by earning another MVP award on the strength of a season that featured 46 home runs and 123 RBIs. The Giants failed to make the playoffs, though, losing the honor to the Atlanta Braves on the last day of the season.

Although Bonds has continued to post strong numbers through the remainder of the 1990s, his team has made the playoffs only twice, in 1997 and 2000. Bonds's continued success during the regular season is remarkable in light of the fact that opposing pitchers do not often offer him decent pitches. They would rather walk Bonds than risk giving up an extra base hit against him.

In 1998 Bonds became the first player with more than 400 home runs and 400 stolen bases in a career; at the beginning of the 2002 season, he needed only 16 stolen bases to gain lone membership in the "500/500 Club." In the 2001 season Bonds amassed an amazing 73 home runs, three more than the previous record. Not only did many consider the record of 70 homers in a season unmatchable, but Bonds hit his 73 with limited at bats as most managers instructed their pitchers to intentionally walk him rather than face the prospect of giving up an extra-base hit. Also at the end of the 2001 season, he won his fourth MVP award, becoming the first player in MLB history to win the award more than three times. On August 12, 2002, he hit his 600th home run, making him only the fourth player in Major League Baseball history to do so.

Lou Brock (1939–)
Baseball Player, Baseball Coach, Business Executive

Born in El Dorado, Arkansas, Lou Brock is the second-highest base stealer in baseball history. He stole 938 bases during his 19-year career with the Chicago Cubs and St. Louis Cardinals. In 1977, Brock collected his 893rd steal, eclipsing the mark that had been held by Ty Cobb for 49 years. In 1974, at the age of 35, Brock's 114 steals broke Maury Wills's single season record. Brock registered at least 50 steals in 12 consecutive seasons and at the time of his retirement was the only player to hold both the Major League single season and career record in any major statistical category.

In 1967, Brock led the league in at-bats, runs scored, and steals. The following season he set the pace in triples and steals, leading the Cardinals to pennants both seasons. With Brock, St. Louis also won World Championships in 1964 and 1967.

Brock went on to become a coach and business executive and was presented with the Jackie Robinson Award by *Ebony* magazine. He won the Roberto Clemente Award in 1975. He was also the recipient of the B'nai B'rith Brotherhood Award and was voted Man of the Year by the St. Louis Jaycees. Brock was inducted into the Baseball Hall of Fame in 1985.

Jim Brown (1936–)
Football Player, Actor, Community Activist

James Nathaniel Brown was born February 17, 1936, on St. Simon Island, Georgia, but moved to Manhasset, Long Island, New York, when he was seven. While at

Jim Brown.

Manhasset High School he became an outstanding competitor in baseball, football, track and field, basketball, and lacrosse and following graduation had a choice of 42 college scholarships, as well as professional offers from both the New York Yankees and the Boston Braves. Brown chose to attend Syracuse University. An All-American performer in both football and lacrosse, he turned down the opportunity to compete in the decathlon at the 1956 Olympic games because it would have conflicted with his football schedule. He also spurned a three-year $150,000 offer to become a professional fighter.

In 1957 Brown began his professional football career with the Cleveland Browns. In his rookie season, he led the league in rushing, helped Cleveland to a division championship, and was unanimously named Rookie of the Year. Brown broke the single season and lifetime rushing and scoring records and was an All-League fullback. His records included most yards gained, lifetime (12,312), and most touchdowns, lifetime (106). He was voted Football Back of the Decade for 1950–1960.

Brown announced his retirement in the summer of 1966, deciding to devote his attention to his movie and business careers. He has made several films including *Rio Conchos, The Dirty Dozen,* and *100 Rifles.* In addition to his film activities, he is president and founder of Amer-I-can and an outspoken activist in issues relating to African Americans and sports.

Roy Campanella (1921–1993)
Baseball Player

Roy Campanella was born on November 19, 1921, in Philadelphia, and began playing semi-professional baseball at the age of 15 with the Bacharach Giants. In 1946, Campanella was signed by the Brooklyn Dodgers. Over the next eight years, the Dodger catcher played with five National League pennant winners and one world championship team. He played on seven consecutive National League All-Star teams (1949 to 1955) and won three Most Valuable Player Awards (1951, 1953, and 1955).

In January 1958, Campanella's career was ended by an automobile accident which left him paralyzed and confined to a wheelchair. In 1969, he was inducted into the Baseball Hall of Fame and into the Black Athletes Hall of Fame in 1975. Campanella died on June 26, 1993.

Wilt Chamberlain (1936–1999)
Basketball Player

Wilt Chamberlain was born in Philadelphia on August 21, 1936. By the time he entered high school, he was already 6'11". When he graduated from high school, he had his choice of 77 major colleges, and 125 smaller schools. He chose Kansas University, but left after his junior year after being a two-time All-American and playing in the 1957 Final Four.

Before entering the NBA in 1959, Chamberlain played with the Harlem Globetrotters. Although dominating the sport statistically from his rookie season, Chamberlain was a member of only two championship teams, the 1967 Philadelphia 76ers and the 1972 Los Angeles Lakers. For his efforts in defeating the Knicks in the 1972 series, including playing the final game with both hands painfully injured, he was voted MVP. At the start of the 1974 season, he left the Lakers to become player-coach of the San Diego Conquistadors (ABA) for a reported $500,000 contract.

Wilt Chamberlain still holds most major records for a single game including most points (100); field goals made (36); free throws (28); and rebounds (55). His season records include: highest scoring average (50.4); highest field goal percentage (.727); and most rebounds per game (27.2).

Chamberlain was inducted into the Basketball Hall of Fame in 1978 and owned various businesses after leaving professional basketball. He was involved with various charitable groups and appeared in several motion pictures. In 1991, Chamberlain published his autobiography, *View from Above.* The book caused quite a controversy due to revelations about his sexual relations. Chamberlain died of a heart attack on October 12, 1999 in Los Angeles.

Alice Coachman (1923–)
Track and Field Athlete

Born in Albany, Georgia, on November 9, 1923, Coachman made a name for herself when, as a seventh grader, she high jumped 5'4 1/2", less than an inch from the world record. On August 7, 1948, Alice Coachman became the first African American woman to win an Olympic gold medal. She did it by setting a world record in the high jump. In college, she attended both the Tuskegee Institute (now University) and Albany State University where she won the Amateur Athletic Union (AAU) Outdoor 50-meters title four times; 100-meters three times; and the high jump ten times. Coachman won the 50-meters twice and the high jump three times during AAU indoor meets. She was also an outstanding basketball player, earning All-American honors as a guard at Tuskegee.

Coachman's ten consecutive victories, between 1939 and 1948, remains an AAU record. She is a member of eight different halls of fame including the National Track and Field Hall of Fame, the Black Athletes Hall of Fame, the Tuskegee Hall of Fame, and the Georgia State Hall of Fame. A 2002 edition of *Ebony* magazine, named her as one of the ten greatest women athletes of all time and received recognition as one of America's 100 greatest Olympic athletes at the 1996 Summer Games held in Atlanta, Georgia.

Leonard S. Coleman Jr. (1949–)
Former-National League of Professional Baseball Clubs President, State Government Official, Business Executive

Leonard Coleman Jr. was born in Newark, but he grew up in Montclair, New Jersey. At Montclair High School, Coleman played baseball and football. He was named all-state and all-American during his senior year. He continued playing baseball and football as an undergraduate at Princeton University, becoming the first African American to score a touchdown for that prestigious Ivy League school. As a sophomore, he

Cynthia Cooper.

joined two other African American players in a protest, charging the Princeton football program with violations of the university's policy of equal opportunity for minorities. When the complaints drew national attention, Coleman and his two friends were dismissed from the team, but a panel charged with investigating the incident urged greater sensitivity toward minority students in the athletic program. Coleman attributes that experience to helping him develop a keen social consciousness.

After earning his bachelor's degree from Princeton in 1971, Coleman moved on to Harvard University, where he pursued dual master's degrees in public administration and education. In 1976, he accepted a position as a missionary to Africa for the Protestant Episcopal Church. All told he spent four years in Africa, serving in 17 different countries and cultivating a close friendship with South African Archbishop Desmond Tutu.

Returning to the United States in 1980, Coleman first served as president of the Greater Newark Urban Coalition. In 1982, he was appointed commissioner of the New Jersey Department of Energy. In 1986, Coleman was named commissioner of the New Jersey Department of Community Affairs. In 1988, he left the public sector for a job as an investment banker with Kidder, Peabody & Co. Eventually, he was named vice president of municipal finance.

In 1991, Coleman accepted his first position with Major League Baseball, as director of marketing development. In that position, he was credited with further encouraging the Reviving Baseball in the Inner Cities (R.B.I.) initiative, aimed at keeping city teenagers active in baseball after they leave the Little Leagues. In 1994, Coleman was unanimously chosen to succeed Bill White as president of the National League.

During his tenure, he carried out his vision for professional baseball—less drug abuse among players including the discouragement of chewing tobacco; less fighting during games; and promotion of baseball as entertainment for the whole family. Coleman also acted as a crusader for the rights of African American baseball players, especially former Negro League participants and their spouses. In 1996, Coleman was named chairman of the Jackie Robinson Foundation.

Coleman resigned from the position of National League president in 1999. He then took over as president of Newark Sports & Entertainment, Inc., and on November 15, 2001, was named director of Churchill Downs Incorporated.

Cynthia Cooper (1963–)
Basketball Player, Coach

Cynthia Cooper was born in Chicago, Illinois, in 1963. She played college basketball at the University of Southern California. Her team at USC is one of the greatest in the history of women's college basketball. It included Hall of Famer Cheryl Miller and won NCAA titles in 1983 and 1984.

Following college, Cooper spent many years playing professional basketball in Europe. In 1988 she was on the U.S. Olympic team that captured a gold medal at the Seoul Olympiad. She was also a member of the bronze medal team in 1992 at the Barcelona Olympiad.

With the formation of the Women's National Basketball Association in 1997, Cooper had the chance to compete professionally in the United States. The 5'10" guard was a member of the Houston Comets. Cooper became one of the most prominent players in the league, winning the WNBA's first two MVP awards. In addition, she led the Comets to four-straight league titles and was named the MVP of the four championship games in which she played.

Cooper retired as a player following the 2000 season. In January 2001, she was named the head coach of the WNBA's Phoenix Mercury, a post she held for less than two seasons, as she resigned in June 2002.

Dominique Dawes (1976–)
Gymnast, Actress

Dawes was born in Silver Springs, Maryland, in 1976. She is the first African American to excel in gymnastics, becoming only the second African American to qualify for the U.S. Olympic team for gymnastics in 1992. Dawes also holds a record for winning the most national championships since 1963 (15) of any athlete, male or female.

Dawes began competing in gymnastics at the age of five. In 1992 at the Barcelona Olympiad she was a member of the U.S. team awarded the bronze medal. At the U.S. National Championships in 1994, Dawes became the first African American to win the all-around title as best gymnast. In 1996 at the Atlanta Olympiad she won two individual bronze medals as well as being a member of the U.S. team awarded the gold medal. Dawes was also a member of the U.S. team at the 2000 Sydney Olympiad.

Dawes currently attends the University of Maryland. She also appears as an analyst for televised gymnastic events, including coverage of the 2001 Goodwill Games for TNT. Her acting credits include a 1996 role in the Broadway musical *Grease* and an appearance on the Disney television series, *The Jersey*.

Lee Elder (1934–)
Golfer, Entrepreneur

Lee Elder was born in Washington, DC, on July 14, 1934. He first was involved with golf as a caddie at the age of 15. After his father's death during World War II, Elder and his mother moved to Los Angeles, where he met the famed African American golfer Ted Rhodes. He was later drafted by the U.S. Army, where he sharpened his skills as captain of the golf team.

Following his discharge from the army, he began to teach golf. In 1962, he debuted as a professional, winning the United Golf Association (an African American organization) national title. Elder played 17 years with the United Golf Association before his debut with the PGA in November of 1967. Elder was the first African American professional golfer to reach $1 million in earnings and, in 1975, was the first to play at the Masters. Elder won eight tournaments on the Senior

PGA Tour, and has been inducted into the NCAA Hall of Fame for his work with predominantly-black colleges.

In 1997, when Tiger Woods became the first African American to win the Masters, Elder was present and was thanked by Woods for his pioneering efforts in the integration of the PGA Tour and the Masters.

Julius Erving (1950–)
Basketball Player, Television Analyst, Basketball Executive

Julius Erving was born in Hempstead, Long Island, on February 22, 1950. As a player at Roosevelt High School, Erving made the All-County and All-Long Island teams. He was awarded an athletic scholarship to the University of Massachusetts, and after completing his junior year, signed a $500,000, four-year contract with the Virginia Squires of the ABA. Voted Rookie of the Year in 1972, he eventually signed with the New Jersey Nets for $2.8 million over four years.

In his first season with the Nets, Erving led the league in scoring for the second consecutive year and led his team to the ABA championship. After being traded to the Philadelphia 76ers, Erving became a favorite with fans, leading the team to the NBA championship in 1983. He became the 13th player to score 20,000 points. Erving retired following the 1986–1987 season. He is credited with popularizing the slam dunk. Erving, who was elected to the National Basketball Hall of Fame in 1992, served as a broadcaster for NBC, and in 1997 was named executive vice president of the Orlando Magic.

George Foreman (1948–)
Boxer, Minister

Born in Marshall, Texas, George Foreman emerged as one of boxing's most endearing figures. During his childhood in Houston, Foreman was a truant, snatching purses and participating in petty larcenies. His early success in boxing included a gold medal performance at the 1968 summer Olympic Games. After turning pro, he quickly became a top contender, recording 42 knockouts in his first 47 bouts.

Foreman captured the heavyweight title with his victory over Joe Frazier, in Kingston, Jamaica, on January 22, 1973. Having twice defended his belt successfully, he prepared to face Muhammad Ali on October 30, 1974, in Kinshasa, Zaire. The fight became known as the "Rumble in the Jungle." Despite being a 4–1 favorite, Foreman was out-fought by Ali who used his "rope-a-dope" tactic to tire Foreman and knock him out in the eighth round.

Foreman soon retired to become a minister and transformed his image into that of a congenial and very popular ex-champion. He initiated a comeback and recaptured the heavyweight crown when he defeated Michael Moorer on November 5, 1994. Foreman, thereby, became the oldest man in history to win the heavyweight championship of the world. He retired shortly thereafter to his gym in Houston.

Althea Gibson (1927–)
Tennis Player

Althea Gibson was born on August 25, 1927, in Silver, South Carolina, but was raised in Harlem. She began her tennis career when she entered and won the Department of Parks Manhattan Girls' Tennis Championship. In 1942, she began to receive professional coaching at the Cosmopolitan Tennis Club, and a year later, won the New York State Negro Girls Singles Title. In 1945 and 1946, she won the National Negro Girls Singles championship, and in 1948 won the title in the Women's Division.

A year later Gibson entered Florida A&M, where she played tennis and basketball. In 1950, she was runner-up for the National Indoor Championship, and became the first African American to play at the U.S. Open at the Forest Hills Country Club. The following year she became the first African American to play at Wimbledon.

In 1957 Gibson won the Wimbledon singles crown, and teamed with Darlene Hard to win the doubles championship. In 1957 and 1958, Gibson won the U.S. Open Women's Singles title. In 1963, just five years after she retired from tennis, Gibson became the first African American on the Ladies Professional Golfers Association (LPGA).

Gibson has served as a recreation manager, a member of the New Jersey State Athletic Control Board, on the Governor's Council on Physical Fitness, and as a sports consultant. She is also the author of the book *I Always Wanted to be Somebody*. In 1997, her 70th birthday was celebrated and her groundbreaking career was honored by the U.S. Tennis Association during the dedication of Arthur Ashe Stadium, where the U.S. Open tournament is held. A 2002 edition of *Ebony* magazine, named her as one of the ten greatest women athletes of all time.

Bob Gibson (1935–)
Baseball Player, Baseball Coach, Radio Announcer

Bob Gibson was born in Omaha, Nebraska, into poverty. Fatherless, he was one of seven children who

George Foreman.

lived in a four-room wooden shack. Denied a spot on Omaha Technical High School's baseball team because he was African American, he was permitted to join the track and field and basketball teams. He attended Creighton University in Omaha and became the first African American athlete to play both basketball and baseball.

Gibson's skill at basketball allowed him to play with the Harlem Globetrotters. While with them, he accepted an offer to join the St. Louis Cardinals' minor league team at Omaha for a salary of $3,000 and a $1,000 bonus. Gibson debuted with the Cardinals in 1959, beginning a Hall of Fame career that lasted 17 seasons and included five 20-victory seasons and 13 consecutive winning seasons. His highlights include a 1968 campaign in which he recorded a remarkable 13 shutouts, 22 victories, 268 strikeouts, and an Earned Run Average of 1.12, still a modern-era Major League record.

During his career, Gibson recorded 3,117 strikeouts and finished with an ERA of 2.91. He won seven and lost two games in three World Series appearances, with an ERA of 1.89. In Game 1 of the 1968 series he struck out 17 Detroit Tigers. Gibson pitched the Cardinals to

World Championships in 1964 and 1967. He was elected to the Baseball Hall of Fame in 1981.

Gibson has served as pitching coach with the New York Mets and Atlanta Braves and has been a special pitching consultant to many teams. He has also broadcast for the St. Louis Cardinals.

Josh Gibson (1911–1947)
Baseball Player

Gibson was born in Buena Vista, Georgia, in 1911, and moved to Pittsburgh, where he left school at the age of 14 to work for Gimbels Department store. Gimbels had a baseball team, which is where Gibson first attracted attention.

Josh Gibson was a catcher whose entire 16-year career was spent in the Negro League. His career began in 1929. With the exception of a stint with the Pittsburgh Crawfords between 1934 and 1936, and one season in Mexico in 1941, Gibson played with the Homestead Grays. His first game with Homestead took place on July 25, 1929, when, as a spectator, he was called out of the stands to replace an injured starter in a game against the Kansas City Monarchs.

Gibson was known for his legendary power. Playing at Yankee Stadium, he once hit a home run over the left field bullpen and out of the stadium. Gibson also hit a 580-foot home run over the top of the bleachers. Though accurate records are unavailable, Gibson is credited with hitting as many as 800 home runs in his career, including one season (1936) in which he hit 84.

Gibson died in 1947, from a stroke thought to be brought on by his alcoholism. He was elected to the Hall of Fame in 1972.

Ken Griffey Jr. (1969–)
Baseball Player

Ken Griffey Jr. was one of the most famous professional athletes in America at the turn of the century. Griffey's talents and flair have made him one of the most popular baseball players in today's game as evidenced by his 11 All-Star Game appearances.

Griffey was drafted first overall in 1987 by the Seattle Mariners while still in high school in Cincinnati. He broke into Major League Baseball in 1989 at the age of 19. He has won ten gold gloves for his play in centerfield and has driven in more than 100 runs eight times. In 1997, Griffey was unanimously selected as the league MVP, and in 1998, he accomplished the rare feat of hitting 50 home runs in back-to-back years. His chase of the single season home run record with Mark McGwire and Sammy Sosa in the summer of 1998 caught the attention of the entire nation. A vote of fellow major league players gave Griffey the title of Player of the Decade for the 1990s.

In 2000, Griffey signed what was, at the time, the richest contract in the history of major league baseball, a nine-year, $112.5 million deal, with the Cincinnati Reds. The trade brought Griffey back to his hometown.

Griffey's skills on the field have translated into many corporate sponsorships, making him one of the nation's most visible athletes.

Lusia Harris (1955–)
Basketball Player, Basketball Coach, Motivational Speaker

Lusia Harris was born in 1955, in Minter City, Mississippi, and participated on the silver medal-winning Olympic basketball team in 1976. She was high scorer at the Olympics and at the 1975 World University and Pan American Games. In college, she led Delta State University to three Association for Intercollegiate Athletics for Women titles from 1975 to 1977. She was named Mississippi's first amateur athlete of the year in 1976. Harris was selected as Delta State's homecoming queen, the first African American so honored.

Harris, the dominant female player of her era, broke hundreds of records and won countless American and international awards. As a graduate student, she became assistant basketball coach and admissions counselor at Delta State. She played briefly with the Houston Angels of the Women's Professional League in 1980.

In the 1990s, Harris coached basketball and taught physical education in Mississippi. In 1992, along with Nera White, Harris became the first woman inducted into the Basketball Hall of Fame. She is also a motivational speaker.

Chamique Holdsclaw (1977–)
Basketball Player

Holdsclaw was born in 1977 in Queens, New York. Holdsclaw left New York to attend the University of Tennessee and play for coach Pat Summitt.

Chamique Holdsclaw playing for the University of Tennessee.

At Tennessee, Holdsclaw became the most honored female basketball player since Cheryl Miller. Holdsclaw was a three-time All-American, two-time player-of-the-year award winner, and winner of three NCAA titles. In 1998 Holdsclaw became the first African American female basketball player to win the Sullivan Award. This award is given to the top amateur athlete in America.

Holdsclaw, a 6'2" forward, has been compared to both Cheryl Miller and Michael Jordan. She is being viewed as the commercial and athletic star to increase the visibility of the WNBA.

Holdsclaw was the first pick in the 1999 WNBA draft by the Washington Mystics, and was named Rookie of the Year following her first season. She has been selected as a starter in the WNBA All-Star game for three consecutive years. In the 2000 Summer Olympics, Holdsclaw led the U.S. Women's basketball team to the gold medal.

Larry Holmes (1949–)
Boxer

Holmes was born in Cuthberth, Georgia, and turned professional at the age of twenty-four after serving as sparring partner for Muhammad Ali. On June 9, 1978, he won the World Boxing Council heavyweight title from Ken Norton. On October 2, 1980, in Las Vegas, he defeated Ali by a technical knockout.

Holmes defended his title 12 times until losing to Michael Spinks on September 22, 1985, and again on April 19, 1986, in 15-round decisions. In all, Holmes held the heavyweight title for seven years, three months, and 13 days. A brief comeback attempt ended in a knockout by Mike Tyson on February 22, 1988. Holmes, who was voted one of the ten Most Outstanding Men in America by the Junior Chamber of Commerce, launched a second comeback in 1991. He fought and lost title bids against Evander Holyfield in 1992 and Oliver McCall in 1995. The former champion, who continues to fight due to monetary difficulties stemming from his relationship with his former promoter Don King, has amassed a career record of 68 wins and 6 losses.

Evander Holyfield (1962–)
Boxer

Evander Holyfield is known for his championship boxing ability, his devout religious faith, and his humble demeanor. In boxing, a sport dominated by braggadocio and large egos, Holyfield has become a popular champion due to his talent and humility.

Holyfield was born and still resides in Atlanta, Georgia. In the 1984 Olympics, he won the bronze medal in the light heavyweight division. He immediately turned professional and in 1986 won the cruiserweight title from Dwight Muhammad Qawi. By 1989 he was the undisputed cruiserweight champion.

Holyfield entered the heavyweight division that same year and in 1990 defeated Buster Douglas to win the heavyweight title. After several defenses of his title, Holyfield was defeated by Riddick Bowe in 1992 and retired due to health problems.

Holyfield, a natural light heavyweight, has always undergone strenuous training to be able to fight against the bigger fighters in the heavyweight division. In 1993 he came out of retirement to defeat Bowe and regain his title. After losing his title to Michael Moorer, Holyfield finally fought heavyweight champion Mike Tyson in 1996. Holyfield upset Tyson to regain the heavyweight title and then defeated Tyson the next year when Tyson bit Holyfield twice and was disqualified.

With the WBA heavyweight title his, Holyfield next faced Michael Moorer in Las Vegas on November 8, 1997. An eighth round TKO gave Holyfield the victory and unified the WBA and IBF heavyweight championships. After successful defenses of the titles, Holyfield lost both in a 1999 rematch against Lennox Lewis.

Holyfield managed to regain the WBA title in his next fight, as he defeated John Ruiz in August 2000. The two have fought twice since, with the second fight resulting in a loss for Holyfield and the third being ruled a draw. Holyfield continues to successfully pursue the heavyweight title, defeating another former heavyweight champion, Hasim Rahman, on June 1, 2002.

Reggie Jackson (1946–)
Baseball Player

Because of his outstanding performance in postseason play, Reggie Jackson became known as "Mr. October." During his years with the Oakland Athletics and New York Yankees, Jackson captured or tied 13 World Series records to become baseball's top record holder in Series play.

Born in Wynecote, Pennsylvania, on May 18, 1946, he followed his father's encouragement to become an all-around athlete while at Cheltenham High School. He ran track, played halfback in football, and was a star hitter on the school baseball team. An outstanding football and baseball player at Arizona State University, he left after his sophomore year to join the Athletics (then located in Kansas City).

In 1968, his first full season with the Athletics, Jackson hit 29 homers and batted in 74 runs, but made

18 errors and struck out 171 times, the worst seasonal total by a left handed hitter in baseball history. After playing a season of winter ball under Frank Robinson's direction, his performance continued to improve, and, in 1973, he batted .293, led the league in home runs (32), RBIs (117), and slugging average (.531), and was selected Most Valuable Player.

While with Oakland, Jackson helped the Athletics to three straight World Series championships, from 1972 to 1974. Later, with the New York Yankees, Jackson won the World Series in 1977 and 1978. The Yankees also won the American League pennant in 1981. In 1977, he was named Series MVP, after hitting five home runs—including three on three consecutive pitches, in the sixth and deciding game.

The first of the big money free agents, Jackson hit 144 homers, drove in 461 runs, and boosted his total career home runs to 425 while with the Yankees. Jackson retired in 1987 and has occasionally served as a commentator during baseball broadcasts. His tumultuous relationship with Yankees owner George Steinbrenner has continued through the various jobs Jackson has held with the organization. He was elected to the Baseball Hall of Fame in 1993.

Earvin "Magic" Johnson (1959–)
Basketball Player, Basketball Coach, Sports Executive, Talk Show Host, Entrepreneur

Earvin Johnson Jr. was born August 14, 1959, in Lansing, Michigan, and attended Everett High School. While playing for Everett he picked up the nickname "Magic" because of his ball-handling abilities. While in high school, Johnson made the All-State Team and for three years was named the United Press International Prep-Player of the Year in Michigan.

In 1977, Johnson enrolled at Michigan State University and led the Spartans to the national championship in 1979. He then turned professional and was selected by the Los Angeles Lakers in the National Basketball Association draft. He led the Lakers to five NBA titles in the 1980s. Johnson played with the Lakers until his retirement in 1991 when he tested positive for the HIV/AIDS virus.

Johnson was the recipient of many awards and was chosen to play on many postseason all-star teams. In college, he was named to the All-Big Ten Team in 1977 and chosen as the NCAA Tournament-Most Valuable Player. He was also a consensus All-American selection (1979). During his professional career, he was a three-time league MVP (1987, 1989, 1990) and was named to the NBA All-Rookie Team (1980) and the All-NBA Team (1982–1989, 1991). He was also recognized as the NBA

Earvin "Magic" Johnson at a press conference before an international game in Brazil.

Finals MVP (1987) and the NBA All-Star Game MVP (1990, 1992).

During his retirement, Johnson played on the U.S. Olympic Basketball Team in 1992 and in the 1992 NBA All-Star game, where he won another MVP award. He also coached the Lakers briefly at the end of the 1994 season, became team vice president, and had an ownership stake in the Lakers, which he was forced to surrender upon his short-lived return in 1996 as a player. Johnson hosted a late night talk show in 1998, but it was cancelled shortly afterwards. In 2001 he was honored with a star on the Hollywood Walk of Fame.

Jack Johnson (1878–1946)
Boxer

Jack Johnson became the first African American heavyweight champion by winning the crown from Tommy Burns in Sydney, Australia, on December 26, 1908.

Johnson was born in Galveston, Texas, on March 31, 1878. He was so tiny as a boy that he was nicknamed "Li'l Arthur," a name that stuck with him throughout his career. As a young man, he drifted around the country, making his way through Chicago, Boston, and New York. He learned to box by working out with veteran professionals whenever he could. When he finally got his chance at the title, he had already been fighting for nine years and had lost only 3 of 100 bouts.

With his victory over Burns, Johnson became the center of a bitter racial controversy, as his flamboyant lifestyle and outspokenness aroused white resentment. Public pressure forced former champion Jim Jeffries to come out of retirement and challenge Johnson for the title. When the two fought on July 4, 1910, in Reno, Nevada, Johnson knocked out Jeffries in the 14th round.

In 1913, Johnson left the United States due to legal difficulties. Two years later he defended his title against Jess Willard in Havana, Cuba, and was knocked out in the 26th round. His career record was 107 wins, 6 losses.

Johnson died on June 10, 1946, in an automobile crash in North Carolina. He was inducted into the Boxing Hall of Fame in 1954.

Marion Jones (1975–)
Track and Field Athlete

Marion Lois Jones was born in Los Angeles on October 12, 1975. As a child living in Thousand Oaks, California, Jones participated in many sports, but she was first attracted to running and jumping while watching track superstars Evelyn Ashford, Carl Lewis, and Jackie Joyner-Kersee on television as they competed in the 1984 Olympics. By the time she had finished high school she had received two High School Athlete of the Year awards for her performance in the 100-meter and 200-meter dashes as well as being named California Division I Player of the Year for basketball during her senior year.

Jones went on to play basketball for the University of North Carolina and took the team to three Atlantic Coast Conference championships and a national title. Her love, however, was still track and field: she had dreams of running in the Olympics. She decided to forgo playing basketball during her junior year of college to focus purely on her running in preparation for the 1996 Summer Olympics. A broken foot bone ended her aspirations in late 1995, though. After the 1996 Olympics, Jones rededicated herself to her goal of running in the Olympics by training with Jamaican track star Trevor Graham.

Jones trained during 1996 and in 1997 she won both the 100-meter title and the long jump title at the USA Outdoor Championships becoming the first woman in nine years to win both events. She won a gold medal in the 100-meter sprint and was on the gold winning 4x100-meter relay team at the Outdoor World Championships later that same year. Jones continued to dominate the world of women's track by setting an American record in the 60-meter sprint in the Gunma International competition in Japan in 1998. She also anchored the Nike International team to a new American record in the 4x200-meter relay at the Penn Relays in Philadelphia that same year. Shortly after, she became the second fastest woman in the world behind Florence Griffith Joyner when she ran 10.71 seconds in the 100-meter sprint at a meet in Chengdu, China. By the end of 1999, Jones had won 37 consecutive races at international and national track and field competitions, including the World Cup and the USA Outdoor Championships. She was also named *Track and Field News* Top Woman Athlete of the year for three consecutive years.

In Sydney, Australia, host to the 2000 Summer Games, Jones took home three gold medals and two bronze medals fulfilling her dream of not only running in but winning at the Olympics. Her victories were momentarily overshadowed by the publicity surrounding her husband's use of steriods in the shot put event. Still, Jones was honored with numerous awards after her Olympic victories, including being named Athlete of the Year by the International Amateur Athletic Federation. Jones continued to compete in track and field, winning a gold medal in the 100-meter race in the 2001 Goodwill Games.

Michael Jordan (1963–)
Basketball Player

Michael Jordan was born in Brooklyn, New York, on February 17, 1963, and attended the University of North Carolina. He won the NCAA championship as a freshman with the Tar Heels. As a rookie with the Chicago Bulls in 1985, Jordan was named to the All-Star team. A skilled ball handler and a slam dunk artist, he became the second NBA player in history to score more than 3,000 points in a single season in 1986.

Jordan was the NBA's individual scoring champ from 1987 through 1993. He was also named the NBA's Most Valuable Player at the end of the 1987–1988 season. In 1991, Jordan led the Chicago Bulls to their first NBA Championship and was the league's Most Valuable Player. Under Jordan's leadership, the Bulls repeated as champions in 1992 and 1993. In 1992 Jordan played for the U.S. Olympic basketball "Dream Team," which captured the gold medal in Barcelona.

In October of 1993, Jordan announced his retirement from basketball to pursue another lifelong dream—to become a professional baseball player. Jordan began his professional baseball career in 1994 with the Chicago White Sox's Class A team, the Birmingham Barons. Despite having only a .202 batting average for the year, Jordan was voted the most popular man in baseball in a national poll and remained at the top of *Forbes* magazine's list of the world's top paid athletes for the third consecutive year, mostly due to endorsements.

In March of 1995, Jordan returned to the NBA with the Bulls. He was named the 1996 All-Star game MVP. Jordan led the Bulls to three straight titles from 1996 to 1998. The 1996 team set a NBA record for most wins (72) in a season. After hitting the shot that won the 1998 NBA Championship, Jordan retired again.

In 2000, Michael Jordan took on yet another role, as it was announced that he would serve as part owner and president of basketball operations for the NBA's Washington Wizards. It was a position that Jordan would only hold for so long, as he decided in September 2001 to come out of retirement once again, this time as a player for the Wizards. Jordan's return was met with much enthusiasm by fans and media. On January 4, 2002, facing his former team, the Chicago Bulls, Jordan became only the fourth NBA player to reach 30,000 career points. Just a few months later, Jordan was placed on the injured list with a painful knee injury that shortened his first season. Despite the setback, Jordan still plans to play through the 2003 season.

Florence Griffith Joyner (1959–1998)
Track and Field Athlete

Born in Los Angeles on December 21, 1959, Florence Griffith started in track at an early age. She first attended California State University-Northridge, but later transferred with her coach Bob Kersee when he moved to UCLA. In 1987 she married 1984 Olympic gold medalist Al Joyner.

At the 1984 Olympic games she won a silver medal. She returned to the Olympic games in 1988, winning a gold medal in the 100-meter, 200-meter, 400-meter relay, and 1600-meter relay races. She set the world record for the 100-meter and 200-meter races that year.

Nicknamed "Flo-Jo," she was inducted into the Track and Field Hall of Fame in 1995. In 1998, she died suddenly in her sleep of an apparent heart seizure.

Jackie Joyner-Kersee holds the gold medal that she won at the 1992 Olympic Games in Barcelona.

Jackie Joyner-Kersee (1962–)
Track and Field Athlete, Community Activist, Sports Agent

Often touted as the world's greatest female athlete, Jackie Joyner-Kersee won two gold medals at the 1988 Olympic games and a gold and a bronze medal at the 1992 games.

Joyner-Kersee was born on March 3, 1962, in East St. Louis, Illinois. Prior to winning the 1988 gold medal, she participated in the 1984 Olympics and won the silver medal for the heptathlon despite a torn hamstring muscle.

The only woman to gain more than 7,000 points in the heptathlon four times, she set a world record with 7,215 points at the 1988 Olympic trials. Joyner-Kersee also earned another gold medal in the heptathlon and a bronze medal in the long jump at the 1992 Olympics in Barcelona, Spain. In 1996 at the Atlanta Olympics she won a bronze medal in the long jump, her sixth medal, the most in the history of U.S. women's track and field.

Joyner-Kersee briefly played professional basketball in the ABL, before retiring from sports to devote time to charitable causes. In addition, Joyner-Kersee is one of the few female sports agents in the United States.

"Sugar" Ray Leonard (1956–)
Boxer, Television Analyst

One of the flashiest and most popular fighters of the modern era, Sugar Ray Leonard brought fame to the lighter divisions of boxing which traditionally have not garnered the same amount of attention as the heavyweight division. Leonard was born in Wilmington, North Carolina, and won the gold medal in the light welterweight division at the 1976 Montreal Olympics.

Leonard rose through the professional ranks, winning the welterweight title from Wilfred Benitez in 1979. His fights with Roberto Duran and Tommy Hearns established his fame. After losing his first fight and his title to Duran, Leonard used a taunting style and flamboyant ring persona to force Duran to quit in the middle of their second fight. In 1981 he defeated Hearns in the 14th round by technical knockout, rallying from a point deficit. He retired shortly thereafter due to a detached retina.

In 1987, Leonard made a comeback by upsetting middleweight champion "Marvelous" Marvin Hagler. The upset prolonged his career, but he was unable to fight at his former level and retired shortly thereafter.

Leonard's public persona has led to many sponsorship deals. In addition, he serves as a boxing analyst for HBO and ESPN Classic Sports.

Carl Lewis (1961–)
Track and Field Athlete

Carl Lewis was born on July 1, 1961, in Birmingham, Alabama. In the 1984 Olympics in Los Angeles, Lewis became the first athlete since Jesse Owens in 1936 to win four gold medals in the same Olympic competition.

An often controversial track and field performer, the New Jersey native went into the 1984 competition with the burden of tremendous expectations as the result of intense pre-Olympic publicity. He did not set any Olympic records, and despite his four gold medals, found himself criticized in the media.

Lewis went to the 1988 Olympics in Seoul, South Korea, hoping to duplicate his four gold medal wins. He was the focus of interest as he faced off against his Canadian archrival Ben Johnson. Lewis won gold medals in the long jump and the 100-meter dash (after Johnson was disqualified for steroid use) and a silver medal in the 200-meter dash. At the 1992 Olympics in

Carl Lewis.

Barcelona, Lewis won a gold medal for the long jump and in the 4x100-meter relay. He won his final gold medal at the 1996 Atlanta Olympiad in the long jump.

Lewis was inducted into the USA Track & Field Hall of Fame in 2001.

Joe Louis (1914–1981)
Boxer

Joe Louis held the heavyweight championship for the longest stretch in history—more than 11 years, and defended the title more often than any other heavyweight champion. His 25 title fights were more than the combined total of the eight champions who preceded him.

Born on May 13, 1914, in a sharecropper's shack in Lexington, Alabama, Louis moved to Detroit as a small boy. Taking up boxing as an amateur, he won 50 out of 59 bouts (43 by knockout), before turning professional in 1934.

In 1935 Lewis fought Primo Carnera, a former boxing champion. Louis knocked out Carnera in six rounds, earning his nickname, "The Brown Bomber." After knocking out ex-champion Max Baer, Louis suffered his lone pre-championship defeat at the hands of Max Schmeling, who knocked him out in the twelfth round. Less than a month later, Louis knocked out another former champion, Jack Sharkey, in three rounds. He later won a rematch with Schmeling in a racially charged fight that earned him national attention. After defeating a number of other challengers, he was given a title fight with Jim Braddock on June 22, 1937. He stopped Braddock in the eighth round to gain the title.

After winning a disputed decision over Joe Walcott in 1947, Louis knocked out Walcott six months later, and then went into retirement. Monetary problems forced Louis into several comebacks that resulted in losses to new heavyweight champions Ezzard Charles and Rocky Marciano. These monetary difficulties were a problem for Louis for the rest of his life. He died April 12, 1981 at the age of 67.

Willie Mays (1931–)
Baseball Player

During his 21 seasons with the Giants, Willie Mays hit more than 600 home runs. Besides being a solid hitter, Mays also was one of the game's finest defensive outfielder and baserunners.

Born in Fairfield, Alabama, on May 6, 1931, Mays made his professional debut on July 4, 1948, with the Birmingham Black Barons. He was signed by the New York Giants in 1950 and reached the major leagues in 1951. He was named the National League's Rookie of the Year for his 20 home runs, 68 RBIs, and fielding, all of which contributed to the Giants pennant victory.

After two years in the U.S. Army, Mays returned to lead the Giants to the World Championship in 1954, gaining recognition as the league's Most Valuable Player for his 41 homers, 110 RBIs, and .345 batting average.

When the Giants moved to San Francisco, Mays continued his home run hitting, and led his team to a 1962 pennant. A year later, *Sport* magazine named him "the greatest player of the decade." He won the MVP award again in 1965, after hitting 52 home runs and batting .317.

Traded to the New York Mets before the 1972 season, he continued to play outfield and first base. At the end of the 1973 season, his statistics included 2,992 games, 3,283 hits, and 660 home runs—third all-time. Willie Mays is one of only 14 ballplayers to hit four home runs in a single game. After acting as a coach for the Mets, Mays left baseball to pursue a business

career. He was elected to the Baseball Hall of Fame in 1979. In 2001 the San Francisco Giants dedicated a plaza and statue to him outside their new stadium.

Cheryl Miller (1964–)
Basketball Player, Television Analyst, Basketball Coach

Cheryl Miller was born and raised in Riverside, California. She has occasionally been overshadowed by her brother, Reggie, a guard with the Indiana Pacers. Another brother, Darrell, played baseball professionally with the California Angels in the late 1980s.

The 6'3" Cheryl Miller began attracting notice in high school, having once scored 105 points in a game at Polytechnic High School. Miller was offered nearly 250 scholarships before deciding to enroll at the University of Southern California (USC). There she led the Trojans to two national titles, was All-American four times, and was named National Player of the Year three times.

Miller was a member of numerous national teams including the U.S. Junior National Team in 1981 and the National Team the following year. She participated in the World Championships and the Pan American Games in 1983. In 1984, she won an Olympic gold medal.

Following her playing career, Miller worked as a television basketball commentator. In 1993, she became the women's head basketball coach at her alma mater, USC, but announced her retirement in 1995. In the previous year, she was elected into the Basketball Hall of Fame. Miller held the post of head coach of the WNBA's Phoenix Mercury from 1997–2000 and also served as the team's general manager.

Edwin Moses (1955–)
Track and Field Athlete, Olympic Committee Chairperson

Born in Dayton, Ohio, in 1955, Edwin Moses became an internationally known track star in hurdles. Having attended Morehouse College, he was the top ranked intermediate hurdler in the world by 1976. That same year he earned a gold medal at the Olympic Games, a feat to be duplicated eight years later. Moses also won a bronze medal at the 1988 Games. A world record holder in the 400-meter hurdles, he recorded 122 consecutive victories in competition. *Sports Illustrated* presented Moses with its Athlete of the Year award in 1984, one year after he won the Sullivan Award, given annually to America's best amateur athlete. He was elected to the USA Track & Field Hall of Fame in 1994.

Moses received his M.B.A. from Pepperdine University in 1994 and is currently a financial consultant. He has served as the chairperson of the U.S. Olympic Committee Substance Abuse Center as well on the International Olympic Committee Athletes Commission.

Shaquille O'Neal (1972–)
Basketball Player

Born in Newark, New Jersey in 1972 to a military family, Shaquille O'Neal has become one of the most famous athletes in America. O'Neal has also appeared in movies and has released his own rap albums.

O'Neal's size and talent attracted attention while he was in high school. While attending Louisiana State University, he was named a collegiate All-American in 1992 and left school to pursue a professional career. He was the first pick of the 1992 NBA draft by the Orlando Magic and starred for them until 1996. He led the Magic to the 1995 NBA finals. In 1996 he signed a free agent contract with the Los Angeles Lakers.

O'Neal has enjoyed great success with the Lakers, leading them to a third straight NBA Championship title in 2002. He has been named Finals MVP in each of the three series, and was named the league's MVP for the 2000 season. O'Neal has been selected as an NBA All-Star nine times, and has led the league in scoring twice (1995 and 2000).

O'Neal has recorded several rap albums and appeared in various movies. In 1996 he was the star of the film *Kazaam*.

Jesse Owens (1913–1980)
Track and Field Athlete

The track and field records Jesse Owens set have all been eclipsed, but his reputation as one of the first great athletes with the combined talents of a sprinter, low hurdler, and broad jumper has not diminished.

Born James Cleveland Owens in Danville, Alabama, on September 12, 1913, Jesse and his family moved to Ohio when he was still young. In 1932, while attending East Technical High School in Cleveland, Owens was clocked at 10.3 seconds in the 100-meter dash. Two years later, Owens entered Ohio State University and became known as "The Ebony Antelope." While competing in the Big Ten Championships at Ann Arbor, Michigan, on May 25, 1935, Owens had what has been called "the greatest single day in the history of man's athletic achievements." In the space of about seventy

Jesse Owens (center) salutes the American flag while standing atop the podium at the 1936 Olympic Games in Berlin.

minutes, he tied the world record for the 100-yard dash and surpassed the world record for five other events including the broad jump, the 220-yard low hurdles, and the 220-yard dash.

In 1936, at the Berlin Olympics, Owens won four gold medals, at that time the most universally acclaimed feat in the history of the games. However, he still faced discrimination in the United States after his victories. He never graduated from Ohio State but did eventually found his own public relations firm.

Satchel Paige (1906–1982)
Baseball Player, Baseball Coach

Long before Jackie Robinson broke the color barrier of "organized baseball," Leroy Robert "Satchel" Paige was the most famous African American baseball player. As an outstanding performer in the Negro Leagues, Paige had become a legendary figure whose encounters with Major League Baseball players added considerably to his athletic reputation.

Paige was born in Mobile, Alabama, on July 7, 1906. He began playing semi-professional ball while working as an iceman and porter. In the mid-1920s, he became a professional player with the Birmingham Black Barons, and later, while playing at Chattanooga, acquired the sobriquet "Satchel" because of his "Satchel-sized feet."

For the next two decades, Paige was the dominant pitcher in Negro League baseball. In 1933, he won 31 games and lost 4. Paige also dominated winter ball in Latin America during the 1930s. In 1942, Paige led the Kansas City Monarchs to victory in the Negro World Series, and four years later he helped them to the pennant by allowing only two runs in 93 innings, a performance which included a string of 64 straight scoreless innings.

In 1948, he was brought up to the major leagues. Despite being well past his prime, he still was able to contribute six victories in Cleveland's pennant drive and pitched in the World Series. Four years later, while pitching for the St. Louis Browns, he was named to the American League All-Star squad.

Until the 1969 baseball season, Paige was active on the barnstorming circuit with the Harlem Globetrotters and a host of other exhibition teams. In 1969 the Atlanta Braves, in an attempt to make Paige eligible for baseball's pension plan, signed him to a one-year contract as coach. Paige died in June of 1982.

Walter Payton (1954–1999)
Football Player, Entrepreneur

Walter Payton was born on July 25, 1954, in Columbia, Mississippi. When he retired as a running back for the Chicago Bears after the 1986 season, he was the National Football League's all-time leading rusher, breaking a record held for many years by Jim Brown.

A graduate of Jackson State University, Payton played his entire career in Chicago, receiving numerous awards and helping to lead the Bears to a victory in Super Bowl XX. He broke O. J. Simpson's single game rushing record after gaining 275 yards during a game with the Minnesota Vikings in 1977. Seven years later, during a game against the New Orleans Saints, he surpassed Jim Brown's career rushing record. He concluded his career with a total of 16,726 yards rushing.

Payton funded several auto racing teams and fronted a group of businessmen in an attempt to bring a professional football team to the city of St. Louis. He was elected to the Pro Football Hall of Fame in 1993. In 1998 Payton was diagnosed with a fatal liver disease. He died on November 1, 1999.

Calvin Peete (1943–)
Golfer

Calvin Peete was born in Detroit, on July 18, 1943. During World War II, Peete moved with his family to Pahikee, Florida. One of 19 children, as a youth he was a farm laborer and itinerant peddler, selling wares to farmers along the East Coast.

He began golfing at the age of 23 and soon realizing that he possessed some aptitude for the sport. Unlike other African American golfers of his era who were forced into caddying as a means of gaining entrance into the sport, Peete was able to move directly toward a professional career. Peete did, however, face the handicap of a left arm that he was unable to completely straighten, leading experts to tell him that he would never be successful.

After turning pro in 1971, Peete struggled. In 1978, he placed 108th in total money winnings on the PGA tour. Peete's first tour victory came at the 1979 Greater Milwaukee Open, which he won again in 1982, along with the Anheuser-Busch Classic, BC Open, and the Pensacola Open. In 1981 and 1982, he finished first on the tour in the categories of driving accuracy and greens reached in regulation.

Despite his success, Peete was not considered fully accredited because the PGA does not recognize a golfer unless he has obtained a high school diploma. This was a requirement toward obtaining a spot on the prestigious Ryder Cup team. In 1982, with the assistance of his wife, Peete passed the Michigan General Equivalency examination 24 years after leaving high school. *Ebony* magazine rewarded him with a Black Achievement award, and, in 1983, Peete was presented with the Jackie Robinson Award.

Peete captured two more PGA titles in 1983—the Georgia-Pacific Atlanta Classic and the Anheuser-Busch Classic. He was also asked to represent the United States as a member of the Ryder Cup team. That same year, he won the Ben Hogan Award. The following year, Peete had the best scoring average on the PGA tour. He is now a member of the PGA's Senior Tour.

Jerry Rice (1962–)
Football Player

Jerry Rice was born in Starkville, Mississippi, on October 13, 1962. At a collegian at Mississippi Valley State, Rice set 18 Division II records. Drafted in the first round by the 49ers in 1985, Rice combined with quarterbacks Joe Montana and Steve Young to form the most elite pass-catching combination in pro football history. He traces the development of his superb hands to his childhood, during which his father would toss him bricks during construction work.

Rice currently holds the career record for touchdowns. His ten straight seasons with more than 1,000 receiving yards is also a league record. His best season was the strike-shortened 1987 campaign, during which he scored 22 touchdowns in only 12 regular season games. In that same year, Rice scored touchdowns in 13 straight games. In a 1990 contest with the Atlanta Falcons, Rice scored five touchdowns. He was named to the Pro Bowl every season until slowed by an injury in 1997. He was named the NFL's Player of the year by the *Sporting News* in 1987 and 1990. Rice was Most Valuable Player in the 49ers' Super Bowl XXIII victory over the Cincinnati Bengals.

Rice helped lead the 49ers to Super Bowl victories after the 1988, 1989, and 1994 seasons. Rice ended his 16-year career as a wide receiver with the San Francisco 49ers following the 2000 season. In 2001, he signed a multi-year contract with the Oakland Raiders.

Oscar Robertson (1938–)
Basketball Player, Business Executive, Community Activist

Oscar Robertson was born in Charlotte, Tennessee, in 1938, before moving to Indiana and attending Indianapolis' Crispus Attucks High School. He led his team to the prestigious Indiana state basketball title on two occasions and shortly thereafter became the first African American to play at the University of Cincinnati. He helped Cincinnati reach the Final Four in 1959 and 1960, was named the United Press International college player of the year for three consecutive seasons, and set 14 major collegiate records. He also became the first to lead the NCAA in scoring for three consecutive seasons.

In 1960, and after participating on the U.S. gold medal winning Olympic basketball team as co-captain, Robertson signed a $100,000 contract with the Cincinnati Royals, earning Rookie of the Year honors during his initial season in the NBA. At 6'5", 210 pounds, he would become the NBA's first true "big guard." The multidimensional Robertson, known as the "Big O," was a textbook fundamental player and unyieldingly physical. During the 1962 season he led the NBA in assists, at 11.4 per game. His best season was the 1964 campaign in which he averaged 31.4 points per game and was named the league's Most Valuable Player.

Over the course of five separate seasons, Robertson, averaged more than 20 points and 10 assists per game,

something no other player in NBA history has accomplished. He was the Most Valuable Player of the 1961, 1964, and 1969 All-Star games. Late in his career, Robertson joined the Milwaukee Bucks and led Milwaukee to its only NBA championship in 1971.

Robertson became the president of the NBA Players Association. Under his leadership, the NBAPA established collective bargaining with the league's owners. He was elected to the Basketball Hall of Fame in 1979, and was named to the NBA's 35th anniversary all-time team in 1980. Robertson was also elected to the Olympic Hall of Fame in 1984.

Robertson has remained visible off the court, becoming a successful chemical company executive as president/CEO of ORCHEM, Inc. in 1981, and starting Oscar Robertson and Associates in 1983. He is a member of the NAACP Sports Board, a trustee of the Indiana High School and Basketball Halls of Fame, the National Director of the Pepsi-Cola Hot Shot Program, and the President of the NBA Retired Players Association. Robertson was also the developer of affordable housing units in Cincinnati and Indianapolis. He served in the U.S. Army for eight years.

Eddie G. Robinson (1919–)
College Football Coach

Eddie Gay Robinson was born on February 13, 1919, in Jackson, Louisiana. As a gifted athlete in high school, Robinson earned a scholarship to Leland College in Louisiana. A star quarterback, Robinson got involved in his first coaching clinic there. After obtaining his bachelor's degree, Robinson took his first college coaching job in 1941. Though only 22 years old at the time, Grambling State gave Robinson the opportunity to coach.

The early success of Grambling State's football team established Robinson as a fixture at Grambling State. He coached numerous NFL stars and successful teams during his tenure as coach. In 1985, Robinson had surpassed Bear Bryant as the career leader in victories by a head coach. He retired following the 1997 season. Two years later his autobiography, *Never Before, Never Again*, was published.

Frank Robinson (1935–)
Baseball Player, Baseball Manager, Sports Executive

Born in Beaumont, Texas, in 1936, Frank Robinson moved to Oakland, California, at the age of five. During his teens, he was a football and baseball star at

Eddie Robinson.

McClyronds High School. After graduation in 1953, he signed with the Cincinnati Reds.

In 1956, Robinson debuted in Major League Baseball, hitting 38 homers and winning Rookie of the Year honors. During the next eight years, he hit 259 homers and had 800 RBIs. In 1961, Robinson was named Most Valuable Player for leading Cincinnati to the National League pennant. Five years later, Robinson won the American League's Triple Crown and became the first player to win the MVP in both leagues. He retired as an active player after the 1976 season with a lifetime batting average of .294 in 2,808 games along with 2,943 hits, 1,829 runs, and 1,812 RBIs. His 586 home runs rank fourth all-time.

Frank Robinson was Major League Baseball's first African American manager. He was named to the head post of the Cleveland Indians in 1975. Robinson left the Indians in 1977, and became the manager of the Rochester Red Wings, a minor league team, in 1978. In 1981, Robinson was hired by the San Francisco Giants, where he managed the team until 1984. He also managed the Baltimore Orioles during the late 1980s. He later became the assistant general manager of that team. He is currently the manager of the Montreal Expos, a position he accepted in 2002 after serving three years as vice-president of on-field operations for Major League Baseball. Robinson was elected to the National Baseball Hall of Fame in 1982.

Jackie Robinson (1919–1972)
Baseball Player, Business Executive, Community Activist

Born in Cairo, Georgia, on January 31, 1919, Robinson was raised in Pasadena, California. At UCLA he gained All-American honorable mention as a halfback, but he left college in his junior year to play professional football for the Los Angeles Bulldogs. After serving as a U.S. Army lieutenant during World War II, Robinson returned to civilian life with the hope of becoming a physical education coach. He began to play in the Negro Baseball League to establish himself.

In 1945, while he was playing with the Kansas City Monarchs, Branch Rickey of the Brooklyn Dodgers signed him to a contract. In 1946 he played for the Dodgers top minor league in Montreal. On April 10, 1947, the Dodgers announced that they had purchased Robinson's contract and the following day he began his Major League Baseball career. During a ten-year career, he hit .311 in 1,382 games with 1,518 hits, 947 runs, 273 doubles, and 734 RBIs. He won the National League's Most Valuable Player award in 1949, and played on six National League pennant winners, as well as one world championship team. Robinson was inducted into the National Baseball Hall of Fame in 1962.

After his retirement from baseball, Robinson became a bank official, president of a land development firm, and a director of programs to combat drug addiction. He died on October 24, 1972 in Stamford, Connecticut.

"Sugar Ray" Robinson (1921–1989)
Boxer

Born Walker Smith, in Detroit on May 3, 1921, he took the name Robinson from the certificate of an amateur boxer whose identity enabled him to meet the age requirements for getting a match in Michigan.

As a youth, Robinson had watched a Detroit neighbor, Joe Louis, train for an amateur boxing career. When Robinson moved to New York two years later, he began to spend most of his time at local gyms in preparation for his own amateur career. After winning all 89 of his amateur bouts and the 1939 Golden Gloves featherweight championship, he turned professional in 1940 at Madison Square Garden.

Robinson beat Tommy Bell in an elimination title bout in December 1946 to win the welterweight title. He successfully defended the title for five years, and on February 14, 1951, took the middleweight crown from Jake LaMotta.

In July of 1951, he lost the title to Randy Turpin, only to win it back two months later. Retiring for a time, Robinson subsequently fought a series of exciting battles with Carl "Bobo" Olsen, Carmen Basilio, and Gene Fullmer before retiring permanently on December 10, 1965, having won six titles.

Suffering from diabetes, hypertension, and Alzheimer's disease, Robinson died of natural causes at the Brotman Medical Center in Culver City, California, on April 12, 1989. Over his career, he won 174 of 201 professional bouts and titles in three weight classes.

Wilma Rudolph (1940–1994)
Track and Field Athlete, Track and Field Coach, Community Activist, Lecturer

Rudolph was born on June 23, 1940, in St. Bethlehem, Tennessee, the 17th of 19 children. At an early age, she survived polio and scarlet fever. Through daily leg massages administered in turn by different members of her family, she progressed to the point where she was able to walk with the aid of a special shoe. Three years later, however, she discarded the shoe, and began joining her brother in backyard basketball games. At Burt High School in Clarksville, Rudolph broke the state basketball record for girls. As a sprinter, she was undefeated high school track meets.

In 1957, Rudolph enrolled at Tennessee State University and began training for the Olympic games in Rome. She gained national recognition in college meets, setting the world record for 200-meters in July of 1960. In the Olympics, she earned the title of the "World's Fastest Woman" by winning gold medals for the 100-meter dash, the 200-meter dash (setting an Olympic record), and for anchoring the 400-meter relay (setting a world record). She was named by the Associated Press as the U.S. Female Athlete of the Year for 1960 and also won United Press Athlete of the Year honors.

Rudolph served as a track coach, an athletic consultant, and assistant director of athletics for the Mayor's Youth Foundation in Chicago. She was also the founder of the Wilma Rudolph Foundation. Rudolph also was a talk show hostess and active on the lecture circuit. On November 12, 1994, Wilma Rudolph died at her home in Brentwood, Tennessee, of a brain tumor.

Bill Russell (1934–)
Basketball Player, Basketball Coach, Sports Executive, Television Commentator

Bill Russell, who led the Boston Celtics to 11 titles including eight in a row, is regarded as the finest defensive basketball player in the game's history. The 6'10" star is also the first African American to coach a National Basketball Association team.

Russell was born on February 12, 1934, in Monroe, Louisiana. The family settled in Oakland, California, when Russell was a youth. At McClyronds High School, Russell proved to be an awkward but determined basketball player who eventually received a scholarship to the nearby University of San Francisco.

In his sophomore year he became the most publicized athlete on the West Coast. Over the next two years, his fame spread across the nation as he led his team to a record 60 consecutive victories and two straight NCAA titles.

The Celtics had never won an NBA Championship before Russell's arrival in 1957. With the help of Russell's defensive capabilities, the Celtics became the most successful team in the history of professional sports, winning the world championship eight years in a row. Russell himself was named Most Valuable Player on five separate occasions (1958, 1961 to 1963, 1965). In 1966, Russell became the Celtics player/coach.

After the 1968–1969 season, having led the Celtics to their 11th NBA crown, Russell retired as both coach and player. He left the game as its all-time leader in minutes played (40,726). In 1980, the Professional Basketball Writers Association of America selected Russell as the greatest player in NBA history.

After retirement, Russell was a color commentator on NBC-TV's NBA Game of the Week. In 1974, he accepted a lucrative contract to become head coach and general manager of the Seattle Supersonics and was inducted into the Basketball Hall of Fame. He remained at Seattle's helm through 1977 and returned to the coaching ranks ten years later for a one-year stint with the Sacramento Kings. He also served as the team's director of player personnel in 1988.

Deion Sanders (1967–)
Football Player

Deion Sanders was born in Fort Myers, Florida, and first achieved fame as an All-American defensive back at Florida State University. Sanders was also a baseball star at the school, and after leaving college in 1989 pursued professional careers in both sports.

Sanders was drafted by the football Atlanta Falcons and has also played for the San Francisco 49ers, the Dallas Cowboys, and the Washington Redskins. He was selected as an All-Pro seven times and was named the top defensive player in the league in 1994. Sanders won Super Bowls with San Francisco in 1994 and Dallas in 1995. He announced his retirement from football in July 2001.

Sanders's baseball career has also been successful. He was drafted and played with the New York Yankees until traded to the Atlanta Braves in 1991. He played in two World Series with the Braves and has also played with the San Francisco Giants and Cincinnati Reds. Sanders's baseball career has been cut short by injuries suffered while playing football.

Sanders is known for his fun-loving image, evidenced by his nickname, "Prime Time." Known for flashy clothing and on-field theatrics, Sanders became one of the most visible athletes in the United States. However, a brush with depression caused him to change his image and rediscover his Christian faith in 1998.

Gale Sayers (1943–)
Football Player, Athletic Director, Community Activist, Entrepreneur

Gale Sayers was born in Wichita, Kansas, on May 30, 1943. He participated in football and track while in high school and enrolled at Kansas University. He signed with the Chicago Bears before graduating but returned to finish and also earned a master's degree.

Sayers garnered All-Pro honors in his rookie season of 1965 and three of the next four seasons. Sayers led the league in rushing in 1969. In a 1965 game against the San Francisco 49ers, he tied an NFL record by scoring six touchdowns.

Sayers's career was ended after the 1971 season due to a knee injury. His final totals included 56 touchdowns—39 rushing, 9 receiving, six on kickoff returns (including a 103 yarder in 1967), and two on punt returns. He was named to the "All-NFL 1960–1984 All-Star Team" as a kick returner. Despite his brief career, he was inducted into the Pro Football Hall of Fame in 1977.

Following his playing career, Sayers was named assistant to the athletic director at Kansas and in 1981, became the athletic director at Southern Illinois University. Active in the community, Sayers has been the commissioner of the Chicago Park District; the co-chairperson of the Legal Defense Fund for Sports, NAACP Coordinator; and an honorary chairman of the American Cancer Society in addition to his involvement in the Reach Out Program. In 1982, Sayers founded

his own computer supplies firm. The Kansas University School of Education's Gale Sayers Microcomputer Center was dedicated in 2000.

Charlie Sifford (1922–)
Golfer

Charlotte, North Carolina, native Charlie Sifford was the first African American to participate in a predominately white golf event, the 1957 Long Beach Open. Sifford's entry into golf began as a caddie at the age of nine. At 13, he won a caddie tournament shooting a 70. After moving to Philadelphia, Sifford worked as a teaching professional and chauffeur.

Sifford became the first African American to be awarded a PGA card as an approved player in 1959 when the tour lifted its "Caucasian only" clause. He was also the first to win a major PGA event, the Hartford Open, in 1967. On the Seniors Tour, Sifford triumphed at the PGA Seniors Open (1975), and the Suntree Seniors Open (1980). He also won the Negro National Title six times, including five consecutively from 1952 to 1956. Sifford's autobiography, *Just Let Me Play: The Story of Charlie Sifford, The First Black PGA Golfer*, was published in 1992, in which he exposed the racism that remained after joining the PGA Tour.

O.J. Simpson (1947–)
Football Player, Television Commentator, Actor

Born in San Francisco on July 9, 1947, Simpson starred at the University of Southern California, winning the Heisman Trophy in 1968. One year prior to that, he was a member of the USC relay team that set a world record of 38.6 seconds in the 440-yard run. ABC Sports voted him College Player of the Decade. He signed with the Buffalo Bills in 1969, and three years later won his first rushing title.

Simpson enjoyed his finest season in 1973. On opening day, he rushed for 250 yards against the New England Patriots, breaking the record of 247 yards held by Willie Ellison. His yardage total of 2,003 for the entire season surpassed the previous mark of 1,863 held by Jim Brown. In addition, he scored 12 touchdowns, averaged six yards per carry, and had more rushing yardage than 15 other NFL clubs. He was named Player of the Year and won the Jim Thorpe Trophy.

Simpson retired from football in 1978. He has appeared in several feature films and worked as a sports commentator for ABC-TV and NBC-TV. In 1995, a jury found Simpson not guilty of charges that he had brutally slain his ex-wife and a male friend. The decision

O.J. Simpson.

was rejected by many Americans, and Simpson has since been forced to live a reclusive lifestyle.

Lawrence Taylor (1959–)
Football Player

Born in Williamsburg, Virginia, Lawrence Taylor revolutionized the linebacker position in the NFL by virtue of his strength and speed.

After an outstanding career at the University of North Carolina where he was named Atlantic Coast Conference Player of the Year in 1980, Taylor was taken by the New York Giants with the second pick of the 1981 draft. Taylor amassed 132.5 career sacks and was an integral part of two Giants Super Bowl championships, following the 1986 and 1990 seasons. He was named to the NFL's All-Decade team for the 1980s.

Problems with substance abuse and taxes have marked his post-football career, at one point leading him to attempt a professional wrestling career in order to earn money. Despite these troubles, Taylor is still acknowledged as one of the finest linebackers in the

history of the NFL. He was voted into the Pro Football Hall of Fame in January of 1999.

Marshall W. "Major" Taylor (1878–1932)
Cyclist

Marshall W. "Major" Taylor became America's first African American U.S. National Champion in 1899. Born in Indianapolis in 1878, the son of a coachman, he worked at a bicycle store part-time as a teen. After attending his first race, his boss suggested that Major enter a couple of races. He won a ten-mile race and proceeded to compete as an amateur.

By the time he was 16, he went to work in a factory owned by a former champion and, with his new boss's encouragement, competed in races in Canada, Europe, Australia and New Zealand. During nearly 16 years of competition, he won numerous championships and set several world records. Taylor is a member of the Bicycle Hall of Fame. He died in 1932.

Debi Thomas (1967–)
Figure Skater

Born in Poughkeepsie, New York, Debi Thomas was the first African American figure skater to win a major championship. Thomas was the winner at the 1985 National Sports Festival in Baton Rouge, Louisiana. The following year she captured the U.S. and World figure skating titles, becoming the first African American to capture an international singles meet.

Thomas won a bronze medal at the 1988 Olympic Games in Calgary, becoming the first African American to win an Olympic medal in a winter sport. Dividing her time between collegiate studies and a professional skating career as a member of "Stars on Ice," Thomas earned her bachelor's degree from Stanford in 1991. She retired from the sport the following year to pursue a career in medicine. In 1997, Thompson completed medical studies at Northwestern University.

John Thompson (1941–)
College Basketball Coach

John Thompson was born in Washington, DC, in 1941. He played college basketball at Providence College and graduated in 1964. Thompson played with the Boston Celtics of the NBA from 1964 to 1966. He won

John Thompson announcing his resignation as head coach of the Georgetown University basketball team in 1999.

NBA titles each season and played behind Hall of Fame center Bill Russell.

In 1966 Thompson began coaching St. Anthony's High School in Washington, DC. In 1972 he was offered the head coaching job at Georgetown University. Thompson turned Georgetown into a national powerhouse. In 1982 he led the Hoyas to the national championship game, becoming the first African American to coach in the Final Four. The Hoyas won the championship in 1984 and were runner-up the next season. Thompson's Hoyas won six Big East titles and he developed star players such as Patrick Ewing, Alonzo Mourning, Dikembe Mutombo, and Allen Iverson.

In 1988, Thompson coached the U.S. Olympic basketball team to a bronze medal at the Seoul Olympiad. He frequently criticized the NCAA for tighter academic standards which he felt discriminated against African Americans. Several times he walked off the court before games to protest increasing test scores for freshman students. Thompson resigned in the middle of the 1999 season due to personal problems. He was elected to the National Basketball Hall of Fame in 1999.

Gene Upshaw (1945–)
Football Player, Executive Director of the NFLPA, Community Activist

Born in Robstown, Texas, Upshaw attended Texas A & I University. He was named All-Pro eight times and inducted into the Pro Football Hall of Fame in 1987.

Upshaw is currently the executive director of the National Football League Players Association, a post he has held since 1982. Under his leadership, the organization has expended considerable resources on education and rehabilitation for substance abuse. Upshaw is also the president of the Federation of Professional Athletes AFL-CIO, as well as a member on the California Governor's Council on Wellness and Physical Fitness. He is the coordinator for voter registration and fund-raising in Alameda County (California) and has served as the planning commissioner for that same county.

Upshaw was the recipient of the Byron (Whizzer) White Humanitarian award as voted by the NFL players in 1980. In 1982, he was presented with the A. Philip Randolph Award.

Bill White (1934–)
Baseball Player, Baseball Announcer, Former National League of Professional Baseball Clubs President

William DeKova White was born in Lakewood, Florida, on January 28, 1934. He began his Major League Baseball career with the New York Giants in 1956 and spent 13 years as a player with the San Francisco Giants, St. Louis Cardinals, and the Philadelphia Phillies. During his career, White was named to the National League All-Star team six times and won seven Gold Gloves. He retired from baseball in 1969 and in 1971 joined Phil Rizzuto as a television announcer for the New York Yankees.

On April 1, 1989, Bill White became the first African American president of the National League. He held the post until he was succeeded in 1994 by another African American, Leonard Coleman.

Lenny Wilkens (1937–)
Basketball Player, Basketball Coach

Lenny Wilkens was born in 1937 in New York City. He developed his game on the city's streets and then starred at Providence College. Wilkens was drafted by the St. Louis Hawks of the NBA in 1960. Wilkens was

Lenny Wilkins holds the NBA record for most wins as a coach.

named to All-Star teams and was MVP of the 1971 game while a member of the Seattle SuperSonics.

Wilkens returned to Seattle as coach in 1978 and led the Sonics to the NBA championship in 1979. He coached with the Sonics until 1986, when left to coach the Cleveland Cavaliers. In 1993, Wilkens was named coach of the Atlanta Hawks, and on January 6, 1995 won his 939th game, breaking Red Auerbach's record for most victories by an NBA head coach. Wilkens coached the Hawks for seven seasons until taking head coaching position with the Toronto Raptors before the start of the 2000–2001 season.

In 1996, Wilkens coached the men's basketball team that won the gold medal at the Atlanta Olympiad. He was inducted into the Basketball Hall of Fame as both a player and coach in 1998.

Serena Williams (1981–)
Tennis Player

The Williams sisters, Venus and Serena, were tennis prodigies in the mid-1990s under the coaching of their father Richard. Featured in various articles and televisions shows, Richard Williams refused to let his daughters join the professional tennis tour until he thought they were ready. In 1997, in just her fifth professional tournament, the 304th-ranked Serena showed the tennis world a glimpse of what was to come as she defeated two of the world's top ten players.

Serena's success on the circuit continued, and by June 1998 she had entered the Women's Tennis Association Top 20. Early in 1999, Serena won her first WTA tour title at the Open de Gaz de France. She went on to take three more titles that year, including her first Grand Slam singles title at the U.S. Open.

A victory over her sister in the finals of the 2002 French Open brought Serena her second Grand Slam singles title. With the victory, which was her 15th professional tournament title overall, Serena became the second-ranked player in the world, one spot behind her older sister. When she defeated her again at Wimbledon that same year, the sisters swapped rankings.

Serena has enjoyed success in doubles competition, as well. She has teamed with Venus to win Grand Slam titles in the French Open (1999 and 2002), the U.S. Open (1999), Wimbledon (2000 and 2002), and the Australian Open (2001). In addition to their growing number of accomplishments on the professional tour, the sisters won the Olympic gold medal for women's doubles at the 2000 Sydney Games. Serena paired with Max Mirnyi in 1997 to win the Wimbledon mixed doubles competition.

Venus Williams (1980–)
Tennis Player

Venus Williams made her professional debut in 1994. In her first tournament, the 14 year old Williams nearly beat Arantxa Sanchez Vicario, the second highest-ranked player in the world at the time. The showing stunned both fans and media, but came as no surprise to Richard Williams, her father and coach, who had predicted that his oldest daughter would one day become the world's greatest tennis player.

In her first few years on the pro circuit, Venus was guided along slowly, playing only a small number of tournaments. Despite her limited schedule, by 1997 Venus had reached number 64 in the world rankings. She won her first singles title on March 1, 1998 at the IGA Tennis Classic, and quickly followed it up with a victory at the Lipton Championships in Key Biscayne, Florida.

Since then, Venus has won over 20 more singles titles, including back-to-back Wimbledon and U.S. Open championships in 2000 and 2001. She won the gold medal at the 2000 Sydney Olympics in the women's singles event. On February 25, 2002, Venus became the top-ranked player in the world.

Venus has combined with her sister, Serena, to claim doubles titles at each of the four Grand Slam titles: the French Open (1999 and 2002), the U.S. Open (1999), Wimbledon (2000 and 2002), and the Australian Open (2001). The team also won the Olympic gold medal for women's doubles at the 2000 Games.

Tiger Woods (1975–)
Golfer

Despite his age, Tiger Woods is already one of the most successful athletes in history. He was born in Long Beach, California, and was a child prodigy in the golf. He became the first player to win the U.S. Amateur title three straight years, from 1994 to 1996, while a student at Stanford University.

In 1996, Woods turned professional. In the spring of 1997, Woods won the Masters Tournament, becoming the first African American to win a Grand Slam event. He has gone on to dominate the PGA Tour, winning over 40 tournaments to date, including the 2001 and 2002 Masters Tournaments, 1999 and 2000 PGA Championships, 2000 and 2002 U.S. Open Championship, and 2000 British Open Championship.

Woods became the youngest player, and only the fifth in history, to complete the career Grand Slam of professional major championships when he won the 2000 British Open. He is already the all-time career money leader on the PGA Tour with winnings in excess of $30 million.

◆ WINNERS OF SELECT PRIZES AND TOURNAMENTS

(The table of Olympic medal winners appears in the Appendix.)

Australian Open (Tennis)

Men's Singles
1970: Arthur Ashe

Men's Doubles
1977: Arthur Ashe (with Tony Roche)

Women's Doubles
1957: Althea Gibson (with Shirley Fry)
2001: Serena Williams and Venus Williams

Mixed Doubles
1987: Zina Garrison (with Sherwood Stewart)

1998: Venus Williams (with Justin Gimelstob)

French Open (Tennis)

Men's Doubles
1971: Arthur Ashe

Women's Singles
1956: Althea Gibson
2002: Serena Williams

Women's Doubles
1956: Althea Gibson (with Angela Buxton)
1999: Venus Williams and Serena Williams

Heisman Memorial Trophy
1961: Ernie Davis, Syracuse University, TB
1965: Michael Garrett, University of Southern California, TB
1968: O. J. Simpson, University of Southern California, TB
1972: Johnny Rodgers, University of Nebraska, FL
1974: Archie Griffin, University of Ohio State, HB
1975: Archie Griffin, University of Ohio State, HB
1976: Anthony (Tony) Dorsett, University of Pittsburgh, HB
1977: Earl Campbell, University of Texas, FB
1978: Billy Sims, University of Oklahoma, HB
1979: Charles White, University of Southern California, TB
1980: George Rogers, University of South Carolina, HB
1981: Marcus Allen, University of Southern California, TB
1982: Herschel Walker, University of Georgia, HB
1983: Mike Rozier, University of Nebraska, TB
1985: Bo Jackson, Auburn University, TB
1987: Tim Brown, University of Notre Dame, FL
1988: Barry Sanders, Oklahoma State University, HB
1989: Andre Ware, University of Houston, QB
1991: Desmond Howard, University of Michigan, WR
1993: Charlie Ward, Florida State University, QB
1994: Rashaan Salaam, Colorado, RB
1995: Eddie George, Ohio State, RB
1997: Charles Woodson, University of Michigan, DB/R
1998: Ricky Williams, University of Texas at Austin, TB
1999: Ron Dayne, University of Wisconsin, TB

Ms. Olympia—International Federation of Bodybuilders, Women's Bodybuilding Champions
1983: Carla Dunlap

1990–1995: Lenda Murray

Mr. Olympia—International Federation of Bodybuilders, Men's Bodybuilding Champions

1967–1968: Sergio Oliva
1982: Chris Dickerson
1984–1991: Lee Haney
1998–2001: Ronnie Coleman

National Track and Field Hall of Fame

1974: Ralph Boston; Lee Calhoun; Harrison Dillard;
    Rafer Johnson; Jesse Owens; Wilma Rudolph;
    Malvin Whitfield
1975: Ralph Metcalfe; Alice Coachman
1976: Robert Hayes; Hayes Jones; Heriwentha
    Mae Faggs
1977: Robert Beamon; Andrew W. Stanfield
1978: Tommie Smith; John Woodruff
1979: Jim Hines; William DeHart Hubbard;
    Edith McGuire
1980: Dave Albritton; Wyomia Tyus
1981: Willye White
1982: Willie Davenport; Eddie Tolan
1983: Lee Evans; LeRoy Walker
1984: Madeline Manning Mims; Joe Yancey
1986: Norwood Barney Ewell
1987: Eulace Peacock; Martha Watson
1988: Gregory Bell; Barbara Ferrell
1989: Milt Campbell; Edward Temple; Nell Jackson
1990: Charles Dumas
1993: Stan Wright
1994: Cornelius Johnson; Edwin Moses
1995: Valerie Brisco; Florence Griffith Joyner
1997: Evelyn Ashford; Henry Carr; Renaldo
    Nehemiah
1998: Greg Foster
1999: Willie Banks; Larry Ellis
2000: Chandra Cheeseborough
2001: Carl Lewis; Larry Myricks

Sullivan Award—Amateur Athletic Union

1960: Rafer Johnson (track)
1961: Wilma Rudolph (track)
1981: Carl Lewis (track)
1983: Edwin Moses (track)

1986: Jackie Joyner-Kersee (track)
1988: Florence Griffith-Joyner (track)
1991: Mike Powell (track)
1993: Charlie Ward (football)
1996: Michael Johnson (track)
1998: Chamique Holdsclaw (basketball)

U.S. Open (Tennis)

Men's Singles
1968: Arthur Ashe

Women's Singles
1957: Althea Gibson
1958: Althea Gibson
1999: Serena Williams
2000: Venus Williams
2001: Venus Williams
2002: Serena Williams

Women's Doubles
1999: Serena Williams and Venus Williams

Mixed Doubles
1957: Althea Gibson (with Kurt Neilsen)
1998: Serena Williams (with Max Mirnyi)

Wimbledon (Tennis)

Men's Singles
1975: Arthur Ashe

Ladies' Singles
1957: Althea Gibson
1958: Althea Gibson
2000: Venus Williams
2001: Venus Williams
2002: Serena Williams

Ladies' Doubles
1956: Althea Gibson (with Angela Buxton)
1957: Althea Gibson (with Darlene Hard)
1958: Althea Gibson (with Maria Bueno)
2000: Venus Williams and Serena Williams
2002: Venus Williams and Serena Williams

Mixed Doubles
1988: Zena Garrison (with S. E. Stewart)
1990: Zena Garrison (with Rick Leach)
1998: Serena Williams (with Max Mirnyi)

㉙

Military

♦ The Colonial Period ♦ The Revolutionary War (1775–1783)
♦ The War of 1812 (1812–1815) ♦ The Civil War (1861–1865)
♦ The Indian Campaigns (1866–1890) ♦ The Spanish-American War (1898)
♦ World War I (1914–1918) ♦ The Interwar Years (1919–1940)
♦ World War II (1941–1945) ♦ The Desegregation of the Military (1946–1949)
♦ The Korean War (1950–1953) ♦ The Vietnam War (1964–1973)
♦ Military Participation in the 1970s and 1980s ♦ The Persian Gulf War (1991)
♦ An Evolving Institution ♦ The War on Terrorism ♦ Outstanding Military Figures
♦ African American Medal of Honor Recipients ♦ Military Statistics

by Kevin C. Kretschmer

As with other aspects of U.S. society, the role of the African American in the nation's armed forces has been evolutionary. The infant republic was shaped by a white majority that embraced, then rejected slavery. Next came an adolescent "separate but equal" era of racial segregation. Finally, the United States matured— as an increasingly multicultural society—in its understanding of race and racism.

Sadly, a nation's history is often shaped by its wars. Insofar as African Americans and the U.S. military are concerned, the historic linkage extends from before the Revolutionary War to the current War on Terrorism.

♦ THE COLONIAL PERIOD

Based on European experiences, the early American colonists were wary of the military. As a result, much of early U.S. military history revolves around the locally recruited militias—which are today's state or territory–controlled National Guard units.

Fearful of Indian warfare and slave insurrection, colonial governments sought to reduce the risk of a confederation between Indians and slaves. Some colonial governments promised freedom and various other inducements to African American slaves willing to help fight Indians, meanwhile paying Indians to hunt down and return escaped slaves. As early as 1703, South

Carolina authorities began to enlist slaves into its colonial militia. The Massachusetts Bay government required African American men, free and slave alike, to undergo militia training. Less concerned with Indian attacks than slave uprisings, Virginia forbid the arming of slaves. Though few in number, both enslaved and free African Americans served in colonial militias and fought in the French and Indian War, 1754–1763.

As tensions mounted between Great Britain and the American colonies, confrontation led to the bloodshed in the Boston Massacre of March 5, 1770. In protest against the manner of British taxation and authority, a crowd of angry Bostonians confronted a group of British soldiers. One of the soldiers fired on the crowd and an escaped slave named Crispus Attucks was struck. Attucks fell dead at the feet of the British soldiers, followed by four white citizens who, with him, became martyrs to the cause of American independence.

♦ THE REVOLUTIONARY WAR (1775–1783)

In 1775, African American men joined whites in fighting the British during the battles of Lexington and Concord, the first battles of the Revolutionary War. An African American, Salem Poore, fought in the Battle of Bunker Hill and is credited with firing the shot that killed Major John Pitcairn, commander of the British force. For this, Poore received a commendation for gallantry. He would later serve with George Washington at Valley Forge.

Although a number of African Americans were serving in New England units and proving themselves both capable and brave, Southern slave holders objected to their presence. In response to these critics, General Washington and his principal officers agreed to reject all slaves and bar free African American veterans from reenlisting, a policy quickly ratified by the Continental Congress.

French and Spanish forces allied with the American colonists did not hesitate to enlist African Americans into their ranks. The English also did not object to this valuable source of military manpower. When Lord Dunmore, the royal governor of Virginia, promised freedom to slaves who joined His Majesty's troops, he was able to organize an Ethiopian Regiment composed of approximately 300 men.

As it became increasingly difficult for the colonial militias and the Continental Army to meet recruiting needs, George Washington began to reconsider his earlier agreement to prohibit African Americans from serving. The success of the British in attracting African American volunteers seeking to earn their freedom was a matter of concern. With troop strength dangerously low following the brutal winter at Valley Forge, Washington reversed his earlier policies and welcomed both free and enslaved African Americans into the Continental Army.

By 1778, the Continental Army was racially integrated. On average, each brigade contained 42 African American soldiers. In the naval service, African American sailors were engaged in nearly every phase of shipboard operations. In addition to cooking and cleaning, African American seamen manned guns, joined boarding parties, and served as sharpshooters in Marine detachments. Ultimately, 5,000 African Americans served in the war for American independence. Some won their freedom, while others gained respect in their communities and a measure of economic security.

The Revolutionary War presented the idea that, through military service, African Americans could secure freedom and liberty. The War also established a trend, in times of military need, of government promises to African Americans, promises that were soon forgotten once a crisis ended. The only places where African Americans obtained any form of freedom were in those that had abolished slavery.

A memorial to the African Americans who served the colonial cause during the Revolutionary War will be erected on the Mall in Washington, D.C. Ironically, the long-in-the-planning Black Patriots Memorial will be dedicated after similar recognition of the nineteenth century's "Buffalo Soldiers" at Fort Leavenworth, Kansas and the twentieth century's Tuskegee Airmen at the U.S. Air Force Academy.

◆ THE WAR OF 1812 (1812–1815)

Following the Revolutionary War, the exclusion of African Americans from military service was reinstated. In 1792, Congress restricted military service to "free able-bodied white males." Six years later, the Secretary of War ordered the commandant of the Marine Corps that "no Negro, mulatto or Indian is to be enlisted." Nevertheless, when the need arose for recruits during the War of 1812, African American sailors made up approximately 20 percent of Navy crews. Commodore Oliver Hazard Perry welcomed African American sailors who served in his armada, which defeated the British on Lake Erie.

While the Army and Marine Corps continued to exclude African Americans, the Louisiana legislature authorized enlistments of free African American landowners. The combat bravery of these African American troops was a key factor in the U.S. victory at the Battle of New Orleans. As African Americans were not authorized to serve in the Army, their contributions went unrecognized by the U.S. Army.

◆ THE CIVIL WAR (1861–1865)

Only weeks after the Confederate assault on Fort Sumter in 1861, which initiated the Civil War, African Americans from Ohio's Wilberforce College answered Abraham Lincoln's call for volunteers to help subdue the Confederacy. Similar offers quickly came from Washington, D.C., and New York, where the governor was offered three African American regiments to serve for the duration of the war, with their weapons, clothing, equipment, pay and provisions all to be provided by the African American population of the state. These and other such requests to serve were rejected because the war was expected to be short.

Although some Union leaders such as Major General John C. Fremont wanted to recruit African Americans as soldiers, the Lincoln administration refused permission to proceed with the effort. Fearful that such action would antagonize slave-holding border states loyal to the Union, President Lincoln made it clear that this was a war to preserve the Union, not to free the slaves. Union General Benjamin Butler, who would later command African American troops, offered Union soldiers

Service records have revealed that over 18,000 African Americans served as seamen during the Civil War.

to suppress a rumored slave uprising in Maryland. Meanwhile, the Confederacy enjoyed the fruits of slave labor in constructing fortifications and related combat service-support roles. As early as June of 1861, some Southern states recruited free African Americans for military service.

Though prohibited from enlisting African Americans for military duty as troops, some Union generals began using African American fugitives from slave territory as teamsters, cooks, and laborers. Only after important military setbacks, as well as considerable debate in the press and Congress, did the legislature authorize the employment of African American soldiers with the Militia Act of July 17, 1862. The War Department had not yet given permission to recruit African American soldiers when General Jim Lane organized and trained the 1st Kansas Colored Volunteers and sent them into action against Confederate troops near Butler, Missouri, in late October of 1862. The success of African American troops in their first engagements in as part of the Union Army, helped to reduce opposition to their recruitment.

U.S. Colored Troops (USCT)

Following the Emancipation Proclamation of September 22, 1862, systematic recruitment of African Americans began throughout the country. Massachusetts organized the 54th and 55th Massachusetts Infantry Regiments. Raised by Colonel Robert Gould Shaw, the 54th led the Union attack on Fort Wagner, South Carolina on July 18, 1863. This strategically-located Confederate position on Morris Island dominated the shipping channel leading into the harbor at Charleston. Although access to Fort Wagner was restricted to a narrow road, and subject to fire from three Confederate forts and batteries nearby, Union General Truman Seymour boasted that he could take it in one night. A reporter for the *New York Tribune* quoted the general as saying that he would have General George C. Strong's brigade take the lead and ". . . put those damned niggers from Massachusetts in the advance; we might as well get rid of them one time as another."

Under intense fire, the 54th made their charge with Shaw urging his men over an earthwork and into the fort. The African American soldiers were met with a barrage of artillery, rifle fire, and grenades. As he crossed the fort's parapet, Shaw was shot dead. Half of the officers and men of his regiment were killed, wounded, or captured in the battle. Although eventually driven away from the fort, the 54th Massachusetts Infantry came to symbolize the courage and determination of African American troops.

Despite repeated demonstrations of their ability and courage, skepticism regarding the usefulness of African American soldiers remained. General Benjamin Butler was determined to prove the African American troops under his command were fit to bear arms. On the dawn of September 29, 1864, Butler ordered his troops of the XVII Corps to storm a fortified Confederate position at New Market Heights, Virginia. The bayonet attack drove the Confederates from their position on the high ground at great cost. Butler recorded in his memoirs that "the capacity of the Negro race for soldiers had then and there been fully settled forever."

By July of 1863, more than 30 African American regiments were being organized or were already on the field. These units and others previously organized, except for the 54th and 55th Massachusetts, were designated as U.S. Colored Troops (USCT). Following the establishment of USCT regiments, African Americans fought and died in every major Civil War action. For a period, they did so with substantially less pay than white troops. While white privates received $13 per month plus $3.50 in clothing allowance, African

Union military camp of the "Colored Battery" in Jacksonville, Tennessee.

American troops of any rank were paid only $10 per month. In some units, African American soldiers would not accept the lesser pay. Several men from an African American Rhode Island artillery unit on duty in Texas were sentenced to hard labor for refusing their pay. When Sergeant William Walker persuaded the men of his South Carolina regiment company to refuse to perform any duty unless they received pay equal to that of white troops, he was brought up on charges of mutiny and executed by firing squad. After vigorous protests by prominent officers of African American troops, newspaper editors, and legislators, the 1864 Army Appropriation Act was enacted to provide identical pay scales for all soldiers.

The passions of the Civil War resulted in the ignoring of the then-emerging doctrines of land warfare on such issues as treatment of noncombatants and prisoners of war. The most serious documented breaches of land warfare standards were committed by the Confederacy. African American soldiers who fell into Confederate hands were either re-enslaved or summarily killed. One of the bloodiest such events was the Confederate butchery at Fort Pillow, Tennessee. Congressional Report No. 65, "Fort Pillow Massacre" (April 24, 1864),

identified the Confederate leader responsible as General Nathan Bedford Forrest, who would later organize the Ku Klux Klan. According to the report:

> . . . the rebels commenced an indiscriminate slaughter, sparing neither age nor sex, white or black, soldier or civilian. The officers and men seemed to vie with each other in the devilish work; men, women, and even children, wherever found, were deliberately shot down, beaten, and hacked with sabers; some of the children not more than ten years old were forced to stand up and face their murderers while being shot; the sick and wounded were butchered without mercy, the rebels even entering the hospital building and dragging them out to be shot or killing them as they lay there unable to offer the least resistance.

Although somewhat exaggerated in the interest of propaganda, the report clearly established that African American troops were murdered while attempting to surrender. The slaughter at Fort Pillow and the murder of captured and wounded African American troops at the Battle of Poison Spring, Arkansas, would not go unanswered. African American troops assaulted their Confederate enemy with ferocious intensity as they shouted their battle cry, "Remember Fort Pillow!" and "Remember Poison Spring!"

Many African American men served in the Union cause, but very few were permitted to do so as officers. Despite strident public opposition and War Department policy unfavorable to the appointment of African American officers, nearly 100 African American men held commissions during the course of the Civil War. Over three-fourths of these commissions were awarded in General Butler's Louisiana regiments. Many African Americans gained their appointment as officers in state militias. A few African American surgeons and a large number of chaplains also received appointments. After Martin R. Delany, a Harvard-trained physician, had an audience with Abraham Lincoln, the president directed his secretary of war to meet this "most remarkable black man." On February 26, 1865, Martin R. Delany was commissioned a Major of Infantry, making him the highest-ranking African American field officer during the war. Before Delany had an opportunity to organize and command an *armee d'Afrique*, the Civil War ended. He retained the rank of major until 1868.

One African American officer, Robert Smalls, was commissioned in the U.S. Colored Troops, but served with the Navy. Smalls earned his commission by stealing the Confederate ship he was serving on as a slave-sailor. Aided by seven fellow slave-sailors, Smalls took the helm of the 300-ton side-wheel steamer *Planter* in the early morning of May 13, 1862, and sailed it out of Charleston Harbor, delivering it to the U.S. Navy's blockade offshore. Fitted with two guns and carrying four others as cargo, the *Planter* was a welcome addition to the Union fleet. Having demonstrated his ability and leadership, Smalls served as pilot of the *Planter* for a time before piloting the gunboat *Keokuk*. During Reconstruction, the former slave was elected to the United States Congress as a representative from the state of South Carolina and was made a major general in the state militia.

While not accepted into the Union forces, African American women also played an important role during the War. Many endured great hardships in their efforts to keep their families together as their husbands, fathers, and sons marched off to war. While some African American women served as volunteer nurses, others took a more aggressive role in support of the Union cause. Both Sojourner Truth and Harriet Tubman used their knowledge of Underground Railroad routes to guide federal forces operating in hostile territory. In one such instance, Tubman led 300 Union cavalrymen on a raid in South Carolina that freed 800 slaves and destroyed cotton valuable to the Confederacy.

The Medal of Honor

America's highest decoration for valor was established during the Civil War when Congress authorized issuance of a Medal of Honor on December 21, 1861. Issuance was initially limited to enlisted men of the Navy and the Marine Corps, but the award was expanded to include the Army on July 12, 1862. On March 3, 1863, commissioned officers also became eligible for the Medal of Honor. During the Civil War, 1,523 Medals of Honor were awarded, 23 to African American servicemen. The first African American recipient was Sergeant William H. Carney of the 54th Massachusetts Infantry for combat valor on July 18, 1863, at Fort Wagner, South Carolina. 13 of the medals were awarded to African American soldiers who fought in the battle of New Market Heights, Virginia on September 29–30, 1864.

Although the Union did not actively recruit African Americans until 1863, their numbers proved significant during the Civil War. U.S. Colored Troops constituted

Christian A. Fleetwood received the Congressional Medal of Honor during the Civil War.

13 percent of the Army, while African American sailors accounted for about 8 percent of the Union Navy. By the end of the war, more than 37,000 African American servicemen had died, constituting nearly 35 percent of all African Americans who served in combat.

◆ THE INDIAN CAMPAIGNS (1866–1890)

Post-Civil War America acquired a new appreciation for the importance of military power. In 1866, the 39th Congress passed legislation to "increase and fix the Military Establishment of the United States." The peacetime army would have five artillery regiments, ten cavalry regiments and 45 infantry regiments. This legislation also stipulated "That to the six regiments of cavalry now in service shall be added four regiments, two of which shall be composed of colored men. . . ." Consequently, the nation gained its first African American regular Army regiments: The 9th and 10th Cavalry, and the 24th and 25th Infantry, which would become known as the "Buffalo Soldiers." This nickname was bestowed upon the soldiers by Plains Indians who saw a resemblance between their hair and that of the buffalo, an animal the Indians considered sacred. Although the term "Buffalo Soldiers" initially denoted those four post-Civil War regiments, it was later proudly adopted by veterans of all racially segregated African American Army ground units of the 1866–1950 era.

The general perception today of the makeup of the U.S. Army during the post-Civil War westward expansion does not reflect its true composition. Approximately 20 percent of army soldiers on duty in the West were African American. The mythology of the cavalry riding to rescue of endangered settlers does not reflect that many of these armed horsemen were African American. Despite often working with rejected horses, inadequate rations, and deteriorating equipment—compounded by the hostility often shown them by many white settlers, as well as some of their own officers—the African American regiments enjoyed the lowest desertion rates of all Army units.

The heroism of African American soldiers is attested to by the 18 Medals of Honor they earned during what historians termed both "The Indian Campaigns" and "The Plains War." Nevertheless, as 370 Medals of Honor were awarded during that era of military history, the 18 given to African American soldiers certainly does not reflect a number proportional to those received by whites, when considering their percentage of all soldiers serving. The first Medal of Honor awarded to an African American soldier during the period was presented to First Sergeant Emanuel Stance of Company

F, 9th Cavalry for actions occurring on May 20, 1870, in the battle of Kickapoo Springs, Texas.

African American participation in the war against Native Americans was embedded in historical ironies, both in terms of fighting another race subjugated by Anglo-Americans, and in terms of anti-African American sentiment within the United States military itself. One of many painful episodes for the original "Buffalo Soldiers" was the case of Second Lieutenant Henry Ossian Flipper. Born in Thomasville, Georgia on March 21, 1856, Flipper was the first African American to graduate from the U.S. Military Academy at West Point, New York. He ranked 50th among the 76 members of the Class of 1887 and became the only African American commissioned officer in the regular Army. Assigned initially to Fort Sill, Oklahoma Territory, Lieutenant Flipper was eventually sent to Fort Davis, Texas. He was assigned the duties routine to a newly-commissioned officer, such as surveying and supervising construction projects. Flipper also acquired some combat experience fighting Apache Indians led by Chief Victoria.

In August of 1881, Lieutenant Flipper was arrested and charged with failing to mail $3,700 in checks to the

Lieutenant Henry O. Flipper, the first African American to graduate from West Point.

Army Chief of Commissary. The young lieutenant was tried for embezzlement and conduct unbecoming an officer. He was acquitted of the first charge (the checks were found in his quarters), but convicted of the second. Upon confirmation of his sentence by President Chester Arthur, Flipper was dismissed from the service on June 30, 1882. Returning to civilian life, Flipper used his West Point education as a surveyor and engineer in working for mining companies. He also published his memoirs as well as technical books dealing with both Mexican and Venezuelan laws. Additionally, Flipper served as a translator for the Senate Committee on Foreign Relations, and became a special assistant to the Secretary of the Interior.

Nearly a century after Flipper left West Point, a review of his record indicated that he had been framed by his fellow officers. His records were corrected, and he was granted an honorable discharge from the Army. On the 100th anniversary of his graduation, a memorial bust and alcove were dedicated in his honor in the cadet library at the U.S. Military Academy.

There were only two other nineteenth century African American graduates of West Point: John H. Alexander (1864–1894), in the Class of 1887, and Charles A. Young (1864–1922), in the Class of 1889. It would be 47 years before another African American cadet graduated from the U.S. Military Academy.

◆ THE SPANISH-AMERICAN WAR (1898)

America's "Ten Week War" with Spain marked the nation's emergence as a global colonial power. Although the United States had just completed its own "Indian Campaigns," the tension between the two nations arose from Spain's treatment of Cuba's indigenous population. In 1885, open rebellion by the Cuban people resulted in brutal suppression by the Spanish. The battleship *USS Maine* was sent to Cuba to protect U.S. interests there and as a reminder of America's intention to enforce the Monroe Doctrine.

On the evening of February 15, 1898, a gigantic explosion rocked the warship. It sank rapidly in the Havana harbor, killing 266 U.S. sailors—22 of them African Americans. The cause of the Maine's sinking was undetermined, but inflamed American passions were demonstrated by the slogan, "Remember the Maine, to hell with Spain."

On March 29, the United States issued an ultimatum to Spain, demanding the release of Cubans from brutal detention camps, the declaration of an armistice, and preparations for peace negotiations mediated by President McKinley. The Spanish government did not comply and, on April 19, the United States Congress proclaimed Cuba free and independent. In its proclamation,

Congress authorized the president to use U.S. troops to remove Spanish forces from Cuba.

In the annals of U.S. military history, the Spanish-American War was of special significance for the African American officer. It was the first time that African American men served in every Army grade below general officer. This opportunity arose because of a geographically-determined national security strategy. Separated from both Europe and Asia by oceans, the United States understood that those waters also provided a mobilization time cushion. Any perceived threat from either direction had to overcome United States naval power before touching the mainland. Thus, the Navy became the "first line of defense." The small U.S. Army was really a cadre force. Time would permit recruitment, training, and deployment of volunteers or draftees who would fight on United States soil led by experienced regulars. An additional mobilization asset was the various state militias comprising part-time citizen soldiers.

The war with Spain was an expeditionary campaign requiring maritime deployment to foreign soil. Instead of a mobilize-and-defend situation, the United States had to mobilize and transport before deploying on foreign soil. It was the nation's first large-scale exposure to the complex logistics of overseas operations, an experience that would evolve into occupation duty and related counterinsurgency warfare.

The regular Army of only 28,000 men included the African American 9th and 10th Cavalry Regiments, and the 24th and 25th Infantry Regiments. On June 24, 1898, one squadron of the 10th Cavalry, two squadrons of Rough Riders, which were a regiment of U.S. cavalry volunteers recruited by Theodore Roosevelt, and a squadron from the regular Army's 1st Cavalry, attacked and defeated twice their number of Spanish soldiers. When Rough Riders were pinned down by Spanish fire while crossing open ground near Las Guasimas, 10th Cavalry troops and soldiers from the 1st Cavalry regiment arrived and relieved the pressure. John J. "Black Jack" Pershing, the 10th Cavalry's regimental quartermaster, credited his men with "relieving the Rough Riders from the volleys that were being poured into them from that portion of the Spanish line."

The 25th Infantry also took part in the action, storming the village of El Caney on the morning of July 1. Armed with a battery of Hotchkiss automatic guns, the 10th Cavalry figured prominently in taking Kettle Hill, while the 24th Infantry, along with the 71st New York Volunteers, stormed San Juan Hill. African American soldiers also manned trenches around Santiago de Cuba, which capitulated in mid-July, ending the war in Cuba. The end of the war, however, did not end the danger to the occupying troops.

The 24th Negro Infantry distinguised itself during Spanish-American War campaigns.

Although hostilities between the United States and Spain were officially ended, U.S. troops in Cuba faced a challenge more deadly than the Spanish forces. More than three of every four deaths among U.S. troops were attributed to disease, particularly typhoid and yellow fever. In the mistaken belief that peoples of African descent had a natural immunity to tropical disease, troops of the 24th Infantry were assigned work details at a hospital treating victims of typhoid and yellow fever. Roughly half of the African American troops assigned to the hospital contracted the illnesses. Many of the African American female volunteer nurses who cared for the sick and dying also became victims.

African Americans also served in the U.S. Volunteer Infantry (USVI), a manpower augmentation of 175,000 troops from the federalized national guard reserves. The USVI was to include the nation's oldest African American national guard unit, which had its organizational roots in Chicago, Illinois. Formed in the wake of the 1871 Chicago fire, it was originally known as the Hannibal Guards. It became an Illinois militia unit on May 5, 1890, as the 9th Battalion, commanded by Major Benjamin G. Johnson, an African American. When the

Spanish-American War erupted, other African American militia regiments were organized: the 3rd Alabama, the 23rd Kansas, the 3rd North Carolina, the 9th Ohio, and the 6th Virginia.

Until converted into artillery battalions in World War II, the 8th Illinois USVI was always commanded by an African American officer; Colonel John R. Marshall was the highest-ranking African American officer of the Spanish-American War and commanded the 8th Illinois until 1914. Marshall was born on March 15, 1859, in Alexandria, Virginia. After attending public schools in Alexandria and Washington, D.C., he became an apprentice bricklayer. After moving to Chicago, he was appointed deputy clerk of Cook County. Marshall joined the Illinois National Guard, organized a battalion, and served in it as a lieutenant and major. In June of 1892, he was commissioned a colonel and assumed command of the 8th Illinois USVI Regiment. He led the regiment to Cuba where it joined with the 23rd Kansas and 3rd North Carolina in occupation duty.

The Spanish-American War provided a small increase in the number of African American regular Army officers. Benjamin O. Davis served as a lieutenant in the

8th Illinois USVI. Upon his discharge, he enlisted in the regular Army on June 14, 1899, as a private in the 9th Cavalry. He was promoted to corporal and then to sergeant major. Davis was commissioned a U.S. Army second lieutenant of cavalry on February 2, 1901. Also commissioned as regular Army officers that year were John R. Lynch and John E. Green. As the twentieth century began, the U.S. Army had four African American commissioned officers (excluding chaplains): Captain Charles Young, and Lieutenants Davis, Green, and Lynch. In 1940, Davis would become the nation's first African American general officer.

Although only 10 weeks long, the Spanish-American War produced 52 Medal of Honor recipients, among them six African Americans. Five were from the 10th Cavalry, which fought as infantry in Cuba, while the sixth was an African American sailor stationed aboard the *USS Iowa*, which saw action in the waters off Santiago, Cuba.

◆ WORLD WAR I (1914–1918)

The nation's entry into World War I raised the question of how to utilize African American troops. The Army's existing African American units were kept on patrol in the Southwest or sent for duty in the Philippines. The majority of African American draftees or enlistees were assigned to stevedore units at ports or to labor units as quartermaster troops. Of the more than 400,000 African American soldiers who served during the war, only about 10 percent saw combat duty, assigned to either of two infantry divisions: the 92nd Infantry Division and the 93rd Infantry Division (Provisional). The 92nd was mainly comprising draftees, while the 93rd had three regiments made up of National Guard units from Connecticut, Illinois, Maryland, Massachusetts, New York, Ohio, Tennessee and the District of Columbia, with a fourth regiment made up of draftees. Neither infantry division trained together as a unit in the United States. As many white citizens feared arming a substantial number of African Americans in a single location, the Army stationed the individual regiments of each division in widely-separated areas of the country. The regiments did not link up together as divisions until they reached France.

The most difficult problem for the War Department was the demand that African Americans be trained as commissioned officers. Initially, the idea was dismissed as ludicrous, as it was said to be "common knowledge" that African Americans inherently lacked leadership qualities. Only the persistence of the NAACP, the Urban League and such African American newspapers as *The Chicago Defender* helped change War Department policy. An African American Officer Training School was established at Fort Des Moines, Iowa. On October 14, 1917, the school graduated and commissioned the first class of 639 African American officers. By the close of the war, 1,200 African American officer candidates had earned commissions from the school. Although that number was far greater than had been commissioned in prior wars, it still represented only seven-tenths of 1 percent of the officer corps. By comparison, African American troops accounted for 13 percent of the total active duty force. In addition, the War Department had an ironclad rule that no African American officer could command white officers or enlisted men.

To comply with this rule, the War Department needed to find a way of skirting the problem posed by Lieutenant Colonel Charles Young, the Army's highest-ranking African American officer and a West Point graduate. Young had trained African American troops for combat and led them in action, causing some white officers to fear that he would assume command of the 10th Cavalry, which was otherwise commanded by whites. Pressured by these officers, the United States senators who represented them in Congress, and President Wilson, the War Department developed a strategy to eliminate Young from consideration. Young, who had contracted Bright's disease, but whose physical health appeared excellent otherwise, was given a medical examination in July of 1917. The medical report was forwarded to a retiring board that recommended that he be removed from active duty due to ill health; the War Department concurred.

To prove his fitness for active duty, Colonel Young rode on horseback (walking a quarter of the distance for good measure) from Xenia, Ohio to Washington, D.C. Starting on June 6, 1918, he covered the 497-mile distance in 16 days, taking just one day off to rest. While Young received support from the African American press and many powerful friends, the War Department relented only five days before the end of World War I. Though he was promoted to full colonel while in retirement, he was called to active service to command a company of trainees at Camp Grant, Illinois—an assignment usually given to officers at the rank of captain. Young never was given the opportunity to command troops in Europe, which likely would have resulted in his promotion to brigadier general. Though he remained on active duty until his death on January 8, 1922, Young never received another promotion.

One solution used by the military to solve the issue of utilizing African American officers and soldiers during the war was to offer African American regiments to foreign forces. The 93rd Infantry Division was attached to the allied French Army and used French weapons, wore French helmets, and ate French rations—only their uniforms were provided by the U.S. Army. Colonel

A group of African American World War I sailors.

William Hayward, commander of New York's 369th Infantry Regiment that constituted one of the four regiments of the 93rd, criticized General John J. Pershing for this decision. Colonel Hayward charged that Pershing "simply put the black orphan in a basket, set it on the doorstep of the French, pulled the bell, and went away."

Despite this status, it was the 369th Infantry Regiment (15th New York) that established the best World War I record of any U.S. Army infantry regiment. Attached to the French 4th Army, the 369th served for 191 consecutive days in the trenches, longer than any other U.S. unit. In that time they never lost a foot of ground to the enemy, nor had a single soldier taken prisoner by the Germans. The 369th gathered many nicknames. They called themselves the "Black Rattlers," while the French dubbed them the "Men of Bronze" and the Germans labeled them the "Harlem Hell Fighters."

In 1919, Columbia University President Nicholas Murray Butler gave *Harper's Weekly* his assessment of the 369th Infantry Regiment, "No American soldier saw harder or more constant fighting and none gave better accounts of themselves. When fighting was to be done, this regiment was there."

Unlike the 93rd Infantry Division, which only came together as a unit in France before being broken up and parceled out to various French commands, the 92nd Infantry Division remained intact. Unfortunately, the 92nd did not fare nearly as well as did the 93rd. The commander, Major General Charles C. Ballou, shared the prejudices of many white officers and rarely stood up for his African American troops. Ballou seldom insured that the soldiers of the 92nd were provided with proper training, equipment, and support services. Upon their arrival in France, the ill-prepared African American soldiers under his command were immediately sent into the fray. Led by white senior officers and unseasoned African American junior officers, the disorganized regiments suffered heavy casualties during several key offenses late in the war.

Ballou's response to the failings of the 92nd was to blame his junior officers, bringing 30 up for court-martial on charges of cowardice. Several officers were convicted by an all-white court-martial board and given harsh sentences before the trials were suspended with the transfer of the 92nd to the command of Lieutenant General Robert L. Bullard. Under Bullard, the morale and training of the 92nd increased, as did its fighting effectiveness. Nevertheless, the damage was done. Bullard was unhappy with the general performance of the division and worried about its reflection on him as a leader. As soon as the war ended, he recommended the immediate transfer of the division back to the United States. The result of the 92nd Infantry's substandard performance was to bolster the already negative opinions of critics of African American units.

Despite the "Jim Crow" atmosphere, African American soldiers still earned an impressive number of awards for combat bravery in defeating German troops. Sergeant Henry Johnson and Private Needham Roberts of New York's 369th Infantry Regiment were the first Americans, black or white, to receive the French Croix de Guerre. France awarded its Croix de Guerre to 34 African American officers and 89 African American enlisted men during the war. In the 92nd Infantry, 14 African American officers and 43 African American enlisted men earned the U.S. Army's Distinguished Service Cross (DSC). Some 10 officers and 34 enlisted men of the 93rd Infantry were DSC recipients.

The African American presence in the U.S. Navy during World War I was negligible. Restricted to ratings in the messmen branch (cooks, stewards, mess attendants), few African Americans enlisted in the Navy. Of a total naval strength of 435,398, only 5,328 were African American by June 30, 1918. Thus, African Americans accounted for only 1.2 percent of the Navy. Continuing its policy of preventing African Americans from earning commissions, the naval officer corps remained completely white. In addition, some naval captains refused to transport African American army troops home after the war.

Although they were not permitted to serve in the Armed Forces, African American women contributed to America's efforts in World War I. They made bandages, worked in hospitals and troop centers, and promoted the purchase of Liberty Bonds to finance the war effort. They also served in the Red Cross, YWCA, and other relief organizations.

Posthumous Medal of Honor Awarded

No Medal of Honor was awarded to an African American serviceman during World War I. In 1988, the Department of the Army researched the National Archives to determine whether racial barriers had prevented the awarding of the nation's highest decoration for valor to an African American. The archives search produced evidence that Corporal Freddie Stowers of Anderson County, South Carolina, had been recommended for the award. For "unknown reasons," the recommendation had not been processed. Stowers was a squad leader in Company C, 371st Infantry Regiment, 93rd Infantry Division. On September 28, 1918, he led his squad through heavy machine-gun fire and destroyed the gun position on Hill 188 in the Champagne Marne Sector, France. Mortally wounded, Stowers led his men through a second trench line. Unable to proceed any further, Stowers continued to yell encouragement to his comrades until dying on the field of battle. On April 24, 1991, President George Bush belatedly presented Stowers' Medal of Honor to his surviving sisters in a White House ceremony.

♦ THE INTERWAR YEARS (1919–1940)

With the end of the war, the nation generally returned to applying the *Plessy v. Ferguson* doctrine. Some senior white Army officers advocated barring enlistment or re-enlistment of African Americans all together, an action that would have eventually abolished the four African American regular Army regiments by attrition.

A focal point of the Army's discriminatory sentiment was the African American commissioned officer. Despite countless well-documented cases of superb combat leadership, most African American officers were eliminated from active duty following World War I. An effective tool against retaining African American officers was their alleged poor performance that was buttressed by criticism of the African American Officer Training School (OTS) at Des Moines, Iowa. One of the severest critics was Major General Ballou, commander of the 92nd Infantry Division during World War I. Ballou emphasized that while white candidates were required to be college graduates, "only high school educations were required for. . . the colored. . . and in many cases these high school educations would have been a disgrace to any grammar school. For the parts of a machine requiring the finest steel, pot metal was provided."

Nevertheless, there were combat-experienced white officers who held a decidedly different view of African American officer training, such as Major Thomas A. Roberts. "As I understand the question," Roberts wrote in April of 1920, "what the progressive Negro desires today is the removal of discrimination against him; that this can be accomplished in a military sense I believe to be largely possible, but not if men of the two races are segregated." Noting his appreciation of the "tremendous force of the prejudice against association between Negroes and whites," Roberts declared "my experience has made me believe that the better element among the Negroes desires the removal of the restriction rather than the association itself."

The exclusionary campaign was also evident in the Army's civilian components, the National Guard and Officers Reserve. New York's 369th Infantry Regiment was maintained at full strength, though the 8th Illinois lost one battalion.

As for commissioned officers, the Reserve Officers Training Corps (ROTC) detachments at Howard and Wilberforce Universities provided the bulk of new African American second lieutenants. With no allocations for African American officers to attend service schools, the lack of opportunity to maintain proficiency caused considerable attrition in the number of African American reserve officers. To retain their commissions, other officers took advantage of correspondence and specially-organized seminar courses.

♦ WORLD WAR II (1941–1945)

Less than two months after war began in Europe, the nation's preeminent African American organizations, the NAACP and the National Urban League, mobilized in an effort to defeat U.S. racial segregation as well as Axis fascism. The African American community foresaw that the United States would eventually ally itself with Britain and France in war against Germany, Italy, and Japan.

Military mobilization began on August 27, 1940, with the federalizing of the National Guard and activation of the Organized Reserve. When Japan attacked Pearl Harbor on December 7, 1941, there were 120,000 officers and 1,523,000 enlisted men on active duty in the Army and its air corps. On September 16, 1940, the nation began its first peacetime draft. By the end of World War II, the Selective Service System had inducted 10,110,104 men, of which 1,082,539 (10.7 percent) were African American.

America's war effort required rapid expansion of both military and industrial power. Victory depended on the constant provision of ammunition, guns, planes, tanks, naval vessels, and merchant ships. The nation would have to unite to survive. A minority number of African Americans, including Nation of Islam founder Elijah Muhammad, openly favored a Japanese victory; Muhammad's stance led to a four-year term in the U.S. Penitentiary at Milan, Michigan.

Essential to the desegregation activism of both the NAACP and the Urban League was the impact of African American-owned weekly newspapers, such as Robert S. Abbott's *Chicago Defender* and Robert Vann's

Pittsburgh Courier. The rallying slogan was the "Double V"—victory against fascism abroad and racial discrimination at home. The goal was equal opportunity in the armed services and within the civilian defense industries.

Soon, the NAACP and the Urban League were joined by the African American activists of the March on Washington movement, led by A. Philip Randolph of the Brotherhood of Sleeping Car Porters and Maids. Randolph predicted that upwards of 100,000 African Americans would march on Washington demanding equal employment opportunities in defense plant employment. On June 25, 1941, a week before the scheduled march, President Franklin D. Roosevelt forestalled the event by issuing Executive Order 8802. The President's order established a Committee on Fair Employment Practice "to provide for the full and equitable participation of all workers in defense industries, without discrimination." Of course, the executive order did not apply to the armed services.

The necessity of winning the war opened the economy to millions of African American men and women who surged into defense plants and earned the same wages as their white counterparts. Thus, the war years brought economic upward mobility to many African American civilians. The postwar benefits of the G.I. Bill of Rights also played a major role, causing the number of African American college graduates and home owners to increase dramatically.

The U.S. Army had actually taken its first steps toward racial integration early in World War II. The obvious waste of duplicated facilities caused the Army to operate all of its 24 officer candidate schools as racially-integrated institutions, where the primary quality sought was proven leadership capacity. The "ninety-day wonders," who survived the standard three-month course, were commissioned as second lieutenants from each of the 24 Army branches, ranging from the Army Air Forces Administrative School (Miami, Florida) to the Tank Destroyer School (Camp Hood, Texas). Nevertheless, upon graduation, African American officers were only assigned to African American units.

The Army Air Force (AAF)

The exception in racially-integrated Army officer procurement during World War II was the Army Air Force Aviation Cadet program, which trained pilots, bombardiers, and navigators. Ironically, African American non-flying officers graduated from the integrated AAF Officer Candidate School at Miami Beach.

A total of 926 African American pilots earned their commissions and wings at the segregated Tuskegee

Members of the 92nd Division marching in Ponsacco, Italy. during World War II.

Army Air Field (TAAF) near Chehaw, Alabama. The 673 single-engine TAAF pilot graduates would eventually form the four squadrons of the 332nd Fighter Group.

Led by Lieutenant Colonel Benjamin O. Davis Jr., a 1936 West Point graduate, the 99th Fighter Squadron was assigned to the 33rd Fighter Group commanded by Colonel William M. Momyer. The 99th's first operational mission was a June 2, 1943, strafing attack on the Italian island of Pantelleria. On that date, Captain Charles B. Hall scored the squadron's first air victory by shooting down an FW-190 and damaging an ME-109. The 99th then settled into normal operations.

In September, Colonel Davis was recalled to take command of the 332nd Fighter Group. It was at that point that he and the African American community discovered that the "Tuskegee Experiment" was about to be labeled a failure. To that effect, Colonel Momyer submitted an extremely negative appraisal of the 99th Fighter Squadron:

Based on the performance of the 99th Fighter Squadron to date, it is my opinion that they are not of the fighting caliber of any squadron in this group. They have failed to display the aggressiveness and daring for combat that are necessary to a first class fighting organization. It may be expected that we will get less work and less operational time out of the 99th Fighter Squadron than any squadron in this group.

On October 16, 1943, squadron commander Davis appeared before the War Department's Committee on Special [Negro] Troop Policies to answer his group commander's allegations. In his 1991 autobiography, written after his retirement as an Air Force lieutenant general, Davis described the problem he faced at the Pentagon as a lieutenant colonel. He wrote, "It would have been hopeless for me to stress the hostility and racism of whites as the motive behind the letter, although that was clearly the case. Instead, I had to adopt a quiet, reasoned approach, presenting the facts about the 99th in a way that would appeal to fairness and win out over ignorance and racism."

Davis presented such a convincing factual case that Army Chief of Staff General George C. Marshall ordered a G-3 [operations] study of the African American

Some who could not serve in the military during World War II chose to contribute their labor to the war effort, like the riveter pictured here.

Trained in Tuskegee, Alabama, and later based in southern Italy, the Tuskegee Airmen flew sorties into southern Europe and North Africa during World War II.

squadron. The study's title "Operations of the 99th Fighter Squadron Compared with Other P-40 Squadrons in the Mediterranean Theatre of Operations" precisely describes its contents. In his book, General Davis described the G-3 study: "It rated the 99th according to readiness, squadron missions, friendly losses versus enemy losses, and sorties dispatched." The opening statement in the report was the clincher: "An examination of the record of the 99th Fighter Squadron reveals no significant general difference between this squadron and the balance of the P-40 squadrons in the Mediterranean Theatre of Operations."

On October 13, 1942, the Army had activated the 100th, 301st, and 302nd Fighter Squadrons. Combined with the 99th, the four squadrons became the 332nd Fighter Group. Colonel Robert R. Selway Jr., a white pilot, was its initial commanding officer. With the 99th vindicated by the G-3 study, Davis assumed command of the Fighter Group at Selfridge Army Air Field, Michigan. The three squadrons of the 332nd previously based in the United States departed for Italy on January 3,

1944, absorbing the 99th as its fourth squadron upon arrival.

During the period that the 99th was deployed and the 332nd was organizing, the TAAF program expanded to training two-engine B-25 pilots. While the fighter pilot fought alone, the B-25 "Mitchell" medium bomber required a five to six-man crew that included two pilots, a bombardier, and a navigator. The 253 medium bomber pilots trained at TAAF, as well as 393 African American navigators and bombardiers from Hondo and Midland Fields in Texas, formed the nation's second African American flying organization when the Army Air Force activated the four-squadron 477th Bombardment Group (Medium) in June of 1943.

The 477th was plagued from the start by a shortage of enlisted aircrew members, ground technicians, and even airplanes. 15 months after activation, the 477th was still short 26 pilots, 43 copilots, two bombardier-navigators, and all of its authorized 288 gunners. Moving from base to base for "operational training," the 477th logged 17,875 flying hours in one year without a major accident. Although finally earmarked for duty in the Pacific, the war ended before the 477th was deployed overseas.

As for the 332nd Fighter Group, it became a famous flying escort for heavy bombers. It was the only AAF fighter group that never lost an escorted bomber to enemy planes. The wartime record of the 332nd Fighter Group was 103 enemy aircraft destroyed during 1,578 combat missions. In addition to more than 100 Distinguished Flying Crosses, the 332nd also earned three Distinguished Unit Citations.

The "Tuskegee Experiment" thus proved that African American could fly advanced aircraft and could also conduct highly successful combat operations meeting AAF standards. The fruit of the Tuskegee Airmen's efforts would be harvested in less than three years—the 1948 racial desegregation of the U.S. Armed Forces.

The Ground War

During World War II, the U.S. Army fielded two major African American combat organizations: the 92nd Infantry Division in Europe and the 93rd Infantry Division in the Pacific.

Just as in World War I, the 93rd Infantry Division suffered from fragmentation. Major General Raymond G. Lehman's headquarters sailed from San Francisco on January 11, 1944, while the artillery and infantry battalions and division headquarters assembled on Guadalcanal at the end of February. This would be the last time all of the components of the division would be in the same place. The division would spend the rest of the war island-hopping, relieving units that had defeated Japanese troops. World War II casualties sustained by the 93rd were 12 killed in action, 121 wounded in action and five who died of wounds. The usual after-action comments were made concerning the lack of initiative by junior officers, but overall, the 93rd was described as well-disciplined and with morale.

The 92nd Infantry Division, in contrast, gained a reputation as a chaotic outfit. During its preparation for deployment overseas, portions of the 92nd were sprinkled across the United States. While the division headquarters were at Fort Huachuca, Arizona, subordinate units were stationed at Fort McClellan, Alabama; Camp Robinson, Arkansas; Camp Breckinridge, Kentucky; and Camp Atterbury, Indiana. The division's World War II casualty figures were vastly different from those of the 93rd: 548 killed in action, 2,187 wounded in action, and 68 who died of wounds. From its training in the United States through combat in Europe, the division's main problem seemed to be its commander, Major General Edward M. Almond. Many veterans of the 92nd

continue to blame General Almond for the division's reputation and casualties.

It appears that "Ned" Almond was racist. In a 1984 interview, retired Lieutenant General William P. Ennis Jr. gave a "warts and all" description of Almond. As a World War II brigadier general, Ennis had commanded the corps artillery that supported the 92nd Infantry Division. According to Ennis, Almond and many white Southern officers in the division were selected because "in theory, they knew more about handling Negroes than anybody else, though I can't imagine why because [Almond] just despised the ground they walked on." One African American officer, Captain Hondon B. Hargrove, was a 1938 Wilberforce University ROTC graduate. After his wartime service in the division's 597th Field Artillery Battalion, he commented that Almond did not believe "any black, no matter what his file showed, or how much training he had, was able in an officer's position. . . . He firmly believed only white officers could get the best out of [Negro troops]. . . [and] just could not countenance black officers leading them."

While Almond denigrated the competence of African American officers, Officer Candidate School (OCS) commandants generally held opposite views. For example, Brigadier General H. T. Mayberry, who commanded the Tank Destroyer OCS, observed in a 1945 interview that "a considerable number of young, potentially outstanding Negro officers were graduated. It was surprising—to me, at least—how high the Negroes (those who graduated) stood in the classes." Lieutenant Colonel Robert C. Ross, a field artillery battalion commander in the 92nd Infantry Division, reported to Almond on five African American officers who completed the basic artillery course. Three were made course instructors, while two were selected "as outstanding students from the entire 48 officers, both white and colored, from the first Officers Basic School."

General Almond established his headquarters at Viareggio, Italy on October 5, 1944. Two days later, the division's 370th Infantry Regiment began its assault on Massa. Professor Lee described the 92nd Infantry Division's major weakness: "It was a problem in faith and lack of it—the wavering faith of commanders in the ability and determination of subordinates and enlisted men, and the continuation in the minds of enlisted men of training period convictions that they could not trust their leaders." Thus, the Massa attack degenerated into chaos. In what was to be a major charge against the division, the men began to "melt away" from the fighting. After Massa, there were increasing cases of mutinous behavior toward both black and white officers.

In February 1945, the 92nd became the focus of serious Pentagon scrutiny. Truman K. Gibson Jr., an

African American insurance company lawyer from Chicago and Civilian Aide to Secretary of War Henry L. Stimpson, examined the situation. In his assessment, Gibson refused to generalize about the capabilities of African American soldiers based on the performance of General Almond's division. In a March 14 news conference in Rome, Gibson maintained that "If the division proves anything, it does not prove that Negroes can't fight. There is no question in my mind about the courage of Negro officers or soldiers and any generalization on the basis of race is entirely unfounded."

On May 14, 1945, a week after Germany surrendered, Lieutenant Colonel Marcus H. Ray wrote a letter to Gibson. A Chicagoan, as was Gibson, Colonel Ray was a National Guard officer of the 8th Illinois when it mobilized in 1940, and ended the war as commanding officer of the 600th Field Artillery Battalion of the 92nd Infantry Division. Colonel Ray closed his letter to Gibson by observing that "those who died in the proper performance of their assigned duties are our men of the decade and all honor should be paid them. They were Americans before all else. Racially, we have been the victims of an unfortunate chain of circumstances backgrounded by the unchanged American attitude as regards the proper 'place' of the Negro. . . . I do not believe the 92nd a complete failure as a combat unit, but when I think of what it might have been, I am heartsic. . . ."

The 761st Tank Battalion

The most highly acclaimed African American ground combat unit of World War II was the 761st Tank Battalion. As an organization, it enjoyed substantially better circumstances than the 92nd Infantry Division. Before the United States entered World War II, some white U.S. Army officers favored opening opportunities for black soldiers. They rejected the dogma of their colleagues who declared that modern weaponry was "too technical" for African Americans. One such officer, Lieutenant General Lesley James McNair, became the commanding general of Army ground forces. In that post he spent most of his time visiting the nationwide array of ground forces training camps. When he visited the 761st at Camp Claiborne, Louisiana, he openly praised and encouraged the Army's first African American tankers. When the 761st went ashore in France on October 10, 1944, the men believed, rightly, that their outfit's existence was due mainly to McNair. (General McNair was killed by United States "friendly fire" on July 25, 1944, in France. The Joint Chiefs of Staff National Defense University is located at Fort Lesley J. McNair, named in his honor, in Washington, D.C.)

The 761st joined the 26th Division on October 31 and was welcomed by the division commander, Major General Willard S. Paul: "I am damned glad to have you with us. We have been expecting you for a long time, and I am sure you are going to give a good account of yourselves." Two days later, Lieutenant General George S. Patton visited and welcomed the 761st. Equipped with Sherman Tanks, the 761st saw its initial combat experience on November 8, 1944 at Athaniville, France— the first of 183 continuous days of combat for the battalion. The battalion is credited with killing 6,266 enemy soldiers and capturing 15,818. Despite its outstanding combat record, the 761st did not receive a Presidential Unit Citation until January 24, 1978.

One veteran of the 761st Tank Battalion, Company A, was posthumously awarded the Medal of Honor in January of 1997. Staff Sergeant Ruben Rivers, of Tecumseh, Oklahoma, was severely wounded on November 16, 1944, when his tank hit a German mine at a railroad crossing outside of Guebling, France. With his lower thigh sliced to the bone, Rivers declined a morphine injection and refused evacuation. Instead, he took command of another tank at the head of the column and led the advance toward their next objective, Bourgaltroff. Three days later, fierce fighting ensued when Company A was met at Bourgaltroff by enemy tanks and anti-tank weapons. Under heavy fire, his company commander ordered his tanks to pull back below the crest of a hill. Rivers had spotted the enemy positions, however, and he radioed his commander that he would press the fight. Rivers continued firing until the tank was hit in the turret by an armor-piercing round, killing him and wounding the other members of the crew.

Smaller African American combat units made significant contributions in combat operations in both Europe and the Pacific. Fire from African American artillerymen helped dislodge German troops as U.S. forces fought to cross the Rhine River. For its defense of Bastogne, a strategic city in Belgium, the 969th Field Artillery Battalion received a Distinguished Unit Citation for meritorious service performed while attached to a white organization. Company C of the 614th Tank Destroyer Battalion became the first African American ground unit to win that honor in World War II for driving off a German force that blocked the 411th Infantry in its advance on Climbach, Germany. African American anti-aircraft outfits protected outposts in the Pacific and shot down German aircraft in Europe.

Because of a policy of racial segregation and discrimination, most of the one million African Americans in uniform during World War II were not assigned combat duty. Instead, they were assigned duty in the Service of Supply (SOS). In this capacity, they proved instrumental in the outcome of the war by operating bulldozers and cranes, setting up communications systems, and transporting essential supplies to the front. More than 70 percent of the truck companies in the Army's Motor Transport Service were African American. Their role was critical in Europe because the railroads in France were destroyed by retreating German forces. Therefore, Allied forces had to be supplied by truck. The "Red Ball Express" was formed to meet this need in August of 1944, with an original route between Saint Lo and Paris. On a normal day, 899 vehicles on the Red Ball Express traveled 1,504,616 miles on the trip that took an average time of 54 hours.

The White Ball Route replaced the Red Ball Express in November of 1944. Four of the nine truck companies transporting supplies from Le Havre and Rouen to forward areas were African American. They also saw duty on the Antwerp-Brussels-Charleroi Route and the Green Diamond Route between Normandy and the Brest peninsula. The 3917th Gasoline Supply Company supplied the Third Army with up to 165,000 gallons of gas a day. African American truckers were also well represented among the 12 amphibian truck companies. Though assigned transport duty, African American truckers were subject to hostile fire and were called upon to fight in emergencies. A number received military honors from both the United States and France for courage and meritorious service in combat.

The Women's Auxiliary Army Corps

With the creation of the Women's Auxiliary Army Corps on May 14, 1942, African American women could serve in the U.S. military in greater numbers than ever before. Many of the 4,000 black volunteers, however, were assigned duties unlike their white counterparts. While white women typically typed in offices, most African American women were assigned to cleanup details, laundry, and mess duty. Nevertheless, there were notable exceptions in the branch that would soon be renamed the Women's Army Corps. Overseas, the 6888th Postal Battalion was commanded by African American Major Charity Adams, who arrived in England in 1945. The unit was later sent to the European mainland where it improved the mail delivery system, a system invaluable to troop morale.

African American women also served in the Army Nurse Corps. Initially, African American nurses were only permitted to care for African American patients, but that policy proved impractical. The resentment generated when African American women were assigned to care for German prisoners of war ultimately led to a change in policy, enabling African American nurses to care for wounded Americans, regardless of race.

The Sea Services

Following a decade of excluding African Americans from enlistment, the U.S. Navy decided upon a separate African American branch in 1932. The branch was known as the Stewards' Service, though it was referred to in the African American community as the "sea-going bell hops." In 1940, the Navy consisted of 170,000 men, of whom 4,007 (or 2.3 percent) were African Americans in the Stewards' Service. In addition to African Americans, Navy stewards were also recruited from among Filipinos and other Asian American populations.

The advent of World War II transformed the situation. President Franklin D. Roosevelt had served as assistant secretary of the Navy during World War I and considered it "his branch" of the armed services. Therefore, his January 9, 1942, memo to the Navy had tremendous impact. The president noted to Secretary of the Navy Frank Knox: "I think that with all the Navy activities, Bureau of Navy might invent something that colored enlistees could do in addition to the rating of messman." The Navy relented on April 7, 1942, by announcing it would accept 14,000 African American enlistees in all ratings and branches. The initial training of African American sailors was conducted at the Great Lakes Naval Training Station, north of Chicago, Illinois.

It was at that station that the Navy finally made a breakthrough in regard to African American personnel. In January of 1944, 16 African American petty officers began a special and intensive course of instruction that was conducted without public announcement. Three months later, the Navy announced the commissioning of 12 African American ensigns and one warrant officer, the Navy's "Golden Thirteen."

Shortly after the "Golden Thirteen" were commissioned, the Navy opened the V-12 officer training programs to African American. Among the V-12 graduates who became Navy officers in World War II were Samuel L. Gravely Jr. and Carl T. Rowan. Gravely became the Navy's first African American admiral while Rowan is a syndicated columnist and broadcaster.

By the end of World War II, 165,000 African Americans had served in the Navy; 17,000 in the Marine Corps; 5,000 in the Coast Guard; 12,000 in Construction Battalions (Sea Bees); and 24,000 in the Merchant Marine. These African American soldiers served with distinction. Notable among them was mess steward Doris Miller, who on December 7, 1941, manned a machine gun aboard the *USS West Virginia* as Japanese aircraft attacked Pearl Harbor. Miller was credited with destroying four planes before being ordered to abandon the sinking ship. After some delay, Miller was personally awarded the Navy Cross by Admiral Chester W. Nimitz. He was also promoted to mess attendant first class. Miller died when the escort aircraft carrier *USS Liscombe Bay* was sunk on November 24, 1943. Three other African American mess attendants received the Navy Cross during World War II: Eli Benjamin (*USS Intrepid*); Leonard Harmon (*USS San Francisco*); and William Pinkney (*USS Enterprise*). Doris Miller is memorialized by one of three Navy warships named for African Americans: the frigates *USS Miller* and *USS Jesse L. Brown* and the missile submarine *USS George Washington Carver*.

Belated Recognition for African American Heroes

Despite their many accomplishments, African American soldiers were not sufficiently honored for their heroics during World War II. Even though 1.2 million African Americans served in the U.S. Armed Forces during war, not one received the nation's highest military award at the time, the Medal of Honor. Additionally, only nine were awarded the military's second highest honor, the Distinguished Service Cross. This was scant recognition, considering that more than 142,000 African Americans died in the war.

In 1992, the U.S. Army contracted with Shaw University for a group of professional military historians to comb the nation's archives and the memories of its veterans, both black and white, to discover why no African Americans had received a Medal of Honor during World War II and to determine whether some deserved the honor. After a 15-month study, the historians cited the racist climate of the Army for the lack of African American recognition and identified ten soldiers who might be deserving of that ultimate military honor. They passed the list of names onto a special Army Senior Officer Awards Board, which narrowed the list to nine, then to the Joint Chiefs of Staff, who reduced it to seven. The Pentagon then sent those seven names to the U.S. Congress and to the White House. As the time limit for awarding the medal had expired in 1952, Congress included a waiver for the seven in the 1997 defense authorization bill. Congress approved a resolution to honor the nominees and sent it on to the president.

At a White House ceremony on January 13, 1997, President Bill Clinton presented Medals of Honor to the families of Staff Sergeant Edward A. Carter Jr., First Lieutenant John R. Fox, Private First Class Willy F.

James Jr., Staff Sergeant Ruben Rivers, First Lieutenant Charles L. Thomas, Private George Watson, and to the lone survivor, First Lieutenant Vernon J. Baker. The 76-year-old Baker, a 28-year Army veteran, was most gracious in accepting the honor, stating that he had long ago resolved any bitterness that he had felt toward the Army for its past racial discrimination.

◆ THE DESEGREGATION OF THE MILITARY (1946–1949)

As the Allied victory of World War II approached, the highest levels of the United States government recognized that a new era of domestic racial relations had emerged. The war to defeat Fascism had, indeed, involved the entire U.S. population.

One impetus for a change in military policy regarding African Americans was an August 5, 1945-letter from Colonel Noel F. Parrish, commander of Tuskegee Army Air Field, to Brigadier General William E. Hall, Headquarters Army Air Forces. Colonel Parrish recommended "that future policy, instead of retreating defensibly further and further, with more and more group concessions, openly progress by slow and reasonable but definite steps toward the employment and treatment of Negroes as individuals which law requires and military efficiency demands."

Although Secretary of War Henry L. Stimson often revealed racist tendencies, his assistant, John R. McCloy, was considerably more liberal. When Robert P. Patterson succeeded Stimson, he adopted McCloy's suggestion for a study on the future use of African Americans in the military. A board of three Army generals conducted the study: Lieutenant General Alvan C. Gillem Jr., a former corps commander; Major General Lewis A. Pick, who built the Ledo Road in Burma; and Brigadier General Winslow C. Morse of the Army Air Force. During a six-week period, the "Gillem Board" took testimony from more than 50 witnesses in forming the Army's postwar racial policy. Two key individuals who worked with the Gillem Board were the two African American Chicagoans who served sequentially as civilian aide to the secretary of war: Truman K. Gibson Jr. and the recently discharged Lieutenant Colonel Marcus H. Ray.

The Gillem Board's findings leaned toward more efficient use of African American manpower, but did not advocate actual desegregation. That ambiguity reactivated the prewar coalition of the NAACP, the National Urban League, and the grassroots labor forces led by A. Philip Randolph.

The advent of the Cold War led to the National Security Act of 1947. The new law provided for the establishment of the Department of Defense (DOD), with the subordinate departments of Army, Navy, and Air Force. The act also created the Central Intelligence Agency (CIA).

In the continuing movement toward desegregation of the Armed Forces, 1947 brought two important African American personnel shifts within the Department of Defense: Lieutenant Colonel Marcus H. Ray returned to active duty as senior advisor on racial matters in Europe, and in the Pentagon, Dr. James C. Evans, a Howard University professor and Department of Army official, moved to the new post of special assistant to the secretary of defense. As the highest-ranking African American civilian in the Department of Defense, Dr. Evans served under 10 secretaries of defense until his retirement in 1970.

The demand for desegregation of the military became a key political issue in black America. As preparations for the 1948 presidential election intensified, President Harry Truman faced a campaign against Republican Thomas E. Dewey, states rights segregationist Strom Thurmond, and the Progressive Party of former Vice President Henry A. Wallace. In such a fragmented situation, the African American vote became crucial. By May of 1948, President Truman had decided to desegregate the Armed Forces by executive order. Nevertheless, the decision required two political concessions. First, no deadlines would be imposed. Second, the order would not denounce racial segregation. On July 26 President Truman issued Executive Order 9981, which signaled an end to segregation in the military.

In June of 1949, Wesley A. Brown became the first African American ever to graduate from the U.S. Naval Academy in Annapolis, Maryland. Brown, who had excelled as a student at Washington, DC's Dunbar High School, was appointed to the academy by New York Congressman Adam Clayton Powell Jr. in June of 1945. Since Annapolis had opened in 1850, only five African Americans had been admitted to the school. All had either resigned or been dismissed for alleged academic or disciplinary reasons. Despite harassment by classmates and hostility from instructors, Brown became the 20,699th midshipman to earn a commission from the naval academy.

◆ THE KOREAN WAR (1950–1953)

On June 25, 1950, North Korean forces surged across the 38th parallel and invaded South Korea. They routed U.S. ground forces in Korea and drove them south. At the start of the Korean War, the Air Force was the only completely desegregated branch of the military.

The first victory by U.S. troops in the Korean War occurred July 20, 1950, at Yechon thanks to the African American soldiers of the 24th Infantry Regiment. Group commander Captain Charles M. Bussey, a World War II Tuskegee Airman, earned a Silver Star for his role in the battle. Two African American soldiers received posthumous Medals of Honor during the Korean War: Private First Class William Thompson and Sergeant Cornelius H. Charlton, both of the 24th Infantry Regiment.

Thompson distinguished himself by bravery and determination above and beyond the call of duty in action on August 6, 1950, near Haman, Korea. While his platoon was reorganizing under cover of darkness, enemy forces overwhelmed the unit with a surprise attack. Johnson set up his machine gun in the path of the onslaught and swept the enemy with fire, momentarily halting their advance and thus permitting the remainder of his platoon to withdraw to a more secure position. Although hit repeatedly by grenade fragments and small-arms fire, he resisted his comrades' efforts to induce him to withdraw. Steadfast at his machine gun, he continued to deliver fire until he was mortally wounded by an enemy grenade.

Charlton, a member of Company C, distinguished himself in action on June 2, 1951, near Chipo-Ri, Korea. During an attack on heavily defended positions on an enemy-held ridge line, his platoon leader was wounded and evacuated. Charlton assumed command, rallied the men, and spearheaded the assault up the hill. Personally eliminating two hostile positions and killing six of the enemy with rifle fire and grenades, he continued up the slope until the unit stalled with heavy casualties. Regrouping the men, he led them forward, only to be forced back again by a shower of grenades. Despite a severe chest wound, Charlton refused medical attention and led a third charge that advanced to the crest of the ridge. He then charged a remaining enemy position on a nearby slope alone and, though hit by a grenade, raked the position with fire that routed the defenders. He died of wounds received during his daring exploits.

The first African American naval officer to lose his life in combat during the Korean War was Ensign Jesse L. Brown, who was also the first African American to earn naval aviator's wings. Brown, a Navy pilot, was shot down shortly after takeoff from the aircraft carrier *USS Leyte* on December 4, 1950. He crash-landed his plane on a snow-covered mountain near North Korea's Chosin Reservoir, but was unable to remove himself from the wreckage. A white pilot landed his aircraft near Brown's, but failed to pull him free. Other flyers radioed for help and, though a rescue helicopter made it to the location, the tangled metal could not be cut

African American members of the 2nd Infantry Division crouching in a foxhole during the Korean War.

away quickly enough to save the life of the injured airman. Brown, who had previously flown 20 air combat missions, was posthumously awarded a Distinguished Flying Cross and a Purple Heart. On March 18, 1972, the U.S. Navy launched the destroyer escort *USS Jesse L. Brown*, marking the first time a Navy ship was ever named in honor of an African American naval officer.

The Korean War Evolution

The early defeats that U.S. forces experienced in Korea prompted President Truman to replace his close friend, Secretary of Defense Louis A. Johnson with retired General of the Army George C. Marshall, who had been Truman's secretary of state during from 1947 to 1949. One of Marshall's first acts as secretary of defense was the creation of a new entity: the Office of Assistant Secretary of Defense for Manpower and Reserves (OASD MPR). Marshall appointed Anna M. Rosenberg, a 48-year-old New York City labor and public relations consultant, as head of the office. In 1944, she had persuaded President Franklin D. Roosevelt to have Congress enact the education provisions of

the World War II G. I. Bill of Rights. Dr. James C. Evans' Office of Special Assistant became a part of the OASD (MPR), which brought together two individuals knowledgeable in the rigors of discrimination—a Hungarian Jewish immigrant and an African American college professor. Known affectionately in the Pentagon as "Aunt Anna," Rosenberg's OASD (MPR) was responsible for industrial and military manpower including Selective Service System policies. Secretary Rosenberg viewed military desegregation as an impetus for societal reform observing that, "In the long run, I don't think a man can live and fight next to one of another race and share experiences where life is at stake, and not have a strong feeling of understanding when he comes home."

The effective implementation of Executive Order 9981 turned on how well African American military personnel could use their opportunities. Many African American generals and admirals owe their stars to the wise counsel of Dr. James C. Evans, who often mentored young African American officers by suggesting advantageous career paths in the military. By the close of the Korean War, racial segregation had been totally removed from the U.S. Armed Forces. In the years preceding the Vietnam War, African Americans entered the military and opted for full careers in increasing numbers. Between 1953 and 1961, there was a slow increase in the number of African American career officers in each branch of the service.

◆ THE VIETNAM WAR (1964–1973)

During the brief cease-fire period between the end of the Korean War and the heightening of conflict in Vietnam, the Kennedy Administration—prompted by Congressman Adam Clayton Powell Jr. and others—sought to end any remaining discrimination in the U.S. Armed Forces. Through Secretary of Defense Robert McNamara, Kennedy stressed to military leaders the need for fostering equal opportunities for African American servicemen, both on and off base.

Extensive U.S. involvement in Vietnam began during the summer of 1964 following an attack on the *USS Maddox* by North Vietnamese naval vessels in the Gulf of Tonkin. Within four months, the United States had 23,000 soldiers fighting in Vietnam. Shortly thereafter, the Army, Navy, and Marine Corps were all engaged in the action in ever-increasing numbers. While the U.S. fighting force in Vietnam comprised all of the nation's racial and ethnic groups, African Americans were disproportionately represented. Furthermore, they were more likely to be placed in combat units. Although African Americans constituted about 10.5 percent of the Army, they accounted for nearly 13 percent of those killed or wounded. By 1965, the conflict in Vietnam had escalated into a full-scale war, mounted to support the democracy of South Vietnamese and to protect U.S. interests in Southeast Asia. The Vietnam War proved deadlier than the Korean War and lasted longer than any other war in U.S. history.

The uncertain objectives of the Vietnam War, the high casualty rates, and the disproportionate number of African American soldiers in Vietnam caused tremendous controversy in the African American community. In 1965, Malcolm X claimed that the U.S. government was "causing American soldiers to be murdered every day, for no reason at all." Martin Luther King Jr. criticized African American involvement in Vietnam, remarking that "we are taking young black men who have been crippled by our society and sending them 8,000 miles away to guarantee liberties in Southeast Asia which they have not found in southwest Georgia or East Harlem."

With the assassinations of Dr. King and Senator Robert Kennedy in 1968, some African American soldiers became increasingly demoralized and disenchanted. Their anger intensified as racial prejudice remained common in Vietnam, on stateside military bases, and aboard the aircraft carriers *USS Kitty Hawk, USS Constellation,* and *USS Franklin D. Roosevelt.* One of the most famous African American protesters of the Vietnam War was heavyweight champion Muhammad Ali. An African American Muslim, Ali declared himself a conscientious objector in 1968 on religious grounds. He was convicted of violating the Selective Service Act, stripped of his heavyweight boxing championship, and threatened with an extensive jail term. In 1970, the U.S. Supreme Court overturned his conviction.

Still, most young African American men were willing to answer the draft board's call. Private First Class Milton Olive of Chicago was typical of African Americans who risked, and sometimes lost, their lives during the war. Olive was killed by an exploding grenade on which he had fallen in order to save the lives of his comrades; the government acknowledged his heroism by posthumously awarding him a Medal of Honor. By mid-1969, nine other African Americans had joined Olive as recipients of the Medal of Honor: Private First Class James Anderson Jr., Sergeant Rodney M. Davis, Specialist Five Lawrence Joel, Specialist Five Dwight H. Johnson, Sergeant Matthew Leonard, Sergeant Donald R. Long, Captain Riley L. Pitts, First Lieutenant Ruppert L. Sargent, Specialist Five Clarence E. Sasser. According to *New York Times* reporter Thomas Johnson, officers in the Military Assistance Command said that the 173rd Airborne Brigade, a crack outfit with a heavy African American representation, was "the best performing unit in Vietnam." In such elite combat units, one out of every four soldiers was an African American man.

In 1973, the United States withdrew all troops from Vietnam and South Vietnam collapsed in 1975.

◆ MILITARY PARTICIPATION IN THE 1970S AND 1980S

In 1972, a year before the final withdrawal of U.S. troops from Vietnam, the Defense Department issued the report "The Search for Military Justice." This report recognized that discrimination still existed in the military. In particular, it found that a disproportionate number of disciplinary incidents involved African Americans and Hispanics who were often punished more severely than whites. In the 1970s, African Americans represented about 13 percent of discharged servicemen, but received 33 percent of dishonorable discharges, 21 percent of bad conduct discharges, 16 percent of undesirable discharges and 20 percent of general discharges. Less than honorable discharges can negatively affect a person for life, threatening one's civilian career, earning ability, and level of veterans benefits.

An African American member of the 25th Infantry Division is greeted in 1966 by the Vietnamese.

High-ranking government and military officials moved to eliminate racial prejudices and barriers. Unquestionably, this became easier as African Americans, despite their relatively low numbers in the officer ranks, rose to the highest levels of the military. In 1975, Daniel "Chappie" James became the first African American to be promoted to full general in the U.S. Air Force. Two years later, President Jimmy Carter appointed lawyer/politician Clifford L. Alexander Jr. to be secretary of the Army, making him the first African American to hold that post. Alexander had previously served in the administrations of John F. Kennedy, Lyndon B. Johnson, and Richard Nixon. As Army secretary, Alexander was responsible for 1.9 million soldiers and a budget of $34 billion. He served in the post until 1980.

By the 1980s, the military was demonstrably less discriminatory than civilian life. The decade also saw increasing numbers of women joining the military, working side-by-side with men in many jobs. These advancements facilitated the breakdown of gender, as well as racial, obstacles to success in the military. By the end of the decade, African Americans represented 28 percent of the total enlisted Army force, while African American women numbered nearly 45 percent of enlisted women in the Armed Forces' largest branch. Recruiting African American officer candidates continued to be difficult, however, due in part to competition from industry and from private sector jobs that offered talented African American men and women higher salaries than were available in the military.

In August of 1989, President George Bush appointed General Colin L. Powell, U.S. Army, to be chairman of the Joint Chiefs of Staff, the nation's highest military post. Powell became the first African American in U.S. Armed Forces history to hold that title, as well as the youngest.

◆ THE PERSIAN GULF WAR (1991)

African Americans divided over U.S. involvement in

the Gulf War, with almost 50 percent of those polled at the time opposed to it. Several African American leaders, including Representative Charles Rangel of New York, were especially concerned about the high number of African Americans fighting to liberate Kuwait from Iraq. General Colin Powell, himself, initially favored economic sanctions (embargoes) over military action, until war became the stated policy of President George Bush. From then on, Powell drafted and put into action a brilliant military campaign—beginning with a large-scale air attack—that minimized the loss of U.S. lives. U.S. military objectives were met in just a few weeks time.

About 104,000 of the 400,000 troops serving in the Persian Gulf War were African American. According to the Department of Defense, African Americans accounted for 30 percent of Army, 21 percent of Navy, 17 percent of Marine Corps, and 14 percent of Air Force personnel stationed in the Persian Gulf (in 1991, African Americans comprised 12.4 percent of the U.S. population). For Powell, the high participation of African Americans, as shown by the Gulf War numbers, was a positive, rather than a negative: "To those who question the proportion of blacks in the armed services, my answer is simple. The military of the United States is the greatest equal opportunity employer around."

◆ AN EVOLVING INSTITUTION

During the 1990s, African Americans continued to make strides in rising to the highest military ranks. The percentage of African American officers in the U.S. Armed Forces remained on an upward trend, rising above 7 percent by 1994. In 1993, Togo D. West Jr. became the second African American to hold the president-appointed post of secretary of the Army. West served in that position until late 1997, when President Bill Clinton tabbed him to replace Jesse Brown as secretary of Veterans Affairs. Brown, who had vacated the post in July of 1997, was the first African American to serve as the department's secretary. A decorated Marine who served in Vietnam, Brown held the post for more than four years. The Department of Veteran's Affairs is the presidential Cabinet's second-largest department, with 215,000 employees and an annual budget of $41 billion. Another important African American first was the selection of Command Sergeant Major Gene C. McKinney to become the sergeant major of the Army in 1995. That singular post represents the highest-ranking noncommissioned officer in the U.S. Army. McKinney, the former command sergeant major of the U.S. Army Europe, became the tenth enlisted man to hold the title. The sergeant major of the Army's job is to

advise the Army chief of staff on issues concerning the organization's 420,000 enlisted personnel.

Since the end of the Persian Gulf War, African American military men and women have been well-represented in peacekeeping missions in Somalia, Haiti, and the republics of the former Yugoslavia. Polls of African American service personnel indicate that the vast majority regards the U.S. Armed Forces as the U.S. institution most free of racism and discrimination, while offering the greatest opportunity for career advancement. Statistical evidence bears out these assertions.

Nevertheless, a pair of scandals chiefly involving African American enlisted men rocked the Army during the latter half of the decade, causing some to question the fairness of military justice. The first of the two scandals took place at Maryland's Aberdeen Proving Ground and involved 11 African American enlisted men and one African American officer accused of sexual misconduct in multiple incidents with white female recruits. All of the enlisted men were drill sergeants, who allegedly took advantage of the recruits under their direct supervision during basic training. The charges included both consensual sex and rape; in the military, consensual sex between soldiers of unequal rank in cases involving direct subordinates is a crime for both parties. The first charges came out in September of 1996, though a number of the recruits were slow to point fingers and admitted willing participation in the acts. Army investigators later faced allegations that they had themselves tried to influence recruits to make the more serious charge of rape. Though some of the rape charges were dropped, several of the men were convicted and sentenced, while others had their military careers effectively ended.

The second scandal involved Sergeant Major of the Army Gene C. McKinney. The scandal became public in February of 1997 when McKinney's former public relations aide, retired Sergeant Major Brenda Hoster, charged him with sexual harassment. Eventually, five other women—four subordinates and one officer—came forward to accuse McKinney of additional sexual abuse charges. All of the women were white. On March 13, 1998, a military jury of four Army officers (including two women) and four enlisted men acquitted McKinney of 18 of the 19 charges, including all of the sexual misconduct charges. McKinney was only found guilty of a related obstruction of justice charge. McKinney was demoted one rank, though he was not given prison time. Many in the media concluded that the Pentagon had allowed a "show trial" in an effort to declare to the country its policy of "zero tolerance" of sexual harassment. Others conjectured that McKinney had been singled out, as white defendants in other Army sexual abuse cases occurring concurrently had been quietly slapped on the wrist.

In 1997, the Defense Manpower Data Center (DMDC) released the Armed Forces Equal Opportunity Survey (EOS), which was the first of its kind for the military. The EOS was conducted by the DMDC from September 1996 through February 1997. In general, the survey detected major differences in the perceptions of service members of different racial/ethnic groups in respect to equal opportunity. Significantly, whites, who comprise the majority population in the U.S. Armed Forces, were more positive than minority members regarding racial/ethnic issues in the military. The survey contained a wide range of items measuring members' perceptions and actions relating to race relations. For the most part, race relations on military installations/ships were perceived to be better than those in local civilian communities. Those perceptions, however, were not expressed in equally strong measure by whites and African Americans. Although more members said that race relations both in the military and in the nation were better at that time than five years previous, African Americans were less likely than other racial/ethnic group members to make those same claims. Despite the survey's lesser positive response rates among African Americans, compared to those of other racial/ethnic groups, the relative levels of satisfaction among African Americans in the U.S. Armed Forces appeared to indicate an overall favorable impression of the military by the group. Still, the EOS indicated areas of concern that could be addressed by military leadership.

The U.S. Armed Forces has continued to provide a primary avenue of upward mobility for those who are ambitious and willing to apply themselves. The overall percentage of African Americans in the military indicates that many are attempting to take that road to success. As of 1995 (the most recent year for which figures are available), the combined personnel strength of the Army, Navy, Marine Corps and Air Force was 1,518,000, of which 298,000 (or 19.6 percent) were African American. African American officers and enlisted personnel combined for 26.9 percent of the Army, 17.2 percent of the Navy, 16.0 percent of the Marine Corps and 14.5 percent of the Air Force; African Americans accounted for 12.6 percent of the U.S. population in 1995.

◆ THE WAR ON TERRORISM

The September 11, 2001 terrorist attacks on the World Trade Centers in New York City and the Pentagon in Arlington, Virginia, caught America off-guard. President George W. Bush immediately declared a War on Terrorism, stating that the United States would use whatever force was necessary to ensure internal security and dismantle the external terrorist threat. That threat was quickly identified as being directed by Osama Bin Laden and his Afghanistan-based al Qaeda terrorist network. In spite of early success by coalition-backed U.S. forces against the so-called Islamic "Jihad," the terrorist threat remained real as top-level al Qaeda leaders were rumored to escape to other Islamic nations. To date, American casualties and individual heroes have been limited. At home, African American support for the war has been strong, even among Muslims, who feel that Bin Laden does not represent the spirit and truth of Islam.

◆ OUTSTANDING MILITARY FIGURES

(To locate biographical profiles more readily, please consult the index at the back of the book.)

Clara L. Adams-Ender (1939–)
Brigadier General, Army Nurse Corps

Clara Mae Leach was born July 11, 1939, near Willow Springs in Wake County, North Carolina. She was the fourth child of ten born to sharecroppers Otha Leach and Caretha Bell (Sapp) Leach. Although her parents did not complete their education, they placed a high value on the education of their children. She attended Fuquay Springs Consolidated High School, which comprised primary grades through high school. From age five until entering college, Leach worked on the farm while going to school. In 1956 she graduated from high school at the age of 16 and entered the School of Nursing at North Carolina Agricultural and Technical State University, located in Greensboro. During her college years, she joined an army program that financed her junior and senior years. As an army reservist in college, she started as a private, later gaining a commission as a second lieutenant in March 1961, three months prior to graduation. Upon graduation, she entered the active U.S. Army Nurse Corps.

Leach began her active army career as a general duty nurse at Walson Army Hospital in Fort Dix, New Jersey, where was assigned from 1961 to 1963. She next the spent 13 months overseas when she was stationed in Ascom, Korea with the 121st Evacuation Hospital. During that assignment, she learned a great deal about nursing administration, leading nursing assistants, and managing nursing practice. She also discovered that she had an affinity for teaching. She was able to develop her teaching skills, when she was assigned to the U.S. Army Medical Training Center at Fort Sam Houston, Texas as a nursing instructor from 1965 until 1967. During 1967, she became the first female in the Army to earn the Expert Field Medical Badge. She also began graduate studies at the University of Minnesota, majoring in medical surgical nursing. After graduating with a Master's degree in nursing in 1969, she was assigned to the Walter Reed Army Institute of Nursing Center of the University of Maryland in Washington, D.C., where she was originally a nursing instructor, then an assistant professor.

For a year, beginning in 1974, she served as assistant chief of the department of nursing at Kimborough Army Hospital, Fort Meade, Maryland. She then entered the U.S. Army Command and General Staff College at Fort Leavenworth, Kansas, and completed a Master of Military Arts and Sciences degree in 1976. Subsequently, she was assigned to Headquarters, Health Services Command at Fort Sam Houston as inspector general.

She began her second overseas assignment at the Army Regional Medical Center in Frankfurt, West Germany, in 1978. She began as the assistant chief of the department of nursing, then, after a year, became chief. At just 39 years of age, she was promoted to full colonel. While in Germany, she took part in a collaborative working relationship with German nurses at a nearby trauma hospital, while learning the German language, local customs, and culture. She also met her husband, a German doctor, Heinz Ender, whom she married in 1981, three months after returning to the States.

In 1981, Adams-Ender was assigned to the U.S. Army Recruiting Command in Fort Sheridan, Illinois, as chief of the Army Nurse Corps division. Despite heavy job responsibilities, she continued to seek educational opportunities whenever possible. When she graduated from the U.S. Army War College in 1982, she became the first black Army Nurse Corps officer to do so. In 1984, she was appointed chief of the department of nursing at Walter Reed Army Medical Center, where she engaged in clinical practice, teaching, nursing administration, and nursing research. Her experiences and education provided a broad base for her next assignment. In 1987, she was appointed to the Office of the Surgeon General as the 18th Chief of the U.S. Army Nurse Corps, with it came a promotion to brigadier general. As the surgeon general's director for medical personnel during the 1991 Gulf War, Adams-Ender was responsible for more than 25,000 military health care professionals who served in the region of conflict. Ordinarily, the holder of that prestigious title retires after her assignment ends, but Adam-Ender added another highlight to her distinguished military career before retiring. In 1991, she became the commanding general at Fort Belvoir, Virginia, while simultaneously serving as deputy commanding officer of the Military District of Washington. Such high-profile appointments

were a rarity for both black females and nursing corps officers. She held those posts until her retirement in August 1993. For her retirement ceremony, composer Marge Wheeler wrote *The General Adams-Ender March* in her honor.

Following her retirement from the military, Adams-Ender founded her own management consulting agency, Caring About People with Enthusiasm (CAPE) Associates, Inc. As president and CEO of CAPE, she specializes in personnel and organizational management issues and is a frequent speaker and lecturer. Adams-Ender chronicled her life story in *My Rise to the Stars: How a Sharecropper's Daughter Became an Army General*, which she wrote with Blair S. Walker. The autobiography was self-published in 2001. Adams-Ender is involved with numerous professional organizations. She is a member of the American Nurses Association, Council of Nursing Administration, American Red Cross Nurses, Chi Eta Phi Nursing Sorority, National Association for Female Executives, and National League of Nursing, to name a few. Among many charitable organizations, she is a life member of the NAACP, and a member of the National Council of Negro Women.

During her military career, Adams-Ender was awarded a Distinguished Service Medal with oak leaf cluster, a Legion of Merit, a Meritorious Service Medal with three oak leaf Clusters, and an Army Commendation Medal. She has been honored with many civilian awards, including the Roy Wilkins Meritorious Service Award by the NAACP, the Gertrude E. Rush Award for Leadership from the National Bar Association, the Regents' Distinguished Graduate Award from the University of Minnesota. In 1993, she was recognized for career achievement when she was selected to be in Dominion's Strong Men and Women: Excellence in Leadership series.

Crispus Attucks. *See* **Africans in America chapter.**

Guion Bluford. *See* **Science & Technology chapter.**

Charles Bolden. *See* **Science & Technology chapter.**

Ensign Jesse L. Brown (1926–1950)
Naval Aviator

Jesse Leroy Brown was born on October 13, 1926, in Hattiesburg, Mississippi. He graduated from Eureka High School in 1944 and studied engineering at Ohio

State University from 1944 to 1947. In 1946, he joined the U.S. Naval Reserve and became an aviation cadet the following year.

Brown's flight training occurred at Pensacola, Florida, and in 1948 he became the first African American to fly for the Navy. In 1949, Brown worked aboard the aircraft carrier *USS Leyte*, earning an Air Medal and a Korean Service Medal for his 20 air combat missions. On December 4, 1950, while flying air support for Marines at the Battle of the Chosin Reservoir, his plane was hit by enemy fire. He crash-landed his aircraft, but was trapped inside and died before rescue efforts could cut through the wreckage to extract him. He was posthumously awarded a Purple Heart and a Distinguished Flying Cross for exceptional courage, airmanship, and devotion to duty. Brown was the first African American naval officer to lose his life in combat during the Korean War.

In March of 1972, a destroyer escort, the *USS Jesse L. Brown*, was named in his honor and launched at the Avondale Shipyards at Westwege, Louisiana. It marked the first time that a ship was named for an African American naval officer.

Sherian G. Cadoria (1940–)
Military Officer

Born to a poor rural family on January 26, 1940, in Marksville, Louisiana, Sherian Grace Cadoria credits her mother with instilling within her the qualities of discipline, honesty, and perseverance. From an early age, she helped supplement the family income by picking cotton, lugging 100-pound capacity bags through the fields. To attend school, she and her two siblings walked five miles each way, passed daily by a "whites only" school bus that traveled the same route. After high school, Cadoria attended Southern University in Baton Rouge. During her junior year she was recruited for a four-week Women's Army Corps (WAC) training program. Though she was actually more interested in joining the navy, she attended the WAC program, which was conducted at Fort McClellan, Alabama, during the summer of 1960. After graduating with a B.S. in Business Education in 1961, she decided to make the Army her career.

It wasn't long before Cadoria realized that, to many in the Army, she had two strikes against her: being both African American and female. At Fort McClellan in the early 1960s, she suffered numerous indignities and missed out on several advancement opportunities as a result of her race. As she progressed through the ranks, however, she faced greater resistance because of her gender, than because of her race. Cadoria was not content to take either of the typical paths open for female advancement, such as administration and nursing. Instead, she rose through the ranks of the military police.

From 1967–1969, while U.S. involvement in Vietnam was at its peak, Cadoria spent 33 months in the Southeast Asian country. The severity of the experience almost caused Cadoria to give up her military career and she seriously considered joining a convent on her return. The turning point came in December of 1969 when she was selected to attend the Command and General Staff College, becoming the first African American woman to be chosen for the school.

Even the dissolution of the WAC in 1978 and the integration of its members into the regular Army did not slow her ascent. Among her marks of distinction, Cadoria was the first woman to command a male battalion; the first African American director of manpower and personnel for the Joint Chiefs of Staff (a position that required her to fill openings in all branches of the armed services, both active and reserve); and the first woman to achieve the rank of general apart from the nursing corps. She is also a graduate of the U.S. Army War College and the National Defense University. Cadoria even managed to find enough time outside her busy career to attend the University of Oklahoma, where she earned an M.A. in social work in 1974. In 1985, Cadoria was promoted to brigadier general, becoming only the second African American female, and the first in the regular U.S. Army, to attain the rank. Cadoria retired from the military on November 30, 1990.

Following her retirement from the military, Cadoria returned to Louisiana. She is the president of her own company, Cadoria Speaker and Consultancy Service, and is a much-in-demand keynote/inspirational/motivational speaker. During the late-1990s, Cadoria put her business on hold for two years to serve as volunteer principal of Holy Ghost Catholic School in her native Marksville. Currently, she is a member of the Louisiana Gaming Control Board and is the Senior Army Representative on the Advisory Board of Vietnam Women Veterans, Inc. Cadoria was named Woman of the Year by the national organization of Business and Professional Women in 1995, was a National Athena Award winner in 1998, and was among the honorees of Dominion's Strong Men and Women: Excellence in Leadership series in 1999.

During nearly three decades of military service, Cadoria was awarded an Air Medal, an Army Commendation Medal with three oak leaf clusters, a Bronze Star with two oak leaf clusters, a Defense Superior Service Medal, a Distinguished Service Medal, a Meritorious

Service Medal with oak leaf cluster, and a Joint Chiefs of Staff Identification Badge.

Sergeant William H. Carney (1840–1908)
First African American Medal of Honor Recipient

William H. Carney was born in Norfolk, Virginia in 1840. At 14, he attended a secret school run by a local minister. In 1856, his father moved the family to New Bedford, Massachusetts. Carney, a man of growing religious conviction, considered becoming a minister, but the Civil War disrupted his plans. Instead, he enlisted in the 54th Massachusetts Colored Infantry Regiment on February 17, 1863.

As a member of Company C of the 54th, Sergeant Carney was part of the force assigned to lead the advance on Fort Wagner, South Carolina, on July 18, 1863. Fort Wagner, a vital Confederate position in the defense of Charleston, was heavily fortified. Led by Colonel Robert Gould Shaw, a white commander, the African American troops attempted a valiant, but ultimately disastrous, assault in the late afternoon. During the attack, the flag bearer was wounded, but before the stars and stripes fell to the ground, Carney grabbed the staff and continued onward. With most of his comrades falling around him, Carney led the charge. He wound up at the fort's entrance—alone. Hiding in the shadows of the fort, Carney avoided rounds and shells falling around him, while clutching the flag. Eventually, a Confederate squad stumbled upon his position and he was forced to flee. Shot twice, he still managed to escape, later joining up with a white soldier who bandaged his wounds. Together, they retreated to the safety of the Union lines, but not before another shot grazed Carney's head. After further medical treatment, Carney returned to his regiment, where his fellow troops cheered his return, flag in hand. "Boys, the old flag never touched the ground," he proclaimed proudly. Unfortunately, approximately half of Carney's comrades, as well as Colonel Shaw, met their end in the unsuccessful undertaking. For his actions, Carney was awarded the Medal of Honor. Among African American soldiers or sailors who were awarded a Medal of Honor for actions during the Civil War, Carney's occurred earliest, though he was not issued his medal until May 23, 1900.

On June 30, 1864, Sergeant Carney was discharged from the infantry at Black Island, South Carolina. He was granted disability for lingering medical problems resulting from the wounds he received in the famed battle. After a short sojourn to California, Carney returned to New Bedford, where he served as a mail carrier for 32 years. After retirement, he moved to Boston to accept a job as a messenger in the State House. He was injured in an elevator accident on November 23, 1908 and died on December 9. Carney was buried in New Bedford.

William H. Carney, Medal of Honor recipient for his role in the Civil War.

General Benjamin O. Davis Jr. (1912–)
First African American Brigadier General in the U.S. Air Force

Born in Washington, D.C., on December 18, 1912, Benjamin Oliver Davis Jr., the son of a career U.S. Army officer, moved often in his early years. Stops included Alabama (where his father taught military science at Tuskegee Institute) and Cleveland, where he graduated as president of his high school class. Davis attended both Western Reserve University and the University of Chicago before accepting an appointment to the U.S. Military Academy in 1932, having been nominated by longtime Chicago Congressman Oscar DePriest.

When Davis entered West Point, no African American had graduated from the academy in 43 years. In an attempt to get Davis to resign, his fellow cadets forced him to endure four years of "silencing." That behavior, encouraged by superiors who also wanted Davis to fail, consisted of no one speaking to him (except to issue an order), room with him (though he lived in a two-man room), or eat with him for his entire stay at the academy. Nevertheless, Davis excelled, graduating 35th in a class of 276 in 1936. Although the Army generally allowed West Point graduates with high class rank to choose their branch of preference, Davis was denied his choice, the U.S. Army Air Corps. Instead, he was assigned to Fort Benning, Georgia as an infantry officer, where he experienced further institutional and de facto racism.

After five years in the infantry, and following a stint at Fort Riley, Kansas, Davis finally got his wish when just months before the United States entered World War II in 1941, he was allowed to transfer to the Army Air Corps. The transfer was part of a daring military experiment championed by President Franklin D. Roosevelt: the creation of an African American flying unit. The 66th Air Force Training Detachment was based at the Tuskegee, Alabama Army Air Field, and Davis was in the first training class. On September 2, 1941, he became the first African American to officially fly solo as an Army Air Corps officer. Shortly after graduation in 1942, Davis—as the only previously commissioned officer—became commander of the African American 99th Pursuit Squadron (later renamed the 99th Fighter Squadron). Davis quickly earned promotions, rising to the rank of lieutenant colonel by the time the 99th arrived in French Morocco for combat duty on April 24, 1943.

In late August of 1943, Davis returned to the U.S. to command the African American 332nd Fighter Group, made up of three squadrons and later the 99th. In April of 1944, the 332nd arrived in Italy, where it flew missions deep into France and Germany. The sterling record of the 332nd contributed to Davis' promotion to full colonel just a few months later. In 200 escort missions, the unit never lost a bomber to Nazi aircraft fire. During World War II, Davis flew 60 missions and logged 224 combat hours. For individual heroism, he was honored with several decorations including a Silver Star (pinned to his uniform by his father, Brigadier General Benjamin O. Davis Sr.) and a Distinguished Flying Cross, the Corps' highest award.

Davis' post-World War II career may not have been as glamorous, but it was no less significant. He played a leading role in the integration of the military in 1949. During the Korean War, he commanded the 51st Fighter Interceptor Wing, later serving as director of operations and training for the Far East Air Forces. His promotion to brigadier general in 1954 made him the

first African American general in U.S. Air Force history, as well as the highest-ranking African American in the U.S. military at the time. Other notable assignments included being named deputy chief of staff of the U.S. Air Force in Europe in 1957; director of manpower and organization for the U.S. Air Force headquarters in 1961; and chief of staff of the United Nations Command and U.S. Forces in Korea in 1965. Davis became a major general in 1957 and a lieutenant general in 1965, becoming the first African American to hold either rank in the U.S. Armed Forces. Named to command the Philippines-based 13th Air Force in August of 1967, Davis was responsible for all Air Force units in Southeast Asia, which included those serving in the Vietnam War. Davis retired from active duty in 1970.

After retiring from the military, Davis served under President Richard M. Nixon as Assistant Secretary of Transportation for Environment, Safety and Consumer Affairs. In 1991, Smithsonian Institution Press published his memoirs as *Benjamin O. Davis Jr., American: An Autobiography*. On December 9, 1998, in order to right a perceived wrong, President Bill Clinton bestowed upon Davis a fourth star, bringing his rank to full general. He currently lives in Arlington, Virginia with his wife, Agatha.

Among Davis' many military decorations are a Distinguished Service Medal with two oak leaf clusters, an Army and an Air Force Silver Star, a Distinguished Flying Cross, a Legion of Merit with two oak leaf clusters, and an Air Medal with five oak leaf clusters.

Brigadier General Benjamin O. Davis Sr. (1877–1970)
First African American Brigadier General in the U.S. Armed Forces

Born in Washington, D.C., on June 1, 1877, Benjamin Oliver Davis Sr. came from a middle-class family largely employed in the civil service. Davis, however, was not interested in pursuing a career in the federal bureaucracy. Instead, he wanted to become a soldier. In high school, he was a member of the Cadet Corps, an extracurricular organization that introduced him to military training and procedure. Following high school, Davis attended classes at Howard University, but despite his parents' objections, he left college in 1898 for an opportunity to fight in the Spanish-American War.

Hoping to see action in Cuba, Davis bounced from the District of Columbia National Guard, in which he was elected a second lieutenant of Company D, to the 8th U.S. Volunteer Infantry, where he accepted a temporary commission as a First Lieutenant in Company G.

Benjamin O. Davis Sr., the first African American brigadier general in the U.S. armed forces.

Neither unit, however, made it out of the states. After the conclusion of the war, Davis sought an Army commission through other avenues. Despite his failure to accomplish his goal at the time, he did not give up his dream of becoming an Army officer.

On June 14, 1899, he enlisted as a private in the Troop I, 9th U.S. Cavalry, an African American regular Army unit. Though openly discouraged by most whites and African Americans, in August of the following year he submitted an application to take the competitive officer candidate examination. A few months later he took the battery of tests and finished among the top candidates. On February 2, 1901, he was commissioned a second lieutenant in the regular Army. His first assignment was with Troop F, 10th U.S. Cavalry, then stationed in the Philippines.

Over the next three decades, Davis received a number of assignments designed to keep him from being in a position to command white soldiers. He served as a military attache to Liberia from 1909 to 1911, commanding officer of a supply troop in the Philippines from 1917 to 1920, and instructor of the 372nd Infantry

of the Ohio National Guard from 1924 to 1929. Between such service assignments, he taught military science and tactics at Wilberforce and Tuskegee Universities. Promotions for African American officers were rare in those years, but Davis rose through the ranks until he became a full colonel on February 18, 1930. In 1938, Davis took command of the African American 369th Cavalry, New York National Guard.

Davis' promotion to brigadier general on October 25, 1940, marked the first time an African American had been promoted to general in the history of the U.S. Armed Forces. The promotion was seen by many detractors as a political ploy by President Franklin D. Roosevelt to garner African American votes in an election year. Davis had spent a 40-year military career, however, in assignments that offered him few opportunities to shine. The promotion was a capping to a difficult career marred by perpetual discrimination. Davis retired just a few months later, having reached the official retirement age of 64.

The ink was not yet dry on Davis' retirement paperwork when he was called back to active service in early 1941 to supervise the introduction of 100,000 African American soldiers into the Army, an institution rampant with unofficial but effective policies of segregation. During World War II, Davis inspected African American units, heard racial complaints, and handled public relations duties throughout the European military theater as a member of the Washington-based inspector general's staff. Davis' strenuous efforts on behalf of African American servicemen made the normally publicity-shy officer a very visible figure in the African American press.

After the war, Davis served as assistant to the inspector general of the Army from 1945 to 1947, then as special assistant to the secretary of the Army from 1947 to 1948. His focus throughout that period was the orderly integration of units in the military's largest branch (President Harry Truman's Executive Order 9981, the historic order that led to the integration of the entire military, was issued six days after Davis' retirement). On July 20, 1948, Davis retired from the Army a second and final time at a special White House ceremony during which his career was lauded by President Truman himself.

Among his later activities, Davis was a member of the American Battle Monuments Commission. Deteriorating eyesight and health problems brought his public life to an end in 1960. Davis died of leukemia on November 26, 1970, in North Chicago, Illinois, and was buried in Arlington National Cemetery. Davis' military honors included a Bronze Star and a Distinguished Service Medal, as well as such foreign decorations as the Croix de Guerre with Palm (from France) and the

Grade of Commander of the Order of the Star of Africa (from Liberia).

Lieutenant Colonel Charity Adams Earley (1918–2002)

First African American Woman Commissioned in the Women's Auxiliary Army Corps

Charity Edna Adams was born in Columbia, South Carolina, in 1918. She was the valedictorian of her high school class and continued her studies at Ohio's Wilberforce University, where she was awarded a B.A. in 1938. Back in Columbia, she taught high school math while studying for a master's degree in psychology.

In the fall of 1941, the War Department began considering ways in which women could be used in support roles so that soldiers in non-combat specialties could be freed up for combat. The result of their brainstorming was the creation of an organization they named the Women's Auxiliary Army Corps (WAAC). By early 1942, recruitment for the new branch was underway. One method used to recruit officer candidates was to ask colleges to compile lists of names for consideration. Wilberforce University submitted a list on which the name Charity E. Adams appeared. At the time, Adams was enrolled at Ohio State University, working on a Master's degree in vocational psychology. In June of that year, Adams filled out and mailed back the application sent her.

Within a month, Adams was at Fort Des Moines, Iowa, as a member of the first WAAC officer candidate school class. Though Adams and the 38 other African American officer candidates trained alongside white officer candidates, they were surprised to find all non-training facilities rigidly segregated, such as housing assignments and mess hall seating. Adams graduated from basic training on August 30, 1942, and became the first African American woman to be commissioned in the WAAC. She was then appointed commander of the basic training company for enlisted females, where her administrative abilities quickly impressed the post's commanding officer.

Adams was soon promoted to captain and was assigned to Fort Des Moines' Plans and Training Section. Her new responsibilities included supervising and training recruits in such skills as office administration, photography, and radio operation. As part of her job, she made frequent trips to duty stations in other states including Massachusetts, New Jersey, and North Carolina. She even had occasion to visit the newly completed Pentagon, located just outside Washington, D.C. By mid-1943, the WAAC was renamed the Women's Army Corps (WAC), and Adams had received a promotion to major.

Despite Adams's stellar record, neither she nor any other African American WACs were being posted overseas. Finally, in December of 1944, Adams became the first African American WAC to be selected for overseas duty. She flew to Birmingham, England, to command the newly-formed 6888th Central Postal Battalion. The all black 850-woman unit was responsible for directing all incoming and outgoing mail for the seven million U.S. Armed Forces personnel, Seabees, and American Red Cross workers serving in the European Theater of Operations. Several months of backed-up mail awaited the new arrivals. Adams quickly organized her command into five companies, then set the women into eight-hour, round-the-clock shifts. She also created lists to track units, sought means to differentiate between persons with similar names, and traced persons whose whereabouts were unknown. In May of 1945, as the war in Europe ended, the 6888th was moved to Rouen, France, later relocating to Paris, where it continued its duties with reduced personnel. Adams was relieved of command in December and sent back to the U.S. for discharge. At the separation center, Adams was promoted to lieutenant colonel just days before leaving the service. Such promotions were a courtesy to service personnel who were deemed deserving of elevated rank, but had not been promoted on active duty. At separation, Adams was the highest-ranking African American officer in the WAC.

Within weeks of her discharge, Adams was back at Ohio State University, where she completed her Master's program in 1946. She married Dr. Stanley A. Earley, M.D. in 1949, at which point she took the name Charity Adams Earley. Among her postwar positions were registration officer at the Cleveland office of the Veterans Administration, personnel officer at both Tennessee A&I University, in Nashville, and Georgia State College, in Savannah, and employment and personnel counselor, YWCA, New York City. Earley recalled her wartime experiences in the 1989 book *One Woman's Army: A Black Officer Remembers the WAC*. In 1991, she received honorary doctorates from Wilberforce University and the University of Dayton. Earley died January 13, 2002 in Dayton, Ohio, her longtime home. She was 83.

Lieutenant Henry O. Flipper (1856–1940)

First African American Graduate of the U.S. Military Academy

Henry Ossian Flipper was born a slave in Thomasville, Georgia, on March 21, 1856. After the Civil War, his father moved the family to Atlanta. Flipper's father was a skilled shoemaker who created a successful business

Major Charity Adams Earley reviewing her troops during World War II, the first black female troops to go overseas.

that allowed him to educate his two sons. In 1866, Flipper began attending schools established by the American Missionary Association and, in 1869, he started taking classes at Atlanta University. In 1873, he received an appointment to the U.S. Military Academy at West Point, New York. Though Flipper was the fifth African American to enter the academy, he was the first to withstand the intense discriminatory practices of the institution, graduating 50th in a class of 76 in June of 1877. He also has the distinction of being the first African American graduate of an engineering school in the United States. A year after graduation his surprisingly restrained memoir of the experience was published as *The Colored Cadet at West Point*.

Upon graduation, Flipper was commissioned a second lieutenant and received his assignment of choice: the African American 10th U.S. Cavalry. The regiment was one of two units that Native Americans had nicknamed "Buffalo Soldiers." Flipper served at various

frontier installations in the Southwest during the next few years including Fort Sill, Oklahoma, and Fort Concho, Texas. An incident that occurred at the latter duty station may have played a role in ending Flipper's military career a short time later: he was seen riding with an attractive white woman. Racist white officers, incensed that Flipper might have been focusing his attentions on a white female, sought ways to remove him from the Army. In 1882, while serving as Commissary Officer at Fort Davis, Texas, Flipper was brought up on charges by his commander, who accused him of embezzling funds and of conduct unbecoming an officer and a gentleman. At the court-martial trial, Flipper was acquitted of the former charge, but was found guilty of the latter and dismissed from the Army, as was required by the conviction.

To his death, Flipper protested his innocence, and he constantly attempted to clear his name. His battle went all the way to the halls of Congress, where he hoped a bill introduced by Wisconsin Congressman Michael Griffen in 1898 would restore him to the duty, grade, rank, pay, and station in the Army he would have attained had he not been unjustifiably turned out. This and numerous other trips to Washington to vindicate himself met with failure.

Flipper's dismissal from the Army, however, did not cause him to fail in civilian life. He went on to become a notable figure in the American Southwest and in Mexico, working as a civil and military engineer. He became much sought after by both private and governmental bodies as a surveyor, engineer, and consultant. He later became a translator of Spanish land grants. His work *Spanish and Mexican Land Laws: New Spain and Mexico* was published by the Department of Justice in 1895. As his reputation spread, job opportunities increased. He served as consulting engineer to the builders of one of the earliest railroads to be constructed in the Alaska Territory, worked for an oil company pioneering the industry in Venezuela, and was an aide to the United States Senate Committee on Foreign Relations. In the course of his career, he befriended such prominent Washington officials as Senator A.B. Fall of New Mexico. When Fall became secretary of the interior, Flipper became his assistant until the infamous Teapot Dome scandal severed their relationship in the mid-1920s. Flipper returned to Atlanta at the close of his career, living with his brother, until his death on May 3, 1940.

In 1978, Flipper's body was disinterred and moved from Atlanta to Thomasville, where he was given a full military funeral attended by nearly 500 people. In 1997, the Texas Christian University Press published *Black Frontiersman: The Memoirs of Henry O. Flipper, First Black Graduate of West Point*, which was compiled and edited from Flipper's papers by Theodore D. Harris.

Though Flipper died before he could be absolved, others took up his fight. In 1976, descendants and supporters approached the Army Board for the Correction of Military Records on his behalf. Although the board stated that it did not have the authority to overturn Flipper's conviction, it found the penalty imposed "unduly harsh and unjust" and recommended that Flipper's dismissal be commuted to a good conduct discharge. Subsequently, with other appropriate approvals, the Department of the Army issued an honorable discharge in Flipper's name, dated June 30, 1882, the date he had been dismissed from the Army. On October 21, 1997, a private law firm filed an application of pardon in Flipper's name with the secretary of the Army. After several months of review by U.S. Army and

Department of Justice personnel, President Bill Clinton pardoned Flipper on February 19, 1999.

Vice Admiral Samuel L. Gravely Jr. (1922–)
First African American Admiral

Samuel Lee Gravely Jr. was born in Richmond, Virginia, on June 4, 1922. Enrolled at Virginia Union University when the U.S. entered World War II, Gravely quit school to enlist in the U.S. Naval Reserve on September 15, 1942. He received recruit training at Great Lakes (Illinois) Naval Training Center and skill training at the Service School, Hampton (Virginia) Institute. To become an officer, he attended the Officer Training Camp at the University of California, Los Angeles, the Pre-Midshipmen School in Asbury Park, New Jersey, and the Midshipmen School at Columbia University in New York City, where he trained from August to December of 1944. The first African American graduate of a midshipman school, Gravely was commissioned an ensign in the U.S. Naval Reserve, on December 14, 1944.

Gravely's initial assignment was as the assistant battalion commander at the Great Lakes Naval Training Center. Later, he became the first African American officer to be assigned shipboard duty when he held such titles as communications officer, electronics officer, executive officer, and personnel officer aboard the submarine chaser *USS PC-1264*. After a brief stint as communications watch officer with the Fleet Training Group, in Norfolk, Virginia, Gravely was released from active duty on April 16, 1946. He then returned to college and received a B.A. in history from Virginia Union University in 1948. Though he had plans of becoming a teacher and coach, he took a job in Richmond as a railway postal clerk following graduation.

In 1948, Harry Truman's historic Executive Order 9981 forced the U.S. Armed Forces to integrate and the military began increasing the recruitment of African Americans. On August 30, 1949, Gravely returned to duty as assistant to the officer in charge of recruiting at the Naval Recruiting Station, Washington, D.C. After attending the Communications Officers Short Course, Gravely saw active duty aboard a pair of ships that engaged the enemy during the Korean War: first as radio operator on the battleship *USS Iowa* and later as communications officer on the cruiser *USS Toledo*. His reputation as a communications expert played a vital role in subsequent assignments. After more than a decade in the military, Gravely finally decided to make the navy his career and he formally transferred from the Naval Reserve to the regular Navy on August 16, 1955. From that point on, Gravely frequently shifted between land-based administrative positions and shipboard assignments, occasionally punctuated by training course instruction.

Steadily promoted through the ranks, Gravely was the touchstone for African American achievement in the Navy. He became the first African American officer to command a U.S. Navy ship on January 15, 1961, when he assumed temporary command of the destroyer *USS Theodore E. Chandler*. When he accepted command of the destroyer escort *USS Falgout* on January 31, 1962, he became the first African American to command a fighting ship. From August of 1963 to June 1964, Gravely attended the senior course in naval warfare at the Naval War College in Newport, Rhode Island. He was then tabbed program manager for the National Command Center and the National Emergency Airborne Command Post at the Defense Communications Agency in Arlington, Virginia. In 1966, when Gravely guided the *USS Taussig* into direct offensive action during the Vietnam War, he became the first African American naval officer to command a U.S. warship under combat conditions since the Civil War.

On June 2, 1971, the day he was relieved of command of the guided missile frigate *USS Jouett*, Gravely became the first African American to be promoted to the rank of rear admiral. In mid-July of that year, he was made commander of the Naval Communications Command and director of the Naval Communications Divisions under the chief of naval operations, dual posts he held for two years. In August 1975, Admiral Gravely assumed duties as commander of the Eleventh Naval District. On August 28, 1976, he was promoted to vice admiral, another first as an African American naval officer. The next month, he was placed in command of the U.S. Navy's Third Fleet, making him the first African American to command a U.S. Navy fleet. As commander of the Third Fleet, Gravely was in charge of 100 ships and 60,000 officers overseeing 50 million miles of ocean (approximately a quarter of the earth's surface). His final naval assignment was as director of the Defense Communications Agency, a post he held from September 15, 1978, until his retirement on August 1, 1980.

After retiring from the U.S. Navy, Gravely worked for several private sector companies. He was senior corporate advisor for Potomac Systems Engineering, director of the Command Support Division for Automated Business Systems and Services, Inc., and vice president for Navy programs at CTEC. He was also a member of the board of directors for Draper Laboratory, where he continues as member emeritus. In 1991,

he was named an aide-de-camp to then-Virginia Governor L. Douglas Wilder. Currently, he is chairman of the Tredegar National Civil War Center Foundation Board. In 2002, he was among those honored for Dominion's Strong Men and Women: Excellence in Leadership series. Gravely lives on a rural, two-acre estate in Haymarket, Virginia.

While in the Navy, Gravely received numerous decorations, including a Legion of Merit with gold star, a Bronze Star, a Meritorious Service Medal, a Joint Service Commendation Medal, a Navy Commendation Medal, a World War II Victory Medal, a Naval Reserve Medal, and an American Campaign Medal. Additional decorations included a Korean Presidential Unit Citation, a National Defense Medal with one bronze star, a China Service Medal, a Korean Service Medal with two bronze stars, a United Nations Service Medal, an Armed Forces Expeditionary Medal, a Vietnam Service Medal with six bronze stars, and an Antarctic Service Medal. Gravely has also received many civilian awards, including Savannah State College's Major Richard R. Wright Award of Excellence (1974), the Prince Hall Founding Fathers Military Commanders Award (1975), and the Virginia Press Association's Virginian of the Year (1979). He received an honorary doctor of laws degree from his alma mater, Virginia Union University, in 1979.

Major General Marcelite Harris (1943–)
Two-Star General, U.S. Air Force

Marcelite Jordan was born on January 16, 1943, in Houston, Texas. She attended Houston public schools, graduating from Kashmere Gardens Junior-Senior High School in 1960. At Spelman College in Atlanta, Jordan studied speech and drama in hopes of becoming an actress. During college she took part in a USO tour of Germany and France. The experience gave her an opportunity to find out about the military, but it did not spark any career interest within her at the time. After earning a B.A. in 1964, she struggled to find stage work. She took a job with a Headstart program at a Houston YMCA, while taking law classes at night. Finding it difficult to maintain that pace, Jordan decided to look into other career options and chose the U.S. Air Force.

Jordan began at the Officer Training School at Lackland Air Force Base in Texas in September of 1965 and was commissioned a second lieutenant on December 21 of that year. Her first assignment was as assistant director for administration with the 60th Airlift Wing at California's Travis Air Force Base. In January of 1967, she received her first promotion and transferred to Bitburg Air Base in West Germany. At Bitburg, Jordan

Marcelite J. Harris.

served as administrative officer of the 71st Tactical Missile Squadron for two years. Then, in May 1969, at the suggestion of a superior, she changed career tracks to maintenance. She was reassigned as maintenance analysis officer of the 36th Tactical Fighter Wing, also based at Bitburg. As the first female Air Force officer in a "man's field," Jordan faced hostility from many of the men under her command. In order to gain credibility with the maintenance crews that she supervised, Jordan decided to learn more about aircraft engineering. She applied for the Aircraft Maintenance Officer Course, but was turned down at first. Jordan persisted and was later accepted to the eight-month course, graduating in May 1971.

Jordan' next assignment took her to Thailand's Korat Royal Thai Air Force Base, where she was maintenance supervisor of the 49th Tactical Fighter Squadron from August of 1971 to May of 1972. Despite initial resistance from the maintenance crews under her command, Jordan forged a cooperative relationship with her personnel. The result was a superb performance record for the aircraft piloted by a tactical fighter squadron flying sorties over Vietnam.

Jordan returned to Travis Air Force Base for a three-year stint before accepting a very visible assignment in Washington, D.C., in September 1975. For more than two and a half years, Jordan served as personnel staff officer and White House social aide during the Ford and Carter administrations. A late-1970s stop at the U.S. Air Force Academy in Colorado Springs, Colorado was followed by a transfer to McConnell Air Force Base in Kansas. On November 29, 1980, in the midst of three consecutive assignments at McConnell, she married Maurice Anthony Harris, taking his surname. Harris' last assignment on foreign soil was a three and a half year stretch as director of maintenance at the Pacific Air Forces Logistic Support Center at Kadena Air Base in Japan starting in November of 1982. While in Japan, Harris earned a B.S. in business management from the University of Maryland University College's Asian Division in 1986.

Returning to the United States in March of 1986, Harris became deputy commander of maintenance at Keesler Air Force Base in Mississippi. Meanwhile, she continued her climb up the career ladder, reaching full colonel on September 1, 1986. In December of 1988 she was named commander of the 3300th Technical Training Wing at Keesler, becoming the third female to attain that level in the history of the U.S. Air Force. On May 1, 1991, while stationed at Tinker Air Force Base in Oklahoma, Harris became the first African American woman to attain the rank of brigadier general in the Air Force. Following a short stint at Randolph Air Force Base in Texas, she became director of maintenance at U.S. Air Force Headquarters, Washington, D.C., in September of 1994. On May 25, 1995, Harris became the first African American female to be promoted to the rank of major general. Her promotion not only made her the highest-ranking African American woman in the Air Force, but in the Department of Defense as a whole. In her role as director of maintenance and deputy chief of staff, logistics, she was accountable for the maintenance operations of every Air Force installation, commanding a workforce of more than 125,000 and maintaining an aerospace weapons system inventory worth more than $260 billion. Harris retired from the U.S. Air Force on February 22, 1997.

Upon retirement from the Air Force, Harris settled in Merritt Island, Florida, and joined aerospace industry firm United Space Alliance as Florida site director. Currently, she also serves on the Advisory Committee on Women Veterans, a special 14-member panel that advises the Secretary of Veterans Affairs.

Among the decorations awarded to Harris during her 31-year career are a Legion of Merit with oak leaf cluster, a Bronze Star, a Meritorious Service Medal with three oak leaf clusters, an Air Force Commendation Medal with oak leaf cluster, a Presidential Unit Citation, an Air Force Outstanding Unit Award with "V" device with eight oak leaf clusters, a National Defense Service Medal with oak leaf cluster, and a Vietnam Service Medal with three oak leaf clusters. Among her many civilian honors are *Dollars and Sense* magazine's Most Prestigious Individual (1991), Journal Recording Publishing Co.'s Woman of Enterprise (1992), the National Federation of Black Women Business Owners' Black Woman of Courage (1995), the Ellis Island Medal of Honor (1996), the Women's International Center's Living Legacy Patriot Award (1998) and the University of Maryland University College's Distinguished Alumna Award (2000).

General Daniel James Jr. (1920–1978)
First African American Four-Star General, U.S. Air Force

Daniel James Jr. was born on February 11, 1920, in Pensacola, Florida. The youngest boy in a large family, he grew up in a home with strict parents who stressed education, hard work, and honesty as means to success. At an early age, James borrowed the nickname "Chappie" from an older brother, a star athlete whom he idolized. James was educated in the private school run by his mother until secondary school age, when he attended Washington High. At Tuskegee (Alabama) Institute, James worked for the college in exchange for credit hours. A physical education major, he was expelled for fighting just two months before he would have graduated in 1941.

During his senior year of college, James enrolled in the Civilian Pilot Training Program. Indirectly sponsored by the War Department, the program operated at six African American colleges to train African American pilots under segregated conditions. James quickly earned his pilot's license and proved himself among the more capable flyers. Upon expulsion from college, he was hired to train the first class of cadets selected for the "Tuskegee Experiment"; among that first class of flyers was Benjamin O. Davis Jr., who would become the first African American Air Force general. Captivated by flying, James turned his attention away from academics to focus on becoming an Air Force officer. He applied for the Aviation Cadet Program and was accepted in January of 1943. Graduating in July of that year, James was commissioned a second lieutenant in the U.S. Air Force. He was then assigned to the 617th Bombardment Squadron, 477th Bombardment Group at Selfridge Field, Michigan, for combat training on B-25 bombers. During World War II, however, racially-motivated bureaucratic waffling kept most African American pilots from being assigned overseas, and James never left the United States.

In the fall of 1949, James received his first overseas assignment. He became flight leader of the 12th Fighter Bomber Squadron, 18th Fighter Wing at Clark Air Force Base in the Philippines. During the Korean War, the 12th was based in Japan and Korea. Usually in F-51 Mustangs, James flew 101 combat missions during the war, most during the early days of the conflict. One such mission, in support of United Nations ground forces, resulted in James being awarded a Distinguished Flying Cross. Leading four bombers through heavy enemy fire and low visibility on October 15, 1950, James was credited with personally killing more than 100 enemy troops.

Following Korea, James was assigned to a base near Rome, New York, where a racist commanding officer boasted he would rid the unit of the African American flyer. Despite the forced integration of the military, which had begun several years earlier, racism still played a major role in duty assignments at the time. Subsequently, James was reassigned to Otis Air Force Base on Cape Cod, Massachusetts. Among his assignments at Otis, James was given command of the all-white 437th Fighter Interceptor Squadron in the Air Defense Command in April of 1953. His loyal and supportive leadership style, as well as his insistence on excellence, earned his mens' allegiance and his superiors' respect. In 1957, he graduated from the Air Command and Staff College at Maxwell Air Force Base in Alabama. His next assignment was at the Pentagon in the Air Defense Division, a job he admitted not particularly enjoying though he understood the importance of it.

James spent the early 1960s at the Royal Air Force Base at Bentwaters, England, where he held three assignments with the 81st Fighter Wing. He returned to the U.S. in the fall of 1964 and held several command positions at Davis-Monthan Air Force Base in Arizona, during which time he was promoted to colonel. In 1966, during the early stages of the Vietnam War, James was assigned to the 8th Tactical Fighter Wing at Thailand's Ubon Royal Thai Air Force Base. He flew 78 missions over Vietnam in F-4C Phantom jets as deputy commander for operations, then vice commander, of the unit, popularly known as the "Wolf Pack." His next assignment brought him just 50 miles from his hometown to Florida's Eglin Air Force Base. After Eglin, he was sent out of the country once again, assuming command of the 7272nd Fighter Training Wing at Wheelus Air Base in Libya. His stay there was shortened, however, when Colonel Moammar Khadafy deposed King Idris and pushed for the closing of the base. Despite James' objections, the U.S. Embassy in Libya decided to shut Wheelus down. James then distinguished himself by overseeing an orderly removal of U.S. personnel and equipment from the base.

Upon his return to the U.S., James was quickly promoted through the upper echelons of the U.S. Air Force. On March 31, 1970, he was sworn in as a deputy assistant of defense for public affairs by Secretary of Defense Melvin R. Laird. James quickly became a much-in-demand speaker and the Pentagon eagerly used his talents by sending him around the country to make speeches in support of military policies. James was rewarded for his willingness to appear before the public, especially since some of that public used his appearances as a venue to demonstrate against the Vietnam War. He was promoted to brigadier general that summer and his rise through the general ranks proved exceedingly swift. He was made a major general on August 1, 1972, and less than a year later, on June 1, 1973, he was elevated to lieutenant general.

James left the Pentagon in August of 1974 and became vice commander of Military Airlift Command the next month. James earned his final promotion on August 29, 1975, when he became the first African American to become a four-star general. The next day he took command of the North American Air Defense Command (NORAD), the bi-national defense force of 65,000 servicemen assigned the task of protecting the United States and Canada from surprise nuclear attack, and NORAD's American subunit, the U.S. Air Force Aerospace Defense Command, both of which are headquartered at Colorado Springs, Colorado. In September of 1977, James suffered a heart attack. After 35 years of service, he retired from the U.S. Air Force on January 26, 1978. One month later, on February 25, 1978, he suffered a second, fatal heart attack. James was buried with highest military honors at Arlington National Cemetery, in Arlington, Virginia.

One of the most highly-decorated servicemen in Air Force history, among the awards James received were a Distinguished Service Medal with oak leaf cluster, a Legion of Merit with oak leaf cluster, a Distinguished Flying Cross with two oak leaf clusters, a Meritorious Service Medal, an Air Medal with 13 oak leaf clusters, an American Defense Service Medal, an American Campaign Medal, a World War II Victory Medal, a Korean Service Medal with four service stars, and a Vietnam Service Medal with four service stars. James received awards from an astounding number of civilian organizations including the Arnold Air Society, the Phoenix Urban League, Kappa Alpha Psi Fraternity, the American Legion, the Veterans of Foreign Wars, the Capital Press Club, and the United Negro College Fund, to name a few. He also received honorary degrees from the University of West Florida, the University of Akron,

Virginia State College, Delaware State College, and St. Louis University.

General Hazel W. Johnson-Brown (1927–)
First Female African American Brigadier General, U.S. Army

Hazel Winifred Johnson was born on October 10, 1927, in West Chester, Pennsylvania. She grew up on a farm near Malvern in Chester County and attended high school in nearby Berwyn. She received her registered nurse diploma in New York City at Harlem Hospital's School of Nursing in 1950 and enlisted in the U.S. Army Nurse Corps in 1955. Johnson used civilian educational opportunities to rapidly advance through the ranks of the nurse corps. She earned a bachelor's degree in nursing from Villanova University in 1959, and was commissioned a second lieutenant by direct appointment on May 11, 1960. Three years later she earned a master's degree in nursing education from Teachers College, Columbia University in New York City.

Johnson was a staff member of the U.S. Medical Research and Development Command in Washington,

Hazel W. Johnson, the first African American woman to become a brigadier general.

D.C., from 1967 to 1973, and dean of the Walter Reed Army Institute of Nursing at the famed Walter Reed Army Medical Center also in Washington, D.C., from 1976 to 1978. She earned a Ph.D. in educational administration from Catholic University of America in 1978 before a brief assignment as chief nurse with the U.S. Army Medical Command in Korea. On September 1, 1979, Johnson became the first African American female in U.S. military history to advance to the rank of brigadier general. At that time, she was also made chief of the Army Nurse Corps, Office of the Surgeon General in Washington, D.C. She held that post until August 31, 1983, when she retired from the U.S. Army.

Johnson-Brown served as director of the government affairs division of the American Nursing Association from 1983 until 1986, when she joined the faculty of Virginia's George Mason University as a professor of nursing. She is now Professor Emerita of Nursing at that institution, where she chairs the college's Board of Advisors and advises doctoral candidates. Currently, she is serving as a member of the Villanova University Board of Trustees. Among her military decorations are a Distinguished Service Medal, a Legion of Merit, a Meritorious Service Medal, and an Army Commendation Medal with oak leaf cluster. In 1997, Johnson-Brown received an honorary degree from Long Island University's Brooklyn Campus.

Sergeant Henry Johnson (1897?–1929)
369th Infantry Regiment, 93rd Division, U.S. Army

Henry Johnson was born around 1897 in Winston-Salem, North Carolina, and grew up in Albany, New York. Upon America's entrance into World War I, Johnson enlisted in the Army on June 5, 1917. He was mustered into Company C, 15th National Guard of New York (later renamed the 369th Infantry Regiment) as a private on July 25. The unit received its training at Camp Wadsworth in Spartanburg, South Carolina.

The 369th landed in Brest, France on January 1, 1918. In March, the 369th was attached to the 16th Division of the French Army, making it the first African American unit to reach the war zone. According to his muster roll, Johnson was promoted to the rank of sergeant on May 1. Several days later, U.S. troops captured a German-held bridge near the Aisne River, and Johnson's unit was assigned to guard it. In the early morning hours of May 14, a force of about 32 Germans tried to retake the bridge. Johnson and fellow soldier Needham Roberts were on sentry duty at the time, armed with pistols and a few hand grenades. The two groups exchanged fire, and Johnson was wounded three times, while Roberts was injured twice. After the pair ran out of ammunition, the Germans rushed them,

capturing Roberts. Johnson pulled a bolo knife and, along with the butt of his pistol, fought hand-to-hand, rescuing his badly wounded compatriot. The startled Germans retreated, preventing them from launching a surprise attack that would likely have inflicted heavy casualties on the regiment. When the skirmish was over, Johnson was credited with killing at least four Germans and wounding ten or more others.

Johnson was hospitalized for several weeks with serious wounds to his back, left arm, face and feet, most of which were inflicted by knives or bayonets. For his heroics, the government of France awarded him a Croix de Guerre with gold leaf, while Roberts also received a Croix de Guerre. In the process, they became the first two Americans to receive the French medal for individual heroism in combat. Johnson was cited by the French as a "magnificent example of courage and energy." The U.S. Army did not award Johnson any decoration for his part in the incident— not even a purple heart.

Despite his injuries, Johnson received no disability allowance when he was discharged from the Army on February 14, 1919. On his return to Albany he received a hero's welcome. New York Governor Alfred E. Smith and other state officials greeted Johnson's arrival at the Albany train station with a homecoming reception. For a while after the war, Johnson's celebrity allowed him to tour the country promoting the sale of Liberty Bonds. Afterwards, his injuries proved too disabling, however, for him to return to regular work. Johnson died in poverty at Walter Reed Army Hospital in Washington, D.C., on July 2, 1929. He was buried with full military honors in Arlington National Cemetery in Arlington, Virginia.

Doris (Dorie) Miller (1919–1943)
Mess Attendant, First Class, U.S. Navy

The son of sharecroppers, Doris Miller was born on a farm near Waco, Texas, on October 12, 1919. Working in the fields with his parents, Miller grew into a solidly-built young man. He went on to become a star fullback on the football team at Waco's Moore High School. At 19 years of age, Miller enlisted in the U.S. Navy as a messman, the only job open to African American naval recruits at the time.

Assigned to the battleship *USS West Virginia*, Mess Attendant Second-Class Miller was nearing the end of his first hitch when, on December 7, 1941, he was thrust into one of the most important events in U.S. history: Japan's surprise attack on the U.S. naval base at Pearl Harbor on Oahu Island, Hawaii. At 7:55 a.m. on that typically quiet Sunday morning, Miller was below deck collecting laundry. Suddenly, the crew heard a midship

Dorie Miller.

explosion. The blast knocked Miller down. Sirens soon called the crew to their battle stations. Miller arrived on deck to witness Japanese planes in full attack on the U.S. Pacific Fleet. Bombing runs were supplemented by machine-gun fire as Japanese aircraft swooped down on virtually undefended ships. In the confusion, sailors ran in all directions, many of them jumping overboard to avoid strafing runs by the enemy flyers. Amid walls of smoke and flame, Miller made his way to his assigned post on the signal bridge. When he arrived, Miller found the ship's commander lying on deck, bleeding from his stomach and chest. He dragged the mortally-wounded officer out of direct fire to a place where a medic and other sailors attempted to treat him. Miller then fought his way back to the bridge, where he spotted an unmanned machine gun. Without any prior weaponry training, Miller started firing the anti-aircraft gun. He brought down four Japanese planes before exhausting the gun's ammunition and being ordered to abandon the sinking ship. For his heroism, Miller was awarded the Navy Cross, which was conferred on him by the commander in chief of the Pacific Fleet, Admiral Chester W. Nimitz. Miller was commended for "distinguished

devotion to duty, extreme courage, and disregard of his personal safety during attack." He also received a Purple Heart and was subsequently promoted to mess attendant first class.

Miller became the first African American hero of the war and traveled around the nation to promote the sale of war bonds. After that tour of duty ended, he was sent to Bremerton, Washington, to qualify as a cook. Though he had shown enormous ability as a gunner, navy policy still restricted African Americans to the Stewards Branch. Miller later served as a mess attendant on the light aircraft carrier *USS Liscombe Bay*. A Japanese submarine torpedoed the vessel on November 24, 1943. The resulting explosion killed most of the crew including Miller before the vessel sank in the South Pacific.

After the war, legislation was introduced on two occasions to posthumously award Miller the Congressional Medal of Honor for his Pearl Harbor heroics, but it was defeated both times. Nevertheless, the Navy honored Miller in succeeding years by naming several things after him, most notably, the destroyer escort *USS Miller*, which was christened in 1973. In so doing, the Navy made Miller the first African American enlisted man to have a ship named after him.

General Frank E. Petersen (1932–)
First African American General in the U.S. Marine Corps

Frank Emmanuel Petersen Jr. was born March 2, 1932, in Topeka, Kansas, where he attended public schools and graduated from Topeka High School in 1949. He attended Topeka's Washburn University for a year before dropping out to enlist in the U.S. Navy Reserve in June of 1950 as an apprentice seaman, serving as an electronics technician. While attending the Navy's electronics school, he applied for admission to the Naval Aviation Cadet Program. He was accepted and, while in flight training at the U.S. Naval Air Station in Pensacola, Florida, applied for a commission in the U.S. Marine Corps. Petersen earned his wings and accepted a second lieutenant's commission in the Corps on October 22, 1952, becoming the branch's first African American aviator.

Petersen received further training at the Marine Corps Air Station El Toro in Santa Ana, California, before being sent to Korea in 1953. Petersen flew a total of 64 combat missions during the latter stages of the Korean War, building a reputation as a superb fighter pilot. In July of 1954, he returned to the Marine Corps' Santa Ana, California facility, where he remained until January of 1960. In February of 1955, Petersen formally transferred from the U.S. Navy Reserve to the U.S. Marine Corps. During the 1960s and 1970s, Petersen took advantage of many civilian and military educational opportunities. He twice attended George Washington University, where he earned a B.S. in 1967 and an M.S. in 1973. He also attended several service schools including the Marine Corps Amphibious Assault School, the Aviation Safety Officers' Course, and the National War College. Petersen has the distinction of being the first African American corpsman to attend the latter school.

At the height of the Vietnam War, Petersen became the first African American officer to command a squadron in the U.S. Navy or Marine Corps. In June of 1968, he took command of VMF-314, Marine Aircraft Group 13, Republic of Vietnam. The unit, popularly known as the "Black Knights," excelled with Petersen as commander, being named the most outstanding fighter squadron in the entire Marine Corps during the year he was in charge. Petersen also was a fighter pilot and flew more than 200 missions in F-4 Phantom jets.

Earlier in the 1960s, during a short stay at the Marine Corps Air Station in Iwakuri, Japan, Petersen took on the role of "race counselor" to calm the racial tensions existing not only between black and white Marines, but between white Americans and the native Japanese. After Vietnam, he performed a similar function, only on a much larger scale, as special assistant for minority affairs to the Marine commandant. In this role Petersen traveled to Germany and Japan to investigate racial conditions among corps members. His straightforward report nearly destroyed his career when senior officers would not accept its damning contents. Events occurring in the U.S. at large, however, lent credence to his findings, and the Corps soon adopted changes.

Petersen became the first African American to reach the rank of brigadier general in the U.S. Marine Corps in February of 1979. While assigned to Marine Corps headquarters in Washington, D.C., during the early to mid-1980s, promotions to major general and lieutenant general followed. Starting in 1985, Petersen served as senior ranking pilot in the U.S. Navy and U.S. Marine Corps, and was the senior pilot of the entire U.S. Armed Forces from 1986 until his retirement on August 1, 1988. In all, he flew more than 350 combat missions covering 4,000 hours in the air.

In 1989, Petersen became vice president, Corporate Aviation at DuPont Denemours, Inc., where he remained for a decade before becoming an independent corporate consultant. Petersen's affiliations with boards and organizations are numerous. Among them are the Tuskegee Airmen, the National Marrow Donor Foundation (for which he served as board chair from 1998–2000), the National Aviation Research and Education Foundation, the Higher Education Assistance Foundation, Opportunity Skyway, the Institute for the Study of

American Wars, the Montford Point Marines, the Educational Credit Management Corporation, and Business Executives for National Security. Petersen is also a frequent public speaker and lecturer. In 1998, *Into the Tiger's Jaw: America's First Black Marine Aviator*, Petersen's autobiography (written with assistance from J. Alfred Phelps) was published. The father of five children, he is divorced from their mother, Eleanor Petersen. He currently lives in Stevenville, Maryland.

Petersen is a recipient of more than 20 individual medals for combat valor, including a Distinguished Flying Cross, an Air Medal with silver star, a Meritorious Service Medal, a Legion of Merit with Combat V, a Navy Commendation Medal with Combat V, a National Defense Service Medal with bronze star, an Air Force Commendation Medal, and a Purple Heart.

General Colin L. Powell (1937–)
First African American Chairman of the Joint Chiefs of Staff

Colin Luther Powell was born in New York City on April 5, 1937, and graduated from Morris High School in the South Bronx in 1954. In 1958, he received a B.S. in geology from City College of New York, where he was very active in the ROTC program, from which he graduated first in his class. He also attained the highest ROTC rank of cadet colonel.

On June 9, 1958, Powell was commissioned a second lieutenant in the U.S. Army. He attended Infantry Officers Basic Training, as well as the Airborne and Ranger schools at Fort Benning, Georgia, before receiving his first regular duty assignment. In 1959, he went to West Germany, where he was a platoon leader, executive officer, and a rifle company commander during his three-year stay. In 1962, he was assigned as a military advisor to a South Vietnamese infantry battalion. In the second year of that tour he was wounded by a Vietcong booby trap and was awarded a Purple Heart. Powell returned to Vietnam in 1968 as an infantry officer, serving in such capacities as battalion executive officer and division operations officer. That tour ended prematurely when he was injured in a helicopter crash, in which he rescued two fellow soldiers from the burning wreckage.

Returning to the United States, Powell enrolled in the M.B.A. program at George Washington University and graduated in 1971. In 1972, he was named a White House fellow and served as assistant to the deputy director of the Office of Management and Budget. From

1973 to 1975, he commanded the 1st Battalion, 32nd Infantry in South Korea. Powell was already receiving relatively high-profile assignments before graduating from the National War College in June of 1976, but from that point on his career accelerated. He next commanded the 2nd Brigade, 101st Airborne Division (Air Assault) at Fort Campbell, Kentucky from 1976 to 1977. Several appointments in Washington, D.C., followed. He was executive to the special assistant to the secretary and deputy secretary of defense starting in 1977, executive assistant to the secretary of energy for several months in 1979 and senior military assistant to the deputy secretary of defense later that year. Powell he was promoted to brigadier general on June 1 of that same year.

Powell served as assistant commander of the 4th Infantry Division at Fort Carson, Colorado, from 1981 to 1983. He then returned to the nation's capital as senior military adviser to the secretary of defense from 1983 to 1985. Powell went back to West Germany in 1986 to become commanding general of the U.S. V Corps. In 1987, he returned to Washington, D.C., first as deputy to the national security adviser, then as national security adviser himself. In April of 1989, he was promoted to four-star general. In August of that year, Powell was named chairman of the Joint Chiefs of Staff, the highest military post in the United States. Powell not only became the first African American in U.S. Armed Forces history to hold that title, but also the youngest. From that position, Powell received international recognition as one of the chief architects of the successful 1989 assault on Panamanian dictator Manuel Noriega and the 1991 Persian Gulf War against Iraq. Both military actions achieved swift and thorough victories with minimal U.S. casualties, while arousing little opposition domestically. Powell retired from the U.S. Army on September 30, 1993.

The public acclaim Powell received for those one-sided military victories opened to him the possibility of a future in nationally-elected political office. Powell wrote his memoir *My American Journey* and embarked on a nationwide tour to promote the book in 1995. During the tour, there was widespread speculation that he would seek the nomination for president the next year. On November 9, 1995, however, Powell held a press conference to announce that he would not enter the presidential race. The decision not to seek the office surprised many who considered Powell a strong potential candidate.

Shying away from the political arena, Powell turned his attention to public-service activities. In 1996, he was named to the board of trustees at Howard University. Then, in April 1997, in a move that stunned many,

Powell helped found America's Promise—The Alliance for Youth, becoming its very hands-on chairman. The Arlington, Virginia-based nonprofit organization works to improve the lives of at-risk youths by increasing their employability. After some initial difficulties, Powell was able to get the organization running smoothly and able to fulfill its own promise.

Powell stepped back into the national spotlight on July 31, 2000, when he delivered a keynote address at the Republican National Convention in Philadelphia. In what was considered a highlight of the convention, Powell endorsed Republican presidential candidate George W. Bush, saying that he believed the candidate "can help bridge our racial divides." Later that year, on December 16, 2000, President-elect George W. Bush nominated Powell to become the 65th Secretary of State. Following a unanimous confirmation by the U.S. Senate, Powell was sworn in on January 20, 2001. He is the first African American to hold that post. As secretary of state, he has been constantly visible, especially in relation to the United States' continuing War on Terrorism, which began in September 2001. Powell is married to the former Alma Vivian Johnson of Birmingham, Alabama. Their family includes son Michael, daughters Linda and Annemarie, daughter-in-law Jane, and grandsons Jeffrey and Bryan.

During his tenure in the military, Powell was the recipient of numerous decorations, including a Purple Heart, a Bronze Star, a Legion of Merit with oak leaf cluster, a Soldier's Medal, an Air Medal, a Distinguished Service Medal, a Defense Superior Service Medal, a Joint Service Commendation Medal, and an Army Commendation Medal. He has received many civilian honors as well, including two Presidential Medals of Freedom, the President's Citizens Medal, the Congressional Gold Medal, the Secretary of State Distinguished Service Medal, the Secretary of Energy Distinguished Service Medal, and the Ronald Reagan Freedom Award. Powell has also been the recipient of honorary degrees from universities and colleges from across the nation and several schools and other institutions have been named in his honor.

Admiral J. Paul Reason (1943–)
First African American Four-Star Admiral, U.S. Navy

Joseph Paul Reason was born on March 22, 1943, in Washington, D.C., where he attended primary and secondary school. After high school, he attended Howard

J. Paul Reason.

officer. From there, he became an assignment officer at the Bureau of Naval Personnel. In late 1976, Reason was named naval aide to the White House for the Gerald Ford administration, a position he kept after Jimmy Carter assumed the presidency in January of 1977. In 1979, he was assigned to the *USS Mississippi* as the ship's executive officer. After a six-year stay aboard that ship, Reason was given command of his own ship, the *USS Coontz*, in 1985. Shortly afterward, he became commander of a nuclear-powered guided missile cruiser, the *USS Bainbridge.*

From 1986 to 1988, Reason was commander of Naval Base Seattle, where he was responsible for all naval activities in Oregon, Washington, and Alaska. His next assignment put him in command of Cruiser-Destroyer Group One, which he led from 1988 to 1994. During that time, he also commanded Battle Group Romeo through operations in the Pacific and Indian Oceans, as well as in the Persian Gulf. Reason was promoted to vice admiral in early 1994 and put in charge of the Naval Surface Force of the U.S. Atlantic Fleet. In August of that year, he was made deputy chief of naval operations for plans, policy, and operations, a post he held for two years.

In May 1996, President Bill Clinton nominated Reason for a promotion and assignment as commander in chief of the U.S. Atlantic Fleet, based in Norfolk, Virginia. His promotion in December of 1996 made him the U.S. Navy's first African American four-star admiral. As chief of the Atlantic fleet, Reason commanded roughly half of the U.S. Navy, or more than 124,000 service personnel. He oversaw an annual budget of $19.5 billion and the operations of 195 warships and 1,357 aircraft based at 18 major shore facilities. Reason retired from active duty in November 1999.

Following his retirement from the military, Reason became President and Chief Operating Officer of Metro Machine Corporation of Norfolk, Virginia. In January 2000, he joined the NASA's Aerospace Safety Advisory Panel as a consultant. Currently, Reason is on the board of directors of Norfolk Southern, Amgen Inc. and Wal-Mart Stores, Inc. He is married to Dianne F. Reason.

Among Reason's many military decorations are a Distinguished Service Medal, a Legion of Merit, a Navy Commendation Medal, a Venezuelan LaMedalla Naval Almirante Luis Brion Medal a National Defense Service Medal, an Armed Forces Expeditionary Medal, a Republic of Vietnam Honor Medal, an Armed Forces Expeditionary Medal, a Vietnam Service Medal, a Sea Service Deployment Ribbon, and a Republic of Vietnam Campaign Medal. In 1998, Reason was among those honored for Dominion's Strong Men and Women: Excellence in Leadership series.

University for three years before receiving nomination to the U.S. Naval Academy from Michigan Congressman Charles Diggs.

While at the Naval Academy, Reason applied to the Navy's nuclear propulsion program, run by Vice Admiral Hyman G. Rickover, "father" of the nuclear submarine. Rickover interviewed Reason and accepted him into the program. Rickover, the first Jewish admiral, took a special interest in Reason as an officer, monitoring Reason's progress from behind the scenes and ensuring that he received fair treatment during his career. Reason's initial assignment was on the destroyer escort *USS J.D. Blackwood*, but after completing the nuclear propulsion program in 1968, he transferred to the nuclear-powered missile cruiser *USS Truxtun*. In 1970, he earned a master's degree in computer systems management.

In 1971, Reason began a four-year stint on the nuclear-powered aircraft carrier *USS Enterprise*, during which he was twice deployed to the Southeast Asia/Indian Ocean region during the Vietnam War. He rejoined the *USS Truxtun* in 1975 as the combat systems

Roscoe Robinson Jr. was the first African American 4-star general in the U.S. Army.

General Roscoe Robinson Jr. (1928–1993)
First African American Four Star General, U.S. Army

Roscoe Robinson Jr. was born on October 28, 1928, in St. Louis, Missouri, where he graduated from Charles Sumner High School. He received an appointment to the U.S. Military Academy at West Point, New York and graduated with a B.S. in military engineering in 1951.

On June 1, 1951, Robinson was commissioned a second lieutenant in the U.S. Army. He attended the Associate Infantry Officer Course and the Basic Airborne Course at Fort Benning, Georgia, before joining the 11th Airborne Division at Fort Campbell, Kentucky. In October of 1952, he was assigned to the 31st Infantry Regiment, 7th Infantry Division in Korea. During the Korean War, his unit saw combat action and Robinson received a bronze star for bravery as commander of a rifle company. Among his assignments in the late 1950s was a tour with the U.S. military mission to Liberia.

From 1965 to 1967, Robinson was the personnel management officer of the Infantry Branch, Officer Personnel Directorate, Office of Personnel Operations, U.S. Army, in Washington, D.C. Starting in 1968, Robinson commanded the Second Battalion, Seventh Cavalry, the historic African American unit that was part of the regular Army in 1866 as Company B, Seventh Cavalry. The unit, part of the First Cavalry Division (Airmobile), U.S. Army Pacific, Vietnam, engaged in fighting during the war with Robinson being awarded a silver star for valor. In the early 1970s, Robinson served with the U.S. Pacific Command in Hawaii, including executive to the chief of staff.

In addition to battlefield heroics, Robinson helped his career by expanding his education. He earned a master's degree in international affairs from the University of Pittsburgh and received further military training at the U.S. Army Command and General Staff College at Fort Leavenworth, Kansas, and at the National War College in Washington, D.C.

In 1972, Robinson became commanding officer of the 2nd Brigade, 82nd Airborne Division at Fort Bragg, North Carolina. He was promoted to the rank of brigadier general on July 1, 1973, and was made deputy commander of the U.S. Army Garrison, Okinawa Base Command. Robinson became a two-star general on July 1, 1976, and, in November of that year, returned to Fort Bragg to become commanding general of the 82nd Airborne Division. In 1978, he was made deputy chief of staff for operations, U.S. Army Europe and the Seventh Army. On June 1, 1980, he was promoted to lieutenant general and became commanding general of the U.S. Army, Japan IX Corps. Robinson became the first African American four-star general in the history of the U.S. Army and the second in the U.S. Armed Forces on August 30, 1982. From 1982 to 1985, he served as the United States representative to the North Atlantic Treaty Organization, becoming the nation's first African American to serve in that capacity. Robinson retired from active military service in 1985.

After his retirement from the Army, Robinson served on the boards of several companies including Comsat, Giant Food, Metropolitan Life, and the parent company of Northwest Airlines. In 1987, he was named to oversee the work of a panel designated with the task of reviewing the Korean War performance records of certain African American Army units that had been criticized at the time. On July 22, 1993, Robinson died of leukemia at the Walter Reed Army Medical Center in Washington, D.C. He is buried in Arlington National Cemetery in Arlington, Virginia.

During his 34-year career, Robinson was the recipient of numerous military awards including a Silver Star with oak leaf cluster, a Legion of Merit with two oak leaf clusters, a Distinguished Flying Cross, a Bronze Star, ten Air Medals, a Defense Distinguished Service Medal, and an Army Commendation Medal.

Roderick K. von Lipsey (1959–)
Fighter Pilot, U.S. Marine Corps

Roderick K. von Lipsey was born on January 13, 1959, in Philadelphia, Pennsylvania. Beginning in third grade, he was educated in private schools, first at Norwood Academy, then at La Salle College High School, where he graduated in 1976. He attended the U.S. Naval Academy in Annapolis, Maryland, majoring in English literature. Upon graduation, von Lipsey joined the U.S. Marine Corps and was commissioned a second lieutenant in May of 1980.

In January of 1981, after completing basic Marine Corps training, von Lipsey went to Pensacola, Florida, and Kingsville, Texas, to master aircraft that would earn him the "naval aviator" designation. Then, starting in September of 1982, he spent an additional six months at the Marine Corps base at Yuma, Arizona, to become combat ready on the F-4 Phantom fighter jet.

In 1983, von Lipsey was assigned to Fort Beaufort, South Carolina, to gain experience in aircraft maintenance and maintenance quality assurance. The following year, he became the officer in charge of aircraft maintenance for F-4 Phantoms at the base. Von Lipsey began training on the F/A-18 Hornet fighter jet in 1985. In 1986, he was deployed to NATO exercises in Europe and the Mediterranean, for which he was awarded a Navy Commendation medal for his performance of logistics responsibilities. In January of 1987, von Lipsey was sent to the prestigious Navy Fighter Weapons School at Naval Station Miramar in California. Informally known as TOPGUN, the grueling six-week training program hones the technique of experienced fighter pilots and teaches them how to use newly-developed skills to instruct others. In 1989, von Lipsey was stationed at the Marine Fighter Attack Squadron at Kaneohe Bay, Hawaii. Also in 1989, he completed work on a master of arts degree in international affairs from Catholic University.

On August 2, 1990, Iraq invaded Kuwait. Von Lipsey was quickly sent to Saudi Arabia to take part in Operation Desert Shield, a measure designed to prevent further Iraqi aggression. While in the Middle East, von Lipsey joined Marine Fighter/Attack Squadron 235. On January 20, 1991, at the start of Operation Desert Storm against Iraqi forces in Kuwait, von Lipsey led an attack of 35 aircraft from the Third Marine Aircraft Wing. The daring 600-mile journey to a secret air base in eastern Iraq resulted in the demolition of the base's maintenance and repair hangars, as well as the network of railroad tracks that were its supply lines. All of the planes under von Lipsey's command returned safely. For his meritorious service in the execution of this highly successful mission, he was awarded the Distinguished Flying Cross. That attack was just one of more than 40 sorties flown by von Lipsey during the Gulf War.

Following his return from the Middle East in 1991, von Lipsey was chosen as one of two aides-de-camp to Chairman of the Joint Chiefs of Staff General Colin L. Powell. Initially the junior aide, and later the senior, von Lipsey helped orchestrate the general's busy travel schedule, which included trips to such countries as Belgium, Czechoslovakia, Hungary, Jamaica, Poland, and Somalia. He remained in that assignment until 1993, when he was awarded a White House fellowship, serving as a special assistant in the areas of foreign and security policy to White House Chief of Staff Thomas F. McLarty III. Often traveling on Air Force One as a member of President Clinton's entourage, von Lipsey provided national security updates and background information for McLarty at high-level meetings with foreign political leaders. Von Lipsey was awarded a second fellowship in 1994 with the Council on Foreign Relations. In December of that year, von Lipsey was honored by *Time* magazine as one of America's most promising leaders under 40 years of age in a special report titled "Fifty for the Future."

When the fellowship ended in mid-1995, von Lipsey was assigned to Marine Corps Air Squadron El Toro, based in Santa Ana, California. He received a promotion to lieutenant colonel shortly afterward. In 1997, he edited and contributed to the book *Breaking the Cycle: A Framework for Conflict Resolution*, which presented new ways of dealing with countries plagued by violent, intergroup disputes. That same year, von Lipsey was selected by the Rockefeller Foundation for its first cohort (1997–1999) of Next Generation Leadership Fellows. Also in 1997, he became Planning Officer at Marine Corps Headquarters, then in 1998 he was assigned to the National Security Council as Director for Defense Policy and Arms Control. He remained in that post through 1999, when he retired from the U.S. Marine Corps after 20 years of service.

In 2000, von Lipsey was named Vice President and Chief Operating Officer, Investment Management Services at Goldman, Sachs Private Wealth Management, Washington, D.C. He is on the board of directors of the Atlantic Council of the United States, Aspen Institute Berlin, Public Allies, and New York City Outward Bound Center. He is also a member of the Council on Foreign Relations, the International Institute for Strategic Studies and the Distinguished Flying Cross Society. Von

Lipsey resides in both Northern Virginia and New York with his wife, Professor Kori N. Schake of the National Defense University, Institute for National Security Studies.

In addition to the Distinguished Flying Cross with Combat V, von Lipsey has received a Defense Meritorious Service Medal, a Single Mission Air Medal with Combat V, a Strike/Flight Air Medal with Numeral 4, a Joint Service Commendation Medal, and two Navy Commendation Medals.

◆ AFRICAN AMERICAN MEDAL OF HONOR RECIPIENTS

Civil War

Army

William H. Barnes, Private, Company C, 38th U.S. Colored Troops

Powhatan Beaty, First Sergeant, Company G, 5th U.S. Colored Troops

James H. Bronson, First Sergeant, Company D, 5th U.S. Colored Troops

William H. Carney, Sergeant, Company C, 54th Massachusetts Infantry, U.S. Colored Troops

Decatur Dorsey, Sergeant, Company B, 39th U.S. Colored Troops

Christian A. Fleetwood, Sergeant Major, 4th U.S. Colored Troops

James Gardiner, Private, Company 1, 36th U.S. Colored Troops

James H. Harris, Sergeant, Company B, 38th U.S. Colored Troops

Thomas R. Hawkins, Sergeant Major, 6th U.S. Colored Troops

Alfred B. Hilton, Sergeant, Company H, 4th U.S. Colored Troops

Milton M. Holland, Sergeant, 5th U.S. Colored Troops

Alexander Kelly, First Sergeant, Company F, 6th U.S. Colored Troops

Robert Pinn, First Sergeant, Company I, 5th U.S. Colored Troops

Edward Radcliff, First Sergeant, Company C, 38th U.S. Colored Troops

Charles Veal, Private, Company D, 4th U.S. Colored Troops

Navy

Aaron Anderson, Landsman, *USS Wyandank*

Robert Blake, Powder Boy, *USS Marblehead*

William H. Brown, Landsman, *USS Brooklyn*

Wilson Brown, *USS Hartford*

John Lawson, Landsman, *USS Hartford*

James Mifflin, Engineer's Cook, *USS Brooklyn*

Joachim Pease, Seaman, *USS Kearsarge*

Interim Period

Navy

Daniel Atkins, Ship's Cook, First Class, *USS Cushing*

John Davis, Seaman, *USS Trenton*

Alphonse Girandy, Seaman, *USS Tetrel*

John Johnson, Seaman, *USS Kansas*

William Johnson, Cooper, *USS Adams*

Joseph B. Noil, Seaman, *USS Powhatan*

John Smith, Seaman, *USS Shenandoah*

Robert Sweeney, Seaman, *USS Kearsage, USS Jamestown*

Western Campaigns

Army

Thomas Boyne, Sergeant, Troop C, 9th U.S. Cavalry

Benjamin Brown, Sergeant, Company C, 24th U.S. Infantry

John Denny, Sergeant, Troop C, 9th U.S. Cavalry

Pompey Factor, Seminole Negro Indian Scouts

Clinton Greaves, Corporal, Troop C, 9th U.S. Cavalry

Henry Johnson, Sergeant, Troop D, 9th U.S. Cavalry

George Jordan, Sergeant, Troop K, 9th U.S. Cavalry

William McBreyar, Sergeant, Troop K, 10th U.S. Cavalry

Isaiah Mays, Corporal, Company B, 24th U.S. Infantry

Issac Payne, Private (Trumpeteer) Seminole Negro Indian Scouts

Thomas Shaw, Sergeant, Troop K, 9th U.S. Cavalry

Emanuel Stance, Sergeant, Troop F, 9th U.S. Cavalry

Augustus Walley, Private, Troop 1, 9th U.S. Cavalry

John Ward, Sergeant, Seminole Negro Indian Scouts

Moses Williams, First Sergeant, Troop 1, 9th U.S. Cavalry

William O. Wilson, Corporal, Troop 1, 9th U.S. Cavalry

Brent Woods, Sergeant, Troop B, 9th U.S. Cavalry

Spanish-American War

Army

Edward L. Baker Jr., Sergeant Major, 10th U.S. Cavalry

Dennis Bell, Private, Troop H, 10th U.S. Cavalry

Fitz Lee, Private, Troop M, 10th U.S. Cavalry

William H. Thompkins, Private, Troop G, 10th U.S. Cavalry

George H. Wanton, Sergeant, Troop M, 10th U.S.
Cavalry

Navy

Joseph B. Noil, Non-combatant Service, *USS Powhatan*

Robert Penn, Fireman, First Class, *USS Iowa*

World War I

Army

Freddie Stowers, Corporal, Company C, 371st
Infantry Regiment, 93rd Infantry Division

World War II

Army

Vernon Baker, First Lieutenant
Edward A. Carter Jr., Staff Sergeant
John R. Fox, First Lieutenant
Willy F. James Jr., Private First Class
Ruben Rivers, Staff Sergeant
Charles L. Thomas, First Lieutenant
George Watson, Private

Korean War

Army

Cornelius H. Charlton, Sergeant, 24th Infantry
Regiment, 25th Division

William Thompson, Private, 24th Infantry Regiment,
25th Division

Vietnam War

Army

Webster Anderson, Sergeant, Battery A, 2nd
Battalion, 320th Artillery, 101st Airborne Division

Eugene Ashley Jr., Sergeant, Company C, 5th Special
Forces Group (Airborne), 1st Special Forces

William M. Bryant, Sergeant First Class, Company A,
5th Special Forces Group, 1st Special Forces

Lawrence Joel, Specialist Sixth Class, Headquarters
and Headquarters Company, 1st Battalion, 173d
Airborne Brigade

Dwight H. Johnson, Specialist Fifth Class, Company
B, 1st Battalion, 69th Armor, 4th Infantry Division

Garfield M. Langhorn, Private First Class, Troop C,
7th Squadron, 17th Cavalry, 1st Aviation Brigade

Matthew Leonard, Platoon Sergeant, Company B, 1st
Battalion, 16th Infantry, 1st Infantry Division

Donald R. Long, Sergeant, Troop C, 1st Squadron,
4th Cavalry, 1st Infantry Division

Milton L. Olive III, Private First Class, Company
B, 2nd Battalion 503d Infantry, 173d Airborne
Brigade

Riley L. Pitts, Captain, Company C, 2nd Battalion,
27th Infantry, 25th Infantry Division

Charles C. Rogers, Lieutenant Colonel, 1st Battalion,
5th Infantry, 1st Infantry Division

Rupert L. Sargent, First Lieutenant, Company B, 4th
Battalion, 9th Infantry, 25th Infantry Division

Clarence E. Sasser, Specialist 5th Class,
Headquarters Company, 3rd Battalion, 60th
Infantry, 90th Infantry Division

Clifford C. Sims, Staff Sergeant, Company D, 2nd
Battalion, 501st Infantry, 101st Airborne Division

John E. Warren Jr., First Lieutenant, Company C,
2nd Battalion, 22d Infantry, 25th Infantry Division

Marines

James A. Anderson Jr., Private First Class, 2nd
Platoon, Company F, 2nd Battalion, 3rd Marine
Division

Oscar P. Austin, Private First Class, Company E, 7th
Marines, 1st Marine Division

Rodney M. Davis, Company B, First Battalion, 5th
Marines, 1st Marine Division

Robert H. Jenkins Jr., Private First Class, 3rd
Reconnaissance Battalion, 3rd Marine Division

Ralph H. Johnson, Private First Class, Company A,
1st Reconnaissance Battalion, 1st Marine Division

Department of Defense Manpower: 1980 to 1997

[In thousands (1,459 represents 1,459,000). As of end of fiscal year. Includes National Guard, Reserve, and retired regular personnel on extended or continuous active duty. Excludes Coast Guard. Other officer candidates are included under enlisted personnel]

Year	Total[1,2]	Army					Navy[3]					Marine corps					Air Force				
		Total[2]	White	Black	Officers	Enlisted	Total[2]	White	Black	Officers	Enlisted	Total[2]	White	Black	Officers	Enlisted	Total[2]	White	Black	Officers	Enlisted
1980	2,051	777	503	229	99	674	527	436	55	63	460	188	142	39	18	170	558	460	80	98	456
1981	2,083	781	502	232	102	675	540	443	58	65	470	191	145	39	18	172	570	468	83	99	467
1982	2,109	780	504	230	103	673	553	450	62	67	481	192	149	38	19	173	583	476	87	102	476
1983	2,123	780	512	220	106	669	558	462	66	68	485	194	152	37	20	174	592	483	88	105	483
1984	2,138	780	520	215	108	668	565	455	67	69	491	196	153	36	20	176	597	486	89	106	486
1985	2,151	781	523	211	110	667	571	459	70	71	495	198	152	37	20	178	602	488	90	108	489
1986	2,169	781	524	210	110	667	581	464	75	72	504	199	151	38	20	179	608	491	92	109	495
1987	2,174	781	519	212	108	668	587	467	81	72	510	200	150	38	20	179	607	489	92	107	495
1988	2,138	772	507	213	107	660	593	466	85	72	516	197	147	38	20	177	576	462	88	105	467
1989	2,130	770	497	218	107	658	593	461	91	72	516	197	146	38	20	177	571	458	87	104	463
1990	2,044	732	466	213	104	624	579	446	93	72	503	197	145	38	20	177	535	428	82	100	431
1991	1,986	711	452	204	104	603	570	439	92	71	495	194	144	36	20	174	510	409	77	97	409
1992	1,807	610	388	173	95	511	542	415	88	69	468	185	138	32	19	165	470	377	70	90	376
1993	1,705	572	365	158	88	480	510	390	84	66	439	178	134	30	18	160	444	357	65	84	356
1994	1,610	541	344	147	85	452	469	355	78	62	403	174	131	28	18	156	426	341	62	81	341
1995	1,518	509	322	137	83	422	435	326	75	59	372	175	130	28	18	157	400	318	58	78	318
1996	1,472	491	(NA)	(NA)	81	407	417	(NA)	(NA)	57	355	175	(NA)	(NA)	18	157	389	(NA)	(NA)	76	309
1997	1,439	492	(NA)	(NA)	79	408	396	(NA)	(NA)	56	335	174	(NA)	(NA)	18	156	377	(NA)	(NA)	74	299

NA Not available.

[1] Beginning 1980, excludes Navy Reserve personnel on active duty for Training and Administration of Reserves (TARS). From 1969, the full-time Guard and Reserve.

[2] Includes Cadets and other not shown separately.

[3] Prior to 1980, includes Navy Reserve personnel on active duty for Training and Administration of Reserves (TARS).

SOURCE: U.S. Dept. of Defense, *Selected Manpower Statistics*, annual.

Ready Reserve Personnel Profile by Race and Sex: 1990 to 1999

[As of end of fiscal year. Excludes U.S. Coast Guard Reserve. The ready reserve includes selected reservists who are intended to assist active forces in a war and the individual ready reserve who, in a major war, would be used to fill out active and reserve units and later would be a source of combat replacements; a portion of the ready reserve serves in an active status. The standby reserve cannot be called to active duty unless the Congress gives its explicit approval. The retired reserve represents a low potential for mobilization]

Item	Race					Percent distribution			
	Total	White	Black	Asian	American Indian	White	Black	Asian	American Indian
1990	1,641,475	1,289,367	271,470	14,616	7,695	78.5	16.5	0.9	0.5
1993	1,840,650	1,425,255	309,699	21,089	9,068	77.4	16.8	1.1	0.5
1994	1,779,436	1,366,387	297,519	22,190	8,870	76.8	16.7	1.2	0.5
1995	1,633,497	1,254,592	273,847	21,792	8,591	76.8	16.8	1.3	0.5
1996	1,522,451	1,166,628	249,114	21,240	8,226	76.6	16.4	1.4	0.5
1997	1,437,722	1,102,234	229,950	21,412	8,115	76.7	16.0	1.5	0.6
1998	1,340,557	1,022,851	209,814	21,411	7,531	76.3	15.7	1.6	0.6
1999, total[1]	1,276,190	969,248	201,969	22,293	7,349	75.9	15.8	1.7	0.6
Male	1,065,979	833,945	145,969	18,714	5,846	78.2	13.7	1.8	0.5
Officers	164,885	139,328	11,188	2,270	456	84.5	6.8	1.4	0.3
Enlisted	901,094	694,617	134,781	16,444	5,390	77.1	15.0	1.8	0.6
Female	209,830	135,291	55,996	3,578	1,503	64.5	26.7	1.7	0.7
Officers	38,135	28,153	5,956	564	123	73.8	15.6	1.5	0.3
Enlisted	171,695	107,138	50,040	3,014	1,380	62.4	29.1	1.8	0.8

[1] Includes unknown sex.

SOURCE: U.S. Dept. of Defense, *Official Guard and Reserve Manpower Strengths and Statistics,* annual.

Appendix

◆ African American Recipients of Selected Awards
◆ African American Olympic Medalists

◆ AFRICAN AMERICAN RECIPIENTS OF SELECTED AWARDS

Congressional Gold Medal

1977: Marian Anderson
1982: Joe Louis
1984: Roy Wilkins
1988: Jesse Owens
1991: Colin L. Powell
1998: Little Rock Nine: Jean Brown Trickey, Carlotta Walls LaNier, Melba Patillo Beals, Terrence Roberts, Gloria Ray Karlmark, Thelma Mothershed Wair, Ernest Green, Elizabeth Eckford, and Jefferson Thomas
1999: Rosa Parks

Kennedy Center Honors

1978: Marian Anderson
1979: Ella Fitzgerald
1980: Leontyne Price
1981: William "Count" Basie
1983: Katherine Dunham
1984: Lena Horne
1986: Ray Charles
1987: Sammy Davis Jr.
1988: Alvin Ailey
1989: Harry Belafonte
1990: Dizzy Gillespie
1991: Fayard and Harold Nicholas

1992: Lionel Hampton
1993: Arthur Mitchell; Marion Williams
1994: Aretha Franklin
1995: B. B. King; Sidney Poitier
1996: Benny Carter
1997: Jessye Norman
1998: Bill Cosby
1999: Judith Jamison; Stevie Wonder
2000: Chuck Berry
2001: Quincy Jones

Martin Luther King Jr. Nonviolent Peace Prize

1973: Andrew Young
1974: César Chávez
1975: John Lewis
1976: Randolph Blackwell
1977: Benjamin E. Mays
1978: Kenneth D. Kaunda; Stanley Levison
1979: Jimmy Carter
1980: Rosa Parks
1981: Ivan Allen Jr.
1982: Harry Belafonte
1983: Sir Richard Attenborough; Martin Luther King Sr
1985: Bishop Desmond Tutu
1987: Corazon Aquino
1990: Joseph E. Lowery
1991: Mikhail Gorbachev
1993: Jesse Jackson
1999: John Hume

Miss America

1984: Vanessa Williams (New York); Suzette Charles (New Jersey)
1990: Debbye Turner (Missouri)
1991: Marjorie Vincent (Illinois)
1994: Kimberly Clarice Aiken (South Carolina)

Miss Black America

1968: Sandy Williams (Pennsylvania)
1969: G. O. Smith (New York)
1970: Stephanie Clark (District of Columbia)
1971: Joyce Warner (Florida)
1972: Linda Barney (New Jersey)
1973: Arnice Russell (New York)
1974: Von Gretchen Sheppard (California)
1975: Helen Ford (Mississippi)
1976: Twanna Kilgore (District of Columbia)
1977: Claire Ford (Tennessee)
1978: Lydia Jackson (New Jersey)
1979: Veretta Shankle (Mississippi)
1980: Sharon Wright (Illinois)
1981: Pamela Jenks (Massachusetts)
1982: Phyllis Tucker (Florida)
1983: Sonia Robinson (Wisconsin)
1984: Lydia Garrett (South Carolina)
1985: Amina Fakir (Michigan)
1986: Rachel Oliver (Massachusetts)
1987: Leila McBride (Colorado)
1989: Paula Swynn (District of Columbia)
1990: Rosie Jones (Connecticut)
1991: Sharmelle Sullivan (Indiana)
1992: Marilyn DeShields
1993: Pilar Ginger Fort
1994: Karen Wallace
1995: Asheera Ahmad

Miss USA

1990: Carole Gist (Michigan)
1992: Shannon Marketic (California)
1993: Kenya Moore (Michigan)
1994: Frances Louise "Lu" Parker (South Carolina)
1995: Chelsi Smith (Texas)
1996: Ali Landry (Louisiana)
2000: Lynnette Cole (Tennessee)
2002: Shauntay Linton (District of Columbia)

National Medal of Arts

1985: Ralph Ellison (writer); Leontyne Price (singer)
1986: Marian Anderson (singer)

1987: Romare Bearden (artist); Ella Fitzgerald (singer)
1988: Gordon Parks (photographer and film director)
1989: Katherine Dunham (choreographer); Dizzy Gillespie (musician)
1990: Riley "B. B." King (musician)
1991: James Earl Jones (actor); Billy Taylor (musician)
1994: Harry Belafonte (singer)
1995: Gwendolyn Brooks (poet); Ossie Davis (actor); Ruby Dee (actress)
1996: The Harlem Boys Choir (chorale); Lionel Hampton (musician)
1997: Betty Carter (singer)
1998: Fats Domino (singer)
1999: Aretha Franklin (singer); Odetta (singer); Rosetta LeNoire (actress)
2000: Maya Angelou (poet); Benny Carter (musician)
2001: Judith Jamison (choreographer/dancer)

National Society of Arts and Letters Gold Medal of Merit Award

1982: André Watts (music)

Nobel Peace Prize

1950: Ralph J. Bunche
1964: Martin Luther King Jr.

Presidential Medal of Freedom

1963: Marian Anderson; Ralph J. Bunche
1964: John L. Lewis; Leontyne Price; A. Philip Randolph
1969: Edward Kennedy "Duke" Ellington; Ralph Ellison; Roy Wilkins; Whitney M. Young Jr.
1976: Jesse Owens
1977: Martin Luther King Jr. (posthumously)
1980: Clarence Mitchell
1981: James H. "Eubie" Blake; Andrew Young
1983: James Cheek; Mabel Mercer
1984: Jack Roosevelt "Jackie" Robinson (posthumously)
1985: William "Count" Basie (posthumously); Jerome "Brud" Holland (posthumously)
1987: Frederick Douglass Patterson
1988: Pearl Bailey
1991: Colin L. Powell
1992: Ella Fitzgerald
1993: Arthur Ashe Jr. (posthumously); Thurgood Marshall (posthumously); Colin L. Powell
1994: Dorothy Height; Barbara Jordan

1995: William Thaddeus Coleman Jr.; John Hope
Franklin; A. Leon Higginbotham Jr.
1996: John H. Johnson; Rosa Parks
1998: James Farmer
2000: Marian Wright Edelman; Jesse Jackson Sr.;
Gardner Taylor

Spingarn Medal

1915: Ernest E. Just—head of the department of
physiology at Howard University Medical School
1916: Charles Young—major in the U.S. Army
1917: Harry T. Burleigh—composer, pianist, singer
1918: William Stanley Braithwaite—poet, literary
critic, editor
1919: Archibald H. Grimké—former U.S. Consul in
Santo Domingo, president of the American Negro
Academy, author, president of the District of
Columbia branch of the NAACP
1920: W. E. B. Du Bois—author, editor, organizer of
the first Pan-African Congress
1921: Charles S. Gilpin—actor
1922: Mary B. Talbert—former president of the
National Association of Colored Women
1923: George Washington Carver—head of research
and director of the experiment station at
Tuskegee Institute
1924: Roland Hayes—singer
1925: James Weldon Johnson—former U.S. Consul in
Venezuela and Nicaragua, author, editor, poet;
secretary of the NAACP
1926: Carter G. Woodson—editor, historian; founder
of the Association for the Study of Negro Life and
History
1927: Anthony Overton—businessman; president of
the Victory Life Insurance Company (the first
African American organization permitted to do
business under the rigid requirements of the State
of New York)
1928: Charles W. Chesnutt—author
1929: Mordecai Wyatt Johnson—the first African
American president of Howard University
1930: Henry A. Hunt—principal of Fort Valley High
and Industrial School, Fort Valley, Georgia
1931: Richard Berry Harrison—actor
1932: Robert Russa Moton—principal of Tuskegee
Institute
1933: Max Yergan—secretary of the YMCA in
South Africa
1934: William Taylor Burwell Williams—dean of
Tuskegee Institute
1935: Mary McLeod Bethune—founder and president
of Bethune Cookman College
1936: John Hope—president of Atlanta University

1937: Walter White—executive secretary of
the NAACP
1939: Marian Anderson—singer
1940: Louis T. Wright—surgeon
1941: Richard Wright—author
1942: A. Philip Randolph—labor leader, international
president of the Brotherhood of Sleeping Car
Porters
1943: William H. Hastie—jurist, educator
1944: Charles Drew—scientist
1945: Paul Robeson—singer, actor
1946: Thurgood Marshall—special counsel of
the NAACP
1947: Percy Julian—research chemist
1948: Channing H. Tobias—minister, educator
1949: Ralph J. Bunche—international civil servant,
acting United Nations mediator in Palestine
1950: Charles Hamilton Houston—chairman of the
NAACP Legal Committee
1951: Mabel K. Staupers—leader of the National
Association of Colored Graduate Nurses
1952: Harry T. Moore—state leader of the
Florida NAACP
1953: Paul R. Williams—architect
1954: Theodore K. Lawless—physician, educator,
philanthropist
1955: Carl Murphy—editor, publisher, civic leader
1956: Jackie Robinson—athlete
1957: Martin Luther King Jr.—minister, civil
rights leader
1958: Daisy Bates and the Little Rock Nine—for
their pioneer role in upholding the basic ideals of
American democracy in the face of continuing
harassment and constant threats of bodily injury
1959: "Duke" Ellington—composer, musician,
orchestra leader
1960: Langston Hughes—poet, author, playwright
1961: Kenneth B. Clark—professor of psychology at
the City College of the City University of New
York, founder and director of the Northside
Center for Child Development, prime mobilizer of
the resources of modern psychology in the attack
upon racial segregation
1962: Robert C. Weaver—administrator of the
Housing and Home Finance Agency
1963: Medgar Evers—NAACP field secretary for
Mississippi, World War II veteran
1964: Roy Wilkins—executive director of the NAACP
1965: Leontyne Price—singer
1966: John H. Johnson—founder and president of
the Johnson Publishing Company
1967: Edward W. Brooke III—the first African
American to win popular election to the
U.S. Senate

1968: Sammy Davis Jr.—performer, civil rights activist

1969: Clarence M. Mitchell Jr.—director of the Washington Bureau of the NAACP, civil rights activist

1970: Jacob Lawrence—artist, teacher, humanitarian

1971: Leon H. Sullivan—minister

1972: Gordon Parks—writer, photographer, filmmaker

1973: Wilson C. Riles—educator

1974: Damon Keith—jurist

1975: Hank Aaron—athlete

1976: Alvin Ailey—dancer, choreographer, artistic director

1977: Alex Haley—author, biographer, lecturer

1978: Andrew Young—U.S. Ambassador to the United Nations, diplomat, cabinet member, civil rights activist, minister

1979: Rosa Parks—community activist

1980: Rayford W. Logan—educator, historian, author

1981: Coleman A. Young—mayor of Detroit, public servant, labor leader, civil rights activist

1982: Benjamin E. Mays—educator, theologian, humanitarian)

1983: Lena Horne—performer, humanitarian

1984: Tom Bradley—government executive, public servant, humanitarian

1985: Bill Cosby—comedian, actor, educator, humanitarian

1986: Benjamin L. Hooks—executive director of the NAACP

1987: Percy E. Sutton—public servant, businessman, community leader

1988: Frederick Douglass Patterson—doctor of veterinary medicine, educator, humanitarian, founder of the United Negro College Fund

1989: Jesse Jackson Sr.—minister, political leader, civil rights activist

1990: L. Douglas Wilder—governor of Virginia

1991: Colin L. Powell—general in the U.S. Army, chairman of the Joint Chiefs of Staff

1992: Barbara C. Jordan—educator, former congresswoman

1993: Dorothy L. Height—president of the National Council of Negro Women

1994: Maya Angelou—poet, author, performing artist

1995: John Hope Franklin—historian

1996: A. Leon Higginbotham Jr.—jurist, judge

1997: Carl T. Rowan—journalist

1998: Myrlie Evers-Williams—former chair, board of directors, NAACP

1999: Earl G. Graves—publisher and media executive

2000: Oprah Winfrey—television personality and executive

2001: Vernon E. Jordan—former head of National Urban League and United Negro College Fund

U.S. Postal Service Stamps on African American History

Louis Armstrong
Benjamin Banneker
William "Count" Basie
James Pierson Beckwourth
Mary McLeod Bethune
James Hubert "Eubie" Blake
Ralph Johnson Bunche
George Washington Carver
Nat "King" Cole
Bessie Coleman
John Coltrane
Allison Davis
Benjamin O. Davis Sr
Frederick Douglass
Charles Richard Drew
W. E. B. Du Bois
Jean Baptiste Pointe Du Sable
Paul Laurence Dunbar
Edward Kennedy "Duke" Ellington
Erroll Garner
W. C. Handy
Patricia Roberts Harris
Coleman Hawkins
Matthew Alexander Henson
Billie Holiday
Langston Hughes
Mahalia Jackson
James Price Johnson
James Weldon Johnson
Robert Johnson
Scott Joplin
Percy Lavon Julian
Ernest Everett Just
Martin Luther King Jr.
Joe Louis
Leadbelly (Hudson William Ledbetter)
Malcolm X
Roberta Martin
Jan E. Matzeliger
Clyde McPhatter
Charles Mingus
Thelonious Sphere Monk
Ferdinand "Jelly Roll" Morton
Jesse Owens
Charlie "Bird" Parker
Bill Pickett
Salem Poor
Gertrude "Ma" Rainey

A. Philip Randolph
Otis Redding
John Roosevelt "Jackie" Robinson
James Andrew "Jimmy" Rushing
Bessie Smith
Henry Ossawa Tanner
Sonny Terry
Sister Rosetta Tharpe
Sojourner Truth
Harriet Tubman
Madame C. J. Walker
Clara Ward
Booker T. Washington
Dinah Washington
Ethel Waters
Muddy Waters
Ida Bell Wells-Barnett
Josh White
Roy Wilkins
Howlin' Wolf
Carter G. Woodson
Whitney Moore Young

◆ AFRICAN AMERICAN OLYMPIC MEDALISTS

St. Louis, 1904

Men's 200 M Hurdles

George Poage, Bronze

Men's 400 M Hurdles

George Poage, Bronze

London, 1908

Men's 1600 M Relay

J. B. Taylor, Gold (3:29.4)

Paris, 1924

Men's Long Jump

Dehart Hubbard, Gold (24' 5.125")
Edward Gourdin, Silver (23' 10")

Los Angeles, 1932

Men's 100 M Dash

Eddie Tolan, Gold (10.3)
Ralph Metcalfe, Silver (10.3)

Men's 200 M Dash

Eddie Tolan, Gold (21.2)
Ralph Metcalfe, Bronze (21.5)

Men's Long Jump

Edward Gordon, Gold (25' .75")

Berlin, 1936

Men's 100 M Dash

Jesse Owens, Gold (10.3)
Ralph Metcalfe, Silver (10.4)

Men's 200 M Dash

Jesse Owens, Gold (20.7)
Matthew Robinson, Silver (21.1)

Men's 400 M Dash

Archie Williams, Gold (46.5)
James DuValle, Silver (46.8)

Men's 800 M Run

John Woodruff, Gold (1:52.9)

Men's 110 M Hurdles

Fritz Pollard Jr., Bronze (14.4)

Men's 400 M Relay

Jesse Owens, Gold (39.8)
Ralph Metcalfe, Gold (39.8)

Men's High Jump

Cornelius Johnson, Gold (6'8")

Men's Long Jump

Jesse Owens, Gold (26' 5.75")

London, 1948

Men's 100 M Dash

Harrison Dillard, Gold (10.3)
Norwood Ewell, Silver (10.4)

Men's 200 M Dash

Norwood Ewell, Gold (21.1)

Women's 200 M Dash

Audrey Patterson, Bronze (25.2)

Men's 400 M Dash

Mal Whitfield, Bronze (46.9)

Men's 400 M Relay

Lorenzo Wright, Gold (40.6)

Men's 1600 M Relay

Harrison Dillard, Gold (3:10.4)
Norwood Ewell, Gold (3:10.4)
Mal Whitfield, Gold (3:10.4)

Women's High Jump

Alice Coachman, Gold (5' 6.125")

Men's Long Jump

Willie Steele, Gold (25' 8")
Herbert Douglass, Bronze (25' 3")

Helsinki, 1952

Men's 200 M Dash

Andrew Stanfield, Gold (20.7)

Men's 400 M Dash

Ollie Matson, Bronze (46.8)

Men's 800 M Run

Mal Whitfield, Gold (1:49.2)

Men's 110 M Hurdles

Harrison Dillard, Gold (13.7)

Men's 400 M Relay

Harrison Dillard, Gold (40.1)
Andrew Stanfield, Gold (40.1)
Ollie Matson, Gold (40.1)

Women's 400 M Relay

Barbara Jones, Gold (45.9)

Men's Long Jump

Jerome Biffle, Gold (24' 10")
Meredith Gourdine, Silver (24' 8.125")

Decathlon

Milton Campbell, Silver (6,975 pts.)

Javelin

Bill Miller, Silver (237)

Boxing: Flyweight

Nathan Brooks, Gold

Boxing: Light Welterweight

Charles Adkins, Gold

Boxing: Middleweight

Floyd Patterson, Gold

Boxing: Light Heavyweight

Norvel Lee, Gold

Melbourne, 1956

Men's 200 M Dash

Andrew Stanfield, Silver (20.7)

Men's 400 M Dash

Charles Jenkins, Gold (46.7)

Men's 110 M Hurdles

Lee Calhoun, Gold (13.5)

Men's 400 M Relay

Ira Murchison, Gold (39.5)
Leamon King, Gold (39.5)
Charles Jenkins, Gold (39.5)

Women's 400 M Relay

Margaret Matthews, Bronze (44.9)
Isabelle Daniels, Bronze (44.9)
Mae Faggs, Bronze (44.9)
Wilma Rudolph, Bronze (44.9)

Men's 1600 M Relay

Lou Jones, Gold (3:04.8)

Men's High Jump

Charles Dumas, Gold (6' 11.25")

Women's High Jump

Mildred McDaniel, Gold (5' 9.25")

Men's Long Jump

Gregory Bell, Gold (25' 8.25")
Willye White, Silver (19' 11.75")

Decathlon

Milton Campbell, Gold (7,937 pts.)
Rafer Johnson, Silver (7,587 pts.)

Men's Basketball

K.C. Jones, Gold
Bill Russell, Gold

Boxing: Light Heavyweight

James Boyd, Gold

Rome, 1960

Women's 100 M Dash

Wilma Rudolph, Gold (11.0)

Men's 200 M Dash

Les Carney, Silver (20.6)

Women's 200 M Dash

Wilma Rudolph, Gold (24.0)

Men's 400 M Dash

Otis Davis, Gold (44.9)

Men's 110 M Hurdles

Lee Calhoun, Gold (13.8)
Willie May, Silver (13.8)
Hayes Jones, Bronze (14.0)

Women's 400 M Relay

Martha Judson, Bronze (44.5)
Lucinda Williams, Bronze (44.5)
Barbara Jones, Bronze (44.5)
Wilma Rudolph, Bronze (44.5)

Men's 1600 M Relay

Otis Davis, Gold (3:02.2)

Men's High Jump

John Thomas, Bronze (7' .25")

Men's Long Jump

Ralph Boston, Gold (26' 7.75")

Irvin Robertson, Silver (26' 7.25")

Decathlon

Rafer Johnson, Gold (8,392 pts.)

Women's Shot Put

Earlene Brown, Bronze (53' 10.25")

Men's Basketball

Oscar Robertson, Gold
Walt Bellamy, Gold
Bob Boozer, Gold

Boxing: Light Welterweight

Quincelon Daniels, Bronze

Boxing: Light Middleweight

Wilbert McClure, Gold

Boxing: Middleweight

Edward Crook, Gold

Boxing: Light Heavyweight

Cassius Clay, Gold

Tokyo, 1964

Men's 100 M Dash

Robert Hayes, Gold (9.9)

Women's 100 M Dash

Wyomia Tyus, Gold (11.4)
Edith McGuire, Silver (11.6)

Men's 200 M Dash

Henry Carr, Gold (20.3)
Paul Drayton, Silver (20.5)

Women's 200 M Dash

Edith McGuire, Gold (23.0)

Men's 110 M Hurdles

Hayes Jones, Gold (13.6)

Men's 400 M Relay

Robert Hayes, Gold (39.0)
Paul Drayton, Gold (39.0)
Richard Stebbins, Gold (39.0)

Women's 400 M Relay

Wyomia Tyus, Silver (43.9)
Edith McGuire, Silver (43.9)
Willye White, Silver (43.9)
Marilyn White, Silver (43.9)

Men's High Jump

John Thomas, Silver (7' 1.75")
John Rambo, Bronze (7' 1")

Men's Long Jump

Ralph Boston, Silver (26' 4")

Men's Basketball

Walt Hazzard, Gold
Lucius Jackson, Gold

Boxing: Flyweight

Robert Carmody, Bronze

Boxing: Featherweight

Charles Brown, Bronze

Boxing: Lightweight

Ronald Harris, Bronze

Boxing: Heavyweight

Joe Frazier, Gold

Mexico City, 1968

Men's 100 M Dash

Jim Hines, Gold (9.9)
Charles Greene, Bronze (10.0)

Women's 100 M Dash

Wyomia Tyus, Gold (11.0)
Barbara Ferrell, Silver (11.1)

Men's 200 M Dash

Tommie Smith, Gold (19.8)
John Carlos, Bronze (20.0)

Men's 400 M Dash

Lee Evans, Gold (43.8)
Larry James, Silver (43.9)
Ron Freeman, Bronze (44.4)

Women's 800 M Run

Madeline Manning, Gold (2:00.9)

Men's 110 M Hurdles

Willie Davenport, Gold (13.3)
Ervin Hall, Silver (13.4)

Men's 400 M Relay

Jim Hines, Gold (38.2)
Charles Greene, Gold (38.2)
Mel Pender, Gold (38.2)
Ronnie Ray Smith, Gold (38.2)

Women's 400 M Relay

Wyomia Tyus, Gold (42.8)
Barbara Ferrell, Gold (42.8)
Margaret Bailes, Gold (42.8)
Mildrette Netter, Gold (42.8)

Men's 1600 M Relay

Lee Evans, Gold (2:56.1)
Vince Matthews, Gold (2:56.1)
Ron Freeman, Gold (2:56.1)
Larry James, Gold (2:56.1)

Men's High Jump

Edward Caruthers, Silver (7' 3.5")

Men's Long Jump

Bob Beamon, Gold (29' 2.5")
Ralph Boston, Bronze (26' 9.25")

Men's Basketball

Spencer Haywood, Gold
Charlie Scott, Gold
Michael Barrett, Gold
James King, Gold
Calvin Fowler, Gold

Boxing: Featherweight

Albert Robinson, Silver

Boxing: Lightweight

Ronald Harris, Gold

Boxing: Light Welterweight

James Wallington, Bronze

Boxing: Light Middleweight

John Baldwin, Bronze

Boxing: Middleweight

Alfred Jones, Bronze

Boxing: Heavyweight

George Foreman, Gold

Munich, 1972

Men's 100 M Dash

Robert Taylor, Silver (10.24)

Men's 200 M Dash

Larry Black, Silver (20.19)

Men's 400 M Dash

Vince Matthews, Gold (44.66)
Wayne Collett, 400 M Run Silver (44.80)

Men's 110 M Hurdles

Rod Milburn, Gold (13.24)

Men's 400 M Relay

Eddie Hart, Gold (38.19)
Robert Taylor, Gold (38.19)
Larry Black, Gold (38.19)
Gerald Tinker, Gold (38.19)

Women's 1600 M Relay

Cheryl Toussain, Silver (3:25.2)
Mable Fergerson, Silver (3:25.2)
Madeline Manning, Silver (3:25.2)

Men's Long Jump

Randy Williams, Gold (27' .25")
Arnie Robinson, Bronze (26' 4")

Decathlon

Jeff Bennet, Bronze (7,974 pts.)

Boxing: Light Welterweight

Ray Seales, Gold

Boxing: Middleweight

Marvin Johnson, Bronze

Montreal, 1976

Men's 200 M Dash

Millard Hampton, Silver (20.29)
Dwayne Evans, Bronze (20.43)

Men's 400 M Dash

Fred Newhouse, Silver (44.40)
Herman Frazier, Bronze (44.95)

Men's 110 M Hurdles

Willie Davenport, Bronze (13.38)

Men's 400 M Hurdles

Edwin Moses, Gold (47.64)

Men's 400 M Relay

Millard Hampton, Gold (38.83)
Steve Riddick, Gold (38.83)
Harvey Glance, Gold (38.83)
John Jones, Gold (38.83)

Men's 1600 M Relay

Herman Frazier, Gold (2:58.7)
Benny Brown, Gold (2:58.7)
Maxie Parks, Gold (2:58.7)
Fred Newhouse, Gold (2:58.7)

Women's 1600 M Relay

Rosalyn Bryant, Silver (3:22.8)
Shelia Ingram, Silver (3:22.8)
Pamela Jiles, Silver (3:22.8)
Debra Sapenter, Silver (3:22.8)

Men's Long Jump

Arnie Robinson, Gold (27' 4.75")
Randy Williams, Silver (26' 7.25")

Men's Triple Jump

James Butts, Silver (56 8.5")

Men's Basketball

Phil Ford, Gold
Adrian Dantley, Gold
Walter Davis, Gold
Quinn Buckner, Gold
Kenneth Carr, Gold
Scott May, Gold
Philip Hubbard, Gold

Women's Basketball

Lusia Harris, Silver
Charlotte Lewis, Silver

Boxing: Flyweight

Leo Randolph, Gold

Boxing: Lightweight

Howard David, Gold

Boxing: Light Welterweight

Sugar Ray Leonard, Gold

Boxing: Middleweight

Michael Spinks, Gold

Boxing: Light Heavyweight

Leon Spinks, Gold

Boxing: Heavyweight

Johnny Tate, Bronze

Los Angeles, 1984

Men's 100 M Dash

Carl Lewis, Gold (9.9)
Sam Graddy, Silver (10.19)

Women's 100 M Dash

Evelyn Ashford, Gold (10.97)
Alice Brown, Silver (11.14)

Men's 200 M Dash

Carl Lewis, Gold (19.80)
Kirk Baptiste, Silver (19.96)

Women's 200 M Dash

Valerie Brisco-Hooks, Gold (21.81)
Florence Griffith, Silver (22.04)

Men's 400 M Dash

Alonzo Babers, Gold (44.27)
Antonio McKay, Bronze (44.71)

Women's 400 M Dash

Valerie Brisco-Hooks, Gold (48.83)
Chandra Cheeseborough, Silver (49.05)

Men's 800 M Run

Earl Jones, Bronze (1:43.83)

Women's 800 M Run

Kim Gallagher, Silver (1:58.63)

Women's 100 M Hurdles

Benita Fitzgerald-Brown, Gold (12.84)
Kim Turner, Silver (12.88)

Men's 110 M Hurdles

Roger Kingdom, Gold (13.20)
Greg Foster, Silver (13.23)

Men's 400 M Hurdle

Edwin Moses, Gold (47.75)
Danny Harris, Silver (48.13)

Women's 400 M Hurdles

Judi Brown, Silver (55.20)

Men's 400 M Relay

Sam Graddy, Gold (37.83)
Ron Brown, Gold (37.83)
Calvin Smith, Gold (37.83)
Carl Lewis, Gold (37.83)

Men's 1600 M Relay

Sunder Nix, Gold (2:57.91)
Roy Armstead, Gold (2:57.91)
Alonzo Babers, Gold (2:57.91)
Antonio McKay, Gold (2:57.91)

Women's 1600 M Relay

Valerie Brisco-Hooks, Gold (3:18.29)
Chandra Cheeseborough, Gold (3:18.29)
Lillie Leatherwood, Gold (3:18.29)
Sherri Howard, Gold (3:18.29)

Men's Long Jump

Carl Lewis, Gold (28' .25")

Men's Triple Jump

Al Joyner, Gold (56' 7.5")
Mike Conley, Silver (56' 4.5")

Heptathlon

Jackie Joyner, Silver (6,386 pts.)

Men's Shot Put

Michael Carter, Gold (69" 2.5")

Men's Basketball

Patrick Ewing, Gold
Vern Fleming, Gold
Michael Jordan, Gold
Sam Perkins, Gold
Alvin Robertson, Gold
Wayman Tisdale, Gold
Leon Wood, Gold

Women's Basketball

Cathy Boswell, Gold
Teresa Edwards, Gold
Janice Lawrence, Gold
Pamela McGee, Gold
Cheryl Miller, Gold
Lynette Woodard, Gold

Boxing: Flyweight

Steven McCrory, Gold

Boxing: Featherweight

Meldrick Taylor, Gold

Boxing: Lightweight

Pernell Whitaker, Gold

Boxing: Light Welterweight

Jerry Page, Gold

Boxing: Welterweight

Mark Breland, Gold

Boxing: Light Middleweight

Frank Tate, Gold

Boxing: Middleweight

Virgil Hill, Silver

Boxing: Light Heavyweight

Evander Holyfield, Bronze

Boxing: Heavyweight

Henry Tillman, Gold

Boxing: Super Heavyweight

Tyrell Biggs, Gold

Seoul, 1988

Men's 100 M Dash

Carl Lewis, Gold (9.92)
Calvin Smith, Silver (9.99)

Women's 100 M Dash

Florence Griffith-Joyner, Gold (10.54)
Evelyn Ashford, Silver (10.83)

Men's 200 M Dash

Joe DeLoach, Gold (19.75)
Carl Lewis, Silver (19.79)

Women's 200 M Dash

Florence Griffith-Joyner, Gold (21.34)

Men's 400 M Dash

Steve Lewis, Gold (43.87)
Butch Reynolds, Silver (43.93)
Danny Everett, Bronze (44.09)

Women's 800 M Run

Kim Gallagher, Bronze (1:56.91)

Men's 110 M Hurdles

Roger Kingdom, Gold (12.98)
Tonie Campbell, Bronze (13.38)

Men's 400 M Hurdles

Andre Phillips, Gold (47.19)
Edwin Moses, Bronze (47.56)

Women's 400 M Relay

Shelia Echols, Gold (41.98)
Florence Griffith-Joyner, Gold (41.98)
Evelyn Ashford, Gold (41.98)
Alice Brown, Gold (41.98)

Men's 1600 M Relay

Butch Reynolds, Gold (2:56.16)
Steve Lewis, Gold (2:56.16)
Antonio McKay, Gold (2:56.16)
Danny Everett, Gold (2:56.16)

Women's 1600 M Relay

Denean Howard-Hill, Silver (3:15.51)
Valerie Brisco, Silver (3:15.51)
Diane Dixon, Silver (3:15.51)
Florence Griffith-Joyner, Silver (3:15.51)

Men's Long Jump

Carl Lewis, Gold (28' 7.25")
Mike Powell, Silver (27' 10.25")
Larry Myricks, Bronze (27' 1.75")

Women's Long Jump

Jackie Joyner-Kersee, Gold (24' 3.5")

Heptathlon

Jackie Joyner-Kersee, Gold (7,291 pts.)

Baseball

Tom Goodwin, Gold
Ty Griffin, Gold

Men's Basketball

Willie Anderson, Bronze
Stacey Augmon, Bronze
Bimbo Coles, Bronze
Jeff Grayer, Bronze
Hersey Hawkins, Bronze
Danny Manning, Bronze
J.R. Reid, Bronze
Mitch Richmond, Bronze
David Robinson, Bronze
Charles E. Smith, Bronze

Women's Basketball

Cindy Brown, Gold
Vicky Bullett, Gold
Cynthia Cooper, Gold
Teresa Edwards, Gold
Jennifer Gillom, Gold
Bridgette Gordon, Gold
Katrina McClain, Gold
Teresa Weatherspoon, Gold

Boxing: Bantamweight

Kennedy McKinney, Gold

Boxing: Middleweight

Roy Jones, Silver

Boxing: Light Heavyweight

Andrew Maynard, Gold

Boxing: Heavyweight

Ray Mercer, Gold

Boxing: Super Heavyweight

Riddick Bowe, Silver

Tennis: Women's Singles

Zina Garrison, Bronze

Tennis: Women's Doubles

Zina Garrison, Gold

Wrestling: Lightweight (Freestyle)

Nate Carr, Bronze

Wrestling: Welterweight (Freestyle)

Kenny Monday, Gold

Barcelona, 1992

Men's 100 M Dash

Dennis Mitchell, Bronze (10.04)

Women's 100 M Dash

Gail Devers, Gold (10.82)

Men's 200 M Dash

Mike Marsh, Gold (20.01)
Michael Bates, Bronze (20.38)

Women's 200 M Dash

Gwen Torrence, Gold (21.81)

Men's 400 M Dash

Quincy Watts, Gold (43.50)
Steve Lewis, Silver (44.21)

Men's 800 M Run

Johnny Gray, Bronze (1:43.97)

Men's 110 M Hurdles

Tony Dees, Silver (13.24)

Men's 400 M Hurdles

Kevin Young, Gold (46.78)

Women's 400 M Hurdles

Sandra Farmer, Silver (53.69)
Janeene Vickers, Bronze (54.31)

Men's 400 M Relay

Mike Marsh, Gold (37.40)
Leroy Burrell, Gold (37.40)
Dennis Mitchell, Gold (37.40)
Carl Lewis, Gold (37.40)

Women's 400 M Relay

Evelyn Ashford, Gold (42.11)
Esther Jones, Gold (42.11)
Carlette Guidry-White, Gold (42.11)
Gwen Torrence, Gold (42.11)

Men's 800 M Relay

Andrew Valmon, Gold (2:55.74)
Quincy Watts, Gold (2:55.74)
Michael Johnson, Gold (2:55.74)
Steve Lewis, Gold (2:55.74)

Women's 800 M Relay

Natasha Kaiser, Silver (3:20.92)
Gwen Torrence, Silver (3:20.92)
Jearl Miles, Silver (3:20.92)
Rochelle Stevens, Silver (3:20.92)

Men's High Jump

Hollis Conway, Bronze (7' 8")

Men's Long Jump

Carl Lewis, Gold (28' 5.5")
Mike Powell, Silver (28' 4.25")
Joe Greene, Bronze (27' 4.5")

Women's Long Jump

Jackie Joyner-Kersee, Bronze (23' 2.5")

Men's Triple Jump

Mike Conley, Gold (59' 7.5")
Charlie Simpkins, Silver (57' 9")

Heptathlon

Jackie Joyner-Kersee, Gold (7,044 pts.)

Men's Basketball

Charles Barkley, Gold
Clyde Drexler, Gold
Patrick Ewing, Gold
Magic Johnson, Gold
Michael Jordan, Gold
Karl Malone, Gold
Scottie Pippen, Gold
David Robinson, Gold

Women's Basketball

Vicky Bullett, Bronze
Daedra Charles, Bronze
Cynthia Cooper, Bronze
Teresa Edwards, Bronze
Carolyn Jones, Bronze
Katrina McClain, Bronze
Vickie Orr, Bronze
Teresa Weatherspoon, Bronze

Boxing: Flyweight

Tim Austin, Bronze

Boxing: Middleweight

Chris Byrd, Silver

Wrestling: Middleweight (Freestyle)

Kevin Jackson, Gold

Wrestling: Welterweight (Freestyle)

Kenny Monday, Silver

Atlanta, 1996

Women's 100 M Dash

Gail Devers, Gold (10.94)
Gwen Torrence, Bronze (10.96)

Men's 200 M Dash

Michael Johnson, Gold (19.32)

Men's 400 M Dash

Michael Johnson, Gold (43.49)

Men's 110 M Hurdles

Allen Johnson Gold (12.95)
Mark Crear, Silver (13.09)

Men's 400 M Hurdles

Derrick Adkins, Gold (47.54)
Calvin Davis, Bronze (47.96)

Women's 400 M Hurdles

Kim Batten, Silver (53.08)
Tonja Buford-Bailey, Bronze (53.22)

Men's 400 M Relay

Tim Harden, Silver (38.05)
Jon Drummond, Silver (38.05)
Michael Marsh, Silver (38.05)
Dennis Mitchell, Silver (38.05)

Women's 400 M Relay

Gail Devers, Gold (41.95)
Chryste Gaines, Gold (41.95)
Gwen Torrence, Gold (41.95)
Inger Miller, Gold (41.95)

Men's 1600 M Relay

LaMont Smith, Gold (2:55.99)
Alvin Harrison, Gold (2:55.99)
Derek Mills, Gold (2:55.99)
Anthuan Maybank, Gold (2:55.99)

Women's 1600 M Relay

Rochelle Stevens, Gold (3:20.91)
Maicel Malone, Gold (3:20.91)
Kim Graham, Gold (3:20.91)
Jearl Miles, Gold (3:20.91)

Men's High Jump

Charles Austin, Gold (7' 10")

Men's Long Jump

Carl Lewis, Gold (27' 10.75")
Joe Greene, Bronze (27' .50")

Women's Long Jump

Jackie Joyner-Kersee, Bronze (22' 11")

Men's Triple Jump

Kenny Harrison, Gold (59' 4")

Decathlon

Dan O'Brien, Gold (8,824 pts.)

Baseball

Jacque Jones, Bronze

Men's Basketball

Mitch Richmond, Gold
Scottie Pippen, Gold
Gary Payton, Gold
Charles Barkley, Gold
Hakeem Olajuwon, Gold
David Robinson, Gold
Penny Hardaway, Gold
Grant Hill, Gold
Karl Malone, Gold
Reggie Miller, Gold

Women's Basketball

Teresa Edwards, Gold
Ruth Bolton, Gold
Lisa Leslie, Gold
Katrina McClain, Gold
Sheryl Swoopes, Gold
Nikki McCray, Gold
Dawn Staley, Gold
Venus Lacey, Gold
Carla McGhee, Gold

Women's Gymnastics: Floor Exercise

Dominique Dawes, Bronze

Women's Gymnastics: Team

Dominique Dawes, Gold

Boxing: Featherweight

Floyd Mayweather, Bronze

Boxing: Lightweight

Terrance Cauthen, Bronze

Boxing: Light Middleweight

David Reid, Gold

Boxing: Middleweight

Rhoshii Wells, Bronze

Boxing: Light Heavyweight

Antonio Tarver, Bronze

Boxing: Heavyweight

Nate Jones, Bronze

Sydney, 2000

Men's 100 M Dash

Maurice Green, Gold (9.87)

Women's 100 M Dash

Marion Jones, Gold (10.75)

Women's 200 M Dash

Marion Jones, Gold (21.84)

Men's 400 M Dash

Michael Johnson, Gold (43.83)
Alvin Harrison, Silver (44.40)

Women's 100 M Hurdles

Melissa Morrison, Bronze (12.65)

Men's 110 M Hurdles

Terrance Trammell, Silver (13.16)
Mark Crear, Bronze (13.22)

Men's 400 M Hurdles

Angelo Taylor, Gold (47.50)

Men's 400 M Relay

Maurice Green, Gold (37.61)
Jonathan Drummond, Gold (37.61)
Brian Lewis, Gold (37.61)
Bernard Williams, Gold (37.61)

Women's 400 M Relay

Marion Jones, Bronze (42.20)
Torri Edwards, Bronze (42.20)
Chryste Gaines, Bronze (42.20)
Nanceen Perry, Bronze (42.20)

Men's 1600 M Relay

Michael Johnson, Gold (2:56.35)
Alvin Harrison, Gold (2:56.35)
Antonio Pettigrew, Gold (2:56.35)
Calvin Harrison, Gold (2:56.35)

Women's 1600 M Relay

Marion Jones, Gold (3:22.62)
La Tasha Colander-Richardson, Gold (3:22.62)
Monique Hennagan, Gold (3:22.62)
Jearl Miles-Clark, Gold (3:22.62)

Women's Long Jump

Marion Jones, Bronze (22' 8.25")

Decathlon

Chris Huffins, Bronze (8,595 pts.)

Men's Pole Vault

Lawrence Johnson, Silver (19' 4.25")

Baseball

Travis Dawkins, Gold
Anthony Sanders, Gold
Ernie Young, Gold

Men's Basketball

Shareef Abdur-Rahim, Gold
Ray Allen, Gold
Vin Baker, Gold
Vince Carter, Gold
Kevin Garnett, Gold
Tim Hardaway, Gold
Allan Houston, Gold
Jason Kidd, Gold
Antonio McDyess, Gold
Alonzo Mourning, Gold
Gary Payton, Gold
Steve Smith, Gold

Women's Basketball

Ruth Bolton-Holifield, Gold
Teresa Edwards, Gold
Yolanda Griffith, Gold
Chamique Holdsclaw, Gold
Lisa Leslie, Gold
Nikki McCray, Gold
DeLisha Milton, Gold
Dawn Staley, Gold
Natalie Williams, Gold

Boxing: Bantamweight

Clarence Vinson, Bronze

Boxing: Light Middleweight

Jermain Taylor, Bronze

Boxing: Light Welterweight

Ricardo Williams Jr., Silver

Tennis: Women's Singles

Venus Williams, Gold

Tennis: Women's Doubles

Serena Williams, Gold
Venus Williams, Gold

Men's Beach Volleyball

Dain Blanton, Gold

Salt Lake City, 2002

Bobsled: Two-woman

Vonetta Flowers, Gold

Bobsled: Four-man

Garrett Hines, Silver
Randy Jones, Silver
Bill Schuffenhauer, Silver

Bibliography

This bibliography is arranged according to the topics covered in *African American Almanac*. It contains recommended books, as well as noteworthy magazine and journal articles, published between 1998 and 2002. All of these sources should be easily accessible in undergraduate libraries or through public library networks. Also included are Internet sites related to this volume's topics, all verified as of July 2002.

Compiled by Geraldine Azzatta

Chronology

"The African-American Mosaic: A Library of Congress Resource Guide for the Study of Black History and Culture." Available online at <lcweb.loc.gov/exhibits/african/intro.html> (cited July 19, 2002).

"African American World Timeline." Available online at <www.pbs.org/aaworld/timeline.html> (cited July 19, 2002).

"Black Facts Online!" Available online at <www.blackfacts.com> (cited July 19, 2002).

"Charles H. Wright Museum of African American History." Available online at <www.maah-detroit.org> (cited July 19, 2002).

Christian, Charles Melvin. *Black Saga: The African American Experience: A Chronology.* New York: Basic Civitas Books, 1999.

"Encyclopaedia Britannica Guide to Black History." Available online at <blackhistory.eb.com/> (cited July 19, 2002).

Kullen, Allan S. *The Peopling of America: A Timeline of Events That Helped Shape Our Nation.* Beltsville, MD: Portfolio Project, 1998.

The New York Public Library African American Desk Reference. New York: John Wiley, 1999.

African American Firsts

"The Internet African American History Challenge." Available online at <www.brightmoments.com/blackhistory> (cited July 19, 2002).

"The MUNIRAH Chronicle of Black Historical Events and Facts." Available online at <maelstrom.stjohns.edu/archives/Munirah.html> (cited July 19, 2002).

The New York Public Library African American Desk Reference. New York: John Wiley, 1999.

Smith, Jessie Carney. *Black Firsts: 4,000 Ground-Breaking and Pioneering Events.* Canton, MI: Visible Ink, 2002.

Webster, Raymond B. *African American Firsts in Science and Technology.* Detroit: Gale, 1999.

Significant Documents in African American History

"Afro-American Almanac Historical Documents." Available online at <toptags.com/aama/docs/docs.html> (cited July 19, 2002).

Boyd, Herb, ed. *Autobiography of a People: Three Centuries of African American History Told by Those Who Lived It.* New York: Doubleday, 2000.

Douglass, Frederick. *Frederick Douglass: Selected Speeches and Writings.* Chicago: Lawrence Hill Books, 1999.

Dunbar, Alice Moore, ed. *Masterpieces of Negro Eloquence, 1818–1913.* Mineola, NY: Dover Publications, 2000.

"Exhibit Hall: The Emancipation Proclamation." Available online at <www.archives.gov/exhibit_hall/featured_documents/emancipation_proclamation.html> (cited July 19, 2002).

Frazier, Thomas R. *Readings in African-American History.* Belmont, CA: Wadsworth/Thomson Learning, 2001.

"Freedmen's Bureau Records." Available online at <www.freedmensbureau.com> (cited July 19, 2002).

Green, Robert P., Jr., ed. *Equal Protection and the African American Constitutional Experience: A Documentary History.* Westport, CT: Greenwood Press, 2000.

"Historic Documents and Books on the Internet: African American." Available online at <www.usc.edu/isd/archives/ethnicstudies/historicdocs/> (cited July 19, 2002).

Sigler, Jay A. *Civil Rights in America: 1500 to the Present.* Detroit: Gale Research, 1998.

African American Landmarks

"African American Civil War Memorial Museum." Available online at <www.afroamcivilwar.org> (cited July 19, 2002).

"Black Heritage Hideaways," *Ebony,* February 1998.

Edison-Swift, Anne. "On the Trail: Discovering African American History in Virginia," *Humanities,* November-December 2001.

Eskridge, Ann E. "Discovering the Power of History," *American Visions,* October-November 1998.

Fitzpatrick, Sandra. *The Guide to Black Washington: Places and Events of Historical and Cultural Significance in the Nation's Capital.* New York: Hippocrene Books, 2001.

"The National Underground Railroad Freedom Center." Available online at <www.undergroundrailroad.org> (cited July 19, 2002).

"Our Sacred History: African American Heritage; National Parks." Available online at <www.cr.nps.gov/aahistory/parks/parks.htm> (cited July 19, 2002).

Robinson, Wayne C. *The African-American Travel Guide.* Edison, NJ: Hunter Publishing, 1998.

Africa and the Black Diaspora

"Africa Online." Available online at <www.africaonline.com> (cited July 19, 2002).

"AfricaNews Wire." Available online at <www.africanews.org> (cited July 19, 2002).

Appiah, Kwame Anthony, and Henry Louis Gates, Jr., eds. *Africana: The Encyclopedia of the African and African American Experience.* New York: Basic Civitas Books, 1999.

Appiah, Kwame Anthony, and Henry Louis Gates, Jr., eds. *Microsoft Encarta Africana 2000* [multimedia optical discs]. Redmond, WA: Microsoft, 1999.

Asante, Molefi K. *The African-American Atlas: Black History and Culture.* New York: Macmillan, 1998.

Bracks, Lean'tin L. *Writings on Black Women of the Diaspora: History, Language, and Identity.* New York: Garland, 1998.

Gates, Henry Louis, Jr. *Wonders of the African World.* New York: Knopf, 1999.

Kasule, Samuel. *The History Atlas of Africa.* New York: Macmillan, 1998.

Okpewho, Isidore, ed. *African Diaspora: African Origins and New World Identities.* Bloomington, IN: Indiana University Press, 2001.

Price, Sally. *Maroon Arts: Cultural Vitality in the African Diaspora.* Boston: Beacon Press, 1999.

Scott, William R., and William G. Shade, eds. *Upon These Shores: Themes in the African-American Experience, 1600 to the Present.* New York: Routledge, 2000.

"The Universal Black Pages." Available online at <www.ubp.com> (cited July 19, 2002).

Africans in America: 1600 to 1900

"African-American Pioneers." Available online at <afgen.com/pioneer.html > (cited July 19, 2002).

"Africans in America." Available online at <www.pbs.org/wgbh/aia/> (cited July 19, 2002).

"American Slave Narratives: An Online Anthology." Available online at <xroads.virginia.edu/~HYPER/wpa/wpahome.html> (cited July 19, 2002).

"The Amistad Research Center." Available online at <www.tulane.edu/~amistad> (cited July 19, 2002).

Appiah, Kwame Anthony, and Henry Louis Gates, Jr., eds. *Africana: The Encyclopedia of the African and African American Experience.* New York: Basic Civitas Books, 1999.

Appiah, Kwame Anthony, and Henry Louis Gates, Jr., eds. *Microsoft Encarta Africana 2000* [multimedia optical discs]. Redmond, WA: Microsoft, 1999.

Boyd, Herb, ed. *Autobiography of a People: Three Centuries of African American History Told by Those Who Lived it.* New York: Doubleday, 2000.

Franklin, John Hope. *From Slavery to Freedom: A History of African Americans.* 8th ed. New York: Knopf, 2000.

Govenar, Alan B. *African American Frontiers: Slave Narratives and Oral Histories.* Santa Barbara, CA: ABC-CLIO, 2000.

Horton, James Oliver, and Lois E. Horton. *Hard Road to Freedom: The Story of African America.* New Brunswick, NJ: Rutgers University Press, 2001.

"Images of 19th Century African Americans." Available online at <digital.nypl.org/schomburg/images_aa19> (cited July 19, 2002).

Johnson, Charles Richard, and Patricia Smith. *Africans in America: America's Journey Through Slavery.* New York: Harcourt Brace, 1998.

Kelley, Robin D., and Earl Lewis, eds. *To Make Our World Anew: A History of African Americans.* New York: Oxford University Press, 2000.

Schwartz, Marie Jenkins. *Born in Bondage: Growing Up Enslaved in the Antebellum South.* Cambridge, MA: Harvard University Press, 2000.

Scott, William R., and William G. Shade, eds. *Upon These Shores: Themes in the African-American Experience, 1600 to the Present.* New York: Routledge, 2000.

Thompson, Kathleen, and Hilary MacAustin, eds. *The Face of Our Past: Images of Black Women from Colonial America to the Present.* Bloomington, IN: Indiana University Press, 1999.

Wilkins, Roger W. *Jefferson's Pillow: The Founding Fathers and the Dilemma of Black Patriotism.* Boston: Beacon Press, 2001.

Civil Rights

"African American Odyssey." Available online at <memory.loc.gov/ammem/aaohtml/aohome.html> (cited July 19, 2002).

"African-American Pioneers." Available online at <afgen.com/pioneer.html> (cited July 19, 2002).

Allison, Robert J., ed. *American Social and Political Movements 1945–2000: Pursuit of Liberty.* Detroit: St. James Press, 2000.

Ball, Howard. *A Defiant Life: Thurgood Marshall and the Persistence of Racism in America.* New York: Crown Publishers, 1998.

"Black History." Available online at <www.nyise.org/blackhistory/index.html> (cited July 19, 2002).

Branch, Taylor. *Pillar of Fire: America in the King Years, 1963–65.* New York: Simon and Schuster, 1998.

Collier-Thomas, Bettye, and V.P. Franklin, eds. *Sisters in the Struggle: African American Women in the Civil Rights-Black Power Movement.* New York: New York University Press, 2001.

Davis, Townsend. *Weary Feet, Rested Souls: A Guided History of the Civil Rights Movement.* New York: W.W. Norton, 1998.

Fairclough, Adam. *Better Day Coming: Blacks and Equality, 1890–2000.* New York: Viking, 2001.

Green, Robert P., Jr., ed. *Equal Protection and the African American Constitutional Experience: A Documentary History.* Westport, CT: Greenwood Press, 2000.

Honey, Michael K. *Black Workers Remember: An Oral History of Segregation, Unionism, and the Freedom Struggle.* Berkeley: University of California Press, 1999.

Lewis, David L. *W.E.B. Du Bois: The Fight for Equality and the American Century, 1919–1963.* New York: H. Holt, 2000.

Litwack, Leon F. *Trouble in Mind: Black Southerners in the Age of Jim Crow.* New York: Knopf, 1998.

Martin, Waldo E., Jr., and Patricia Sullivan, eds. *Civil Rights in the United States.* New York: Macmillan Reference, 2000.

McWhorter, Diane. *Carry Me Home: Birmingham, Alabama, the Climactic Battle of the Civil Rights Revolution.* New York: Simon and Schuster, 2002.

Meacham, Jon, ed. *Voices in Our Blood: America's Best on the Civil Rights Movement.* New York: Random House, 2001.

"National Civil Rights Museum." Available online at <www.civilrightsmuseum.org> (cited July 19, 2002).

Patterson, James T. *Brown v. Board of Education: A Civil Rights Milestone and Its Troubled Legacy.* New York: Oxford University Press, 2001.

Pinkney, Andrea Davis. *Let It Shine: Stories of Black Women Freedom Fighters.* New York: Harcourt Brace, 2000.

Sigler, Jay A., ed. *Civil Rights in America: 1500 to the Present.* Detroit: Gale Research, 1998.

Terborg-Penn, Rosalyn. *African American Women in the Struggle for the Vote, 1850–1920.* Bloomington, IN: Indiana University Press, 1998.

Wexler, Sanford. *An Eyewitness History of the Civil Rights Movement.* New York: Checkmark Books, 1999.

Winters, Paul A., ed. *The Civil Rights Movement.* San Diego, CA: Greenhaven Press, 2000.

Black Nationalism

Adeleke, Tunde. *UnAfrican American: Nineteenth-Century Black Nationalists and the Civilizing Mission.* Lexington, KY: University Press of Kentucky, 1998.

Alexander, Amy, ed. *The Farrakhan Factor: African-American Writers on Leadership, Nationhood, and Minister Louis Farrakhan.* New York: Grove Press, 1998.

Collier-Thomas, Bettye, and V.P. Franklin, eds. *Sisters in the Struggle: African American Women in the Civil Rights-Black Power Movement.* New York: New York University Press, 2001.

Dixon, Chris. *African America and Haiti: Emigration and Black Nationalism in the Nineteenth Century.* Westport, CT: Greenwood Press, 2000.

"Dr. Huey P. Newton Foundation/The Black Panther Party." Available online at <www.blackpanther.org> (cited July 19, 2002).

Evanzz, Karl. *The Messenger: The Rise and Fall of Elijah Muhammad.* New York: Pantheon Books, 1999.

Gates, Henry Louis., Jr. *The African-American Century: How Black Americans Have Shaped Our Country.* New York: Free Press, 2000.

Jones, Charles E., ed. *The Black Panther Party.* Baltimore: Black Classic Press, 1998.

"Nation of Islam Online." Available online at <www.noi.org> (cited July 19, 2002).

Woodard, Komozi. *A Nation Within a Nation: Amiri Baraka (Leroi Jones) and Black Power Politics.* Chapel Hill, NC: University of North Carolina Press, 1999.

National Organizations

Bell, Janet Cheatham. *Till Victory Is Won: Famous Black Quotations from the NAACP.* New York: Simon and Schuster, 2002.

Dickerson, Dennis C. *Militant Mediator: Whitney M. Young, Jr.* Lexington, KY: University Press of Kentucky, 1998.

Fairclough, Adam. *Better Day Coming: Blacks and Equality, 1890–2000.* New York: Viking, 2001.

Garrow, David J. *Bearing the Cross: Martin Luther King, Jr., and the Southern Christian Leadership Conference.* New York: Quill, 1999 (reprint).

Jordan, Vernon E. *Vernon Can Read! A Memoir.* New York: PublicAffairs, 2001.

"NAACP Online." Available online at <www.naacp.org> (cited July 19, 2002).

"National Society of Black Engineers." Available online at <www.nsbe.org> (cited July 19, 2002).

"National Urban League." Available online at <www.nul.org> (cited July 19, 2002).

"100+ Organization Leaders," *Ebony,* May 2000.

Wedin, Carolyn. *Inheritors of the Spirit: Mary White Ovington and the Founding of the NAACP.* New York: John Wiley, 1998.

Law

Allison, Robert J., ed. *American Social and Political Movements 1945–2000: Pursuit of Liberty.* Detroit: St. James Press, 2000.

Asim, Jabari, ed. *Not Guilty: Twelve Black Men Speak Out on Law, Justice, and Life.* New York: Amistad, 2001.

Ball, Howard. *A Defiant Life: Thurgood Marshall and the Persistence of Racism in America.* New York: Crown Publishers, 1998.

Green, Robert P., Jr., ed. *Equal Protection and the African American Constitutional Experience: A Documentary History.* Westport, CT: Greenwood Press, 2000.

Horowitz, David. *Uncivil Wars: The Controversy Over Reparations for Slavery.* San Francisco: Encounter Books, 2002.

Markowitz, Michael W., and Delores D. Jones-Brown, eds. *The System in Black and White: Exploring the Connections Between Race, Crime, and Justice.* Westport, CT: Praeger, 2000.

"The Minority Business Enterprise Legal Defense and Education Fund." Available online at <www.mbeldef.org> (cited July 19, 2002).

Motley, Constance Baker. *Equal Justice Under Law: An Autobiography.* New York: Farrar, Straus, and Giroux, 1998.

"NAACP Legal Defense and Educational Fund." Available online at <www.naacpldf.org> (cited July 19, 2002).

"The National Bar Association." Available online at <www.nationalbar.org> (cited July 19, 2002).

O'Brien, Gail Williams. *The Color of the Law: Race, Violence, and Justice in the Post-World War II South.* Chapel Hill, NC: University of North Carolina Press, 1999.

Patterson, James T. *Brown v. Board of Education: A Civil Rights Milestone and Its Troubled Legacy.* New York: Oxford University Press, 2001.

Sollors, Werner, ed. *Interracialism: Black-White Intermarriage in American History, Literature, and Law.* New York: Oxford University Press, 2000.

Spann, Girardeau A. *The Law of Affirmative Action: Twenty-Five Years of Supreme Court Decisions on Race and Remedies.* New York: New York University Press, 2000.

Williams, Juan. *Thurgood Marshall: American Revolutionary.* New York: Times Books, 1998.

Politics

Alexander, Amy, ed. *The Farrakhan Factor: African-American Writers on Leadership, Nationhood, and Minister Louis Farrakhan.* New York: Grove Press, 1998.

"Black History." Available online at <www.nyise.org/blackhistory/index.html> (cited July 19, 2002).

Brandt, Eric, ed. *Dangerous Liaisons: Blacks, Gays, and the Struggle for Equality.* New York: New Press, 1999.

Colburn, David R., and Jeffrey S. Adler, eds. *African-American Mayors: Race, Politics, and the American City.* Urbana, IL: University of Illinois Press, 2001.

Collier-Thomas, Bettye, and V.P. Franklin, eds. *Sisters in the Struggle: African American Women in the Civil Rights-Black Power Movement.* New York: New York University Press, 2001.

"Congressional Black Caucus Foundation." Available online at <www.cbcfonline.org> (cited July 19, 2002).

Dailey, Jane, Glenda Elizabeth Gilmore, and Bryant Simon, eds. *Jumpin' Jim Crow: Southern Politics from Civil War to Civil Rights.* Princeton, NJ: Princeton University Press, 2000.

Haskins, James. *Distinguished African American Political and Governmental Leaders.* Phoenix, AZ: Oryx Press, 1999.

Marable, Manning. *Black Leadership.* New York: Columbia University Press, 1998.

"Minority On-Line Information Service (MOLIS)." Available online at <www.lights.com/hytelnet/oth/oth023.html> (cited July 19, 2002).

"National Organization of Blacks in Government." Available online at <www.bignet.org> (cited July 19, 2002).

Reed, Adolph L. *Stirrings in the Jug: Black Politics in the Post-Segregation Era.* Minneapolis: University of Minnesota Press, 1999.

West, Cornel. *The Cornel West Reader.* New York: Basic Civitas Books, 1999.

Population

"Black Population Surged During '90s: U.S. Census," *Jet,* August 27, 2001.

Cohn, D'Vera. "Reversing a Long Pattern, Blacks Are Heading South," *Washington Post,* May 5, 2001.

Frey, William H. "Minority Majorities," *American Demographics,* October 1998.

Hornor, Louise L., ed. *Black Americans: A Statistical Sourcebook.* Palo Alto, CA: Information Publications, 2000.

Sigelman, Lee, and Richard G. Niemi. "Innumeracy about Minority Populations; African Americans and Whites Compared," *Public Opinion Quarterly,* Spring 2001.

"U.S. Black Population Is Younger, Growing Faster, Census Bureau Reports," *Jet,* February 28, 2000.

"U.S. Census Bureau: The Black Population in the U.S." Available online at <www.census.gov/population/www/socdemo/race/black.html> (cited July 19, 2002).

Employment and Income

Arnesen, Eric. *Brotherhoods of Color: Black Railroad Workers and the Struggle for Equality.* Cambridge, MA: Harvard University Press, 2001.

Browne, Irene. *Latinas and African American Women at Work: Race, Gender, and Economic Inequality.* New York: Russell Sage Foundation, 1999.

"Coalition of Black Investors." Available online at <www.cobinvest.com> (cited July 19, 2002).

Honey, Michael K. *Black Workers Remember: An Oral History of Segregation, Unionism, and the Freedom Struggle.* Berkeley: University of California Press, 1999.

Hornor, Louise L., ed. *Black Americans: A Statistical Sourcebook.* Palo Alto, CA: Information Publications, 2000.

Jones, Jacqueline. *American Work: Four Centuries of Black and White Labor.* New York: W.W. Norton, 1998.

Nelson, Bruce. *Divided We Stand: American Workers and the Struggle for Black Equality.* Princeton, NJ: Princeton University Press, 2001.

Sigler, Jay A., ed. *Civil Rights in America: 1500 to the Present.* Detroit: Gale Research, 1998.

"The State of Black Male America: 1998." Available online at <www.ritesofpassage.org/genstb98.htm> (cited July 19, 2002).

Venkatesh, Sudhir Alladi. *American Project: The Rise and Fall of a Modern Ghetto.* Cambridge, MA: Harvard University Press, 2000.

Entrepreneurship

Barber, John T., and Alice A. Tait, eds. *The Information Society and the Black Community.* Westport, CT: Praeger, 2001.

"blackenterprise.com: The Virtual Desktop for African Americans." Available online at <www.blackenterprise.com> (cited July 19, 2002).

Broussard, Cheryl D. *Sister CEO: The Black Woman's Guide to Starting Her Own Business.* New York: Penguin, 1998.

Bundles, A'Lelia Perry. *On Her Own Ground: The Life and Times of Madam C.J. Walker.* New York: Scribner, 2001.

Clarke, Caroline V. *Take a Lesson: Today's Black Achievers on How They Made It and What They Learned Along the Way*. New York: John Wiley, 2001.

Dingle, Derek T. *Black Enterprise Titans of the B.E. 100s: Black CEOs Who Redefined and Conquered American Business*. New York: John Wiley, 1999.

Fraser, George C. *Race for Success: The Ten Best Business Opportunities for Blacks in America*. New York: W. Morrow, 1998.

Hunt, Martin K. and Jacqueline E. *History of Black Business: The Coming of America's Largest African-American-owned Businesses*. Chicago: Knowledge Express, 1998.

Mitchell, Niki Butler. *The New Color of Success: Twenty Young Black Millionaires Tell You How They're Making It*. Rocklin, CA: Prima, 2000.

"The Network Journal: Black Professional and Small Business News." Available online at <www.tnj.com> (cited July 19, 2002).

Walker, Juliet E.K. *The History of Black Business in America: Capitalism, Race, Entrepreneurship*. New York: Macmillan Reference, 1998.

Family and Health

"African American Web Connection." Available online at <www.aawc.com> (cited July 19, 2002).

"African Wedding Guide." Available online at <www.melanet.com/awg/start.html> (cited July 19, 2002).

Alexander, Adele Logan. *Homelands and Waterways: The American Journey of the Bond Family*. New York: Pantheon Books, 1999.

Ball, Edward. *Slaves in the Family*. New York: Farrar, Straus and Giroux, 1998.

"Black Family Network." Available online at <www.blackfamilynet.net> (cited July 19, 2002).

"The BlackStripe." Available online at <www.blackstripe.com> (cited July 19, 2002).

Burroughs, Tony. *Black Roots: A Beginner's Guide to Tracing the African American Family Tree*. New York: Fireside Books, 2001.

Harris, Phyllis Y. *From the Soul: Stories of Great Black Parents and the Lives They Gave Us*. New York: G.P. Putnam's Sons, 2001.

Henry, Neil. *Pearl's Secret: A Black Man's Search for His White Family*. Berkeley: University of California Press, 2001.

"Kwanzaa Information Center." Available online at <www.melanet.com/kwanzaa/> (cited July 19, 2002).

Lanier, Shannon. *Jefferson's Children: The Story of One American Family*. New York: Random House, 2000.

Lee, Essie E. *Nurturing Success: Successful Women of Color and Their Daughters*. Westport, CT: Praeger, 2000.

Rushdy, Ashraf H.A. *Remembering Generations: Race and Family in Contemporary African American Fiction*. Chapel Hill, NC: University of North Carolina Press, 2001.

Scruggs, Afi. *Claiming Kin: Confronting the History of an African American Family*. New York: St. Martin's Press, 2002.

Sollors, Werner, ed. *Interracialism: Black-White Intermarriage in American History, Literature, and Law*. New York: Oxford University Press, 2000.

Wamba, Philippe E. *Kinship: A Family's Journey in Africa and America*. New York: Plume, 2000.

Wiencek, Henry. *The Hairstons: An American Family in Black and White*. New York: St. Martin's Press, 1999.

Young, Yolanda. *On Our Way to Beautiful: A Family Memoir*. New York: Villard, 2002.

Education

"The Carter G. Woodson Institute for Afro-American and African Studies." Available online at <minerva.acc.virginia.edu/~woodson> (cited July 19, 2002).

Fairclough, Adam. *Teaching Equality: Black Schools in the Age of Jim Crow*. Athens, GA: University of Georgia Press, 2001.

Fraser, James W. *Between Church and State: Religion and Public Education in a Multicultural America*. New York: St. Martin's Press, 1999.

Hale, Janice E. *Learning While Black: Creating Educational Excellence for African American Children.* Baltimore: Johns Hopkins University Press, 2001.

Hrabowski, Freeman A. *Beating the Odds: Raising Academically Successful African American Males.* New York: Oxford University Press, 1998.

Hrabowski, Freeman A. *Overcoming the Odds: Raising Academically Successful African American Young Women.* New York: Oxford University Press, 2002.

Jackson, Cynthia L. *African American Education: A Reference Handbook.* Santa Barbara, CA: ABC-CLIO, 2001.

McWhorter, John H. *Losing the Race: Self-Sabotage in Black America.* New York: Free Press, 2000.

"Morehouse College." Available online at <www.morehouse.edu> (cited July 19, 2002).

Patterson, James T. *Brown v. Board of Education: A Civil Rights Milestone and its Troubled Legacy.* New York: Oxford University Press, 2001.

Perry, Theresa, and Lisa Delpit, eds. *The Real Ebonics Debate: Power, Language, and the Education of African-American Children.* Boston: Beacon Press, 1998.

Wilson, Erlene B. *The 100 Best Colleges for African-American Students.* Rev. and updated ed. New York: Plume, 1998.

Religion

Best, Felton O., ed. *Black Religious Leadership from the Slave Community to the Million Man March: Flames of Fire.* Lewiston, NY: Edwin Mellen Press, 1998.

Billingsley, Andrew. *Mighty Like a River: The Black Church and Social Reform.* New York: Oxford University Press, 1999.

"Black Catholic Information Mall." Available online at <www.bcimall.org> (cited July 19, 2002).

Bolden, Tonya. *Rock of Ages: A Tribute to the Black Church.* New York: Knopf, 2001.

Bridges, Flora Wilson. *Resurrection Song: African-American Spirituality.* Maryknoll, NY: Orbis Books, 2001.

Evanzz, Karl. *The Messenger: The Rise and Fall of Elijah Muhammad.* New York: Pantheon Books, 1999.

Fraser, James W. *Between Church and State: Religion and Public Education in a Multicultural America.* New York: St. Martin's Press, 1999.

Glazier, Stephen D., ed. *The Encyclopedia of African and African-American Religions.* New York: Routledge, 2001.

"National Baptist Convention, U.S.A." Available online at <www.nationalbaptist.com/> (cited July 19, 2002).

Olupona, Jacob K., ed. *African Spirituality: Forms, Meanings, and Expressions.* New York: Crossroad, 2000.

Raboteau, Albert J. *Canaan Land: A Religious History of African Americans.* New York: Oxford University Press, 2001.

Literature

"African American Literature Book Club." Available online at <aalbc.com> (cited July 19, 2002).

"African American Writers: Online E-Texts." Available online at <falcon.jmu.edu/~ramseyil/afroonline.htm > (cited July 19, 2002).

Andrews, William L., Frances Smith Foster, and Trudier Harris, eds. *The Concise Oxford Companion to African American Literature.* New York: Oxford University Press, 2001.

Bascom, Lionel C., ed. *A Renaissance in Harlem: Lost Voices of an American Community.* New York: Bard, 1999.

Berry, Faith, ed. *From Bondage to Liberation: Writings By and About Afro-Americans from 1700 to 1918.* New York: Continuum, 2001.

"Black Americans in Publishing." Available online at <www.bwip.org> (cited July 19, 2002).

Chapman, Abraham, ed. *Black Voices: An Anthology of African-American Literature.* Updated ed. New York: Signet Classic, 2001.

Dance, Daryl Cumber, ed. *From My People: 400 Years of African American Folklore.* New York: W.W. Norton, 2002.

Gabbin, Joanne V., ed. *The Furious Flowering of African American Poetry.* Charlottesville, VA: University Press of Virginia, 1999.

Glasrud, Bruce A., and Laurie Champion, eds. *The African American West: A Century of Short Stories.* Boulder, CO: University Press of Colorado, 2000.

Harper, Michael S., and Anthony Walton, eds. *The Vintage Book of African American Poetry.* New York: Vintage Books, 2000.

Harris, Trudier. *Saints, Sinners, Saviors: Strong Black Women in African American Literature.* New York: Palgrave, 2001.

Hatch, Shari Dorantes, and Michael R. Strickland, eds. *African-American Writers: A Dictionary.* Santa Barbara, CA: ABC-CLIO, 2000.

Helbling, Mark Irving. *The Harlem Renaissance: The One and the Many.* Westport, CT: Greenwood Press, 1999.

Howes, Kelly King, and Christine Slovey, eds. *Harlem Renaissance.* Detroit: UXL, 2001.

Hurston, Zora Neale. *Zora Neale Hurston: A Life in Letters.* New York: Doubleday, 2001.

Nelson, Emmanuel S., ed. *African American Authors, 1745–1945: Bio-bibliographical Critical Sourcebook.* Westport, CT: Greenwood Press, 2000.

Powell, Kevin, ed. *Step into a World: A Global Anthology of the New Black Literature.* New York: John Wiley, 2000.

Richards, Phillip M., and Neil Schlager, eds. *Best Literature By and About Blacks.* Detroit: Gale Research, 2000.

Rodgers, Marie E. *The Harlem Renaissance: An Annotated Reference Guide for Student Research.* Englewood, CO: Libraries Unlimited, 1998.

Rodriguez, Max, Angeli R. Rasbury, and Carol Taylor, eds. *Sacred Fire: The QBR 100 Essential Black Books.* New York: John Wiley, 1999.

Rushdy, Ashraf H.A. *Remembering Generations: Race and Family in Contemporary African American Fiction.* Chapel Hill, NC: University of North Carolina Press, 2001.

Smith, Valerie, ed. *African American Writers.* New York: Charles Scribner's Sons, 2001.

Sollors, Werner, ed. *Interracialism: Black-White Intermarriage in American History, Literature, and Law.* New York: Oxford University Press, 2000.

"Voices from the Gaps: Women Writers of Color." Available online at <voices.cla.umn.edu> (cited July 19, 2002).

Wideman, John Edgar. *My Soul Has Grown Deep: Classics of Early African-American Literature.* Philadelphia: Running Press, 2001.

Wilson, Sondra Kathryn, ed. *The Messenger Reader: Stories, Poetry, and Essays from The Messenger Magazine.* New York: Modern Library, 2000.

Young, Kevin, ed. *Giant Steps: The New Generation of African American Writers.* New York: Perennial, 2000.

Wilkinson, Brenda Scott, ed. *African American Women Writers.* New York: John Wiley, 2000.

Media

"Africana.com." Available online at <www.africana.com> (cited July 19, 2002).

Barber, John T., and Alice A. Tait, eds. *The Information Society and the Black Community.* Westport, CT: Praeger, 2001.

Barlow, William. *Voice Over: The Making of Black Radio.* Philadelphia: Temple University Press, 1999.

"Black Entertainment Network." Available online at <bet.com> (cited July 19, 2002).

"Black Voices." Available online at <www.blackvoices.com> (cited July 19, 2002).

"The Black World Today." Available online at <www.tbwt.com> (cited July 19, 2002).

Coleman, Robin R. Means, ed. *Say It Loud! African-American Audiences, Media, and Identity.* New York: Routledge, 2002.

Entman, Robert M. *The Black Image in the White Mind: Media and Race in America.* Chicago: University of Chicago Press, 2001.

Jacobs, Ronald N. *Race, Media, and the Crisis of Civil Society: From Watts to Rodney King.* New York: Cambridge University Press, 2000.

Kamalipour, Yahya R., and Theresa Carilli, eds. *Cultural Diversity and the U.S. Media.* Albany, NY: State University of New York Press, 1998.

Newkirk, Pamela. *Within the Veil: Black Journalists, White Media.* New York: New York University Press, 2000.

Ward, Brian, ed. *Media, Culture, and the Modern African American Freedom Struggle.* Gainesville: University Press of Florida, 2001.

"The World of Essence Online." Available online at <www.essence.com> (cited July 19, 2002).

Film and Television

Bernardi, Daniel, ed. *Classic Hollywood, Classic Whiteness.* Minneapolis: University of Minnesota Press, 2001.

Berry, S. Torriano, and Venise T. Berry. *The 50 Most Influential Black Films: A Celebration of African-American Talent, Determination, and Creativity.* New York: Citadel Press/Kensington, 2001.

"Black Entertainment Network." Available online at <bet.com> (cited July 19, 2002).

"Black Film Center/Archive Home Page." Available online at <www.indiana.edu/~bfca> (cited July 19, 2002).

Bobo, Jacqueline, ed. *Black Women Film and Video Artists.* New York: Routledge, 1998.

Bogle, Donald. *Prime Time Blues: African Americans on Network Television.* New York: Farrar, Straus and Giroux, 2001.

Bogle, Donald. *Toms, Coons, Mulattoes, Mammies, and Bucks: An Interpretive History of Blacks in American Films.* 4th ed. New York: Continuum, 2001.

Chadwick, Bruce. *The Reel Civil War: Mythmaking in American Film.* New York: Knopf, 2001.

Everett, Anna. *Returning the Gaze: A Genealogy of Black Film Criticism, 1909–1949.* Durham, NC: Duke University Press, 2001.

"HBO Soul." Available online at <www.hbo.com/soul> (cited July 19, 2002).

Sampson, Henry T. *That's Enough, Folks: Black Images in Animated Cartoons, 1900–1960.* Lanham, MD: Scarecrow Press, 1998.

Torres, Sasha, ed. *Living Color: Race and Television in the United States.* Durham, NC: Duke University Press, 1998.

Ward, Brian, ed. *Media, Culture, and the Modern African American Freedom Struggle.* Gainesville, FL: University Press of Florida, 2001.

Zook, Kristal Brent. *Color by Fox: The Fox Network and the Revolution in Black Television.* New York: Oxford University Press, 1999.

Drama, Comedy, and Dance

Ailey, Alvin. *Revelations: The Autobiography of Alvin Ailey.* Secaucus, NJ: Replica Books, 2000.

Curtis, Susan. *The First Black Actors on the Great White Way.* Columbia, MO: University of Missouri Press, 1998.

DeFrantz, Thomas, ed. *Dancing Many Drums: Excavations in African American Dance.* Madison, WI: University of Wisconsin Press, 2001.

Dunning, Jennifer. *Alvin Ailey: A Life in Dance.* New York: Da Capo Press, 1998.

Elam, Harry J., and David Krasner, eds. *African-American Performance and Theater History: A Critical Reader.* New York: Oxford University Press, 2001.

Gavin, Christy, ed. *African American Women Playwrights: A Research Guide.* New York: Garland, 1999.

Gill, Glenda Eloise. *No Surrender! No Retreat! African American Pioneer Performers of Twentieth-Century American Theater.* New York: St. Martin's Press, 2000.

Gottschild, Brenda Dixon. *Digging the Africanist Presence in American Performance: Dance and Other Contexts.* Westport, CT: Praeger, 2001.

Gottschild, Brenda Dixon. *Waltzing in the Dark: African American Vaudeville and Race Politics in the Swing Era.* New York: Palgrave Macmillan, 2000.

"It's Showtime at the Apollo!" Available online at <www.apolloshowtime.com> (cited July 19, 2002).

Johnson, Anne E. *Jazz Tap: From African Drums to American Feet.* New York: Rosen Publishing Group, 1999.

"Jomandi Productions: Keeping Black Theatre Alive." Available online at <www.jomandi.com> (cited July 19, 2002).

Peterson, Bernard L. *Profiles of African American Stage Performers and Theatre People, 1816–1960.* Westport, CT: Greenwood Press, 2001.

"Soul in Motion Players, Inc." Available online at <www.us.net/simpinc> (cited July 19, 2002).

Swanson, Meg, ed. *Playwrights of Color.* Yarmouth, ME: Intercultural Press, 1999.

Watkins, Mel. *On the Real Side: A History of African American Comedy.* Chicago: Lawrence Hill, 1999.

Classical Music

Boyle, Sheila Tully. *Paul Robeson: The Years of Promise and Achievement.* Amherst, MA: University of Massachusetts Press, 2001.

Floyd, Samuel A., Jr., ed. *International Dictionary of Black Composers.* Chicago: Fitzroy Dearborn, 1999.

Keiler, Allan. *Marian Anderson: A Singer's Journey.* New York: Scribner, 2000.

Nicholls, David, ed. *The Cambridge History of American Music.* New York: Cambridge University Press, 1998.

Robeson, Paul. *The Undiscovered Paul Robeson: An Artist's Journey, 1898–1939.* New York: John Wiley, 2001.

Sacred Music Traditions

"The Black Gospel Music Clef." Available online at <www.blackgospel.com> (cited July 19, 2002).

Carpenter, Delores, and Nolan E. Williams, eds. *African American Heritage Hymnal.* Chicago: GIA Publications, 2001.

Crawford, Richard. *America's Musical Life: A History.* New York: W.W. Norton, 2001.

"GospelForce.com." Available online at <www.gospelforce.com> (cited July 19, 2002).

Newman, Richard. *Go Down Moses: A Celebration of the African-American Spiritual.* New York: Clarkson Potter, 1998.

Nicholls, David, ed. *The Cambridge History of American Music.* New York: Cambridge University Press, 1998.

Reagon, Bernice Johnson. *If You Don't Go, Don't Hinder Me: The African American Sacred Song Tradition.* Lincoln, NE: University of Nebraska Press, 2001.

Santelli, Robert, Holly George-Warren, and Jim Brown, eds. *American Roots Music.* New York: H.N. Abrams, 2001.

Warren, Gwendolyn Sims. *Ev'ry Time I Feel the Spirit: 101 Best-Loved Psalms, Gospel Hymns, and Spiritual Songs of the African-American Church.* New York: Owl Books/Henry Holt, 1999.

Blues and Jazz

Bjorn, Lars. *Before Motown: A History of Jazz in Detroit, 1920–60.* Ann Arbor, MI: University of Michigan Press, 2001.

"The Blue Highway." Available online at <www.thebluehighway.com> (cited July 19, 2002).

"Blue Note Records." Available online at <www.bluenote.com> (cited July 19, 2002).

"The Blues Foundation." Available online at <www.blues.org> (cited July 19, 2002).

Conyers, James L., Jr. ed. *African American Jazz and Rap.* Jefferson, NC: McFarland, 2001.

Crawford, Richard. *America's Musical Life: A History.* New York: W.W. Norton, 2001.

Dalton, David. *Been Here and Gone: A Memoir of the Blues.* New York: William Morrow, 2000.

Davis, Angela Yvonne. *Blues Legacies and Black Feminism: Gertrude "Ma" Rainey, Bessie Smith, and Billie Holiday.* New York: Pantheon Books, 1998.

Dicaire, David. *Blues Singers: Biographies of 50 Legendary Artists of the Early 20th Century.* Jefferson, NC: McFarland, 1999.

Gerard, Charley. *Jazz in Black and White: Race, Culture, and Identity in the Jazz Community.* Westport, CT: Greenwood Press, 1998.

Hasse, John Edward, ed. *Jazz: The First Century.* New York: William Morrow, 2000.

Jasen, David A. *That American Rag: The Story of Ragtime from Coast to Coast.* New York: Schirmer Books, 2000.

Jasen, David A., and Gene Jones. *Black Bottom Stomp: Eight Masters of Ragtime and Early Jazz.* New York: Routledge, 2002.

Kirchner, Bill, ed. *The Oxford Companion to Jazz.* New York: Oxford University Press, 2000.

Nicholls, David, ed. *The Cambridge History of American Music.* New York: Cambridge University Press, 1998.

Ward, Geoffrey C. *Jazz: A History of America's Music.* New York: Knopf, 2000.

Popular Music

Bond, Julian, and Sondra Kathryn Wilson, eds. *Lift Every Voice and Sing: A Celebration of the Negro National Anthem.* New York: Random House, 2000.

Conyers, James L., Jr. ed. *African American Jazz and Rap.* Jefferson, NC: McFarland, 2001.

Crawford, Richard. *America's Musical Life: A History.* New York: W.W. Norton, 2001.

"EURWEB: The Urban Cyberstation." Available online at <www.eurweb.com> (cited July 19, 2002).

Forman, Murray. *The 'Hood Comes First: Race, Space, and Place in Rap and Hip-Hop.* Middletown, CT: Wesleyan University Press, 2002.

George, Nelson. *Hip Hop America.* New York: Viking, 1998.

"Malaco Music Group." Available online at <www.malaco.com/> (cited July 19, 2002).

Nicholls, David, ed. *The Cambridge History of American Music.* New York: Cambridge University Press, 1998.

Ogg, Alex. *The Hip Hop Years: A History of Rap.* New York: Fromm International, 2001.

"Peeps Republic; The Source for Hip-Hop Culture News." Available online at <www.peeps.com> (cited July 19, 2002).

Richardson, C. Perry, ed. *"What'd I Say?" The Atlantic Story: 50 Years of Music.* New York: Welcome Rain Publishers, 2001.

Roberts, John Storm. *Black Music of Two Worlds: African, Caribbean, Latin, and African-American Traditions.* 2nd ed. New York: Schirmer Books, 1998.

Smith, Suzanne E. *Dancing in the Street: Motown and the Cultural Politics of Detroit.* Cambridge, MA: Harvard University Press, 1999.

Stewart, Earl L. *African American Music: An Introduction.* New York: Schirmer Books, 1998.

"Vibe Online." Available online at <www.vibe.com> (cited July 19, 2002).

Winfield, Betty Houchin, and Sandra Davidson, eds. *Bleep! Censoring Rock and Rap Music.* Westport, CT: Greenwood Press, 1999.

Visual and Applied Arts

"ArtNoir Showcase." Available online at <www.artnoir.com> (cited July 19, 2002).

"California African American Museum." Available online at <www.caam.ca.gov> (cited July 19, 2002).

Collins, Lisa Gail. *The Art of History: African American Women Artists Engage the Past.* New Brunswick, NJ: Rutgers University Press, 2002.

"Genesis Art Line." Available online at <www.genesisartline.com> (cited July 19, 2002).

"National Museum of African Art." Available online at <www.si.edu/nmafa> (cited July 19, 2002).

The New York Public Library African American Desk Reference. New York: John Wiley, 1999.

Patton, Sharon F. *African-American Art.* New York: Oxford University Press, 1998.

Visona, Monica Blackmun, et al., eds. *A History of Art in Africa.* New York: Harry N. Abrams, 2001.

Willis, Deborah. *Reflections in Black: A History of Black Photographers, 1840 to the Present.* New York: W.W. Norton, 2000.

Science and Technology

"The African World Community Network." Available online at <www.he.net/ˆawe/> (cited July 19, 2002).

Barber, John T., and Alice A. Tait, eds. *The Information Society and the Black Community.* Westport, CT: Praeger, 2001.

Bedini, Silvio A. *The Life of Benjamin Banneker: The First African-American Man of Science.* Baltimore: Maryland Historical Society, 1999.

"The Conduit: The Definitive Technological Guide for the African in America." Available online at <www.theconduit.com> (cited July 19, 2002).

"The Faces of Science: African Americans in the Sciences." Available online at <www.princeton.edu/ˆmcbrown/display/faces.html> (cited July 19, 2002).

Krapp, Kristine, ed. *Notable Black American Scientists.* Detroit: Gale Research, 1999.

Warren, Wini. *Black Women Scientists in the United States.* Bloomington, IN: Indiana University Press, 1999.

Webster, Raymond B., ed. *African American Firsts in Science and Technology.* Detroit: Gale Research, 1999.

Sports

Adelson, Bruce. *Brushing Back Jim Crow: The Integration of Minor-League Baseball in the American South.* Charlottesville, VA: University Press of Virginia, 1999.

Collins, Ace. *Blackball Superstars: Legendary Players of the Negro Baseball Leagues.* Greensboro, NC: Avisson Press, 1999.

Halberstam, David. *Playing for Keeps: Michael Jordan and the World He Made.* New York: Random House, 1999.

"Harlem Globetrotters." Available online at <www.harlemglobetrotters.com> (cited July 19, 2002).

Hotaling, Edward. *The Great Black Jockeys: The Lives and Times of the Men Who Dominated America's First National Sport.* Rocklin, CA: Forum, 1999.

"National Association of Black Scuba Divers." Available online at <www.nabsdivers.org> (cited July 19, 2002).

"Negro Baseball Leagues." Available online at <www.blackbaseball.com> (cited July 19, 2002).

"National Brotherhood of Skiers." Available online at <www.nbs.org> (cited July 19, 2002).

"Negro League Baseball Online." Available online at <www.negroleaguebaseball.com/> (cited July 19, 2002).

Remnick, David. *King of the World: Muhammad Ali and the Rise of an American Hero.* New York: Random House, 1998.

Ross, Charles Kenyatta. *Outside the Lines: African Americans and the Integration of the National Football League.* New York: New York University Press, 1999.

Sailes, Gary A., ed. *African Americans in Sport: Contemporary Themes.* New Brunswick, NJ: Transaction Publishers, 1998.

Sinnette, Calvin H. *Forbidden Fairways: African Americans and the Game of Golf.* Chelsea, MI: Sleeping Bear Press, 1998.

Military

"African-American Civil War Memorial." Available online at <www.afroamcivilwar.org/> (cited July 19, 2002).

Astor, Gerald. *The Right to Fight: A History of African Americans in the Military.* Novato, CA: Presidio, 1998.

Buckley, Gail Lumet. *American Patriots: The Story of Blacks in the Military from the Revolution to Desert Storm.* New York: Random House, 2001.

Clinton, Catherine. *The Black Soldier: 1492 to the Present.* Boston: Houghton Mifflin, 2000.

Edgerton, Robert B. *Hidden Heroism: Black Soldiers in America's Wars.* Boulder, CO: Westview Press, 2001.

Haskins, James. *African American Military Heroes.* New York: John Wiley, 1998.

"366th Infantry Homepage." Available online at <www.wiz-worx.com/366th> (cited July 19, 2002).

Trudeau, Noah Andre. *Like Men of War: Black Troops in the Civil War, 1862–1865.* Boston: Little Brown, 1998.

Index

Personal names, place names, events, organizations, subjects, and keywords contained in *The African American Almanac* are listed in this index with corresponding page numbers indicating text references. Page numbers in **boldface** identify major treatments of topics, such as biographical profiles and organizational entries. *Italicized* page numbers refer to photographs; page references for tables are followed by *t*; and an *f* denotes that the page locator is for a non-tabular graphic.

C

E

X